WHITAKER'S
2015

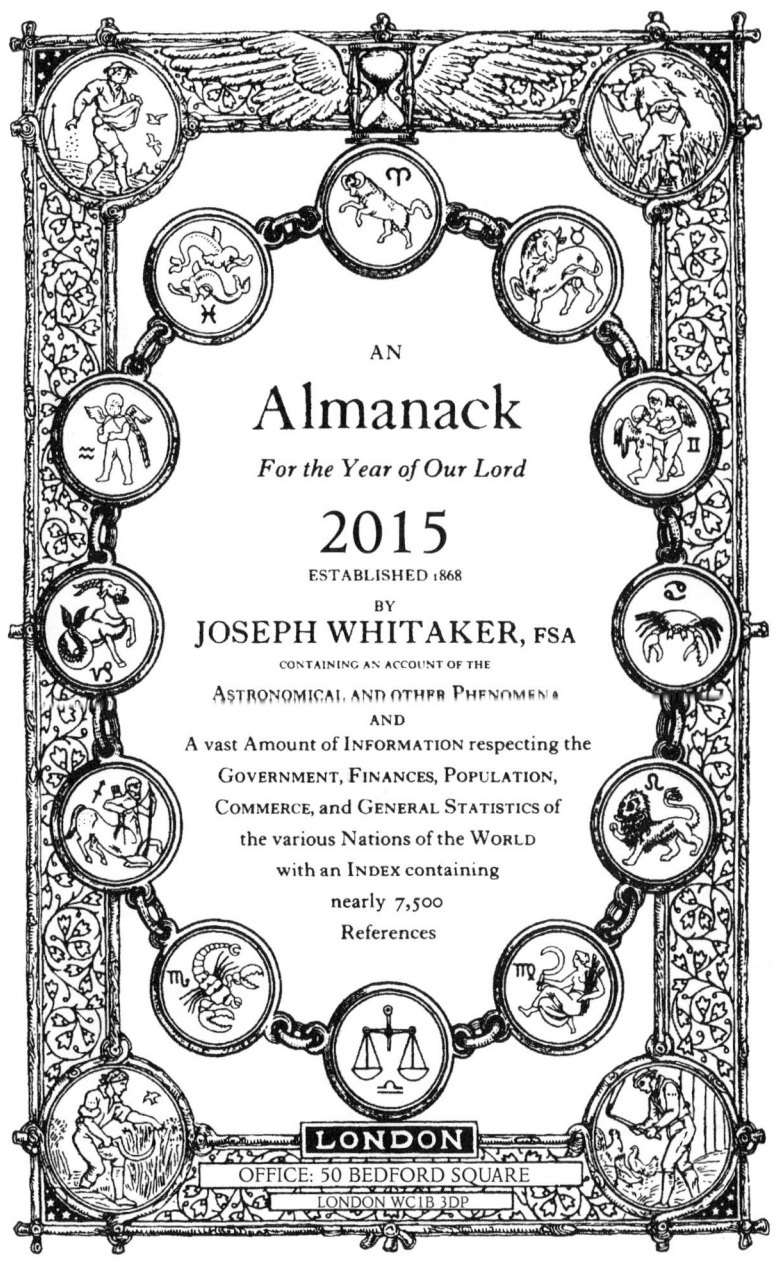

AN

Almanack

For the Year of Our Lord

2015

ESTABLISHED 1868

BY

JOSEPH WHITAKER, FSA

CONTAINING AN ACCOUNT OF THE

ASTRONOMICAL AND OTHER PHENOMENA

AND

A vast Amount of INFORMATION respecting the
GOVERNMENT, FINANCES, POPULATION,
COMMERCE, and GENERAL STATISTICS of
the various Nations of the WORLD
with an INDEX containing
nearly 7,500
References

LONDON

OFFICE: 50 BEDFORD SQUARE
LONDON WC1B 3DP

The traditional design of the title page for Whitaker's Almanack which has appeared in each edition since 1868

B L O O M S B U R Y
LONDON · NEW DELHI · NEW YORK · SYDNEY

Bloomsbury Publishing Plc.
50 Bedford Square, London WC1B 3DP

Whitaker's Almanack published annually since 1868
147th edition © 2014 Bloomsbury Publishing Plc.

www.bloomsbury.com
Bloomsbury Publishing, London, New Delhi, New York
and Sydney

STANDARD EDITION
Cloth covers
978-1-4729-0929-9

CONCISE EDITION
Paperback
978-1-4729-0931-2

JACKET PHOTOGRAPHS
Main image: Crowds of 'No' campaigners attend a 'Better Together' rally in Trafalgar Square, London ahead of the Scottish independence referendum. © Jonathan Brady/PA Wire/Press Association Images
Spine: The Whitaker's trident, *Whitaker's Almanack 1869*
Top, from left to right:
1. Nelson Mandela during a state visit to Sweden in 1999. © Jan Collsioo/TT News Agency/Press Association Images
2. FIFA World Cup 2014: In the Uruguay v England match, Uruguay's Luis Suarez (centre) celebrates scoring their first goal of the game with team mates. © EMPICS Sport/Press Association Images
3. Russian President Vladimir Putin holds a globe presented to him during a visit to a youth educational forum at a youth camp near Lake Seliger, Russia on 29 August 2014. © Mikhail Klimentyev/AP/Press Association Images
4. Syrian People's Protection Units fight against Islamic State (IS) in Rabia, Mosul, Iraq on 6 August 2014. © AA / TT/TT News Agency/Press Association Images

Typeset in the UK by RefineCatch Ltd, Bungay, Suffolk NR35 1EF

Printed and bound in Italy by L.E.G.O. S.p.A.

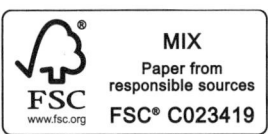

MIX
Paper from responsible sources
FSC
www.fsc.org
FSC® C023419

WHITAKER'S, the 'W' Trident logo and the Diana logo are trademarks of Bloomsbury Publishing Plc.

Whitaker's was compiled with the assistance of Amnesty International; HM Revenue and Customs; Keesing's Worldwide; Oxford Cartographers; Press Association; Transparency International: the global coalition against corruption; UK Hydrographic Office; and WM/Reuters.

Material was reproduced from (in addition to that indicated): *CIA World Factbook 2014*; *Human Development Indicators 2013* published by the UN Development Programme and *UN Statistics* published by UN Data; *World Economic Outlook Database 2013* © International Monetary Fund; *World Development Indicators 2014* published by The World Bank; Stockholm International Peace Research Institute (SIPRI) 2014; Press Freedom Score 2014 © Reporters Without Borders. Crown copyright material is reproduced with the permission of the Controller of Her Majesty's Stationery Office.

Government cabinet lists and embassy details are sourced from *People in Power* ©, Cambridge International Reference on Current Affairs Ltd (W www.circaworld.com). *People in Power* provides a constantly updated service at www.peopleinpower.com

A CIP catalogue record for this book is available from the British Library.

EDITORIAL STAFF
Executive Editor: Ruth Northey
Senior Project Editor/Infographic Design: Oli Lurie
Editorial Assistants: James McCall (International); Rachel Nickolds; Lydia Wassan
Head of Yearbooks: Katy McAdam

Thanks to Omer Ali, Lucy Beevor; John Bromham; Rob Hardy; Stephen Kershaw; Elizabeth Kingston; Peter Macdonald; Hilary Marsden; Graham Relf

Special thanks to Gordon Taylor

CONTRIBUTORS (where not listed)
Sheridan Williams (Astronomy); Anthea Lipsett, Caroline Macready (Education); Clive Longhurst (Insurance); Graham Bartram (Flags); Duncan Murray, Chris Priestley (Legal Notes); Matthew Chorley (Sport); Jill Papworth (Taxation); and Philip Eden (Weather)

REF
AY
754
W5

CONTENTS

2015

4

At the start of 2014, when the process of updating Whitaker's was already well underway, the Scottish referendum on independence seemed an awfully long way off, and all thoughts (and hopes) were firmly on the World Cup in Brazil. Despite England's 2–1 defeat by Italy, nobody really thought they would be out in the group stage and the mood was confident prior to their match against Uruguay, particularly as the weather was forecast to be rainy and 16°C! However, it was not to be, and it seemed that while everyone's focus had been on the world sporting arena the 'yes' campaign for an independent Scotland had gathered a considerable amount of momentum.

Internationally, the political landscape was also changing rapidly. Following internal civil unrest in the Ukraine at the start of the year, events took an unexpected turn when Russia annexed Crimea on 18 March; amid signs of a build-up of Russian forces on Ukraine's eastern border, US President Barack Obama urged Moscow to 'move back its troops' and lower tensions. In Syria, the civil war moved to a new level as Islamic State (IS) increased their campaign of terror causing prime minister David Cameron to raise the UK security threat level to 'severe' on 29 August, while US-led strikes on IS targets extended from Iraq into Syria on 22 September.

In the end, the result of the Scottish referendum was a 'no' to independence, but the 'yes' campaign had an unexpected level of support, forcing the 'Better Together' campaigners to pull out all the stops in the weeks leading up to polling day. When the no result was declared on 19 September the Scottish National Party leader Alex Salmond felt he had no option but to resign as first minister and step down from the leadership of the SNP. Nevertheless, the referendum has changed the UK's political thinking, with serious questions already being raised about further devolving powers to the regions.

The *Whitaker's* team has worked very hard as always to bring you this fully updated 147th edition, spending many thousands of hours gathering the information, checking facts and qualifying data. I would like to take this opportunity to welcome our new astronomy contributor Sheridan Williams on board and draw attention to the new page in the astronomy chapter detailing the solar eclipse which will take place on 20 March 2015. I would also like to say a special thank you to Sheridan's predecessor, Gordon Taylor, for his lengthy contribution to *Whitaker's*.

Ruth Northey
Executive Editor

THE YEAR 2015

CHRONOLOGICAL CYCLES AND ERAS

Dominical Letter	D
Epact	10
Golden Number (Lunar Cycle)	II
Julian Period	6728
Roman Indiction	8
Solar Cycle	8

	Beginning
*Muslim year AH 1436	25 Oct 2014
Japanese year Heisei 27	1 Jan
Roman year 2768 AUC	14 Jan
Regnal year 64	6 Feb
Chinese year of the Goat or Sheep	19 Feb
Sikh new year	14 Mar
Hindu new year (Chaitra)	21 Mar
Indian (Saka) year 1937	22 Mar
*Jewish year AM 5776	14 Sep

* Year begins at sunset on the previous day

RELIGIOUS CALENDARS

CHRISTIAN

Epiphany	6 Jan
Presentation of Christ in the Temple	2 Feb
Ash Wednesday	18 Feb
The Annunciation	25 Mar
Palm Sunday	29 Mar
Maundy Thursday	2 Apr
Good Friday	3 Apr
Easter Day (western churches)	5 Apr
Easter Day (Eastern Orthodox)	12 Apr
Rogation Sunday	10 May
Ascension Day	14 May
Pentecost (Whit Sunday)	24 May
Trinity Sunday	31 May
Corpus Christi	4 Jun
All Saints' Day	1 Nov
Advent Sunday	29 Nov
Christmas Day	25 Dec

HINDU

Makar Sankranti	14 Jan
Vasant Panchami (Sarasvati Puja)	24 Jan
Shivaratri	17 Feb
Holi	6 Mar
Chaitra (Spring new year)	21 Mar
Ram Navami	28 Mar
Raksha-bandhan	29 Aug
Krishna Janmashtami	5 Sep
Ganesh Chaturthi, first day	17 Sep
Navaratri festival (Durga Puja), first day	13 Oct
Dussehra	22 Oct
Diwali (New Year festival of lights), first day	11 Nov

JEWISH

Purim	5 Mar
Pesach (Passover), first day	4 Apr
Shavuot (Feast of Weeks), first day	24 May
Rosh Hashanah (Jewish new year)	14 Sep
Yom Kippur (Day of Atonement)	23 Sep
Succot (Feast of Tabernacles), first day	28 Sep
Hanukkah, first day	7 Dec

MUSLIM

Al-Hijra (Muslim new year)	25 Oct 2014
Ashura	3 Nov 2014
Ramadan, first day	18 Jun
Eid-ul-Fitr	17 Jul
Hajj	21 Sep
Eid-ul-Adha	23 Sep

SIKH

Birthday of Guru Gobind Singh Ji	5 Jan
1 Chet (Sikh new year)	14 Mar
†Hola Mohalla	14 Apr
Baisakhi	13 Apr
‡Birthday of Guru Nanak Dev Ji	14 Apr
Martyrdom of Guru Arjan Dev Ji	16 Jun
Martyrdom of Guru Tegh Bahadur Ji	24 Nov

† This festival is currently celebrated according to the lunar calendar: 6 Mar in 2015
‡ This festival is also celebrated according to the lunar calendar: 25 Nov in 2015

CIVIL CALENDAR

Duchess of Cambridge's birthday	9 Jan
Countess of Wessex's birthday	20 Jan
Accession of the Queen	6 Feb
Duke of York's birthday	19 Feb
St David's Day	1 Mar
Commonwealth Day	9 Mar
Earl of Wessex's birthday	10 Mar
St Patrick's Day	17 Mar
Birthday of the Queen	21 Apr
St George's Day	23 Apr
Europe Day	9 May
Coronation Day	2 Jun
Duke of Edinburgh's birthday	10 Jun
The Queen's Official Birthday	13 Jun
Duke of Cambridge's birthday	21 Jun
Duchess of Cornwall's birthday	17 Jul
Princess Royal's birthday	15 Aug
Remembrance Sunday	8 Nov
Lord Mayor's Day	14 Nov
Prince of Wales' birthday	14 Nov
Wedding Day of the Queen	20 Nov
St Andrew's Day	30 Nov

LEGAL CALENDAR

LAW TERMS

Hilary Term	12 Jan to 1 Apr
Easter Term	14 Apr to 22 May
Trinity Term	2 Jun to 31 Jul
Michaelmas Term	1 Oct to 21 Dec

QUARTER DAYS	TERM DAYS
England, Wales and Northern Ireland	*Scotland*
Lady – 25 Mar	Candlemas – 28 Feb
Midsummer – 24 Jun	Whitsunday – 28 May
Michaelmas – 29 Sep	Lammas – 28 Aug
Christmas – 25 Dec	Martinmas – 28 Nov

2015

JANUARY
Sunday		4	11	18	25
Monday		5	12	19	26
Tuesday		6	13	20	27
Wednesday		7	14	21	28
Thursday	1	8	15	22	29
Friday	2	9	16	23	30
Saturday	3	10	17	24	31

FEBRUARY
Sunday	1	8	15	22
Monday	2	9	16	23
Tuesday	3	10	17	24
Wednesday	4	11	18	25
Thursday	5	12	19	26
Friday	6	13	20	27
Saturday	7	14	21	28

MARCH
Sunday	1	8	15	22	29
Monday	2	9	16	23	30
Tuesday	3	10	17	24	31
Wednesday	4	11	18	25	
Thursday	5	12	19	26	
Friday	6	13	20	27	
Saturday	7	14	21	28	

APRIL
Sunday		5	12	19	26
Monday		6	13	20	27
Tuesday		7	14	21	28
Wednesday	1	8	15	22	29
Thursday	2	9	16	23	30
Friday	3	10	17	24	
Saturday	4	11	18	25	

MAY
Sunday		3	10	17	24	31
Monday		4	11	18	25	
Tuesday		5	12	19	26	
Wednesday		6	13	20	27	
Thursday		7	14	21	28	
Friday	1	8	15	22	29	
Saturday	2	9	16	23	30	

JUNE
Sunday		7	14	21	28
Monday	1	8	15	22	29
Tuesday	2	9	16	23	30
Wednesday	3	10	17	24	
Thursday	4	11	18	25	
Friday	5	12	19	26	
Saturday	6	13	20	27	

JULY
Sunday		5	12	19	26
Monday		6	13	20	27
Tuesday		7	14	21	28
Wednesday	1	8	15	22	29
Thursday	2	9	16	23	30
Friday	3	10	17	24	31
Saturday	4	11	18	25	

AUGUST
Sunday		2	9	16	23	30
Monday		3	10	17	24	31
Tuesday		4	11	18	25	
Wednesday		5	12	19	26	
Thursday		6	13	20	27	
Friday		7	14	21	28	
Saturday	1	8	15	22	29	

SEPTEMBER
Sunday		6	13	20	27
Monday		7	14	21	28
Tuesday	1	8	15	22	29
Wednesday	2	9	16	23	30
Thursday	3	10	17	24	
Friday	4	11	18	25	
Saturday	5	12	19	26	

OCTOBER
Sunday		4	11	18	25
Monday		5	12	19	26
Tuesday		6	13	20	27
Wednesday		7	14	21	28
Thursday	1	8	15	22	29
Friday	2	9	16	23	30
Saturday	3	10	17	24	31

NOVEMBER
Sunday	1	8	15	22	29
Monday	2	9	16	23	30
Tuesday	3	10	17	24	
Wednesday	4	11	18	25	
Thursday	5	12	19	26	
Friday	6	13	20	27	
Saturday	7	14	21	28	

DECEMBER
Sunday		6	13	20	27
Monday		7	14	21	28
Tuesday	1	8	15	22	29
Wednesday	2	9	16	23	30
Thursday	3	10	17	24	31
Friday	4	11	18	25	
Saturday	5	12	19	26	

PUBLIC HOLIDAYS

	England and Wales	Scotland	Northern Ireland
New Year	1 January†	1, 2† January	1 January†
St Patrick's Day	—	—	17 March
*Good Friday	3 April	3 April	3 April
Easter Monday	6 April	—	6 April
Early May	4 May†	4 May	4 May†
Spring	25 May	25 May†	25 May
Battle of the Boyne	—	—	13 July‡
Summer	31 August	3 August	31 August
St Andrew's Day	—	30 November§	—
*Christmas	25, 28 December	25†, 28 December	25, 28 December

* In England, Wales and Northern Ireland, Christmas Day and Good Friday are common law holidays

† Subject to royal proclamation

‡ Subject to proclamation by the Secretary of State for Northern Ireland

§ The St Andrew's Day Holiday (Scotland) Bill was approved by parliament on 29 November 2006; it does not oblige employers to change their existing pattern of holidays but provides the legal framework in which the St Andrew's Day bank holiday could be substituted for an existing local holiday from another date in the year

Note: In the Channel Islands, Liberation Day is a bank and public holiday

2016

JANUARY							
Sunday		3	10	17	24	31	
Monday		4	11	18	25		
Tuesday		5	12	19	26		
Wednesday		6	13	20	27		
Thursday		7	14	21	28		
Friday	1	8	15	22	29		
Saturday	2	9	16	23	30		

FEBRUARY						
Sunday			7	14	21	28
Monday	1	8	15	22	29	
Tuesday	2	9	16	23		
Wednesday	3	10	17	24		
Thursday	4	11	18	25		
Friday	5	12	19	26		
Saturday	6	13	20	27		

MARCH						
Sunday			6	13	20	27
Monday			7	14	21	28
Tuesday	1	8	15	22	29	
Wednesday	2	9	16	23	30	
Thursday	3	10	17	24	31	
Friday	4	11	18	25		
Saturday	5	12	19	26		

APRIL					
Sunday		3	10	17	24
Monday		4	11	18	25
Tuesday		5	12	19	26
Wednesday		6	13	20	27
Thursday		7	14	21	28
Friday	1	8	15	22	29
Saturday	2	9	16	23	30

MAY					
Sunday	1	8	15	22	29
Monday	2	9	16	23	30
Tuesday	3	10	17	24	31
Wednesday	4	11	18	25	
Thursday	5	12	19	26	
Friday	6	13	20	27	
Saturday	7	14	21	28	

JUNE					
Sunday		5	12	19	26
Monday		6	13	20	27
Tuesday		7	14	21	28
Wednesday	1	8	15	22	29
Thursday	2	9	16	23	30
Friday	3	10	17	24	
Saturday	4	11	18	25	

JULY						
Sunday		3	10	17	24	31
Monday		4	11	18	25	
Tuesday		5	12	19	26	
Wednesday		6	13	20	27	
Thursday		7	14	21	28	
Friday	1	8	15	22	29	
Saturday	2	9	16	23	30	

AUGUST						
Sunday			7	14	21	28
Monday	1	8	15	22	29	
Tuesday	2	9	16	23	30	
Wednesday	3	10	17	24	31	
Thursday	4	11	18	25		
Friday	5	12	19	26		
Saturday	6	13	20	27		

SEPTEMBER					
Sunday		4	11	18	25
Monday		5	12	19	26
Tuesday		6	13	20	27
Wednesday		7	14	21	28
Thursday	1	8	15	22	29
Friday	2	9	16	23	30
Saturday	3	10	17	24	

OCTOBER						
Sunday	2	9	16	23	30	
Monday	3	10	17	24	31	
Tuesday	4	11	18	25		
Wednesday	5	12	19	26		
Thursday	6	13	20	27		
Friday	7	14	21	28		
Saturday	1	8	15	22	29	

NOVEMBER						
Sunday			6	13	20	27
Monday			7	14	21	28
Tuesday	1	8	15	22	29	
Wednesday	2	9	16	23	30	
Thursday	3	10	17	24		
Friday	4	11	18	25		
Saturday	5	12	19	26		

DECEMBER						
Sunday			4	11	18	25
Monday			5	12	19	26
Tuesday			6	13	20	27
Wednesday			7	14	21	28
Thursday	1	8	15	22	29	
Friday	2	9	16	23	30	
Saturday	3	10	17	24	31	

PUBLIC HOLIDAYS	England and Wales	Scotland	Northern Ireland
New Year	1 January†	1, 4† January	1 January†
St Patrick's Day	—	—	17 March
*Good Friday	25 March	25 March	25 March
Easter Monday	28 March	—	28 March
Early May	2 May†	2 May	2 May†
Spring	30 May	30 May†	30 May
Battle of the Boyne	—	—	12 July‡
Summer	29 August	1 August	29 August
St Andrew's Day	—	28 November§	—
*Christmas	26, 27 December	26†, 27 December	26, 27 December

* In England, Wales and Northern Ireland, Christmas Day and Good Friday are common law holidays

† Subject to royal proclamation

‡ Subject to proclamation by the Secretary of State for Northern Ireland

§ The St Andrew's Day Holiday (Scotland) Bill was approved by parliament on 29 November 2006; it does not oblige employers to change their existing pattern of holidays but provides the legal framework in which the St Andrew's Day bank holiday could be substituted for an existing local holiday from another date in the year

Note: In the Channel Islands, Liberation Day is a bank and public holiday

FORTHCOMING EVENTS

* Provisional dates

JANUARY 2015
9–18	London Boat Show, Excel, London Docklands
9–18	London Short Film Festival
15–1 Feb	Celtic Connections Music Festival, Glasgow
20–22	UK Open Dance Championships, Bournemouth
21–25	London Art Fair, Business Design Centre
23–31	Big Burns Supper, Dumfries

FEBRUARY
*2–11	Bath Literature Festival
4–22	Leicester Comedy Festival
8	British Academy Film Awards, Royal Opera House, London
13–15	London Motorcycle Show, Excel, London Docklands
14–22	31st Jorvik Viking Festival, Jorvik Viking Centre, York

MARCH
5	World Book Day
5–8	Crufts Dog Show, NEC, Birmingham
8	International Women's Day
13–22	National Science and Engineering Week
17	St Patrick's Day Parade, Piccadilly, London
18–24	BADA Antiques and Fine Art Fair, Duke of York Square, London
20–6 Apr	Ideal Home Show, Olympia, London
21	World Poetry Day
*28–5 Apr	Oxford Literary Festival

APRIL
14–16	London Book Fair, Olympia, London
17–19	Ceramic Art London, Royal College of Art
22	Earth Day

MAY
19–23	RHS Chelsea Flower Show, Royal Hospital, Chelsea, London
21–30 Aug	81st Glyndebourne Festival
21–31	28th Hay Festival of Literature and the Arts, Hay-on-Wye
*25	Belfast Titanic Maritime Festival
29	Word Festival, Aberdeen

JUNE
14	Trooping the Colour, Horse Guards Parade, London
24–28	Glastonbury Festival of Contemporary Performing Arts, Somerset
24–4 Jul	New Designers Exhibition, Business Design Centre, London
30–5 Jul	RHS Hampton Court Palace Flower Show, Surrey
30–11 Jul	Cheltenham Music Festival

JULY
3–11	York Early Music Festival
10–25	Buxton Festival, Derbyshire
Mid-Jul–Mid-Sep	BBC Promenade Concerts, Royal Albert Hall, London
22–26	RHS Flower Show, Tatton Park, Cheshire
Mid-Jul	The Welsh Proms, St David's Hall, Cardiff
23–26	WOMAD Festival, Charlton Park, Wiltshire
25–1 Aug	Three Choirs Festival, Gloucester
30–2 Aug	Cambridge Folk Festival

AUGUST
1–8	National Eisteddfod of Wales, Montgomeryshire
7–29	Edinburgh Military Tattoo, Edinburgh Castle
7–31	Edinburgh International Festival
*24–25	Notting Hill Carnival, London
Late Aug–Late Oct	Blackpool Illuminations, Blackpool Promenade

SEPTEMBER
2–7	RHS Wisley Flower Show, RHS Garden, Wisley
6	Braemar Royal Highland Gathering, Aberdeenshire
8	International Literacy Day
10–13	Heritage Open Days, England
Mid-Sep	TUC Annual Congress
19–23	Liberal Democrat Party Conference, Bournemouth
Sep–Oct	Labour Party Conference, Brighton
Sep–Oct	Conservative Party Conference, Manchester

OCTOBER
8–11	Frieze Art Fair, Regent's Park, London
Mid-Oct	Booker Prize
Mid-Oct	BFI London Film Festival

NOVEMBER
Early-Nov	London to Brighton Veteran Car Run
14 Nov	Lord Mayor's Procession and Show, City of London
Mid-Nov	CBI Annual Conference

SPORTS EVENTS

JANUARY 2015

11–18	Snooker: Masters, Alexandra Palace, London
17–8 Feb	Football: Africa Cup of Nations, Morocco
19–1 Feb	Tennis: Australian Open, Melbourne, Australia

FEBRUARY

1	American Football: Superbowl XLIX, Arizona, USA
6–21 March	Rugby Union: Six Nations Championship
9–15	Squash: British National Championships, Manchester
14–29	Cricket: ICC Cricket World Cup, Australia and New Zealand

MARCH

1	Football: League Cup Final: Wembley Stadium, London
6–8	Athletics: World Indoor Championships, Prague, Czech Republic

APRIL

9–11	Horse racing: Grand National, Aintree, Liverpool
9–12	Golf: Masters, Augusta, Georgia, USA
11	Rowing: The Boat Race, Putney to Mortlake, London
18–4 May	Snooker: World Championship, Crucible Theatre, Sheffield
26	Athletics: London Marathon

MAY

2	Rugby Union: The European Rugby Champions Cup, Twickenham
6–10	Equestrian: Badminton Horse Trials, Badminton
Early May	Horse racing: Guineas Festival, Newmarket
13–17	Equestrian: Royal Windsor Horse Show, Home Park, Windsor
24–7 Jun	Tennis: French Open, Paris
27	Football: UEFA Europa League Final, Warsaw, Poland
28–31	Golf: Royal Irish Open, Royal County Down Golf Club, N. Ireland
30	Football: FA Cup Final, Wembley Stadium, London
30	Football: Scottish Cup Final, Hampden Park, Glasgow
30–12 Jun	Motorcycling: TT Races, Isle of Man

JUNE

6	Football: UEFA Champions League Final, Berlin, Germany
6	Horse racing: The Derby, Epsom Downs
15–20	Golf: British Amateur Golf Championship, Carnoustie, Angus
15–21	Golf: US Open, Chambers Way, Washington State
16–20	Horse racing: Royal Ascot
29–12 Jul	Tennis: Wimbledon Championship, All England Lawn Tennis Club, London

JULY

1–5	Rowing: Henley Royal Regatta, Henley-on-Thames
3–5	Motor Sport: British Formula 1 Grand Prix, Silverstone
4–26	Cycling: Tour de France
9–12	Cricket: Ashes First Test, Cardiff
12–19	Golf: Open Championship, St Andrews
16–20	Cricket: Ashes Second Test, Lord's
29–2 Aug	Cricket: Ashes Third Test, Edgbaston
30–2 Aug	Golf: Women's British Open, Turnberry
Late Jul	Horse racing: King George VI and Queen Elizabeth Diamond Stakes, Ascot

AUGUST

5–16	Swimming: World Masters Championships, Kazan, Russia
6–10	Cricket: Ashes Fourth Test, Trent Bridge
8–15	Sailing: Cowes Week, Isle of Wight
13–16	Golf: PGA Championship, Whistling Straights, Wisconsin, USA
20–24	Cricket: Ashes Fifth Test, Kia Oval
22–30	Athletics: 15th IAAF World Championships, Beijing, China
29	Rugby League: Challenge Cup Final, Wembley Stadium, London
31–13 Sep	Tennis: US Open, New York
Late Aug–Sep	Athletics: 11th All African Games, Brazzaville, Republic of the Congo

SEPTEMBER

Early Sep	Equestrian: Burghley Horse Trials, Stamford, Lincolnshire
Early Sep	Horse racing: St Leger, Doncaster
18–31 Oct	Rugby Union: 2015 Rugby World Cup, England
Late Sep–Early Oct	Horse racing: Cambridgeshire Meeting, Newmarket
Late Sep–Early Oct	Athletics: Great North Run, Newcastle

OCTOBER

Early Oct	Equestrian: Horse of the Year Show, NEC, Birmingham
Early–Mid-Oct	Rugby League: Super League Final, Old Trafford, Manchester
Mid-Oct	Horse racing: Champions Meeting, Newmarket

NOVEMBER

Mid-Nov	Tennis: ATP World Tour Finals, O2 Arena, London

CENTENARIES

2015

1515
22 Sep   Anne of Cleves, fourth wife of Henry VIII, born

1715
1 Sep   Louis XIV ('the Sun King'), King of France 1643–1715, died
23 Oct   Peter II, Emperor of Russia 1727–30, born

1815
11 Jan   Sir John Macdonald, first prime minister of Canada, born
15 Jan   Emma, Lady Hamilton, mistress of Horatio Nelson, died
1 Apr   Otto von Bismarck, first chancellor of the German Empire, born
24 Apr   Anthony Trollope, novelist, born

1915
11 Jan   Lt.-Col. Robert Blair 'Paddy' Mayne, founding member of the Special Air Service (SAS), born
30 Jan   John Profumo, CBE, Conservative minister at the centre of the Profumo Affair scandal, born
1 Feb   Sir Stanley Matthews, footballer who won the first Ballon d'Or, born
4 Feb   Sir Norman Wisdom, comedian, born
21 Feb   Ann Sheridan, American film actor, born
23 Feb   Paul Tibbetts, Jr., American pilot of the *Enola Gay* aircraft, born
7 Apr   Billie Holiday, American jazz singer and songwriter, born
10 Apr   Harry Morgan, American actor who starred in *M*A*S*H*, born
22 Apr   Second Battle of Ypres began
23 Apr   Rupert Brooke, war poet, died
25 Apr   Anzac forces landed at Gallipoli.
6 May   Orson Welles, American actor and director, born
7 May   RMS *Lusitania* torpedoed and sunk by a German U-boat
10 May   Sir Denis Thatcher, husband of former prime minister Margaret Thatcher, born
9 Jun   Les Paul, American guitarist and inventor of the solid-body electric guitar, born
10 Jun   Saul Bellow, American Pulitzer and Nobel Prize winning author, born
29 Aug   Ingrid Bergman, Swedish actor, born
15 Sep   Helmut Schön, West German football manager whose team won the 1974 World Cup, born
12 Oct   Edith Cavell, nurse and heroine of the First World War, died
17 Oct   Arthur Miller, American playwright, born
23 Oct   William Gilbert 'W. G.' Grace, England cricketer, died

24 Oct   Bob Kane, American comic book artist who did the original drawings for *Batman*, born
25 Nov   Gen. Augusto Pinochet, president of Chile 1974–90, born
12 Dec   Frank Sinatra, American singer and film actor, born
19 Dec   Édith Piaf, French singer, born

2016

1716
20 Jan   King Charles III of Spain, born
5 Aug   Silahdar Damat Ali Pasha, Grand Vizier of the Ottoman Empire 1713–16, died

1816
20 Mar   Queen Maria I of Portugal, died.
21 Apr   Charlotte Brontë, novelist and poet, born
5 Jun   Giovanni Paisiello, Italian composer, died
30 Jun   Richard Lindon, inventor of the rugby ball, born
9 Jul   Argentina declared independence from Spain
13 Dec   Ernst Werner von Siemens, German inventor and industrialist, born

1916
6 Feb   Rubén Darío, Nicaraguan writer, died
21 Feb   Battle of Verdun began
28 Feb   Henry James, writer, died
6 Mar   German car manufacturer BMW, founded
11 Mar   Harold Wilson, prime minister 1974–6, born
5 Apr   Gregory Peck, American actor, born
22 Apr   Yehudi Menuhin, violinist, born
24 Apr   Easter Rising began in Ireland
31 May   Battle of Jutland began
4 Jun   The Brusilov Offensive began
5 Jun   Lord Kitchener (1st Earl Kitchener), Secretary of State for War (1914–16), died
8 Jun   Francis Crick, molecular biologist and co-discoverer of the structure of DNA, born
1 Jul   Battle of the Somme began
23 Jul   Sir William Ramsay, Scottish chemist, born
13 Sep   Roald Dahl, children's author, born
11 Oct   King Otto of Bavaria, died
21 Oct   Karl von Stürgkh, Austrian prime minister, assassinated
26 Oct   François Mitterand, President of France 1981–95, born
21 Nov   Emperor Franz Joseph I of Austria, died
22 Nov   Jack London, American author, died
9 Dec   Kirk Douglas, American actor, born
17 Dec   Grigori Rasputin, Russian mystic and private adviser to the Romanovs, murdered

THE UNITED KINGDOM

THE UK IN FIGURES

The United Kingdom comprises Great Britain (England, Wales and Scotland) and Northern Ireland. The Isle of Man and the Channel Islands are Crown dependencies with their own legislative systems and are not part of the UK.

ABBREVIATIONS

ONS	Office for National Statistics
NISRA	Northern Ireland Statistics and Research Agency

All data is for the UK unless otherwise stated.

AREA OF THE UNITED KINGDOM

	Sq. km	Sq. miles
United Kingdom	243,122	93,870
England	130,280	50,301
Wales	20,733	8,005
Scotland	77,958	30,100
Northern Ireland	14,150	5,463

Source: ONS (Crown copyright)

POPULATION

The first official census of population in England, Wales and Scotland was taken in 1801 and a census has been taken every ten years since, except in 1941 when there was no census because of the Second World War. The last official census in the UK was taken on 27 March 2011.

The first official census of population in Ireland was taken in 1841. However, all figures given below refer only to the area which is now Northern Ireland. Figures for Northern Ireland in 1921 and 1931 are estimates based on the censuses taken in 1926 and 1937 respectively.

Estimates of the population of England before 1801, calculated from the number of baptisms, burials and marriages, are:

1570	4,160,221	1670	5,773,646
1600	4,811,718	1700	6,045,008
1630	5,600,517	1750	6,517,035

Further details are available on the ONS website (W www.ons.gov.uk).

CENSUS RESULTS *Thousands*

	United Kingdom			England and Wales			Scotland			Northern Ireland		
	Total	Male	Female	Total	Male	Female	Total	Male	Female	Total	Male	Female
1801	—	—	—	8,893	4,255	4,638	1,608	739	869	—	—	—
1811	13,368	6,368	7,000	10,165	4,874	5,291	1,806	826	980	—	—	—
1821	15,472	7,498	7,974	12,000	5,850	6,150	2,092	983	1,109	—	—	—
1831	17,835	8,647	9,188	13,897	6,771	7,126	2,364	1,114	1,250	—	—	—
1841	20,183	9,819	10,364	15,914	7,778	8,137	2,620	1,242	1,378	1,649	800	849
1851	22,259	10,855	11,404	17,928	8,781	9,146	2,889	1,376	1,513	1,443	698	745
1861	24,525	11,894	12,631	20,066	9,776	10,290	3,062	1,450	1,612	1,396	668	728
1871	27,431	13,309	14,122	22,712	11,059	11,653	3,360	1,603	1,757	1,359	647	712
1881	31,015	15,060	15,955	25,974	12,640	13,335	3,736	1,799	1,936	1,305	621	684
1891	34,264	16,593	17,671	29,003	14,060	14,942	4,026	1,943	2,083	1,236	590	646
1901	38,237	18,492	19,745	32,528	15,729	16,799	4,472	2,174	2,298	1,237	590	647
1911	42,082	20,357	21,725	36,070	17,446	18,625	4,761	2,309	2,452	1,251	603	648
1921	44,027	21,033	22,994	37,887	18,075	19,811	4,882	2,348	2,535	1,258	610	648
1931	46,038	22,060	23,978	39,952	19,133	20,819	4,843	2,326	2,517	1,243	601	642
1951	50,225	24,118	26,107	43,758	21,016	22,742	5,096	2,434	2,662	1,371	668	703
1961	52,709	25,481	27,228	46,105	22,304	23,801	5,179	2,483	2,697	1,425	694	731
1971	55,515	26,952	28,562	48,750	23,683	25,067	5,229	2,515	2,714	1,536	755	781
1981	55,848	27,104	28,742	49,155	23,873	25,281	5,131	2,466	2,664	1,533*	750	783
1991	56,467	27,344	29,123	49,890	24,182	25,707	4,999	2,392	2,607	1,578	769	809
2001	58,789	28,581	30,208	52,042	25,327	26,715	5,062	2,432	2,630	1,685	821	864
2011	63,182	31,028	32,153	56,076	27,574	28,502	5,295	2,567	2,728	1,810	887	923

* Figure includes 44,500 non-enumerated persons

ISLANDS

	Isle of Man			Jersey			Guernsey		
	Total	Male	Female	Total	Male	Female	Total	Male	Female
1901	54,752	25,496	29,256	52,576	23,940	28,636	40,446	19,652	20,794
1921	60,284	27,329	32,955	49,701	22,438	27,263	38,315	18,246	20,069
1951	55,123	25,749	29,464	57,296	27,282	30,014	43,652	21,221	22,431
1971	56,289	26,461	29,828	72,532	35,423	37,109	51,458	24,792	26,666
1991	69,788	33,693	36,095	84,082	40,862	43,220	58,867	28,297	30,570
2001	76,315	37,372	38,943	87,186	42,485	44,701	59,807	29,138	30,669
2006	80,058	39,523	40,535	—	—	—	—	—	—
2011	84,497	41,971	42,526	97,857	48,296	49,561	62,915	31,025	31,890

Source: Guernsey Annual Publication Bulletin, Isle of Man Government, States of Jersey Statistics Unit

RESIDENT POPULATION, 2013

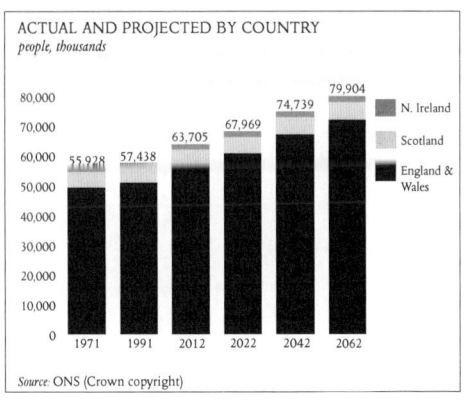

ACTUAL AND PROJECTED BY COUNTRY
people, thousands

Source: ONS (Crown copyright)

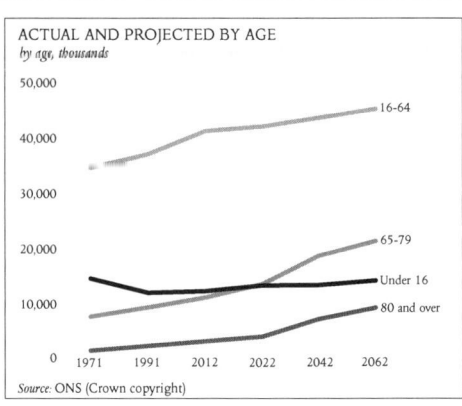

ACTUAL AND PROJECTED BY AGE
by age, thousands

Source: ONS (Crown copyright)

NON-UK BORN RESIDENTS BY COUNTRY OF BIRTH
thousands

	2001	2011
India	468	722
Poland	61	654
Pakistan	321	503
Republic of Ireland	534	468
Germany	266	300
Bangladesh	154	214
South Africa	141	203
Nigeria	88	201
USA	158	197
China	53	170

Source: National Records of Scotland, NISRA, ONS (Crown Copyright)

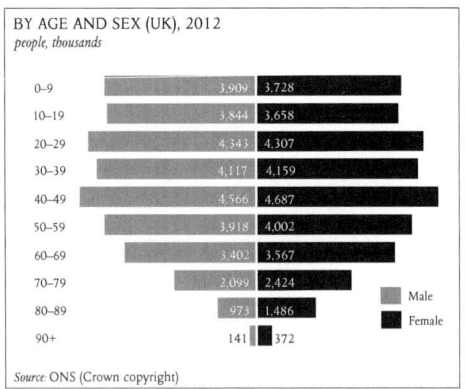

BY AGE AND SEX (UK), 2012
people, thousands

	Male	Female
0–9	3,909	3,728
10–19	3,844	3,658
20–29	4,343	4,307
30–39	4,117	4,159
40–49	4,566	4,687
50–59	3,918	4,002
60–69	3,402	3,567
70–79	2,099	2,424
80–89	973	1,486
90+	141	372

Source: ONS (Crown copyright)

MIGRATION

UK ENTRANCE VISAS ISSUED
by geographical region

	2012	2013
Europe	197,613	207,901
Africa	230,403	239,507
Americas	249,085	259,815
Asia	1,127,243	1,081,017
Middle East	197,613	207,901
Oceania	101,128	97,283
ALL NATIONALITIES	2,061,139	2,056,593

Source: ONS (Crown copyright)

BIRTHS

	Live births	Birth rate*
United Kingdom	779,795	12.2
England and Wales	698,512	12.3
Scotland	56,014	10.5
†Northern Ireland	25,269	13.9

* Live births per 1,000 population
† Northern Ireland figures are for 2012; England, Wales and Scotland figures are for 2013
Source: General Register Office for Scotland, NISRA, ONS (Crown copyright)

FERTILITY RATES
Total fertility rate is the average number of children which would be born to a woman if she experienced the age-specific fertility rates of the period in question throughout her child-bearing life span. The figures for the years 1960–2 are estimates.

	1960–2	2000	2013
United Kingdom	3.07	1.65	1.83
England and Wales	2.77	1.72	1.85
Scotland	2.98	1.48	1.61
Northern Ireland	3.47	1.75	*2.03

* Figure for 2012
Source: General Register Office for Scotland, NISRA, ONS (Crown copyright)

MATERNITY RATES FOR ENGLAND AND WALES 2012

	All maternities*	Singleton	All multiple†	Twins	Triplets
All ages	721,574	710,133	11,441	11,228	208
<20	33,805	33,579	226	225	1
20–24	131,863	130,624	1,239	1,217	21
25–29	200,636	198,004	2,632	2,594	38
30–34	213,333	209,573	3,760	3,701	56
35–39	112,715	110,090	2,625	2,568	56
40–44	27,439	26,686	753	726	27
45+	1,783	1,577	206	197	9

* Includes stillbirths
† Total includes rates for twins, triplets, quads and above
Source: ONS (Crown copyright)

TOP TEN BABY NAMES (ENGLAND AND WALES)

	1914		2013	
	Girls	*Boys*	*Girls*	*Boys*
1	Mary	John	Amelia	Oliver
2	Margaret	William	Olivia	Jack
3	Doris	George	Emily	Harry
4	Dorothy	Thomas	Ava	Jacob
5	Kathleen	James	Isla	Charlie
6	Florence	Arthur	Jessica	Thomas
7	Elsie	Frederick	Poppy	Oscar
8	Edith	Albert	Isabella	William
9	Elizabeth	Charles	Sophie	James
10	Winifred	Robert	Mia	George

Source: ONS (Crown copyright)

LIVE BIRTHS (ENGLAND AND WALES)
by age of mother and registration type

Outside marriage/civil partnership

Year	under 20	20–29	30–39	40+	All ages
1938	4,730	14,158	6,403	1,088	26,379
1952	5,123	16,962	9,041	1,423	32,549
1972	21,737	30,926	8,821	1,027	62,511
1992	40,074	132,961	39,852	2,338	215,225
2012	32,520	198,644	103,947	11,374	346,485

Within marriage/civil partnership

Year	under 20	20–29	30–39	40+	All ages
1938	20,680	332,448	216,226	25,471	594,825
1952	24,025	386,782	207,950	22,429	641,186
1972	57,350	465,859	129,739	9,981	662,929
1992	7,787	275,148	183,637	7,859	474,431
2012	1,295	136,182	227,092	18,620	383,189

Source: ONS (Crown copyright)

MARRIAGE AND DIVORCE

	Marriages	Divorces
United Kingdom	*301,254	130,284
England and Wales	*262,240	118,140
Scotland	30,534	†9,700
Northern Ireland	8,480	2,444

* Provisional figures

Source: NISRA, ONS (Crown copyright), Scottish Government

LEGAL ABORTIONS

	2002	2013
England and Wales	175,932	185,331
Scotland	11,870	11,777

Source: Department of Health, NHS Scotland

DEATHS

INFANT MORTALITY RATE 2012*

United Kingdom	3.7
England and Wales	4.0
Scotland	3.7
Northern Ireland	3.5

* Deaths of infants under one year of age per 1,000 live births

Source: NISRA, ONS (Crown copyright), Scottish Government

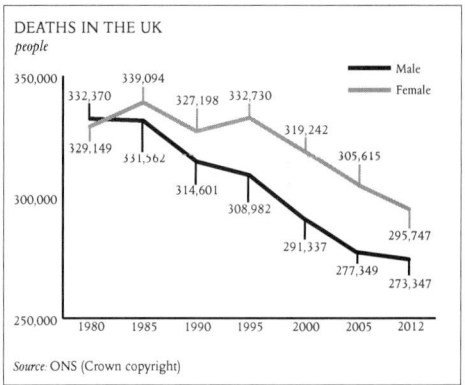

DEATHS IN THE UK
people

Source: ONS (Crown copyright)

EMPLOYMENT

MEDIAN FULL-TIME GROSS ANNUAL EARNINGS
BY REGION (£)

Region	2000	2013
UK	18,848	27,017
England	19,107	27,376
North East	17,430	24,084
North West	17,863	25,097
Yorkshire and the Humber	17,503	24,954
East Midlands	17,352	24,918
West Midlands	17,812	25,341
East	19,020	26,483
London	24,204	35,238
South East	19,992	28,400
South West	17,847	25,251
Wales	17,157	24,182
Scotland	18,029	26,472
Northern Ireland	16,355	23,904

Source: ONS (Crown Copyright)

HOUSE PRICES

Average Price

Year	£	Year	£
1930	1,000	2000	102,000
1950	2,000	2005	191,000
1960	3,000	2009	226,000
1970	5,000	2010	251,000
1980	24,000	2011	245,000
1990	60,000	2012	246,000
1995	66,000	2013	251,000

Source: ONS (Crown Copyright)

ORIGINS OF UK FOOD

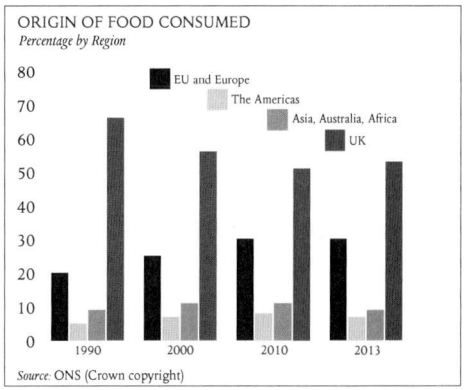

ORIGIN OF FOOD CONSUMED
Percentage by Region

Source: ONS (Crown copyright)

DEATHS BY CAUSE, 2013

	England and Wales	Scotland	N. Ireland*
Total deaths	506,790	54,700	14,756
Deaths from natural causes	487,869	52,114	14,019
Certain infectious and parasitic diseases	5,305	754	166
Intestinal infectious diseases	1,578	142	46
Respiratory and other tuberculosis	280	31	9
Meningococcal infection	45	7	2
Viral hepatitis	234	28	4
Human immunodeficiency virus (HIV)	208	14	3
Neoplasms	145,344	16,161	4,260
Malignant neoplasms	141,909	15,858	4,134
Malignant neoplasm of trachea, bronchus and lung	30,437	4,120	957
Malignant melanoma of skin	2,109	180	44
Malignant neoplasm of breast	10,230	1,020	292
Malignant neoplasm of cervix uteri	774	91	22
Malignant neoplasm of prostate	9,726	876	267
Leukaemia	4,269	378	107
Diseases of the blood and blood-forming organs and certain			
disorders involving the immune mechanism	956	113	37
Endocrine, nutritional and metabolic diseases	6,778	938	240
Diabetes mellitus	4,974	708	174
Mental and behavioural disorders	38,233	3,912	1,092
Vascular and unspecified dementia	37,325	3,623	1,014
Diseases of the nervous system	22,504	2,434	806
Meningitis (excluding meningococcal)	147	12	5
Alzheimer's disease	9,787	1,196	406
Diseases of the circulatory system	140,301	15,568	4,001
Ischaemic heart diseases	63,872	7,239	1,975
Cerebrovascular diseases	34,764	4,446	1,077
Diseases of the respiratory system	74,229	7,025	2,023
Influenza	140	59	2
Pneumonia	26,626	1,996	807
Bronchitis, emphysema and other chronic obstructive pulmonary			
diseases	27,393	2,943	728
Asthma	1,113	105	31
Diseases of the digestive system	24,358	2,868	670
Gastric and duodenal ulcer	1,976	114	34
Diseases of the liver	7,522	1,024	229
Diseases of the skin and subcutaneous tissue	1,720	162	25
Diseases of the musculo-skeletal system and connective tissue	4,221	363	91
Osteoporosis	1,260	58	11
Diseases of the genitourinary system	9,631	1,081	358
Complications of pregnancy, childbirth and the puerperium	47	3	0
Certain conditions originating in the perinatal period†	167	102	41
Congenital malformations, deformations and chromosomal			
abnormalities†	1,126	148	78
Symptoms, signs and abnormal findings not classified elsewhere	11,018	476	131
Senility	9,365	288	104
Sudden infant death syndrome	160	17	2
Deaths from external causes	18,921	2,586	737
Suicide and intentional self-harm	3,977	601	203
Assault	‡309	58	26

* Figures for Northern Ireland are for 2012

† Excludes neonatal deaths (those at age under 28 days): for England and Wales neonatal deaths are included in the total number of deaths but excluded from the cause figures

‡ This will not be a true figure as registration of homicide and assault deaths in England and Wales is often delayed by adjourned inquests

Source: General Register Office for Scotland, NISRA, ONS (Crown copyright)

THE NATIONAL FLAG

The national flag of the United Kingdom is the Union Flag, generally known as the Union Jack.

The Union Flag is a combination of the cross of St George, patron saint of England, the cross of St Andrew, patron saint of Scotland and the cross of St Patrick, patron saint of Ireland.

Cross of St George: cross Gules in a field Argent (red cross on a white ground)

Cross of St Andrew: saltire Argent in a field Azure (white diagonal cross on a blue ground)

Cross of St Patrick: saltire Gules in a field Argent (red diagonal cross on a white ground)

A flag combining the cross of St George and the cross of St Andrew was first introduced by royal decree in 1606 following the conjoining of the English and Scottish crowns in 1603. In 1707 this flag became the flag of Great Britain after the parliaments of the two kingdoms were united. The cross of St Patrick was added in 1801 after the union of Great Britain and Ireland.

See also Flags of the World colour plates.

FLYING THE UNION FLAG

The correct orientation of the Union Flag when flying is with the broader diagonal band of white uppermost in the hoist (ie near the pole) and the narrower diagonal band of white uppermost in the fly (ie furthest from the pole).

The flying of the Union Flag on government buildings is decided by the Department for Culture, Media and Sport (DCMS) at the Queen's command. There is no formal definition of a government building but it is generally accepted to mean a building owned or used by the Crown and/or predominantly occupied or used by civil servants or the Armed Forces.

The Scottish or Welsh governments are responsible for drawing up their own flag-flying guidance for their buildings. In Northern Ireland, the flying of flags is constrained by The Flags Regulations (Northern Ireland) 2000 and the Police Emblems and Flag Regulations (Northern Ireland) 2002. Individuals, local authorities and other organisations may fly the Union Flag whenever they wish, subject to compliance with any local planning requirement.

FLAGS AT HALF-MAST

Flags are flown at half-mast (ie two-thirds up between the top and bottom of the flagstaff) on the following occasions:
• from the announcement of the death of the sovereign until the funeral
• the death or funeral of a member of the royal family*
• the funerals of foreign rulers*
• the funerals of prime ministers and ex-prime ministers of the UK*
• the funerals of first ministers and ex-first ministers of Scotland, Wales and Northern Ireland (unless otherwise commanded by the sovereign, this only applies to flags in their respective countries)*
• other occasions by special command from the Queen

* By special command from the Queen in each case

DAYS FOR FLYING FLAGS

On 25 March 2008 the DCMS announced that UK government departments in England, Scotland and Wales may fly the Union Flag on their buildings whenever they choose and not just on the designated days listed below. In addition, on the patron saints' days of Scotland and Wales, the appropriate national flag may be flown alongside the Union Flag on UK government buildings in the wider Whitehall area. When flying on designated days flags are hoisted from 8am to sunset.

Duchess of Cambridge's birthday	9 Jan
Countess of Wessex's birthday	20 Jan
Accession of the Queen	6 Feb
Duke of York's birthday	19 Feb
St David's Day (in Wales only)*	1 Mar
Commonwealth Day (2015)	9 Mar
Earl of Wessex's birthday	10 Mar
St Patrick's Day (in Northern Ireland only)†	17 Mar
The Queen's birthday	21 Apr
St George's Day (in England only)*	23 Apr
Europe Day†	9 May
Coronation Day	2 Jun
Duke of Edinburgh's birthday	10 Jun
The Queen's official birthday (2015)	13 Jun
Duke of Cambridge's birthday	21 Jun
Duchess of Cornwall's birthday	17 Jul
Princess Royal's birthday	15 Aug
Remembrance Day (2015)	8 Nov
Prince of Wales' birthday	14 Nov
Wedding Day of the Queen	20 Nov
St Andrew's Day (in Scotland only)*	30 Nov
Opening of parliament by the Queen‡	
Prorogation of parliament by the Queen‡	

* The appropriate national flag, or the European flag, may be flown in addition to the Union Flag (where there are two or more flagpoles), but not in a superior position
† Only the Union Flag should be flown
‡ Only in the Greater London area, whether or not the Queen performs the ceremony in person

THE ROYAL STANDARD

The Royal Standard comprises four quarterings – two for England (three lions passant), one for Scotland* (a lion rampant) and one for Ireland (a harp).

The Royal Standard is flown when the Queen is in residence at a royal palace, on transport being used by the Queen for official journeys and from Victoria Tower when the Queen attends parliament. It may also be flown on any building (excluding ecclesiastical buildings) during a visit by the Queen. If the Queen is to be present in a building, advice on flag flying can be obtained from the DCMS.

The Royal Standard is never flown at half-mast, even after the death of the sovereign, as the new monarch immediately succeeds to the throne.

* In Scotland a version with two Scottish quarterings is used

THE ROYAL FAMILY

THE SOVEREIGN

ELIZABETH II, by the Grace of God, of the United Kingdom of Great Britain and Northern Ireland and of her other Realms and Territories Queen, Head of the Commonwealth, Defender of the Faith
Her Majesty Elizabeth Alexandra Mary of Windsor, elder daughter of King George VI and of HM Queen Elizabeth the Queen Mother
Born 21 April 1926, at 17 Bruton Street, London W1
Ascended the throne 6 February 1952
Crowned 2 June 1953, at Westminster Abbey
Married 20 November 1947, in Westminster Abbey, HRH the Prince Philip, Duke of Edinburgh
Official residences Buckingham Palace, London SW1A 1AA; Windsor Castle, Berks; Palace of Holyroodhouse, Edinburgh
Private residences Sandringham, Norfolk; Balmoral Castle, Aberdeenshire

HUSBAND OF THE QUEEN

HRH THE PRINCE PHILIP, DUKE OF EDINBURGH, KG, KT, OM, GBE, Royal Victorian Chain, AC, QSO, PC, Ranger of Windsor Park
Born 10 June 1921, son of Prince and Princess Andrew of Greece and Denmark, naturalised a British subject 1947, created Duke of Edinburgh, Earl of Merioneth and Baron Greenwich 1947

CHILDREN OF THE QUEEN

HRH THE PRINCE OF WALES (Prince Charles Philip Arthur George), KG, KT, GCB, OM and Great Master of the Order of the Bath, AK, QSO, PC, ADC(P)
Born 14 November 1948, created Prince of Wales and Earl of Chester 1958, succeeded as Duke of Cornwall, Duke of Rothesay, Earl of Carrick and Baron Renfrew, Lord of the Isles and Great Steward of Scotland 1952
Married (1) 29 July 1981 Lady Diana Frances Spencer (Diana, Princess of Wales (1961–97), youngest daughter of the 8th Earl Spencer and the Hon. Mrs Shand Kydd), marriage dissolved 1996; (2) 9 April 2005 Mrs Camilla Rosemary Parker Bowles, now HRH the Duchess of Cornwall, GCVO (*born* 17 July 1947, daughter of Major Bruce Shand and the Hon. Mrs Rosalind Shand)
Residences Clarence House, London SW1A 1BA; Highgrove, Doughton, Tetbury, Glos GL8 8TN; Birkhall, Ballater, Aberdeenshire
Issue
1. HRH Duke of Cambridge (Prince William Arthur Philip Louis), KG, KT *born* 21 June 1982, *created* Duke of Cambridge, Earl of Strathearn and Baron Carrickfergus 2011 *married* 29 April 2011 Catherine Elizabeth Middleton, now HRH the Duchess of Cambridge (*born* 9 January 1982, elder daughter of Michael and Carole Middleton), and has issue, HRH Prince George of Cambridge (Prince George Alexander Louis), *born* 22 July 2013
Residence Kensington Palace, London W8 4PU; Amner Hall, Norfolk PE31 6RW
2. HRH Prince Henry of Wales (Prince Henry Charles Albert David), *born* 15 September 1984
Residence Nottingham Cottage, Kensington Palace, London W8 4PU

HRH THE PRINCESS ROYAL (Princess Anne Elizabeth Alice Louise), KG, KT, GCVO
Born 15 August 1950, declared the Princess Royal 1987
Married (1) 14 November 1973 Captain Mark Anthony Peter Phillips, CVO (*born* 22 September 1948); marriage dissolved 1992; (2) 12 December 1992 Vice-Adm. Sir Timothy James Hamilton Laurence, KCVO, CB, ADC (P) (*born* 1 March 1955)
Residence Gatcombe Park, Minchinhampton, Glos GL6 9AT
Issue
1. Peter Mark Andrew Phillips, *born* 15 November 1977, *married* 17 May 2008 Autumn Patricia Kelly, and has issue, Savannah Phillips, *born* 29 December 2010; Isla Elizabeth Phillips, *born* 29 March 2012
2. Zara Anne Elizabeth Tindall, MBE, *born* 15 May 1981, *married* 30 July 2011 Michael James Tindall, MBE, and has issue, Mia Grace Tindall, *born* 17 January 2014

HRH THE DUKE OF YORK (Prince Andrew Albert Christian Edward), KG, GCVO, ADC(P)
Born 19 February 1960, created Duke of York, Earl of Inverness and Baron Killyleagh 1986
Married 23 July 1986 Sarah Margaret Ferguson, now Sarah, Duchess of York (*born* 15 October 1959, younger daughter of Major Ronald Ferguson and Mrs Hector Barrantes), marriage dissolved 1996
Residence Royal Lodge, Windsor Great Park, Berks
Issue
1. HRH Princess Beatrice of York (Princess Beatrice Elizabeth Mary), *born* 8 August 1988
2. HRH Princess Eugenie of York (Princess Eugenie Victoria Helena), *born* 23 March 1990

HRH THE EARL OF WESSEX (Prince Edward Antony Richard Louis), KG, GCVO, ADC(P)
Born 10 March 1964, created Earl of Wessex, Viscount Severn 1999
Married 19 June 1999 Sophie Helen Rhys-Jones, now HRH the Countess of Wessex, GCVO (*born* 20 January 1965, daughter of Mr and Mrs Christopher Rhys-Jones)
Residence Bagshot Park, Bagshot, Surrey GU19 5HS
Issue
1. Lady Louise Mountbatten-Windsor (Louise Alice Elizabeth Mary Mountbatten-Windsor), *born* 8 November 2003
2. Viscount Severn (James Alexander Philip Theo Mountbatten-Windsor), *born* 17 December 2007

NEPHEW AND NIECE OF THE QUEEN

Children of HRH the Princess Margaret, Countess of Snowdon and the Earl of Snowdon (*see* House of Windsor):

DAVID ALBERT CHARLES ARMSTRONG-JONES, VISCOUNT LINLEY, *born* 3 November 1961, *married* 8 October 1993 Hon. Serena Alleyne Stanhope, and has issue, Hon. Charles Patrick Inigo Armstrong-Jones, *born* 1 July 1999; Hon. Margarita Elizabeth Alleyne Armstrong-Jones, *born* 14 May 2002

LADY SARAH CHATTO (Sarah Frances Elizabeth), *born* 1 May 1964, *married* 14 July 1994 Daniel Chatto, and has issue, Samuel David Benedict Chatto, *born* 28 July 1996; Arthur Robert Nathaniel Chatto, *born* 5 February 1999

COUSINS OF THE QUEEN

Child of HRH the Duke of Gloucester and HRH Princess Alice, Duchess of Gloucester (*see* House of Windsor):
HRH THE DUKE OF GLOUCESTER (Prince Richard Alexander Walter George), KG, GCVO, Grand Prior of the Order of St John of Jerusalem
Born 26 August 1944
Married 8 July 1972 Birgitte Eva van Deurs, now HRH the Duchess of Gloucester, GCVO (*born* 20 June 1946, daughter of Asger Henriksen and Vivian van Deurs)
Residence Kensington Palace, London W8 4PU
Issue
1.   Earl of Ulster (Alexander Patrick Gregers Richard), *born* 24 October 1974 *married* 22 June 2002 Dr Claire Alexandra Booth, and has issue, Lord Culloden (Xan Richard Anders), *born* 12 March 2007; Lady Cosima Windsor (Cosima Rose Alexandra), *born* 20 May 2010
2.   Lady Davina Lewis (Davina Elizabeth Alice Benedikte), *born* 19 November 1977 *married* 31 July 2004 Gary Christie Lewis, and has issue, Senna Kowhai Lewis, *born* 22 June 2010; Tane Mahuta Lewis, *born* 25 May 2012
3.   Lady Rose Gilman (Rose Victoria Birgitte Louise), *born* 1 March 1980 *married* 19 July 2008 George Edward Gilman, and has issue, Lyla Beatrix Christabel Gilman, *born* 30 May 2010; Rufus Gilman, *born* October/November 2012

Children of HRH the Duke of Kent and Princess Marina, Duchess of Kent (*see* House of Windsor):

HRH THE DUKE OF KENT (Prince Edward George Nicholas Paul Patrick), KG, GCMG, GCVO, ADC(P)
Born 9 October 1935
Married 8 June 1961 Katharine Lucy Mary Worsley, now HRH the Duchess of Kent, GCVO (*born* 22 February 1933, daughter of Sir William Worsley, Bt.)
Residence Wren House, Palace Green, London W8 4PY
Issue
1.   Earl of St Andrews (George Philip Nicholas), *born* 26 June 1962, *married* 9 January 1988 Sylvana Tomaselli, and has issue, Lord Downpatrick (Edward Edmund Maximilian George), *born* 2 December 1988; Lady Marina-Charlotte Windsor (Marina-Charlotte Alexandra Katharine Helen), *born* 30 September 1992; Lady Amelia Windsor (Amelia Sophia Theodora Mary Margaret), *born* 24 August 1995

2.   Lady Helen Taylor (Helen Marina Lucy), *born* 28 April 1964, *married* 18 July 1992 Timothy Verner Taylor, and has issue, Columbus George Donald Taylor, *born* 6 August 1994; Cassius Edward Taylor, *born* 26 December 1996; Eloise Olivia Katharine Taylor, *born* 3 March 2003; Estella Olga Elizabeth Taylor, *born* 21 December 2004
3.   Lord Nicholas Windsor (Nicholas Charles Edward Jonathan), *born* 25 July 1970, *married* 4 November 2006 Princess Paola Doimi de Lupis Frankopan Subic Zrinski, and has issue, Albert Louis Philip Edward Windsor, *born* 22 September 2007; Leopold Ernest Augustus Guelph Windsor, *born* 8 September 2009; Louis Arthur Nicholas Felix Windsor, *born* 27 May 2014

HRH PRINCESS ALEXANDRA, THE HON. LADY OGILVY (Princess Alexandra Helen Elizabeth Olga Christabel), KG, GCVO
Born 25 December 1936
Married 24 April 1963 the Rt. Hon. Sir Angus Ogilvy, KCVO (1928–2004), second son of 12th Earl of Airlie
Residence Thatched House Lodge, Richmond Park, Surrey TW10 5HP
Issue
1.   James Robert Bruce Ogilvy, *born* 29 February 1964, *married* 30 July 1988 Julia Rawlinson, and has issue, Flora Alexandra Ogilvy, *born* 15 December 1994; Alexander Charles Ogilvy, *born* 12 November 1996
2.   Marina Victoria Alexandra Ogilvy, *born* 31 July 1966, *married* 2 February 1990 Paul Julian Mowatt (marriage dissolved 1997), and has issue, Zenouska May Mowatt, *born* 26 May 1990; Christian Alexander Mowatt, *born* 4 June 1993

HRH PRINCE MICHAEL OF KENT (Prince Michael George Charles Franklin), GCVO
Born 4 July 1942
Married 30 June 1978 Baroness Marie-Christine Agnes Hedwig Ida von Reibnitz, now HRH Princess Michael of Kent (*born* 15 January 1945, daughter of Baron Gunther von Reibnitz)
Residence Kensington Palace, London W8 4PU
Issue
1.   Lord Frederick Windsor (Frederick Michael George David Louis), *born* 6 April 1979, *married* 12 September 2009 Sophie Winkleman, and has issue, Maud Elizabeth Daphne Marina, *born* 15 August 2013
2.   Lady Gabriella Windsor (Gabriella Marina Alexandra Ophelia), *born* 23 April 1981

ORDER OF SUCCESSION

The Succession to the Crown Act 2013, received royal assent on 25 April 2013 and makes provision for the order of succession to the Crown not to be dependent on gender and for those members of the royal family married to a Roman Catholic to retain the right of succession to the throne. The Act will come into force after all the remaining 15 Realms of the Commonwealth have enacted similar legislation and an order is issued by the Lord President of the Council.

When the Succession to the Crown Act 2013 commences HRH Prince Michael of Kent, the Earl of St Andrews and HRH Prince Michael of Kent will be restored to the succession. In addition, all male members of the royal family born after 28 October 2011 will no longer precede any elder female siblings; and their place in the order of succession will change accordingly.

The following list includes all those members of the royal family listed on pages 20 and 21 who are entitled to succeed to the Crown under the current legislation (the living descendants of the sons of King George V). Lord Nicholas Windsor, Lord Downpatrick and Lady Marina-Charlotte Windsor renounced their rights to the throne on converting to Roman Catholicism in 2001, 2003 and 2008 respectively. Their children remain in succession provided that they are in communion with the Church of England.

1	HRH the Prince of Wales	27	Lady Davina Lewis
2	HRH the Duke of Cambridge	28	Tane Lewis
3	HRH Prince George of Cambridge	29	Senna Lewis
4	HRH Prince Henry of Wales	30	Lady Rose Gilman
5	HRH the Duke of York	31	Rufus Gilman
6	HRH Princess Beatrice of York	32	Lyla Gilman
7	HRH Princess Eugenie of York	33	HRH the Duke of Kent
8	HRH the Earl of Wessex	34	Lady Amelia Windsor
9	Viscount Severn	35	Albert Windsor
10	Lady Louise Mountbatten-Windsor	36	Leopold Windsor
11	HRH the Princess Royal	37	Louis Windsor
12	Peter Phillips	38	Lady Helen Taylor
13	Savannah Phillips	39	Columbus Taylor
14	Isla Phillips	40	Cassius Taylor
15	Zara Tindall	41	Eloise Taylor
16	Mia Tindall	42	Estella Taylor
17	Viscount Linley	43	Lord Frederick Windsor
18	Hon. Charles Armstrong-Jones	44	Maud Windsor
19	Hon. Margarita Armstrong-Jones	45	Lady Gabriella Windsor
20	Lady Sarah Chatto	46	HRH Princess Alexandra, the Hon. Lady Ogilvy
21	Samuel Chatto	47	James Ogilvy
22	Arthur Chatto	48	Alexander Ogilvy
23	HRH the Duke of Gloucester	49	Flora Ogilvy
24	Earl of Ulster	50	Marina Ogilvy
25	Lord Culloden	51	Christian Mowatt
26	Lady Cosima Windsor	52	Zenouska Mowatt

ROYAL HOUSEHOLD

The PRIVATE SECRETARY is responsible for:

- informing and advising the Queen on constitutional, governmental and political matters in the UK, her other Realms and the wider Commonwealth, including communications with the prime minister and government departments
- organising the Queen's domestic and overseas official programme
- the Queen's speeches, messages, patronage, photographs, portraits and official presents
- communications in connection with the role of the royal family
- dealing with correspondence to the Queen from members of the public
- royal travel policy
- coordinating and initiating research to support engagements by members of the royal family

The DIRECTOR OF ROYAL COMMUNICATIONS is in charge of Buckingham Palace's communications office and reports to the private secretary. The director is responsible for:

- developing communications strategies to enhance the public understanding of the role of the monarchy
- briefing the British and international media on the role and duties of the Queen and issues relating to the royal family
- responding to media enquiries
- arranging media facilities in the UK and overseas to support royal functions and engagements
- the management of the royal website

The private secretary is keeper of the royal archives and is responsible for the care of the records of the sovereign and the royal household from previous reigns, preserved in the royal archives at Windsor. As keeper, it is the private secretary's responsibility to ensure the proper management of the records of the present reign with a view to their transfer to the archives as and when appropriate. The private secretary is an *ex officio* trustee of the Royal Collection Trust.

The KEEPER OF THE PRIVY PURSE AND TREASURER to the Queen is responsible for:

- the Sovereign Grant, which is the money paid from the government's Consolidated Fund to meet official expenditure relating to the Queen's duties as head of state and head of the Commonwealth and is provided by the government in return for the net surplus from the Crown Estate and other hereditary revenues (*see also* Royal Finances)
- through the director of personnel, the planning and management of personnel policy across the royal household, the administration of all its pension schemes and private estates employees, and the allocation of employee and pensioner housing
- information technology systems
- property services at occupied royal palaces in England, comprising Buckingham Palace, St James's Palace, Clarence House, Marlborough House Mews, the residential and office areas of Kensington Palace, Windsor Castle and buildings in the Home and Great Parks of Windsor and Hampton Court Mews and Paddocks
- internal audit services
- health and safety; insurance matters
- the privy purse, which is mainly financed by the net income of the Duchy of Lancaster, and meets both official and private expenditure incurred by the Queen

- liaison with other members of the royal family and their households on financial matters
- the Queen's private estates at Sandringham and Balmoral, the Queen's Racing Establishment and the Royal Studs and liaison with the Ascot Authority
- the Home Park at Windsor and liaison with the Crown Estate Commissioners concerning the Home Park and the Great Park at Windsor
- the Royal Philatelic Collection
- administrative aspects of the Military Knights of Windsor
- administration of the Royal Victorian Order, of which the keeper of the privy purse is secretary, Long and Faithful Service Medals, and the Queen's cups, medals and prizes, and policy on commemorative medals

The keeper of the privy purse is one of three royal trustees (in respect of his responsibilities for the Sovereign Grant) and is receiver-general of the Duchy of Lancaster and a member of the Duchy's Council.

The keeper of the privy purse is an *ex officio* trustee of the Historic Royal Palaces Trust and the Royal Collection Trust.

The DIRECTOR OF THE PROPERTY SECTION has day-to-day responsibility for the royal household's property section:

- fire and health and safety
- repairs and refurbishment of buildings and new building work
- utilities and telecommunications
- putting up stages, tents and other work in connection with ceremonial occasions, garden parties and other official functions

The property section is also responsible, on a sub-contract basis from the DCMS, for the maintenance of Marlborough House (which is occupied by the Commonwealth Secretariat).

The MASTER OF THE HOUSEHOLD is responsible for:

- delivering the majority of the official and private entertaining in the Queen's annual programme at residences in the UK, and on occasion overseas
- periodic support for entertaining by other members of the royal family
- furnishings and internal decorative refurbishment in conjunction with the director of the Royal Collection and Property Services
- housekeeping, catering and service provision for the royal household

The COMPTROLLER, LORD CHAMBERLAIN'S OFFICE is responsible for:

- the organisation of all ceremonial engagements, including state visits to the Queen in the UK, royal weddings and funerals, the state opening of parliament, Guards of Honour at Buckingham Palace, investitures, and the Garter and Thistle ceremonies
- garden parties at Buckingham Palace and the Palace of Holyroodhouse (except for catering and tents)
- the Crown Jewels, which are part of the Royal Collection, when they are in use on state occasions
- coordination of the arrangements for the Queen to be represented at funerals and memorial services and at the arrival and departure of visiting heads of state
- delivery of all official and approved travel operations

- advising on matters of precedence, style and titles, dress, flying of flags, gun salutes, mourning and other ceremonial issues
- supervising the applications from tradesmen for Royal Warrants of Appointment
- advising on the commercial use of royal emblems and contemporary royal photographs
- the ecclesiastical household, the medical household, the bodyguards and certain ceremonial appointments such as Gentlemen Ushers and Pages of Honour
- the lords in waiting, who represent the Queen on various occasions and escort visiting heads of state during incoming state visits
- the Queen's bargemaster and watermen and the Queen's swans
- the Royal Almonry

The comptroller is also responsible for the Royal Mews, assisted by the CROWN EQUERRY, who has day-to-day responsibility for:

- the provision of carriage processions for the state opening of parliament, state visits, Trooping of the Colour, Royal Ascot, the Garter Ceremony, the Thistle Service, the presentation of credentials to the Queen by incoming foreign ambassadors and high commissioners, and other state and ceremonial occasions
- the provision of chauffeur-driven cars
- coordinating travel arrangements by road in respect of the royal household
- supervision and administration of the Royal Mews at Buckingham Palace, Windsor Castle, Hampton Court and the Palace of Holyroodhouse

The comptroller also has overall responsibility for the MARSHAL OF THE DIPLOMATIC CORPS, who is responsible for the relationship between the royal household and the Diplomatic Heads of Mission in London; and the SECRETARY OF THE CENTRAL CHANCERY OF THE ORDERS OF KNIGHTHOOD, who administers the Orders of Chivalry, makes arrangements for investitures and the distribution of insignia, and ensures the proper public notification of awards through *The London Gazette;* and the HEAD OF ROYAL TRAVEL, who is responsible for the provision of travel arrangements by air and rail.

The DIRECTOR OF THE ROYAL COLLECTION is responsible for:

- the administration and custodial control of the Royal Collection in all royal residences
- the care, display, conservation and restoration of items in the collection
- initiating and assisting research into the collection and publishing catalogues and books on the collection
- making the collection accessible to the public and educating and informing the public about the collection

The Royal Collection, which contains a large number of works of art, is held by the Queen as sovereign in trust for her successors and the nation and is not owned by her as an individual. The administration, conservation and presentation of the Royal Collection are funded by the Royal Collection Trust solely from income from visitors to Windsor Castle, Buckingham Palace and the Palace of Holyroodhouse. The Royal Collection Trust is chaired by the Prince of Wales. The Lord Chamberlain, the private secretary and the keeper of the privy purse are *ex officio* trustees and there are three external trustees appointed by the Queen.

The director of the Royal Collection is also at present

the SURVEYOR OF THE QUEEN'S WORKS OF ART. The ROYAL LIBRARIAN is responsible for all books, manuscripts, coins and medals, insignia and works of art on paper including the watercolours, prints and drawings in the Print Room at Windsor Castle, and the SURVEYOR OF THE QUEEN'S PICTURES is responsible for pictures and miniatures.

Royal Collection Enterprises Limited is the trading subsidiary of the Royal Collection Trust. The company, whose chair is the Keeper of the Privy Purse, is responsible for:

- managing access by the public to Windsor Castle (including Frogmore House), Buckingham Palace (including the Royal Mews and the Queen's Gallery) and the Palace of Holyroodhouse (including the Queen's Gallery)
- running shops at each location
- managing the images and intellectual property rights of the Royal Collection

The director of the Royal Collection is also an *ex officio* trustee of the Historic Royal Palaces Trust.

PRIVATE SECRETARIES

THE QUEEN
Office: Buckingham Palace, London SW1A 1AA T 020-7930 4832
Private Secretary to the Queen, Rt. Hon. Sir Christopher Geidt, KCB, KCVO, OBE

PRINCE PHILIP, THE DUKE OF EDINBURGH
Office: Buckingham Palace, London SW1A 1AA T 020-7930 4832
Private Secretary, Brig. Archie Miller-Bakewell

THE PRINCE OF WALES AND THE DUCHESS OF CORNWALL
Office: Clarence House, London SW1A 1BA T 020-7930 4832
Principal Private Secretary, William Nye

THE DUKE AND DUCHESS OF CAMBRIDGE AND PRINCE HENRY OF WALES
Office: Kensington Palace, Palace Green, London W8 4PU T 020-7930 4832
Principal Private Secretary, James Lowther-Pinkerton, LVO, MBE

THE DUKE OF YORK
Office: Buckingham Palace, London SW1A 1AA T 020-7024 4227
Private Secretary, Amanda Thirsk, LVO

THE EARL AND COUNTESS OF WESSEX
Office: Bagshot Park, Surrey GU19 5PL T 01276-707040
Private Secretary, Tim Roberts

THE PRINCESS ROYAL
Office: Buckingham Palace, London SW1A 1AA T 020-7024 4199
Private Secretary, Capt. N. P. Wright, CVO, RN

THE DUKE AND DUCHESS OF GLOUCESTER
Office: Kensington Palace, London W8 4PU T 020-7368 1000
Private Secretary, Lt.-Col. Alastair Todd

THE DUKE OF KENT
Office: York House, St James's Palace, London SW1A 1BQ T 020-7930 4872
Private Secretary, Nicholas Marden

THE DUCHESS OF KENT
Office: Wren House, Palace Green, London W8 4PY T 020-7937 2730
Personal Secretary, Chloe Hill

PRINCE AND PRINCESS MICHAEL OF KENT
Office: Kensington Palace, London W8 4PU
W www.princemichael.org.uk
Private Secretary, Nicholas Chance, CVO

PRINCESS ALEXANDRA, THE HON. LADY OGILVY
Office: Buckingham Palace, London SW1A 1AA **T** 020-7024 4270
Private Secretary, Diane Duke, LVO

SENIOR MANAGEMENT OF THE ROYAL HOUSEHOLD

Lord Chamberlain, Earl Peel, GCVO, PC
HEADS OF DEPARTMENT
Private Secretary to The Queen, Rt. Hon. Sir Christopher Geidt, KCB, KCVO, OBE
Keeper of the Privy Purse, Sir Alan Reid, GCVO
Master of the Household, Vice-Adm. Tony Johnstone-Burt, CB, OBE
Comptroller, Lord Chamberlain's Office, Lt.-Col. Sir Andrew Ford, KCVO
Director of the Royal Collection, Jonathan Marsden, CVO
NON-EXECUTIVE MEMBERS
Private Secretary to the Duke of Edinburgh, Brig. Archie Miller-Bakewell
Principal Private Secretary to the Prince of Wales and the Duchess of Cornwall, William Nye

ASTRONOMER ROYAL

The post of Astronomer Royal dates back to 1675, when astronomy had many practical applications in navigation. Today the post is largely honorary, although the Astronomer Royal is expected to be available for consultation on scientific matters for as long as the holder remains a professional astronomer. The Astronomer Royal receives a stipend of £100 a year and is a member of the royal household.

Astronomer Royal, Lord Rees of Ludlow, OM, *apptd* 1995

MASTER OF THE QUEEN'S MUSIC

The office of Master of the Queen's Music is an honour conferred on a musician of great distinction. The office was first created in 1626, when the master was responsible for the court musicians. Since the reign of King George V, the position has had no fixed duties, although the Master may choose to produce compositions to mark royal or state occasions. The Master of the Queen's Music is paid an annual stipend of £15,000. In 2004 the length of appointment was changed from life tenure to a ten-year term.

Master of the Queen's Music, Judith Weir, CBE, *apptd* 2014

POET LAUREATE

The post of Poet Laureate was officially established when John Dryden was appointed by royal warrant as Poet Laureate and Historiographer Royal in 1668. The post is attached to the royal household and was originally conferred on the holder for life; in 1999 the length of appointment was changed to a ten-year term. It is customary for the Poet Laureate to write verse to mark events of national importance. The postholder currently receives an honorarium of £5,750 a year.

The Poet Laureate, Carol Ann Duffy, *apptd* 2009

ROYAL FINANCES

Dating back to the late 17th century the Civil List was originally used by the sovereign to supplement hereditary revenues for paying the salaries of judges, ambassadors and other government officers as well as the expenses of the royal household. In 1760, on the accession of George III, it was decided that the Civil List would be provided by parliament to cover all relevant expenditure in return for the king surrendering the hereditary revenues of the Crown. At that time parliament undertook to pay the salaries of judges, ambassadors etc. In 1831 parliament agreed also to meet the costs of the royal palaces in return for a reduction in the Civil List.

Until 1 April 2012 the Civil List met the central staff costs and running expenses of the Queen's official household. Annual grants-in-aid provided for the maintenance of the occupied royal palaces (see Royal Household for a list of occupied palaces) and royal travel.

THE SOVEREIGN GRANT
Under the Sovereign Grant Act 2011, which came into force on 1 April 2012, the funding previously provided by the Civil List and the grants-in-aid was consolidated in the Sovereign Grant, which was set at £36.1m for 2013–14. It is provided by HM Treasury from public funds in exchange for the surrender by the Queen of the revenue of the Crown Estate.

Official expenditure met by the Sovereign Grant in 2013–14 amounted to £35.7m, an increase of £1.9m (5.7 per cent) compared with 2012–13. Royal travel accounted for £4.2m of the expenditure and property maintenance for £13.3m. The excess of Sovereign Grant over expenditure of £0.4m was transferred to the Sovereign Grant reserve. The Sovereign Grant is calculated based on 15 per cent of the income account net surplus of the Crown Estate for the two financial years previous. The Crown Estate surplus for the financial year 2011–12 amounted to £240.2m, providing for a Sovereign Grant of £36.1m for 2013–14.

The legislative requirement is for Sovereign Grant accounts to be audited by the Comptroller and Auditor-General, scrutinised by the National Audit Office, and submitted to parliament annually. They are then subjected to the same audit scrutiny as for any other government department. The annual report for the year to 31 March 2014, was published in June 2014.

	2012–13	2013–14
Sovereign Grant	£31,000,000	£36,100,000
Draw-down from/		
(transfer to) the reserve	£2,300,000	(£400,000)
Net Funding Receipts	£33,300,000	£35,700,000
Net Expenditure	(£33,300,000)	(£35,700,000)

PARLIAMENTARY ANNUITIES
The Civil List acts provided for other members of the royal family to receive parliamentary annuities from government funds to meet the expenses of carrying out their official duties. Since 1993 these annuities have been a statutory anomaly as the Queen reimbursed HM Treasury for all of them except those paid to the late Queen Elizabeth the Queen Mother and the Duke of Edinburgh. The Sovereign Grant Act 2011 repealed all the parliamentary annuities paid to the royal family, with the exception of the Duke of Edinburgh. The Duke of Edinburgh's annuity (£359,000) is now paid directly from the Consolidated Fund.

THE PRIVY PURSE
The funds received by the privy purse pay for official expenses incurred by the Queen as head of state and for some of the Queen's private expenditure. The revenues of the Duchy of Lancaster are the principal source of income for the privy purse. The revenues of the Duchy were retained by George III in 1760 when the hereditary revenues were surrendered. The Duchy Council reports to the Chancellor of the Duchy of Lancaster, who is accountable directly to the sovereign rather than to parliament. However the chancellor does answer parliamentary questions on matters relating to the Duchy's responsibilities.

THE DUCHY OF LANCASTER, 1 Lancaster Place, London WC2E 7ED W www.duchyoflancaster.co.uk
Chancellor of the Duchy of Lancaster, Rt. Hon. Oliver Letwin, MP apptd 2014
Chair of the Council, Lord Shuttleworth, KCVO
Chief Executive and Clerk, Nathan Thompson
Receiver-General, Sir Alan Reid, GCVO
Attorney-General, Robert Miles, QC

PERSONAL INCOME
The Queen's personal income derives mostly from investments, and is used to meet private expenditure.

PRINCE OF WALES' FUNDING
The Duchy Estate was created in 1337 by Edward III for his son and heir Prince Edward (the Black Prince) who became the Duke of Cornwall. The Duchy's primary function is to provide an income from its assets for the Prince of Wales. Under a 1337 charter, confirmed by subsequent legislation, the Prince of Wales is not entitled to the proceeds or profit on the sale of Duchy assets but only to the annual income which is generated. The Duchy is responsible for the sustainable and commercial management of its properties, investment portfolio and around 53,134 hectares of land, based mostly in the south-west of England. The Prince of Wales has chosen to use a proportion of his income to meet the cost of his public and charitable work. The Duchy also funds the public, charitable and private activities of the Duchess of Cornwall, the Duke and Duchess of Cambridge and Prince Henry of Wales.

THE DUCHY OF CORNWALL, 10 Buckingham Gate, London SW1E 6LA T 020-7834 7346 W www.duchyofcornwall.org
Lord Warden of the Stannaries, Sir Nicholas Bacon, Bt., OBE
Receiver-General, Hon. James Leigh-Pemberton, CVO
Attorney-General, Jonathan Crow, QC
Secretary and Keeper of the Records, Alastair Martin

TAXATION
The sovereign is not legally liable to pay income tax or capital gains tax. In 1992 the Queen offered to pay income and capital gains tax on a voluntary basis from 6 April 1993, and the Prince of Wales offered to pay tax on a voluntary basis on his income from the Duchy of Cornwall (he was already taxed in all other respects).

The main provisions for the Queen and the Prince of Wales to pay tax, set out in a Memorandum of Understanding on Royal Taxation presented to parliament on 11 February 1993, are that the Queen will pay income tax and capital gains tax in respect of her private income and assets, and on the proportion of the income and capital gains of the Privy Purse used for private purposes. Inheritance tax will be paid on the Queen's assets, except for those which pass to the next sovereign, whether automatically or by gift or bequest. The Prince of Wales will pay income tax on income from the Duchy of Cornwall used for private purposes.

ROYAL SALUTES

ENGLAND

The basic royal salute is 21 rounds with an extra 20 rounds fired at Hyde Park because it is a royal park. At the Tower of London 62 rounds are fired on royal anniversaries (21 plus a further 20 because the Tower is a royal palace and a further 21 'for the City of London') and 41 on other occasions. When the Queen's official birthday coincides with the Duke of Edinburgh's birthday, 124 rounds are fired from the Tower (62 rounds for each birthday). Gun salutes occur on the following royal anniversaries:

• Accession Day
• The Queen's birthday
• Coronation Day
• Duke of Edinburgh's birthday
• The Queen's Official Birthday
• The Prince of Wales' birthday
• State opening of parliament

Gun salutes also occur when parliament is prorogued by the sovereign, on royal births and when a visiting head of state meets the sovereign in London, Windsor or Edinburgh.

In London, salutes are fired at Hyde Park and the Tower of London although on some occasions (state visits, state opening of parliament and the Queen's birthday parade) Green Park is used instead of Hyde Park. Other military saluting stations in England are at Colchester, Dover, Plymouth, Woolwich and York.

Constable of the Royal Palace and Fortress of London, Gen. Lord Dannatt, GCB, CBE, MC
Lieutenant of the Tower of London, Lt. Gen. Peter Pearson, CB, CBE
Master Gunner of St James's Park, Gen. Sir Timothy Granville-Chapman, GBE, KCB, ADC
Resident Governor and Keeper of the Jewel House, Col. Richard Harrold, OBE
Master Gunner within the Tower, HRH Prince Michael of Kent, GCVO

SCOTLAND

Royal salutes are authorised at Edinburgh Castle and Stirling Castle. A salute of 21 guns is fired on the following occasions:

• the anniversaries of the birth, accession and coronation of the sovereign
• the anniversary of the birth of the Duke of Edinburgh

A salute of 21 guns is fired in Edinburgh on the occasion of the opening of the general assembly of the Church of Scotland. A salute of 21 guns may also be fired in Edinburgh on the arrival of HM The Queen or a member of the royal family who is a Royal Highness on an official visit.

Military saluting stations are also situated at Cardiff Castle in Wales, Hillsborough Castle in Northern Ireland and in Gibraltar.

MILITARY RANKS AND TITLES

THE QUEEN
ARMY
Colonel-in-Chief
  The Life Guards; The Blues and Royals (Royal Horse Guards and 1st Dragoons); The Royal Scots Dragoon Guards (Carabiniers and Greys); The Royal Lancers; Royal Tank Regiment; Corps of Royal Engineers; Grenadier Guards; Coldstream Guards; Scots Guards; Irish Guards; Welsh Guards; The Royal Regiment of Scotland; The Duke of Lancaster's Regiment (King's, Lancashire and Border); The Royal Welsh; Adjutant General's Corps; The Governor General's Horse Guards (of Canada); The King's Own Calgary Regiment (Royal Canadian Armoured Corps); Canadian Military Engineering Branch; Royal 22e Regiment (of Canada); Governor General's Foot Guards (of Canada); The Canadian Grenadier Guards; The Stormont, Dundas and Glengarry Highlanders; Le Régiment de la Chaudière (of Canada); The Royal New Brunswick Regiment; 48th Highlanders of Canada; The Argyll and Sutherland Highlanders of Canada (Princess Louise's); The Calgary Highlanders; Royal Australian Engineers; Royal Australian Infantry Corps; Royal Australian Army Ordnance Corps; Royal Australian Army Nursing Corps; The Corps of Royal New Zealand Engineers; Royal New Zealand Infantry Regiment; The Malawi Rifles
Affiliated Colonel-in-Chief
  The Queen's Gurkha Engineers
Captain-General
  Royal Regiment of Artillery; The Honourable Artillery Company; Combined Cadet Force; Royal Regiment of Canadian Artillery; Royal Regiment of Australian Artillery; Royal Regiment of New Zealand Artillery; Royal New Zealand Armoured Corps
Royal Colonel
  Balaklava Company, 5th Battalion The Royal Regiment of Scotland
Patron
  Royal Army Chaplains' Department
ROYAL AIR FORCE
Air Commodore-in-Chief
  Royal Auxiliary Air Force; Royal Air Force Regiment; Air Reserve of Canada; Royal Australian Air Force Reserve; Territorial Air Force (of New Zealand)
Commandant-in-Chief
  RAF College, Cranwell
Royal Honorary Air Commodore
  RAF Marham; 603 (City of Edinburgh) Squadron Royal Auxiliary Air Force

PRINCE PHILIP, DUKE OF EDINBURGH
ROYAL NAVY
Lord High Admiral of the United Kingdom
Admiral of the Fleet
Admiral of the Fleet, Royal Australian Navy
Admiral of the Fleet, Royal New Zealand Navy
Admiral, Royal Canadian Navy
Admiral, Royal Canadian Sea Cadets
ROYAL MARINES
Captain-General
ARMY
Field Marshal
Field Marshal, Australian Military Forces
Field Marshal, New Zealand Army
General, Royal Canadian Army

Colonel-in-Chief
  The Queen's Royal Hussars (Queen's Own and Royal Irish); The Rifles; Corps of Royal Electrical and Mechanical Engineers; Intelligence Corps; Army Cadet Force Association; The Royal Canadian Regiment; The Royal Hamilton Light Infantry (Wentworth Regiment of Canada); The Cameron Highlanders of Ottawa; The Queen's Own Cameron Highlanders of Canada; The Seaforth Highlanders of Canada; The Royal Canadian Army Cadets; The Royal Australian Corps of Electrical and Mechanical Engineers; The Australian Army Cadet Corps
Colonel
  Grenadier Guards
Royal Colonel
  The Highlanders, 4th Battalion The Royal Regiment of Scotland
Honorary Colonel
  City of Edinburgh University Officers' Training Corps; The Trinidad and Tobago Regiment
Member
  Honourable Artillery Company
ROYAL AIR FORCE
Marshal of the Royal Air Force
Marshal of the Royal Australian Air Force
Marshal of the Royal New Zealand Air Force
General, Royal Canadian Air Force
Air Commodore-in-Chief
  Air Training Corps; Royal Canadian Air Cadets
Honorary Air Commodore
  RAF Northolt

THE PRINCE OF WALES
ROYAL NAVY
Admiral of the Fleet
Commodore-in-Chief
  Royal Naval Command Plymouth
ARMY
Field Marshal
Colonel-in-Chief
  The Royal Dragoon Guards; The Parachute Regiment; The Royal Gurkha Rifles; Army Air Corps; The Royal Canadian Dragoons; Lord Strathcona's Horse (Royal Canadians); The Royal Regiment of Canada; Royal Winnipeg Rifles; Royal Australian Armoured Corps; The Royal Pacific Islands Regiment; 1st The Queen's Dragoon Guards; The Black Watch (Royal Highland Regiment) of Canada; The Toronto Scottish Regiment (Queen Elizabeth The Queen Mother's Own); The Mercian Regiment
Royal Colonel
  The Black Watch, 3rd Battalion The Royal Regiment of Scotland; 51st Highland, 7th Battalion The Royal Regiment of Scotland (Territorial Army)
Colonel
  The Welsh Guards
Royal Honorary Colonel
  The Queen's Own Yeomanry
ROYAL AIR FORCE
Marshal of the RAF
Honorary Air Commodore
  RAF Valley
Air Commodore-in-Chief
  Royal New Zealand Air Force
Colonel-in-Chief
  Air Reserve Canada

THE DUCHESS OF CORNWALL
ROYAL NAVY
Commodore-in-Chief
Royal Naval Medical Services; Naval Chaplaincy Services
ARMY
Colonel-in-Chief
Queen's Own Rifles of Canada
Royal Colonel
4th Battalion The Rifles
ROYAL AIR FORCE
Honorary Air Commodore
RAF Halton; RAF Leeming

THE DUKE OF CAMBRIDGE
ROYAL NAVY
Lieutenant
Commodore-in-Chief
Scotland Command; Submarines Command
ARMY
Colonel
Irish Guards
Captain
The Blues and Royals (Royal Horse Guards and 1st Dragoons)
ROYAL AIR FORCE
Flight Lieutenant
Honorary Air Commandant
RAF Coningsby

PRINCE HENRY OF WALES
ROYAL NAVY
Commodore-in-Chief
Small Ships and Diving Command
ARMY
Captain
The Blues and Royals (Royal Horse Guards and 1st Dragoons)
ROYAL AIR FORCE
Honorary Air Commandant
RAF Honington

THE DUKE OF YORK
ROYAL NAVY
Rear Admiral
Commodore-in-Chief
Fleet Air Arm
Admiral of the Marine Society and Sea Cadets
ARMY
Colonel-in-Chief
The Royal Irish Regiment (27th (Inniskilling), 83rd, 87th and The Ulster Defence Regiment); The Yorkshire Regiment; Small Arms School Corps; The Queen's York Rangers (First Americans); Royal New Zealand Army Logistics Regiment; The Royal Highland Fusiliers of Canada; The Princess Louise Fusiliers (Canada)
Royal Colonel
The Royal Highland Fusiliers, 2nd Battalion The Royal Regiment of Scotland
ROYAL AIR FORCE
Honorary Air Commodore
RAF Lossiemouth

THE EARL OF WESSEX
ROYAL NAVY
Commodore-in-Chief
Royal Fleet Auxiliary
Patron
Royal Fleet Auxiliary Association

ARMY
Colonel-in-Chief
Hastings and Prince Edward Regiment; Saskatchewan Dragoons; Prince Edward Island Regiment
Royal Colonel
2nd Battalion, The Rifles
Royal Honorary Colonel
Royal Wessex Yeomanry; The London Regiment
ROYAL AIR FORCE
Honorary Air Commodore
RAF Waddington

THE COUNTESS OF WESSEX
ARMY
Colonel-in-Chief
Queen Alexandra's Royal Army Nursing Corps; The Lincoln and Welland Regiment; South Alberta Light Horse Regiment
Royal Colonel
5th Battalion, The Rifles
Patron
Corps of Army Music; Queen Alexandra's Royal Army Nursing Corps Association
ROYAL AIR FORCE
Honorary Air Commodore
RAF Wittering
ROYAL NAVY
Sponsor
HMS *Daring*

THE PRINCESS ROYAL
ROYAL NAVY
Admiral (Chief Commandant for Women in the Royal Navy)
Commodore-in-Chief
HM Naval Base Portsmouth
ARMY
Colonel-in-Chief
The King's Royal Hussars; Royal Corps of Signals; Royal Logistic Corps; The Royal Army Veterinary Corps; 8th Canadian Hussars (Princess Louise's); Royal Newfoundland Regiment; Canadian Forces Communications and Electronics Branch; The Grey and Simcoe Foresters (Royal Canadian Armoured Corps); The Royal Regina Rifle Regiment; Canadian Forces Medical Branch; Royal Australian Corps of Signals; Royal Australian Corps of Transport; Royal New Zealand Corps of Signals; Royal New Zealand Nursing Corps
Affiliated Colonel-in-Chief
The Queen's Gurkha Signals; The Queen's Own Gurkha Transport Regiment
Royal Colonel
1st Battalion The Royal Regiment of Scotland; 52nd Lowland, 6th Battalion The Royal Regiment of Scotland
Colonel
The Blues and Royals (Royal Horse Guards and 1st Dragoons)
Honorary Colonel
University of London Officers' Training Corps
Commandant-in-Chief
First Aid Nursing Yeomanry (Princess Royal's Volunteer Corps)
ROYAL AIR FORCE
Honorary Air Commodore
RAF Brize Norton; University of London Air Squadron

THE DUKE OF GLOUCESTER
ARMY
Colonel-in-Chief
The Royal Anglian Regiment; Royal Army Medical Corps; Royal New Zealand Army Medical Corps

Deputy Colonel-in-Chief
  The Royal Logistic Corps
Royal Colonel
  6th Battalion, The Rifles
Honorary Royal Colonel
  Royal Monmouthshire Royal Engineers (Militia)
ROYAL AIR FORCE
Honorary Air Marshal
Honorary Air Commodore
  RAF Odiham; No. 501 (County of Gloucester) Logistic
  Support Squadron

THE DUCHESS OF GLOUCESTER
ARMY
Colonel-in-Chief
  Royal Army Dental Corps; Royal Australian Army
  Educational Corps; Royal New Zealand Army Educational
  Corps; Royal Canadian Dental Corps; The Bermuda
  Regiment
Deputy Colonel-in-Chief
  Adjutant-General's Corps
Royal Colonel
  7th Battalion, The Rifles
Vice-Patron
  Adjutant General's Corps Regimental Association
Patron
  Royal Army Educational Corps Association; Army
  Families Federation

THE DUKE OF KENT
ARMY
Field Marshal
Colonel-in-Chief
  The Royal Regiment of Fusiliers; Lorne Scots (Peel,
  Dufferin and Hamilton Regiment)
Deputy Colonel-in-Chief
  The Royal Scots Dragoon Guards (Carabiniers and Greys)
Royal Colonel
  1st Battalion The Rifles
Colonel
  Scots Guards

ROYAL AIR FORCE
Honorary Air Chief Marshal

THE DUCHESS OF KENT
ARMY
Deputy Colonel-in-Chief
  The Royal Dragoon Guards; Adjutant-General's Corps;
  The Royal Logistic Corps

PRINCE MICHAEL OF KENT
ROYAL NAVY
Honorary Rear Admiral of the Royal Naval Reserves
Commodore-in-Chief of the Maritime Reserves
ARMY
Colonel-in-Chief
  Essex and Kent Scottish Regiment (Ontario)
Royal Honorary Colonel
  Honourable Artillery Company
Senior Colonel
  King's Royal Hussars
ROYAL AIR FORCE
Honorary Air Marshal
  RAF Benson

PRINCESS ALEXANDRA, THE HON. LADY OGILVY
ROYAL NAVY
Patron
  Queen Alexandra's Royal Naval Nursing Service
ARMY
Colonel-in-Chief
  The Canadian Scottish Regiment (Princess Mary's)
Deputy Colonel-in-Chief
  The Queen's Royal Lancers
Royal Colonel
  3rd Battalion The Rifles
Royal Honorary Colonel
  The Royal Yeomanry
ROYAL AIR FORCE
Patron and Air Chief Commandant
  Princess Mary's RAF Nursing Service

KINGS AND QUEENS

ENGLISH KINGS AND QUEENS 927 TO 1603

HOUSES OF CERDIC AND DENMARK

Reign

927–939   **ÆTHELSTAN**   Son of Edward the Elder, by Ecgwynn, and grandson of Alfred *acceded* to Wessex and Mercia *c.*924, established direct rule over Northumbria 927, effectively creating the Kingdom of England *reigned* 15 years

939–946   **EDMUND I**   *born* 921, son of Edward the Elder, by Eadgifu *married* (1) Ælfgifu (2) Æthelflæd *killed* aged 25 *reigned* 6 years

946–955   **EADRED**   Son of Edward the Elder, by Eadgifu *reigned* 9 years

955–959   **EADWIG**   *born* before 943, son of Edmund and Ælfgifu *married* Ælfgifu *reigned* 3 years

959–975   **EDGAR I**   *born* 943, son of Edmund and Ælfgifu *married* (1) Æthelflæd (2) Wulfthryth (3) Ælfthryth *died* aged 32 *reigned* 15 years

975–978   **EDWARD I (the Martyr)**   *born c.*962, son of Edgar and Æthelflæd *assassinated* aged *c.*16 *reigned* 2 years

978–1016   **ÆTHELRED (the Unready)**   *born* 968/9, son of Edgar and Ælfthryth *married* (1) Ælfgifu (2) Emma, daughter of Richard I, Count of Normandy, 1013–14 dispossessed of kingdom by Swegn Forkbeard (King of Denmark 987–1014) *died* aged *c.*47, *reigned* 38 years

1016 (Apr–Nov)   **EDMUND II (Ironside)**   *born* before 993, son of Æthelred and Ælfgifu *married* Ealdgyth died aged over 23 *reigned* 7 months

1016–1035   **CNUT (Canute)**   *born c.*995, son of Swegn Forkbeard, King of Denmark, and Gunhild *married* (1) Ælfgifu (2) Emma, widow of Æthelred the Unready. Gained submission of West Saxons 1015, Northumbrians 1016, Mercia 1016, King of all England after Edmund's death, King of Denmark 1019–35, King of Norway 1028–35 *died* aged *c.*40 *reigned* 19 years

1035–1040   **HAROLD I (Harefoot)**   *born* 1016/17, son of Cnut and Ælfgifu *married* Ælfgifu 1035 recognised as regent for himself and his brother Harthacnut; 1037 recognised as king *died* aged *c.*23 *reigned* 4 years

1040–1042   **HARTHACNUT (Harthacanute)**   *born c.*1018, son of Cnut and Emma. Titular king of Denmark from 1028, acknowledged King of England 1035–7 with Harold I as regent; effective king after Harold's death *died* aged *c.*24 *reigned* 2 years

1042–1066   **EDWARD II (the Confessor)**   *born* between 1002 and 1005, son of Æthelred the Unready and Emma *married* Eadgyth, daughter of Godwine, Earl of Wessex *died* aged over 60 *reigned* 23 years

1066 (Jan–Oct)   **HAROLD II (Godwinesson)**   *born c.*1020, son of Godwine, Earl of Wessex, and Gytha *married* (1) Eadgyth (2) Ealdgyth *killed* in battle aged *c.*46 *reigned* 10 months

THE HOUSE OF NORMANDY

1066–1087   **WILLIAM I (the Conqueror)**   *born* 1027/8, son of Robert I, Duke of Normandy; obtained the Crown by conquest *married* Matilda, daughter of Baldwin, Count of Flanders *died* aged *c.*60, *reigned* 20 years

1087–1100   **WILLIAM II (Rufus)**   *born* between 1056 and 1060, third son of William I; succeeded his father in England only *killed* aged *c.*40 *reigned* 12 years

1100–1135   **HENRY I (Beauclerk)**   *born* 1068, fourth son of William I *married* (1) Edith or Matilda, daughter of Malcolm III of Scotland (2) Adela, daughter of Godfrey, Count of Louvain *died* aged 67 *reigned* 35 years

1135–1154   **STEPHEN**   *born* not later than 1100, third son of Adela, daughter of William I, and Stephen, Count of Blois *married* Matilda, daughter of Eustace, Count of Boulogne. Feb–Nov 1141 held captive by adherents of Matilda, daughter of Henry I, who contested the Crown until 1153 *died* aged over 53 *reigned* 18 years

THE HOUSE OF ANJOU (PLANTAGENETS)

1154–1189   **HENRY II (Curtmantle)**   *born* 1133, son of Matilda, daughter of Henry I, and Geoffrey, Count of Anjou *married* Eleanor, daughter of William, Duke of Aquitaine, and divorced queen of Louis VII of France *died* aged 56 *reigned* 34 years

1189–1199   **RICHARD I (Coeur de Lion)**   *born* 1157, third son of Henry II *married* Berengaria, daughter of Sancho VI, King of Navarre *died* aged 42 *reigned* 9 years

1199–1216   **JOHN (Lackland)**   *born* 1167, fifth son of Henry II *married* (1) Isabella or Avisa, daughter of William, Earl of Gloucester (divorced) (2) Isabella, daughter of Aymer, Count of Angoulême *died* aged 48 *reigned* 17 years

1216–1272   **HENRY III**   *born* 1207, son of John and Isabella of Angoulême *married* Eleanor, daughter of Raymond, Count of Provence *died* aged 65 *reigned* 56 years

1272–1307   **EDWARD I (Longshanks)**   *born* 1239, eldest son of Henry III *married* (1) Eleanor, daughter of Ferdinand III, King of Castile (2) Margaret, daughter of Philip III of France *died* aged 68 *reigned* 34 years

1307–1327   **EDWARD II**   *born* 1284, eldest surviving son of Edward I and Eleanor *married* Isabella, daughter of Philip IV of France *deposed* Jan 1327 *killed* Sep 1327 aged 43 *reigned* 19 years

1327–1377   **EDWARD III**   *born* 1312, eldest son of Edward II *married* Philippa, daughter of William, Count of Hainault *died* aged 64 *reigned* 50 years

1377–1399   **RICHARD II**   *born* 1367, son of Edward (the Black Prince), eldest son of Edward III *married* (1) Anne, daughter of Emperor Charles IV (2) Isabelle, daughter of Charles VI of France *deposed* Sep 1399 *killed* Feb 1400 aged 33 *reigned* 22 years

THE HOUSE OF LANCASTER

1399–1413 **HENRY IV** *born* 1366, son of John of Gaunt, fourth son of Edward III, and Blanche, daughter of Henry, Duke of Lancaster *married* (1) Mary, daughter of Humphrey, Earl of Hereford (2) Joan, daughter of Charles, King of Navarre, and widow of John, Duke of Brittany *died* aged *c.*47 *reigned* 13 years

1413–1422 **HENRY V** *born* 1387, eldest surviving son of Henry IV and Mary *married* Catherine, daughter of Charles VI of France *died* aged 34 *reigned* 9 years

1422–1471 **HENRY VI** *born* 1421, son of Henry V *married* Margaret, daughter of René, Duke of Anjou and Count of Provence *deposed* Mar 1461 *restored* Oct 1470 *deposed* Apr 1471 *killed* May 1471 aged 49 *reigned* 39 years

THE HOUSE OF YORK

1461–1483 **EDWARD IV** *born* 1442, eldest son of Richard of York (grandson of Edmund, fifth son of Edward III; and son of Anne, great-granddaughter of Lionel, third son of Edward III) *married* Elizabeth Woodville, daughter of Richard, Lord Rivers, and widow of Sir John Grey *acceded* Mar 1461 *deposed* Oct 1470 *restored* Apr 1471 *died* aged 40 *reigned* 21 years

1483   **EDWARD V** *born* 1470, eldest son of
(Apr–Jun) Edward IV *deposed* Jun 1483, *died* probably Jul–Sep 1483, aged 12 *reigned* 2 months

1483–1485 **RICHARD III** *born* 1452, fourth son of Richard of York *married* Anne Neville, daughter of Richard, Earl of Warwick, and widow of Edward, Prince of Wales, son of Henry VI *killed* in battle aged 32 *reigned* 2 years

THE HOUSE OF TUDOR

1485–1509 **HENRY VII** *born* 1457, son of Margaret Beaufort (great-granddaughter of John of Gaunt, fourth son of Edward III) and Edmund Tudor, Earl of Richmond *married* Elizabeth, daughter of Edward IV *died* aged 52 *reigned* 23 years

1509–1547 **HENRY VIII** *born* 1491, second son of Henry VII *married* (1) Catherine, daughter of Ferdinand II, King of Aragon, and widow of his elder brother Arthur (divorced) (2) Anne, daughter of Sir Thomas Boleyn (executed) (3) Jane, daughter of Sir John Seymour (died in childbirth) (4) Anne, daughter of John, Duke of Cleves (divorced) (5) Catherine Howard, niece of the Duke of Norfolk (executed) (6) Catherine, daughter of Sir Thomas Parr and widow of Lord Latimer *died* aged 55 *reigned* 37 years

1547–1553 **EDWARD VI** *born* 1537, son of Henry VIII and Jane Seymour *died* aged 15 *reigned* 6 years

1553   **JANE** *born* 1537, daughter of Frances
*(6/10–   (daughter of Mary Tudor, the younger
19 Jul)   daughter of Henry VII) and Henry Grey, Duke of Suffolk *married* Lord Guildford Dudley, son of the Duke of Northumberland *deposed*

Jul 1553 *executed* Feb 1554 aged 16 *reigned* 13/9 days

1553–1558 **MARY I** *born* 1516, daughter of Henry VIII and Catherine of Aragon *married* Philip II of Spain *died* aged 42 *reigned* 5 years

1558–1603 **ELIZABETH I** *born* 1533, daughter of Henry VIII and Anne Boleyn *died* aged 69 *reigned* 44 years

BRITISH KINGS AND QUEENS SINCE 1603

THE HOUSE OF STUART

Reign

1603–1625 **JAMES I (VI OF SCOTLAND)** *born* 1566, son of Mary, Queen of Scots (granddaughter of Margaret Tudor, elder daughter of Henry VII), and Henry Stewart, Lord Darnley *married* Anne, daughter of Frederick II of Denmark *died* aged 58 *reigned* 22 years

1625–1649 **CHARLES I** *born* 1600, second son of James I *married* Henrietta Maria, daughter of Henry IV of France *executed* 1649 aged 48 *reigned* 23 years

INTERREGNUM 1649–1660

1649–1653 Government by a council of state
1653–1658 Oliver Cromwell, Lord Protector
1658–1659 Richard Cromwell, Lord Protector

Reign

1660–1685 **CHARLES II** *born* 1630, eldest son of Charles I *married* Catherine, daughter of John IV of Portugal *died* aged 54 *reigned* 24 years

1685–1688 **JAMES II (VII OF SCOTLAND)** *born* 1633, second son of Charles I *married* (1) Lady Anne Hyde, daughter of Edward, Earl of Clarendon (2) Mary, daughter of Alphonso, Duke of Modena reign ended with flight from kingdom Dec 1688 *died* 1701 aged 67 *reigned* 3 years

INTERREGNUM
11 Dec 1688 to 12 Feb 1689

Reign

1689–1702 **WILLIAM III** *born* 1650, son of William II, Prince of Orange, and Mary Stuart, daughter of Charles I *married* Mary, elder daughter of James II *died* aged 51 *reigned* 13 years

and

1689–1694 **MARY II** *born* 1662, elder daughter of James II and Anne *died* aged 32 *reigned* 5 years

1702–1714 **ANNE** *born* 1665, younger daughter of James II and Anne *married* Prince George of Denmark, son of Frederick III of Denmark *died* aged 49 *reigned* 12 years

THE HOUSE OF HANOVER

1714–1727 **GEORGE I (Elector of Hanover)** *born* 1660, son of Sophia (daughter of Frederick, Elector Palatine, and Elizabeth Stuart, daughter of James I) and Ernest Augustus, Elector of Hanover *married* Sophia Dorothea, daughter of George William, Duke of Lüneburg-Celle *died* aged 67 *reigned* 12 years

1727–1760 **GEORGE II** *born* 1683, son of George I *married* Caroline, daughter of John Frederick, Margrave of Brandenburg-Anspach *died* aged 76 *reigned* 33 years

* Depending on whether the date of her predecessor's death (6 July) or that of her official proclamation as Queen (10 July) is taken as the beginning of her reign

1760–1820   **GEORGE III**   *born* 1738, son of Frederick, eldest son of George II *married* Charlotte, daughter of Charles Louis, Duke of Mecklenburg-Strelitz *died* aged 81 *reigned* 59 years

REGENCY 1811–1820
Prince of Wales regent owing to the insanity of George III

Reign
1820–1830   **GEORGE IV**   *born* 1762, eldest son of George III *married* Caroline, daughter of Charles, Duke of Brunswick-Wolfenbüttel *died* aged 67 *reigned* 10 years

1830–1837   **WILLIAM IV**   *born* 1765, third son of George III *married* Adelaide, daughter of George, Duke of Saxe-Meiningen *died* aged 71 *reigned* 7 years

1837–1901   **VICTORIA**   *born* 1819, daughter of Edward, fourth son of George III *married* Prince Albert of Saxe-Coburg and Gotha *died* aged 81 *reigned* 63 years

THE HOUSE OF SAXE-COBURG AND GOTHA
1901–1910   **EDWARD VII**   *born* 1841, eldest son of Victoria and Albert *married* Alexandra, daughter of Christian IX of Denmark *died* aged 68 *reigned* 9 years

THE HOUSE OF WINDSOR
1910–1936   **GEORGE V**   *born* 1865, second son of Edward VII *married* Victoria Mary, daughter of Francis, Duke of Teck *died* aged 70 *reigned* 25 years

1936   **EDWARD VIII**   *born* 1894, eldest son of
(20 Jan–   George V *married* (1937) Mrs Wallis Simpson
11 Dec)   *abdicated* 1936 *died* 1972 aged 77 *reigned* 10 months

1936–1952   **GEORGE VI**   *born* 1895, second son of George V *married* Lady Elizabeth Bowes-Lyon, daughter of 14th Earl of Strathmore and Kinghorne *died* aged 56 *reigned* 15 years

1952–   **ELIZABETH II**   *born* 1926, elder daughter of George VI *married* Philip, son of Prince Andrew of Greece

KINGS AND QUEENS OF SCOTS 1016 TO 1603

Reign
1016–1034   **MALCOLM II**   *born* c.954, son of Kenneth II *acceded* to Alba 1005, secured Lothian c.1016, obtained Strathclyde for his grandson Duncan c.1016, thus reigning over an area approximately the same as that governed by later rulers of Scotland *died* aged c.80 *reigned* 18 years

THE HOUSE OF ATHOLL
1034–1040   **DUNCAN I**   son of Bethoc, daughter of Malcolm II, and Crinan, Mormaer of Atholl *married* a cousin of Siward, Earl of Northumbria *reigned* 5 years

1040–1057   **MACBETH**   *born* c.1005, son of a daughter of Malcolm II and Finlaec, Mormaer of Moray *married* Gruoch, granddaughter of Kenneth III *killed* aged c.52 *reigned* 17 years

1057–1058   **LULACH**   *born* c.1032, son of Gillacomgan,
(Aug–Mar)   Mormaer of Moray, and Gruoch (and stepson of Macbeth) *died* aged c.26 *reigned* 7 months

1058–1093   **MALCOLM III (Canmore)**   *born* c.1031, elder son of Duncan I *married* (1) Ingibiorg (2) Margaret (St Margaret), granddaughter of Edmund II of England *killed* in battle aged c.62 *reigned* 35 years

1093–1097   **DONALD III BÁN**   *born* c.1033, second son of Duncan I *deposed* May 1094 *restored* Nov 1094 *deposed* Oct 1097 *reigned* 3 years

1094   **DUNCAN II**   *born* c.1060, elder son of
(May–Nov)   Malcolm III and Ingibiorg *married* Octreda of Dunbar *killed* aged c.34 *reigned* 6 months

1097–1107   **EDGAR**   *born* c.1074, second son of Malcolm III and Margaret *died* aged c.32 *reigned* 9 years

1107–1124   **ALEXANDER I (the Fierce)**   *born* c.1077, fifth son of Malcolm III and Margaret *married* Sybilla, illegitimate daughter of Henry I of England *died* aged c.47 *reigned* 17 years

1124–1153   **DAVID I (the Saint)**   *born* c.1085, sixth son of Malcolm III and Margaret *married* Matilda, daughter of Waltheof, Earl of Huntingdon *died* aged c.68 *reigned* 29 years

1153–1165   **MALCOLM IV (the Maiden)**   *born* c.1141, son of Henry, Earl of Huntingdon, second son of David I *died* aged c.24 *reigned* 12 years

1165–1214   **WILLIAM I (the Lion)**   *born* c.1142, brother of Malcolm IV *married* Ermengarde, daughter of Richard, Viscount of Beaumont *died* aged c.72 *reigned* 49 years

1214–1249   **ALEXANDER II**   *born* 1198, son of William I *married* (1) Joan, daughter of John, King of England (2) Marie, daughter of Ingelram de Coucy *died* aged 50 *reigned* 34 years

1249–1286   **ALEXANDER III**   *born* 1241, son of Alexander II and Marie *married* (1) Margaret, daughter of Henry III of England (2) Yolande, daughter of the Count of Dreux *killed* accidentally aged 44 *reigned* 36 years

1286–1290   **MARGARET (the Maid of Norway)**   *born* 1283, daughter of Margaret (daughter of Alexander III) and Eric II of Norway *died* aged 7 *reigned* 4 years

FIRST INTERREGNUM 1290–1292
Throne disputed by 13 competitors. Crown awarded to John Balliol by adjudication of Edward I of England

THE HOUSE OF BALLIOL
Reign
1292–1296   **JOHN (Balliol)**   *born* c.1250, son of Dervorguilla, great-great-granddaughter of David I, and John de Balliol *married* Isabella, daughter of John, Earl of Surrey *abdicated* 1296 *died* 1313 aged c.63 *reigned* 3 years

SECOND INTERREGNUM 1296–1306
Edward I of England declared John Balliol to have forfeited the throne for contumacy in 1296 and took the government of Scotland into his own hands

THE HOUSE OF BRUCE
Reign
1306–1329   **ROBERT I (Bruce)**   *born* 1274, son of Robert Bruce and Marjorie, Countess of Carrick, and great-grandson of the second daughter of David, Earl of Huntingdon,

brother of William I *married* (1) Isabella, daughter of Donald, Earl of Mar (2) Elizabeth, daughter of Richard, Earl of Ulster *died* aged 54 *reigned* 23 years

1329–1371 **DAVID II**   *born* 1324, son of Robert I and Elizabeth *married* (1) Joanna, daughter of Edward II of England (2) Margaret Drummond, widow of Sir John Logie (divorced) *died* aged 46 *reigned* 41 years
1332 (Sep–Dec) Edward Balliol, son of John Balliol
1333–1336 Edward Balliol

THE HOUSE OF STEWART

1371–1390 **ROBERT II (Stewart)**   *born* 1316, son of Marjorie (daughter of Robert I) and Walter, High Steward of Scotland *married* (1) Elizabeth, daughter of Sir Robert Mure of Rowallan (2) Euphemia, daughter of Hugh, Earl of Ross *died* aged 74 *reigned* 19 years

1390–1406 **ROBERT III**   *born* c.1337, son of Robert II and Elizabeth *married* Annabella, daughter of Sir John Drummond of Stobhall *died* aged c.69 *reigned* 16 years

1406–1437 **JAMES I**   *born* 1394, son of Robert III *married* Joan Beaufort, daughter of John, Earl of Somerset *assassinated* aged 42 *reigned* 30 years

1437–1460 **JAMES II**   *born* 1430, son of James I *married* Mary, daughter of Arnold, Duke of Gueldres *killed* accidentally aged 29 *reigned* 23 years

1460–1488 **JAMES III**   *born* 1452, son of James II *married* Margaret, daughter of Christian I of Denmark *assassinated* aged 36 *reigned* 27 years

1488–1513 **JAMES IV**   *born* 1473, son of James III *married* Margaret Tudor, daughter of Henry VII of England *killed* in battle aged 40 *reigned* 25 years

1513–1542 **JAMES V**   *born* 1512, son of James IV *married* (1) Madeleine, daughter of Francis I of France (2) Mary of Lorraine, daughter of the Duc de Guise *died* aged 30 *reigned* 29 years

1542–1567 **MARY**   *born* 1542, daughter of James V and Mary *married* (1) the Dauphin, afterwards Francis II of France (2) Henry Stewart, Lord Darnley (3) James Hepburn, Earl of Bothwell *abdicated* 1567, prisoner in England from 1568, *executed* 1587 *reigned* 24 years

1567–1625 **JAMES VI (and I of England)**   *born* 1566, son of Mary, Queen of Scots, and Henry, Lord Darnley *acceded* 1567 to the Scottish throne *reigned* 58 years *succeeded* 1603 to the English throne, so joining the English and Scottish crowns in one person. The two kingdoms remained distinct until 1707 when the parliaments of the kingdoms became conjoined

WELSH SOVEREIGNS AND PRINCES

Wales was ruled by sovereign princes from the earliest times until the death of Llywelyn in 1282. The first English Prince of Wales was the son of Edward I, who was born in Caernarvon town on 25 April 1284. According to a discredited legend, he was presented to the Welsh chieftains as their prince, in fulfilment of a promise that they should have a prince who 'could not speak a word of English' and should be native born. This son, who afterwards became Edward II, was created 'Prince of Wales and Earl of Chester' at the Lincoln Parliament on 7 February 1301.

The title Prince of Wales is borne after individual conferment and is not inherited at birth, though some Princes have been declared and styled Prince of Wales but never formally so created (*s.*). The title was conferred on Prince Charles by the Queen on 26 July 1958. He was invested at Caernarvon on 1 July 1969.

INDEPENDENT PRINCES AD 844 TO 1282

844–878	Rhodri the Great
878–916	Anarawd, son of Rhodri
916–950	Hywel Dda, the Good
950–979	Iago ab Idwal (or Ieuaf)
979–985	Hywel ab Ieuaf, the Bad
985–986	Cadwallon, his brother
986–999	Maredudd ab Owain ap Hywel Dda
999–1005	Cynan ap Hywel ab Ieuaf
1005–1018	Aeddan ap Blegywryd
1018–1023	Llywelyn ap Seisyll
1023–1039	Iago ab Idwal ap Meurig
1039–1063	Gruffydd ap Llywelyn ap Seisyll
1063–1075	Bleddyn ap Cynfyn
1075–1081	Trahaern ap Caradog
1081–1137	Gruffydd ap Cynan ab Iago
1137–1170	Owain Gwynedd
1170–1194	Dafydd ab Owain Gwynedd
1194–1240	Llywelyn Fawr, the Great
1240–1246	Dafydd ap Llywelyn
1246–1282	Llywelyn ap Gruffydd ap Llywelyn

ENGLISH PRINCES SINCE 1301

1301	Edward (Edward II)
1343	Edward the Black Prince, son of Edward III
1376	Richard (Richard II), son of the Black Prince
1399	Henry of Monmouth (Henry V)
1454	Edward of Westminster, son of Henry VI
1471	Edward of Westminster (Edward V)
1483	Edward, son of Richard III (*d.* 1484)
1489	Arthur Tudor, son of Henry VII
1504	Henry Tudor (Henry VIII)
1610	Henry Stuart, son of James I (*d.* 1612)
1616	Charles Stuart (Charles I)
c.1638 (*s.*)	Charles Stuart (Charles II)
1688 (*s.*)	James Francis Edward Stuart (The Old Pretender), son of James II (*d.* 1766)
1714	George Augustus (George II)
1729	Frederick Lewis, son of George II (*d.* 1751)
1751	George William Frederick (George III)
1762	George Augustus Frederick (George IV)
1841	Albert Edward (Edward VII)
1901	George (George V)
1910	Edward (Edward VIII)
1958	Charles, son of Elizabeth II

PRINCESSES ROYAL

The style Princess Royal is conferred at the sovereign's discretion on his or her eldest daughter. It is an honorary title, held for life, and cannot be inherited or passed on. It was first conferred on Princess Mary, daughter of Charles I, in approximately 1642.

c.1642	Princess Mary (1631–60), daughter of Charles I
1727	Princess Anne (1709–59), daughter of George II
1766	Princess Charlotte (1766–1828), daughter of George III
1840	Princess Victoria (1840–1901), daughter of Victoria
1905	Princess Louise (1867–1931), daughter of Edward VII
1932	Princess Mary (1897–1965), daughter of George V
1987	Princess Anne (*b.* 1950), daughter of Elizabeth II

THE HOUSE OF WINDSOR

King George V assumed by royal proclamation (17 July 1917) for his House and family, as well as for all descendants in the male line of Queen Victoria who are subjects of these realms, the name of Windsor.

KING GEORGE V
(George Frederick Ernest Albert), second son of King Edward VII *born* 3 June 1865 *married* 6 July 1893 HSH Princess Victoria Mary Augusta Louise Olga Pauline Claudine Agnes of Teck (Queen Mary *born* 26 May 1867 *died* 24 March 1953) *succeeded* to the throne 6 May 1910 *died* 20 January 1936. *Issue*

1. HRH PRINCE EDWARD Albert Christian George Andrew Patrick David *born* 23 June 1894 *succeeded* to the throne as King Edward VIII, 20 January 1936 *abdicated* 11 December 1936 *created* Duke of Windsor 1937 *married* 3 June 1937 Mrs Wallis Simpson (Her Grace The Duchess of Windsor *born* 19 June 1896 *died* 24 April 1986) *died* 28 May 1972

2. HRH PRINCE ALBERT Frederick Arthur George *born* 14 December 1895 *created* Duke of York 1920 *married* 26 April 1923 Lady Elizabeth Bowes-Lyon, youngest daughter of the 14th Earl of Strathmore and Kinghorne (HM Queen Elizabeth the Queen Mother *born* 4 August 1900 *died* 30 March 2002) *succeeded* to the throne as King George VI, 11 December 1936 *died* 6 February 1952. *Issue*
   (1) HRH Princess Elizabeth Alexandra Mary *succeeded* to the throne as Queen Elizabeth II, 6 February 1952 (*see* Royal Family)
   (2) HRH Princess Margaret Rose (later HRH The Princess Margaret, Countess of Snowdon) *born* 21 August 1930 *married* 6 May 1960 Anthony Charles Robert Armstrong-Jones, GCVO *created* Earl of Snowdon 1961 (marriage dissolved 1978) *died* 9 February 2002, having had issue (*see* Royal Family)

3. HRH PRINCESS (Victoria Alexandra Alice) MARY *born* 25 April 1897 *created* Princess Royal 1932 *married* 28 February 1922 Viscount Lascelles, later the 6th Earl of Harewood (1882–1947) *died* 28 March 1965. *Issue*

(1) George Henry Hubert Lascelles, 7th Earl of Harewood, KBE *born* 7 February 1923 *died* 11 July 2011 *married* (1) 1949 Maria (Marion) Stein (marriage dissolved 1967) *issue (a)* David Henry George, 8th Earl of Harewood *born* 1950 *(b)* James Edward *born* 1953 *(c)* (Robert) Jeremy Hugh *born* 1955 (2) 1967 Patricia Tuckwell *issue (d)* Mark Hubert *born* 1964
(2) Gerald David Lascelles *born* 21 August 1924 *died* 27 February 1998 *married* (1) 1952 Angela Dowding (marriage dissolved 1978) *issue (a)* Henry Ulick *born* 1953 (2) 1978 Elizabeth Collingwood (Elizabeth Colvin) *issue (b)* Martin David *born* 1962

4. HRH PRINCE HENRY William Frederick Albert *born* 31 March 1900 *created* Duke of Gloucester, Earl of Ulster and Baron Culloden 1928 *married* 6 November 1935 Lady Alice Christabel Montagu-Douglas-Scott, daughter of the 7th Duke of Buccleuch and Queensberry (HRH Princess Alice, Duchess of Gloucester *born* 25 December 1901 *died* 29 October 2004) *died* 10 June 1974. *Issue*
   (1) HRH Prince William Henry Andrew Frederick *born* 18 December 1941 accidentally *killed* 28 August 1972
   (2) HRH Prince Richard Alexander Walter George (HRH The Duke of Gloucester, *see* Royal Family)

5. HRH PRINCE GEORGE Edward Alexander Edmund *born* 20 December 1902 *created* Duke of Kent, Earl of St Andrews and Baron Downpatrick 1934 *married* 29 November 1934 HRH Princess Marina of Greece and Denmark (*born* 30 November 1906 *died* 27 August 1968) *killed* on active service 25 August 1942. *Issue*
   (1) HRH Prince Edward George Nicholas Paul Patrick (HRH The Duke of Kent, *see* Royal Family)
   (2) HRH Princess Alexandra Helen Elizabeth Olga Christabel (HRH Princess Alexandra, the Hon. Lady Ogilvy, *see* Royal Family)
   (3) HRH Prince Michael George Charles Franklin (HRH Prince Michael of Kent, *see* Royal Family)

6. HRH PRINCE JOHN Charles Francis *born* 12 July 1905 *died* 18 January 1919

DESCENDANTS OF QUEEN VICTORIA

I. HRH Princess Victoria Adelaide Mary Louisa, Princess Royal (1840–1901) m Friedrich III (1831–88), later German Emperor	II. HRH Prince Albert Edward (HM KING EDWARD VII) (1841–1910) succeeded 22 Jan 1901 m HRH Princess Alexandra of Denmark (1844–1925)	III. HRH Princess Alice Maud Mary (1843–78) m Prince Ludwig (1837–92), later Grand Duke of Hesse	IV. HRH Prince Alfred Ernest Albert, Duke of Edinburgh (1844–1900) succeeded as Duke of Saxe-Coburg and Gotha 1893 m Grand Duchess Marie Alexandrovna of Russia (1853–1920)

1. HIM Wilhelm II (1859–1941), later German Emperor m (1) Princess Augusta Victoria of Schleswig-Holstein-Sonderburg-Augustenburg (1858–1921) (2) Princess Hermine of Reuss (1887–1947). *Issue* Wilhelm (1882–1951); Eitel-Friedrich (1883–1942); Adalbert (1884–1948); August Wilhelm (1887–1949); Oskar (1888–1958); Joachim (1890–1920); Viktoria Luise (1892–1980)

2. Charlotte (1860–1919) m Bernhard, Duke of Saxe-Meiningen (1851–1928). *Issue* Feodora (1879–1945)

3. Heinrich (1862–1929) m Princess Irene of Hesse (*see* III.3). *Issue* Waldemar (1889–1945); Sigismund (1896–1978); Heinrich (1900–4)

1. Albert Victor, Duke of Clarence and Avondale (1864–92)

2. George (HM KING GEORGE V) (1865–1936) (*see* House of Windsor)

3. Louise (1867–1931), later Princess Royal m 1st Duke of Fife (1849–1912). *Issue* Alexandra (1891–1959); Maud (1893–1945)

4. Victoria (1868–1935)

5. Maud (1869–1938) m Prince Carl of Denmark (1872–1957), later King Haakon VII of Norway. *Issue* Olav V (1903–91)

6. Alexander (6–7 Apr 1871)

1. Victoria (1863–1950) m Prince Louis of Battenberg (1854–1921), later 1st Marquess of Milford Haven. *Issue* Alice (1885–1969); Louise (1889–1965); George (1892–1938); Louis (1900–79)

2. Elizabeth (1864–1918) m Grand Duke Sergius of Russia (1857–1905)

3. Irene (1866–1953) m Prince Heinrich of Prussia (*see* I.3)

4. Ernst Ludwig (1868–1937), Grand Duke of Hesse, m (1) Princess Victoria Melita of Saxe-Coburg (see IV.3) (2) Princess Eleonore of Solms-Hohensolms-Lich (1871–1937). *Issue* Elizabeth (1895–1903); George (1906–37); Ludwig (1908–68)

5. Frederick William (1870–3)

6. Alix (Tsaritsa of Russia) (1872–1918) m Nicholas II, Tsar of All the Russias (1868–1918). *Issue* Olga (1895–1918); Tatiana (1897–1918); Marie (1899–1918); Anastasia (1901–18); Alexis (1904–18)

7. Marie (1874–8)

4. Sigismund (1864–6)

5. Victoria (1866–1929) m (1) Prince Adolf of Schaumburg-Lippe (1859–1916) (2) Alexander Zubkov (1900–36)

6. Waldemar (1868–79)

7. Sophie (1870–1932) m Constantine I (1868–1923), later King of the Hellenes. *Issue* George II (1890–1947); Alexander I (1893–1920); Helena (1896–1982); Paul I (1901–64); Irene (1904–74); Katherine (1913–2007)

8. Margarethe (1872–1954) m Prince Friedrich Karl of Hesse (1868–1940). *Issue* Friedrich Wilhelm (1893–1916); Maximilian (1894–1914); Philipp (1896–1980); Wolfgang (1896–1989); Richard (1901–69); Christoph (1901–43)

QUEEN VICTORIA (Alexandrina Victoria) (1819–1901) *succeeded* 20 Jun 1837 *m* (Francis) Albert Augustus Charles Emmanuel, Duke of Saxony, Prince of Saxe-Coburg and Gotha (HRH Albert, Prince Consort) (1819–61)

| VI. HRH Princess Louise Caroline Alberta (1848–1939) *m* Marquess of Lorne (1845–1914), later 9th Duke of Argyll | VII. HRH Prince Arthur William Patrick Albert, Duke of Connaught (1850–1942) *m* Princess Louisa of Prussia (1860–1917) | VIII. HRH Prince Leopold George Duncan Albert, Duke of Albany (1853–84) *m* Princess Helena of Waldeck (1861–1922) | IX. HRH Princess Beatrice Mary Victoria Feodore (1857–1944) *m* Prince Henry of Battenberg (1858–96) |

1. Alfred, Prince of Saxe-Coburg (1874–99)

2. Marie (1875–1938) *m* Ferdinand (1865–1927), later King of Roumania. *Issue* Carol II (1893–1953); Elisabeth (1894–1956); Marie (1900–61); Nicolas (1903–78); Ileana (1909–91); Mircea (1913–16)

3. Victoria Melita (1876–1936) *m* (1) Grand Duke Ernst Ludwig of Hesse (see III.4) (2) Grand Duke Kirill of Russia (1876–1938). *Issue* Marie (1907–51); Kira (1909–67); Vladimir (1917–92)

4. Alexandra (1878–1942) *m* Ernst, Prince of Hohenlohe Langenburg (1863–1950). *Issue* Gottfried (1897–1960); Maria (1899–1967); Alexandra (1901–63); Irma (1902–86)

5. Beatrice (1884–1966) *m* Alfonso of Orleans, Infante of Spain (1886–1975). *Issue* Alvaro (1910–97); Alonso (1912–36); Ataulfo (1913–74)

1. Margaret (1882–1920) *m* Crown Prince Gustaf Adolf (1882–1973), later King of Sweden. *Issue* Gustaf Adolf (1906–47); Sigvard (1907–2002); Ingrid (1910–2000); Bertil (1912–97); Count Carl Bernadotte (1916–2012)

2. Arthur (1883–1938) *m* HH Duchess of Fife (1891–1959). *Issue* Alastair Arthur (1914–43)

3. (Victoria) Patricia (1886–1974) *m* Adm. Hon. Sir Alexander Ramsay (1881–1972). *Issue* Alexander (1919–2000)

1. Alice (1883–1981) *m* Prince Alexander of Teck (1874–1957), later 1st Earl of Athlone. *Issue* May (1906–94); Rupert (1907–28); Maurice (Mar–Sep 1910)

2. Charles Edward (1884–1954), Duke of Albany until title suspended 1917, Duke of Saxe-Coburg-Gotha *m* Princess Victoria Adelheid of Schleswig-Holstein-Sonderburg-Glücksburg (1885–1970) *Issue* Johann Leopold (1906–72); Sibylla (1908–72); Dietmar Hubertus (1909–43); Caroline (1912–83); Friedrich Josias (1918–98)

1. Alexander, 1st Marquess of Carisbrooke (1886–1960) *m* Lady Irene Denison (1890–1956). *Issue* Iris (1920–82)

2. Victoria Eugénie (1887–1969) *m* Alfonso XIII, King of Spain (1886–1941). *Issue* Alfonso (1907–38); Jaime (1908–75); Beatriz (1909–2002); Maria (1911–96); Juan (1913–93); Gonzalo (1914–34)

3. Maj. Lord Leopold Mountbatten (1889–1922)

4. Maurice (1891–1914)

V. HRH Princess Helena Augusta Victoria (1846–1923) *m* Prince Christian of Schleswig-Holstein-Sonderburg-Augustenburg (1831–1917)

1. Christian Victor (1867–1900)

2. Albert (1869–1931), later Duke of Schleswig-Holstein

3. Helena (1870–1948)

4. Marie Louise (1872–1956), *m* Prince Aribert of Anhalt (1864–1933)

5. Harold (12–20 May 1876)

PRECEDENCE

ENGLAND AND WALES

The Sovereign
The Prince Philip, Duke of Edinburgh
The Prince of Wales
The Sovereign's younger sons
The Sovereign's grandsons
The Sovereign's cousins
Archbishop of Canterbury
Lord High Chancellor
Archbishop of York
The Prime Minister
Lord President of the Council
Speaker of the House of Commons
Speaker of the House of Lords
President of the Supreme Court
Lord Chief Justice of England and
  Wales
Lord Privy Seal
Ambassadors and High Commissioners
Lord Great Chamberlain
Earl Marshal
Lord Steward of the Household
Lord Chamberlain of the Household
Master of the Horse
Dukes, according to their patent of
  creation:
  1. of England
  2. of Scotland
  3. of Great Britain
  4. of Ireland
  5. those created since the Union
Eldest sons of Dukes of the Blood
  Royal
Ministers, Envoys, and other important
  overseas visitors
Marquesses, according to their patent
  of creation:
  1. of England
  2. of Scotland
  3. of Great Britain
  4. of Ireland
  5. those created since the Union
Dukes' eldest sons
Earls, according to their patent of
  creation:
  1. of England
  2. of Scotland
  3. of Great Britain
  4. of Ireland
  5. those created since the Union
Younger sons of Dukes of Blood Royal
Marquesses' eldest sons

Dukes' younger sons
Viscounts, according to their patent of
  creation:
  1. of England
  2. of Scotland
  3. of Great Britain
  4. of Ireland
  5. those created since the Union
Earls' eldest sons
Marquesses' younger sons
Bishop of London
Bishop of Durham
Bishop of Winchester
Other English Diocesan Bishops,
  according to seniority of
  consecration
Retired Church of England Diocesan
  Bishops, according to seniority of
  consecration
Suffragan Bishops, according to
  seniority of consecration
Secretaries of State, if of the degree of a
  Baron
Barons, according to their patent of
  creation:
  1. of England
  2. of Scotland (Lords of Parliament)
  3. of Great Britain
  4. of Ireland
  5. those created since the Union,
    including Life Barons
Master of the Rolls
Deputy President of the Supreme
  Court
Justices of the Supreme Court,
  according to seniority of
  appointment
Treasurer of the Household
Comptroller of the Household
Vice-Chamberlain of the Household
Secretaries of State under the degree of
  Baron
Viscounts' eldest sons
Earls' younger sons
Barons' eldest sons
Knights of the Garter
Privy Counsellors
Chancellor of the Order of the Garter
Chancellor of the Exchequer
Chancellor of the Duchy of Lancaster
President of the Queen's Bench
  Division
President of the Family Division

Chancellor of the High Court
Lord Justices of Appeal, according to
  seniority of appointment
Judges of the High Court, according to
  seniority of appointment
Viscounts' younger sons
Barons' younger sons
Sons of Life Peers
Baronets, according to date of patent
Knights of the Thistle
Knights Grand Cross of the Bath
Knights Grand Cross of St Michael and
  St George
Knights Grand Cross of the Royal
  Victorian Order
Knights Grand Cross of the British
  Empire
Knights Commanders of the Bath
Knights Commanders of St Michael
  and St George
Knights Commanders of the Royal
  Victorian Order
Knights Commanders of the British
  Empire
Knights Bachelor
Circuit Judges, according to priority
  and order of their respective
  appointments
Master of the Court of Protection
Companions of the Bath
Companions of St Michael and St
  George
Commanders of the Royal Victorian
  Order
Commanders of the British Empire
Companions of the Distinguished
  Service Order
Lieutenants of the Royal Victorian
  Order
Officers of the British Empire
Companions of the Imperial Service
  Order
Eldest sons of younger sons of peers
Baronets' eldest sons
Eldest sons of knights, in the same
  order as their fathers
Members of the Royal Victorian Order
Members of the British Empire
Baronets' younger sons
Knights' younger sons, in the same
  order as their fathers
Esquires
Gentlemen

WOMEN

Women take the same rank as their husbands or as their brothers; but the daughter of a peer marrying a commoner retains her title as Lady or Honourable. Daughters of peers rank next immediately after the wives of their elder brothers, and before their younger brothers' wives. Daughters of peers marrying peers of a lower degree take the same order of precedence as that of their husbands; thus the daughter of a Duke marrying a Baron becomes of the rank of Baroness only, while her sisters married to commoners retain their rank and take precedence over the Baroness. Merely official rank on the husband's part does not give any similar precedence to the wife.

Peeresses in their own right take the same precedence as peers of the same rank, ie from their date of creation.

SCOTLAND

The Sovereign
The Prince Philip, Duke of Edinburgh
The Lord High Commissioner to the
  General Assembly of the Church of
  Scotland (while that assembly is
  sitting)
The Duke of Rothesay (eldest son of
  the Sovereign)
The Sovereign's younger sons
The Sovereign's grandsons
The Sovereign's nephews
Lord-Lieutenants
Lord Provosts, during their term of
  office*
Sheriffs Principal, during their term of
  office and within the bounds of their
  respective sheriffdoms
Lord Chancellor of Great Britain
Moderator of the General Assembly of
  the Church of Scotland
Keeper of the Great Seal of Scotland
  (the First Minister)
Presiding Officer
The Secretary of State for Scotland
Hereditary High Constable of Scotland
Hereditary Master of the Household in
  Scotland
Dukes, as in England
Eldest sons of Dukes of the Blood Royal

Marquesses, as in England
Dukes' eldest sons
Earls, as in England
Younger sons of Dukes of Blood Royal
Marquesses' eldest sons
Dukes' younger sons
Lord Justice General
Lord Clerk Register
Lord Advocate
The Advocate General
Lord Justice Clerk
Viscounts, as in England
Earls' eldest sons
Marquesses' younger sons
Lords of Parliament or Barons, as in
  England
Eldest sons of Viscounts
Earls' younger sons
Eldest sons of Lords of Parliament or
  Barons
Knights and Ladies of the Garter
Knights and Ladies of the Thistle
Privy Counsellors
Senators of the College of Justice
  (Lords of Session)
Viscounts' younger sons
Younger sons of Lords of Parliament or
  Barons
Baronets
Knights and Dames Grand Cross of
  orders, as in England

Knights and Dames Commanders of
  orders, as in England
Solicitor-General for Scotland
Lord Lyon King of Arms
Sheriffs Principal, when not within
  own county
Knights Bachelor
Sheriffs
Companions of Orders, as in England
Commanders of the Royal Victorian
  Order
Commanders of the British Empire
Lieutenants of the Royal Victorian
  Order
Companions of the Distinguished
  Service Order
Officers of the British Empire
Companions of the Imperial Service
  Order
Eldest sons of younger sons of peers
Eldest sons of baronets
Eldest sons of knights, as in England
Members of the Royal Victorian
  Order
Members of the British Empire
Baronets' younger sons
Knights' younger sons
Queen's Counsel
Esquires
Gentlemen

* The Lord Provosts of Aberdeen, Dundee, Edinburgh and Glasgow are Lord-Lieutenants for these cities *ex officio* and take precedence as such

THE PEERAGE

S.	Scottish title	*c.p.*	civil partnership
I.	Irish title	*w.*	widower or widow
**	hereditary peer remaining in the House of Lords	M.	minor
°	there is no 'of' in the title	†	heir not ascertained at time of going to press
b.	born	F_	represents forename
s.	succeeded	S_	represents surname
m.	married	cr.	created
§	life peer disqualified from sitting in the House of Lords as a member of the juidiciary	¶	life peer who has resigned permanently from the House of Lords

The rules which govern the creation and succession of peerages are extremely complicated. There are, technically, five separate peerages, the Peerage of England, of Scotland, of Ireland, of Great Britain, and of the United Kingdom. The Peerage of Great Britain dates from 1707 when an Act of Union combined the two kingdoms of England and Scotland and separate peerages were discontinued. The Peerage of the United Kingdom dates from 1801 when Great Britain and Ireland were combined under an Act of Union. Some Scottish peers have received additional peerages of Great Britain or of the UK since 1707, and some Irish peers additional peerages of the UK since 1801.

The Peerage of Ireland was not entirely discontinued from 1801 but holders of Irish peerages, whether pre-dating or created subsequent to the Union of 1801, were not entitled to sit in the House of Lords if they had no additional English, Scottish, Great Britain or UK peerage. However, they are eligible for election to the House of Commons and to vote in parliamentary elections. An Irish peer holding a peerage of a lower grade which enabled him to sit in the House of Lords was introduced there by the title which enabled him to sit, though for all other purposes he was known by his higher title.

In the Peerage of Scotland there is no rank of Baron; the equivalent rank is Lord of Parliament, abbreviated to 'Lord' (the female equivalent is 'Lady').

All peers of England, Scotland, Great Britain or the UK who are 21 years or over, and of British, Irish or Commonwealth nationality were entitled to sit in the House of Lords until the House of Lords Act 1999, when hereditary peers lost the right to sit. However, section two of the act provided an exception for 90 hereditary peers plus the holders of the office of Earl Marshal and Lord Great Chamberlain to remain as members of the House of Lords for their lifetime or pending further reform. Of the 90 hereditary peers, 75 were elected by the hereditary peers in their political party, or Crossbench grouping, and the remaining 15 by the whole house. Until 7 November 2002 any vacancy arising due to the death of one of the 90 excepted hereditary peers was filled by the runner-up to the original election. From 7 November 2002 any vacancy due to a death has been filled by holding a by-election. By-elections are conducted in accordance with arrangements made by the Clerk of the Parliaments and have to take place within three months of a vacancy occurring. If the vacancy is among the 75, only the excepted hereditary peers in the relevant party or Crossbench grouping are entitled to vote. If the vacancy is among the other 15, the whole house is entitled to vote.

In the list below, peers currently holding one of the 92 hereditary places in the House of Lords are indicated by **.

HEREDITARY WOMEN PEERS

Most hereditary peerages pass on death to the nearest male heir, but there are exceptions, and several are held by women.

A woman peer in her own right retains her title after marriage, and if her husband's rank is the superior she is designated by the two titles jointly, the inferior one second. Her hereditary claim still holds good in spite of any marriage whether higher or lower. No rank held by a woman can confer any title or even precedence upon her husband but the rank of a hereditary woman peer in her own right is inherited by her eldest son (or in some cases daughter).

After the Peerage Act 1963, hereditary women peers in their own right were entitled to sit in the House of Lords, subject to the same qualifications as men, until the House of Lords Act 1999.

LIFE PEERS

From 1876 to 2009 non-hereditary or life peerages were conferred on certain eminent judges to enable the judicial functions of the House of Lords to be carried out. These lords were known as Lords of Appeal in Ordinary or law lords. The judicial role of the House of Lords as the highest appeal court in the UK ended on 30 July 2009 and since 1 October 2009, under the Constitutional Reform Act 2005, any peer who holds a senior judicial office is disqualified from sitting in the House of Lords until they retire from that office. In the list of life peerages which follows, members of the judiciary who are currently disqualified from sitting and voting in the House of Lords until retirement, are marked by a '§'.

Under the Constitutional Reform and Governance Act 2010, five peers permanently resigned from the House of Lords. These are indicated in the following list by a '¶'.

Since 1958 life peerages have been conferred upon distinguished men and women from all walks of life, giving them seats in the House of Lords in the degree of Baron or Baroness. They are addressed in the same way as hereditary lords and barons, and their children have similar courtesy titles.

HOUSE OF LORD REFORM ACT 2014

The House of Lords Reform Act 2014 makes provision for a member of the House of Lords who is a peer to retire or resign by giving notice in writing to the Clerk of Parliaments. Resignations may not be rescinded. The Act also makes provision for the expulsion of peers who do not attend the House of Lords for an entire parliamentary session which is longer than six months. Peers on leave of absence or subject to a suspension or disqualification which results in absenteeism for an entire session will not be expelled. The House can also resolve that a peer should not be expelled by reason of special circumstances.

PEERAGES EXTINCT SINCE THE LAST EDITION

LIFE PEERAGES: Attenborough (cr. 1993); Ballyedmond (cr. 2004); Bannside (cr. 2010); Bilston (cr. 2005); Hayhoe (cr. 1992); Jacobs (cr. 1997); Kimball (cr. 1985); Kingsdown (cr. 1993); Lewis of Newnham (cr. 1989); McAlpine of West Green (cr. 1984); Macaulay of Bragar (cr. 1988); Miller of Hendon (cr. 1993); Roberts of Conwy (cr. 1997); Templeman (cr. 1982)

DISCLAIMER OF PEERAGES

The Peerage Act 1963 enables peers to disclaim their peerages for life. Peers alive in 1963 could disclaim within twelve months after the passing of the act (31 July 1963); a person subsequently succeeding to a peerage may disclaim within 12 months (one month if an MP) after the date of succession, or of reaching 21, if later. The disclaimer is irrevocable but does not affect the descent of the peerage after the disclaimant's death, and children of a disclaimed peer may, if they wish, retain their precedence and any courtesy titles and styles borne as children of a peer. The disclaimer permitted the disclaimant to sit in the House of Commons if elected as an MP. As the House of Lords Act 1999 removed hereditary peers from the House of Lords, they are now entitled to sit in the House of Commons without having to disclaim their titles.

The following peerages are currently disclaimed:

EARLDOM: Selkirk (1994)
BARONIES: Merthyr (1977); Reith (1972); Sanderson of Ayot (1971); Silkin (2002)
PEERS WHO ARE MINORS (ie under 21 years of age)
BARONS: Glenconner (b. 1994); Hawke (b. 1995); Rodney (b. 1999)

FORMS OF ADDRESS

Forms of address are given under the style for each individual rank of the peerage. Both formal and social forms of address are given where usage differs; nowadays, the social form is generally preferred to the formal, which increasingly is used only for official documents and on very formal occasions.

ROLL OF THE PEERAGE

Crown Office, House of Lords, London SW1A 0PW

The Roll of the Peerage is kept at the Crown Office and maintained by the Registrar and Assistant Registrar of the Peerage in accordance with the terms of a 2004 royal warrant. The roll records the names of all living life peers and hereditary peers who have proved their succession to the satisfaction of the Lord Chancellor. The Roll of the Peerage is maintained in addition to the Clerk of the Parliaments' register of hereditary peers eligible to stand for election in House of Lords' by-elections.

A person whose name is not entered on the Roll of the Peerage can not be addressed or mentioned by the title of a peer in any official document.

Registrar, Ian Denyer, MVO
Assistant Registrar, Grant Bavister

HEREDITARY PEERS

as at 31 August 2014

PEERS OF THE BLOOD ROYAL

Style, His Royal Highness the Duke of _/His Royal Highness the Earl of_/His Royal Highness the Lord_
Style of address (formal) May it please your Royal Highness; *(informal)* Sir

Created	Title, order of succession, name, etc	Heir
	Dukes	
1947	*Edinburgh (1st)*, HRH the Prince Philip, Duke of Edinburgh	The Prince of Wales *
1337	*Cornwall*, HRH the Prince of Wales, s. 1952	‡
1398 S.	*Rothesay*, HRH the Prince of Wales, s. 1952	‡
2011	*Cambridge (1st)*, HRH Prince William of Wales	HRH Prince George of Cambridge
1986	*York (1st)*, Prince Andrew, HRH the Duke of York	None
1928	*Gloucester (2nd)*, Prince Richard, HRH the Duke of Gloucester, s. 1974	Earl of Ulster
1934	*Kent (2nd)*, Prince Edward, HRH the Duke of Kent, s. 1942	Earl of St Andrews
	Earl	
1999	*Wessex (1st)*, Prince Edward, HRH the Earl of Wesex	Viscount Severn

* In June 1999 Buckingham Palace announced that the current Earl of Wessex will be granted the Dukedom of Edinburgh when the title reverts to the Crown. The title will only revert to the Crown on both the death of the current Duke of Edinburgh and the Prince of Wales' succession as king
‡ The title is held by the sovereign's eldest son from the moment of his birth or the sovereign's accession

DUKES

Coronet, Eight strawberry leaves

Style, His Grace the Duke of _
  Envelope (formal), His Grace the Duke of _; *(social),* The Duke of _. *Letter (formal),* My Lord Duke; *(social),* Dear Duke.
Spoken (formal), Your Grace; *(social),* Duke
Wife's style, Her Grace the Duchess of _
  Envelope (formal), Her Grace the Duchess of _; *(social),* The Duchess of _. *Letter (formal),* Dear Madam; *(social),* Dear
Duchess. *Spoken,* Duchess
Eldest son's style, Takes his father's second title as a courtesy title (*see* Courtesy Titles)
Younger sons' style, 'Lord' before forename (F_) and surname (S_)
  Envelope, Lord F_ S_. *Letter (formal),* My Lord; *(social),* Dear Lord F_. *Spoken (formal),* My Lord; *(social),* Lord F_.
Daughters' style, 'Lady' before forename (F_) and surname (S_)
  Envelope, Lady F_ S_. *Letter (formal),* Dear Madam; *(social),* Dear Lady F_. *Spoken,* Lady F_

Created	Title, order of succession, name, etc	Heir
1868 I.	*Abercorn (5th),* James Hamilton, KG, *b.* 1934, *s.* 1979, *m.*	Marquess of Hamilton, *b.* 1969
1701 S.	*Argyll (13th),* Torquhil Ian Campbell, *b.* 1968, *s.* 2001, 1979, *m.*	Marquess of Lorne, *b.* 2004
1703 S.	*Atholl (12th),* Bruce George Ronald Murray, *b.* 1960, *s.* 2012, *m.*	Marquis of Tullibardine, *b.* 1985
1682	*Beaufort (11th),* David Robert Somerset, *b.* 1928, *s.* 1984, *m.*	Marquess of Worcester, *b.* 1952
1694	*Bedford (15th),* Andrew Ian Henry Russell, *b.* 1962, *s.* 2003, *m.*	Marquess of Tavistock, *b.* 2005
1663 S.	*Buccleuch (10th) and Queensberry (12th) (S. 1684),* Richard Walter John Montagu Douglas Scott, KBE, *b.* 1954, *s.* 2007, *m.*	Earl of Dalkeith, *b.* 1984
1694	*Devonshire (12th),* Peregrine Andrew Morny Cavendish, KCVO, CBE, *b.* 1944, *s.* 2004, *m.*	Earl of Burlington, *b.* 1969
1900	*Fife (3rd),* James George Alexander Bannerman Carnegie, *b.* 1929, *s.* 1959	Earl of Southesk, *b.* 1961
1675	*Grafton (12th),* Henry Oliver Charles FitzRoy, *b.* 1978, *s.* 2011, *m.*	Earl of Euston, *b.* 2012
1643 S.	*Hamilton (16th) and Brandon (13th) (1711),* Alexander Douglas Douglas-Hamilton, *b.* 1978, *s.* 2010, *m. Premier Peer of Scotland*	Marquess of Douglas and Clydesdale, *b.* 2012
1766 I.	*Leinster (9th),* Maurice FitzGerald, *b.* 1948, *s.* 2004, *m. Premier Duke, Marquess and Earl of Ireland*	Lord John F., *b.* 1952
1719	*Manchester (13th),* Alexander Charles David Drogo Montagu, *b.* 1962, *s.* 2002, *m.*	Lord Kimble W. D. M., *b.* 1964
1702	*Marlborough (11th),* John George Vanderbilt Henry Spencer-Churchill, *b.* 1926, *s.* 1972, *m.*	Marquess of Blandford, *b.* 1955
1707 S.	** *Montrose (8th),* James Graham, *b.* 1935, *s.* 1992, *m.*	Marquis of Graham, *b.* 1973
1483	** *Norfolk (18th),* Edward Wiliam Fitzalan-Howard, *b.* 1956, *s.* 2002, *m. Premier Duke and Earl Marshal*	Earl of Arundel and Surrey, *b.* 1987
1766	*Northumberland (12th),* Ralph George Algernon Percy, *b.* 1956, *s.* 1995, *m.*	Earl Percy, *b.* 1984
1675	*Richmond (10th) and Gordon (5th) (1876),* Charles Henry Gordon Lennox, *b.* 1929, *s.* 1989, *m.*	Earl of March and Kinrara, *b.* 1955
1707 S.	*Roxburghe (10th),* Guy David Innes-Ker, *b.* 1954, *s.* 1974, *m. Premier Baronet of Scotland*	Marquis of Bowmont and Cessford, *b.* 1981
1703	*Rutland (11th),* David Charles Robert Manners, *b.* 1959, *s.* 1999, *m.*	Marquess of Granby, *b.* 1999
1684	*St Albans (14th),* Murray de Vere Beauclerk, *b.* 1939, *s.* 1988, *m.*	Earl of Burford, *b.* 1965
1547	*Somerset (19th),* John Michael Edward Seymour, *b.* 1952, *s.* 1984, *m.*	Lord Seymour, *b.* 1982
1833	*Sutherland (7th),* Francis Ronald Egerton, *b.* 1940, *s.* 2000, *m.*	Marquess of Stafford, *b.* 1975
1814	*Wellington (8th),* Arthur Valerian Wellesley, KG, LVO, OBE, MC, *b.* 1915, *s.* 1972, *w.*	Marquess of Douro, *b.* 1945
1874	*Westminster (6th),* Gerald Cavendish Grosvenor, KG, CB, CVO, OBE, TD, *b.* 1951, *s.* 1979, *m.*	Earl Grosvenor, *b.* 1991

MARQUESSES

Coronet, Four strawberry leaves alternating with four silver balls

Style, The Most Hon. the Marquess (of) _ . In Scotland the spelling 'Marquis' is preferred for pre-Union creations
  Envelope (formal), The Most Hon. the Marquess of _; *(social),* The Marquess of _. *Letter (formal),* My Lord; *(social),* Dear
Lord _. *Spoken (formal),* My Lord; *(social),* Lord _
Wife's style, The Most Hon. the Marchioness (of) _
  Envelope (formal), The Most Hon. the Marchioness of _; *(social),* The Marchioness of _. *Letter (formal),* Madam;
(social), Dear Lady _. *Spoken,* Lady _
Eldest son's style, Takes his father's second title as a courtesy title *(see* Courtesy Titles)
Younger sons' style, 'Lord' before forename and surname, as for Duke's younger sons
Daughters' style, 'Lady' before forename and surname, as for Duke's daughter

Created	Title, order of succession, name, etc	Heir
1916	Aberdeen and Temair (7th), Alexander George Gordon, b. 1955, s. 2002, m.	Earl of Haddo, b. 1983
1876	Abergavenny (6th), Christopher George Charles Nevill, b. 1955, s. 2000, m.	To Earldom only, David M. R. N., b. 1941
1821	Ailesbury (8th), Michael Sidney Cedric Brudenell-Bruce, b. 1926, s. 1974	Earl of Cardigan, b. 1952
1831	Ailsa (8th), Archibald Angus Charles Kennedy, b. 1956, s. 1994	Lord David T. K., b. 1958
1815	Anglesey (8th), Charles Alexander Vaughan Paget, b. 1950, s. 2013, m.	Earl of Uxbridge, b. 1986
1789	Bath (7th), Alexander George Thynn, b. 1932, s. 1992, m.	Viscount Weymouth, b. 1974
1826	Bristol (8th), Frederick William Augustus Hervey, b. 1979, s. 1999	Timothy H. H., b. 1960
1796	Bute (7th), John Colum Crichton-Stuart, b. 1958, s. 1993, m.	Earl of Dumfries, b. 1989
1812	° Camden (6th), David George Edward Henry Pratt, b. 1930, s. 1983	Earl of Brecknock, b. 1965
1815	** Cholmondeley (7th), David George Philip Cholmondeley, KCVO, b. 1960, s. 1990, m. Lord Great Chamberlain	Earl of Rocksavage, b. 2010
1816 I.	° Conyngham (8th), Henry Vivian Pierpoint Conyngham, b. 1951, s. 2009, m.	Earl of Mount Charles, b. 1975
1791 I.	Donegall (8th), Arthur Patrick Chichester, b. 1952, s. 2007, m.	Earl of Belfast, b. 1990
1789 I.	Downshire (9th), (Arthur Francis) Nicholas Wills Hill, b. 1959, s. 2003, m.	Earl of Hillsborough, b. 1996
1801 I.	Ely (9th), Charles John Tottenham, b. 1943, s. 2006, m.	Lord Timothy C. T., b. 1948
1801	Exeter (8th), (William) Michael Anthony Cecil, b. 1935, s. 1988, m.	Lord Burghley, b. 1970
1800 I.	Headfort (7th), Thomas Michael Ronald Christopher Taylour, b. 1959, s. 2005, m.	Earl of Bective, b. 1989
1793	Hertford (9th), Henry Jocelyn Seymour, b. 1958, s. 1997, m.	Earl of Yarmouth, b. 1993
1599 S.	Huntly (13th), Granville Charles Gomer Gordon, b. 1944, s. 1987, m. Premier Marquess of Scotland	Earl of Aboyne, b. 1973
1784	Lansdowne (9th), Charles Maurice Mercer Nairne Petty-Fitzmaurice, LVO b. 1941, s. 1999, m.	Earl of Kerry, b. 1970
1902	Linlithgow (4th), Adrian John Charles Hope, b. 1946, s. 1987, m.	Earl of Hopetoun, b. 1969
1816 I.	Londonderry (10th), Frederick Aubrey Vane-Tempest-Stewart, b. 1972, s. 2012	Lord Reginald A. V-T-S, b. 1977
1701 S.	Lothian (13th) and Baron Kerr of Monteviot (life peerage, 2010), Michael Andrew Foster Jude Kerr (Michael Ancram), PC, QC, b. 1945, s. 2004, m.	Lord Ralph W. F. J. K., b. 1957
1917	Milford Haven (4th), George Ivar Louis Mountbatten, b. 1961, s. 1970, m.	Earl of Medina, b. 1991
1838	Normanby (5th), Constantine Edmund Walter Phipps, b. 1954, s. 1994, m.	Earl of Mulgrave, b. 1994
1812	Northampton (7th), Spencer Douglas David Compton, b. 1946, s. 1978, m.	Earl Compton, b. 1973
1682 S.	Queensberry (12th), David Harrington Angus Douglas, b. 1929, s. 1954, m.	Viscount Drumlanrig, b. 1967
1926	Reading (4th), Simon Charles Henry Rufus Isaacs, b. 1942, s. 1980, m.	Viscount Erleigh, b. 1986
1789	Salisbury (7th) and Baron Gascoyne-Cecil (life peerage, 1999), Robert Michael James Gascoyne-Cecil, KCVO, PC, b. 1946, s. 2003, m.	Viscount Cranborne, b. 1970
1800 I.	Sligo (12th), Sebastian Ulick Browne, b. 1964, s. 2014, m.	Earl of Altamont, b. 1988
1787	° Townshend (8th), Charles George Townshend, b. 1945, s. 2010, m.	Viscount Raynham, b. 1977
1694 S.	Tweeddale (14th), Charles David Montagu Hay, b. 1947, s. 2005	(Lord) Alistair J. M. H., b. 1955
1789 I.	Waterford (8th), John Hubert de la Poer Beresford, b. 1933, s. 1934, m.	Earl of Tyrone, b. 1958
1551	Winchester (18th), Nigel George Paulet, b. 1941, s. 1968, m. Premier Marquess of England	Earl of Wiltshire, b. 1969
1892	Zetland (4th), Lawrence Mark Dundas, b. 1937, s. 1989, m.	Earl of Ronaldshay, b. 1965

EARLS

Coronet, Eight silver balls on stalks alternating with eight gold strawberry leaves

Style, The Rt. Hon. the Earl (of) _
    Envelope (formal), The Rt. Hon. the Earl (of) _; *(social),* The Earl (of) _. *Letter (formal),* My Lord; *(social),* Dear Lord
    _. *Spoken (formal),* My Lord; *(social),* Lord _.
Wife's style, The Rt. Hon. the Countess (of) _
    Envelope (formal), The Rt. Hon. the Countess (of) _; *(social),* The Countess (of) _. *Letter (formal),* Madam; *(social),*
    Lady _. *Spoken (formal),* Madam; *(social),* Lady _.
Eldest son's style, Takes his father's second title as a courtesy title (*see* Courtesy Titles)
Younger sons' style, 'The Hon.' before forename and surname, as for Baron's children
Daughters' style, 'Lady' before forename and surname, as for Duke's daughter

Created	Title, order of succession, name, etc	Heir
1639 S.	Airlie (13th), David George Coke Patrick Ogilvy, KT, GCVO, PC, Royal Victorian Chain, *b.* 1926, *s.* 1968, *m.*	Lord Ogilvy, *b.* 1958
1696	Albemarle (10th), Rufus Arnold Alexis Keppel, *b.* 1965, *s.* 1979, *m.*	Viscount Bury, *b.* 2003
1952	° Alexander of Tunis (2nd), Shane William Desmond Alexander, *b.* 1935, *s.* 1969, *m.*	Hon. Brian J. A., *b.* 1939
1662 S.	Annandale and Hartfell (11th), Patrick Andrew Wentworth Hope Johnstone, *b.* 1941, *s.* 1983, *m.* claim established 1985	Lord Johnstone, *b.* 1971
1789 I.	° Annesley (12th), Michael Robert Annesley, *b.* 1933, *s.* 2011, *m.*	Viscount Glerawly, *b.* 1957
1785 I.	Antrim (9th), Alexander Randal Mark McDonnell, *b.* 1935, *s.* 1977, *m.*	Viscount Dunluce, *b.* 1967
1762 I.	** Arran (9th), Arthur Desmond Colquhoun Gore, *b.* 1938, *s.* 1983, *m.*	William H. G., *b.* 1950 (to the Earldom)
1955	° ** Attlee (3rd), John Richard Attlee, *b.* 1956, *s.* 1991, *m.*	None
1714	Aylesford (12th), Charles Heneage Finch-Knightley, *b.* 1947, *s.* 2008, *m.*	Lord Guernsey, *b.* 1985
1937	** Baldwin of Bewdley (4th), Edward Alfred Alexander Baldwin, *b.* 1938, *s.* 1976, *w.*	Viscount Corvedale, *b.* 1973
1922	Balfour (5th), Roderick Francis Arthur Balfour, *b.* 1948, *s.* 2003, *m.*	Charles G. Y. B., *b.* 1951
1772	° Bathurst (9th), Allen Christopher Bertram Bathurst, *b.* 1961, *s.* 2011, *m.*	Lord Apsley, *b.* 1990
1919	° Beatty (3rd), David Beatty, *b.* 1946, *s.* 1972, *m.*	Viscount Borodale, *b.* 1973
1797 I.	° Belmore (8th), John Armar Lowry-Corry, *b.* 1951, *s.* 1960, *m.*	Viscount Corry, *b.* 1985
1739 I.	Bessborough (12th), Myles Fitzhugh Longfield Ponsonby, *b.* 1941, *s.* 2002, *m.*	Viscount Duncannon, *b.* 1974
1815	Bradford (7th), Richard Thomas Orlando Bridgeman, *b.* 1947, *s.* 1981, *m.*	Viscount Newport, *b.* 1980
1469 S.	Buchan (17th), Malcolm Harry Erskine, *b.* 1930, *s.* 1984, *m.*	Lord Cardross, *b.* 1960
1746	Buckinghamshire (10th), (George) Miles Hobart-Hampden, *b.* 1944, *s.* 1983, *m.*	Sir John V. Hobart, Bt., *b.* 1945
1800	° Cadogan (8th), Charles Gerald John Cadogan, KBE, *b.* 1937, *s.* 1997, *m.*	Viscount Chelsea, *b.* 1966
1878	° Cairns (6th), Simon Dallas Cairns, CVO, CBE, *b.* 1939, *s.* 1989, *m.*	Viscount Garmoyle, *b.* 1965
1455 S.	** Caithness (20th), Malcolm Ian Sinclair, PC, *b.* 1948, *s.* 1965, *w.*	Lord Berriedale, *b.* 1981
1800 I.	Caledon (7th), Nicholas James Alexander, *b.* 1955, *s.* 1980, *m.*	Viscount Alexander, *b.* 1990
1661	Carlisle (13th), George William Beaumont Howard, *b.* 1949, *s.* 1994	Hon. Philip C. W. H., *b.* 1963
1793	Carnarvon (8th), George Reginald Oliver Molyneux Herbert, *b.* 1956, *s.* 2001, *m.*	Lord Porchester, *b.* 1992
1748 I.	Carrick (11th), Arion Thomas Piers Hamilton Butler, *b.* 1975, *s.* 2008, *m.*	Hon. Piers E. T. L. B., *b.* 1979
1800 I.	° Castle Stewart (8th), Arthur Patrick Avondale Stuart, *b.* 1928, *s.* 1961, *m.*	Viscount Stuart, *b.* 1953
1814	°** Cathcart (7th), Charles Alan Andrew Cathcart, *b.* 1952, *s.* 1999, *m.*	Lord Greenock, *b.* 1986
1647 I.	Cavan (13th), Roger Cavan Lambart, *b.* 1944, *s.* 1988 (claim to the peerage not yet established)	Cavan C. E. L., *b.* 1957
1827	° Cawdor (7th), Colin Robert Vaughan Campbell, *b.* 1962, *s.* 1993, *m.*	Viscount Emlyn, *b.* 1998
1801	Chichester (9th), John Nicholas Pelham, *b.* 1944, *s.* 1944, *m.*	Richard A. H. P., *b.* 1952
1803 I.	** Clancarty (9th), Nicholas Power Richard Le Poer Trench, *b.* 1952, *s.* 1995, *m.*	None
1776 I.	Clanwilliam (8th), Patrick James Meade, *b.* 1960, *s.* 2009, *m.*	Lord Gillford, *b.* 1998
1776	Clarendon (8th), George Edward Laurence Villiers, *b.* 1976, *s.* 2009, *m.*	Lord Hyde, *b.* 2008
1620 I.	Cork and Orrery (15th), John Richard Boyle, *b.* 1945, *s.* 2003, *m.*	Viscount Dungarvan, *b.* 1978
1850	Cottenham (9th), Mark John Henry Pepys, *b.* 1983, *s.* 2000	Hon. Sam R. P., *b.* 1986
1762 I.	** Courtown (9th), James Patrick Montagu Burgoyne Winthrop Stopford, *b.* 1954, *s.* 1975, *m.*	Viscount Stopford, *b.* 1988
1697	Coventry (13th), George William Coventry, *b.* 1939, *s.* 2004, *m.*	David D. S. C., *b.* 1973
1857	° Cowley (7th), Garret Graham Wellesley, *b.* 1934, *s.* 1975, *m.*	Viscount Dangan, *b.* 1965

1892	*Cranbrook (5th)*, Gathorne Gathorne-Hardy, *b.* 1933, *s.* 1978, *m.*	Lord Medway, *b.* 1968
1801	*Craven (9th)*, Benjamin Robert Joseph Craven, *b.* 1989, *s.* 1990	Rupert J. E. C., *b.* 1926
1398 S.	*Crawford (29th) and Balcarres (12th) (S. 1651) and Baron Balniel (life peerage, 1974)*, Robert Alexander Lindsay, KT, GCVO, PC, *b.* 1927, *s.* 1975, *m.* Premier Earl on Union Roll	Lord Balniel, *b.* 1958
1861	*Cromartie (5th)*, John Ruaridh Blunt Grant Mackenzie, *b.* 1948, *s.* 1989, *m.*	Viscount Tarbat, *b.* 1987
1901	*Cromer (4th)*, Evelyn Rowland Esmond Baring, *b.* 1946, *s.* 1991, *m.*	Viscount Errington, *b.* 1994
1633 S.	*Dalhousie (17th)*, James Hubert Ramsay, *b.* 1948, *s.* 1999, *m.* Lord Steward	Lord Ramsay, *b.* 1981
1725 I.	*Darnley (11th)*, Adam Ivo Stuart Bligh, *b.* 1941, *s.* 1980, *m.*	Lord Clifton, *b.* 1968
1711	*Dartmouth (10th)*, William Legge, *b.* 1949, *s.* 1997, *m.*	Hon. Rupert L., *b.* 1951
1761	° *De La Warr (11th)*, William Herbrand Sackville, *b.* 1948, *s.* 1988, *m.*	Lord Buckhurst, *b.* 1979
1622	*Denbigh (12th) and Desmond (11th) (I. 1622)*, Alexander Stephen Rudolph Feilding, *b.* 1970, *s.* 1995, *m.*	Viscount Feilding, *b.* 2005
1485	*Derby (19th)*, Edward Richard William Stanley, *b.* 1962, *s.* 1994, *m.*	Lord Stanley, *b.* 1998
1553	*Devon (18th)*, Hugh Rupert Courtenay, *b.* 1942, *s.* 1998, *m.*	Lord Courtenay, *b.* 1975
1800 I.	*Donoughmore (8th)*, Richard Michael John Hely-Hutchinson, *b.* 1927, *s.* 1981, *w.*	Viscount Suirdale, *b.* 1952
1661 I.	*Drogheda (12th)*, Henry Dermot Ponsonby Moore, *b.* 1937, *s.* 1989, *m.*	Viscount Moore, *b.* 1983
1837	*Ducie (7th)*, David Leslie Moreton, *b.* 1951, *s.* 1991, *m.*	Lord Moreton, *b.* 1981
1860	*Dudley (5th)*, William Humble David Jeremy Ward, *b.* 1947, *s.* 2013	Hon. Leander G. D. W., *b.* 1971
1660 S.	** *Dundee (12th)*, Alexander Henry Scrymgeour, *b.* 1949, *s.* 1983, *m.*	Lord Scrymgeour, *b.* 1982
1669 S.	*Dundonald (15th)*, Iain Alexander Douglas Blair Cochrane, *b.* 1961, *s.* 1986, *m.*	Lord Cochrane, *b.* 1991
1686 S.	*Dunmore (12th)*, Malcolm Kenneth Murray, *b.* 1946, *s.* 1995, *m.*	Hon. Geoffrey C. M., *b.* 1949
1833	*Durham (7th)*, Edward Richard Lambton, *b.* 1961, *s.* 2006, *m.*	Viscount Lambton, *b.* 1985
1643 S.	*Dysart (13th)*, John Peter Grant of Rothiemurchus, *b.* 1946, *s.* 2011, *m.*	Lord Huntingtower, *b.* 1977
1837	*Effingham (7th)*, David Mowbray Algernon Howard, *b.* 1939, *s.* 1996, *m.*	Lord Howard of Effingham, *b.* 1971
1507 S.	*Eglinton (18th) and Winton (9th) (S. 1600)*, Archibald George Montgomerie, *b.* 1939, *s.* 1966, *m.*	Lord Montgomerie, *b.* 1966
1821	*Eldon (5th)*, John Joseph Nicholas Scott, *b.* 1937, *s.* 1976, *m.*	Viscount Encombe, *b.* 1962
1633 S.	*Elgin (11th) and Kincardine (15th) (S. 1647)*, Andrew Douglas Alexander Thomas Bruce, KT, *b.* 1924, *s.* 1968, *m.*	Lord Bruce, *b.* 1961
1789 I.	*Enniskillen (7th)*, Andrew John Galbraith Cole, *b* 1942, *s.* 1989, *m.*	Berkeley A. C., *b.* 1949
1789 I.	*Erne (6th)*, Henry George Victor John Crichton, KCVO, *b.* 1937, *s.* 1940, *m.*	Viscount Crichton, *b.* 1971
1452 S.	** *Erroll (24th)*, Merlin Sereld Victor Gilbert Hay, *b.* 1948, *s.* 1978, *m.* Hereditary Lord High Constable and Knight Marischal of Scotland	Lord Hay, *b.* 1984
1661	*Essex (11th)*, Frederick Paul de Vere Capell, *b.* 1944, *s.* 2005	William J. C., *b.* 1952
1711	° *Ferrers (14th)*, Robert William Saswalo Shirley, *b.* 1952, *s.* 2012, *m.*	Viscount Tamworth, *b.* 1984
1789	° *Fortescue (8th)*, Charles Hugh Richard Fortescue, *b.* 1951, *s.* 1993, *m.*	John A. F. F., *b.* 1955
1841	*Gainsborough (6th)*, Anthony Baptist Noel, *b.* 1950, *s.* 2009, *m.*	Viscount Campden, *b.* 1977
1623 S.	*Galloway (13th)*, Randolph Keith Reginald Stewart, *b.* 1928, *s.* 1978, *w.*	Andrew C. S., *b.* 1949
1703 S.	** *Glasgow (10th)*, Patrick Robin Archibald Boyle, *b.* 1939, *s.* 1984, *m.*	Viscount of Kelburn, *b.* 1978
1806 I.	*Gosford (7th)*, Charles David Nicholas Alexander John Sparrow Acheson, *b.* 1942, *s.* 1966, *m.*	Nicholas H. C. A., *b.* 1947
1945	*Gowrie (2nd)*, Alexander Patrick Greysteil Hore Ruthven, PC, *b.* 1939, *s.* 1955, *m.*	Viscount Ruthven of Canberra, *b.* 1964
1684 I.	*Granard (10th)*, Peter Arthur Edward Hastings Forbes, *b.* 1957, *s.* 1992, *m.*	Viscount Forbes, *b.* 1981
1833	° *Granville (6th)*, Granville George Fergus Leveson-Gower, *b.* 1959, *s.* 1996, *m.*	Lord Leveson, *b.* 1999
1806	° *Grey (7th)*, Philip Kent Grey, *b.* 1940, *s.* 2013, *m.*	Viscount Howick, *b.* 1968
1752	*Guilford (10th)*, Piers Edward Brownlow North, *b.* 1971, *s.* 1999, *m.*	Lord North, *b.* 2002
1619 S.	*Haddington (13th)*, John George Baillie-Hamilton, *b.* 1941, *s.* 1986, *m.*	Lord Binning, *b.* 1985
1919	° *Haig (3rd)*, Alexander Douglas Derrick Haig, *b.* 1961, *s.* 2009, *m.*	None
1944	*Halifax (3rd)*, Charles Edward Peter Neil Wood, *b.* 1944, *s.* 1980, *m.*	Lord Irwin, *b.* 1977
1754	*Hardwicke (10th)*, Joseph Philip Sebastian Yorke, *b.* 1971, *s.* 1974, *m.*	Viscount Royston, *b.* 2009
1812	*Harewood (8th)*, David Henry George Lascelles, *b.* 1950, *s.* 2011, *m.*	Viscount Lascelles, *b.* 1978
1742	*Harrington (12th)*, Charles Henry Leicester Stanhope, *b.* 1945, *s.* 2009, *m.*	Viscount Petersham, *b.* 1967
1809	*Harrowby (8th)*, Dudley Adrian Conroy Ryder, *b.* 1951, *s.* 2007, *m.*	Viscount Sandon, *b.* 1981
1605 S.	** *Home (15th)*, David Alexander Cospatrick Douglas-Home, KT, CVO, CBE, *b.* 1943, *s.* 1995, *m.*	Lord Dunglass, *b.* 1987
1821	° ** *Howe (7th)*, Frederick Richard Penn Curzon, PC, *b.* 1951, *s.* 1984, *m.*	Viscount Curzon, *b.* 1994
1529	*Huntingdon (16th)*, William Edward Robin Hood Hastings Bass, LVO, *b.* 1948, *s.* 1990, *m.*	Hon. Simon A. R. H. H. B., *b.* 1950
1885	*Iddesleigh (5th)*, John Stafford Northcote, *b.* 1957, *s.* 2004, *m.*	Viscount St Cyres, *b.* 1985
1756	*Ilchester (10th)*, Robin Maurice Fox-Strangways, *b.* 1942, *s.* 2006, *m.*	Lord Stavordale, *b.* 1972
1929	*Inchcape (4th)*, (Kenneth) Peter (Lyle) Mackay, *b.* 1943, *s.* 1994, *m.*	Viscount Glenapp, *b.* 1979
1919	*Iveagh (4th)*, Arthur Edward Rory Guinness, *b.* 1969, *s.* 1992, *m.*	Viscount Elveden, *b.* 2003
1925	° *Jellicoe (3rd)*, Patrick John Bernard Jellicoe, *b.* 1950, *s.* 2007	Hon. Nicholas C. J., *b.* 1953

1697	*Jersey (10th),* George Francis William Child Villiers, *b.* 1976, *s.* 1998 *m.*	Hon. Jamie C. C. V., *b.* 1994
1822 I.	*Kilmorey (6th),* Sir Richard Francis Needham, PC, *b.* 1942, *s.* 1977, *m,* (Does not use title)	Viscount Newry and Mourne, *b.* 1966
1866	*Kimberley (5th),* John Armine Wodehouse, *b.* 1951, *s.* 2002, *m.*	Lord Wodehouse, *b.* 1978
1768 I.	*Kingston (12th),* Robert Charles Henry King-Tenison, *b.* 1969, *s.* 2002, *m.*	Viscount Kingsborough, *b.* 2000
1633 S.	*Kinnoull (16th),* Charles William Harley Hay, *b.* 1962, *s.* 2013, *m.*	Viscount Dupplin, *b.* 2011
1677 S.	*Kintore (14th),* James William Falconer Keith, *b.* 1976, *s.* 2004 *m*	Lord Inverurie, *b.* 2010
1624 S.	*Lauderdale (18th),* Ian Maitland, *b.* 1937, *s.* 2008, *m.*	Viscount Maitland, *b.* 1965
1837	*Leicester (7th),* Edward Douglas Coke, *b.* 1936, *s.* 1994, *m.*	Viscount Coke, *b.* 1965
1641 S.	*Leven (15th) and Melville (14th) (S. 1690),* Alexander Ian Leslie Melville, *b.* 1984, *s.* 2012	Hon. Archibald R. L. M., *b.* 1957
1831	*Lichfield (6th),* Thomas William Robert Hugh Anson, *b.* 1978, *s.* 2005, *m.*	Viscount Anson, *b.* 2011
1803 I.	*Limerick (7th),* Edmund Christopher Pery, *b.* 1963, *s.* 2003, *m.*	Viscount Glentworth, *b.* 1991
1572	*Lincoln (19th),* Robert Edward Fiennes-Clinton, *b.* 1972, *s.* 2001	Hon. William J. Howson, *b.* 1980
1633 S.	** *Lindsay (16th),* James Randolph Lindesay-Bethune, *b.* 1955, *s.* 1989, *m.*	Viscount Garnock, *b.* 1990
1626	*Lindsey (14th) and Abingdon (9th) (1682),* Richard Henry Rupert Bertie, *b.* 1931, *s.* 1963, *m.*	Lord Norreys, *b.* 1958
1776 I.	*Lisburne (9th),* David John Francis Malet Vaughan, *b.* 1945, *s.* 2014, *m.*	Viscount Vaughan, *b.* 1973
1822 I.	** *Listowel (6th),* Francis Michael Hare, *b.* 1964, *s.* 1997, *m.*	Hon. Timothy P. H., *b.* 1966
1905	** *Liverpool (5th),* Edward Peter Bertram Savile Foljambe, *b.* 1944, *s.* 1969, *m.*	Viscount Hawkesbury, *b.* 1972
1945	° *Lloyd George of Dwyfor (4th),* David Richard Owen Lloyd George, *b.* 1951, *s.* 2010, *m.*	Viscount Gwynedd, *b.* 1986
1785 I.	*Longford (8th),* Thomas Frank Dermot Pakenham, *b.* 1933, *s.* 2001, *m.* (Does not use title)	Edward M. P., *b.* 1970
1807	*Lonsdale (8th),* Hugh Clayton Lowther, *b.* 1949, *s.* 2006, *m.*	Hon. William J. L., *b.* 1957
1633 S.	*Loudoun (15th),* Simon Michael Abney-Hastings, *b.* 1974, *s.* 2012, *m.*	Hon. Marcus W. A.-H., *b.* 1981
1838	*Lovelace (5th),* Peter Axel William Locke King, *b.* 1951, *s.* 1964, *m.*	None
1795 I.	*Lucan (7th),* Richard John Bingham, *b.* 1934, *s.* 1964, *m.* (missing since 8 November 1974)	Lord Bingham, *b.* 1967
1880	** *Lytton (5th),* John Peter Michael Scawen Lytton, *b.* 1950, *s.* 1985, *m.*	Viscount Knebworth, *b.* 1989
1721	*Macclesfield (9th),* Richard Timothy George Mansfield Parker, *b.* 1943, *s.* 1992, *m.*	Hon. J. David G. P., *b.* 1945
1800	*Malmesbury (7th),* James Carleton Harris, *b.* 1946, *s.* 2000, *m.*	Viscount FitzHarris, *b.* 1970
1776	*Mansfield and Mansfield (8th) (1792),* William David Mungo James Murray, *b.* 1930, *s.* 1971, *m.*	Viscount Stormont, *b.* 1956
1565 S.	*Mar (14th) and Kellie (16th) (S. 1616) and Baron Erskine of Alloa Tower (life peerage, 2000),* James Thorne Erskine, *b.* 1949, *s.* 1994, *m.*	Hon. Alexander D. E., *b.* 1952
1785 I.	*Mayo (11th),* Charles Diarmuidh John Bourke, *b.* 1953, *s.* 2006, *m.*	Lord Naas, *b.* 1985
1627 I.	*Meath (15th),* John Anthony Brabazon, *b.* 1941, *s.* 1998, *m.*	Lord Ardee, *b.* 1977
1766 I.	*Mexborough (8th),* John Christopher George Savile, *b.* 1931, *s.* 1980, *m.*	Viscount Pollington, *b.* 1959
1813	*Minto (7th),* Gilbert Timothy George Lariston Elliot-Murray-Kynynmound, *b.* 1953, *s.* 2005, *m.*	Viscount Melgund, *b.* 1984
1562 S.	*Moray (21st),* John Douglas Stuart, *b.* 1966, *s.* 2011, *m.*	Lord Doune, *b.* 2002
1815	*Morley (6th),* John St Aubyn Parker, KCVO, *b.* 1923, *s.* 1962, *m.*	Viscount Boringdon, *b.* 1956
1458 S.	*Morton (22nd),* John Charles Sholto Douglas, *b.* 1927, *s.* 1976, *m.*	Lord Aberdour, *b.* 1952
1789	*Mount Edgcumbe (8th),* Robert Charles Edgcumbe, *b.* 1939, *s.* 1982	Piers V. E., *b.* 1946
1805	° *Nelson (10th),* Simon John Horatio Nelson, *b.* 1971, *s.* 2009, *m.*	Viscount Merton, *b.* 1994
1660 S.	*Newburgh (12th),* Don Filippo Giambattista Camillo Francesco Aldo Maria Rospigliosi, *b.* 1942, *s.* 1986, *m.*	Princess Donna Benedetta F. M. R., *b.* 1974
1827 I.	*Norbury (7th),* Richard James Graham-Toler, *b.* 1967, *s.* 2000	None
1806 I.	*Normanton (6th),* Shaun James Christian Welbore Ellis Agar, *b.* 1945, *s.* 1967, *m.*	Viscount Somerton, *b.* 1982
1647 S.	*Northesk (15th),* Patrick Charles Carnegy, *b.* 1940, *s.* 2010	Hon. Colin D. C., *b.* 1942
1801	*Onslow (8th),* Rupert Charles William Bullard Onslow, *b.* 1967, *s.* 2011, *m.*	Anthony E. E. O., *b.* 1955
1696 S.	*Orkney (9th),* (Oliver) Peter St John, *b.* 1938, *s.* 1998, *m.*	Viscount Kirkwall, *b.* 1969
1328 I.	*Ormonde and Ossory (I. 1527),* The 25th/18th Earl (7th Marquess) died in 1988	†Viscount Mountgarret *b.* 1961 (*see* that title)
1925	*Oxford and Asquith (3rd),* Raymond Benedict Bartholomew Michael Asquith, OBE, *b.* 1952, *s.* 2011, *m.*	Viscount Asquith, *b.* 1979
1929	° ** *Peel (3rd),* William James Robert Peel, GCVO, PC, *b.* 1947, *s.* 1969, *m.* Lord Chamberlain	Viscount Clanfield, *b.* 1976
1551	*Pembroke (18th) and Montgomery (15th) (1605),* William Alexander Sidney Herbert, *b.* 1978, *s.* 2003, *m.*	Lord Herbert *b.* 2012
1605 S.	*Perth (18th),* John Eric Drummond, *b.* 1935, *s.* 2002, *m.*	Viscount Strathallan, *b.* 1965
1905	*Plymouth (3rd),* Other Robert Ivor Windsor-Clive, *b.* 1923, *s.* 1943, *m.*	Viscount Windsor, *b.* 1951
1785	*Portarlington (7th),* George Lionel Yuill Seymour Dawson-Damer, *b.* 1938, *s.* 1959, *m.*	Viscount Carlow, *b.* 1965
1689	*Portland (12th),* Count Timothy Charles Robert Noel Bentinck, *b.* 1953, *s.* 1997, *m.*	Viscount Woodstock, *b.* 1984

1743	*Portsmouth (10th)*, Quentin Gerard Carew Wallop, *b.* 1954, *s.* 1984, *m.*	Viscount Lymington, *b.* 1981
1804	*Powis (8th)*, John George Herbert, *b.* 1952, *s.* 1993, *m.*	Viscount Clive, *b.* 1979
1765	*Radnor (9th)*, William Pleydell-Bouverie, *b.* 1955, *s.* 2008, *m.*	Viscount Folkestone, *b.* 1999
1831 I.	*Ranfurly (7th)*, Gerald Françoys Needham Knox, *b.* 1929, *s.* 1988, *m.*	Viscount Northland, *b.* 1957
1771 I.	*Roden (10th)*, Robert John Jocelyn, *b.* 1938, *s.* 1993, *m.*	Viscount Jocelyn, *b.* 1989
1801	*Romney (8th)*, Julian Charles Marsham, *b.* 1948, *s.* 2004, *m.*	Viscount Marsham, *b.* 1977
1703 S.	*Rosebery (7th)*, Neil Archibald Primrose, *b.* 1929, *s.* 1974, *m.*	Lord Dalmeny, *b.* 1967
1806 I.	*Rosse (7th)*, William Brendan Parsons, *b.* 1936, *s.* 1979, *m.*	Lord Oxmantown, *b.* 1969
1801	** *Rosslyn (7th)*, Peter St Clair-Erskine, QPM, *b.* 1958, *s.* 1977, *m.*	Lord Loughborough, *b.* 1986
1457 S.	*Rothes (22nd)*, James Malcolm David Leslie, *b.* 1958, *s.* 2005, *m.*	Hon. Alexander J. L., *b.* 1962
1861	° *Russell (7th)*, John Francis Russell, *b.* 1971, *s.* 2014, *m.*	None
1915	° *St Aldwyn (3rd)*, Michael Henry Hicks Beach, *b.* 1950, *s.* 1992, *m.*	Hon. David S. H. B., *b.* 1955
1815	*St Germans (10th)*, Peregrine Nicholas Eliot, *b.* 1941, *s.* 1988, *m.*	Lord Eliot, *b.* 2004
1660	** *Sandwich (11th)*, John Edward Hollister Montagu, *b.* 1943, *s.* 1995, *m.*	Viscount Hinchingbrooke, *b.* 1969
1690	*Scarbrough (13th)*, Richard Osbert Lumley, *b.* 1973, *s.* 2004, *m.*	Hon. Thomas H. L., *b.* 1980
1701 S.	*Seafield (13th)*, Ian Derek Francis Ogilvie-Grant, *b.* 1939, *s.* 1969, *m.*	Viscount Reidhaven, *b.* 1963
1882	** *Selborne (4th)*, John Roundell Palmer, GBE, *b.* 1940, *s.* 1971, *m.*	Viscount Wolmer, *b.* 1971
1646 S.	*Selkirk (11th)*, Disclaimed for life 1994 (*see* Lord Selkirk of Douglas, Life Peers)	Master of Selkirk, *b.* 1978
1672	*Shaftesbury (12th)*, Nicholas Edmund Anthony Ashley-Cooper, *b.* 1979, *s.* 2005, *m.*	Lord Ashley, *b.* 2011
1756 I.	*Shannon (10th)*, Richard Henry John Boyle, *b.* 1960, *s.* 2013	Robert F. B., *b.* 1930
1442	** *Shrewsbury and Waterford (22nd) (I. 1446)*, Charles Henry John Benedict Crofton Chetwynd Chetwynd-Talbot, *b.* 1952, *s.* 1980, *m. Premier Earl of England and Ireland*	Viscount Ingestre, *b.* 1978
1961	*Snowdon (1st) and Baron Armstrong-Jones (life peerage, 1999)*, Antony Charles Robert Armstrong-Jones, GCVO, *b.* 1930, *m.*	Viscount Linley, *b.* 1961
1765	° *Spencer (9th)*, Charles Edward Maurice Spencer, *b.* 1964, *s.* 1992, *m.*	Viscount Althorp, *b.* 1994
1703 S.	** *Stair (14th)*, John David James Dalrymple, *b.* 1961, *s.* 1996, *m.*	Viscount Dalrymple, *b.* 2008
1984	*Stockton (2nd)*, Alexander Daniel Alan Macmillan, *b.* 1943, *s.* 1986, *m.*	Viscount Macmillan of Ovenden, *b.* 1974
1821	*Stradbroke (6th)*, Robert Keith Rous, *b.* 1937, *s.* 1983, *m.*	Viscount Dunwich, *b.* 1961
1847	*Strafford (8th)*, Thomas Edmund Byng, *b.* 1936, *s.* 1984, *m.*	Viscount Enfield, *b.* 1964
1606 S.	*Strathmore and Kinghorne (18th) (S. 1677)*, Michael Fergus Bowes Lyon, *b.* 1957, *s.* 1987, *m.*	Lord Glamis, *b.* 1986
1603	*Suffolk (21st) and Berkshire (14th) (1626)*, Michael John James George Robert Howard, *b.* 1935, *s.* 1941, *m.*	Viscount Andover, *b.* 1974
1955	*Swinton (3rd)*, Nicholas John Cunliffe-Lister, *b.* 1939, *s.* 2006, *m.*	Lord Masham *b.* 1970
1714	*Tankerville (10th)*, Peter Grey Bennet, *b.* 1956, *s.* 1980	Adrian G. B., *b.* 1958
1822	° *Temple of Stowe (9th)*, James Grenville Temple-Gore-Langton, *b.* 1955, *s.* 2013, *m.*	Hon. Robert C. H. T.-G.-L., *b.* 1957
1815	*Verulam (7th)*, John Duncan Grimston, *b.* 1951, *s.* 1973, *m.*	Viscount Grimston, *b.* 1978
1729	° *Waldegrave (13th)*, James Sherbrooke Waldegrave, *b.* 1940, *s.* 1995, *m.*	Viscount Chewton, *b.* 1986
1759	*Warwick (9th) and Brooke (9th) (1746)*, Guy David Greville, *b.* 1957, *s.* 1996, *m.*	Lord Brooke, *b.* 1982
1633 S.	*Wemyss (13th) and March (9th) (S. 1697)*, James Donald Charteris, *b.* 1948, *s.* 2008, *m.*	Lord Elcho, *b.* 1984
1621 I.	*Westmeath (13th)*, William Anthony Nugent, *b.* 1928, *s.* 1971, *m.*	Sean C. W. N., *b.* 1965
1624	*Westmorland (16th)*, Anthony David Francis Henry Fane, *b.* 1951, *s.* 1993, *m.*	Hon. Harry St C. F., *b.* 1953
1876	*Wharncliffe (5th)*, Richard Alan Montagu Stuart Wortley, *b.* 1953, *s.* 1987, *m.*	Viscount Carlton, *b.* 1980
1801	*Wilton (8th)*, Francis Egerton Grosvenor, *b.* 1934, *s.* 1999, *m.*	Viscount Grey de Wilton, *b.* 1959
1628	*Winchilsea (17th) and Nottingham (12th) (1681)*, Daniel James Hatfield Finch Hatton, *b.* 1967, *s.* 1999, *m.*	Viscount Maidstone, *b.* 1998
1766	° *Winterton (8th)*, (Donald) David Turnour, *b.* 1943, *s.* 1991, *m.*	Robert C. T., *b.* 1950
1956	*Woolton (3rd)*, Simon Frederick Marquis, *b.* 1958, *s.* 1969, *m.*	None
1837	*Yarborough (8th)*, Charles John Pelham, *b.* 1963, *s.* 1991, *m.*	Lord Worsley, *b.* 1990

COUNTESSES IN THEIR OWN RIGHT

Style, The Rt. Hon. the Countess (of) _
  Envelope (formal), The Rt. Hon. the Countess (of) _; *(social),* The Countess (of) _. *Letter (formal),* Madam; *(social),*
  Lady _. *Spoken (formal),* Madam; *(social),* Lady _.
Husband, Untitled
Children's style, As for children of an Earl

Created	Title, order of succession, name, etc	Heir
c.1115 S.	** *Mar (31st),* Margaret of Mar, *b.* 1940, *s.* 1975, *m. Premier Earldom of Scotland*	Mistress of Mar, *b.* 1963
1947	° *Mountbatten of Burma (2nd),* Patricia Edwina Victoria Knatchbull, CBE, *b.* 1924, *s.* 1979, *w.*	Lord Romsey, (*also* Lord Brabourne (8th) *see* that title)
c.1235 S.	*Sutherland (24th),* Elizabeth Millicent Sutherland, *b.* 1921, *s.* 1963, *w.*	Lord Strathnaver, *b.* 1947

VISCOUNTS

Coronet, Sixteen silver balls

Style, The Rt. Hon. the Viscount _
  Envelope (formal), The Rt. Hon. the Viscount _; *(social),* The Viscount _. *Letter (formal),* My Lord; *(social),* Dear Lord
  _. *Spoken,* Lord _.
Wife's style, The Rt. Hon. the Viscountess _
  Envelope (formal), The Rt. Hon. the Viscountess _; *(social),* The Viscountess _. *Letter (formal),* Madam; *(social),* Dear
  Lady _. *Spoken,* Lady _.
Children's style, 'The Hon.' before forename and surname, as for Baron's children
In Scotland, the heir apparent to a Viscount may be styled 'The Master of _ (title of peer)'

Created	Title, order of succession, name, etc	Heir
1945	*Addison (4th),* William Matthew Wand Addison, *b.* 1945, *s.* 1992, *m.*	Hon. Paul W. A., *b.* 1973
1946	*Alanbrooke (3rd),* Alan Victor Harold Brooke, *b.* 1932, *s.* 1972	None
1919	** *Allenby (3rd),* Lt.-Col. Michael Jaffray Hynman Allenby, *b.* 1931, *s.* 1984, *m.*	Hon. Henry J. H. A., *b.* 1968
1911	*Allendale (4th),* Wentworth Peter Ismay Beaumont, *b.* 1948, *s.* 2002, *m.*	Hon. Wentworth A. I. B., *b.* 1979
1642 S.	*of Arbuthnott (17th),* John Keith Oxley Arbuthnott, *b.* 1950, *s.* 2012, *m.*	Master of Arbuthnott, *b.* 1977
1751 I.	*Ashbrook (11th),* Michael Llowarch Warburton Flower, *b.* 1935, *s.* 1995, *m.*	Hon. Rowland F. W. F., *b.* 1975
1917	** *Astor (4th),* William Waldorf Astor, *b.* 1951, *s.* 1966, *m.*	Hon. William W. A., *b.* 1979
1781 I.	*Bangor (8th),* William Maxwell David Ward, *b.* 1948, *s.* 1993, *m.*	Hon. E. Nicholas W., *b.* 1953
1925	*Bearsted (5th),* Nicholas Alan Samuel, *b.* 1950, *s.* 1996, *m.*	Hon. Harry R. S., *b.* 1988
1963	*Blakenham (2nd),* Michael John Hare, *b.* 1938, *s.* 1982, *m.*	Hon. Caspar J. H., *b.* 1972
1935	*Bledisloe (4th),* Rupert Edward Ludlow Bathurst, *b.* 1964, *s.* 2009, *m.*	Hon. Benjamin B., *b.* 2004
1712	*Bolingbroke (9th) and St John (10th) (1716),* Nicholas Alexander Mowbray St John, *b.* 1974, *s.* 2011, *m.*	Walter W. St J., *b.* 1921
1960	*Boyd of Merton (2nd),* Simon Donald Rupert Neville Lennox-Boyd, *b.* 1939, *s.* 1983, *m.*	Hon. Benjamin A. L.-B., *b.* 1964
1717 I.	*Boyne (11th),* Gustavus Michael Stucley Hamilton-Russell, *b.* 1965, *s.* 1995, *m.*	Hon. Gustavus A. E. H.-R., *b.* 1999
1929	*Brentford (4th),* Crispin William Joynson-Hicks, *b.* 1933, *s.* 1983, *m.*	Hon. Paul W. J.-H., *b.* 1971
1929	** *Bridgeman (3rd),* Robin John Orlando Bridgeman, *b.* 1930, *s.* 1982, *m.*	Hon. Luke R. O. B., *b.* 1971
1868	*Bridport (4th) and 7th Duke, Bronte in Sicily, 1799,* Alexander Nelson Hood, *b.* 1948, *s.* 1969, *m.*	Hon. Peregrine A. N. H., *b.* 1974
1952	** *Brookeborough (3rd),* Alan Henry Brooke, *b.* 1952, *s.* 1987, *m.*	Hon. Christopher A. B., *b.* 1954
1933	*Buckmaster (4th),* Adrian Charles Buckmaster, *b.* 1949, *s.* 2007, *m.*	Hon. Andrew N. B., *b.* 1980
1939	*Caldecote (3rd),* Piers James Hampden Inskip, *b.* 1947, *s.* 1999, *m.*	Hon. Thomas J. H. I., *b.* 1985
1941	*Camrose (4th),* Adrian Michael Berry, *b.* 1937, *s.* 2001, *m.*	Hon. Jonathan W. B., *b.* 1970
1954	*Chandos (3rd) and Baron Lyttelton of Aldershot (life peerage, 2000),* Thomas Orlando Lyttelton, *b.* 1953, *s.* 1980, *m.*	Hon. Oliver A. L., *b.* 1986

1665 I. *Charlemont (15th)*, John Dodd Caulfeild, *b.* 1966, *s.* 2001, *m.*   Hon. Shane A. C., *b.* 1996

1921 *Chelmsford (4th)* Frederic Corin Piers Thesiger, *b.* 1962, *s.* 1999, *m.*   Hon. Frederic T. *b.* 2006

1717 I. *Chetwynd (10th)*, Adam Richard John Casson Chetwynd, *b.* 1935, *s.* 1965, *m.*   Hon. Adam D. C., *b.* 1969

1911 *Chilston (4th)*, Alastair George Akers-Douglas, *b.* 1946, *s.* 1982, *m.*   Hon. Oliver I. A.-D., *b.* 1973

1902 *Churchill (3rd) and 5th UK Baron Churchill (1815)*, Victor George Spencer, *b.* 1934, *s.* 1973   To Barony only, Richard H. R. S., *b.* 1926

1718 *Cobham (12th)*, Christopher Charles Lyttelton, *b.* 1947, *s.* 2006, *m.*   Hon. Oliver C. L., *b.* 1976

1902 ** *Colville of Culross (5th)*, Charles Mark Townshend Colville, *b.* 1959, *s.* 2010   Master of Colville, *b.* 1961

1826 *Combermere (6th)*, Thomas Robert Wellington Stapleton-Cotton, *b.* 1969, *s.* 2000, *m.*   Hon. Laszlo M. W. S.-C., *b.* 2010

1917 *Cowdray (4th)*, Michael Orlando Weetman Pearson, *b.* 1944, *s.* 1995, *m.*   Hon. Peregrine J. D. P., *b.* 1994

1927 ** *Craigavon (3rd)*, Janric Fraser Craig, *b.* 1944, *s.* 1974   None

1943 *Daventry (4th)*, James Edward FitzRoy Newdegate, *b.* 1960, *s.* 2000, *m.*   Hon. Humphrey J. F. N., *b.* 1995

1937 *Davidson (3rd)*, Malcolm William Mackenzie Davidson, *b.* 1934, *s.* 2012, *m.*   Hon. John N. A. D., *b.* 1971

1956 *De L'Isle (2nd)*, Philip John Algernon Sidney, MBE, *b.* 1945, *s.* 1991, *m.*   Hon. Philip W. E. S., *b.* 1985

1776 I. *de Vesci (7th)*, Thomas Eustace Vesey, *b.* 1955, *s.* 1983, *m.*   Hon. Oliver I. V., *b.* 1991

1917 *Devonport (3rd)*, Terence Kearley, *b.* 1944, *s.* 1973, *m.*   Chester D. H. K., *b.* 1932

1964 *Dilhorne (2nd)*, John Mervyn Manningham-Buller, *b.* 1932, *s.* 1980, *m.*   Hon. James E. M.-B., *b.* 1956

1622 I. *Dillon (22nd)*, Henry Benedict Charles Dillon, *b.* 1973, *s.* 1982   Hon. Richard A. L. D., *b.* 1948

1785 I. *Doneraile (10th)*, Richard Allen St Leger, *b.* 1946, *s.* 1983, *m.*   Hon. Nathaniel W. R. St J. St L., *b.* 1971

1680 I. *Downe (12th)*, Richard Henry Dawnay, *b.* 1967, *s.* 2002   Thomas P. D., *b.* 1978

1959 *Dunrossil (3rd)*, Andrew William Reginald Morrison, *b.* 1953, *s.* 2000, *m.*   Hon. Callum A. B. M., *b.* 1994

1964 ** *Eccles (2nd)*, John Dawson Eccles, CBE, *b.* 1931, *s.* 1999, *m.*   Hon. William D. E., *b.* 1960

1897 *Esher (5th)*, Christopher Lionel Baliol Brett, *b.* 1936, *s.* 2004, *m.*   Hon. Matthew C. A. B., *b.* 1963

1816 *Exmouth (10th)*, Paul Edward Pellew, *b.* 1940, *s.* 1970, *m.*   Hon. Edward F. P., *b.* 1978

1620 S. ** *of Falkland (15th)*, Lucius Edward William Plantagenet Cary, *b.* 1935, *s.* 1984, *m. Premier Scottish Viscount on the Roll*   Master of Falkland, *b.* 1963

1720 *Falmouth (9th)*, George Hugh Boscawen, *b.* 1919, *s.* 1962, *w.*   Hon. Evelyn A. H. B., *b.* 1955

1720 I. *Gage (8th)*, (Henry) Nicolas Gage, *b.* 1934, *s.* 1993, *m.*   Hon. Henry W. G., *b.* 1975

1727 I. *Galway (12th)*, George Rupert Monckton-Arundell, *b.* 1922, *s.* 1980, *m.*   Hon. J. Philip M., *b.* 1952

1478 I. *Gormanston (17th)*, Jenico Nicholas Dudley Preston, *b.* 1939, *s.* 1940, *m. Premier Viscount of Ireland*   Hon. Jenico F. T. P., *b.* 1974

1016 I. *Gort (9th)*, Foley Robert Standish Prendergast Vereker, *b.* 1951, *s.* 1995, *m.*   Hon. Robert F. P. V. *b.* 1993

1900 ** *Goschen (4th)*, Giles John Harry Goschen, *b.* 1965, *s.* 1977, *m.*   Hon. Alexander J. E. G., *b.* 2001

1849 *Gough (5th)*, Shane Hugh Maryon Gough, *b.* 1941, *s.* 1951   None

1929 *Hailsham (3rd)*, Douglas Martin Hogg, PC, QC, *b.* 1945, *s.* 2001, *m.*   Hon. Quintin J. N. M. H., *b.* 1973

1891 *Hambleden (5th)*, William Henry Bernard Smith, *b.* 1955, *s.* 2012, *m.*   Hon. Bernardo J. S., *b.* 1957

1884 *Hampden (7th)*, Francis Anthony Brand, *b.* 1970, *s.* 2008, *m.*   Hon. Lucian A. B., *b.* 2005

1936 ** *Hanworth (3rd)*, David Stephen Geoffrey Pollock, *b.* 1946, *s.* 1996, *m.*   Harold W. C. P., *b.* 1988

1791 I. *Harberton (11th)*, Henry Robert Pomeroy, *b.* 1958, *s.* 2004, *m.*   Hon. Patrick C. P., *b.* 1995

1846 *Hardinge (8th)*, Thomas Henry de Montarville Hardinge, *b.* 1993, *s.* 2014   Hon. Jamie A. D. H., *b.* 1996

1791 I. *Hawarden (9th)*, (Robert) Connan Wyndham Leslie Maude, *b.* 1961, *s.* 1991, *m.*   Hon. Varian J. C. E. M., *b.* 1997

1960 *Head (2nd)*, Richard Antony Head, *b.* 1937, *s.* 1983, *m.*   Hon. Henry J. H., *b.* 1980

1550 *Hereford (19th)*, Charles Robin De Bohun Devereux, *b.* 1975, *s.* 2004, *m. Premier Viscount of England*   Hon. Edward M. de B. D., *b.* 1977

1842 *Hill (9th)*, Peter David Raymond Charles Clegg-Hill, *b.* 1945, *s.* 2003, *m.*   Hon. Michael C. D. C.-H., *b.* 1988

1796 *Hood (8th)*, Henry Lyttleton Alexander Hood, *b.* 1958, *s.* 1999, *m.*   Hon. Archibald L. S. H., *b.* 1993

1945 *Kemsley (3rd)*, Richard Gomer Berry, *b.* 1951, *s.* 1999, *m.*   Hon. Luke G. B., *b.* 1998

1911 *Knollys (3rd)*, David Francis Dudley Knollys, *b.* 1931, *s.* 1966, *m.*   Hon. Patrick N. M. K., *b.* 1962

1895 *Knutsford (6th)*, Michael Holland-Hibbert, *b.* 1926, *s.* 1986, *m.*   Hon. Henry T. H.-H., *b.* 1959

1954 *Leathers (3rd)*, Christopher Graeme Leathers, *b.* 1941, *s.* 1996, *m.*   Hon. James F. L., *b.* 1969

1781 I. *Lifford (9th)*, (Edward) James Wingfield Hewitt, *b.* 1949, *s.* 1987, *m.*   Hon. James T. W. H., *b.* 1979

1921 *Long (4th)*, Richard Gerard Long, CBE, *b.* 1929, *s.* 1967, *m.*   Hon. James R. L., *b.* 1960

1957 *Mackintosh of Halifax (3rd)*, (John) Clive Mackintosh, *b.* 1958, *s.* 1980, *m.*   Hon. Thomas H. G. M., *b.* 1985

1955 *Malvern (3rd)*, Ashley Kevin Godfrey Huggins, *b.* 1949, *s.* 1978   Hon. M. James H., *b.* 1928

1945 *Marchwood (3rd)*, David George Staveley Penny, *b.* 1936, *s.* 1979, *w.*   Hon. Peter G. W. P., *b.* 1965

1942 *Margesson (2nd)*, Francis Vere Hampden Margesson, *b.* 1922, *s.* 1965, *m.*   Capt. Hon. Richard F. D. M., *b.* 1960

1660 I. *Massereene (14th) and Ferrard (7th) (I. 1797)*, John David Clotworthy Whyte-Melville Foster Skeffington, *b.* 1940, *s.* 1992, *m.*   Hon. Charles J. C. W.-M. F. S., *b.* 1973

1802 *Melville (10th)*, Robert Henry Kirkpatrick Dundas, *b.* 1984, *s.* 2011   Hon. James D. B. D., *b.* 1986

1916 *Mersey (5th)*, Edward John Hallam Bigham, *b.* 1966, *s.* 2006, *m.*   Hon. David E. H. B., *b.* 1938 (to Viscountcy); Mistress of Nairne, *b.* 2003 (to Lordship of Nairne)

1717 I.	*Midleton (12th)*, Alan Henry Brodrick, *b.* 1949, *s.* 1988, *m.*	Hon. Ashley R. B., *b.* 1980
1962	*Mills (3rd)*, Christopher Philip Roger Mills, *b.* 1956, *s.* 1988, *m.*	None
1716 I.	*Molesworth (12th)*, Robert Bysse Kelham Molesworth, *b.* 1959, *s.* 1997	Hon. William J. C. M., *b.* 1960
1801 I.	*Monck (7th)*, Charles Stanley Monck, *b.* 1953, *s.* 1982 (Does not use title)	Hon. George S. M., *b.* 1957
1957	*Monckton of Brenchley (3rd)*, Christopher Walter Monckton, *b.* 1952, *s.* 2006, *m.*	Hon. Timothy D. R. M., *b.* 1955
1946	** *Montgomery of Alamein (2nd)*, David Bernard Montgomery, CMG, CBE, *b.* 1928, *s.* 1976, *m.*	Hon. Henry D. M., *b.* 1954
1550 I.	*Mountgarret (18th)*, Piers James Richard Butler, *b.* 1961, *s.* 2004	Hon. Edmund H. R. B., *b.* 1962
1952	*Norwich (2nd)*, John Julius Cooper, CVO, *b.* 1929, *s.* 1954, *m.*	Hon. Jason C. D. B. C., *b.* 1959
1651 S.	*of Oxfuird (14th)*, Ian Arthur Alexander Makgill, *b.* 1969, *s.* 2003, *m.*	Master of Oxfuird, *b.* 2012
1873	*Portman (10th)*, Christopher Edward Berkeley Portman, *b.* 1958, *s.* 1999, *m.*	Hon. Luke O. B. P., *b.* 1984
1743 I.	*Powerscourt (10th)*, Mervyn Niall Wingfield, *b.* 1935, *s.* 1973, *m.*	Hon. Mervyn A. W., *b.* 1963
1900	** *Ridley (5th)*, Matthew White Ridley, *b.* 1958, *s.* 2012, *m.*	Hon. Matthew W. R., *b.* 1993
1960	*Rochdale (2nd)*, St John Durival Kemp, *b.* 1938, *s.* 1993, *m.*	Hon. Jonathan H. D. K., *b.* 1961
1919	*Rothermere (4th)*, (Harold) Jonathan Esmond Vere Harmsworth, *b.* 1967, *s.* 1998, *m.*	Hon. Vere R. J. H. H., *b.* 1994
1937	*Runciman of Doxford (3rd)*, Walter Garrison Runciman (Garry), CBE, *b.* 1934, *s.* 1989, *m.*	Hon. David W. R., *b.* 1967
1918	*St Davids (4th)*, Rhodri Colwyn Philipps, *b.* 1966, *s.* 2009, *m.*	Hon. Roland A. J. E. P., *b.* 1970
1801	*St Vincent (8th)*, Edward Robert James Jervis, *b.* 1951, *s.* 2006, *m.*	Hon. James R. A. J., *b.* 1982
1937	*Samuel (3rd)*, David Herbert Samuel, OBE, PHD, *b.* 1922, *s.* 1978, *m.*	Hon. Dan J. S., *b.* 1925
1911	*Scarsdale (4th)*, Peter Ghislain Nathaniel Curzon, *b.* 1949, *s.* 2000, *m.*	Hon. David J. N. C., *b.* 1958
1905	*Selby (6th)*, Christopher Rolf Thomas Gully, *b.* 1993, *s.* 2001	Hon. (James) Edward H. G. G., *b.* 1945
1805	*Sidmouth (8th)*, Jeremy Francis Addington, *b.* 1947, *s.* 2005, *w.*	Hon. John A., *b.* 1990
1940	** *Simon (3rd)*, Jan David Simon, *b.* 1940, *s.* 1993, *m.*	None
1960	** *Slim (2nd)*, John Douglas Slim, OBE, *b.* 1927, *s.* 1970, *m.*	Hon. Mark W. R. S., *b.* 1960
1954	*Soulbury (4th)*, Oliver Peter Ramsbotham, *b.* 1943, *s.* 2010, *m.*	Hon. Edward H. R., *b.* 1966
1776 I.	*Southwell (7th)*, Pyers Anthony Joseph Southwell, *b.* 1930, *s.* 1960, *m.*	Hon. Richard A. P. S., *b.* 1956
1942	*Stansgate (3rd)*, Stephen Michael Wedgwood Benn, *b.* 1951, *s.* 2014, *m.*	Hon. Daniel J. W. B., *b.* 1991
1959	*Stuart of Findhorn (3rd)*, Dominic Stuart, *b.* 1948, *s.* 1999, *m.*	Hon. Andrew M. S., *b.* 1957
1957	** *Tenby (3rd)*, William Lloyd George, *b.* 1927, *s.* 1983, *m.*	Hon. Timothy H. G. L. G., *b.* 1962
1952	*Thurso (3rd)*, John Archibald Sinclair, PC, MP, *b.* 1953, *s.* 1995, *m.*	Hon. James A. R. S., *b.* 1984
1721	*Torrington (11th)*, Timothy Howard St George Byng, *b.* 1943, *s.* 1961, *m.*	Colin H. Cranmer-Byng, *b.* 1960
1936	** *Trenchard (3rd)*, Hugh Trenchard, *b.* 1951, *s.* 1987, *m.*	Hon. Alexander T. T., *b.* 1978
1921	** *Ullswater (2nd)*, Nicholas James Christopher Lowther, LVO, PC, *b.* 1942, *s.* 1949, *m.*	Hon. Benjamin J. L., *b.* 1975
1642 I.	*Valentia (16th)*, Frances William Dighton Annesley, *b.* 1959, *s.* 2005, *m.*	Hon. Peter J. A., *b.* 1967
1952	** *Waverley (3rd)*, John Desmond Forbes Anderson, *b.* 1949, *s.* 1990	Hon. Forbes A. R. A., *b.* 1996
1938	*Weir (3rd)*, William Kenneth James Weir, *b.* 1933, *s.* 1975, *m.*	Hon. James W. H. W., *b.* 1965
1918	*Wimborne (4th)*, Ivor Mervyn Vigors Guest, *b.* 1968, *s.* 1993	Hon. Julian J. G., *b.* 1945
1923	** *Younger of Leckie (5th)*, James Edward George Younger, *b.* 1955, *s.* 2003, *m.*	Hon. Alexander W. G. Y., *b.* 1993

BARONS/LORDS

Coronet, Six silver balls

Style, The Rt. Hon. the Lord _
   Envelope (formal), The Rt. Hon. Lord _; *(social),* The Lord _. *Letter (formal),* My Lord; *(social),* Dear Lord _. *Spoken,* Lord _.
In the Peerage of Scotland there is no rank of Baron; the equivalent rank is Lord of Parliament and Scottish peers should always be styled 'Lord', never 'Baron'.
Wife's style, The Rt. Hon. the Lady _
   Envelope (formal), The Rt. Hon. Lady _; *(social),* The Lady _. *Letter (formal),* My Lady; *(social),* Dear Lady _. *Spoken,* Lady _
Children's style, 'The Hon.' before forename (F_) and surname (S_)
   Envelope, The Hon. F_ S_. *Letter,* Dear Mr/Miss/Mrs S_. *Spoken,* Mr/Miss/Mrs S_
In Scotland, the heir apparent to a Lord may be styled 'The Master of _ (title of peer)'

Created	Title, order of succession, name, etc	Heir
1911	*Aberconway (4th)*, (Henry) Charles McLaren, *b.* 1948, *s.* 2003, *m.*	Hon. Charles S. M., *b.* 1984
1873	** *Aberdare (5th)*, Alastair John Lyndhurst Bruce, *b.* 1947, *s.* 2005, *m.*	Hon. Hector M. N. B., *b.* 1974

1835	*Abinger (9th)*, James Harry Scarlett, *b.* 1959, *s.* 2002, *m.*	Hon. Peter R. S., *b.* 1961
1869	*Acton (5th)*, John Charles Ferdinand Harold Lyon-Dalberg-Acton, *b.* 1966, *s.* 2010, *m.*	Hon. John C. L.-D.-A., *b.* 1943
1887	** *Addington (6th)*, Dominic Bryce Hubbard, *b.* 1963, *s.* 1982	Hon. Michael W. L. H., *b.* 1965
1896	*Aldenham (6th) and Hunsdon of Hunsdon (4th) (1923)*, Vicary Tyser Gibbs, *b.* 1948, *s.* 1986, *m.*	Hon. Humphrey W. F. G., *b.* 1989
1962	*Aldington (2nd)*, Charles Harold Stuart Low, *b.* 1948, *s.* 2000, *m.*	Hon. Philip T. A. L., *b.* 1990
1945	*Altrincham (3rd)*, Anthony Ulick David Dundas Grigg, *b.* 1934, *s.* 2001, *m.*	Hon. (Edward) Sebastian G., *b.* 1965
1929	*Alvingham (2nd)*, Maj.-Gen. Robert Guy Eardley Yerburgh, CBE, *b.* 1926, *s.* 1955, *m.*	Capt. Hon. Robert R. G. Y., *b.* 1956
1892	*Amherst of Hackney (5th)*, Hugh William Amherst Cecil, *b.* 1968, *s.* 2009, *m.*	Hon. Jack W. A. C., *b.* 2001
1881	*Ampthill (5th)*, David Whitney Erskine Russell, *b.* 1947, *s.* 2011	Hon. Anthony J. M. R., *b.* 1952
1947	*Amwell (3rd)*, Keith Norman Montague, *b.* 1943, *s.* 1990, *m.*	Hon. Ian K. M., *b.* 1973
1863	*Annaly (6th)*, Luke Richard White, *b.* 1954, *s.* 1990, *m.*	Hon. Luke H. W., *b.* 1990
1885	*Ashbourne (4th)*, Edward Barry Greynville Gibson, *b.* 1933, *s.* 1983, *m.*	Hon. Edward C. d'O. G., *b.* 1967
1835	*Ashburton (7th)*, John Francis Harcourt Baring, KG, KCVO, *b.* 1928, *s.* 1991, *m.*	Hon. Mark F. R. B., *b.* 1958
1892	*Ashcombe (5th)*, Mark Edward Cubitt, *b.* 1964, *s.* 2013, *m.*	Hon. Richard R. A. C., *b.* 1995
1911	** *Ashton of Hyde (4th)*, Thomas Henry Ashton, *b.* 1958, *s.* 2008, *m.*	Hon. John E. A., *b.* 1966
1800 I.	*Ashtown (8th)*, Roderick Nigel Godolphin Trench, *b.* 1944, *s.* 2010, *m.*	Hon. Timothy R. H. T., *b.* 1968
1956	** *Astor of Hever (3rd)*, John Jacob Astor, *b.* 1946, *s.* 1984, *m.*	Hon. Charles G. J. A., *b.* 1990
1789 I.	*Auckland (10th) and Auckland (10th) (1793)*, Robert Ian Burnard Eden, *b.* 1962, *s.* 1997, *m.*	Henry V. E., *b.* 1958
1313	*Audley*, Barony in abeyance between three co-heiresses since 1997	
1900	** *Avebury (4th)*, Eric Reginald Lubbock, *b.* 1928, *s.* 1971, *m.*	Hon. Lyulph A. J. L., *b.* 1954
1718 I.	*Aylmer (14th)*, (Anthony) Julian Aylmer, *b.* 1951, *s.* 2006, *m.*	Hon. Michael H. A., *b.* 1991
1929	*Baden-Powell (3rd)*, Robert Crause Baden-Powell, *b.* 1936, *s.* 1962, *w.*	Hon. David M. B.-P., *b.* 1940
1780	*Bagot (10th)*, (Charles Hugh) Shaun Bagot, *b.* 1944, *s.* 2001, *m.*	Richard C. V. B., *b.* 1941
1953	*Baillieu (3rd)*, James William Latham Baillieu, *b.* 1950, *s.* 1973, *m.*	Hon. Robert L. B., *b.* 1979
1607 S.	*Balfour of Burleigh (8th)*, Robert Bruce, *b.* 1927, *s.* 1967, *m.*	Hon. Victoria B., *b.* 1973
1924	*Banbury of Southam (3rd)*, Charles William Banbury, *b.* 1953, *s.* 1981, *m.*	None
1698	*Barnard (11th)*, Harry John Neville Vane, TD, *b.* 1923, *s.* 1964	Hon. Henry F. C. V., *b.* 1959
1887	*Basing (6th)*, Stuart Anthony Whitfield Sclater-Booth, *b.* 1969, *s.* 2007, *m.*	Hon. Luke W. S.-B., *b.* 2000
1917	*Beaverbrook (3rd)*, Maxwell William Humphrey Aitken, *b.* 1951, *s.* 1985, *m.*	Hon. Maxwell F. A., *b.* 1977
1647 S.	*Belhaven and Stenton (13th)*, Robert Anthony Carmichael Hamilton, *b.* 1927, *s.* 1961, *m.*	Master of Belhaven, *b.* 1953
1848 I.	*Bellew (8th)*, Bryan Edward Bellew, *b.* 1943, *s.* 2010, *m.*	Hon. Anthony R. B. B., *b.* 1972
1856	*Belper (5th)*, Richard Henry Strutt, *b.* 1941, *s.* 1999, *m.*	Hon. Michael H. S., *b.* 1969
1421	*Berkeley (18th) and Gueterbock (life peerage, 2000)*, Anthony Fitzhardinge Gueterbock, OBE, *b.* 1939, *s.* 1992, *m.*	Hon. Thomas F. G., *b.* 1969
1922	*Bethell (5th)*, James Nicholas Bethell, *b.* 1967, *s.* 2007, *m.*	Hon. Jacob N. D. B., *b.* 2006
1938	*Bicester (3rd)*, Angus Edward Vivian Smith, *b.* 1932, *s.* 1968	Hugh C. V. S., *b.* 1934
1903	*Biddulph (5th)*, (Anthony) Nicholas Colin Maitland Biddulph, *b.* 1959, *s.* 1988, *m.*	Hon. Robert J. M. B., *b.* 1994
1938	*Birdwood (3rd)*, Mark William Ogilvie Birdwood, *b.* 1938, *s.* 1962, *m.*	None
1958	*Birkett (2nd)*, Michael Birkett, *b.* 1929, *s.* 1962, *w.*	Hon. Thomas B., *b.* 1982
1907	*Blyth (5th)*, James Audley Ian Blyth, *b.* 1970, *s.* 2009, *m.*	Hon. Hugo A. J. B., *b.* 2006
1797	*Bolton (8th)*, Harry Algar Nigel Orde-Powlett, *b.* 1954, *s.* 2001, *m.*	Hon. Thomas O.-P., *b.* 1979
1452 S.	*Borthwick (24th)*, John Hugh Borthwick, *b.* 1940, *s.* 1996, *m.*	Hon. James H. A. B. of Glengelt, *b.* 1940
1922	** *Borwick (5th)*, (Geoffrey Robert) James Borwick, *b.* 1955, *s.* 2007, *m.*	Hon. Edwin D. W. B., *b.* 1984
1761	*Boston (11th)*, George William Eustace Boteler Irby, *b.* 1971, *s.* 2007, *m.*	Hon. Thomas W. G. B. I., *b.* 1999
1942	** *Brabazon of Tara (3rd)*, Ivon Anthony Moore-Brabazon, PC, *b.* 1946, *s.* 1974, *m.*	Hon. Benjamin R. M.-B., *b.* 1983
1880	*Brabourne (8th)*, Norton Louis Philip Knatchbull, *b.* 1947, *s.* 2005, *m.* (*also* Lord Romsey heir to Countess Mountbatten of Burma, *see* that title)	Hon. Nicholas L. C. N. K., *b.* 1981
1925	*Bradbury (3rd)*, John Bradbury, *b.* 1940, *s.* 1994, *m.*	Hon. John B., *b.* 1973
1962	*Brain (3rd)*, Michael Cottrell Brain, *b.* 1928, *s.* 2014, *m.*	Hon. Thomas R. B., *b.* 1965
1938	*Brassey of Apethorpe (3rd)*, David Henry Brassey, OBE, *b.* 1932, *s.* 1967, *m.*	Hon. Edward B., *b.* 1964
1788	*Braybrooke (10th)*, Robin Henry Charles Neville, *b.* 1932, *s.* 1990, *m.*	Richard R. N., *b.* 1977
1957	** *Bridges (2nd)*, Thomas Edward Bridges, GCMG, *b.* 1927, *s.* 1969, *m.*	Hon. Mark T. B., *b.* 1954
1945	*Broadbridge (4th)*, Martin Hugh Broadbridge, *b.* 1929, *s.* 2000, *w.*	Hon. Richard J. M. B., *b.* 1959
1933	*Brocket (3rd)*, Charles Ronald George Nall-Cain, *b.* 1952, *s.* 1967, *w.*	Hon. Alexander C. C. N.-C., *b.* 1984
1860	** *Brougham and Vaux (5th)*, Michael John Brougham, CBE, *b.* 1938, *s.* 1967	Hon. Charles W. B., *b.* 1971
1776	*Brownlow (7th)*, Edward John Peregrine Cust, *b.* 1936, *s.* 1978, *m.*	Hon. Peregrine E. Q. C., *b.* 1974

1942	*Bruntisfield (3rd)*, Michael John Victor Warrender, *b.* 1949, *s.* 2007, *m.*	Hon. John M. P. C. W., *b.* 1996
1950	*Burden (4th)*, Fraser William Elsworth Burden, *b.* 1964, *s.* 2000, *m.*	Hon. Ian S. B., *b.* 1967
1529	*Burgh (8th)*, (Alexander) Gregory Disney Leith, *b.* 1958, *s.* 2001, *m.*	Hon. Alexander J. S. L., *b.* 1986
1903	*Burnham (7th)*, Harry Frederick Alan Lawson, *b.* 1968, *s.* 2005	None
1897	*Burton (4th)*, Evan Michael Ronald Baillie, *b.* 1949, *s.* 2013, *m.*	Hon. James E. B., *b.* 1975
1643	*Byron (13th)*, Robert James Byron, *b.* 1950, *s.* 1989, *m.*	Hon. Charles R. G. B., *b.* 1990
1937	*Cadman (3rd)*, John Anthony Cadman, *b.* 1938, *s.* 1966, *m.*	Hon. Nicholas A. J. C., *b.* 1977
1945	*Calverley (3rd)*, Charles Rodney Muff, *b.* 1946, *s.* 1971, *m.*	Hon. Jonathan E. B., *b.* 1975
1383	*Camoys (7th)*, (Ralph) Thomas Campion George Sherman Stonor, GCVO, PC, *b.* 1940, *s.* 1976, *m.*	Hon. R. William R. T. S., *b.* 1974
1715 I.	*Carbery (12th)*, Michael Peter Evans-Freke, *b.* 1942, *s.* 2012, *m.*	Hon. Dominic R. C. E.-F., *b.* 1969
1834 I.	*Carew (7th) and Carew (7th) (1838)*, Patrick Thomas Conolly-Carew, *b.* 1938, *s.* 1994, *m.*	Hon. William P. C.-C., *b.* 1973
1916	*Carnock (5th)*, Adam Nicolson, *b.* 1957, *s.* 2008, *m.*	Hon. Thomas N., *b.* 1984
1796 I.	*Carrington (6th) and Carrington (6th) (1797) and Carington of Upton (life peerage, 1999)*, Peter Alexander Rupert Carington, KG, GCMG, CH, MC, PC, *b.* 1919, *s.* 1938, *w.*	Hon. Rupert F. J. C., *b.* 1948
1812 I.	*Castlemaine (8th)*, Roland Thomas John Handcock, MBE, *b.* 1943, *s.* 1973, *m.*	Hon. Ronan M. E. H., *b.* 1989
1936	*Catto (3rd)*, Innes Gordon Catto, *b.* 1950, *s.* 2001, *m.*	Hon. Alexander G. C., *b.* 1952
1918	*Cawley (4th)*, John Francis Cawley, *b.* 1946, *s.* 2001, *m.*	Hon. William R. H. C., *b.* 1981
1858	*Chesham (7th)*, Charles Gray Compton Cavendish, *b.* 1974, *s.* 2009, *m.*	Hon. Oliver N. B. C., *b.* 2007
1945	*Chetwode (2nd)*, Philip Chetwode, *b.* 1937, *s.* 1950, *m.*	Hon. Roger C., *b.* 1968
1945	** *Chorley (2nd)*, Roger Richard Edward Chorley, *b.* 1930, *s.* 1978, *m.*	Hon. Nicholas R. D. C., *b.* 1966
1858	*Churston (5th)*, John Francis Yarde-Buller, *b.* 1934, *s.* 1991, *m.*	Hon. Benjamin F. A. Y.-B., *b.* 1974
1800 I.	*Clanmorris (8th)*, Simon John Ward Bingham, *b.* 1937, *s.* 1988, *m.*	Robert D. de B. B., *b.* 1942
1672	*Clifford of Chudleigh (14th)*, Thomas Hugh Clifford, *b.* 1948, *s.* 1988, *m.*	Hon. Alexander T. H. C., *b.* 1985
1299	*Clinton (22nd)*, Gerard Nevile Mark Fane Trefusis, *b.* 1934, *s.* 1965, *m.*	Hon. Charles P. R. F. T., *b.* 1962
1955	*Clitheroe (2nd)*, Ralph John Assheton, *b.* 1929, *s.* 1984, *m.*	Hon. Ralph C. A., *b.* 1962
1919	*Clwyd (4th)*, (John) Murray Roberts, *b.* 1971, *s.* 2006	Hon. Jeremy T. R., *b.* 1973
1948	*Clydesmuir (3rd)*, David Ronald Colville, *b.* 1949, *s.* 1996, *m.*	Hon. Richard C., *b.* 1980
1960	** *Cobbold (2nd)*, David Antony Fromanteel Lytton Cobbold, *b.* 1937, *s.* 1987, *m.*	Hon. Henry F. L. C., *b.* 1962
1919	*Cochrane of Cults (4th)*, (Ralph Henry) Vere Cochrane, *b.* 1926, *s.* 1990, *m.*	Hon. Thomas H. V. C., *b.* 1957
1954	*Coleraine (2nd)*, (James) Martin (Bonar) Law, *b.* 1931, *s.* 1980, *m.*	Hon. James P. B. L., *b.* 1975
1873	*Coleridge (5th)*, William Duke Coleridge, *b.* 1937, *s.* 1984, *m.*	Hon. James D. C., *b.* 1967
1946	*Colgrain (4th)*, Alastair Colin Leckie Campbell, *b.* 1951, *s.* 2008, *m.*	Hon. Thomas C. D. C., *b.* 1984
1917	** *Colwyn (3rd)*, (Ian) Anthony Hamilton-Smith, CBE, *b.* 1942, *s.* 1966, *m.*	Hon. Craig P. H.-S., *b.* 1968
1956	*Colyton (2nd)*, Alisdair John Munro Hopkinson, *b.* 1958, *s.* 1996, *m.*	Hon. James P. M. H., *b.* 1983
1841	*Congleton (8th)*, Christopher Patrick Parnell, *b.* 1930, *s.* 1967, *m.*	Hon. John P. C. P., *b.* 1959
1927	*Cornwallis (4th)*, Fiennes Wykeham Jeremy Cornwallis, *b.* 1946, *s.* 2010, *m.*	Hon. Fiennes A. W. M. C., *b.* 1987
1874	*Cottesloe (5th)*, John Tapling Fremantle, *b.* 1927, *s.* 1994, *w.*	Hon. Thomas F. H. F., *b.* 1966
1929	*Craigmyle (4th)*, Thomas Columba Shaw, *b.* 1960, *s.* 1998, *m.*	Hon. Alexander F. S., *b.* 1988
1899	*Cranworth (3rd)*, Philip Bertram Gurdon, *b.* 1940, *s.* 1964, *m.*	Hon. Sacha W. R. G., *b.* 1970
1959	** *Crathorne (2nd)*, Charles James Dugdale, KCVO, *b.* 1939, *s.* 1977, *w.*	Hon. Thomas A. J. D., *b.* 1977
1892	*Crawshaw (5th)*, David Gerald Brooks, *b.* 1934, *s.* 1997, *m.*	Hon. John P. B., *b.* 1938
1940	*Croft (3rd)*, Bernard William Henry Page Croft, *b.* 1949, *s.* 1997, *m.*	None
1797 I.	*Crofton (8th)*, Edward Harry Piers Crofton, *b.* 1988, *s.* 2007	Hon. Charles M. G. C., *b.* 1988
1375	** *Cromwell (7th)*, Godfrey John Bewicke-Copley, *b.* 1960, *s.* 1982, *m.*	Hon. David G. B.-C., *b.* 1997
1947	*Crook (3rd)*, Robert Douglas Edwin Crook, *b.* 1955, *s.* 2001, *m.*	Hon. Matthew R. C., *b.* 1990
1920	*Cullen of Ashbourne (3rd)*, Edmund Willoughby Marsham Cokayne, *b.* 1916, *s.* 2000, *w.*	(Hon.) John O'B. M. C., *b.* 1920
1914	*Cunliffe (3rd)*, Roger Cunliffe, *b.* 1932, *s.* 1963, *m.*	Hon. Henry C., *b.* 1962
1332	*Darcy de Knayth (19th)*, Caspar David Ingrams, *b.* 1962, *s.* 2008, *m.*	Hon. Thomas R. I., *b.* 1999
1927	*Daresbury (4th)*, Peter Gilbert Greenall, *b.* 1953, *s.* 1996, *m.*	Hon. Thomas E. G., *b.* 1984
1924	*Darling (3rd)*, (Robert) Julian Henry Darling, *b.* 1944, *s.* 2003, *m.*	Hon. Robert J. C. D., *b.* 1972
1946	*Darwen (4th)*, Paul Davies, *b.* 1962, *s.* 2011	Hon. Benjamin D., *b.* 1966
1932	*Davies (3rd)*, David Davies, *b.* 1940, *s.* 1944, *m.*	Hon. David D. D., *b.* 1975
1812 I.	*Decies (7th)*, Marcus Hugh Tristram de la Poer Beresford, *b.* 1948, *s.* 1992, *m.*	Hon. Robert M. D. de la P. B., *b.* 1988
1299	*de Clifford (27th)*, John Edward Southwell Russell, *b.* 1928, *s.* 1982, *m.*	Miles E. S. R., *b.* 1966
1851	*De Freyne (8th)*, Fulke Charles Arthur John French, *b.* 1957, *s.* 2009	Hon. Alexander J. C. F., *b.* 1988
1821	*Delamere (5th)*, Hugh George Cholmondeley, *b.* 1934, *s.* 1979, *m.*	Hon. Thomas P. G. C., *b.* 1968
1838	** *de Mauley (7th)*, Rupert Charles Ponsonby, *b.* 1957, *s.* 2002, *m.*	Ashley G. P., *b.* 1959
1937	** *Denham (2nd)*, Bertram Stanley Mitford Bowyer, KBE, PC, *b.* 1927, *s.* 1948, *m.*	Hon. Richard G. G. B., *b.* 1959

1834	*Denman (6th)*, Richard Thomas Stewart Denman, *b.* 1946, *s.* 2012, *m.*	Hon. Robert D., *b.* 1995
1887	*De Ramsey (4th)*, John Ailwyn Fellowes, *b.* 1942, *s.* 1993, *m.*	Hon. Freddie J. F., *b.* 1978
1264	*de Ros (28th)*, Peter Trevor Maxwell, *b.* 1958, *s.* 1983, *m. Premier Baron of England*	Hon. Finbar J. M., *b.* 1988
1881	*Derwent (5th)*, Robin Evelyn Leo Vanden-Bempde-Johnstone, LVO, *b.* 1930, *s.* 1986, *m.*	Hon. Francis P. H. V.-B.-J., *b.* 1965
1831	*de Saumarez (7th)*, Eric Douglas Saumarez, *b.* 1956, *s.* 1991, *m.*	Hon. Victor T. S., *b.* 1956
1910	*de Villiers (4th)*, Alexander Charles de Villiers, *b.* 1940, *s.* 2001, *m.*	None
1930	*Dickinson (2nd)*, Richard Clavering Hyett Dickinson, *b.* 1926, *s.* 1943, *m.*	Hon. Martin H. D., *b.* 1961
1620 I.	*Digby (12th) and Digby (5th) (1765)*, Edward Henry Kenelm Digby, KCVO, *b.* 1924, *s.* 1964, *m.*	Hon. Henry N. K. D., *b.* 1954
1615	*Dormer (17th)*, Geoffrey Henry Dormer, *b.* 1920, *s.* 1995, *m.*	Hon. William R. D., *b.* 1960
1943	*Dowding (3rd)*, Piers Hugh Tremenheere Dowding, *b.* 1948, *s.* 1992	Hon. Mark D. J. D., *b.* 1949
1439	*Dudley (15th)*, Jim Anthony Hill Wallace, *b.* 1930, *s.* 2002, *m.*	Hon. Jeremy W. G. W., *b.* 1964
1800 I.	*Dufferin and Clandeboye (11th)*, John Francis Blackwood, *b.* 1944, *s.* 1991 (claim to the peerage not yet established), *m.*	Hon. Francis S. B., *b.* 1979
1929	*Dulverton (3rd)*, (Gilbert) Michael Hamilton Wills, *b.* 1944, *s.* 1992, *m.*	Hon. Robert A. H. W., *b.* 1983
1800 I.	*Dunalley (7th)*, Henry Francis Cornelius Prittie, *b.* 1948, *s.* 1992, *m.*	Hon. Joel H. P., *b.* 1981
1324 I.	*Dunboyne (30th)*, Richard Pierce Theobald Butler, *b.* 1983, *s.* 2013, *m.*	Michael J. B., *b.* 1944
1892	*Dunleath (6th)*, Brian Henry Mulholland, *b.* 1950, *s.* 1997, *m.*	Hon. Andrew H. M., *b.* 1981
1439 I.	*Dunsany (21st)*, Randal Plunkett, *b.* 1983, *s.* 2011	Hon. Oliver P., *b.* 1985
1780	*Dynevor (10th)*, Hugo Griffith Uryan Rhys, *b.* 1966, *s.* 2008	Robert D. A. R., *b.* 1963
1963	*Egremont (2nd) and Leconfield (7th) (1859)*, John Max Henry Scawen Wyndham, *b.* 1948, *s.* 1972, *m.*	Hon. George R. V. W., *b.* 1983
1643 S.	*Elibank (14th)*, Alan D'Ardis Erskine-Murray, *b.* 1923, *s.* 1973, *w.*	Master of Elibank, *b.* 1964
1802	*Ellenborough (9th)*, Rupert Edward Henry Law, *b.* 1955, *s.* 2013, *m.*	Hon. James R. T. L., *b.* 1983
1509 S.	*Elphinstone (19th) and Elphinstone (5th) (1885)*, Alexander Mountstuart Elphinstone, *b.* 1980, *s.* 1994, *m.*	Master of Elphinstone, *b.* 2011
1934	** *Elton (2nd)*, Rodney Elton, TD, *b.* 1930, *s.* 1973, *m.*	Hon. Edward P. E., *b.* 1966
1627 S.	*Fairfax of Cameron (14th)*, Nicholas John Albert Fairfax, *b.* 1956, *s.* 1964, *m.*	Hon. Edward N. T. F., *b.* 1984
1961	*Fairhaven (3rd)*, Ailwyn Henry George Broughton, *b.* 1936, *s.* 1973, *m.*	Maj. Hon. James H. A. B., *b.* 1963
1916	*Faringdon (3rd)*, Charles Michael Henderson, KCVO, *b.* 1937, *s.* 1977, *m.*	Hon. James H. H., *b.* 1961
1756 I.	*Farnham (13th)*, Simon Kenlis Maxwell, *b* 1933, *s.* 2001, *w.*	Hon. Robin S. M., *b.* 1965
1856 I.	*Fermoy (6th)*, Maurice Burke Roche, *b.* 1967, *s.* 1984, *m.*	Hon. E. Hugh B. R., *b.* 1972
1826	*Feversham (7th)*, Jasper Orlando Slingsby Duncombe, *b.* 1968, *s.* 2009	Hon. Jake B. D., *b.* 1972
1798 I.	*ffrench (8th)*, Robuck John Peter Charles Mario ffrench, *b.* 1956, *s.* 1986, *m.*	Hon. John C. M. J. F. ff., *b.* 1928
1909	*Fisher (4th)*, Patrick Vavasseur Fisher, *b.* 1953, *s.* 2012, *m.*	Hon. John C. V. F., *b.* 1979
1295	*Fitzwalter (22nd)*, Julian Brook Plumptre, *b.* 1952, *s.* 2004, *m.*	Hon. Edward B. P., *b.* 1989
1776	*Foley (9th)*, Thomas Henry Foley, *b.* 1961, *s.* 2012	Rupert T. F., *b.* 1970
1445 S.	*Forbes (23rd)*, Malcolm Nigel Forbes, *b.* 1946, *s.* 2013, *m. Premier Lord of Scotland*	Master of Forbes, *b.* 1970
1821	*Forester (9th)*, Charles Richard George Weld-Forester, *b.* 1975, *s.* 2004, *m.*	Wolstan W. W.-F., *b.* 1941
1922	*Forres (4th)*, Alastair Stephen Grant Williamson, *b.* 1946, *s.* 1978, *m.*	Hon. George A. M. W., *b.* 1972
1917	*Forteviot (4th)*, John James Evelyn Dewar, *b.* 1938, *s.* 1993, *w.*	Hon. Alexander J. E. D., *b.* 1971
1951	** *Freyberg (3rd)*, Valerian Bernard Freyberg, *b.* 1970, *s.* 1993, *m.*	Hon. Joseph J. F., *b.* 2007
1917	*Gainford (4th)*, George Pease, *b.* 1926, *s.* 2013, *m.*	Hon. Adrian C. P., *b.* 1960
1818 I.	*Garvagh (6th)*, Spence George Stratford de Redcliffe Canning, *b.* 1953, *s.* 2013, *w.*	Hon. Stratford G. E. de R. C., *b.* 1990
1942	** *Geddes (3rd)*, Euan Michael Ross Geddes, *b.* 1937, *s.* 1975, *m.*	Hon. James G. N. G., *b.* 1969
1876	*Gerard (5th)*, Anthony Robert Hugo Gerard, *b.* 1949, *s.* 1992, *m.*	Hon. Rupert B. C. G., *b.* 1981
1824	*Gifford (6th)*, Anthony Maurice Gifford, QC, *b.* 1940, *s.* 1961, *m.*	Hon. Thomas A. G., *b.* 1967
1917	*Gisborough (3rd)*, Thomas Richard John Long Chaloner, *b.* 1927, *s.* 1951, *m.*	Hon. T. Peregrine L. C., *b.* 1961
1960	*Gladwyn (2nd)*, Miles Alvery Gladwyn Jebb, *b.* 1930, *s.* 1996	None
1899	*Glanusk (5th)*, Christopher Russell Bailey, *b.* 1942, *s.* 1997, *m.*	Hon. Charles H. B., *b.* 1976
1918	** *Glenarthur (4th)*, Simon Mark Arthur, *b.* 1944, *s.* 1976, *m.*	Hon. Edward A. A., *b.* 1973
1911 M.	*Glenconner (4th)*, Cody Charles Edward Tennant, *b.* 1994, *s.* 2010	Euan L. T., *b.* 1983
1964	*Glendevon (3rd)*, Jonathan Charles Hope, *b.* 1952, *s.* 2009	None
1922	*Glendyne (4th)*, John Nivison, *b.* 1960, *s.* 2008	None
1939	** *Glentoran (3rd)*, (Thomas) Robin (Valerian) Dixon, CBE, *b.* 1935, *s.* 1995, *m.*	Hon. Daniel G. D., *b.* 1959
1909	*Gorell (5th)*, John Picton Gorell Barnes, *b.* 1959, *s.* 2007, *m.*	Hon. Oliver G. B., *b.* 1993
1953	** *Grantchester (3rd)*, Christopher John Suenson-Taylor, *b.* 1951, *s.* 1995, *m.*	Hon. Jesse D. S.-T., *b.* 1977
1782	*Grantley (8th)*, Richard William Brinsley Norton, *b.* 1956, *s.* 1995	Hon. Francis J. H. N., *b.* 1960
1794 I.	*Graves (10th)*, Timothy Evelyn Graves, *b.* 1960, *s.* 2002	None
1445 S.	*Gray (23rd)*, Andrew Godfrey Diarmid Stuart Campbell-Gray, *b.* 1964, *s.* 2003, *m.*	Master of Gray, *b.* 1996
1950	*Greenhill (3rd)*, Malcolm Greenhill, *b.* 1924, *s.* 1989	None
1927	** *Greenway (4th)*, Ambrose Charles Drexel Greenway, *b.* 1941, *s.* 1975, *m.*	Hon. Nigel. P. G., *b.* 1944

1902	*Grenfell (3rd) and Grenfell of Kilvey (life peerage, 2000)*, Julian Pascoe Francis St Leger Grenfell, *b.* 1935, *s.* 1976, *m.*	Richard A. St L. G., *b.* 1966
1944	*Gretton (4th)*, John Lysander Gretton, *b.* 1975, *s.* 1989	Hon. John F. B. G., *b.* 2008
1397	*Grey of Codnor (6th)*, Richard Henry Cornwall-Legh, *b.* 1936, *s.* 1996, *m.*	Hon. Richard S. C. C.-L., *b.* 1976
1955	*Gridley (3rd)*, Richard David Arnold Gridley, *b.* 1956, *s.* 1996, *m.*	Peter A. C. G., *b.* 1940
1964	*Grimston of Westbury (3rd)*, Robert John Sylvester Grimston, *b.* 1951, *s.* 2003, *m.*	Hon. Gerald C. W. G., *b.* 1953
1886	*Grimthorpe (5th)*, Edward John Beckett, *b.* 1954, *s.* 2003, *m.*	Hon. Harry M. B., *b.* 1993
1945	*Hacking (3rd)*, Douglas David Hacking, *b.* 1938, *s.* 1971, *m.*	Hon. Douglas F. H., *b.* 1968
1950	*Haden-Guest (5th)*, Christopher Haden-Guest, *b.* 1948, *s.* 1996, *m.*	Hon. Nicholas H.-G., *b.* 1951
1886	*Hamilton of Dalzell (5th)*, Gavin Goulburn Hamilton, *b.* 1968, *s.* 2006, *m.*	Hon. Francis A. J. G. H., *b.* 2009
1874	*Hampton (7th)*, John Humphrey Arnott Pakington, *b.* 1964, *s.* 2003, *m.*	Hon. Charles R. C. P., *b.* 2005
1939	*Hankey (3rd)*, Donald Robin Alers Hankey, *b.* 1938, *s.* 1996, *m.*	Hon. Alexander M. A. H., *b.* 1947
1958	*Harding of Petherton (2nd)*, John Charles Harding, *b.* 1928, *s.* 1989, *w.*	Hon. William A. J. H., *b.* 1969
1910	*Hardinge of Penshurst (4th)*, Julian Alexander Hardinge, *b.* 1945, *s.* 1997	Hon. Hugh F. H., *b.* 1948
1876	*Harlech (6th)*, Francis David Ormsby-Gore, *b.* 1954, *s.* 1985, *m.*	Hon. Jasset D. C. O.-G., *b.* 1986
1939	*Harmsworth (3rd)*, Thomas Harold Raymond Harmsworth, *b.* 1939, *s.* 1990, *m.*	Hon. Dominic M. E. H., *b.* 1973
1815	*Harris (8th)*, Anthony Harris, *b.* 1942, *s.* 1996, *m.*	Rear-Adm. Michael G. T. H., *b.* 1941
1954	*Harvey of Tasburgh (3rd)*, Charles John Giuseppe Harvey, *b.* 1951, *s.* 2010, *m.*	Hon. John H., *b.* 1993
1295	*Hastings (23rd)*, Delaval Thomas Harold Astley, *b.* 1960, *s.* 2007, *m.*	Hon. Jacob A. A., *b.* 1991
1835	*Hatherton (8th)*, Edward Charles Littleton, *b.* 1950, *s.* 1985, *m.*	Hon. Thomas E. L., *b.* 1977
1776 M.	*Hawke (12th)*, William Martin Theodore Hawke, *b.* 1995, *s.* 2010	None
1927	*Hayter (4th)*, George William Michael Chubb, *b.* 1943, *s.* 2003, *m.*	Hon. Thomas F. F. C., *b.* 1986
1945	*Hazlerigg (3rd)*, Arthur Grey Hazlerigg, *b.* 1951, *s.* 2002, *m.*	Hon. Arthur W. G. H. *b.* 1987
1943	*Hemingford (3rd)*, (Dennis) Nicholas Herbert, *b.* 1934, *s.* 1982, *m.*	Hon. Christopher D. C. H., *b.* 1973
1906	*Hemphill (6th)*, Charles Andrew Martyn Martyn-Hemphill, *b.* 1954, *s.* 2012, *m.*	Hon. Richard P. L. M.-H., *b.* 1990
1799 I.	** *Henley (8th) and Northington (6th) (1885)*, Oliver Michael Robert Eden, PC, *b.* 1953, *s.* 1977, *m.*	Hon. John W. O. E., *b.* 1988
1800 I.	*Henniker (9th) and Hartismere (6th) (1866)*, Mark Ian Philip Chandos Henniker-Major, *b.* 1947, *s.* 2004, *m.*	Hon. Edward G. M. H.-M., *b.* 1985
1461	*Herbert (19th)*, David John Seyfried Herbert, *b.* 1952, *s.* 2002, *m.* Title called out of abeyance 2002	Hon. Oliver R. S. H., *b.* 1976
1935	*Hesketh (3rd)*, Thomas Alexander Fermor-Hesketh, KBE, PC, *b.* 1950, *s.* 1955, *m.*	Hon. Frederick H. F.-H., *b.* 1988
1828	*Heytesbury (7th)*, James William Holmes à Court, *b.* 1967, *s.* 2004, *m.*	Peter M. H.. H. à. C., *b.* 1968
1886	*Hindlip (6th)*, Charles Henry Allsopp, *b.* 1940, *s.* 1993, *w.*	Hon. Henry W. A., *b.* 1973
1950	*Hives (3rd)*, Matthew Peter Hives, *b.* 1971, *s.* 1997	Hon. Michael B. H., *b.* 1926
1912	*Hollenden (4th)*, Ian Hampden Hope-Morley, *b.* 1946, *s.* 1999, *m.*	Hon. Edward H.-M., *b.* 1981
1897	*Holm Patrick (4th)*, Hans James David Hamilton, *b.* 1955, *s.* 1991, *m.*	Hon. Ion H. J. H., *b.* 1956
1797 I.	*Hotham (8th)*, Henry Durand Hotham, *b.* 1940, *s.* 1967, *m.*	Hon. William B. H., *b.* 1972
1881	*Hothfield (6th)*, Anthony Charles Sackville Tufton, *b.* 1939, *s.* 1991, *m.*	Hon. William S. T., *b.* 1977
1930	*Howard of Penrith (3rd)*, Philip Esme Howard, *b.* 1945, *s.* 1999, *m.*	Hon. Thomas Philip H., *b.* 1974
1960	*Howick of Glendale (2nd)*, Charles Evelyn Baring, *b.* 1937, *s.* 1973, *m.*	Hon. David E. C. B., *b.* 1975
1796 I.	*Huntingfield (7th)*, Joshua Charles Vanneck, *b.* 1954, *s.* 1994, *w.*	Hon. Gerard C. A. V., *b.* 1985
1866	** *Hylton (5th)*, Raymond Hervey Jolliffe, *b.* 1932, *s.* 1967, *m.*	Hon. William H. M. J., *b.* 1967
1933	*Iliffe (3rd)*, Robert Peter Richard Iliffe, *b.* 1944, *s.* 1996, *m.*	Hon. Edward R. I., *b.* 1968
1543 I.	*Inchiquin (18th)*, Conor Myles John O'Brien, *b.* 1943, *s.* 1982, *m.*	Conor J. A. O'B., *b.* 1952
1962	*Inchyra (3rd)*, Christian James Charles Hoyer Millar, *b.* 1962, *s.* 2011, *m.*	Hon. Jake C. R. M., *b.* 1996
1964	** *Inglewood (2nd)*, (William) Richard Fletcher-Vane, *b.* 1951, *s.* 1989, *m.*	Hon. Henry W. F. F.-V., *b.* 1990
1919	*Inverforth (4th)*, Andrew Peter Weir, *b.* 1966, *s.* 1982	Hon. Benjamin A. W., *b.* 1997
1941	*Ironside (2nd)*, Edmund Oslac Ironside, *b.* 1924, *s.* 1959, *m.*	Hon. Charles E. G. I., *b.* 1956
1952	*Jeffreys (3rd)*, Christopher Henry Mark Jeffreys, *b.* 1957, *s.* 1986, *m.*	Hon. Arthur M. H. J., *b.* 1989
1906	*Joicey (5th)*, James Michael Joicey, *b.* 1953, *s.* 1993, *m.*	Hon. William J. J., *b.* 1990
1937	*Kenilworth (4th)*, (John) Randle Siddeley, *b.* 1954, *s.* 1981, *m.*	Hon. William R. J. S., *b.* 1992
1935	*Kennet (3rd)*, William Aldus Thoby Young, *b.* 1957, *s.* 2009, *m.*	Hon. Archibald W. K. Y., *b.* 1992
1776 I.	*Kensington (8th) and Kensington (5th) (1886)*, Hugh Ivor Edwardes, *b.* 1933, *s.* 1981, *m.*	Hon. W. Owen A. E., *b.* 1964
1951	*Kenswood (2nd)*, John Michael Howard Whitfield, *b.* 1930, *s.* 1963, *m.*	Hon. Michael C. W., *b.* 1955
1788	*Kenyon (6th)*, Lloyd Tyrell-Kenyon, *b.* 1947, *s.* 1993, *m.*	Hon. Lloyd N. T.-K., *b.* 1972
1947	*Kershaw (4th)*, Edward John Kershaw, *b.* 1936, *s.* 1962, *m.*	Hon. John C. E. K., *b.* 1971
1943	*Keyes (3rd)*, Charles William Packe Keyes, *b.* 1951, *s.* 2005, *m.*	Hon. (Leopold R.) J. K., *b.* 1956
1909	*Kilbracken (4th)*, Christopher John Godley, *b.* 1945, *s.* 2006, *m.*	Hon. James J. G., *b.* 1972

1900	*Killanin (4th)*, (George) Redmond Fitzpatrick Morris, *b.* 1947, *s.* 1999, *m.*	Hon. Luke M. G. M., *b.* 1975
1943	*Killearn (3rd)*, Victor Miles George Aldous Lampson, *b.* 1941, *s.* 1996, *w.*	Hon. Miles H. M. L., *b.* 1977
1789 I.	*Kilmaine (8th)*, John Francis Sandford Browne, *b.* 1983, *s.* 2013	Revd Aubrey R. C. B., *b.* 1931
1831	*Kilmarnock (8th)*, Dr Robin Jordan Boyd, *b.* 1941, *s.* 2009, *m.*	Hon. Simon J. B., *b.* 1978
1941	*Kindersley (4th)*, Rupert John Molesworth Kindersley, *b.* 1955, *s.* 2013, *m.*	Hon. Frederick H. M. K., *b.* 1987
1223 I.	*Kingsale (36th)*, Nevinson Mark de Courcy, *b.* 1958, *s.* 2005, *m.*, *Premier Baron of Ireland*	Joseph K. C. de C., *b.* 1955
1902	*Kinross (5th)*, Christopher Patrick Balfour, *b.* 1949, *s.* 1985, *m.*	Hon. Alan I. B., *b.* 1978
1951	*Kirkwood (3rd)*, David Harvie Kirkwood, PHD, *b.* 1931, *s.* 1970, *m.*	Hon. James S. K., *b.* 1937
1800 I.	*Langford (9th)*, Col. Geoffrey Alexander Rowley-Conwy, OBE, *b.* 1912, *s.* 1953, *m.*	Hon. Owain G. R.-C., *b.* 1958
1942	*Latham (2nd)*, Dominic Charles Latham, *b.* 1954, *s.* 1970	Anthony M. L., *b.* 1954
1431	*Latymer (9th)*, Crispin James Alan Nevill Money-Coutts, *b.* 1955, *s.* 2003, *m.*	Hon. Drummond W. T. M.-C., *b.* 1986
1869	*Lawrence (5th)*, David John Downer Lawrence, *b.* 1937, *s.* 1968	None
1947	*Layton (3rd)*, Geoffrey Michael Layton, *b.* 1947, *s.* 1989, *m.*	Jonathan F. L., *b.* 1942
1839	*Leigh (6th)*, Christopher Dudley Piers Leigh, *b.* 1960, *s.* 2003, *m.*	Hon. Rupert D. L., *b.* 1994
1962	*Leighton of St Mellons (3rd)*, Robert William Henry Leighton Seager, *b.* 1955, *s.* 1998	Hon. Simon J. L. S., *b.* 1957
1797	*Lilford (8th)*, Mark Vernon Powys, *b.* 1975, *s.* 2005	Robert C. L. P., *b.* 1930
1945	*Lindsay of Birker (3rd)*, James Francis Lindsay, *b.* 1945, *s.* 1994, *m.*	Alexander S. L., *b.* 1940
1758 I.	*Lisle (9th)*, (John) Nicholas Geoffrey Lysaght, *b.* 1960, *s.* 2003	Hon. David J. L., *b.* 1963
1850	*Londesborough (9th)*, Richard John Denison, *b.* 1959, *s.* 1968, *m.*	Hon. James F. D., *b.* 1990
1541 I.	*Louth (17th)*, Jonathan Oliver Plunkett, *b.* 1952, *s.* 2013	Hon. Matthew O. P., *b.* 1982
1458 S.	*Lovat (16th) and Lovat (5th) (1837)*, Simon Fraser, *b.* 1977, *s.* 1995	Hon. Jack F., *b.* 1984
1946	*Lucas of Chilworth (3rd)*, Simon William Lucas, *b.* 1957, *s.* 2001, *m.*	Hon. John R. M. L., *b.* 1995
1663	** *Lucas (11th) and Dingwall (14th) (S. 1609)*, Ralph Matthew Palmer, *b.* 1951, *s.* 1991	Hon. Lewis E. P., *b.* 1987
1929	** *Luke (3rd)*, Arthur Charles St John Lawson Johnston, *b.* 1933, *s.* 1996, *m.*	Hon. Ian J. St J. L. J., *b.* 1963
1914	** *Lyell (3rd)*, Charles Lyell, *b.* 1939, *s.* 1943	None
1859	*Lyveden (7th)*, Jack Leslie Vernon, *b.* 1938, *s.* 1999, *m.*	Hon. Colin R. V., *b.* 1967
1959	*MacAndrew (3rd)*, Christopher Anthony Colin MacAndrew, *b.* 1945, *s.* 1989, *m.*	Hon. Oliver C. J. M., *b.* 1983
1776 I.	*Macdonald (8th)*, Godfrey James Macdonald of Macdonald, *b.* 1947, *s.* 1970, *m.*	Hon. Godfrey E. H. T. M., *b.* 1982
1937	*McGowan (4th)*, Harry John Charles McGowan, *b.* 1971, *s.* 2003, *m.*	Hon. Dominic J. W. M., *b.* 1951
1922	*Maclay (3rd)*, Joseph Paton Maclay, *b.* 1942, *s.* 1969, *m.*	Hon. Joseph P. M., *b.* 1977
1955	*McNair (3rd)*, Duncan James McNair, *b.* 1947, *s.* 1989, *m.*	Hon. William S. A. M., *b.* 1958
1951	*Macpherson of Drumochter (3rd)*, James Anthony Macpherson, *b.* 1979, *s.* 2008	Hon. Daniel T. M., *b.* 2013
1937	** *Mancroft (3rd)*, Benjamin Lloyd Stormont Mancroft, *b.* 1957, *s.* 1987, *m.*	Hon. Arthur L. S. M., *b.* 1995
1807	*Manners (6th)*, John Hugh Robert Manners, *b.* 1956, *s.* 2008, *m.*	Hon. John A. D. M., *b.* 2011
1922	*Manton (4th)*, Miles Ronald Marcus Watson, *b.* 1958, *s.* 2003, *m.*	Hon. Thomas N. C. D. W., *b.* 1985
1908	*Marchamley (4th)*, William Francis Whiteley, *b.* 1968, *s.* 1994, *m.*	Hon. Leon W., *b.* 2004
1964	*Margadale (3rd)*, Alastair John Morrison, *b.* 1958, *s.* 2003, *m.*	Hon. Declan J. M., *b.* 1993
1961	*Marks of Broughton (3rd)*, Simon Richard Marks, *b.* 1950, *s.* 1998, *m.*	Hon. Michael M., *b.* 1989
1964	*Martonmere (2nd)*, John Stephen Robinson, *b.* 1963, *s.* 1989	Hon. James I. R., *b.* 2003
1776 I.	*Massy (10th)*, David Hamon Somerset Massy, *b.* 1947, *s.* 1995	Hon. John H. M., *b.* 1950
1935	*May (4th)*, Jasper Bertram St John May, *b.* 1965, *s.* 2006	None
1928	*Melchett (4th)*, Peter Robert Henry Mond, *b.* 1948, *s.* 1973	None
1925	*Merrivale (4th)*, Derek John Philip Duke, *b.* 1948, *s.* 2007, *m.*	Hon. Thomas D., *b.* 1980
1911	*Merthyr (4th)*, Trevor Oswin Lewis, CBE, *b.* 1935, *s.* 1977, *m.* Disclaimed for life 1977.	David T. L., *b.* 1977
1919	*Meston (3rd)*, James Meston, QC, *b.* 1950, *s.* 1984, *m.*	Hon. Thomas J. D. M., *b.* 1977
1838	*Methuen (8th)*, James Paul Archibald Methuen-Campbell, *b.* 1952, *s.* 2014	Thomas R. M. M.-C., *b.* 1977
1711	*Middleton (13th)*, Michael Charles James Willoughby, *b.* 1948, *s.* 2011, *m.*	Hon. James W. M. W., *b.* 1976
1939	*Milford (4th)*, Guy Wogan Philipps, QC, *b.* 1961, *s.* 1999, *m.*	Hon. Archie S. P., *b.* 1997
1933	*Milne (3rd)*, George Alexander Milne, *b.* 1941, *s.* 2005	Hon. Iain C. L. M., *b.* 1949
1951	*Milner of Leeds (3rd)*, Richard James Milner, *b.* 1959, *s.* 2003, *m.*	None
1947	*Milverton (2nd)*, Revd Fraser Arthur Richard Richards, *b.* 1930, *s.* 1978, *m.*	Hon. Michael H. R., *b.* 1936
1873	*Moncreiff (6th)*, Rhoderick Harry Wellwood Moncreiff, *b.* 1954, *s.* 2002, *m.*	Hon. Harry J. W. M., *b.* 1986
1884	*Monk Bretton (3rd)*, John Charles Dodson, *b.* 1924, *s.* 1933, *m.*	Hon. Christopher M. D., *b.* 1958
1885	*Monkswell (5th)*, Gerard Collier, *b.* 1947, *s.* 1984, *m.*	Hon. James A. C., *b.* 1977
1728	*Monson (12th)*, Nicholas John Monson, *b.* 1955, *s.* 2011, *m.*	Hon. Andrew A. J. M., *b.* 1959
1885	** *Montagu of Beaulieu (3rd)*, Edward John Barrington Douglas-Scott-Montagu, *b.* 1926, *s.* 1929, *m.*	Hon. Ralph D.-S.-M., *b.* 1961
1839	*Monteagle of Brandon (7th)*, Charles James Spring Rice, *b.* 1953, *s.* 2013, *m.*	Hon. Michael S. R., *b.* 1935

1943	*Moran (3rd),* James McMoran Wilson, *b.* 1952, *s.* 2014, *m.*	Hon. David A. M. W., *b.* 1990
1918	*Morris (4th),* Thomas Anthony Salmon Morris, *b.* 1982, *s.* 2011	Hon. John M. M., *b.* 1983
1950	*Morris of Kenwood (3rd),* Jonathan David Morris, *b.* 1968, *s.* 2004, *m.*	Hon. Benjamin J. M., *b.* 1998
1831	*Mostyn (7th),* Gregory Philip Roger Lloyd-Mostyn, *b.* 1984, *s.* 2011	Roger Hugh L.-M., *b.* 1941
1933	*Mottistone (6th),* Christopher David Peter Seely, *b.* 1974, *s.* 2013	Hon. Richard W. A. S., *b.* 1988
1945	*Mountevans (3rd),* Edward Patrick Broke Evans, *b.* 1943, *s.* 1974, *m.*	Hon. Jeffrey de C. R. E., *b.* 1948
1283	*Mowbray (27th), Segrave (28th) (1295) and Stourton (24th) (1448),* Edward William Stephen Stourton, *b.* 1953, *s.* 2006, *m.*	Hon. James C. P. 3., *b.* 1991
1932	*Moyne (3rd),* Jonathan Bryan Guinness, *b.* 1930, *s.* 1992, *m.*	Hon. Valentine G. B. G., *b.* 1959
1929	** *Moynihan (4th),* Colin Berkeley Moynihan, *b.* 1955, *s.* 1997, *m.*	Hon. Nicholas E. B. M., *b.* 1994
1781 I.	*Muskerry (9th),* Robert Fitzmaurice Deane, *b.* 1948, *s.* 1988, *m.*	Hon. Jonathan F. D., *b.* 1986
1627 S.	*Napier (15th) and Ettrick (6th) (1872),* Francis David Charles Napier, *b.* 1962, *s.* 2012, *m.*	Master of Napier, *b.* 1996
1868	*Napier of Magdala (6th),* Robert Alan Napier, *b.* 1940, *s.* 1987, *m.*	Hon. James R. N., *b.* 1966
1940	*Nathan (3rd),* Rupert Harry Bernard Nathan, *b.* 1957, *s.* 2007, *m.*	None
1960	*Nelson of Stafford (4th),* Alistair William Henry Nelson, *b.* 1973, *s.* 2006	Hon. James J. N., *b.* 1947
1959	*Netherthorpe (3rd),* James Frederick Turner, *b.* 1964, *s.* 1982, *m.*	Hon. Andrew J. E. T., *b.* 1993
1946	*Newall (2nd),* Francis Storer Eaton Newall, *b.* 1930, *s.* 1963, *m.*	Hon. Richard H. E. N., *b.* 1961
1776 I.	*Newborough (8th),* Robert Vaughan Wynn, *b.* 1949, *s.* 1998, *m.*	Antony C. V. W., *b.* 1949
1892	*Newton (5th),* Richard Thomas Legh, *b.* 1950, *s.* 1992, *m.*	Hon. Piers R. L., *b.* 1979
1930	*Noel-Buxton (4th),* Charles Connal Noel-Buxton, *b.* 1975, *s.* 2013, *m.*	Hon. Simon C. N.-B., *b.* 1943
1957	*Norrie (2nd),* (George) Willoughby Moke Norrie, *b.* 1936, *s.* 1977, *m.*	Hon. Mark W. J. N., *b.* 1972
1884	** *Northbourne (5th),* Christopher George Walter James, *b.* 1926, *s.* 1982, *m.*	Hon. Charles W. H. J., *b.* 1960
1866	** *Northbrook (6th),* Francis Thomas Baring, *b.* 1954, *s.* 1990, *m.*	To the Baronetcy, Peter B. *b.* 1939
1878	*Norton (8th),* James Nigel Arden Adderley, *b.* 1947, *s.* 1993, *m.*	Hon. Edward J. A. A., *b.* 1982
1906	*Nunburnholme (6th),* Stephen Charles Yanath Wilson, *b.* 1973, *s.* 2000	Hon. David M. W., *b.* 1954
1950	*Ogmore (3rd),* Morgan Rees-Williams, *b.* 1937, *s.* 2004, *m.*	Hon. Tudor D. R.-W., *b.* 1991
1870	*O'Hagan (4th),* Charles Towneley Strachey, *b.* 1945, *s.* 1961	Hon. Richard T. S., *b.* 1950
1868	*O'Neill (4th),* Raymond Arthur Clanaboy O'Neill, KCVO, TD, *b.* 1933, *s.* 1944, *m.*	Hon. Shane S. C. O'N., *b.* 1965
1836 I.	*Oranmore and Browne (5th) and Mereworth (3rd) (1926),* Dominick Geoffrey Thomas Browne, *b.* 1929, *s.* 2002	Shaun D. B., *b.* 1964
1933	** *Palmer (4th),* Adrian Bailie Nottage Palmer, *b.* 1951, *s.* 1990, *m.*	Hon. Hugo B. R. P., *b.* 1980
1914	*Parmoor (5th),* Michael Leonard Seddon Cripps, *b.* 1942, *s.* 2008, *m.*	Hon. Henry W. A. C., *b.* 1976
1937	*Pender (3rd),* John Willoughby Denison-Pender, *b.* 1933, *s.* 1965, *w.*	Hon. Henry J. R. D.-P., *b.* 1968
1866	*Penrhyn (7th),* Simon Douglas-Pennant, *b.* 1938, *s.* 2003, *m.*	Hon. Edward S. D.-P., *b.* 1966
1603	*Petre (18th),* John Patrick Lionel Petre, *b.* 1942, *s.* 1989, *m.*	Hon. Dominic W. P., *b.* 1966
1918	*Phillimore (5th),* Francis Stephen Phillimore, *b.* 1944, *s.* 1994, *m.*	Hon. Tristan A. S. P., *b.* 1977
1945	*Piercy (3rd),* James William Piercy, *b.* 1946, *s.* 1981	Hon. Mark E. P. P., *b.* 1953
1827	*Plunket (9th),* Tyrone Shaun Terence Plunket, *b.* 1966, *s.* 2013, *m.*	Hon. Rory P., *b.* 2001
1831	*Poltimore (7th),* Mark Coplestone Bampfylde, *b.* 1957, *s.* 1978, *m.*	Hon. Henry A. W. B., *b.* 1985
1690 S.	*Polwarth (11th),* Andrew Walter Hepburne-Scott, *b.* 1947, *s.* 2005, *m.*	Master of Polwarth, *b.* 1973
1930	*Ponsonby of Shulbrede (4th) and Ponsonby of Roehampton (life peerage, 2000),* Frederick Matthew Thomas Ponsonby, *b.* 1958, *s.* 1990, *m.*	Hon. Cameron J. J. P., *b.* 1995
1958	*Poole (2nd),* David Charles Poole, *b.* 1945, *s.* 1993, *m.*	Hon. Oliver J. P., *b.* 1972
1852	*Raglan (6th),* Geoffrey Somerset, *b.* 1932, *s.* 2010, *m.*	Iggy F. S., *b.* 2004
1932	*Rankeillour (5th),* Michael Richard Hope, *b.* 1940, *s.* 2005, *m.*	James F. H., *b.* 1968
1953	*Rathcavan (3rd),* Hugh Detmar Torrens O'Neill, *b.* 1939, *s.* 1994, *m.*	Hon. François H. N. O'N., *b.* 1984
1916	*Rathcreedan (3rd),* Christopher John Norton, *b.* 1949, *s.* 1990, *m.*	Hon. Adam G. N., *b.* 1952
1868 I.	*Rathdonnell (5th),* Thomas Benjamin McClintock-Bunbury, *b.* 1938, *s.* 1959, *m.*	Hon. William L. M.-B., *b.* 1966
1911	*Ravensdale (3rd),* Nicholas Mosley, MC, *b.* 1923, *s.* 1966, *m.*	Daniel N. M., *b.* 1982
1821	*Ravensworth (9th),* Thomas Arthur Hamish Liddell, *b.* 1954, *s.* 2004, *m.*	Hon. Henry A. T. L., *b.* 1987
1821	*Rayleigh (6th),* John Gerald Strutt, *b.* 1960, *s.* 1988, *m.*	Hon. John F. S., *b.* 1993
1937	** *Rea (3rd),* John Nicolas Rea, MD, *b.* 1928, *s.* 1981, *m.*	Hon. Matthew J. R., *b.* 1956
1628 S.	*Reay (15th),* Aeneas Simon Mackay, *b.* 1965, *s.* 2013, *m.*	Master of Reay, *b.* 2010
1902	*Redesdale (6th) and Mitford (life peerage, 2000),* Rupert Bertram Mitford, *b.* 1967, *s.* 1991, *m.*	Hon. Bertram D. M., *b.* 2000
1940	*Reith (2nd),* Christopher John Reith, *b.* 1928, *s.* 1971, *m.* Disclaimed for life 1972.	Hon. James H. J. R., *b.* 1971
1928	*Remnant (3rd),* James Wogan Remnant, CVO, *b.* 1930, *s.* 1967, *m.*	Hon. Philip J. R., *b.* 1954
1806 I.	*Rendlesham (9th),* Charles William Brooke Thellusson, *b.* 1954, *s.* 1999, *m.*	Hon. Peter R. T., *b.* 1920
1933	*Rennell (4th),* James Roderick David Tremayne Rodd, *b.* 1978, *s.* 2006	None
1964	*Renwick (2nd),* Harry Andrew Renwick, *b.* 1935, *s.* 1973, *m.*	Hon. Robert J. R., *b.* 1966
1885	*Revelstoke (7th),* Alexander Rupert Baring, *b.* 1970, *s.* 2012	Hon. Thomas J. B., *b.* 1971
1905	*Ritchie of Dundee (6th),* Charles Rupert Rendall Ritchie, *b.* 1958, *s.* 2008, *m.*	Hon. Sebastian R., *b.* 2004
1935	*Riverdale (3rd),* Anthony Robert Balfour, *b.* 1960, *s.* 1998	Arthur M. B., *b.* 1938

1961	*Robertson of Oakridge (3rd)*, William Brian Elworthy Robertson, *b.* 1975, *s.* 2009, *m.*	None
1938	*Roborough (3rd)*, Henry Massey Lopes, *b.* 1940, *s.* 1992, *m.*	Hon. Massey J. H. L., *b.* 1969
1931	*Rochester (2nd)*, Foster Charles Lowry Lamb, *b.* 1916, *s.* 1955, *w.*	Hon. David C. L., *b.* 1944
1934	*Rockley (4th)*, Anthony Robert Cecil, *b.* 1961, *s.* 2011, *m.*	Hon. William E. C., *b.* 1996
1782 M.	*Rodney (11th)*, John George Brydges Rodney, *b.* 1999, *s.* 2011	Nicholas S. H. R., *b.* 1947
1651 S.	*Rollo (14th) and Dunning (5th) (1869)*, David Eric Howard Rollo, *b.* 1943, *s.* 1997, *m.*	Master of Rollo, *b.* 1972
1959	*Rootes (3rd)*, Nicholas Geoffrey Rootes, *b.* 1951, *s.* 1992, *m.*	William B. R., *b.* 1944
1796 I.	*Rossmore (7th) and Rossmore (6th) (1838)*, William Warner Westenra, *b.* 1931, *s.* 1958, *m.*	Hon. Benedict W. W., *b.* 1983
1939	** *Rotherwick (3rd)*, (Herbert) Robin Cayzer, *b.* 1954, *s.* 1996, *m.*	Hon. H. Robin C., *b.* 1989
1885	*Rothschild (4th)*, (Nathaniel Charles) Jacob Rothschild, OM, GBE, *b.* 1936, *s.* 1990, *m.*	Hon. Nathaniel P. V. J. R., *b.* 1971
1911	*Rowallan (4th)*, John Polson Cameron Corbett, *b.* 1947, *s.* 1993	Hon. Jason W. P. C. C., *b.* 1972
1947	*Rugby (3rd)*, Robert Charles Maffey, *b.* 1951, *s.* 1990, *m.*	Hon. Timothy J. H. M., *b.* 1975
1919	*Russell of Liverpool (3rd)*, Simon Gordon Jared Russell, *b.* 1952, *s.* 1981, *m.*	Hon. Edward C. S. R., *b.* 1985
1876	*Sackville (7th)*, Robert Bertrand Sackville-West, *b.* 1958, *s.* 2004, *m.*	Hon. Arthur S-W., *b.* 2000
1964	*St Helens (2nd)*, Richard Francis Hughes-Young, *b.* 1945, *s.* 1980, *m.*	Hon. Henry T. H.-Y., *b.* 1986
1559	** *St John of Bletso (21st)*, Anthony Tudor St John, *b.* 1957, *s.* 1978, *m.*	Hon. Oliver B. St J., *b.* 1995
1887	*St Levan (5th)*, James Piers Southwell St Aubyn, *b.* 1950, *s.* 2013, *m.*	Hon. Hugh J. St A., *b.* 1983
1885	*St Oswald (6th)*, Charles Rowland Andrew Winn, *b.* 1959, *s.* 1999, *m.*	Hon. Rowland C. S. H. W., *b.* 1986
1960	*Sanderson of Ayot (2nd)*, Alan Lindsay Sanderson, *b.* 1931, *s.* 1971, *m.* Disclaimed for life 1971.	Hon. Michael S., *b.* 1959
1945	*Sandford (3rd)*, James John Mowbray Edmondson, *b.* 1949, *s.* 2009, *m.*	Hon. Devon J. E., *b.* 1986
1871	*Sandhurst (6th)*, Guy Rees John Mansfield, QC, *b.* 1949, *s.* 2002, *m.*	Hon. Edward J. M., *b.* 1982
1888	*Savile (4th)*, John Anthony Thornhill Lumley-Savile, *b.* 1947, *s.* 2008, *m.*	Hon. James G. A. L-S., *b.* 1975
1447	*Saye and Sele (21st)*, Nathaniel Thomas Allen Fiennes, *b.* 1920, *s.* 1968, *m.*	Hon. Martin G. F., *b.* 1961
1826	*Seaford (6th)*, Colin Humphrey Felton Ellis, *b.* 1946, *s.* 1999, *m.*	Hon. Benjamin F. T. E., *b.* 1976
1932	** *Selsdon (3rd)*, Malcolm McEacharn Mitchell-Thomson, *b.* 1937, *s.* 1963, *m.*	Hon. Callum M. M. M.-T., *b.* 1969
1489 S.	*Sempill (21st)*, James William Stuart Whitemore Sempill, *b.* 1949, *s.* 1995, *m.*	Master of Sempill, *b.* 1979
1916	*Shaughnessy (5th)*, Charles George Patrick Shaughnessy, *b* 1955, *s.* 2007, *m.*	David J. S., *b.* 1957
1946	*Shepherd (3rd)*, Graham George Shepherd, *b.* 1949, *s.* 2001, *m.*	Hon. Patrick M. S., *b.* 1980
1964	*Sherfield (3rd)*, Dwight William Makins, *b.* 1951, *s.* 2006, *m.*	None
1902	*Shuttleworth (5th)*, Charles Geoffrey Nicholas Kay-Shuttleworth, KCVO, *b.* 1948, *s.* 1975, *m.*	Hon. Thomas E. K.-S., *b.* 1976
1950	*Silkin (3rd)*, Christopher Lewis Silkin, *b.* 1947, *s.* 2001. Disclaimed for life 2002.	Rory L. S., *b.* 1954
1963	*Silsoe (3rd)*, Simon Rupert Trustram Eve *b.* 1966, *s.* 2005	Hon. Peter N. T. E., *b.* 1930
1947	*Simon of Wythenshawe (3rd)*, Matthew Simon, *b.* 1955, *s.* 2002	Martin S., *b.* 1944
1449 S.	*Sinclair (18th)*, Matthew Murray Kennedy St Clair *b.* 1968, *s.* 2004, *m.*	Master of Sinclair, *b.* 2007
1957	*Sinclair of Cleeve (3rd)*, John Lawrence Robert Sinclair, *b.* 1953, *s.* 1985	None
1919	*Sinha (6th)*, Arup Kumar Sinha, *b.* 1966, *s.* 1999	Hon. Dilip K. S., *b.* 1967
1828	** *Skelmersdale (7th)*, Roger Bootle-Wilbraham, *b.* 1945, *s.* 1973, *m.*	Hon. Andrew B.-W., *b.* 1977
1916	*Somerleyton (4th)*, Hugh Francis Saville Crossley, *b.* 1971, *s.* 2012, *m.*	Hon. John de B. T. S. C., *b.* 2010
1784	*Somers (9th)*, Philip Sebastian Somers Cocks, *b.* 1948, *s.* 1995	Jonathan B. C., *b.* 1985
1780	*Southampton (6th)*, Charles James FitzRoy, *b.* 1928, *s.* 1989, *m.*	Hon. Edward C. F., *b.* 1955
1959	*Spens (4th)*, Patrick Nathaniel George Spens, *b.* 1968, *s.* 2001, *m.*	Hon. Peter L. S., *b.* 2000
1640	*Stafford (15th)*, Francis Melfort William Fitzherbert, *b.* 1954, *s.* 1986, *m.*	Hon. Benjamin J. B. F., *b.* 1983
1938	*Stamp (4th)*, Trevor Charles Bosworth Stamp, MD, *b.* 1935, *s.* 1987, *m.*	Hon. Nicholas C. T. S., *b.* 1978
1839	*Stanley of Alderley (9th)*, Sheffield (9th) (I. 1738) and Eddisbury (8th) (1848), Richard Oliver Stanley, *b.* 1956, *s.* 2013, *m.*	Hon. Charles E. S., *b.* 1960
1318	*Strabolgi (12th)*, Andrew David Whitley Kenworthy, *b.* 1967, *s.* 2010, *m.*	Hon. Joel B. K., *b.* 2004
1954	*Strang (2nd)*, Colin Strang, *b.* 1922, *s.* 1978, *m.*	None
1628	*Strange (17th)*, Adam Humphrey Drummond of Megginch, *b.* 1953, *s.* 2005, *m.*	Hon. John A. H. D. of M. *b.* 1992
1955	*Strathalmond (3rd)*, William Roberton Fraser, *b.* 1947, *s.* 1976, *m.*	Hon. William G. F., *b.* 1976
1936	*Strathcarron (3rd)*, Ian David Patrick Macpherson, *b.* 1949, *s.* 2006, *m.*	Hon. Rory D. A. M., *b.* 1982
1955	** *Strathclyde (2nd)*, Thomas Galloway Dunlop du Roy de Blicquy Galbraith, CH, PC, *b.* 1960, *s.* 1985, *m.*	Hon. Charles W. du R. de B. G., *b.* 1962
1900	*Strathcona and Mount Royal (4th)*, Donald Euan Palmer Howard, *b.* 1923, *s.* 1959, *m.*	Hon. D. Alexander S. H., *b.* 1961
1836	*Stratheden (7th) and Campbell (7th) (1841)*, David Anthony Campbell, *b.* 1963, *s.* 2011, *m.*	None
1884	*Strathspey (6th)*, James Patrick Trevor Grant of Grant, *b.* 1943, *s.* 1992, *m.*	Hon. Michael P. F. G., *b.* 1953
1838	*Sudeley (7th)*, Merlin Charles Sainthill Hanbury-Tracy, *b.* 1939, *s.* 1941	Nicholas E. J. H.-T., *b.* 1959

1786	*Suffield (12th)*, Charles Anthony Assheton Harbord-Hamond, *b.* 1953, *s.* 2011, *m.*	Hon. John E. R. H.-H., *b.* 1956
1893	*Swansea (5th)*, Richard Anthony Hussey Vivian, *b.* 1957, *s.* 2005, *m.*	Hon. James H. H. V., *b.* 1999
1907	*Swaythling (5th)*, Charles Edgar Samuel Montagu, *b.* 1954, *s.* 1998, *m.*	Rupert A. S. M., *b.* 1965
1919	** *Swinfen (3rd)*, Roger Mynors Swinfen Eady, *b.* 1938, *s.* 1977, *m.*	Hon. Charles R. P. S. E., *b.* 1971
1831 I.	*Talbot of Malahide (10th)*, Reginald John Richard Arundell, *b.* 1931, *s.* 1987, *m.*	Hon. Richard J. T. A., *b.* 1957
1946	*Tedder (3rd)*, Robin John Tedder, *b.* 1955, *s.* 1994, *m.*	Hon. Benjamin J. T., *b.* 1985
1884	*Tennyson (6th)*, David Harold Alexander Tennyson, *b.* 1960, *s.* 2006	Alan J. D. T., *b.* 1965
1918	*Terrington (6th)*, Christopher Richard James Woodhouse, MB, *b.* 1946, *s.* 2001, *m.*	Hon. Jack H. L. W., *b.* 1978
1940	*Teviot (2nd)*, Charles John Kerr, *b.* 1934, *s.* 1968, *m.*	Hon. Charles R. K., *b.* 1971
1616	*Teynham (20th)*, John Christopher Ingham Roper-Curzon, *b.* 1928, *s.* 1972, *m.*	Hon. David J. H. I. R.-C., *b.* 1965
1964	*Thomson of Fleet (3rd)*, David Kenneth Roy Thomson, *b.* 1957, *s.* 2006, *m.*	Hon. Benjamin T., *b.* 2006
1792	*Thurlow (9th)*, Roualeyn Robert Hovell-Thurlow-Cumming-Bruce, *b.* 1952, *s.* 2013, *m.*	Hon. Nicholas E. H.-T.-C.-B., *b.* 1986
1876	*Tollemache (5th)*, Timothy John Edward Tollemache, *b.* 1939, *s.* 1975, *m.*	Hon. Edward J. H. T., *b.* 1976
1564 S.	*Torphichen (15th)*, James Andrew Douglas Sandilands, *b.* 1946, *s.* 1975, *m.*	Robert P. S., *b.* 1950
1947	** *Trefgarne (2nd)*, David Garro Trefgarne, PC, *b.* 1941, *s.* 1960, *m.*	Hon. George G. T., *b.* 1970
1921	*Trevethin (5th) and Oaksey (3rd) (1947)*, Patrick John Tristram Lawrence, QC, *b.* 1960, *s.* 2012, *m.*	Hon. Oliver J. T. L., *b.* 1990
1880	*Trevor (5th)*, Marke Charles Hill-Trevor, *b.* 1970, *s.* 1997, *m.*	Hon. Iain R. H.-T., *b.* 1971
1461 I.	*Trimlestown (21st)*, Raymond Charles Barnewall, *b.* 1930, *s.* 1997	None
1940	*Tryon (3rd)*, Anthony George Merrik Tryon, *b.* 1940, *s.* 1976	Hon. Charles G. B. T., *b.* 1976
1935	*Tweedsmuir (4th)*, John William de l'Aigle (Toby) Buchan, *b.* 1950, *s.* 2008, *m.*	Hon. John A. G. B., *b.* 1986
1523	*Vaux of Harrowden (11th)*, Anthony William Gilbey, *b.* 1940, *s.* 2002, *m.*	Hon. Richard H. G. G., *b.* 1965
1800 I.	*Ventry (8th)*, Andrew Wesley Daubeny de Moleyns, *b.* 1943, *s.* 1987, *m.*	Hon. Francis W. D. de M., *b.* 1965
1762	*Vernon (11th)*, Anthony William Vernon-Harcourt, *b.* 1939, *s.* 2000, *m.*	Hon. Simon A. V.-H., *b.* 1969
1922	*Vestey (3rd)*, Samuel George Armstrong Vestey, KCVO, *b.* 1941, *s.* 1954, *m.*	Hon. William G. V., *b.* 1983
1841	*Vivian (7th)*, Charles Crespigny Hussey Vivian, *b.* 1966, *s.* 2004	Thomas C. B. V., *b.* 1971
1934	*Wakehurst (3rd)*, (John) Christopher Loder, *b.* 1925, *s.* 1970, *m.*	Hon. Timothy W. L., *b.* 1958
1723	** *Walpole (10th) and Walpole of Wolterton (8th) (1756)*, Robert Horatio Walpole, *b.* 1938, *s.* 1989, *m.*	Hon. Jonathan R. H. W., *b.* 1967
1780	*Walsingham (9th)*, John de Grey, MC, *b.* 1925, *s.* 1965, *m.*	Hon. Robert de. G., *b.* 1969
1936	*Wardington (3rd)*, William Simon Pease, *b.* 1925, *s.* 2005, *m.*	None
1792 I.	*Waterpark (8th)*, Roderick Alexander Cavendish, *b.* 1959, *s.* 2013, *m.*	Hon. Luke F. C., *b.* 1990
1942	*Wedgwood (5th)*, Antony John Wedgwood, *b.* 1944, *s.* 2014, *m.*	Hon. Thomas W., *b.* 1978
1861	*Westbury (6th)*, Richard Nicholas Bethell, MBE, *b.* 1950, *s.* 2001, *m.*	Hon. Alexander B., *b.* 1986
1944	*Westwood (3rd)*, (William) Gavin Westwood, *b.* 1944, *s.* 1991, *m.*	Hon. W. Fergus W., *b.* 1972
1544/5	*Wharton (12th)*, Myles Christopher David Robertson, *b.* 1964, *s.* 2000, *m.*	Hon. Meghan Z. M. R., *b.* 2006
1935	*Wigram (2nd)*, (George) Neville (Clive) Wigram, MC, *b.* 1915, *s.* 1960, *w.*	Maj. Hon. Andrew F. C. W., *b.* 1949
1491	** *Willoughby de Broke (21st)*, Leopold David Verney, *b.* 1938, *s.* 1986, *m.*	Hon. Rupert G. V., *b.* 1966
1937	*Windlesham (4th)*, James Rupert Hennessy, *b.* 1968, *s.* 2010, *m.*	Hon. George R. J. H., *b.* 2006
1951	*Wise (3rd)*, Christopher John Clayton Wise, *b.* 1949, *s.* 2012	Hon. Martin H. W., *b.* 1950
1869	*Wolverton (8th)*, Miles John Glyn, *b.* 1966, *s.* 2011	Jonathan C. G., *b.* 1990
1928	*Wraxall (3rd)*, Eustace Hubert Beilby Gibbs, KCVO, CMG, *b.* 1929, *s.* 2001, *m.*	Hon. Anthony H. G., *b.* 1958
1915	*Wrenbury (3rd)*, Revd John Burton Buckley, *b.* 1927, *s.* 1940, *m.*	Hon. William E. B., *b.* 1966
1838	*Wrottesley (6th)*, Clifton Hugh Lancelot de Verdon Wrottesley, *b.* 1968, *s.* 1977, *m.*	Hon. Victor E. F. de V. W., *b.* 2004
1829	*Wynford (9th)*, John Philip Robert Best, *b.* 1950, *s.* 2002, *m.*	Hon. Harry R. F. B., *b.* 1987
1308	*Zouche (18th)*, James Assheton Frankland, *b.* 1943, *s.* 1965, *m.*	Hon. William T. A. F., *b.* 1984

BARONESSES/LADIES IN THEIR OWN RIGHT

Style, The Rt. Hon. the Lady _ , *or* The Rt. Hon. the Baroness _ , according to her preference. Either style may be used, except in the case of Scottish titles (indicated by S.), which are not baronies (*see* page 44) and whose holders are always addressed as Lady.

Envelope, may be addressed in same way as a Baron's wife or, if she prefers *(formal)*, The Rt. Hon. the Baroness _;   *(social)*, The Baroness _. Otherwise as for a Baron's wife

Husband, Untitled

Children's style, As for children of a Baron

Created	Title, order of succession, name, etc	Heir
1664	*Arlington (11th)*, Jennifer Jane Forwood, *b.* 1939, *s.* 1999, *w.* Title called out of abeyance 1999	Hon. Patrick J. D. F., *b.* 1967
1455	*Berners (16th)*, Pamela Vivien Kirkham, *b.* 1929, *s.* 1995, *m.* Title called out of abeyance 1995	Hon. Rupert W. T. K., *b.* 1953
1529	*Braye (8th)*, Mary Penelope Aubrey-Fletcher, *b.* 1941, *s.* 1985, *m.*	Linda K. C. Fothergill, *b.* 1930
1321	*Dacre (29th)*, Emily Douglas-Home, *b.* 1983, *s.* 2014	Three co-heiresses
1283	*Fauconberg (10th) and Conyers (16th) (1509)*, Baronies in abeyance between two co-heiresses since 2013	
1490 S.	*Herries of Terregles (14th)*, Anne Elizabeth Fitzalan-Howard, *b.* 1938, *s.* 1975, *w.*	Lady Mary Mumford, *b.* 1940
1597	*Howard de Walden (10th)*, Mary Hazel Caridwen Czernin, *b.* 1935, *s.* 2004, *m.* Title called out of abeyance 2004	Hon. Peter J. J. C., *b.* 1966
1602 S.	*Kinloss (13th)*, Teresa Mary Nugent Freeman-Grenville, *b.* 1957, *s.* 2012	Hon. Hester J. A. Haworth, *b.* 1960
1445 S.	** *Saltoun (20th)*, Flora Marjory Fraser, *b.* 1930, *s.* 1979, *w.*	Hon. Katharine I. M. I. F., *b.* 1957
1313	*Willoughby de Eresby (27th)*, (Nancy) Jane Marie Heathcote-Drummond-Willoughby, *b.* 1934, *s.* 1983	Two co-heirs

LIFE PEERS

Style, The Rt. Hon. the Lord _ / The Rt. Hon. the Lady _ , *or* The Rt. Hon. the Baroness _ , according to her preference *Envelope (formal)*, The Rt. Hon. Lord _/Lady_/ Baroness_; *(social)*, The Lord _/Lady_/Baroness_ *Letter (formal)*, My Lord/Lady; *(social)*, Dear Lord/ Lady _. *Spoken*, Lord/Lady _
Wife's style, The Rt. Hon. the Lady _
Husband, Untitled
Children's style, 'The Hon.' before forename (F_) and surname (S_)
Envelope, The Hon. F_ S_. *Letter*, Dear Mr/Miss/Mrs S_. *Spoken*, Mr/Miss/Mrs S_

NEW LIFE PEERAGES

1 September 2013 to 31 August 2014:
Karen Brady, CBE; Martin Callanan; Michael Cashman, CBE; Carlyn Chisholm; Andrew Cooper; Natalie Evans; Michael Stahel Farmer; Chris Fox; David Goddard; Dido (Diana Mary) Harding; William Hay; Arminka Helic; Barbara Janke; Chris Lennie; Nosheena Mobarik, CBE; Kath Pinnock; Dame Gail Ruth Rebuck, DBE; Gen. Sir David Julian Richards, GCB, CBE, DSO; Sir Stuart Alan Ransom Rose; Paul Scriven; Joanna Shields, OBE; Dr Julie Smith; Ranbir Suri; Rt. Hon. Sir Roger John Laugharne Thomas

SYMBOLS
* Hereditary peer who has been granted a life peerage. For further details, please refer to the Hereditary Peers section. For example, life peer *Balniel* can be found under his hereditary title *Earl of Crawford and Balcarres*
§ Members of the Judiciary currently disqualified from sitting or voting in the House of Lords until they retire from that office. For further information *see* Law Courts and Offices
‡ Title not confirmed at time of going to press
¶ Peer who has permanently resigned from the House of Lords

CREATED UNDER THE APPELLATE JURISDICTION ACT 1876 (AS AMENDED)

BARONS
Created
2004   *Brown of Eaton-under-Heywood*, Simon Denis Brown, PC, *b.* 1937, *m.*
1991   *Browne-Wilkinson*, Nicolas Christopher Henry Browne-Wilkinson, PC, *b.* 1930, *m.*
2004   *Carswell*, Robert Douglas Carswell, PC, *b.* 1934, *m.*
2009   *Collins of Mapesbury*, Lawrence Antony Collins, PC, *b.* 1941
1986   *Goff of Chieveley*, Robert Lionel Archibald Goff, PC, *b.* 1926, *m.*
1985   *Griffiths*, (William) Hugh Griffiths, MC, PC, *b.* 1923, *m.*
1995   *Hoffmann*, Leonard Hubert Hoffmann, PC, *b.* 1934, *m.*
1997   *Hutton*, (James) Brian (Edward) Hutton, PC, *b.* 1931, *m.*
2009   §*Kerr of Tonaghmore*, Brian Francis Kerr, PC, *b.* 1948, *m.*
1993   *Lloyd of Berwick*, Anthony John Leslie Lloyd, PC, *b.* 1929, *m.*

2005   §*Mance*, Jonathan Hugh Mance, PC, *b.* 1943, *m.*
1998   *Millett*, Peter Julian Millett, PC, *b.* 1932, *m.*
1992   *Mustill*, Michael John Mustill, PC, *b.* 1931, *m.*
2007   §*Neuberger of Abbotsbury*, David Edmond Neuberger, PC, *b.* 1948, *m.*
1994   *Nicholls of Birkenhead*, Donald James Nicholls, PC, *b.* 1933, *m.*
1999   *Phillips of Worth Matravers*, Nicholas Addison Phillips, KG, PC, *b.* 1938, *m.*
1997   *Saville of Newdigate*, Mark Oliver Saville, PC, *b.* 1936, *m.*
2000   *Scott of Foscote*, Richard Rashleigh Folliott Scott, PC, *b.* 1934, *m.*
1995   *Steyn*, Johan van Zyl Steyn, PC, *b.* 1932, *m.*
2003   *Walker of Gestingthorpe*, Robert Walker, PC, *b.* 1938, *m.*
1992   *Woolf*, Harry Kenneth Woolf, PC, *b.* 1933, *m.*

BARONESSES
2004   §*Hale of Richmond*, Brenda Marjorie Hale, DBE, PC, *b.* 1945, *m.*

CREATED UNDER THE LIFE PEERAGES ACT 1958

BARONS
Created
2001   *Adebowale*, Victor Olufemi Adebowale, CBE, *b.* 1962
2005   *Adonis*, Andrew Adonis, PC, *b.* 1963, *m.*
2011   *Ahmad of Wimbledon*, Tariq Mahmood Ahmad, *b.* 1968, *m.*
1998   *Ahmed*, Nazir Ahmed, *b.* 1957, *m.*
1996   *Alderdice*, John Thomas Alderdice, *b.* 1955, *m.*
2010   *Allan of Hallam*, Richard Beecroft Allan, *b.* 1966
2013   *Allen of Kensington*, Charles Lamb Allen, CBE, *b.* 1957
1998   *Alli*, Waheed Alli, *b.* 1964
2004   *Alliance*, David Alliance, CBE, *b.* 1932
1997   *Alton of Liverpool*, David Patrick Paul Alton, *b.* 1951, *m.*
2005   *Anderson of Swansea*, Donald Anderson, PC, *b.* 1939, *m.*
1992   *Archer of Weston-super-Mare*, Jeffrey Howard Archer, *b.* 1940, *m.*
1988   *Armstrong of Ilminster*, Robert Temple Armstrong, GCB, CVO, *b.* 1927, *m.*
1999   *Armstrong-Jones*, Earl of Snowdon, GCVO, *b.* 1930, *m.* (*see* Hereditary Peers)
2000   *Ashcroft*, Michael Anthony Ashcroft, KCMG, PC, *b.* 1946, *m.*
2001   *Ashdown of Norton-sub-Hamdon*, Jeremy John Durham (Paddy) Ashdown, GCMG, KBE, PC, *b.* 1941, *m.*
1998   *Bach*, William Stephen Goulden Bach, *b.* 1946, *m.*
1997   ¶*Bagri*, Raj Kumar Bagri, CBE, *b.* 1930, *m.*
1997   *Baker of Dorking*, Kenneth Wilfred Baker, CH, PC, *b.* 1934, *m.*
2013   *Balfe*, Richard Andrew Balfe, *b.* 1944, *m.*
1974   *Balniel*, The Earl of Crawford and Balcarres, KT, GCVO, PC *b.* 1927, *m.* (*see* Hereditary Peers)
2013   *Bamford*, Anthony Paul Bamford *b.* 1945, *m.*

1992   *Barber of Tewkesbury*, Derek Coates Barber, b. 1918, m.
1983   *Barnett*, Joel Barnett, PC, b. 1923, m.
1997   *Bassam of Brighton*, (John) Steven Bassam, PC, b. 1953
2008   *Bates*, Michael Walton Bates, b. 1961
2010   *Beecham*, Jeremy Hugh Beecham, b. 1944, m.
1998   *Bell*, Timothy John Leigh Bell, b. 1941, m.
2013   *Berkeley of Knighton*, Michael Fitzhardinge Berkeley, CBE, b. 1948, m.
2001   *Best*, Richard Stuart Best, OBE, b. 1945, m.
2007   *Bew*, Prof. Paul Anthony Elliott Bew, b. 1950, m.
2001   *Bhatia*, Amirali Alibhai Bhatia, OBE, b. 1932, m.
2004   *Bhattacharyya*, Prof. (Sushantha) Kumar Bhattacharyya, CBE b. 1932, m.
2010   *Bichard*, Michael George Bichard, KCB, b. 1947
2006   *Bilimoria*, Karan Faridoon Bilimoria, CBE, b. 1961, m.
2000   *Birt*, John Francis Hodgess Birt, b. 1944, m.
2010   *Black of Brentwood*, Guy Vaughan Black, b. 1964, c. p.
2001   *Black of Crossharbour*, Conrad Moffat Black, PC (Canadian), b. 1944, m.
1997   *Blackwell*, Norman Roy Blackwell, b. 1952, m.
2010   *Blair of Boughton*, Ian Warwick Blair, QPM b. 1953, m.
2011   *Blencathra*, David John Maclean, PC, b. 1953
1995   *Blyth of Rowington*, James Blyth, b. 1940, m.
2010   *Boateng*, Paul Yaw Boateng, PC, b. 1951, m.
1996   *Borrie*, Gordon Johnson Borrie, QC, b. 1931, w.
2010   *Boswell of Aynho*, Timothy Eric Boswell, b. 1942, m.
2013   *Bourne of Aberystwyth*, Nicholas Henry Bourne, b. 1952
1996   *Bowness*, Peter Spencer Bowness, CBE, b. 1943, m.
2003   *Boyce*, Michael Boyce, KG, GCB, OBE, b. 1943, m.
2006   §*Boyd of Duncansby*, Colin David Boyd, PC, b. 1953, m.
2006   *Bradley*, Keith John Charles Bradley, PC, b. 1950, m.
1999   *Bradshaw*, William Peter Bradshaw, b. 1936, m.
1998   *Bragg*, Melvyn Bragg, b. 1939, m.
1987   *Bramall*, Edwin Noel Westby Bramall, KG, GCB, OBE, MC, b. 1923, m.
2000   *Brennan*, Daniel Joseph Brennan, QC, b. 1942, m.
1976   *Briggs*, Asa Briggs, FBA, b. 1921, m.
2000   *Brittan of Spennithorne*, Leon Brittan, PC, QC, b. 1939, m.
2004   *Broers*, Prof. Alec (Nigel) Broers, b. 1938, m.
1997   *Brooke of Alverthorpe*, Clive Brooke, b. 1942, m.
2001   *Brooke of Sutton Mandeville*, Peter Leonard Brooke, CH, PC, b. 1934, m.
1998   *Brookman*, David Keith Brookman, b. 1937, m.
1979   *Brooks of Tremorfa*, John Edward Brooks, b. 1927, m.
2006   *Browne of Belmont*, Wallace Hamilton Browne, b. 1947
2010   *Browne of Ladyton*, Desmond Henry Browne, PC, b. 1952
2001   *Browne of Madingley*, Edmund John Phillip Browne, b. 1948
2006   *Burnett*, John Patrick Aubone Burnett, b. 1945, m.
1998   *Burns*, Terence Burns, GCB, b. 1944, m.
1998   *Butler of Brockwell*, (Frederick Edward) Robin Butler, KG, GCB, CVO, PC, b. 1938, m.
2014   ‡*Callanan*, Martin John Callanan, b. 1961, m.
2004   *Cameron of Dillington*, Ewen (James Hanning) Cameron, b. 1949, m.
1984   *Cameron of Lochbroom*, Kenneth John Cameron, PC, b. 1931, m.
2001   *Campbell-Savours*, Dale Norman Campbell-Savours, b. 1943, m.

2002   *Carey of Clifton*, Rt. Revd George Leonard Carey, PC, Royal Victorian Chain, b. 1935, m.
1999   *Carington of Upton*, Lord Carrington, KG, GCMG, CH, MC, PC, b. 1919, w. (*see* Hereditary Peers)
1999   *Carlile of Berriew*, Alexander Charles Carlile, QC, b. 1948, m
2013   *Carrington of Fulham*, Matthew Hadrian Marshall Carrington, b. 1947, m.
2008   *Carter of Barnes*, Stephen Andrew Carter, CBE, b. 1964, m.
2004   *Carter of Coles*, Patrick Robert Carter, b. 1946, m.
2014   ‡*Cashman*, Michael Maurice Cashman, CBE, b. 1950
1990   *Cavendish of Furness*, (Richard) Hugh Cavendish, b. 1941, m.
1996   *Chadlington*, Peter Selwyn Gummer, b. 1942, m.
1964   *Chalfont*, (Alun) Arthur Gwynne Jones, OBE, MC, PC, b. 1919, w.
2005   *Chidgey*, David William George Chidgey, b. 1942, m.
1998   *Christopher*, Anthony Martin Grosvenor Christopher, CBE, b. 1925, m.
2001   *Clark of Windermere*, David George Clark, PC, PHD, b. 1939, m.
1998   *Clarke of Hampstead*, Anthony James Clarke, CBE, b. 1932, m.
2009   §*Clarke of Stone-Cum-Ebony*, Anthony Peter Clarke, PC, b. 1943, m.
1998   *Clement-Jones*, Timothy Francis Clement-Jones, CBE, b. 1949, m.
1990   *Clinton-Davis*, Stanley Clinton Clinton-Davis, PC, b. 1928, m.
2000   *Coe*, Sebastian Newbold Coe, CH, KBE, b. 1956, m.
2011   *Collins of Highbury*, Raymond Edward Harry Collins, b. 1954
2001   *Condon*, Paul Leslie Condon, QPM, b. 1947, m.
2014   *Cooper of Windrush*, Andrew Timothy Cooper, b. 1963, m.
1997   *Cope of Berkeley*, John Ambrose Cope, PC, b. 1937, m.
2010   *Cormack*, Patrick Thomas Cormack, b. 1939, m.
2006   *Cotter*, Brian Joseph Michael Cotter, b. 1939, m.
1991   *Craig of Radley*, David Brownrigg Craig, GCB, OBE, b. 1929, m.
1987   *Crickhowell*, (Roger) Nicholas Edwards, PC, b. 1934, m.
2006   *Crisp*, (Edmund) Nigel (Ramsay) Crisp, KCB, b. 1952, m.
2003   *Cullen of Whitekirk*, William Douglas Cullen, KT, PC, b. 1935, m.
2005   *Cunningham of Felling*, John Anderson Cunningham, PC, b. 1939, m.
1996   *Currie of Marylebone*, David Anthony Currie, b. 1946, m.
2011   *Curry of Kirkharle*, Donald Thomas Younger Curry, CBE, b. 1944, m.
2011   *Dannatt*, (Francis) Richard Dannatt, GCB, CBE, MC, b. 1950, m.
2007   *Darzi of Denham*, Ara Warkes Darzi, KBE, PC, b. 1960, m.
2006   *Davidson of Glen Clova*, Neil Forbes Davidson, QC, b. 1950, m.
2009   *Davies of Abersoch*, Evan Mervyn Davies, CBE, b. 1952, m.
1997   *Davies of Coity*, (David) Garfield Davies, CBE, b. 1935, m.
1997   *Davies of Oldham*, Bryan Davies, PC, b. 1939, m.
2010   *Davies of Stamford*, John Quentin Davies, b. 1944, m.
2006   *Dear*, Geoffrey (James) Dear, QPM, b. 1937, m.
2010   *Deben*, John Selwyn Gummer, PC, b. 1939, m.

2012   *Deighton,* Paul Clive Deighton, KBE, *b.* 1956, *m.*
1991   *Desai,* Prof. Meghnad Jagdishchandra Desai, PHD,
        b. 1940, *m.*
1997   *Dholakia,* Navnit Dholakia, OBE, PC, *b.* 1937, *m.*
1997   *Dixon,* Donald Dixon, PC, *b.* 1929, *m.*
1993   *Dixon-Smith,* Robert William Dixon-Smith,
        b. 1934, *m.*
2010   *Dobbs,* Michael John Dobbs, *b.* 1948, *m.*
1985   *Donoughue,* Bernard Donoughue, DPHIL,
        b. 1934
2004   *Drayson,* Paul Rudd Drayson, PC, *b.* 1960, *m.*
1994   *Dubs,* Alfred Dubs, *b.* 1932, *m.*
2004   *Dykes,* Hugh John Maxwell Dykes, *b.* 1939, *m.*
1995   *Eames,* Rt. Revd Robert Henry Alexander Eames,
        OM, PHD, *b.* 1937, *m.*
1992   *Eatwell,* John Leonard Eatwell, PHD, *b.* 1945
1983   *Eden of Winton,* John Benedict Eden, PC,
        b. 1925, *m.*
2011   *Edmiston,* Robert Norman Edmiston, *b.* 1946, *m.*
1999   *Elder,* Thomas Murray Elder, *b.* 1950
1992   *Elis-Thomas,* Dafydd Elis Elis-Thomas, PC,
        b. 1946, *m.*
1981   *Elystan-Morgan,* Dafydd Elystan Elystan-Morgan,
        b. 1932, *w.*
2011   *Empey,* Reginald Norman Morgan Empey, OBE,
        b. 1947, *m.*
2000   *Erskine of Alloa Tower,* Earl of Mar and Kellie,
        b. 1949, *m.* (*see* Hereditary Peers)
1997   *Evans of Parkside,* John Evans, *b.* 1930, *m.*
2000   *Evans of Temple Guiting,* Matthew Evans, CBE,
        b. 1941, *m.*
1998   *Evans of Watford,* David Charles Evans, *b.* 1942, *m.*
1983   *Ezra,* Derek Ezra, MBE, *b.* 1919, *m.*
1997   *Falconer of Thoroton,* Charles Leslie Falconer, PC,
        QC, *b.* 1951, *m.*
2014   *Farmer,* Michael Stahel Farmer, *b.* 1944, *m.*
1999   *Faulkner of Worcester,* Richard Oliver Faulkner,
        b. 1946, *m.*
2010   *Faulks,* Edward Peter Lawless Faulks, QC,
        b. 1950, *m.*
2001   *Fearn,* Ronald Cyril Fearn, OBE, *b.* 1931, *m.*
1996   *Feldman,* Basil Feldman, *b.* 1926, *m.*
2010   *Feldman of Elstree,* Andrew Simon Feldman,
        b. 1966, *m.*
1999   *Fellowes,* Robert Fellowes, GCB, GCVO, PC,
        b. 1941, *m.*
2011   *Fellowes of West Stafford,* Julian Alexander Fellowes,
        b. 1949, *m.*
1999   *Filkin,* David Geoffrey Nigel Filkin, CBE, *b.* 1944
2011   *Fink,* Stanley Fink, *b.* 1957, *m.*
2013   *Finkelstein,* Daniel William Finkelstein, OBE,
        b. 1962, *m.*
2011   *Flight,* Howard Emerson Flight, *b.* 1948, *m.*
1999   *Forsyth of Drumlean,* Michael Bruce Forsyth, PC,
        b. 1954, *m.*
2005   *Foster of Bishop Auckland,* Derek Foster, PC,
        b. 1937, *m.*
1999   ¶*Foster of Thames Bank,* Norman Robert Foster, OM,
        b. 1935, *m.*
2005   *Foulkes of Cumnock,* George Foulkes, PC,
        b. 1942, *m.*
2001   *Fowler,* (Peter) Norman Fowler, PC, *b.* 1938, *m.*
2014   *Fox,* Christopher Francis Fox, *b.* 1957, *m.*
2011   *Framlingham,* Michael Nicholson Lord, *b.* 1938, *m.*
1997   *Freeman,* Roger Norman Freeman, PC, *b.* 1942, *m.*
2009   *Freud,* David Anthony Freud, *b.* 1950 *m.*
2010   *Gardiner of Kimble,* John Gardiner, *b.* 1956, *m.*
1997   *Garel-Jones,* (William Armand) Thomas Tristan
        Garel-Jones, PC, *b.* 1941, *m.*

1999   *Gascoyne-Cecil,* The Marquess of Salisbury, KCVO,
        PC, *b.* 1946, *m.* (*see* Hereditary Peers)
1999   *Gavron,* Robert Gavron, CBE, *b.* 1930, *m.*
2010   *German,* Michael James German, OBE, *b.* 1945, *m.*
2004   *Giddens,* Prof. Anthony Giddens, *b.* 1938, *m.*
2011   *Glasman,* Maurice Mark Glasman, *b.* 1961, *m.*
2011   *Glendonbrook,* Michael David Bishop, CBE,
        b. 1942
2014   *Goddard of Stockport,* David Goddard
2011   *Gold,* David Laurence Gold, *b.* 1951, *m.*
1999   *Goldsmith,* Peter Henry Goldsmith, PC, QC,
        b. 1950, *m.*
1997   *Goodhart,* William Howard Goodhart, QC,
        b. 1933, *m.*
2005   *Goodlad,* Alastair Robertson Goodlad, KCMG,
        b. 1943, *m.*
1997   *Gordon of Strathblane,* James Stuart Gordon, CBE,
        b. 1936, *m.*
1999   *Grabiner,* Anthony Stephen Grabiner, QC,
        b. 1945, *m.*
2011   *Grade of Yarmouth,* Michael Ian Grade, CBE,
        b. 1943, *m.*
1983   *Graham of Edmonton,* (Thomas) Edward Graham,
        PC, *b.* 1925, *m.*
2000   *Greaves,* Anthony Robert Greaves, *b.* 1942, *m.*
2010   *Green of Hurstpierpoint,* Stephen Keith Green,
        b. 1948, *m.*
2000   *Grenfell of Kilvey,* Lord Grenfell, *b.* 1935, *m.* (*see*
        Hereditary Peers)
2004   *Griffiths of Burry Port,* Revd Dr Leslie John
        Griffiths, *b.* 1942, *m.*
1991   *Griffiths of Fforestfach,* Brian Griffiths, *b.* 1941, *m.*
2001   *Grocott,* Bruce Joseph Grocott, PC, *b.* 1940, *m.*
2000   *Gueterbock,* Lord Berkeley, OBE, *b.* 1939, *m.* (*see*
        Hereditary Peers)
2000   *Guthrie of Craigiebank,* Charles Ronald Llewelyn
        Guthrie, GCB, LVO, OBE, *b.* 1938, *m.*
1995   *Habgood,* Rt. Revd John Stapylton Habgood, PC,
        PHD, *b.* 1927, *m.*
2010   *Hall of Birkenhead,* Anthony William Hall, CBE,
        b. 1951, *m.*
2007   *Hameed,* Dr Khalid Hameed, *b.* 1941, *m.*
2005   *Hamilton of Epsom,* Archibald Gavin Hamilton, PC,
        b. 1941, *m.*
2001   *Hannay of Chiswick,* David Hugh Alexander
        Hannay, GCMG, CH, *b.* 1935, *m.*
1998   *Hanningfield,* Paul Edward Winston White, *b.* 1940
1997   *Hardie,* Andrew Rutherford Hardie, PC, QC,
        b. 1946, *m.*
2006   *Harries of Pentregarth,* Rt. Revd Richard Douglas
        Harries, *b.* 1936, *m.*
1998   *Harris of Haringey,* (Jonathan) Toby Harris,
        b. 1953, *m.*
1996   *Harris of Peckham,* Philip Charles Harris, *b.* 1942, *m.*
1999   *Harrison,* Lyndon Henry Arthur Harrison,
        b. 1947, *m.*
2004   *Hart of Chilton,* Garry Richard Rushby Hart,
        b. 1940, *m.*
1993   *Haskel,* Simon Haskel, *b.* 1934, *m.*
1998   *Haskins,* Christopher Robin Haskins, *b.* 1937, *m.*
2005   *Hastings of Scarisbrick,* Michael John Hastings,
        CBE, *b.* 1958, *m.*
1997   *Hattersley,* Roy Sidney George Hattersley, PC,
        b. 1932
2013   *Haughey,* William Haughey, OBE, *b.* 1956, *m.*
2004   *Haworth,* Alan Robert Haworth, *b.* 1948, *m.*
2014   *Hay,* William Hay, *b.* 1950, *m.*
1992   *Healey,* Denis Winston Healey, CH, MBE, PC,
        b. 1917, *w.*

2010	*Hennessy of Nympsfield,* Prof. Peter John Hennessy, *b.* 1947, *m.*
2001	*Heseltine,* Michael Ray Dibdin Heseltine, CH, PC, *b.* 1933, *m.*
1997	*Higgins,* Terence Langley Higgins, KBE, PC, *b.* 1928, *m.*
2010	*Hill of Oareford,* Jonathan Hopkin Hill, CBE, PC, *b.* 1960, *m.*
2000	*Hodgson of Astley Abbotts,* Robin Granville Hodgson, CBE, *b.* 1942, *m.*
1991	*Hollick,* Clive Richard Hollick, *b.* 1945, *m.*
2013	*Holmes of Richmond,* Christopher Holmes, MBE, *b.* 1971
1995	*Hope of Craighead,* (James Arthur) David Hope, KT, PC, *b.* 1938, *m.*
2005	*Hope of Thornes,* Rt. Revd David Michael Hope, KCVO, PC, *b.* 1940
2013	*Horam,* John Rhodes Horam, *b.* 1939, *m.*
2010	*Howard of Lympne,* Michael Howard, CH, PC, QC, *b.* 1941, *m.*
2004	*Howard of Rising,* Greville Patrick Charles Howard, *b.* 1941, *m.*
2005	*Howarth of Newport,* Alan Thomas Howarth, CBE, PC, *b.* 1944
1992	*Howe of Aberavon,* (Richard Edward) Geoffrey Howe, CH, PC, QC, *b.* 1926, *m.*
1997	*Howell of Guildford,* David Arthur Russell Howell, PC, *b.* 1936, *m.*
1978	*Howie of Troon,* William Howie, *b.* 1924, *w.*
1997	*Hoyle,* (Eric) Douglas Harvey Hoyle, *b.* 1930, *w.*
1997	*Hughes of Woodside,* Robert Hughes, *b.* 1932, *m.*
2000	*Hunt of Chesterton,* Julian Charles Roland Hunt, CBE, *b.* 1941, *m.*
1997	*Hunt of Kings Heath,* Philip Alexander Hunt, OBE, PC, *b.* 1949, *m.*
1997	*Hunt of Wirral,* David James Fletcher Hunt, MBE, PC, *b.* 1942, *m.*
1997	*Hurd of Westwell,* Douglas Richard Hurd, CH, CBE, PC, *b.* 1930, *w.*
2011	*Hussain,* Qurban Hussain, *b.* 1956, *m.*
1978	*Hutchinson of Lullington,* Jeremy Nicolas Hutchinson, QC, *b.* 1915, *w.*
2010	*Hutton of Furness,* John Matthew Patrick Hutton, PC, *b.* 1955, *m.*
1999	*Imbert,* Peter Michael Imbert, CVO, QPM, *b.* 1933, *m.*
1997	*Inge,* Peter Anthony Inge, KG, GCB, PC, *b.* 1935, *m.*
1987	*Irvine of Lairg,* Alexander Andrew Mackay Irvine, PC, QC, *b.* 1940, *m.*
2006	*James of Blackheath,* David Noel James, CBE, *b.* 1937, *m.*
1997	*Janner of Braunstone,* Greville Ewan Janner, QC, *b.* 1928, *m.*
2007	*Janvrin,* Robin Berry Janvrin, GCB, GCVO, PC, *b.* 1946, *m.*
2006	*Jay of Ewelme,* Michael (Hastings) Jay, GCMG, *b.* 1946, *m.*
1987	*Jenkin of Roding,* (Charles) Patrick (Fleeming) Jenkin, PC, *b.* 1926, *m.*
2000	*Joffe,* Joel Goodman Joffe, CBE, *b.* 1932, *m.*
2001	*Jones,* (Stephen) Barry Jones, *b.* 1937, *m.*
2007	*Jones of Birmingham,* Digby Marritt Jones, *b.* 1955, *m.*
2005,	*Jones of Cheltenham,* Nigel David Jones, *b.* 1948, *m.*
1997	*Jopling,* (Thomas) Michael Jopling, PC, *b.* 1930, *m.*
2000	*Jordan,* William Brian Jordan, CBE, *b.* 1936, *m.*
1991	*Judd,* Frank Ashcroft Judd, *b.* 1935, *m.*
2008	*Judge,* Igor Judge, PC, *b.* 1941, *m.*

2010	*Kakkar,* Prof. Ajay Kumar Kakkar, *b.* 1964
2004	*Kalms,* Harold Stanley Kalms, *b.* 1931, *m.*
2010	*Kennedy of Southwark,* Roy Francis Kennedy, *b.* 1962
2004	*Kerr of Kinlochard,* John (Olav) Kerr, GCMG, *b.* 1942, *m.*
2010	**Kerr of Monteviot,* Marquess of Lothian (Michael Ancram), PC, QC, *b.* 1945, *m.* (*see* Hereditary Peers)
2011	*Kestenbaum,* Jonathan Andrew Kestenbaum, *b.* 1959, *m.*
2001	*Kilclooney,* John David Taylor, PC (NI), *b.* 1937, *m.*
1996	*Kilpatrick of Kincraig,* Robert Kilpatrick, CBE, *b.* 1926, *m.*
2001	*King of Bridgwater,* Thomas Jeremy King, CH, PC, *b.* 1933, *m.*
2013	*King of Lothbury,* Mervyn Allister King, KG, GBE, *b.* 1948
2005	*Kinnock,* Neil Gordon Kinnock, PC, *b.* 1942, *m.*
1999	*Kirkham,* Graham Kirkham, *b.* 1944, *m.*
1975	*Kirkhill,* John Farquharson Smith, *b.* 1930, *m.*
2005	*Kirkwood of Kirkhope,* Archibald Johnstone Kirkwood, *b.* 1946, *m.*
2010	*Knight of Weymouth,* James Philip Knight, PC, *b.* 1965, *m.*
1987	*Knights,* Philip Douglas Knights, CBE, QPM, *b.* 1920, *m.*
2007	*Krebs,* Prof. John (Richard) Krebs, FRS, *b.* 1945, *m.*
2004	¶*Laidlaw,* Irvine Alan Stewart Laidlaw, *b.* 1942, *m.*
1999	*Laird,* John Dunn Laird, *b.* 1944, *m.*
1998	*Laming,* (William) Herbert Laming, PC, CBE, *b.* 1936, *m.*
1998	*Lamont of Lerwick,* Norman Stewart Hughson Lamont, PC, *b.* 1942, *m.*
1997	*Lang of Monkton,* Ian Bruce Lang, PC, *b.* 1940, *m.*
1992	*Lawson of Blaby,* Nigel Lawson, PC, *b.* 1932, *m.*
2000	*Layard,* Peter Richard Grenville Layard, *b.* 1934, *m.*
1999	*Lea of Crondall,* David Edward Lea, OBE, *b.* 1937
2006	*Leach of Fairford,* Charles Guy Rodney Leach, *b.* 1934, *m.*
2006	*Lee of Trafford,* John Robert Louis Lee, *b.* 1942, *m.*
2013	*Leigh of Hurley,* Howard Darryl Leigh, *b.* 1959, *m.*
2004	*Leitch,* Alexander Park Leitch, *b.* 1947, *m.*
2014	‡*Lennie,* Chris Lennie, *b.* 1953, *m.*
1993	*Lester of Herne Hill,* Anthony Paul Lester, QC, *b.* 1936, *m.*
1997	*Levene of Portsoken,* Peter Keith Levene, KBE, *b.* 1941, *m.*
1997	*Levy,* Michael Abraham Levy, *b.* 1944, *m.*
2010	*Lexden,* Alistair Basil Cooke, OBE, *b.* 1945
2010	*Liddle,* Roger John Liddle, *b.* 1947, *m.*
2010	*Lingfield,* Robert George Alexander Balchin, *b.* 1942, *m.*
1999	*Lipsey,* David Lawrence Lipsey, *b.* 1948, *m.*
2013	*Livingston of Parkhead,* Ian Paul Livingston, *b.* 1964, *m.*
1997	*Lloyd-Webber,* Andrew Lloyd Webber, *b.* 1948, *m.*
2011	*Loomba,* Rajinder Paul Loomba, CBE, *b.* 1943, *m.*
2006	*Low of Dalston,* Prof. Colin MacKenzie Low, CBE, *b.* 1942, *m.*
2000	*Luce,* Richard Napier Luce, KG, GCVO, PC, *b.* 1936, *m.*
2000	**Lyttelton of Aldershot,* The Viscount Chandos, *b.* 1953, *m.* (*see* Hereditary Peers)
2010	*McAvoy,* Thomas McLaughlin McAvoy, PC, *b.* 1943, *m.*
1976	*McCluskey,* John Herbert McCluskey, *b.* 1929, *m.*
1989	*McColl of Dulwich,* Ian McColl, CBE, FRCS, FRCSE, *b.* 1933, *m.*

2010   *McConnell of Glenscorrodale,* Dr Jack Wilson
McConnell, PC, *b.* 1960, *m.*
2010   *Macdonald of River Glaven,* Kenneth Donald John
Macdonald, QC, *b.* 1953, *m.*
1998   *Macdonald of Tradeston,* Angus John Macdonald,
CBE, PC, *b.* 1940, *m.*
2010   *McFall of Alcluith,* John Francis McFall, PC,
h 1944 *m*
1991   *Macfarlane of Bearsden,* Norman Somerville
Macfarlane, KT, FRSE, *b.* 1926, *m.*
2001   *MacGregor of Pulham Market,* John Roddick
Russell MacGregor, CBE, PC, *b.* 1937, *m.*
1979   *Mackay of Clashfern,* James Peter Hymers Mackay,
KT, PC, FRSE, *b.* 1927, *m.*
1995   *Mackay of Drumadoon,* Donald Sage Mackay, PC,
b. 1946, *m.*
1998   *MacKenzie of Culkein,* Hector Uisdean MacKenzie,
b. 1940
1999   *Mackenzie of Framwellgate,* Brian Mackenzie, OBE,
b. 1943, *m.*
2004   *McKenzie of Luton,* William David McKenzie,
b. 1946, *m.*
1974   *Mackie of Benshie,* George Yull Mackie, CBE, DSO,
DFC, *b.* 1919, *m.*
1996   *MacLaurin of Knebworth,* Ian Charter MacLaurin,
b. 1937, *m.*
2001   *Maclennan of Rogart,* Robert Adam Ross
Maclennan, PC, *b.* 1936, *m.*
1995   *McNally,* Tom McNally, PC, *b.* 1943, *m.*
2011   *Magan of Castletown,* George Morgan Magan,
b. 1945, *m.*
2001   *Maginnis of Drumglass,* Kenneth Wiggins Maginnis,
b. 1938, *m.*
2007   *Malloch-Brown,* George Mark Malloch Brown,
KCMG, PC, *b.* 1953, *m.*
2008   *Mandelson,* Peter Benjamin Mandelson, PC, *b.* 1953
2011   *Marks of Henley-on-Thames,* Jonathan Clive Marks,
QC, *b.* 1952, *m.*
2006   *Marland,* Jonathan Peter Marland, *b.* 1956, *m.*
1991   *Marlesford,* Mark Shuldham Schreiber, *b.* 1931, *m.*
2009   *Martin of Springburn,* Michael Martin, PC,
b. 1945, *m.*
1987   *Mason of Barnsley,* Roy Mason, PC, *b.* 1924, *m.*
2005   *Mawhinney,* Brian Stanley Mawhinney, PC,
b. 1940, *m.*
2007   *Mawson,* Revd Andrew Mawson, OBE, *b.* 1954, *m.*
2004   *Maxton,* John Alston Maxton, *b.* 1936, *m.*
2001   *May of Oxford,* Robert McCredie May, OM,
b. 1936, *m.*
1997   *Mayhew of Twysden,* Patrick Barnabas Burke
Mayhew, PC, QC, *b.* 1929, *m.*
2013   *Mendelsohn,* Jonathan Neil Mendelsohn,
b. 1966, *m.*
2000   *Mitchell,* Parry Andrew Mitchell, *b.* 1943, *m.*
2000   **Mitford,* Lord Redesdale, *b.* 1967, *m.* (*see*
Hereditary Peers)
2008   *Mogg,* John (Frederick) Mogg, KCMG, *b.* 1943 *m.*
1997   *Molyneaux of Killead,* James Henry Molyneaux,
KBE, PC, *b.* 1920
2010   *Monks,* John Stephen Monks, *b.* 1945, *m.*
2005   *Moonie,* Dr. Lewis George Moonie, *b.* 1947, *m.*
1992   *Moore of Lower Marsh,* John Edward Michael
Moore, PC, *b.* 1937, *w.*
2000   *Morgan,* Kenneth Owen Morgan, *b.* 1934, *m.*
2001   *Morris of Aberavon,* John Morris, KG, PC, QC,
b. 1931, *m.*
2006   *Morris of Handsworth,* William Manuel Morris,
b. 1938, *m.*
2006   *Morrow,* Maurice George Morrow, *b.* 1948, *m.*

2001   *Moser,* Claus Adolf Moser, KCB, CBE, *b.* 1922, *m.*
2008   *Myners,* Paul Myners, CBE, *b.* 1948, *m.*
1997   *Naseby,* Michael Wolfgang Laurence Morris, PC,
b. 1936, *m.*
2013   *Nash,* John Alfred Stoddard Nash, *b.* 1949
1997   *Neill of Bladen,* (Francis) Patrick Neill, QC,
b. 1926, *m.*
1997   *Newby,* Richard Mark Newby, PC, OBE,
b. 1953, *m.*
1994   *Nickson,* David Wigley Nickson, KBE, FRSE,
b. 1929, *m.*
2011   *Noon,* Gulam Kaderbhoy Noon, MBE, *b.* 1936, *m.*
1998   *Norton of Louth,* Philip Norton, *b.* 1951
2000   *Oakeshott of Seagrove Bay,* Matthew Alan
Oakeshott, *b.* 1947, *m.*
2012   *O'Donnell,* Augustine Thomas (Gus) O'Donnell,
GCB, *b.* 1952, *m.*
2005   *O'Neill of Clackmannan,* Martin John O'Neill,
b. 1945, *m.*
2001   *Ouseley,* Herman George Ouseley, *b.* 1945, *m.*
1992   *Owen,* David Anthony Llewellyn Owen, CH, PC,
b. 1938, *m.*
1999   *Oxburgh,* Ernest Ronald Oxburgh, KBE, FRS,
PHD, *b.* 1934, *m.*
2013   *Paddick,* Brian Leonard Paddick, *b.* 1958, *m.*
2011   *Palmer of Childs Hill,* Monroe Edward Palmer,
OBE, *b.* 1938, *m.*
1991   *Palumbo,* Peter Garth Palumbo, *b.* 1935, *m.*
2013   *Palumbo of Southwark,* James Rudolph Palumbo,
b. 1963
2008   *Pannick,* David Philip Pannick, QC, *b.* 1956, *m.*
2000   *Parekh,* Bhikhu Chhotalal Parekh, *b.* 1935, *m.*
1992   *Parkinson,* Cecil Edward Parkinson, PC, *b.* 1931, *m.*
1999   *Patel,* Narendra Babubhai Patel, *b.* 1938
2000   *Patel of Blackburn,* Adam Hafejee Patel, *b.* 1940
2006   *Patel of Bradford,* Prof. Kamlesh Kumar Patel, OBE,
b. 1960 *m.*
1997   *Patten,* John Haggitt Charles Patten, PC,
b. 1945, *m.*
2005   *Patten of Barnes,* Christopher Francis Patten, CH,
PC, *b.* 1944, *m.*
1996   *Paul,* Swraj Paul, PC, *b.* 1931, *m.*
1990   *Pearson of Rannoch,* Malcolm Everard MacLaren
Pearson, *b.* 1942, *m.*
2001   *Pendry,* Thomas Pendry, PC, *b.* 1934, *m.*
1987   *Peston,* Maurice Harry Peston, *b.* 1931, *m.*
1998   *Phillips of Sudbury,* Andrew Wyndham Phillips,
OBE, *b.* 1939, *m.*
1992   *Plant of Highfield,* Prof. Raymond Plant, PHD,
b. 1945, *m.*
1987   *Plumb,* (Charles) Henry Plumb, *b.* 1925, *m.*
2000   **Ponsonby of Roehampton,* Lord Ponsonby of
Shulbrede, *b.* 1958 (*see* Hereditary Peers)
2010   *Popat,* Dolar Amarshi Popat, *b.* 1953, *m.*
2000   *Powell of Bayswater,* Charles David Powell, KCMG,
b. 1941
2010   *Prescott,* John Leslie Prescott, *b.* 1938, *m.*
1987   *Prior,* James Michael Leathes Prior, PC, *b.* 1927, *m.*
1982   *Prys-Davies,* Gwilym Prys Prys-Davies, *b.* 1923, *m.*
2013   *Purvis of Tweed,* Jeremy Purvis, *b.* 1974
1997   *Puttnam,* David Terence Puttnam, CBE, *b.* 1941, *m.*
1994   *Quirk,* Prof. (Charles) Randolph Quirk, CBE, FBA,
b. 1920, *m.*
2001   *Radice,* Giles Heneage Radice, PC, *b.* 1936
2005   *Ramsbotham,* David John Ramsbotham, GCB, CBE,
b. 1934, *m.*
2004   *Rana,* Dr Diljit Singh Rana, MBE, *b.* 1938, *m.*
1997   *Razzall,* (Edward) Timothy Razzall, CBE,
b. 1943, *m.*

2005	*Rees of Ludlow,* Prof. Martin John Rees, OM, *b.* 1942, *m.*
2010	*Reid of Cardowan,* Dr John Reid, PC, *b.* 1947, *m.*
1991	*Renfrew of Kaimsthorn,* (Andrew) Colin Renfrew, FBA, *b.* 1937, *m.*
1999	*Rennard,* Christopher John Rennard, MBE, *b.* 1960
1997	*Renton of Mount Harry,* (Ronald) Timothy Renton, PC, *b.* 1932, *m.*
1997	*Renwick of Clifton,* Robin William Renwick, KCMG, *b.* 1937, *m.*
2010	*Ribeiro,* Bernard Francisco Ribeiro, CBE, *b.* 1944, *m.*
1990	*Richard,* Ivor Seward Richard, PC, QC, *b.* 1932, *m.*
2014	*Richards of Herstmonceux,* David Julian Richards, GCB, CBE, DSO, *b.* 1952, *m.*
2010	*Risby,* Richard John Grenville Spring, *b.* 1946, *m.*
1992	*Rix,* Brian Norman Roger Rix, CBE, *b.* 1924, *w.*
2004	*Roberts of Llandudno,* Revd John Roger Roberts, *b.* 1935, *m.*
1999	*Robertson of Port Ellen,* George Islay MacNeill Robertson, KT, GCMG, PC, *b.* 1946, *m.*
1992	*Rodgers of Quarry Bank,* William Thomas Rodgers, PC, *b.* 1928, *w.*
1999	*Rogan,* Dennis Robert David Rogan, *b.* 1942, *m.*
1996	*Rogers of Riverside,* Richard George Rogers, CH, RA, RIBA, *b.* 1933, *m.*
2001	*Rooker,* Jeffrey William Rooker, PC, *b.* 1941, *m.*
2000	*Roper,* John Francis Hodgess Roper, PC, *b.* 1935, *m.*
2014	*Rose of Monewden,* Stuart Alan Ransom Rose, *b.* 1949
2004	*Rosser,* Richard Andrew Rosser, *b.* 1944, *m.*
2006	*Rowe-Beddoe,* David (Sydney) Rowe-Beddoe, *b.* 1937, *m.*
2004	*Rowlands,* Edward Rowlands, CBE, *b.* 1940, *m.*
1997	*Ryder of Wensum,* Richard Andrew Ryder, OBE, PC, *b.* 1949, *m.*
1996	*Saatchi,* Maurice Saatchi, *b.* 1946, *w.*
2009	*Sacks,* Chief Rabbi Dr Jonathan Henry Sacks, *b.* 1948, *m.*
1989	*Sainsbury of Preston Candover,* John Davan Sainsbury, KG, *b.* 1927, *m.*
1997	*Sainsbury of Turville,* David John Sainsbury, *b.* 1940, *m.*
1997	*Sandberg,* Michael Graham Ruddock Sandberg, CBE, *b.* 1927, *m.*
1985	*Sanderson of Bowden,* Charles Russell Sanderson, *b.* 1933, *m.*
2010	*Sassoon,* James Meyer Sassoon, *b.* 1955, *m.*
1998	*Sawyer,* Lawrence (Tom) Sawyer, *b.* 1943
2014	‡*Scriven,* Paul James Scriven, *b.* 1966
1997	*Selkirk of Douglas,* James Alexander Douglas-Hamilton, PC, QC, *b.* 1942, *m.*
1996	*Sewel,* John Buttifant Sewel, CBE, *b.* 1946
2010	*Sharkey,* John Kevin Sharkey, *b.* 1947, *m.*
1999	*Sharman,* Colin Morven Sharman, OBE, *b.* 1943, *m.*
1994	*Shaw of Northstead,* Michael Norman Shaw, *b.* 1920, *m.*
2006	*Sheikh,* Mohamed Iltaf Sheikh, *b.* 1941, *m.*
2001	*Sheldon,* Robert Edward Sheldon, PC, *b.* 1923, *m.*
1994	*Sheppard of Didgemere,* Allan John George Sheppard, KCVO, *b.* 1932, *m.*
2013	*Sherbourne of Didsbury,* Stephen Ashley Sherbourne, CBE, *b.* 1945
2010	*Shipley,* John Warren Shipley, OBE, *b.* 1946
2000	*Shutt of Greetland,* David Trevor Shutt, OBE, PC, *b.* 1942
1997	*Simon of Highbury,* David Alec Gwyn Simon, CBE, *b.* 1939, *m.*
1997	*Simpson of Dunkeld,* George Simpson, *b.* 1942, *m.*

2011	*Singh of Wimbledon,* Indarjit Singh, CBE, *b.* 1932, *m.*
1991	*Skidelsky,* Robert Jacob Alexander Skidelsky, DPHIL, *b.* 1939, *m.*
1997	*Smith of Clifton,* Trevor Arthur Smith, *b.* 1937, *m.*
2005	*Smith of Finsbury,* Christopher Robert Smith, PC, *b.* 1951
2008	*Smith of Kelvin,* Robert (Haldane) Smith, KT, *b.* 1944, *m.*
1999	*Smith of Leigh,* Peter Richard Charles Smith, *b.* 1945, *m.*
2004	*Snape,* Peter Charles Snape, *b.* 1942
2005	*Soley,* Clive Stafford Soley, *b.* 1939
1990	*Soulsby of Swaffham Prior,* Ernest Jackson Lawson Soulsby, PHD, *b.* 1926, *m.*
2010	*Spicer,* (William) Michael Hardy Spicer, PC, *b.* 1943, *m.*
1997	*Steel of Aikwood,* David Martin Scott Steel, KT, KBE, PC, *b.* 1938, *m.*
2011	*Stephen,* Nicol Ross Stephen, *b.* 1960, *m.*
1991	*Sterling of Plaistow,* Jeffrey Maurice Sterling, GCVO, CBE, *b.* 1934, *m.*
2007	*Stern of Brentford,* Nicholas Herbert Stern, *b.* 1946, *m.*
2005	*Stevens of Kirkwhelpington,* John Arthur Stevens, QPM, *b.* 1942, *m.*
1987	*Stevens of Ludgate,* David Robert Stevens, *b.* 1936, *m.*
2010	*Stevenson of Balmacara,* Robert Wilfrid Stevenson, *b.* 1947, *m.*
1999	*Stevenson of Coddenham,* Henry Dennistoun Stevenson, CBE, *b.* 1945, *m.*
1992	*Stewartby,* (Bernard Harold) Ian (Halley) Stewart, RD, PC, FBA, FRSE, *b.* 1935, *m.*
2011	*Stirrup,* Graham Eric Stirrup, KG, GCB, AFC, *b.* 1949, *m.*
1983	*Stoddart of Swindon,* David Leonard Stoddart, *b.* 1926, *m.*
1997	*Stone of Blackheath,* Andrew Zelig Stone, *b.* 1942, *m.*
2011	*Stoneham of Droxford,* Benjamin Russell Mackintosh Stoneham 1940, *m.*
2011	*Storey,* Michael John Storey, CBE, *b.* 1949
2011	*Strasburger,* Paul Cline Strasburger, *b.* 1946
2009	*Sugar,* Alan Michael Sugar, *b.* 1947, *m.*
2014	*Suri,* Ranbir Singh Suri, *b.* 1935
2001	*Sutherland of Houndwood,* Stewart Ross Sutherland, KT, *b.* 1941, *m.*
1971	*Tanlaw,* Simon Brooke Mackay, *b.* 1934, *m.*
1996	*Taverne,* Dick Taverne, QC, *b.* 1928, *m.*
1978	*Taylor of Blackburn,* Thomas Taylor, CBE, *b.* 1929, *m.*
2010	*Taylor of Goss Moor,* Matthew Owen John Taylor, *b.* 1963, *m.*
2006	*Taylor of Holbeach,* John Derek Taylor, CBE, *b.* 1943, *m.*
1996	*Taylor of Warwick,* John David Beckett Taylor, *b.* 1952, *m.*
1992	*Tebbit,* Norman Beresford Tebbit, CH, PC, *b.* 1931, *m.*
2001	*Temple-Morris,* Peter Temple-Morris, *b.* 1938, *m.*
2006	*Teverson,* Robin Teverson, *b.* 1952, *m.*
2013	§*Thomas of Cwmgiedd,* Roger John Laugharne Thomas, PC, *b.* 1947, *m., Lord Chief Justice of England and Wales*
1996	*Thomas of Gresford,* Donald Martin Thomas, OBE, QC, *b.* 1937, *m.*
1997	*Thomas of Macclesfield,* Terence James Thomas, CBE, *b.* 1937, *m.*

1981	*Thomas of Swynnerton,* Hugh Swynnerton Thomas, *b.* 1931, *m.*
1990	*Tombs,* Francis Leonard Tombs, FENG, *b.* 1924, *w.*
1998	*Tomlinson,* John Edward Tomlinson, *b.* 1939
1994	*Tope,* Graham Norman Tope, CBE, *b.* 1943, *m.*
1981	*Tordoff,* Geoffrey Johnson Tordoff, *b.* 1928, *m.*
2010	*Touhig,* James Donnelly Touhig, PC, *b.* 1947, *m.*
2012	*Trees,* Alexander John Trees, PHD, *b.* 1946, *m.*
2004	*Triesman,* David Maxim Triesman, *b.* 1943
2006	*Trimble,* William David Trimble, PC, *b.* 1944, *m.*
2010	*True,* Nicholas Edward True, CBE, *b.* 1951, *m.*
2004	*Truscott,* Dr Peter Derek Truscott, *b.* 1959, *m.*
1993	*Tugendhat,* Christopher Samuel Tugendhat, *b.* 1937, *m.*
2004	*Tunnicliffe,* Denis Tunnicliffe, CBE, *b.* 1943, *m.*
2000	*Turnberg,* Leslie Arnold Turnberg, MD, *b.* 1934, *m.*
2005	*Turnbull,* Andrew Turnbull, KCB, CVO, *b.* 1945, *m.*
2005	*Turner of Ecchinswell,* (Jonathan) Adair Turner, *b.* 1955, *m.*
2005	*Tyler,* Paul Archer Tyler, PC, CBE, *b.* 1941, *m.*
2013	*Verjee,* Rumi Verjee, CBE, *b.* 1957
2004	*Vallance of Tummel,* Iain (David Thomas) Vallance, *b.* 1943, *m.*
1996	*Vincent of Coleshill,* Richard Frederick Vincent, GBE, KCB, DSO, *b.* 1931, *m.*
1985	*Vinson,* Nigel Vinson, LVO, *b.* 1931, *m.*
1990	*Waddington,* David Charles Waddington, GCVO, PC, QC, *b.* 1929, *m.*
1990	*Wade of Chorlton,* (William) Oulton Wade, *b.* 1932, *m.*
1992	*Wakeham,* John Wakeham, PC, *b.* 1932, *m.*
1999	*Waldegrave of North Hill,* William Arthur Waldegrave, PC, *b.* 1946, *m.*
2007	*Walker of Aldringham,* Michael John Dawson Walker, GCB, CMG, CBE, *b.* 1944, *m.*
1995	*Wallace of Saltaire,* William John Lawrence Wallace, PC, PHD, *b.* 1941, *m.*
2007	*Wallace of Tankerness,* James Robert Wallace, PC, QC, *b.* 1954, *m.*
1989	*Walton of Detchant,* John Nicholas Walton, TD, FRCP, *b.* 1922, *w.*
1998	*Warner,* Norman Reginald Warner, PC, *b.* 1940, *m.*
2011	*Wasserman,* Gordon Joshua Wasserman, *b.* 1938
1997	*Watson of Invergowrie,* Michael Goodall Watson, *b.* 1949, *m.*
1999	*Watson of Richmond,* Alan John Watson, CBE, *b.* 1941, *m.*
2010	*Wei,* Nathanael Ming-Yan Wei, *b.* 1977, *m.*
1976	*Weidenfeld,* (Arthur) George Weidenfeld, GBE, *b.* 1919, *m.*
2007	*West of Spithead,* Alan William John West, GCB, DSC, PC, *b.* 1948, *m.*
2013	*Whitby,* Michael John Whitby, *b.* 1948
1996	*Whitty,* John Lawrence (Larry) Whitty, PC, *b.* 1943, *m.*
2011	*Wigley,* Dafydd Wynne Wigley, PC, *b.* 1943, *m.*
2010	*Williams of Baglan,* Michael Charles Williams, *b.* 1949
1985	*Williams of Elvel,* Charles Cuthbert Powell Williams, CBE, PC, *b.* 1933, *m.*
2013	*Williams of Oystermouth,* Rt. Revd Rowan Douglas Williams, Royal Victorian Chain, PC, DPHIL, *b.* 1950, *m.*
1999	*Williamson of Horton,* David (Francis) Williamson, GCMG, CB, PC, *b.* 1934, *m.*
2010	*Willis of Knaresborough,* George Philip Willis, *b.* 1941, *m.*
2010	*Wills,* Michael David Wills, PC, *b.* 1952, *m.*
2002	*Wilson of Dinton,* Richard Thomas James Wilson, GCB, *b.* 1942, *m.*
1992	*Wilson of Tillyorn,* David Clive Wilson, KT, GCMG, PHD, *b.* 1935, *m.*
1995	*Winston,* Robert Maurice Lipson Winston, FRCOG, *b.* 1940, *m.*
2010	*Wolfson of Aspley Guise,* Simon Adam Wolfson, *b.* 1967
1991	*Wolfson of Sunningdale,* David Wolfson, *b.* 1935, *m.*
2011	*Wood of Anfield,* Stewart Martin Wood, *b.* 1968, *m.*
1999	*Woolmer of Leeds,* Kenneth John Woolmer, *b.* 1940, *m.*
2013	*Wrigglesworth,* Ian William Wrigglesworth, *b.* 1939, *m.*
1994	*Wright of Richmond,* Patrick Richard Henry Wright, GCMG, *b.* 1931, *m.*
1984	*Young of Graffham,* David Ivor Young, PC, *b.* 1932, *m.*
2004	*Young of Norwood Green,* Anthony (Ian) Young, *b.* 1942, *m.*

BARONESSES

Created

2005	*Adams of Craigielea,* Katherine Patricia Irene Adams, *b.* 1947, *w.*
2007	*Afshar,* Prof. Haleh Afshar, OBE, *b.* 1944, *m.*
1997	*Amos,* Valerie Ann Amos, PC, *b.* 1954
2000	*Andrews,* Elizabeth Kay Andrews, OBE, *b.* 1943, *m.*
1996	*Anelay of St Johns,* Joyce Anne Anelay, DBE, PC, *b.* 1947, *m.*
2010	*Armstrong of Hill Top,* Hilary Jane Armstrong, PC, *b.* 1945, *m.*
1999	*Ashton of Upholland,* Catherine Margaret Ashton, PC, *b.* 1956, *m.*
2011	*Bakewell,* Joan Dawson Bakewell, DBE, *b.* 1933
2013	*Bakewell of Hardington Mandeville,* Catherine Mary Bakewell, MBE, *b.* 1949
1999	*Barker,* Elizabeth Jean Barker, *b.* 1961
2010	*Benjamin,* Floella Karen Yunies Benjamin, OBE, *b.* 1949, *m.*
2011	*Berridge,* Elizabeth Rose Berridge, *b.* 1972
2000	*Billingham,* Angela Theodora Billingham, DPHIL, *b.* 1939, *w.*
1987	*Blackstone,* Tessa Ann Vosper Blackstone, PC, PHD, *b.* 1942
1999	*Blood,* May Blood, MBE, *b.* 1938
2004	*Bonham-Carter of Yarnbury,* Jane Bonham Carter, *b.* 1957, *w.*
2000	*Boothroyd,* Betty Boothroyd, OM, PC, *b.* 1929
2005	*Bottomley of Nettlestone,* Virginia Hilda Brunette Maxwell Bottomley, PC, *b.* 1948, *m.*
2014	‡*Brady,* Karren Brady, CBE, *b.* 1969, *m.*
2011	*Brinton,* Sarah Virginia Brinton, *b.* 1955, *m.*
2010	*Browning,* Angela Frances Browning, *b.* 1946, *m.*
1998	*Buscombe,* Peta Jane Buscombe, *b.* 1954, *m.*
2006	*Butler-Sloss,* (Ann) Elizabeth (Oldfield) Butler-Sloss, GBE, PC *b.* 1933, *m.*
1996	*Byford,* Hazel Byford, DBE, *b.* 1941, *w.*
2008	*Campbell of Loughborough,* Susan Catherine Campbell, CBE, *b.* 1948
2007	*Campbell of Surbiton,* Jane Susan Campbell, DBE, *b.* 1959, *m.*
1992	*Chalker of Wallasey,* Lynda Chalker, PC, *b.* 1942
2014	*Chisholm of Owlpen,* Carlyn Elizabeth Chisholm, *b.* 1951, *m.*
2005	§*Clark of Calton,* Dr Lynda Margaret Clark, PC, *b.* 1949
2000	*Cohen of Pimlico,* Janet Cohen, *b.* 1940, *m.*
2005	*Corston,* Jean Ann Corston, PC, *b.* 1942, *w.*

2007	*Coussins,* Jean Coussins, *b.* 1950
1982	*Cox,* Caroline Anne Cox, *b.* 1937, *m.*
1998	*Crawley,* Christine Mary Crawley, *b.* 1950, *m.*
1990	*Cumberlege,* Julia Frances Cumberlege, CBE, *b.* 1943, *m.*
1993	*Dean of Thornton-le-Fylde,* Brenda Dean, PC, *b.* 1943, *m.*
2005	*Deech,* Ruth Lynn Deech, DBE, *b.* 1943, *m.*
2010	*Donaghy,* Rita Margaret Donaghy, CBE, *b.* 1944, *m.*
2010	*Doocey,* Elizabeth Deirdre Doocey, OBE, *b.* 1948, *m. Lord Speaker*
2010	*Drake,* Jean Lesley Patricia Drake, CBE, *b.* 1948
2004	*D'Souza,* Dr Frances Gertrude Claire D'Souza, CMG, PC, *b.* 1944, *m.*
1990	¶*Dunn,* Lydia Selina Dunn, DBE, *b.* 1940, *m.*
2010	*Eaton,* Ellen Margaret Eaton, DBE, *b.* 1942, *m.*
1990	*Eccles of Moulton,* Diana Catherine Eccles, *b.* 1933, *m.*
1997	*Emerton,* Audrey Caroline Emerton, DBE, *b.* 1935
2014	*Evans of Bowes Park,* Natalie Jessica Evans, *b.* 1975, *m.*
1974	*Falkender,* Marcia Matilda Falkender, CBE, *b.* 1932
2004	*Falkner of Margravine,* Kishwer Falkner, *b.* 1955, *m.*
1994	*Farrington of Ribbleton,* Josephine Farrington, *b.* 1940, *m.*
2001	*Finlay of Llandaff,* Ilora Gillian Finlay, *b.* 1949, *m.*
1990	*Flather,* Shreela Flather, *b.* 1934, *m.*
1997	*Fookes,* Janet Evelyn Fookes, DBE, *b.* 1936
2006	*Ford,* Margaret Anne Ford, *b.* 1957, *m.*
2005	*Fritchie,* Irene Tordoff Fritchie, DBE, *b.* 1942, *m.*
1999	*Gale,* Anita Gale, *b.* 1940
2007	*Garden of Frognal,* Susan Elizabeth Garden, *b.* 1944, *w.*
1981	*Gardner of Parkes,* (Rachel) Trixie (Anne) Gardner, *b.* 1927, *w.*
2000	*Gibson of Market Rasen,* Anne Gibson, OBE, *b.* 1940, *m.*
2013	*Goldie,* Annabel MacNicholl Goldie, *b.* 1950
2001	*Golding,* Llinos Golding, *b.* 1933, *m.*
1998	*Goudie,* Mary Teresa Goudie, *b.* 1946, *m.*
1993	*Gould of Potternewton,* Joyce Brenda Gould, *b.* 1932, *m.*
2001	*Greenfield,* Susan Adele Greenfield, CBE, *b.* 1950, *m.*
2000	*Greengross,* Sally Ralea Greengross, OBE, *b.* 1935, *m.*
2013	*Grender,* Rosalind Mary Grender, MBE, *b.* 1962
2010	*Grey-Thompson,* Tanni Carys Davina Grey-Thompson, DBE, *b.* 1969, *m.*
1991	*Hamwee,* Sally Rachel Hamwee, *b.* 1947
1999	*Hanham,* Joan Brownlow Hanham, CBE, *b.* 1939, *m.*
2014	*Harding of Winscombe,* Diana Mary (Dido) Harding, *b.* 1967, *m.*
1999	*Harris of Richmond,* Angela Felicity Harris, *b.* 1944
1996	*Hayman,* Helene Valerie Hayman, GBE, PC, *b.* 1949, *m.*
2010	*Hayter of Kentish Town,* Dr Dianne Hayter, *b.* 1949, *m.*
2014	‡*Helic,* Arminka Helic
2010	*Healy of Primrose Hill,* Anna Healy, *b.* 1955, *m.*
2004	*Henig,* Ruth Beatrice Henig, CBE, *b.* 1943, *m.*
2011	*Heyhoe-Flint,* Rachel Heyhoe Flint, OBE, *b.* 1939, *m.*
1991	*Hilton of Eggardon,* Jennifer Hilton, QPM, *b.* 1936
2013	*Hodgson of Abinger,* Fiona Ferelith Hodgson, CBE, *b.* 1954, *m.*
1995	*Hogg,* Sarah Elizabeth Mary Hogg, *b.* 1946, *m.*
2010	*Hollins,* Prof. Sheila Clare Hollins, *b.* 1946, *m.*
1990	*Hollis of Heigham,* Patricia Lesley Hollis, PC, DPHIL, *b.* 1941, *m.*
1985	*Hooper,* Gloria Dorothy Hooper, CMG, *b.* 1939
2001	*Howarth of Breckland,* Valerie Georgina Howarth, OBE, *b.* 1940
2001	*Howe of Idlicote,* Elspeth Rosamond Morton Howe, CBE, *b.* 1932, *m.*
1999	*Howells of St Davids,* Rosalind Patricia-Anne Howells, *b.* 1931, *m.*
2010	*Hughes of Stretford,* Beverley Hughes, PC, *b.* 1950, *m.*
2013	*Humphreys,* Christine Mary Humphreys
2010	*Hussein-Ece,* Meral Hussein Ece, OBE, *b.* 1953
1991	*James of Holland Park,* Phyllis Dorothy White (P. D. James), OBE, *b.* 1920, *w.*
2014	‡*Janke,* Barbara Janke, *b.* 1947, *m.*
1992	*Jay of Paddington,* Margaret Ann Jay, PC, *b.* 1939, *m.*
2011	*Jenkin of Kennington,* Anne Caroline Jenkin, *b.* 1955, *m.*
2010	*Jolly,* Judith Anne Jolly, *b.* 1951, *m.*
2013	*Jones of Moulsecoomb,* Jennifer Helen Jones, *b.* 1949
2006	*Jones of Whitchurch,* Margaret Beryl Jones, *b.* 1955
2013	*Kennedy of Cradley,* Alicia Pamela Kennedy, *b.* 1969, *m.*
1997	*Kennedy of the Shaws,* Helena Ann Kennedy, QC, *b.* 1950, *m.*
2012	*Kidron,* Beeban Tania Kidron, OBE, *b.* 1961 *m.*
2011	*King of Bow,* Oona Tamsyn King, *b.* 1967, *m.*
2006	*Kingsmill,* Denise Patricia Byrne Kingsmill, CBE, *b.* 1947, *m.*
2009	*Kinnock of Holyhead,* Glenys Elizabeth Kinnock, *b.* 1944, *m.*
1997	*Knight of Collingtree,* (Joan Christabel) Jill Knight, DBE, *b.* 1927, *w.*
2010	*Kramer,* Susan Veronica Kramer, *b.* 1950, *w.*
2013	*Lane-Fox of Soho,* Martha Lane Fox, CBE, *b.* 1973
2013	*Lawrence of Clarendon,* Doreen Delceita Lawrence, OBE, *b.* 1952
2010	*Liddell of Coatdyke,* Helen Lawrie Liddell, PC, *b.* 1950, *m.*
1997	*Linklater of Butterstone,* Veronica Linklater, *b.* 1943, *m.*
2011	*Lister of Burtersett,* Margot Ruth Aline Lister, CBE, *b.* 1949, *m.*
1978	*Lockwood,* Betty Lockwood, *b.* 1924, *w.*
1997	*Ludford,* Sarah Ann Ludford, *b.*1951 disqualified as MEP
2004	*McDonagh,* Margaret Josephine McDonagh, *b.* 1961
1999	*McIntosh of Hudnall,* Genista Mary McIntosh, *b.* 1946
1997	*Maddock,* Diana Margaret Maddock, *b.* 1945, *m.*
1991	*Mallalieu,* Ann Mallalieu, QC, *b.* 1945
2008	*Manningham-Buller,* Elizabeth (Lydia) Manningham-Buller, KG, DCB, *b.* 1948, *m.*
2013	*Manzoor,* Zahida Parveen Manzoor, CBE, *b.* 1958, *m.*
1970	*Masham of Ilton,* Susan Lilian Primrose Cunliffe-Lister, *b.* 1935, *w.*
1999	*Massey of Darwen,* Doreen Elizabeth Massey, *b.* 1938, *m.*
2006	*Meacher,* Molly Christine Meacher, *b.* 1940, *m.*
1998	*Miller of Chilthorne Domer,* Susan Elizabeth Miller, *b.* 1954
2014	‡*Mobarik,* Nosheena Mobarik, CBE, *b.* 1957, *m.*
2004	*Morgan of Drefelin,* Delyth Jane Morgan, *b.* 1961, *m.*
2011	*Morgan of Ely,* Mair Eluned Morgan, *b.* 1967, *m.*
2001	*Morgan of Huyton,* Sally Morgan, *b.* 1959, *m.*

2004   *Morris of Bolton,* Patricia Morris, OBE, *b.* 1953
2005   *Morris of Yardley,* Estelle Morris, PC, *b.* 1952
2004   *Murphy,* Elaine Murphy, *b.* 1947, *m.*
2004   *Neuberger,* Rabbi Julia (Babette Sarah) Neuberger, DBE, *b.* 1950, *m.*
2007   *Neville-Jones,* (Lilian) Pauline Neville-Jones, DCMG, PC, *b.* 1939
2013   *Neville-Rolfe,* Lucy Jeanne Neville-Rolfe, DBE, CMG, *b.* 1953, *m.*
2010   *Newlove,* Helen Margaret Newlove, *b.* 1961, *w.*
1997   *Nicholson of Winterbourne,* Emma Harriet Nicholson, *b.* 1941, *m.*
1982   *Nicol,* Olive Mary Wendy Nicol, *b.* 1923, *m.*
2000   *Noakes,* Sheila Valerie Masters, DBE, *b.* 1949, *m.*
2000   *Northover,* Lindsay Patricia Granshaw, *b.* 1954
2010   *Nye,* Susan Nye, *b.* 1955, *m.*
1991   *O'Cathain,* Detta O'Cathain, OBE, *b.* 1938, *w.*
2009   *O'Loan,* Nuala Patricia O'Loan, DBE, *b.* 1951, *m.*
1999   *O'Neill of Bengarve,* Onora Sylvia O'Neill, CH, CBE, DRS, FBA, *b.* 1941
1989   *Oppenheim-Barnes,* Sally Oppenheim-Barnes, PC, *b.* 1930, *m.*
2006   *Paisley of St George's,* Eileen Emily Paisley, *b.* 1931, *m.*
2010   *Parminter,* Kathryn Jane Parminter, *b.* 1964, *m.*
1991   *Perry of Southwark,* Pauline Perry, *b.* 1931, *m.*
2014   ‡*Pinnock,* Kath Pinnock, *m.*
1997   *Pitkeathley,* Jill Elizabeth Pitkeathley, OBE, *b.* 1940
1981   *Platt of Writtle,* Beryl Catherine Platt, CBE, FENG, *b.* 1923, *m.*
1999   *Prashar,* Usha Kumari Prashar, CBE, PC, *b.* 1948, *m.*
2004   *Prosser,* Margaret Theresa Prosser, OBE, *b.* 1937
2006   *Quin,* Joyce Gwendoline Quin, PC *b.* 1944
1996   *Ramsay of Cartvale,* Margaret Mildred (Meta) Ramsay, *b.* 1936
2011   *Randerson,* Jennifer Elizabeth Randerson, *b.* 1948, *m.*
1994   *Rawlings,* Patricia Elizabeth Rawlings, *b.* 1939
2014   ‡*Rebuck,* Gail Ruth Rebuck, DBE, *b.* 1952, *w.*
1997   *Rendell of Babergh,* Ruth Barbara Rendell, CBE, *b.* 1930, *m.*
1998   *Richardson of Calow,* Kathleen Margaret Richardson, OBE, *b.* 1938, *m.*
2004   *Royall of Blaisdon,* Janet Anne Royall, PC, *b.* 1955, *m.*
1997   *Scotland of Asthal,* Patricia Janet Scotland, PC, QC, *b.* 1955, *m.*
2000   *Scott of Needham Market,* Rosalind Carol Scott, *b.* 1957
1991   *Seccombe,* Joan Anna Dalziel Seccombe, DBE, *b.* 1930, *m.*
2010   *Shackleton of Belgravia,* Fiona Sara Shackleton, LVO, *b.* 1956, *m.*
1998   *Sharp of Guildford,* Margaret Lucy Sharp, *b.* 1938, *m.*
1973   *Sharples,* Pamela Sharples, *b.* 1923, *w.*
2005   *Shephard of Northwold,* Gillian Patricia Shephard, PC, *b.* 1940, *m.*

2010   *Sherlock,* Maeve Christina Mary Sherlock, OBE, *b.* 1960
2014   *Shields,* Joanna Shields, OBE, *b.* 1962, *m.*
2010   *Smith of Basildon,* Angela Evans Smith, PC, *b.* 1959, *m.*
1995   *Smith of Gilmorehill,* Elizabeth Margaret Smith, *b.* 1940, *w.*
2014   *Smith of Newnham,* Dr Julie Elizabeth Smith, *b.* 1969
2010   *Stedman-Scott,* Deborah Stedman-Scott, OBE, *b.* 1955
1999   *Stern,* Vivien Helen Stern, CBE, *b.* 1941
2011   *Stowell of Beeston,* Tina Wendy Stowell, PC, MBE, *b.* 1967
2013   *Suttie,* Alison Mary Suttie
1996   *Symons of Vernham Dean,* Elizabeth Conway Symons, PC, *b.* 1951, *m.*
2005   *Taylor of Bolton,* Winifred Ann Taylor, PC, *b.* 1947, *m.*
1994   *Thomas of Walliswood,* Susan Petronella Thomas, OBE, *b.* 1935, *m.*
2006   *Thomas of Winchester,* Celia Marjorie Thomas, MBE, *b.* 1945
1998   *Thornton,* (Dorothea) Glenys Thornton, *b.* 1952, *m.*
2005   *Tonge,* Dr. Jennifer Louise Tonge, *b.* 1941, *m.*
1980   *Trumpington,* Jean Alys Barker, DCVO, PC, *b.* 1922, *w.*
1985   *Turner of Camden,* Muriel Winifred Turner, *b.* 1927, *m.*
2011   *Tyler of Enfield,* Claire Tyler, *b.* 1957
1998   *Uddin,* Manzila Pola Uddin, *b.* 1959, *m.*
2007   *Vadera,* Shriti Vadera, PC, *b.* 1962
2005   *Valentine,* Josephine Clare Valentine, *b.* 1958, *m.*
2006   *Verma,* Sandip Verma, *b.* 1959, *m.*
2004   *Wall of New Barnet,* Margaret Mary Wall, *b.* 1941, *m.*
2000   *Walmsley,* Joan Margaret Walmsley, *b.* 1943
1985   *Warnock,* Helen Mary Warnock, DBE, *b.* 1924, *w.*
2007   *Warsi,* Sayeeda Hussain Warsi, PC, *b.* 1971
1999   *Warwick of Undercliffe,* Diana Mary Warwick, *b.* 1945, *m.*
2010   *Wheatcroft,* Patience Jane Wheatcroft, *b.* 1951, *m.*
2010   *Wheeler,* Margaret Eileen Joyce Wheeler, MBE, *b.* 1949
1999   *Whitaker,* Janet Alison Whitaker, *b.* 1936
1996   *Wilcox,* Judith Ann Wilcox, *b.* 1940, *w.*
1999   *Wilkins,* Rosalie Catherine Wilkins, *b.* 1946
1993   *Williams of Crosby,* Shirley Vivien Teresa Brittain Williams, PC, *b.* 1930, *w.*
2013   *Williams of Trafford,* Susan Frances Maria Williams, *b.* 1967, *m.*
2011   *Worthington,* Bryony Katherine Worthington, *b.* 1971, *m.*
2004   *Young of Hornsey,* Prof. Margaret Omolola Young, OBE, *b.* 1951, *m.*
1997   *Young of Old Scone,* Barbara Scott Young, *b.* 1948

LORDS SPIRITUAL

The Lords Spiritual are the Archbishops of Canterbury and York and 24 diocesan bishops of the Church of England. The Bishops of London, Durham and Winchester always have seats in the House of Lords; the other 21 seats are filled by the remaining diocesan bishops in order of seniority. The Bishop of Sodor and Man and the Bishop of Gibraltar are not eligible to sit in the House of Lords.

ARCHBISHOPS

Style, The Most Revd and Rt. Hon. the Lord Archbishop of_
Addressed as Archbishop *or* Your Grace

INTRODUCED TO HOUSE OF LORDS
2012   *Canterbury* (105th), Justin Portal Welby, *b.* 1956, *m., cons.* 2011, *elected* 2012, *trans.* 2013
2005   *York* (97th), John Mugabi Tucker Sentamu, PC, PHD, *b.* 1949, *m., cons.* 1996, *elected* 2005, *trans.* 2005

BISHOPS

Style, The Rt. Revd the Lord Bishop of _
Addressed as My Lord
elected date of confirmation as diocesan bishop

INTRODUCED TO HOUSE OF LORDS
as at November 2014

1996   *London* (132nd), Richard John Carew Chartres, KCVO, PC, *b.* 1947, *m., cons.* 1992, *elected* 1995
2013   *Durham* (74th), Paul Roger Butler, *b.* 1955, *m., cons.* 2004, *elected* 2013, *trans.* 2014
2012   *Winchester* (97th), Timothy John Dakin, *b.* 1958, *m., cons.* 2012, *elected* 2012
2001   *Chester* (40th), Peter Robert Forster, PHD, *b.* 1950, *m., cons.* 1996, *elected* 1996
2003   *Leicester* (6th), Timothy John Stevens, *b.* 1946, *m., cons.* 1995, *elected* 1999
2004   *Norwich* (71st), Graham Richard James, *b.* 1951, *m., cons.* 1993, *elected* 1999
2009   *Bristol* (55th), Michael Arthur Hill, *b.* 1947, *m., cons.* 1998, *elected* 2003
2009   *Lichfield* (98th), Jonathan Michael Gledhill, *b.* 1949, *m., cons.* 1996, *elected* 2003
2009   *Gloucester* (40th), Michael Francis Perham, *b.* 1947, *m., cons.* 2004, *elected* 2004
2010   *Derby* (7th), Alastair Llewellyn John Redfern, PHD, *b.* 1948, *m., cons.* 1997, *elected* 2005
2010   *Birmingham* (9th), David Andrew Urquhart, *b.* 1952, *cons.* 2000, *elected* 2006

2012   *Worcester* (113th), John Geoffrey Inge, PHD, *b.* 1955, *m., cons.* 2003, *elected* 2007
2013   *Coventry* (9th), Christopher John Cocksworth, PHD, *b.* 1959, *m., cons.* 2008, *elected* 2008
2013   *Truro* (15th), Timothy Martin Thornton, *b.* 1957, *m., cons.* 2001, *elected* 2008
2013   *Sheffield* (7th), Stephen John Lindsey Croft, PHD, *b.* 1957, *m., cons.* 2009, *elected* 2009
2013   *Carlisle* (66th), James William Scobie Newcome, *b.* 1953, *m., cons.* 2002, *elected* 2009
2013   *St Albans* (10th), Alan Gregory Clayton Smith, PHD, *b.* 1957, *cons.* 2001, *elected* 2009
2014   *Peterborough* (38th), Donald Spargo Allister, *b.* 1952, *m., cons.* 2010, *elected* 2010
2014   *Portsmouth* (9th), Christopher Richard James Foster, *b.* 1953, *m., cons.* 2001, *elected* 2010
2014   *Chelmsford* (10th), Stephen Geoffrey Cottrell, *b.* 1958, *m., cons.* 2004, *elected* 2010
2014   *Rochester* (107th), James Henry Langstaff, *b.* 1956, *m., cons.* 2004, *elected* 2010
2014   *Ely* (69th), Stephen David Conway, *b.* 1957, *cons.* 2006, *elected* 2010
2014   *Southwark* (10th), Christopher Thomas James Chessun, *b.* 1956, *cons.* 2005, *elected* 2011
2014   *Leeds* (1st), Nicholas Baines, *b.* 1957, *m., cons.* 2003, *elected* 2014

BISHOPS AWAITING SEATS, in order of seniority
as at November 2014

Salisbury (78th), Nicholas Roderick Holtam, *b.* 1954, *m., cons.* 2011, *elected* 2011
Lincoln (71st), Christopher Lowson, *b.* 1953, *m., cons.* 2011, *elected* 2011
Chichester (103rd), Martin Clive Warner, PHD, *b.* 1958, *cons.* 2010, *elected* 2012
Blackburn (9th), Julian Tudor Henderson, *b.* 1954, *m., cons.* 2013, *elected* 2013
Manchester (12th), David Stuart Walker, *b.* 1957, *m., cons.* 2000, *elected* 2013
Bath and Wells (79th), Peter Hancock, *b.* 1955, *m., cons.* 2010, *elected* 2014
Exeter (71st), Robert Ronald Atwell, *b.* 1954, *cons.* 2008, *elected* 2014
Liverpool (8th), Paul Bayes, *b.* 1953, *m., cons.* 2010, *elected* 2014
Hereford (105th), Richard Michael Cokayne Frith, *b.* 1949, *m., cons.* 1998, *elected* 2014
Guildford (10th), vacant
St Edmundsbury and Ipswich (11th), vacant
Southwell and Nottingham (12th), vacant
Newcastle (12th), vacant
Oxford (43rd), vacant
Gloucester (41st), vacant

COURTESY TITLES

The heir apparent to a Duke, Marquess or Earl uses the highest of his father's other titles as a courtesy title. For example, the Marquess of Blandford is heir to the Dukedom of Marlborough, and Viscount Amberley to the Earldom of Russell. Titles of second heirs (when in use) are also given, and the courtesy title of the father of a second heir is indicated by * eg Earl of Mornington, eldest son of *Marquess of Douro.

The holder of a courtesy title is not styled 'the Most Hon.' or 'the Rt. Hon.', and in correspondence 'the' is omitted before the title. The heir apparent to a Scottish title may use the title 'Master'.

MARQUESSES

*Blandford – *Marlborough, D.*
Bowmont and Cessford – *Roxburghe, D.*
Douglas and Clydesdale – *Hamilton and Brandon, D.*
*Douro – *Wellington, D.*
Graham – *Montrose, D.*
Granby – *Rutland, D.*
*Hamilton – *Abercorn, D.*
Lorne – *Argyll, D.*
Stafford – *Sutherland, D.*
Tavistock – *Bedford, D.*
Tullibardine – *Atholl, D.*
*Worcester – *Beaufort, D.*

EARLS

*Aboyne – *Huntly, M.*
Altamont – *Sligo, M.*
Arundel and Surrey – *Norfolk, D.*
Bective – *Headfort, M.*
Belfast – *Donegall, M.*
Brecknock – *Camden, M.*
*Burford – *St Albans, D.*
*Burlington – *Devonshire, D.*
*Cardigan – *Ailesbury, M.*
Compton – *Northampton, M.*
*Dalkeith – *Buccleuch, D.*
Dumfries – *Bute, M.*
Euston – *Grafton, D.*
Glamorgan – **Worcester, M.*
Grosvenor – *Westminster, D.*
*Haddo – *Aberdeen and Temair, M.*
Hillsborough – *Downshire, M.*
*Hopetoun – *Linlithgow, M.*
Kerry – *Lansdowne, M.*
*March and Kinrara – *Richmond, D.*
Medina – *Milford Haven, M.*
*Mount Charles – *Conyngham, M.*
*Mornington – **Douro, M.*
Mulgrave – *Normanby, M.*
Percy – *Northumberland, D.*
Rocksavage – *Cholmondley, M.*
Ronaldshay – *Zetland, M.*
*St Andrews – *Kent, D.*

*Southesk – *Fife, D.*
Sunderland – **Blandford, M.*
*Tyrone – *Waterford, M.*
*Ulster – *Gloucester, D.*
Uxbridge – *Anglesey, M.*
*Wiltshire – *Winchester, M.*
Yarmouth – *Hertford, M.*

VISCOUNTS

Aithrie – **Hopetoun, E.*
Alexander – *Caledon, E.*
Althorp – *Spencer, E.*
Andover – *Suffolk and Berkshire, E.*
Anson – *Lichfield, E.*
Asquith – *Oxford and Asquith, E.*
Boringdon – *Morley, E.*
Borodale – *Beatty, E.*
Bury – *Albemarle, E.*
Campden – *Gainsborough, E.*
Carlow – *Portarlington, E.*
Carlton – *Wharncliffe, E.*
Chelsea – *Cadogan, E.*
Chewton – *Waldegrave, E.*
Clanfield – *Peel, E.*
Clive – *Powis, E.*
Coke – *Leicester, E.*
Corry – *Belmore, E.*
Corvedale – *Baldwin of Bewdley, E.*
Cranborne – *Salisbury, M.*
Crichton – *Erne, E.*
Curzon – *Howe, E.*
Dalrymple – *Stair, E.*
Dangan – *Cowley, E.*
Drumlanrig – *Queensberry, M.*
Duncannon – *Bessborough, E.*
Dungarvan – *Cork and Orrery, E.*
Dunluce – *Antrim, E.*
Dunwich – *Stradbroke, E.*
Dupplin – *Kinnoull, E.*
Elveden – *Iveagh, E.*
Emlyn – *Cawdor, E*
Encombe – *Eldon, E.*
Enfield – *Strafford, E.*
Erleigh – *Reading, M.*
Errington – *Cromer, E.*

Feilding – *Denbigh and Desmond, E.*
FitzHarris – *Malmesbury, E.*
Folkestone – *Radnor, E.*
Forbes – *Granard, E.*
Formartine – **Haddo, E.*
Garmoyle – *Cairns, E.*
Garnock – *Lindsay, E.*
Glenapp – *Inchcape, E.*
Glentworth – *Limerick, E.*
Glerawly – *Annesley, E.*
Grey de Wilton – *Wilton, E.*
Grimstone – *Verulam, E.*
Gwynedd – *Lloyd George of Dwyfor, E.*
Hawkesbury – *Liverpool, E.*
Hinchingbrooke – *Sandwich, E.*
Howick – *Grey, E.*
Ikerrin – *Carrick, E.*
Ingestre – *Shrewsbury, E.*
Jocelyn – *Roden, E.*
Kelburn – *Glasgow, E.*
Kingsborough – *Kingston, E.*
Kirkwall – *Orkney, E.*
Knebworth – *Lytton, E.*
Lambton – *Durham, E.*
Lascelles – *Harewood, E.*
Linley – *Snowdon, E.*
Lymington – *Portsmouth, E.*
Macmillan of Ovenden – *Stockton, E.*
Maidstone – *Winchilsea, E*
Maitland – *Lauderdale, E.*
Mandeville – *Manchester, D.*
Marsham – *Romney, E.*
Melgund – *Minto, E.*
Merton – *Nelson, E.*
Moore – *Drogheda, E.*
Newport – *Bradford, E.*
Northland – *Ranfurly, E.*
Newry and Mourne – *Kilmorey, E.*
Petersham – *Harrington, E.*
Pollington – *Mexborough, E*
Raynham – *Townshend, M.*
Reidhaven – *Seafield, E.*
Royston – *Hardwicke, E.*
Ruthven of Canberra – *Gowrie, E.*
St Cyres – *Iddesleigh, E.*
Sandon – *Harrowby, E.*
Savernake – **Cardigan, E.*
Severn – *Wessex, E.*
Slane – **Mount Charles, E.*
Somerton – *Normanton, E.*
Stopford – *Courtown, E.*
Stormont – *Mansfield, E.*
Strabane – **Hamilton, M.*
Strathallan – *Perth, E.*
Stuart – *Castle Stewart, E.*
Suirdale – *Donoughmore, E.*
Tamworth – *Ferrers, E.*
Tarbat – *Cromartie, E.*
Vaughan – *Lisburne, E.*

Wellesley – **Mornington, E.*
Weymouth – *Bath, M.*
Windsor – *Plymouth, E.*
Wolmer – *Selborne, E.*
Woodstock – *Portland, E.*

BARONS (LORDS)

Aberdour – *Morton, E.*
Apsley – *Bathurst, E.*
Ardee – *Meath, E.*
Ashley – *Shaftesbury, E.*
Balniel – *Crawford and Balcarres, E.*
Berriedale – *Caithness, E.*
Bingham – *Lucan, E.*
Binning – *Haddington, E.*
Brooke – *Warwick, E.*
Bruce – *Elgin, E.*
Buckhurst – *De La Warr, E.*
Burghley – *Exeter, M.*
Cardross – *Buchan, E.*
Carnegie – **Southesk, E.*
Cavendish – **Burlington, E.*
Clifton – *Darnley, E.*
Cochrane – *Dundonald, E.*
Courtenay – *Devon, E.*
Culloden – **Ulster, E.*
Dalmeny – *Rosebery, E.*
Doune – *Moray, E.*
Downpatrick – **St Andrews, E.*
Dunglass – *Home, E.*
Elcho – *Wemyss and March, E.*
Eliot – *St Germans, E.*
Gillford – *Clanwilliam, E.*
Glamis – *Strathmore, E.*
Greenock – *Cathcart, E.*
Guernsey – *Aylesford, E.*
Hay – *Erroll, E.*
Herbert – *Pembroke and Montgomery, E.*
Howard of Effingham – *Effingham, E.*
Huntingtower – *Dysart, E.*
Hyde – *Clarendon, E.*
Inverurie – *Kintore, E.*
Irwin – *Halifax, E.*
Johnstone – *Annandale and Hartfell, E.*
Le Poer – **Tyrone, E.*
Leveson – *Granville, E*
Loughborough – *Rosslyn, E.*
Masham – *Swinton, E.*
Medway – *Cranbrook, E.*
Montgomerie – *Eglinton and Winton, E.*
Moreton – *Ducie, E.*
Naas – *Mayo, E.*
Norreys – *Lindsey and Abingdon, E.*
North – *Guilford, E.*
Ogilvy – *Airlie, E.*
Oxmantown – *Rosse, E.*
Porchester – *Carnarvon, E.*

Ramsay – *Dalhousie, E.*
Romsey – *Mountbatten of Burma, C.*
St. John – **Wiltshire, E.*

Scrymgeour – *Dundee, E.*
Settrington – **March and Kinrara, E.*
Seymour – *Somerset, D.*

Stanley – *Derby, E.*
Stavordale – *Ilchester, E.*
Strathavon – **Aboyne, E.*
Strathnaver – *Sutherland, C.*

Vere of Hanworth – **Burford, E.*
Wodehouse – *Kimberley, E.*
Worsley – *Yarborough, E.*

PEERS' SURNAMES

The following symbols indicate the rank of the peer holding each title:
C.   Countess
D.   Duke
E.   Earl
M.   Marquess
V.   Viscount
*   Life Peer
Where no designation is given, the title is that of a hereditary Baron or Baroness.

Abney-Hastings – *Loudoun, E.*
Acheson – *Gosford, E.*
Adams – *A. of Craigielea**
Adderley – *Norton*
Addington – *Sidmouth, V.*
Agar – *Normanton, E.*
Ahmad – *A. of Wimbledon**
Aitken – *Beaverbrook*
Akers-Douglas – *Chilston, V.*
Alexander – *A. of Tunis, E.*
Alexander – *Caledon, E.*
Allan – *A. of Hallam**
Allen – *A. of Kensington**
Allsopp – *Hindlip*
Alton – *A. of Liverpool**
Ancram – *Kerr of Monteviot**
Anderson – *A. of Swansea**
Anderson – *Waverley, V.*
Anelay – *A. of St Johns**
Annesley – *Valentia, V.*
Anson – *Lichfield, E.*
Archer – *A. of Weston-super-Mare**
Armstrong – *A. of Hill Top**
Armstrong – *A. of Ilminster**
Armstrong-Jones – *Snowdon, E.*
Arthur – *Glenarthur*
Arundell – *Talbot of Malahide*
Ashdown – *A. of Norton-sub-Hamdon**
Ashley-Cooper – *Shaftesbury, E.*
Ashton – *A. of Hyde*
Ashton – *A. of Upholland**
Asquith – *Oxford and Asquith, E.*
Assheton – *Clitheroe*
Astley – *Hastings*
Astor – *A. of Hever*
Aubrey-Fletcher – *Braye*
Bailey – *Glanusk*
Baillie – *Burton*
Baillie Hamilton – *Haddington, E.*
Baker – *B. of Dorking**

Bakewell – *B. of Hardington Mandeville**
Balchin – *Lingfield**
Baldwin – *B. of Bewdley, E.*
Balfour – *Kinross*
Balfour – *Riverdale*
Bampfylde – *Poltimore*
Banbury – *B. of Southam*
Barber – *B. of Tewkesbury**
Baring – *Ashburton*
Baring – *Cromer, E.*
Baring – *Howick of Glendale*
Baring – *Northbrook*
Baring – *Revelstoke*
Barker – *Trumpington**
Barnes – *Gorell*
Barnewall – *Trimlestown*
Bassam – *B. of Brighton**
Bathurst – *Bledisloe, V.*
Beauclerk – *St Albans, D.*
Beaumont – *Allendale, V.*
Beckett – *Grimthorpe*
Benn – *Stansgate, V.*
Bennet – *Tankerville, E.*
Bentinck – *Portland, E.*
Beresford – *Decies*
Beresford – *Waterford M*
Berkeley – *B. of Knighton**
Berry – *Camrose, V.*
Berry – *Kemsley, V.*
Bertie – *Lindsey and Abingdon, E.*
Best – *Wynford*
Bethell – *Westbury*
Bewicke-Copley – *Cromwell*
Bigham – *Mersey, V.*
Bingham – *Clanmorris*
Bingham – *Lucan, E.*
Bishop – *Glendonbrook**
Black – *B. of Brentwood**
Black – *B. of Crossharbour**
Blair – *B. of Boughton**
Bligh – *Darnley, E.*
Blyth – *B. of Rowington**
Bonham Carter – *B.-C. of Yarnbury**
Bootle-Wilbraham – *Skelmersdale*
Boscawen – *Falmouth, V.*
Boswell – *B. of Aynho**
Bottomley – *B. of Nettlestone**
Bourke – *Mayo, E.*
Bourne – *B. of Aberystwyth**
Bowes Lyon – *Strathmore and Kinghorne, E.*
Bowyer – *Denham*
Boyd – *B. of Duncansby**
Boyd – *Kilmarnock*
Boyle – *Cork and Orrery, E.*
Boyle – *Glasgow, E.*

Boyle – *Shannon, E.*
Brabazon – *Meath, E.*
Brand – *Hampden, V.*
Brassey – *B. of Apethorpe*
Brett – *Esher, V.*
Bridgeman – *Bradford, E.*
Brittan – *B. of Spennithorne**
Brodrick – *Midleton, V.*
Brooke – *Alanbrooke, V.*
Brooke – *B. of Alverthorpe**
Brooke – *B. of Sutton Mandeville**
Brooke – *Brookeborough, V.*
Brooks – *B. of Tremorfa**
Brooks – *Crawshaw*
Brougham – *Brougham and Vaux*
Broughton – *Fairhaven*
Brown – *B. of Eaton-under-Heywood**
Browne – *B. of Belmont**
Browne – *B. of Ladyton**
Browne – *B. of Madingley**
Browne – *Kilmaine*
Browne – *Oranmore and Browne*
Browne – *Sligo, M*
Bruce – *Aberdare*
Bruce – *Balfour of Burleigh*
Bruce – *Elgin and Kincardine, E.*
Brudenell-Bruce – *Ailesbury, M.*
Buchan – *Tweedsmuir*
Buckley – *Wrenbury*
Butler – *B. of Brockwell**
Butler – *Carrick, E.*
Butler – *Dunboyne*
Butler – *Mountgarret, V.*
Byng – *Strafford, E.*
Byng – *Torrington, V.*
Cameron – *C. of Dillington**
Cameron – *C. of Lochbroom**
Campbell – *Argyll, D.*
Campbell – *C. of Loughborough**
Campbell – *C. of Surbiton**
Campbell – *Cawdor, E.*
Campbell – *Colgrain*
Campbell – *Stratheden and Campbell*
Campbell-Gray – *Gray*
Canning – *Garvagh*
Capell – *Essex, E.*
Carey – *C. of Clifton**
Carington – *Carrington*
Carlile – *C. of Berriew**
Carnegie – *Fife, D.*
Carnegy – *Northesk, E.*
Carrington – *C. of Fulham**
Carter – *C. of Barnes**

Carter – *C. of Coles**
Cary – *Falkland, V.*
Caulfeild – *Charlemont, V.*
Cavendish – *C. of Furness**
Cavendish – *Chesham*
Cavendish – *Devonshire, D.*
Cavendish – *Waterpark*
Cayzer – *Rotherwick*
Cecil – *Amherst of Hackney*
Cecil – *Exeter, M.*
Cecil – *Rockley*
Chalker – *C. of Wallasey**
Chaloner – *Gisborough*
Charteris – *Wemyss and March, E.*
Chetwynd-Talbot – *Shrewsbury and Waterford, E.*
Chichester – *Donegall, M.*
Child Villiers – *Jersey, E.*
Chisholm – *C. of Owlpen**
Cholmondeley – *Delamere*
Chubb – *Hayter*
Clark – *C. of Calton**
Clarke – *C. of Hampstead**
Clarke – *C. of Stone Cum Ebony**
Clegg-Hill – *Hill, V.*
Clifford – *C. of Chudleigh*
Cochrane – *C. of Cults*
Cochrane – *Dundonald, E.*
Cocks – *Somers*
Cohen – *C. of Pimlico**
Cokayne – *Cullen of Ashbourne*
Coke – *Leicester, E.*
Cole – *Enniskillen, E.*
Collier – *Monkswell*
Collins – *C. of Highbury**
Collins – *C. of Mapesbury**
Colville – *Clydesmuir*
Colville – *C. of Culross, V.*
Compton – *Northampton, M.*
Conolly-Carew – *Carew*
Cooke – *Lexden**
Cooper – *C. of Windrush*
Cooper – *Norwich, V.*
Cope – *C. of Berkeley**
Corbett – *Rowallan*
Cornwall-Legh – *Grey of Codnor*
Courtenay – *Devon, E.*
Craig – *C. of Radley**
Craig – *Craigavon, V.*
Crichton – *Erne, E.*
Crichton-Stuart – *Bute, M.*
Cripps – *Parmoor*
Crossley – *Somerleyton*
Cubitt – *Ashcombe*
Cunliffe-Lister – *Masham of Ilton**

Howard – *H. of Penrith*
Howard – *H. of Rising*⋆
Howard – *Strathcona and Mount Royal*
Howard – *Suffolk and Berkshire, E.*
Howarth – *H. of Breckland*⋆
Howarth – *H. of Newport*⋆
Howe – *H. of Aberavon*⋆
Howe – *H. of Idlicote*⋆
Howell – *H. of Guildford*⋆
Howells – *H. of St. Davids*⋆
Howie – *H. of Troon*⋆
Hubbard – *Addington*
Huggins – *Malvern, V.*
Hughes – *H. of Stretford*⋆
Hughes – *H. of Woodside*⋆
Hughes-Young – *St Helens*
Hunt – *H. of Chesterton*⋆
Hunt – *H. of Kings Heath*⋆
Hunt – *H. of Wirral*⋆
Hurd – *H. of Westwell*⋆
Hutchinson – *H. of Lullington*⋆
Hutton – *H. of Furness*⋆
Ingrams – *Darcy de Knayth*
Innes-Ker – *Roxburghe, D.*
Inskip – *Caldecote, V.*
Irby – *Boston*
Irvine – *I. of Lairg*⋆
Isaacs – *Reading, M.*
James – *J. of Blackheath*⋆
James – *J. of Holland Park*⋆
James – *Northbourne*
Janner – *J. of Braunstone*⋆
Jay – *J. of Ewelme*⋆
Jay – *J. of Paddington*⋆
Jebb – *Gladwyn*
Jenkin – *J. of Kennington*⋆
Jenkin – *J. of Roding*⋆
Jervis – *St Vincent, V.*
Jocelyn – *Roden, E.*
Jolliffe – *Hylton*
Jones – *J. of Birmingham*⋆
Jones – *J. of Cheltenham*⋆
Jones – *J. of Moulsecoomb*⋆
Jones – *J. of Whitchurch*⋆
Joynson-Hicks – *Brentford, V.*
Kay-Shuttleworth – *Shuttleworth*
Kearley – *Devonport, V.*
Keith – *Kintore, E.*
Kemp – *Rochdale, V.*
Kennedy – *Ailsa, M.*
Kennedy – *K. of Cradley*⋆
Kennedy – *K. of Southwark*⋆
Kennedy – *K. of the Shaws*⋆
Kenworthy – *Strabolgi*
Keppel – *Albemarle, E.*
Kerr – *K. of Kinlochard*⋆
Kerr – *K. of Tonaghmore*⋆
Kerr – *Lothian, M.*
Kerr – *Teviot*
Kilpatrick – *K. of Kincraig*⋆
King – *K. of Bow*⋆
King – *K. of Lothbury*⋆
King – *Lovelace, E.*
King-Tenison – *Kingston, E.*

Kinnock – *K. of Holyhead*⋆
Kirkham – *Berners*
Kirkwood – *K. of Kirkhope*⋆
Knatchbull – *Brabourne*
Knatchbull – *Mountbatten of Burma, C.*
Knight – *K. of Collingtree*⋆
Knight – *K. of Weymouth*⋆
Knox – *Ranfurly, E.*
Lamb – *Rochester*
Lambton – *Durham, E.*
Lamont – *L. of Lerwick*⋆
Lampson – *Killearn*
Lane Fox – *L.-F. of Soho*⋆
Lang – *L. of Monkton*⋆
Lascelles – *Harewood, E.*
Law – *Coleraine*
Law – *Ellenborough*
Lawrence – *L. of Clarendon*⋆
Lawrence – *Trevethin and Oaksey*
Lawson – *Burnham*
Lawson – *L. of Blaby*⋆
Lawson Johnston – *Luke*
Lea – *L. of Crondall*⋆
Leach – *L. of Fairford*⋆
Lee – *L. of Trafford*⋆
Legge – *Dartmouth, E.*
Legh – *Newton*
Leigh – *L. of Hurley*⋆
Leith – *Burgh*
Lennox-Boyd – *Boyd of Merton, V.*
Le Poer Trench – *Clancarty, E.*
Leslie   *Rothes, E.*
Leslie Melville – *Leven and Melville, E.*
Lester – *L. of Herne Hill*⋆
Levene – *L. of Portsoken*⋆
Leveson-Gower – *Granville, E.*
Lewis – *Merthyr*
Liddell – *L. of Coatdyke*⋆
Liddell – *Ravensworth*
Lindesay-Bethune – *Lindsay, E.*
Lindsay – *Crawford and Balcarres, E.*
Lindsay – *L. of Birker*
Linklater – *L. of Butterstone*⋆
Lister – *L. of Burtersett*⋆
Littleton – *Hatherton*
Livingston – *L. of Parkhead*⋆
Lloyd – *L. of Berwick*⋆
Lloyd George – *Lloyd George of Dwyfor, E.*
Lloyd George – *Tenby, V.*
Lloyd-Mostyn – *Mostyn*
Loder – *Wakehurst*
Lopes – *Roborough*
Lord – *Framlingham*⋆
Low – *Aldington*
Low – *L. of Dalston*⋆
Lowry-Corry – *Belmore, E.*
Lowther – *Lonsdale, E.*
Lowther – *Ullswater, V.*
Lubbock – *Avebury*
Lucas – *L. of Chilworth*

Lumley – *Scarbrough, E.*
Lumley-Savile – *Savile*
Lyon-Dalberg-Acton – *Acton*
Lysaght – *Lisle*
Lyttelton – *Chandos, V.*
Lyttelton – *Cobham, V.*
Lytton Cobbold – *Cobbold*
McClintock-Bunbury – *Rathdonnell*
McColl – *M. of Dulwich*⋆
McConnell – *M. of Glenscorrodale*⋆
MacDonald – *M. of River Glaven*⋆
Macdonald – *M. of Tradeston*⋆
McDonnell – *Antrim, E.*
McFall – *M. of Alcluith*⋆
Macfarlane – *M. of Bearsden*⋆
MacGregor – *M. of Pulham Market*⋆
McIntosh – *M. of Hudnall*⋆
Mackay – *Inchcape, E.*
Mackay – *M. of Clashfern*⋆
Mackay – *M. of Drumadoon*⋆
Mackay – *Reay*
Mackay – *Tanlaw*⋆
Mackenzie – *Cromartie, E.*
MacKenzie – *M. of Culkein*⋆
Mackenzie – *M. of Framwellgate*⋆
McKenzie – *M. of Luton*⋆
Mackie – *M. of Benshie*⋆
Mackintosh – *M. of Halifax, V.*
McLaren – *Aberconway*
MacLaurin – *M. of Knebworth*⋆
Maclean – *Blencathra*⋆
Maclennan – *M. of Rogart*⋆
Macmillan – *Stockton, E.*
Macpherson – *M. of Drumochter*
Macpherson – *Strathcarron*
Maffey – *Rugby*
Magan – *M. of Castletown*⋆
Maginnis – *M. of Drumglass*⋆
Maitland – *Lauderdale, E.*
Makgill – *Oxfuird, V.*
Makins – *Sherfield*
Manners – *Rutland, D.*
Manningham-Buller – *Dilhorne, V.*
Mansfield – *Sandhurst*
Marks – *M. of Broughton*
Marks – *M. of Henley-on-Thames*⋆
Marquis – *Woolton, E.*
Marsham – *Romney, E.*
Martin – *M. of Springburn*⋆
Martyn-Hemphill – *Hemphill*
Mason – *M. of Barnsley*⋆
Massey – *M. of Darwen*⋆
Masters – *Noakes*⋆
Maude – *Hawarden, V.*
Maxwell – *de Ros*
Maxwell – *Farnham*

May – *M. of Oxford*⋆
Mayhew – *M. of Twysden*⋆
Meade – *Clanwilliam, E.*
Mercer Nairne Petty-Fitzmaurice – *Lansdowne, M.*
Methuen-Campbell – *Methuen*
Millar – *Inchyra*
Miller – *M. of Chilthorne Domer*⋆
Milner – *M. of Leeds*
Mitchell-Thomson – *Selsdon*
Mitford – *Redesdale*
Molyneaux – *M. of Killead*⋆
Monckton – *M. of Brenchley, V.*
Monckton-Arundell – *Galway, V.*
Mond – *Melchett*
Money-Coutts – *Latymer*
Montagu – *Manchester, D.*
Montagu – *Sandwich, E.*
Montagu – *Swaythling*
Montagu Douglas Scott – *Buccleuch and Queensberry, D.*
Montagu Stuart Wortley – *Wharncliffe, E.*
Montague – *Amwell*
Montgomerie – *Eglinton and Winton, E.*
Montgomery – *M. of Alamein, V.*
Moore   *Drogheda, E.*
Moore – *M. of Lower Marsh*⋆
Moore-Brabazon – *Brabazon of Tara*
Moreton – *Ducie, E*
Morgan – *M. of Drefelin*⋆
Morgan – *M. of Ely*⋆
Morgan – *M. of Huyton*⋆
Morris – *Killanin*
Morris – *M. of Aberavon*⋆
Morris – *M. of Bolton*⋆
Morris – *M. of Handsworth*⋆
Morris – *M. of Kenwood*
Morris – *M. of Yardley*⋆
Morris – *Naseby*⋆
Morrison – *Dunrossil, V.*
Morrison – *Margadale*
Mosley – *Ravensdale*
Mountbatten – *Milford Haven, M.*
Muff – *Calverley*
Mulholland – *Dunleath*
Murray – *Atholl, D.*
Murray – *Dunmore, E.*
Murray – *Mansfield and Mansfield, E.*
Nall-Cain – *Brocket*
Napier – *Napier and Ettrick*
Napier – *N. of Magdala*
Needham – *Kilmorey, E.*
Neill – *N. of Bladen*⋆
Nelson – *N. of Stafford*
Neuberger – *N. of Abbotsbury*⋆

Nevill – Abergavenny, M.
Neville – Braybrooke
Nicholls – N. of Birkenhead*
Nicolson – Carnock
Nicholson – N. of Winterbourne*
Nivison – Glendyne
Noel – Gainsborough, E.
North – Guilford, E.
Northcote – Iddesleigh, E.
Norton – Grantley
Norton – N. of Louth*
Norton – Rathcreedan
Nugent – Westmeath, E.
Oakeshott – O. of Seagrove Bay*
O'Brien – Inchiquin
Ogilvie-Grant – Seafield, E.
Ogilvy – Airlie, E.
O'Neill – O'N. of Bengarve*
O'Neill – O'N. of Clackmannan*
O'Neill – Rathcavan
Orde-Powlett – Bolton
Ormsby-Gore – Harlech
Paget – Anglesey, M.
Paisley – P. of St George's*
Pakenham – Longford, E.
Pakington – Hampton
Palmer – Lucas and Dingwall
Palmer – P. of Childs Hill*
Palmer – Selborne, E.
Palumbo – P. of Southwark*
Parker – Macclesfield, E.
Parker – Morley, E.
Parnell – Congleton
Parsons – Rosse, E.
Patel – P. of Blackburn*
Patel – P. of Bradford*
Patten – P. of Barnes*
Paulet – Winchester, M.
Pearson – Cowdray, V.
Pearson – P. of Rannoch*
Pease – Gainford
Pease – Wardington
Pelham – Chichester, E.
Pelham – Yarborough, E.
Pellew – Exmouth, V
Penny – Marchwood, V.
Pepys – Cottenham, E.
Percy – Northumberland, D.
Perry – P. of Southwark*
Pery – Limerick, E.
Philipps – Milford
Philipps – St Davids, V.
Phillips – P. of Sudbury*
Phillips – P. of Worth Matravers*
Phipps – Normanby, M.
Plant – P. of Highfield*
Platt – P. of Writtle*
Pleydell-Bouverie – Radnor, E.
Plumptre – Fitzwalter
Plunkett – Dunsany
Plunkett – Louth
Pollock – Hanworth, V.
Pomeroy – Harberton, V.
Ponsonby – Bessborough, E.

Ponsonby – de Mauley
Ponsonby – P. of Shulbrede
Powell – P. of Bayswater*
Powys – Lilford
Pratt – Camden, M.
Preston – Gormanston, V.
Primrose – Rosebery, E.
Prittie – Dunalley
Purvis – P. of Tweed*
Ramsay – Dalhousie, E.
Ramsay – R. of Cartvale*
Ramsbotham – Soulbury, V.
Rees – R. of Ludlow*
Rees-Williams – Ogmore
Reid – R. of Cardowan*
Rendell – R. of Babergh*
Renfrew – R. of Kaimsthorn*
Renton – R. of Mount Harry*
Renwick – R. of Clifton*
Rhys – Dynevor
Richards – Milverton
Richards – R. of Herstmonceux*
Richardson – R. of Calow*
Ritchie – R. of Dundee
Roberts – Clwyd
Roberts – R. of Llandudno*
Robertson – R. of Oakridge
Robertson – R. of Port Ellen*
Robertson – Wharton
Robinson – Martonmere
Roche – Fermoy
Rodd – Rennell
Rodgers – R. of Quarry Bank*
Rogers – R. of Riverside*
Roper-Curzon – Teynham
Rose – R. of Monewden*
Rospigliosi – Newburgh, E.
Rous – Stradbroke, E.
Rowley-Conwy – Langford
Royall – R. of Blaisdon*
Runciman – R. of Doxford, V.
Russell – Ampthill
Russell – Bedford, D.
Russell – de Clifford
Russell – R. of Liverpool
Ryder – Harrowby, E.
Ryder – R. of Wensum*
Sackville – De La Warr, E.
Sackville-West – Sackville
Sainsbury – S. of Preston Candover*
Sainsbury – S. of Turville*
St Aubyn – St Levan
St Clair – Sinclair
St Clair-Erskine – Rosslyn, E.
St John – Bolingbroke and St John, V.
St John – St John of Bletso
St Leger – Doneraile, V.
Samuel – Bearsted, V.
Sanderson – S. of Ayot
Sanderson – S. of Bowden*
Sandilands – Torphichen

Saumarez – de Saumarez
Savile – Mexborough, E.
Saville – S. of Newdigate*
Scarlett – Abinger
Schreiber – Marlesford*
Sclater-Booth – Basing
Scotland – S. of Asthal*
Scott – Eldon, E.
Scott – S. of Foscote*
Scott – S. of Needham Market*
Scrymgeour – Dundee, E.
Seager – Leighton of St Mellons
Seely – Mottistone
Seymour – Hertford, M.
Seymour – Somerset, D.
Shackleton – S. of Belgravia*
Sharp – S. of Guildford*
Shaw – Craigmyle
Shaw – S. of Northstead*
Shephard – S. of Northwold*
Sheppard – S. of Didgemere*
Sherbourne – S. of Didbury*
Shirley – Ferrers, E.
Shutt – S. of Greetland*
Siddeley – Kenilworth
Sidney – De L'Isle, V.
Simon – S. of Highbury*
Simon – S. of Wythenshawe
Simpson – S. of Dunkeld*
Sinclair – Caithness, E.
Sinclair – S. of Cleeve
Sinclair – Thurso, V.
Singh – S. of Wimbledon*
Skeffington – Massereene and Ferrard, V.
Smith – Bicester
Smith – Hambleden, V.
Smith – Kirkhill*
Smith – S. of Basildon*
Smith – S. of Clifton*
Smith – S. of Finsbury*
Smith – S. of Gilmorehill*
Smith – S. of Kelvin*
Smith – S. of Leigh*
Smith – S. of Newnham*
Somerset – Beaufort, D.
Somerset – Raglan
Soulsby – S. of Swaffham Prior*
Spencer – Churchill, V.
Spencer-Churchill – Marlborough, D.
Spring – Risby*
Spring Rice – Monteagle of Brandon
Stanhope – Harrington, E.
Stanley – Derby, E.
Stanley – S. of Alderley and Sheffield
Stapleton-Cotton – Combermere, V.
Steel – S. of Aikwood*
Sterling – S. of Plaistow*
Stern – S. of Brentford*
Stevens – S. of Kirkwhelpington*
Stevens – S. of Ludgate*

Stevenson – B. of Balmacara*
Stevenson – S. of Coddenham*
Stewart – Galloway, E.
Stewart – Stewartby*
Stoddart – S. of Swindon*
Stone – S. of Blackheath*
Stoneham – S. of Droxford*
Stonor – Camoys
Stopford – Courtown, E.
Stourton – Mowbray, Segrave and S.
Stowell – S. of Beeston*
Strachey – O'Hagan
Strutt – Belper
Strutt – Rayleigh
Stuart – Castle Stewart, E.
Stuart – Moray, E.
Stuart – S. of Findhorn, V.
Suenson-Taylor – Grantchester
Sutherland – S. of Houndwood*
Symons – S. of Vernham Dean*
Taylor – Kilclooney*
Taylor – T. of Blackburn*
Taylor – T. of Bolton*
Taylor – T. of Goss Moor*
Taylor – T. of Holbeach*
Taylor – T. of Warwick*
Taylour – Headfort, M.
Temple-Gore-Langton – Temple of Stowe, E
Tennant – Glenconner
Thellusson – Rendlesham
Thesiger – Chelmsford, V.
Thomas – T. of Cwmgiedd*
Thomas – T. of Gresford*
Thomas – T. of Macclesfield*
Thomas – T. of Swynnerton*
Thomas – T. of Walliswood*
Thomas – T. of Winchester*
Thomson – T. of Fleet
Thynn – Bath, M.
Tottenham – Ely, M.
Trefusis – Clinton
Trench – Ashtown
Tufton – Hothfield
Turner – Netherthorpe
Turner – T. of Camden*
Turner – T. of Ecchinswell*
Turnour – Winterton, E.
Tyler – T. of Enfield*
Tyrell-Kenyon – Kenyon
Vallance – V. of Tummel*
Vanden-Bempde-Johnstone – Derwent
Vane – Barnard
Vane-Tempest-Stewart – Londonderry, M.
Vanneck – Huntingfield
Vaughan – Lisburne, E.
Vereker – Gort, V.
Verney – Willoughby de Broke
Vernon – Lyveden
Vesey – de Vesci, V.

Villiers – *Clarendon, E.*
Vincent – *V. of Coleshill**
Vivian – *Swansea*
Wade – *W. of Chorlton**
Waldegrave – *W. of North Hill**
Walker – *W. of Aldringham**
Walker – *W. of Gestingthorpe**
Wall – *W. of New Barnet**
Wallace – *Dudley*
Wallace – *W. of Saltaire**
Wallace – *W. of Tankerness**
Wallop – *Portsmouth, E.*
Walton – *W. of Detchant**
Ward – *Bangor, V.*
Ward – *Dudley, E.*
Warrender – *Bruntisfield*
Warwick – *W. of Undercliffe**

Watson – *Manton*
Watson – *W. of Invergowrie**
Watson – *W. of Richmond**
Webber – *Lloyd-Webber**
Weir – *Inverforth*
Weld-Forester – *Forester*
Wellesley *Cowley, E.*
Wellesley – *Wellington, D.*
West – *W. of Spithead**
Westenra – *Rossmore*
White – *Annaly*
White – *Hanningfield**
Whiteley – *Marchamley*
Whitfield – *Kenswood*
Williams – *W. of Baglan**
Williams – *W. of Crosby**
Williams – *W. of Elvel**
Williams – *W. of Oystermouth**
Williams – *W. of Trafford**

Williamson – *Forres*
Williamson – *W. of Horton**
Willis – *W. of Knaresborough**
Willoughby – *Middleton*
Wills – *Dulverton*
Wilson – *Moran*
Wilson – *Nunburnholme*
Wilson – *W. of Dinton**
Wilson – *W. of Tillyorn**
Windsor – *Gloucester, D.*
Windsor – *Kent, D.*
Windsor-Clive – *Plymouth, E.*
Wingfield – *Powerscourt, V.*
Winn – *St Oswald*
Wodehouse – *Kimberley, E.*
Wolfson – *W. of Aspley Guise**

Wolfson – *W. of Sunningdale**
Wood – *Halifax, E.*
Wood – *W. of Anfield**
Woodhouse – *Terrington*
Woolmer – *W. of Leeds**
Wright – *W. of Richmond**
Wyndham – *Egremont and Leconfield*
Wynn – *Newborough*
Yarde-Buller – *Churston*
Yerburgh – *Alvingham*
Yorke – *Hardwicke, E.*
Young – *Kennet*
Young – *Y. of Graffham**
Young – *Y. of Hornsey**
Young – *Y. of Norwood Green**
Young – *Y. of Old Scone**
Younger – *Y. of Leckie, V.*

ORDERS OF CHIVALRY

THE MOST NOBLE ORDER OF THE GARTER (1348)

KG
Ribbon, Blue
Motto, Honi soit qui mal y pense
(Shame on him who thinks evil of it)

The number of Knights and Ladies Companion is limited to 24

SOVEREIGN OF THE ORDER
The Queen

LADIES OF THE ORDER
HRH The Princess Royal, 1994
HRH Princess Alexandra, The Hon. Lady Ogilvy, 2003

ROYAL KNIGHTS
HRH The Prince Philip, Duke of Edinburgh, 1947
HRH The Prince of Wales, 1958
HRH The Duke of Kent, 1985
HRH The Duke of Gloucester, 1997
HRH The Duke of York, 2006
HRH The Earl of Wessex, 2006
HRH The Duke of Cambridge, 2008

EXTRA KNIGHTS COMPANION AND LADIES
Grand Duke Jean of Luxembourg, 1972
HM The Queen of Denmark, 1979
HM The King of Sweden, 1983
HM King Juan Carlos of Spain, 1988
HRH Princess Beatrix of the Netherlands, 1989
HIM The Emperor of Japan, 1998
HM The King of Norway, 2001

KNIGHTS AND LADIES COMPANION
Lord Carrington, 1985
Duke of Wellington, 1990
Lord Bramall, 1990
Lord Sainsbury of Preston Candover, 1992
Lord Ashburton, 1994
Sir Ninian Stephen, 1994
Sir Timothy Colman, 1996
Duke of Abercorn, 1999
Sir William Gladstone, 1999
Lord Inge, 2001
Sir Anthony Acland, 2001
Duke of Westminster, 2003
Lord Butler of Brockwell, 2003
Lord Morris of Aberavon, 2003
Sir John Major, 2005

Lord Luce, 2008
Sir Thomas Dunne, 2008
Lord Phillips of Worth Matravers, 2011
Lord Boyce, 2011
Lord Stirrup, 2013
Lady Manningham-Buller, 2014
Lord King of Lothbury, 2014

Prelate, Bishop of Winchester
Chancellor, Duke of Abercorn, KG
Register, Dean of Windsor
Garter King of Arms, Thomas Woodcock, CVO
Gentleman Usher of the Black Rod, Lt.-Gen. David Leakey, CMG, CBE
Secretary, Patric Dickinson, LVO

THE MOST ANCIENT AND MOST NOBLE ORDER OF THE THISTLE (REVIVED 1687)

KT
Ribbon, Green
Motto, Nemo me impune lacessit
(No one provokes me with impunity)

The number of Knights and Ladies of the Thistle is limited to 16

SOVEREIGN OF THE ORDER
The Queen

ROYAL KNIGHTS
HRH The Prince Philip, Duke of Edinburgh, 1952
HRH The Prince of Wales, Duke of Rothesay, 1977
HRH The Duke of Cambridge, Earl of Strathearn, 2012

ROYAL LADY OF THE ORDER
HRH The Princess Royal, 2000

KNIGHTS AND LADIES
Earl of Elgin and Kincardine, 1981
Earl of Airlie, 1985
Earl of Crawford and Balcarres, 1996
Lady Marion Fraser, 1996
Lord Macfarlane of Bearsden, 1996
Lord Mackay of Clashfern, 1997
Lord Wilson of Tillyorn, 2000
Lord Sutherland of Houndwood, 2002
Sir Eric Anderson, 2002
Lord Steel of Aikwood, 2004
Lord Robertson of Port Ellen, 2004
Lord Cullen of Whitekirk, 2007
Lord Hope of Craighead, 2009

Lord Patel, 2009
Earl of Home, 2013
Lord Smith of Kelvin, 2013

Chancellor, Earl of Airlie, KT, GCVO, PC
Dean, Very Revd Iain Torrance
Lord Lyon King of Arms, Dr Joseph Morrow
Gentleman Usher of the Green Rod, Rear-Adm. Christopher Layman, CB, DSO, LVO
Secretary, Mrs C. Roads, LVO

THE MOST HONOURABLE ORDER OF THE BATH (1725)

GCB *Military* GCB *Civil*

GCB	Knight (or Dame) Grand Cross
KCB	Knight Commander
DCB	Dame Commander
CB	Companion

Ribbon, Crimson
Motto, Tria juncta in uno
(Three joined in one)

Remodelled 1815, and enlarged many times since. The order is divided into civil and military divisions. Women became eligible for the order from 1 January 1971.

THE SOVEREIGN

GREAT MASTER AND FIRST OR PRINCIPAL KNIGHT GRAND CROSS
HRH The Prince of Wales, KG, KT, GCB, OM

Dean of the Order, Dean of Westminster
Bath King of Arms, Adm. Lord Boyce, KG, GCB, OBE
Registrar and Secretary, Rear-Adm. Iain Henderson, CB, CBE
Genealogist, Thomas Woodcock, CVO
Gentleman Usher of the Scarlet Rod, Maj.-Gen. Charles Vyvyan, CB, CBE
Deputy Secretary, Secretary of the Central Chancery of the Orders of Knighthood
Chancery, Central Chancery of the Orders of Knighthood, St James's Palace, London SW1A 1BH

THE ORDER OF MERIT (1902)

OM *Military*   OM *Civil*

OM

Ribbon, Blue and crimson

This order is designed as a special distinction for eminent men and women without conferring a knighthood upon them. The order is limited in numbers to 24, with the addition of foreign honorary members.

THE SOVEREIGN

HRH The Prince Philip, Duke of
  Edinburgh, 1968
Revd Prof. Owen Chadwick, KBE,
  1983
Sir Michael Atiyah, 1992
Sir Aaron Klug, 1995
Lord Foster of Thames Bank, 1997
Prof. Sir Roger Penrose, 2000
Sir Tom Stoppard, 2000
HRH The Prince of Wales, 2002
Lord May of Oxford, 2002
Lord Rothschild, 2002
Sir David Attenborough, 2005
Baroness Boothroyd, 2005
Sir Michael Howard, 2005
Sir Timothy Berners-Lee, KBE, 2007
Lord Eames, 2007
Lord Rees of Ludlow, 2007
Rt. Hon. Jean Chrétien, QC, 2009
Robert Neil MacGregor, 2010
Hon. John Howard, 2012
David Hockney, 2012
Sir Simon Rattle, 2013
Dr Martin West, 2013
Prof. Sir Magdi Yacoub, 2013

Secretary and Registrar, Lord Fellowes,
  GCB, GCVO, PC, QSO
Chancery, Central Chancery of the Orders
  of Knighthood, St James's Palace,
  London SW1A 1BH

THE MOST DISTINGUISHED ORDER OF ST MICHAEL AND ST GEORGE (1818)

GCMG   KCMG

GCMG   Knight (or Dame) Grand
          Cross
KCMG   Knight Commander
DCMG   Dame Commander
CMG   Companion

Ribbon, Saxon blue, with scarlet centre
Motto, Auspicium melioris aevi
(Token of a better age)

THE SOVEREIGN

GRAND MASTER
HRH The Duke of Kent, KG, GCMG,
  GCVO, ADC

Prelate, Rt. Revd David Urquhart
Chancellor, Lord Robertson of Port
  Ellen, KT, GCMG, PC
Secretary, Permanent Under-Secretary
  of State at the Foreign and
  Commonwealth Office and Head of
  the Diplomatic Service
Registrar, Sir David Manning, GCMG,
  CVO
King of Arms, Sir Jeremy Greenstock,
  GCMG
Gentleman Usher of the Blue Rod, Sir
  Anthony Figgis, KCVO, CMG
Dean, Dean of St Paul's
Deputy Secretary, Secretary of the
  Central Chancery of the Orders of
  Knighthood
Hon. Genealogist, Timothy Duke
Chancery, Central Chancery of the Orders
  of Knighthood, St James's Palace,
  London SW1A 1BH

THE IMPERIAL ORDER OF THE CROWN OF INDIA (1877) FOR LADIES

CI

Badge, the royal cipher of Queen
Victoria in jewels within an oval,
surmounted by an heraldic crown and
attached to a bow of light blue watered
ribbon, edged white

The honour does not confer any rank
or title upon the recipient

No conferments have been made since
1947

HM The Queen, 1947

THE ROYAL VICTORIAN ORDER (1896)

GCVO   KCVO

GCVO   Knight or Dame Grand
          Cross
KCVO   Knight Commander
DCVO   Dame Commander
CVO   Commander
LVO   Lieutenant
MVO   Member

Ribbon, Blue, with red and white edges
Motto, Victoria

THE SOVEREIGN
GRAND MASTER
HRH The Princess Royal, KG, KT,
  GCVO

Chancellor, Lord Chamberlain
Secretary, Keeper of the Privy Purse
Registrar, Secretary of the Central
  Chancery of the Orders of
  Knighthood
Chaplain, Chaplain of the Queen's
  Chapel of the Savoy
Hon. Genealogist, David White

THE MOST EXCELLENT ORDER OF THE BRITISH EMPIRE (1917)

GBE   KBE

The order was divided into military and civil divisions in December 1918

GBE   Knight or Dame Grand Cross
KBE   Knight Commander
DBE   Dame Commander
CBE   Commander
OBE   Officer
MBE   Member

Ribbon, Rose pink edged with pearl grey with vertical pearl stripe in centre (military division); without vertical pearl stripe (civil division)
Motto, For God and the Empire

THE SOVEREIGN

GRAND MASTER
HRH The Prince Philip, Duke of Edinburgh, KG, KT, OM, GBE, PC

Prelate, Bishop of London
King of Arms, Adm. Sir Peter Abbott, GBE, KCB
Registrar, Secretary of the Central Chancery of the Orders of Knighthood
Secretary, Secretary of the Cabinet and Head of the Home Civil Service
Dean, Dean of St Paul's
Lady Usher of the Purple Rod, Dame Amelia Chilcott Fawcett, DBE
Chancery, Central Chancery of the Orders of Knighthood, St James's Palace, London SW1A 1BH

ORDER OF THE COMPANIONS OF HONOUR (1917)

CH

Ribbon, Carmine, with gold edges

This order consists of one class only and carries with it no title. The number of awards is limited to 65 (excluding honorary members).

Anthony, Rt. Hon. John, 1981
Attenborough, Sir David, 1995
Baker, Dame Janet, 1993
Baker of Dorking, Lord, 1992
Birtwistle, Sir Harrison, 2000
Brenner, Sydney, 1986
Brook, Peter, 1998
Brooke of Sutton Mandeville, Lord, 1992
Campbell, Rt. Hon. Sir Menzies, 2013
Carrington, Lord, 1983
Clarke, Rt. Hon. Kenneth, 2014
Coe, Lord, 2012
De Chastelain, Gen. John, 1999
Dench, Dame Judi, 2005
Fraser, Rt. Hon. Malcolm, 1977
Hannay of Chiswick, Lord, 2003
Hawking, Prof. Stephen, 1989
Healey, Lord, 1979
Heseltine, Lord, 1997
Higgs, Prof. Peter, 2012
Hockney, David, 1997
Hodgkin, Sir Howard, 2002
Howard, Sir Michael, 2002
Howard of Lympne, Lord, 2011
Howe of Aberavon, Lord, 1996
Hurd of Westwell, Lord, 1995
King of Bridgwater, Lord, 1992
Lovelock, Prof. James, 2002
McKellen, Sir Ian Murray, 2008
McKenzie, Prof. Dan Peter, 2003
Major, Rt. Hon. Sir John, 1998
Maxwell Davies, Sir Peter, 2013
O'Neill of Bengarve, Lady, 2013
Owen, Lord, 1994
Patten of Barnes, Lord, 1997
Riley, Bridget, 1998
Rogers of Riverside, Lord, 2008
Serota, Sir Nicholas, 2013
Smith, Dame Margaret (Maggie), 2014
Somare, Rt. Hon. Sir Michael, 1978
Strathclyde, Lord, 2013
Tebbit, Lord, 1987
Young, Rt. Hon. Sir George, 2012

Honorary Members, Lee Kuan Yew, 1970; Prof. Amartya Sen, 2000; Bernard Haitink, 2002
Secretary and Registrar, Secretary of the Central Chancery of the Orders of Knighthood

THE DISTINGUISHED SERVICE ORDER (1886)

DSO

Ribbon, Red, with blue edges

Bestowed in recognition of especial services in action of commissioned officers in the Navy, Army and Royal Air Force and (since 1942) Mercantile Marine. The members are Companions only. A bar may be awarded for any additional act of service.

THE IMPERIAL SERVICE ORDER (1902)

ISO

Ribbon, Crimson, with blue centre

Appointment as companion of this order is open to members of the civil services whose eligibility is determined by the grade they hold. The order consists of the sovereign and companions to a number not exceeding 1,900, of whom 1,300 may belong to the home civil services and 600 to overseas civil services. The then prime minister announced in March 1993 that he would make no further recommendations for appointments to the order.

Secretary, Head of the Home Civil Service
Registrar, Secretary of the Central Chancery of the Orders of Knighthood

THE ROYAL VICTORIAN CHAIN (1902)

It confers no precedence on its holders

HM THE QUEEN

HM The King of Thailand, 1960
HM The Queen of Denmark, 1974
HM The King of Sweden, 1975
HRH Princess Beatrix of the Netherlands, 1982
Gen. Antonio Eanes, 1985
HM King Juan Carlos of Spain, 1986
Dr Richard von Weizsäcker, 1992
HM The King of Norway, 1994
Earl of Airlie, 1997
Rt. Revd and Rt. Hon. Lord Carey of Clifton, 2002
HRH Prince Philip, Duke of Edinburgh, 2007
HM The King of Saudi Arabia, 2007
HM The Sultan of Oman, 2010
Rt. Revd and Rt. Hon. Lord Williams of Oystermouth, 2012

BARONETAGE AND KNIGHTAGE

BARONETS

Style, 'Sir' before forename and surname, followed by 'Bt'.
  Envelope, Sir F_ S_, Bt. *Letter (formal),* Dear Sir; *(social),* Dear Sir F_. *Spoken,* Sir F_
Wife's style, 'Lady' followed by surname
  Envelope, Lady S_. *Letter (formal),* Dear Madam; *(social),* Dear Lady S_. *Spoken,* Lady S_
Style of Baroness, 'Dame' before forename and surname, followed by 'Btss.' (*see also* Dames)

There are five different creations of baronetcies: Baronets of England (creations dating from 1611); Baronets of Ireland (creations dating from 1619); Baronets of Scotland or Nova Scotia (creations dating from 1625); Baronets of Great Britain (creations after the Act of Union 1707 which combined the kingdoms of England and Scotland); and Baronets of the United Kingdom (creations after the union of Great Britain and Ireland in 1801).

Badge of Baronets of the United Kingdom   *Badge of Baronets of Nova Scotia*

Badge of Ulster

The patent of creation limits the destination of a baronetcy, usually to male descendants of the first baronet, although special remainders allow the baronetcy to pass, if the male issue of sons fail, to the male issue of daughters of the first baronet. In the case of baronetcies of Scotland or Nova Scotia, a special remainder of 'heirs male and of tailzie' allows the baronetcy to descend to heirs general, including women. There are four existing Scottish baronets with such a remainder.

The Official Roll of the Baronetage is kept at the Crown Office and maintained by the Registrar and Assistant Registrar of the Baronetage. Anyone who considers that he or she is entitled to be entered on the roll may apply through the Crown Office to prove their succession. Every person succeeding to a baronetcy must exhibit proofs of succession to the Lord Chancellor. A person whose name is not entered on the official roll will not be addressed or mentioned by the title of baronet or baronetess in any official document, nor will he or she be accorded precedence as a baronet or baronetess.

BARONETCY EXTINCT SINCE THE LAST EDITION
Reade (cr. 1661); Speelman (cr. 1686); Staples (cr. 1628); Thomas (cr. 1918)

OFFICIAL ROLL OF THE BARONETAGE, Crown Office, House of Lords, London SW1A 0PW T 020-7219 2632
Registrar, Ian Denyer, MVO
Assistant Registrar, Grant Bavister

KNIGHTS

Style, 'Sir' before forename and surname, followed by appropriate post-nominal initials if a Knight Grand Cross or Knight Commander
  Envelope, Sir F_ S_. *Letter (formal),* Dear Sir; *(social),* Dear Sir F_. *Spoken,* Sir F_
Wife's style, 'Lady' followed by surname
  Envelope, Lady S_. *Letter (formal),* Dear Madam; *(social),* Dear Lady S_. *Spoken,* Lady S_

The prefix 'Sir' is not used by knights who are clerics of the Church of England, who do not receive the accolade. Their wives are entitled to precedence as the wife of a knight but not to the style of 'Lady'.

ORDERS OF KNIGHTHOOD
Knight Grand Cross and Knight Commander are the higher classes of the Orders of Chivalry (*see* Orders of Chivalry). Honorary knighthoods of these orders may be conferred on men who are citizens of countries of which the Queen is not head of state. As a rule, the prefix 'Sir' is not used by honorary knights.

KNIGHTS BACHELOR

The Knights Bachelor do not constitute a royal order, but comprise the surviving representation of the ancient state orders of knighthood. The Register of Knights Bachelor, instituted by James I in the 17th century, lapsed, and in 1908 a voluntary association under the title of the Society of Knights (now the Imperial Society of Knights Bachelor) was formed with the primary objectives of continuing the various registers dating from 1257 and obtaining the uniform registration of every created Knight Bachelor. In 1926 a design for a badge to be worn by Knights Bachelor was approved and adopted; in 1974 a neck badge and miniature were added.

THE IMPERIAL SOCIETY OF KNIGHTS BACHELOR, Magnesia House, 56 Playhouse Yard, London EC4V 5EX
Knight Principal, Sir Colin Berry
Prelate, Rt. Revd and Rt. Hon. Bishop of London
Registrar, Sir Gavyn Arthur
Hon. Treasurer, Sir Jeremy Elwes, CBE
Clerk to the Council, Col. Simon Doughty

LIST OF BARONETS AND KNIGHTS *as at 31 August 2014*

†		Not registered on the Official Roll of the Baronetage at the time of going to press
( )		The date of creation of the baronetcy is given in parentheses
I		Baronet of Ireland
NS		Baronet of Nova Scotia
S		Baronet of Scotland

A full entry in italic type indicates that the recipient of a knighthood died during the year in which the honour was conferred. The name is included for purposes of record. Peers are not included in this list.

Aaronson, Sir Michael John, Kt., CBE

Abbott, *Adm.* Sir Peter Charles, GBE, KCB

†Abdy, Sir Robert Etienne Eric, Bt. (1850)

Abed, *Dr* Sir Fazle Hasan, KCMG

Acher, Sir Gerald, Kt., CBE, LVO

Ackroyd, Sir Timothy Robert Whyte, Bt. (1956)

Acland, Sir Antony Arthur, KG, GCMG, GCVO

Acland, *Lt.-Col.* Sir (Christopher) Guy (Dyke), Bt. (1890), MVO

†Acland, Sir Dominic Dyke, Bt. (1678)

Adam, Sir Kenneth Hugo, Kt., OBE

Adams, Sir Geoffrey Doyne, KCMG

Adams, Sir William James, KCMG

Adsetts, Sir William Norman, Kt., OBE

Adye, Sir John Anthony, KCMG

Aga Khan IV, HH Prince Karim, KBE

Agnew, Sir Crispin Hamlyn, Bt. (S. 1629)

Agnew, Sir George Anthony, Bt. (1895)

Agnew, Sir Rudolph Ion Joseph, Kt.

Agnew-Somerville, Sir James Lockett Charles, Bt. (1957)

Ah Koy, Sir James Michael, KBE

Aikens, *Rt. Hon.* Sir Richard John Pearson, Kt.

Ainslie, Sir Charles Benedict, Kt., CBE

†Ainsworth, Sir Anthony Thomas Hugh, Bt. (1917)

Aird, Sir (George) John, Bt. (1901)

Airy, *Maj.-Gen.* Sir Christopher John, KCVO, CBE

Aitchison, Sir Charles Walter de Lancey, Bt. (1938)

Ajegbo, Sir Keith Onyema, Kt., OBE

Akenhead, *Hon.* Sir Robert, Kt.

Akers-Jones, Sir David, KBE, CMG

Alberti, *Prof.* Sir Kurt George Matthew Mayer, Kt.

Albu, Sir George, Bt. (1912)

Alcock, *Air Chief Marshal* Sir (Robert James) Michael, GCB, KBE

Aldous, *Rt. Hon.* Sir William, Kt.

Aldridge, Sir Rodney Malcolm, Kt., OBE

Alexander, Sir Douglas, Bt. (1921)

Alexander, Sir Richard, Bt. (1945)

Allan, Sir Alexander Claud Stuart, KCB

Allen, Sir Errol Newton Fitzrose, KCMG

Allen, *Prof.* Sir Geoffrey, Kt., PHD, FRS

Allen, Sir John Derek, Kt., CBE

Allen, Sir Mark John Spurgeon, Kt., CMG

Allen, *Hon.* Sir Peter Austin Philip Jermyn, Kt.

Allen, Sir Thomas Boaz, Kt., CBE

Allen, *Hon.* Sir William Clifford, KCMG

Allen, Sir William Guilford, Kt.

Alleyne, Sir George Allanmoore Ogarren, Kt.

Alleyne, *Revd* John Olpherts Campbell, Bt. (1769)

Allinson, Sir (Walter) Leonard, KCVO, CMG

Alliott, *Hon.* Sir John Downes, Kt.

Allison, *Air Chief Marshal* Sir John Shakespeare, KCB, CBE

Amet, *Hon.* Sir Arnold Karibone, Kt.

Amory, Sir Ian Heathcoat, Bt. (1874)

Anderson, *Dr* Sir James Iain Walker, Kt., CBE

Anderson, Sir John Anthony, KBE

Anderson, Sir Leith Reinsford Steven, Kt., CBE

Anderson, *Prof.* Sir Roy Malcolm, Kt.

Anderson, *Air Marshal* Sir Timothy Michael, KCB, DSO

Anderson, Sir (William) Eric Kinloch, KT

Anderton, Sir (Cyril) James, Kt., CBE, QPM

Andrew, Sir Robert John, KCB

Andrews, Sir Derek Henry, KCB, CBE

Andrews, Sir Ian Charles Franklin, Kt., CBE, TD

Annesley, Sir Hugh Norman, Kt., QPM

Anson, *Vice-Adm.* Sir Edward Rosebery, KCB

Anson, Sir John, KCB

Anson, *Rear-Adm.* Sir Peter, Bt. (1831), CB

Anstruther, Sir Sebastian Paten Campbell, Bt. (S. 1694 and S. 1700)

Anstruther-Gough-Calthorpe, Sir Euan Hamilton, Bt. (1929)

Antrobus, Sir Edward Philip, Bt. (1815)

Appleyard, Sir Leonard Vincent, KCMG

Appleyard, Sir Raymond Kenelm, KBE

Arbib, Sir Martyn, Kt.

Arbuthnot, Sir Keith Robert Charles, Bt. (1823)

Arbuthnot, Sir William Reierson, Bt. (1964)

Arbuthnott, *Prof.* Sir John Peebles, Kt., PHD, FRSE

†Archdale, Sir Nicholas Edward, Bt. (1928)

Arculus, Sir Ronald, KCMG, KCVO

Arculus, Sir Thomas David Guy, Kt.

Armitage, *Air Chief Marshal* Sir Michael John, KCB, CBE

Armitt, Sir John Alexander, Kt., CBE

Armour, *Prof.* Sir James, Kt., CBE

Armstrong, Sir Christopher John Edmund Stuart, Bt. (1841), MBE

Armstrong, Sir Patrick John, Kt., CBE

Armstrong, Sir Richard, Kt., CBE

Armytage, Sir John Martin, Bt. (1738)

Arnold, *Hon.* Sir Richard David, Kt.

Arnold, Sir Thomas Richard, Kt.

Arnott, Sir Alexander John Maxwell, Bt. (1896)

†Arthur, Sir Benjamin Nathan, Bt. (1841)

Arthur, Sir Gavyn Farr, Kt.

Arthur, *Lt.-Gen.* Sir (John) Norman Stewart, KCB, CVO

Arthur, Sir Michael Anthony, KCMG

Arulkumaran, *Prof.* Sir Sabaratnam, Kt.

Asbridge, Sir Jonathan Elliott, Kt.

Ash, *Prof.* Sir Eric Albert, Kt., CBE, FRS, FRENG

Ashburnham, Sir James Fleetwood, Bt. (1661)

Ashmore, *Admiral of the Fleet* Sir Edward Beckwith, GCB, DSC

Ashworth, *Dr* Sir John Michael, Kt.

Aske, Sir Robert John Bingham, Bt. (1922)

Askew, Sir Bryan, Kt.

Asquith, *Hon.* Sir Dominic Anthony Gerard, KCMG

Astill, *Hon.* Sir Michael John, Kt.

Astley-Cooper, Sir Alexander Paston, Bt. (1821)

Astwood, *Hon.* Sir James Rufus, KBE

Atcherley, Sir Harold Winter, Kt.

Atiyah, Sir Michael Francis, Kt., OM, PHD, FRS

Atkins, *Rt. Hon.* Sir Robert James, Kt.

Atkinson, *Prof.* Sir Anthony Barnes, Kt.

Atkinson, Sir Frederick John, KCB

Atkinson, Sir John Alexander, KCB, DFC

Atkinson, Sir Robert, Kt., DSC, FRENG

Atkinson, Sir William Samuel, Kt.

Atopare, Sir Sailas, GCMG

Attenborough, Sir David Frederick, Kt., OM, CH, CVO, CBE, FRS

Aubrey-Fletcher, Sir Henry Egerton, Bt. (1782)

Audland, Sir Christopher John, KCMG

Augier, *Prof.* Sir Fitzroy Richard, Kt.

Auld, *Rt. Hon.* Sir Robin Ernest, Kt.

Austin, Sir Anthony Leonard, Bt. (1894)

Austin, *Air Marshal* Sir Roger Mark, KCB, AFC

Austen-Smith, *Air Marshal* Sir Roy David, KBE, CB, CVO, DFC

Avei, Sir Moi, KBE

Ayckbourn, Sir Alan, Kt., CBE

Aykroyd, Sir Henry Robert George, Bt. (1920)

Aykroyd, Sir James Alexander Frederic, Bt. (1929)

Aylmer, Sir Richard John, Bt. (I. 1622)
Aylward, *Prof.* Sir Mansel, Kt., CB
Aynsley-Green, *Prof.* Sir Albert, Kt.

Bacha, Sir Bhinod, Kt., CMG
Backhouse, Sir Alfred James Stott, Bt. (1901)
Bacon, Sir Nicholas Hickman Ponsonby, Bt., OBE (1611 and 1627), *Premier Baronet of England*
Baddeley, Sir John Wolsey Beresford, Bt. (1922)
Badge, Sir Peter Gilmour Noto, Kt.
Baer, Sir Jack Mervyn Frank, Kt.
Bagge, Sir (John) Jeremy Picton, Bt. (1867)
Bagnall, *Air Chief Marshal* Sir Anthony, GBE, KCB
Bai, Sir Brown, KBE
Bailey, Sir Alan Marshall, KCB
Bailey, Sir Brian Harry, Kt., OBE
Bailey, Sir John Bilsland, KCB
†Bailey, Sir John Richard, Bt. (1919)
Bailhache, Sir Philip Martin, Kt.
Baillie, Sir Adrian Louis, Bt. (1823)
Bain, *Prof.* Sir George Sayers, Kt.
Baird, Sir Charles William Stuart, Bt. (1809)
†Baird, Sir James Andrew Gardiner, Bt. (S. 1695)
Baird, *Air Marshal* Sir John Alexander, KBE
Baird, *Vice-Adm.* Sir Thomas Henry Eustace, KCB
Bairsto, *Air Marshal* Sir Peter Edward, KBE, CB
Baker, Sir Bryan William, Kt.
Baker, *Hon.* Sir Jeremy Russell, Kt.
Baker, *Prof.* Sir John Hamilton, Kt., QC
Baker, Sir John William, Kt., CBE
Baker, *Hon.* Sir Jonathan Leslie, Kt.
Baker, *Rt. Hon.* Sir (Thomas) Scott (Gillespie), Kt.
Balderstone, Sir James Schofield, Kt.
Baldry, Sir Antony Brian, Kt.
Baldwin, *Prof.* Sir Jack Edward, Kt., FRS
Ball, Sir Christopher John Elinger, Kt.
Ball, *Prof.* Sir John Macleod, Kt.
Ball, Sir Richard Bentley, Bt. (1911)
Ball, *Prof.* Sir Robert James, Kt., PHD
Ballantyne, *Dr* Sir Frederick Nathaniel, GCMG
Band, *Adm.* Sir Jonathon, GCB
Banham, Sir John Michael Middlecott, Kt.
Bannerman, Sir David Gordon, Bt. (S. 1682), OBE
Bannister, Sir Roger Gilbert, Kt., CBE, DM, FRCP
Barber, Sir Brendan, Kt.
Barber, Sir Michael Bayldon, Kt.
Barber, Sir (Thomas) David, Bt. (1960)
Barbour, *Very Revd* Robert Alexander Stewart, KCVO, MC
Barclay, Sir David Rowat, Kt.
Barclay, Sir Frederick Hugh, Kt.
Barclay, Sir Robert Colraine, Bt. (S. 1668)
Barder, Sir Brian Leon, KCMG
Baring, Sir John Francis, Bt. (1911)
Barker, Sir Colin, Kt.
Barker, *Hon.* Sir (Richard) Ian, Kt.

Barling, *Hon.* Sir Gerald Edward, Kt.
Barlow, Sir Christopher Hilaro, Bt. (1803)
Barlow, Sir Frank, Kt., CBE
Barlow, Sir James Alan, Bt. (1902)
Barlow, Sir John Kemp, Bt. (1907)
Barnes, *The Most Revd* Brian James, KBE
Barnes, Sir (James) David (Francis), Kt., CBE
Barnett, *Hon.* Sir Michael Lancelot Patrick, Kt.
Barnewall, Sir Reginald Robert, Bt. (I. 1623)
Baron, Sir Thomas, Kt., CBE
†Barran, Sir John Ruthven, Bt. (1895)
Barrett, Sir Stephen Jeremy, KCMG
Barrett-Lennard, Sir Peter John, Bt. (1801)
Barrington, Sir Benjamin, Bt. (1831)
Barrington, Sir Nicholas John, KCMG, CVO
Barrington-Ward, *Rt. Revd* Simon, KCMG
Barron, Sir Donald James, Kt.
Barron, *Rt. Hon.* Sir Kevin, Kt.
Barrons, *Gen.* Sir Richard, KCB, CBE, ADC
Barrow, Sir Anthony John Grenfell, Bt. (1835)
Barry, Sir (Lawrence) Edward (Anthony Tress), Bt. (1899)
Barter, Sir Peter Leslie Charles, Kt., OBE
Bartlett, Sir Andrew Alan, Bt. (1913)
Barttelot, *Col.* Sir Brian Walter de Stopham, Bt. (1875), OBE
Bates, Sir James Geoffrey, Bt. (1880)
Bates, Sir Richard Dawson Hoult, Bt. (1937)
Bateson, *Prof.* Sir Patrick, Kt.
Bather, Sir John Knollys, KCVO
Batho, Sir Peter Ghislain, Bt. (1928)
Bathurst, *Admiral of the Fleet* Sir (David) Benjamin, GCB
Battersby, *Prof.* Sir Alan Rushton, Kt., FRS
Battishill, Sir Anthony Michael William, GCB
Baulcombe, *Prof.* Sir David Charles, Kt., FRS
Baxendell, Sir Peter Brian, Kt., CBE, FRENG
Bayly, *Prof.* Sir Christopher Alan, Kt.
Bayne, Sir Nicholas Peter, KCMG
Baynes, Sir Christopher Rory, Bt. (1801)
Bazalgette, Sir Peter Lytton, Kt.
Bazley, Sir Thomas John Sebastian, Bt. (1869)
Beach, *Gen.* Sir (William Gerald) Hugh, GBE, KCB, MC
Beache, *Hon.* Sir Vincent Ian, KCMG
Beale, *Lt.-Gen.* Sir Peter John, KBE, FRCP
Beamish, Sir Adrian John, KCMG
Bean, *Dr* Sir Charles Richard, Kt.
Bean, *Hon.* Sir David Michael, Kt.
Bear, Sir Michael David, Kt.
Beatson, *Rt. Hon.* Sir Jack, Kt.
Beavis, *Air Chief Marshal* Sir Michael Gordon, KCB, CBE, AFC
Beck, Sir Edgar Philip, Kt.

Beckett, Sir Richard Gervase, Bt. (1921), QC
Beckwith, Sir John Lionel, Kt., CBE
Beddington, *Prof.* Sir John Rex, Kt., CMG
Beecham, Sir Robert Adrian, Bt. (1914)
Beetham, *Marshal of the Royal Air Force* Sir Michael James, GCB, CBE, DFC, AFC
Beevor, Sir Thomas Agnew, Bt. (1784)
Beith, *Rt. Hon.* Sir Alan James, Kt.
Beldam, *Rt. Hon.* Sir (Alexander) Roy (Asplan), Kt.
Belgrave, *HE* Sir Elliott Fitzroy, GCMG
Belich, Sir James, Kt.
Bell, Sir David Charles Maurice, Kt.
Bell, Sir David Robert, KCB
Bell, *Prof.* Sir John Irving, Kt.
Bell, Sir John Lowthian, Bt. (1885)
Bell, *Prof.* Sir Peter Robert Frank, Kt.
Bell, *Hon.* Sir Rodger, Kt.
Bellamy, *Hon.* Sir Christopher William, Kt.
Bellingham, Sir Anthony Edward Norman, Bt. (1796)
Bender, Sir Brian Geoffrey, KCB
Benn, Sir (James) Jonathan, Bt. (1914)
Bennett, *Air Vice-Marshal* Sir Erik Peter, KBE, CB
Bennett, *Hon.* Sir Hugh Peter Derwyn, Kt.
Bennett, *Gen.* Sir Phillip Harvey, KBE, DSO
Bennett, Sir Ronald Wilfrid Murdoch, Bt. (1929)
Benson, Sir Christopher John, Kt.
Beresford, Sir (Alexander) Paul, Kt.
Beresford-Peirse, Sir Henry Njers de la Poer, Bt. (1814)
Berghuser, *Hon.* Sir Eric, Kt., MBE
Beringer, *Prof.* Sir John Evelyn, Kt., CBE
Berman, Sir Franklin Delow, KCMG
Berners-Lee, Sir Timothy John, OM, KBE, FRS
Bernard, Sir Dallas Edmund, Bt. (1954)
Berney, Sir Julian Reedham Stuart, Bt. (1620)
Bernstein, Sir Howard, Kt.
Berridge, *Prof.* Sir Michael John, Kt., FRS
Berriman, Sir David, Kt.
Berry, *Prof.* Sir Colin Leonard, Kt., FRCPATH
Berry, *Prof.* Sir Michael Victor, Kt., FRS
Berthoud, Sir Martin Seymour, KCVO, CMG
Berwick, *Prof.* Sir George Thomas, Kt., CBE
Best-Shaw, Sir Thomas Joshua, Bt. (1665)
Bethel, Sir Baltron Benjamin, KCMG
Bethlehem, Sir Daniel, KCMG
Bett, Sir Michael, Kt., CBE
Bettison, Sir Norman George, Kt., QPM
Bevan, Sir James David, KCMG
Bevan, Sir Martyn Evan Evans, Bt. (1958)
Bevan, Sir Nicolas, Kt., CB
Bevan, Sir Timothy Hugh, Kt.
Beverley, *Lt.-Gen.* Sir Henry York La Roche, KCB, OBE, RM

Bibby, Sir Michael James, Bt. (1959)

Bickersteth, *Rt. Revd* John Monier, KCVO

Biddulph, Sir Ian D'Olier, Bt. (1664)

Biggam, Sir Robin Adair, Kt.

Bilas, Sir Angmai Simon, Kt., OBE

Bill, *Lt.-Gen.* Sir David Robert, KCB

Billière, *Gen.* Sir Peter Edgar de la Cour de la, KCB, KBE, DSO, MC

Bindman, Sir Geoffrey Lionel, Kt.

Bingham, *Hon.* Sir Eardley Max, Kt.

Birch, Sir John Allan, KCVO, CMG

Birch, Sir Roger, Kt., CBE, QPM

Bird, *Prof.* Sir Adrian Peter, Kt., CBE, FRS, FRSE

Bird, Sir Richard Geoffrey Chapman, Bt. (1922)

Birkett, Sir Peter, Kt.

Birkin, Sir John Christian William, Bt. (1905)

Birkin, Sir (John) Derek, Kt., TD

Birkmyre, Sir James, Bt. (1921)

Birrell, Sir James Drake, Kt.

Birss, *Hon.* Sir Colin Ian, Kt.

Birt, Sir Michael, Kt.

Birtwistle, Sir Harrison, Kt., CH

Bischoff, Sir Winfried Franz Wilhelm, Kt.

Black, *Adm.* Sir (John) Jeremy, GBE, KCB, DSO

Black, Sir Robert David, Bt. (1922)

Blackburn, *Vice-Adm.* Sir David Anthony James, KCVO, CB

Blackburne, *Hon.* Sir William Anthony, Kt.

Blackett, Sir Hugh Francis, Bt. (1673)

Blackham, *Vice-Adm.* Sir Jeremy Joe, KCB

Blackman, Sir Frank Milton, KCVO, OBE

†Blair, Sir Patrick David Hunter, Bt. (1786)

Blair, *Hon.* Sir William James Lynton, Kt.

Blake, Sir Anthony Teilo Bruce, Bt. (I. 1622)

Blake, Sir Francis Michael, Bt. (1907)

Blake, *Hon.* Sir Nicholas John Gorrod, Kt.

Blake, Sir Peter Thomas, Kt., CBE

Blake, Sir Quentin Saxby, Kt., CBE

Blakemore, *Prof.* Sir Colin Brian, Kt., FRS

Blaker, Sir John, Bt. (1919)

Blakiston, Sir Ferguson Arthur James, Bt. (1763)

Blanch, Sir Malcolm, KCVO

Bland, Sir (Francis) Christopher (Buchan), Kt.

Bland, *Lt.-Col.* Sir Simon Claud Michael, KCVO

Blank, Sir Maurice Victor, Kt.

Blatherwick, Sir David Elliott Spiby, KCMG, OBE

Blelloch, Sir John Nial Henderson, KCB

Blennerhassett, Sir (Marmaduke) Adrian Francis William, Bt. (1809)

Blewitt, *Maj.* Sir Shane Gabriel Basil, GCVO

Blofeld, *Hon.* Sir John Christopher Calthorpe, Kt.

Blois, Sir Charles Nicholas Gervase, Bt. (1686)

Blom-Cooper, Sir Louis Jacques, Kt., QC

Blomefield, Sir Thomas Charles Peregrine, Bt. (1807)

Bundell, *Prof.* Sir Richard William, Kt., CBE, FBA

Bloom, *Prof.* Sir Stephen Robert, Kt

Bloomfield, Sir Kenneth Percy, KCB

Blundell, *Prof.* Sir Richard William, Kt., CBE, FBA

Blundell, Sir Thomas Leon, Kt., FRS

†Blunden, Sir Hubert Chisholm, Bt. (I. 1766)

Blunt, Sir David Richard Reginald Harvey, Bt. (1720)

Blyth, Sir Charles (Chay), Kt., CBE, BEM

Boardman, *Prof.* Sir John, Kt., FSA, FBA

Bodey, *Hon.* Sir David Roderick Lessiter, Kt.

Bodmer, Sir Walter Fred, Kt., PHD, FRS

Body, Sir Richard Bernard Frank Stewart, Kt.

Bogle, Sir Nigel, Kt.

Bogan, Sir Nagora, KBE

Boileau, Sir Nicolas Edmond George, Bt. (1838)

†Boles, Sir Richard Fortescue, Bt. (1922)

Bona, Sir Kina, KBE

Bonallack, Sir Michael Francis, Kt., OBE

Bond, Sir John Reginald Hartnell, Kt.

Bond, *Prof.* Sir Michael Richard, Kt., FRCPSYCH, FRCPGLAS, FRCSE

Bone, *Prof.* Sir (James) Drummond, Kt., FRSE

Bone, Sir Roger Bridgland, KCMG

Bonfield, Sir Peter Leahy, Kt., CBE, FRENG

Bonham, Sir George Martin Antony, Bt. (1852)

Bonington, Sir Christian John Storey, Kt., CVO, CBE

Bonsall, Sir Arthur Wilfred, KCMG, CBE

Bonsor, Sir Nicholas Cosmo, Bt. (1925)

Boord, Sir Nicolas John Charles, Bt. (1896)

Boorman, *Lt.-Gen.* Sir Derek, KCB

Booth, Sir Clive, Kt.

Booth, Sir Douglas Allen, Bt. (1916)

Booth, Sir Gordon, KCMG, CVO

Boothby, Sir Brooke Charles, Bt. (1660)

Bore, Sir Albert, Kt.

Boreel, Sir Stephan Gerard, Bt. (1645)

Borthwick, Sir Anthony Thomas, Bt. (1908)

Borysiewicz, *Prof.* Sir Leszek Krzysztof, Kt.

Bosher, Sir Robin, Kt.

Bossom, *Hon.* Sir Clive, Bt. (1953)

Boswell, *Lt.-Gen.* Sir Alexander Crawford Simpson, KCB, CBE

Botham, Sir Ian Terence, Kt., OBE

Bottomley, Sir Peter James, Kt.

Bottoms, *Prof.* Sir Anthony Edward, Kt.

Boughey, Sir John George Fletcher, Bt. (1798)

Boulton, Sir Clifford John, GCB

†Boulton, Sir John Gibson, Bt. (1944)

Bouraga, Sir Phillip, KBE

Bourn, Sir John Bryant, KCB

Bowater, Sir Euan David Vansittart, Bt. (1939)

†Bowater, Sir Michael Patrick, Bt. (1914)

Bowden, Sir Andrew, Kt., MBE

Bowden, Sir Nicholas Richard, Bt. (1915)

Bowen, Sir Barry Manfield, KCMG

Bowen, Sir Geoffrey Fraser, Kt.

Bowen, Sir George Edward Michael, Bt. (1921)

Bowes Lyon, Sir Simon Alexander, KCVO

Bowlby, Sir Richard Peregrine Longstaff, Bt. (1923)

Bowman, Sir Edwin Geoffrey, KCB

Bowman, Sir Jeffery Haverstock, Kt.

Bowman-Shaw, Sir (George) Neville, Kt.

Bowness, Sir Alan, Kt., CBE

Bowyer-Smyth, Sir Thomas Weyland, Bt. (1661)

Boyce, Sir Graham Hugh, KCMG

Boyce, Sir Robert Charles Leslie, Bt. (1952)

Boyd, Sir Alexander Walter, Bt. (1916)

Boyd, Sir John Dixon Iklé, KCMG

Boyd, Sir Michael, Kt.

Boyd, *Prof.* Sir Robert David Hugh, Kt.

Boyd-Carpenter, Sir (Marsom) Henry, KCVO

Boyd-Carpenter, *Lt.-Gen. Hon.* Sir Thomas Patrick John, KBE

Boyle, *Prof.* Sir Roger Michael, Kt., CBE

Boyle, Sir Stephen Gurney, Bt. (1904)

Bracewell-Smith, Sir Charles, Bt. (1947)

Bradbeer, Sir John Derek Richardson, Kt., OBE, TD

Bradfield, *Dr* Sir John Richard Grenfell, Kt., CBE

Bradford, Sir Edward Alexander Slade, Bt. (1902)

Bradshaw, *Lt-Gen.* Sir Adrian, KCB, OBE

Brady, *Prof.* Sir John Michael, Kt., FRS

Brailsford, Sir David John, Kt., CBE

Braithwaite, Sir Rodric Quentin, GCMG

Bramley, *Prof.* Sir Paul Anthony, Kt.

Branagh, Sir Kenneth Charles, Kt.

Branson, Sir Richard Charles Nicholas, Kt.

Braithwaite, *Rt. Hon.* Sir Nicholas Alexander, Kt., OBE

Bratza, *Hon.* Sir Nicolas Dušan, Kt.

Breckenridge, *Prof.* Sir Alasdair Muir, Kt., CBE

Brennan, *Hon.* Sir (Francis) Gerard, KBE

Brenton, Sir Anthony Russell, KCMG

Brewer, Sir David William, Kt., CMG

Brierley, Sir Ronald Alfred, Kt.

Briggs, *Rt. Hon.* Sir Michael Townley Featherstone, Kt.

Brighouse, *Prof.* Sir Timothy Robert Peter, Kt.

Bright, Sir Graham Frank James, Kt.

Bright, Sir Keith, Kt.
Brigstocke, *Adm.* Sir John Richard, KCB
Brinckman, Sir Theodore George Roderick, Bt. (1831)
†Brisco, Sir Campbell Howard, Bt. (1782)
Briscoe, Sir Brian Anthony, Kt.
Briscoe, Sir John Geoffrey James, Bt. (1910)
Brittan, Sir Samuel, Kt.
Britton, Sir Paul John James, Kt., CB
†Broadbent, Sir Andrew George, Bt. (1893)
Broadbent, Sir Richard John, KCB
Brocklebank, Sir Aubrey Thomas, Bt. (1885)
Brodie, Sir Benjamin David Ross, Bt. (1834)
Bromhead, Sir John Desmond Gonville, Bt. (1806)
Bromley, Sir Michael Roger, KBE
Bromley, Sir Rupert Charles, Bt. (1757)
Bromley-Davenport, Sir William Arthur, KCVO
Brook, *Prof.* Sir Richard John, Kt. OBE
Brooke, Sir Alistair Weston, Bt. (1919)
Brooke, Sir Francis George Windham, Bt. (1903)
Brooke, *Rt. Hon.* Sir Henry, Kt.
Brooke, Sir Richard Christopher, Bt. (1662)
Brooke, Sir Rodney George, Kt., CBE
Brooking, Sir Trevor David, Kt., CBE
Brooksbank, Sir (Edward) Nicholas, Bt. (1919)
Broomfield, Sir Nigel Hugh Robert Allen, KCMG
†Broughton, Sir David Delves, Bt. (1661)
Broughton, Sir Martin Faulkner, Kt.
Broun, Sir Wayne Hercules, Bt. (S. 1686)
Brown, Sir (Austen) Patrick, KCB
Brown, *Adm.* Sir Brian Thomas, KCB, CBE
Brown, Sir David, Kt.
Brown, *Hon.* Sir Douglas Dunlop, Kt.
Brown, Sir Ewan, Kt., CBE
Brown, Sir George Francis Richmond, Bt. (1863)
Brown, Sir Mervyn, KCMG, OBE
Brown, Sir Peter Randolph, Kt.
Brown, *Rt. Hon.* Sir Stephen, GBE
Brown, Sir Stephen David Reid, KCVO
Brownrigg, Sir Nicholas (Gawen), Bt. (1816)
Browse, *Prof.* Sir Norman Leslie, Kt., MD, FRCS
Bruce, Sir (Francis) Michael Ian, Bt. (S. 1628)
Bruce, *Rt. Hon.* Sir Malcolm Gray Bruce, Kt.
Bruce-Clifton, Sir Hervey Hamish Peter, Bt. (1804)
Bruce-Gardner, Sir Robert Henry, Bt. (1945)
Brunner, Sir Hugo Laurence Joseph, KCVO
Brunner, Sir John Henry Kilian, Bt. (1895)
Brunton, Sir Gordon Charles, Kt.

†Brunton, Sir James Lauder, Bt. (1908)
Bryant, *Air Chief Marshal* Sir Simon, KCB, CBE, ADC
Bubb, Sir Stephen John Limrick, Kt.
Buchan-Hepburn, Sir John Alastair Trant Kidd, Bt. (1815)
Buchanan, Sir Andrew George, Bt. (1878), KCVO
Buchanan, *Dr* Sir John Gordon St Clair, Kt.
Buchanan, Sir Robert Wilson (Robin), Kt.
Buchanan-Jardine, Sir John Christopher Rupert, Bt. (1885)
Buckland, Sir Ross, Kt.
Buckley, *Dr* Sir George William, Kt.
Buckley, Sir Michael Sidney, Kt.
Buckley, *Lt.-Cdr.* Sir (Peter) Richard, KCVO
Buckley, *Hon.* Sir Roger John, Kt.
Bucknall, *Lt.-Gen.* Sir James Jeffrey Corfield, KCB, CBE
Buckworth-Herne-Soame, Sir Charles John, Bt. (1697)
Budd, Sir Alan Peter, GBE
Budd, Sir Colin Richard, KCMG
Bull, Sir George Jeffrey, Kt.
Bull, Sir Simeon George, Bt. (1922)
Bullock, Sir Stephen Michael, Kt.
Bultin, Sir Bato, Kt., MBE
Bunbury, Sir Michael William, Bt. (1681), KCVO
Bunyard, Sir Robert Sidney, Kt., CBE, QPM
Burbidge, Sir Peter Dudley, Bt. (1916)
Burden, Sir Anthony Thomas, Kt., QPM
Burdett, Sir Savile Aylmer, Bt. (1665)
Burgen, Sir Arnold Stanley Vincent, Kt., FRS
Burgess, *Gen.* Sir Edward Arthur, KCB, OBE
Burgess, Sir (Joseph) Stuart, Kt., CBE, PHD, FRSC
Burgess, *Prof.* Sir Robert George, Kt.
Burke, Sir James Stanley Gilbert, Bt. (I. 1797)
Burke, Sir (Thomas) Kerry, Kt.
Burn, *Prof.* Sir John, Kt.
Burnell-Nugent, *Vice-Adm.* Sir James Michael, KCB, CBE, ADC
Burnett, Sir Charles David, Bt., (1913)
Burnett, *Hon.* Sir Ian Duncan, Kt.
Burnett, Sir Walter John, Kt.
Burney, Sir Nigel Dennistoun, Bt. (1921)
Burns, *Dr* Sir Henry, Kt.
Burns, Sir (Robert) Andrew, KCMG
Burnton, *Rt. Hon.* Sir Stanley Jeffrey, Kt.
Burrell, Sir Charles Raymond, Bt. (1774)
Burridge, *Air Chief Marshal* Sir Brian Kevin, KCB, CBE, ADC
Burston, Sir Samuel Gerald Wood, Kt., OBE
Burt, Sir Peter Alexander, Kt.
Burton, Sir Carlisle Archibald, Kt., OBE
Burton, *Lt.-Gen.* Sir Edmund Fortescue Gerard, KBE
Burton, Sir Graham Stuart, KCMG

Burton, *Hon.* Sir Michael John, Kt.
Burton, Sir Michael St Edmund, KCVO, CMG
Butler, *Hon.* Sir Arlington Griffith, KCMG
Butler, *Dr* Sir David Edgeworth, Kt., CBE
Butler, Sir Percy James, Kt., CBE
†Butler, Sir Reginald Richard Michael, Bt. (1922)
Butler, Sir Richard Pierce, Bt. (I. 1628)
Butterfield, *Hon.* Sir Alexander Neil Logie, Kt.
Butterfill, Sir John Valentine, Kt.
†Buxton, Sir Crispin Charles Gerard, Bt. (1840)
Buxton, *Rt. Hon.* Sir Richard Joseph, Kt.
Buzzard, Sir Anthony Farquhar, Bt. (1929)
Byatt, Sir Ian Charles Rayner, Kt.
Byford, Sir Lawrence, Kt., CBE, QPM
Byron, *Rt. Hon.* Sir Charles Michael Dennis, Kt.

†Cable-Alexander, Sir Patrick Desmond William, Bt. (1809)
Cadbury, Sir (George) Adrian (Hayhurst), Kt.
Cadbury, Sir (Nicholas) Dominic, Kt.
Cadogan, *Prof.* Sir John Ivan George, Kt., CBE, FRS, FRSE
Cahn, Sir Albert Jonas, Bt. (1934)
Cahn, Sir Andrew Thomas, KCMG
Caine, Sir Michael (Maurice Micklewhite), Kt., CBE
Caines, Sir John, KCB
Cairns, *Very Revd* John Ballantyne, KCVO
Caldwell, Sir Edward George, KCB
Callaghan, Sir William Henry, Kt.
Callan, Sir Ivan Roy, KCVO, CMG
Callman, *His Hon.* Sir Clive Vernon, Kt.
Calman, *Prof.* Sir Kenneth Charles, KCB, MD, FRCP, FRCS, FRSE
Calne, *Prof.* Sir Roy Yorke, Kt., FRS
Calvert-Smith, Sir David, Kt., QC
Cameron, Sir Hugh Roy Graham, Kt., QPM
Campbell, *Prof.* Sir Colin Murray, Kt.
Campbell, Sir Ian Tofts, Kt., CBE, VRD
Campbell, Sir Ilay Mark, Bt. (1808)
Campbell, Sir James Alexander Moffat Bain, Bt. (S. 1668)
Campbell, Sir Lachlan Philip Kemeys, Bt. (1815)
Campbell, Sir Roderick Duncan Hamilton, Bt. (1831)
Campbell, Sir Robin Auchinbreck, Bt. (S. 1628)
Campbell, *Rt. Hon.* Sir Walter Menzies, Kt., CH, CBE, QC
Campbell, *Rt. Hon.* Sir William Anthony, Kt.
Campbell-Orde, Sir John Alexander, Bt. (1790)
Cannadine, *Prof.* Sir David Nicholas, Kt.
Capewell, *Lt-Gen.* Sir David Andrew, KCB, OBE, RM
†Carden, Sir Christopher Robert, Bt. (1887)

†Carden, Sir John Craven, Bt. (I. 1787)
Carew, Sir Rivers Verain, Bt. (1661)
Carey, Sir de Vic Graham, Kt.
Carleton-Smith, *Maj.-Gen.* Sir Michael Edward, Kt., CBE
Carlisle, Sir James Beethoven, GCMG
Carlisle, Sir John Michael, Kt.
Carlisle, Sir Kenneth Melville, Kt.
Carnegie, Sir Roderick Howard, Kt.
Carnwath, *Rt. Hon.* Sir Robert John Anderson, Kt., CVO
Carr, Sir (Albert) Raymond (Maillard), Kt.
Carr, *Very Revd Dr* Arthur Wesley, KCVO
Carr, Sir Peter Derek, Kt., CBE
Carr, Sir Roger Martyn, Kt.
Carrick, *Hon.* Sir John Leslie, KCMG
Carrick, Sir Roger John, KCMG, LVO
Carruthers, Sir Ian James, Kt., OBE
Carsberg, *Prof.* Sir Bryan Victor, Kt.
Carter, Sir Andrew Nicholas, Kt., OBE
Carter, Sir David Anthony, Kt.
Carter, *Prof.* Sir David Craig, Kt., FRCSE, FRCSGLAS, FRCPE
Carter, Sir John Alexander, Kt.
Carter, Sir John Gordon Thomas, Kt.
Carter, *Lt-Gen.* Sir Nicholas Patrick, KCB, CBE, DSO
Carter, Sir Philip David, Kt., CBE
Cartledge, Sir Bryan George, KCMG
Caruna, *Hon.* Sir Peter Richard, KCMG, QC
†Cary, Sir Nicholas Robert Hugh, Bt. (1955)
Cash, Sir Andrew John, Kt., OBE
Cash, Sir William Nigel Paul, Kt.
Cass, Sir Geoffrey Arthur, Kt.
Cassel, Sir Timothy Felix Harold, Bt. (1920)
Cassels, Sir John Seton, Kt., CB
Cassels, *Adm.* Sir Simon Alastair Cassillis, KCB, CB
Cassidi, *Adm.* Sir (Arthur) Desmond, GCB
Castell, Sir William Martin, Kt.
Castledine, *Prof.* Sir George, Kt.
Catherwood, Sir (Henry) Frederick (Ross), Kt.
Catto, *Prof.* Sir Graeme Robertson Dawson, Kt.
Cave, Sir John Charles, Bt. (1896)
Cave-Browne-Cave, Sir John Robert Charles, Bt. (1641)
Cayley, Sir Digby William David, Bt. (1661)
Cazalet, *Hon.* Sir Edward Stephen, Kt.
Cazalet, Sir Peter Grenville, Kt.
Cecil, *Rear-Adm.* Sir (Oswald) Nigel Amherst, KBE, CB
Chadwick, *Rt. Hon.* Sir John Murray, Kt.
Chadwick, Sir Joshua Kenneth Burton, Bt. (1935)
Chadwick, *Revd Prof.* (William) Owen, OM, KBE, FBA
Chadwyck-Healey, Sir Charles Edward, Bt. (1919)
Chakrabarti, Sir Sumantra, KCB
Chalmers, Sir Iain Geoffrey, Kt.
Chalmers, Sir Neil Robert, Kt.
Chalstrey, Sir (Leonard) John, Kt., MD, FRCS

Chan, *Rt. Hon.* Sir Julius, GCMG, KBE
Chan, Sir Thomas Kok, Kt., OBE
Chance, Sir (George) Jeremy ffolliott, Bt. (1900)
Chandler, Sir Colin Michael, Kt.
Chantler, *Prof.* Sir Cyril, Kt., MD, FRCP
Chaplin, Sir Malcolm Hilbery, Kt., CBE
Chapman, Sir David Robert Macgowan, Bt. (1958)
Chapman, Sir Frank, Kt.
Chapman, Sir George Alan, Kt.
Chapman, Sir Sydney Brookes, Kt.
Chapple, *Field Marshal* Sir John Lyon, GCB, CBE
Charles, *Hon.* Sir Arthur William Hessin, Kt.
Charlton, Sir Robert (Bobby), Kt., CBE
Charnley, Sir (William) John, Kt., CB, FRENG
Chartres, *Rt. Revd and Rt. Hon.* Richard John Carew, KCVO
†Chaytor, Sir Bruce Gordon, Bt. (1831)
Checketts, *Sqn. Ldr.* Sir David John, KCVO
Checkland, Sir Michael, Kt.
Cheshire, Sir Ian Michael, Kt.
Cheshire, *Air Chief Marshal* Sir John Anthony, KBE, CB
Chessells, Sir Arthur David (Tim), Kt.
†Chetwynd, Sir Peter James Talbot, Bt. (1795)
Cheyne, Sir Patrick John Lister, Bt. (1908)
Chichester, Sir James Henry Edward, Bt. (1641)
Chichester-Clark, Sir Robin, Kt.
Chilcot, *Rt. Hon.* Sir John Anthony, GCB
Child, Sir (Coles John) Jeremy, Bt. (1919)
Chilwell, *Hon.* Sir Muir Fitzherbert, Kt.
Chinn, Sir Trevor Edwin, Kt., CVO
†Chinubhai, Sir Prashat, Bt. (1913)
Chipperfield, *Prof.* Sir David Alan, Kt., CBE
Chipperfield, Sir Geoffrey Howes, KCB
Chisholm, Sir John Alexander Raymond, Kt., FRENG
†Chitty, Sir Andrew Edward Willes, Bt. (1924)
Cholmeley, Sir Hugh John Frederick Sebastian, Bt. (1806)
Chow, Sir Chung Kong, Kt.
Chow, Sir Henry Francis, Kt., OBE
Christopher, Sir Duncan Robin Carmichael, KBE, CMG
Chung, Sir Sze-yuen, GBE, FRENG
Clark, Sir Francis Drake, Bt. (1886)
Clark, Sir John Arnold, Kt.
Clark, Sir Jonathan George, Bt. (1917)
Clark, Sir Terence Joseph, KBE, CMG, CVO
Clark, Sir Timothy Charles, KBE
Clarke, Sir (Charles Mansfield) Tobias, Bt. (1831)
Clarke, *Hon.* Sir Christopher Simon Courtenay Stephenson, Kt.
Clarke, *Hon.* Sir David Clive, Kt.
Clarke, Sir Jonathan Dennis, Kt.

Clarke, Sir Paul Robert Virgo, KCVO
Clarke, Sir Robert Cyril, Kt.
†Clarke, Sir Rupert Grant Alexander, Bt. (1882)
Clay, Sir Edward, KCMG
Clay, Sir Richard Henry, Bt. (1841)
Clayton, Sir David Robert, Bt. (1732)
Cleaver, Sir Anthony Brian, Kt.
Clementi, Sir David Cecil, Kt.
Clerk, Sir Robert Maxwell, Bt. (S. 1679), OBE
Clerke, Sir Francis Ludlow Longueville, Bt. (1660)
Clifford, Sir Roger Joseph, Bt. (1887)
Clifford, Sir Timothy Peter Plint, Kt.
Coates, Sir Anthony Robert Milnes, Bt. (1911)
Coates, Sir David Frederick Charlton, Bt. (1921)
Coats, Sir Alastair Francis Stuart, Bt. (1905)
Cobb, *Hon.* Sir Stephen William Scott, Kt.
Cochrane, Sir (Henry) Marc (Sursock), Bt. (1903)
Cockburn, Sir John Elliot, Bt. (S. 1671)
Cockburn-Campbell, Sir Alexander Thomas, Bt. (1821)
Cockell, Sir Merrick, Kt.
Cockshaw, Sir Alan, Kt., FRENG
†Codrington, Sir Christopher George Wayne, Bt. (1876)
Codrington, Sir Giles Peter, Bt. (1721)
Codron, Sir Michael Victor, Kt., CBE
Coghill, Sir Patrick Kendal Farley, Bt. (1778)
Coghlin, *Rt. Hon.* Sir Patrick, Kt.
Cohen, Sir Ivor Harold, Kt., CBE, TD
Cohen, *Prof.* Sir Philip, Kt., PHD, FRS
Cohen, Sir Ronald, Kt.
Cole, Sir (Robert) William, Kt.
Coleman, Sir Robert John, KCMG
Coleridge, *Hon.* Sir Paul James Duke, Kt.
Coles, Sir (Arthur) John, GCMG
Colfox, Sir Philip John, Bt. (1939)
Collas, Sir Richard John, Kt.
Collett, Sir Ian Seymour, Bt. (1934)
Collier, Sir Paul, Kt., CBE
Collins, Sir Alan Stanley, KCVO, CMG
Collins, *Hon.* Sir Andrew David, Kt.
Collins, Sir Bryan Thomas Alfred, Kt., OBE, QFSM
Collins, Sir John Alexander, Kt
Collins, Sir Kenneth Darlingston, Kt.
Collins, *Prof.* Sir Rory Edwards, Kt.
Collyear, Sir John Gowen, Kt.
Colman, *Hon.* Sir Anthony David, Kt.
Colman, Sir Michael Jeremiah, Bt. (1907)
Colman, Sir Timothy, KG
Colquhoun of Luss, Sir Malcolm Rory, Bt. (1786)
Colt, Sir Edward William Dutton, Bt. (1694)
Colthurst, Sir Charles St John, Bt. (I. 1744)
Conant, Sir John Ernest Michael, Bt. (1954)
Conner, *Rt. Revd* David John, KCVO
Connery, Sir Sean, Kt.

Connor, Sir William Joseph, Kt.

Conran, Sir Terence Orby, Kt.

Cons, *Hon.* Sir Derek, Kt.

Constantinou, Sir Theophilus George, Kt., CBE

Conway, *Prof.* Sir Gordon Richard, KCMG, FRS

Cook, Sir Christopher Wymondham Rayner Herbert, Bt. (1886)

Cook, *Prof.* Sir Peter Frederic Chester, Kt.

Cooke, *Col.* Sir David William Perceval, Bt. (1661)

Cooke, *Hon.* Sir Jeremy Lionel, Kt.

Cooke, *Prof.* Sir Ronald Urwick, Kt.

Cooksey, Sir David James Scott, GBE

Cooper, *Prof.* Sir Cary Lynn, Kt., CBE

Cooper, *Gen.* Sir George Leslie Conroy, GCB, MC

Cooper, Sir Richard Adrian, Bt. (1905)

Cooper, Sir Robert Francis, KCMG, MVO

Cooper, *Maj.-Gen.* Sir Simon Christie, GCVO

Cooper, Sir William Daniel Charles, Bt. (1863)

Coote, Sir Christopher John, Bt. (I. 1621), *Premier Baronet of Ireland*

Copisarow, Sir Alcon Charles, Kt.

Corbett, *Maj.-Gen.* Sir Robert John Swan, KCVO, CB

Cordy-Simpson, *Lt.-Gen.* Sir Roderick Alexander, KBE, CB

Corfield, Sir Kenneth George, Kt., FRENG

Corness, Sir Colin Ross, Kt.

Cortazzi, Sir (Henry Arthur) Hugh, GCMG

Cory, Sir (Clinton Charles) Donald, Bt. (1919)

Cory-Wright, Sir Richard Michael, Bt. (1903)

Cossons, Sir Neil, Kt., OBE

Cotter, Sir Patrick Laurence Delaval, Bt. (I. 1763)

Cotterell, Sir John Henry Geers, Bt. (1805)

†Cotts, Sir Richard Crichton Mitchell, Bt. (1921)

Coulson, *Hon.* Sir Peter David William, Kt.

Couper, Sir James George, Bt. (1841)

Courtenay, Sir Thomas Daniel, Kt.

Cousins, *Air Chief Marshal* Sir David, KCB, AFC

Coville, *Air Marshal* Sir Christopher Charles Cotton, KCB

Cowan, *Gen.* Sir Samuel, KCB, CBE

Coward, *Lt-Gen.* Sir Gary Robert, KBE, CB, OBE

Coward, *Vice-Adm.* Sir John Francis, KCB, DSO

Cowper-Coles, Sir Sherard Louis, KCMG, LVO

Cox, Sir Alan George, Kt., CBE

Cox, *Prof.* Sir David Roxbee, Kt.

Cox, Sir George Edwin, Kt.

Craft, *Prof.* Sir Alan William, Kt.

Cragnolini, Sir Luciano, Kt.

Craig, Sir (Albert) James (Macqueen), GCMG

Craig-Cooper, Sir (Frederick Howard) Michael, Kt., CBE, TD

Crane, *Prof.* Sir Peter Robert, Kt.

Cranston, *Hon.* Sir Ross Frederick, Kt.

Craufurd, Sir Robert James, Bt. (1781)

Craven, Sir John Anthony, Kt.

Craven, Sir Philip Lee, Kt., MBE

Crawford, *Prof.* Sir Frederick William, Kt., FRENG

Crawford, Sir Robert William Kenneth, Kt. CBE

Crawley-Boevey, Sir Thomas Michael Blake, Bt. (1784)

Cresswell, *Hon.* Sir Peter John, Kt.

Crew, Sir (Michael) Edward, Kt., QPM

Crewe, *Prof.* Sir Ivor Martin, Kt.

Crisp, Sir John Charles, Bt. (1913)

Critchett, Sir Charles George Montague, Bt. (1908)

Crittin, *Hon.* Sir John Luke, KBE

Croft, Sir Owen Glendower, Bt. (1671)

Croft, Sir Thomas Stephen Hutton, Bt. (1818)

†Crofton, Sir Hugh Denis, Bt. (1801)

†Crofton, Sir Julian Malby, Bt. (1838)

Crombie, Sir Alexander, Kt.

Crompton, Sir Dan, Kt., CBE, QPM

Cropper, Sir James Anthony, KCVO

Crossley, Sir Sloan Nicholas, Bt. (1909)

Crowe, Sir Brian Lee, KCMG

Cruickshank, Sir Donald Gordon, Kt.

Cruthers, Sir James Winter, Kt.

Cubbon, Sir Brian Crossland, GCB

Cubie, *Dr* Sir Andrew, Kt., CBE

Cubitt, Sir Hugh Guy, Kt., CBE

Cubitt, *Maj.-Gen.* Sir William George, KCVO, CBE

Cullen, Sir (Edward) John, Kt., FRENG

Culme-Seymour, Sir Michael Patrick, Bt. (1809)

Culpin, Sir Robert Paul, Kt.

Cummins, Sir Michael John Austin, Kt.

Cunliffe, *Prof.* Sir Barrington, Kt., CBE

Cunliffe, Sir David Ellis, Bt. (1759)

Cunliffe, Sir Jonathan Stephen, Kt., CB

Cunliffe-Owen, Sir Hugo Dudley, Bt. (1920)

Cunningham, *Lt.-Gen.* Sir Hugh Patrick, KBE

Cunningham, *Prof.* Sir John, KCVO

Cunningham, Sir Roger Keith, Kt., CBE

Cunningham, Sir Thomas Anthony, Kt.

Cunynghame, Sir Andrew David Francis, Bt. (S. 1702)

†Currie, Sir Donald Scott, Bt. (1847)

Curtain, Sir Michael, KBE

Curtis, Sir Barry John, Kt.

Curtis, *Hon.* Sir Richard Herbert, Kt.

Curtis, Sir Edward Philip, Bt. (1802)

Cuschieri, *Prof.* Sir Alfred, Kt.

Dain, Sir David John Michael, KCVO

Dales, Sir Richard Nigel, KCVO

Dalrymple-Hay, Sir Malcolm John Robert, Bt. (1798)

†Dalrymple-White, Sir Jan Hew, Bt. (1926)

Dalton, Sir David Nigel, Kt.

Dalton, *Vice-Adm.* Sir Geoffrey Thomas James Oliver, GCB

Dalton, Sir Richard John, KCMG

Dalton, *Air Chief Marshal* Sir Stephen Gary George, GCB

Dalyell, Sir Tam (Thomas), Bt. (NS 1685)

Dancer, Sir Eric, KCVO, CBE

Daniel, Sir John Sagar, Kt., DSC

Darell, Sir Guy Jeffrey Adair, Bt. (1795)

Darrington, Sir Michael John, Kt.

Darroch, Sir Nigel Kim, KCMG

Dasgupta, *Prof.* Sir Partha Sarathi, Kt.

Dashwood, *Prof.* Sir (Arthur) Alan, KCMG, CBE, QC

Dashwood, Sir Edward John Francis, Bt. (1707), *Premier Baronet of Great Britain*

Dashwood, Sir Frederick George Mahon, Bt. (1684)

Daunt, Sir Timothy Lewis Achilles, KCMG

David, Sir Jean Marc, Kt., CBE, QC

David, *His Hon.* Sir Robin (Robert) Daniel George, Kt.

Davidson, Sir Martin Stuart, KCMG

Davies, Sir (Charles) Noel, Kt.

Davies, *Prof.* Sir David Evan Naughton, Kt., CBE, FRS, FRENG

Davies, *Hon.* Sir (David Herbert) Mervyn, Kt., MC, TD

Davies, Sir David John, Kt.

Davies, Sir Frank John, Kt., CBE

Davies, *Prof.* Sir Graeme John, Kt., FRENG

Davies, Sir John Howard, Kt.

Davies, Sir John Michael, KCB

Davies, Sir Rhys Everson, Kt., QC

Davis, Sir Andrew Frank, Kt., CBE

Davis, Sir Crispin Henry Lamert, Kt.

Davis, Sir John Gilbert, Bt. (1946)

Davis, *Rt. Hon.* Sir Nigel Anthony Lambert, Kt.

Davis, Sir Peter John, Kt.

Davis-Goff, Sir Robert (William), Bt. (1905)

Davison, *Rt. Hon.* Sir Ronald Keith, GBE, CMG

†Davson, Sir George Trenchard Simon, Bt. (1927)

Dawanincura, Sir John Norbert, Kt., OBE

Dawbarn, Sir Simon Yelverton, KCVO, CMG

Dawson, *Hon.* Sir Daryl Michael, KBE, CB

Dawson, Sir Nicholas Antony Trevor, Bt. (1920)

Dawtry, Sir Alan (Graham), Kt., CBE, TD

Day, Sir Barry Stuart, Kt., OBE

Day, Sir Derek Malcolm, KCMG

Day, *Air Chief Marshal* Sir John Romney, KCB, OBE, ADC

Day, Sir (Judson) Graham, Kt.

Day, Sir Michael John, Kt., OBE

Day, Sir Simon James, Kt.

Day-Lewis, Sir Daniel Michael Blake, Kt.

Deane, *Hon.* Sir William Patrick, KBE

Dearlove, Sir Richard Billing, KCMG, OBE

†Debenham, Sir Thomas Adam, Bt. (1931)

de Deney, Sir Geoffrey Ivor, KCVO

Deegan, Sir Michael, Kt., CBE

Deeny, *Hon.* Sir Donnell Justin Patrick, Kt.

De Haan, Sir Roger Michael, Kt., CBE

De Halpert, *Rear-Adm.* Sir Jeremy Michael, KCVO, CB

de Hoghton, Sir (Richard) Bernard (Cuthbert), Bt. (1611)

De la Bère, Sir Cameron, Bt. (1953)

de la Rue, Sir Andrew George Ilay, Bt. (1898)

Dellow, Sir John Albert, Kt., CBE

Delves, *Lt.-Gen.* Sir Cedric Norman George, KBE

Denholm, Sir John Ferguson (Ian), Kt., CBE

Denison-Smith, *Lt.-Gen.* Sir Anthony Arthur, KBE

Denny, Sir Charles Alistair Maurice, Bt. (1913)

†Denny, Sir Piers Anthony de Waltham, Bt. (I. 1782)

Derbyshire, Sir Andrew George, Kt.

De Silva, *Rt. Hon.* Sir (George) Desmond Lorenz, Kt., QC

de Trafford, Sir John Humphrey, Bt. (1841)

Deverell, *Gen.* Sir John Freegard, KCB, OBE

De Ville, Sir Harold Godfrey Oscar, Kt., CBE

Devine, *Prof.* Sir Thomas Martin, Kt., OBE, FRSE

Devitt, Sir James Hugh Thomas, Bt. (1916)

de Waal, Sir (Constant Henrik) Henry, KCB, QC

Dewey, Sir Anthony Hugh, Bt. (1917)

De Witt, Sir Ronald Wayne, Kt.

Diamond, *Prof.* Sir Ian David, Kt., FRSE

Dick-Lauder, Sir Piers Robert, Bt. (S. 1690)

Dilke, Revd Charles John Wentworth, Bt. (1862)

Dilnot, Sir Andrew William, Kt., CBE

Dillon, Sir Andrew Patrick, Kt., CBE

Dilley, Sir Philip Graham, Kt.

Dillwyn-Venables-Llewelyn, Sir John Michael, Bt. (1890)

Dingemans, *Hon.* Sir James Michael, Kt.

Dixon, Sir Jeremy, Kt.

Dixon, Sir Jonathan Mark, Bt. (1919)

Dixon, *Dr* Sir Michael, Kt.

Dixon, Sir Peter John Bellett, Kt.

Djanogly, Sir Harry Ari Simon, Kt., CBE

Dobson, *Vice-Adm.* Sir David Stuart, KBE

Dodds, Sir Ralph Jordan, Bt. (1964)

Dollery, Sir Colin Terence, Kt.

Don-Wauchope, Sir Roger (Hamilton), Bt. (S. 1667)

Donald, Sir Alan Ewen, KCMG

Donald, *Air Marshal* Sir John George, KBE

Donaldson, *Prof.* Sir Liam Joseph, Kt.

Donaldson, *Prof.* Sir Simon Kirwan, Kt.

Donne, Sir John Christopher, Kt.

Donnelly, Sir Joseph Brian, KBE, CMG

Dorey, Sir Graham Martyn, Kt.

Dorman, Sir Philip Henry Keppel, Bt. (1923)

Doughty, Sir William Roland, Kt.

Douglas, *Prof.* Sir Neil James, Kt.

Douglas, *Hon.* Sir Roger Owen, Kt.

Dowell, Sir Anthony James, Kt., CBE

Dowling, Sir Robert, Kt.

Downey, Sir Gordon Stanley, KCB

Downward, *Maj.-Gen.* Sir Peter Aldcroft, KCVO, CB, DSO, DFC

Doyle, Sir Reginald Derek Henry, Kt., CBE

D'Oyly, Sir Hadley Gregory Bt. (1663)

Drewry, *Lt.-Gen.* Sir Christopher Francis, KCB, CBE

Drinkwater, Sir John Muir, Kt., QC

Dryden, Sir John Stephen Gyles, Bt. (1733 and 1795)

du Cann, *Rt. Hon.* Sir Edward Dillon Lott, KBE

Duckworth, Sir James Edward Dyce, Bt. (1909)

†du Cros, Sir Julian Claude Arthur Mallet, Bt. (1916)

Dudley-Williams, Sir Alastair Edgcumbe James, Bt. (1964)

Duff, *Prof.* Sir Gordon William, Kt.

Duff-Gordon, Sir Andrew Cosmo Lewis, Bt. (1813)

Duffell, *Lt.-Gen.* Sir Peter Royson, KCB, CBE, MC

Duffy, Sir (Albert) (Edward) Patrick, Kt., PHD

Dugdale, Sir William Stratford, Bt. (1936), CBE, MC

Duggin, Sir Thomas Joseph, Kt.

Dunbar, Sir Archibald Ranulph, Bt. (S. 1700)

Dunbar, Sir James Michael, Bt. (S. 1694)

Dunbar, Sir Robert Drummond Cospatrick, Bt. (S. 1698)

Dunbar of Hempriggs, Sir Richard Francis, Bt. (S. 1706)

Dunbar-Nasmith, *Prof.* Sir James Duncan, Kt., CBE

Duncan, Sir James Blair, Kt.

Dunford, *Dr* Sir John Ernest, Kt., OBE

Dunlop, Sir Thomas, Bt. (1916)

Dunne, Sir Martin, KCVO

Dunne, Sir Thomas Raymond, KG, KCVO

Dunning, Sir Simon William Patrick, Bt. (1930)

Dunnington-Jefferson, Sir John Alexander, Bt. (1958)

Dunstone, Sir Charles William, Kt.

Dunt, *Vice-Adm.* Sir John Hugh, KCB

Duntze, Sir Daniel Evans, Bt. (1774)

Dupre, Sir Tumun, Kt., MBE

Durand, Sir Edward Alan Christopher David Percy, Bt. (1892)

Durant, Sir (Robert) Anthony (Bevis), Kt.

Durie, Sir David Robert Campbell, KCMG

Durrant, Sir William Alexander Estridge, Bt. (1784)

Duthie, *Prof.* Sir Herbert Livingston, Kt.

Duthie, Sir Robert Grieve (Robin), Kt., CBE

Dutton, *Lt-Gen.* Sir James Benjamin, KCB, CBE

Dwyer, Sir Joseph Anthony, Kt.

Dyke, Sir David William Hart, Bt. (1677)

Dymock, *Vice-Adm.* Sir Anthony Knox, KBE, CB

Dyson, Sir James, Kt., CBE

Dyson, *Rt. Hon.* Sir John Anthony, Kt.

Eady, *Hon.* Sir David, Kt.

Eardley-Wilmot, Sir Michael John Assheton, Bt. (1821)

Earle, Sir (Hardman) George (Algernon), Bt. (1869)

Eastwood, *Prof.* Sir David Stephen, Kt.

Eaton, *Adm.* Sir Kenneth John, GBE, KCB

Eberle, *Adm.* Sir James Henry Fuller, GCB

Ebrahim, Sir (Mahomed) Currimbhoy, Bt. (1910)

Eddington, Sir Roderick Ian, Kt.

Eder, *Hon.* Sir Henry Bernard, Kt.

Edge, *Capt.* Sir (Philip) Malcolm, KCVO

†Edge, Sir William, Bt. (1937)

Edmonstone, Sir Archibald Bruce Charles, Bt. (1774)

Edward, *Rt. Hon.* Sir David Alexander Ogilvy, KCMG

Edwardes, Sir Michael Owen, Kt.

Edwards, Sir Christopher John Churchill, Bt. (1866)

Edwards, *Prof.* Sir Christopher Richard Watkin, Kt.

Edwards, Sir Llewellyn Roy, Kt.

Edwards, *Prof.* Sir Michael, OBE

Edwards, Sir Robert Paul, Kt.

Edwards, *Prof.* Sir Samuel Frederick, Kt., FRS

†Edwards-Moss, Sir David John, Bt. (1868)

Edwards-Stuart, *Hon.* Sir Antony James Cobham, Kt.

Egan, Sir John Leopold, Kt.

Egerton, Sir William de Malpas, Bt. (1617)

Ehrman, Sir William Geoffrey, KCMG

Eichelbaum, *Rt. Hon.* Sir Thomas, GBE

Elder, Sir Mark Philip, Kt., CBE

Eldon, Sir Stewart Graham, KCMG, OBE

Elias, *Rt. Hon.* Sir Patrick, Kt.

Eliott of Stobs, Sir Charles Joseph Alexander, Bt. (S. 1666)

Elliot, Sir Gerald Henry, Kt.

Elliott, Sir Clive Christopher Hugh, Bt. (1917)

Elliott, Sir David Murray, KCMG, CB

Elliott, *Prof.* Sir John Huxtable, Kt., FBA

Elliott, *Prof.* Sir Roger James, Kt., FRS

Ellis, Sir Herbert Douglas, Kt., OBE

Ellis, Sir Vernon James, Kt.

Ellwood, Sir Peter Brian, Kt., CBE

Elphinstone, Sir John, Bt. (S. 1701)

Elphinstone, Sir John Howard Main, Bt. (1816)

Elton, Sir Arnold, Kt., CBE

Elton, Sir Charles Abraham Grierson, Bt. (1717)

Elvidge, Sir John, KCB

Elwes, *Dr* Sir Henry William, KCVO

Elwes, Sir Jeremy Vernon, Kt., CBE

Elwood, Sir Brian George Conway, Kt., CBE

Elworthy, *Air Cdre. Hon.* Sir Timothy Charles, KCVO, CBE

Enderby, *Prof.* Sir John Edwin, Kt. CBE, FRS

Engle, Sir George Lawrence Jose, KCB, QC

English, Sir Terence Alexander Hawthorne, KBE, FRCS

Ennals, Sir Paul Martin, Kt., CBE

Epstein, *Prof.* Sir (Michael) Anthony, Kt., CBE, FRS

Errington, *Col.* Sir Geoffrey Frederick, Bt. (1963), OBE

Erskine, Sir (Thomas) Peter Neil, Bt. (1821)

Erskine-Hill, Sir Alexander Rodger, Bt. (1945)

Esmonde, Sir Thomas Francis Grattan, Bt. (I. 1629)

Esplen, Sir John Graham, Bt. (1921)

Esquivel, *Rt. Hon.* Sir Manuel, KCMG

Essenhigh, *Adm.* Sir Nigel Richard, GCB

Etherington, Sir Stuart James, Kt.

Etherton, *Rt. Hon.* Sir Terence Michael Elkan Barnet, Kt.

Evans, Sir Anthony Adney, Bt. (1920)

Evans, *Rt. Hon.* Sir Anthony Howell Meurig, Kt., RD

Evans, *Prof.* Sir Christopher Thomas, Kt., OBE

Evans, *Air Chief Marshal* Sir David George, GCB, CBE

Evans, *Hon.* Sir David Roderick, Kt.

Evans, Sir Harold Matthew, Kt.

Evans, *Prof.* Sir John Grimley, Kt., FRCP

Evans, Sir John Stanley, Kt., QPM

Evans, Sir Jonathan, KCB

Evans, *Prof.* Sir Martin John, Kt., FRS

Evans, Sir Richard Harry, Kt., CBE

Evans, *Prof.* Sir Richard John, Kt.

Evans, Sir Robert, Kt., CBE, FRENG

Evans-Lombe, *Hon.* Sir Edward Christopher, Kt.

†Evans-Tipping, Sir David Gwynne, Bt. (1913)

Eveleigh, *Rt. Hon.* Sir Edward Walter, Kt., ERD

Everard, Sir Henry Peter Charles, Bt. (1911)

Every, Sir Henry John Michael, Bt. (1641)

Ewart, Sir William Michael, Bt. (1887)

Eyre, Sir Reginald Edwin, Kt.

Eyre, Sir Richard Charles Hastings, Kt., CBE

Fagge, Sir John Christopher Frederick, Bt. (1660)

Fahy, Sir Peter, Kt., QPM

Fairbairn, Sir (James) Brooke, Bt. (1869)

Fairlie-Cuninghame, Sir Robert Henry, Bt. (S. 1630)

Fairweather, Sir Patrick Stanislaus, KCMG

Faldo, Sir Nicholas Alexander, Kt., MBE

†Falkiner, Sir Benjamin Simon Patrick, Bt. (I. 1778)

Fall, Sir Brian James Proetel, GCVO, KCMG

Fang, *Prof.* Sir Harry, Kt., CBE

Fareed, Sir Djamil Sheik, Kt.

Farmer, Sir Thomas, Kt., CVO, CBE

Farquhar, Sir Michael Fitzroy Henry, Bt. (1796)

Farquharson, Sir Angus Durie Miller, KCVO, OBE

Farrell, Sir Terence, Kt., CBE

Farrer, Sir (Charles) Matthew, GCVO

Farrington, Sir Henry William, Bt. (1818)

Fat, Sir (Maxime) Edouard (Lim Man) Lim, Kt.

Faulkner, Sir (James) Dennis (Compton), Kt., CBE, VRD

Fay, Sir (Humphrey) Michael Gerard, Kt.

Fayrer, Sir John Lang Macpherson, Bt. (1896)

Feachem, *Prof.* Sir Richard George Andrew, KBE

Fean, Sir Thomas Vincent, KCVO

Feilden, Sir Henry Rudyard, Bt. (1846)

Feldmann, *Prof.* Sir Marc, Kt.

Fell, Sir David, KCB

Fender, Sir Brian Edward Frederick, Kt., CMG, PHD

Fenn, Sir Nicholas Maxted, GCMG

Fenwick, Sir Leonard Raymond, Kt., CBE

Fergus, Sir Howard Archibald, KBE

Ferguson, Sir Alexander Chapman, Kt., CBE

Ferguson-Davie, Sir Michael, Bt. (1847)

Fergusson of Kilkerran, Sir Charles, Bt. (S. 1703)

Fergusson, Sir Ewan Alastair John, GCMG, GCVO

Ferris, *Hon.* Sir Francis Mursell, Kt., TD

Fersht, *Prof.* Sir Alan Roy, Kt., FRS

ffolkes, Sir Robert Francis Alexander, Bt. (1774), OBE

Field, Sir Malcolm David, Kt.

Field, *Hon.* Sir Richard Alan, Kt.

Fielding, Sir Leslie, KCMG

Fields, Sir Allan Clifford, KCMG

Fieldsend, *Hon.* Sir John Charles Rowell, KBE

Fiennes, Sir Ranulph Twisleton-Wykeham, Bt. (1916), OBE

Figg, Sir Leonard Clifford William, KCMG

Figgis, Sir Anthony St John Howard, KCVO, CMG

Finch, Sir Robert Gerard, Kt.

Finlay, Sir David Ronald James Bell, Bt. (1964)

Finlayson, Sir Garet Orlando, KCMG, OBE

Fish, *Hon.* Sir David Royden, Kt.

†Fison, Sir Charles William, Bt. (1905)

FitzGerald, Sir Adrian James Andrew, Bt. (1880)

†Fitzgerald, *Revd* Daniel Patrick, Bt. (1903)

FitzHerbert, Sir Richard Ranulph, Bt. (1784)

Fitzpatrick, *Air Marshal* Sir John Bernard, KBE, CB

Flanagan, Sir Maurice, KBE

Flanagan, Sir Ronald, GBE, QPM

Flaux, *Hon.* Sir Julian Martin, Kt.

Floud, *Prof.* Sir Roderick Castle, Kt.

Floyd, *Rt. Hon.* Sir Christopher David, Kt.

Floyd, Sir Giles Henry Charles, Bt. (1816)

Foley, *Lt.-Gen.* Sir John Paul, KCB, OBE, MC

Follett, *Prof.* Sir Brian Keith, Kt., FRS

Forbes of Craigievar, Sir Andrew Iain Ochoncar, Bt. (S. 1630)

Forbes, *Adm.* Sir Ian Andrew, KCB, CBE

Forbes, Sir James Thomas Stewart, Bt. (1823)

Forbes, *Vice-Adm.* Sir John Morrison, KCB

Forbes, *Hon.* Sir Thayne John, Kt.

†Forbes Adam, Revd Stephen Timothy Beilby, Bt. (1917)

Forbes-Leith, Sir George Ian David, Bt. (1923)

Ford, *Lt-Col.* Sir Andrew Charles, KCVO

Ford, Sir Andrew Russell, Bt. (1929)

Ford, Sir David Robert, KBE, LVO

Ford, Sir John Archibald, KCMG, MC

Ford, *Gen.* Sir Robert Cyril, GCB, CBE

Forestier-Walker, Sir Michael Leolin, Bt. (1835)

Forrest, *Prof.* Sir (Andrew) Patrick (McEwen), Kt.

Forsyth-Johnson, Sir Bruce Joseph, Kt., CBE (Bruce Forsyth)

Forte, *Hon.* Sir Rocco John Vincent, Kt.

Forwood, Sir Peter Noel, Bt. (1895)

Foskett, *Hon.* Sir David Robert, Kt.

Foster, Sir Andrew William, Kt.

Foster, *Prof.* Sir Christopher David, Kt.

†Foster, Sir Saxby Gregory, Bt. (1930)

Foulkes, Sir Arthur Alexander, GCMG

Fountain, *Hon.* Sir Cyril Stanley Smith, Kt.

Fowke, Sir David Frederick Gustavus, Bt. (1814)

Fowler, Sir (Edward) Michael Coulson, Kt.

Fox, Sir Christopher, Kt., QPM

Fox, Sir Paul Leonard, Kt., CBE

France, Sir Christopher Walter, GCB

Francis, Sir Horace William Alexander, Kt., CBE, FRENG

Francis, Sir Robert Anthony, Kt., QC

Frank, Sir Robert Andrew, Bt. (1920)

Franklin, Sir Michael David Milroy, KCB, CMG

Fraser, Sir Charles Annand, KCVO

Fraser, Sir Iain Michael Duncan, Bt. (1943)

Fraser, Sir James Murdo, KBE

Fraser, Sir Simon James, KCMG

Fraser, Sir William Kerr, GCB

Frayling, *Prof.* Sir Christopher John, Kt.

Frederick, Sir Christopher St John, Bt. (1723)

Freedman, *Rt. Hon. Prof.* Sir Lawrence David, KCMG, CBE

Freeman, Sir James Robin, Bt. (1945)

French, *Air Marshal* Sir Joseph Charles, KCB, CBE

Frere, *Vice-Adm.* Sir Richard Tobias, KCB

Fretwell, Sir (Major) John (Emsley), GCMG

Friend *Prof.* Sir Richard Henry, Kt.

Froggatt, Sir Peter, Kt.

Fry, Sir Graham Holbrook, KCMG

Fry, Sir Peter Derek, Kt.

Fry, *Lt.-Gen.* Sir Robert Allan, KCB, CBE

Fry, *Dr* Sir Roger Gordon, Kt., OBE

Fulford, *Rt. Hon.* Sir Adrian Bruce, Kt.

Fuller, Sir James Henry Fleetwood, Bt. (1910)

Fulton, *Lt.-Gen.* Sir Robert Henry Gervase, KBE

Furness, Sir Stephen Roberts, Bt. (1913)

Gage, *Rt. Hon.* Sir William Marcus, Kt., QC

Gains, Sir John Christopher, Kt.

Gainsford, Sir Ian Derek, Kt.

Gale, Sir Roger James, Kt.

Galsworthy, Sir Anthony Charles, KCMG

Galway, Sir James, Kt., OBE

Gamble, Sir David Hugh Norman, Bt. (1897)

Gambon, Sir Michael John, Kt., CBE

Gammell, Sir William Benjamin Bowring, Kt.

Gardiner, Sir John Eliot, Kt., CBE

Gardner, *Prof.* Sir Richard Lavenham, Kt.

Gardner, Sir Roy Alan, Kt.

Garland, *Hon.* Sir Patrick Neville, Kt.

Garland, *Hon.* Sir Ransley Victor, KBE

Garland, *Dr* Sir Trevor, KBE

Garner, Sir Anthony Stuart, Kt.

Garnett, *Adm.* Sir Ian David Graham, KCB

Garnier, Sir Edward Henry, Kt., QC

Garnier, *Rear-Adm.* Sir John, KCVO, CBE

Garrard, Sir David Eardley, Kt.

Garrett, Sir Anthony Peter, Kt., CBE

Garrick, Sir Ronald, Kt., CBE, FRENG

Garthwaite, Sir (William) Mark (Charles), Bt. (1919)

Gaskell, Sir Richard Kennedy Harvey, Kt.

Gass, Sir Simon Lawrance, KCMG, CVO

Geidt, *Rt. Hon.* Sir Christopher, KCB, KCVO, OBE

Geim, *Prof.* Sir Andre Konstantin, Kt.

Geno, Sir Makena Viora, KBE

Gent, Sir Christopher Charles, Kt.

George, *Prof.* Sir Charles Frederick, Kt., MD, FRCP

George, Sir Richard William, Kt., CVO

Gerken, *Vice-Adm.* Sir Robert William Frank, KCB, CBE

Gershon, Sir Peter Oliver, Kt., CBE

Gethin, Sir Richard Joseph St Lawrence, Bt. (I. 1665)

Gibbings, Sir Peter Walter, Kt.

Gibbons, Sir William Edward Doran, Bt. (1752)

Gibbs, *Hon.* Sir Richard John Hedley, Kt.

Gibbs, Sir Roger Geoffrey, Kt.

†Gibson, *Revd* Christopher Herbert, Bt. (1931)

Gibson, Sir Ian, Kt., CBE

Gibson, Sir Kenneth Archibald, Kt.

Gibson, *Rt. Hon.* Sir Peter Leslie, Kt.

Gibson-Craig-Carmichael, Sir David Peter William, Bt. (S. 1702 and 1831)

Gieve, Sir Edward John Watson, KCB

Giffard, Sir (Charles) Sydney (Rycroft), KCMG

Gifford, Sir Michael Roger, Kt.

Gilbart, *Hon.* Sir Andrew James, Kt., QC

Gilbart-Denham, *Lt.-Col.* Sir Seymour Vivian, KCVO

Gilbert, *Air Chief Marshal* Sir Joseph Alfred, KCB, CBE

Gilbert, *Rt. Hon.* Sir Martin John, Kt., CBE

†Gilbey, Sir Walter Gavin, Bt. (1893)

Gill, Sir Anthony Keith, Kt.

Gill, Sir Robin Denys, KCVO

Gillam, Sir Patrick John, Kt.

Gillen, *Hon.* Sir John de Winter, Kt.

Gillett, Sir Nicholas Danvers Penrose, Bt. (1959)

Gillinson, Sir Clive Daniel, Kt., CBE

Gilmore, *Prof.* Sir Ian Thomas, Kt.

Gilmour, *Hon.* Sir David Robert, Bt. (1926)

Gilmour, Sir John Nicholas, Bt. (1897)

Gina, Sir Lloyd Maepeza, KBE

Giordano, Sir Richard Vincent, KBE

Girolami, Sir Paul, Kt.

Girvan, *Rt. Hon.* Sir (Frederick) Paul, Kt.

Gladstone, Sir (Erskine) William, Bt. (1846), KG

Glean, Sir Carlyle Arnold, GCMG

Glidewell, *Rt. Hon.* Sir Iain Derek Laing, Kt.

Globe, *Hon.* Sir Henry Brian, Kt.

Glover, Sir Victor Joseph Patrick, Kt.

Glyn, Sir Richard Lindsay, Bt. (1759 and 1800)

Gobbo, Sir James Augustine, Kt., AC

Goldberg, *Prof.* Sir David Paul Brandes, Kt.

Goldring, *Rt. Hon.* Sir John Bernard, Kt.

Gomersall, Sir Stephen John, KCMG

Gonsalves-Sabola, *Hon.* Sir Joaquim Claudino, Kt

Gooch, Sir Arthur Brian Sherlock Heywood, Bt. (1746)

Gooch, Sir Miles Peter, Bt. (1866)

Good, Sir John James Griffen, Kt. CBE

Goodall, Sir (Arthur) David Saunders, GCMG

Goodall, *Air Marshal* Sir Roderick Harvey, KBE, CB, AFC

Goode, *Prof.* Sir Royston Miles, Kt., CBE, QC

Goodenough, Sir Anthony Michael, KCMG

Goodenough, Sir William McLernon, Bt. (1943)

Goodhart, Sir Philip Carter, Kt.

Goodhart, Sir Robert Anthony Gordon, Bt. (1911)

Goodison, Sir Nicholas Proctor, Kt.

Goodman, Sir Patrick Ledger, Kt., CBE

Goodson, Sir Mark Weston Lassam, Bt. (1922)

Goodwin, Sir Frederick, KBE

Goody, *Prof.* Sir John Rankine, Kt.

Goold, Sir George William, Bt. (1801)

Gordon, Sir Donald, Kt.

Gordon, Sir Gerald Henry, Kt., CBE, QC

Gordon, Sir Robert James, Bt. (S. 1706)

Gordon-Cumming, Sir Alexander Penrose, Bt. (1804)

Gore, Sir Hugh Frederick Corbet, Bt. (I. 1622)

Gore-Booth, Sir Josslyn Henry Robert, Bt. (I. 1760)

Goring, Sir William Burton Nigel, Bt. (1678)

Gormley, sir Antony Mark David, Kt., OBE CBE, MC

Gormley, Sir Paul Brendan, KCMG, MBE

Goschen, Sir (Edward) Alexander, Bt. (1916)

Gosling, Sir (Frederick) Donald, KCVO

Goulden, Sir (Peter) John, GCMG

Goulding, Sir (William) Lingard Walter, Bt. (1904)

Gourlay, Sir Simon Alexander, Kt.

Gowans, Sir James Learmonth, Kt., CBE, FRCP, FRS

Gowers, *Prof.* Sir William Timothy, Kt.

Gozney, Sir Richard Hugh Turton, KCMG

Graaff, Sir David de Villiers, Bt. (1911)

Grabham, Sir Anthony Henry, Kt.

Graham, Sir Alexander Michael, GBE

Graham, Sir James Bellingham, Bt. (1662)

Graham, Sir James Fergus Surtees, Bt. (1783)

Graham, Sir James Thompson, Kt., CMG

Graham, Sir John Alexander Noble, Bt. (1906), GCMG

Graham, Sir John Alistair, Kt.

Graham, Sir John Moodie, Bt. (1964)

Graham, Sir Peter, KCB, QC

Graham, *Lt.-Gen.* Sir Peter Walter, KCB, CBE

†Graham, Sir Ralph Stuart, Bt. (1629)

Graham-Moon, Sir Peter Wilfred Giles, Bt. (1855)

Graham-Smith, *Prof.* Sir Francis, Kt.

Grange, Sir Kenneth Henry, Kt., CBE

Grant, Sir Archibald, Bt. (S. 1705)

Grant, Sir Clifford, Kt.

Grant, Sir Ian David, Kt., CBE

Grant, Sir (John) Anthony, Kt.

Grant, Sir John Douglas Kelso, KCMG

Grant, *Prof.* Sir Malcolm John, Kt., CBE

Grant, Sir Patrick Alexander Benedict, Bt. (S. 1688)

Grant, Sir Paul Joseph Patrick, Kt.

Grant, *Lt.-Gen.* Sir Scott Carnegie, KCB

Grant-Suttie, Sir James Edward, Bt. (S. 1702)

Granville-Chapman, *Gen.* Sir Timothy John, GBE, KCB, ADC

Grattan-Bellew, Sir Henry Charles, Bt. (1838)

Gray, *Hon.* Sir Charles Anthony St John, Kt.

Gray, Sir Charles Ireland, Kt., CBE

Gray, *Prof.* Sir Denis John Pereira, Kt., OBE, FRCGP

Gray, *Dr.* Sir John Armstrong Muir, Kt., CBE

Gray, Sir Robert McDowall (Robin), Kt.

Gray, Sir William Hume, Bt. (1917)

Graydon, *Air Chief Marshal* Sir Michael James, GCB, CBE

Grayson, Sir Jeremy Brian Vincent Harrington, Bt. (1922)

Green, Sir Allan David, KCB, QC

Green, Sir Andrew Fleming, KCMG

Green, Sir Edward Patrick Lycett, Bt. (1886)

Green, Sir Gregory David, KCMG

Green, *Hon.* Sir Guy Stephen Montague, KBE

Green, *Prof.* Sir Malcolm, Kt.

Green, *Hon.* Sir Nicholas Nigel, Kt., QC

Green, Sir Owen Whitley, Kt.

Green, Sir Philip Green, Kt.

Green-Price, Sir Robert John, Bt. (1874)

Greenaway, *Prof.* Sir David, Kt.

Greenaway, Sir John Michael Burdick, Bt. (1933)

Greenbury, Sir Richard, Kt.

Greener, Sir Anthony Armitage, Kt.

Greengross, Sir Alan David, Kt.

Greenstock, Sir Jeremy Quentin, GCMG

Greenwell, Sir Edward Bernard, Bt. (1906)

Greenwood, *Prof.* Sir Brian Mellor, Kt., CBE

Greenwood, *Prof.* Sir Christopher John, Kt., CMG

Gregory, *Prof.* Sir Michael John, Kt., CBE

Gregson, Sir Peter John, Kt.

Gregson, Sir Peter Lewis, GCB

Grey, Sir Anthony Dysart, Bt. (1814)

Grierson, Sir Ronald Hugh, Kt.

Griffiths, Sir Michael, Kt.

Grigson, *Hon.* Sir Geoffrey Douglas, Kt.

Grimshaw, Sir Nicholas Thomas, Kt., CBE

Grimstone, Sir Gerald Edgar, Kt.

Grimwade, Sir Andrew Sheppard, Kt., CBE

Grose, *Vice-Adm.* Sir Alan, KBE

Gross, *Rt. Hon.* Sir Peter Henry, Kt.

Grossart, Sir Angus McFarlane McLeod, Kt., CBE

Grotrian, Sir Philip Christian Brent, Bt. (1934)

Grove, Sir Charles Gerald, Bt. (1874)

Grundy, Sir Mark, Kt.

Guinness, Sir Howard Christian Sheldon, Kt., VRD

Guinness, Sir John Ralph Sidney, CB

Guinness, Sir Kenelm Edward Lee, Bt. (1867)

Guise, Sir Christopher James, Bt. (1783)

Gull, Sir Rupert William Cameron, Bt. (1872)

Gumbs, Sir Emile Rudolph, Kt.

Gunn, Sir Robert Norman, Kt.

Gunning, Sir Charles Theodore, Bt. (1778)

Gunston, Sir John Wellesley, Bt. (1938)

Gurdon, *Prof.* Sir John Bertrand, Kt., DPHIL, FRS

Guthrie, Sir Malcolm Connop, Bt. (1936)

Haddacks, *Vice-Adm.* Sir Paul Kenneth, KCB

Haddon-Cave, *Hon.* Sir Charles Anthony, Kt.

Hadlee, Sir Richard John, Kt., MBE

Hagart-Alexander, Sir Claud, Bt. (1886)

Hague, *Prof.* Sir Douglas Chalmers, Kt., CBE

Haines, *Prof.* Sir Andrew Paul, Kt.

Haji-Ioannou, Sir Stelios, Kt.

Halberg, Sir Murray Gordon, Kt., MBE

Hall, *Dr* Sir Andrew James, Kt.

Hall, Sir David Christopher, Bt. (1923)

Hall, *Prof.* Sir David Michael Baldock, Kt.

Hall, Sir Ernest, Kt., OBE

Hall, Sir Geoffrey, Kt.

Hall, Sir Graham Joseph, Kt.

Hall, Sir Iain Robert, Kt.

Hall, Sir John, Kt.

Hall, Sir John Bernard, Bt. (1919)

Hall, Sir John Douglas Hoste, Bt. (S. 1687)

Hall, HE *Prof.* Sir Kenneth Octavius, GCMG

Hall, Sir Peter Edward, KBE, CMG

Hall, Sir Peter Reginald Frederick, Kt., CBE

Hall, *Revd* Wesley Winfield, Kt.

Hall, Sir William Joseph, KCVO

Halpern, Sir Ralph Mark, Kt.

Halsey, *Revd* John Walter Brooke, Bt. (1920)

Halstead, Sir Ronald, Kt., CBE

Hamblen, *Hon.* Sir Nicholas Archibald, Kt.

Hambling, Sir Herbert Peter Hugh, Bt. (1924)

Hamilton, Sir Andrew Caradoc, Bt. (S. 1646)

Hamilton, Sir Nigel, KCB

Hamilton-Dalrymple, *Maj.* Sir Hew Fleetwood, Bt. (S. 1698), GCVO

Hamilton-Spencer-Smith, Sir John, Bt. (1804)

†Hammick, Sir Jeremy Charles, Bt. (1834)

Hammond, Sir Anthony Hilgrove, KCB, QC

Hampel, Sir Ronald Claus, Kt.

Hampson, Sir Stuart, Kt.

Hampton, Sir (Leslie) Geoffrey, Kt.

Hampton, Sir Philip Roy, Kt.

Hanbury-Tenison, Sir Richard, KCVO

Hanham, Sir William John Edward, Bt. (1667)

Hankes-Drielsma, Sir Claude Dunbar, KCVO

Hanley, *Rt. Hon.* Sir Jeremy James, KCMG

Hanmer, Sir Wyndham Richard Guy, Bt. (1774)

Hannam, Sir John Gordon, Kt.

Hanson, Sir (Charles) Rupert (Patrick), Bt. (1918)

Hanson, Sir John Gilbert, KCMG, CBE

Harcourt-Smith, *Air Chief Marshal* Sir David, GBE, KCB, DFC

Hardie Boys, *Rt. Hon.* Sir Michael, GCMG

Harding, Sir George William, KCMG, CVO

Harding, *Marshal of the Royal Air Force* Sir Peter Robin, GCB

Hardy, Sir David William, Kt.

Hardy, Sir James Gilbert, Kt., OBE

Hardy, Sir Richard Charles Chandos, Bt. (1876)

Hare, Sir David, Kt., FRSL

Hare, Sir Nicholas Patrick, Bt. (1818)

Haren, *Dr* Sir Patrick Hugh, Kt.

Harford, Sir Mark John, Bt. (1934)

Harington, Sir Nicholas John, Bt. (1611)

Harkness, *Very Revd* James, KCVO, CB, OBE

Harley, *Gen.* Sir Alexander George Hamilton, KBE, CB

Harman, *Hon.* Sir Jeremiah LeRoy, Kt.

Harman, Sir John Andrew, Kt.

Harmsworth, Sir Hildebrand Harold, Bt. (1922)

Harper, *Air Marshal* Sir Christopher Nigel, KBE

Harper, Sir Ewan William, Kt., CBE

Harper, *Prof.* Sir Peter Stanley, Kt., CBE

Harris, Sir Christopher John Ashford, Bt. (1932)

Harris, *Prof.* Sir Henry, Kt., FRCP, FRCPATH, FRS

Harris, *Air Marshal* Sir John Hulme, KCB, CBE

Harris, *Prof.* Sir Martin Best, Kt., CBE

Harris, Sir Michael Frank, Kt.

Harris, Sir (Theodore) Wilson, Kt.

Harris, Sir Thomas George, KBE, CMG

Harrison, *Prof.* Sir Brian Howard, Kt.

Harrison, Sir David, Kt., CBE, FRENG

Harrison, *Hon.* Sir Michael Guy Vicat, Kt.

Harrison, Sir Michael James Harwood, Bt. (1961)

Harrison, Sir (Robert) Colin, Bt. (1922)

Harrison, Sir Terence, Kt., FRENG

Harrop, Sir Peter John, KCB

Hart, *Hon.* Sir Anthony Ronald, Kt.

Hart, Sir Graham Allan, KCB

Hartwell, Sir (Francis) Anthony Charles Peter, Bt. (1805)

Harvey, Sir Charles Richard Musgrave, Bt. (1933)

Harvey, Sir Nicholas Barton, Kt.

Harvie, Sir John Smith, Kt., CBE

Harvie-Watt, Sir James, Bt. (1945)

Harwood, Sir Ronald, Kt., CBE

Haselhurst, *Rt. Hon.* Sir Alan Gordon Barraclough, Kt.

Haskard, Sir Cosmo Dugal Patrick Thomas, KCMG, MBE

Hastie, *Cdre* Sir Robert Cameron, KCVO, CBE, RD

Hastings, Sir Max Macdonald, Kt.

Hastings, *Dr* Sir William George, Kt., CBE

Hatter, Sir Maurice, Kt.

Havelock-Allan, Sir (Anthony) Mark David, Bt. (1858)

Hawkes, Sir John Garry, Kt., CBE

Hawkhead, Sir Anthony Gerard, Kt., CBE

Hawkins, Sir Richard Caesar, Bt. (1778)

†Hawley, Sir Henry Nicholas, Bt. (1795)

Hawley, Sir James Appleton, KCVO, TD

Haworth, Sir Philip, Bt. (1911)

Hay, Sir David Russell, Kt., CBE, FRCP, MD

Hay, Sir John Erroll Audley, Bt. (S. 1663)

†Hay, Sir Ronald Frederick Hamilton, Bt. (S. 1703)

Hayden, *Hon.* Sir Anthony Paul, Kt.

Hayes, Sir Brian, Kt., CBE, QPM

Hayes, Sir Brian David, GCB

Hayman-Joyce, *Lt.-Gen.* Sir Robert John, KCB, CBE

Hayter, Sir Paul David Grenville, KCB, LVO

Hayward, Sir Jack Arnold, Kt., OBE

Head, Sir Richard Douglas Somerville, Bt. (1838)

Heald, Sir Oliver, Kt.

Heap, Sir Peter William, KCMG

Heap, *Prof.* Sir Robert Brian, Kt., CBE, FRS

Hearne, Sir Graham James, Kt., CBE

†Heathcote, Sir Mark Simon Robert, Bt. (1733), OBE

†Heathcote, Sir Timothy Gilbert, Bt. (1733)

Heatley, Sir Peter, Kt., CBE

Heber-Percy, Sir Algernon Eustace Hugh, KCVO

Hedley *Hon.* Sir Mark, Kt.

Hegarty, Sir John Kevin, Kt.

Heiser, Sir Terence Michael, GCB

Heller, Sir Michael Aron, Kt.

Henderson, Sir Denys Hartley, Kt.

Henderson, *Hon.* Sir Launcelot Dinadan James, Kt.

Henderson, *Maj.* Sir Richard Yates, KCVO

Hendry, *Prof.* Sir David Forbes, Kt.

Hendy, Sir Peter Gerard, Kt., CBE

Hennessy, Sir James Patrick Ivan, KBE, CMG

†Henniker, Sir Adrian Chandos, Bt. (1813)

Henniker-Heaton, Sir Yvo Robert, Bt. (1912)

Henriques, *Hon.* Sir Richard Henry Quixano, Kt.

†Henry, Sir Patrick Denis, Bt. (1923)

Henshaw, Sir David George, Kt.

Hepple, *Prof.* Sir Bob Alexander, Kt.

Herbecq, Sir John Edward, KCB

Herbert, *Adm.* Sir Peter Geoffrey Marshall, KCB, OBE

Heron, Sir Conrad Frederick, KCB, OBE

Heron-Maxwell, Sir Nigel Mellor, Bt. (S. 1683)

Hervey, Sir Roger Blaise Ramsay, KCVO, CMG

Hervey-Bathurst, Sir Frederick William John, Bt. (1818)

Heseltine, *Rt. Hon.* Sir William Frederick Payne, GCB, GCVO

Hewetson, Sir Christopher Raynor, Kt., TD

Hewett, Sir Richard Mark John, Bt. (1813)

Hewitt, Sir (Cyrus) Lenox (Simson), Kt., OBE

Hewitt, Sir Nicholas Charles Joseph, Bt. (1921)

Heygate, Sir Richard John Gage, Bt. (1831)

Heywood, Sir Jeremy John, KCB, CVO

Heywood, Sir Peter, Bt. (1838)

Hickey, sir John Tongri, Kt., CBE

Hickinbottom, *Hon.* Sir Gary Robert, Kt.

Hickman, Sir (Richard) Glenn, Bt. (1903)

Hicks, Sir Robert, Kt.

Hidden, *Hon.* Sir Anthony Brian, Kt.

Hielscher, Sir Leo Arthur, Kt.

Higgins, Sir David Hartmann, Kt.

Higgins, *Rt. Hon.* Sir Malachy Joseph, Kt.

Hildyard, *Hon.* Sir Robert Henry Thoroton, Kt.

Hill, Sir Brian John, Kt.

Hill, *Prof.* Sir Geoffrey William, Kt.

Hill, Sir James Frederick, Bt. (1917)

Hill, Sir John Alfred Rowley, Bt. (I. 1779)

Hill, *Vice-Adm.* Sir Robert Charles Finch, KBE, FRENG

Hill-Norton, *Vice-Adm. Hon.* Sir Nicholas John, KCB

Hill-Wood, Sir Samuel Thomas, Bt. (1921)

Hillhouse, Sir (Robert) Russell, KCB

Hillier, *Air Marshal* Sir Stephen John, KCB, CBE, DFC

Hills, Sir John Robert, Kt., CBE

Hilly, Sir Francis Billy, KCMG

Hine, *Air Chief Marshal* Sir Patrick Bardon, GCB, GBE

Hintze, Sir Michael, Kt.

Hirsch, *Prof.* Sir Peter Bernhard, Kt., PHD, FRS

Hirst, Sir Michael William, Kt.

Hoare, *Prof.* Sir Charles Anthony Richard, Kt., FRS

Hoare, Sir Charles James, Bt. (I. 1784)

Hoare, Sir David John, Bt. (1786)

Hobart, Sir John Vere, Bt. (1914)

Hobbs, *Maj.-Gen.* Sir Michael Frederick, KCVO, CBE

Hobday, Sir Gordon Ivan, Kt.

Hobhouse, Sir Charles John Spinney, Bt. (1812)

Hobson, Sir Ronald, KCVO

†Hodge, Sir Andrew Rowland, Bt. (1921)

Hodge, Sir James William, KCVO, CMG

Hodgkin, Sir (Gordon) Howard (Eliot), Kt., CH, CBE

Hodgkinson, Sir Michael Stewart, Kt.

Hodgson, Sir Maurice Arthur Eric, Kt., FRENG

Hodson, Sir Michael Robin Adderley, Bt. (I. 1789)

Hogan-Howe, Sir Bernard, Kt., QPM

Hogg, Sir Christopher Anthony, Kt.

Hogg, Sir Piers Michael James, Bt. (1846)

Hohn, Sir Christopher, KCMG

Holcroft, Sir Charles Anthony Culcheth, Bt. (1921)

Holden, Sir John David, Bt. (1919)

Holden, Sir Paul, Bt. (1893)

Holden-Brown, Sir Derrick, Kt.

Holder, Sir John Henry, Bt. (1898)

Holderness, Sir Martin William, Bt. (1920)

Holdgate, Sir Martin Wyatt, Kt., CB, PHD

Holland, *Hon.* Sir Alan Douglas, Kt.

Holland, *Hon.* Sir Christopher John, Kt.

Holland, Sir Geoffrey, KCB

Holland, Sir John Anthony, Kt.

Holliday, *Prof.* Sir Frederick George Thomas, Kt., CBE, FRSE

Holm, Sir Ian (Holm Cuthbert), Kt., CBE

Holman, *Hon.* Sir (Edward) James, Kt.

Holman, *Prof.* Sir John Stranger, Kt.

Holmes, Sir John Eaton, GCVO, KBE, CMG

Holroyd, Sir Michael De Courcy Fraser, Kt., CBE

Holroyde, *Hon.* Sir Timothy Victor, Kt.

Home, Sir William Dundas, Bt. (S. 1671)

Honywood, Sir Filmer Courtenay William, Bt. (1660)

†Hood, Sir John Joseph Harold, Bt. (1922)

Hooper, *Rt. Hon.* Sir Anthony, Kt.

Hope, Sir Alexander Archibald Douglas, Bt. (S. 1628)

Hope, Sir Colin Frederick Newton, Kt.

Hope-Dunbar, Sir David, Bt. (S. 1664)

Hopkin, *Prof.* Sir Deian Rhys, Kt.

Hopkin, Sir Royston Oliver, KCMG

Hopkins, Sir Anthony Philip, Kt., CBE

Hopkins, Sir Michael John, Kt., CBE, RA, RIBA

Hopwood, *Prof.* Sir David Alan, Kt., FRS

Hordern, *Rt. Hon.* Sir Peter Maudslay, Kt.

Horlick, *Vice-Adm.* Sir Edwin John, KBE, FRENG

Horlick, Sir James Cunliffe William, Bt. (1914)

Horlock, *Prof.* Sir John Harold, Kt., FRS, FRENG

Horn-Smith, Sir Julian Michael, Kt.

Horne, Sir Alan Gray Antony, Bt. (1929)

Horne, *Dr* Sir Alistair Allan, Kt. CBE

Horner, *Hon.* Sir Thomas Mark, Kt.

Horsbrugh-Porter, Sir Andrew Alexander Marshall, Bt. (1902)

Horsfall, Sir Edward John Wright, Bt. (1909)

Hort, Sir Andrew Edwin Fenton, Bt. (1767)

Hosker, Sir Gerald Albery, KCB, QC

Hoskins, *Prof.* Sir Brian John, Kt. CBE, FRS

†Hoskyns, Sir Edwyn Wren, Bt. (1676)

Hoskyns, Sir John Austin Hungerford Leigh, Kt.

Hotung, Sir Joseph Edward, Kt.

Houghton, *Gen.* Sir John Nicholas Reynolds, GCB, CBE

Houghton, Sir John Theodore, Kt., CBE, FRS

Houghton, Sir Stephen Geoffrey, Kt., CBE

Houldsworth, Sir Richard Thomas Reginald, Bt. (1887)

Hourston, Sir Gordon Minto, Kt.

Housden, Sir Peter James, KCB

House, Sir Stephen, Kt., QPM

Houssemayne du Boulay, Sir Roger William, KCVO, CMG

Houstoun-Boswall, Sir (Thomas) Alford, Bt. (1836)

Howard, Sir David Howarth Seymour, Bt. (1955)

Howard, *Prof.* Sir Michael Eliot, Kt., OM, CH, CBE, MC

Howard-Lawson, Sir John Philip, Bt. (1841)

Howarth, Sir (James) Gerald Douglas, Kt.

Howells, Sir Eric Waldo Benjamin, Kt., CBE

Howes, Sir Christopher Kingston, KCVO, CB

Howlett, *Gen.* Sir Geoffrey Hugh Whitby, KBE, MC

Hoy, Sir Christopher Andrew, Kt., MBE

Hugh-Jones, Sir Wynn Normington, Kt., LVO

Hughes, *Rt. Hon.* Sir Anthony Philip Gilson, Kt.

Hughes, Sir Thomas Collingwood, Bt. (1773)

Hughes, Sir Trevor Poulton, KCB

Hughes-Hallett, Sir Thomas Michael Sydney, Kt.

Hughes-Morgan, Sir (Ian) Parry David, Bt. (1925)

Hull, *Prof.* Sir David, Kt.

Hulse, Sir Edward Jeremy Westrow, Bt. (1739)

Hum, Sir Christopher Owen, KCMG

Humphreys, *Prof.* Sir Colin John, Kt., CBE

Hunt, Sir John Leonard, Kt.

Hunt, *Dr* Sir Richard Timothy, Kt.

Hunt-Davis, *Brig.* Sir Miles Garth, GCVO, CBE

Hunte, *Dr* Sir Julian Robert, KCMG, OBE

Hunter, Sir Alistair John, KCMG

Hunter, *Prof.* Sir Laurence Colvin, Kt., CBE, FRSE

Hunter, *Dr* Sir Philip John, Kt., CBE

Hunter, Sir Thomas Blane, Kt.

†Huntington-Whiteley, Sir John Miles, Bt. (1918)

Hurn, Sir (Francis) Roger, Kt.

Hurst, Sir Geoffrey Charles, Kt., MBE

Husbands, Sir Clifford Straugh, GCMG

Hutchison, *Rt. Hon.* Sir Michael, Kt.

Hutchison, Sir Peter Craft, Bt. (1956), CBE

Hutchison, Sir Robert, Bt. (1939)

Hutt, Sir Dexter Walter, Kt.

Huxtable, *Gen.* Sir Charles Richard, KCB, CBE

Hytner, Sir Nicholas, Kt.

Iacobescu, Sir George, Kt., CBE

Ibbotson, *Vice-Adm.* Sir Richard Jeffrey, KBE, CB, DSC

Imbert-Terry, Sir Michael Edward Stanley, Bt. (1917)

Imray, Sir Colin Henry, KBE, CMG

Ingham, Sir Bernard, Kt.

Ingilby, Sir Thomas Colvin William, Bt. (1866)

Inglis, Sir Brian Scott, Kt.

Inglis of Glencorse, Sir Roderick John, Bt. (S. 1703)

Ingram, Sir James Herbert Charles, Bt. (1893)

Ingram, Sir John Henderson, Kt., CBE

Innes, Sir Alastair Charles Deverell, Bt. (NS 1686)

Innes of Edingight, Sir Malcolm Rognvald, KCVO

Innes, Sir Peter Alexander Berowald, Bt. (S. 1628)

Insall, Sir Donald William, Kt., CBE

Irvine, Sir Donald Hamilton, Kt., CBE, MD, FRCGP

Irving, *Prof.* Sir Miles Horsfall, Kt., MD, FRCS, FRCSE

Irwin, *Lt.-Gen.* Sir Alistair Stuart Hastings, KCB, CBE

Irwin, *Hon.* Sir Stephen John, Kt.

Isaacs, Sir Jeremy Israel, Kt.

Isham, Sir Norman Murray Crawford, Bt. (1627)

Italeli, *HE* Sir Iakoba Taeia, GCMG

Ive, Sir Jonathan Paul, KBE

Ivory, Sir Brian Gammell, Kt., CBE

Jack, Sir Malcolm Roy, KCB

Jack, *Hon.* Sir Raymond Evan, Kt.

Jackling, Sir Roger Tustin, KCB, CBE

Jackson, Sir Barry Trevor, Kt.

Jackson, Sir Kenneth Joseph, Kt.

Jackson, *Gen.* Sir Michael David, GCB, CBE

Jackson, Sir Michael Roland, Bt. (1902)

†Jackson, Sir Neil Keith, Bt. (1815)

Jackson, Sir Nicholas Fane St George, Bt. (1913)

Jackson, *Hon.* Sir Peter Arthur Brian, Kt.

Jackson, *Rt. Hon.* Sir Rupert Matthew, Kt.

Jackson, Sir (William) Roland Cedric, Bt. (1869)

Jacob, *Rt. Hon.* Sir Robert Raphael Hayim (Robin), Kt.

Jacobi, Sir Derek George, Kt., CBE

Jacobs, Sir Cecil Albert, Kt., CBE

Jacobs, *Rt. Hon.* Sir Francis Geoffrey, KCMG, QC

Jacobs, *Hon.* Sir Kenneth Sydney, KBE

Jacomb, Sir Martin Wakefield, Kt.

Jaffray, Sir William Otho, Bt. (1892)

Jagger, Sir Michael Philip, Kt.

James, Sir Jeffrey Russell, KBE

James, Sir John Nigel Courtenay, KCVO, CBE

Jardine, Sir Andrew Colin Douglas, Bt. (1916)

Jardine of Applegirth, Sir William Murray, Bt. (S. 1672)

Jarman, *Prof.* Sir Brian, Kt., OBE

Jarratt, Sir Alexander Anthony, Kt., CB

Jawara, *Hon.* Sir Dawda Kairaba, Kt.

Jay, Sir Antony Rupert, Kt., CVO

Jay, *Hon.* Sir Robert Maurice, Kt.

Jeewoolall, Sir Ramesh, Kt.

Jeffrey, Sir William Alexander, KCB

Jeffreys, *Prof.* Sir Alec John, Kt., FRS

Jeffries, *Hon.* Sir John Francis, Kt.

Jehangir, Sir Cowasji, Bt. (1908)

†Jejeebhoy, Sir Jehangir, Bt. (1857)

Jenkins, Sir Brian Garton, GBE

Jenkins, Sir Elgar Spencer, Kt., OBE

Jenkins, Sir James Christopher, KCB, QC

Jenkins, Sir John, KCMG, LVO

Jenkins, Sir Michael Nicholas Howard, Kt., OBE

Jenkins, Sir Paul Christopher, KCB

Jenkins, Sir Simon, Kt.

Jenkinson, Sir John Banks, Bt. (1661)

Jenks, Sir (Richard) Peter, Bt. (1932)

Jenner, *Air Marshal* Sir Timothy Ivo, KCB

Jennings, Sir John Southwood, Kt., CBE, FRSE

Jennings, Sir Peter Neville Wake, Kt., CVO

Jephcott, Sir David Welbourn, Bt. (1962)

Jessel, Sir Charles John, Bt. (1883)

Jewkes, Sir Gordon Wesley, KCMG

Job, Sir Peter James Denton, Kt.

John, Sir David Glyndwr, KCMG

John, Sir Elton Hercules (Reginald Kenneth Dwight), Kt., CBE

Johns, *Vice-Adm.* Sir Adrian James, KCB, CBE, ADC

Johns, *Air Chief Marshal* Sir Richard Edward, GCB, KCVO, OBE

Johnson, Sir Colpoys Guy, Bt. (1755)

Johnson, *Gen.* Sir Garry Dene, KCB, OBE, MC

Johnson, Sir John Rodney, KCMG

†Johnson, Sir Patrick Eliot, Bt. (1818)

Johnson, *Hon.* Sir Robert Lionel, Kt.

Johnson-Ferguson, Sir Ian Edward, Bt. (1906)

Johnston, *Lt.-Gen.* Sir Maurice Robert, KCB, CVO, OBE

Johnston, Sir Thomas Alexander, Bt. (S. 1626)

Johnston, Sir William Ian Ridley, Kt., CBE, QPM

Johnstone, Sir Geoffrey Adams Dinwiddie, KCMG

Johnstone, Sir (George) Richard Douglas, Bt. (S. 1700)

Johnstone, Sir (John) Raymond, Kt., CBE

Jolliffe, Sir Anthony Stuart, GBE

Jolly, Sir Arthur Richard, KCMG

Jonas, Sir John Peter, Kt., CBE

Jones, Sir Alan Jeffrey, Kt.

Jones, Sir David Charles, Kt., CBE

Jones, Sir Derek William, KCB

Jones, Sir Harry George, Kt., CBE

Jones, Sir John Francis, Kt.

Jones, Sir Kenneth Lloyd, Kt., QPM

Jones, Sir Lyndon, Kt.

Jones, Sir Mark Ellis Powell, Kt.

Lawson-Tancred, Sir Andrew Peter, Bt. (1662)

Lawton, *Prof.* Sir John Hartley, Kt., CBE, FRS

Layard, *Adm.* Sir Michael Henry Gordon, KCB, CBE

Lea, *Vice-Adm.* Sir John Stuart Crosbie, KBE

Lea, Sir Thomas William, Bt. (1892)

Leahy, Sir Daniel Joseph, Kt.

Leahy, Sir John Henry Gladstone, KCMG

Leahy, Sir Terence Patrick, Kt.

Learmont, *Gen.* Sir John Hartley, KCB, CBE

Leaver, Sir Christopher, GBE

Le Cheminant, *Air Chief Marshal* Sir Peter de Lacey, GBE, KCB, DFC

Lechler, *Prof.* Sir Robert Ian, Kt.

Lechmere, Sir Nicholas Anthony Hungerford, Bt. (1818)

Lee, Sir Christopher Frank Carandini, Kt., CBE

†Leeds, Sir John Charles Hildyard, Bt. (1812)

Lees, Sir David Bryan, Kt.

Lees, Sir Thomas Edward, Bt. (1897)

Lees, Sir Thomas Harcourt Ivor, Bt. (1804)

Lees, Sir (William) Antony Clare, Bt. (1937)

Leese, Sir Richard Charles, Kt., CBE

Leeson, *Air Marshal* Sir Kevin James, KCB, CBE

le Fleming, Sir David Kelland, Bt. (1705)

Legard, Sir Charles Thomas, Bt. (1660)

Legg, Sir Thomas Stuart, KCB, QC

Leggatt, *Rt. Hon.* Sir Andrew Peter, Kt.

Leggatt, *Hon.* George Andrew Midsomer, Kt.

Leggett, *Prof.* Sir Anthony James, KBE

Leigh, Sir Edward Julian Egerton, Kt.

Leigh, Sir Geoffrey Norman, Kt.

Leigh, *Dr* Sir Michael, KCMG

Leigh, Sir Richard Henry, Bt. (1918)

Leighton, Sir John Mark Nicholas, Kt.

Leighton, Sir Michael John Bryan, Bt. (1693)

Leith-Buchanan, Sir Gordon Kelly McNicol, Bt. (1775)

Le Marchant, Sir Francis Arthur, Bt. (1841)

Lennox-Boyd, *Hon.* Sir Mark Alexander, Kt.

Leon, Sir John Ronald, Bt. (1911)

Lepping, Sir George Geria Dennis, GCMG, MBE

Leslie, Sir John Norman Ide, Bt. (1876)

Lester, Sir James Theodore, Kt.

Lethbridge, Sir Thomas Periam Hector Noel, Bt. (1804)

Lever, Sir Jeremy Frederick, KCMG, QC

Lever, Sir Paul, KCMG

Lever, Sir (Tresham) Christopher Arthur Lindsay, Bt. (1911)

Leveson, *Rt. Hon.* Sir Brian Henry, Kt.

Levi, Sir Wasangula Noel, Kt., CBE

Levinge, Sir Richard George Robin, Bt. (I. 1704)

Lewinton, Sir Christopher, Kt.

Lewis, *Hon.* Sir Clive Buckland, Kt.

Lewis, Sir David Thomas Rowell, Kt.

Lewis, Sir John Anthony, Kt., OBE

Lewis, Sir Lawrence Vernon Harcourt, KCMG, GCM

Lewis, Sir Leigh Warren, KCB

Lewis, Sir Terence Murray, Kt., OBE, GM, QPM

Lewison, *Rt. Hon.* Sir Kim Martin Jordan, Kt.

Ley, Sir Ian Francis, Bt. (1905)

Li, Sir Ka-Shing, KBE

Lickiss, Sir Michael Gillam, Kt.

Liddington, Sir Bruce, Kt.

Lightman, *Hon.* Sir Gavin Anthony, Kt.

Lighton, Sir Thomas Hamilton, Bt. (I. 1791)

Likierman, *Prof.* Sir John Andrew, Kt.

Lilleyman, *Prof.* Sir John Stuart, Kt.

Linacre, Sir (John) Gordon (Seymour), Kt., CBE, AFC, DFM

Lindblom, *Hon.* Sir Keith John, Kt.

†Lindsay, Sir James Martin Evelyn, Bt. (1962)

Lindsay, *Hon.* Sir John Edmund Frederic, Kt.

†Lindsay-Hogg, Sir Michael Edward, Bt. (1905)

Lipton, Sir Stuart Anthony, Kt.

Lipworth, Sir (Maurice) Sydney, Kt.

Lister-Kaye, Sir John Phillip Lister, Bt. (1812)

Lithgow, Sir William James, Bt. (1925)

Llewellyn, Sir Roderic Victor, Bt. (1922)

Llewellyn-Smith, *Prof.* Sir Christopher Hubert, Kt.

Lloyd, *Prof.* Sir Geoffrey Ernest Richard, Kt., FBA

Lloyd, Sir Nicholas Markley, Kt.

Lloyd, *Rt. Hon.* Sir Peter Robert Cable, Kt.

Lloyd, Sir Richard Ernest Butler, Bt. (1960)

Lloyd, *Rt. Hon.* Sir Timothy Andrew Wigram, Kt.

Lloyd-Edwards, *Capt.* Sir Norman, KCVO, RD

Lloyd Jones, *Rt. Hon.* Sir David, Kt.

Loader, *Air Marshal* Sir Clive Robert, KCB, OBE

Lobban, Sir Iain Robert, KCMG, CB

Lobo, Sir Rogerio Hyndman, Kt., CBE

Lockett, Sir Michael Vernon, KCVO

Lockhead, Sir Moir, Kt., OBE

Loder, Sir Edmund Jeune, Bt. (1887)

Logan, Sir David Brian Carleton, KCMG

Longmore, *Rt. Hon.* Sir Andrew Centlivres, Kt.

Lorimer, Sir (Thomas) Desmond, Kt.

Los, *Hon.* Sir Kubulan, Kt., CBE

Loughran, Sir Gerald Finbar, KCB

Lourdenadin, Sir Ninian Mogan, KCMG, KBE

Lovill, Sir John Roger, Kt., CBE

Lowa, *Rt. Revd* Sir Samson, KBE

Lowe, *Air Chief Marshal* Sir Douglas Charles, GCB, DFC, AFC

Lowe, Sir Frank Budge, Kt.

Lowe, Sir Philip Martin, KCMG

Lowe, Sir Thomas William Gordon, Bt. (1918)

Lowson, Sir Ian Patrick, Bt. (1951)

Lowther, *Col.* Sir Charles Douglas, Bt. (1824)

Loyd, Sir Julian St John, KCVO

Lu, Sir Tseng Chi, Kt.

Lucas, *Prof.* Sir Colin Renshaw, Kt.

Lucas, Sir Thomas Edward, Bt. (1887)

Lucas-Tooth, Sir (Hugh) John, Bt. (1920)

Luff, Sir Peter James, Kt.

Lumsden, Sir David James, Kt.

Lushington, Sir John Richard Castleman, Bt. (1791)

Lyall Grant, Sir Mark Justin, KCMG

Lyle, Sir Gavin Archibald, Bt. (1929)

Lynch-Blosse, *Capt.* Sir Richard Hely, Bt. (I. 1622)

Lynch-Robinson, Sir Dominick Christopher, Bt. (1920)

Lyne, *Rt. Hon.* Sir Roderic Michael John, KBE, CMG

Lyons, Sir John, Kt.

Lyons, Sir Michael Thomas, Kt.

McAllister, Sir Ian Gerald, Kt., CBE

McAlpine, Sir William Hepburn, Bt. (1918)

McCaffrey, Sir Thomas Daniel, Kt.

McCamley, Sir Graham Edward, KBE

McCarthy, Sir Callum, Kt.

McCartney, *Rt. Hon.* Sir Ian, Kt.

McCartney, Sir (James) Paul, Kt., MBE

Macartney, Sir John Ralph, Bt. (I. 1799)

McClement, *Vice-Admiral* Sir Timothy Pentreath, KCB, OBE

McClintock, Sir Eric Paul, Kt.

McCloskey, *Hon.* Sir John Bernard, Kt.

McColl, Sir Colin Hugh Verel, KCMG

McColl, *Gen.* Sir John Chalmers, KCB, CBE, DSO

McCollum, *Rt. Hon.* Sir William, Kt.

McCombe, *Rt. Hon.* Sir Richard George Bramwell, Kt.

McConnell, Sir Robert Shean, Bt. (1900)

†McCowan, Sir David William, Bt. (1934)

MacCulloch, *Prof.* Sir Diarmaid Ninian John, Kt.

McCulloch, *Rt. Revd* Nigel Simeon, KCVO

McCullough, *Hon.* Sir (Iain) Charles (Robert), Kt.

MacDermott, *Rt. Hon.* Sir John Clarke, Kt.

Macdonald, Sir Alasdair Uist, Kt., CBE

McDonald of Sleat, Sir Ian Godfrey Bosville, Bt. (S. 1625)

Macdonald, *Prof.* Sir James, Kt.

Macdonald, Sir Kenneth Carmichael, KCB

McDonald, Sir Simon Gerard, KCMG

McDonald, Sir Trevor, Kt., OBE

McDowell, Sir Eric Wallace, Kt., CBE

MacDuff, *Hon.* Sir Alistair Geoffrey, Kt.

Mace, *Lt.-Gen.* Sir John Airth, KBE, CB

McEwen, Sir John Roderick Hugh, Bt. (1953)

MacFadyen *Air Marshal* Sir Ian David, KCVO, CB, OBE

McFarland, Sir John Talbot, Bt. (1914)

MacFarlane, *Prof.* Sir Alistair George James, Kt., CBE, FRS

McFarlane, *Rt. Hon.* Sir Andrew Ewart, Kt.

Macfarlane, Sir (David) Neil, Kt.

McGeechan, Sir Ian Robert, Kt., OBE

McGrath, Sir Brian Henry, GCVO

Macgregor, Sir Ian Grant, Bt. (1828)

McGregor, Sir James David, Kt., OBE

MacGregor of MacGregor, Sir Malcolm Gregor Charles, Bt. (1795)

McGrigor, Sir James Angus Rhoderick Neil, Bt. (1831)

McIntosh, Sir Neil William David, Kt., CBE

McIntosh, Sir Ronald Robert Duncan, KCB

McIntyre, Sir Donald Conroy, Kt., CBE

McIntyre, Sir Meredith Alister, Kt.

Mackay, *Hon.* Sir Colin Crichton, Kt.

MacKay, *Prof.* Sir Donald Iain, Kt.

MacKay, Sir Francis Henry, Kt.

McKay, Sir Neil Stuart, Kt., CB

McKay, Sir William Robert, KCB

Mackay-Dick, *Maj.-Gen.* Sir Iain Charles, KCVO, MBE

Mackechnie, Sir Alistair John, Kt.

McKellen, Sir Ian Murray, Kt., CH, CBE

Mackenzie, Sir (James William) Guy, Bt. (1890)

Mackenzie, *Gen.* Sir Jeremy John George, GCB, OBE

†Mackenzie, Sir Peter Douglas, Bt. (S. 1673)

†Mackenzie, Sir Roderick McQuhae, Bt. (S. 1703)

Mackeson, Sir Rupert Henry, Bt. (1954)

McKillop, Sir Thomas Fulton Wilson, Kt.

McKinnon, *Rt. Hon.* Sir Donald Charles, GCVO

McKinnon, Sir James, Kt.

McKinnon, *Hon.* Sir Stuart Neil, Kt.

Mackintosh, Sir Cameron Anthony, Kt.

Mackworth, Sir Digby (John), Bt. (1776)

McLaughlin, Sir Richard, Kt.

Maclean of Dunconnell, Sir Charles Edward, Bt. (1957)

Maclean, *Hon.* Sir Lachlan Hector Charles, Bt., CVO (NS 1631)

Maclean, Sir Murdo, Kt.

†McLeod, Sir James Roderick Charles, Bt. (1925)

MacLeod, Sir (John) Maxwell Norman, Bt. (1924)

Macleod, Sir (Nathaniel William) Hamish, KBE

McLintock, Sir Michael William, Bt. (1934)

Maclure, Sir John Robert Spencer, Bt. (1898)

McMahon, Sir Brian Patrick, Bt. (1817)

McMahon, Sir Christopher William, Kt.

McMaster, Sir Brian John, Kt., CBE

McMichael, *Prof.* Sir Andrew James, Kt., FRS

MacMillan *Very Rvd.* Gilleasbuig Iain, KCVO

MacMillan, *Lt.-Gen.* Sir John Richard Alexander, KCB, CBE

McMullin, *Rt. Hon.* Sir Duncan Wallace, Kt.

McMurtry, Sir David, Kt., CBE

Macnaghten, Sir Malcolm Francis, Bt. (1836)

McNair-Wilson, Sir Patrick Michael Ernest David, Kt.

Macnaughton, *Prof.* Sir Malcolm Campbell, Kt.

McNee, Sir David Blackstock, Kt., QPM

McNulty, Sir (Robert William) Roy, Kt., CBE

MacPhail, Sir Bruce Dugald, Kt.

MacPherson, Sir Nicholas, KCB

Macpherson, Sir Ronald Thomas Steward (Tommy), CBE, MC, TD

Macpherson of Cluny, *Hon.* Sir William Alan, Kt., TD

McQuarrie, Sir Albert, Kt.

MacRae, Sir (Alastair) Christopher (Donald Summerhayes), KCMG

Macready, Sir Nevil John Wilfrid, Bt. (1923), CBE

MacSween, *Prof.* Sir Roderick Norman McIver, Kt.

Mactaggart, Sir John Auld, Bt. (1938)

McVicar, Sir David, Kt.

McWilliam, Sir Michael Douglas, KCMG

McWilliams, Sir Francis, GBE

Madden, Sir Charles Jonathan, Bt. (1919)

Madden, Sir David Christopher Andrew, KCMG

Maddison, *Hon.* Sir David George, Kt.

Madejski, Sir John Robert, Kt., OBE

Madel, Sir (William) David, Kt.

Magee, Sir Ian Bernard Vaughan, Kt., CB

Magnus, Sir Laurence Henry Philip, Bt. (1917)

Maguire, *Hon.* Sir Paul Richard, Kt.

Mahon, Sir William Walter, Bt. (1819), LVO

Maiden, Sir Colin James, Kt., DPHIL

Maini, *Prof.* Sir Ravinder Nath, Kt.

Maino, Sir Charles, KBE

†Maitland, Sir Charles Alexander, Bt. (1818)

Major, *Rt. Hon.* Sir John, KG, CH

Malbon, *Vice-Adm.* Sir Fabian Michael, KBE

Malcolm, Sir Alexander James Elton, Bt. (S. 1665), OBE

Malcolm, *Dr* Noel Robert, Kt., FBA

Males, *Hon.* Sir Stephen Martin, Kt.

Malet, Sir Harry Douglas St Lo, Bt. (1791)

Mallaby, Sir Christopher Leslie George, GCMG, GCVO

Mallick, *Prof.* Sir Netar Prakash, Kt.

Mallinson, Sir William James, Bt. (1935)

Malpas, Sir Robert, Kt., CBE

Mancham, Sir James Richard Marie, KBE

Mander, Sir (Charles) Nicholas, Bt. (1911)

Manduell, Sir John, Kt., CBE

Mann, *Hon.* Sir George Anthony, Kt.

Mann, Sir Rupert Edward, Bt. (1905)

Manning, Sir David Geoffrey, GCMG, CVO

Mano, Sir Koitaga, Kt., MBE

Mans, *Lt-Gen.* Sir Mark Francis Noel, KCB, CBE

Mansel, Sir Philip, Bt. (1622?)

Mansfield, *Prof.* Sir Peter, Kt.

Manuella, Sir Tulaga, GCMG, MBE

Manzie, Sir (Andrew) Gordon, KCB

Mara, Sir Ratu Naiqama, KBE

Margetson, Sir John William Denys, KCMG

Margetts, Sir Robert John, Kt., CBE

Markesinis, *Prof.* Sir Basil Spyridonos, Kt. QC

Markham, *Prof.* Sir Alexander Fred, Kt.

Markham, Sir (Arthur) David, Bt. (1911)

Marling, Sir Charles William Somerset, Bt. (1882)

Marmot, *Prof.* Sir Michael Gideon, Kt.

Marr, Sir Leslie Lynn, Bt. (1919)

Marriner, Sir Neville, Kt., CBE

†Marsden, Sir Tadgh Orlando Denton, Bt. (1924)

Marsh, *Prof.* Sir John Stanley, Kt., CBE

Marshall, Sir Michael John, Kt., CBE

Marshall, *Prof.* Sir (Oshley) Roy, Kt., CBE

Marshall, Sir Peter Harold Reginald, KCMG

Marshall, *Prof. Emeritus* Sir Woodville Kemble, Kt.

Martin, Sir Clive Haydon, Kt., OBE

Martin, Sir George Henry, Kt., CBE

Martin, Sir Gregory Michael Gerard, Kt.

Martin, *Prof.* Sir Laurence Woodward, Kt.

Martin, Sir (Robert) Bruce, Kt., QC

Marychurch, Sir Peter Harvey, KCMG

Masefield, Sir Charles Beech Gordon, Kt.

Mason, *Hon.* Sir Anthony Frank, KBE

Mason, Sir (Basil) John, Kt., CB, DSC, FRS

Mason, *Prof.* Sir David Kean, Kt., CBE

Mason, Sir John Peter, Kt., CBE

Mason, Sir Peter James, KBE

Mason, *Prof.* Sir Ronald, KCB, FRS

Massey, *Vice-Adm.* Sir Alan, KCB, CBE, ADC

Massie, Sir Herbert William, Kt., CBE

Matane, HE Sir Paulias Nguna, GCMG, OBE

Matheson of Matheson, Sir Fergus John, Bt. (1882)

Mathews, *Vice-Adm.* Sir Andrew David Hugh, KCB

Mathewson, Sir George Ross, Kt., CBE, PHD, FRSE

Matthews, Sir Terence Hedley, Kt., OBE

Maughan, Sir Deryck, Kt.

Mawer, Sir Philip John Courtney, Kt.

Maxwell, Sir Michael Eustace George, Bt. (S. 1681)

Maxwell Davies, Sir Peter, Kt., CH, CBE

Maxwell Macdonald (formerly Stirling-Maxwell), Sir John Ronald, Bt. (NS 1682)

Maxwell-Scott, Sir Dominic James, Bt. (1642)
May, *Rt. Hon.* Sir Anthony Tristram Kenneth, Kt.
Mayall, *Lt-Gen.* Sir Simon Vincent, KBE, CB
Mayfield, Sir Andrew Charles, Kt.
Meadow, *Prof.* Sir (Samuel) Roy, Kt., FRCP, FRCPE
Meale, Sir Joseph Alan, Kt.
Medlycott, Sir Mervyn Tregonwell, Bt. (1808)
Meeran, *His Hon.* Sir Goolam Hoosen Kader, Kt.
Meldrum, Sir Graham, Kt., CBE, QFSM
Melhuish, Sir Michael Ramsay, KBE, CMG
Mellars, *Prof.* Sir Paul Anthony, Kt., FBA
Mellon, Sir James, KCMG
Melmoth, Sir Graham John, Kt.
Melville, *Prof.* Sir David, Kt., CBE
Merifield, Sir Anthony James, KCVO, CB
Metcalf, *Prof.* Sir David Harry, Kt., CBE
†Meyer, Sir (Anthony) Ashley Frank, Bt. (1910)
Meyer, Sir Christopher John Rome, KCMG
†Meyrick, Sir Timothy Thomas Charlton, Bt. (1880)
Miakwe, *Hon.* Sir Akepa, KBE
Michael, Sir Duncan, Kt.
Michael, *Dr* Sir Jonathan, Kt.
Michael, Sir Peter Colin, Kt., CBE
Michels, Sir David Michael Charles, Kt.
Middleton, Sir John Maxwell, Kt.
Middleton, Sir Peter Edward, GCB
Miers, Sir (Henry) David Alastair Capel, KBE, CMG
Milbank, Sir Anthony Frederick, Bt. (1882)
Milborne-Swinnerton-Pilkington, Sir Thomas Henry, Bt. (S. 1635)
Milburn, Sir Anthony Rupert, Bt. (1905)
†Miles, Sir Philip John, Bt. (1859)
Millais, Sir Geoffrey Richard Everett, Bt. (1885)
Millar, *Prof.* Sir Fergus Graham Burtholme, Kt.
Miller, Sir Albert Joel, KCMG, LVO, MBE, QPM, CPM
Miller, Sir Donald John, Kt., FRSE, FRENG
Miller, *Air Marshal* Sir Graham Anthony, KBE
Miller, Sir Anthony Thomas, Bt. (1705)
Miller, Sir Hilary Duppa (Hal), Kt.
Miller, Sir Jonathan Wolfe, Kt., CBE
Miller, Sir Peter North, Kt.
Miller, Sir Robin Robert William, Kt.
Miller, Sir Ronald Andrew Baird, Kt., CBE
Miller of Glenlee, Sir Stephen William Macdonald, Bt. (1788)
Mills, Sir Ian, Kt.
Mills, Sir Jonathan Edward Harland (John), Kt., FRSE
Mills, Sir Keith Edward, GBE

Mills, Sir Peter Frederick Leighton, Bt. (1921)
Milman, Sir David Patrick, Bt. (1800)
Milne, Sir John Drummond, Kt.
Milne-Watson, Sir Andrew Michael, Bt. (1937)
Milner, Sir Timothy William Lycett, Bt. (1717)
Mirrlees, *Prof.* Sir James Alexander, Kt., FBA
Mitchell, *Rt. Hon.* Sir James FitzAllen, KCMG
Mitchell, *Very Revd* Patrick Reynolds, KCVO
Mitchell, *Hon.* Sir Stephen George, Kt.
Mitting, *Hon.* Sir John Edward, Kt.
Moate, Sir Roger Denis, Kt.
Moberly, Sir Patrick Hamilton, KCMG
Moffat, Sir Brian Scott, Kt., OBE
Moffat, *Lt.-Gen.* Sir (William) Cameron, KBE
Moir, Sir Christopher Ernest, Bt. (1916)
Molesworth-St Aubyn, Sir William, Bt. (1689)
Molony, Sir Thomas Desmond, Bt. (1925)
Moncada, *Prof.* Sir Salvador, Kt.
Montagu, Sir Nicholas Lionel John, KCB
Montagu-Pollock, Sir Giles Hampden, Bt. (1872)
Montague, Sir Adrian Alastair, Kt., CBE
Montgomery, Sir (Basil Henry) David, Bt. (1801), CVO
Montgomery, *Vice-Adm.* Sir Charles Percival Ross, KBE, ADC
Montgomery-Cuninghame, Sir John Christopher Foggo, Bt. (NS 1672)
Moody-Stuart, Sir Mark, KCMG
Moollan, Sir Abdool Hamid Adam, Kt.
†Moon, Sir Roger, Bt. (1887)
Moor, *Hon.* Sir Philip Drury, Kt.
Moorcroft, Sir William, KBE
Moore, *Most Revd* Desmond Charles, KBE
Moore, Sir Francis Thomas, Kt.
Moore, Sir John Michael, KCVO, CB, DSC
Moore, *Vice Adm.* Sir Michael Antony Claës, KBE, LVO
Moore, *Prof.* Sir Norman Winfrid, Bt. (1919)
Moore, Sir Patrick William Eisdell, Kt., OBE
Moore, Sir Roger George, KBE
Moore, Sir William Roger Clotworthy, Bt. (1932), TD
Moore-Bick, *Rt. Hon.* Sir Martin James, Kt.
Moores, Sir Peter, Kt., CBE
Morauta, Sir Mekere, KCMG
Mordaunt, Sir Richard Nigel Charles, Bt. (1611)
Morgan, *Vice-Adm.* Sir Charles Christopher, KBE
Morgan, *Rt. Hon.* Sir (Charles) Declan, Kt.
Morgan, Sir Graham, Kt.
Morgan, *Hon.* Sir Paul Hyacinth, Kt.
Morison, *Hon.* Sir Thomas Richard Atkin, Kt.
Moritz, Sir Michael Jonathan, KBE

Morland, *Hon.* Sir Michael, Kt.
Morland, Sir Robert Kenelm, Kt.
†Morris, Sir Allan Lindsay, Bt. (1806)
Morris, *Air Marshal* Sir Arnold Alec, KBE, CB
Morris, Sir Derek James, Kt.
Morris, Sir Keith Elliot Hedley, KBE, CMG
Morris, *Prof.* Sir Peter John, Kt.
Morris, Sir Trefor Alfred, Kt., CBE, QPM
Morrison, Sir (Alexander) Fraser, Kt., CBE
Morrison, Sir Kenneth Duncan, Kt., CBE
Morrison-Bell, Sir William Hollin Dayrell, Bt. (1905)
Morrison-Low, Sir Richard Walter, Bt. (1908)
Morritt, *Rt. Hon.* Sir (Robert) Andrew, Kt., CVO
Morse, Sir Amyas Charles Edward, KCB
Morse, Sir Christopher Jeremy, KCMG
Moses, *Rt. Hon.* Sir Alan George, Kt.
Moses, *Very Revd* Dr John Henry, KCVO
Moss, Sir David Joseph, KCVO, CMG
Moss, Sir Stephen Alan, Kt.
Moss, Sir Stirling Craufurd, Kt., OBE
Mostyn, *Hon.* Sir Nicholas Anthony Joseph Ghislain, Kt.
Mostyn, Sir William Basil John, Bt. (1670)
Motion, Sir Andrew, Kt.
Mott, Sir John Harmer, Bt. (1930)
Mottram, Sir Richard Clive, GCB
†Mount, Sir (William Robert) Ferdinand, Bt. (1921)
Mountain, Sir Edward Brian Stanford, Bt. (1922)
Mowbray, Sir John Robert, Bt. (1880)
Moylan, *Hon.* Sir Andrew John Gregory, Kt.
Moynihan, *Dr* Sir Daniel, Kt.
†Muir, Sir Richard James Kay, Bt. (1892)
Muir-Mackenzie, Sir Alexander Alwyne Henry Charles Brinton, Bt. (1805)
Mulcahy, Sir Geoffrey John, Kt.
Mummery, *Rt. Hon.* Sir John Frank, Kt.
Munby, *Rt. Hon.* Sir James Lawrence, Kt.
Munro, Sir Alan Gordon, KCMG
†Munro, Sir Ian Kenneth, Bt. (S. 1634)
†Munro, Sir Keith Gordon Ian, Bt. (1825)
Muria, *Hon.* Sir Gilbert John Baptist, Kt.
Murphy, Sir Jonathan Michael, Kt., QPM
Murray, Sir David Edward, Kt.
Murray, *Rt. Hon.* Sir Donald Bruce, Kt.
Murray, Sir Nigel Andrew Digby, Bt. (S. 1628)
Murray, Sir Patrick Ian Keith, Bt. (S. 1673)
Murray, Sir Robert Sydney, Kt., CBE
Murray, Sir Robin MacGregor, Kt.
†Murray, Sir Rowland William, Bt. (S. 1630)

Musgrave, Sir Christopher John Shane, Bt. (1782)
Musgrave, Sir Christopher Patrick Charles, Bt. (1611)
Myers, Sir Derek John, Kt.
Myers, *Prof.* Sir Rupert Horace, KBE
Mynors, Sir Richard Baskerville, Bt. (1964)

Naipaul, Sir Vidiadhar Surajprasad, Kt.
Nairn, Sir Michael, Bt. (1904)
Naish, Sir (Charles) David, Kt.
Nalau, Sir Jerry Kasip, KBE
Nall, Sir Edward William Joseph Bt. (1954)
Namaliu, *Rt. Hon.* Sir Rabbie Langanai, KCMG
Napier, Sir Charles Joseph, Bt. (1867)
Napier, Sir John Archibald Lennox, Bt. (S. 1627)
Narey, Sir Martin James, Kt.
Naylor, Sir Robert, Kt.
Naylor-Leyland, Sir Philip Vyvyan, Bt. (1895)
Neal, Sir Eric James, Kt., CVO
Neale, Sir Gerrard Anthony, Kt.
Neave, Sir Paul Arundell, Bt. (1795)
Neill, *Rt. Hon.* Sir Brian Thomas, Kt.
Neill, Sir (James) Hugh, KCVO, CBE, TD
†Nelson, Sir Jamie Charles Vernon Hope, Bt. (1912)
Nelson, *Hon.* Sir Robert Franklyn, Kt.
New, *Maj.-Gen.* Sir Laurence Anthony Wallis, Kt., CB, CBE
Newall, Sir Paul Henry, Kt., TD
Newbigging, Sir David Kennedy, Kt., OBE
Newby, *Prof.* Sir Howard Joseph, Kt., CBE
Newey, *Hon.* Sir Guy Richard, Kt.
Newington, Sir Michael John, KCMG
Newman, Sir Francis Hugh Cecil, Bt. (1912)
Newman, Sir Geoffrey Robert, Bt. (1836)
Newman, *Hon.* Sir George Michael, Kt.
Newman, Sir Kenneth Leslie, GBE, QPM
Newman, *Vice-Adm.* Sir Roy Thomas, KCB
Newman Taylor, *Prof.* Sir Anthony John, Kt., CBE
Newsam, Sir Peter Anthony, Kt.
Newson-Smith, Sir Peter Frank Graham, Bt. (1944)
Newton, *Revd* George Peter Howgill, Bt. (1900)
Newton, Sir John Garnar, Bt. (1924)
Newton, *Lt-Gen.* Sir Paul Raymond, KBE
Nice, Sir Geoffrey, Kt., QC
Nicol, *Hon.* Sir Andrew George Lindsay, Kt.
Nichol, Sir Duncan Kirkbride, Kt., CBE
Nicholas, Sir David, Kt., CBE
Nicholas, Sir John William, KCVO, CMG
Nicholls, Sir Nigel Hamilton, KCVO, CBE
Nichols, Sir Richard Everard, Kt.
Nicholson, Sir Bryan Hubert, GBE, Kt.

Nicholson, Sir Charles Christian, Bt. (1912)
Nicholson, Sir David, KCB, CBE
Nicholson, *Rt. Hon.* Sir Michael, Kt.
Nicholson, Sir Paul Douglas, KCVO, Kt.
Nicholson, Sir Robin Buchanan, Kt., PHD, FRS, FRENG
Nicoll, Sir William, KCMG
Nightingale, Sir Charles Manners Gamaliel, Bt. (1628)
Nixon, Sir Simon Michael Christopher, Bt. (1906)
Noble, Sir David Brunel, Bt. (1902)
Noble, Sir Timothy Peter, Bt. (1923)
Nombri, Sir Joseph Karl, Kt., ISO, BEM
Norman, Sir Nigel James, Bt. (1915)
Norman, Sir Ronald, Kt., OBE
Norman, Sir Torquil Patrick Alexander, Kt., CBE
Normington, Sir David John, GCB
Norrington, Sir Roger Arthur Carver, Kt., CBE
Norris, *Hon.* Sir Alastair Hubert, Kt.
Norriss, *Air Marshal* Sir Peter Coulson, KBE, CB, AFC
North, Sir Peter Machin, Kt., CBE, QC, DCL, FBA
North, Sir Thomas Lindsay, Kt.
North, Sir (William) Jonathan (Frederick), Bt. (1920)
Norton, *Maj.-Gen.* Sir George Pemberton Ross, KCVO, CBE
Norton-Griffiths, Sir John, Bt. (1922)
Nossal, Sir Gustav Joseph Victor, Kt., CBE
Nott, *Rt. Hon.* Sir John William Frederic, KCB
Nourse, *Rt. Hon.* Sir Martin Charles, Kt.
Novoselov, *Prof.* Sir Konstantin, Kt.
Nugee, *Hon.* Sir Chrisstopher George, Kt.
†Nugent, Sir Christopher George Ridley, Bt. (1806)
Nugent, Sir Nicholas Myles John, Bt. (I. 1795)
Nugent, Sir (Walter) Richard Middleton, Bt. (1831)
Nunn, Sir Trevor Robert, Kt., CBE
Nunneley, Sir Charles Kenneth Roylance, Kt.
Nursaw, Sir James, KCB, QC
Nurse, Sir Paul Maxime, Kt.
Nuttall, Sir Harry, Bt. (1922)
Nutting, Sir John Grenfell, Bt. (1903), QC

Oakeley, Sir John Digby Atholl, Bt. (1790)
Oakes, Sir Christopher, Bt. (1939)
†Oakshott, Sir Thomas Hendrie, Bt. (1959)
Oates, Sir Thomas, Kt., CMG, OBE
O'Brien, Sir Robert Stephen, Kt., CBE
O'Brien, Sir Timothy John, Bt. (1849)
O'Brien, Sir William, Kt.
O'Brien, *Adm.* Sir William Donough, KCB, DSC
O'Connell, Sir Bernard, Kt.
O'Connell, Sir Maurice James Donagh MacCarthy, Bt. (1869)

O'Connor, Sir Denis Francis, Kt., CBE, QPM
Odell, Sir Stanley John, Kt.
Odgers, Sir Graeme David William, Kt.
O'Donnell, Sir Christopher John, Kt.
O'Donoghue, *Lt.-Gen.* Sir Kevin, KCB, CBE
O'Dowd, Sir David Joseph, Kt., CBE, QPM
Ogden, *Dr* Sir Peter James, Kt.
Ogden, Sir Robert, Kt., CBE
Ogilvy, Sir Francis Gilbert Arthur, Bt. (S. 1626)
Ogilvy-Wedderburn, Sir Andrew John Alexander, Bt. (1803)
Ogio, *HE* Sir Michael, GCMG, CBE
Ognall, *Hon.* Sir Harry Henry, Kt.
Ohlson, Sir Brian Eric Christopher, Bt. (1920)
Oldham, *Dr* Sir John, Kt., OBE
Oliver, Sir James Michael Yorrick, Kt.
Oliver, Sir Stephen John Lindsay, Kt., QC
O'Hara *Hon.* Sir John Ailbe
†O'Loghlen, Sir Michael, Bt. (1838)
Olver, Sir Richard Lake, Kt.
Omand, Sir David Bruce, GCB
Ondaatje, Sir Christopher, Kt., CBE
O'Nions, Prof. Sir Robert Keith, Kt., FRS, PHD
Onslow, Sir Richard Paul Atherton, Bt. (1797)
Oppenheimer, Sir Michael Bernard Grenville, Bt. (1921)
Oppenshaw, Sir Charles Peter Lawford, Kt., QC
O'Rahilly, *Prof.* Sir Stephen Patrick, Kt., FRS
Orde, Sir Hugh Stephen Roden, Kt., OBE, QPM
O'Regan, *Dr* Sir Stephen Gerard (Tipene), Kt.
O'Reilly, Sir Anthony John Francis, Kt.
O'Reilly, *Prof.* Sir John James, Kt.
Orr, Sir John, Kt., OBE
Orr-Ewing, Sir (Alistair) Simon, Bt. (1963)
Orr-Ewing, Sir Archibald Donald, Bt. (1886)
Osborn, Sir John Holbrook, Kt.
Osborn, Sir Richard Henry Danvers, Bt. (1662)
Osborne, Sir Peter George, Bt. (I. 1629)
O'Shea, *Prof.* Sir Timothy Michael Martin, Kt.
Osmotherly, Sir Edward Benjamin Crofton, Kt., CB
O'Sullevan, Sir Peter John, Kt., CBE
Oswald, Sir (William Richard) Michael, KCVO
Ottaway *Rt. Hon.* Sir Richard Geoffrey James, Kt.
Otton, Sir Geoffrey John, KCB
Otton, *Rt. Hon.* Sir Philip Howard, Kt.
Oulton, Sir Antony Derek Maxwell, GCB, QC
Ouseley, *Hon.* Sir Brian Walter, Kt.
Outram, Sir Alan James, Bt. (1858)
Owen, Sir Geoffrey, Kt.
Owen, *Prof.* Sir Michaael John, Kt.

Owen, *Hon.* Sir Robert Michael, Kt.

Owen-Jones, Sir Lindsay Harwood, KBE

Packer, Sir Richard John, KCB

Paget, Sir Julian Tolver, Bt. (1871), CVO

Paget, Sir Richard Herbert, Bt. (1886)

Paice, *Rt. Hon.* Sir James Edward Thornton, Kt.

Pakenham, *Hon.* Sir Michael Aiden, KBE, CMG

Palin, *Air Chief Marshal* Sir Roger Hewlett, KCB, OBE

Palmer, Sir Albert Rocky, Kt.

Palmer, Sir (Charles) Mark, Bt. (1886)

Palmer, Sir Geoffrey Christopher John, Bt. (1660)

Palmer, *Rt. Hon.* Sir Geoffrey Winston Russell, KCMG

Palmer, *Prof.* Sir Godfrey Henry Oliver, Kt., OBE

Palmer, Sir John Edward Somerset, Bt. (1791)

Palmer, *Maj.-Gen.* Sir (Joseph) Michael, KCVO

Palmer, Sir Reginald Oswald, GCMG, MBE

Panter, Sir Howard Hugh, Kt.

Pappano, Sir Antonio, Kt.

Parbo, Sir Arvi Hillar, Kt.

Park, *Hon.* Sir Andrew Edward Wilson, Kt.

Parker, Sir Alan, Kt.

Parker, Sir Alan William, Kt., CBE

Parker, *Rt. Hon.* Sir Jonathan Frederic, Kt.

Parker, *Hon.* Sir Kenneth Blades, Kt.

Parker, *Maj.* Sir Michael John, KCVO, CBE

Parker, *Gen.* Sir Nicholas Ralph, KCB, CBE

Parker, Sir Richard (William) Hyde, Bt. (1681)

Parker, Sir (Thomas) John, GBE

Parker, Sir William Peter Brian, Bt. (1844)

Parkes, Sir Edward Walter, Kt., FRENG

Parkinson, Sir Michael, Kt., CBE

Parry, *Prof.* Sir Eldryd Hugh Owen, KCMG, OBE

Parry, Sir Emyr Jones, GCMG

Parry-Evans, *Air Chief Marshal* Sir David, GCB, CBE

Parsons, Sir John Christopher, KCVO

Parsons, Sir Richard Edmund (Clement Fownes), KCMG

Partridge, Sir Michael John Anthony, KCB

Partridge, Sir Nicholas Wyndham, Kt., OBE

Pascoe, *Gen.* Sir Robert Alan, KCB, MBE

Pasley, Sir Robert Killigrew Sabine, Bt. (1794)

Paston-Bedingfeld, Sir Henry Edgar, Bt. (1661)

Paterson, Sir Dennis Craig, Kt.

Patey, Sir William Charters, KCMG

Patten, *Rt. Hon.* Sir Nicholas John, Kt.

Pattie, *Rt. Hon.* Sir Geoffrey Edwin, Kt.

Pattison, *Prof.* Sir John Ridley, Kt., DM, FRCPATH

Pattullo, Sir (David) Bruce, Kt., CBE

Pauncefort-Duncombe, Sir David Philip Henry, Bt. (1859)

Payne, *Prof.* Sir David Neil, Kt., CBE, FRS

Peace, Sir John Wilfrid, Kt.

Peach, Sir Leonard Harry, Kt.

Peach, *Air Chief Marshal* Sir Stuart William, KCB, CBE

Pearce, Sir (Daniel Norton) Idris, Kt., CBE, TD

Pearse, Sir Brian Gerald, Kt.

Pearson, Sir Francis Nicholas Fraser, Bt. (1964)

Pearson, Sir Keith, Kt.

Pearson, *Gen.* Sir Thomas Cecil Hook, KCB, CBE, DSO

Peart, *Prof.* Sir William Stanley, Kt., MD, FRS

Pease, Sir Joseph Gurney, Bt. (1882)

Pease, Sir Richard Thorn, Bt. (1920)

Peat, Sir Gerrard Charles, KCVO

Peat, Sir Michael Charles Gerrard, GCVO

Peckham, *Prof.* Sir Michael John, Kt.,

Peek, Sir Richard Grenville, Bt. (1874)

Pelgen, Sir Harry Friedrich, Kt., MBE

Pelham, *Dr* Sir Hugh Reginald Brentnall, Kt., FRS

Pelly, Sir Richard John, Bt. (1840)

Pendry, *Prof.* Sir John Brian, Kt., FRS

Penrose, *Prof.* Sir Roger, Kt., OM, FRS

Penry-Davey, *Hon.* Sir David Herbert, Kt.

Pepper, *Dr.* Sir David Edwin, KCMG

Pepper, *Prof.* Sir Michael, Kt.

Pepys, *Prof.* Sir Mark Brian, Kt.

Perowne, *Vice-Adm.* Sir James Francis, KBE

Perring, Sir John Raymond, Bt. (1963)

Perris, Sir David (Arthur), Kt., MBE

Perry, Sir David Howard, KCB

Perry, Sir Michael Sydney, GBE

Pervez, Sir Mohammed Anwar, Kt., OBE

Peters, *Prof.* Sir David Keith, Kt., FRCP

Pethica, *Prof.* Sir John Bernard, Kt., FRS

Petit, Sir Dinshaw Manockjee, Bt. (1890)

Peto, Sir Francis Michael Morton, Bt. (1855)

Peto, Sir Henry Christopher Morton Bampfylde, Bt. (1927)

Peto, *Prof.* Sir Richard, Kt., FRS

Petrie, Sir Peter Charles, Bt. (1918), CMG

Pettigrew, Sir Russell Hilton, Kt.

†Philipson-Stow, Sir (Robert) Matthew, Bt. (1907)

Phillips, Sir (Gerald) Hayden, GCB

Phillips, Sir John David, Kt., QPM

Phillips, Sir Jonathan, KCB

Phillips, Sir Peter John, Kt., OBE

Phillips, Sir Robin Francis, Bt. (1912)

Phillips *Hon.* Sir Stephen Edmund, Kt.

Phillips, Sir Tom Richard Vaughan, KCMG

Pickard, Sir (John) Michael, Kt.

Pickthorn, Sir James Francis Mann, Bt. (1959)

Pidgeon, Sir John Allan Stewart, Kt.

†Piers, Sir James Desmond, Bt. (I. 1661)

Piggott-Brown, Sir William Brian, Bt. (1903)

Pigot, Sir George Hugh, Bt. (1764)

Pigott, *Lt.-Gen.* Sir Anthony David, KCB, CBE

Pigott, Sir Berkeley Henry Sebastian, Bt. (1808)

Pike, *Lt.-Gen.* Sir Hew William Royston, KCB, DSO, MBE

Pike, Sir Michael Edmund, KCVO, CMG

Pile, Sir Anthony John Devereux, Bt. (1900)

Pilditch, Sir John Richard, Bt. (1929)

Pill, *Rt. Hon.* Sir Malcolm Thomas, Kt.

Pilling, Sir Joseph Grant, KCB

Pinsent, Sir Christopher Roy, Bt. (1938)

Pinsent, Sir Matthew Clive, Kt., CBE

Pissarides, *Prof.* Sir Christopher Antoniou, Kt., FBA

Pitcher, Sir Desmond Henry, Kt.

Pitchers, *Hon.* Sir Christopher (John), Kt.

Pitchford, *Rt. Hon.* Sir Christopher John, Kt.

Pitoi, Sir Sere, Kt., CBE

Pitt, Sir Michael Edward, Kt.

Plastow, Sir David Arnold Stuart, Kt.

Platt, Sir Martin Philip, Bt. (1959)

Pledger, *Air Chief Marshal* Sir Malcolm David, KCB, OBE, AFC

Plender, *Hon.* Sir Richard Owen, Kt.

Plumbly, Sir Derek John, KCMG

Pohai, Sir Timothy, Kt., MBE

Pole, Sir John Chandos, Bt. (1791)

Pole, Sir (John) Richard (Walter Reginald) Carew, Bt. (1628)

Polkinghorne, *Revd Canon* John Charlton, KBE, FRS

Pollard, Sir Charles, Kt.

†Pollen, Sir Richard John Hungerford, Bt. (1795)

Pollock, Sir George Frederick, Bt. (1866)

Pomeroy, Sir Brian Walter, Kt., CBE

Ponder, *Prof.* Sir Bruce Anthony John, Kt.

†Ponsonby, Sir Charles Ashley, Bt. (1956)

Poore, Sir Roger Ricardo, Bt. (1795)

Popplewell, *Hon.* Sir Andrew John, Kt.

Popplewell, *Hon.* Sir Oliver Bury, Kt.

†Porritt, *Hon.* Sir Jonathon Espie, Bt. (1963), CBE

Portal, Sir Jonathan Francis, Bt. (1901)

Porter, *Prof.* Sir Keith Macdonald, Kt.

Potter, *Rt. Hon.* Sir Mark Howard, Kt.

Pound, Sir John David, Bt. (1905)

Povey, Sir Keith, Kt., QPM

Powell, Sir John Christopher, Kt.

Powell, Sir Nicholas Folliott Douglas, Bt. (1897)

Power, Sir Alastair John Cecil, Bt. (1924)

Pownall, Sir Michael Graham, KCB

Prance, *Prof.* Sir Ghillean Tolmie, Kt., FRS

Pratchett, Sir Terence David John, Kt., OBE
Prendergast, Sir (Walter) Kieran, KCVO, CMG
Prescott, Sir Mark, Bt. (1938)
Preston, Sir Philip Charles Henry Hulton, Bt. (1815)
Prevost, Sir Christopher Gerald, Bt. (1805)
Price, Sir Francis Caradoc Rose, Bt. (1815)
Price, Sir Frank Leslie, Kt.
†Prichard-Jones, Sir David John Walter, Bt. (1910)
Priestly, Sir Julian Gordon, KCMG
†Primrose, Sir John Ure, Bt. (1903)
Pringle, *Hon.* Sir John Kenneth, Kt.
†Pringle, Sir Simon Robert, Bt. (S. 1683)
Proby, Sir William Henry, Bt. (1952)
Proctor-Beauchamp, Sir Christopher Radstock, Bt. (1745)
Prosser, Sir David John, Kt.
Prosser, Sir Ian Maurice Gray, Kt.
Pryke, Sir Christopher Dudley, Bt. (1926)
Puapua, *Rt. Hon.* Sir Tomasi, GCMG, KBE
Pulford, *Air Marshal* Sir Andrew Douglas, KCB, CBE
Purves, Sir William, Kt., CBE, DSO
Purvis, *Vice-Adm.* Sir Neville, KCB

Quan, Sir Henry (Francis), KBE
†Quilter, Sir Guy Raymond Cuthbert, Bt. (1897)

Radcliffe, Sir Sebastian Everard, Bt. (1813)
Radda, *Prof.* Sir George Karoly, Kt., CBE, FRS
Rae, Sir William, Kt., QPM
Raeburn, Sir Michael Edward Norman, Bt. (1923)
Rake, Sir Michael Derek Vaughan, Kt.
Ralli, Sir David Charles, Bt. (1912)
Ramakrishnan, *Dr* Sir Venkatraman, Kt.
Ramdanee, Sir Mookteswar Baboolall Kailash, Kt.
Ramphal, Sir Shridath Surendranath, GCMG
Ramphul, Sir Baalkhristna, Kt.
Ramphul, Sir Indurduth, Kt.
Ramsay, Sir Alexander William Burnett, Bt. (1806)
Ramsay, Sir Allan John (Hepple), KBE, CMG
Ramsay-Fairfax-Lucy, Sir Edmund John William Hugh, Bt. (1836)
Ramsden, Sir John Charles Josslyn, Bt. (1689)
Ramsey, *Dr* Sir Frank Cuthbert, KCMG
Ramsey, *Hon.* Sir Vivian Arthur, Kt.
Randall, *Rt. Hon.* Sir (Alexander) John, Kt.
Rankin, Sir Ian Niall, Bt. (1898)
Rasch, Sir Simon Anthony Carne, Bt. (1903)
Rashleigh, Sir Richard Harry, Bt. (1831)
Ratcliffe, *Prof.* Sir Peter John, Kt., FRS
Ratford, Sir David John Edward, KCMG, CVO

Rattee, *Hon.* Sir Donald Keith, Kt.
Rattle, Sir Simon Dennis, Kt., OM, CBE
Rawlins, *Hon.* Sir Hugh Anthony, Kt.
Rawlins, *Prof.* Sir Michael David, Kt., FRCP, FRCPED
Rawlinson, Sir Anthony Henry John, Bt. (1891)
Rea, *Prof.* Sir Desmond, Kt., OBE
Read, *Air Marshal* Sir Charles Frederick, KBE, CB, DFC, AFC
Read, *Prof.* Sir David John, Kt.
Read, Sir John Emms, Kt.
Reardon-Smith, Sir (William) Antony (John), Bt. (1920)
Reddaway, Sir David Norman, KCMG, MBE
Redgrave, Sir Steven Geoffrey, Kt., CBE
Redmayne, Sir Giles Martin, Bt. (1964)
Redmond, Sir Anthony Gerard, Kt.
Redwood, Sir Peter Boverton, Bt. (1911)
Reed, *Prof.* Sir Alec Edward, Kt., CBE
Reedie, Sir Craig Collins, Kt., CBE
Rees, Sir David Allan, Kt., PHD, DSC, FRS
Rees, Sir Richard Ellis Meuric, Kt., CBE
Reeve, Sir Anthony, KCMG, KCVO
Reffell, *Adm.* Sir Derek Roy, KCB
Reich, Sir Erich Arieh, Kt.
Reid, Sir Alexander James, Bt. (1897)
Reid, Sir David Edward, Kt.
Reid, *Rt. Hon.* Sir George, Kt.
Reid, Sir (Philip) Alan, GCVO
Reid, Sir Robert Paul, Kt.
Reid, Sir William Kennedy, KCB
Reiher, Sir Frederick Bernard Carl, KCMG, KBE
Reilly, *Lt.-Gen.* Sir Jeremy Calcott, KCB, DSO
Renals, Sir Stanley, Bt. (1895)
Renouf, Sir Clement William Bailey, Kt.
Renshaw, Sir John David Bine, Bt. (1903)
Renwick, Sir Richard Eustace, Bt. (1921)
Reporter, Sir Shapoor Ardeshirji, KBE
Reynolds, Sir David James, Bt. (1923)
Reynolds, Sir Peter William John, Kt., CBE
Rhodes, Sir John Christopher Douglas, Bt. (1919)
Rice, *Prof.* Sir Charles Duncan, Kt.
Rice, *Maj.-Gen.* Sir Desmond Hind Garrett, KCVO, CBE
Rice, Sir Timothy Miles Bindon, Kt.
Richard, Sir Cliff, Kt., OBE
Richards, Sir Brian Mansel, Kt., CBE, PHD
Richards, *Hon.* Sir David Anthony Stewart, Kt.
Richards, Sir David Gerald, Kt.
Richards, Sir Francis Neville, KCMG, CVO
Richards, *Prof.* Sir Michael Adrian, Kt., CBE
Richards, Sir Rex Edward, Kt., DSC, FRS
Richards, *Rt. Hon.* Sir Stephen Price, Kt.

Richardson, Sir Anthony Lewis, Bt. (1924)
Richardson, *Rt. Hon.* Sir Ivor Lloyd Morgan, Kt,
Richardson, Sir John Patrick, KBE
Richardson, *Lt.-Gen.* Sir Robert Francis, KCB, CVO, CBE
Richardson, Sir Thomas Legh, KCMG
Richardson-Bunbury, Sir (Richard David) Michael, Bt. (I. 1787)
Richmond, Sir David Frank, KBE, CMG
Richmond, *Prof.* Sir Mark Henry, Kt., FRS
Ricketts, Sir Peter Forbes, GCMG, GCVO
Ricketts, Sir Stephen Tristram, Bt. (1828)
Ricks, *Prof.* Sir Christopher Bruce, Kt.
Riddell, Sir Walter John, Bt. (S. 1628)
Ridgway, *Lt.-Gen.* Sir Andrew Peter, KBE, CB
Ridley, Sir Adam (Nicholas), Kt.
Ridley, Sir Michael Kershaw, KCVO
Rifkind, *Rt. Hon.* Sir Malcolm Leslie, KCMG
Rigby, Sir Anthony John, Bt. (1929)
Rigby, Sir Peter, Kt.
Rimer, *Rt. Hon.* Sir Colin Percy Farquharson, Kt.
Ripley, Sir William Hugh, Bt. (1880)
Ritako, Sir Thomas Baha, Kt., MBE
Ritblat, Sir John Henry, Kt.
Ritchie, *Prof.* Sir Lewis Duthie, Kt., OBE
Rivett-Carnac, Sir Jonathan James, Bt. (1836)
Rix, *Rt. Hon.* Sir Bernard Anthony, Kt.
Robb, Sir John Weddell, Kt.
Roberts, Sir Derek Harry, Kt., CBE, FRS, FRENG
Roberts, *Prof.* Sir Edward Adam, KCMG
Roberts, Sir Gilbert Howland Rookehurst, Bt. (1809)
Roberts, Sir Hugh Ashley, GCVO
Roberts, Sir Ivor Anthony, KCMG
Roberts, *Dr* Sir Richard John, Kt.
Roberts, Sir Samuel, Bt. (1919)
Roberts, *Maj.-Gen.* Sir Sebastian John Lechmere, KCVO, OBE
†Roberts-Buchanan, Sir James Elton Denby, Bt. (1909)
Robertson, Sir Simon Manwaring, Kt.
Robins, Sir Ralph Harry, Kt., FRENG
Robinson, Sir Anthony, Kt.
Robinson, Sir Bruce, KCB
†Robinson, Sir Christopher Philipse, Bt. (1854)
Robinson, Sir Gerrard Jude, Kt.
Robinson, Sir Ian, Kt.
Robinson, Sir John James Michael Laud, Bt. (1660)
Robinson, *Dr* Sir Kenneth, Kt.
Robinson, Sir Peter Frank, Bt. (1908)
Robson, Sir John Adam, KCMG
Robson, Sir Stephen Arthur, Kt., CB
Roch, *Rt. Hon.* Sir John Ormond, Kt.
Roche, Sir David O'Grady, Bt. (1838)
Roche, Sir Henry John, Kt.
Rodgers, Sir (Andrew) Piers (Wingate Aikin-Sneath), Bt. (1964)

Rodley, *Prof.* Sir Nigel, KBE
Rogers, *Air Chief Marshal* Sir John Robson, KCB, CBE
Rogers, Sir Peter, Kt.
Rogers, Sir Robert James, KCB
Rollo, *Lt.-Gen.* Sir William Raoul, KCB, CBE
Ropner, Sir John Bruce Woollacott, Bt. (1952)
Ropner, Sir Robert Clinton, Bt. (1904)
Rose, Sir Arthur James, Kt., CBE
Rose, *Rt. Hon.* Sir Christopher Dudley Roger, Kt.
Rose, Sir Clive Martin, GCMG
Rose, Sir David Lancaster, Bt. (1874)
Rose, *Gen.* Sir (Hugh) Michael, KCB, CBE, DSO, QGM
Rose, Sir John Edward Victor, Kt.
Rose, Sir Julian Day, Bt. (1872 and 1909)
Rosenthal, Sir Norman Leon, Kt.
Ross, *Maj.* Sir Andrew Charles Paterson, Bt. (1960)
Ross, *Lt.-Gen.* Sir Robert Jeremy, KCB, OBE
Ross, *Lt.-Col.* Sir Walter Hugh Malcolm, GCVO, OBE
Ross, Sir Walter Robert Alexander, KCVO
Rossi, Sir Hugh Alexis Louis, Kt.
Roth, *Hon.* Sir Peter Marcel, Kt.
Rothschild, Sir Evelyn Robert Adrian de, Kt.
Rove, *Revd* Ikan, KBE
Rowe, *Rear-Adm.* Sir Patrick Barton, KCVO, CBE
Rowe Ham, Sir David Kenneth, CBE
Rowland, Sir Geoffrey Robert, Kt.
Rowland, Sir (John) David, Kt.
Rowley, Sir Charles Robert, Bt. (1786 and 1836)
Rowling, Sir John Reginald, Kt.
Rowlinson, *Prof.* Sir John Shipley, Kt., FRS
Royce, *Hon.* Sir Roger John, Kt.
Royden, Sir Christopher John, Bt. (1905)
Rubin, *Prof.* Sir Peter Charles, Kt.
Rudd, Sir (Anthony) Nigel (Russell), Kt.
Ruddock, Sir Paul, Kt.
Rudge, Sir Alan Walter, Kt., CBE, FRS
Rugge-Price, Sir James Keith Peter, Bt. (1804)
Ruggles-Brise, Sir Timothy Edward, Bt. (1935)
Rumbold, Sir Henry John Sebastian, Bt. (1779)
Rushdie, Sir (Ahmed) Salman, Kt.
†Russell, Sir (Arthur) Mervyn, Bt. (1812)
Russell, Sir Charles Dominic, Bt. (1916)
Russell, Sir George, Kt., CBE
Russell, Sir Muir, KCB
Russell, Sir Robert, Kt.
Rutter, *Prof.* Sir Michael Llewellyn, Kt., CBE, MD, FRS
Ryan, Sir Derek Gerald, Bt. (1919)
Rycroft, Sir Richard John, Bt. (1784)
Ryder, *Rt. Hon.* Sir Ernest Nigel, Kt., TD

Sacranie, Sir Iqbal Abdul Karim Mussa, Kt., OBE
Sainsbury, *Rt. Hon.* Sir Timothy Alan Davan, Kt.
St Clair-Ford, Sir Robin Sam, Bt. (1793)
St George, Sir John Avenel Bligh, Bt. (I. 1766)
St John-Mildmay, Sir Walter John Hugh, Bt. (1772)
St Omer, *Hon. Dr* Sir Dunstan Gerbert Raphael, KCMG
Sainty, Sir John Christopher, KCB
Sakora, *Hon.* Sir Bernard Berekia, KBE
Sales, *Hon.* Sir Philip James, Kt.
Salika, Sir Gibuna Gibbs, KBE
Salisbury, Sir Robert William, Kt.
Salt, Sir Patrick MacDonnell, Bt. (1869)
Salt, Sir (Thomas) Michael John, Bt. (1899)
Salusbury-Trelawny, Sir John William Richard, Bt. (1628)
Salz, Sir Anthony Michael Vaughan, Kt.
Sampson, Sir Colin, Kt., CBE, QPM
Samuel, Sir John Michael Glen, Bt. (1898)
Samuelson, Sir James Francis, Bt. (1884)
Samuelson, Sir Sydney Wylie, Kt., CBE
Samworth, Sir David Chetwode, Kt., CBE
Sanders, Sir Robert Tait, KBE, CMG
Sanders, Sir Ronald Michael, KCMG
Sanderson, Sir Frank Linton, Bt. (1920)
Sands, Sir Roger Blakemore, KCB
Sants, Sir Hector William Hepburn, Kt.
Sarei, Sir Alexis Holyweek, Kt., CBE
Sargent, Sir William Desmond, Kt., CBE
Satchwell, Sir Kevin Joseph, Kt.
Saunders, Sir Bruce Joshua, KBE
Saunders, *Hon.* Sir John Henry Boulton, Kt.
Savill, *Prof.* Sir John Stewart, Kt.
Savory, Sir Michael Berry, Kt.
Sawers, Sir Robert John, KCMG
Saxby, *Prof.* Sir Robin Keith, Kt.
Scarlett, Sir John McLeod, KCMG, OBE
Schiemann, *Rt. Hon.* Sir Konrad Hermann Theodor, Kt.
Schiff, Sir András, Kt.
Scholar, Sir Michael Charles, KCB
Scholey, Sir David Gerald, Kt., CBE
Schubert, Sir Sydney, Kt.
Scipio, Sir Hudson Rupert, Kt.
Scott, Sir Anthony Percy, Bt. (1913)
Scott, Sir David Richard Alexander, Kt., CBE
Scott, *Prof.* Sir George Peter, Kt.
Scott, Sir James Jervoise, Bt. (1962)
Scott, Sir John Hamilton, KCVO
Scott, Sir Kenneth Bertram Adam, KCVO, CMG
Scott, Sir Oliver Christopher Anderson, Bt. (1909)
Scott, *Prof.* Sir Philip John, KBE
Scott, Sir Ridley, Kt.
Scott, Sir Robert David Hillyer, Kt.
Scott, Sir Walter John, Bt. (1907)

Scott-Lee, Sir Paul Joseph, Kt., QPM
Seale, Sir Clarence David, Kt.
Seale, Sir John Henry, Bt. (1838)
Sebastian, Sir Cuthbert Montraville, GCMG, OBE
†Sebright, Sir Rufus Hugo Giles, Bt. (1626)
Seccombe, Sir (William) Vernon Stephen, Kt.
Seconde, Sir Reginald Louis, KCMG, CVO
Sedley, *Rt. Hon.* Sir Stephen John, Kt.
Seely, Sir Nigel Edward, Bt. (1896)
Seeto, Sir Ling James, Kt., MBE
Seeyave, Sir Rene Sow Choung, Kt., CBE
Seldon, *Dr* Sir Anthony Francis, Kt.
Semple, Sir John Laughlin, KCB
Sergeant, Sir Patrick, Kt.
Serota, *Hon.* Sir Nicholas Andrew, Kt., CH
Setchell, Sir Marcus Edward, KCVO
†Seton, Sir Charles Wallace, Bt. (S. 1683)
Seton, Sir Iain Bruce, Bt. (S. 1663)
Severne, *Air Vice-Marshal* Sir John de Milt, KCVO, OBE, AFC
Seymour, Sir Julian Roger, Kt., CBE
Shadbolt, *Prof.* Sir Nigel Richard, Kt.
Shaffer, Sir Peter Levin, Kt., CBE
Shakerley, Sir Nicholas Simon Adam, Bt. (1838)
Shakespeare, Sir Thomas William, Bt. (1942)
Sharp, Sir Adrian, Bt. (1922)
Sharp, Sir Leslie, Kt., QPM
Sharp, Sir Sheridan Christopher Robin, Bt. (1920)
Sharples, Sir James, Kt., QPM
Shaw, Sir Charles De Vere, Bt. (1821)
Shaw, *Prof.* Sir John Calman, Kt., CBE
Shaw, Sir Neil McGowan, Kt.
Shaw-Stewart, Sir Ludovic Houston, Bt. (S. 1667)
Shebbeare, Sir Thomas Andrew, KCVO
Sheehy, Sir Patrick, Kt.
Sheffield, Sir Reginald Adrian Berkeley, Bt. (1755)
Shehadie, Sir Nicholas Michael, Kt., OBE
Sheil, *Rt. Hon.* Sir John, Kt.
Sheinwald, Sir Nigel Elton, GCMG
Shelley, Sir John Richard, Bt. (1611)
Shepherd, Sir Colin Ryley, Kt.
Shepherd, Sir John Alan, KCVO, CMG
Shepherd, Sir Richard Charles Scrimgeour, Kt.
Sher, Sir Antony, KBE
Sherlock, Sir Nigel, KCVO, OBE
Sherston-Baker, Sir Robert George Humphrey, Bt. (1796)
Shiffner, Sir Henry David, Bt. (1818)
Shinwell, Sir (Maurice) Adrian, Kt.
Shirreff, *Gen.* Sir Alexander Richard David, KCB, CBE
Shock, Sir Maurice, Kt.
Shortridge, Sir Jon Deacon, KCB
Shuckburgh, Sir James Rupert Charles, Bt. (1660)
Sieff, *Hon.* Sir David, Kt.
Silber, *Rt. Hon.* Sir Stephen Robert, Kt.
†Simeon, Sir Stephen George Barrington, Bt. (1815)

Simmonds, *Rt. Hon. Dr* Sir Kennedy Alphonse, KCMG

Simmons, *Air Marshal* Sir Michael George, KCB, AFC

Simmons, Sir Stanley Clifford, Kt.

Simms, Sir Neville Ian, Kt., FRENG

Simon, *Hon.* Sir Peregrine Charles Hugh, Kt.

Simonet, *Sir* Louis Marcel Pierre, Kt., CBE

Simpson, Sir Peter Austin, Kt., OBE

Simpson, *Dr* Sir Peter Jeffery, Kt.

Sims, Sir Roger Edward, Kt.

Sinclair, Sir Clive Marles, Kt.

Sinclair, Sir Robert John, Kt.

Sinclair, Sir William Robert Francis, Bt. (S. 1704)

Sinclair-Lockhart, Sir Simon John Edward Francis, Bt. (S. 1636)

Singer, *Hon.* Sir Jan Peter, Kt.

Singh, *His Hon.* Sir Mota, Kt., QC

Singh, Sir Pritpal, Kt.

Singh, *Hon.* Sir Rabinder, Kt.

Singleton, Sir Roger, Kt., CBE

Sione, Sir Tomu Malaefone, GCMG, OBE

Sissons, *Prof.* Sir (John Gerald) Patrick, Kt.

†Sitwell, Sir George Reresby Sacheverell, Bt. (1808)

Skeggs, Sir Clifford George, Kt.

Skehel, Sir John James, Kt., FRS

Skingsley, *Air Chief Marshal* Sir Anthony Gerald, GBE, KCB

Skinner, Sir (Thomas) Keith (Hewitt), Bt. (1912)

Skipwith, Sir Patrick Alexander d'Estoteville, Bt. (1622)

Slack, Sir William Willatt, KCVO, FRCS

Slade, Sir Benjamin Julian Alfred, Bt. (1831)

Slade, *Rt. Hon.* Sir Christopher John, Kt.

Slaney, *Prof.* Sir Geoffrey, KBE

Slater, *Adm.* Sir John (Jock) Cunningham Kirkwood, GCB, LVO

Sleight, Sir Richard, Bt. (1920)

Smiley, *Lt.-Col.* Sir John Philip, Bt. (1903)

Smith, *Prof.* Sir Adrian Frederick Melhuish, Kt., FRS

Smith, *Hon.* Sir Andrew Charles, Kt.

Smith, Sir Andrew Thomas, Bt. (1897)

Smith, *Prof.* Sir David Cecil, Kt., FRS

Smith, Sir David Iser, KCVO

Smith, Sir Dudley (Gordon), Kt.

Smith, *Prof.* Sir Eric Brian, Kt., PHD

Smith, Sir John Alfred, Kt., QPM

Smith, Sir Joseph William Grenville, Kt.

Smith, Sir Kevin, Kt., CBE

Smith, Sir Martin Gregory, Kt.

Smith, Sir Michael John Llewellyn, KCVO, CMG

Smith, Sir (Norman) Brian, Kt., CBE, PHD

Smith, Sir Paul Brierley, Kt., CBE

Smith, *Hon.* Sir Peter (Winston), Kt.

Smith, Sir Robert Courtney, Kt., CBE

Smith, Sir Robert Hill, Bt. (1945)

Smith, *Gen.* Sir Rupert Anthony, KCB, DSO, OBE, QGM

Smith, Sir Steven Murray, Kt.

Smith-Dodsworth, Sir David John, Bt. (1784)

Smith-Gordon, Sir (Lionel) Eldred (Peter), Bt. (1838)

Smith-Marriott, Sir Peter Francis, Bt. (1774)

Smurfit, *Dr.* Sir Michael William Joseph, KBE

Smyth, *Sir* Timothy John, Bt. (1956)

Snowden, *Prof.* Sir Christopher Maxwell, Kt.

Snyder, Sir Michael John, Kt.

Soames, *Rt. Hon.* Sir (Arthur) Nicholas Winston, Kt.

Soar, *Adm.* Sir Trevor Alan, KCB, OBE

Sobers, Sir Garfield St Auburn, Kt.

Solomon, Sir Harry, Kt.

Somare, *Rt. Hon.* Sir Michael Thomas, GCMG, CH

Somerville, *Brig.* Sir John Nicholas, Kt., CBE

Songo, Sir Bernard Paul, Kt., CMG, OBE

Sorabji, *Prof.* Sir Richard Rustom Kharsedji, Kt., CBE

Sorrell, Sir John William, Kt., CBE

Sorrell, Sir Martin Stuart, Kt.

Sosa, Sir Manuel, Kt.

Soulsby, Sir Peter Alfred, Kt.

Soutar, *Air Marshal* Sir Charles John Williamson, KBE

Souter, Sir Brian, Kt.

Southby, Sir John Richard Bilbe, Bt. (1937)

Southern, *Prof.* Sir Edwin Mellor, Kt.

Southgate, Sir Colin Grieve, Kt.

Southgate, Sir William David, Kt.

Southward, *Dr* Sir Nigel Ralph, KCVO

Sowrey, *Air Marshal* Sir Frederick Beresford, KCB, CBE, AFC

Sparrow, Sir John, Kt.

Spearman, Sir Alexander Young Richard Mainwaring, Bt. (1840)

Speed, Sir (Herbert) Keith, Kt., RD

Spencer, Sir Derek Harold, Kt., QC

Spencer, *Vice-Adm.* Sir Peter, KCB

Spencer, *Hon.* Sir Robin Godfrey, Kt.

Spencer-Nairn, Sir Robert Arnold, Bt. (1933)

Spicer, Sir James Wilton, Kt.

Spicer, Sir Nicholas Adrian Albert, Bt. (1906)

Spiegelhalter *Prof.* Sir David John, Kt., OBE, FRS

Spiers, Sir Donald Maurice, Kt., CB, TD

Spooner, Sir James Douglas, Kt.

Spring, Sir Dryden Thomas, Kt.

Spurling, Sir John Damian, KCVO, OBE

Squire, *Air Chief Marshal* Sir Peter Ted, GCB, DFC, AFC, ADC

Stadlen, *Hon.* Sir Nicholas Felix, Kt.

Stagg, Sir Charles Richard Vernon, KCMG

Staite, Sir Richard John, Kt., OBE

†Stamer, Sir Peter Tomlinson, Bt. (1809)

Stanhope, *Adm.* Sir Mark, GCB, OBE, ADC

Stanier, Sir Beville Douglas, Bt. (1917)

Stanley, *Rt. Hon.* Sir John Paul, Kt.

Starkey, Sir John Philip, Bt. (1935)

Starmer, Sir Keir, KCB, QC

Staughton, *Rt. Hon.* Sir Christopher Stephen Thomas Jonathan Thayer, Kt.

Stear, *Air Chief Marshal* Sir Michael James Douglas, KCB, CBE

Steel, *Hon.* Sir David William, Kt.

Steer, Sir Alan William, Kt.

Stephen, *Rt. Hon.* Sir Ninian Martin, KG, GCMG, GCVO, KBE

Stephens, Sir (Edwin) Barrie, Kt.

Stephens, Sir Jonathan Andrew de Sievrac, KCB

Stephens, Sir William Benjamin Synge, Kt.

Stephenson, Sir Henry Upton, Bt. (1936)

Stephenson, Sir Paul Robert, Kt., QPM

Sterling, Sir Michael John Howard, Kt.

Sternberg, Sir Sigmund, Kt.

Stevens, Sir Jocelyn Edward Greville, Kt., CVO

Stevenson, Sir Hugh Alexander, Kt.

Stevenson, Sir Simpson, Kt.

Stewart, Sir Alan d'Arcy, Bt. (I. 1623)

Stewart, Sir Brian John, Kt., CBE

Stewart, Sir David James Henderson, Bt. (1957)

Stewart, Sir David John Christopher, Bt. (1803)

Stewart, Sir James Moray, KCB

Stewart, Sir (John) Simon (Watson), Bt. (1920)

Stewart, Sir John Young, Kt., OBE

Stewart, Sir Patrick, Kt., OBE

Stewart, *Lt.-Col.* Sir Robert Christie, KCVO, CBE, TD

Stewart, Sir Robin Alastair, Bt. (1960)

Stewart, *Hon.* Sir Stephen Paul, Kt.

Stewart, *Prof.* Sir William Duncan Paterson, Kt., FRS, FRSE

Stewart-Clark, Sir John, Bt. (1918)

Stewart-Richardson, Sir Simon Alaisdair, Bt. (S. 1630)

Stilgoe, Sir Richard Henry Simpson, Kt., OBE

Stirling, Sir Angus Duncan Aeneas, Kt.

Stirling of Garden, *Col.* Sir James, KCVO, CBE, TD

Stirling-Hamilton, Sir Malcolm William Bruce, Bt. (S. 1673)

Stockdale, Sir Thomas Minshull, Bt. (1960)

Stoddart, *Prof.* Sir James Fraser, Kt.

Stone, Sir Christopher, Kt.

Stonhouse, *Revd* Michael Philip, Bt. (1628 and 1670)

Stonor, *Air Marshal* Sir Thomas Henry, KCB

Stoppard, Sir Thomas, Kt., OM, CBE

Storey, *Hon.* Sir Richard, Bt., CBE (1960)

Stothard, Sir Peter Michael, Kt.

Stott, Sir Adrian George Ellingham, Bt. (1920)

Stoute, Sir Michael Ronald, Kt.

Stowe, Sir Kenneth Ronald, GCB, CVO

Stracey, Sir John Simon, Bt. (1818)

Strachan, Sir Curtis Victor, Kt., CVO

Strachan, Sir Hew Francis Anthony, Kt.

Strachey, Sir Charles, Bt. (1801)

Straker, Sir Louis Hilton, KCMG

Strang Steel, Sir (Fiennes) Michael, Bt. (1938), CBE
Stratton, *Prof.* Sir Michael Rudolf, Kt., FRS
Street, *Hon.* Sir Laurence Whistler, KCMG
Streeton, Sir Terence George, KBE, CMG
Strickland-Constable, Sir Frederic, Bt. (1641)
Stringer, Sir Donald Edgar, Kt., CBE
Stringer, Sir Howard, Kt.
Strong, Sir Roy Colin, Kt., PHD, FSA
Stronge, Sir James Anselan Maxwell, Bt. (1803)
Stuart, Sir James Keith, Kt.
Stuart, Sir Kenneth Lamonte, Kt.
†Stuart, Sir Phillip Luttrell, Bt. (1660)
†Stuart-Forbes, Sir William Daniel, Bt. (S. 1626)
Stuart-Menteth, Sir Charles Greaves, Bt. (1838)
Stuart-Paul, *Air Marshal* Sir Ronald Ian, KBE
Stuart-Smith, *Hon.* Sir Jeremy Hugh, Kt.
Stuart-Smith, *Rt. Hon.* Sir Murray, KCMG, Kt.
Stubbs, Sir William Hamilton, Kt., PHD
Stucley, *Lt.* Sir Hugh George Coplestone Bampfylde, Bt. (1859)
Studd, Sir Edward Fairfax, Bt. (1929)
Studholme, Sir Henry William, Bt. (1956)
Stunell, *Rt. Hon.* Sir Robert Andrew, Kt., OBE
Sturridge, Sir Nicholas Anthony, KCVO
Stuttard, Sir John Boothman, Kt.
†Style, Sir William Frederick, Bt. (1627)
Sullivan, *Rt. Hon.* Sir Jeremy Mirth, Kt.
Sullivan, Sir Richard Arthur, Bt. (1804)
Sulston, Sir John Edward, Kt.
Sunderland, Sir John Michael, Kt.
Supperstone, *Hon.* Sir Michael Alan, Kt.
Sutherland, Sir John Brewer, Bt. (1921)
Sutherland, Sir William George MacKenzie, Kt.
Sutton, *Air Marshal* Sir John Matthias Dobson, KCB
Sutton, Sir Richard Lexington, Bt. (1772)
Swaffield, Sir James Chesebrough, Kt., CBE, RD
Swan, Sir Conrad Marshall John Fisher, KCVO, PHD
Swan, Sir John William David, KBE
Swann, Sir Michael Christopher, Bt. (1906), TD
Sweeney, Sir George, Kt.
Sweeney, *Hon.* Sir Nigel Hamilton, Kt.
Sweeting, *Prof.* Sir Martin Nicholas, Kt., OBE, FRS
Swinburn, *Lt.-Gen.* Sir Richard Hull, KCB
Swinnerton-Dyer, *Prof.* Sir (Henry) Peter (Francis), Bt. (1678), KBE, FRS
Swinton, *Maj.-Gen.* Sir John, KCVO, OBE
Swire, Sir Adrian Christopher, Kt.

Swire, Sir John Anthony, Kt., CBE
Sykes, Sir David Michael, Bt. (1921)
Sykes, Sir Francis John Badcock, Bt. (1781)
Sykes, Sir Hugh Ridley, Kt.
Sykes, *Prof.* Sir (Malcolm) Keith, Kt.
Sykes, Sir Richard, Kt.
Sykes, Sir Tatton Christopher Mark, Bt. (1783)
Symons, *Vice-Adm.* Sir Patrick Jeremy, KBE
†Synge, Sir Allen James Edward, Bt. (1801)

Tang, Sir David Wing-cheung, KBE
Tanner, Sir David Whitlock, Kt., CBE
Tapps-Gervis-Meyrick, Sir George Christopher Cadafael, Bt. (1791)
Tapsell, *Rt. Hon.* Sir Peter Hannay Bailey, Kt.
†Tate, Sir Edward Nicolas, Bt. (1898)
Taureka, *Dr* Sir Reubeh, KBE
Tauvasa, Sir Joseph James, KBE
Tavare, Sir John, Kt., CBE
Taylor, Sir Cyril Julian Hebden, GBE
Taylor, Sir Edward Macmillan (Teddy), Kt.
Taylor, Sir Hugh Henderson, KCB
Taylor, *Rt. Revd* John Bernard, KCVO
Taylor, *Dr* Sir John Michael, Kt., OBE
Taylor, *Prof.* Sir Martin John, Kt., FRS
Taylor, Sir Nicholas Richard Stuart, Bt. (1917)
Taylor, *Prof.* Sir William, Kt., CBE
Taylor, Sir William George, Kt.
Teagle, *Vice-Adm.* Sir Somerford Francis, KBE
Teare, *Hon.* Sir Nigel John Martin, Kt.
Teasdale, *Prof.* Sir Graham Michael, Kt.
Tebbit, Sir Kevin Reginald, KCB, CMG
Temple, *Prof.* Sir John Graham, Kt.
Temple, Sir Richard Carnac Chartier, Bt. (1876)
Temu, *Hon. Dr* Sir Puka, KBE, CMG
Tennyson-D'Eyncourt, Sir Mark Gervais, Bt. (1930)
Terry, *Air Marshal* Sir Colin George, KBE, CB
Terry, *Air Chief Marshal* Sir Peter David George, GCB, AFC
Thatcher, *Hon.* Sir Mark, Bt. (1990)
Thomas, Sir David John Godfrey, Bt. (1694)
Thomas, Sir Derek Morison David, KCMG
Thomas, *Prof.* Sir Eric Jackson, Kt.
Thomas, Sir Gilbert Stanley, Kt., OBE
Thomas, Sir Jeremy Cashel, KCMG
Thomas, Sir (John) Alan, Kt.
Thomas, *Prof.* Sir John Meurig, Kt., FRS
Thomas, Sir Keith Vivian, Kt.
Thomas, *Dr* Sir Leton Felix, KCMG, CBE
Thomas, Sir Philip Lloyd, KCVO, CMG
Thomas, Sir Quentin Jeremy, Kt., CB
Thomas, *Rt. Hon.* Sir Swinton Barclay, Kt.
Thomas, Sir William Michael, Bt. (1919)
Thompson, Sir Christopher Peile, Bt. (1890)

Thompson, Sir Clive Malcolm, Kt.
Thompson, Sir David Albert, KCMG
Thompson, *Prof.* Sir Michael Warwick, Kt., DSc
Thompson, Sir Nicholas Annesley, Bt. (1963)
Thompson, Sir Nigel Cooper, KCMG, CBE
Thompson, Sir Paul Anthony, Bt. (1963)
Thompson, Sir Peter Anthony, Kt.
Thompson, *Dr* Sir Richard Paul Hepworth, KCVO
Thompson, Sir Thomas d'Eyncourt John, Bt. (1806)
Thomson, Sir Adam McClure, KCMG
Thomson, Sir (Frederick Douglas) David, Bt. (1929)
Thomson, Sir John Adam, GCMG
Thomson, Sir Mark Wilfrid Home, Bt. (1925)
Thomson, Sir Thomas James, Kt., CBE, FRCP
Thorne, Sir Neil Gordon, Kt., OBE, TD
Thornton, *Air Marshal* Sir Barry Michael, KCB
Thornton, Sir (George) Malcolm, Kt.
†Thorold, Sir (Anthony) Oliver, Bt. (1642)
Thorpe, *Rt. Hon.* Sir Mathew Alexander, Kt.
Thurecht, Sir Ramon Richard, Kt., OBE
Thwaites, Sir Bryan, Kt., PHD
Tickell, Sir Crispin Charles Cervantes, GCMG, KCVO
Tidmarsh, Sir James Napier, KCVO, MBE
Tilt, Sir Robin Richard, Kt.
Tiltman, Sir John Hessell, KCVO
Timmins, *Col.* Sir John Bradford, KCVO, OBE, TD
Tims, Sir Michael David, KCVO
Tindle, Sir Ray Stanley, Kt., CBE
Tirvengadum, Sir Harry Krishnan, Kt.
Tjoeng, Sir James Neng, KBE
Tod, *Vice-Adm.* Sir Jonathan James Richard, KCB, CBE
Todd, *Prof.* Sir David, Kt., CBE
Todd, Sir Ian Pelham, KBE, FRCS
Toka, Sir Mahuru Dadi, Kt., MBE
Tollemache, Sir Lyonel Humphry John, Bt. (1793)
Tomkys, Sir (William) Roger, KCMG
Tomlinson, *Prof.* Sir Bernard Evans, Kt., CBE
Tomlinson, Sir John Rowland, Kt., CBE
Tomlinson, Sir Michael John, Kt., CBE
Tomlinson, *Rt. Hon.* Sir Stephen Miles, Kt.
Tooke, *Prof.* Sir John Edward, Kt.
Tooley, Sir John, Kt.
ToRobert, Sir Henry Thomas, KBE
Torpy, *Air Chief Marshal* Sir Glenn Lester, GCB, CBE, DSO
Torry, Sir Peter James, GCVO, KCMG
Touche, Sir Anthony George, Bt. (1920)
Touche, Sir Rodney Gordon, Bt. (1962)
Toulson, *Rt. Hon.* Sir Roger Grenfell, Kt.

Tovadek, Sir Martin, Kt. CMG
Tovey, Sir Brian John Maynard, KCMG
Tovua, Sir Paul Joshua, KCMG
ToVue, Sir Ronald, Kt., OBE
Towneley, Sir Simon Peter Edmund
  Cosmo William, KCVO
Traill, Sir Alan Towers, GBE
Trainor, *Prof.* Sir Richard Hughes, KBE
Treacher, *Adm.* Sir John Devereux,
  KCB
Treacy, *Rt. Hon.* Sir Colman Maurice,
  Kt.
Treacy, *Hon.* Sir (James Mary) Seamus,
  Kt.
Treitel, *Prof.* Sir Guenter Heinz, Kt.,
  FBA, QC
Trescowthick, Sir Donald Henry, KBE
†Trevelyan, Sir Andrew John, Bt.
  (1662 and 1874)
Trezise, Sir Kenneth Bruce, Kt., OBE
Trippier, Sir David Austin, Kt., RD
Tritton, Sir Jeremy Ernest, Bt. (1905)
Trollope, Sir Anthony Simon, Bt.
  (1642)
Trotman-Dickenson, Sir Aubrey
  Fiennes, Kt.
Trotter, Sir Neville Guthrie, Kt.
Troubridge, Sir Thomas Richard, Bt.
  (1799)
Trousdell, *Lt.-Gen.* Sir Philip Charles
  Cornwallis, KBE, CB
Truscott, Sir Ralph Eric Nicholson, Bt.
  (1909)
Tsang, Sir Donald Yam-keun, KBE
Tuck, Sir Bruce Adolph Reginald, Bt.
  (1910)
Tucker, Sir Paul, Kt.
Tucker, *Hon.* Sir Richard Howard, Kt.
Tuckey, *Rt. Hon.* Sir Simon Lane, Kt.
Tugendhat, *Hon.* Sir Michael George,
  Kt.
Tuite, Sir Christopher Hugh, Bt.
  (I. 1622), PHD
Tuivaga, Sir Timoci Uluiburotu, Kt.
Tully, Sir William Mark, KBE
Tunstall, Sir Craig, Kt.
Tupper, Sir Charles Hibbert, Bt. (1888)
Turbott, Sir Ian Graham, Kt., CMG,
  CVO
Turing, Sir John Dermot, Bt. (S. 1638)
Turner, *Hon.* Sir Mark George, Kt.
Turner, *Hon.* Sir Michael John, Kt.
Turnquest, Sir Orville Alton, GCMG,
  QC
Tusa, Sir John, Kt.
Tweedie, *Prof.* Sir David Philip, Kt.
Tyree, Sir (Alfred) William, Kt., OBE
Tyrwhitt, Sir Reginald Thomas
  Newman, Bt. (1919)

Udny-Lister, Sir Edward Julian, Kt.
Underhill, *Rt. Hon.* Sir Nicholas
  Edward, Kt.
Underwood, *Prof.* Sir James Cressee
  Elphinstone, Kt.
Unwin, Sir (James) Brian, KCB
Ure, Sir John Burns, KCMG, LVO
Urquhart, Sir Brian Edward, KCMG,
  MBE
Urwick, Sir Alan Bedford, KCVO,
  CMG
Usher, Sir Andrew John, Bt. (1899)
Utting, Sir William Benjamin, Kt., CB

Vardy, Sir Peter, Kt.
Varney, Sir David Robert, Kt.
Vassar-Smith, Sir John Rathbone, Bt.
  (1917)
Vavasour, Sir Eric Michael Joseph
  Marmaduke, Bt. (1828)
Veness, Sir David, Kt., CBE, QPM
Venner, Sir Kenneth Dwight Vincent,
  KBE
Vereker, Sir John Michael Medlicott,
  KCB
†Verney, Sir John Sebastian, Bt.
  (1946)
Verney, Sir Edmund Ralph, Bt. (1818)
Vernon, Sir James William, Bt. (1914)
Vestey, Sir Paul Edmund, Bt. (1921)
Vickers, *Prof.* Sir Brian William, Kt.
Vickers, Sir John Stuart, Kt.
Vickers, *Lt.-Gen.* Sir Richard Maurice
  Hilton, KCB, CVO, OBE
Vickers, Sir Roger Henry, KCVO
Viggers, *Lt-Gen.* Sir Frederick Richard,
  KCB, CMG, MBE
Viggers, Sir Peter John, Kt.
Vincent, Sir William Percy Maxwell,
  Bt. (1936)
Vineall, Sir Anthony John Patrick, Kt.
Virdee, *Prof.* Sir Tejinder Singh, Kt.
Vos, *Hon.* Sir Geoffrey Michael, Kt.
†Vyvyan, Sir Ralph Ferrers Alexander,
  Bt. (1645)

Wade-Gery, Sir Robert Lucian, KCMG,
  KCVO
Waena, Sir Nathaniel Rahumaea,
  GCMG
Waine, *Rt. Revd* John, KCVO
Waite, *Rt. Hon.* Sir John Douglas, Kt.
Waka, Sir Lucas Joseph, Kt., OBE
Wake, Sir Hereward, Bt. (1621), MC
Wakefield, Sir (Edward) Humphry
  (Tyrell), Bt. (1962)
Wakefield, Sir Norman Edward, Kt.
Wakeford, Sir Geoffrey Michael
  Montgomery, Kt., OBE
Wakeham, *Prof.* Sir William Arnot, Kt.
†Wakeley, Sir Nicholas Jeremy, Bt.
  (1952)
Wald, *Prof.* Sir Nicholas John, Kt.
Wales, Sir Robert Andrew, Kt.
Waley-Cohen, Sir Stephen Harry, Bt.
  (1961)
Walford, Sir Christopher Rupert, Kt.
Walker, *Gen.* Sir Antony Kenneth
  Frederick, KCB
Walker, Sir Christopher Robert
  Baldwin, Bt. (1856)
Walker, Sir David Alan, Kt.
Walker, *Air Vice-Marshal* Sir David
  Allan, KCVO, OBE
Walker, Sir Harold Berners, KCMG
Walker, Sir John Ernest, Kt., DPHIL,
  FRS
Walker, *Air Marshal* Sir John Robert,
  KCB, CBE, AFC
Walker, Sir Miles Rawstron, Kt., CBE
Walker, Sir Patrick Jeremy, KCB
Walker, *Hon.* Sir Paul James, Kt.
Walker, Sir Rodney Myerscough, Kt.
Walker, Sir Roy Edward, Bt. (1906)
Walker, *Hon.* Sir Timothy Edward, Kt.
Walker, Sir Victor Stewart Heron, Bt.
  (1868)

Walker-Okeover, Sir Andrew Peter
  Monro, Bt. (1886)
Walker-Smith, *Hon.* Sir John Jonah,
  Bt. (1960)
Wall, Sir (John) Stephen, GCMG, LVO
Wall, *Rt. Hon.* Sir Nicholas Peter
  Rathbone, Kt.
Wall, *Gen.* Sir Peter Anthony, GCB,
  CBE, ADC
Wallace, *Lt.-Gen.* Sir Christopher
  Brooke Quentin, KBE
Wallace, *Prof.* Sir David James, Kt.,
  CBE, FRS
Waller, *Rt. Hon.* Sir (George) Mark, Kt.
Waller, Sir John Michael, Bt. (I. 1780)
Wallis, Sir Peter Gordon, KCVO
Wallis, Sir Timothy William, Kt.
Walmsley, *Vice-Adm.* Sir Robert, KCB
Walport, *Dr* Sir Mark Jeremy, Kt.
†Walsham, Sir Gerald Percy Robert,
  Bt. (1831)
Walters, Sir Dennis Murray, Kt., MBE
Walters, Sir Frederick Donald, Kt.
Walters, Sir Peter Ingram, Kt.
Wamiri, Sir Akapite, KBE
Ward, *Rt. Hon.* Sir Alan Hylton, Kt.
Ward, Sir Austin, Kt., QC
Ward, *Hon.* Sir (Frederik) Gordon
  (Roy), Kt., OBE
Ward, *Prof.* Sir John MacQueen, Kt.,
  CBE
Ward, Sir Joseph James Laffey, Bt.
  (1911)
Ward, Sir Timothy James, Kt.
Wardale, Sir Geoffrey Charles, KCB
Wardlaw, Sir Henry Justin, Bt.
  (NS. 1631)
Waring, Sir (Alfred) Holburt, Bt. (1935)
Warmington, Sir Rupert Marshall, Bt.
  (1908)
Warner, Sir Gerald Chierici, KCMG
Warner, Sir Philip Courtenay
  Thomas, Bt. (1910)
Warren, Sir David Alexander, KCMG
Warren, Sir (Frederick) Miles, KBE
Warren, Sir Kenneth Robin, Kt.
Warren, Sir Nicholas Roger, Kt.
Wass, Sir Douglas William Gretton,
  GCB
Waterlow, Sir Christopher Rupert, Bt.
  (1873)
Waterlow, Sir (Thomas) James, Bt.
  (1930)
Waters, *Gen.* Sir (Charles) John, GCB,
  CBE
Waters, Sir (Thomas) Neil (Morris), Kt.
Waterworth, Sir Alan William, KCVO
Wates, Sir Christopher Stephen, Kt.
Watson, *Prof.* Sir David John, Kt., PHD
Watson, Sir Graham Robert, Kt.
Watson, Sir (James) Andrew, Bt. (1866)
Watson, *Prof.* Sir Robert Tony, Kt.,
  CMG
Watson, Sir Ronald Matthew, Kt., CBE
Watson, Sir Simon Conran Hamilton,
  Bt. (1895)
Watt, *Gen.* Sir Charles Redmond, KCB,
  KCVO, CBE, ADC
Watts, Sir John Augustus Fitzroy,
  KCMG, CBE
Watts, Sir Philip Beverley, KCMG
Weatherall, *Prof.* Sir David John, Kt.,
  FRS

Weatherall, *Vice-Adm.* Sir James Lamb, KCVO, KBE

Weatherup, *Hon.* Sir Ronald Eccles, Kt.

Webb, *Prof.* Sir Adrian Leonard, Kt.

Webb-Carter, *Maj.-Gen.* Sir Evelyn John, KCVO, OBE

Webster, *Vice-Adm.* Sir John Morrison, KCB

Wedgwood, Sir Ralph Nicholas, Bt. (1942)

Weekes, Sir Everton DeCourcey, KCMG, OBE

Weinberg, Sir Mark Aubrey, Kt.

Weir, *Hon.* Sir Reginald George, Kt.

Weir, Sir Roderick Bignell, Kt.

Welby, Sir (Richard) Bruno Gregory, Bt. (1801)

Welch, Sir John Reader, Bt. (1957)

Weldon, Sir Anthony William, Bt. (I. 1723)

Wellend, *Prof.* Sir Mark Edward, Kt.

†Wells, Sir Christopher Charles, Bt. (1944)

Wells, Sir John Julius, Kt.

Wells, Sir William Henry Weston, Kt., FRICS

Wesker, Sir Arnold, Kt.

Wessely, *Prof.* Sir Simon Charles, Kt.

Westmacott, Sir Peter John, KCMG

Weston, Sir Michael Charles Swift, KCMG, CVO

Weston, Sir (Philip) John, KCMG

Whalen, Sir Geoffrey Henry, Kt., CBE

Wheeler, Sir Harry Anthony, Kt., OBE

Wheeler, *Rt. Hon.* Sir John Daniel, Kt.

Wheeler, Sir John Frederick, Bt. (1920)

Wheeler, *Gen.* Sir Roger Neil, GCB, CBE

Wheeler-Booth, Sir Michael Addison John, KCB

Wheler, Sir Trevor Woodford, Bt. (1660)

Whitaker, Sir John James Ingham (Jack), Bt. (1936)

Whitbread, Sir Samuel Charles, KCVO

Whitchurch, Sir Graeme Ian, Kt., OBE

White, *Prof.* Sir Christopher John, Kt., CVO

White, Sir Christopher Robert Meadows, Bt. (1937)

White, Sir David (David Jason), Kt., OBE

White, Sir David Harry, Kt.

White, Sir George Stanley James, Bt. (1904)

White, Sir John Woolmer, Bt. (1922)

White, Sir Nicholas Peter Archibald, Bt. (1802)

White, Sir Willard Wentworth, Kt., CBE

White-Spunner, *Lt.-Gen.* Sir Barnabas William Benjamin, KCB, CBE

Whitehead, Sir Philip Henry Rathbone, Bt. (1889)

Whiteley, *Gen.* Sir Peter John Frederick, GCB, OBE, RM

Whitfield, Sir William, Kt., CBE

Whitmore, Sir Clive Anthony, GCB, CVO

Whitmore, Sir John Henry Douglas, Bt. (1954)

Whitson, Sir Keith Roderick, Kt.

Wickerson, Sir John Michael, Kt.

Wicks, Sir Nigel Leonard, GCB, CVO, CBE

Wigan, Sir Michael Iain, Bt. (1898)

Wiggin, Sir Alfred William (Jerry), Kt., TD

Wiggin, Sir Richard Edward John, Bt. (1892)

Wiggins, Sir Bradley Marc, Kt., CBE

Wigram, Sir John Woolmore, Bt. (1805)

Wilbraham, Sir Richard Baker, Bt. (1776)

Wild, Sir John Ralston, Kt., CBE

Wiles, *Prof.* Sir Andrew John, KBE

Wilkie, *Hon.* Sir Alan Fraser, Kt.

Wilkins, Sir Michael, Kt.

Wilkinson, Sir (David) Graham (Brook) Bt. (1941)

Wilkinson, *Prof.* Sir Denys Haigh, Kt., FRS

Willcocks, Sir David Valentine, Kt., CBE, MC

Willcocks, *Lt.-Gen.* Sir Michael Alan, KCB, CVO

Williams, Sir (Arthur) Gareth Ludovic Emrys Rhys, Bt. (1918)

Williams, Sir Charles Othniel, Kt.

Williams, Sir Daniel Charles, GCMG, QC

Williams, Sir David Reeve, Kt., CBE

Williams, Sir Donald Mark, Bt. (1866)

Williams, *Prof.* Sir (Edward) Dillwyn, Kt., FRCP

Williams, Sir Francis Owen Garbett, Kt., CBE

Williams, *Hon.* Sir (John) Griffith, Kt.

Williams, Sir (Lawrence) Hugh, Bt. (1798)

Williams, Sir Nicholas Stephen, Kt.

Williams, Sir Paul Michael, Kt., OBE

Williams, Sir Peter Michael, Kt.

Williams, Sir (Robert) Philip Nathaniel, Bt. (1915)

Williams, Sir Anthony Geraint, Bt. (1953)

Williams, *Prof.* Sir Roger, Kt.

Williams, Sir (William) Maxwell (Harries), Kt.

Williams, *Hon.* Sir Wyn Lewis, Kt.

Williams-Bulkeley, Sir Richard Thomas, Bt. (1661)

Williams-Wynn, Sir David Watkin, Bt. (1688)

Williamson, Sir George Malcolm, Kt.

Williamson, *Marshal of the Royal Air Force* Sir Keith Alec, GCB, AFC

Williamson, Sir Robert Brian, Kt., CBE

Willink, Sir Edward Daniel, Bt. (1957)

Wills, Sir David James Vernon, Bt. (1923)

Wills, Sir David Seton, Bt. (1904)

Wilmot, Sir David, Kt., QPM

Wilmot, Sir Henry Robert, Bt. (1759)

Wilmut, *Prof.* Sir Ian, Kt., OBE

Wilsey, *Gen.* Sir John Finlay Willasey, GCB, CBE

Wilshaw, Sir Michael, Kt.

Wilson, *Prof.* Sir Alan Geoffrey, Kt.

Wilson, *Vice-Adm.* Sir Barry Nigel, KCB

†Wilson, Sir Thomas David, Bt. (1920)

Wilson, Sir David Mackenzie, Kt.

Wilson, Sir James William Douglas, Bt. (1906)

Wilson, *Brig.* Sir Mathew John Anthony, Bt. (1874), OBE, MC

Wilson, *Rt. Hon.* Sir Nicholas Allan Roy, Kt.

Wilson, *Prof.* Sir Robert James Timothy, Kt.

Wilson, Sir Robert Peter, KCMG

Wilson, *Air Chief Marshal* Sir (Ronald) Andrew (Fellowes), KCB, AFC

Wingate, *Capt.* Sir Miles Buckley, KCVO

Winkley, Sir David Ross, Kt.

Winnington, Sir Anthony Edward, Bt. (1755)

Winship, Sir Peter James Joseph, Kt., CBE

Winter, *Dr* Sir Gregory Winter, Kt., CBE

Winterton, Sir Nicholas Raymond, Kt.

Wiseman, Sir John William, Bt. (1628)

Witty, Sir Andrew, Kt.

Wolfendale, *Prof.* Sir Arnold Whittaker, Kt., FRS

Wolseley, Sir Charles Garnet Richard Mark, Bt. (1628)

†Wolseley, Sir James Douglas, Bt. (I. 1745)

†Wombwell, Sir George Philip Frederick, Bt. (1778)

Womersley, Sir Peter John Walter, Bt. (1945)

Woo, Sir Leo Joseph, Kt., MBE

Woo, Sir Po-Shing, Kt.

Wood, Sir Andrew Marley, GCMG

Wood, Sir Anthony John Page, Bt. (1837)

Wood, Sir Ian Clark, Kt., CBE

Wood, Sir James Sebastian Lamin, KCMG

Wood, Sir Martin Francis, Kt., OBE

Wood, Sir Michael Charles, KCMG

Wood, *Hon.* Sir Roderic Lionel James, Kt.

Woodard, *Rear Adm.* Sir Robert Nathaniel, KCVO

Woodhead, *Vice-Adm.* Sir (Anthony) Peter, KCB

Woodhead, Sir Christopher Anthony, Kt.

Woods, *Prof.* Sir Kent Linton, Kt.

Woods, Sir Robert Kynnersley, Kt., CBE

Woodward, Sir Clive Ronald, Kt., OBE

Woodward, Sir Thomas Jones (Tom Jones), Kt., OBE

Wootton, Sir David Hugh, Kt.

Worsley, Sir William Ralph, Bt. (1838)

Worsthorne, Sir Peregrine Gerard, Kt.

Worthington, Sir Mark, Kt., OBE

Wratten, *Air Chief Marshal* Sir William John, GBE, CB, AFC

Wraxall, Sir Charles Frederick Lascelles, Bt. (1813)

Wrey, Sir George Richard Bourchier, Bt. (1628)

Wright, Sir Allan Frederick, KBE

Wright, Sir David John, GCMG, LVO

Wright, *Hon.* Sir (John) Michael, Kt.

Wright, *Prof.* Sir Nicholas Alcwyn, Kt.
Wright, Sir Peter Robert, Kt., CBE
Wright, *Air Marshal* Sir Robert Alfred, KBE, AFC
Wright, Sir Stephen John Leadbetter, KCMG
Wrightson, Sir Charles Mark Garmondsway, Bt. (1900)
Wrigley, *Prof.* Sir Edward Anthony (Sir Tony), Kt., PHD, PBA
Wrixon-Becher, Sir John William Michael, Bt. (1831)
Wroughton, Sir Philip Lavallin, KCVO
Wu, Sir Gordon Ying Sheung, KCMG
Wynne, Sir Graham Robert, Kt., CBE

Yacoub, *Prof.* Sir Magdi Habib, Kt., OM, FRCS
Yaki, Sir Roy, KBE
Yang, *Hon.* Sir Ti Liang, Kt.

Yarrow, Sir Eric Grant, Bt. (1916), MBE
Yassaie, *Dr* Sir Hossein, Kt.
Yocklunn, Sir John (Soong Chung), KCVO
Yoo Foo, Sir (François) Henri, Kt.
Young, Sir Brian Walter Mark, Kt.
Young, Sir Colville Norbert, GCMG, MBE
Young, Sir Dennis Charles, KCMG
Young, *Rt. Hon.* Sir George Samuel Knatchbull, Bt. (1813), CH
Young, Sir Jimmy Leslie Ronald, Kt., CBE
Young, Sir John Kenyon Roe, Bt. (1821)
Young, Sir John Robertson, GCMG
Young, Sir Leslie Clarence, Kt., CBE
Young, Sir Nicholas Charles, Kt.
Young, Sir Robin Urquhart, KCB

Young, Sir Roger William, Kt.
Young, Sir Stephen Stewart Templeton, Bt. (1945)
Young, Sir William Neil, Bt. (1769)
Younger, *Capt.* Sir John David Bingham, KCVO
Younger, Sir Julian William Richard, Bt. (1911)
Yuwi, Sir Matiabe, KBE

Zambellas, *Adm.* Sir George Michael, KCB, DSC
Zeeman, *Prof.* Sir (Erik) Christopher, Kt., FRS
Zissman, Sir Bernard Philip, Kt.
Zunz, Sir Gerhard Jacob (Jack), Kt., FRENG
Zurenuoc, Sir Manasupe Zure, Kt., OBE
Zurenuoc, Sir Zibang, KBE

THE ORDER OF ST JOHN

THE MOST VENERABLE ORDER OF THE HOSPITAL OF ST JOHN OF JERUSALEM (1888)

GCStJ	Bailiff/Dame Grand Cross
KStJ	Knight of Justice/Grace
DStJ	Dame of Justice/Grace
CStJ	Commander
OStJ	Officer
SBStJ	Serving Brother
SSStJ	Serving Sister

Motto, Pro Fide, Pro Utilitate Hominum
(For the faith and in the service of humanity)

The Order of St John, founded in the early 12th century in Jerusalem, was a religious order with a particular duty to care for the sick. In Britain the order was dissolved by Henry VIII in 1540 but the British branch was revived in the early 19th century. The branch was not accepted by the Grand Magistracy of the Order in Rome but its search for a role in the tradition of the hospitallers led to the founding of the St John Ambulance Association in 1877 and later the St John Ambulance Brigade; in 1882 the St John Ophthalmic Hospital was founded in Jerusalem. A royal charter was granted in 1888 establishing the Order of St John as a British Order of Chivalry with the sovereign as its head.

Since October 1999 the whole order worldwide has been governed by a Grand Council which includes a representative from each of the ten priories (England, Scotland, Wales, Kenya, Singapore, South Africa, New Zealand, Canada, Australia and the USA). In addition there are also five commanderies in Northern Ireland, Jersey, Guernsey, the Isle of Man and Western Australia. There are also branches in about 30 other Commonwealth countries. Apart from St John Ambulance, the Order is also responsible for the Jerusalem Eye Hospital. Admission to the order is usually conferred in recognition of service to either one of these institutions. Membership does not confer any rank, style, title or precedence on a recipient.

SOVEREIGN HEAD OF THE ORDER
HM The Queen

GRAND PRIOR
HRH The Duke of Gloucester, KG, GCVO

Lord Prior, Dr Neil Raymond Conn
Prelate, Rt. Revd John Nicholls
Sub Prior, Stuart Shilson, LVO
Chancellor, Patrick Burgess, MBE
Secretary General, Vice-Adm. Sir Paul Lambert, KCB
International Office, 3 Charterhouse Mews, London EC1M 6BB
    T 020-7251 3292 **W** www.orderofstjohn.org

DAMES

Style, 'Dame' before forename and surname, followed by appropriate post-nominal initials. Where such an award is made to a lady already in possession of a higher title, the appropriate initials follow her name
Envelope, Dame F_ S_, followed by appropriate post-nominal letters. *Letter (formal),* Dear Madam; *(social),* Dear Dame F_. *Spoken,* Dame F_
Husband, Untitled

Dame Grand Cross and Dame Commander are the higher classes for women of the Order of the Bath, the Order of St Michael and St George, the Royal Victorian Order, and the Order of the British Empire. Dames Grand Cross rank after the wives of Baronets and before the wives of Knights Grand Cross. Dames Commanders rank after the wives of Knights Grand Cross and before the wives of Knights Commanders.
   Honorary damehoods may be conferred on women who are citizens of countries of which the Queen is not head of state.

LIST OF DAMES *As at 31 August 2014*

Women peers in their own right and life peers are not included in this list. Female members of the royal family are not included in this list; details of the orders they hold can be found within the Royal Family section.
   If a dame has a double barrelled or hyphenated surname, she is listed under the first element of the name.

Abaijah, Dame Josephine, DBE
Abramsky, Dame Jennifer Gita, DBE
Acland Hood Gass, Lady (Elizabeth Periam), DCVO
Airlie, The Countess of, DCVO
Alexander, Dame Helen Anne, DBE
Allen, *Prof.* Dame Ingrid Victoria, DBE
Andrews, *Hon.* Dame Geraldine Mary, DBE
Andrews, Dame Julie, DBE
Angiolini, *Rt. Hon.* Dame Elish, DBE, QC
Anglesey, Shirley, Marchioness of, DBE
Anson, Lady (Elizabeth Audrey), DBE
Anstee, Dame Margaret Joan, DCMG
Archer, *Dr* Dame Mary Doreen, DBE
Arden, *Rt. Hon.* Dame Mary Howarth (Mrs Mance), DBE
Asplin, *Hon.* Dame Sarah Jane (Mrs Sherwin), DBE
Atkins, Dame Eileen, DBE
August, Dame Kathryn, DBE
Bacon, Dame Patricia Anne, DBE
Bailey, *Prof.* Dame Susan Mary, DBE
Baker, Dame Janet Abbott (Mrs Shelley), CH, DBE
Barbour, Dame Margaret (Mrs Ash), DBE
Barker, Dame Katharine Mary, DBE
Barker-Welch, *Hon.* Dame Maizie Irene, DBE
Barrow, Dame Jocelyn Anita (Mrs Downer), DBE
Barstow, Dame Josephine Clare (Mrs Anderson), DBE
Bassey, Dame Shirley, DBE
Beasley, *Prof.* Dame Christine Joan, DBE
Beaurepaire, Dame Beryl Edith, DBE
Beckett, *Rt. Hon.* Dame Margaret Mary, DBE
Beer, *Prof.* Dame Gillian Patricia Kempster, DBE, FBA
Begg, Dame Anne, DBE
Beral, *Prof.* Dame Valerie, DBE
Bertschinger, *Dr* Dame Claire, DBE
Bevan, Dame Yasmin, DBE
Bewley, Dame Beulah Rosemary, DBE
Bibby, Dame Enid, DBE

Black, *Prof.* Dame Carol Mary, DBE
Black, *Rt. Hon.* Dame Jill Margaret, DBE
Blackadder, Dame Elizabeth Violet, DBE
Blaize, Dame Venetia Ursula, DBE
Blaxland, Dame Helen Frances, DBE
Blume, Dame Hilary Sharon Braverman, DBE
Booth, *Hon.* Dame Margaret Myfanwy Wood, DBE
Bourne, Dame Susan Mary (Mrs Bourne), DBE
Bowe, *Dr* Dame (Mary) Colette, DBE
Bowtell, Dame Ann Elizabeth, DCB
Braddock, *Dr* Dame Christine, DBE
Brain, Dame Margaret Anne (Mrs Wheeler), DBE
Breakwell, *Prof.* Dame Glynis Marie, DBE
Brennan, Dame Maureen, DBE
Brennan, Dame Ursula, DCB
Brewer, *Dr* Dame Nicola Mary, DCMG
Bridges, Dame Mary Patricia, DBE
Brindley, Dame Lynne Janie, DBE
Brittan, Dame Diana (Lady Brittan of Spennithorne), DBE
Browne, Lady Moyra Blanche Madeleine, DBE
Buckland, Dame Yvonne Helen Elaine, DBE
Burnell, *Prof.* Dame Susan Jocelyn Bell, DBE
Burslem, Dame Alexandra Vivien, DBE
Butler, Dame Rosemary Janet Mair, DBE
Byatt, Dame Antonia Susan, DBE, FRSL
Caldicott, Dame Fiona, DBE, FRCP, FRCPSYCH
Cameron, *Prof.* Dame Averil Millicent, DBE
Campbell-Preston, Dame Frances Olivia, DCVO
Carnall, Dame Ruth, DBE
Carnwath, Dame Alison Jane, DBE
Carr, *Hon.* Dame Sue Lascelles (Mrs Birch), DBE
Cartwright, Dame Silvia Rose, DBE
Clark, *Prof.* Dame Jill MacLeod, DBE
Clark, *Prof.* Dame (Margaret) June, DBE, PHD
Cleverdon, Dame Julia Charity, DCVO, CBE
Coates, Dame Sally, DBE
Collarbone, Dame Patricia, DBE
Contreras, *Prof.* Dame Marcela, DBE
Corner, *Prof.* Dame Jessica Lois, DBE
Corsar, *Hon.* Dame Mary Drummond, DBE
Coward, Dame Pamela Sarah, DBE
Cowley, *Prof.* Dame Sarah Ann, DBE
Cox, *Hon.* Dame Laura Mary, DBE
Cramp, *Prof.* Dame Rosemary Jean, DBE
Cullum, *Prof.* Dame Nicola Anne, DBE
Dacon, Dame Monica Jessie, DBE, CMG
Davies, *Prof.* Dame Kay Elizabeth, DBE
Davies, Dame Laura Jane, DBE
Davies, *Hon.* Dame Nicola Velfor, DBE
Davies, *Prof.* Dame Sally Claire, DBE
Davies, Dame Wendy Patricia, DBE
Davis, Dame Karlene Cecile, DBE
Dawson, *Prof.* Dame Sandra Jane Noble, DBE
De Souza, Dame Rachel Mary, DBE
Dell, Dame Miriam Patricia, DBE
Dench, Dame Judith Olivia (Mrs Williams), CH, DBE
Descartes, Dame Marie Selipha Sesenne, DBE, BEM
Devonshire, Deborah, The Duchess of, DCVO
Digby, The Lady, DBE
Dobbs, *Hon.* Dame Linda Penelope, DBE
Docherty, Dame Jacqueline, DBE
Donald, *Prof.* Dame Athene Margaret, DBE, FRS
Dowling, *Prof.* Dame Ann Patricia, DBE
Duffield, Dame Vivien Louise, DBE

Dumont, Dame Ivy Leona, DCMG
Dunnell, Dame Karen, DCB
Dyche, Dame Rachael Mary, DBE
Elcoat, Dame Catherine Elizabeth, DBE
Ellis, Dame Diana Margaret (Mrs Ellis), DBE
Ellison, Dame Jill, DBE
Elton, Dame Susan Richenda (Lady Elton), DCVO
Engel, Dame Pauline Frances (Sister Pauline Engel), DBE
Esteve-Coll, Dame Elizabeth Anne Loosemore, DBE
Evans, Dame Anne Elizabeth Jane, DBE
Evans, Dame Madeline Glynne Dervel, DBE, CMG
Fagan, Dame (Florence) Mary, DCVO
Farnham, Dame Marion (Lady Farnham), DCVO
Fawcett, Dame Amelia Chilcott, DBE
Fenner, Dame Peggy Edith, DBE
Fielding, Dame Pauline, DBE
Finch, *Prof.* Dame Janet Valerie, DBE
Fisher, Dame Jacqueline, DBE
Forgan, Dame Elizabeth Anne Lucy, DBE
Fradd, Dame Elizabeth, DBE
Fraser, Lady Antonia, DBE
Fraser, Dame Dorothy Rita, DBE
Fry, Dame Margaret Louise, DBE
Furse, Dame Clara Hedwig Frances, DBE
Gaymer, Dame Janet Marion, DBE, QC
Ghosh, Dame Helen Frances, DCB
Gibb, Dame Moira Margaret, DBE
Glen-Haig, Dame Mary Alison, DBE
Glenn, *Prof.* Dame Hazel Gillian, DBE
Glennie, *Dr* Dame Evelyn Elizabeth Ann, DBE
Gloster, *Rt. Hon.* Dame Elizabeth (Lady Popplewell), DBE
Glover, Dame Audrey Frances, DBE, CMG
Goad, Dame Sarah Jane Frances, DCVO
Goodall, *Dr* Dame (Valerie) Jane, DBE
Goodfellow, *Prof.* Dame Julia Mary, DBE
Gordon, Dame Minita Elmira, GCMG, GCVO
Gordon, *Hon.* Dame Pamela Felicity, DBE
Gow, Dame Jane Elizabeth (Mrs Whiteley), DBE
Grafton, Ann, The Duchess of, GCVO
Grant, Dame Mavis, DBE
Green, Dame Pauline, DBE
Grey, Dame Beryl Elizabeth (Mrs Svenson), DBE
Griffiths, Dame Anne, DCVO
Grimthorpe, Elizabeth, The Lady, DCVO
Guilfoyle, Dame Margaret Georgina Constance, DBE
Guthardt, *Revd Dr* Dame Phyllis Myra, DBE
Hadid, Dame Zaha, DBE
Hakin, *Dr* Dame Barbara Ann, DBE
Hall, *Prof.* Dame Wendy, DBE
Hallett, *Rt. Hon.* Dame Heather Carol, DBE
Hallett, Dame Nancy Karen, DBE
Harbison, Dame Joan Irene, DBE
Harper, Dame Elizabeth Margaret Way, DBE
Harris, Dame Pauline (Lady Harris of Peckham), DBE
Hassan, Dame Anna Patricia Lucy, DBE
Hay, Dame Barbara Logan, DCMG, MBE
Henderson, Dame Fiona Douglas, DCVO
Hercus, *Hon.* Dame (Margaret) Ann, DCMG
Higgins, *Prof.* Dame Joan Margaret, DBE
Higgins, *Prof.* Dame Julia Stretton, DBE, FRS
Higgins, *Prof.* Dame Rosalyn, DBE, QC
Hill, *Air Cdre* Dame Felicity Barbara, DBE
Hill, *Prof.* Dame Judith Eileen, DBE
Hine, Dame Deirdre Joan, DBE, FRCP
Hodgson, Dame Patricia Anne, DBE
Hogg, *Hon.* Dame Mary Claire (Mrs Koops), DBE
Holborow, Lady Mary Christina, DCVO
Hollows, Dame Sharon, DBE
Holmes, Dame Kelly, DBE

Holroyd, Lady (Margaret Drabble), DBE
Holt, Dame Denise Mary, DCMG
Hoodless, Dame Elisabeth Anne, DBE
Hoyles, *Prof.* Dame Celia Mary, DBE
Hufton, *Prof.* Dame Olwen, DBE
Humphrey, *Prof.* Dame Caroline (Lady Rees of Ludlow), DBE
Husband, *Prof.* Dame Janet Elizabeth Siarey, DBE
Hussey, Dame Susan Katharine (Lady Hussey of North Bradley), GCVO
Hutton, Dame Deirdre Mary, DBE
Hyde, Dame Helen, DBE
Imison, Dame Tamsyn, DBE
Ion, *Dr* Dame Susan Elizabeth, DBE
Isaacs, Dame Albertha Madeline, DBE
James, Dame Naomi Christine (Mrs Haythorne), DBE
Jenkins, Dame (Mary) Jennifer (Lady Jenkins of Hillhead), DBE
John, Dame Susan, DBE
Johnson, *Prof.* Dame Anne Mandall, DBE
Jones, Dame Gwyneth (Mrs Haberfeld-Jones), DBE
Jordan, *Prof.* Dame Carole, DBE
Joseph, Dame Monica Theresa, DBE
Jowell, *Rt. Hon.* Dame Tessa Jane, DBE
Julius, *Dr* Dame DeAnne Shirley, DCMG, CBE
Karika, Dame Pauline Margaret Rakera George (Mrs Taripo), DBE
Keeble, *Dr* Dame Reena, DBE
Keegan, Dame Elizabeth Mary, DBE
Keegan, Dame Geraldine Mary Marcella, DBE
Keith, Dame Penelope Anne Constance (Mrs Timson), DBE
Kekedo, Dame Rosalina Violet, DBE
Kelleher, Dame Joan, DBE
Kelly, Dame Barbara Mary, DBE
Kelly, Dame Lorna May Boreland, DBE
Kershaw, Dame Janet Elizabeth Murray (Dame Betty), DBE
Kettlewell, *Comdt.* Dame Marion Mildred, DBE
Khemka, Dame Asha, DBE
Kidu, Lady, DBE
King, *Hon.* Dame Eleanor Warwick, DBE
King, *Prof.* Dame Julia Elizabeth, DBE
Kinnair, Dame Donna, DBE
Kirby, Dame Carolyn Emma, DBE
Kirby, Dame Georgina Kamiria, DBE
Kirwan, *Prof.* Dame Frances Clare, DBE, FRS
Kramer, *Prof.* Dame Leonie Judith, DBE
La Grenade, *HE.* Dame Cécile Ellen Fleurette, GCMG, OBE
Laine, Dame Cleo (Clementine) Dinah (Lady Dankworth), DBE
Lake-Tack, *HE* Dame Louise Agnetha, GCMG
Lamb, Dame Dawn Ruth, DBE
Lang, *Hon.* Dame Beverley Ann Macnaughton, DBE
Lansbury Shaw, Dame Angela Brigid, DBE
Lavender, *Prof.* Dame Tina, DBE
Leather, Dame Susan Catherine, DBE
Lee, *Prof.* Dame Hermione, DBE
Leslie, Dame Alison Mariot, DCMG
Leslie, Dame Ann Elizabeth Mary, DBE
Lewis, Dame Edna Leofrida (Lady Lewis), DBE
Lively, Dame Penelope Margaret, DBE
Lott, Dame Felicity Ann Emwhyla (Mrs Woolf), DBE
Louisy, Dame (Calliopa) Pearlette, GCMG
Lynn, Dame Vera (Mrs Lewis), DBE
Lynne, Dame Gillian Barbara, DBE
MacArthur, Dame Ellen Patricia, DBE
Macdonald, Dame Mary Beaton, DBE
McDonald, Dame Mavis, DCB
MacIntyre, *Prof.* Dame Sarah Jane, DBE
Macmillan of Ovenden, Katharine, Viscountess, DBE
Macur, *Rt. Hon.* Dame Julia Wendy, DBE

McVittie, Dame Joan Christine, DBE
Mayhew, Jonas, Dame Judith, DBE
Major, Dame Malvina Lorraine (Mrs Fleming), DBE
Major, Dame Norma Christina Elizabeth, DBE
Makin, *Dr* Dame Pamela Louise, DBE
Mantel, *Dr.* Dame Hiliary Mary, DBE
Marsden, *Dr* Dame Rosalind Mary, DCMG
Marsh, Dame Mary Elizabeth, DBE
Mason, Dame Monica Margaret, DBE
Matheson, Dame Jilian Norma, DCB
Mellor, Dame Julie Thérèse Mellor, DBE
Metge, *Dr* Dame (Alice) Joan, DBE
Middleton, Dame Elaine Madoline, DCMG, MBE
Mirren, Dame Helen, DBE
Monroe, *Prof.* Dame Barbara, DBE
Moore, Dame Julie, DBE
Moores, Dame Yvonne, DBE
Morgan, *Dr* Dame Gillian Margaret, DBE
Morris, Dame Sylvia Ann, DBE
Morrison, *Hon.* Dame Mary Anne, GCVO
Muirhead, Dame Lorna Elizabeth Fox, DBE
Muldoon, Lady (Thea Dale), DBE, QSO
Mullally, *Revd* Dame Sarah Elisabeth, DBE
Mumford, Lady Mary Katharine, DCVO
Murray, Dame Jennifer Susan, DBE
Nelson, *Prof.* Dame Janet Laughland, DBE
Nelson-Taylor, Dame Nicola Jane, DBE
Neville, Dame Elizabeth, DBE, QPM
Newell, Dame Priscilla Jane, DBE
Ogilvie, Dame Bridget Margaret, DBE, PHD, DSc
Oliver, Dame Gillian Frances, DBE
Owers, Dame Anne Elizabeth (Mrs Cook), DBE
Oxenbury, Dame Shirley Ann, DBE
Palmer, Dame Felicity Joan, DBE
Paraskeva, *Rt. Hon.* Dame Janet, DBE
Park, Dame Merle Florence (Mrs Bloch), DBE
Parslow, *Hon.* Dame Judith Mary Frances, DBE
Partridge, *Prof.* Dame Linda, DBE
Patel, Dame Indira, DBE
Paterson, Dame Vicki, DBE
Patterson, *Hon.* Dame Frances Silvia, DBE
Pauffley, *Hon.* Dame Anna Evelyn Hamilton, DBE
Peacock, Dame Alison Margaret, DBE
Pearce, *Prof.* Dame Shirley, DBE
Penhaligon, Dame Annette (Mrs Egerton), DBE
Pereira, *Hon.* Dame Janice Mesadis, DBE
Perkins, Dame Mary Lesley, DBE
Peters, Dame Mary Elizabeth, DBE
Pienaar, Dame Erica, DBE
Pindling, Lady (Marguerite M.), DCMG
Platt, Dame Denise, DBE
Plowright, Dame Joan Ann, DBE
Poole, Dame Avril Anne Barker, DBE
Porter, Dame Shirley (Lady Porter), DBE
Powell, Dame Sally Ann Vickers, DBE
Primarolo, *Rt. Hon.* Dame Dawn, DBE
Pringle, Dame Anne Fyfe, DCMG
Proudman, *Hon.* Dame Sonia Rosemary Susan, DBE
Pugh, *Dr* Dame Gillian Mary, DBE
Quinn, Dame Sheila Margaret Imelda, DBE
Rafferty, *Rt. Hon.* Dame Anne Judith, DBE
Rawson, *Prof.* Dame Jessica Mary, DBE
Rees, *Prof.* Dame Judith Anne, DBE
Rees, *Prof.* Dame Lesley Howard, DBE
Reeves, Dame Helen May, DBE
Rego, Dame Paula Figueiroa, DBE
Reid, Dame Seona Elizabeth, DBE
Reynolds, Dame Fiona Claire, DBE
Rhodes, Dame Zandra Lindsey, DBE

Richard, Dame Alison (Fettes), DBE
Richardson, Dame Mary, DBE
Rigg, Dame Diana, DBE
Rimington, Dame Stella, DCB
Ritterman, Dame Janet, DBE
Roberts, Dame Jane Elisabeth, DBE
Roberts, *Hon.* Dame Priscilla Jane Stephanie (Lady Roberts), DCVO
Robins, Dame Ruth Laura, DBE
Robinson, *Prof.* Dame Carol Vivien, DBE
Robottom, Dame Marlene, DBE
Roe, Dame Marion Audrey, DBE
Roe, Dame Raigh Edith, DBE
Ronson, Dame Gail, DBE
Rose, *Hon.* Dame Vivien Judith, DBE
Ross-Wawrzynski, Dame Dana (Mrs Ross-Wawrzynski), DBE
Rothwell, *Prof.* Dame Nancy Jane, DBE
Ruddock, *Rt. Hon.* Dame Joan Mary, DBE
Runciman of Doxford, The Viscountess, DBE
Russell, *Hon.* Dame Alison Hunter, DBE, QC
Russell, *Dr* Dame Philippa Margaret, DBE
Sackler, Dame Theresa, DBE
Salas, Dame Margaret Laurence, DBE
Salmond, *Prof.* Dame Mary Anne, DBE
Savill, Dame Rosalind Joy, DBE
Sawyer, *Rt. Hon.* Dame Joan Augusta, DBE
Scardino, Dame Marjorie, DBE
Scott, Dame Catherine Margaret (Mrs Denton), DBE
Seward, Dame Margaret Helen Elizabeth, DBE
Sharp, *Rt. Hon.* Dame Victoria Madeleine, DBE
Shaw, *Prof.* Dame Pamela Jean, DBE
Sheldrick, *Dr* Dame Daphne Marjorie, DBE
Shirley, Dame Stephanie, DBE
Shovelton, Dame Helena, DBE
Sibley, Dame Antoinette (Mrs Corbett), DBE
Silver, *Dr* Dame Ruth Muldoon, DBE
Simler, *Hon.* Dame Ingrid Ann (Mrs Bernstein), DBE
Slade, *Hon.* Dame Elizabeth Ann, DBE
Slingo, *Prof.* Dame Julia Mary, DBE
Smith, Dame Dela, DBE
Smith, *Rt. Hon.* Dame Janet Hilary (Mrs Mathieson), DBE
Smith, *Hon.* Dame Jennifer Meredith, DBE
Smith, Dame Margaret Natalie (Maggie) (Mrs Cross), DBE, CH
Southgate, *Prof.* Dame Lesley Jill, DBE
Spencer, Dame Rosemary Jane, DCMG
Steel, *Hon.* Dame (Anne) Heather (Mrs Beattie), DBE
Stocking, Dame Barbara Mary, DBE
Storey, Dame Sarah Joanne, DBE
Strachan, Dame Valerie Patricia Marie, DCB
Strathern, *Prof.* Dame Anne Marilyn, DBE
Street, Dame Susan Ruth, DCB
Stringer, *Prof.* Dame Joan Kathleen, DBE
Sutherland, Dame Veronica Evelyn, DBE, CMG
Suzman, Dame Janet, DBE
Swift, *Hon.* Dame Caroline Jane (Mrs Openshaw), DBE
Symonds, Dame Olga Patricia, DBE
Tanner, *Dr* Dame Mary Elizabeth, DBE
Taylor, Dame Meg, DBE
Te Kanawa, Dame Kiri Janette, DBE
Theis, *Hon.* Dame Lucy Morgan, DBE
Thirlwall, *Hon.* Dame Kathryn Mary, DBE
Thomas, *Prof.* Dame Jean Olwen, DBE
Thomas, Dame Maureen Elizabeth (Lady Thomas), DBE
Thornton, *Prof.* Dame Janet Maureen, DBE
Tickell, Dame Clare Oriana, DBE
Tinson, Dame Sue, DBE
Tizard, Dame Catherine Anne, GCMG, GCVO, DBE
Tokiel, Dame Rosa, DBE

Townsend, Lady Juliet Margaret, DCVO
Trotter, Dame Janet Olive, DBE
Turner-Warwick, Dame Margaret Elizabeth Harvey, DBE,
   FRCP, FRCPED
Twelftree, Dame Marcia, DBE
Uchida, Dame Mitsuko, DBE
Uprichard, Dame Mary Elizabeth, DBE
Varley, Dame Joan Fleetwood, DBE
Wagner, Dame Gillian Mary Millicent (Lady Wagner), DBE
Wall, Dame (Alice) Anne, (Mrs Michael Wall), DCVO
Wallace, *Prof.* Dame Helen Sarah, DBE, CMG
Wallis, Dame Sheila Ann, DBE
Walter, Dame Harriet Mary, DBE
Warburton, Dame Anne Marion, DCVO, CMG
Waterhouse, Dr Dame Rachel Elizabeth, DBE

Waterman, *Dr* Dame Fanny, DBE
Watkinson, Dame Angela Eileen, DBE
Webb, *Prof.* Dame Patricia, DBE
Weir, Dame Gillian Constance (Mrs Phelps), DBE
Weller, Dame Rita, DBE
Weston, Dame Margaret Kate, DBE
Westwood, Dame Vivienne Isabel, DBE
Whitehead, *Hon.* Dame Annabel Alice Hoyer, DCVO
Williams, Dame Josephine, DBE
Wilson, Dame Jacqueline, DBE
Wilson-Barnett, *Prof.* Dame Jenifer, DBE
Winstone, Dame Dorothy Gertrude, DBE, CMG
Wolfson de Botton, Dame Janet (Mrs Wolfson de Botton), DBE
Wong Yick-ming, Dame Rosanna, DBE
Zaffar, Dame Naila, DBE

DECORATIONS AND MEDALS

PRINCIPAL DECORATIONS AND MEDALS
IN ORDER OF WEAR

VICTORIA CROSS (VC), 1856 (*see* below)
GEORGE CROSS (GC), 1940 (*see* below)

BRITISH ORDERS OF KNIGHTHOOD (*see also* Orders of Chivalry)
Order of the Garter
Order of the Thistle
Order of St Patrick
Order of the Bath
Order of Merit
Order of the Star of India
Order of St Michael and George
Order of the Indian Empire
Order of the Crown of India
Royal Victorian Order (Classes I, II and III)
Order of the British Empire (Classes I, II and III)
Order of the Companions of Honour
Distinguished Service Order
Royal Victorian Order (Class IV)
Order of the British Empire (Class IV)
Imperial Service Order
Royal Victorian Order (Class V)
Order of the British Empire (Class V)

BARONET'S BADGE

KNIGHT BACHELOR'S BADGE

INDIAN ORDER OF MERIT (MILITARY)

DECORATIONS
Conspicuous Gallantry Cross (CGC), 1995
Royal Red Cross Class I (RRC), 1883
Distinguished Service Cross (DSC), 1914
Military Cross (MC), December 1914
Distinguished Flying Cross (DFC), 1918
Air Force Cross (AFC), 1918
Royal Red Cross Class II (ARRC)
Order of British India
Kaisar-i-Hind Medal
Order of St John

MEDALS FOR GALLANTRY AND DISTINGUISHED CONDUCT
Union of South Africa Queen's Medal for Bravery, in Gold
Distinguished Conduct Medal (DCM), 1854
Conspicuous Gallantry Medal (CGM), 1874
Conspicuous Gallantry Medal (Flying)
George Medal (GM), 1940
Queen's Police Medal for Gallantry
Queen's Fire Service Medal for Gallantry
Royal West African Frontier Force Distinguished Conduct Medal
King's African Rifles Distinguished Conduct Medal
Indian Distinguished Service Medal
Union of South Africa Queen's Medal for Bravery, in Silver
Distinguished Service Medal (DSM), 1914
Military Medal (MM), 1916
Distinguished Flying Medal (DFM), 1918
Air Force Medal (AFM)

Constabulary Medal (Ireland)
Medal for Saving Life at Sea (Sea Gallantry Medal)
Indian Order of Merit (Civil)
Indian Police Medal for Gallantry
Ceylon Police Medal for Gallantry
Sierra Leone Police Medal for Gallantry
Sierra Leone Fire Brigades Medal for Gallantry
Overseas Territories Police Medal for Gallantry
Queen's Gallantry Medal (QGM), 1974
Royal Victorian Medal (RVM), Gold, Silver and Bronze
British Empire Medal (BEM)
Canada Medal
Queen's Police Medal for Distinguished Service (QPM)
Queen's Fire Service Medal for Distinguished Service (QFSM)
Queen's Volunteer Reserves Medal
Queen's Medal for Chiefs

CAMPAIGN MEDALS AND STARS
    Including authorised United Nations, European Community/Union and North Atlantic Treaty Organisation medals (in order of date of campaign for which awarded)

Iraq Reconstruction Service Medal
Civilian Service Medal (Afghanistan)

POLAR MEDALS (in order of date)

IMPERIAL SERVICE MEDAL

POLICE MEDALS FOR VALUABLE SERVICE
Indian Police Medal for Meritorious Service
Ceylon Police Medal for Merit
Sierra Leone Police Medal for Meritorious Service
Sierra Leone Fire Brigades Medal for Meritorious Service
Overseas Territories Police Medal for Meritorious Service

BADGE OF HONOUR

JUBILEE, CORONATION AND DURBAR MEDALS
Queen Victoria, King Edward VII, King George V, King George VI, Queen Elizabeth II, Visit Commemoration and Long and Faithful Service Medals

EFFICIENCY AND LONG SERVICE DECORATIONS AND MEDALS
Medal for Meritorious Service
Accumulated Campaign Service Medal
Medal for Long Service and Good Conduct (Military)
Naval Long Service and Good Conduct Medal
Medal for Meritorious Service (Royal Navy 1918–28)
Indian Long Service and Good Conduct Medal
Indian Meritorious Service Medal
Royal Marines Meritorious Service Medal (1849–1947)
Royal Air Force Meritorious Service Medal (1918–1928)
Royal Air Force Long Service and Good Conduct Medal
Medal for Long Service and Good Conduct (Ulster Defence Regiment)
Indian Long Service and Good Conduct Medal
Royal West African Frontier Force Long Service and Good Conduct Medal
Royal Sierra Leone Military Forces Long Service and Good Conduct Medal

King's African Rifles Long Service and Good Conduct Medal
Indian Meritorious Service Medal
Police Long Service and Good Conduct Medal
Fire Brigade Long Service and Good Conduct Medal
African Police Medal for Meritorious Service
Royal Canadian Mounted Police Long Service Medal
Ceylon Police Long Service Medal
Ceylon Fire Services Long Service Medal
Sierra Leone Police Long Service Medal
Overseas Territories Police Long Service Medal
Sierra Leone Fire Brigades Long Service Medal
Mauritius Police Long Service and Good Conduct Medal
Mauritius Fire Services Long Service and Good Conduct Medal
Mauritius Prisons Service Long Service and Good Conduct
  Medal
Overseas Territories Fire Brigades Long Service Medal
Overseas Territories Prison Service Medal
Hong Kong Disciplined Services Medal
Army Emergency Reserve Decoration (ERD)
Volunteer Officers' Decoration (VD)
Volunteer Long Service Medal
Volunteer Officers' Decoration (for India and the Colonies)
Volunteer Long Service Medal (for India and the Colonies)
Colonial Auxiliary Forces Officers' Decoration
Colonial Auxiliary Forces Long Service Medal
Medal for Good Shooting (Naval)
Militia Long Service Medal
Imperial Yeomanry Long Service Medal
Territorial Decoration (TD), 1908
Ceylon Armed Services Long Service Medal
Efficiency Decoration (ED)
Territorial Efficiency Medal
Efficiency Medal
Special Reserve Long Service and Good Conduct Medal
Decoration for Officers of the Royal Navy Reserve (RD), 1910
Decoration for Officers of the Royal Naval Volunteer Reserve
  (VRD)
Royal Naval Reserve Long Service and Good Conduct Medal
Royal Naval Volunteer Reserve Long Service and Good Conduct
  Medal
Royal Naval Auxiliary Sick Berth Reserve Long Service and
  Good Conduct Medal
Royal Fleet Reserve Long Service and Good Conduct Medal
Royal Naval Wireless Auxiliary Reserve Long Service and Good
  Conduct Medal
Royal Naval Auxiliary Service Medal
Air Efficiency Award (AE), 1942
Volunteer Reserves Service Medal
Ulster Defence Regiment Medal
Northern Ireland Home Service Medal
Queen's Medal (for Champion Shots of the RN and RM)
Queen's Medal (for Champion Shots of the New Zealand
  Naval Forces)
Queen's Medal (for Champion Shots in the Military Forces)
Queen's Medal (for Champion Shots of the Air Forces)
Cadet Forces Medal, 1950
HM Coastguard Long Service and Good Conduct Medal
Special Constabulary Long Service Medal
Canadian Forces Decoration
Royal Observer Corps Medal
Civil Defence Long Service Medal
Ambulance Service (Emergency Duties) Long Service and Good
  Conduct Medal
Royal Fleet Auxiliary Service Medal
Prison Services (Operational Duties) Long Service and Good
  Conduct Medal
Rhodesia Medal
Royal Ulster Constabulary Service Medal
Northern Ireland Prison Service Medal

Union of South Africa Commemoration Medal
Indian Independence Medal
Pakistan Medal
Ceylon Armed Services Inauguration Medal
Ceylon Police Independence Medal (1948)
Sierra Leone Independence Medal
Jamaica Independence Medal
Uganda Independence Medal
Malawi Independence Medal
Fiji Independence Medal
Papua New Guinea Independence Medal
Solomon Islands Independence Medal
Service Medal of the Order of St John
Badge of the Order of the League of Mercy
Voluntary Medical Service Medal (1932)
Women's Royal Voluntary Service Medal
South African Medal for War Services
Overseas Territories Special Constabulary Medal

HONORARY MEMBERSHIP OF COMMONWEALTH
ORDERS

OTHER COMMONWEALTH MEMBERS' ORDERS,
DECORATIONS AND MEDALS

FOREIGN ORDERS

FOREIGN DECORATIONS

FOREIGN MEDALS

THE VICTORIA CROSS (1856)
FOR CONSPICUOUS BRAVERY

VC

Ribbon, Crimson, for all Services (until 1918 it was blue for
  the Royal Navy)

Instituted on 29 January 1856, the Victoria Cross was
awarded retrospectively to 1854, the first being held by Lt.
C. D. Lucas, RN, for bravery in the Baltic Sea on 21 June
1854 (gazetted 24 February 1857). The first 62 crosses were
presented by Queen Victoria in Hyde Park, London, on 26
June 1857.

The Victoria Cross is worn before all other decorations,
on the left breast, and consists of a cross-pattée of bronze,
3.8cm in diameter, with the royal crown surmounted by
a lion in the centre, and beneath there is the inscription *For
Valour*. Holders of the VC currently receive a tax-free annuity
of £2,000, irrespective of need or other conditions. In 1911,
the right to receive the cross was extended to Indian soldiers,
and in 1920 to matrons, sisters and nurses, the staff of the
nursing services and other services pertaining to hospitals
and nursing, and to civilians of either sex regularly or
temporarily under the orders, direction or supervision of the
naval, military, or air forces of the crown.

SURVIVING RECIPIENTS OF THE VICTORIA CROSS
as at 31 August 2014

Apiata, *Cpl.* B. H., VC (New Zealand Special Air Service)
  2004 *Afghanistan*
Beharry, *LSgt.* J. G., VC (Princess of Wales's Royal Regiment)
  2005 *Iraq*

Cruickshank, *Flt. Lt.* J. A., VC (RAFVR)
1944 *World War*
Donaldson, *Cpl.* M. G. S., VC (Australian Special Air Service)
2008 *Afghanistan*
Keighran, *Cpl.* D. A., VC (Royal Australian Regiment)
2012 *Afghanistan*
Payne, *WO* K., VC, DSC (USA) (Australian Army Training
Team)
1969 *Vietnam*
Rambahadur Limbu, *Capt.,* VC, MVO (10th Princess Mary's
Gurkha Rifles)
1965 *Sarawak*
Roberts-Smith, *Cpl.* B., VC (Australian Special Air Service)
2010 *Afghanistan*
Speakman, *Sgt.* W., VC (Black Watch, attached KOSB)
1951 *Korea*

THE GEORGE CROSS (1940)
FOR GALLANTRY

GC

Ribbon, Dark blue, threaded through a bar adorned with
laurel leaves
Instituted 24 September 1940 (with amendments,
3 November 1942)

The George Cross is worn before all other decorations
(except the VC) on the left breast (when worn by a woman it
may be worn on the left shoulder from a ribbon of the same
width and colour fashioned into a bow). It consists of a plain
silver cross with four equal limbs, the cross having in the
centre a circular medallion bearing a design showing St
George and the Dragon. The inscription *For Gallantry*
appears round the medallion and in the angle of each limb of
the cross is the royal cypher 'G VI' forming a circle
concentric with the medallion. The reverse is plain and bears
the name of the recipient and the date of the award. The
cross is suspended by a ring from a bar adorned with laurel
leaves on dark blue ribbon 3.8cm wide.

The cross is intended primarily for civilians; awards to the
fighting services are confined to actions for which purely
military honours are not normally granted. It is awarded only
for acts of the greatest heroism or of the most conspicuous
courage in circumstances of extreme danger. From 1 April
1965, holders of the cross have received a tax-free annuity,
which is currently £2,000. The cross has twice been awarded
collectively rather than to an individual: to Malta (1942) and
the Royal Ulster Constabulary (1999).

In October 1971 all surviving holders of the Albert Medal
and the Edward Medal exchanged those decorations for the
George Cross.

SURVIVING RECIPIENTS OF THE GEORGE CROSS
as at 31 August 2014

If the recipient originally received the Albert Medal (AM) or
the Edward Medal (EM), this is indicated by the initials in
parentheses.

Archer, *Col.* B. S. T., GC, OBE, ERD, 1941
Bamford, J., GC, 1952
Beaton, J., GC, CVO, 1974
Butson, *Lt.-Col.* A. R. C., GC, CD, MD (AM), 1948
Croucher, *Lance Cpl.* M., GC, 2008
Finney, C., GC, 2003
Flintoff, H. H., GC (EM), 1944
Gledhill, A. J., GC, 1967
Gregson, J. S., GC (AM), 1943
Hughes, *WO2* K. S., GC, 2010
Johnson, *WO1 (SSM)* B., GC, 1990
Kinne, D. G., GC, 1954
Lowe, A. R., GC (AM), 1949
Norton, *Maj.* P. A., GC, 2006
Pratt, M. K., GC, 1978
Purves, Mrs M., GC (AM), 1949
Raweng, Awang anak, GC, 1951
Stevens, H. W., GC, 1958
Walker, C., GC, 1972
Wooding, E. A., GC (AM), 1945

THE ELIZABETH CROSS (2009)

EC

Instituted 1 July 2009

The Elizabeth Cross consists of a silver cross with a laurel
wreath passing between the arms, which bear the floral
symbols of England (rose), Scotland (thistle), Ireland
(shamrock) and Wales (daffodil). The centre of the cross bears
the royal cypher and the reverse is inscribed with the name
of the person for whom it is in honour. The cross is
accompanied by a memorial scroll and a miniature.

The cross was created to commemorate UK armed forces
personnel who have died on operations or as a result of an
act of terrorism. It may be granted to and worn by the next of
kin of any eligible personnel who died from 1 January 1948
to date. It offers the wearer no precedence. Those that are
eligible include the next of kin of personnel who died while
serving on a medal earning operation, as a result of an act of
terrorism, or on a non-medal earning operation where death
was caused by the inherent high risk of the task.

The Elizabeth Cross is not intended as a posthumous
medal for the fallen but as an emblem of national recognition
of the loss and sacrifice made by the personnel and their
families.

CHIEFS OF CLANS IN SCOTLAND

Only chiefs of whole Names or Clans are included, except certain special instances (marked *) who, though not chiefs of a whole Name, were or are for some reason (eg the Macdonald forfeiture) independent. Under decision (*Campbell-Gray,* 1950) that a bearer of a 'double or triple-barrelled' surname cannot be held chief of a part of such, several others cannot be included in the list at present.

THE ROYAL HOUSE: HM The Queen

AGNEW: Sir Crispin Agnew of Lochnaw, Bt., QC
ANSTRUTHER: Tobias Anstruther of Anstruther and Balcaskie
ARBUTHNOTT: Viscount of Arbuthnott
BANNERMAN: Sir David Bannerman of Elsick, Bt.
BARCLAY: Peter C. Barclay of Towie Barclay and of that Ilk
BORTHWICK: Lord Borthwick
BOYLE: Earl of Glasgow
BRODIE: Alexander Brodie of Brodie
BROUN OF COLSTOUN: Sir Wayne Broun of Colstoun, Bt.
BRUCE: Earl of Elgin and Kincardine, KT
BUCHAN: David Buchan of Auchmacoy
BURNETT: J. C. A. Burnett of Leys
CAMERON: Donald Cameron of Lochiel
CAMPBELL: Duke of Argyll
CARMICHAEL: Richard Carmichael of Carmichael
CARNEGIE: Duke of Fife
CATHCART: Earl Cathcart
CHARTERIS: Earl of Wemyss and March
CLAN CHATTAN: K. Mackintosh of Clan Chattan
CHISHOLM: Hamish Chisholm of Chisholm (*The Chisholm*)
COCHRANE: Earl of Dundonald
COLQUHOUN: Sir Malcolm Rory Colquhoun of Luss, Bt.
CRANSTOUN: David Cranstoun of that Ilk
CUMMING: Sir Alastair Cumming of Altyre, Bt.
DARROCH: Duncan Darroch of Gourock
DEWAR: Michael Dewar of that Ilk and Vogrie
DRUMMOND: Earl of Perth
DUNBAR: Sir James Dunbar of Mochrum, Bt.
DUNDAS: David Dundas of Dundas
DURIE: Andrew Durie of Durie, CBE
ELIOTT: Mrs Margaret Eliott of Redheugh
ERSKINE: Earl of Mar and Kellie
FARQUHARSON: Capt. A. Farquharson of Invercauld, MC
FERGUSSON: Sir Charles Fergusson of Kilkerran, Bt.
FORBES: Lord Forbes
FORSYTH: Alistair Forsyth of that Ilk
FRASER: Lady Saltoun
*FRASER (OF LOVAT): Lord Lovat
GAYRE: R. Gayre of Gayre and Nigg
GORDON: Marquess of Huntly
GRAHAM: Duke of Montrose
GRANT: Lord Strathspey
GUTHRIE: Alexander Guthrie of Guthrie
HAIG: Earl Haig
HALDANE: Martin Haldane of Gleneagles
HANNAY: David Hannay of Kirkdale and of that Ilk
HAY: Earl of Erroll

HENDERSON: Alistair Henderson of Fordell
HUNTER: Pauline Hunter of Hunterston
IRVINE OF DRUM: David Irvine of Drum
JARDINE: Sir William Jardine of Applegirth, Bt.
JOHNSTONE: Earl of Annandale and Hartfell
KEITH: Earl of Kintore
KENNEDY: Marquess of Ailsa
KERR: Marquess of Lothian, PC
KINCAID: Madam Arabella Kincaid of Kincaid
LAMONT: Revd Peter Lamont of that Ilk
LEASK: Jonathan Leask of that Ilk
LENNOX: Edward Lennox of that Ilk
LESLIE: Earl of Rothes
LINDSAY: Earl of Crawford and Balcarres, KT, GCVO, PC
LIVINGSTONE (or MACLEA): Niall Livingstone of the Bachuil
LOCKHART: Angus Lockhart of the Lee
LUMSDEN: Gillem Lumsden of that Ilk and Blanerne
MACALESTER: William St J. McAlester of Loup and Kennox
MACARTHUR; John MacArthur of that Ilk
MCBAIN: J. H. McBain of McBain
MACDONALD: Lord Macdonald (*The Macdonald of Macdonald*)
*MACDONALD OF CLANRANALD: Ranald Macdonald of Clanranald
*MACDONALD OF KEPPOCH: Ranald MacDonald of Keppoch
*MACDONALD OF SLEAT (CLAN HUSTEAIN): Sir Ian Macdonald of Sleat, Bt.
*MACDONELL OF GLENGARRY: Ranald MacDonell of Glengarry
MACDOUGALL: Morag MacDougall of MacDougall
MACDOWALL: Fergus Macdowall of Garthland
MACGREGOR: Sir Malcolm MacGregor of MacGregor, Bt.
MACINTYRE: Donald MacIntyre of Glenoe
MACKAY: Lord Reay
MACKENZIE: Earl of Cromartie
MACKINNON: Anne Mackinnon of Mackinnon
MACKINTOSH: John Mackintosh of Mackintosh (*The Mackintosh of Mackintosh*)
MACLACHLAN: Euan MacLachlan of MacLachlan
MACLAREN: Donald MacLaren of MacLaren and Achleskine
MACLEAN: Hon. Sir Lachlan Maclean of Duart, Bt., CVO
MACLENNAN: Ruaraidh MacLennan of MacLennan
MACLEOD: Hugh MacLeod of MacLeod
MACMILLAN: George MacMillan of MacMillan

MACNAB: J. W. A. Macnab of Macnab (*The Macnab*)
MACNAGHTEN: Sir Malcolm Macnaghten of Macnaghten and Dundarave, Bt.
MACNEACAIL: John Macneacail of Macneacail and Scorrybreac
MACNEIL OF BARRA: Rory Macneil of Barra (*The Macneil of Barra*)
MACPHERSON: Hon. Sir William Macpherson of Cluny, TD
MACTAVISH: Steven MacTavish of Dunardry
MACTHOMAS: Andrew MacThomas of Finegand
MAITLAND: Earl of Lauderdale
MAKGILL: Viscount of Oxfuird
MALCOLM (MACCALLUM): Robin N. L. Malcolm of Poltalloch
MAR: Countess of Mar
MARJORIBANKS: Andrew Marjoribanks of that Ilk
MATHESON: Maj. Sir Fergus Matheson of Matheson, Bt.
MENZIES: David Menzies of Menzies
MOFFAT: Madam Moffat of that Ilk
MONCREIFFE: Hon. Peregrine Moncreiffe of that Ilk
MONTGOMERIE: Earl of Eglinton and Winton
MORRISON: Dr John Ruairidh Morrison of Ruchdi
MUNRO: Hector Munro of Foulis
MURRAY: Duke of Atholl
NESBITT (or NISBET): Mark Nesbitt of that Ilk
OGILVY: Earl of Airlie, KT, GCVO, PC
OLIPHANT: Richard Oliphant of that Ilk
RAMSAY: Earl of Dalhousie
RIDDELL: Sir Walter Riddell of Riddell, Bt.
ROBERTSON: Alexander Robertson of Struan (*Struan-Robertson)*
ROLLO: Lord Rollo
ROSE: David Rose of Kilravock
ROSS: David Ross of that Ilk and Balnagowan
RUTHVEN: Earl of Gowrie, PC
SCOTT: Duke of Buccleuch and Queensberry, KBE
SCRYMGEOUR: Earl of Dundee
SEMPILL: Lord Sempill
SHAW: John Shaw of Tordarroch
SINCLAIR: Earl of Caithness, PC
SKENE: Danus Skene of Skene
STIRLING: Fraser Stirling of Cader
STRANGE: Maj. Timothy Strange of Balcaskie
SUTHERLAND: Countess of Sutherland
SWINTON: John Swinton of that Ilk
TROTTER: Alexander Trotter of Mortonhall, CVO
URQUHART: Wilkins F. Urquhart of Urquhart
WALLACE: Ian Wallace of that Ilk
WEDDERBURN: Master of Dundee
WEMYSS: Michael Wemyss of that Ilk

THE PRIVY COUNCIL

The sovereign in council, or Privy Council, was the chief source of executive power until the system of cabinet government developed in the 18th century. Now the Privy Council's main functions are to advise the sovereign and to exercise its own statutory responsibilities independent of the sovereign in council.

Membership of the Privy Council is automatic upon appointment to certain government and judicial positions in the UK, eg cabinet ministers must be Privy Counsellors and are sworn in on first assuming office. Membership is also accorded by the Queen to eminent people in the UK and independent countries of the Commonwealth of which she is Queen, on the recommendation of the prime minister. Membership of the council is retained for life, except for very occasional removals.

The administrative functions of the Privy Council are carried out by the Privy Council Office under the direction of the president of the council, who is always a member of the cabinet. (*See also* Parliament)
President of the Council, Rt. Hon. Nick Clegg
Clerk of the Council, Richard Tilbrook

Style The Right (or Rt.) Hon._
  *Envelope, The Right (or Rt.) Hon. F_ S_*
  *Letter, Dear Mr/Miss/Mrs S_*
  *Spoken, Mr/Miss/Mrs S_*
It is incorrect to use the letters PC after the name in conjunction with the prefix The Rt. Hon., unless the Privy Counsellor is a peer below the rank of Marquess and so is styled The Rt. Hon. because of his/her rank.

MEMBERS *as at August 2014*

HRH The Duke of Edinburgh, 1951
HRH The Prince of Wales, 1977

Abernethy, *Hon.* Lord (Alastair Cameron), 2005
Adonis, Lord, 2009
Aikens, Sir Richard, 2008
Airlie, Earl of, 1984
Aldous, Sir William, 1995
Alebua, Ezekiel, 1988
Alexander, Douglas, 2005
Alexander, Danny, 2010
Amos, Baroness, 2003
Anderson of Swansea, Lord, 2000
Anelay of St Johns, Baroness, 2009
Angiolini, Dame Elish, 2006
Anthony, Douglas, 1971
Arbuthnot, James, 1998
Arden, Dame Mary, 2000
Armstrong of Hill Top, Baroness, 1999
Arthur, *Hon.* Owen, 1995
Ashdown of Norton-sub-Hamdon, Lord, 1989
Ashcroft, Lord, 2012
Ashton of Upholland, Baroness, 2006
Atkins, Sir Robert, 1995
Auld, Sir Robin, 1995
Baker, Norman, 2014
Baker, Sir Thomas, 2002
Baker of Dorking, Lord, 1984
Baldry, Sir Tony, 2013
Balls, Ed, 2007
Barker, Gregory, 2012
Barnett, Lord, 1975
Barron, Sir Kevin, 2001
Bassam of Brighton, Lord, 2009
Battle, John, 2002
Beatson, Sir Jack, 2013
Beckett, Dame Margaret, 1993
Beith, Sir Alan, 1992
Beldam, Sir Roy, 1989
Benn, Hilary, 2003
Bercow, John, 2009
Birch, William, 1992
Black, Dame Jill, 2011

Blackstone, Baroness, 2001
Blair, Anthony, 1994
Blanchard, Peter, 1998
Blears, Hazel, 2005
Blencathra, Lord, 1995
Blunkett, David, 1997
Boateng, Lord, 1999
Bolger, James, 1991
Bonomy, *Hon.* Lord (Iain Bonomy), 2010
Boothroyd, Baroness, 1992
Bottomley of Nettlestone, Baroness, 1992
Boyd of Duncansby, Lord, 2000
Brabazon of Tara, Lord, 2013
Bracadale, *Hon.* Lord (Alistair Campbell), 2013
Bradley, Lord, 2001
Bradshaw, Ben, 2009
Brake, Thomas, 2011
Brathwaite, Sir Nicholas, 1991
Briggs, Sir Michael, 2013
Brittan of Spennithorne, Lord, 1981
Brodie, *Hon.* Lord (Philip Brodie), 2013
Brooke, Annette, 2014
Brooke, Sir Henry, 1996
Brooke of Sutton Mandeville, Lord, 1988
Brown, Gordon, 1996
Brown, Nicholas, 1997
Brown, Sir Stephen, 1983
Brown of Eaton-under-Heywood, Lord, 1992
Browne of Ladyton, Lord, 2005
Browne-Wilkinson, Lord, 1983
Bruce, Sir Malcolm, 2006
Burnham, Andy, 2007
Burns, Simon, 2011
Burnton, Sir Stanley, 2008
Burstow, Paul, 2012
Burt, Alistair, 2013
Butler of Brockwell, Lord, 2004
Butler-Sloss, Baroness, 1988
Buxton, Sir Richard, 1997

Byers, Stephen, 1998
Byrne, Liam, 2008
Byron, Sir Dennis, 2004
Cable, Vincent, 2010
Caborn, Richard, 1999
Caithness, Earl of, 1990
Cameron, David, 2005
Cameron of Lochbroom, Lord, 1984
Camoys, Lord, 1997
Campbell, Alan, 2014
Campbell, Sir Walter Menzies, 1999
Campbell, Sir William, 1999
Canterbury, Archbishop of, 2013
Carey of Clifton, Lord, 1991
Carloway, *Hon.* Lord (Colin Sutherland), 2008
Carmichael, Alistair, 2010
Carnwath of Notting Hill, Lord, 2002
Carrington, Lord, 1959
Carswell, Lord, 1993
Chadwick, Sir John, 1997
Chalfont, Lord, 1964
Chalker of Wallasey, Baroness, 1987
Chan, Sir Julius, 1981
Chilcot, Sir John, 2004
Christie, Perry, 2004
Clark, Greg, 2010
Clark, Helen, 1990
Clark of Carlton, Baroness, 2013
Clark of Windermere, Lord, 1997
Clarke, Charles, 2001
Clarke, Sir Christopher, 2013
Clarke, Kenneth, 1984
Clarke, *Hon.* Lord (Matthew Clarke), 2008
Clarke, Thomas, 1997
Clarke of Stone-Cum-Ebony, Lord, 1998
Clegg, Nicholas, 2008
Clinton-Davis, Lord, 1998
Clwyd, Ann, 2004
Coghlin, Sir Patrick, 2009
Collins of Mapesbury, Lord, 2007
Cooper, Yvette, 2007
Cope of Berkeley, Lord, 1988
Corston, Baroness, 2003

Sandiford, Erskine, 1989
Saville of Newdigate, Lord, 1994
Sawyer, Dame Joan, 2004
Schiemann, Sir Konrad, 1995
Scotland of Asthal, Baroness, 2001
Scott of Foscote, Lord, 1991
Seaga, Edward, 1981
Sedley, Sir Stephen, 1999
Selkirk of Douglas, Lord, 1996
Shapps, Grant, 2010
Sharp, Dame Victoria, 2013
Sheldon, Lord, 1977
Shephard of Northwold, Baroness, 1992
Sheil, Sir John, 2005
Shipley, Jennifer, 1998
Short, Clare, 1997
Shutt of Greetland, Lord, 2009
Simmonds, Kennedy Sir, 1984
Sinclair, Ian, 1977
Slade, Sir Christopher, 1982
Smith, Andrew, 1997
Smith, Dame Janet, 2002
Smith, Hon. Lady (Anne Smith), 2013
Smith, Jacqueline, 2003
Smith of Basildon, Baroness, 2009
Smith of Finsbury, Lord, 1997
Soames, Hon. (Arthur) Nicholas, 2011
Somare, Sir Michael, 1977
Spellar, John, 2001
Spelman, Caroline, 2010
Spicer, Lord, 2013
Stanley, Sir John, 1984
Staughton, Sir Christopher, 1988
Steel of Aikwood, Lord, 1977
Stephen, Sir Ninian, 1979
Stewartby, Lord, 1989
Steyn, Lord, 1992
Stowell of Beeston, Baroness, 2014
Strang, Gavin, 1997

Strathclyde, Lord, 1995
Straw, Jack, 1997
Stuart, Freundel, 2013
Stuart-Smith, Sir Murray, 1988
Stunnell, Sir Andrew, 2012
Sullivan, Sir Jeremy, 2009
Sumption, Lord, 2011
Sutherland, Hon. Lord (Ranald Sutherland), 2000
Swayne, Desmond, 2011
Swire, Hugo, 2010
Symons of Vernham Dean, Baroness, 2001
Tapsell, Sir Peter, 2011
Taylor of Bolton, Baroness, 1997
Tebbit, Lord, 1981
Thomas, Edmund, 1996
Thomas, Sir Swinton, 1994
Thomas of Cwmgiedd, Lord, 2003
Thorpe, Jeremy, 1967
Thorpe, Sir Matthew, 1995
Thurso, Viscount, 2014
Timms, Stephen, 2006
Tipping, Andrew, 1998
Tizard, Robert, 1986
Tomlinson, Sir Stephen, 2011
Touhig, Lord, 2006
Toulson, Lord, 2007
Treacy, Sir Colman, 2012
Trefgarne, Lord, 1989
Trimble, Lord, 1997
Trumpington, Baroness, 1992
Tuckey, Sir Simon, 1998
Tyler, Lord, 2014
Ullswater, Viscount, 1994
Underhill, Sir Nicholas, 2013
Upton, Simon, 1999
Vadera, Baroness, 2009
Vaz, Keith, 2006
Villiers, Theresa, 2010
Vos, Sir Geoffrey, 2013

Waddington, Lord, 1987
Waite, Sir John, 1993
Wakeham, Lord, 1983
Waldegrave of North Hill, Lord, 1990
Walker of Gestingthorpe, Lord, 1997
Wall, Sir Nicholas, 2004
Wallace of Saltaire, Lord, 2012
Wallace of Tankerness, Lord, 2000
Waller, Sir Mark, 1996
Ward, Sir Alan, 1995
Warner, Lord, 2006
Warsi, Baroness, 2010
Webb, Steve, 2014
West of Spithead, Lord, 2010
Wheatley, Hon. Lord (John Wheatley), 2007
Wheeler, Sir John, 1993
Whitty, Lord, 2005
Widdecombe, Ann, 1997
Wigley, Lord, 1997
Willetts, David, 2010
Williams, Alan, 1977
Williams of Crosby, Baroness, 1974
Williams of Elvel, Lord, 2013
Williams of Oystermouth, Lord, 2002
Williamson of Horton, Lord, 2007
Wills, Lord, 2008
Wilson, Brian, 2003
Wilson of Culworth, Lord, 2005
Winterton, Rosie, 2006
Wingti, Paias, 1987
Withers, Reginald, 1977
Woodward, Shaun, 2007
Woolf, Lord, 1986
Wright, Jeremy, 2014
York, Archbishop of, 2005
Young, Sir George, 1993
Young of Graffham, Lord, 1984
Zacca, Edward, 1992

PRIVY COUNCIL OF NORTHERN IRELAND

The Privy Council of Northern Ireland had responsibilities in Northern Ireland similar to those of the Privy Council in Great Britain until the Northern Ireland Act 1974. Membership of the Privy Council of Northern Ireland is retained for life. Since the Northern Ireland Constitution Act 1973 no further appointments have been made. The postnominal initials PC (NI) are used to differentiate its members from those of the Privy Council.

MEMBERS *as at August 2014*
Bailie, Robin, 1971
Bleakley, David, 1971
Dobson, John, 1969
Kilclooney, Lord, 1970

PARLIAMENT

The UK constitution is not contained in any single document but has evolved over time, formed by statute, common law and convention. A constitutional monarchy, the UK is governed by ministers of the crown in the name of the sovereign, who is head both of the state and of the government.

The organs of government are the legislature (parliament), the executive and the judiciary. The executive comprises HM government (the cabinet and other ministers), government departments and local authorities (*see* Government Departments, Public Bodies and Local Government). The judiciary (*see* Law Courts and Offices) pronounces on the law, both written and unwritten, interprets statutes and is responsible for the enforcement of the law; the judiciary is independent of both the legislature and the executive.

THE MONARCHY

The sovereign personifies the state and is, in law, an integral part of the legislature, head of the executive, head of the judiciary, commander-in-chief of all armed forces of the crown and supreme governor of the Church of England. In the Channel Islands and the Isle of Man, which are crown dependencies, the sovereign is represented by a lieutenant-governor. In the member states of the Commonwealth of which the sovereign is head of state, her representative is a governor-general; in UK overseas territories the sovereign is usually represented by a governor, who is responsible to the British government.

Although in practice the powers of the monarchy are now very limited, and restricted mainly to the advisory and ceremonial, there are important acts of government which require the participation of the sovereign. These include summoning, proroguing and dissolving parliament, giving royal assent to bills passed by parliament, appointing important office-holders, eg government ministers, judges, bishops and governors, conferring peerages, knighthoods and other honours, and granting pardon to a person wrongly convicted of a crime. The sovereign appoints the prime minister; by convention this office is held by the leader of the political party which enjoys, or can secure, a majority of votes in the House of Commons. In international affairs the sovereign, as head of state, has the power to declare war and make peace, to recognise foreign states and governments, to conclude treaties and to annex or cede territory. However, as the sovereign entrusts executive power to ministers of the crown and acts on the advice of her ministers, which she cannot ignore, royal prerogative powers are in practice exercised by ministers, who are responsible to parliament.

Ministerial responsibility does not diminish the sovereign's importance to the smooth working of government. She holds meetings of the Privy Council (*see* below), gives audiences to her ministers and other officials at home and overseas, receives accounts of cabinet decisions, reads dispatches and signs state papers; she must be informed and consulted on every aspect of national life; and she must show complete impartiality.

COUNSELLORS OF STATE

If the sovereign travels abroad for more than a few days or suffers from a temporary illness, it is necessary to appoint members of the royal family, known as counsellors of state, under letters patent to carry out the chief functions of the monarch, including the holding of Privy Councils and giving royal assent to acts passed by parliament. The normal procedure is to appoint three or four members of the royal family among those members remaining in the UK, provided they are over 21. There are currently five counsellors of state.

In the event of the sovereign on accession being under the age of 18 years, or by infirmity of mind or body, rendered incapable of performing the royal functions, provision is made for a regency.

THE PRIVY COUNCIL

The sovereign in council, or Privy Council, was the chief source of executive power until the system of cabinet government developed. Its main function today is to advise the sovereign on the approval of various statutory functions and acts of the royal prerogative. These powers are exercised through orders in council and royal proclamations, approved by the Queen at meetings of the Privy Council. The council is also able to exercise a number of statutory duties without approval from the sovereign, including powers of supervision over the registering bodies for the medical and allied professions. These duties are exercised through orders of council.

Although appointment as a privy counsellor is for life, only those who are currently government ministers are involved in the day-to-day business of the council. A full council is summoned only on the death of the sovereign or when the sovereign announces his or her intention to marry. (For a full list of privy counsellors, *see* the Privy Council section.)

There are a number of advisory Privy Council committees whose meetings the sovereign does not attend. Some are prerogative committees, such as those dealing with legislative matters submitted by the legislatures of the Channel Islands and the Isle of Man or with applications for charters of incorporation; and some are provided for by statute, eg those for the universities of Oxford and Cambridge and some Scottish universities.

Administrative work is carried out by the Privy Council Office under the direction of the Lord President of the Council, a cabinet minister.

JUDICIAL COMMITTEE OF THE PRIVY COUNCIL
Supreme Court Building, Parliament Square, London SW1P 3BD
T 020-7960 1500 W www.jcpc.uk

The Judicial Committee of the Privy Council is the court of final appeal from courts of the UK dependencies, courts of independent Commonwealth countries which have retained the right of appeal and courts of the Channel Islands and the Isle of Man. It also hears very occasional appeals from a number of ancient and ecclesiastical courts.

The committee is composed of privy counsellors who hold, or have held, high judicial office. Only three or five judges hear each case, and these are usually justices of the supreme court.
Chief Executive, Jenny Rowe, CB

PARLIAMENT

Parliament is the supreme law-making authority and can legislate for the UK as a whole or for any parts of it separately (the Channel Islands and the Isle of Man are crown dependencies and not part of the UK). The main functions of parliament are to pass laws, to enable the government to raise taxes and to scrutinise government policy and administration, particularly proposals for expenditure. International treaties and agreements are customarily presented to parliament before ratification.

Parliament can trace its roots to two characteristics of Anglo-Saxon rule: the *witan* (a meeting of the king, nobles and advisors) and the *moot* (county meetings where local matters were discussed). However, it was the parliament that Simon de Montfort called in 1265 that is accepted as the forerunner to modern parliament, as it included non-noble representatives from counties, cities and towns alongside the nobility. The nucleus of early parliaments at the beginning of the 14th century were the officers of the king's household and the king's judges, joined by such ecclesiastical and lay magnates as the king might summon to form a prototype 'House of Lords', and occasionally by the knights of the shires, burgesses and proctors of the lower clergy. By the end of Edward III's reign a 'House of Commons' was beginning to appear; the first known Speaker was elected in 1377.

Parliamentary procedure is based on custom and precedent, partly formulated in the standing orders of both houses of parliament. Each house has the right to control its own internal proceedings and to commit for contempt. The system of debate in the two houses is similar; when a motion has been moved, the Speaker proposes the question as the subject of a debate. Members speak from wherever they have been sitting. Questions are decided by a vote on a simple majority. Draft legislation is introduced, in either house, as a bill. Bills can be introduced by a government minister or a private member, but in practice the majority of bills which become law are introduced by the government. To become law, a bill must be passed by each house (for parliamentary stages, *see* Parliamentary Information) and then sent to the sovereign for the royal assent, after which it becomes an act of parliament.

Proceedings of both houses are public, except on extremely rare occasions. The minutes (called *Votes and Proceedings in the Commons,* and *Minutes of Proceedings in the Lords)* and the speeches *(The Official Report of Parliamentary Debates,* Hansard) are published daily. Proceedings are also recorded for transmission on radio and television and stored in the Parliamentary Recording Unit before transfer to the National Sound Archive. Television cameras have been allowed into the House of Lords since 1985 and into the House of Commons since 1989; committee meetings may also be televised.

The Fixed Term Parliament Act 2011 fixed the duration of a parliament at five years in normal circumstances, the term being reckoned from the date given on the writs for the new parliament. The term of a parliament has been prolonged by legislation in such rare circumstances as the two World Wars (31 January 1911 to 25 November 1918; 26 November 1935 to 15 June 1945). The life of a parliament is divided into sessions, usually of one year in length, beginning and ending most often in May.

DEVOLUTION

The Scottish parliament and the National Assembly for Wales have legislative power over all devolved matters, ie matters not reserved to Westminster or otherwise outside its powers. The Northern Ireland Assembly has legislative authority in the fields previously administered by the Northern Ireland departments. The assembly was suspended in October 2002 and dissolved in April 2003, before being reinstated on 8 May 2007. For further information, *see* Regional Government.

THE HOUSE OF LORDS

London SW1A 0PW
T 020-7219 3000 **Information Office** 020-7219 3107
E hlinfo@parliament.uk **W** www.parliament.uk

The House of Lords is the second chamber, or 'Upper House', of the UK's bicameral parliament. Until the beginning of the 20th century, the House of Lords had considerable power, being able to veto any bill submitted to it by the House of Commons. Since 1911, however, it has no powers over money bills and its power of veto over public legislation has been reduced over time to the power to delay bills for up to one session of parliament (usually one year). Today the main functions of the House of Lords are to contribute to the legislative process, to act as a check on the government, and to provide a forum of expertise. Its judicial role as final court of appeal ended in 2009 with the establishment of a new UK Supreme Court (*see* Law Courts and Offices section).

The House of Lords has a number of select committees. Some relate to the internal affairs of the house – such as its management and administration – while others carry out important investigative work on matters of public interest. The main areas of work are: Europe, science, the economy, the constitution, communications and the media. House of Lords' investigative committees look at broad issues and do not mirror government departments as the select committees in the House of Commons do.

The Constitutional Reform Act 2005 significantly altered the judicial function of the House of Lords and the role of the Lord Chancellor as a judge and its presiding officer. The Lord Chancellor is no longer the presiding officer of the House of Lords nor head of the judiciary in England and Wales, but remains a cabinet minister (the Lord Chancellor and Secretary of State for Justice), and is currently a member of the House of Commons. The function of the presiding officer of the House of Lords was devolved to the newly created post of the Speaker of the House of Lords, commonly known as Lord Speaker. The Rt. Hon. Baroness Hayman was elected as the first Lord Speaker by the house on 4 July 2006.

Membership of the House of Lords comprises mainly of life peers created under the Life Peerages Act 1958, along with 92 hereditary peers and a small number of Lords of Appeal in Ordinary, ie law lords, who were created under the Appellate Jurisdiction Act 1876*. The Archbishops of Canterbury and York, the Bishops of London, Durham and Winchester, and the 21 senior diocesan bishops of the Church of England are also members.

The House of Lords Act 1999 provides for 92 hereditary peers to remain in the House of Lords until further reform of the House has been carried out. Of these, 75 (42 Conservative, 28 crossbench, three Liberal Democrat and two Labour) are elected by hereditary peers in their political party or crossbench grouping. Elections for each of the party groups and the crossbenches were held in October and November 1999. In addition, 15 office holders were elected by the whole house. Two hereditary peers with royal duties, the Earl Marshal and the Lord Great Chamberlain, have also remained members. Since November 2002, by-elections have been held to fill vacancies left by deaths of hereditary peers; the by-elections take place under the Alternative Vote System and must occur within three months of the death of the hereditary peer (*see also* The Peerage).

Peers are disqualified from sitting in the house if they are:

• aliens, ie any peer who is not a British citizen, a Commonwealth citizen (under the British Nationality Act 1981) or a citizen of the Republic of Ireland

- under the age of 21
- undischarged bankrupts or, in Scotland, those whose estate is sequestered
- holders of a disqualifying judicial office
- members of the European Parliament
- convicted of treason

Bishops cease to be members of the house when they retire.

Members who do not wish to attend sittings of the House of Lords may apply for leave of absence for the duration of a parliament. Since the passage of the House of Lords Reform Act 2014, members of the House may also retire permanently by giving notice in writing to the Clerk of the Parliaments.

Members of the House of Lords, who are not paid a salary, may claim a flat-rate daily attendance allowance of £300 (for peers that attend for a full sitting day) or £150 (for those peers that attend for less than a full sitting day), or may choose to make no claim for each sitting day they attend the house.

* Although the office of Lord of Appeal in Ordinary no longer exists, law lords created under the Appellate Jurisdiction Act 1876 remain members of the House. Those in office at the time of the establishment of the Supreme Court became justices of the UK Supreme Court and are not permitted to sit or vote in the House of Lords until they retire.

COMPOSITION *as at 1 September2014*

Archbishops and bishops	26
Life peers under the Appellate Jurisdiction Act 1876 and the Life Peerages Act 1958	665
Peers under the House of Lords Act 1999	87
Total	778

STATE OF THE PARTIES *as at 1 September 2014*†

Conservative	221
Labour	216
Liberal Democrat	101
Crossbench	180
Archbishops and bishops	26
Other	34
Total	778

† Excluding 43 peers on leave of absence, one who is suspended and eight disqualified as senior members of the judiciary.

HOUSE OF LORDS PAY BANDS FOR SENIOR STAFF
Senior staff are placed in the following pay bands according to their level of responsibility and taking account of other factors such as experience and marketability.

Judicial group 4	£174,881
Senior band 3	£103,000–£145,629
Senior band 2	£84,000–£135,970
Senior band 1A	£69,000–£113,202
Senior band 1	£60,000–£100,374
Band A1	£57,290–£73,516
Band A2	£47,636–£60,824

OFFICERS AND OFFICIALS
The house is presided over by the Lord Speaker, whose powers differ from those of the Speaker of the House of Commons. The Lord Speaker has no power to rule on matters of order because the House of Lords is self-regulating. The maintenance of the rules of debate is the responsibility of all the members who are present.

A panel of deputy speakers is appointed by Royal Commission. The first deputy speaker is the Chair of Committees, a salaried officer of the house appointed at the beginning of each session. He or she chairs a number of 'domestic' committees relating to the internal affairs of the house. The first deputy speaker is assisted by a panel of deputy chairs, headed by the salaried Principal Deputy Chair of Committees, who is also chair of the European Union Committee of the house.

The Clerk of the Parliaments is the accounting officer and the chief permanent official responsible for the administration of the house. The Gentleman Usher of the Black Rod is responsible for security and other services and also has royal duties as secretary to the Lord Great Chamberlain.

Lord Speaker (£101,038), Rt. Hon. Baroness D'Souza, CMG
Chair of Committees (£84,524), Lord Sewel, CBE
Principal Deputy Chair of Committees (£79,076), Lord Boswell of Aynho
Clerk of the Parliaments (Judicial Group 4), D. R. Beamish
Clerk Assistant (Senior Band 3), E. C. Ollard
Reading Clerk and Clerk of the Overseas Office (Senior Band 3), S. P. Burton
Clerk of Committees (Senior Band 2), Dr F. P. Tudor
Director of Facilities (Senior Band 2), C. V. Woodall
Finance Director (Senior Band 1A), A. Makower
Director of Human Resources (Senior Band 1A), T. V. Mohan
Registrar of Members' Interests (Senior Band 1A), B. P. Keith
Director of Information Services and Librarian (Senior Band 2), Dr E. Hallam Smith
Clerk of Legislation (Senior Band 1A), J. A. Vaughan
Principal Clerk of Select Committees (Senior Band 1A), Dr C. S. Johnson
Editor of the Official Report (Senior Band 1), J. S. Vice
Director of Parliamentary Archives (Senior Band 1), Dr C. Shenton
Deputy Finance Director and Head of Finance (Senior Band 1), J. P. Smith
Director of Public Information (Band A1), B. Hiscock
Counsel to the Chair of Committees (Senior Band 2), P. Hardy; P. Milledge
Legal Adviser to the Human Rights Committee (Senior Band 2), M. Hunt
Change Manager (Senior Band 1), Mrs M. E. Ollard
Clerk of the European Union Committee (Senior Band 1A), A. J. Mackersie
Clerks of Select Committees (Senior Band 1), A. J. Mackersie; D. Sagar
Gentleman Usher of the Black Rod and Serjeant-at-Arms (Senior Band 2), Lt.-Gen. David Leakey, CMG, CBE
Yeoman Usher of the Black Rod and Deputy Serjeant-at-Arms (Band A1), N. Baverstock

LORD GREAT CHAMBERLAIN'S OFFICE
Lord Great Chamberlain, Marquess of Cholmondeley, KCVO
Secretary to the Lord Great Chamberlain, Lt.-Gen. David Leakey, CMG, CBE

SELECT COMMITTEES
The main House of Lords select committees, as at July 2014, are as follows:
Administration and Works – *Chair,* Lord Sewel, CBE; *Clerk,* Chris Atkinson
Affordable Childcare – *Chair,* Lord Sutherland of Houndwood, KT, *Clerk,* Judith Brooke
Arctic – *Chair,* Lord Teverson, *Clerk,* Susannah Street
Communications – *Chair,* Lord Best, OBE; *Clerk,* Anna Murphy
Constitution – *Chair,* Rt. Hon. Lord Lang of Monkton, *Clerk,* Nicolas Besly

Delegated Powers and Regulatory Reform – Chair, Baroness
  Thomas of Winchester, MBE; *Clerk,* Christine Salmon
  Percival
Digital Skills – Chair, Baroness Morgan of Huyton, *Clerk,*
  Aaron Speer
Economic Affairs – Chair, Lord Hollick; *Clerk,*
  Bill Sinton
European Union – Chair, Lord Boswell of Aynho; *Clerk,*
  Chris Johnson
European Union – Sub-committees:
  A Economic and Financial Affairs) – Chair, Lord Harrison;
    Clerk, Stuart Stoner
  B (Internal Market, Infrastructure and Employment) – Chair,
    Baroness O'Cathain, OBE; *Clerk,* Nicole Mason
  C (External Affairs) – Chair, Lord Tugendhat; *Clerk,*
    Sarah Jones
  D (Agriculture, Fisheries, Environment and Energy) –
    Chair, Baroness Scott of Needham Market;
    Clerk, Patrick Milner
  E (Justice, Institutions and Consumer Protection) – Chair,
    Rt. Hon. Baroness Corston; *Clerk,* Luke Hussey
  F (Home Affairs, Health and Education) – Chair,
    Rt. Hon. Baroness Prashar, CBE; *Clerk,* Michael Collon
Extradition Law – Chair, Lord Inglewood, *Clerk,*
  James Whittle
House Committee – Chair, Rt. Hon. Baroness D'Souza, CMG;
  Clerk, vacant
Liaison Committee – Chair, Lord Sewel, CBE; *Clerk,* Philippa
  Tudor
Privileges and Conduct – Chair, Lord Sewel; *Clerk,*
  Chloe Mawson
Refreshment Committee – Chair, Lord Sewel, CBE; *Clerk,*
  Sarah Jones
Science and Technology – Chair, Lord Earl of Selborne, GBE;
  Clerk, Chris Clarke
Secondary Legislation Scrutiny Committee – Chair,
  Rt. Hon. Lord Goodlad, KCMG; *Clerk,*
  Christine Salmon Percival
Selection Committee – Chair, Lord Sewel, CBE; *Clerk,* vacant
Joint Committees
Human Rights – Chair, Dr Hywel Francis, MP; *Clerks,*
  Mike Hennessy *(Commons)*; Megan Conway *(Lords)*
National Security Strategy – Chair, Rt. Hon. Dame Margaret
  Beckett, DBE, MP; *Clerks,* Philippa Helme *(Commons)*;
  Duncan Sagar *(Lords)*
Statutory Instruments – Chair, George Mudie, MP; *Clerks,*
  Sarah Petit *(Commons);* Jane White *(Lords)*

THE HOUSE OF COMMONS

London SW1A 0AA
T 020-7219 3000 W www.parliament.uk

HOUSE OF COMMONS INFORMATION OFFICE

14 Tothill Street, London SW1H 9NB
T 020-7219 4272 E hcinfo@parliament.uk

The members of the House of Commons are elected by
universal adult suffrage. For electoral purposes, the UK is
divided into constituencies, each of which returns one
member to the House of Commons, the member being the
candidate who obtains the largest number of votes cast in
the constituency. To ensure equitable representation, the four
Boundary Commissions keep constituency boundaries under
review and recommend any redistribution of seats which
may seem necessary because of population movements etc. At
the 2010 general election the number of seats increased from
646 to 650. Of the present 650 seats, there are 533 for
England, 40 for Wales, 59 for Scotland and 18 for Northern
Ireland.

NUMBER OF SEATS IN THE HOUSE OF COMMONS BY COUNTRY

	2005	2010
England	529	533
Wales	40	40
Scotland	59	59
Northern Ireland	18	18
Total	646	650

ELECTIONS

Elections are by secret ballot, each elector casting one vote;
voting is not compulsory. (For entitlement to vote in
parliamentary elections, *see* Legal Notes.) When a seat
becomes vacant between general elections, a by-election is
held.

British subjects and citizens of the Irish Republic can
stand for election as MPs provided they are 18 or over and
not subject to disqualification. Those disqualified from sitting
in the house include:
• undischarged bankrupts
• people sentenced to more than one year's imprisonment
• members of the House of Lords (but hereditary peers not
  sitting in the Lords are eligible)
• holders of certain offices listed in the House of Commons
  Disqualification Act 1975, eg members of the judiciary,
  civil service, regular armed forces, police forces, some local
  government officers and some members of public
  corporations and government commissions

A candidate does not require any party backing but his or her
nomination for election must be supported by the signatures
of ten people registered in the constituency. A candidate must
also deposit £500 with the returning officer, which is forfeit
if the candidate does not receive more than 5 per cent of the
votes cast. All election expenses at a general election, except
the candidate's personal expenses, are subject to a statutory
limit of £7,150, plus five pence for each elector in a borough
constituency or seven pence for each elector in a county
constituency.

See pages 135–172 for an alphabetical list of MPs and
results of the general election in 2010.

STATE OF THE PARTIES *as at 1 September 2014**

Party	Seats
Conservative	304
Labour	256
Liberal Democrats	56
Democratic Unionist Party	8
Scottish National Party	6
Sinn Fein (have not taken their seats)	5
Plaid Cymru	3
Social Democratic & Labour Party	3
Alliance	1
Green	1
Respect	1
Independent	3
The Speaker	1
Vacant	2
Total	650

* Working majority of 79; 304 Conservative and 56 Liberal
Democrat MPs less 281 of all other parties (excluding the speaker,
deputy speakers and Sinn Fein)

BUSINESS

The week's business of the house is outlined each Thursday
by the leader of the house, after consultation between the
chief government whip and the chief opposition whip.
A quarter to a third of the time will be taken up by the

government's legislative programme and the rest by other business. As a rule, bills likely to raise political controversy are introduced in the Commons before going on to the Lords, and the Commons claims exclusive control in respect of national taxation and expenditure. Bills such as the finance bill, which imposes taxation, and the consolidated fund bills, which authorise expenditure, must begin in the Commons. A bill of which the financial provisions are subsidiary may begin in the Lords, and the Commons may waive its rights in regard to Lords' amendments affecting finance.

The Commons has a public register of MPs' financial and certain other interests; this is published annually as a House of Commons paper. Members must also disclose any relevant financial interest or benefit in a matter before the house when taking part in a debate, in certain other proceedings of the house, or in consultations with other MPs, with ministers or with civil servants.

MEMBERS' PAY AND ALLOWANCES
Since 1911 members of the House of Commons have received salary payments; facilities for free travel were introduced in 1924. Salary rates for the last 30 years are as follows:

1985 Jan	£16,904	2000 Apr	£48,371
1986 Jan	17,702	2001 Apr	49,822
1987 Jan	18,500	2002 Apr	55,118
1988 Jan	22,548	2003 Apr	56,358
1989 Jan	24,107	2004 Apr	57,485
1990 Jan	26,701	2005 Apr	59,095
1991 Jan	28,970	2006 Apr	59,686
1992 Jan	30,854	2007 Apr	61,181
1993 Jan	30,854	2008 Apr	63,291
1994 Jan	31,687	2009 Apr	64,766
1995 Jan	33,189	2010 Apr	65,738
1996 Jan	34,085	2011 Apr	65,738
1996 Jul	43,000	2012 Apr	65,738
1997 Apr	43,860	2013 Apr	66,396
1998 Apr	45,066	2014 Apr	67,060
1999 Apr	47,008	2015	74,000*

* Provisional amount recommended by IPSA (*see* below) subject to statutory review and approval following the 2015 General Election

The Independent Parliamentary Standards Authority (IPSA) was established under the Parliamentary Standards Act 2009 and is responsible for the independent regulation and administration of the MPs' Scheme of Business Costs and Expenses, as well as for paying the salaries of MPs and their staff members. Since May 2011, the IPSA has also been responsible for determining MPs' pay and setting the level of any increase to their salary.

For 2014–15, the office costs expenditure budget is £25,900 for London area MPs and £23,250 for non-London area MPs. The maximum annual staff budget for London area MPs is £145,500 and £138,600 for non-London area MPs.

Since 1972 MPs have been able to claim reimbursement for the additional cost of staying overnight away from their main residence while on parliamentary business. This is not payable to London area MPs and those MPs who reside in 'grace and favour' accommodation. Accommodation expenses for MPs claiming rental payments is capped at £20,600 per year; for MPs who own their own homes, mortgage interest and associated expenses up to £8,850 are payable.

For ministerial salaries *see* Government Departments.

MEMBERS' PENSIONS
Pension arrangements for MPs were first introduced in 1964. Under the Parliamentary Contributory Pension Fund (PCPF), MPs receive a pension on retirement based upon their salary in their final year, and upon their number of years' service as an MP. Members may pay a contribution rate of 7.75, 9.75 or 13.75 per cent and build up a pension of 1.6, 2 or 2.5 per cent of salary for each year of service. Pensions are normally payable upon retirement at age 65; the pension payable is subject to a maximum of 66.6 per cent of salary, inclusive of pensions from employment or self-employment prior to becoming an MP. There are provisions in place for: early retirement for those MPs who cease to serve between the ages of 55 and 65; MPs of any age who retire due to ill health; and pensions for widows/widowers of MPs. All pensions are index-linked. There is also an Exchequer contribution; currently 20.2 per cent of an MP's salary.

The House of Commons Members' Fund provides for annual or lump sum grants to ex-MPs, their widows or widowers, and children of those who either ceased to serve as an MP prior to the PCPF being established or who are experiencing hardship. Members contribute £24 a year and the Exchequer £215,000 a year to the fund.

HOUSE OF COMMONS PAY BANDS FOR SENIOR STAFF
Senior Staff are placed in the following Senior Civil Service pay bands. These pay bands apply to the most senior staff in departments and agencies.

Pay Band 1	£58,200–£93,380
Pay Band 1A	£67,600–£105,560
Pay Band 2	£82,900–£124,845
Pay Band 3	£101,500–£139,849

OFFICERS AND OFFICIALS
The House of Commons is presided over by the Speaker, who has considerable powers to maintain order. A deputy speaker, called the Chairman of Ways and Means, and two deputy chairs may preside over sittings of the House of Commons; they are elected by the house, and, like the Speaker, neither speak nor vote other than in their official capacity.

The staff of the house are employed by a commission chaired by the Speaker. The heads of the six House of Commons departments are permanent officers of the house, not MPs. The Clerk of the House is the principal adviser to the Speaker on the privileges and procedures of the house, the conduct of the business of the house, and committees. The Serjeant-at-Arms is responsible for security and ceremonial functions of the house.

Speaker (£142,162)*, Rt. Hon. John Bercow, MP
Chairman of Ways and Means (£107,108),
    Rt. Hon. Lindsay Hoyle, MP
First Deputy Chairman of Ways and Means (£102,098),
    Nigel Evans, MP
Second Deputy Chairman of Ways and Means (£102,098),
    Rt. Hon. Dawn Primarolo, MP
Parliamentary Commissioner for Standards, Kathryn Hudson
* Salaries in parentheses are the maximum available. The Speaker and Deputies have opted not to take the statutory increases awarded to them each year as office holders.

OFFICES OF THE SPEAKER AND CHAIRMAN OF WAYS AND MEANS
Speaker's Secretary, Peter Barratt
Chaplain to the Speaker, Revd Rose Hudson-Wilkin

Secretary to the Chairman of Ways and Means, Sara Howe
Clerk of the House of Commons and Chief Executive,
  Sir Robert Rogers, KCB

OFFICE OF THE CHIEF EXECUTIVE
Head of Office, Matthew Hamlyn
Director of Internal Audit, Paul Dillon-Robinson

DEPARTMENT OF CHAMBER AND COMMITTEE
SERVICES
Director-General and Clerk Assistant, David Natzler
Principal Clerk, Overseas Office, Crispin Poyser
Director of Departmental Services, Elizabeth Hunt

VOTE OFFICE
Deliverer of the Vote, Catherine Fogarty
Head of Procedural Publishing, Tom McVeagh (Production)
Deputy Deliverer of the Vote, Owen Sweeney (Parliamentary)

COMMITTEE DIRECTORATE
Clerk of Committees, Andrew Kennon
Principal Clerk and Deputy Head of Committee Office,
  Philippa Helme
Clerk of Domestic Committees/Secretary to the Commission,
  Robert Twigger
Select Committees, Mark Hutton; Colin Lee; Simon Patrick
Head of Scrutiny Unit, Jessica Mulley

LEGISLATION DIRECTORATE
Clerk of Legislation, Jacqy Sharpe
Principal Clerks
  Table Office, Paul Evans
  Journals, Liam Laurence Smyth
  Bills, Matthew Hamlyn
  National Parliament Office (Brussels), Alison Groves
  Ways and Means Office, Sara Howe

OFFICIAL REPORT DIRECTORATE
Editor, Lorraine Sutherland
Deputy Editor, Alex Newton
Director of Parliamentary Audio and Video, John Angeli

SERJEANT-AT-ARMS DIRECTORATE
Serjeant-at-Arms, Lawrence Ward
Deputy Serjeant-at-Arms, Richard Latham
Assistant Serjeant-at-Arms, Lesley Scott

OFFICE OF SPEAKER'S COUNSEL
Speaker's Counsel and Head of Legal Services Office,
  Michael Carpenter, CB
Counsel for European Legislation, Arnold Ridout
Assistant Counsel for European Legislation, Joanne Dee
Counsel for Domestic Legislation, Peter Davis
Deputy Counsel for Domestic Legislation, Peter Brooksbank;
  Peter Davies; Daniel Greenberg
Principal Assistant Counsel, Helen Emes
Legal Assistants, Klara Banaszak

DEPARTMENT OF FACILITIES
Director-General, John Borley
Director of Business Management, Della Herd
Parliamentary Director of Estates, Mel Barlex
Director of Accommodation Services, James Robertson
Director of Facilities Finance, Philip Collins
Executive Officer, Katherine Gray
Director of Catering Services, Richard Tapner-Evans
Operations Manager, Robert Gibbs
Executive Chef, Mark Hill

DEPARTMENT OF FINANCE
Director of Finance, Myfanwy Barrett
Director of Financial Management, Chris Ridley
Director of Commercial Services, Veronica Daly
Head of Pensions and Payroll, Lucy Tindal

DEPARTMENT OF HUMAN RESOURCES AND
CHANGE
Director General of HR and Change, Andrew J. Walker
Director of Business Management and Delivery, Janet Rissen
Director of Change, Selven Naicker
Head of Occupational Safety, Health and Wellbeing Service,
  Dr Marianne McDougall

DEPARTMENT OF INFORMATION SERVICES
Director-General and Librarian, John Pullinger, CB
Directors, John Benger (Service Delivery); Prof. David Cope
  (Parliamentary Office of Science and Technology); Adam
  Mellows-Facer (Research); Aileen Walker (Public
  Engagement); Steve Wise (Information Management);
  Edward Wood (Public Information)
Head of Media and Communications Service, Lee Bridges
Head of Public Information and Outreach, Claire Cowan
Visitor Services, Deborah Newman

PARLIAMENTARY INFORMATION AND
COMMUNICATION TECHNOLOGY (ICT)
Director of Parliamentary ICT, Joan Miller
Director of Technology Directorate, Steve O'Connor
Director of Operations and Members Services,
  Matthew Taylor
Director of Resources, Fergus Reid
Director of Programmes and Projects, Rebecca Elton
Director of Network Programme, Innis Montgomery

SELECT COMMITTEES
The more significant committees, as at July 2014 are:

DEPARTMENTAL COMMITTEES
Business, Innovation and Skills – Chair, Adrian Bailey, MP;
  Clerk, James Davies
Communities and Local Government – Chair, Clive Betts, MP;
  Clerk, Glen McKee
Culture, Media and Sport – Chair, John Whittingdale, OBE,
  MP; Clerk, Elizabeth Flood
Defence – Chair, Rory Stewart, MP; Clerk, James Rhys
Education – Chair, Graham Stuart, MP; Clerk,
  Dr Lynn Gardner
Energy and Climate Change – Chair, Tim Yeo, MP; Clerk,
  Sarah Hartwell-Naguib
Environment, Food and Rural Affairs – Chair,
  Anne McIntosh, MP; Clerk, David Weir
Foreign Affairs – Chair, Rt. Hon. Sir Richard Ottaway, MP;
  Clerk, Kenneth Fox
Health – Chair, Dr Sarah Wollaston, MP; Clerk,
  David Lloyd
Home Affairs – Chair, Rt. Hon. Keith Vaz, MP; Clerk,
  Tom Healey
International Development – Chair, Rt. Hon.
  Sir Malcolm Bruce, MP; Clerk, Dr David Harrison
Justice – Chair, Rt. Hon. Sir Alan Beith, MP; Clerk,
  Nick Walker
Northern Ireland Affairs – Chair, Laurence Robertson, MP;
  Clerk, Mike Clark
Scottish Affairs – Chair, Ian Davidson, MP; Clerk,
  Eliot Wilson
Transport – Chair, Louise Ellman, MP; Clerk,
  Gordon Clarke
Treasury – Chair, Andrew Tyrie, MP; Clerk, Chris Stanton

Welsh Affairs – *Chair,* David T. C. Davies, MP; *Clerk,*
    Markek Kubala
Work and Pensions – *Chair,* Dame Anne Begg, DBE, MP;
    Clerk, Carol Oxborough

NON-DEPARTMENTAL COMMITTEES
Environmental Audit – *Chair,* Joan Walley, MP; *Clerk,*
    Simon Fiander
Political and Constitutional Reform – *Chair,* Graham Allen,
    MP; *Clerk,* Joanna Dodd
Procedure – *Chair,* Charles Walker, MP; *Clerk,*
    Huw Yardley
Public Accounts – *Chair,* Rt. Hon. Margaret Hodge, MBE,
    MP; *Clerk,* Adrian Jenner
Public Administration – *Chair,* Bernard Jenkin, MP; *Clerks,*
    Catherine Tyack; Sian Woodward
Science and Technology – *Chair,* Andrew Miller, MP; *Clerk,*
    Dr Stephen McGinness

NATIONAL AUDIT OFFICE
157–197 Buckingham Palace Road, London SW1W 9SP
T 020-7798 7000
E enquiries@nao.gsi.gov.uk W www.nao.org.uk

The National Audit Office came into existence under the
National Audit Act 1983 to replace and continue the
work of the former Exchequer and Audit Department. The
act reinforced the office's total financial and operational
independence from the government and brought its head, the
Comptroller and Auditor-General, into a closer relationship
with parliament as an officer of the House of Commons.

The National Audit Office (NAO) scrutinises public
spending on behalf of parliament, helping it to hold
government departments to account and helping public
service managers improve performance and service delivery.
The NAO audits the financial statements of all government
departments and a wide range of other public bodies.
It regularly publishes 'value for money' reports on the
efficiency and effectiveness of how public resources are used.
Comptroller and Auditor-General, Amyas Morse
Assistant Auditors-General, Gabrielle Cohen; Sue Higgins;
    Sally Howes; Martin Sinclair; John Thorpe
Chief Operating Officer, Michael Whitehouse

PARLIAMENTARY INFORMATION

The following is a short glossary of aspects of the work of
parliament. Unless otherwise stated, references are to House
of Commons procedures.

BILL – Proposed legislation is termed a bill. The stages
of a public bill (for private bills, *see* below) in the House of
Commons are as follows:
First reading: This stage introduces the legislation to the
house and, for government bills, merely constitutes an order
to have the bill printed.
Second reading: The debate on the principles of the bill.
Committee stage: The detailed examination of a bill, clause
by clause. In most cases this takes place in a public bill
committee, or the whole house may act as a committee.
Public bill committees may take evidence before embarking
on detailed scrutiny of the bill. Very rarely, a bill may be
examined by a select committee.
Report stage: Detailed review of a bill as amended in
committee, on the floor of the house, and an opportunity to
make further changes.
Third reading: Final debate on the full bill in the
Commons.
Public bills go through the same stages in the House of
Lords, but with important differences: the committee stage

is taken in committee of the whole house or in a grand
committee, in which any peer may participate. There are
no time limits, all amendments are debated, and further
amendments can be made at third reading.

A bill may start in either house, and has to pass through
both houses to become law. Both houses have to agree the
final text of a bill, so that amendments made by the second
house are then considered in the originating house, and
if not agreed, sent back or themselves amended, until
agreement is reached.

CHILTERN HUNDREDS – A nominal office of profit
under the crown, the acceptance of which requires an MP
to vacate his/her seat. The Manor of Northstead is similar.
These are the only means by which an MP may resign.

CONSOLIDATED FUND BILL – A bill to authorise the
issue of money to maintain government services. The bill is
dealt with without debate.

EARLY DAY MOTION – A motion put on the notice
paper by an MP without, in general, the real prospect of its
being debated. Such motions are expressions of back-bench
opinion.

FATHER OF THE HOUSE – The MP whose continuous
service in the House of Commons is the longest. The present
Father of the House is Sir Peter Tapsell, MP.

GRAND COMMITTEES – There are three grand
committees in the House of Commons, one each for
Northern Ireland, Scotland and Wales; they consider matters
relating specifically to that country. In the House of Lords,
bills may be sent to a grand committee instead of a
committee of the whole house (*see also* Bill).

HOURS OF MEETING – The House of Commons
normally meets on Mondays at 2.30pm, Tuesdays and
Wednesdays at 11.30am, Thursdays at 9.30am and some
Fridays at 9.30am. (*See also* Westminster Hall Sittings, below.)
The House of Lords normally meets at 2.30pm Mondays and
Tuesdays, 3pm on Wednesdays and at 11am on Thursdays.
The House of Lords occasionally sits on Fridays at 10am.

LEADER OF THE OPPOSITION – In 1937 the office
of leader of the opposition was recognised and a salary
was assigned to the post. In 2014–15 this is £130,158
(including a parliamentary salary of £67,060). The present
leader of the opposition is the Rt. Hon. Ed Miliband, MP.

THE LORD CHANCELLOR – The office of Lord High
Chancellor of Great Britain was significantly altered by the
Constitutional Reform Act 2005. Previously, the Lord
Chancellor was (*ex officio*) the Speaker of the House of
Lords, and took part in debates and voted in divisions in the
House of Lords. The Department for Constitutional Affairs
was created in 2003, and became the Ministry of Justice in
2007, incorporating most of the responsibilities of the Lord
Chancellor's department. The role of Speaker has been
transferred to the post of Lord Speaker. The Constitutional
Reform Act 2005 also brought to an end the Lord
Chancellor's role as head of the judiciary. A Judicial
Appointments Commission was created in April 2006, and
a supreme court (separate from the House of Lords) was
established in 2009.

THE LORD GREAT CHAMBERLAIN – The Lord Great
Chamberlain is a Great Officer of State, the office being
hereditary since the grant of Henry I to the family of De
Vere, Earls of Oxford. It is now a joint hereditary office
rotating on the death of the sovereign between the
Cholmondeley, Carington and Ancaster families.

The Lord Great Chamberlain, currently the Marquess of
Cholmondeley, is responsible for the royal apartments in the
Palace of Westminster, the Royal Gallery, the administration
of the Chapel of St Mary Undercroft and, in conjunction
with the Lord Speaker and the Speaker of the House of
Commons, Westminster Hall. The Lord Great Chamberlain

has the right to perform specific services at a coronation and has particular responsibility for the internal administrative arrangements within the House of Lords for state openings of parliament.

THE LORD SPEAKER – The first Lord Speaker of the House of Lords, the Rt. Hon. Baroness Hayman, took up office on 4 July 2006. The Lord Speaker is independent of the government and elected by members of the House of Lords rather than appointed by the prime minister. Although the Lord Speaker's primary role is to preside over proceedings in the House of Lords, she does not have the same powers as the Speaker of the House of Commons. For example, the Lord Speaker is not responsible for maintaining order during debates, as this is the responsibility of the house as a whole. The Lord Speaker sits in the Lords on one of the woolsacks, which are couches covered in red cloth and stuffed with wool.

OPPOSITION DAY – A day on which the topic for debate is chosen by the opposition. There are 20 such days in a normal session. On 17 days, subjects are chosen by the leader of the opposition; on the remaining three days by the leader of the next largest opposition party.

PARLIAMENT ACTS 1911 AND 1949 – Under these acts, bills may become law without the consent of the Lords, though the House of Lords has the power to delay a public bill for a parliamentary session.

PRIME MINISTER'S QUESTIONS – The prime minister answers questions from 12 to 12.30pm on Wednesdays.

PRIVATE BILL – A bill promoted by a body or an individual to give powers additional to, or in conflict with, the general law, and to which a special procedure applies to enable people affected to object.

PRIVATE MEMBER'S BILL – A public bill promoted by an MP or peer who is not a member of the government.

PRIVATE NOTICE QUESTION – A question adjudged of urgent importance on submission to the Speaker (in the Lords, the Lord Speaker), answered at the end of oral questions.

PRIVILEGE – The House of Commons has rights and immunities to protect it from obstruction in carrying out its duties. These are known as parliamentary privilege and enable Members of Parliament to debate freely. The most important privilege is that of freedom of speech. MPs cannot be prosecuted for sedition or sued for libel or slander over anything said during proceedings in the house. This enables them to raise in the house questions affecting the public good which might be difficult to raise outside owing to the possibility of legal action against them. The House of Lords has similar privileges.

QUESTION TIME – Oral questions are answered by ministers in the Commons from 2.30 to 3.30pm on Mondays, 11.30am to 12.30pm on Tuesdays and Wednesdays, and 9.30 to 10.30am on Thursdays. Questions are also taken for half an hour at the start of the Lords sittings.

ROYAL ASSENT – The royal assent is signified by letters patent to such bills and measures as have passed both Houses of Parliament (or bills which have been passed under the Parliament Acts 1911 and 1949). The sovereign has not given royal assent in person since 1854. On occasion, for instance in the prorogation of parliament, royal assent may be pronounced to the two houses by Lords Commissioners. More usually royal assent is notified to each house sitting separately in accordance with the Royal Assent Act 1967. The old French formulae for royal assent are then endorsed on the acts by the Clerk of the Parliaments.

The power to withhold assent resides with the sovereign but has not been exercised in the UK since 1707.

SELECT COMMITTEES – Consisting usually of 10 to 15 members of all parties, select committees are a means used by both houses in order to investigate certain matters.

Most select committees in the House of Commons are tied to departments; each committee investigates subjects within a government department's remit. There are other select committees dealing with matters such as public accounts (ie the spending by the government of money voted by parliament) and European legislation, and also committees advising on procedures and domestic administration of the house. Major select committees usually take evidence in public; their evidence and reports are published on the parliament website and in hard copy by The Stationery Office (TSO). House of Commons select committees are reconstituted after a general election.

In the House of Lords, select committees do not mirror government departments but cover broader issues. There is a select committee on the European Union (EU), which has six sub-committees dealing with specific areas of EU policy, a select committee on science and technology, a select committee on economic affairs and also one on the constitution. There is also a select committee on delegated powers and regulatory reform and one on privileges and conduct. In addition, *ad hoc* select committees have been set up from time to time to investigate specific subjects. There are also joint committees of the two houses, eg the committees on statutory instruments and on human rights.

THE SPEAKER – The Speaker of the House of Commons is the spokesperson and chair of the Chamber. He or she is elected by the house at the beginning of each parliament or when the previous Speaker retires or dies. The Speaker neither speaks in debates nor votes in divisions except when the voting is equal.

VACANT SEATS – When a vacancy occurs in the House of Commons during a session of parliament, the writ for the by-election is moved by a whip of the party to which the member whose seat has been vacated belonged. If the house is in recess, the Speaker can issue a warrant for a writ, should two members certify to him that a seat is vacant.

WESTMINSTER HALL SITTINGS – Following a report by the Modernisation of the House of Commons Select Committee, the Commons decided in May 1999 to set up a second debating forum. It is known as 'Westminster Hall' and sittings are in the Grand Committee Room on some Mondays from 4.30pm to 7.30pm, Tuesdays and Wednesdays from 9.30am to 11.30am and from 2pm to 5pm, and Thursdays from 1.30pm to 4.30pm. Sittings are open to the public at the times indicated.

WHIPS – In order to secure the attendance of members of a particular party in parliament, particularly on the occasion of an important vote, whips (originally known as 'whippers-in') are appointed. The written appeal or circular letter issued by them is also known as a 'whip', its urgency being denoted by the number of times it is underlined. Failure to respond to a three-line whip is tantamount in the Commons to secession (at any rate temporarily) from the party. Whips are provided with office accommodation in both houses, and government and some opposition whips receive salaries from public funds.

PARLIAMENTARY ARCHIVES

Houses of Parliament, London SW1A 0PW
T 020-7219 3074 E archives@parliament.uk
W www.parliament.uk/archives

Since 1497, the records of parliament have been kept within the Palace of Westminster. They are in the custody of the Clerk of Parliaments. In 1946 the House of Lords Record Office, which became the Parliamentary Archives in 2006, was established to supervise their preservation and their availability to the public. Some 3 million documents are preserved, including acts of parliament from 1497, journals of the House of Lords from 1510, minutes and committee proceedings from 1610, and papers laid before parliament from 1531. Among the records are the Petition of Right, the death warrant of Charles I, the Declaration of Breda, and the Bill of Rights. Records are made available through a public search room.

Director of the Parliamentary Archives, Dr Caroline Shenton

GOVERNMENT OFFICE

The government is the body of ministers responsible for the administration of national affairs, determining policy and introducing into parliament any legislation necessary to give effect to government policy. The majority of ministers are members of the House of Commons but members of the House of Lords, or of neither house, may also hold ministerial responsibility. The prime minister is, by current convention, always a member of the House of Commons.

THE PRIME MINISTER

The office of prime minister, which had been in existence for nearly 200 years, was officially recognised in 1905 and its holder was granted a place in the table of precedence. The prime minister, by tradition also First Lord of the Treasury and Minister for the Civil Service, is appointed by the sovereign and is usually the leader of the party which enjoys, or can secure, a majority in the House of Commons. Other ministers are appointed by the sovereign on the recommendation of the prime minister, who also allocates functions among ministers and has the power to dismiss ministers from their posts.

The prime minister informs the sovereign on state and political matters, advises on the dissolution of parliament, and makes recommendations for important crown appointments, ie the award of honours, etc.

As the chair of cabinet meetings and leader of a political party, the prime minister is responsible for translating party policy into government activity. As leader of the government, the prime minister is responsible to parliament and to the electorate for the policies and their implementation.

The prime minister also represents the nation in international affairs, eg summit conferences.

THE CABINET

The cabinet developed during the 18th century as an inner committee of the Privy Council, which was the chief source of executive power until that time. The cabinet is composed of about 20 ministers chosen by the prime minister, usually the heads of government departments (generally known as secretaries of state unless they have a special title, eg Chancellor of the Exchequer), the leaders of the two houses of parliament, and the holders of various traditional offices.

The cabinet's functions are the final determination of policy, control of government and coordination of government departments. The exercise of its functions is dependent upon the incumbent party's (or parties') majority support in the House of Commons. Cabinet meetings are held in private, taking place once or twice a week during parliamentary sittings and less often during a recess. Proceedings are confidential, the members being bound by their oath as privy counsellors not to disclose information about the proceedings.

The convention of collective responsibility means that the cabinet acts unanimously even when cabinet ministers do not all agree on a subject. The policies of departmental ministers must be consistent with the policies of the government as a

whole, and once the government's policy has been decided, each minister is expected to support it or resign.

The convention of ministerial responsibility holds a minister, as the political head of his or her department, accountable to parliament for the department's work. Departmental ministers usually decide all matters within their responsibility, although on matters of political importance they normally consult their colleagues collectively. A decision by a departmental minister is binding on the government as a whole.

POLITICAL PARTIES

Before the reign of William and Mary, the principal officers of state were chosen by and were responsible to the sovereign alone and not to parliament or the nation at large. Such officers acted sometimes in concert with one another but more often independently, and the fall of one did not, of necessity, involve that of others, although all were liable to be dismissed at any moment.

In 1693 the Earl of Sunderland recommended to William III the advisability of selecting a ministry from the political party which enjoyed a majority in the House of Commons, and the first united ministry was drawn in 1696 from the Whigs, to which party the king owed his throne. This group became known as the 'junto' and was regarded with suspicion as a novelty in the political life of the nation, being a small section meeting in secret apart from the main body of ministers. It may be regarded as the forerunner of the cabinet and in the course of time it led to the establishment of the principle of joint responsibility of ministers, so that internal disagreement caused a change of personnel or resignation of the whole body of ministers.

The accession of George I, who was unfamiliar with the English language, led to a disinclination on the part of the sovereign to preside at meetings of his ministers and caused the emergence of a prime minister, a position first acquired by Robert Walpole in 1721 and retained by him without interruption for 20 years and 326 days. The office of prime minister was formally recognised in 1905 when it was established by royal warrant.

DEVELOPMENT OF PARTIES

In 1828 the Whigs became known as Liberals, a name originally given by opponents to imply laxity of principles, but gradually accepted by the party to indicate its claim to be pioneers and champions of political reform and progressive legislation. In 1861 a Liberal Registration Association was founded and Liberal Associations became widespread. In 1877 a National Liberal Federation was formed, with its headquarters in London. The Liberal Party was in power for long periods during the second half of the 19th century and for several years during the first quarter of the 20th century, but after a split in the party in 1931, the numbers elected remained small. In 1988 a majority of the Liberals agreed on a merger with the Social Democratic Party under the title Social and Liberal Democrats; since 1989 they have been known as the Liberal Democrats. A minority continue separately as the Liberal Party.

Soon after the change from Whig to Liberal, the Tory Party became known as Conservative, a name believed to have been invented by John Wilson Croker in 1830 and to have been generally adopted around the time of the passing of the Reform Act of 1832 – to indicate that the preservation of national institutions was the leading principle of the party. After the Home Rule crisis of 1886 the dissentient Liberals entered into a compact with the Conservatives, under which the latter undertook not to contest their seats, but a separate

Liberal Unionist organisation was maintained until 1912, when it was united with the Conservatives.

Labour candidates for parliament made their first appearance at the general election of 1892, when there were 27 standing as Labour or Liberal-Labour. In 1900 the Labour Representation Committee (LRC) was set up in order to establish a distinct Labour group in parliament, with its own whips, its own policy, and a readiness to cooperate with any party which might be engaged in promoting legislation in the direct interests of labour. In 1906 the LRC became known as the Labour Party.

The Green Party was founded in 1973 and campaigns for social and environmental justice. The party began as 'People', was renamed the Ecology Party, and became the Green Party in 1985.

The UK Independence Party (UKIP) was founded in 1993 by members of the Anti-Federalist League. It is a right-wing populist party with one key policy – to leave the European Union. In the 2014 European elections, UKIP became the first party, other than the Conservatives or Labour to win a national election in over a century.

The Respect Party was founded in 2004 as a left-wing alternative to the three major political parties. It has a broad socialist agenda, opposing war and privatisation.

Plaid Cymru was founded in 1926 to provide an independent political voice for Wales and to campaign for self-government in Wales.

The Scottish National Party (SNP) was founded in 1934 to campaign for independence for Scotland.

The Social Democratic and Labour Party (SDLP) was founded in 1970, emerging from the civil rights movement of the 1960s, with the aim of promoting reform, reconciliation and partnership across the sectarian divide in Northern Ireland, and of opposing violence from any quarter.

The Democratic Unionist Party (DUP) was founded in 1971 to resist moves by the Ulster Unionist Party which were considered a threat to the Union. Its aim is to maintain Northern Ireland as an integral part of the UK.

The Alliance Party of Northern Ireland was formed in 1970 as a non-sectarian unionist party.

Sinn Fein first emerged in the 1900s as a federation of nationalist clubs. It is a left-wing republican and labour party that seeks to end British governance in Ireland and achieve a 32-county republic.

GOVERNMENT AND OPPOSITION

The government is formed by the party which wins the largest number of seats in the House of Commons at a general election, or which has the support of a majority of members in the House of Commons. By tradition, the leader of the majority party is asked by the sovereign to form a government, while the largest minority party becomes the official opposition with its own leader and a shadow cabinet. Leaders of the government and opposition sit on the front benches of the Commons with their supporters (the back-benchers) sitting behind them.

FINANCIAL SUPPORT

Financial support for opposition parties in the House of Commons was introduced in 1975 and is commonly known as Short Money, after Edward Short, the leader of the house at that time, who introduced the scheme. Short Money is only payable to those parties that secured either one or two seats and more than 150,000 votes at the previous general election, and is only intended to provide assistance for parliamentary duties. Short Money allocations for 2014–15 are:

DUP	£166,250
Green	£66,020
Labour	£6,684,794
Plaid Cymru	£79,858
SDLP	£70,528
SNP	£187,294
*Sinn Fein	£115,283

* The sum paid to Sinn Fein and any other party that may choose not to take their seats in the House of Commons is calculated on the same basis as Short Money, but is known as Representative Money.

A specific allocation for the leader of the opposition's office was introduced in April 1999 and has been set at £777,538 for the year 2014–15.

Financial support for opposition parties in the House of Lords was introduced in 1996 and is commonly known as Cranborne Money, after former leader of the house, Viscount Cranborne. In 2014–15 the Labour Party's Cranborne Money allocation is £572,717, while the Convenor of Crossbench Peers' allocation is £73,565.

The following list of political parties are those with at least one MP or sitting member of the House of Lords in the present parliament.

ALLIANCE PARTY OF NORTHERN IRELAND

88 University Street, Belfast BT7 1HE
T 028-9032 4274 E alliance@allianceparty.org
W www.allianceparty.org
Party Leader, David Ford
Deputy Party Leader, Naomi Long, MP
President, Billy Webb
Chair, Andrew Muir
Hon. Treasurers, Mervyn Jones; Dan McGuinness

CONSERVATIVE PARTY

Conservative Campaign Headquarters, 4 Matthew Parker Street, London SW1H 9HQ
T 020-7222 9000 W www.conservatives.com
Parliamentary Party Leader, Rt. Hon. David Cameron, MP
Leader in the Lords and Chancellor of the Duchy of Lancaster, Rt. Hon. Lord Hill of Oareford, CBE
Leader in the Commons and Lord Privy Seal, Rt. Hon. Andrew Lansley, CBE, MP
Chairs, Lord Feldman of Elstree; Rt. Hon. Grant Shapps, MP
Party Treasurer, Michael Farmer

GREEN PARTY

Development House, 56–64 Leonard Street, London, EC2A 4LT
T 020-7549 0310 E office@greenparty.org.uk
W www.greenparty.org.uk
Party Leader, Natalie Bennett
Deputy Leader, Will Duckworth
Chair of Party Executive, Tim Dawes
Finance Coordinator, Michael Coffey

LABOUR PARTY

1 Brewer's Green, London SW1H 0RH
T 0845-092 2299 W www.labour.org.uk
General Secretary, Iain McNicol
General Secretary, Welsh Labour, Dave Hagendyk
General Secretary, Scottish Labour Party, Ian Price

SHADOW CABINET *AS AT JUNE 2014*
Leader of the Opposition, Rt. Hon. Ed Miliband, MP
Deputy Leader, Party Chair and Secretary of State for Culture, Media and Sport, Rt. Hon. Harriet Harman, QC, MP
Chancellor of the Exchequer, Rt. Hon. Ed Balls, MP

Secretary of State for Foreign and Commonwealth Affairs,
Rt. Hon. Douglas Alexander, MP
Secretary of State for the Home Department, Rt. Hon.
Yvette Cooper, MP
Secretary of State for Business, Innovation and Skills,
Chuka Umunna, MP
Minister for the Cabinet Office, Michael Dugher, MP
Secretary of State for Communities and Local Government,
Rt. Hon. Hilary Benn, MP
Secretary of State for Defence, Vernon Coaker, MP
Secretary of State for Education, Tristram Hunt, MP
Secretary of State for Energy and Climate Change, Rt. Hon.
Caroline Flint, MP
Secretary of State for Environment, Food and Rural Affairs,
Maria Eagle, MP
Secretary of State for Health, Rt. Hon. Andy Burnham, MP
Secretary of State for International Development, Rt. Hon.
Jim Murphy, MP
Lord Chancellor and Secretary of State for Justice, Rt. Hon.
Sadiq Khan, MP
Secretary of State for Northern Ireland, Ivan Lewis, MP
Secretary of State for Scotland, Margaret Curran, MP
Secretary of State for Transport, Mary Creagh, MP
Chief Secretary to the Treasury, Chris Leslie, MP
Minister for Women and Equalities, Gloria de Piero, MP
Secretary of State for Wales, Owen Smith, MP
Secretary of State for Work and Pensions, Rachel Reeves, MP
Leader of the House of Commons, Angela Eagle, MP
Leader of the House of Lords,
Rt. Hon. Baroness Royall of Blaisdon
Policy Review Coordinator, Jon Cruddas, MP
Attorney-General, Emily Thornberry, MP
Minister for Care and Older People, Liz Kendall, MP
Minister without Portfolio, Jon Trickett, MP
Minister without Portfolio, Lord Wood of Anfield
* Attends shadow cabinet meetings but is not a cabinet member

LABOUR WHIPS
Commons Chief Whip, Rt. Hon. Rosie Winterton, MP
Lords Chief Whip, Rt. Hon. Lord Bassam of Brighton

LIBERAL DEMOCRATS
8–10 Great George Street, London SW1P 3AE
T 020-7222 7999 E info@libdems.org.uk W www.libdems.org.uk
Parliamentary Party Leader, Rt. Hon. Nick Clegg, MP
Deputy Party Leader, Rt. Hon. Malcolm Bruce, MP
Leader in the Lords, Rt. Hon. Lord Wallace
Deputy Leader in the Commons, Rt. Hon. Tom Brake, MP
President, Tim Farron, MP
Chief Executive, Tim Gordon
Hon. Treasurer, Lord Wrigglesworth

NORTHERN IRELAND DEMOCRATIC UNIONIST PARTY
91 Dundela Avenue, Belfast BT4 3BU
T 028-9047 1155
E info@mydup.com W www.mydup.com
Parliamentary Party Leader, Rt. Hon. Peter Robinson, MLA
Deputy Leader, Rt. Hon Nigel Dodds, OBE, MP, MLA
Chair, Lord Morrow, MLA

PLAID CYMRU – THE PARTY OF WALES
Ty Gwynfor, Anson Court, Atlantic Wharf, Caerdydd CF10 4AL
T 029-2047 2272 E post@plaidcymru.org
W www.partyofwales.org
Party Leader, Leanne Wood, AM

Hon. Party President, Rt. Hon. Lord Wigley
Parliamentary Group Leader, Rt. Hon. Elfyn Llwyd, MP
Chair, Dafydd Trystan Davies
Chief Executive, Rhuanedd Richards

RESPECT PARTY
PO Box 167, Manchester M19 0AH
E contact@respectparty.org W www.respectparty.org
Party Leader, George Galloway
Deputy Party Leader, Dawud Islam
Chair, Abjol Miah
National Secretary, Chris Chilvers

SCOTTISH NATIONAL PARTY
Gordon Lamb House, 3 Jackson's Entry, Edinburgh EH8 8PJ
T 0800-633 5432 E info@snp.org W www.snp.org
Westminster Parliamentary Party Leader,
Angus Robertson, MP
Westminster Parliamentary Party Chief Whip,
Stewart Hosie, MP
Scottish Parliamentary Party Leader and Leader of the SNP,
Rt. Hon. Alex Salmond, MSP
Deputy Leader and Deputy First Minister of Scotland,
Nicola Sturgeon, MSP
Party President, Ian Hudghton, MEP
National Treasurer, Colin Beattie, MSP
Chief Executive, Peter Murrell

* On 19 September 2014 Alex Salmond announced he would step
down as Leader of the SNP from November 2014

SINN FEIN
53 Falls Road, Belfast BT12 4PD
T 028-9034 7350 E admin@sinnfein.ie W www.sinnfein.ie
Party President, Gerry Adams
Vice-President, Mary Lou McDonald
Chair, Declan Kearney

SOCIAL DEMOCRATIC AND LABOUR PARTY
121 Ormeau Road, Belfast BT7 1SH
T 028-9024 7700 E info@sdlp.ie W www.sdlp.ie
Parliamentary Party Leader, Dr Alisdair McDonnell,
MP, MLA
Deputy Leader, Dolores Kelly, MLA
Party Whip, Pat Ramsey, MLA
Chair, Joe Byrne, MLA
Treasurer, Peter McEvoy
General Secretary, Gerry Cosgrove

ULSTER UNIONIST PARTY
Strandtown Hall, 2–4 Belmont Road, Belfast BT4 2AN
T 028-9047 4630
E uup@uup.org W www.uup.org
Party Leader, Mike Nesbitt, MLA
Chair, Lord Empey of Shandon, OBE
Hon. Treasurer, Cllr Mark Cosgrove

UK INDEPENDENCE PARTY
PO Box 408, Newton Abbot, Devon TQ12 9BG
T 0800-587 6587
E mail@ukip.org W www.ukip.org
Party Leader, Nigel Farage, MEP
Deputy Leader, Paul Nuttall
Chief Executive, Will Gilpin
Treasurer, Stuart Wheeler

MEMBERS OF PARLIAMENT *as at September 2014*

* Denotes new MP at the 2010 General Election
† MP for another seat in previous Parliament
‡ MP for another party in previous Parliament
§ Elected at a by-election since the 2010 General Election
¶ Currently suspended from the parliamentary Labour Party
** Currently suspended from the parliamentary Liberal Democrats

Abbott, Diane (*b.* 1953) *Lab., Hackney North & Stoke Newington*, Maj. 14,461
§Abrahams, Deborah (*b.* 1960) *Lab., Oldham East & Saddleworth*, Maj. 3,558
*Adams, Nigel (*b.* 1966) *C., Selby & Ainsty*, Maj. 12,265
Afriyie, Adam (*b.* 1965) *C., Windsor*, Maj. 19,054
Ainsworth, Rt. Hon. Robert (*b.* 1952) *Lab., Coventry North East*, Maj. 11,775
*Aldous, Peter (*b.* 1961) *C., Waveney*, Maj. 769
†Alexander, Rt. Hon. Danny (*b.* 1972) *LD, Inverness, Nairn, Badenoch & Strathspey*, Maj. 8,765
Alexander, Rt. Hon. Douglas (*b.* 1967) *Lab., Paisley & Renfrewshire South*, Maj. 16,614
*Alexander, Heidi (*b.* 1975) *Lab., Lewisham East*, Maj. 6,216
*Ali, Rushanara (*b.* 1975) *Lab., Bethnal Green & Bow*, Maj. 11,574
Allen, Graham (*b.* 1953) *Lab., Nottingham North*, Maj. 8,138
Amess, David (*b.* 1952) *C., Southend West*, Maj. 7,270
Anderson, David (*b.* 1953) *Lab., Blaydon*, Maj. 9,117
*Andrew, Stuart (*b.* 1971) *C., Pudsey*, Maj. 1,659
Arbuthnot, Rt. Hon. James (*b.* 1952) *C., Hampshire North East*, Maj. 18,597
§Ashworth, Jon (*b.* 1978) *Lab., Leicester South*, Maj. 12,078
Austin, Ian (*b.* 1965) *Lab., Dudley North*, Maj. 649
Bacon, Richard (*b.* 1962) *C., Norfolk South*, Maj. 10,940
Bailey, Adrian (*b.* 1945) *Lab. (Co-op), West Bromwich West*, Maj. 5,651
Bain, William (*b.* 1972) *Lab., Glasgow North East*, Maj. 15,942
Baker, Rt. Hon. Norman (*b.* 1957) *LD, Lewes*, Maj. 7,647
*Baker, Steven (*b.* 1971) *C., Wycombe*, Maj. 9,560
Baldry, Rt. Hon. Sir Tony (*b.* 1950) *C., Banbury*, Maj. 18,227
*Baldwin, Harriett (*b.* 1960) *C., West Worcestershire*, Maj. 6,804
Balls, Rt. Hon. Ed (*b.* 1967) *Lab. (Co-op), Morley & Outwood*, Maj. 1,101
Banks, Gordon (*b.* 1955) *Lab., Ochil & Perthshire South*, Maj. 5,187
*Barclay, Stephen (*b.* 1972) *C., Cambridgeshire North East*, Maj. 16,425
Barker, Rt. Hon. Gregory (*b.* 1966) *C., Bexhill & Battle*, Maj. 12,880
Baron, John (*b.* 1959) *C., Basildon & Billericay*, Maj. 12,398
Barron, Rt. Hon. Sir Kevin (*b.* 1946) *Lab., Rother Valley*, Maj. 5,866
*Barwell, Gavin (*b.* 1972) *C., Croydon Central*, Maj. 2,969
Bayley, Hugh (*b.* 1952) *Lab., York Central*, Maj. 6,451
*Bebb, Guto (*b.* 1968) *C., Aberconwy*, Maj. 3,398
Beckett, Rt. Hon. Dame Margaret (*b.* 1943) *Lab., Derby South*, Maj. 6,122
Begg, Dame Anne (*b.* 1955) *Lab., Aberdeen South*, Maj. 3,506
Beith, Rt. Hon. Sir Alan (*b.* 1943) *LD, Berwick-upon-Tweed*, Maj. 2,690
Bellingham, Henry (*b.* 1955) *C., Norfolk North West*, Maj. 14,810
Benn, Rt. Hon. Hilary (*b.* 1953) *Lab., Leeds Central*, Maj. 10,645
Benton, Joe (*b.* 1933) *Lab., Bootle*, Maj. 21,181

Benyon, Richard (*b.* 1960) *C., Newbury*, Maj. 12,248
Bercow, Rt. Hon. John (*b.* 1963) *The Speaker, Buckingham*, Maj. 12,529
Beresford, Sir Paul (*b.* 1946) *C., Mole Valley*, Maj. 15,653
*Berger, Luciana (*b.* 1981) *Lab. (Co-op), Liverpool Wavertree*, Maj. 7,167
*Berry, Jake (*b.* 1978) *C., Rossendale & Darwen*, Maj. 4,493
Betts, Clive (*b.* 1950) *Lab., Sheffield South East*, Maj. 10,505
*Bingham, Andrew (*b.* 1962) *C., High Peak*, Maj. 4,677
Binley, Brian (*b.* 1942) *C., Northampton South*, Maj. 6,004
*Birtwistle, Gordon (*b.* 1943) *LD, Burnley*, Maj. 1,818
*Blackman, Bob (*b.* 1956) *C., Harrow East*, Maj. 3,403
Blackman-Woods, Dr Roberta (*b.* 1957) *Lab., Durham, City of*, Maj. 3,067
*Blackwood, Nicola (*b.* 1979) *C., Oxford West & Abingdon*, Maj. 176
Blears, Rt. Hon. Hazel (*b.* 1956) *Lab., Salford & Eccles*, Maj. 5,725
*Blenkinsop, Tom (*b.* 1980) *Lab., Middlesbrough South & East Cleveland*, Maj. 1,677
*Blomfield, Paul (*b.* 1953) *Lab., Sheffield Central*, Maj. 165
Blunkett, Rt. Hon. David (*b.* 1947) *Lab., Sheffield, Brightside & Hillsborough*, Maj. 13,632
Blunt, Crispin (*b.* 1960) *C., Reigate*, Maj. 13,591
*Boles, Nick (*b.* 1965) *C., Grantham & Stamford*, Maj. 14,826
Bone, Peter (*b.* 1952) *C., Wellingborough*, Maj. 11,787
Bottomley, Sir Peter (*b.* 1944) *C., Worthing West*, Maj. 11,729
*Bradley, Karen (*b.* 1970) *C., Staffordshire Moorlands*, Maj. 6,689
Bradshaw, Rt. Hon. Ben (*b.* 1960) *Lab., Exeter*, Maj. 2,721
Brady, Graham (*b.* 1967) *C., Altrincham & Sale West*, Maj. 11,595
Brake, Rt. Hon. Tom (*b.* 1962) *LD, Carshalton & Wallington*, Maj. 5,260
*Bray, Angie (*b.* 1953) *C., Ealing Central &Acton*, Maj. 3,716
Brazier, Julian (*b.* 1953) *C., Canterbury*, Maj. 6,048
Brennan, Kevin (*b.* 1959) *Lab., Cardiff West*, Maj. 4,750
*Bridgen, Andrew (*b.* 1964) *C., Leicestershire North West*, Maj. 7,511
*Brine, Steve (*b.* 1974) *C., Winchester*, Maj. 3,048
†Brokenshire, James (*b.* 1968) *C., Old Bexley & Sidcup*, Maj. 15,857
Brooke, Rt. Hon. Annette (*b.* 1947) *LD, Dorset Mid & Poole North*, Maj. 269
Brown, Rt. Hon. Gordon (*b.* 1951) *Lab., Kirkcaldy & Cowdenbeath*, Maj. 23,009
Brown, Lyn (*b.* 1960) *Lab., West Ham*, Maj. 22,534
Brown, Rt. Hon. Nicholas (*b.* 1950) *Lab., Newcastle upon Tyne East*, Maj. 4,453
Brown, Russell (*b.* 1951) *Lab., Dumfries & Galloway*, Maj. 7,449
Browne, Jeremy (*b.* 1970) *LD, Taunton Deane*, Maj. 3,993
*Bruce, Fiona (*b.* 1957) *C., Congleton*, Maj. 7,063
Bruce, Rt. Hon. Sir Malcolm (*b.* 1944) *LD, Gordon*, Maj. 6,748
Bryant, Chris (*b.* 1962) *Lab., Rhondda*, Maj. 11,553
Buck, Karen (*b.* 1958) *Lab., Westminster North*, Maj. 2,126
*Buckland, Robert (*b.* 1968) *C., Swindon South*, Maj. 3,544
Burden, Richard (*b.* 1954) *Lab., Birmingham Northfield*, Maj. 2,782
*Burley, Aidan (*b.* 1979) *C., Cannock Chase*, Maj. 3,195
Burnham, Rt. Hon. Andy (*b.* 1970) *Lab., Leigh*, Maj. 15,011
*Burns, Conor (*b.* 1972) *C., Bournemouth West*, Maj. 5,583

Burns, Rt. Hon. Simon (*b.* 1952) *C., Chelmsford,* Maj. 5,110

Burrowes, David (*b.* 1969) *C., Enfield Southgate,* Maj. 7,626

Burstow, Rt. Hon. Paul (*b.* 1962) *LD, Sutton & Cheam,* Maj. 1,608

Burt, Rt. Hon. Alistair (*b.* 1955) *C., Bedfordshire North East,* Maj. 18,942

Burt, Lorely (*b.* 1957) *LD, Solihull,* Maj. 175

*Byles, Daniel (*b.* 1974) *C., Warwickshire North,* Maj. 54

Byrne, Rt. Hon. Liam (*b.* 1970) *Lab., Birmingham Hodge Hill,* Maj. 10,302

Cable, Rt. Hon. Dr Vincent (*b.* 1943) *LD, Twickenham,* Maj. 12,140

*Cairns, Alun (*b.* 1970) *C., Vale of Glamorgan,* Maj. 4,307

Cameron, Rt. Hon. David (*b.* 1966) *C., Witney,* Maj. 22,740

Campbell, Alan (*b.* 1957) *Lab., Tynemouth,* Maj. 5,739

Campbell, Gregory (*b.* 1953) *DUP, Londonderry East,* Maj. 5,355

Campbell, Rt. Hon. Sir Menzies (*b.* 1941) *LD, Fife North East,* Maj. 9,048

Campbell, Ronnie (*b.* 1943) *Lab., Blyth Valley,* Maj. 6,668

Carmichael, Rt. Hon. Alistair (*b.* 1965) *LD, Orkney & Shetland,* Maj. 9,928

*Carmichael, Neil (*b.* 1961) *C., Stroud,* Maj. 1,299

Cash, William (*b.* 1940) *C., Stone,* Maj. 13,292

Caton, Martin (*b.* 1951) *Lab., Gower,* Maj. 2,683

§Champion, Sarah (*b.* 1969) *Lab., Rotherham,* Maj. 5,318

*Chapman, Jenny (*b.* 1973) *Lab., Darlington,* Maj. 3,388

*Chishti, Rehman (*b.* 1978) *C., Gillingham & Rainham,* Maj. 8,680

Chope, Christopher (*b.* 1947) *C., Christchurch,* Maj. 15,410

Clappison, James (*b.* 1956) *C., Hertsmere,* Maj. 17,605

Clark, Rt. Hon. Greg (*b.* 1967) *C., Tunbridge Wells,* Maj. 15,576

Clark, Katy (*b.* 1967) *Lab., Ayrshire North & Arran,* Maj. 9,895

Clarke, Rt. Hon. Kenneth (*b.* 1940) *C., Rushcliffe,* Maj. 15,811

Clarke, Rt. Hon. Thomas (*b.* 1941) *Lab., Coatbridge, Chryston & Bellshill,* Maj. 20,714

Clegg, Rt. Hon. Nick (*b.* 1967) *LD, Sheffield Hallam,* Maj. 15,284

Clifton-Brown, Geoffrey (*b.* 1953) *C., The Cotswolds,* Maj. 12,864

Clwyd, Rt. Hon. Ann (*b.* 1937) *Lab., Cynon Valley,* Maj. 9,617

Coaker, Vernon (*b.* 1953) *Lab., Gedling,* Maj. 1,859

Coffey, Ann (*b.* 1946) *Lab., Stockport,* Maj. 6,784

*Coffey, Thérèse (*b.* 1971) *C., Suffolk Coastal,* Maj. 9,128

*Collins, Damian (*b.* 1974) *C., Folkestone & Hythe,* Maj. 10,122

*Colvile, Oliver (*b.* 1959) *C., Plymouth Sutton & Devonport,* Maj. 1,149

Connarty, Michael (*b.* 1947) *Lab., Linlithgow & Falkirk East,* Maj. 12,553

Cooper, Rosie (*b.* 1950) *Lab., Lancashire West,* Maj. 4,343

Cooper, Rt. Hon. Yvette (*b.* 1969) *Lab., Normanton, Pontefract & Castleford,* Maj. 10,979

Corbyn, Jeremy (*b.* 1949) *Lab., Islington North,* Maj. 12,401

Cox, Geoffrey (*b.* 1960) *C., Devon West & Torridge,* Maj. 2,957

Crabb, Rt. Hon. Stephen (*b.* 1973) *C., Preseli Pembrokeshire,* Maj. 4,605

Crausby, David (*b.* 1946) *Lab., Bolton North East,* Maj. 4,084

Creagh, Mary (*b.* 1967) *Lab., Wakefield,* Maj. 1,613

*Creasy, Stella (*b.* 1977) *Lab. (Co-op), Walthamstow,* Maj. 9,478

*Crockart, Mike (*b.* 1966) *LD, Edinburgh West,* Maj. 3,803

*Crouch, Tracey (*b.* 1975) *C., Chatham & Aylesford,* Maj. 6,069

Cruddas, Jonathan (*b.* 1965) *Lab., Dagenham & Rainham,* Maj. 2,630

*Cryer, John (*b.* 1964) *Lab., Leyton & Wanstead,* Maj. 6,416

*Cunningham, Alex (*b.* 1955) *Lab., Stockton North,* Maj. 6,676

Cunningham, Jim (*b.* 1941) *Lab., Coventry South,* Maj. 3,845

Cunningham, Sir Tony (*b.* 1952) *Lab., Workington,* Maj. 4,575

*Curran, Margaret (*b.* 1958) *Lab., Glasgow East,* Maj. 11,840

*Dakin, Nic (*b.* 1955) *Lab., Scunthorpe,* Maj. 2,549

*Danczuk, Simon (*b.* 1966) *Lab., Rochdale,* Maj. 889

Darling, Rt. Hon. Alistair (*b.* 1953) *Lab., Edinburgh South West,* Maj. 8,447

Davey, Rt. Hon. Edward (*b.* 1965) *LD, Kingston & Surbiton,* Maj. 7,560

David, Wayne (*b.* 1957) *Lab., Caerphilly,* Maj. 10,775

Davidson, Ian (*b.* 1950) *Lab. (Co-op), Glasgow South West,* Maj. 14,671

Davies, David (*b.* 1970) *C., Monmouth,* Maj. 10,425

*Davies, Geraint (*b.* 1960) *Lab. (Co-op), Swansea West,* Maj. 504

*Davies, Glyn (*b.* 1944) *C., Montgomeryshire,* Maj. 1,184

Davies, Philip (*b.* 1972) *C., Shipley,* Maj. 9,944

Davis, Rt. Hon. David (*b.* 1948) *C., Haltemprice & Howden,* Maj. 11,602

*de Bois, Nick (*b.* 1959) *C., Enfield North,* Maj. 1,692

*De Piero, Gloria (*b.* 1972) *Lab., Ashfield,* Maj. 192

Denham, Rt. Hon. John (*b.* 1953) *Lab., Southampton Itchen,* Maj. 192

*Dinenage, Caroline (*b.* 1971) *C., Gosport,* Maj. 14,413

Djanogly, Jonathan (*b.* 1965) *C., Huntingdon,* Maj. 10,019

Dobson, Rt. Hon. Frank (*b.* 1940) *Lab., Holborn & St Pancras,* Maj. 9,942

*Docherty, Thomas (*b.* 1975) *Lab., Dunfermline & Fife West,* Maj. 5,470

Dodds, Rt. Hon. Nigel (*b.* 1958) *DUP, Belfast North,* Maj. 2,224

Doherty, Pat (*b.* 1945) *SF, Tyrone West,* Maj. 10,685

†Donaldson, Rt. Hon. Jeffrey (*b.* 1962) *DUP, Lagan Valley,* Maj. 10,486

Donohoe, Brian (*b.* 1948) *Lab., Ayrshire Central,* Maj. 12,007

Doran, Frank (*b.* 1949) *Lab., Aberdeen North,* Maj. 8,361

Dorrell, Rt. Hon. Stephen (*b.* 1952) *C., Charnwood,* Maj. 15,029

Dorries, Nadine (*b.* 1958) *C., Bedfordshire Mid,* Maj. 15,152

§Doughty, Stephen (*b.* 1980) *Lab. (Co-op), Cardiff South and Penarth,* Maj. 5,334

Dowd, Jim (*b.* 1951) *Lab., Lewisham West & Penge,* Maj. 5,828

*Doyle, Gemma (*b.* 1981) *Lab. (Co-op), Dunbartonshire West,* Maj. 17,408

*Doyle-Price, Jackie (*b.* 1969) *C., Thurrock,* Maj. 92

*Drax, Richard (*b.* 1958) *C., Dorset South,* Maj. 7,443

*Dromey, Jack (*b.* 1948) *Lab., Birmingham Erdington,* Maj. 3,277

Duddridge, James (*b.* 1971) *C., Rochford & Southend East,* Maj. 11,050

*Dugher, Michael (*b.* 1975) *Lab., Barnsley East,* Maj. 11,090

Duncan, Rt. Hon. Sir Alan (*b.* 1957) *C., Rutland & Melton,* Maj. 14,000

Duncan Smith, Rt. Hon. Iain (*b.* 1954) *C., Chingford & Woodford Green,* Maj. 12,963

Dunne, Philip (*b.* 1958) *C., Ludlow,* Maj. 9,749

Durkan, Mark (*b.* 1960) *SDLP, Foyle,* Maj. 4,824

Eagle, Angela (*b.* 1961) *Lab., Wallasey,* Maj. 8,507

Eagle, Maria (*b.* 1961) *Lab., Garston & Halewood,*
Maj. 16,877
*Edwards, Jonathan (*b.* 1976) *PC, Carmarthen East &*
Dinefwr, Maj. 3,481
Efford, Clive (*b.* 1958) *Lab., Eltham,* Maj. 1,663
*Elliott, Julie (*b.* 1963) *Lab., Sunderland Central,* Maj. 6,725
*Ellis, Michael (*b.* 1967) *C., Northampton*
North Maj. 1,936
*Ellison, Jane (*b.* 1964) *C., Battersea,* Maj. 5,977
Ellman, Louise (*b.* 1945) *Lab. (Co-op), Liverpool Riverside,*
Maj. 14,173
Ellwood, Tobias (*b.* 1966) *C., Bournemouth East,* Maj. 7,728
*Elphicke, Charlie (*b.* 1971) *C., Dover,* Maj. 5,274
Engel, Natascha (*b.* 1967) *Lab., Derbyshire North East,*
Maj. 2,445
*Esterson, Bill (*b.* 1966) *Lab., Sefton Central,* Maj. 3,862
*Eustice, George (*b.* 1971) *C., Camborne & Redruth,* Maj. 66
*Evans, Chris (*b.* 1976) *Lab. (Co-op), Islwyn,* Maj. 12,215
*Evans, Graham (*b.* 1963) *C., Weaver Vale,* Maj. 991
*Evans, Jonathan (*b.* 1950) *C., Cardiff North,* Maj. 194
Evans, Nigel (*b.* 1957) *Ind., Ribble Valley,* Maj. 14,769
Evennett, David (*b.* 1949) *C., Bexleyheath & Crayford,*
Maj. 10,344
Fabricant, Michael (*b.* 1950) *C., Lichfield,* Maj. 17,683
Fallon, Rt. Hon. Michael (*b.* 1952) *C., Sevenoaks,*
Maj. 17,515
Farrelly, Paul (*b.* 1962) *Lab., Newcastle-under-Lyme,*
Maj. 1,552
Farron, Tim (*b.* 1970) *LD, Westmorland & Lonsdale,*
Maj. 12,264
Featherstone, Rt. Hon. Lynne (*b.* 1951) *LD, Hornsey &*
Wood Green, Maj. 6,875
Field, Rt. Hon. Frank (*b.* 1942) *Lab., Birkenhead,*
Maj. 15,195
Field, Mark (*b.* 1964) *C., Cities of London & Westminster,*
Maj. 11,076
Fitzpatrick, Jim (*b.* 1952) *Lab., Poplar & Limehouse,*
Maj. 6,030
Flello, Robert (*b.* 1966) *Lab., Stoke-on-Trent South,*
Maj. 4,130
Flint, Rt. Hon. Caroline (*b.* 1961) *Lab., Don Valley,*
Maj. 3,595
Flynn, Paul (*b.* 1935) *Lab., Newport West,* Maj. 3,544
Foster, Rt. Hon. Don (*b.* 1947) *LD, Bath,* Maj. 11,883
*Fovargue, Yvonne (*b.* 1956) *Lab., Makerfield,* Maj. 12,490
Fox, Rt. Hon. Dr Liam (*b.* 1961) *C., Somerset North,*
Maj. 7,862
Francis, Dr Hywel (*b.* 1946) *Lab., Aberavon,* Maj. 11,039
Francois, Rt. Hon. Mark (*b.* 1965) *C., Rayleigh &*
Wickford, Maj. 22,338
*Freeman, George (*b.* 1967) *C., Norfolk Mid,* Maj. 13,856
*Freer, Mike (*b.* 1960) *C., Finchley & Golders Green,*
Maj. 5,809
*Fullbrook, Lorraine (*b.* 1959) *C., Ribble South,* Maj. 5,554
*Fuller, Richard (*b.* 1962) *C., Bedford,* Maj. 1,353
Gale, Sir Roger (*b.* 1943) *C., Thanet North,* Maj. 13,528
†‡§Galloway, George (*b.* 1954) *Respect, Bradford West,*
Maj. 10,140
Gapes, Mike (*b.* 1952) *Lab. (Co-op), Ilford South,* Maj. 11,297
Gardiner, Barry (*b.* 1957) *Lab., Brent North,* Maj. 8,028
Garnier, Sir Edward (*b.* 1952) *C., Harborough,* Maj. 9,877
*Garnier, Mark (*b.* 1963) *C., Wyre Forest,* Maj. 2,643
Gauke, David (*b.* 1971) *C., Hertfordshire South West,*
Maj. 14,920
George, Andrew (*b.* 1958) *LD, St Ives,* Maj. 1,719
Gibb, Nick (*b.* 1960) *C., Bognor Regis & Littlehampton,*
Maj. 13,063
*Gilbert, Stephen (*b.* 1976) *LD, St Austell & Newquay,*
Maj. 1,312

Gildernew, Michelle (*b.* 1970) *SF, Fermanagh & South*
Tyrone, Maj. 4
Gillan, Rt. Hon. Cheryl (*b.* 1952) *C., Chesham & Amersham,*
Maj. 16,710
*Gilmore, Sheila (*b.* 1950) *Lab., Edinburgh East,*
Maj. 9,181
*Glass, Pat (*b.* 1956) *Lab., Durham North West,* Maj. 7,612
*Glen, John (*b.* 1974) *C., Salisbury,* Maj. 5,966
*Glindon, Mary (*b.* 1957) *Lab., Tyneside North,* Maj. 12,884
Godsiff, Roger (*b.* 1946) *Lab., Birmingham Hall Green,*
Maj. 3,799
*Goldsmith, Zac (*b.* 1975) *C., Richmond Park,* Maj. 4,091
Goodman, Helen (*b.* 1958) *Lab., Bishop Auckland,*
Maj. 5,218
Goodwill, Robert (*b.* 1956) *C., Scarborough & Whitby,*
Maj. 8,130
Gove, Rt. Hon. Michael (*b.* 1967) *C., Surrey Heath,*
Maj. 17,289
*Graham, Richard (*b.* 1958) *C., Gloucester,* Maj. 2,420
*Grant, Helen (*b.* 1961) *C., Maidstone & The Weald,*
Maj. 5,889
Gray, James (*b.* 1954) *C., Wiltshire North,* Maj. 7,483
Grayling, Rt. Hon. Chris (*b.* 1962) *C., Epsom & Ewell,*
Maj. 16,134
*Greatrex, Tom (*b.* 1974) *Lab. (Co-op), Rutherglen &*
Hamilton West, Maj. 21,002
Green, Rt. Hon. Damian (*b.* 1956) *C., Ashford,* Maj. 17,297
*Green, Kate (*b.* 1960) *Lab., Stretford & Urmston,*
Maj. 8,935
Greening, Rt. Hon. Justine (*b.* 1969) *C., Putney,* Maj. 10,053
*Greenwood, Lilian (*b.* 1966) *Lab., Nottingham South,*
Maj. 1,772
Grieve, Rt. Hon. Dominic (*b.* 1956) *C., Beaconsfield,*
Maj. 21,782
Griffith, Nia (*b.* 1956) *Lab., Llanelli,* Maj. 4,701
*Griffiths, Andrew (*b.* 1970) *C., Burton,* Maj. 6,304
*Gummer, Ben (*b.* 1978) *C., Ipswich,* Maj. 2,079
Gwynne, Andrew (*b.* 1974) *Lab., Denton & Reddish,*
Maj. 9,831
*Gyimah, Sam (*b.* 1976) *C., Surrey East,* Maj. 16,874
Hague, Rt. Hon. William (*b.* 1961) *C., Richmond (Yorks),*
Maj. 23,336
Hain, Rt. Hon. Peter (*b.* 1950) *Lab., Neath,* Maj. 9,775
*Halfon, Robert (*b.* 1969) *C., Harlow,* Maj. 4,925
*Hames, Duncan (*b.* 1977) *LD, Chippenham,* Maj. 2,470
Hamilton, David (*b.* 1950) *Lab., Midlothian,* Maj. 4,545
Hamilton, Fabian (*b.* 1955) *Lab., Leeds North East,*
Maj. 10,349
Hammond, Rt. Hon. Philip (*b.* 1955) *C., Runnymede &*
Weybridge, Maj. 16,509
Hammond, Stephen (*b.* 1962) *C., Wimbledon,* Maj. 11,408
*Hancock, Rt. Hon. Matthew (*b.* 1978) *C., Suffolk West,*
Maj. 13,050
**Hancock, Mike (*b.* 1946) *Ind., Portsmouth South,*
Maj. 5,200
Hands, Greg (*b.* 1965) *C., Chelsea & Fulham,* Maj. 16,722
Hanson, Rt. Hon. David (*b.* 1957) *Lab., Delyn,* Maj. 2,272
Harman, Rt. Hon. Harriet (*b.* 1950) *Lab., Camberwell &*
Peckham, Maj. 17,187
Harper, Mark (*b.* 1970) *C., Forest of Dean,* Maj. 11,064
*Harrington, Richard (*b.* 1957) *C., Watford,* Maj. 1,425
*Harris, Rebecca (*b.* 1967) *C., Castle Point,* Maj. 7,632
Harris, Tom (*b.* 1964) *Lab., Glasgow South,* Maj. 12,658
*Hart, Simon (*b.* 1963) *C., Carmarthen West & Pembrokeshire*
South, Maj. 3,423
Harvey, Sir Nick (*b.* 1961) *LD, Devon North,* Maj. 5,821
Haselhurst, Rt. Hon. Sir Alan (*b.* 1937) *C., Saffron Walden,*
Maj. 15,242
Havard, Dai (*b.* 1949) *Lab., Merthyr Tydfil & Rhymney,*
Maj. 4,056

Hayes, Rt. Hon. John (*b.* 1958) *C., South Holland & The Deepings*, Maj. 21,880

Heald, Sir Oliver (*b.* 1954) *C., Hertfordshire North East*, Maj. 15,194

Healey, Rt. Hon. John (*b.* 1960) *Lab., Wentworth & Dearne*, Maj. 13,920

Heath, David (*b.* 1954) *LD, Somerton & Frome*, Maj. 1,817

***Heaton-Harris**, Chris (*b.* 1967) *C., Daventry*, Maj. 19,188

Hemming, John (*b.* 1960) *LD, Birmingham Yardley*, Maj. 3,002

***Henderson**, Gordon (*b.* 1948) *C., Sittingbourne & Sheppey*, Maj. 12,383

Hendrick, Mark (*b.* 1958) *Lab. (Co-op), Preston*, Maj. 7,733

Hendry, Charles (*b.* 1959) *C., Wealden*, Maj. 17,179

Hepburn, Stephen (*b.* 1959) *Lab., Jarrow*, Maj. 12,908

Herbert, Rt. Hon. Nick (*b.* 1963) *C., Arundel & South Downs*, Maj. 16,691

Hermon, Lady (Sylvia) (*b.* 1956) *Ind., Down North*, Maj. 14,364

Heyes, David (*b.* 1946) *Lab., Ashton-under-Lyne*, Maj. 9,094

Hillier, Meg (*b.* 1969) *Lab. (Co-op), Hackney South & Shoreditch*, Maj. 14,288

***Hilling**, Julie (*b.* 1955) *Lab., Bolton West*, Maj. 92

***Hinds**, Damian (*b.* 1969) *C., Hampshire East*, Maj. 13,497

Hoban, Mark (*b.* 1964) *C., Fareham*, Maj. 17,092

Hodge, Rt. Hon. Margaret (*b.* 1944) *Lab., Barking*, Maj. 16,555

Hodgson, Sharon (*b.* 1966) *Lab., Washington & Sunderland West*, Maj. 11,458

Hoey, Kate (*b.* 1946) *Lab., Vauxhall*, Maj. 10,651

***Hollingbery**, George (*b.* 1963) *C., Meon Valley*, Maj. 12,125

Hollobone, Philip (*b.* 1964) *C., Kettering*, Maj. 9,094

Holloway, Adam (*b.* 1965) *C., Gravesham*, Maj. 9,312

Hood, Jim (*b.* 1948) *Lab., Lanark & Hamilton East*, Maj. 13,478

Hopkins, Kelvin (*b.* 1941) *Lab., Luton North*, Maj. 7,520

***Hopkins**, Kris (*b.* 1963) *C., Keighley*, Maj. 2,940

Horwood, Martin (*b.* 1962) *LD, Cheltenham*, Maj. 4,920

Hosie, Stewart (*b.* 1963) *SNP, Dundee East*, Maj. 1,821

Howarth, Rt. Hon. George (*b.* 1949) *Lab., Knowsley*, Maj. 25,690

Howarth, Sir Gerald (*b.* 1947) *C., Aldershot*, Maj. 5,586

Howell, John (*b.* 1955) *C., Henley*, Maj. 16,588

Hoyle, Rt. Hon. Lindsay (*b.* 1957) *Lab., Deputy Speaker, Chorley*, Maj. 2,593

Hughes, Rt. Hon. Simon (*b.* 1951) *LD, Bermondsey & Old Southwark*, Maj. 8,530

Hunt, Rt. Hon. Jeremy (*b.* 1966) *C., Surrey South West*, Maj. 16,318

***Hunt**, Tristram (*b.* 1974) *Lab., Stoke-on-Trent Central*, Maj. 5,566

Hunter, Mark (*b.* 1957) *LD, Cheadle*, Maj. 3,272

***Huppert**, Julian (*b.* 1978) *LD, Cambridge*, Maj. 6,792

Hurd, Nick (*b.* 1962) *C., Ruislip, Northwood & Pinner*, Maj. 19,060

Irranca-Davies, Huw (*b.* 1963) *Lab., Ogmore*, Maj. 13,246

Jackson, Glenda (*b.* 1936) *Lab., Hampstead & Kilburn*, Maj. 42

Jackson, Stewart (*b.* 1965) *C., Peterborough*, Maj. 4,861

***James**, Margot (*b.* 1957) *C., Stourbridge*, Maj. 5,164

James, Siân (*b.* 1959) *Lab., Swansea East*, Maj. 10,838

***Jamieson**, Cathy (*b.* 1956) *Lab. (Co-op), Kilmarnock & Loudoun*, Maj. 12,378

§**Jarvis**, Dan (*b.* 1972) *Lab., Barnsley Central*, Maj. 11,771

***Javid**, Sajid (*b.* 1969) *C., Bromsgrove*, Maj. 11,308

Jenkin, Bernard (*b.* 1959) *C., Harwich & Essex North*, Maj. 11,447

§**Jenrick**, Robert (*b.* 1982) *C., Newark*, Maj. 7,403

Johnson, Rt. Hon. Alan (*b.* 1950) *Lab., Hull West & Hessle*, Maj. 5,740

Johnson, Diana (*b.* 1966) *Lab., Hull North*, Maj. 641

***Johnson**, Gareth (*b.* 1969) *C., Dartford*, Maj. 10,628

***Johnson**, Joseph (*b.* 1971) *C., Orpington*, Maj. 17,200

***Jones**, Andrew (*b.* 1963) *C., Harrogate & Knaresborough*, Maj. 1,039

Jones, Rt. Hon. David (*b.* 1952) *C., Clwyd West*, Maj. 6,419

***Jones**, Graham (*b.* 1966) *Lab., Hyndburn*, Maj. 3,090

Jones, Helen (*b.* 1954) *Lab., Warrington North*, Maj. 6,771

Jones, Kevan (*b.* 1964) *Lab., Durham North*, Maj. 12,076

***Jones**, Marcus (*b.* 1974) *C., Nuneaton*, Maj. 2,069

***Jones**, Susan (*b.* 1968) *Lab., Clwyd South*, Maj. 2,834

Jowell, Rt. Hon. Dame Tessa (*b.* 1947) *Lab., Dulwich & West Norwood*, Maj. 9,365

¶ **Joyce**, Eric (*b.* 1960) *Ind., Falkirk*, Maj. 7,843

§**Kane**, Michael (*b.* 1969) *Lab., Wythenshawe & Sale East*, Maj. 8,960

Kaufman, Rt. Hon. Sir Gerald (*b.* 1930) *Lab., Manchester Gorton*, Maj. 6,703

Kawczynski, Daniel (*b.* 1972) *C., Shrewsbury & Atcham*, Maj. 7,944

Keeley, Barbara (*b.* 1952) *Lab., Worsley & Eccles South*, Maj. 4,337

***Kelly**, Chris (*b.* 1978) *C., Dudley South*, Maj. 3,856

***Kendall**, Liz (*b.* 1971) *Lab., Leicester West*, Maj. 4,017

Kennedy, Rt. Hon. Charles (*b.* 1959) *LD, Ross, Skye & Lochaber*, Maj. 13,070

Khan, Rt. Hon. Sadiq (*b.* 1970) *Lab., Tooting*, Maj. 2,524

***Kirby**, Simon (*b.* 1964) *C., Brighton Kemptown*, Maj. 1,328

Knight, Rt. Hon. Sir Greg (*b.* 1949) *C., Yorkshire East*, Maj. 13,486

***Kwarteng**, Kwasi (*b.* 1975) *C., Spelthorne*, Maj. 10,019

Laing, Eleanor (*b.* 1958) *C., Deputy Speaker, Epping Forest*, Maj. 15,131

Lamb, Rt. Hon. Norman (*b.* 1957) *LD, Norfolk North*, Maj. 11,626

Lammy, Rt. Hon. David (*b.* 1972) *Lab., Tottenham*, Maj. 16,931

Lancaster, Mark (*b.* 1970) *C., Milton Keynes North*, Maj. 8,961

Lansley, Rt. Hon. Andrew (*b.* 1956) *C., Cambridgeshire South*, Maj. 7,838

***Latham**, Pauline (*b.* 1948) *C., Derbyshire Mid*, Maj. 11,292

***Lavery**, Ian (*b.* 1962) *Lab., Wansbeck*, Maj. 7,031

Laws, Rt. Hon. David (*b.* 1965) *LD, Yeovil*, Maj. 13,036

Lazarowicz, Mark (*b.* 1953) *Lab. (Co-op), Edinburgh North & Leith*, Maj. 1,724

***Leadsom**, Andrea (*b.* 1963) *C., Northamptonshire South*, Maj. 20,478

***Lee**, Jessica (*b.* 1976) *C., Erewash*, Maj. 2,501

***Lee**, Phillip (*b.* 1970) *C., Bracknell*, Maj. 15,074

Leech, John (*b.* 1971) *LD, Manchester Withington*, Maj. 1,850

***Lefroy**, Jeremy (*b.* 1959) *C., Stafford*, Maj. 5,460

Leigh, Sir Edward (*b.* 1950) *C., Gainsborough*, Maj. 10,559

***Leslie**, Charlotte (*b.* 1978) *C., Bristol North West*, Maj. 3,274

***Leslie**, Chris (*b.* 1972) *Lab. (Co-op), Nottingham East*, Maj. 6,969

Letwin, Rt. Hon. Oliver (*b.* 1956) *C., Dorset West*, Maj. 3,923

§**Lewell-Buck**, Emma (*b.* 1978) *Lab., South Shields*, Maj. 6,505

***Lewis**, Brandon (*b.* 1971) *C., Great Yarmouth*, Maj. 4,276

Lewis, Ivan (*b.* 1967) *Lab., Bury South*, Maj. 3,292

Lewis, Dr Julian (*b.* 1951) *C., New Forest East*, Maj. 11,307

Liddell-Grainger, Ian (*b.* 1959) *C., Bridgwater & Somerset West*, Maj. 9,249

Lidington, Rt. Hon. David (*b.* 1956) *C., Aylesbury,*
Maj. 12,618
Lilley, Rt. Hon. Peter (*b.* 1943) *C., Hitchin & Harpenden,*
Maj. 15,271
*****Lloyd**, Stephen (*b.* 1957) *LD, Eastbourne,* Maj. 3,435
Llwyd, Rt. Hon. Elfyn (*b.* 1951) *PC, Dwyfor Meirionnydd,*
Maj. 6,367
*****Long**, Naomi (*b.* 1971) *All., Belfast East,* Maj. 1,533
*****Lopresti,** Jack (*b.* 1969) *C., Filton & Bradley Stoke,*
Maj. 6,914
*****Lord**, Jonathan (*b.* 1962) *C., Woking,* Maj. 6,807
Loughton, Tim (*b.* 1962) *C., Worthing East & Shoreham,*
Maj. 11,105
Love, Andy (*b.* 1949) *Lab. (Co-op), Edmonton,* Maj. 9,613
*****Lucas**, Caroline (*b.* 1960) *Green, Brighton Pavilion,*
Maj. 1,252
Lucas, Ian (*b.* 1960) *Lab., Wrexham,* Maj. 3,658
Luff, Sir Peter (*b.* 1955) *C., Worcestershire Mid,*
Maj. 15,864
*****Lumley**, Karen (*b.* 1964) *C., Redditch,* Maj. 5,821
McCabe, Steve (*b.* 1955) *Lab., Birmingham Selly Oak,*
Maj. 3,482
*****McCann**, Michael (*b.* 1964) *Lab., East Kilbride, Strathaven*
& Lesmahagow, Maj. 14,503
McCarthy, Kerry (*b.* 1965) *Lab., Bristol East,* Maj. 3,722
*****McCartney**, Jason (*b.* 1968) *C., Colne Valley,* Maj. 4,837
*****McCartney**, Karl (*b.* 1968) *C., Lincoln,* Maj. 1,058
*****McClymont**, Gregg (*b.* 1976) *Lab., Cumbernauld, Kilsyth*
& Kirkintilloch East, Maj. 13,755
McCrea, Revd Dr William (*b.* 1948) *DUP, Antrim South,*
Maj. 1,183
McDonagh, Siobhain (*b.* 1960) *Lab., Mitcham & Morden,*
Maj. 13,666
§**McDonald**, Andy (*b.* 1958) *Lab., Middlesbrough,*
Maj. 8,211
McDonnell, Dr Alasdair (*b.* 1949) *SDLP, Belfast South,*
Maj. 5,926
McDonnell, John (*b.* 1951) *Lab., Hayes & Harlington,*
Maj. 10,824
McFadden, Rt. Hon. Pat (*b.* 1965) *Lab., Wolverhampton*
South East, Maj. 6,593
*****McGovern**, Alison (*b.* 1980) *Lab., Wirral South,* Maj. 531
McGovern, Jim (*b.* 1956) *Lab., Dundee West,* Maj. 7,278
McGuire, Rt. Hon. Anne (*b.* 1949) *Lab., Stirling,* Maj. 8,354
McIntosh, Anne (*b.* 1954) *C., Thirsk and Malton,*
Maj. 11,281
McKechin, Ann (*b.* 1961) *Lab., Glasgow North,* Maj. 3,898
§**McKenzie**, Iain (*b.* 1959) *Lab., Inverclyde,* Maj. 5,838
*****McKinnell**, Catherine (*b.* 1976) *Lab., Newcastle upon Tyne*
North, Maj. 3,414
*****Macleod**, Mary (*b.* 1969) *C., Brentford & Isleworth,*
Maj. 1,958
McLoughlin, Rt. Hon. Patrick (*b.* 1957) *C., Derbyshire*
Dales, Maj. 13,866
MacNeil, Angus (*b.* 1970) *SNP, Na h-Eileanan an Iar,*
Maj. 1,885
*****McPartland**, Stephen (*b.* 1976) *C., Stevenage,* Maj. 3,578
Mactaggart, Fiona (*b.* 1953) *Lab., Slough,* Maj. 5,523
*****McVey**, Esther (*b.* 1967) *C., Wirral West,* Maj. 2,436
Mahmood, Khalid (*b.* 1961) *Lab., Birmingham Perry Barr,*
Maj. 11,908
*****Mahmood**, Shabana (*b.* 1980) *Lab., Birmingham Ladywood,*
Maj. 10,105
Main, Anne (*b.* 1957) *C., St Albans,* Maj. 2,305
§**Malhotra**, Seema (*b.* 1972) *Lab. (Co-op), Feltham &*
Heston, Maj. 6,203
Mann, John (*b.* 1960) *Lab., Bassetlaw,* Maj. 8,215
Marsden, Gordon (*b.* 1953) *Lab., Blackpool South,*
Maj. 1,852

§**Maskey**, Paul (*b.* 1967) *SF, Belfast West,* Maj. 13,123
Maude, Rt. Hon. Francis (*b.* 1953) *C., Horsham,*
Maj. 11,460
May, Rt. Hon. Theresa (*b.* 1956) *C., Maidenhead,*
Maj. 16,769
*****Maynard**, Paul (*b.* 1975) *C., Blackpool North & Cleveleys,*
Maj. 2,150
Meacher, Rt. Hon. Michael (*b.* 1939) *Lab., Oldham West*
& Royton, Maj. 9,352
Meale, Sir Alan (*b.* 1949) *Lab., Mansfield,* Maj. 6,012
*****Mearns**, Ian (*b.* 1957) *Lab., Gateshead,* Maj. 12,549
*****Menzies**, Mark (*b.* 1971) *C., Fylde,* Maj. 13,185
*****Metcalfe**, Stephen (*b.* 1966) *C., Basildon South & Thurrock*
East, Maj. 5,772
Miliband, Rt. Hon. Edward (*b.* 1969) *Lab., Doncaster North,*
Maj. 10,909
Miller, Andrew (*b.* 1949) *Lab., Ellesmere Port & Neston,*
Maj. 4,331
Miller, Rt. Hon. Maria (*b.* 1964) *C., Basingstoke,*
Maj. 13,176
*****Mills**, Nigel (*b.* 1974) *C., Amber Valley,* Maj. 536
Milton, Anne (*b.* 1955) *C., Guildford,* Maj. 7,782
Mitchell, Rt. Hon. Andrew (*b.* 1956) *C., Sutton Coldfield,*
Maj. 17,005
Mitchell, Austin (*b.* 1934) *Lab., Great Grimsby,* Maj. 714
§**Molloy**, Francie (*b.* 1950) *SF, Ulster Mid,* Maj. 4,681
Moon, Madeleine (*b.* 1950) *Lab., Bridgend,* Maj. 2,263
Moore, Rt. Hon. Michael (*b.* 1965) *LD, Berwickshire,*
Roxburgh & Selkirk, Maj. 5,675
*****Mordaunt**, Penny (*b.* 1973) *C., Portsmouth North,*
Maj. 7,289
Morden, Jessica (*b.* 1968) *Lab., Newport East,* Maj. 1,650
*****Morgan**, Nicky (*b.* 1972) *C., Loughborough,* Maj. 3,744
*****Morrice**, Graeme (*b.* 1959) *Lab., Livingston,* Maj. 10,791
*****Morris**, Anne Marie (*b.* 1957) *C., Newton Abbot,* Maj. 523
*****Morris**, David (*b.* 1966) *C., Morecambe & Lunesdale,*
Maj. 866
*****Morris**, Grahame (*b.* 1961) *Lab., Easington,* Maj. 14,982
*****Morris**, James (*b.* 1967) *C., Halesowen & Rowley Regis,*
Maj. 2,023
*****Mosley**, Stephen (*b.* 1972) *C., Chester, City of,* Maj. 2,583
*****Mowat**, David (*b.* 1957) *C., Warrington South,* Maj. 1,553
Mudie, George (*b.* 1945) *Lab., Leeds East,* Maj. 10,293
Mulholland, Greg (*b.* 1970) *LD, Leeds North West,*
Maj. 9,103
Mundell, Rt. Hon. David (*b.* 1962) *C., Dumfriesshire,*
Clydesdale & Tweeddale, Maj. 4,194
Munn, Meg (*b.* 1959) *Lab. (Co-op), Sheffield Heeley,*
Maj. 5,807
*****Munt**, Tessa (*b.* 1959) *LD, Wells,* Maj. 800
Murphy, Conor (*b.* 1963) *SF, Newry & Armagh,* Maj. 8,331
Murphy, Rt. Hon. Jim (*b.* 1967) *Lab., Renfrewshire East,*
Maj. 10,420
Murphy, Rt. Hon. Paul (*b.* 1948) *Lab., Torfaen,* Maj. 9,306
*****Murray**, Ian (*b.* 1976) *Lab., Edinburgh South,* Maj. 316
*****Murray**, Sheryll (*b.* 1956) *C., Cornwall South East,*
Maj. 3,220
Murrison, Dr Andrew (*b.* 1961) *C., Wiltshire South West,*
Maj. 10,367
*****Nandy**, Lisa (*b.* 1979) *Lab., Wigan,* Maj. 10,487
*****Nash**, Pamela (*b.* 1984) *Lab., Airdrie & Shotts,* Maj. 12,408
Neill, Robert (*b.* 1952) *C., Bromley & Chislehurst,*
Maj. 13,900
Newmark, Brooks (*b.* 1958) *C., Braintree,* Maj. 16,121
*****Newton**, Sarah (*b.* 1962) *C., Truro & Falmouth,* Maj. 435
*****Nokes**, Caroline (*b.* 1972) *C., Romsey & Southampton*
North, Maj. 4,156
*****Norman**, Jesse (*b.* 1962) *C., Hereford & Herefordshire*
South, Maj. 2,481

*Nuttall, David (*b.* 1962) *C., Bury North,* Maj. 2,243
O'Brien, Rt. Hon. Stephen (*b.* 1957) *C., Eddisbury,* Maj. 13,255
*O'Donnell, Fiona (*b.* 1960) *Lab., East Lothian,* Maj. 12,258
*Offord, Matthew (*b.* 1969) *C., Hendon,* Maj. 106
*Ollerenshaw, Eric (*b.* 1950) *C., Lancaster & Fleetwood,* Maj. 333
*Onwurah, Chi (*b.* 1965) *Lab., Newcastle upon Tyne Central,* Maj. 7,464
*Opperman, Guy (*b.* 1965) *C., Hexham,* Maj. 5,788
Osborne, Rt. Hon. George (*b.* 1971) *C., Tatton,* Maj. 14,487
Osborne, Sandra (*b.* 1956) *Lab., Ayr, Carrick & Cumnock,* Maj. 9,911
Ottaway, Rt. Hon. Sir Richard (*b.* 1945) *C., Croydon South,* Maj. 15,818
Owen, Albert (*b.* 1960) *Lab., Ynys Mon,* Maj. 2,461
Paice, Rt. Hon. Sir James (*b.* 1949) *C., Cambridgeshire South East,* Maj. 5,946
*Paisley Jr, Ian (*b.* 1966) *DUP, Antrim North,* Maj. 12,558
*Parish, Neil (*b.* 1956) *C., Tiverton & Honiton,* Maj. 9,320
*Patel, Priti (*b.* 1972) *C., Witham,* Maj. 15,196
Paterson, Rt. Hon. Owen (*b.* 1956) *C., Shropshire North,* Maj. 15,828
*Pawsey, Mark (*b.* 1957) *C., Rugby,* Maj. 6,000
*Pearce, Teresa (*b.* 1955) *Lab., Erith & Thamesmead,* Maj. 5,703
Penning, Mike (*b.* 1957) *C., Hemel Hempstead,* Maj. 13,406
Penrose, John (*b.* 1964) *C., Weston-super-Mare,* Maj. 2,691
*Percy, Andrew (*b.* 1977) *C., Brigg & Goole,* Maj. 5,147
*Perkins, Toby (*b.* 1970) *Lab., Chesterfield,* Maj. 549
*Perry, Claire (*b.* 1964) *C., Devizes,* Maj. 13,005
*Phillips, Stephen (*b.* 1970) *C., Sleaford & Hykeham North,* Maj. 19,905
*Phillipson, Bridget (*b.* 1983) *Lab., Houghton & Sunderland South,* Maj. 10,990
Pickles, Rt. Hon. Eric (*b.* 1952) *C., Brentwood & Ongar,* Maj. 16,920
*Pincher, Christopher (*b.* 1969) *C., Tamworth,* Maj. 6,090
*Poulter, Daniel (*b.* 1978) *C., Suffolk Central & Ipswich North,* Maj. 13,786
Pound, Stephen (*b.* 1948) *Lab., Ealing North,* Maj. 9,301
§Powell, Lucy (*b.* 1974) *Lab., Manchester Central,* Maj. 9,936
Primarolo, Rt. Hon. Dame Dawn, DBE (*b.* 1954) *Lab., Deputy Speaker, Bristol South,* Maj. 4,734
Prisk, Mark (*b.* 1962) *C., Hertford & Stortford,* Maj. 15,437
Pritchard, Mark (*b.* 1966) *C., The Wrekin,* Maj. 9,450
Pugh, Dr John (*b.* 1948) *LD, Southport,* Maj. 6,024
*Qureshi, Yasmin (*b.* 1963) *Lab., Bolton South East,* Maj. 8,634
*Raab, Dominic (*b.* 1974) *C., Esher & Walton,* Maj. 18,593
Randall, Rt. Hon. Sir John (*b.* 1955) *C., Uxbridge & Ruislip South,* Maj. 11,216
Raynsford, Rt. Hon. Nick (*b.* 1945) *Lab., Greenwich & Woolwich,* Maj. 10,153
*Reckless, Mark (*b.* 1970) *C., Rochester & Strood,* Maj. 9,953
Redwood, Rt. Hon. John (*b.* 1951) *C., Wokingham,* Maj. 13,492
Reed, Jamie (*b.* 1973) *Lab., Copeland,* Maj. 3,833
§Reed, Steve (*b.* 1963) *Lab., Croydon North,* Maj. 11,761
*Rees-Mogg, Jacob (*b.* 1969) *C., Somerset North East,* Maj. 4,914
*Reevell, Simon (*b.* 1966) *C., Dewsbury,* Maj. 1,526
*Reeves, Rachel (*b.* 1979) *Lab., Leeds West,* Maj. 7,016
Reid, Alan (*b.* 1954) *LD, Argyll & Bute,* Maj. 3,431
*Reynolds, Emma (*b.* 1977) *Lab., Wolverhampton North East,* Maj. 2,484
*Reynolds, Jonathan (*b.* 1980) *Lab. (Co-op), Stalybridge & Hyde,* Maj. 2,744

Rifkind, Rt. Hon. Sir Malcolm (*b.* 1946) *C., Kensington,* Maj. 8,616
Riordan, Linda (*b.* 1953) *Lab. (Co-op), Halifax,* Maj. 1,472
*Ritchie, Margaret (*b.* 1958) *SDLP, South Down,* Maj. 8,412
Robathan, Rt. Hon. Andrew (*b.* 1951) *C., Leicestershire South,* Maj. 15,524
Robertson, Angus (*b.* 1969) *SNP, Moray,* Maj. 5,590
Robertson, Rt. Hon. Sir Hugh (*b.* 1962) *C., Faversham & Kent Mid,* Maj. 17,088
Robertson, John (*b.* 1952) *Lab., Glasgow North West,* Maj. 13,611
Robertson, Laurence (*b.* 1958) *C., Tewkesbury,* Maj. 6,310
Robinson, Geoffrey (*b.* 1938) *Lab., Coventry North West,* Maj. 6,288
Rogerson, Dan (*b.* 1975) *LD, Cornwall North,* Maj. 2,981
Rosindell, Andrew (*b.* 1966) *C., Romford,* Maj. 16,954
*Rotheram, Steve (*b.* 1961) *Lab., Liverpool Walton,* Maj. 19,818
Roy, Frank (*b.* 1958) *Lab., Motherwell & Wishaw,* Maj. 16,806
Roy, Lindsay (*b.* 1949) *Lab., Glenrothes,* Maj. 16,455
Ruane, Chris (*b.* 1958) *Lab., Vale of Clwyd,* Maj. 2,509
*Rudd, Amber (*b.* 1963) *C., Hastings & Rye,* Maj. 1,993
Ruddock, Rt. Hon. Dame Joan (*b.* 1943) *Lab., Lewisham Deptford,* Maj. 12,499
Ruffley, David (*b.* 1962) *C., Bury St Edmunds,* Maj. 12,380
Russell, Sir Bob (*b.* 1946) *LD, Colchester,* Maj. 6,982
*Rutley, David (*b.* 1961) *C., Macclesfield,* Maj. 11,959
Sanders, Adrian (*b.* 1959) *LD, Torbay,* Maj. 4,078
*Sandys, Laura (*b.* 1964) *C., Thanet South,* Maj. 7,617
*Sarwar, Anas (*b.* 1983) *Lab., Glasgow Central,* Maj. 10,551
§Sawford, Andy (*b.* 1976) *Lab. (Co-op), Corby,* Maj. 7,791
Scott, Lee (*b.* 1956) *C., Ilford North,* Maj. 5,404
Seabeck, Alison (*b.* 1954) *Lab., Plymouth Moor View,* Maj. 1,588
Selous, Andrew (*b.* 1962) *C., Bedfordshire South West,* Maj. 16,649
*Shannon, Jim (*b.* 1955) *DUP, Strangford,* Maj. 5,876
Shapps, Rt. Hon. Grant (*b.* 1968) *C., Welwyn Hatfield,* Maj. 7,423
*Sharma, Alok (*b.* 1967) *C., Reading West,* Maj. 6,004
Sharma, Virendra (*b.* 1947) *Lab., Ealing Southall,* Maj. 9,291
Sheerman, Barry (*b.* 1940) *Lab. (Co-op), Huddersfield,* Maj. 4,472
*Shelbrooke, Alec (*b.* 1976) *C., Elmet & Rothwell,* Maj. 4,521
Shepherd, Sir Richard (*b.* 1942) *C., Aldridge-Brownhills,* Maj. 15,256
Sheridan, Jim (*b.* 1952) *Lab., Paisley & Renfrewshire North,* Maj. 15,280
*Shuker, Gavin (*b.* 1981) *Lab. (Co-op), Luton South,* Maj. 2,329
Simmonds, Mark (*b.* 1964) *C., Boston & Skegness,* Maj. 12,426
Simpson, David (*b.* 1959) *DUP, Upper Bann,* Maj. 3,361
†Simpson, Keith (*b.* 1949) *C., Broadland,* Maj. 7,292
*Skidmore, Chris (*b.* 1981) *C., Kingswood,* Maj. 2,445
Skinner, Dennis (*b.* 1932) *Lab., Bolsover,* Maj. 11,182
Slaughter, Andrew (*b.* 1960) *Lab., Hammersmith,* Maj. 3,549
Smith, Rt. Hon. Andrew (*b.* 1951) *Lab., Oxford East,* Maj. 4,581
Smith, Angela C. (*b.* 1961) *Lab., Penistone & Stocksbridge,* Maj. 3,049
Smith, Chloe (*b.* 1982) *C., Norwich North,* Maj. 3,901
*Smith, Henry (*b.* 1969) *C., Crawley,* Maj. 5,928
*Smith, Julian (*b.* 1971) *C., Skipton & Ripon,* Maj. 9,950
*Smith, Nick (*b.* 1960) *Lab., Blaenau Gwent,* Maj. 10,516

GENERAL ELECTION RESULTS

The results of voting in each parliamentary division at the general election of 6 May 2010 are given below.

BOUNDARY CHANGES
The constituency boundaries were redrawn for the 2010 election in England, Wales and Northern Ireland. As a result of the review the number of constituencies increased from 646 to 650, with four new seats in England. Only 138 constituencies had no boundary changes, 59 of them in Scotland.

For the majority of constituencies where a boundary change has taken place, it is not appropriate to make a direct comparison between the results of 2005 and 2010. The seat of Hammersmith, for example, comprises 60 per cent of the old Hammersmith and Fulham constituency and 40 per cent

of the old Ealing and Shepherds Bush constituency; it cannot therefore be described as a simple hold for the Labour party. The term 'notional' used here refers to a theoretical set of results, published by Professors Rallings and Thrasher of Plymouth University, which estimates the way each new constituency might have voted in the 2005 general election.

KEY
* New MP
† Previously MP in another seat
‡ Previously MP for another party
§ Notional result; see explanation of boundary changes
¶ By-election held since 2010 general election
E. Electorate   T. Turnout

Abbreviations

		DUP	Democratic Unionist Party	Macc. Ind.	The Macclesfield Independent
		Elvis	Elvis Loves Pets	Magna Carta	The Magna Carta Party
AD	Apolitical Democrats	Eng. Dem.	English Democrats	Mansfield	Mansfield Independent
Alliance	Alliance	Eng. Ind.	English Independence	Ind.	Forum
Animals	Animals Count		Party	Meb. Ker.	Mebyon Kernow
Anti-War	Fight for an Anti-War	F and R	For Freedom and	Med. Ind.	Medway Independent
	Government		Responsibility	Mid. England	Middle England Party
APP	Animal Protection Party	FDP	Fancy Dress Party	MP Expense	A Vote Against MP Expense
Battersea	Putting the People of	Good	The Common Good		Abuse
	Battersea First	Green	Green	MRP	Money Reform Party
BB	A Better Britain for All	Green Belt	Independent Save Our	Nat. Dem.	National Democrat
BB&C	Beer, Baccy and Crumpet		Green Belt	ND	No Description
BCP	Basingstoke Common Man	Green Soc.	Alliance for Green Socialism	New Party	The New Party
Bean	New Millennium Bean	Humanity	Humanity	NF	National Front
Beer	Reduce Tax on Beer Party	Impact	Impact Party	NFP	Nationwide Reform Party
Best	The Best of a Bad Bunch	Ind.	Independent	NHA	National Health Action
BIB	Bushra Irfan of Blackburn	Ind. CCF	New Independent	Nine11	Nine Eleven Was An Inside
BIC	Bromsgrove Independent		Conservative Chelsea		Job
	Conservative		and Fulham	No Vote	No Candidate Deserves
Blaenau	Blaenau Gwent People's	Ind. CHC	Independent Community		My Vote
Voice	Voice		and Health Concern	Nobody	Nobody Party
Blue	Blue Environment Party	Ind. EACPS	Independent Ealing Action	NSPS	Northampton – Save Our
BNP	British National Party		Communities Public		Public Services
BP Elvis	Bus-Pass Elvis Party		Services	Parenting	Equal Parenting Alliance
C.	Conservative	Ind. Fed.	Independents Federation UK	PBP	People Before Profit
Ch. M.	Christian Movement for	Ind. People	Independent People	PC	Plaid Cymru
	Great Britain		Together	Peace	Peace Party
Ch. P.	Christian Party	Ind. Rantzen	Independent Rantzen	PDP	People's Democratic Party
Christian	Christian	Ind. Voice	Independent Voice for	Pirate	Pirate Party UK
CIP	Campaign for		Halifax	PNDP	People's National
	Independent Politicians	Integrity	Integrity UK		Democratic Party
City Ind.	City Independent	ISP	Independent Socialist Party	Poetry	The True English (Poetry)
Clause 28	Clause 28, Children's	IZB	Islam Zinda Baad Platform		Party
	Protection Christian	J & AC	Justice & Anti-Corruption	PP Essex	Peoples Party Essex
	Democrats		Party	PPN-V	Peace Party Non-Violence
CLR	Cannabis Law Reform	Jacobite	Scottish Jacobite Party		Justice Environment
CME	Church of the Militant	Joy	The Joy of Talk	PSP	Patriotic Socialist Party
	Elvis	JP	Justice Party	R and E	Citizens for Undead Rights
CNBPG	Community Need Before	King George	Save King George Hospital		and Equality
	Private Greed	Lab.	Labour	RA	Solihull and Meriden
Comm.	Communist Party	Lab. (Co-op)	Labour and Co-operative		Residents' Association
Comm. Brit.	Communist Party of Britain	Land	Land is Power	RAL	Residents' Association of
Comm. Lge	Communist League	LD	Liberal Democrat		London
Cornish D.	Cornish Democrats	Leave EU	Independent Leave the EU	Reform	Reform 2000
CPA	Christian People's Alliance		Alliance	Respect	Respect the Unity Coalition
CSP	Common Sense Party	Lib.	Liberal	RP	The Restoration Party
CUP	Communities United Party	Libertarian	Libertarian Party	RRG	Radical Reform Group
Currency	Virtue Currency Cognitive	Lincs. Ind.	Lincolnshire Independents	SACL	Scotland Against Crooked
	Appraisal Party	LLPBPP	Local Liberals People Before		Lawyers
D. Nat.	Democratic Nationalist		Politics Party	Save QM	Independents to Save
DDP	Direct Democracy Party	Loony	Monster Raving Loony Party		Queen Mary's Hospital
Deficit	Cut the Deficit Party	LPBP	London People Before Profit	Science	The Science Party
Dem. 2015	Democracy 2015	LTT	Lawfulness Trustworthiness	SDLP	Social Democratic and
Dem. Lab.	Democratic Labour Party		and Transparency		Labour Party

SEP	Socialist Equality Party
SF	Sinn Fein
SMA	Scrap Members Allowances
Snouts	Get Snouts Out The Trough
SNP	Scottish National Party
Soc.	Socialist Party
Soc. Alt.	Socialist Alternative Party
Soc. Dem.	Social Democratic Party
Soc. Lab.	Socialist Labour Party
South	All the South Party
Speaker	The Speaker
SSP	Scottish Socialist Party
Staffs Ind.	Staffordshire Independent Group
Stop	Stop Commercial Banks Owning Britain's Money

Tendring	Tendring First
TOC	Tamsin Omond to the Commons
Trust	Trust
TUSC	Trade Unionist and Socialist Coalition
TUV	Traditional Unionist Voice
UCUNF	Ulster Conservatives and Unionists – New Force
UK Integrity	Independents Federation UK – Honest Integrity Democracy
UKIP	UK Independence Party
UPP	United People's Party

UPS	Unity for Peace and Socialism
Voice	United Voice
Wessex Reg.	Wessex Regionalist
Workers Lib.	Alliance for Workers Liberty
WP	Workers' Party
WR	Wessex Regionalists
WRP	Workers' Revolutionary Party
You	You Party
Youth	Youth Party
YP	Go Mad and Vote For Yourself Party
YPP	Young People's Party
YRDPL	Your Right to Democracy Party Limited

PARLIAMENTARY CONSTITUENCIES AS AT 6 MAY 2010 GENERAL ELECTION

UK Turnout
E. 45,533,536 T. 29,643,522 (65.1%)

ENGLAND

§ALDERSHOT
E. 71,469   T. 45,384 (63.50%)   C. hold
Gerald Howarth, C.   21,203
Adrian Collett, LD   15,617
Jonathan Slater, Lab.   5,489
Robert Snare, UKIP   2,041
Gary Crowd, Eng. Ind.   803
Juliana Brimicombe, Ch. P.   231
C. majority 5,586 (12.31%)
Notional 1.41% swing C. to LD
(2005: C. majority 6,345 (15.12%))

§ALDRIDGE-BROWNHILLS
E. 59,355   T. 38,634 (65.09%)   C. hold
Richard Shepherd, C.   22,913
Ashiq Hussain, Lab.   7,647
Ian Jenkins, LD   6,833
Karl Macnaughton, Green   847
Sue Gray, Ch. P.   394
C. majority 15,266 (39.51%)
Notional 12.01% swing Lab. to C.
(2005: C. majority 5,732 (15.49%))

§ALTRINCHAM & SALE WEST
E. 71,254   T. 49,393 (69.32%)   C. hold
Graham Brady, C.   24,176
Jane Brophy, LD   12,581
Tom Ross, Lab.   11,073
Kenneth Bullman, UKIP   1,563
C. majority 11,595 (23.47%)
Notional 0.83% swing C. to LD
(2005: C. majority 7,618 (17.57%))

§AMBER VALLEY
E. 70,171   T. 45,958 (65.49%)   C. gain
*Nigel Mills, C.   17,746
Judy Mallaber, Lab.   17,210
Tom Snowdon, LD   6,636
Michael Clarke, BNP   3,195
Sue Ransome, UKIP   906
Sam Thing, Loony   265
C. majority 536 (1.17%)
Notional 6.85% swing Lab. to C.
(2005: Lab. majority 5,512 (12.53%))

§ARUNDEL & SOUTH DOWNS
E. 77,564   T. 55,982 (72.18%)   C. hold
Nick Herbert, C.   32,333
Derek Deedman, LD   15,642
Tim Lunnon, Lab.   4,835
Stuart Bower, UKIP   3,172
C. majority 16,691 (29.81%)
Notional 3.00% swing LD to C.
(2005: C. majority 12,291 (23.81%))

§ASHFIELD
E. 77,379   T. 48,196 (62.29%)   Lab. hold
*Gloria De Piero, Lab.   16,239
Jason Zadrozny, LD   16,047
Garry Hickton, C.   10,698
Edward Holmes, BNP   2,781
Tony Ellis, Eng. Dem.   1,102
Terry Coleman, UKIP   933
Eddie Smith, Ind.   396
Lab. majority 192 (0.40%)
Notional 17.23% swing Lab. to LD
(2005: Lab. majority 10,370 (24.28%))

§ASHFORD
E. 81,269   T. 55,185 (67.90%)   C. hold
Damian Green, C.   29,878
Chris Took, LD   12,581
Chris Clark, Lab.   9,204
Jeffrey Elenor, UKIP   2,508
Steve Campkin, Green   1,014
C. majority 17,297 (31.34%)
Notional 2.25% swing C. to LD
(2005: C. majority 12,268 (25.02%))

§ASHTON UNDER LYNE
E. 67,564   T. 38,432 (56.88%)   Lab. hold
David Heyes, Lab.   18,604
Seema Kennedy, C.   9,510
Paul Larkin, LD   5,703
David Lomas, BNP   2,929
Angela McManus, UKIP   1,686
Lab. majority 9,094 (23.66%)
Notional 7.34% swing Lab. to C.
(2005: Lab. majority 13,199 (38.33%))

§AYLESBURY
E. 77,934   T. 53,162 (68.21%)   C. hold
David Lidington, C.   27,736
Steven Lambert, LD   15,118
Kathryn White, Lab.   6,695
Chris Adams, UKIP   3,613
C. majority 12,618 (23.73%)
Notional 2.12% swing LD to C.
(2005: C. majority 9,314 (19.49%))

§BANBURY
E. 86,986   T. 56,241 (64.66%)   C. hold
Tony Baldry, C.   29,703
David Rundle, LD   11,476
Les Sibley, Lab.   10,773
Dr David Fairweather, UKIP   2,806
Alastair White, Green   959
Roseanne Edwards, Ind.   524
C. majority 18,227 (32.41%)
Notional 1.51% swing LD to C.
(2005: C. majority 10,090 (18.79%))

§BARKING
E. 73,864   T. 45,343 (61.39%)   Lab. hold
Margaret Hodge, Lab.   24,628
Simon Marcus, C.   8,073
Nick Griffin, BNP   6,620
Dominic Carman, LD   3,719
Frank Maloney, UKIP   1,300
George Hargreaves, Ch. P.   482
Jayne Forbes, Green   317
Crucial Chris Dowling, Loony   82
Thomas Darwood, Ind.   77
Dapo Sijuwola, RP   45
Lab. majority 16,555 (36.51%)
Notional 1.73% swing C. to Lab.
(2005: Lab. majority 12,183 (33.04%))

§¶BARNSLEY CENTRAL
E. 65,543   T. 37,001 (56.45%)   Lab. hold
Eric Illsley, Lab.   17,487
Christopher Wiggin, LD   6,394
Piers Tempest, C.   6,388
Ian Sutton, BNP   3,307
David Silver, UKIP   1,727
Donald Wood, Ind.   732
Tony Devoy, Ind.   610
Terry Robinson, Soc. Lab.   356
Lab. majority 11,093 (29.98%)
Notional 4.17% swing Lab. to LD
(2005: Lab. majority 11,839 (38.32%))

§BARNSLEY EAST
E. 68,435   T. 38,386 (56.09%)   Lab. hold
*Michael Dugher, Lab.   18,059
John Brown, LD   6,969
James Hockney, C.   6,329
Colin Porter, BNP   3,301
Tony Watson, UKIP   1,731
Kevin Hogan, Ind.   712
Eddie Devoy, Ind.   684
Ken Capstick, Soc. Lab.   601
Lab. majority 11,090 (28.89%)
Notional 14.02% swing Lab. to LD
(2005: Lab. majority 18,298 (56.94%))

§BARROW & FURNESS
E. 68,758 T. 44,124 (64.17%)
Lab. Co-op hold
*John Woodcock, Lab. Co-op   21,226
John Gough, C.   16,018
Barry Rabone, LD   4,424
John Smith, UKIP   841
Mike Ashburner, BNP   840
Christopher Loynes, Green   530
Brian Greaves, Ind.   245
Lab. Co-op majority 5,208 (11.80%)
Notional 0.37% swing Lab. to C.
(2005: Lab. Co-op majority 4,843 (12.54%))

§BASILDON & BILLERICAY
E. 65,482 T. 41,569 (63.48%) C. hold
John Baron, C.   21,922
Allan Davies, Lab.   9,584
Mike Hibbs, LD   6,538
Irene Bateman, BNP   1,934
Alan Broad, UKIP   1,591
C. majority 12,338 (29.68%)
Notional 9.23% swing Lab. to C.
(2005: C. majority 4,559 (11.22%))

§BASILDON SOUTH & THURROCK
EAST
E. 71,815 T. 44,735 (62.29%) C. gain
*Stephen Metcalfe, C.   19,624
Angela Smith, Lab. Co-op   13,852
Geoff Williams, LD   5,977
Kerry Smith, UKIP   2,639
Chris Roberts, BNP   2,518
None Of The Above X, ND   125
C. majority 5,772 (12.90%)
Notional 7.52% swing Lab. to C.
(2005: Lab. majority 905 (2.14%))

§BASINGSTOKE
E. 75,470 T. 50,654 (67.12%) C. hold
Maria Miller, C.   25,590
John Shaw, LD   12,414
Funda Pepperell, Lab.   10,327
Stella Howell, UKIP   2,076
Steve Saul, BCP   247
C. majority 13,176 (26.01%)
Notional 4.55% swing LD to C.
(2005: C. majority 2,651 (6.27%))

§BASSETLAW
E. 76,542 T. 49,577 (64.77%) Lab. hold
John Mann, Lab.   25,018
Keith Girling, C.   16,803
David Dobbie, LD   5,570
Andrea Hamilton, UKIP   1,779
Grahame Whithurst, Ind.   407
Lab. majority 8,215 (16.57%)
Notional 0.67% swing Lab. to C.
(2005: Lab. majority 8,256 (17.92%))

§BATH
E. 65,603 T. 47,086 (71.77%) LD hold
Don Foster, LD   26,651
Fabian Richter, C.   14,768
Hattie Ajderian, Lab.   3,251
Eric Lucas, Green   1,120
Ernie Warrender, UKIP   890
Steve Hewett, Ch. P.   250
ANON, ND   69
Sean Geddis, Ind.   56
Robert Craig, South   31
LD majority 11,883 (25.24%)
Notional 5.84% swing C. to LD
(2005: LD majority 5,624 (13.56%))

§BATLEY & SPEN
E. 76,732 T. 51,109 (66.61%) Lab. hold
Mike Wood, Lab.   21,565
Janice Small, C.   17,159
Neil Bentley, LD   8,095
David Exley, BNP   3,685
Matt Blakeley, Green   605
Lab. majority 4,406 (8.62%)
Notional 2.46% swing Lab. to C.
(2005: Lab. majority 6,060 (13.54%))

§BATTERSEA
E. 74,300 T. 48,792 (65.67%) C. gain
*Jane Ellison, C.   23,103
Martin Linton, Lab.   17,126
Layla Moran, LD   7,176
Guy Evans, Green   559
Christopher MacDonald, UKIP   505
Hugh Salmon, Battersea   168
Tom Fox, Ind.   155
C. majority 5,977 (12.25%)
Notional 6.53% swing Lab. to C.
(2005: Lab. majority 332 (0.81%))

§BEACONSFIELD
E. 74,982 T. 52,490 (70.00%) C. hold
Dominic Grieve, C.   32,053
John Edwards, LD   10,271
Jeremy Miles, Lab.   6,135
Delphine Gray-Fisk, UKIP   2,597
Jem Bailey, Green   768
Andrew Cowen, MP Expense   475
Quentin Baron, Ind.   191
C. majority 21,782 (41.50%)
Notional 4.70% swing LD to C.
(2005: C. majority 14,794 (32.09%))

§BECKENHAM
E. 66,219 T. 47,686 (72.01%) C. hold
*Bob Stewart, C.   27,597
Steve Jenkins, LD   9,813
Damien Egan, Lab.   6,893
Owen Brolly, UKIP   1,551
Roger Tonks, BNP   1,001
Ann Garrett, Green   608
Dan Eastgate, Eng. Dem.   223
C. majority 17,784 (37.29%)
Notional 3.15% swing C. to LD
(2005: C. majority 16,913 (40.40%))

§BEDFORD
E. 68,491 T. 45,102 (65.85%) C. gain
*Richard Fuller, C.   17,546
Patrick Hall, Lab.   16,193
Henry Vann, LD   8,957
Mark Adkin, UKIP   1,136
William Dewick, BNP   757
Ben Foley, Green   393
Samrat Bhandari, Ind.   120
C. majority 1,353 (3.00%)
Notional 5.52% swing Lab. to C.
(2005: Lab. majority 3,413 (8.04%))

§BEDFORDSHIRE MID
E. 76,023 T. 54,897 (72.21%) C. hold
Nadine Dorries, C.   28,815
Linda Jack, LD   13,663
David Reeves, Lab.   8,108
Bill Hall, UKIP   2,826
Malcolm Bailey, Green   773
John Cooper, Eng. Dem.   712
C. majority 15,152 (27.60%)
Notional 2.26% swing LD to C.
(2005: C. majority 11,593 (23.08%))

§BEDFORDSHIRE NORTH EAST
E. 78,060 T. 55,552 (71.17%) C. hold
Alistair Burt, C.   30,989
Mike Pitt, LD   12,047
Edward Brown, Lab.   8,957
Brian Capell, UKIP   2,294
Ian Seeby, BNP   1,265
C. majority 18,942 (34.10%)
Notional 2.55% swing LD to C.
(2005: C. majority 12,128 (24.59%))

BEDFORDSHIRE SOUTH WEST
E. 76,559 T. 50,774 (66.32%) C. hold
Andrew Selous, C.   26,815
Rod Cantrill, LD   10,166
Jennifer Bone, Lab.   9,948
Martin Newman, UKIP   2,142
Mark Tolman, BNP   1,703
C. majority 16,649 (32.79%)
0.69% swing LD to C.
(2005: C. majority 8,277 (18.07%))

§BERMONDSEY & OLD SOUTHWARK
E. 77,623 T. 44,651 (57.52%) LD hold
Simon Hughes, LD   21,590
Val Shawcross, Lab.   13,060
Loanna Morrison, C.   7,638
Stephen Tyler, BNP   1,370
Tom Chance, Green   718
Alan Kirkby, Ind.   155
Steve Freeman, ND   120
LD majority 8,530 (19.10%)
Notional 1.55% swing Lab. to LD
(2005: LD majority 5,769 (16.00%))

§BERWICK-UPON-TWEED
E. 57,403 T. 38,439 (66.96%) LD hold
Sir Alan Beith, LD   16,806
Anne-Marie Trevelyan, C.   14,116
Alan Strickland, Lab.   5,061
Michael Weatheritt, UKIP   1,243
Peter Mailer, BNP   1,213
LD majority 2,690 (7.00%)
Notional 8.29% swing LD to C.
(2005: LD majority 8,585 (23.58%))

§BETHNAL GREEN & BOW
E. 81,243 T. 50,728 (62.44%) Lab. gain
*Rushanara Ali, Lab.   21,784
Ajmal Masroor, LD   10,210
Abjol Miah, Respect   8,532
Zakir Khan, C.   7,071
Jeffrey Marshall, BNP   1,405
Farid Bakht, Green   856
Patrick Brooks, Ind.   277
Alexander Van Terheyden, Pirate   213
Hasib Hikmat, Voice   209
Haji Choudhury, Ind.   100
Ahmed Malik, Ind.   71
Lab. majority 11,574 (22.82%)
Notional 14.11% swing Respect to Lab.
(2005: Respect majority 804 (2.10%))

§BEVERLEY & HOLDERNESS
E. 79,611 T. 53,199 (66.82%) C. hold
Graham Stuart, C.   25,063
Craig Dobson, LD   12,076
Ian Saunders, Lab.   11,224
Neil Whitelam, BNP   2,080
Andrew Horsfield, UKIP   1,845
Bill Rigby, Green   686
Ron Hughes, Ind.   225
C. majority 12,987 (24.41%)
Notional 1.58% swing LD to C.
(2005: C. majority 3,097 (6.23%))

§BEXHILL & BATTLE
E. 79,208 T. 54,587 (68.92%) C. hold
Greg Barker, C.   28,147
Mary Varrall, LD   15,267
James Royston, Lab.   6,524
Stuart Wheeler, Trust   2,699
Neil Jackson, BNP   1,950
C. majority 12,880 (23.60%)
Notional 3.96% swing C. to LD
(2005: C. majority 15,893 (31.52%))

§BEXLEYHEATH & CRAYFORD
E. 64,985   T. 43,182 (66.45%)   C. hold
David Evennett, C.   21,794
Howard Dawber, Lab.   11,450
Karelia Scott, LD   5,502
Stephen James, BNP   2,042
John Dunford, UKIP   1,557
John Griffiths, Eng. Dem.   466
Adrian Ross, Green   371
C. majority 10,344 (23.95%)
Notional 5.81% swing Lab. to C.
(2005: C. majority 5,167 (12.33%))

§BIRKENHEAD
E. 62,773   T. 35,323 (56.27%)   Lab. hold
Frank Field, Lab.   22,082
Andrew Gilbert, C.   6,687
Stuart Kelly, LD   6,554
Lab. majority 15,395 (43.58%)
Notional 2.34% swing Lab. to C.
(2005: Lab. majority 14,638 (46.21%))

§BIRMINGHAM EDGBASTON
E. 68,573   T. 41,571 (60.62%)   Lab. hold
Gisela Stuart, Lab.   16,894
Deirdre Alden, C.   15,620
Roger Harmer, LD   6,387
Trevor Lloyd, BNP   1,196
Greville Warwick, UKIP   732
Phil Simpson, Green   469
Harry Takhar, Impact   146
Charith Fernando, Ch. P.   127
Lab. majority 1,274 (3.06%)
Notional 0.47% swing Lab. to C.
(2005: Lab. majority 1,555 (4.01%))

§BIRMINGHAM ERDINGTON
E. 66,405   T. 35,546 (53.53%)   Lab. hold
*Jack Dromey, Lab.   14,869
Robert Alden, C.   11,592
Ann Holtom, LD   5,742
Kevin McHugh, BNP   1,815
Maria Foy, UKIP   842
Tony Tomkins, Ind.   240
Terry Williams, NF   229
Timothy Gray, Ch. P.   217
Lab. majority 3,277 (9.22%)
Notional 10.43% swing Lab. to C.
(2005: Lab. majority 9,677 (30.07%))

§BIRMINGHAM HALL GREEN
E. 76,580   T. 48,727 (63.63%)   Lab. hold
Roger Godsiff, Lab.   16,039
Salma Yaqoob, Respect   12,240
Jerry Evans, LD   11,988
Jo Barker, C.   7,320
Alan Blumenthal, UKIP   950
Andrew Gardner, Ind.   190
Lab. majority 3,799 (7.80%)
Notional 11.07% swing Lab. to Respect
(2005: Lab. majority 6,649 (15.90%))

§BIRMINGHAM HODGE HILL
E. 75,040   T. 42,472 (56.60%)   Lab. hold
Liam Byrne, Lab.   22,077
Tariq Khan, LD   11,775
Shailesh Parekh, C.   4,936
Richard Lumby, BNP   2,333
Waheed Rafiq, UKIP   714
Peter Johnson, Soc. Dem.   637
Lab. majority 10,302 (24.26%)
Notional 3.61% swing LD to Lab.
(2005: Lab. majority 7,063 (17.05%))

§BIRMINGHAM LADYWOOD
E. 73,646   T. 35,833 (48.66%)   Lab. hold
*Shabana Mahmood, Lab.   19,950
Ayoub Khan, LD   9,845
Nusrat Ghani, C.   4,277
Christopher Booth, UKIP   902
Peter Beck, Green   859
Lab. majority 10,105 (28.20%)
Notional 2.49% swing LD to Lab.
(2005: Lab. majority 6,804 (23.23%))

§BIRMINGHAM NORTHFIELD
E. 71,338   T. 41,814 (58.61%)   Lab. hold
Richard Burden, Lab.   16,841
Keely Huxtable, C.   14,059
Mike Dixon, LD   6,550
Les Orton, BNP   2,290
John Borthwick, UKIP   1,363
Susan Pearce, Green   406
Dick Rodgers, Good   305
Lab. majority 2,782 (6.65%)
Notional 6.64% swing Lab. to C.
(2005: Lab. majority 7,879 (19.93%))

§BIRMINGHAM PERRY BARR
E. 71,304   T. 42,045 (58.97%)   Lab. hold
Khalid Mahmood, Lab.   21,142
Karen Hamilton, LD   9,234
William Norton, C.   8,960
Melvin Ward, UKIP   1,675
John Tyrrell, Soc. Lab.   527
Deborah Hey-Smith, Ch. P.   507
Lab. majority 11,908 (28.32%)
Notional 4.05% swing LD to Lab.
(2005: Lab. majority 7,825 (20.22%))

§BIRMINGHAM SELLY OAK
E. 74,805   T. 46,563 (62.25%)   Lab. hold
Steve McCabe, Lab.   17,950
Nigel Dawkins, C.   14,468
David Radcliffe, LD   10,371
Lynette Orton, BNP   1,820
Jeffrey Burgess, UKIP   1,131
James Burn, Green   664
Samuel Leeds, Ch. P.   159
Lab. majority 3,482 (7.48%)
Notional 4.83% swing Lab. to C.
(2005: Lab. majority 7,564 (17.14%))

§BIRMINGHAM YARDLEY
E. 72,321   T. 40,850 (56.48%)   LD hold
John Hemming, LD   16,162
Lynnette Kelly, Lab.   13,160
Meirion Jenkins, C.   7,836
Tanya Lumby, BNP   2,153
Graham Duffen, UKIP   1,190
Paul Morris, NF   349
LD majority 3,002 (7.35%)
Notional 0.02% swing Lab. to LD
(2005: LD majority 2,864 (7.30%))

§BISHOP AUCKLAND
E. 68,370   T. 41,136 (60.17%)   Lab. hold
Helen Goodman, Lab.   16,023
Barbara Harrison, C.   10,805
Mark Wilkes, LD   9,189
Adam Walker, BNP   2,036
Sam Zair, LLPBPP   1,964
Dave Brothers, UKIP   1,119
Lab. majority 5,218 (12.68%)
Notional 7.20% swing Lab. to C.
(2005: Lab. majority 10,047 (26.35%))

§BLACKBURN
E. 72,331   T. 45,499 (62.90%)   Lab. hold
Jack Straw, Lab.   21,751
Michael Law-Riding, C.   11,895
Paul English, LD   6,918
Robin Evans, BNP   2,158
Bushra Irfanullah, BIB   1,424
Bobby Anwar, UKIP   942
Grace Astley, Ind.   238
Janis Sharp, Ind.   173
Lab. majority 9,856 (21.66%)
Notional 1.11% swing C. to Lab.
(2005: Lab. majority 8,048 (19.45%))

§BLACKLEY & BROUGHTON
E. 69,489   T. 34,204 (49.22%)   Lab. hold
Graham Stringer, Lab.   18,563
James Edsberg, C.   6,260
William Hobhouse, LD   4,861
Derek Adams, BNP   2,469
Kay Phillips, Respect   996
Bob Willescroft, UKIP   894
Shafiq-Uz Zaman, Ch. P.   161
Lab. majority 12,303 (35.97%)
Notional 6.74% swing Lab. to C.
(2005: Lab. majority 13,060 (43.35%))

§BLACKPOOL NORTH & CLEVELEYS
E. 65,888   T. 40,591 (61.61%)   C. gain
*Paul Maynard, C.   16,964
Penny Martin, Lab.   14,814
Bill Greene, LD   5,400
Roy Hopwood, UKIP   1,659
James Clayton, BNP   1,556
Tony Davies, Loony   198
C. majority 2,150 (5.30%)
Notional 6.89% swing Lab. to C.
(2005: Lab. majority 3,241 (8.48%))

§BLACKPOOL SOUTH
E. 63,025   T. 35,191 (55.84%)   Lab. hold
Gordon Marsden, Lab.   14,448
Ron Bell, C.   12,597
Doreen Holt, LD   5,082
Roy Goodwin, BNP   1,482
Hamish Howitt, UKIP   1,352
Si Thu Tun, Integrity   230
Lab. majority 1,851 (5.26%)
Notional 6.21% swing Lab. to C.
(2005: Lab. majority 5,911 (17.67%))

§BLAYDON
E. 67,808   T. 44,913 (66.24%)   Lab. hold
Dave Anderson, Lab.   22,297
Neil Bradbury, LD   13,180
Glenn Hall, C.   7,159
Keith McFarlane, BNP   2,277
Lab. majority 9,117 (20.30%)
Notional 3.28% swing LD to Lab.
(2005: Lab. majority 5,748 (13.75%))

BLYTH VALLEY
E. 64,263   T. 38,566 (60.01%)   Lab. hold
Ronnie Campbell, Lab.   17,156
Jeffrey Reid, LD   10,488
Barry Flux, C.   6,412
Steve Fairbairn, BNP   1,699
James Condon, UKIP   1,665
Barry Elliott, Ind.   819
Allan White, Eng. Dem.   327
Lab. majority 6,668 (17.29%)
3.27% swing Lab. to LD
(2005: Lab. majority 8,527 (23.84%))

§BOGNOR REGIS & LITTLEHAMPTON
E. 70,812   T. 46,852 (66.16%)   C. hold
Nick Gibb, C.   24,087
Simon McDougall, LD   11,024
Michael Jones, Lab.   6,580
Douglas Denny, UKIP   3,036
Andrew Moffat, BNP   1,890
Melissa Briggs, Ind.   235
C. majority 13,063 (27.88%)
Notional 2.31% swing LD to C.
(2005: C. majority 8,617 (20.15%))

§BOLSOVER
E. 72,766   T. 43,988 (60.45%)   Lab. hold
Dennis Skinner, Lab.   21,994
Lee Rowley, C.   10,812
Denise Hawksworth, LD   6,821
Martin Radford, BNP   2,640
Ray Calladine, UKIP   1,721
Lab. majority 11,182 (25.42%)
Notional 11.23% swing Lab. to C.
(2005: Lab. majority 19,260 (47.68%))

§BOLTON NORTH EAST
E. 67,281   T. 43,277 (64.32%)   Lab. hold
David Crausby, Lab.   19,870
Deborah Dunleavy, C.   15,786
Paul Ankers, LD   5,624
Neil Johnson, UKIP   1,815
Norma Armston, You   182
Lab. majority 4,084 (9.44%)
Notional 1.27% swing Lab. to C.
(2005: Lab. majority 4,527 (11.99%))

§BOLTON SOUTH EAST
E. 69,928   T. 39,604 (56.64%)   Lab. hold
*Yasmin Qureshi, Lab.   18,782
Andy Morgan, C.   10,148
Donal O'Hanlon, LD   6,289
Sheila Spink, BNP   3,013
Ian Sidaway, UKIP   1,564
Alan Johnson, Green   614
Navaid Syed, CPA   195
Lab. majority 8,634 (21.80%)
Notional 5.61% swing Lab. to C.
(2005: Lab. majority 11,483 (33.03%))

§BOLTON WEST
E. 71,250   T. 47,576 (66.77%)   Lab. hold
*Julie Hilling, Lab.   18,327
Susan Williams, C.   18,235
Jackie Pearcey, LD   8,177
Harry Lamb, UKIP   1,901
Rachel Mann, Green   545
Jimmy Jones, Ind.   254
Doug Bagnall, You   137
Lab. majority 92 (0.19%)
Notional 5.88% swing Lab. to C.
(2005: Lab. majority 5,041 (11.95%))

§BOOTLE
E. 71,426   T. 41,277 (57.79%)   Lab. hold
Joe Benton, Lab.   27,426
James Murray, LD   6,245
Sohail Qureshi, C.   3,678
Paul Nuttall, UKIP   2,514
Charles Stewart, BNP   942
Pete Glover, TUSC   472
Lab. majority 21,181 (51.31%)
Notional 1.59% swing Lab. to LD
(2005: Lab. majority 20,125 (54.48%))

§BOSTON & SKEGNESS
E. 70,529   T. 43,125 (61.15%)   C. hold
Mark Simmonds, C.   21,325
Paul Kenny, Lab.   8,899
Philip Smith, LD   6,371
Christopher Pain, UKIP   4,081
David Owens, BNP   2,278
Peter Wilson, Ind.   171
C. majority 12,426 (28.81%)
Notional 7.00% swing Lab. to C.
(2005: C. majority 6,391 (14.81%))

§BOSWORTH
E. 77,296   T. 54,274 (70.22%)   C. hold
David Tredinnick, C.   23,132
Michael Mullaney, LD   18,100
Rory Palmer, Lab.   8,674
John Ryde, BNP   2,458
Dutch Veldhuizen, UKIP   1,098
James Lampitt, Eng. Dem.   615
Michael Brooks, Science   197
C. majority 5,032 (9.27%)
Notional 5.87% swing C. to LD
(2005: C. majority 5,335 (10.72%))

§BOURNEMOUTH EAST
E. 71,125   T. 44,024 (61.90%)   C. hold
Tobias Ellwood, C.   21,320
Lisa Northover, LD   13,592
David Stokes, Lab.   5,836
David Hughes, UKIP   3,027
Steven Humphrey, Ind.   249
C. majority 7,728 (17.55%)
Notional 1.76% swing LD to C.
(2005: C. majority 5,874 (14.04%))

§BOURNEMOUTH WEST
E. 71,753   T. 41,659 (58.06%)   C. hold
*Conor Burns, C.   18,808
Alasdair Murray, LD   13,225
Sharon Carr-Brown, Lab.   6,171
Philip Glover, UKIP   2,999
Harvey Taylor, Ind.   456
C. majority 5,583 (13.40%)
Notional 2.92% swing LD to C.
(2005: C. majority 2,766 (7.55%))

§BRACKNELL
E. 76,885   T. 52,140 (67.82%)   C. hold
*Phillip Lee, C.   27,327
Ray Earwicker, LD   11,623
John Piasecki, Lab.   8,755
Murray Barter, UKIP   2,297
Mark Burke, BNP   1,253
David Young, Green   825
Dan Haycocks, SMA   60
C. majority 15,704 (30.12%)
Notional 0.97% swing C. to LD
(2005: C. majority 10,037 (21.96%))

§BRADFORD EAST
E. 65,116   T. 40,457 (62.13%)   LD gain
*David Ward, LD   13,637
Terry Rooney, Lab.   13,272
Mohammed Riaz, C.   10,860
Neville Poynton, BNP   1,854
Raja Hussain, Ind.   375
Peter Shields, Ind.   237
Gerry Robinson, NF   222
LD majority 365 (0.90%)
Notional 7.57% swing Lab. to LD
(2005: Lab. majority 5,227 (14.24%))

§BRADFORD SOUTH
E. 63,580   T. 37,995 (59.76%)   Lab. hold
Gerry Sutcliffe, Lab.   15,682
Matt Palmer, C.   11,060
Alun Griffiths, LD   6,948
Sharon Sutton, BNP   2,651
Jamie Illingworth, UKIP   1,339
James Lewthwaite, D. Nat.   315
Lab. majority 4,622 (12.16%)
Notional 5.91% swing Lab. to C.
(2005: Lab. majority 8,444 (23.99%))

§¶BRADFORD WEST
E. 62,519   T. 40,576 (64.90%)   Lab. hold
Marsha Singh, Lab.   18,401
Zahid Iqbal, C.   12,638
David Hall-Matthews, LD   4,732
Jenny Sampson, BNP   1,370
Arshad Ali, Respect   1,245
David Ford, Green   940
Jason Smith, UKIP   812
Neil Craig, D. Nat.   438
Lab. majority 5,763 (14.20%)
Notional 2.93% swing C. to Lab.
(2005: Lab. majority 3,050 (8.34%))

§BRAINTREE
E. 71,162   T. 49,203 (69.14%)   C. hold
Brooks Newmark, C.   25,901
Bill Edwards, Lab.   9,780
Steve Jarvis, LD   9,247
Michael Ford, UKIP   2,477
Paul Hooks, BNP   1,080
Daisy Blench, Green   718
C. majority 16,121 (32.76%)
Notional 6.74% swing Lab. to C.
(2005: C. majority 8,658 (19.28%))

§BRENT CENTRAL
E. 74,076   T. 45,324 (61.19%)   LD gain
Sarah Teather, LD   20,026
Dawn Butler, Lab.   18,681
Sachin Rajput, C.   5,068
Shahar Ali, Green   668
Errol Williams, Ch. P.   488
Abdi Duale, Respect   230
Dean McCastree, Ind.   163
LD majority 1,345 (2.97%)
Notional 10.99% swing Lab. to LD
(2005: Lab. majority 7,469 (19.02%))

§BRENT NORTH
E. 83,896   T. 52,298 (62.34%)   Lab. hold
Barry Gardiner, Lab.   24,514
Harshadbhai Patel, C.   16,486
James Allie, LD   8,879
Atiq Malik, Ind.   734
Martin Francis, Green   725
Sunita Webb, UKIP   380
Jannen Vamadeva, Ind.   333
Arvind Tailor, Eng. Dem.   247
Lab. majority 8,028 (15.35%)
Notional 2.35% swing Lab. to C.
(2005: Lab. majority 8,830 (20.04%))

§BRENTFORD & ISLEWORTH
E. 83,546   T. 53,765 (64.35%)   C. gain
*Mary Macleod, C.   20,022
Ann Keen, Lab.   18,064
Andrew Dakers, LD   12,718
Jason Hargreaves, UKIP   863
John Hunt, Green   787
Paul Winnet, BNP   704
David Cunningham, Eng. Dem.   230
Aamir Bhatti, Ch. P.   210
Evangeline Pillai, CPA   99
Teresa Vanneck-Surplice, Ind.   68
C. majority 1,958 (3.64%)
Notional 5.96% swing Lab. to C.
(2005: Lab. majority 3,633 (8.29%))

§BRENTWOOD & ONGAR
E. 73,224   T. 50,592 (69.09%)   C. hold
Eric Pickles, C.   28,793
David Kendall, LD   11,872
Heidi Benzing, Lab.   4,992
Michael McGough, UKIP   2,037
Paul Morris, BNP   1,447
Jess Barnecutt, Green   584
Robin Tilbrook, Eng. Dem.   491
James Sapwell, Ind.   263
Danny Attfield, ND   113
C. majority 16,921 (33.45%)
Notional 3.12% swing LD to C.
(2005: C. majority 12,522 (27.21%))

§BRIDGWATER & SOMERSET WEST
E. 76,560   T. 54,493 (71.18%)   C. hold
Ian Liddell-Grainger, C.   24,675
Theo Butt Philip, LD   15,426
Kathryn Pearce, Lab.   9,332
Peter Hollings, UKIP   2,604
Donna Treanor, BNP   1,282
Charles Graham, Green   859
Bob Cudlipp, Ind.   315
C. majority 9,249 (16.97%)
Notional 2.88% swing C. to LD
(2005: C. majority 10,081 (19.77%))

§BRIGG & GOOLE
E. 67,345   T. 43,874 (65.15%)   C. gain
*Andrew Percy, C.   19,680
Ian Cawsey, Lab.   14,533
Richard Nixon, LD   6,414
Nigel Wright, UKIP   1,749
Stephen Ward, BNP   1,498
C. majority 5,147 (11.73%)
Notional 9.79% swing Lab. to C.
(2005: Lab. majority 3,217 (7.84%))

§BRIGHTON KEMPTOWN
E. 66,017   T. 42,705 (64.69%)   C. gain
*Simon Kirby, C.   16,217
Simon Burgess, Lab. Co-op   14,889
Juliet Williams, LD   7,691
Ben Duncan, Green   2,330
James Chamberlain-Webber, UKIP   1,384
Dave Hill, TUSC   194
C. majority 1,328 (3.11%)
Notional 3.97% swing Lab. to C.
(2005: Lab. majority 1,853 (4.83%))

§BRIGHTON PAVILION
E. 74,004   T. 51,834 (70.04%) Green gain
*Dr Caroline Lucas, Green   16,238
Nancy Platts, Lab.   14,986
Charlotte Vere, C.   12,275
Bernadette Millam, LD   7,159
Nigel Carter, UKIP   948
Ian Fyvie, Soc. Lab.   148
Soraya Kara, R and E   61
Leo Atreides, ND   19
Green majority 1,252 (2.42%)
Notional 8.45% swing Lab. to Green
(2005: Lab. majority 5,867 (13.11%))

§BRISTOL EAST
E. 69,448   T. 45,017 (64.82%)   Lab. hold
Kerry McCarthy, Lab.   16,471
Adeela Shafi, C.   12,749
Mike Popham, LD   10,993
Brian Jenkins, BNP   1,960
Philip Collins, UKIP   1,510
Glenn Vowles, Green   803
Stephen Wright, Eng. Dem.   347
Rae Lynch, TUSC   184
Lab. majority 3,722 (8.27%)
Notional 4.54% swing Lab. to C.
(2005: Lab. majority 7,335 (17.35%))

§BRISTOL NORTH WEST
E. 73,469   T. 50,336 (68.51%)   C. gain
*Charlotte Leslie, C.   19,115
Paul Harrod, LD   15,841
Sam Townend, Lab.   13,059
Robert Upton, UKIP   1,175
Ray Carr, Eng. Dem.   635
Alex Dunn, Green   511
C. majority 3,274 (6.50%)
Notional 8.86% swing Lab. to C.
(2005: Lab. majority 2,781 (5.69%))

§BRISTOL SOUTH
E. 78,579   T. 48,377 (61.56%)   Lab. hold
Dawn Primarolo, Lab.   18,600
Mark Wright, LD   13,866
Mark Lloyd Davies, C.   11,086
Colin Chidsey, BNP   1,739
Colin McNamee, UKIP   1,264
Charlie Bolton, Green   1,216
Craig Clarke, Eng. Dem.   400
Tom Baldwin, TUSC   206
Lab. majority 4,734 (9.79%)
Notional 7.53% swing Lab. to LD
(2005: Lab. majority 10,928 (24.86%))

§BRISTOL WEST
E. 82,728   T. 55,347 (66.90%)   LD hold
Stephen Williams, LD   26,593
Paul Smith, Lab.   15,227
Nick Yarker, C.   10,169
Ricky Knight, Green   2,090
Chris Lees, UKIP   655
Danny Kushlick, Ind.   343
Jon Baker, Eng. Dem.   270
LD majority 11,366 (20.54%)
Notional 9.00% swing Lab. to LD
(2005: LD majority 1,147 (2.55%))

§BROADLAND
E. 73,168   T. 52,676 (71.99%)   C. hold
Keith Simpson, C.   24,338
Daniel Roper, LD   17,046
Allyson Barron, Lab.   7,287
Stuart Agnew, UKIP   2,382
Edith Crowther, BNP   871
Susan Curran, Green   752
C. majority 7,292 (13.84%)
Notional 0.06% swing C. to LD
(2005: C. majority 6,573 (13.97%))

§BROMLEY & CHISLEHURST
E. 65,427   T. 44,037 (67.31%)   C. hold
Bob Neill, C.   23,569
Sam Webber, LD   9,669
Chris Kirby, Lab.   7,295
Emmett Jenner, UKIP   1,451
Rowena Savage, BNP   1,070
Roisin Robertson, Green   607
Jon Cheeseman, Eng. Dem.   376
C. majority 13,900 (31.56%)
Notional 5.13% swing LD to C.
(2005: C. majority 8,236 (20.57%))

§BROMSGROVE
E. 73,086   T. 51,630 (70.64%)   C. hold
*Sajid Javid, C.   22,558
Sam Burden, Lab.   11,250
Philip Ling, LD   10,124
Steven Morson, UKIP   2,950
Adrian Kriss, BIC   2,182
Elizabeth Wainwright, BNP   1,923
Mark France, Ind.   336
Ken Wheatley, Ind.   307
C. majority 11,308 (21.90%)
0.41% swing Lab. to C.
(2005: C. majority 10,080 (21.08%))

BROXBOURNE
E. 71,391   T. 45,658 (63.95%)   C. hold
Charles Walker, C.   26,844
Michael Watson, Lab.   8,040
Allan Witherick, LD   6,107
Steve McCole, BNP   2,159
Martin Harvey, UKIP   1,890
Debbie LeMay, Eng. Dem.   618
C. majority 18,804 (41.18%)
6.43% swing Lab. to C.
(2005: C. majority 11,509 (28.33%))

§BROXTOWE
E. 72,042   T. 52,727 (73.19%)   C. gain
*Anna Soubry, C.   20,585
Nick Palmer, Lab.   20,196
David Watts, LD   8,907
Mike Shore, BNP   1,422
Chris Cobb, UKIP   1,194
David Mitchell, Green   423
C. majority 389 (0.74%)
Notional 2.59% swing Lab. to C.
(2005: Lab. majority 2,139 (4.44%))

§BUCKINGHAM
E. 74,996 T. 48,335 (64.45%)
                                Speaker hold
John Bercow, Speaker   22,860
John Stevens, Ind.   10,331
Nigel Farage, UKIP   8,401
Patrick Phillips, Ind.   2,394
Debbie Martin, Ind.   1,270
Lynne Mozar, BNP   980
Colin Dale, Loony   856
Geoff Howard, Ind.   435
David Hews, Ch. P.   369
Anthony Watts, Ind.   332
Simon Strutt, Deficit   107
Speaker majority 12,529 (25.92%)
(2005: C. majority 18,716 (37.83%))

BURNLEY
E. 66,616   T. 41,845 (62.82%)   LD gain
*Gordon Birtwistle, LD   14,932
Julie Cooper, Lab.   13,114
Richard Ali, C.   6,950
Sharon Wilkinson, BNP   3,747
Andrew Brown, Ind.   1,876
John Wignall, UKIP   929
Andrew Hennessey, Ind.   297
LD majority 1,818 (4.34%)
9.58% swing Lab. to LD
(2005: Lab. majority 5,778 (14.82%))

§BURTON
E. 74,874   T. 49,823 (66.54%)   C. gain
*Andrew Griffiths, C.   22,188
Ruth Smeeth, Lab.   15,884
Michael Rodgers, LD   7,891
Alan Hewitt, BNP   2,409
Philip Lancaster, UKIP   1,451
C. majority 6,304 (12.65%)
Notional 8.73% swing Lab. to C.
(2005: Lab. majority 2,132 (4.81%))

§BURY NORTH
E. 66,759   T. 44,961 (67.35%)   C. gain
*David Nuttall, C.   18,070
Maryam Khan, Lab.   15,827
Richard Baum, LD   7,645
John Maude, BNP   1,825
Stephen Evans, UKIP   1,282
Bill Brison, Ind.   181
Graeme Lambert, Pirate   131
C. majority 2,243 (4.99%)
Notional 5.02% swing Lab. to C.
(2005: Lab. majority 2,059 (5.05%))

§BURY ST EDMUNDS
E. 84,727   T. 58,718 (69.30%)   C. hold
David Ruffley, C. 27,899
David Chappell, LD 15,519
Kevin Hind, Lab. 9,776
John Howlett, UKIP 3,003
Mark Ereira-Guyer, Green 2,521
C. majority 12,380 (21.08%)
Notional 2.76% swing C. to LD
(2005: C. majority 10,080 (19.03%))

§BURY SOUTH
E. 73,544   T. 48,267 (65.63%)   Lab. hold
Ivan Lewis, Lab. 19,508
Michelle Wiseman, C. 16,216
Vic D'Albert, LD 8,796
Jean Purdy, BNP 1,743
Paul Chadwick, UKIP 1,017
Valerie Morris, Eng. Dem. 494
George Heron, Green 493
Lab. majority 3,292 (6.82%)
Notional 8.01% swing Lab. to C.
(2005: Lab. majority 9,779 (22.84%))

§CALDER VALLEY
E. 76,903   T. 51,780 (67.33%)   C. gain
*Craig Whittaker, C. 20,397
Steph Booth, Lab. 13,966
Hilary Myers, LD 13,037
John Gregory, BNP 1,823
Greg Burrows, UKIP 1,173
Kate Sweeny, Green 858
Tim Cole, Ind. 194
Barry Greenwood, Ind. 175
Paul Rogan, Eng. Dem. 157
C. majority 6,431 (12.42%)
Notional 7.58% swing Lab. to C.
(2005: Lab. majority 1,303 (2.73%))

§CAMBERWELL & PECKHAM
E. 78,618   T. 46,659 (59.35%)   Lab. hold
Harriet Harman, Lab. 27,619
Columba Blango, LD 10,432
Andy Stranack, C. 6,080
Jenny Jones, Green 1,361
Yohara Robby Munilla, Eng. Dem. 435
Joshua Ogunleye, WRP 211
Margaret Sharkey, Soc. Lab. 184
Decima Francis, Ind. 93
Steven Robbins, Ind. 87
Patricia Knox, ND 82
Jill Mountford, Workers Lib 75
Lab. majority 17,187 (36.84%)
Notional 3.00% swing Lab. to LD
(2005: Lab. majority 16,608 (42.83%))

§CAMBORNE & REDRUTH
E. 63,968   T. 42,493 (66.43%)   C. gain
*George Eustice, C. 15,969
Julia Goldsworthy, LD 15,903
Jude Robinson, Lab. 6,945
Derek Elliott, UKIP 2,152
Loveday Jenkin, Meb. Ker. 775
Euan McPhee, Green 581
Robert Hawkins, Soc. Lab. 168
C. majority 66 (0.16%)
Notional 5.21% swing LD to C.
(2005: LD majority 2,733 (7.08%))

§CAMBRIDGE
E. 77,081   T. 50,130 (65.04%)   LD hold
*Julian Huppert, LD 19,621
Nick Hillman, C. 12,829
Daniel Zeichner, Lab. 12,174
Tony Juniper, Green 3,804
Peter Burkinshaw, UKIP 1,195
Martin Booth, TUSC 362
Holborn Old, Ind. 145
LD majority 6,792 (13.55%)
Notional 6.98% swing LD to C.
(2005: LD majority 5,834 (12.27%))

§CAMBRIDGESHIRE NORTH EAST
E. 73,224   T. 52,264 (71.38%)   C. hold
*Stephen Barclay, C. 26,862
Lorna Spenceley, LD 10,437
Peter Roberts, Lab. 9,274
Robin Talbot, UKIP 2,991
Susan Clapp, BNP 1,747
Debra Jordan, Ind. 566
Graham Murphy, Eng. Dem. 387
C. majority 16,425 (31.43%)
Notional 0.79% swing LD to C.
(2005: C. majority 7,726 (16.30%))

§CAMBRIDGESHIRE NORTH WEST
E. 88,857   T. 58,283 (65.59%)   C. hold
Shailesh Vara, C. 29,425
Kevin Wilkins, LD 12,748
Chris York, Lab. 9,877
Robert Brown, UKIP 4,826
Stephen Goldspink, Eng. Dem. 1,407
C. majority 16,677 (28.61%)
Notional 2.64% swing LD to C.
(2005: C. majority 10,925 (20.62%))

§CAMBRIDGESHIRE SOUTH
E. 78,995   T. 59,056 (74.76%)   C. hold
Andrew Lansley, C. 27,995
Sebastian Kindersley, LD 20,157
Tariq Sadiq, Lab. 6,024
Robin Page, Ind. 1,968
Helene Davies-Green, UKIP 1,873
Simon Saggers, Green 1,039
C. majority 7,838 (13.27%)
Notional 2.46% swing C. to LD
(2005: C. majority 9,634 (18.20%))

§CAMBRIDGESHIRE SOUTH EAST
E. 83,068   T. 57,602 (69.34%)   C. hold
Jim Paice, C. 27,629
Jonathan Chatfield, LD 21,683
John Cowan, Lab. 4,380
Andy Monk, UKIP 2,138
Simon Sedgwick-Jell, Green 766
Geoffrey Woollard, Ind. 517
Daniel Bell, CPA 489
C. majority 5,946 (10.32%)
Notional 2.67% swing C. to LD
(2005: C. majority 8,110 (15.66%))

§CANNOCK CHASE
E. 74,509   T. 45,559 (61.15%)   C. gain
*Aidan Burley, C. 18,271
Susan Woodward, Lab. 15,076
Jon Hunt, LD 7,732
Terence Majorowicz, BNP 2,168
Malcolm McKenzie, UKIP 1,580
Ron Turville, Ind. 380
Royston Jenkins, Snouts 259
Mike Walters, Ind. 93
C. majority 3,195 (7.01%)
Notional 14.01% swing Lab. to C.
(2005: Lab. majority 8,726 (21.00%))

§CANTERBURY
E. 76,808   T. 49,209 (64.07%)   C. hold
Julian Brazier, C. 22,050
Guy Voizey, LD 16,002
Jean Samuel, Lab. 7,940
Howard Farmer, UKIP 1,907
Geoff Meaden, Green 1,137
Anne Belsey, MRP 173
C. majority 6,048 (12.29%)
Notional 5.36% swing C. to LD
(2005: C. majority 7,579 (16.37%))

§CARLISLE
E. 65,263   T. 42,200 (64.66%)   C. gain
*John Stevenson, C. 16,589
Michael Boaden, Lab. 15,736
Neil Hughes, LD 6,567
Paul Stafford, BNP 1,086
Michael Owen, UKIP 969
John Reardon, Green 614
John Metcalfe, TUSC 376
Peter Howe, ND 263
C. majority 853 (2.02%)
Notional 7.74% swing Lab. to C.
(2005: Lab. majority 5,085 (13.46%))

§CARSHALTON & WALLINGTON
E. 66,520   T. 45,918 (69.03%)   LD hold
Tom Brake, LD 22,180
Dr Ken Andrew, C. 16,920
Shafi Khan, Lab. 4,015
Frank Day, UKIP 1,348
Charlotte Lewis, BNP 1,100
George Dow, Green 355
LD majority 5,260 (11.46%)
Notional 4.26% swing C. to LD
(2005: LD majority 1,225 (2.93%))

CASTLE POINT
E. 67,284   T. 45,026 (66.92%)   C. gain
*Rebecca Harris, C. 19,806
Bob Spink, Green Belt 12,174
Julian Ware-Lane, Lab. 6,609
Brendan D'Cruz, LD 4,232
Philip Howell, BNP 2,205
C. majority 7,632 (16.95%)
(2005: C. majority 8,201 (17.91%))

§CHARNWOOD
E. 74,473   T. 53,542 (71.89%)   C. hold
Stephen Dorrell, C. 26,560
Robin Webber-Jones, LD 11,531
Eric Goodyer, Lab. 10,536
Cathy Duffy, BNP 3,116
Miles Storier, UKIP 1,799
C. majority 15,029 (28.07%)
Notional 0.10% swing C. to LD
(2005: C. majority 8,613 (18.05%))

§CHATHAM & AYLESFORD
E. 71,122   T. 43,807 (61.59%)   C. gain
*Tracey Crouch, C. 20,230
Jonathan Shaw, Lab. 14,161
John McClintock, LD 5,832
Colin McCarthy-Stewart, BNP 1,365
Steve Newton, UKIP 1,314
Sean Varnham, Eng. Dem. 400
Dave Arthur, Green 396
Maureen Smith, Ch. P. 109
C. majority 6,069 (13.85%)
Notional 11.05% swing Lab. to C.
(2005: Lab. majority 3,289 (8.25%))

§CHEADLE
E. 72,458   T. 52,512 (72.47%)   LD hold
Mark Hunter, LD   24,717
Ben Jeffreys, C.   21,445
Martin Miller, Lab.   4,920
Tony Moore, UKIP   1,430
LD majority 3,272 (6.23%)
Notional 0.59% swing LD to C.
(2005: LD majority 3,672 (7.41%))

§CHELMSFORD
E. 77,529   T. 54,593 (70.42%)   C. hold
Simon Burns, C.   25,207
Stephen Robinson, LD   20,097
Peter Dixon, Lab.   5,980
Ken Wedon, UKIP   1,527
Mike Bateman, BNP   899
Angela Thomson, Green   476
Claire Breed, Eng. Dem.   254
Ben Sherman, Beer   153
C. majority 5,110 (9.36%)
Notional 0.08% swing LD to C.
(2005: C. majority 4,358 (9.20%))

§CHELSEA & FULHAM
E. 66,295   T. 39,856 (60.12%)   C. hold
Greg Hands, C.   24,093
Alexander Hilton, Lab.   7,371
Dirk Hazell, LD   6,473
Julia Stephenson, Green   671
Timothy Gittos, UKIP   478
Brian McDonald, BNP   388
Roland Courtenay, Ind. CCF   196
George Roseman, Eng. Dem.   169
Godfrey Spickernell, Blue   17
C. majority 16,722 (41.96%)
Notional 6.08% swing Lab. to C.
(2005: C. majority 10,253 (29.79%))

§CHELTENHAM
E. 78,998   T. 52,786 (66.82%)   LD hold
Martin Horwood, LD   26,659
Mark Coote, C.   21,739
James Green, Lab.   2,703
Peter Bowman, UKIP   1,192
Dancing Ken Hanks, Loony   493
LD majority 4,920 (9.32%)
Notional 4.33% swing C. to LD
(2005: LD majority 316 (0.66%))

§CHESHAM & AMERSHAM
E. 70,333   T. 52,444 (74.57%)   C. hold
Cheryl Gillan, C.   31,658
Tim Starkey, LD   14,948
Anthony Gajadharsingh, Lab.   2,942
Alan Stevens, UKIP   2,129
Nick Wilkins, Green   767
C. majority 16,710 (31.86%)
Notional 2.28% swing LD to C.
(2005: C. majority 12,974 (27.31%))

§CHESTER, CITY OF
E. 68,874   T. 46,790 (67.94%)   C. gain
*Stephen Mosley, C.   18,995
Christine Russell, Lab.   16,412
Elizabeth Jewkes, LD   8,930
Allan Weddell, UKIP   1,225
Ed Abrams, Eng. Dem.   594
Tom Barker, Green   535
John Whittingham, Ind.   99
C. majority 2,583 (5.52%)
Notional 3.86% swing Lab. to C.
(2005: Lab. majority 973 (2.20%))

§CHESTERFIELD
E. 71,878   T. 45,839 (63.77%)   Lab. gain
*Toby Perkins, Lab.   17,891
Paul Holmes, LD   17,342
Carolyn Abbott, C.   7,214
David Phillips, UKIP   1,432
Ian Jerram, Eng. Dem.   1,213
Duncan Kerr, Green   600
John Noneoftheabove Daramy, Ind.   147
Lab. majority 549 (1.20%)
Notional 3.78% swing LD to Lab.
(2005: LD majority 2,733 (6.36%))

§CHICHESTER
E. 81,462   T. 56,787 (69.71%)   C. hold
Andrew Tyrie, C.   31,427
Martin Lury, LD   15,550
Simon Holland, Lab.   5,937
Andrew Moncrieff, UKIP   3,873
C. majority 15,877 (27.96%)
Notional 3.82% swing LD to C.
(2005: C. majority 10,457 (20.32%))

CHINGFORD & WOODFORD GREEN
E. 64,831   T. 43,106 (66.49%)   C. hold
Iain Duncan Smith, C.   22,743
Cath Arakelian, Lab.   9,780
Geoffrey Seeff, LD   7,242
Julian Leppert, BNP   1,288
Nick Jones, UKIP   1,133
Lucy Craig, Green   650
None of The Above, Ind.   202
Barry White, Ind.   68
C. majority 12,963 (30.07%)
1.27% swing Lab. to C.
(2005: C. majority 10,641 (27.53%))

§CHIPPENHAM
E. 72,105   T. 52,385 (72.65%)   LD hold
*Duncan Hames, LD   23,970
Wilfred Emmanuel-Jones, C.   21,500
Greg Lovell, Lab.   3,620
Julia Reid, UKIP   1,783
Michael Simpkins, BNP   641
Samantha Fletcher, Green   446
John Maguire, Eng. Dem.   307
Richard Sexton, Ch. P.   118
LD majority 2,470 (4.72%)
Notional 0.01% swing C. to LD
(2005: LD majority 2,183 (4.70%))

§CHIPPING BARNET
E. 77,798   T. 50,608 (65.05%)   C. hold
Theresa Villiers, C.   24,700
Damien Welfare, Lab.   12,773
Stephen Barber, LD   10,202
James Fluss, UKIP   1,442
Kate Tansley, Green   1,021
Philip Clayton, Ind.   470
C. majority 11,927 (23.57%)
Notional 5.77% swing Lab. to C.
(2005: C. majority 5,457 (12.02%))

§CHORLEY
E. 70,950   T. 49,774 (70.15%)   Lab. hold
Lindsay Hoyle, Lab.   21,515
Alan Cullens, C.   18,922
Stephen Fenn, LD   6,957
Nick Hogan, UKIP   2,021
Chris Curtis, Ind.   359
Lab. majority 2,593 (5.21%)
Notional 5.60% swing Lab. to C.
(2005: Lab. majority 7,285 (16.41%))

§CHRISTCHURCH
E. 68,861   T. 49,416 (71.76%)   C. hold
Christopher Chope, C.   27,888
Martyn Hurll, LD   12,478
Robert Deeks, Lab.   4,849
David Williams, UKIP   4,201
C. majority 15,410 (31.18%)
Notional 0.05% swing C. to LD
(2005: C. majority 14,640 (31.28%))

§CITIES OF LONDON & WESTMINSTER
E. 66,489   T. 36,931 (55.54%)   C. hold
Mark Field, C.   19,264
David Rowntree, Lab.   8,188
Naomi Smith, LD   7,574
Dr Derek Chase, Green   778
Paul Weston, UKIP   664
Frank Roseman, Eng. Dem.   191
Dennis Delderfield, Ind.   98
Jack Nunn, Pirate   90
Mad Cap'n Tom, Ind.   84
C. majority 11,076 (29.99%)
Notional 3.51% swing Lab. to C.
(2005: C. majority 7,352 (22.96%))

§CLACTON
E. 67,194   T. 43,123 (64.18%)   C. hold
Douglas Carswell, C.   22,867
Ivan Henderson, Lab.   10,799
Michael Green, LD   5,577
Jim Taylor, BNP   1,975
Terry Allen, Tendring   1,078
Chris Southall, Green   535
Christopher Humphrey, Ind.   292
C. majority 12,068 (27.99%)
Notional 9.74% swing Lab. to C.
(2005: C. majority 3,629 (8.50%))

CLEETHORPES
E. 70,214   T. 44,966 (64.04%)   C. gain
*Martin Vickers, C.   18,939
Shona McIsaac, Lab.   14,641
Malcolm Morland, LD   8,192
Stephen Harness, UKIP   3,194
C. majority 4,298 (9.56%)
7.81% swing Lab. to C.
(2005: Lab. majority 2,642 (6.06%))

§COLCHESTER
E. 74,042   T. 46,139 (62.30%)   LD hold
Bob Russell, LD   22,151
Will Quince, C.   15,169
Jordan Newell, Lab.   5,680
John Pitts, UKIP   1,350
Sidney Chaney, BNP   705
Peter Lynn, Green   694
Eddie Bone, Eng. Dem.   335
Garryck Noble, PP Essex   35
Paul Shaw, ND   20
LD majority 6,982 (15.13%)
Notional 0.24% swing LD to C.
(2005: LD majority 6,388 (15.60%))

§COLNE VALLEY
E. 80,062   T. 55,296 (69.07%)   C. gain
*Jason McCartney, C.   20,440
Nicola Turner, LD   15,603
Debbie Abrahams, Lab.   14,589
Barry Fowler, BNP   1,893
Melanie Roberts, UKIP   1,163
Chas Ball, Green   867
Dr Jackie Grunsell, TUSC   741
C. majority 4,837 (8.75%)
Notional 6.55% swing Lab. to C.
(2005: Lab. majority 1,267 (2.51%))

CONGLETON
E. 73,692   T. 50,780 (68.91%)   C. hold
*Fiona Bruce, C.   23,250
Peter Hirst, LD   16,187
David Bryant, Lab.   8,747
Lee Slaughter, UKIP   2,147
Paul Edwards, Ind.   276
Paul Rothwell, ND   94
Adam Parton, Ind.   79
C. majority 7,063 (13.91%)
2.30% swing C. to LD
(2005: C. majority 8,246 (17.66%))

§COPELAND
E. 63,291   T. 42,787 (67.60%)   Lab. hold
Jamie Reed, Lab.   19,699
Christopher Whiteside, C.   15,866
Frank Hollowell, LD   4,365
Clive Jefferson, BNP   1,474
Ted Caley-Knowles, UKIP   994
Jill Perry, Green   389
Lab. majority 3,833 (8.96%)
Notional 2.14% swing Lab. to C.
(2005: Lab. majority 5,157 (13.24%))

¶CORBY
E. 78,305   T. 54,236 (69.26%)   C. gain
*Louise Bagshawe, C.   22,886
Phil Hope, Lab.   20,991
Portia Wilson, LD   7,834
Roy Davies, BNP   2,525
C. majority 1,895 (3.49%)
3.31% swing Lab. to C.
(2005: Lab. (Co-op) majority 1,517
(3.13%))

§CORNWALL NORTH
E. 68,662   T. 46,844 (68.22%)   LD hold
Dan Rogerson, LD   22,512
Sian Flynn, C.   19,531
Miriel O'Connor, UKIP   2,300
Janet Hulme, Lab.   1,971
Joanie Willett, Meb. Ker.   530
LD majority 2,981 (6.36%)
Notional 0.25% swing LD to C.
(2005: LD majority 2,892 (6.87%))

§CORNWALL SOUTH EAST
E. 72,237   T. 49,617 (68.69%)   C. gain
*Sheryll Murray, C.   22,390
Karen Gillard, LD   19,170
Michael Sparling, Lab.   3,507
Stephanie McWilliam, UKIP   3,083
Roger Creagh-Osborne, Green   826
Roger Holmes, Meb. Ker.   641
C. majority 3,220 (6.49%)
Notional 9.13% swing LD to C.
(2005: LD majority 5,485 (11.77%))

§COTSWOLDS, THE
E. 76,728   T. 54,832 (71.46%)   C. hold
Geoffrey Clifton-Brown, C.   29,075
Mike Collins, LD   16,211
Mark Dempsey, Lab.   5,886
Adrian Blake, UKIP   2,292
Kevin Lister, Green   940
Alex Steel, Ind.   428
C. majority 12,864 (23.46%)
Notional 1.08% swing LD to C.
(2005: C. majority 10,742 (21.29%))

§COVENTRY NORTH EAST
E. 73,035   T. 43,383 (59.40%)   Lab. hold
Bob Ainsworth, Lab.   21,384
Hazel Noonan, C.   9,609
Russell Field, LD   7,210
Tom Gower, BNP   1,863
Dave Nellist, Soc. Alt.   1,592
Chris Forbes, UKIP   1,291
Ron Lebar, Ch. M.   434
Lab. majority 11,775 (27.14%)
Notional 5.47% swing Lab. to C.
(2005: Lab. majority 14,621 (38.08%))

§COVENTRY NORTH WEST
E. 72,871   T. 46,560 (63.89%)   Lab. hold
Geoffrey Robinson, Lab.   19,936
Gary Ridley, C.   13,648
Vincent McKee, LD   8,344
Edward Sheppard, BNP   1,666
Mark Nattrass, UKIP   1,295
John Clarke, Ind.   640
Justin Wood, Green   497
Nikki Downes, Soc. Alt.   370
William Sidhu, Ch. M.   164
Lab. majority 6,288 (13.51%)
Notional 3.92% swing Lab. to C.
(2005: Lab. majority 8,934 (21.35%))

§COVENTRY SOUTH
E. 73,652   T. 45,924 (62.35%)   Lab. hold
Jim Cunningham, Lab.   19,197
Kevin Foster, C.   15,352
Brian Patton, LD   8,278
Mark Taylor, UKIP   1,767
Judy Griffiths, Soc. Alt.   691
Stephen Gray, Green   639
Lab. majority 3,845 (8.37%)
Notional 3.41% swing Lab. to C.
(2005: Lab. majority 6,237 (15.18%))

CRAWLEY
E. 72,781   T. 47,504 (65.27%)   C. gain
*Henry Smith, C.   21,264
Chris Oxlade, Lab.   15,336
John Vincent, LD   6,844
Richard Trower, BNP   1,672
Chris French, UKIP   1,382
Phil Smith, Green   598
Arshad Khan, JP   265
Andrew Hubner, Ind.   143
C. majority 5,928 (12.48%)
6.28% swing Lab. to C.
(2005: Lab. majority 37 (0.09%))

§CREWE & NANTWICH
E. 77,460   T. 51,084 (65.95%)   C. hold
Edward Timpson, C.   23,420
David Williams, Lab.   17,374
Roy Wood, LD   7,656
James Clutton, UKIP   1,414
Phil Williams, BNP   1,043
Mike Parsons, Ind.   177
C. majority 6,046 (11.84%)
Notional 13.67% swing Lab. to C.
(2005: Lab. majority 6,999 (15.50%))

§CROYDON CENTRAL
E. 78,880   T. 49,757 (63.08%)   C. gain
*Gavin Barwell, C.   19,657
Gerry Ryan, Lab. (Co-op)   16,688
Peter Lambell, LD   6,553
Andrew Pelling, Ind.   3,239
Cliff Le May, BNP   1,448
Ralph Atkinson, UKIP   997
Bernice Golberg, Green   581
James Gitau, Ch. P.   264
John Cartwright, Loony   192
Michael Castle, Ind.   138
C. majority 2,969 (5.97%)
Notional 3.34% swing Lab. to C.
(2005: Lab. majority 328 (0.72%))

§¶CROYDON NORTH
E. 85,212   T. 51,678 (60.65%)   Lab. hold
Malcolm Wicks, Lab.   28,949
Jason Hadden, C.   12,466
Gerry Jerome, LD   7,226
Shasha Khan, Green   1,017
Jonathan Serter, UKIP   891
Novlette Williams, Ch. P.   586
Mohommad Shaikh, Respect   272
Ben Stevenson, Comm.   160
Mohamed Seyed, Ind.   111
Lab. majority 16,483 (31.90%)
Notional 0.27% swing C. to Lab.
(2005: Lab. majority 14,185 (31.37%))

§CROYDON SOUTH
E. 81,301   T. 56,322 (69.28%)   C. hold
Richard Ottaway, C.   28,684
Simon Rix, LD   12,866
Jane Avis, Lab.   11,287
Jeffrey Bolter, UKIP   2,504
Gordon Ross, Green   981
C. majority 15,818 (28.08%)
Notional 1.75% swing C. to LD
(2005: C. majority 14,228 (27.95%))

§DAGENHAM & RAINHAM
E. 69,764   T. 44,232 (63.40%)   Lab. hold
Jon Cruddas, Lab.   17,813
Simon Jones, C.   15,183
Michael Barnbrook, BNP   4,952
Joseph Bourke, LD   3,806
Craig Litwin, UKIP   1,569
Gordon Kennedy, Ind.   308
Paula Watson, Ch. P.   305
Debbie Rosaman, Green   296
Lab. majority 2,630 (5.95%)
Notional 4.87% swing Lab. to C.
(2005: Lab. majority 6,372 (15.69%))

§DARLINGTON
E. 69,352   T. 42,896 (61.85%)   Lab. hold
*Jenny Chapman, Lab.   16,891
Edward Legard, C.   13,503
Mike Barker, LD   10,046
Amanda Foster, BNP   1,262
Charlotte Bull, UKIP   1,194
Lab. majority 3,388 (7.90%)
Notional 9.14% swing Lab. to C.
(2005: Lab. majority 10,417 (26.18%))

§DARTFORD
E. 76,271   T. 50,080 (65.66%)   C. gain
*Gareth Johnson, C.   24,428
John Adams, Lab.   13,800
James Willis, LD   7,361
Gary Rogers, Eng. Dem.   2,178
Richard Palmer, UKIP   1,842
Stephane Tindame, Ind.   264
John Crockford, FDP   207
C. majority 10,628 (21.22%)
Notional 11.56% swing Lab. to C.
(2005: Lab. majority 860 (1.90%))

§DAVENTRY
E. 71,451   T. 51,774 (72.46%)   C. hold
*Chris Heaton-Harris, C.   29,252
Christopher McGlynn, LD   10,064
Paul Corazzo, Lab.   8,168
Jim Broomfield, UKIP   2,333
Alan Bennett-Spencer, Eng. Dem.   1,187
Steve Whiffen, Green   770
C. majority 19,188 (37.06%)
Notional 0.71% swing C. to LD
(2005: C. majority 11,776 (25.15%))

§DENTON & REDDISH
E. 64,765   T. 37,635 (58.11%)   Lab. hold
Andrew Gwynne, Lab.   19,191
Julie Searle, C.   9,360
Stephen Broadhurst, LD   6,727
William Robinson, UKIP   2,060
Jeff Dennis, Ind.   297
Lab. majority 9,831 (26.12%)
Notional 6.25% swing Lab. to C.
(2005: Lab. majority 13,128 (38.62%))

§DERBY NORTH
E. 71,484   T. 45,080 (63.06%)   Lab. hold
*Chris Williamson, Lab.   14,896
Stephen Mold, C.   14,283
Lucy Care, LD   12,638
Peter Cheeseman, BNP   2,000
Elizabeth Ransome, UKIP   829
David Gale, Ind.   264
David Geraghty, Pirate   170
Lab. majority 613 (1.36%)
Notional 7.39% swing Lab. to C.
(2005: Lab. majority 5,691 (14.58%))

§DERBY SOUTH
E. 71,012   T. 41,188 (58.00%)   Lab. hold
Margaret Beckett, Lab.   17,851
Jack Perschke, C.   11,729
David Batey, LD   8,430
Stephen Fowke, UKIP   1,821
Alan Graves, Ind.   1,357
Lab. majority 6,122 (14.86%)
Notional 9.26% swing Lab. to C.
(2005: Lab. majority 11,655 (28.99%))

§DERBYSHIRE DALES
E. 63,367   T. 46,780 (73.82%)   C. hold
Patrick McLoughlin, C.   24,378
Joe Naitta, LD   10,512
Colin Swindell, Lab.   9,061
Ian Guiver, UKIP   1,779
Josh Stockell, Green   772
Nick The Flying Brick Delves,
Loony   228
Amila Y'mech, Humanity   50
C. majority 13,866 (29.64%)
Notional 3.74% swing LD to C.
(2005: C. majority 8,810 (20.82%))

§DERBYSHIRE MID
E. 66,297   T. 47,342 (71.41%)   C. hold
*Pauline Latham, C.   22,877
Hardyal Dhindsa, Lab.   11,585
Sally McIntosh, LD   9,711
Lewis Allsebrook, BNP   1,698
Anthony Kay, UKIP   1,252
RU Seerius, Loony   219
C. majority 11,292 (23.85%)
Notional 5.66% swing Lab. to C.
(2005: C. majority 5,329 (12.54%))

§DERBYSHIRE NORTH EAST
E. 71,422   T. 47,034 (65.85%)   Lab. hold
Natascha Engel, Lab.   17,948
Huw Merriman, C.   15,503
Richard Bull, LD   10,947
James Bush, UKIP   2,636
Lab. majority 2,445 (5.20%)
Notional 8.56% swing Lab. to C.
(2005: Lab. majority 9,564 (22.31%))

§DERBYSHIRE SOUTH
E. 70,610   T. 50,419 (71.40%)   C. gain
*Heather Wheeler, C.   22,935
Michael Edwards, Lab.   15,807
Alexis Diouf, LD   8,012
Peter Jarvis, BNP   2,193
Charles Swabey, UKIP   1,206
Paul Liversuch, Soc. Lab.   266
C. majority 7,128 (14.14%)
Notional 9.80% swing Lab. to C.
(2005: Lab. majority 2,436 (5.45%))

§DEVIZES
E. 67,374   T. 46,340 (68.78%)   C. hold
*Claire Perry, C.   25,519
Fiona Hornby, LD   12,514
Jurab Ali, Lab.   4,711
Patricia Bryant, UKIP   2,076
Mark Fletcher, Green   813
Martin Houlden, Ind.   566
Nic Coombe, Libertarian   141
C. majority 13,005 (28.06%)
Notional 0.33% swing C. to LD
(2005: C. majority 12,259 (28.63%))

§DEVON CENTRAL
E. 71,204   T. 53,873 (75.66%)   C. hold
*Mel Stride, C.   27,737
Philip Hutty, LD   18,507
Moira Macdonald, Lab.   3,715
Bob Edwards, UKIP   2,870
Colin Mathews, Green   1,044
C. majority 9,230 (17.13%)
Notional 6.07% swing LD to C.
(2005: C. majority 2,338 (4.99%))

§DEVON EAST
E. 73,109   T. 53,092 (72.62%)   C. hold
Hugo Swire, C.   25,662
Paull Robathan, LD   16,548
Gareth Manson, Lab.   5,721
Mike Amor, UKIP   4,346
Sharon Pavey, Green   815
C. majority 9,114 (17.17%)
Notional 1.03% swing C. to LD
(2005: C. majority 9,168 (19.23%))

§DEVON NORTH
E. 74,508   T. 51,321 (68.88%)   LD hold
Nick Harvey, LD   24,305
Philip Milton, C.   18,484
Stephen Crowther, UKIP   3,720
Mark Cann, Lab.   2,671
L'Anne Knight, Green   697
Gary Marshall, BNP   614
Rodney Cann, Ind.   588
Nigel Vidler, Eng. Dem.   146
Gerrard Sables, Comm. Brit.   96
LD majority 5,821 (11.34%)
Notional 0.32% swing C. to LD
(2005: LD majority 5,276 (10.71%))

§DEVON SOUTH WEST
E. 70,059   T. 49,860 (71.17%)   C. hold
Gary Streeter, C.   27,908
Anna Pascoe, LD   12,034
Luke Pollard, Lab.   6,193
Hugh Williams, UKIP   3,084
Vaughan Brean, Green   641
C. majority 15,874 (31.84%)
Notional 5.64% swing LD to C.
(2005: C. majority 9,442 (20.12%))

§DEVON WEST & TORRIDGE
E. 76,574   T. 55,257 (72.16%)   C. hold
Geoffrey Cox, C.   25,230
Adam Symons, LD   22,273
Robin Julian, UKIP   3,021
Darren Jones, Lab.   2,917
Cathrine Simmons, Green   1,050
Nick Baker, BNP   766
C. majority 2,957 (5.35%)
Notional 0.01% swing C. to LD
(2005: C. majority 2,732 (5.37%))

§DEWSBURY
E. 78,901   T. 54,008 (68.45%)   C. gain
*Simon Reevell, C.   18,898
Shahid Malik, Lab.   17,372
Andrew Hutchinson, LD   9,150
Khizar Iqbal, Ind.   3,813
Roger Roberts, BNP   3,265
Adrian Cruden, Green   849
Michael Felse, Eng. Dem.   661
C. majority 1,526 (2.83%)
Notional 5.85% swing Lab. to C.
(2005: Lab. majority 3,999 (8.88%))

§DON VALLEY
E. 73,214   T. 43,430 (59.32%)   Lab. hold
Caroline Flint, Lab.   16,472
Matthew Stephens, C.   12,877
Edward Simpson, LD   7,422
Erwin Toseland, BNP   2,112
William Shaw, UKIP   1,904
Bernie Aston, Eng. Dem.   1,756
Martin Williams, Ind.   887
Lab. majority 3,595 (8.28%)
Notional 10.64% swing Lab. to C.
(2005: Lab. majority 11,333 (29.56%))

§DONCASTER CENTRAL
E. 75,207   T. 41,745 (55.51%)   Lab. hold
Rosie Winterton, Lab.   16,569
Gareth Davies, C.   10,340
Patrick Wilson, LD   8,795
Lawrence Parramore, Eng. Dem.   1,816
John Bettney, BNP   1,762
Michael Andrews, UKIP   1,421
Scott Pickles, Ind.   970
Derek Williams, R and E   72
Lab. majority 6,229 (14.92%)
Notional 8.72% swing Lab. to C.
(2005: Lab. majority 10,325 (27.33%))

§DONCASTER NORTH
E. 72,381   T. 41,483 (57.31%)   Lab. hold
Ed Miliband, Lab.   19,637
Sophie Brodie, C.   8,728
Edward Sanderson, LD   6,174
Pamela Chambers, BNP   2,818
Wayne Crawshaw, Eng. Dem.   2,148
Liz Andrews, UKIP   1,797
Bill Rawcliffe, TUSC
Lab. majority 10,909 (26.30%)
Notional 2.77% swing Lab. to C.
(2005: Lab. majority 12,027 (31.85%))

§DORSET MID & POOLE NORTH
E. 72,647 T. 46,788 (64.40%) LD hold
Annette Brooke, LD   21,100
Nick King, C.   20,831
Darren Brown, Lab.   2,748
Dave Evans, UKIP   2,109
LD majority 269 (0.57%)
Notional 6.27% swing LD to C.
(2005: LD majority 5,931 (13.12%))

§DORSET NORTH
E. 73,698 T. 54,141 (73.46%) C. hold
Bob Walter, C.   27,640
Emily Gasson, LD   20,015
Mike Bunney, Lab.   2,910
Jeremy Nieboer, UKIP   2,812
Anna Hayball, Green   546
Roger Monksummers, Loony   218
C. majority 7,625 (14.08%)
Notional 2.75% swing LD to C.
(2005: C. majority 4,200 (8.58%))

DORSET SOUTH
E. 73,838 T. 50,310 (68.14%) C. gain
*Richard Drax, C.   22,667
Jim Knight, Lab.   15,224
Ros Kayes, LD   9,557
Mike Hobson, UKIP   2,034
Brian Heatley, Green   595
Andy Kirkwood, YP   233
C. majority 7,443 (14.79%)
9.26% swing Lab. to C.
(2005: Lab. majority 1,812 (3.73%))

DORSET WEST
E. 76,869 T. 57,337 (74.59%) C. hold
Oliver Letwin, C.   27,287
Sue Farrant, LD   23,364
Dr Steve Bick, Lab.   3,815
Oliver Chisholm, UKIP   2,196
Susan Greene, Green   675
C. majority 3,923 (6.84%)
1.11% swing LD to C.
(2005: C. majority 2,461 (4.62%))

§DOVER
E. 71,832 T. 50,385 (70.14%) C. gain
*Charlie Elphicke, C.   22,174
Gwyn Prosser, Lab.   16,900
John Brigden, LD   7,962
Victor Matcham, UKIP   1,747
Dennis Whiting, BNP   1,104
Michael Walters, Eng. Dem.   216
David Clark, CPA   200
George Lee-Delisle, Ind.   82
C. majority 5,274 (10.47%)
Notional 10.43% swing Lab. to C.
(2005: Lab. majority 5,005 (10.40%))

§DUDLEY NORTH
E. 60,838 T. 38,602 (63.45%) Lab. hold
Ian Austin, Lab.   14,923
Graeme Brown, C.   14,274
Mike Beckett, LD   4,066
Malcolm Davis, UKIP   3,267
Ken Griffiths, BNP   1,899
Kevin Inman, NF   173
Lab. majority 649 (1.68%)
Notional 4.73% swing Lab. to C.
(2005: Lab. majority 4,106 (11.14%))

§DUDLEY SOUTH
E. 60,572 T. 38,165 (63.01%) C. gain
*Chris Kelly, C.   16,450
Rachel Harris, Lab.   12,594
Jonathan Bramall, LD   5,989
Philip Rowe, UKIP   3,132
C. majority 3,856 (10.10%)
Notional 9.51% swing Lab. to C.
(2005: Lab. majority 3,222 (8.91%))

§DULWICH & WEST NORWOOD
E. 72,817 T. 48,214 (66.21%) Lab. hold
Tessa Jowell, Lab.   22,461
Jonathan Mitchell, LD   13,096
Kemi Adegoke, C.   10,684
Shane Collins, Green   1,266
Elizabeth Jones, UKIP   707
Lab. majority 9,365 (19.42%)
Notional 0.84% swing Lab. to LD
(2005: Lab. majority 7,853 (19.75%))

DURHAM, CITY OF
E. 68,832 T. 46,252 (67.20%) Lab. hold
Roberta Blackman-Woods, Lab.   20,496
Carol Woods, LD   17,429
Nick Varley, C.   6,146
Ralph Musgrave, BNP   1,153
Nigel Coghill-Marshall, UKIP   856
Jonathan Collings, Ind.   172
Lab. majority 3,067 (6.63%)
0.37% swing Lab. to LD
(2005: Lab. majority 3,274 (7.38%))

§DURHAM NORTH
E. 67,548 T. 40,967 (60.65%) Lab. hold
Kevan Jones, Lab.   20,698
David Skelton, C.   8,622
Ian Lindley, LD   8,617
Pete Molloy, BNP   1,686
Bruce Reid, UKIP   1,344
Lab. majority 12,076 (29.48%)
Notional 8.93% swing Lab. to C.
(2005: Lab. majority 16,781 (44.94%))

§DURHAM NORTH WEST
E. 70,618 T. 43,815 (62.05%) Lab. hold
*Pat Glass, Lab.   18,539
Owen Temple, LD   10,927
Michelle Tempest, C.   8,766
Watts Stelling, Ind.   2,472
Michael Stewart, BNP   1,852
Andrew McDonald, UKIP   1,259
Lab. majority 7,612 (17.37%)
Notional 8.33% swing Lab. to LD
(2005: Lab. majority 13,443 (34.03%))

§EALING CENTRAL & ACTON
E. 63,489 T. 47,200 (74.34%) C. gain
*Angie Bray, C.   17,944
Bassam Mahfouz, Lab.   14,228
Jon Ball, LD   13,041
Julie Carter, UKIP   765
Sarah Edwards, Green   737
Suzanne Fernandes, Ch. P.   295
Sam Akaki, Ind. EACPS   190
C. majority 3,716 (7.87%)
Notional 5.02% swing Lab. to C.
(2005: Lab. majority 839 (2.16%))

§EALING NORTH
E. 67,902 T. 47,678 (70.22%) Lab. hold
Stephen Pound, Lab.   24,023
Ian Gibb, C.   14,722
Chris Lucas, LD   6,283
Dave Furness, BNP   1,045
Ian De Wulverton, UKIP   685
Christopher Warleigh-Lack, Green   505
Petar Ljubisic, Ch. P.   415
Lab. majority 9,301 (19.51%)
Notional 0.45% swing C. to Lab.
(2005: Lab. majority 8,126 (18.61%))

§EALING SOUTHALL
E. 60,379 T. 42,756 (70.81%) Lab. hold
Virendra Sharma, Lab.   22,024
Gurcharan Singh, C.   12,733
Nigel Bakhai, LD   6,383
Suneil Basu, Green   705
Mehboob Anil, Ch. P.   503
Sati Chaggar, Eng. Dem.   408
Lab. majority 9,291 (21.73%)
Notional 8.30% swing Lab. to C.
(2005: Lab. majority 13,140 (38.33%))

§EASINGTON
E. 63,873 T. 34,914 (54.66%) Lab. hold
*Grahame Morris, Lab.   20,579
Tara Saville, LD   5,597
Richard Harrison, C.   4,790
Cheryl Dunn, BNP   2,317
Martyn Aiken, UKIP   1,631
Lab. majority 14,982 (42.91%)
Notional 7.74% swing Lab. to LD
(2005: Lab. majority 18,874 (58.39%))

§EAST HAM
E. 90,675 T. 50,373 (55.55%) Lab. hold
Stephen Timms, Lab.   35,471
Paul Shea, C.   7,645
Chris Brice, LD   5,849
Barry O'Connor, Eng. Dem.   822
Judy Maciejowska, Green   586
Lab. majority 27,826 (55.24%)
Notional 7.71% swing C. to Lab.
(2005: Lab. majority 13,649 (33.08%))

§EASTBOURNE
E. 77,840 T. 52,124 (66.96%) LD gain
*Stephen Lloyd, LD   24,658
Nigel Waterson, C.   21,223
Dave Brinson, Lab.   2,497
Stephen Shing, Ind.   1,327
Roger Needham, UKIP   1,305
Colin Poulter, BNP   939
Michael Baldry, Ind.   101
Keith Gell, Ind.   74
LD majority 3,435 (6.59%)
Notional 4.00% swing C. to LD
(2005: C. majority 672 (1.41%))

§¶EASTLEIGH
E. 77,435 T. 53,650 (69.28%) LD hold
Chris Huhne, LD   24,966
Maria Hutchings, C.   21,102
Leo Barraclough, Lab.   5,153
Ray Finch, UKIP   1,933
Tony Stephen Pewsey, Eng. Dem.   249
Dave Stone, Ind.   154
Keith Low, Nat. Dem.   93
LD majority 3,864 (7.20%)
Notional 3.04% swing C. to LD
(2005: LD majority 534 (1.12%))

§EDDISBURY
E. 65,306   T. 45,414 (69.54%)   C. hold
Stephen O'Brien, C.   23,472
Robert Thompson, LD   10,217
Pat Merrick, Lab.   9,794
Charles Dodman, UKIP   1,931
C. majority 13,255 (29.19%)
Notional 0.13% swing LD to C.
(2005: C. majority 6,408 (14.83%))

§EDMONTON
E. 63,902   T. 40,377 (63.19%)
                      Lab. (Co-op) hold
Andy Love, Lab. (Co-op)   21,665
Andrew Charalambous, C.   12,052
Iarla Kilbane-Dawe, LD   4,252
Roy Freshwater, UKIP   1,036
Jack Johnson, Green   516
Erol Basarik, Reform   379
Clive Morrison, Ch. P.   350
David Mclean, Ind.   127
Lab. (Co-op) majority 9,613 (23.81%)
Notional 2.26% swing Lab. (Co-op) to C.
(2005: Lab. (Co-op) majority 10,312
(28.33%))

§ELLESMERE PORT & NESTON
E. 63,097   T. 44,233 (70.10%)   Lab. hold
Andrew Miller, Lab.   19,750
Stuart Penketh, C.   15,419
Denise Aspinall, LD   6,663
Henry Crocker, UKIP   1,619
Jonathan Starkey, Ind.   782
Lab. majority 4,331 (9.79%)
Notional 3.10% swing Lab. to C.
(2005: Lab. majority 6,713 (15.99%))

§ELMET & ROTHWELL
E. 77,724   T. 55,789 (71.78%)   C. gain
*Alec Shelbrooke, C.   23,778
James Lewis, Lab.   19,257
Stewart Golton, LD   9,109
Sam Clayton, BNP   1,802
Darren Oddy, UKIP   1,593
Christopher Nolan, Ind.   250
C. majority 4,521 (8.10%)
Notional 9.77% swing Lab. to C.
(2005: Lab. majority 6,078 (11.43%))

§ELTHAM
E. 62,590   T. 41,964 (67.05%)   Lab. hold
Clive Efford, Lab.   17,416
David Gold, C.   15,753
Steven Toole, LD   5,299
Roberta Woods, BNP   1,745
Ray Adams, UKIP   1,011
Arthur Hayles, Green   419
Mike Tibby, Eng. Dem.   217
Andrew Graham, Ind.   104
Lab. majority 1,663 (3.96%)
Notional 1.82% swing Lab. to C.
(2005: Lab. majority 2,904 (7.60%))

§ENFIELD NORTH
E. 66,258   T. 44,453 (67.09%)   C. hold
*Nick de Bois, C.   18,804
Joan Ryan, Lab.   17,112
Paul Smith, LD   5,403
Tony Avery, BNP   1,228
Madge Jones, UKIP   938
Bill Linton, Green   489
Anthony Williams, Ch. P.   161
Raquel Weald, Eng. Dem.   131
Anna Athow, WRP   96
Gonul Daniels, Ind.   91
C. majority 1,692 (3.81%)
Notional 0.73% swing Lab. to C.
(2005: C. majority 937 (2.35%))

§ENFIELD SOUTHGATE
E. 64,138   T. 44,352 (69.15%)   C. hold
David Burrowes, C.   21,928
Bambos Charalambous, Lab.   14,302
Johar Khan, LD   6,124
Peter Krakowiak, Green   632
Bob Brock, UKIP   505
Dr Asit Mukhopadhyay, Ind.   391
Samad Billoo, Respect   174
Ben Weald, Eng. Dem.   173
Mal Malakounides, ND   88
Jeremy Sturgess, BB   35
C. majority 7,626 (17.19%)
Notional 7.24% swing Lab. to C.
(2005: C. majority 1,127 (2.72%))

§EPPING FOREST
E. 72,198   T. 46,584 (64.52%)   C. hold
Eleanor Laing, C.   25,148
Ann Haigh, LD   10,017
Katie Curtis, Lab.   6,641
Pat Richardson, BNP   1,982
Andrew Smith, UKIP   1,852
Simon Pepper, Green   659
Kim Sawyer, Eng. Dem.   285
C. majority 15,131 (32.48%)
Notional 1.08% swing C. to LD
(2005: C. majority 13,473 (31.33%))

§EPSOM & EWELL
E. 78,104   T. 54,955 (70.36%)   C. hold
Chris Grayling, C.   30,868
Jonathan Lees, LD   14,734
Craig Montgomery, Lab.   6,538
Elizabeth Wallace, UKIP   2,549
Peter Ticher, RRG   266
C. majority 16,134 (29.36%)
Notional 2.05% swing C. to LD
(2005: C. majority 16,342 (33.47%))

§EREWASH
E. 69,654   T. 47,642 (68.40%)   C. gain
*Jessica Lee, C.   18,805
Cheryl Pidgeon, Lab.   16,304
Martin Garnett, LD   8,343
Mark Bailey, BNP   2,337
Jodie Sutton, UKIP   855
Lee Fletcher, Green   534
Luke Wilkins, Ind.   464
C. majority 2,501 (5.25%)
Notional 10.45% swing Lab. to C.
(2005: Lab. majority 6,782 (15.66%))

§ERITH & THAMESMEAD
E. 69,918   T. 42,476 (60.75%)   Lab. hold
*Teresa Pearce, Lab.   19,068
Colin Bloom, C.   13,365
Alexander Cunliffe, LD   5,116
Kevin Saunders, BNP   2,184
Pamela Perrin, UKIP   1,139
Laurence Williams, Eng. Dem.   465
Abbey Akinoshun, ND   438
Sid Cordle, CPA   379
Marek Powley, Green   322
Lab. majority 5,703 (13.43%)
Notional 6.34% swing Lab. to C.
(2005: Lab. majority 9,870 (26.11%))

ESHER & WALTON
E. 75,338   T. 54,543 (72.40%)   C. hold
*Dominic Raab, C.   32,134
Lionel Blackman, LD   13,541
Francis Eldergill, Lab.   5,829
Bernard Collignon, UKIP   1,783
Tony Popham, Ind.   378
Chinners Chinnery, Loony   341
Mike Kearsley, Eng. Dem.   307
Andy Lear, Best   230
C. majority 18,593 (34.09%)
8.97% swing LD to C.
(2005: C. majority 7,727 (16.14%))

§EXETER
E. 77,157   T. 52,247 (67.72%)   Lab. hold
Ben Bradshaw, Lab.   19,942
Hannah Foster, C.   17,221
Graham Oakes, LD   10,581
Keith Crawford, UKIP   1,930
Chris Gale, Lib.   1,108
Paula Black, Green   792
Robert Farmer, BNP   673
Lab. majority 2,721 (5.21%)
Notional 6.03% swing Lab. to C.
(2005: Lab. majority 8,559 (17.27%))

FAREHAM
E. 75,878   T. 54,345 (71.62%)   C. hold
Mark Hoban, C.   30,037
Alex Bentley, LD   12,945
James Carr, Lab.   7,719
Steve Richards, UKIP   2,235
Peter Doggett, Green   791
Joe Jenkins, Eng. Dem.   618
C. majority 17,092 (31.45%)
1.73% swing LD to C.
(2005: C. majority 11,702 (24.09%))

§FAVERSHAM & KENT MID
E. 68,858   T. 46,712 (67.84%)   C. hold
Hugh Robertson, C.   26,250
David Naghi, LD   9,162
Ash Rehal, Lab.   7,748
Sarah Larkins, UKIP   1,722
Tim Valentine, Green   890
Graham Kemp, NF   542
Hairy Knorm Davidson, Loony   398
C. majority 17,088 (36.58%)
Notional 1.62% swing LD to C.
(2005: C. majority 8,927 (21.00%))

§¶FELTHAM & HESTON
E. 81,058 T. 48,526 (59.87%)
                      Lab. (Co-op) hold
Alan Keen, Lab. (Co-op)   21,174
Mark Bowen, C.   16,516
Munira Wilson, LD   6,669
John Donnelly, BNP   1,714
Jerry Shadbolt, UKIP   992
Elizabeth Anstis, Green   530
Dharmendra Tripathi, Ind.   505
Asa Khaira, Ind.   180
Roger Williams, Ind.   168
Matthew Linley, WRP   78
Lab. (Co-op) majority 4,658 (9.60%)
Notional 4.83% swing Lab. (Co-op) to C.
(2005: Lab. (Co-op) majority 7,598
(19.25%))

§FILTON & BRADLEY STOKE
E. 69,003 T. 48,301 (70.00%) C. hold
*Jack Lopresti, C. 19,686
Ian Boulton, Lab. 12,772
Peter Tyzack, LD 12,197
John Knight, UKIP 1,506
David Scott, BNP 1,328
Jon Lucas, Green 441
Ruth Johnson, Ch. P. 199
Vote Zero None of the Above, ND 172
C. majority 6,914 (14.31%)
Notional 6.37% swing Lab. to C.
(2005: C. majority 653 (1.58%))

§FINCHLEY & GOLDERS GREEN
E. 77,198 T. 47,157 (61.09%) C. hold
*Mike Freer, C. 21,688
Alison Moore, Lab. 15,879
Laura Edge, LD 8,036
Susan Cummins, UKIP 817
Donald Lyven, Green 737
C. majority 5,809 (12.32%)
Notional 5.81% swing Lab. to C.
(2005: C. majority 294 (0.70%))

§FOLKESTONE & HYTHE
E. 78,003 T. 52,800 (67.69%) C. hold
*Damian Collins, C. 26,109
Lynne Beaumont, LD 15,987
Donald Worsley, Lab. 5,719
Frank McKenna, UKIP 2,439
Harry Williams, BNP 1,662
Penny Kemp, Green 637
David Plumstead, Ind. 247
C. majority 10,122 (19.17%)
Notional 2.58% swing C. to LD
(2005: C. majority 12,446 (24.33%))

FOREST OF DEAN
E. 68,419 T. 48,763 (71.27%) C. hold
Mark Harper, C. 22,853
Bruce Hogan, Lab. 11,789
Chris Coleman, LD 10,676
Tim Congdon, UKIP 2,522
James Greenwood, Green 923
C. majority 11,064 (22.69%)
9.19% swing Lab. to C.
(2005: C. majority 2,049 (4.30%))

§FYLDE
E. 65,917 T. 43,690 (66.28%) C. hold
*Mark Menzies, C. 22,826
Bill Winlow, LD 9,641
Liam Robinson, Lab. 8,624
Martin Bleeker, UKIP 1,945
Philip Mitchell, Green 654
C. majority 13,185 (30.18%)
Notional 4.15% swing C. to LD
(2005: C. majority 11,117 (28.67%))

§GAINSBOROUGH
E. 72,144 T. 49,251 (68.27%) C. hold
Edward Leigh, C. 24,266
Pat O'Connor, LD 13,707
Jamie McMahon, Lab. 7,701
Steve Pearson, UKIP 2,065
Malcolm Porter, BNP 1,512
C. majority 10,559 (21.44%)
Notional 1.80% swing LD to C.
(2005: C. majority 7,895 (17.73%))

§GARSTON & HALEWOOD
E. 71,312 T. 42,825 (60.05%) Lab. hold
Maria Eagle, Lab. 25,493
Paula Keaveney, LD 8,616
Richard Downey, C. 6,908
Tony Hammond, UKIP 1,540
Diana Raby, Respect 268
Lab. majority 16,877 (39.41%)
Notional 5.74% swing LD to Lab.
(2005: Lab. majority 10,814 (27.92%))

§GATESHEAD
E. 66,492 T. 38,257 (57.54%) Lab. hold
*Ian Mearns, Lab. 20,712
Frank Hindle, LD 8,163
Hazel Anderson, C. 5,716
Kevin Scott, BNP 1,787
John Tennant, UKIP 1,103
Andy Redfern, Green 379
Elaine Brunskill, TUSC 266
David Walton, Ch. P. 131
Lab. majority 12,549 (32.80%)
Notional 3.94% swing Lab. to LD
(2005: Lab. majority 14,245 (40.68%))

§GEDLING
E. 70,590 T. 48,190 (68.27%) Lab. hold
Vernon Coaker, Lab. 19,821
Bruce Laughton, C. 17,962
Julia Bateman, LD 7,350
Stephen Adcock, BNP 1,598
Dave Marshall, UKIP 1,459
Lab. majority 1,859 (3.86%)
Notional 2.89% swing Lab. to C.
(2005: Lab. majority 4,335 (9.63%))

§GILLINGHAM & RAINHAM
E. 70,865 T. 46,786 (66.02%) C. gain
*Rehman Chishti, C. 21,624
Paul Clark, Lab. 12,944
Andrew Stamp, LD 8,484
Robert Oakley, UKIP 1,515
Brian Ravenscroft, BNP 1,149
Dean Lacey, Eng. Dem. 464
Trish Marchant, Green 356
Gordon Bryan, ND 141
George Meegan, Med. Ind. 109
C. majority 8,680 (18.55%)
Notional 9.29% swing Lab. to C.
(2005: Lab. majority 15 (0.03%))

§GLOUCESTER
E. 79,322 T. 50,764 (64.00%) C. gain
*Richard Graham, C. 20,267
Parmjit Dhanda, Lab. 17,847
Jeremy Hilton, LD 9,767
Mike Smith, UKIP 1,808
Alan Platt, Eng. Dem. 564
Bryan Meloy, Green 511
C. majority 2,420 (4.77%)
Notional 8.86% swing Lab. to C.
(2005: Lab. majority 6,063 (12.95%))

GOSPORT
E. 72,720 T. 46,939 (64.55%) C. hold
*Caroline Dinenage, C. 24,300
Rob Hylands, LD 9,887
Graham Giles, Lab. 7,944
Andrew Rice, UKIP 1,496
Barry Bennett, BNP 1,004
Bob Shaw, Eng. Dem. 622
Andrea Smith, Green 573
David Smith, Ind. 493
Charles Read, Ind. 331
Brian Hart, Ind. 289
C. majority 14,413 (30.71%)
1.27% swing LD to C.
(2005: C. majority 5,730 (13.32%))

§GRANTHAM & STAMFORD
E. 78,000 T. 52,799 (67.69%) C. hold
*Nicholas Boles, C. 26,552
Harrish Bisnauthsing, LD 11,726
Mark Bartlett, Lab. 9,503
Christopher Robinson, BNP 2,485
Tony Wells, UKIP 1,604
Mark Horn, Lincs Ind. 929
C. majority 14,826 (28.08%)
Notional 1.18% swing C. to LD
(2005: C. majority 7,308 (15.77%))

GRAVESHAM
E. 70,195 T. 47,303 (67.39%) C. hold
Adam Holloway, C. 22,956
Kathryn Smith, Lab. (Co-op) 13,644
Anna Arrowsmith, LD 6,293
Geoffrey Clark, UKIP 2,265
Steven Uncles, Eng. Dem. 1,005
Richard Crawford, Green 675
Alice Dartnell, Ind. 465
C. majority 9,312 (19.69%)
9.12% swing Lab. (Co-op) to C.
(2005: C. majority 654 (1.45%))

GREAT GRIMSBY
E. 61,229 T. 32,954 (53.82%) Lab. hold
Austin Mitchell, Lab. 10,777
Victoria Ayling, C. 10,063
Andrew de Freitas, LD 7,388
Henry Hudson, UKIP 2,043
Steve Fyfe, BNP 1,517
Ernie Brown, Ind. 835
Adrian Howe, PNDP 331
Lab. majority 714 (2.17%)
10.53% swing Lab. to C.
(2005: Lab. majority 7,654 (23.22%))

GREAT YARMOUTH
E. 70,315 T. 45,037 (61.25%) C. gain
*Brandon Lewis, C. 18,571
Tony Wright, Lab. 14,295
Simon Partridge, LD 6,188
Alan Baugh, UKIP 2,066
Bosco Tann, BNP 1,421
Laura Biggart, Green 416
Margaret McMahon-Morris, LTT 100
C. majority 4,276 (9.93%)
8.66% swing Lab. to C.
(2005: Lab. majority 3,055 (7.38%))

§GREENWICH & WOOLWICH
E. 65,489 T. 41,188 (62.89%) Lab. hold
Nick Raynsford, Lab. 20,262
Spencer Drury, C. 10,109
Joseph Lee, LD 7,498
Lawrence Rustem, BNP 1,151
Andy Hewett, Green 1,054
Edward Adeleye, Ch. P. 443
Topo Wresniwiro, Eng. Dem. 339
Onay Kasab, TUSC 267
Dr Tammy Alingham, Ind. 65
Lab. majority 10,153 (24.65%)
Notional 5.12% swing Lab. to C.
(2005: Lab. majority 11,638 (32.77%))

§GUILDFORD
E. 77,082 T. 55,567 (72.09%) C. hold
Anne Milton, C. 29,618
Sue Doughty, LD 21,836
Tim Shand, Lab. 2,812
Mazhar Manzoor, UKIP 1,021
John Morris, PPN-V 280
C. majority 7,782 (14.00%)
Notional 6.91% swing LD to C.
(2005: C. majority 89 (0.17%))

§HACKNEY NORTH & STOKE
NEWINGTON
E. 73,874   T. 46,488 (62.93%)   Lab. hold
Diane Abbott, Lab.   25,553
Keith Angus, LD   11,092
Darren Caplan, C.   6,759
Matt Sellwood, Green   2,133
Maxine Hargreaves, Ch. P.   299
Suzanne Moore, ND   285
Knigel Knapp, Loony   182
Paul Shaer, Ind.   96
Alessandra Williams, Ind.   61
Dr Jack Pope-De-Locksley, Magna
  Carta   28
Lab. majority 14,461 (31.11%)
Notional 2.61% swing LD to Lab.
(2005: Lab. majority 8,002 (25.88%))

§HACKNEY SOUTH & SHOREDITCH
E. 72,816   T. 42,858 (58.86%)   Lab. hold
Meg Hillier, Lab.   23,888
Dave Raval, LD   9,600
Simon Nayyar, C.   5,800
Polly Lane, Green   1,493
Michael King, UKIP   651
Ben Rae, Lib.   539
John Williams, Ch. P.   434
Nusret Sen, DDP   202
Paul Davies, Comm. Lge   110
Denny De La Haye, Ind.   95
Jane Tuckett, Ind.   26
Michael Spinks, Ind.   20
Lab. majority 14,288 (33.34%)
Notional 0.99% swing LD to Lab.
(2005: Lab. majority 9,629 (31.37%))

§HALESOWEN & ROWLEY REGIS
E. 63,693   T. 43,979 (69.05%)   C. gain
*James Morris, C.   18,115
Sue Hayman, Lab.   16,092
Philip Tibbets, LD   6,515
Derek Baddeley, UKIP   2,824
Derek Thompson, Ind.   433
C. majority 2,023 (4.60%)
Notional 7.13% swing Lab. to C.
(2005: Lab. majority 4,010 (9.66%))

§HALIFAX
E. 70,380   T. 43,555 (61.89%)   Lab. hold
Linda Riordan, Lab.   16,278
Philip Allott, C.   14,806
Elisabeth Wilson, LD   8,335
Tom Bates, BNP   2,760
Diane Park, Ind. Voice   722
Jay Sangha, UKIP   654
Lab. majority 1,472 (3.38%)
Notional 2.69% swing Lab. to C.
(2005: Lab. majority 3,481 (8.75%))

§HALTEMPRICE & HOWDEN
E. 70,403   T. 48,737 (69.23%)   C. hold
David Davis, C.   24,486
Jon Neal, LD   12,884
Danny Marten, Lab.   7,630
James Cornell, BNP   1,583
Joanne Robinson, Eng. Dem.   1,485
Shan Oakes, Green   669
C. majority 11,602 (23.81%)
Notional 6.64% swing LD to C.
(2005: C. majority 5,080 (10.52%))

§HALTON
E. 68,884   T. 41,338 (60.01%)   Lab. hold
Derek Twigg, Lab.   23,843
Ben Jones, C.   8,339
Frank Harasiwka, LD   5,718
Andrew Taylor, BNP   1,563
John Moore, UKIP   1,228
Jim Craig, Green   647
Lab. majority 15,504 (37.51%)
Notional 2.87% swing Lab. to C.
(2005: Lab. majority 16,060 (43.25%))

§HAMMERSMITH
E. 72,348   T. 47,452 (65.59%)   Lab. hold
Andy Slaughter, Lab.   20,810
Shaun Bailey, C.   17,261
Merlene Emerson, LD   7,567
Rollo Miles, Green   696
Vanessa Crichton, UKIP   551
Lawrence Searle, BNP   432
Stephen Brennan, Ind.   135
Lab. majority 3,549 (7.48%)
Notional 0.48% swing Lab. to C.
(2005: Lab. majority 3,673 (8.44%))

§HAMPSHIRE EAST
E. 72,250   T. 51,317 (71.03%)   C. hold
*Damian Hinds, C.   29,137
Adam Carew, LD   15,640
Jane Edbrooke, Lab.   4,043
Hugh McGuinness, UKIP   1,477
Matt Williams, Eng. Dem.   710
Don Jerrard, J & AC   310
C. majority 13,497 (26.30%)
Notional 6.61% swing LD to C.
(2005: C. majority 5,968 (13.09%))

§HAMPSHIRE NORTH EAST
E. 72,196   T. 52,939 (73.33%)   C. hold
James Arbuthnot, C.   32,075
Denzil Coulson, LD   13,478
Barry Jones, Lab.   5,173
Ruth Duffin, UKIP   2,213
C. majority 18,597 (35.13%)
Notional 4.52% swing LD to C.
(2005: C. majority 11,189 (26.09%))

§HAMPSHIRE NORTH WEST
E. 76,040   T. 53,292 (70.08%)   C. hold
Sir George Young, C.   31,072
Thomas McCann, LD   12,489
Sarah Evans, Lab.   6,980
Stan Oram, UKIP   2,751
C. majority 18,583 (34.87%)
Notional 4.67% swing LD to C.
(2005: C. majority 12,683 (25.53%))

§HAMPSTEAD & KILBURN
E. 79,713   T. 52,822 (66.27%)   Lab. hold
Glenda Jackson, Lab.   17,332
Chris Philp, C.   17,290
Edward Fordham, LD   16,491
Bea Campbell, Green   759
Magnus Nielsen, UKIP   408
Victoria Moore, BNP   328
Tamsin Omond, TOC   123
Gene Alcantara, Ind.   91
Lab. majority 42 (0.08%)
Notional 6.65% swing Lab. to C.
(2005: Lab. majority 474 (1.14%))

§HARBOROUGH
E. 77,917   T. 54,945 (70.52%)   C. hold
Edward Garnier, C.   26,894
Zuffar Haq, LD   17,097
Kevin McKeever, Lab.   6,981
Geoff Dickens, BNP   1,715
Marrietta King, UKIP   1,462
David Ball, Eng. Dem.   568
Jeff Stephenson, Ind.   228
C. majority 9,797 (17.83%)
Notional 4.73% swing LD to C.
(2005: C. majority 4,047 (8.38%))

§HARLOW
E. 67,439   T. 43,878 (65.06%)   C. gain
*Robert Halfon, C.   19,691
Bill Rammell, Lab.   14,766
David White, LD   5,990
Eddy Butler, BNP   1,739
John Croft, UKIP   1,591
Oluyemi Adeeko, Ch. P.   101
C. majority 4,925 (11.22%)
Notional 5.90% swing Lab. to C.
(2005: Lab. majority 230 (0.58%))

§HARROGATE & KNARESBOROUGH
E. 75,269   T. 53,134 (70.59%)   C. gain
*Andrew Jones, C.   24,305
Claire Kelley, LD   23,266
Kevin McNerney, Lab.   3,413
Steven Gill, BNP   1,094
John Upex, UKIP   1,056
C. majority 1,039 (1.96%)
Notional 9.09% swing LD to C.
(2005: LD majority 7,980 (16.22%))

§HARROW EAST
E. 68,554   T. 48,006 (70.03%)   C. gain
*Bob Blackman, C.   21,435
Tony McNulty, Lab.   18,032
Nahid Boethe, LD   6,850
Abhijit Pandya, UKIP   896
Madeleine Atkins, Green   793
C. majority 3,403 (7.09%)
Notional 6.99% swing Lab. to C.
(2005: Lab. majority 2,934 (6.89%))

§HARROW WEST
E. 71,510   T. 46,116 (64.49%)
                              Lab. (Co-op) hold
Gareth Thomas, Lab. (Co-op)   20,111
Dr Rachel Joyce, C.   16,968
Christopher Noyce, LD   7,458
Herbert Crossman, UKIP   954
Rowan Langley, Green   625
Lab. (Co-op) majority 3,143 (6.82%)
Notional 5.72% swing Lab. (Co-op) to C.
(2005: Lab. (Co-op) majority 7,742
(18.26%))

HARTLEPOOL
E. 68,923   T. 38,242 (55.49%)   Lab. hold
Iain Wright, Lab.   16,267
Alan Wright, C.   10,758
Reg Clark, LD   6,533
Stephen Allison, UKIP   2,682
Ronnie Bage, BNP   2,002
Lab. majority 5,509 (14.41%)
12.82% swing Lab. to C.
(2005: Lab. majority 7,478 (21.10%))

§HARWICH & ESSEX NORTH
E. 70,743   T. 49,000 (69.26%)   C. hold
Bernard Jenkin, C.   23,001
James Raven, LD   11,554
Darren Barrenger, Lab.   9,774
Simon Anselmi, UKIP   2,527
Stephen Robey, BNP   1,065
Chris Fox, Green   909
Peter Thompson Bates, Ind.   170
C. majority 11,447 (23.36%)
Notional 0.00% swing C. to LD
(2005: C. majority 5,583 (11.73%))

§HASTINGS & RYE
E. 78,000   T. 49,814 (63.86%)   C. gain
*Amber Rudd, C.   20,468
Michael Foster, Lab.   18,475
Nicholas Perry, LD   7,825
Anthony Smith, UKIP   1,397
Nicholas Prince, BNP   1,310
Rodney Bridger, Eng. Dem.   339
C. majority 1,993 (4.00%)
Notional 3.27% swing Lab. to C.
(2005: Lab. majority 1,156 (2.54%))

§HAVANT
E. 69,712   T. 43,903 (62.98%)   C. hold
David Willetts, C.   22,433
Alex Payton, LD   10,273
Robert Smith, Lab.   7,777
Gary Kerrin, UKIP   2,611
Fungus Addams, Eng. Dem.   809
C. majority 12,160 (27.70%)
Notional 1.79% swing LD to C.
(2005: C. majority 6,395 (15.58%))

§HAYES & HARLINGTON
E. 70,233   T. 42,637 (60.71%)   Lab. hold
John McDonnell, Lab.   23,377
Scott Seaman-Digby, C.   12,553
Satnam Kaur Khalsa, LD   3,726
Chris Forster, UKIP   1,520
Andrew Cripps, NF   566
Cliff Dixon, Eng. Dem.   464
Jessica Lee, Green   348
Aneel Shahzad, Ch. P.   83
Lab. majority 10,824 (25.39%)
Notional 1.65% swing Lab. to C.
(2005: Lab. majority 10,594 (28.68%))

§HAZEL GROVE
E. 63,074   T. 41,981 (66.56%)   LD hold
Andrew Stunell, LD   20,485
Annesley Abercorn, C.   14,114
Richard Scorer, Lab.   5,234
John Whittaker, UKIP   2,148
LD majority 6,371 (15.18%)
Notional 2.37% swing LD to C.
(2005: LD majority 7,694 (19.92%))

§HEMEL HEMPSTEAD
E. 72,754   T. 49,471 (68.00%)   C. hold
Mike Penning, C.   24,721
Dr Richard Grayson, LD   11,315
Ayfer Orhan, Lab.   10,295
Janet Price, BNP   1,615
David Alexander, UKIP   1,254
Mick Young, Ind.   271
C. majority 13,406 (27.10%)
Notional 1.94% swing LD to C.
(2005: C. majority 168 (0.36%))

§HEMSWORTH
E. 72,552   T. 43,840 (60.43%)   Lab. hold
Jon Trickett, Lab.   20,506
Ann Myatt, C.   10,662
Alan Belmore, LD   5,667
Ian Womersley, Ind.   3,946
Ian Kitchen, BNP   3,059
Lab. majority 9,844 (22.45%)
Notional 7.03% swing Lab. to C.
(2005: Lab. majority 14,026 (36.51%))

§HENDON
E. 78,923   T. 46,374 (58.76%)   C. gain
*Matthew Offord, C.   19,635
Andrew Dismore, Lab.   19,529
Matthew Harris, LD   5,734
Robin Lambert, UKIP   958
Andrew Newby, Green   518
C. majority 106 (0.23%)
Notional 4.14% swing Lab. to C.
(2005: Lab. majority 3,231 (8.06%))

§HENLEY
E. 75,005   T. 53,520 (71.36%)   C. hold
John Howell, C.   30,054
Andrew Crick, LD   13,466
Richard McKenzie, Lab.   5,835
Laurence Hughes, UKIP   1,817
Mark Stevenson, Green   1,328
John Bews, BNP   1,020
C. majority 16,588 (30.99%)
Notional 1.93% swing LD to C.
(2005: C. majority 13,366 (27.13%))

§HEREFORD & HEREFORDSHIRE
SOUTH
E. 71,435   T. 48,381 (67.73%)   C. gain
*Jesse Norman, C.   22,366
Sarah Carr, LD   19,885
Philippa Roberts, Lab.   3,506
Valentine Smith, UKIP   1,638
John Oliver, Green   986
C. majority 2,481 (5.13%)
Notional 3.76% swing LD to C.
(2005: LD majority 1,089 (2.39%))

§HEREFORDSHIRE NORTH
E. 66,525   T. 47,568 (71.50%)   C. hold
Bill Wiggin, C.   24,631
Lucy Hurds, LD   14,744
Neil Sabharwal, Lab.   3,373
Jonathan Oakton, UKIP   2,701
Felicity Norman, Green   1,533
John King, Ind.   586
C. majority 9,887 (20.78%)
Notional 3.82% swing LD to C.
(2005: C. majority 12,688 (28.43%))

§HERTFORD & STORTFORD
E. 78,459   T. 55,377 (70.58%)   C. hold
Mark Prisk, C.   29,810
Andrew Lewin, LD   14,373
Steve Terry, Lab.   7,620
David Sodey, UKIP   1,716
Roy Harris, BNP   1,297
Loucas Xenophontos, Ind.   325
Martin Adams, Ind.   236
C. majority 15,437 (27.88%)
Notional 1.95% swing C. to LD
(2005: C. majority 12,756 (25.95%))

§HERTFORDSHIRE NORTH EAST
E. 72,200   T. 50,425 (69.84%)   C. hold
Oliver Heald, C.   26,995
Hugh Annand, LD   11,801
David Kirkman, Lab.   8,291
Adrianne Smyth, UKIP   2,075
Rosemary Bland, Green   875
Richard Campbell, Ind.   209
David Ralph, YRDPL   143
Philip Reichardt, Ind.   36
C. majority 15,194 (30.13%)
Notional 1.19% swing LD to C.
(2005: C. majority 9,510 (19.75%))

§HERTFORDSHIRE SOUTH WEST
E. 78,248   T. 56,750 (72.53%)   C. hold
David Gauke, C.   30,773
Christopher Townsend, LD   15,853
Harry Mann, Lab.   6,526
Mark Benson, UKIP   1,450
Deirdre Gates, BNP   1,302
James Hannaway, Ind.   846
C. majority 14,920 (26.29%)
Notional 4.66% swing LD to C.
(2005: C. majority 8,640 (16.97%))

HERTSMERE
E. 73,062   T. 47,270 (64.70%)   C. hold
James Clappison, C.   26,476
Sam Russell, Lab.   8,871
Anthony Rowlands, LD   8,210
David Rutter, UKIP   1,712
Daniel Seabrook, BNP   1,397
Arjuna Krishna-Das, Green   604
C. majority 17,605 (37.24%)
5.59% swing Lab. to C.
(2005: C. majority 11,093 (26.06%))

§HEXHAM
E. 61,175   T. 43,403 (70.95%)   C. hold
*Guy Opperman, C.   18,795
Andrew Duffield, LD   13,007
Antoine Tinnion, Lab.   8,253
Steve Ford, Ind.   1,974
Quentin Hawkins, BNP   1,205
Colin Moss, Ind.   249
C. majority 5,788 (13.31%)
Notional 1.70% swing C. to LD
(2005: C. majority 4,957 (12.03%))

§HEYWOOD & MIDDLETON
E. 80,171   T. 46,125 (57.53%)   Lab. hold
Jim Dobbin, Lab.   18,499
Michael Holly, C.   12,528
Wera Hobhouse, LD   10,474
Peter Greenwood, BNP   3,239
Victoria Cecil, UKIP   1,215
Chrissy Lee, Ind.   170
Lab. majority 5,971 (12.95%)
Notional 6.82% swing Lab. to C.
(2005: Lab. majority 11,034 (26.58%))

§HIGH PEAK
E. 71,973   T. 50,337 (69.94%)   C. gain
*Andrew Bingham, C.   20,587
Caitlin Bisknell, Lab.   15,910
Alistair Stevens, LD   10,993
Sylvia Hall, UKIP   1,690
Peter Allen, Green   922
Lance Dowson, Ind.   161
Tony Alves, ND   74
C. majority 4,677 (9.29%)
Notional 6.54% swing Lab. to C.
(2005: Lab. majority 1,750 (3.80%))

§HITCHIN & HARPENDEN
E. 73,851   T. 54,707 (74.08%)   C. hold
Peter Lilley, C.   29,869
Nigel Quinton, LD   14,598
Oliver de Botton, Lab.   7,413
Graham Wilkinson, UKIP   1,663
Richard Wise, Green   807
Margaret Henderson, Ind.   109
Simon Byron, R and E   108
Eric Hannah, TRDPL   90
Peter Rigby, Ind.   50
C. majority 15,271 (27.91%)
Notional 2.50% swing LD to C.
(2005: C. majority 11,064 (22.90%))

§HOLBORN & ST PANCRAS
E. 86,863   T. 54,649 (62.91%)   Lab. hold
Frank Dobson, Lab.   25,198
Jo Shaw, LD   15,256
George Lee, C.   11,134
Natalie Bennett, Green   1,480
Robert Carlyle, BNP   779
Max Spencer, UKIP   587
John Chapman, Ind.   96
Mikel Susperregi, Eng. Dem.   75
Iain Meek, Ind.   44
Lab. majority 9,942 (18.19%)
Notional 0.38% swing Lab. to LD
(2005: Lab. majority 8,348 (18.95%))

§HORNCHURCH & UPMINSTER
E. 78,487   T. 53,390 (68.02%)   C. hold
Angela Watkinson, C.   27,469
Kath McGuirk, Lab.   11,098
Karen Chilvers, LD   7,426
William Whelpley, BNP   3,421
Lawrence Webb, UKIP   2,848
Melanie Collins, Green   542
David Durant, Ind.   305
Johnson Olukotun, Ch. P.   281
C. majority 16,371 (30.66%)
Notional 7.14% swing Lab. to C.
(2005: C. majority 8,058 (16.38%))

HORNSEY & WOOD GREEN
E. 79,916   T. 55,042 (68.87%)   LD hold
Lynne Featherstone, LD   25,595
Karen Jennings, Lab.   18,720
Richard Merrin, C.   9,174
Pete McAskie, Green   1,261
Stephane De Roche, Ind.   201
Rohen Kapur, Ind.   91
LD majority 6,875 (12.49%)
3.72% swing Lab. to LD
(2005: LD majority 2,395 (5.06%))

§HORSHAM
E. 76,835   T. 55,841 (72.68%)   C. hold
Francis Maude, C.   29,447
Godfrey Newman, LD   17,987
Andrew Skudder, Lab.   4,189
Harry Aldridge, UKIP   2,839
Nick Fitter, Green   570
Steve Lyon, Ch. P.   469
Jim Duggan, PPN-V   253
Derek Kissach, Ind.   87
C. majority 11,460 (20.52%)
Notional 0.57% swing C. to LD
(2005: C. majority 10,780 (21.66%))

§HOUGHTON & SUNDERLAND SOUTH
E. 68,729   T. 38,021 (55.32%)   Lab. hold
*Bridget Phillipson, Lab.   19,137
Robert Oliver, C.   8,147
Chris Boyle, LD   5,292
Colin Wakefield, Ind.   2,462
Karen Allen, BNP   1,961
Richard Elvin, UKIP   1,022
Lab. majority 10,990 (28.91%)
Notional 0.44% swing Lab. to C.
(2005: Lab. majority 16,986 (45.78%))

§HOVE
E. 71,708   T. 49,819 (69.47%)   C. gain
*Mike Weatherley, C.   18,294
Celia Barlow, Lab.   16,426
Paul Elgood, LD   11,240
Ian Davey, Green   2,568
Paul Perrin, UKIP   1,206
Brian Ralfe, Ind.   85
C. majority 1,868 (3.75%)
Notional 2.37% swing Lab. to C.
(2005: Lab. majority 448 (1.00%))

§HUDDERSFIELD
E. 66,316   T. 40,524 (61.11%)   Lab. hold
Barry Sheerman, Lab.   15,725
Karen Tweed, C.   11,253
James Blanchard, LD   10,023
Andrew Cooper, Green   1,641
Rachel Firth, BNP   1,563
Paul Cooney, TUSC   319
Lab. majority 4,472 (11.04%)
Notional 7.14% swing Lab. to C.
(2005: Lab. majority 7,883 (22.29%))

§HULL EAST
E. 67,530   T. 34,184 (50.62%)   Lab. hold
*Karl Turner, Lab.   16,387
Jeremy Wilcock, LD   7,790
Christine Mackay, C.   5,667
Mike Hookem, UKIP   2,745
Joe Uttley, NF   880
Mike Burton, Eng. Dem.   715
Lab. majority 8,597 (25.15%)
Notional 5.35% swing Lab. to LD
(2005: Lab. majority 11,740 (35.84%))

§HULL NORTH
E. 64,082   T. 33,291 (51.95%)   Lab. hold
Diana Johnson, Lab.   13,044
Denis Healy, LD   12,403
Victoria Aitken, C.   4,365
John Mainprize, BNP   1,443
Paul Barlow, UKIP   1,358
Martin Deane, Green   478
Michael Cassidy, Eng. Dem.   200
Lab. majority 641 (1.93%)
Notional 12.18% swing Lab. to LD
(2005: Lab. majority 7,384 (26.29%))

§HULL WEST & HESSLE
E. 69,017   T. 31,505 (45.65%)   Lab. hold
Alan Johnson, Lab.   13,378
Mike Ross, LD   7,636
Gary Shores, C.   6,361
Ken Hordon, UKIP   1,688
Edward Scott, BNP   1,416
Peter Mawer, Eng. Dem.   876
Keith Gibson, TUSC   150
Lab. majority 5,742 (18.23%)
Notional 7.92% swing Lab. to LD
(2005: Lab. majority 9,430 (34.06%))

§HUNTINGDON
E. 83,557   T. 54,266 (64.94%)   C. hold
Jonathan Djanogly, C.   26,516
Martin Land, LD   15,697
Anthea Cox, Lab.   5,982
Ian Curtis, UKIP   3,258
Jonathan Salt, Ind.   1,432
John Clare, Green   652
Lord Toby Jug, Loony   548
Carrie Holliman, APP   181
C. majority 10,819 (19.94%)
Notional 2.08% swing C. to LD
(2005: C. majority 11,652 (24.10%))

§HYNDBURN
E. 67,221   T. 42,672 (63.48%)   Lab. hold
*Graham Jones, Lab.   17,531
Karen Buckley, C.   14,441
Andrew Rankine, LD   5,033
David Shapcott, BNP   2,137
Granville Barker, UKIP   1,481
The Revd Kevin Logan, CPA   795
Kerry Gormley, Green   463
Christopher Reid, Eng. Dem.   413
Craig Hall, Ind.   378
Lab. majority 3,090 (7.24%)
Notional 3.28% swing Lab. to C.
(2005: Lab. majority 5,528 (13.80%))

§ILFORD NORTH
E. 71,995   T. 47,018 (65.31%)   C. hold
Lee Scott, C.   21,506
Sonia Klein, Lab.   16,102
Alex Berhanu, LD   5,966
Danny Warville, BNP   1,545
Henri van der Stighelen, UKIP   871
Caroline Allen, Green   572
The Revd Robert Hampson, CPA   456
C. majority 5,404 (11.49%)
Notional 3.68% swing Lab. to C.
(2005: C. majority 1,735 (4.14%))

ILFORD SOUTH
E. 75,246 T. 51,191 (68.03%)
                          Lab. (Co-op) hold
Mike Gapes, Lab. (Co-op)   25,301
Toby Boutle, C.   14,014
Anood Al-Samerai, LD   8,679
Wilson Chowdhry, Green   1,319
Terry Murray, UKIP   1,132
John Jestico, King George   746
Lab. (Co-op) majority 11,287 (22.05%)
0.22% swing C. to Lab. (Co-op)
(2005: Lab. (Co-op) majority 9,228
(21.61%))

§IPSWICH
E. 78,371   T. 46,941 (59.90%)   C. gain
*Benedict Gummer, C.   18,371
Chris Mole, Lab.   16,292
Mark Dyson, LD   8,556
Chris Streatfield, UKIP   1,365
Dennis Boater, BNP   1,270
Tim Glover, Green   775
Kim Christofi, Ch. P.   149
Peter Turtill, Ind.   93
Sally Wainman, Ind.   70
C. majority 2,079 (4.43%)
Notional 8.12% swing Lab. to C.
(2005: Lab. majority 5,235 (11.81%))

ISLE OF WIGHT
E. 109,966 T. 70,264 (63.90%) C. hold
Andrew Turner, C. 32,810
Jill Wareham, LD 22,283
Mark Chiverton, Lab. 8,169
Mike Tarrant, UKIP 2,435
Geoff Clynch, BNP 1,457
Ian Dunsire, Eng. Dem. 1,233
Bob Keats, Green 931
Paul Martin, Mid. England 616
Pete Harris, Ind. 175
Paul Randle-Jolliffe, Ind. 89
Edward Corby, Ind. 66
C. majority 10,527 (14.98%)
2.22% swing C. to LD
(2005: C. majority 12,978 (19.42%))

ISLINGTON NORTH
E. 68,120 T. 44,554 (65.41%) Lab. hold
Jeremy Corbyn, Lab. 24,276
Rhodri Jamieson-Ball, LD 11,875
Adrian Berrill-Cox, C. 6,339
Emma Dixon, Green 1,348
Dominic Lennon, UKIP 716
Lab. majority 12,401 (27.83%)
3.25% swing LD to Lab.
(2005: Lab. majority 6,716 (21.32%))

ISLINGTON SOUTH & FINSBURY
E. 67,649 T. 43,555 (64.38%) Lab. hold
Emily Thornberry, Lab. 18,407
Bridget Fox, LD 14,838
Antonia Cox, C. 8,449
James Humphreys, Green 710
Rose-Marie McDonald, UKIP 701
John Dodds, Eng. Dem. 301
Richard Deboo, Animals 149
Lab. majority 3,569 (8.19%)
3.32% swing LD to Lab.
(2005: Lab. majority 484 (1.56%))

§JARROW
E. 64,350 T. 38,784 (60.27%) Lab. hold
Stephen Hepburn, Lab. 20,910
Jeffrey Milburn, C. 8,002
Tom Appleby, LD 7,163
Andy Swaddle, BNP 2,709
Lab. majority 12,908 (33.28%)
Notional 6.38% swing Lab. to C.
(2005: Lab. majority 12,749 (36.35%))

KEIGHLEY
E. 65,893 T. 47,692 (72.38%) C. gain
*Kris Hopkins, C. 20,003
Jane Thomas, Lab. 17,063
Nader Fekri, LD 7,059
Andrew Brons, BNP 1,962
Paul Latham, UKIP 1,470
Steven Smith, NF 135
C. majority 2,940 (6.16%)
8.32% swing Lab. to C.
(2005: Lab. majority 4,852 (10.48%))

§KENILWORTH & SOUTHAM
E. 59,630 T. 48,431 (81.22%) C. hold
Jeremy Wright, C. 25,945
Nigel Rock, LD 13,393
Nicholas Milton, Lab. 6,949
John Moore, UKIP 1,214
James Harrison, Green 568
Joe Rukin, Ind. 362
C. majority 12,552 (25.92%)
Notional 1.20% swing C. to LD
(2005: C. majority 10,956 (24.80%))

§KENSINGTON
E. 65,961 T. 35,150 (53.29%) C. hold
Sir Malcolm Rifkind, C. 17,595
Sam Gurney, Lab. 8,979
Robin Meltzer, LD 6,872
Lady Caroline Pearson, UKIP 754
Zahra-Melan Ebrahimi-Fardouee,
Green 753
Eddie Adams, Green Soc. 197
C. majority 8,616 (24.51%)
Notional 5.19% swing Lab. to C.
(2005: C. majority 4,540 (14.13%))

§KETTERING
E. 68,837 T. 47,328 (68.75%) C. hold
Philip Hollobone, C. 23,247
Phil Sawford, Lab. 14,153
Chris Nelson, LD 7,498
Clive Skinner, BNP 1,366
Derek Hilling, Eng. Dem. 952
Dave Bishop, BP Elvis 112
C. majority 9,094 (19.21%)
Notional 9.41% swing Lab. to C.
(2005: C. majority 176 (0.39%))

§KINGSTON & SURBITON
E. 81,116 T. 57,111 (70.41%) LD hold
Edward Davey, LD 28,428
Helen Whately, C. 20,868
Max Freedman, Lab. 5,337
Jonathan Greensted, UKIP 1,450
Chris Walker, Green 555
Monkey the Drummer, Loony 247
Anthony May, CPA 226
LD majority 7,560 (13.24%)
Notional 2.43% swing LD to C.
(2005: LD majority 9,084 (18.11%))

§KINGSWOOD
E. 66,361 T. 47,906 (72.19%) C. gain
*Chris Skidmore, C. 19,362
Roger Berry, Lab. 16,917
Sally Fitzharris, LD 8,072
Neil Dowdney, UKIP 1,528
Michael Carey, BNP 1,311
Nick Foster, Green 383
Michael Blundell, Eng. Dem. 333
C. majority 2,445 (5.10%)
Notional 9.43% swing Lab. to C.
(2005: Lab. majority 6,145 (13.76%))

§KNOWSLEY
E. 79,561 T. 44,658 (56.13%) Lab. hold
George Howarth, Lab. 31,650
Flo Clucas, LD 5,964
David Dunne, C. 4,004
Steven Greenhalgh, BNP 1,895
Anthony Rundle, UKIP 1,145
Lab. majority 25,686 (57.52%)
Notional 0.25% swing Lab. to LD
(2005: Lab. majority 24,333 (58.02%))

LANCASHIRE WEST
E. 75,975 T. 48,473 (63.80%) Lab. hold
Rosie Cooper, Lab. 21,883
Adrian Owens, C. 17,540
John Gibson, LD 6,573
Damon Noone, UKIP 1,775
Peter Cranie, Green 485
David Braid, Clause 28 217
Lab. majority 4,343 (8.96%)
2.57% swing Lab. to C.
(2005: Lab. majority 6,084 (14.10%))

§LANCASTER & FLEETWOOD
E. 69,908 T. 42,701 (61.08%) C. gain
*Eric Ollerenshaw, C. 15,404
Clive Grunshaw, Lab. 15,071
Stuart Langhorn, LD 8,167
Gina Dowding, Green 1,888
Fred McGlade, UKIP 1,020
Debra Kent, BNP 938
Keith Riley, Ind. 213
C. majority 333 (0.78%)
Notional 4.80% swing Lab. to C.
(2005: Lab. majority 3,428 (8.82%))

§LEEDS CENTRAL
E. 64,698 T. 37,394 (57.80%) Lab. hold
Hilary Benn, Lab. 18,434
Michael Taylor, LD 7,789
Alan Lamb, C. 7,541
Kevin Meeson, BNP 3,066
Dave Procter, Ind. 409
We Beat The Scum One-Nil, ND 155
Lab. majority 10,645 (28.47%)
Notional 4.76% swing Lab. to LD
(2005: Lab. majority 12,916 (37.98%))

§LEEDS EAST
E. 65,067 T. 37,813 (58.11%) Lab. hold
George Mudie, Lab. 19,056
Barry Anderson, C. 8,763
Andrew Tear, LD 6,618
Trevor Brown, BNP 2,947
Michael Davies, Green Soc. 429
Lab. majority 10,293 (27.22%)
Notional 5.49% swing Lab. to C.
(2005: Lab. majority 13,689 (38.21%))

§LEEDS NORTH EAST
E. 67,899 T. 47,535 (70.01%) Lab. hold
Fabian Hamilton, Lab. 20,287
Matthew Lobley, C. 15,742
Aqila Choudhry, LD 9,310
Warren Hendon, UKIP 842
Tom Redmond, BNP 758
Celia Foote, Green Soc. 596
Lab. majority 4,545 (9.56%)
Notional 2.97% swing Lab. to C.
(2005: Lab. majority 6,762 (15.51%))

§LEEDS NORTH WEST
E. 65,399 T. 43,483 (66.49%) LD hold
Greg Mulholland, LD 20,653
Julia Mulligan, C. 11,550
Judith Blake, Lab. 9,132
Geoffrey Bulmer, BNP 766
Mark Thackray, UKIP 600
Martin Hemingway, Green 508
Alan Procter, Eng. Dem. 153
Trevor Bavage, Green Soc. 121
LD majority 9,103 (20.93%)
Notional 5.44% swing C. to LD
(2005: LD majority 2,064 (4.96%))

§LEEDS WEST
E. 67,453 T. 38,752 (57.45%) Lab. hold
*Rachel Reeves, Lab. 16,389
Ruth Coleman, LD 9,373
Joe Marjoram, C. 7,641
Joanna Beverley, BNP 2,377
David Blackburn, Green 1,832
Jeff Miles, UKIP 1,140
Lab. majority 7,016 (18.10%)
Notional 10.36% swing Lab. to LD
(2005: Lab. majority 13,699 (38.83%))

§LEICESTER EAST
E. 72,986   T. 47,995 (65.76%)   Lab. hold
Keith Vaz, Lab.   25,804
Jane Hunt, C.   11,722
Ali Asghar, LD   6,817
Colin Gilmore, BNP   1,700
Mo Taylor, Green   733
Felicity Ransome, UKIP   725
Avtar Sadiq, UPS   494
Lab. majority 14,082 (29.34%)
Notional 4.77% swing Lab. to C.
(2005: Lab. majority 16,400 (38.89%))

§¶LEICESTER SOUTH
E. 77,175   T. 47,124 (61.06%)   Lab. hold
Sir Peter Soulsby, Lab.   21,479
Parmjit Singh Gill, LD   12,671
Ross Grant, C.   10,066
Adrian Waudby, BNP   1,418
Dave Dixey, Green   770
Christopher Lucas, UKIP   720
Lab. majority 8,808 (18.69%)
Notional 4.96% swing LD to Lab.
(2005: Lab. majority 3,727 (8.78%))

§LEICESTER WEST
E. 64,900   T. 35,819 (55.19%)   Lab. hold
*Elizabeth Kendall, Lab.   13,745
Celia Harvey, C.   9,728
Peter Coley, LD   8,107
Gary Reynolds, BNP   2,158
Stephen Ingall, UKIP   883
Geoff Forse, Green   639
Steven Huggins, Ind.   181
Steve Score, TUSC   157
Shaun Dyer, Pirate   113
David Bowley, Ind.   108
Lab. majority 4,017 (11.21%)
Notional 7.60% swing Lab. to C.
(2005: Lab. majority 8,539 (26.42%))

LEICESTERSHIRE NORTH WEST
E. 71,219   T. 51,952 (72.95%)   C. gain
*Andrew Bridgen, C.   23,147
Ross Willmott, Lab. (Co-op)   15,636
Paul Reynolds, LD   8,639
Ian Meller, BNP   3,396
Martin Green, UKIP   1,134
C. majority 7,511 (14.46%)
11.98% swing Lab. (Co-op) to C.
(2005: Lab. (Co-op) majority 4,477
(9.50%))

§LEICESTERSHIRE SOUTH
E. 76,639   T. 54,577 (71.21%)   C. hold
Andrew Robathan, C.   27,000
Aladdin Ayesh, LD   11,476
Sally Gimson, Lab.   11,392
Paul Preston, BNP   2,721
John Williams, UKIP   1,988
C. majority 15,524 (28.44%)
Notional 1.03% swing LD to C.
(2005: C. majority 7,704 (15.77%))

§LEIGH
E. 76,350   T. 44,332 (58.06%)   Lab. hold
Andy Burnham, Lab.   21,295
Shazia Awan, C.   9,284
Chris Blackburn, LD   8,049
Gary Chadwick, BNP   2,724
Mary Lavelle, UKIP   1,535
Norman Bradbury, Ind.   988
Terry Dainty, Ind.   320
Ryan Hessell, Ch. P.   137
Lab. majority 12,011 (27.09%)
Notional 7.17% swing Lab. to C.
(2005: Lab. majority 15,098 (38.73%))

§LEWES
E. 68,708   T. 50,088 (72.90%)   LD hold
Norman Baker, LD   26,048
Jason Sugarman, C.   18,401
Hratche Koundarjian, Lab.   2,508
Peter Charlton, UKIP   1,728
Susan Murray, Green   729
David Lloyd, BNP   594
Ondrej Soucek, Ind.   80
LD majority 7,647 (15.27%)
Notional 0.81% swing LD to C.
(2005: LD majority 7,889 (16.89%))

§LEWISHAM DEPTFORD
E. 67,058   T. 41,220 (61.47%)   Lab. hold
Joan Ruddock, Lab.   22,132
Tam Langley, LD   9,633
Gemma Townsend, C.   5,551
Darren Johnson, Green   2,772
Ian Page, Soc. Alt.   645
Malcolm Martin, CPA   487
Lab. majority 12,499 (30.32%)
Notional 3.56% swing Lab. to LD
(2005: Lab. majority 13,012 (37.43%))

§LEWISHAM EAST
E. 65,926   T. 41,719 (63.28%)   Lab. hold
*Heidi Alexander, Lab.   17,966
Pete Pattisson, LD   11,750
Jonathan Clamp, C.   9,850
Roderick Reed, UKIP   771
Priscilla Cotterell, Green   624
James Rose, Eng. Dem.   426
George Hallam, CNBPG   332
Lab. majority 6,216 (14.90%)
Notional 6.41% swing Lab. to LD
(2005: Lab. majority 8,758 (23.31%))

§LEWISHAM WEST & PENGE
E. 69,022   T. 45,028 (65.24%)   Lab. hold
Jim Dowd, Lab.   18,501
Alex Feakes, LD   12,673
Chris Phillips, C.   11,489
Peter Staveley, UKIP   1,117
Romayne Phoenix, Green   931
Stephen Hammond, CPA   317
Lab. majority 5,828 (12.94%)
Notional 3.10% swing Lab. to LD
(2005: Lab. majority 7,779 (19.15%))

§LEYTON & WANSTEAD
E. 63,541   T. 40,159 (63.20%)   Lab. hold
*John Cryer, Lab.   17,511
Farooq Qureshi, LD   11,095
Ed Northover, C.   8,928
Graham Wood, UKIP   1,080
Ashley Gunstock, Green   562
Jim Clift, BNP   561
Sonika Bhatti, Ch. P.   342
Martin Levin, Ind. Fed.   80
Lab. majority 6,416 (15.98%)
Notional 2.57% swing Lab. to LD
(2005: Lab. majority 7,253 (21.11%))

§LICHFIELD
E. 72,586   T. 51,563 (71.04%)   C. hold
Michael Fabricant, C.   28,048
Ian Jackson, LD   10,365
Steve Hyden, Lab.   10,230
Karen Maunder, UKIP   2,920
C. majority 17,683 (34.29%)
Notional 0.74% swing LD to C.
(2005: C. majority 7,791 (16.49%))

§LINCOLN
E. 73,540   T. 45,721 (62.17%)   C. gain
*Karl McCartney, C.   17,163
Gillian Merron, Lab.   16,105
Reg Shore, LD   9,256
Robert West, BNP   1,367
Nick Smith, UKIP   1,004
Ernest Coleman, Eng. Dem.   604
Gary Walker, Ind.   222
C. majority 1,058 (2.31%)
Notional 5.89% swing Lab. to C.
(2005: Lab. majority 3,806 (9.47%))

§LIVERPOOL RIVERSIDE
E. 74,539   T. 38,801 (52.05%)   Lab. hold
Louise Ellman, Lab.   22,998
Richard Marbrow, LD   8,825
Kegang Wu, C.   4,243
Tom Crone, Green   1,355
Peter Stafford, BNP   706
Pat Gaskell, UKIP   674
Lab. majority 14,173 (36.53%)
Notional 0.30% swing LD to Lab.
(2005: Lab. majority 11,731 (35.93%))

§LIVERPOOL WALTON
E. 62,612   T. 34,335 (54.84%)   Lab. hold
*Steve Rotheram, Lab.   24,709
Patrick Moloney, LD   4,891
Adam Marsden, C.   2,241
Peter Stafford, BNP   1,104
Joe Nugent, UKIP   898
John Manwell, CPA   297
Daren Ireland, TUSC   195
Lab. majority 19,818 (57.72%)
Notional 1.47% swing LD to Lab.
(2005: Lab. majority 17,611 (54.77%))

§LIVERPOOL WAVERTREE
E. 62,518 T. 37,914 (60.64%)
                               Lab. (Co-op) hold
*Luciana Berger, Lab. (Co-op)   20,132
Colin Eldridge, LD   12,965
Andrew Garnett, C.   2,830
Neil Miney, UKIP   890
Rebecca Lawson, Green   598
Kim Singleton, Soc. Lab.   200
Steven McEllenborough, BNP   150
Frank Dunne, Ind.   149
Lab. (Co-op) majority 7,167 (18.90%)
Notional 5.00% swing LD to Lab. (Co-op)
(2005: Lab. (Co-op) majority 2,911
(8.91%))

§LIVERPOOL WEST DERBY
E. 63,082 T. 35,784 (56.73%)
                               Lab. (Co-op) hold
*Stephen Twigg, Lab. (Co-op)   22,953
Paul Twigger, LD   4,486
Stephen Radford, Lib   3,327
Pamela Hall, C.   3,311
Hilary Jones, UKIP   1,093
Kai Andersen, Soc. Lab.   614
Lab. (Co-op) majority 18,467 (51.61%)
Notional 3.16% swing LD to Lab. (Co-op)
(2005: Lab. (Co-op) majority 13,874
(45.29%))

§LOUGHBOROUGH
E. 77,502   T. 52,838 (68.18%)   C. gain
*Nicky Morgan, C.   21,971
Andy Reed, Lab. (Co-op)   18,227
Mike Willis, LD   9,675
Kevan Stafford, BNP   2,040
John Foden, UKIP   925
C. majority 3,744 (7.09%)
Notional 5.48% swing Lab. (Co-op) to C.
(2005: Lab. (Co-op) majority 1,816
(3.88%))

§LOUTH & HORNCASTLE
E. 77,650   T. 50,494 (65.03%)   C. hold
Sir Peter Tapsell, C. 25,065
Fiona Martin, LD 11,194
Patrick Mountain, Lab. 8,760
Julia Green, BNP 2,199
Pat Nurse, UKIP 2,183
Daniel Simpson, Lincs Ind. 576
Colin Mair, Eng. Dem. 517
C. majority 13,871 (27.47%)
Notional 0.80% swing LD to C.
(2005: C. majority 9,813 (21.08%))

LUDLOW
E. 66,631   T. 48,732 (73.14%)   C. hold
Philip Dunne, C. 25,720
Heather Kidd, LD 15,971
Anthony Hunt, Lab. 3,272
Christopher Gill, UKIP 2,127
Christina Evans, BNP 1,016
Jacqui Morrish, Green 447
Alan Powell, Loony 179
C. majority 9,749 (20.01%)
7.82% swing LD to C.
(2005: C. majority 2,027 (4.36%))

§LUTON NORTH
E. 65,062   T. 43,018 (66.12%)   Lab. hold
Kelvin Hopkins, Lab. 21,192
Jeremy Brier, C. 13,672
Rabi Martins, LD 4,784
Colin Brown, UKIP 1,564
Shelley Rose, BNP 1,316
Simon Hall, Green 490
Lab. majority 7,520 (17.48%)
Notional 0.55% swing C. to Lab.
(2005: Lab. majority 6,439 (16.39%))

§LUTON SOUTH
E. 59,962 T. 42,216 (70.40%)
                         Lab. (Co-op) hold
*Gavin Shuker, Lab. (Co-op) 14,725
Nigel Huddleston, C. 12,396
Qurban Hussain, LD 9,567
Esther Rantzen, Ind. Rantzen 1,872
Tony Blakey, BNP 1,299
Charles Lawman, UKIP 975
Stephen Rhodes, Ind. 463
Marc Scheimann, Green 366
Joe Hall, Ind. 264
Faruk Choudhury, Ind. 130
Stephen Lathwell, Ind. 84
Frank Sweeney, WRP 75
Lab. (Co-op) majority 2,329 (5.52%)
Notional 4.59% swing Lab. (Co-op) to C.
(2005: Lab. (Co-op) majority 5,698
(14.71%))

§MACCLESFIELD
E. 73,417   T. 50,059 (68.18%)   C. hold
*David Rutley, C. 23,503
Roger Barlow, LD 11,544
Adrian Heald, Lab. 10,164
Brendan Murphy, Macc. Ind. 2,590
Jacqueline Smith, UKIP 1,418
John Knight, Green 840
C. majority 11,959 (23.89%)
Notional 3.11% swing C. to LD
(2005: C. majority 9,464 (20.66%))

§MAIDENHEAD
E. 72,844   T. 53,720 (73.75%)   C. hold
Theresa May, C. 31,937
Tony Hill, LD 15,168
Pat McDonald, Lab. 3,795
Kenneth Wight, UKIP 1,243
Tim Rait, BNP 825
Peter Forbes, Green 482
Peter Prior, F and R 270
C. majority 16,769 (31.22%)
Notional 7.82% swing LD to C.
(2005: C. majority 7,650 (15.58%))

§MAIDSTONE & THE WEALD
E. 71,041   T. 48,928 (68.87%)   C. hold
*Helen Grant, C. 23,491
Peter Carroll, LD 17,602
Rav Seeruthun, Lab. 4,769
Gareth Kendall, UKIP 1,637
Stuart Jeffery, Green 655
Gary Butler, NF 643
Heidi Simmonds, Ch. P. 131
C. majority 5,889 (12.04%)
Notional 8.48% swing C. to LD
(2005: C. majority 12,922 (28.99%))

§MAKERFIELD
E. 73,641   T. 43,771 (59.44%)   Lab. hold
*Yvonne Fovargue, Lab. 20,700
Itrat Ali, C. 8,210
David Crowther, LD 7,082
Bob Brierley, Ind. 3,424
Ken Haslam, BNP 3,229
John Mather, Ind. 1,126
Lab. majority 12,490 (28.53%)
Notional 9.98% swing Lab. to C.
(2005: Lab. majority 17,903 (48.49%))

§MALDON
E. 68,861   T. 47,895 (69.55%)   C. hold
John Whittingdale, C. 28,661
Elfreda Tealby-Watson, LD 9,254
Swatantra Nandanwar, Lab. 6,070
Jesse Pryke, UKIP 2,446
Len Blaine, BNP 1,464
C. majority 19,407 (40.52%)
Notional 0.40% swing C. to LD
(2005: C. majority 13,631 (32.13%))

§¶MANCHESTER CENTRAL
E. 90,110   T. 39,927 (44.31%)   Lab. hold
Tony Lloyd, Lab. 21,059
Marc Ramsbottom, LD 10,620
Suhail Rahuja, C. 4,704
Tony Trebilcock, BNP 1,636
Gayle O'Donovan, Green 915
Nicola Weatherill, UKIP 607
Ron Sinclair, Soc. Lab. 153
John Cartwright, Ind. 120
Jonty Leff, WRP 59
Robert Skelton, SEP 54
Lab. majority 10,439 (26.15%)
Notional 6.11% swing Lab. to LD
(2005: Lab. majority 11,636 (38.36%))

§MANCHESTER GORTON
E. 75,933   T. 38,325 (50.47%)   Lab. hold
Gerald Kaufman, Lab. 19,211
Qassim Afzal, LD 12,508
Caroline Healy, C. 4,224
Justine Hall, Green 1,048
Karen Reissman, TUSC 507
Mohammed Zulfikar, Respect 337
Peter Harrison, Ch. P. 254
Tim Dobson, Pirate 236
Lab. majority 6,703 (17.49%)
Notional 1.06% swing Lab. to LD
(2005: Lab. majority 6,355 (19.61%))

§MANCHESTER WITHINGTON
E. 74,371   T. 45,031 (60.55%)   LD hold
John Leech, LD 20,110
Lucy Powell, Lab. 18,216
Christopher Green, C. 5,005
Brian Candeland, Green 798
Bob Gutfreund-Walmsley, UKIP 698
Yasmin Zalzala, Ind. 147
Marcus Farmer, Ind. 57
LD majority 1,894 (4.21%)
Notional 1.41% swing Lab. to LD
(2005: LD majority 531 (1.39%))

§MANSFIELD
E. 80,069   T. 48,395 (60.44%)   Lab. hold
Joseph Meale, Lab. 18,753
Tracy Critchlow, C. 12,741
Michael Wyatt, LD 7,469
Andre Camilleri, Mansfield Ind. 4,339
David Hamilton, UKIP 2,985
Rachel Hill, BNP 2,108
Lab. majority 6,012 (12.42%)
Notional 9.49% swing Lab. to C.
(2005: Lab. majority 13,776 (31.39%))

§MEON VALLEY
E. 70,488   T. 51,238 (72.69%)   C. hold
*George Hollingbery, C. 28,818
Liz Leffman, LD 16,693
Howard Linsley, Lab. 3,266
Steve Harris, UKIP 1,490
Pat Harris, Eng. Dem. 582
Sarah Coats, APP 255
Graeme Quar, Ind. 134
C. majority 12,125 (23.66%)
Notional 9.38% swing LD to C.
(2005: C. majority 2,378 (4.91%))

§MERIDEN
E. 83,876   T. 52,162 (62.27%)   C. hold
Caroline Spelman, C. 26,956
Ed Williams, Lab. 10,703
Simon Slater, LD 9,278
Frank O'Brien, BNP 2,511
Barry Allcock, UKIP 1,378
Elly Stanton, Green 678
Nikki Sinclaire, RA 658
C. majority 16,253 (31.16%)
Notional 7.90% swing Lab. to C.
(2005: C. majority 7,412 (15.37%))

§¶MIDDLESBROUGH
E. 65,148   T. 33,455 (51.35%)   Lab. hold
Sir Stuart Bell, Lab. 15,351
Chris Foote-Wood, LD 6,662
John Walsh, C. 6,283
Joan McTigue, Ind. 1,969
Michael Ferguson, BNP 1,954
Robert Parker, UKIP 1,236
Lab. majority 8,689 (25.97%)
Notional 6.45% swing Lab. to LD
(2005: Lab. majority 12,476 (38.87%))

§MIDDLESBROUGH SOUTH &
CLEVELAND EAST
E. 72,664   T. 46,214 (63.60%)   Lab. hold
*Tom Blenkinsop, Lab. 18,138
Paul Bristow, C. 16,461
Nick Emmerson, LD 7,340
Stuart Lightwing, UKIP 1,881
Shaun Gatley, BNP 1,576
Mike Allen, Ind. 818
Lab. majority 1,677 (3.63%)
Notional 7.44% swing Lab. to C.
(2005: Lab. majority 8,096 (18.51%))

§MILTON KEYNES NORTH
E. 85,841   T. 53,888 (62.78%)   C. gain
Mark Lancaster, C.   23,419
Andrew Pakes, Lab.   14,458
Jill Hope, LD   11,894
Michael Phillips, UKIP   1,772
Richard Hamilton, BNP   1,154
Alan Francis, Green   733
Revd John Lennon, CPA   206
Matt Bananamatt Fensome, Loony   157
Anant Vyas, Ind.   95
C. majority 8,961 (16.63%)
Notional 9.17% swing Lab. to C.
(2005: Lab. majority 848 (1.71%))

§MILTON KEYNES SOUTH
E. 90,487   T. 55,333 (61.15%)   C. gain
*Iain Stewart, C.   23,034
Phyllis Starkey, Lab.   17,833
Peter Jones, LD   9,787
Philip Pinto, UKIP   2,074
Matthew Tait, BNP   1,502
Katrina Deacon, Green   774
Suzanne Nti, CPA   245
Jonathan Worth, NFP   84
C. majority 5,201 (9.40%)
Notional 6.22% swing Lab. to C.
(2005: Lab. majority 1,497 (3.04%))

§MITCHAM & MORDEN
E. 65,939   T. 43,797 (66.42%)   Lab. hold
Siobhain McDonagh, Lab.   24,722
Melanie Hampton, C.   11,056
Diana Coman, LD   5,202
Tony Martin, BNP   1,386
Andrew Mills, UKIP   857
Smarajit Roy, Green   381
Rathy Alagaratnam, Ind.   155
Ernest Redgrave, Ind.   38
Lab. majority 13,666 (31.20%)
Notional 0.44% swing Lab. to C.
(2005: Lab. majority 12,739 (32.08%))

MOLE VALLEY
E. 72,612   T. 54,324 (74.81%)   C. hold
Sir Paul Beresford, C.   31,263
Alice Humphreys, LD   15,610
James Dove, Lab.   3,804
Leigh Jones, UKIP   2,752
Rob Sedgwick, Green   895
C. majority 15,653 (28.81%)
2.27% swing LD to C.
(2005: C. majority 11,997 (24.28%))

§MORECAMBE & LUNESDALE
E. 69,965   T. 43,616 (62.34%)   C. gain
*David Morris, C.   18,035
Geraldine Smith, Lab.   17,169
Leslie Jones, LD   5,971
Mark Knight, UKIP   1,843
Chris Coates, Green   598
C. majority 866 (1.99%)
Notional 6.86% swing Lab. to C.
(2005: Lab. majority 4,849 (11.74%))

§MORLEY & OUTWOOD
E. 74,200 T. 48,856 (65.84%)
                                   Lab. (Co-op) hold
Ed Balls, Lab. (Co-op)   18,365
Antony Calvert, C.   17,264
James Monaghan, LD   8,186
Chris Beverley, BNP   3,535
David Daniel, UKIP   1,506
Lab. (Co-op) majority 1,101 (2.25%)
Notional 9.35% swing Lab. (Co-op) to C.
(2005: Lab. (Co-op) majority 8,669
(20.95%))

§NEW FOREST EAST
E. 72,858   T. 50,036 (68.68%)   C. hold
Julian Lewis, C.   26,443
Terry Scriven, LD   15,136
Peter Sopowski, Lab.   4,915
Peter Day, UKIP   2,518
Beverley Golden, Green   1,024
C. majority 11,307 (22.60%)
Notional 3.20% swing LD to C.
(2005: C. majority 7,653 (16.21%))

§NEW FOREST WEST
E. 68,332   T. 47,572 (69.62%)   C. hold
Desmond Swayne, C.   27,980
Mike Plummer, LD   11,084
Janice Hurne, Lab.   4,666
Martin Lyon, UKIP   2,783
Janet Richards, Green   1,059
C. majority 16,896 (35.52%)
Notional 0.60% swing C. to LD
(2005: C. majority 16,183 (36.71%))

§¶NEWARK
E. 71,785   T. 51,228 (71.36%)   C. hold
Patrick Mercer, C.   27,590
Dr Ian Campbell, Lab.   11,438
Pauline Jenkins, LD   10,246
Tom Irvine, UKIP   1,954
C. majority 16,152 (31.53%)
Notional 4.68% swing Lab. to C.
(2005: C. majority 10,077 (22.17%))

§NEWBURY
E. 83,411   T. 58,589 (70.24%)   C. hold
Richard Benyon, C.   33,057
David Rendel, LD   20,809
Hannah Cooper, Lab.   2,505
David Black, UKIP   1,475
Adrian Hollister, Green   490
Brian Burgess, Ind.   158
David Yates, AD   95
C. majority 12,248 (20.90%)
Notional 7.24% swing LD to C.
(2005: C. majority 3,452 (6.42%))

NEWCASTLE-UNDER-LYME
E. 69,433   T. 43,191 (62.21%)   Lab. hold
Paul Farrelly, Lab.   16,393
Robert Jenrick, C.   14,841
Nigel Jones, LD   8,466
David Nixon, UKIP   3,491
Lab. majority 1,552 (3.59%)
8.39% swing Lab. to C.
(2005: Lab. majority 8,108 (20.38%))

§NEWCASTLE UPON TYNE CENTRAL
E. 60,507   T. 34,157 (56.45%)   Lab. hold
*Chinyelu Onwurah, Lab.   15,694
Gareth Kane, LD   8,228
Nick Holder, C.   6,611
Ken Booth, BNP   2,302
Martin Davies, UKIP   754
John Pearson, Green   568
Lab. majority 7,466 (21.86%)
Notional 0.60% swing Lab. to LD
(2005: Lab. majority 7,509 (23.07%))

§NEWCASTLE UPON TYNE EAST
E. 64,487   T. 37,840 (58.68%)   Lab. hold
Nicholas Brown, Lab.   17,043
Wendy Taylor, LD   12,590
Dominic Llewellyn, C.   6,068
Alan Spence, BNP   1,342
Andrew Gray, Green   620
Martin Levy, Comm.   177
Lab. majority 4,453 (11.77%)
Notional 4.60% swing Lab. to LD
(2005: Lab. majority 6,987 (20.97%))

§NEWCASTLE UPON TYNE NORTH
E. 67,110   T. 43,946 (65.48%)   Lab. hold
*Catherine McKinnell, Lab.   17,950
Ronald Beadle, LD   14,536
Stephen Parkinson, C.   7,966
Terry Gibson, BNP   1,890
Ian Proud, UKIP   1,285
Anna Heyman, Green   319
Lab. majority 3,414 (7.77%)
Notional 4.54% swing Lab. to LD
(2005: Lab. majority 6,878 (16.84%))

§NEWTON ABBOT
E. 69,343   T. 48,283 (69.63%)   C. gain
*Anne-Marie Morris, C.   20,774
Richard Younger-Ross, LD   20,251
Patrick Canavan, Lab.   3,387
Jackie Hooper, UKIP   3,088
Corinne Lindsey, Green   701
Keith Sharp, Ind.   82
C. majority 523 (1.08%)
Notional 5.79% swing LD to C.
(2005: LD majority 4,830 (10.50%))

§NORFOLK MID
E. 74,260   T. 50,765 (68.36%)   C. hold
*George Freeman, C.   25,123
David Newman, LD   11,267
Elizabeth Hughes, Lab.   8,857
Toby Coke, UKIP   2,800
Tim Birt, Green   1,457
Christine Kelly, BNP   1,261
C. majority 13,856 (27.29%)
Notional 0.02% swing C. to LD
(2005: C. majority 7,793 (16.29%))

§NORFOLK NORTH
E. 67,841   T. 49,661 (73.20%)   LD hold
Norman Lamb, LD   27,554
Trevor Ivory, C.   15,928
Phil Harris, Lab.   2,896
Michael Baker, UKIP   2,680
Andrew Boswell, Green   508
Simon Mann, Ind.   95
LD majority 11,626 (23.41%)
Notional 3.06% swing C. to LD
(2005: LD majority 8,575 (17.28%))

§NORFOLK NORTH WEST
E. 73,207   T. 47,800 (65.29%)   C. hold
Henry Bellingham, C.   25,916
William Summers, LD   11,106
Manish Sood, Lab.   6,353
John Gray, UKIP   1,841
David Fleming, BNP   1,839
Michael de Whalley, Green   745
C. majority 14,810 (30.98%)
Notional 2.09% swing C. to LD
(2005: C. majority 8,417 (18.34%))

§NORFOLK SOUTH
E. 76,165   T. 54,993 (72.20%)   C. hold
Richard Bacon, C.   27,133
Jacky Howe, LD   16,193
Mick Castle, Lab.   7,252
Evan Heasley, UKIP   2,329
Helen Mitchell, BNP   1,086
Jo Willcott, Green   1,000
C. majority 10,940 (19.89%)
Notional 3.25% swing LD to C.
(2005: C. majority 6,719 (13.39%))

§NORFOLK SOUTH WEST
E. 74,298   T. 49,150 (66.15%)   C. hold
*Elizabeth Truss, C.   23,753
Stephen Gordon, LD   10,613
Peter Smith, Lab.   9,119
Kay Hipsey, UKIP   3,061
Dennis Pearce, BNP   1,774
Lori Allen, Green   830
C. majority 13,140 (26.73%)
Notional 0.48% swing LD to C.
(2005: C. majority 6,817 (15.00%))

§NORMANTON, PONTEFRACT &
CASTLEFORD
E. 82,239   T. 46,239 (56.23%)   Lab. hold
Yvette Cooper, Lab.   22,293
Nick Pickles, C.   11,314
Chris Rush, LD   7,585
Graham Thewlis-Hardy, BNP   3,864
Gareth Allen, Ind.   1,183
Lab. majority 10,979 (23.74%)
Notional 12.49% swing Lab. to C.
(2005: Lab. majority 20,608 (48.73%))

§NORTHAMPTON NORTH
E. 64,230   T. 40,271 (62.70%)   C. gain
*Michael Ellis, C.   13,735
Sally Keeble, Lab.   11,799
Andrew Simpson, LD   11,250
Ray Beasley, BNP   1,316
Jim Macarthur, UKIP   1,238
Tony Lochmuller, Green   443
Eamonn Fitzpatrick, Ind.   334
Timothy Webb, Ch. P.   98
Malcolm Mildren, Ind.   58
C. majority 1,936 (4.81%)
Notional 6.90% swing Lab. to C.
(2005: Lab. majority 3,340 (9.00%))

§NORTHAMPTON SOUTH
E. 66,923   T. 38,978 (58.24%)   C. gain
*Brian Binley, C.   15,917
Clyde Loakes, Lab.   9,913
Paul Varnsverry, LD   7,579
Tony Clarke, Ind.   2,242
Derek Clark, UKIP   1,897
Kevin Sills, Eng. Dem.   618
Julie Hawkins, Green   363
Dave Green, NSPS   325
Kevin Willsher, Ind.   65
Liam Costello, SMA   59
C. majority 6,004 (15.40%)
Notional 9.59% swing Lab. to C.
(2005: Lab. majority 1,445 (3.78%))

§NORTHAMPTONSHIRE SOUTH
E. 82,032   T. 59,890 (73.01%)   C. hold
*Andrea Leadsom, C.   33,081
Scott Collins, LD   12,603
Matthew May, Lab.   10,380
Barry Mahoney, UKIP   2,406
Tony Tappy, Eng. Dem.   735
Marcus Rock, Green   685
C. majority 20,478 (34.19%)
Notional 0.12% swing C. to LD
(2005: C. majority 11,356 (22.85%))

§NORWICH NORTH
E. 65,258   T. 42,573 (65.24%)   C. gain
Chloe Smith, C.   17,280
John Cook, Lab.   13,379
John Stephen, LD   7,783
Glenn Tingle, UKIP   1,878
Jessica Goldfinch, Green   1,245
Thomas Richardson, BNP   747
Bill Holden, Ind.   143
Andrew Holland, Ch. P.   118
C. majority 3,901 (9.16%)
Notional 12.88% swing Lab. to C.
(2005: Lab. majority 6,769 (16.60%))

§NORWICH SOUTH
E. 73,649   T. 47,551 (64.56%)   LD gain
*Simon Wright, LD   13,960
Charles Clarke, Lab.   13,650
Antony Little, C.   10,902
Adrian Ramsay, Green   7,095
Steve Emmens, UKIP   1,145
Leonard Heather, BNP   697
Gabriel Polley, WRP   102
LD majority 310 (0.65%)
Notional 4.03% swing Lab. to LD
(2005: Lab. majority 3,023 (7.40%))

§NOTTINGHAM EAST
E. 58,707   T. 33,112 (56.40%)
                                   Lab. (Co-op) hold
*Christopher Leslie, Lab. (Co-op)   15,022
Sam Boote, LD   8,053
Ewan Lamont, C.   7,846
Pat Wolfe, UKIP   1,138
Benjamin Hoare, Green   928
Parvaiz Sardar, Ch. P.   125
Lab. (Co-op) majority 6,969 (21.05%)
Notional 1.89% swing Lab. (Co-op) to LD
(2005: Lab. (Co-op) majority 7,083
(24.22%))

§NOTTINGHAM NORTH
E. 63,240   T. 34,285 (54.21%)   Lab. hold
Graham Allen, Lab.   16,646
Martin Curtis, C.   8,508
Tim Ball, LD   5,849
Bob Brindley, BNP   1,944
Irenea Marriott, UKIP   1,338
Lab. majority 8,138 (23.74%)
Notional 8.65% swing Lab. to C.
(2005: Lab. majority 12,870 (41.04%))

§NOTTINGHAM SOUTH
E. 67,441   T. 40,789 (60.48%)   Lab. hold
*Lilian Greenwood, Lab.   15,209
Rowena Holland, C.   13,437
Tony Sutton, LD   9,406
Tony Woodward, BNP   1,140
Ken Browne, UKIP   967
Matthew Butcher, Green   630
Lab. majority 1,772 (4.34%)
Notional 7.43% swing Lab. to C.
(2005: Lab. majority 6,665 (19.20%))

§NUNEATON
E. 67,837   T. 44,646 (65.81%)   C. gain
*Marcus Jones, C.   18,536
Jayne Innes, Lab.   16,467
Christina Jebb, LD   6,846
Martyn Findley, BNP   2,797
C. majority 2,069 (4.63%)
Notional 7.19% swing Lab. to C.
(2005: Lab. majority 3,894 (9.74%))

§OLD BEXLEY & SIDCUP
E. 65,665   T. 45,492 (69.28%)   C. hold
James Brokenshire, C.   24,625
Rick Everitt, Lab.   8,768
Duncan Borrowman, LD   6,996
John Brooks, BNP   2,132
David Coburn, UKIP   1,532
Elaine Cheeseman, Eng. Dem.   520
John Hemming-Clark, Save QM   393
Jonathan Rooks, Green   371
Napoleon Dynamite, Loony   155
C. majority 15,857 (34.86%)
Notional 6.43% swing Lab. to C.
(2005: C. majority 9,309 (22.00%))

§¶OLDHAM EAST & SADDLEWORTH
E. 72,765   T. 44,520 (61.18%)   Lab. hold
Phil Woolas, Lab.   14,186
Elwyn Watkins, LD   14,083
Kashif Ali, C.   11,773
Alwyn Stott, BNP   2,546
David Bentley, UKIP   1,720
Gulzar Nazir, Ch. P.   212
Lab. majority 103 (0.23%)
Notional 5.08% swing Lab. to LD
(2005: Lab. majority 4,245 (10.39%))

§OLDHAM WEST & ROYTON
E. 72,651   T. 42,910 (59.06%)   Lab. hold
Michael Meacher, Lab.   19,503
Kamran Ghafoor, C.   10,151
Mark Alcock, LD   8,193
David Joines, BNP   3,049
Helen Roberts, UKIP   1,387
Shahid Miah, Respect   627
Lab. majority 9,352 (21.79%)
Notional 2.74% swing Lab. to C.
(2005: Lab. majority 10,454 (27.13%))

§ORPINGTON
E. 67,732   T. 48,911 (72.21%)   C. hold
*Joseph Johnson, C.   29,200
David McBride, LD   12,000
Stephen Morgan, Lab.   4,400
Mick Greenhough, UKIP   1,360
Tess Culnane, BNP   1,241
Tamara Galloway, Green   511
Chriss Snape, Eng. Dem.   199
C. majority 17,200 (35.17%)
Notional 12.19% swing LD to C.
(2005: C. majority 5,221 (10.79%))

§OXFORD EAST
E. 81,886   T. 51,651 (63.08%)   Lab. hold
Andrew Smith, Lab.   21,938
Steve Goddard, LD   17,357
Edward Argar, C.   9,727
Sushila Dhall, Green   1,238
Julia Gasper, UKIP   1,202
David O'Sullivan, SEP   116
Roger Crawford, Parenting   73
Lab. majority 4,581 (8.87%)
Notional 4.07% swing LD to Lab.
(2005: Lab. majority 332 (0.73%))

§OXFORD WEST & ABINGDON
E. 86,458   T. 56,480 (65.33%)   C. gain
*Nicola Blackwood, C.   23,906
Evan Harris, LD   23,730
Richard Stevens, Lab.   5,999
Paul Williams, UKIP   1,518
Chris Goodall, Green   1,184
Keith Mann, APP   143
C. majority 176 (0.31%)
Notional 6.87% swing LD to C.
(2005: LD majority 6,816 (13.43%))

PENDLE

E. 66,417   T. 45,045 (67.82%)   C. gain

*Andrew Stephenson, C.	17,512
Gordon Prentice, Lab.	13,927
Afzal Anwar, LD	9,095
James Jackman, BNP	2,894
Graham Cannon, UKIP	1,476
Richard Masih, Ch. P.	141

C. majority 3,585 (7.96%)
6.63% swing Lab. to C.
(2005: Lab. majority 2,180 (5.30%))

§PENISTONE & STOCKSBRIDGE

E. 68,501   T. 46,516 (67.91%)   Lab. hold

Angela Smith, Lab.	17,565
Spencer Pitfield, C.	14,516
Ian Cuthbertson, LD	9,800
Paul James, BNP	2,207
Grant French, UKIP	1,936
Paul McEnhill, Eng. Dem.	492

Lab. majority 3,049 (6.55%)
Notional 7.45% swing Lab. to C.
(2005: Lab. majority 8,617 (20.43%))

§PENRITH & THE BORDER

E. 64,548   T. 45,087 (69.85%)   C. hold

*Rory Stewart, C.	24,071
Peter Thornton, LD	12,830
Barbara Cannon, Lab.	5,834
John Stanyer, UKIP	1,259
Chris Davidson, BNP	1,093

C. majority 11,241 (24.93%)
Notional 0.32% swing C. to LD
(2005: C. majority 10,795 (25.58%))

§PETERBOROUGH

E. 70,316   T. 44,927 (63.89%)   C. hold

Stewart Jackson, C.	18,133
Ed Murphy, Lab.	13,272
Nick Sandford, LD	8,816
Frances Fox, UKIP	3,007
Rob King, Eng. Dem.	770
Fiona Radic, Green	523
John Swallow, Ind.	406

C. majority 4,861 (10.82%)
Notional 0.94% swing Lab. to C.
(2005: C. majority 4,005 (8.93%))

§PLYMOUTH MOOR VIEW

E. 67,261   T. 41,526 (61.74%)   Lab. hold

Alison Seabeck, Lab.	15,433
Matthew Groves, C.	13,845
Stuart Bonar, LD	7,016
Bill Wakeham, UKIP	3,188
Roy Cook, BNP	1,438
Wendy Miller, Green	398
David Marchesi, Soc. Lab.	208

Lab. majority 1,588 (3.82%)
Notional 7.77% swing Lab. to C.
(2005: Lab. majority 7,740 (19.37%))

§PLYMOUTH SUTTON & DEVONPORT

E. 71,035   T. 43,894 (61.79%)   C. gain

*Oliver Colvile, C.	15,050
Linda Gilroy, Lab. (Co-op)	13,901
Judy Evans, LD	10,829
Andrew Leigh, UKIP	2,854
Tony Brown, Green	904
Brian Gerrish, Ind.	233
Robert Hawkins, Soc. Lab.	123

C. majority 1,149 (2.62%)
Notional 6.86% swing Lab. (Co-op) to C.
(2005: Lab. (Co-op) majority 4,472 (11.11%))

§POOLE

E. 64,661   T. 47,436 (73.36%)   C. hold

Robert Syms, C.	22,532
Philip Eades, LD	14,991
Jason Sanderson, Lab.	6,041
Nick Wellstead, UKIP	2,507
David Holmes, BNP	1,188
Ian Northover, Ind.	177

C. majority 7,541 (15.90%)
Notional 0.79% swing LD to C.
(2005: C. majority 6,035 (14.32%))

§POPLAR & LIMEHOUSE

E. 74,956   T. 46,700 (62.30%)   Lab. hold

Jim Fitzpatrick, Lab.	18,679
Tim Archer, C.	12,649
George Galloway, Respect	8,160
Jonathan Fryer, LD	5,209
Wayne Lochner, UKIP	565
Andrew Osborne, Eng. Dem.	470
Chris Smith, Green	449
Kabir Mahmud, Ind.	293
Mohammed Hoque, Ind.	167
Jim Thornton, Ind.	59

Lab. majority 6,030 (12.91%)
Notional 1.04% swing C. to Lab.
(2005: Lab. majority 3,823 (10.84%))

§PORTSMOUTH NORTH

E. 70,329   T. 44,118 (62.73%)   C. gain

*Penny Mordaunt, C.	19,533
Sarah McCarthy-Fry, Lab. (Co-op)	12,244
Darren Sanders, LD	8,874
Mike Fitzgerald, UKIP	1,812
David Knight, Eng. Dem.	1,040
Iain Maclennan, Green	461
Mick Tosh, TUSC	154

C. majority 7,289 (16.52%)
Notional 8.64% swing Lab. (Co-op) to C.
(2005: Lab. (Co-op) majority 315 (0.77%))

§PORTSMOUTH SOUTH

E. 70,242   T. 41,264 (58.75%)   LD hold

Mike Hancock, LD	18,921
Flick Drummond, C.	13,721
John Ferrett, Lab.	5,640
Christopher Martin, UKIP	876
Geoff Crompton, BNP	873
Tim Dawes, Green	716
Ian DuCane, Eng. Dem.	400
Les Cummings, J & AC	117

LD majority 5,200 (12.60%)
Notional 2.30% swing C. to LD
(2005: LD majority 2,955 (8.00%))

§PRESTON

E. 62,460   T. 32,505 (52.04%)   Lab. (Co-op) hold

Mark Hendrick, Lab. (Co-op)	15,668
Mark Jewell, LD	7,935
Nerissa Warner-O'Neill, C.	7,060
Richard Muirhead, UKIP	1,462
George Ambroze, Ch. P.	272
Krishna Tayya, Ind.	108

Lab. (Co-op) majority 7,733 (23.79%)
Notional 2.50% swing Lab. (Co-op) to LD
(2005: Lab. (Co-op) majority 8,338 (27.67%))

§PUDSEY

E. 69,257   T. 49,083 (70.87%)   C. gain

*Stuart Andrew, C.	18,874
Jamie Hanley, Lab.	17,215
Jamie Matthews, LD	10,224
Ian Gibson, BNP	1,549
David Dews, UKIP	1,221

C. majority 1,659 (3.38%)
Notional 7.56% swing Lab. to C.
(2005: Lab. majority 5,204 (11.74%))

§PUTNEY

E. 63,370   T. 40,785 (64.36%)   C. hold

Justine Greening, C.	21,223
Stuart King, Lab.	11,170
James Sandbach, LD	6,907
Bruce Mackenzie, Green	591
Peter Darby, BNP	459
Hugo Wareham, UKIP	435

C. majority 10,053 (24.65%)
Notional 9.92% swing Lab. to C.
(2005: C. majority 1,723 (4.80%))

§RAYLEIGH & WICKFORD

E. 75,905   T. 52,343 (68.96%)   C. hold

Mark Francois, C.	30,257
Susan Gaszczak, LD	7,919
Michael Le-Surf, Lab.	7,577
John Hayter, Eng. Dem.	2,219
Tino Callaghan, UKIP	2,211
Anthony Evennett, BNP	2,160

C. majority 22,338 (42.68%)
Notional 2.13% swing LD to C.
(2005: C. majority 12,983 (27.37%))

§READING EAST

E. 74,922   T. 49,985 (66.72%)   C. hold

Rob Wilson, C.	21,269
Gareth Epps, LD	13,664
Anneliese Dodds, Lab.	12,729
Adrian Pitfield, UKIP	1,086
Rob White, Green	1,069
Joan Lloyd, Ind.	111
Michael Turberville, Ind.	57

C. majority 7,605 (15.21%)
Notional 1.97% swing LD to C.
(2005: C. majority 739 (1.71%))

§READING WEST

E. 72,118   T. 47,530 (65.91%)   C. gain

*Alok Sharma, C.	20,523
Naz Sarkar, Lab.	14,519
Daisy Benson, LD	9,546
Bruce Hay, UKIP	1,508
Howard Thomas, CSP	852
Adrian Windisch, Green	582

C. majority 6,004 (12.63%)
Notional 12.05% swing Lab. to C.
(2005: Lab. majority 4,931 (11.47%))

REDCAR

E. 67,125   T. 41,963 (62.51%)   LD gain

*Ian Swales, LD	18,955
Vera Baird, Lab.	13,741
Steve Mastin, C.	5,790
Martin Bulmer, UKIP	1,875
Kevin Broughton, BNP	1,475
Hannah Walter, TUSC	127

LD majority 5,214 (12.43%)
21.80% swing Lab. to LD
(2005: Lab. majority 12,116 (31.18%))

§REDDITCH

E. 68,550   T. 44,018 (64.21%)   C. gain

*Karen Lumley, C.	19,138
Jacqui Smith, Lab.	13,317
Nicholas Lane, LD	7,750
Anne Davis, UKIP	1,497
Andy Ingram, BNP	1,394
Kevin White, Green	393
Vincent Schittone, Eng. Dem.	255
Scott Beverley, Ch. P.	101
Paul Swansborough, Ind.	100
Derek Fletcher, Nobody	73

C. majority 5,821 (13.22%)
Notional 9.21% swing Lab. to C.
(2005: Lab. majority 2,163 (5.20%))

§REIGATE
E. 71,604   T. 49,978 (69.80%)   C. hold
Crispin Blunt, C.   26,688
Jane Kulka, LD   13,097
Robert Hull, Lab.   5,672
Joe Fox, UKIP   2,089
Keith Brown, BNP   1,345
Jonathan Essex, Green   1,087
C. majority 13,591 (27.19%)
Notional 0.89% swing LD to C.
(2005: C. majority 11,093 (25.41%))

§RIBBLE VALLEY
E. 78,068   T. 52,287 (66.98%)   C. hold
Nigel Evans, C.   26,298
Paul Foster, Lab.   11,529
Allan Knox, LD   10,732
Stephen Rush, UKIP   3,496
Tony Johnson, ND   232
C. majority 14,769 (28.25%)
Notional 6.58% swing Lab. to C.
(2005: C. majority 6,953 (15.09%))

§RICHMOND (YORKS)
E. 79,478   T. 53,412 (67.20%)   C. hold
William Hague, C.   33,541
Lawrence Meredith, LD   10,205
Eileen Driver, Lab.   8,150
Leslie Rowe, Green   1,516
C. majority 23,336 (43.69%)
Notional 0.64% swing LD to C.
(2005: C. majority 19,450 (38.73%))

§RICHMOND PARK
E. 77,060   T. 59,268 (76.91%)   C. gain
*Zac Goldsmith, C.   29,461
Susan Kramer, LD   25,370
Eleanor Tunnicliffe, Lab.   2,979
Peter Dul, UKIP   669
James Page, Green   572
Susan May, CPA   133
Charles Hill, Ind.   84
C. majority 4,091 (6.90%)
Notional 7.00% swing LD to C.
(2005: LD majority 3,613 (7.09%))

§ROCHDALE
E. 78,952   T. 45,907 (58.15%)   Lab. hold
*Simon Danczuk, Lab.   16,699
Paul Rowen, LD   15,810
Mudasir Dean, C.   8,305
Chris Jackson, NF   2,236
Colin Denby, UKIP   1,999
Mohammed Salim, IZB   545
John Whitehead, Ind.   313
Lab. majority 889 (1.94%)
Notional 0.79% swing LD to Lab.
(2005: Lab. majority 149 (0.35%))

§ROCHESTER & STROOD
E. 73,882   T. 47,971 (64.93%)   C. hold
*Mark Reckless, C.   23,604
Teresa Murray, Lab.   13,651
Geoffrey Juby, LD   7,800
Ron Sands, Eng. Dem.   2,182
Simon Marchant, Green   734
C. majority 9,953 (20.75%)
Notional 9.81% swing Lab. to C.
(2005: C. majority 503 (1.14%))

§ROCHFORD & SOUTHEND EAST
E. 71,080   T. 41,631 (58.57%)   C. hold
James Duddridge, C.   19,509
Kevin Bonavia, Lab.   8,459
Graham Longley, LD   8,084
James Moyies, UKIP   2,405
Geoff Strobridge, BNP   1,856
Andrew Vaughan, Green   707
Anthony Chytry, Ind.   611
C. majority 11,050 (26.54%)
Notional 6.37% swing Lab. to C.
(2005: C. majority 5,307 (13.80%))

§ROMFORD
E. 71,193   T. 46,481 (65.29%)   C. hold
Andrew Rosindell, C.   26,031
Rachel Voller, Lab.   9,077
Helen Duffett, LD   5,572
Robert Bailey, BNP   2,438
Gerard Batten, UKIP   2,050
Dr Peter Thorogood, Eng. Dem.   603
Gary Haines, Green   447
Philip Hyde, Ind.   151
David Sturman, Ind.   112
C. majority 16,954 (36.48%)
Notional 3.94% swing Lab. to C.
(2005: C. majority 12,120 (28.59%))

§ROMSEY & SOUTHAMPTON NORTH
E. 66,901   T. 48,939 (73.15%)   C. gain
*Caroline Nokes, C.   24,345
Sandra Gidley, LD   20,189
Aktar Beg, Lab.   3,116
John Meropoulos, UKIP   1,289
C. majority 4,156 (8.49%)
Notional 4.48% swing LD to C.
(2005: LD majority 204 (0.46%))

§ROSSENDALE & DARWEN
E. 73,003   T. 47,128 (64.56%)   C. gain
*Jake Berry, C.   19,691
Janet Anderson, Lab.   15,198
Robert Sheffield, LD   8,541
David Duthie, UKIP   1,617
Kevin Bryan, NF   1,062
Michael Johnson, Eng. Dem.   663
Tony Melia, Impact   243
Mike Sivieri, Ind.   113
C. majority 4,493 (9.53%)
Notional 8.94% swing Lab. to C.
(2005: Lab. majority 3,696 (8.35%))

§ROTHER VALLEY
E. 72,841   T. 46,758 (64.19%)   Lab. hold
Kevin Barron, Lab.   19,147
Lynda Donaldson, C.   13,281
Wesley Paxton, LD   8,111
Will Blair, BNP   3,606
Tina Dowdall, UKIP   2,613
Lab. majority 5,866 (12.55%)
Notional 7.96% swing Lab. to C.
(2005: Lab. majority 11,558 (28.47%))

§¶ROTHERHAM
E. 63,565   T. 37,506 (59.00%)   Lab. hold
Denis MacShane, Lab.   16,741
Jackie Whiteley, C.   6,279
Rebecca Taylor, LD   5,994
Marlene Guest, BNP   3,906
Peter Thirlwall, Ind.   2,366
Caven Vines, UKIP   2,220
Lab. majority 10,462 (27.89%)
Notional 8.27% swing Lab. to C.
(2005: Lab. majority 13,865 (41.33%))

§RUGBY
E. 68,914   T. 47,468 (68.88%)   C. gain
*Mark Pawsey, C.   20,901
Andy King, Lab.   14,901
Jerry Roodhouse, LD   9,434
Mark Badrick, BNP   1,375
Roy Sandison, Green   451
Barry Milford, UKIP   406
C. majority 6,000 (12.64%)
Notional 8.92% swing Lab. to C.
(2005: Lab. majority 2,397 (5.20%))

§RUISLIP, NORTHWOOD & PINNER
E. 70,873   T. 50,205 (70.84%)   C. hold
Nick Hurd, C.   28,866
Anita McDonald, Lab.   9,806
Thomas Papworth, LD   8,345
Jason Pontey, UKIP   1,351
Ian Edward, NF   899
Graham Lee, Green   740
Ruby Akhtar, Ch. P.   198
C. majority 19,060 (37.96%)
Notional 3.63% swing Lab. to C.
(2005: C. majority 13,274 (30.71%))

RUNNYMEDE & WEYBRIDGE
E. 72,566   T. 48,150 (66.35%)   C. hold
Philip Hammond, C.   26,915
Andrew Falconer, LD   10,406
Paul Greenwood, Lab.   6,446
Toby Micklethwait, UKIP   3,146
Jenny Gould, Green   696
David Sammons, Ind.   541
C. majority 16,509 (34.29%)
0.38% swing LD to C.
(2005: C. majority 12,349 (28.37%))

§RUSHCLIFFE
E. 72,955   T. 53,687 (73.59%)   C. hold
Kenneth Clarke, C.   27,470
Karrar Khan, LD   11,659
Andrew Clayworth, Lab.   11,128
Matthew Faithfull, UKIP   2,179
Richard Mallender, Green   1,251
C. majority 15,811 (29.45%)
Notional 0.63% swing C. to LD
(2005: C. majority 9,932 (20.60%))

§RUTLAND & MELTON
E. 77,185   T. 55,220 (71.54%)   C. hold
Alan Duncan, C.   28,228
Grahame Hudson, LD   14,228
John Morgan, Lab.   7,893
Peter Baker, UKIP   2,526
Keith Addison, BNP   1,757
Leigh Higgins, Ind.   588
C. majority 14,000 (25.35%)
Notional 3.65% swing C. to LD
(2005: C. majority 12,998 (26.29%))

§SAFFRON WALDEN
E. 76,035   T. 54,369 (71.51%)   C. hold
Sir Alan Haselhurst, C.   30,155
Peter Wilcock, LD   14,913
Barbara Light, Lab.   5,288
Roger Lord, UKIP   2,228
Christine Mitchell, BNP   1,050
Reza Hossain, Green   735
C. majority 15,242 (28.03%)
Notional 3.39% swing LD to C.
(2005: C. majority 10,483 (21.25%))

§ST ALBANS
E. 70,058   T. 52,835 (75.42%)   C. hold
Anne Main, C.   21,533
Sandy Walkington, LD   19,228
Roma Mills, Lab.   9,288
John Stocker, UKIP   2,028
Jack Easton, Green   758
C. majority 2,305 (4.36%)
Notional 3.74% swing C. to LD
(2005: C. majority 1,334 (2.94%))

§ST AUSTELL & NEWQUAY
E. 76,346   T. 47,238 (61.87%)   LD hold
*Stephen Gilbert, LD   20,189
Caroline Righton, C.   18,877
Lee Jameson, Lab.   3,386
Dick Cole, Meb. Ker.   2,007
Clive Medway, UKIP   1,757
James Fitton, BNP   1,022
LD majority 1,312 (2.78%)
Notional 4.83% swing LD to C.
(2005: LD majority 5,723 (12.44%))

§ST HELENS NORTH
E. 74,985   T. 44,556 (59.42%)   Lab. hold
Dave Watts, Lab.   23,041
Paul Greenall, C.   9,940
John Beirne, LD   8,992
Gary Robinson, UKIP   2,100
Stephen Whatham, Soc. Lab.   483
Lab. majority 13,101 (29.40%)
Notional 4.55% swing Lab. to C.
(2005: Lab. majority 15,265 (36.49%))

§ST HELENS SOUTH & WHISTON
E. 77,975   T. 46,081 (59.10%)   Lab. hold
Shaun Woodward, Lab.   24,364
Brian Spencer, LD   10,242
Val Allen, C.   8,209
James Winstanley, BNP   2,040
John Sumner, UKIP   1,226
Lab. majority 14,122 (30.65%)
Notional 1.94% swing LD to Lab.
(2005: Lab. majority 10,987 (26.76%))

§ST IVES
E. 66,930   T. 45,921 (68.61%)   LD hold
Andrew George, LD   19,619
Derek Thomas, C.   17,900
Philippa Latimer, Lab.   3,751
Mick Faulkner, UKIP   2,560
Tim Andrewes, Green   1,308
Jonathan Rogers, Cornish D.   396
Simon Reed, Meb. Ker.   387
LD majority 1,719 (3.74%)
Notional 10.39% swing LD to C.
(2005: LD majority 10,711 (24.52%))

§SALFORD & ECCLES
E. 75,482   T. 41,533 (55.02%)   Lab. hold
Hazel Blears, Lab.   16,655
Norman Owen, LD   10,930
Matthew Sephton, C.   8,497
Tina Wingfield, BNP   2,632
Duran O'Dwyer, UKIP   1,084
David Henry, TUSC   730
Stephen Morris, Eng. Dem.   621
Richard Carvath, Ind.   384
Lab. majority 5,725 (13.78%)
Notional 9.43% swing Lab. to LD
(2005: Lab. majority 10,707 (32.64%))

§SALISBURY
E. 67,429   T. 48,481 (71.90%)   C. hold
*John Glen, C.   23,859
Nick Radford, LD   17,893
Tom Gann, Lab.   3,690
Frances Howard, UKIP   1,392
Sean Witheridge, BNP   765
Nick Startin, Green   506
King Arthur, Ind.   257
John Holme, Ind.   119
C. majority 5,966 (12.31%)
Notional 3.60% swing C. to LD
(2005: C. majority 8,860 (19.50%))

SCARBOROUGH & WHITBY
E. 75,443   T. 49,282 (65.32%)   C. hold
Robert Goodwill, C.   21,108
Annajoy David, Lab.   12,978
Tania Exley-Moore, LD   11,093
Michael James, UKIP   1,484
Trisha Scott, BNP   1,445
Dilys Cluer, Green   734
Peter Popple, Ind.   329
Juliet Boddington, Green Soc.   111
C. majority 8,130 (16.50%)
6.92% swing Lab. to C.
(2005: C. majority 1,245 (2.65%))

§SCUNTHORPE
E. 63,089   T. 37,034 (58.70%)   Lab. hold
*Nic Dakin, Lab.   14,640
Caroline Johnson, C.   12,091
Neil Poole, LD   6,774
Jane Collins, UKIP   1,686
Douglas Ward, BNP   1,447
Natalie Hurst, Green   396
Lab. majority 2,549 (6.88%)
Notional 9.18% swing Lab. to C.
(2005: Lab. majority 8,638 (25.24%))

§SEDGEFIELD
E. 64,727   T. 40,222 (62.14%)   Lab. hold
Phil Wilson, Lab.   18,141
Neil Mahapatra, C.   9,445
Alan Thompson, LD   8,033
Mark Walker, BNP   2,075
Brian Gregory, UKIP   1,479
Paul Gittins, Ind.   1,049
Lab. majority 8,696 (21.62%)
Notional 11.60% swing Lab. to C.
(2005: Lab. majority 18,198 (44.82%))

§SEFTON CENTRAL
E. 67,512   T. 48,463 (71.78%)   Lab. hold
*Bill Esterson, Lab.   20,307
Debi Jones, C.   16,445
Richard Clein, LD   9,656
Peter Harper, UKIP   2,055
Lab. majority 3,862 (7.97%)
Notional 2.03% swing Lab. to C.
(2005: Lab. majority 4,950 (12.02%))

§SELBY & AINSTY
E. 72,789   T. 51,728 (71.07%)   C. hold
*Nigel Adams, C.   25,562
Jan Marshall, Lab.   13,297
Tom Holvey, LD   9,180
Darren Haley, UKIP   1,635
Duncan Lorriman, BNP   1,377
Graham Michael, Eng. Dem.   677
C. majority 12,265 (23.71%)
Notional 9.70% swing Lab. to C.
(2005: C. majority 2,060 (4.31%))

§SEVENOAKS
E. 69,591   T. 49,408 (71.00%)   C. hold
Michael Fallon, C.   28,076
Alan Bullion, LD   10,561
Gareth Siddorn, Lab.   6,541
Chris Heath, UKIP   1,782
Paul Golding, BNP   1,384
Louise Uncles, Eng. Dem.   806
Mark Ellis, Ind,   258
C. majority 17,515 (35.45%)
Notional 3.13% swing LD to C.
(2005: C. majority 13,060 (29.19%))

§SHEFFIELD BRIGHTSIDE &
HILLSBOROUGH
E. 68,186   T. 38,914 (57.07%)   Lab. hold
David Blunkett, Lab.   21,400
Jonathan Harston, LD   7,768
John Sharp, C.   4,468
John Sheldon, BNP   3,026
Pat Sullivan, UKIP   1,596
Maxine Bowler, TUSC   656
Lab. majority 13,632 (35.03%)
Notional 10.77% swing Lab. to LD
(2005: Lab. majority 18,801 (56.58%))

§SHEFFIELD CENTRAL
E. 69,519   T. 41,468 (59.65%)   Lab. hold
*Paul Blomfield, Lab.   17,138
Paul Scriven, LD   16,973
Andrew Lee, C.   4,206
Jillian Creasy, Green   1,556
Tracey Smith, BNP   903
Jeffrey Shaw, UKIP   652
Rod Rodgers, Ind.   40
Lab. majority 165 (0.40%)
Notional 7.36% swing Lab. to LD
(2005: Lab. majority 5,025 (15.12%))

§SHEFFIELD HALLAM
E. 69,378   T. 51,135 (73.70%)   LD hold
Nick Clegg, LD   27,324
Nicola Bates, C.   12,040
Jack Scott, Lab.   8,228
Nigel James, UKIP   1,195
Steve Barnard, Green   919
David Wildgoose, Eng. Dem.   586
Martin Fitzpatrick, Ind.   429
Ray Green, Ch. P.   250
Mark Adshead, Loony   164
LD majority 15,284 (29.89%)
Notional 6.86% swing C. to LD
(2005: LD majority 7,416 (16.17%))

§SHEFFIELD HEELEY
E. 65,869   T. 40,871 (62.05%)   Lab. hold
Meg Munn, Lab.   17,409
Simon Clement-Jones, LD   11,602
Anne Crampton, C.   7,081
John Beatson, BNP   2,260
Charlotte Arnott, UKIP   1,530
Gareth Roberts, Green   989
Lab. majority 5,807 (14.21%)
Notional 9.23% swing Lab. to LD
(2005: Lab. majority 12,340 (32.67%))

§SHEFFIELD SOUTH EAST
E. 67,284   T. 41,408 (61.54%)   Lab. hold
Clive Betts, Lab.   20,169
Gail Smith, LD   9,664
Nigel Bonson, C.   7,202
Christopher Hartigan, BNP   2,345
Jonathan Arnott, UKIP   1,889
Steven Andrew, Comm. Brit.   139
Lab. majority 10,505 (25.37%)
Notional 9.00% swing Lab. to LD
(2005: Lab. majority 15,843 (43.36%))

§SHERWOOD
E. 71,043   T. 48,954 (68.91%)   C. gain
*Mark Spencer, C.   19,211
Emilie Oldknow, Lab.   18,997
Kevin Moore, LD   7,283
James North, BNP   1,754
Margot Parker, UKIP   1,490
Russ Swan, Ind.   219
C. majority 214 (0.44%)
Notional 8.17% swing Lab. to C.
(2005: Lab. majority 6,869 (15.90%))

§SHIPLEY
E. 67,689   T. 49,427 (73.02%)   C. hold
Philip Davies, C.   24,002
Susan Hinchcliffe, Lab.   14,058
John Harris, LD   9,890
Kevin Warnes, Green   1,477
C. majority 9,944 (20.12%)
Notional 9.58% swing Lab. to C.
(2005: C. majority 450 (0.97%))

SHREWSBURY & ATCHAM
E. 75,438   T. 53,045 (70.32%)   C. hold
Daniel Kawczynski, C.   23,313
Charles West, LD   15,369
Jon Tandy, Lab.   10,915
Peter Lewis, UKIP   1,627
James Whittall, BNP   1,168
Alan Whittaker, Green   565
James Gollings, Impact   88
C. majority 7,944 (14.98%)
0.06% swing LD to C.
(2005: C. majority 1,808 (3.59%))

SHROPSHIRE NORTH
E. 78,926   T. 51,869 (65.72%)   C. hold
Owen Paterson, C.   26,692
Ian Croll, LD   10,864
Ian McLaughlan, Lab.   9,406
Sandra List, UKIP   2,432
Phil Reddall, BNP   1,667
Steve Boulding, Green   808
C. majority 15,828 (30.52%)
0.33% swing LD to C.
(2005: C. majority 11,020 (23.69%))

§SITTINGBOURNE & SHEPPEY
E. 75,354   T. 48,578 (64.47%)   C. hold
*Gordon Henderson, C.   24,313
Angela Harrison, Lab.   11,930
Keith Nevols, LD   7,943
Ian Davison, UKIP   2,610
Lawrence Tames, BNP   1,305
Mad Mike Young, Loony   319
David Cassidy, Ind.   158
C. majority 12,383 (25.49%)
Notional 12.72% swing Lab. to C.
(2005: C. majority 22 (0.05%))

§SKIPTON & RIPON
E. 77,381   T. 54,724 (70.72%)   C. hold
*Julian Smith, C.   27,685
Helen Flynn, LD   17,735
Claire Hazelgrove, Lab.   5,498
Rodney Mills, UKIP   1,909
Bernard Allen, BNP   1,403
Roger Bell, Ind.   315
Dylan Gilligan, Youth   95
Robert Leakey, Currency   84
C. majority 9,950 (18.18%)
Notional 2.63% swing C. to LD
(2005: C. majority 11,596 (23.43%))

§SLEAFORD & NORTH HYKEHAM
E. 85,550   T. 59,530 (69.59%)   C. hold
*Stephen Phillips, C.   30,719
David Harding-Price, LD   10,814
James Normington, Lab.   10,051
Marianne Overton, Lincs Ind.   3,806
Rodger Doughty, UKIP   2,163
Mike Clayton, BNP   1,977
C. majority 19,905 (33.44%)
Notional 0.46% swing LD to C.
(2005: C. majority 12,687 (24.15%))

§SLOUGH
E. 77,068   T. 47,742 (61.95%)   Lab. hold
Fiona Mactaggart, Lab.   21,884
Diana Coad, C.   16,361
Chris Tucker, LD   6,943
Peter Mason-Apps, UKIP   1,517
Miriam Kennet, Green   542
Sunil Chaudhary, Ch. P.   495
Lab. majority 5,523 (11.57%)
Notional 4.14% swing Lab. to C.
(2005: Lab. majority 7,924 (19.86%))

§SOLIHULL
E. 77,863   T. 55,129 (70.80%)   LD gain
Lorely Burt, LD   23,635
Maggie Throup, C.   23,460
Sarah-Jayne Merrill, Lab.   4,891
Andrew Terry, BNP   1,624
John Ison, UKIP   1,200
Neill Watts, RA   319
LD majority 175 (0.32%)
Notional 0.28% swing C. to LD
(2005: C. majority 124 (0.25%))

§SOMERSET NORTH
E. 77,304   T. 57,941 (74.95%)   C. hold
Dr Liam Fox, C.   28,549
Brian Mathew, LD   20,687
Steven Parry-Hearn, Lab.   6,448
Susan Taylor, UKIP   2,257
C. majority 7,862 (13.57%)
Notional 0.98% swing LD to C.
(2005: C. majority 6,007 (11.61%))

§SOMERSET NORTH EAST
E. 67,412   T. 51,203 (75.96%)   C. hold
*Jacob Rees-Mogg, C.   21,130
Dan Norris, Lab.   16,216
Gail Coleshill, LD   11,433
Peter Sandell, UKIP   1,754
Michael Jay, Green   670
C. majority 4,914 (9.60%)
Notional 4.57% swing Lab. to C.
(2005: C. majority 212 (0.46%))

§SOMERTON & FROME
E. 81,548   T. 60,612 (74.33%)   LD hold
David Heath, LD   28,793
Annunziata Rees-Mogg, C.   26,976
David Oakensen, Lab.   2,675
Barry Harding, UKIP   1,932
Niall Warry, Leave EU   236
LD majority 1,817 (3.00%)
Notional 0.94% swing C. to LD
(2005: LD majority 595 (1.12%))

§SOUTH HOLLAND & THE DEEPINGS
E. 76,243   T. 50,188 (65.83%)   C. hold
John Hayes, C.   29,639
Jennifer Conroy, LD   7,759
Gareth Gould, Lab.   7,024
Richard Fairman, UKIP   3,246
Roy Harban, BNP   1,796
Ashley Baxter, Green   724
C. majority 21,880 (43.60%)
Notional 0.27% swing C. to LD
(2005: C. majority 15,127 (32.48%))

§SOUTH RIBBLE
E. 75,822   T. 51,458 (67.87%)   C. gain
*Lorraine Fullbrook, C.   23,396
David Borrow, Lab.   17,842
Peter Fisher, LD   7,271
David Duxbury, UKIP   1,895
Rosalind Gauci, BNP   1,054
C. majority 5,554 (10.79%)
Notional 8.11% swing Lab. to C.
(2005: Lab. majority 2,528 (5.42%))

§¶SOUTH SHIELDS
E. 63,294   T. 36,518 (57.70%)   Lab. hold
David Miliband, Lab.   18,995
Karen Allen, C.   7,886
Stephen Psallidas, LD   5,189
Donna Watson, BNP   2,382
Shirley Ford, Green   762
Siamak Kaikavoosi, Ind.   729
Victor Thompson, Ind.   316
Sam Navabi, Ind.   168
Roger Nettleship, Anti-War   91
Lab. majority 11,109 (30.42%)
Notional 6.36% swing Lab. to C.
(2005: Lab. majority 13,368 (41.61%))

§SOUTHAMPTON ITCHEN
E. 74,532   T. 44,412 (59.59%)   Lab. hold
John Denham, Lab.   16,326
Royston Smith, C.   16,134
David Goodall, LD   9,256
Alan Kebbell, UKIP   1,928
John Spottiswoode, Green   600
Tim Cutter, TUSC   168
Lab. majority 192 (0.43%)
Notional 10.28% swing Lab. to C.
(2005: Lab. majority 8,479 (21.00%))

§SOUTHAMPTON TEST
E. 71,931   T. 44,187 (61.43%)   Lab. hold
Alan Whitehead, Lab.   17,001
Jeremy Moulton, C.   14,588
David Callaghan, LD   9,865
Pearline Hingston, UKIP   1,726
Chris Bluemel, Green   881
Charles Sanderson, Ind.   126
Lab. majority 2,413 (5.46%)
Notional 6.86% swing Lab. to C.
(2005: Lab. majority 7,817 (19.17%))

§SOUTHEND WEST
E. 66,527   T. 43,606 (65.55%)   C. hold
David Amess, C.   20,086
Peter Welch, LD   12,816
Thomas Flynn, Lab.   5,850
Garry Cockrill, UKIP   1,714
Tony Gladwin, BNP   1,333
Barry Bolton, Green   644
Dr Vel, Ind.   617
Terry Phillips, Eng. Dem.   546
C. majority 7,270 (16.67%)
Notional 2.77% swing C. to LD
(2005: C. majority 9,008 (22.20%))

SOUTHPORT
E. 67,202   T. 43,757 (65.11%)   LD hold
John Pugh, LD   21,707
Brenda Porter, C.   15,683
Jim Conalty, Lab.   4,116
Terry Durrance, UKIP   2,251
LD majority 6,024 (13.77%)
2.23% swing C. to LD
(2005: LD majority 3,838 (9.32%))

SPELTHORNE
E. 70,479   T. 47,304 (67.12%)   C. hold
*Kwasi Kwarteng, C.   22,261
Mark Chapman, LD   12,242
Adam Tyler-Moore, Lab.   7,789
Christopher Browne, UKIP   4,009
Ian Swinglehurst, Ind.   314
Rod Littlewood, Best   244
Paul Couchman, TUSC   176
John Gore, CIP   167
Grahame Leon-Smith, Ind. Fed.   102
C. majority 10,019 (21.18%)
6.11% swing C. to LD
(2005: C. majority 9,936 (23.20%))

§STAFFORD
E. 70,587   T. 50,239 (71.17%)   C. gain
*Jeremy Lefroy, C.   22,047
David Kidney, Lab.   16,587
Barry Stamp, LD   8,211
Roy Goode, UKIP   1,727
Roland Hynd, BNP   1,103
Mike Shone, Green   564
C. majority 5,460 (10.87%)
Notional 7.44% swing Lab. to C.
(2005: Lab. majority 1,852 (4.01%))

§STAFFORDSHIRE MOORLANDS
E. 62,071   T. 43,815 (70.59%)   C. hold
*Karen Bradley, C.   19,793
Charlotte Atkins, Lab.   13,104
Henry Jebb, LD   7,338
Steve Povey, UKIP   3,580
C. majority 6,689 (15.27%)
Notional 5.71% swing Lab. to C.
(2005: C. majority 1,618 (3.86%))

§STAFFORDSHIRE SOUTH
E. 73,390   T. 50,440 (68.73%)   C. hold
*Gavin Williamson, C.   26,834
Kevin McElduff, Lab.   10,244
Sarah Fellows, LD   8,427
Mike Nattrass, UKIP   2,753
David Bradnock, BNP   1,928
Andrew Morris, Ind.   254
C. majority 16,590 (32.89%)
Notional 1.12% swing Lab. to C.
(2005: C. majority 8,346 (30.65%))

§STALYBRIDGE & HYDE
E. 69,037   T. 40,879 (59.21%)   Lab. hold
*Jonathan Reynolds, Lab.   16,189
Rob Adlard, C.   13,445
John Potter, LD   6,965
Anthony Jones, BNP   2,259
John Cooke, UKIP   1,342
Ruth Bergan, Green   679
Lab. majority 2,744 (6.71%)
Notional 8.47% swing Lab. to C.
(2005: Lab. majority 8,455 (23.64%))

§STEVENAGE
E. 68,937   T. 44,651 (64.77%)   C. gain
*Stephen McPartland, C.   18,491
Sharon Taylor, Lab. (Co-op)   14,913
Julia Davies, LD   7,432
Marion Mason, UKIP   2,004
Andrew Green, BNP   1,007
Charles Vickers, Eng. Dem.   366
Stephen Phillips, No Vote   327
David Cox, Ind.   80
Andrew Ralph, YRDPL   31
C. majority 3,578 (8.01%)
Notional 8.03% swing Lab. (Co-op) to C.
(2005: Lab. (Co-op) majority 3,288
(8.05%))

§STOCKPORT
E. 63,525   T. 39,128 (61.59%)   Lab. hold
Ann Coffey, Lab.   16,697
Stephen Holland, C.   9,913
Stuart Bodsworth, LD   9,778
Duncan Warner, BNP   1,201
Mike Kelly, UKIP   862
Peter Barber, Green   677
Lab. majority 6,784 (17.34%)
Notional 5.74% swing Lab. to C.
(2005: Lab. majority 9,982 (28.82%))

§STOCKTON NORTH
E. 67,363   T. 39,498 (58.63%)   Lab. hold
*Alex Cunningham, Lab.   16,923
Ian Galletley, C.   10,247
Philip Latham, LD   6,342
James Macpherson, BNP   1,724
Frank Cook, Ind.   1,577
Gordon Parkin, UKIP   1,556
Ian Saul, Eng. Dem.   1,129
Lab. majority 6,676 (16.90%)
Notional 8.35% swing Lab. to C.
(2005: Lab. majority 12,742 (33.60%))

§STOCKTON SOUTH
E. 74,552   T. 50,284 (67.45%)   C. gain
*James Wharton, C.   19,577
Dari Taylor, Lab.   19,245
Jacquie Bell, LD   7,600
Neil Sinclair, BNP   1,553
Peter Braney, UKIP   1,471
Yvonne Hossack, Ind.   536
Ted Strike, Ch. P.   302
C. majority 332 (0.66%)
Notional 7.05% swing Lab. to C.
(2005: Lab. majority 5,834 (13.44%))

§STOKE-ON-TRENT CENTRAL
E. 60,995   T. 32,470 (53.23%)   Lab. hold
*Tristram Hunt, Lab.   12,605
John Redfern, LD   7,039
Norsheen Bhatti, C.   6,833
Simon Darby, BNP   2,502
Carol Lovatt, UKIP   1,402
Paul Breeze, Ind.   959
Gary Elsby, Ind.   399
Brian Ward, City Ind.   303
Alby Walker, Ind.   295
Matthew Wright, TUSC   133
Lab. majority 5,566 (17.14%)
Notional 8.33% swing Lab. to LD
(2005: Lab. majority 9,717 (33.80%))

§STOKE-ON-TRENT NORTH
E. 72,052   T. 40,196 (55.79%)   Lab. hold
Joan Walley, Lab.   17,815
Andy Large, C.   9,580
John Fisher, LD   7,120
Melanie Baddeley, BNP   3,196
Geoffrey Locke, UKIP   2,485
Lab. majority 8,235 (20.49%)
Notional 8.77% swing Lab. to C.
(2005: Lab. majority 13,666 (38.03%))

§STOKE-ON-TRENT SOUTH
E. 68,031   T. 39,852 (58.58%)   Lab. hold
Rob Flello, Lab.   15,446
James Rushton, C.   11,316
Zulfiqar Ali, LD   6,323
Michael Coleman, BNP   3,762
Mark Barlow, UKIP   1,363
Terry Follows, Staffs Ind.   1,208
Mark Breeze, Ind.   434
Lab. majority 4,130 (10.36%)
Notional 6.15% swing Lab. to C.
(2005: Lab. majority 8,324 (22.67%))

§STONE
E. 66,979   T. 47,229 (70.51%)   C. hold
Bill Cash, C.   23,890
Christine Tinker, LD   10,598
Jo Lewis, Lab.   9,770
Andrew Illsley, UKIP   2,481
Damon Hoppe, Green   490
C. majority 13,292 (28.14%)
Notional 0.81% swing C. to LD
(2005: C. majority 8,191 (18.72%))

§STOURBRIDGE
E. 69,637   T. 47,234 (67.83%)   C. gain
*Margot James, C.   20,153
Lynda Waltho, Lab.   14,989
Christopher Bramall, LD   7,733
Maddy Westrop, UKIP   2,103
Robert Weale, BNP   1,696
Will Duckworth, Green   394
Alun Nicholas, Ind.   166
C. majority 5,164 (10.93%)
Notional 6.93% swing Lab. to C.
(2005: Lab. majority 1,280 (2.92%))

§STRATFORD-ON-AVON
E. 69,516   T. 50,542 (72.71%)   C. hold
*Nadhim Zahawi, C.   26,052
Martin Turner, LD   14,706
Robert Johnston, Lab.   4,809
Brett Parsons, UKIP   1,846
George Jones, BNP   1,097
Neil Basnett, Ind.   1,032
Karen Varga, Green   527
Fred Bishop, Eng. Dem.   473
C. majority 11,346 (22.45%)
Notional 0.72% swing C. to LD
(2005: C. majority 10,928 (23.90%))

§STREATHAM
E. 74,531   T. 46,837 (62.84%)   Lab. hold
*Chuka Umunna, Lab.   20,037
Chris Nicholson, LD   16,778
Rahoul Bhansali, C.   8,578
Rebecca Findlay, Green   861
Geoffrey Macharia, Ch. P.   237
Janus Polenceus, Eng. Dem.   229
Paul Lepper, WRP   117
Lab. majority 3,259 (6.96%)
Notional 5.25% swing Lab. to LD
(2005: Lab. majority 6,584 (17.47%))

§STRETFORD & URMSTON
E. 70,091   T. 44,910 (64.07%)   Lab. hold
*Kate Green, Lab.   21,821
Alex Williams, C.   12,886
Steve Cooke, LD   7,601
David Owen, UKIP   1,508
Margaret Westbrook, Green   916
Samuel Jacob, Ch. P.   178
Lab. majority 8,935 (19.90%)
Notional 0.69% swing Lab. to C.
(2005: Lab. majority 8,310 (21.28%))

§STROUD
E. 78,305   T. 57,973 (74.03%)   C. gain
*Neil Carmichael, C.   23,679
David Drew, Lab. (Co-op)   22,380
Dennis Andrewartha, LD   8,955
Martin Whiteside, Green   1,542
Steve Parker, UKIP   1,301
Alan Lomas, Ind.   116
C. majority 1,299 (2.24%)
Notional 2.05% swing Lab. (Co-op) to C.
(2005: Lab. (Co-op) majority 996 (1.85%))

§SUFFOLK CENTRAL & IPSWICH
NORTH
E. 75,848   T. 53,420 (70.43%)   C. hold
*Daniel Poulter, C.   27,125
Andrew Aalders-Dunthorne, LD   13,339
Bhavna Joshi, Lab.   8,636
Roy Philpot, UKIP   2,361
Andrew Stringer, Green   1,452
Mark Trevitt, Ind.   389
Richard Vass, New Party   118
C. majority 13,786 (25.81%)
Notional 0.76% swing LD to C.
(2005: C. majority 7,786 (16.07%))

§SUFFOLK COASTAL
E. 76,687   T. 54,893 (71.58%)   C. hold
*Therese Coffey, C.   25,475
Daisy Cooper, LD   16,347
Adam Leeder, Lab.   8,812
Prof. Stephen Bush, UKIP   3,156
Rachel Fulcher, Green   1,103
C. majority 9,128 (16.63%)
Notional 2.91% swing C. to LD
(2005: C. majority 9,674 (18.43%))

§SUFFOLK SOUTH
E. 72,498   T. 51,416 (70.92%)   C. hold
Tim Yeo, C.   24,550
Nigel Bennett, LD   15,861
Emma Bishton, Lab.   7,368
David Campbell Bannerman,
   UKIP   3,637
C. majority 8,689 (16.90%)
Notional 1.63% swing LD to C.
(2005: C. majority 6,664 (13.64%))

§SUFFOLK WEST
E. 74,413   T. 48,089 (64.62%)   C. hold
*Matthew Hancock, C.   24,312
Belinda Brooks-Gordon, LD   11,262
Ohid Ahmed, Lab.   7,089
Ian Smith, UKIP   3,085
Ramon Johns, BNP   1,428
Andrew Appleby, Ind.   540
Colin Young, CPA   373
C. majority 13,050 (27.14%)
Notional 2.28% swing C. to LD
(2005: C. majority 8,735 (19.92%))

§SUNDERLAND CENTRAL
E. 74,485   T. 42,463 (57.01%)   Lab. hold
*Julie Elliott, Lab.   19,495
Lee Martin, C.   12,770
Paul Dixon, LD   7,191
John McCaffrey, BNP   1,913
Pauline Featonby-Warren, UKIP   1,094
Lab. majority 6,725 (15.84%)
Notional 4.85% swing Lab. to C.
(2005: Lab. majority 9,464 (25.53%))

SURREY EAST
E. 76,855   T. 54,640 (71.09%)   C. hold
*Sam Gyimah, C.   31,007
David Lee, LD   14,133
Mathew Rodda, Lab.   4,925
Helena Windsor, UKIP   3,770
Martin Hogbin, Loony   422
Sandy Pratt, Ind.   383
C. majority 16,874 (30.88%)
0.72% swing C. to LD
(2005: C. majority 15,921 (32.32%))

SURREY HEATH
E. 77,690   T. 54,347 (69.95%)   C. hold
Michael Gove, C.   31,326
Alan Hilliar, LD   14,037
Matthew Willey, Lab.   5,552
Mark Stroud, UKIP   3,432
C. majority 17,289 (31.81%)
4.58% swing LD to C.
(2005: C. majority 10,845 (22.66%))

§SURREY SOUTH WEST
E. 77,980   T. 57,259 (73.43%)   C. hold
Jeremy Hunt, C.   33,605
Mike Simpson, LD   17,287
Richard Mollet, Lab.   3,419
Roger Meekins, UKIP   1,486
Cherry Allan, Green   690
Helen Hamilton, BNP   644
Luke Leighton, Pirate   94
Arthur Price, Ind.   34
C. majority 16,318 (28.50%)
Notional 8.63% swing LD to C.
(2005: C. majority 5,969 (11.23%))

§SUSSEX MID
E. 77,182   T. 55,855 (72.37%)   C. hold
Nicholas Soames, C.   28,329
Serena Tierney, LD   20,927
David Boot, Lab.   3,689
Marc Montgomery, UKIP   1,423
Paul Brown, Green   645
Stuart Minihane, BNP   583
Baron Von Thunderclap, Loony   259
C. majority 7,402 (13.25%)
Notional 0.32% swing LD to C.
(2005: C. majority 6,462 (12.62%))

§SUTTON & CHEAM
E. 66,658   T. 48,508 (72.77%)   LD hold
Paul Burstow, LD   22,156
Philippa Stroud, C.   20,548
Kathy Allen, Lab.   3,376
John Clarke, BNP   1,014
David Pickles, UKIP   950
Peter Hickson, Green   246
John Dodds, Eng. Dem.   106
Matthew Connolly, CPA   52
Martin Cullip, Libertarian   41
Dr Brian Hammond, UK Integrity   19
LD majority 1,608 (3.31%)
Notional 1.45% swing LD to C.
(2005: LD majority 2,689 (6.22%))

§SUTTON COLDFIELD
E. 74,489   T. 50,589 (67.91%)   C. hold
Andrew Mitchell, C.   27,303
Robert Pocock, Lab.   10,298
Richard Brighton, LD   9,117
Robert Grierson, BNP   1,749
Edward Siddall-Jones, UKIP   1,587
Joe Rooney, Green   535
C. majority 17,005 (33.61%)
Notional 3.44% swing Lab. to C.
(2005: C. majority 12,318 (26.72%))

§SWINDON NORTH
E. 78,391   T. 50,295 (64.16%)   C. gain
*Justin Tomlinson, C.   22,408
Victor Agarwal, Lab.   15,348
Jane Lock, LD   8,668
Stephen Halden, UKIP   1,842
Reginald Bates, BNP   1,542
Bill Hughes, Green   487
C. majority 7,060 (14.04%)
Notional 10.14% swing Lab. to C.
(2005: Lab. majority 2,675 (6.25%))

§SWINDON SOUTH
E. 72,622   T. 47,119 (64.88%)   C. gain
*Robert Buckland, C.   19,687
Anne Snelgrove, Lab.   16,143
Damon Hooton, LD   8,305
Robin Tingey, UKIP   2,029
Jenni Miles, Green   619
Alastair Kirk, Ch. P.   176
Karsten Evans, Ind.   160
C. majority 3,544 (7.52%)
Notional 5.51% swing Lab. to C.
(2005: Lab. majority 1,493 (3.50%))

TAMWORTH
E. 72,693   T. 46,390 (63.82%)   C. gain
*Christopher Pincher, C.   21,238
Brian Jenkins, Lab.   15,148
Jenny Pinkett, LD   7,516
Paul Smith, UKIP   2,253
Charlene Detheridge, Ch. P.   235
C. majority 6,090 (13.13%)
9.50% swing Lab. to C.
(2005: Lab. majority 2,569 (5.87%))

§TATTON
E. 65,689   T. 45,231 (68.86%)   C. hold
George Osborne, C.   24,687
David Lomax, LD   10,200
Richard Jackson, Lab.   7,803
Sarah Flannery, Ind.   2,243
Michael Gibson, Poetry   298
C. majority 14,487 (32.03%)
Notional 1.17% swing LD to C.
(2005: C. majority 11,537 (27.73%))

§TAUNTON DEANE
E. 82,537   T. 58,150 (70.45%)   LD hold
Jeremy Browne, LD   28,531
Mark Formosa, C.   24,538
Martin Jevon, Lab.   2,967
Tony McIntyre, UKIP   2,114
LD majority 3,993 (6.87%)
Notional 1.78% swing C. to LD
(2005: LD majority 1,868 (3.30%))

§TELFORD
E. 65,061   T. 41,310 (63.49%)   Lab. hold
David Wright, Lab.   15,974
Tom Biggins, C.   14,996
Phil Bennion, LD   6,399
Denis Allen, UKIP   2,428
Phil Spencer, BNP   1,513
Lab. majority 978 (2.37%)
Notional 6.32% swing Lab. to C.
(2005: Lab. majority 5,651 (15.01%))

§TEWKESBURY
E. 76,655   T. 53,961 (70.39%)   C. hold
Laurence Robertson, C.   25,472
Alistair Cameron, LD   19,162
Stuart Emmerson, Lab.   6,253
Brian Jones, UKIP   2,230
Matthew Sidford, Green   525
George Ridgeon, Loony   319
C. majority 6,310 (11.69%)
Notional 4.04% swing C. to LD
(2005: C. majority 9,130 (19.78%))

§THANET NORTH
E. 69,432   T. 43,343 (62.43%)   C. hold
Roger Gale, C.   22,826
Michael Britton, Lab.   9,298
Laura Murphy, LD   8,400
Rosamund Parker, UKIP   2,819
C. majority 13,528 (31.21%)
Notional 7.94% swing Lab. to C.
(2005: C. majority 6,118 (15.33%))

§THANET SOUTH
E. 71,596   T. 45,933 (64.16%)   C. hold
*Laura Sandys, C.   22,043
Dr Stephen Ladyman, Lab.   14,426
Peter Bucklitsch, LD   6,935
Trevor Shonk, UKIP   2,529
C. majority 7,617 (16.58%)
Notional 7.41% swing Lab. to C.
(2005: C. majority 810 (1.76%))

§THIRSK & MALTON
E. 76,231   T. 38,142 (50.03%)   C. hold
Anne McIntosh, C.   20,167
Howard Keal, LD   8,886
Jonathan Roberts, Lab.   5,169
Toby Horton, UKIP   2,502
John Clark, Lib.   1,418
C. majority 11,281 (29.58%)
Notional 1.75% swing C. to LD
(2005: C. majority 14,117 (28.50%))

§THORNBURY & YATE
E. 64,092   T. 48,226 (75.24%)   LD hold
Steve Webb, LD   25,032
Matthew Riddle, C.   17,916
Roxanne Egan, Lab.   3,385
Jenny Knight, UKIP   1,709
Thomas Beacham, Ind. Fed.   126
Anthony Clements, ND   58
LD majority 7,116 (14.76%)
Notional 4.35% swing LD to C.
(2005: LD majority 11,060 (23.45%))

§THURROCK
E. 92,390   T. 45,821 (49.60%)   C. gain
*Jackie Doyle-Price, C.   16,869
Carl Morris, Lab.   16,777
Carys Davis, LD   4,901
Emma Colgate, BNP   3,618
Clive Broad, UKIP   3,390
Arinola Araba, Ch. P.   266
C. majority 92 (0.20%)
Notional 6.61% swing Lab. to C.
(2005: Lab. majority 5,358 (13.02%))

§TIVERTON & HONITON
E. 76,810   T. 54,894 (71.47%)   C. hold
*Neil Parish, C.   27,614
Jon Underwood, LD   18,294
Vernon Whitlock, Lab.   4,907
Daryl Stanbury, UKIP   3,277
Cathy Connor, Green   802
C. majority 9,320 (16.98%)
Notional 0.28% swing C. to LD
(2005: C. majority 9,007 (17.55%))

TONBRIDGE & MALLING
E. 71,790   T. 51,314 (71.48%)   C. hold
Sir John Stanley, C.   29,723
Elizabeth Simpson, LD   11,545
Daniel Griffiths, Lab.   6,476
David Waller, UKIP   1,911
Steve Dawe, Green   764
Mike Easter, NF   505
Lisa Rogers, Eng. Dem.   390
C. majority 18,178 (35.43%)
1.02% swing LD to C.
(2005: C. majority 13,352 (28.99%))

§TOOTING
E. 73,836   T. 50,655 (68.60%)   Lab. hold
Sadiq Khan, Lab.   22,038
Mark Clarke, C.   19,514
Nasser Butt, LD   7,509
Strachan McDonald, UKIP   624
Roy Vickery, Green   609
Susan John-Richards, Ind.   190
Shereen Paul, Ch. P.   171
Lab. majority 2,524 (4.98%)
Notional 3.60% swing Lab. to C.
(2005: Lab. majority 5,169 (12.17%))

§TORBAY
E. 76,151   T. 49,210 (64.62%)   LD hold
Adrian Sanders, LD   23,126
Marcus Wood, C.   19,048
David Pedrick-Friend, Lab.   3,231
Julien Parrott, UKIP   2,628
Ann Conway, BNP   709
Sam Moss, Green   468
LD majority 4,078 (8.29%)
Notional 1.14% swing C. to LD
(2005: LD majority 2,727 (6.01%))

§TOTNES
E. 67,937   T. 47,843 (70.42%)   C. hold
*Dr Sarah Wollaston, C.   21,940
Julian Brazil, LD   17,013
Carole Whitty, Lab.   3,538
Jeff Beer, UKIP   2,890
Lydia Somerville, Green   1,181
Mike Turner, BNP   624
Simon Drew, Ind.   390
Dr Stephen Hopwood, Ind.   267
C. majority 4,927 (10.30%)
Notional 2.27% swing LD to C.
(2005: C. majority 2,693 (5.76%))

TOTTENHAM
E. 69,933   T. 40,687 (58.18%)   Lab. hold
David Lammy, Lab.   24,128
David Schmitz, LD   7,197
Sean Sullivan, C.   6,064
Jenny Sutton, TUSC   1,057
Anne Gray, Green   980
Winston McKenzie, UKIP   466
Neville Watson, Ind. People   265
Abimbola Kadara, Ch. P.   262
Sheik Thompson, Ind.   143
Errol Carr, Ind.   125
Lab. majority 16,931 (41.61%)
0.22% swing LD to Lab.
(2005: Lab. majority 13,034 (41.16%))

§TRURO & FALMOUTH
E. 70,598   T. 48,768 (69.08%)   C. gain
*Sarah Newton, C.   20,349
Terrye Teverson, LD   19,914
Charlotte Mackenzie, Lab.   4,697
Harry Blakeley, UKIP   1,911
Loic Rich, Meb. Ker.   1,039
Ian Wright, Green   858
C. majority 435 (0.89%)
Notional 5.07% swing LD to C.
(2005: LD majority 3,931 (9.25%))

§TUNBRIDGE WELLS
E. 72,042   T. 50,320 (69.85%)   C. hold
Greg Clark, C.   28,302
David Hallas, LD   12,726
Gary Heather, Lab.   5,448
Victor Webb, UKIP   2,054
Hazel Dawe, Green   914
Andrew McBride, BNP   704
Farel Bradbury, Ind.   172
C. majority 15,576 (30.95%)
Notional 2.79% swing LD to C.
(2005: C. majority 11,572 (25.38%))

TWICKENHAM
E. 79,861   T. 59,721 (74.78%)   LD hold
Vince Cable, LD   32,483
Deborah Thomas, C.   20,343
Brian Tomlinson, Lab.   4,583
Brian Gilbert, UKIP   868
Steve Roest, Green   674
Chris Hurst, BNP   654
Harry Cole, R and E   76
Paul Armstrong, Magna Carta   40
LD majority 12,140 (20.33%)
0.52% swing C. to LD
(2005: LD majority 9,965 (19.28%))

§TYNEMOUTH
E. 75,680   T. 52,668 (69.59%)   Lab. hold
Alan Campbell, Lab.   23,860
Wendy Morton, C.   18,121
John Appleby, LD   7,845
Dorothy Brooke, BNP   1,404
Natasha Payne, UKIP   900
Julia Erskine, Green   538
Lab. majority 5,739 (10.90%)
Notional 0.38% swing Lab. to C.
(2005: Lab. majority 5,490 (11.65%))

§TYNESIDE NORTH
E. 77,690   T. 46,405 (59.73%)   Lab. hold
*Mary Glindon, Lab.   23,505
David Ord, LD   10,621
Gagan Mohindra, C.   8,514
John Burrows, BNP   1,860
Claudia Blake, UKIP   1,306
Bob Batten, NF   599
Lab. majority 12,884 (27.76%)
Notional 4.81% swing Lab. to LD
(2005: Lab. majority 14,929 (37.38%))

§UXBRIDGE & RUISLIP SOUTH
E. 71,168   T. 45,076 (63.34%)   C. hold
John Randall, C.   21,758
Sidharath Garg, Lab.   10,542
Michael Cox, LD   8,995
Dianne Neal, BNP   1,396
Mark Wadsworth, UKIP   1,234
Mike Harling, Green   477
Roger Cooper, Eng. Dem.   403
Francis Mcallister, NF   271
C. majority 11,216 (24.88%)
Notional 3.44% swing Lab. to C.
(2005: C. majority 7,178 (18.01%))

§VAUXHALL
E. 74,811   T. 43,191 (57.73%)   Lab. hold
Kate Hoey, Lab.   21,498
Caroline Pidgeon, LD   10,847
Glyn Chambers, C.   9,301
Joseph Healy, Green   708
Jose Navarro, Eng. Dem.   289
Lana Martin, Ch. P.   200
Daniel Lambert, Soc.   143
Jeremy Drinkall, WP   109
James Kapetanos, APP   96
Lab. majority 10,651 (24.66%)
Notional 0.06% swing LD to Lab.
(2005: Lab. majority 8,503 (24.54%))

§WAKEFIELD
E. 70,834   T. 44,444 (62.74%)   Lab. hold
Mary Creagh, Lab.   17,454
Alex Story, C.   15,841
David Smith, LD   7,256
Ian Senior, BNP   2,581
Miriam Hawkins, Green   873
Mark Harrop, Ind.   439
Lab. majority 1,613 (3.63%)
Notional 6.94% swing Lab. to C.
(2005: Lab. majority 7,349 (17.50%))

§WALLASEY
E. 65,915   T. 41,654 (63.19%)   Lab. hold
Angela Eagle, Lab.   21,578
Leah Fraser, C.   13,071
Steve Pitt, LD   5,693
Derek Snowden, UKIP   1,205
Emmanuel Mwaba, Ind.   107
Lab. majority 8,507 (20.42%)
Notional 1.78% swing Lab. to C.
(2005: Lab. majority 9,130 (23.98%))

§WALSALL NORTH
E. 65,183   T. 36,187 (55.52%)   Lab. hold
David Winnick, Lab.   13,385
Helyn Clack, C.   12,395
Nadia Fazal, LD   4,754
Christopher Woodall, BNP   2,930
Elizabeth Hazell, UKIP   1,737
Peter Smith, Dem. Lab.   842
Babar Shakir, Ch. P.   144
Lab. majority 990 (2.74%)
Notional 9.03% swing Lab. to C.
(2005: Lab. majority 6,901 (20.79%))

§WALSALL SOUTH
E. 64,830   T. 40,882 (63.06%)   Lab. hold
*Valerie Vaz, Lab.   16,211
Richard Hunt, C.   14,456
Dr Murli Sinha, LD   5,880
Derek Bennett, UKIP   3,449
Gulzaman Khan, Ch. P.   482
Mohammed Mulia, ND   404
Lab. majority 1,755 (4.29%)
Notional 8.24% swing Lab. to C.
(2005: Lab. majority 7,910 (20.77%))

WALTHAMSTOW
E. 64,625   T. 40,994 (63.43%)   Lab. hold
*Stella Creasy, Lab.   21,252
Farid Ahmed, LD   11,774
Andy Hemsted, C.   5,734
Judith Chisholm-Benli, UKIP   823
Daniel Perrett, Green   767
Nancy Taaffe, TUSC   279
Ashar Mall, Ch. P.   248
Paul Warburton, Ind.   117
Lab. majority 9,478 (23.12%)
0.04% swing Lab. to LD
(2005: Lab. majority 7,993 (23.21%))

WANSBECK
E. 63,045   T. 38,273 (60.71%)   Lab. hold
*Ian Lavery, Lab.   17,548
Simon Reed, LD   10,517
Campbell Storey, C.   6,714
Stephen Finlay, BNP   1,418
Linda Lee-Stokoe, UKIP   974
Nic Best, Green   601
Malcolm Reid, Ind.   359
Michael Flynn, Ch. P.   142
Lab. majority 7,031 (18.37%)
5.19% swing Lab. to LD
(2005: Lab. majority 10,581 (28.75%))

§WANTAGE
E. 80,456   T. 56,341 (70.03%)   C. hold
Ed Vaizey, C.   29,284
Alan Armitage, LD   15,737
Steven Mitchell, Lab.   7,855
Jacqueline Jones, UKIP   2,421
Adam Twine, Green   1,044
C. majority 13,547 (24.04%)
Notional 4.30% swing LD to C.
(2005: C. majority 8,039 (15.44%))

§WARLEY
E. 63,106   T. 38,270 (60.64%)   Lab. hold
John Spellar, Lab.   20,240
Jasbir Parmar, C.   9,484
Edward Keating, LD   5,929
Nigel Harvey, UKIP   2,617
Lab. majority 10,756 (28.11%)
Notional 1.94% swing Lab. to C.
(2005: Lab. majority 11,206 (31.99%))

§WARRINGTON NORTH
E. 71,601   T. 44,211 (61.75%)   Lab. hold
Helen Jones, Lab.   20,135
Paul Campbell, C.   13,364
David Eccles, LD   9,196
Albert Scott, Ind.   1,516
Lab. majority 6,771 (15.32%)
Notional 6.61% swing Lab. to C.
(2005: Lab. majority 11,382 (28.53%))

§WARRINGTON SOUTH
E. 80,506   T. 54,874 (68.16%)   C. gain
*David Mowat, C.   19,641
Nick Bent, Lab.   18,088
Jo Crotty, LD   15,094
James Ashington, UKIP   1,624
Steph Davies, Green   427
C. majority 1,553 (2.83%)
Notional 6.00% swing Lab. to C.
(2005: Lab. majority 4,337 (9.17%))

§WARWICK & LEAMINGTON
E. 58,030   T. 49,032 (84.49%)   C. gain
*Chris White, C.   20,876
James Plaskitt, Lab.   17,363
Alan Beddow, LD   8,977
Christopher Lenton, UKIP   926
Ian Davison, Green   693
Jim Cullinane, Ind.   197
C. majority 3,513 (7.16%)
Notional 8.76% swing Lab. to C.
(2005: Lab. majority 4,393 (10.35%))

§WARWICKSHIRE NORTH
E. 70,143   T. 47,265 (67.38%)   C. gain
*Dan Byles, C.   18,993
Mike O'Brien, Lab.   18,939
Stephen Martin, LD   5,481
Jason Holmes, BNP   2,106
Steven Fowler, UKIP   1,335
David Lane, Eng. Dem.   411
C. majority 54 (0.11%)
Notional 7.69% swing Lab. to C.
(2005: Lab. majority 6,684 (15.27%))

§WASHINGTON & SUNDERLAND WEST
E. 68,910   T. 37,334 (54.18%)   Lab. hold
Sharon Hodgson, Lab.   19,615
Ian Cuthbert, C.   8,157
Peter Andras, LD   6,382
Ian McDonald, BNP   1,913
Linda Hudson, UKIP   1,267
Lab. majority 11,458 (30.69%)
Notional 11.56% swing Lab. to C.
(2005: Lab. majority 17,060 (52.56%))

§WATFORD
E. 80,798   T. 55,208 (68.33%)   C. gain
*Richard Harrington, C.   19,291
Sal Brinton, LD   17,866
Claire Ward, Lab.   14,750
Andrew Emerson, BNP   1,217
Graham Eardley, UKIP   1,199
Ian Brandon, Green   885
C. majority 1,425 (2.58%)
Notional 6.08% swing Lab. to C.
(2005: Lab. majority 1,151 (2.33%))

§WAVENEY
E. 78,532   T. 51,141 (65.12%)   C. gain
*Peter Aldous, C.   20,571
Bob Blizzard, Lab.   19,802
Alan Dean, LD   6,811
Jack Tyler, UKIP   2,684
Graham Elliott, Green   1,167
Louis Barfe, Ind.   106
C. majority 769 (1.50%)
Notional 6.75% swing Lab. to C.
(2005: Lab. majority 5,950 (12.00%))

§WEALDEN
E. 76,537   T. 54,969 (71.82%)   C. hold
Charles Hendry, C.   31,090
Chris Bowers, LD   13,911
Lorna Blackmore, Lab.   5,266
Dan Docker, UKIP   3,319
David Jonas, Green   1,383
C. majority 17,179 (31.25%)
Notional 2.79% swing LD to C.
(2005: C. majority 12,812 (25.66%))

§WEAVER VALE
E. 66,538   T. 43,990 (66.11%)   C. gain
*Graham Evans, C.   16,953
John Stockton, Lab.   15,962
Peter Hampson, LD   8,196
Colin Marsh, BNP   1,063
Paul Remfry, UKIP   1,018
Howard Thorp, Green   338
Mike Cooksley, Ind.   270
Tom Reynolds, Ind.   133
Will Charlton, Ind.   57
C. majority 991 (2.25%)
Notional 8.14% swing Lab. to C.
(2005: Lab. majority 5,277 (14.03%))

§WELLINGBOROUGH
E. 76,857   T. 51,661 (67.22%)   C. hold
Peter Bone, C.   24,918
Jayne Buckland, Lab.   13,131
Kevin Barron, LD   8,848
Adrian Haynes, UKIP   1,636
Rob Walker, BNP   1,596
Terry Spencer, Eng. Dem.   530
Jonathan Hornett, Green   480
Paul Crofts, TUSC   249
Gary Donaldson, Ind.   240
Marcus Lavin, Ind.   33
C. majority 11,787 (22.82%)
Notional 10.78% swing Lab. to C.
(2005: C. majority 610 (1.25%))

WELLS
E. 79,432   T. 55,864 (70.33%)   LD gain
*Tessa Munt, LD   24,560
David Heathcoat-Amory, C.   23,760
Andy Merryfield, Lab.   4,198
Jake Baynes, UKIP   1,711
Richard Boyce, BNP   1,004
Chris Briton, Green   631
LD majority 800 (1.43%)
3.59% swing C. to LD
(2005: C. majority 3,040 (5.74%))

WELWYN HATFIELD
E. 72,058   T. 48,972 (67.96%)   C. hold
Grant Shapps, C.   27,894
Mike Hobday, Lab.   10,471
Paul Zukowskyj, LD   8,010
David Platt, UKIP   1,643
Jill Weston, Green   796
Nigel Parker, Ind.   158
C. majority 17,423 (35.58%)
11.14% swing Lab. to C.
(2005: C. majority 5,946 (13.30%))

§WENTWORTH & DEARNE
E. 72,586   T. 42,106 (58.01%)   Lab. hold
John Healey, Lab.   21,316
Michelle Donelan, C.   7,396
Nick Love, LD   6,787
John Wilkinson, UKIP   3,418
George Baldwin, BNP   3,189
Lab. majority 13,920 (33.06%)
Notional 7.49% swing Lab. to C.
(2005: Lab. majority 17,551 (45.55%))

§WEST BROMWICH EAST
E. 62,824   T. 37,950 (60.41%)   Lab. hold
Tom Watson, Lab.   17,657
Alistair Thompson, C.   10,961
Ian Garrett, LD   4,993
Terry Lewin, BNP   2,205
Mark Cowles, Eng. Dem.   1,150
Steve Grey, UKIP   984
Lab. majority 6,696 (17.64%)
Notional 7.68% swing Lab. to C.
(2005: Lab. majority 11,947 (33.00%))

§WEST BROMWICH WEST
E. 65,013   T. 36,171 (55.64%)   Lab. hold
Adrian Bailey, Lab.   16,263
Andrew Hardie, C.   10,612
Sadie Smith, LD   4,336
Russ Green, BNP   3,394
Mac Ford, UKIP   1,566
Lab. majority 5,651 (15.62%)
Notional 7.64% swing Lab. to C.
(2005: Lab. majority 9,821 (30.90%))

§WEST HAM
E. 85,313   T. 46,951 (55.03%)   Lab. hold
Lyn Brown, Lab.   29,422
Virginia Morris, C.   6,888
Martin Pierce, LD   5,392
Stan Gain, CPA   1,327
Kamran Malik, Ind.   1,245
Michael Davidson, NF   1,089
Kim Gandy, UKIP   766
Jane Lithgow, Green   645
Grace Agbogun-Toko, Ind.   177
Lab. majority 22,534 (47.99%)
Notional 4.16% swing C. to Lab.
(2005: Lab. majority 12,274 (31.76%))

§WESTMINSTER NORTH
E. 66,739   T. 39,598 (59.33%)   Lab. hold
Karen Buck, Lab.   17,377
Joanne Cash, C.   15,251
Mark Blackburn, LD   5,513
Tristan Smith, Green   478
Stephen Curry, BNP   334
Jasna Badzak, UKIP   315
Dr Ali Bahaijoub, Ind.   101
Edward Roseman, Eng. Dem.   99
Gabriela Fajardo, Ch. P.   98
Abby Dharamsey, Ind.   32
Lab. majority 2,126 (5.37%)
Notional 0.61% swing Lab. to C.
(2005: Lab. majority 2,120 (6.59%))

§WESTMORLAND & LONSDALE
E. 67,881   T. 51,487 (75.85%)   LD hold
Tim Farron, LD   30,896
Gareth McKeever, C.   18,632
Jonathan Todd, Lab.   1,158
John Mander, UKIP   801
LD majority 12,264 (23.82%)
Notional 11.06% swing C. to LD
(2005: LD majority 806 (1.70%))

§WESTON-SUPER-MARE
E. 78,487   T. 52,716 (67.17%)   C. hold
John Penrose, C.   23,356
Mike Bell, LD   20,665
David Bradley, Lab.   5,772
Paul Spencer, UKIP   1,406
Peryn Parsons, BNP   1,098
John Peverelle, Eng. Dem.   275
Steve Satch, Ind.   144
C. majority 2,691 (5.10%)
Notional 0.42% swing LD to C.
(2005: C. majority 2,088 (4.26%))

§WIGAN
E. 75,564   T. 44,140 (58.41%)   Lab. hold
*Lisa Nandy, Lab.   21,404
Michael Winstanley, C.   10,917
Mark Clayton, LD   6,797
Alan Freeman, UKIP   2,516
Charles Mather, BNP   2,506
Lab. majority 10,487 (23.76%)
Notional 7.69% swing Lab. to C.
(2005: Lab. majority 15,501 (39.15%))

§WILTSHIRE NORTH
E. 66,313   T. 48,699 (73.44%)   C. hold
James Gray, C.   25,114
Mike Evemy, LD   17,631
Jason Hughes, Lab.   3,239
Charles Bennett, UKIP   1,908
Phil Chamberlain, Green   599
Philip Allnatt, Ind.   208
C. majority 7,483 (15.37%)
Notional 0.01% swing LD to C.
(2005: C. majority 6,888 (15.34%))

§WILTSHIRE SOUTH WEST
E. 71,645   T. 49,018 (68.42%)   C. hold
Andrew Murrison, C.   25,321
Trevor Carbin, LD   14,954
Rebecca Rennison, Lab.   5,613
Michael Cuthbert-Murray, UKIP   2,684
Crispin Black, Ind.   446
C. majority 10,367 (21.15%)
Notional 1.15% swing LD to C.
(2005: C. majority 8,568 (18.85%))

§WIMBLEDON
E. 65,723   T. 47,395 (72.11%)   C. hold
Stephen Hammond, C.   23,257
Shas Sheehan, LD   11,849
Andrew Judge, Lab.   10,550
Mark McAleer, UKIP   914
Rajeev Thacker, Green   590
David Martin, Ch. P.   235
C. majority 11,408 (24.07%)
Notional 0.42% swing LD to C.
(2005: C. majority 2,480 (5.69%))

§WINCHESTER
E. 73,806   T. 55,955 (75.81%)   C. gain
*Steve Brine, C.   27,155
Martin Tod, LD   24,107
Patrick Davies, Lab.   3,051
Jocelyn Penn-Bull, UKIP   1,139
Mark Lancaster, Eng. Dem.   503
C. majority 3,048 (5.45%)
Notional 9.09% swing LD to C.
(2005: LD majority 6,524 (12.74%))

§WINDSOR
E. 69,511   T. 49,588 (71.34%)   C. hold
Adam Afriyie, C.   30,172
Julian Tisi, LD   11,118
Amanjit Jhund, Lab.   4,910
John-Paul Rye, UKIP   1,612
Peter Phillips, BNP   950
Derek Wall, Green   628
Peter Hooper, Ind.   198
C. majority 19,054 (38.42%)
Notional 8.05% swing LD to C.
(2005: C. majority 9,605 (22.32%))

§WIRRAL SOUTH
E. 56,099   T. 39,906 (71.13%)   Lab. hold
*Alison McGovern, Lab.   16,276
Jeff Clarke, C.   15,745
Jamie Saddler, LD   6,611
David Scott, UKIP   1,274
Lab. majority 531 (1.33%)
Notional 3.98% swing Lab. to C.
(2005: Lab. majority 3,538 (9.30%))

§WIRRAL WEST
E. 55,050   T. 39,372 (71.52%)   C. hold
*Esther McVey, C.   16,726
Phillip Davies, Lab.   14,290
Peter Reisdorf, LD   6,630
Philip Griffiths, UKIP   899
David Kirwan, Ind.   506
David James, CSP   321
C. majority 2,436 (6.19%)
Notional 2.34% swing Lab. to C.
(2005: C. majority 569 (1.51%))

§WITHAM
E. 66,750   T. 46,835 (70.16%)   C. hold
*Priti Patel, C.   24,448
Margaret Phelps, LD   9,252
John Spademan, Lab.   8,656
David Hodges, UKIP   3,060
James Abbott, Green   1,419
C. majority 15,196 (32.45%)
Notional 1.06% swing C. to LD
(2005: C. majority 7,241 (17.29%))

§WITNEY
E. 78,766   T. 57,769 (73.34%)   C. hold
David Cameron, C.   33,973
Dawn Barnes, LD   11,233
Joe Goldberg, Lab.   7,511
Stuart Macdonald, Green   2,385
Nikolai Tolstoy, UKIP   2,001
Howling Hope, Loony   234
Paul Wesson, Ind.   166
Johnnie Cook, Ind.   151
Colin Bex, Wessex Reg.   62
Aaron Barschak, Ind.   53
C. majority 22,740 (39.36%)
Notional 6.29% swing LD to C.
(2005: C. majority 13,874 (26.78%))

WOKING
E. 73,838   T. 52,786 (71.49%)   C. hold
*Jonathan Lord, C.   26,551
Rosie Sharpley, LD   19,744
Tom Miller, Lab.   4,246
Rob Burberry, UKIP   1,997
Julie Roxburgh, PPN-V   204
Ruth Temple, Magna Carta   44
C. majority 6,807 (12.90%)
0.73% swing C. to LD
(2005: C. majority 6,612 (14.36%))

§WOKINGHAM
E. 76,219 T. 54,528 (71.54%) C. hold
John Redwood, C. 28,754
Prue Bray, LD 15,262
George Davidson, Lab. 5,516
Mark Ashwell, Ind. 2,340
Ann Zebedee, UKIP 1,664
Marjory Bisset, Green 567
Top Cat Owen, Loony 329
Robin Smith, Ind. 96
C. majority 13,492 (24.74%)
Notional 4.65% swing LD to C.
(2005: C. majority 7,257 (15.44%))

§WOLVERHAMPTON NORTH EAST
E. 59,324 T. 34,894 (58.82%) Lab. hold
*Emma Reynolds, Lab. 14,448
Julie Rook, C. 11,964
Colin Ross, LD 4,711
Simon Patten, BNP 2,296
Paul Valdmanis, UKIP 1,138
Shangara Bhatoe, Soc. Lab. 337
Lab. majority 2,484 (7.12%)
Notional 9.00% swing Lab. to C.
(2005: Lab. majority 8,628 (25.12%))

§WOLVERHAMPTON SOUTH EAST
E. 60,450 T. 34,707 (57.41%) Lab. hold
Pat McFadden, Lab. 16,505
Ken Wood, C. 9,912
Richard Whitehouse, LD 5,277
Gordon Fanthom, UKIP 2,675
Sudhir Handa, Ind. 338
Lab. majority 6,593 (19.00%)
Notional 8.79% swing Lab. to C.
(2005: Lab. majority 12,309 (36.58%))

§WOLVERHAMPTON SOUTH WEST
E. 59,160 T. 40,160 (67.88%) C. gain
*Paul Uppal, C. 16,344
Rob Marris, Lab. 15,653
Robin Lawrence, LD 6,430
Amanda Mobberley, UKIP 1,487
Raymond Barry, Parenting 246
C. majority 691 (1.72%)
Notional 3.52% swing Lab. to C.
(2005: Lab. majority 2,114 (5.31%))

WORCESTER
E. 72,831 T. 48,974 (67.24%) C. gain
*Robin Walker, C. 19,358
Michael Foster, Lab. 16,376
Jackie Alderson, LD 9,525
Jack Bennett, UKIP 1,360
Spencer Lee Kirby, BNP 1,219
Louis Stephen, Green 735
Andrew Robinson, Pirate 173
Peter Nielsen, Ind. 129
Andrew Christian-Brookes, Ind. 99
C. majority 2,982 (6.09%)
6.43% swing Lab. to C.
(2005: Lab. majority 3,144 (6.78%))

§WORCESTERSHIRE MID
E. 72,171 T. 50,931 (70.57%) C. hold
Peter Luff, C. 27,770
Margaret Rowley, LD 11,906
Robin Lunn, Lab. 7,613
John White, UKIP 3,049
Gordon Matthews, Green 593
C. majority 15,864 (31.15%)
Notional 0.04% swing LD to C.
(2005: C. majority 12,906 (27.33%))

§WORCESTERSHIRE WEST
E. 73,270 T. 54,093 (73.83%) C. hold
*Harriett Baldwin, C. 27,213
Richard Burt, LD 20,459
Penelope Barber, Lab. 3,661
Caroline Bovey, UKIP 2,119
Malcolm Victory, Green 641
C. majority 6,754 (12.49%)
Notional 3.23% swing LD to C.
(2005: C. majority 3,053 (6.03%))

§WORKINGTON
E. 59,607 T. 39,259 (65.86%) Lab. hold
Tony Cunningham, Lab. 17,865
Judith Pattinson, C. 13,290
Stan Collins, LD 5,318
Martin Wingfield, BNP 1,496
Stephen Lee, UKIP 876
Rob Logan, Eng. Dem. 414
Lab. majority 4,575 (11.65%)
Notional 5.66% swing Lab. to C.
(2005: Lab. majority 8,226 (22.97%))

§WORSLEY & ECCLES SOUTH
E. 72,473 T. 41,701 (57.54%) Lab. hold
Barbara Keeley, Lab. 17,892
Iain Lindley, C. 13,555
Richard Gadsden, LD 6,883
Andrew Townsend, UKIP 2,037
Paul Whitelegg, Eng. Dem. 1,334
Lab. majority 4,337 (10.40%)
Notional 7.61% swing Lab. to C.
(2005: Lab. majority 10,001 (25.62%))

§WORTHING EAST & SHOREHAM
E. 74,001 T. 48,397 (65.40%) C. hold
Tim Loughton, C. 23,458
James Doyle, LD 12,353
Emily Benn, Lab. 8,087
Mike Glennon, UKIP 2,984
Susan Board, Green 1,126
Clive Maltby, Eng. Dem. 389
C. majority 11,105 (22.95%)
Notional 1.70% swing LD to C.
(2005: C. majority 8,180 (18.37%))

§WORTHING WEST
E. 75,945 T. 49,123 (64.68%) C. hold
Peter Bottomley, C. 25,416
Hazel Thorpe, LD 13,687
Ian Ross, Lab. 5,800
John Wallace, UKIP 2,924
David Aherne, Green 996
Stuart Dearsley, Christian 300
C. majority 11,729 (23.88%)
Notional 1.50% swing LD to C.
(2005: C. majority 9,383 (20.89%))

§WREKIN, THE
E. 65,544 T. 45,968 (70.13%) C. hold
Mark Pritchard, C. 21,922
Paul Kalinauckas, Lab. (Co-op) 12,472
Ali Cameron-Daw, LD 8,019
Malcolm Hurst, UKIP 2,050
Susan Harwood, BNP 1,505
C. majority 9,450 (20.56%)
Notional 8.85% swing Lab. (Co-op) to C.
(2005: C. majority 1,187 (2.85%))

§WYCOMBE
E. 74,502 T. 48,151 (64.63%) C. hold
*Steven Baker, C. 23,423
Steve Guy, LD 13,863
Andrew Lomas, Lab. 8,326
John Wiseman, UKIP 2,123
Madassar Khokar, Ind. 228
David Fitton, Ind. 188
C. majority 9,560 (19.85%)
Notional 4.83% swing C. to LD
(2005: C. majority 7,597 (17.29%))

§WYRE & PRESTON NORTH
E. 71,201 T. 51,308 (72.06%) C. hold
*Ben Wallace, C. 26,877
Danny Gallagher, LD 11,033
Cat Smith, Lab. 10,932
Nigel Cecil, UKIP 2,466
C. majority 15,844 (30.88%)
Notional 3.86% swing C. to LD
(2005: C. majority 12,082 (27.51%))

§WYRE FOREST
E. 76,711 T. 50,899 (66.35%) C. gain
*Mark Garnier, C. 18,793
Dr Richard Taylor, Ind. CHC 16,150
Nigel Knowles, Lab. 7,298
Neville Farmer, LD 6,040
Michael Wrench, UKIP 1,498
Gordon Howells, BNP 1,120
C. majority 2,643 (5.19%)
Notional 7.35% swing Ind. CHC to C.
(2005: Ind. CHC majority 4,613 (9.51%))

¶WYTHENSHAWE & SALE EAST
E. 79,923 T. 40,751 (50.99%) Lab. hold
Paul Goggins, Lab. 17,987
Janet Clowes, C. 10,412
Martin Eakins, LD 9,107
Bernard Todd, BNP 1,572
Chris Cassidy, UKIP 1,405
Lynn Worthington, TUSC 268
Lab. majority 7,575 (18.59%)
5.67% swing Lab. to C.
(2005: Lab. majority 10,827 (29.92%))

§YEOVIL
E. 82,314 T. 57,160 (69.44%) LD hold
David Laws, LD 31,843
Kevin Davis, C. 18,807
Lee Skevington, Lab. 2,991
Nigel Pearson, UKIP 2,357
Robert Baehr, BNP 1,162
LD majority 13,036 (22.81%)
Notional 2.74% swing C. to LD
(2005: LD majority 8,779 (17.33%))

§YORK CENTRAL
E. 74,908 T. 46,483 (62.05%) Lab. hold
Hugh Bayley, Lab. 18,573
Susan Wade Weeks, C. 12,122
Christian Vassie, LD 11,694
Andy Chase, Green 1,669
Jeff Kelly, BNP 1,171
Paul Abbott, UKIP 1,100
Eddie Vee, Loony 154
Lab. majority 6,451 (13.88%)
Notional 6.02% swing Lab. to C.
(2005: Lab. majority 10,344 (25.92%))

§YORK OUTER
E. 74,965   T. 53,300 (71.10%)   C. gain
*Julian Sturdy, C.   22,912
Madeleine Kirk, LD   19,224
James Alexander, Lab.   9,108
Judith Morris, UKIP   1,100
Cathy Smurthwaite, BNP   956
C. majority 3,688 (6.92%)
Notional 3.68% swing LD to C.
(2005: LD majority 203 (0.44%))

§YORKSHIRE EAST
E. 80,342   T. 51,254 (63.79%)   C. hold
Greg Knight, C.   24,328
Robert Adamson, LD   10,842
Paul Rounding, Lab.   10,401
Chris Daniels, UKIP   2,142
Gary Pudsey, BNP   1,865
Ray Allerston, Soc. Dem.   914
Michael Jackson, Green   762
C. majority 13,486 (26.31%)
Notional 0.06% swing C. to LD
(2005: C. majority 6,284 (13.31%))

WALES

ABERAVON
E. 50,789   T. 30,958 (60.95%)   Lab. hold
Hywel Francis, Lab.   16,073
Keith Davies, LD   5,034
Caroline Jones, C.   4,411
Paul Nicholls-Jones, PC   2,198
Kevin Edwards, BNP   1,276
Andrew Tutton, Ind.   919
Captain Beany, Bean   558
Joe Callan, UKIP   489
Lab. majority 11,039 (35.66%)
5.32% swing Lab. to LD
(2005: Lab. majority 13,937 (46.30%))

§ABERCONWY
E. 44,593   T. 29,966 (67.20%)   C. gain
*Guto Bebb, C.   10,734
Ronald Hughes, Lab.   7,336
Mike Priestley, LD   5,786
Phil Edwards, PC   5,341
Mike Wieteska, UKIP   632
Louise Wynne-Jones, Ch. P.   137
C. majority 3,398 (11.34%)
Notional 7.63% swing Lab. to C.
(2005: Lab. majority 1,070 (3.93%))

ALYN & DEESIDE
E. 60,931   T. 39,923 (65.52%)   Lab. hold
Mark Tami, Lab.   15,804
Will Gallagher, C.   12,885
Paul Brighton, LD   7,308
Maurice Jones, PC   1,549
John Walker, BNP   1,368
James Howson, UKIP   1,009
Lab. majority 2,919 (7.31%)
8.15% swing Lab. to C.
(2005: Lab. majority 8,378 (23.60%))

§ARFON
E. 41,198   T. 26,078 (63.30%)   PC gain
Hywel Williams, PC   9,383
Alan Pugh, Lab.   7,928
Robin Millar, C.   4,416
Sarah Green, LD   3,666
Elwyn Williams, UKIP   685
PC majority 1,455 (5.58%)
Notional 3.70% swing Lab. to PC
(2005: Lab. majority 456 (1.82%))

BLAENAU GWENT
E. 52,438   T. 32,395 (61.78%)   Lab. gain
*Nick Smith, Lab.   16,974
Dai Davies, Blaenau Voice   6,458
Matt Smith, LD   3,285
Liz Stevenson, C.   2,265
Rhodri Davies, PC   1,333
Anthony King, BNP   1,211
Mike Kocan, UKIP   488
Alyson O'Connell, Soc. Lab.   381
Lab. majority 10,516 (32.46%)
29.2% swing Blaenau Voice to Lab.
(2005: Ind. Law majority 9,121
(25.87%))(2006: Ind. Davies majority
2,484 (9.14%))

BRECON & RADNORSHIRE
E. 53,589   T. 38,845 (72.49%)   LD hold
Roger Williams, LD   17,929
Suzy Davies, C.   14,182
Christopher Lloyd, Lab.   4,096
Janet Davies, PC   989
Clive Easton, UKIP   876
Dorienne Robinson, Green   341
Jeffrey Green, Ch. P.   222
Lord Offa, Loony   210
LD majority 3,747 (9.65%)
0.27% swing LD to C.
(2005: LD majority 3,905 (10.18%))

§BRIDGEND
E. 58,700   T. 38,347 (65.33%)   Lab. hold
Madeleine Moon, Lab.   13,931
Helen Baker, C.   11,668
Wayne Morgan, LD   8,658
Nick Thomas, PC   2,269
Brian Urch, BNP   1,020
David Fulton, UKIP   801
Lab. majority 2,263 (5.90%)
Notional 5.98% swing Lab. to C.
(2005: Lab. majority 6,089 (17.87%))

§CAERPHILLY
E. 62,134   T. 38,992 (62.75%)   Lab. hold
Wayne David, Lab.   17,377
Maria Caulfield, C.   6,622
Lindsay Whittle, PC   6,460
Kay David, LD   5,988
Laurence Reid, BNP   1,635
Tony Jenkins, UKIP   910
Lab. majority 10,755 (27.58%)
Notional 6.57% swing Lab. to C.
(2005: Lab. majority 13,517 (37.32%))

CARDIFF CENTRAL
E. 61,162   T. 36,151 (59.11%)   LD hold
Jenny Willott, LD   14,976
Jenny Rathbone, Lab.   10,400
Karen Robson, C.   7,799
Chris Williams, PC   1,246
Susan Davies, UKIP   765
Sam Coates, Green   575
Ross Saunders, TUSC   162
Mark Beech, Loony   142
Alun Mathias, Ind.   86
LD majority 4,576 (12.66%)
1.41% swing LD to Lab.
(2005: LD majority 5,593 (15.48%))

CARDIFF NORTH
E. 65,553   T. 47,630 (72.66%)   C. gain
*Jonathan Evans, C.   17,860
Julie Morgan, Lab.   17,666
John Dixon, LD   8,724
Llywelyn Rhys, PC   1,588
Lawrence Gwynn, UKIP   1,130
Christopher von Ruhland, Green   362
Derek Thomson, Ch. P.   300
C. majority 194 (0.41%)
1.47% swing Lab. to C.
(2005: Lab. majority 1,146 (2.53%))

§¶CARDIFF SOUTH & PENARTH
E. 73,704 T. 44,370 (60.20%)
                            Lab. (Co-op) hold
Alun Michael, Lab. (Co-op)   17,263
Simon Hoare, C.   12,553
Dominic Hannigan, LD   9,875
Farida Aslam, PC   1,851
Simon Zeigler, UKIP   1,145
George Burke, Ind.   648
Matt Townsend, Green   554
Clive Bate, Ch. P.   285
Robert Griffiths, Comm   196
Lab. (Co-op) majority 4,710 (10.62%)
Notional 6.03% swing Lab. (Co-op) to C.
(2005: Lab. (Co-op) majority 8,955
(22.68%))

§CARDIFF WEST
E. 62,787   T. 40,957 (65.23%)   Lab. hold
Kevin Brennan, Lab.   16,893
Angela Jones-Evans, C.   12,143
Rachael Hitchinson, LD   7,186
Mohammed Sarul Islam, PC   2,868
Mike Henessey, UKIP   1,117
Jake Griffiths, Green   750
Lab. majority 4,750 (11.60%)
Notional 5.33% swing Lab. to C.
(2005: Lab. majority 8,361 (22.25%))

§CARMARTHEN EAST & DINEFWR
E. 52,385   T. 38,011 (72.56%)   PC hold
*Jonathan Edwards, PC   13,546
Christine Gwyther, Lab.   10,065
Andrew Morgan, C.   8,506
Bill Powell, LD   4,609
John Atkinson, UKIP   1,285
PC majority 3,481 (9.16%)
Notional 4.19% swing PC to Lab.
(2005: PC majority 6,551 (17.54%))

§CARMARTHEN WEST &
PEMBROKESHIRE SOUTH
E. 57,519   T. 40,507 (70.42%)   C. gain
*Simon Hart, C.   16,649
Nick Ainger, Lab.   13,226
John Gossage, LD   4,890
John Dixon, PC   4,232
Ray Clarke, UKIP   1,146
Henry Langen, Ind.   364
C. majority 3,423 (8.45%)
Notional 6.88% swing Lab. to C.
(2005: Lab. majority 2,043 (5.32%))

§CEREDIGION
E. 59,043   T. 38,258 (64.80%)   LD hold
Mark Williams, LD   19,139
Penri James, PC   10,815
Luke Evetts, C.   4,421
Richard Boudier, Lab.   2,210
Elwyn Williams, UKIP   977
Leila Kiersch, Green   696
LD majority 8,324 (21.76%)
Notional 10.57% swing PC to LD
(2005: LD majority 218 (0.61%))

§CLWYD SOUTH
E. 53,748 T. 34,681 (64.53%) Lab. hold
*Susan Elan Jones, Lab.   13,311
John Bell, C.   10,477
Bruce Roberts, LD   5,965
Janet Ryder, PC   3,009
Sarah Hynes, BNP   1,100
Nick Powell, UKIP   819
Lab. majority 2,834 (8.17%)
Notional 5.83% swing Lab. to C.
(2005: Lab. majority 6,220 (19.84%))

§CLWYD WEST
E. 57,913 T. 38,111 (65.81%) C. hold
David Jones, C.   15,833
Donna Hutton, Lab.   9,414
Llyr Huws Gruffydd, PC   5,864
Michele Jones, LD   5,801
Warwick Nicholson, UKIP   864
Revd Dr David Griffiths, Ch. P. 239
Joe Blakesley, Ind.   96
C. majority 6,419 (16.84%)
Notional 8.35% swing Lab. to C.
(2005: C. majority 51 (0.14%))

§CYNON VALLEY
E. 50,656 T. 29,876 (58.98%) Lab. hold
Ann Clwyd, Lab.   15,681
Dafydd Trystan Davies, PC   6,064
Lee Thacker, LD   4,120
Juliette Ash, C.   3,010
Frank Hughes, UKIP   1,001
Lab. majority 9,617 (32.19%)
Notional 8.65% swing Lab. to PC
(2005: Lab. majority 14,390 (49.48%))

DELYN
E. 53,470 T. 36,984 (69.17%) Lab. hold
David Hanson, Lab.   15,083
Antoinette Sandbach, C.   12,811
Bill Brereton, LD   5,747
Peter Ryder, PC   1,844
Jennifer Matthys, BNP   844
Andrew Haigh, UKIP   655
Lab. majority 2,272 (6.14%)
6.70% swing Lab. to C.
(2005: Lab. majority 6,644 (19.54%))

§DWYFOR MEIRIONNYDD
E. 45,354 T. 28,906 (63.73%) PC hold
Elfyn Llwyd, PC   12,814
Simon Baynes, C.   6,447
Alwyn Humphreys, Lab.   4,021
Steve Churchman, LD   3,538
Louise Hughes, Ind.   1,310
Frank Wykes, UKIP   776
PC majority 6,367 (22.03%)
Notional 7.28% swing PC to C.
(2005: PC majority 8,706 (29.02%))

§GOWER
E. 61,696 T. 41,671 (67.54%) Lab. hold
Martin Caton, Lab.   16,016
Byron Davies, C.   13,333
Mike Day, LD   7,947
Darren Price, PC   2,760
Adrian Jones, BNP   963
Gordon Triggs, UKIP   652
Lab. majority 2,683 (6.44%)
Notional 5.26% swing Lab. to C.
(2005: Lab. majority 6,703 (16.95%))

§ISLWYN
E. 54,826 T. 34,690 (63.27%)
                  Lab. (Co-op) hold
*Christopher Evans, Lab. (Co-op) 17,069
Daniel Thomas, C.   4,854
Steffan Lewis, PC   4,518
Asghar Ali, LD   3,597
Dave Rees, Ind.   1,495
John Voisey, BNP   1,320
Jason Crew, UKIP   936
Paul Taylor, Ind.   901
Lab. (Co-op) majority 12,215 (35.21%)
Notional 9.05% swing Lab. (Co-op) to C.
(2005: Lab. (Co-op) majority 17,582
(51.91%))

LLANELLI
E. 55,637 T. 37,461 (67.33%) Lab. hold
Nia Griffith, Lab.   15,916
Myfanwy Davies, PC   11,215
Christopher Salmon, C.   5,381
Myrddin Edwards, LD   3,902
Andrew Marshall, UKIP   1,047
Lab. majority 4,701 (12.55%)
3.96% swing Lab. to PC
(2005: Lab. majority 7,234 (20.47%))

MERTHYR TYDFIL & RHYMNEY
E. 54,715 T. 32,076 (58.62%) Lab. hold
Dai Havard, Lab.   14,007
Amy Kitcher, LD   9,951
Maria Hill, C.   2,412
Clive Tovey, Ind.   1,845
Glyndwr Cennydd Jones, PC   1,621
Richard Barnes, BNP   1,173
Adam Brown, UKIP   872
Alan Cowdell, Soc. Lab.   195
Lab. majority 4,056 (12.64%)
16.92% swing Lab. to LD
(2005: Lab. majority 13,934 (46.48%))

MONMOUTH
E. 62,768 T. 46,519 (74.11%) C. hold
David Davies, C.   22,466
Hamish Sandison, Lab.   12,041
Martin Blakebrough, LD   9,026
Jonathan Clark, PC   1,273
Derek Rowe, UKIP   1,126
Steve Millson, Green   587
C. majority 10,425 (22.41%)
6.25% swing Lab. to C.
(2005: C. majority 4,527 (9.92%))

§MONTGOMERYSHIRE
E. 48,730 T. 33,813 (69.39%) C. gain
*Glyn Davies, C.   13,976
Lembit Opik, LD   12,792
Heledd Fychan, PC   2,802
Nick Colbourne, Lab.   2,407
David Rowlands, UKIP   1,128
Milton Ellis, NF   384
Bruce Lawson, Ind.   324
C. majority 1,184 (3.50%)
Notional 13.15% swing LD to C.
(2005: LD majority 7,048 (22.80%))

§NEATH
E. 57,186 T. 37,122 (64.91%) Lab. hold
Peter Hain, Lab.   17,172
Alun Llewelyn, PC   7,397
Frank Little, LD   5,535
Emmeline Owens, C.   4,847
Michael Green, BNP   1,342
James Bevan, UKIP   829
Lab. majority 9,775 (26.33%)
Notional 4.58% swing Lab. to PC
(2005: Lab. majority 12,710 (35.49%))

NEWPORT EAST
E. 54,437 T. 34,448 (63.28%) Lab. hold
Jessica Morden, Lab.   12,744
Ed Townsend, LD   11,094
Dawn Parry, C.   7,918
Keith Jones, BNP   1,168
Fiona Cross, PC   724
David Rowlands, UKIP   677
Liz Screen, Soc. Lab.   123
Lab. majority 1,650 (4.79%)
8.35% swing Lab. to LD
(2005: Lab. majority 6,838 (21.49%))

NEWPORT WEST
E. 62,111 T. 39,720 (63.95%) Lab. hold
Paul Flynn, Lab.   16,389
Matthew Williams, C.   12,845
Veronica German, LD   6,587
Timothy Windsor, BNP   1,183
Hugh Moelwyn Hughes, UKIP   1,144
Jeff Rees, PC   1,122
Pippa Bartolotti, Green   450
Lab. majority 3,544 (8.92%)
3.18% swing Lab. to C.
(2005: Lab. majority 5,458 (15.27%))

§OGMORE
E. 55,527 T. 34,650 (62.40%) Lab. hold
Huw Irranca-Davies, Lab.   18,644
Emma Moore, C.   5,398
Jackie Radford, LD   5,260
Danny Clark, PC   3,326
Kay Thomas, BNP   1,242
Carolyn Passey, UKIP   780
Lab. majority 13,246 (38.23%)
Notional 4.28% swing Lab. to C.
(2005: Lab. majority 14,839 (46.29%))

§PONTYPRIDD
E. 58,219 T. 36,671 (62.99%) Lab. hold
*Owen Smith, Lab.   14,220
Michael Powell, LD   11,435
Lee Gonzalez, C.   5,932
Ioan Bellin, PC   2,673
David Bevan, UKIP   1,229
Simon Parsons, Soc. Lab.   456
Donald Watson, Ch. P.   365
John Matthews, Green   361
Lab. majority 2,785 (7.59%)
Notional 13.31% swing Lab. to LD
(2005: Lab. majority 11,694 (34.21%))

§PRESELI PEMBROKESHIRE
E. 57,419 T. 39,602 (68.97%) C. hold
Stephen Crabb, C.   16,944
Mari Rees, Lab.   12,339
Nick Tregoning, LD   5,759
Henry Jones-Davies, PC   3,654
Richard Lawson, UKIP   906
C. majority 4,605 (11.63%)
Notional 5.05% swing Lab. to C.
(2005: C. majority 601 (1.53%))

RHONDDA
E. 51,554 T. 31,072 (60.27%) Lab. hold
Chris Bryant, Lab.   17,183
Geraint Davies, PC   5,630
Paul Wasley, LD   3,309
Philip Howe, Ind.   2,599
Juliet Henderson, C.   1,993
Taffy John, UKIP   358
Lab. majority 11,553 (37.18%)
7.48% swing Lab. to PC
(2005: Lab. majority 16,242 (52.14%))

SWANSEA EAST
E. 59,823 T. 32,676 (54.62%) Lab. hold
Sian James, Lab.   16,819
Robert Speht, LD   5,981
Christian Holliday, C.   4,823
Dic Jones, PC   2,181
Clive Bennett, BNP   1,715
David Rogers, UKIP   839
Tony Young, Green   318
Lab. majority 10,838 (33.17%)
1.66% swing Lab. to LD
(2005: Lab. majority 11,249 (36.48%))

SWANSEA WEST
E. 61,334 T. 35,593 (58.03%) Lab. hold
*Geraint Davies, Lab.   12,335
Peter May, LD   11,831
Rene Kinzett, C.   7,407
Harri Roberts, PC   1,437
Alan Bateman, BNP   910
Tim Jenkins, UKIP   716
Keith Ross, Green   404
Ian McCloy, Ind.   374
Rob Williams, TUSC   179
Lab. majority 504 (1.42%)
5.74% swing Lab. to LD
(2005: Lab. majority 4,269 (12.90%))

TORFAEN
E. 61,178 T. 37,640 (61.53%) Lab. hold
Paul Murphy, Lab.   16,847
Jonathan Burns, C.   7,541
David Morgan, LD   6,264
Rhys ab Elis, PC   2,005
Jennifer Noble, BNP   1,657
Fred Wildgust, Ind.   1,419
Gareth Dunn, UKIP   862
Richard Turner-Thomas, Ind.   607
Owen Clarke, Green   438
Lab. majority 9,306 (24.72%)
8.19% swing Lab. to C.
(2005: Lab. majority 14,791 (41.11%))

§VALE OF CLWYD
E. 55,781 T. 35,534 (63.70%) Lab. hold
Chris Ruane, Lab.   15,017
Matt Wright, C.   12,508
Paul Penlington, LD   4,472
Caryl Wyn Jones, PC   2,068
Ian Si'Ree, BNP   827
Tom Turner, UKIP   515
Mike Butler, Green Soc.   127
Lab. majority 2,509 (7.06%)
Notional 3.56% swing Lab. to C.
(2005: Lab. majority 4,629 (14.18%))

§VALE OF GLAMORGAN
E. 70,262 T. 48,667 (69.27%) C. gain
*Alun Cairns, C.   20,341
Alana Davies, Lab.   16,034
Eluned Parrott, LD   7,403
Ian Johnson, PC   2,667
Kevin Mahoney, UKIP   1,529
Rhodri Thomas, Green   457
John Harrold, Ch. P.   236
C. majority 4,307 (8.85%)
Notional 6.11% swing Lab. to C.
(2005: Lab. majority 1,574 (3.37%))

WREXHAM
E. 50,872 T. 32,976 (64.82%) Lab. hold
Ian Lucas, Lab.   12,161
Tom Rippeth, LD   8,503
Gareth Hughes, C.   8,375
Arfon Jones, PC   2,029
Melvin Roberts, BNP   1,134
John Humberstone, UKIP   774
Lab. majority 3,658 (11.09%)
5.67% swing Lab. to LD
(2005: Lab. majority 6,819 (22.44%))

YNYS MON
E. 50,075 T. 34,444 (68.78%) Lab. hold
Albert Owen, Lab.   11,490
Dylan Rees, PC   9,029
Anthony Ridge-Newman, C.   7,744
Matt Wood, LD   2,592
Peter Rogers, Ind.   2,225
Elaine Gill, UKIP   1,201
The Rev David Owen, Ch. P.   163
Lab. majority 2,461 (7.14%)
1.82% swing PC to Lab.
(2005: Lab. majority 1,242 (3.50%))

SCOTLAND

ABERDEEN NORTH
E. 64,808 T. 37,701 (58.17%) Lab. hold
Frank Doran, Lab.   16,746
Joanna Strathdee, SNP   8,385
Kristian Chapman, LD   7,001
Stewart Whyte, C.   4,666
Roy Jones, BNP   635
Ewan Robertson, SSP   268
Lab. majority 8,361 (22.18%)
1.00% swing SNP to Lab.
(2005: Lab. majority 6,795 (18.55%))

ABERDEEN SOUTH
E. 64,031 T. 43,034 (67.21%) Lab. hold
Anne Begg, Lab.   15,722
John Sleigh, LD   12,216
Amanda Harvie, C.   8,914
Mark McDonald, SNP   5,102
Susan Ross, BNP   529
Rhonda Reekie, Green   413
Robert Green, SACL   138
Lab. majority 3,506 (8.15%)
2.45% swing LD to Lab.
(2005: Lab. majority 1,348 (3.24%))

ABERDEENSHIRE WEST &
KINCARDINE
E. 66,110 T. 45,195 (68.36%) LD hold
Sir Robert Smith, LD   17,362
Alex Johnstone, C.   13,678
Dennis Robertson, SNP   7,086
Greg Williams, Lab.   6,159
Gary Raikes, BNP   513
Anthony Atkinson, UKIP   397
LD majority 3,684 (8.15%)
4.89% swing LD to C.
(2005: LD majority 7,471 (17.94%))

AIRDRIE & SHOTTS
E. 62,364 T. 35,849 (57.48%) Lab. hold
*Pamela Nash, Lab.   20,849
Sophia Coyle, SNP   8,441
Ruth Whitfield, C.   3,133
John Love, LD   2,898
John McGeechan, Ind.   528
Lab. majority 12,408 (34.61%)
3.93% swing Lab. to SNP
(2005: Lab. majority 14,084 (42.48%))

ANGUS
E. 62,863 T. 37,960 (60.39%) SNP hold
Mike Weir, SNP   15,020
Alberto Costa, C.   11,738
Kevin Hutchens, Lab.   6,535
Sanjay Samani, LD   4,090
Martin Gray, UKIP   577
SNP majority 3,282 (8.65%)
2.22% swing C. to SNP
(2005: SNP majority 1,601 (4.20%))

ARGYLL & BUTE
E. 67,165 T. 45,207 (67.31%) LD hold
Alan Reid, LD   14,292
Gary Mulvaney, C.   10,861
David Graham, Lab.   10,274
Michael MacKenzie, SNP   8,563
Elaine Morrison, Green   789
George Doyle, Ind.   272
John Black, Jacobite   156
LD majority 3,431 (7.59%)
2.72% swing LD to C.
(2005: LD majority 5,636 (13.04%))

AYR, CARRICK & CUMNOCK
E. 73,320 T. 45,893 (62.59%) Lab. hold
Sandra Osborne, Lab.   21,632
William Grant, C.   11,721
Charles Brodie, SNP   8,276
James Taylor, LD   4,264
Lab. majority 9,911 (21.60%)
0.30% swing Lab. to C.
(2005: Lab. majority 9,997 (22.19%))

AYRSHIRE CENTRAL
E. 68,352 T. 43,915 (64.25%) Lab. hold
Brian Donohoe, Lab.   20,950
Maurice Golden, C.   8,943
John Mullen, SNP   8,364
Andrew Chamberlain, LD   5,236
James McDaid, Soc. Lab.   422
Lab. majority 12,007 (27.34%)
1.51% swing C. to Lab.
(2005: Lab. majority 10,423 (24.31%))

AYRSHIRE NORTH & ARRAN
E. 74,953 T. 46,116 (61.53%) Lab. hold
Katy Clark, Lab. 21,860
Patricia Gibson, SNP 11,965
Philip Lardner, C. 7,212
Gillian Cole-Hamilton, LD 4,630
Louise McDaid, Soc. Lab. 449
Lab. majority 9,895 (21.46%)
2.26% swing Lab. to SNP
(2005: Lab. majority 11,296 (25.55%))

BANFF & BUCHAN
E. 64,300 T. 38,466 (59.82%) SNP hold
*Eilidh Whiteford, SNP 15,868
Jimmy Buchan, C. 11,841
Glen Reynolds, Lab. 5,382
Galen Milne, LD 4,365
Richard Payne, BNP 1,010
SNP majority 4,027 (10.47%)
10.67% swing SNP to C.
(2005: SNP majority 11,837 (31.81%))

BERWICKSHIRE, ROXBURGH & SELKIRK
E. 73,826 T. 49,014 (66.39%) LD hold
Michael Moore, LD 22,230
John Lamont, C. 16,555
Ian Miller, Lab. 5,003
Paul Wheelhouse, SNP 4,497
Sherry Fowler, UKIP 595
Chris Black, Jacobite 134
LD majority 5,675 (11.58%)
0.71% swing LD to C.
(2005: LD majority 5,901 (13.00%))

CAITHNESS, SUTHERLAND & EASTER ROSS
E. 47,257 T. 28,768 (60.88%) LD hold
John Thurso, LD 11,007
John Mackay, Lab. 7,081
Jean Urquhart, SNP 5,516
Alastair Graham, C. 3,744
Gordon Campbell, Ind. 520
LD majority 4,826 (16.78%)
6.38% swing LD to Lab.
(2005: LD majority 8,168 (29.53%))

COATBRIDGE, CHRYSTON & BELLSHILL
E. 70,067 T. 41,635 (59.42%) Lab. hold
Tom Clarke, Lab. 27,728
Frances McGlinchey, SNP 7,014
Kenneth Elder, LD 3,519
Fiona Houston, C. 3,374
Lab. majority 20,714 (49.75%)
0.58% swing Lab. to SNP
(2005: Lab. majority 19,519 (50.90%))

CUMBERNAULD, KILSYTH & KIRKINTILLOCH EAST
E. 64,037 T. 41,150 (64.26%) Lab. hold
*Gregg McClymont, Lab. 23,549
Julie Hepburn, SNP 9,794
Rod Ackland, LD 3,924
Stephanie Fraser, C. 3,407
William O'Neill, SSP 476
Lab. majority 13,755 (33.43%)
1.92% swing SNP to Lab.
(2005: Lab. majority 11,562 (29.58%))

DUMFRIES & GALLOWAY
E. 74,581 T. 52,173 (69.95%) Lab. hold
Russell Brown, Lab. 23,950
Peter Duncan, C. 16,501
Andrew Wood, SNP 6,419
Richard Brodie, LD 4,608
William Wright, UKIP 695
Lab. majority 7,449 (14.28%)
4.27% swing C. to Lab.
(2005: Lab. majority 2,922 (5.74%))

DUMFRIESSHIRE, CLYDESDALE & TWEEDDALE
E. 66,627 T. 45,892 (68.88%) C. hold
David Mundell, C. 17,457
Claudia Beamish, Lab. 13,263
Catriona Bhatia, LD 9,080
Aileen Orr, SNP 4,945
Steven McKeane, UKIP 637
Alis Ballance, Green 510
C. majority 4,194 (9.14%)
2.62% swing Lab. to C.
(2005: C. majority 1,738 (3.90%))

DUNBARTONSHIRE EAST
E. 63,795 T. 47,948 (75.16%) LD hold
Jo Swinson, LD 18,551
Mary Galbraith, Lab. 16,367
Mark Nolan, C. 7,431
Iain White, SNP 5,054
James Beeley, UKIP 545
LD majority 2,184 (4.55%)
2.07% swing LD to Lab.
(2005: LD majority 4,061 (8.69%))

DUNBARTONSHIRE WEST
E. 66,085 T. 42,266 (63.96%)
Lab. (Co-op) hold
*Gemma Doyle, Lab. (Co-op) 25,905
Graeme McCormick, SNP 8,497
Helen Watt, LD 3,434
Martyn McIntyre, C. 3,242
Mitch Sorbie, UKIP 683
Katharine McGavigan, Soc. Lab. 505
Lab. (Co-op) majority 17,408 (41.19%)
5.50% swing SNP to Lab. (Co-op)
(2005: Lab. (Co-op) majority 12,553
(30.18%))

DUNDEE EAST
E. 65,471 T. 40,568 (61.96%) SNP hold
Stewart Hosie, SNP 15,350
Katrina Murray, Lab. 13,529
Chris Bustin, C. 6,177
Clive Sneddon, LD 4,285
Shiona Baird, Green 542
Mike Arthur, UKIP 431
Angela Gorrie, SSP 254
SNP majority 1,821 (4.49%)
1.76% swing Lab. to SNP
(2005: SNP majority 383 (0.97%))

DUNDEE WEST
E. 63,013 T. 37,126 (58.92%) Lab. hold
Jim McGovern, Lab. 17,994
Jim Barrie, SNP 10,716
John Barnett, LD 4,233
Colin Stewart, C. 3,461
Andy McBride, Ind. 365
Jim McFarlane, TUSC 357
Lab. majority 7,278 (19.60%)
2.52% swing SNP to Lab.
(2005: Lab. majority 5,379 (14.56%))

DUNFERMLINE & FIFE WEST
E. 73,769 T. 48,947 (66.35%) Lab. gain
*Thomas Docherty, Lab. 22,639
Willie Rennie, LD 17,169
Joe McCall, SNP 5,201
Belinda Hacking, C. 3,305
Otto Inglis, UKIP 633
Lab. majority 5,470 (11.18%)
8.05% swing Lab. to LD
(2005: Lab. majority 11,562
(27.27%))(2006: LD majority 1,800
(5.21%))

EAST KILBRIDE, STRATHAVEN & LESMAHAGOW
E. 76,534 T. 50,946 (66.57%) Lab. hold
*Michael McCann, Lab. 26,241
John McKenna, SNP 11,738
Graham Simpson, C. 6,613
John Loughton, LD 5,052
Kirsten Robb, Green 1,003
John Houston, Ind. 299
Lab. majority 14,503 (28.47%)
1.19% swing Lab. to SNP
(2005: Lab. majority 14,723 (30.84%))

EAST LOTHIAN
E. 73,438 T. 49,161 (66.94%) Lab. hold
*Fiona O'Donnell, Lab. 21,919
Michael Veitch, C. 9,661
Stuart Ritchie, LD 8,288
Andrew Sharp, SNP 7,883
James Mackenzie, Green 862
Jon Lloyd, UKIP 548
Lab. majority 12,258 (24.93%)
0.28% swing Lab. to C.
(2005: Lab. majority 7,620 (16.65%))

EDINBURGH EAST
E. 60,941 T. 39,805 (65.42%) Lab. hold
*Sheila Gilmore, Lab. 17,314
George Kerevan, SNP 8,133
Beverley Hope, LD 7,751
Martin Donald, C. 4,358
Robin Harper, Green 2,035
Gary Clark, TUSC 274
Lab. majority 9,181 (23.03%)
0.01% swing SNP to Lab.
(2005: Lab. majority 6,202 (15.62%))

EDINBURGH NORTH & LEITH
E. 69,204 T. 47,356 (68.43%)
Lab. (Co-op) hold
Mark Lazarowicz, Lab. (Co-op) 17,740
Kevin Lang, LD 16,016
Iain McGill, C. 7,079
Calum Cashley, SNP 4,568
Kate Joester, Green 1,062
John Hein, Lib. 389
Willie Black, TUSC 233
David Jacobsen, Soc. Lab. 141
Cameron MacIntyre, Ind. 128
Lab. Co-op majority 1,724 (3.64%)
0.70% swing Lab. (Co-op) to LD
(2005: Lab. (Co-op) majority 2,153
(5.05%))

EDINBURGH SOUTH
E. 59,354 T. 43,801 (73.80%) Lab. hold
*Ian Murray, Lab. 15,215
Fred Mackintosh, LD 14,899
Neil Hudson, C. 9,452
Sandy Howat, SNP 3,354
Steve Burgess, Green 881
Lab. majority 316 (0.72%)
0.11% swing Lab. to LD
(2005: Lab. majority 405 (0.95%))

EDINBURGH SOUTH WEST
E. 66,359   T. 45,462 (68.51%)   Lab. hold
Alistair Darling, Lab.   19,473
Jason Rust, C.   11,026
Tim McKay, LD   8,194
Kaukab Stewart, SNP   5,530
Clare Cooney, Green   872
Colin Fox, SSP   319
Caroline Bellamy, Comm. Lge   48
Lab. majority 8,447 (18.58%)
1.05% swing C. to Lab.
(2005: Lab. majority 7,242 (16.49%))

EDINBURGH WEST
E. 65,161   T. 46,447 (71.28%)   LD hold
*Michael Crockart, LD   16,684
Cameron Day, Lab.   12,881
Stewart Geddes, C.   10,767
Sheena Cleland, SNP   6,115
LD majority 3,803 (8.19%)
11.35% swing LD to Lab.
(2005: LD majority 13,600 (30.05%))

FALKIRK
E. 81,869   T. 50,777 (62.02%)   Lab. hold
Eric Joyce, Lab.   23,207
John McNally, SNP   15,364
Katie Mackie, C.   5,698
Kieran Leach, LD   5,225
Brian Goldie, UKIP   1,283
Lab. majority 7,843 (15.45%)
7.00% swing Lab. to SNP
(2005: Lab. majority 13,475 (29.45%))

FIFE NORTH EAST
E. 62,969   T. 40,064 (63.62%)   LD hold
Sir Menzies Campbell, LD   17,763
Miles Briggs, C.   8,715
Mark Hood, Lab.   6,869
Rod Campbell, SNP   5,685
Mike Scott-Hayward, UKIP   1,032
LD majority 9,048 (22.58%)
5.01% swing LD to C.
(2005: LD majority 12,571 (32.60%))

GLASGOW CENTRAL
E. 60,062   T. 30,580 (50.91%)   Lab. hold
*Anas Sarwar, Lab.   15,908
Osama Saeed, SNP   5,357
Chris Young, LD   5,010
John Bradley, C.   2,158
Alastair Whitelaw, Green   800
Ian Holt, BNP   616
James Nesbitt, SSP   357
Ramsay Urquhart, UKIP   246
Finlay Archibald, Pirate   128
Lab. majority 10,551 (34.50%)
0.54% swing SNP to Lab.
(2005: Lab. majority 8,531 (30.43%))

GLASGOW EAST
E. 61,516   T. 32,164 (52.29%)   Lab. gain
*Margaret Curran, Lab.   19,797
John Mason, SNP   7,957
Kevin Ward, LD   1,617
Hamira Khan, C.   1,453
Joseph Finnie, BNP   677
Frances Curran, SSP   454
Arthur Thackeray, UKIP   209
Lab. majority 11,840 (36.81%)
3.42% swing Lab. to SNP
(2005: Lab. majority 13,507
(43.66%))(2008: SNP majority 365
(1.39%))

GLASGOW NORTH
E. 51,416   T. 29,613 (57.59%)   Lab. hold
Ann McKechin, Lab.   13,181
Katy Gordon, LD   9,283
Patrick Grady, SNP   3,330
Erin Boyle, C.   2,089
Martin Bartos, Green   947
Thomas Main, BNP   296
Angela McCormick, TUSC   287
Lab. majority 3,898 (13.16%)
0.60% swing LD to Lab.
(2005: Lab. majority 3,338 (11.96%))

GLASGOW NORTH EAST
E. 59,859   T. 29,409 (49.13%)   Lab. hold
Willie Bain, Lab.   20,100
Billy McAllister, SNP   4,158
Eileen Baxendale, LD   2,262
Ruth Davidson, C.   1,569
Walter Hamilton, BNP   798
Graham Campbell, TUSC   187
Kevin McVey, SSP   179
Jim Berrington, Soc. Lab.   156
Lab. majority 15,942 (54.21%)
9.3% swing SNP to Lab.
(2005: Speaker majority 10,134
(35.66%))(2009: Lab. majority 8,111
(39.38%))

GLASGOW NORTH WEST
E. 60,968   T. 35,582 (58.36%)   Lab. hold
John Robertson, Lab.   19,233
Natalie McKee, LD   5,622
Mags Park, SNP   5,430
Richard Sullivan, C.   3,537
Moira Crawford, Green   882
Scott Mclean, BNP   699
Marc Livingstone, Comm.   179
Lab. majority 13,611 (38.25%)
4.31% swing LD to Lab.
(2005: Lab. majority 10,093 (29.63%))

GLASGOW SOUTH
E. 65,029   T. 40,094 (61.66%)   Lab. hold
Tom Harris, Lab.   20,736
Malcolm Fleming, SNP   8,078
Shabnum Mustapha, LD   4,739
Davena Rankin, C.   4,592
Marie Campbell, Green   961
Mike Coyle, BNP   637
Brian Smith, TUSC   351
Lab. majority 12,658 (31.57%)
1.51% swing Lab. to SNP
(2005: Lab. majority 10,832 (28.19%))

GLASGOW SOUTH WEST
E. 58,182   T. 31,781 (54.62%)
                               Lab. (Co-op) hold
Ian Davidson, Lab. (Co-op)   19,863
Chris Stephens, SNP   5,192
Isabel Nelson, LD   2,870
Maya Henderson Forrest, C.   2,084
Tommy Sheridan, TUSC   931
David Orr, BNP   841
Lab. (Co-op) majority 14,671 (46.16%)
0.65% swing SNP to Lab. (Co-op)
(2005: Lab. (Co-op) majority 13,896
(44.86%))

GLENROTHES
E. 67,893   T. 40,501 (59.65%)   Lab. hold
Lindsay Roy, Lab.   25,247
David Alexander, SNP   8,799
Harry Wills, LD   3,108
Sheila Low, C.   2,922
Kris Seunarine, UKIP   425
Lab. majority 16,448 (40.61%)
6.04% swing SNP to Lab.
(2005: Lab. majority 10,664
(28.54%))(2008: Lab. majority 6,737
(18.61%))

GORDON
E. 73,420   T. 48,775 (66.43%)   LD hold
Malcolm Bruce, LD   17,575
Richard Thomson, SNP   10,827
Barney Crockett, Lab.   9,811
Ross Thomson, C.   9,111
Sue Edwards, Green   752
Elise Jones, BNP   699
LD majority 6,748 (13.83%)
7.61% swing LD to SNP
(2005: LD majority 11,026 (24.81%))

¶**INVERCLYDE**
E. 59,209   T. 37,502 (63.34%)   Lab. hold
David Cairns, Lab.   20,993
Innes Nelson, SNP   6,567
Simon Hutton, LD   5,007
David Wilson, C.   4,502
Peter Campbell, UKIP   433
Lab. majority 14,426 (38.47%)
3.64% swing SNP to Lab.
(2005: Lab. majority 11,259 (31.19%))

**INVERNESS, NAIRN, BADENOCH &
STRATHSPEY**
E. 72,528   T. 47,086 (64.92%)   LD hold
Danny Alexander, LD   19,172
Mike Robb, Lab.   10,407
John Finnie, SNP   8,803
Jim Ferguson, C.   6,278
Dr Donald Boyd, Ch. P.   835
Donnie MacLeod, Green   789
Ross Durance, UKIP   574
George MacDonald, TUSC   135
Kit Fraser, Joy   93
LD majority 8,765 (18.61%)
4.62% swing Lab. to LD
(2005: LD majority 4,148 (9.37%))

KILMARNOCK & LOUDOUN
E. 74,131   T. 46,553 (62.80%)
                               Lab. (Co-op) hold
*Cathy Jamieson, Lab. (Co-op)   24,460
George Leslie, SNP   12,082
Janette McAlpine, C.   6,592
Sebastian Tombs, LD   3,419
Lab. (Co-op) majority 12,378 (26.59%)
3.49% swing SNP to Lab. (Co-op)
(2005: Lab. (Co-op) majority 8,703
(19.61%))

KIRKCALDY & COWDENBEATH
E. 73,665   T. 45,802 (62.18%)   Lab. hold
Gordon Brown, Lab.   29,559
Douglas Chapman, SNP   6,550
John Mainland, LD   4,269
Lindsay Paterson, C.   4,258
Peter Adams, UKIP   760
Susan Archibald, Ind.   184
Donald MacLaren of MacLaren, Ind.   165
Derek Jackson, Land   57
Lab. majority 23,009 (50.24%)
3.33% swing SNP to Lab.
(2005: Lab. majority 18,216 (43.58%))

LANARK & HAMILTON EAST
E. 74,773 T. 46,554 (62.26%) Lab. hold
Jim Hood, Lab.   23,258
Clare Adamson, SNP   9,780
Colin McGavigan, C.   6,981
Douglas Herbison, LD   5,249
Duncan McFarlane, Ind.   670
Rob Sale, UKIP   616
Lab. majority 13,478 (28.95%)
0.34% swing SNP to Lab.
(2005: Lab. majority 11,947 (27.41%))

LINLITHGOW & FALKIRK EAST
E. 80,907 T. 51,450 (63.59%) Lab. hold
Michael Connarty, Lab.   25,634
Tam Smith, SNP   13,081
Stephen Glenn, LD   6,589
Andrea Stephenson, C.   6,146
Lab. majority 12,553 (24.40%)
0.13% swing SNP to Lab.
(2005: Lab. majority 11,202 (24.15%))

LIVINGSTON
E. 75,924 T. 47,907 (63.10%) Lab. hold
*Graeme Morrice, Lab.   23,215
Lis Bardell, SNP   12,424
Charles Dundas, LD   5,316
Alison Adamson-Ross, C.   5,158
David Orr, BNP   960
Alistair Forrest, UKIP   443
Ally Hendry, SSP   242
Jim Slavin, Ind.   149
Lab. majority 10,791 (22.52%)
3.51% swing Lab. to SNP
(2005: Lab. majority 13,097 (29.54%);
2005 by-election: Lab. majority 2,680
(9.09%))

MIDLOTHIAN
E. 61,307 T. 39,012 (63.93%) Lab. hold
David Hamilton, Lab.   18,449
Colin Beattie, SNP   8,100
Ross Laird, LD   6,711
James Callander, C.   4,661
Ian Baxter, Green   595
Gordon Norrie, UKIP   364
George McCleery, Ind.   196
Willie Duncan, TUSC   166
Lab. majority 10,349 (26.37%)
1.07% swing Lab. to SNP
(2005: Lab. majority 7,265 (19.27%))

MORAY
E. 65,925 T. 41,004 (62.20%) SNP hold
Angus Robertson, SNP   16,273
Douglas Ross, C.   10,683
Kieron Green, Lab.   7,007
James Paterson, LD   5,956
Donald Gatt, UKIP   1,085
SNP majority 5,590 (13.63%)
0.50% swing SNP to C.
(2005: SNP majority 5,676 (14.63%))

MOTHERWELL & WISHAW
E. 66,918 T. 39,123 (58.46%) Lab. hold
Frank Roy, Lab.   23,910
Marion Fellows, SNP   7,104
Stuart Douglas, LD   3,840
Patsy Gilroy, C.   3,660
Ray Gunnion, TUSC   609
Lab. majority 16,806 (42.96%)
0.97% swing SNP to Lab.
(2005: Lab. majority 15,222 (41.02%))

NA H-EILEANAN AN IAR
E. 22,266 T. 14,717 (66.10%) SNP hold
Angus MacNeil, SNP   6,723
Donald John MacSween, Lab.   4,838
Murdo Murray, Ind.   1,412
Jean Davis, LD   1,097
Sheena Norquay, C.   647
SNP majority 1,885 (12.81%)
1.20% swing Lab. to SNP
(2005: SNP majority 1,441 (10.41%))

OCHIL & PERTHSHIRE SOUTH
E. 75,115 T. 50,469 (67.19%) Lab. hold
Gordon Banks, Lab.   19,131
Annabelle Ewing, SNP   13,944
Gerald Michaluk, C.   10,342
Graeme Littlejohn, LD   5,754
David Bushby, UKIP   689
Hilary Charles, Green   609
Lab. majority 5,187 (10.28%)
4.40% swing SNP to Lab.
(2005: Lab. majority 688 (1.47%))

ORKNEY & SHETLAND
E. 33,085 T. 19,346 (58.47%) LD hold
Alistair Carmichael, LD   11,989
Mark Cooper, Lab.   2,061
John Mowat, SNP   2,042
Frank Nairn, C.   2,032
Robert Smith, UKIP   1,222
LD majority 9,928 (51.32%)
6.98% swing Lab. to LD
(2005: LD majority 6,627 (37.35%))

PAISLEY & RENFREWSHIRE NORTH
E. 63,704 T. 43,707 (68.61%) Lab. hold
Jim Sheridan, Lab.   23,613
Mags MacLaren, SNP   8,333
Alistair Campbell, C.   6,381
Ruaraidh Dobson, LD   4,597
Gary Pearson, Ind.   550
Chris Rollo, SSP   233
Lab. majority 15,280 (34.96%)
4.03% swing SNP to Lab.
(2005: Lab. majority 11,001 (26.91%))

PAISLEY & RENFREWSHIRE SOUTH
E. 61,197 T. 39,998 (65.36%) Lab. hold
Douglas Alexander, Lab.   23,842
Andy Doig, SNP   7,228
Gordon McCaskill, C.   3,979
Ashay Ghai, LD   3,812
Paul Mack, Ind.   513
Jimmy Kerr, SSP   375
William Hendry, Ind.   249
Lab. majority 16,614 (41.54%)
3.27% swing SNP to Lab.
(2005: Lab. majority 13,232 (34.95%))

PERTH & PERTHSHIRE NORTH
E. 72,141 T. 48,268 (66.91%) SNP hold
Pete Wishart, SNP   19,118
Peter Lyburn, C.   14,739
Jamie Glackin, Lab.   7,923
Peter Barrett, LD   5,954
Douglas Taylor, Trust   534
SNP majority 4,379 (9.07%)
2.88% swing C. to SNP
(2005: SNP majority 1,521 (3.31%))

RENFREWSHIRE EAST
E. 66,249 T. 51,181 (77.26%) Lab. hold
Jim Murphy, Lab.   25,987
Richard Cook, C.   15,567
Gordon Macdonald, LD   4,720
Gordon Archer, SNP   4,535
Donald MacKay, UKIP   372
Lab. majority 10,420 (20.36%)
3.16% swing C. to Lab.
(2005: Lab. majority 6,657 (14.04%))

ROSS, SKYE & LOCHABER
E. 51,836 T. 34,838 (67.21%) LD hold
Charles Kennedy, LD   18,335
John McKendrick, Lab.   5,265
Alasdair Stephen, SNP   5,263
Donald Cameron, C.   4,260
Eleanor Scott, Green   777
Philip Anderson, UKIP   659
Ronnie Campbell, Ind.   279
LD majority 13,070 (37.52%)
3.14% swing LD to Lab.
(2005: LD majority 14,249 (43.79%))

RUTHERGLEN & HAMILTON WEST
E. 76,408 T. 46,981 (61.49%)
                         Lab. (Co-op) hold
*Tom Greatrex, Lab. (Co-op)   28,566
Graeme Horne, SNP   7,564
Ian Robertson, LD   5,636
Malcolm Macaskill, C.   4,540
Janice Murdoch, UKIP   675
Lab. (Co-op) majority 21,002 (44.70%)
1.51% swing SNP to Lab. (Co-op)
(2005: Lab. (Co-op) majority 16,112
(37.24%))

STIRLING
E. 66,080 T. 46,791 (70.81%) Lab. hold
Anne McGuire, Lab.   19,558
Bob Dalrymple, C.   11,204
Alison Lindsay, SNP   8,091
Graham Reed, LD   6,797
Mark Ruskell, Green   746
Paul Henke, UKIP   395
Lab. majority 8,354 (17.85%)
3.47% swing C. to Lab.
(2005: Lab. majority 4,767 (10.91%))

NORTHERN IRELAND

§ANTRIM EAST
E. 60,204 T. 30,502 (50.66%)

		DUP hold
Sammy Wilson, DUP	13,993	
Rodney McCune, UCUNF	7,223	
Gerry Lynch, Alliance	3,377	
Oliver McMullan, SF	2,064	
Justin McCamphill, SDLP	2,019	
Samuel Morrison, TUV	1,826	

DUP majority 6,770 (22.20%)
Notional 0.2% swing UCUNF to DUP
(2005: DUP majority 6,996 (21.76%))

§ANTRIM NORTH
E. 73,338 T. 42,397 (57.81%)

		DUP hold
*Ian Paisley Junior, DUP	19,672	
Jim Allister, TUV	7,114	
Daithi McKay, SF	5,265	
Irwin Armstrong, UCUNF	4,634	
Declan O'Loan, SDLP	3,738	
Jayne Dunlop, Alliance	1,368	
Lyle Cubitt, ND	606	

DUP majority 12,558 (29.62%)
(2005: DUP majority 18,486 (41.80%))

§ANTRIM SOUTH
E. 63,054 T. 34,009 (53.94%)

		DUP hold
Revd William McCrea, DUP	11,536	
Sir Reg Empey, UCUNF	10,353	
Mitchel McLaughlin, SF	4,729	
Michelle Byrne, SDLP	2,955	
Alan Lawther, Alliance	2,607	
Melwyn Lucas, TUV	1,829	

DUP majority 1,183 (3.48%)
Notional 3.6% swing DUP to UCUNF
(2005: DUP majority 3,778 (10.74%))

§BELFAST EAST
E. 59,007 T. 34,488 (58.45%)

		Alliance gain
*Naomi Long, Alliance	12,839	
Peter Robinson, DUP	11,306	
Trevor Ringland, UCUNF	7,305	
David Vance, TUV	1,856	
Niall Donnelly, SF	817	
Mary Muldoon, SDLP	365	

Alliance majority 1,533 (4.45%)
Notional 22.87% swing DUP to Alliance
(2005: DUP majority 7,900 (22.87%))

§BELFAST NORTH
E. 65,504 T. 36,993 (56.47%)

		DUP hold
Nigel Dodds, DUP	14,812	
Gerry Kelly, SF	12,588	
Alban Maginness, SDLP	4,544	
Fred Cobain, UCUNF	2,837	
William Webb, Alliance	1,809	
Martin McAuley, Ind.	403	

DUP majority 2,224 (6.01%)
Notional 5.00% swing DUP to SF
(2005: DUP majority 5,832 (16.02%))

§BELFAST SOUTH
E. 59,524 T. 34,186 (57.43%)

		SDLP hold
Dr Alasdair McDonnell, SDLP	14,026	
Jimmy Spratt, DUP	8,100	
Paula Bradshaw, UCUNF	5,910	
Anna Lo, Alliance	5,114	
Adam McGibbon, Green	1,036	

SDLP majority 5,926 (17.33%)
Notional 8.41% swing DUP to SDLP
(2005: SDLP majority 188 (0.52%))

§¶BELFAST WEST
E. 59,522 T. 32,133 (53.99%)   SF hold

Gerry Adams, SF	22,840
Alex Attwood, SDLP	5,261
William Humphrey, DUP	2,436
Bill Manwaring, UCUNF	1,000
Maire Hendron, Alliance	596

SF majority 17,579 (54.71%)
Notional 1.07% swing SDLP to SF
(2005: SF majority 19,527 (52.57%))

DOWN NORTH
E. 60,698 T. 33,481 (55.16%)

		Ind. gain
Lady (Sylvia) Hermon, Ind.	21,181	
Ian Parsley, UCUNF	6,817	
Stephen Farry, Alliance	1,876	
Mary Kilpatrick, TUV	1,634	
Steven Agnew, Green	1,043	
Liam Logan, SDLP	680	
Vincent Parker, SF	250	

Ind. majority 14,364 (42.90%)
(2005: UUP majority 4,944 (15.31%))

§DOWN SOUTH
E. 70,784 T. 42,589 (60.17%)

		SDLP hold
*Margaret Ritchie, SDLP	20,648	
Caitriona Ruane, SF	12,236	
Jim Wells, DUP	3,645	
John McCallister, UCUNF	3,093	
Ivor McConnell, TUV	1,506	
Cadogan Enright, Green	901	
David Griffin, Alliance	560	

SDLP majority 8,412 (19.75%)
Notional 0.06% swing SDLP to SF
(2005: SDLP majority 8,801 (19.87%))

FERMANAGH & SOUTH TYRONE
E. 67,908 T. 46,803 (68.92%)   SF hold

Michelle Gildernew, SF	21,304
Rodney Connor, Ind.	21,300
Fearghal McKinney, SDLP	3,574
Vasundhara Kamble, Alliance	437
John Stevenson, Ind.	188

SF majority 4 (0.01%)
(2005: SF majority 4,582 (9.39%))

§FOYLE
E. 65,843 T. 37,889 (57.54%)

		SDLP hold
Mark Durkan, SDLP	16,922	
Martina Anderson, SF	12,098	
Maurice Devenney, DUP	4,489	
Eammon McCann, PBP	2,936	
David Harding, UCUNF	1,221	
Keith McGrellis, Alliance	223	

SDLP majority 4,824 (12.73%)
Notional 0.17% swing SF to SDLP
(2005: SDLP majority 5,570 (13.08%))

§LAGAN VALLEY
E. 65,257 T. 36,540 (55.99%)

		DUP hold
Jeffrey Donaldson, DUP	18,199	
Daphne Trimble, UCUNF	7,713	
Trevor Lunn, Alliance	4,174	
Keith Harbinson, TUV	3,154	
Brian Heading, SDLP	1,835	
Paul Butler, SF	1,465	

DUP majority 10,486 (28.70%)
Notional 3.3% swing DUP to UCUNF
(2005: DUP majority 13,493 (35.33%))

§LONDONDERRY EAST
E. 63,220 T. 34,950 (55.28%)

		DUP hold
Gregory Campbell, DUP	12,097	
Cathal O hOisin, SF	6,742	
Lesley Macaulay, UCUNF	6,218	
Thomas Conway, SDLP	5,399	
William Ross, TUV	2,572	
Bernard Fitzpatrick, Alliance	1,922	

DUP majority 5,355 (15.32%)
Notional 4.13% swing DUP to SF
(2005: DUP majority 8,192 (21.26%))

NEWRY & ARMAGH
E. 74,308 T. 44,906 (60.43%)   SF hold

Conor Murphy, SF	18,857
Dominic Bradley, SDLP	10,526
Danny Kennedy, UCUNF	8,558
William Irwin, DUP	5,764
William Frazer, Ind.	656
Andrew Muir, Alliance	545

SF majority 8,331 (18.55%)
1.19% swing SDLP to SF
(2005: SF majority 8,195 (16.16%))

§STRANGFORD
E. 60,539 T. 32,505 (53.69%)

		DUP hold
*Jim Shannon, DUP	14,926	
Mike Nesbitt, UCUNF	9,050	
Deborah Girvan, Alliance	2,828	
Claire Hanna, SDLP	2,164	
Terry Williams, TUV	1,814	
Michael Coogan, SF	1,161	
Barbara Haig, Green	562	

DUP majority 5,876 (18.08%)
Notional 7.6% swing DUP to UCUNF
(2005: DUP majority 10,934 (33.32%))

TYRONE WEST
E. 61,148 T. 37,275 (60.96%)   SF hold

Pat Doherty, SF	18,050
Thomas Buchanan, DUP	7,365
Ross Hussey, UCUNF	5,281
Joe Byrne, SDLP	5,212
Michael Bower, Alliance	859
Ciaran McClean, Ind.	508

SF majority 10,685 (28.67%)
3.79% swing DUP to SF
(2005: SF majority 5,005 (11.51%))

¶ULSTER MID
E. 64,594 T. 40,842 (63.23%)   SF hold

Martin McGuinness, SF	21,239
Ian McCrea, DUP	5,876
Tony Quinn, SDLP	5,826
Sandra Overend, UCUNF	4,509
Walter Millar, TUV	2,995
Ian Butler, Alliance	397

SF majority 15,363 (37.62%)
6.73% swing DUP to SF
(2005: SF majority 10,976 (24.16%))

UPPER BANN
E. 74,732 T. 41,383 (55.38%)

		DUP hold
David Simpson, DUP	14,000	
Harry Hamilton, UCUNF	10,639	
John O'Dowd, SF	10,237	
Dolores Kelly, SDLP	5,276	
Brendan Heading, Alliance	1,231	

DUP majority 3,361 (8.12%)
Notional 1.9% swing DUP to UCUNF
(2005: DUP majority 5,298 (11.93%))

BY-ELECTIONS 2010–14

For a list of party abbreviations *see* General Election results:

BARNSLEY CENTRAL
3 March 2011
E. 65,471 T. 24,219 (36.99%)   Lab. hold
Dan Jarvis, Lab.   14,724
Jane Collins, UKIP   2,953
James Hockney, C.   1,999
Enis Dalton, BNP   1,463
Tony Devoy, Ind.   1,266
Dominic Carman, LD   1,012
Kevin Riddiough, Eng. Dem.   544
Howling 'Laud' Hope, Loony   198
Michael Val Davies, Ind.   60
Lab. maj. 11,771 (48.60%)
13.3% swing LD to Lab.
(2010: Lab. maj. 11,093 (29.98%))

BELFAST WEST
9 June 2011
E. 61,441 T. 22,951 (37.35%)   SF hold
Paul Maskey, SF   16,211
Alex Atwood, SDLP   3,088
Gerry Carroll, PBP   1,751
Brian Kingston, DUP   1,393
Bill Manwaring, UUP   386
Aaron McIntyre, Alliance   122
SF maj. 13,123 (50.6%)
1.2% swing SDLP to SF
(2010: SF maj. 17,579 (54.71%))

BRADFORD WEST
29 March 2012
E. 64,613 T. 32,814 (50.79%)Respect gain
George Galloway, Respect   18,341
Imran Hussain, Lab.   8,201
Jackie Whiteley, C.   2,746
Jeanette Sunderland, LD   1,505
Sonja McNally, UKIP   1,085
Dawud Islam, Green   481
Neil Craig, D. Nat   344
Howling 'Laud' Hope, Loony   111
Respect maj. 10,140 (30.90%)
36.6% swing Lab. to Respect
(2010: Lab. maj. 5,763 (14.20%))

CARDIFF SOUTH AND PENARTH
15 November 2012
E. 75,764 T. 19,436 (25.65%)   Lab. hold
Stephen Doughty, Lab.   9,193
Craig Williams, C.   3,859
Bablin Molik, LD   2,103
Luke Nichols, PC   1,854
Simon Zeigler, UKIP   1,179
Anthony Slaughter, Green   800
Andrew Jordan, Soc. Lab.   235
Robert Griffiths, Comm.   213
Lab. maj. 5,334 (27.44%)
8.4% swing C. to Lab.
(2010: Lab. maj. 4,710 (10.62%))

CORBY
15 November 2012
E. 79,878 T. 35,665 (44.65%)   Lab. gain
Andy Sawford, Lab.   17,267
Christine Emmett, C.   9,476
Margot Parker, UKIP   5,108
Jill Hope, LD   1,770
Gordon Riddell, BNP   614
David Wickham, Eng. Dem.   432
Jonathan Hornett, Green   378
Ian Gillman, Ind.   212
Peter Reynolds, CLR   137
David Bishop, CME   99
Mr Mozzarella, Ind.   73
Rohen Kapur, Young   39

Adam Lotun, Dem. 2015.   35
Christopher Scotton, UPP   25
Lab.maj. 7,791 (21.84%)
12.7% swing C. to Lab.
(2010: C. maj. 1,895 (3.49%))

CROYDON NORTH
29 November 2012
E. 93,036 T. 24,568 (26.41%)   Lab. hold
Steve Reed, Lab.   15,898
Andrew Stranack, C.   4,137
Winston McKenzie, UKIP   1,400
Marisha Ray, LD   860
Shasha Khan, Green   855
Lee Jasper, Respect   707
Stephen Hammond, CPA   192
Richard Edmonds, NF   161
Ben Stevenson, Comm.   119
John Cartwright, Loony   110
Simon Lane, Nine11   66
Robin Smith, Young   63
Lab. maj. 11,761 (47.87%)
8.0% swing C. to Lab.
(2010: Lab. maj. 16,483 (31.90%))

EASTLEIGH
28 February 2013
E. 79,004 T. 41,616 (52.68%)   LD hold
Mike Thornton, LD   13,342
Diane James, UKIP   11,571
Maria Hutchings, C.   10,559
John O'Farrell, Lab.   4,088
Danny Stupple, Ind.   768
Iain Maclennan, NHA   392
Ray Hall. BB&C   235
Kevin Milburn, CPA   163
Howling 'Laud' Hope, Loony   136
Jim Duggan, Peace   128
David Bishop, Elvis   72
Mike Walters, Eng. Dem.   70
Daz Procter, TUSC   62
Colin Bex, WR   30
LD maj. 1,771 (4.26%)
19.3% swing LD to UKIP
(2010: LD maj. 3,864 (7.20%))

FELTHAM AND HESTON
15 December 2011
E. 80,813 T. 23,224 (28.74%)   Lab. hold
Seema Malhotra, Lab.   12,639
Mark Bowen, C.   6,436
Roger Crouch, LD   1,364
Andrew Charalambous, UKIP   1,276
Dave Furness, BNP   540
Daniel Goldsmith, Green   426
Roger Cooper, Eng. Dem.   322
George Hallam, PBPA   128
David Bishop, BP Elvis   93
Lab. maj. 6,203 (26.71%)
8.6% swing C. to Lab.
(2010: Lab. maj. 4,658 (9.60%))

INVERCLYDE
30 June 2011
E. 61,856 T. 28,097 (45.42%)   Lab. hold
Iain McKenzie, Lab.   15,118
Anne McLaughlin, SNP   9,280
David Wilson, C.   2,784
Sophie Bridger, LD   627
Mitch Sorbie, UKIP   288
Lab. maj. 5,838 (20.78%)
8.9% swing Lab. to SNP
(2010: Lab. maj. 14,426 (38.47%))

LEICESTER SOUTH
5 May 2011
E. 77,880 T. 34,180 (43.89%)   Lab. hold
Jon Ashworth, Lab.   19,771
Zuffar Haq, LD   7,693
Jane Hunt, C.   5,169
Adhijit Pandya, UKIP   994
Howling 'Laud' Hope, Loony   553
Lab. maj. 12,078 (35.34%)
8.4% swing LD to Lab.
(2010: Lab. maj. 8,808 (18.69%))

MANCHESTER CENTRAL
15 November 2012
E. 91,692 T. 16,648 (18.16%)   Lab. hold
Lucy Powell, Lab.   11,507
Marc Ramsbottom, LD   1,571
Matthew Sephton, C.   754
Christopher Cassidy, UKIP   749
Tom Dylan, Green   652
Eddy O'Sullivan, BNP   492
Loz Kaye, Pirate   308
Alex Davidson, TUSC   220
Catherine Higgins, Respect   182
Howling 'Laud' Hope, Loony   78
Lee Holmes, PDP   71
Peter Clifford, Comm. Lge   64
Lab. maj. 9,936 (59.68%)
16.8% swing LD to Lab.
(2010: Lab. maj. 10,439 (26.15%))

MIDDLESBROUGH
29 November 2012
E. 65,095 T. 16,866 (25.91%)   Lab. hold
Andy McDonald, Lab.   10,201
Richard Livin, UKIP   1,990
George Selmer, LD   1,672
Ben Houchen, C.   1,063
Imdad Hussain, Peace   1,060
Peter Foreman, BNP   328
John Malcolm, TUSC   277
Mark Helsehurst, ND   275
Lab. maj. 8,211 (47.7%)
3.3% swing UKIP to Lab.
(2010: Lab. maj. 8,689 (26.0%))

MID ULSTER
7 March 2013
E. 67,192 T. 37,208 (55.38%)   SF hold
Francie Molloy, SF   17,462
Nigel Lutton, Ind.   12,781
Patsy McGlone, SDLP   6,478
Eric Bullick, Alliance   487
SF maj. 4,681 (12.58%)
3.4% swing SF to Ind.
(2010: SF maj. 15,363 (37.62%))

NEWARK
5 June 2014
E. 73,486 T. 38,707 (52.7%)   C. hold
Robert Jenrick, C.   17,431
Roger Helmer, UKIP   10,028
Michael Payne, Lab.   6,842
Paul Baggaley, Ind.   1,891
David Kirwan, Green   1,057
David Watts, LD   1,004
Nick 'The Flying Brick', Loony   168
Andy Hayes, Ind.   117
David Bishop, BP Elvis   87
Dick Rodgers, Stop   64
Lee Woods, PSP   18
C. maj. 7,403 (19.1%)
15.46% swing C. to UKIP
(2010: C. maj. 16,152 (31.53%))

OLDHAM EAST & SADDLEWORTH
13 January 2011

E. 72,788 T. 34,786 (47.79%)		Lab. hold
Debbie Abrahams, Lab.	14,718	
Elwyn Watkins, LD	11,160	
Kashif Ali, C.	4,481	
Paul Nuttall, UKIP	2,029	
Derek Adams, BNP	1,560	
Peter Allen, Green	530	
The Flying Brick, Loony	143	
Stephen Saul, Pirate	96	
David Bishop, BP Elvis	67	

Lab. maj. 3,558 (10.23%)
5.0% swing LD to Lab.
(2010: Lab. maj. 103 (0.23%))

ROTHERHAM
29 November 2012

E. 63,420 T. 21,450 (33.82%)		Lab. hold
Sarah Champion, Lab.	9,966	
Jane Collins, UKIP	4,648	
Marlene Guest, BNP	1,804	
Yvonne Ridley, Respect	1,778	
Simon Wilson, C.	1,157	
David Wildgoose, Eng. Dem.	703	
Simon Copley, Ind.	582	
Michael Beckett, LD	451	
Ralph Dyson, TUSC	281	
Paul Dickson, Ind.	51	
Clint Bristow, ND	29	

Lab. maj. 5,318 (24.79%)
7.0% swing Lab. to UKIP
(2010: Lab. maj. 10,462 (27.9%))

SOUTH SHIELDS
2 May 2013

E. 62,979 T. 24,736 (39.28%)		Lab. hold
Emma Lewell-Buck, Lab.	12,493	
Richard Elvin, UKIP	5,988	
Karen Allen, C.	2,857	
Ahmed Khan, Ind.	1,331	
Phil Brown, ISP	750	
Lady Dorothy Brookes, UKIP	711	
Hugh Annand, LD	352	
Howling 'Laud' Hope, Loony	197	
Thomas Darwood, Ind.	57	

Lab. maj. 6,505 (26.30%)
12.9% swing Lab. to UKIP
(2010: Lab. maj. 11,109 (30.42%))

WYTHENSHAWE AND SALE EAST
13 February 2014

E. 85,058 T. 23,865 (28.06%)		Lab. hold
Michael Kane, Lab.	13,261	
John Bickley, UKIP	4,301	
Daniel Critchlow, C.	3,479	
Mary Di Mauro, LD	1,176	
Nigel Woodcock, Green	748	
Eddy O'Sullivan, BNP	700	
Cpt Chaplington-Smythe, Loony	200	

Lab. maj. 8,960 (37.54%)
1.6% swing Lab. to UKIP
(2010: Lab. maj. 7,575 (18.59%))

THE GOVERNMENT

A coalition government formed of the Conservative Party and Liberal Democrat Party (since 12 May 2010)

as at 1 September 2014

* Liberal Democrats

THE CABINET

Prime Minister, First Lord of the Treasury and Minister for the Civil Service
Rt. Hon. David Cameron, MP
Deputy Prime Minister, Lord President of the Council (with special responsibility for political and constitutional reform)
*Rt. Hon. Nick Clegg, MP
Chancellor of the Exchequer
Rt. Hon. George Osborne, MP
First Secretary of State, Secretary of State for Foreign and Commonwealth Affairs
Rt. Hon. Philip Hammond, MP
Secretary of State for the Home Department
Rt. Hon. Theresa May, MP
First Secretary of State, Leader of the House of Commons
Rt. Hon. William Hague, MP
Secretary of State for Business, Innovation and Skills and President of the Board of Trade
*Rt. Hon. Dr Vincent Cable, MP
Secretary of State for Communities and Local Government and Minister for Faith
Rt. Hon. Eric Pickles, MP
Secretary of State for Culture, Media and Sport
Rt. Hon. Sajid Javid, MP
Secretary of State for Defence
Rt. Hon. Michael Fallon, MP
Secretary of State for Education and Minister for Women and Equalities
Rt. Hon. Nicky Morgan, MP
Secretary of State for Energy and Climate Change
*Rt. Hon. Edward Davey, MP
Secretary of State for Environment, Food and Rural Affairs
Rt. Hon. Elizabeth Truss, MP
Secretary of State for Health
Rt. Hon. Jeremy Hunt, MP
Secretary of State for International Development
Rt. Hon. Justine Greening, MP
Secretary of State for Justice and Lord Chancellor
Rt. Hon. Chris Grayling, MP
Secretary of State for Northern Ireland
Rt. Hon. Theresa Villiers, MP
Secretary of State for Scotland
*Rt. Hon. Alistair Carmichael, MP
Secretary of State for Transport
Rt. Hon. Patrick McLoughlin, MP
Secretary of State for Wales
Rt. Hon. Stephen Crabb, MP
Secretary of State for Work and Pensions
Rt. Hon. Iain Duncan Smith, MP
Chief Secretary to the Treasury
*Rt. Hon. Danny Alexander, MP

ALSO ATTENDING CABINET MEETINGS

Leader of the House of Lords and Lord Privy Seal
Rt. Hon. Baroness Stowell of Beeston, MBE
Attorney-General
†Rt. Hon. Jeremy Wright, QC, MP
Minister for the Cabinet Office and Paymaster General
Rt. Hon. Francis Maude, MP
Minister for Government Policy and Chancellor for the Duchy of Lancaster
Rt. Hon. Oliver Letwin, MP
‡*Minister of State for the Cabinet Office and Minister of State for Schools*
*Rt. Hon. David Laws, MP
Minister of State for Universities, Science and Cities
Rt. Hon. Greg Clark, MP
Minister without Portfolio
Rt. Hon. Grant Shapps, MP
Parliamentary Secretary to the Treasury and Chief Whip
Rt. Hon. Michael Gove, MP
Minister of State at the Foreign and Commonwealth Office
Rt. Hon. Baroness Anelay of St Johns, DBE
Minister of State for Employment
Rt. Hon. Esther McVey, MP
Minister of State for Energy, Minister of State for Business and Enterprise and Minister for Portsmouth
Rt. Hon. Matthew Hancock, MP

† only attends cabinet meetings when ministerial responsibilities are on the agenda
‡ position held jointly with the Department for Education

LAW OFFICERS

Attorney-General
Rt. Hon. Jeremy Wright, QC, MP
Solicitor-General
Robert Buckland, QC, MP
Advocate-General for Scotland
*Rt. Hon. Lord Wallace of Tankerness, QC

MINISTERS OF STATE

Business, Innovation and Skills
Rt. Hon. Greg Clark, MP
†Lord Livingston of Parkhead
Rt. Hon. Matthew Hancock, MP
‡Ed Vaizey, MP
§Nick Boles, MP
Cabinet Office
*Rt. Hon. David Laws, MP
Rt. Hon. Greg Clark, MP
Jo Johnson, MP

Communities and Local Government
Brandon Lewis, MP
Culture, Media and Sport
¶Ed Vaizey, MP
Defence
Rt. Hon. Mark Francois, MP
Anna Soubry, MP
Education
*Rt. Hon. David Laws, MP
¶Nick Boles, MP
Nick Gibb, MP
Energy and Climate Change
Rt. Hon. Matthew Hancock, MP
Foreign and Commonwealth Office
¶Lord Livingston of Parkhead
Rt. Hon. David Lidington, MP
Rt. Hon. Hugo Swire, MP
**Rt. Hon. Baroness Anelay of St Johns, DBE
Health
*Norman Lamb, MP
Home Office
*Rt. Hon. Norman Baker, MP
Rt. Hon. Mike Penning, MP
James Brokenshire, MP
International Development
Rt. Hon. Desmond Swayne, TD, MP
Justice
*Rt. Hon. Simon Hughes, MP
Rt. Hon. Mike Penning, MP
Rt. Hon. Lord Edward Faulks, QC
Transport
Rt. Hon. John Hayes, MP
*Baroness Kramer
Work and Pensions
Rt. Hon. Esther McVey, MP
*Rt. Hon. Steve Webb, MP
Mark Harper, MP
UK Export Finance
**Lord Livingston of Parkhead

† position held jointly with the Foreign and Commonwealth Office (FCO)
‡ position held jointly with the Department for Culture, Media and Sport
§ position held jointly with the Department for Education
¶ position held jointly with the Department for Business, Innovation and Skills (BIS)
** position held jointly between the FCO and the BIS

UNDER-SECRETARIES OF STATE

Business, Innovation and Skills
†George Freeman, MP
Baroness Neville-Rolfe, DBE, CMG
*‡Jo Swinson, MP
Communities and Local Government
*Stephen Williams, MP
Kris Hopkins, MP
Penny Mordaunt, MP
Lord Ahmad of Wimbledon
Culture, Media and Sport
Helen Grant, MP

Defence
Lord Astor of Hever
Philip Dunne, MP
Julian Brazier, MP
Education
Sam Gyimah, MP
Lord Nash
Edward Timpson, MP
*§Jo Swinson, MP
Energy and Climate Change
Baroness Verma
Amber Rudd, MP
Environment, Food and Rural Affairs
*Dan Rogerson, MP
Lord de Mauley
George Eustice, MP
Foreign and Commonwealth Office
James Duddridge, MP
Tobias Ellwood, MP
Health
Rt. Hon. Earl Howe
Dr Daniel Poulter, MP
Jane Ellison, MP
§George Freeman, MP
Home Office
Karen Bradley, MP
Lord Bates
International Development
*Lynne Featherstone, MP
Justice
Shailesh Vara, MP
Andrew Selous, MP
Northern Ireland Office
Dr Andrew Murrison, MP
Scotland Office
Rt. Hon. David Mundell, MP
Transport
Robert Goodwill, MP
Claire Perry, MP
Wales Office
¶Alun Cairns, MP
*Baroness Randerson
Work and Pensions
Lord Freud

† Jointly with the Department for Health
‡ Jointly with the Department for Education
§ Jointly with BIS
¶ alongside role as Lord Commissioner of HM Treasury (Whip)

OTHER MINISTERS

Cabinet Office
Sam Gyimah, MP *(Parliamentary Secretary)*
Brooks Newmark, MP *(Parliamentary Secretary)*
Rt. Hon. Grant Shapps *(Minister without Portfolio)*
Office of the Leader of the House of Commons
*Rt. Hon. Tom Brake, MP *(Parliamentary Secretary and Deputy Leader of the Commons)*
Treasury
Priti Patel, MP *(Exchequer Secretary)*
David Gauke, MP *(Financial Secretary)*
Andrea Leadsom, MP *(Economic Secretary)*
Lord Deighton, KBE *(Commercial Secretary)*

GOVERNMENT WHIPS

HOUSE OF LORDS

Lords Chief Whip and Captain of the Honourable Corps of Gentlemen-at-Arms
  Lord Taylor of Holbeach, CBE
Deputy Chief Whip and Captain of the Queen's Bodyguard of the Yeomen of the Guard
  *Lord Newby, OBE
Lords-in-Waiting
  Lord Ashton of Hyde
  Lord Bourne of Aberystwyth
  Lord Gardiner of Kimble
  Lord Popat of Harrow
  *Rt. Hon. Lord Wallace of Saltaire
Baronesses-in-Waiting
  *Baroness Jolly
  *Baroness Northover
  Baroness Williams of Trafford

HOUSE OF COMMONS

Chief Whip and Parliamentary Secretary to the Treasury
  Rt. Hon. Michael Gove, MP
Deputy Chief Whip and Treasurer of HM Household
  Rt. Hon. Greg Hands, MP
Deputy Chief Whip and Comptroller of HM Household
  *Rt. Hon. Don Foster, MP
Government Whip and Vice-Chamberlain of HM Household
  Anne Milton, MP
Lords Commissioners of HM Treasury (Whips)
  Mark Lancaster, TD, MP; David Evennett, MP; John Penrose, MP; Gavin Barwell, MP; Harriett Baldwin, MP; †Alun Cairns, MP
Assistant Whips
  Andrew Selous, MP; Therese Coffey, MP; Mel Stride, MP; Ben Wallace, MP; Damian Hinds, MP; *Mark Hunter, MP; *Jenny Willott, MP

† alongside role as Under-Secretary of State at the Wales Office

GOVERNMENT DEPARTMENTS

THE CIVIL SERVICE

The civil service helps the government develop and deliver its policies as effectively as possible. It works in three types of organisations – departments, executive agencies, and non-departmental government bodies (NDPBs). Under the Next Steps programme, launched in 1988, many semi-autonomous executive agencies were established to carry out much of the work of the civil service. Executive agencies operate within a framework set by the responsible minister which specifies policies, objectives and available resources. All executive agencies are set annual performance targets by their minister. Each agency has a chief executive, who is responsible for the day-to-day operations of the agency and who is accountable to the minister for the use of resources and for meeting the agency's targets. The minister accounts to parliament for the work of the agency.

There are currently 411,000 civil servants on a full-time equivalent (FTE) basis. FTE is a measure that counts staff according to the proportion of full-time hours that they work. Of these, the senior civil service comprises just under 3,700 staff from permanent secretary to the former grade 5 level, including all agency chief executives. Almost three-quarters of all civil servants work outside London and the south-east. All government departments and executive agencies are responsible for their own pay and grading systems for civil servants outside the senior civil service.

SALARIES 2014–15

MINISTERIAL SALARIES *from 1 April 2014*
Ministers who are members of the House of Commons receive a parliamentary salary of £67,060 in addition to their ministerial salary.

Prime minister	£75,440
Cabinet minister (Commons)	£67,505
Cabinet minister (Lords)	£101,038
Minister of state (Commons)	£31,680
Minister of state (Lords)	£78,891
Parliamentary under-secretary (Commons)	£22,375
Parliamentary under-secretary (Lords)	£68,710

SPECIAL ADVISERS' SALARIES *from 1 April 2014*
Special advisers to government ministers are paid out of public funds; their salaries are negotiated individually, but are usually in the range of £40,352 to £106,864.

CIVIL SERVICE SALARIES *from 1 April 2014*

Senior Civil Servants	
Permanent secretary	£142,000–£200,000
Band 3	£104,000–£208,100
Band 2	£85,000–£162,500
Band 1A	£67,600–£128,900
Band 1	£62,000–£117,800

Staff are placed in pay bands according to their level of responsibility and taking account of other factors such as experience and marketability. Movement within and between bands is based on performance. Following the delegation of responsibility for pay and grading to government

departments and agencies from 1 April 1996, it is no longer possible to show service-wide pay rates for staff outside the Senior Civil Service.

GOVERNMENT DEPARTMENTS

For more information on government departments, *see* W www.gov.uk/government/ministers

ATTORNEY-GENERAL'S OFFICE

Attorney-General's Office, 20 Victoria Street, London SW1H 0NF
T 020-7271 2492
E correspondence@attorneygeneral.gsi.gov.uk
W www.gov.uk/government/organisations/attorney-generals-office

The law officers of the crown for England and Wales are the Attorney-General and the Solicitor-General. The Attorney-General, assisted by the Solicitor-General, is the chief legal adviser to the government and is also ultimately responsible for all crown litigation. He has overall responsibility for the work of the Law Officers' Departments (the Treasury Solicitor's Department, the Crown Prosecution Service – incorporating the Revenue and Customs Prosecutions Office – and the Serious Fraud Office, and HM Crown Prosecution Service Inspectorate). The Attorney-General also oversees the armed forces' prosecuting authority and the government legal service. He has a specific statutory duty to superintend the discharge of their duties by the Director of Public Prosecutions (who heads the Crown Prosecution Service) and the Director of the Serious Fraud Office. The Attorney-General has specific responsibilities for the enforcement of the criminal law and also performs certain public interest functions, eg protecting charities and appealing unduly lenient sentences. He also deals with questions of law arising in bills and with issues of legal policy.

Following the devolution of power to the Northern Ireland Assembly on 12 April 2010, the assembly now appoints the Attorney General for Northern Ireland. The Attorney General for England and Wales holds the office of Advocate General for Northern Ireland, with significantly reduced responsibilities in Northern Ireland.
Attorney-General, Rt. Hon. Jeremy Wright, QC, MP
Parliamentary Private Secretary, Heather Wheeler, MP
Solicitor-General, Robert Buckland, QC, MP
Director-General, Rowena Collins Rice

DEPARTMENT FOR BUSINESS, INNOVATION AND SKILLS

1 Victoria Street, London SW1H 0ET
T 020-7215 5000
W www.gov.uk/government/organisations/department-for-business-innovation-skills

The Department for Business, Innovation and Skills (BIS) was established in June 2009 by merging the Department for Business, Enterprise and Regulatory Reform and the Department for Innovation, Universities and Skills. Its purpose is to connect people to opportunity and prosperity right across the country and help businesses succeed. The department and its partner bodies provide expertise across a wide range of areas including skills development, investment in new business ideas and technologies, regulation, consumer rights, building Britain's research base and higher education.

Secretary of State for Business, Innovation and Skills and President of the Board of Trade, Rt. Hon. Dr Vince Cable, MP
Principal Private Secretary, Hannah Wiskin
Senior Private Secretary, Emily Hamblin
Special Advisers, Ashley Lumsden; Emily Walch
Minister of State, Rt. Hon. Greg Clark, MP *(Universities and Science)*
Parliamentary Private Secretary, David Mowat, MP
Senior Private Secretary, Alex Williams
Minister of State, Lord Livingston of Parkhead *(Trade and Investment)**
Parliamentary Private Secretary, Stephen McPartland, MP
Senior Private Secretary, John Frew
Minister of State, Rt. Hon. Mattew Hancock, MP *(Business and Enterprise)†*
Parliamentary Private Secretary, Nicola Blackwood, MP
Private Secretary, Phillip Carr
Minister of State, Ed Vaizey, MP *(Culture and the Digital Economy)*
Parliamentary Private Secretary, Justin Tomlinson, MP
Minister of State, Nick Boles, MP *(Skills and Equalities)‡*
Parliamentary Private Secretary, Mike Freer, MP
Private Secretary, Lucy Yates
Parliamentary Under-Secretary of State, Jo Swinson, MP *(Employment Relations and Consumer Affairs)‡*
Private Secretary, Emily Cloke
Parliamentary Under-Secretary of State, George Freeman, MP *(Life Sciences)§*
Private Secretary, Rebecca Molyneux
Parliamentary Under-Secretary of State, Baroness Neville-Rolfe, DBE, CMG *(Business, Innovation and Skills)*
Permanent Secretary, Martin Donnelly
Private Secretary, Jamie Ballantyne
Head of Parliamentary Unit, Ian Webster

* Jointly with the Foreign and Commonwealth Office
† Jointly with the Department for Energy and Climate Change
‡ Jointly with the Department for Education
§ Jointly with the Department of Health

DEPARTMENTAL BOARD
Chair, Rt. Hon. Dr Vince Cable, MP *(Secretary of State)*
Members, Sam Beckett *(Economics and Markets)*; Martin Donnelly *(Permanent Secretary)*; Dominic Jermey *(Chief Executive, UK Trade and Investment)*; Bernadette Kelly *(Business and Local Growth)*; Philippa Lloyd *(People and Strategy)*; Howard Orme *(Finance and Commercial)*; Sir John O'Reilly *(Knowledge and Innovation)*; Mark Russell *(Chief Executive, Shareholder Executive)*; Rachel Sandby-Thomas, CB *(Enterprise and Skills)*
Non-Executive Members, Alan Aubrey; Alan Cook *(Lead)*; Prof. Dame Ann Dowling, DBE; Dale Murray; Dalton Philips; Prof. Wendy Purcell

BETTER REGULATION EXECUTIVE
1 Victoria Street, London SW1 0ET
T 020-7215 5000 E betterregulation@bis.gsi.gov.uk
W www.gov.uk/government/policy-teams/better-regulation-executive

The Better Regulation Executive (BRE) is part of BIS. It leads on delivering the coalition's commitment to reduce the overall burden of regulation on business over the lifetime of the current parliament in order to increase growth and create jobs. Each government department is responsible for delivering its part of this agenda within a framework maintained by BRE.

BRE is managing a series of reviews, announced in the Budget of March 2012, through which poor practice in the enforcement of regulation will be challenged.
Non-Executive Chair, Lord Curry of Kirkharle, CBE
Chief Executive, Graham Turnock, CBE

SHAREHOLDER EXECUTIVE
1 Victoria Street, London SW1H 0ET
T 020-7215 6689
W www.shareholderexecutive.gov.uk

The Shareholder Executive was set up in September 2003 to work with other departments in government to improve the government's capabilities and performance as a shareholder, and to offer corporate finance expertise and advice across government. Its goal is to create a climate of ownership that, while challenging, is genuinely supportive and provides the framework for the 28 businesses under its remit to be successful. In addition, the Shareholder Executive's Government Property Unit is responsible for maximising value from the state's property portfolio.
Chair, Patrick O'Sullivan
Chief Executive, Mark Russell

CABINET OFFICE
70 Whitehall, London SW1A 2AS
T 020-7276 1234; Switchboard 020-7276 3000
W www.gov.uk/government/organisations/cabinet-office

The Cabinet Office, alongside the Treasury, sits at the centre of the government, with an overarching purpose of making government work better. It supports the prime minister and the cabinet, helping to ensure effective development, coordination and implementation of policy and operations across all government departments. The Cabinet Office also leads work to ensure that the Civil Service provides the most effective and efficient support to the government to meet its objectives. The department is headed by the Minister for the Cabinet Office.
Prime Minister, First Lord of the Treasury and Minister for the Civil Service, Rt. Hon. David Cameron, MP
Principal Private Secretary, Chris Martin
Deputy Prime Minister, Rt. Hon. Nick Clegg, MP
Principal Private Secretary, Lucy Smith
Minister for the Cabinet Office and Paymaster General, Rt. Hon. Francis Maude, MP
Parliamentary Private Secretary, Stuart Andrew, MP
Principal Private Secretary, Daniel Gieve
Private Secretaries, Victoria James; William Newton; Joanna Shayer
Minister for Government Policy and Chancellor of the Duchy of Lancaster, Rt. Hon. Oliver Letwin, MP
Parliamentary Private Secretary, Paul Maynard, MP
Private Secretary, Guy Horsington
Minister for Civil Society, Brooks Newmark
Private Secretary, Lara Bogie
Minister of State for Cabinet Office, Rt. Hon. David Laws, MP
Private Secretary, Nick Donlevy
Minister of State for Universities, Science and Cities, Rt. Hon. Greg Clark, MP
Parliamentary Private Secretary, David Mowat, MP
Private Secretary, Alex Williams
Minister without Portfolio, Rt. Hon. Grant Shapps, MP
Parliamentary Private Secretary, Jake Berry, MP
Private Secretary, Christopher Maxsted
Minister of State for Cabinet Office, Jo Johnson, MP
Minister for the Constitution, Sam Gyimah, MP*
Private Secretary, Luke Montague

* Jointly with the Department for Education

Cabinet Secretary, Sir Jeremy Heywood, KCB, CVO
Head of the Civil Service, Sir Bob Kerslake
Principal Private Secretary, Rachel Hopcroft
Private Secretaries, Scott Bailey; Mark Doran; Becky Wyse
Permanent Secretary and First Parliamentary Counsel, Richard
  Heaton, CB
Private Secretary (CO), Hannah Boardman
Private Secretary (OPC), John Healey

MANAGEMENT BOARD
Chair, Rt. Hon. Francis Maude, MP
Board Members, Melanie Dawes *(Director-General, Economic
  and Domestic Affairs Secretariat);* Sue Gray *(Director
  General, Propriety and Ethics Team, and Head of Private
  Offices Group);* Richard Heaton, CB *(Permanent
  Secretary and First Parliamentary Counsel);* Sir Jeremy
  Heywood, KCB, CVO *(Cabinet Secretary);* Nick Hurd,
  MP *(Minister for Civil Society);* Bruce Mann, CB
  (Finance Director)
Non-Executive Directors, Lord Browne of Madingley;
  Ian Davis; Rona Fairhead; Dame Barbara Stocking, DBE

HONOURS AND APPOINTMENTS SECRETARIAT
Room G-39, Horse Guards Road, London SW1A 2HQ
T 020-7276 2777
Head, Richard Tilbrook

OFFICE OF THE LEADER OF THE HOUSE OF
COMMONS
1 Horse Guards Road, London SW1A 2HQ
T 020-7276 1005 E leader@commonsleader.x.gsi.gov.uk
W www.gov.uk/government/organisations/the-office-of-the-
leader-of-the-house-of-commons

The Office of the Leader of the House of Commons is
responsible for the arrangement of government business in the
House of Commons and for planning and supervising the
government's legislative programme. The Leader of the House
of Commons upholds the rights and privileges of the house
and acts as a spokesperson for the government as a whole.
  The leader reports regularly to the cabinet on
parliamentary business and the legislative programme. In
his capacity as leader of the house, he is a member of the
House of Commons Commission. He also chairs the cabinet
committee on the legislative programme. As Lord Privy Seal,
he is chair of the board of trustees of the Chevening Estate.
  The Deputy Leader of the House of Commons supports
the leader in handling the government's business in the
house. He is responsible for monitoring MPs' and peers'
correspondence.
Leader of the House of Commons and Lord Privy Seal,
  Rt. Hon. William Hague, MP
Parliamentary Private Secretary, Margot James, MP
Head of Office, Mike Winter
Deputy Head of Office, Christine Hill
Assistant Private Secretaries, Niall Clarke-Petty *(Parliamentary
  Business);* Mark Fernandes *(Parliamentary Reform)*
Deputy Leader of the House of Commons, Rt. Hon. Tom Brake,
  MP
Private Secretary (acting), Lagle Heinla

OFFICE OF THE LEADER OF THE HOUSE OF LORDS
House of Lords, London SW1A 0PW
T 020-7219 3200
E pslseaderofthelords@cabinet-office.x.gsi.gov.uk
W www.gov.uk/government/organisations/office-of-the-leader-
of-the-house-of-lords

The Office of the Leader of the House of Lords provides
support to the leader in their parliamentary and ministerial

duties, which include leading the government benches in the
House of Lords; the delivery of the government's business in
the Lords; taking part in formal ceremonies such as the state
opening of parliament; and giving guidance to the House of
Lords on matters of procedure and order.
Lord Privy Seal, Leader of the House of Lords, Rt. Hon.
  Baroness Stowell of Beeston, MBE
Parliamentary Private Secretary, Mark Spencer, MP
Deputy Leader of the House of Lords, Rt. Hon. Lord Wallace of
  Tankerness, QC

GOVERNMENT POLICY
PRIME MINISTER'S OFFICE
10 Downing Street, London SW1A 2AA
T 020-7930 4433
W www.number-10.gov.uk
Prime Minister, Rt. Hon. David Cameron, MP
Parliamentary Private Secretary, Gavin Williamson, MP
Principal Private Secretary, Chris Martin
Private Secretaries, Emma Boggis; John Casson; Gus Jaspert;
  Claire Lombardelli
Speech Writer to the Prime Minister, Tim Kiddell
Chief Operating Officer, Helen Lederer
Director of Communications, Craig Oliver
Prime Minister's Official Spokesman, Steve Field
Head of News and Deputy Spokesperson, Vickie Sheriff
Chief of Staff (Political), Ed Llewellyn
Deputy Chief of Staff (Political), Catherine Fall
Political Press Secretary to the Prime Minister, Gabby Bertin

POLICY AND IMPLEMENTATION UNIT
Head of Policy Unit, Paul Kirby
Head of Implementation Unit, Kris Murrin
Head of Analytics Team, Ivan Collister

DEPUTY PRIME MINISTER'S OFFICE
Principal Private Secretary to the Deputy Prime Minister,
  Lucy Smith
Parliamentary Private Secretary to the Deputy Prime Minister,
  Duncan Hames, MP
*Head of Communications and Official Spokesman to the Deputy
  Prime Minister,* James Sorene
Deputy Prime Minister's Chief of Staff, Jonny Oates
Deputy Prime Minister's Special Adviser for Economic Affairs,
  Chris Saunders
Head of the Deputy Prime Minister's Office, Philip Rycroft, CB

CONSTITUTION GROUP
Director, Ciaran Martin

ECONOMIC AND DOMESTIC AFFAIRS
Director-General, Melanie Dawes
*Head of Implementation Unit, Open Public Services and
  Regulatory Reform,* Will Cavendish

EUROPEAN AND GLOBAL ISSUES
Head, Ivan Rogers

GOVERNMENT IN PARLIAMENT
Head, Richard Heaton, CB

PRIVATE OFFICES GROUP
Director-General, Propriety and Ethics, Sue Gray

NATIONAL SECURITY
Comprises the National Security Secretariat (consisting of
the Civil Contingencies Secretariat; Office of Cyber Security
and Information Assurance; Intelligence and Security; and
the Foreign and Defence Policy Secretariat) and the Joint
Intelligence Organisation

NATIONAL SECURITY SECRETARIAT
National Security Adviser, Sir Kim Darroch, KCMG
Deputy Security Advisers, Julian Miller, CB; Olly Robbins
Head of Civil Contigencies Secretariat, Christina Scott
Head of Office of Cyber Security and Information Assurance,
James Quinault
Head of Intelligence and Security Secretariat, Dominic
Wilson
Head of Foreign and Defence Policy Secretariat, Liane
Saunders

JOINT INTELLIGENCE ORGANISATION
Chair, Joint Intelligence Committee, Jon Day
Head of the Joint Intelligence Organisation, Paul Rimmer

EFFICIENCY AND REFORM GROUP
Chief Procurement Officer, Bill Crothers, CB
Deputy Chief Procurement Officer, Sally Collier
Executive Directors, Mike Bracken *(Head of Government
Digital Service);* Katharine Davidson *(Strategy Team);*
William Jordan *(Executive Director);* John McCready
(Head of Government Property Unit); Liam Maxwell
(Chief Information Officer); David Shields *(Managing
Director Government Procurement Service)*

CIVIL SERVICE REFORM
Director-General, Katherine Kerswell

GOVERNMENT SERVICES
Head of Government HR, Chris Last

CABINET OFFICE CORPORATE SERVICES
Head of HR, Melanie Steel
Executive Director, Government Communications, Alex Aiken
Finance Director, Bruce Mann, CB
Chief Economist, Liz McKeown

INDEPENDENT OFFICES

CIVIL SERVICE COMMISSION
1 Horse Guards Road, London SW1A 2HQ
T 020-7271 0831
W http://civilservicecommission.independent.gov.uk

The Civil Service Commission regulates the requirement
that selection for appointment to the Civil Service must be
on merit on the basis of fair and open competition; the
commission publishes its recruitment principles and audit
departments and agencies' performance against these.
Commissioners personally chair competitions for the most
senior jobs in the civil service. In addition, the commission
hears complaints from civil servants under the Civil Service
Code.
The commission was established as a statutory body in
November 2010 under the provisions of the Constitutional
Reform and Governance Act 2010.
First Commissioner (part-time), Sir David Normington, GCB
Commissioners, Jonathan Baume; Kathryn Bishop; Adele Biss;
Peter Blausten; Christine Farnish, CBE; Andrew Flanagan;
Dame Moira Gibb, DBE; Wanda Goldwag; Eliza
Hermann; Angela Sarkis, CBE

THE COMMISSIONER FOR PUBLIC APPOINTMENTS
G/8, 1 Horse Guards Road, London SW1A 2HQ
T 020-7271 0831 E publicappointments@csc.gsi.gov.uk
W http://publicappointmentscommissioner.independent.gov.uk

The Commissioner for Public Appointments is responsible
for monitoring, regulating and reporting on ministerial
appointments (including those made by Welsh government

ministers) to public bodies. The commissioner can investigate
complaints about the way in which appointments were made.
Commissioner for Public Appointments, Sir David Normington,
GCB
Principal Policy Adviser, Terry Willows

OFFICE OF THE PARLIAMENTARY COUNSEL
1 Horse Guards Road, London SW1A 2HQ
T 02-7276 6586 E goodlaw@cabinet-office.gsi.gov.ukk
W www.gov.uk/government/organisations/office-of-the-
parliamentary-counsel

The Office of the Parliamentary Counsel is a group of
government lawyers who specialise in drafting government
bills; advising departments on the rules and procedures of
Parliament; reviewing orders and regulations which amend
Acts of Parliament; and assisting the government on a range
of legal and constitutional issues.
First Parliamentary Counsel, Richard Heaton, CB
Chief Executive, Jim Barron, CBE

DEPARTMENT FOR COMMUNITIES AND LOCAL GOVERNMENT
2 Marsham Street, London SW1P 4DF
T 0303-444 0000
W www.gov.uk/government/organisations/department-for-
communities-and-local-government

The Department for Communities and Local Government
was formed in May 2006 with a remit to promote
community cohesion and prevent extremism, and was given
responsibility for housing, urban regeneration and planning.
It unites the communities and civil renewal functions
previously undertaken by the Home Office, with
responsibility for regeneration, neighbourhood renewal and
local government (previously held by the Office of the
Deputy Prime Minister, which was abolished following a
cabinet reshuffle in May 2006). The department ensures
that the Fire and Rescue services have the resources they
need to reduce the number of deaths from fire, promote
fire prevention activity and respond swiftly to national
emergencies. The department also has responsibility for
equality policy on race and faith (functions that were
previously split between several government departments).
*Secretary of State for Communities and Local Government and
Minister for Faith,* Rt. Hon. Eric Pickles, MP
Principal Private Secretary, Alex Powell
Parliamentary Private Secretary, John Glen, MP
Special Advisers, Zoe Thorogood; Sheridan Westlake
Minister of State, Brandon Lewis, MP *(Housing and Planning)*
Private Secretary, Lee Burge
Parliamentary Private Secretary, Julian Sturdy, MP
Private Secretary, Peter Fenn
Parliamentary Under-Secretary of State, Stephen Williams,
MP
Private Secretary, Kerr McKendrick
Parliamentary Under-Secretary of State, Kris Hopkins, MP
Private Secretary, Peter Fenn
Parliamentary Under-Secretary of State, Penny Mordaunt, MP
Private Secretary, Kerida Allaway
Parliamentary Under-Secretary of State, Lord Ahmad of
Wimbledon
Permanent Secretary, Sir Bob Kerslake
Principal Private Secretary, Leigh Bura
Private Secretary, Lucy Rigler
Chief Scientific Adviser, Stephen Aldridge, CB

MANAGEMENT BOARD
Chair, Rt. Hon. Eric Pickles, MP

Members, Nick Boles; Andrew Campbell, CB; Louise Casey, CB; Helen Edwards, CBE; David Hill; Kris Hopkins, MP; Sir Bob Kerslake *(Permanent Secretary);* Brandon Lewis; David Rossington; Peter Schofield; Baroness Stowell of Beeston, MBE; Stephen Williams, MP

Non-Executive Members, Stephen Hay; Nick Markham; Grenville Turner; Sara Weller *(Lead)*

DEPARTMENT FOR CULTURE, MEDIA AND SPORT

100 Parliament Street, London SW1A 2BQ
T 020-7211 6000 E enquiries@culture.gov.uk
W www.gov.uk/government/organisations/department-for-culture-media-sport

The Department for Culture, Media and Sport (DCMS) was established in July 1997 and aims to improve the quality of life for all those in the UK through cultural and sporting activities while championing the tourism, creative and leisure industries. It is responsible for government policy relating to the arts, sport, the National Lottery, tourism, libraries, museums and galleries, broadcasting, creative industries – including film and the music industry – press freedom and regulation, licensing, gambling, the historic environment, telecommunications and online and media ownership and mergers.

The department is also responsible for 44 agencies and public bodies that help deliver the department's strategic aims and objectives, the listing of historic buildings and scheduling of ancient monuments, the export licensing of cultural goods, and the management of the Government Art Collection and the Royal Parks (its sole executive agency). It has the responsibility for humanitarian assistance in the event of a disaster, as well as for the organisation of the annual Remembrance Day ceremony at the Cenotaph. In September 2012, the Government Equalities Office became part of DCMS, having previously been part of the Home Office.

Secretary of State for Culture, Media and Sport and Minister for Women and Equalities, Rt. Hon. Sajid Javid, MP
Principal Private Secretary, Paul Williams
Parliamentary Private Secretary, Marcus Jones, MP
Minister of State, Ed Vaizey, MP *(Culture and Digital Industries)*
Parliamentary Private Secretary, Justin Tomlinson, MP
Private Secretary, Jack Hindley
Parliamentary Under-Secretary of State, Helen Grant, MP *(Sport, Tourism and Equalities)*
Private Secretary, Alana Jabobs
Permanent Secretary, Sue Owen

MANAGEMENT BOARD

Chair, Sue Owen
Members, David Brooker *(Sport and Olympic Legacy);* Rachel Clark *(Government Equalities Office);* Samantha Foley *(Finance and Commercial; Lottery and Gambling);* Rita French; Helen McNamara *(Media; Strategy; Change);* Clare Pillman *(Culture and Heritage; People);* Jon Zeff *(Broadband; Digital Economy; Departmental Communications)*
Non-Executive Members, Ajay Chowdhury; Dr Tracy Long; Ruby McGregor-Smith, CBE; David Verey

GOVERNMENT EQUALITIES OFFICE (GEO)

100 Parliament Street, London SW1A 2BQ T 020-7211 6000
E enquiries@culture.gsi.gov.uk
W www.gov.uk/government/organisations/government-equalities-office

The GEO is responsible for the government's overall strategy on equality. Its work includes leading the development of a more integrated approach on equality across government with the aim of improving equality and reducing discrimination and disadvantage for all. The office is also responsible for leading policy on gender equality, sexual orientation and transgender equality matters.

Minister for Women and Equality, Rt. Hon. Nicky Morgan, MP
Minister of State, Nick Boles, MP *(Skills and Equalities)*
Parliamentary Under-Secretary of State Jo Swinson, MP *(Women and Equalities),*
Director, Rachel Clark

MINISTRY OF DEFENCE

see Defence chapter

DEPARTMENT FOR EDUCATION

Piccadilly Gate, Store Street, Manchester M1 2WD
T 0370-000 2288
W www.gov.uk/government/organisations/department-for-education

The Department for Education (DfE) was established in May 2010 in place of the Department for Children, Schools and Families (DCSF), in order to refocus the department on its core purpose of supporting teaching and learning. The department is responsible for education and children's services, while the Department for Business, Innovation and Skills is responsible for higher education. The DfE is supported by nine executive agencies and public bodies.

The department's objectives include the expansion of the academies programme, to allow schools to apply to become independent of their local authority, and the introduction of the free schools programme, to allow any suitable proposers, such as parents, businesses or charities, to set up their own school.

Secretary of State for Education, Rt. Hon. Nicky Morgan, MP
Principal Private Secretary, Pamela Dow
Deputy Principal Private Secretary, Elin Jones
Senior Private Secretary, Louise Evans
Private Secretaries, Elizabeth Kelly; Victoria Woodcock
Special Advisers, Chris Wilkins; Luke Tryl
Parliamentary Private Secretaries, Caroline Dinenage, MP; Ben Gummer, MP
Minister of State, Rt. Hon. David Laws, MP *(Schools)**
Senior Private Secretary, Lydia Mulholland
Parliamentary Private Secretaries, Gavin Barwell, MP; Simon Wright, MP
Minister of State, Nick Boles, MP *(Skills and Equalities)*
Parliamentary Private Secretary, Mike Freer, MP
Minister of State, Nick Gibb, MP *(School Reform),*
Parliamentary Private Secretary, Rehman Chishti, MP
Parliamentary Under-Secretary of State, Edward Timpson, MP *(Children and Families)*
Private Secretary, Holly Jones
Parliamentary Under-Secretary of State, Lord Nash *(Schools)*
Private Secretary, Bonnie Wang
Parliamentary Under-Secretary of State, Jo Swinson, MP *(Women and Equalities)**
Private Secretary, vacant
Parliamentary Under-Secretary of State, Sam Gyimah, MP *(Childcare and Education)†*
Private Secretary, Matthew Edwards
Parliamentary Clerk, Eligio Cerval-Pena
Spokesperson in the House of Lords, Lord Nash
Permanent Secretary, Chris Wormald
Private Secretaries, Hannah Lewis; Kris Nursiah

* Jointly with the Department for Business, Innovation and Skills
† Jointly with the Cabinet Office

MANAGEMENT BOARD
Chair, Chris Wormald *(Permanent Secretary)*
Members, Shona Dunn (Director-General, Education Standards); Janette Durbin; Tom Jeffery; Simon Judge; Peter Lauener; Andrew McCully; Tom Shinner
Non-Executive Members, Theodore Agnew; Paul Marshall *(Lead);* David Meller; Jim O'Neill

DEPARTMENT OF ENERGY AND CLIMATE CHANGE

3 Whitehall Place, London SW1A 2AW
T 0300-060 4000 E correspondence@decc.gsi.gov.uk
W www.gov.uk/government/organisations/department-of-energy-climate-change

The Department of Energy and Climate Change (DECC) was formed in 2008 to ensure that the UK has secure, clean, affordable energy supplies and to promote international action to mitigate climate change.
Secretary of State for the Department of Energy and Climate Change, Rt. Hon. Ed Davey, MP
Private Secretary, Ross Gribbin
Parliamentary Private Secretary, Stephen Lloyd, MP
Minister of State, Rt. Hon. Matthew Hancock, MP *(Energy)*
Parliamentary Private Secretary, Nicola Blackwood, MP
Private Secretary, Athith Shetty
Parliamentary Under-Secretary of State, Amber Rudd, MP
Private Secretary, Grace Carey
Parliamentary Under-Secretary of State, Baroness Verma
Private Secretary, Stephen Burke

EXECUTIVE COMMITTEE
Permanent Secretary, Stephen Lovegrove
Private Secretary, Jessica Ayers
Members, Prof. David Mackay *(Chief Scientific Adviser);* Clive Maxwell *(Director-General, Consumers and Households);* Angie Ridgwell *(Director-General, Finance and Corporate Services);* Simon Virley *(Director-General, Markets and Infrastructure);* Katrina Williams *(Director-General, International, Science and Resilience)*

DEPARTMENT FOR ENVIRONMENT, FOOD AND RURAL AFFAIRS

Nobel House, 17 Smith Square, London SW1P 3JR
T 03459-335577
E defra.helpline@defra.gsi.gov.uk
W www.gov.uk/government/organisations/department-for-environment-food-rural-affairs

The Department for Environment, Food and Rural Affairs (DEFRA) is responsible for government policy on the environment, rural matters and farming and food production. In association with the agriculture departments of the Scottish government, the National Assembly for Wales and the Northern Ireland Office, the department is responsible for negotiations in the EU on the common agricultural and fisheries policies, and for single European market questions relating to its responsibilities. Its remit includes international agricultural and food trade policy.

The department's five strategic priorities are climate change adaptation; sustainable consumption and production; the protection of natural resources and the countryside; sustainable rural communities; and sustainable farming and food, including animal health and welfare. DEFRA, which is supported by 35 executive agencies and public bodies, is also the lead government department for emergencies in animal and plant diseases, flooding, food and water supply, dealing with the consequences of a chemical, biological, radiological or nuclear incident, and other threats to the environment.

Secretary of State for Environment, Food and Rural Affairs, Rt. Hon. Elizabeth Truss, MP
Parliamentary Private Secretary, Robin Walker, MP
Principal Private Secretary, Dr Jeremy Marlow
Senior Private Secretary, Mike Barrett
Private Secretaries, Jamie Brothwell; Sarah Cundy; Emma Southard; Adam Stevens
Parliamentary Under-Secretary of State, Dan Rogerson, MP *(Water, Forestry, Rural Affairs and Resource Management)*
Senior Private Secretary, Suzie Pinkett
Private Secretaries, David How; Lucy Johnson; Sally Viner
Parliamentary Under-Secretary of State, George Eustice, MP *(Farming, Food and Marine Environment)*
Senior Private Secretary, Matthew Sabsarin
Private Secretaries, Rose Macfarlane; Amy Bell
Permanent Secretary, Bronwyn Hill, CBE
Senior Private Secretary, David Read
Private Secretaries, Lisa Austin; Stratos Ttofis

SUPERVISORY BOARD
Chair, Bronwyn Hill *(Permanent Secretary)*
Members, Prof Ian Boyd *(Chief Scientific Adviser);* Alastair Bridges *(Finance);* Nick Joicey *(Strategy, International and Biosecurity);* Peter Unwin *(Policy Delivery)*
Non-Executive Members, Catherine Doran; Iain Ferguson; Sir Tony Hawkhead, CBE; Paul Rew

FOREIGN AND COMMONWEALTH OFFICE

King Charles Street, London SW1A 2AH
T 020-7008 1500
W www.gov.uk/government/organisations/foreign-commonwealth-office

The Foreign and Commonwealth Office (FCO) provides the means of communication between the British government and other governments – and international governmental organisations – on all matters falling within the field of international relations. The FCO employs over 14,000 in nearly 270 places across the world through a network of embassies and consulates, which help to protect and promote national interests. FCO diplomats are skilled in understanding and influencing what is happening abroad, supporting British citizens who are travelling and living overseas, helping to manage migration into Britain, promoting British trade and other interests abroad and encouraging foreign investment in the UK. The FCO is supported by 11 executive agencies and public bodies.
Secretary of State for Foreign and Commonwealth Affairs, Rt. Hon. Philip Hammond, MP
Principal Private Secretary, Thomas Drew
Special Advisers, Graham Hark; Hayden Allan
Parliamentary Private Secretary, Damian Collins, MP
Minister of State, Rt. Hon. David Lidington, MP *(Europe)*
Parliamentary Private Secretary, David Rutley, MP
Private Secretary, Jennifer McNaughton
Minister of State, Rt. Hon. Hugo Swire, MP
Parliamentary Private Secretary, Alec Shelbrooke, MP
Private Secretary, Fergus Eckereley
Minister of State, Lord Livingston of Parkhead *(Trade and Investment)*★
Parliamentary Private Secretary, Stephen McPartland, MP
Private Secretary, Nick Whittingham
Minister of State, Rt. Hon. Baroness Anelay of St Johns, DBE
Parliamentary Under-Secretary of State, James Duddridge, MP
Private Secretary, Ben Wastnage
Parliamentary Under-Secretary of State, Tobias Ellwood, MP

Private Secretary, Sharon Wilkins
Permanent Under-Secretary of State and Head of HM Diplomatic Service, Sir Simon Fraser, KCMG
Private Secretary, Tamsin Heath
Special Representatives, Sir Andrew Burns *(Post-Holocaust Issues);* Simon Gass *(Afghanistan and Pakistan);* Matt Cannell *(Sudan and South Sudan);* Sir David King *(Climate Change)*

* Jointly with the Department for Business, Innovation and Skills

BOARD
Chair, Sir Simon Fraser, KCMG
Members, Nick Baird *(Chief Executive, UK Trade and Investment);* Sir Simon Gass *(Political);* Julian King *(Economic and Consular);* Sara Mackintosh *(Defence and Intelligence);* Shan Morgan *(HM Ambassador, Buenos Aires);* Menna Rawlings *(Human Resources);* Matthew Rycroft *(Chief Operating Officer);* Iain Walker *(Finance)*
Non-Executive Members, Julia Bond; Rudy Markham

DEPARTMENT OF HEALTH
Richmond House, 79 Whitehall, London SW1A 2NS
T 020-7210 4850
W https://www.gov.uk/government/organisations/department-of-health

The Department of Health (DH) leads, shapes and funds health and care in England, making sure people have the support, care and treatment they need and that this is delivered in a compassionate, respectful and dignified manner.

The DH leads across health and care by creating national policies and legislation to meet current and future challenges. It provides funding, assures the delivery and continuity of services and accounts to parliament in a way that represents the best interests of the patient, public and taxpayer. Twenty-three executive agencies and public bodies support the DH.

Secretary of State for Health, Rt. Hon. Jeremy Hunt, MP
Parliamentary Private Secretaries, Andrew Jones, MP; Simon Kirby, MP
Principal Private Secretary, Kristen McLeod
Private Secretary, Rebecca Besalel
Minister of State, Norman Lamb, MP *(Care and Support)*
Private Secretary, Claire McAvinchey
Parliamentary Under-Secretary of State, Dr Daniel Poulter, MP *(Health)*
Private Secretary, Andrew Edmunds
Parliamentary Under-Secretary of State, Jane Ellison, MP *(Public Health)*
Parliamentary Under-Secretary of State, Earl Howe *(Quality)*
Private Secretary, Ilarie Regondi
Parliamentary Under-Secretary of State, George Freeman, MP *(Life Sciences)*
Private Secretary, Rebecca Molyneux
Permanent Secretary, Una O'Brien, CB

* Jointly with the Department for Business, Innovation and Skills

DEPARTMENTAL BOARD
Chair, Rt. Hon. Jeremy Hunt, MP
Members, Will Cavendish *(Innovation, Growth and Technology);* Prof. Dame Sally Davies, DBE *(Chief Medical Officer);* Richard Douglas, CB *(Finance and NHS);* Jane Ellison, MP; Felicity Harvey, CBE *(Public Health);* Earl Howe; Norman Lamb, MP; Charlie Massey, *(Strategy and External Relations);* Una O'Brien *(Permanent Secretary);* Dr Daniel Poulter, MP; Jon Rouse *(Social Care, Local Government and Care Partnerships);* Anna Soubry, MP

Non-Executive Members, Dr Catherine Bell; Chris Pilling; Peter Sands *(Lead);* Mike Wheeler

HOME OFFICE
2 Marsham Street, London SW1P 4DF
T 020-7035 4848 E public.enquiries@homeoffice.gsi.gov.uk
W www.gov.uk/government/organisations/home-office

The Home Office deals with those internal affairs in England and Wales which have not been assigned to other government departments. The Secretary of State for the Home Department is the link between the Queen and the public, and exercises certain powers on her behalf, including that of the royal pardon.

The Home Office aims to build a safe, just and tolerant society and to maintain and enhance public security and protection; to support and mobilise communities so that they are able to shape policy and improvement for their locality, overcome nuisance and anti-social behaviour, maintain and enhance social cohesion and enjoy their homes and public spaces peacefully; to deliver departmental policies and responsibilities fairly, effectively and efficiently; and to make the best use of resources. These objectives reflect the priorities of the government and the home secretary in areas of crime, citizenship and communities, namely to reduce crime and the fear of crime through visible, responsive and accountable policing; to reduce organised and international crime; to combat terrorism and other threats to national security; to ensure the effective delivery of justice; to reduce re-offending and protect the public; to reduce the availability and abuse of dangerous drugs; to regulate entry to, and settlement in, the UK in the interests of sustainable growth and social inclusion; and to support strong, active communities in which people of all races and backgrounds are valued and participate on equal terms.

The Home Office delivers these aims through the immigration services, its 27 executive agencies and non-departmental public bodies, and by working with partners in private, public and voluntary sectors, individuals and communities. The home secretary is also the link between the UK government and the governments of the Channel Islands and the Isle of Man.

Secretary of State for the Home Department, Rt. Hon. Theresa May, MP
Parliamentary Private Secretary, George Hollingbery, MP
Principal Private Secretary, Jonathan Nancekivell-Smith
Deputy Private Secretary, Matt Lewsey
Special Advisers, Fiona Cunningham; Nick Timothy; Stephen Parkinson
Minister of State (Crime Prevention), Norman Baker, MP
Private Secretary, Alice Matthews
Minister of State (Policing, Criminal Justice and Victims), Rt. Hon. Mike Penning, MP*
Parliamentary Private Secretary, Steve Brine, MP
Private Secretary, Emma Ross
Minister of State (Modern Slavery and Organised Crime), Karen Bradley, MP
Private Secretary, Pamal Hayre
Minister of State (Security and Immigration), James Brokenshire, MP
Parliamentary Private Secretary, Guy Opperman
Private Secretary, Stephen Knight
Minister of State (Criminal Information), Lord Bates
Private Secretary, Moore Flannery
Permanent Secretary, Mark Sedwill
Private Secretary, Mark Williams

* Jointly with the Ministry of Justice

MANAGEMENT BOARD

Chair, Mark Sedwill

Members, Mike Anderson *(International and Immigration Policy Group);* Mary Calam *(Crime and Policing Group);* Mandie Campbell *(Immigration Enforcement);* Charles Farr *(Office for Security and Counter Terrorism);* Peter Fish *(Legal);* Sir Charles Montgomery *(Border Force);* Mike Parsons *(Chief Operating Officer, Home Office);* Sarah Rapson *(UK Visas and Immigration);* Prof. Bernard Silverman *(Chief Scientific Adviser);* Kevin White, CB *(Human Resources);* Simon Wren *(Communications)*

DEPARTMENT FOR INTERNATIONAL DEVELOPMENT

22 Whitehall, London SW1A 2EG

T 020-7023 0000

Abercrombie House, Eaglesham Road, East Kilbride, Glasgow G75 8EA **T** 01355-844000 **Public Enquiries** 0845-300 4100

E enquiry@dfid.gov.uk

W www.gov.uk/government/organisations/department-for-international-development

The Department for International Development (DFID) is responsible for promoting sustainable development and reducing poverty. The central focus of the government's policy, based on the 1997, 2000, 2006 and 2009 white papers on international development, is a commitment to the internationally agreed Millennium Development Goals, to be achieved by 2015. These seek to eradicate extreme poverty and hunger; achieve universal primary education; promote gender equality and empower women; reduce child mortality; improve maternal health; combat HIV/AIDS, malaria and other diseases; improve sanitation and access to clean water; ensure environmental sustainability; and encourage a global partnership for development.

DFID's assistance is concentrated in the poorest countries of sub-Saharan Africa and Asia, but also contributes to poverty reduction and sustainable development in middle-income countries, including those in Latin America and Eastern Europe. It also responds to overseas emergencies. The department works in partnership with governments of developing countries, charities, non-governmental organisations and businesses. It also works with multilateral institutions, including the World Bank, United Nations agencies and the European Commission. The department, which is supported by two executive agencies and public bodies, has headquarters in London and East Kilbride, offices in many developing countries, and staff based in British embassies and high commissions around the world.

Secretary of State for International Development, Rt. Hon. Justine Greening, MP

Principal Private Secretary, Vel Gnanendran

Parliamentary Private Secretary, Julian Smith

Special Advisers, Simon Bishop; Victoria Crawford

Parliamentary Clerk, Rob Foot

Minister of State, Rt. Hon. Desmond Swayne, TD, MP

Private Secretary, Jonny Hall

Parliamentary Private Secretary, Jack Lopresti, MP

Parliamentary Under-Secretary of State, Lynne Featherstone, MP

Private Secretary, Emily Travis

House of Lords Spokesperson, Baroness Northover

Permanent Secretary, Mark Lowcock

Principal Private Secretary, Sarah Metcalf

MANAGEMENT BOARD

Chair, Rt. Hon. Justine Greening, MP

Members, Richard Calvert *(Finance and Corporate*

Performance); Rt. Hon. Alan Duncan, MP; Nick Dyer *(acting Policy and Global Programmes);* Lynne Featherstone, MP; Joy Hutcheon *(Country Programmes);* Mark Lowcock *(Permanent Secretary);* Moazzam Malik *(Humanitarian, Security, Conflict and International Finance);* Baroness Northover

Non-Executive Members, Vivienne Cox *(Lead);* Richard Keys; Tim Robinson; Eric Salama

CDC GROUP

123 Victoria Street, London SW1E 6DE

T 020-7963 4700 E enquiries@cdcgroup.com

W www.cdcgroup.com

Founded in 1948, CDC is a government-owned Development Finance Institution that invests in the creation and growth of viable private businesses in the poorest countries in order to contribute to economic growth and reduce poverty. In 2013 CDC made 26 new investment commitments which totalled £608.3m across Africa and South Asia. CDC is a public limited company with the Department for International Development as its 100 per cent shareholder.

Chair, Graham Wrigley

Chief Executive, Diana Noble

MINISTRY OF JUSTICE

102 Petty France, London SW1H 9AJ

T 020-3334 3555 E general.queries@justice.gsi.gov.uk

W www.justice.gov.uk

The Ministry of Justice (MoJ) was established in May 2007. MoJ is headed by the Lord Chancellor and Secretary of State for Justice who is responsible for improvements to the justice system so that it better serves the public. He is also responsible for some areas of constitutional policy (those not covered by the Deputy Prime Minister).

The MoJ established five key priorities for 2014. These were to reduce reoffending by using the skills of the public, private and voluntary sectors; reduce youth crime by putting education at the centre of youth justice; build a prison system that delivers maximum value for money; reduce the cost of legal aid and ensure it helps those cases that genuinely require it; and to improve the way the courts are run and put the needs of victims first. The MoJ has a budget of around £9bn and is supported by 39 executive agencies and public bodies to achieve its targets.

The Lord Chancellor and Secretary of State for Justice is the government minister responsible to parliament for the judiciary, the court system and prisons and probation. The Lord Chief Justice has been the head of the judiciary since 2006.

MoJ incorporates the National Offender Management Service; the HM Prison Service and the National Probation Service; Her Majesty's Courts and Tribunals Service; the Legal Aid Agency; and the Youth Justice Board.

MoJ has several associated departments, non-departmental public bodies and executive agencies, including the National Archives and the Office of the Public Guardian.

Lord Chancellor and Secretary of State for Justice, Rt. Hon. Chris Grayling, MP

Principal Private Secretary, James Crawforth

Parliamentary Private Secretary, Lee Scott, MP

Minister of State, Rt. Hon. Simon Hughes, MP *(Justice and Civil Liberties)*

Private Secretary, Chris Beal

Minister of State, Rt. Hon. Mike Penning, MP

Private Secretary, Emma Ross

Minister of State, Lord Edward Faulks, QC *(Civil Justice and Legal Policy)*

Private Secretary, Elaine Cobb
Parliamentary Under-Secretary of State, Shailesh Vara, MP
  (Courts and Legal Aid)
Private Secretary, Stephen Donby
Parliamentary Under-Secretary of State, Andrew Selous, MP
  (Prisons, Probation and Rehabilitation)
Private Secretary, Kathryn Matheson
Permanent Secretary, Dame Ursula Brennan, DCB
Private Secretary, Matthew Nicholes
Parliamentary Clerk, Ann Nixon

MANAGEMENT BOARD
Chair, Rt. Hon. Chris Grayling, MP *(Lord Chancellor and
  Secretary of State for Justice)*
Members, Ann Beasley *(Director-General, Finance);* Ursula
  Brennan *(Permanent Secretary);* Matthew Coats
  *(Director-General, Legal Aid Agency & Corporate
  Services Group);* Peter Handcock, CBE *(Chief Executive,
  HM Courts and Tribunals Service);* Catherine Lee
  (Director-General, Law and Access to Justice Group);
  Antonia Romeo *(Director-General, Criminal Justice);*
  Michael Spurr *(Chief Executive, National Offender
  Management Service),* MP
Non-Executive Members, Tim Breedon *(Lead);* Bill
  Griffiths; Dame Sue Street, DCB; Fields Wicker-Miurin,
  OBE

NORTHERN IRELAND OFFICE
1 Horse Guards Road, London SW1A 2HQ
Stormont House, Stormont Estate, Belfast BT4 3SH
T 028-9052 0700 E nioweb.editor@nio.x.gsi.gov.uk
W www.gov.uk/government/organisations/northern-ireland-office

The Northern Ireland Office was established in 1972, when
the Northern Ireland (Temporary Provisions) Act transferred
the legislative and executive powers of the Northern Ireland
parliament and government to the UK parliament and a
secretary of state. Under the terms of the 1998 Good Friday
Agreement, power was devolved to the Northern Ireland
Assembly in 1999. The assembly took on responsibility for
the relevant areas of work previously undertaken by the
departments of the Northern Ireland Office, covering
agriculture and rural development, the environment, regional
development, social development, education, higher
education, training and employment, enterprise, trade and
investment, culture, arts and leisure, health, social services,
public safety and finance and personnel. In October 2002
the Northern Ireland Assembly was suspended and Northern
Ireland returned to direct rule, but despite repeated setbacks,
devolution was restored on 8 May 2007. For further details,
see Regional Government.
  The Northern Ireland Office is supported by three
executive agencies and public bodies and is currently
responsible for overseeing the devolution settlement;
representing Northern Ireland interests within the UK
government and similarly representing the UK government
in Northern Ireland; working in partnership with the
Northern Ireland Executive for a stable, prosperous Northern
Ireland; and supporting and implementing political
agreements to increase stability.
Secretary of State for Northern Ireland, Rt. Hon. Theresa
  Villiers, MP
Parliamentary Private Secretary, Mary Macleod, MP
Parliamentary Under-Secretary of State, Dr Andrew Murrison,
  MP
Permanent Secretary, Sir Jonathan Stephens

OFFICE OF THE ADVOCATE-GENERAL FOR SCOTLAND
Dover House, Whitehall, London SW1A 2AU
T 020-7270 6810
Office of the Solicitor to the Advocate-General, Victoria Quay,
Edinburgh EH6 6QQ
T 0131-244 0359 E enquiries@advocategeneral.gsi.gov.uk
W www.gov.uk/government/organisations/office-of-the-advocate-
general-for-scotland

The Advocate-General for Scotland is one of the three law
officers of the crown, alongside the Attorney-General and
the Solicitor-General for England and Wales. He is the legal
adviser to the UK government on Scottish law and is
supported by staff in the Office of the Advocate-General for
Scotland. The office is divided into the Legal Secretariat,
based mainly in London, and the Office of the Solicitor to
the Advocate-General, based in Edinburgh.
  The post was created as a consequence of the
constitutional changes set out in the Scotland Act 1998,
which created a devolved Scottish parliament. The Lord
Advocate and the Solicitor-General for Scotland then became
part of the Scottish government and the Advocate-General
took over their previous role as legal adviser to the UK
government on Scots law. *See also* Regional Government
and Ministry of Justice.
Advocate-General for Scotland, Rt. Hon. Lord Wallace of
  Tankerness, QC
Private Secretary, Craig Chalcraft
Direcor and Solicitor, Michael Chalmers

SCOTLAND OFFICE
Dover House, Whitehall, London SW1A 2AU
T 020-7270 6754
1 Melville Crescent, Edinburgh EH3 7HW
T 0131-244 9010
E sofsscotland@scotlandoffice.gsi.gov.uk
W www.gov.uk/government/organisations/scotland-office

The Scotland Office is the department of the Secretary of
State for Scotland which represents Scottish interests
within the UK government in matters reserved to the UK
parliament. The Secretary of State for Scotland maintains the
stability of the devolution settlement for Scotland; delivers
secondary legislation under the Scotland Act 1998; is
responsible for the conduct and funding of the Scottish
parliament elections; manages the Scottish vote provision and
authorises the monthly payment of funds from the UK
consolidated fund to the Scottish consolidated fund; and
publishes regular information on the state of the Scottish
economy.
  Matters reserved to the UK parliament include the
constitution, foreign affairs, defence, international
development, the civil service, financial and economic
matters, national security, immigration and nationality,
misuse of drugs, trade and industry, various aspects of energy
regulation (eg coal, electricity, oil, gas and nuclear energy),
various aspects of transport, social security, employment,
abortion, genetics, surrogacy, medicines, broadcasting and
equal opportunities. Devolved matters include health
and social work, education and training, local government
and housing, justice and police, agriculture, forestry, fisheries,
the environment, tourism, sports, heritage, economic development and internal transport. *See also* Regional Government
and Ministry of Justice.
Secretary of State for Scotland, Rt. Hon. Alistair Carmichael,
  MP
Principal Private Secretary, Colin Faulkner
Parliamentary Under-Secretary of State, Rt. Hon. David
  Mundell, MP

Private Secretary, Jennifer Manton
Advocate-General and Spokesperson in the House of Lords,
    Rt. Hon. Lord Wallace of Tankerness, QC
Private Secretary, Craig Chalcraft

DEPARTMENT FOR TRANSPORT
Great Minster House, 33 Horseferry Road, London SW1P 4DR
T 0300-330 3000
W www.gov.uk/government/organisations/department-for-transport

The Department for Transport (DfT) is tasked with ensuring that Britain has an efficient transport network that is an engine for sustainable economic growth. Its main responsibilities include aviation, public transport, freight, regional and local transport, social inclusion, railways, roads and road safety, science and research, shipping and vehicles and sustainable travel. Among its current projects is the delivery of a new high-speed rail network, alongside reforming the existing railways and looking at new strategies for roads and aviation. The DfT is supported by 21 executive agencies and public bodies.

Secretary of State for Transport, Rt. Hon. Patrick McLoughlin, MP
Parliamentary Private Secretary, Iain Stewart, MP
Principal Private Secretary, Phil West
Minister of State, Rt. Hon. John Hayes, MP
Parliamentary Private Secretary, Neil Parish, MP
Private Secretary, Rosa Estevez
Minister of State, Baroness Kramer
Parliamentary Under-Secretary of State, Robert Goodwill, MP
Private Secretary, Alex Philpott
Parliamentary Under-Secretary of State, Claire Perry, MP
Private Secretary, Tom Newman-Taylor
Permanent Secretary, Philip Rutnam
Private Secretary, Natalie Golding

MANAGEMENT BOARD
Chair, Rt. Hon. Patrick McLoughlin, MP *(Secretary of State)*
Members, Lucy Chadwick *(Director-General, International, Security and Environment);* Steve Gooding *(Director-General, Roads, Traffic and Local);* Robert Goodwill, MP; John Hayes, MP; Baroness Kramer; Claire Moriarty *(Director-General, Rail);* Jonathan Moor, CBE *(Director-General, Resources and Strategy);* Nick Olley *(General Counsel);* Claire Perry, MP; David Prout *(Director-General, High Speed 2);* Philip Rutnam *(Permanent Secretary)*

HM TREASURY
1 Horse Guards Road, London SW1A 2HQ
T 020-7270 5000 E public.enquiries@hmtreasury.gsi.gov.uk
W www.gov.uk/government/organisations/hm-treasury

HM Treasury is the country's economics and finance ministry, and is responsible for formulating and implementing the government's financial and economic policy. It aims to raise the rate of sustainable growth, boost prosperity, and provide the conditions necessary for universal economic and employment opportunities. The Office of the Lord High Treasurer has been continuously in commission for over 200 years. The Lord High Commissioners of HM Treasury are the First Lord of the Treasury (who is also the prime minister), the Chancellor of the Exchequer and five junior lords. This board of commissioners is assisted at present by the chief secretary, the parliamentary secretary (who is also the government chief whip in the House of Commons), the financial secretary, the economic secretary, the exchequer secretary and the commercial secretary. The prime minister as first lord is not primarily concerned with the day-to-day aspects of Treasury business; neither are the parliamentary secretary and the junior lords as government whips. Treasury business is managed by the Chancellor of the Exchequer and the other Treasury ministers, assisted by the permanent secretary.

The chief secretary is responsible for public expenditure, including spending reviews and strategic planning; in-year control; public-sector pay and pensions; Annually Managed Expenditure and welfare reform; efficiency in public services; procurement and capital investment. He also has responsibility for the Treasury's interest in devolution.

The financial secretary has responsibility for financial services policy including banking and financial services reform and regulation; financial stability; city competitiveness; wholesale and retail markets in the UK, Europe and internationally; and the Financial Services Authority. His other responsibilities include banking support; bank lending; UK Financial Investments; Equitable Life; and personal savings and pensions policy. He also provides support to the chancellor on EU and wider international finance issues.

The exchequer secretary is a title only used occasionally, normally when the post of paymaster-general is allocated to a minister outside of the Treasury (as it is at present; Francis Maude, MP was appointed paymaster-general and minister of the Cabinet Office in May 2010). The exchequer secretary's responsibilities include strategic oversight of the UK tax system; corporate and small business taxation, with input from the commercial secretary; departmental minister for HM Revenue and Customs and the Valuation Office Agency; and lead minister on European and international tax issues.

The economic secretary's responsibilities include environmental issues such as taxation of transport, international climate change and energy; North Sea oil taxation; tax credits and child poverty, assisting the chief secretary on welfare reform; charities and the voluntary sector; excise duties and gambling; stamp duty land tax; EU Budget; the Royal Mint; and departmental minister for HM Treasury Group.

The role of commercial secretary was created in 2010. Responsibilities include enterprise and productivity; corporate finance; assisting the financial secretary on financial services, banking policy promoting the government's financial services policies and the competitiveness of the UK; asset freezing and financial crime; foreign exchange reserves and debt management policy; National Savings and Investments; and the Debt Management Office. The commercial secretary is also the treasury spokesperson in the House of Lords.

Prime Minister and First Lord of the Treasury, Rt. Hon. David Cameron, MP
Chancellor of the Exchequer, Rt. Hon. George Osborne, MP
Parliamentary Private Secretary, Robert Halfon, MP
Private Secretary, Melanie Pitt
Special Advisers to the Chancellor of the Exchequer, Ramesh Chhabra; Thea Rogers
Chief Economic Adviser, Dave Ramsden
Council of Economic Advisers, Rupert Harrison; Neil O'Brien; Eleanor Wolfson; Jennifer Donnellan
Chief Secretary to the Treasury, Rt. Hon. Danny Alexander, MP
Special Advisers to the Chief Secretary, John Foster; Will de Peyer; Peter Carroll
Private Secretary, Will Garton
Financial Secretary to the Treasury, David Gauke, MP
Parliamentary Private Secretary, Gareth Johnson, MP
Exchequer Secretary to the Treasury, Priti Patel, MP
Private Secretary, Oliver Haydon
Economic Secretary to the Treasury, Andrea Leadsom, MP
Private Secretary, Miranda Claremont

Commercial Secretary to the Treasury, Lord Deighton, KBE
Private Secretary, Emily Marsh, KBE
Permanent Secretary to the Treasury, Sir Nicholas Macpherson
Private Secretary and Speechwriter, Juliet Palfrey
Lords Commissioners of HM Treasury (Whips), Harriett
  Baldwin, MP; Gavin Barwell, MP; Alun Cairns, MP;
  Mark Lancaster, TD, MP; John Penrose, MP
Assistant Whips, Therese Coffey, MP; Damien Hinds, MP;
  Mark Hunter, MP; Andrew Selous, MP; Mel Stride, MP;
  Ben Wallace, MP; Jenny Willott, MP

MANAGEMENT BOARD
Chair, Sir Nicholas Macpherson (Permanent Secretary)
Executive Members, Mark Bowman (Director-General,
  International and EU); John Kingman (Second Permanent
  Secretary); Indra Morris (Director-General, Tax and
  Welfare); Dave Ramsden (Chief Economic Adviser);
  Charles Roxburgh (Director-General, Financial Services);
  Sharon White (Second Permanent Secretary)

ROYAL MINT LTD
PO Box 500, Llantrisant, Pontyclun CF72 8YT
T 01443-222111
W www.royalmint.com

From 1975 the Royal Mint operated as a trading fund and
was established as an executive agency in 1990. Since 2010
it has operated as Royal Mint Ltd, a company 100 per cent
owned by HM Treasury, with an exclusive contract to supply
all coinage for the UK.

The Royal Mint actively competes in world markets for a
share of the available circulating coin business and about half
of the coins and blanks it produces annually are exported.
It is the leading export mint, accounting for around 15 per
cent of the world market. The Royal Mint also manufactures
special proof and uncirculated quality coins in gold, silver
and other metals; military and civil decorations and medals;
commemorative and prize medals; and royal and official
seals.
Master of the Mint, Chancellor of the Exchequer (ex officio)
Chair, Peter Warry
Chief Executive, Adam Lawrence

UK EXPORT FINANCE
1 Horse Guards Road, London SW1A 2HQ
T 020-7271 8001 E enquiries@ukef.gsi.gov.uk
W www.gov.uk/government/organisations/uk-export-finance

UK Export Finance is the UK's export credit agency. It
helps UK exporters by providing insurance to them and
guarantees to banks to share the risks of providing export
finance. Additionally, it can make loans to overseas buyers
of goods and services from the UK. UK Export Finance
is the operating name of the Export Credits Guarantee
Department.

The priorities of UK Export Finance are to fulfil its
statutory remit to support exports; operate within the policy
and financial objectives established by the government,
which includes international obligations; and to recover the
maximum amount of debt in respect of claims paid, taking
account of the government's policy n debt forgiveness.
Secretary of State for Business, Innovation and Skills and
  President of the Board of Trade, Rt. Hon. Dr Vince Cable,
  MP
Minister of State, Lord Livingston of Parkhead (Trade and
  Investment)

MANAGEMENT BOARD
Members, Steve Dodgson (Business Group); Cameron Fox
  (Finance); David Godfrey (Chief Executive); David

Havelock (Credit Risk Group); Lucy Wylde (General
  Counsel)
Non-Executive Members, Guy Beringer; Jon Harding; David
  Harrison, CBE; Fiona-Jane MacGregor; Amin Mawji,
  OBE; Sir Eric Peacock

WALES OFFICE
Gwydyr House, Whitehall, London SW1A 2NP
T 029-2092 4220
E correspondence@walesoffice.gsi.gov.uk
W www.gov.uk/wales-office

The Wales Office was established in 1999 when most of the
powers of the Welsh Office were handed over to the National
Assembly for Wales. It is the department of the Secretary of
State for Wales, who is the key government figure liaising
with the devolved government in Wales and who represents
Welsh interests in the cabinet and parliament. The secretary
of state has the right to attend and speak at sessions of
the National Assembly (and must consult the assembly on the
government's legislative programme). See also Regional
Government and Ministry of Justice.
Secretary of State for Wales, Rt. Hon. Stephen Crabb, MP
Parliamentary Private Secretary, David Morris, MP
Principal Private Secretary, Sian Oborne
Parliamentary Under-Secretary of State, Alun Cairns, MP
Parliamentary Under-Secretary of State, Baroness Randerson
Director of Office, Glynne Jones

DEPARTMENT FOR WORK AND PENSIONS
Caxton House, Tothill Street, London SW1H 9NA
T 020-7340 4000 E ministers@dwp.gsi.gov.uk
W www.gov.uk/government/organisations/department-for-work-
pensions

The Department for Work and Pensions was formed in June
2001 from parts of the former Department of Social Security,
the Department for Education and Employment and the
Employment Service. The department helps unemployed
people of working age into work, helps employers to fill their
vacancies and provides financial support to people unable
to help themselves, through back-to-work programmes. The
department also administers the child support system,
social security benefits and the social fund. In addition, the
department has reciprocal social security arrangements with
other countries.
Secretary of State for Work and Pensions, Rt. Hon. Iain Duncan
  Smith, MP
Parliamentary Private Secretary, Charlie Elphicke, MP
Principal Private Secretary, Paul McComb
Private Secretaries, Kate Davies; David Slovak
Minister of State (Employment), Esther McVey, MP
Parliamentary Private Secretary, James Morris, MP
Private Secretary, Mike Maynard
Assistant Private Secretaries, Tia Priest; Jack Purchase;
  Nicholas Slim
Minister of State (Pensions), Steve Webb, MP
Private Secretary, Michael Dynan-Oakley
Assistant Private Secretaries, Yasna Hawksley; Gemma
  Gargent; Victoria Price
Minister of State, Mark Harper, MP (Disabled People)
Parliamentary Private Secretary, Caroline Nokes, MP
Private Secretary, Jack Goodwin
Assistant Private Secretaries, Ellie Tack; Harry Elks
Parliamentary Under-Secretary of State (Welfare Reform),
  Lord Freud
Private Secretary, Rob Cook
Assistant Private Secretaries, Becky Richards; Gemma Alcorn;
  Chris Ramm
Permanent Secretary, Robert Devereux

MANAGEMENT BOARD
Permanent Secretary and Head of Department, Robert Devereux
Members, Kevin Cunnington *(Director-General, Digital Transformation);* Mike Driver *(Director-General, Finance);* Jeremy Moore *(Director-General, Strategy);* Steve Riley *(Director-General, IT);* Noel Shanahan *(Director-General, Operations);* Howard Shiplee, CBE *(Director-General, Universal Credit)*

EXECUTIVE AGENCIES

Executive agencies are well-defined business units that carry out services with a clear focus on delivering specific outputs within a framework of accountability to ministers. They can be set up or disbanded without legislation, and they are organisationally independent from the department they are answerable to. In the following list the agencies are shown in the accounts of their sponsor departments. Legally they act on behalf of the relevant secretary of state. Their chief executives also perform the role of accounting officers, which means they are responsible for the money spent by their organisations. Staff employed by agencies are civil servants.

DEPARTMENT FOR BUSINESS, INNOVATION AND SKILLS

COMPANIES HOUSE
Crown Way, Cardiff CF14 3UZ
T 0303-123 4500
E enquiries@companies-house.gov.uk
W www.companies-house.gov.uk

Companies House incorporates and dissolves companies, examines and stores company information delivered under the Companies Act and related legislation; and makes this information available to the public.
Registrar of Companies for England and Wales and Chief Executive, Tim Moss
Registrar of Companies for Scotland, Dorothy Blair
Registrar of Companies for Northern Ireland, Helen Shilliday

THE INSOLVENCY SERVICE
4 Abbey Orchard Street, London SW1P 2HT
T 0300-678 0015
E redundancyclaims@insolvency.gsi.gov.uk
W www.bis.gov.uk/insolvency

The role of the service includes administration and investigation of the affairs of bankrupts, individuals subject to debt relief orders, partnerships and companies in compulsory liquidation; dealing with the disqualification of directors in all corporate failures; authorising and regulating the insolvency profession; providing banking and investment services for bankruptcy and liquidation estate funds; assessing and paying statutory entitlement to redundancy payments when an employer cannot, or will not, pay its employees; and advising ministers on insolvency, redundancy and related issues. The service has around 1,900 staff, operating from 31 locations across Great Britain.
Inspector-General and Chief Executive, Dr Richard Judge
Deputy Chief Executive, Graham Horne

INTELLECTUAL PROPERTY OFFICE
Concept House, Cardiff Road, Newport NP10 8QQ
T 0300-300 2000 E information@ipo.gov.uk
W www.ipo.gov.uk

The Intellectual Property Office (an operating name of the Patent Office) was set up in 1852 to act as the UK's sole office for the granting of patents. It was established as an executive agency in 1990 and became a trading fund in 1991. The office is responsible for the granting of intellectual property (IP) rights which include patents, trade marks, designs and copyright.
Comptroller-General and Chief Executive, John Alty

MET OFFICE
FitzRoy Road, Exeter, Devon EX1 3PB
T 01392-885680 E enquiries@metoffice.gov.uk
W www.metoffice.gov.uk

The Met Office is the UK's National Weather Service, operating as an executive agency of BIS, having transferred from the MoD in July 2011. It is a world leader in providing weather and climate services, using over 10 million weather observations a day, and employs more than 1,800 people at 60 locations throughout the world.
Chief Executive, John Hirst

NATIONAL MEASUREMENT OFFICE
Stanton Avenue, Teddington, Middx TW11 0JZ
T 020-8943 7272 E info@nmo.gov.uk
W www.gov.uk/nmo

The National Measurement Office (NMO) was created in April 2009, merging the functions of the National Weights and Measures Laboratory and the National Measurement System. NMO is responsible for providing policy support to ministers on measurement issues and a measurement infrastructure to enable innovation and growth, promote trade and facilitate fair competition and the protection of consumers, health and the environment.
Chief Executive (acting), Richard Sanders

SKILLS FUNDING AGENCY
Cheylesmore House, Quinton Road, Coventry CV1 2WT
T 0845-377 5000 E info@skillsfundingagency.bis.gov.uk
W www.gov.uk/sfa

The Skills Funding Agency (SFA) funds skills training for further education (FE) in England, including traineeships and apprenticeships. The SFA supports over 1,000 colleges, private training organisations and employers with more than £4bn of funding annually. It is responsible for giving colleges, training organisations and employers the right funding to help adults, young people, the unemployed and those with low skill levels the opportunity to obtain the skills they require for employment..
Chief Executive (acting), Barbara Spicer

UK SPACE AGENCY
Polaris House, North Star Avenue, Swindon, Wiltshire SN2 1SZ
T 020-7215 5000 E info@ukspaceagency.bis.gsi.gov.uk
W www.gov.uk/ukspaceagency

The UK Space Agency was established on 23 March 2010 and became an executive agency on 1 April 2011. It was created to provide a single voice for UK space ambitions, and is responsible for all strategic decisions on the UK civil space programme. Responsibilities of the UK Space Agency include coordinating UK civil space activity; supporting academic research; nurturing the UK space industry; raising the profile of UK space activities at home and abroad; working to increase understanding of space science and its practical benefits; and inspiring the next generation of UK scientists and engineers.
Chief Executive, Dr David Parker

CABINET OFFICE

CROWN COMMERCIAL SERVICE
Floor 9, The Capital Building, Old Hall Street, Liverpool L3 9PP
T 0345-410 2222 E info@ccs.gsi.gov.uk
W http://ccs.cabinetoffice.gov.uk

The Crown Commercial Service is an executive agency of the Cabinet Office, providing a professional procurement and commercial service to central government and the UK public sector including local government, health, education, devolved administrations, emergency services, defence and not-for-profit organisations to ensure maximum value is extracted from every commercial relationship and to improve the quality of service delivery.
Chair, Bill Crothers, CB
Chief Executive, Sally Collier

DEPARTMENT FOR COMMUNITIES AND LOCAL GOVERNMENT

PLANNING INSPECTORATE
Room 3/13, Temple Quay House, 2 The Square, Temple Quay, Bristol BS1 6PN
T 0303-444 5000
E enquiries@pins.gsi.gov.uk
W www.gov.uk/government/organisations/planning-inspectorate
Crown Buildings, Cathays Park, Cardiff CF10 3NQ
T 029-2082 3866 E wales@pins.gsi.gov.uk
W http://planninginspectorate.wales.gov.uk

The main work of the inspectorate consists of national infrastructure planning under the Planning Act 2008 as amended by the Localism Act 2011, the processing of planning and enforcement appeals, and holding examinations into development plan documents. It also deals with listed building consent appeals; advertisement appeals; rights of way cases; cases arising from the Environmental Protection and Water acts, the Transport and Works Act 1992 and other highways legislation; and reporting on planning applications called in for decision by the Department for Communities and Local Government and the Welsh government.
Chief Executive, Simon Ridley

THE QUEEN ELIZABETH II CONFERENCE CENTRE
Broad Sanctuary, London SW1P 3EE
T 020-7798 4426
W www.qeiicc.co.uk

The centre provides secure conference facilities for national and international government and private sector use.
Chief Executive, Mark Taylor

DEPARTMENT FOR CULTURE, MEDIA AND SPORT

THE ROYAL PARKS
The Old Police House, Hyde Park, London W2 2UH
T 0300-061 2000 E hq@royalparks.gsi.gov.uk
W www.royalparks.org.uk

Royal Parks is responsible for maintaining and developing over 2,000 hectares (5,000 acres) of urban parkland contained within the eight royal parks in London: Bushy Park (with the Longford river); Green Park; Greenwich Park; Hyde Park; Kensington Gardens; Regent's Park (with Primrose Hill); Richmond Park and St James's Park.
Chief Executive, Linda Lennon, CBE

MINISTRY OF DEFENCE
see Defence chapter

DEPARTMENT FOR EDUCATION

THE EDUCATION FUNDING AGENCY
Sanctuary Buildings, 20 Great Smith Street, London SW1P 3BT
T 0370-000 2288
W www.gov.uk/government/organisations/education-funding-agency

Formed on 1 April 2012, the Education Funding Agency (EFA) is the DFE's delivery agency for funding and compliance. It manages £54m of funding each year for education for learners aged between 3 and 19 years, or aged between 3 and 25 years for those with learning difficulties and disabilities. The EFA also supports the delivery of building and maintenance programmes for schools, academies, free schools and sixth-form colleges.
Chief Executive, Peter Lauener

NATIONAL COLLEGE FOR TEACHING AND LEADERSHIP
Piccadilly Gate, Store Street, Manchester M1 2WD
T 0370-000 2288 E enquiries@nationalcollege.org.uk
W www.gov.uk/government/organisations/national-college-for-teaching-and-leadership

On 1 April 2013 the National College merged with the Teaching Agency to become the National College for Teaching and Leadership. It has two key aims: improving the quality of the workforce; and helping schools to help each other to improve. It is also the awarding body for Qualified Teacher Status (QTS).
Chief Executive, Charlie Taylor

STANDARDS AND TESTING AGENCY
53–55 Butts Road, Earlsdon Park, Coventry CV1 3BH
T 0300-303 3013 E assessments@education.gov.uk
W www.gov.uk/government/organisations/standards-and-testing-agency

The Standards and Testing Agency (STA) opened on 1 October 2011 and is responsible for the development and delivery of all statutory assessments from early years to the end of Key Stage 3.
Chief Executive, Ian Todd

DEPARTMENT FOR ENVIRONMENT, FOOD AND RURAL AFFAIRS

ANIMAL HEALTH AND VETERINARY LABORATORIES AGENCY
Woodham Lane, New Haw, Addlestone, Surrey KT15 3NB
T 01932-341 111 E AH.corporate_centre@ahvla.gsi.gov.uk
W www.gov.uk/government/organisations/animal-health-and-veterinary-laboratories-agency

The Animal Health and Veterinary Laboratories Agency (AHVLA) is an executive agency of DEFRA. It was formed on 1 April 2011 following the merger of Animal Health and the Veterinary Laboratories Agency.

The agency is responsible, on behalf of DEFRA, the Welsh government and the Scottish government for protecting the health and welfare of farmed animals, including playing a key role in the prevention, detection and management of exotic and endemic diseases in animals. It is also responsible for delivering research and laboratory services for animal and public health and for advising policy departments regarding the veterinary evidence base for policy development.

The AHVLA's services include a wide range of core functions covering veterinary research, disease surveillance, specialised testing and an emergency response capability. This includes protecting the welfare of farmed animals; the eradication of endemic disease; import and export certification; animal by-product regulation; and preparedness for managing exotic animal diseases.

The AHVLA is also reponsible for licensing the trade in endangered species for conservation purposes; for ensuring that eggs are correctly labelled and that marketing regulations are being complied with.

In April 2014, DEFRA announced that a new executive agency would be formed bringing together AHVLA, the Bee Inspectorate, the Plant Health and Seeds Inspectorate, the Plant Variety and Seeds Group, and the GM Inspectorate from the Food and Environment Research Agency. The new agency was set to be established in late 2014.
Chief Executive, Chris Hadkiss

CENTRE FOR ENVIRONMENT, FISHERIES AND AQUACULTURE SCIENCE (CEFAS)
Pakefield Road, Lowestoft, Suffolk NR33 0HT
T 01502-562244 W www.cefas.defra.gov.uk

Established in April 1997, the agency provides research and consultancy services in fisheries science and management, aquaculture, fish health and hygiene, environmental impact assessment, and environmental quality assessment.
Chief Executive, Mike Waldock

FOOD AND ENVIRONMENT RESEARCH AGENCY
Sand Hutton, York YO41 1LZ
T 01904-462000 E info@fera.gsi.gov.uk W www.fera.defra.gov.uk

The Food and Environment Research Agency was formed on 1 April 2009 from the merger of the Central Science Laboratory, the Government Decontamination Service, and DEFRA's Plant Health division and Plant Varieties office. The agency's purpose is to support and develop a sustainable food chain, a healthy natural environment, and to protect the community from biological and chemical risks. It does this by providing evidence, analysis and professional advice to the government, international organisations and the private sector. The agency brings together expertise in multi-disciplinary science to rapidly diagnose threats, evaluate risk and inform policy in food and environmental areas; and in responding to and recovering from unforeseen or emergency situations.
Chief Executive, Adrian Belton

RURAL PAYMENTS AGENCY
PO Box 69, Reading RG1 3YD
T 0845-603 7777
E csc@rpa.gsi.gov.uk
W www.gov.uk/government/organisations/rural-payments-agency

The RPA was established in 2001. It is the single paying agency responsible for Common Agricultural Policy (CAP) schemes in England and for certain other schemes throughout the UK; it is also responsible for operating cattle tracing services across Great Britain, conducting inspections of farms, processing plants and fresh produce markets in England, and managing the Rural Land Register.
Chief Executive, Mark Grimshaw

VETERINARY MEDICINES DIRECTORATE
Woodham Lane, New Haw, Addlestone, Surrey KT15 3LS
T 01932-336911 E postmaster@vmd.defra.gsi.gov.uk
W www.gov.uk/government/organisations/veterinary-medicines-directorate

The Veterinary Medicines Directorate is responsible for all aspects of the authorisation and control of veterinary medicines, including post-authorisation surveillance of residues in animals and animal products. It is also responsible for the development and enforcement of legislation concerning veterinary medicines and the provision of policy advice to ministers.
Chief Executive, Prof. Pete Borriello

FOREIGN AND COMMONWEALTH OFFICE

FCO SERVICES
Hanslope Park, Milton Keynes MK19 7BH
T 01908-515 789 E fcoservices.customercontactcentre@fco.gov.uk
W www.fcoservices.gov.uk

FCO Services was established as an executive agency in April 2006 and became a trading fund in April 2008. It operates as the service delivery arm of the FCO, keeping their people, assets and information across the globe safe and secure from the threats they face. FCO Services also works with central government departments, law enforcement, HM government abroad, local government and the UK's critical national infrastructure.
Chief Executive, Chris Moxey

WILTON PARK CONFERENCE CENTRE
Wiston House, Steyning, W. Sussex BN44 3DZ
T 01903-815020 W www.wiltonpark.org.uk

Wilton Park organises international affairs conferences and is hired out to government departments and commercial users.
Chair, Iain Ferguson
Chief Executive, Richard Burge

DEPARTMENT OF HEALTH

MEDICINES AND HEALTHCARE PRODUCTS REGULATORY AGENCY (MHRA)
151 Buckingham Palace Road, London SW1W 9SS
E info@mhra.gsi.gov.uk W www.mhra.gov.uk

The MHRA is a centre of the Medicines and Healthcare Products Regulatory Agency which also includes the National Institute for Biological Standards and Control (NIBSC) and the Clinical Practice Research Datalink (CPRD). The MHRA is responsible for regulating all medicines and medical devices in the UK by ensuring they work and are acceptably safe.
Chair, Sir Gordon Duff
Chief Executive, Dr Ian Hudson

PUBLIC HEALTH ENGLAND
Wellington House, 133–155 Waterloo Road, London SE1 8UG
T 020-7654 8000 E enquiries@phe.gov.uk
W www.gov.uk/government/organisations/public-health-england

Public Health England began operating on 1 April 2013 with a remit to protect and improve the health and wellbeing of people within the UK, and reducing health inequalities. Its key priorities for 2014–15 are to protect the public's health from infectious diseases and other hazards to health; to improve the public's health and wellbeing, and reduce health inequalities; to improve population health through sustainable health and care services; to build the capability and capacity of the public health system; and to deliver expertise to its partners.
Chair, Prof. David Heymann, CBE
Chief Executive, Duncan Selbie

HOME OFFICE

HM PASSPORT OFFICE
2 Marsham Street, London SW1P 4DF
Passport Advice Line 0300-222 0000
General Register Office 0300-123 1837
W www.gov.uk/government/organisations/hm-passport-office

HM Passport Office (formerly known as the Identity and Passport Service) is an executive agency of the Home Office. The agency incorporates the General Register Office. HM Passport Office issues, renews and amends passports for UK nationals both at home and abroad. The General Register Office is responsible for overseeing the system of civil registration in England and Wales, which involves administering the marriage laws; securing an effective system for the registration of births, adoptions, civil partnerships, marriages and deaths; maintaining an archive of births, civil partnerships, marriages and deaths; maintaining the adopted children's register, adoption contact register and other registers; and supplying certificates from the registers and the archives for research or family history purposes.

Chief Executive, Paul Pugh

MINISTRY OF JUSTICE

CRIMINAL INJURIES COMPENSATION AUTHORITY (CICA)

Tay House, 300 Bath Street, Glasgow G2 4LN
T 0300-003 3601
W www.gov.uk/goverment/organisations/criminal-injuries-compensation-authority

CICA is the executive agency responsible for administering the Criminal Injuries Compensation Scheme in England, Scotland and Wales (separate arrangements apply in Northern Ireland). CICA handles up to 40,000 applications for compensation each year, covering every aspect of compensation under the 1996, 2001 and 2008 Criminal Injuries Compensation Schemes and can make awards of between £1,000 and £500,000. Appeals against decisions made by CICA can be put to the First-tier Tribunal (Criminal Injuries Compensation) (*see* Tribunals).

Chief Executive, Carole Oatway

HER MAJESTY'S COURTS AND TRIBUNALS SERVICE
see Law Courts and Offices

LEGAL AID AGENCY

102 Petty France, London SW1H 9AJ
T 0300-200 2020 E legal.queries@legalaid.gsi.gov.uk
W www.gov.uk/government/organisations/legal-aid-agency

The Legal Aid Agency provides civil and criminal legal aid and advice in England and Wales. Formed on 1 April 2013 as part of the Legal Aid, Sentencing and Punishment of Offenders Act 2012, the agency replaces the Legal Services Commission, a non-departmental public body of the MoJ.

Chief Executive, Matthew Coats

NATIONAL OFFENDER MANAGEMENT SERVICE
see The Prison Service

OFFICE OF THE PUBLIC GUARDIAN

PO Box 16185, Birmingham B2 2WH
T 0300-456 0300 E customerservices@publicguardian.gsi.gov.uk

The Office of the Public Guardian (OPG) works within the Mental Capacity Act 2005 to support and protect those who lack the mental capacity to make decisions for themselves. It supports the Public Guardian in the registration of Enduring Powers of Attorney (EPA) and Lasting Powers of Attorney (LPA), and the supervision of deputies appointed by the Court of Protection. The OPG also has responsibility for investigating and acting on allegations of abuse by attorneys and deputies. The OPG's responsibility extends across England and Wales.

Chief Executive and Public Guardian, Alan Eccles

DEPARTMENT FOR TRANSPORT

DRIVER AND VEHICLE LICENSING AGENCY (DVLA)

Longview Road, Swansea SA6 7JL
T 0300 790 6901
W www.gov.uk/government/organisations/driver-and-vehicle-licensing-agency

The DVLA, established as an executive agency in 1990, maintains registers of drivers and vehicles in Great Britain. The information collated by the DVLA helps to improve road safety, reduce vehicle related crime, support environmental initiatives and limit vehicle tax evasion. The DVLA is responsible for collection and enforcement of vehicle excise duty (£6bn in 2013–14). The agency also maintains records of all those who are entitled to drive various types of vehicle, in addition to their endorsements, disqualifications and medical conditions. The DVLA maintains records of over 37 million vehicles currently registered in the UK.

Chief Executive, Oliver Morley

DRIVER AND VEHICLE STANDARDS AGENCY

Driver Enquiries: PO Box 280, Newcastle-Upon-Tyne NE99 1FP
T 0300-200 1122 E customer.services@dsa.gsi.gov.uk
Vehicle Enquiries: The Ellipse, Padley Road, Swansea SA1 8AN
T 0300-123 9000 E enquiries@vosa.gov.uk
W www.gov.uk/government/organisations/driver-and-vehicle-standards-agency

Formed by the merger of the Driving Standards Agency and the Vehicle and Operator Services Agency in 2014, the Driver and Vehicle Standards Agency (DVSA) is responsible for improving road safety in the UK by setting standards for driving and motorcycling, and ensuring drivers, vehicle operators and MOT garages understand and comply with roadworthiness standards. It additionally provides a range of licensing, testing, education and enforcement services.

Chief Executive, Alastair Peoples

HIGHWAYS AGENCY

Federated House, London Road, Dorking RH4 1SZ
T 0300-123 5000
E ha_info@highways.gsi.gov.uk
W www.gov.uk/government/organisations/highways-agency

The Highways Agency is responsible for operating, maintaining and improving England's strategic road network which comprises approximately 4,300 miles of motorways and all-purpose trunk roads valued at £109bn.

Chief Executive, Graham Dalton

MARITIME AND COASTGUARD AGENCY

Spring Place, 105 Commercial Road, Southampton SO15 1EG
T 023-8032 9100
W www.gov.uk/government/organisations/maritime-and-coastguard-agency

The agency's aims are to prevent loss of life, continuously improve maritime safety and protect the marine environment.

Chief Executive, Sir Alan Massey
Chief Coastguard (acting), Richard Martin, OBE

VEHICLE CERTIFICATION AGENCY

1 Eastgate Office Centre, Eastgate Road, Bristol BS5 6XX
T 0300-330 5797 E enquiries@vca.gov.uk
W www.gov.uk/government/organisations/vehicle-certification-agency

The agency is the UK authority responsible for ensuring that new road vehicles, agricultural tractors, off-road vehicles and vehicle parts have been designed and constructed to meet

internationally agreed standards of safety and environmental protection.
Chief Executive, Paul Markwick

HM TREASURY

UK DEBT MANAGEMENT OFFICE
Eastcheap Court, 11 Philpot Lane, London EC3M 8UD
T 020-7862 6500 W www.dmo.gov.uk

The UK Debt Management Office (DMO) was launched as an executive agency of HM Treasury in April 1998. The Chancellor of the Exchequer determines the policy and financial framework within which the DMO operates, but delegates operational decisions on debt and cash management and the day-to-day running of the office to the chief executive. The DMO's remit is to carry out the government's debt management policy of minimising financing costs over the long term, and to minimise the cost of offsetting the government's net cash flows over time, while operating at a level of risk approved by ministers in both cases. The DMO is also responsible for providing loans to local authorities through the Public Works Loan Board, and for managing the assets of certain public-sector bodies through the Commissioners for the Reduction of the National Debt.
Chief Executive, Robert Stheeman

NON-MINISTERIAL GOVERNMENT DEPARTMENTS

Non-ministerial government departments are part of central government but are not headed by a minister and are not funded by a sponsor department. They are created to implement specific legislation, but do not have the ability to change it. Departments may have links to a minister, but the minister is not responsible for the department's overall performance. Staff employed by non-ministerial departments are civil servants.

CHARITY COMMISSION
PO Box 1227, Liverpool L69 3UG
T 0845-300 0218 W www.charitycommission.gov.uk

The Charity Commission is established by law as the independent regulator and registrar of charities in England and Wales. Its aim is to provide the best possible regulation of these charities in order to ensure their legal compliance and increase their efficiency, accountability and effectiveness, as well as to encourage public trust and confidence in them. The commission maintains a register of over 160,000 charities. It is accountable to both parliament and the First-tier Tribunal (Charity), and the chamber of the Upper Tribunal or high court for decisions made in exercising the commission's legal powers. The Charity Commission has offices in London, Liverpool, Taunton and Newport.
Chair, William Shawcross, CVO
Chief Executive, Paula Sussex

COMPETITION AND MARKETS AUTHORITY
Victoria House, Southampton Row, London WC1B 4AD
T 020-3738 6000 E general.enquiries@cma.gsi.gov.uk
W www.gov.uk/cma

The Competition and Markets Authority (CMA) was established under the Enterprise and Regulatory Reform Act 2013 and acquired its powers on 1 April 2014 when it took over the functions of the Competition Commission and the Office of Fair Trading. The CMA works to promote competition for the benefit of consumers, within and outside of the UK. The CMA's aim is to make markets work well for consumers, businesses and the economy.

The authority's responsibilities include, but are not limited to: investigating mergers which could restrict competition; investigating possible breaches of UK or EU prohibitions against anti-competitive agreements and abuses of dominant positions; enforcing consumer protection legislation and cooperating with sector regulators.
Chair, David Currie
Chief Executive, Alex Chisholm

CROWN PROSECUTION SERVICE
Rose Court, 2 Southwark Bridge Road, London SE1 9HS
T 020-3357 0000 E enquiries@cps.gsi.gov.uk
W www.cps.gov.uk

The Crown Prosecution Service (CPS) is the independent body responsible for prosecuting people in England and Wales. The CPS was established as a result of the Prosecution of Offences Act 1985. It works closely with the police to advise on lines of inquiry and to decide on appropriate charges and other disposals in all but minor cases. *See also* Law Courts and Offices.
Director of Public Prosecutions, Alison Saunders, CB
Chief Executive, Peter Lewis, CB

FOOD STANDARDS AGENCY
Aviation House, 125 Kingsway, London WC2B 6NH
T 020-7276 8829
E helpline@foodstandards.gsi.gov.uk
W www.food.gov.uk

Established in April 2000, the FSA is a UK-wide non-ministerial government body responsible for food safety and hygiene. The agency has the general function of developing policy in these areas and provides information and advice to the government, other public bodies and consumers. The FSA also works with local authorities to enforce food safety regulations and has staff working in UK meat plants to check that the requirements of the regulations are being met.
Chair, Tim Bennett
Chief Executive, Catherine Brown

FOOD STANDARDS AGENCY NORTHERN IRELAND,
10C Clarendon Road, Belfast BT1 3BG T 028-9041 7700
E infosani@foodstandards.gsi.gov.uk
FOOD STANDARDS AGENCY SCOTLAND, 6th Floor,
St Magnus House, 25 Guild Street, Aberdeen AB11 6NJ
T 01224-285100 E scotland@foodstandards.gsi.gov.uk
FOOD STANDARDS AGENCY WALES, 11th Floor, South
Gate House, Wood Street, Cardiff CF10 1EW T 029-2067 8999
E wales@foodstandards.gsi.gov.uk

FORESTRY COMMISSION
Silvan House, 231 Corstorphine Road, Edinburgh EH12 7AT
T 0300-067 5000 E enquiries@forestry.gsi.gov.uk
W www.forestry.gov.uk

The Forestry Commission is the government department responsible for forestry policy in England and Scotland. It is divided into Forestry Commission England and Forestry Commission Scotland, which report to forestry ministers (the Secretary of State for Environment, Food & Rural Affairs in the UK government, and to ministers in the Scottish government), to whom it is responsible for advice on and implementation of forestry policy. It has an agency, Forest Research, which carries out scientific research and technical development relevant to forestry. The public forests are managed through two additional executive agencies, known as Forest Enterprise England and Forest Enterprise Scotland.

On 1 April 2013 the functions of its Welsh division, Forestry Commission Wales, were subsumed into Natural Resources Wales, a new body established by the Welsh government to regulate and manage natural resources in Wales.

The commission's principal objectives are to protect and expand England's and Scotland's forests and woodlands; enhance the economic value of forest resources; conserve and improve the biodiversity, landscape and cultural heritage of forests and woodlands; develop opportunities for woodland recreation; and increase public understanding of, and community participation in, forestry. It does this by managing public forests in its care to implement these objectives; by supporting other woodland owners with grants, regulation, advice and tree felling licences; and, through its Forest Research agency, by carrying out scientific research and technical development in support of these objectives.

Chair (2014–17), Sir Harry Studholme, Bt.
Deputy Chair and Director, England, Ian Gambles
Forestry Commissioner Scotland, Dr Bob McIntosh

FORESTRY COMMISSION ENGLAND, 620 Bristol Business Park, Coldharbour Lane, Bristol BS16 1EJ T 0117-906 6000
FORESTRY COMMISSION SCOTLAND, Silvan House, 231 Corstorphine Road, Edinburgh EH12 7AT T 0845-367 3787

GOVERNMENT ACTUARY'S DEPARTMENT

Finlaison House, 15–17 Furnival Street, London EC4A 1AB
T 020-7211 2601
Belford House, 59 Belford Road, Edinburgh EH4 3UE
T 0131-467 0324
E enquiries@gad.gov.uk W www.gov.uk/gad

The Government Actuary's Department (GAD) was established in 1919 and provides actuarial advice to the public sector in the UK and overseas, and also to the private sector, where consistent with government policy. The GAD provides advice on occupational pension schemes, social security and National Insurance, investement and strategic risk management, insurance analysis and advice, financial risk management, and healthcare financing.

Government Actuary, Martin Clarke
Deputy Government Actuaries, George Russell; Colin Wilson
Chief Actuaries, Sandra Bell; Ian Boonin; Dermot Grenham; Adrian Hale; Stephen Humphrey; Ken Kneller; Aidan Smith; Sue Vivian

HM REVENUE AND CUSTOMS (HMRC)

100 Parliament Street, London SW1A 2BQ
Income Tax Enquiries 0300-200 3300
National Insurance Enquiries 0300-200 3500
VAT Enquiries 0300-200 3700
W www.gov.uk/government/organisations/hm-revenue-customs

HMRC was formed following the integration of the Inland Revenue and HM Customs and Excise, which was made formal by parliament in April 2005. It collects and administers direct taxes (capital gains tax, corporation tax, income tax, inheritance tax and national insurance contributions) and indirect taxes (excise duties, insurance premium tax, petroleum revenue tax, stamp duty, stamp duty land tax, stamp duty reserve tax and value-added tax). HMRC also pays and administers child benefit, tax credits and the Child Trust Fund, in addition to being responsible for environmental taxes, national minimum wage enforcement, recovery of student loans, the climate change levy and landfill tax. HMRC also administers the Government Banking Service.

Lead Non-Executive, Ian Barlow
Chief Executive and Permanent Secretary, Lin Homer
Tax Assurance Commissioner and Second Permanent Secretary, Edward Troup

VALUATION OFFICE AGENCY

Wingate House, 93–107 Shaftesbury Avenue, London W1D 5BU
T 0300-561700
W www.voa.gov.uk

Established in 1991, the Valuation Office is an executive agency of HM Revenue and Customs. It is responsible for compiling and maintaining the business rating and council tax valuation lists for England and Wales; valuing property throughout Great Britain for the purposes of taxes administered by HMRC; providing statutory and non-statutory property valuation services in England, Wales and Scotland; and giving policy advice to ministers on property valuation matters. In April 2009 the VOA assumed responsibility for the functions of The Rent Service, which provided a rental valuation service to local authorities in England, and fair rent determinations for landlords and tenants.

Chief Executive, Penny Ciniewicz

LAND REGISTRY

Trafalgar House, 1 Bedford Park, Croydon CR0 2AQ
T 0300-006 0411 E customersupport@landregistry.gsi.gov.uk
W www.landregistry.gov.uk

A government department and trading fund of BIS, Land Registry maintains the Land Register – the definitive source of information for more than 23 million property titles in England and Wales. The Land Register has been open to public inspection since 1990.

Chief Land Registrar and Chief Executive, Ed Lester

NATIONAL ARCHIVES

NATIONAL ARCHIVES
Kew, Richmond, Surrey TW9 4DU
T 020-8876 3444 W www.nationalarchives.gov.uk

The National Archives is a non-ministerial government department of the Ministry of Justice. It incorporates the Public Record Office, Historical Manuscripts Commission, Office of Public Sector Information and Her Majesty's Stationery Office. As the official archive of the UK government, it preserves, protects and makes accessible the historical collection of official records.

The National Archives also manages digital information including the UK government web archive which contains over one billion digital documents, and devises solutions for keeping government records readable now and in the future.

The organisation administers the UK's public records system under the Public Records Acts of 1958 and 1967. The records it holds span 1,000 years – from the Domesday Book to the latest government papers to be released – and fill more than 167km (104 miles) of shelving.

Chief Executive and Keeper, Oliver Morley

NATIONAL CRIME AGENCY

Units 1–6 Citadel Place, Tinworth Street, London SE11 5EF
T 0370-496 7622 E communication@nca.x.gsi.gov.uk
W www.nationalcrimeagency.gov.uk

The National Crime Agency (NCA) is an operational crime fighting agency introduced under the Crime and Courts Act 2013, which became fully operational in October 2013. The NCA's remit is to fight organised crime, strengthen UK borders, tackle fraud and cyber crime and protect children and young people. The agency employs over 4,000 officers and provides leadership through its organised crime, border policing, economic crime and Child Exploitation and Online Protection Centre commands, the National Cyber Crime Unit and specialist capability teams.

Chair, Keith Bristow, QPM

NATIONAL SAVINGS AND INVESTMENTS
Glasgow G58 1SB
T 0500-007 007 W www.nsandi.com

NS&I (National Savings and Investments) came into being in 1861 when the Palmerston government set up the Post Office Savings Bank, a savings scheme which aimed to encourage ordinary wage earners 'to provide for themselves against adversity and ill health'. NS&I was established as a government department in 1969. It is responsible for the design, marketing and administration of savings and investment products for personal savers and investors. It has over 26 million customers and almost £100bn invested. See also Banking and Finance, National Savings.

Chief Executive, Jane Platt

OFFICE OF GAS AND ELECTRICITY MARKETS (OFGEM)
9 Millbank, London SW1P 3GE
T 020-7901 7295 W www.ofgem.gov.uk

OFGEM is the regulator for Britain's gas and electricity industries. Its role is to protect and advance the interests of consumers by promoting competition where possible, and through regulation only where necessary. OFGEM operates under the direction and governance of the Gas and Electricity Markets Authority, which makes all major decisions and sets policy priorities for OFGEM. OFGEM's powers are provided for under the Gas Act 1986 and the Electricity Act 1989, as amended by the Utilities Act 2000. It also has enforcement powers under the Competition Act 1998 and the Enterprise Act 2002.

Chair, David Gray
Chief Executive, Dermot Nolan

OFFICE OF QUALIFICATIONS AND EXAMINATIONS REGULATION (OFQUAL)
OFQUAL, Spring Place, Herald Avenue, Coventry CV5 6UB
T 0300-303 3346 E info@ofqual.gov.uk
W www.ofqual.gov.uk

OFQUAL became the independent regulator of qualifications, examinations and assessments on 1 April 2010. It is responsible for maintaining standards, improving confidence and distributing information about qualifications and examinations, as well as regulating general and vocational qualifications in England and vocational qualifications in Northern Ireland.

Chief Executive, Glenys Stacey

OFFICE OF RAIL REGULATION
1 Kemble Street, London WC2B 4AN
T 020-7282 2000 E contact.cct@orr.gsi.gov.uk
W www.orr.gov.uk

The Office of the Rail Regulator was set up under the Railways Act 1993. It became the Office of Rail Regulation (ORR) in July 2004 under the provisions of the Railways and Transport Safety Act 2003. On 1 April 2006, in addition to its role as economic regulator, the ORR became the health and safety regulator for the rail industry. This transfer of responsibility from the Health and Safety Executive was given effect under the Railways Act 2005. ORR has a board and chair who are appointed by the Secretary of State for Transport. ORR is also a competition and consumer authority and has powers under the Enterprise Act 2002 and Competitions Act 1998.

The ORR's key roles are to ensure that Network Rail, the owner and operator of the national railway infrastructure, manages the network efficiently and in a way that meets the needs of its users; to encourage continuous improvement in health and safety performance while securing compliance with relevant health and safety law, including taking enforcement action as necessary, and to develop policy and enhance relevant railway health and safety legislation. The ORR is also the economic regulator for HS1. The ORR is responsible for licensing operators of railways assets, setting the terms for access by operators to the network and other railways facilities, and enforcing competition law in the rail sector.

Chair, Anna Walker
Chief Executive, Richard Price

OFFICE FOR STANDARDS IN EDUCATION, CHILDREN'S SERVICES AND SKILLS (OFSTED)
Piccadilly Gate, Store Street, Manchester M1 2WD
T 0300-123 1231 E enquiries@ofsted.gov.uk
W www.ofsted.gov.uk

Ofsted was established under the Education (Schools Act) 1992 and was relaunched on 1 April 2007 with a wider remit, bringing together four formerly separate inspectorates. It works to raise standards in services through the inspection and regulation of care for children and young people, and inspects education and training for children of all ages. See also Education.

HM Chief Inspector, Sir Michael Wilshaw
Chair, David Hoare

ORDNANCE SURVEY
Adanac Drive, Southampton SO16 0AS
T 0845-605 0505
E customerservices@ordnancesurvey.co.uk
W www.ordnancesurvey.co.uk

Ordnance Survey is the national mapping agency for Great Britain. It is a government department and executive agency operating as a trading fund since 1999.

Director-General and Chief Executive (acting), Neil Ackroyd

SERIOUS FRAUD OFFICE
2–4 Cockspur Street, London SW1Y 5BS
T 020-7239 7272 E public.enquiries@sfo.gsi.gov.uk
W www.sfo.gov.uk

The Serious Fraud Office is an independent government department that investigates and, where appropriate, prosecutes serious or complex fraud, bribery and corruption. It is part of the UK criminal justice system with jurisdiction over England, Wales and Northern Ireland but not Scotland, the Isle of Man or the Channel Islands. The office is headed by a director who is accountable to the Attorney-General.

Director, David Green, CB, QC

SUPREME COURT OF THE UNITED KINGDOM
see Law Courts and Offices

TREASURY SOLICITOR'S DEPARTMENT
1 Kemble Street, London WC2B 4TS
T 020-7210 3000
E thetreasurysolicitor@tsol.gsi.gov.uk
W www.gov.uk/tsol

The Treasury Solicitor's Department provides legal services for many government departments and other publicly funded bodies, and is answerable to the Attorney-General. Those departments and bodies without their own lawyers are provided with legal advice and litigation services. The Treasury Solicitor is also the Queen's Proctor, and is responsible for collecting ownerless goods *(bona vacantia)* on behalf of the crown.

HM Procurator-General and Treasury Solicitor, Jonathan Jones
Directors-General, Stephen Braviner-Roman; Peter Fish;
   Claire Johnston
Head of Bona Vacantia, Zane Denton

UK STATISTICS AUTHORITY
1 Drummond Gate, London SW1V 2QQ
T 0845-604 1857 E authority.enquiries@statistics.gsi.gov.uk
W www.statisticsauthority.gov.uk

The UK Statistics Authority was established on 1 April 2008 by the Statistics and Registration Service Act 2007 as an independent body operating at arm's length from government, reporting to the UK parliament and the devolved legislatures. Its overall objective is to promote and safeguard the production and publication of official statistics and ensure their quality and comprehensiveness. The authority's main functions are the oversight of the Office for National Statistics (ONS); monitoring and reporting on all UK official statistics, which includes around 30 central government departments and the devolved administrations; and the production of a code of practice for statistics and the assessment of official statistics against the code.

BOARD
Chair, Sir Andrew Dilnot, CBE
Board Members, Dr Dame Colette Bowe, DBE; Carolyn
   Fairbairn; Dame Moira Gibb, DBE; Prof. David Hand;
   Ed Humpherson *(Head of Assessment);* Dr David Levy;
   John Pullinger *(National Statistician);* Prof. David Rhind,
   CBE, FRS, FBA *(Deputy Chair, Official Statistics);*
   Prof. Sir Adrian Smith, FRS *(Deputy Chair, ONS);*
   Glen Watson *(Director-General, ONS)*

OFFICE FOR NATIONAL STATISTICS (ONS)
Cardiff Road, Newport NP10 8XG
T 0845-601 3034 E info@statistics.gov.uk
W www.ons.gov.uk

The ONS was created in 1996 by the merger of the Central Statistical Office and the Office of Population Censuses and Surveys. On 1 April 2008 it became the executive office of the UK Statistics Authority. As part of these changes, the office's responsibility for the General Register Office transferred to HM Passport Office of the Home Office.

The ONS is responsible for preparing, interpreting and publishing key statistics on the government, economy and society of the UK. Its key responsibilities include designing, managing and running the Census and providing statistics on health and other demographic matters in England and Wales; the production of the UK National Accounts and other economic indicators; the organisation of population censuses in England and Wales and surveys for government departments and public bodies.

National Statistician, John Pullinger
Director-General, Glen Watson

UK TRADE AND INVESTMENT
1 Victoria Street, London SW1H 0ET
T 020-7215 5000
W www.gov.uk/government/organisations/uk-trade-investment

UK Trade and Investment is a government organisation that helps UK-based companies succeed in international markets. It assists overseas companies to bring high quality investment to the UK economy.

Chief Executive, Dominic Jermey

WATER SERVICES REGULATION AUTHORITY (OFWAT)
Centre City Tower, 7 Hill Street, Birmingham B5 4UA
T 0121-644 7500 E mailbox@ofwat.gsi.gov.uk
W www.ofwat.gov.uk

OFWAT is the independent economic regulator of the water and sewerage companies in England and Wales. It is responsible for ensuring that the water industry in England and Wales provides household and business customers with a good quality service and value for money. This is done by ensuring that the companies provide customers with a good quality, efficient service at a fair price; limiting the prices companies can charge; monitoring the companies' performance and taking action, including enforcement, to protect customers' interests; settting the companies efficiency targets; making sure the companies deliver the best for consumers and the environment in the long term; and encouraging competition where it benefits consumers.

Chair, Jonson Cox
Chief Executive, Cathryn Ross

PUBLIC BODIES

The following section is a listing of public bodies and other civil service organisations: it is not a complete list of these organisations.

Whereas executive agencies are either part of a government department or are one in their own right (*see* Government Departments), public bodies carry out their functions to a greater or lesser extent at arm's length from central government. Ministers are ultimately responsible to parliament for the activities of the public bodies sponsored by their department and in almost all cases (except where there is separate statutory provision) ministers make the appointments to their boards. Departments are responsible for funding and ensuring good governance of their public bodies.

The term 'public body' is a general one which includes public corporations, such as the BBC; NHS bodies; and non-departmental public bodies (NDPBs).

In October 2010, the government announced proposals to drastically reform public bodies or 'quangos' (quasi-autonomous non-governmental organisations, another term for NDPBs). In total, 901 bodies were reviewed – 679 NDPBs and 222 other statutory bodies. Consequently, the government introduced the Public Bodies Bill, which received royal assent on 14 December 2011 and became the Public Bodies act 2011, allowing the government to abolish, merge or transfer the functions of the public bodies listed in the appropriate schedules to the Act.

ADJUDICATOR'S OFFICE
PO Box 10280, Nottingham NG2 9PF
T 0300-057 1111 W www.adjudicatorsoffice.gov.uk

The Adjudicator's Office investigates complaints from individuals and businesses about the way that HM Revenue and Customs, the Valuation Office Agency and the Insolvency Service have handled a person's affairs. The Adjudicator's Office will only consider a complaint after the respective organisation's internal complaints procedure has been exhausted.
The Adjudicator, Judy Clements, OBE

ADVISORY, CONCILIATION AND ARBITRATION SERVICE (ACAS)
22nd Floor, Euston Tower, 286 Euston Road, London NW1 3JJ
Helpline 0300-123 1100 W www.acas.org.uk

The Advisory, Conciliation and Arbitration Service was set up under the Employment Protection Act 1975 (the provisions now being found in the Trade Union and Labour Relations (Consolidation) Act 1992.

ACAS is largely funded by the Department for Business, Innovation and Skills. A council sets its strategic direction, policies and priorities, and ensures that the agreed strategic objectives and targets are met. It consists of a chair and 7 employer, trade union and independent members, appointed by the Secretary of State for Business, Innovation and Skills.

ACAS aims to improve organisations and working life through better employment relations, to provide up-to-date information, independent advice and high-quality training, and to work with employers and employees to solve problems and improve performance.

ACAS has regional offices, in Birmingham, Bristol, Bury St Edmunds, Cardiff, Fleet, Glasgow, Leeds, Liverpool, Manchester, Newcastle upon Tyne and Nottingham. The head office is in London.
Chair, Brendan Barber
Chief Executive, Anne Sharp

ADVISORY COUNCIL ON NATIONAL RECORDS AND ARCHIVES
The National Archives, Kew, Surrey TW9 4DU
T 020-8392 5337
W www.nationalarchives.gov.uk/advisorycouncil

The Advisory Council on National Records and Archives advises the Lord Chancellor on issues relating to public records that are over 30 years old including public access to them. The council meets four times a year, and its main task is to consider requests for the extended closure of public records; it also reaches decisions regarding government departments that want to keep records.

The Forum on Historical Manuscripts and Academic Research, a sub-committee of the Advisory Council, provides advice to the Lord Chancellor on matters relating to historical manuscripts, records and archives, other than public records.
Chair, Rt. Hon.Lord Dyson, PC *(Master of the Rolls)*

AGRICULTURE AND HORTICULTURE DEVELOPMENT BOARD
Stoneleigh Park, Kenilworth, Warwickshire CV8 2TL
T 02476-692051 E info@ahdb.org.uk W www.ahdb.org.uk

The Agriculture and Horticulture Development Board (AHDB) is funded by the agriculture and horticulture industries through statutory levies, with the duty to improve efficiency and competitiveness within six sectors: pig meat in England; milk in Great Britain; beef and lamb in England; commercial horticulture in Great Britain; cereals and oilseeds in the UK; and potatoes in Great Britain. The AHDB represents about 75 per cent of total UK agricultural output. Levies raised from the six sectors are ring-fenced to ensure that they can only be used to the benefit of the sectors from which they were raised.
Chair, Peter Kendall
Independent members, Lorraine Clinton; Tim Kelly; Will Lifford
Sector members, Neil Bragg *(horticulture);* John Cross *(beef and lamb);* Stewart Houston *(pig meat);* Fiona Fell *(potatoes);* Jonathan Tipples *(cereals and oilseeds);* vacant *(milk)*
Chief Executive, Tom Taylor

ARCHITECTURE AND DESIGN SCOTLAND
Bakehouse Close, 146 Canongate, Edinburgh EH8 8DD
T 0131-556 6699
W www.ads.org.uk

Architecture and Design Scotland (A+DS) was established in 2005 by the Scottish government as the national champion for good architecture, urban design and planning in the built environment; it works with a wide range of organisations at national, regional and local levels.
Chair, Karen Anderson
Chief Executive, Jim MacDonald

ARMED FORCES' PAY REVIEW BODY
6th Floor, Victoria House, Southampton Row, London WC1B 4AD
T 020-7271 0469 W www.ome.uk.com

The Armed Forces' Pay Review Body was appointed in 1971. It advises the prime minister and the Secretary of State for Defence on the pay and allowances of members of naval, military and air forces of the Crown.
Chair, John Steele
Members, Mary Carter; Prof. Peter Dolton; Very Revd. Dr Graham Forbes, CBE; Vice-Adm. Sir Richard Ibbotson, KBE, CB; Paul Kernaghan, CBE, QPM; Judy McKnight, CBE; John Steele

ARTS COUNCIL ENGLAND
14 Great Peter Street, London SW1P 3NQ
T 0845-300 6200
W www.artscouncil.org.uk

Arts Council England is the national development agency for the arts in England. Using public money from government and the National Lottery, it supports a range of artistic activities, including theatre, music, literature, dance, photography, digital art, carnival and crafts. Between 2010 and 2015, Arts Council England is investing £1.9bn of public money from the government and around £1.1bn from the National Lottery.

The governing body, the national council, comprises 14 members, who are appointed by the Secretary of State for Culture, Media and Sport usually for a term of four years. There are also five councils, responsible for the agreement of area strategies, plans and priorities for action within the national framework.
National Council Chair, Sir Peter Bazalgette
National Council Members, Maria Balshaw; Matthew Bowcock, CBE; David Bryan; Prof. Jon Cook; Joe Docherty; Sheila Healy; David Joseph; Sir Nicholas Kenyon; Nazo Moosa; Peter Phillips; Alistair Spalding, CBE; Rosemary Squire, OBE; Veronica Wadley
Chief Executive, Alan Davey

ARTS COUNCIL OF NORTHERN IRELAND
77 Malone Road, Belfast BT9 6AQ
T 028-9038 5200 E info@artscouncil-ni.org
W www.artscouncil-ni.org

The Arts Council of Northern Ireland is the prime distributor of government funds in support of the arts in Northern Ireland. It is funded by the Department of Culture, Arts and Leisure and from National Lottery funds.
Chair, Bob Collins
Members, David Alderdice; Anna Carragher; Damien Coyle *(Vice-Chair);* Eibhlinn Ni Dhochartaigh; Noelle McAlinden; Katherine McCloskey; Prof. Ian Montgomery; Paul Mullan; Prof. Paul Seawright; Conor Shields; Brian Sore; Nisha Tandon
Chief Executive, Roisin McDonough

ARTS COUNCIL OF WALES
Bute Place, Cardiff CF10 5AL
T 0845-873 4900 E information@artswales.org.uk
W www.artswales.org.uk

The Arts Council of Wales was established in 1994 by royal charter and is the development body for the arts in Wales. It funds arts organisations with funding from the Welsh government and is the distributor of National Lottery funds to the arts in Wales. Grant-in-aid allocated by the Welsh government for 2013–14 totalled £34.25m.
Chair, Prof. Dai Smith
Members, Emma Evans; John Geraint; Michael Griffiths; Melanie Hawthorne; Dr Lesley Hodgson; Margaret Jervis;

MBE; Marian Wyn Jones; Andrew Miller; Osi Rhys Osmond; Richard Turner; Alan Watkin; Prof. Gerwyn Wiliams; John Carey Williams; Dr Kate Woodward
Chief Executive, Nick Capaldi

AUDIT SCOTLAND
110 George Street, Edinburgh EH2 4LH
T 0845-146 1010 E info@audit-scotland.gov.uk
W www.audit-scotland.gov.uk

Audit Scotland was set up in 2000 to provide services to the Accounts Commission and the Auditor-General for Scotland. Together they help to ensure that public-sector bodies in Scotland are held accountable for the proper, efficient and effective use of public funds.

Audit Scotland's work covers about 200 bodies including local authorities; health boards; further education colleges; Scottish Water; the Scottish government; government agencies such as the Prison Service and non-departmental public bodies such as the Scottish Police Authority and the Scottish Fire and Rescue Service.

Audit Scotland carries out financial and regularity audits to ensure that public-sector bodies adhere to the highest standards of financial management and governance. It also carries out performance audits to ensure that these bodies achieve the best value for money. All of Audit Scotland's work in connection with local authorities is carried out for the Accounts Commission; its other work is undertaken for the Auditor-General.
Auditor-General, Caroline Gardner
Chair of the Accounts Commission, Douglas Sinclair

BANK OF ENGLAND
Threadneedle Street, London EC2R 8AH
T 020-7601 4444 E enquiries@bankofengland.co.uk
W www.bankofengland.co.uk

The Bank of England was incorporated in 1694 under royal charter. It was nationalised in 1946 under the Bank of England Act of that year which gave HM Treasury statutory powers over the bank. It is the banker of the government and it manages the issue of banknotes. Since 1998 it has been operationally independent and its Monetary Policy Committee has been responsible for setting short-term interest rates to meet the government's inflation target. Its responsibility for banking supervision was transferred to the Financial Services Authority in the same year. As the central reserve bank of the country, the Bank of England keeps the accounts of British banks, and of most overseas central banks; the larger banks and building societies are required to maintain with it a proportion of their cash resources. The bank's core purposes are monetary stability and financial stability. The Banking Act 2009 increased the responsibilities of the bank, including giving it a new financial stability objective and creating a special resolution regime for dealing with failing banks.

In 2013, through the Prudential Regulation Authority (PRA), the bank became responsible for the prudential regulation and supervision of banks, building societies, credit unions, insurers and major investment firms.
Governor, Mark Carney
Deputy Governors, Andrew Bailey; Dr Ben Broadbent; Sir John Cunliffe; Nemat Shafik
Court of Directors, The Governor; the Deputy Governors; Michael Cohrs; Bradley Fried; Tim Frost; Anthony Habgood; Diana Harding; Dave Prentis; Don Robert; John Stewart; Dorothy Thompson
Monetary Policy Committee, The Governor; Dr Ben Broadbent; Sir Jon Cunliffe; Andy Haldane; Kristin Forbes; Paul Fisher; Ian McCafferty; Prof. David Miles; Dr Martin Weale

Financial Policy Committee, The Governor; the Deputy
Governors; Dame Clara Furse; Donald Kohn; Richard
Sharp; Martin Taylor; Martin Wheatley
Chief Legal Adviser, Graham Nicholson
Director for Banknotes and Chief Cashier, Victoria Cleland
The Auditor, Stephen Brown

BIG LOTTERY FUND

1 Plough Place, London EC4A 1DE
T 020-7211 1800 **Advice Line** 0845-410 2030
E general.enquiries@biglotteryfund.org.uk
W www.biglotteryfund.org.uk

The Big Lottery Fund was launched in 2004, merging the
New Opportunities Fund and the Lottery Charities Board
(Community Fund). The fund is responsible for giving out
40 per cent of all funds raised for good causes by the National
Lottery, amounting to around £600m a year. The money
is distributed to charitable, benevolent and philanthropic
organisations in the voluntary and community sectors, as well
as health, education and environmental projects.
Chair, Peter Ainsworth
Vice-Chair, Tony Burton, CBE
Regional Chairs, Frank Hewitt *(Northern Ireland);* Maureen
McGinn *(Scotland);* Nat Sloane *(England);* Sir Adrian
Webb *(Wales)*
Chief Executive, Dawn Austwick

BOUNDARY COMMISSIONS

ENGLAND
Room 3/21, 1 Horse Guards Road, London SW1A 2HQ
T 020-7276 1102 **E** information@bcommengland.gsi.gov.uk
W www.independent.gov.uk/boundarycommissionforengland
Deputy Chair, Hon. Mr Justice Sales

WALES
Hastings House, Fitzalan Court, Cardiff CF24 0BL
T 029-2046 4819 **E** bcomm.wales@wales.gsi.gov.uk
W www.bcomm-wales.gov.uk
Deputy Chair, Hon. Mr Justice Williams

SCOTLAND
Thistle House, 91 Haymarket Terrace, Edinburgh EH12 5HD
T 0131-538 7510 **E** bcs@scottishboundaries.gov.uk
W www.bcomm-scotland.gov.uk
Deputy Chair, Hon. Lord Woolman

NORTHERN IRELAND
Forestview, Purdy's Lane, Belfast BT8 7AR
T 028-9069 4800 **E** bcni@belfast.org.uk
W www.boundarycommission.org.uk
Deputy Chair, Hon. Mr Justice McCloskey

The commissions, established in 1944, are constituted under
the Parliamentary Constituencies Act 1986 (as amended).
The Speaker of the House of Commons is the *ex officio* chair
of all four commissions in the UK.

The next reviews of UK parliament constituencies will be
undertaken using the electoral register from 1 September
2015; these reviews must be submitted during September
2018.

BRITISH BROADCASTING CORPORATION (BBC)

BBC Broadcasting House, Portland Place, London W1A 1AA
W www.bbc.co.uk

The BBC was incorporated under royal charter in 1926 as
successor to the British Broadcasting Company Ltd. The BBC's
current charter, which came into force on 1 January 2007 and

extends to 31 December 2016, recognises the BBC's editorial
independence and sets out its public purposes. The BBC Trust
was formed under the new charter and replaces the Board of
Governors; it sets the strategic direction of the BBC and has a
duty to represent the interests of licence fee payers. The chair,
vice-chair and other trustees are appointed by the Queen-in-
Council. The BBC is financed by television licence revenue
and by grant-in-aid from parliament for the World Service
(radio). *See* Broadcasting.

BBC TRUST MEMBERS
Chair, Rona Fairhead
National Trustees, Alison Hastings *(England);* Aideen
McGinley, OBE *(Northern Ireland);* Bill Matthews
(Scotland); Elan Closs Stephens *(Wales)*
Trustees, Sonita Alleyne, OBE; Richard Ayre; David
Liddiment; Nicholas Prettejohn; Suzanna Taverne;
Lord Williams of Baglan

EXECUTIVE BOARD
Director-General, Tony Hall
Directors, Lucy Adams *(HR, BBC Academy and Internal
Communications);* Helen Boaden *(Radio);* Anne Bulford,
OBE *(Finance and Operations);* Danny Cohen *(Television);*
Tim Davie *(CEO: BBC Worldwide, Director: Global);*
James Harding *(News and Current Affairs);* James Purnell
(Strategy & Digital)
Non-Executive Directors, Simon Burke; Nicholas Hytner;
Alice Perkins; Dame Fiona Reynolds, DBE; Sir Howard
Stringer

STATION CONTROLLERS
BBC1, Charlotte Moore
BBC2 and BBC4, Kim Shillinglaw
BBC3, Zai Bennett
BBC News Channel, Sam Taylor
BBC Parliament, Peter Knowles
BBC Northern Ireland, Peter Johnston
BBC Scotland, Ken MacQuarrie
BBC Wales, Rhodri Talfan-Davies
CBBC, Damian Kavanagh
CBeebies, Kay Benbow
Radio 1 and 1Xtra, Ben Cooper
Radio 2, 6 Music and Asian Network, Bob Shennan
Radio 3, vacant
Radio 4, Gwyneth Williams
Radio 5 Live and 5 Live Sports Extra, Jonathan Wall

BRITISH COUNCIL

Bridgewater House, 58 Whitworth Street, Manchester M1 6BB
T 0161-957 7755 **E** general.enquiries@britishcouncil.org
W www.britishcouncil.org

The British Council was established in 1934, incorporated
by royal charter in 1940 and granted a supplemental charter
in 1993. It is an independent, non-political organisation
which promotes Britain abroad and is the UK's international
organisation for educational and cultural relations. The
British Council is represented in over 200 towns and cities in
over 100 countries.
Chair, Sir Vernon Ellis
Chief Executive, Sir Martin Davidson, KCMG

BRITISH FILM INSTITUTE

21 Stephen Street, London W1T 1LN
T 020-7255 1444 **W** www.bfi.org.uk

The BFI, established in 1933, offers opportunities for people
throughout the UK to experience, learn and discover more
about the world of film and moving image culture. It

incorporates the BFI National Archive, the BFI Reuben Library, BFI Southbank, BFI Distribution, the annual BFI London Film Festival as well as the BFI London Lesbian and Gay Film Festival, and the BFI IMAX cinema. It also publishes the monthly *Sight and Sound* magazine and provides advice and support for regional cinemas and film festivals across the UK.

Following the closure of the UK Film Council in April 2011, the BFI became the lead body for film in the UK, in charge of allocating lottery money for the development and production of new British films.

Chair, Greg Dyke
Chief Executive, Amanda Nevill

BRITISH LIBRARY

96 Euston Road, London NW1 2DB
T 0843-208 1144 E customer-services@bl.uk
W www.bl.uk

The British Library was established in 1973. It is the UK's national library and occupies a key position in the library and information network. It aims to serve scholarship, research, industry, commerce and all other major users of information. Its services are based on a collection of over 150 million separate items, including books, journals, manuscripts, maps, stamps, music, patents, newspapers and sound recordings in all written and spoken languages. The library is now based at three sites: London (St Pancras and Colindale) and Boston Spa, W. Yorks. The library's sponsoring department is the Department for Culture, Media and Sport.

Access to the reading rooms at St Pancras is limited to holders of a British Library reader's pass; information about eligibility is available from the reader admissions office. The exhibition galleries and public areas are open to all, free of charge.

BRITISH LIBRARY BOARD
Chair, Rt. Hon. Baroness Blackstone
Members, David Barclay; Dr Robert Black, CBE, FRSA, FRSE; Prof. Sir Kenneth Calman, KCB; Rt. Hon. Lord Fellowes, GCB, GCVO; Prof. Dame Wendy Hall, DBE; Roly Keating; Prof. Kate McLuskie; Dr Stephen Page; Patrick Plant; Maggie Semple, OBE

EXECUTIVE
Chief Executive, Roly Keating
Director, Collections, Caroline Brazier
Director, Audiences, Frances Brindle
Chief Operating Officer, Phil Spence
Chief Digital Officer, Richard Boulderstone
Chief Financial Officer, Steve Morris

BRITISH LIBRARY NEWSPAPERS
Colindale Avenue, London NW9 5HE
T 020-7412 7353

BRITISH LIBRARY, BOSTON SPA
Boston Spa, Wetherby, W. Yorks LS23 7BQ
T 01937-546070

BRITISH MUSEUM

Great Russell Street, London WC1B 3DG
T 020-7323 8000 E information@britishmuseum.org
W www.britishmuseum.org

The British Museum houses the national collection of antiquities, ethnography, coins and paper money, medals, prints and drawings. The British Museum dates from 7 June 1753, when parliament approved the holding of a public

lottery to raise funds for the purchase of the collections of Sir Hans Sloane and the Harleian manuscripts, and for their proper housing and maintenance. The building (Montagu House) was opened in 1759. The existing buildings were erected between 1823 and the present day, and the original collection has increased to its current dimensions by gifts and purchases. Total government grant-in-aid for 2013–14 is £43.9m.

Chair, Niall Fitzgerald, KBE
Trustees, Karen Armstrong; Prof. Sir Christopher Bayly; Hon. Nigel Boardman; Cheryl Carolus; Dame Liz Forgan, DBE; Prof. Clive Gamble; Anthony Gormley, OBE; Penny Hughes, CBE; Sir George Iacobescu, CBE; James Lupton, CBE; John Micklethwait; Sir Paul Nurse, PRS; Gavin Patterson; Prof. Amartya Sen; Sir Martin Sorrell; Ahdaf Soueif; Lord Stern of Brentford, FBA; Lord Turner of Ecchinswell; Baroness Wheatcroft

OFFICERS
Director, Neil MacGregor, OM, FSA
Deputy Directors, Joanna Mackle; Jonathan Williams; Christopher Yates

KEEPERS
Keeper of Africa, Oceania and the Americas, Lissant Bolton
Keeper of Ancient Egypt and Sudan, Neal Spencer
Keeper of Asia, Jan Stuart
Keeper of Coins and Medals, Philip Attwood
Keeper of Greece and Rome, J. Lesley Fitton
Keeper of the Middle East, Jonathan Tubb
Keeper of Britain, Europe and Prehistory, Roger Bland
Keeper of Prints and Drawings, Hugo Chapman
Keeper of Conservation and Scientific Research, David Saunders

BRITISH PHARMACOPOEIA COMMISSION

151 Buckingham Palace Road, London SW1W 9SZ
T 020-3080 6561 E bpcom@mhra.gsi.gov.uk
W www.pharmacopoeia.com

The British Pharmacopoeia Commission sets standards for medicinal products used in human and veterinary medicines and is responsible for publication of the *British Pharmacopoeia* (a publicly available statement of the standard that a medicinal substance or product must meet throughout its shelf-life), the *British Pharmacopoeia (Veterinary)* and the *British Approved Names.* It has 17 members, including two lay members, who are appointed on behalf of the Secretary of State for Health by the Department of Health.

Chair, Prof. Kevin Taylor
Vice-Chair, Prof. A. Davidson
Secretary and Scientific Director, Dr Samantha Atkinson

CARE QUALITY COMMISSION

Finsbury Tower, 103–105 Bunhill Row, London EC1Y 8TG
T 0300-061 6161 E enquiries@cqc.org.uk W www.cqc.org.uk

The Care Quality Commission (CQC) is the independent regulator of health and adult social care services in England, including care provided by the NHS, local authorities, private companies and voluntary organisations. It is also in CQC's remit to protect the interests of people whose rights are restricted under the Mental Health Act.

Chair, David Prior
Board Members, Prof. Louis Appleby; Anna Bradley; Camilla Cavendish; Paul Corrigan; Dr Jennifer Dixon; Sir Robert Francis, QC; Michael Mire; Kay Sheldon
Chief Executive, David Behan, CBE

CENTRAL ARBITRATION COMMITTEE

22nd Floor, Euston Tower, 286 Euston Road, London NW1 3JJ
T 020-7904 2300 E enquiries@cac.gov.uk W www.cac.gov.uk

The Central Arbitration Committee (CAC) is a permanent independent body with statutory powers whose main function is to adjudicate on applications relating to the statutory recognition and de-recognition of trade unions for collective bargaining purposes, where such recognition or de-recognition cannot be agreed voluntarily. In addition, the CAC has a statutory role in determining disputes between trade unions and employers over the disclosure of information for collective bargaining purposes, and in resolving applications and complaints under the information and consultation regulations, and performs a similar role in relation to the legislation on the European Works Council, European companies, European cooperative societies and cross-border mergers. The CAC and its predecessors have also provided voluntary arbitration in collective disputes, but this role has not been used for some years.
Chair, Sir Michael Burton
Chief Executive, Simon Gouldstone

CERTIFICATION OFFICE FOR TRADE UNIONS AND EMPLOYERS' ASSOCIATIONS

Euston Tower, 286 Euston Road, London NW1 3JJ
T 020-7210 3734 E info@certoffice.org
W www.certoffice.org

The Certification Office is an independent statutory authority. The Certification Officer is appointed by the Secretary of State for Business, Innovation and Skills and is responsible for maintaining a list of trade unions and employers' associations; ensuring compliance with statutory requirements and keeping available for public inspection annual returns from trade unions and employers' associations; determining complaints concerning trade union elections, certain ballots and certain breaches of trade union rules; ensuring observance of statutory requirements governing mergers between trade unions and employers' associations; overseeing the political funds and finances of trade unions and employers' associations; and for certifying the independence of trade unions.
The Certification Officer, David Cockburn

CHURCH COMMISSIONERS

Church House, Great Smith Street, London SW1P 3AZ
T 020-7898 1000 E commissioners.enquiry@churchofengland.org
W www.churchofengland.org/about-us/structure/
churchcommissioners

The Church Commissioners were established in 1948 by the amalgamation of Queen Anne's Bounty (established 1704) and the Ecclesiastical Commissioners (established 1836). They are responsible for the management of some of the Church of England's assets, the income from which is predominantly used to help pay for the stipend and pension of the clergy and to support the church's work throughout the country. The commissioners own UK and global company shares, over 43,000ha (106,000 acres) of agricultural land, a residential estate in central London, and commercial property across Great Britain, plus an interest in overseas property via managed funds. They also carry out administrative duties in connection with pastoral reorganisation and closed churches.

The 33 commissioners are: the Archbishops of Canterbury and of York; eleven people elected by the General Synod, comprising four bishops, three clergy and four lay persons; three Church Estates Commissioners; two cathedral deans;

nine people appointed by the crown and the archbishops; six holders of state office, comprising the Prime Minister, the Lord Chancellor, the Lord President of the Council, the Secretary of State for Culture, Media and Sport, the Speaker of the House of Commons and the Lord Speaker.

CHURCH ESTATES COMMISSIONERS
First, Andreas Whittam Smith, CBE
Second, Rt. Hon. Sir Tony Baldry, MP
Third, Andrew Mackie

OFFICERS
Chief Executive, Secretary, Andrew Brown
Official Solicitor, Stephen Slack

COAL AUTHORITY

200 Lichfield Lane, Mansfield, Notts NG18 4RG
T 01623-637000 E thecoalauthority@coal.gov.uk
W coal.decc.gov.uk

The Coal Authority was established under the Coal Industry Act 1994 to manage certain functions previously undertaken by British Coal, including ownership of unworked coal. It is responsible for licensing coal mining operations and for providing information on coal reserves and past and future coal mining. It settles subsidence damage claims which are not the responsibility of licensed coal mining operators. It deals with the management and disposal of property and with surface hazards such as abandoned coal mine entries and mine water discharges. The Coal Authority's powers were extended alongside the Energy Act 2011 to enable it to deal with metal mine subsidence issues and deliver a metal mine water treatment programme when the necessary funding is made available.
Chair, Stephen Dingle
Chief Executive, Philip Lawrence

COMMITTEE ON STANDARDS IN PUBLIC LIFE

1 Horseguards Road, London SW1A 2HQ
T 020-7271 2948 E public@standards.gsi.gov.uk
W www.public-standards.org.uk

The Committee on Standards in Public Life was set up in October 1994. It is formed of 10 people appointed by the prime minister, comprising the chair, three political members nominated by the leaders of the three main political parties and six independent members. The committee's remit is to examine concerns about standards of conduct of all holders of public office, including arrangements relating to financial and commercial activities, and to make recommendations as to any changes in present arrangements which might be required to ensure the highest standards of propriety in public life. It is also charged with reviewing issues in relation to the funding of political parties. The committee does not investigate individual allegations of misconduct.
Chair, Lord Bew
Members, Lord John Alderdice; Rt. Hon. Dame Margaret Beckett, DBE, MP; Dame Denise Platt, DBE; David Prince, CBE; Patricia Moberly; Sheila Drew Smith, OBE; Richard Thomas; Dame Angela Watkinson, DBE, MP

COMMONWEALTH WAR GRAVES COMMISSION

2 Marlow Road, Maidenhead, Berks SL6 7DX
T 01628-634221 W www.cwgc.org

The Commonwealth War Graves Commission (formerly Imperial War Graves Commission) was founded by royal charter in 1917. It is responsible for the commemoration of around 1.7 million members of the forces of the Commonwealth who lost their lives in the two world wars. More than one million graves are maintained in over 23,000 burial grounds across 153 countries. Over three-quarters of a million men and women who have no known grave or who were cremated are commemorated by name on memorials built by the commission.

The funds of the commission are derived from the six participating governments: the UK, Canada, Australia, New Zealand, South Africa and India.

President, HRH The Duke of Kent, KG, GCMG, GCVO, ADC

Chair, Secretary of State for Defence (UK)

Vice-Chair, Air Chief Marshal Sir Joe French, KCB, CBE

Members, High Commissioners in London for Australia, Canada, India, New Zealand and South Africa; Edward Chaplin, CMG, OBE; Robert Fox, MBE; Kevan Jones, MP; Hon. Ros Kelly; Vice-Adm. Sir Tim Laurence, KCVO, CB; Lt.-Gen. Sir William Rollo, KCB, CBE; Keith Simpson, MP; Prof. Sir Hew Strachan, FRSE

Director-General and Secretary to the Commission, Brian Davidson, MBE

Director of Legal Services, Gillian Stedman

COMPETITION SERVICE

Victoria House, Bloomsbury Place, London WC1A 2EB
T 020-7979 7979 E info@catribunal.org.uk
W www.catribunal.org.uk

The Competition Service is the financial corporate body by which the Competition Appeal Tribunal is administered and through which it receives funding for the performance of its judicial functions.

Registrar, Charles Dhanowa, OBE, QC

CONSUMER COUNCIL FOR WATER

Victoria Square House, Victoria Square, Birmingham B2 4AJ
T 0121-345 1000 E enquiries@ccwater.org.uk
W www.ccwater.org.uk

The Consumer Council for Water was established in 2005 under the Water Act 2003 to represent consumers' interests in respect of price, service and value for money from their water and sewerage services, and to investigate complaints from customers about their water company. There are four regional committees in England and one in Wales.

Chair, Dame Yvonne Buckland, DBE

CORPORATION OF TRINITY HOUSE

Trinity House, Tower Hill, London EC3N 4DH
T 020-7481 6900 E enquiries@thls.org
W www.trinityhouse.co.uk

The Corporation of Trinity House is the General Lighthouse Authority for England, Wales and the Channel Islands, and was granted its first charter by Henry VIII in 1514. Its remit is to assist the safe passage of a variety of vessels through some of the busiest sea-lanes in the world; it does this by deploying and maintaining approximately 600 aids to navigation, ranging from lighthouses to a satellite navigation service. The corporation also has certain statutory jurisdiction over aids to navigation maintained by local harbour authorities and is responsible for marking or dispersing wrecks dangerous to navigation, except those occurring within port limits or wrecks of HM ships.

The statutory duties of Trinity House are funded by the General Lighthouse Fund, which is provided from light dues levied on ships calling at ports of the UK and the Republic of Ireland. The corporation is a deep-sea pilotage authority, authorised by the Secretary of State for Transport to license deep-sea pilots. In addition Trinity House is a charitable organisation that maintains a number of retirement homes for mariners and their dependants, funds a four-year training scheme for those seeking a career in the merchant navy, and also dispenses grants to a wide range of maritime charities. The charity work is wholly funded by its own activities.

The corporation is controlled by a board of Elder Brethren; a separate board controls the Lighthouse Service. The Elder Brethren also act as nautical assessors in marine cases in the Admiralty Division of the High Court.

ELDER BRETHREN

Master, HRH The Princess Royal, KG, KT, GCVO

Deputy Master, Capt. Ian McNaught

Wardens, Simon Sherrard *(Nether);* Cdre David Squire, CBE, FNI, FCMI *(Rental)*

Elder Brethren, HRH The Duke of Edinburgh, KG, KT, OM, GBE; HRH The Prince of Wales, KG, KT, GCB; HRH The Duke of York, KG, GCVO, ADC; Capt. Roger Barker; Adm. Lord Boyce, KG, GCB, OBE; Lord Browne of Madingley; Capt. John Burton-Hall, RD; Lord Carrington, KG, GCMG, CH, PC; Viscount Cobham; Capt. Sir Malcolm Edge, KCVO; Capt. Ian Gibb, MBE; Capt. Duncan Glass, OBE; Capt. Stephen Gobbi; Lord Greenway; Rear-Adm. Sir Jeremy de Halpert, KCVO, CB; Capt. Nigel Hope, RD; Lord Mackay of Clashfern, KT, PC; Sir John Major, KG, CH; Capt. Peter Mason, CBE; Cdre. Peter Melson, CVO, CBE, RN; Capt. David Orr; Capt. Nigel Palmer, OBE; Sir John Parker, GBE, FRENG; Douglas Potter; Capt. Nigel Pryke; Capt. Derek Richards, RD, RNR; Lord Robertson of Port Ellen, KT, GCMG, PC; Rear-Adm. Sir Patrick Rowe, KCVO, CBE; Cdre. Jim Scorer; Simon Sherrard; Adm. Sir Jock Slater, GCB, LVO; Rear-Adm. David Snelson, CB, FNI; Cdre. David Squire, CBE, RFA; Rear-Adm. Lord Sterling of Plaistow, GCVO, CBE, RNR; Capt. Colin Stewart, LVO; Sir Adrian Swire, KT, AE; Capt. Sir Miles Wingate, KCVO; Capt. Thomas Woodfield, OBE; Capt. Richard Woodman, LVO

OFFICERS

Secretary, Cdr Graham Hockley

Director of Finance, Jerry Wedge

Director of Navigation, Capt. Roger Barker

Director of Operations, Cdre. Jim Scorer

CREATIVE SCOTLAND

Waverley Gate, 2–4 Waterloo Place, Edinburgh EH1 3EG
T 0330-333 2000 E enquiries@creativescotland.com
W www.creativescotland.com

Creative Scotland is the organisation tasked with leading the development of the arts, creative and screen industries across Scotland. It was created in 2010 as an amalgamation of the Scottish Arts Council and Scottish Screen, and it encourages and sustains the arts through investment in the form of grants, bursaries, loans and equity. It aims to invest in talent; artistic production; audiences, access and participation; and the cultural economy. Total Scottish government grant-in-aid for 2014–15 is £53m.

Chair, Sir Sandy Crombie

Board, Steve Grimmond; Sandra Gunn; Prof. Robin MacPherson; May Miller; Fergus Muir; Barclay Price; Richard Scott; Dr Gary West; Ruth Wishart

Chief Executive, Janet Archer

CRIMINAL CASES REVIEW COMMISSION
5 Philip's Place, Birmingham B3 2PW
T 0121-233 1473 E info@ccrc.gov.uk
W www.ccrc.gov.uk

The Criminal Cases Review Commission is the independent body set up under the Criminal Appeal Act 1995. It is a non-departmental public body reporting to parliament via the Lord Chancellor and Secretary of State for Justice. It is responsible for investigating possible miscarriages of justice in England, Wales and Northern Ireland, and deciding whether or not to refer cases back to an appeal court. Members of the commission are appointed in accordance with the Commissioner for Public Appointments' code of practice.
Chair, Richard Foster, CBE
Members, Penelope Barrett; Liz Calderbank; Jim England; Julie Goulding; Celia Hughes; Stephen Leach; Alexandra Marks; Dr Sharon Persaud; Andrew Rennison; David Smith; Ewen Smith; Ranjit Sondhi
Chief Executive, Karen Kneller

CROFTING COMMISSION
Great Glen House, Leachkin Road, Inverness IV3 8NW
T 01463-663450 E info@croftingscotland.gov.uk
W www.croftingscotland.gov.uk

The Crofting Commission was established on 1 April 2012, taking over the regulation of crofting from the Crofters Commission. The aim of the Crofting Commission is to regulate crofting, to promote the occupancy of crofts, active land use, and shared management of the land by crofters, as a means of sustaining and enhancing rural communities in Scotland.
Chief Executive, Catriona Maclean

CROWN ESTATE
16 New Burlington Place, London W1S 2HX
T 020-7851 5000 E enquiries@thecrownestate.co.uk
W www.thecrownestate.co.uk

The Crown Estate is part of the hereditary possessions of the sovereign 'in right of the crown', managed under the provisions of the Crown Estate Act 1961. It had a capital value of £9.9bn in 2014, and includes substantial blocks of urban property, primarily in London, almost 144,000 hectares (356,000 acres) of rural land, over half of the foreshore, and the seabed out to the 12 nautical mile territorial limit throughout the UK. The Crown Estate has a duty to maintain and enhance the capital value of estate and the income obtained from it. Under the terms of the act, the estate pays its revenue surplus to the Treasury every year.
Chair and First Commissioner, Sir Stuart Hampson
Chief Executive and Second Commissioner, Alison Nimmo, CBE, FRICS

DISCLOSURE AND BARRING SERVICE
PO Box 110, Liverpool L69 3EF
T 0870-909 0811 E customerservices@dbs.gsi.gov.uk
W https://www.gov.uk/government/organisations/disclosure-and-barring-service

The Disclosure and Barring Service (DBS) is an executive non-departmental public body of the Home Office. It helps employers make safer recruitment decisions and prevent unsuitable people from working with vulnerable groups, including children. It was formed on 1 December 2012 and replaces the Criminal Records Bureau (CRB) and Independent Safeguarding Authority (ISA). The DBS is responsible for the children's barred list and adults' barred list for England, Wales and Northern Ireland.

Chair, Bill Griffiths
Chief Executive, Adriènne Kelbie

ENGLISH HERITAGE (HISTORIC BUILDINGS AND MONUMENTS COMMISSION FOR ENGLAND)
1 Waterhouse Square, 138–142 Holborn, London EC1N 2ST
T 020-7973 3000 W www.english-heritage.org.uk

English Heritage was established under the National Heritage Act 1983. On 1 April 1999 it merged with the Royal Commission on the Historical Monuments of England to become the new lead body for England's historic environment. It is sponsored by the Department for Culture, Media and Sport and its duties are to carry out and sponsor archaeological, architectural and scientific surveys and research designed to increase the understanding of England's past and its changing condition; to identify buildings, monuments and landscapes for protection while also offering expert advice, skills and grants to conserve these sites; to encourage town planners to make imaginative re-use of historic buildings to aid regeneration of the centres of cities, towns and villages; to manage and curate selected sites; and to curate and make publicly accessible the English Heritage Archive (formerly known as the National Monuments Record), whose records of over one million historic sites and buildings, and extensive collections of photographs, maps, drawings and reports, constitute the central database and archive of England's historic environment.
Chair, Sir Laurie Magnus
Commissioners, Lynda Addison, OBE; Sally Balcombe; Alex Balfour; Victoria Barnsley, OBE; Prof. Martin Daunton; Peter Draper; Prof. Michael Fulford, CBE; Victoria Harley Vice-Adm. Sir Tim Laurence, KCVO, CB, ADC; Martin Moore; Graham Morrison; Michael Morrison; Baroness Young of Hornsey, OBE
Chief Executive, Dr Simon Thurley

ENVIRONMENT AGENCY
PO Box 544, Rotherham S60 1BY
T 0370-850 6506 E enquiries@environment-agency.gov.uk,
Incident Hotline 0800-807060
W www.environment-agency.gov.uk

Established in 1996 under the Environment Act 1995, the Environment Agency is a non-departmental public body sponsored by the Department for Environment, Food and Rural Affairs. On 1 April 2013, Natural Resources Wales took over the Environment Agency's responsibilities in Wales. Around 70 per cent of the agency's funding is from the government, with the rest raised from various charging schemes. The agency is responsible for pollution prevention and control in England and for the management and use of water resources, including flood defences, fisheries and navigation. Its remit also includes: scrutinising potentially hazardous business operations; helping businesses to use resources more efficiently; taking action against those who do not take environmental responsibilities seriously; looking after wildlife; working with farmers; helping people get the most out of their environment; and improving the quality of inner city areas and parks by restoring rivers and lakes.

The Environment Agency has head offices in London, Bristol and six regional offices. Its total grant-in-aid for 2014–15 is £676m.
Chair, Rt. Hon. Lord Smith of Finsbury
Deputy Chair, Robert Light
Board Members, Peter Ainsworth; Karen Burrows; Dr Clive Elphick; Emma Howard Boyd; Richard Leafe; Richard MacDonald; John Varley; Jeremy Walker
Chief Executive, Dr Paul Leinster, CBE

EQUALITY AND HUMAN RIGHTS COMMISSION

Arndale House, The Arndale Centre, Manchester M4 3AQ
T 0161 829 8100 E correspondence@equalityhumanrights.com
W www.equalityhumanrights.com

The Equality and Human Rights Commission (EHRC) is a statutory body, established under the Equality Act 2006 and launched in October 2007. It inherited the responsibilities of the Commission for Racial Equality, the Disability Rights Commission and the Equal Opportunities Commission. The EHRC's purpose is to reduce inequality, eliminate discrimination, strengthen relations between people, and promote and protect human rights. It enforces equality legislation on age, disability and health, gender, race, religion and belief, sexual orientation or transgender status, and encourages compliance with the Human Rights Act 1998 throughout England, Wales and Scotland.

Chair, Baroness O'Neill of Bengarve, CH, CBE, PHD, FBA
Deputy Chair, Caroline Waters, OBE
Commissioners, Sarah Anderson, CBE; Evelyn Asante-Mensah, OBE; Ann Beynon, OBE; Laura Carstensen; Lord Holmes of Richmond, MBE; Kaliani Lyle; Prof. Sarwan Singh; Sarah Veale, CBE
Chief Executive, Mark Hammond

EQUALITY COMMISSION FOR NORTHERN IRELAND

Equality House, 7–9 Shaftesbury Square, Belfast BT2 7DP
T 028-9050 0600 Textphone 028-9050 0589
E information@equalityni.org W www.equalityni.org

The Equality Commission was set up in 1999 under the Northern Ireland Act 1998 and is responsible for promoting equality, keeping the relevant legislation under review, eliminating discrimination on the grounds of race, disability, sexual orientation, gender (including marital and civil partner status, gender reassignment, pregnancy and maternity), age, religion and political opinion and for overseeing the statutory duties on public authorities to promote equality of opportunity and good relations.

Chief Commissioner, Dr Michael Wardlow
Deputy Chief Commissioner, Jane Morrice
Chief Executive, Evelyn Collins, CBE, FRSA

GAMBLING COMMISSION

Victoria Square House, Victoria Square, Birmingham B2 4BP
T 0121-230 6666
E info@gamblingcommission.gov.uk
W www.gamblingcommission.gov.uk

The Gambling Commission was established under the Gambling Act 2005, and took over the role previously occupied by the Gaming Board for Great Britain in regulating and licensing all commercial gambling – apart from spread betting and the National Lottery – ie casinos, bingo, betting, remote gambling, gaming machines and lotteries. It also advises local and central government on related issues, and is responsible for the protection of children and the vulnerable from being harmed by gambling. In October 2013, the Gambling Commission took over all the responsibilities of the National Lottery Commission in regulating the National Lottery. The commission is sponsored by the Department for Culture, Media and Sport, with its work funded by licence fees paid by the gambling industry.

Chair, Philip Graf
Chief Executive, Jenny Williams

HEALTH AND SAFETY EXECUTIVE

Redgrave Court, Merton Road, Bootle, Merseyside L20 7HS
Incident Centre 0845-300 9923 W www.hse.gov.uk

The Health and Safety Commission (HSC) and the Health and Safety Executive (HSE) merged on 1 April 2008 to form a single national regulatory body – the HSE – responsible for promoting the cause of better health and safety at work. The HSE is sponsored by the Department for Work and Pensions.

HSE regulates all industrial and commercial sectors except operations in the air and at sea. This includes agriculture, construction, manufacturing, services, transport, mines, offshore oil and gas, quarries and major hazard sites in chemicals and petrochemicals.

HSE is responsible for developing and enforcing health and safety law; providing guidance and advice; commissioning research; conducting inspections and accident and ill-health investigations; developing standards; and licensing or approving some work activities such as asbestos removal. The HSE's nuclear directorate merged with a number of other bodies on 1 April 2011 to form the Office for Nuclear Regulation, an agency of the HSE.

Chair, Judith Hackitt, CBE
Board Members, Nick Baldwin; Jonathan Baume; George Brechin; Isobel Garner; David Gartside; Paul Kenny; John Morgan; Frances Outram; Prof. Richard Taylor; Sarah Veale, CBE
Acting Chief Executive, Kevin Myers

HER MAJESTY'S OFFICERS OF ARMS

COLLEGE OF ARMS (HERALDS' COLLEGE)
130 Queen Victoria Street, London EC4V 4BT
T 020-7248 2762 E enquiries@college-of-arms.gov.uk
W www.college-of-arms.gov.uk

The Sovereign's Officers of Arms (Kings, Heralds and Pursuivants of Arms) were first incorporated by Richard III in 1484. The powers vested by the crown in the Earl Marshal (the Duke of Norfolk) with regard to state ceremonial are largely exercised through the college. The college is also the official repository of the arms and pedigrees of English, Welsh, Northern Irish and Commonwealth (except Canadian) families and their descendants, and its records include official copies of the records of the Ulster King of Arms, the originals of which remain in Dublin. The 13 officers of the college specialise in genealogical and heraldic work for their respective clients.

Arms have long been, and still are, granted by letters patent from the Kings of Arms. A right to arms can only be established by the registration in the official records of the College of Arms of a pedigree showing direct male line descent from an ancestor already appearing therein as being entitled to arms, or by making application through the College of Arms for a grant of arms. Grants are made to corporations as well as to individuals.

Earl Marshal, Duke of Norfolk

KINGS OF ARMS
Garter, Thomas Woodcock, CVO, FSA
Clarenceux, Patric Dickinson, LVO
Norroy and Ulster, Timothy Duke

HERALDS
Chester, vacant
Lancaster, Robert Noel
Windsor, William Hunt, TD
Somerset (and Registrar), David White
Richmond (and Earl Marshal's Secretary), Clive Cheesman, FSA
York, M. P. D. O'Donoghue

PURSUIVANTS
Portcullis, Hon. Christopher Fletcher-Vane
Rouge Croix, John Allen-Petrie

COURT OF THE LORD LYON
HM New Register House, Edinburgh EH1 3YT
T 0131-556 7255 W www.lyon-court.com

Her Majesty's Officers of Arms in Scotland perform ceremonial duties and in addition may be consulted by members of the public on heraldic and genealogical matters in a professional capacity.

KING OF ARMS
Lord Lyon King of Arms, Dr Joseph Morrow

HERALDS
Rothesay, Sir Crispin Agnew of Lochnaw, Bt., QC
Snawdoun, Elizabeth Roads, LVO, FSA, FSA SCOT
Marchmont, The Hon. Adam Bruce, WS

PURSUIVANTS
Ormond, Mark Dennis
Dingwall, Yvonne Holton
Unicorn, John Malden

EXTRAORDINARY OFFICERS
Orkney Herald Extraordinary, Sir Malcolm Innes of
   Edingight, KCVO, WS
Angus Herald Extraordinary, Robin Blair, CVO, WS
Islay Herald Extraordinary, David Sellar, MVO
Ross Herald Extraordinary, Charles Burnett, FSA SCOT

HERALD PAINTER
Herald Painter, Yvonne Holton

HIGHLANDS AND ISLANDS ENTERPRISE
Fraser House, Friar's Lane, Inverness IV1 1BA
T 01463-234171 E info@hient.co.uk W www.hie.co.uk

Highlands and Islands Enterprise (HIE) was set up under the Enterprise and New Towns (Scotland) Act 1991. Its role is to deliver community and economic development in line with the Scottish government economic strategy. It focuses on helping high-growth businesses, improving regional competitiveness and strengthening communities. HIE's draft budget for 2014–15 is £96.9m.
Chair, Prof. Lorne Crerar
Chief Executive, Alex Paterson

HISTORIC ROYAL PALACES
Apartment 39A, Hampton Court Palace, Surrey KT8 9AU
T 0844-482 7777 E operators@hrp.org.uk W www.hrp.org.uk

Historic Royal Palaces was established in 1998 as a royal charter body with charitable status and is contracted by the Secretary of State for Culture, Media and Sport to manage the palaces on his behalf. The palaces – the Tower of London, Hampton Court Palace, the Banqueting House, Kensington Palace and Kew Palace – are owned by the Queen on behalf of the nation.

The organisation is governed by a board comprising a chair and 10 non-executive trustees. The chief executive is accountable to the board of trustees and ultimately to parliament. Historic Royal Palaces receives no funding from the government or the Crown.

TRUSTEES
Chair, Charles Mackay, CBE
Appointed by the Queen, Val Gooding, CBE; Sir Trevor

McDonald, OBE; Jonathan Marsden, CVO, FSA;
   Sir Alan Reid, GCVO *(Deputy Chair)*
Appointed by the Secretary of State, Sophie Andreae, DSG,
   FSA; Dawn Austwick, OBE; Bruce Carnegie-Brown;
   Liz Cleaver; Louise Wilson, FRSA
Ex officio, Gen. Lord Dannatt, GCB, CBE, MC *(159th
   Constable of the Tower of London)*

OFFICER
Chief Executive, Michael Day

HOMES AND COMMUNITIES AGENCY
Maple House, 149 Tottenham Court Road, London W1T 7BN
T 0300-1234 500 E mail@homesandcommunities.co.uk
W www.homesandcommunities.co.uk

The Homes and Communities Agency (HCA) is the national housing regeneration agency for England. With a capital investment budget of around £4bn for 2012–15, the HCA contributes to economic growth by delivering high-quality affordable housing. The HCA also provides investment to improve existing social housing as well as identifying and regenerating surplus public-sector land.
Chair, Robert Napier, CBE
Chief Executive, Andy Rose

HUMAN TISSUE AUTHORITY (HTA)
2nd Floor, 151 Buckingham Palace Road, London SW1W 9SZ
T 020-7269 1900 E enquiries@hta.gov.uk
W www.hta.gov.uk

The Human Tissue Authority (HTA) was established on 1 April 2005 under the Human Tissue Act 2004, and is sponsored and part-funded by the Department of Health. It regulates organisations that remove, store and use tissue for research, medical treatment, post-mortem examination, teaching and display in public. The HTA also gives approval for organ and bone marrow donations from living people. Under the EU tissues and cells directives, the HTA is one of the two designated competent authorities for the UK responsible for regulating tissues and cells. The HTA is also the sole competent authority for the UK under the EU organ donation directive.
Chair, Sharmila Nebhrajani, OBE
Chief Executive, Dr Alan Clamp

IMPERIAL WAR MUSEUMS (IWM)
Lambeth Road, London SE1 6HZ
T 020-7416 5000 E mail@iwm.org.uk
W www.iwm.org.uk

IWM is the world's leading authority on conflict and its impact, focusing on Britain, its former empire and the Commonwealth, from the First World War to the present. IWM aims to enrich people's understanding of the causes, course and consequences of war and conflict.

IWM comprises the organisation's flagship, IWM London; IWM North in Trafford, Manchester; IWM Duxford in Cambridgeshire; the Churchill War Rooms in Whitehall; and HMS *Belfast* in the Pool of London.

The total grant-in-aid (including grants for special projects) for 2013–14 is £20.28m.

OFFICERS
Chair, Sir Francis Richards, KCMG, CVO
Trustees, Rt. Hon. Lord Ashcroft, KCMG; Lord Black of
   Brentwood; HE Gordon Campbell; Hon. Alexander
   Downer; HE Wajid Shamsul Hasan; HE Rt. Hon. Sir
   Lockwood Smith; Prof. Sir Miles Irving, FRCS; Lt.-Gen.
   Sir John Kiszely, KCB, MC; Bronwen Maddox; HE Ranjan

Mathai; Dame Judith Mayhew Jonas, DBE; HE Obed
Mlaba; HE Dr Chris Nonis; Air Chief Marshal Sir Stuart
Peach, KCB, CBE, FRAES; Sir John Scarlett, KCMG,
OBE; Rt. Hon. Lord West of Spithead,GCB, DSC;
Prof. Sir Hew Strachan, FRSE; Peter Watkins, CBE;
Jonathan Watkins; Sir Nick Williams
Director-General, Diane Lees
Directors, Richard Ashton *(IWM Duxford);* Graham Boxer
(IWM North), Jon Card *(Secretary, Business and
Governance);* Sue Coleman *(Marketing and Development);*
Samantha Heywood *(Learning and Interpretation);*
Phil Reed *(Churchill War Rooms and HMS Belfast);*
Alan Stoneman *(Corporate Services);* Mark Whitmore
(Collections and Research)

INFORMATION COMMISSIONER'S OFFICE

Wycliffe House, Water Lane, Wilmslow, Cheshire SK9 5AF
T 0303-123 1113 W www.ico.org.uk

The Information Commissioner's Office (ICO) oversees and
enforces the Freedom of Information Act 2000 and the Data
Protection Act 1998, with the objective of promoting public
access to official information and protecting personal
information.

The Data Protection Act 1998 sets out rules for the
processing of personal information and applies to records
held on computers and some paper files. The Freedom of
Information Act 2000 is designed to help end the culture
of unnecessary secrecy and open up the inner workings of
the public sector to citizens and businesses.

The ICO also enforces and oversees the privacy and
electronic communications regulations 2003 and the environmental regulations 2004. It also has limited responsibilities
under the INSPIRE regulations 2009.

The Information Commissioner reports annually to parliament on the performance of his/her functions under the acts
and has obligations to assess breaches of the acts. As of April
2010, the ICO has been able to fine organisations up to
£500,000 for serious breaches of the Data Protection Act.
The budget for 2013–14 was £20m.
Information Commissioner, Christopher Graham

INDUSTRIAL INJURIES ADVISORY COUNCIL

Second Floor, Caxton House, Tothill Street, London SW1H 9NA
T 020-7449 5618 E iiac@dwp.gsi.gov.uk
W www.iiac.independent.gov.uk

The Industrial Injuries Advisory Council was established
under the National Insurance (Industrial Injuries) Act 1946,
which came into effect on 5 July 1948. Statutory provisions
governing its work are set out in the Social Security Administration Act 1992 and corresponding Northern Ireland
legislation. The council currently consists of 17 independent
members appointed by the Secretary of State for Work and
Pensions, and has three roles: to advise on the prescription
of diseases; to consider and advise on draft regulations and
proposals concerning the industrial injuries disablement
benefit scheme referred to it by the Secretary of State for
Work and Pensions or the Department for Social Development in Northern Ireland; and to advise on any other matter
concerning the scheme or its administration.
Chair, Prof. Keith Palmer

JOINT NATURE CONSERVATION COMMITTEE

Monkstone House, City Road, Peterborough PE1 1JY
T 01733-562626 E communications@jncc.gov.uk
W www.jncc.defra.gov.uk

The committee was established under the Environmental
Protection Act 1990 and was reconstituted by the Natural
Environment and Rural Communities Act 2006. It advises
the government and devolved administrations on UK and
international nature conservation issues. Its work contributes
to maintaining and enriching biological diversity, conserving
geological features and sustaining natural systems.
Chair, Prof. Chris Gilligan
Deputy Chair, Judith Webb, MBE

LAW COMMISSION

1st Floor, Tower, 52 Queen Anne's Gate, London SW1H 9AG
T 020-3334 0200 E enquiries@lawcommission.gsi.gov.uk
W www.lawcom.gov.uk

The Law Commission was set up under the Law
Commissions Act 1965 to make proposals to the government
for the examination of the law in England and Wales and for
its revision where it is unsuited for modern requirements,
obscure or otherwise unsatisfactory. It recommends to the
lord chancellor programmes for the examination of different
branches of the law and suggests whether the examination
should be carried out by the commission itself or by some
other body. The commission is also responsible for the
preparation of Consolidation and Statute Law (Repeals) Bills.
Chair, Rt. Hon. Lord Justice Lloyd Jones
Commissioners, Prof. Elizabeth Cooke; David Hertzell;
    Prof. David Ormerod QC; Nicholas Paines, QC
Chief Executive, Elaine Lorimer

NATIONAL ARMY MUSEUM

Royal Hospital Road, London SW3 4HT
T 020-7730 0717 E info@nam.ac.uk
W www.nam.ac.uk

The National Army Museum explores the impact of the
British Army on the story of Britain, Europe and the world.
It was established by royal charter in 1960 and moved to its
current site in Chelsea in 1970. The museum houses a wide
array of artefacts, paintings, photographs, uniforms and
equipment.
Chair, General Sir Jack Deverell, KCB, OBE
Council Members, Keith Baldwin; Patrick Bradley; Algy Cluff;
    Brig. Douglas Erskine Crum; Rt. Hon. Lord Hamilton of
    Epsom; Prof. William Philpott; Lt.-Gen Sir Barney White-
    Spunner; Maj.-Gen. Charles Vyvyan, CB, CBE; Deborah
    Younger
Director-General, Janice Murray, FRSA

NATIONAL GALLERIES OF SCOTLAND

73 Belford Road, Edinburgh EH4 3DS
T 0131-624 6200 E enquiries@nationalgalleries.org
W www.nationalgalleries.org

The National Galleries of Scotland comprise three galleries
in Edinburgh: the National Gallery of Scotland, the Scottish
National Portrait Gallery and the Scottish National Gallery
of Modern Art. There are also partner galleries at Paxton
House, Berwickshire, and Duff House, Banffshire.

TRUSTEES
Chair, Ben Thomson
Trustees, Tricia Bey; Richard Burns; Alistair Dodds;
    Edward Green; Benny Higgins; Prof. Ian Howard;
    Lesley Knox; Tari Lang; Ray Macfarlane; Alasdair Morton;
    Catherine Muirden; Nicky Wilson

OFFICERS
Director-General, Sir John Leighton
Directors, Christopher Baker *(Scottish National Portrait
    Gallery);* Michael Clarke, CBE *(National Gallery of*

Scotland); Nicola Catterall *(Chief Operating Officer);* Dr Simon Groom *(Scottish National Gallery of Modern Art);* Jacqueline Ridge *(Keeper of Conservation)*

NATIONAL GALLERY

Trafalgar Square, London WC2N 5DN
T 020-7747 2885 E information@ng-london.org.uk
W www.nationalgallery.org.uk

The National Gallery, which houses a collection of paintings in the western European tradition from the 13th to the 20th century, was founded in 1824, following a parliamentary grant of £60,000 for the purchase and exhibition of the Angerstein collection of pictures. The present site was first occupied in 1838; an extension to the north of the building with a public entrance in Orange Street was opened in 1975; the Sainsbury Wing was opened in 1991; and the Getty Entrance opened off Trafalgar Square at the east end of the main building in 2004. Total government grant-in-aid for 2014–15 is £25.47m.

BOARD OF TRUSTEES
Chair, Mark Getty
Trustees, Lance Batchelor; Gautam Dalal; Prof. Dexter Dalwood; Lady Heseltine; Sir Michael Hintze; Prof. Anya Hurlbert; John Nelson; Hannah Rothschild; Charles Sebag-Montefiore; Monisha Shah; John Singer; Caroline Thomson

OFFICERS
Director, Dr Nicholas Penny
Director of Public Engagement and Deputy Director, Dr Susan Foister
Director of Finance and Operations, Chris Walker
Director of Collections, Dr Ashok Roy

NATIONAL HERITAGE MEMORIAL FUND

7 Holbein Place, London SW1W 8NR
T 020-7591 6042 E NHMF_Enquiries@nhmf.org.uk
W www.nhmf.org.uk

The National Heritage Memorial Fund was set up under the National Heritage Act 1980 in memory of people who have given their lives for the United Kingdom. The fund provides grants to organisations based in the UK, mainly so that they can buy items of outstanding interest and of importance to the national heritage. These must either be at risk or have a memorial character. The fund is administered by a chair and 14 trustees who are appointed by the prime minister.

The National Heritage Memorial Fund receives an annual grant from the Department for Culture, Media and Sport. Under the National Lottery etc Act 1993, the trustees of the fund became responsible for the distribution of funds for both the National Heritage Memorial Fund and the Heritage Lottery Fund.

Chair, Dame Jenny Abramsky, DBE
Trustees, David Heathcoat-Amory; Dr Manon Antoniazzi; Dr Angela Dean; Sandie Dawe, MBE; Kim Evans; Sir Roger De Haan; Hilary Lade; Steve Miller; Richard Morris; Atul Patel; Dame Seona Reid, DBE; Virginia Tandy; Dr Tom Tew
Chief Executive, Carole Souter, CBE

NATIONAL LIBRARY OF SCOTLAND

George IV Bridge, Edinburgh EH1 1EW
T 0131-623 3700 E enquiries@nls.uk W www.nls.uk

The library, which was founded as the Advocates' Library in 1682, became the National Library of Scotland (NLS) in 1925. Funded by the Scottish government, it contains

about 24 million printed items: two million maps, 25,000 newspaper and magazine titles and over 100,000 manuscripts, including the John Murray Archive. The library receives around 320,000 new items every year and has material in 490 languages. It has an unrivalled Scottish collection as well as online catalogues and digital resources which can be accessed through the NLS website. Material can be consulted in the reading rooms, which are open to anyone with a valid library card.

The National Library of Scotland Act 2012 modernised the make-up and responsibilities of the board of trustees. At present there are 14, one of whom is nominated by the Faculty of Advocates. All of them are appointed by the Scottish ministers.

Chair, James Boyle
National Librarian and Chief Executive, Martyn Wade
Heads of Department, John Coll *(Access);* Graeme Forbes *(Ingest);* Anthony Gillespie *(Finance);* Murat Guven *(Resources);* Alexandra Miller *(Communications and Enterprise);* Robin Smith *(Collections and Interpretation)*

NATIONAL LIBRARY OF WALES/ LLYFRGELL GENEDLAETHOL CYMRU

Aberystwyth, Ceredigion, Wales SY23 3BU
T 01970-632800 W www.llgc.org.uk

The National Library of Wales was founded by royal charter in 1907, and is funded by the Welsh government. It contains about five million printed books, 40,000 manuscripts, four million deeds and documents, numerous maps, prints and drawings, and a sound and moving image collection. It specialises in manuscripts and books relating to Wales and the Celtic peoples. It is the repository for pre-1858 Welsh probate records, manorial records and tithe documents, and certain legal records. Admission is by reader's ticket to the reading rooms but entry to the exhibition programme is free.

Total grant-in-aid from the Welsh government for 2014–15 is £14.4m.

Trustees, Lord Aberdare; David Barker; Tricia Carter; Roy Evans; John Gittins; Sir Deian Hopkin *(President);* Colin John *(Treasurer);* Wyn Penri Jones; Enid Morgan; Roy Roberts; David Hugh Thomas; Michael Trickey; Gareth Haulfryn Williams; Huw Williams
Librarian and Chief Executive, Aled Gruffydd Jones
Heads of Departments, Manon Foster Evans *(Interim Head of Public Services);* Avril Jones *(Collection Services);* David Michael *(Corporate Services)*

NATIONAL LOTTERY COMMISSION

4th Floor, Victoria Square House, Victoria Square, Birmingham B2 4BP
T 0121-230 6750 E info@natlotcomm.gov.uk
W www.natlotcomm.gov.uk

The National Lottery Commission replaced the Office of the National Lottery (OFLOT) in 1999 under the National Lottery Act 1998. The commission is responsible for the granting, varying and enforcing of licences to run the National Lottery. Its duties are to ensure that the National Lottery is run with all due propriety, that the interests of players are protected and, subject to these two objectives, that returns to the good causes are maximised. The commission does not have a role in the distribution of funds to good causes: this is undertaken by 16 distributors.

The Department for Culture, Media and Sport sponsors the National Lottery Commission, which in turn regulates Camelot, the lottery operator. Camelot, was granted a third licence to run the lottery from 1 February 2009 for ten years.

Following the Public Bodies Order 2013, the functions of the National Lottery Commission will be subsumed by the Gambling Commission in late 2013.

Chair, Dr Anne Wright, CBE

Commissioners, Mary Chapman; Robert Foster; James Froomberg; Mark Harris *(Chief Executive);* Deep Sagar; Sarah Thane, CBE

NATIONAL MUSEUM OF THE ROYAL NAVY
HM Naval Base (PP66), Portsmouth PO1 3NH
T 023-9272 7574
W www.nmrn.org.uk

The National Museum of the Royal Navy comprises six museums: HMS *Victory* , the National Museum of the Royal Navy Portsmouth, the Fleet Air Arm Museum, the Royal Navy Submarine Museum, the Royal Marines Museum and Explosion! Museum of Naval Firepower. The Fleet Air Museum is located at RNAS Yeovilton, Somerset, while the other four are situated in Portsmouth and Gosport.

Chair, Adm. Sir Jonathon Band, GCB

Trustees, John Brookes, OBE; Prof. John Craven; Sir Robert Crawford, CBE; Neil Davidson, FCA; Lieut.-Gen. Sir Robert Fulton, KBE; Rear-Adm. Terry Loughran, CB; Vice-Adm. Sir Tim McClement, KCB, OBE; Kim Marshall; Tim Schadla-Hall; Dr Caroline Williams

Director-General, Prof. Dominic Tweddle

NATIONAL MUSEUM WALES/AMGUEDDFA CYMRU
Cathays Park, Cardiff CF10 3NP
T 029-2039 7951
W www.museumwales.ac.uk

National Museum Wales – Amgueddfa Cymru aims to provide a complete illustration of the geology, mineralogy, zoology, botany, ethnography, archaeology, art, history and special industries of Wales. It comprises National Museum Cardiff; St Fagans: National History Museum; Big Pit: National Coal Museum, Blaenafon; National Roman Legion Museum, Caerleon; National Slate Museum, Llanberis; National Wool Museum, Dre-fach Felindre; National Waterfront Museum, Swansea; and National Collections Centre, Nantgarw. Total funding from the Welsh government for 2013–14 is £26.1m.

Trustees, Elisabeth Elias *(President);* Prof. Tony Atkins; Dr Carol Bell; Carole-Anne Davies; Dr Haydn Edwards; Laurence Pavelin; Miriam Hazel Griffiths; Dr Glenda Jones; Emeritus Prof. Richard G. Wyn Jones, FLSW; Christina Macaulay; J. Peter W. Morgan, FCA *(Treasurer);* Prof. Jonathan Osmond; Prof. Robert Pickard; Victoria Mary Provis; Keshav Singhal, MBE; David Beresford Vokes

Director-General, David Anderson

NATIONAL MUSEUMS LIVERPOOL
127 Dale Street, Liverpool L2 2JH
T 0151-207 0001 W www.liverpoolmuseums.org.uk

National Museums Liverpool is a group of museums and collections including the World Museum, the Merseyside Maritime Museum (also home to the Border Force National Museum), the Lady Lever Art Gallery, the Walker Art Gallery, Sudley House, the International Slavery Museum and the Museum of Liverpool.

Chair, Prof. Phil Redmond, CBE

Trustees, Prof. John Ashton, CBE; Carmel Booth; Laura Carstensen; Sir Robert Crawford, CBE; Clive Elphick; Joe Godwin; Nisha Katona; Norma Kurland; Andrew McCluskey; Philip Price; Deborah Shackleton, CBE; Dr Nicola Thorp

Director, Dr David Fleming, OBE

Director of Art Galleries, Sandra Penketh
Director, World Museum Liverpool, Steve Judd
Director, Museum of Liverpool, Janet Dugdale
Head of International Slavery Museum, Dr Richard Benjamin

NATIONAL MUSEUMS NORTHERN IRELAND
Cultra, Holywood, Northern Ireland BT18 0EU
T 0845 608 0000
W www.nmni.com

Across four unique sites National Museums Northern Ireland cares for and presents inspirational collections reflecting the creativity, innovation, history, culture and people of Northern Ireland and beyond.

Together the Ulster Museum, Ulster Folk and Transport Museum, Ulster American Folk Park and Armagh County Museum offer a unique opportunity to experience the heritage and way of life of Northern Ireland.

Chair, Miceal McCoy

Trustees, Prof. Michael Catto; Prof. Garth Earls; Prof. Karen Fleming; Hazel Francey; Daphne Harshaw; Dr Rosemary Kelly; Dr Leon Litvack; Alan McFarland; Dr George McIlroy; Catherine Molloy; Annette Moor; Joseph Rice; Dr Margaret Ward

Director and Chief Executive, Tim Cooke

NATIONAL MUSEUMS SCOTLAND
Chambers Street, Edinburgh EH1 1JF
T 0300-123 6789 E info@nms.ac.uk W www.nms.ac.uk

National Museums Scotland provides advice, expertise and support to the museums community across Scotland, and undertakes fieldwork that often involves collaboration at local, national and international levels. National Museums Scotland comprises the National Museum of Scotland, the National War Museum, the National Museum of Rural Life, the National Museum of Flight, the National Museum of Costume and the National Museums Collection Centre. Its collections represent more than two centuries of collecting and include Scottish and classical archaeology, decorative and applied arts, world cultures and social history and science, technology and the natural world.

Up to 15 trustees can be appointed by the Minister for Culture and External Affairs for a term of four years, and may serve a second term.

Chair, Bruce Minto

Trustees, Prof. Chris Breward; Dr Isabel Bruce, OBE, FRSSA; Gordon Drummond; Chris Fletcher; Dr Anna Gregor, CBE, FRCR, FRCP; Andrew Holmes; Miller McLean, FCIBS, FIB; Prof. Walter Nimmo, FRCA, FRCP, FRSE; James Troughton, RIBA; Iain Watt, FCIBS

Director, Dr Gordon Rintoul

NATIONAL PORTRAIT GALLERY
St Martin's Place, London WC2H 0HE
T 020-7306 0055 W www.npg.org.uk

The National Portrait Gallery was formed after a grant was made in 1856 to form a gallery of the portraits of the most eminent persons in British history. Today the gallery collects portraits of those who have made, or are making, a significant contribution to British history and culture. The collection includes works across all media, from painting and sculpture to photography and digital portraits. The present building was opened in 1896 and the Ondaatje Wing (including the Balcony Gallery, Tudor Gallery, Digital Space, Ondaatje Wing Theatre and roof-top Portrait Restaurant) opened in May 2000. There are three regional partnerships displaying portraits at Montacute House, Beningbrough Hall and Bodelwyddan Castle. Total government grant-in-aid for 2014–15 is £6.96m.

BOARD OF TRUSTEES

Chair, Sir William Proby, Bt., CBE

Trustees, Dr Brian Allen; Allegra Berman; Prof. Dame Carol Black, DBE; Dr Rosalind P. Blakesley; Dr Augustus Casely-Hayford; Kim Evans, OBE; Rt. Hon. Nick Clegg, MP; Rt. Hon. Lord Janvrin, GCB, GCVO, QSO; Christopher Le Brun, PRA; Mary McCartney; David Ross; Stephan Shakespeare; Marina Warner, CBE, FBA

Director, Sandy Nairne

NATURAL ENGLAND

Foundry House, 3 Millsands, Riverside Exchange, Sheffield S3 8NH
T 0845-600 3078 **E** enquiries@naturalengland.org.uk
W www.naturalengland.org.uk

Natural England is the government's adviser on the natural environment, providing practical advice, grounded in science, on how best to safeguard England's natural wealth for the benefit of everyone.

The organisation's remit is to ensure that the natural environment is conserved, enhanced and managed for the benefit of present and future generations, thereby contributing to sustainable development. Its priorities are to reconnect people with nature; protect natural assets; and maximise the opportunities offered by a greener economy.

Natural England works with farmers and land managers; business and industry; planners and developers; national and local government; charities and conservationists; interest groups and local communities to help them improve their local environment.

Chair, Andrew Sells

Chief Executive, Dave Webster

NATURAL HISTORY MUSEUM

Cromwell Road, London SW7 5BD
T 020-7942 5000 **W** www.nhm.ac.uk

The Natural History Museum, which houses 70 million natural history specimens, originates from the natural history departments of the British Museum, which grew extensively during the 19th century; in 1860 it was agreed that the natural history collections should be separated from the British Museum's collections of books, manuscripts and antiquities. Part of the site of the 1862 International Exhibition in South Kensington was acquired for the new museum, and the museum opened to the public in 1881. In 1963 the Natural History Museum became completely independent with its own board of trustees. The Natural History Museum at Tring, bequeathed by the second Lord Rothschild, has formed part of the museum since 1937. The Geological Museum merged with the Natural History Museum in 1985. In September 2009 the Natural History Museum opened the Darwin Centre, which contains public galleries, a high-tech interactive area known as the Attenborough Studio, scientific research facilities and storage for 28 million zoological specimens, 17 million entomology specimens and three million botanical specimens. Total government grant-in-aid for 2014–15 is £43.8m

Chair, Lord Green of Hurstpierpoint

Trustees, Prof. Sir Roy Anderson, FRS, FMEDSCI; Prof. Sir John Beddington, CMG, FRS; Prof. David Drewry; Prof. Christopher Gilligan; Prof. Sir John Holman; Dr Derek Langslow, CBE; Dr Kim Winser, OBE

Museum Director, Dr Michael Dixon

Directors, Neil Greenwood *(Finance and Corporate Services);* Dr Justin Morris *(Public Engagement);* Prof. Ian Owens *(Science)*

NATURAL RESOURCES WALES

Ty Cambria, 29 Newport Road, Cardiff CF24 0TP
T 0300-065 3000 **E** enquiries@naturalresourceswales.gov.uk
W www.naturalresourceswales.gov.uk

Natural Resources Wales is the principal adviser to the Welsh government on the environment. It became operational on 1 April 2013 following a merger of the Countryside Council for Wales, Environment Agency Wales and the Forestry Commission Wales. It is responsible for ensuring that the natural resources of Wales are sustainably maintained, enhanced and used; now and in the future.

Chair, Prof. Peter Matthews, FRSC, FCIWEM, FIWO

Board Members, Harry Legge-Bourke; Dr Mike Brooker; Revd Hywel Davies; Dr Ruth Hall; Dr Madeleine Havard; Andy Middleton; Nigel Reader, CBE; Dr Emyr Roberts *(Chief Executive);* Prof. Lynda Warren; Sir Paul Williams, OBE

NHS PAY REVIEW BODY

6th Floor, Victoria House, Southampton Row, London WC1B 4AD
T 020-7271 0490
W www.gov.uk/government/organisations/nhs-pay-review-body

The NHS Pay Review Body (NHSPRB) makes recommendations to the prime minister, Secretary of State for Health and ministers in Scotland, Wales and Northern Ireland on the remuneration of all paid staff under agenda for change and employed in the NHS. The review body was established in 1983 for nurses and allied health professionals. Its remit has since expanded to cover over 1.8 million staff; ie almost all staff in the NHS, with the exception of dentists, doctors and very senior managers.

Chair, Jerry Cope

Members, Prof. David Blackaby; Dame Denise Holt, DCMG; Joan Ingram; Graham Jagger; Colin Kennedy; Janet Rubin; Prof. Anna Vignoles

NORTHERN IRELAND HUMAN RIGHTS COMMISSION

Temple Court, 39 North Street, Belfast BT1 1NA
T 028-9024 3987 **E** information@nihrc.org **W** www.nihrc.org

The Northern Ireland Human Rights Commission is a non-departmental public body, established by the Northern Ireland Act 1998 and set up in March 1999. Its purpose is to protect and promote human rights in Northern Ireland. Its main functions include reviewing the law and practice relating to human rights, advising government and the Northern Ireland Assembly, and promoting an awareness of human rights. It can also investigate human rights violations and take cases to court. The members of the commission are appointed by the Secretary of State for Northern Ireland.

Interim Chair, John Corey

Commissioners, Christine Collins; Milton Kerr, QPM; Grainia Long; Alan McBride; Marion Reynolds; Paul Yam

Director, Virginia McVea

NORTHERN LIGHTHOUSE BOARD

84 George Street, Edinburgh EH2 3DA
T 0131-473 3100 **E** enquiries@nlb.org.uk
W www.nlb.org.uk

The Northern Lighthouse Board is the general lighthouse authority for Scotland and the Isle of Man and owes its origin to an act of parliament passed in 1786. At present there are 19 commissioners who operate under the Merchant Shipping Act 1995.

The commissioners control 205 lighthouses, many lighted and unlighted buoys, a DGPS (differential global positioning system) station and an ELORAN (long-range navigation) system. *See also* Transport.

Chair, Capt. H. Michael Close

Commissioners, Lord Advocate; Solicitor-General for Scotland; Lord Provosts of Edinburgh, Glasgow and Aberdeen; Convener of Highland Council; Convener of Argyll and Bute Council; Sheriffs-Principal of North Strathclyde, Tayside, Central and Fife, Grampian, Highlands and Islands, South Strathclyde, Dumfries and Galloway, Lothians and Borders and Glasgow and Strathkelvin; Capt. Alastair Beveridge; Capt. Michael Brew; Graham Crerar; Alistair MacKenzie; John Ross, CBE

Chief Executive, Mike Bullock, MBE

NUCLEAR DECOMMISSIONING AUTHORITY

Herdus House, Westlakes Science and Technology Park, Moor Row, Cumbria CA24 3HU

T 01925-802001 E enquiries@nda.gov.uk W www.nda.gov.uk

The Nuclear Decommissioning Authority (NDA) was created under the Energy Act 2004. It is a strategic authority that owns 19 sites and associated civil nuclear liabilities and assets of the public sector, previously under the control of the UK Energy Authority and British Nuclear Fuels. The NDA's responsibilities include decommissioning and cleaning up civil nuclear facilities; ensuring the safe management of waste products, both radioactive and non-radioactive; implementing government policy on the long-term management of nuclear waste; and developing UK-wide low-level waste strategy plans.

Total planned expenditure for 2014–15 is £3.2bn, with total grant-in-aid standing at £2.2bn. The remaining £1bn will come from commercial operations.

Chair, Stephen Henwood

Chief Executive, John Clarke

OFFICE FOR BUDGET RESPONSIBILITY

20 Victoria Street, London SW1H 0NF

T 020-7271 2520 E obrenquiries@obr.gsi.gov.uk

W budgetresponsibility.org.uk

The Office for Budget Responsibility (OBR) was created in 2010 to provide independent and authoritative analysis of the UK's public finances. It has four main roles: producing forecasts for the economy and public finances; judging progress towards the government's fiscal targets; assessing the long-term sustainability of the public finances; and scrutinising HM Treasury's costing of tax and welfare spending measures.

Chair, Robert Chote

Committee Members, Steve Nickell, CBE; Graham Parker, CBE

OFFICE OF COMMUNICATIONS (OFCOM)

Riverside House, 2A Southwark Bridge Road, London SE1 9HA

T 0300-123 3000 W www.ofcom.org.uk

OFCOM was established in 2003 under the Office of Communications Act 2002 as the independent regulator and competition authority for the UK communications industries with responsibility for television, radio, telecommunications and wireless communications services.

Following the passing of the Postal Services Act 2011, OFCOM has assumed regulatory responsibility for postal services from Postcomm, the Postal Services Commission.

Chair, Dame Patricia Hodgson, DBE

Deputy Chair, Baroness Noakes, DBE

Board Members, Jill Ainscough; Dame Lynne Brindley, DBE; Tim Gardam; Stephen Hill; Graham Mather; Mike McTighe

Chief Executive, Ed Richards

OFFICE OF TAX SIMPLIFICATION

HM Treasury, 1 Horse Guards Road, London SW1A 2HQ

E ots@ots.gsi.gov.uk

W www.gov.uk/government/organisations/office-of-tax-simplification

The chancellor and exchequer secretary to HM Treasury launched the Office of Tax Simplification (OTS) on 20 July 2010 to provide the government with independent advice on simplifying the UK tax system.

The Office has been established as an independent office of HM Treasury for the life of the current parliament and draws together expertise from across the tax and legal professions, the business community and other interested parties.

Chair, Rt. Hon. Michael Jack

Tax Director, John Whiting

OFFICE OF MANPOWER ECONOMICS (OME)

6th Floor, Victoria House, Southampton Row, London WC1B 4AD

T 020-7271 0497

W www.gov.uk/government/organisations/office-of-manpower-economics

The Office of Manpower Economics (OME) was established in 1971. It is an independent non-statutory organisation which is responsible for servicing independent review bodies that advise on the pay of various public sector groups, the Police Negotiating Board and the Police Advisory Board for England and Wales. The OME is also responsible for servicing *ad hoc* bodies of inquiry and for undertaking research into pay and associated matters as requested by the government.

OME Director, Geoff Dart

Directors, Jenny Eastabrook *(National Crime Agency Remuneration Review Body, Police Negotiating Board, Police Advisory Board for England and Wales, and School Teachers' Review Body);* Margaret McEvoy *(Chief Economist and Research and Analysis Group);* Stuart Sarson *(Prison Service Pay Review Body and Armed Forces' Pay Review Body);* vacant *(Senior Salaries Review Body, NHS Pay Review Body, and Review Body on Doctors' and Dentists' Remuneration)*

PARADES COMMISSION

Windsor House, 9–15 Bedford Street, Belfast BT2 7EL

T 028-9089 5900 E info@paradescommissionni.org

W www.paradescommission.org

The Parades Commission was set up under the Public Processions (Northern Ireland) Act 1998. Its function is to encourage and facilitate local accommodation of contentious parades; where this is not possible, the commission is empowered to make legal determinations about such parades, which may include imposing conditions on aspects of the notified parade (such as restrictions on routes/areas and exclusion of certain groups with a record of bad behaviour).

The chair and members are appointed by the Secretary of State for Northern Ireland; the membership must, as far as is practicable, be representative of the community in Northern Ireland.

Chair, Anne Henderson

Members, Sarah Havlin; Paul Hutchinson; Colin Kennedy; Frances McCartney

PAROLE BOARD FOR ENGLAND AND WALES

Grenadier House, 99–105 Horseferry Road, London SW1P 2DX

T 0300-047 4600 E info@paroleboard.gov.uk

W www.justice.gov.uk/about/parole-board

The Parole Board was established in 1968 under the Criminal Justice Act 1967 and became an independent executive non-departmental public body on 1 July 1996 under the Criminal Justice and Public Order Act 1994. It is the body that protects the public by making risk assessments about prisoners to decide who may safely be released into the community and who must remain in, or be returned to, custody. Board decisions are taken at two main types of panels of up to three members: 'paper panels' for the majority of cases, or oral hearings for decisions concerning prisoners serving life or indeterminate sentences for public protection. The budget for 2014–15 is £14.2m.
Chair, Sir David Calvert-Smith
Chief Executive, Claire Bassett

PAROLE BOARD FOR SCOTLAND

Saughton House, Broomhouse Drive, Edinburgh EH11 3XD
T 0131-244 8373
E paroleboardforscotlandexecutive@scotland.gsi.gov.uk
W www.scottishparoleboard.gov.uk

The board directs and advises the Scottish ministers on the release of prisoners on licence, and related matters.
Chair, John Watt
Vice-Chair, Terry Powell

PENSION PROTECTION FUND (PPF)

Renaissance, 12 Dingwall Road, Croydon CR0 2NA
T 0845-600 2541 E information@ppf.gsi.gov.uk
W www.pensionprotectionfund.org.uk

The PPF became operational in 2005. It was established to pay compensation to members of eligible defined-benefit pension schemes where a qualifying insolvency event in relation to the employer occurs and where there is a lack of sufficient assets in the pension scheme. The PPF also administers the Financial Assistance Scheme, which helps members whose schemes wound-up before 2005. It is also responsible for the Fraud Compensation Fund (which provides compensation to occupational pension schemes that suffer a loss that can be attributed to dishonesty). The chair and board of the PPF are appointed by, and accountable to, the Secretary of State for Work and Pensions, and are responsible for paying compensation, calculating annual levies (which help fund the PPF), and setting and overseeing investment strategy.
Chair, Lady Judge, CBE
Chief Executive, Alan Rubenstein

PENSIONS REGULATOR

Napier House, Trafalgar Place, Brighton BN1 4DW
T 0845-600 0707 E customersupport@tpr.gov.uk
W www.thepensionsregulator.gov.uk

The Pensions Regulator was established in 2005 as the regulator of work-based pension schemes in the UK, replacing the Occupational Pensions Regulatory Authority (OPRA). It aims to protect the benefits of occupational and personal pension scheme members by working with trustees, employers, pension providers and advisors. The regulator's work focuses on encouraging better management and administration of schemes, ensuring that final salary schemes have a sensible funding plan, and encouraging money purchase schemes to provide members with the information that they need to make informed choices about their pension fund. The Pensions Act 2004 and the Pensions Act 2008 gave the regulator a range of powers which can be used to protect scheme members, but a strong emphasis is placed on educating and enabling those responsible for managing pension schemes, and powers are used only where necessary.

The regulator offers three free online resources to help trustees, employers, professionals and advisors understand their role, duties and obligations.
Chair, Mark Boyle
Interim Chief Executive, Stephen Soper

POLICE ADVISORY BOARD FOR ENGLAND AND WALES

6th Floor, Victoria House, Southampton Row, London WC1B 4AD
T 020-7271 0472
W www.gov.uk/government/organisations/police-advisory-board-for-england-and-wales

The Police Advisory Board for England and Wales was established in 1965 and provides advice to the home secretary on general questions affecting the police in England and Wales. It also considers draft regulations which the secretary of state proposes to make with respect to matters other than hours of duty, leave, pay and allowances or the issue, use and return of police clothing, personal equipment and other effects.
Independent Chair, Elizabeth France
Independent Deputy Chair, Prof. Gillian Morris

POLICE NEGOTIATING BOARD (PNB)

6th Floor, Victoria House, Southampton Row, London WC1B 4AD
T 020-7271 0472
W www.gov.uk/government/organisations/police-negotiating-board

The PNB was established in 1980 to negotiate pay; allowances; hours of duty; the issue, use and return of police clothing, personal equipment and accoutrements; leave; and pensions of UK police officers, and to make recommendations on these matters to the home secretary, the Northern Ireland secretary and Scottish ministers.
Independent Chair, John Randall
Independent Deputy Chair, Prof. Gillian Morris

PRISON SERVICE PAY REVIEW BODY

6th Floor, Victoria House, Southampton Row, London WC1B 4AD
T 020-7271 0465
W www.gov.uk/government/organisations/prison-services-pay-review-body

The Prison Service Pay Review Body was set up in 2001. It makes independent recommendations on the pay of prison governors, operational managers, prison officers and related grades for the Prison Service in England and Wales and for the Northern Ireland Prison Service.
Chair, Dr Peter Knight, CBE
Members, Prof. John Beath; Karen Heaton; Ann Jarvis; Esmond Lindop; Peter Maddison

PRIVY COUNCIL OFFICE

2 Carlton Gardens, London SW1Y 5AA
T 020-7747 5310 E pcosecretariat@pco.x.gsi.gov.uk
W http://privycouncil.independent.gov.uk

The primary function of the office is to act as the secretariat to the Privy Council. It is responsible for the arrangements leading to the making of all royal proclamations and orders in council; for certain formalities connected with ministerial changes; for considering applications for the granting (or amendment) of royal charters; for the scrutiny and approval of by-laws and statutes of chartered institutions and the governing instruments of universities and colleges; and for the appointment of high sheriffs and Privy Council appointments to governing bodies. Under the relevant acts, the office is responsible for the approval of certain regulations and rules made by the regulatory bodies of the medical and certain allied professions.

The Lord President of the Council is the ministerial head of the office and presides at meetings of the Privy Council. The Clerk of the Council is the administrative head of the Privy Council office.

Lord President of the Council and Deputy Prime Minister, Rt. Hon. Nick Clegg, MP

Clerk of the Council, Richard Tilbrook

Head of Secretariat and Deputy Clerk, Ceri King

Deputy Clerk, Christopher Berry

REVIEW BODY ON DOCTORS' AND DENTISTS' REMUNERATION

6th Floor, Victoria House, Southampton Row, London WC1B 4AD

T 020-7271 0486

W www.gov.uk/government/organisations/review-body-on-doctors-and-dentists-remuneration

The Review Body on Doctors' and Dentists' Remuneration was set up in 1971. It advises the prime minister, first ministers in Scotland, Wales and Northern Ireland, and the ministers for Health, in England, Scotland, Wales and Northern Ireland on the remuneration of doctors and dentists taking any part in the National Health Service.

Chair, Prof. Paul Curnan

Members, Lucinda Bolton; Mark Butler; John Glennie, OBE; Alan Henry, OBE; Prof. Kevin Lee; Prof. Steve Thompson; Nigel Turner, OBE

ROYAL AIR FORCE MUSEUM

Grahame Park Way, London NW9 5LL

T 020-8205 2266 E london@rafmuseum.org

W www.rafmuseum.org.uk

The museum has two sites, one at the former airfield at Hendon and the second at Cosford, in the West Midlands, both of which illustrate the development of aviation from before the Wright brothers to the present-day RAF. The museum's collection across both sites consists of over 170 aircraft, as well as artefacts, aviation memorabilia, fine art and photographs.

Chair, Air Chief Marshal Sir Glen Torpy, GCB, CBE, DSO

Trustees, Dr Carol Cole; Brendan Connor; Alan Coppin; Dr Rodney Eastwood, MBE; Lord Hutton of Furness; Gerry Grimstone; Richard Holman; Hon. John Michaelson; Andrew Reid; Michael Schindler; Robin Southwell; Alan Spence; Malcolm G. F. White, OBE

Director-General, Air Vice-Marshal Peter Dye, OBE

ROYAL BOTANIC GARDEN EDINBURGH

20A Inverleith Row, Edinburgh EH3 5LR

T 0131-552 7171 W www.rbge.org.uk

The Royal Botanic Garden Edinburgh (RBGE) originated as the Physic Garden, established in 1670 beside the Palace of Holyroodhouse. The garden moved to its present 28 ha site at Inverleith, Edinburgh, in 1821. There are also three regional gardens: Benmore Botanic Garden, near Dunoon, Argyll; Logan Botanic Garden, near Stranraer, Wigtownshire; and Dawyck Botanic Garden, near Stobo, Peeblesshire. Since 1986 RBGE has been administered by a board of trustees established under the National Heritage (Scotland) Act 1985. It receives an annual grant from the Scottish government's Rural and Environmental Research and Analysis Directorate.

The RBGE is an international centre for scientific research on plant diversity and for horticulture education and conservation. It has an extensive library, a herbarium with almost three million preserved plant specimens, and over 15,000 species in the living collections.

Chair, Sir Muir Russell, KCB, FRSE

Trustees, Prof. Iain Gordon, FRSE; Patricia Henton, FRSE; Angela McNaught; Prof. Thomas Meagher; Diana Murray; Tim Rollinson, CBE; Prof. Janet Sprent, OBE, FRSE; Dr Ian Sword, CBE, FRSE

Regius Keeper and Queen's Botanist in Scotland, Simon Milne, MBE

ROYAL BOTANIC GARDENS, KEW

Kew Gardens, Richmond, Surrey TW9 3AB

T 020-8332 5655 E info@kew.org

Wakehurst, Ardingly, W. Sussex RH17 6TN

T 01444-894066

E wakehurstinfo@kew.org W www.kew.org

Kew Gardens was originally laid out as a private garden for the now demolished White House for George III's mother, Princess Augusta, in 1759. The gardens were much enlarged in the 19th century, notably by the inclusion of the grounds of the former Richmond Lodge. In 1965 Kew acquired the gardens at Wakehurst on a long lease from the National Trust. Under the National Heritage Act 1983 a board of trustees was set up to administer the gardens, which in 1984 became an independent body supported by grant-in-aid from the Department for Environment, Food and Rural Affairs.

The functions of RBG, Kew are to carry out research into plant sciences, to disseminate knowledge about plants and to provide the public with the opportunity to gain knowledge and enjoyment from the gardens' collections. There are extensive national reference collections of living and preserved plants and a comprehensive library and archive. The main emphasis is on plant conservation and biodiversity; Wakehurst houses the Millennium Seed Bank Partnership, which is the largest *ex situ* conservation project in the world – its aim is to save seed from 25 per cent of the earth's wild plant species by 2020.

Chair, Marcus Agius

Trustees, Prof. Michael Crawley; Prof. Jonathan Drori, CBE; Valerie Gooding; Ian Karet; Dr Geoffrey Hawtin; Sir Henry Keswick; George Loudon; Sir Derek Myers; Prof. Malcolm Press; Prof. Nicola Spence; Ms Jennifer Ullman; Sir Ferrers Vyvyan

Director, Richard Deverell

ROYAL COMMISSION ON THE ANCIENT AND HISTORICAL MONUMENTS OF SCOTLAND

John Sinclair House, 16 Bernard Terrace, Edinburgh EH8 9NX

T 0131-662 1456

W www.rcahms.gov.uk

The Royal Commission on the Ancient and Historical Monuments of Scotland (RCAHMS) was established by a royal warrant in 1908, which was revised in 1992, and is appointed to provide for the collecting, recording and interpretation of information on the architectural, industrial, archaeological and maritime heritage of Scotland, to give a picture of the human influence on Scotland's places from the earliest times to the present day. It is funded by the Scottish government. More than 15 million items, including photographs, maps, drawings and documents, are available through the search room, and online databases provide access to over 600,000 images and information on 300,000 buildings and sites. RCAHMS also holds Scotland's national collection of historical aerial photography as well as The Aerial Reconnaissance Archives (TARA) of international wartime photography.

Chair, Prof. John Hume, OBE, FSA SCOT

Commissioners, Dr Kate Byrne, FRSA; Tom Dawson, FSA SCOT; Mark Hopton, FSA SCOT; Dr Jeremy Huggett, FSA, FSA SCOT; Prof. John Hunter, OBE, FSA, FSA

SCOT; Paul Jardine; Dr Gordon Masterton, OBE, FICE, FIES; Jude Quartson-Mochrie; Elspeth Reid
Chief Executive, Diana Murray, FSA, FSA SCOT

ROYAL COMMISSION ON THE ANCIENT AND HISTORICAL MONUMENTS OF WALES

Crown Building, Plas Crug, Aberystwyth SY23 1NJ
T 01970-621200 E nmr.wales@rcahmw.gov.uk
W www.rcahmw.gov.uk

The Royal Commission on the Ancient and Historical Monuments of Wales, established in 1908, is the investigation body and national archive for the historic environment of Wales. It has the lead role in ensuring that Wales's archaeological, built and maritime heritage is authoritatively recorded, and seeks to promote the understanding and appreciation of this heritage nationally and internationally. The commission is funded by the Welsh government.
Chair, Dr Eurwyn Wiliam, FSA
Vice-Chair, Henry Owen-John, FSA
Commissioners, Ms Catherine S. Hardman; Jonathan Hudson; Thomas O. S. Lloyd, OBE, FSA; Dr Mark Redknap, FSA; Prof. Christopher Williams, FRHISTS
Chief Executive. Hilary Malaws

ROYAL MUSEUMS GREENWICH

National Maritime Museum, Greenwich, London SE10 9NF
T 020-8858 4422 W www.rmg.co.uk

Royal Museums Greenwich comprises the National Maritime Museum, the Queen's House and the Royal Observatory Greenwich. It also works in collaboration with the Cutty Sark Trust. The National Maritime Museum provides information on the maritime history of Great Britain and is the largest institution of its kind in the world, with over two million items in its collections related to seafaring, navigation and astronomy. Originally the home of Charles I's Queen, Henrietta Maria, the Queen's House was designed by Inigo Jones and built between 1616–18, although it was structurally altered between 1629–35. It now contains a fine-art collection. The Royal Observatory, Greenwich is the home of Greenwich Mean Time and the prime meridian of the world. It also contains London's only planetarium, Harrison's timekeepers and the UK's largest refracting telescope.
Director, Kevin Fewster, FRSA
Chair, Sir Charles Dunstone
Trustees, Eleanor Boddington; Sir Robert Crawford, CBE; Linda Hutchinson; Dr Christopher Lintott; Joyce Bridges, CBE; Carol Marlow; Jonathan Ofer; Eric Reynolds; Gerald Russell

SCHOOL TEACHERS' REVIEW BODY

6th Floor, Victoria House, Southampton Row, London WC1B 4AD
T 020-7271 0474
W www.gov.uk/government/organisations/school-teachers-review-body

The School Teachers' Review Body was set up under the School Teachers' Pay and Conditions Act 1991. It is required to examine and report on such matters relating to the statutory conditions of employment of school teachers in England and Wales as may be referred to it by the education secretary.
Chair, Dr Patricia Rice
Members, Peter Batley; Jonathan Crossley-Holland; Daniel Flint; Debbie Meech; Jill Pullen; Mike Redhouse

SCIENCE MUSEUM

Exhibition Road, London SW7 2DD
T 0870-870 4868 E info@sciencemuseum.org.uk
W www.sciencemuseum.org.uk

The Science Museum, part of the Science Museum Group (SMG), houses the national collections of science, technology, industry and medicine. The museum began as the science collection of the South Kensington Museum and first opened in 1857. In 1883 it acquired the collections of the Patent Museum and in 1909 the science collections were transferred to the new Science Museum, leaving the art collections with the Victoria and Albert Museum. The Wellcome Wing was opened in July 2000.

The SMG also incorporates the National Railway Museum, York; the National Media Museum, Bradford; Locomotion: the National Railway Museum at Shildon; and the Museum of Science and Industry, Manchester.

Total government grant-in-aid for 2014–15 was £42.39m.
Chair, Dr Gill Samuels, CBE
Trustees, Lady Chisholm; Howard Covington; Prof. Dame Athene Donald, DBE, FRS; Andreas Goss; Lord Grade of Yarmouth, CBE; Lord Faulkner of Worcester; Prof. Ludmilla Jordanova; Simon Linnett; Prof. Averil Macdonald; Sir Howard Newby, CBE; Dr Gill Samuels, CBE; James Smith; Christopher Swinson, OBE
Director of SMG, Ian Blatchford
Director of Science Museum, Ian Blatchford
Director of Museum of Science & Industry, Jean Franczyk
Director of National Media Museum, Jo Quinton-Tulloch
Director of National Railway Museum, Paul Kirkman

SCOTTISH CRIMINAL CASES REVIEW COMMISSION

5th Floor, Portland House, 17 Renfield Street, Glasgow G2 5AH
T 0141-270 7030 E info@sccrc.org.uk W www.sccrc.org.uk

The commission is a non-departmental public body, funded by the Scottish Government Criminal Justice Directorate, and established by Act of Parliament in April 1999. It assumed the role previously performed by the Secretary of State for Scotland to consider alleged miscarriages of justice in Scotland and refer cases meeting the relevant criteria to the high court for determination. Members are appointed by the Queen on the recommendation of the first minister; senior executive staff are appointed by the commission.
Chair, Jean Couper, CBE
Members, Gerrard Bann; Prof. Brian Caddy; Stewart Campbell; Peter Ferguson, QC; Prof. George Irving, CBE; Gerard McClay; Frances McMenamin, QC
Chief Executive, Gerard Sinclair

SCOTTISH ENTERPRISE

Atrium Court, 50 Waterloo Street, Glasgow G2 6HQ
T 0845-607 8787 E enquiries@scotent.co.uk
W www.scottish-enterprise.com

Scottish Enterprise was established in 1991 and its purpose is to stimulate the sustainable growth of Scotland's economy. It is mainly funded by the Scottish government and is responsible to the Scottish ministers. Working in partnership with the private and public sectors, Scottish Enterprise will invest £330m in 2014–15 to further the development of Scotland's economy by helping ambitious and innovative businesses grow and become more successful. Scottish Enterprise is particularly interested in supporting companies that provide renewable energy, encourage trade overseas, increase innovation, and those that will help Scotland

become a low-carbon economy. Its grant-in-aid allocation (capital and resource allocation) for 2014–15 is £254.5m.
Chair, Crawford Gillies
Chief Executive, Dr Lena Wilson

SCOTTISH ENVIRONMENT PROTECTION AGENCY (SEPA)
Erskine Court, Castle Business Park, Stirling FK9 4TZ
T 01786-457700 Hotline 0800-807060
W www.sepa.org.uk

SEPA was established in 1996 and is the public body responsible for environmental protection in Scotland. It regulates pollution to land, air and water; the storage, transport and disposal of controlled waste; and the safekeeping and disposal of radioactive materials. It does this within a complex legislative framework of acts of parliament, EU directives and regulations, granting licences to operations of industrial processes and waste disposal. SEPA also operates Floodline (T 0845-988 1188), a public service providing information on the possible risk of flooding 24 hours a day, 365 days a year.
Chair, David Sigsworth
Chief Executive, Prof. James Curran, MBE
Directors, Calum MacDonald *(Operations);* David Pirie *(Science and Strategy)*

SCOTTISH LAW COMMISSION
140 Causewayside, Edinburgh EH9 1PR
T 0131-668 2131 E info@scotlawcom.gsi.gov.uk
W www.scotlawcom.gov.uk

The Scottish Law Commission, established in 1965, keeps the law in Scotland under review and makes proposals for its development and reform. It is responsible to the Scottish ministers through the Scottish government law and courts directorate.
Chair (part-time), Lord Pentland
Chief Executive, M. McMillan
Commissioners, Ms L. Dunlop, QC; P. Layden, QC, TD; Prof. H. MacQueen; Dr A. Steven

SCOTTISH LEGAL AID BOARD
44 Drumsheugh Gardens, Edinburgh EH3 7SW
T 0131-226 7061 Helpline 0845-122 8686
E general@slab.org.uk W www.slab.org.uk

The Scottish Legal Aid Board was set up under the Legal Aid (Scotland) Act 1986 to manage legal aid in Scotland. It reports to the Scottish government. Board members are appointed by Scottish ministers.
Chair, Iain Robertson, CBE
Members, Les Campbell; Rani Dhir; Alastair Kinroy, QC; Denise Loney; Ray MacFarlane; Vincent McGovern; Bill McQueen, CBE; Ros Micklem; Derek Ogg, QC; Sheriff Ray Small; Graham Watson
Chief Executive, Lindsay Montgomery, CBE

SCOTTISH NATURAL HERITAGE (SNH)
Great Glen House, Leachkin Road, Inverness IV3 8NW
T 01463-725000 E enquiries@snh.gov.uk
W www.snh.org.uk

SNH was established in 1992 under the Natural Heritage (Scotland) Act 1991. It is the government's adviser on all aspects of nature and landscape across Scotland and its role is to help the public understand, value and enjoy Scotland's nature, as well as to support those people and organisations that manage it.
Chair, Ian Ross
Chief Executive, Ian Jardine

Directors, Andrew Bachell *(Operations);* Ron Macdonald *(Policy and Advice);* Joe Moore *(Corporate Services)*

SEAFISH
18 Logie Mill, Logie Green Road, Edinburgh EH7 4HS
T 0131-558 3331 E seafish@seafish.co.uk
W www.seafish.org

Established under the Fisheries Act 1981, Seafish works with all sectors of the UK seafood industry to satisfy consumers, raise standards, improve efficiency and secure a sustainable and profitable future. Services range from research and development, economic consulting, market research and training and accreditation through to legislative advice for the seafood industry. It is sponsored by the four UK fisheries departments, which appoint the board, and is funded by a levy on seafood.
Chair, Elaine Hayes
Chief Executive, Dr Paul Williams

SECURITY AND INTELLIGENCE SERVICES
GOVERNMENT COMMUNICATIONS HEADQUARTERS (GCHQ)
Hubble Road, Cheltenham GL51 0EX
T 01242-221491
W www.gchq.gov.uk

GCHQ produces signals intelligence in support of national security and the UK's economic wellbeing, and in the prevention or detection of serious crime. Additionally, GCHQ's Information Security arm, CESG, is the national technical authority for information assurance, and provides advice and assistance to government departments, the armed forces and other national infrastructure bodies on the security of their communications and information systems. GCHQ was placed on a statutory footing by the Intelligence Services Act 1994 and is headed by a director who is directly accountable to the foreign secretary.
Director, Sir Iain Lobban, KCMG, CB

SECRET INTELLIGENCE SERVICE (MI6)
PO Box 1300, London SE1 1BD
W www.sis.gov.uk

Established in 1909 as the Foreign Section of the Secret Service Bureau, the Secret Intelligence Service produces secret intelligence in support of the government's security, defence, foreign and economic policies. It was placed on a statutory footing by the Intelligence Services Act 1994 and is headed by a chief, known as 'C', who is directly accountable to the foreign secretary.
Chief, Sir John Sawers

SECURITY SERVICE (MI5)
PO Box 3255, London SW1P 1AE
T 020-7930 9000
W www.mi5.gov.uk

The Security Service is responsible for security intelligence work against covertly organised threats to the UK. It is organised into seven branches, each with dedicated areas of responsibility, which include countering terrorism, espionage and the proliferation of weapons of mass destruction. The Security Service also provides security advice to a wide range of organisations to help reduce vulnerability to threats from individuals, groups or countries hostile to UK interests. The home secretary has parliamentary accountability for the Security Service. There is a network of regional offices around the UK plus a Northern Ireland headquarters.
Director-General, Andrew Parker

SENIOR SALARIES REVIEW BODY

6th Floor, Victoria House, Southampton Row, London WC1B 4AD
T 020-7271 0494 W www.ome.uk.com

The Senior Salaries Review Body (formerly the Top Salaries Review Body) was set up in 1971 to advise the prime minister on the remuneration of the judiciary, senior civil servants, senior officers of the armed forces and very senior managers in the NHS. In 1993 its remit was extended to cover the pay, pensions and allowances of MPs, ministers and others whose pay is determined by the Ministerial and Other Salaries Act 1975, and also the allowances of peers. If asked, it advises on the pay of officers and members of the devolved parliament and assemblies.
Chair, Bill Cockburn, CBE, TD
Members, Margaret Edwards; Dame Hazel Glenn, DBE, QC; Prof. David Metcalf, CBE; John Steele; Bruce Warman

STUDENT LOANS COMPANY LTD

100 Bothwell Street, Glasgow G2 7JD
T 0141-306 2000 W www.slc.co.uk

The Student Loans Company (SLC) is owned by the Department for Business, Innovation and Skills and the Secretary of State for Scotland. It processes and administers financial assistance, in the form of grants and loans, for undergraduates who have secured a place at university or college. The SLC also provides loans for tuition fees, which are paid directly to the university or college. In the year 2013–14 the SLC supported around 1.43 million students.
Chair, Christian Brodie
Chief Executive, Mick Laverty

TATE

W www.tate.org.uk

TATE BRITAIN

Millbank, London SW1P 4RG
T 020-7887 8888 E visiting.britain@tate.org.uk

TATE MODERN

Bankside, London SE1 9TG
T 020-7887 8888 E visiting.modern@tate.org.uk

TATE LIVERPOOL

Albert Dock, Liverpool L3 4BB
T 0151-702 7400 E visiting.liverpool@tate.org.uk

TATE ST IVES

Porthmeor Beach, St Ives, Cornwall TR26 1TG
T 01736-796226 E visiting.stives@tate.org.uk

Tate comprises four art galleries: Tate Britain and Tate Modern in London, Tate Liverpool and Tate St Ives.
   Tate Britain, which opened in 1897, displays the national collection of British art from 1500 to the present day – with special attention and dedicated space given to Blake, Turner and Constable. A £45m renovation of Tate Britain was completed in 2013.
   Opened in May 2000, Tate Modern displays the Tate collection of international modern art dating from 1900 to the present day. It includes works by Dalí, Picasso, Matisse and Warhol as well as many contemporary works. It is housed in the former Bankside Power Station in London, which was redesigned by the Swiss architects Herzog and de Meuron.
   Tate Liverpool opened in 1988 and houses mainly 20th-century art and Tate St Ives, which features work by artists from and working in St Ives and includes the Barbara Hepworth Museum and Sculpture Garden, opened in 1993.

BOARD OF TRUSTEES

Chair, Lord Browne of Madingley
Trustees, Tomma Abts; Lionel Barber; Tom Bloxham, MBE; Mala Gaonkar; Maja Hoffman; Lisa Milroy; Elisabeth Murdoch; Franck Petitgas; Dame Seona Reid, DBE; Hannah Rothschild; Monisha Shah; Gareth Thomas; Wolfgang Tillmans

OFFICERS

Director, Tate, Sir Nicholas Serota, CH
Directors, Dr Penelope Curtis *(Tate Britain);* Chris Dercon *(Tate Modern);* Caroline Collier *(Tate National);* Andrea Nixon *(Tate Liverpool);* Mark Osterfield *(Tate St Ives)*

TOURISM BODIES

Visit Britain, Visit Scotland, Visit Wales and the Northern Ireland Tourist Board are responsible for developing and marketing the tourist industry in their respective regions. Visit Wales is not listed here as it is part of the Welsh government, within the Department for Heritage, and not a public body.

VISITBRITAIN

Sanctuary Buildings, 20 Great Smith Street, London SW1P 3BT
T 020-7578 1000 E industry.relations@visitbritain.org
W www.visitbritain.com
Chair, Christopher Rodrigues, CBE
Chief Executive (interim), Keith Beecham

VISIT SCOTLAND

Ocean Point One, 94 Ocean Drive, Edinburgh EH6 6JH
T 0131-472 2222
E info@visitscotland.com W www.visitscotland.com
Chair, Dr Mike Cantlay
Chief Executive, Malcolm Roughead, OBE

NORTHERN IRELAND TOURIST BOARD

59 North Street, Belfast BT1 1NB T 028-9023 1221
W www.discovernorthernireland.com
Chair, Dr Howard Hastings
Chief Executive, Alan Clarke

TRANSPORT FOR LONDON (TFL)

Windsor House, 42–50 Victoria Street, London SW1H 0TL
E enquire@tfl.gov.uk W www.tfl.gov.uk

TfL was created in July 2000 and is the integrated body responsible for the capital's transport system. Its role is to implement the Mayor of London's transport strategy and manage the transport services across London for which the mayor has responsibility. These services include London's buses, London Underground, London Overground, the Docklands Light Railway (DLR), Tramlink, London River Services and Victoria Coach Station. TfL also runs the Emirates Air Line and the London Transport Museum.
   TfL is responsible for managing the Congestion Charging scheme and for maintaining 360 miles (580km) of main roads and all of London's 6,000 traffic lights. It also regulates the city's taxis and private hire vehicles. TfL runs Barclays Cycle Hire and the Dial-a-ride scheme, a door-to-door service for disabled people unable to use buses, trams or the London Underground.
Chair, Boris Johnson
Members, Peter Anderson; Sir John Armitt, CBE; Sir Brendan Barber; Richard Barnes; Charles Belcher; Roger Burnley; Brian Cooke; Isabel Dedring; Baroness Grey-Thompson, DBE; Angela Knight; Michael Liebreich; Eva Lindholm; Daniel Moylan; Bob Oddy; Keith Williams; Steve Wright, MBE
Commissioner, Sir Peter Hendy, CBE

UK ATOMIC ENERGY AUTHORITY

Culham Science Centre, Abingdon, Oxfordshire OX14 3DB
T 01235-528822 W www.gov.uk/government/organisations/uk-atomic-energy-authority

The UK Atomic Energy Authority (UKAEA) was established by the Atomic Energy Authority Act 1954 and took over responsibility for the research and development of the civil nuclear power programme. The UKAEA reports to the Department for Business, Innovation and Skills and is responsible for managing UK fusion research including operating the Joint European Torus (JET) on behalf of the UKAEA's European partners at its site in Culham, Oxfordshire. In October 2009, as part of the government's Operation Efficiency Programme, the authority sold its commercial arm, UKAEA Limited; as a result, the UKAEA no longer provides nuclear decommissioning services.
Chair, Prof. Roger Cashmore
Chief Executive, Prof. Steven Cowley

UK SPORT

40 Bernard Street, London WC1N 1ST
T 020-7211 5100 E info@uksport.gov.uk W www.uksport.gov.uk

UK Sport was established by royal charter in 1997 and is accountable to parliament through the Department for Culture, Media and Sport. Its mission is to lead sport in the UK to world-class success. This means working with partner organisations to deliver medals at the Olympic and Paralympic Games and organising, bidding for and staging major sporting events in the UK; increasing the UK's sporting activity and influence overseas; and promoting sporting conduct, ethics and diversity in society. UK Sport is funded by a mix of grant-in-aid and National Lottery income. For 2014–15 projected grant-in-aid and National Lottery funding will amount to approximately £111m.
Chair, Rod Carr, CBE
Chief Executive, Liz Nicholl, OBE

VICTORIA AND ALBERT MUSEUM

Cromwell Road, London SW7 2RL
T 020-7942 2000 W www.vam.ac.uk

The Victoria and Albert Museum (V&A) is the national museum of fine and applied art and design. It descends directly from the Museum of Manufactures, which opened in Marlborough House in 1852 after the Great Exhibition of 1851. The museum was moved in 1857 to become part of the South Kensington Museum. It was renamed the Victoria and Albert Museum in 1899. It also houses the National Art Library and Print Room.

The museum administers the V&A Museum of Childhood at Bethnal Green, which opened in 1872; the building is the most important surviving example of the type of glass and iron construction used by Joseph Paxton for the Great Exhibition. Total government grant-in-aid for 2013–14 is £39m.
Chair, Sir Paul Ruddock
Trustees, Joao Baptista; Nicholas Coleridge, CBE; Mark Damazer, CBE; Prof. Margot Finn; Andrew Hochhauser, QC; Stephen McGuckin; Michelle Ogundehin; Dame Theresa Sackler, DBE; Mark Sebba; Caroline Silver; Samir Shah, OBE; Sir John Sorrell; Bob Stefanowski; Dr Paul Thompson; Edmund de Waal, OBE; Prof. Evelyn Welch
Director, Prof. Martin Roth

WALLACE COLLECTION

Hertford House, Manchester Square, London W1U 3BN
T 020-7563 9500 E collections@wallacecollection.org
W www.wallacecollection.org

The Wallace Collection was bequeathed to the nation by the widow of Sir Richard Wallace, in 1897, and Hertford House was subsequently acquired by the government. The collection contains works by Titian and Rembrandt, and includes porcelain, furniture and an array of arms and armour.
Chair, Sir John Ritblat
Trustees, Prof. Jasper Conran, OBE; Prof. Frances Corner, OBE; Duke of Devonshire, KCVO, CBE; Jennifer Eady, QC; Rupert Hambro; Jagdip Jagpal; Denise Lewis; Jessica Pulay; Sir Hugh Roberts, GCVO, FSA; Kate de Rothschild Agius; Dr Ashok Roy; Adrian Sassoon; TImothy Schrofer
Director, Dr Christoph Vogtherr

REGIONAL GOVERNMENT

LONDON

GREATER LONDON AUTHORITY (GLA)
City Hall, The Queen's Walk, London SE1 2AA
T 020-7983 4000 E mayor@london.gov.uk
W www.london.gov.uk

On 7 May 1998 London voted in favour of the formation of the Greater London Authority (GLA). The first elections to the GLA took place on 4 May 2000 and the new authority took over its responsibilities on 3 July 2000. In July 2002 the GLA moved to one of London's most spectacular buildings, newly built on a brownfield site on the south bank of the Thames, adjacent to Tower Bridge. The fourth and most recent election to the GLA took place on 3 May 2012.

The structure and objectives of the GLA stem from its main areas of responsibility: transport, policing, fire and emergency planning, economic development, planning, culture and health. There are four functional bodies which form part of the wider GLA group and report to the GLA: the Mayor's Office for Policing and Crime (MOPAC), Transport for London (TfL), the London Fire and Emergency Planning Authority (LFEPA) and the London Legacy Development Corporation, established in 2012.

The GLA consists of a directly elected mayor, the Mayor of London, and a separately elected assembly, the London Assembly. The mayor has the key role of decision making, with the assembly performing the tasks of regulating and scrutinising these decisions, and investigating issues of importance to Londoners. In addition, the GLA has around 600 permanent staff to support the activities of the mayor and the assembly, which are overseen by a head of paid service. The mayor may appoint two political advisers and not more than ten other members of staff, though he does not necessarily exercise this power, but he does not appoint the chief executive, the monitoring officer or the chief finance officer. These must be appointed jointly by the assembly and the mayor.

Every aspect of the assembly and its activities must be open to public scrutiny and therefore accountable. The assembly holds the mayor to account through scrutiny of his strategies, decisions and actions. Mayor's Question Time, conducted on ten occasions a year at City Hall, is carried out by direct questioning at assembly meetings and by conducting detailed investigations in committee.

People's Question Time and Talk London give Londoners the chance to question the mayor and the assembly about plans, priorities and policies for London. People's Question Time is held twice a year, and Talk London is held four times a year in venues across London.

The role of the mayor can be broken down into a number of key areas:
• to represent and promote London at home and abroad and speak up for Londoners
• to devise strategies and plans to tackle London-wide issues, such as crime, transport, housing, planning, economic development and regeneration, environment, public services, society and culture, sport and health; and to set budgets for TfL, MOPAC, LFEPA and the London Legacy Development Corporation
• the mayor is chair of TfL, and is responsible for the Metropolitan Police's priorities and performance

The role of the assembly can be broken down into a number of key areas:
• to hold the mayor to account by examining his decisions and actions
• to have the power to amend the mayor's budget by a majority of two-thirds
• to have the power to summon the mayor, senior staff of the GLA and functional bodies
• to investigate issues of London-wide significance and make proposals to appropriate stakeholders
• to examine the work of MOPAC and to review the police and crime plan for London through the newly formed Police and Crime Committee

Mayor, Boris Johnson
Deputy Mayors, Victoria Borwick *(Statutory Deputy Mayor);* Richard Blakeway *(Housing, Land and Property);* Isabel Dedring *(Transport);* Stephen Greenhalgh *(Policing and Crime);* Sir Edward Lister *(Policy and Planning, and Chief of Staff);* Kit Malthouse *(Business and Enterprise);* Munira Mirza *(Education and Culture)*
Chair of the London Assembly, Roger Evans
Deputy Chair of the Assembly, Jennette Arnold, OBE

ELECTIONS AND VOTING SYSTEMS
The assembly is elected every four years at the same time as the mayor, and consists of 25 members. There is one member from each of the 14 GLA constituencies topped up with 11 London-wide members who are either representatives of political parties or individuals standing as independent candidates. The last election was on 3 May 2012.

Two distinct voting systems are used to appoint the existing mayor and the assembly. The mayor is elected using the supplementary vote system (SVS). With SVS, electors have two votes: one to give a first choice for mayor and one to give a second choice; they cannot vote twice for the same candidate. If one candidate gets more than half of all the first-choice votes, he or she becomes mayor. If no candidate gets more than half of the first-choice votes, the two candidates with the most first-choice votes remain in the election and all the other candidates drop out. The second-choice votes on the ballot papers for the candidates who are then counted. Where these second-choice votes are for the two remaining candidates they are added to the first-choice votes these candidates already have. The candidate with the most first- and second-choice votes combined becomes the Mayor of London.

The assembly is appointed using the additional member system (AMS). Under AMS, electors have two votes. The first vote is for a constituency candidate. The second vote is for a party list or individual candidate contesting the London-wide assembly seats. The 14 constituency members are elected under the first-past-the-post system, the same system used in general and local elections. Electors vote for one candidate and the candidate with the most votes wins. The additional members are drawn from party lists or are independent candidates who stand as London members; they are chosen using a form of proportional representation.

The Greater London Returning Officer (GLRO) is the independent official responsible for running the election in London. He is supported in this by returning officers in each of the 14 London constituencies.
GLRO, Jeff Jacobs

TRANSPORT FOR LONDON (TFL)

TfL is the integrated body responsible for London's transport system. Its role is to implement the mayor's transport strategy for London and manage transport services across the capital for which the mayor has responsibility. TfL is directed by a management board whose members are chosen for their understanding of transport matters and are appointed by the mayor, who chairs the board. TfL's role is:

- to manage the London Underground, buses, Croydon Tramlink, London Overground and the Docklands Light Railway (DLR)
- to manage a 580km network of main roads and all 6,000 of London's traffic lights
- to regulate taxis and minicabs
- to run the London River Services, Victoria Coach Station and London Transport Museum
- to help to coordinate the Dial-a-Ride, Capital Call and Taxicard schemes for door-to-door services for transport users with mobility problems

The London Borough Councils maintain the role of highway and traffic authorities for 95 per cent of London's roads. A congestion charge for motorists driving into central London between the hours of 7am and 6.30pm, Monday to Friday (excluding public holidays) was introduced on 17 February 2003. On 19 February 2007, the charge zone roughly doubled in size after a westward expansion and the charging hours were shortened, to finish at 6pm. On 4 January 2011, the westward expansion was removed from the charging zone and an automated payment system was also introduced. As at September 2014 the daily congestion charge was £11.50 (£10.50 if paid via the automated service).

TfL introduced a low emission zone (LEZ) for London on 4 February 2008 which is in constant operation. Following tougher emissions standards introduced on 3 January 2012 there is a daily charge for polluting vehicles entering the zone (which covers most of Greater London) that do not meet Euro 3 or Euro 4 emissions standards. With the exception of minibuses, vehicles over three-and-a-half tonnes such as lorries, buses and coaches, face a daily charge of £200. Vehicles up to three-and-a-half tonnes and minibuses (with more than eight passenger seats) up to five tonnes pay a daily charge of £100. For further information see W www.tfl.gov.uk/lez

Since 2 January 2009, Londoners over pensionable age (or over 60 if born before 1950) and those with eligible disabilities are entitled to free travel on the capital's transport network at any time. War veterans who are receiving on-going payments under the war pensions scheme, or those receiving guaranteed income payments under the armed forces compensation scheme can travel free at any time on bus, underground, DLR, tram and London Overground services and at certain times on National Rail services.

In the summer of 2010, the London cycle hire scheme launched with 6,000 new bicycles for hire from 400 docking stations across eight boroughs, the City and the Royal parks. The scheme has been expanded and there are now around 10,000 bicycles available.

Commissioner of Transport for London, Sir Peter Hendy, CBE

MAYOR'S OFFICE FOR POLICING AND CRIME (MOPAC)

The Mayor's Office for Policing and Crime (MOPAC) was set up in response to the Police Reform and Social Responsibility Act 2011, replacing the Metropolitan Police Authority. MOPAC is headed by the mayor, or the appointed statutory deputy mayor for policing and crime. Operational responsibility for policing in London belongs to the Metropolitan Police Commissioner. The major areas of focus of MOPAC are:

- operational policing and crime reduction including counter terrorism
- ensuring the Metropolitan Police effectively reduce gang crime and violence in London and coordinating support for communities and local organisations to prevent gang activities
- criminal justice, including preventing reoffending, reducing crime and decreasing demand within the criminal justice system in addition to reducing alcohol and drug abuse.

The Police and Crime Committee consisting of nine elected members of the London Assembly scrutinises the work of MOPAC and meets regularly to hold to account the Deputy Mayor for Policing and Crime.

Deputy Mayor for Policing and Crime, Stephen Greenhalgh

LONDON FIRE AND EMERGENCY PLANNING AUTHORITY (LFEPA)

In July 2000 the London Fire and Civil Defence Authority became the London Fire and Emergency Planning Authority. It consists of 17 members, eight drawn from the assembly, seven from the London boroughs and two mayoral appointees. The role of the LFEPA is:

- to set the strategy for the provision of fire services
- to ensure that the fire brigade can meet all the normal requirements efficiently
- to ensure that effective arrangements are made for the fire brigade to receive emergency calls and deal with them promptly
- to ensure members of the fire brigade are properly trained and equipped
- to ensure that information useful to the development of the fire brigades is gathered
- to ensure arrangements for advice and guidance on fire protection are made

Chair, James Cleverly

LONDON LEGACY DEVELOPMENT CORPORATION

Following the London 2012 Olympic Games, the London Legacy Development Corporation was made responsible for the long-term planning, development, management and maintenance of the Queen Elizabeth Olympic Park (formerly the Olympic Park) and its facilities. The organisation is tasked with transforming the area into a thriving neighbourhood.

Chair, Boris Johnson

SALARIES *as at July 2014*	
Mayor	£143,911
Deputy Mayors	
Victoria Borwick	£97,053
Richard Blakeway	£129,062
Isabel Dedring	£129,062
Stephen Greenhalgh	£129,062
Sir Edward Lister	£150,000
Kit Malthouse	£129,062
Munira Mirza	£129,062
Chair of the Assembly	£64,744
Assembly Members	£53,973

LONDON ASSEMBLY COMMITTEES

Chair, Audit Panel, John Biggs
Chair, Budget and Performance Committee, John Biggs
Chair, Budget Monitoring Sub-Committee, John Biggs
Chair, Confirmation Hearings Committee, various
Chair, Economy Committee, Jenny Jones
Chair, Education Panel, Jennette Arnold, OBE
Chair, Environment Committee, Stephen Knight
Chair, GLA Oversight Committee, Len Duvall

Chair, Health Committee, Onkar Sahota
Chair, Housing Committee, Darren Johnson
Chair, Planning Committee, Nicky Gavron
Chair, Police and Crime Committee, Joanne McCartney
Chair, Regeneration Committee, Gareth Bacon
Chair, Taser Working Group, Joanne McCartney
Chair, Transport Committee, Caroline Pidgeon, MBE

LONDON ASSEMBLY MEMBERS
as at 3 May 2012

Arbour, Tony, *C., South West,* Maj. 19,262
Arnold, Jennette, *Lab. North East,* Maj. 66,188
Bacon, Gareth, *C., London List*
Biggs, John, *Lab., City and East,* Maj. 82,744
Boff, Andrew, *C., London List*
Borwick, Victoria, *C., London List*
Cleverly, James, *C., Bexley and Bromley,* Maj. 47,768
Copley, Tom, *Lab. London List*
Dismore, Andrew, *Lab., Barnet and Camden,* Maj. 21,299
Duvall, Len, *Lab., Greenwich and Lewisham,* Maj. 38,037
Evans, Roger, *C., Havering and Redbridge,* Maj. 3,899
Gavron, Nicky, *Lab., London List*
Johnson, Darren, *Green, London List*
Jones, Jenny, *Green, London List*
Knight, Stephen, *LD, London List*
Malthouse, Kit, *C., West Central,* Maj. 29,131
McCartney, Joanne, *Lab., Enfield and Haringey,* Maj. 36,741
O'Connell, Steve, *C., Croydon and Sutton,* Maj. 9,418
Pidgeon, Caroline, *LD, London List*
Qureshi, Murad, *Lab., London List*
Sahota, Onkar, *Lab., Ealing and Hillingdon,* Maj. 3,110
Shah, Navin, *Lab., Brent and Harrow,* Maj. 29,796
Shawcross, Valerie, *Lab., Lambeth and Southwark,* Maj. 52,702
Tracey, Richard, *C., Merton and Wandsworth,* Maj. 9,981
Twycross, Fiona, *Lab., London List*

STATE OF THE PARTIES *as at 3 May 2012*

Party	Seats
Conservative (C.)	9
Labour (Lab.)	12
Liberal Democrats (LD)	2
Green	2

MAYORAL ELECTION RESULTS
as at 3 May 2012

Electorate 5,910,460   Turnout 38%

Change in turnout from 2008: -7.33%
Good votes: 1st choice 2,208,475 (98.21%); 2nd choice 1,763,009 (79.83%)
Rejected votes: 1st choice 40,210 (1.79%); 2nd choice 445,466 (20.17%)

First	Party	Votes	%
Boris Johnson	C.	971,931	44.01
Ken Livingstone	Lab.	889,918	40.30
Jenny Jones	Green	98,913	4.48
Brian Paddick	LD	91,774	4.16
Siobhan Benita	Ind.	83,914	3.80
Lawrence Webb	UKIP	43,274	1.96
Carlos Cortiglia	BNP	28,751	1.30

Second	Party	Votes	%
Brian Paddick	LD	363,692	20.63
Jenny Jones	Green	363,193	20.60
Ken Livingstone	Lab.	335,398	19.02
Boris Johnson	C.	253,709	14.39
Siobhan Benita	Ind.	212,412	12.05
Lawrence Webb	UKIP	161,252	9.15
Carlos Cortiglia	BNP	73,353	4.16

LONDON ASSEMBLY ELECTION RESULTS
as at 3 May 2012
E. Electorate T. Turnout
See General Election Results for a list of party abbreviations

CONSTITUENCIES
E. 5,910,460 T. 38%

BARNET AND CAMDEN
E. 446,248 T. 38%

Andrew Dismore, Lab.	74,677
Brian Coleman, C.	53,378
Audrey Poppy, Green	17,904
Chris Richards, LD	13,800
Michael Corby, UKIP	7,331
Lab. majority 21,299	

BEXLEY AND BROMLEY
E. 447,465 T. 38.1%

James Cleverly, C.	88,482
Josie Channer, Lab.	40,714
Sam Webber, LD,	11,396
David Cobum, UKIP	10,771
Jonathan Rooks, Green	9,209
Donna Treanor, BNP	7,563
C. majority 47,768	

BRENT AND HARROW
E. 389,737 T. 38%

Navin Shah, Lab.	70,400
Sachin Rajput, C.	40,604
Charlotte Henry, LD	15,690
Shahrar Ali, Green	10,546
Mick McGough, UKIP	7,830
Lab. majority 29,796	

CITY AND EAST
E. 500,427 T. 34.8%

John Biggs, Lab.	107,667
John Moss, C.	24,923
Chris Smith, Green	10,891
Richard Macmillan, LD	7,351
Paul Borg, BNP	7,031
Kamran Malik, CUP	6,774
Steven Woolfe, UKIP	5,243
Paul Davies, Comm. Lge	1,108
Lab. majority 82,744	

CROYDON AND SUTTON
E. 436,451 T. 35.7%

Stephen O'Connell, C.	60,152
Louisa Woodley, Lab.	50,734
Abigail Lock, LD	21,889
Winston McKenzie, UKIP	10,757
Gordon Ross, Green	10,287
C. majority 9,418	

EALING AND HILLINGDON
E. 439,143 T. 37.9%

Onkar Sahota, Lab.	65,584
Richard Barnes, C.	62,474
Michael Cox, LD	11,805
Mike Harling, Green	10,877
Helen Knight, UKIP	6,750
Dave Furness, BNP	4,284
Ian Edward, NF	2,035
Lab. majority 3,110	

ENFIELD AND HARINGEY
E. 383,623 T. 38.3%

Joanne McCartney, Lab.	74,034
Andy Hemsted, C.	37,293
Dawn Barnes, LD	13,601
Peter Krakowiak, Green	12,278
Peter Staveley, UKIP	4,298
Marie Nicholas, BNP	3,081

Lab. majority 36,741

GREENWICH AND LEWISHAM
E. 359,742 T. 37.2%

Len Duvall, Lab.	65,366
Alex Wilson, C.	27,329
Roger Sedgley, Green	12,427
John Russell, LD	9,393
Barbara Raymond, PBP	6,873
Paul Oakley, UKIP	4,997
Roberta Woods, BNP	3,551
Tess Culnane, NF	1,816

Lab. majority 38,037

HAVERING AND REDBRIDGE
E. 389,814 T. 36.9%

Roger Evans, C.	53,285
Mandy Richards, Lab.	49,386
Lawrence Webb, UKIP	9,471
Melvin Brown, RAL	8,239
Farrukh Islam, LD	6,435
Robert Taylor, BNP	5,234
Haroon Saad, Green	5,207
Mark Twiddy, Eng. Dem.	2,573
Richard Edmonds, NF	1,936

C. majority 3,899

LAMBETH AND SOUTHWARK
E. 422,981 T. 37.8%

Valerie Shawcross, Lab.	83,239
Michael Mitchell, C.	30,537
Rob Blackie, LD	18,359
Jonathan Bartley, Green	18,144
James Fluss, UKIP	4,395
Daniel Lambert, Soc.	2,938

Lab. majority 52,702

MERTON AND WANDSWORTH
E. 376,365 T. 40.9%

Richard Tracey, C.	65,197
Leonie Cooper, Lab.	55,216
Lisa Smart, LD	11,904
Roy Vickery, Green	11,307
Mazhar Manzoor, UKIP	3,717
Thamilini Kulendran, Ind.	2,424
James Martin, Soc.	1,343

C. majority 9,981

NORTH EAST
E. 499,418 T. 39.1%

Jennette Arnold, Lab.	101,902
Naomi Newstead, C.	35,714
Caroline Allen, Green	29,677
Farooq Qureshi, LD	13,237
Paul Wiffen, UKIP	6,623
Ijaz Hayat, Ind.	4,842

Lab. majority 66,188

SOUTH WEST
E. 437,945 T. 40.2%

Tony Arbour, C.	69,151
Lisa Homan, Lab.	49,889
Munira Wilson, LD	28,947
Daniel Goldsmith, Green	17,070
Jeff Bolter, UKIP	8,505

C. majority 19,262

WEST CENTRAL
E. 381,101 T. 39.2%

Kit Malthouse, C.	73,761
Todd Foreman, Lab.	44,630
Susanna Rustin, Green	12,799
Layla Moran, LD	10,035
Elizabeth Jones, UKIP	5,161

C. majority 29,131

LONDON-WIDE MEMBERS

Conservative	*Labour Party*
Gareth Bacon	Tom Copley
Andrew Boff	Nicky Gavron
Victoria Borwick	Murad Qureshi
	Fiona Twycross

Green Party	*Liberal Democrat*
Darren Johnson	Stephen Knight
Jenny Jones	Caroline Pidgeon

WALES

WELSH GOVERNMENT

Cathays Park, Cardiff CF10 3NQ
T 0845-010 3300 W http://wales.gov.uk

The Welsh government is the devolved government of Wales. It is accountable to the National Assembly for Wales, the Welsh legislature which represents the interests of the people of Wales, and makes laws for Wales. The Welsh government and the National Assembly for Wales were established as separate institutions under the Government of Wales Act 2006.

The Welsh government comprises the first minister, who is usually the leader of the largest party in the National Assembly for Wales; up to 14 ministers and deputy ministers; and a counsel general (the chief legal adviser).

Following the referendum on 3 March 2011 on granting further law-making powers to the National Assembly, the Welsh government's functions now include the ability to propose bills to the National Assembly on subjects within 20 set areas of policy. Subject to limitations prescribed by the Government of Wales Act 2006, acts of the National Assembly may make any provision that could be made by act of parliament. The 20 areas of responsibility devolved to the National Assembly for Wales (and within which Welsh ministers exercise executive functions) are: agriculture, fisheries, forestry and rural development; ancient monuments and historic buildings; culture; economic development; education and training; environment; fire and rescue services and promotion of fire safety; food; health and health services; highways and transport; housing; local government; the National Assembly for Wales; public administration; social welfare; sport and recreation; tourism; town and county planning; water and flood defence; and the Welsh language.

First Minister of Wales, Rt. Hon. Carwyn Jones, AM
Minister for Communities and Tackling Poverty, Jeff Cuthbert, AM
Minister for Culture and Sport, John Griffiths, AM
Minister for Economy, Science and Transport, Edwina Hart, MBE, AM
Minister for Education and Skills, Huw Lewis, AM
Minister for Finance and Leader of the House, Jane Hutt, AM
Minister for Health and Social Services, Mark Drakeford, AM
Minister for Housing, Regeneration and Planning, Carl Sargeant, AM
Minister for Local Government and Government Business, Lesley Griffiths, AM
Minister for Natural Resources and Food, Alun Davies, AM
Deputy Minister for Communities and Tackling Poverty, Vaughan Gething, AM
Deputy Minister for Children and Social Services, Gwenda Thomas, AM
Deputy Minister for Skills and Technology, Ken Skates, AM
Counsel General of Wales, Theodore Huckle, QC
Chief Whip, Janice Gregory, AM

MANAGEMENT BOARD

Permanent Secretary, Sir Derek Jones, KCB
Director-General, Finance and Corporate Services, Michael Hearty
Director-General, Economy, Science and Transport, James Price
Director-General, Education and Skills, Owen Evans
Director-General, Health, Social Services and Children and Chief Executive of NHS Wales, Andrew Goodhall
Director-General, Local Government and Communities, Dr June Milligan
Director-General, People, Places and Corporate Services, Bernard Galton

Director-General, Sustainable Futures, Gareth Jones (acting)
Non-Executive Directors, Elan Closs Stephens; James Turner; Adrian Webb

DEPARTMENTS

Department for Education and Skills
Department for Health, Social Services and Children
Department for Economy, Science and Transport
Department for Strategic Planning, Finance and Performance
Local Government and Communities
People, Places and Corporate Services
Permanent Secretary's Division (Office of the First Minister; Legal Services Department; European and External Affairs Division; Constitutional Affairs and Inter-governmental Relations Division)
Sustainable Futures

ASSEMBLY COMMITTEES

Children and Young People
Communities, Equality and Local Government
Constitutional and Legislative Affairs
Enterprise and Business
Environment and Sustainability
Finance
Health and Social Care
Petitions
Public Accounts
Scrutiny of the First Minister
Standards of Conduct

ASSEMBLY COMMISSION

The Assembly Commission was created under the Government of Wales Act 2006 to ensure that the assembly is provided with the property, staff and services required for it to carry out its functions. The commission also sets the National Assembly's strategic aims, objectives, standards and values. The Assembly Commission consists of the presiding officer, plus four other assembly members, one nominated by each of the four party groups. The five commissioners are accountable to the National Assembly.

Presiding Officer, Dame Rosemary Butler, DBE, AM
Commissioners, Peter Black, Angela Burns, Rhodri Glyn Thomas, Sandy Mewies
Chief Executive and Clerk of the Assembly, Claire Clancy

NATIONAL ASSEMBLY FOR WALES

Cardiff Bay, Cardiff CF99 1NA
T 0845-010 5500 W www.assemblywales.org

In July 1997 the government announced plans to establish a National Assembly for Wales. In a referendum in September 1997 about 50 per cent of the electorate voted, of whom 50.3 per cent voted in favour of a national assembly. Elections are held every four years and the first election took place on 6 May 1999. The fourth election took place on 5 May 2011. There has been a minority Labour administration since the 2011 elections.

National Assembly members are elected using the additional member system. Voters are given two votes: one for a constituency member and one for a regional member. The constituency members are elected under the first-past-the-post system, also used to elect constituency members to the London Assembly. Four regional members in each of the five constituencies are then chosen from party lists or independent candidates using a form of proportional representation.

Until 2007 the National Assembly for Wales was a corporate body comprising both the executive and legislative branches of government. It had no primary law-making powers and only had responsibility for exercising and implementing ministerial functions which had previously been vested in the Secretary of State for Wales.

The Government of Wales Act 2006 introduced a radical change to the functions and status of the National Assembly for Wales. With effect from 25 May 2007 the act formally separated the National Assembly for Wales (the legislature – made up of 60 elected assembly members) and the Welsh government (the executive – comprising the first minister, Welsh ministers, deputy Welsh ministers and the counsel general). It also made changes to the electoral process: candidates are no longer permitted to stand as both constituency and regional members. The act enabled the National Assembly for Wales to formulate its own legislation (assembly measures) on the 20 devolved areas for which it has responsibility (see Welsh government); the assembly was given legislative competence (the legal authority to pass measures) on a case-by-case basis by the UK parliament.

The act also included a mechanism that would allow for full transfer of legislative powers relating to all devolved matters to the National Assembly, provided that the people of Wales voted for such a proposal in a referendum. In a referendum held on 3 March 2011, 63.5 per cent voted in favour of giving the National Assembly full legislative powers for all devolved matters. The National Assembly for Wales can now pass legislation (assembly acts) on the 20 devolved areas for which it has responsibility. An assembly act has the same powers as an act of the UK parliament and may be proposed by the Welsh government, assembly committees, an assembly member or the assembly commission.

The National Assembly for Wales also scrutinises and monitors the Welsh government. It meets in plenary in the Senedd debating chamber. The 60 assembly members examine and approve assembly bills and approve certain items of subordinate legislation; approve the Welsh government and assembly commission's budget; hold Welsh ministers to account; and analyse and debate their decisions and policies.

Presiding Officer, Dame Rosemary Butler, DBE, AM

SALARIES *2013–14*	
First Minister*	£78,575
Minister/Presiding Officer*	£40,759
Deputy Minister/Deputy Presiding Officer*	£24,411
Assembly Members (AM)†	£53,852

* Also receives the assembly member salary
† Reduced by two-thirds if the member is already an MP or an MEP

MEMBERS OF THE NATIONAL ASSEMBLY FOR WALES
as at 1 July 2014

Andrews, Leighton, *Lab., Rhondda,* Maj. 6,739
Antoniw, Mick, *Lab., Pontypridd,* Maj. 7,694
ap Iorweth, Rhun, *PC, Ynys Môn,* Maj. 9,166
Asghar, Mohammad, *C., South Wales East region*
Black, Peter, *LD, South Wales West region*
Burns, Angela, *C., Carmarthen West and South Pembrokeshire,* Maj. 1,504
Butler, Rosemary, *Lab., Newport W.,* Maj. 4,220
Chapman, Christine, *Lab., Cynon Valley,* Maj. 6,515
Cuthbert, Jeff, *Lab., Caerphilly,* Maj. 4,924
Davies, Alun, *Lab., Blaenau Gwent,* Maj. 9,120
Davies, Andrew R. T., *C., South Wales Central region*
Davies, Byron, *C., South Wales West region*
Davies, Jocelyn, *PC, South Wales East region*
Davies, Keith, *Lab., Llanelli,* Maj. 80
Davies, Paul, *C., Preseli Pembrokeshire,* Maj. 2,175
Davies, Suzy, *C., South Wales West region*
Drakeford, Mark, *Lab., Cardiff West,* Maj. 5,901
Elis-Thomas, Rt. Hon. Lord, *PC, Dwyfor Meirionnydd,* Maj. 5,417
Evans, Rebecca, *Lab., Mid and West Wales region*
Finch-Saunders, Janet, *C., Aberconwy,* Maj. 1,567
George, Russell, *C., Montgomeryshire,* Maj. 2,324
Gething, Vaughan, *Lab., Cardiff South and Penarth,* Maj. 6,259
Graham, William, *C., South Wales East region*
Gregory, Janice, *Lab., Ogmore,* Maj. 9,576
Griffiths, John, *Lab., Newport East,* Maj. 5,388
Griffiths, Lesley, *Lab., Wrexham,* Maj. 3,337
Hart, Edwina, *Lab., Gower,* Maj. 4,864
Hedges, Mike, *Lab., Swansea East,* Maj. 8,281
Hutt, Jane, *Lab., Vale of Glamorgan,* Maj. 3,775
Huws Gruffydd, Llyr, *PC, North Wales region*
Isherwood, Mark, *C., North Wales region*
James, Julie, *Lab., Swansea West,* Maj. 4,654
Jenkins, Bethan, *PC, South Wales West region*
Jones, Alun Ffred, *PC, Arfon,* Maj. 5,394
Jones, Ann, *Lab., Vale of Clwyd,* Maj. 4,011
Jones, Rt. Hon. Carwyn, *Lab., Bridgend,* Maj. 6,775
Jones, Elin, *PC, Ceredigion,* Maj. 1,777
Lewis, Huw, *Lab., Merthyr Tydfil and Rhymney,* Maj. 7,051
Melding, David, *C., South Wales Central region*
Mewies, Sandra, *Lab., Delyn,* Maj. 2,881
Millar, Darren, *C., Clwyd West,* Maj. 4,248
Morgan, Julie, *Lab., Cardiff North,* Maj. 1,782
Neagle, Lynne, *Lab., Torfaen,* Maj. 6,088
Parrott, Eluned, *LD, South Wales Central region*
Powell, William, *LD, Mid and West Wales region*
Price, Gwyn, *Lab., Islwyn,* Maj. 7,589
Ramsay, Nicholas, *C., Monmouth,* Maj. 6,117
Rathbone, Jenny, *Lab., Cardiff Central,* Maj. 38
Rees, David, *Lab., Aberavon,* Maj. 9,311
Roberts, Aled, *LD, North Wales region*
Sandbach, Antoinette, *C., North Wales region*
Sargeant, Carl, *Lab., Alyn and Deeside,* Maj. 5,581
Skates, Ken, *Lab., Clwyd South,* Maj. 2,659
Thomas, Gwenda, *Lab., Neath,* Maj. 6,390
Thomas, Rhodri Glyn, *PC, Carmarthen East and Dinefwr,* Maj. 4,148
Thomas, Simon, *PC, Mid and West Wales region*
Watson, Joyce, *Lab., Mid and West Wales region*
Whittle, Lindsay, *PC, South Wales East region*
Williams, Kirsty, *LD, Brecon and Radnorshire,* Maj. 2,757
Wood, Leanne, *PC, South Wales Central region*
Wyn Jones, Ieuan, *PC, Ynys Mon,* Maj. 2,937

STATE OF THE PARTIES
as at 1 July 2014

	Constituency AMs	Regional AMs	AM total
Labour (Lab.)	28*	2	30
Conservative (C.)	6	8†	14
Plaid Cymru (PC)	5	6	11
Liberal Democrats (LD)	1	4	5
Total	40	20	60

* Includes the Presiding Officer
† Includes the Deputy Presiding Officer

NATIONAL ASSEMBLY ELECTION RESULTS

As at 5 May 2011
E. Electorate T. Turnout
See General Election Results for a list of party abbreviations

CONSTITUENCIES
E. 2,289,555 T. 41.5%

ABERAVON (S. WALES WEST)
E. 50,754 T. 18,879 (37.20%)
David Rees, Lab.   12,104
Paul Nicholls-Jones, PC   2,793
Tamojen Morgan, C.   2,704
Helen Ceri Clarke, LD   1,278
Lab. majority 9,311 (49.32%)
8.65% swing PC to Lab.

ABERCONWY (WALES N.)
E. 44,978 T. 20,288 (45.11%)
Janet Finch-Saunders, C.   6,888
Iwan Huws, PC   5,321
Eifion Wyn Williams, Lab.   5,206
Mike Priestley, LD   2,873
C. majority 1,567 (7.72%)
7.95% swing PC to C.

ALYN AND DEESIDE (WALES N.)
E. 61,751 T. 22,769 (36.87%)
Carl Sargeant, Lab.   11,978
John Bell, C.   6,397
Pete Williams, LD   1,725
Shane Brennan, PC   1,710
Michael Whitby, BNP   959
Lab. majority 5,581 (24.51%)
4.29% swing C. to Lab.

ARFON (WALES N.)
E. 41,093 T. 17,664 (42.99%)
Alun Ffred Jones, PC   10,024
Christina Rees, Lab.   4,630
Aled Davies, C.   2,209
Rhys Jones, LD   801
PC majority 5,394 (30.54%)
2.45% swing Lab. to PC

**BLAENAU GWENT
(S. WALES EAST)**
E. 53,230 T. 20,211 (37.97%)
Alun Davies, Lab.   12,926
Jayne Sullivan, Ind.   3,806
Darren Jones, PC   1,098
Bob Hayward, C.   1,066
Brian Urch, BNP   948
Martin Blakeborough, LD   367
Lab. majority 9,120 (45.12%)
33.95% swing Ind. to Lab.

**BRECON AND RADNORSHIRE
(WALES MID AND W.)**
E. 53,546 T. 28,348 (52.94%)
Kirsty Williams, LD   12,201
Chris Davies, C.   9,444
Christopher Lloyd, Lab.   4,797
Gary Price, PC   1,906
LD majority 2,757 (9.73%)
4.45% swing LD to C.

BRIDGEND (S. WALES WEST)
E. 59,104 T. 24,035 (40.67%)
Carwyn Jones, Lab.   13,499
Alex Williams, C.   6,724
Tim Thomas, PC   2,076
Briony Davies, LD   1,736
Lab. majority 6,775 (28.19%)
8.89% swing C. to Lab.

CAERPHILLY (S. WALES EAST)
E. 62,049 T. 25,570 (41.21%)
Jeff Cuthbert, Lab.   12,521
Ron Davies, PC   7,597
Owen Meredith, C.   3,368
Kay David, LD   1,062
Anthony King, BNP   1,022
Lab. majority 4,924 (19.26%)
5.25% swing PC to Lab.

**CARDIFF CENTRAL
(S. WALES CENTRAL)**
E. 64,347 T. 23,628 (36.72%)
Jenny Rathbone, Lab.   8,954
Nigel Howells, LD   8,916
Matt Smith, C.   3,559
Chris Williams, PC   1,690
Mathab Khan, Ind.   509
Lab. majority 38 (0.16%)
14.74% swing LD to Lab.

**CARDIFF NORTH
(S. WALES CENTRAL)**
E. 66,934 T. 34,431 (51.44%)
Julie Morgan, Lab.   16,384
Jonathan Morgan, C.   14,602
Ben Foday, PC   1,850
Matt Smith, LD   1,595
Lab. majority 1,782 (5.18%)
9.77% swing C. to Lab.

**CARDIFF SOUTH AND PENARTH
(S. WALES CENTRAL)**
E. 75,038 T. 27,479 (36.62%)
Vaughan Gething, Lab.   13,814
Ben Gray, C.   7,555
Liz Musa, PC   3,324
Sian Cliff, LD   2,786
Lab. majority 6,259 (22.78%)
6.24% swing C. to Lab.

**CARDIFF WEST
(S. WALES CENTRAL)**
E. 64,219 T. 27,726 (43.17%)
Mark Drakeford, Lab.   13,067
Craig Williams, C.   7,167
Neil McEvoy, PC   5,551
David Morgan, LD   1,942
Lab. majority 5,901 (21.28%)
3.77% C. to Lab.

**CARMARTHEN EAST AND
DINEFWR (WALES MID AND W.)**
E. 54,243 T. 27,828 (51.30%)
Rhodri Glyn Thomas, PC   12,501
Anthony Jones, Lab.   8,353
Henrietta Hensher, C.   5,635
Will Griffiths, LD   1,339
PC majority 4,148 (14.91%)
7.01% swing PC to Lab.

**CARMARTHEN WEST AND
SOUTH PEMBROKESHIRE
(WALES MID AND W.)**
E. 58,435 T. 28,156 (48.18%)
Angela Burns, C.   10,095
Christine Gwyther, Lab.   8,591
Nerys Evans, PC   8,373
Selwyn Runnett, LD   1,097
C. majority 1,504 (5.34%)
2.50% swing Lab. to C.

**CEREDIGION
(WALES MID AND W.)**
E. 56,983 T. 29,076 (51.03%)
Elin Jones, PC   12,020
Liz Evans, LD   10,243
Luke Evetts, C.   2,755
Richard Boudier, Lab.   2,544
Chris Simpson, Green   1,514
PC majority 1,777 (6.11%)
3.51% swing PC to LD

CLWYD SOUTH (WALES N.)
E. 54,499 T. 19,498 (37.59%)
Ken Skates, Lab.   8,500
Paul Rogers, C.   5,841
Mabon ap Gwynfor, PC   3,719
Bruce Roberts, LD   1,977
Lab. majority 2,659 (13.27%)
3.77% swing C. to Lab.

CLWYD WEST (WALES N.)
E. 57,980 T. 25,153 (43.38%)
Darren Millar, C.   10,890
Crispin Jones, Lab.   6,642
Eifion Lloyd Jones, PC   5,775
Brian Cossey, LD   1,846
C. majority 4,248 (16.89%)
5.40% swing Lab. to C.

**CYNON VALLEY
(S. WALES CENTRAL)**
E. 52,133 T. 18,760 (35.98%)
Christine Chapman, Lab.   11,626
Dafydd Trystan Davies, PC   5,111
Dan Saxton, C.   1,531
Ian Walton, LD   492
Lab. majority 6,515 (34.73%)
2.96% swing PC to Lab.

DELYN (WALES N.)
E. 53,996 T. 23,194 (42.96%)
Sandy Mewies, Lab.   10,695
Matt Wright, C.   7,814
Carrie Harper, PC   2,918
Michele Jones, LD   1,767
Lab. majority 2,881 (12.42%)
5.03% swing C. to Lab.

DWYFOR MEIRONNYDD (WALES MID AND W.)
E. 44,669 T. 20,743 (46.44%)

Dafydd Elis-Thomas, PC	9,656
Simon Baynes, C	4,239
Louise Hughes, Llais Gwynedd	3,225
Martyn Stuart Singleton, Lab.	2,623
Steven William Churchman, LD	1,000

PC majority 5,417 (26.11%)
6.99% swing PC to C.

GOWER (S. WALES WEST)
E. 61,909 T. 26,773 (43.25%)

Edwina Hart, Lab.	12,866
Caroline Jones, C.	8,002
Darren Price, PC	3,249
Peter May, LD	2,656

Lab. majority 4,864 (18.17%)
6.92% swing C. to Lab.

ISLWYN (S. WALES EAST)
E. 54,893 T. 20,908 (38.09%)

Gwyn Price, Lab.	12,116
Steffan Lewis, PC	4,527
David Chipp, C.	2,497
Peter Whalley, BNP	1,115
Tom Sullivan, LD	653

Lab. majority 7,589 (36.30%)
10.09% swing PC to Lab.

LLANELLI (WALES MID AND W.)
E. 58,838 T. 26,070 (44.31%)

Keith Davies, Lab.	10,359
Helen Mary Jones, PC	10,279
Andrew Morgan, C.	2,880
Sian Caiach, Putting Llanelli First	2,004
Cheryl Philpott, LD	548

Lab. majority 80 (0.31%)
7.19% swing PC to Lab.

MERTHYR TYDFIL AND RHYMNEY (S. WALES EAST)
E. 55,031 T. 19,320 (35.11%)

Huw Lewis, Lab.	10,483
Tony Rogers, Ind.	3,432
Amy Kitcher, LD	2,480
Noel Turner, PC	1,701
Chris O'Brien, C.	1,224

Lab. majority 7,051 (36.50%)
0.14% swing Ind. to Lab.

MONMOUTH (S. WALES EAST)
E. 64,857 T. 30,001 (46.26%)

Nick Ramsay, C.	15,087
Mark Whitcutt, Lab.	8,970
Janet Ellard, LD	2,937
Fiona Cross, PC	2,263
Steve Uncles, Eng. Dem.	744

C. majority 6,117 (20.39%)
4.13% swing C. to Lab.

MONTGOMERYSHIRE (WALES MID AND W.)
E. 48,675 T. 22,933 (47.11%)

Russell George, C.	10,026
Wyn Williams, LD	7,702
Nick Colbourne, Lab.	2,609
David Senior, PC	2,596

C. majority 2,324 (10.13%)
9.50% swing LD to C.

NEATH (S. WALES WEST)
E. 57,533 T. 23,849 (41.45%)

Gwenda Thomas, Lab.	12,736
Alun Llewelyn, PC	6,346
Alex Powell, C.	2,780
Michael Green, BNP	1,004
Mathew McCarthy, LD	983

Lab. majority 6,390 (26.79%)
9.34% swing PC to Lab.

NEWPORT EAST (S. WALES EAST)
E. 55,120 T. 19,460 (35.30%)

John Griffiths, Lab.	9,888
Nick Webb, C.	4,500
Ed Townsend, LD	3,703
Chris Paul, PC	1,369

Lab. majority 5,388 (27.69%)
9.11% swing C. to Lab.

NEWPORT WEST (S. WALES EAST)
E. 63,180 T. 23,014 (36.43%)

Rosemary Butler, Lab.	12,011
David Williams, C.	7,791
Lyndon Binding, PC	1,626
Liz Newton, LD	1,586

Lab. majority 4,220 (18.34%)
6.21% swing C. to Lab.

OGMORE (S. WALES WEST)
E. 55,442 T. 20,264 (36.55%)

Janice Gregory, Lab.	12,955
Danny Clark, PC	3,379
Martyn Hughes, C.	2,945
Gerald Francis, LD	985

Lab. majority 9,576 (47.26%)
6.28% swing PC to Lab.

PONTYPRIDD (S. WALES CENTRAL)
E. 60,028 T. 23,333 (38.87%)

Mick Antoniw, Lab.	11,864
Michael Powell, LD	4,170
Joel James, C.	3,659
Ioan Bellin, PC	3,139
Ken Owen, ND	501

Lab. majority 7,694 (32.97%)
9.28% swing LD to Lab.

PRESELI PEMBROKESHIRE (WALES MID AND W.)
E. 57,758 T. 27,218 (47.12%)

Paul Davies, C.	11,541
Terry Mills (Lab.)	9,366
Rhys Sinnett, PC	4,226
Rob Kilmister, LD	2,085

C. majority 2,175 (7.99%)
1.58% swing C. to Lab.

RHONDDA (S. WALES CENTRAL)
E. 52,532 T. 20,027 (38.12%)

Leighton Andrews, Lab.	12,650
Sarah Evans-Fear, PC	5,911
James Jeffreys, C.	969
George Summers, LD	497

Lab. majority 6,739 (33.65%)
2.77% swing PC to Lab.

SWANSEA EAST (S. WALES WEST)
E. 60,246 T. 18,910 (58.36%)

Mike Hedges, Lab.	11,035
Daniel Boucher, C.	2,754
Dic Jones, PC	2,346
Sam Samuel, LD.	1,673
Joanne Shannon, BNP	1,102

Lab. majority 8,281 (43.79%)
0.05% swing C. to Lab.

SWANSEA WEST (S. WALES WEST)
E. 62,345 T. 21,805 (34.97%)

Julie James, Lab.	9,885
Steve Jenkins, C.	5,231
Rob Speht, LD	3,654
Carl Harris, PC	3,035

Lab. majority 4,654 (21.34%)
4.09% swing C. to Lab.

TORFAEN (S. WALES EAST)
E. 61,126 T. 22,328 (36.53%)

Lynne Neagle, Lab.	10,318
Elizabeth Haynes, Ind.	4,230
Natasha Asghar, C.	3,306
Jeff Rees, PC	2,716
Susan Harwood, BNP	906
Will Griffiths, LD	852

Lab. majority 6,088 (27.27%)
0.52% swing Lab. to Ind.

VALE OF CLWYD (WALES N.)
E. 56,232 T. 23,056 (41.00%)

Ann Jones, Lab.	11,691
Ian Gunning, C.	7,680
Alun Lloyd Jones, PC	2,597
Heather Prydderch, LD	1,088

Lab. majority 4,011 (17.40%)
8.49% swing C. to Lab.

VALE OF GLAMORGAN (S. WALES CENTRAL)
E. 71,602 T. 33,254 (46.80%)

Jane Hutt, Lab.	15,746
Angela Jones-Evans, C.	11,971
Ian Johnson, PC	4,024
Damian Chick, LD	1,513

Lab. majority 3,775 (11.35%)
5.55% swing C. to Lab.

WREXHAM (WALES N.)
E. 53,516 T. 18,687 (34.92%)

Lesley Griffiths, Lab.	8,368
John Marek, C.	5,031
Bill Brereton	2,692
Marc Jones, PC	2,596

Lab. majority 3,337 (17.86%)
3.15% swing C. to Lab.

YNYS MON (WALES N.)
E. 49,431 T. 24,067 (48.69%)

Ieuan Wyn Jones, PC	9,969
Paul Williams, C.	7,032
Joe Lock, Lab.	6,307
Rhys Taylor, LD	759

PC majority 2,937 (12.20%)
7.27% swing PC to C.

REGIONS
E. 2,289,555 T. 41.4%

MID AND WEST WALES
E. 433,147 T. 210,352 (48.56%)

PC	56,384	(26.7%)
C.	52,905	(25.1%)
Lab.	47,348	(22.5%)
LD	26,847	(12.7%)
UKIP	9,211	(4.4%)
Green	8,660	(4.1%)
Soc. Lab.	3,951	(1.9%)
BNP	2,821	(1.3%)
Welsh Christian Party	1,630	(0.8%)
Comm. Brit.	595	(0.3%)

PC majority 3,479 (1.65%)
3.25% swing PC to C. (2007 PC majority 17,652)

ADDITIONAL MEMBERS
Rebecca Evans, *Lab.*	William Powell, *LD*
Joyce Watson, *Lab.*	Simon Thomas, *PC*

NORTH WALES
E. 473,296 T. 194,798 (41.16%)

Lab.	62,677	(32.2%)
C.	52,201	(26.8%)
PC	41,701	(21.4%)
LD	11,507	(5.9%)
UKIP	9,608	(4.9%)
Soc. Lab.	4,895	(2.5%)
BNP	4,785	(2.5%)
Green	4,406	(2.3%)
Welsh Christian Party	1,401	(0.7%)
Ind.	1,094	(0.6%)
Comm. Brit.	523	(0.3%)

Lab. majority 10,476 (5.38%)
5.05% swing PC to Lab. (2007 Lab. majority 1,273)

ADDITIONAL MEMBERS
Mark Isherwood, *C.*	Aled Roberts, *LD*
Antoinette Sandbach, *C.*	Llyr Huws Griffiths, *PC*

SOUTH WALES CENTRAL
E. 506,293 T. 208,333 (41.15%)

Lab.	85,445	(41.0%)
C.	45,751	(22.0%)
PC	28,606	(13.7%)
LD	16,514	(7.9%)
Green	10,774	(5.2%)
UKIP	8,292	(4.0%)
Soc. Lab.	4,690	(2.3%)
BNP	3,805	(1.8%)
Welsh Christian Party	1,873	(0.9%)
Loony	1,237	(0.6%)
TUSC	830	(0.4%)
Comm. Brit.	516	(0.2%)

Lab. majority 39,694 (19.05%)
6.55% swing LD to C. (2007 Lab. majority 25,652)

ADDITIONAL MEMBERS
David Melding, *C.*	Leanne Wood, *PC*
Andrew Davies, *C.*	John Dixon, *LD*

SOUTH WALES EAST
E. 469,486 T. 181,024 (38.56%)

Lab.	82,699	(45.7%)
C.	35,459	(19.6%)
PC	21,851	(12.1%)
LD	10,798	(6.0%)
UKIP	9,526	(5.3%)
BNP	6,485	(3.6%)
Green	4,857	(2.7%)
Soc. Lab.	4,427	(2.4%)
Welsh Christian Party	2,441	(1.3%)
Eng. Dem.	1,904	(1.1%)
Comm. Brit.	578	(0.3%)

Lab. majority 47,240 (26.10%)
5.95% swing LD to Lab. (2007 Lab. majority 30,063)

ADDITIONAL MEMBERS
William Graham, *C.*	Jocelyn Davies, *PC*
Mohammad Asghar, *C.*	Lindsay Whittle, *PC*

SOUTH WALES WEST
E. 407,333 T. 154,381 (37.90%)

Lab.	71,766	(46.5%)
Con.	27,457	(17.8%)
PC	21,258	(13.8%)
LD	10,683	(6.9%)
UKIP	6,619	(4.3%)
Soc. Lab.	5,057	(3.3%)
BNP	4,714	(3.1%)
Green	3,952	(2.6%)
Welsh Christian Party	1,602	(1.0%)
TUSC	809	(0.5%)
Comm. Brit.	464	(0.3%)

Lab. majority 44,309 (28.70%)
8.10% swing LD to Lab. (2007 Lab. majority 29,528)

ADDITIONAL MEMBERS
Suzy Davies, *C.*	Peter Black, *LD*
Byron Davies, *C.*	Bethan Jenkins, *PC*

SCOTLAND

SCOTTISH GOVERNMENT

St Andrew's House, Regent Road, Edinburgh EH1 3DG
T 0845-774 1741 **Enquiry Line** 0131-556 840
E ceu@scotland.gsi.gov.uk **W** www.scotland.gov.uk

The devolved government for Scotland is responsible for most of the issues of day-to-day concern to the people of Scotland, including health, education, justice, rural affairs and transport.

The Scottish government was known as the Scottish executive when it was established in 1999, following the first elections to the Scottish parliament. There has been a majority Scottish National Party administration since the elections in May 2011.

The government is led by a first minister who is nominated by the parliament and in turn appoints the other Scottish ministers who make up the cabinet.

Civil servants in Scotland are accountable to Scottish ministers, who are themselves accountable to the Scottish parliament.

CABINET

First Minister, Rt. Hon. Alex Salmond, MSP
Deputy First Minister and Cabinet Secretary for Infrastructure, Investment and Cities, Nicola Sturgeon, MSP
Cabinet Secretary for Commonwealth Games, Sport, Equalities and Pensioners' Rights, Shona Robison, MSP
Cabinet Secretary for Culture and External Affairs, Fiona Hyslop, MSP
Cabinet Secretary for Education and Lifelong Learning, Michael Russell, MSP
Cabinet Secretary for Finance, Employment and Sustainable Growth, John Swinney, MSP
Cabinet Secretary for Health and Wellbeing, Alex Neil, MSP
Cabinet Secretary for Rural Affairs and the Environment, Richard Lochhead, MSP
Cabinet Secretary for Justice, Kenny MacAskill, MSP
Cabinet Secretary for Training Youth and Women's Employment, Angela Constance, MSP
Minister for Children and Young People, Aileen Campbell, MSP
Minister for Community Safety and Legal Affairs, Roseanna Cunningham, MSP
Minister for Energy, Enterprise and Tourism, Fergus Ewing, MSP
Minister for Environment and Climate Change, Paul Wheelhouse, MSP
Minister for External Affairs and International Development, Humza Yousaf, MSP
Minister for Housing and Welfare, Margaret Burgess, MSP
Minister for Learning, Science and Scotland's Languages, Alasdair Allan, MSP
Minister for Local Government and Planning, Derek Mackay, MSP
Minister for Parliamentary Business, Joe Fitzpatrick, MSP
Minister for Public Health, Michael Matheson, MSP
Minister for Transport and Veterans, Keith Brown, MSP

* Alex Salmonod announced on 19 September 2014, following the referendum, that he would resign as First Minister in November 2014.

LAW OFFICERS

Lord Advocate, Frank Mulholland, QC
Solicitor-General for Scotland, Lesley Thomson

STRATEGIC BOARD

Permanent Secretary, Sir Peter Housden, KCB
Director-General Communities, Sarah Davidson
Director-General, Enterprise, Environment and Digital, Graeme Dickson
Director-General, Finance, Alyson Stafford
Director-General, Health and Social Care, Paul Gray
Director-General, Learning and Justice, Leslie Evans
Director-General, Strategy and External Affairs, Ken Thomson

GOVERNMENT DEPARTMENTS

DIRECTOR-GENERAL ENTERPRISE, ENVIRONMENT AND INNOVATION

St Andrew's House, Edinburgh EH1 3DG
Directorates: Agriculture, Food and Rural Affairs; Business; Chief Scientific Adviser for Rural Affairs and the Environment; Chief Economist; Energy and Climate Change; Environment and Forestry; Marine Scotland; Scottish Development International
Director-General, Graeme Dickson
Executive Agencies
Accountant in Bankruptcy
Drinking Water Quality Regulator
James Hutton Institute
Moredun Research Institute
Scottish Agricultural College
Transport Scotland
Waterwatch

DIRECTOR-GENERAL FINANCE

Victoria Quay, Edinburgh EH6 6QQ
Directorates: Legal Services, Finance; Office of the Scottish Parliamentary Counsel; Scottish Procurement and Commercial
Director-General, Alyson Stafford
Executive Agencies
Audit Scotland
Scottish Public Pensions Agency

DIRECTOR-GENERAL COMMUNITIES

Saughton House, Broomhouse Drive, Edinburgh, EH11 3XD
Directorates: Digital; Housing, Regeneration and Welfare; Local Government and Communities
Director-General, Sarah Davidson
Executive Agency
Scottish Housing Regulator

DIRECTOR-GENERAL HEALTH AND SOCIAL CARE

St Andrew's House, Regent Road, Edinburgh EH1 3DG
Directorates: Chief Medical Officer and Public Health; Chief Nursing Officer, Patients, Public and Health Professions; Children and Families; Commonwealth Games and Sport; Health and Pharmaceuticals; Health and Social Care Integration; Health Workforce and Performance; The Quality Unit
Director-General Health and Social Care and Chief Executive, Paul Gray
Executive Agencies
Disclosure Scotland
Scottish Children's Reporters Administration

DIRECTOR-GENERAL LEARNING AND JUSTICE

St Andrew's House, Edinburgh EH1 3DG
Directorates: Education Analytical Services; Employability, Skills and Lifelong Learning; Justice; Learning; Safer Communities
Director-General, Leslie Evans
Executive Agencies
Education Scotland
HM Chief Inspector of Prosecution in Scotland
HM Inspectorate of Constabulary

HM Inspectorate of Prisons
Justices of the Peace Advisory Committee
Scottish Prison Service
Student Awards Agency for Scotland
Visiting Committees for Scottish Penal Establishments

DIRECTOR-GENERAL STRATEGY AND EXTERNAL AFFAIRS
St Andrew's House, Edinburgh EH1 3DG
Directorates: Communications and Ministerial Support; Culture and Heritage; External Affairs; HR and Organisational Development; Strategy and Constitution
Executive Agency
Historic Scotland

NON-MINISTERIAL DEPARTMENTS

NATIONAL RECORDS OF SCOTLAND
General Register House, 2 Princes Street, Edinburgh EH1 3YY
T 0131-535 1314 W www.nrscotland.gov.uk
Registrar General and Keeper of the Records of Scotland,
  Tim Ellis

OFFICE OF THE SCOTTISH CHARITY REGULATOR
2nd Floor, Quadrant House, 9 Riverside Drive, Dundee DD1 4NY
T 01382-220 446 W www.oscr.org.uk
Chief Executive, David Robb

REGISTERS OF SCOTLAND
Meadowbank House, 153 London Road, Edinburgh, Midlothian
EH8 7AU T 0845-607 0161 W www.ros.gov.uk
Keeper, Sheena Adams

SCOTTISH HOUSING REGULATOR
Highlander House, 58 Waterloo Street, Glasgow G2 7DA
T 0141-271 3810 W www.scottishhousingregulator.gov.uk
Chief Executive, Michael Cameron

NON-DEPARTMENTAL OFFICES

AUDIT SCOTLAND
110 George Street, Edinburgh EH2 4LH
T 0131-625 1500 E info@audit-scotland.gov.uk
W www.audit-scotland.gov.uk
Auditor-General, Caroline Gardner
Accounts Commission Chair, Douglas Sinclair

CROWN OFFICE AND PROCURATOR FISCAL SERVICE
25 Chambers Street, Edinburgh EH1 1LA
T 0844-561 3000
Chief Executive and Crown Agent, Catherine Dyer

OFFICE OF THE PERMANENT SECRETARY
St Andrew's House, Regent Road, Edinburgh EH1 3DG
T 0131-556 8400
Permanent Secretary, Sir Peter Housden, KCB

SCOTTISH PARLIAMENT

Edinburgh EH99 1SP
T 0131-348 5000 **Textphone** 0800-092 7100
E sp.info@scottish.parliament.uk
W www.scottish.parliament.uk

In July 1997 the government announced plans to establish a Scottish parliament. In a referendum on 11 September 1997 about 60 per cent of the electorate voted. Of those who voted, 74.3 per cent voted in favour of the parliament and 63.5 per cent voted in support of granting the parliament having tax-raising powers. Elections are held every four years. The first elections were held on 6 May 1999, when around 59 per cent of the electorate voted. The first meeting was held on 12 May 1999 and the Scottish parliament was officially opened on 1 July 1999 at the Assembly Hall, Edinburgh. A new building to house parliament was opened, in the presence of the Queen, at Holyrood on 9 October 2004. On 5 May 2011 the fourth elections to the Scottish parliament took place.

The Scottish parliament has 129 members (including the presiding officer), comprising 73 constituency members and 56 additional regional members, mainly from party lists. It can introduce primary legislation and has the power to raise or lower the basic rate of income tax by up to three pence in the pound. Members of the Scottish parliament are elected using the additional member system, the same system used to elect London Assembly and Welsh Assembly members.

The areas for which the Scottish parliament is responsible include: education; health; law; environment; economic development; local government; housing; police; fire services; planning; financial assistance to industry; tourism; heritage and the arts; agriculture; social work; sports; public registers and records; forestry; food standards; and some transport.

SALARIES *as at 1 April 2014*	
First Minister*	£85,002
Cabinet Secretaries*	£44,097
Lord Advocate*	£57,609
Solicitor-General for Scotland*	£41,659
Ministers*	£27,622
MSPs†	£58,678
Presiding Officer*	£44,097
Deputy Presiding Officer*	£27,622

* In addition to the MSP salary
† Reduced by two-thirds if the member is already an MP or an MEP

MEMBERS OF THE SCOTTISH PARLIAMENT

as at 1 July 2014
Adam, George, *SNP, Paisley,* Maj. 248
Adamson, Clare, *SNP, Central Scotland region*
Allan, Alasdair, *SNP, Na h-Eileanan an Iar,* Maj. 4,772
Allard, Christian, *SNP, North East Scotland region*
Baillie, Jackie, *Lab., Dumbarton,* Maj. 1,639
Baker, Claire, *Lab., Mid Scotland and Fife region*
Baker, Richard, *Lab., North East Scotland region*
Baxter, Jayne, *Lab., Mid Scotland and Fife region*
Beamish, Claudia, *Lab., South Scotland region*
Beattie, Colin, *SNP, Midlothian North and Musselburgh,* Maj. 2,996
Biagi, Marco, *SNP, Edinburgh Central,* Maj. 237
Bibby, Neil, *Lab., West Scotland region*
Boyack, Sarah, *Lab., Lothian region*
Brodie, Chic, *SNP, South Scotland region*
Brown, Gavin, *C., Lothian region*
Brown, Keith, *SNP, Clackmannanshire and Dunblane,* Maj. 3,609
Buchanan, Cameron, *C., Lothian Region*
Burgess, Margaret, *SNP, Cunninghame South,* Maj. 2,348
Campbell, Aileen, *SNP, Clydesdale,* Maj. 4,216
Campbell, Roderick, *SNP, North East Fife,* Maj. 2,592
Carlaw, Jackson, *C., West Scotland region*
Chisholm, Malcolm, *Lab., Edinburgh Northern and Leith,* Maj. 595
Coffey, Willie, *SNP, Kilmarnock and Irvine Valley,* Maj. 5,993
Constance, Angela, *SNP, Almond Valley,* Maj. 5,542
Crawford, Bruce, *SNP, Stirling,* Maj. 5,671
Cunningham, Roseanna, *SNP, Perthshire South and Kinross-shire,* Maj. 7,166
Davidson, Ruth, *C., Glasgow region*

Dey, Graeme, *SNP, Angus South,* Maj. 10,583

Don, Nigel, *SNP, Angus North and Mearns,* Maj. 7,286

Doris, Bob, *SNP, Glasgow region*

Dornan, James, *SNP, Glasgow Cathcart,* Maj. 1,592

Dugdale, Kezia, *Lab., Lothian region*

Eadie, Helen, *Lab., Cowdenbeath,* Maj. 1,247

Eadie, Jim, *SNP, Edinburgh Southern,* Maj. 693

Ewing, Annabelle, *SNP, Mid Scotland and Fife region*

Ewing, Fergus, *SNP, Inverness and Nairn,* Maj. 9,745

Fabiani, Linda, *SNP, East Kilbride,* Maj. 1,949

Fee, Mary, *Lab., West Scotland region*

Ferguson, Patricia, *Lab., Glasgow Maryhill and Springburn,* Maj. 1,252

Fergusson, Rt. Hon. Alex, *C., Galloway and West Dumfries,* Maj. 862

Findlay, Neil, *Lab., Lothian region*

Finnie, John, *Ind., Highlands and Islands region*

FitzPatrick, Joe, *SNP, Dundee City West,* Maj. 6,405

Fraser, Murdo, *C., Mid Scotland and Fife region*

Gibson, Kenneth, *SNP, Cunninghame North,* Maj. 6,117

Gibson, Rob, *SNP, Caithness, Sutherland and Ross,* Maj. 7,458

Goldie, Baroness, *C., West Scotland region*

Grahame, Christine, *SNP, Midlothian South, Tweeddale and Lauderdale,* Maj. 4,924

Grant, Rhoda, *Lab., Highlands and Islands region*

Gray, Iain, *Lab., East Lothian,* Maj. 151

Griffin, Mark, *Lab., Central Scotland region*

Harvie, Patrick, *Green, Glasgow region*

Henry, Hugh, *Lab., Renfrewshire South,* Maj. 2,577

Hepburn, Jamie, *SNP, Cumbernauld and Kilsyth,* Maj. 3,459

Hilton, Cara, *Lab., Dunfermline*

Hume, Jim, *LD, South Scotland region*

Hyslop, Fiona, *SNP, Linlithgow,* Maj. 4,091

Ingram, Adam, *SNP, Carrick, Cumnock and Doon Valley,* Maj. 2,581

Johnstone, Alex, *C., North East Scotland region*

Johnstone, Alison, *Green, Lothian region*

Keir, Colin, *SNP, Edinburgh West,* Maj. 2,689

Kelly, James, *Lab., Rutherglen,* Maj. 1,779

Kidd, Bill, *SNP, Glasgow Anniesland,* Maj. 7

Lamont, Johann, *Lab., Glasgow Pollok,* Maj. 623

Lamont, John, *C., Ettrick, Roxburgh and Berwickshire,* Maj. 5,334

Lochhead, Richard, *SNP, Moray,* Maj. 10,944

Lyle, Richard, *SNP, Central Scotland region*

McAlpine, Joan, *SNP, South Scotland region*

McArthur, Liam, *LD, Orkney,* Maj. 860

MacAskill, Kenny, *SNP, Edinburgh Eastern,* Maj. 2,233

McCulloch, Margaret, *Lab., Central Scotland region*

MacDonald, Angus, *SNP, Falkirk East,* Maj. 3,535

MacDonald, Gordon, *SNP, Edinburgh Pentlands,* Maj. 1,758

Macdonald, Lewis, *Lab., North East Scotland region*

McDonald, Mark, *SNP, Aberdeen Donside,* Maj. 2,025

McDougall, Margaret, *Lab., West Scotland region*

McGrigor, Jamie, *C., Highlands and Islands region*

McInnes, Alison, *LD, North East Scotland region*

Macintosh, Ken, *Lab., Eastwood,* Maj. 2,012

Mackay, Derek, *SNP Renfrewshire North and West,* Maj. 1,564

McKelvie, Christina, *SNP, Hamilton, Larkhall and Stonehouse,* Maj. 2,213

MacKenzie, Mike, *SNP, Highlands and Islands region*

McLeod, Aileen, *SNP, South Scotland region*

McLeod, Fiona, *SNP, Strathkelvin and Bearsden,* Maj. 1,802

McMahon, Michael, *Lab., Uddingston and Bellshill,* Maj. 714

McMahon, Siobhan, *Lab., Central Scotland region*

McMillan, Stuart, *SNP, West Scotland region*

McNeil, Duncan, *Lab., Greenock and Inverclyde,* Maj. 511

McTaggart, Anne, *Lab., Glasgow region*

Malik, Hanzala, *Lab., Glasgow region*

Marra, Jenny, *Lab., North East Scotland region*

Martin, Paul, *Lab., Glasgow Provan,* Maj. 2,079

Marwick, Rt. Hon. Tricia, *SNP, Mid Fife and Glenrothes,* Maj. 4,188

Mason, John, *SNP, Glasgow Shettleston,* Maj. 586

Matheson, Michael, *SNP, Falkirk West,* Maj. 5,745

Maxwell, Stewart, *SNP, West Scotland region*

Milne, Nanette, *C., North East Scotland region*

Mitchell, Margaret, *C., Central Scotland region*

Murray, Elaine, *Lab., Dumfriesshire,* Maj. 3,156

Neil, Alex, *SNP, Airdrie and Shotts,* Maj. 2,001

Paterson, Gil, *SNP, Clydebank and Milngavie,* Maj. 714

Pearson, Graeme, *Lab, South Scotland region*

Pentland, John, *Lab., Motherwell and Wishaw,* Maj. 587

Rennie, Willie, *LD, Mid Scotland and Fife region*

Robertson, Dennis, *SNP, Aberdeenshire West,* Maj. 4,112

Robison, Shona, *SNP, Dundee City East,* Maj. 10,679

Rowley, Alex, *Lab., Cowdenbeath,* Maj. 5,488

Russell, Michael, *SNP, Argyll and Bute,* Maj. 8,543

Salmond, Rt. Hon. Alex, *SNP, Aberdeenshire East,* Maj. 15,295

Scanlon, Mary, *C., Highlands and Islands region*

Scott, John, *C., Ayr,* Maj. 1,113

Scott, Tavish, *LD, Shetland Islands,* Maj. 1,617

Simpson, Richard, *Lab., Mid Scotland and Fife region*

Smith, Drew, *Lab., Glasgow region*

Smith, Elaine, *Lab., Coatbridge and Chryston,* Maj. 2,741

Smith, Liz, *C., Mid Scotland and Fife region*

Stevenson, Stewart, *SNP, Banffshire and Buchan Coast,* Maj. 12,220

Stewart, David, *Lab., Highlands and Islands region*

Stewart, Kevin, *SNP, Aberdeen Central,* Maj. 617

Sturgeon, Nicola, *SNP, Glasgow Southside,* Maj. 4,349

Swinney, John, *SNP, Perthshire North,* Maj. 10,353

Thompson, Dave, *SNP, Skye, Lochaber and Badenoch* Maj. 4,995

Torrance, David, *SNP, Kirkcaldy,* Maj. 182

Urquhart, Jean, *Ind., Highlands and Islands region*

Watt, Maureen, *SNP, Aberdeen South and North Kincardine,* Maj. 6,323

Wheelhouse, Paul, *SNP, South Scotland region*

White, Sandra, *SNP, Glasgow Kelvin,* Maj. 882

Wilson, John, *SNP, Central Scotland region*

Yousaf, Humza, *SNP, Glasgow region*

STATE OF THE PARTIES
as at 1 September 2014

	Constituency MSPs	Regional MSPs	Total
Scottish National Party (SNP)	51	14	65
Scottish Labour Party (Lab.)	16	22	38
Scottish Conservative and Unionist Party (C.)	3	12	15
Scottish Liberal Democrats (LD)	2	3	5
Scottish Green Party (Green)	0	2	2
Independent (Ind.)	0	2	2
‡Presiding Officer	1	0	1
Total	73	56	129

‡The presiding officer was elected as a constituency member for the SNP but has no party allegiance while in post

The Presiding Officer, Rt. Hon. Tricia Marwick, MSP

Deputy Presiding Officers, John Scott, MSP *(C.)*; Elaine Smith, MSP *(Lab.)*

SCOTTISH PARLIAMENT ELECTION RESULTS

as at 5 May 2011
E. Electorate T. Turnout
See General Election Results for a list of party abbreviations

CONSTITUENCIES
E. 3,985,161 T. 50.4%

ABERDEEN CENTRAL
(Scotland North East Region)
E. 57,396 T. 25,149 (43.82%)
Kevin Stewart, SNP   10,058
Lewis Macdonald, Lab.   9,441
Sandy Wallace, C.   3,100
Sheila Thomson, LD   2,349
Mike Phillips, NF   201
SNP majority 617 (2.45%)
0.54% swing Lab. to SNP

ABERDEEN DONSIDE
(Scotland North East Region)
E. 56,145 T. 26,761 (47.66%)
Brian Adam, SNP   14,790
Barney Crockett, Lab.   7,615
Ross Thomson, C.   2,166
Millie McLeod, LD.   1,606
David Henderson, Ind.   371
Christopher Willett, NF   213
SNP majority 7,175 (26.81%)
6.87% swing Lab. to SNP

**ABERDEEN SOUTH AND
KINCARDINE NORTH**
(Scotland North East Region)
E. 54,338 T. 28,697 (52.81%)
Maureen Watt, SNP   11,947
Greg Williams, Lab.   5,624
John Sleigh, LD   4,994
Stewart Whyte, C.   4,058
SNP majority 6,323 (22.03%)
15.77% swing LD to SNP

ABERDEENSHIRE EAST
(Scotland North East Region)
E. 57,591 T. 30,286 (52.59%)
Alex Salmond, SNP   19,533
Alison McInnes, LD   4,238
Geordie Burnett Stuart, C.   4,211
Peter Smyth, Lab.   2,304
SNP majority 15,295 (50.5%)
19.53% swing LD to SNP

ABERDEENSHIRE WEST
(Scotland North East Region)
E. 53,779 T. 28,636 (53.25%)
Dennis Robertson, SNP   12,186
Mike Rumbles, LD   8,074
Nanette Milne, C.   6,027
Jean Morrison, Lab.   2,349
SNP majority 4,112 (14.36%)
13.45% swing LD to SNP

AIRDRIE AND SHOTTS
(Scotland Central Region)
E. 51,336 T. 23,894 (46.54%)
Alex Neil, SNP   11,984
Karen Whitefield, Lab.   9,983
Robert Crozier, C.   1,396
John Love, LD   531
SNP majority 2,001 (8.37%)
5.50% swing Lab. to SNP

ALMOND VALLEY
(Lothian Region)
E. 59,896 T. 30,737 (51.32%)
Angela Constance, SNP   16,704
Lawrence Fitzpatrick, Lab. 11,162
Andrew Hardie, C.   1,886
Emma Sykes, LD   656
Neil McIvor, NF   329
SNP majority 5,542 (18.03%)
9.01% swing Lab. to SNP

ANGUS NORTH AND MEARNS
(Scotland North East Region)
E. 52,124 T. 24,920 (47.81%)
Nigel Don, SNP   13,660
Alex Johnstone, C.   6,374
Kevin Hutchens, Lab.   3,160
Sanjay Samani, LD   1,726
SNP majority 7,286 (29.24%)
4.15% swing C. to SNP

ANGUS SOUTH
(Scotland North East Region)
E. 54,922 T. 27,643 (50.33%)
Graeme Dey, SNP   16,164
Hughie Campbell
   Adamson, C.   5,581
William Campbell, Lab.   3,703
David Fairweather, AIR   1,321
Clive Sneddon, LD   874
SNP majority 10,583 (38.28%)
9.31% swing C. to SNP

ARGYLL AND BUTE
(Highlands and Islands Region)
E. 49,028 T. 26,476 (54.00%)
Michael Russell, SNP   13,390
Jamie McGrigor, C.   4,847
Mick Rice, Lab.   4,041
Alison Hay, LD   3,220
George Doyle, Ind.   542
George White, Lib.   436
SNP majority 8,543 (32.27%)
8.52% swing C. to SNP

AYR
(Scotland South Region)
E. 61,563 T. 33,373 (54.21%)
John Scott, C.   12,997
Chic Brodie, SNP   11,884
Gordon McKenzie, Lab.   7,779
Eileen Taylor, LD   713
C. majority 1,113 (3.34%)
5.16% swing C. to SNP

**BANFFSHIRE AND BUCHAN
COAST**
(Scotland North East Region)
E. 53,698 T. 25,004 (46.56%)
Stewart Stevenson, SNP   16,812
Michael Watt, C.   4,592
Alan Duffill, Lab.   2,642
Galen Milne, LD   958
SNP majority 12,220 (48.87%)
3.48% swing C. to SNP

**CAITHNESS, SUTHERLAND AND
ROSS**
(Highlands and Islands Region)
E. 55,116 T. 28,600 (51.89%)
Rob Gibson, SNP   13,843
Robbie Rowantree, LD   6,385
John MacKay, Lab.   5,438
Edward Mountain, C.   2,934
SNP majority 7,458 (26.08%)
17.32% swing LD to SNP

**CARRICK, CUMNOCK AND
DOON VALLEY**
(Scotland South Region)
E. 59,368 T. 28,703 (48.35%)
Adam Ingram, SNP   13,250
Richard Leonard, Lab.   10,669
Peter Kennerley, C.   4,160
Andrew Chamberlain, LD   624
SNP majority 2,581 (8.99%)
11.77% swing Lab. to SNP

**CLACKMANNANSHIRE &
DUNBLANE**
(Mid Scotland and Fife Region)
E. 49,415 T. 27,416 (55.48%)
Keith Brown, SNP   13,253
Richard Simpson, Lab.   9,644
Callum Campbell, C.   3,501
Tim Brett, LD   1,018
SNP majority 3,609 (13.16%)
5.20% swing Lab. to SNP

CLYDEBANK AND MILNGAVIE
(Scotland West Region)
E. 53,018 T. 28,369 (53.51%)

Gils Paterson, SNP	12,278
Des McNulty, Lab.	11,564
Alice Struthers, C.	2,758
John Duncan, LD	1,769

SD majority 714 (2.52%)
6.56% swing Lab. to SNP

CLYDESDALE
(Scotland South Region)
E. 56,828 T. 29,937 (52.68%)

Aileen Campbell, SNP	14,931
Karen Gillon, Lab.	10,715
Colin McGavigan, C.	4,291

SNP majority 4,216 (14.08%)
8.89% swing Lab. to SNP

COATBRIDGE AND CHRYSTON
(Scotland Central Region)
E. 51,206 T. 23,279 (45.46%)

Elaine Smith, Lab.	12,161
John Wilson, SNP	9,420
Jason Lingiah, C.	1,317
Rod Ackland, LD	381

Lab. majority 2,741 (11.77%)
3.28% swing Lab. to SNP

COWDENBEATH
(Mid Scotland and Fife Region)
E. 54,284 T. 25,670 (47.29%)

Helen Eadie, Lab.	11,926
Ian Chisholm, SNP	10,679
Belinda Don, C.	1,792
Keith Legg, LD	997
Mike Heenan, Land Party	276

Lab. majority 1,247 (4.86%)
4.85% swing Lab. to SNP

CUMBERNAULD AND KILSYTH
(Scotland Central Region)
E. 48,006 T. 25,254 (52.61%)

Jamie Hepburn, SNP	13,595
Cathie Craigie, Lab.	10,136
James Boswell, C.	1,156
Martin Oliver, LD	367

SNP majority 3,459 (13.7%)
10.79% Lab. to SNP

CUNNINGHAME NORTH
(Scotland West Region)
E. 56,548 T. 29,536 (52.23%)

Kenneth Gibson, SNP	15,539
Allan Wilson, Lab.	9,422
Maurice Golden, C.	4,032
Mallika Punukollu, LD	543

SNP majority 6,117 (20.71%)
10.29% swing Lab. to SNP

CUNNINGHAME SOUTH
(Scotland South Region)
E. 50,926 T. 22,056 (43.31%)

Margaret Burgess, SNP	10,993
Irene Oldfather, Lab.	8,645
Alistair Haw, C.	1,871
Ruby Kirkwood, LD	547

SNP majority 2,348 (10.65%)
9.93% swing Lab. to SNP

DUMBARTON
(Scotland West Region)
E. 53,470 T. 28,508 (53.32%)

Jackie Baillie, Lab.	12,562
Iain Robertson, SNP	10,923
Graham Smith, C.	3,395
Helen Watt, LD	858
George Rice, Ind.	770

Lab. majority 1,639 (5.75%)
0.24% swing SNP to Lab.

DUMFRIESSHIRE
(Scotland South Region)
E. 59,716 T. 31,895 (53.41%)

Elaine Murray, Lab.	12,624
Gill Dykes, C.	9,468
Aileen Orr, SNP	8,384
Richard Brodie, LD	1,419

Lab. majority 3,156 (9.89%)
5.99% swing C. to Lab.

DUNDEE EAST
(Scotland North East Region)
E. 54,404 T. 25,753 (47.34%)

Shona Robison, SNP	16,541
Mohammed Asif, Lab.	5,862
Brian Docherty, C.	2,550
Allan Petrie, LD	800

SNP majority 10,679 (41.47%)
12.47% swing Lab. to SNP

DUNDEE WEST
(Scotland North East Region)
E. 53,841 T. 24,461 (45.43%)

Joe Fitzpatrick, SNP	14,089
Richard McCready, Lab.	7,684
Colin Stewart, C.	1,625
Alison Burns, LD	1,063

SNP majority 6,405 (26.18%)
8.88% swing Lab. to SNP

DUNFERMLINE
(Scotland Mid and Fife Region)
E. 55,479 T. 29,299 (52.81%)

Bill Walker, SNP	11,010
Alex Rowley, Lab.	10,420
Jim Tolson, LD	5,776
James Reekie, C.	2,093

SNP majority 599 (2.01%)
13.41% swing LD to SNP

EAST KILBRIDE
(Scotland Central Region)
E. 58,251 T. 29,911 (51.35%)

Linda Fabiani, SNP	14,359
Andy Kerr, Lab.	12,410
Graham Simpson, C.	2,260
Douglas Herbison, LD	468
John Houston, Ind.	414

SNP majority 1,949 (6.52%)
6.64% swing Lab. to SNP

EAST LOTHIAN
(Scotland South Region)
E. 56,333 T. 32,177 (57.12%)

Iain Gray, Lab.	12,536
David Berry, SNP	12,385
Derek Brownlee, C.	5,344
Ettie Spencer, LD	1,912

Lab. majority 151 (0.47%)
3.12% swing Lab to SNP

EASTWOOD
(Scotland West Region)
E. 50,476 T. 31,924 (63.25%)

Ken Macintosh, Lab.	12,662
Jackson Carlaw, C.	10,650
Stewart Maxwell, SNP	7,777
Gordon Cochrane, LD	835

Lab. majority 2,012 (6.3%)
8.74% swing C. to Lab.

EDINBURGH CENTRAL
(Lothian Region)
E. 53,606 T. 29,014 (54.12%)

Marco Biagi, SNP	9,480
Sarah Boyack, Lab.	9,243
Alex Cole-Hamilton, LD	5,937
Iain McGill, C.	4,354

SNP majority 237 (0.82%)
10.16% swing Lab. to SNP

EDINBURGH EASTERN
(Lothian Region)
E. 55,773 T. 30,728 (55.09%)

Kenny MacAskill, SNP	14,552
Ewan Aitken, Lab.	12,319
Cameron Buchanan, C.	2,630
Martin Veart, LD	1,227

SNP majority 2,233 (7.27%)
4.53% swing Lab. to SNP

EDINBURGH NORTHERN AND LEITH
(Lothian Region)
E. 59,138 T. 30,885 (52.23%)

Malcolm Chisholm, Lab.	12,858
Shirley-Anne Somerville, SNP	12,263
Sheila Low, C.	2,928
Don Farthing, LD	2,836

Lab. majority 595 (1.93%)
2.66% swing Lab. to SNP

EDINBURGH PENTLANDS
(Lothian Region)
E. 52,620 T. 30,049 (57.11%)

Gordon MacDonald, SNP	11,197
David McLetchie, C.	9,439
Ricky Henderson, Lab.	7,993
Simon Clark, LD	1,420

SNP majority 1,758 (5.85%)
7.42% swing C. to SNP

EDINBURGH SOUTHERN
(Lothian Region)
E. 54,868 T. 33,796 (61.60%)

Jim Eadie, SNP	9,947
Paul Godzik, Lab.	9,254
Mike Pringle, LD	8,297
Gavin Brown, C.	6,298

SNP majority 693 (2.05%)
12.06% swing LD to SNP

EDINBURGH WESTERN
(Lothian Region)
E. 56,338 T. 33,452 (59.38%)

Colin Keir, SNP	11,965
Margaret Smith, LD	9,276
Lesley Hinds, Lab.	7,164
Gordon Lindhurst, C.	5,047

SNP majority 2,689 (8.04%)
12.60% swing LD to SNP

**ETTRICK, ROXBURGH AND
BERWICKSHIRE**
(Scotland South Region)
E. 54,327 T. 28,816 (53.04%)

John Lamont, C.	12,933
Paul Wheelhouse, SNP	7,599
Euan Robson, LD	4,990
Rab Stewart, Lab.	2,986
Jesse Rae, Ind.	308

C. majority 5,334 (18.51%)
1.39% swing C. to SNP

FALKIRK EAST
(Scotland Central Region)
E. 56,408 T. 28,168 (49.94%)

Angus MacDonald, SNP	14,302
Cathy Peattie, Lab.	10,767
Lynn Munro, C.	2,372
Ross Laird, LD	727

SNP majority 3,535 (12.55%)
9.33% swing Lab. to SNP

FALKIRK WEST
(Scotland Central Region)
E. 55,739 T. 28,199 (50.59%)

Michael Matheson, SNP	15,607
Dennis Goldie, Lab.	9,862
Allan Finnie, C.	2,086
Callum Chomczuk, LD	644

SNP majority 5,745 (20.37%)
8.91% swing Lab. to SNP

FIFE MID AND GLENROTHES
(Scotland Mid and Fife Region)
E. 53,701 T. 26,313 (49.0%)

Tricia Marwick, SNP	13,761
Claire Baker, Lab.	9,573
Allan Smith, C.	1,676
Jim Parker, ASPP	673
Callum Leslie, LD	630

SNP majority 4,188 (15.92%)
3.43% swing Lab. to SNP

FIFE NORTH EAST
(Scotland Mid and Fife Region)
E. 58,858 T. 29,676 (50.42%)

Roderick Campbell, SNP	11,029
Iain Smith, LD	8,437
Miles Briggs, C.	5,618
Colin Davidson, Lab.	3,613
Mike Scott-Hayward, UKIP	979

SNP majority 2,592 (8.73%)
15.02% swing LD to SNP

**GALLOWAY AND WEST
DUMFRIES**
(Scotland South Region)
E. 56,611 T. 29,997 (52.99%)

Alex Fergusson, C.	11,071
Aileen McLeod, SNP	10,209
Willie Scobie, Lab.	7,954
Joe Rosiejak, LD	763

C. majority 862 (2.87%)
2.40% swing C. to SNP

GLASGOW ANNIESLAND
(Glasgow Region)
E. 55,411 T. 23,918 (43.16%)

Bill Kidd, SNP	10,329
Bill Butler, Lab.	10,322
Matthew Smith, C.	2,011
Paul McGarry, LD	1,000
Marc Livingstone, Comm. Brit.	256

SNP majority 7 (0.03%)
10.09% swing Lab. to SNP

GLASGOW CATHCART
(Glasgow Region)
E. 58,525 T. 26,222 (44.8%)

James Dornan, SNP	11,918
Charlie Gordon, Lab.	10,326
Richard Sullivan, C.	2,410
Eileen Baxendale, LD	1,118
John McKee, Ind.	450

SNP majority 1,592 (6.07%)
6.53% swing Lab. to SNP

GLASGOW KELVIN
(Glasgow Region)
E. 61,893 T. 24,548 (39.66%)

Sandra White, SNP	10,640
Pauline McNeil, Lab.	9,758
Natalie McKee, LD	1,900
Ruth Davidson, C.	1,845
Tom Muirhead, Ind.	405

SNP majority 882 (3.59%)
4.03% swing Lab. to SNP

**GLASGOW MARYHILL AND
SPRINGBURN**
(Glasgow Region)
E. 56,622 T. 20,531 (36.26%)

Patricia Ferguson, Lab.	9,884
Bob Doris, SNP	8,592
Stephanie Murray, C.	1,222
Sophie Bridger, LD	833

Lab. majority 1,292 (6.29%)
5.43% swing Lab. to SNP

GLASGOW POLLOK
(Glasgow Region)
E. 58,429 T. 22,915 (39.22%)

Johann Lamont, Lab.	10,875
Chris Stephens, SNP	10,252
Andrew Morrison, C.	1,298
Isabel Nelson, LD	490

Lab. majority 623 (2.72%)
8.53% swing Lab. to SNP

GLASGOW PROVAN
(Glasgow Region)
E. 55,118 T. 19,185 (34.81%)

Paul Martin, Lab.	10,037
Anne McLaughlin, SNP	7,958
Majid Hussain, C.	777
Michael O'Donnell, LD	413

Lab. majority 2,079 (10.84%)
8.68% swing Lab. to SNP

GLASGOW SHETTLESTON
(Glasgow Region)
E. 55,874 T. 21,204 (37.95%)

John Mason, SNP	10,128
Frank McAveety, Lab.	9,542
David Wilson, C.	1,163
Ruaraidh Dobson, LD	371

SNP majority 586 (2.76%)
12.61% swing Lab. to SNP

GLASGOW SOUTHSIDE
(Glasgow Region)
E. 52,325 T. 22,608 (43.21%)

Nicola Sturgeon, SNP	12,306
Stephen Curran, Lab.	7,957
David Meikle, C.	1,733
Kenneth Elder, LD	612

SNP majority 4,349 (19.24%)
9.68% swing Lab. to SNP

GREENOCK AND INVERCLYDE
(Scotland West Region)
E. 56,989 T. 28,298 (49.50%)

Duncan McNeil, Lab.	12,387
Stuart McMillan, SNP	11,876
Graeme Brooks, C.	2,011
Ross Finnie, LD	1,934

Lab. majority 511 (1.81%)
6.90% swing Lab. to SNP

**HAMILTON, LARKHALL AND
STONEHOUSE**
(Scotland Central Region)
E. 56,123 T. 25,354 (45.18%)

Christina McKelvie, SNP	12,202
Tom McCabe, Lab.	9,989
Margaret Mitchell, C.	2,547
Ewan Hoyle, LD	616

SNP majority 2,213 (8.73%)
10.99% swing Lab. to SNP

INVERNESS & NAIRN
(Highlands and Islands Region)
E. 62,168 T. 32,731 (52.65%)

Fergus Ewing, SNP	16,870
David Stewart, Lab.	7,125
Mary Scanlon, C.	3,797
Christine Jardine, LD	3,763
Donald Boyd, Christian Party	646
Ross Durance, UKIP	530

SNP majority 9,745 (29.77%)
4.85% swing Lab. to SNP

KILMARNOCK AND IRVINE VALLEY
(Scotland Central Region)
E. 63,257 T. 31,858 (50.36%)

Willie Coffey, SNP	16,964
Matt McLaughlin, Lab.	10,971
Grant Fergusson, C.	3,309
Robbie Simpson, LD	614

SNP majority 5,993 (18.81%)
7.40% swing Lab. to SNP

KIRKCALDY
(Scotland Mid and Fife Region)
E. 60,079 T. 27,803 (46.28%)

David Torrance, SNP	12,579
Marilyn Livingstone, Lab.	12,397
Ian McFarlane, C.	2,007
John Mainland, LD	820

SNP majority 182 (0.65%)
6.19% swing Lab. to SNP

LINLITHGOW
(Lothian Region)
E. 65,025 T. 34,182 (52.57%)

Fiona Hyslop, SNP	17,027
Mary Mulligan, Lab.	12,936
Christopher Donnelly, C.	2,646
Jennifer Lang, LD	1,015
Mike Coyle, NF	558

SNP majority 4,091 (11.97%)
6.42% swing Lab. to SNP

MIDLOTHIAN NORTH AND MUSSELBURGH
(Lothian Region)
E. 58,246 T. 29,818 (51.19%)

Colin Beattie, SNP	14,079
Bernard Harkins, Lab.	11,083
Scott Douglas, C.	2,541
Ian Younger, LD	1,254
Alan Hay, Ind.	861

SNP majority 2,996 (10.05%)
7.61% swing Lab. to SNP

MIDLOTHIAN SOUTH, TWEEDDALE AND LAUDERDALE
(Lothian Region)
E. 57,781 T. 31,841 (55.11%)

Christine Grahame, SNP	13,855
Jeremy Purvis, LD	8,931
Ian Miller, Lab.	5,312
Peter Duncan, C.	3,743

SNP majority 4,924 (15.46%)
5.87% swing LD to SNP

MORAY
(Highlands and Islands Region)
E. 56,215 T. 28,596 (50.87%)

Richard Lochhead, SNP	16,817
Douglas Ross, C.	5,873
Kieron Green, Lab.	3,580
Jamie Paterson, LD	1,327
Donald Gatt, UKIP	999

SNP majority 10,944 (38.27%)
6.19% swing C. to SNP

MOTHERWELL AND WISHAW
(Scotland Central Region)
E. 53,610 T. 24,451 (45.61%)

John Pentland, Lab.	10,713
Clare Adamson, SNP	10,126
Bob Burgess, C.	1,753
John Swinburne, ASPP	945
Tom Selfridge, Christian Party	547
Beverley Hope, LD	367

Lab. majority 587 (2.4%)
10.20% swing Lab. to SNP

NA H-EILEANAN AN IAR
(Highlands and Islands Region)
E. 21,834 T. 13,011 (59.59%)

Alasdair Allan, SNP	8,496
Donald Crichton, Lab.	3,724
Charlie McGrigor, C.	563
Peter Morrison, LD	228

SNP majority 4,772 (36.68%)
15.82% swing Lab. to SNP

ORKNEY
(Highlands and Islands Region)
E. 16,393 T. 8,152 (49.73%)

Liam McArthur, LD	2,912
James Stockan, Ind.	2,052
George Adam, SNP	2,044
Jamie Halcro Johnston, C.	686
William Sharkey, Lab.	458

LD majority 860 (10.55%)
17.70% swing LD to Ind.

PAISLEY
(Scotland West Region)
E. 52,066 T. 25,590 (49.15%)

George Adam, SNP	10,913
Evan Williams, Lab.	10,665
Malcolm MacAskill, C.	2,229
Eileen McCartin, LD	1,783

SNP majority 248 (0.97%)
7.80% swing Lab. to SNP

PERTHSHIRE NORTH
(Scotland and Mid Fife Region)
E. 53,412 T. 29,953 (56.08%)

John Swinney, SNP	18,219
Murdo Fraser, C.	7,866
Pete Cheema, Lab.	2,672
Victor Clements, LD	1,196

SNP majority 10,353 (34.56%)
6.53% swing C. to SNP

PERTHSHIRE SOUTH AND KINROSS-SHIRE
(Scotland and Mid Fife Region)
E. 58,093 T. 31,216 (53.73%)

Roseanna Cunningham, SNP	16,073
Liz Smith, C.	8,907
Tricia Duncan, Lab.	3,980
Willie Robertson, LD	2,256

SNP majority 7,166 (22.96%)
9.25% swing C. to SNP

RENFREWSHIRE NORTH AND WEST
(Scotland West Region)
E. 49,060 T. 27,495 (56.04%)

Derek Mackay, SNP	11,510
Stuart Clark, Lab.	9,946
Annabel Goldie, C.	5,489
Andrew Page, LD	550

SNP majority 1,564 (5.69%)
8.42% swing Lab. to SNP

RENFREWSHIRE SOUTH
(Scotland West Region)
E. 50,221 T. 26,908 (53.58%)

Hugh Henry, Lab.	12,933
Andrew Doig, SNP	10,356
Alistair Campbell, C.	2,917
Gordon Anderson, LD	702

Lab. majority 2,577 (9.58%)
5.41% swing Lab. to SNP

RUTHERGLEN
(Glasgow Region)
E. 57,777 T. 27,122 (46.94%)

James Kelly, Lab.	12,489
Jim McGuigan, SNP	10,710
Martyn McIntyre, C.	2,096
Lisa Strachan, LD	1,174
Caroline Johnstone, Ind.	633

Lab. majority 1,779 (6.56%)
7.43% swing Lab. to SNP

SHETLAND ISLANDS
(Highlands and Islands Region)
E. 17,505 T. 9,391 (53.65%)

Tavish Scott, LD	4,462
Billy Fox, Ind.	2,845
Jean Urquhart, SNP	1,134
Jamie Kerr, Lab.	620
Sandy Cross, C.	330

LD majority 1,617 (17.22%)
5.5% swing LD to Ind.

SKYE, LOCHABER AND BADENOCH
(Highlands and Islands Region)
E. 57,024 T. 31,915 (55.97%)

Dave Thompson, SNP	14,737
Alan MacRae, LD	9,742
Linda Stewart, Lab.	4,112
Kerensa Carr, C.	2,834
Ronnie Campbell, Ind.	490

SNP majority 4,995 (15.65%)
12.97% swing LD to SNP

STIRLING
(Scotland and Mid Fife Region)
E. 51,458 T. 30,406 (59.09%)

Bruce Crawford, SNP	14,859
John Hendry, Lab.	9,188
Neil Benny, C.	4,610
Graham Reed, LD	1,296
Jack Black, Ind.	454

SNP majority 5,671 (18.65%)
9.93% swing Lab. to SNP

STRATHKELVIN AND BEARSDEN
(Scotland West Region)
E. 59,323 T. 33,752 (56.90%)

Fiona McLeod, SNP	14,258
David Whitton, Lab.	12,456
Jean Turner, Ind.	6,742
Stephanie Fraser, C.	4,438
Gordon Macdonald, LD	2,600

SNP majority 1,802 (5.34%)
7.69% swing Lab. to SNP

UDDINGSTON AND BELLSHILL
(Central Scotland Region)
E. 55,584 T. 24,995 (44.97%)

Michael McMahon, Lab.	11,531
Richard Lyle, SNP	10,817
Mark Brown, C.	2,117
Fraser Macgregor, LD	530

Lab majority 714 (2.86%)
9.04% swing Lab. to SNP

REGIONS
E. 3,985,161 T. 50.4%

GLASGOW
E. 514,393 T. 208,712 (40.57%)

SNP	83,109	(39.8%)
Lab.	73,031	(35.0%)
C.	12,749	(6.1%)
Green	12,454	(6.0%)
Respect	6,972	(3.3%)
LD	5,312	(2.5%)
ASPP	3,750	(1.8%)
BNP	2,424	(1.2%)
Socialist Labour	2,276	(1.1%)
Christian Party	1,501	(0.7%)
Scottish Unionist Party	1,447	(0.7%)
SSP	1,362	(0.7%)
UKIP	1,123	(0.5%)
Pirate	581	(0.3%)
Ind. Johnstone	338	(0.2%)
SHP	283	(0.1%)

Lab. majority 10,078 (4.83%)
8.04% swing Lab. to SNP (2007 Lab. majority 23,006)

ADDITIONAL MEMBERS
Humza Yousaf, SNP
Bob Doris, SNP
Hanzala Malik, Lab.
Drew Smith, Lab.
Anne McTaggert, Lab.
Ruth Davidson, C.
Patrick Harvie, Green

HIGHLANDS AND ISLANDS
E. 337,588 T. 179,010 (53.03%)

SNP	85,082	(47.5%)
Lab.	25,884	(14.5%)
C.	21,729	(12.1%)
LD	20,843	(11.6%)
Green	9,076	(5.1%)
Christian Party	3,541	(2%)
UKIP	3,372	(1.9%)
ASPP	2,770	(1.5%)
Ban Bankers Bonuses	1,764	(1%)
Lib.	1,696	(0.9%)
Soc. Lab.	1,406	(0.8%)
BNP	1,134	(0.6%)
SSP	509	(0.3%)
Solidarity	204	(0.1%)

SNP majority 59,198 (33.07%)
8.16% swing Lab. to SNP (2007 SNP majority 26,978)

ADDITIONAL MEMBERS
John Finnie, SNP
Jean Urquhart, SNP
Mike MacKenzie, SNP
Rhoda Grant, Lab.
David Stewart, Lab.
Jamie McGrigor, C.
Mary Scanlon, C.

LOTHIAN
E. 515,978 T. 283,203 (54.89%)

SNP	110,953	(39.2%)
Lab.	70,544	(24.9%)
C.	33,019	(11.7%)
Green	21,505	(7.6%)
Ind. MacDonald	18,732	(6.6%)
LD	15,588	(5.5%)
ASPP	3,218	(1.1%)
BNP	1,978	(0.7%)
UKIP	1,822	(0.6%)
Soc. Lab.	1,681	(0.6%)
SSP	1,183	(0.4%)
Christian Party	914	(0.3%)
Lib.	697	(0.2%)
CPA	553	(0.2%)
Solidarity	327	(0.1%)
Ind. Hogg	294	(0.1%)
Ind. O'Neill	134	(0.1%)
Ind. Brown	61	(0.1%)

SNP majority 40,409 (14.27%)
7.0% swing Lab. to SNP (2007 SNP majority 524)

ADDITIONAL MEMBERS
Sarah Boyack, Lab.
Kezia Dugdale, Lab.
Neil Findlay, Lab.
David McLetchie, C.
Gavin Brown, C.
Alison Johnstone, Green
Margo MacDonald, Ind.

SCOTLAND CENTRAL
E. 497,737 T. 233,560 (46.92%)

SNP	108,261	(46.4%)
Lab.	82,459	(35.3%)
C.	14,870	(6.4%)
ASPP	5,793	(2.5%)
Green	5,634	(2.4%)
LD	3,318	(1.4%)
Christian Party	3,173	(1.4%)
Soci. Lab.	2,483	(1.1%)
BNP	2,214	(0.9%)
Scottish Unionist Party	1,555	(0.7%)
UKIP	1,263	(0.5%)
Ind. O'Donnell	821	(0.4%)
SSP	820	(0.4%)
Solidarity	559	(0.2%)
SHP	337	(0.1%)

Lab. majority 25,802 (11.05%)
10.08% swing Lab. to SNP (2007 Lab. majority 23,386)

ADDITIONAL MEMBERS
Richard Lyle, SNP
John Wilson, SNP
Clare Adamson, SNP
Siobhan McMahon, Lab.
Mark Griffin, Lab.
Margaret McCulloch, Lab.
Margaret Mitchell, C.

SCOTLAND MID AND FIFE
E. 503,559 T. 258,163 (51.27%)

SNP	116,691	(45.2%)
Lab.	64,623	(25.0%)
C.	36,458	(14.1%)
LD	15,103	(5.9%)
Green	10,914	(4.2%)
ASPP	4,113	(1.6%)
UKIP	2,838	(1.1%)
Soc. Lab.	1,771	(0.7%)
BNP	1,726	(0.7%)
Ind. Rodger	1,466	(0.6%)
SSP	834	(0.3%)
Christian Party	786	(0.3%)
CPA	638	(0.2%)
Solidarity	202	(0.1%)

SNP majority 52,068 (10.9%)
7.43% swing Lab. to SNP (2007 Lab. majority 18,168)

ADDITIONAL MEMBERS
Annabelle Ewing, *SNP*
John Park, *Lab.*
Claire Baker, *Lab.*
Richard Simpson, *Lab.*
Murdo Fraser, *C.*
Liz Smith, *C.*
Willie Rennie, *LD*

SCOTLAND NORTH EAST
E. 550,162 T. 267,045 (48.54%)

SNP	140,749	(52.7%)
Lab.	43,893	(16.4%)
C.	37,681	(14.1%)
LD	18,178	(6.8%)
Green	10,407	(3.9%)
ASPP	4,420	(1.7%)
UKIP	2,477	(0.9%)
Christian Party	2,159	(0.8%)
BNP	1,925	(0.7%)
Soc. Lab.	1,459	(0.5%)
Ind. Cox	758	(0.3%)
NF	640	(0.2%)
AIR	471	(0.2%)
Solidarity	286	(0.1%)
Ind. Henderson	237	(0.1%)
Ind. McBride	190	(0.1%)

SNP majority 96,856 (36.27%)
7.68% swing Lab. to SNP (2007 SNP majority 53,140)

ADDITIONAL MEMBERS
Mark McDonald, *SNP*
Richard Baker, *Lab.*
Jenny Marra, *Lab.*
Lewis McDonald, *Lab.*
Alex Johnstone, *C.*
Nanette Milne, *C.*
Alison McInnes, *LD*

SCOTLAND SOUTH
E. 529,682 T. 278,987 (52.67%)

SNP	114,270	(41.0%)
Lab.	70,595	(25.3%)
C.	54,352	(19.5%)
LD	15,096	(5.4%)
Green	8,656	(3.1%)
ASPP	4,418	(1.6%)
UKIP	3,243	(1.2%)
Soc. Lab.	2,906	(1.0%)
BNP	2,017	(0.7%)
Christian Party	1,924	(0.7%)
Solidarity	813	(0.3%)
SSP	697	(0.2%)

SNP majority 43,675 (15.66%)
7.95% swing Lab. to SNP (2007 Lab. majority 2,709)

ADDITIONAL MEMBERS
Joan McAlpine, *SNP*
Aileen McLeod, *SNP*
Paul Wheelhouse, *SNP*
Chic Brodie, *SNP*
Claudia Beamish, *Lab.*
Graeme Pearson, *Lab.*
Jim Hume, *LD*

SCOTLAND WEST
E. 536,062 T. 282,371 (52.68%)

SNP	117,306	(41.5%)
Lab.	92,530	(32.8%)
C.	35,995	(12.7%)
LD	9,148	(3.2%)
Green	8,414	(3.0%)
ASPP	4,771	(1.7%)
Soc. Lab.	2,865	(1.0%)
Christian Party	2,468	(0.9%)
BNP	2,162	(0.8%)
UKIP	2,000	(0.7%)
SSP	1,752	(0.6%)
Ban Bankers Bonuses	1,204	(0.4%)
Pirate	850	(0.3%)
Ind. Vassie	460	(0.2%)
Solidarity	446	(0.2%)

SNP majority 24,776 (8.77%)
7.4% swing Lab. to SNP (2007 Lab. majority 15,772)

ADDITIONAL MEMBERS
Stewart Maxwell, *SNP*
Stuart McMillan, *SNP*
Mary Fee, *Lab.*
Neil Bibby, *Lab.*
Margaret McDougall, *Lab.*
Annabel Goldie, *C.*
Jackson Carlaw, *C.*

THE SCOTTISH REFERENDUM

THE ROAD TO REFERENDUM

Following the establishment of a majority Scottish National Party (SNP) government at Holyrood in May 2011, the SNP officially launched its independence bid at its annual party conference in October the same year. In May 2012 the UK government published the results of the Scottish referendum consultation, which showed strong levels of support for a single clear question on independence. On 25 May 2012 the 'Yes Scotland' campaign launched with the aim of encouraging 1 million Scots to sign a declaration of independence prior to a referendum.

THE EDINBURGH AGREEMENT

A series of talks between the Scottish government's deputy first minister Nicola Sturgeon and the Secretary of State for Scotland Michael Moore resulted in the Edinburgh Agreement. The agreement was signed by prime minister David Cameron and first minister Alex Salmond on 15 October 2012 and set out a timetable for a referendum vote to be held in autumn 2014.

SHOULD SCOTLAND BE AN INDEPENDENT COUNTRY?

On 30 January 2013 the wording of the independence referendum question was finalised as a simple yes/no question: 'Should Scotland be an independent country?'

THOSE AGED 16 GET TO VOTE

The Scottish independence referendum (franchise) bill was brought before parliament to ensure that all those aged 16 and over on the date of the referendum were entitled to vote.

THE DATE IS SET

On 21 March 2013 the date of the referendum was revealed as 18 September 2014. On 26 November 2013 Alex Salmond launched his government's independence blueprint, a 667-page white paper entitled *Scotland's Future: Your guide to an Independent Scotland*. On 13 February 2014 the UK Chancellor of the Exchequer, George Osborne ruled out a formal currency union in the event of independence. The formal 16-week campaign period, during which the amount of money registered campaigners can spend was limited, began at the start of May 2014.

REFERENDUM RESULTS *18 September 2014*

SHOULD SCOTLAND BE AN INDEPENDENT COUNTRY?

NO	YES
2,001,926 votes	1,617,989 votes
(55.3%)	(44.7%)
Turnout 84.6%	

PERCENTAGE OF VOTE BY REGION

Only four of the 32 Scottish local authority areas voted in favour of independence: Dundee City, Glasgow, North Lanarkshire and West Dunbartonshire.

Local Authority Area	No (%)	Yes (%)
Aberdeen City	58.6	41.4
Aberdeenshire	60.4	39.6
Angus	56.3	43.7
Argyll and Bute	58.5	41.5
Clackmannanshire	53.8	46.2
Dumfries and Galloway	65.7	34.3
Dundee City	42.7	57.3
East Ayrshire	52.8	47.2
East Dunbartonshire	61.2	38.8
East Lothian	61.7	38.3
East Renfrewshire	63.2	36.8
Edinburgh City	61.1	38.9
Falkirk	53.5	46.5
Fife	55.0	45.0
Glasgow City	46.5	53.5
Highland	52.9	47.1
Inverclyde	50.1	49.9
Midlothian	56.3	43.7
Moray	57.6	42.4
North Ayrshire	51.0	49.0
North Lanarkshire	48.9	51.1
Orkney	67.2	32.8
Perth and Kinross	60.2	39.8
Renfrewshire	52.8	47.2
Scottish Borders	66.6	33.4
Shetland	63.7	36.3
South Ayrshire	57.9	42.1
South Lanarkshire	54.7	45.3
Stirling	59.8	40.2
West Dunbartonshire	46.0	54.0
Western Isles (Eilean Siar)	53.4	46.6
West Lothian	55.2	44.8

NORTHERN IRELAND

NORTHERN IRELAND EXECUTIVE
Stormont Castle, Stormont, Belfast BT4 3TT
T 028-9052 8400
W www.northernireland.gov.uk

The first minister and deputy first minister head the executive committee of ministers and, acting jointly, determine the total number of ministers in the executive. First and deputy first ministers are elected by Northern Ireland assembly members through a formula of parallel consent that requires a majority of designated unionists, a majority of designated nationalists and a majority of the whole assembly to vote in favour. The parties elected to the assembly select ministerial portfolios in proportion to party strengths using the d'Hondt nominating procedure.

The executive committee includes five DUP ministers, four SF ministers, two Alliance members, one Social Democratic and Labour Party minister and one Ulster Unionist minister alongside the first minister Peter Robinson, MLA of the DUP and the deputy first minister, Martin McGuinness, MLA, of SF.

EXECUTIVE COMMITTEE
First Minister, Rt. Hon. Peter Robinson, MLA
Deputy First Minister, Martin McGuinness, MLA
Junior Ministers, Jennifer McCann, MLA; Jonathan Bell, MLA
Minister for Agriculture and Rural Development, Michelle O'Neill, MLA
Minister for Culture, Arts and Leisure, Carál Ní Chuilín, MLA
Minister for Education, John O'Dowd, MLA
Minister for Employment and Learning, Dr Stephen Farry, MLA
Minister for Enterprise, Trade and Investment, Arlene Foster, MLA
Minister for Environment, Mark Durkan, MLA
Minister for Finance and Personnel, Simon Hamilton, MLA
Minister for Health, Social Services and Public Safety, Edwin Poots, MLA
Minister for Justice, David Ford, MLA
Minister for Regional Development, Danny Kennedy, MLA
Minister for Social Development, Nelson McCausland, MLA

OFFICE OF THE FIRST MINISTER AND DEPUTY FIRST MINISTER
Stormont Castle, Stormont, Belfast BT4 3TT
T 028-9052 8400 W www.ofmdfmni.gov.uk

DEPARTMENT OF AGRICULTURE AND RURAL DEVELOPMENT
Dundonald House, Upper Newtownards Road, Belfast BT4 3SB
T 028-9052 0100 W www.dardni.gov.uk

EXECUTIVE AGENCIES
Forest Service
Veterinary Service

DEPARTMENT OF CULTURE, ARTS AND LEISURE
Causeway Exchange, 1–7 Bedford Street, Belfast BT1 7FB
T 028-9025 8825 W www.dcalni.gov.uk

DEPARTMENT OF EDUCATION
Rathgael House, Balloo Road, Bangor, Co. Down BT19 7PR
T 028-9127 9279 W www.deni.gov.uk

DEPARTMENT FOR EMPLOYMENT AND LEARNING
Adelaide House, 39–49 Adelaide Street, Belfast BT2 8FD
T 028-9025 7777 W www.delni.gov.uk

DEPARTMENT OF ENTERPRISE, TRADE AND INVESTMENT
Netherleigh, Massey Avenue, Belfast BT4 2JP T 028-9052 9900
W www.detini.gov.uk

EXECUTIVE AGENCIES
General Consumer Council for Northern Ireland
Health and Safety Executive
Invest Northern Ireland
Northern Ireland Tourist Board

DEPARTMENT OF THE ENVIRONMENT
Goodwood House, 45–58 May Street, Belfast BT1 4NN
W www.doeni.gov.uk

EXECUTIVE AGENCIES
Driver and Vehicle Agency (Northern Ireland)
NI Environment Agency

DEPARTMENT OF FINANCE AND PERSONNEL
Rathgael House, Balloo Road, Bangor BT19 7NA T 028-9185 8111
W www.dfpni.gov.uk

EXECUTIVE AGENCIES
Northern Ireland Statistics and Research Agency (Incorporates Land Registers of Northern Ireland and Ordnance Survey of Northern Ireland)

DEPARTMENT OF HEALTH, SOCIAL SERVICES AND PUBLIC SAFETY
Castle Buildings, Stormont, Belfast BT4 3SJ T 028-9052 0500
W www.dhsspsni.gov.uk

DEPARTMENT FOR REGIONAL DEVELOPMENT
Clarence Court, 10–18 Adelaide Street, Belfast BT2 8GB
T 028-9054 0540 W www.drdni.gov.uk

DEPARTMENT FOR SOCIAL DEVELOPMENT
Lighthouse Building, 1 Cromac Place, Gasworks Business Park, Ormeau Road, Belfast BT7 2JB T 028-9082 9000
W www.dsdni.gov.uk

EXECUTIVE AGENCIES
Charity Commission for Northern Ireland
Northern Ireland Housing Executive

DEPARTMENT OF JUSTICE
Block B, Castle Buildings, Stormont Estate, Belfast BT4 3SG
T 028-9076 3000 W www.dojni.gov.uk

EXECUTIVE AGENCIES
Forensic Service Northern Ireland
Northern Ireland Courts and Tribunals Service
Northern Ireland Prison Service
Youth Justice Agency

NORTHERN IRELAND AUDIT OFFICE
106 University Street, Belfast BT7 1EU
T 028-9025 1000 E info@niauditoffice.gov.uk
W www.niauditoffice.gov.uk
Comptroller and Auditor-General, Kieran Donnelly

NORTHERN IRELAND AUTHORITY FOR UTILITY REGULATION
Queens House, 14 Queen Street, Belfast BT1 6ED
T 028-9031 1575 E info@uregni.gov.uk W www.uregni.gov.uk
Chair, Dr Bill Emery

NORTHERN IRELAND ASSEMBLY

Parliament Buildings, Stormont, Belfast BT4 3XX
T 028-9052 1137 E info@niassembly.gov.uk
W www.niassembly.gov.uk

The Northern Ireland Assembly was established as a result of the Belfast Agreement (also known as the Good Friday Agreement) in April 1998. The agreement was endorsed through a referendum held in May 1998 and subsequently given legal force through the Northern Ireland Act 1998.

The Northern Ireland Assembly has full legislative and executive authority for all matters that are the responsibility of the government's Northern Ireland departments – known as transferred matters. Excepted and reserved matters are defined in schedules 2 and 3 of the Northern Ireland Act 1998 and remain the responsibility of UK parliament.

The first assembly election occurred on 25 June 1998 and the 108 members elected met for the first time on 1 July 1998. Members of the Northern Ireland Assembly are elected by the single transferable vote system from 18 constituencies – six per constituency. Under the single transferable vote system every voter has a single vote that can be transferred from one candidate to another. Voters number their candidates in order of preference. Where candidates reach their quota of votes and are elected, surplus votes are transferred to other candidates according to the next preference on each voter's ballot slip. The candidate in each round with the fewest votes is eliminated and their surplus votes are redistributed according to the voter's next preference. The process is repeated until the required number of members are elected.

On 29 November 1999 the assembly appointed ten ministers as well as the chairs and deputy chairs for the ten statutory departmental committees. Devolution of powers to the Northern Ireland Assembly occurred on 2 December 1999, following several delays concerned with Sinn Fein's inclusion in the executive while Irish Republican Army (IRA) weapons were yet to be decommissioned.

Since the devolution of powers, the assembly has been suspended by the Secretary of State for Northern Ireland on four occasions. The first was between 11 February and 30 May 2000, with two 24-hour suspensions on 10 August and 22 September 2001 – all owing to a lack of progress in decommissioning. The final suspension took place on 14 October 2002 after unionists walked out of the executive following a police raid on Sinn Fein's office investigating alleged intelligence gathering.

The assembly was formally dissolved in April 2003 in anticipation of an election, which eventually took place on 26 November 2003. The results of the election changed the balance of power between the political parties, with an increase in the number of seats held by the Democratic Unionist Party (DUP) and Sinn Fein (SF), so that they became the largest parties. The assembly was restored to a state of suspension following the November election while political parties engaged in a review of the Belfast Agreement aimed at fully restoring the devolved institutions.

In July 2005 the leadership of the IRA formally ordered an end to its armed campaign; it authorised a representative to engage with the Independent International Commission on Decommissioning in order to verifiably put the arms beyond use. On 26 September 2005 General John de Chastelain, the chair of the commission, along with two independent church witnesses confirmed that the IRA's entire arsenal of weapons had been decommissioned.

Following the passing of the Northern Ireland Act 2006 the secretary of state created a non-legislative fixed-term assembly, whose membership consisted of the 108 members elected in the 2003 election. It first met on 15 May 2006 with the remit of making preparations for the restoration of devolved government; its discussions informed the next round of talks called by the British and Irish governments held at St Andrews. The St Andrews agreement of 13 October 2006 led to the establishment of the transitional assembly.

The Northern Ireland (St Andrews Agreement) Act 2006 set out a timetable to restore devolution, and also set the date for the third election to the assembly as 7 March 2007. The DUP and SF had the largest number of Members of the Legislative Assembly (MLAs) elected, and although the initial restoration deadline of 26 March was missed, the leaders of the DUP and SF (Revd Dr Ian Paisley, MP, MLA and Gerry Adams, MLA, respectively) took part in a historic meeting and made a joint commitment to establish an executive committee in the assembly to which devolved powers were restored on 8 May 2007. After completing a full four-year mandate, new assembly elections took place on 5 May 2011 to elect the 108 members of the legislative assembly.

SALARIES	
	2014–15
First Minister/Deputy First Minister	£120,000
Minister	£86,000
MLA	£48,000

NORTHERN IRELAND ASSEMBLY MEMBERS

* New Member of the Legislative Assembly (MLA)
† Previously MLA for another party
as at September 2014

Agnew, Steven, *Green, North Down*
Allister, Jim, *TUV, North Antrim*
Anderson, Sydney, *DUP, Upper Bann*
Attwood, Alex, *SDLP, Belfast West*
Beggs, Roy, *UUP, East Antrim*
Bell, Jonathan, *DUP, Strangford*
Boylan, Cathal, *SF, Newry and Armagh*
Boyle, Michaela, *SF, West Tyrone*
Bradley, Dominic, *SDLP, Newry and Armagh*
Bradley, Paula, *DUP, Belfast North*
Brady, Mickey, *SF, Newry and Armagh*
Buchanan, Thomas, *DUP, West Tyrone*
Byrne, Joe, *SDLP, West Tyrone*
Cameron, Pam, *DUP, South Antrim*
Campbell, Gregory, *DUP, East Londonderry*
Clarke, Trevor, *DUP, South Antrim*
Cochrane, Judith, *Alliance, Belfast East*
Copeland, Michael, *UUP, Belfast East*
Craig, Jonathan, *DUP, Lagan Valley*
Cree, Leslie, *UUP, North Down*
Dallat, John, *SDLP, East Londonderry*
Dickson, Stewart, *Alliance, East Antrim*
Dobson, Jo-Anne, *UUP, Upper Bann*
Douglas, Sammy, *DUP, Belfast East*
Dunne, Gordon, *DUP, North Down*
Durkan, Mark, *SDLP, Foyle*
Easton, Alex, *DUP, North Down*
Eastwood, Colum, *SDLP, Foyle*
Elliot, Tom, *UUP, Fermanagh and South Tyrone*
Farry, Stephen, *Alliance, North Down*
*Fearon, Megan, *SF, Newry and Armagh*
Flanagan, Phil, *SF, Fermanagh and South Tyrone*
Ford, David, *Alliance, South Antrim*
Foster, Arlene, *DUP, Fermanagh and South Tyrone*
Frew, Paul, *DUP, North Antrim*
Gardiner, Samuel, *UUP, Upper Bann*
Girvan, Paul, *DUP, South Antrim*

Givan, Paul, *DUP, Lagan Valley*
Hale, Brenda, *DUP, Lagan Valley*
Hamilton, Simon, *DUP, Strangford*
Hay, William, *DUP, Foyle*
Hazzard, Chris, *SF, South Down*
Hilditch, David, *DUP, East Antrim*
Humphrey, William, *DUP, Belfast North*
Hussey, Ross, *UUP, West Tyrone*
Irwin, William, *DUP, Newry and Armagh*
Kelly, Dolores, *SDLP, Upper Bann*
Kelly, Gerry, *SF, Belfast North*
Kennedy, Danny, *UUP, Newry and Armagh*
Kinahan, Danny, *UUP, South Antrim*
Lo, Anna, *Alliance, Belfast South*
Lunn, Trevor, *Alliance, Lagan Valley*
Lynch, Sean, *SF, Fermanagh and South Tyrone*
Lyttle, Chris, *Alliance, Belfast East*
Maginness, Alban, *SDLP, Belfast North*
Maskey, Alex, *SF, Belfast South*
*McAleer, Declan, *SF, West Tyrone*
†McCallister, John, *NI21, South Down*
McCann, Fra, *SF, Belfast West*
McCann, Jennifer, *SF, Belfast West*
McCarthy, Kieran, *Alliance, Strangford*
McCartney, Raymond, *SF, Foyle*
McCausland, Nelson, *DUP, Belfast North*
McClarty, David, *Ind., East Londonderry*
*McCorley, Rosaleen, *SF, Belfast West*
†McCrea, Basil, *NI21, Lagan Valley*
McCrea, Ian, *DUP, Mid Ulster*
McDevitt, Conall, *SDLP, Belfast South*
McDonnell, Dr Alasdair, *SDLP, Belfast South*
McElduff, Barry, *SF, West Tyrone*
*McGahan, Bronwyn, *SF, Fermanagh and South Tyrone*
McGimpsey, Michael, *UUP, Belfast South*
McGlone, Patsy, *SDLP, Mid Ulster*
McGuinness, Martin, *SF, Mid Ulster*
McIlveen, David, *DUP, North Antrim*
McIlveen, Michelle, *DUP, Strangford*
McKay, Daithi, *SF, North Antrim*
McKevitt, Karen, *SDLP, South Down*
McKinney, Fearghal, *SDLP, Belfast South*
McLaughlin, Maeve, *SF, Foyle*
McLaughlin, Mitchel, *SF, South Antrim*
McMullan, Oliver, *SF, East Antrim*
†McNarry, David, *UKIP, Strangford*
McQuillan, Adrian, *DUP, East Londonderry*
*Milne, Ian, *SF, Mid Ulster*
Morrow, Lord, *DUP, Fermanagh and South Tyrone*
Moutray, Stephen, *DUP, Upper Bann*
Nesbitt, Mike, *UUP, Strangford*
Newton, Robin, *DUP, Belfast East*
Ni Chuilin, Caral, *SF, Belfast North*
O'Dowd, John, *SF, Upper Bann*
O'Neill, Michelle, *SF, Mid Ulster*
O hOisin, Cathal, *SF, East Londonderry*
Overend, Sandra, *UUP, Mid Ulster*
Poots, Edwin, *DUP, Lagan Valley*
Ramsey, Pat, *SDLP, Foyle*
Ramsey, Sue, *SF, Belfast West*
Robinson, George, *DUP, East Londonderry*
Robinson, Rt. Hon. Peter, *DUP, Belfast East*
Rodgers, Sean, *SDLP, South Down*
Ross, Alastair, *DUP, East Antrim*
Ruane, Caitriona, *SF, South Down*
Sheehan, Pat, *SF, Belfast West*
Spratt, Jimmy, *DUP, Belfast South*
Storey, Mervyn, *DUP, North Antrim*
Sugden, Claire, *Ind., East Londonderry*

Swann, Robin, *UUP, North Antrim*
Weir, Peter, *DUP, North Down*
Wells, Jim, *DUP, South Down*
Wilson, Sammy, *DUP, East Antrim*

STATE OF THE PARTIES *as at 1 September 2014*

Party	Seats
Democratic Unionist Party (DUP)	38
Sinn Fein (SF)	29
Social Democratic and Labour Party (SDLP)	14
Ulster Unionist Party (UUP)	13
Alliance Party (Alliance)	8
NI21	2
Green Party	1
Independent (Ind.)	1
Traditional Unionist Voice (TUV)	1
UK Independence Party (UKIP)	1
Total	108

NORTHERN IRELAND ASSEMBLY ELECTION RESULTS
As at 5 May 2011
E. 1,210,009 T. 55.64%

E. Electorate T. Turnout
First = first-preference votes
Final = final total for that candidate, after all necessary transfers of lower-preference votes
R. = round
* = eliminated last
See General Election Results for a list of party abbreviations

ANTRIM EAST
E. 61,617 T. 29,430 (47.76%)

	First	Final	Elected (R.)
Sammy Wilson, DUP	7,181	7,181	First (1)
David Hilditch, DUP	3,288	4,219	Second (2)
Roy Beggs, UUP	3,042	4,194	Fifth (9)
Stewart Dickson, Alliance	2,889	4,777	Fourth (9)
Oliver McMullan, SF	2,369	3,389	Sixth (10)
*Rodney McCune, UUP	1,851	2,890	
Gerardine Mulvenna, Alliance	1,620		
Alastair Ross, DUP	1,608	4,267	Third (6)
Ruth Wilson, TUV	1,346		
Justin McCamphill, SDLP	1,333		
Gordon Lyons, DUP	1,321		
Daniel Donnelly, Green	664		
Steven Moore, BNP	511		

ANTRIM NORTH
E. 74,760 T. 40,983 (54.82%)

	First	Final	Elected (R.)
Paul Frew, DUP	6,581	6,581	First (1)
Daithi McKay, SF	6,152	6,152	Second (1)
Mervyn Storey, DUP	6,083	6,083	Third (1)
Jim Allister, TUV	4,061	5,430	Sixth (9)
*Declan O'Loan, SDLP	3,682	4,816	
David McIlveen, DUP	3,275	6,594	Fourth (8)
Evelyne Robinson, DUP	3,256		
Robin Swann, UUP	2,518	5,557	Fifth (9)
Bill Kennedy, UUP	2,189		
Jayne Dunlop, Alliance	1,848		
Audrey Patterson, TUV	668		

ANTRIM SOUTH
E. 65,231 T. 32,652 (50.06%)

	First	Final	Elected (R.)
Paul Girvan, DUP	4,844	4,844	First (1)
Mitchel McLaughlin, SF	4,662	4,662	Second (1)
Trevor Clarke, UUP	4,607	4,607	Third (1)
David Ford, Alliance	4,554	4,660	Fourth (2)
Danny Kinahan, UUP	3,445	5,585	Fifth (3)
*Thomas Burns, SDLP	3,406	3,591	
Pam Lewis, DUP	2,866	4,668	Sixth (4)
Adrian Cochrane-Watson, UUP	2,285		
Mel Lucas, TUV	1,091		
Stephen Parkes, BNP	404		

BELFAST EAST
E. 61,263 T. 32,828 (53.59%)

	First	Final	Elected (R.)
Peter Robinson, DUP	9,149	9,149	First (1)
Judith Cochrane, Alliance	4,329	4,755	Third (7)
Chris Lyttle, Alliance	4,183	4,696	Fourth (9)
Sammy Douglas, DUP	2,668	4,783	Fifth (11)
Robin Newton, DUP	2,436	4,801	Second (2)
Michael Copeland, UUP	2,194	3,723	Sixth (11)
*Dawn Purvis, Ind.	1,702	2,789	
Brian Ervine, PUP	1,493		
Niall O'Donnghaile, SF	1,030		
Philip Robinson, UUP	943		
Harry Toan, TUV	712		
Martin Gregg, Green	572		
Ann Cooper, BNP	337		
Magdalena Wolska, SDLP	250		
Tommy Black, SP	201		
Kevin McNally, WP	102		
Stephen Stewart, Ind.	46		

BELFAST NORTH
E. 68,119 T. 34,280 (50.32%)

	First	Final	Elected (R.)
Gerry Kelly, SF	6,674	6,674	First (1)
Nelson McCausland, DUP	5,200	5,200	Second (1)
Alban Maginness, SDLP	4,025	5,004	Fourth (6)
William Humphrey, DUP	3,724	4,332	Fifth (7)
Paula Bradley, DUP	3,488	4,065	Sixth (7)
Caral Ni Chuilin, SF	2,999	4,868	Third (6)
*Fred Cobain, UUP	2,758	3,623	
Billy Webb, Alliance	2,096		
Raymond McCord, Ind.	1,176		
JJ Magee, SF	998		
John Lavery, WP	332		

BELFAST SOUTH
E. 62,484 T. 32,752 (52.42%)

	First	Final	Elected (R.)
Anna Lo, Alliance	6,390	6,390	First (1)
Dr Alasdair McDonnell, SDLP	4,527	4,916	Second (2)
Jimmy Spratt, DUP	4,045	4,281	Sixth (5)
Alex Maskey, SF	4,038	4,452	Fourth (5)
*Ruth Patterson, DUP	3,800	4,163	
Connall McDevitt, SDLP	3,191	4,445	Fifth (5)
Michael McGimpsey, UUP	2,988	4,622	Third (5)
Mark Finlay, UUP	1,394		
Claire Bailey, Green	889		
Brian Faloon, PBP	414		
Paddy Meehan, SP	234		
Nico Torregrosa, UKIP	234		
Paddy Lynn, WP	135		
Charles Smyth, Pro-Capitalism	29		

BELFAST WEST
E. 61,520 T. 35,618 (57.89%)

	First	Final	Elected (R.)
Paul Maskey, SF	5,343	5,343	First (1)
Jennifer McCann, SF	5,239	5,239	Second (1)
Fra McCann, SF	4,481	5,167	Third (10)
Sue Ramsey, SF	4,116	4,823	Fifth (11)
Alex Attwood, SDLP	3,765	5,152	Fourth (10)
Pat Sheehan, SF	3,723	4,327	Sixth (11)
*Brian Kingston, DUP	2,587	3,867	
Gerry Carroll, PBP	1,661		
Bill Manwaring, UUP	1,471		
Colin Keenan, SDLP	802		
John Lowry, WP	586		
Pat Lawlor, SP	384		
Dan McGuinness, Alliance	365		
Brian Pelan, Ind.	122		

DOWN NORTH
E. 62,170 T. 28,528 (45.89%)

	First	Final	Elected (R.)
Alex Easton, DUP	5,175	5,175	First (1)
Gordon Dunne, DUP	3,741	4,121	Second (2)
Peter Weir, DUP	3,496	4,101	Third (2)
Stephen Farry, Alliance	3,131	4,078	Fourth (10)
Steven Agnew, Green	2,207	3,229	Sixth (11)
*Anne Wilson, Alliance	2,100	3,130	
Alan McFarland, Ind.	1,879		
Alan Chambers, Ind.	1,765		
Leslie Cree, UUP	1,585	4,015	Fifth (10)
Colin Breen, UUP	1,343		
Liam Logan, SDLP	768		
Fred McGlade, UKIP	615		
Conor Keenan, SF	293		

DOWN SOUTH
E. 73,240 T. 42,551 (58.10%)

	First	Final	Elected (R.)
Margaret Ritchie, SDLP	8,506	8,506	First (1)
Catriona Ruane, SF	5,955	6,192	Second (2)
Jim Wells, DUP	5,200	6,543	Third (5)
John McCallister, UUP	4,409	6,240	Fourth (6)
Willie Clarke, SF	3,882	6,777	Fifth (7)
Karen McKevitt, SDLP	3,758	5,347	Sixth (9)
Naomi Bailie, SF	3,050		
*Eamonn O'Neill, SDLP	2,663	4,883	
Henry Reilly, UKIP	2,332		
Cadogan Enright, Green	1,107		
David Griffin, Alliance	864		

FERMANAGH AND SOUTH TYRONE
E. 70,985 T. 48,949 (68.96%)

	First	Final	Elected (R.)
Michelle Gildernew, SF	9,110	9,110	First (1)
Tom Elliott, UUP	6,896	6,896	Second (1)
Arlene Foster, DUP	6,876	6,876	Third (3)
Sean Lynch, SF	5,146	6,476	Fifth (6)
Phil Flanagan, SF	5,082	6,137	Sixth (6)
Maurice Morrow, DUP	4,844	7,229	Fourth (5)
*Tommy Gallagher, SDLP	4,606	6,075	
Kenny Donaldson, UUP	2,366		
Alex Elliott, TUV	1,231		
Pat Cox, Ind.	997		
Hannah Su, Alliance	845		

FOYLE
E. 68,663 T. 39,686 (57.80%)

	First	Final	Elected (R.)
William Hay, DUP	7,154	7,154	First (1)
Martina Anderson, SF	6,950	6,950	Second (1)
Mark Durkan, SDLP	4,970	5,794	Third (4)
Raymond McCartney, SF	3,638	6,245	Fourth (7)
Pat Ramsey, SDLP	3,138	4,876	Sixth (7)
*Eamonn McCann (PBP)	3,120	3,916	
Colum Eastwood, SDLP	2,967	5,563	Fifth (7)
Pol Callaghan, SDLP	2,624		
Paul Fleming, SF	2,612		
Paul McFadden, Ind.	1,280		
Keith McGrellis, Alliance	334		
Terry Doherty, Ind.	60		

LAGAN VALLEY
E. 67,532 T. 35,842 (53.07%)

	First	Final	Elected (R.)
Edwin Poots, DUP	7,329	7,329	First (1)
Basil McCrea, UUP	5,771	5,771	Second (1)
Trevor Lunn, Alliance	4,389	5,120	Fourth (6)
Paul Givan, DUP	4,352	5,518	Fifth (7)
Jonathan Craig, DUP	4,263	5,081	Third (5)
Brenda Hale, DUP	2,910	4,791	Sixth (7)
*Pat Catney, SDLP	2,165	3,406	
Mark Hill, UUP	1,482		
Mary-Kate Quinn, SF	1,203		
Lyle Rea, TUV	1,031		
Conor Quinn, Green	592		

LONDONDERRY EAST
E. 65,226 T. 35,303 (54.12%)

	First	Final	Elected (R.)
Gregory Campbell, DUP	6,319	6,319	First (1)
Cathal O hOisin, SF	4,681	4,962	Third (6)
George Robinson, DUP	3,855	4,823	Fourth (7)
David McClarty (Ind.)	3,003	4,405	Fifth (7)
John Dallat, SDLP	2,967	5,207	Second (6)
Bernadette Archibald, SF	2,639		
Adrian McQuillan, DUP	2,633	3,782	Sixth (7)
Thomas Conway	2,222		
Barney Fitzpatrick, Alliance	1,905		
Boyd Douglas, TUV	1,568		
Lesley Macaulay, UUP	1,472		
*David Harding, UUP	1,458	3,460	

NEWRY AND ARMAGH
E. 77,544 T. 47,562 (61.34%)

	First	Final	Elected (R.)
Conor Murphy, SF	9,127	9,127	First (1)
Danny Kennedy, UUP	8,718	8,718	Second (1)
Dominic Bradley, SDLP	7,123	7,123	Third (1)
Cathal Boylan, SF	6,614	8,092	Fourth (2)
William Irwin, DUP	6,101	7,502	Fifth (3)
*Thomas O'Hanlon, SDLP	3,825	5,014	
Mickey Brady, SF	3,254	5,625	Sixth (6)
Barrie Halliday, TUV	830		
David Murphy, Alliance	734		
Robert Woods, UKIP	98		
James Malone, ND	90		

STRANGFORD
E. 62,178 T. 30,186 (48.55%)

	First	Final	Elected (R.)
Michelle McIlveen, DUP	4,573	4,573	First (1)
Kieran McCarthy, Alliance	4,284	4,284	Second (1)
Jonathan Bell, DUP	4,265	4,265	Third (1)
Simon Hamilton, DUP	3,456	5,745	Fourth (5)
Mike Nesbitt, UUP	3,273	4,072	Fifth (6)
David McNarry, UUP	2,733	3,767	Sixth (6)
*Joe Boyle, SDLP	2,525	3,308	
Billy Walker, DUP	2,175		
Mickey Coogan, SF	902		
Terry Williams, TUV	841		
Cecil Andrews, UKIP	601		

TYRONE WEST
E. 62,970 T. 40,323 (64.04%)

	First	Final	Elected (R.)
Barry McElduff, SF	6,008	6,008	First (1)
Pat Doherty, SF	5,630	5,630	Second (1)
Michaela Boyle, SF	5,053	7,792	Third (4)
Tom Buchanan, DUP	5,027	5,162	Fifth (5)
Ross Hussey, UUP	4,072	4,398	Sixth (5)
*Allan Bresland, DUP	4,059	4,124	
Joe Byrne, SDLP	3,353	5,321	Fourth (5)
Declan McAleer, SF	3,008		
Paddy McGowan, Ind.	1,145		
Eugene McMenamin, Ind.	1,096		
Eric Bullick, Ind.	852		

ULSTER MID
E. 66,602 T. 43,522 (65.35%)

	First	Final	Elected (R.)
Martin McGuinness, SF	8,957	8,957	First (1)
Ian McCrea, DUP	7,127	7,127	Second (1)
Michelle O'Neill, SF	5,178	5,735	Sixth (7)
Patsy McGlone, SDLP	5,065	6,110	Third (5)
Sandra Overend, UUP	4,409	7,130	Fourth (6)
Francie Molloy, SF	4,263	5,191	Fifth (7)
*Ian Milne, SF	2,635	4,412	
Walter Millar, TUV	2,075		
Austin Kelly, SDLP	1,214		
Hugh McCloy, Ind.	933		
Michael McDonald, Alliance	398		
Harry Hutchinson, PBP	243		
Gary McCann, Ind.	241		

UPPER BANN
E. 77,905 T. 43,113 (55.34%)

	First	Final	Elected (R.)
John O'Dowd, SF	6,649	6,649	First (1)
Sydney Anderson, DUP	5,584	6,163	Second (5)
Stephen Moutray, DUP	5,645	6,085	Third (5)
*Johnny McGibbon, SF	4,879	5,438	
Dolores Kelly, SDLP	4,846	5,787	Sixth (7)
Sam Gardiner, UUP	3,676	6,012	Fourth (7)
Colin McCusker, UUP	3,402		
Joanne Dobson, UUP	3,348	5,827	Fifth (7)
Harry Hamilton, Alliance	1,979		
David Vance, TUV	1,026		
Sheila McQuaid, Alliance	786		
Barbara Trotter, UKIP	272		

EUROPEAN PARLIAMENT

European parliament elections take place at five-yearly intervals; the first direct elections to the parliament were held in 1979. In mainland Britain, members of the European parliament (MEPs) were elected in all constituencies on a first-past-the-post basis until 1999, when a regional system of proportional representation was introduced; in Northern Ireland three MEPs have been elected by the single transferable vote system of proportional representation since 1979. Under the terms of the Lisbon Treaty, the UK gained an extra seat in December 2011, taking the total to 73. This seat was added to the West Midlands region and filled by the highest-ranked losing candidate standing for the region in the 2009 European parliament elections.

At the 2014 European parliament elections all UK MEPs were elected under a 'closed-list' regional system of proportional representation, with England being divided into nine regions (residents of Gibraltar vote in the South West region) and Scotland, Wales and Northern Ireland each constituting a single region each. Parties submitted a list of candidates for each region in their own order of preference. Votes were cast for a party or an independent candidate, and the first seat in each region was allocated to the party or candidate with the highest number of votes. The rest of the seats in each region were then allocated broadly in proportion to each party's share of the vote. Each region returned the following number of members: East Midlands, 5; Eastern, 7; London, 8; North East, 3; North West, 8; South East, 10; South West, 6; West Midlands, 7; Yorkshire and the Humber, 6; Wales, 4; Northern Ireland, 3; Scotland, 6.

If a vacancy occurs due to the resignation or death of an MEP, it is filled by the next available person on that party's list. If an independent MEP resigns or dies, a by-election is held. Where an MEP leaves the party on whose list he/she was elected, there is no requirement to resign the post of MEP.

British subjects and nationals of member states of the European Union are eligible for election to the European parliament provided they are aged 18 or over and not subject to disqualification. Since 1994, eligible citizens have had the right to vote in elections to the European parliament in the UK as long as they are entered on the electoral register.

MEPs previously received a salary set at the level of the national parliamentary salary of their country. In July 2009 an MEP statute introduced a uniform salary for all MEPs, set at a rate of 38.5 per cent of the basic salary of a European court of justice judge. In 2014 this approximated an annual salary of €95,484 (£78,444).

The 2014 UK component of the European parliament was won by the United Kingdom Independence Party (UKIP), who claimed 24 seats. It was the first time a party other than the Conservatives or Labour had won the largest number of seats in a general election since the December 1910 general election.

The next elections to the European parliament will take place in 2019. For further information visit the UK's European parliament website (W www.europarl.org.uk).

UK MEMBERS *as at June 2014*

* Denotes membership of the last European parliament
† Previously sat as a member of the Conservative party
‡ Previously sat as a member of UKIP
§ Previously sat as a member of UCUNF

*Agnew, Stuart (b. 1949), UKIP, Eastern
Aker, Tim (b. 1985), UKIP, Eastern
Anderson, Lucy, Lab., London
*Anderson, Martina (b. 1962), SF, Northern Ireland
Arnott, Jonathan (b. 1981), UKIP, North East
*Ashworth, Richard (b. 1947), C., South East
Atkinson, Janice (b. 1962), UKIP, South East
Bashir, Amjad (b. 1952), UKIP, Yorkshire and the Humber
*Batten, Gerard (b. 1954), UKIP, London
*Bearder, Catherine (b. 1949), LD, South East
Bours, Louise (b. 1968), UKIP, North West
*Bradbourn, Philip, OBE (b. 1951), C., West Midlands
Brannen, Paul (b. 1962), Lab., North East
*‡Campbell Bannerman, David (b. 1960), C., Eastern
Carver, Jim (b. 1969), UKIP, West Midlands
Coburn, David (b. 1958), UKIP, Scotland
Collins, Jane (b. 1962), UKIP, Yorkshire and the Humber
Corbett, Richard (b. 1955), Lab., Yorkshire and the Humber
Dance, Seb (b. 1981), Lab., London
*Dartmouth, Earl of (b. 1949), UKIP, South West
*Deva, Nirj (b. 1948), C., South East
Dodds, Anneliese (b. 1978), Lab., South East
*Dodds, Diane (b. 1958), DUP, Northern Ireland
Duncan, Ian (b. 1973), C., Scotland
Etheridge, Bill (b. 1970), UKIP, West Midlands
*Evans, Jill (b. 1959), PC, Wales
*Farage, Nigel (b. 1964), UKIP, South East
Finch, Ray (b. 1963), UKIP, South East
*Ford, Vicky (b. 1967), C., Eastern
*Foster, Jacqueline (b. 1947), C., North West
*Fox, Ashley (b. 1969), C., South West
Gill, Nathan (b. 1973), UKIP, Wales
Gill, Neena (b. 1957), Lab., West Midlands
*Girling, Julie (b. 1956), C., South East
Griffin, Theresa (b. 1962), Lab., North West
*Hannan, Daniel (b. 1971), C., South East
*†Helmer, Roger (b. 1944), UKIP, East Midlands
*Honeyball, Mary (b. 1952), Lab., London
Hookem, Mike (b. 1953), UKIP, Yorkshire and the Humber
*Howitt, Richard (b. 1961), Lab., Eastern
*Hudghton, Ian (b. 1951), SNP, Scotland
James, Diane (b. 1959), UKIP, South East
*Kamall, Dr Syed (b. 1967), C., London
*Karim, Sajjad (b. 1970), C., North West
Khan, Afzal (b. 1960), Lab., North West
*Kirkhope, Timothy (b. 1945), C., Yorkshire and the Humber
Kirton-Darling, Judith (b. 1977), Lab., North East
*Lambert, Jean (b. 1950), Green, London
Lewer, Andrew (b. 1971), C., East Midlands
*McAvan, Linda (b. 1962), Lab., Yorkshire and the Humber
*McClarkin, Emma (b. 1978), C., East Midlands
*McIntyre, Anthea (b. 1954), C., West Midlands
*Martin, David (b. 1954), Lab., Scotland
Moody, Clare (b. 1965), Lab., South West
*Moraes, Claude (b. 1965), Lab., London
*Nicholson, Jim (b. 1945), UUP, Northern Ireland
*Nuttall, Paul (b. 1976), UKIP, North West
O'Flynn, Patrick (b. 1965), UKIP, Eastern
Parker, Margaret (b. 1943), UKIP, East Midlands
Reid, Julia (b. 1952), UKIP, South West
Scott Cato, Molly (b. 1963), Green, South West
Seymour, Jill (b. 1958), UKIP, West Midlands
Simon, Siôn (b. 1968), Lab., West Midlands
*Smith, Alyn (b. 1973), SNP, Scotland

*Stihler, Catherine (b. 1973), Lab., Scotland
*Swinburne, Dr Kay (b. 1967), C., Wales
*Tannock, Dr Charles (b. 1957), C., London
*Taylor, Keith (b. 1953), Green, South East
*Van Orden, Geoffrey (b. 1945), C., Eastern
*Vaughan, Derek (b. 1961), Lab., Wales
Ward, Julie (b. 1957), Lab., North West
*Willmott, Glenis (b. 1951), Lab., East Midlands
Woolfe, Steven (b. 1967), UKIP, North West

STATE OF THE PARTIES as at June 2014

Party	Seats
UK Independence Party (UKIP)	24
Labour (Lab.)	20
Conservative (C.)	19
Green Party (Green)	3
Scottish National Party (SNP)	2
Others*	5
Total	73

* The Democratic Unionist Party (DUP), Liberal Democrats (LD), Plaid Cymru (PC), the Ulster Unionist Party (UUP) and Sinn Fein (SF) have one seat each.

UK REGIONS as at 22 May 2014 election

Abbreviations

4FP	4 Freedoms Party (UK EPP)
AIFE	An Independence from Europe
AW	Animal Welfare
BF	Britain First
CPA	Christian Peoples Alliance
EP	Europeans Party
Harmony	Harmony Party
Liberty	Liberty GB
NLP	National Liberal Party
NI21	NI21
No2EU	No2EU Yes to Democracy
Peace	Peace Party
Roman	Roman Party
SGB	Socialist Party of Great Britain
SLP	Socialist Labour Party
TUV	Traditional Unionist Voice (NI)
UUP	Ulster Unionist Party
WDR	We Demand a Referendum
Your	YOURvoice
YF	Yorkshire First

For other abbreviations, see UK General Election Results.

E. 46,615,585   T. 35.32%

EASTERN
(Bedfordshire, Cambridgeshire, Essex, Hertfordshire, Luton, Norfolk, Peterborough, Southend-on-Sea, Suffolk, Thurrock)

E. 4,369,382	T. 36.19%
UKIP	542,812 (34.5%)
C.	446,569 (28.4%)
Lab.	271,601 (17.2%)
Green	133,331 (8.5%)
LD	108,010 (6.9%)
AIFE	26,564 (1.7%)
Eng. Dem.	16,497 (1.0%)
BNP	12,465 (0.8%)
CPA	11,627 (0.7%)
No2EU	4,870 (0.3%)
UKIP majority	96,243

(June 2009, C. maj. 186,410)

MEMBERS ELECTED
1. P. O'Flynn, UKIP 2. *V. Ford, C.
3. *R. Howitt, Lab. 4. *S. Agnew, UKIP
5. *G. Van Orden, C. 6. T. Aker, UKIP
7. *‡ D. Campbell Bannerman, C.

EAST MIDLANDS
(Derby, Derbyshire, Leicester, Leicestershire, Lincolnshire, Northamptonshire, Nottingham, Nottinghamshire, Rutland)

E. 3,437,794	T. 32.6%
UKIP	368,734 (32.9%)
C.	291,270 (26.0%)
Lab.	279,363 (24.9%)
Green	67,066 (6.0%)
LD	60,773 (5.4%)
AIFE	21,384 (1.9%)
BNP	18,326 (1.6%)
Eng. Dem.	11,612 (1.0%)
Harmony	2,194 (0.2%)
UKIP majority	77,464

(June 2009, C. maj. 163,330)

MEMBERS ELECTED
1. *†R. Helmer, UKIP 2. *E. McClarkin, C. 3. *G. Willmott, Lab. 4. M. Parker, UKIP 5. A. Lewer, C.

LONDON

E. 5,490,248	T. 40.5%
Lab.	806,959 (36.7%)
C.	495,639 (22.5%)
UKIP	371,133 (16.9%)
Green	196,419 (8.9%)
LD	148,013 (6.7%)
4FP	28,014 (1.3%)
AIFE	26,675 (1.2%)
CPA	23,702 (1.1%)
NHA	23,253 (1.1%)
AW	21,092 (1.0%)
BNP	19,246 (0.9%)
EP	10,712 (0.5%)
Eng. Dem.	10,142 (0.5%)
CUP	6,951 (0.3%)
NLP	6,736 (0.3%)
No2EU	3,804 (0.2%)
Harmony	1,985 (0.1%)
Lab. majority	311,320

(June 2009, C. maj. 106,447)

MEMBERS ELECTED
1. *C. Moraes, Lab. 2. *S. Kamall, C.
3. *M. Honeyball, Lab. 4. *G. Batten, UKIP 5. L. Anderson, Lab.
6. *C. Tannock, C. 7. S. Dance, Lab.
8. *J. Lambert, Green

NORTH EAST
(Co. Durham, Darlington, Hartlepool, Middlesbrough, Northumberland, Redcar and Cleveland, Stockton-on-Tees, Tyne and Wear)

E. 1,968,780	T. 31.0%
Lab.	221,988 (36.5%)
UKIP	177,660 (29.2%)
C.	107,733 (17.7%)
LD	36,093 (5.9%)
Green	31,605 (5.2%)
AIFE	13,934 (2.3%)
BNP	10,360 (1.7%)
Eng. Dem.	9,279 (1.5%)
Lab. majority	44,328

(June 2009, Lab. maj. 30,427)

MEMBERS ELECTED
1. J. Darling, Lab. 2. J. Arnott, UKIP
3. P. Brannen, Lab.

NORTHERN IRELAND
(Northern Ireland forms a three-member seat with a single transferable vote system)

E. 1,225,771	T. 51.84%
	1st Pref. Votes
Martina Anderson, SF	159,813 (25.5%)
Diane Dodds, DUP	131,163 (20.9%)
Jim Nicholson, UUP	83,438 (13.3%)
Alex Attwood, SDLP	81,594 (13%)
Jim Allister, TUV	75,806 (12.1%)
Anna Lo, Alliance	44,432 (7.1%)
Henry Reilly, UKIP,	24,584 (3.9%)
Ross Brown, Green	10,598 (1.7%)
Tina McKenzie, NI21	10,553 (1.7%)
Mark Brotherston, C.	4,144 (0.7%)

MEMBERS ELECTED
1. *M. Anderson, SF 2. *D. Dodds, DUP 3. *§ J. Nicholson, UUP

NORTH WEST
(Blackburn-with-Darwen, Blackpool, Cheshire, Cumbria, Greater Manchester, Halton, Lancashire, Merseyside, Warrington)

E. 5,267,777	T. 33.68%
Lab.	594,063 (33.9%)
UKIP	401,932 (27.5%)
C.	351,985 (20.1%)
Green	123,075 (7.0%)
LD	105,487 (6.0%)
BNP	32,826 (1.9%)
AIFE	26,731 (1.5%)
Eng. Dem.	19,522 (1.1%)
Pirate	8,597 (0.5%)
No2EU	5,402 (0.3%)
SEP	5,067 (0.3%)
Lab. majority	112,131
(June 2009, C. maj. 86,343)

MEMBERS ELECTED
1. T. Griffin, Lab. 2.*P. Nuttall, UKIP
3. *J. Foster, C. 4. A. Khan, Lab.
5. L. Bours, UKIP 6. J. Ward, Lab.
7. *S. Karim, C. 8. S. Woolfe, UKIP

SCOTLAND

E. 4,016,735	T. 33.5%
SNP	389,503 (29.0%)
Lab.	348,219 (25.9%)
C.	231,330 (17.2%)
UKIP	140,534 (10.5%)
Green	108,305 (8.7%)
LD	95,319 (7.1%)
BF	13,639 (1.0%)
BNP	10,216 (0.8%)
No2EU	6,418 (0.5%)
SNP majority	41,284
(June 2009, SNP. maj. 91,154)

MEMBERS ELECTED
1. *I. Hudghton, SNP 2. *D. Martin, Lab. 3. I. Duncan, C. 4. *A. Smith, SNP
5. *C. Stihler, Lab. 6. D. Coburn, UKIP

SOUTH EAST
(Bracknell Forest, Brighton and Hove, Buckinghamshire, East Sussex, Hampshire, Isle of Wight, Kent, Medway, Milton Keynes, Newbury, Oxfordshire, Portsmouth, Reading, Slough, Southampton, Surrey, West Sussex, Windsor and Maidenhead, Wokingham)

E. 6,441,003	T. 36.46%
UKIP	751,439 (32.1%)
C.	723,571 (31.0%)
Lab.	342,775 (14.7%)
Green	211,706 (9.1%)
LD	187,876 (8.0%)

AIFE	45,199 (1.9%)
Eng. Dem.	17,771 (0.8%)
BNP	16,909 (0.7%)
CPA	14,893 (0.6%)
Peace	10,130 (0.4%)
SGB	5,454 (0.2%)
Roman	2,997 (0.1%)
Your	2,932 (0.1%)
Liberty	2,194 (0.1%)
Harmony	1,904 (0.1%)
UKIP majority	27,868
(June 2009, C. maj. 372,286)

MEMBERS ELECTED
1. *N. Farage, UKIP 2. *D. Hannan, C.
3. J. Atkinson, UKIP 4. *N. Deva, C.
5. A. Dodds, Lab. 6. D. James, UKIP
7. *R. Ashworth, C. 8. *K.Taylor, Green
9. * C. Bearder, LD 10. R. Finch, UKIP

SOUTH WEST
(Bath and North East Somerset, Bournemouth, Bristol, Cornwall, Devon, Dorset, Gloucestershire, North Somerset, Plymouth, Poole, Somerset, South Gloucestershire, Swindon, Torbay, Wiltshire, Isles of Scilly, Gibraltar)

E. 4,059,889	T. 37.03%
UKIP	484,184 (32.3%)
C.	433,151 (28.9%)
Lab.	206,124 (13.8%)
Green	166,447 (11.1%)
LD	160,376 (10.7%)
AIFE	23,169 (1.6%)
Eng. Dem.	15,081 (1.0%)
BNP	10,910 (0.7%)
UKIP majority	51,033
(June 2009, C. maj. 126,627)

MEMBERS ELECTED
1. *W. Dartmouth, UKIP 2. *A. Fox, C.
3. J. Reid, UKIP 4. *J. Girling, C.
5. C. Moody, Lab. 6. M. Scott Cato, Green

WALES

E. 2,327,175	T. 31.50%
Lab.	206,332 (28.2%)
UKIP	201,983 (27.6%)
C.	127,742 (17.4%)
PC	111,864 (15.3%)
Green	33,275 (4.5%)
LD	28,930 (4.0%)
BNP	7,655 (1.0%)
BF	6,633 (0.9%)
SLP	4,459 (0.6%)
No2EU	2,803 (0.4%)
SGB	1,384 (0.2%)
Lab. majority	4,349
(June 2004, Lab. maj. 120,039)

MEMBERS ELECTED
1. *D. Vaughan, Lab. 2. N. Gill, UKIP
3. *K. Swinburne, C. 4. *J. Evans, PC

WEST MIDLANDS
(Herefordshire, Shropshire, Staffordshire, Stoke-on-Trent, Telford and Wrekin, Warwickshire, West Midlands Metropolitan area, Worcestershire)

E. 4,105,305	T. 33.31%
UKIP	428,010 (28.1%)
Lab.	363,033 (21.3%)
C.	330,470 (17.0%)
LD	75,648 (12.0%)
Green	71,464 (8.6%)
AIFE	27,171 (6.2%)
WDR	23,426 (2.3%)
BNP	20,643 (1.3%)
Eng. Dem.	12,832 (1.0%)
No2EU	4,653 (0.9%)
Harmony	1,857 (0.6%)
UKIP majority	64,977
(June 2009, C. maj. 96,016)

MEMBERS ELECTED
1. J Seymour, UKIP 2. N. Gill, Lab.
3. *P. Bradbourn, C. 4. J. Carver, UKIP
5. S. Simon, Lab. 6. *A. McIntyre, C.
7. B. Etheridge, UKIP

YORKSHIRE AND THE HUMBER
(East Riding of Yorkshire, Kingston-upon-Hull, North East Lincolnshire, North Lincolnshire, North Yorkshire, South Yorkshire, West Yorkshire, York)

E. 3,905,726	T. 33.2%
UKIP	403,630 (31.1%)
Lab.	380,189 (29.3%)
C.	248,945 (19.2%)
Green	102,282 (7.9%)
LD	81,108 (6.3%)
AIFE	24,297 (1.9%)
BNP	20,138 (1.6%)
YF	19,017 (1.5%)
Eng. Dem.	13,288 (1.0%)
No2EU	3,807 (0.3%)
UKIP majority	23,441
(June 2009, C. maj. 69,793)

MEMBERS ELECTED
1. J. Collins, UKIP 2. *L. McAvan, Lab.
3. *T. Kirkhope, C. 4. A. Bashir, UKIP
5. R. Corbett, Lab. 6. M. Hookem, UKIP

LOCAL GOVERNMENT

Major changes in local government were introduced in England and Wales in 1974 and in Scotland in 1975 by the Local Government Act 1972 and the Local Government (Scotland) Act 1973. Further significant alterations were made in England by the Local Government Acts of 1985, 1992 and 2000.

The structure in England was based on two tiers of local authorities (county councils and district councils) in the non-metropolitan areas; and a single tier of metropolitan councils in the six metropolitan areas of England and London borough councils in London.

Following reviews of the structure of local government in England by the Local Government Commission (now the Boundary Commission for England), 46 unitary (all-purpose) authorities were created between April 1995 and April 1998 to cover certain areas in the non-metropolitan counties. The remaining county areas continue to have two tiers of local authorities. The county and district councils in the Isle of Wight were replaced by a single unitary authority on 1 April 1995; the former counties of Avon, Cleveland, Humberside and Berkshire were replaced by unitary authorities; and Hereford and Worcester was replaced by a new county council for Worcestershire (with district councils) and a unitary authority for Herefordshire. On 1 April 2009 the county areas of Cornwall, Durham, Northumberland, Shropshire and Wiltshire were given unitary status and two new unitary authorities were created for Bedfordshire (Bedford and Central Bedfordshire) and Cheshire (Cheshire East and Cheshire West & Chester), replacing the two-tier county/district system in these areas.

The Local Government (Wales) Act 1994 and the Local Government etc (Scotland) Act 1994 abolished the two-tier structure in Wales and Scotland with effect from 1 April 1996, replacing it with a single tier of unitary authorities.

In Northern Ireland a reform programme to reduce the number of local authorities from 26 to 11 began in 2012 when legislation finalising the boundaries of the new 11 local government district authorities was approved by the Northern Ireland Assembly. The Local Government Act (Northern Ireland) 2014 received royal assent on 12 May 2014, providing the legislative framework for the 11 new councils. The process is expected to be completed by April 2015 when functions which are currently the responsibilty of the Northern Ireland executive fully transfer to the new district authorities.

ELECTIONS

Local elections are normally held on the first Thursday in May. Generally, all citizens of the UK, the Republic of Ireland, Commonwealth and other European Union citizens who are 18 years or over and resident on the qualifying date in the area for which the election is being held, are entitled to vote at local government elections. A register of electors is prepared and published annually by local electoral registration officers.

A returning officer has the overall responsibility for an election. Voting takes place at polling stations, arranged by the local authority and under the supervision of a presiding officer specially appointed for the purpose. Candidates, who are subject to various statutory qualifications and disqualifications designed to ensure that they are suitable to hold office, must be nominated by electors for the electoral area concerned.

In England, the Local Government Boundary Commission for England is responsible for carrying out periodic reviews of electoral arrangements, to consider whether the boundaries of wards or divisions within a local authority need to be altered to take account of changes in electorate; structural reviews, to consider whether a single, unitary authority should be established in an area instead of an existing two-tier system; and administrative boundary reviews of district or county authorities.

The Local Democracy and Boundary Commission for Wales, the Local Government Boundary Commission for Scotland and the local government boundary commissioner for Northern Ireland (appointed when required by the Boundary Commission for Northern Ireland) are responsible for reviewing the electoral arrangements and boundaries of local authorities within their respective regions.

The Local Government Act 2000 provided for the secretary of state to change the frequency and phasing of elections in England and Wales.

LOCAL GOVERNMENT BOUNDARY COMMISSION FOR ENGLAND, Layden House, 76–86 Turnmill Street, London EC1M 5LG T 020-7664 8534 E reviews@lgbce.org.uk W www.lgbce.org.uk

LOCAL DEMOCRACY AND BOUNDARY COMMISSION FOR WALES, Ground Floor, Hastings House, Fitzalan Court, Cardiff CF24 0BL T 029-2046 4819 E ldbc.wales@wales.gsi.gov.uk W www.lgbc-wales.gov.uk

LOCAL GOVERNMENT BOUNDARY COMMISSION FOR SCOTLAND, Thistle House, 91 Haymarket Terrace, Edinburgh EH12 5HD T 0131 538 7510 E lgbcs@scottishboundaries.gov.uk W www.lgbc-scotland.gov.uk

BOUNDARY COMMISSION FOR NORTHERN IRELAND, Forestview, Purdy's Lane, Belfast BT8 7AR T 028-9069 4800 E bcni@belfast.org.uk W www.boundarycommission.org.uk

INTERNAL ORGANISATION

The council as a whole is the final decision-making body within any authority. Councils are free to a great extent to make their own internal organisational arrangements. The Local Government Act, given royal assent on 28 July 2000, allows councils to adopt one of three broad categories of constitution which include a separate executive:
• A directly elected mayor with a cabinet selected by that mayor
• A cabinet, either elected by the council or appointed by its leader
• A directly elected mayor and council manager
Normally, questions of policy are settled by the full council, while the administration of the various services is the responsibility of committees of councillors. Day-to-day decisions are delegated to the council's officers, who act within the policies laid down by the councillors.

FINANCE

Local government in England, Wales and Scotland is financed from four sources: council tax, non-domestic rates, government grants and income from fees and charges for services.

COUNCIL TAX

Council tax is a local tax levied by each local council. Liability for the council tax bill usually falls on the owner-occupier or tenant of a dwelling which is their sole or main residence. Council tax bills may be reduced because of the personal circumstances of people resident in a property and there are discounts in the case of dwellings occupied by fewer than two adults.

In England, unitary and metropolitan authorities are responsible for collecting their own council tax. In areas where there are two tiers of local authority, each county and district authority sets its own council tax rate; the district authorities collect the combined council tax and the county councils claim their share from the district councils' collection funds. In Wales, each unitary authority sets its own council tax rate and is responsible for collection. In Scotland, each local authority sets its own rate of council tax.

The tax relates to the value of the dwelling. In England and Scotland each dwelling is placed in one of eight valuation bands, ranging from A to H, based on the property's estimated market value as at 1 April 1991. In Wales there are nine bands, ranging from A to I, based on the estimated market value of property as at 1 April 2003.

The valuation bands and ranges of values in England, Wales and Scotland are:

England

A	Up to £40,000	E	£88,001–£120,000
B	£40,001–£52,000	F	£120,001–£160,000
C	£52,001–£68,000	G	£160,001–£320,000
D	£68,001–£88,000	H	Over £320,001

Wales

A	Up to £44,000	F	£162,001–£223,000
B	£44,001–£65,000	G	£223,001–£324,000
C	£65,001–£91,000	H	£324,001–£424,000
D	£91,001–£123,000	I	Over £424,001
E	£123,001–£162,000		

Scotland

A	Up to £27,000	E	£58,001–£80,000
B	£27,001–£35,000	F	£80,001–£106,000
C	£35,001–£45,000	G	£106,001–£212,000
D	£45,001–£58,000	H	Over £212,001

The council tax within a local area varies between the different bands according to proportions laid down by law. The charge attributable to each band as a proportion of the Band D charge set by the council is approximately:

A	67%	F	144%
B	78%	G	167%
C	89%	H	200%
D	100%	I	233%*
E	122%		

* Wales only

The average Band D council tax bill for each authority area is given in the tables starting on page 263. There may be variations from the given figure within each district council area because of different parish or community precepts being levied.

NON-DOMESTIC RATES

Non-domestic (business) rates are collected by billing authorities; these are the district councils in those areas of England with two tiers of local government and are unitary authorities in other parts of England, in Wales and in Scotland. In respect of England and Wales, the Local Government Finance Act 1988 provides for liability for rates to be assessed on the basis of a poundage (multiplier) tax on the rateable value of property (hereditaments). Separate multipliers are set by the Department for Communities and Local Government (CLG) in England, the Welsh government and the Scottish government. Rates are collected by the billing authority for the area where a property is located. Rate income collected by billing authorities is paid into a national non-domestic rating (NNDR) pool and redistributed to individual authorities on the basis of the adult population figure as prescribed by CLG, the Welsh government or the Scottish government. The rates pools are maintained separately in England, Wales and Scotland. Actual payment of rates in certain cases is subject to transitional arrangements, to phase in the larger increases and reductions in rates resulting from the effects of the latest revaluation.

Rateable values for the 2010 rating lists came into effect on 1 April 2010. They are derived from the rental value of property as at 1 April 2003 and determined on certain statutory assumptions by the Valuation Office Agency in England and Wales, and by local area assessors in Scotland. New property which is added to the list, and significant changes to existing property, necessitate amendments to the rateable value on the same basis. Rating lists (valuation rolls in Scotland) remain in force until the next general revaluation, which usually take place every five years to reflect changes in the property market. The next revaluations for England, Wales and Scotland are scheduled for 2017 and in 2015 for Northern Ireland.

Certain types of property are exempt from rates, eg agricultural land and buildings, certain businesses and some places of public religious worship. Charities and other non-profit-making organisations may receive full or partial relief. Empty commercial property in England and Wales is exempt from business rates for the first three months that the property is vacant (six months for some types of property such as industrial premises and listed buildings), after which full business rates are normally payable. In Scotland an empty commercial property is exempt from business rates for the first three months and entitled to a 10 per cent discount thereafter, except for empty industrial and listed buildings and properties with a rateable value of less than £1,700, which are entirely exempt.

COMPLAINTS

ENGLAND

In England the Local Government Ombudsman investigates complaints of injustice arising from maladministration by local authorities and certain other bodies. The Local Government Ombudsman will not usually consider a complaint unless the local authority concerned has had an opportunity to investigate and reply to a complainant.

LOCAL GOVERNMENT OMBUDSMAN, PO Box 4771,
   Coventry CV4 0EH T 0300-061 0614 W www.lgo.org.uk
   Ombudsman, Jane Martin

WALES

The office of Public Services Ombudsman for Wales came into force on 1 April 2006, incorporating the functions of the Local Government Ombudsman for Wales.

PUBLIC SERVICES OMBUDSMAN FOR WALES,
   1 Ffordd yr Hen Gae, Pencoed CF35 5LJ T 0300-790 0203
   W www.ombudsman-wales.org.uk
   Ombudsman, Nick Bennett

SCOTLAND

The Scottish Public Services Ombudsman is responsible for complaints regarding the maladministration of local government in Scotland.

SCOTTISH PUBLIC SERVICES OMBUDSMAN,
4 Melville Street, Edinburgh EH3 7NS T 0800-377 7330
W www.spso.org.uk
Ombudsman, Jim Martin

NORTHERN IRELAND

The Northern Ireland Commissioner for Complaints fulfils a similar function in Northern Ireland, investigating complaints about local authorities and certain public bodies. Complaints are made to the relevant local authority in the first instance but may also be made directly to the commissioner.

NORTHERN IRELAND COMMISSIONER FOR
COMPLAINTS, Freepost BEL 1478, Belfast BT1 6BR
T 0800-343424 E ombudsman@ni-ombudsman.org.uk
W www.ni-ombudsman.org.uk
NI Commissioner for Complaints, Tom Frawley, CBE

THE QUEEN'S REPRESENTATIVES

The lord-lieutenant of a county is the permanent local representative of the Crown in that county. The appointment of lord-lieutenants is now regulated by the Lieutenancies Act 1997. They are appointed by the sovereign on the recommendation of the prime minister. The retirement age is 75. The office of lord-lieutenant dates from 1551, and its holder was originally responsible for maintaining order and for local defence in the county. The duties of the post include attending on royalty during official visits to the county, performing certain duties in connection with the armed forces (and in particular the reserve forces), and making presentations of honours and awards on behalf of the Crown. In England, Wales and Northern Ireland, the lord-lieutenant usually also holds the office of *Custos Rotulorum.* As such, he or she acts as head of the county's commission of the peace (which recommends the appointment of magistrates).

The office of sheriff (from the Old English *shire-reeve*) of a county was created in the tenth century. The sheriff was the special nominee of the sovereign, and the office reached the peak of its influence under the Norman kings. The Provisions of Oxford (1258) laid down a yearly tenure of office. Since the mid-16th century the office has been purely civil, with military duties taken over by the lord-lieutenant of the county. The sheriff (commonly known as 'high sheriff') attends on royalty during official visits to the county, acts as the returning officer during parliamentary elections in county constituencies, attends the opening ceremony when a high court judge goes on circuit, executes high court writs, and appoints under-sheriffs to act as deputies. The appointments and duties of the sheriffs in England and Wales are laid down by the Sheriffs Act 1887.

The serving high sheriff submits a list of names of possible future sheriffs to a tribunal, which chooses three names to put to the sovereign. The tribunal nominates the high sheriff annually on 12 November and the sovereign picks the name of the sheriff to succeed in the following year. The term of office runs from 25 March to the following 24 March (the civil and legal year before 1752). No person may be chosen twice in three years if there is any other suitable person in the county.

CIVIC DIGNITIES

District councils in England and local councils in Wales may petition for a royal charter granting borough or 'city' status to the council.

In England and Wales the chair of a borough or county borough council may be called a mayor, and the chair of a city council may be called a lord mayor (if lord mayoralty has been conferred on that city). Parish councils in England and community councils in Wales may call themselves 'town councils', in which case their chair is the town mayor.

In Scotland the chair of a local council may be known as a convenor; a provost is the mayoral equivalent. The chair of the councils for the cities of Aberdeen, Dundee, Edinburgh and Glasgow are lord provosts.

ENGLAND

There are 27 counties, divided into 201 districts, 55 unitary authorities (plus the Isles of Scilly) and 36 metropolitan boroughs.

The populations of most of the unitary authorities are in the range of 100,000 to 300,000. The district councils have populations broadly in the range of 60,000 to 100,000; some, however, have larger populations, because of the need to avoid dividing large towns, and some in mainly rural areas have smaller populations.

The main conurbations outside Greater London – Tyne and Wear, West Midlands, Merseyside, Greater Manchester, West Yorkshire and South Yorkshire – are divided into 36 metropolitan boroughs, most of which have a population of over 200,000.

There are also around 9,500 town and parish councils.

ELECTIONS

For districts, counties and for around 8,700 parishes, there are elected councils, consisting of directly elected councillors. The councillors elect one of their number as chair annually.

In general, councils can have whole council elections, elections by thirds or elections by halves. However all metropolitan authorities must hold elections by thirds. The electoral cycle of any new unitary authority is specified in the appropriate statutory order under which it is established.

FUNCTIONS

In areas with a two-tier system of local governance, functions are divided between the district and county authorities, with those functions affecting the larger area or population generally being the responsibility of the county council. A few functions continue to be exercised over the larger area by joint bodies, made up of councillors from each authority within the area.

Generally the allocation of functions is as follows:

County councils: education; strategic planning; traffic, transport and highways; fire service; consumer protection; refuse disposal; smallholdings; social care; libraries

District councils: local planning; housing; highways (maintenance of certain urban roads and off-street car parks); building regulations; environmental health; refuse collection; cemeteries and crematoria; collection of council tax and non-domestic rates

Unitary and metropolitan councils: their functions are all those listed above, except that the fire service is exercised by a joint body

Concurrently by county and district councils: recreation (parks, playing fields, swimming pools); museums; encouragement of the arts, tourism and industry

PARISH COUNCILS

Parish or town councils are the most local tier of government in England. There are currently around 10,000 parishes in England, of which around 9,500 have councils served by approximately 100,000 councillors. Since 15 February 2008 local councils have been able to create new parish councils without seeking approval from the government. Around 80 per cent of parish councils represent populations of less than 2,500; parishes with no parish council can be grouped with neighbouring parishes under a common parish council. A parish council comprises at least five members, the number being fixed by the district council. Elections are held every four years, at the time of the election of the district councillor for the ward including the parish. Full parish councils must be formed for those parishes with more than 999 electors – below this number, parish meetings comprising the electors of the parish must be held at least twice a year.

Parish council functions include: allotments; encouragement of arts and crafts; community halls, recreational facilities (eg open spaces, swimming pools), cemeteries and crematoria; and many minor functions. They must also be given an opportunity to comment on planning applications. They may, like county and district councils, spend limited sums for the general benefit of the parish. They levy a precept on the district councils for their funds. Parish precepts for 2014–15 totalled £389m, an increase of 6 per cent on 2013–14.

FINANCE

Local government revenue expenditure is budgeted to be £98.8bn in 2014–15; of this £24bn is to be raised through council tax, £11.1bn from the business rate retention scheme and £61.3bn from government grants. The remainder will be drawn down from local authority reserves.

Since April 2013 local authorities retain a share of business rates and keep the growth on that share (the 'rate retention scheme'). Revenue support grant is paid to local authorities to enable all authorities in the same class to broadly set the same council tax; in 2014–15 revenue support grant totals £12.7bn. In addition central government pays specific grants in support of revenue expenditure on particular services. Police grant totals £7.8bn in 2014–15.

In England, the average council tax per dwelling for 2014–15 is £1,051. The average council tax bill for a Band D dwelling (occupied by two adults, including parish precepts) for 2014–15 is £1,468, an increase of 0.9 per cent from 2013–14. The average Band D council tax is £1,527 in shire districts, £1,434 in metropolitan areas, £1,502 in unitary authority areas and £1,296 in London. Since 2006–7 the London figure has included a levy to fund the 2012 Olympic Games, which equates to a £20 a year increase on a Band D council tax. This levy is expected to continue until 2016.

The non-domestic rating multiplier for England for 2014–15 is 48.2p (47.1p for small businesses). The City of London is able to set a different multiplier from the rest of England; for 2014–15 this is 48.6p (47.5p for small businesses).

Under the Local Government and Housing Act 1989, local authorities have four main ways of paying for capital expenditure: borrowing and other forms of extended credit; capital grants from central government towards some types of capital expenditure; 'usable' capital receipts from the sale of land, houses and other assets; and revenue.

The amount of capital expenditure which a local authority can finance by borrowing (or other forms of credit) is effectively limited by the credit approvals issued to it by central government. Most credit approvals can be used for any kind of local authority capital expenditure; these are known as basic credit approvals. Others (supplementary credit approvals) can be used only for the kind of expenditure specified in the approval, and so are often given to fund particular projects or services.

Local authorities can use all capital receipts from the sale of property or assets for capital spending, except in the case of sales of council houses. Generally, the usable part of a local authority's capital receipts consists of 25 per cent of receipts from the sale of council houses and 50 per cent of other housing assets such as shops or vacant land. The balance has to be set aside as provision for repaying debt and meeting other credit liabilities.

EXPENDITURE

Budgeted revenue expenditure for 2014–15 is:

Service	£ million
*Education	35,835
Highways and transport	4,814
Social care	22,090
Public Health	2,849
Housing (excluding HRA)	1,945
Cultural, environment and planning	9,029
Police	11,121
Fire and rescue	2,123
Central services	3,686
Mandatory housing benefits	21,001
Other services	224
Less appropriations from accumulated absences account	(4)
Net current expenditure	114,711
Capital financing	4,482
Capital expenditure charged to revenue account	3,120
Discretionary non-domestic rate relief	–
Bad debt provision	61
Flood defence payments to Environment Agency	31
Private Finance Initiative schemes	75
Carbon Reduction Commitment	28
Less adjustments permitted by regulation	(19)
Less interest receipts	(744)
Less specific grants outside AEF	(22,617)
Less Business Rates Supplement	(335)
Less Community Infrastructure Levy	(40)
REVENUE EXPENDITURE	98,753

HRA = Housing Revenue Account

AEF = aggregate external finance

* Education expenditure is not comparable to previous years due to a number of schools becoming centrally funded academies

LONDON

The Greater London Council was abolished in 1986 and London was divided into 32 borough councils, which have a status similar to the metropolitan borough councils in the rest of England, and the City of London Corporation.

In March 1998 the government announced proposals for a Greater London Authority (GLA) covering the area of the 32 London boroughs and the City of London, which would comprise a directly elected mayor and a 25-member assembly. A referendum was held in London on 7 May 1998 and 72 per cent of voters balloted in favour of the GLA. A London mayor was elected on 4 May 2000 and the authority assumed its responsibilities on 3 July 2000 (*see also* Regional Government).

LONDON BOROUGH COUNCILS

The London boroughs have whole council elections every four years, in the year immediately following the county council election year. The most recent elections took place on 22 May 2014.

The borough councils have responsibility for the following functions: building regulations, cemeteries and crematoria, consumer protection, education, youth employment, environmental health, electoral registration, food, drugs, housing, leisure services, libraries, local planning, local roads, museums, parking, recreation (parks, playing fields, swimming pools), refuse collection and street cleaning, social services, town planning and traffic management.

CITY OF LONDON CORPORATION

The City of London Corporation is the local authority for the City of London. Its legal definition is the 'Mayor and Commonalty and Citizens of the City of London'. It is governed by the court of common council, which consists of the lord mayor, 25 other aldermen and 100 common councilmen. The lord mayor and two sheriffs are nominated annually by the City guilds (the livery companies) and elected by the court of aldermen. Aldermen and councilmen are elected from the 25 wards into which the City is divided; councilmen must stand for re-election annually. The council is a legislative assembly, and there are no political parties.

The corporation has the same functions as the London borough councils. In addition, it runs the City of London Police; is the health authority for the Port of London; has health control of animal imports throughout Greater London, including at Heathrow airport; owns and manages public open spaces throughout Greater London; runs the central criminal court; and runs Billingsgate, Smithfield and Spitalfields markets.

THE CITY GUILDS (LIVERY COMPANIES)

The livery companies of the City of London grew out of early medieval religious fraternities and began to emerge as trade and craft guilds, retaining their religious aspect, in the 12th century. From the early 14th century, only members of the trade and craft guilds could call themselves citizens of the City of London. The guilds began to be called livery companies, because of the distinctive livery worn by the most prosperous guild members on ceremonial occasions, in the late 15th century.

By the early 19th century the power of the companies within their trades had begun to wane, but those wearing the livery of a company continued to play an important role in the government of the City of London. Liverymen still have the right to nominate the lord mayor and sheriffs, and most members of the court of common council are liverymen.

WALES

The Local Government (Wales) Act 1994 abolished the two-tier structure of eight county and 37 district councils which had existed since 1974, and replaced it, from 1 April 1996, with 22 unitary authorities. The new authorities were elected in May 1995. Each unitary authority inherited all the functions of the previous county and district councils, except fire services (which are provided by three combined fire authorities, composed of representatives from the unitary authorities) and national parks (which are the responsibility of three independent national park authorities).

COMMUNITY COUNCILS

In Wales communities are the equivalent of parishes in England. Unlike England, where many areas are not in any parish, communities have been established for the whole of Wales, approximately 865 communities in all. Community meetings may be convened as and when desired.

Community or town councils exist in around 730 of the communities and further councils may be established at the request of a community meeting. Community councils have broadly the same range of powers as English parish councils. Community councillors are elected for a term of four years.

ELECTIONS

Elections take place every four years; the last elections took place in May 2012.

FINANCE

Total budgeted revenue expenditure for 2014–15 is £7.9bn, a decrease of 0.2 per cent on 2013–14. Total budget requirement, which excludes expenditure financed by specific and special government grants and any use of reserves, is £6.1bn. This comprises revenue support grant of £3.4bn, support from the national non-domestic rate pool of £1bn, police grant of £236m and £1.5bn to be raised through council tax. The non-domestic rating multiplier for Wales for 2014–15 is 47.3p. The average Band D council tax levied in Wales for 2014–15 is £1,276, comprising unitary authorities £1,043, police and crime commissioners £205 and community councils £28.

EXPENDITURE

Local authority budgeted net expenditure for 2014–15 is:

Service	£ million
Education	2,630.2
Social services	1,599.0
Council fund housing	1,139.5
Local environmental services	412.7
Roads and transport	302.2
Libraries, culture, heritage, sport and recreation	242.7
Planning, economic and community development	110.1
Council tax collection	40.4
Debt financing	337.4
Central administrative and other revenue expenditure	294.7
Police	667.6
Fire	148.4
National parks	15.4
Gross revenue expenditure	7,940.1
Less specific and special government grants	(1,981.1)
Net revenue expenditure	5,959.0
Less appropriations from reserves	(72.2)
Council tax reduction scheme	247.3
BUDGET REQUIREMENT	6,134.1

SCOTLAND

The Local Government etc (Scotland) Act 1994 abolished the two-tier structure of nine regional and 53 district councils which had existed since 1975 and replaced it, from 1 April 1996, with 29 unitary authorities on the mainland; the three islands councils remained. The new authorities were elected in April 1995.

In July 1999 the Scottish parliament assumed responsibility for legislation on local government.

ELECTIONS

The unitary authorities consist of directly elected councillors. The Scottish Local Government (Elections) Act 2002 moved elections from a three-year to a four-year cycle, but to avoid the local authority elections coinciding with the Scottish parliament elections in May 2011, the last local authority elections took place in May 2012.

FUNCTIONS

The functions of the councils and islands councils are: education; social work; strategic planning; the provision of infrastructure such as roads; consumer protection; flood prevention; coast protection; valuation and rating; the police and fire services; civil defence; electoral registration; public transport; registration of births, deaths and marriages;

housing; leisure and recreation; development and building control; environmental health; licensing; allotments; public conveniences; and the administration of district courts.

COMMUNITY COUNCILS
Scottish community councils differ from those in England and Wales. Their purpose as defined in statute is to ascertain and express the views of the communities they represent, and to take in the interests of their communities such action as appears to be expedient or practicable. Around 1,200 community councils have been established under schemes drawn up by local authorities in Scotland.

FINANCE
Budgeted total revenue support for 2014–15 is £9.8bn, comprising £7.1bn general resource grant, non-domestic rate income of £2.6bn and specific revenue grants of £90.9m. As a consequence of the creation of the Scottish Police Services Authority and the Scottish Fire and Rescue Service on 1 April 2013, police and fire services are no longer funded through the local government settlement. The non-domestic rate multiplier or poundage for 2014–15 is 47.1p. Larger businesses in 2014–15 (rateable value in excess of £35,000) pay a poundage supplement of 1.1p, which contributes towards the cost of the small business bonus scheme. All non-domestic properties with a rateable value of £18,000 or less may be eligible for non-domestic rates relief of up to 100 per cent from the small business bonus scheme. The average Band D council tax for 2014–15 is £1,149.

EXPENDITURE
Local authority budgeted net expenditure for 2014–15 is:

Service	£ million
Education	4,614.5
Cultural and related services	619.4
Social work services	3,018.1
Roads and transport	449.2
Environmental services	681.6
Planning and development services	298.3
Other	2,107.3
TOTAL	11,788.4

NORTHERN IRELAND

In 2012 a reform programme began to reduce the number of district councils from 26 to 11. The Local Government Act (Northern Ireland) received royal assent on 12 May 2014 providing new governance arrangements for local councils and made transitional provisions for the transfer of staff, assets and liabilities etc to the new 11 councils; the process is expected to be completed by 1 April 2015.

ELECTIONS
Elections to the 11 new councils took place on 22 May 2014 and they are now operating in shadow form.

FUNCTIONS
The 11 new shadow councils are responsible for approving business and financial plans, setting domestic and non-domestic rates for 2015–16, appointing senior staff and leading the cooperation between merging councils in preparation for taking on full powers and responsibilities in April 2015. In addition to the responsibilities outlined below, further functions will transfer from central to local government in April 2015. These include powers in planning, roads, urban regeneration, community development, housing, local economic development and local tourism. The transfer will also include spot listing of buildings and greater involvement of local government in local sports decisions.

Currently the district councils have three main roles. These are:

Executive: responsibility for a wide range of local services including building regulations; community services; consumer protection; cultural facilities; environmental health; miscellaneous licensing and registration provisions, including dog control; litter prevention; recreational and social facilities; refuse collection and disposal; street cleaning; and tourist development

Representative: nominating representatives to sit as members of the various statutory bodies responsible for the administration of regional services such as drainage, education, fire, health and personal social services, housing, and libraries

Consultative: acting as the medium through which the views of local people are expressed on the operation in their area of other regional services – notably conservation (including water supply and sewerage services), planning and roads – provided by those departments of central government which have an obligation, statutory or otherwise, to consult the district councils about proposals affecting their areas

FINANCE
Government in Northern Ireland is part-funded by a system of rates, which supplement the Northern Ireland budget from the UK government. The ratepayer receives a combined tax bill consisting of the regional rate, set by the Northern Ireland executive, and the district rate, which is set by each district council. The regional and district rates are both collected by the Land and Property Services Agency (formerly the Rate Collection Agency). The product of the district rates is paid over to each council while the product of the regional rate supports expenditure by the departments of the executive and assembly.

Since April 2007 domestic rates bills have been based on the capital value of a property, rather than the rental value. The capital value is defined as the price the property might reasonably be expected to realise had it been sold on the open market on 1 January 2005. Non-domestic rates bills are based on 2001 rental values.

Rate bills are calculated by multiplying the property's net annual rental value (in the case of non-domestic property), or capital value (in the case of domestic property), by the regional and district rate poundages respectively.

For 2014–15 the overall average domestic poundage is 0.7387p compared to 0.7227p in 2013–14. The overall average non-domestic rate poundage in 2014–15 is 59.17p compared to 58.12p in 2013–14.

POLITICAL COMPOSITION OF LOCAL COUNCILS

as at May 2014

Abbreviations

All.	Alliance
BNP	British National Party
C.	Conservative
DUP	Democratic Unionist Party
Green	Green
Ind.	Independent
Ind. Un.	Independent Unionist
Lab.	Labour
LD	Liberal Democrat
Lib.	Liberal
O.	Other
PC	Plaid Cymru
PUP	Progressive Unionist Party of Northern Ireland
R.	Residents Associations/Ratepayers
SD	Social Democrat
SDLP	Social Democratic and Labour Party
SF	Sinn Fein
SNP	Scottish National Party
Soc.	Socialist
TUV	Traditional Unionist Voice
UKIP	UK Independence Party
UUP	Ulster Unionist Party
v.	vacant

Total number of seats is given in parentheses after council name.

ENGLAND

COUNTY COUNCILS

Buckinghamshire (49)	C. 36; UKIP 6; LD 4; Ind. 1; Lab. 1; O. 1
Cambridgeshire (69)	C. 32; LD 14; UKIP 12; Lab. 7; Ind. 4
Cumbria (84)	Lab. 36; C. 26; LD 15; Ind. 5; O. 2
Derbyshire (64)	Lab. 43; C. 18; LD 3
Devon (62)	C. 38; LD 9; Lab. 7; UKIP 4; Ind. 3; Green 1
Dorset (45)	C. 27; LD 12; Lab. 5; UKIP 1
East Sussex (49)	C. 20; LD 10; Lab. 7; UKIP 7; Ind. 3; O. 2
Essex (75)	C. 42; Lab. 9; LD 9; UKIP 9; Ind. 4; Green 2
Gloucestershire (52)	C. 23; LD 14; Lab. 9; UKIP 3; Green 1; Ind. 1; O. 1
Hampshire (78)	C. 46; LD 16; UKIP 10; Lab. 4; O. 1; Ind. 1
Hertfordshire (77)	C. 46; LD 16; Lab. 15
Kent (84)	C. 45; UKIP 17; Lab. 13; LD 7; O. 2
Lancashire (84)	Lab. 39; C. 35; LD 6; Ind. 3; Green 1
Leicestershire (55)	C. 30; LD 13; Lab. 10; UKIP 2
Lincolnshire (77)	C. 35; Lab. 12; O. 12; UKIP 11; LD 4; Ind. 3
Norfolk (84)	C. 40; Lab. 14; UKIP 13; LD 10; Green 4; Ind. 3
North Yorkshire (72)	C. 45; O. 7; Lab. 7; LD 7; Lib. 3; UKIP 2; Ind. 1
Northamptonshire (57)	C. 33; Lab. 11; LD 6; UKIP 3; Ind. 2; v. 2
Nottinghamshire (67)	Lab. 34; C. 21; LD 8; O. 3; Ind. 1
Oxfordshire (63)	C. 31; Lab. 15; LD 11; Ind. 4; Green 2

Somerset (55)	C. 29; LD 18; Lab. 3; Ind. 3; UKIP 2
Staffordshire (62)	C. 34; Lab. 24; Ind. 2; UKIP 2
Suffolk (75)	C. 39; Lab. 15; UKIP 9; LD 7; Ind. 3; Green 2
Surrey (81)	C. 58; LD 9; R. 9; UKIP 3; Green 1; Lab. 1
Warwickshire (62)	C. 26; Lab. 22; LD 9; Ind. 3; Green 2
West Sussex (71)	C. 46; UKIP 10; LD 7; Lab. 6; Ind. 2
Worcestershire (57)	C. 31; Lab. 7; Ind. 5; O. 5; LD 3; Green 2; UKIP 2; Lib. 1; R. 1

DISTRICT COUNCILS

Adur (29)	C. 20; UKIP 6; Ind. 2; Lab. 1
Allerdale (56)	Lab. 27; C. 12; Ind. 8; O. 5; UKIP 4
Amber Valley (45)	Lab. 23; C. 21; v. 1
Arun (56)	C. 45; LD 4; Ind. 4; Lab. 3
Ashfield (33)	Lab. 23; LD 4; O. 4; Ind. 2
Ashford (43)	C. 30; Lab. 5; O. 5; LD 2; Ind. 1
Aylesbury Vale (59)	C. 35; LD 17; UKIP 3; Lab. 2; Ind. 2
Babergh (43)	C. 17; LD 12; Ind. 9; Lab. 3; O. 2
Barrow-in-Furness (36)	Lab. 29; C. 7
Basildon (42)	C. 17; UKIP 12; Lab. 10; O. 2; LD 1
Basingstoke and Deane (60)	C. 29; Lab. 17; LD 8; Ind. 4; UKIP 2
Bassetlaw (48)	Lab. 35; C. 10; Ind. 3
Blaby (39)	C. 27; Lab. 6; LD 5; UKIP 1
Bolsover (37)	Lab. 31; O. 3; Ind. 2; v. 1
Boston (32)	C. 17; Ind. 9; Lab. 3; UKIP 2; O. 1
Braintree (60)	C. 45; Lab. 11; Green 2; Ind. 1; R. 1
Breckland (54)	C. 47; Lab. 4; Ind. 2; O. 1
Brentwood (37)	C. 18; LD 11; O. 4; Lab. 3; Ind. 1
Broadland (47)	C. 31; LD 14; Lab. 1; Ind. 1
Bromsgrove (39)	C. 25; Lab. 10; Ind. 4
Broxbourne (30)	C. 26; Lab. 3; UKIP 1
Broxtowe (44)	C. 18; Lab. 17; LD 9
Burnley (45)	Lab. 28; LD 12; C. 5
Cambridge (42)	Lab. 25; LD 14; Ind. 2; C. 1
Cannock Chase (41)	Lab. 25; UKIP 6; C. 5; LD 3; Ind. 2
Canterbury (50)	C. 34; LD 11; Lab. 3; UKIP 2
Carlisle (52)	Lab. 29; C. 19; LD 2; Ind. 2
Castle Point (41)	C. 20; Ind. 15; UKIP 5; v. 1
Charnwood (52)	C. 31; Lab. 15; LD 2; Ind. 2; BNP 1; v. 1
Chelmsford (57)	C. 40; LD 15; Lab. 1; O. 1
Cheltenham (40)	LD 24; C. 12; O. 4
Cherwell (50)	C. 40; Lab. 7; LD 2; Ind. 1
Chesterfield (48)	Lab. 38; LD 8; Ind. 2
Chichester (48)	C. 36; LD 8; Ind. 4
Chiltern (40)	C. 33; LD 5; Ind. 2
Chorley (47)	Lab. 32; C. 13; Ind. 2
Christchurch (24)	C. 22; Ind. 2
Colchester (60)	LD 24; C. 23; Lab. 8; Ind. 4; v. 1
Copeland (51)	Lab. 34; C. 15; Ind. 2
Corby (29)	Lab. 23; C. 4; LD 2
Cotswolds (44)	C. 28; LD 11; Ind. 5

Craven (30) C. 18; Ind. 9; LD 2; v. 1
Crawley (37) Lab. 20; C. 16; UKIP 1
Dacorum (51) C. 43; LD 7; Lab. 1
Dartford (44) C. 30; Lab. 11; R 3
Daventry (36) C. 28; Lab. 4; UKIP 3; LD 1
Derbyshire Dales (39) C. 29; Lab. 5; LD 4; Ind. 1
Dover (45) C. 26; Lab. 19
East Cambridgeshire (39) C. 22; LD 10; Ind. 6; v. 1
East Devon (59) C. 42; LD 10; Ind. 7
East Dorset (36) C. 30; LD 6
East Hampshire (44) C. 39; LD 3; Ind. 2
East Hertfordshire (50) C. 45; O. 3; LD 2
East Lindsey (60) C. 29; Ind. 15; Lab. 11; LD 3; UKIP 2
East Northamptonshire (40) C. 35; Ind. 3; Lab. 2
East Staffordshire (39) C. 18; Lab. 16; Ind. 4; LD 1
Eastbourne (27) LD 15; C. 12
Eastleigh (44) LD 40; C. 4
Eden (38) C. 15; LD 10; Ind. 9; O. 4
Elmbridge (60) C. 32; R. 21; LD 6; O. 1
Epping Forest (58) C. 37; R. 12; LD 3; Ind. 2; UKIP 2; Green 1; Lab. 1
Epsom and Ewell (38) R. 26; LD 6; C. 3; Lab. 3
Erewash (51) C. 26; Lab. 25
Exeter (40) Lab. 27; C. 10; LD 3
Fareham (31) C. 23; LD 5; Ind. 2; UKIP 1
Fenland (40) C. 34; Ind. 3; O. 2; LD 1
Forest Heath (27) C. 23; Ind. 2; Lab. 1; LD 1
Forest of Dean (48) C. 18; Lab. 17; Ind. 11; LD 1; UKIP 1
Fylde (51) C. 28; Ind. 17; LD 3; O. 3
Gedling (50) Lab. 32; C. 15; LD 3
Gloucester (36) C. 18; Lab. 9; LD 9
Gosport (34) C. 21; Lab. 6; LD 6; UKIP 1
Gravesham (44) Lab. 25; C. 19
Great Yarmouth (39) Lab. 15; C. 14; UKIP 10
Guildford (48) C. 34; LD 12; Lab. 2
Hambleton (44) C. 37; Ind. 5; LD 2
Harborough (37) C. 25; LD 9; Ind. 3
Harlow (33) Lab. 17; C. 11; UKIP 5
Harrogate (54) C. 34; LD 14; Ind. 3; O. 2; v. 1
Hart (33) C. 14; LD 9; O. 9; Ind. 1
Hastings (32) Lab. 24; C. 8
Havant (38) C. 31; Lab. 4; UKIP 2; LD 1
Hertsmere (39) C. 34; Lab. 5
High Peak (43) Lab. 21; C. 13; LD 3; Ind. 3; O. 3
Hinckley and Bosworth (34) LD 18; C. 14; Lab. 1; O. 1
Horsham (44) C. 33; LD 7; Ind. 3; UKIP 1
Huntingdonshire (52) C. 34; UKIP 7; LD 5; Ind. 4; Lab. 1; v. 1
Hyndburn (35) Lab. 23; C. 8; Ind. 2; UKIP 2
Ipswich (48) Lab. 35; C. 10; LD 3
Kettering (36) C. 25; Lab. 9; Ind. 1; UKIP 1
King's Lynn and West Norfolk (62) C. 40; Lab. 12; Ind. 6; LD 2; UKIP 1; v. 1
Lancaster (60) Lab. 21; C. 15; Green 10; Ind. 10; O. 4
Lewes (41) LD 19; C. 18; Ind. 2; UKIP 2
Lichfield (56) C. 46; Lab. 10
Lincoln City (33) Lab. 27; C. 6
Maidstone (55) C. 24; LD 20; Ind. 5; UKIP 4; Lab. 2
Maldon (31) C. 27; Ind. 3; Lab. 1
Malvern Hills (38) C. 19; LD 7; Ind. 6; Green 3; O. 1; UKIP 1; v. 1
Mansfield (36) Lab. 24; O. 11; v. 1
Melton (28) C. 18; Lab. 5; Ind. 4; O. 1

Mendip (47) C. 31; LD 13; Ind. 2; Lab. 1
Mid Devon (42) C. 25; Ind. 13; LD 3; Lib. 1
Mid Suffolk (40) C. 22; LD 6; Ind. 5; Green 4; O. 2; Lab. 1
Mid Sussex (54) C. 45; LD 6; Ind. 2; Lab. 1
Mole Valley (41) C. 19; LD 15; Ind. 6; UKIP 1
New Forest (60) C. 52; LD 6; UKIP 2
Newark and Sherwood (46) C. 21; Lab. 14; Ind. 4; LD 3; O. 2; v. 2
Newcastle-under-Lyme (60) Lab. 32; C. 16; LD 6; UKIP 5; Green 1
North Devon (43) C. 18; LD 14; Ind. 11;
North Dorset (33) C. 22; LD 7; Ind. 4
North East Derbyshire (53) Lab. 34; C. 17; Ind. 2
North Hertfordshire (49) C. 34; Lab. 12; LD 3
North Kesteven (43) C. 27; O. 11; LD 3; Ind. 2
North Norfolk (48) C. 28; LD 17; Ind. 2; UKIP 1
North Warwickshire (35) Lab. 18; C. 16; Ind. 1
North West Leicestershire (38) C. 20; Lab. 16; Ind. 1; LD 1
Northampton (45) C. 26; Lab. 14; LD 4; UKIP 1
Norwich (39) Lab. 21; Green 15; LD 3
Nuneaton and Bedworth (34) Lab. 28; C. 3; O. 3
Oadby and Wigston (26) LD 22; C. 2; O. 2
Oxford (48) Lab. 32; LD 8; Green 6; Ind. 1; v. 1
Pendle (49) C. 19; Lab. 18; LD 10; BNP 1; v. 1
Preston (57) Lab. 32; C. 19; LD 5; Ind. 1
Purbeck (24) C. 12; LD 11; Ind. 1
Redditch (29) Lab. 17; C. 9; Ind. 1; UKIP 1; v. 1
Reigate and Banstead (51) C. 37; R. 7; Green 3; LD 2; Ind. 1; UKIP 1
Ribble Valley (40) C. 33; LD 6; Ind. 1
Richmondshire (34) Ind. 18; C. 13; LD 2; UKIP 1
Rochford (39) C. 27; LD 3; O. 3; UKIP 3; Green 2; Lab. 1
Rossendale (36) Lab. 24; C. 10; Ind. 1; O. 1
Rother (38) C. 23; LD 5; O. 4; Ind. 2; Lab. 2; v. 2
Rugby (42) C. 23; Lab. 10; LD 7; Ind. 2
Runnymede (42) C. 35; Ind. 6; UKIP 1
Rushcliffe (50) C. 36; LD 6; Lab. 5; Green 2; Ind. 1
Rushmoor (39) C. 24; Lab. 12; UKIP 3
Ryedale (30) C. 18; Lib. 5; Ind. 3; LD 3; O. 1
St Albans (58) C. 29; LD 17; Lab. 10; Green 1; Ind. 1
St Edmundsbury (45) C. 35; Lab. 3; O. 3; UKIP 2; Green 1; Ind. 1
Scarborough (50) C. 25; Ind. 12; Lab. 9; Green 1; LD 1; O. 1; UKIP 1
Sedgemoor (48) C. 31; Lab. 13; Ind. 2; LD 2
Selby (41) C. 29; Lab. 10; Ind. 2
Sevenoaks (54) C. 47; Lab. 4; LD 2; UKIP 1
Shepway (46) C. 42; O. 2; LD 1; UKIP 1
South Bucks (40) C. 38; Ind. 2
South Cambridgeshire (57) C. 35; LD 13; Ind. 8; Lab. 1
South Derbyshire (36) C. 19; Lab. 17
South Hams (40) C. 30; LD 4; Green 3; Ind. 2; Lab. 1
South Holland (37) C. 25; Ind. 12
South Kesteven (58) C. 38; Ind. 13; Lab. 7
South Lakeland (51) LD 33; C. 14; Lab. 3; Ind. 1
South Norfolk (46) C. 35; LD 8; O. 2; Ind. 1

South Northamptonshire (42) C. 32; Ind. 7; LD 3

South Oxfordshire (48) C. 32; Ind. 4; Lab. 4; LD 4; R 2; O. 1; UKIP 1

South Ribble (55) C. 32; Lab. 21; LD 2

South Somerset (60) LD 31; C. 25; Ind. 4

South Staffordshire (49) C. 41, Ind. 6, Lab. 2

Spelthorne (39) C. 26; O. 8; LD 4; Ind. 1

Stafford (59) C. 35; Lab. 18; O. 3; Ind. 2; Green 1

Staffordshire Moorlands (56) C. 35; Lab. 8; O. 7; LD 4; Ind. 2

Stevenage (39) Lab. 33; C. 3; LD 3

Stratford-on-Avon (53) C. 36; LD 12; Ind. 2; O. 2; Lab. 1

Stroud (51) C. 21; Lab. 20; Green 6; LD 3; O. 1

Suffolk Coastal (55) C. 44; LD 5; Lab. 4; Ind. 2

Surrey Heath (40) C. 35; Ind. 2; Lab. 1; LD 1; v. 1

Swale (47) C. 31; Lab. 13; Ind. 2; O. 1

Tamworth (30) C. 16; Lab. 12; Ind. 1; UKIP 1

Tandridge (42) C. 34; LD 6; Ind. 2

Taunton Deane (56) C. 27; LD 21; Ind. 5; Lab. 3

Teignbridge (46) C. 24; Ind. 11; LD 10; UKIP 1

Tendring (60) C. 32; Lab. 9; Ind. 7; O. 6; R. 3; LD 2; v. 1

Test Valley (48) C. 35; LD 12; Ind. 1

Tewkesbury (38) C. 23; LD 10; Ind. 3; O. 2

Thanet (56) Lab. 26; C. 23; Ind. 3; O. 2; UKIP 2

Three Rivers (39) LD 23; C. 13; Lab. 3

Tonbridge and Malling (53) C. 47; LD 4; Lab. 1; Ind. 1

Torridge (36) Ind. 16; C. 15; LD 4; v. 1

Tunbridge Wells (48) C. 38; Lab. 3; LD 3; Ind. 2; UKIP 2

Uttlesford (44) C. 34; LD 7; Ind. 3

Vale of White Horse (51) C. 28; LD 21; Ind. 1; Lab. 1

Warwick (46) C. 22; LD 9; Lab. 8; Ind. 7

Watford (37) LD 24; Lab. 11; C. 1; Green 1

Waveney (48) C. 24; Lab. 22; Green 1; Ind. 1

Waverley (57) C. 53; UKIP 3; Ind. 1

Wealden (55) C. 47; O. 4; LD 3; Ind. 1

Wellingborough (36) C. 26; Lab. 8; Ind. 2

Welwyn and Hatfield (48) C. 31; Lab. 14; LD 2; Ind. 1

West Devon (31) C. 15; Ind. 10; O. 4; LD 2

West Dorset (48) C. 32; LD 11; O. 4; Ind. 1

West Lancashire (54) C. 27; Lab. 27

West Lindsey (37) C. 20; LD 10; Ind. 5; Lab. 2

West Oxfordshire (49) C. 40; Lab. 5; LD 3; Ind. 1

West Somerset (28) C. 19; Ind. 7; Lab. 2

Weymouth and Portland (36) Lab. 15; C. 11; LD 7; Ind. 2; UKIP 1

Winchester (57) C. 28; LD 25; Lab. 3; Ind. 1

Woking (36) C. 23; LD 11; Ind. 1; Lab. 1

Worcester (35) C. 17; Lab. 14; Green 1; Ind. 1; LD 1; O. 1

Worthing (37) C. 27; LD 7; Green 1; Ind. 1; UKIP 1

Wychavon (45) C. 37; LD 5; Ind. 2; Lab. 1

Wycombe (60) C. 42; LD 9; Lab. 5; Ind. 3; UKIP 1

Wyre (55) C. 40; Lab. 15

Wyre Forest (42) C. 16; O. 12; Lab. 9; UKIP 5

LONDON BOROUGH COUNCILS

Barking and Dagenham (51) Lab. 51

Barnet (63) C. 32; Lab. 30; LD 1

Bexley (63) C. 45; Lab. 15; UKIP 3

Brent (63) Lab. 56; C. 6; LD 1

Bromley (60) C. 51; Lab. 7; UKIP 2

Camden (54) Lab. 40; C. 12; Green 1; LD 1

Croydon (70) Lab. 40; C. 30

Ealing (69) Lab. 53, C. 12, LD 4

Enfield (63) Lab. 41; C. 22

Greenwich (51) Lab. 43; C. 8

Hackney (57) Lab. 50; C. 4; LD 3

Hammersmith and Fulham (46) Lab. 26; C. 20

Haringey (57) Lab. 48; LD 9

Harrow (63) Lab. 34; C. 26; Ind. 2; LD 1

Havering (54) C. 22; Ind. 19; UKIP 7; R. 5; Lab. 1

Hillingdon (65) C. 42; Lab. 23

Hounslow (60) Lab. 48; C. 11; Ind. 1

Islington (48) Lab. 47; Green 1

Kensington and Chelsea (50) C. 37; Lab. 12; LD 1

Kingston upon Thames (48) C. 28; LD 18; Lab. 2

Lambeth (63) Lab. 59; C. 3; Green 1

Lewisham (55) Lab. 54; Green 1

Merton (60) Lab. 36; C. 20; R. 3; Ind. 1

Newham (60) Lab. 60

Redbridge (63) Lab. 35; C. 25; LD 3

Richmond upon Thames (54) C. 39; LD 15

Southwark (63) Lab. 48; LD 13; C. 2

Sutton (54) LD 45; C. 9

Tower Hamlets (45) Lab. 22; O. 18; C. 5

Waltham Forest (60) Lab. 44; C. 16

Wandsworth (60) C. 41; Lab. 19

Westminster (60) C. 44; Lab. 16

METROPOLITAN BOROUGHS

Barnsley (63) Lab. 52; Ind. 6; C. 4; v. 1

Birmingham (120) Lab. 77; C. 31; LD 12

Bolton (60) Lab. 40; C. 15; LD 3; Ind. 2

Bradford (90) Lab. 46; C. 21; O. 10; LD 8; Green 3; Ind. 1; UKIP 1

Bury (51) Lab. 38; C. 11; Ind. 1; LD 1

Calderdale (51) Lab. 25; C. 19; LD 6; Ind. 1

Coventry (54) Lab. 43; C. 11

Doncaster (63) Lab. 48; C. 8; Ind. 3; LD 2; O. 1; UKIP 1

Dudley (72) Lab. 40; C. 22; UKIP 9; Green 1

Gateshead (66) Lab. 55; LD 11

Kirklees (69) Lab. 32; C. 18; LD 11; Green 5; Ind. 3

Knowsley (63) Lab. 63

Leeds (99) Lab. 63; C. 18; LD 9; O. 5; Green 3; Ind. 1

Liverpool (90) Lab. 79; Green 4; LD 3; Lib. 3; Ind. 1

Manchester (96) Lab. 95; O. 1

Newcastle-upon-Tyne (78) Lab. 52; LD 24; Ind. 2

North Tyneside (60) Lab. 44; C. 12; LD 4

Oldham (60) Lab. 45; LD 10; C. 2; UKIP 2; Ind. 1

Rochdale (60) Lab. 46; C. 11; O. 2; LD 1

Rotherham (63) Lab. 50; UKIP 10; C. 2; Ind. 1

St Helens (48) Lab. 42; C. 3; LD 3

Salford (60) Lab. 52; C. 8

Sandwell (72) Lab. 70; C. 1; UKIP 1

Sefton (66) Lab. 40; LD 17; C. 7; Ind. 2

Sheffield (84)   Lab. 59; LD 18; Green 4; UKIP 3
Solihull (51)   C. 29; Green 10; LD 8; Lab. 2;
                          Ind. 1; UKIP 1
South Tyneside (54)   Lab. 49; O. 2; C. 1; Ind. 1;
                          UKIP 1
Stockport (63)   LD 28; Lab. 22; C. 10; Ind. 3
Sunderland (75)   Lab. 63; C. 8; Ind. 4
Tameside (57)   Lab. 52; C. 5
Trafford (63)   C. 33; Lab. 27; LD 3
Wakefield (63)   Lab. 54; C. 6; UKIP 2; Ind. 1
Walsall (60)   Lab. 29; C. 21; Ind. 3; LD 3;
                          UKIP 3; v. 1
Wigan (75)   Lab. 63; Ind. 10; C. 2
Wirral (66)   Lab. 38; C. 21; LD 6; Green 1
Wolverhampton (60)   Lab. 46; C. 11; LD 2; UKIP 1

UNITARY COUNCILS

Bath and North East   LD 28; C. 26; Ind. 5; Lab. 4;
  Somerset (65)   Ind. 2
Bedford (40)   C. 12; Lab. 12; LD 12; Ind. 4
Blackburn with Darwen   Lab. 48; C. 12; LD 4
  (64)
Blackpool (42)   Lab. 27; C. 13; LD 1; v. 1
Bournemouth (54)   C. 45; Ind. 4; Lab. 3; LD 2
Bracknell Forest (42)   C. 38; Ind. 2; Lab. 2
Brighton and Hove (54)   Green 21; C. 18; Lab. 14; Ind. 1
Bristol (70)   Lab. 31; LD 16; C. 15; Green 6;
                          Ind. 1; UKIP 1
Central Bedfordshire   C. 47; Ind. 6; LD 4; Lab. 1; O. 1
  (59)
Cheshire East (82)   C. 50; Lab. 15; Ind. 12; LD 4;
                          UKIP 1
Cheshire West and   C. 42; Lab. 30; LD 1; v. 2
  Chester (75)
Cornwall (123)   Ind. 37; LD 36; C. 31; Lab. 8;
                          UKIP 6; O. 4; Green 1
Darlington (53)   Lab. 33; C. 15; LD 5
Derby (51)   Lab. 27; C. 14; LD 7; UKIP 2;
                          Ind. 1
Durham (126)   Lab. 94; Ind. 18; LD 9; C. 4; v. 1
East Riding of Yorkshire C. 53; Lab. 6; Ind. 4; LD 3; SD 1
  (67)
Halton (56)   Lab. 51; LD 3; C. 2
Hartlepool (33)   Lab. 19; O. 5; Ind. 4; C. 3;
                          UKIP 2
Herefordshire (58)   C. 27; Ind. 14; O. 11; LD 3;
                          Green 1; v. 2
*Isles of Scilly (21)   Ind. 20; v. 1
Isle of Wight (40)   Ind. 20; C. 15; Lab. 2; UKIP 2;
                          LD 1
Kingston-upon-Hull   Lab. 39; LD 15; C. 2; Ind. 2;
  (59)   UKIP 1
Leicester (54)   Lab. 50; O. 2; C. 1; LD 1
Luton (48)   Lab. 36; LD 8; C. 4
Medway (55)   C. 34; Lab. 17; LD 3; Ind. 1
Middlesbrough (49)   Lab. 25; O. 10; Ind. 8; C. 4;
                          Green 1; LD 1
Milton Keynes (57)   Lab. 25; C. 18; LD 13; UKIP 1
North East Lincolnshire   Lab. 21; C. 10; UKIP 8; LD 3
  (42)
North Lincolnshire (43)   C. 23; Lab. 20
North Somerset (61)   C. 40; Ind. 10; LD 6; Lab. 5
Northumberland (67)   Lab. 32; C. 21; LD 9; Ind. 4;
                          v. 1
Nottingham (55)   Lab. 49; C. 4; Ind. 2
Peterborough (57)   C. 28; Lab. 12; O. 10; LD 4;
                          UKIP 3
Plymouth (57)   Lab. 29; C. 24; UKIP 3; Ind. 1
Poole (42)   C. 19; LD 18; O. 4; UKIP 1

Portsmouth (42)   LD 19; C. 12; UKIP 6; Lab. 4;
                          Ind. 1
Reading (46)   Lab. 31; C. 10; Green 3; LD 2
Redcar and Cleveland   Lab. 29; LD 11; O. 11; C. 6;
  (59)   Ind. 2
Rutland (26)   C. 16; Ind. 5; UKIP 3; Green 1;
                          LD 1
Shropshire (74)   C. 47; LD 13; Lab. 9; O. 4; Ind. 1
Slough (42)   Lab. 33; C. 8; UKIP 1
South Gloucestershire   C. 33; LD 21; Lab. 15; UKIP 1
  (70)
Southampton (48)   Lab. 28; C. 18; O. 2
Southend-on-Sea (51)   C. 19; Ind. 13; Lab. 9; LD 5;
                          UKIP 5
Stockton-on-Tees (56)   Lab. 27; O. 13; C. 11; LD 4;
                          UKIP 1
Stoke-on-Trent (44)   Lab. 31; O. 10; C. 2; Ind. 1
Swindon (57)   C. 30; Lab. 23; LD 4
Telford and Wrekin (54)   Lab. 33; C. 17; LD 3; Ind. 1
Thurrock (49)   Lab. 23; C. 18; UKIP 6; Ind. 2
Torbay (37)   C. 21; LD 9; Ind. 5; Lab. 1;
                          UKIP 1
Warrington (57)   Lab. 43; LD 11; C. 3
West Berkshire (52)   C. 39; LD 13
Wiltshire (98)   C. 59; LD 24; Ind. 10; Lab. 4;
                          UKIP 1
Windsor and   C. 47; Ind. 4; LD 3; UKIP 2; v. 1
  Maidenhead (57)
Wokingham (54)   C. 44; LD 7; Ind. 3
York (47)   Lab. 24; C. 9; LD 9; Ind. 3;
                          Green 2

* Thirteen councillors are elected by the residents of the isle of St
Mary's and two councillors each are elected by the residents of the
four other islands (Bryher, St Agnes, St Martins and Tresco).

WALES

Blaenau Gwent (42)   Lab. 32; Ind. 10
Bridgend (54)   Lab. 39; Ind. 6; O. 4; LD 3; C. 1;
                          PC 1
Caerphilly (73)   Lab. 50; PC 20; Ind. 3
Cardiff (75)   Lab. 47; LD 16; C. 7; Ind. 3; PC 2
Carmarthenshire (74)   PC 28; Ind. 22; Lab. 22; O. 2
Ceredigion (42)   PC 19; Ind. 11; LD 7; O. 5
Conwy (59)   Ind. 19; C. 13; PC 12; Lab. 10;
                          LD 5
Denbighshire (47)   Lab. 18; Ind. 13; C. 8; PC 8
Flintshire (70)   Lab. 31; O. 17; C. 8; LD 7; Ind. 6
                          v. 1
Gwynedd (75)   PC 37; Ind. 18; O. 14; Lab. 4;
                          LD 2
Merthyr Tydfil (33)   Lab. 25; Ind. 6; O. 1; v. 1
Monmouthshire (43)   C. 19; Lab. 11; Ind. 10; LD 3
Neath Port Talbot (64)   Lab. 49; PC 8; Ind. 4; O. 2; v. 1
Newport (50)   Lab. 37; C. 10; Ind. 2; LD 1
Pembrokeshire (60)   Ind. 33; O. 13; Lab. 7; PC 4; C. 3
Powys (73)   O. 47; C. 10; LD 8; Lab. 6; Ind. 2
Rhondda Cynon Taff   Lab. 59; PC 9; Ind. 4; C. 1; LD 1;
  (75)   v. 1
Swansea (72)   Lab. 49; LD 12; Ind. 7; C. 4
Torfaen (44)   Lab. 30; Ind. 8; C. 4; PC 2
Vale of Glamorgan (47)   Lab. 21; C. 11; PC 6; Ind. 4; O. 4;
                          UKIP 1
Wrexham (52)   Lab. 23; Ind. 19; C. 5; LD 4;
                          PC 1
Ynys Mon (Isle of   Ind. 14; PC 12; Lab. 2; O. 2;
  Anglesey) (30)

SCOTLAND

Aberdeen (43)	Lab. 17; SNP 15; LD 5; Ind. 4; C. 2
Aberdeenshire (68)	SNP 27; Ind. 15; C. 14; LD 9; Lab. 2; Green 1
Angus (29)	SNP 14; Ind. 9; C. 4; LD 1; Lab. 1
Argyll and Bute (36)	Ind. 18; SNP 7; C. 4; LD 4; Lab. 1; O. 1; v. 1
Clackmannanshire (18)	Lab. 8; SNP 8; C. 1; Ind. 1
Dumfries and Galloway (47)	Lab. 15; C. 14; SNP 10; Ind. 5; O. 3
Dundee (29)	SNP 16; Lab. 10; C. 1; Ind. 1; LD 1
East Ayrshire (32)	SNP 15; Lab. 14; C. 2; Ind. 1
East Dunbartonshire (24)	Lab. 9; SNP 8; LD 3; C. 2; Ind. 2
East Lothian (23)	Lab. 10; SNP 8; C. 3; Ind. 2
East Renfrewshire (20)	Lab. 8; C. 6; SNP 4; Ind. 2
Edinburgh (58)	Lab. 20; SNP 17; C. 11; Green 6; LD 3; Ind. 1
Eilean Siar (Western Isles) (31)	Ind. 22; SNP 6; Lab. 3
Falkirk (32)	Lab. 14; SNP 13; Ind. 3; C. 2
Fife (78)	Lab. 35; SNP 26; LD 10; C. 3; Ind. 3; O. 1
Glasgow (79)	Lab. 45; SNP 26; Green 5; C. 1; LD 1; O. 1
Highland (80)	Ind. 34; SNP 21; LD 14; Lab. 8; O. 3
Inverclyde (20)	Lab. 10; SNP 6; LD 2; C. 1; Ind. 1
Midlothian (18)	SNP 8; Lab. 7; Ind. 2; Green 1
Moray (26)	Ind. 11; SNP 9; C. 3; Lab. 3
North Ayrshire (30)	SNP 12; Lab. 11; Ind. 6; O. 1
North Lanarkshire (70)	Lab. 41; SNP 25; Ind. 3; O. 1
Orkney Islands (21)	Ind. 21
Perth and Kinross (41)	SNP 18; C. 10; LD 5; Lab. 4; Ind. 4
Renfrewshire (40)	Lab. 22; SNP 15; C. 1; Ind. 1; LD 1
Scottish Borders (34)	Ind. 10; C. 9; SNP 9; LD 6
Shetland Islands (22)	Ind. 22
South Ayrshire (30)	C. 9; Lab. 9; SNP 9; Ind. 3
South Lanarkshire (67)	Lab. 38; SNP 22; C. 3; Ind. 3; LD 1
Stirling (22)	SNP 9; Lab. 8; C. 4; Green 1
West Dunbartonshire (22)	Lab. 12; SNP 6; Ind. 3; O. 1
West Lothian (33)	Lab. 16; SNP 15; C. 1; Ind. 1

NORTHERN IRELAND*

Antrim and Newtownabbey (40)	DUP 15; UUP 12; All. 4; SDLP 4; SF 3; TUV 2
Armagh, Banbridge and Craigavon (41)	DUP 13; UUP 12; SF 8; SDLP 6; Ind. 1; UKIP 1
Belfast (60)	SF 19; DUP 13; All. 8; SDLP 7; UUP 7; PUP 3; O. 1; TUV 1
Causeway Coast and Glens (40)	DUP 11; UUP 10; SF 7; SDLP 6; TUV 3; All. 1; Ind. 1; PUP 1
Derry and Strabane (40)	SF 16; SDLP 10; DUP 8; Ind. 4; UUP 2
Fermanagh and Omagh (40)	SF 17; UUP 9; SDLP 8; DUP 5; Ind. Un. 1
Lisburn and Castlereagh (40)	DUP 20; UUP 8; All. 7; SDLP 3; O. 1; TUV 1
Mid and East Antrim (40)	DUP 16; UUP 9; TUV 5; All. 3; SF 3; Ind. 2; SDLP 1; UKIP 1
Mid Ulster (40)	SF 18; DUP 8; SDLP 6; UUP 7; Ind. 1
Newry, Mourne and Down (41)	SDLP 14; SF 14; DUP 4; Ind. 3; UUP 3; All. 2; UKIP 1
North Down and Ards (40)	DUP 17; UUP 9; All. 7; Green 3; Ind. 2; SDLP 1; TUV 1

* Elections for Northern Ireland's 11 new district councils were held on 22 May 2014. For further information on the reform of local government in Northern Ireland *see* page 250 and for a map of the local council areas *see* page 284.

ENGLAND

The country of England lies between 55° 46' and 49° 57' 30" N. latitude (from a few miles north of the mouth of the Tweed to the Lizard), and between 1° 46' E. and 5° 43' W. longitude (from Lowestoft to Land's End). England is bounded on the north by the Cheviot Hills; on the south by the English Channel; on the east by the Straits of Dover (Pas de Calais) and the North Sea; and on the west by the Atlantic Ocean, Wales and the Irish Sea. It has a total area of 130,432 sq. km (50,360 sq. miles): land 130,279 sq. km (50,301 sq. miles); inland water 153 sq. km (59 sq. miles).

POPULATION
The population at the 2011 census was 53,012,456 (men 26,069,148; women 26,943,308). The average density of the population in 2011 was 406 persons per sq. km (1,053 per sq. mile).

FLAG
The flag of England is the cross of St George, a red cross on a white field (cross gules in a field argent). The cross of St George, the patron saint of England, has been used since the 13th century.

RELIEF
There is a marked division between the upland and lowland areas of England. In the extreme north the Cheviot Hills (highest point, the Cheviot, 815m/2,674ft) form a natural boundary with Scotland. Running south from the Cheviots, though divided from them by the Tyne Gap, is the Pennine range (highest point, Cross Fell, 893m/2,930ft), the main orological feature of the country. The Pennines culminate in the Peak District of Derbyshire (Kinder Scout, 636m/2,088ft). West of the Pennines are the Cumbrian mountains, which include Scafell Pike (978m/3,210ft), the highest peak in England, and to the east are the Yorkshire Moors, their highest point being Urra Moor (454m/1,490ft).

In the west, the foothills of the Welsh mountains extend into the bordering English counties of Shropshire (the Wrekin, 407m/1,334ft; Long Mynd, 516m/1,694ft) and Hereford and Worcester (the Malvern Hills – Worcestershire Beacon, 425m/1,394ft). Extensive areas of highland and moorland are also to be found in the south-western peninsula formed by Somerset, Devon and Cornwall, principally Exmoor (Dunkery Beacon, 519m/1,704ft), Dartmoor (High Willhays, 621m/2,038ft) and Bodmin Moor (Brown Willy, 420m/1,377ft). Ranges of low, undulating hills run across the south of the country, including the Cotswolds in the Midlands and south-west, the Chilterns to the north of London, and the North (Kent) and South (Sussex) Downs of the south-east coastal areas.

The lowlands of England lie in the Vale of York, East Anglia and the area around the Wash. The lowest-lying are the Cambridgeshire Fens in the valleys of the Great Ouse and the river Nene, which are below sea-level in places. Since the 17th century extensive drainage has brought much of the Fens under cultivation. The North Sea coast between the Thames and the Humber, low-lying and formed of sand and shingle for the most part, is subject to erosion and defences against further incursion have been built along many stretches.

HYDROGRAPHY
The Severn is the longest river in Great Britain, rising on the north-eastern slopes of Plynlimon (Wales) and entering England in Shropshire, with a total length of 354km (220

miles) from its source to its outflow into the Bristol Channel, where it receives the Bristol Avon on the east and the Wye on the west; its other tributaries are the Vyrnwy, Tern, Stour, Teme and Upper (or Warwickshire) Avon. The Severn is tidal below Gloucester, and a high bore or tidal wave sometimes reverses the flow as high as Tewkesbury (21.75km/13.5 miles above Gloucester). The scenery of the greater part of the river is very picturesque, and the Severn is a noted salmon river, with some of its tributaries being famous for trout. Navigation is assisted by the Gloucester and Berkeley Ship Canal (26km/16.25 miles), which admits vessels of 350 tons to Gloucester. The Severn Tunnel was begun in 1873 and completed in 1886 at a cost of £2m and after many difficulties caused by flooding. It is 7km (4 miles 628 yards) in length (of which 3.67km/2.25 miles are under the river). The Severn road bridge between Haysgate, Gwent, and Almondsbury, Glos, with a centre span of 988m (3,240ft), was opened in 1966.

The longest river wholly in England is the Thames, with a total length of 346km (215 miles) from its source in the Cotswold hills to the Nore, and is navigable by ocean-going ships to London Bridge. The Thames is tidal to Teddington (111km/69 miles from its mouth) and forms county boundaries almost throughout its course; on its banks are situated London, Windsor Castle, Eton College and Oxford University. Of the remaining English rivers, those flowing into the North Sea are the Tyne, Wear, Tees, Ouse and Trent from the Pennine Range, the Great Ouse (257km/160 miles), which rises in Northamptonshire, and the Orwell and Stour from the hills of East Anglia. Flowing into the English Channel are the Sussex Ouse from the Weald, the Itchen from the Hampshire hills, and the Axe, Teign, Dart, Tamar and Exe from the Devonian hills. Flowing into the Irish Sea are the Mersey, Ribble and Eden from the western slopes of the Pennines and the Derwent from the Cumbrian mountains.

The English Lakes, notable for their picturesque scenery and poetic associations, lie in Cumbria's Lake District; the largest are Windermere (14.7 sq. km/5.7 sq. miles), Ullswater (8.8 sq. km/3.4 sq. miles) and Derwent Water (5.3 sq. km/2.0 sq. miles).

ISLANDS
The Isle of Wight is separated from Hampshire by the Solent. The capital, Newport, stands at the head of the estuary of the Medina, and Cowes (at the mouth) is the chief port. Other centres are Ryde, Sandown, Shanklin, Ventnor, Freshwater, Yarmouth, Totland Bay, Seaview and Bembridge.

Lundy (the name is derived from the Old Norse for 'puffin island'), 18km (11 miles) north-west of Hartland Point, Devon, is around 5km (3 miles) long and almost 1km (half a mile) wide on average, with a total area of around 452 hectares (1,116 acres), and a population of 27. It became the property of the National Trust in 1969 and is now principally a bird sanctuary and the UK's first marine conservation zone.

The Isles of Scilly comprise around 140 islands and skerries (total area, 10 sq. km/6 sq. miles) situated 45 km (28 miles) south-west of Land's End in Cornwall. Only five are inhabited: St Mary's, St Agnes, Bryher, Tresco and St Martin's. The population at the 2011 census was 2,200. The entire group has been designated an Area of Outstanding Natural Beauty because of its unique flora and fauna. Tourism and the winter/spring flower trade for the home market form the basis of the economy of the islands. The island group is a recognised rural development area.

EARLY HISTORY

Archaeological evidence suggests that England has been inhabited since at least the Palaeolithic period, though the extent of the various Palaeolithic cultures was dependent upon the degree of glaciation. The succeeding Neolithic and Bronze Age cultures have left abundant remains throughout the country; the best-known of these are the henges and stone circles of Stonehenge (ten miles north of Salisbury, Wilts) and Avebury (Wilts), both of which are believed to have been of religious significance. In the latter part of the Bronze Age the Goidels, a people of the Celtic race, invaded the country and brought with them Celtic civilisation and dialects; as a result place names in England bear witness to the spread of the invasion across the whole region.

THE ROMAN CONQUEST

The Roman conquest of Gaul (57–50 BC) brought Britain into close contact with Roman civilisation, but although Julius Caesar raided the south of Britain in 55 and 54 BC, conquest was not undertaken until nearly 100 years later. In AD 43 the Emperor Claudius dispatched Aulus Plautius, with a well-equipped force of 40,000, and himself followed with reinforcements in the same year. Success was delayed by the resistance of Caratacus (Caractacus), the British leader from AD 48–51, who was finally captured and sent to Rome, and by a great revolt in AD 61 led by Boudicca (Boadicea), Queen of the Iceni, but the south of Britain was secured by AD 70, and Wales and the area north to the Tyne by about AD 80.

In AD 122, the Emperor Hadrian visited Britain and built a continuous rampart, since known as Hadrian's Wall, from Wallsend to Bowness (Tyne to Solway). The work was entrusted by the Emperor Hadrian to Aulus Platorius Nepos, legate of Britain from AD 122 to 126, and it was intended to form the northern frontier of the Roman Empire.

The Romans administered Britain as a province under a governor, with a well-defined system of local government, each Roman municipality ruling itself and its surrounding territory, while London was the centre of the road system and the seat of the financial officials of the Province of Britain. Colchester, Lincoln, York, Gloucester and St Albans stand on the sites of five Roman municipalities, and Wroxeter, Caerleon, Chester, Lincoln and York were at various times the sites of legionary fortresses. Well-preserved Roman towns have been uncovered at or near Silchester (Calleva Atrebatum), ten miles south of Reading, Wroxeter (Viroconium Cornoviorum), near Shrewsbury, and St Albans (Verulamium) in Hertfordshire.

Four main groups of roads radiated from London, and a fifth (the Fosse) ran obliquely from Lincoln through Leicester, Cirencester and Bath to Exeter. Of the four groups radiating from London, one ran south-east to Canterbury and the coast of Kent, a second to Silchester and thence to parts of western Britain and south Wales, a third (later known as Watling Street) ran through St Albans to Chester, with various branches, and the fourth reached Colchester, Lincoln, York and the eastern counties.

In the fourth century Britain was subjected to raids along the east coast by Saxon pirates, which led to the establishment of a system of coastal defences from the Wash to Southampton Water, with forts at Brancaster, Burgh Castle (Yarmouth), Walton (Felixstowe), Bradwell, Reculver, Richborough, Dover, Lympne, Pevensey and Porchester (Portsmouth). The Irish (Scoti) and Picts in the north were also becoming more aggressive and from around AD 350 incursions became more frequent and more formidable. As the Roman Empire came increasingly under attack towards the end of the fourth century, many troops were removed from Britain for service in other parts of the empire. The island was eventually cut off from Rome by the Teutonic conquest of Gaul, and with the withdrawal of the last Roman garrison early in the fifth century, the Romano-British were left to themselves.

SAXON SETTLEMENT

According to legend, the British King Vortigern called in the Saxons to defend his lands against the Picts. The Saxon chieftains Hengist and Horsa landed at Ebbsfleet, Kent, and established themselves in the Isle of Thanet, but the events during the one-and-a-half centuries between the final break with Rome and the re-establishment of Christianity are unclear. However, it would appear that over the course of this period the raids turned into large-scale settlement by invaders traditionally known as Angles (England north of the Wash and East Anglia), Saxons (Essex and southern England) and Jutes (Kent and the Weald), which pushed the Romano-British into the mountainous areas of the north and west. Celtic culture outside Wales and Cornwall survives only in topographical names. Various kingdoms established at this time attempted to claim overlordship of the whole country, hegemony finally being achieved by Wessex (with the capital at Winchester) in the ninth century. This century also saw the beginning of raids by the Vikings (Danes), which were resisted by Alfred the Great (871–899), who fixed a limit on the advance of Danish settlement by the Treaty of Wedmore (878), giving them the area north and east of Watling Street on the condition that they adopt Christianity.

In the tenth century the kings of Wessex recovered the whole of England from the Danes, but subsequent rulers were unable to resist a second wave of invaders. England paid tribute (Danegeld) for many years, and was invaded in 1013 by the Danes and ruled by Danish kings (including Cnut) from 1016 until 1042, when Edward the Confessor was recalled from exile in Normandy. On Edward's death in 1066 Harold Godwinson (brother-in-law of Edward and son of Earl Godwin of Wessex) was chosen to be King of England. After defeating (at Stamford Bridge, Yorkshire, 25 September 1066) an invading army under Harald Hadraada, King of Norway (aided by the outlawed Earl Tostig of Northumbria, Harold's brother), Harold was himself defeated at the Battle of Hastings on 14 October 1066, and the Norman conquest secured the throne of England for Duke William of Normandy, a cousin of Edward the Confessor.

CHRISTIANITY

Christianity reached the Roman province of Britain from Gaul in the third century (or possibly earlier). Alban, traditionally Britain's first martyr, was put to death as a Christian during the persecution of Diocletian (22 June 303) at his native town Verulamium, and the bishops of Londinium, Eboracum (York), and Lindum (Lincoln) attended the Council of Arles in 314. However, the Anglo-Saxon invasions submerged the Christian religion in England until the sixth century: conversion was undertaken in the north from 563 by Celtic missionaries from Ireland led by St Columba, and in the south by a mission sent from Rome in 597 which was led by St Augustine, who became the first archbishop of Canterbury. England appears to have been converted again by the end of the seventh century and followed, after the Council of Whitby in 663, the practices of the Roman Church, which brought the kingdom into the mainstream of European thought and culture.

PRINCIPAL CITIES

There are 51 cities in England and space constraints prevent us from including profiles of them all. Below is a selection of

England's principal cities with the date on which city status was conferred in parentheses. Other cities are Bradford (pre-1900), Chelmsford (2012), Chichester (pre-1900), Coventry (pre-1900), Derby (1977), Ely (pre-1900), Exeter (pre-1900), Gloucester (pre-1900), Hereford (pre-1900), Kingston-upon-Hull (pre-1900), Lancaster (1937), Lichfield (pre-1900), London (pre-1900), Peterborough (pre-1900), Plymouth (1928), Portsmouth (1926), Preston (2002), Ripon (pre-1900), Salford (1926), Stoke-on-Trent (1925), Sunderland (1992), Truro (pre-1900), Wakefield (pre-1900), Wells (pre-1900), Westminster (pre-1900), Wolverhampton (2000) and Worcester (pre-1900).

Certain cities have also been granted a lord mayoralty – this grant confers no additional powers or functions and is purely honorific. Cities with lord mayors are Birmingham, Bradford, Bristol, Canterbury, Chester, Coventry, Exeter, Kingston-upon-Hull, Leeds, Leicester, Liverpool, London, Manchester, Newcastle-upon-Tyne, Norwich, Nottingham, Oxford, Plymouth, Portsmouth, Sheffield, Stoke-on-Trent, Westminster and York.

BATH (PRE-1900)
Bath stands on the river Avon between the Cotswold hills to the north and the Mendips to the south. Originally a small Roman town *(Aquae Sulis)* with a baths and temple complex built around naturally occurring hot springs. In the early 18th century Bath became England's premier spa town where the rich and celebrated members of fashionable society gathered to 'take the waters' and enjoy the town's theatres and concert rooms. During this period the architect John Wood laid the foundations of a new Georgian city built using the honey-coloured stone for which Bath is famous today. Since 1987 the city has been listed as a UNESCO World Heritage Site.

Contemporary Bath is a thriving tourist destination and remains a leading cultural, religious and historical centre with many art galleries and historic sites including the Pump Room (1790); the Royal Crescent (1767); the Circus (1754); the 18th-century Assembly Rooms (housing the Museum of Costume); Pulteney Bridge (1771); the Guildhall and the Abbey, now over 500 years old, which is built on the site of a Saxon monastery. In 2006 the Bath Thermae Spa was completed and the hot springs reopened to the public for the first time since 1978.

BIRMINGHAM (PRE-1900)
Birmingham is Britain's second largest city, with a population of over one million. The generally accepted derivation of 'Birmingham' is the *ham* (dwelling-place) of the *ing* (family) of *Beorma,* presumed to have been Saxon. During the Industrial Revolution the town grew into a major manufacturing centre, known as the 'city of a thousand trades', and in 1889 was granted city status. By the 18th century, Birmingham was the main European producer of items such as buckles, medals and coins. Today, around 40 per cent of all the UK's handmade jewellery is produced in Birmingham's Jewellery Quarter. Another product of the Industrial Revolution are the city's 34 miles (56km) of canals.

Recent developments include Millennium Point, which houses Thinktank, the Birmingham science museum, and Brindleyplace, a development of shops, offices and leisure facilities on a former industrial site clustered around canals. In 2003 the Bullring shopping centre was officially opened as part of the city's urban regeneration programme.

The principal buildings are the Town Hall (1834–50), the Council House (1879), Victoria Law Courts (1891), the University of Birmingham (1906–9), the 13th-century Church of St Martin in the Bull Ring (rebuilt 1873), the

cathedral (formerly St Philip's Church) (1711), the Roman Catholic cathedral of St Chad (1839–41), the Assay Office (1773), the Rotunda (1964) and the National Exhibition Centre (1976).

BRIGHTON AND HOVE (2000)
Brighton and Hove is situated on the south coast of England, around 96 km (60 miles) south of London. Originally a fishing village called Brighthelmstone, it was transformed into a fashionable seaside resort in the 18th century when Dr Richard Russell popularised the benefits of his 'sea-water cure'; as one of the closest beaches to London, Brighton began to attract wealthy visitors. One of these was the Prince Regent (the future King George IV), who first visited in 1783 and became so fond of the city that in 1807 he bought the former farmhouse he had been renting, and gradually turned it into Brighton's most recognisable building, the Royal Pavilion. The Pavilion is renowned for its Indo-Saracenic exterior, featuring minarets and an enormous central dome designed by John Nash, combined with the lavish chinoiserie of Frederick Crace's and Robert Jones' interiors. Queen Victoria sold the Pavilion to Brighton's municipal authority in 1850.

Brighton and Hove's Regency heritage can also be seen in the numerous elegant squares and crescents designed by Amon Wilds and Augustin Busby that dominate the seafront.

BRISTOL (PRE-1900)
Bristol was a royal borough before the Norman conquest. The earliest form of the name is *Bricgstow.* Due to the city's position close to the mouth of the River Avon, it was an important location for marine trade for centuries and prospered greatly from the transatlantic slave trade during the 18th century.

The principal buildings include the 12th-century Cathedral with Norman chapter house and gateway; the 14th-century Church of St Mary Redcliffe; Wesley's Chapel, Broadmead; the Merchant Venturers' Almshouses; the Council House (1956); the Guildhall; the Exchange (erected from the designs of John Wood in 1743); Cabot Tower; University and Clifton College.

The Clifton Suspension Bridge, with a span of 214m (702ft) over the Avon, was projected by Isambard Kingdom Brunel in 1836 but was not completed until 1864. Brunel's SS *Great Britain,* the first ocean-going propeller-driven ship, now forms a museum at the Western Dockyard, from where she was originally launched in 1843. The docks themselves have been extensively restored and redeveloped; the 19th-century two-storey former tea warehouse is now the Arnolfini centre for contemporary arts, and an 18th-century sail-loft houses the Architecture Centre. On Princes Wharf, 1950s transit sheds have been renovated and converted into the museum of Bristol, M Shed, which opened in 2011.

CAMBRIDGE (1951)
Cambridge, a settlement far older than its ancient university, lies on the River Cam (or Granta). Its industries include technology research and development, and biotechnology. Among its open spaces are Jesus Green, Sheep's Green, Coe Fen, Parker's Piece, Christ's Pieces, the University Botanic Garden, and the 'Backs' – lawns and gardens through which the Cam winds behind the principal line of college buildings. Historical sites east of the Cam include King's Parade, Great St Mary's Church, Gibbs' Senate House and King's College Chapel.

University and college buildings provide the outstanding features of Cambridge's architecture but several churches (especially St Bene't's, the oldest building in the city, and Holy Sepulchre or the Round Church) are also notable. The

Guildhall (1937) stands on a site of which at least part has held municipal buildings since 1224. In 2009 the University of Cambridge celebrated its 800th anniversary.

CANTERBURY (PRE-1900)

Canterbury, seat of the Archbishop of Canterbury, the primate of the Church of England, dates back to prehistoric times. It was the Roman *Durovernum Cantiacorum* and the Saxon *Cant-wara-byrig* (stronghold of the men of Kent). It was here in 597 that St Augustine began the conversion of the English to Christianity, when Ethelbert, King of Kent, was baptised.

Of the Benedictine St Augustine's Abbey, burial place of the Jutish kings of Kent, only ruins remain. According to Bede, St Martin's Church, on the eastern outskirts of the city, was the place of worship of Queen Bertha, the Christian wife of King Ethelbert, before the advent of St Augustine.

In 1170 the rivalry of Church and State culminated in the murder in Canterbury Cathedral, by Henry II's knights, of Archbishop Thomas Becket. His shrine became a great centre of pilgrimage, as described in Chaucer's *Canterbury Tales*. After the Reformation pilgrimages ceased, but the prosperity of the city was strengthened by an influx of Huguenot refugees, who introduced weaving. The poet and playwright Christopher Marlowe was born and raised in Canterbury and the city is home to the 1,200-seat Marlowe Theatre, which reopened to the public in 2011, following an extensive £25m rebuild.

The cathedral, its architecture ranging from the 11th to the 15th centuries, is famous worldwide. Visitors are attracted particularly to the Martyrdom, the Black Prince's Tomb and the Warriors' Chapel.

The medieval city walls are built on Roman foundations and the 14th-century West Gate is one of the finest buildings of its kind in the country.

CHESTER (PRE-1900)

Chester is situated on the River Dee. Its recorded history dates from the first century when the Romans founded the fortress of *Deva*. The city's name is derived from the Latin *castra* (a camp or encampment). During the Middle Ages, Chester was the principal port of north-west England but declined with the silting of the Dee estuary and competition from Liverpool. The city was also an important military centre, notably during Edward I's Welsh campaigns and the Elizabethan Irish campaigns. During the Civil War, Chester supported the King and was besieged from 1643 to 1646. Chester's first charter was granted *c*.1175 and the city was incorporated in 1506. The office of sheriff is the earliest created in the country (1120s), and in 1992 the mayor, who also enjoys the title 'Admiral of the Dee', was made a lord mayor.

The city's architectural features include the city walls (an almost complete two-mile circuit), the unique 13th-century Rows (covered galleries above the street-level shops), the Victorian Gothic town hall (1869), the castle (rebuilt 1788 and 1822) and numerous half-timbered buildings. The cathedral was a Benedictine abbey until the dissolution of the monasteries. Chester racecourse is the oldest racecourse in Britain, believed to have origins in the 13th century. The first recorded horserace was in 1539, during the reign of Henry VIII. Chester also houses the ruins of a Roman amphitheatre, built in the late first century AD.

DURHAM (PRE-1900)

The city of Durham's prominent Norman cathedral and castle are set high on a wooded peninsula overlooking the river Wear. The cathedral was founded as a shrine for the body of St Cuthbert in 995. The present building dates from 1093 and among its many treasures is the tomb of the Venerable Bede (673–735). Durham's prince bishops had unique powers up to 1836, being lay rulers as well as religious leaders. As a palatinate, Durham could have its own army, nobility, coinage and courts. The castle was the main seat of the prince bishops for nearly 800 years; it is now used as a college by the University of Durham. The university, founded in the early 19th century on the initiative of Bishop William Van Mildert, is England's third oldest.

Annual events include Durham's regatta in June (claimed to be the oldest rowing event in Britain) and the annual Gala (formerly Durham Miners' Gala) in July. Durham County Cricket Club was established in 1882.

LEEDS (PRE-1900)

Leeds, situated in the lower Aire valley, was first incorporated by Charles I in 1626. The earliest forms of the name are *Loidis* or *Ledes,* the origins of which are obscure.

The principal buildings are the Civic Hall (1933), the Town Hall (1858), the Municipal Buildings and Art Gallery (1884) with the Henry Moore Gallery (1982), the Corn Exchange (1863) and the University. The parish church of St Peter was rebuilt in 1841 and granted minster status in 2012. The 17th-century St John's Church has a fine interior with a famous English Renaissance screen; the last remaining 18th-century church in the city is Holy Trinity in Boar Lane (1727). Kirkstall Abbey (about three miles from the centre of the city), founded by Henry de Lacy in 1152, is one of the most complete examples of a Cistercian house now remaining. The Royal Armouries Museum forms part of a group of museums that house the national collection of antique arms and armour. The Grand Theatre and Opera House is home to Northern Ballet and Opera North.

LEICESTER (1919)

Leicester is situated in central England. The city was an important Roman settlement and also one of the five 'burghs' or boroughs of the Danelaw. In 1485 Richard III was buried in Leicester following his death at the nearby Battle of Bosworth. In 1589 Queen Elizabeth I granted a charter to the city and the ancient title was confirmed by letters patent in 1919.

The textile industry was responsible for Leicester's early expansion and the city still maintains a strong manufacturing base. Cotton mills and factories are now undergoing extensive regeneration and are being converted into offices, apartments, bars and restaurants. The principal buildings include the two universities (the University of Leicester and De Montfort University), as well as the Town Hall, the 13th-century Guildhall, De Montfort Hall, Leicester Cathedral, the Jewry Wall (the UK's highest standing Roman wall), St Nicholas Church and St Mary de Castro church. The motte and Great Hall of Leicester can be seen from the castle gardens, situated next to the River Soar.

LINCOLN (PRE-1900)

Situated 64km (40 miles) inland on the river Witham, Lincoln derives its name from a contraction of *Lindum Colonia,* the settlement founded in AD 48 by the Romans to command the crossing of Ermine Street and Fosse Way. Sections of the third-century Roman city wall can be seen, including an extant gateway (Newport Arch). The Romans also drained the surrounding fenland and created a canal system, laying the foundations of Lincoln's agricultural prosperity and also the city's importance in the medieval wool trade as a port and staple town.

As one of the five 'burghs' or boroughs of the Danelaw, Lincoln was an important trading centre in the ninth and tenth centuries and prosperity from the wool trade lasted until the 14th century. This wealth enabled local merchants to build parish churches, of which three survive, and there are also remains of a 12th-century Jewish community. However, the removal of the staple to Boston in 1369 heralded a decline, from which the city only recovered fully in the 19th century, when improved fen drainage made Lincoln agriculturally important. Improved canal and rail links led to industrial development, mainly in the manufacture of machinery and engineering products.

The castle was built shortly after the Norman Conquest and is unusual in having two mounds; on one motte stands a keep (Lucy's Tower) added in the 12th century. It currently houses one of the four surviving copies of the Magna Carta. The cathedral was begun c.1073 but was mostly destroyed by fire and earthquake in the 12th century. Rebuilding was begun by St Hugh and completed over a century later. Other notable architectural features are the 12th-century High Bridge, the oldest in Britain still to carry buildings, and the Guildhall, situated above the 15th-century Stonebow gateway.

LIVERPOOL (PRE-1900)

Liverpool, on the north bank of the river Mersey, 5km (3 miles) from the Irish Sea, is the UK's foremost port for Atlantic trade.

There are 2,100 acres of dockland on both sides of the river and the Gladstone and Royal Seaforth Docks can accommodate tanker-sized vessels. Liverpool Free Port was opened in 1984.

Liverpool was created a free borough in 1207 and a city in 1880. From the early 18th century it expanded rapidly with the growth of industrialisation and the transatlantic slave trade. Surviving buildings from this period include the Bluecoat Chambers (1717, formerly the Bluecoat School), and the Town Hall (1754, rebuilt to the original design 1795). Notable from the 19th and 20th centuries are the Anglican cathedral (built from the designs of Sir Giles Gilbert Scott, it took 74 years to construct), and the Catholic Metropolitan Cathedral (designed by Sir Frederick Gibberd, consecrated 1967). Both of these cathedrals are situated on Hope Street, named after the merchant William Hope, which is the only street in the UK with a cathedral at either end. The refurbished Albert Dock (designed by Jesse Hartley) contains the Merseyside Maritime Museum, the International Slavery Museum, the Beatles Story and the Tate Liverpool art gallery. The Museum of Liverpool opened in 2011.

MANCHESTER (PRE-1900)

Manchester (the *Mamucium* of the Romans, who occupied it in AD 79) is a commercial and industrial centre connected with the sea by the Manchester Ship Canal, 57km (35.5 miles) long, opened in 1894, and accommodating ships up to 15,000 tons. During the Industrial Revolution the city had a thriving cotton industry and by 1853 there were over 100 cotton mills which dominated the city's landscape.

The principal buildings are the Town Hall, erected in 1877 from the designs of Alfred Waterhouse, with a large extension of 1938; the Royal Exchange (1869, enlarged 1921); the Central Library (1934); Heaton Hall; the 17th-century Chetham Library; the Rylands Library (1900), which includes the Althorp collection; the university precinct; the 15th-century cathedral (formerly the parish church); the Manchester Central conference and exhibition centre and the Bridgewater Hall (1996) concert venue. Manchester is the home of the Hallé Orchestra, the Royal Northern College of Music, the Royal Exchange Theatre and numerous public art galleries.

The town received its first charter of incorporation in 1838 and was created a city in 1853.

NEWCASTLE UPON TYNE (PRE-1900)

Newcastle upon Tyne, on the north bank of the River Tyne, is 13km (8 miles) from the North Sea. A cathedral and university city, it is the administrative, commercial and cultural centre for north-east England and the principal port.

The principal buildings include the Castle Keep (12th century), Black Gate (13th century), Blackfriars (13th century), West Walls (13th century), St Nicholas's Cathedral (15th century, fine lantern tower), St Andrew's Church (12th–14th century), St John's (14th–15th century), All Saints (1786 by Stephenson), St Mary's Roman Catholic Cathedral (1844), Trinity House (17th century), Sandhill (16th-century houses), Guildhall (Georgian), Grey Street (1834–9), Central Station (1846–50) and the Central Library (1969). Open spaces include the Town Moor (927 acres).

Numerous bridges span the Tyne at Newcastle, including the Tyne Bridge (1928) and the tilting Millennium Bridge (2001) which links the city with Gateshead to the south.

The city's name is derived from the 'new castle' (1080) erected as a defence against the Scots. In 1265 defensive walls over two miles in length were built around the city as further protection; parts of these walls remain today and can be found to the west of the city centre.

NORWICH (PRE-1900)

Norwich grew from an early Anglo-Saxon settlement near the confluence of the rivers Yare and Wensum, and now serves as the provincial capital for the predominantly agricultural region of East Anglia. The name is thought to relate to the most northerly of a group of Anglo-Saxon villages or *wics*. The city's first known charter was granted in 1158 by Henry II.

Norwich serves its surrounding area as a market town and commercial centre. From the 14th century until the Industrial Revolution, Norwich was the regional centre of the woollen industry. Now the biggest single industry is financial services and principal trades are engineering, printing and shoemaking. The University of East Anglia is on the city's western boundary and admitted its first students in 1963. Norwich is accessible to seagoing vessels by means of the river Yare, entered at Great Yarmouth, 32km (20 miles) to the east.

Among many historic buildings are the cathedral (completed in the 12th century and surmounted by a 15th-century spire 96m (315ft) in height); the keep of the Norman castle (now a museum and art gallery); the 15th-century flint-walled Guildhall; some 30 medieval parish churches; St Andrew's and Blackfriars' Halls; the Tudor houses preserved in Elm Hill and the Georgian Assembly House.

NOTTINGHAM (PRE-1900)

Nottingham stands on the river Trent. *Snotingaham* or *Notingeham,* the 'homestead of the people of Snot', is the Anglo-Saxon name for the Celtic settlement of *Tigguocobauc,* or the house of caves. In 878, Nottingham became one of the five 'burghs' or boroughs of the Danelaw. William the Conqueror ordered the construction of Nottingham Castle, while the town itself developed rapidly under Norman rule. Its laws and rights were formally recognised by Henry II's charter in 1155. The castle became a favoured residence of King John. In 1642 Charles I raised his personal standard at Nottingham Castle at the start of the Civil War.

Architecturally, Nottingham has a wealth of notable buildings, particularly those designed in the Victorian era by T. C. Hine and Watson Fothergill. The city council owns the castle, of Norman origin but restored in 1878, Wollaton Hall (1580–8), Newstead Abbey (once the home of Lord Byron), the Guildhall (1888) and the Council House (1929). St Mary's, St Peter's and St Nicholas' churches are of interest, as is the Roman Catholic cathedral (Pugin, 1842–4). Nottingham was granted city status in 1897.

OXFORD (PRE-1900)

Oxford is a university city, an important industrial centre and a market town.

Oxford is known for its architecture, its oldest specimens being the reputedly Saxon tower of St Michael's Church, the remains of the Norman castle and city walls, and the Norman church at Iffley. It also has many Gothic buildings, such as the Divinity Schools, the Old Library at Merton College, William of Wykeham's New College, Magdalen and Christ Church colleges and many other college buildings. Later centuries are represented by the Laudian quadrangle at St John's College, the Renaissance Sheldonian Theatre by Wren, Trinity College Chapel, All Saints Church, Hawksmoor's mock-Gothic at All Souls College, and the 18th-century Queen's College. In addition to individual buildings, High Street and Radcliffe Square both form interesting architectural compositions. Most of the colleges have gardens, those of Magdalen, New College, St John's and Worcester being the largest.

The Oxford University Museum of Natural History, renowned for its spectacular neo-gothic architecture, houses the university's scientific collections of zoological, entomological and geological specimens and is attached to the neighbouring Pitt Rivers Museum, which houses ethnographic and archaeological objects from around the world. The Ashmolean is the city's museum of art and archaeology and Modern Art Oxford hosts a programme of contemporary art exhibitions.

ST ALBANS (PRE-1900)

The origins of St Albans, situated on the river Ver, stem from the Roman town of *Verulamium.* Named after the first Christian martyr in Britain, who was executed there, St Albans has developed around the Norman abbey and cathedral church (consecrated 1115), built partly of materials from the old Roman city. The museums house Iron Age and Roman artefacts and the Roman theatre, unique in Britain, has a stage as opposed to an amphitheatre. Archaeological excavations in the city centre have revealed evidence of pre-Roman, Saxon and medieval occupation.

The town's significance grew to the extent that it was a signatory and venue for the drafting of the Magna Carta. It was also the scene of riots during the Peasants' Revolt, the French King John was imprisoned there after the Battle of Poitiers, and heavy fighting took place there during the Wars of the Roses.

Previously controlled by the Abbot, the town achieved a charter in 1553 and city status in 1877. The street market, first established in 1553, is still an important feature of the city, as are many hotels and inns, surviving from the days when St Albans was an important coach stop. St Albans is also noted for its Clock Tower, built between 1403 and 1412, the only remaining medieval town belfry in England.

SALISBURY (PRE-1900)

The history of Salisbury centres around the cathedral and cathedral close. The city evolved from an Iron Age camp a mile to the north of its current position which was strengthened by the Romans and called *Serviodunum.* The Normans built a castle and cathedral on the site and renamed it Sarum. In 1220 Bishop Richard Poore and the architect Elias de Derham decided to build a new Gothic-style cathedral. The cathedral was completed 38 years later and a community known as New Sarum, now called Salisbury, grew around it. Originally the cathedral had a squat tower; the 123m (404ft) spire that makes the cathedral the tallest medieval structure in the world was added c.1315. A walled

close with houses for the clergy was built around the cathedral; the Medieval Hall still stands today, alongside buildings dating from the 13th to the 20th century, including some designed by Sir Christopher Wren.

A prosperous wool and cloth trade allowed Salisbury to flourish until the 17th century. When the wool trade declined new crafts were established, including cutlery, leather and basket work, saddlery, lacemaking, joinery and malting. By 1750 it had become an important road junction and coaching centre and in the Victorian era the railways enabled a new age of expansion and prosperity.

SHEFFIELD (PRE-1900)

Sheffield is situated at the confluence of the rivers Sheaf, Porter, Rivelin and Loxley with the river Don and was created a city in 1893.

The parish church of St Peter and St Paul, founded in the 12th century, became the cathedral church of the diocese of Sheffield in 1914. The Roman Catholic Cathedral Church of St Marie (founded 1847) was created a cathedral for the new diocese of Hallam in 1980; parts of the present building date from c.1435. The principal buildings are the Town Hall (1897), the Cutlers' Hall (1832), City Hall (1932), Graves Art Gallery (1934), Mappin Art Gallery, the Crucible Theatre and the restored Lyceum theatre, which dates from 1897 and was reopened in 1990. Three major sporting and entertainment venues were opened between 1990 and 1991: Sheffield Arena, Don Valley Stadium (closed 2013) and Pond's Forge. The Millennium Galleries opened in 2001. The Leadmill, Sheffield's longest-running independent live music venue, opened in 1980.

SOUTHAMPTON (1964)

Southampton is a major seaport on the south coast of England, situated between the mouths of the Test and Itchen rivers. Southampton's natural deep-water harbour has made the area an important settlement since the Romans built the first port (known as *Clausentum*) in the first century, and Southampton's port has witnessed several important departures, including those of Henry V in 1415 for the Battle of Agincourt, RMS *Titanic* in 1912, and the *Mayflower* in 1620.

The city's strategic importance, not only as a seaport but also as a centre for aircraft production, meant that it was heavily bombed during the Second World War; however, many historically significant structures remain, including the Wool House, dating from 1417 and now used as the Maritime Museum; parts of the Norman city walls, which are among the most complete in the UK; the Bargate, which was originally the main gateway into the city; God's House Tower, now the Museum of Archaeology; St Michael's, the city's oldest church; and the Tudor Merchants Hall.

WINCHESTER (PRE-1900)

Winchester, the ancient capital of England, is situated on the river Itchen. The city is rich in architecture of all types, and especially notable is the cathedral. Built in 1079–93 the cathedral exhibits examples of Norman, early English and Perpendicular styles and is the burial place of author Jane Austen. Winchester College, founded in 1382, is one of the country's most famous public schools, and the original building (1393) remains largely unaltered. St Cross Hospital, another great medieval foundation, lies one mile south of the city. The almshouses were founded in 1136 by Bishop Henry de Blois, and Cardinal Henry Beaufort added a new almshouse of 'Noble Poverty' in 1446. The chapel and dwellings are of great architectural interest, and visitors may still receive the 'Wayfarer's Dole' of bread and ale, a tradition now 900 years old.

Excavations have done much to clarify the origins and development of Winchester. Part of the forum and several of the streets from the Roman town have been discovered. Excavations in the cathedral close have uncovered the entire site of the Anglo-Saxon cathedral (known as the Old Minster) and parts of the New Minster which was built by Alfred the Great's son, Edward the Elder, and is the burial place of the Alfredian dynasty. The original burial place of St Swithun, before his remains were translated to a site in the present cathedral, was also uncovered.

Excavations in other parts of the city have thrown much light on Norman Winchester, notably on the site of the Royal Castle (adjacent to which the new Law Courts have been built) and in the grounds of Wolvesey Castle, where the great house built by Bishops Giffard and Henry de Blois in the 12th century has been uncovered. The Great Hall, built by Henry III between 1222 and 1236, survives and houses the Arthurian Round Table.

YORK (PRE-1900)

The city of York is an archiepiscopal seat. Its recorded history dates from AD 71, when the Roman Ninth Legion established a base under Petilius Cerealis that would later become the fortress of *Eburacum,* or *Eboracum.* In Anglo-Saxon times the city was the royal and ecclesiastical centre of Northumbria, and after capture by a Viking army in AD 866 it became the capital of the Viking kingdom of Jorvik. By the 14th century the city had become a great mercantile centre, mainly because of its control of the wool trade, and was used as the chief base against the Scots. Under the Tudors its fortunes declined, although Henry VIII made it the headquarters of the Council of the North. Excavations on many sites, including Coppergate, have greatly expanded knowledge of Roman, Viking and medieval urban life.

The city is rich in examples of architecture of all periods. The earliest church was built in AD 627 and, from the 12th to 15th centuries, the present Minster was built in a succession of styles.

LORD-LIEUTENANTS AND HIGH SHERIFFS

Area	Lord-Lieutenant	High Sheriff (2014–15)
Bedfordshire	Helen Nellis	Colin Osborne, MBE
Berkshire	Hon. Mary Bayliss	Christopher Teik-Kooi Khoo
Bristol	Mary Prior, MBE	Henry Bothamley
Buckinghamshire	Sir Henry Aubrey-Fletcher	Joseph Gurney Barclay
Cambridgeshire	Hugh Duberly, CBE	Linda Fairbrother
Cheshire	David Briggs, MBE	Susan Sellers
Cornwall	Col. Edward Bolitho, OBE	Charles Williams
Cumbria	Claire Hensman	Martyn Telford
Derbyshire	William Tucker	David Coleman, QPM
Devon	Sir Eric Dancer, KCVO, CBE	Hon. John Rous
Dorset	Angus Campbell	Jane Sitchbury, CBE, QPM
Durham	Susan Snowdon	Gerald Osborne
East Riding of Yorkshire	Hon. Susan Cunliffe-Lister	Gail Mettyear
East Sussex	Peter Field	Christopher Gebbie, OBE
Essex	Lord Petre	Nicholas Charrington
Gloucestershire	Dame Janet Trotter, DBE	Thomas Fortescue Frost
Greater London	Sir David Brewer, CMG	Kevin McGrath
Greater Manchester	Warren Smith	Paul Lee
Hampshire	Dame Mary Fagan, DCVO	Maj.-Gen. James Balfour, CBE
Herefordshire	Countess of Darnley	Maj. Patrick Darling
Hertfordshire	Countess of Verulam	Fergus McMullen
Isle of Wight	Maj.-Gen. Martin White, CB, CBE	Claire Locke
Kent	Viscount De L'Isle, MBE	Hugo Fenwick
Lancashire	Lord Shuttleworth, KCVO	James Johnson
Leicestershire	Lady Gretton	Richard Clowes
Lincolnshire	Anthony Worth	Earl of Yarborough
Merseyside	Dame Lorna Fox Muirhead, DBE	Mrs Abila Pointing, MBE
Norfolk	Richard Jewson	Lady Dannatt
North Yorkshire	Lord Crathorne, KCVO	Thomas Ponsonby Ramsden
Northamptonshire	David Laing	Virginia Burnett
Northumberland	Duchess of Northumberland	John Carr-Ellison
Nottinghamshire	Sir John Peace	Graham Cartledge, CBE
Oxfordshire	Tim Stevenson, OBE	Anthony Stratton
Rutland	Dr Laurence Howard, OBE	Air Cdre Simon Williamson-Noble
Shropshire	Sir Algernon Heber-Percy, KCVO	Robert Bowring Bland
Somerset	Lady Gass, DCVO	Richard Ayshford Lloyd
South Yorkshire	David Moody	John Bramah
Staffordshire	Ian Dudson, CBE	Ann Fisher
Suffolk	Lord Tollemache	Nicholas Wingfield Digby
Surrey	Dame Sarah Goad, DCVO	Peter Gorringe Lee
Tyne and Wear	Sir Nigel Sherlock, KCVO, OBE	Ruth Thompson, OBE
Warwickshire	Timothy Cox	Clare Hopkinson
West Midlands	Paul Sabapathy, CBE	Timothy Watts
West Sussex	Susan Pyper	Jonathan Lucas
West Yorkshire	Dr Ingrid Roscoe	Hon. Mrs Dent
Wiltshire	Sarah Troughton	Peter Addington
Worcestershire	Lt.-Col. Patrick Holcroft, LVO, OBE	John Waller Hogan

COUNTY COUNCILS

Council & Administrative Headquarters	Telephone	Population*	Council Tax†	Chief Executive‡
Buckinghamshire, Aylesbury	01296-395000	511,488	£1,094	Chris Williams
Cambridgeshire, Cambridge	0345-045 5200	628,339	£1,122	Mark Lloyd
Cumbria, Carlisle	01228-606060	499,104	£1,162	Diane Wood
Derbyshire, Matlock	01629-580000	773,522	£1,099	Ian Stephenson
Devon, Exeter	0345-155 1015	753,157	£1,139	Phil Norrey
Dorset, Dorchester	01305-221000	414,940	£1,192	Debbie Ward
East Sussex, Lewes	0345-608 0190	531,201	£1,181	Becky Shaw
Essex, Chelmsford	0845-7430 430	1,406,517	£1,087	Joanna Killian
Gloucestershire, Gloucester	01452-425000	602,159	£1,091	Peter Bungard
Hampshire, Winchester	01962-841841	1,330,153	£1,038	Andrew Smith, OBE
Hertfordshire, Hertford	01992-555555	1,129,096	£1,119	John Wood
Kent, Maidstone	0300-041 4141	1,480,166	£1,069	David Cockburn
Lancashire, Preston	0300-123 6701	1,175,979	£1,108	Jo Turton
Leicestershire, Leicester	0116-232 3232	656,698	£1,063	John Sinnott
Lincolnshire, Lincoln	01522-552222	718,838	£1,066	Tony McArdle
Norfolk, Norwich	0344-800 8020	865,302	£1,145	Anne Gibson (acting)
North Yorkshire, Northallerton	01609-780780	602,628	£1,079	Richard Flinton
Northamptonshire, Northampton	0300-126 1000	700,576	£1,049	Paul Blantern
Nottinghamshire, Nottingham	0115-982 3823	790,173	£1,217	Mick Burrows
Oxfordshire, Oxford	01865-792422	660,772	£1,208	Joanna Simons
Somerset, Taunton	0845-345 9166	534,950	£1,027	Patrick Flaherty
Staffordshire, Stafford	0300-111 8000	852,123	£1,027	Nick Bell
Suffolk, Ipswich	08456-066 067	732,332	£1,127	Deborah Cadman
Surrey, Kingston upon Thames	0845-600 9009	1,143,509	£1,196	David McNulty
Warwickshire, Warwick	01926-410410	547,974	£1,178	Jim Graham
West Sussex, Chichester	01243-777100	815,119	£1,162	Diane Ashby
Worcestershire, Worcester	01905-763763	569,032	£1,059	Clare Marchant

* Source: Office for National Statistics – Mid-2012 Population Estimates (Crown copyright)
† Average 2014–15 Band D council tax in the county area exclusive of precepts for fire and police authorities. County councils claim their share of the combined council tax from the collection funds of the district authorities within their area. Average Band D council tax bills for the billing authority are given on the following pages
‡ Or equivalent postholder

LONDON BOROUGH COUNCILS

Council	Telephone	Population*	Council Tax†	Chief Executive‡
Barking and Dagenham	020-8592 4500	190,560	£1,315	Graham Farrant
Barnet	020-8359 2000	363,956	£1,401	Andrew Travers
Bexley	020-8303 7777	234,271	£1,428	Will Tuckley
Brent	020-8937 1234	314,660	£1,358	Christine Gilbert (acting)
Bromley	020-8464 3333	314,036	£1,309	Doug Patterson
Camden	020-7974 4444	224,962	£1,321	Mike Cooke
CITY OF LONDON CORPORATION	020-7606 3030	7,604	£942	John Barradell, OBE
Croydon	020-8726 6000	368,886	£1,470	Nathan Elvery
Ealing	020-8825 5000	340,671	£1,359	Martin Smith
Enfield	020-8379 1000	317,287	£1,399	Rob Leak
Greenwich	020-8854 8888	260,068	£1,280	Mary Ney
Hackney	020-8356 5000	252,142	£1,297	Tim Shields
Hammersmith and Fulham	020-8748 3020	179,850	£1,034	Nicholas Holgate (acting)
Haringey	020-8489 0000	258,912	£1,483	Nick Walkley
Harrow	020-8863 5611	242,377	£1,509	Paul Najsarek (acting)
Havering	01708-434343	239,733	£1,494	Cheryl Coppell
Hillingdon	01895-250111	281,756	£1,412	Fran Beasley
Hounslow	020-8583 2000	259,052	£1,379	Mary Harpley
Islington	020-7527 2000	211,047	£1,261	Lesley Seary
Kensington and Chelsea	020-7361 3000	155,930	£1,082	Nicholas Holgate (acting)
Kingston upon Thames	020-8547 5757	163,906	£1,679	Bruce McDonald
Lambeth	020-7926 1000	310,200	£1,224	Derrick Anderson, CBE
Lewisham	020-8314 6000	281,556	£1,359	Barry Quirk, CBE
Merton	020-8543 2222	202,225	£1,406	Ged Curran
Newham	020-8430 2000	314,084	£1,245	Kim Bromley-Derry
Redbridge	020-8554 5000	284,617	£1,395	Roger Hampson
Richmond upon Thames	020-8891 1411	189,145	£1,586	Gillian Norton
Southwark	020-7525 5000	293,530	£1,211	Eleanor Kelly
Sutton	020-8770 5000	193,630	£1,440	Niall Bolger
Tower Hamlets	020-7364 5000	263,003	£1,185	Stephen Halsey
Waltham Forest	020-8496 3000	262,566	£1,451	Martin Esom
Wandsworth	020-8871 6000	308,312	£687	Paul Martin
WESTMINSTER	020-7641 6000	223,858	£678	Charlie Parker

DISTRICT COUNCILS

District Council	Telephone	Population*	Council Tax†	Chief Executive‡
Adur	01903-239999	61,929	£1,593	Alex Bailey
Allerdale	01900-702702	96,268	£1,580	Ian Frost
Amber Valley	01773-570222	122,746	£1,531	Sylvia Delahay & Julian Townsend
Arun	01903-737500	151,384	£1,526	Nigel Lynn
Ashfield	01623-450000	120,131	£1,639	Philip Marshall
Ashford	01233-331111	120,116	£1,455	John Bunnett
Aylesbury Vale	01296-585858	177,793	£1,523	Andrew Grant
Babergh	01473-822801	87,917	£1,511	Charlie Adan
Barrow-in-Furness	01229-876300	68,446	£1,592	Phil Huck
Basildon	01268-533333	176,474	£1,557	Bala Mahendran
Basingstoke and Deane	01256-844844	170,492	£1,376	Tony Curtis
Bassetlaw	01909-533533	113,178	£1,644	Neil Taylor
Blaby	0116-275 0555	94,593	£1,516	Sandra Whiles
Bolsover	01246-240000	76,447	£1,608	Wesley Lumley
Boston	01205-314200	64,793	£1,446	Richard Harbord
Braintree	01376-552525	148,384	£1,491	Nicola Beach
Breckland	01362-656870	131,857	£1,495	Anna Graves
Brentwood	01277-312500	74,020	£1,475	Alison Crowe
Broadland	01603-431133	125,215	£1,527	Phil Kirby
Bromsgrove	01527-881288	94,285	£1,538	Kevin Dicks
Broxbourne	01992-785555	94,497	£1,380	Jeff Stack
Broxtowe	0115-917 7777	110,716	£1,645	Ruth Hyde, OBE
Burnley	01282-425011	87,127	£1,597	Steve Rumbelow
CAMBRIDGE	01223-457000	125,155	£1,541	Antoinette Jackson
Cannock Chase	01543-462621	97,940	£1,495	Stephen Brown
CANTERBURY	01227-862000	153,399	£1,480	Colin Carmichael
CARLISLE	01228-817000	107,952	£1,577	Jason Gooding
Castle Point	01268-882200	88,218	£1,539	David Marchant
Charnwood	01509-263151	168,779	£1,476	Geoff Parker
CHELMSFORD	01245-606606	169,335	£1,505	Steve Packham
Cheltenham	01242-262626	116,080	£1,490	Andrew North
Cherwell	01295-252535	142,822	£1,575	Sue Smith
Chesterfield	01246-345345	103,782	£1,495	Huw Bowen
Chichester	01243-785166	114,521	£1,490	Diane Shepherd
Chiltern	01494-729000	92,954	£1,533	Alan Goodrum
Chorley	01257-515151	109,077	£1,522	Gary Hall
Christchurch	01202-495000	47,987	£1,628	David McIntosh
Colchester	01206-282222	176,008	£1,493	Adrian Pritchard
Copeland	0845-054 8600	70,329	£1,582	Paul Walker
Corby	01536-464000	63,073	£1,427	Norman Stronach
Cotswold	01285-623000	83,562	£1,491	David Neudegg
Craven	01756-700600	55,457	£1,556	Paul Shevlin
Crawley	01293-438000	108,302	£1,491	Lee Harris
Dacorum	01442-228000	146,727	£1,455	Sally Marshall
Dartford	01322-343434	98,940	£1,478	Graham Harris
Daventry	01327-871100	78,281	£1,446	Ian Vincent
Derbyshire Dales	01629-761100	71,336	£1,573	Dorcas Bunton
Dover	01304-821199	111,765	£1,510	Nadeem Aziz
East Cambridgeshire	01353-665555	85,097	£1,568	John Hill
East Devon	01395-516551	134,359	£1,542	Mark Williams
East Dorset	01202-886201	87,755	£1,688	David McIntosh
East Hampshire	01730-266551	116,400	£1,456	Sandy Hopkins
East Hertfordshire	01279-655261	139,458	£1,487	George Robertson
East Lindsey	01507-601111	136,596	£1,415	Stuart Davy
East Northamptonshire	01832-742000	87,365	£1,456	David Oliver
East Staffordshire	01283-508000	114,388	£1,483	Andy O'Brien
Eastbourne	01323-410000	100,049	£1,630	Robert Cottrill
Eastleigh	023-8068 8000	126,764	£1,442	Nick Tustian
Eden	01768-817817	52,656	£1,576	Robin Hooper
Elmbridge	01372-474474	131,512	£1,611	Robert Moran
Epping Forest	01992-564000	126,080	£1,507	Glen Chipp
Epsom and Ewell	01372-732000	76,052	£1,581	Frances Rutter
Erewash	0115-907 2244	112,809	£1,511	Jeremy Jaroszek
EXETER	01392-277888	119,397	£1,514	Karime Hassan
Fareham	01329-236100	112,802	£1,394	Peter Grimwood
Fenland	01354-654321	95,996	£1,645	Paul Medd
Forest Heath	01638-719000	60,735	£1,514	Ian Gallin
Forest of Dean	01594-810000	82,731	£1,523	Sue Pangbourne
Fylde	01253-658658	76,020	£1,542	Allan Oldfield

District Council	Telephone	Population*	Council Tax†	Chief Executive‡
Gedling	0115-901 3901	114,052	£1,5629	John Robinson
GLOUCESTER	01452-522232	123,439	£1,484	vacant
Gosport	023-9258 4242	83,276	£1,456	Ian Lycett
Gravesham	01474-337000	102,764	£1,468	David Hughes
Great Yarmouth	01493-856100	97,570	£1,508	vacant
Guildford	01483-505050	139,710	£1,581	Sue Sturgeon
Hambleton	01619-779977	89,748	£1,476	Phillip Morton
Harborough	01858-828282	86,389	£1,503	vacant
Harlow	01279-446655	82,676	£1,557	Malcolm Morley
Harrogate	01423-500600	158,610	£1,581	Wallace Sampson
Hart	01252-622122	92,162	£1,465	Daryl Phillips
Hastings	01424 451066	90,345	£1,641	Neil Dart
Havant	023-9247 4174	121,271	£1,446	Sandy Hopkins
Hertsmere	020-8207 2277	100,710	£1,448	Donald Graham
High Peak	0845-129 7777	91,118	£1,530	Simon Baker
Hinckley and Bosworth	01455-238141	106,046	£1,453	Steve Atkinson
Horsham	01403-215100	132,160	£1,486	Tom Crowley
Huntingdonshire	01480-388388	171,023	£1,585	Jo Lancaster
Hyndburn	01254-388111	80,190	£1,558	David Welsby
Ipswich	01473-432000	134,466	£1,615	Russell Williams
Kettering	01536-410333	94,841	£1,458	David Cook, MBE
King's Lynn and West Norfolk	01553-616200	148,628	£1,511	Ray Harding
LANCASTER	01524-582000	139,665	£1,541	Mark Cullinan
Lewes	01273-471600	98,690	£1,676	Jenny Rowlands
Lichfield	01543-308000	101,186	£1,463	Diane Tilley
LINCOLN	01522-881188	94,588	£1,505	Andrew Taylor
Maidstone	01622-602000	157,927	£1,536	Alison Broom
Maldon	01621-854477	61,918	£1,518	Fiona Marshall
Malvern Hills	01684-862151	74,980	£1,512	Chris Bocock
Mansfield	01623-463463	104,737	£1,648	Ruth Marlow
Melton	01664-502502	50,770	£1,506	Lynn Aisbett
Mendip	0300-3038588	109,938	£1,491	Stuart Brown
Mid Devon	01884-255255	78,335	£1,602	Kevin Finan
Mid Suffolk	01449-720711	97,611	£1,507	Charlie Adan
Mid Sussex	01444-458166	141,162	£1,512	Kathryn Hall
Mole Valley	01306-885001	85,846	£1,569	Yvonne Rees
New Forest	023-8028 5000	177,382	£1,478	David Yates
Newark and Sherwood	01636-650000	115,761	£1,688	Andrew Muter
Newcastle-under-Lyme	01782-717717	124,183	£1,458	John Sellgren
North Devon	01271-327711	93,847	£1,594	Mike Mansell
North Dorset	01258-454111	69,348	£1,644	Liz Goodall
North East Derbyshire	01246-231111	99,325	£1,608	Wes Lumley
North Hertfordshire	01462-474000	128,428	£1,490	David Scholes
North Kesteven	01529-414155	109,263	£1,473	Ian Fytche
North Norfolk	01263-513811	101,790	£1,533	Sheila Oxtoby
North Warwickshire	01827-715341	62,200	£1,615	Jerry Hutchinson
North West Leicestershire	01530-454545	94,018	£1,524	Christine Fisher
Northampton	01604-837837	214,566	£1,471	David Kennedy
NORWICH	0344-980 3333	134,264	£1,585	Laura McGillivray
Nuneaton and Bedworth	024-7637 6376	125,805	£1,570	Alan Franks
Oadby and Wigston	0116-288 8961	56,103	£1,501	Mark Hall
OXFORD	01865-249811	152,527	£1,646	Peter Sloman
Pendle	01282-661661	89,613	£1,593	Stephen Barnes
PRESTON	01772-906900	140,540	£1,612	Lorraine Norris
Purbeck	01929-556561	45,289	£1,683	Steve Mackenzie
Redditch	01527-534123	84,419	£1,530	Kevin Dicks
Reigate and Banstead	01737-276000	139,888	£1,615	John Jory
Ribble Valley	01200-425111	57,596	£1,485	Marshal Scott
Richmondshire	01748-829100	53,935	£1,580	Tony Clark
Rochford	01702-546366	83,869	£1,546	Amar Dave
Rossendale	01706-217777	68,366	£1,583	Helen Lockwood
Rother	01424-787999	91,088	£1,620	Malcolm Johnston & Anthony Leonard
Rugby	01788-533533	100,751	£1,551	Ian Davis & Adam Norburn
Runnymede	01932-838383	82,189	£1,549	Paul Turrell
Rushcliffe	0115-981 9911	111,598	£1,641	Allen Graham
Rushmoor	01252-398398	94,870	£1,438	Andrew Lloyd
Ryedale	01653-600666	52,102	£1,563	Janet Waggott
ST ALBANS	01727-866100	141,899	£1,474	James Blake
St Edmundsbury	01284-763233	111,610	£1,514	Ian Gallin
Scarborough	01723-232323	108,632	£1,581	Jim Dillon
Sedgemoor	0845-408 2540	116,071	£1,464	Mr Kerry Rickards

District Council	Telephone	Population*	Council Tax†	Chief Executive‡
Selby	01757-705101	84,144	£1,564	Mary Weastell
Sevenoaks	01732-227000	116,400	£1,545	Dr Pav Ramewal
Shepway	01303-853000	108,700	£1,570	Alistair Stewart
South Bucks	01895-837200	67,435	£1,517	Alan Goodrum
South Cambridgeshire	0345-045 0500	151,068	£1,566	Jean Hunter
South Derbyshire	01283-221000	95,959	£1,508	Frank McArdle
South Hams	01803-861234	83,597	£1,571	Alan Robinson & Tracy Winser
South Holland	01775-761161	88,518	£1,446	Anna Graves
South Kesteven	01476-406080	135,033	£1,431	Beverly Agass
South Lakeland	01539-733333	103,453	£1,576	Lawrence Conway
South Norfolk	01508-533633	125,978	£1,546	Sandra Dinneen
South Northamptonshire	01327-322322	86,350	£1,485	Sue Smith
South Oxfordshire	01491-823000	135,541	£1,559	David Buckle
South Ribble	01772-421491	108,971	£1,543	Mike Nuttall
South Somerset	01935-462462	163,012	£1,498	Mark Williams
South Staffordshire	01902-696000	108,441	£1,416	Steve Winterflood
Spelthorne	01784-451499	96,744	£1,586	Roberto Tambini
Stafford	01785-619000	131,630	£1,436	Ian Thompson
Staffordshire Moorlands	01538-483483	97,237	£1,456	Simon Baker
Stevenage	01438-242242	84,798	£1,455	Nick Parry
Stratford-on-Avon	01789-267575	120,578	£1,543	Paul Lankester
Stroud	01453-766321	113,363	£1,552	David Hagg
Suffolk Coastal	01394-383789	124,323	£1,499	Stephen Baker
Surrey Heath	01276-707100	86,614	£1,619	Karen Whelan
Swale	01795-417850	137,670	£1,463	Abdool Kara
Tamworth	01827-709709	77,118	£1,428	Tony Goodwin
Tandridge	01883-722000	83,693	£1,620	Louise Round
Taunton Deane	01823-356356	111,370	£1,428	Penny James
Teignbridge	01626-361101	125,020	£1,583	Nicola Bulbeck
Tendring	01255-686868	138,285	£1,476	Ian Davidson
Test Valley	01264-368000	117,032	£1,411	Roger Tetstall
Tewkesbury	01684-295010	82,984	£1,448	Michael Dawson
Thanet	01843-577000	135,661	£1,512	Dr Sue McGonigal
Three Rivers	01923-776611	88,801	£1,463	Dr Steven Halls
Tonbridge and Malling	01732-844522	121,912	£1,509	Julie Beilby
Torridge	01237-428700	64,743	£1,573	Jenny Wallace
Tunbridge Wells	01892-526121	115,542	£1,480	William Benson
Uttlesford	01799-510510	81,250	£1,514	John Mitchell
Vale of White Horse	01235-520202	122,764	£1,548	David Buckle
Warwick	01926-450000	138,640	£1,534	Chris Elliott
Watford	01923-226400	91,732	£1,516	Manny Lewis
Waveney	01502-562111	115,670	£1,457	Stephen Baker
Waverley	01483-523333	121,884	£1,617	Paul Wenham
Wealden	01323-443322	151,029	£1,664	Charles Lant
Wellingborough	01933-229777	76,100	£1,397	John Campbell
Welwyn & Hatfield	01707-357000	112,046	£1,502	Michel Saminaden
West Devon	01822-813600	53,859	£1,643	Alan Robinson
West Dorset	01305-251010	99,532	£1,650	Matt Prosser
West Lancashire	01695-577177	110,925	£1,525	Gill Rowe & Kim Webber
West Lindsey	01427-676676	90,047	£1,504	Manjeet Gill
West Oxfordshire	01993-861000	107,118	£1,522	David Neudegg
West Somerset	01643-703704	34,559	£1,475	Penny James
Weymouth and Portland	01305-838000	65,029	£1,726	Matt Prosser
WINCHESTER	01962-840222	117,702	£1,447	Simon Eden
Woking	01483-755855	99,377	£1,620	Ray Morgan, OBE
WORCESTER	01905-723471	99,604	£1,486	Duncan Sharkey
Worthing	01903-239999	105,661	£1,519	Alex Bailey
Wychavon	01386-565000	117,670	£1,468	Jack Hegarty
Wycombe	01494-461000	173,306	£1,480	Karen Satterford
Wyre	01253-891000	107,889	£1,521	Garry Payne
Wyre Forest	01562-732928	98,074	£1,533	Ian Miller

METROPOLITAN BOROUGH COUNCILS

Metropolitan Borough Council	Telephone	Population*	Council Tax†	Chief Executive‡
Barnsley	01226-770770	233,671	£1,443	Diana Terris
BIRMINGHAM	0121-303 9944	1,085,417	£1,294	Mark Rogers
Bolton	01204-333333	278,984	£1,492	Sean Harriss
BRADFORD	01274-432001	524,619	£1,339	Tony Reeves
Bury	0161-253 5000	186,199	£1,514	Mike Kelly
Calderdale	01422-357257	205,293	£1,455	Merran McRae
COVENTRY	0500-834 333	323,132	£1,508	Martin Reeves
Doncaster	01302-734444	302,739	£1,358	Jo Miller
Dudley	0300-555 2345	313,589	£1,284	John Polychronakis
Gateshead	0191-433 3000	200,153	£1,603	Jane Robinson
Kirklees	01484-221000	425,517	£1,443	Adrian Lythgo
Knowsley	0151-489 6000	145,936	£1,502	Sheena Ramsey
LEEDS	0113-222 4444	757,655	£1,349	Tom Riordan
LIVERPOOL	0151-233 3000	469,690	£1,584	Ged Fitzgerald
MANCHESTER	0161-234 5000	510,772	£1,382	Sir Howard Bernstein
NEWCASTLE UPON TYNE	0191-278 7878	282,442	£1,516	Pat Ritchie
North Tyneside	0191-643 5991	201,446	£1,488	Patrick Melia
Oldham	0161-911 3000	225,875	£1,607	Carolyn Wilkins
Rochdale	01706-647474	212,020	£1,540	Linda Fisher (acting)
Rotherham	01709-382121	258,352	£1,497	Martin Kimber
St Helens	01744-676789	176,114	£1,422	Carole Hudson, CBE
SALFORD	0161-794 4711	237,085	£1,536	Jim Taylor
Sandwell	0121-569 2200	311,304	£1,334	Jan Britton
Sefton	0151-922 4040	273,697	£1,530	Margaret Carney
SHEFFIELD	0114-273 4567	557,382	£1,497	John Mothersole
Solihull	0121-704 6000	207,380	£1,348	Nick Page
South Tyneside	0191-427 1717	148,428	£1,451	Martin Swales
Stockport	0161-480 4949	283,897	£1,607	Eamonn Boylan
SUNDERLAND	0191-520 5555	275,743	£1,346	Dave Smith
Tameside	0161-342 8355	220,241	£1,420	Steven Pleasant
Trafford	0161-912 2000	228,466	£1,316	Theresa Grant
WAKEFIELD	0845-8506 506	327,627	£1,367	Joanne Roney, OBE
Walsall	01922-650000	270,924	£1,569	Paul Sheehan
Wigan	01942-244991	318,670	£1,403	Donna Hall
Wirral	0151-606 2000	320,229	£1,505	Graham Burgess
WOLVERHAMPTON	01902-551155	250,970	£1,501	Simon Warren

UNITARY COUNCILS

Unitary Council	Telephone	Population*	Council Tax†	Chief Executive‡
Bath and North East Somerset	01225-477000	177,643	£1,474	Dr Jo Farrar
Bedford	01234-267422	159,207	£1,575	Philip Simpkins
Blackburn with Darwen	01254-585585	147,713	£1,491	Harry Catherall
Blackpool	01253-477477	141,976	£1,526	Neil Jack
Bournemouth	01202-451451	186,744	£1,499	Tony Williams
Bracknell Forest	01344-352000	115,058	£1,380	Timothy Wheadon
BRIGHTON AND HOVE	01273-290000	275,762	£1,538	Penny Thompson, CBE
BRISTOL	0117-922 2000	432,451	£1,629	Nicola Yates
Central Bedfordshire	0300-300 8000	259,969	£1,660	Richard Carr
Cheshire East	0300-123 5500	372,146	£1,473	Mike Suarez
Cheshire West and Chester	0300-123 8123	330,200	£1,520	Steve Robinson
Cornwall	0300-123 4100	537,914	£1,512	Andrew Kerr
Darlington	01325-380651	105,248	£1,494	Ada Burns
DERBY	01332-293111	250,568	£1,405	Adam Wilkinson
DURHAM	0300-026000	514,348	£1,641	George Garlick
East Riding of Yorkshire	01482-887700	335,887	£1,514	Nigel Pearson
Halton	0303-333 4300	125,692	£1,406	David Parr
Hartlepool	01429-266522	92,238	£1,691	Dave Stubbs
Herefordshire	01432-260000	184,932	£1,552	Alastair Neill
Isle of Wight	01983-821000	138,748	£1,513	Dave Burbage
Isles of Scilly§	01720-422537	2,264	£1,217	Theo Leijser
KINGSTON-UPON-HULL	01482-609100	257,204	£1,394	Darryl Stephenson
LEICESTER	0116-254 9922	331,606	£1,512	Andy Keeling
Luton	01582-546000	205,843	£1,469	Trevor Holden
Medway	01634-333333	268,218	£1,382	Neil Davies
Middlesbrough	01642-245432	138,744	£1,627	Mike Robinson
Milton Keynes	01908-691691	252,358	£1,424	Carole Mills
North East Lincolnshire	01472-313131	159,727	£1,540	Rob Walsh (acting)
North Lincolnshire	01724-296296	168,372	£1,566	Simon Driver
North Somerset	01934-888888	204,385	£1,453	Mike Jackson
Northumberland	01670-533000	316,116	£1,559	Steven Mason
NOTTINGHAM	0115-915 5555	308,735	£1,676	Ian Curryer
PETERBOROUGH	01733-747474	186,372	£1,382	Gillian Beasley
PLYMOUTH	01752-668000	258,026	£1,538	Tracey Lee
Poole	01202-633633	148,615	£1,463	Andrew Floackhart (acting)
PORTSMOUTH	023-9282 2251	206,836	£1,387	David Williams
Reading	0118-937 3737	157,112	£1,559	Ian Wardle
Redcar and Cleveland	0164-277 4774	134,998	£1,677	Amanda Skelton
Rutland	01572-722577	37,015	£1,705	Helen Briggs
Shropshire	0345-678 9000	308,207	£1,496	Clive Wright
Slough	01753-475111	141,838	£1,400	Ruth Bagley, OBE
South Gloucestershire	01454-868686	266,147	£1,545	Amanda Deeks
SOUTHAMPTON	023-8083 3000	239,428	£1,504	Dawn Baxendale
Southend-on-Sea	01702-215000	174,838	£1,354	Robert Tinlin
Stockton-on-Tees	01642-393939	192,406	£1,596	Neil Schneider
STOKE-ON-TRENT	01782-234567	249,903	£1,429	John van de Laarschot
Swindon	01793-445500	211,934	£1,399	Gavin Jones
Telford and Wrekin	01952-380000	167,682	£1,486	Richard Partington
Thurrock	01375-652652	159,533	£1,335	Graham Farrant
Torbay	01803-201201	131,492	£1,509	Steve Parrock
Warrington	01925-444400	203,652	£1,427	Steven Broomhead (acting)
West Berkshire	01635-42400	154,486	£1,542	Nick Carter
Wiltshire	0300-456 0100	476,816	£1,527	C. Brand, C. Godfrey & M. Rae
Windsor and Maidenhead	01628-683800	145,822	£1,166	Mike McGaughrin
Wokingham	0118-974 6000	156,663	£1,522	Andy Couldrick
YORK	01904-551550	200,018	£1,447	Kersten England

* *Source:* Office for National Statistics – *Mid-2012 Population Estimates* (Crown copyright)
† Average Band D council tax bill for 2014–15
‡ Or equivalent postholder
§ Under the Isles of Scilly Clause the council has additional functions to other unitary authorities
Councils in CAPITAL LETTERS have city status

MAP OF COUNCILS IN ENGLAND

1 Stockton-on-Tees
2 Middlesbrough
3 Blackpool
4 Blackburn
   with Darwen
5 Bolton
6 Bury
7 Rochdale
8 Salford
9 Oldham
10 Liverpool
11 Knowsley
12 St Helens
13 Halton
14 Warrington
15 Trafford
16 Manchester
17 Tameside
18 Stockport
19 Nottingham
20 Telford and
   Wrekin
21 Wolverhampton

22 Walsall
23 Sandwell
24 Dudley
25 Birmingham
26 Solihull
27 Coventry
28 Peterborough
29 South Glos
30 Bristol
31 Bath and
   NE Somerset
32 Windsor and
   Maidenhead
33 Slough
34 Reading
35 Wokingham
36 Bracknell Forest
37 Thurrock
38 Southend
39 Medway
40 Plymouth
41 Torbay
42 Bournemouth

LONDON

1 Hillingdon
2 Harrow
3 Barnet
4 Enfield
5 Waltham Forest
6 Redbridge
7 Barking and Dagenham
8 Havering
9 Ealing
10 Brent
11 Camden
12 Haringey
13 Islington
14 Hackney
15 Newham
16 Hounslow
17 Hammersmith and Fulham

18 Kensington and Chelsea
19 City of Westminster
20 City of London
21 Tower Hamlets
22 Richmond upon Thames
23 Wandsworth
24 Lambeth
25 Southwark
26 Lewisham
27 Greenwich
28 Bexley
29 Kingston upon Thames
30 Merton
31 Sutton
32 Croydon
33 Bromley

LONDON

THE CITY OF LONDON CORPORATION

The City of London is the historic centre at the heart of London known as 'the square mile' around which the vast metropolis has grown over the centuries. The City's residential population was 7,400 at the 2011 census and in addition, around 400,000 people work in the City. The civic government is carried on by the City of London Corporation through the court of Common Council.

The City is an international financial and business centre, generating about £30bn a year for the British economy. It includes the head offices of the principal banks, insurance companies and mercantile houses, in addition to buildings ranging from the historic Roman Wall and the 15th-century Guildhall, to the massive splendour of St Paul's Cathedral and the architectural beauty of Wren's spires.

The City of London was described by Tacitus in AD 62 as 'a busy emporium for trade and traders'. Under the Romans it became an important administration centre and hub of the road system. Little is known of London in Saxon times, when it formed part of the kingdom of the East Saxons. In 886 Alfred recovered London from the Danes and reconstituted it a burgh under his son-in-law. In 1066 the citizens submitted to William the Conqueror who in 1067 granted them a charter, which is still preserved, establishing them in the rights and privileges they had hitherto enjoyed.

THE MAYORALTY

The mayoralty was probably established about 1189, the first mayor being Henry Fitz Ailwyn who filled the office for 23 years and was succeeded by Fitz Alan (1212–14). A new charter was granted by King John in 1215, directing the mayor to be chosen annually, which has been done ever since, though in early times the same individual often held the office more than once. A familiar instance is that of 'Whittington, thrice Lord Mayor of London' (in reality four times: 1397, 1398, 1406 and 1419); and many modern cases have occurred. The earliest instance of the phrase 'lord mayor' in English is in 1414. It was used more generally in the latter part of the 15th century and became invariable from 1535 onwards. At Michaelmas the liverymen in Common Hall choose two aldermen who have served the office of sheriff for presentation to the Court of Aldermen, and one is chosen to be lord mayor for the following mayoral year.

LORD MAYOR'S DAY

The lord mayor of London was previously elected on the feast of St Simon and St Jude (28 October), and from the time of Edward I, at least, was presented to the King or to the Barons of the Exchequer on the following day, unless that day was a Sunday. The day of election was altered to 16 October in 1346, and after some further changes was fixed for Michaelmas Day in 1546, but the ceremonies of admittance and swearing-in of the lord mayor continued to take place on 28 and 29 October respectively until 1751. In 1752, at the reform of the calendar, the lord mayor was continued in office until 8 November, the 'new style' equivalent of 28 October. The lord mayor is now presented to the lord chief justice at the royal courts of justice on the second Saturday in November to make the final declaration of office, having been sworn in at Guildhall on the preceding day. The procession to the royal courts of justice is popularly known as the Lord Mayor's Show.

REPRESENTATIVES

Aldermen are mentioned in the 11th century and their office is of Saxon origin. They were elected annually between 1377 and 1394, when an act of parliament of Richard II directed them to be chosen for life. Aldermen now serve a six-year term of office before submitting themselves for re-election.

The Common Council was, at an early date, substituted for a popular assembly called the *Folkmote*. At first only two representatives were sent from each ward, but now each of the City's 25 wards is represented by an alderman and at least two Common Councilmen (the number depending on the size of the ward). Common Councilmen are elected every four years.

OFFICERS

Sheriffs were Saxon officers; their predecessors were the *wic-reeves* and *portreeves* of London and Middlesex. At first they were officers of the Crown, and were named by the Barons of the Exchequer; but Henry I (in 1132) gave the citizens permission to choose their own sheriffs, and the annual election of sheriffs became fully operative under King John's charter of 1199. The citizens lost this privilege, as far as the election of the sheriff of Middlesex was concerned, by the Local Government Act 1888; but the liverymen continue to choose two sheriffs of the City of London, who are appointed on Midsummer Day and take office at Michaelmas.

The office of chamberlain is an ancient one, the first contemporary record of which is 1237. The town clerk (or common clerk) is first mentioned in 1274.

ACTIVITIES

The work of the City of London Corporation is assigned to a number of committees which present reports to the Court of Common Council. These committees are: Audit and Risk Management; Barbican Centre; Barbican Residential; Board of Governors of the City of London Freeman's School, the City of London School, the City of London School for Girls, the Guildhall School of Music and Drama and the Museum of London; City Bridge Trust; Community and Children's Services; Culture, Heritage and Libraries; Education; Epping Forest and Commons; Establishment; Finance; Freedom Applications; Gresham (City Side); Guildhall Improvement; Hampstead Heath, Highgate Wood and Queen's Park; Health and Wellbeing; Investment; Licensing; Livery; Markets; Open Spaces and City Gardens; Planning and Transportation; Police; Policy and Resources; Port Health and Environmental Services; Standards Committees; and West Ham Park.

The City's estate, in the possession of which the City of London Corporation differs from other municipalities, is managed by the City Lands and Bridge House Estates Committee, the chairmanship of which carries with it the title of chief commoner.

The Honourable the Irish Society, which manages the City Corporation's estates in Ulster, consists of a governor and five other aldermen, the recorder, and 19 common councilmen, of whom one is elected deputy governor.

THE LORD MAYOR 2014–15
The Rt. Hon. the Lord Mayor, Alan Yarrow*
Private Secretary, William Chapman
* Provisional at time of going to press

THE SHERIFFS 2014–15
Alderman Andrew Parmley (Vintry); Fiona Adler

OFFICERS, ETC
Town Clerk, John Barradell
Chamberlain, Peter Kane
Chief Commoner (2014), John Bennett
Clerk, The Honourable the Irish Society, C. Fisher

THE ALDERMEN
with office held and date of appointment to that office

Name and Ward	Common Councilman	Alderman	Sheriff	Lord Mayor
Sir David Howard, Bt., *Cornhill*	1972	1986	1997	2000
Ian Luder, *Castle Baynard*	1998	2005	2007	2008
Nicholas Anstee, *Aldersgate*	1987	1996	2003	2009
Sir Michael Bear, *Portsoken*	2003	2005	2007	2010
Sir David Wootton, *Langbourn*	2002	2005	2009	2011
Sir Roger Gifford, *Cordwainer*	–	2004	2008	2012
Fiona Woolf, CBE, *Candlewick*	–	2007	2010	2013
Alan Yarrow, *Bridge & Bridge Wt.*	–	2007	2011	2014

All the above have passed the Civic Chair

Dr Andrew Parmley, *Vintry*	1992	2001	–
Alison Gowman, *Dowgate*	1991	2002	–
Gordon Haines, *Queenhithe*	–	2004	–
Jeffrey Evans, *Cheap*	–	2007	2012
Sir Paul Judge, *Tower*	–	2007	2013
David Graves, *Cripplegate*	–	2008	–
John Garbutt, *Walbrook*	–	2009	–
Neil Redcliffe, *Bishopsgate*	–	2009	–
Peter Hewitt, *Aldgate*	–	2012	–
Timothy Hailes, *Bassishaw*	–	2013	–
Julian Malins, QC, *Farringdon Wt.*	–	2013	–
Matthew Richardson, *Billingsgate*	2009	2012	–
William Russell, *Bread Street*	–	2013	–
Peter Estlin, *Coleman Street*	–	2013	–
Charles Bowman, *Lime Street*	–	2013	–
Vincent Keaveny, *Farringdon Wn*	–	2013	–

THE COMMON COUNCIL
Deputy: each common councilman so described serves as deputy to the alderman of her/his ward.

Abrahams, G. C. (2000)	*Farringdon Wt.*
Absalom, J. D. (1994)	*Farringdon Wt.*
Ayers, *Deputy* K. E., MBE (1996)	*Bassishaw*
Anderson, R. K. (2013)	*Aldersgate*
Bain-Stewart, A. (2005)	*Farringdon Wn.*
Barker, *Deputy* J. A., OBE (1981)	*Cripplegate Wn.*
Barrow, *Deputy* D. (2007)	*Aldgate*
Bennett, *Deputy* J. A. (2005)	*Broad Street*
Boden, C. P. (2013)	*Castle Baynard*
Benstead-Smith, N. M. (2014)	*Cheap*
Boleat, M. J. (2002)	*Cordwainer*
Bradshaw, D. J. (1991)	*Cripplegate Wn.*
Campbell-Taylor, Revd W. G. (2014)	*Portsoken*
Cassidy, *Deputy* M. J., CBE (1989)	*Coleman Street*
Chadwick, R. A. H. (1994)	*Tower*
Challis, N. K. (2005)	*Castle Baynard*
Chapman, J. D. (2006)	*Langbourn*
Colthurst, H. N. A. (2013)	*Lime Street*
Cotgrove, D. (1991)	*Lime Street*
Deane, A. J. (2011)	*Farringdon Wt.*
Dostalova, K. (2013)	*Farringdon Wn.*
Dove, W. H., MBE (1993)	*Bishopsgate*
Duckworth, S. D. (2000)	*Bishopsgate*
Dudley, Revd Dr M. R. (2002)	*Aldersgate*
Dunphy, P. G. (2009)	*Cornhill*
Edham, E. (2014)	*Castle Baynard*
Eskenzi, *Deputy* A. N., CBE (1970)	*Farringdon Wn.*
Everett, K. M. (1984)	*Candlewick*
Fernandes, S. A. (2009)	*Coleman Street*
Fletcher, J. W. (2011)	*Portsoken*
Fraser, S. J. (1993)	*Coleman Street*
Fraser, *Deputy* W. B., OBE (1981)	*Vintry*
Fredericks, M. B. (2008)	*Tower*
Frew, L. (2013)	*Walbrook*
Gillon, G. M. F. (1995)	*Cordwainer*
Ginsburg, *Deputy* S. (1990)	*Bishopsgate*
Haines, *Deputy* Revd S. D. (2005)	*Cornhill*
Harris, B. N. (2004)	*Bridge*
Haywood, C. M. (2013)	*Broad Street*
Hoffman, T. D. D. (2002)	*Vintry*
Holmes, A. (2013)	*Farringdon Wn.*
Howard, R. P. (2011)	*Lime Street*
Hudson, M. (2007)	*Castle Baynard*
Hyde, W. (2011)	*Bishopsgate*
Ingham Clark, J. (2013)	*Billingsgate*
James, Clare (2008)	*Farringdon Wn.*
Jones, G. P., QC (2013)	*Farringdon Wt.*
Jones, *Deputy* H. L. M. (2004)	*Portsoken*
King, *Deputy* A. J. N. (1999)	*Queenhithe*
Knowles, *Deputy* S. K., MBE (1984)	*Candlewick*
Lawrence, *Deputy* G. A. (2002)	*Farringdon Wt.*
Littlechild, V. (2009)	*Cripplegate Wn.*
Lodge, O. A. W., TD (2009)	*Bread Street*
Lord, C. E., OBE (2009)	*Farringdon Wt.*
Lumley, J. S. P. (2013)	*Aldersgate*
McGuinness, *Deputy* C. S. (1997)	*Castle Baynard*
McMurtie, A. S. (2013)	*Coleman Street*
Martinelli, P. J. (2009)	*Farringdon Wt.*
Mayhew, J. P. (1996)	*Aldersgate*
Mead, Mrs W. (1997)	*Farringdon Wt.*
Merrett, R. A. (2009)	*Bassishaw*
Mooney, B. D. F. (1998)	*Queenhithe*
Moore, G. W. (2009)	*Cripplegate Wn.*
Morris, H. F. (2008)	*Aldgate*
Moss, Deputy A. M. (2013)	*Cheap*

Moys, Mrs S. D. (2001) — *Aldgate*
Nash, *Deputy* Mrs J. C., OBE (1983) — *Aldersgate*
Newman, Mrs B. P., CBE (1989) — *Aldersgate*
Owen-Ward, *Deputy* J. R., MBE (1983) — *Bridge*
Packham, G. D. (2013) — *Castle Baynard*
Patel, D. (2013) — *Aldgate*
Pembroke, Mrs A. M. F. (1978) — *Cheap*
Pleasance, J. L. (2013) — *Langbourn*
Pollard, J. H. G. (2002) — *Dowgate*
Price, E. C. L. (2013) — *Farringdon Wt.*
Priest, H. J. S. (2009) — *Castle Baynard*
Pulman, *Deputy* G. A. G. (1983) — *Tower*
Punter, C. (1993) — *Cripplegate Wn.*
Quilter, S. D. (2013) — *Cripplegate*
Regan, *Deputy* R. D. (1998) — *Farringdon Wn.*
Regis, D. (2009) — *Portsoken*
Richardson, A. F. M. (2013) — *Farringdon Wt.*
Richardson, M. C. (2009) — *Coleman Street*
Rogula, E. (2008) — *Lime Street*
Rounding, V. (2011) — *Farringdon Wn.*
Scott, J. G. S. (1999) — *Broad Street*
Seaton, I. (2009) — *Bassishaw*
Shilson, *Deputy*, G. R. E., DPHIL (2009) — *Bread Street*
Simons, J. L. (2004) — *Castle Baynard*
Sleigh, T. (2013) — *Bishopsgate*
Smith, G. M. (2013) — *Farringdon Wn.*
Snyder, *Deputy* Sir Michael (1986) — *Cordwainer*
Starling, Mrs A. J. (2006) — *Cripplegate Wt.*
Streeter, P. T. (2013) — *Bishopsgate*
Thompson, D. J. (2004) — *Aldgate*
Thomson, *Deputy* J. M. D. (2013) — *Walbrook*
Tomlinson, J. (2004) — *Cripplegate Wt.*
Tumbridge, J. R. (2009) — *Tower*
Welbank, *Deputy* M. (2005) — *Billingsgate*
Wheatley, M. R. P. (2013) — *Dowgate*
Woodhouse, P. (2013) — *Langbourn*

THE CITY GUILDS (LIVERY COMPANIES)

The constitution of the livery companies has been unchanged for centuries. There are three ranks of membership: freemen, liverymen and assistants. A person can become a freeman by patrimony (through a parent having been a freeman); by servitude (through having served an apprenticeship to a freeman); or by redemption (by purchase).

Election to the livery is the prerogative of the company, who can elect any of its freemen as liverymen. Assistants are usually elected from the livery and form a Court of Assistants which is the governing body of the company. The master (in some companies called the prime warden) is elected annually from the assistants.

The register for 2014–15 lists 25,335 liverymen of the guilds entitled to vote at elections at Common Hall.

The order of precedence, omitting extinct companies, is given in parentheses after the name of each company in the list below. In certain companies the election of master or prime warden for the year does not take place until the autumn. In such cases the master or prime warden for 2013–14, rather than 2014–15, is given.

THE TWELVE GREAT COMPANIES
In order of civic precedence

MERCERS *(1)*. *Hall*, Mercers' Hall, Ironmonger Lane, London EC2V 8HE *Livery*, 237. *Clerk*, Menna McGregor *Master*, Deborah Ounsted, CBE

GROCERS *(2)*. *Hall*, Grocers' Hall, Princes Street, London EC2R 8AD *Livery*, 348. *Clerk*, Brig. Robert Pridham, OBE *Master*, James Roundell

DRAPERS *(3)*. *Hall*, Drapers' Hall, Throgmorton Avenue, London EC2N 2DQ *Livery*, 317. *Clerk*, Col. Richard Winstanley, OBE *Master*, Nicholas Alexander Bence-Trower

FISHMONGERS *(4)*. *Hall*, Fishmongers' Hall, London Bridge, London EC4R 9EL *Livery*, 388. *Clerk*, Maj.-Gen. Colin Boag, CB, CBE *Prime Warden*, James Fforde

GOLDSMITHS *(5)*. *Hall*, Goldsmiths' Hall, Foster Lane, London EC2V 6BN *Livery*, 313. *Clerk*, Rear-Adm. Richard Melly *Prime Warden*, William Parente

MERCHANT TAYLORS *(6/7)*. *Hall*, Merchant Taylors' Hall, 30 Threadneedle Street, London EC2R 8JB *Livery*, 330. *Clerk*, Rear-Adm. Nicholas Harris, CB, MBE *Master*, Peter Howard Watkins

SKINNERS *(6/7)*. *Hall*, Skinners' Hall, 8 Dowgate Hill, London EC4R 2SP *Livery*, 400. *Clerk*, Maj.-Gen. Brian Plummer, CBE *Master*, John Hitchins

HABERDASHERS *(8)*. *Hall*, Haberdashers' Hall, 18 West Smithfield, London EC1A 9HQ *Livery*, 320. *Clerk*, Cdre Philip Thicknesse, RN *Master*, Audley Twiston-Davies

SALTERS *(9)*. *Hall*, Salters' Hall, 4 Fore Street, London EC2Y 5DE *Livery*, 185. *Clerk*, Capt. David Morris, RN *Master*, Chris Russell

IRONMONGERS *(10)*. *Hall*, Ironmongers' Hall, 1 Shaftesbury Place, London EC2Y 8AA *Livery*, 112. *Clerk*, Col. Hamon Massey *Master*, A. M. Carter-Clout

VINTNERS *(11)*. *Hall*, Vintners' Hall, Upper Thames Street, London EC4V 3BG *Livery*, 369. *Clerk*, Brig. Jonathan Bourne-May *Master*, Rupert Clevely

CLOTHWORKERS *(12)*. *Hall*, Clothworkers' Hall, Dunster Court, Mincing Lane, London EC3R 7AH *Livery*, 200. *Clerk*, Andrew Blessley *Master*, Michael Howell

OTHER CITY GUILDS
In alphabetical order

ACTUARIES *(91)*. Cheapside House, 138 Cheapside, London EC2V 6BW *Livery*, 234. *Clerk*, David Johnson *Master*, Martin Miles

AIR PILOTS AND AIR NAVIGATORS *(81)*. *Hall*, Cobham House, 9 Warwick Court, Gray's Inn, London WC1R 5DJ *Livery*, 600. *Clerk*, Paul Tacon *Grand Master*, HRH the Duke of York, KG, GCVO, ADC(P) *Master*, Dorothy Saul-Pooley

APOTHECARIES *(58)*. *Hall*, Apothecaries' Hall, 14 Black Friars Lane, London EC4V 6EJ *Livery*, 1,215. *Clerk*, A. Wallington-Smith *Master*, Dr J. C. Moore-Gillon

ARBITRATORS *(93)*. 98 Elm Road, Kingston-upon-Thames, Surrey KT2 6HU *Livery*, 180. *Clerk*, Elinor Pritchard *Master*, Prof. John Uff, CBE

ARMOURERS AND BRASIERS *(22)*. *Hall*, Armourers' Hall, 81 Coleman Street, London EC2R 5BJ *Livery*, 128. *Clerk*, Peter Bateman *Master*, Dr Simon Alexander Archer

ART SCHOLARS *(110)*. Furniture Makers' Hall, 12 Austin Friars, London EC2N 2HE *Livery*, 85. *Clerk*, Georgina Gough *Master*, Alderman Ian Luder, CBE

BAKERS *(19)*. *Hall*, Bakers' Hall, 9 Harp Lane, London EC3R 6DP *Livery*, 350. *Clerk*, Cdre M. W. Westwood, RN *Master*, Paul Heygate

BARBERS *(17)*. *Hall*, Barber-Surgeons' Hall, Monkwell Square, Wood Street, London EC2Y 5BL *Livery*, 220. *Clerk*, Col. Peter Durrant, MBE *Master*, Sir Roger Vickers, KCVO, FRCS

BASKETMAKERS *(52)*. 56 Victoria Way, Liphook, Hampshire GU30 7NJ *Livery*, 300. *Clerk*, Fiona Janczur *Prime Warden*, Edward F. C. Donaldson

BLACKSMITHS *(40)*. 9 Little Trinity Lane, London EC4V 2AD *Livery*, 235. *Clerk*, Martin Heath *Prime Warden*, Michael Shepherd

BOWYERS *(38)*. 46 The Haydens, Tonbridge, Kent TN9 1NS *Livery*, 88. *Clerk*, Richard Sawyer *Master*, Revd John Hayton, TD

BREWERS *(14). Hall,* Brewers' Hall, Aldermanbury Square, London EC2V 7HR *Livery,* 193. *Clerk,* Col. Michael Gillespie Carew O'Dwyer, OBE *Master,* James Rixon Arkell, TD

BRODERERS *(48).* Ember House, 35–37 Creek Road, East Molesey, Surrey KT8 9BE *Livery,* 126. *Clerk,* Peter J. C. Crouch *Master,* Lt. Col. D. Hugh Toler, MBE

BUILDERS MERCHANTS *(88).* 4 College Hill, London EC4R 2RB *Livery,* 187. *Clerk,* T. Statham *Master,* Gill Moore

BUTCHERS *(24). Hall,* Butchers' Hall, 87 Bartholomew Close, London EC1A 7EB *Livery,* 633. *Clerk,* Jeffrey Mason, MBE *Master,* Nicholas J. Anstee

CARMEN *(77).* Five Kings House, 1 Queen Street Place, London EC4R 1QS *Livery,* 500. *Clerk,* Walter Gill *Master,* Lt. Col. Paul Holder, RLC

CARPENTERS *(26). Hall,* Carpenters' Hall, 1 Throgmorton Avenue, London EC2N 2JJ *Livery,* 150. *Clerk,* Brig. Tim Gregson, MBE *Master,* Michael Felton

CHARTERED ACCOUNTANTS *(86).* Larksfield, Kent Hatch Road, Crockham Hill, Edenbridge, Kent TN8 6SX *Livery,* 365. *Clerk,* Peter Dickinson *Master,* David Illingworth

CHARTERED ARCHITECTS *(98).* 164 Stockbridge Road, Winchester SO22 6RW *Livery,* 165. *Clerk,* Ian Head *Master,* Dr Geoffrey Purves

CHARTERED SECRETARIES AND ADMINISTRATORS *(87).* 3rd Floor, Saddlers' House, 40 Gutter Lane, London EC2V 6BR *Livery,* 270. *Clerk,* Erica Lee (Acting) *Master,* Sandra Worsdall

CHARTERED SURVEYORS *(85).* 75 Meadway Drive, Horsell, Woking, Surrey GU21 4TF *Livery,* 365. *Clerk,* Amanda Jackson *Master,* Sarah Chase

CLOCKMAKERS *(61).* 1 Throgmorton Avenue, London EC2N 2BY *Livery,* 289. *Clerk,* Wr. Col. O. P. Bartrum, MBE *Master,* Jonathan Betts, MBE

COACHMAKERS AND COACH-HARNESS MAKERS *(72).* The Old Barn, Church Lane, Glentham, Market Rasen, Lincolnshire LN8 2EL *Livery,* 500. *Clerk,* Cdr Mark Leaning, RN *Master,* Ian Smith

CONSTRUCTORS *(99).* 5 Delft Close, Locks Heath, Southampton SO31 7TQ *Livery,* 138. *Clerk,* Kim Tyrrell *Master,* Victoria Russell

COOKS *(35).* 18 Solent Drive, Warsash, Southampton SO31 9HB *Livery,* 75. *Clerk,* Vice-Adm. P. J. Wilkinson, CB, CVO *Master,* Dr. S. D. Gibson, MBE

COOPERS *(36). Hall,* Coopers' Hall, 13 Devonshire Square, London EC2M 4TH *Livery,* 260. *Clerk,* Lt.-Col. Adrian Carroll Amer, Dr Ian Frood

CORDWAINERS *(27).* Clothworkers' Hall, Dunster Court, Mincing Lane, London EC3R 7AH *Livery,* 170. *Clerk,* John Miller *Master,* Lance Shaw

CURRIERS *(29).* Oak Lodge, 4 Greenhill Lane, Wimborne, Dorset BH21 2RN *Livery,* 102. *Clerk,* Adrian Rafferty *Master,* Mark Henders

CUTLERS *(18). Hall,* Cutlers' Hall, Warwick Lane, London EC4M 7BR *Livery,* 100. *Clerk,* Rupert Meacher *Master,* Richard James Herbert

DISTILLERS *(69).* 1 The Sanctuary, Westminster, London SW1P 3JT *Livery,* 260. *Clerk,* Edward Macey-Dare *Master,* Allan Cheesman

DYERS *(13). Hall,* Dyers' Hall, 10 Dowgate Hill, London EC4R 2ST *Livery,* 136. *Clerk,* J. R. Vaizey *Prime Warden,* J. N. Crockatt

EDUCATORS *(109).* PO Box 484, Sevenoaks, Kent TN13 9LD *Livery,* 275. *Clerk,* Keith Lawrey *Master,* Peter Williams, CBE

ENGINEERS *(94).* Wax Chandlers' Hall, 6 Gresham Street, London EC2V 7AD *Livery,* 330. *Clerk,* Tony Willenbruch *Master,* John Baxter, FRSE FRENG

ENVIRONMENTAL CLEANERS *(97).* 10 Seaton Close, Lynden Gate, Putney, London SW15 3TJ *Livery,* 185. *Clerk,* Keith Lambert *Master,* Issa Tahhan

FAN MAKERS *(76).* Skinners' Hall, 8 Dowgate Hill, London EC4R 2SP *Livery,* 202. *Clerk,* Martin Davies *Master,* Douglas Clasby

FARMERS *(80). Hall,* The Farmers' and Fletchers' Hall, 3 Cloth Street, London EC1A 7LD *Livery,* 350. *Clerk,* Col. David King, OBE *Master,* A. J. Alston

FARRIERS *(55).* 19 Queen Street, Chipperfield, Kings Langley, Herts WD4 9BT *Livery,* 351. *Clerk,* Charlotte Clifford *Master,* Wayne Upton

FELTMAKERS *(63).* Post Cottage, Greywell, Hook, Hants RG29 1DA *Livery,* 180. *Clerk,* Maj. J. T. H. Coombs *Master,* Edward Hutton

FIREFIGHTERS *(103).* The Insurance Hall, 20 Aldermanbury, London EC2V 7GF *Livery,* 121. *Clerk,* Steven Tamcken *Master,* Bryan Spearman

FLETCHERS *(39). Hall,* The Farmers' and Fletchers' Hall, 3 Cloth Street, London EC1A 7LD *Livery,* 146. *Clerk,* Kate Pink *Master,* A. C. McMillan

FOUNDERS *(33). Hall,* Founders' Hall, 1 Cloth Fair, London EC1A 7JQ *Livery,* 175. *Clerk,* J. P. Knight *Master,* P. A. Draycott

FRAMEWORK KNITTERS *(64).* The Grange, Kimcote, Lutterworth LE17 5RU *Livery,* 200. *Clerk,* Capt. Shaun Mackaness *Master,* Linda Smith

FRUITERERS *(45).* Chapelstones, 84 High Street, Codford St Mary, Warminster BA12 0ND *Livery,* 283. *Clerk,* Lt.-Col. L. French *Master,* Peter Cooper

FUELLERS *(95).* Skinners' Hall, 8 Dowgate Hill, London EC4R 2SP *Livery,* 141. *Clerk,* Sir Anthony Reardon Smith, Bt. *Master,* Dennis Woods

FURNITURE MAKERS *(83). Hall,* Furniture Makers' Hall, 12 Austin Friars, London EC2N 2HE *Livery,* 205. *Clerk,* Jonny Westbrooke *Master,* Paul von der Heyde

GARDENERS *(66).* 25 Luke Street, London EC2A 4AR *Livery,* 298. *Clerk,* Maj. Jeremy Herrtage *Master,* Stephen Bernhard

GIRDLERS *(23). Hall,* Girdlers' Hall, Basinghall Avenue, London EC2V 5DD *Livery,* 80. *Clerk,* Brig. Ian Rees *Master,* Hon. Robin Neill

GLASS SELLERS *(71).* North Farm House, High Road, Loughton IG10 4JJ *Livery,* 230. *Clerk,* Vincent Emms *Master,* Gwenllian Rhys

GLAZIERS AND PAINTERS OF GLASS *(53). Hall,* Glaziers' Hall, 9 Montague Close, London SE1 9DD *Livery,* 292. *Clerk,* Cdr Andrew Gordon-Lennox *Master,* John Dallimore

GLOVERS *(62).* Seniors Farmhouse, Semley, Shaftesbury, Dorset SP7 9AX *Livery,* 245. *Clerk,* M. T. D. Butler *Master,* Ann Esslemont

GOLD AND SILVER WYRE DRAWERS *(74).* 9A Prince of Wales Mansions, Prince of Wales Drive, London SW11 4BG *Livery,* 280. *Clerk,* Cdr. R. House *Master,* Michael F. Powell

GUNMAKERS *(73).* The Proof House, 48–50 Commercial Road, London E1 1LP *Livery,* 350. *Clerk,* John Allen *Master,* J. F. Jackman

HACKNEY CARRIAGE DRIVERS *(104).* 25 The Grove, Parkfield, Latimer, Bucks HP5 1UE *Livery,* 109. *Clerk,* Mary Whitworth *Master,* Malcolm Paice

HORNERS *(54).* 12 Coltsfoot Close, Ixworth, Suffolk IP31 2NJ *Livery,* 225. *Clerk,* Jack E. B. Bunyer

INFORMATION TECHNOLOGISTS *(100). Hall,* Information Technologists' Hall, 39A Bartholomew Close, London EC1A 7JN *Livery,* 349. *Clerk,* Mike Jenkins *Master,* Nicholas Birtles

INNHOLDERS *(32). Hall,* Innholders' Hall, 30 College Street, London EC4R 2RH *Livery,* 149. *Clerk,* Dougal Bulger *Master,* A. F. Groom

INSURERS *(92).* Insurance Hall, 20 Aldermanbury, London EC2V 7HY *Livery,* 418. *Clerk,* Sarah Clark *Master,* G. G. Dickinson

INTERNATIONAL BANKERS *(106)*. 12 Austin Friars, London EC2N 2HE *Livery*, 223. *Clerk*, Nicholas Westgarth *Master*, Mark Seligman

JOINERS AND CEILERS *(41)*. 75 Meadway Drive, Horsell, Woking, Surrey GU21 4TF *Livery*, 115. *Clerk*, Amanda Jackson *Master*, Derek Woods

LAUNDERERS *(89)*. *Hall*, Launderers' Hall, 9 Montague Close, London Bridge, London SE1 9DD *Livery*, 215. *Clerk*, Terry Winter *Master*, John Shonfeld

LEATHERSELLERS *(15)*. 21 Garlick Hill, London EC4V 2AU *Livery*, 150. *Clerk*, Brig. David Santa-Olalla *Master*, Dr Anthony Watson, CBE

LIGHTMONGERS *(96)*. 1 Manor House Garden, High Street, Wanstead, London E11 2RU *Livery*, 168. *Clerk*, Phillip Hyde *Master*, William Wright

LORINERS *(57)*. 30 Elm Park, Royal Wootton Bassett, Wiltshire SN4 7TA *Livery*, 400. *Clerk*, Honor Page *Master*, His Hon. Peter Beaumont, CBE, QC

MAKERS OF PLAYING CARDS *(75)*. 256 St David's Square, London E14 3WE *Livery*, 147. *Clerk*, David Barrett *Master*, Tony Carter

MANAGEMENT CONSULTANTS *(105)*. Skinners' Hall, 8 Dowgate Hill, London EC4R 2SP *Livery*, 170. *Clerk*, Adèle Thorpe *Master*, Patrick Chapman

MARKETORS *(90)*. Plaisterers' Hall, One London Wall, London EC2Y 5JU *Livery*, 250. *Clerk*, John Hammond *Master*, Michael Harrison, FCIM

MASONS *(30)*. 22 Cannon Hill, Southgate, London N14 6LG *Livery*, 163. *Clerk*, Maj. Giles Clapp *Master*, R. A. H. Morrow

MASTER MARINERS *(78)*. *Hall*, HQS Wellington, Temple Stairs, Victoria Embankment, London WC2R 2PN *Livery*, 160. *Clerk*, Cdre Angus Menzies, RN *Master*, Capt. Sam Judah, MBE *Admiral*, HRH Prince Philip, Duke of Edinburgh, Lord High Admiral of the UK, KG KT OM

MUSICIANS *(50)*. 1 Speed Highwalk, Barbican, London EC2Y 8DX *Livery*, 420. *Clerk*, Hugh Lloyd *Master*, Kathleen Duncan, OBE

NEEDLEMAKERS *(65)*. PO Box 3682, Windsor, Berkshire SL4 3WR *Livery*, 200. *Clerk*, Philip Grant *Master*, Sue Kent

PAINTER-STAINERS *(28)*. *Hall*, Painters' Hall, 9 Little Trinity Lane, London EC4V 2AD *Livery*, 310. *Clerk*, C. J. Twyman *Master*, C. J. Goodman

PATTENMAKERS *(70)*. 3 The High Street, Sutton Valence, Kent ME17 3AG *Livery*, 200. *Clerk*, Col. R. W. Murfin, TD *Master*, Christopher Hayward

PAVIORS *(56)*. Paviors' House, Charter House, Charterhouse Square, London, EC1M 6AN *Livery*, 285. *Clerk*, John Freestone *Master*, Nigel Kempner

PEWTERERS *(16)*. *Hall*, Pewterers' Hall, Oat Lane, London EC2V 7DE *Livery*, 124. *Clerk*, Capt. Paddy Watson, RN *Master*, Robin Edward Furber

PLAISTERERS *(46)*. *Hall*, Plaisterers' Hall, 1 London Wall, London EC2Y 5JU *Livery*, 236. *Clerk*, Nigel Bamping *Master*, Michael Jones

PLUMBERS *(31)*. Wax Chandlers' Hall, 6 Gresham Street, London EC2V 7AD *Livery*, 360. *Clerk*, Air Cdre Paul Nash, OBE *Master*, Stephen Hodkinson

POULTERS *(34)*. 57 Cullum Welch House, Golden Lane Estate, London EC17 0SH *Livery*, 204. *Clerk*, Vernon Ashford *Master*, Alistair Bassett Cross

SADDLERS *(25)*. *Hall*, Saddlers' Hall, 40 Gutter Lane, London EC2V 6BR *Livery*, 75. *Clerk*, Col. N. Lithgow, CBE *Master*, M. P. Farmar

SCIENTIFIC INSTRUMENT MAKERS *(84)*. 9 Montague Close, London SE1 9DD *Livery*, 185. *Clerk*, Neville Watson *Master*, Prof. Tony Wilson

SCRIVENERS *(44)*. HQS Wellington, Temple Stairs, Victoria Embankment, London WC2R 2PN *Livery*, 186. *Clerk*, Giles Cole *Master*, Revd Michael Lovegrove

SECURITY PROFESSIONALS *(108)*. 34 Tye Green, Glemsford, Suffolk CO10 7RG *Livery*, 150. *Clerk*, Tricia Boswell *Master*, Barrie Stewart

SHIPWRIGHTS *(59)*. Ironmongers Hall, Shaftesbury Place, London EC2Y 8AA *Livery*, 450. *Clerk*, Lt.-Col. Andy Milne, RM *Prime Warden*, Lord Clarke of Stone-Cum-Ebony, PC *Grand Master*, HRH the Prince of Wales, KG, KT, GCB

SOLICITORS *(79)*. 4 College Hill, London EC4R 2RB *Livery*, 350. *Clerk*, Neil Cameron *Master*, Andrew Vincent Keaveny

SPECTACLE MAKERS *(60)*. Apothecaries' Hall, Black Friars Lane, London EC4V 6EL *Livery*, 390. *Clerk*, Lt.-Col. John Salmon, OBE *Master*, Dr C. M. Tomkins, FRCS, FRCPATH, FRCP

STATIONERS AND NEWSPAPER MAKERS *(47)*. *Hall*, Stationers' Hall, Ave Maria Lane, London EC4M 7DD *Livery*, 520. *Clerk*, William Alden, MBE *Master*, Ian Locks

TAX ADVISERS *(107)*. 191 West End Road, Ruislip, Middx HA4 6LD *Freemen*, 145. *Clerk*, Paul Herbage, MBE *Master*, Michael Godbee

TALLOW CHANDLERS *(21)*. *Hall*, Tallow Chandlers' Hall, 4 Dowgate Hill, London EC4R 2SH *Livery*, 180. *Clerk*, Brig. D. Homer, MBE *Master*, Ian McIntyre

TIN PLATE WORKERS (ALIAS WIRE WORKERS) *(67)*. PO Box 71002, London W4 9FH *Livery*, 220. *Clerk*, Piers Baker *Master*, Jeremy Balcombe

TOBACCO PIPE MAKERS AND TOBACCO BLENDERS *(82)*. 14 Montpelier Road, Sutton, Surrey SM1 4QE *Livery*, 132. *Clerk*, Sandra Stocker *Master*, Mark Gower-Smith

TURNERS *(51)*. Skinner's Hall, 8 Dowgate Hill, London EC4R 2SP *Livery*, 186. *Clerk*, Alex Robertson *Master*, Col. John Bridgeman, CBE TD

TYLERS AND BRICKLAYERS *(37)*. 3 Farmers' Way, Seer Green, Bucks HP9 2YY *Livery*, 155. *Clerk*, John Brooks *Master*, Roger Westbrook, CMG

UPHOLDERS *(49)*. clerk@upholders.co.uk, *Livery*, 175. *Clerk*, Susan Nevard *Master*, Derek Thornton

WATER CONSERVATORS *(102)*. The Lark, 2 Bell Lane, Worlington, Bury St Edmunds, Suffolk IP28 8SE *Livery*, 212. *Clerk*, Ralph Riley *Master*, Roger North

WAX CHANDLERS *(20)*. *Hall*, Wax Chandlers' Hall, 6 Gresham Street, London EC2V 7AD *Livery*, 110. *Clerk*, Georgina Brown *Master*, Heather Hawker, MBE

WEAVERS *(42)*. Saddlers' House, Gutter Lane, London EC2V 6BR *Livery*, 125. *Clerk*, John Snowdon *Upper Bailiff*, Edward Martineau

WHEELWRIGHTS *(68)*. 16 Gordon Avenue, Twickenham TW1 1NQ *Livery*, 220. *Clerk*, Bridget Hynard *Master*, G. I. A. Armfield

WOOLMEN *(43)*. The Old Post Office, 56 Lower Way, Great Brickhill, Bucks MK17 9AG *Livery*, 150. *Clerk*, Gillian Wilson *Master*, Richard Excell

WORLD TRADERS *(101)*. 13 Hall Gardens, Colney Heath, St. Albans, Herts AL4 0QF *Livery*, 240. *Clerk*, Mrs Gaye Duffy *Master*, Mark Hardy

PARISH CLERKS (*No Livery**). Acreholt, 33 Medstead Road, Beech, Alton, Hants GU34 4AD *Members*, 91. *Clerk*, Alana Coombes *Master*, Michael Cooper

WATERMEN AND LIGHTERMEN (*No Livery**). *Hall*, Watermen's Hall, 16–18 St Mary at Hill, London EC3R 8EF *Craft Owning Freemen*, 387. *Clerk*, Colin Middlemiss *Master*, Jeremy D. Randall

---

* Parish Clerks and Watermen and Lightermen have requested to remain with no livery

WALES

Cymru

The principality of Wales (Cymru) occupies the extreme west of the central southern portion of the island of Great Britain, with a total area of 20,778 sq. km (8,022 sq. miles): land 20,733 sq. km (8,005 sq. miles); inland water 45 sq. km (17 sq. miles). It is bordered in the north by the Irish Sea, in the south by the Bristol Channel, in the east by the English counties of Cheshire West and Chester, Shropshire, Herefordshire and Gloucestershire, and in the west by St George's Channel.

Across the Menai Straits is Ynys Mon (Isle of Anglesey) (715 sq. km/276 sq. miles), communication with which is facilitated by the Menai Suspension Bridge (305m/1,000ft long) built by Telford in 1826, and by the Britannia Bridge (351m/1,151ft), a two-tier road and rail truss arch design, rebuilt in 1972 after a fire destroyed the original tubular railway bridge built by Stephenson in 1850. Holyhead harbour, on Holy Isle (north-west of Anglesey), provides ferry services to Dublin (113km/70 miles).

POPULATION
The population at the 2011 census was 3,063,456 (men 1,504,228; women 1,559,228). The average density of population in 2011 was 147 persons per sq. km (382 per sq. mile).

RELIEF
Wales is a country of extensive tracts of high plateau and shorter stretches of mountain ranges deeply dissected by river valleys. Lower-lying ground is largely confined to the coastal belt and the lower parts of the valleys. The highest mountains are those of Snowdonia in the north-west (Snowdon, 1,085m/3,559ft and Aran Fawddwy, 906m/2,971ft). Snowdonia is also home to Cader Idris (Pen y Gadair, 892m/2,928ft). Other high peaks are to be found in the Cambrian range (Plynlimon, 752m/2,467ft), and the Black Mountains, Brecon Beacons and Black Forest ranges in the south-east (Pen y Fan, 886m/2,906ft; Waun Fâch, 811m/2,660ft; Carmarthen Van, 802m/2,630ft).

HYDROGRAPHY
The principal river in Wales is the Severn, which flows from the slopes of Plynlimon to the English border. The Wye (209km/130 miles) also rises on the slopes of Plynlimon. The Usk (90km/56 miles) flows into the Bristol Channel through Gwent. The Dee (113km/70 miles) rises in Bala Lake and flows through the Vale of Llangollen, where an aqueduct (built by Telford in 1805) carries the Pontcysyllte branch of the Shropshire Union Canal across the valley. The estuary of the Dee is the navigable portion; it is 23km (14 miles) in length and about 8km (5 miles) in breadth. The Towy (109km/68 miles), Teifi (80km/50 miles), Taff (64km/40 miles), Dovey (48km/30 miles), Taf (40km/25 miles) and Conway (39km/24 miles) are wholly Welsh rivers.

The largest natural lake is Bala (Llyn Tegid) in Gwynedd, nearly 7km (4 miles) long and 1.6km (1 mile) wide. Lake Vyrnwy is an artificial reservoir, about the size of Bala, and forms the water supply of Liverpool; Birmingham's water is supplied from reservoirs in the Elan and Claerwen valleys.

WELSH LANGUAGE
According to the 2011 census results, the percentage of people aged three years and over who are able to speak Welsh is:

Blaenau Gwent	7.8	Neath Port Talbot	15.3
Bridgend	9.7	Newport	9.3
Caerphilly	11.2	Pembrokeshire	19.2
Cardiff	11.1	Powys	18.6
Carmarthenshire	43.9	Rhondda Cynon Taf	12.3
Ceredigion	47.3	Swansea	11.4
Conwy	27.4	Torfaen	9.8
Denbighshire	24.6	Vale of Glamorgan	10.8
Flintshire	13.2	Wrexham	12.9
Gwynedd	65.4	Ynys Mon	
Merthyr Tydfil	8.9	(Isle of Anglesey)	57.2
Monmouthshire	9.9	*Total in Wales*	19.0

FLAG
The flag of Wales, the Red Dragon *(Y Ddraig Goch)*, is a red dragon on a field divided white over green (per fess argent and vert a dragon passant gules). The flag was augmented in 1953 by a royal badge on a shield encircled with a riband bearing the words *Ddraig Goch Ddyry Cychwyn* and imperially crowned, but this augmented flag is rarely used.

EARLY HISTORY

The earliest inhabitants of whom there is any record appear to have been subdued or exterminated by the Goidels (a people of Celtic race) in the Bronze Age. A further invasion of Celtic Brythons and Belgae followed in the ensuing Iron Age. The Roman conquest of southern Britain and Wales was for some time successfully opposed by Caratacus (Caractacus or Caradog), chieftain of the Catuvellauni and son of Cunobelinus (Cymbeline). South-east Wales was subjugated and the legionary fortress at Caerleon-on-Usk established by around AD 75–7; the conquest of Wales was completed by Agricola around AD 78. Communications were opened up by the construction of military roads from Chester to Caerleon-on-Usk and Caerwent, and from Chester to Conwy (and thence to Carmarthen and Neath). Christianity was introduced in the fourth century, during the Roman occupation.

ANGLO-SAXON ATTACKS
The Anglo-Saxon invaders of southern Britain drove the Celts into the mountain stronghold of Wales, and into Strathclyde (Cumberland and south-west Scotland) and Cornwall, giving them the name of *Waelisc* (Welsh), meaning 'foreign'. The West Saxons' victory of Deorham (AD 577) isolated Wales from Cornwall and the battle of Chester (AD 613) cut off communication with Strathclyde and northern Britain. In the eighth century the boundaries of the Welsh were further restricted by the annexations of Offa, King of Mercia, and counter-attacks were largely prevented by the construction of an artificial boundary from the Dee to the Wye (Offa's Dyke).

In the ninth century Rhodri Mawr (844–878) united the country and successfully resisted further incursions of the Saxons by land and raids of Norse and Danish pirates by sea, but at his death his three provinces of Gwynedd (north), Powys (central) and Deheubarth (south) were divided among his three sons, Anarawd, Mervyn and Cadell. Cadell's son Hywel Dda ruled a large part of Wales and codified its laws but the provinces were not united again until the rule of Llewelyn ap Seisyllt (husband of the heiress of Gwynedd) from 1018 to 1023.

THE NORMAN CONQUEST

After the Norman conquest of England, William I created palatine counties along the Welsh frontier, and the Norman barons began to make encroachments into Welsh territory. The Welsh princes recovered many of their losses during the civil wars of Stephen's reign (1135–54), and in the early 13th century Owen Gruffydd, prince of Gwynedd, was the dominant figure in Wales. Under Llywelyn ap Iorwerth (1194–1240) the Welsh united in powerful resistance to English incursions and Llywelyn's privileges and *de facto* independence were recognised in the Magna Carta. His grandson, Llywelyn ap Gruffydd, was the last native prince; he was killed in 1282 during hostilities between the Welsh and English, allowing Edward I of England to establish his authority over the country. On 7 February 1301, Edward of Caernarvon, son of Edward I, was created Prince of Wales, a title subsequently borne by the eldest son of the sovereign.

Strong Welsh national feeling continued, expressed in the early 15th century in the rising led by Owain Glyndwr, but the situation was altered by the accession to the English throne in 1485 of Henry VII of the Welsh House of Tudor. Wales was politically annexed by England under the Act of Union of 1535, which extended English laws to the principality and gave it parliamentary representation for the first time.

EISTEDDFOD

The Welsh are a distinct nation, with a language and literature of their own; the national bardic festival (Eisteddfod), instituted by Prince Rhys ap Griffith in 1176, is still held annually.

PRINCIPAL CITIES

There are six cities in Wales (with date city status conferred): Bangor (pre-1900), Cardiff (1905), Newport (2002), St Asaph (2012), St David's (1994) and Swansea (1969).

Cardiff and Swansea have also been granted lord mayoralities.

CARDIFF

Cardiff *(Caerdydd)*, at the mouth of the rivers Taff, Rhymney and Ely, is the capital city of Wales and at the 2011 census had a population of 346,090. The city has changed dramatically in recent years following the regeneration of Cardiff Bay and construction of a barrage, which has created a permanent freshwater lake and waterfront for the city. As the capital city, Cardiff is home to the National Assembly for Wales and is a major administrative, retail, business and cultural centre.

The city is home to many fine buildings, including the City Hall, Cardiff Castle, Llandaff Cathedral, the National Museum of Wales, university buildings, law courts and the Temple of Peace and Health. The Millennium Stadium opened in 1999 and has hosted high-profile events since 2001.

SWANSEA

Swansea *(Abertawe)* is a seaport with a population of 239,023 at the 2011 census. The Gower peninsula was brought within the city boundary under local government reform in 1974.

The principal buildings are the Norman castle (rebuilt *c.*1330), the Royal Institution of South Wales, founded in 1835 (including library), the University of Wales Swansea at Singleton and the Guildhall, containing Frank Brangwyn's British Empire panels. The Dylan Thomas Centre, formerly the old Guildhall, was restored in 1995. More recent buildings include the County Hall, the Maritime Quarter Marina, the Wales National Pool and the National Waterfront Museum.

Swansea was chartered by the Earl of Warwick (1158–84), and further charters were granted by King John, Henry III, Edward II, Edward III and James II, Oliver Cromwell and the Marcher lord William de Breos. It was formally invested with city status in 1969.

LORD-LIEUTENANTS AND HIGH SHERIFFS

Area	Lord-Lieutenant	High Sheriff (2014–15)
Clwyd	Henry Fetherstonhaugh, OBE	John Jones
Dyfed	Hon. Robin Lewis, OBE	Rachel Jones
Gwent	Simon Boyle	Gillian Sheddick, OBE
Gwynedd	Edmund Bailey	David Lea-Wilson
Mid Glamorgan	Kate Thomas, CVO	Elizabeth Singer
Powys	Hon. Mrs E. Legge-Bourke, LVO	Philip Bowen
South Glamorgan	Dr Peter Beck, MD, FRCP	David Jenkins
West Glamorgan	D. Byron Lewis	Martyn Jenkins

LOCAL COUNCILS

Council	Administrative Headquarters	Telephone	Population*	Council Tax†	Chief Executive
Blaenau Gwent	Ebbw Vale	01495-311556	69,822	£1,591	David Waggett
Bridgend	Bridgend	01656-643643	139,740	£1,413	Darren Mepham
Caerphilly	Hengoed	01443-815588	179,022	£1,169	Stuart Rosser *(interim)*
CARDIFF	Cardiff	029-2087 2087	348,493	£1,166	Paul Orders
Carmarthenshire	Carmarthen	01267-234567	184,317	£1,307	Mark James, CBE
Ceredigion	Aberaeron	01545-570881	76,046	£1,259	Bronwen Morgan
Conwy	Conwy	01492-574000	115,515	£1,229	Iwan Davies
Denbighshire	Ruthin	01824-706101	94,066	£1,380	Dr Mohammed Mehmet
Flintshire	Mold	01352-752121	152,743	£1,255	Colin Everett
Gwynedd	Caernarfon	01766-771000	122,142	£1,371	Harry Thomas
Merthyr Tydfil	Merthyr Tydfil	01685-725000	58,898	£1,486	Gareth Chapman
Monmouthshire	Cwmbran	01633-644644	91,659	£1,285	Paul Matthews
Neath Port Talbot	Port Talbot	01639-686868	140,108	£1,542	Steven Phillips
NEWPORT	Newport	01633-656656	146,106	£1,101	Will Godfrey
Pembrokeshire	Haverfordwest	01437-764551	123,035	£1,005	Bryn Parry-Jones
Powys	Llandrindod Wells	01597-827460	132,952	£1,255	Jeremy Patterson
Rhondda Cynon Taff	Tonypandy	01443-424000	235,599	£1,461	Steve Merritt
SWANSEA	Swansea	01792-636000	239,633	£1,280	Jack Straw
Torfaen	Pontypool	01495-762200	91,372	£1,294	Alison Ward
Vale of Glamorgan	Barry	01446-700111	126,831	£1,261	Siân Davies
Wrexham	Wrexham	01978-292000	135,919	£1,238	Dr Helen Paterson
Ynys Mon (Isle of Anglesey)	Ynys Mon	01248-750057	70,049	£1,242	Richard Parry Jones

* *Source:* Office for National Statistics – *Mid-2012 Population Estimates* (Crown copyright)
† Average Band D council tax bill 2014–15
Councils in CAPITAL LETTERS have city status

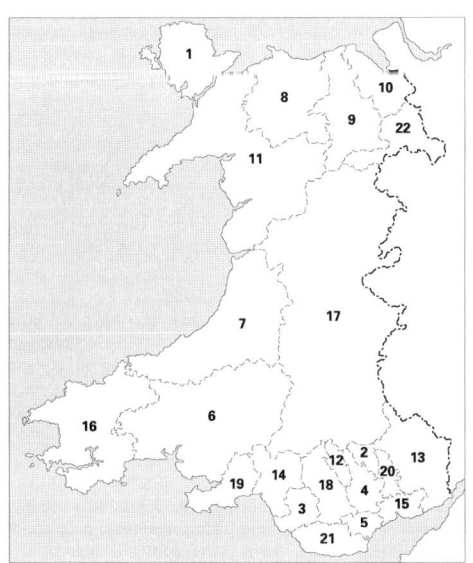

Key	Council	Key	Council
1	Anglesey (Ynys Mon)	12	Merthyr Tydfil
2	Blaenau Gwent	13	Monmouthshire
3	Bridgend	14	Neath Port Talbot
4	Caerphilly	15	Newport
5	Cardiff	16	Pembrokeshire
6	Carmarthenshire	17	Powys
7	Ceredigion	18	Rhondda Cynon Taff
8	Conwy	19	Swansea
9	Denbighshire	20	Torfaen
10	Flintshire	21	Vale of Glamorgan
11	Gwynedd	22	Wrexham

SCOTLAND

Scotland occupies the northern portion of the main island of Great Britain and includes the Inner and Outer Hebrides, Orkney, Shetland and many other islands. It lies between 60° 51′ 30″ and 54° 38′ N. latitude and between 1° 45′ 32″ and 6° 14′ W. longitude, with England to the south-east, the North Channel and the Irish Sea to the south-west, the Atlantic Ocean on the north and west, and the North Sea on the east.

The greatest length of the mainland (Cape Wrath to the Mull of Galloway) is 441km (274 miles), and the greatest breadth (Buchan Ness to Applecross) is 248km (154 miles). The customary measurement of the island of Great Britain is from the site of John o' Groats house, near Duncansby Head, Caithness, to Land's End, Cornwall, a total distance of 970km (603 miles) in a straight line and approximately 1,448km (900 miles) by road.

The total area of Scotland is 78,807 sq. km (30,427 sq. miles): land 77,907 sq. km (30,080 sq. miles), inland water 900 sq. km (347 sq. miles).

POPULATION
The population at the 2011 census was 5,295,403 (men 2,567,444; women 2,727,959). The average density of the population in 2011 was 67 persons per sq. km (174 per sq. mile).

RELIEF
There are three natural orographic divisions of Scotland. The southern uplands have their highest points in Merrick (843m/2,766ft), Rhinns of Kells (814m/2,669ft) and Cairnsmuir of Carsphairn (797m/2,614ft), in the west; and the Tweedsmuir Hills in the east (Broad Law 840m/2,756ft; Dollar Law 817m/2,682ft; Hartfell 808m/2,651ft).

The central lowlands, formed by the valleys of the Clyde, Forth and Tay, divide the southern uplands from the Highlands, which extend from close to the extreme north of the mainland to the central lowlands, and are divided into a northern and a southern system by the Great Glen.

The Grampian Mountains, the southern Highland system, include in the west Ben Nevis (1,343m/4,406ft), the highest point in the British Isles, and in the east the Cairngorm Mountains (Ben Macdui 1,309m/4,296ft; Braeriach 1,295m/4,248ft; Cairn Gorm 1,245m/4,084ft). The north-west Highlands contain the mountains of Wester and Easter Ross (Carn Eige 1,183m/3,880ft; Sgurr na Lapaich 1,151m/3,775ft).

Created, like the central lowlands, by a major geological fault, the Great Glen (97km/60 miles long) runs between Inverness and Fort William, and contains Loch Ness, Loch Oich and Loch Lochy. These are linked to each other and to the north-east and south-west coasts of Scotland by the Caledonian Canal, providing a navigable passage between the Moray Firth and the Inner Hebrides.

HYDROGRAPHY
The western coast is fragmented by peninsulas and islands, and indented by fjords (sea-lochs), the longest of which is Loch Fyne (68km/42 miles long) in Argyll. Although the east coast tends to be less fractured and lower, there are several great drowned inlets (firths), including the Firth of Forth, Firth of Tay and the Moray Firth, as well as the Firth of Clyde in the west.

The lochs are the principal hydrographic feature. The largest in Scotland and in Britain is Loch Lomond (70 sq. km/

27 sq. miles), in the Grampian valleys, and the longest and deepest is Loch Ness (39km/24 miles long and 244m/800ft deep), in the Great Glen.

The longest river is the Tay (188km/117 miles), noted for its salmon. It flows into the North Sea, with Dundee on the estuary, which is spanned by the Tay Bridge (3,136m/10,289ft) opened in 1887 and the Tay Road Bridge (2,245m/7,365ft) opened in 1966. Other noted salmon rivers are the Dee (145km/90 miles) which flows into the North Sea at Aberdeen, and the Spey (177km/110 miles), the swiftest flowing river in the British Isles, which flows into the Moray Firth. The Tweed, which gave its name to the woollen cloth produced along its banks, marks in the lower stretches of its 154km (96 mile) course the border between Scotland and England.

The most important river commercially is the Clyde (171km/106 miles), formed by the junction of the Daer and Portrail water, which flows through the city of Glasgow to the Firth of Clyde. During its course it passes over the picturesque Falls of Clyde, Bonnington Linn (9m/30ft), Corra Linn (26m/84ft), Dundaff Linn (3m/10ft) and Stonebyres Linn (24m/80ft), above and below Lanark. The Forth (106km/66 miles), upon which stands Edinburgh, the capital, is spanned by the Forth Railway Bridge (1890), which is 1,625m (5,330ft) long, and the Forth Road Bridge (1964), which has a total length of 1,876m (6,156ft) (over water) and a single span of 914m (3,000ft).

The highest waterfall in Scotland, and the British Isles, is Eas a'Chùal Aluinn with a total height of 201m (658ft), which falls from Glas Bheinn in Sutherland. The Falls of Glomach, on a head-stream of the Elchaig in Wester Ross, have a drop of 113m (370ft).

GAELIC LANGUAGE
According to the 2011 census, 1.1 per cent (58,000 people) of the population of Scotland aged three and over were able to speak the Scottish form of Gaelic. This was a slight decrease from the 1.2 per cent recorded at the 2001 census.

LOWLAND SCOTTISH LANGUAGE
Several regional lowland Scottish dialects, known variously as Scots, Lallans or Doric, are widely spoken. According to the 2011 census, 43 per cent of the population of Scotland aged three and over stated they could do one or a combination of read, write, speak or understand Scots. A question on Scots was not included in the 2001 census.

FLAG
The flag of Scotland is known as the Saltire. It is a white diagonal cross on a blue field (saltire argent in a field azure) and represents St Andrew, the patron saint of Scotland.

THE SCOTTISH ISLANDS

ORKNEY
The Orkney Islands (total area 972 sq. km/376 sq. miles) lie about 10km (six miles) north of the mainland, separated from it by the Pentland Firth. Of the 90 islands and islets (holms and skerries) in the group, about one-third are inhabited.

The total population at the 2011 census was 21,349; the 2011 populations of the islands shown here include those of smaller islands forming part of the same council district.

Mainland, 17,162	Inner Holm, 1
Auskerry, 4	North Ronaldsay, 72
Burray, 409	Papa Westray, 90
Eday, 160	Rousay, 216
Egilsay, 26	Sanday, 494
Flotta, 8	Shapinsay, 307
Gairsay, 3	South Ronaldsay, 909
Graemsay, 28	Stronsay, 349
Holm of Grimbister, 3	Westray, 588
Hoy, 419	Wyre, 29

The islands are rich in prehistoric and Scandinavian remains, the most notable being the Stone Age village of Skara Brae, the burial chamber of Maes Howe, the many brochs (towers) and the 12th-century St Magnus Cathedral. Scapa Flow, between the Mainland and Hoy, was the war station of the British Grand Fleet from 1914 to 1919 and the scene of the scuttling of the surrendered German High Seas Fleet (21 June 1919).

Most of the islands are low-lying and fertile, and farming (principally beef cattle) is the main industry. Flotta, to the south of Scapa Flow, is the site of the oil terminal for the Piper, Claymore and Tartan fields in the North Sea.

The capital is Kirkwall (population 7,045) situated on Mainland.

SHETLAND

The Shetland Islands have a total area of 1,427 sq. km (551 sq. miles) and had a population at the 2011 census of 23,167. They lie about 80km (50 miles) north of the Orkneys, with Fair Isle about half way between the two groups. Out Stack, off Muckle Flugga, 1.6km (one mile) north of Unst, is the most northerly part of the British Isles (60° 51′ 30″ N. lat.).

There are over 100 islands, of which 16 are inhabited. Populations at the 2011 census were:

Mainland, 18,765	Muckle Roe, 130
Bressay, 368	Papa Stour, 15
Bruray, 24	Trondra, 135
East Burra, 76	Unst, 632
Fair Isle, 68	Vaila, 2
Fetlar, 61	West Burra, 776
Foula, 38	Whalsay, 1,061
Housay, 50	Yell, 966

Shetland's many archaeological sites include Jarlshof, Mousa and Clickhimin, and its long connection with Scandinavia has resulted in a strong Norse influence on its place names and dialect.

Industries include fishing, knitwear and farming. In addition to the fishing fleet there are fish processing factories, and the traditional handknitting of Fair Isle and Unst is now supplemented with machine-knitted garments. Farming is mainly crofting, with sheep being raised on the moorland and hills of the islands. Latterly the islands have become a centre of the North Sea oil industry, with pipelines from the Brent and Ninian fields running to the terminal at Sullom Voe, the largest of its kind in Europe.

The capital is Lerwick (population 6,958) situated on Mainland. Lerwick is the main centre for supply services for offshore oil exploration and development.

THE HEBRIDES

Until the late 13th century the Hebrides included other Scottish islands in the Firth of Clyde, the peninsula of Kintyre (Argyll), the Isle of Man and the (Irish) Isle of Rathlin. The origin of the name is probably the Greek *Eboudai*, latinised as *Hebudes* by Pliny, and corrupted to its present form. The Norwegian name *Sudreyjar* (Southern

Islands) was latinised as *Sodorenses*, a name that survives in the Anglican bishopric of Sodor and Man.

There are over 500 islands and islets, of which about 100 are inhabited, though mountainous terrain and extensive peat bogs mean that only a fraction of the total area is under cultivation. Stone, Bronze and Iron Age settlement has left many remains, including those at Callanish on Lewis, and Norse colonisation influenced language, customs and place names. Occupations include farming (mostly crofting and stock-raising), fishing and the manufacture of tweeds and other woollens. Tourism is also an important part of the economy.

The Inner Hebrides lie off the west coast of Scotland and are relatively close to the mainland. The largest and best-known is Skye (area 1,665 sq. km/643 sq. miles; pop. 10,008; chief town, Portree), which contains the Cuillin Hills (Sgurr Alasdair, 993m/3,257ft), Bla Bheinn (928m/3,046ft), the Storr (719m/2,358ft) and the Red Hills (Beinn na Caillich 732m/2,403ft). Other islands in the Highland council area include Raasay (pop. 161), Eigg (pop. 83), Muck (pop. 27) and Rhum (pop. 22).

Further south the Inner Hebridean islands include Arran (pop. 4,629), containing Goat Fell (874m/2,868ft); Coll (pop. 195) and Tiree (pop. 653); Colonsay (pop. 124) and Oronsay (pop. 8); Easdale (pop. 59); Gigha (pop. 163); Islay (area 608 sq. km/235 sq. miles; pop. 3,228); Jura (area 414 sq. km/160 sq. miles; pop. 196), with a range of hills culminating in the Paps of Jura (Beinn-an-Oir, 785m/2,576ft, and Beinn Chaolais, 755m/2,477ft); Lismore (pop. 192); Luing (pop. 195); and Mull (area 950 sq. km/367 sq. miles; pop. 2,800; chief town Tobermory), containing Ben More (967m/3,171ft).

The Outer Hebrides, separated from the mainland by the Minch, now form the Eilean Siar (Western Isles) council area (area 2,897 sq. km/1,119 sq. miles; pop. 27,684). The main islands are Lewis with Harris (area 1,994 sq. km/770 sq. miles, pop. 21,031), whose chief town, Stornoway, is the administrative headquarters; North Uist (pop. 1,254); South Uist (pop. 1,754); Benbecula (pop. 1,303) and Barra (pop. 1,174). Other inhabited islands include Great Bernera (252), Berneray (138), Eriskay (143), Grimsay (169), Scalpay (291) and Vatersay (90).

EARLY HISTORY

There is evidence of human settlement in Scotland dating from the third millennium BC, the earliest settlers being Mesolithic hunters and fishermen. Early in the second millennium BC, Neolithic farmers began to cultivate crops and rear livestock; their settlements were on the west coast and in the north, and included Skara Brae and Maeshowe (Orkney). Settlement by the early Bronze Age 'Beaker Folk', so-called from the shape of their drinking vessels, in eastern Scotland dates from about 1800 BC. Further settlement is believed to have occurred from 700 BC onwards, as tribes were displaced from further south by new incursions from the Continent and the Roman invasions from AD 43.

Julius Agricola, the Roman governor of Britain AD 77–84, extended the Roman conquests in Britain by advancing into Caledonia, culminating with a victory at Mons Graupius, probably in AD 84; he was recalled to Rome shortly afterwards and his forward policy was not pursued. Hadrian's Wall, mostly completed by AD 30, marked the northern frontier of the Roman empire except for the period between about AD 144 and 190 when the frontier moved north to the Forth-Clyde isthmus and a turf wall, the Antonine Wall, was manned.

After the Roman withdrawal from Britain, there were centuries of warfare between the Picts, Scots, Britons, Angles and Vikings. The Picts, generally accepted to be descended from the indigenous Iron Age people of northern Scotland, occupied the area north of the Forth. The Scots, a Gaelic-speaking people of northern Ireland, colonised the area of Argyll and Bute (the kingdom of Dalriada) in the fifth century AD and then expanded eastwards and northwards. The Britons, speaking a Brythonic Celtic language, colonised Scotland from the south from the first century BC; they lost control of south eastern Scotland (incorporated into the kingdom of Northumbria) to the Angles in the early seventh century but retained Strathclyde (south-western Scotland and Cumbria). Viking raids from the late eighth century were followed by Norse settlement in the western and northern isles, Argyll, Caithness and Sutherland from the mid-ninth century onwards.

UNIFICATION
The union of the areas which now comprise Scotland began in AD 843 when Kenneth mac Alpin, king of the Scots from c.834, also became king of the Picts, joining the two lands to form the kingdom of Alba (comprising Scotland north of a line between the Forth and Clyde rivers). Lothian, the eastern part of the area between the Forth and the Tweed, seems to have been leased to Kenneth II of Alba (reigned 971–995) by Edgar of England c.973, and Scottish possession was confirmed by Malcolm II's victory over a Northumbrian army at Carham c.1016. At about this time Malcolm II (reigned 1005–34) placed his grandson Duncan on the throne of the British kingdom of Strathclyde, bringing under Scots rule virtually all of what is now Scotland.

The Norse possessions were incorporated into the kingdom of Scotland from the 12th century onwards. An uprising in the mid-12th century drove the Norse from most of mainland Argyll. The Hebrides were ceded to Scotland by the Treaty of Perth in 1266 after a Norwegian expedition in 1263 failed to maintain Norse authority over the islands. Orkney and Shetland fell to Scotland in 1468–9 as a pledge for the unpaid dowry of Margaret of Denmark, wife of James III, although Danish claims of suzerainty were relinquished only with the marriage of Anne of Denmark to James VI in 1590.

From the 11th century, there were frequent wars between Scotland and England over territory and the extent of England's political influence. The failure of the Scottish royal line with the death of Margaret of Norway in 1290 led to disputes over the throne which were resolved by the adjudication of Edward I of England. He awarded the throne to John Balliol in 1292 but Balliol's refusal to be a puppet king led to war. Balliol surrendered to Edward I in 1296 and Edward attempted to rule Scotland himself. Resistance to Scotland's loss of independence was led by William Wallace, who defeated the English at Stirling Bridge (1297), and Robert Bruce, crowned in 1306, who held most of Scotland by 1311 and routed Edward II's army at Bannockburn (1314). England recognised the independence of Scotland in the Treaty of Northampton in 1328. Subsequent clashes include the disastrous battle of Flodden (1513) in which James IV and many of his nobles fell.

THE UNION
In 1603 James VI of Scotland succeeded Elizabeth I on the throne of England (his mother, Mary Queen of Scots, was the great-granddaughter of Henry VII), his successors reigning as sovereigns of Great Britain. Political union of the two countries did not occur until 1707.

THE JACOBITE REVOLTS
After the abdication (by flight) in 1688 of James VII and II, the crown devolved upon William III (grandson of Charles I) and Mary II (elder daughter of James VII and II). In 1689 Graham of Claverhouse roused the Highlands on behalf of James VII and II, but died after a military success at Killiecrankie.

After the death of Anne (younger daughter of James VII and II), the throne devolved upon George I (great-grandson of James VI and I). In 1715, armed risings on behalf of James Stuart (the Old Pretender, son of James VII and II) led to the indecisive battle of Sheriffmuir, and the Jacobite movement died down until 1745, when Charles Stuart (the Young Pretender) defeated the Royalist troops at Prestonpans and advanced to Derby (1746). From Derby, the adherents of 'James VIII and III' (the title claimed for his father by Charles Stuart) fell back on the defensive and were finally crushed at Culloden (16 April 1746) by an army led by the Duke of Cumberland, son of George II.

PRINCIPAL CITIES

ABERDEEN
Aberdeen, 209km (130 miles) north-east of Edinburgh, received its charter as a Royal Burgh in 1124. Scotland's third largest city, Aberdeen lies between two rivers, the Dee and the Don, facing the North Sea; the city has a strong maritime history and is today a major centre for offshore oil exploration and production. It is also an ancient university town and distinguished research centre. Other industries include engineering, food processing, textiles, paper manufacturing and chemicals.

Places of interest include King's College, St Machar's Cathedral, Brig o' Balgownie, Duthie Park and Winter Gardens, Hazlehead Park, the Kirk of St Nicholas, Mercat Cross, Marischal College and Marischal Museum, Provost Skene's House, Aberdeen Art Gallery, Gordon Highlanders Museum, Satrosphere Science Centre, and Aberdeen Maritime Museum.

DUNDEE
The Royal Burgh of Dundee is situated on the north bank of the Tay estuary. The city's port and dock installations are important to the offshore oil industry and the airport also provides servicing facilities. Principal industries include textiles, biotechnology and digital media, lasers, printing, tyre manufacture, food processing, engineering and tourism.

The unique City Churches – three churches under one roof, together with the 15th-century St Mary's Tower – are the most prominent architectural feature. Dundee is home to two historic ships: the Dundee-built RRS *Discovery* which took Capt. Scott to the Antarctic lies alongside Discovery Quay, and the frigate *Unicorn*, the only British-built wooden warship still afloat, is moored in Victoria Dock. Places of interest include Mills Public Observatory, the Tay road and rail bridges, Dundee Contemporary Arts centre, McManus Galleries, Claypotts Castle, Broughty Castle, Verdant Works (textile heritage centre) and the Sensation Science Centre.

EDINBURGH
Edinburgh is the capital city and seat of government in Scotland. The new Scottish parliament building designed by Enric Miralles was completed in 2004 and is open to visitors. The city is built on a group of hills and both the Old and New Towns are inscribed on the UNESCO World Cultural and Natural Heritage List for their cultural significance.

Other places of interest include the castle, which houses the Stone of Scone and also includes St Margaret's Chapel, the oldest building in Edinburgh, and near it, the Scottish National War Memorial; the Palace of Holyroodhouse, the Queen's official residence in Scotland; Parliament House, the present seat of the judicature; Princes Street; three

universities (Edinburgh, Heriot-Watt, Napier); St Giles'
Cathedral; St Mary's (Scottish Episcopal) Cathedral (Sir
George Gilbert Scott); the General Register House (Robert
Adam); the National and Signet libraries; the National
Gallery of Scotland; the Royal Scottish Academy; the
Scottish National Portrait Gallery and the Edinburgh
International Conference Centre.

GLASGOW
Glasgow, a Royal Burgh, is Scotland's largest city and its
principal commercial and industrial centre. The city occupies
the north and south banks of the Clyde, formerly one of the
chief commercial estuaries in the world. The main industries
include engineering, electronics, finance, chemicals and
printing. The city is also a key tourist and conference
destination.

The chief buildings are the 13th-century Gothic cathedral,
the university (Sir George Gilbert Scott), the City Chambers,
the Royal Concert Hall, St Mungo Museum of Religious Life
and Art, Pollok House, the School of Art (Charles Rennie
Mackintosh), Kelvingrove Art Gallery and Museum, the
Gallery of Modern Art, the Riverside Museum: Scotland's
Museum of Transport and Travel (Zaha Hadid), the Burrell
Collection museum and the Mitchell Library. The city is
home to the Royal Scottish National Orchestra, Scottish
Opera, Scottish Ballet, BBC Scotland and Scottish Television
(STV).

INVERNESS
Inverness was granted city status in 2000. The city's name is
derived from the Gaelic for 'the mouth of the Ness', referring
to the river on which it lies. Inverness is recorded as being
at the junction of trade routes since AD 565. Today the city
is the main administrative centre for the north of Scotland
and is the capital of the Highlands. Tourism is one of the
city's main industries.

Among the city's most notable buildings is Abertarff
House, built in 1593 and the oldest secular building
remaining in Inverness. Balnain House, built as a town house
in 1726, is a fine example of early Georgian architecture. The
Old High Church, on St Michael's Mount, is the original
parish church of Inverness and is built on the site of the
earliest Christian church in the city. Parts of the church date
back to the 14th century.

Stirling was granted city status in 2002 and Perth in 2012.
Aberdeen, Dundee, Edinburgh and Glasgow have also been
granted lord mayoralty/lord provostship status.

LORD-LIEUTENANTS

Title	Name
Aberdeen City*	Lord Provost George Adam
Aberdeenshire	James Ingleby
Angus	Georgiana Osborne
Argyll and Bute	Patrick Stewart, MBE
Ayrshire and Arran	John Duncan, QPM
Banffshire	Clare Russell
Berwickshire	Jeannna Swan
Caithness	M. Anne Dunnett
Clackmannanshire	Lt.-Col. John Stewart
Dumfries	Jean Tulloch
Dunbartonshire	Rear-Adm. Michael Gregory, OBE
Dundee City*	Lord Provost Robert Duncan
East Lothian	Maj. Michael Williams, MBE
Edinburgh City*	Rt. Hon. Lord Provost Donald Wilson
Eilean Siar (Western Isles)	Alexander Matheson, OBE
Fife	Margaret Dean, CVO
Glasgow City*	Rt. Hon. Lord Provost Sadie Docherty
Inverness	Donald Cameron of Lochiel
Kincardineshire	Carol Kinghorn
Lanarkshire	Mushtaq Ahmad, OBE
Midlothian	Sir Robert Maxwell Clerk, Bt., OBE
Moray	Grenville Shaw Johnston, OBE, TD
Nairn	Ewen Brodie of Lethan
Orkney	Bill Spence
Perth and Kinross	Brig. Melville Jameson, CBE
Renfrewshire	Guy Clark
Ross and Cromarty	Janet Bowen
Roxburgh, Ettrick and Lauderdale	Capt. Hon. Gerald Maitland-Carew
Shetland	Robert Hunter
Stirling and Falkirk	Marjory McLachlan
Sutherland	Dr Monica Main
The Stewartry of Kirkcudbright	Lt.-Col. Sir Malcolm Ross, GCVO, OBE
Tweeddale	Prof. Sir Hew Strachan
West Lothian	Isobel Brydie, MBE
Wigtown	Marion Brewis, CVO

* The Lord Provosts of the four cities of Aberdeen, Dundee,
Edinburgh and Glasgow are Lord-Lieutenants *ex officio* for those
districts

LOCAL COUNCILS

Council	Administrative Headquarters	Telephone	Population*	Council Tax†	Chief Executive
ABERDEEN	Aberdeen	0845-608 0910	224,970	£1,230	Angela Scott
Aberdeenshire	Aberdeen	01467-620981	255,540	£1,141	Colin Mackenzie
Angus	Forfar	0845-277 7778	116,210	£1,072	Richard Stiff
Argyll and Bute	Lochgilphead	01546-602127	86,900	£1,178	Sally Loudon
Clackmannanshire	Alloa	01259-450000	51,280	£1,148	Elaine McPherson
Dumfries and Galloway	Dumfries	030-3333 3000	150,830	£1,049	Gavin Stevenson
DUNDEE	Dundee	01382-434000	147,800	£1,211	David Dorward
East Ayrshire	Kilmarnock	01563-576000	122,720	£1,189	Fiona Lees
East Dunbartonshire	Kirkintilloch	0300-123 4510	105,880	£1,142	Gerry Cornes
East Lothian	Haddington	01620-827827	100,850	£1,118	Angela Leitch
East Renfrewshire	Giffnock	0141-577 3000	91,030	£1,126	Lorraine McMillan
EDINBURGH	Edinburgh	0131-200 2000	482,640	£1,169	Sue Bruce
Eilean Siar (Western Isles)	Stornoway	01851-703773	27,560	£1,024	Malcolm Burr
Falkirk	Falkirk	01324-506070	156,800	£1,070	Mary Pitcaithly, OBE
Fife	Glenrothes	0345-155 0000	366,220	£1,118	Steve Grimmond
GLASGOW	Glasgow	0141-287 2000	595,080	£1,213	George Black
Highland	Inverness	01349-856606	232,910	£1,163	Steve Barron
Inverclyde	Greenock	01475-717171	80,680	£1,198	John Mundell
Midlothian	Dalkeith	0131-270 7500	84,240	£1,210	Kenneth Lawrie
Moray	Elgin	01343-543451	92,910	£1,135	Roddy Burns
North Ayrshire	Irvine	01294-310000	137,560	£1,152	Elma Murray
North Lanarkshire	Motherwell	01698-302222	337,870	£1,098	Gavin Whitefield
Orkney	Kirkwall	01856-873535	21,530	£1,037	Alistair Buchan
Perth and Kinross	Perth	01738-475000	147,740	£1,158	Bernadette Malone
Renfrewshire	Paisley	0300-300 0300	174,310	£1,165	David Martin
Scottish Borders	Melrose	01835-824000	113,710	£1,084	Tracey Logan
Shetland	Lerwick	01595-693535	23,210	£1,053	Mark Boden
South Ayrshire	Ayr	0300-123 0900	112,910	£1,154	Eileen Howat
South Lanarkshire	Hamilton	0303-123 1015	314,360	£1,101	Lindsay Freeland
STIRLING	Stirling	0845-277 7000	91,020	£1,197	Stewart Carruth
West Dunbartonshire	Dumbarton	01389-737000	90,340	£1,163	Joyce White
West Lothian	Livingston	01506-280000	175,990	£1,128	Graham Hope

Key	Council	Key	Council
1	Aberdeen City	17	Inverclyde
2	Aberdeenshire	18	Midlothian
3	Angus	19	Moray
4	Argyll and Bute	20	North Ayrshire
5	City of Edinburgh	21	North Lanarkshire
6	Clackmannanshire	22	Orkney
7	Dumfries and Galloway	23	Perth and Kinross
8	Dundee City	24	Renfrewshire
9	East Ayrshire	25	Scottish Borders
10	East Dunbartonshire	26	Shetland
11	East Lothian	27	South Ayrshire
12	East Renfrewshire	28	South Lanarkshire
13	Falkirk	29	Stirling
14	Fife	30	West Dunbartonshire
15	Glasgow City	31	Western Isles (Eilean Siar)
16	Highland	32	West Lothian

* *Source:* Office for National Statistics – *Mid-2012 Population Estimates* (Crown copyright)
† Average Band D council tax bill 2014–15
Councils in CAPITAL LETTERS have city status

NORTHERN IRELAND

Northern Ireland has a total area of 14,149 sq. km (5,463 sq. miles): land, 13,576 sq. km (5,242 sq. miles); inland water, 573 sq. km (221 sq. miles).

The population of Northern Ireland at the 2011 census was 1,810,863 (men 887,323; women 923,540). The average density of population in 2011 was 128 persons per sq. km (331 per sq. mile).

FLAG

The official national flag of Northern Ireland is the Union Flag.

PRINCIPAL CITIES

In addition to Belfast and Londonderry, three other places in Northern Ireland have been granted city status: Armagh (1994), Lisburn (2002) and Newry (2002).

BELFAST

Belfast, the administrative centre of Northern Ireland, is situated at the mouth of the River Lagan at its entrance to Belfast Lough. The city grew to be a great industrial centre, owing to its easy access by sea to Scottish coal and iron.

The principal buildings are of a relatively young age and include the parliament buildings at Stormont, the City Hall, Waterfront Hall, the Law Courts, the Public Library and the Museum and Art Gallery. In March 2012, a new museum, Titanic Belfast, opened on the banks of the Lagan River, the site where RMS Titanic was built and launched. The museum forms the centrepiece of a new mixed-use maritime quarter.

Belfast received its first charter of incorporation in 1613 and was created a city in 1888; the title of lord mayor was conferred in 1892.

LONDONDERRY

Londonderry (originally Derry) is situated on the River Foyle, and has important associations with the City of London. The Irish Society was created by the City of London in 1610, and under its royal charter of 1613 it fortified the city and was for a long time closely associated with its administration. Because of this connection the city was incorporated in 1613 under the new name of Londonderry.

The city is famous for the great siege of 1688–9, when for 105 days the town held out against the forces of James II. The city walls are still intact and form a circuit of 1.6 km (one mile) around the old city.

Interesting buildings are the Protestant cathedral of St Columb's (1633) and the Guildhall, reconstructed in 1912 and containing a number of beautiful stained glass windows, many of which were presented by the livery companies of London.

CONSTITUTIONAL HISTORY

Northern Ireland is subject to the same fundamental constitutional provisions which apply to the rest of the UK. It had its own parliament and government from 1921 to 1972, but after increasing civil unrest the Northern Ireland (Temporary Provisions) Act 1972 transferred the legislative and executive powers of the Northern Ireland parliament and government to the UK parliament and a secretary of state. The Northern Ireland Constitution Act 1973 provided for devolution in Northern Ireland through an assembly and executive, but a power-sharing executive formed by the Northern Ireland political parties in January 1974 collapsed in May 1974. Following the collapse of the power-sharing executive Northern Ireland returned to direct rule governance under the provisions of the Northern Ireland Act 1974, placing the Northern Ireland department under the direction and control of the Northern Ireland secretary.

In December 1993 the British and Irish governments published the Joint Declaration complementing their political talks, and making clear that any settlement would need to be founded on principles of democracy and consent.

On 12 January 1998 the British and Irish governments issued a joint document, *Propositions on Heads of Agreement*, proposing the establishment of various new cross-border bodies; further proposals were presented on 27 January. A draft peace settlement was issued by the talks' chairman, US Senator George Mitchell, on 6 April 1998 but was rejected by the Unionists the following day. On 10 April agreement was reached between the British and Irish governments and the eight Northern Ireland political parties still involved in the talks (the Good Friday Agreement). The agreement provided for an elected Northern Ireland Assembly, a North/South Ministerial Council, and a British-Irish Council comprising representatives of the British, Irish, Channel Islands and Isle of Man governments and members of the new assemblies for Scotland, Wales and Northern Ireland. Further points included the abandonment of the Republic of Ireland's constitutional claim to Northern Ireland; the decommissioning of weapons; the release of paramilitary prisoners and changes in policing.

The agreement was ratified in referendums held in Northern Ireland and the Republic of Ireland on 22 May 1998. In the UK, the Northern Ireland Act received royal assent in November 1998.

On 28 April 2003 the secretary of state again assumed responsibility for the direction of the Northern Ireland departments on the dissolution of the Northern Ireland Assembly, following its initial suspension from midnight on 14 October 2002. In 2006, following the passing of the Northern Ireland Act, the secretary of state created a non-legislative fixed-term assembly which would cease to operate either when the political parties agreed to restore devolution, or on 24 November 2006 (whichever occurred first). In October 2006 a timetable to restore devolution was drawn up (St Andrews Agreement) and a transitional Northern Ireland Assembly was formed on 24 November. The transitional assembly was dissolved in January 2007 in preparation for elections to be held on 7 March; following the elections a power-sharing executive was formed and the new 108-member Northern Ireland Assembly became operational on 8 May 2007.

See also Regional Government.

LORD-LIEUTENANTS AND HIGH SHERIFFS

County	Lord-Lieutenant	High Sheriff (2014)
Antrim	Joan Christie, OBE	Hon. Shane O'Neill
Armagh	The Earl of Caledon	Paul Reaney
Belfast City	Fionnuala Mary Jay-O'Boyle, CBE	Lydia Patterson
Down	David Lindsay	Simon Brien
Fermanagh	Viscount Brookeborough	Henry Robinson
Londonderry	Denis Desmond, CBE	John O'Neill
Londonderry City	Dr Angela Josepha Garvey	Robert Dunn
Tyrone	Robert Scott, OBE	Kathleen Adams

LOCAL COUNCILS

Council*	Telephone	Population†	Chief Executive
Antrim & Newtownabbey	028-9448 1311	139,536	Jacqui Dixon
Armagh, Banbridge & Craigavon	028-3752 9600	203,757	Roger Wilson
Belfast	028-9032 0202	335,133	Suzanne Wylie
Causeway Coast & Glens	028-7034 7034	141,699	David Jackson
Derry & Strabane	028-7138 2204	148,632	John Kelpie
Fermanagh & Omagh	028-6632 5050	114,365	Brendan Hegarty
Lisburn & Castlereagh	028-9250 9250	136,808	Theresa Donaldson
Mid & East Antrim	028-9335 8000	135,997	Anne Donaghy
Mid Ulster	028-8772 0300	141,329	Anthony Tohill
Newry, Mourne & Down	028-3031 3037	174,829	Liam Hannaway
North Down & Ards	028-9127 8034	157,640	Stephen Reid

* Transitional shadow councils due to take on their full functions by April 2015 *see* pages 245 and 250 for further information
† *Source: NISRA – Mid-year Population Estimates 2013*

THE ISLE OF MAN

Ellan Vannin

The Isle of Man is an island situated in the Irish Sea, at latitude 54° 3′–54° 25′ N. and longitude 4° 18′–4° 47′ W., nearly equidistant from England, Scotland and Ireland. Although the early inhabitants were of Celtic origin, the Isle of Man was part of the Norwegian Kingdom of the Hebrides until 1266, when this was ceded to Scotland. Subsequently granted to the Stanleys (Earls of Derby) in the 15th century and later to the Dukes of Atholl, it was brought under the administration of the Crown in 1765. The island forms the bishopric of Sodor and Man.

The total land area is 572 sq. km (221 sq. miles). The 2011 census showed a resident population of 84,497 (men, 41,971; women, 42,526). The main language in use is English. Around 1,660 people are able to speak the Manx Gaelic language.

CAPITAL – ΨDouglas; population, 27,938 (2011). ΨCastletown (3,097) is the ancient capital; the other towns are ΨPeel (5,093) and ΨRamsey (7,821)

FLAG – A red flag charged with three conjoined armoured legs in white and gold

NATIONAL DAY – 5 July (Tynwald Day)

GOVERNMENT

The Isle of Man is a self-governing Crown dependency, with its own parliamentary, legal and administrative system. The British government is responsible for international relations and defence. Under the UK Act of Accession, Protocol 3, the island's relationship with the European Union is limited to trade alone and does not extend to financial aid. The Lieutenant-Governor is the Queen's personal representative on the island.

The legislature, Tynwald, is the oldest parliament in the world in continuous existence. It has two branches: the Legislative Council and the House of Keys. The council consists of the President of Tynwald, the Bishop of Sodor and Man, the Attorney-General (who does not have a vote) and eight members elected by the House of Keys. The House of Keys has 24 members, elected by universal adult suffrage. The branches sit separately to consider legislation and sit together, as Tynwald Court, for most other parliamentary purposes.

The presiding officer of Tynwald Court is the President of Tynwald, elected by the members, who also presides over sittings of the Legislative Council. The presiding officer of the House of Keys is the Speaker, who is elected by members of the house.

The principal members of the Manx government are the chief minister and eight departmental ministers, who comprise the Council of Ministers.

Lieutenant-Governor, HE Adam Wood
President of Tynwald, Hon. Clare Christian

Speaker, House of Keys, Hon. Steve Rodan, SHK
The First Deemster and Clerk of the Rolls, His Hon. David Doyle
Clerk of Tynwald, Secretary to the House of Keys and Counsel to the Speaker, Roger Phillips
Clerk of the Legislative Council and Deputy Clerk of Tynwald, Jonathan King
Attorney-General, Stephen Harding
Chief Minister, Hon. Allan Bell, MHK
Chief Secretary, Will Greenhow

ECONOMY

Most of the income generated in the island is earned in the services sector with financial and professional services accounting for just over half of the national income. Tourism and manufacturing are also major generators of income while the island's other traditional industries of agriculture and fishing now play a smaller role in the economy. Under the terms of protocol 3, the island has tariff-free access to EU markets for its goods.

In June 2014 the island's unemployment rate was 2.1 per cent and the rate of inflation (RPI) was 2.8 per cent.

FINANCE

The budget for 2014–15 provides for net revenue expenditure of £543.6m. The principal sources of government revenue are taxes on income and expenditure. Income tax is payable at a rate of 10 per cent on the first £10,500 of taxable income for single resident individuals and 20 per cent on the balance, after personal allowances of £9,500. These bands are doubled for married couples. The rate of income tax for trading companies is zero per cent except for income from banking, land and property and major retail operations which is taxed at 10 per cent. By agreement with the British government, the island keeps most of its rates of indirect taxation (VAT and duties) the same as those in the UK. However, VAT on tourist accommodation, property, repairs and renovations is charged at 5 per cent. A reciprocal agreement on national insurance benefits and pensions exists between the governments of the Isle of Man and the UK. Taxes are also charged on property (rates), but these are comparatively low.

The major government expenditure items are social care, health and education, which account for 50 per cent of the government budget. The island makes an annual contribution to the UK for defence and other external services.

The island has a special relationship with the European Union and neither contributes money to nor receives funds from the EU budget.

Ψ = sea port

THE CHANNEL ISLANDS

The Channel Islands, situated off the north-west coast of France (at a distance of 16km (10 miles) at their closest point), are the only portions of the Dukedom of Normandy still belonging to the Crown, to which they have been attached since the Norman Conquest of 1066. They were the only British territory to come under German occupation during the Second World War, following invasion on 30 June and 1 July 1940. Guernsey and Jersey were relieved by British forces on 9 May 1945, Sark on 10 May 1945 and Alderney on 16 May 1945; 9 May (Liberation Day) is now observed as a bank and public holiday in Guernsey and Jersey.

The islands consist of Jersey (11,630ha/28,717 acres), Guernsey (6,340ha/15,654 acres), and the dependencies of Guernsey: Alderney (795ha/1,962 acres), Brecqhou (30ha/74 acres), Great Sark (419ha/1,035 acres), Little Sark (97ha/239 acres), Herm (130ha/320 acres), Jethou (18ha/44 acres) and Lihou (15ha/38 acres) – a total of 19,474ha/48,083 acres, or 195 sq. km/75 sq. miles.

The 2011 census (taken in March) showed the population of Jersey as 97,857. Guernsey did not complete the same census, but the most recent official records for Guernsey and Alderney estimated the populations at 62,732 and 1,903 respectively. Sark's population is estimated to be around 600. The official language is English but French is often used for ceremonial purposes. In country districts of Jersey and Guernsey and throughout Sark a Norman-French *patois* is also in use, though to a lesser extent.

GOVERNMENT

The islands are Crown dependencies with their own legislative assemblies (the States of Jersey and the States of Alderney, the States of Deliberation in Guernsey and the Chief Pleas in Sark), systems of local administration and law, and their own courts. *Projets de Loi* (Acts) passed by the States require the sanction of the Queen-in-council. The UK government is responsible for defence and international relations, although the islands are increasingly entering into agreements with other countries in their own right. The Channel Islands are not members of the European Union but, under protocol 3 of the UK's Treaty of Accession, have trading rights with the free movement of goods within the EU. A common customs tariff, levies and agricultural and import measures apply to trade between the islands and non-member countries.

In both Jersey and Guernsey bailiwicks the Lieutenant-Governor and Commander-in-Chief, who is appointed by the Crown, is the personal representative of the Queen and the official channel of communication between the Crown (via the Privy Council) and the islands' governments.

The head of government in both Jersey and Guernsey is the Chief Minister. Jersey has a ministerial system of government; the executive comprises the Council of Ministers and consists of a chief minister and nine other ministers. The ministers are assisted by up to 12 assistant ministers. Members of the States who are not in the executive are able to sit on a number of scrutiny panels and the Public Accounts Committee to examine the policy of the executive and hold ministers to account. Guernsey is administered by a number of departments and committees. There are ten States departments with mandated responsibilities, each department is constituted of a minister and four members of the States. Each of the ministers has a seat on the Policy Council

which is presided over by the Chief Minister. The States of Deliberation, the island's parliamentary assembly, is the overarching executive. There are also five parliamentary committees, each led by a chair, responsible for scrutinising policy, finance and legislation, parliamentary procedural matters and public sector pay negotiations. Alderney has a legislature comprising a President and ten members elected by universal suffrage. Sark has a directly elected legislature of 28 members *(conseillers)* who serve on a number of committees.

Justice is administered by the royal courts of Jersey and Guernsey, each consisting of the bailiff and 12 elected jurats. The bailiffs of Jersey and Guernsey, appointed by the Crown, are presidents of the royal courts of their respective islands. Each bailiff is the *ex-officio* presiding officer in their respective parliaments and, by convention, the civic head.

Each bailiwick constitutes a deanery under the administration of the Diocese of Winchester. Since January 2014 episcopal oversight for the Channel Islands has been delegated, on a temporary basis, to the Bishop of Dover (Diocese of Canterbury).

ECONOMY

A mild climate and good soil have led to the development of intensive systems of agriculture and horticulture, which form a significant part of the economy. Equally important are earnings from tourism and banking and finance: the low rates of income and corporation tax and the absence of death duties make the islands an important offshore financial centre. The financial services sector contributes over 50 per cent of GDP in Jersey and around 40 per cent in Guernsey. In addition, there is no VAT or equivalent tax in Guernsey and only small goods and services tax in Jersey (5 per cent since 1 June 2011). The Channel Islands stock exchange is located in Guernsey, which also has a thriving e-gaming sector.

Principal exports are agricultural produce and flowers; imports are chiefly machinery, manufactured goods, food, fuel and chemicals. Trade with the UK is regarded as internal.

British currency is legal tender in the Channel Islands but each bailiwick issues its own coins and notes *(see Currency section)*. They also issue their own postage stamps; UK stamps are not valid.

JERSEY

Lieutenant-Governor and Commander-in-Chief of Jersey,
  HE Gen. Sir John McColl, KCB, CBE, DSO, *apptd* 2011
Secretary and ADC, Lt.-Col. A. Woodrow, LVO, OBE, MC
Bailiff of Jersey, Sir Michael Birt
Deputy Bailiff, William. J. Bailhache
Attorney-General, Timothy J. Le Cocq, QC
Receiver-General, David Pett
Solicitor-General, Howard Sharp, QC
Greffier of the States, Michael N. de la Haye, OBE
States Treasurer, Laura Rowley
Chief Minister, Senator Ian Gorst

FINANCE*	2012	2013
Revenue income	£1,093,520,000	£1,241,343,000
Revenue expenditure	£923,524,000	£978,813,000
Capital expenditure	£36,844,000	£51,507,000

* A change in accounting rules means that for the first time the 2013 States of Jersey Financial Statement of Accounts includes the Social Security Funds. Figures for 2012 have been restated by the States Treasury in accordance with this accounting change in order that an accurate comparison can be made between figures for 2013 and 2012.

CHIEF TOWN – Ψ St Helier, on the south coast

FLAG – A white field charged with a red saltire cross, and the arms of Jersey in the upper centre

GUERNSEY AND DEPENDENCIES

Lieutenant-Governor and Commander-in-Chief of the Bailiwick of Guernsey and its Dependencies, HE Air Marshal Peter Walker, CB, CBE, *apptd* 2011

Presiding Officer of the Royal Court and of the States of Deliberation, Bailiff Richard Collas

Deputy Presiding Officer of the Royal Court and States of Deliberation, Richard McMahon, QC

HM Procureur and Receiver-General (Attorney-General), Howard Roberts, QC

HM Comptroller (Solicitor-General), Megan Pullum, QC

GUERNSEY

Chief Minister, Deputy Jonathan Le Tocq

Chief Executive, Paul Whitfield

FINANCE	2012	2013
Revenue income	£362,343,000	£361,257,000
Revenue expenditure	£341,712,000	£345,698,000
Capital expenditure	£16,361,000	£13,362,000

CHIEF TOWNS – Ψ St Peter Port, on the east coast of Guernsey; St Anne on Alderney

FLAG – White, bearing a red cross of St George, with a gold cross of Normandy overall in the centre

ALDERNEY

President of the States, Stuart Trought

Chief Executive, Victor Brownlees

Greffier, Sarah Kelly

SARK

Sark was the last European territory to abolish feudal parliamentary representation. Elections for a democratic legislative assembly took place in December 2008, with the *conseillers* taking their seats in the newly constituted Chief Pleas in January 2009.

Seigneur of Sark, John Beaumont, OBE

Seneschal, Jeremy la Trobe-Bateman

President, Lt.-Col. Reg Guille, MBE

Greffier, Trevor Hamon

OTHER DEPENDENCIES

Herm and Lihou are owned by the States of Guernsey; Herm is leased, Lihou is uninhabited. Jethou is leased by the Crown to the States of Guernsey and is sub-let by the States. Brecqhou is within the legislative and judicial territory of Sark.

Ψ = seaport

LAW COURTS AND OFFICES

SUPREME COURT OF THE UNITED KINGDOM

The Supreme Court of the United Kingdom is the highest domestic judicial authority; it replaced the appellate committee of the House of Lords (the house functioning in its judicial capacity) on 1 October 2009. It is the final court of appeal for cases heard in Great Britain and Northern Ireland (except for criminal cases from Scotland). Cases concerning the interpretation and application of European Union law, including preliminary rulings requested by British courts and tribunals, which are decided by the Court of Justice of the European Union (CJEU) (*see* European Union), and the supreme court can make a reference to the CJEU in appropriate cases. Additionally, in giving effect to rights contained in the European Convention on Human Rights, the supreme court must take account of any decision of the European Court of Human Rights.

The supreme court also assumed jurisdiction in relation to devolution matters under the Scotland Act 1998 (now partly superseded by the Scotland Act 2012), the Northern Ireland Act 1988 and the Government of Wales Act 2006; these powers were transferred from the Judicial Committee of the Privy Council. Ten of the 12 Lords of Appeal in Ordinary (Law Lords) from the House of Lords transferred to the 12-member supreme court when it came into operation (at the same time one law lord retired and another was appointed Master of the Rolls). All new justices of the supreme court are now appointed by an independent selection commission, and, although styled Rt. Hon. Lord, are not members of the House of Lords. Peers who are members of the judiciary are disqualified from sitting or voting in the House of Lords until they retire from their judicial office. *See* Life Peers (page 60) for a list of such peers (§).

President of the Supreme Court (£218,470), Rt. Hon. Lord Neuberger of Abbotsbury, *born* 1948, *apptd* 2012
Deputy President of the Supreme Court (£211,015), Rt. Hon. Lady Hale of Richmond, *born* 1945, *apptd* 2013

JUSTICES OF THE SUPREME COURT *as at September 2014* (each £211,015)
Style, The Rt. Hon. Lord/Lady–

Rt. Hon. Lord Mance, *born* 1943, *apptd* 2005
Rt. Hon. Lord Kerr of Tonaghmore, *born* 1948, *apptd* 2009
Rt. Hon. Lord Clarke of Stone-cum-Ebony, *born* 1943, *apptd* 2009
Rt. Hon. Lord Wilson of Culworth, *born* 1945, *apptd* 2011
Rt. Hon. Lord Sumption, *born* 1948, *apptd* 2012
Rt. Hon. Lord Reed, *born* 1956, *apptd* 2012
Rt. Hon. Lord Carnwath of Notting Hill, CVO, *born* 1945, *apptd* 2012
Rt. Hon. Lord Hughes of Ombersley, *born* 1948, *apptd* 2013
Rt. Hon. Lord Toulson, *born* 1946, *apptd* 2013
Rt. Hon. Lord Hodge, *born* 1953, *apptd* 2013

UNITED KINGDOM SUPREME COURT
Parliament Square, London SW1P 3BD T 020-7960 1900
Chief Executive, Jenny Rowe, CB

JUDICATURE OF ENGLAND AND WALES

The legal system in England and Wales is divided into criminal law and civil law. Criminal law is concerned with

acts harmful to the community and the rules laid down by the state for the benefit of citizens, whereas civil law governs the relationships and transactions between individuals. Administrative law is a kind of civil law usually concerning the interaction of individuals and the state, and most cases are heard in tribunals specific to the subject (*see* Tribunals section). Scotland and Northern Ireland possess legal systems that differ from the system in England and Wales in law, judicial procedure and court structure, but retain the distinction between criminal and civil law.

Under the provisions of the Criminal Appeal Act 1995, a commission was set up to direct and supervise investigations into possible miscarriages of justice and to refer cases to the appeal courts on the grounds of conviction and sentence; these functions were formerly the responsibility of the home secretary.

SENIOR COURTS OF ENGLAND AND WALES
The senior courts of England and Wales (until September 2009 known as the supreme court of judicature of England and Wales) comprise the high court, the crown court and the court of appeal. The President of the Courts of England and Wales, a new title given to the Lord Chief Justice under the Constitutional Reform Act 2005, is the head of the judiciary.

The high court was created in 1875 and combined many previously separate courts. Sittings are held at the royal courts of justice in London or at around 120 district registries outside the capital. It is the superior civil court and is split into three divisions – the chancery division, the Queen's bench division and the family division – each of which is further divided. The chancery division is headed by the Chancellor of the High Court and is concerned mainly with equity, trusts, tax and bankruptcy, while also including two specialist courts, the patents court and the companies court. The Queen's bench division (QBD) is the largest of the three divisions, and is headed by its own president. It deals with common law (ie tort, contract, debt and personal injuries), some tax law, eg VAT tribunal appeals, and encompasses the admiralty court and the commercial court. The QBD also administers the technology and construction court. The family division was created in 1970 and is headed by its own president, who is also Head of Family Justice, and hears cases concerning divorce, access to and custody of children, and other family matters. The divisional court of the high court sits in the family and chancery divisions, and hears appeals from the magistrates' courts and county courts.

The crown court was set up in 1972 and sits at 77 centres throughout England and Wales. It deals with more serious (indictable) criminal offences, which are triable before a judge and jury, including treason, murder, rape, kidnapping, armed robbery and Official Secrets Act offences. It also handles cases transferred from the magistrates' courts where the magistrate decides his or her own power of sentence is inadequate, or where someone appeals against a magistrate's decision, or in a case that is triable 'either way' where the accused has chosen a jury trial. The crown court centres are divided into three tiers: high court judges, circuit judges and sometimes recorders (part-time circuit judges), sit in first-tier centres, hearing the most serious criminal offences (eg murder, treason, rape, manslaughter) and some civil high court cases. The second-tier centres are presided over by high court judges, circuit judges or recorders and also deal with the most serious criminal cases. Third-tier courts deal

HIERARCHY OF ENGLISH AND WELSH COURTS

with the remaining criminal offences, with circuit judges or recorders presiding.

The court of appeal hears appeals against both fact and law, and was last restructured in 1966 when it replaced the court of criminal appeal. It is split into the civil division (which hears appeals from the high court, tribunals and in certain cases, the county courts) and the criminal division (which hears appeals from the crown court). Cases are heard by Lords Justices of Appeal and high court judges if deemed suitable for reconsideration.

The Constitutional Reform Act 2005 instigated several key changes to the judiciary in England and Wales. These included the establishment of the independent supreme court, which opened in October 2009; the reform of the post of Lord Chancellor, transferring its judicial functions to the President of the Courts of England and Wales; a duty on government ministers to uphold the independence of the judiciary by barring them from trying to influence judicial decisions through any special access to judges; the formation of a fully transparent and independent Judicial Appointments Commission that is responsible for selecting candidates to recommend for judicial appointment to the Lord Chancellor and Secretary of State for Justice; and the creation of the post of Judicial Appointments and Conduct Ombudsman.

CRIMINAL CASES
In criminal matters the decision to prosecute (in the majority of cases) rests with the Crown Prosecution Service (CPS), which is the independent prosecuting body in England and Wales. The CPS is headed by the director of public prosecutions, who works under the superintendence of the Attorney-General. Certain categories of offence continue to require the Attorney-General's consent for prosecution.

Most minor criminal cases (summary offences) are dealt with in magistrates' courts, usually by a bench of three unpaid lay magistrates (justices of the peace) sitting without a jury and assisted on points of law and procedure by a legally trained clerk. There were around 21,500 justices of the peace. In some courts a full-time, salaried and legally qualified district judge (magistrates' court) – formerly known

as a stipendiary judge – presides alone. There are 150 district judges (magistrates' courts). Magistrates' courts oversee the completion of 95 per cent of all criminal cases. Magistrates' courts also house some family proceedings courts (which deal with relationship breakdown and childcare cases) and youth courts. Cases of medium seriousness (known as 'offences triable either way') where the defendant pleads not guilty can be heard in the crown court for a trial by jury, if the defendant so chooses. Preliminary proceedings in a serious case to decide whether there is evidence to justify committal for trial in the crown court are dealt with in the magistrates' courts.

The 77 centres that the crown court sits in are divided into seven regions. There are 653 circuit judges and around 1,200 recorders (part-time circuit judges); they must sit a minimum of 15 days per year and are usually subject to a maximum of 30. A jury is present in all trials that are contested.

Appeals from magistrates' courts against sentence or conviction are made to the crown court, and appeals upon a point of law are made to the high court, which may ultimately be appealed to the supreme court. Appeals from the crown court, either against sentence or conviction, are made to the court of appeal (criminal division). Again, these appeals may be brought to the supreme court if a point of law is contested, and if the house considers it is of sufficient importance.

CIVIL CASES
Most minor civil cases – including contract, tort (especially personal injuries), property, divorce and other family matters, bankruptcy etc – are dealt with by the county courts, of which there are around 215 (see W www.justice.gov.uk for further details). Cases are heard by circuit judges, recorders or district judges. For cases involving small claims (with certain exceptions, where the amount claimed is £5,000 or less) there are informal and simplified procedures designed to enable parties to present their cases themselves without recourse to lawyers. Where there are financial limits on county court jurisdiction, claims that exceed those limits may be tried in the county courts with the consent of the parties,

subject to the court's agreement, or in certain circumstances on transfer from the high court. Outside London, bankruptcy proceedings can be heard in designated county courts. Magistrates' courts also deal with certain classes of civil case, and committees of magistrates license public houses, clubs and betting shops. For the implementation of the Children Act 1989, a new structure of hearing centres was set up in 1991 for family proceedings cases, involving magistrates' courts (family proceedings courts), divorce county courts, family hearing centres and care centres.

Appeals in certain family matters heard in the family proceedings courts go to the family division of the high court. Appeals from county courts may be heard in the court of appeal (civil division) or the high court, and may go on to the supreme court.

CORONERS' COURTS
The coroners' courts investigate violent and unnatural deaths or sudden deaths where the cause is unknown. Doctors, the police, various public authorities or members of the public may bring cases before a local coroner (a senior lawyer or doctor), in order to determine whether further criminal investigation is necessary. Where a death is sudden and the cause is unknown, the coroner may order a post-mortem examination to determine the cause of death rather than hold an inquest in court. An inquest must be held, however, if a person died in a violent or unnatural way, or died in prison or other unusual circumstances. If the coroner suspects murder, manslaughter or infanticide, he or she must summon a jury.

SENIOR JUDICIARY OF ENGLAND AND WALES
Lord Chief Justice of England and Wales and Head of Criminal Justice (£244,665), Rt. Hon. Lord Thomas of Cwmgiedd, *born* 1947, *apptd* 2013
Master of the Rolls and Head of Civil Justice (£218,470), Rt. Hon. Lord Dyson, *born* 1943, *apptd* 2012
President of the Queen's Bench Division (£211,015), Sir Brian Leveson, *born* 1949, *apptd* 2013
President of the Family Division and Head of Family Justice (£211,015), Rt. Hon. Sir James Munby, *born* 1948, *apptd* 2013
Chancellor of the High Court (£211,015), Rt. Hon. Sir Terence Etherton, *born* 1951, *apptd* 2013

SENIOR COURTS OF ENGLAND AND WALES
COURT OF APPEAL
Presiding Judge, Criminal Division, Lord Chief Justice of England and Wales
Presiding Judge, Civil Division, Master of the Rolls
Vice-President, Civil Division (£200,661), Rt. Hon. Sir Martin Moore-Bick, *born* 1946, *apptd* 2014
Vice-President, Criminal Division (£200,661), Rt. Hon. Dame Heather Hallett, DBE, *born* 1949, *apptd* 2013

LORD JUSTICES OF APPEAL *as at September 2014* (each £200,661)
Style, The Rt. Hon. Lord/Lady Justice [surname]

Rt. Hon. Sir John Laws, *born* 1945, *apptd* 1999
Rt. Hon. Dame Mary Arden, DBE, *born* 1947, *apptd* 2000
Rt. Hon. Sir Andrew Longmore, *born* 1944, *apptd* 2001
Rt. Hon. Sir Timothy Lloyd, *born* 1946, *apptd* 2005
Rt. Hon. Sir Martin Moore-Bick, *born* 1948, *apptd* 2005
Rt. Hon. Sir Stephen Richards, *born* 1950, *apptd* 2005
Rt. Hon. Dame Heather Hallett, DBE, *born* 1949, *apptd* 2005
Rt. Hon. Sir Colin Rimer, *born* 1944, *apptd* 2007
Rt. Hon. Sir Rupert Jackson, *born* 1948, *apptd* 2008
Rt. Hon. Sir John Goldring, *born* 1944, *apptd* 2008

Rt. Hon. Sir Richard Aikens, *born* 1948, *apptd* 2008
Rt. Hon. Sir Jeremy Sullivan, *born* 1945, *apptd* 2009
Rt. Hon. Sir Patrick Elias, *born* 1947, *apptd* 2009
Rt. Hon. Sir Nicholas Patten, *born* 1950, *apptd* 2009
Rt. Hon. Sir Christopher Pitchford, *born* 1947, *apptd* 2010
Rt. Hon. Dame Jill Black, DBE, *born* 1954, *apptd* 2010
Rt. Hon. Sir Stephen Tomlinson, *born* 1952, *apptd* 2010
Rt. Hon. Sir Peter Gross, *born* 1952, *apptd* 2010
Rt. Hon. Dame Anne Rafferty, DBE, *born* 1950, *apptd* 2011
Rt. Hon. Sir Andrew McFarlane, *born* 1954, *apptd* 2011
Rt. Hon. Sir Nigel Davis, *born* 1951, *apptd* 2011
Rt. Hon. Sir Kim Lewison, *born* 1952, *apptd* 2011
Rt. Hon. Sir David Kitchin, *born* 1955, *apptd* 2011
Rt. Hon. Sir David Lloyd Jones, *born* 1952, *apptd* 2012
Rt. Hon. Sir Colman Treacy, *born* 1949, *apptd* 2012
Rt. Hon. Sir Richard McCombe, *born* 1952, *apptd* 2012
Rt. Hon. Sir Jack Beatson, *born* 1948, *apptd* 2013
Rt. Hon. Dame Elizabeth Gloster, DBE, *born* 1949, *apptd* 2013
Rt. Hon. Sir Ernest Ryder, TD, *born* 1957, *apptd* 2013
Rt. Hon. Sir Nicholas Underhill, *born* 1952, *apptd* 2013
Rt. Hon. Sir Michael Briggs, *born* 1954, *apptd* 2013
Rt. Hon. Sir Christopher Floyd, *born* 1951, *apptd* 2013
Rt. Hon. Sir Adrian Fulford, *born* 1953, *apptd* 2013
Rt. Hon. Dame Julia Macur, DBE, *born* 1957, *apptd* 2013
Rt. Hon. Sir Christopher Clarke, *born* 1947, *apptd* 2013
Rt. Hon. Dame Victoria Sharp, DBE, *born* 1956, *apptd* 2013
Rt. Hon. Sir Geoffrey Vos, *born* 1955, *apptd* 2013
Ex Officio Judges, Lord Chief Justice of England and Wales; Master of the Rolls; President of the Queen's Bench Division; President of the Family Division; Chancellor of the High Court

COURTS-MARTIAL APPEAL COURT
Judges, Lord Chief Justice of England and Wales; Master of the Rolls; Lord Justices of Appeal; Judges of the High Court of Justice

HIGH COURT
CHANCERY DIVISION
Chancellor of the High Court (£211,015), Rt. Hon. Sir Terence Etherton, *born* 1951, *apptd* 2013
Personal Secretary, Elaine Harbert
Legal Secretary, Vannina Ettori
Clerk, Amanda Collins

JUDGES *as at September 2014* (each £176,226)
Style, The Hon. Mr/Mrs Justice [surname]

Hon. Sir Peter Smith, *born* 1952, *apptd* 2002
Hon. Sir David Richards, *born* 1951, *apptd* 2003
Hon. Sir George Mann, *born* 1951, *apptd* 2004
Hon. Sir Nicholas Warren, *born* 1949, *apptd* 2005
Hon. Sir Launcelot Henderson, *born* 1951, *apptd* 2007
Hon. Sir Paul Morgan, *born* 1952, *apptd* 2007
Hon. Sir Alastair Norris, *born* 1950, *apptd* 2007
Hon. Sir Gerald Barling, *born* 1949, *apptd* 2007
Hon. Sir Philip Sales, *born* 1962, *apptd* 2008
Hon. Dame Sonia Proudman, DBE, *born* 1949, *apptd* 2008
Hon. Sir Richard Arnold, *born* 1961, *apptd* 2008
Hon. Sir Peter Roth, *born* 1952, *apptd* 2009
Hon. Sir Guy Newey, *born* 1959, *apptd* 2010
Hon. Sir Robert Hildyard, *born* 1952, *apptd* 2011
Hon. Dame Sarah Asplin, DBE, *born* 1959, *apptd* 2012
Hon. Sir Colin Birss, *born* 1964, *apptd* 2013
Hon. Dame Vivien Rose, DBE, *born* 1960, *apptd* 2013
Hon. Sir Christopher Nugee, *born* 1959, *apptd* 2013

The Chancery Division also includes three specialist courts: the Companies Court, the Patents Court and the Bankruptcy Court.

QUEEN'S BENCH DIVISION
President (£211,015), Rt. Hon. Sir Brian Leveson, *born* 1949, *apptd* 2013
Vice-President (£200,661), Rt. Hon. Sir Nigel Davies, *born* 1951, *apptd* 2014

JUDGES *as at September 2014* (each £176,226)
Style, The Hon. Mr/Mrs Justice [surname]

Hon. Sir Andrew Collins, *born* 1942, *apptd* 1994
Hon. Sir William Charles, *born* 1948, *apptd* 1998
Hon. Sir Michael Burton, *born* 1946, *apptd* 1998
Hon. Sir Andrew Smith, *born* 1947, *apptd* 2000
Hon. Sir Duncan Ouseley, *born* 1950, *apptd* 2000
Hon. Sir John Mitting, *born* 1947, *apptd* 2001
Hon. Sir Jeremy Cooke, *born* 1949, *apptd* 2001
Hon. Sir Richard Field, *born* 1947, *apptd* 2002
Hon. Sir Peregrine Simon, *born* 1950, *apptd* 2002
Hon. Dame Laura Cox, DBE, *born* 1951, *apptd* 2002
Hon. Sir David Bean, *born* 1954, *apptd* 2004
Hon. Sir Alan Wilkie, *born* 1947, *apptd* 2004
Hon. Sir Paul Walker, *born* 1954, *apptd* 2004
Hon. Sir Charles Openshaw, *born* 1947, *apptd* 2005
Hon. Dame Caroline Swift, DBE, *born* 1955, *apptd* 2005
Hon. Sir Brian Langstaff, *born* 1948, *apptd* 2005
Hon. Sir Vivian Ramsey, *born* 1950, *apptd* 2005
Hon. Sir Stephen Irwin, *born* 1953, *apptd* 2006
Hon. Sir Nigel Teare, *born* 1952, *apptd* 2006
Hon. Sir Griffith Williams, *born* 1944, *apptd* 2007
Hon. Sir Wyn Williams, *born* 1951, *apptd* 2007
Hon. Sir Timothy King, *born* 1949, *apptd* 2007
Hon. Sir John Saunders, *born* 1949, *apptd* 2007
Hon. Sir Julian Flaux, *born* 1955, *apptd* 2007
Hon. Sir David Foskett, *born* 1949, *apptd* 2007
Hon. Sir Nicholas Blake, *born* 1949, *apptd* 2007
Hon. Sir Ross Cranston, *born* 1948, *apptd* 2007
Hon. Sir Peter Coulson, *born* 1958, *apptd* 2008
Hon. Sir William Blair, *born* 1950, *apptd* 2008
Hon. Sir Alistair MacDuff, *born* 1945, *apptd* 2008
Hon. Sir Ian Burnett, *born* 1958, *apptd* 2008
Hon. Sir Nigel Sweeney, *born* 1954, *apptd* 2008
Hon. Dame Elizabeth Slade, DBE, *born* 1949, *apptd* 2008
Hon. Sir Nicholas Hamblen, *born* 1957, *apptd* 2008
Hon. Sir Gary Hickinbottom, *born* 1955, *apptd* 2009
Hon. Sir Timothy Holroyde, *born* 1955, *apptd* 2009
Hon. Sir Andrew Nicol, *born* 1951, *apptd* 2009
Hon. Sir Kenneth Parker, *born* 1945, *apptd* 2009
Hon. Sir Antony Edwards-Stuart, *born* 1946, *apptd* 2009
Hon. Dame Nicola Davies, DBE, *born* 1953, *apptd* 2010
Hon. Dame Kathryn Thirlwall, DBE, *born* 1957, *apptd* 2010
Hon. Sir Michael Supperstone, *born* 1950, *apptd* 2010
Hon. Sir Robin Spencer, *born* 1955, *apptd* 2010
Hon. Sir Keith Lindblom, *born* 1956, *apptd* 2010
Hon. Sir Henry Bernard Eder, *born* 1952, *apptd* 2011
Hon. Sir Henry Globe, *born* 1949, *apptd* 2011
Hon. Sir Andrew Popplewell, *born* 1959, *apptd* 2011
Hon. Sir Rabinder Singh, *born* 1964, *apptd* 2011
Hon. Dame Beverley Lang, DBE, *born* 1955, *apptd* 2011
Hon. Sir Charles Haddon-Cave, *born* 1956, *apptd* 2011
Hon. Sir Stephen Males, *born* 1955, *apptd* 2012
Hon. Sir Jeremy Stuart-Smith, *born* 1955, *apptd* 2012
Hon. Sir George Leggatt, *born* 1957, *apptd* 2012
Hon. Sir Mark Turner, *born* 1959, *apptd* 2013
Hon. Sir Jeremy Baker, *born* 1958, *apptd* 2013
Hon. Sir Stephen Stewart, *born* 1953, *apptd* 2013
Hon. Sir Robert Jay, QC, *born* 1959, *apptd* 2013
Hon. Sir James Dingemans, *born* 1964, *apptd* 2013
Hon. Sir Clive Lewis, *born* 1960, *apptd* 2013
Hon. Dame Sue Carr, DBE, *born* 1964, *apptd* 2013

Hon. Sir Stephen Phillips, *born* 1961, *apptd* 2013
Hon. Dame Geraldine Andrews, DBE, *born* 1959, *apptd* 2013
Hon. Dame Frances Patterson, DBE, *born* 1955, *apptd* 2013
Hon. Dame Ingrid Simler, DBE, *born* 1963, *apptd* 2013
Hon. Sir Nicholas Green, QC, *born* 1958, *apptd* 2013
Hon. Sir William Davis, QC, *born* 1954, *apptd* 2014
Hon. Dame Elisabeth Laing, DBE, *born* 1956, *apptd* 2014
Hon. Sir Mark Warby, QC, *born* 1958, *apptd* 2014

The Queen's Bench Division also includes the Divisional Court, the Admiralty Court, Commercial Court and Technology and Construction Court.

FAMILY DIVISION
President (£211,015), Rt. Hon. Sir James Munby, *born* 1948, *apptd* 2013
Secretary, Mrs Sarah Leung
Clerk, George Pitchley

JUDGES *as at September 2014* (each £176,226)
Style, The Hon. Mr/Mrs Justice [surname]

Hon. Sir Edward Holman, *born* 1947, *apptd* 1995
Hon. Dame Mary Hogg, DBE, *born* 1947, *apptd* 1995
Hon. Sir David Bodey, *born* 1947, *apptd* 1999
Hon. Dame Anna Pauffley, DBE, *born* 1956, *apptd* 2003
Hon. Sir Roderic Wood, *born* 1951, *apptd* 2004
Hon. Sir Andrew Moylan, *born* 1953, *apptd* 2007
Hon. Dame Eleanor King, DBE, *born* 1957, *apptd* 2008
Hon. Dame Judith Parker, DBE, *born* 1950, *apptd* 2008
Hon. Sir Jonathan Baker, *born* 1955, *apptd* 2009
Hon. Sir Nicholas Mostyn, *born* 1957, *apptd* 2010
Hon. Sir Peter Arthur Jackson, *born* 1955, *apptd* 2010
Hon. Dame Lucy Theis, DBE, *born* 1960, *apptd* 2010
Hon. Sir Philip Moor, *born* 1959, *apptd* 2011
Hon. Sir Stephen Cobb, *born* 1960, *apptd* 2013
Hon. Sir Michael Keehan, *born* 1960, *apptd* 2013
Hon. Sir Anthony Hayden, *born* 1961, *apptd* 2013
Hon. Dame Alison Russell, DBE, *born* 1958, *apptd* 2014
Hon. Roderick Newton, *born* 1958, *apptd* 2014
Hon. Dame Jennifer Roberts, *born* 1953, *apptd* 2014

DEPARTMENTS AND OFFICES OF THE SENIOR COURTS OF ENGLAND AND WALES
Royal Courts of Justice, London WC2A 2LL
T 020-7947 6000

ADMINISTRATIVE COURT OFFICE
T 020-7947 6655
Judge in charge of the Administrative Court (£176,226), Hon. Sir Duncan Ouseley
Master of the Crown Office, and Queen's Coroner and Attorney (£104,990), M. Egan, QC
Deputy Master of the Crown Office, Mrs L. G. Knapman
Court Manager, Miss A. Lee

ADMIRALTY, COMMERCIAL AND LONDON MERCANTILE COURT
Ground Floor, 7 Rolls Building, Fetter Lane, London EC4A 1NL
T 020-7947 6112
Registrar (£104,990), J. Kay, QC
Admiralty Marshal, M. Parker
Admiralty Court Manager, W. Lusty
Judge in charge of Commercial Court (£176,226), Hon. Sir Jeremy Cooke
Commercial Court Senior Lists Officer, J. Kelly

BANKRUPTCY AND COMPANIES COURT REGISTRY
7 Rolls Building, Fetter Lane, London EC4A 1NL T 020-7947 6294
Chief Registrar (£130,875), S. Baister

Bankruptcy Registrars (£104,990), S. Barber; C. Derrett;
C. Jones
Court Manager, T. Pollen

CENTRAL OFFICE OF THE QUEEN'S BENCH DIVISION
Senior Master and Queen's Remembrancer (£130,875), H. J.
Leslie *(acting)*
Masters of the Queen's Bench Division (£104,990),
J. D. Cooke; R. Eastman; B. J. F. Fontaine; J. K. Kay, QC;
V. McCloud; R. R. Roberts; B. Yoxall
Court Manager, Miss A. Lee

CHANCERY CHAMBERS
T 020-7947 6148
Chief Master (£130,875), M. Marsh
Masters of the Senior Courts (£104,990), T. J. Bowles;
N. W. Bragge; N. S. Price; P. R. Teverson
Court Manager, T. Pollen

COSTS OFFICE
T 020-7947 6423

Senior Costs Judge (£130,875), P. T. Hurst
Masters of the Senior Courts (£104,990), C. D. N. Campbell;
A. Gordon-Saker; P. Haworth; C. Leonard; J. E. O'Hare;
J. Rowley; J. Simons
Court Manager, S. Christou

COURT OF APPEAL CIVIL DIVISION
T 020-7947 6915
Deputy Registrars, Marie Bancroft-Rimer; Sally Meacher
Court Manager, Miss K. Langan

COURT OF APPEAL CRIMINAL DIVISION
T 020-7947 6011
Registrar (£104,990), M. Egan, QC
Deputy Registrar, Mrs L. G. Knapman
Court Manager, Miss C. Brownbill

COURT OF PROTECTION
First Avenue House, 42–49 High Holborn, London WC1V 6NP
T 0300-456 4600
Senior Judge (£130,875), D. Lush
Court Manager, J. Matthews

ELECTION PETITIONS OFFICE
Room E113, Royal Courts of Justice, Strand, London WC2A 2LL
T 020-7947 6877

The office accepts petitions and deals with all matters
relating to the questioning of parliamentary, European
Parliament, local government and parish elections, and with
applications for relief under the 'representation of the people'
legislation.
Prescribed Officer, The Senior Master and Senior Remembrancer
(£129,579), vacant
Chief Clerk, Geraint Evans

EXAMINERS OF THE COURT
Empowered to take examination of witnesses in all divisions
of the High Court.
Examiners, His Hon. M. W. M. Chism; A. G. Dyer;
A. W. Hughes; Mrs G. M. Keene; R. M. Planterose

PRINCIPAL REGISTRY (FAMILY DIVISION)
First Avenue House, 42–49 High Holborn, London WC1V 6NP
T 020-7947 6000
Senior District Judge (£130,875), P. Waller
District Judges (£104,990), Mrs A. Aitken; Ms Y. Gibson;
Mrs L. Gordon-Saker; E. Hess; Ms H. MacGregor;
R. Robinson; C. Simmonds; Ms S. Walker

TECHNOLOGY AND CONSTRUCTION COURT (TCC)
Ground Floor, 7 Rolls Building, Fetter Lane, London EC4A 1NL
T 020-7947 6022
Judge in charge of the TCC (£176,226), Hon. Sir Robert
Akenhead
Court Manager, T. Pollen
List Officer, S. Gibbon

COURT FUNDS OFFICE
Glasgow G58 1AB T 0845-223 8500

The Court Funds Office (CFO), established in 1726,
provides a banking and administration service for the civil
courts throughout England and Wales, including the High
Court.
Head of CFO, Eddie Bloomfield

OFFICIAL SOLICITOR AND PUBLIC TRUSTEE
Victory House, 30–34 Kingsway, London WC2B 6EX

The Official Solicitor and the Public Trustee are independent
statutory office holders. Their office (OSPT) is an arms-
length body of the Ministry of Justice that exists to support
their work. The Official Solicitor provides access to the
justice system to those who are vulnerable by virtue of
minority or lack of mental capacity. The Public Trustee acts
as executor or administrator of estates and as the appointed
trustee of settlements, providing an effective executor and
trustee service of last resort.
Official Solicitor to the Senior Courts, Alistair Pitblado
Public Trustee, Eddie Bloomfield

PROBATE SERVICE
London Probate Department
PRFD, 7th Floor, First Avenue House, 42–49 High Holborn,
London WC1V 6NP T 020-7421 8500
Probate Manager, Ms T. Constantinou

DISTRICT PROBATE REGISTRARS/MANAGERS
Birmingham District Registrar, Miss P. Walbeoff
Brighton District Probate Manager, M. Hussain
Bristol District Registrar, Mrs B. Phillips
Cardiff District (Wales) Registrar, Mrs F. Herdman
Ipswich District Registrar, Miss H. Whitby
Leeds District Probate Manager, Mrs S. Holding
Liverpool District Probate Manager, Mrs D. Shone
Manchester District Registrar, K. Murphy
Newcastle District Registrar, Mrs M. C. Riley
Oxford District Registrar, Mrs F. Herdman
Winchester District Registrar, A. Butler

JUDGE ADVOCATES GENERAL
The Judge Advocate General is the judicial head of the
Service justice system, and the leader of the judges who
preside over trials in the court martial and other Service
courts. The defendants are service personnel from the Royal
Navy, the army and the Royal Air Force, and civilians
accompanying them overseas.

JUDGE ADVOCATE GENERAL OF THE FORCES
9th Floor, Thomas More Building, Royal Courts of Justice, Strand,
London WC2A 2LL T 020-7218 8095
Judge Advocate General (£149,616), His Hon. Judge
Blackett
Vice Judge Advocate General (£123,213), Michael Hunter
Assistant Judge Advocates General (£104,990), J. P. Camp;
M. R. Elsom; R. D. Hill; A. M. Large; A. J. B. McGrigor;
E. Peters
Style, Judge [surname]

HIGH COURT AND CROWN COURT CENTRES

First-tier centres deal with both civil and criminal cases and are served by high court and circuit judges. Second-tier centres deal with criminal cases only and are served by high court and circuit judges. Third-tier centres deal with criminal cases only and are served only by circuit judges.

LONDON REGION
First-tier – None
Second-tier – Central Criminal Court
Third-tier – Blackfriars, Croydon, Harrow, Inner London, Isleworth, Kingston upon Thames, Snaresbrook, Southwark, Wood Green, Woolwich
Delivery Director, Sheila Proudlock, 3rd Floor, Rose Court, 2 Southwark Bridge, London SE1 9HS
Heads of Departments, Martin John *(Civil, Family and Tribunals);* Dave Weston *(Crime London)*

The high court (first-tier) in Greater London sits at the Royal Courts of Justice.

MIDLANDS REGION
First-tier – Birmingham, Lincoln, Nottingham, Stafford, Warwick
Second-tier – Leicester, Northampton, Shrewsbury, Worcester, Wolverhampton
Third-tier – Coventry, Derby, Hereford, Stoke on Trent
Delivery Director, Lucy Garrod, 6th Floor, Temple Court, Bull Street, Birmingham B4 6WF

NORTH-EAST REGION
First-tier – Leeds, Newcastle upon Tyne, Sheffield, Teesside
Second-tier – Bradford, York
Third-tier – Doncaster, Durham, Kingston upon Hull, Great Grimsby
Delivery Director, Mark Swales, 17th Floor, West Riding House, Albion Street, Leeds LS1 5AA **T** 0113-251 1204
Head of Crime (interim), Graham Goldsmith

NORTH-WEST REGION
First-tier – Carlisle, Chester, Liverpool, Manchester (Crown Square), Preston
Third-tier – Barrow in Furness, Bolton, Burnley, Knutsford, Lancaster, Manchester (Minshull Street), Warrington
Delivery Director, Gill Hague, Manchester Civil Justice Centre, 1 Bridge Street West, Manchester M60 1UR **T** 0161-240 5000
Heads of Departments, Sue Brooks *(Regional Support Unit);* Paul McGladrigan *(Crime);* Simon Vowles *(Civil, Family and Tribunals)*

SOUTH-EAST REGION
First-tier – Cambridge, Chelmsford, Lewes, Norwich, Oxford
Second-tier – Guildford, Ipswich, Luton, Maidstone, Reading, St Albans
Third-tier – Aylesbury, Basildon, Canterbury, Chichester, Croydon, King's Lynn, Peterborough, Southend
Delivery Director, Chris Jennings, 9th Floor, 102 Petty France, London SW1H 9AJ **T** 020-3206 0627
Cluster Managers, Philip Densham *(Thames Valley);* Dr Jim Doherty *(Kent);* Yvonne Mckenna-Young *(Cambridgeshire and Essex);* Dave Manning *(Surrey and Sussex);* Ian Miller *(Norfolk and Suffolk);* Mark Stewart *(Bedfordshire and Hertfordshire)*

SOUTH-WEST REGION
First-tier – Bristol, Exeter, Truro, Winchester
Second-tier – Dorchester & Weymouth, Gloucester, Plymouth
Third-tier – Barnstaple, Bournemouth, Newport (IoW), Portsmouth, Salisbury, Southampton, Swindon, Taunton

Delivery Director, Sandra Aston, PO Box 484, Queensway House, Weston-super-Mare, N. Somerset BS23 7BJ **T** 01934 528668

WALES REGION
First-tier – Caernarfon, Cardiff, Merthyr Tydfil, Mold, Swansea
Second-tier – Carmarthen, Newport, Welshpool
Third-tier – Dolgellau, Haverfordwest
Delivery Director, Luigi Strinati, Wales Support Unit, Churchill House, Churchill Way, Cardiff CF10 4HH **T** 029-2067 8311

CIRCUIT JUDGES

Circuit judges are barristers of at least seven years' standing or recorders of at least five years' standing. Circuit judges serve in the county courts and the crown court.
Style, His/Her Hon. Judge [surname]
Senior Presiding Judge, Rt. Hon. Lord Justice Gross
Senior Circuit Judges, each £141,332
Circuit Judges at the Central Criminal Court, London (Old Bailey Judges), each £141,332
Circuit Judges, each £130,875

MIDLAND CIRCUIT
Presiding Judges, Hon. Mr Justice Haddon-Cave; Hon. Mrs Justice Thirlwall

NORTH-EASTERN CIRCUIT
Presiding Judges, Hon. Mr Justice Coulson; Hon. Mr Justice Globe

NORTHERN CIRCUIT
Presiding Judges, Hon. Mr Justice Holroyde; Hon. Mr Justice Turner

SOUTH-EASTERN CIRCUIT
Presiding Judges, Hon. Mr Justice Nicol; Hon. Mr Justice Singh; Hon. Mr Justice Spencer; Hon. Mr Justice Sweeney

WALES CIRCUIT
Presiding Judges, Hon. Mrs Justice Davies; Hon. Mr Justice Wyn Williams

WESTERN CIRCUIT
Presiding Judges, Hon. Mr Justice Burnett; Hon. Mr Justice Teare

DISTRICT JUDGES

District judges, formerly known as registrars of the court, are solicitors of at least seven years' standing and serve in county courts.
District Judges, each £104,990

DISTRICT JUDGES (MAGISTRATES' COURTS)

District judges (magistrates' courts), formerly known as stipendiary magistrates, serve in magistrates courts where they hear criminal cases, youth cases and some civil proceedings. Many also hear family cases in the single family court. Some may be authorised to handle extradition proceedings and terrorist cases. District judges (magistrates' courts) are appointed following competition conducted by the Judicial Appointments Commission.
District Judges (Magistrates' Courts), each £104,990

OFFICE OF THE CHIEF MAGISTRATE
181 Marylebone Road, London NW1 5BR
T 020-3126 3100

The Chief Magistrate (senior district judge) is responsible for hearing many of the sensitive or complex cases – extradition and special jurisdiction cases in particular – in the magistrates' courts. The Chief Magistrate also supports and guides district judges (magistrates' court), and liaises with the senior judiciary and presiding judges on matters pertaining to magistrates' courts.

The Office of the Chief Magistrate provides administrative support to both the Chief Magistrate and to all the district judges sitting at magistrates' courts in England and Wales.
Chief Magistrate, Howard Riddle
Deputy Chief Magistrate, Emma Arbuthnot

CROWN PROSECUTION SERVICE

Rose Court, 2 Southwark Bridge Road, London SE1 9HS
T 020-3357 0000 E enquiries@cps.gsi.gov.uk W www.cps.gov.uk

The Crown Prosecution Service (CPS) is responsible for prosecuting cases investigated by the police in England and Wales, with the exception of cases conducted by the Serious Fraud Office and certain minor offences.

The CPS is headed by the director of public prosecutions (DPP), who works under the superintendence of the attorney-general. The service is divided into 13 areas across England and Wales, with each area led by a chief crown prosecutor.
Director of Public Prosecutions, Alison Saunders, CB
Chief Executive, Peter Lewis
Chief Operating Officer, Jim Brisbane
Principal Legal Adviser, Alison Levitt, QC
Directors, Nick Hunt *(Strategy and Policy);* Helen Kershaw
  (Private Office); Joanne Millington *(Communication);*
  Dale Simon *(Public Accountability and Inclusion);*
  Paul Staff *(Business Information Systems and Finance);*
  Mark Summerfield *(Human Resources)*

CPS AREAS
EAST MIDLANDS, 2 King Edward Court, King Edward Street,
  Nottingham NG1 1EL T 0115-852 3300
  Chief Crown Prosecutor, Steve Chappell
EASTERN, County House, 100 New London Road, Chelmsford,
  Essex CM2 0RG T 01245-455800
  Chief Crown Prosecutor (acting), Frank Ferguson
LONDON, 5th Floor, Rose Court, 2 Southwark Bridge,
  London SE1 9HS T 020-3357 0000
  Chief Crown Prosecutor, Baljit Ubhey, OBE
MERSEY–CHESHIRE, 7th Floor, Royal Liver Building,
  Pier Head, Liverpool L3 1HN T 0151-239 6400
  Chief Crown Prosecutor, Claire Lindley
NORTH EAST, St Ann's Quay, 112 Quayside,
  Newcastle Upon Tyne, NE1 3BD T 0191-260 4200
  Chief Crown Prosecutor, Wendy Williams
NORTH WEST, 1st Floor, Stocklund House, Castle Street,
  Carlisle CA3 8SY T 01228-882900
  Chief Crown Prosecutor, Nazir Afzal, OBE
SOUTH EAST, 29 Union Street, Maidstone, Kent ME14 1PT
  T 01622-356300
  Chief Crown Prosecutor, Jaswant Narwal
SOUTH WEST, 5th Floor, Kite Wing, Temple Quay House,
  2 The Square, Bristol BS1 6PN T 0117-930 2800
  Chief Crown Prosecutor, Barry Hughes
THAMES AND CHILTERN, Eaton Court, 112 Oxford Road,
  Reading, Berks RG1 7LL T 0118-951 3600
  Chief Crown Prosecutor, Adrian Foster
WALES, 20th Floor, Capital Tower, Greyfriars Road, Cardiff
  CF10 3PL T 029-2080 3800
  Chief Crown Prosecutor, Ed Beltrami
WESSEX, 3rd Floor, Black Horse House, 8–10 Leigh Road,
  Eastleigh, Hants SO50 9FH T 02380-673 800
  Chief Crown Prosecutor, Kate Brown
WEST MIDLANDS, Colmore Gate, 2 Colmore Row,
  Birmingham B3 2QA T 0121-262 1300
  Chief Crown Prosecutor, Grace Ononiwu, OBE

YORKSHIRE AND HUMBERSIDE, 27 Park Place,
  Leeds LS1 2SZ T 0113-290 2700
  Chief Crown Prosecutor, Martin Goldman

HER MAJESTY'S COURTS AND TRIBUNALS SERVICE

1st Floor, 102 Petty France, London SW1H 9AJ
W www.justice.gov.uk

Her Majesty's Courts Service and the Tribunals Service merged on 1 April 2011 to form HM Courts and Tribunals Service. It is an agency of the Ministry of Justice, operating as a partnership between the Lord Chancellor, the Lord Chief Justice and the Senior President of Tribunals. It is responsible for administering the criminal, civil and family courts and tribunals in England and Wales and non-devolved tribunals in Scotland and Northern Ireland.
Chief Executive, Peter Handcock, CBE

JUDICIAL APPOINTMENTS COMMISSION

5th Floor, Zone A, 102 Petty France, London SW1H 9AJ
T 020-3334 0123 E jaas@jac.gsi.gov.uk W jjac.judiciary.gov.uk

The Judicial Appointments Commission was established as an independent non-departmental public body in April 2006 by the Constitutional Reform Act 2005. Its role is to select judicial office holders independently of government (a responsibility previously held by the Lord Chancellor) for courts and tribunals in England and Wales, and for some tribunals whose jurisdiction extends to Scotland or Northern Ireland. It has a statutory duty to encourage diversity in the range of persons available for selection and is sponsored by the Ministry of Justice and accountable to parliament through the Lord Chancellor. It is made up of 15 commissioners, including a chair.
Chair, Christopher Stephens
Commissioners, Martin Forde, QC; Debra van Gene;
  Prof. Emily Jackson; Prof. Noel Lloyd, CBE; Rt. Hon.
  Dame Julia Macur, DBE; Alexandra Marks; Katharine
  Rainsford; Lt.-Gen. Sir Andrew Ridgway, KBE, CB;
  Lucy Scott-Moncrieff; District Judge Simmonds;
  Valerie Strachan; Hon. Sir Alan Wilkie
Chief Executive, Nigel Reeder

DIRECTORATE OF JUDICIAL OFFICES

The Judicial Office was established in April 2006 to support the judiciary in discharging its responsibilities under the Constitutional Reform Act 2005. It is led by a chief executive, who reports to the Lord Chief Justice rather than to ministers, and its work is directed by the judiciary rather than by the administration of the day. The Judicial Office incorporates the Judicial College, sponsorship of the Family and Civil Justice Councils, the Office for Judicial Complaints and Office of the Chief Coroner.

CHIEF EXECUTIVE'S OFFICE
T 020-7947 7598
Chief Executive Officer, Jillian Kay

JUDICIAL COMMITTEE OF THE PRIVY COUNCIL

The Judicial Committee of the Privy Council is the final court of appeal for the United Kingdom overseas territories (*see* UK Overseas Territories section), crown dependencies and those independent Commonwealth countries which have retained this avenue of appeal and the sovereign base areas of Akrotiri and Dhekelia in Cyprus. The committee also hears appeals against pastoral schemes under the Pastoral Measure 1983, and deals with appeals from veterinary disciplinary bodies.

Until October 2009, the Judicial Committee of the Privy Council was the final arbiter in disputes as to the legal competence of matters done or proposed by the devolved legislative and executive authorities in Scotland, Wales and Northern Ireland. This is now the responsibility of the UK Supreme Court.

In 2013–14 the Judicial Committee heard a total of 51 appeals and dealt with 60 petitions for special leave to appeal.

The members of the Judicial Committee are the justices of the supreme court, and Privy Counsellors who hold or have held high judicial office in the United Kingdom or in certain designated courts of Commonwealth countries from which appeals are taken to committee.

JUDICIAL COMMITTEE OF THE PRIVY COUNCIL
Parliament Square, London SW1A 2AJ T 020-7960 1500
W www.jcpc.uk
Registrar of the Privy Council, Louise di Mambro
Chief Clerk, Jackie Lindsay

SCOTTISH JUDICATURE

Scotland has a legal system separate from, and differing greatly from, the English legal system in enacted law, judicial procedure and the structure of courts.

In Scotland the system of public prosecution is headed by the Lord Advocate and is independent of the police, who have no say in the decision to prosecute. The Lord Advocate, discharging his functions through the Crown Office in Edinburgh, is responsible for prosecutions in the high court, sheriff courts and justice of the peace courts. Prosecutions in the high court are prepared by the Crown Office and conducted in court by one of the law officers, by an advocate-depute, or by a solicitor advocate. In the inferior courts the decision to prosecute is made and prosecution is preferred by procurators fiscal, who are lawyers and full-time civil servants subject to the directions of the Crown Office. A permanent legally qualified civil servant, known as the crown agent, is responsible for the running of the Crown Office and the organisation of the Procurator Fiscal Service, of which he or she is the head.

Scotland is divided into six sheriffdoms, each with a full-time sheriff principal. The sheriffdoms are further divided into sheriff court districts, each of which has a legally qualified resident sheriff or sheriffs, who are the judges of the court.

In criminal cases sheriffs principal and sheriffs have the same powers; sitting with a jury of 15 members, they may try more serious cases under indictment, or, sitting alone, may try lesser cases under summary procedure. Minor summary offences are dealt with in justice of the peace courts, which replaced district courts formerly operated by local authorities, and presided over by lay justices of the peace (of whom some 500 regularly sit in court) and, in Glasgow only, by stipendiary magistrates. Juvenile offenders (children under 16) may be brought before an informal children's hearing comprising three local lay people. The superior criminal court is the high court of justiciary which is both a trial and an appeal court. Cases on indictment are tried by a high court judge, sitting with a jury of 15, in Edinburgh and on circuit in other towns. Appeals from the lower courts against conviction or sentence are also heard by the high court, which sits as an appeal court only in Edinburgh. There is no further appeal to the UK supreme court in criminal cases.

In civil cases the jurisdiction of the sheriff court extends to most kinds of action. Appeals against decisions of the sheriff may be made to the sheriff principal and thence to the court of session, or direct to the court of session, which sits only in Edinburgh. The court of session is divided into the inner and the outer house. The outer house is a court of first instance in which cases are heard by judges sitting singly, sometimes with a jury of 12. The inner house, itself subdivided into two divisions of equal status, is mainly an appeal court. Appeals may be made to the inner house from the outer house as well as from the sheriff court. An appeal may be made from the inner house to the UK supreme court.

The judges of the court of session are the same as those of the high court of justiciary, with the Lord President of the court of session also holding the office of Lord Justice General in the high court. Senators of the College of Justice are Lords Commissioners of Justiciary as well as judges of the court of session. On appointment, a senator takes a judicial title, which is retained for life. Although styled The Hon./ Rt. Hon. Lord, the senator is not a peer, although some judges are peers in their own right.

The office of coroner does not exist in Scotland. The local procurator fiscal inquires privately into sudden or suspicious deaths and may report findings to the crown agent. In some cases a fatal accident inquiry may be held before the sheriff.

COURT OF SESSION AND HIGH COURT OF JUSTICIARY
The Lord President and Lord Justice General (£218,470),
Rt. Hon. Lord Gill, *born* 1942, *apptd* 2012
Private Secretary, P. Gilmour

INNER HOUSE
Lords of Session (each £200,661)

FIRST DIVISION
The Lord President

Rt. Hon. Lord Eassie (Ronald Mackay), *born* 1945, *apptd* 2006
Rt. Hon. Lord Menzies (Duncan Menzies), *born* 1953, *apptd* 2012
Rt. Hon. Lady Smith (Anne Smith), *born* 1955, *apptd* 2012
Rt. Hon. Lord Brodie (Philip Brodie), *born* 1950, *apptd* 2012
Rt. Hon. Lady Clark of Calton (Lynda Clark), *born* 1949, *apptd* 2013

SECOND DIVISION
Lord Justice Clerk (£211,015), Rt. Hon. Lord Carloway, *born* 1954, *apptd* 2012
Rt. Hon. Lady Paton (Ann Paton), *born* 1952, *apptd* 2007
Rt. Hon. Lady Dorrian (Leona Dorrian), *born* 1957, *apptd* 2012
Rt. Hon. Lord Bracadale (Alistair Campbell), *born* 1949, *apptd* 2013
Rt. Hon. Lord Drummond Young (James Drummond Young), *born* 1950, *apptd* 2001

OUTER HOUSE
Lords of Session (each £176,226)
Hon. Lord Glennie (Angus Glennie), *born* 1950, *apptd* 2005
Hon. Lord Kinclaven (Alexander F. Wylie), *born* 1951, *apptd* 2005
Hon. Lord Turnbull (Alan Turnbull), *born* 1958, *apptd* 2006
Hon. Lord Brailsford (Sidney Brailsford), *born* 1954, *apptd* 2006
Hon. Lord Uist (Roderick Macdonald), *born* 1951, *apptd* 2006

Hon. Lord Malcolm (Colin M. Campbell), *born* 1953,
    apptd 2007
Hon. Lord Matthews (Hugh Matthews), *born* 1953, *apptd*
    2007
Hon. Lord Woolman (Stephen Woolman), *born* 1953,
    apptd 2008
Hon. Lord Pentland (Paul Cullen), *born* 1957, *apptd* 2008
Hon. Lord Bannatyne (Iain Peebles), *born* 1954, *apptd* 2008
Hon. Lady Stacey (Valerie E. Stacey), *born* 1954,
    apptd 2009
Hon. Lord Tyre (Colin Tyre), *born* 1956, *apptd* 2010
Hon. Lord Doherty (Raymond Doherty), *born* 1958,
    apptd 2010
Hon. Lord Stewart (Angus Stewart), *born* 1946, *apptd* 2010
Rt. Hon. Lord Boyd of Duncansby (Colin Boyd), *born* 1953,
    apptd 2012
Hon. Lord Jones (Michael Jones), *born* 1948, *apptd* 2012
Hon. Lord Burns (David Burns), *born* 1952, *apptd* 2012
Hon. Lady Scott (Margaret Scott), *born* 1960, *apptd* 2012
Hon. Lady Wise (Morag Wise), *born* 1963, *apptd* 2013
Hon. Lord Armstrong (Iain Armstrong), *born* 1956,
    apptd 2013
Hon. Lady Rae (Rita Rae), *born* 1950, *apptd* 2014
Hon. Lady Wolffe (Sarah Wolffe), *apptd* 2014

COURT OF SESSION AND HIGH COURT OF JUSTICIARY
Parliament House, Parliament Square, Edinburgh EH1 1RQ
T 0131-225 2595
Principal Clerk of Session and Justiciary, G. Marwick
Deputy Principal Clerk of Session and Principal Extractor,
    G. Prentice
Deputy Principal Clerk of Justiciary, J. Moyes
Depute in Charge of Offices of Court, Y. Anderson
Officer in Charge of Justiciary Office, Roddy MacPherson
Keeper of the Rolls, G. Combe
Depute Clerks, D. Cullen; A. Hutchison; C. Reid
Appeal Manager, A. Mackay
Clerking Service Manager, D. MacLeod
Depute Clerks of Session and Justiciary, L. Alexander; N. Boyle;
    R. Broome; G. Burton; Z. Conway; L. Curran; H. Fraser;
    A. Galloway; K. Keir; T. Kell; A. Lynch; N. Marchant;
    R. Martin; M. McGrane; G. McLeod; L. McNamara;
    L. Morgan; D. Morrison; C. Munn; K. Neal; R. Newlands;
    K. O'Hare; C. Scott; G. Scott; L. Sexto; C. Stark; P. Weir

JUDICIAL APPOINTMENTS BOARD FOR SCOTLAND
38–39 Drumsheugh Gardens, Edinburgh EH3 7SW
T 0131-528 5101 W www.judicialappointmentsscotland.org.uk

The board's remit is to provide the first minister with the
names of candidates recommended for appointment to the
posts of senator of the college of justice, chair of the Scottish
Land Court, sheriff principal, sheriff and part-time sheriff.
Chair, Sir Muir Russell, KCB, FRSE

JUDICIAL OFFICE FOR SCOTLAND
Parliament House, Edinburgh EH1 1RQ
T 0131-240 6677 W www.scotland-judiciary.org.uk

The Judicial Office for Scotland came into being on 1 April
2010 as part of the changes introduced by the Judiciary and
Courts (Scotland) Act 2008. It provides support for the Lord
President in his role as head of the Scottish judiciary with
responsibility for the training, welfare, deployment and
conduct of judges and the efficient disposal of business in the
courts.
Executive Director, Steve Humphreys

SCOTTISH COURT SERVICE
Saughton House, Broomhouse Drive, Edinburgh EH11 3XD
T 0131-444 3300 W www.scotcourts.gov.uk

The Scottish Court Service is responsible for the provision of
staff, buildings and technology to support Scotland's courts,
the independent judiciary, the courts' Rules Councils and the
Office of the Public Guardian. On 1 April 2010 it was
established by the Judiciary and Courts (Scotland) Act 2008
as an independent body, governed by a corporate board and
chaired by the Lord President.
Chief Executive, Eric McQueen

SCOTTISH GOVERNMENT JUSTICE DIRECTORATE
Legal System Division, Room 2W, St Andrew's House, Edinburgh
EH1 3DG
T 0131-556 8400

The Justice Directorate is responsible for the appointment of
judges and sheriffs to meet the needs of the business of the
supreme and sheriffs court in Scotland. It is also responsible
for providing resources for the efficient administration of
certain specialist courts and tribunals.
Deputy Director, Bridget Campbell

SCOTTISH LAND COURT
126 George Street, Edinburgh EH2 4HH
T 0131-271 4360

The court deals with disputes relating to agricultural and
crofting land in Scotland.
Chair (£141,332), Hon. Lord McGhie (James McGhie), QC
Deputy Chair, R. J. Macleod
Members, D. J. Houston; A. Macdonald *(part-time)*; J. A. Smith
    (part-time)
Principal Clerk, Barbara Brown

SHERIFF COURT OF CHANCERY
27 Chambers Street, Edinburgh EH1 1LB
T 0131-225 2525

The court deals with service of heirs and completion of title
in relation to heritable property.
Sheriff of Chancery, M. Stephen

SHERIFF COURTS
The majority of cases in Scotland are handled by one of the
49 sheriff courts. Criminal cases are heard by a sheriff and a
jury (solemn procedure) but can be heard by a sheriff alone
(summary procedure). Civil cases are heard by a single sheriff.
    Scotland is split into six sheriffdoms, each headed by a
sheriff principal.

SALARIES
Sheriff Principal, £141,332
Sheriff, £130,875

SHERIFFDOMS
GLASGOW AND STRATHKELVIN
    Sheriff Principal, C. A. L. Scott
GRAMPIAN, HIGHLAND AND ISLANDS
    Sheriff Principal, D. Pyle
LOTHIAN AND BORDERS
    Sheriff Principal, M. M. Stephen
NORTH STRATHCLYDE
    Sheriff Principal, D. Murray
SOUTH STRATHCLYDE, DUMFRIES AND GALLOWAY
    Sheriff Principal, B. A. Lockhart
TAYSIDE, CENTRAL AND FIFE
    Sheriff Principal, R. A. Dunlop, QC

JUSTICE OF THE PEACE COURTS

Justice of the peace courts replaced district courts and are a unique feature of Scotland's judicial system. Justices of the peace are lay magistrates who either sit alone, or in a bench of three, and deal with summary crimes such as speeding and careless driving. In court, justices have access to solicitors, who fulfill the role of legal advisers or clerks of court.

A justice of the peace court can be presided over by a stipendiary magistrate – a legally qualified solicitor or advocate who sits alone. They deal with more serious summary business similar to sheriffs, such as drink driving and assault. All sheriffs principal have powers to appoint stipendiary magistrates, but at present they have only been appointed in the justice of the peace court in the Sheriffdom of Glasgow and Strathkelvin.

CROWN OFFICE AND PROCURATOR FISCAL SERVICE

CROWN OFFICE
25 Chambers Street, Edinburgh EH1 1LA
T 0844-561 1020 W www.crownoffice.gov.uk
Chief Executive and Crown Agent, Catherine Dyer

PROCURATORS FISCAL

PAY BAND SALARY SCALE: £75,000–£162,500

NORTH FEDERATION
  Area Procurator Fiscal, Liam Murphy
EAST FEDERATION
  Area Procurator Fiscal, John Dunn
WEST FEDERATION
  Area Procurator Fiscal, David Harvie
NATIONAL FEDERATION
  Director of Serious Casework, John Logue

COURT OF THE LORD LYON

HM New Register House, Edinburgh EH1 3YT
T 0131-556 7255 W www.lyon-court.com

The Court of the Lord Lyon is the Scottish Court of Chivalry (including the genealogical jurisdiction of the *Ri-Sennachie* of Scotland's Celtic kings). The Lord Lyon King of Arms has jurisdiction, subject to appeal to the Court of Session and the House of Lords, in questions of heraldry and the right to bear arms. The court also administers the Public Register of All Arms and Bearings and the Public Register of All Genealogies in Scotland. Pedigrees are established by decrees of Lyon Court and by letters patent. As Royal Commissioner in Armory, the Lord Lyon grants patents of arms to virtuous and well-deserving Scots and to petitioners (personal or corporate) in the Queen's overseas realms of Scottish connection, and also issues birthbrieves. For information on Her Majesty's Officers of Arms in Scotland, *see* the Court of the Lord Lyon in the Public Bodies section.
Lord Lyon King of Arms, Dr Joseph J. Morrow
Lyon Clerk and Keeper of the Records, Mrs C. G. W. Roads, LVO, FSA SCOT, FSA
Procurator Fiscal, Alexander M. S. Green
Macer, Roderick Macpherson

NORTHERN IRELAND JUDICATURE

In Northern Ireland the legal system and the structure of courts closely resemble those of England and Wales; there are, however, often differences in enacted law.

The court of judicature of Northern Ireland comprises the court of appeal, the high court of justice and the crown court. The practice and procedure of these courts is similar to that in England. The superior civil court is the high court of

justice, from which an appeal lies to the Northern Ireland court of appeal; the UK supreme court is the final civil appeal court.

The crown court, served by high court and county court judges, deals with criminal trials on indictment. Cases are heard before a judge and, except those certified by the Director of Public Prosecutions under the Justice and Security Act 2007, a jury. Appeals from the crown court against conviction or sentence are heard by the Northern Ireland court of appeal; the UK supreme court is the final court of appeal.

The decision to prosecute in criminal cases in Northern Ireland rests with the Director of Public Prosecutions.

Minor criminal offences are dealt with in magistrates' courts by a legally qualified district judge (magistrates' courts) and, where an offender is under the age of 18, by youth courts each consisting of a district judge (magistrates' courts) and two lay magistrates (at least one of whom must be a woman). As at 1 June 2014 there were 174 lay magistrates in Northern Ireland. Appeals from magistrates' courts are heard by the county court, or by the court of appeal on a point of law or an issue as to jurisdiction.

Magistrates' courts in Northern Ireland can deal with certain classes of civil case but most minor civil cases are dealt with in county courts. Judgments of all civil courts are enforceable through a centralised procedure administered by the Enforcement of Judgments Office.

COURT OF JUDICATURE

The Royal Courts of Justice, Chichester Street, Belfast BT1 3JF
T 0300-200 7812
Lord Chief Justice of Northern Ireland (£218,470),
  Rt. Hon. Sir Declan Morgan, *born* 1952, *apptd* 2009
Principal Private Secretary, Laurene McAlpine

LORDS JUSTICES OF APPEAL (£200,661)
Style, The Rt. Hon. Lord Justice [surname]

Rt. Hon. Sir Paul Girvan, *born* 1948, *apptd* 2007
Rt. Hon. Sir Patrick Coghlin, *born* 1945, *apptd* 2008
Rt. Hon. Sir John Gillen, *born* 1947, *apptd* 2014

HIGH COURT JUDGES (£176,226)
Style, The Hon. Mr Justice [surname]

Hon. Sir John Gillen, *born* 1947, *apptd* 1999
Hon. Sir Ronald Weatherup, *born* 1947, *apptd* 2001
Hon. Sir Reginald Weir, *born* 1947, *apptd* 2003
Hon. Sir Donnell Deeny, *born* 1950, *apptd* 2004
Hon. Sir Benjamin Stephens, *born* 1954, *apptd* 2007
Hon. Sir Seamus Treacy, *born* 1956, *apptd* 2007
Hon. Sir Bernard McCloskey, *born* 1956, *apptd* 2008
Hon. Sir Paul Maguire, *born* 1952, *apptd* 2012
Hon. Sir Mark Horner, *born* 1956, *apptd* 2012
Hon. Sir John O'Hara, *born* 1956, *apptd* 2013
*Hon. Sir Thomas Burgess, *born* 1943, *apptd* 2012

* Temporary appointment

MASTERS OF THE HIGH COURT (£104,990)
Master, Queen's Bench and Appeals, C. J. McCorry
Master, Office of Care and Protection, H. Wells
Master, Chancery and Probate, I. Haaarastaff
Master, Matrimonial, C. W. G. Redpath
Master, Queen's Bench and Matrimonial, E. Bell
Master, Taxing Office, A. Wells
Master, Bankruptcy, F. Kelly

OFFICIAL SOLICITOR
Official Solicitor to the Court of Judicature, Miss B. M. Donnelly

COUNTY COURTS

JUDGES (£130,875†)
Style, His/Her Hon. Judge [surname]

Judge Babington; Judge Devlin; Judge Finnegan, QC; Judge Fowler, QC; Judge Grant; Judge Kerr, QC; Judge Kinney; Judge Lynch, QC; Judge McColgan; Judge McFarland; Judge McReynolds, Judge Marrinan, Judge Miller, QC; Judge Philpott, QC; Judge Ramsay; Judge Sherrard; Judge Smyth

† County court judges are paid £141,332 so long as they are required to carry out significantly different work from their counterparts elsewhere in the UK

RECORDERS
Belfast (£152,639), Judge McFarland
Londonderry (£141,332), Judge Babington

DISTRICT JUDGES (£104,990)
Only barristers and solicitors with ten years' standing are eligible to become district judges. There are four district judges in Northern Ireland.

MAGISTRATES' COURTS

DISTRICT JUDGES (MAGISTRATES' COURTS)
(£104,990)
There are 21 district judges (magistrates' courts) in Northern Ireland.

NORTHERN IRELAND COURTS AND TRIBUNALS SERVICE
23–27 Oxford Street, Belfast BT1 3LA
T 0300-200 7812 W www.courtsni.gov.uk
Chief Executive, J. Durkin

CROWN SOLICITOR'S OFFICE
Royal Courts of Justice, Chichester Street, Belfast BT1 3JE
T 028-9054 2555
Crown Solicitor, J. Conn

PUBLIC PROSECUTION SERVICE
93 Chichester Street, Belfast BT1 3JR
T 028-9054 2444 W www.ppsni.gov.uk
Director of Public Prosecutions, Barra McGrory, QC

TRIBUNALS

Information on all the tribunals listed here, with the exception of the independent tribunals and the tribunals based in Scotland, Wales and Northern Ireland, can be found on the Ministry of Justice website (W www.justice.gov.uk/tribunals).

HM COURTS AND TRIBUNALS SERVICE

102 Petty France, London SW1H 9AJ
W www.justice.gov.uk
W https://courttribunalfinder.service.gov.uk

HM Courts Service and the Tribunals Service merged on 1 April 2011 to form HM Courts and Tribunals Service, an integrated agency providing support for the administration of justice in courts and tribunals. It is an agency within the Ministry of Justice, operating as a partnership between the Lord Chancellor, the Lord Chief Justice and the Senior President of Tribunals. It is responsible for the administration of the criminal, civil and family courts and tribunals in England and Wales and non-devolved tribunals in Scotland and Northern Ireland. The agency's work is overseen by a board headed by an independent chair working with non-executive, executive and judicial members.

A two-tier tribunal system, comprising the First-tier Tribunal and Upper Tribunal, was established on 3 November 2008 as a result of radical reform under the Tribunals, Courts and Enforcement Act 2007. Both of these tiers are split into a number of separate chambers. These chambers group together individual tribunals (also known as 'jurisdictions') which deal with similar work or require similar skills. Cases start in the First-tier Tribunal and there is a right of appeal to the Upper Tribunal. Some tribunals transferred to the new two-tier system immediately, with more transferring between 2009 and 2011. The exception is employment tribunals, which remain outside this structure. The Act also allowed legally qualified tribunal chairs and adjudicators to swear the judicial oath and become judges.
Senior President, Rt. Hon. Sir Jeremy Sullivan
Chief Executive, Peter Handcock, CBE

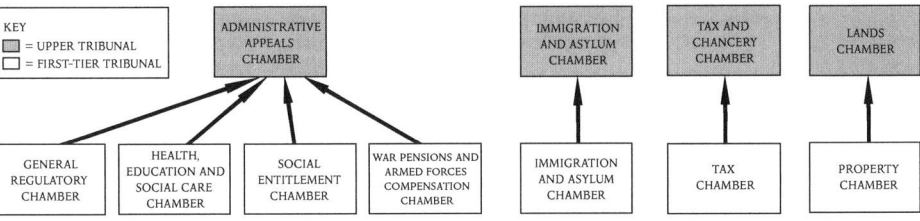

FIRST-TIER TRIBUNAL

The main function of the First-tier Tribunal is to hear appeals by citizens against decisions of the government. In most cases appeals are heard by a panel made up of one judge and two specialists in their relevant field, known as 'members'. Both judges and members are appointed through the Independent Judicial Appointments Commission. Most of the tribunals administered by central government are part of the First-tier Tribunal, which is split into seven separate chambers.

GENERAL REGULATORY CHAMBER

For all jurisdictions except Transport: General Regulatory Chamber, HMCTS, PO Box 9300, Leicester LE1 8DJ
T 0300-123 4504 E grc@hmcts.gsi.gov.uk
Immigration Services imset@hmcts.gsi.gov.uk
For First-tier Tribunal (Transport): 5th Floor Rolls Building, 7 Rolls Building, Fetter Lane, London EC4A 1NL
T 020-7947 7422 E transport@hmcts.gsi.gov.uk
Chamber President, Judge Warren*
Judicial Leads, Judge Brodrick (Transport); Judge Alison McKenna (Charity); His Hon. Judge Wulwik (Estate Agents)

* Acts as judicial lead for all jurisdictions with the exception of the ones specified above

CHARITY
Under the Charities Act 2011 (only applicable to England and Wales), First-tier Tribunal (Charity) hears appeals against the decisions of the Charity Commission, applications for the review of decisions made by the Charity Commission and considers references from the Attorney-General or the Charity Commission on points of law.

CLAIMS MANAGEMENT SERVICES
Under the Compensation Act 2006, Claims Management Services hears appeals pertaining to decisions made by the claims regulator in relation to personal injury; criminal injuries compensation; employment matters; housing disrepair; financial products and services; and industrial injury disablement benefits.

COMMUNITY RIGHT TO BID
The Community Right to Bid jurisdiction of the General Regulatory Chamber was established in January 2013 and currently hears appeals against review decisions made by local authorities under the Localism Act 2011.

ELECTRONIC COMMUNICATIONS AND POSTAL SERVICES
Hears appeals against decisions made by the Interception of Communications Commissioner under the Regulation of Investigatory Powers (Monetary Penalty Notices and Consents for Interceptions) Regulations 2011.

ENVIRONMENT
First-tier Tribunal (Environment) was created to decide appeals regarding civil sanctions made by environmental regulators. Established in April 2010, the jurisdiction of the tribunal extends to England and Wales.

ESTATE AGENTS
First-tier Tribunal (Estate Agents) hears appeals, under the Estate Agents Act 1979, against decisions made by the Office of Fair Trading pertaining to orders prohibiting a person from being employed as an estate agent when that person has been, for example, convicted of fraud or another offence

involving dishonesty. The tribunal also hears appeals relating to decisions refusing to revoke or vary a prohibition order or warning order, as well as appeals regarding the issuing of a warning order when a person has not fulfilled their obligations under the Act.

EXAM BOARD

Under the Education Act 1997 regulated awarding organisations can appeal to the Exam Board tribunal if they disagree with a decision by OFQUAL or the Welsh government to impose a fine, the amount of the fine, or to recover the costs of taking enforcement action. The board is an independent tribunal and hears appeals across England and Wales.

FOOD

The food jurisdiction of the General Regulatory Chamber was established in January 2013 and hears appeals against some of the decisions taken by the Food Standards Agency, Department for Environment, Food and Rural Affairs and local authority trading standards departments. It also deals with appeals against decisions under the Fish Labelling (England) Regulations.

GAMBLING

First-tier Tribunal (Gambling) hears and decides appeals against decisions made by the Gambling Commission under the Gambling Act 2005.

IMMIGRATION SERVICES

First-tier Tribunal (Immigration Services) is an independent judicial body established in 2000. It hears appeals against decisions made by the Office of the Immigration Services Commissioner and considers disciplinary charges brought against immigration advisers by the Commissioner. The tribunal does not deal with immigration and asylum cases.

INFORMATION RIGHTS

First-tier Tribunal (Information Rights) determines appeals against notices issued by the Information Commissioner under the Freedom of Information Act 2000 and other regulations.

When a minister of the crown issues a certificate on the grounds of national security, the appeal must be transferred to the Administrative Appeals Chamber of the Upper Tribunal on receipt.

PENSIONS

First-tier Tribunal (Pensions) hears appeals against decisions made by the Pensions Regulator under section 44 of the Pensions Act 2008. Appeals under section 102 of the Act are heard by the Tax and Chancery Chamber of the Upper Tribunal.

PROFESSIONAL REGULATION

The professional regulation jurisdiction, which replaced the Alternative Business Structures jurisdiction in 2013, was created to deal with appeals made against decisions of professional regulatory bodies. Currently it hears appeals made by the Council for Licensed Conveyancers under the Legal Services Act 2007.

TRANSPORT

First-tier Tribunal (Transport) hears appeals against decisions of the Registrar of Approved Driving Instructors, hears and decides appeals for London service permits against decisions made by Transport for London and is able to resolve disputes over postal charges under the Postal Services Act 2000. Its jurisdiction covers England, Scotland and Wales.

HEALTH, EDUCATION AND SOCIAL CARE CHAMBER

Chamber President, His Hon. Judge Sycamore
Judicial Leads, Judge Aitken (Care Standards, Primary Health Lists, Special Educational Needs and Disability); Judge Hinchliffe (Mental Health)

CARE STANDARDS

Mowden Hall, Staindrop Road, Darlington, Co. Durham DL3 9BG
T 01325-392712 E cst@hmcts.gsi.gov.uk
First-tier Tribunal (Care Standards) was established under the Protection of Children Act 1999 and considers appeals in relation to decisions made about the inclusion of individuals' names on the list of those considered unsuitable to work with children or vulnerable adults, restrictions from teaching and employment in schools/further education institutions, and the registration of independent schools. It also deals with general registration decisions made about care homes, children's homes, childcare providers, nurses' agencies, social workers, residential family centres, independent hospitals and fostering agencies.

MENTAL HEALTH

Secretariat: PO Box 8793, 5th Floor, Leicester LE1 8BN
T 0300-123 2201 E mhrtenquiries@hmcts.gsi.gov.uk
The First-tier Tribunal (Mental Health) hears applications and references for people detained under the Mental Health Act 1983 (as amended by the Mental Health Act 2007). There are separate mental health tribunals for Wales and Scotland.

PRIMARY HEALTH LISTS

Mowden Hall, Staindrop Road, Darlington, Co. Durham DL3 9BG
T 01325-391130
First-tier Tribunal (Primary Health Lists) took over the role of the Family Health Services Appeal Authority on 18 January 2010. The tribunal is independent of the Department of Health and considers appeals resulting from decisions made by the NHS regarding occupations such as GPs, dentists, optometrists and some pharmacists.

SPECIAL EDUCATIONAL NEEDS AND DISABILITY

Ground Floor, Mowden Hall, Staindrop Road, Darlington,
Co. Durham DL3 9BG
T 01325-392760 E sendistqueries@hmcts.gsi.gov.uk
First-tier Tribunal (Special Educational Needs and Disability) considers parents' appeals against the decisions of local authorities about children's special educational needs if parents cannot reach agreement with the local authority. It also considers claims of disability discrimination in schools.

IMMIGRATION AND ASYLUM CHAMBER

Chamber President, Judge Clements
PO Box 6987, Leicester LE11 2XZ
T 0300-123 1711 E customer.service@hmcts.gsi.gov.uk
The Immigration and Asylum Chamber replaced the Asylum and Immigration Tribunal in February 2010. It is an independent tribunal dealing with appeals against decisions made by the Home Secretary and their officials concerning immigration, asylum and nationality matters.

PROPERTY CHAMBER

Chamber President, Judge McGrath
10 Alfred Place, London WC1E 7LR
T 020-7446 7700 E rplondon@hmcts.gsi.gov.uk
The First-tier Tribunal (Property Chamber) Residential Property serves the private-rented and leasehold property market in England by resolving disputes between leaseholders, tenants and landlords.

SOCIAL ENTITLEMENT CHAMBER
Chamber President, His Hon. Judge Martin
Judicial Leads, His Hon. Judge Martin (Social Security and Child Support); Sehba Storey (Asylum Support); Tony Summers (Criminal Injuries Compensation)

ASYLUM SUPPORT
2nd Floor, Anchorage House, 2 Clove Crescent, London E14 2BE
T 020-7538 6171
First-tier Tribunal (Asylum Support) deals with appeals against decisions made by the Home Office. The Home Office decides whether asylum seekers, failed asylum seekers and/or their dependants are entitled to support and accommodation on the grounds of destitution, as provided by the Immigration and Asylum Act 1999. The tribunal can only consider appeals against a refusal or termination of support. It can, if appropriate, require the Secretary of State for the Home Department to reconsider the original decision, substitute the original decision with the tribunal's own decision or dismiss the appeal.

CRIMINAL INJURIES COMPENSATION
Head Office, Wellington House, 134–136 Wellington Street, Glasgow G2 2XL T 0141-354 8555
E enquiries-cicap@tribunals.gsi.gov.uk
Judicial Review Enquiries, 5th Floor, Field House, 15–25 Breams Buildings, London EC4A 1DZ T 020-7073 4124
First-tier Tribunal (Criminal Injuries Compensation) determines appeals against review decisions made by the Criminal Injuries Compensation Authority on applications for compensation made by victims of violent crime. It only considers appeals on claims made on or after 1 April 1996 under the Criminal Injuries Compensation Scheme.

SOCIAL SECURITY AND CHILD SUPPORT
Administrative Support Centre, PO Box 14620, Birmingham B16 6FR T 0300-123 1142
First-tier Tribunal (Social Security and Child Support) arranges and hears appeals on a range of decisions made by the Department for Work and Pensions, HM Revenue and Customs, and local authorities. Appeals considered include those concerned with income support, jobseeker's allowance, child support, tax credits, retirement pensions, housing benefit, council tax benefit, personal independence payment, vaccine damage and compensation recovery.
The tribunal also contains an executive agency responsible for the administration of appeals, headed by the chief executive of HM Courts and Tribunals Service.

TAX CHAMBER
Chamber President, Judge Bishopp

MP EXPENSES
3rd Floor, Temple Court, 35 Bull Street, Birmingham B4 6EQ
T 0845-223 8080 E taxappeals@tribunals.gsi.gov.uk
First-tier Tribunal (MP Expenses) hears appeals against certain decisions made by the Compliance Officer, an independent office holder appointed by the Independent Parliamentary Standards Authority, the organisation responsible for determining and paying MP expenses. Appeals can be made by current or former MPs under the Parliamentary Standards Act 2009. The jurisdiction is UK-wide.

TAX
3rd Floor, Temple Court, 35 Bull Street, Birmingham B4 6EQ
T 0845-223 8080 E taxappeals@tribunals.gsi.gov.uk
First-tier Tribunal (Tax) hears most appeals against decisions of HM Revenue and Customs in relation to income tax, corporation tax, capital gains tax, inheritance tax, stamp duty land tax, national insurance contributions and VAT or duties. Appeals can be made by individuals or organisations, single taxpayers or large multinational companies. The jurisdiction is UK-wide.

WAR PENSIONS AND ARMED FORCES COMPENSATION CHAMBER
Acting Chamber President, Judge Horrocks
5th Floor, Fox Court, 14 Gray's Inn Road, London WC1X 8HN
T 020-3206 0701 E armedforces.chamber@hmcts.gsi.gov.uk
The War Pensions and Armed Forces Compensation Chamber of the First-tier Tribunal is the successor to the Pensions Appeal Tribunal which has existed in different forms since the War Pensions Act 1919. The tribunal hears appeals brought by ex-servicemen and women against decisions of the Secretary of State for Defence under the war pensions legislation for injuries sustained before 5 April 2005, and under the armed forces compensation scheme for injuries after that date. Under the war pensions legislation, the tribunal decides on entitlement to a war pension, the degree of disablement and entitlement to certain allowances (eg for mobility needs). Under the armed forces compensation scheme, the tribunal decides both the entitlement to an award and the tariff level of the award. The tribunal's jurisdiction covers England and Wales.

UPPER TRIBUNAL

Comprising four separate chambers, the Upper Tribunal deals mostly with appeals from, and enforcement of, decisions taken by the First-tier Tribunal, but it also handles some cases that do not go through the First-tier Tribunal. Additionally, it has assumed some of the supervisory powers of the courts to deal with the actions of tribunals, government departments and some other public authorities. All the decision-makers of the Upper Tribunal are judges or expert members sitting in a panel chaired by a judge, and are specialists in the areas of law they handle. Over time their decisions are expected to build comprehensive case law for each area covered by the tribunals.

ADMINISTRATIVE APPEALS CHAMBER
Chamber President, Hon. Sir Arthur Charles
5th Floor, 7 Rolls Buildings, Fetter Lane, London EC4A 1NL
T 020-7071 5662 E adminappeals@hmcts.gsi.gov.uk
The Administrative Appeals Chamber considers appeals against most of the decisions of the following First-tier chambers: Social Entitlement; Health, Education and Social Care; General Regulatory; and War Pensions and Armed Forces Compensation. It also considers appeals against decisions of the Independent Safeguarding Authority (England and Wales), Traffic Commissioners (England, Wales and Scotland) and appeals from decisions of a number of independent tribunals in Northern Ireland, Scotland and Wales. Its judges also decide Forfeiture Act references (England, Wales and Scotland).
For England and Wales, the Administrative Appeals Chamber considers applications for judicial review of the First-tier Tribunal in certain cases.

IMMIGRATION AND ASYLUM CHAMBER
Chamber President, Hon. Sir Nicholas Blake
PO Box 6987, Leicester LE1 6ZX
T 0845-600 0877 E customer.service@hmcts.gsi.gov.uk
The Immigration and Asylum Chamber was created on 15 February 2010. It hears appeals against decisions made by the Immigration and Asylum Chamber in the First-tier Tribunal in matters of immigration, asylum and nationality.

LANDS CHAMBER

Chamber President, Hon. Sir Keith Lindblom
45 Bedford Square, London WC1B 3AS
T 020 7612 9710 E lands@hmcts.gsi.gov.uk
W www.justice.gov.uk/tribunals/lands

The Lands Chamber determines questions relating to the valuation of land, rating appeals from valuation tribunals, appeals from the First-tier (Property Chamber), applications to discharge or modify restrictions on the use of land, and compulsory purchase compensation. The tribunal may also arbitrate under a reference by consent.

TAX AND CHANCERY CHAMBER

Chamber President, Hon. Sir Nicholas Warren
45 Bedford Square, London WC1B 3DN
T 020-7612 9700 E financeandtaxappeals@tribunals.gsi.gov.uk

The Tax and Chancery Chamber decides applications for permission to appeal and appeals on point of law from decisions of the First-tier Tribunal in tax or charity cases. The jurisdiction of the former Financial Services and Markets tribunal transferred to the chamber in April 2010. As a result the chamber hears appeals against decisions issued by the Financial Conduct Authority (FCA), the Prudential Regulation Authority and from the Pensions Regulator. For charity and land registration cases, since 1 July 2013, its jurisdiction extends to England and Wales. In references against decisions of the Pensions Regulator it has jurisdiction in England, Wales and Scotland.

SPECIAL IMMIGRATION APPEALS COMMISSION

15–25 Bream's Buildings, London EC4A 1DZ
T 0300-123 1711 E customer.service@hmcts.gsi.gov.uk

The commission was set up under the Special Immigration Appeals Commission Act 1997. It remains separate from the First-tier and Upper Tribunal structure but is part of HM Courts and Tribunals Service. Its main function is to consider appeals against orders for deportations in cases which involve, in the main, considerations of national security or the public interest. The commission also hears appeals against decisions to deprive persons of citizenship status.

Chair, Hon. Sir Stephen Irwin

EMPLOYMENT TRIBUNALS

ENGLAND AND WALES

Public Enquiry Line: 0300-123 1024

Employment Tribunals for England and Wales sit in 12 regions. The tribunals deal with matters of employment law, redundancy, dismissal, contract disputes, sexual, racial and disability discrimination and related areas of dispute which may arise in the workplace. Its public register of judgments is held at 100 Southgate Street, Bury St Edmunds, Suffolk IP33 2AQ.
President, David John Latham

SCOTLAND

Central Office, Eagle Building, 215 Bothwell Street, Glasgow G2 7TS T 0141-204 0730

Tribunals in Scotland have the same remit as those in England and Wales. Employment judges are appointed by the Lord President of the Court of Session and lay members by the Lord Chancellor. A public register of judgments made in employment tribunals in Scotland is held at the Glasgow office.
President, Shona Simon

EMPLOYMENT APPEAL TRIBUNAL

London Office, 2nd Floor, Fleetbank House, 2–6 Salisbury Square, London EC4Y 8AE T 020-7273 1041
E londoneat@hmcts.gsi.gov.uk
Edinburgh Office, 52 Melville Street, Edinburgh EH3 7HF
T 0131-225 3963 E edinburgheat@hmcts.gsi.gov.uk

The Employment Appeal Tribunal hears appeals (on points of law only) arising from decisions made by employment tribunals.

President, Hon. Sir Brian Langstaff
Registrar, Pauline Donleavy, OBE

SCOTTISH TRIBUNALS SERVICE

First Floor, Bothwell House, Hamilton Business Park, Caird Park, Hamilton ML3 0QA T 0800-345 7060 W www.scotland.gov.uk
Chief Executive, Martin McKenna

The Scottish Tribunals Service currently provides administrative support for the following Scottish tribunals:

THE ADDITIONAL SUPPORT NEEDS TRIBUNAL FOR SCOTLAND, Europa Building, 450 Argyle Street, Glasgow G2 8LH T 0845-120 2906
E asntsinquiries@scotland.gsi.gov.uk
W www.asntscotland.gov.uk
President, Dr Joe Morrow

COUNCIL TAX REDUCTION REVIEW PANEL, Europa Building, 450 Argyle Street, Glasgow G2 8LH
T 0141-242 0223 E ctrrpadmin@scotland.gsi.gov.uk
W www.counciltaxreductionreview.scotland.gov.uk
Senior Convener, Donald Ferguson

HOMEOWNER HOUSING PANEL, Europa Building, 450 Argyle Street, Glasgow G2 8LH T 0141-242 0175
E hohpadmin@scotland.gsi.gov.uk
W www.hohp.scotland.gov.uk
President, Aileen Devanny

THE LANDS TRIBUNAL FOR SCOTLAND, George House, 126 George Street, Edinburgh EH2 4HH T 0131-271 4350
E mailbox@lands-tribunal-scotland.org.uk
W www.lands-tribunal-scotland.org.uk
President, Hon. Lord McGhie, QC

THE MENTAL HEALTH TRIBUNAL FOR SCOTLAND, Bothwell House, First Floor, Hamilton Business Park, Caird Park, Hamilton ML3 0QA T 0800-345 7060
E mhts@scotland.gsi.gov.uk
W www.mhtscotland.gov.uk
President, Dr Joe Morrow

THE PENSIONS APPEAL TRIBUNAL SCOTLAND, George House, 126 George Street, Edinburgh EH2 4HH
T 0131-271 4340 E info@patscotland.org.uk
W www.patscotland.org.uk
President, Marion Caldwell, QC

THE PRIVATE RENTED HOUSING PANEL, Europa Building, 450 Argyle Street, Glasgow G2 8LH
T 0141-242 0142
E prhpadmin@scotland.gsi.gov.uk
W www.prhpscotland.gov.uk
President, Aileen Devanny

THE SCOTTISH CHARITY APPEALS PANEL, George House, 126 George Street, Edinburgh EH2 4HH
T 0131-271 4340 E scap@scotland.gsi.gov.uk
W www.scap.gov.uk
Chairs, Saria Akhter; Aileen Devanny; Joseph Hughes; Gary McIlravey; John Walker

NORTHERN IRELAND COURTS AND TRIBUNALS SERVICE

Laganside House, 23–27 Oxford Street, Belfast BT1 3LA
T 028-9032 8594 W www.courtsni.gov.uk
Lord Chief Justice of Northern Ireland, Rt. Hon. Sir Declan Morgan

The Northern Ireland Courts and Tribunals Service currently provides administrative support for the following Northern Ireland tribunals:

THE APPEALS SERVICE, Cleaver House, 3 Donegall Square North, Belfast BT1 5GA T 028-9051 8518
E appeals.service.belfast@dsdni.gov.uk
President of the Appeal Tribunals, Conall Maclynn
THE CARE TRIBUNAL, 3rd Floor, Bedford House, 16–22 Bedford Street, Belfast BT2 7FD T 028-9072 4893
E tribunalsunit@courtsni.gov.uk
Chairs, W. Harry Black; Diane Drennan
THE CHARITY TRIBUNAL, 3rd Floor, Bedford House, 16–22 Bedford Street, Belfast BT2 7FD T 028-9072 4892
E tribunalsunit@courts.ni.gov.uk
President, Damien McMahon
CRIMINAL INJURIES COMPENSATION APPEALS PANEL NORTHERN IRELAND, 3rd Floor, Bedford House, 16–22 Bedford Street, Belfast BT1 2LG T 028-9072 4823
E cicapnicustomer@courtsni.gov.uk
Chair, John Duffy
LANDS TRIBUNAL, Royal Courts of Justice, 2nd Floor, Chichester Street, Belfast BT1 3JJ T 028-9032 7703
E landstribunal@courtsni.gov.uk
President, Rt. Hon. Sir Patrick Coghlin
MENTAL HEALTH REVIEW TRIBUNAL, 3rd Floor, Bedford House, 16–22 Bedford Street, Belfast BT2 7FD
T 028-9072 4843 E tribunalsunit@courtsni.gov.uk
Chair, Fraser Elliott, QC
NORTHERN IRELAND HEALTH AND SAFETY TRIBUNAL, 3rd Floor, Bedford House, 16–22 Bedford Street, Belfast BT2 7FD T 028-9072 4892
E tribunalsunit@courtsni.gov.uk
Chairs, James Leonard; Damien McMahon; Petra Shiels
NORTHERN IRELAND TRAFFIC PENALTY TRIBUNAL, 3rd Floor, Bedford House, 16–22 Bedford Street, Belfast BT2 7FD T 028-9072 4892 E tribunalsunit@courtsni.gov.uk
Adjudicators, Michael Bready; Maura Hutchinson; Peter King; Robin Steer
NORTHERN IRELAND VALUATION TRIBUNAL, 3rd Floor, Bedford House, 16–22 Bedford Street, Belfast BT2 7FD T 028-9072 4887 E tribunalsunit@courtsni.gov.uk
President, James Leonard
OFFICE OF SOCIAL SECURITY COMMISSIONERS AND CHILD SUPPORT COMMISSIONERS, 3rd Floor, Bedford House, 16–22 Bedford Street, Belfast BT2 7FD
T 028-9072 4883 E tribunalsunit@courtsni.gov.uk
Chief Commissioner, Dr Kenneth Mullan
PAROLE COMMISSIONERS FOR NORTHERN IRELAND, Linum Chambers, 9th Floor, 2 Bedford Square, Bedford Street BT2 7ES T 028-9054 5900
E info@parolecomni.org.uk W www.parolecomni.org.uk
Chief Commissioner, Ms Christine Glenn
PENSIONS APPEAL COMMISSIONERS, 3rd Floor, Bedford House, 16–22 Bedford Street, Belfast BT2 7FD
T 028-9072 4884 E tribunalsunit@courtsni.gov.uk
Chief Commissioner, Dr Kenneth Mullan
PENSIONS APPEAL TRIBUNALS, 3rd Floor, Bedford House, 16–22 Bedford Street, Belfast BT2 7FD T 028-9072 4886
E tribunalsunit@courtsni.gsi.gov.uk
President, Dr Kenneth Mullan

RENT ASSESSMENT PANEL, Cleaver House, 3 Donegall Square North, Belfast BT1 5GA T 028-9051 8518
E appeals.service.belfast@dsdni.gov.uk
SPECIAL EDUCATIONAL NEEDS AND DISABILITY TRIBUNAL, 3rd Floor, Bedford House, 16–22 Bedford Street, Belfast BT2 7FD T 028-9072 4887
E tribunalsunit@courtsni.gov.uk
President, Damian G. McCormick

INDEPENDENT TRIBUNALS

The following represents a selection of tribunals not administered by HM Courts and Tribunals Service.

CIVIL AVIATION AUTHORITY
CAA House, 45–59 Kingsway, London WC2B 6TE
T 020-7379 7311 E infoservices@caa.co.uk
W www.caa.co.uk
The Civil Aviation Authority (CAA) does not have a separate tribunal department as such, but for certain purposes the CAA must conform to tribunal requirements, for example, to deal with appeals against the refusal or revocation of aviation licences and certificates issued by the CAA, and the allocation of routes outside of the EU to airlines.

The chair and four non-executive members who may sit on panels for tribunal purposes are appointed by the Secretary of State for Transport.
Chair, Dame Deirdre Hutton, DBE

COMPETITION APPEAL TRIBUNAL
Victoria House, Bloomsbury Place, London WC1A 2EB
T 020-7979 7979 E info@catribunal.org.uk
W www.catribunal.org.uk
The Competition Appeal Tribunal (CAT) is a specialist tribunal established to hear certain cases in the sphere of UK competition and economic regulatory law. It hears appeals against decisions of the Competition and Markets Authority (CMA) and the sectoral regulators in respect of infringements of competition law and with respect to mergers and markets. The CAT also has jurisdiction to award damages in respect of infringements of EU or UK competition law and to hear appeals against decisions of the Office of Communications (OFCOM) in telecommunications matters.
President, Hon. Sir Peter Roth

COPYRIGHT TRIBUNAL
4 Abbey Orchard Street, London SW1P 2HT
T 020-7034 2836 E copyright.tribunal@ipo.gov.uk
W www.ipo.gov.uk/ctribunal
The Copyright Tribunal resolves disputes over the terms and conditions of licences offered by, or licensing schemes operated by, collective management organisations in the copyright and related rights area. Its decisions are appealable to the high court on points of law only.
Chair, Hon. Mr Justice Hacon

INDUSTRIAL TRIBUNALS AND THE FAIR EMPLOYMENT TRIBUNAL (NORTHERN IRELAND)
Killymeal House, 2 Cromac Quay, Ormeau Road, Belfast BT7 2JD
T 028-9032 7666 E mail@employmenttribunalsni.org
W www.employmenttribunalsni.co.uk
The industrial tribunal system in Northern Ireland was set up in 1965 and has a similar remit to the employment tribunals in the rest of the UK. There is also a Fair Employment Tribunal, which hears and determines individual cases of alleged religious or political discrimination in employment. Employers can appeal to the Fair Employment Tribunal if they consider the directions of the Equality Commission to be unreasonable, inappropriate or unnecessary, and the

Equality Commission can make application to the tribunal for the enforcement of undertakings or directions with which an employer has not complied.
President, Eileen McBride

INVESTIGATORY POWERS TRIBUNAL

PO Box 33220, London SW1H 9ZQ

T 020-7035 3711 E info@ipt-uk.com W www.ipt-uk.com

The Investigatory Powers Tribunal replaced the Interception of Communications Tribunal, the Intelligence Services Tribunal, the Security Services Tribunal and the complaints function of the commissioner appointed under the Police Act 1997.

The Regulation of Investigatory Powers Act 2000 (RIPA) provides for a tribunal made up of senior members of the legal profession, independent of the government and appointed by the Queen, to consider all complaints against the intelligence services and those against public authorities in respect of powers covered by RIPA; and to consider proceedings brought under section 7 of the Human Rights Act 1998 against the intelligence services and law enforcement agencies in respect of these powers.
President, Sir Michael Burton

NATIONAL HEALTH SERVICE TRIBUNAL (SCOTLAND)

Anderson Strathern LLP, Lomond House, 9 George Square, Glasgow G2 1DY

T 0141-242 7974 E nhstribunal@nhs.net

The Scottish National Health Service Tribunal considers representations that the continued inclusion of a family health service practitioner (eg a doctor, dentist, optometrist or pharmacist) on a health board's list would be prejudicial to the efficiency of the service concerned, by virtue either of fraudulent practices or unsatisfactory personal or professional conduct. If this is established, the tribunal has the power to disqualify practitioners from working in the NHS family health services.
Chair, J. Michael D. Graham

SOLICITORS' DISCIPLINARY TRIBUNAL

3rd Floor, Gate House, 1 Farringdon Street, London EC4M 7LG

T 020-7329 4808 E enquiries@solicitorsdt.com

W www.solicitorstribunal.org.uk

The Solicitors' Disciplinary Tribunal is an independent statutory body whose members are appointed by the Master of the Rolls. The tribunal adjudicates upon alleged breaches of the rules and regulations applicable to solicitors and their firms, including the Solicitors' Code of Conduct 2007. It also decides applications by former solicitors for restoration to the Roll.
President, Andrew Spooner

SOLICITORS' DISCIPLINE TRIBUNAL (SCOTTISH)

Unit 3.5, The Granary Business Centre, Coal Road, Cupar, Fife KY15 5YQ

T 01334-659088 E enquiries@ssdt.org.uk W www.ssdt.org.uk

The Scottish Solicitors' Discipline Tribunal is an independent statutory body with a panel of 24 members, 12 of whom are solicitors appointed by the Lord President

of the Court of Session. Its principal function is to consider complaints of misconduct against solicitors in Scotland.
Chair, A. Cockburn

TRAFFIC PENALTY TRIBUNAL

Springfield House, Water Lane, Wilmslow, Cheshire SK9 5BG

T 01625-445555 E info@trafficpenaltytribunal.gov.uk

W www.trafficpenaltytribunal.gov.uk

The Traffic Penalty Tribunal considers appeals from motorists against penalty charge notices issued by Civil Enforcement Authorities in England (outside London) and Wales under the Traffic Management Act 2004, and considers appeals against bus lane contraventions in England (outside London) under the Bus Lane Contraventions Regulations 2005. Parking adjudicators are appointed with the express consent of the Lord Chancellor and must be lawyers of five years' standing.
Head of Service, Louise Hutchinson

VALUATION TRIBUNAL SERVICE

2nd Floor, Black Lion House, 45 Whitechapel Road, London E1 1DU

T 0300-123 2035 W www.valuationtribunal.gov.uk

The Valuation Tribunal Service (VTS) was created as a corporate body by the Local Government Act 2003, and is responsible for providing or arranging the services required for the operation of the Valuation Tribunal for England. The VTS board consists of a chair and members appointed by the secretary of state. The VTS is sponsored by the Department for Communities and Local Government.
Chair, Anne Galbraith, CBE

VALUATION TRIBUNAL FOR ENGLAND

President's Office, 2nd Floor, Black Lion House, 45 Whitechapel Road, London E1 1DU

T 020-7246 3900 W www.valuationtribunal.gov.uk

The Valuation Tribunal for England (VTE) came into being on 1 October 2009, replacing 56 valuation tribunals in England. Provision for the VTE was made in the Local Government and Public Involvement in Health Act 2007. The VTE hears appeals concerning council tax and non-domestic (business) rates, as well as a small number of appeals against drainage boards' assessments of drainage rates. A separate panel is constituted for each hearing, and consists of a chair and one or two other members.
President, Prof. Graham Zellick CBE, QC

VALUATION TRIBUNAL SERVICE FOR WALES

Government Buildings, Block A (L1), Sarn Mynach, Llandudno Junction LL31 9RZ

T 0300-062 5350 E VTWalesnorth@vtw.gsi.gov.uk

W www.valuation-tribunals-wales.org.uk

The Valuation Tribunal for Wales (VTW) was established by the Valuation Tribunal for Wales Regulations 2010, and hears and determines appeals concerning council tax, non-domestic rating and drainage rates in Wales. The governing council, comprising the president, four regional representatives and one member who is appointed by the Welsh government, performs the management functions on behalf of the tribunal.
Chief Executive, Andrew Shipsides

OMBUDSMAN SERVICES

The following section is a listing of selected ombudsman services. Ombudsmen are a free, independent and impartial means of resolving certain disputes outside of the courts. These disputes are, in the majority of cases, concerned with whether something has been badly or unfairly handled (for example owing to delay, neglect, inefficiency or failure to follow proper procedures). Most ombudsman schemes are established by statute; they cover various public and private bodies and generally examine matters only after the relevant body has been given a reasonable opportunity to deal with the complaint.

After conducting an investigation an ombudsman will usually issue a written report, which normally suggests a resolution to the dispute and often includes recommendations concerning the improvement of procedures.

OMBUDSMAN ASSOCIATION

PO Box 308, Twickenham TW1 9BE
T 020-8894 9272 E secretary@ombudsmanassociation.org
W www.ombudsmanassociation.org

The Ombudsman Association was established in 1994 and exists to provide information to the government, public bodies and the public about ombudsmen and other complaint-handling services in the United Kingdom and Ireland. An ombudsman scheme must meet four criteria in order to attain full Ombudsman Association membership: independence from the organisations the ombudsman has the power to investigate, fairness, effectiveness and public accountability. Complaint Handler membership is open to complaint-handling bodies that do not meet these criteria in full. Ombudsman schemes from the UK, Ireland, British crown dependencies and overseas territories may apply to the Ombudsman Association for membership. The Ombudsman Association publishes a triannual newsletter containing news about ombudsmen and complaint-handling services in the UK, Ireland and overseas, along with topical articles of interest to members of the Association.
Secretary, Ian Pattison

The following is a selection of organisations that are members of the Ombudsman Association.

FINANCIAL OMBUDSMAN SERVICE

Exchange Tower, London E14 9SR
T 020-7964 1000 E complaint.info@financial-ombudsman.org.uk
W www.financial-ombudsman.org.uk

The Financial Ombudsman Service settles individual disputes between businesses providing financial services and their customers. The service answers around a million enquiries every year and deals with over 250,000 disputes. The service examines complaints about most financial matters, including banking, insurance, mortgages, pensions, savings, loans and credit cards. *See also* Banking and Finance.
Chief Ombudsman and Chief Executive, Caroline Wayman

HOUSING OMBUDSMAN SERVICE

81 Aldwych, London WC2B 4HN
T 0300-111 3000 E info@housing-ombudsman.org.uk
W www.housing-ombudsman.org.uk

The Housing Ombudsman Service was established in 1997 to deal with complaints and disputes involving tenants and housing associations and social landlords, certain private-sector landlords and managing agents. The ombudsman has a statutory jurisdiction over all registered social landlords in England. Private and other landlords can join the service on a voluntary basis. On 1 April 2013 a new Housing Ombudsman Service was launched with an extended jurisdiction covering all housing associations and local authorities.
Ombudsman, Dr Mike Biles

INDEPENDENT POLICE COMPLAINTS COMMISSION (IPCC)

90 High Holborn, London WC1V 6BH
T 0300-020 0096 E enquiries@ipcc.gsi.gov.uk
W www.ipcc.gov.uk

The IPCC succeeded the Police Complaints Authority in 2004. It was established under the Police Reform Act 2002. The IPCC is responsible for carrying out independent investigations into serious incidents or allegations of misconduct by those serving with the police in England and Wales. The IPCC's chair and commissioners must not have worked for the police in any capacity prior to their appointment. It has the power to initiate, undertake and oversee investigations and is also responsible for the way in which complaints are handled by local police forces. The IPCC is also responsible for serious complaints and conduct matters relating to staff at the National Crime Agency (NCA), Her Majesty's Revenue and Customs (HMRC), and the Home Office immigration and enforcement staff. In 2011 the IPCC became responsible for investigating allegations against the Police and Crime Commissioner for each police force area in England and Wales (established 2011) and against the equivalent for the Metropolitan Police, the Mayor's Office for Policing and Crime (MOPAC), set up in 2012.
Chair, Dame Anne Owers
Deputy Chairs, Rachel Cerfontyne; Sarah Green
Chief Executive (acting), Amanda Kelly

LEGAL OMBUDSMAN

PO Box 6806, Wolverhampton WV1 9WJ
T 0300-555 0333 E enquiries@legalombudsman.org.uk
W www.legalombudsman.org.uk

The Legal Ombudsman was set up by the Office for Legal Complaints under the Legal Services Act 2007 and is the single body for all consumer legal complaints in England and Wales. It replaced the Office of the Legal Services Ombudsman in 2010. The Legal Ombudsman aims to resolve disputes between individuals and authorised legal practitioners, including barristers, law cost draftsmen, legal executives, licensed conveyancers, notaries, patent attorneys, probate practitioners, registered European lawyers, solicitors and trade mark attorneys. The Legal Ombudsman is an independent and impartial organisation and deals with various types of complaints against legal services, such as wills, family issues, personal injury and buying or selling a house.
Chief Ombudsman, Adam Sampson

LOCAL GOVERNMENT OMBUDSMAN

Advice Team, PO Box 4771, Coventry CV4 0EH
T 0300-061 0614 W www.lgo.org.uk

The Local Government Ombudsman deals with complaints about councils and service failure by local authorities, schools and care providers.

There are two ombudsmen in England, each with responsibility for different regions; they aim to provide satisfactory redress for complainants and better administration by the authorities The ombudsmen investigate complaints about most council matters, including housing, planning, education, social care, housing benefit, transport and highways, environment and waste, and council tax. *See also* Local Government.

Local Government Ombudsmen, Dr Jane Martin

OFFICE OF THE PENSIONS OMBUDSMAN
11 Belgrave Road, London SW1V 1RB
T 020-7630 2200 E enquiries@pensions-ombudsman.org.uk
W www.pensions-ombudsman.org.uk

The Pensions Ombudsman is appointed by the Secretary of State for Work and Pensions, under the Pension Schemes Act 1993 as amended by the Pensions Act 1995. He investigates and decides complaints and disputes about the way that personal and occupational pension schemes are run and between members of pensions schemes and their beneficiaries, employers, trustees, managers and scheme administrators. As the ombudsman for the Board of the Pension Protection Fund, he can deal with disputes about the decisions made by the board or the actions of their staff. He also deals with appeals against decisions made by the scheme manager under the Financial Assistance Scheme.

Pensions Ombudsman, Tony King
Deputy Pensions Ombudsman, Jane Irvine

OMBUDSMAN SERVICES
Brew House, Wilderspool Park, Greenalls Avenue, Warrington WA4 6HL
W www.ombudsman-services.org

Ombudsman Services was founded in 2002 and provides independent dispute resolution for the communications, copyright licensing, energy and property sectors.

Ombudsman Services: Communications investigates complaints from consumers about companies which provide communication services to the public.

Ombudsman Services: Copyright Licensing helps to resolve complaints about bodies that either own or administer, on behalf of third parties, the licensing of copyright materials.

Ombudsman Services: Energy helps to resolve complaints from consumers about energy (gas and electricity companies). This service is also responsible for handling investigations concerning the government's Green Deal policy, which launched in 2013, and offers long-term loans towards energy-saving home improvements.

Ombudsman Services: Property investigates complaints from consumers about chartered surveying companies, surveyors, estate agents and other property professionals.

Chair, Dame Janet Finch
Chief Ombudsman, Lewis Shand Smith

OMBUDSMAN SERVICES: COMMUNICATIONS
PO Box 730, Warrington WA4 6WU
T 0330-440 1614

OMBUDSMAN SERVICES: COPYRIGHT LICENSING
PO Box 1124, Warrington WA4 9GH
T 0330-440 1601

OMBUDSMAN SERVICES: ENERGY
PO Box 966, Warrington WA4 9DF
T 0330-440 1624

OMBUDSMAN SERVICES: PROPERTY
PO Box 1021, Warrington WA4 9FE
T 0330-440 1634

PARLIAMENTARY AND HEALTH SERVICE OMBUDSMAN
Millbank Tower, Millbank, London SW1P 4QP
T 0345-015 4033 E phso.enquiries@ombudsman.org.uk
W www.ombudsman.org.uk

The Parliamentary Commissioner for Administration (commonly known as the Parliamentary Ombudsman) is independent of government and is an officer of Parliament. She is responsible for investigating complaints referred to her by MPs from members of the public who claim to have sustained injustice in consequence of maladministration by or on behalf of government departments and certain non-departmental public bodies in the UK. Certain types of action by government departments or bodies are excluded from investigation.

The Health Service Ombudsman is responsible for investigating complaints about services funded by the National Health Service in England that have not been dealt with by the service providers to the satisfaction of the complainant. This includes complaints about doctors, dentists, pharmacists and opticians. Complaints can be referred directly by the member of the public who claims to have sustained injustice or hardship in consequence of the failure in a service provided by a relevant organisation.

The two offices of the Parliamentary and Health Service Ombudsman are traditionally held by the same person.

Parliamentary Ombudsman and Health Service Ombudsman,
   Dame Julie Mellor, DBE

PRISONS AND PROBATION OMBUDSMAN
PO Box 70769, London SE1P 4XY
T 020-7633 4100 E mail@ppo.gsi.gov.uk
W www.ppo.gov.uk

The Prisons and Probation Ombudsman investigates complaints from prisoners, people on probation and immigration detainees, deaths of prisoners, residents of probation-service Approved Premises and those held in immigration removal centres. The ombudsman is appointed by the Secretary of State for Justice and works closely with the Ministry of Justice. All deaths that occur in prison are investigated and an anonymised fatal incident report is written after each investigation.

Ombudsman, Nigel Newcomen, CBE

PROPERTY OMBUDSMAN
Milford House, 43–55 Milford Street, Salisbury SP1 2BP
T 01722-333306 E admin@tpos.co.uk
W www.tpos.co.uk

The Property Ombudsman (TPO) scheme was established in 1998 and provides a free, impartial and independent service for dealing with unresolved disputes between property agents and buyers, sellers, tenants and landlords of property in the UK.

The ombudsman's role is to consider complaints against the agents' obligation to act in accordance with the TPO codes of practice and to propose a full and final resolution of the dispute. Consumers are not bound by the ombudsman's decision, but, registered agents are.

With over 12,800 estate agent offices and 11,500 lettings offices registered, TPO is the primary dispute-resolution service for the property industry.

Ombudsman, Christopher Hamer

PUBLIC SERVICES OMBUDSMAN FOR WALES

1 Ffordd yr Hen Gae, Pencoed CF35 5LJ
T 0300-790 0203
W www.ombudsman-wales.org.uk

The office of Public Services Ombudsman for Wales was established, with effect from 1 April 2006, by the Public Services Ombudsman (Wales) Act 2005. The ombudsman, who is appointed by the Queen, investigates complaints of injustice caused by maladministration or service failure by public services such as the Assembly Commission (and public bodies sponsored by the assembly); Welsh government; National Health Service bodies, including GPs, family health service providers and hospitals; registered social landlords; local authorities, including community councils; fire and rescue authorities; police authorities; the Arts Council of Wales; national park authorities; and countryside and environmental organisations.
Ombudsman, Nick Bennett

REMOVALS INDUSTRY OMBUDSMAN SCHEME

PO Box 6412, Leighton Buzzard, Beds LU7 6EG
T 01525-850054 E ombudsman@removalsombudsman.co.uk
W www.removalsombudsman.org.uk

The Removals Industry Ombudsman Scheme was established to resolve disputes between removal companies that are members of the scheme and their clients, both domestic and commercial. It comprises a board of four members, only one of whom has any connection with the removals industry. The ombudsman investigates complaints such as breaches of contract, unprofessional conduct, delays, excessive charges or breaches in the code of practice. The National Guild of Removers and Storers is currently the principal member.
Ombudsman, Lynne Stone

SCOTTISH PUBLIC SERVICES OMBUDSMAN

4 Melville Street, Edinburgh EH3 7NS
T 0800-377 7300 E www.spso.org.uk/contact-us
W www.spso.org.uk

The Scottish Public Services Ombudsman (SPSO) was established in 2002. The SPSO is the final stage for complaints about public services in Scotland. Its service is free and independent. SPSO investigates complaints about the Scottish government, its agencies and departments; the Scottish Parliamentary Corporate Body; colleges and universities; councils; housing associations; NHS Scotland; prisons; some water and sewerage service providers; and most other Scottish public bodies. The ombudsman looks at complaints regarding poor service or administrative failure and can usually only look at those that have been through the formal complaints process of the organisation concerned. It also has a statutory function in improving complaints handling in public services, which it carries out through its Complaints Standards Authority.
Scottish Public Services Ombudsman, Jim Martin

WATERWAYS OMBUDSMAN

PO Box 854, Altrincham WA15 5JS
T 0161-980 4858 E enquiries@waterways-ombudsman.org
W www.waterways-ombudsman.org

From July 2012, the Waterways Ombudsman investigates complaints about the Canal and River Trust and its subsidiaries (such as British Waterways Marinas Limited). The ombudsman does not consider complaints about canals in Scotland, which are the responsibility of the Scottish Public Services Ombudsman.
Ombudsman, Andrew Walker

THE POLICE SERVICE

There are 45 police forces in the United Kingdom: 43 in England and Wales, including the Metropolitan Police and the City of London Police, Police Scotland and the Police Service of Northern Ireland. The Isle of Man, Jersey and Guernsey have their own forces responsible for policing in their respective islands and bailiwicks. The National Crime Agency, which became operational in October 2013, is responsible for preventing organised crime and strengthening UK borders.

Since 1964, police authorities – separate independent bodies for each police force – were responsible for the supervision of local policing in England and Wales. Following the government's white paper *Policing in the 21st Century* it was concluded that, in order to make the police more accountable, police authorities should be replaced with a directly elected commissioner for each force, supported by a police and crime panel. In November 2012, following the enactment of the Police Reform and Social Responsibility Act 2011, elections were held in 41 police force areas across England and Wales. The PCCs are responsible for appointing the chief constable of their force, establishing local priorities and setting budgets. The PCCs are not in place to run their local force but rather to hold them to account. The Mayor of London, supported by the Mayor's Office for Policing and Crime (MOPAC), acts as the PCC for the Metropolitan Police. The City of London Corporation acts as the police authority for the City of London Police.

In England the police and crime panels are made up of representatives from each local authority in a police force area. In Wales they are independent public bodies, established and maintained by the secretary of state, rather than local authority committees.

Under the Police and Fire Reform (Scotland) Act 2012, Police Scotland was established on 1 April 2013, merging the eight separate territorial police forces, the Scottish Crime and Drug Enforcement Agency and the Association of Chief Police Officers in Scotland. Responsible for policing the whole of Scotland, Police Scotland is the second largest force in the UK after the Metropolitan Police. The service is led by a chief constable who is supported by a team of four deputy constables, assistant chief constables and three directors. The Scottish Police Authority, established in October 2012, is responsible for maintaining policing, promoting policing principles, the continuous improvement of policing and holds the Chief Constable to account. In Northern Ireland, the Northern Ireland Policing Board, an independent public body consisting of 19 political and independent members, fulfils a similar role.

Police forces in England, Scotland and Wales are financed by central and local government grants and a precept on the council tax. The Police Service of Northern Ireland is wholly funded by central government.

The home secretary, the Scottish government and the Northern Ireland Minister of Justice are responsible for the organisation, administration and operation of the police service. They regulate police ranks, discipline, hours of duty and pay and allowances. All police forces are subject to inspection by HM Inspectorate of Constabulary, which reports to the home secretary and the Northern Ireland Minister of Justice. Police forces in Scotland are inspected by HM Inspectorate of Constabulary for Scotland which operates independently of the Scottish government.

COMPLAINTS

The Independent Police Complaints Commission (IPCC) was established under the Police Reform Act 2002. The IPCC is responsible for carrying out independent investigations into serious incidents or allegations of misconduct by those serving with the police in England and Wales. It has the power to initiate, undertake and oversee investigations and is also responsible for the way in which complaints are handled by local police forces. In addition the IPCC is responsible for dealing with serious complaints and conduct matters relating to staff at the National Crime Agency, HM Revenue and Customs and Home Office immigration and enforcement staff. The most recent responsibility assigned to the IPCC is to decide whether investigations should be made regarding any allegations of criminal offence against MOPAC, the PCCs or their deputies.

If a complaint is relatively minor, the police force will attempt to resolve it internally and an official investigation might not be required. In more serious cases the IPCC or police force may refer the case to the Crown Prosecution Service, which will decide whether to bring criminal charges against the officers involved. An officer who is dismissed, required to resign or reduced in rank, whether as a result of a complaint or not, can appeal to a police appeals tribunal established by the relevant police authority.

Following the Police and Fire Reform (Scotland) Act 2012 which brought together Scotland's eight police services into the single Police Service of Scotland, the remit of the Police Complaints Commissioner for Scotland (PCCS) was expanded to include investigations into the most serious incidents concerning the police. In relation to the change, the PCCS was renamed the Police Investigations and Review Commissioner (PIRC).

The Police Ombudsman for Northern Ireland provides an independent police complaints system for Northern Ireland, dealing with all stages of the complaints procedure. Complaints that cannot be resolved informally are investigated and the ombudsman recommends a suitable course of action to the Chief Constable of the Police Service of Northern Ireland or the Northern Ireland Policing Board based on the investigation's findings. The ombudsman may recommend that a police officer be prosecuted, but the decision to prosecute a police officer rests with the Director of Public Prosecutions.

INDEPENDENT POLICE COMPLAINTS
COMMISSION, PO Box 473, Sale M33 0BW
T 0300-020 0096 E enquiries@ipcc.gsi.gov.uk
W www.ipcc.gov.uk
POLICE INVESTIGATIONS AND REVIEW
COMMISSIONER, Hamilton House, Hamilton Business Park,
Caird Park, Hamilton ML3 0QA T 0808-178 5577
E enquiries@pirc.gsi.gov.uk W www.pirc.scotland.gov.uk
Police Investigations and Review Commissioner,
Kate Frame
POLICE OMBUDSMAN FOR NORTHERN IRELAND,
New Cathedral Buildings, 11 Church Street, Belfast BT1 1PG
T 028-9082 8600 E info@policeombudsman.org
W www.policeombudsman.org
Police Ombudsman, Dr Michael Maguire

POLICE SERVICES

COLLEGE OF POLICING

Leamington Road, Ryton-on-Dunsmore, Coventry CV8 3EN
T 0800-496 3322 E contactus@college.pnn.police.uk
W www.college.police.uk

The College of Policing was established in December 2012 as the first professional body set up for policing. It works on behalf of the public to raise professional standards in policing and to assist forces to reduce crime and protect the public. It engages with the public through the Police and Crime Commissioners to ensure that it is responsive to the issues of greatest concern.

The government has designated the college as a centre for reviewing and testing practices and interventions to identify which are effective in reducing crime. It makes this information accessible for all in policing, particularly frontline practitioners. The college also supports continuous professional development and sets national standards for promotion and progression.

Chief Executive, Alex Marshall, QPM
Chair, Prof. Dame Shirley Pearce, DBE

NATIONAL CRIME AGENCY

Units 1–6 Citadel Place, Tinworth Street, London SE11 5EF
T 0370-496 7622
E communication@nca.x.gsi.gov.uk
W www.nationalcrimeagency.gov.uk

Established under the Crime and Courts Act 2013 the National Crime Agency (NCA) became fully operational in October 2013. The NCA is a non-ministerial government department.

In order to carry out its remit is to fight organised crime, strengthen UK borders, tackle fraud and cyber crime and protect children and young people the agency is organised into four separate commands: Border Policing, Child Exploitation and Online Protection, Economic Crime and Organised Crime; and a specialist National Cyber Crime Unit.

The director-general has independent operational direction and control over the NCA's activities and, through the home secretary, is accountable to parliament.

Director-General, Keith Bristow, QPM

UK MISSING PERSONS BUREAU

Bramshill, Hook, Hampshire RG27 0JW T 0845-000 5481
E missingpersonsbureau@nca.x.gsi.gov.uk
W www.missingpersons.police.uk

The UK Missing Persons Bureau, which is now part of the National Crime Agency, acts as the centre for the exchange of information connected with the search for missing persons nationally and internationally alongside the police and other related organisations. The unit focuses on cross-matching missing persons with unidentified persons or bodies by maintaining records, including a dental index of ante-mortem chartings of long-term missing persons and post-mortem chartings from unidentified bodies.

Information is supplied and collected for all persons who have been missing in the UK for over 72 hours (or fewer where police deem appropriate), foreign nationals reported missing in the UK, UK nationals reported missing abroad and all unidentified bodies and persons found within the UK.

SPECIALIST FORCES

BRITISH TRANSPORT POLICE

25 Camden Road, London NW1 9LN T 0800-405040
W www.btp.police.uk
Strength (March 2014), 2,912

British Transport Police is the national police force for the railways in England, Wales and Scotland, including the London Underground system, Docklands Light Railway, Glasgow Subway, Midland Metro tram system, Sunderland Metro, Croydon Tramlink and the Emirates Air Line cable car. The chief constable reports to the British Transport Police Authority. The members of the authority are appointed by the transport secretary and include representatives from the rail industry as well as independent members. Officers are paid the same salary as those in other police forces.

Chief Constable, Paul Crowther, OBE

CIVIL NUCLEAR CONSTABULARY

Building F6, Culham Science Centre, Abingdon,
Oxfordshire OX14 3DB T 01235-466606 W www.gov.uk/
government/organisations/civil-nuclear-constabulary
Strength (July 2014), c.1,500

The Civil Nuclear Constabulary (CNC) operates under the strategic direction of the Department of Energy and Climate Change. The CNC is a specialised armed force that protects civil nuclear sites and nuclear materials. The constabulary is responsible for policing UK civil nuclear industry facilities and for escorting nuclear material between establishments within the UK and worldwide.

Chief Constable, Michael Griffiths, CBE
Deputy Chief Constable, Simon Chesterton, QPM

MINISTRY OF DEFENCE POLICE

Ministry of Defence Police HQ, Wethersfield, Braintree, Essex
CM7 4AZ T 01371-854000 W www.mod.police.uk
Strength (July 2014), 2,467

Part of the Ministry of Defence Police and Guarding Agency, the Ministry of Defence Police is a statutory civil police force with particular responsibility for the security and policing of the MoD environment. It contributes to the physical protection of property and personnel within its jurisdiction and provides a comprehensive police service to the MoD as a whole.

Chief Constable, Alf Hitchcock, QPM
Deputy Chief Constable, Gerard McAuley

THE SPECIAL CONSTABULARY

Darby House, 162 Bletchingley Road, Merstham, Surrey RH1 3DN
W www.policespecials.com
Strength (June 2014), c.20,000

The Special Constabulary is a force of trained volunteers who support and work with their local police force, usually for a minimum of 16 hours a month. Special constables are thoroughly grounded in the basic aspects of police work, such as self-defence, powers of arrest, common crimes and preparing evidence for court, before they can begin to carry out any police duties. Once they have completed their training, they have the same powers as a regular officer and wear a similar uniform.

POLICE FORCES

The telephone number for each local police force in England, Wales and Scotland is T 101

ENGLAND*

Force	Strength†	Chief Constable	Police and Crime Commissioner
Avon and Somerset	2,800	Nick Gargan, QPM	Sue Mountstevens
Bedfordshire	1,019	Colette Paul, QPM	Olly Martins
Cambridgeshire	1,370	Simon Parr, QPM	Sir Graham Bright
Cheshire	1,925	Simon Byrne	John Dwyer
Cleveland	1,382	Jacqui Cheer, QPM	Barry Coppinger
Cumbria	1,150	Bernard Lawson, QPM	Richard Rhodes
Derbyshire	1,788	Mick Creedon, QPM	Alan Charles
Devon and Cornwall	3,096	Shaun Sawyer	Tony Hogg
Dorset	1,217	Debbie Simpson, QPM	Martyn Underhill
Durham	1,288	Mike Barton, QPM	Ron Hogg
Essex	3,196	Stephen Kavanagh	Nick Alston
Gloucestershire	1,188	Suzette Davenport	Martin Surl
Greater Manchester	6,997	Sir Peter Fahy, QPM	Tony Lloyd
Hampshire	3,247	Andy Marsh	Simon Hayes
Hertfordshire	1,927	Andy Bliss, QPM	David Lloyd
Humberside	1,701	Justine Curran, QPM	Matthew Grove
Kent	3,268	Alan Pughsley	Ann Barnes
Lancashire	3,074	Steve Finnigan, CBE, QPM	Clive Grunshaw
Leicestershire	2,043	Simon Cole, QPM	Sir Clive Loader
Lincolnshire	1,091	Neil Rhodes	Alan Hardwick
Merseyside	3,954	Jon Murphy, QPM	Jane Kennedy
Norfolk	1,582	Simon Bailey	Stephen Bett
North Yorkshire	1,408	Dave Jones	Julia Mulligan
Northamptonshire	1,239	Adrian Lee	Adam Simmonds
Northumbria	3,646	Sue Sim	Vera Baird
Nottinghamshire	2,158	Chris Eyre, QPM	Paddy Tipping
South Yorkshire	2,722	David Crompton, QPM	vacant
Staffordshire	1,729	Mike Cunningham, QPM	Matthew Ellis
Suffolk	1,226	Douglas Paxton, QPM	Tim Passmore
Surrey	1,938	Lynne Owens, QPM	Kevin Hurley
Sussex	2,805	Martin Richards, QPM	Katy Bourne
Thames Valley	4,346	Sara Thornton, CBE, QPM	Anthony Stansfeld
Warwickshire	802	Andy Parker, QPM	Ron Ball
West Mercia	1,966	David Shaw	Bill Longmore
West Midlands	7,288	Chris Sims, QPM	Bob Jones
West Yorkshire	4,857	Mark Gilmore, QPM	Mark Burns-Williamson
Wiltshire	1,020	Patrick Geenty	Angus Macpherson
WALES			
Dyfed-Powys	1,123	Simon Prince	Christopher Salmon
Gwent	1,330	Jeffrey Farrar, QPM	Ian Johnston
North Wales	1,464	Mark Polin, QPM	Winston Roddick
South Wales	2,861	Peter Vaughan, QPM	Rt. Hon. Alun Michael

Force	Strength	Chief Constable	Telephone
POLICE SCOTLAND	17,436	Sir Stephen House, QPM	–
POLICE SERVICE OF NORTHERN IRELAND	7,033	Matt Baggott, CBE, QPM	0845-600 8000
ISLANDS			
Isle of Man	236	Gary Roberts	01624-631212
States of Jersey	237	Mike Bowron, QPM	01534-612612
Guernsey	148	Patrick Rice	01481-725111

* For the City of London Police and the Metropolitan Police Service see London Forces
† Size of force (full-time equivalent) as at March 2014
Sources: R. Hazell & Co, Sweet & Maxwell Police and Constabulary Almanac 2014; Home Office

STAFF ASSOCIATIONS

Police officers are not permitted to join a trade union or to strike. All ranks have their own staff associations.
CHIEF POLICE OFFICERS' STAFF ASSOCIATION,
10 Victoria Street, London SW1H 0NN T 020-7084 8950
President, Sir Hugh Orde

ENGLAND AND WALES
POLICE FEDERATION OF ENGLAND AND WALES,
Federation House, Highbury Drive, Leatherhead, Surrey
KT22 7UY T 01372-352000 W www.polfed.org
General Secretary, Andy Fittes

POLICE SUPERINTENDENTS' ASSOCIATION OF
ENGLAND AND WALES, 67A Reading Road, Pangbourne,
Reading RG8 7JD T 0118-984 4005 W www.policesupers.com
President, Chief Supt. Irene Curtis
National Secretary, Chief Supt. Tim Jackson

SCOTLAND
ASSOCIATION OF SCOTTISH POLICE
SUPERINTENDENTS, Scottish Police College, Tulliallan
Castle, Kincardine, Fife FK10 4BE T 0141-532 4022
W www.scottishpolicesupers.org.uk
General Secretary, Carol Forfar
SCOTTISH POLICE FEDERATION, 5 Woodside Place,
Glasgow G3 7QF T 0300-303 0027 W www.spf.org.uk
General Secretary, Calum Steele

NORTHERN IRELAND
POLICE FEDERATION FOR NORTHERN IRELAND,
77–79 Garnerville Road, Belfast BT4 2NX T 028-9076 4200
W www.policefed-ni.org.uk
Secretary, Marty Whittle
SUPERINTENDENTS' ASSOCIATION OF NORTHERN
IRELAND, PSNI College, Garnerville Road, Belfast BT4 2NX
T 028-9092 2201 W www.policesuperintendentsni.org
President, Chief Supt. Nigel Grimshaw
Hon. Secretary, Supt. Jonathan Kearney

LONDON FORCES

CITY OF LONDON POLICE
37 Wood Street, London EC2P 2NQ T 020-7601 2222
W www.cityoflondon.police.uk
Strength (March 2014), 746

The City of London has one of the most important financial
centres in the world and the force has particular expertise in
fraud investigation. The force concentrates on economic
crime, counter terrorism and community policing. It has
a wholly elected police authority, the police committee
of the City of London Corporation, which appoints the
commissioner.
Commissioner, Adrian Leppard, QPM
Assistant Commissioner, Ian Dyson
Commanders, Wayne Chance *(Operations);* Steve Head
    (Economic Crime)

METROPOLITAN POLICE SERVICE
New Scotland Yard, Broadway, London SW1H 0BG
T 020-7230 1212 W www.met.police.uk
Strength (March 2014), 30,932
Commissioner, Sir Bernard Hogan-Howe, QPM
Deputy Commissioner, Craig Mackey, QPM

The Metropolitan Police Service is divided into three main
areas for operational purposes:
TERRITORIAL POLICING
Most of the day-to-day policing of London is carried out by
32 borough operational command units operating within the
same boundaries as the London borough councils.
Assistant Commissioner, Helen King
SPECIALIST CRIME AND OPERATIONS (SC&O)
SC&O provides two main services: reducing the harm caused
by serious crime and criminal networks and providing
specialist policing services across London. SC&O provides
specialist training to detectives, and conducts forensic
examinations of crime scenes in the capital.
Assistant Commissioner, Cressida Dick, QPM

SPECIALIST OPERATIONS
• *Counter Terrorism Command* is responsible for the prevention
and disruption of terrorist activity, domestic extremism and
related offences within London and nationally. It provides an
explosives disposal and chemical, biological, radiological
and nuclear capability within London, assists the security
services in fulfilling their roles and provides a point of contact
for international partners in counter-terrorism matters.
• *Protection Command* is responsible for the protection and
security of high-profile persons, including the royal family
and the prime minister. It is responsible for protecting royal
residences and embassies, providing residential protection for
visiting heads of states, governments and foreign ministers
and advising the diplomatic community on security.
• *Security Command* works with authorities at the Houses of
Parliament to provide security for peers, MPs, employees
and visitors to the Palace of Westminster. It also operates at
Heathrow and London City airports.
Assistant Commissioner, Mark Rowley, QPM
PROFESSIONALISM
The Directorate of Professionalism's key aims are to uphold
and improve professionalism across the service. The
directorate works with the IPCC to establish good practice,
reduce bureaucracy and review decision making. It also
works with the Crown Prosecution Service to ensure timely
and professional investigations of complaints and conduct
matters.
Assistant Commissioner, Martin Hewitt

RATES OF PAY *as at August 2014*

Chief Constables of Greater Manchester	
and West Midlands*	£181,455
Chief Constable	£130,044–£169,359
Deputy Chief Constable	£108,873–£139,119
Assistant Chief Constable and	
Commanders	£90,726–£105,849
Chief Superintendent	£74,394–£78,636
Superintendent Range 2[†]	£71,331–£75,909
Superintendent	£62,298–£72,585
Chief Inspector[‡§]	£51,789 (£53,853)–£53,919 (£55,980)
Inspector[‡§]	£46,788 (£48,840)–£50,751 (£52,818)
Sergeant[‡]	£36,519–£41,040
Constable[‡]	£19,000–£36,519
Metropolitan Police	
Commissioner	£260,088
Deputy Commissioner	£214,722
City of London Police	
Commissioner	£160,902
Assistant Commissioner	£132,714
Police Scotland	
Chief Constable	£127,017
Deputy Chief Constable	£108,873
Police Service of Northern Ireland	
Chief Constable	£193,548
Deputy Chief Constable	£157,257

* Also applicable to the four Assistant Commissioners of the
Metropolitan Police Service
† For Superintendents who were not given the rank of Chief
Superintendent on its re-introduction on 1 January 2002
‡ For officers in receipt of a competence-related threshold payment
(£600 in 2014–15). Will be phased out by April 2016
§ London salary in parentheses. All other police officers (not
Metropolitan or City of London Commissioners) in London receive
an additional payment of £2,277 per annum

THE PRISON SERVICE

The prison services in the UK are the responsibility of the Secretary of State for Justice, the Scottish Secretary for Justice and the Minister of Justice in Northern Ireland. The chief executive (director-general in Northern Ireland), officers of the National Offender Management Service (NOMS), the Scottish Prison Service (SPS) and the Northern Ireland Prison Service are responsible for the day-to-day running of the system.

There are 122 prison establishments in England and Wales, 15 in Scotland and three in Northern Ireland. Convicted prisoners are classified according to their assessed security risk and are housed in establishments appropriate to that level of security. There are no open prisons in Northern Ireland. Female prisoners are housed in women's establishments or in separate wings of mixed prisons. Remand prisoners are, where possible, housed separately from convicted prisoners. Offenders under the age of 21 are usually detained in a Young Offender Institution, which may be a separate establishment or part of a prison. Appellant and failed asylum seekers are held in Immigration Removal Centres, or in separate units of other prisons.

Fourteen prisons are now run by the private sector in England and Wales, and in England, Wales and Scotland all escort services have been contracted out to private companies. In Scotland, two prisons (Kilmarnock and Addiewell) were built and financed by the private sector and are being operated by private contractors.

There are independent prison inspectorates in England, Wales and Scotland which report annually on conditions and the treatment of prisoners. The Chief Inspector of Criminal Justice in Northern Ireland and HM Inspectorate of Prisons for England and Wales perform an inspectorate role for prisons in Northern Ireland. Every prison establishment also has an independent monitoring board made up of local volunteers.

Any prisoner whose complaint is not satisfied by the internal complaints procedures may complain to the prisons and probation ombudsman for England and Wales, the Scottish public services ombudsman or the prisoner ombudsman for Northern Ireland. The prisons and probation inspectors, the prisons ombudsman and the independent monitoring boards report to the home secretary and to the Minister of Justice in Northern Ireland.

PRISON STATISTICS

The projected 'high scenario' prison population for 2019 in England and Wales is 86,600; the 'low scenario' is 77,300.

PRISON POPULATION (UK) *as at June 2014*

	Remand	Sentenced	Other
ENGLAND AND WALES	12,197	71,481	1,831
Male	11,503	68,274	1,803
Female	694	3,207	28
SCOTLAND*	1,203	5,846	–
Male	1,138	5,530	–
Female	65	316	–
N. IRELAND	404	1,463	0
Male	383	1,416	0
Female	21	47	0
UK TOTAL	13,804	78,790	1,831

* Figures from August 2014

Sources: MoJ; Scottish Prison Service; NI Prison Service

PRISON CAPACITY (ENGLAND AND WALES)
as at August 2014

Male prisoners	81,930
Female prisoners	3,904
Total	85,834
Useable operational capacity	87,362
Under home detention curfew supervision	2,118

Source: MoJ – *Prisons and Probation Statistics*

SENTENCED PRISON POPULATION BY SEX
AND OFFENCE (ENGLAND AND WALES)
as at 30 June 2014

	Male	Female
Violence against the person	18,694	902
Sexual offences	11,100	92
Burglary	6,926	215
Robbery	8,210	297
Theft, handling	3,852	525
Fraud and forgery	1,189	163
Drugs offences	9,866	440
Motoring offences	794	26
Other offences	7,142	502
Offence not recorded	390	36
*Total**	68,163	3,198

* Figures do not include civil (non-criminal) prisoners or fine defaulters

Source: MoJ – *Prisons and Probation Statistics*

SENTENCED POPULATION BY LENGTH OF
SENTENCE (ENGLAND AND WALES)
as at 30 June 2014

	British	Foreign and Not Recorded
Less than 12 months	5,707	943
12 months to less than 4 years	17,548	2,041
4 years to less than life	24,384	2,891
Indeterminate	11,495	1,092
*Total**	59,134	6,967

* Figures do not include civil (non-criminal) prisoners or fine defaulters

Source: MoJ – *Prisons and Probation Statistics*

AVERAGE DAILY POPULATION BY TYPE OF
CUSTODY 2013–14 (SCOTLAND)

Remand: sub total	1,476
Persons under sentence: sub total	6,375
Under 4 years	3,540
4 years and over	2,835
Total	7,851

Source: SPS – *Annual Report and Accounts 2013–14*

SUICIDES IN PRISON IN 2013 (ENGLAND AND
WALES)

Male	72
Female	2
Total	74

Source: MoJ

THE PRISON SERVICES

NATIONAL OFFENDER MANAGEMENT SERVICE

Clive House, 70 Petty France, London SW1H 9EX
T 0300-047 6325 E public.enquiries@noms.gsi.gov.uk
W www.gov.uk/government/organisations/national-offender-management-service

HM Prison Service became part of the National Offender Management Service (NOMS) on 1 April 2008 as part of the reorganisation of the Ministry of Justice (MoJ).

SALARIES *as at March 2014*

Senior manager A	£64,765–£82,892
Senior manager B	£60,980–£80,458
Senior manager C	£56,920–£72,458
Senior manager D	£45,700–£61,038
Manager E	£33,335–£46,024
Manager F	£29,685–£39,041
Manager G	£25,105–£32,140

THE NOMS BOARD

Chief Executive, Michael Spurr
Director of Commissioning and Commercial, Ian Blakeman
Director of Probation, Colin Allars
Director of National Operational Services, Digby Griffith
Director of Public Sector Prisons, Phil Copple
Director of Human Resources, Carol Carpenter
Director, National Offender Management Service in Wales, Sarah Payne
Director of Finance and Analysis, Andrew Emmett

DEPUTY DIRECTORS OF CUSTODY

Ian Mulholland (Public Service Prisons); Paul Baker *(East Midlands);* Adrian Smith *(East of England),* Michelle Jarman Howe *(Kent and Sussex);* Nick Pascoe *(London);* Alan Tallentire *(North-East and Youth Justice);* Alan Scott *(North-West);* Claudia Sturt *(South-Central);* Ferdie Parker *(South-West);* Ian Mullholland *(Wales);* Luke Serjeant *(West Midlands);* Amy Rice *(Yorkshire and Humberside);* Richard Vince *(High Security)*

OPERATING COSTS OF NOMS 2013–14

Staff costs	£2,206,782,000
Other operating costs	£2,076,965,000
Operating income	(£364,073,000)
Net operating costs (before tax)	£3,755,943,000
Net operating costs (after tax)	£3,756,836,000

Source: NOMS – *Annual Report 2013–14*

SCOTTISH PRISON SERVICE (SPS)

Calton House, 5 Redheughs Rigg, Edinburgh EH12 9HW
T 0131-244 8745 E gaolinfo@sps.pnn.gov.uk
W www.sps.gov.uk

SALARIES *as at March 2014*
Senior managers in the Scottish Prison Service, including governors and deputy governors of prisons, are paid across three pay bands depending on the size of the establishment:

Band I	£54,930–£68,433
Band H	£43,601–£56,704
Band G	£34,333–£47,149

SPS BOARD

Chief Executive, Colin McConnell
Directors, Ian Davidson *(Strategy and Innovation);* Eric Murch *(Operations);* Catherine Topley *(Corporate Services)*
Non-Executive Directors, Harry McGuigan; Jane Martin; Susan Matheson, OBE; Zoe Van Zwanenberg

OPERATING COSTS OF SPS 2013–14

Total income	(£7,518,000)
Total expenditure	£260,343,000
Staff costs	£150,176,000
Running costs	£78,235,000
Other current expenditure	£31,932,000
Operating cost	£252,825,000
Interest payable and similar charges	£11,302,000
Net operating cost	£264,127,000

Source: SPS – *Annual Report and Accounts 2013–14*

NORTHERN IRELAND PRISON SERVICE

Dundonald House, Upper Newtownards Road, Belfast BT4 3SU
T 028-9052 5065 E info@niprisonservice.gov.uk
W www.dojni.gov.uk

SALARIES *as at April 2014*

Governor 1	£74,747–£80,550
Governor 2	£67,983–£72,183
Governor 3	£58,874–£62,766
Governor 4	£51,156–£55,407
Governor 5	£44,934–£50,396

SENIOR STAFF

Director-General, Sue McAllister
Executive, Mark Adam *(Human Resources, Organisational Development, Finance and Corporate Services);* Paul Cawkwell *(Offender Policy and Operations);* Brian McCaughey *(Rehabilitation);* Max Murray *(Estates Management)*

OPERATING COSTS OF NORTHERN IRELAND PRISON SERVICE 2012–13

Staff costs	£84,531,000
Net running costs	£30,311,000
Depreciation and Amortisation	£11,829,000
Operating expenditure	£126,671,000
Net operating costs for the year	£173,660,000

Source: NI Prison Service – *Annual Report and Accounts 2012–13*

PRISON ESTABLISHMENTS

ENGLAND AND WALES *as at July 2014*

Prison	Address	Capacity	Prisoners	Governor/Director
ALTCOURSE (private prison)	Liverpool L9 7WU	1,133	1,132	Bob McColm
ASHFIELD (private prison)	Bristol BS16 9QJ	400	396	Ray Duckworth
*‡ASKHAM GRANGE	York YO23 3FT	128	99	Diane Pellew
‡AYLESBURY	Bucks HP20 1EH	444	439	Kevin Leggett
BEDFORD	Bedford MK40 1HG	506	503	Ian Blakeman
BELMARSH	London SE28 0EB	930	875	Phil Wragg
BIRMINGHAM	Birmingham B18 4AS	1,450	1,441	Peter Small
BLANTYRE HOUSE	Kent TN17 2NH	122	113	James Bourke
†‡BRINSFORD	Wolverhampton WV10 7PY	521	441	Carl Hardwick
‡BRISTOL	Bristol BS7 8PS	614	612	Andrea Albutt
‡BRIXTON	London SW2 5XF	798	533	Edmond Tullett
*BRONZEFIELD (private prison)	Middlesex TW15 3JZ	527	482	Charlotte Pattison-Rideout
BUCKLEY HALL	Lancs OL12 9DP	445	444	Susan Kennedy
BULLINGDON	Oxon OX25 1PZ	1,114	1,104	Ian Young
BURE	Norfolk NR10 5GB	624	623	Sue Doolan
†CARDIFF	Cardiff CF24 0UG	814	812	Steve Cross
CHANNINGS WOOD	Devon TQ12 6DW	731	727	Gavin O'Malley
‡CHELMSFORD	Essex CM2 6LQ	726	741	Helen Carter
COLDINGLEY	Surrey GU24 9EX	513	509	Glenn Knight
‡COOKHAM WOOD	Kent ME1 3LU	143	150	Jonathan French
DARTMOOR	Devon PL20 6RR	659	649	Terry Witton
‡DEERBOLT	Co. Durham DL12 9BG	513	480	Gabrielle Lee
‡DONCASTER (private prison)	Doncaster DN5 8UX	1,145	1,139	John Biggin
DOVEGATE (private prison)	Staffs ST14 8XR	1,133	1,119	Craig Thomson
§DOVER	Kent CT17 9DR	401	370	Sara Pennington
*DOWNVIEW	Surrey SM2 5PD	0	0	Jonathan French
*‡DRAKE HALL	Staffs ST21 6LQ	315	311	Paul Newton
DURHAM	Durham DH1 3HU	995	953	Tim Allen *(acting)*
*‡EAST SUTTON PARK	Kent ME17 3DF	100	79	James Bourke
*‡EASTWOOD PARK	Glos GL12 8DB	363	343	Simon Beecroft
ELMLEY	Kent ME12 4DZ	1,252	1,247	Jim Carmichael
ERLESTOKE	Wilts SN10 5TU	491	489	Andy Rogers
†‡EXETER	Devon EX4 4EX	561	535	Jeannine Hendrick
FEATHERSTONE	Wolverhampton WV10 7PU	687	683	Deborah Butler
†‡FELTHAM	Middx TW13 4ND	650	573	Glenn Knight
FORD	W. Sussex BN18 0BX	531	516	Sharon Williams
‡FOREST BANK (private prison)	Manchester M27 8FB	1,460	1,455	Trevor Shortt
*FOSTON HALL	Derby DE65 5DN	310	283	Ken Kan
FRANKLAND	Durham DH1 5YD	788	770	Paddy Fox
FULL SUTTON	York YO41 1PS	616	603	Paul Foweather
GARTH	Preston PR26 8NE	766	775	Steve Lawrence
GARTREE	Leics LE16 7RP	708	707	Ian Telfer
†‡GLEN PARVA	Leicester LE18 4TN	728	710	Michael Wood
GRENDON/SPRING HILL	Bucks HP18 0TL	554	521	Jamie Bennett
‡GUYS MARSH	Dorset SP7 0AH	579	563	Duncan Burles
§HASLAR	Hampshire PO12 2AW	170	151	Paul Millett
HAVERIGG	Cumbria LA18 4NA	644	641	Tony Corcoran
HEWELL	Worcs B97 6QS	1,301	1,269	Nigel Atkinson
HIGH DOWN	Surrey SM2 5PJ	1,163	1,162	Ian Bickers
HIGHPOINT	Suffolk CB8 9YG	1,331	1,326	Nigel Smith
†‡HINDLEY	Lancs WN2 5TH	367	274	Peter Francis
‡HOLLESLEY BAY	Suffolk IP12 3JW	434	431	Declan Moore
*‡HOLLOWAY	London N7 0NU	591	543	Julia Killick
HOLME HOUSE	Stockton-on-Tees TS18 2QU	1,210	1,208	Jenny Mooney
‡HULL	Hull HU9 5LS	762	755	Norman Griffin
HUMBER	E. Yorks HU15	1,062	1,061	Ed Commell
‡HUNTERCOMBE	Oxon RG9 5SB	417	405	Nigel Atkinson
ISIS	Thamesmead SE28 0NZ	622	612	Grahame Hawkings
ISLE OF WIGHT	Isle of Wight PO30 5RS	1,139	1,132	Andy Lattimore
KENNET	Merseyside L31 1HX	342	304	Steve Valentine
KIRKHAM	Lancs PR4 2RN	634	619	Graham Beck
KIRKLEVINGTON GRANGE	Cleveland TS15 9PA	303	296	Steve Robson
†‡LANCASTER FARMS	Lancaster LA1 3QZ	416	355	Derek Harrison
LEEDS	Leeds LS12 2TJ	1,212	1,216	Susan Kennedy
LEICESTER	Leicester LE2 7AJ	411	365	Ali Dodds
‡LEWES	E. Sussex BN7 1EA	729	688	Nigel Foote
LEYHILL	Glos GL12 8BT	527	490	Chantel King
LINCOLN	Lincoln LN2 4BD	729	701	Peter Wright
LINDHOLME	Doncaster DN7 6EE	1,010	1,009	Mahala McGuffie
LITTLEHEY	Cambs PE28 0SR	1,206	931	David Taylor
LIVERPOOL	Liverpool L9 3DF	1,442	1,241	John Illingsworth
LONG LARTIN	Worcs WR11 8TZ	622	613	Nick Dann
*‡LOW NEWTON	Durham DH1 5YA	329	321	Alan Richer

Prison	Address	Capacity	Prisoners	Governor/Director
LOWDHAM GRANGE (private prison)	Notts NG14 7DA	920	912	Trish Mithcell
MAIDSTONE	Kent ME14 1UZ	600	587	Dave Atkinson
MANCHESTER	Manchester M60 9AH	1,286	1,164	Hannah Lane (acting)
‡MOORLAND/HATFIELD	Doncaster DN7 6BW	1,272	1,281	David Bamford
§MORTON HALL	Lincoln LN6 9PT	392	352	Karen Head
MOUNT	Herts HP3 0NZ	782	781	Steven Bradford
*‡NEW HALL	W. Yorks WF4 4XX	425	404	Diane Pellew
NORTH SEA CAMP	Lincs PE22 0QX	420	399	Paul Yates
‡NORTHUMBERLAND	Northumberland NE65 9XF	1,348	1,324	Matt Spencer
‡NORWICH	Norfolk NR1 4LU	769	744	Will Styles
NOTTINGHAM	Notts NG5 3AG	1,100	1,091	James Shanley
OAKWOOD	W. Midlands WV10 7QD	1,605	1,593	John McLaughlin
ONLEY	Warks CV23 8AP	682	680	Stephen Ruddy
†‡PARC (private prison)	Bridgend CF35 6AP	1,434	1,415	Janet Wallsgrove
‡PENTONVILLE	London N7 8TT	1,310	1,325	Kevin Reilly
*†PETERBOROUGH (private prison)	Peterborough PE3 7PD	1,008	960	Nick Leader
‡PORTLAND	Dorset DT5 1DL	580	574	James Lucas
PRESTON	Lancs PR1 5AB	800	699	Paul Holland
RANBY	Notts DN22 8EU	1,098	1,094	Susan Howard
RISLEY	Cheshire WA3 6BP	1,095	1,095	Jerry Spencer
‡ROCHESTER	Kent ME1 3QS	742	741	Andy Hudson
RYE HILL (private prison)	Warks CV23 8SZ	625	573	Dave Thompson, OBE
*SEND	Surrey GU23 7EJ	282	280	Dave Charity (acting)
STAFFORD	Stafford ST16 3AW	741	708	Bridie Oakes-Richards
STANDFORD HILL	Kent ME12 4AA	464	450	Sarah Coccia
STOCKEN	Leics LE15 7RD	843	831	Michael Wood
‡STOKE HEATH	Shropshire TF9 2JL	642	630	John Huntington
*‡STYAL	Cheshire SK9 4HR	460	443	John Hewitson
SUDBURY	Derbys DE6 5HW	600	579	Adrian Turner
SWALESIDE	Kent ME12 4AX	1,112	1,108	Sarah Coccia
†‡SWANSEA	Swansea SA1 3SR	455	450	Lauren Watson
‡SWINFEN HALL	Staffs WS14 9QS	594	593	Teresa Clarke
THAMESIDE	London SE28 0FJ	900	891	Guy Baulf
‡THORN CROSS	Cheshire WA4 4RL	331	325	Pia Sinha
USK/PRESCOED	Monmouthshire NP15 1XP	523	474	Darren Hughes
VERNE	Dorset DT5 1EQ	416	217	David Ward
WAKEFIELD	W. Yorks WF2 9AG	749	742	Susan Howard
WANDSWORTH	London SW18 3HS	1,628	1,634	Kenny Brown
‡WARREN HILL	Suffolk IP12 3JW	195	173	Bev Bevan
WAYLAND	Norfolk IP25 6RL	1,001	996	Steve Rodford, OBE
WEALSTUN	W. Yorks LS23 7AZ	807	802	Andrew Dickinson
‡WERRINGTON	Stoke-on-Trent ST9 0DX	160	110	Babafemi Dada
‡WETHERBY	W. Yorks LS22 5ED	276	199	Sara Snell
WHATTON	Nottingham NG13 9FQ	841	837	Lynn Saunders
WHITEMOOR	Cambs PE15 0PR	458	450	Paul Cawkwell
WINCHESTER	Winchester SO22 5DF	685	678	David Rogers
WOODHILL	Bucks MK4 4DA	819	812	Rob Davis
WORMWOOD SCRUBS	London W12 0AE	1,279	1,262	Gary Monaghan
WYMOTT	Preston PR26 8LW	1,111	1,100	Terry Williams

SCOTLAND as at April 2014

Prison	Address	Average Daily	Maximum Number	Governor/Director
ADDIEWELL(private prison)	West Lothian EH55 8QA	699	710	Audrey Park
†BARLINNIE	Glasgow G33 2QX	1,306	1,453	Ian Whitehead
*†‡CORNTON VALE	Stirling FK9 5NU	213	292	Allister Purdie
†DUMFRIES	Dumfries DG2 9AX	188	207	Rhona Hotchkiss
†EDINBURGH	Edinburgh EH11 3LN	890	932	Teresa Medhurst
GLENOCHIL	Tullibody FK10 3AD	684	737	Nigel Ironside
GRAMPIAN	Aberdeenshire AB42 2YY	16	–	Jim Farish
†‡GREENOCK	Greenock PA16 9AH	242	252	William Stuart
*†INVERNESS	Inverness IV2 3HH	129	148	Caroline Johnston
†‡KILMARNOCK (private prison)	Kilmarnock KA1 5AA	501	510	Craig Thomson
LOW MOSS	Glasgow G64 2PZ	730	788	Michael Stoney
OPEN ESTATE	Angus DD8 3QY	236	258	Jacqui Clinton
†PERTH	Perth PH2 8AT	656	704	Fraser Munro
†‡POLMONT	Falkirk FK2 0AB	617	604	Sue Brookes
SHOTTS	Lanarkshire ML7 4LE	532	543	James Kerr

NORTHERN IRELAND as at June 2014

Prison	Address	Prisoners		Governor/Director
*†‡HYDEBANK WOOD	Belfast BT8 8NA	227		Austin Treacy
†§MAGHABERRY	Co. Antrim BT28 2NF	1,083		Pat Maguire
MAGILLIGAN	Co. Londonderry BT49 0LR	557		Alan Longwell

PRISON ESTABLISHMENTS KEY: * Women's establishment or establishment with units for women; † Remand Centre or establishment with units for remand prisoners; ‡ Young Offender Institution or establishment with units for young offenders; § Immigration Removal Centre or establishment with units for immigration detainees

DEFENCE

The armed forces of the UK comprise the Royal Navy, the Army and the Royal Air Force (RAF). The Queen is Commander-in-Chief of all the armed forces. The Secretary of State for Defence is responsible for the formulation and content of defence policy and for providing the means by which it is conducted. The formal legal basis for the conduct of defence in the UK rests on a range of powers vested by statute and letters patent in the Defence Council, chaired by the Secretary of State for Defence. Beneath the ministers lies the top management of the Ministry of Defence (MoD), headed jointly by the Permanent Secretary and the Chief of Defence Staff. The Permanent Secretary is the government's principal civilian adviser on defence and has the primary responsibility for policy, finance, management and administration. The Permanent Secretary is also personally accountable to parliament for the expenditure of all public money allocated to defence purposes. The Chief of the Defence Staff is the professional head of the armed forces in the UK and the principal military adviser to the secretary of state and the government.

The Defence Board is the executive of the Defence Council. Chaired by the Permanent Secretary, it acts as the main executive board of the Ministry of Defence, providing senior level leadership and strategic management of defence.

The Central Staff, headed by the Vice-Chief of the Defence Staff and the Second Permanent Under-Secretary of State, is the policy core of the department. Defence Equipment and Support, headed by the Chief of Defence Materiel, is responsible for purchasing defence equipment and providing logistical support to the armed forces.

A permanent Joint Headquarters for the conduct of joint operations was set up at Northwood in 1996. The Joint Headquarters connects the policy and strategic functions of the MoD head office with the conduct of operations and is intended to strengthen the policy/executive division.

The UK pursues its defence and security policies through its membership of NATO (to which most of its armed forces are committed), the European Union, the Organisation for Security and Cooperation in Europe and the UN (see International Organisations section).

STRENGTH OF THE REGULAR ARMED FORCES

	Royal Navy	Army	RAF	All Services
1975 strength	76,200	167,100	95,000	338,300
2000 strength	42,850	110,050	54,720	207,620
2005 strength	39,940	109,290	51,870	201,100
2006 strength	39,390	107,730	48,730	195,850
2007 strength	38,850	106,340	45,480	190,670
2008 strength	38,560	104,980	43,370	186,910
2009 strength	38,340	106,700	43,560	188,600
2010 strength	38,730	108,920	44,050	191,700
2011 strength	37,660	106,240	42,460	186,360
2012 strength	35,540	104,250	40,000	179,790
2013 strength	33,960	99,730	37,030	170,710
2014 strength	33,080	89,480	34,940	157,490

Source: MoD – Defence Statistics (Tri-Service)

SERVICE PERSONNEL BY RANK AND GENDER

	Males	Females
Officers	24,230	3,530
Other Ranks	117,480	12,250

Source: MoD – Defence Statistics (Tri-Service)

UK regular forces include trained and untrained personnel and nursing services, but exclude Gurkhas, full-time reserve service personnel, mobilised reservists and naval activated reservists. As at 1 July 2014 these groups provisionally numbered:

All Gurkhas	2,830
Full-time reserve service	3,340
Mobilised reservists	
Army	430
RAF	210
Naval activated reservists	40

Source: MoD – Defence Statistics (Tri-Service)

CIVILIAN PERSONNEL

2000 level	121,300
2001 level	118,200
2002 level	110,100
2003 level	107,600
2004 level	108,990
2005 level	107,680
2006 level	102,970
2007 level	95,790
2008 level	88,690
2009 level	86,620
2010 level	85,850
2011 level	83,060
2012 level	70,940
2013 level	65,400
2014 level	62,340

Source: MoD – Defence Statistics (Tri-Service)

UK REGULAR FORCES: DEATHS

In 2013 there were a total of 86 deaths among the UK regular armed forces, of which 13 were serving in the Royal Navy and Royal Marines, 63 in the Army and 10 in the RAF. The largest single cause of death was cancer, which accounted for 19 deaths (22 per cent of the total) in 2013. Land transport accidents accounted for 15 deaths (17 per cent) and other accidents accounted for a further 18 deaths (21 per cent). Nine deaths (10 per cent) were as a result of hostile action. Suicides and open verdicts accounted for five deaths.

NUMBER OF DEATHS AND MORTALITY RATES

	2009	2010	2011	2012	2013
Total number	205	187	132	129	86
Royal Navy	23	30	19	19	13
Army	158	136	98	95	63
RAF	24	21	15	15	10
Mortality rates per thousand					
Tri-service rate	1.07	0.97	0.69	0.71	0.50
Navy	0.58	0.78	0.52	0.55	0.42
Army	1.33	1.16	0.89	0.89	0.65
RAF	0.55	0.50	0.33	0.42	0.23

Source: MoD National Statistics

NUCLEAR FORCES

The Vanguard Class SSBN (ship submersible ballistic nuclear) provides the UK's strategic nuclear deterrent. Each Vanguard Class submarine is capable of carrying 16 Trident D5 missiles equipped with nuclear warheads.

There is a ballistic missile early warning system station at RAF Fylingdales in North Yorkshire.

ARMS CONTROL

The 1990 Conventional Armed Forces in Europe (CFE) Treaty, which commits all NATO and former Warsaw Pact members to limiting their holdings of five major classes of conventional weapons, has been adapted to reflect the changed geo-strategic environment and negotiations continue for its implementation. The Open Skies Treaty, which the UK signed in 1992 and entered into force in 2002, allows for the overflight of states parties by other states parties using unarmed observation aircraft.

The UN Convention on Certain Conventional Weapons (as amended 2001), which bans or restricts the use of specific types of weapons that are considered to cause unnecessary or unjustifiable suffering to combatants, or to affect civilians indiscriminately, was ratified by the UK in 1995. In 1968 the UK signed and ratified the Nuclear Non-Proliferation Treaty, which came into force in 1970 and was indefinitely and unconditionally extended in 1995. In 1996 the UK signed the Comprehensive Nuclear Test Ban Treaty and ratified it in 1998. The UK is a party to the 1972 Biological and Toxin Weapons Convention, which provides for a worldwide ban on biological weapons, and the 1993 Chemical Weapons Convention, which came into force in 1997 and provides for a verifiable worldwide ban on chemical weapons.

DEFENCE BUDGET DEPARTMENTAL EXPENDITURE LIMITS £ billion

	Resource budget	Capital budget	Total DEL
2013–14	27.1	7.7	34.8
2014–15 (forecast)	25.3	9.0	34.3
2015–16 (forecast)	23.6	9.3	32.9

Source: HM Treasury – Budget 2014 (Crown copyright)

MINISTRY OF DEFENCE

Main Building, Whitehall, London SW1A 2HB
T 020-7218 9000
W www.gov.uk/government/organisations/ministry-of-defence

Secretary of State for Defence, Rt. Hon. Michael Fallon, MP
Parliamentary Private Secretary, Graham Evans, MP
Private Secretary, Luke Dearden
Special Adviser, James Wise
Minister of State (Armed Forces), Rt. Hon. Mark Francois, MP
Parliamentary Private Secretary, Andrew Bingham, MP
Private Secretary, Gareth Martin
Minister of State (Defence Personnel, Welfare and Veterans), Anna Soubry, MP
Parliamentary Private Secretary, Mark Pawsey, MP
Private Secretary, Charles Seeley
Parliamentary Under-Secretary of State and Minister for Defence Equipment, Support and Technolgy, Philip Dunne, MP
Private Secretary, Tom Burden
Parliamentary Under-Secretary of State and Minister for Reserves, Julian Brazier, MP
Private Secretary, Emma Frost
Parliamentary Under-Secretary of State and Lords Spokesman, Lord Astor of Hever
Private Secretary, Alan Lawson

CHIEFS OF STAFF

Chief of the Defence Staff, Gen. Sir Nicholas Houghton, GCB, CBE, ADC
Vice Chief of the Defence Staff, Air Chief Marshal Sir Stuart Peach, KCB, CBE, ADC
Chief of the Naval Staff and First Sea Lord, Adm. Sir George Zambellas, KCB, DSC, ADC
Second Sea Lord and Chief of Naval Personnel and Training, and Chief Naval Logistics Officer, Vice-Adm. David Steel, CBE
Chief of the General Staff, Gen. Sir Peter Wall, GCB, CBE, ADC
Assistant Chief of the General Staff, Maj.-Gen. David Cullen, OBE
Chief of the Air Staff, Air Chief Marshal Sir Andrew Pulford, KCB, CBE, ADC
Assistant Chief of the Air Staff, Air Vice-Marshal Edward Stringer, CBE

SENIOR OFFICIALS

Permanent Under-Secretary of State, Jon Thompson
Second Permanent Under-Secretary of State, vacant
Chief of Defence Materiel, Bernard Gray
Chief Scientific Adviser, Prof. Vernon Gibson, FRS
Director-General Finance, David Williams

THE DEFENCE COUNCIL

The Defence Council is the senior committee of the MoD, and was established by royal prerogative under letters patent in April 1964. The letters patent confer on the Defence Council the command over all of the armed forces and charge the council with such matters relating to the administration of the armed forces as the Secretary of State for Defence should direct them to execute. It consists of the Secretary of State for Defence, the Minister of State for the Armed Forces, the Parliamentary Under-Secretary of State and Minister for Defence Personnel, Welfare and Veterans, the Parliamentary Under-Secretary of State and Minister for Defence Equipment, Support and Technology, the Parliamentary Under-Secretary of State and Minister for International Security Strategy, the Parliamentary Under-Secretary of State and Lords Spokesman on Defence, the Chief of the Defence Staff, the Permanent Under-Secretary of State of the MoD, the Chief of the Naval Staff and First Sea Lord, the Chief of the General Staff, the Chief of the Air Staff, the Vice-Chief of the Defence Staff, the Commander Joint Forces Command, the Chief of Defence Materiel, the Chief Scientific Adviser and the Director-General Finance.

CENTRAL STAFF

Vice-Chief of the Defence Staff, Air Chief Marshal Sir Stuart Peach, KCB, CBE, ADC

JOINT FORCES COMMAND

Commander Joint Forces Command, Gen. Sir Richard Barrons, KCB, CBE, ADC
Chief of Joint Operations, Lt.-Gen. John Lorimer, MBE, DSO
Chief of Staff (Operations), Air Vice-Marshal Stuart Atha, DSO
Chief of Staff HQ, Rear-Adm. Paul Bennett, OBE

FLEET COMMAND

First Sea Lord, Adm. Sir George Zambellas, KCB, DSC, ADC
Fleet Commander and Deputy Chief of Naval Staff, Vice-Adm. Sir Philip Jones, KCB

NAVAL HOME COMMAND

Second Sea Lord and Chief of Naval Personnel and Training, and Chief Naval Logistics Officer, Vice-Adm. David Steel, CBE

Naval Secretary and Assistant Chief of Naval Staff (Personnel),
Rear-Admiral (Simon) Jonathan Woodcock, OBE

LAND FORCES
Commander Land Forces, Lt.-Gen. Sir Nicholas Carter, KCB,
CBE, DSO
Chief of Staff Land Forces, Maj.-Gen. Tyrone Urch, CBE

AIR COMMAND
Deputy Commander Operations, Air Marshal Greg Bagwell,
CB, CBE
*Deputy Commander Capability and Air Member for Personnel
and Capability,* Air Marshal Barry North, OBE

DEFENCE EQUIPMENT AND SUPPORT
Chief of Defence Materiel, Bernard Gray
Chief of Materiel (Fleet), Vice-Adm. Simon Lister, CB, OBE
Chief of Materiel (Land), Lt.-Gen. Christopher Deverell,
MBE
Chief of Materiel (Air), Air Marshal Simon Bollom, CB

EXECUTIVE AGENCIES

DEFENCE SCIENCE AND TECHNOLOGY
LABORATORY
Porton Down, Salisbury, Wiltshire SP4 0JQ **T** 01980-613000
E centralenquiries@dstl.gov.uk
W www.gov.uk/government/organisations/defence-science-and-
technology-laboratory
Chief Executive, Jonathan Lyle

DEFENCE SUPPORT GROUP
Sedgemoor Building, Monxton Road, Andover, Hampshire
SP11 8HT **T** 01264-383295 **E** info@dsg.mod.uk
W www.dsg.mod.uk
Chief Executive, Archie Hughes

UK HYDROGRAPHIC OFFICE
Admiralty Way, Taunton, Somerset TA1 2DN **T** 01823-337900
E customerservices@ukho.gov.uk
W www.gov.uk/government/organisations/uk-hydrographic-office
Chief Executive, Ian Moncrieff, CBE

ARMED FORCES TRAINING AND
RECRUITMENT
Flag Officer Sea Training (FOST) is responsible for all
Royal Navy and Royal Fleet Auxiliary training. FOST's
International Defence Training provides the focal point for
all aspects of naval training. Training is divided into five
streams: Naval Core Training (responsible for new entry,
command, leadership and management training); Royal
Marine; Submarine; Surface and Aviation.

The Army Recruiting and Training Division (ARTD) is
responsible for the four key areas of army training: soldier
initial training, at the School of Infantry or at one of the
army's four other facilities; officer initial training at the Royal
Military Academy Sandhurst; trade training at one of the
army's specialist facilities; and resettlement training for those
about to leave the army. Trade training facilities include: the
Armour Centre; the Defence College of Logistics and
Personnel Administration; the Royal School of Artillery; the
Royal School of Military Engineering and the Army Aviation
Centre.

The Royal Air Force No. 22 (Training) Group exists to
recruit RAF personnel and provide trained specialist
personnel to the armed forces as a whole, such as providing
the army air corps with trained helicopter pilots. The group is
split into eight areas: RAF College Cranwell and Inspectorate
of Recruiting; the Directorate of Flying Training (DFT); the
Directorate of Joint Technical Training (DJTT); the Air Cadet
Organisation (ACO); Core Headquarters; the Defence
College of Aeronautical Engineering (DCAE); the Defence
College of Communications and Information Systems
(DCCIS) and the Defence College of Electro-Mechanical
Engineering (DCEME).

USEFUL WEBSITES
W www.royalnavy.mod.uk
W www.army.mod.uk
W www.raf.mod.uk

THE ROYAL NAVY

In Order of Seniority

LORD HIGH ADMIRAL OF THE UNITED KINGDOM
HRH The Prince Philip, Duke of Edinburgh, KG, KT, OM, GBE, AC, QSO, PC, *apptd* 2011

ADMIRALS OF THE FLEET
HRH The Prince Philip, Duke of Edinburgh, KG, KT, OM, GBE, AC, QSO, PC, *apptd* 1953
Sir Edward Ashmore, GCB, DSC, *apptd* 1977
Sir Benjamin Bathurst, GCB, *apptd* 1995
HRH The Prince of Wales, KG, KT, GCB, OM, AK, QSO, PC, ADC, *apptd* 2012
Lord Boyce, KG, GCB, OBE, *apptd* 2014

ADMIRALS
(Former Chiefs or Vice Chiefs of Defence Staff and First Sea Lords who remain on the active list)
Slater, Sir Jock, GCB, LVO, *apptd* 1991
Abbott, Sir Peter, GBE, KCB, *apptd* 1995
Essenhigh, Sir Nigel, GCB, *apptd* 1998
West of Spithead, Lord, GCB, DSC, PC, *apptd* 2000
Band, Sir Jonathon, GCB, *apptd* 2002
Stanhope, Sir Mark, GCB, OBE, *apptd* 2004

ADMIRALS
HRH The Princess Royal, KG, KT, GCVO, QSO *(Cdre-in-Chief HM Naval Base Portsmouth)*
Zambellas, Sir George, KCB, DSC, ADC *(First Sea Lord and Chief of Naval Staff)*

VICE-ADMIRALS
Jones, Sir Philip, KCB *(Fleet Commander, Deputy Chief of Naval Staff and Chief Naval Warfare Officer)*
Richards, Alan, CB *(Chief of Defence Intelligence)*
Steel, David, CBE *(Second Sea Lord, Chief of Naval Personnel and Training and Chief Naval Logistics Officer)*
Hudson, Peter, CBE *(Cdr Maritime Command)*
Corder, Ian, CB *(UK Military Representative to NATO and the EU)*
Lister, Simon, CB, OBE *(Chief of Materiel (Fleet), Chief of Fleet Support to the Navy Board and Chief Naval Engineering Officer)*
Potts, Duncan, CB *(Director-General Joint Force Development and Director Defence Academy)*

REAR-ADMIRALS
HRH The Duke of York, KG, GCVO, ADC *(Adm. of the Sea Cadet Corps and Cdre-in-Chief Fleet Air Arm)*
Harding, Russell, OBE *(Assistant Chief of Naval Staff (Aviation and Carriers) and Rear-Adm. Fleet Air Arm (Head of Fighting Arm))*
Johnstone, Clive, CBE *(Assistant Chief of Naval Staff (Policy))*
Parr, Matthew, CB *(Cdr (Operations) and Rear-Adm. Submarines (Head of Fighting Arm))*
Fraser, Timothy *(Assistant Chief of Defence Staff (Capability and Force Design))*
Parker, Henry *(Director Ship Acquisition and Deputy Director Ships)*
Jess, Ian *(Assistant Chief of Naval Staff (Support))*
Beverstock, Mark *(Assistant Chief of Defence Staff (Nuclear and Chemical, Biological))*
Morse, James *(Assistant Chief of Naval Staff (Capability) and Controller of the Navy)*
Woodcock, (Simon) Jonathan, OBE *(Naval Secretary and Assistant Chief of Naval Staff (Personnel))*
Lowe, Timothy *(Deputy Cdr Strike Force NATO)*

Williams, Simon *(Defence Services Secretary and Assistant Chief of Defence Staff (Personnel and Training))*
Karsten, Thomas *(National Hydrographer and Deputy Chief Executive (Hydrography))*
Bennett, Paul, OBE *(Chief of Staff Joint Forces Command)*
Key, Benjamin *(Flag Officer Sea Training)*
Wareham, Michael *(Director Submarines)*
Cree, Malcolm *(Chief of Staff (Integrated Change Programme))*
Ancona, Simon *(Assistant Chief of Defence Staff (Military Strategy))*
Kingwell, John *(Director Concepts and Doctrine)*
Mackay, Graeme *(Programme Director Carrier Strike)*
Clink, John, OBE *(Flag Officer Scotland, Northern England and Northern Ireland and Flag Officer Reserve Forces)*
Beckett, K., CBE *(Chief Strategic Systems Executive)*
Radakin, A., *(Cdr UK Maritime Forces)*

MEDICAL
McArthur, Calum, QHP *(Surgeon Rear-Adm., Cdr Joint Medical Command, Chief Naval Medical Officer and Medical Director-General (Naval))*
Walker, Alasdair, OBE, QHS *(Surgeon Rear-Adm., Director Medical Policy and Operational Capability)*

ROYAL MARINES
CAPTAIN-GENERAL
HRH The Prince Philip, Duke of Edinburgh, KG, KT, OM, GBE, AC, QSO, PC

LIEUTENANT-GENERAL
Capewell, Sir David, KCB, OBE *(Hudson Fellowship)*
Messenger, Gordon, DSO*, OBE *(Deputy Chief of Defence Staff (Military Strategic Operations))*
Davis, Edward, CB, CDE *(Deputy Cdr Land Command Izmir)*

MAJOR-GENERALS
Howes, (F. H. R.) Buster, CB, OBE *(Head of the British Defence Staff, USA and Defence Attaché)*
Smith, Martin, MBE *(Cdr UK Amphibious Forces and Commandant-General Royal Marines)*

The Royal Marines were formed in 1664 and are part of the Naval Service. Their primary purpose is to conduct amphibious and land warfare. The principal operational units are:
• Three Commando Brigade, an amphibious all-arms brigade trained to operate in arduous environments (a core element of the UK's Joint Rapid Reaction Force). The commando units, 40 Commando, 42 Commando and 45 Commando each have a strength of around 700 and are based in Taunton, Plymouth and Arbroath, respectively. 43 Commando Fleet Protection Group is over 500 strong and is based at HM Naval Base Clyde on the west coast of Scotland.
• 1 Assault Group, which has its headquarters located in Devonport, Plymouth is responsible for ten landing craft training squadron at Poole, Dorset and 11 amphibious trials and training squadron at Instow, Devon
The Royal Marines also provide detachments for warships and land-based naval parties as required.

ROYAL MARINES RESERVES (RMR)
The Royal Marines Reserve is a commando-trained volunteer force with the principal role, when mobilised, of supporting the Royal Marines. The RMR consists of approximately 600 trained ranks who are distributed between the four RMR

centres in the UK. Approximately 10 per cent of the RMR are working with the regular corps on long-term attachments within all of the Royal Marines regular units.

OTHER PARTS OF THE NAVAL SERVICE
FLEET AIR ARM
The Fleet Air Arm (FAA) provides the Royal Navy with a multi-role aviation combat capability able to operate autonomously at short notice worldwide in all environments, over the sea and land. The FAA numbers some 6,200 people, which comprises 11.5 per cent of the total Royal Naval strength. It operates some 200 combat aircraft and more than 50 support/training aircraft.

ROYAL FLEET AUXILIARY SERVICE (RFA)
The Royal Fleet Auxiliary Service is a civilian-manned flotilla of 13 ships owned by the MoD. Its primary role is to supply the Royal Navy and host nations while at sea with fuel, ammunition, food and spares, enabling them to maintain operations away from their home ports. It also provides amphibious support and secure sea transport for military units and their equipment. The ships routinely support and embark Royal Naval Air Squadrons.

ROYAL NAVAL RESERVE (RNR)
The Royal Naval Reserve is an integral part of the Naval Service. It is a part-time force of 2,300 trained men and women who are deployed with the Royal Navy in times of tension, humanitarian crisis or conflict.

The Royal Naval Reserve has 18 units throughout the UK; 17 of these provide initial training while one other specialist unit, HMS *Ferret,* provides intelligence training. Basic training is provided at HMS *Raleigh,* Torpoint in Cornwall for ratings and at the Britannia Royal Naval College, Dartmouth in Devon for officers; both these and most other RNR courses are of two weeks' duration or less.

QUEEN ALEXANDRA'S ROYAL NAVAL NURSING SERVICE
The first nursing sisters were appointed to naval hospitals in 1884 and the Queen Alexandra's Royal Navy Nursing Service (QARNNS) gained its current title in 1902. Nursing ratings were introduced in 1960 and men were integrated into the service in 1982; QARNNS recruits qualified nurses as both officers and ratings, and student nurse training can be undertaken in the service.

Patron, HRH Princess Alexandra, the Hon. Lady Ogilvy, KG, GCVO
Director of Naval Nursing Services and Matron-in-Chief, Capt. Inga Kennedy, QHNS, QARNNS

HM FLEET
as at September 2014

Submarines	
Vanguard Class	Vanguard, Vengeance, Victorious, Vigilant
Trafalgar Class	Talent, Tireless, Torbay, Trenchant, Triumph
Astute Class	Astute, Ambush
Landing Platform Helicopter	Ocean, Illustrious
Landing Platform Dock	Albion, Bulwark
Destroyers	
Type 45	Daring, Dauntless, Defender, Diamond, Dragon, Duncan
Frigates	
Type 23	Argyll, Iron Duke, Kent, Lancaster, Monmouth, Montrose, Northumberland, Portland, Richmond, St Albans, Somerset, Sutherland, Westminster
Mine Warfare Vessels	
Hunt Class	Atherstone, Brocklesby, Cattistock, Chiddingfold, Hurworth, Ledbury, Middleton, Quorn
Sandown Class	Bangor, Blyth, Grimsby, Pembroke, Penzance, Ramsey, Shoreham
Patrol Vessels	
Archer Class P2000 Training Boats	Archer, Biter, Blazer, Charger, Dasher, Example, Exploit, Explorer, Express, Puncher, Pursuer, Raider, Ranger, Smiter, Tracker, Trumpeter
Gibraltar Squadron 16m Fast Patrol Boats	Sabre, Scimitar
River Class	Mersey, Severn, Tyne, Clyde
Survey Vessels	
Ice Patrol Ships	Protector
Ocean Survey Vessel	Scott
Coastal Survey Vessel	Gleaner
Multi-Role Survey Vessels	Echo, Enterprise

ROYAL FLEET AUXILIARY

Landing Ship Dock (Auxiliary)	RFA Cardigan Bay, RFA Mounts Bay, RFA Lyme Bay
Wave Class	RFA Wave Knight, RFA Wave Ruler
Rover Class	RFA Black Rover, RFA Gold Rover
Leaf Class	RFA Orangeleaf
Fort Class	RFA Fort Austin, RFA Fort Rosalie, RFA Fort Victoria
Forward Repair Ship	RFA Diligence
Joint Casualty Treatment Ship/Maritime Afloat Training Capability	RFA Argus

THE ARMY

In Order of Seniority

THE QUEEN

FIELD MARSHALS
HRH The Prince Philip, Duke of Edinburgh, KG, KT, OM, GBE, AC, QSO, PC, *apptd* 1953
Lord Bramall, KG, GCB, OBE, MC, *apptd* 1982
Lord Vincent of Coleshill, GBE, KCB, DSO, *apptd* 1991

Sir John Chapple, GCB, CBE, *apptd* 1992
HRH The Duke of Kent, KG, GCMG, GCVO, ADC, *apptd* 1993
Lord Inge, KG, GCB, PC, *apptd* 1994
HRH The Prince of Wales, KG, KT, GCB, OM, AK, QSO, PC, ADC, *apptd* 2012
Lord Guthrie of Craigiebank, GCB, LVO, OBE, *apptd* 2012
Lord Walker of Aldringham, GCB, CMG, CBE, *apptd* 2014

FORMER CHIEFS OF STAFF
Gen. Sir Roger Wheeler, GCB, CBE, *apptd* 1997
Gen. Sir Mike Jackson, GCB, CBE, DSO, *apptd* 2003
Gen. Sir Timothy Granville-Chapman, GBE, KCB, *apptd* 2005
Gen. Lord Dannatt, GCB, CBE, MC, *apptd* 2006
Gen. Lord Richards of Herstmonceux, GCB, CBE, DSO, ADC *apptd* 2009

GENERALS
Houghton, Sir Nicholas, GCB, CBE, ADC *(Chief of the Defence Staff)*
Wall, Sir Peter, GCB, CBE, ADC *(Chief of the General Staff)*
Shirreff, Sir Richard, KCB, CBE *(pending retirement)*
Barrons, Sir Richard, KCB, CBE, ADC *(Cdr Joint Force Command)*
Bradshaw Sir Adrian, KCB, OBE *(Deputy Supreme Allied Cdr Europe)*

LIEUTENANT-GENERALS
Mayall, Sir Simon, KBE, CB *(Defence Senior Adviser to the Middle East)*
Carter, Sir Nicholas, KCB, CBE, DSO *(Cdr Land Forces)*
Page, J., CB, OBE *(pending retirement)*
Deverell, C., MBE *(Chief of Materiel (Land) and Quartermaster General)*
Berragan, G., CB *(Adjutant-General)*
Everard, J., CBE *(Deputy Chief of Defence Staff (Military Strategy and Operations))*
Gregory, A., CB *(Chief of Defence Personnel)*
Lorimer, J., MBE, DSO *(Chief of Joint Operations, Permanent Joint HQ)*
Evans, T., CBE, DSO *(Cdr Allied Rapid Reaction Corps)*
Jones, P., CBE *(Chief of Staff Supreme Allied Command Transformation)*
Poffley, M., OBE *(Cdr Force Development and Capability)*

MAJOR-GENERALS
Gordon, J., CB, CBE *(Senior British Loan Service Officer, Oman)*
Foster, A., CMG, MBE *(Deputy Military Adviser UNHQ)*
Beckett, T., CBE *(pending assignment)*
Conway, M. *(Director-General Army Legal Services)*
Davis, R., CBE *(Director-General Personnel)*
Jaques, P., CBE *(Director Land Equipment, Defence Equipment and Support)*
Burley, S., CB, MBE *(Military Secretary)*
Bashall, J., CBE *(pending assignment)*

Pope, N., CBE *(Director Land Capability Transformation and Master General of the Ordnance)*
Norton, Sir George, KCVO, CBE *(Deputy Cdr NATO Rapid Deployment Corps, Naples)*
Woodhouse, Revd J., CB, QHC, CF *(Chaplain General)*
Ashmore, N., OBE *(Head Strategic Asset Management and Programme Team)*
Storrie, A., CBE *(Deputy Commandant, Royal College of Defence Studies)*
Cullen, D., OBE *(Assistant Chief of the General Staff)*
Rowan, J., OBE, QHS *(Assistant Chief of Defence Staff (Health))*
Radford, T., DSO, OBE *(GOC Theatre Troops Command)*
Eeles, N., DSO *(GOC Scotland)*
Riddell-Webster, M., CBE, DSO *(pending retirement)*
Carleton-Smith, M., CBE *(appointment withheld)*
Free, J., CBE *(Chief of Staff, HQ Allied Rapid Reaction Corps)*
Nugee, R., CBE *(Chief of Staff, HQ International Security Assistance Force, Afghanistan)*
Abraham, K., CB *(Director-General Army Reform)*
Weighill, R., CBE *(Deputy Chief of Staff (Plans) Joint Force Command, Naples)*
Henderson, J., CB *(GOC – British Forces, Germany)*
Carmichael, E., CBE, QHDS *(Director-General Army Medical Services)*
Munro, R., CBE, TD *(Deputy Cdr Land Forces (Reserves))*
Chiswell, J., CBE, MC *(GOC 1st (UK) Armoured Division)*
Fox, P., CBE *(Director Customer Design)*
Smyth-Osbourne, E., CBE *(GOC London District and Maj.-Gen. Commanding the Household Division)*
Urch, T., CBE *(Chief of Staff Land Forces)*
Cripwell, R., CBE *(Cdr British Forces Cyprus)*
Sanders, P., CBE, DSO *(Assistant Chief of Defence Staff (Operations))*
Crackett, J., TD *(Assistant Chief of Defence Staff (Reserves and Cadets))*
Cowan, J., CBE, DSO *(GOC 3rd (UK) Division)*
Hockenhull, J., OBE *(pending assignment)*
Nitsch, R., CBE *(GOC Support Command)*
Skeates, S., CBE *(Commandant Royal Military Academy Sandhurst)*
Tickell, C., CBE *(Director-General Army Recruiting and Training)*
Semple, R., CBE *(Director-General Logistics, Support and Equipment)*
Felton, R., CBE *(Cdr Joint Helicopter Command)*
Talbot Rice, R. *(head of Armoured Vehicle Programmes)*
Bathurst, B., OBE *(Director MoD Ministerial Advisory Group, HQ International Security Assistance Force, Afghanistan)*
Dickinson, A. *(Director-General Army Basing and Infrastructure)*

CONSTITUTION OF THE ARMY
The army consists of the Regular Army, the Regular Reserve and the Territorial Army (TA). It is commanded by the Chief of the General Staff, who is the professional Head of Service and Chair of the Executive Committee of the Army Board, which provides overall strategic policy and direction to the Commander Land Forces (formerly Commander-in-Chief, Land Forces). There are four subordinate commands that report to the Commander Land Forces: the Field Army; Support Command, headed by the Adjutant-General; Force Development and Capability Command and the Joint Helicopter Command. The army is divided into functional arms and services, subdivided into regiments and corps

(listed below in order of precedence). During 2008, as part of the Future Army Structure (FAS) reform programme, the infantry was re-structured into large multi-battalion regiments, which involved amalgamations and changes in title for some regiments. The 2010 Strategic Defence and Security Review laid out the commitments expected of the UK Armed Forces and, as a result, Army 2020 was created to replace FAS. The main changes at divisional, brigade and unit level will occur largely between mid-2014 and mid-2015.

All enquiries with regard to records of serving personnel (Regular and Territorial Army) should be directed to The Army Personnel Centre Help Desk, Kentigern House, 65 Brown Street, Glasgow G2 8EX T 0845-600 9663. Enquirers should note that the Army is governed in the release of personal information by various acts of parliament.

ORDER OF PRECEDENCE OF CORPS AND REGIMENTS OF THE BRITISH ARMY

ARMS

HOUSEHOLD CAVALRY
The Life Guards
The Blues and Royals (Royal Horse Guards and 1st Dragoons)

ROYAL HORSE ARTILLERY
(when on parade, the Royal Horse Artillery take precedence over the Household Cavalry)

ROYAL ARMOURED CORPS
1st the Queen's Dragoon Guards
The Royal Scots Dragoon Guards (Carabiniers and Greys)
The Royal Dragoon Guards
The Queen's Royal Hussars (The Queen's Own and Royal Irish)
The Royal Lancers
The King's Royal Hussars
The Light Dragoons
1st Royal Tank Regiment
2nd Royal Tank Regiment

ROYAL REGIMENT OF ARTILLERY
(with the exception of the Royal Horse Artillery (*see* above))

CORPS OF ROYAL ENGINEERS
ROYAL CORPS OF SIGNALS
REGIMENTS OF FOOT GUARDS
Grenadier Guards
Coldstream Guards
Scots Guards
Irish Guards
Welsh Guards

REGIMENTS OF INFANTRY
The Royal Regiment of Scotland
The Princess of Wales' Royal Regiment (Queen and Royal Hampshire's)
The Duke of Lancaster's Regiment (King's, Lancashire and Border)
The Royal Regiment of Fusiliers
The Royal Anglian Regiment
The Rifles
The Yorkshire Regiment
The Mercian Regiment
The Royal Welsh

The Royal Irish Regiment
The Parachute Regiment
The Royal Gurkha Rifles

SPECIAL AIR SERVICE
ARMY AIR CORPS
SERVICES

ROYAL ARMY CHAPLAINS' DEPARTMENT
THE ROYAL LOGISTIC CORPS
ROYAL ARMY MEDICAL CORPS
CORPS OF ROYAL ELECTRICAL AND MECHANICAL ENGINEERS
ADJUTANT-GENERAL'S CORPS
ROYAL ARMY VETERINARY CORPS
SMALL ARMS SCHOOL CORPS
ROYAL ARMY DENTAL CORPS
INTELLIGENCE CORPS
ARMY PHYSICAL TRAINING CORPS
QUEEN ALEXANDRA'S ROYAL ARMY NURSING CORPS
CORPS OF ARMY MUSIC
THE ROYAL MONMOUTHSHIRE ROYAL ENGINEERS (MILITIA) (THE ARMY RESERVE)
THE HONOURABLE ARTILLERY COMPANY (THE ARMY RESERVE)
REST OF THE ARMY RESERVE

THE ARMY RESERVE
The Army Reserve (formerly the Territorial Army (TA)) is part of the UK's reserve land forces and provides support to the regular army at home and overseas. The Army Reserve is divided into three types of unit: national, regional, and sponsored. Army Reserve soldiers serving in regional units complete a minimum of 27 days training a year, comprising some evenings, weekends and an annual two-week camp. National units normally specialise in a specific role or trade, such as logistics, IT, communications or medical services. Members of national units have a lower level of training commitment and complete 19 days training a year. Sponsored reserves are individuals who will serve, as members of the workforce of a company contracted to the MoD, in a military capacity and have agreed to accept a reserve liability to be called up for active service in a crisis. In 2012 the Secretary of State for Defence issued a consultation paper *Future Reserves 2020: Delivering the Nation's Security Together,* which outlined plans to invest an additional £1.8bn in the Reserve Forces over the next ten years, for the Reserve Forces to be more integrated with the regular forces and to have a more significant role within the armed forces as a whole.

QUEEN ALEXANDRA'S ROYAL ARMY NURSING CORPS
The Queen Alexandra's Royal Army Nursing Corps (QARANC) was founded in 1902 as Queen Alexandra's Imperial Military Nursing Service and gained its present title in 1949. The QARANC has trained nurses for the register since 1950 and also trains and employs health care assistants up to diploma level 3 in Health and Social Care. The corps recruits qualified nurses as officers and other ranks and in 1992 male nurses already serving in the army were transferred to the QARANC.
Colonel-in-Chief, HRH The Countess of Wessex, GCVO
Colonels Commandant, Col. Rosemary Kennedy, TD; Col. Sue Bush

THE ROYAL AIR FORCE

In Order of Seniority

THE QUEEN

MARSHALS OF THE ROYAL AIR FORCE
HRH The Prince Philip, Duke of Edinburgh, KG, KT, OM, GBE, AC, QSO, PC, *apptd* 1953
HRH The Prince of Wales, KG, KT, GCB, OM, AK, QSO, PC, ADC, *apptd* 2012

FORMER CHIEFS OF THE AIR STAFF

MARSHALS OF THE ROYAL AIR FORCE
Sir Michael Beetham, GCB, CBE, DFC, AFC, *apptd* 1982
Sir Keith Williamson, GCB, AFC, *apptd* 1985
Lord Craig of Radley, GCB, OBE, *apptd* 1988
Lord Stirrup, KG, GCB, AFC, *apptd* 2003

AIR CHIEF MARSHALS
Sir Michael Graydon, GCB, CBE, *apptd* 1991
Sir Richard Johns, GCB, KCVO, OBE, *apptd* 1994
Sir Peter Squire, GCB, DFC, AFC, *apptd* 1999
Sir Glenn Torpy, GCB, CBE, DSO, *apptd* 2006
Sir Stephen Dalton, GCB, *apptd* 2009

AIR RANK LIST

AIR CHIEF MARSHALS
Peach, Sir Stuart, KCB, CBE, ADC *(Vice Chief of the Defence Staff)*
Pulford, Sir Andrew KCB, CBE, ADC *(Chief of the Air Staff)*

AIR MARSHALS
Harper, Sir Christopher, KBE *(Director-General International Military Staff)*
Garwood, R., CB, CBE, DFC *(Director-General of the Military Aviation Authority)*
Hillier, Sir Stephen, KCB, CBE, DFC *(Deputy Chief of the Defence Staff (Military Capability))*
Bollom, S., CB *(Chief of Materiel (Air) and Air Member for Materiel)*
Bagwell, G., CB, CBE *(Deputy Cdr Operations and Air Member for Operations)*
Stacey, G., CB, MBE *(Deputy Cdr Joint Force Command, Brunssum)*
North, B., OBE *(Deputy Cdr Capability and Air Member for Personnel and Capability)*
Evans, C., CB, QHP *(Surgeon-General HQ Joint Medical Command)*

AIR VICE-MARSHALS
Dixon, C., CB, OBE *(Cdr Joint Helicopter Command)*
Irvine, L., CB *(Director RAF Legal Services)*
Young, J., CB, OBE *(Director Technical, Defence Equipment and Support)*
Chafferty, J., QHC *(Chaplain Chief and Director-General Chaplaincy Services)*
Osborn, P., CBE *(Director Capability Joint Forces Command)*
Howard, G., CB *(Assistant Chief of the Defence Staff Logistics Operations)*
Atha, S., DSO *(Chief of Staff (Operations), Permanent Joint HQ)*

Morrison, I., CBE *(Director-General, Saudi Armed Forces Project)*
Judson, R. *(Director Joint Warfare, Joint Forces Command)*
Mozumder, A., QHP *(Cdr Defence Primary Healthcare, HQ Surgeon-General)*
Rigby, J., CBE *(Director Cyber, Intelligence and Information Integration)*
Clark, M. *(Director Technical in the Military Aviation Authority)*
Farnell, G., OBE *(General-Manager, NATO Eurofighter and Typhoon Management Agency)*
Atherton, P., OBE *(Director Operations, Military Aviation Authority)*
Brecht, M. *(Chief of Staff Capability, Air Command)*
Ewen, P. *(Director Air Support, Defence Equipment and Support)*
Reynolds, S., CBE, DFC *(Air Officer Commanding No. 2 Group and Chief of Staff (Operations))*
Stringer, E., CBE *(Assistant Chief of the Air Staff)*
Bishop, T., OBE *(Air Officer Commanding No. 38 Group)*
Evans, S., CBE *(Senior British Military Adviser to the United States Central Command, Tampa)*
Gray, S., OBE *(Director Combat Air, Defence Equipment and Support)*
Turner, A., CBE *(Air Officer Commanding No. 22 Group and Chief of Staff Training)*
Stubbs, D., OBE *(Chief of Staff Personnel and Air Secretary)*
West, M., CBE *(Director of Projects and Programme Delivery, Defence Infrastructure Organisation)*
Waterfall, G., CBE *(Air Officer Commanding No. 1 Group)*

CONSTITUTION OF THE RAF

The RAF consists of a single command, Air Command, based at RAF High Wycombe. RAF Air Command was formed on 1 April 2007 from the amalgamation of Strike Command and Personnel and Training Command.

Air Command consists of three groups, each organised around specific operational duties. No. 1 Group is the coordinating organisation for the tactical fast-jet forces responsible for attack, offensive support and air defence operations. No. 2 Group provides air combat support including air transport and air to air refuelling; intelligence surveillance; targeting and reconnaissance; and force protection. No. 22 (Training) Group recruits personnel and provides trained specialist personnel to the RAF, as well as to the Royal Navy and the Army *(see also* Armed Forces Training and Recruitment).

RAF EQUIPMENT
AIRCRAFT

Combat Aircraft	Lightening II, Tornado GR4, Typhoon FGR4
Training Aircraft	Hawk T1, Hawk T2, King Air B200, Tucano T1, Tutor T1, Vigilant T1, Viking T1
Surveillance Aircraft	Reaper MQ9A RPAS, Sentinel R1, E-3D Sentry AEW1, Shadow R1

HELICOPTERS

Helicopters	Chinook, Griffin HAR2, Merlin HC3, Puma HC2, Sea King HAR3/3A
Training Helicopters	Griffin HT1, Squirrel HT1

ROYAL AUXILIARY AIR FORCE

The Auxiliary Air Force was formed in 1924 to train an elite corps of civilians to serve their country in flying squadrons in their spare time. In 1947 the force was awarded the prefix 'royal' in recognition of its distinguished war service and the Sovereign's Colour for the Royal Auxiliary Air Force (RAuxAF) was presented in 1989. The RAuxAF continues to recruit civilians who undertake military training in their spare time to support the Royal Air Force in times of emergency or war. Reserves commit a minimum of 27 days a year on a renewable five-year basis.

Air Commodore-in-Chief, HM The Queen
Honorary Inspector-General (Air Vice-Marshal) Royal Auxiliary Air Force, Lord Beaverbrook
Inspector Royal Auxiliary Air Force, Gp Capt. Gary Bunkell, QVRM, AE, ADC

PRINCESS MARY'S ROYAL AIR FORCE NURSING SERVICE

The Princess Mary's Royal Air Force Nursing Service (PMRAFNS) was formed on 1 June 1918 as the Royal Air Force Nursing Service. In June 1923, His Majesty King George V gave his royal assent for the Royal Air Force Nursing Service to be known as the Princess Mary's Royal Air Force Nursing Service. Men were integrated into the PMRAFNS in 1980.

Patron and Air Chief Commandant, HRH Princess Alexandra, The Hon. Lady Ogilvy, KG, GCVO
Director of Nursing Services and Matron-in-Chief, Gp Capt. Phil Spragg

SERVICE SALARIES

The following rates of pay apply from 1 April 2014 and are rounded to the nearest pound.

The pay rates shown are for army personnel. The rates also apply to personnel of equivalent rank and pay band in the other services (*see* below for table of relative ranks).

Rank	Annual salary
SECOND LIEUTENANT	£25,220
LIEUTENANT	
On appointment	£30,314
After 1 year in rank	£31,115
After 2 years in rank	£31,912
After 3 years in rank	£32,705
After 4 years in rank	£33,507
CAPTAIN	
On appointment	£38,848
After 1 year in rank	£39,888
After 2 years in rank	£40,941
After 3 years in rank	£41,999
After 4 years in rank	£43,043
After 5 years in rank	£44,097
After 6 years in rank	£45,141
After 7 years in rank	£45,674
After 8 years in rank	£46,199
MAJOR	
On appointment	£48,934
After 1 year in rank	£50,142
After 2 years in rank	£51,342
After 3 years in rank	£52,559
After 4 years in rank	£53,763
After 5 years in rank	£54,980
After 6 years in rank	£56,100
After 7 years in rank	£57,392
After 8 years in rank	£58,605
LIEUTENANT-COLONEL	
On appointment	£68,679
After 1 year in rank	£69,589
After 2 years in rank	£70,491
After 3 years in rank	£71,394
After 4 years in rank	£72,296
After 5 years in rank	£76,448
After 6 years in rank	£77,467
After 7 years in rank	£78,496
After 8 years in rank	£79,524
COLONEL	
On appointment	£83,205
After 1 year in rank	£84,236
After 2 years in rank	£85,272
After 3 years in rank	£86,303
After 4 years in rank	£87,334
After 5 years in rank	£88,365
After 6 years in rank	£89,396
After 7 years in rank	£90,431
After 8 years in rank	£91,466
BRIGADIER	
On appointment	£99,154
After 1 year in rank	£100,156
After 2 years in rank	£101,158
After 3 years in rank	£102,156
After 4 years in rank	£103,167

PAY SYSTEM FOR SENIOR MILITARY OFFICERS

Pay rates effective from 1 April 2014 for all military officers of 2* rank and above (excluding medical and dental officers). All pay rates are rounded to the nearest pound.

Rank	Annual salary
MAJOR-GENERAL (2*)	
Scale 1	£110,463
Scale 2	£112,621
Scale 3	£114,824
Scale 4	£117,070
Scale 5	£119,361
Scale 6	£121,697
LIEUTENANT-GENERAL (3*)	
Scale 1	£128,526
Scale 2	£134,826
Scale 3	£141,441
Scale 4	£146,998
Scale 5	£151,332
Scale 6	£155,797
GENERAL (4*)	
Scale 1	£168,606
Scale 2	£172,821
Scale 3	£177,142
Scale 4	£181,571
Scale 5	£185,202
Scale 6	£188,906

Field Marshal – appointments to this rank will not usually be made in peacetime. The salary for holders of the rank is equivalent to the salary of a 5-star General, a salary created only in times of war. In peacetime, the equivalent rank to Field Marshal is the Chief of the Defence Staff. From 1 April 2014, the annual salary range for the Chief of the Defence Staff is £242,909–£257,777.

OFFICERS COMMISSIONED FROM THE SENIOR RANKS

Rank	Annual salary
Level 15	£51,926
Level 14	£51,586
Level 13	£51,229
Level 12	£50,537
Level 11	£49,849
Level 10	£49,152
Level 9	£48,460
Level 8	£47,768
Level 7*	£46,903
Level 6	£46,371
Level 5	£45,829
Level 4†	£44,760
Level 3	£44,226
Level 2	£43,681
Level 1‡	£42,615

* Officers commissioned from the ranks with more than 15 years' service enter on level 7

† Officers commissioned from the ranks with between 12 and 15 years' service enter on level 4

‡ Officers commissioned from the ranks with less than 12 years' service enter on level 1

SOLDIERS' SALARIES

Under the Pay 2000 scheme, personnel are paid in either a high or low band in accordance with how their trade has been allocated to those bands at each rank. Pay is based on trade and rank, not on individual appointment, or in response to temporary changes in role.

Rates of pay effective from 1 April 2014 (rounded to the nearest pound) are:

Rank	Lower band	Higher band
PRIVATE		
Level 1	£17,945	£17,945
Level 2	£18,428	£19,305
Level 3	£18,910	£21,260
Level 4	£20,521	£22,308
LANCE CORPORAL (levels 5–7 also applicable to Privates)		
Level 5	£21,600	£24,666
Level 6	£21,969	£25,866
Level 7	£22,908	£27,054
Level 8	£23,957	£28,270
Level 9	£24,826	£29,651
CORPORAL		
Level 1	£27,054	£28,270
Level 2	£28,270	£29,651
Level 3	£29,651	£31,103
Level 4	£29,877	£31,828
Level 5	£30,112	£32,596
Level 6	£30,352	£33,272
Level 7	£30,574	£33,998

Rank	Lower band	Higher band
SERGEANT		
Level 1	£30,750	£33,561
Level 2	£31,556	£34,430
Level 3	£32,349	£35,302
Level 4	£32,676	£35,747
Level 5	£33,528	£36,444
Level 6	£34,686	£37,140
Level 7	£34,950	£37,836
STAFF SERGEANT		
Level 1	£34,039	£37,862
Level 2	£34,484	£38,776
Level 3	£35,604	£39,704
Level 4	£36,439	£40,622
WARRANT OFFICER II (levels 5–7 also applicable to Staff Sergeants)		
Level 5	£36,934	£41,546
Level 6	£38,604	£42,464
Level 7	£39,196	£43,077
Level 8	£39,704	£43,690
Level 9	£40,602	£44,315
WARRANT OFFICER I		
Level 1	£39,548	£43,115
Level 2	£40,316	£43,962
Level 3	£41,130	£44,718
Level 4	£41,944	£45,540
Level 5	£42,762	£46,354
Level 6	£43,962	£47,180
Level 7	£45,204	£47,902

RELATIVE RANK – ARMED FORCES

Royal Navy	Army	Royal Air Force
1 Admiral of the Fleet	1 Field Marshal	1 Marshal of the RAF
2 Admiral (Adm.)	2 General (Gen.)	2 Air Chief Marshal
3 Vice-Admiral (Vice-Adm.)	3 Lieutenant-General (Lt.-Gen.)	3 Air Marshal
4 Rear-Admiral (Rear-Adm.)	4 Major-General (Maj.-Gen.)	4 Air Vice-Marshal
5 Commodore (Cdre)	5 Brigadier (Brig.)	5 Air Commodore (Air Cdre)
6 Captain (Capt.)	6 Colonel (Col.)	6 Group Captain (Gp Capt.)
7 Commander (Cdr)	7 Lieutenant-Colonel (Lt.-Col.)	7 Wing Commander (Wg Cdr)
8 Lieutenant-Commander (Lt.-Cdr)	8 Major (Maj.)	8 Squadron Leader (Sqn Ldr)
9 Lieutenant (Lt.)	9 Captain (Capt.)	9 Flight Lieutenant (Flt Lt)
10 Sub-Lieutenant (Sub-Lt.)	10 Lieutenant (Lt.)	10 Flying Officer (FO)
11 Midshipman	11 Second Lieutenant (2nd Lt.)	11 Pilot Officer (PO)

SERVICE RETIRED PAY *on compulsory retirement*

Those who leave the services having served at least five years, but not long enough to qualify for the appropriate immediate pension, now qualify for a preserved pension and terminal grant, both of which are payable at age 60. The tax-free resettlement grants shown below are payable on release to those who qualify for a preserved pension and who have completed nine years' service from age 21 (officers) or 12 years from age 18 (other ranks).

The annual rates for army personnel are given. The rates also apply to personnel of equivalent rank in the other services, including the nursing services.

OFFICERS

Applicable to officers who give full pay service on the active list on or after 31 March 2014. Pensionable earnings for senior officers (*) is defined as the total amount of basic pay received during the year ending on the day prior to retirement, or the amount of basic pay received during any 12-month period within three years prior to retirement, whichever is the higher. Figures for senior officers are percentage rates of pensionable earnings on final salary arrangements on or after 31 March 2014.

No. of years reckonable service	Capt. and below	Major	Lt.-Col.	Colonel	Brigadier	Major-General*	Lieutenant-General*	General*
16	£12,865	£15,323	£20,090	£24,302	£28,830	—	—	—
17	£13,458	£16,050	£21,117	£25,417	£29,954	—	—	—
18	£14,051	£16,778	£22,143	£26,531	£31,078	—	—	—
19	£14,644	£17,506	£23,170	£27,645	£32,202	—	—	—
20	£15,237	£18,234	£24,197	£28,760	£33,326	—	—	—
21	£15,830	£18,962	£25,223	£29,874	£35,450	—	—	—
22	£16,423	£19,690	£26,250	£30,989	£35,574	—	—	—
23	£17,016	£20,417	£27,276	£32,103	£36,698	—	—	—
24	£17,609	£21,145	£28,303	£33,217	£37,822	38.5%	—	—
25	£18,202	£21,873	£29,330	£34,332	£38,946	39.7%	—	—
26	£18,795	£22,601	£30,356	£35,446	£40,070	40.8%	—	—
27	£19,388	£23,329	£31,383	£36,560	£41,194	42.0%	42.0%	—
28	£19,981	£24,057	£32,410	£37,675	£42,318	43.1%	43.1%	—
29	£20,574	£24,784	£33,436	£38,789	£43,442	44.3%	44.3%	—
30	£21,167	£25,512	£34,463	£39,904	£44,566	45.4%	45.4%	45.4%
31	£21,760	£26,240	£35,489	£41,018	£45,690	46.6%	46.6%	46.6%
32	£22,353	£26,968	£36,516	£42,132	£46,814	47.7%	47.7%	47.7%
33	£22,946	£27,696	£37,543	£43,247	£47,938	48.9%	48.9%	48.9%
34	£23,539	£28,424	£38,569	£44,361	£49,062	50.0%	50.0%	50.0%

WARRANT OFFICERS, NCOS AND PRIVATES
(Applicable to soldiers who give full pay service on or after 31 March 2014)

No. of years reckonable service	Below Corporal	Corporal	Sergeant	Staff Sergeant	Warrant Officer Level II	Warrant Officer Level I
22	£7,614	£9,821	£10,768	£12,266	£13,095	£13,924
23	£7,879	£10,164	£11,144	£12,694	£13,552	£14,410
24	£8,145	£10,507	£11,519	£13,122	£14,009	£14,896
25	£8,411	£10,850	£11,895	£13,550	£14,466	£15,383
26	£8,677	£11,193	£12,271	£13,978	£14,923	£15,869
27	£8,942	£11,535	£12,647	£14,406	£15,380	£16,355
28	£9,208	£11,878	£13,023	£14,834	£15,837	£16,841
29	£9,474	£12,221	£13,399	£15,262	£16,294	£17,327
30	£9,740	£12,564	£13,774	£15,691	£16,752	£17,813
31	£10,005	£12,907	£14,150	£16,119	£17,209	£18,299
32	£10,271	£13,250	£14,526	£16,547	£17,666	£18,785
33	£10,537	£13,592	£14,902	£16,975	£18,123	£19,271
34	£10,803	£13,935	£15,278	£17,403	£18,580	£19,757
35	£11,068	£14,278	£15,654	£17,831	£19,037	£20,243
36	£11,334	£14,621	£16,030	£18,259	£19,494	£20,729
37	£11,600	£14,964	£16,405	£18,687	£19,951	£21,215

GRANTS AND GRATUITIES

Terminal grants are in each case three times the rate of retired pay or pension. There are special rates of retired pay for certain other ranks not shown above. Lower rates are payable in cases of voluntary retirement.

A gratuity of £4,370 is payable for officers with short service commissions for each year completed. Resettlement grants are £15,047 for officers and £10,284 for other ranks.

EDUCATION

THE UK EDUCATION SYSTEM

The structure of the education system in the UK is a devolved matter with each of the countries of the UK having separate systems under separate governments. There are differences between the school systems in terms of the curriculum, examinations and final qualifications and, at university level, in terms of the nature of some degrees and in the matter of tuition fees. The systems in England, Wales and Northern Ireland are similar and have more in common with one another than the Scottish system, which differs significantly.

Education in England is overseen by the Department for Education (DfE) and the Department for Business, Innovation and Skills (BIS).

In Wales, responsibility for education lies with the Department for Education and Skills (DfES) within the Welsh government. Ministers in the Scottish government are responsible for education in Scotland, led by the directorates of Learning and Lifelong Learning, while in Northern Ireland responsibility lies with the Department of Education (DENI) and the Department for Employment and Learning (DELNI) within the Northern Ireland government.

DEPARTMENT FOR EDUCATION T 0370-000 2288
  W www.gov.uk/government/organisations/department-for-education
DEPARTMENT FOR BUSINESS, INNOVATION AND SKILLS T 020-7215 5000
  W www.gov.uk/government/organisations/department-for-business-innovation-skills
DEPARTMENT FOR EDUCATION AND SKILLS (DFES)
  T 0300-060 3300; 0845-010 3300
  W www.wales.gov.uk/topics/educationandskills
SCOTTISH GOVERNMENT – EDUCATION
  T 08457-741741; 0131-556 8400
  W www.scotland.gov.uk/Topics/Education
DEPARTMENT OF EDUCATION (NI) T 028-9127 9279
  W www.deni.gov.uk
DEPARTMENT FOR EMPLOYMENT AND LEARNING
  (NI) T 028-9025 7777 W www.delni.gov.uk

RECENT DEVELOPMENTS

England announced further stages of curriculum reform and changes to vocational education, while elsewhere in the UK new strategies and qualifications bedded down. Changes made or announced include:

ENGLAND
• Free school meals available for all infants (in Reception and Years 1 and 2) from September 2014
• From 2015, new funding of £50m will extend to 3- and 4-year-olds in nursery schools with the pupil premium already available to primary school children from poorer families
• Reformed GCSEs in English and maths will be available for first teaching in schools from September 2015, with the first examinations being sat in summer 2017. These new GCSEs will be introduced into post-16 education in phases between 2015 and 2020. By 2020, adults aged 19 and over and apprentices of all ages will work toward gaining the new English and maths GCSEs
• From September 2015, Technical Awards will be the first step on a new vocational route available to 14- to 19-year-

olds. From 14 to 16, pupils will be able to study Technical Awards alongside GCSEs. From 16 to 19, students will be able to study Tech Levels alongside or instead of A-levels or as part of the TechBacc, which also comprises an advanced maths qualification and extended research project. The government's aim is that after completing school or college these young people will be ready for an advanced apprenticeship, university or skilled employment
• New Substantial Vocational Qualifications will provide 16- to 19-year old students wishing to specialise in a specific industry or occupation with intermediate (level 2) technical qualifications that are valued by employers
• New assessment arrangements for primary schools willl be introduced in stages starting in September 2015. These will include a new assessment in Reception year as a baseline for judging pupils' subsequent progress, more challenging tests and an expectation that all schools will help at least 85 per cent of their pupils to achieve a new higher standard by the end of primary school
• From 2016 early years education providers will no longer have to assess children by completing the Foundation Stage Profile, though they will still be expected to meet statutory Early Years Foundation Stage requirements
• In higher education, the government announced 30,000 more student places for 2014–15 and that from 2015–16 there will be no cap on the numbers of students publicly funded institutions can recruit

WALES
• The Education (Wales) Act 2014, passed in May 2014, replaced the General Teaching Council for Wales with a reconfigured body known as the Education Workforce Council. This will introduce a new, more robust registration and regulation system for teachers and the wider education workforce. Further Education teachers, learning support workers and school learning support workers will have to register with the Education Workforce Council and school term dates will be harmonised across all maintained schools in Wales
• Ministers announced reviews of education in Wales: from Foundation Phase to Key Stage 4, linking directly to Wales' new qualifications system; and of higher education and student finance in Wales, which will report in 2016
• A £1.4bn 5-year programme to modernise classrooms – *21st Century Schools* – was announced

SCOTLAND
• The Children and Young People (Scotland) Act, passed in February 2014, increased funding for early learning and childcare from 475 to at least 600 hours a year for 3 and 4-year-olds and the most vulnerable 2-year-olds. All children in primary 1 to 3 also have the option of a free school lunch from January 2015
• Some 1,400 of Scotland's teachers will undertake Masters level learning through 18 programmes backed by £1.7m Scottish government funding in 2014
• A report on vocational education in June 2014 called for youth unemployment to be reduced by 40 per cent, enhanced careers education in primary school, the opportunity to prepare for a Modern Apprenticeship (MA) in the senior phase of school and closer links between employers and schools and colleges

- The Scottish government sought to allay fears about the future of higher education research in an independent Scotland

NORTHERN IRELAND
- Some 40 schools will benefit from the School Enhancement Programme established in January 2013 to refurbish or extend school buildings with up to £134m from the Northern Ireland Executive
- *Learning to Learn – A Framework for Early Years Education and Learning* sets out a number of actions to ensure consistently high quality services for young children and their families, including: a review of Sure Start, the establishment of early years education support clusters, and renewed emphasis on the use of extended schools funding across nursery schools and units

STATE SCHOOL SYSTEM

PRE-SCHOOL

Pre-school education is not compulsory. In England, a free place is available for every 3- and 4-year-old whose parents want one, although parents may use as little or as much of their entitlement as they choose. All 3- and 4-year-olds, and disadvantaged 2-year-olds, are entitled to 15 hours a week of free early education over 38 weeks of the year until they reach compulsory school age (the term following their fifth birthday). This is delivered flexibly over a minimum of two days each week during normal term times. Free places are funded by local authorities and are delivered by a range of providers in the maintained and non-maintained sectors – nursery schools; nursery classes in primary schools; private schools; private day nurseries; voluntary playgroups; pre-schools; and registered childminders. In order to receive funding, providers must be working towards the early learning goals and other features of the Early Years Foundation Stage curriculum, must be inspected on a regular basis by Ofsted and must meet any conditions set by the local authority.

In Wales, every child is entitled to receive free Foundation Phase education for a minimum of two hours a day from the term following their third birthday.

In Scotland, councils have a duty to provide a pre-school education for all 3- and 4-year-olds whose parents request one. From August 2014, education authorities must offer each child at least 600 hours of free pre-school education a year (*see* Recent Developments), although they may provide more if they choose.

In Northern Ireland, the Department of Education aims to provide a funded place for all 3- and 4-year-old children in their final pre-school year. All places offer 2.5 hours a day, five days a week for at least 38 weeks a year.

PRIMARY AND SECONDARY SCHOOLS

By law, full-time education starts at the age of five for children in England, Scotland and Wales and at the age of four in Northern Ireland. In practice, most children in the UK start school before their fifth birthday: in England all children are entitled to a primary school place from the September after their fourth birthday.

Children in England are required to stay in education or training until the end of the academic year in which they turn 17 (from 2013) or 18 (from 2015). In all other parts of the UK, compulsory schooling ends at age 16, but children born between certain dates may leave school before their 16th birthday. Most young people stay in some form of education until 17 or 18.

Primary education consists mainly of infant schools for children aged 5 to 7, junior schools for those aged 7 to 11,

and combined infant and junior schools for both age groups.

First schools in some parts of England cater for ages 5 to 10 as the first stage of a three-tier system of first (lower), middle and secondary (upper) schools. Scotland has only primary schools with no infant/junior division.

Children usually leave primary school and move on to secondary school at the age of 11 (or 12 in Scotland). In the few areas of England that have a three-tier system of schools, middle schools cater for children after they leave first schools for three to four years between the ages of 8 and 14, depending on the local authority.

Secondary schools cater for children aged 11 to 16 and, if they have a sixth form, for those who choose to stay on to the age of 17 or 18. From the age of 16, students may move instead to further education colleges or work-based training. Most UK secondary schools are co-educational. The largest secondary schools have more than 1,500 pupils and around 60 per cent of secondary pupils in the UK are in schools that take more than 1,000 pupils.

Most state-maintained secondary schools in England, Wales and Scotland are comprehensive schools, which admit pupils without reference to ability. In England there remain some areas with grammar schools, catering for pupils aged 11 to 18, which select pupils on the basis of high academic ability. Over half of state secondary schools in England (57 per cent in June 2013) are now academies: academies are funded directly by the state rather than being maintained by local authorities. Northern Ireland still has 68 grammar schools; the 11-plus has been officially discontinued but schools, or consortia of schools, use their own unregulated entry tests.

More than 90 per cent of pupils in the UK attend publicly funded schools and receive free education. The rest attend privately funded 'independent' schools, which charge fees, or are educated at home.

The bulk of the UK government's expenditure on school education is through local authorities (Education and Library Boards (ELBs) in Northern Ireland), who pass on state funding to schools and other educational institutions.

SPECIAL EDUCATION

Schools and local authorities in England and Wales, Education and Library Boards (ELBs) in Northern Ireland and education authorities in Scotland are required to identify and secure provision for children with special educational needs and to involve parents in decisions. The majority of children with special educational needs are educated in ordinary mainstream schools, sometimes with supplementary help from outside specialists. Parents of children with special educational needs (referred to as additional support needs in Scotland) have a right of appeal to independent tribunals if their wishes are not met.

Special educational needs provision may be made in maintained special schools, special units attached to mainstream schools or in mainstream classes themselves, all funded by local authorities. There are also non-maintained special schools run by voluntary bodies, mainly charities, who may receive grants from central government for capital expenditure and equipment but whose other costs are met primarily from the fees charged to local authorities for pupils placed in the schools. Some independent schools also provide education wholly or mainly for children with special educational needs.

ADDITIONAL SUPPORT NEEDS TRIBUNALS FOR
SCOTLAND T 0845-120 2906 W www.asntscotland.gov.uk
FIRST-TIER TRIBUNAL (SPECIAL EDUCATIONAL
NEEDS AND DISABILITY) T 01325-392760
W www.justice.gov.uk/tribunals/send

NATIONAL PARENT PARTNERSHIP NETWORK
    T 0207 843 6058 W www.parentpartnership.org.uk
SPECIAL EDUCATIONAL NEEDS TRIBUNAL FOR
    WALES T 01597-829800 W sentw.gov.uk

HOME EDUCATION

In England and Wales parents have the right to educate their children at home and do not have to be qualified teachers to do so. Home-educated children do not have to follow the National Curriculum or take national tests nor do they need a fixed timetable, formal lessons or to observe school hours, days or terms. However, by law parents must ensure that the home education provided is full-time and suitable for the child's age, ability and aptitude and, if appropriate, for any special educational needs. Parents have no legal obligation to notify the local authority that a child is being educated at home, but if they take a child out of school, they must notify the school in writing and the school must report this to the local authority. Local authorities can make informal enquiries of parents to establish that a suitable education is being provided. For children in special schools, parents must seek the consent of the local authority before taking steps to educate them at home.

In Northern Ireland, ELBs monitor the quality of home provision and provide general guidance on appropriate materials and exam types through regular home visits.

The home schooling law in Scotland is similar to that of England. One difference, however, is that if parents wish to take a child out of school they must have permission from the local education authority.

HOME EDUCATION ADVISORY SERVICE
    T 01707-371854 W www.heas.org.uk
HOME EDUCATION IN NORTHERN IRELAND
    W www.hedni.org
SCHOOLHOUSE HOME EDUCATION ASSOCIATION
    (SCOTLAND) T 01307-463120 W www.schoolhouse.org.uk

FURTHER EDUCATION

In the UK, further education (FE) is generally understood as post-secondary education, ie any education undertaken after an individual leaves school that is below higher education level. FE therefore embraces a wide range of general and vocational study undertaken by people of all ages from 16 upwards, full-time or part-time, who may be self-funded, employer-funded or state-funded.

FE in the UK is often undertaken at further education colleges, although some takes place on employers' premises. Many of these colleges offer some courses at higher education level; some FE colleges teach certain subjects to 14- to 16-year-olds under collaborative arrangements with schools. Colleges' income comes from public funding, student fees and work for and with employers.

HIGHER EDUCATION

Higher education (HE) in the UK describes courses of study, provided in universities, specialist colleges of higher education and in some FE colleges, where the level of instruction is above that of A-level or equivalent exams.

All UK universities and colleges that provide HE are autonomous bodies with their own internal systems of governance. They are not owned by the state. However, most receive a portion of their income from state funds distributed by the separate HE funding councils for England, Scotland and Wales, and the Department for Employment and Learning in Northern Ireland. The rest of their income comes from a number of sources including fees from home and overseas students, government funding for research, endowments and work with or for business.

EXPENDITURE

UK-MANAGED EXPENDITURE ON EDUCATION
(Real terms adjusted to 2013–14 price levels) £bn

2004–5	79.7	2009–10	95.5
2005–6	83.0	2010–11	96.2
2006–7	85.3	2011–12	89.3
2007–8	89.7	2012–13	88.5
2008–9	92.0	2013–14 (est)	90.2

Source: Public Expenditure Statistical Analyses (PESA) 2014

SCHOOLS

ENGLAND AND WALES

In England and Wales, publicly funded schools are referred to as 'state schools'. The four main categories of state school – Community, Foundation, Voluntary-aided and Voluntary-controlled – are maintained by local authorities, which have a duty to ensure there is a suitable place for every school-age child resident in their area. Each school has a governing body, made up of volunteers elected or appointed by parents, staff, the community and the local authority, which is responsible for strategic management, ensuring accountability, monitoring school performance, setting budgets and appointing the headteacher and senior staff. The headteacher is responsible for the school's day-to-day management and operations and for decisions requiring professional teaching expertise.

In *Community schools,* which are non-denominational, local authorities are the employers of the staff, own the land and buildings and set the admissions criteria.

In *Foundation schools,* the governing body employs the staff and sets the admissions criteria. The land and buildings are usually owned by the governing body or a charitable foundation. A Foundation school may have a religious character, although most do not. A *Trust school* is a distinct type of foundation school that forms a charitable trust with an outside partner – for example, a business, a university, an educational charity or simply another school – that shares the school's aspirations. The decision to become a Trust school is taken by the governing body while taking account of parents' views. Community schools can take on Foundation status and set up a trust in a single process.

Most *Voluntary-aided schools* are religious schools founded by Christian denominations or other faiths. As with Foundation schools, the governing body employs the staff and sets the admissions criteria, which may include priority for members of the faith or denomination. The school buildings and land are normally owned and provided by a charitable foundation, often a religious organisation, which appoints a majority of the school's governors and makes a small contribution to major building costs.

Voluntary-controlled schools are similar to Voluntary-aided schools in that they often have a particular religious ethos, commonly Church of England, and the school land and buildings are normally owned by a charity. However, as with Community schools, the local authority employs the school's staff, sets the admissions criteria and bears all the costs.

Among the local authority-maintained schools are some with particular characteristics:

• *Community and Foundation Special schools* cater for children with specific special educational needs, which may include physical disabilities or learning difficulties

• *Grammar schools* are secondary schools catering for pupils aged 11 to 18 that select all of their pupils based on academic ability. In England there are 164 grammar schools, concentrated in certain local authority areas. Wales has none

• *Maintained boarding schools* are state-funded and offer free tuition but charge fees for board and lodging

In Wales, Welsh-medium primary and secondary schools were first established in the 1950s and 1960s, originally in response to the wishes of Welsh-speaking parents who wanted their children to be educated through the medium of the Welsh language. Now, many children who are not from Welsh-speaking homes also attend Welsh-medium and bilingual schools throughout Wales. There are 452 Welsh-medium primary schools, where the main or sole medium of instruction is in the Welsh language, two Welsh-medium middle schools and 53 Welsh-medium secondary schools, where more than half of foundation subjects (other than English and Welsh) and religious education are taught wholly or partly in Welsh.

England now has increasing numbers of *Academies*. Those set-up before the Academies Act 2010 were sponsored by business, faith or voluntary groups who contributed to funding their land and buildings, while the government covered the running costs at a level comparable to other local schools. The Academies Act 2010 streamlined the process of becoming an academy, enabled high-performing schools to convert without a sponsor and allowed primary and special schools to become academies. All academies now receive funding from central government at the level they would have received if still maintained by their local authority, with extra funding only to cover those services the local authority no longer provides. Academies have greater freedoms over how they use their budgets, set staff pay and conditions and deliver the curriculum. As at June 2014 there were 3,923 academies, of which 1,761 were primaries.

SCOTLAND

Most schools in Scotland, known as 'publicly funded' schools, are state-funded and charge no fees. Funding is met from resources raised by the Scottish local authorities and from an annual grant from the Scottish government. Scotland does not have school governing bodies like the rest of the UK: local authorities retain greater responsibility for the management and performance of publicly funded schools. Headteachers manage at least 80 per cent of a school's budget, covering staffing, furnishings, repairs, supplies, services and energy costs. Spending on new buildings, modernisation projects and equipment is financed by the local authority within the limits set by the Scottish government.

Scotland has 370 state-funded *faith schools*, the majority of which are Catholic. It has no grammar schools.

Integrated community schools form part of the Scottish government's strategy to promote social inclusion and to raise educational standards. They encourage closer and better joint working among education, health and social work agencies and professionals, greater pupil and parental involvement in schools, and improved support and service provision for vulnerable children and young people.

Scotland has a number of *grant-aided schools* that are independent of local authorities but supported financially by the Scottish government. These schools are managed by boards and most of them provide education for children and young people with special educational needs.

NORTHERN IRELAND

Most schools in Northern Ireland are maintained by the state and generally charge no fees, though fees may be charged in preparatory departments of some grammar schools. There are different types of state-funded schools, each under the control of management committees, which also employ the teachers.

Controlled schools (nursery, primary, special, secondary and grammar schools) are managed by Northern Ireland's five ELBs through boards of governors consisting of teachers,

parents, members of the ELB and transferor representatives (mainly from the Protestant churches).

Catholic maintained schools (nursery, primary, special and secondary) are under the management of boards of governors consisting of teachers, parents and members nominated by the employing authority, the Council for Catholic Maintained Schools (CCMS).

Other maintained schools (primary, special and secondary) are, in the main, Irish-medium schools that provide education in an Irish-speaking environment. The Department of Education has a duty to encourage and facilitate the development of Irish-medium education. Northern Ireland has 29 standalone Irish-medium schools, most of them primary schools, and ten Irish-medium units attached to English-medium host schools.

Voluntary schools are mainly grammar schools, which select most pupils according to academic ability. They are managed by boards of governors consisting of teachers, parents and, in most cases, representatives from the Department of Education and the ELB.

Integrated schools (primary and secondary) educate pupils from both the Protestant and Catholic communities as well as those of other faiths and no faith; each school is managed by a board of governors. There are at present 62 integrated schools maintained by the state, 24 of which are controlled schools.

From 2013 all pupils are guaranteed access to a much wider range of courses, with a minimum of 24 courses at Key Stage 4, and 27 at post-16. At least one-third of the courses on offer will be academic and another third will be vocational. Schools are working with other schools, FE colleges and other providers to offer the wider range of courses.

INDEPENDENT SCHOOLS

Around 6 per cent of UK schoolchildren are educated by privately funded 'independent' schools that charge fees and set their own admissions policies. Independent schools are required to meet certain minimum standards but need not teach the National Curriculum. *See also* Independent Schools.

UK SCHOOLS BY CATEGORY (2012–13)

	England	Wales
Maintained nursery schools	417	20
*Maintained primary and secondary schools	17,418	1,594
Community	10,143	–
Voluntary-aided	3,901	–
Voluntary-controlled	2,464	–
Foundation	910	–
Pupil Referral Units	400	–
Maintained Special schools	961	42
†Non-maintained Special schools	71	–
†Academies	2,647	–
Independent schools	2,413	68
Total	24,327	1,724

* Includes four middle schools in Wales
† Includes City Technology Colleges and free schools; excludes voluntary and private pre-school education centres
‡ Figure includes two hospital schools
Source: DfE; Welsh government

Scotland	
Publicly funded schools	2,569
Primary	2,056
Secondary	364
Special	149
Independent schools	102
Total	2,671

Source: Scottish government

Northern Ireland

State-maintained nursery schools	96
State-maintained primary and secondary schools	1,035
Controlled	440
Voluntary	51
Catholic maintained	452
Other maintained	30
Integrated	62
Special schools	40
Independent schools	15
Total	1,186

Source: DENI

INSPECTION

ENGLAND

The Office for Standards in Education, Children's Services and Skills (Ofsted) is the main body responsible for inspecting education in English schools. As well as inspecting all publicly funded and some independent schools, Ofsted inspects a range of other services in England, including childcare, children's homes, pupil referral units, local authority children's services, further education, initial teacher training and publicly funded adult skills training.

Ofsted is an independent, non-ministerial government department that reports directly to parliament, headed by Her Majesty's Chief Inspector (HMCI). Ofsted is required to promote improvement in the public services that it inspects; ensure that these services focus on the interests of their users – children, parents, learners and employers; and see that these services are efficient, effective and promote value for money. The inspection regime changed in 2012 to focus on four areas: achievement, teaching, leadership and behaviour.

Ofsted publishes the findings of its inspection reports, its recommendations and statistical information on its website.

OFFICE FOR STANDARDS IN EDUCATION,
    CHILDREN'S SERVICES AND SKILLS T 0300-123 1231
    W www.ofsted.gov.uk

WALES

Estyn is the office of Her Majesty's Inspectorate for Education and Training in Wales. It is independent of, but funded by, the Welsh government and is led by Her Majesty's Chief Inspector of Education and Training in Wales.

Estyn's role is to inspect quality and standards in education and training in Wales, including in primary, secondary, special and independent schools, and pupil referral units, publicly funded nursery schools and settings, further education, adult community-based and work-based learning, local authorities and teacher education and training.

Estyn also provides advice on quality and standards in education and training to the Welsh government and others and its remit includes making public good practice based on inspection evidence. Estyn publishes the findings of its inspection reports, its recommendations and statistical information on its website.

HER MAJESTY'S INSPECTORATE FOR EDUCATION
    AND TRAINING IN WALES T 029-2044 6446
    W www.estyn.gov.uk

SCOTLAND

HM Inspectorate of Education (HMIE) merged with Learning and Teaching Scotland in July 2011 to become Education Scotland, an executive agency of the Scottish government. Education Scotland operates independently and impartially while being directly accountable to Scottish ministers for the standards of its work. The agency's core business is inspection and review. It is responsible for delivering measurable year-on-year improvements, with maximum efficiency, by promoting excellence, building on strengths, and identifying and addressing under-performance.

Inspection reports and reviews, recommendations, examples of good practice and statistical information are published on Education Scotland's website.

EDUCATION SCOTLAND T 0141 282 5000
    W www.educationscotland.gov.uk

NORTHERN IRELAND

The Education and Training Inspectorate (ETINI) provides inspection services for the Department of Education and Employment and Learning Northern Ireland.

ETINI carries out inspections of all schools, pre-school services, special education, further education colleges, initial teacher training, training organisations, and curriculum advisory and support services. Since September 2013 regional colleges of further education have received four weeks' notification of inspection, while all other organisations have received two weeks' notification of inspection.

The inspectorate's role is to improve services and it provides evidence-based advice to ministers in order to assist in the formulation of policies. It publishes the findings of its inspection reports, its recommendations and statistical information on its website.

EDUCATION AND TRAINING INSPECTORATE
    T 028-9127 9726 W www.etini.gov.uk

THE NATIONAL CURRICULUM

ENGLAND

The National Curriculum, first introduced in 1988, is mandatory in all state schools for children from age 5 onwards.

Until age 5, or the end of Reception Year in primary school, children are in the Early Years Foundation Stage (EYFS), which has its own learning and development requirements for children in nursery and primary schools. Changes to the EYFS came into effect in September 2012 and a further revised EYFS came into force on 1 September 2014. These included simplifying the statutory assessment of children's development at age five; reducing the number of early learning goals from 69 to 17; focusing on seven areas of learning and development (prime areas: communication and language, physical development and personal, social and emotional development; and specific areas: literacy, mathematics, understanding the world, and expressive arts and design) and, for parents, a new progress check at age two on their child's development.

Following the EYFS, the National Curriculum is organised into 'Key Stages', and sets out the core subjects that must be taught and the standards or attainment targets for each subject at each Key Stage.

• Key Stage 1 covers Years 1 and 2 of primary school, for children aged 5–7
• Key Stage 2 covers Years 3 to 6 of primary school, for children aged 7–11
• Key Stage 3 covers Years 7 to 9 of secondary school, for children aged 11–14
• Key Stage 4 covers Years 10 and 11 of secondary school, for children aged 14–16

Within the framework of the National Curriculum, schools may plan and organise teaching and learning in the way that best meets the needs of their pupils, but maintained schools are expected to follow the programmes of study associated with particular subjects. The programmes of study describe the subject knowledge, skills and understanding that pupils are expected to have developed by the end of each Key Stage.

The new National Curriculum for England is to be taught in all maintained primary and secondary schools from September 2014. However, in the academic year 2014–15, pupils in Years 2 and 6 will be taught the current programmes of study in English, mathematics and science and sit the current Key Stage 1 and 2 tests respectively. New tests will be available from 2016. Similarly, pupils in Years 10 and 11 will be taught the current programmes of study in English, mathematics and science because reformed GCSEs in these subjects will not be available for teaching until September 2015.

KEY STAGES 1 AND 2 COMPULSORY SUBJECTS	
English	Design and technology
Mathematics	Geography
Science	History
Art and design	Music
Computing	Physical education

Foreign languages will be compulsory in Key Stage 2, but not Key Stage 1: schools can choose from French, German, Italian, Mandarin, Spanish, Latin or Ancient Greek.

In Key Stage 3, compulsory subjects include those listed above for Key Stage 2 (though the language taught should be a modern foreign language) plus citizenship.

Pupils in Key Stage 4 study a mix of compulsory and optional subjects in preparation for national examinations such as GCSEs. Pupils at this key stage also have to undertake careers education and work-related learning. In addition, schools must offer at least one subject from each of four 'entitlement' areas: arts (art and design, music, dance, drama and media arts); design and technology; humanities (history and geography); and modern foreign languages. To meet the entitlement requirements, schools must ensure that courses in these areas lead to approved qualifications, and allow pupils to take courses in all four areas if they wish to do so.

KEY STAGE 4 COMPULSORY SUBJECTS	
English	Citizenship
Mathematics	Computing
Science	Physical education

Schools must teach religious education (RE) at all key stages, although parents have the right to withdraw children for all or part of the RE curriculum. Secondary schools must provide sex and relationship education.

Statutory assessment must be undertaken for all pupils in publicly funded schools in the relevant years. It first takes place towards the end of the Early Years Foundation Stage, when children's level of development is compared to and recorded against a Foundation Stage Profile (this will no longer be a statutory requirement from September 2016 see Recent Developments). Pupils receive a phonics screening check at the end of the first year in Key Stage 1, repeated the following year if necessary. Teacher assessments in English, mathematics and science take place at the end of Key Stage 1 (Year 2) and Key Stage 2 (Year 6); at the end of Key Stage 3 (Year 9) teachers assess progress in all subjects being studied. National tests in English and mathematics take place in Year 6. At Key Stage 4, national examinations are the main form of assessment.

The assessment process for English at the end of Key Stage 2 now involves three elements. Reading comprehension is assessed by an external national test. Written comprehension is subject only to teacher assessment. Grammar, punctuation and spelling are assessed by a new external test introduced in May 2013.

Each year the DfE publishes on its website achievement and attainment tables, showing performance measures for every school and local authority. The tables for primary schools are based mainly on the results of the tests taken by children at the end of Key Stage 2 when they are usually aged 11; since 2010 the tables also include teacher assessment results. The tables for secondary schools and for attainment post-16 rely mainly on the results of national examinations. All tables include indicators of the progress that pupils have made since their last assessment.
DEPARTMENT FOR EDUCATION T 0370-000 2288
W www.education.gov.uk

WALES

Wales is reviewing its National Curriculum and assessment from Foundation Phase to Key Stage 4 (*see* Recent Developments). It originally introduced a Foundation Phase curriculum for 3- to 7-year-olds from September 2008. The emphasis is on learning-by-doing and children's skills and knowledge are planned across seven areas of learning. They are:
• Personal and social development, well-being and cultural diversity
• Language, literacy and communication skills
• Mathematical development
• Welsh language development
• Knowledge and understanding of the world
• Physical development
• Creative development

Full details of the Foundation Phase can be found in *Framework for Children's Learning for 3- to 7-year-olds in Wales*, available on the Welsh government website (*see* below).

The National Curriculum exists for 7- to 16-year-olds. Originally it was broadly similar to that of England, with distinctive characteristics for Wales reflected in the programmes of study. From September 2008 a revised school curriculum was implemented, consisting of the National Curriculum subjects together with non-statutory frameworks for personal and social education, the world of work, religious education and skills.

The National Curriculum in Wales includes the following subjects:
• *Key Stage 2* – English, Welsh, mathematics, science, design and technology, ICT, history, geography, art and design, music, and physical education
• *Key Stage 3* – as Key Stage 2, plus a modern foreign language
• *Key Stage 4* – English, Welsh, mathematics, science and physical education

Welsh is compulsory for pupils at all key stages, either as a first or as a second language. In 2010, 16.5 per cent of pupils were taught Welsh as a first language. In April 2012, the Minister for Education and Skills approved the implementation of an action plan to raise standards and attainment in Welsh second language education. A comprehensive review of the strategy is due in 2015.

Statutory testing at the end of Key Stage 2 was removed for pupils in Wales from 2004–5. Only statutory teacher assessment remains. It is also done at the end of Key Stage 1 (in future, the Foundation Phase) and Key Stage 3, and is being strengthened by moderation and accreditation arrangements.

The new National Literacy and Numeracy Framework (LNF), outlining the skills 5- to 15-year-olds are expected to acquire, became statutory from September 2013. For literacy, this means children should become accomplished in reading for information, writing for information and expressing themselves fluently and grammatically in speech.

In numeracy, children are expected to develop numerical reasoning and use number skills, measuring skills and data skills.

New national reading and numeracy tests for pupils in Years 2 to 9 took place for the first time in Wales in May 2013. The tests are designed to give teachers a clearer insight into a learner's development and progress, to allow them to intervene at an earlier stage if learners are falling behind.

The reading test includes a statutory 'core' test, and a set of optional test materials to help teachers to investigate learners' strengths and development needs in more depth.

The numeracy test is split into two papers: numerical procedures and numerical reasoning. The procedural paper consists of a set of questions designed to assess the basic, essential numeracy skills such as addition, multiplication and division.

The numerical reasoning paper was introduced in May 2014. It will assess learners' ability to find the most effective ways to solve everyday numeracy problems.

Learners in Welsh medium schools will take a reading test in Welsh only in Years 2 and 3, but in both English and Welsh from Year 4 onwards. Schools will have the option to use both tests in Year 3. Learners will take the numeracy test in either English or Welsh.

THE WELSH GOVERNMENT – EDUCATION AND SKILLS
W www.wales.gov.uk/topics/educationandskills/schoolshome/curriculuminwales/arevisedcurriculumforwales
W www.learning.wales.gov.uk

SCOTLAND

The curriculum in Scotland is not prescribed by statute but is the responsibility of education authorities and individual schools. However, schools and authorities are expected to follow the Scottish government's guidance on management and delivery of the curriculum.

Advice and guidance are provided by the Scottish government primarily through Education Scotland.

Scotland is now implementing *Curriculum for Excellence*, which aims to provide more autonomy for teachers, greater choice and opportunity for pupils and a single coherent curriculum for all children and young people aged 3 to 18.

The purpose of Curriculum for Excellence is encapsulated in 'the four capacities': to enable each child or young person to be a successful learner, a confident individual, a responsible citizen and an effective contributor. It focuses on providing a broad curriculum that develops skills for learning, skills for life and skills for work, with a sustained focus on literacy and numeracy. The period of education from pre-school through to the end of secondary stage 3, when pupils reach age 14, has the particular purpose of providing each young person in Scotland with this broad general education.

Curriculum for Excellence sets out 'experiences and outcomes', which describe broad areas of learning and what is to be achieved within them. They are:
- Expressive arts (including art and design, dance, drama, music)
- Health and wellbeing (including physical education, food and health, relationships and sexual health and mental, physical and social wellbeing)
- Languages
- Mathematics
- Religious and moral education
- Sciences
- Social studies (including history, geography, society and economy)
- Technologies (including business, computing, food and textiles, craft, design, engineering and graphics)

The experiences and outcomes are written at five levels with progression to examinations and qualifications during the senior phase, which covers secondary stages 4 to 6 when students are generally aged 14 to 17. The framework is designed to be flexible so that pupils can progress at their own pace.

Level	Stage
Early	The pre-school years and primary 1 (ages 3–5), or later for some
First	To the end of primary 4 (age 8), but earlier or later for some
Second	To the end of primary 7 (age 11), but earlier or later for some
Third and Fourth	Secondary 1 to secondary 3 (ages 12–14), but earlier for some. The fourth level experiences and outcomes are intended to provide possibilities for choice and young people's programmes will not include all of the fourth level outcomes
Senior phase	Secondary 4 to secondary 6 (ages 15–18), and college or other means of study

Under the new curriculum, assessment of students' progress and achievements from ages 3 to 15 is carried out by teachers who are required to base their assessment judgments on a range of evidence rather than single assessment instruments such as tests. Teachers have access to an online National Assessment Resource (NAR), which provides a range of assessment material and national exemplars across the curriculum areas.

In the senior phase, young people aged 16 to 18, including those studying outside school, build up a portfolio of national qualifications, awarded by the Scottish Qualifications Authority (SQA).

Provision is made for teaching in Gaelic in many parts of Scotland and the number of pupils, from nursery to secondary, in Gaelic-medium education is growing.

EDUCATION SCOTLAND T 0141-282 5000
W www.educationscotland.gov.uk
SCOTTISH QUALIFICATIONS AUTHORITY
T 0845-279 1000 W www.sqa.org.uk

NORTHERN IRELAND

In September 2009 Northern Ireland put in place across Years 1 to 12 a revised statutory curriculum placing greater emphasis on developing skills and preparing young people for life and work.

This curriculum includes a new Foundation Stage to cover Years 1 and 2 of primary school, so as to allow a more appropriate learning style for the youngest pupils and to ease the transition from pre-school. Key Stage 1 covers primary Years 3 and 4, until children are 8, and Key Stage 2 covers primary Years 5, 6 and 7, until children are 11. Post-primary, Key Stage 3 covers Years 8, 9 and 10 and Key Stage 4 Years 11 and 12.

The current primary curriculum is made up of the following areas of learning:
- Language and literacy
- Mathematics and numeracy
- The arts
- The world around us
- Physical education
- Religeous education

The current post-primary curriculum includes a new area of learning for life and work, made up of employability, personal development, local and global citizenship and home economics (at Key Stage 3). In addition, it is made up of RE and the following areas of learning:

- English
- Mathematics
- Modern languages
- The arts
- Environment and society
- Physical education
- Science and technology

At Key Stage 4, there are nine areas of learning of which the statutory requirements have been significantly reduced to learning for life and work, physical education and RE. The aim is to provide greater choice and flexibility for pupils and allow them access to a wider range of academic and vocational courses provided under the revised curriculum's 'Entitlement Framework' (EF).

Since September 2013, schools have been required to provide pupils with access to at least 18 courses at Key Stage 4 and 21 courses at post-16. This will increase to 24 and 27 courses respectively by September 2015. At least one third of the courses must be 'general' with one third 'applied'. The remaining third is at the discretion of each school. Individual pupils decide on the number and mix of courses they wish to follow.

RE is a compulsory part of the Northern Ireland curriculum, although parents have the right to withdraw their children from part or all of RE or collective worship. Schools have to provide RE in accordance with a core syllabus drawn up by the province's four main churches (Church of Ireland, Presbyterian, Methodist and Roman Catholic) and specified by the Department of Education.

Revised assessment and reporting arrangements were introduced when the curriculum was revised. The focus from Foundation to Key Stage 3 is on 'Assessment for Learning'. This programme includes classroom-based teacher assessment, computer-based assessment of literacy and numeracy and pupils deciding on their strengths and weaknesses and how they might progress to achieve their potential. Assessment information is given to parents in an annual report. Pupils at Key Stage 4 and beyond continue to be assessed through public examinations.

The Council for the Curriculum, Examinations and Assessment (CCEA), a non-departmental public body reporting to the Department of Education in Northern Ireland, is unique in the UK in combining the functions of a curriculum advisory body, an awarding body and a qualifications regulatory body. It advises the government on what should be taught in Northern Ireland's schools and colleges, ensures that the qualifications and examinations offered by awarding bodies in Northern Ireland are of an appropriate quality and standard and, as the leading awarding body itself, offers a range of qualifications including GCSEs, A-levels and AS-levels.

The CCEA hosts a dedicated curriculum website covering all aspects of the revised curriculum, assessment and reporting.

COUNCIL FOR THE CURRICULUM, EXAMINATIONS
AND ASSESSMENT T 028-9026 1200 W www.ccea.org.uk
NORTHERN IRELAND CURRICULUM T 028-9028 1200
W www.nicurriculum.org.uk

QUALIFICATIONS

ENGLAND, WALES AND NORTHERN IRELAND

There is a very wide range of public examinations and qualifications available, accredited by the Office of Qualifications and Examinations Regulation (OFQUAL) in England, the Department for Education and Skills (DfES) in Wales, and the Council for the Curriculum, Examinations and Assessment (CCEA) in Northern Ireland. Up-to-date

information on all accredited qualifications and awarding bodies is available online at the Register of Regulated Qualifications website.

Four main qualification frameworks group all accredited qualifications into levels (from entry level to level 8). All the qualifications within a level place similar demands on individuals as learners. Entry level, for example, covers basic knowledge and skills in English, maths and ICT not geared towards specific occupations, while level 3 includes qualifications such as A-levels which are appropriate for those wishing to go to university, and level 7 covers Master's degrees and vocational qualifications appropriate for senior professionals and managers.

Young people aged 14 to 19 in schools or (post-16) colleges or apprenticeships may gain academic qualifications such as GCSEs, AS-levels and A-levels; qualifications linked to particular career fields, like diplomas, vocational qualifications such as BTECs and NVQs; and functional key or basic skills qualifications. The frameworks in England, Wales and Northern Ireland are:
- National Qualifications Framework (NQF)
- Qualifications and Credit Framework (QCF) in England and Northern Ireland
- Credit and Qualifications Framework for Wales (CQFW)
- Framework for Higher Education Qualifications (FHEQ)

NQF AND QCF QUALIFICATIONS
Courses in these frameworks range from entry level up to level 8. QCF courses are vocational and use a credit system so that learners can study units at their own pace and build these up into qualifications over time.

NQF and QCF qualifications include: English for Speakers of Other Languages (ESOL); Skills for Life; GCSEs and A-levels; International Baccalaureate; BTEC courses; Foundation Learning; National Vocational Qualifications (NVQs); Cambridge Nationals; Higher National Certificates (HNC); and Higher National Diplomas (HND).

FRAMEWORK FOR HIGHER EDUCATION QUALIFICATIONS (FHEQ)
This framework starts at level 4 and goes up to level 8 and includes the following qualifications: Certificate of Higher Education; Diploma of Higher Education; Bachelor's degrees; Master's degrees; and Doctoral degrees.

COUNCIL FOR THE CURRICULUM, EXAMINATIONS
    AND ASSESSMENT (NORTHERN IRELAND)
    T 028-9026 1200 W www.ccea.org.uk
DEPARTMENT FOR EDUCATION AND SKILLS (DfES)
    T 0300-0603300; 0845-010 3300
    W http://wales.gov.uk/topics/educationandskills
REGISTER OF REGULATED QUALIFICATIONS
    T 0300-303 3346 W http://register.ofqual.gov.uk
OFFICE OF QUALIFICATIONS AND EXAMINATIONS
    REGULATION (OFQUAL) T 0300-303 3344
    W www.ofqual.gov.uk

GCSE
The vast majority of pupils in their last year of compulsory schooling in England, Wales and Northern Ireland take at least one General Certificate of Secondary Education (GCSE) exam, though GCSEs may be taken at any age. GCSEs assess the performance of pupils on a subject-specific basis and are mostly taken after a two-year course. They are available in more than 50 subjects, most of them academic subjects, though some, known as vocational or applied GCSEs, involve the study of a particular area of employment and the development of work-related skills. Some subjects are also offered as short-course qualifications, equivalent to half a standard GCSE, or as double awards, equivalent to two GCSEs.

GCSEs have traditionally been assessed by exams at the end of the course and by coursework completed by students during the course. GCSE certificates are awarded on an eight-point scale from A* to G. In most subjects two different papers, foundation and higher, are provided for different ranges of ability, with grades A*–D available to students taking the higher paper and grades C–G available from the foundation paper.

Major changes to GCSEs are planned in England. From 2015, GCSEs will no longer involve modules and coursework, just exams at the end of the two-year course. The pass mark will be higher and the qualifications will be graded 9 to 1, rather than A* to G. There will no longer be controlled assessments (coursework done under exam conditions) and final exams will be essay-based. Changes will initially be for nine core GCSE subjects. Revised GCSEs in English language, English literature and mathematics will be taught from September 2015. Revised GCSEs in chemistry, biology, physics, science (double award), geography, history and modern foreign languages will be taught in schools from September 2016. Revised GCSEs in art and design, computer science, citizenship, dance, design and technology, drama, music, physical education and religious studies will also be ready for teaching from September 2016. The remaining subjects will either be reformed for teaching from 2017 or withdrawn.
W www.gov.uk/government/collections/gcse-subject-content

All GCSE specifications, assessments and grading procedures are monitored by OFQUAL, DfES and the CCEA.

Since September 2010 the government has allowed state schools to offer pupils International GCSE (iGCSE) exams in key subjects including English, mathematics, science and ICT. The iGCSEs do not include coursework and some experts consider them more rigorous than traditional GCSEs.

GCE A-LEVEL AND AS-LEVEL
GCE (General Certificate of Education) Advanced levels (A-levels) are the qualifications used by most young people in England, Wales and Northern Ireland to gain entry to university.

A-levels are subject-based qualifications. They are mostly taken by UK students aged 16 to 19 over a two-year course in school sixth forms or at college, but can be taken at any age. They are available in more than 45, mostly academic, subjects, though there are some A-levels in vocational areas, often termed 'applied A-levels'.

An A-level qualification consists of advanced subsidiary (AS) and A2 units. The AS is a standalone qualification and is worth half a full A-level qualification. It normally consists of two units, assessed at the standard expected for a learner half way through an A-level course, that together contribute 50 per cent towards the full A-level.

The A2 is the second half of a full A-level qualification. It normally consists of two units, assessed at the standard expected for a learner at the end of a full A-level course, that together are worth 50 per cent of the full A-level qualification. Most units are assessed by examination. Each unit is graded A–E. Revised A-level specifications were introduced in September 2008, with a new A* grade awarded from 2010 to reward exceptional candidates.

An extended project was introduced in September 2008 as a separate qualification. It is a single piece of work on a topic of the student's own choosing that requires a high degree of planning, preparation, research and autonomous working. Awards are graded A–E and the extended project is accredited as half an A-level.

Since September 2013, students in England in their first or second year of A-level studies can no longer sit A-level exams in January. A-levels will still be examined unit by unit, but all exams will be taken in the summer

OFQUAL is working on reforming the way A-levels are assessed so that all assessment takes place at the end of the two-year course. The AS will become a standalone qualification rather than contributing to a full A-level qualification.

Revised content for A and AS levels in English language, English literature, English literature and language, science (biology, chemistry, physics and psychology), art and design, business, computer science, economics, history and sociology was published in April 2014, for first teaching from September 2015.

Revised content for A-level mathematics, further mathematics, geography and languages is expected in time for first teaching from September 2016.
W www.gov.uk/government/collections/gce-as-and-a-level-subject-content

INTERNATIONAL BACCALAUREATE
The International Baccalaureate (IB) offers four educational programmes for students aged 3 to 19: IB primary years programme, IB middle years programme, IB diploma programme, IB career-related certificate.

Some 155 'IB World Schools' in the UK offer at least one IB programme.

The IB diploma programme for students aged 16 to 19 is based around detailed academic study of a wide range of subjects, including languages, the arts, science, maths, history and geography, this leads to a single qualification recognised by UK universities.

The IB diploma is made up of a compulsory 'core' plus six separate subjects where individuals have some choice over what they study. The compulsory core contains three elements: theory of knowledge; creativity, action and service; and a 4,000-word extended essay.

The diploma normally takes two years to complete and most of the assessment is done through externally marked examinations. Candidates are awarded points for each part of the programme, up to a maximum of 45. A candidate must score 24 points or more to achieve a full diploma.

Successfully completing the diploma earns points on the 'UCAS tariff', the UK system for allocating points to qualifications used for entry to higher education. An IB diploma total of 24 points is worth 260 UCAS points – the same as a B and two C grades at A-level. The maximum of 45 points earns 720 UCAS points – equivalent to six A-levels at grade A.

WELSH BACCALAUREATE
The Welsh Baccalaureate Qualification (WBQ), available for 14- to 19-year-olds in Wales, combines a compulsory core, which incorporates personal development skills, with options from existing academic and vocational qualifications, such as A-levels, GCSEs and NVQs, to make one broader award. The WBQ can be studied in English or Welsh, or a combination of the two. Candidates who meet the requirements of the compulsory core and options relevant to each level of the qualification are awarded the Welsh Baccalaureate Foundation, Intermediate or Advanced Diploma as appropriate.

WJEC (Welsh Joint Education Committee), which administers the WBQ, has also developed two new WBQs at level 1 and level 2 suitable for delivery over one year and with a particular focus on employability. These are currently only available as a pilot in some colleges or work-based learning providers.

BTECS, OCR NATIONALS AND OTHER VOCATIONAL QUALIFICATIONS

Vocational qualifications can range from general qualifications where a person learns skills relevant to a variety of jobs, to specialist qualifications designed for a particular sector. They are available from several awarding bodies, such as City & Guilds, Edexcel and OCR, and can be taken at many different levels.

BTEC qualifications and OCR Nationals are particular types of work-related qualifications, available in a wide range of subjects, including: art and design, business, health and social care, information technology, media, public services, science and sport. The qualifications offer a mix of theory and practice, can include work experience and can take the form of (or be part of) a technical certificate, one of the key components of an Apprenticeship. They can be studied full-time at college or school, or part-time at college. BTEC qualifications are available at various levels on the National Qualifications Framework (NQF), including Higher National Certificates and Diplomas (HNCs and HNDs), at higher education level; OCR Nationals are achieved at levels 1 to 3.

Learners complete a range of assignments, case studies and practical activities, as well as a portfolio of evidence that shows what work has been completed. Assessment is usually done by the teacher or trainer, sometimes externally. BTEC and OCR Nationals are graded as pass, merit or distinction. BTEC and OCR Nationals at level 3 can qualify the learner for university entry.

All vocational and work-related qualifications fit into the Qualifications and Credit Framework (QCF). QCF qualifications are made up of units that can be studied at each individual's own pace and built up to full qualifications over time. Every qualification and unit on the QCF has a credit value, showing how long it takes to complete. One credit is equivalent to ten hours. When an individual takes QCF units or qualifications, their learning is 'banked' and stored on their personal learner record, showing what they have completed and how they can progress further.

There are thousands of vocational qualifications on the QCF, available in a broad range of subjects from a wide range of learning providers and some employers. Available in England, Northern Ireland and Wales, they are also recognised in Scotland.

NVQS

A National Vocational Qualification (NVQ) is a 'competence-based' qualification that is recognised by employers. Individuals learn practical, work-related tasks designed to help them develop the skills and knowledge to do a particular job effectively. NVQs can be taken in school, at college or by people already in work. There are more than 1,300 different NVQs available from the vast majority of business sectors. NVQs exist at levels 1 to 5 on the NQF and as new vocational qualifications on the QCF, though some will continue to be called NVQs. An NVQ qualification at level 2 or 3 can also be taken as part of an apprenticeship.

FUNCTIONAL SKILLS

Functional skills are a new set of qualifications launched across England during 2010, available for all learners aged 14 and above. They test the practical skills in English, mathematics and ICT that allow people to work confidently, effectively and independently in life. These skills are an integral part of the secondary school curriculum and of other qualifications and apprenticeships. Stand-alone functional skills qualifications are also available. These skills are assessed mainly by a set of practical tasks completed within a given time limit, though new ways of assessment such as electronic and online methods are being considered. Functional skills replace previous skills for life qualifications and the three main key skills qualifications in England. In Wales these new qualifications are known as 'essential skills'. They are currently under review by OFQUAL.

APPRENTICESHIPS

An apprenticeship combines on-the-job training with nationally recognised qualifications, allowing individuals to gain skills and qualifications while working and earning a wage. More than 200 different types of apprenticeships are available, offering over 1,200 job roles; they take between one and four years to complete. There are three levels available:

- Intermediate Level Apprenticeships – at level 2 on the National Qualifications Framework (NQF), they are equivalent to five good GCSE passes
- Advanced Level Apprenticeships – at level 3 on the NQF, they are equivalent to two A-level passes
- Higher Apprenticeships – lead to qualifications at NVQ Level 4 or, in some cases, a foundation degree

In England, the National Apprenticeship Service (NAS), launched in 2009, has responsibility for the delivery of apprenticeships including the provision of an online vacancy matching system. In 2012–13, some 510,000 young people started apprenticeships in England. The Welsh government and the Department for Employment and Learning (DEL) are responsible for the apprenticeship programmes in Wales and Northern Ireland respectively.

NATIONAL APPRENTICESHIP SERVICE (NAS)
T 02476-826482 W www.apprenticeships.org.uk

SCOTLAND

Scotland has its own system of public examinations and qualifications. The Scottish Qualifications Authority (SQA) is Scotland's national body for qualifications, responsible for developing, accrediting, assessing and certificating all Scottish qualifications apart from university degrees and some professional body qualifications.

There are qualifications at all levels of attainment. Almost all school candidates gain SQA qualifications in the fourth year of secondary school and most obtain further qualifications in the fifth or sixth year or in further education colleges. Increasingly, people also take them in the workplace.

SQA, with partners such as Universities Scotland, has introduced the Scottish Credit and Qualifications Framework (SCQF) as a way of comparing and understanding Scottish qualifications. It includes qualifications across academic and vocational sectors and compares them by giving a level and credit points. There are 12 levels in the SCQF, level 1 being the least difficult and level 12 the most difficult. The number of SCQF credit points shows how much learning has to be done to achieve the qualification. For instance, one SCQF credit point equals about 10 hours of learning including assessment.

- Standard Grades which are taken over the third and fourth years at secondary school. Students often choose to study seven or eight subjects, of which Mathematics and English are compulsory. There are three levels of study at Standard Grade: Foundation, General and Credit. Students usually sit exams at two levels – either Foundation/General or General/Credit – to ensure they have the best chance of achieving as high a grade as possible.
- National Units are the building blocks of National Courses, but they are also recognised qualifications in their own right and are designed to take approximately 40 hours of teaching time to complete.

National Courses usually comprise three National Units and an externally marked assessment. National Courses are available at a number of levels including Access 1, Access 2, Access 3, Intermediate 1, Intermediate 2, Higher and Advanced Higher.

- Skills for Work courses encourage school pupils to become familiar with the world of work. They involve a strong element of learning through involvement in practical and vocational activities and develop knowledge, skills and experience that are related to employment. They are available at a number of levels and are frequently delivered in partnership between schools and colleges.
- Wider Achievement qualifications provide young people with the opportunity to have learning and skills formally recognised, whether developed in or outside the classroom. Available at a number of levels in subjects including Employability, Leadership and Enterprise, these qualifications help schools deliver skills for learning, life and work.
- Scottish Baccalaureates consist of a coherent group of Higher and Advanced Higher qualifications and, uniquely, an interdisciplinary project of candidates' own choosing which is marked at Advanced Higher level in one of four broad topics – languages, science, expressive arts or social studies. Aimed at high-achieving candidates in their sixth year, the Scottish Baccalaureate is designed to encourage personalised, in-depth study and interdisciplinary learning in the later stages of secondary school.

As part of the Curriculum for Excellence programme (see above) SQA has developed new National qualifications that became available in schools from August 2013, replacing Standard Grade, Intermediate and Access qualifications at all levels. New Higher qualifications became available from August 2014 and Advanced Higher qualifications will be available from August 2015 respectively:

SCQF Level	New national qualifications	Replaces
1 and 2	National 1 and 2	Access 1 and Access 2
3	National 3	Access 3 Standard Grade (Foundation Level)
4	National 4	Standard Grade (General Level) Intermediate 1
5	National 5	Standard Grade (Credit Level) Intermediate 2
6	Higher (new)	Higher
7	Advanced Higher (new)	Advanced Higher

All new qualifications will run concurrently with existing qualifications until 2015/16.

SQA has also developed five new Awards – in modern languages, personal achievement, personal development, religion and wellbeing – that cover work from across different subject areas, and are shorter than traditional courses and recognise success across different levels of difficulty. These started in August 2012 and are marked and assessed by schools and colleges rather than by external assessment or exams. New Awards in Cycling and Scottish Studies began in August 2013.

SQA QUALIFICATIONS

HIGHER NATIONAL CERTIFICATES AND HIGHER NATIONAL DIPLOMAS
Higher National Certificates and Higher National Diplomas (HNCs and HNDs) are offered by colleges, some universities and many other training providers – including employers. Both HNCs and HNDs are comprised of Higher National Units and cover a wide range of subject areas. Many HNDs

allow the holder entry to the second or third year of a degree course. HNCs are available at SCQF level 7, HNDs at level 8.

SCOTTISH VOCATIONAL QUALIFICATIONS
Scottish Vocational Qualifications (SVQs) are based on national standards drawn up by people from industry, commerce and education. Possession of an SVQ demonstrates ability to perform in a job to agreed national standards. Primarily delivered to candidates in full-time employment, SVQs are available at SCQF levels 4 to 12.

PROFESSIONAL DEVELOPMENT AWARDS
Professional Development Awards (PDAs) are designed to develop and deliver high-level skills in a sharp, flexible and focused way. They are for people already in work who wish to extend or broaden their skills. Candidates often take a PDA after completing a degree or vocational qualification. PDAs are available at SCQF levels 6 to 12.

THE SCOTTISH QUALIFICATIONS AUTHORITY (SQA)
T 0845-279 1000 W www.sqa.org.uk
SCOTTISH CREDIT AND QUALIFICATIONS
FRAMEWORK (SCQF) T 0845-270 7371
W www.scqf.org.uk

FURTHER EDUCATION AND LIFELONG LEARNING

ENGLAND
The further education (FE) system in England provides a wide range of education and training opportunities for young people and adults. From the age of 16, young people who wish to remain in education, but not in a school setting, can undertake further education (including skills training) in an FE college. There are two main types of college in the FE sector: sixth form colleges and general further education (GFE) colleges. Some FE colleges focus on a particular area, such as art and design or agriculture and horticulture. Each institution decides its own range of subjects and courses. Students at FE colleges can study for a wide and growing range of academic and/or work-related qualifications, from entry level to higher education level.

Though the Department for Business, Innovation and Skills is responsible for the FE sector and for funding FE for adults (19 or over), the Department for Education funds all education and training for 16- to 18-year-olds.

The proportion of 16- to 18-year-olds in education or training has risen steadily over recent years. Those in full-time education increased from 68.6 per cent in 2012 to 70 per cent in 2013, driven by increase in state-funded schools and higher education. By the time that England's education-leaving age rises to 18 in 2015, 100 per cent should be in education or training. It is assumed that most of the additional students will go into FE or work-based training rather than staying on as school.

The 'September Guarantee', introduced in 2007, offers a place in post-16 education or training to all 16- and 17-year-olds who want one. In 2013, 92.1 per cent of 16- and 17-year-olds received an offer of a place. A new Education Funding Agency (EFA) was established in April 2012 as an executive agency of the Department for Education (DfE). It is responsible for education funding for 16- to 19-year-olds as well as academies.

The FE sector in England, as in other parts of the UK, also provides a range of opportunities for adults.

The Skills Funding Agency (SFA), part of the Department for Business, Innovation and Skills, is presently responsible for funding and regulating education and training for adults. It will invest government funding of £4.07bn in FE and skills training places in 2014–15.

In November 2010, the government announced a new strategy for FE, including more adult apprenticeships (provision for 200,000 adults by 2014–15); fully funded training for 19- to 24-year-olds undertaking their first full level 2 (GCSE equivalent) or first level 3 qualification when they do not already have one; and fully funded basic skills for people who left school without basic skills in reading, writing and mathematics. 'Train to Gain', the programme that funded trainees sponsored by employers, was replaced in July 2011 by a programme focused on helping small employers to train low-skilled staff. This was followed in December 2011 by a plan to reform FE that focuses on students and in April 2012 by the creation of a National Careers Service.

In April 2013, the government announced plans to make vocational qualifications more 'rigorous' (removing up to 2,550 qualifications), to make the skills system more 'responsive' and to create new traineeships.

From 2014, Tech-levels will take as long to complete as A-Levels and will need to be endorsed by either a professional association or by five employers registered with Companies House. These qualifications will focus on hands-on practical training leading to recognised occupations for example in engineering, computing, accounting or hospitality.

Applied General Qualifications will take the same time to complete as AS-levels and will focus on broader study of a technical area, not directly linked to an occupation. These qualifications will need backing from three universities to count in the school and college performance tables.

A Tech-level along with a core maths qualification, for example AS-level maths, and an extended project will amount to an over-arching Technical Baccalaureate.

New Substantial Vocational Qualifications at level 2 will provide 16- to 19-year old students seeking entry at a more basic level to a skilled trade or occupation with qualifications that are valued by employers.

There are currently 19 centres of training excellence called National Skills Academies, led, funded and designed by employers, in various stages of development. Each academy offers specialist training in a key sector of the economy, working in partnership with colleges, schools and independent training providers.

Among the many voluntary bodies providing adult education, the Workers' Educational Association (WEA) is the UK's largest, operating throughout England and Scotland. It provides part-time courses to adults in response to local need in community centres, village halls, schools, pubs or workplaces. Similar but separate WEA organisations operate in Wales and Northern Ireland.

The National Institute of Adult Continuing Education (NIACE), a charitable non-governmental organisation, promotes lifelong learning opportunities for adults in England and Wales.

NATIONAL INSTITUTE OF ADULT CONTINUING
EDUCATION (NIACE) T 0116-204 4200
    W www.niace.org.uk
THE SKILLS FUNDING AGENCY T 0345-377 5000
    W www.gov.uk/government/organisations/skills-funding-agency
WORKERS' EDUCATIONAL ASSOCIATION (WEA)
    T 020-7426 3450 W www.wea.org.uk

WALES

In Wales, the aims and makeup of the FE system are similar to those outlined for England. The Welsh government funds a wide range of learning programmes for young people through its 15 FE colleges, and local authorities and private organisations. The Welsh government has set out plans to improve learning opportunities for all post-16 learners in the shortest possible time, to increase the engagement of disadvantaged young people in the learning process, and to transform the learning network to increase learner choice, reduce duplication of provision and encourage higher-quality learning and teaching in all post-16 provision. One goal is to ensure that, by 2015, 95 per cent of young people will be ready for high-skilled employment or higher education by the age of 25.

In Wales, responsibility for adult and continuing education lies with the Department for Education and Skills (DfES) within the Welsh government. Wales operates a range of programmes to support skills development, including subsidised work-based training courses for employees and the Workforce Development Programme, where employers can use the free services of experienced skills advisers to develop staff training plans.

COLLEGES WALES T 029-2052 2500
    W www.collegeswales.ac.uk
COLEG HARLECH WEA T 01248-353254
    W www.harlech.ac.uk/en
NIACE DYSGU CYMRU T 029-2037 0900
    W www.niacedc.org.uk
WEA SOUTH WALES T 029-2023 5277
    W www.swales.wea.org.uk

SCOTLAND

Scotland's 41 FE colleges (known simply as colleges) are at the forefront of lifelong learning, education, training and skills in Scotland. Colleges cater for the needs of learners both in and out of employment at all stages in their lives from middle secondary school and earlier to retirement. Colleges' courses span much of the range of learning needs, from specialised vocational education and training through to general educational programmes. The level of provision ranges from essential life skills and provision for students with learning difficulties to HNCs and HNDs. Some colleges, notably those in the Highlands and Islands, also deliver degrees and postgraduate qualifications.

A shift in study patterns is taking place within the college sector as colleges concentrate on full-time courses aimed at helping people gain employment and no longer fund short courses lasting less than ten hours. Overall figures are stable but this change has led to a decline in part-time study and an increase in full-time study.

The Scottish Funding Council (SFC) is the statutory body responsible for funding teaching and learning provision, research and other activities in Scotland's colleges. Overall strategic direction for the sector is provided by the Lifelong Learning Directorate of the Scottish government, which provides annual guidance to the SFC and liaises closely with bodies such as Scotland's Colleges, the Scottish Qualifications Authority and the FE colleges themselves to ensure that its policies remain relevant and practical.

The Scottish government takes responsibility for community learning and development in Scotland while Skills Development Scotland, a non-departmental public body, is charged with improving Scotland's skills performance by linking skills supply and demand and helping people and organisations to learn, develop and make use of these skills to greater effect. ILA Scotland is a Scottish government scheme delivered by Skills Development Scotland that provides funding for training to individuals over the age of 16 with an income of less than £22,000 a year.

ILA SCOTLAND T 0808-100 1090 W www.ilascotland.org.uk
SCOTLAND'S COLLEGES T 01786-892000
    W www.scotlandscolleges.ac.uk
SCOTTISH FUNDING COUNCIL T 0131-313 6500
    W www.sfc.ac.uk

SKILLS DEVELOPMENT SCOTLAND T 0141-285 6000
  W www.skillsdevelopmentscotland.co.uk

NORTHERN IRELAND

FE in Northern Ireland is provided through six regional multi-campus colleges and the College of Agriculture, Food and Rural Affairs (CAFRE). Most secondary schools also have a sixth form which students may attend for two additional years to complete their AS levels and A levels.

Colleges Northern Ireland (CNI) acts as the representative body for the six FE colleges which, like their counterparts in the rest of the UK, are independent corporate bodies each managed by their own governing body. The range of courses that they offer spans essential skills, a wide choice of vocational and academic programmes and higher education programmes. Most full-time students in the six colleges are aged 16 to 19, while most part-time students are over 19.

The Department for Employment and Learning (DELNI) is responsible for the policy, strategic development and financing of the statutory FE sector and for lifelong learning, and also provides support to a small number of non-statutory FE providers. The Educational Guidance Service for Adults (EGSA), an independent, not-for-profit organisation, has a network of local offices based across Northern Ireland which provide services to adult learners, learning advisers, providers, employers and others interested in improving access to learning for adults.

COLLEGES NORTHERN IRELAND (CNI) T 028-9068 2296
  W www.anic.ac.uk

THE EDUCATIONAL GUIDANCE SERVICE FOR
  ADULTS T 028-9024 4274 W www.egsa.org.uk

WEA NORTHERN IRELAND T 028-9032 9718
  W www.wea-ni.com

FINANCIAL SUPPORT

England has a bursary scheme of up to £1,200 a year for full-time 16- to 19-year-old students facing financial hardship. Two types of bursary exist: vulnerable student bursary and discretionary bursary. Help with transport costs is also possible for some students. This scheme replaced the Education Maintenance Allowance (EMA) which gave 16- to 19-year-olds from low-income families a weekly allowance to continue in education.

There are EMA schemes in Scotland, Wales and Northern Ireland, but with slightly different eligibility conditions. Students must apply to the EMA scheme for the part of the UK where they intend to study. In Northern Ireland 16- to 19-year-old students, who meet the relevant criteria, and live in a household that has an annual income of £20,500 or less a year (£22,500 if there is more than one young person in the household who qualifies for child benefit) automatically get £30 a week in 2014–15.

Colleges and learning providers award learner support funds directly to new students aged 19 and over.

Care to Learn is available in England to help young parents under the age of 20 who are caring for their own child or children with the costs of childcare and travel while they are in some form of publicly funded learning (below higher education level). The scheme is not income assessed and pays up to £160 a week (£175 in London) to cover costs.

Dance and Drama Awards (DaDA) are state-funded scholarships for students over the age of 16 enrolled at one of 19 private dance and drama schools in England, who are taking specified courses at National Certificate or National Diploma level. Awards, based on household income, cover some of students' tuition fees and up to £5,185 maintenance in 2014–15.

Young people studying away from home because their chosen course is not available locally may qualify for the *Residential Support Scheme.*

Information and advice on funding support and applications are available from the Learner Support helpline (T 0800-121 8989) or on the GOV.UK website *(see* below).

Discretionary Support Funds (DSF) are available in colleges and school sixth forms to help students who have trouble meeting the costs of participating in further education.

In Wales, students aged 19 or over on FE courses may be eligible for the *Assembly Learning Grant for Further Education* (ALG (FE)). This is a means-tested payment of up to £1,500 for full-time students and up to £750 for those studying part-time. *Discretionary Financial Contingency Funds* are also available to all students in Wales suffering hardship and are administered by the institutions themselves.

In Scotland, FE students can apply to their college for discretionary support in the form of *Further Education Bursaries.* These can include allowances for maintenance, travel, study, childcare and additional support needs. *Individual Learning Accounts* provide up to £200 for those with incomes of less than £22,000.

In Northern Ireland, FE students may be eligible for *Further Education Awards,* non-refundable assistance administered on behalf of the five Education and Library Boards by the Western Education and Library Board.

UK FE students over 18 whose costs are not fully met from the grants described above may also be eligible for *Professional and Career Development Loans.* These loans – also available to HE students – cover up to 80 per cent of course fees (up to 100 per cent for those unemployed for three months); other course costs, such as books, travel and childcare; and living expenses, such as rent, food and clothing (for those who are unemployed or working fewer than 30 hours a week). The loans, of between £300 and £10,000, are available from participating high street banks – currently Barclays and the Co-operative. The Skills Funding Agency (SFA) pays the interest on the loan while the student is studying and for one month afterwards. Once students complete their courses, they must pay interest at the rate fixed when they took out the loan, which will be competitive with other commercially available 'unsecured' personal loans.

CAREERS SCOTLAND
  W www.careers-scotland.org.uk/Education/Funding/Funding.asp
GOV.UK W www.gov.uk/further-education-courses/financial-help
STUDENT FINANCE WALES T 0845-602 8845
  W www.studentfinancewales.co.uk
WESTERN EDUCATION AND LIBRARY BOARD
  T 028-8241 1411 W www.welbni.org

HIGHER EDUCATION

Publicly funded higher education (HE) in the UK is provided in more than 300 universities, higher education colleges and other specialist HE institutions, and a significant number of FE colleges offering higher education courses.

The Higher Education Funding Council for England (HEFCE) funds teaching and research in 128 English higher education institutions (HEIs) and 187 FE colleges.

The Higher Education Funding Council for Wales (HEFCW) distributes funding for HE in Wales through Wales's 10 HEIs and some FE colleges.

The Scottish Funding Council (SFC) – which is also responsible for FE in Scotland – is the national strategic body responsible for funding HE teaching and research in Scotland's 19 HEIs and 41 colleges.

In Northern Ireland, HE is provided by two universities, two university colleges, six regional institutes of further and higher education and the Open University (OU), which operates UK-wide. Unlike other parts of the UK, Northern Ireland has no higher education funding council; the Department for Employment and Learning fulfils that role.

All UK universities and a number of HE colleges award their own degrees and other HE qualifications. HE providers who do not have their own degree-awarding powers offer degrees under 'validation arrangements' with other institutions that do have those powers. The OU, for example, runs a validation service which enables a number of other institutions to award OU degrees, after the OU has assured itself that the academic standards of their courses are as high as the OU's own standards.

Each HE institution is responsible for the standards of the awards it makes and the quality of the education it provides to its students, and each has its own internal quality assurance procedures. External quality assurance for HE institutions throughout the UK is provided by the Quality Assurance Agency for Higher Education (QAA).

The QAA is independent of government, funded by subscriptions from all publicly funded UK universities and colleges of HE. Its main role is to safeguard the standards of HE qualifications. It does this by defining standards for HE through a framework known as the academic infrastructure. QAA also carries out reviews of the quality of UK HE institutions via a system known as 'institutional audits'. QAA also advises government on a range of HE quality issues, including applications for the grant of degree-awarding powers. It publishes reports on its review activities on its website.

DEPARTMENT FOR EMPLOYMENT AND LEARNING
T 028-9025 7777 W www.delni.gov.uk
HIGHER EDUCATION FUNDING COUNCIL FOR
ENGLAND T 0117-931 7317 W www.hefce.ac.uk
HIGHER EDUCATION FUNDING COUNCIL FOR
WALES T 029-2076 1861 W www.hefcw.ac.uk
SCOTTISH FUNDING COUNCIL T 0131-313 6500
W www.sfc.ac.uk
THE QUALITY ASSURANCE AGENCY FOR HIGHER
EDUCATION T 01452-557000 W www.qaa.ac.uk
See also Universities for information on the Research Assessment Exercise (being replaced from 2014 by the Research Excellence Framework) and listings of universities in the UK.

STUDENTS APPLYING TO UNIVERSITY			
	2013	2014	Difference
Total applicants	635,910	659,030	4%
Source: UCAS			

STUDENTS IN HIGHER EDUCATION (2012–13)*			
	Full-time	Part-time	Total
HE students	1,682,145	658,130	2,340,275
Postgraduate students	296,470	239,965	536,435
Undergraduate students	1,385,675	418,165	1,803,840
*Includes UK, EU and non-EU students			
Source: Higher Education Statistics Agency (HESA) 2013			

UK HIGHER EDUCATION QUALIFICATIONS AWARDED (2012–13)		
	Full-time	Part-time
First degrees	302,370	35,285
Other undergraduate qualifications	52,070	53,285
Postgraduate Certificate in Education (PGCE)	16,875	1,380
Other postgraduate qualifications	10,820	27,525
Total higher degrees including doctorates	122,870	38,445
Source: HESA 2013		

COURSES

HE institutions in the UK mainly offer courses leading to the following qualifications. These qualifications go from levels 4 to 8 on England's National Qualifications Framework, levels 7 to 12 on Scotland's Credit and Qualifications Framework. Individual HEIs may not offer all of these.

Certificates of Higher Education (CertHE), awarded after one year's full-time study (or equivalent). If available to students on longer courses, they certify that students have reached a minimum standard in their first year.

Diplomas of Higher Education (DipHE) *and other Higher Diplomas,* awarded after two to three years' full-time study (or equivalent). They certify that a student has achieved a minimum standard in first- and second-year courses and, in the case of nursing, third-year courses. They can often be used for entry to the third year of a related degree course.

Foundation degrees, awarded after two years of full-time study (or equivalent). These degrees combine academic study with work-based learning, and have been designed jointly by universities, colleges and employers with a particular area of work in mind. They are usually accepted as a basis for entry to the third year of a related degree course.

Bachelor's degrees, also referred to as *first degrees.* There are different titles; Bachelor of Arts (BA) and Bachelor of Science (BSc) being the most common. In England, Wales and Northern Ireland most Bachelor's degree courses are typically 'with Honours' and awarded after three years of full-time study, although in some subjects the courses last longer. In Scotland, where young people often leave school and go to university a year younger, HE institutions typically offer Ordinary Bachelor's degrees after three years' study and Bachelor's degrees with Honours after four years. Honours degrees are graded as first, upper-second (2:1), lower second (2:2), or third. HEIs in England, Wales and Northern Ireland may allow students who fail the first year of an Honours degree by a small margin to transfer to an Ordinary degree course, if they have one. Ordinary degrees may also be awarded to Honours degree students who do not finish an Honours degree course but complete enough of it to earn a pass.

Postgraduate or *Higher degrees.* Graduates may go on to take *Master's degrees,* which involve one or two years' work and can be taught or research-based. They may also take one-year postgraduate diplomas and certificates, often linked to a specific profession, such as the *Postgraduate Certificate in Education* (PGCE) required to become a state school teacher. A *doctorate,* leading to a qualification such as a Doctor of Philosophy – a PHD or DPHIL – usually involves at least three years of full-time research.

The framework for HE qualifications in England, Wales and Northern Ireland (FHEQ) and the framework for qualifications of HE institutions in Scotland, can both be found on the QAA website (W www.qaa.ac.uk/academicinfrastructure/FHEQ/SCQF/), which describes the achievement represented by HE qualifications.

ADMISSIONS

When preparing to apply to a university or other HE college, individuals can compare facts and figures on institutions and courses using the government's Unistats website. This includes details of students' views from the annual National Student Survey.

For the vast majority of full-time undergraduate courses, individuals need to apply online through UCAS, the organisation responsible for managing applications to HE courses in the UK. More than half a million people wanting to study at a university or college each year use this UCAS service, which has useful online tools to help students find the right course.

UCAS also provides two specialist applications services used by more than 50,000 people each year: the Conservatoires UK Admissions Service (CUKAS), for those applying to UK music conservatoires, and the Graduate Teacher Training Registry (GTTR), for postgraduate applications for initial teacher training courses in England and Wales and some in Scotland. Details of initial teacher training courses in Scotland can also be obtained from Universities Scotland and from Teach in Scotland, the website created by the Scottish government to promote teaching.

Each university or college sets its own entry requirements. These can be in terms of particular exam grades or total points on the 'UCAS tariff' (UCAS's system for allocating points to different qualifications on a common basis), or be non-academic, like having a health check. HEIs will make 'firm offers' to candidates who have already gained the qualifications they present for entry, and 'conditional offers' to those who have yet to take their exams or obtain their results. Conditional offers often require a minimum level of achievement in a specified subject, for example '300 points to include grade A at A-level Chemistry'. If candidates' achievements are lower than specified in their conditional offers, the university or college may not accept them; then, if they still wish to go into HE, they need to find another institution through the UCAS 'clearing' process.

The OU conducts its own admissions. It is the UK's only university dedicated to distance learning and the UK's largest for part-time HE. Because it is designed to be 'open' to all, no qualifications are needed for entry to the majority of its courses.

Individuals can search over 58,000 UK postgraduate courses and research opportunities on UK graduate careers website Prospects. The application process for postgraduate places can vary between institutions. Most universities and colleges accept direct applications and many accept applications through UKPASS, a free, centralised online service run by UCAS that allows individuals to submit up to ten different applications, track their progress and attach supporting material, such as references.

UNISTATS W http://unistats.direct.gov.uk
UCAS T 0371-468 0468 W www.ucas.com
UNIVERSITIES SCOTLAND T 0131-226 1111
    W www.universities-scotland.ac.uk
TEACH IN SCOTLAND T 0845-345 4745
    W www.teachinginscotland.com
PROSPECTS T 0161-277 5200 W www.prospects.ac.uk
UKPASS T 0371-334 4447 W http://ukpass.ac.uk

TUITION FEES AND STUDENT SUPPORT
TUITION FEES
HE institutions in England, Wales and Northern Ireland are allowed to charge variable tuition fees for full-time HE courses. Although students from outside the EU can be charged the full cost of their courses, the amount that HEIs may charge students from the UK and other EU countries was capped from 2006 at £3,000 a year plus inflationary increases. From September 2012, universities have been able to charge up to £9,000 a year in tuition fees. The exact fee depends on the course studied and the institution attended. Full-time students do not have to pay their fees before or during their course, as tuition fee loans are available to cover the full cost; these do not have to be repaid until the student is working (see below).

In recent years, Scottish HE institutions have charged flat rate fees, set by the Scottish government, to undergraduate students classed as being ordinarily resident in England, Wales or Northern Ireland; though, as explained above, they can get repayable tuition fee loans to cover the cost. Since 2012 universities can set their own fees, up to £9,000 a year, for undergraduates starting courses. On average, Scottish universities have opted to charge £6,841. However, undergraduate students classed as being ordinarily resident in Scotland or another EU country do not have to pay tuition fees at Scottish HE institutions. All tuition fees are paid on their behalf by the Scottish government through the Student Awards Agency for Scotland (SAAS); students must apply for this funding every year.

STUDENT LOANS, GRANTS AND BURSARIES
ENGLAND
All students starting a full-time HE course in 2014–15 can apply through Student Finance England for financial support. Two student loans are available from the government: a *tuition fee loan* of up to £9,000 for 2014–15; and a *maintenance loan* (for students aged under 60) to help with living expenses of up to £5,555 for those living away from home (£7,751 if studying away from home in London) and £4,418 for those living with their parents during term time, or £6,600 if living and studying abroad for at least one term.

The tuition fee loan is not affected by household income and is paid directly to the relevant HE institution. A proportion (currently 65 per cent) of the maximum maintenance loan is available irrespective of household income while the rest depends on an income assessment. Student Finance England usually pays the money into the student's own bank account in three instalments, one at the start of each term.

Repayment of both loans does not start until the April after the student has left university or college and is earning more than £21,000 a year. At this point the individual's employer will take 9 per cent of any salary above the starting limit through the Pay As You Earn (PAYE) system. The self-employed make repayments through their tax returns. Someone earning £21,702 a year, the average starting salary for graduates entering full-time employment, will have to pay back £5.27 a week. Student loans accrue interest from the date they are paid out, up until they are repaid in full. Generally, the interest rate for student loans is set in September each year. The latest rate can be found online (W www.studentloanrepayment.co.uk/interest).

Students can also apply for a *maintenance grant* towards living expenses which does not have to be repaid. The maximum grant available for 2014–15 is £3,387 for the academic year. This is available to full-time HE students with a household income of £25,000 or under. Those with a household income of £42,620 or under receive a partial grant. The exact amount paid depends upon income. Students eligible for help through the maintenance grant receive some of it instead of the maintenance loan. The amount they are eligible for through the maintenance loan is reduced by £1 for every £1 of maintenance grant that they are entitled to (up to a maximum of £1,354). This means that students from lower income households generally have less to repay when they finish studying and start work.

Certain groups of students who claim means-tested state benefits can get the *special support grant*, also worth up to £3,387, instead of the maintenance grant. Likely recipients include single parents and students with certain disabilities. If a student receives the special support grant, it does not affect the amount of maintenance loan that he or she receives.

Bursaries are an additional source of help available from universities and colleges. They do not have to be repaid.

Students can use the student finance calculator on the Student Finance England website to work out what financial support they may get.

Part-time Higher Education Students in England are entitled to tuition fee loans (which replaced grants) of up to £6,750 in 2014–15. Following government changes to student finance, the maximum universities and colleges can charge part-time students in tuition fees is £6,750. Part-time students who earn over £21,000 a year have to start paying back their loans after four years even if their course has not finished.

Details are available on the Student Finance England website.

If the student's chosen HE institution runs the *additional fee support scheme*, it could provide extra financial help if the student is on a low income and in certain other circumstances. Help may also be available through the institution's *access to learning fund*, for students in financial difficulty.

STUDENT FINANCE ENGLAND T 0300-100 0607
W www.sfengland.slc.co.uk

WALES
Welsh students starting a full-time HE course in 2014–15 can apply through Student Finance Wales for the forms of financial support described below.

A similar system of tuition fee and maintenance loans and grants operates in Wales as in England but Welsh students can also receive a substantial tuition *fee grant*. Maximum maintenance loans are: up to £5,202 for students living away from home (£7,288 if studying away from home in London) and £4,027 for those living with their parents during term time. From September 2014, eligible Welsh students can access a non means-tested tuition fee loan of up to £3,685 and grant of up to £5,315 to cover the exact amount that the institution charges for a course.

Welsh-domiciled students may apply for an *assembly learning grant* (ALG) of up to £5,161 to help meet general living costs. This is paid in three instalments, one at the start of each term, like the student maintenance loan. The amount that a student gets depends on household income. The maximum ALG is available to those with a household income of £18,370 or under. Those with an income of £50,020 or under receive a partial grant. The amount of maintenance loan a student can receive is reduced by 50p for every £1 of ALG they receive up to a maximum of £2,575.

There is also a *Welsh government learning grant* (or *special support grant*) for those receiving benefits, which is worth up to £5,161 a year (in 2014/15). It is paid directly to students and is not offset against student loan borrowing.

Students needing extra help may also be entitled to receive adult dependants' grant (ADG), childcare grant (CCG), parents' learning allowance (PLA) and disabled students' allowance (DSA).

Students can use the student finance calculator on the Student Finance Wales website to work out what financial support they may be entitled to.

Welsh HE institutions also hold financial contingency funds to provide discretionary assistance to students experiencing financial difficulties.

From September 2014 part-time undergraduate higher education students studying at least 50 per cent of an equivalent full-time course are entitled to receive a fee loan of £2,625 (£6,750 for a course at a publicly funded university or college elsewhere in the UK, or £4,500 at a private university or college).

A *course grant* of up to £1,155 for books, travel and other course-related costs are available for part-time students. This grant depends on household income.

Like the *fee grant*, you must be studying at an average course intensity of at least 50 per cent to get a *course grant*. The *course grant* is paid into the recipient's bank account in one lump sum. The *course grant* is not usually available to those who already have a UK honours degree.

Continuing part-time students get a *fee grant* of up to £1,025, depending on their household income (partial fee grant is available for those with household incomes up to £25,435). Students needing extra help may also be entitled to receive *adult dependants' grant* (ADG), *childcare grant* (CCG), *parents' learning allowance* (PLA) and *disabled students' allowance* (DSA). Part-time students can also apply for a course-related grant worth up to £1,155 (partial course grant is available for those with household incomes up to £28,180).

STUDENT FINANCE WALES T 0300-200 4050
W www.studentfinancewales.co.uk

SCOTLAND
All students starting a full-time HE course in 2014–15 can apply through the Student Awards Agency for Scotland for financial support. Living cost support is mainly provided through a *student loan*, the majority of which is income-assessed. The maximum loan for 2014–15 is £5,500.

The *young students' bursary* (YSB) is available to young students from low-income backgrounds and is non-repayable. Eligible students receive this bursary instead of part of the student loan, thus reducing their level of repayable debt. In 2014–15 the maximum annual support provided through YSB is £1,750 if household income is £17,000 or less a year.

The *independent students' bursary* (ISB) similarly replaces part of the loan and reduces repayable debt for low-income students classed as 'independent' of parental support. The maximum paid is £750 a year to those whose household income is £17,000 or less a year.

Travel expenses are included within the student loan. There are also *supplementary grants* available to certain categories of students such as lone parents (£2,640) and those with dependants (£1,305). Extra help is also available to those who have a disability, learning difficulty or mental health problem.

STUDENT AWARDS AGENCY FOR SCOTLAND
T 0300-555 0505
W www.saas.gov.uk/forms/funding_guide.pdf

NORTHERN IRELAND
All students starting a full-time HE course in 2014–15 can apply through Student Finance Northern Ireland for financial support. The arrangements for both full-time and part-time students are similar to those for England. The main difference is that the income-assessed *maintenance grant* (or *special support grant* for students on certain income-assessed benefits) for new full-time students studying at UK universities and colleges is worth up to £3,475. Loans for living costs of £3,750 for study in Northern Ireland, £4,840 elsewhere in the UK (£6,780 in London) and £4,840 in the Republic of Ireland are available.

STUDENT FINANCE NORTHERN IRELAND
T 0300-100 0077 W www.studentfinanceni.co.uk

DISABLED STUDENTS' ALLOWANCES
Disabled Students' Allowances (DSAs) are grants available throughout the UK to help meet the extra course costs that students can face as a direct result of a disability, ongoing health condition, mental health condition or specific learning difficulty. They help disabled people to study in HE on an equal basis with other students. They are paid on top of the standard student finance package and do not have to be repaid. The amount that an individual gets depends on the type of extra help needed, not on household income. This amounts to £5,212 for specialist equipment for the entire

course, men medical helper allowance of £20,723 a year and a general allowance of £1,741 a year. Eligible individuals should apply as early as possible to their relevant UK awarding authority.

POSTGRADUATE AWARDS

In general, postgraduate students do not qualify for mandatory support like student loans. An exception to this is students taking a Postgraduate Certificate in Education (PGCE), who can qualify for the finance package usually available only to undergraduates.

There is heavy competition for any postgraduate funding available. Individuals can search for postgraduate awards and scholarships on two websites: Hot Courses and Prospects. They can also search for grants available from educational trusts, often reserved for students from poorer backgrounds or for those who have achieved academic excellence, on the Educational Grants Advisory Service (EGAS) website. Otherwise they need to fund their own fees and living expenses.

Postgraduates from Scotland can get £3,400 towards tuition fees but no support for living costs. In Northern Ireland, the Department for Employment and Learning and the Education and Library Boards provide postgraduate funding for certain courses. Postgraduate students with an impairment, health condition or learning difficulty can apply for disabled students' allowances (see above) for both taught courses and research places. For both full-time and part-time postgraduate students there is a single allowance of up to £10,362 a year.

DEPARTMENT FOR EMPLOYMENT AND LEARNING (DELNI) T 028-9025 7777 W www.delni.gov.uk
EDUCATIONAL GRANTS ADVISORY SERVICE (EGAS) T 020-7254 6251 W www.family-action.org.uk
HOT COURSES W www.scholarship-search.org.uk
PROSPECTS W www.prospects.ac.uk
STUDENT AWARDS AGENCY FOR SCOTLAND (SAAS) T 0300-555 0505 W www.student-support-saas.gov.uk

TEACHER TRAINING

See Professional Education.

EMPLOYEES AND SALARIES

EMPLOYEES
QUALIFIED TEACHERS IN MAINTAINED SCHOOLS (NOVEMBER 2012–13)
Full-time equivalent, thousands

	England	Wales	Scotland	NI	UK
Nursery and primary schools	200.0*	13.6	24.2	8.0	245.8
Secondary schools	204.9*	12.8	23.7	9.5	250.9
Special schools	14.6	0.7	2.0	0.8	18.1
Total	419.5	27.1	49.9	18.3	514.8

* Includes academies and city technology colleges in England

SUPPORT STAFF IN MAINTAINED SCHOOLS, ENGLAND AND WALES (2012–13)
Full-time equivalent, thousands

	England	Wales
Total support staff	384.2*	23.5
Teaching assistants	243.7	–
Other support staff	140.5*	–

* Includes academies and city technology colleges in England

INSTITUTIONS (2012–13)

	Full-time	Part-time	Total
Professors	14,785	3,100	17,880
Non-professors	121,000	61,940	190,935
Teaching only	10,730	36,065	46,795
Teaching and research	75,710	18,890	94,600
Research only	34,810	7,540	42,350
Neither teaching or research	1,250	590	1,840

Source: HESA 2014

SALARIES
State school teachers in England and Wales are employed by local authorities or the governing bodies of their schools, but their conditions, and pay until 2014, are set nationally.

There are teaching and learning responsibility payments for specific posts, special needs work and recruitment and retention factors which may be awarded at the discretion of the school governing body or the local authority. Schemes for 'Excellent Teachers' and 'Advanced Skills Teachers' came to an end in August 2013. Headteachers and other school leaders are paid on a separate leadership pay spine. All teachers are eligible for membership of the Teachers' Pension Scheme.

Academies are free to set their own salaries. In 2013, the average pay of full-time regular qualified classroom teachers in maintained secondary schools was £39,600 compared with £39,000 in secondary academies and £36,600 in maintained nursery and primary schools, compared with £35,800 in primary academies.

All teachers in England and Wales received a 1 per cent pay rise in September 2013, after the government accepted recommendations made by the School Teachers Review Body. From September 2013 every school needs to have revised its pay and appraisal policies, setting out how pay progression will, in future, be linked to a teacher's performance. The first decisions on pay progression under the new provisions were for September 2014, based on appraisals at the end of the 2013–14 cycle.

After completing initial teacher training (ITT) and achieving qualified teacher status (QTS), newly qualified teachers (NQTs) in maintained schools can expect to start on a salary of £21,804 a year in England and Wales (or £27,270 in inner London). The current pay ranges for teachers in England and Wales are:

Main pay range (including NQTs)	
London fringe	£22,853–£32,914
Outer London	£25,369–£35,468
Inner London	£27,270–£36,751
Rest of England and Wales	£21,804–£31,868
Upper pay range	
London fringe	£35,571–£38,173
Outer London	£37,975–£40,838
Inner London	£41,912–£45,450
Rest of England and Wales	£34,523–£37,124

In March 2014 the Scottish Negotiating Committee for Teachers agreed a two-year pay deal, backdated to 1 April 2013. The agreement provides for pay increases of 1 per cent from 1 April 2013, followed by a 1 per cent increase from 1 April 2014. Teachers are paid on a seven-point scale where the entry point is for newly qualified teachers undertaking their probationary year. There is no equivalent in Scotland of the upper pay spine operated in England and Wales. Experienced, ambitious teachers who reach the top of the main pay scale are eligible to become chartered teachers and earn more on a separate pay spine. However, to do so they must study for further professional qualifications. Headteachers and deputies have a separate pay spine as do 'principals' or heads of department. Additional allowances are payable to teachers under a range of circumstances, such as working in distant islands and remote schools.

As at September 2014, salary scales for teachers in Scotland are:

Headteacher/deputy headteacher	£43,137–£84,201
Principal teacher	£38,034–£49,086
Chartered teacher	£35,964–£42,768
Main grade	£21,867–£34,887

Teachers in Northern Ireland have broadly similar payscales to teachers in England and Wales, although there is neither an Advanced Skills Teacher grade nor an Excellent Teacher scheme. Classroom teachers who take on teaching and learning responsibilities outside their normal classroom duties may be awarded one of five teaching allowances.

Salary scales for teachers in Northern Ireland have been frozen since 2011, except for those earning £21,000 or less, who receive an increase of at least £250 a year. As at September 2014, salary scales in Northern Ireland are:

Principal (headteacher)	£42,379–£105,379
Classroom teacher (upper pay scale)	£34,181–£36,756
Classroom teacher (main pay scale)	£21,588–£31,552
Associate teachers	£13,734
Teaching allowances	£1,847–£11,911

Since 2007, most academic staff in HE across the UK are paid on a single national pay scale as a result of a national framework agreement negotiated by the HE unions and HE institutions. Staff are paid according to rates on a 51-point national pay spine and academic and academic-related staff are graded according to a national grading structure. In 2014–15 the pay spine ranged from £13,953 to £58,172. As HE institutions are autonomous employers, precise job grades and salaries may vary but the following table outlines salaries that typically tally with certain job roles in HE.

Principal lecturer	£47,328–£54,841
Senior lecturer	£37,394–£45,954
Lecturer	£31,342–£36,309
Junior researcher	£24,775–£30,434

UNIVERSITIES

The following is a list of universities, which are those institutions that have been granted degree-awarding powers by either a royal charter or an act of parliament, or have been permitted to use the word 'university' (or 'university college') by the Privy Council. There are other recognised bodies in the UK with degree-awarding powers, as well as institutions offering courses leading to a degree from a recognised body. Further information is available at W www.gov.uk/recognised-uk-degrees

Student figures represent the number of undergraduate (UG) and postgraduate (PG) students based on information available at June 2014.

For information on tuition fees and student loans, *see* Education, Higher Education.

RESEARCH ASSESSMENT EXERCISE

The research assessment exercise (RAE) gives a rating to each university department or specialist college put forward for evaluation, based on the quality of its research. It enables the higher education funding bodies to distribute public funds for research selectively on the basis of quality. Institutions conducting the best research receive a larger proportion of the available grant so that the infrastructure for the top level of research in the UK is protected and developed. The table below shows the top five universities or specialist colleges for each discipline based on the mean average ranking of the overall quality of their research. The research excellence framework (REF) is the new system for assessing the quality of research in UK higher education institutions. It will replace the RAE and is due to be published in December 2014.

Subject	Universities or university colleges
Anthropology	LSE (1), SOAS (1), Cambridge (3), Roehampton (4), UCL (5)
Archaeology	Durham (1), Reading (2), Cambridge (3), Oxford (3), Liverpool (5)
Biological sciences	Institute of Cancer Research (1), Manchester (2), Oxford (2), Sheffield (2), Dundee (5), RHUL (5)
Business and management	London Business School (1), Imperial (2), Cambridge (3), Cardiff (4), Bath (5), King's (5), Lancaster (5), LSE (5), Oxford (5), Warwick (5)
Chemistry	Cambridge (1), Nottingham (2), Oxford (3), Bristol (4), Edinburgh (4), St Andrews (4)
Classics	Cambridge (1), Oxford (2), UCL (3), Durham (4), King's (4), Warwick (4)
Communication and media studies	Westminster (1), East Anglia (2), Goldsmiths (3), LSE (3), Cardiff (5)
Computer science	Cambridge (1), Edinburgh (2), Imperial (2), Southampton (2), Manchester (5), Oxford (5), UCL (5)
Dentistry	Manchester (1), Queen Mary (2), King's (3), Sheffield (4), Bristol (5), Cardiff (5)
Drama and performing arts	Queen Mary (1), St Andrews (1), Manchester (3), Warwick (4), Bristol (5), King's (5)
Economics	LSE (1), UCL (2), Essex (3), Oxford (3), Warwick (3)

Engineering (electronic)	Leeds (1), Bangor (2), Manchester (2), Surrey (2), Imperial (5)
Engineering (general)	Cambridge (1), Oxford (2), Leeds (3), Nottingham (3), Imperial (5), Swansea (5)
English	York (1), Edinburgh (2), Manchester (2), Queen Mary (2), Exeter (5), Nottingham (5), Oxford (5)
French	Oxford (1), King's (2), Warwick (2), Aberdeen (4), Cambridge (4), St Andrews (4)
Geography	Bristol (1), Cambridge (1), Durham (1), Oxford (1), Queen Mary (1)
German, Dutch and Scandinavian	Oxford (1), Cambridge (2), Durham (2), King's (2), Leeds (2), RHUL (2), St Andrews (2)
History	Imperial (1), Essex (2), Kent (2), Liverpool (2), Oxford (2), Warwick (2)
Law	LSE (1), UCL (2), Oxford (3), Durham (4), Nottingham (4)
Mathematics (applied)	Cambridge (1), Oxford (1), Bristol (3), Bath (4), Portsmouth (4), St Andrews (4)
Mathematics (pure)	Imperial (1), Warwick (2), Oxford (3), Cambridge (4), Bristol (5), Edinburgh (5), Heriot-Watt (5)
Music	RHUL (1), Birmingham (2), Manchester (2), Cambridge (4), King's (4), Sheffield (4), Southampton (4)
Philosophy	UCL (1), St Andrews (1), King's (3), Reading (3), Sheffield (3)
Physics	Lancaster (1), Bath (2), Cambridge (2), Nottingham (2), St Andrews (2)
Politics	Essex (1), Sheffield (1), Aberystwyth (3), Oxford (4), LSE (5)
Psychology	Cambridge (1), Oxford (2), Birmingham (3), UCL (4), Birkbeck (5), Cardiff (5)
Sociology	Essex (1), Goldsmiths (1), Manchester (1), York (1), Lancaster (5)
Sports-related subjects	Birmingham (1), Loughborough (1), Bristol (3), Liverpool John Moores (4), Stirling (5)
Theology and religious studies	Durham (1), Aberdeen (2), Cambridge (3), Oxford (3), UCL (3)

UNIVERSITY OF ABERDEEN (1495)

King's College, Aberdeen AB24 3FX T 01224-272000
W www.abdn.ac.uk
Fee: £9,000 *Students:* 11,890 UG; 3,430 PG
Chancellor, HRH the Duchess of Rothesay
Vice-Chancellor, Prof. Sir Ian Diamond
University Secretary, Caroline Inglis

UNIVERSITY OF ABERTAY DUNDEE (1994)

Bell Street, Dundee DD1 1HG T 01382-308000
W www.abertay.ac.uk
Fee: £7,000 *Students:* 4,415 UG; 420 PG
Chancellor, Lord Cullen of Whitekirk, KT, PC, FRSE
Vice-Chancellor, Prof. Nigel Seaton, FRENG
Registrar, Susan Campbell

ABERYSTWYTH UNIVERSITY (1872)
Penglais, Aberystwyth SY23 3FL T 01970-623111
W www.aber.ac.uk
Fee: £9,000 *Students:* 9,840 UG; 1,775 PG
Vice-Chancellor, Prof. April McMahon, FRSE, FBA
University Secretary, Geraint Pugh

ANGLIA RUSKIN UNIVERSITY (1992)
Chelmsford Campus, Bishop Hall Lane, Chelmsford CM1 1SQ
T 0845-271 3333 W www.anglia.ac.uk
Fee: £8,300 *Students:* 17,650 UG; 3,420 PG
Chancellor, Lord Ashcroft, KCMG
Vice-Chancellor, Prof. Michael Thorne, FRS, PHD
Secretary and Clerk, Stephen Bennett

UNIVERSITY OF THE ARTS LONDON (2003)
(Formerly The London Institute (1986), renamed 2004)
272 High Holborn, London WC1V 7EY T 020-7514 6000
W www.arts.ac.uk
Fee: £9,000 *Students:* 13,985 UG; 3,060 PG
Chancellor, Kwame Kwei-Armah
Vice-Chancellor, Nigel Carrington
Secretary and Registrar, Stephen Marshall

COLLEGES
CAMBERWELL COLLEGE OF ARTS (1898)
Peckham Road, London SE5 8UF T 020-7514 6302
W www.arts.ac.uk/camberwell
Head of College, Prof. Chris Wainwright
CENTRAL SAINT MARTINS COLLEGE OF ART AND
DESIGN (1854)
Granary Building, 1 Granary Square, London N1C 4AA
T 020-7514 7444 W www.arts.ac.uk/csm
Head of College, Jeremy Till
CHELSEA COLLEGE OF ARTS (1895)
John Islip Street, London SW1P 4JU T 020-7514 7751
W www.arts.ac.uk/chelsea
Head of College, Prof. Chris Wainwright
LONDON COLLEGE OF COMMUNICATION (1894)
Elephant and Castle, London SE1 6SB T 020-7514 6500
W www.arts.ac.uk/lcc
Head of College, Natalie Brett
LONDON COLLEGE OF FASHION (1963)
20 John Prince's Street, London W1G 0BJ T 020-7514 7400
W www.arts.ac.uk/fashion
Head of College, Prof. Frances Corner, OBE
WIMBLEDON COLLEGE OF ART (1930)
Merton Hall Road, London SW19 3QA T 020-7514 9641
W www.arts.ac.uk/wimbledon
Head of College, Chris Wainwright

ASTON UNIVERSITY (1966)
Aston Triangle, Birmingham B4 7ET T 0121-204 3000
W www.aston.ac.uk
Fee: £9,000 *Students:* 7,875 UG; 2,115 PG
Chancellor, Sir John Sunderland
Vice-Chancellor, Prof. Dame Julia King, DBE, FRENG, FRSA
Registrar, Judith Whitaker

BANGOR UNIVERSITY (1884)
Gwynedd LL57 2DG T 01248-351151 W www.bangor.ac.uk
Fee: £9,000 *Students:* 8,460 UG; 2,900 PG
Vice-Chancellor, Prof. John Hughes
Secretary and Registrar, Dr David Roberts

UNIVERSITY OF BATH (1966)
Claverton Down, Bath BA2 7AY T 01225-388388
W www.bath.ac.uk
Fee: £9,000 *Students:* 10,580 UG; 4,480 PG
Chancellor, HRH the Earl of Wessex, KG, GCVO, ADC(P)
Vice-Chancellor, Prof. Dame Glynis Breakwell, DBE, FRSA
University Secretary, Mark Humphriss

BATH SPA UNIVERSITY (2005)
Newton Park, Newton St Loe, Bath BA2 9BN T 01225-875875
W www.bathspa.ac.uk
Fee: £9,000 *Students:* 5,365 UG; 2,500 PG
Vice-Chancellor, Prof. Christina Slade
Academic Registrar, Christopher Ellicott

UNIVERSITY OF BEDFORDSHIRE (1993)
University Square, Luton LU1 3JU T 01234-400400
W www.beds.ac.uk
Fee: £9,000 *Students:* 14,185 UG; 6,130 PG
Chancellor, Baroness Howells of St Davids, OBE
Vice-Chancellor, Bill Rammell
Registrar, Richard Middleton

UNIVERSITY OF BIRMINGHAM (1900)
Edgbaston, Birmingham B15 2TT T 0121-414 3344
W www.birmingham.ac.uk
Fee: £9,000 *Students:* 18,785 UG; 11,915 PG
Chancellor, Lord Bilimoria, CBE
Vice-Chancellor and Principal, Prof. David Eastwood
Registrar and Secretary, Lee Sanders

BIRMINGHAM CITY UNIVERSITY (1992)
City North Campus, Birmingham B42 2SU T 0121-331 5000
W www.bcu.ac.uk
Fee: £9,000 *Students:* 18,515 UG; 3,570 PG
Chancellor, Lord Mayor of Birmingham (Mike Leddy,
   2013–14)
Vice-Chancellor, Prof. Cliff Allan
University Secretary, Ms Christine Abbott

UNIVERSITY OF BOLTON (2005)
Deane Road, Bolton BL3 5AB T 01204-900600
W www.bolton.ac.uk
Fee: £8,400 *Students:* 6,125 UG; 1,170 PG
Chancellor, Lord Justice Ryder, PC
Vice-Chancellor, Prof George Holmes
Registrar and Secretary, Sue Duncan

BOURNEMOUTH UNIVERSITY (1992)
Fern Barrow, Poole, Dorset BH12 5BB T 01202-524111
W www.bournemouth.ac.uk
Fee: £9,000 *Students:* 15,005 UG; 2,965 PG
Chancellor, Lord Phillips of Worth Matravers, PC, QC
Vice-Chancellor, Prof. John Vinney
Clerk, Noel Richardson

UNIVERSITY OF BRADFORD (1966)
Richmond Road, Bradford BD7 1DP T 01274-232323
W www.bradford.ac.uk
Fee: £9,000 *Students:* 10,420 UG; 2,775 PG
Chancellor, Imran Khan
Vice-Chancellor and Principal, Prof. Brian Cantor, CBE
University Secretary, Adrian Pearce

UNIVERSITY OF BRIGHTON (1992)
Mithras House, Lewes Road, Brighton BN2 4AT T 01273-600900
W www.brighton.ac.uk
Fee: £9,000 *Students:* 17,155 UG; 4,160 PG
Vice-Chancellor, Prof. Julian Crampton
Registrar, Carol Burns

UNIVERSITY OF BRISTOL (1909)
Senate House, Tyndall Avenue, Bristol BS8 1TH T 0117-928 9000
W www.bris.ac.uk
Fee: £9,000 *Students:* 14,040 UG; 5,430 PG
Chancellor, Baroness Hale of Richmond, DBE, PC
Vice-Chancellor, Prof. Eric Thomas
Registrar, Robin Geller

BRUNEL UNIVERSITY (1966)
Uxbridge, Middx UB8 3PH T 01895-274000 W www.brunel.ac.uk
Fee: £9,000 *Students:* 10,035 UG; 5,275 PG
Chancellor, Sir Richard Sykes
Vice-Chancellor, Prof. Julia Buckingham
Registrar, Helen Emerson

UNIVERSITY OF BUCKINGHAM (1983)
Buckingham MK18 1EG T 01280-814080
W www.buckingham.ac.uk
Fee: £9,000 *Students:* 1,360 UG; 730 PG
Chancellor, Lady Keswick
Vice-Chancellor, Prof. Terence Kealey, DPHIL
Registrar, Anne Miller

BUCKINGHAMSHIRE NEW UNIVERSITY (2007)
High Wycombe Campus, Queen Alexandra Road, High Wycombe
HP11 2JZ T 0800-0565 660 W www.bucks.ac.uk
Fee: £8,000 *Students:* 8,200 UG; 1,005 PG
Vice-Chancellor, Prof. Ruth Farwell
Director of Academic Quality, Ellie Smith

UNIVERSITY OF CAMBRIDGE (1209)
The Old Schools, Trinity Lane, Cambridge CB2 1TN
T 01223-337733 W www.cam.ac.uk
Fee: £9,000 *Students:* 12,140 UG; 7,245 PG
Chancellor, Lord Sainsbury of Turville, FRS (King's)
Vice-Chancellor, Prof. Sir Leszek Borysiewicz, FRS (Wolfson)
High Steward, Lord Watson of Richmond, CBE (Jesus)
Deputy High Steward, Mrs A. Lonsdale, CBE (Murray Edwards)
Commissary, Lord Mackay of Clashfern, KT, PC, FRSE
   (Trinity)
Pro-Vice-Chancellors, Dr J. C. Barnes (Murray Edwards); Prof.
   L. F. Gladden, CBE, FRS (Trinity); Prof. J. M. Rallison
   (Trinity); Prof. J. K. M. Sanders, FRS (Selwyn); Prof. S. J.
   Young, FRENG (Emmanuel)
Proctors, Revd Dr J. M. Holmes (Queens'); R. K. Taplin,
   MBE (Downing)
Orator, Dr R. J. E. Thompson (Selwyn)
Registrar, Dr J. W. Nicholls (Emmanuel)
Librarian, Mrs A. E. Jarvis (Wolfson)
Director of the Fitzwilliam Museum, T. Knox (Gonville and
   Caius)
Academic Secretary, G. P. Allen (Wolfson)
Director of Finance, A. M. Reid (Wolfson)
Executive Director of Development, Ms A. Traub
Esquire Bedells, Mrs N. Hardy (Jesus); Ms S. V. Scarlett
   (Lucy Cavendish)
University Advocate, Dr R. E. Thornton (Emmanuel)

COLLEGES AND HALLS *with dates of foundation*
CHRIST'S (1505)
Master, Prof. F. P. Kelly, CBE, FRS
CHURCHILL (1960)
Master, Prof. Sir David Wallace, CBE, FRS
CLARE (1326)
Master, Prof. A. J. Badger
CLARE HALL (1966)
President, Prof. D. J. Ibbetson, FBA
CORPUS CHRISTI (1352)
Master, Mr S. Laing

DARWIN (1964)
Master, C. M. R. Fowler
DOWNING (1800)
Master, Prof. G. R. Grimmett
EMMANUEL (1584)
Master, Dame Fiona Reynolds, DBE
FITZWILLIAM (1966)
Master, Mrs N. M. Padfield
GIRTON (1869)
Mistress, Prof. S. J. Smith, FBA
GONVILLE AND CAIUS (1348)
Master, Prof. Sir Alan Fersht, FRS
HOMERTON (1976)
Principal, Prof. G. Ward
HUGHES HALL (1885)
President, Mrs S. L. Squire
JESUS (1496)
Master, Prof. I. H. White
KING'S (1441)
Provost, Prof. M. R. E. Proctor, FRS
LUCY CAVENDISH (1965)
President, Prof. J. M. Todd, OBE
MAGDALENE (1542)
Master, Rt. Revd Lord Williams of Oystermouth, PC, DPHIL,
   FBA
MURRAY EDWARDS (1954)
President, Dame Barbara Stocking, DBE
NEWNHAM (1871)
Principal, Prof. Dame Carol Black, DBE, FRCP
PEMBROKE (1347)
Master, Sir Richard Dearlove, KCMG, OBE
PETERHOUSE (1284)
Master, Prof. A. K. Dixon, FRCP
QUEENS' (1448)
President, Prof. Lord Eatwell
ROBINSON (1979)
Warden, Prof. A. D. Yates
ST CATHARINE'S (1473)
Master, Prof. Dame Jean Thomas, DBE, FRS
ST EDMUND'S (1896)
Master, Prof. J. P. Luzio, FRCPATH
ST JOHN'S (1511)
Master, Prof. C. M. Dobson, FRS
SELWYN (1882)
Master, Roger Mosey
SIDNEY SUSSEX (1596)
Master, Prof. R. V. Penty
TRINITY (1546)
Master, Sir Gregory Winter, CBE, FRS
TRINITY HALL (1350)
Master, Prof. M. J. Daunton, FBA
WOLFSON (1965)
President, Prof. Sir Richard Evans, FBA

CANTERBURY CHRIST CHURCH UNIVERSITY
(2005)
North Holmes Road, Canterbury CT1 1QU T 01227-767700
W www.canterbury.ac.uk
Fee: £8,500 *Students:* 14,195 UG; 3,845 PG
Chancellor, Most Revd and Rt. Hon. Archbishop of
   Canterbury
Vice-Chancellor, Prof. Rama Thirunamachandran
Academic Registrar, Lorri Curri

CARDIFF METROPOLITAN UNIVERSITY (2011)
Western Avenue, Cardiff CF5 2YB T 029-2041 6138
W www.cardiffmet.ac.uk
Fee: £7,800 *Students:* 8,570 UG; 3,870 PG
Vice-Chancellor and Principal, Prof. Anthony Chapman

CARDIFF UNIVERSITY (1883)
Cardiff CF10 3XQ **T** 029-2087 4000 **W** www.cardiff.ac.uk
Fee: £9,000 *Students:* 21,020 UG; 7,520 PG
Chancellor, Prof. Sir Martin Evans, FRS
Vice-Chancellor, Prof. Colin Riordan
Chief Operating Officer, Jayne Dowden

UNIVERSITY OF CENTRAL LANCASHIRE (1992)
Preston PR1 2HE **T** 01772-201201 **W** www.uclan.ac.uk
Fee: £9,000 *Students:* 24,005 UG; 4,715 PG
Chancellor, Sir Richard Evans, CBE
Vice-Chancellor, Prof. Gerry Kelleher

UNIVERSITY OF CHESTER (2005)
Parkgate Road, Chester CH1 4BJ **T** 01244-511000
W www.chester.ac.uk
Fee: £9,000 *Students:* 10,775 UG; 3,575 PG
Chancellor, Duke of Westminster, KG, CB, CVO
Vice-Chancellor, Canon Prof. Tim Wheeler
Registrar, Jonathan Moores

UNIVERSITY OF CHICHESTER (2005)
College Lane, Chichester PO19 6PE **T** 01243-816000
W www.chi.ac.uk
Fee: £8,500 *Students:* 4,700 UG; 850 PG
Vice-Chancellor, Prof. Clive Behagg, PHD
Secretary, Isabel Cherrett

CITY UNIVERSITY LONDON (1966)
Northampton Square, London EC1V 0HB **T** 020-7040 5060
W www.city.ac.uk
Fee: £9,000 *Students:* 9,430 UG; 7,090 PG
Chancellor, Fiona Woolf, CBE
Vice-Chancellor, Prof. Paul Curran
Secretary, Frank Toop

COVENTRY UNIVERSITY (1992)
Priory Street, Coventry CV1 5FB **T** 024-7688 7688
W www.coventry.ac.uk
Fee: £9,000 *Students:* 22,020 UG; 5,250 PG
Chancellor, Sir John Egan
Vice-Chancellor, John Latham
Registrar, Kate Quantrell

CRANFIELD UNIVERSITY (1969)
Cranfield, Bedfordshire MK43 0AL **T** 01234-750111
W www.cranfield.ac.uk
Students: 3,920 PG (postgraduate only)
Chancellor, Baroness Young of Old Scone
Vice-Chancellor, Prof. Sir Peter Gregson

UNIVERSITY FOR THE CREATIVE ARTS (2008)
Falkner Road, Farnham, Surrey GU9 7DS **T** 01252-722441
W www.ucreative.ac.uk
Fee: £8,500 *Students:* 5,050 UG; 295 PG
Chancellor, Zandra Rhodes, CBE
Vice-Chancellor, Dr Simon Ofield-Kerr
University Secretary, Marion Wilks

UNIVERSITY OF CUMBRIA (2007)
Fusehill Street, Carlisle CA1 2HH **T** 01228-616234
W www.cumbria.ac.uk
Fee: £9,000 *Students:* 7,925 UG; 1,675 PG
Chancellor, Most Revd and Rt. Hon. Archbishop of York
Vice-Chancellor, Prof. Peter Strike
Registrar and Secretary, Neil Harris

DE MONTFORT UNIVERSITY (1992)
The Gateway, Leicester LE1 9BH **T** 0116-255 1551
W www.dmu.ac.uk

Fee: £9,000 *Students:* 16,750 UG; 3,565 PG
Chancellor, Lord Waheed Alli
Vice-Chancellor, Prof. Dominic Shellard
University Secretary, Helen Chan

UNIVERSITY OF DERBY (1992)
Kedleston Road, Derby DE22 1GB **T** 01332-590500
W www.derby.ac.uk
Fee: £9,000 *Students:* 13,595 UG; 2,695 PG
Chancellor, Duke of Devonshire, KCVO, CBE
Vice-Chancellor, Prof. John Coyne
Registrar, June Hughes

UNIVERSITY OF DUNDEE (1967)
Nethergate, Dundee DD1 4HN **T** 01382-383000
W www.dundee.ac.uk
Fee: £9,000 *Students:* 10,550 UG; 5,155 PG
Chancellor, Lord Patel, KT, FRSE
Vice-Chancellor and Principal, Prof. Pete Downes, OBE,
FRSE
University Secretary, Dr Jim McGeorge

DURHAM UNIVERSITY (1832)
The Palatine Centre, Stockton Road, Durham DH1 3LE
T 0191-334 2000 **W** www.dur.ac.uk
Fee: £9,000 *Students:* 12,085 UG; 4,715 PG
Chancellor, Sir Thomas Allen, CBE
Vice-Chancellor, Prof. Christopher Higgins, FRSE,
FMEDSCI
Registrar and Treasurer (acting), Paulina Lubacz

COLLEGES
COLLINGWOOD (1972)
Principal, Prof. J. Elliott
GREY (1959)
Master, Prof. T. Allen
HATFIELD (1846)
Master, Prof. T. P. Burt
JOHN SNOW (2001)
Principal, Prof. C. Summerbell
JOSEPHINE BUTLER (2006)
Principal, A. Simpson
ST AIDAN'S (1947)
Principal, Dr S. F. Frenk
ST CHAD'S (1904)
Principal, Revd Dr J. P. M. Cassidy
ST CUTHBERT'S SOCIETY (1888)
Principal, Prof. E. Archibald
ST HILD AND ST BEDE (1839)
Principal, Prof. C. Hutchison
ST JOHN'S (1909)
Principal, Revd Dr D. Wilkinson
ST MARY'S (1899)
Principal, Prof. S. Hackett
STEPHENSON (2001)
Principal, Prof. J. Ashworth
TREVELYAN (1966)
Principal, Prof. H. M. Evans
UNIVERSITY (1832)
Master, Prof. D. Held
USTINOV
Principal, Prof. G. McGregor
VAN MILDERT (1965)
Principal, Prof. D. Harper

UNIVERSITY OF EAST ANGLIA (1963)
Norwich Research Park, Norwich NR4 7TJ **T** 01603-456161
W www.uea.ac.uk

Fee: £9,000 Students: 12,360 UG; 4,860 PG
Chancellor, Rose Tremain, CBE
Vice-Chancellor, Prof. Edward Acton
Registrar and Secretary, Brian Summers

UNIVERSITY OF EAST LONDON (1898)
University Way, London E16 2RD T 020-8223 3000
W www.uel.ac.uk
Fee: £9,000 Students: 15,025 UG; 4,570 PG
Vice-Chancellor, Prof. John Joughin
Deputy Vice-Chancellor, Dusty Amroliwala

EDGE HILL UNIVERSITY (2006)
St Helens Road, Ormskirk, Lancs L39 4QP T 01695-575171
W www.edgehill.ac.uk
Fee: £9,000 Students: 12,990 UG; 5,545 PG
Chancellor, Prof. Tanya Byron
Vice-Chancellor, Dr John Cater
Registrar, Ian Jones

UNIVERSITY OF EDINBURGH (1583)
Old College, South Bridge, Edinburgh EH8 9YL T 0131-650 1000
W www.ed.ac.uk
Fee: £9,000 Students: 19,125 UG; 8,565 PG
Chancellor, HRH the Princess Royal, KG, KT, GCVO
Vice-Chancellor and Principal, Prof. Sir Timothy O'Shea, FRSE
University Secretary, Sarah Smith

EDINBURGH NAPIER UNIVERSITY (1992)
Sighthill Campus, Edinburgh EH11 4BN T 0333-900 6040
W www.napier.ac.uk
Fee: £6,630 Students: 10,720 UG; 2,130 PG
Chancellor, Tim Waterstone
Vice-Chancellor, Prof. Andrea Nolan, OBE
Secretary, Dr Gerry Webber

UNIVERSITY OF ESSEX (1965)
Wivenhoe Park, Colchester CO4 3SQ T 01206-873333
W www.essex.ac.uk
Fee: £9,000 Students: 11,425 UG; 3,245 PG
Chancellor, Shami Chakrabarti
Vice-Chancellor, Prof. Anthony Forster, DPHIL
Registrar, Bryn Morris

UNIVERSITY OF EXETER (1955)
Stocker Road, Exeter EX4 4PY T 01392-661000
W www.exeter.ac.uk
Fee: £9,000 Students: 14,235 UG; 4,630 PG
Chancellor, Baroness Benjamin, OBE
Vice-Chancellor and Chief Executive, Prof. Sir Steve Smith, PhD
Chief Operating Officer, Geoff Pringle

UNIVERSITY OF GLASGOW (1451)
University Avenue, Glasgow G12 8QQ T 0141-330 2000
W www.gla.ac.uk
Fee: £9,000 Students: 20,010 UG; 6,625 PG
Chancellor, Prof. Sir Kenneth Calman, KCB, FRCS
Vice-Chancellor, Prof. Anton Muscatelli, FRSE
Registrar, David Bennion

GLASGOW CALEDONIAN UNIVERSITY (1993)
City Campus, Cowcaddens Road, Glasgow G4 0BA
T 0141-331 3000 W www.gcu.ac.uk
Fee: £7,000 Students: 13,385 UG; 2,540 PG
Chancellor, Prof. Muhammad Yunus
Vice-Chancellor, Prof. Pamela Gillies, CBE
University Secretary, Jan Hulme

UNIVERSITY OF GLOUCESTERSHIRE (2001)
The Park, Cheltenham GL50 2RH T 0844-801 0001
W www.glos.ac.uk
Fee: £8,250 Students: 6,865 UG; 1,535 PG
Chancellor, Baroness Fritchie, DBE
Vice-Chancellor, Stephen Marston
Registrar, Julie Thackray

GLYNDWR UNIVERSITY (2008)
Mold Road, Wrexham LL11 2AW T 01978-290666
W www.glyndwr.ac.uk
Fee: £8,450 Students: 7,135 UG; 1,385 PG
Vice-Chancellor, Prof. Michael Scott
Academic Registrar, Gillian Bridgett

UNIVERSITY OF GREENWICH (1992)
Old Royal Naval College, Park Row, Greenwich, London SE10 9LS
T 020-8331 8000 W www.gre.ac.uk
Fee: £9,000 Students: 18,620 UG; 5,300 PG
Chancellor, Baroness Scotland of Asthal, PC, QC
Vice-Chancellor, Prof. David Maguire
Secretary, Anne Poulson

HERIOT-WATT UNIVERSITY (1966)
Edinburgh EH14 4AS T 0131-449 5111 W www.hw.ac.uk
Fee: £9,000 Students: 6,830 UG; 4,235 PG
Chancellor, Dr Robert Buchan
Vice-Chancellor and Principal, Prof. Steve Chapman, FRSE
Secretary, Ann Marie Dalton

UNIVERSITY OF HERTFORDSHIRE (1992)
College Lane, Hatfield, Herts AL10 9AB T 01707-284000
W www.herts.ac.uk
Fee: £9,000 Students: 20,010 UG; 5,125 PG
Chancellor, Marquess of Salisbury, KCVO, PC
Vice-Chancellor, Prof. Quintin McKellar, CBE
Registrar, Sue Grant

UNIVERSITY OF HUDDERSFIELD (1992)
Queensgate, Huddersfield HD1 3DH T 01484-422288
W www.hud.ac.uk
Fee: £7,950 Students: 16,510 UG; 3,925 PG
Chancellor, Prof. Sir Patrick Stewart, OBE
Vice-Chancellor, Prof. Bob Cryan, CBE, PHD, DSc
University Secretary, Tony Mears

UNIVERSITY OF HULL (1927)
Cottingham Road, Hull HU6 7RX T 01482-346311
W www.hull.ac.uk
Fee: £9,000 Students: 15,255 UG; 3,620 PG
Chancellor, Baroness Bottomley of Nettlestone, PC
Vice-Chancellor, Prof. Calie Pistorius, PHD
Registrar, Jeannette Strachan

IMPERIAL COLLEGE LONDON (1907)
South Kensington, London SW7 2AZ T 020-7589 5111
W www.imperial.ac.uk
Fee: £9,000 Students: 8,810 UG; 7,195 PG
Rector, Sir Keith O'Nions, FRS
Deputy Rector, Prof. Stephen Richardson
Registrar, John Neilson

KEELE UNIVERSITY (1962)
Keele, Staffs ST5 5BG T 01782-732000 W www.keele.ac.uk
Fee: £9,000 Students: 7,650 UG; 2,585 PG
Chancellor, Jonathon Porritt, CBE
Vice-Chancellor, Prof. Nick Foskett, PHD

UNIVERSITY OF KENT (1965)
Canterbury, Kent CT2 7NZ **T** 01227-764000 **W** www.kent.ac.uk
Fee: £9,000 *Students:* 15,770 UG; 4,045 PG
Chancellor, Gavin Esler
Vice-Chancellor, Prof. Dame Julia Goodfellow, DBE, CBE, PHD
Academic Registrar, Jon Pink

KINGSTON UNIVERSITY (1992)
River House, 53–57 High Street, Kingston upon Thames, Surrey KT1 1LQ **T** 020-8417 9000 **W** www.kingston.ac.uk
Fee: £9,000 *Students:* 19,160 UG; 4,940 PG
Chancellor, Bonnie Greer, OBE
Vice-Chancellor, Prof. Julius Weinberg
Academic Registrar, Marie Sheehan

UNIVERSITY OF LANCASTER (1964)
Bailrigg, Lancaster LA1 4YW **T** 01524-65201
W www.lancaster.ac.uk
Fee: £9,000 *Students:* 9,155 UG; 3,580 PG
Chancellor, Sir Christian Bonington, CVO, CBE
Vice-Chancellor, Prof. Mark E. Smith
University Secretary, Fiona Aiken

UNIVERSITY OF LEEDS (1904)
Leeds LS2 9JT **T** 0113-243 1751 **W** www.leeds.ac.uk
Fee: £9,000 *Students:* 23,295 UG; 7,090 PG
Chancellor, Lord Bragg, PC
Vice-Chancellor, Sir Alan Langlands
University Secretary, J. Roger Gair

LEEDS METROPOLITAN UNIVERSITY (1992)
City Campus, Leeds LS1 3HE **T** 0113-812 0000
W www.leedsmet.ac.uk
Fee: £8,500 *Students:* 22,155 UG; 3,650 PG
Chancellor, Sir Bob Murray, CBE
Vice-Chancellor, Prof. Susan Price
Secretary and Registrar, Jenny Share

LEEDS TRINITY UNIVERSITY (2012)
Brownberrie Lane, Leeds LS18 3HD **T** 0113-283 7100
W www.leedstrinity.ac.uk
Fee: £9,000 *Students:* 2,660 UG; 605 PG
Chancellor, Gabby Logan
Vice-Chancellor, Prof. Margaret House
Secretary, vacant

UNIVERSITY OF LEICESTER (1957)
University Road, Leicester LE1 7RH **T** 0116-252 2522
W www.le.ac.uk
Fee: £9,000 *Students:* 10,880 UG; 6,280 PG
Chancellor, Lord Grocott
Vice-Chancellor, Prof. Sir Robert Burgess, PHD
Registrar, Dave Hall

UNIVERSITY OF LINCOLN (1992)
Brayford Pool, Lincoln LN6 7TS **T** 01522-882000
W www.lincoln.ac.uk
Fee: £9,000 *Students:* 10,695 UG; 2,025 PG
Chancellor, Lord Adebowale, CBE
Vice-Chancellor, Prof. Mary Stuart
Registrar, Chris Spendlove

UNIVERSITY OF LIVERPOOL (1903)
Liverpool L69 3BX **T** 0151-794 2000 **W** www.liv.ac.uk
Fee: £9,000 *Students:* 16,220 UG; 4,655 PG
Chancellor, Prof. Sir David King, PHD, FRS
Vice-Chancellor, Prof. Sir Howard Newby, CBE, PHD
Chief Operating Officer, Patrick Hackett

LIVERPOOL HOPE UNIVERSITY (2005)
Hope Park, Liverpool L16 9JD **T** 0151-291 3000
W www.hope.ac.uk
Fee: £9,000 *Students:* 4,875 UG; 1,665 PG
Chancellor, Lord Guthrie of Craigiebank, GCB, LVO, OBE
Vice-Chancellor and Rector, Prof. Gerald Pillay
University Secretary, Graham Donelan

LIVERPOOL JOHN MOORES UNIVERSITY (1992)
Kingsway House, 2nd Floor, Hatton Garden, Liverpool L3 2AJ
T 0151-231 2121 **W** www.ljmu.ac.uk
Fee: £9,000 *Students:* 19,105 UG; 3,480 PG
Chancellor, Rt. Hon. Sir Brian Leveson
Vice-Chancellor, Prof. Nigel Weatherill, FRENG, DSC
Secretary, Denise Tipping

UNIVERSITY OF LONDON (1836)
Senate House, Malet Street, London WC1E 7HU **T** 020-7862 8000
W www.london.ac.uk
Fee: £9,000
Chancellor, HRH the Princess Royal, KG, KT, GCVO
Vice-Chancellor, Prof. Sir Adrian Smith
University Secretary, Chris Cobb

COLLEGES
BIRKBECK COLLEGE
Malet Street, London WC1E 7HX
Students: 11,485 UG; 4,975 PG
President, Baroness Bakewell, DBE
Master, Prof. David Latchman, PhD
CENTRAL SCHOOL OF SPEECH AND DRAMA
Eton Avenue, London NW3 3HY
Students: 660 UG; 340 PG
President, Michael Grandage, CBE
Principal, Prof. Gavin Henderson, CBE
COURTAULD INSTITUTE OF ART
Somerset House, Strand, London WC2R 0RN
Students: 155 UG; 280 PG
Director, Prof. Deborah Swallow
GOLDSMITHS COLLEGE
New Cross, London SE14 6NW
Students: 4,880 UG; 3,200 PG
Warden, Patrick Loughrey
HEYTHROP COLLEGE
Kensington Square, London W8 5HN
Students: 505 UG; 415 PG
Principal, Michael Holman, SJ
INSTITUTE OF CANCER RESEARCH
15 Cotswold Road, London SM2 5NG
Students: 300 PG (postgraduate only)
Chief Executive, Prof. Alan Ashworth
INSTITUTE OF EDUCATION
20 Bedford Way, London WC1H 0AL
Students: 270 UG; 5,155 PG
Director, Prof. Chris Husbands
KING'S COLLEGE LONDON (includes Guy's, King's and St Thomas's Schools of Medicine, Dentistry and Biomedical Sciences)
Strand, London WC2R 2LS
Students: 16,535 UG; 10,750 PG
Principal, Prof. Sir Richard Trainor, KBE
LONDON BUSINESS SCHOOL
Regent's Park, London NW1 4SA
Students: 1,855 PG (postgraduate only)
Dean, Prof. Sir Andrew Likierman
LONDON SCHOOL OF ECONOMICS AND POLITICAL SCIENCE
Houghton Street, London WC2A 2AE
Students: 3,970 UG; 5,980 PG
Director, Prof. Craig Calhoun

LONDON SCHOOL OF HYGIENE AND TROPICAL
MEDICINE
Keppel Street, London WC1E 7HT
Students: 1,135 PG (postgraduate only)
Director, Prof. Peter Piot, CMG, MD, PHD
QUEEN MARY (incorporating St Bartholomew's and the
London School of Medicine and Dentistry)
Mile End Road, London E1 4NS
Students: 10,985 UG; 4,055 PG
Principal, Prof. Simon Gaskell
ROYAL ACADEMY OF MUSIC
Marylebone Road, London NW1 5HT
Students: 325 UG; 430 PG
Principal, Prof. Jonathan Freeman-Attwood
ROYAL HOLLOWAY
Egham Hill, Egham, Surrey TW20 0EX
Students: 7,250 UG; 2,315 PG
Principal, Prof. Paul Layzell
ROYAL VETERINARY COLLEGE
Royal College Street, London NW1 0TU
Students: 1,605 UG; 550 PG
Principal, Prof. Stuart Reid
ST GEORGE'S
Cranmer Terrace, London SW17 0RE
Students: 4,515 UG; 640 PG
Principal, Prof. Peter Kopelman
SCHOOL OF ORIENTAL AND AFRICAN STUDIES
Thornhaugh Street, Russell Square, London WC1H 0XG
Students: 3,030 UG; 2,385 PG
Director, Prof. Paul Webley
UNIVERSITY COLLEGE LONDON (including UCL
Medical School and School of Pharmacy)
Gower Street, London WC1E 6BT
Students: 14,585 UG; 11,690 PG
Provost and President, Prof. Michael Arthur, FRCP
INSTITUTES
INSTITUTE OF ADVANCED LEGAL STUDIES
Charles Clore House, 17 Russell Square, London WC1B 5DR
Dean and Chief Executive, Prof. Roger Kain, CBE, FBA
INSTITUTE OF CLASSICAL STUDIES
Senate House, Malet Street, London WC1E 7HU
Director, Prof. John North
INSTITUTE OF COMMONWEALTH STUDIES
Senate House, Malet Street, London WC1E 7HU
Director, Prof. Philip Murphy
INSTITUTE OF ENGLISH STUDIES
Senate House, Malet Street, London WC1E 7HU
Director, Prof. Warwick Gould
INSTITUTE OF GERMANIC AND ROMANCE STUDIES
Senate House, Malet Street, London WC1E 7HU
Director, Prof. Bill Marsall
INSTITUTE OF HISTORICAL RESEARCH
Senate House, Malet Street, London WC1E 7HU
Director, Prof. Miles Taylor
INSTITUTE OF MUSICAL RESEARCH
Senate House, Malet Street, London WC1E 7HU
Director, Dr Paul Archbold
INSTITUTE OF PHILOSOPHY
Senate House, Malet Street, London WC1E 7HU
Director, Prof. Colin Blakemore
INSTITUTE FOR THE STUDY OF THE AMERICAS
Senate House, Malet Street, London WC1E 7HU
Director, Prof. Linda Newson
SCHOOL OF ADVANCED STUDY
Senate House, Malet Street, London WC1E 7HU
Dean and Chief Executive, Prof. Roger Kain, CBE, FBA
UNIVERSITY OF LONDON INSTITUTE IN PARIS
9–11 rue de Constantine, 75340 Paris Cedex 07, France
Dean, Prof. Andrew Hussey, OBE

WARBURG INSTITUTE
Woburn Square, London WC1H 0AB
Director, Prof. Roger Kain, CBE, FBA

LONDON METROPOLITAN UNIVERSITY (2002)
166–220 Holloway Road, London N7 8DB T 020-7423 0000
W www.londonmet.ac.uk
Fee: £9,000 *Students:* 14,290 UG; 3,815 PG
Patron, HRH the Duke of York, KG, GCVO
Vice-Chancellor, Prof. Malcolm Gillies
University Secretary, Alison Wells

LONDON SOUTH BANK UNIVERSITY (1992)
103 Borough Road, London SE1 0AA T 020-7815 7815
W www.lsbu.ac.uk
Fee: £8,450 *Students:* 15,105 UG; 4,695 PG
Chancellor, Richard Farleigh
Vice-Chancellor, Prof. David Phoenix
University Secretary, James Stevenson

LOUGHBOROUGH UNIVERSITY (1966)
Epinal Way, Loughborough, Leics LE11 3TU T 01509-222222
W www.lboro.ac.uk
Fee: £9,000 *Students:* 11,475 UG; 3,985 PG
Chancellor, Sir Nigel Rudd, CBE, FRSE, PHD
Vice-Chancellor and President, Prof. Robert Allison
Chief Operating Officer, Richard Taylor

UNIVERSITY OF MANCHESTER (2004)
(Formed by the amalgamation of Victoria University of
Manchester (1851; reorganised 1880 and 1903) and the
University of Manchester Institute of Science and
Technology (1824))
Oxford Road, Manchester M13 9PL T 0161-306 6000
W www.manchester.ac.uk
Fee: £9,000 *Students:* 27,080 UG; 11,350 PG
Chancellor, Tom Bloxham, MBE
Vice-Chancellor, Prof. Dame Nancy Rothwell, DBE, FRS
Registrar, Will Spinks

MANCHESTER METROPOLITAN UNIVERSITY (1992)
All Saints, Manchester M15 6BH T 0161-247 2000
W www.mmu.ac.uk
Fee: £9,000 *Students:* 26,555 UG; 5,910 PG
Chancellor, Dianne Thompson, CBE
Vice-Chancellor, Prof. John Brooks, DSC
Registrar, Karen Moore

MIDDLESEX UNIVERSITY (1992)
Hendon Campus, The Burroughs, London NW4 4BT
T 020-8411 5555 W www.mdx.ac.uk
Fee: £9,000 *Students:* 16,750 UG; 4,380 PG
Chancellor, Dame Janet Ritterman, DBE
Vice-Chancellor, Prof. Michael Driscoll

NEWCASTLE UNIVERSITY (1963)
Newcastle upon Tyne NE1 7RU T 0191-222 6000 W www.ncl.ac.uk
Fee: £9,000 *Students:* 15,515 UG; 5,680 PG
Chancellor, Prof. Sir Liam Donaldson
Vice-Chancellor, Prof. Chris Brink, FRS, DPHIL
Registrar, Dr John Hogan

UNIVERSITY OF NORTHAMPTON (2005)
Park Campus, Boughton Green Road, Northampton NN2 7AL
T 01604-735500 W www.northampton.ac.uk
Fee: £8,750 *Students:* 11,590 UG; 2,445 PG
Chancellor, Baroness Falkner of Margravine
Vice-Chancellor, Prof. Nick Petford, PHD, DSC
Director of Academic Services, Jane Bunce

NORTHUMBRIA UNIVERSITY AT NEWCASTLE (1992)
Ellison Building, Ellison Place, Newcastle upon Tyne NE1 8ST
T 0191-232 6002 W www.northumbria.ac.uk
Fee: £9,000 *Students:* 23,200 UG; 4,615 PG
Chancellor, Lord Stevens of Kirkwhelpington, QPM
Vice-Chancellor, Prof. Andrew Wathey, DPHIL
Chief Operating Officer, Chris Reilly

UNIVERSITY OF NOTTINGHAM (1948)
University Park, Nottingham NG7 2RD T 0115-951 5151
W www.nottingham.ac.uk
Fee: £9,000 *Students:* 25,130 UG; 10,410 PG
Chancellor, Sir Andrew Witty
Vice-Chancellor, Prof. David Greenaway
Registrar, Dr Paul Greatrix

NOTTINGHAM TRENT UNIVERSITY (1992)
Burton Street, Nottingham NG1 4BU T 0115-941 8418
W www.ntu.ac.uk
Fee: £8,750 *Students:* 21,740 UG; 5,130 PG
Chancellor, Sir Michael Parkinson, CBE
Vice-Chancellor, Prof. Neil Gorman, PHD
Registrar, David Samson

OPEN UNIVERSITY (1969)
Walton Hall, Milton Keynes MK7 6AA T 01908-274066
W www.open.ac.uk
Fee: £6,000 *Students:* 156,975 UG; 11,240 PG
Chancellor, Baroness Lane-Fox of Soho, CBE
Vice-Chancellor, Martin Bean
University Secretary, Fraser Woodburn

UNIVERSITY OF OXFORD (*c.*12th century)
University Offices, Wellington Square, Oxford OX1 2JD
T 01865-270000 W www.ox.ac.uk
Fee: £9,000 *Students:* 16,745 UG; 8,925 PG
Chancellor, Lord Patten of Barnes, CH, PC (Balliol, St Antony's)
Vice-Chancellor, Prof. Andrew Hamilton, FRS (Harris
   Manchester, Kellogg, Wolfson)
Pro-Vice-Chancellors, Dr S. J. Goss (Wadham); Prof. W. James
   (Brasenose); Prof. S. L. Mapstone (St Hilda's); Prof. J. N. P.
   Rawlins (Wolfson); Prof. I. A. Walmsley (St. Hugh's)
Registrar, Prof. E. G. McKendrick (Lady Margaret Hall)
Deputy Registrar, M. D. Sibly (St Anne's)
Public Orator, R. H. A. Jenkyns (Lady Margaret Hall)
Director of University Library Services and Bodley's Librarian,
   R. Ovenden (Balliol)
Director of the Ashmolean Museum, Dr A. Sturgis (Worcester)
Keeper of Archives, S. Bailey (Linacre)
Director of Estates, P. Goffin
Director of Finance, G. F. B. Kerr (Keble)

COLLEGES AND HALLS *with dates of foundation*
ALL SOULS (1438)
Warden, Prof. Sir John Vickers, FBA
BALLIOL (1263)
Master, Prof. Sir Drummond Bone, FRSE
BLACKFRIARS (1221)
Regent, Very Revd Dr Simon Gaine
BRASENOSE (1509)
Principal, Prof. Alan K. Bowman, FBA, FSA
CAMPION HALL (1896)
Master, Revd James Hanvey
CHRIST CHURCH (1546)
Dean, Very Revd Christopher Lewis
CORPUS CHRISTI (1517)
President, Prof. Richard Carwardine, FBA
EXETER (1314)
Rector, Prof. Sir Rick Trainor, KBE
GREEN TEMPLETON (2008)
Principal, Prof. Sir David Watson

HARRIS MANCHESTER (1889)
Principal, Revd Dr Ralph Waller, FRSE
HERTFORD (1740)
Principal, Will Hutton
JESUS (1571)
Principal, Lord Krebs, FRS, FMEDSCI
KEBLE (1870)
Warden, Sir Jonathan Phillips, KCB
KELLOGG (1990)
President, Prof. Jonathan M. Michie
LADY MARGARET HALL (1878)
Principal, Dr Frances Lannon
LINACRE (1962)
Principal, Dr Nick Brown
LINCOLN (1427)
Rector, Prof. Henry Woudhuysen, FBA
MAGDALEN (1458)
President, Prof. David Clary, FRS
MANSFIELD (1886)
Principal, Baroness Kennedy of the Shaws, QC
MERTON (1264)
Warden, Prof. Sir Martin Taylor, FRS
NEW COLLEGE (1379)
Warden, Prof. Sir Curtis Price, KBE
NUFFIELD (1958)
Warden, Sir Andrew Dilnot, CBE
ORIEL (1326)
Provost, Moira Wallace, OBE
PEMBROKE (1624)
Master, Dame Lynne Brindley, DBE
QUEEN'S (1341)
Provost, Prof. Paul Madden, FRS, FRSE
REGENT'S PARK (1810)
Principal, Revd Dr Robert Ellis
ST ANNE'S (1878)
Principal, Tim Gardam
ST ANTONY'S (1953)
Warden, Prof. Margaret MacMillan
ST BENET'S HALL (1897)
Master, Prof. Werner Jeanrond
ST CATHERINE'S (1963)
Master, Prof. Roger Ainsworth
ST CROSS (1965)
Master, Sir Mark Jones, FRSE
ST EDMUND HALL (*C.*1278)
Principal, Prof. Keith Gull, CBE, FRS, FMEDSCI
ST HILDA'S (1893)
Principal, Prof. Sir Gordon Duff, FRCP, FMEDSCI, FRSE
ST HUGH'S (1886)
Principal, Dame Elish Angiolini, DBE, QC
ST JOHN'S (1555)
President, Prof. Margaret J. Snowling, FBA, FMEDSCI
ST PETER'S (1929)
Principal, Mark Damazer, CBE
ST STEPHEN'S HOUSE (1876)
Principal, Revd Dr Robin Ward
SOMERVILLE (1879)
Principal, Dr Alice Prochaska
TRINITY (1554)
President, Sir Ivor Roberts, KCMG
UNIVERSITY (1249)
Master, Sir Ivor Crewe
WADHAM (1610)
Warden, Lord Macdonald of River Glaven, QC
WOLFSON (1981)
President, Prof. Dame Hermione Lee, DBE, FBA, FRSL
WORCESTER (1714)
Provost, Prof. Jonathan Bate, CBE, FBA, FRSL
WYCLIFFE HALL (1877)
Principal, Revd Michael Lloyd

OXFORD BROOKES UNIVERSITY (1992)
Gipsy Lane, Oxford OX3 0BP T 01865-741111
W www.brookes.ac.uk
Fee: £9,000 *Students:* 13,625 UG; 4,240 PG
Chancellor, Shami Chakrabarti, CBE
Vice-Chancellor, Prof. Janet Beer
Registrar, Paul Large

UNIVERSITY OF PLYMOUTH (1992)
Drake Circus, Plymouth PL4 8AA T 01752-600600
W www.plymouth.ac.uk
Fee: £9,000 *Students:* 24,675 UG; 3,955 PG
Vice-Chancellor and Chief Executive, Prof. Wendy Purcell
University Secretary, Jane Hopkinson

UNIVERSITY OF PORTSMOUTH (1992)
University House, Winston Churchill Avenue, Portsmouth PO1 2UP
T 023-9284 8484 W www.port.ac.uk
Fee: £9,000 *Students:* 18,980 UG; 3,715 PG
Chancellor, Sandi Toksvig
Vice-Chancellor, Prof. Graham Galbraith, PHD
University Secretary, Sally Hartley

QUEEN MARGARET UNIVERSITY (2007)
Musselburgh, Edinburgh EH21 6UU T 0131-474 0000
W www.qmu.ac.uk
Fee: £6,750 *Students:* 3,430 UG; 1,905 PG
Chancellor, Sir Tom Farmer, CVO, CBE
Vice-Chancellor, Prof. Petra Wend
Secretary, Irene Hynd

QUEEN'S UNIVERSITY BELFAST (1908)
University Road, Belfast BT7 1NN T 028-9024 5133
W www.qub.ac.uk
Fee: £9,000 *Students:* 18,075 UG; 4,625 PG
Chancellor, HE Kamalesh Sharma
Vice-Chancellor, Prof. Patrick Johnston
Registrar, James O'Kane

UNIVERSITY OF READING (1926)
Whiteknights, PO Box 217, Reading RG6 6AH T 0118-987 5123
W www.reading.ac.uk
Fee: £9,000 *Students:* 8,910 UG; 4,525 PG
Chancellor, Sir John Madejski, OBE
Vice-Chancellor, Sir David Bell, KCB
University Secretary, Keith Hodgson

ROBERT GORDON UNIVERSITY (1992)
Schoolhill, Aberdeen AB10 1FR T 01224-262000
W www.rgu.ac.uk
Fee: £8,500 *Students:* 9,060 UG; 3,950 PG
Chancellor, Sir Ian Wood, CBE
Vice-Chancellor, Prof. Ferdinand von Prondzynski
Academic Registrar, Hilary Douglas

ROEHAMPTON UNIVERSITY (2004)
Erasmus House, Roehampton Lane, London SW15 5PU
T 020-8392 3000 W www.roehampton.ac.uk
Fee: £8,500 *Students:* 6,375 UG; 2,685 PG
Chancellor, John Simpson, CBE
Vice-Chancellor, Prof. Paul O'Prey
Registrar, Laurence Benson

ROYAL COLLEGE OF ART (1967)
Kensington Gore, London SW7 2EU T 020-7590 4444
W www.rca.ac.uk
Fee: £9,000 *Students:* 1,465 PG (postgraduate only)
Provost, Sir James Dyson, CBE
Rector, Dr Paul Thompson
Academic Registrar, Corinne Smith

ROYAL COLLEGE OF MUSIC (1882)
Prince Consort Road, London SW7 2BS T 020-7591 4300
W www.rcm.ac.uk
Fee: £9,000 *Students:* 385 UG; 345 PG
President, HRH the Prince of Wales, KG, KT, GCB
Director, Prof. Colin Lawson
Deputy Director, Kevin Porter

UNIVERSITY OF ST ANDREWS (1413)
St Andrews, Fife KY16 9AJ T 01334-476161
W www.st-andrews.ac.uk
Fee: £9,000 *Students:* 7,415 UG; 2,050 PG
Chancellor, Sir Menzies Campbell, CBE, QC
Vice-Chancellor and Principal, Prof. Louise Richardson, FRSE
Academic Registrar, Ester Ruskuc

UNIVERSITY OF SALFORD (1967)
The Crescent, Salford, Greater Manchester M5 4WT
T 0161-295 5000 W www.salford.ac.uk
Fee: £9,000 *Students:* 15,510 UG; 3,650 PG
Chancellor, Dr Irene Khan
Vice-Chancellor, Prof. Martin Hall

UNIVERSITY OF SHEFFIELD (1905)
Western Bank, Sheffield S10 2TN T 0114-222 2000
W www.sheffield.ac.uk
Fee: £9,000 *Students:* 18,105 UG; 7,435 PG
Chancellor, Sir Peter Middleton, GCB
Vice-Chancellor, Prof. Sir Keith Burnett, CBE, DPHIL, FRS
Registrar and Secretary, Dr Philip Harvey

SHEFFIELD HALLAM UNIVERSITY (1992)
City Campus, Howard Street, Sheffield S1 1WB T 0114-225 5555
W www.shu.ac.uk
Fee: £9,000 *Students:* 27,040 UG; 7,680 PG
Chancellor, Prof. Lord Winston, FMEDSCI, FRCOG, FRCP
Vice-Chancellor, Prof. Philip Jones
Secretary & Registrar, Elizabeth Winders

UNIVERSITY OF SOUTH WALES (1992)
Pontypridd CF37 1DL T 0845-5767 778 W www.southwales.ac.uk
Fee: £9,000 *Students:* 24,505 UG; 5,620 PG
Chancellor, Rt. Revd Lord Williams of Oystermouth, PC, DPHIL, FBA
Vice-Chancellor, Prof. Julie Lydon
Registrar, William Callaway

UNIVERSITY OF SOUTHAMPTON (1952)
University Road, Southampton SO17 1BJ T 023-8059 5000
W www.southampton.ac.uk
Fee: £9,000 *Students:* 16,055 UG; 7,060 PG
Chancellor, Dame Helen Alexander, DBE
Vice-Chancellor, Prof. Don Nutbeam
Registrar, Tessa Harrison

SOUTHAMPTON SOLENT UNIVERSITY (2005)
East Park Terrace, Southampton SO14 0YN T 023-8031 9039
W www.solent.ac.uk
Fee: £7,800 *Students:* 11,515 UG; 575 PG
Chancellor, Adm. Lord West of Spithead, GCB, DSC, PC
Vice-Chancellor, Prof. Van Gore

STAFFORDSHIRE UNIVERSITY (1992)
College Road, Stoke-on-Trent ST4 2DE T 01782-294000
W www.staffs.ac.uk
Fee: £8,490 *Students:* 17,480 UG; 3,540 PG
Chancellor, Lord Stafford
Vice-Chancellor and Chief Executive, Prof. Michael Gunn
University Secretary, Ken Sproston

UNIVERSITY OF STIRLING (1967)
Stirling FK9 4LA T 01786-473171 W www.stir.ac.uk
Fee: £6,750 *Students:* 7,285 UG; 3,450 PG
Chancellor, James Naughtie, OBE
Vice-Chancellor, Prof. Gerry McCormac, FRSE
University Secretary, Eileen Schofield

UNIVERSITY OF STRATHCLYDE (1964)
16 Richmond Street, Glasgow G1 1XQ T 0141-552 4400
W www.strath.ac.uk
Fee: £9,000 *Students:* 14,180 UG; 5,670 PG
Chancellor, Lord Smith of Kelvin, KT
Vice-Chancellor, Prof. Sir Jim McDonald, FRENG, FRSE
Chief Operating Officer, Hugh Hall

UNIVERSITY OF SUNDERLAND (1992)
Edinburgh Building, Chester Road, Sunderland SR1 3SD
T 0191-515 2000 W www.sunderland.ac.uk
Fee: £8,500 *Students:* 11,740 UG; 3,215 PG
Chancellor, Steve Cram, MBE
Vice-Chancellor, Shirley Atkinson

UNIVERSITY OF SURREY (1966)
Guildford GU2 7XH T 01483-300800 W www.surrey.ac.uk
Fee: £9,000 *Students:* 9,800 UG; 4,095 PG
Chancellor, HRH the Duke of Kent, KG, GCMG, GCVO
Vice-Chancellor, Prof. Sir Christopher Snowden, FRS, FREng

UNIVERSITY OF SUSSEX (1961)
Sussex House, Brighton BN1 9RH T 01273-606755
W www.sussex.ac.uk
Fee: £9,000 *Students:* 9,590 UG; 3,555 PG
Chancellor, Sanjeev Bhaskar, OBE
Vice-Chancellor, Prof. Michael Farthing, FRCP
Academic Registrar, John Duffy

SWANSEA UNIVERSITY (1920)
Singleton Park, SA2 8PP T 01792-205678 W www.swansea.ac.uk
Fee: £9,000 *Students:* 11,910 UG; 2,450 PG
Vice-Chancellor, Richard Davies
Academic Registrar, Huw Morris

UNIVERSITY OF TEESSIDE (1992)
Middlesbrough, Tees Valley TS1 3BA T 01642-218121
W www.tees.ac.uk
Fee: £8,450 *Students:* 17,830 UG; 2,135 PG
Chancellor, Lord Sawyer of Darlington
Vice-Chancellor, Prof. Graham Henderson, CBE

UNIVERSITY OF ULSTER (1984)
Cromore Road, Coleraine, Co. Londonderry BT52 1SA
T 028-7012 3456 W www.ulster.ac.uk
Fee: £6,000 *Students:* 20,655 UG; 5,800 PG
Chancellor, James Nesbitt
Vice-Chancellor, Prof. Richard Barnett
Administrative Manager, Norma Cameron

UNIVERSITY OF WALES, TRINITY SAINT DAVID (1828)
42 The Parade, Roath, Cardiff CF24 3AD T 01267-676767
W www.uwtsd.ac.uk
Fee: £9,000
Chancellor, HRH the Prince of Wales, KG, KT, GCB
Vice-Chancellor, Prof. Medwin Hughes

UNIVERSITY OF WARWICK (1965)
Coventry CV4 7AL T 024-7652 3523 W www.warwick.ac.uk
Fee: £9,000 *Students:* 16,370 UG; 9,780 PG
Chancellor, Sir Richard Lambert
Vice-Chancellor, Prof. Nigel Thrift, FBA, PHD, DSc
Registrar, Ken Sloan

UNIVERSITY OF WEST LONDON (1992)
St Mary's Road, Ealing, London W5 5RF T 0800-036 8888
W www.uwl.ac.uk
Fee: £8,200 *Students:* 10,175 UG; 1,405 PG
Chancellor, Laurence Geller
Vice-Chancellor, Prof. Peter John
University Secretary, Maureen Skinner

UNIVERSITY OF WESTMINSTER (1992)
309 Regent Street, London W1B 2HW T 020-7911 5000
W www.westminster.ac.uk
Fee: £9,000 *Students:* 15,760 UG; 4,410 PG
Chancellor, Lord Paul, PC
Vice-Chancellor and Rector, Prof. Geoffrey Petts
Registrar and Secretary, Carole Mainstone

UNIVERSITY OF THE WEST OF ENGLAND (1992)
Frenchay Campus, Coldharbour Lane, Bristol BS16 1QY
T 0117-965 6261 W www.uwe.ac.uk
Fee: £9,000 *Students:* 22,185 UG; 5,245 PG
Chancellor, Sir Ian Carruthers, OBE
Vice-Chancellor, Prof. Steve West
Academic Registrar, Rachel Cowie

UNIVERSITY OF THE WEST OF SCOTLAND (2007)
(Formed by merger of University of Paisley (1992) with Bell
College, Hamilton)
Paisley PA1 2BE T 0141-848 3000 W www.uws.ac.uk
Fee: £7,250 *Students:* 13,800 UG; 1,575 PG
Chancellor, Dame Elish Angiolini, DBE, QC
Vice-Chancellor and Principal, Prof. Craig Mahoney
Registrar and Secretary, Donna McMillan

UNIVERSITY OF WINCHESTER (2005)
Winchester SO22 4NR T 01962-841515 W www.winchester.ac.uk
Fee: £8,500 *Students:* 5,370 UG; 1,025 PG
Chancellor, Dame Mary Fagan, DCVO
Vice Chancellor, Prof. Joy Carter
Director of Student Recruitment and Marketing, Dr Karen
  Pendlebury

UNIVERSITY OF WOLVERHAMPTON (1992)
Wulfruna Street, Wolverhampton WV1 1LY T 01902-321000
W www.wlv.ac.uk
Fee: £8,650 *Students:* 16,420 UG; 3,530 PG
Chancellor, Lord Paul, PC
Vice-Chancellor, Prof. Geoff Layer, OBE, FRSA
Registrar, Helen Lloyd Wildman

UNIVERSITY OF WORCESTER (2005)
Henwick Grove, Worcester WR2 6AJ T 01905-855000
W www.worcester.ac.uk
Fee: £8,650 *Students:* 8,735 UG; 1,575 PG
Chancellor, HRH the Duke of Gloucester, KG, GCVO
Vice-Chancellor, Prof. David Green
Registrar, John Ryan

UNIVERSITY OF YORK (1963)
Heslington, York YO10 5DD T 01904-320000 W www.york.ac.uk
Fee: £9,000 *Students:* 12,180 UG; 3,970 PG
Chancellor, Greg Dyke
Vice-Chancellor, Prof. Koen Lamberts
Registrar, Dr David Duncan

YORK ST JOHN UNIVERSITY (2006)
Lord Mayor's Walk, York YO31 7EX T 01904-624624
W www.yorksj.ac.uk
Fee: £9,000 *Students:* 5,235 UG; 815 PG
Chancellor, Most Revd and Rt. Hon. Archbishop of York
Vice-Chancellor, Prof. David Fleming
Registrar, Alison Kennell

PROFESSIONAL EDUCATION

The organisations selected below provide specialist training, conduct examinations or are responsible for maintaining a register of those with professional qualifications in their sector, thereby controlling entry into a profession.

EU RECOGNITION

It is possible for those with professional qualifications obtained in the UK to have these recognised in other European countries. Further information can be obtained from:

UK NCP, Oriel House, Oriel Road, Cheltenham GL50 1XP
T 0871-330 7033 W www.ecctis.co.uk

ACCOUNTANCY

Salary range for chartered accountants:
Certified £15,000–£25,000 (starting) rising to £25,000–£45,000+ (qualified), £40,000–£100,000+ at senior levels
Management £29,000 (starting), £58,000 (average), £45,000–£120,000+ at senior levels
Public finance £18,000–£30,000 (starting), £32,000–£65,000 (qualified), £80,000+ at senior levels

Most chartered accountancy trainees are graduates, although some contracts are available to school-leavers. The undergraduate degree is followed by a three-year training contract with an approved employer culminating in professional exams provided by the Institute of Chartered Accountants in England and Wales (ICAEW), the Institute of Chartered Accountants of Scotland (ICAS) or the Institute of Chartered Accountants in Ireland (ICAI). Success in the examination and membership of one of the institutes allows the use of the designation 'chartered accountant' and the letters ACA or CA.

The Association of Chartered Certified Accountants (ACCA) is the global body for professional accountants. The ACCA aims to offer business-relevant qualifications to students in a range of business sectors and countries seeking a career in accountancy, finance and management. The ACCA Qualification consists of up to 14 examinations, practical experiences and a professional ethics module. Chartered certified accountants can use the designatory letters ACCA.

Chartered global management accountants focus on accounting for businesses, and most do not work in accountancy practices but in industry, commerce, not-for-profit and public-sector organisations. Graduates who have not studied a business or accounting degree must complete the Chartered Institute of Management Accountants (CIMA) Certificate in Business Accounting before progressing to the CIMA Professional Qualification, which requires three years of practical experience, nine examinations and a pass in the Institute's Test of Professional Competence in Management Accounting (TOPCIMA). In May 2011, CIMA and the American Institute of Certified Public Accountants (AICPA) agreed on the creation of a new professional designation, the Chartered Global Management Accountant (CGMA), which will represent a worldwide standard of professional excellence in management accounting.

The Chartered Institute of Public Finance and Accountancy (CIPFA) is the professional body for people working in public finance. Chartered public finance accountants usually work for public bodies, but they can also work in the private sector. To gain chartered public finance

accountant status (CPFA), trainees must complete a professional qualification in public sector accountancy. In addition, CIPFA also offers a postgraduate diploma for those already working in leadership positions.

ASSOCIATION OF CHARTERED CERTIFIED ACCOUNTANTS (ACCA), 29 Lincoln's Inn Fields, London WC2A 3EE T 020-7059 5000 E info@accaglobal.com W www.accaglobal.com
Chief Executive, Helen Brand

CHARTERED INSTITUTE OF MANAGEMENT ACCOUNTANTS (CIMA), 26 Chapter Street, London SW1P 4NP T 020-8849 2251 E cima.contact@cimaglobal.com W www.cimaglobal.com
Chief Executive, Charles Tilley

CHARTERED INSTITUTE OF PUBLIC FINANCE AND ACCOUNTANCY (CIPFA), 3 Robert Street, London WC2N 6RL T 020-7543 5600 E customerliaison@cipfa.org W www.cipfa.org.uk
Chief Executive, Rob Whiteman

INSTITUTE OF CHARTERED ACCOUNTANTS IN ENGLAND AND WALES (ICAEW), Chartered Accountants' Hall, Moorgate Place, London EC2R 6EA T 020-7920 8100 E contactus@icaew.com W www.icaew.com
Chief Executive, Michael Izza

INSTITUTE OF CHARTERED ACCOUNTANTS IN IRELAND (ICAI), 47–49 Pearse Street, Dublin T 0353-1637 7200 W www.charteredaccountants.ie
Chief Executive, Pat Costello

INSTITUTE OF CHARTERED ACCOUNTANTS OF SCOTLAND (ICAS), CA House, 21 Haymarket Yards, Edinburgh EH12 5BH T 0131-347 0100 E enquiries@icas.org.uk W www.icas.org.uk
Chief Executive, Anton Colella

ACTUARIAL SCIENCE

Salary range: £25,000–£35,000 for graduate trainees; £40,000–£55,000 after qualification; £60,000–£100,000+ for senior roles; £185,000+ for senior directors

Actuaries apply financial and statistical theories to solve business problems. These problems usually involve analysing future financial events in order to assess investment risks. To qualify, graduate trainees must complete 15 exams and three years worth of actuarial work-based training; most graduate trainees take between three and six years to qualify. Students can become Associate members of the Institute and Faculty of Actuaries (IFoA) and gain the right to describe themselves as an actuary and to use the letters AIA or AFA. Members of the profession who wish to continue their studies to an advanced level, or who specialise in a particular actuarial field, may take further specialist exams to qualify as a Fellow and bear the designations FIA or FFA.

The IFoA is the UK's chartered professional body dedicated to educating, developing and regulating actuaries based both in the UK and internationally. The IFoA represent and regulate their members and oversee their education at all stages of qualification and development throughout their careers.

The Financial Reporting Council (FRC) is the unified independent regulator for corporate reporting, auditing, actuarial practice, corporate governance and the professionalism of accountants and actuaries. The FRC's

Board for Actuarial Standards sets and maintains technical actuarial standards independently of the profession, while the Professional Oversight Board of the FRC oversees the regulation of the accountancy and actuarial professions by their respective professional bodies. The Accountancy and Actuarial Discipline Board operates an investigation and discipline scheme in relation to members of the profession who raise issues affecting UK public interest.

FINANCIAL REPORTING COUNCIL (FRC), 8th Floor,
125 London Wall, London EC2Y 5AS **T** 020-7492 2300
E enquiries@frc.org.uk **W** www.frc.org.uk
Chief Executive, Stephen Haddrill

INSTITUTE AND FACULTY OF ACTUARIES, Staple Inn
Hall, High Holborn, London WC1V 7QJ **T** 020-7632 2100
W www.actuaries.org.uk
Chief Executive, Derek Cribb

ARCHITECTURE

Salary range: £15,000–£26,000 during training; newly registered £26,000–£35,000; project architect and senior roles £35,000–£80,000+

It takes a minimum of seven years to become an architect, involving three stages: a three-year first degree, a two-year second degree or diploma and two years of professional experience followed by the successful completion of a professional practice examination.

The Architects Registration Board (ARB) is the independent regulator for the profession. It was set up by an act of parliament in 1997 and is responsible for maintaining the register of UK architects, prescribing qualifications that lead to registration as an architect, investigating complaints about the conduct and competence of architects and ensuring that only those who are registered with ARB offer their services as an architect. It is only following registration with ARB that an architect can apply for chartered membership of the Royal Institute of British Architects (RIBA). RIBA, the UK body for architecture and the architectural profession, received its royal charter in 1837 and validates courses at over 40 schools of architecture in the UK; it also validates overseas courses. RIBA provides support and guidance for its members in the form of training, technical services and events and sets standards for the education of architects.

The Chartered Institute of Architectural Technologists is the international qualifying body for Chartered Architectural Technologists (MCIAT) and Architectural Technicians (TCIAT).

ARCHITECTS REGISTRATION BOARD (ARB)
8 Weymouth Street, London W1W 5BU **T** 020-7580 5861
E info@arb.org.uk **W** www.arb.org.uk
Registrar and Chief Executive, Karen Holmes (interim)

CHARTERED INSTITUTE OF ARCHITECTURAL
TECHNOLOGISTS 397 City Road, London EC1V 1NH
T 020-7278 2206 **E** info@ciat.org.uk **W** www.ciat.org.uk
Chief Executive, Francesca Berriman

ROYAL INCORPORATION OF ARCHITECTS IN
SCOTLAND 15 Rutland Square, Edinburgh EH1 2BE
T 0131-229 7545 **E** info@rias.org.uk **W** www.rias.org.uk
Secretary, Neil Baxter

ROYAL INSTITUTE OF BRITISH ARCHITECTS (RIBA)
66 Portland Place, London W1B 1AD **T** 020-7580 5533
E info@riba.org **W** www.architecture.com
Chief Executive, Harry Rich

ENGINEERING

Salary range:
Civil/structural £23,500–£28,500 (graduate); £40,000–£80,000+ with experience (chartered status, in senior posts);

Chemical £28,000 average (graduate); £53,000 (average); £70,000+ (chartered)
Electrical £20,000–£25,000 (graduate); £28,000–£40,000 with experience; £40,000–£50,000 (chartered)

The Engineering Council holds the national registers of Engineering Technicians (EngTech), Incorporated Engineers (IEng), Chartered Engineers (CEng) and Information and Communication Technology Technicians (ICTTech). It also sets and maintains the internationally recognised standards of competence and ethics that govern the award and retention of these titles.

To apply for the EngTech, IEng, CEng or ICTTech titles, an individual must be a member of one of the 36 engineering institutions and societies (listed below) currently licensed by the Engineering Council to assess candidates. Applicants must demonstrate that they possess a range of technical and personal competences and are committed to keeping these up-to-date.

ENGINEERING COUNCIL, 246 High Holborn, London
WC1V 7EX **T** 020-3206 0500 **E** info@engc.org.uk
W www.engc.org.uk
Chief Executive, Jon Prichard

LICENSED MEMBERS
BCS – The Chartered Institute for IT **W** www.bcs.org
British Institute of Non-Destructive Testing **W** www.bindt.org
Chartered Institute of Plumbing and Heating Engineering
W www.ciphe.org.uk
Chartered Institution of Building Services Engineers
W www.cibse.org
Chartered Institution of Highways and Transportation
W www.ciht.org.uk
Chartered Institution of Water and Environmental Management
W www.ciwem.org.uk
Energy Institute **W** www.energyinst.org.uk
Institute of Acoustics **W** www.ioa.org.uk
Institute of Cast Metals Engineers **W** www.icme.org.uk
Institute of Healthcare Engineering and Estate Management
W www.iheem.org.uk
Institute of Highway Engineers **W** www.theihe.org
Institute of Marine Engineering, Science and Technology
W www.imarest.org
Institute of Materials, Minerals and Mining **W** www.iom3.org
Institute of Measurement and Control **W** www.instmc.org.uk
Institute of Physics **W** www.iop.org
Institute of Physics and Engineering in Medicine
W www.ipem.ac.uk
Institute of Water **W** www.instituteofwater.org.uk
Institution of Agricultural Engineers **W** www.iagre.org
Institution of Chemical Engineers **W** www.icheme.org
Institution of Civil Engineers **W** www.ice.org.uk
Institution of Diesel and Gas Turbine Engineers
W www.idgte.org
Institution of Engineering Designers **W** www.ied.org.uk
Institution of Engineering and Technology **W** www.theiet.org
Institution of Fire Engineers **W** www.ife.org.uk
Institution of Gas Engineers and Managers **W** www.igem.org.uk
Institution of Lighting Professionals **W** www.theilp.org.uk
Institution of Mechanical Engineers **W** www.imeche.org
Institution of Railway Signal Engineers **W** www.irse.org
Institution of Royal Engineers **W** www.instre.org
Institution of Structural Engineers **W** www.istructe.org
Nuclear Institute **W** www.nuclearinst.com
Royal Aeronautical Society **W** www.aerosociety.com
Royal Institution of Naval Architects **W** www.rina.org.uk
Society of Environmental Engineers
W www.environmental.org.uk
Society of Operations Engineers **W** www.soe.org.uk
The Welding Institute **W** www.theweldinginstitute.com

HEALTHCARE
CHIROPRACTIC
Salary range: £20,000–£40,000 starting salary; with own practice £50,000–£70,000

Chiropractors diagnose and treat conditions caused by problems with joints, ligaments, tendons and nerves of the body. The General Chiropractic Council (GCC) is the independent statutory regulatory body for chiropractors and its role and remit is defined in the Chiropractors Act 1994. The GCC sets the criteria for the recognition of chiropractic degrees and for standards of proficiency and conduct. Details of the institutions offering degree programmes are available on the GCC website (*see* below). It is illegal for anyone in the UK to use the title 'chiropractor' unless registered with the GCC.

The British Chiropractic Association, Scottish Chiropractic Association, McTimoney Chiropractic Association and United Chiropractic Association are the representative bodies for the profession and are sources of further information.

BRITISH CHIROPRACTIC ASSOCIATION, 59 Castle Street, Reading RG1 7SN T 0118-950 5950
E enquiries@chiropractic-uk.co.uk
W www.chiropractic-uk.co.uk
Executive Director, Sue Wakefield

GENERAL CHIROPRACTIC COUNCIL (GCC), 44 Wicklow Street, London WC1X 9HL T 020-7713 5155
E enquiries@gcc-uk.org W www.gcc-uk.org
Chief Executive and Registrar, David Howell, CB, OBE, MBE

SCOTTISH CHIROPRACTIC ASSOCIATION, 1 Chisholm Avenue, Bishopton, Renfrewshire PA7 5JH T 0141-404 0260
E admin@sca-chiropractic.org W www.sca-chiropractic.org
Administrator, Morag Cairns

DENTISTRY
Salary range: see Health: Employees and Salaries

The General Dental Council (GDC) is the organisation that regulates dental professionals in the UK. All dentists, dental hygienists, dental therapists, dental technicians, clinical dental technicians, dental nurses and orthodontic therapists must be registered with the GDC to work in the UK.

There are various different routes to qualify for registration as a dentist, including holding a degree from a UK university, completing the GDC's qualifying examination or holding a relevant European Economic Area or overseas diploma. The GDC's purpose is to protect the public through the regulation of UK dental professionals. It keeps up-to-date registers of dental professionals, works to set standards of dental practice, behaviour, education, and helps to protect patients by hearing complaints and taking action against professionals where necessary.

Founded in 1880, the British Dental Association (BDA) is the professional association and trade union for dentists in the UK. The majority of its members are in general practice.

BRITISH DENTAL ASSOCIATION (BDA), 64 Wimpole Street, London W1G 8YS T 020-7935 0875
E enquiries@bda.org W www.bda.org
Chief Executive, Peter Ward

GENERAL DENTAL COUNCIL (GDC), 37 Wimpole Street, London W1G 8DQ T 020-7167 6000 E information@gdc-uk.org
W www.gdc-uk.org
Chief Executive, Evlynne Gilvarry

MEDICINE
Salary range: see Health: Employees and Salaries

The General Medical Council (GMC) regulates medical education and training in the UK. This covers undergraduate study (usually five years), the two-year foundation programme taken by doctors directly after graduation and all subsequent postgraduate study, including specialty and GP training.

All doctors must be registered with the GMC, which is responsible for protecting the public. It does this by promoting high standards of medical education and training, fostering good medical practice, keeping a register of qualified doctors and taking action where a doctor's fitness to practise is in doubt. Doctors are eligible for full registration upon successful completion of the first year of training after graduation.

Following the foundation programme, many doctors undertake specialist training (provided by the colleges and faculties listed below) to become either a consultant or a GP. Once specialist training has been completed, doctors are awarded the Certificate of Completion of Training (CCT) and are eligible to be placed on either the GMC's specialist register or its GP register.

GENERAL MEDICAL COUNCIL (GMC), 350 Euston Road, London NW1 3JN T 0161-923 6602 E gmc@gmc-uk.org
W www.gmc-uk.org
Chief Executive, Niall Dickson

SOCIETY OF APOTHECARIES OF LONDON, Black Friars Lane, London EC4V 6EJ T 020-7236 1189
E clerk@apothecaries.org W www.apothecaries.org
Master, Dr J. Moore-Gillon

SPECIALIST TRAINING COLLEGES AND FACULTIES
College of Emergency Medicine W www.collemergencymed.ac.uk
Faculty of Pharmaceutical Medicine W www.fpm.org.uk
Faculty of Public Health W www.fph.org.uk
Royal College of Anaesthetists W www.rcoa.ac.uk
Royal College of General Practitioners W www.rcgp.org.uk
Royal College of Obstetricians and Gynaecologists
W www.rcog.org.uk
Royal College of Opthalmologists W www.rcophth.ac.uk
Royal College of Paediatrics and Child Health
W www.rcpch.ac.uk
Royal College of Pathologists W www.rcpath.org
Royal College of Physicians, London W www.rcplondon.ac.uk
Royal College of Physicians and Surgeons of Glasgow
W www.rcpsg.ac.uk
Royal College of Physicians of Edinburgh W www.rcpe.ac.uk
Royal College of Psychiatrists W www.rcpsych.ac.uk
Royal College of Radiologists W www.rcr.ac.uk
Royal College of Surgeons of Edinburgh W www.rcsed.ac.uk
Royal College of Surgeons of England W www.rcseng.ac.uk

MEDICINE, SUPPLEMENTARY PROFESSIONS
The standard of professional education for arts therapists, biomedical scientists, chiropodists and podiatrists, clinical scientists, dietitians, hearing aid dispensers, occupational therapists, operating department practitioners, orthoptists, paramedics, physiotherapists, practitioner psychologists, prosthetists and orthotists, radiographers, social workers in England and speech and language therapists are regulated by the Health and Care Professions Council (HCPC), which only registers those practitioners who meet certain standards of training, professional skills, behaviour and health. The HCPC can take action against professionals who do not meet these standards or falsely declare they are registered. Each profession regulated by the HCPC has at least one professional title that is protected by law.

HEALTH AND CARE PROFESSIONS COUNCIL (HCPC), Park House, 184 Kennington Park Road, London SE11 4BU
T 0845-300 6184 E registration@hcpc-uk.org
W www.hcpc-uk.org
Chief Executive and Registrar, Marc Seale

ART, DRAMA AND MUSIC THERAPIES
Salary range: £25,500–£34,500 (starting); £39,000–£47,000 with experience

An art, drama or music therapist encourages people to express their feelings and emotions through art, such as painting and drawing, drama or music. A postgraduate qualification in the relevant therapy is required. Details of accredited training programmes in the UK can be obtained from the following organisations:
BRITISH ASSOCIATION FOR MUSIC THERAPY,
   24–27 White Lion Street, London N1 9PD T 020-7837 6100
   E info@bamt.org W www.bamt.org
   Chair, Donald Wetherick
BRITISH ASSOCIATION OF ART THERAPISTS,
   24–27 White Lion Street, London N1 9PD T 020-7686 4216
   E info@baat.org W www.baat.org
   Chief Executive, Val Huet
BRITISH ASSOCIATION OF DRAMA THERAPISTS,
   Waverley, Battledown Approach, Cheltenham, Gloucestershire
   GL52 6RE T 0124-2235 5155 E info@badth.org.uk
   W www.badth.org.uk
   Chair, John Hazlett Dickinson

BIOMEDICAL SCIENCES
Salary range: £21,000–£28,000 (starting); £26,000–£34,500 with experience; £31,000–41,000 for senior roles

The Institute of Biomedical Science (IBMS) is the professional body for biomedical scientists in the UK. Biomedical scientists carry out investigations on tissue and body fluid samples to diagnose disease and monitor the progress of a patient's treatment. The IBMS sets quality standards for the profession through training, education, assessments, examinations and continuous professional development.
INSTITUTE OF BIOMEDICAL SCIENCE (IBMS),
   12 Coldbath Square, London EC1R 5HL T 020-7713 0214
   E mail@ibms.org W www.ibms.org
   Chief Executive, Jill Rodney

CHIROPODY AND PODIATRY
Salary range: £21,000–£40,500

Chiropodists and podiatrists assess, diagnose and treat problems of the lower leg and foot. The Society of Chiropodists and Podiatrists is the professional body and trade union for the profession. Qualifications granted and degrees recognised by the society are approved by the HCPC. HCPC registration is required in order to use the titles chiropodist and podiatrist.
SOCIETY OF CHIROPODISTS AND PODIATRISTS,
   1 Fellmonger's Path, Tower Bridge Road, London SE1 3LY
   T 020-7234 8620 W www.scpod.org
   Chief Executive, Joanna Brown

CLINICAL SCIENCE
Salary range: £25,500–£97,000+

Clinical scientists conduct tests in laboratories in order to diagnose and manage disease. The Association of Clinical Scientists is responsible for setting the criteria for competence of applicants to the HCPC's register and to present a Certificate of Attainment to candidates following a successful assessment. This certificate will allow direct registration with the HCPC.
ASSOCIATION OF CLINICAL SCIENTISTS, c/o
   Association for Clinical Biochemistry, 130–132 Tooley Street,
   London SE1 2TU T 020-7940 8960 E info@assclinsci.org
   W www.assclinsci.org
   Chair, Prof. Richard Lerski

DIETETICS
Salary range: £21,000–£40,000

Dietitians advise patients on how to improve their health and counter specific health problems through diet. The British Dietetic Association, established in 1936, is the professional association for dietitians. Full membership is open to UK-registered dietitians, who must also be registered with HCPC.
BRITISH DIETETIC ASSOCIATION, 5th Floor, Charles
   House, 148–149 Great Charles Street Queensway, Birmingham
   B3 3HT T 0121-200 8080 E info@bda.uk.com
   W www.bda.uk.com
   Chief Executive, Andy Burman

OCCUPATIONAL THERAPY
Salary range: £21,000–£40,000; £63,000–£79,000 for consultancy roles

Occupational therapists work with people who have physical, mental and/or social problems, either from birth or as a result of accident, illness or ageing, and aim to make them as independent as possible. The professional qualification and eligibility for registration may be obtained upon successful completion of a validated course in any of the educational institutions approved by the College of Occupational Therapists, which is the professional body for occupational therapy in the UK. The courses are normally degree-level and based in higher education institutions.
COLLEGE OF OCCUPATIONAL THERAPISTS,
   106–114 Borough High Street, London SE1 1LB
   T 020-7357 6480 W www.cot.org.uk
   Chief Executive, Julia Scott

MENTAL HEALTH
Salary range:
Clinical psychologist £25,500, rising to £45,500–£81,000+ at senior levels
Counsellor £19,000–£26,000, rising to £30,000–£40,000 with experience
Educational psychologist £22,000, rising to £46,000 (fully qualified) and up to £63,500 at senior levels
Psychotherapist £21,000–£27,500 (starting), rising to £47,000 with experience

Psychologists and counsellors are mental health professionals who can work in a range of settings including prisons, schools and hospitals. The British Psychological Society (BPS) is the representative body for psychology and psychologists in the UK. The BPS is responsible for the development, promotion and application of psychology for the public good. The Association of Educational Psychologists (AEP) represents the interests of educational psychologists. The British Association for Counselling and Psychotherapy (BACP) sets educational standards and provides professional support to counsellors, psychotherapists and others working in counselling, psychotherapy or counselling-related roles. The BPS website provides more information on the different specialisations that may be pursued by psychologists.
ASSOCIATION OF EDUCATIONAL PSYCHOLOGISTS
   (AEP), 4 The Riverside Centre, Frankland Lane, Durham
   DH1 5TA T 0191-384 9512 E enquiries@aep.org.uk
   W www.aep.org.uk
   General Secretary, Kate Fallon
BRITISH ASSOCIATION FOR COUNSELLING AND
   PSYCHOTHERAPY (BACP), BACP House, 15 St John's
   Business Park, Lutterworth, Leicestershire LE17 4HB
   T 01455-883300 E bacp@bacp.co.uk W www.bacp.co.uk
   President, Dr Michael Shooter, CBE

BRITISH PSYCHOLOGICAL SOCIETY (BPS), St Andrews House, 48 Princess Road East, Leicester LE1 7DR
T 0116-254 9568 E enquiries@bps.org.uk W www.bps.org.uk
President, Prof. Dorothy Miell

ORTHOPTICS
Salary range: £21,000 (graduate), rising to £30,000–£80,500 in senior posts

Orthoptists undertake the diagnosis and treatment of all types of squint and other anomalies of binocular vision, working in close collaboration with ophthalmologists. The all-graduate workforce comes from three universities: the University of Liverpool, the University of Sheffield and Glasgow Caledonion University.
BRITISH AND IRISH ORTHOPTIC SOCIETY,
Salisbury House, Station Road, Cambridge CB1 2LA
T 01353-665541 E bios@orthoptics.org.uk
W www.orthoptics.org.uk
Chair, Lesley-Anne Baxter

PARAMEDICAL SERVICES
Salary range: £21,500–£34,500

Paramedics deal with accidents and emergencies, assessing patients and carrying out any specialist treatment and care needed in the first instance. The body that represents ambulance professionals is the College of Paramedics.
COLLEGE OF PARAMEDICS, The Exchange, Express Park,
Bristol Road, Bridgwater TA6 4RR T 01278-420014
E membership@collegeofparamedics.co.uk
W www.collegeofparamedics.co.uk
Chief Executive, Dave Hodge

PHYSIOTHERAPY
Salary range: £21,000–£40,000

Physiotherapists are concerned with movement and function and deal with problems arising from injury, illness and ageing. Full-time three- or four-year degree courses are available at around 36 higher education institutions in the UK. Information about courses leading to state registration is available from the Chartered Society of Physiotherapy.
CHARTERED SOCIETY OF PHYSIOTHERAPY,
14 Bedford Row, London WC1R 4ED T 020-7306 6666
W www.csp.org.uk
Chief Executive, Karen Middleton, CBE

PROSTHETICS AND ORTHOTICS
Salary range: £21,000 on qualification, up to £67,000 as a consultant

Prosthetists provide artificial limbs while orthotists provide devices to support or control a part of the body. It is necessary to obtain an honours degree to become a prosthetist or orthotist. Training is centred at the University of Salford and the University of Strathclyde.
BRITISH ASSOCIATION OF PROSTHETISTS AND
ORTHOTISTS, Sir James Clark Building,
Abbey Mill Business Centre, Paisley PA1 1TJ T 0141-561 7217
E enquiries@bapo.com W www.bapo.com
Chair, Jonathan Bull

RADIOGRAPHY
Salary range: £21,000–£40,000, rising to £67,000 in senior posts

In order to practise both diagnostic and therapeutic radiography in the UK, it is necessary to have successfully completed a course of education and training recognised by the HCPC. Such courses are offered by around 24 universities throughout the UK and lead to the award of a degree in radiography. Further information is available from the Society and College of Radiographers, the trade and professional body which represents the whole of the radiographic workforce in the UK.
SOCIETY AND COLLEGE OF RADIOGRAPHERS,
207 Providence Square, Mill Street, London SE1 2EW
T 020-7740 7200 W www.sor.org
Chief Executive, Richard Evans

SPEECH AND LANGUAGE THERAPY
Salary range: £21,000–£40,000

Speech and language therapists (SLTs) work with people with communication, swallowing, eating and drinking problems. The Royal College of Speech and Language Therapists is the professional body for speech and language therapists and support workers. Alongside the HCPC, it accredits education and training courses leading to qualification.
ROYAL COLLEGE OF SPEECH AND LANGUAGE
THERAPISTS, 2 White Hart Yard, London SE1 1NX
T 020-7378 1200 E info@rcslt.org W www.rcslt.org
Chief Executive, Kamini Gadhok, MBE

NURSING
Salary range: see Health: Employees and Salaries

In order to practise in the UK, all nurses and midwives must be registered with the Nursing and Midwifery Council (NMC). The NMC is a statutory regulatory body that establishes and maintains standards of education, training, conduct and performance for nursing and midwifery. Courses leading to registration are currently at a minimum of degree level. All take a minimum of three years if undertaken full-time. The NMC approves programmes run jointly by higher education institutions with their healthcare service partners who offer clinical placements. The nursing part of the register has four fields of practice: adult, children's (paediatric), learning disability and mental health nursing. In most cases students must select one specific field to study before applying to an institution. Some universities run courses which offer the simultaneous study of two nursing fields. In addition, those studying to become adult nurses gain experience of nursing in relation to medicine, surgery, maternity care and nursing in the home. The NMC also sets standards for programmes leading to registration as a midwife and a range of post-registration courses including specialist practice programmes, nurse prescribing and those for teachers of nursing and midwifery. The NMC has a part of the register for specialist community public health nurses and approves programmes for health visitors, occupational health nurses and school nurses.
The Royal College of Nursing is the largest professional union for nursing in the UK, representing qualified nurses, healthcare assistants and nursing students in the NHS and the independent sector.
NURSING AND MIDWIFERY COUNCIL (NMC),
23 Portland Place, London W1B 1PZ T 020-7637 7181
E communications@nmc-uk.org W www.nmc-uk.org
Chief Executive and Registrar, Jackie Smith
ROYAL COLLEGE OF NURSING,
20 Cavendish Square, London W1G 0RN
T 0345-772 6100 W www.rcn.org.uk
Chief Executive and General Secretary, Dr Peter Carter

OPTOMETRY AND DISPENSING OPTICS

Salary range:
Optometrist £19,500–£53,500, up to £80,000 for consultant posts
Dispensing Optician £14,000–£35,000

There are various routes to qualification as a dispensing optician. Qualification takes three years in total, and can be completed by combining a distance learning course or day release while working as a trainee under the supervision of a qualified and registered optician. Alternatively, students can do a two-year full-time course followed by one year of supervised practice with a qualified and registered optician. Training must be done at a training establishment approved by the regulatory body – the General Optical Council (GOC). There are six training establishments which are approved by the GOC: ABDO (Association of British Dispensing Opticians) College, Anglia Ruskin University, Bradford College, City University, City and Islington College and Glasgow Caledonian University. Students are also able to complete a Foundation or Undergraduate degree in Ophthalmic Dispensing, with both degrees offered by ABDO in association with Canterbury Christ Church University. All routes are concluded by professional qualifying examinations, successful completion of which leads to the awarding of the Fellowship Diploma of the Association of British Dispensing Opticians (FBDO) by ABDO. FBDO holders are able to register with the GOC following the awarding of their diploma, with registration being compulsory for all practising dispensing opticians. After two years post-qualifying experience and the completion of training to fit contact lenses, students have the option to take a career progression course at the University of Bradford that allows them to graduate with a degree in optometry in one calendar year.

Optometrists must obtain an undergraduate optometry degree from one of the nine institutions approved by the GOC (Anglia Ruskin University, Aston University, the University of Bradford, Cardiff University, City University, Glasgow Caledonian University, the University of Manchester, Plymouth University or the University of Ulster). Following graduation, trainees must complete a year of supervised salaried training with a registered optometrist after which they must pass a series of assessments set by the College of Optometrists. As with dispensing opticians, optometrists must be registered with the GOC in order to practise.

Continuing Education and Training (CET) is a statutory requirement for all registered dispensing opticians and optometrists to retain GOC registration.

ASSOCIATION OF BRITISH DISPENSING OPTICIANS (ABDO), Godmersham Park, Godmersham, Canterbury, Kent CT4 7DT **T** 020-7298 5100 **E** general@abdolondon.org.uk
W www.abdo.org.uk
General Secretary, Sir Anthony Garrett, CBE
COLLEGE OF OPTOMETRISTS, 42 Craven Street, London WC2N 5NG **T** 020-7839 6000
W www.college-optometrists.org
Chief Executive, Bryony Pawinska
GENERAL OPTICAL COUNCIL (GOC), 41 Harley Street, London W1G 8DJ **T** 020-7580 3898 **E** goc@optical.org
W www.optical.org
Chief Executive, Samantha Peters

OSTEOPATHY

Salary Range: £20,000–£100,000+

Osteopathy is a system of diagnosis and treatment for a wide range of conditions. It works with the structure and function of the body, and is based on the principle that the well-being of an individual depends on the skeleton, muscles, ligaments and connective tissues functioning smoothly together. The General Osteopathic Council (GOsC) regulates the practice of osteopathy in the UK and maintains a register of those entitled to practise. It is a criminal offence for anyone to describe themselves as an osteopath unless they are registered with the GOsC.

To gain entry to the register, applicants must hold a recognised qualification from an osteopathic education institute accredited by the GOsC; this involves a four-to five-year honours degree programme combined with clinical training.

GENERAL OSTEOPATHIC COUNCIL (GOsC), Osteopathy House, 176 Tower Bridge Road, London SE1 3LU
T 020-7357 6655 **E** info@osteopathy.org.uk
W www.osteopathy.org.uk
Chief Executive and Registrar, Tim Walker

PHARMACY

Salary range: £20,000–£68,000+

Pharmacists are involved in the preparation and use of medicines, from the discovery of their active ingredients to their use by patients. Pharmacists also monitor the effects of medicines, both for patient care and for research purposes.

The General Pharmaceutical Council (GPhC) is the independent regulatory body for pharmacists in England, Scotland and Wales, having taken over the regulating function of the Royal Pharmaceutical Society in 2010. The GPhC maintains the register of pharmacists, pharmacy technicians and pharmacy premises; it also sets national standards for training, ethics, proficiency and continuing professional development. The Pharmaceutical Society of Northern Ireland (PSNI) performs the same role in Northern Ireland. In order to register, students must complete a four-year degree in pharmacy that is accredited by either the GPhC or the PSNI, followed by one year of pre-registration training at an approved pharmacy; they must then pass an entrance examination.

GENERAL PHARMACEUTICAL COUNCIL (GPhC), 129 Lambeth Road, London SE1 7BT **T** 020-3365 3400
W www.pharmacyregulation.org
Chief Executive and Registrar, Duncan Rudkin
PHARMACEUTICAL SOCIETY OF NORTHERN IRELAND (PSNI), 73 University Street, Belfast BT7 1HL
T 028-9032 6927 **W** www.psni.org.uk
Chief Executive, Trevor Patterson
ROYAL PHARMACEUTICAL SOCIETY, 1 Lambeth High Street, London SE1 7JN **T** 020-7572 2737
E support@rpharms.com **W** www.rpharms.com
Chief Executive, Helen Gordon

INFORMATION MANAGEMENT

Salary range: Archivist £21,000–£30,000 (starting); £30,000–£55,000+ in senior posts
Information Officer £17,000–£25,000 (starting); £26,000–£50,000+ in senior posts
Librarian £19,500–£23,500 (newly qualified); £23,500–£30,000 (chartered); £49,000+ in senior posts

The Chartered Institute of Library and Information Professionals (CILIP) is the leading professional body for librarians, information specialists and knowledge managers. The Archives and Records Association is the professional body for archivists and record managers. The Association of Special Libraries and Information Bureau (ASLIB) is a member association for people who manage information and knowledge in organisations across all sectors. ASLIB provides its members with access to leading publications in information and knowledge management, networking opportunities and professional development.

ARCHIVES AND RECORDS ASSOCIATION,
Prioryfield House, 20 Canon Street, Taunton, Somerset
IA1 1SW **T** 01823-327077 **E** ara@archives.org.uk
W www.archives.org.uk
Chief Executive, John Chambers

ASLIB, Howard House, Wagon Lane, Bingley, W. Yorks
BD16 1WA **T** 01274-777700 **E** dheath@aslib.com
W www.aslib.com
Director, Rebecca Marsh

CHARTERED INSTITUTE OF LIBRARY AND INFORMATION PROFESSIONALS (CILIP),
7 Ridgmount Street, London WC1E 7AE **T** 020-7255 0500
E info@cilip.org.uk **W** www.cilip.org.uk
Chief Executive, Annie Mauger

JOURNALISM

Salary range: starting salaries £12,000–£15,000 (trainee); £22,250 for established journalists, rising to £50,000–£85,000 for senior journalists/editors

The National Council for the Training of Journalists (NCTJ) accredits 74 courses for journalists run by a number of different education providers throughout the United Kingdom; it also provides professional support to journalists.

The Broadcast Journalism Training Council (BJTC) is an association of the UK's main broadcast journalism employers and accredits courses in broadcast journalism.

BROADCAST JOURNALISM TRAINING COUNCIL
(BJTC), 18 Miller's Close, Rippingale Nr. Bourne,
Lincolnshire PE10 0TH **T** 0845-600 8789 **E** sec@bjtc.org.uk
W www.bjtc.org.uk
Secretary, Martyn Hurd

NATIONAL COUNCIL FOR THE TRAINING OF JOURNALISTS (NCTJ), The New Granary, Station Road,
Newport, Saffron Walden, Essex CB11 3PL **T** 01799-544014
E info@nctj.com **W** www.nctj.com
Chief Executive, Joanne Butcher

LAW

There are three types of practising lawyers: barristers, notaries and solicitors. Solicitors tend to work as a group in firms, and can be approached directly by individuals. They advise on a variety of legal issues and must decide the most appropriate course of action, if any. Notaries have all the powers of a solicitor other than the conduct of litigation. Most of them are primarily concerned with the preparation and authentication of documents for use abroad. Barristers are usually self-employed. If a solicitor believes that a barrister is required, he or she will instruct one on behalf of the client; the client will not have contact with the barrister without the solicitor being present.

When specialist expertise is needed, barristers give opinions on complex matters of law, and when clients require representation in the higher courts (crown courts, the high court, the court of appeal and the supreme court), barristers provide a specialist advocacy service. However, solicitors – who represent their clients in the lower courts such as magistrates' courts and county courts – can also apply for advocacy rights in the higher courts instead of briefing a barrister.

THE BAR

Salary range: £12,000–£65,000 (pupillage); £25,000–£300,000 (qualified); £1,000,000+ with ten years experience

The governing body of the Bar of England and Wales is the General Council of the Bar, also known as the Bar Council. Since January 2006, the regulatory functions of the Bar Council (including regulating the education and training requirements for those wishing to enter the profession) have been undertaken by the Bar Standards Board.

In the first (or 'academic') stage of training, aspiring barristers must obtain a law degree of a good standard (at least second class). Alternatively, those with a non-law degree (at least second class) may complete a one-year full-time or two-year part-time Common Professional Examination (CPE) or Graduate Diploma in Law (GDL).

The second (vocational) stage is the completion of the Bar Professional Training Course (BPTC), which is available at eight validated institutions in the UK and must be applied for around one year in advance (**W** www.barprofessional training.org.uk). All barristers must join one of the four Inns of Court prior to commencing the BPTC.

Students are 'called to the Bar' by their Inn after completion of the vocational stage, but cannot practise as a barrister until completion of the third stage, which is called 'pupillage'. Being called to the Bar does not entitle a person to practise as a barrister – successful completion of pupillage is now a prerequisite. Pupillage lasts for two six-month periods: the 'non-practising six' and the 'practising six'. The former consists of shadowing an experienced barrister, while the latter involves appearing in court as a barrister.

Admission to the Bar of Northern Ireland is controlled by the General Council of the Bar of Northern Ireland; admission as an Advocate to the Scottish Bar is through the Faculty of Advocates.

FACULTY OF ADVOCATES, Parliament House,
Edinburgh EH1 1RF **T** 0131-226 5071
W www.advocates.org.uk
Dean, Richard Keen, QC

GENERAL COUNCIL OF THE BAR (THE BAR COUNCIL), 289–293 High Holborn, London WC1V 7HZ
T 020-7242 0082 **E** contactus@barcouncil.org.uk
W www.barcouncil.org.uk
Chief Executive, Stephen Crowne

BAR STANDARDS BOARD address as above
E contactus@barstandardsboard.org.uk
W www.barstandardsboard.org.uk
Chair of the Bar Council, Baroness Deech, DBE
Director, Bar Standards Board, Dr Vanessa Davies

GENERAL COUNCIL OF THE BAR OF NORTHERN IRELAND, The Bar Library, 91 Chichester Street,
Belfast BT1 3JQ **T** 028-9024 1523 **E** contatc@barofni.com
W www.barlibrary.com
Chief Executive, David Mulholland

THE INNS OF COURT

HONOURABLE SOCIETY OF GRAY'S INN,
8 South Square, London WC1R 5ET **T** 020-7458 7800
W www.graysinn.org.uk
Under-Treasurer, Brig. Anthony Faith, CBE

HONOURABLE SOCIETY OF LINCOLN'S INN,
Treasury Office, Lincoln's Inn, London WC2A 3TL
T 020-7405 1393 **E** mail@lincolnsinn.org.uk
W www.lincolnsinn.org.uk
Under-Treasurer, Mary Kerr

HONOURABLE SOCIETY OF THE INNER TEMPLE,
Inner Temple, London EC4Y 7HL **T** 020-7797 8250
W www.innertemple.org.uk
Treasurer, Lord Justice Tomlinson

HONOURABLE SOCIETY OF THE MIDDLE TEMPLE,
Middle Temple Lane, London EC4Y 9AT **T** 020-7427 4800
E members@middletemple.org.uk
W www.middletemple.org.uk
Chief Executive, Guy Perricone

NOTARIES PUBLIC

Notaries are qualified lawyers with a postgraduate diploma in notarial practice. Once a potential notary has passed the postgraduate diploma, they can petition the Court of Faculties for a 'faculty'. After the faculty is granted, the notary is able to practise; however, for the first two years this must be under the supervision of an experienced notary. The admission and regulation of notaries in England and Wales is a statutory function of the Faculty Office. This jurisdiction was confirmed by the Courts and Legal Services Act 1990. The Notaries Society of England and Wales is the representative body for practising notaries.

THE FACULTY OFFICE, 1 The Sanctuary, Westminster,
London SW1P 3JT T 020-7222 5381
E faculty.office@1thesanctuary.com
W www.facultyoffice.org.uk
Registrars, Peter Beesley; Howard Dellar
THE NOTARIES SOCIETY OF ENGLAND AND WALES,
PO Box 1023, Ipswitch IP1 9XB T 01394-380436
E admin@thenotariessociety.org.uk
W www.thenotariessociety.org.uk
Secretary, Christopher Vaughan

SOLICITORS

Salary range: £16,500–£19,000 (trainee); £25,000–£75,000 after qualification; £100,000+ (associate or partner)

Graduates from any discipline can train to be a solicitor; however, if the undergraduate degree is not in law, a one-year conversion course – either the Common Professional Examination (CPE) or the Graduate Diploma in Law (GDL) – must be completed. The next stage, and the beginning of the vocational phase, is the Legal Practice Course (LPC), which takes one year and is obligatory for both law and non-law graduates. The LPC provides professional instruction for prospective solicitors and can be completed on a full-time or part-time basis. Trainee solicitors then enter the final stage, which is a paid period of supervised work that lasts two years for full-time contracts. The employer that provides the training contract must be authorised by the Solicitors Regulation Authority (SRA) (the regulatory body of the Law Society of England and Wales), the Law Society of Scotland or the Law Society of Northern Ireland. The SRA also monitors the training contract to ensure that it provides the trainee with the expertise to qualify as a solicitor.

Conveyancers are specialist property lawyers, dealing with the legal processes involved in transferring buildings, land and associated finances from one owner to another. This was the sole responsibility of solicitors until 1987 but under current legislation it is now possible for others to train as conveyancers.

COUNCIL FOR LICENSED CONVEYANCERS (CLC),
16 Glebe Road, Chelmsford, Essex CM1 1QG
T 01245-349599 E clc@clc-uk.org W www.clc-uk.org
Chief Executive, Sheila Kumar
THE LAW SOCIETY OF ENGLAND AND WALES,
The Law Society's Hall, 113 Chancery Lane, London WC2A 1PL
T 020-7242 1222 W www.lawsociety.org.uk
Chief Executive, Des Hudson
LAW SOCIETY OF NORTHERN IRELAND,
96 Victoria Street, Belfast BT1 3GN T 028-9023 1614
W www.lawsoc-ni.org
Chief Executive, Alan Hunter
LAW SOCIETY OF SCOTLAND, 26 Drumsheugh Gardens,
Edinburgh EH3 7YR T 0131-226 7411
E lawscot@lawscot.org.uk W www.lawscot.org.uk
Chief Executive, Lorna Jack
SOLICITORS REGULATION AUTHORITY (SRA),
The Cube, 199 Wharfside Street, Birmingham B1 1RN

T 0370-606 2555 W www.sra.org.uk
Chief Executive, Paul Philip

SOCIAL WORK

Salary range: £25,000–£34,000 (starting), rising to £42,000 as an experienced manager; £57,000+ at senior levels

Social workers tend to specialise in either adult or children's services. The HCPC obtained regulatory responsibility from the General Social Care Council in August 2012 and is responsible for setting standards of conduct and practice for social care workers and their employers; regulating the workforce and social work education and training. A degree or postgraduate qualification is needed in order to become a social worker. For more information *see* Social Welfare.

HEALTH AND CARE PROFESSIONS COUNCIL (HCPC),
Park House, 184 Kennington Park Road, London SE11 4BU
T 0845-300 6184 E registration@hcpc-uk.org
W www.hcpc-uk.org
Chief Executive and Registrar, Marc Seale

SURVEYING

Salary range: £18,000–£26,000 (starting); £45,000 (senior); up to £100,000 (partners and directors)

The Royal Institution of Chartered Surveyors (RICS) is the professional body that represents and regulates property professionals including land surveyors, valuers, auctioneers, quantity surveyors and project managers. Entry to the institution, following completion of a RICS-accredited degree, is through completion of the Assessment of Professional Competence (APC), which involves a period of practical training concluded by a final assessment of competence. Entry as a technical surveyor requires completion of the Assessment of Technical Competence (ATC), which mirrors the format of the APC. The different levels of RICS membership are MRICS (member) or FRICS (fellow) for chartered surveyors, and AssocRICS for associate members.

Relevant courses can also be accredited by the Chartered Institute of Building (CIOB), which represents players working in a range of construction disciplines. The CIOB offers four levels of membership to those who satisfy its requirements: FCIOB (fellow), MCIOB (member), ICIOB (incorporated) and ACIOB (associate).

CHARTERED INSTITUTE OF BUILDING (CIOB),
1 Arlington Square, Downshire Way, Bracknell RG12 1WA
T 01344-630700 E reception@ciob.org.uk W www.ciob.org.uk
Chief Executive, Chris Blythe
ROYAL INSTITUTION OF CHARTERED SURVEYORS
(RICS), RICS HQ, Parliament Square, London SW1P 3AD
T 024-7686 8555 E contactrics@rics.org W www.rics.org
Chief Executive, Sean Tompkins

TEACHING

Salary range: £21,500–£57,000; headteacher £42,000–£113,000 (for more detailed information *see* Education: Employees and Salaries)

The General Teaching Councils (GTCs) for Northern Ireland, Scotland and Wales maintain registers of qualified teachers in their respective countries, and registration is a legal requirement in order to teach in local authority schools. On 1 April 2013, the Teaching Agency merged with the National College to form the National College for Teaching and Leadership (NCTL), an executive agency of the Department for Education, which became the awarding body for Qualified Teacher Status (QTS). UCAS Teacher Training (UTT) has replaced the Graduate Teacher Training Registry (GTTR) as the body through which to apply for postgraduate teacher training in the UK. To become a qualified teacher, all entrants must have a degree and gain QTS, which includes a minimum of 24 weeks in at least two different schools and academic study of teaching. Another route is through School-centred Initial Teacher Training (SCITT), where practical, hands on teacher training is delivered by experienced, practicing teachers in their own government-approved school.

Many courses also award an academic qualification known as the Postgraduate Certificate in Education (PGCE) in England and Wales and the Professional Graduate Diploma in Education (PGDE) in Scotland. Once training is completed, applicants spend a year in school as a newly qualified teacher (NQT).

Teachers in Further Education (FE) need not have QTS, though new entrants to FE may be required to work towards a specified FE qualification by employers. A range of courses are offered and usually require one year of study in addition to 100 hours of teaching experience. Similarly, academic staff in Higher Education require no formal teaching qualification, but are expected to obtain a qualification that meets standards set by the Higher Education Academy.

Details of routes to gaining QTS are available in England from the NCTL, the Department for Education and UTT, in Wales from the Teacher Training & Education Recruitment Forum Wales, in Scotland from Teach in Scotland and in Northern Ireland from the Department of Education.

The College of Teachers, under the terms of its royal charter, provides professional qualifications and membership to teachers and those involved in education in the UK and overseas.

COLLEGE OF TEACHERS, Institute of Education,
20 Bedford Way, London WC1H 0AL T 020-7911 5536
W www.collegeofteachers.ac.uk
Chief Executive and Registrar, Angela McFarlane
DEPARTMENT OF EDUCATION NORTHERN
IRELAND, Rathgael House, Balloo Road, Bangor BT19 7PR
T 028-9127 9279 E mail@deni.gov.uk W www.deni.gov.uk
Permanent Secretary, Paul Sweeney
GENERAL TEACHING COUNCIL FOR NORTHERN
IRELAND, 3rd Floor, Albany House, 73–75 Great Victoria
Street, Belfast BT2 7AF T 028-9033 3390 E info@gtcni.org.uk
W www.gtcni.org.uk
Chair, Ivan Arbuthnot
GENERAL TEACHING COUNCIL FOR SCOTLAND,
Clerwood House, 96 Clermiston Road, Edinburgh EH12 6UT
T 0131-314 6000 E gtcs@gtcs.org.uk W www.gtcs.org.uk
Chief Executive, Kenneth Muir
GENERAL TEACHING COUNCIL FOR WALES, 9th Floor,
Eastgate House, 35–43 Newport Road, Cardiff CF24 0AB
T 029-2046 0099 E information@gtcw.org.uk
W www.gtcw.org.uk
Chair, Angela Jardine

UCAS TEACHER TRAINING (UTT), Rosehill, New Barn
Lane, Cheltenham GL52 3LZ T 0371-468 0469
W www.ucas.com/ucas-teacher-training
Chief Executive, Mary Curnock Cook, OBE
HIGHER EDUCATION ACADEMY, Innovation Way,
York Science Park, Heslington, York YO10 5BR
T 01904-717500 E enquiries@heacademy.ac.uk
W www.heacademy.ac.uk
Chief Executive, Prof. Stephanie Marshall
NATIONAL COLLEGE FOR TEACHING AND
LEADERSHIP, Triumph Road, Nottingham NG8 1DH
T 0345-609 0009 E college.enquiries@bt.com
W www.nationalcollege.org.uk
Chief Executive, Charlie Taylor

VETERINARY MEDICINE
Salary range: £21,000–£53,000+

The regulatory body for veterinary surgeons in the UK is the Royal College of Veterinary Surgeons (RCVS), which keeps the register of those entitled to practise veterinary medicine, the register and list of qualified veterinary nurses and, more recently, veterinary practice premises (on behalf of the Veterinary Medicines Directorate). Holders of recognised degrees from any of the seven UK university veterinary schools or from certain EU or overseas universities are entitled to be registered, and holders of certain other degrees may take a statutory membership examination. The UK's veterinary schools are located at the University of Bristol, the University of Cambridge, the University of Edinburgh, the University of Glasgow, the University of Liverpool, the University of Nottingham and the Royal Veterinary College in London; all veterinary degrees last for five years except that offered at Cambridge, which lasts for six.

The British Veterinary Association is the national representative body for the UK veterinary profession. The British Veterinary Nursing Association is the professional body representing veterinary nurses.

BRITISH VETERINARY ASSOCIATION, 7 Mansfield Street,
London W1G 9NQ T 020-7636 6541 E bvahq@bva.co.uk
W www.bva.co.uk
Secretary General, David Calpin
BRITISH VETERINARY NURSING ASSOCIATION,
82 Greenway Business Centre, Harlow Business Park,
Harlow CM19 5QE T 01279-408644 E bvna@bvna.co.uk
W www.bvna.org.uk
Honorary Secretary, Fiona Andrew
ROYAL COLLEGE OF VETERINARY SURGEONS
(RCVS), Belgravia House, 62–64 Horseferry Road,
London SW1P 2AF T 020-7222 2001 E info@rcvs.org.uk
W www.rcvs.org.uk
Registrar, Nick Stace

INDEPENDENT SCHOOLS

Independent schools (non-maintained mainstream schools) charge fees and are owned and managed under special trusts, with profits being used for the benefit of the schools concerned. In 2012–13 there were 2,598 non-maintained mainstream schools in the UK, educating around 625,000 pupils, or around 6.4 per cent of the total school-age population. The approximate number of pupils at non-maintained mainstream schools in 2012–13 was:

UK	624,750
England	584,000
Wales	8,900
Scotland	31,150
Northern Ireland	700

The Independent Schools Council (ISC), formed in 1974, acts on behalf of the eight independent schools' associations which constitute it. These associations are:

Association of Governing Bodies of Independent Schools (AGBIS)
Council of British International Schools (COBIS)
Girls' Schools Association (GSA)
Headmasters' & Headmistresses' Conference (HMC)
Independent Association of Prep Schools (IAPS)
Independent Schools Association (ISA)
Independent Schools' Bursars Association (ISBA)
The Society of Heads

In 2013–14 there were 511,928 pupils being educated in 1,257 schools in membership of associations within the Independent Schools Council (ISC). Most schools not in membership of an ISC association are likely to be privately owned. The Independent Schools Inspectorate (ISI) was demerged from ISC with effect from 1 January 2008 and is legally and operationally independent of ISC. ISI works as an accredited inspectorate of schools in membership of the ISC associations under a framework agreed with the Department for Education (DfE). A school must pass an ISI accreditation inspection to qualify for membership of an association within ISC.

In 2013 at GCSE 60.4 per cent of all exams taken by candidates in ISC associations' member schools achieved either an A* or A grade (compared to the national average of 23 per cent), and at A-level 18 per cent of entries were awarded an A* grade (national average, 7.6 per cent). In 2013–14 a total of 170,984 (33.4 per cent) pupils at schools in ISC associations received help with their fees, mainly in the form of bursaries and scholarships from the schools. ISC schools provided more than £660m of assistance with fees.

INDEPENDENT SCHOOLS COUNCIL
St Vincent House, 30 Orange Street, London WC2H 7HH
T 020-7766 7070 W www.isc.co.uk

The list of schools below was compiled from the Independent Schools Yearbook 2013–14 (ed. Judy Mott, published by Bloomsbury Publishing) which includes schools whose heads are members of one of the ISC's five Heads' Associations. Further details are available online (W www.isyb.co.uk).

The fees shown below represent the upper limit payable for the year 2013–14.

		Termly Fees		
School	Web Address	Day	Board	Head
ENGLAND				
Abbey Gate College, Cheshire	www.abbeygatecollege.co.uk	£3,625	–	Mrs T. Pollard
The Abbey School, Berks	www.theabbey.co.uk	£4,660	–	Mrs B. Stanley
Abbots Bromley School, Staffs	www.abbotsbromley.net	£5,119	£8,575	Mrs V. Musgrave
Abbot's Hill School, Herts	www.abbotshill.herts.sch.uk	£5,260	–	Mrs E. Thomas
Abbotsholme School, Derbys	www.abbotsholme.co.uk	£6,540	£9,600	S. Fairclough
Abingdon School, Oxon	www.abingdon.org.uk	£5,290	–	Miss O. Lusk
Ackworth School, W. Yorks	www.ackworthschool.com	£4,191	£7,479	Mrs K. Bell
AKS, Lancs	www.arnoldkeqms.com	£3,109	–	J. Keefe
Aldenham School, Herts	www.aldenham.com	£6,500	£9,470	J. Fowler
Alderley Edge School for Girls, Cheshire	www.aesg.co.uk	£3,278	–	Mrs S. Goff
Alleyn's School, Lonodn SE22	www.alleyns.org.uk	£5,289	–	Dr G. Savage
Ampleforth College, N. Yorks	www.college.ampleforth.org.uk	£6,711	£10,088	Revd C. Everitt
Ardingly College, W. Sussex	www.ardingly.com	£7,355	£9,845	P. Green
Ashford School, Kent	www.ashfordschool.co.uk	£4,999	£9,999	M. Buchanan
Ashville College, N. Yorks	www.ashville.co.uk	£4,060	£8,010	D. Lauder
Austin Friars St Monica's Senior School, Cumbria	www.austinfriars.cumbria.sch.uk	£3,999	–	M. Harris
Bablake School, W. Midlands	www.bablake.com	£3,272	–	J. Watson
Badminton School, Bristol	www.badmintonschool.co.uk	£5,640	£10,690	Mrs R. Tear
Bancroft's School, Essex	www.bancrofts.org	£4,710	–	Mrs M. Ireland
Barnard Castle School, Durham	www.barnardcastleschool.org.uk	£3,997	£7,176	A. Stevens
Bearwood College, Berks	www.bearwoodcollege.co.uk	£4,985	£10,075	D. Wilkinson
Bedales School, Hants	www.bedales.org.uk	£8,345	£10,615	K. Budge
Bede's Senior School, E. Sussex	www.bedes.org	£6,480	£9,810	Dr R. Maloney
Bedford Girls' School, Beds	www.bedfordgirlsschool.co.uk	£3,815	–	Miss J. MacKenzie

School	Website	Fee 1	Fee 2	Head
Bedford Modern School, Beds	www.bedmod.co.uk	£3,833	–	M. Hall
Bedford School, Beds	www.bedfordschool.org.uk	£5,558	£9,400	J. Moule
Bedstone College, Shrops	www.bedstone.org	£4,360	£7,900	D. Gajadharsingh
Beechwood Sacred Heart School, Kent	www.beechwood.org.uk	£5,175	£8,590	A. Lennon
Benenden School, Kent	www.benenden.kent.sch.uk	–	£10,800	Mrs S. Price
Berkhamsted School, Herts	www.berkhamstedschool.org	£6,000	£9,553	M. Steed
Bethany School, Kent	www.bethanyschool.org.uk	£5,310	£8,764	M. Healy
Birkdale School, S. Yorks	www.birkdaleschool.org.uk	£3,721	–	Dr P. Owen
Birkenhead School, Merseyside	www.birkenheadschool.co.uk	£3,440	–	D. Clark
Bishop's Stortford College, Herts	www.bishops-stortford-college.herts.sch.uk	£5,484	£7,967	J. Gladwin
Blackheath High School, London SE3	www.blackheathhighschool.gdst.net	£4,470	–	Mrs E. Laws
Bloxham School, Oxon	www.bloxhamschool.com	£7,735	£9,995	P. Sanderson
Blundell's School, Devon	www.blundells.org	£6,310	£9,780	Mrs N. Huggett
Bolton School Boys' Division, Lancs	www.boltonschool.org/seniorboys	£3,499	–	P. Britton
Bolton School Girls' Division, Lancs	www.boltonschool.org/seniorgirls	£3,499	–	Miss S. Hincks
Bootham School, N. Yorks	www.boothamschool.com	£5,330	£9,065	J. Taylor
Bournemouth Collegiate School, Dorset	www.bournemouthcollegiateschool.co.uk	£4,250	£7,862	S. Duckitt
Box Hill School, Surrey	www.boxhillschool.com	£5,560	£9,280	M. Eagers
Bradfield College, Berks	www.bradfieldcollege.org.uk	£8,584	£10,730	S. Henderson
Bradford Grammar School, W. Yorks	www.bradfordgrammar.com	£3,830	–	K. Riley
Brentwood School, Essex	www.brentwoodschool.co.uk	£5,130	£9,795	D. Davies
Brighton & Hove High School, E. Sussex	www.bhhs.gdst.net	£3,950	–	Ms J. Smith
Brighton College, E. Sussex	www.brightoncollege.net	£6,800	£10,930	R. Cairns
Bristol Grammar School, Bristol	www.bristolgrammarschool.co.uk	£4,280	–	R. MacKinnon
Bromley High School, Kent	www.bromleyhigh.gdst.net	£4,674	–	Ms L. Simpson
Bromsgrove School, Worcs	www.bromsgrove-school.co.uk	£4,725	£8,990	C. Edwards
Bruton School for Girls, Somerset	www.brutonschool.co.uk	£4,677		Mrs N. Botterill
Bryanston School, Dorset	www.bryanston.co.uk	£8,805	£10,738	Ms S. Thomas
Burgess Hill School for Girls, W. Sussex	www.burgesshill-school.com	£4,900	£8,650	Mrs A. Aughwane
Bury Grammar School Boys, Lancs	www.bgsboys.co.uk	£3,111	–	R. Marshall
Bury Grammar School Girls, Lancs	www.bgsg.bury.sch.uk	£3,111	–	Mrs R. Georghiou
Canford School, Dorset	www.canford.com	£7,722	£9,880	B. Vessey
Caterham School, Surrey	www.caterhamschool.co.uk	£5,230	£9,759	J. Thomas
Central Newcastle High School, Tyne and Wear	www.newcastlehigh.gdst.net	£3,726	–	Mrs H. French
Channing School, London N6	www.channing.co.uk	£5,085	–	Mrs B. Elliott
Charterhouse, Surrey	www.charterhouse.org.uk	£9,070	£10,975	R. Pleming
Cheadle Hulme School, Cheshire	www.cheadlehulmeschool.co.uk	£3,448	–	Miss L. Pearson
Cheltenham College, Glos	www.cheltenhamcollege.org	£8,256	£10,917	Dr A. Peterken
The Cheltenham Ladies' College, Glos	www.cheltladiescollege.org	£7,749	£11,434	Ms E. Jardine-Young
Chetham's School of Music, Greater Manchester	www.chethams.com	sliding scale	–	Mrs C. Moreland
Chigwell School, Essex	www.chigwell-school.org	£4,995	£8,225	M. Punt
Christ's Hospital, W. Sussex	www.christs-hospital.org.uk	£6,100	£9,400	J. Franklin
Churcher's College, Hants	www.churcherscollege.com	£4,125	–	S. Williams
City of London Freemen's School, Surrey	www.clfs.surrey.sch.uk	£5,022	£8,064	P. MacDonald
City of London School, London EC4	www.clsb.org.uk	£4,601	–	Mrs S. Fletcher
City of London School for Girls, London EC2	www.clsg.org.uk	£4,622	–	Mrs E. Harrop
Claremont Fan Court School, Surrey	www.claremont-school.co.uk	£4,915	–	J. Insall-Reid
Clayesmore School, Dorset	www.clayesmore.com	£7,520	£10,279	M. Cooke
Clifton College, Bristol	www.cliftoncollege.com	£7,755	£10,995	M. Moore
Clifton High School, Bristol	www.cliftonhigh.bristol.sch.uk	£4,145	£7,450	Dr A. Neill
Cobham Hall, Kent	www.cobhamhall.com	£6,367	£9,578	P. Mitchell
Cokethorpe School, Oxon	www.cokethorpe.org.uk	£5,325	–	D. Ettinger
Colfe's School, London SE12	www.colfes.com	£4,728	–	R. Russell
Colston's School, Bristol	www.colstons.bristol.sch.uk	£3,890	–	P. Goodyer
Combe Bank School, Kent	www.combebankschool.co.uk	£5,120	–	Mrs E. Abbotts
Concord College, Shrops	www.concordcollegeuk.com	£4,080	£10,100	N. Hawkins
Cranford House School, Oxon	www.cranfordhouse.net	£4,850	–	Mrs L. Lawson
Cranleigh School, Surrey	www.cranleigh.org	£8,650	£10,610	G. Waller
Croydon High School, Surrey	www.croydonhigh.gdst.net	£4,633	–	Mrs D. Leonard

Culford School, Suffolk	www.culford.co.uk	£5,665	£9,085	J. Johnson-Munday
Dame Allan's Boys' School, Tyne and Wear	www.dameallans.co.uk	£3,594	–	Dr J. Hind
Dame Allan's Girls' School, Tyne and Wear	www.dameallans.co.uk	£3,594	–	Dr J. Hind
Dauntsey's School, Wilts	www.dauntseys.org	£5,455	£9,195	M. Lascelles
Dean Close School, Glos	www.deanclose.org.uk	£7,215	£10,320	J. Lancashire
Denstone College, Staffs	www.denstonecollege.org	£4,392	£7,648	D. Derbyshire
Derby Grammar School, Derbys	www.derbygrammar.co.uk	£3,765	–	R. Paine
Derby High School, Derbys	www.derbyhigh.derby.sch.uk	£3,640	–	Mrs D. Gould
Dodderhill School, Worcs	www.dodderhill.co.uk	£3,250	–	Mrs C. Mawston
Dover College, Kent	www.dovercollege.org.uk	£4,585	£9,050	G. Holden
d'Overbroeck's College, Oxon	www.doverbroecks.com	£6,595	£10,095	S. Cohen
Downe House, Berks	www.downehouse.net	£7,680	£10,610	Mrs E. McKendrick
Dulwich College, London SE21	www.dulwich.org.uk	£5,486	£11,396	Dr J. Spence
Dunottar School, Surrey	www.dunottarschool.com	£4,700	–	Mrs N. Matthews
Durham High School for Girls, Durham	www.dhsfg.org.uk	£3,575	–	Mrs L. Renwick
Durham School, Durham	www.durhamschool.co.uk	£5,150	£7,930	E. George
Eastbourne College, E. Sussex	www.eastbourne-college.co.uk	£6,610	£10,030	S. Davies
Edgbaston High School, W. Midlands	www.edgbastonhigh.co.uk	£3,568	–	Dr R. Weeks
Ellesmere College, Shrops	www.ellesmere.com	£5,460	£9,480	B. Wignall
Eltham College, London SE9	www.eltham-college.org.uk	£4,682	–	P. Henderson
Emanuel School, London SW11	www.emanuel.org.uk	£5,245	–	M. Hanley-Browne
Epsom College, Surrey	www.epsomcollege.org.uk	£7,085	£10,366	J. Piggott
Eton College, Berks	www.etoncollege.com	–	£11,090	A. Little
Ewell Castle School, Surrey	www.ewellcastle.co.uk	£4,340	–	P. Harris
Exeter School, Devon	www.exeterschool.org.uk	£3,619	–	R. Griffin
Farlington School, W. Sussex	www.farlingtonschool.net	£5,280	£8,720	Miss L. Higson
Farnborough Hill, Hants	www.farnborough-hill.org.uk	£4,040	–	Mrs S. Buckle
Farringtons School, Kent	www.farringtons.org.uk	£4,160	£8,200	Mrs C. James
Felsted School, Essex	www.felsted.org	£6,795	£9,395	Dr M. Walker
Forest School, London E17	www.forest.org.uk	£5,027	–	Mrs S. Kerr-Dineen
Framlingham College, Suffolk	www.framcollege.co.uk	£5,791	£9,010	P. Taylor
Francis Holland School, London NW1	www.francisholland.org.uk	£5,270	–	Mrs V. Durham
Francis Holland School, London NW1	www.francisholland.org.uk	£5,375	–	Mrs L . Elphinstone
Frensham Heights, Surrey	www.frensham.org	£5,930	£8,780	A. Fisher
Friends' School, Essex	www.friends.org.uk	£5,305	£8,590	Mrs A. Chaudhri
Fulneck School, W. Yorks	www.fulneckschool.co.uk	£3,855	£7,245	Mrs D. Newman
Gateways School, W. Yorks	www.gatewaysschool.co.uk	£3,795	–	Dr T. Johnson
Giggleswick School, N. Yorks	www.giggleswick.org.uk	£6,540	£9,550	G. Boult
The Godolphin and Latymer School, London W6	www.godolphinandlatymer.com	£5,760	–	Mrs R. Mercer
The Godolphin School, Wilts	www.godolphin.org	£6,176	£9,008	Mrs E. Hattersley
The Grange School, Cheshire	www.grange.org.uk	£3,350	–	C. Jeffery
Greenacre School for Girls, Surrey	www.greenacre.surrey.sch.uk	£4,650	–	Mrs L. Redding
Gresham's School, Norfolk	www.greshams.com	£7,475	£9,750	N. Flower
Guildford High School, Surrey	www.guildfordhigh.surrey.sch.uk	£4,750	–	Mrs F. Boulton
The Haberdashers' Aske's Boys' School, Herts	www.habsboys.org.uk	£5,289	–	P. Hamilton
Haberdashers' Aske's School for Girls, Herts	www.habsgirls.org.uk	£4,518	–	Miss B. O'Connor
Haileybury, Herts	www.haileybury.com	£7,308	£9,730	J. Davies
Halliford School, Middx	www.hallifordschool.co.uk	£4,150	–	P. Cottam
Hampshire Collegiate School, Hants	www.hampshirecs.org.uk	£4,600	£7,792	Mrs E. K. Henry
Hampton School, Middx	www.hamptonschool.org.uk	£5,330	–	K. Knibbs
Harrogate Ladies' College, N. Yorks	www.hlc.org.uk	£4,790	£10,285	Mrs S. Brett
Harrow School, Middx	www.harrowschool.org.uk	–	£11,095	J. Hawkins
Headington School, Oxon	www.headington.org	£5,267	£10,197	Mrs C. Jordan
Heathfield School, Berks	www.heathfieldschool.net	–	£10,347	Mrs J. Heywood
Hereford Cathedral School, Herefords	www.herefordcs.com	£4,090	–	P. Smith
Hethersett Old Hall School, Norfolk	www.hohs.co.uk	£4,150	£7,725	S. Crump
Highgate School, London N6	www.highgateschool.org.uk	£5,825	–	A. Pettitt
Hill House School, S. Yorks	www.hillhouse.doncaster.sch.uk	£3,470	–	D. Holland
Hull Collegiate School, E. Yorks	www.hullcollegiateschool.co.uk	£3,450	–	R. Haworth

School	Website	Day	Boarding	Head
Hurstpierpoint College, W. Sussex	www.hppc.co.uk	£6,775	£9,550	T. Manly
Hymers College, E. Yorks	www.hymerscollege.co.uk	£3,207	–	D. Elstone
Immanuel College, Herts	www.immanuelcollege.co.uk	£4,784	–	C. Dormer
Ipswich High School, Suffolk	www.ipswichhighschool.co.uk	£3,912	–	Ms O. Carlin
Ipswich School, Suffolk	www.ipswich.suffolk.sch.uk	£4,194	–	N. Weaver
James Allen's Girls' School (JAGS), London SE22	www.jags.org.uk	£4,900	–	Mrs M. Gibbs
The John Lyon School, Middx	www.johnlyon.org	£5,180	–	Miss K. Haynes
Kelly College, Devon	www.kellycollege.com	£5,150	£8,995	Dr G. Hawley
Kent College, Kent	www.kentcollege.com	£5,423	£9,912	Dr D. Lamper
Kent College Pembury, Kent	www.kent-college.co.uk	£5,774	£9,308	Mrs S. Huang
Kimbolton School, Cambs	www.kimbolton.cambs.sch.uk	£4,475	£7,405	J. Belbin
King Edward VI High School for Girls, W. Midlands	www.kehs.org.uk	£3,645	–	Mrs A. Clark
King Edward VI School, Hants	www.kes.hants.sch.uk	£4,365	–	A. Thould
King Edward's School, Somerset	www.kesbath.com	£4,050	–	M. Boden
King Edward's School, W. Midlands	www.kes.org.uk	£3,750	–	J. Claughton
King Edward's, Surrey	www.kesw.org	–	£9,275	J. Attwater
King Henry VIII School, W. Midlands	www.khviii.com	£3,272	–	J. Slack
King William's College, Isle of Man	www.kwc.im	£6,582	£9,582	M. Humphreys
Kingham Hill School, Oxon	www.kingham-hill.oxon.sch.uk	£5,460	£9,125	Revd N. Seward
King's College School, London SW19	www.kcs.org.uk	£6,300	–	A. Halls
King's College, Somerset	www.kings-taunton.co.uk	£6,380	£9,480	R. Biggs
King's High School, Warwicks	www.kingshighwarwick.co.uk	£3,484	–	Mrs E. Surber
King's School, Somerset	www.kingsbruton.com	£6,668	£9,316	I. Wilmshurst
The King's School, Kent	www.kings-school.co.uk	£8,090	£10,745	P. Roberts
The King's School, Cheshire	www.kingschester.co.uk	£3,833	–	C. Ramsey
King's Ely, Cambs	www.kingsely.org	£2,818	–	S. Freestone
The King's School, Glos	www.thekingsschool.co.uk	£5,695	–	A. Macnaughton
The King's School, Cheshire	www.kingsmac.co.uk	£3,590	–	Dr S. Hyde
King's Rochester, Kent	www.kings-rochester.co.uk	£5,545	£9,000	J. Walker
The King's School, Worcs	www.ksw.org.uk	£3,894	–	T. Keyes
Kingsley School, Devon	www.kingsleyschoolbideford.co.uk	£4,060	£7,850	S. Woolcott
The Kingsley School, Warwicks	www.thekingsleyschool.com	£3,690	–	Ms H. Owens
Kingston Grammar School, Surrey	www.kgs.org.uk	£5,340	–	J. Wallace
Kingswood School, Somerset	www.kingswood.bath.sch.uk	£4,253	£9,166	S. Morris
Kirkham Grammar School, Lancs	www.kirkhamgrammar.co.uk	£3,225	–	R. Laithwaite
The Lady Eleanor Holles School, Middx	www.lehs.org.uk	£5,400	–	Mrs G. Low
Lancing College, W. Sussex	www.lancingcollege.co.uk	£7,260	£10,340	J. Gillespie
Langley School, Norfolk	www.langleyschool.co.uk	£4,185	£8,505	D. Findlay
Latymer Upper School, London W6	www.latymer-upper.org	£5,495	–	D. Goodhew
Lavant House, W. Sussex	www.lavanthouse.org.uk	£4,560	£7,176	Mrs C. Horton
The Grammar School at Leeds, W. Yorks	www.gsal.org.uk	£3,897	–	M. Gibbons
Leicester Grammar School, Leics	www.leicestergrammar.org.uk	£3,738	–	C. King
Leicester High School for Girls, Leics	www.leicesterhigh.co.uk	£3,500	–	A. Whelpdale
Leighton Park School, Berks	www.leightonpark.com	£6,363	£9,910	N. Williams
Leweston School, Dorset	www.leweston.co.uk	£5,755	£9,120	A. Aylward
The Leys School, Cambs	www.theleys.net	£6,160	£9,260	M. Priestley
Lichfield Cathedral School, Staffs	www.lichfieldcathedralschool.com	£4,480	£5,890	D. Corran
Lincoln Minster School, Lincs	www.lincolnminsterschool.co.uk	£3,999	£7,994	C. Rickart
Longridge Towers School, Northumberland	www.lts.org.uk	£3,894	£7,933	T. Manning
Lord Wandsworth College, Hants	www.lordwandsworth.org	£6,640	£9,380	F. Livingstone
Loughborough Grammar School, Leics	www.lesgrammar.org	£3,575	£9,380	P. Fisher
Loughborough High School, Leics	www.leshigh.org	£3,397	–	Mrs G. Byrom
Luckley House School, Berks	www.luckleyhouseschool.org	£4,812	£8,422	Mrs J. Tudor
LVS Ascot (The Licensed Victuallers' School), Berks	www.lvs.ascot.sch.uk	£4,900	£8,610	Mrs C. Cunniffe
Magdalen College School, Oxon	www.mcsoxford.org	£4,876	–	Dr T. Hands
Malvern College, Worcs	www.malverncollege.org.uk	£7,309	£11,413	A. Clark
The Manchester Grammar School, Greater Manchester	www.mgs.org	£3,685	–	Dr M. Boulton
Manchester High School for Girls, Greater Manchester	www.manchesterhigh.co.uk	£3,429	–	Mrs A. Hewitt

School	Website	Fee 1	Fee 2	Head
Manor House School, Surrey	www.manorhouseschool.org	£4,770	–	Miss Z. Axton
The Marist Senior School, Berks	www.themaristschools.com	£3,950	–	K. McCloskey
Marlborough College, Wilts	www.marlboroughcollege.org	£9,140	£10,760	J. Leigh
Marymount International School, Surrey	www.marymountlondon.com	£6,673	£11,246	Ms S. Gallagher
The Maynard School, Devon	www.maynard.co.uk	£3,756	–	Ms B. Hughes
Merchant Taylors' Boys' School, Merseyside	www.merchanttaylors.com	£3,373	–	D. Cook
Merchant Taylors' Girls' School, Merseyside	www.merchanttaylors.com	£3,373	–	Mrs L. Robinson
Merchant Taylors' School, Middx	www.mtsn.org.uk	£6,935	–	S. Everson
Mill Hill School, London NW7	www.millhill.org.uk	£5,948	£9,398	Dr D. Luckett
Millfield, Somerset	www.millfieldschool.com	£7,270	£10,795	C. Considine
Milton Abbey School, Dorset	www.miltonabbey.co.uk	£7,800	£10,400	M. Bashaarat
Moira House Girls School, E. Sussex	www.moirahouse.co.uk	£5,010	£9,205	J. Sheridan
Monkton Combe School, Somerset	www.monktoncombeschool.com	£6,188	£9,776	R. Backhouse
More House School, London SW1	www.morehouse.org.uk	£5,300	–	Mrs A. Leach
Moreton Hall, Shrops	www.moretonhall.org	£8,030	£9,740	J. Forster
Mount St Mary's College, Derbys	www.msmcollege.com	–	£8,369	L. McKell
The Mount School, London NW7	www.mountschool.com	£4,150	–	Ms C. Cozens
The Mount School, N. Yorks	www.mountschoolyork.co.uk	£5,355	£8,475	Ms J. Lodrick
New Hall School, Essex	www.newhallschool.co.uk	£5,583	£8,571	Mrs K. Jeffrey
Newcastle School for Boys, Tyne and Wear	www.newcastleschool.co.uk	£3,765	–	D. Tickner
Newcastle-under-Lyme School, Staffs	www.nuls.org.uk	£3,493	–	N. Rugg
The Newcastle upon Tyne Church High School, Tyne and Wear	www.churchhigh.com	£3,799	–	Mrs J. Gatenby
North Cestrian Grammar School, Cheshire	www.ncgs.co.uk	£2,992	–	L. Bergin
North London Collegiate School, Middx	www.nlcs.org.uk	£5,543	–	Mrs B. McCabe
Northampton High School, Northants	www.northamptonhigh.gdst.net	£4,116	–	Mrs S. Dixon
Northwood College, Middx	www.northwoodcollege.co.uk	£4,750	–	Miss J. Pain
Norwich High School, Norfolk	www.norwichhigh.gdst.net	£3,897	–	J. Morrow
Norwich School, Norfolk	www.norwich-school.org.uk	£4,389	–	S. Griffiths
Notre Dame Senior School, Surrey	www.notredame.co.uk	£4,675	–	D. Plummer
Notting Hill and Ealing High School, London W13	www.nhehs.gdst.net	£4,994	–	Ms L. Hunt
Nottingham Girls' High School, Notts	www.nottinghamgirlshigh.gdst.net	£3,745	–	Mrs S. Gorham
Nottingham High School, Notts	www.nottinghamhigh.co.uk	£4,097	–	D. Fear
Oakham School, Rutland	www.oakham.rutland.sch.uk	£5,205	£7,985	N. Lashbrook
Ockbrook School, Derbys	www.ockbrooksch.co.uk	£3,250	£6,860	T. Brooksby
Oldham Hulme Grammar Schools, Lancs	www.ohgs.co.uk	£3,215	–	Dr P. Neeson
The Oratory School, Oxon	www.oratory.co.uk	£7,130	£9,845	C. Dytor
Oswestry School, Shrops	www.oswestryschool.org.uk	£4,470	£8,150	D. Robb
Oundle School, Northants	www.oundleschool.org.uk	–	£10,235	C. Bush
Our Lady of Sion School, W. Sussex	www.sionschool.org.uk	£3,604	–	M. Scullion
Our Lady's Abingdon Senior School, Oxon	www.olab.org.uk	£4,133	–	S. Oliver
Oxford High School, Oxon	www.oxfordhigh.gdst.net	£4,096	–	Mrs J. Carlisle
Padworth College, Berks	www.padworth.com	£4,550	£9,100	J. Aguilar
Palmers Green High School, London N21	www.pghs.co.uk	£4,250	–	Mrs C. Edmundson
Pangbourne College, Berks	www.pangbournecollege.com	£6,990	£9,885	T. Garnier
The Perse Upper School, Cambs	www.perse.co.uk	£4,817	–	E. Elliott
The Peterborough School, Cambs	www.thepeterboroughschool.co.uk	£4,352	–	A. Meadows
Pipers Corner School, Bucks	www.piperscorner.co.uk	£4,880	–	Mrs H. Ness-Gifford
Pitsford School, Northants	www.pitsfordschool.com	£3,949	–	N. Toone
Plymouth College, Devon	www.plymouthcollege.com	£3,085	–	Dr S. Wormleighton
Pocklington School, E. Yorks	www.pocklingtonschool.com	£4,150	£7,640	M. Ronan
Polam Hall School, Durham	www.polamhall.com	£4,070	£7,815	J. Moreland
Portland Place School, London W1	www.portland-place.co.uk	£5,750	–	T. Cook
The Portsmouth Grammar School, Hants	www.pgs.org.uk	£4,391	–	J. Priory
Portsmouth High School, Hants	www.portsmouthhigh.co.uk	£3,895	–	Mrs J. Prescott
Princess Helena College, Herts	www.princesshelenacollege.co.uk	£5,855	£8,450	Mrs J. Duncan

School	Website			Head
Princethorpe College, Warwicks	www.princethorpe.co.uk	£3,393	–	E. Hester
Prior Park College, Somerset	www.thepriorfoundation.com	£4,795	£8,875	J. Murphy-O'Connor
Prior's Field, Surrey	www.priorsfieldschool.com	£5,285	£8,525	Mrs J. Roseblade
The Purcell School, Herts	www.purcell-school.org	£8,259	£10,562	D. Thomas
Putney High School, London SW15	www.putneyhigh.gdst.net	£4,986	–	Dr D. Lodge
Queen Anne's School, Berks	www.qas.org.uk	£6,525	£9,615	Mrs J. Harrington
Queen Elizabeth's Grammar School, Lancs	www.qegsblackburn.com	£3,495	–	S. Corns
Queen Elizabeth's Hospital (QEH), Bristol	www.qehbristol.co.uk	£4,078	–	S. Holliday
Queen Margaret's School, N. Yorks	www.queenmargarets.com	£5,877	£9,275	Dr P. Silverwood
Queen Mary's School, N. Yorks	www.queenmarys.org	£5,040	–	Mrs S. Lewis-Beckett
Queen's College, London W1	www.qcl.org.uk	£5,305	–	Dr F. Ramsey
Queen's College, Somerset	www.queenscollege.org.uk	£5,280	£8,650	C. Alcock
Queen's Gate School, London SW7	www.queensgate.org.uk	£5,565	–	Mrs R. Kamaryc
The Queen's School, Cheshire	www.queens.cheshire.sch.uk	£3,800	–	Mrs E. Clark
Queenswood, Herts	www.queenswood.org	£7,890	£10,390	Mrs P. Edgar
Radley College, Oxon	www.radley.org.uk	–	£10,700	A. McPhail
Ratcliffe College, Leics	www.ratcliffe-college.co.uk	–	£7,456	G. Lloyd
The Read School, N. Yorks	www.readschool.co.uk	£3,376	£7,277	J. Sweetman
Reading Blue Coat School, Berks	www.rbcs.org.uk	£4,670	–	M. Windsor
The Red Maids' School, Bristol	www.redmaids.co.uk	£3,900	–	Mrs I. Tobias
Redland High School for Girls, Bristol	www.redlandhigh.com	£3,695	–	Mrs C. Bateson
Reed's School, Surrey	www.reeds.surrey.sch.uk	£7,045	£9,320	D. Jarrett
Reigate Grammar School, Surrey	www.reigategrammar.org	£5,160	–	S. Fenton
Rendcomb College, Glos	www.rendcombcollege.org.uk	£6,675	£9,185	R. Martin
Repton School, Derbys	www.repton.org.uk	£7,528	£10,146	R. Holroyd
Rishworth School, W. Yorks	www.rishworth-school.co.uk	£3,690	£7,805	A. Gloag
Roedean School, E. Sussex	www.roedean.co.uk	£6,300	£10,870	O. Blond
Rossall School, Lancs	www.rossallschool.org.uk	£3,980	£10,980	Ms E. Purves
The Royal Grammar School, Surrey	www.rgs-guildford.co.uk	£4,890	–	Dr J. Cox
Royal Grammar School, Tyne and Wear	www.rgs.newcastle.sch.uk	£3,570	–	Dr B. Trafford
RGS Worcester, Worcs	www.rgsw.org.uk	£3,468	–	A. Rattue
The Royal High School Bath, Somerset	www.royalhighbath.gdst.net	£3,895	£8,095	Mrs R. Dougall
The Royal Hospital School, Suffolk	www.royalhospitalschool.org	£4,592	£8,479	J. Lockwood
The Royal Masonic School for Girls, Herts	www.royalmasonic.herts.sch.uk	£4,900	£7,920	Mrs D. Rose
Royal Russell School, Surrey	www.royalrussell.co.uk	£5,095	£10,080	C. Hutchinson
The Royal School, Wolverhampton, W. Midlands	www.theroyalschool.co.uk	£4,199	£9,149	M. Heywood
Rugby School, Warwicks	www.rugbyschool.net	£6,535	£10,415	P. Derham
Ryde School with Upper Chine, Isle of Wight	www.rydeschool.org.uk	£3,735	–	M. Waldron
Rye St Antony, Oxon	www.ryestantony.co.uk	£3,485	£7,140	Miss A. Jones
St Albans High School for Girls, Herts	www.stahs.org.uk	£4,560	–	Mrs R. Martin
St Albans School, Herts	www.st-albans.herts.sch.uk	£5,098	–	A. Grant
Saint Augustine's Priory School, London W5	www.saintaugustinespriory.org.uk	£3,998	–	Mrs S. Raffray
St Bede's College, Greater Manchester	www.stbedescollege.co.uk	£3,150	–	D. Kearney
St Bees School, Cumbria	www.st-bees-school.org	£5,295	£9,985	J. Davies
St Benedict's School, London W5	www.stbenedicts.org.uk	£4,450	–	C. Cleugh
St Catherine's School, Surrey	www.stcatherines.info	£5,375	–	Mrs A. Phillips
St Catherine's School, Middx	www.stcatherineschool.co.uk	£3,995	–	Sister P. Thomas
St Christopher School, Herts	www.stchris.co.uk	£5,400	£9,550	R. Palmer
St Columba's College, Herts	www.stcolumbascollege.org	£4,185	–	D. Buxton
St Dominic's High School for Girls, Staffs	www.stdominicsschool.co.uk	£3,875	–	H. Trump
St Dominic's Priory School, Staffs	www.stdominicspriory.co.uk	£3,414	£5,414	Mrs M. Adamson
St Dunstan's College, London SE6	www.stdunstans.org.uk	£4,874	–	Mrs J. Davies
St Edmund's College, Herts	www.stedmundscollege.org	£5,315	£8,663	P. Durn
St Edmund's School, Kent	www.stedmunds.org.uk	£6,018	£9,365	Mrs L. Moelwyn-Hughes
St Edward's, Oxford, Oxon	www.stedwardsoxford.org	£8,557	£10,694	S. Jones

School	Website			Head
St Edward's School, Glos	www.stedwards.co.uk	£4,508	–	Mrs P. Clayfield
Saint Felix School, Suffolk	www.stfelix.co.uk	£4,660	£8,140	Miss M. D'Alcorn
St Gabriel's, Berks	www.stgabriels.co.uk	£4,735	–	A. Jones
St George's College, Surrey	www.stgeorgesweybridge.com	£5,380	–	J. Peake
St George's School, W. Midlands	www.sgse.co.uk	£3,255	–	G. Neal
St George's, Ascot, Berks	www.stgeorges-ascot.org.uk	£6,525	£10,020	Mrs R. Owens
St Helen & St Katharine, Oxon	www.shsk.org.uk	£4,340	–	Miss R. Edbrooke
St Helen's School, Middx	www.sthn.co.uk	£4,790	–	Dr M. Short
St James Senior Boys' School, Surrey	www.stjamesboys.co.uk	£4,800	£6,850 Mon–Fri	D. Brazier
St James Senior Girls' School, London W14	www.stjamesgirls.co.uk	£5,050	–	Mrs L. Hyde
St John's College, Hants	www.stjohnscollege.co.uk	£3,400	£7,350	G. Best
St John's School, Surrey	www.stjohnsleatherhead.co.uk	£6,960	£8,790	M. Collier
St Joseph's College, Suffolk	www.stjos.co.uk	£4,365	£8,970	Mrs D. Clarke
St Joseph's College, Berks	www.sjcr.org.uk	£3,960	–	A. Colpus
St Lawrence College, Kent	www.slcuk.com	£5,479	£9,601	A. Spencer
St Leonards-Mayfield School, E. Sussex	www.mayfieldgirls.org	£5,975	£9,550	Miss A. Beary
St Margaret's School, Herts	www.stmargaretsbushey.co.uk	£4,770	£8,889	Mrs L. Crighton
St Margaret's School, NW3	www.st-margarets.co.uk	£3,846	–	M. Webster
St Martha's, Herts	www.st-marthas.co.uk	£4,180	–	M. Burke
Saint Martin's, W. Midlands	www.saintmartins-school.com	£3,665	–	Mrs J. Carwithen
St Mary's College, Berks	www.stmarys.ac	£3,241	–	M. Kennedy
St Mary's Calne, Wilts	www.stmaryscalne.org	£8,050	£10,917	Dr F. Kirk
St Mary's School, Cambs	www.stmaryscambridge.co.uk	£4,507	£9,708	Miss C. Avery
St Mary's School, Essex	www.stmaryscolchester.org.uk	£3,780	–	Mrs H. Vipond
St Mary's School Ascot, Merseyside	www.st-marys-ascot.co.uk	£7,460	£10,480	Mrs M. Breen
St Mary's School, Bucks	www.stmarysschool.co.uk	£4,652	–	Mrs J. Ross
St Mary's School, Dorset	www.st-marys-shaftesbury.co.uk	£5,952	£8,660	R. James
St Nicholas' School, Hants	www.st-nicholas.hants.sch.uk	£4,091	–	R. James
St Paul's Girls' School, London W6	www.spgs.org	£7,056	–	Ms C. Farr
St Paul's School, London SW13	www.stpaulsschool.org.uk	£6,951	–	Prof. M. Bailey
St Peter's School, York, N. Yorks	www.stpetersyork.org.uk	£5,130	£8,395	L. Winkley
St Swithun's School, Hants	www.stswithuns.com	£5,885	£9,430	Ms J. Gandee
St Teresa's Effingham, Surrey	www.st-teresas.com	£4,995	£8,695	M. Farmer
Scarborough College, N. Yorks	www.scarboroughcollege.co.uk	£4,205	£6,898	Mrs I. Nixon
Seaford College, W. Sussex	www.seaford.org	£5,950	£9,300	J. Green
Sedbergh School, Cumbria	www.sedberghschool.org	£7,173	£9,734	A. Fleck
Sevenoaks School, Kent	www.sevenoaksschool.org	£7,299	£11,136	Mrs C. Ricks
Shebbear College, Devon	www.shebbearcollege.co.uk	£3,800	£7,415	S. Weale
Sheffield High School, S. Yorks	www.sheffieldhighschool.org.uk	£3,642	–	Mrs V. Dunsford
Sherborne Girls, Dorset	www.sherborne.com	£7,250	£9,980	Mrs J. Dwyer
Sherborne School, Dorset	www.sherborne.org	£8,545	£10,555	C. Davis
Shiplake College, Oxon	www.shiplake.org.uk	£6,210	£9,205	A. Davies
Shrewsbury High School, Shrops	www.shrewsburyhigh.gdst.net	£3,884	–	M. Getty
Shrewsbury School, Shrops	www.shrewsbury.org.uk	£7,100	£10,140	M. Turner
Sibford School, Oxon	www.sibfordschool.co.uk	£4,151	£8,065	M. Goodwin
Sidcot School, Somerset	www.sidcot.org.uk	£5,050	£9,070	I. Kilpatrick
Silcoates School, W. Yorks	www.silcoates.org.uk	£4,092	–	D. Wideman
Solihull School, W. Midlands	www.solsch.org.uk	£3,633	–	D. Lloyd
South Hampstead High School, London N3	www.shhs.gdst.net	£4,833	–	Miss H. Pike
Stafford Grammar School, Staffs	www.staffordgrammar.co.uk	£3,666	–	M. Darley
Stamford High School, Lincs	www.ses.lincs.sch.uk	£4,343	£7,983	S. Roberts
Stamford School, Lincs	www.ses.lincs.sch.uk	£4,343	£7,983	S. Roberts
The Stephen Perse Foundation, Cambs	www.stephenperse.com	£4,835	–	Miss P. Kelleher
Stockport Grammar School, Cheshire	www.stockportgrammar.co.uk	£3,327	–	A. Chicken
Stonar School, Wilts	www.stonarschool.com	£4,795	£8,655	T. Nutt
Stonyhurst College, Lancs	www.stonyhurst.ac.uk	£5,464	£9,813	A. Johnson
Stover School, Devon	www.stover.co.uk	£5,720	£6,520	Mrs S. Bradley
Stowe School, Bucks	www.stowe.co.uk	£7,500	£10,325	Dr A. Wallersteiner
Streatham & Clapham High School, London SW16	www.schs.gdst.net	£4,775	–	Dr M. Sachania
Sunderland High School, Tyne and Wear	www.sunderlandhigh.co.uk	£2,995	–	Dr A. Slater
Surbiton High School, Surrey	www.surbitonhigh.com	£4,701	–	Ms E. Haydon
Sutton High School, Surrey	www.suttonhigh.co.uk	£4,695	–	Mrs K. Crouch

Sutton Valence School, Kent	www.svs.org.uk	£6,215	£9,470	B. Grindlay
Sydenham High School, London SE26	www.sydenhamhighschool.gdst.net	£4,633	–	Mrs K. Pullen
Talbot Heath, Dorset	www.talbotheath.org	£3,882	–	Mrs A. Holloway
Taunton School, Somerset	www.tauntonschool.co.uk	£5,495	£10,280	Dr J. Newton
Tettenhall College, W. Midlands	www.tettenhallcollege.co.uk	£4,832	£8,506	D. Williams
Thetford Grammar School, Norfolk	www.thetgram.norfolk.sch.uk	£3,876	–	G. Price
Thornton College, Bucks	www.thorntoncollege.com	£3,975	£6,510	Miss A. Williams
Tonbridge School, Kent	www.tonbridge-school.co.uk	£8,534	£11,379	T. Haynes
Tormead School, Surrey	www.tormeadschool.org.uk	£4,380	–	Mrs C. Foord
Trent College, Notts	www.trentcollege.net	£4,996	£8,835	Mrs G. Dixon
Tring Park School for the Performing Arts, Herts	www.tringpark.com	£6,900	£10,330	S. Anderson
Trinity School, Surrey	www.trinity-school.org	£4,572	–	M. Bishop
Trinity School, Devon	www.trinityschool.co.uk	£3,645	£7,960	T. Waters
Truro High School for Girls, Cornwall	www.trurohigh.co.uk	£3,739	–	Mrs M. Smith
Truro School, Cornwall	www.truroschool.com	£4,070	£7,560	A. Gordon-Brown
Tudor Hall, Oxon	www.tudorhallschool.com	£6,202	£9,730	Miss W. Griffiths
University College School, London NW3	www.ucs.org.uk	£5,720	–	M. Beard
Uppingham School, Rutland	www.uppingham.co.uk	£7,366	£10,523	R. Harman
Walthamstow Hall, Kent	www.walthamstow-hall.co.uk	£5,470	–	Mrs J. Milner
Warminster School, Wilts	www.warminsterschool.org.uk	£4,560	£8,530	M. Mortimer
Warwick School, Warwicks	www.warwickschool.org	£3,645	£7,779	A. Lock
Welbeck - The Defence Sixth Form College, Leics	www.dsfc.ac.uk	–	–	J. Middleton
Wellingborough School, Northants	www.wellingboroughschool.org	£4,362	–	G. Bowe
Wellington College, Berks	www.wellingtoncollege.org.uk	£8,110	£10,980	Dr A. Seldon
Wellington School, Somerset	www.wellington-school.org.uk	£4,295	£8,614	M. Reader
Wells Cathedral School, Somerset	www.wellscathedralschool.org	£5,334	£8,926	Mrs E. Cairncross
West Buckland School, Devon	www.westbuckland.devon.sch.uk	£4,250	£7,880	J. Vick
Westfield School, Tyne and Wear	www.westfield.newcastle.sch.uk	£3,820	–	Mrs M. Farndale
Westminster School, London SW1	www.westminster.org.uk	£8,130	£10,830	Dr M. Spurr
Westonbirt School, Glos	www.westonbirt.org	£6,960	£10,995	Mrs N. Dangerfield
Whitgift School, Surrey	www.whitgift.co.uk	£5,452	£10,500	Dr C. Barnett
Wimbledon High School, London SW19	www.wimbledonhigh.gdst.net	£5,008	–	Mrs H. Hanbury
Winchester College, Hants	www.winchestercollege.org	–	£11,250	R. Townsend
Windermere School, Cumbria	www.windermereschool.co.uk	£5,115	–	I. Lavender
Wisbech Grammar School, Cambs	www.wisbechgrammar.com	£3,760	–	N. Hammond
Withington Girls' School, Greater Manchester	www.wgs.org	£3,480	–	Mrs S. Marks
Woldingham School, Surrey	www.woldinghamschool.co.uk	£6,705	£10,815	Mrs J. Triffitt
Wolverhampton Grammar School, W. Midlands	www.wgs.org.uk	£3,998	–	Mrs K. Crewe-Read
Woodbridge School, Suffolk	www.woodbridge.suffolk.sch.uk	£4,800	£8,900	Mr S. Cole
Woodhouse Grove School, W. Yorks	www.woodhousegrove.co.uk	£3,795	£7,710	D. Humphreys
Worksop College, Notts	www.wsnl.co.uk	£5,250	£8,280	G. Horgan
Worth School, W. Sussex	www.worthschool.co.uk	£6,980	£9,650	G. Carminati
Wrekin College, Shrops	www.wrekincollege.com	£5,420	£8,940	R. Chapman
Wychwood School, Oxon	www.wychwoodschool.org	£4,400	£6,870	Mrs A. Johnson
Wycliffe College, Glos	www.wycliffe.co.uk	£5,850	£9,185	Mrs M. Burnet Ward
Wycombe Abbey School, Bucks	www.wycombeabbey.com	£8,325	£11,100	Mrs R. Wilkinson
Wykeham House School, Hants	www.wykehamhouse.com	£3,800	–	Mrs L. Clarke
Yarm School, Cleveland	www.yarmschool.org	£3,758	–	D. Dunn
The Yehudi Menuhin School, Surrey	www.yehudimenuhinschool.co.uk	–	–	Dr R. Hillier

WALES

The Cathedral School Llandaff, Cardiff	www.cathedral-school.co.uk	£3,649	–	S. Morris
Christ College, Brecon	www.christcollegebrecon.com	£5,290	£8,170	Mrs E. Taylor
Haberdashers' Monmouth School for Girls, Monmouth	www.habs-monmouth.org	£4,290	£8,820	Mrs C. Pascoe
Howell's School Llandaff, Cardiff	www.howells-cardiff.gdst.net	£3,971	–	Mrs S. Davis
Monmouth School, Monmouth	www.habs-monmouth.org	£4,591	£8,820	Dr S. Connors
Rougemont School, Newport	www.rougemontschool.co.uk	£3,820	–	Dr J. Tribbick
Ruthin School, Ruthin	www.ruthinschool.co.uk	£3,917	£7,833	T. Belfield
Rydal Penrhos School, Colwyn Bay	www.rydalpenrhos.com	£4,875	£9,715	P. Lee-Browne

SCOTLAND

Dollar Academy, Dollar	www.dollaracademy.org.uk	£3,555	£4,668	D. Knapman
The High School of Dundee, Dundee	www.highschoolofdundee.org.uk	£3,555	–	Dr J. Halliday
The Edinburgh Academy, Edinburgh	www.edinburghacademy.org.uk	£4,042	–	M. Longmore
Fettes College, Edinburgh	www.fettes.com	£7,390	£9,720	M. Spens
George Heriot's School, Edinburgh	www.george-heriots.com	£3,433	–	G. Doodes
The Glasgow Academy, Glasgow	www.theglasgowacademy.org.uk	£3,497	–	P. Brodie
The High School of Glasgow, Glasgow	www.glasgowhigh.com	£3,535	–	C. Mair
Glenalmond College, Perth	www.glenalmondcollege.co.uk	£6,655	£9,765	G. Woods
Hutchesons' Grammar School, Glasgow	www.hutchesons.org	£3,410	–	Dr K. Greig
Kelvinside Academy, Glasgow	www.kelvinsideacademy.org.uk	£3,610	–	R. Karling
Kilgraston, Bridge of Earn	www.kilgraston.com	£4,975	£8,485	F. Thompson
Lomond School, Helensburgh	www.lomondschool.com	£3,360	–	S. Mills
Loretto School, Musselburgh	www.loretto.com	–	£9,530	Ms E. Logan
The Mary Erskine School, Edinburgh	www.esms.org.uk	£3,242	£6,504	J. Gray
Merchiston Castle School, Edinburgh	www.merchiston.co.uk	£6,730	£9,155	A. Hunter
Morrison's Academy, Crieff	www.morrisonsacademy.org	£3,613	–	G. Pengelley
Robert Gordon's College, Aberdeen	www.rgc.aberdeen.sch.uk	£3,728	–	H. Ouston
St Aloysius' College, Glasgow	www.staloysius.org	£3,216	–	J. Browne
St Columba's School, Kilmacolm	www.st-columbas.org	£3,373	–	D. Girdwood
St Leonards School, St Andrews	www.stleonards-fife.org	£3,910	£9,400	Dr M. Carslaw
St Margaret's School for Girls, Aberdeen	www.st-margaret.aberdeen.sch.uk	£3,608	–	Dr J. Land
Stewart's Melville College, Edinburgh	www.esms.org.uk	£3,242	£6,504	J. Gray
Strathallan School, Perth	www.strathallan.co.uk	£6,348	£9,355	B. Thompson

NORTHERN IRELAND

Bangor Grammar School, Bangor	www.bangorgrammarschool.com	–	–	Mrs E. Huddleson
Belfast Royal Academy, Belfast	www.belfastroyalacademy.com	£47	–	J. Dickson
Campbell College, Belfast	www.campbellcollege.co.uk	£767	£3,885	R. Robinson
The Royal School Dungannon, Dungannon	www.royaldungannon.com	£50	£2,750	D. Burnett

CHANNEL ISLANDS

Elizabeth College, Guernsey	www.elizabethcollege.gg	£3,010	–	G. Hartley
Victoria College, Jersey	www.victoriacollege.je	£1,528	–	A. Watkins

NATIONAL ACADEMIES OF SCHOLARSHIP

The national academies are self-governing bodies whose members are elected as a result of achievement and distinction in the academy's field. Within their discipline, the academies provide advice, support education and exceptional scholars, stimulate debate, promote UK research worldwide and collaborate with international counterparts.

Three of the national academies – the Royal Society, the British Academy and the Royal Academy of Engineering – receive grant-in-aid funding from the Department for Business, Innovation and Skills (BIS). The Academy of Medical Sciences receives core funding from the Department of Health, and the Royal Society of Edinburgh is aided by funds provided by the Scottish government. In addition to government funding, the national academies generate additional income from donations, membership contributions, trading and investments.

SCIENCE BUDGET ALLOCATIONS
£ thousands

Royal Society ■
British Academy ▨
Royal Academy of Engineering ▨

Source: BIS/ The Allocation of Science and Research Funding

ACADEMY OF MEDICAL SCIENCES (1998)
41 Portland Place, London W1B 1QH
T 020-3176 2150 W www.acmedsci.ac.uk

Founded in 1998, the Academy of Medical Sciences is the independent body in the UK representing the diversity of medical science. The Academy seeks to improve health through research, as well as to promote medical science and its translation into benefits for society.

The academy is self-governing and receives funding from a variety of sources, including the fellowship, charitable donations, government and industry.

Fellows are elected from a broad range of medical sciences: biomedical, clinical and population based. The academy includes in its remit veterinary medicine, dentistry, nursing, medical law, economics, sociology and ethics. Elections are from nominations put forward by existing fellows.

As at May 2014 there were 1,092 fellows and 36 honorary fellows.
President, Prof. Sir John Tooke, PMEDSCI
Executive Director, Dr Helen Munn

BRITISH ACADEMY (1902)
10–11 Carlton House Terrace, London SW1Y 5AH
T 020-7969 5200 W www.britac.ac.uk

The British Academy is an independent, self-governing learned society for the promotion of the humanities and social sciences. It was founded in 1901 and granted a royal charter in 1902. The British Academy supports advanced academic research and is a channel for the government's support of research in those disciplines.

The fellows are scholars who have attained distinction in one of the branches of study that the academy exists to promote. Candidates must be nominated by existing fellows. There are around 930 fellows, 20 honorary fellows and 300 corresponding fellows overseas.
President, Lord Stern of Brentford
Chief Executive, Dr Robin Jackson

ROYAL ACADEMY OF ENGINEERING (1976)
3 Carlton House Terrace, London SW1Y 5DG
T 020-7766 0600 W www.raeng.org.uk

The Royal Academy of Engineering was established as the Fellowship of Engineering in 1976. It was granted a royal charter in 1983 and its present title in 1992. It is an independent, self-governing body whose object is the pursuit, encouragement and maintenance of excellence in the whole field of engineering, in order to promote advancement of the science, art and practice of engineering for the benefit of the public.

Election to the fellowship is by invitation only, from nominations supported by the body of fellows. As at May 2014 there were 1,370 fellows, 42 honorary fellows and 102 international fellows. The Duke of Edinburgh is the senior fellow and the Princess Royal and the Duke of Kent are both royal fellows.
President, Sir John Parker, GBE, FRENG
Chief Executive, Philip Greenish, CBE

ROYAL SOCIETY (1660)
6–9 Carlton House Terrace, London SW1Y 5AG
T 020-7451 2500 W www.royalsociety.org

The Royal Society is an independent academy promoting the natural and applied sciences. Founded in 1660 and granted a royal charter in 1662, the society has three roles: as the UK academy of science, as a learned society and as a funding agency. It is an independent, self-governing body under a royal charter, promoting and advancing all fields of physical and biological sciences, of mathematics and engineering, medical and agricultural sciences and their application.

Fellows are elected for their contributions to science, both in fundamental research resulting in greater understanding, and also in leading and directing scientific and technological progress in industry and research establishments. Each year up to 52 new fellows, who must be citizens or residents of the Commonwealth or Ireland, and up to ten foreign members may be elected. In addition one honorary fellow may also be elected annually from those not eligible for election as fellows or foreign members. As at May 2014, there were 1,430 fellows, 165 foreign members and six honorary members covering all scientific disciplines. The Queen is the patron of the Royal Society, and there are also six royal fellows.

President, Sir Paul Nurse, PRS

Executive Director, Dr Julie Maxton

ROYAL SOCIETY OF EDINBURGH (1783)

22–26 George Street, Edinburgh FH7 2PQ

T 0131-240 5000 W www.royalsoced.org.uk

The Royal Society of Edinburgh (RSE) is an educational charity and Scotland's national academy. An independent body with charitable status, its multidisciplinary membership represents a knowledge resource for the people of Scotland. Granted its royal charter in 1783 for the 'advancement of learning and useful knowledge', the society organises conferences, debates and lectures; conducts independent inquiries; facilitates international collaboration and showcases the country's research and development capabilities; provides educational activities for primary and secondary school students; and awards prizes and medals. The society also awards over £2m annually to Scotland's top researchers and entrepreneurs working in Scotland.

As at May 2014 there were 1,585 fellows, comprising 1,452 fellows, 67 honorary fellows and 66 corresponding fellows overseas.

President, Prof. Dame Jocelyn Bell Burnell, DBE, FRS, FRSE

General Secretary, Prof. Alan Alexander, OBE, FRSE

PRIVATELY FUNDED ARTS ACADEMIES

The Royal Academy and the Royal Scottish Academy support the visual arts community in the UK, hold educational events and promote interest in the arts. They are entirely privately funded through contributions by 'friends' (regular donors who receive benefits such as free entry, previews and magazines), bequests, corporate donations and exhibitions.

ROYAL ACADEMY OF ARTS (1768)

Burlington House, Piccadilly, London W1J 0BD

T 020-7300 8000 W www.royalacademy.org.uk

Founded by George III in 1768, the Royal Academy of Arts is an independent, self-governing society devoted to the encouragement and promotion of the fine arts.

Membership of the academy is limited to 80 academicians, all of whom are either painters, engravers, printmakers, draughtsmen, sculptors or architects. There must always be at least 14 sculptors, 12 architects and eight printmakers among the academicians. Candidates must be professionally active in the UK and are nominated and elected by the existing academicians. The members are known as royal academicians (RAs) and are responsible for both the governance and direction of the academy. When RAs reach the age of 75, they become senior academicians and can no longer serve as officers or on the committees.

The title of honorary academician is awarded to a small number of distinguished artists who are not resident in the UK; as at April 2014, there were 27 honorary academicians. Unlike the RAs, they do not take part in the governance of the academy and are unable to vote.

President, Christopher Le Brun, PRA

Secretary & Chief Executive, Dr Charles Saumarez Smith, CBE

ROYAL SCOTTISH ACADEMY (1838)

The Mound, Edinburgh EH2 2EL

T 0131-225 6671 W www.royalscottishacademy.org

Founded in 1826 and led by a body of academicians comprising eminent artists and architects, the Royal Scottish Academy (RSA) is an independent voice for cultural advocacy and one of the largest supporters of artists in Scotland. The Academy administers a number of scholarships, awards and residencies and has a historic collection of Scottish artworks, recognised by the Scottish government as being of national significance. The Academy is independent from local or national government funding, relying instead on bequests, legacies, sponsorship and earned income.

Academicians have to be Scots by birth or domicile, and are elected from the disciplines of art and architecure following nominations put forward by the existing membership. There are also a small number of honorary academicians – distinguished artists and architects, writers, historians and musicians – who do not have to be Scottish. As at May 2014 there were 104 academicians and 29 honorary academicians.

President, Arthur Watson, PRSA

Secretary, Marion Smith, RSA

RESEARCH COUNCILS

The government funds basic and applied civil science research, mostly through seven research councils, which are established under royal charter and supported by the Department for Business, Innovation and Skills (BIS). Research Councils UK is the strategic partnership of these seven councils* (for further information *see* W www.rcuk.ac.uk). The councils support research and training in universities and other higher education and research facilities.

The science budget, administered by BIS, is the main source of public sector funding for research councils, with further public funds provided through the Large Facilities Capital Fund and the Higher Education Innovation Fund. Additional funds may also be provided by other government departments, devolved administrations, the European Commission and other international bodies. The councils also receive income for research specifically commissioned by government departments and the private sector, and income from charitable sources.

GOVERNMENT SCIENCE BUDGET
£ thousand

	2013–14	2014–15
Arts and Humanities Research Council	98,522	98,521
Biotechnology and Biological Sciences Research Council	391,271	391,271
Economic and Social Research Council	166,186	166,186
Engineering and Physical Sciences Research Council	781,150	780,150
Medical Research Council	639,645	649,370
Natural Environment Research Council	356,929	347,929
Science and Technology Facilities Council*	516,627	527,708
Large Facilities Capital Fund	47,769	128,132
Higher Education Innovation Fund†	150,000	150,000

* Includes cross-council facilities and international subscriptions, which are managed by STFC on behalf of all research councils
† Includes £37m from the Higher Education Funding Council for England (HEFCE)
Source: BIS – *The Allocation of Science and Research Funding 2011/12–2014/15*

ARTS AND HUMANITIES RESEARCH COUNCIL*
Polaris House, North Star Avenue, Swindon SN2 1FL
T 01793-416000 W www.ahrc.ac.uk

The AHRC is the successor organisation to the Arts and Humanities Research Board and was incorporated by royal charter and established in 2005. It provides funding for postgraduate training and research in the arts and humanities; in any one year, the AHRC makes approximately 700 research awards and around 2,000 postgraduate scholarships. Awards are made after a rigorous peer review system, which ensures the quality of applications.
Chair, Prof. Sir Drummond Bone, FRSE
Chief Executive, Prof. Rick Rylance, FRSA

BIOTECHNOLOGY AND BIOLOGICAL SCIENCES RESEARCH COUNCIL*
Polaris House, North Star Avenue, Swindon SN2 1UH
T 01793-413200 W www.bbsrc.ac.uk

Established by royal charter in 1994, the BBSRC is the UK funding agency for research in the non-clinical life sciences. It funds research into how all living organisms function and behave, benefiting the agriculture, food, health, pharmaceutical and chemical sectors. To deliver its mission, the BBSRC supports research and training in universities and research centres throughout the UK, including providing strategic research grants to the institutes listed below.
Chair, Prof. Sir Tom Blundell
Chief Executive, Prof. Jackie Hunter

INSTITUTES
BABRAHAM INSTITUTE, Babraham Hall, Babraham, Cambridge CB22 3AT T 01223-496000
Director, Prof. Michael Wakelam
GENOME ANALYSIS CENTRE, Norwich Research Park, Colney, Norwich NR4 7UH T 01603-450861
Director, Dr Mario Caccamo
INSTITUTE FOR BIOLOGICAL, ENVIRONMENTAL AND RURAL SCIENCES (ABERYSTWYTH UNIVERSITY), Penglais, Aberystwyth SY23 3DA T 01970-622316
Director (interim), Prof. Chris Thomas
INSTITUTE OF FOOD RESEARCH, Norwich Research Park, Colney Lane, Norwich NR4 7UA T 01603-255000
Director, Prof. David Boxer
JOHN INNES CENTRE, Norwich Research Park, Colney, Norwich NR4 7UH T 01603-450000
Director, Prof. Dale Sanders
PIRBRIGHT INSTITUTE, Pirbright Laboratory, Ash Road, Pirbright, Surrey GU24 0NF T 01483-232441
Director, Prof. John Fazakerley
ROSLIN INSTITUTE (UNIVERSITY OF EDINBURGH), Roslin Biocentre, Roslin, Midlothian EH25 9PS T 0131-651 9100
Director, Prof. David Hume
ROTHAMSTED RESEARCH, Harpenden, Herts AL5 2JQ T 01582-763133
Director, Prof. Achim Dobermann

ECONOMIC AND SOCIAL RESEARCH COUNCIL*
Polaris House, North Star Avenue, Swindon SN2 1UJ
T 01793-413000 E comms@esrc.ac.uk
W www.esrc.ac.uk

The purpose of the ESRC is to promote and support research and postgraduate training in the social sciences. It also provides advice, disseminates knowledge and promotes public understanding in these areas. The ESRC provides core funding to the centres listed below. Further information can be obtained on the ESRC website, including details of centres it funds in collaboration with other research councils.
Chair, Dr Alan Gillespie, CBE
Chief Executive, Prof. Paul Boyle

RESEARCH CENTRES
CENTRE FOR CLIMATE CHANGE, ECONOMICS AND POLICY, LSE, Houghton Street, London WC2A 2AE T 020-7107 5433
Directors, Dr Simon Dietz; Prof. Andy Gouldson

CENTRE FOR COMPETITIVE ADVANTAGE IN THE GLOBAL ECONOMY, Department of Economics, University of Warwick, Coventry CV4 7AL **T** 024-7615 1176
Director, Prof. Nick Crafts
CENTRE FOR CORPUS APPROACHES TO SOCIAL SCIENCE (CASS), FASS Building, Lancaster University, Lancaster LA1 4YW **E** CASS@lancs.ac.uk
Director, Prof. Tony McEnery
CENTRE FOR ECONOMIC PERFORMANCE, LSE, Houghton Street, London WC2A 2AE **T** 020-7955 7673
Director, Prof. John Van Reenen
CENTRE FOR LANGUAGE AND COMMUNICATIVE DEVELOPMENT, University of Manchester, Manchester M13 9PL
Director, Prof. Elena Lieven
CENTRE FOR LONGITUDINAL STUDIES, Institute of Education, 20 Bedford Way, London WC1H 0AL **T** 020-7612 6875
Director, Prof. Jane Elliott
CENTRE FOR MACROECONOMICS, LSE, Houghton Street, London WC2A 2AE **T** 020-3486 2818
Directors, Prof. Wouter Den Haan; Prof. Morten Ravn
CENTRE FOR MICRODATA METHODS AND PRACTICE, Institute for Fiscal Studies, 7 Ridgmount Street, London WC1E 7AE **T** 020-7291 4800
Director, Andrew Chesher
CENTRE OF MICROECONOMIC ANALYSIS OF PUBLIC POLICY, Institute for Fiscal Studies, 7 Ridgmount Street, London WC1E 7AE **T** 020-7291 4800
Director, Prof. Richard Blundell
CENTRE ON DYNAMICS OF ETHNICITY, University of Manchester, Oxford Road, Manchester M13 9PL **T** 0161-275 4579
Director, Prof. James Nazroo
DEAFNESS, COGNITION AND LANGUAGE RESEARCH CENTRE, 49 Gordon Square, London WC1H 0PD **T** 020-7679 8679
Director, Prof. Bencie Woll
ENTERPRISE RESEARCH CENTRE, Warwick Business School, University of Warwick, Coventry CV4 7AL **T** 024-7652 8433
Director, Prof. Stephen Roper
NATIONAL CENTRE FOR RESEARCH METHODS, Social Sciences, Room 4139, Murray Building, University of Southampton, Southampton SO17 1BJ **T** 0238-059 4539
Director, Prof. Patrick Sturgis
SYSTEMIC RISK CENTRE, LSE, Houghton Street, London WC2A 2AE **E** scr@lse.ac.uk
Directors, Dr Jon Danielsson; Dr Jean-Pierre Zigrand
TAX ADMINISTRATION RESEARCH CENTRE, University of Exeter, Streatham Court, Rennes Drive, Exeter EX4 4ST **T** 01392-726286
Director, Prof. Gareth Myles
UK ENERGY RESEARCH CENTRE, 58 Princes Gate, Exhibition Road, London SW7 2PG **T** 020-7594 1574
Executive Director, Prof. John Loughead, OBE, FRENG

ENGINEERING AND PHYSICAL SCIENCES RESEARCH COUNCIL*

Polaris House, North Star Avenue, Swindon SN2 1ET
T 01793-444000 **W** www.epsrc.ac.uk

Formed in 1994 by royal charter, the EPSRC is the UK government's main agency for funding research and training in engineering and the physical sciences in universities and other organisations throughout the UK. It also provides advice, disseminates knowledge and promotes public understanding in these areas.
Chair, Paul Golby, FRENG
Chief Executive, Prof. Philip Nelson, FRENG

MEDICAL RESEARCH COUNCIL*

Polaris House, North Star Avenue, Swindon SN2 1FL
T 01793-416200 **W** www.mrc.ac.uk

The MRC is a publicly funded organisation dedicated to improving human health. The MRC supports research across the entire spectrum of medical sciences, in universities, hospitals, centres and institutes.
Chair, Donald Brydon, CBE
Chief Executive, Prof. Sir John Savill
Chair, Infections and Immunity Board, Prof. Paul Moss
Chair, Molecular and Cellular Medicine Board, Prof. Patrick Maxwell
Chair, Neurosciences and Mental Health Board, Prof. Hugh Perry
Chair, Population and Systems Medicine Board, Prof. David Lomas

MRC UNITS, CENTRES AND INSTITUTES
Anatomical Neuropharmacology Unit **W** www.mrc.ox.ac.uk
Asthma UK Centre in Allergic Mechanisms of Asthma **W** www.asthma-allergy.ac.uk
Behavioural and Clinical Neuroscience Institute (BCNI) **W** http://research.psychol.cam.ac.uk/~bcni
Biostatistics Unit **W** www.mrc-bsu.cam.ac.uk
Cancer Unit **W** www.mrc-cu.cam.ac.uk
Centre for Brain Ageing and Vitality **W** www.ncl.ac.uk/cbav
Centre for Cognitive Ageing and Cognitive Epidemiology **W** www.ccace.ed.ac.uk
Centre for Developmental Neurobiology **W** www.kcl.ac.uk/biohealth/research/divisions/devneuro
Centre for Drug Safety **W** www.liv.ac.uk/drug-safety
Centre for Environment and Health **W** www.environment-health.ac.uk
Centre for Genomics and Global Health **W** www.cggh.org
Centre for Immune Regulation **W** www.birmingham.ac.uk/research/activity/mds/centres/mrc-immune
Centre for Inflammation Research **W** www.cir.ed.ac.uk
Centre for Integrated Research into Musculoskeletal Ageing **W** www.cimauk.org
Centre for Medical Molecular Virology **W** www.ucl.ac.uk/infection-immunity/mrc_ucl-centre
Centre for Molecular Bacteriology and Infection **W** www3.imperial.ac.uk/cmbi
Centre for Mouse Genetics **W** www.har.mrc.ac.uk
Centre for Musculoskeletal Ageing Research **W** www.birmingham.ac.uk/generic/mrc-aruk
Centre for Neuromuscular Diseases **W** www.cnmd.ac.uk
Centre for Neuropsychiatric Genetics and Genomics **W** http://medicine.cardiff.ac.uk/cngg
Centre for Outbreak Analysis and Modelling **W** www1.imperial.ac.uk/medicine/about/institutes/outbreaks
Centre for Regenerative Medicine **W** www.crm.ed.ac.uk
Centre for Reproductive Health (CRH) **W** www.crh.ed.ac.uk
Centre for Transplantation **W** http://transplantation.kcl.ac.uk
Centre for Virus Research **W** www.gla.ac.uk/researchinstitutes/iii/cvr
Clinical Sciences Centre **W** www.csc.mrc.ac.uk
Clinical Trial Services and Epidemiological Studies Unit **W** www.ctsu.ox.ac.uk
Clinical Trials Unit **W** www.ctu.mrc.ac.uk
Cognition and Brain Sciences Unit **W** www.mrc-cbu.cam.ac.uk
Epidemiology Unit **W** www.mrc-epid.cam.ac.uk
Functional Genomics Unit **W** www.mrcfgu.ox.ac.uk
Genome Damage and Stability Centre **W** www.sussex.ac.uk/gdsc
Human Genetics Unit **W** www.hgu.mrc.ac.uk
Human Immunology Unit **W** www.imm.ox.ac.uk
Human Nutrition Research Unit **W** www.mrc-hnr.cam.ac.uk

Institute of Genetics and Molecular Medicine
  W www.igmm.ac.uk
Institute of Hearing Research W www.ihr.mrc.ac.uk
Institute of Radiation Oncology and Biology
  W www.rob.ox.ac.uk
Integrative Epidemiology Unit
  W www.bristol.ac.uk/integrative-epidemiology
Laboratory for Molecular Cell Biology W www.ucl.ac.uk/lmcb
Laboratory of Molecular Biology W www2.mrc-lmb.cam.ac.uk
Lifecourse Epidemiology Unit W www.mrc.soton.ac.uk
Lifelong Health and Ageing Unit W www.nshd.mrc.ac.uk
Metabolic Diseases Unit, W www.mrc-cord.org
Mitochondrial Biology Unit W www.mrc-mbu.cam.ac.uk
Molecular Haemotology Unit
  W www.imm.ox.ac.uk/mrc-molecular-haematology-unit
National Institute for Medical Research (NIMR)
  W www.nimr.mrc.ac.uk
Prion Unit W www.prion.ucl.ac.uk
Protein Phosphorylation and Ubiquitylation Unit
  W www.ppu.mrc.ac.uk
Scottish Collaboration for Public Health Research and Policy
  W www.scphrp.ac.uk
Social and Public Health Sciences Unit W www.sphsu.mrc.ac.uk
Social, Genetic and Developmental Psychiatry Centre
  W www.kcl.ac.uk/iop/depts/mrc
Stem Cell Institute W www.stemcells.cam.ac.uk
Toxicology Unit W www.tox.mrc.ac.uk
Weatherall Institute of Molecular Medicine (WIMM)
  W www.imm.ox.ac.uk

MRC The Gambia W www.mrc.gm
Uganda Research Unit on AIDS W www.mrcuganda.org

NATIONAL PHYSICAL LABORATORY
Hampton Road, Teddington, Middx TW11 0LW
T 020-8977 3222 W www.npl.co.uk

The National Physical Laboratory (NPL) was established in 1900 and is the UK's national measurement institute. It develops, maintains and disseminates national measurement standards for physical quantities such as mass, length, time, temperature, voltage and force. It also conducts underpinning research on engineering materials and information technology, and disseminates good measurement practice.
Managing Director, B. Bowsher

ASSOCIATION OF INDEPENDENT RESEARCH AND TECHNOLOGY ORGANISATIONS LIMITED (AIRTO)
T 020-8943 6600 E enquiries@airto.co.uk W www.airto.co.uk

(AIRTO) is a membership body, based at and run by the NPL, for organisations operating in the UK's research and technology sector. Members' activities span a wide range of disciplines from life sciences to engineering. Their work includes basic research, development and design of innovative products or processes, instrumentation testing and certification, and technology and management consultancy. AIRTO publishes a directory to help clients identify the organisations that might be able to assist them. For a full list of members, *see* AIRTO's website.
President, Prof. Richard Brook, OBE, FRENG

NATURAL ENVIRONMENT RESEARCH COUNCIL*
Polaris House, North Star Avenue, Swindon SN2 1EU
T 01793-411500 W www.nerc.ac.uk

NERC is the leading funder of independent research, training and innovation in environmental science in the UK.

Its work covers the full range of atmospheric, earth, biological, terrestrial and aquatic sciences. NERC invests public money in research explorng how we can sustainably benefit from our natural resources, predict and respond to natural hazards and understand environmental change. NERC works closely with policymakers and industry to support sustainable economic growth in the UK and around the world.
Chair, Sir Anthony Cleaver
Chief Executive, Prof. Duncan Wingham

RESEARCH CENTRES
BRITISH ANTARCTIC SURVEY, High Cross, Madingley Road, Cambridge CB3 OET T 01223-221400
  Director, Prof. Jane Francis
BRITISH GEOLOGICAL SURVEY, Kingsley Dunham Centre, Keyworth, Nottingham NG12 5GG T 0115-936 3100
  Executive Director, Prof. John Ludden
CENTRE FOR ECOLOGY AND HYDROLOGY, Maclean Building, Benson Lane, Crowmarsh Gifford, Wallingford OX10 8BB T 01491-838800
  Director, Prof. Mark J. Bailey
NATIONAL CENTRE FOR ATMOSPHERIC SCIENCE, NCAS Headquarters, School of Earth and Environment, University of Leeds, Leeds LS2 9JT T 0113-343 6408
  Director, Prof. Stephen Mobbs
NATIONAL CENTRE FOR EARTH OBSERVATION, Department of Meteorology, University of Reading, Earley Gate Building 58, Reading RG6 6BB T 0118-378 6728
  Director (interim), Prof. Peter Jan van Leeuwen
NATIONAL OCEANOGRAPHY CENTRE, University of Southampton Waterfront Campus, European Way, Southampton SO14 3ZH T 023-8059 6666
  Director, Prof. Ed Hill, OBE

SCIENCE AND TECHNOLOGY FACILITIES COUNCIL*
Polaris House, North Star Avenue, Swindon SN2 1SZ
T 01793-442000 W www.stfc.ac.uk

Formed by royal charter in 2007 through the merger of the Council for the Central Laboratory of the Research Councils and the Particle Physics and Astronomy Research Council, the STFC is a non-departmental public body reporting to BIS.

The STFC invests in large national and international research facilities, while delivering science and technology expertise for the UK. The council is involved in research projects such as the Diamond Light Source Synchrotron and the Large Hadron Collider, and develops new areas of science and technology. The EPSRC has transferred its responsibility for nuclear physics to the STFC.
Chair, Prof. Michael Sterling, FRENG
Chief Executive, Prof. John Womersley

RESEARCH CENTRES
CHILBOLTON OBSERVATORY, Chilbolton, Stockbridge, Hampshire SO20 6BJ T 01264-860391
DARESBURY LABORATORY, Daresbury Science and Innovation Campus, Warrington WA4 4AD T 01925-603000
RUTHERFORD APPLETON LABORATORY, Harwell Science and Innovation Campus, Didcot OX11 0QX T 01235-445000
UK ASTRONOMY TECHNOLOGY CENTRE, Royal Observatory Edinburgh, Blackford Hill, Edinburgh EH9 3HJ T 0131-668 8100

HEALTH

NATIONAL HEALTH SERVICE

The National Health Service (NHS) came into being on 5 July 1948 under the National Health Service Act 1946, covering England and Wales and, under separate legislation, Scotland and Northern Ireland. The NHS is now administered by the Secretary of State for Health (in England), the Welsh government, the Scottish government and the Northern Ireland Executive.

The function of the NHS is to provide a comprehensive health service designed to secure improvement in the physical and mental health of the people and to prevent, diagnose and treat illness. It was founded on the principle that treatment should be provided according to clinical need rather than ability to pay, and should be free at the point of delivery.

Hospital, mental, dental, nursing, ophthalmic and ambulance services and facilities for the care of expectant and nursing mothers and young children are provided by the NHS to meet all reasonable requirements. Rehabilitation services such as occupational therapy, physiotherapy, speech therapy and surgical and medical appliances are supplied where appropriate. Specialists and consultants who work in NHS hospitals can also engage in private practice, including the treatment of their private patients in NHS hospitals.

STRUCTURE

The structure of the NHS remained relatively stable for the first 30 years of its existence. In 1974, a three-tier management structure comprising regional health authorities, area health authorities and district management teams was introduced in England, and the NHS became responsible for community health services. In 1979, area health authorities were abolished and district management teams were replaced by district health authorities.

The National Health Service and Community Care Act 1990 provided for more streamlined regional health authorities and district health authorities, and for the establishment of family health services authorities (FHSAs) and NHS trusts. The concept of the 'internal market' was introduced into health care, whereby care was provided through NHS contracts where health authorities or boards and GP fundholders (the purchasers) were responsible for buying health care from hospitals, non-fundholding GPs, community services and ambulance services (the providers). The Act also paved the way for the community care reforms, which were introduced in April 1993, and changed the way care is administered for older people, the mentally ill, the physically disabled and people with learning disabilities.

ENGLAND

Under the Health and Social Care Act 2012, which gained royal assent in March 2012, the NHS in England is undergoing a complete operational and budgetary restructure at a cost of approximately £1.4bn. The full implementation of all the changes will not be complete for some time. During the transition period, all vital NHS services in England will continue as normal.

Hospitals will be extensively affected by the overhaul, with the cap on income from private hospital patients rising from 1.5 per cent to 49 per cent. All hospitals will become foundation trusts, competing for treatment contracts from clinical commissioning groups (CCGs).

On 1 April 2013 the new commissioning board, NHS England, took on full statutory responsibilities; at the same time, strategic health authorities (SHAs) and primary care trusts (PCTs) which, alongside the Department of Health, had been responsible for NHS planning and delivery, were abolished. NHS England is an executive non-departmental public body of the Department of Health with a remit to:
- provide national leadership to improve the quality of care
- oversee the operation of clinical commissioning groups
- allocate resources to clinical commissioning groups
- commission primary care and specialist services

The secretary of state has ultimate responsibility for the provision of a comprehensive health service in England and for ensuring the system works to its optimum capacity to meet the needs of its patients. The Department of Health is responsible for strategic leadership of the health and social care systems, but will cease to be the headquarters of the NHS, nor will it directly manage any NHS organisations.

NHS ENGLAND, PO Box 16738, Redditch B97 9PT
T 0300-311 2233 W www.england.nhs.uk
Chief Executive, Simon Stevens

CLINICAL COMMISSIONING GROUPS (CCGS)

On 1 April 2013, PCTs, which controlled 80 per cent of the NHS budget and commissioned most NHS services, were abolished. They were replaced with CCGs which took on many of the functions of the PCTs in addition to some functions previously assumed by the Department of Health. All GP practices now belong to a CCG which also includes other health professionals, such as nurses. CCGs commission most services, including:
- mental health and learning disability services
- planned hospital care
- rehabilitative care
- urgent and emergency care (including out-of-hours)
- most community health services

CCGs can commission any service provider that meets NHS standards and costs. These can be NHS hospitals, social enterprises, charities, or private-sector providers. There are over 200 CCGs, which together are responsible for around 60 per cent of the NHS budget.

HEALTH AND WELLBEING BOARDS

Every upper-tier local authority has established a health and wellbeing board to act as a forum for local commissioners across the NHS, social care, public health and other services. The 153 boards are intended to:
- encourage integrated commissioning of health and social care services
- increase democratic input into strategic decisions about health and wellbeing services
- strengthen working relationships between health and social care

PUBLIC HEALTH ENGLAND (PHE)

This new organisation was established on 1 April 2013. It provides national leadership and expert services to support public health and also works with local government and the NHS to respond to emergencies. PHE's responsibilities are to:
- coordinate a national public health service
- support the public to make healthier choices
- provide leadership to the public health delivery system
- support the development of the public health workforce

REGULATION

Since the restructuring of the NHS in England began in April 2013, some elements of the regulation system have changed. Responsibility for the regulation of particular aspects of care is shared across a number of different bodies, including the Care Quality Commission (CQC), Monitor, and individual professional regulatory bodies, such as the General Medical Council, Nursing and Midwifery Council, General Dental Council and the Health and Care Professions Council.

CARE QUALITY COMMISSION (CQC)

The CQC regulates all health and social care services in England, including those provided by the NHS, local authorities, private companies or voluntary organisations. In addition it protects the interests of people detained under the Mental Health Act. The CQC ensures that all essential standards of quality and safety are met where care is provided, from hospitals to private care homes. By law all NHS providers (such as hospitals and ambulance services) must register with the CQC to show they are protecting people from the risk of infection. The CQC possesses a range of legal powers and duties and will take action if providers do not meet essential standards of quality or safety.

MONITOR

Monitor is the sector regulator for health services in England. Their job is to protect and promote the interests of patients. Monitor's aim is to promote competition, regulate prices and ensure the continuity of services for NHS foundation trusts. Under the new structure, most NHS providers need to be registered with both the CQC and Monitor to be able to legally provide services.

HEALTHWATCH

Healthwatch England was established in October 2012 following the restructuring of the NHS. The organisation functions at a national and local level as an independent consumer body, gathering and representing the views of the public about health and social care services in England.

CARE QUALITY COMMISSION, Finsbury Tower,
103–105 Bunhill Row, London EC1Y 8TG **T** 03000-616161
W www.cqc.org.uk
Chief Executive, David Behan

MONITOR, Wellington House, 133–155 Waterloo Road,
London SE1 8UG **T** 020-3747 0000
W www.monitor-nhsft.gov.uk
Chief Executive, Dr David Bennett

HEALTHWATCH, Citygate, Gallowgate, Newcastle upon Tyne
NE1 4PA **T** 03000-683000 **W** www.healthwatch.co.uk
Chief Executive, Dr Katherine Rake, OBE

AUTHORITIES AND TRUSTS

Overseen by the NHS Trust Development Authority all NHS trusts are expected to become foundation trusts in the next three to five years.

ACUTE TRUSTS

Hospitals in England are managed by acute trusts. There are 171 acute trusts, of which 105 have foundation trust status. Acute trusts ensure hospitals provide high-quality healthcare and spend money efficiently. They employ a large sector of the NHS workforce, including doctors, nurses, pharmacists, midwives, and health visitors. Acute trusts also employ those in supplementary medical professions, such as physiotherapists, radiographers and podiatrists, in addition to many other non-medical staff.

AMBULANCE TRUSTS

There are 10 ambulance services (five foundation trusts) in England, providing emergency services to healthcare.

CLINICAL SENATES AND STRATEGIC CLINICAL NETWORKS

Clinical senates are advisory groups of experts from across health and social care. There are 12 senates covering England comprising clinical leaders from across the healthcare system, in addition to members from social care and public health.

There are 12 strategic clinical networks across England, comprising groups of clinical experts covering a particular disease, patient or professional group. They offer advice to CCGs and NHS England.

Neither organisation is a statutory body, and although they comment on CCG plans to NHS England, they are unable to veto them.

FOUNDATION TRUSTS

NHS foundation trusts are independent legal entities with unique governance arrangements. Each NHS foundation trust has a duty to consult and involve a board of governors in the strategic planning of its organisation. They have financial freedoms and can raise capital from both the public and private sectors within borrowing limits determined by projected cash flows and based on affordability. They are overseen by Monitor.

MENTAL HEALTH TRUSTS

There are 52 mental health trusts in England, 37 of which have reached foundation trust status. They provide health and social care services for people with mental health problems.

NHS TRUST DEVELOPMENT AUTHORITY (TDA)

Following the abolition of SHAs in 2013, the TDA became responsible for overseeing the performance, management and governance of NHS trusts, including clinical quality, and managing their progress towards foundation trust status.

SPECIAL HEALTH AUTHORITIES

Special health authorities are health authorities that have a nationwide remit, such as:
• The National Blood and Transplant Authority
• NHS Business Services Authority
• NHS Litigation Authority

WALES

The NHS Wales was reorganised according to Welsh Assembly commitments laid out in the *One Wales* strategy which came into effect in October 2009. There are now seven local health boards (LHBs) that are responsible for delivering all health care services within a geographical area, rather than the trust and local health board system that existed previously. Community health councils (CHCs) are statutory lay bodies that represent the public for the health service in their region. There are currently eight CHCs.

NHS TRUSTS

There are three NHS trusts in Wales. The Welsh Ambulance Services NHS Trust is for emergency services; the Velindre NHS Trust offers specialist services in cancer care; while Public Health Wales serves as a unified public health organisation for Wales.

LOCAL HEALTH BOARDS

The websites of the seven LHBs, and contact details for community health councils and NHS trusts, are available in the *NHS Wales Directory* on the NHS Wales website (**W** www.wales.nhs.uk).

ABERTAWE BRO MORGANNWG UNIVERSITY
    HEALTH BOARD, One Talbot Gateway, Baglan Energy Park,
    Baglan, Port Talbot SA12 7BR T 01656-752752
    Chief Executive, Paul Roberts
ANEURIN BEVAN HEALTH BOARD, St Cadoc's Hospital,
    Lodge Road, Caerleon, Newport NP18 3XQ T 01633-436700
    Chief Executive (interim), Judith Paget
BETSI CADWALADR UNIVERSITY HEALTH BOARD,
    Ysbyty Gwynedd, Penrhosgarnedd, Bangor, Gwynedd
    LL57 2PW T 01248-384384
    Chief Executive, Prof. Trevor Purt
CARDIFF AND VALE UNIVERSITY HEALTH BOARD,
    Whitchurch Hospital, Park Road, Whitchurch, Cardiff CF14 7XB
    T 029-2074 7747
    Chief Executive, Adam Cairns
CWM TAF HEALTH BOARD, Unit 3, Navigation Park,
    Abercynon CF45 4SN T 01443-744800
    Chief Executive, Allison Williams
HYWEL DDA HEALTH BOARD, Merlin's Court, Winch Lane,
    Haverfordwest, Pembrokeshire SA61 1SB T 01437-771220
    Chief Executive (interim), Karen Howell
POWYS TEACHING HEALTH BOARD, Mansion House,
    Bronllys, Brecon, Powys LD3 0LS T 01874-771661
    Chief Executive, Bob Hudson

SCOTLAND

The Scottish government Health Directorate is responsible
both for NHS Scotland and for the development and implementation of health and community care policy. The chief
executive of NHS Scotland leads the central management of
the NHS, is accountable to ministers for the efficiency and
performance of the service and heads the Health Department
which oversees the work of the 14 regional health boards.
These boards provide strategic management for the entire
local NHS system and are responsible for ensuring that
services are delivered effectively and efficiently.
    In addition to the 11 regional health boards there are a
further seven special boards and one public health body,
which provide national services, such as the Scottish
ambulance service and NHS Health Scotland. Healthcare
Improvement Scotland, was formed on 1 April 2011 by the
Public Services Reform Act 2010 to improve the quality of
Scottish healthcare.

REGIONAL HEALTH BOARDS
AYRSHIRE AND ARRAN, Eglinton House, Ailsa Hospital,
    Dalmellington Road, Ayr KA6 6AB T 0800-169 1441
    W www.nhsaaa.net
    Chief Executive, John Burns
BORDERS, Newstead, Melrose TD6 9DA T 01896-826000
    W www.nhsborders.org.uk
    Chief Executive, Calum Campbell
DUMFRIES AND GALLOWAY, Ryan North, Crichton Hall,
    Dumfries DG1 4TG T 01387-246246
    W www.nhsdg.scot.nhs.uk
    Chief Executive, Jeff Ace
FIFE, Hayfield House, Hayfield Road, Kirkcaldy, Fife KY2 5AH
    T 01592-643355 W www.nhsfife.org
    Chief Executive, John Wilson
FORTH VALLEY, Carseview House, Castle Business Park, Stirling
    FK9 4SW T 01786-463031 W www.nhsforthvalley.com
    Chief Executive, Jane Grant
GRAMPIAN, Summerfield House, 2 Eday Road, Aberdeen
    AB15 6RE T 0845-456 6000 W www.nhsgrampian.org
    Chief Executive, Richard Carey
GREATER GLASGOW AND CLYDE, J B Russell House,
    Gartnavel Royal Hospital Campus, 1055 Great Western Road,
    Glasgow G12 0XH T 0141-201 4444 W www.nhsgg.org.uk
    Chief Executive, Robert Calderwood

HIGHLAND, Assynt House, Beechwood Park, Inverness IV2 3BW
    T 01463-717123 W www.nhshighland.scot.nhs.uk
    Chief Executive, Elaine Mead
LANARKSHIRE, Kirklands, Fallside Road, Bothwell G71 8BB
    T 0845-313 0130 W www.nhslanarkshire.org.uk
    Chief Executive, Ian Ross
LOTHIAN, Waverley Gate, 2–4 Waterloo Place, Edinburgh
    EH1 3EG T 0131-536 9000 W www.nhslothian.scot.nhs.uk
    Chief Executive, Tim Davison
ORKNEY, Balfour Hospital, New Scapa Road, Kirkwall,
    Orkney KW15 1BH T 01856-888000 W www.ohb.scot.nhs.uk
    Chief Executive, Cathie Cowan
SHETLAND, Brevik House, South Road, Lerwick ZE1 0TG
    T 01595-743060 W www.shb.scot.nhs.uk
    Chief Executive, Ralph Roberts
TAYSIDE, Level 10, Ninewells Hospital, Dundee DD1 9SY
    T 01382-660111 W www.nhstayside.scot.nhs.uk
    Chief Executive, Gerry Marr
WESTERN ISLES, 37 South Beach Street, Stornoway, Isle of
    Lewis HS1 2BB T 01851-702997 W www.wihb.scot.nhs.uk
    Chief Executive, Gordon Jamieson

NORTHERN IRELAND

On 1 April 2009 the four health and social services boards
in Northern Ireland were replaced by a single health and
social care board for the whole of Northern Ireland. The new
board together with its local commissioning groups (whose
boundaries are subject to review pending the outcome of local
government reform) are responsible for improving the health
and social wellbeing of people in the area for which they are
responsible, planning and commissioning services, and coordinating the delivery of services in a cost-effective manner.
HEALTH AND SOCIAL CARE BOARD,
    12–22 Linenhall Street, Belfast BT2 8BS T 030-0555 0115
    W www.hscboard.hscni.net
    Chief Executive, Valerie Watts

FINANCE

The NHS is still funded mainly through general taxation,
although in recent years more reliance has been placed on
the NHS element of national insurance contributions, patient
charges and other sources of income.
    Funding for NHS England was set at £96.42bn for 2014–
15. Expenditure for the NHS in Wales, Scotland and
Northern Ireland is set by the devolved governments.

EMPLOYEES AND SALARIES

NHS HEALTH SERVICE STAFF 2014 (ENGLAND)
Full-time equivalent

All hospital, community and dental staff	1,203,892
Consultants	41,950
Registrars	39,464
Qualified nursing and midwifery staff	354,083
Qualified scientific, therapeutic and technical staff	154,658

Source: Health and Social Care Information Centre *NHS Hospital
and Community Health Service: Monthly Workforce Statistics*

SALARIES
Many general practitioners (GPs) are self-employed and hold
contracts, either on their own or as part of a Clinical
Commissioning Group (CCG). The profit of GPs varies
according to the services they provide for their patients
and the way they choose to provide these services. Salaried

GPs who are part of a CCG earn between £54,863 and £82,789 dependent on, among other factors, length of service and experience. Most NHS dentists are self-employed contractors. A contract for dentists was introduced on 1 April 2006 which provides dentists with an annual income in return for carrying out an agreed amount, or units, of work. A salaried dentist employed by the NHS, who works mainly with community dental services earn between £38,095 and £81,480.

BASIC SALARIES FOR HOSPITAL MEDICAL AND DENTAL STAFF*
from 1 April 2014

Consultant (2003 contract)	£75,249–£101,451
Consultant (pre-2003 contract)	£62,477–£80,988
Specialist registrar	£31,301–£47,175
Speciality registrar (full)	£30,002–£47,175
Speciality registrar (fixed term)	£30,002–£39,693
Foundation house officer year 2	£28,076–£31,748
Foundation house officer year 1	£22,636–£25,461

* These figures do not include merit awards, discretionary points or banding supplements

NURSES
From 1 December 2004 the *Agenda for Change* pay system was introduced throughout the UK for all NHS staff with the exception of medical and dental staff, doctors in public health medicine and the community health service. Nurses' salaries are incorporated in the *Agenda for Change* nine pay band structure, which provides additional payments for flexible working such as providing out-of-hours services, working weekends and nights and being 'on-call'. There is also additional payments for those staff who work in 'high-cost' areas such as London.

SALARIES FOR NURSES AND MIDWIVES
from 1 April 2014

Nurse/Midwife consultant	£39,239–£67,805
Modern matron	£39,239–£67,805
Nurse advanced/team manager	£30,764–£40,558
Midwife higher level	£30,764–£40,558
Nurse specialist/team leader	£25,783–£34,530
Hospital/community midwife	£25,783–£34,530
Registered nurse/entry level midwife*	£21,478–£27,901

* Starting salaries in Wales and Northern Ireland are currently the same as in England. The starting salary in Scotland is £21,602.

HEALTH SERVICES

PRIMARY CARE

Primary care comprises the services provided by general practitioners, community health centres, pharmacies, dental practices and opticians. Primary nursing care includes the work carried out by practice nurses, community nurses, community midwives and health visitors.

PRIMARY MEDICAL SERVICES
In England, primary medical services (PMS) are provided by around 60,000 registerd GPs, working in around 8,000 GP practices, with 55 million registered patients.

In Wales, responsibility for primary medical services rests with local health boards (LHBs), in Scotland with the 14 regional health boards and in Northern Ireland with the health and social care board.

Any vocationally trained doctor may provide general or personal medical services. GPs may also have private fee-paying patients, but not if that patient is already an NHS patient on that doctor's patient list.

A person who is ordinarily resident in the UK is eligible to register with a GP (or PMS provider) for free primary care

treatment. Should a patient have difficulty in registering with a doctor, he or she should contact the local CCG for help. When a person is away from home he/she can still access primary care treatment from a GP if they ask to be treated as a temporary resident. In an emergency any doctor in the service will give treatment and advice.

GPs or CCGs are responsible for the care of their patients 24 hours a day, seven days a week, but can fulfil the terms of their contract by delegating or transferring responsibility for out-of-hours care to an accredited provider.

In addition, NHS walk-in centres throughout England are usually open seven days a week, from early in the morning until late in the evening. They are nurse-led and provide treatment for minor illnesses and injuries, health information and self-help advice.

HEALTH COSTS
Some people are exempt from, or entitled to help with, health costs such as prescription charges, ophthalmic and dental costs, and in some cases help towards travel costs to and from hospital.

The following list is intended as a general guide to those who may be entitled to help, or who are exempt from some of the charges relating to the above:
- children under 16 and young people in full-time education who are under 19
- people aged 60 or over
- pregnant women and women who have had a baby in the last 12 months and have a valid maternity exemption certificate (MatEx)
- people, or their partners, who are in receipt of income support, income-based jobseeker's allowance and/or income-based employment and support allowance
- people in receipt of the pension credit
- diagnosed glaucoma patients, people who have been advised by an ophthalmologist that they are at risk of glaucoma and people aged 40 or over who have an immediate family member who is a diagnosed glaucoma patient
- NHS in-patients
- NHS out-patients for all prescribed contraceptives, medication given at a hospital, NHS walk-in centre, personally administered by a GP or supplied at a hospital or primary care trust clinic for the treatment of tuberculosis or a sexually transmissable infection
- out-patients of the NHS Hospital Dental Service
- people registered blind or partially sighted
- people who need complex lenses
- war pensioners whose treatment/prescription is for their accepted disablement and who have a valid exemption certificate
- people who are entitled to, or named on, a valid NHS tax credit exemption or HC2 certificate
- people who have a medical exemption (MedEx) certificate, including those with cancer or diabetes

People in other circumstances may also be eligible for help; *see* booklet HC12 (England) and HCS2 (Scotland) for further information.

WALES
On 1 April 2007 all prescription charges (including those for medical supports and appliances and wigs) for people living in Wales were abolished. The above guide still applies for NHS dental and optical charges although all people aged under 25 living in Wales are also entitled to free dental examinations.

SCOTLAND
On 1 April 2011 all prescription charges in Scotland were abolished. Those entitled to free prescriptions in Scotland include patients registered with a Scottish GP and receiving a prescription from a Scottish pharmacy, and Scottish patients who have an English GP and an entitlement card.

NORTHERN IRELAND

On 1 April 2010 all prescription charges in Northern Ireland were abolished. All prescriptions dispensed in Northern Ireland are free, even for patients visiting from England, Wales or Scotland.

PHARMACEUTICAL SERVICES

Patients may obtain medicines and appliances under the NHS from any pharmacy whose owner has entered into arrangements with the CCG to provide this service. There are also some suppliers who only provide special appliances. In rural areas, where access to a pharmacy may be difficult, patients may be able to obtain medicines, etc, from a dispensing doctor.

In England, a charge of £8.05 is payable for each item supplied (except for contraceptives for which there is no charge), unless the patient is exempt and the declaration on the back of the prescription form is completed. Prescription prepayment certificates (£29.10 valid for three months, £104.00 valid for a year) may be purchased by those patients not entitled to exemption who require frequent prescriptions.

DENTAL SERVICES

Dentists, like doctors, may take part in the NHS and also have private patients. Dentists are responsible to the local health provider in whose areas they provide services. Patients may go to any dentist who is taking part in the NHS and is willing to accept them. On 1 April 2006 the charging system for NHS dentistry in England and Wales was changed. There is now a three-tier payment system based on the individual course of treatment required.

NHS DENTAL CHARGES
from 1 April 2014

	England/Wales
Band 1* – Examination, diagnosis, preventive care (eg x-rays, scale and polish)	£18.50/£13.00
Band 2 – Band 1 + basic additional treatment (eg fillings and extractions)	£50.50/£42.00
Band 3 – Bands 1 and 2 + all other treatment (eg crowns, dentures and bridges)	£219.00/£180.90

* Urgent and out-of-hours treatment is also charged at this payment tier

The cost of individual treatment plans should be known prior to treatment and some dental practices may require payment in advance. There is no charge for writing a prescription or removing stitches and only one charge is payable for each course of treatment even if more than one visit to the dentist is required. If additional treatment is required within two months of visiting the dentist and this is covered by the course of treatment most recently paid for (eg payment was made for the second tier of treatment but an additional filling is required) then this will be provided free of charge.

SCOTLAND AND NORTHERN IRELAND

Scotland and Northern Ireland have yet to simplify their charging systems. NHS dental patients pay 80 per cent of the cost of the individual items of treatment provided up to a maximum of £384. Patients in Scotland are entitled to free basic and extensive examinations.

GENERAL OPHTHALMIC SERVICES

General ophthalmic services are administered by local health providers. Testing of sight may be carried out by any ophthalmic medical practitioner or ophthalmic optician (optometrist). The optician must give the prescription to the patient, who can take this to any supplier of glasses to have them dispensed. Only registered opticians can supply glasses to children and to people registered as blind or partially sighted.

Free eyesight tests and help towards the cost are available to people in certain circumstances. Help is also available for the purchase of glasses or contact lenses (*see* Health Costs). In Scotland eye examinations, which include a sight test, are free to all UK residents. Help is also available for the purchase of glasses or contact lenses to those entitled to help with health costs in the same way it is available to those in England and Wales.

CHILD HEALTH SERVICES

Pre-school services at GP surgeries or child health clinics provide regular monitoring of children's physical, mental and emotional health and development and advise parents on their children's health and welfare.

NHS 111, NHS DIRECT AND NHS 24

NHS Direct Wales is a website and 24-hour nurse-led advice telephone service for Wales. It provides medical advice as well as directing people to the appropriate part of the NHS for treatment if necessary (T 0845 46 47 W www.nhsdirect.wales.nhs.uk). NHS Direct had also operated in England but closed on 31 March 2014. Non-urgent 24-hour nurse-led advice in England can be accessed via the NHS 111 service (T 111).

NHS 24 provides an equivalent service for Scotland (T 0845-424 2424 W www.nhs24.com).

SECONDARY CARE AND OTHER SERVICES

HOSPITALS

NHS hospitals provide acute and specialist care services, treating conditions which normally cannot be dealt with by primary care specialists, and provide for medical emergencies.

NUMBER OF BEDS 2013–14

	Average daily	
	available beds	occupation of beds
England	136,895	119,646
Wales*	11,495	9,920
Scotland*	16,484	14,110
Northern Ireland	6,152	5,088

* Figures are for 2012–13

Sources: NHS England, Welsh government, ISD Scotland, NI Direct

HOSPITAL CHARGES

Acute or foundation trusts can provide hospital accommodation in single rooms or small wards, if not required for patients who need privacy for medical reasons. The patient is still an NHS patient, but there may be a charge for these additional facilities. Acute or foundation trusts can charge for certain patient services that are considered to be additional treatments over and above the normal hospital service provision. There is no blanket policy to cover this and each case is considered in the light of the patient's clinical need. However, if an item or service is considered to be an integral part of a patient's treatment by their clinician, then a charge should not be made.

In some NHS hospitals, accommodation and services are available for the treatment of private patients where it does not interfere with care for NHS patients. Income generated by treating private patients is then put back into local NHS services. Private patients undertake to pay the full costs of medical treatment, accommodation, medication and other related services. Charges for private patients are set locally.

WAITING LISTS

England

In July 2004 a target of an 18-week maximum wait, from start time (ie seeing a GP) to treatment, was introduced. For April 2014, 295,641 referral to treatment (RTT) patients started admitted treatment and 839,956 started non-admitted treatment. Of the admitted patients, 90 per cent were treated within 18 weeks, and for non-admitted patients 96.3 per cent were treated within 18 weeks. The *Revision to the Operating Framework for the NHS in England 2010/11* published in June 2010, abolished the performance management of the 18-week waiting time target although referral-to-treatment data will continue to be published.

Wales

In Wales the main target is for referral to treatment to take no longer than 26 weeks. In June 2014, 78.9 per cent of 87,205 patients were treated within 26 weeks and 92.4 per cent were treated within 36 weeks of the date the referral letter was received in the hospital. There are also operational standards for maximum waiting times for first out-patient appointments and in-patient or day-case treatment but these are not set targets. The standards are 14 weeks for in-patient or day case treatment, and ten weeks for a first out-patient appointment.

Scotland

An 18-week referral to treatment target, due to be delivered from December 2011, was set out in the publication *Better Health, Better Care*. In March 2014, 89.6 per cent of patients on an 18 week referral to treatment pathway were reported as being seen within 18 weeks, a decrease from 90.6 per cent in March 2013.

Northern Ireland

From March 2014 the aim was for at least 70 per cent of patients to wait no longer than nine weeks for a first out-patient appointment, with no patient waiting longer than 18 weeks. The total number of people waiting for a first out-patient appointment at the end of March 2014 was 127,095; of these, 39,768 had been waiting over nine weeks, an increase from 19,764 at the end of March 2013. The number of people waiting for in-patient treatment at the end of March 2014 was 49,341 – of these, 33.1 per cent had been waiting for more than 13 weeks.

AMBULANCE SERVICE

The NHS provides emergency ambulance services free of charge via the 999 emergency telephone service. Air ambulances, provided through local charities and partially funded by the NHS, are used throughout the UK. They assist with cases where access may be difficult or heavy traffic could hinder road progress. Non-emergency ambulance services are provided free to patients who are deemed to require them on medical grounds.

Since 1 April 2001 all services have had a system of call prioritisation. The prioritisation procedures require all emergency calls to be classified as either immediately life threatening (category A) or other emergency (category B). Services are expected to reach 75 per cent of category A calls within eight minutes and 95 per cent of category B calls within 19 minutes.

In April 2014, the NHS employed 1,548 qualified ambulance staff earning between £18,838 (ambulance practitioner) and £34,530 (senior paramedic).

BLOOD AND TRANSPLANT SERVICES

There are four national bodies which coordinate the blood donor programme and transplant and related services in the UK. Donors give blood at local centres on a voluntary basis.

NHS BLOOD AND TRANSPLANT, Oak House, Reeds Crescent, Watford, Herts WD24 4QN T 0300-123 2323
W www.nhsbt.nhs.uk

WELSH BLOOD SERVICE, Ely Valley Road, Talbot Green, Pontyclun CF72 9WB T 01443-622000
W www.welsh-blood.org.uk

SCOTTISH NATIONAL BLOOD TRANSFUSION SERVICE, 21 Ellen's Glen Road, Edinburgh EH17 7QT
T 0131-314536 5510 W www.scotblood.co.uk

NORTHERN IRELAND BLOOD TRANSFUSION SERVICE, Lisburn Road, Belfast BT9 7TS T 028-9032 1414
W www.nibts.org

HOSPICES

Hospice or palliative care may be available for patients with life-threatening illnesses. It may be provided at the patient's home or in a voluntary or NHS hospice or in hospital, and is intended to ensure the best possible quality of life for the patient during their illness, and to provide help and support to both the patient and the patient's family. The National Council for Palliative Care coordinates NHS and voluntary services in England, Wales and Northern Ireland; the Scottish Partnership for Palliative Care performs the same function in Scotland.

NATIONAL COUNCIL FOR PALLIATIVE CARE, The Fitzpatrick Building, 188–194 York Way, London N7 9AS
T 020-7697 1520 W www.ncpc.org.uk

SCOTTISH PARTNERSHIP FOR PALLIATIVE CARE, 1A Cambridge Street, Edinburgh EH1 2DY T 0131-229 0538
W www.palliativecarescotland.org.uk

COMPLAINTS

Patient advice and liaison services (PALS) have been established for every NHS and PCT in England. PALS can give advice on local complaints procedure, or resolve concerns informally. If the case is not resolved locally or the complainant is not satisfied with the way a local NHS body or practice has dealt with their complaint, they may approach the Parliamentary and Health Service Ombudsman in England, the Scottish Public Services Ombudsman, Public Services Ombudsman for Wales or the Northern Ireland Commissioner for Complaints.

HEALTH ADVICE AND MEDICAL TREATMENT ABROAD

IMMUNISATION

Country-by-country guidance is set out on the website W www.fitfortravel.nhs.uk. Health care professionals can obtain information about immunisation recommendations from the Department of Health publication *Health Information for Overseas Travel* (the 'Yellow Book').

RECIPROCAL ARRANGEMENTS

The European Health Insurance Card (EHIC) allows UK residents access to state-provided health care that may become necessary while temporarily travelling in all European Economic Area countries and Switzerland either free or at a reduced cost. A card is free, valid for up to five years and should be obtained before travelling. Applications can be made by telephone (T 0300 330 1350), online (W www.gov.uk/european-health-insurance-card) or by post (a form is available from the post office).

The UK also has bilateral agreements with several other countries, including Australia and New Zealand, for the free provision of urgent medical treatment.

European Economic Area nationals visiting the UK and visitors from other countries with which the UK has bilateral health care agreements are entitled to receive emergency health care on the NHS on the same terms as it is available to UK residents.

SOCIAL WELFARE

SOCIAL SERVICES

The Secretary of State for Health (in England), the Welsh government, the Scottish government and the Secretary of State for Northern Ireland are responsible, under the Local Authority Social Services Act 1970, for the provision of social services for older people, disabled people, families and children, and those with mental disorders. Personal social services are administered by local authorities according to policies, with standards set by central and devolved government. Each authority has a director and a committee responsible for the social services functions placed upon them. Local authorities provide, enable and commission care after assessing the needs of their population. The private and voluntary sectors also play an important role in the delivery of social services, and an estimated 6 million people in the UK provide substantial regular care for a member of their family.

The Care Quality Commission (CQC) was established in April 2009, bringing together the independent regulation of health, mental health and adult social care. Prior to 1 April 2009 this work was carried out by three separate organisations: the Healthcare Commission, the Mental Health Act Commission and the Commission for Social Care Inspection. The CQC is responsible for the registration of health and social care providers, the monitoring and inspection of all health and adult social care, issuing fines, public warnings or closures if standards are not met and for undertaking regular performance reviews. Since April 2007 the Office for Standards in Education, Children's Services and Skills (Ofsted) has been responsible for inspecting and regulating all care services for children and young people in England. Both Ofsted and CQC collate information on local care services and make this information available to the public.

The Care and Social Services Inspectorate Wales (CSSIW), an operationally independent part of the Welsh government, is reponsible for the regulation and inspection of all social care services in Wales. A new unified body, the Care Inspectorate, was established on 1 April 2011, replacing the Scottish Commission for the Regulation of Care (the Care Commission) and is now the independent care services regulator for Scotland.

The Department of Health, Social Services and Public Safety is responsible for social care in Northern Ireland.

CARE QUALITY COMMISSION (CQC), Citygate,
Gallowgate, Newcastle upon Tyne NE1 4PA T 0300-061 6161
W www.cqc.org.uk

OFFICE FOR STANDARDS IN EDUCATION,
CHILDREN'S SERVICES AND SKILLS (Ofsted),
Piccadilly Gate, Store Street, Manchester M1 2WD
T 0300-123 1231 E enquiries@ofsted.gov.uk
W www.ofsted.gov.uk

CARE AND SOCIAL SERVICES INSPECTORATE WALES
(CSSIW), Welsh Government, Rhydcar Business Park, Merthyr
Tydfil CF48 1UZ T 0300-790 0126 E cssiw@wales.gsi.gov.uk
W www.cssiw.org.uk

CARE INSPECTORATE, Compass House, 11 Riverside Drive,
Dundee DD1 4NY T 0845-600 9527
E enquiries@careinspectorate.com W www.scswis.com

DEPARTMENT OF HEALTH, SOCIAL SERVICES AND
PUBLIC SAFETY, Castle Buildings, Stormont, Belfast BT4 3SJ
T 028-9052 0500 E webmaster@dhsspsni.gov.uk
W www.dhsspsni.gov.uk

STAFF

Total Social Services Staff (England, full-time)	150,700
Community	52,600
Residential	33,500
Other	30,600
Domiciliary	19,100
Day	14,800

Source: Department of Health

OLDER PEOPLE
Services for older people are designed to enable them to remain living in their own homes for as long as possible. Local authority services include advice, domestic help, meals in the home, alterations to the home to aid mobility, emergency alarm systems, day and/or night attendants, laundry services and the provision of day centres and recreational facilities. Charges may be made for these services. Respite care may also be provided in order to allow carers temporary relief from their responsibilities.

Local authorities and the private sector also provide 'sheltered housing' for older people, sometimes with resident wardens.

If an older person is admitted to a residential home, charges are made according to a means test; if the person cannot afford to pay, the costs are met by the local authority.

DISABLED PEOPLE
Services for disabled people are designed to enable them to remain living in their own homes wherever possible. Local authority services include advice, adaptations to the home, meals in the home, help with personal care, occupational therapy, educational facilities and recreational facilities. Respite care may also be provided in order to allow carers temporary relief from their responsibilities.

Special housing may be available for disabled people who can live independently, and residential accommodation for those who cannot.

FAMILIES AND CHILDREN
Local authorities are required to provide services aimed at safeguarding the welfare of children in need and, wherever possible, allowing them to be brought up by their families. Services include advice, counselling, help in the home and the provision of family centres. Many authorities also provide short-term refuge accommodation for women and children.

DAY CARE
In allocating day care places to children, local authorities give priority to children with special needs, whether in terms of their health, learning abilities or social needs. Since September 2001, Ofsted has been responsible for the regulation and registration of all early years childcare and education provision in England (previously the responsibility of the local authorities). All day care and childminding services that care for children under eight years of age for more than two hours a day must register with Ofsted and are inspected at least every two years. As at 31 March 2014, there were 92,251 registered childcare providers in England.

CHILD PROTECTION
Children considered to be at risk of physical injury, neglect or sexual abuse are placed on the local authority's child protection register. Local authority social services staff,

schools, health visitors and other agencies work together to prevent and detect cases of abuse. As at 31 March 2013, there was a total of 50,732 children on child protection registers or subject to a child protection plan in the UK. In England, there were 43,140 children on child protection registers, of these, 17,687 were at risk of neglect, 5,047 of physical abuse, 2,071 of sexual abuse and 13,675 of emotional abuse. At 31 March (July in Scotland) 2013 there were 2,950 children on child protection registers in Wales, 2,681 in Scotland and 1,961 in Northern Ireland.

LOCAL AUTHORITY CARE

Local authorities are required to provide accommodation for children who have no parents or guardians or whose parents or guardians are unable or unwilling to care for them. A family proceedings court may also issue a care order where a child is being neglected or abused, or is not attending school; the court must be satisfied that this would positively contribute to the well-being of the child.

The welfare of children in local authority care must be properly safeguarded. Children may be placed with foster families, who receive payments to cover the expenses of caring for the child or children, or in residential care.

Children's homes may be run by the local authority or by the private or voluntary sectors; all homes are subject to inspection procedures. As at 31 March 2013, 68,110 children in the UK were in the care of local authorities, of these, 50,900 were in foster placements and 6,000 were in children's homes, hostels or secure units.

ADOPTION

Local authorities are required to provide an adoption service, either directly or via approved voluntary societies. In 2012–13, there were 2,943 children aged under 18 entered in the adopted children register in the UK. In the year ending 31 March 2013, 3,350 children in local authority care were placed for adoption.

PEOPLE WITH LEARNING DISABILITIES

Services for people with learning disabilities are designed to enable them to remain living in the community wherever possible. Local authority services include short-term care, support in the home, the provision of day care centres, and help with other activities outside the home. Residential care is provided for the severely or profoundly disabled.

MENTALLY ILL PEOPLE

Under the care programme approach, mentally ill people should be assessed by specialist services and receive a care plan. A key worker should be appointed for each patient; regular reviews of the person's progress should be conducted. Local authorities provide help and advice to mentally ill people and their families, and places in day centres and social centres. Social workers can apply for a mentally disturbed person to be compulsorily detained in hospital. Where appropriate, mentally ill people are provided with accommodation in special hospitals, local authority accommodation, or at homes run by private or voluntary organisations. Patients who have been discharged from hospitals may be placed on a supervision register.

NATIONAL INSURANCE

The National Insurance (NI) scheme operates under the Social Security Contributions and Benefits Act 1992 and the Social Security Administration Act 1992, and orders and regulations made thereunder. The scheme is financed by contributions payable by earners, employers and others (*see* below). Money collected under the scheme is used to finance the National Insurance Fund (from which contributory benefits are paid) and to contribute to the cost of the National Health Service.

NATIONAL INSURANCE FUND

Estimated receipts, payments and statement of balances of the National Insurance Fund for 2014–15:

Receipts	£ million
Net national insurance contributions	83,001
Compensation from the Consolidated Fund for statutory sick, maternity, paternity and adoption pay recoveries	2,481
Income from investments	90
State scheme premiums	37
Other receipts	40
TOTAL RECEIPTS	85,648

Payments	£ million
Benefits	
At present rates	89,445
Increase due to proposed rate changes	2,369
Personal and stakeholder pensions contracted-out rebates	6
Age-related rebates for contracted-out money purchase schemes	1
Administration costs	962
Redundancy fund payments	318
Transfer to Northern Ireland	340
Other payments	172
TOTAL PAYMENTS	93,613

Balances	£ million
Balance at the begining of the year	22,033
Excess of receipts over payments	(7,965)
BALANCE AT END OF YEAR	14,068

CONTRIBUTIONS

There are six classes of National Insurance contributions (NICs):

Class 1	paid by employees and their employers
Class 1A	paid by employers who provide employees with certain benefits in kind for private use, such as company cars
Class 1B	paid by employers who enter into a pay as you earn (PAYE) settlement agreement (PSA) with HM Revenue and Customs
Class 2	paid by self-employed people
Class 3	voluntary contributions paid to protect entitlement to the state pension for those who do not pay enough NI contributions in another class
Class 4	paid by the self-employed on their taxable profits over a set limit. These are normally paid by self-employed people in addition to class 2 contributions. Class 4 contributions do not count towards benefits.

The lower and upper earnings limits and the percentage rates referred to below apply from April 2013 to April 2014.

CLASS 1

Class 1 contributions are paid where a person:
- is an employed earner (employee), office holder (eg company director) or employed under a contract of service in Great Britain or Northern Ireland
- is 16 or over and under state pension age
- earns at or above the earnings threshold of £153 per week (including overtime pay, bonus, commission, etc, without deduction of superannuation contributions)

Class 1 contributions are made up of primary and secondary contributions. Primary contributions are those paid by the employee and these are deducted from earnings by the employer. Since 6 April 2001 the employee's and employer's earnings thresholds have been the same and are referred to as the earnings threshold. Primary contributions are not paid on earnings below the earnings threshold of £153.00 per week. However, between the lower earnings limit of £111.00 per week and the earnings threshold of £153.00 per week, NI contributions are treated as having been paid to protect the benefit entitlement position of lower earners. Contributions are payable at the rate of 12 per cent on earnings between the earnings threshold and the upper earnings limit of £805.00 per week (10.6 per cent for contracted-out employment). Above the upper earnings limit 2 per cent is payable.

Some married women or widows pay a reduced rate of 5.85 per cent on earnings between the earnings threshold and upper earnings limits and 2 per cent above this. It is no longer possible to elect to pay the reduced rate but those who had reduced liability before 12 May 1977 may retain it for as long as certain conditions are met.

Secondary contributions are paid by employers of employed earners at the rate of 13.8 per cent on all earnings above the earnings threshold of £153 per week. There is no upper earnings limit for employers' contributions. Employers operating contracted-out salary related schemes pay reduced contributions of 10.4 per cent. The contracted-out rate applies only to that portion of earnings between the earnings threshold and the upper earnings limit. Employers' contributions below and above those respective limits are assessed at the appropriate not contracted-out rate.

CLASS 2
Class 2 contributions are paid where a person is self-employed and is 16 or over and under state pension age. Contributions are paid at a flat rate of £2.75 per week regardless of the amount earned. However, those with earnings of less than £5,885 a year can apply for small earnings exception. Those granted exemption from class 2 contributions may pay class 2 or class 3 contributions voluntarily. Self-employed earners (whether or not they pay class 2 contributions) may also be liable to pay class 4 contributions based on profits. There are special rules for those who are concurrently employed and self-employed.

Married women and widows can no longer choose not to pay class 2 contributions but those who elected not to pay class 2 contributions before 12 May 1977 may retain the right for as long as certain conditions are met.

Class 2 contributions are collected by the national insurance contributions department of HM Revenue and Customs (HMRC), by direct debit or quarterly bills.

CLASS 3
Class 3 contributions are voluntary flat-rate contributions of £13.90 per week payable by persons over the age of 16 who would otherwise be unable to qualify for retirement pension and certain other benefits because they have an insufficient record of class 1 or class 2 contributions. This may include those who are not working, those not liable for class 1 or class 2 contributions, or those excepted from class 2 contributions. Married women and widows who on or before 11 May 1977 elected not to pay class 1 (full rate) or class 2 contributions cannot pay class 3 contributions while they retain this right. Class 3 contributions are collected by HMRC by quarterly bills or direct debit.

CLASS 4
Self-employed people whose profits and gains are over £7,956 a year pay class 4 contributions in addition to class 2

contributions. This applies to self-employed earners over 16 and under the state pension age. Class 4 contributions are calculated at 9 per cent of annual profits or gains between £7,956 and £41,865 and 2 per cent above. Class 4 contributions are assessed and collected by HMRC. It is possible, in some circumstances, to apply for exceptions from liability to pay class 4 contributions or to have the amount of contribution reduced.

PENSIONS

Many people will qualify for a state pension; however, there are further pension choices available, such as workplace, personal and stakeholder pensions. There are also other non-pension savings and investment options. The following section provides background information on existing pension schemes.

STATE PENSION
From April 2016, the system of basic and additional state pension will be replaced with a new scheme for people reaching state pension age after that date (ie men born on or after 6 April 1951, and women born on or after 6 April 1953).

Current pensioners and those reaching state pension age before the introduction of the new state pension will continue to recieve their state pension in line with existing rules. Information about the new state pension can be found online: www.gov.uk/new-state-pension.

The state pension does not have to be claimed at state pension age, people can delay claiming it to earn weekly state pension (new state pension after 6 April 2016) or a lump sum payment.

CURRENT STATE PENSION SCHEME
The current system consists of:
• basic state pension
• additional state pension
People may be able to get both or either when they reach state pension age and meet the qualifying conditions.

Basic State Pension
The amount of basic state pension paid is dependent on the number of 'qualifying years' a person has established during their working life. In 2014–15, the full basic state pension is £113.10 a week (*see also* Benefits, State Pension: Categories A and B).

Working Life
The working life is from the start of the tax year (6 April) in which a person reaches 16 to the end of the tax year (5 April) before the one in which they reach state pension age (*see* State Pension Age).

Qualifying Years
A 'qualifying year' is a tax year in which a person has sufficient earnings upon which they have paid, are treated as having paid, or have been credited with national insurance (NI) contributions (*see* National Insurance Credits section).

From 6 April 2010 to 5 April 2016, a person who has 30 qualifying years will be entitled to a full basic state pension. Someone with less than 30 qualifying years will be entitled to a proportion of the full basic state pension based on the number of qualifying years they have. Just one qualifying year, achieved through paid or credited contributions, will give entitlement to the basic state pension worth one-thirtieth of the full basic state pension.

Until 6 April 2010, women normally needed 39 qualifying years for a full basic state pension (£113.10 in 2014–15) and men normally needed 44 qualifying years. A reduced-rate basic state pension was payable if the number of qualifying years was less than 90 per cent of the working life, but to receive any basic state pension at all, a person must have had enough qualifying years, normally 10 or 11, to receive a basic state pension of at least 25 per cent of the full rate.

The full rate of the new state pension will be finalised closer to its introduction. It will be set at a level that is above the basic level of means-tested support, the standard minimum guarantee in pension credit (£148.35 in 2014–15 for a single person).

The amounts of state pension people will receive under the new system will also be based on their NI record, with NI contributors or credits made prior to 6 April 2016 recognised under transitional arrangements.

NI contributions and credits will be used to calculate a 'starting amount' under the new system. An individual's starting amount will be the higher of either:
• the value of NI contributions under the current state pension rules (basic state pension and additional state pension)
• the value of NI contributions if the new state pension had been in place at the start of their working life
Individuals may be able to add to their starting amount by gaining NI qualifying years after 5 April 2016 (until they reach the full level of the new state pension or state pension age – whichever is first).

A minimum of 10 qualifying years will usually be needed to get any new state pension.

National Insurance Credits
Those in receipt of carer's allowance, working tax credit (with a disability element), jobseeker's allowance, incapacity benefit, employment support allowance, unemployability supplement, statutory sick pay, statutory maternity pay or statutory adoption pay may have class 1 NI contributions credited to them each week. People may also get credits if they are unemployed and looking for work or too sick to work, even if they have not paid enough contributions to receive benefit. Since April 2010, spouses and civil partners of members of HM forces may get credits if they are on an accompanied assignment outside the UK. Persons undertaking certain training courses or jury service or who have been wrongly imprisoned for a conviction which is quashed on appeal may also get class 1 NI credits for each week they fulfil certain conditions. Class 1 credits may also be available to men approaching state pension age. Until 5 April 2010, these credits were awarded for the tax years in which they reached age 60 and continued until age 64, if they were not liable to pay contributions and were not absent from the UK for more than six months in any tax year. Since 6 April 2010 these credits are being phased out in line with the increase in women's state pension age. Class 1 NI credits count toward all future contributory benefits. A class 3 NI credit for basic state pension and bereavement benefit purposes is awarded, where required, for each week the working tax credit (without a disability element) has been received or child benefit, for a child under 12, has been received. Class 3 credits may also be awarded, on application, to approved foster carers and people caring for at least 20 hours a week. Since 6 April 2011, class 3 credits have been available to adults under state pension age who care for a family member under 12. In certain cases people may also get a credit towards their state second pension.

State Pension Age
State pension age is currently 65 for men and between 60 and 65 for women. Women's state pension age will equalise with men's at 65 in 2018 and this will increase to age 66 by October 2020. However, The Pensions Act 2014 makes provision for a regular review of state pension age, based around the principle of maintaining a given proportion of adult life in receipt of state pension, with the proportion to

be set by the government of the day. Further information can be obtained from the online state pension calculator (W www.gov.uk/calculate-state-pension).

Using the NI Contribution Record of Another Person to Claim a State Pension
Married people or civil partners whose own NI record is incomplete may get a lower-rate basic state pension calculated using their partner's NI contribution record. This can be up to £67.80 a week in 2014–15, including any basic state pension of their own. Married men and civil partners may only be able to qualify if their spouse or civil partner was born on or after 6 April 1950. Widows, widowers, surviving civil partners, and people who are divorced or whose civil partnership has been dissolved may qualify for up to a full basic state pension based on their late or ex-spouse's/civil partner's NI contributions.

People who reach state pension age before 6 April 2016 will continue to be able to use these provisions, even if their spouse or civil partner reaches state pension age on or after that date. however, contributions their spouse or civil partner pays, or is credited with, following implementation of the new system will only count towards their own state pension. This means that only the NI record of the spouse or civil partner up to and including 2015–16 will be used to calculate any derived entitlement.

People reaching state pension age on or after 6 April 2016 will not be able to claim state pension on their spouse's or civil partner's NI record. There will be special arrangements for women who had opted to pay the married women's and widows reduced rate contributions before May 1977.

Non-contributory State Pensions
A non-contributory state pension may be payable to those aged 80 or over who live in England, Scotland or Wales, and have done so for a total of ten years or more for any continuous period in the 20 years after their 60th birthday, if they are not entitled to another category of state pension, or are entitled to one below the rate of £67.80 a week in 2014–15 (*see also* Benefits, State Pension for people aged 80 and over).

Graduated Retirement Benefit
Graduated Retirement Benefit (GRB) is based on the amount of graduated NI contributions paid into the GRB scheme between April 1961 and April 1975 (*see also* Benefits, Graduated Retirement Benefit).

Home Responsibilities Protection
From 6 April 1978 until 5 April 2010, it was possible for people who had low income or were unable to work because they cared for children or a sick or disabled person at home to reduce the number of qualifying years required for basic state pension. This was called home responsibilities protection (HRP); the number of years for which HRP was given was deducted from the number of qualifying years needed. HRP could, in some cases, also qualify the recipient for additional state pension. From April 2003 to April 2010 HRP was also available to approved foster carers.

From 6 April 2010, HRP was replaced by weekly credits for parents and carers. A class 3 national insurance credit is given, where eligible, towards basic state pension and bereavement benefits for spouses and civil partners. An earnings factor credit towards additional state pension is also awarded. Any years of HRP accrued before 6 April 2010 have been converted into qualifying years of credits for people reaching state pension age after that date, up to a maximum of 22 years for basic state pension purposes.

Additional State Pension
The amount of additional state pension paid depends on the amount of earnings a person has, or is treated as having,

between the lower and upper earnings limits (from April 2009, the upper accruals point replaced the upper earnings limit for additional pension) for each complete tax year between 6 April 1978 (when the scheme started) and the tax year before they reach state pension age. The right to additional state pension does not depend on the person's right to basic state pension.

From 1978 to 2002, additional state pension was called the State Earnings-Related Pension Scheme (SERPS). SERPS covered all earnings by employees from 6 April 1978 to 5 April 1997 on which standard rate class 1 NI contributions had been paid, and earnings between 6 April 1997 and 5 April 2002 if the standard rate class 1 NI contributions had been contracted-in.

In 2002, SERPS was reformed through the state second pension, by improving the pension available to low and moderate earners and extending access to certain carers and people with long-term illness or disability. If earnings on which class 1 NI contributions have been paid or can be treated as paid are above the annual NI lower earnings limit (£5,772 for 2014–15) but below the statutory low earnings threshold (£15,100 for 2014–15), the state second pension regards this as earnings of £15,000 and it is treated as equivalent. Certain carers and people with long-term illness and disability will be considered as having earned at the low earnings threshold for each complete tax year since 2002–3 even if they do not work at all, or earn less than the annual NI lower earnings limit.

The amount of additional state pension paid also depends on when a person reaches state pension age; changes phased in from 6 April 1999 mean that pensions are calculated differently from that date.

Additional State Pension Inheritance
Men or women widowed before 6 October 2002 may inherit all of their late spouse's SERPS pension. From 6 October 2002, the maximum percentage of SERPS pension that a person can inherit from a late spouse or civil partner depends on their late spouse's or civil partner's date of birth:

Maximum SERPS entitlement	d.o.b (men)	d.o.b (women)
100%	5/10/37 or earlier	5/10/42 or earlier
90%	6/10/37 to 5/10/39	6/10/42 to 5/10/44
80%	6/10/39 to 5/10/41	6/10/44 to 5/10/46
70%	6/10/41 to 5/10/43	6/10/46 to 5/10/48
60%	6/10/43 to 5/10/45	6/10/48 to 5/7/50
50%	6/10/45 or later	6/7/50 or later

The maximum state second pension a person can inherit from a spouse or civil partner is 50 per cent. If a person is bereaved before they have reached their state pension age, inherited SERPS or state second pension can be paid as part of widowed parents allowance (in the case of a person who has dependent children) or otherwise only from state pension age. If they remarry or form a new civil partnership before state pension age they lose the right to inherit any state pension.

New State Pension Inheritance
A person who reaches state pension age before 6 April 2016 will still be able to inherit additional state pension under the existing rules. However, if their late spouse or civil partner reaches state pension age on or after that date, the amount they can inherit will be based on the deceased's contributions up to 5 April 2016 only.

A person reaching state pension age on or after 6 April 2016 will be able to inherit part or all of the additional state pension built-up before 6 April 2016 by their deceased spouse or civil partner under specific circumstances.

In either case, in order to qualify for an inherited amount the marriage or civil partnership must have begun before 6 April 2016; and, in the case of a person widowed under state pension age, they must not remarry or form a new civil partnership before state pension age.

State Pension Statements
The Department for Work and Pensions provide state pension statements. These statements give an estimate of the state pension an individual may get based on their current NI contribution record (W www.gov.uk/state-pension-statement).

There is also an online state pension calculator. Individuals can use this to find out their state pension age and, based on information they provide, get an estimate of their basic state pension (W www.gov.uk/calculate-state-pension).

PRIVATE PENSIONS

CONTRACTED-OUT PENSIONS
'Contracting-out' means leaving the additional state pension and joining a workplace, company or occupational pension scheme to build up benefits into an alternative pension scheme.

Contracting-Out with an Occupational Pension Scheme
An occupational pension scheme is an arrangement some employers set up to give their employees a pension when they retire. The government is gradually introducing a requirement for all employers to provide their workers with a workplace pension. All employers will be included by 2018.

Providing that a company pension scheme meets certain conditions, it can be used to contract employees out of the additional state pension. Employees who join a scheme that is contracted-out will automatically be contracted-out of the additional state pension.

Employers providing such contracted-out schemes pay a lower rate of National Insurance contributions for those employees who join their schemes, and employees themselves also pay reduced-rate contributions.

Contracted-Out Salary-Related (COSR) Scheme
• these schemes (also known as contracted-out defined benefit (DB) or final salary schemes) provide a pension related to earnings and the length of pensionable service
• any notional additional state pension built up from 6 April 1978 to 5 April 1997 will be reduced by the amount of guaranteed minimum pension (GMP) accrued during that period (the contracted-out deduction). GMP is payable at 65 for men and 60 for women
• since 6 April 1997 these schemes no longer provide a GMP. Instead, as a condition of contracting-out they have to ensure that the benefits provided are at least as good as a prescribed standard (known as the Reference Scheme Test)
• when someone contracts-out of the additional state pension through these schemes, both the scheme member and the employer pay a reduced rate of NI contributions (known as the contracted-out rebate) to compensate for the additional state pension given up

Changes to contracted-out pensions from 2012
The rules for contracting-out of the additional state pension changed from 6 April 2012. The changes means contracting-out will not be possible through:
• a money purchase (defined contribution) occupational pension scheme
• a personal pension or stakeholder pension
From that date, employees have not been able to contract-out of the state second pension on a money purchase basis. Anyone contracted-out through this basis from that date was automatically contracted back into the additional state

pension. Those rights built up before the abolition date will be used to provide pension benefits. These changes have not affected contracting-out via a salary-related occupational pension scheme. However, the introduction of the singletier pension scheme in April 2016 will close the additional state pension for those reaching state pension age after this date, and contracting out on a DB basis will end.

STAKEHOLDER PENSION SCHEMES

Introduced in 2001, stakeholder pensions are available to everyone but are principally for moderate earners who do not have access to a good value company pension scheme. Stakeholder pensions must meet minimum standards to make sure they are flexible, portable and annual management charges are capped. The minimum contribution is £20.

As with personal pensions it is possible to invest up to £3,600 (including tax relief) into stakeholder pensions each year without evidence of earnings. Contributions can be made on someone else's behalf, eg a non-working partner.

AUTOMATIC ENROLMENT INTO WORKPLACE PENSIONS

Since October 2012, employers must automatically enrol their workers who meet the age and earnings criteria into a workplace pension. This applies to people who are not already in a workplace pension scheme and who:
• earn over £10,000 per annum
• are aged 22 or over
• are under state pension age
• work in the UK
Employees who meet the above requirements are entitled to opt out of the scheme if they wish to. If remains in the scheme, they, together with their employer, will pay into it every month. The government will also contribute through tax relief. Further information is available at W www.gov.uk/workplace-pensions

COMPLAINTS

The Pensions Advisory Service provides information and guidance to members of the public, on state, company, personal and stakeholder schemes. They also help any member of the public who has a problem, complaint or dispute with their occupational or personal pensions.

There are two bodies for pension complaints. The Financial Ombudsman Service deals with complaints which predominantly concern the sale and/or marketing of occupational, stakeholder and personal pensions. The Pensions Ombudsman deals with complaints which predominantly concern the management (after sale or marketing) of occupational, stakeholder and personal pensions.

The Pensions Regulator is the UK regulator for work-based pension schemes; it concentrates its resources on schemes where there is the greatest risk to the security of members' benefits, promotes good administration practice for all work-based schemes and works with trustees, employers and professional advisers to put things right when necessary.

WAR PENSIONS AND THE ARMED FORCES COMPENSATION SCHEME

The Service Personnel and Veterans Agency (SPVA) is part of the Ministry of Defence. SPVA was formed on 1 April 2007 from the former Armed Forces Personnel Administration Agency and the Veterans Agency to provide services to both serving personnel and veterans.

SPVA is responsible for the administration of the war pensions scheme and the armed forces compensation scheme (AFCS) to members of the armed forces in respect of disablement or death due to service. There is also a scheme

for civilians and civil defence workers in respect of the Second World War, and other schemes for groups such as merchant seamen and Polish armed forces who served under British command during the Second World War. The agency is also responsible for the administration of the armed forces pension scheme (AFPS), which provides occupational pensions for ex-service personnel (see Defence).

THE WAR PENSIONS SCHEME

War disablement pension is awarded for the disabling effects of any injury, wound or disease which was the result of, or was aggravated by, service in the armed forces prior to 6 April 2005. Claims are only considered once the person has left the armed forces. The amount of pension paid depends on the severity of disablement, which is assessed by comparing the health of the claimant with that of a healthy person of the same age and sex. The person's earning capacity or occupation are not taken into account in this assessment. A pension is awarded if the person has a disablement of 20 per cent or more and a lump sum is usually payable to those with a disablement of less than 20 per cent. No award is made for noise-induced sensorineural hearing loss where the assessment of disablement is less than 20 per cent. Where an assessment of disablement is at 40 per cent or more, an age addition is automatically given when the pensioner reaches 65.

A pension is payable to war widows, widowers and surviving civil partners where the spouse's or civil partner's death was due to, or hastened by, service in the armed forces prior to 6 April 2005 or where the spouse or civil partner was in receipt of a war disablement pension constant attendance allowance (or would have been if not in hospital) at the time of death. A pension is also payable to widows, widowers or surviving civil partners if the spouse or civil partner was receiving the war disablement pension at the 80 per cent rate or higher in conjunction with unemployability supplement at the time of death. War widows, widowers and surviving civil partners receive a standard rank-related rate, but a lower weekly rate is payable to war widows, widowers and surviving civil partners of personnel of the rank of Major or below who are under the age of 40, without children and capable of maintaining themselves. This is increased to the standard rate at age 40. Allowances are paid for children and adult dependants. An age allowance is automatically given when the widow, widower or surviving civil partner reaches 65 and increased at ages 70 and 80.

Pensioners living overseas receive the same pension rates as those living in the UK. All war disablement pensions and allowances and pensions for war widows, widowers and surviving civil partners are tax-free in the UK; this does not always apply in overseas countries due to different tax laws.

SUPPLEMENTARY ALLOWANCES

A number of supplementary allowances may be awarded to a war pensioner and are intended to meet various needs. The principal supplementary allowances are unemployability supplement, allowance for lowered standard of occupation, constant attendance allowance and war pensions mobility supplement. Others include exceptionally severe disablement allowance, severe disablement occupational allowance, treatment allowance, comforts allowance, clothing allowance, age allowance and widow/widower/surviving civil partner's age allowance. Rent and children's allowances are also available with pensions for war widows, widowers and surviving civil partners.

ARMED FORCES COMPENSATION SCHEME

The armed forces compensation scheme (AFCS) became effective on 6 April 2005 and covers all regular (including

Gurkhas) and reserve personnel whose injury, ill health or death is caused predominantly by service on or after 6 April 2005. There are time limits under this scheme and generally claims must be made within seven years of the injury occuring or from first seeking medical advice about an illness. There are some exceptions to this time limit, the main one being for a late-onset illness. Claims for a late-onset illness can be made at any time after the event to which it relates, providing the claim is made within three years of medical advice being sought.

The AFCS provides compensation where service in the armed forces is the only or predominant cause of injury, illness or death. Any other personal accident cover held by the individual is not taken into account when determining an AFCS award. Under the terms of the scheme a tax-free lump sum is payable to service or ex-service personnel based on a 15-level tariff, graduated according to the seriousness of the injury. If multiple injuries are sustained in the same incident compensation for each injury, up to the scheme maximum, is awarded. For those with the most serious injuries and illness a tax-free, index-linked monthly payment – a guaranteed income payment or GIP – is paid for life from the point of discharge. A survivor's GIP (SGIP) will also be paid to surviving spouses, civil partners and unmarried partners who meet certain criteria. GIP and SGIP are calculated by multiplying the pensionable pay of the service person by a factor that depends on the age at the person's last birthday. The younger the person, the higher the factor, because there are more years to normal retirement age.

ARMED FORCES INDEPENDENCE PAYMENT
Armed forces independence payment (AFIP) is designed to provide financial support for service personnel and veterans who have been seriously injured to cover the extra costs they may incur as a result of their injury. It is administered by Veterans UK as part of AFCS although payments are made by the Department for Work and Pensions (DWP). It is non-taxable and non-means-tested.

Service personnel and veterans awarded a GIP of 50 per cent or higher under the AFCS are eligible. Those eligible for AFIP are not required to undergo an assessment and will keep the payment for as long as they are entitled to recieve a GIP of 50 per cent or higher.

DEPARTMENT FOR WORK AND PENSIONS BENEFITS
Payments under the AFCS and the war pensions scheme may affect income related benefits from the DWP. In particular any supplementary allowances in payment with war pensions. Any state pension for which a war widow, widower or surviving civil partner qualifies for on their own NI contribution record can be paid in addition to monies received under the war pensions scheme.

CLAIMS AND QUESTIONS
Further information on the war pensions scheme, the AFCS and the nearest Veterans' Welfare Office can be obtained from the Service Personnel and Veterans Agency by telephone (T 0800-169 2277, if calling from the UK or, if living overseas, T (+44) (125) 386-6043).

SERVICE PERSONNEL AND VETERANS AGENCY,
Norcross Lane, Thornton-Cleveleys FY5 3WP
E veterans-uk@mod.uk W www.veterans-uk.info

TAX CREDITS

Tax credits are administered by HM Revenue and Customs (HMRC). They are based on an individual's or couple's household income and current circumstances. Adjustments can be made during the year to reflect changes in income and/or circumstances. Further information regarding the qualifying conditions for tax credits, how to claim and the rates payable is available online on the HMRC website (W www.hmrc.gov.uk/taxcredits).

WORKING TAX CREDIT
Working tax credit is a payment from the government to support people on low incomes. It may be claimed by:
- those aged 25 or over who work at least 30 hours a week
- those aged 16 or over who work at least 16 hours a week, who are responsible for a child or young person, or have a disability that puts them at a disadvantage of getting a job
- those aged 60 or over, who work at least 16 hours a week
- couples who are responsible for a child or young person, who work at least 24 hours per week between them with one partner working at least 16 hours a week

The amount received depends on the circumstances and number of hours worked a week.

WORKING TAX CREDIT FOR INDIVIDUALS WITHOUT CHILDREN 2014–15
The amounts shown are for a selection of incomes and statuses.

Annual Income/Status	Tax Credit per annum
£5,250	
*Single	–
*Couple	–
Single adult with a disability	£4,880
£9,850	
Single	£1,340
Couple	£3,330
Single adult with a disability	£3,475
£10,000	
Single	£1,275
Couple	£3,270
Single adult with a disability	£3,410
£12,000	
Single	£455
Couple	£2,450
Single adult with a disability	£2,590
£16,000	
Single	–
Couple	£810
Single adult with a disability	£950

* No amounts are shown here as this income would be under the minimum wage for 2014–15 of £5328.96 per annum for an adult (aged 21 and above) working 16 hours a week (six months at £6.19/hour (minimum wage April to September 2014), plus six months at £6.50 (minimum wage from October 2014))

CHILDCARE
In families with children where a lone parent works at least 16 hours a week, or couples who work at least 24 hours a week between them with one partner working at least 16 hours a week, or where one partner works at least 16 hours a week and the other is disabled, an in-patient in hospital, or in prison, the family is entitled to the childcare element of working tax credit. Depending on circumstances this payment can contribute up to £175 of childcare costs for one child and up to £300 a week for two or more children. Families can only claim if they use an approved or registered childcare provider.

CHILD TAX CREDIT
Child tax credit combines all income-related support for children and is paid direct to the main carer. The credit is

made up of a main 'family' payment with additional payments for each extra child in the household, for children with a disability and an extra payment for children who are severely disabled. Child tax credit is available to households where:
• there is at least one dependant under 16
• there is at least one dependant between 16 and 20 who is in relevant education or training or is registered for work, education or training with an approved body

BENEFITS

The following is intended as a general guide to the benefits system. Conditions of entitlement and benefit rates change annually and all prospective claimants should check exact entitlements and rates of benefit directly with their local Jobcentre Plus office, pension centre or online (W www.gov.uk). Leaflets relating to the various benefits and contribution conditions for different benefits are available from local Jobcentre Plus offices.

UNIVERSAL CREDIT
From 29 April 2013, Universal Credit began to gradually be introduced in certain areas of the country. Universal Credit is a single new payment for those looking for work or on a low income. Universal Credit will eventually replace:
• Income-based jobseekers allowance
• Income-related employment support allowance
• Income support
• Child tax credit
• Working tax credit
• Housing benefit
For more information go to W www.gov.uk/universalcredit

CONTRIBUTORY BENEFITS
Entitlement to contributory benefits depends on national insurance contribution conditions being satisfied either by the claimant or by someone on the claimant's behalf (depending on the kind of benefit). The class or classes of national insurance contribution relevant to each benefit are:

Jobseeker's allowance (contribution-based)	Class 1
Employment and Support Allowance (contributory)	Class 1 or 2
Widow's benefit and bereavement benefit	Class 1, 2 or 3
State pensions, categories A and B	Class 1, 2 or 3

The system of contribution conditions relates to yearly levels of earnings on which national insurance (NI) contributions have been paid.

JOBSEEKER'S ALLOWANCE
Jobseeker's allowance (JSA) replaced unemployment benefit and income support for unemployed people under state pension age from 7 October 1996. There are two routes of entitlement. Contribution-based JSA is paid at a personal rate (ie additional benefit for dependants is not paid) to those who have made sufficient NI contributions in two particular tax years. Savings and partner's earnings are not taken into account and payment can be made for up to six months. Rates of JSA correspond to income support rates.
    Claims are made through Jobcentre Plus. A person wishing to claim JSA must generally be unemployed or working on average less than 16 hours a week, capable of work and available for any work which he or she can reasonably be expected to do, usually for at least 40 hours a week. The claimant must agree and sign a 'jobseeker's agreement', which will set out his or her plans to find work, and must actively seek work. If the claimant refuses work or training the benefit may be sanctioned for between one and 26 weeks.

A person will be sanctioned from JSA for up to 26 weeks if he or she has left a job voluntarily without just cause or through misconduct. In these circumstances, it may be possible to receive hardship payments, particularly where the claimant or the claimant's family is vulnerable, eg if sick or pregnant, or with children or caring responsibilities.

Weekly Rates from April 2014

Person aged 16–24	£57.35
Person aged 25 to state pension age*	£72.40

* Since October 2003 people aged between 60 and state pension age can choose to claim pension credits instead of JSA

EMPLOYMENT AND SUPPORT ALLOWANCE
From 27 October 2008, employment and support allowance (ESA) replaced incapacity benefit and income support paid on the grounds of incapacity or disability. The benefit consists of two strands, contribution-based benefit and income-related benefit, so that people no longer need to make two claims for benefit in order to gain their full entitlement. Contributory ESA is available to those who have limited capability for work but cannot get statutory sick pay from their employer. Those over pensionable age are not entitled to ESA. Apart from those who qualify under the special provisions for people incapacitated in youth, entitlement to contributory ESA is based on a person's NI contribution record. In order to qualify for contributory ESA, two contribution conditions, based on the last three years before the tax year in which benefit is claimed, must be satisfied. The amount of contributory ESA payable may be reduced where the person receives more than a specified amount of occupational or personal pension. Contributory ESA is paid only in respect of the person claiming the benefit – there are no additional amounts for dependants.
    At the outset, new claimants are paid a basic allowance (the same rate as jobseeker's allowance) for 13 weeks while their medical condition is assessed and a work capability assessment is conducted. Following the completion of the assessment phase those claimants capable of engaging in work-related activities will receive a work-related activity component on top of the basic rate. The work-related activity component can be subject to sanctions if the claimant does not engage in the conditionality requirements without good reason. The maximum sanction is equal to the value of the work-related activity component of the benefit.
    Those with the most severe health conditions or disabilities will receive the support component, which is more than the work-related activity component. Claimants in receipt of the support component are not required to engage in work-related activities, although they can volunteer to do so or undertake permitted work if their condition allows.

Weekly Rates from April 2014

ESA plus work-related activity component	up to £101.15
ESA plus support component	up to £108.15

BEREAVEMENT BENEFITS
Bereavement benefits replaced widow's benefit on 9 April 2001. Those claiming widow's benefit before this date will continue to receive it under the old scheme for as long as they qualify. The new system provides bereavement benefits for widows, widowers and, from 5 December 2005, surviving civil partners (providing that their deceased spouse or civil partner paid NI contributions). The new system offers benefits in three forms:
• *Bereavement payment* – may be received by a man or woman who is under the state pension age at the time of their spouse or civil partner's death, or whose husband, wife or

civil partner was not entitled to a category A retirement pension when he or she died. It is a single tax-free lump sum of £2,000 payable immediately on widowhood or loss of a civil partner

• *Widowed parent's allowance* – a taxable benefit payable to the surviving partner if he or she is entitled or treated as entitled to child benefit, or to a widow if she is expecting her husband's baby at the time of his death

• *Bereavement allowance* – a taxable weekly benefit paid for 52 weeks after the spouse or civil partner's death. If aged over 55 and under state pension age the full allowance is payable, if aged between 45 and 54 a percentage of the full rate is paid. A widow, widower or surviving civil partner may receive this allowance if his or her widowed parent's allowance ends before 52 weeks

It is not possible to receive widowed parent's allowance and bereavement allowance at the same time. Bereavement benefits and widow's benefit, in any form, cease upon remarriage or a new civil partnership or are suspended during a period of cohabitation as partners without being legally married or in a civil partnership.

Weekly Rates from April 2014

Bereavement payment (lump sum)	£2,000
Widowed parent's allowance (or widowed mother's allowance)	£111.20
Bereavement allowance (or widow's pension), full entitlement (aged 55 and over at time of spouse's or civil partner's death)	£111.20

Amount of bereavement allowance (or widow's pension) by age of widow/widower or surviving civil partner at spouse's or civil partner's death:

aged 54	£103.42
aged 53	£95.63
aged 52	£87.85
aged 51	£80.06
aged 50	£72.28
aged 49	£64.50
aged 48	£56.71
aged 47	£48.93
aged 46	£41.14
aged 45	£33.36

STATE PENSION: CATEGORIES A AND B

Category A pension is payable for life to men and women who reach state pension age, who satisfy the contributions conditions and who claim for it. Category B pension may be payable to married women, married men and civil partners who are not entitled to a basic state pension on their own NI contributions or whose own basic state pension entitlement is less than £67.80 a week in 2014–15. It is based on their wife's, husband's or civil partner's NI contributions and is payable when both members of the couple have reached state pension age. Married men and civil partners may only be able to qualify for a category B pension if their wife or civil partner was born on or after 6 April 1950. Category B pension is also payable to widows, widowers and surviving civil partners who are bereaved before state pension age if they were previously entitled to widowed parent's allowance or bereavement allowance based on their late spouse's or civil partner's NI contributions. If they were receiving widowed parent's allowance on reaching state pension age, they could qualify for a category B pension payable at the same rate as their widowed parent's allowance comprising a basic pension, plus, if applicable, the appropriate share of their late spouse's or late civil partner's additional state pension. If their widowed parent's allowance had stopped before they

reached state pension age, or they had been getting bereavement allowance at any time before state pension age, their category B pension will consist of inheritable additional state pension only. No basic state pension is included, although they may qualify for a basic state pension or have their own basic state pension improved by substituting their late spouse's or late civil partner's NI records for their own.

Widows who are bereaved when over state pension age can qualify for a category B pension regardless of the age of their husband when he died. This is payable at the same rate as the basic state pension the widow's late husband was entitled to (or would have been entitled to) at the time of his death. It can also be paid to widowers and civil partners who are bereaved when over state pension age if their wife or civil partner had reached state pension age when they died. Widowers and surviving civil partners who reached state pension age on or after 6 April 2010 and bereaved when over state pension age can qualify for a category B pension regardless of the age of their wife or civil partner when they died.

Where a person is entitled to both a category A and category B pension then they can be combined to give a composite pension, but this cannot be more than the full rate pension. Where a person is entitled to more than one category A or category B pension then only one can be paid. In such cases the person can choose which to get; if no choice is made, the most favourable one is paid.

A person may defer claiming their pension beyond state pension age. In doing so they may earn increments which will increase the weekly amount paid by 1 per cent per five weeks of deferral (equivalent to 10.4 per cent/year) when they claim their state pension. If a person delays claiming for at least 12 months they are given the option of a one-off taxable lump sum, instead of a pension increase, based on the weekly pension deferred, plus interest of at least 2 per cent above the Bank of England base rate. Since 6 April 2010, a category B pension has been treated independently of the spouse's or partner's pension. It is possible to take a category B pension even if the spouse or partner has deferred theirs.

It is no longer possible to claim an increase on a state pension for another adult (known as adult dependency increase). Those who received the increase before April 2010 can keep receiving it until the conditions are no longer met or until 5 April 2020, whichever is first.

Provision for children is made through child tax credits. An age addition of 25p a week is payable with a state pension if a pensioner is aged 80 or over.

Since 1989 pensioners have been allowed to have unlimited earnings without affecting their state pension. *See also* Pensions.

Weekly Rates from April 2014

Category A or B pension for a single person	£113.10
Based on husband's/wife's/civil partner's NI contributions	£67.80

GRADUATED RETIREMENT BENEFIT

Graduated retirement benefit (GRB) is based on the amount of graduated NI contributions paid into the GRB scheme between April 1961 and April 1975; however, it is still paid in addition to any state pension to those who made the relevant contributions. A person will receive graduated retirement benefit based on their own contributions, even if not entitled to a basic state pension. Widows, widowers and surviving civil partners may inherit half of their deceased spouse's or civil partner's entitlement, but none that the deceased spouse or civil partner may have been eligible for from a former spouse or civil partner. If a person defers making a claim beyond state pension age, they may earn an increase or a one-off lump sum payment in respect of their deferred graduated retirement benefit; calculated in the same way as for category A or B state pension.

NON-CONTRIBUTORY BENEFITS

These benefits are paid from general taxation and are not dependent on NI contributions.

JOBSEEKER'S ALLOWANCE (INCOME-BASED)

Those who do not qualify for contribution-based jobseeker's allowance (JSA), those who have exhausted their entitlement to contribution-based JSA or those for whom contribution-based JSA provides insufficient income may qualify for income-based JSA. The amount paid depends on age, whether they are single or a couple, number of dependants and amount of income and savings. Income-based JSA comprises three parts:
• a personal allowance for the jobseeker and his/her partner*
• premiums for people with special needs
• amounts for housing costs

* Since April 2003, child dependants have been provided for through the child tax credit system

The rules of entitlement are the same as for contribution-based JSA.

If one person in a couple was born after 28 October 1957 and neither person in the couple has responsibility for a child or children, then the couple will have to make a joint claim for JSA if they wish to receive income-based JSA.

Weekly Rates from April 2014

Person aged 16–24	£57.35
Person aged 25 to state pension age	£72.40
Couple, both under 18; or, one under 18, one aged 18–24*	£57.35
Couple, one under 18, one aged 25+	£72.40
Couple aged 18 to state pension age	£113.70
Lone parent aged under 18	£57.35
Lone parent aged 18 to state pension age	£72.40
* depending on circumstances	

MATERNITY ALLOWANCE

Maternity allowance (MA) is a benefit available for pregnant women who cannot get statutory maternity pay (SMP) from their employer or have been employed/self-employed during or close to their pregnancy. In order to qualify for payment, a woman must have been employed and/or self-employed for at least 26 weeks in the 66-week period up to and including the week before the baby is due (test period). These weeks do not have to be in a row and any part weeks worked will count towards the 26 weeks. She must also have an average weekly earning of at least £30 (maternity allowance threshold) over any 13 weeks of the woman's choice within the test period.

Self-employed women who pay class 2 NI contributions or who hold a small earnings exception certificate are deemed to have enough earnings to qualify for MA.

A woman can choose to start receiving MA from the 11th week before the week in which the baby is due (if she stops work before then) up to the day following the day of birth. The exact date MA starts will depend on when the woman stops work to have her baby or if the baby is born before she stops work. However, where the woman is absent from work wholly or partly due to her pregnancy in the four weeks before the week the baby is due to be born, MA will start the day following the first day of absence from work. MA is paid for a maximum of 39 weeks.

The woman may be entitled to get extra payments for her husband, civil partner or someone else who looks after her children.

Weekly Rate from April 2014

Standard rate	£138.18 or 90 per cent of the woman's average weekly earnings if less than £138.18

CHILD BENEFIT

Child benefit is payable for virtually all children aged under 16 and for those aged 16 and 17 if they are in relevant education or training or are registered for work, education or training with an approved body.

Weekly Rates at April 2014

Eldest/only child	£20.50
Each subsequent child	£13.55

GUARDIAN'S ALLOWANCE

Guardian's allowance is payable to a person who is bringing up a child or young person because the child's parents have died, or in some circumstances, where only one parent has died. To receive the allowance the person must be in receipt of child benefit for the child or young person, although they do not have to be the child's legal guardian.

Weekly Rate (in addition to child benefit) from April 2014

Each child	£16.35

CARER'S ALLOWANCE

Carer's allowance (CA) is a benefit payable to people who spend at least 35 hours a week caring for a severely disabled person. To qualify for CA a person must be caring for someone in receipt of one of the following benefits:
• attendance allowance
• personal independence payment
• constant attendance allowance, paid at not less than the normal maximum rate with an industrial injuries disablement payment or basic (full-day) rate, under the industrial injuries or war pension schemes.
• armed forces independence payment (AFIP)

Weekly Rate from April 2014

Carer's allowance	£61.35

ATTENDANCE ALLOWANCE

This may be payable to people aged 65 or over who need help with personal care because they are physically or mentally disabled, and who have needed help for a period of at least six months. Attendance allowance has two rates: the lower rate is for day or night care, and the higher rate is for day and night care. People not expected to live for more than six months because of a progressive disease can receive the highest rate of attendance allowance straight away.

Weekly Rates from April 2014

Higher rate	£81.30
Lower rate	£54.45

PERSONAL INDEPENDENCE PAYMENT (PIP)

Personal independence payment (PIP) replaced disability living allowance (DLA) for people aged 16 to 64 on 8 April 2013. PIP has two components: the daily living component and the mobility component, with each offering two different benefit rates: standard and enhanced. Whether one or both components are claimed depends on the requirements of the individual. Claimants are assessed on their ability to carry out everyday activities, with the majority of claims evaluated via an interview. Claimants with a terminal illness automatically receive the enhanced daily living component.

Weekly Rates from April 2014
Daily living component

Standard	£54.45
Enhanced	£81.30

Mobility component

Standard	£21.55
Enhanced	£56.75

STATE PENSION FOR PEOPLE AGED 80 AND OVER

A state pension, also referred to as category D pension, is provided for people aged 80 and over if they are not entitled to another category of pension or are entitled to a state pension that is less than £66.00 a week. The person must also live in Great Britain and have done so for a period of ten years or more in any continuous 20-year period since their 60th birthday.

Weekly Rate from April 2014

Single person	£67.80
Age addition	£0.25

INCOME SUPPORT

Broadly speaking income support is a benefit for those between age 16 and the age they can receive pension credit, whose income is below a certain level, who work on average less than 16 hours a week and who are:

• bringing up children alone
• registered sick or disabled
• a student who is also a lone parent or disabled
• caring for someone who is sick or elderly

Income support is not payable if the claimant, or claimant and partner, have capital or savings in excess of £16,000 – and deductions are made for capital and savings over £6,000. For people permanently in residential care and nursing homes deductions apply for capital in excess of £10,000.

Sums payable depend on fixed allowances laid down by law for people in different circumstances. If both partners are eligible for income support, either may claim it for the couple. People receiving income support may be able to receive housing benefit, help with mortgage or home loan interest and help with healthcare. They may also be eligible for help with exceptional expenses from the Social Fund. Special rates may apply to some people living in residential care or nursing homes.

INCOME SUPPORT PREMIUMS

Income support premiums are extra weekly payments for those with additional needs. People qualifying for more than one premium will normally only receive the highest single premium for which they qualify. However, family premium, disabled child premium, severe disability premium and carer premium are payable in addition to other premiums.

Child tax credit replaced premiums for people with children for all new income support claims from 6 April 2004. People with children who were already in receipt of income support in April 2004 and have not claimed child tax credit may qualify for:

• the family premium if they have at least one child
• the disabled child premium if they have a child who receives disability living allowance or is registered blind
• the enhanced disability child premium if they have a child in receipt of the higher rate disability living allowance care component

Carers may qualify for:

• the carer premium if they or their partner are in receipt of carer's allowance

Long-term sick or disabled people may qualify for:

• the disability premium if they or their partner are receiving certain benefits because they are disabled or cannot work; are registered blind; or if the claimant has been incapable of work or receiving statutory sick pay for at least 364 days (196 days if the person is terminally ill), including periods of incapacity separated by eight weeks or less
• the severe disability premium if the person lives alone and receives the middle or higher rate of disability living allowance care component and no one receives carer's allowance for caring for that person
• the enhanced disability premium if the person is in receipt of the higher rate disability living allowance care component

People with a partner aged over 60 may qualify for:

• the pensioner premium

WEEKLY RATES OF INCOME SUPPORT
from April 2014

Single person

aged 16–24	£57.35
aged 25+	£72.40
aged under 18 and a single parent	£57.35
aged 18+ and a single parent	£72.40

Couples

Both under 18	£57.35
Both under 18, in certain circumstances	£86.65
One under 18, one aged 18–24	£57.35
One under 18, one aged 25+	£72.40
Both aged 18+	£113.70

Premiums

Carer premium	£34.20
Severe disability premium	£61.10
Enhanced disability premium	
Single person	£15.55
Couples	£22.35
Pensioner premium (couple)	£112.80

PENSION CREDIT

Pension credit was introduced on 6 October 2003 and replaced income support for those aged 60 and over. Between April 2010 and April 2020 the pension credit qualifying age is increasing from 60 to 65 alongside the increase in women's state pension age.

There are two elements to pension credit:

THE GUARANTEE CREDIT

The guarantee credit guarantees a minimum income of £148.35 for single people and £226.50 for couples, with additional elements for people who have:

• eligible housing costs
• severe disabilities
• caring responsibilities

Income from state pension, private pensions, earnings, working tax credit and certain benefits are taken into account when calculating the pension credit. For savings and capital in excess of £10,000, £1 for every £500 or part of £500 held is taken into account as income when working out entitlement to pension credit.

People receiving the guarantee credit element of pension credit will be able to receive housing benefit, council tax benefit and help with healthcare costs.

Weekly Rates from April 2014

Additional amount for severe disability	
Single person	£61.10
Couple (one qualifies)	£61.10
Couple (both qualify)	£122.20
Additional amount for carers	£34.20

THE SAVINGS CREDIT

Single people aged 65 or over (and couples where one member is 65 or over) may be entitled to a savings credit which provides additional support for pensioners who have made modest provision towards their retirement. The savings credit is calculated by taking into account any qualifying income above the savings credit threshold. For 2014–15 the threshold is £120.35 for single people and £192.00 for couples. The maximum savings credit is £16.80 per week (£20.70 a week for couples)

Income that qualifies towards the savings credit includes state pensions, earnings, second pensions and income taken into account from capital above £10,000.

Some people will be entitled to the guarantee credit, some to the savings credit and some to both.

Where only the savings credit is in payment, people need to claim standard housing benefit or council tax benefit. Although local authorities take any savings credit into account in the housing benefit or council tax benefit assessment, for people aged 65 and over housing benefit or council tax benefit is enhanced to ensure that gains in pension credit are not depleted.

HOUSING BENEFIT

Housing benefit is designed to help people with rent (including rent for accommodation in guesthouses, lodgings or hostels). It does not cover mortgage payments. The amount of benefit paid depends on:

- the income of the claimant, and partner if there is one, including earned income, unearned income (any other income including some other benefits) and savings
- number of dependants
- certain extra needs of the claimant, partner or any dependants
- number and gross income of people sharing the home who are not dependent on the claimant
- how much rent is paid

Housing benefit is not payable if the claimant, or claimant and partner, have savings in excess of £16,000. The amount of benefit is affected if savings held exceed £6,000 (£10,000 for people living in residential care and nursing homes). Housing benefit is not paid for meals, fuel or certain service charges that may be included in the rent. Deductions are also made for most non-dependants who live in the same accommodation as the claimant (and their partner). If the claimant is living with a partner or civil partner there can only be one claim.

The maximum amount of benefit (which is not necessarily the same as the amount of rent paid) may be paid where the claimant is in receipt of income support, income-based jobseeker's allowance, the guarantee element of pension credit or where the claimant's income is less than the amount allowed for their needs. Any income over that allowed for their needs will mean that their benefit is reduced.

LOCAL HOUSING ALLOWANCE

Local housing allowance (LHA), which was rolled out nationally from 7 April 2008, is a way of calculating the rent element of housing benefit based on the area in which a person lives and household size. It affects people in the deregulated private rented sector who make a new claim for housing benefit or existing recipients who move address. LHA ensures that tenants in similar circumstances in the same area receive the same amount of financial support for their housing costs. It does not affect the way a person's income or capital is taken into account. LHA is paid to the tenant rather than the landlord in most circumstances. A weekly limit on payments is now in place so LHA does not exceed:

- £250 for a one bedroom property
- £290 for a two bedroom property
- £340 for a three bedroom property
- £400 for a four bedroom property

COUNCIL TAX REDUCTION

From April 2013, council tax benefit was replaced by council tax reduction. Nearly all the rules that apply to housing benefit apply to council tax reduction, which helps people on low incomes to pay council tax bills. The amount payable depends on how much council tax is paid and who lives with the claimant. The benefit may be available to those receiving income support, income-based jobseeker's allowance, the guarantee element of pension credit or to those whose income is less than that allowed for their needs. Any income over that allowed for their needs will mean that they will receive less help with their council tax reduction. Deductions are made for non-dependants.

A full council tax bill is based on at least two adults living in a home. Residents may receive a 25 per cent reduction on their bill if they count as an adult for council tax and live on their own. If the property is the resident's main home and there is no-one who counts as an adult, the reduction is 50 per cent.

THE SOCIAL FUND

REGULATED PAYMENTS
Sure Start Maternity Grant

Sure start maternity grant (SSMG) is a one-off payment of £500 to help people on low incomes pay for essential items for new babies that are expected, born, adopted, the subject of a parental order (following a surrogate birth) or, in certain circumstances, the subject of a residency order. SSMG can be claimed any time from within 11 weeks of the expected birth and up to three months after the birth, adoption or date of parental or residency order. Those eligible are people in receipt of income support, income-based jobseeker's allowance, pension credit, child tax credit at a rate higher than the family element or working tax credit where a disability or severe disability element is in payment. Since 11 April 2011, new rules have been applied for babies due, born or adopted on this date. These are that SSMG is only available if there are no other children under 16 in the family or in the case of a dependent child's new baby, SSMG is only available if the dependent is under the age of 20 and has no other children.

Funeral Payments

Payable to help cover the necessary cost of burial or cremation, a new burial plot with an exclusive right of burial (where burial is chosen), certain other expenses, and up to £700 for any other funeral expenses, such as the funeral director's fees, the coffin or flowers. Those eligible are people receiving income support, income-based jobseeker's allowance, pension credit, child tax credit at a higher rate than the family element, working tax credit where a disability or severe disability element is in payment, council tax benefit or housing benefit who have good reason for taking responsibility for the funeral expenses. These payments are recoverable from any estate of the deceased.

Cold Weather Payments

A payment of £25.00 per seven day period between 1 November and 31 March when the average temperature is recorded at or forecast to be 0°C or below over seven consecutive days in the qualifying person's area. Payments are made to people on pension credit or child tax credit with a disability element, those on income support whose benefit includes a pensioner or disability premium, and those on income-based jobseeker's allowance or employment and support allowance who have a child who is disabled or under the age of five. Payments are made automatically and do not have to be repaid.

Winter Fuel Payments
For 2014–15 the winter fuel payment is set at £200 for households with someone aged 62–79 and £300 for households with someone aged 80 or over. The rate paid is based on the person's age and circumstances in the 'qualifying week' between 15 and 21 September 2014. The majority of eligible people are paid automatically before Christmas, although a few need to claim. Payments do not have to be repaid.

Christmas Bonus
The Christmas bonus is a one-off tax-free £10 payment made before Christmas to those people in receipt of a qualifying benefit in the qualifying week.

DISCRETIONARY PAYMENTS
Community Care Grants
These are intended to help people in Northern Ireland (they are no longer available in the rest of the UK) in receipt of income support, income-based jobseeker's allowance or employment and support allowance, pension credit, or payments on account of such benefits (or those likely to receive these benefits within the next six weeks because they are leaving residential or institutional accommodation) to live as independently as possible in the community; ease exceptional pressures on families; care for a prisoner or young offender released on temporary licence; help people set up home as part of a resettlement programme and/or assist with certain travelling expenses. They do not have to be repaid.

Budgeting Loans
These are interest-free loans to people who have been receiving income support, income-based jobseeker's allowance or employment and support allowance, pension credit or payments on account of such benefits for at least 26 weeks, for intermittent expenses that may be difficult to budget for. The smallest amount available to borrow is £100.

Crisis Loans
These are interest-free loans available to anyone in Northern Ireland aged 16 or over (they are no longer available in the rest of the UK), whether receiving benefits or not, who is without resources in an emergency or due to a disaster, where there is no other means of preventing serious damage or serious risk to their or their family members' health or safety.

SAVINGS
Savings over £500 (£1,000 for people aged 60 or over) are taken into account for community care grants and savings of £1,000 (£2,000 for people aged 60 or over) are taken into account for budgeting loans. All savings are taken into account for crisis loans. Savings are not taken into account for sure start maternity grant, funeral payments, cold weather payments, winter fuel payments or the Christmas bonus.

INDUSTRIAL INJURIES AND DISABLEMENT BENEFITS
The Industrial Injuries Scheme, administered under the Social Security Contributions and Benefits Act 1992, provides a range of benefits designed to compensate for disablement resulting from an industrial accident (ie an accident arising out of and in the course of an earner's employment) or from a prescribed disease due to the nature of a person's employment. Those who are self-employed are not covered by this scheme.

INDUSTRIAL INJURIES DISABLEMENT BENEFIT
A person may be able to claim industrial injuries disablement benefit if they are ill or disabled due to an accident or incident that happened at work or in connection with work in England, Scotland or Wales. The amount of benefit awarded depends on the person's age and the degree of disability as assessed by a doctor.

The benefit is payable whether the person works or not and those who are incapable of work are entitled to draw other benefits, such as statutory sick pay or incapacity benefit, in addition to industrial injuries disablement benefit. It may also be possible to claim the following allowances:

• reduced earnings allowance for those who are unable to return to their regular work or work of the same standard and who had their accident (or whose disease started) before 1 October 1990. At state pension age this is converted to retirement allowance
• constant attendance allowance for those with a disablement of 100 per cent who need constant care. There are four rates of allowance depending on how much care the person needs
• exceptionally severe disablement allowance can be claimed in addition to constant care attendance allowance at one of the higher rates for those who need constant care permanently

Weekly Rates of Benefit from April 2014

Degree of disablement	Aged 18+ or with dependants
100 per cent	£166.00
90	£149.40
80	£132.80
70	£116.20
60	£99.60
50	£83.00
40	£66.40
30	£49.80
20	£33.20
Unemployability supplement	£102.60
Reduced earnings allowance (maximum)	£66.40
Retirement allowance (maximum)	£16.60
Constant attendance allowance (normal maximum rate)	£66.40
Exceptionally severe disablement allowance	£66.40

OTHER BENEFITS
People who are disabled because of an accident or disease that was the result of work that they did before 5 July 1948 are not entitled to industrial injuries disablement benefit. They may, however, be entitled to payment under the Workmen's Compensation Scheme or the Pneumoconiosis, Byssinosis and Miscellaneous Diseases Benefit Scheme. People who suffer from certain industrial diseases caused by dust can make a claim for an additional payment under the Pneumoconiosis Act 1979 if they are unable to get damages from the employer who caused or contributed to the disease.

Diffuse Mesothelioma Payment
Since 1 October 2008 any person suffering from the asbestos-related disease, diffuse mesothelioma, who is unable to make a claim under the Pneumoconiosis Act 1979, have not received payment in respect of the disease from an employer, via a civil claim or elsewhere, and are not entitled to compensation from a MoD scheme, can claim a one-off lump sum payment. The scheme covers people whose exposure to asbestos occurred in the UK and was not as a result of their work as an employee (ie they lived near a factory using asbestos). The amount paid depends on the age

of the person when the disease was diagnosed, or the date of the claim if the diagnosis date is not known. The current rate is £85,580 for those aged 37 and under to £13,295 for persons aged 77 and over. From 1 October 2009 claims must be received within 12 months of the date of diagnosis. If the sufferer has died, their dependants may be able to claim, but must do so within 12 months of the date of death.

CLAIMS AND QUESTIONS

Entitlement to benefit and regulated Social Fund payments is determined by a decision maker on behalf of the Secretary of State for the Department for Work and Pensions. A claimant who is dissatisfied with that decision can ask for an explanation. He or she can dispute the decision by applying to have it revised or, in particular circumstances, superseded. The claimant can go to the Social Security and Child Support Tribunal where the case will be heard by an independent tribunal. There is a further right of appeal to a social security commissioner against the tribunal's decision but this is on a point of law only and leave to appeal must first be obtained.

Decisions on claims and applications for housing benefit and council tax benefit are made by local authorities. The explanation, dispute and appeals process is the same as for other benefits.

All decisions on applications to the discretionary Social Fund are made by Jobcentre Plus Social Fund decision makers. Applicants can ask for a review of the decision within 28 days of the date on the decision letter. The Social Fund review officer will review the case and there is a further right of review by an independent Social Fund inspector.

EMPLOYER PAYMENTS

STATUTORY MATERNITY PAY

Employers pay statutory maternity pay (SMP) to pregnant women who have been employed by them full or part-time continuously for at least 26 weeks into the 15th week before the week the baby is due, and whose earnings on average at least equal the lower earnings limit applied to NI contributions (£111 a week if the end of the qualifying week is in the 2014–15 tax year). SMP can be paid for a maximum period of up to 39 weeks. If the qualifying conditions are met women will receive a payment of 90 per cent of their average earnings for the first six weeks, followed by 33 weeks at £138.18 or 90 per cent of the woman's average weekly earnings if this is less than £138.18. SMP can be paid, at the earliest, 11 weeks before the week in which the baby is due, up to the day following the birth. Women can decide when they wish their maternity leave and pay to start and can work until the baby is born. However, where the woman is absent from work wholly or partly due to her pregnancy in the four weeks before the week the baby is due to be born, SMP will start the day following the first day of absence from work.

Employers are reimbursed for 92 per cent of the SMP they pay. Small employers with annual gross NI payments of £45,000 or less recover 103 per cent of the SMP paid out.

STATUTORY PATERNITY PAY

Ordinary Statutory Paternity Pay

Employers pay ordinary statutory paternity pay (OSPP) to employees who are taking leave when a child is born or placed for adoption. To qualify the employee must:
• have responsibility for the child's upbringing
• be the biological father of the child (or the child's adopter), or the spouse/civil partner/partner of the mother or adopter
• have been employed by the same employer for at least 26 weeks ending with the 15th week before the baby is due (or the week in which the adopter is notified of having been matched with a child)

• continue working for the employer up to the child's birth (or placement for adoption)
• be earning an average of at least £111 a week (before tax)
Employees who meet these conditions receive payment of £138.18 or 90 per cent of the employee's average weekly earnings if this is less than £138.18. The employee can choose to be paid for one or two consecutive weeks. The earliest the OSPP period can begin is the date of the child's birth or placement for adoption. The OSPP period must be completed within eight weeks of that date. OSPP is not payable for any week in which the employee works. Employers are reimbursed in the same way as for statutory maternity pay.

ADDITIONAL PATERNITY LEAVE AND PAY

Regulations introduced on 6 April 2010 give parents greater flexibility in how they use their maternity and paternity provisions. For births from 3 April 2011, additional paternity leave (APL) entitles eligible fathers to take up to 26 weeks' additional paternity leave, allowing for up to a total of one year's leave to be shared between the couple. APL entitlement requires the mother to have returned to work; it must also be taken between 20 weeks and one year after the child is born. APL may be paid if taken during the mother's statutory maternity pay period or maternity allowance period.

The APL entitlement will also apply to husbands, partners or civil partners who are not the child's father but expect to have the main responsibility (apart from the mother) for the child's upbringing.

The current rate of additional statutory paternity pay is £138.18 a week or 90 per cent of the emplyee's average weekly earnings if this is less than £138.18.

STATUTORY ADOPTION PAY

Employers pay statutory adoption pay (SAP) to employees taking adoption leave from their employers. To qualify for SAP the employee must:
• be newly matched with a child by an adoption agency
• have been employed by the same employer for at least 26 weeks ending the week in which they have been notified of being matched with a child
• be earning an average of at least £111 a week (before tax)
Employees who meet these conditions receive payment of £138.18 or 90 per cent of their average weekly earnings if this is less than £138.18 for up to 39 weeks. The earliest SAP can be paid from is two weeks before the expected date of placement; the latest it can start is the date of the child's placement. Where a couple adopt a child, only one of them may receive SAP, the other may be able to receive statutory paternity pay if they meet the eligibility criteria. Employers are reimbursed in the same way as for statutory maternity pay.

The additional paternity leave entitlement (*see* above) will also apply to adoptions where adoptive parents are notified of a match on or after 3 April 2011.

STATUTORY SICK PAY

Employers pay statutory sick pay (SSP) for up to a maximum of 28 weeks to any employee incapable of work for four or more consecutive days. Employees must have done some work under their contract of service and have average weekly earnings of at least £111 from April 2014. SSP is a daily payment and is usually paid for the days that an employee would normally work, these days are known as qualifying days. SSP is not paid for the first three qualifying days in a period of sickness. SSP is paid at £87.55 per week and is subject to PAYE and NI contributions. Employees who cannot obtain SSP may be able to claim incapacity benefit. Employers may be able to recover some SSP costs.

THE WATER INDUSTRY

In the UK, the water industry provides clean and safe drinking water for homes and businesses to over 63 million people and has an annual turnover of around £10bn. It supplies around 17 billion litres of water a day to domestic and commercial customers and collects and treats more than 16 billion litres of wastewater a day. It also manages assets that include around 1,400 water treatment and 9,350 wastewater treatment works, 550 impounding reservoirs, over 6,500 service reservoirs/water towers and 800,000km of water mains and sewers.

Water services in England and Wales are provided by private companies. In Scotland and Northern Ireland there are single authorities, Scottish Water and Northern Ireland Water, that are publicly owned companies answerable to their respective governments. In drinking water quality tests carried out in 2013 by the Drinking Water Inspectorate, the water industry in England and Wales achieved 99.97 per cent compliance with the standards required by the EU Drinking Water Directive; Scotland achieved 99.86 per cent and Northern Ireland 99.78 per cent.

Water UK is the industry association that represents all UK water and wastewater service suppliers at national and European level and is funded directly by its members, who are the service suppliers for England, Scotland, Wales and Northern Ireland; every member has a seat on the Water UK Council.

WATER UK, 3rd Floor, 36 Broadway, London SW1H 0BH
T 020 7344 1844 W www.water.org.uk
Chief Executive, Pamela Taylor

ENGLAND AND WALES

In England and Wales, the Secretary of State for Environment, Food and Rural Affairs and the Welsh government have overall responsibility for water policy and oversee environmental standards for the water industry.

The statutory consumer representative body for water services is the Consumer Council for Water.

CONSUMER COUNCIL FOR WATER, 1st Floor, Victoria Square House, Victoria Square, Birmingham B2 4AJ
T 0121-345 1000 E enquiries@ccwater.org.uk
W www.ccwater.org.uk

REGULATORY BODIES

The Water Services Regulation Authority (OFWAT) was established in 1989 when the water and sewerage industry in England and Wales was privatised. Its statutory role and duties are laid out under the Water Industry Act 1991 and it is the independent economic regulator of the water and sewerage companies in England and Wales. OFWAT's main duties are to ensure that the companies can finance and carry out their statutory functions and to protect the interests of water customers. OFWAT is a non-ministerial government department headed by a board following a change in legislation introduced by the Water Act 2003.

Under the Competition Act 1998, from 1 March 2000 the Competition Appeal Tribunal has heard appeals against the regulator's decisions regarding anti-competitive agreements and abuse of a dominant position in the marketplace. The

Water Act 2003 placed a new duty on OFWAT to contribute to the achievement of sustainable development.

The Environment Agency has statutory duties and powers in relation to water resources, pollution control, flood defence, fisheries, recreation, conservation and navigation in England and Wales. It is also responsible for issuing permits, licences, consents and registrations such as industrial licences to extract water and fishing licences.

The Drinking Water Inspectorate (DWI) is the drinking water quality regulator for England and Wales, responsible for assessing the quality of the drinking water supplied by the water companies and investigating any incidents affecting drinking water quality, initiating prosecution where necessary. The DWI science and strategy group provides scientific advice on drinking water policy issues to DEFRA and the Welsh government.

OFWAT, Centre City Tower, 7 Hill Street, Birmingham B5 4UA
T 0121-644 7500 E mailbox@ofwat.gsi.gov.uk
W www.ofwat.gov.uk
Chair, Jonson Cox
Chief Executive, Cathryn Ross

METHODS OF CHARGING

In England and Wales, most domestic customers still pay for domestic water supply and sewerage services through charges based on the rateable value of their property. OFWAT estimates that the proportion of household customers in England and Wales to have metered supplies will be around 50 per cent in 2014–15. Nearly all non-household customers are charged according to consumption.

Under the Water Industry Act 1999, water companies can continue basing their charges on the old rateable value of the property. Domestic customers can continue paying on an unmeasured basis unless they choose to pay according to consumption. After having a meter installed (which is free of charge), a customer can revert to unmeasured charging within 12 months. However, water companies may charge by meter for new homes, or homes where there is a high discretionary use of water. Domestic, school and hospital customers cannot be disconnected for non-payment.

In August 2014, OFWAT set proposals for household water bills between 2014 and 2020. Under the proposals, average bills would on average be 5 per cent lower, before inflation, at the end of 2020.

SCOTLAND

In 2002 the three existing water authorities in Scotland (East of Scotland Water, North of Scotland Water and West of Scotland Water) merged to form Scottish Water. Scottish Water, which serves around 2.4 million households and provides 1.3 billion litres of water per day while removing 840 million litres of waste water, is a public sector company, structured and managed like a private company, but remains answerable to the Scottish parliament. Scottish Water is regulated by the Water Industry Commission for Scotland (established under the Water Services (Scotland) Act 2005), the Scottish Environment Protection Agency (SEPA) and the Drinking Water Quality Regulator for Scotland. The Water Industry Commissioner is responsible for regulating all

AVERAGE HOUSEHOLD BILLS 2014–20 *(£)*

WATER AND SEWERAGE COMPANIES*

	2014–15	2015–16	2016–17	2017–18	2018–19	2019–20
Anglian	408	380	375	370	368	363
Dŵr Cymru	410	405	407	405	398	398
Northumbrian	368	362	362	362	362	362
Severn Trent	315	298	294	294	293	297
South West	516	492	488	485	482	479
Southern	413	381	381	379	378	378
Wessex	459	417	417	417	416	416
Yorkshire	353	338	338	338	337	336

* Thames Water and United Utilities figures were unresolved at the time of publication

WATER ONLY COMPANIES†

	2014–15	2015–16	2016–17	2017–18	2018–19	2019–20
Affinity	174	165	165	159	156	155
Dee Valley	144	136	136	136	136	136
Portsmouth	92	92	92	92	92	92
Sembcorp Bournemouth	145	130	130	129	126	125
South East	190	181	181	180	179	179
South Staffordshire	133	130	129	128	128	128
Sutton and East Surrey	176	180	173	169	165	160

† Bristol Water figures were unresolved at the time of publication
Source: OFWAT

aspects of economic and customer service performance, including water and sewerage charges. SEPA, created under the Environment Act 1995, is responsible for environmental issues, including controlling pollution and promoting the cleanliness of Scotland's rivers, lochs and coastal waters. The Public Services Reform (Scotland) Act 2010 transferred the complaints handling function of Waterwatch Scotland regarding Scottish Water, to the Scottish Public Services Ombudsman. Consumer Futures represented the views and interests of Scottish Water customers but became part of Citizens Advice Scotland on 1 April 2014.

METHODS OF CHARGING
Scottish Water sets charges for domestic and non-domestic water and sewerage provision through charges schemes which are regulated by the Water Industry Commission for Scotland. In February 2004 the harmonisation of all household charges across the country was completed following the merger of the separate authorities under Scottish Water. In November 2009 the Water Industry Commission for Scotland published *The Strategic Review of Charges 2010–2015*, stating that annual price rises would be kept at 5 per cent below the rate of inflation during this five-year period. For the year 2014–15, the combined service charge, covering the water supply and waste water collection, rose by 1.6 per cent. The average household bill for 2014–15 therefore increased to around £339.

CITIZENS ADVICE SCOTLAND, T 0131-550 1000
  W www.cas.org.uk
DRINKING WATER QUALITY REGULATOR FOR
  SCOTLAND, Area 1-D South, Victoria Quay, Edinburgh
  EH6 6QQ T 0131-244 0190 W www.dwqr.org.uk
SCOTTISH ENVIRONMENT PROTECTION AGENCY,
  Erskine Court, Castle Business Park, Stirling FK9 4TZ
  T 01786-457700 W www.sepa.org.uk
SCOTTISH WATER, Castle House, 6 Castle Drive,
  Dunfermline KY11 8GG T 0345-601 8855
  W www.scottishwater.co.uk
  Chief Executive, Douglas Millican
WATER INDUSTRY COMMISSION FOR SCOTLAND,
  First Floor, Moray House, Forthside Way, Stirling FK8 1QZ
  T 01786-430200 W www.watercommission.co.uk

NORTHERN IRELAND

Formerly an executive agency of the Department for Regional Development, Northern Ireland Water is a government-owned company but with substantial independence from government. Northern Ireland Water was set up as a result of government reform of water and sewerage services in April 2007. It is responsible for policy and coordination with regard to the supply, distribution and cleanliness of water, and the provision and maintenance of sewerage services. The Northern Ireland Authority for Utility Regulation (known as the Utility Regulator) is responsible for regulating the water services provided by Northern Ireland Water. The Drinking Water Inspectorate, a unit in the Northern Ireland Environment Agency (NIEA), regulates drinking water quality. Another NIEA unit, the Water Management Unit, has responsibility for the protection of the aquatic environment. The Consumer Council for Northern Ireland is the consumer representative body for water services.

METHODS OF CHARGING
The water and sewerage used by domestic customers in Northern Ireland is currently paid for by the Department for Regional Development (DRD), a system which will continue during 2014–2015. In March 2010, the Northern Ireland Assembly passed the Water and Sewerage Services (Amendment) Act (Northern Ireland) 2010, which ensured that Northern Ireland Water would continue to receive DRD subsidy until at least 2014. Non-domestic customers in Northern Ireland became subject to water and sewerage charges and trade effluent charges where applicable in April 2008.

CONSUMER COUNCIL FOR NORTHERN IRELAND,
  116 Holywood Road, Belfast BT4 1NY T 028-9067 2488
  W www.consumercouncil.org.uk
NORTHERN IRELAND AUTHORITY FOR UTILITY
  REGULATION, Queens House, 14 Queen Street, Belfast
  BT1 6ED T 028-9031 1575 W www.uregni.gov.uk
NORTHERN IRELAND WATER, PO Box 1026, Belfast
  BT1 9DJ T 0845-744 0088 W www.niwater.com
  Chief Executive, Sara Venning

We promise we'll never put down a healthy dog.

Please promise to help us with a gift in your Will.

Every year, Dogs Trust cares for around 17,000 dogs in our 20 rehoming centres across the UK. We never put down a healthy dog. By leaving a gift in your Will, your love of dogs can live on and help us make the world a better place for them.

Call: 020 7837 0006

Email: infopack@dogstrust.org.uk

Please quote "112544"

 DogsTrust

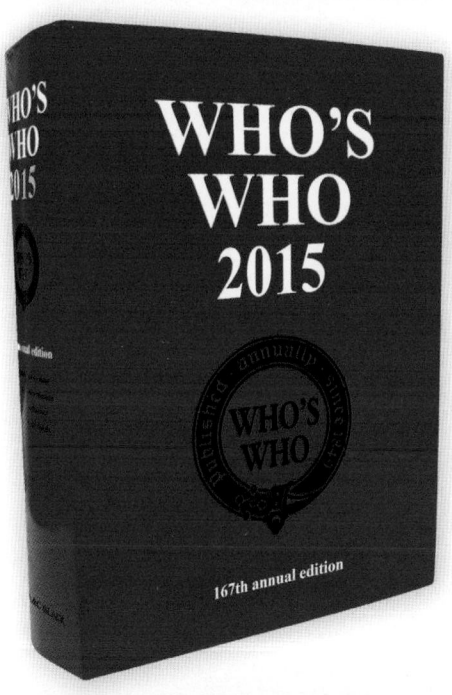

WHITAKER'S ALMANACK 1869

Joseph Whitaker described the first edition of his almanack as 'unusually full and complete' when published in 1868. One hundred and forty six years later *Whitaker's* is still published annually and its remit has remained remarkably unchanged. This facsimile of the very first edition provides a fascinating insight not only into the origins of this extraordinary book, but also into the Victorian World it describes. Alongside the calendar and astronomical data associated with an almanack, it provides a comprehensive overview of all aspects of UK infrastructure, a detailed digest of every country of the world and an overview of the events and discoveries of the past year.

www.bloomsbury.com   £19.99 | ISBN: 9781472907080

WATER SERVICE COMPANIES

(* associate member of Water UK)

AFFINITY WATER, Tamblin Way, Hatfield, Herts AL10 9EZ
T 01707-268111 W www.affinitywater.co.uk

ALBION WATER LTD, Forest House, 3–5 Horndean Road,
Bracknell RG12 0XQ T 0845-604 2355
W www.albionwater.co.uk

ANGLIAN WATER SERVICES LTD, PO Box 10642, Harlow
CM20 9HA T 03457-919155 W www.anglianwater.co.uk

BRISTOL WATER PLC, PO Box 218, Bridgwater Road, Bristol
BS99 7AU T 0345-702 3797 W www.bristolwater.co.uk

CAMBRIDGE WATER PLC, 90 Fulbourn Road, Cambridge
CB1 9JN T 01223-706050 W www.cambridge-water.co.uk

*CHOLDERTON & DISTRICT WATER COMPANY LTD,
Estate Office, Cholderton, Salisbury, Wiltshire SP4 0DR
T 01980-629203 W www.choldertonwater.co.uk

DEE VALLEY WATER PLC, Packsaddle, Wrexham Road,
Rhostyllen, Wrexham LL14 4EH T 01978-846946
W www.deevalleywater.co.uk

DWR CYMRU (WELSH WATER), Pentwyn Road, Nelson,
Treharris, Mid Glamorgan CF46 6LY T 01443-452300
W www.dwrcymru.co.uk

**ESSEX & SUFFOLK WATER PLC (subsidiary of
Northumbrian Water Ltd)**, Customer Centre, PO Box 292,
Durham DH1 9TX T 0845-782 0111 W www.eswater.co.uk

NORTHUMBRIAN WATER LTD, Abbey Road, Pity Me,
Durham DH1 5FJ T 0845-604 7468 W www.nwl.co.uk

PORTSMOUTH WATER PLC, PO Box 8, West Street, Havant,
Hants PO9 1LG T 023-9249 9888
W www.portsmouthwater.co.uk

SEMBCORP BOURNEMOUTH WATER LTD, George
Jessel House, Francis Avenue, Bournemouth, Dorset BH11 8NX
T 01202-591111 W www.sembcorpbw.co.uk

SEVERN TRENT WATER LTD, 2 St Johns Street, Coventry
CV1 2LZ T 024-7771 5000 W www.stwater.co.uk

SOUTH EAST WATER LTD, Rocfort Road, Snodland, Kent
ME6 5AH T 0333-000 0001 W www.southeastwater.co.uk

SOUTH STAFFORDSHIRE WATER PLC, Green Lane,
Walsall WS2 7PD T 0845-607 0456
W www.south-staffs-water.co.uk

SOUTH WEST WATER LTD, Peninsula House, Rydon Lane,
Exeter EX2 7HR T 01392-443020
W www.southwestwater.co.uk

SOUTHERN WATER SERVICES LTD, Southern House,
Yeoman Road, Worthing, Sussex BN13 3NX T 01 903-264444
W www.southernwater.co.uk

SUTTON AND EAST SURREY WATER PLC, London Road,
Redhill, Surrey RH1 1LJ T 01737-772000 W www.waterplc.com

THAMES WATER UTILITIES LTD, PO Box 286, Swindon
SN38 2RA T 0845-920 0800 W www.thameswater.co.uk

UNITED UTILITIES WATER PLC, Haweswater House,
Lingley Mere Business Park, Great Sankey, Warrington WA5 3LP
T 0845-746 2200 W www.unitedutilities.com

WESSEX WATER SERVICES LTD, Claverton Down,
Bath BA2 7WW T 01225-526000 W www.wessexwater.co.uk

YORKSHIRE WATER SERVICES LTD, Western House,
Western Way, Bradford BD6 2LZ T 01274-69111 1
W www.yorkshirewater.com

ISLAND WATER AUTHORITIES
(not members of Water UK)

COUNCIL OF THE ISLES OF SCILLY, Town Hall, St Mary's,
Isles of Scilly TR21 0LW T 01720-424000 W www.scilly.gov.uk

GUERNSEY WATER, PO Box 30, Brickfield House, St Andrew,
Guernsey GY1 3AS T 01481-239500 W www.water.gg

ISLE OF MAN WATER AND SEWERAGE AUTHORITY,
Tromode Road, Douglas, Isle of Man IM2 5PA T 01624-695949
W www.gov.im/water

JERSEY WATER, PO Box 69, Mulcaster House, Westmount
Road, St Helier, Jersey JE1 1DG T 01534-707301
W www.jerseywater.je

ENERGY

The main primary sources of energy in Britain are coal, oil, natural gas, renewables and nuclear power. The main secondary sources are electricity, coke and smokeless fuels and petroleum products. The UK was a net importer of fuels in the 1970s, however as a result of growth in oil and gas production from the North Sea, the UK became a net exporter of energy for most of the 1980s. Output decreased in the late 1980s following the Piper Alpha disaster until the mid-1990s, after which the UK again became a net exporter. Since 2004, the UK reverted back to become a net importer of energy. In 2013, the UK net import gap was 102 million tonnes of oil equivalent, accounting for 47.1 per cent of the total energy used in the UK. In value terms, on an Overseas Trade Statistics (OTS) basis, the total fuel deficit for 2013 was £18.3bn driven by a fall in the deficit of crude oil and petroleum products. The deficit of crude oil and petroleum products, on the same basis, in 2013 was £5.7bn (46 per cent less than in 2012) compared to a £2.2bn surplus in 2004. In value terms, on an OTS basis, the total fuel deficit for 2012 was £22bn. The Department of Energy and Climate Change (DECC) is responsible for promoting energy efficiency.

INDIGENOUS PRODUCTION OF PRIMARY FUELS
Million tonnes of oil equivalent

	2012	2013
Primary oils	48.8	44.5
Natural gas	38.9	36.5
Primary electricity	17.5	18.5
Coal	10.6	8.0
Bioenergy and waste	6.2	6.9
Total	122.0	114.4

Source: DECC

INLAND ENERGY CONSUMPTION BY PRIMARY FUEL
Million tonnes of oil equivalent, temperature adjusted

	2012	2013
Natural gas	73.3	70.5
Petroleum	66.9	65.5
Coal	40.9	38.7
Nuclear electricity	15.2	15.4
Bioenergy and waste	7.7	8.8
Wind and hydro electricity	2.3	3.0
Net Imports	1.0	1.2
Total	207.2	203.2

Source: DECC

TRADE IN FUELS AND RELATED MATERIALS (2013)

	Quantity, million tonnes of oil equivalent	Value £m
Imports		
Crude oil	64.7	25,546
Petroleum products	30.9	18,557
Natural gas	46.0	11,337
Coal and other solid fuel	32.7	3,213
Electricity	1.5	937
Total	178.0	59,590
Exports		
Crude oil	37.0	19,395
Petroleum products	28.7	19,051
Natural gas	9.4	2,511
Coal and other solid fuel	0.5	171
Electricity	0.3	168
Total	76.2	41,926

Source: HMRC/DECC, ONS

OIL

Until the 1960s Britain imported almost all its oil supplies. In 1969 oil was discovered in the Arbroath field in the North Sea. The first oilfield to be brought into production was Argyll in 1975, and since the mid-1970s Britain has been a major producer of crude oil.

To date, the UK has produced around 3.5 billion tonnes of oil. It is estimated that there are around 800 million tonnes remaining to be produced. Licences for exploration and production are granted to companies by the DECC. At the end of 2004, 565 seaward production licences and 101 onshore petroleum exploration and development licenses had been awarded. At the end of 2012, there were a total of 339 offshore oil and gas fields in production. To date, the UK has produced around 27 billion barrels of oil. An estimated 3 to 8 billion barrels remain to be produced. Total UK oil production peaked in 1999 and is now declining. At around a third of the 1999 level, production stood at 44.6 million tonnes in 2012. Profits from oil production are subject to a special tax regime with different taxes applying depending on the date of approval of each field.

DRILLING ACTIVITY (2013)
by number of wells started

	Offshore	Onshore
Exploration	15	47
Appraisal	29	0
Development	120	8

Source: DECC

INDIGENOUS PRODUCTION AND REFINERY RECEIPTS
Thousand tonnes

	2012	2013
Indigenous production	44,561	40,646
Crude oil	42,052	38,456
*NGLs	2,508	2,190
Refinery receipts	74,380	68,575

* Natural Gas Liquids: condensates and petroleum gases derived at onshore treatment plants
Source: DECC

DELIVERIES OF PETROLEUM PRODUCTS FOR INLAND CONSUMPTION BY ENERGY USE
Thousand tonnes

	2012	2013
Transport	47,515	47,104
Industry	4,182	4,063
Domestic	2,433	2,489
Other	1,166	1,113
Total	55,296	54,769

Source: DECC

COAL

Mines were in private ownership until 1947 when they were nationalised and came under the management of the National Coal Board, later the British Coal Corporation. The corporation held a near monopoly on coal production until 1994 when the industry was restructured. Under the Coal Industry Act 1994, the Coal Authority was established to take over ownership of coal reserves and to issue licences to private mining companies. The Coal Authority is also responsible for the physical legacy of mining, eg subsidence damage claims that are not the responsibility of licensees, and for holding and making available all existing records. It also publishes current data on the coal industry on its website (W www.coal.decc.gov.uk).

The mines owned by the British Coal Corporation were sold as five separate businesses in 1994 and coal production is now undertaken entirely in the private sector. Coal output was around 50 million tonnes a year in 1994 but has since declined to around 12.7 million tonnes. As at 31 March 2014, there were four large, two medium-sized and five small underground mines as well as 26 surface mines in production or development in the UK.

The main consumer of coal in the UK is the electricity supply industry. Coal still supplies over a third of the UK's electricity needs but as indigenous production has declined, imports have continued to make up the shortfall and now represent around 82 per cent of UK coal supply, 41 per cent of which is currently supplied from Russia.

UK government policy is to meet the long-term challenges posed by climate change while continuing to ensure secure, clean and affordable energy. Coal's availability, flexibility and reliability compared to other sources mean that it is expected to continue to play an important role in the future generating mix, but its carbon emissions will need to be managed through the introduction of abatement technologies including carbon capture and storage (CCS).

CCS attempts to mitigate the effects of global warming by capturing the carbon dioxide emissions from power stations that burn fossil fuels, preventing the gas from being released into the atmosphere, and storing it in underground geological formations. CCS is still in its infancy and only through its successful demonstration and development will it be possible for coal to remain a part of a low-carbon UK energy mix. The government is committed to public sector investment in CCS technology on four power stations and has made it clear that there can be no new coal power stations in England and Wales without CCS on a defined amount of capacity. As part of a wider package of reforms to the electricity market, the government will also be introducing an Emissions Performance Standard, which will limit the emissions from new fossil fuel power stations.

COAL PRODUCTION AND FOREIGN TRADE
Thousand tonnes

	2012	2013
Surface mining	10,894	8,759
Deep-mined	6,153	4,089
Imports	44,815	49,402
Exports	(488)	(593)
*Total supply	64,340	60,358
TOTAL	64,030	60,405

* Includes an estimate for slurry and stock change
Source: DECC

INLAND COAL USE
Thousand tonnes

	2012	2013
Fuel producers		
Electricity generators	54,901	50,042
Coke manufacture	4,965	5,288
Blast furnaces	987	1,411
Heat generation	461	609
*Other conversion industries	176	214
Final consumption		
Industry	1,826	2,147
Transport	16	14
Domestic	674	646
Public administration	12	22
Commercial	5	5
Agriculture	1	0
Miscellaneous	6	7

* Mainly recycled products
Source: DECC

GAS

From the late 18th century gas in Britain was produced from coal. In the 1960s town gas began to be produced from oil-based feedstocks using imported oil. In 1965 gas was discovered in the North Sea in the West Sole field, which became the first gasfield in production in 1967, and from the late 1960s natural gas began to replace town gas. From October 1998 Britain was connected to the continental European gas system via a pipeline from Bacton, Norfolk to Zeebrugge, Belgium. Gas is transported through 278,000km of mains pipeline including 7,600km of high-pressure gas pipelines owned and operated in the UK by National Grid Gas plc.

The gas industry in Britain was nationalised in 1949 and operated as the Gas Council. The Gas Council was replaced by the British Gas Corporation in 1972 and the industry became more centralised. The British Gas Corporation was privatised in 1986 as British Gas plc. In 1993 the Monopolies and Mergers Commission found that British Gas's integrated business in Great Britain as a gas trader and the owner of the gas transportation system could operate against the public interest. In February 1997 British Gas demerged its trading arm to become two separate companies, BG plc and Centrica plc. BG Group, as the company is now known, is an international natural gas company whose principal business is finding and developing gas reserves and building gas markets. Its core operations are located in the UK, South America, Egypt, Trinidad and Tobago, Kazakhstan and India. Centrica runs the trading and services operations under the British Gas brand name in Great Britain. In October 2000 BG demerged its pipeline business, Transco, which became part of Lattice Group, finally merging with the National Grid Group in 2002 to become National Grid Transco plc.

In July 2005 National Grid Transco plc changed its name to National Grid plc and Transco plc became National Grid Gas plc. In the same year National Grid Gas also completed the sale of four of its eight gas distribution networks. The distribution networks transport gas at lower pressures, which eventually supply the consumers such as domestic customers. The Scotland and south-east of England networks were sold to Scotia Gas Networks. The Wales and south-west network was sold to Wales & West Utilities and the network in the north-east to Northern Gas Networks. This was the biggest change in the corporate structure of gas infrastructure since privatisation in 1986.

Competition was gradually introduced into the industrial gas market from 1986. Supply of gas to the domestic market was opened to companies other than British Gas, starting in April 1996 with a pilot project in the West Country and Wales, with the rest of the UK following soon after.

Declines in UK indigenous gas production and increasing demand led to the UK becoming a net importer of gas once more in 2004. With the depletion of the UK Continental Shelf reserves, UK gas production has seen growing rates of decline. As part of the Energy Act 2008, the government planned to strengthen regulation of the offshore gas supply infrastructure, to allow private sector investment to help maintain UK energy supplies.

BG GROUP PLC, Thames Valley Park Drive, Reading RG6 1PT
T 0118-935 3222 W www.bg-group.com
Executive Chair, Andrew Gould

CENTRICA PLC, Millstream, Maidenhead Road, Windsor, Berkshire SL4 5GD T 01753-494000 W www.centrica.com
Chair, Rick Haythornthwaite
Chief Executive, Sam Laidlaw

NATIONAL GRID PLC, National Grid House, Warwick Technology Park, Gallows Hill, Warwick CV34 6DA
T 01926-653000 W www.nationalgrid.com
Chair, Sir Peter Gershon, CBE
Chief Executive, Steve Holliday

UK GAS CONSUMPTION BY INDUSTRY
GWh

	2012	2013
Domestic	345,080	344,501
Industry	91,524	93,307
Public administration	43,243	44,495
Commercial	57,377	60,286
Agriculture	1,162	1,097
Miscellaneous	11,111	13,871
Total gas consumption	555,268	563,154

Source: DECC

ELECTRICITY

The first power station in Britain generating electricity for public supply began operating in 1882. In the 1930s a national transmission grid was developed and it was reconstructed and extended in the 1950s and 1960s. Power stations were operated by the Central Electricity Generating Board.

Under the Electricity Act 1989, 12 regional electricity companies, responsible for the distribution of electricity from the national grid to consumers, were formed from the former area electricity boards in England and Wales. Four companies were formed from the Central Electricity Generating Board: three generating companies (National Power plc, Nuclear Electric plc and Powergen plc) and the National Grid Company plc, which owned and operated the transmission system in England and Wales. National Power and Powergen were floated on the stock market in 1991.

National Power was demerged in October 2000 to form two separate companies: International Power plc and Innogy plc, which manages the bulk of National Power's UK assets. Nuclear Electric was split into two parts in 1996.

The National Grid Company was floated on the stock market in 1995 and formed a new holding company, National Grid Group. National Grid Group completed a merger with Lattice in 2002 to form National Grid Transco, a public limited company (*see* Gas).

Following privatisation, generators and suppliers in England and Wales traded via the Electricity Pool. A competitive wholesale trading market known as NETA (New Electricity Trading Arrangements) replaced the Electricity Pool in March 2001, and was extended to include Scotland via the British Electricity Transmissions and Trading Arrangements (BETTA) in 2005. As part of BETTA, National Grid became the system operator for all transmission. The introduction of competition into the domestic electricity market was completed in May 1999. Since competition was introduced, over 19 million of Britain's 28 million electricity customers have switched their supplier.

In Scotland, three new companies were formed under the Electricity Act 1989: Scottish Power plc and Scottish Hydro-Electric plc, which were responsible for generation, transmission, distribution and supply; and Scottish Nuclear Ltd. Scottish Power and Scottish Hydro-Electric were floated on the stock market in 1991. Scottish Hydro-Electric merged with Southern Electric in 1998 to become Scottish and Southern Energy plc. Scottish Nuclear was incorporated into British Energy in 1996. BETTA opened the Scottish market to the same competition that had applied in England and Wales.

In Northern Ireland, Northern Ireland Electricity plc (NIE) was set up in 1993 under a 1991 Order in Council. In 1993 it was floated on the stock market and in 1998 it became part of the Viridian Group and was responsible for distribution and supply until NIE was sold to ESB Independent Energy in December 2010. In June 2010, Airtricity became the first new electricity supplier since the Northern Ireland electricity market was opened to competition in 2007.

On 12 July 2011, the government published *Planning Our Electric Future: a White Paper for Secure, Affordable and Low-carbon Electricity* in response to the challenges set by increasing electricity demands. It has been agreed that over £110bn in investment is needed to update the grid and build new power stations. Currently, 16 per cent of the UK electricity supply comes from nuclear reactors. While nuclear power stations will close gradually over the next decade, with only one expected to produce power beyond 2025, there are plans in place for a new generation of reactors to be built, potentially running by 2018.

On 30 September 2003 the Electricity Association, the industry's main trade association, was replaced with three separate trade bodies: the Association of Electricity Producers; the Energy Networks Association; and the Energy Retail Association. In April 2012, following a merger between the Association of Electricity Producers, the Energy Retail Association and the UK Business Council for Sustainable Energy, Energy UK – the new trade association for the gas and electricity sector – was established.

ENERGY NETWORKS ASSOCIATION, 6th floor, Dean Bradley House, 52 Horseferry Road, London SW1P 2AF
T 020-7706 5100 W www.energynetworks.org
Chief Executive, David Smith

ENERGY UK, Charles House, 5–11 Regent Street, London SW1Y 4LR T 020-7930 9390 W www.energy-uk.org.uk
Chief Executive, Angela Knight

ELECTRICITY PRODUCTION, SUPPLY AND CONSUMPTION
GWh

	2012	2013
Electricity produced		
Nuclear	70,405	70,608
Hydro	5,285	4,698
Wind, wave and solar photovoltaics	21,015	30,475
Coal	143,156	130,768
Oil	2,571	2,135
Gas	100,158	95,612
Other renewables	14,913	18,494
Other	2,937	3,462
Total	360,439	356,253
Electricity supplied		
Production	360,349	356,253
*Other sources	2,966	2,898
Imports	13,742	17,533
Exports	(1,871)	(3,103)
Total	375,277	373,581
Electricity consumed		
Industry	97,813	98,007
Transport	4,097	4,109
Other	215,921	215,184
Domestic	114,764	113,453
Public administration	18,913	18,822
Commercial	78,372	79,035
Agriculture	3,871	3,874
Total	317,831	317,300

* Pumped storage production

Source: DECC

GAS AND ELECTRICITY SUPPLIERS

With the gas and electricity markets open, most suppliers offer their customers both services. The majority of gas/electricity companies have become part of larger multi-utility companies, often operating internationally.

As part of measures to reduce the UK's carbon output, the government has outlined plans to introduce 'smart meters' to all UK homes. Smart meters perform the traditional meter function of measuring energy consumption, in addition to more advanced functions such as allowing energy suppliers to communicate directly with their customers and removing the need for meter readings and bill estimates. The meters also allow domestic customers to have direct access to energy consumption information.

ENERGY BILLS 2013–14

Supplier	2013 Average	2014 Average	Average Price Increase (%)
E.ON	£1,226	£1,240	1.1
EDF	£1,190	£1,237	3.9
SSE	£1,211	£1,259	4.0
Scottish Power	£1,230	£1,284	4.4
British Gas	£1,191	£1,265	6.2
Npower	£1,220	£1,299	6.5
Average	£1,212	£1,264	4.3

Source: OFGEM

The following list comprises a selection of suppliers offering gas and electricity. Organisations in italics are subsidiaries of the companies listed in capital letters directly above.

ENGLAND, SCOTLAND AND WALES

CENTRICA PLC, Millstream, Maidenhead Road, Windsor, Berkshire SL4 5GD **T** 01753-494000 **W** www.centrica.com

British Gas, PO Box 4805, Worthing BN11 9QW **T** 0800-048 0202 **W** www.britishgas.co.uk

EDF ENERGY, Osprey House, Osprey Road, Exeter, EX2 7WN **T** 0800-056 7777 **W** www.edfenergy.com

E.ON, 6th Floor, 100 Pall Mall, London SW1Y 5NQ **T** 024-7618 3843 **W** www.eonenergy.com

NORTHERN POWERGRID, Houghton le Spring DH4 7LA **T** 0845-070 7172 **W** www.northernpowergrid.com

NPOWER, PO Box 93, Peterlee SR8 2XX **T** 0800-073 3000 **W** www.npower.com

SCOTTISHPOWER, PO Box 8729, Bellshill ML4 3YD **T** 0845-270 0700 **W** www.scottishpower.com

SSE PLC, Inveralmond House, 200 Dunkeld Road, Perth PH1 3AQ **T** 0800-980 8831 **W** www.sse.co.uk

Scottish Hydro, **T** 0800-980 8754 **W** www.hydro.co.uk

Southern Electric, **T** 0800-980 8476 **W** www.southern-electric.co.uk

SWALEC, **T** 0800-980 9041 **W** www.swalec.co.uk

NORTHERN IRELAND

AIRTRICITY (a member of Scottish and Southern Energy), Red Oak South, South County Business Park, Leopardstown, Dublin 18 **T** 0345-864 3546 **W** www.airtricity.com

ELECTRIC IRELAND, Forsyth House, Cromac Square, Belfast BT2 8LA **T** 0845-600 5335 **W** www.electricireland.ie

VIRIDIAN GROUP PLC, Greenwood House, 64 Newforge Lane, Belfast BT9 5NF **T** 028-9066 8416 **W** www.viridiangroup.co.uk

Energia, 3rd Floor, Mill House, Ashtowngate, Navan Road, Dublin 15 **T** 1850-363744 **W** www.energia.ie

REGULATION OF THE GAS AND ELECTRICITY INDUSTRIES

The Office of the Gas and Electricity Markets (OFGEM) regulates the gas and electricity industries in Great Britain. It was formed in 1999 by the merger of the Office of Gas Supply and the Office of Electricity Regulation. OFGEM's overriding aim is to protect and promote the interests of all gas and electricity customers by promoting competition and regulating monopolies. It is governed by an authority and its powers are provided for under the Gas Act 1986, the Electricity Act 1989, the Competition Act 1998, the Utilities Act 2000 and the Enterprise Act 2002. Energywatch was the independent gas and electricity watchdog, set up in November 2000 through the Utility Act to protect and promote the interests of gas and electricity consumers. In October 2008 Energywatch merged with Postwatch and the National Consumer Council to form a new advocacy body, Consumer Focus. In October 2010 the government announced that Consumer Focus would be abolished and some of its functions would transfer to Citizens Advice, Citizens Advice Scotland and the Consumer Council for Northern Ireland. This transfer began in April 2013 and full responsibility was transferred to Citizens Advice following the abolition of Consumer Focus on 1 April 2014.

CITIZENS ADVICE, 3rd Floor North, 200 Aldersgate Street, London EC1A 4HD **T** 0300-023 1231 **W** www.citizensadvice.org.uk

CITIZENS ADVICE SCOTLAND, 1st Floor, Spectrum House, 2 Powderhall Road, Edinburgh EH7 4GB **T** 0808-800 9060 **W** www.cas.org.uk

CONSUMER COUNCIL FOR NORTHERN IRELAND, 116 Holywood Road, Belfast BT4 1NY **T** 028-9067 2488 **W** www.consumercouncil.org.uk

THE OFFICE OF THE GAS AND ELECTRCITY MARKETS (OFGEM), 9 Millbank, London SW1 3GE **T** 020-7901 7000 **W** www.ofgem.gov.uk

NUCLEAR POWER

Nuclear reactors began to supply electricity to the national grid in 1956. Nuclear power is currently generated in the UK at nine sites: one magnox reactor (Wylfa 1, possible generation extension to December 2015) following the closure of Oldbury nuclear power station in February 2012, seven advanced gas-cooled reactors (AGR) and one pressurised water reactor (PWR), Sizewell 'B' in Suffolk. The AGRs and PWR are owned by a private company, EDF Energy, while the magnox reactor is state-owned by the Nuclear Decommissioning Authority. The first of a series of new-generation plants is expected to come on-line around 2018; all but one of the current sites (Sizewell 'B') will be shut down by 2035.

In April 2005 the responsibility for the decommissioning of civil nuclear reactors and other nuclear facilities used in research and development was handed to the Nuclear Decommissioning Authority (NDA). The NDA is a non-departmental public body, funded mainly by the DECC. The total planned expenditure for the NDA in 2014–15 was £3.2bn. Until April 2007, UK Nirex was responsible for the disposal of intermediate and some low-level nuclear waste. After this date Nirex was integrated into the NDA and renamed the Radioactive Waste Management directorate.

There are currently 17 nuclear sites owned by the NDA that are in various stages of decommissioning, including the world's first commercial power station at Calder Hall on the Sellafield site in Cumbria. The decommissioning of these sites is scheduled for completion within the next 15 to 20 years. In the case of the Dounreay research facility in Scotland, controls on access to contaminated land are expected to remain in place until around 2300.

In 2013 electricity supplied from nuclear sources accounted for 19.8 per cent of the total electricity supply. The 2008 Energy bill paved the way for the construction of up to ten new nuclear power stations by 2020. Eight sites have been assessed as potentially suitable for the development of new power stations in England and Wales before the end of 2025. A number of factors have led to government backing for nuclear power: domestic gas supplies are running low; oil and gas prices are high; carbon emissions must be cut to comply with EU legislation and meet global climate change targets; and a number of coal-fired power stations that fail to meet clean air requirements are due to be closed.

Nuclear power has its advantages: reactors emit virtually no carbon dioxide and uranium prices remain relatively steady. However, the advantages of low emissions are countered by the high costs of construction and difficulties in disposing of nuclear waste. Currently, the only method is to store it securely until it has slowly decayed to safe levels. Public distrust persists despite the advances in safety technology.

SAFETY AND REGULATION

The Office for Nuclear Regulation (ONR), a public corporation of the Department for Work and Pensions, is the nuclear industry's regulator. Operations at all UK nuclear power stations are governed by a site licence which is issued under the Nuclear Installations Act. The ONR monitors compliance and has the jurisdiction to close down a reactor if the terms of the licence are breached. The DECC is responsible for security at all the UK's nuclear power stations, which are policed by the Civil Nuclear Constabulary, a specialised armed force created in April 2005. In 2009 Magnox Electric Ltd was found guilty of breaking the Radioactive Substances Act 2003: it had left a radioactive leak on a holding tank at Bradwell power station, Essex, unchecked for 14 years.

RENEWABLE SOURCES

Renewable sources of energy principally include biofuels, hydro, wind and solar. Renewable sources produced 11.8 million tonnes of oil equivalent for primary energy usage in 2013; of this, about 8.9 million tonnes was used to generate electricity, 1.9 million tonnes to generate heat and 1.1 million tonnes was used as transport fuels. In 2013, the UK generated 14.9 per cent of its total electricity production from renewable sources, up by 3.6 percentage points from 2012.

The government's principal mechanism for developing renewable energy sources is the Renewables Obligation (RO), which aims to increase the contribution of electricity from renewables in the UK. There are separate RO schemes for England and Wales, Scotland and Northern Ireland. For both England and Wales and Scotland, the RO is set so that 9.7 per cent of licensed electricity sales should be from renewable sources eligible for the RO by 2009/10, and 15.4 per cent should be eligible by 2015/16. For Northern Ireland, these figures are 3.5 per cent and 6.3 per cent. In 2013, renewable sources accounted for 14.1 per cent of sales on an RO basis, an increase of 3.3 per cent from 2012.

A Renewables Obligation has been in place in England and Wales since April 2002 to give incentives to generators to supply progressively higher levels of renewable energy over time. These measures included exempting renewable energy sources from the climate change levy, capital grants, enhanced research funding and regional planning to meet renewables targets.

In addition to the RO, in April 2010, the government launched a Feed-in Tariff (FIT) scheme in Great Britain to encourage the uptake of small-scale low carbon electricity generation technologies, principally renewables such as solar photovoltaics, wind and hydro-electricity.

The government approved an EU-wide agreement in March 2007 to generate 20 per cent of energy production from renewable sources by 2020. It has since negotiated down the national share in this target to 15 per cent of energy production by 2020. In July 2009 the government published a Renewable Energy Strategy in order to meet this target. Other impediments to the expansion of renewable energy production include planning restrictions, rising raw material prices, and the possible redirection of funds to develop CCS technology and nuclear energy sources. For further information on renewable energy see The Environment.

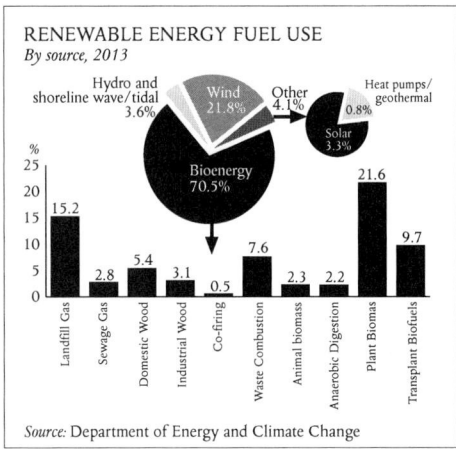

RENEWABLE ENERGY FUEL USE
By source, 2013

Source: Department of Energy and Climate Change

TRANSPORT

CIVIL AVIATION

Since the privatisation of British Airways in 1987, UK airlines have been operated entirely by the private sector. In 2013, total capacity of British airlines amounted to 50 billion tonne-km, of which 41 billion tonne-km was on scheduled services. UK airlines carried around 135 million passengers; 118 million on scheduled services and 17 million on charter flights. Passenger traffic through UK airports increased by 0.3 per cent in 2013. Traffic at the six main London area airports (Gatwick, Heathrow, London City, Luton, Southend and Stansted) increased by 3 per cent over 2013 and other UK regional airports saw an increase of 3 per cent.

Leading British airlines include British Airways, EasyJet, Monarch, Thomas Cook Airlines, Thomson Airways and Virgin Atlantic. Irish airline Ryanair also operates frequent flights from the UK.

There are around 140 licensed civil aerodromes in Britain, with Heathrow and Gatwick handling the highest volume of passengers.

The Civil Aviation Authority (CAA), an independent statutory body, is responsible for the regulation of UK airlines. This includes economic and airspace regulation, air safety, consumer protection and environmental research and consultancy. All commercial airline companies must be granted an air operator's certificate, which is issued by the CAA to operators meeting the required safety standards. The CAA issues airport safety licences, which must be obtained by any airport used for public transport and training flights. All British-registered aircraft must be granted an air-worthiness certificate, and the CAA issues professional licences to pilots, flight crew, ground engineers and air traffic controllers. The CAA also manages the Air Travel Organiser's Licence (ATOL), the UK's principal travel protection scheme. The CAA's costs are met entirely from charges on those whom it regulates; there is no direct government funding of the CAA's work.

The Transport Act 2000 separated the CAA from its subsidiary, National Air Traffic Services (NATS), which provides air traffic control services to aircraft flying in UK airspace and over the eastern part of the North Atlantic. NATS is a public private partnership (PPP) between the Airline Group (a consortium of UK airlines), which holds 42 per cent of the shares; NATS staff, who hold 5 per cent; UK airport operator LHR Airports Limited, which holds 4 per cent, and the government, which holds 49 per cent and a golden share. In 2013–14 NATS handled a total of 2,153,995 flights, an increase of 0.4 per cent on 2012–13 figures.

AIR PASSENGERS 2013

All UK Airports: Total	228,594,686
Aberdeen	3,440,765
Barra (HIAL)	9,410
Belfast City	2,541,759
Belfast International	4,023,336
Benbecula (HIAL)	30,738
Birmingham	9,120,201
Blackpool	262,630
Bournemouth	660,272
Bristol	6,131,896
Cambridge	9,307
Campbeltown (HIAL)	9,550
Cardiff	1,072,062
City of Derry (Eglinton)	384,973
Doncaster Sheffield	690,351
Dundee	27,595
Durham Tees Valley	161,092
East Midlands	4,334,117
Edinburgh	9,775,443
Exeter	741,465
Gatwick	35,444,206
Glasgow	7,363,764
Gloucestershire	14,168
Heathrow	72,367,054
Humberside	236,083
Inverness (HIAL)	608,184
Islay (HIAL)	26,085
Isle of Man	739,683
Isles of Scilly (St Mary's)	89,170
Isles of Scilly (Tresco)	—
Kent International	40,391
Kirkwall (HIAL)	159,325
Lands End (St Just)	46,626
Leeds Bradford	3,318,358
Lerwick (Tingwall)	3,748
Liverpool	4,187,493
London City	3,379,753
Luton	9,697,944
Lydd	670
Manchester	20,751,581
Newcastle	4,420,839
Newquay	174,891
Norwich	463,401
Oxford (Kidlington)	6,847
Penzance Heliport	—
Prestwick	1,145,836
Scatsta	298,308
Shoreham	732
Southampton	1,722,758
Southend	969,912
Stansted	17,852,393
Stornoway (HIAL)	122,758
Sumburgh (HIAL)	212,233
Tiree (HIAL)	8,560
Wick (HIAL)	33,639
Channel Islands Airports: Total	2,403,114
Alderney	62,855
Guernsey	886,396
Jersey	1,453,863

HIAL = Highlands and Islands Airports Ltd
Source: Civil Aviation Authority

CAA, CAA House, 45–59 Kingsway, London WC2B 6TE
T 020-7379 7311 W www.caa.co.uk

Heathrow Airport	T 0844-335 1801
Gatwick Airport	T 0844-892 0322
Manchester Airport	T 0871-271 0711
Stansted Airport	T 0844-335 1803

BRITISH AIRLINES

BRITISH AIRWAYS, PO Box 365, Waterside, Harmondsworth
UB7 0GB T 0844-493 0787 W www.britishairways.com
EASYJET, Hangar 89, London Luton Airport LU2 9PF
T 0330-365 5000 W www.easyjet.com

MONARCH, Prospect House, Prospect Way, London Luton
Airport LU2 9NU **T** 0333-003 0100 **W** www.monarch.co.uk

THOMAS COOK AIRLINES, Thomas Cook Business Park,
Coningsby Road, Peterborough PE3 8SB **T** 01733-224 800
W www.thomascook.com

THOMSON AIRWAYS, Wigmore House, Wigmore Place,
Wigmore Lane, Luton, Beds LU2 9TN **T** 0203-451 2688
W www.thomson.co.uk

VIRGIN ATLANTIC, The Office, Manor Royal, Crawley,
W. Sussex RH10 9NU **T** 0344-811 0000
W www.virgin-atlantic.com

RAILWAYS

The railway network in Britain was developed by private
companies in the 19th century. In 1948 the main railway
companies were nationalised and were run by a public
authority, the British Transport Commission. The commission
was replaced by the British Railways Board in 1963,
operating as British Rail. On 1 April 1994, responsibility for
managing the track and railway infrastructure passed to a
newly formed company, Railtrack plc. In October 2001
Railtrack was put into administration under the Railways
Act 1993. In October 2002 Railtrack was taken out of
administration and replaced by the not-for-profit company
Network Rail. The British Railways Board continued as
operator of all train services until 1996–7, when they were
sold or franchised to the private sector.

The Strategic Rail Authority (SRA) was created to provide
strategic leadership to the rail industry and formally came
into being on 1 February 2001 following the passing of
the Transport Act 2000. In January 2002 it published its
first strategic plan, setting out the strategic priorities for
Britain's railways over the next ten years. In addition to its
coordinating role, the SRA was responsible for allocating
government funding to the railways and awarding and
monitoring the franchises for operating rail services.

On 15 July 2004 the transport secretary announced a new
structure for the rail industry in the white paper *The Future
of Rail*. These proposals were implemented under the
Railways Act 2005, which abolished the SRA, passing
most of its functions to the Department for Transport;
established the Rail Passengers Council as a single national
body, dissolving the regional committees; and gave
devolved governments in Scotland and Wales more say in
decisions at a local level. In addition, responsibility for
railway safety regulation was transferred to the Office of
Rail Regulation from the Health and Safety Executive.

OFFICE OF RAIL REGULATION

The Office of Rail Regulation (ORR) was established on 5
July 2004 by the Railways and Transport Safety Act 2003,
replacing the Office of the Rail Regulator. As the railway
industry's economic and safety regulator, the ORR's
principal function is to regulate Network Rail's stewardship
of the national network. The ORR also licenses operators of
railway assets, approves agreements for access by operators to
track, stations and light maintenance depots, and enforces
domestic competition law. The ORR is led by a board
appointed by the Secretary of State for Transport and chaired
by Anna Walker.

SERVICES

For privatisation, under the Railways Act 1993, domestic
passenger services were divided into 25 train operating units,
which were franchised to private sector operators via a
competitive tendering process. The train operators formed
the Association of Train Operating Companies (ATOC) to act
as the official voice of the passenger rail industry and provide

its members with a range of services enabling them to
comply with conditions imposed on them through their
franchise agreements and operating licences.

As at July 2014 there were 23 passenger train operating
companies: Arriva Trains Wales, c2c, Chiltern Railways,
CrossCountry, East Coast, East Midlands Trains, Eurostar,
First Capital Connect, First Great Western, First Hull Trains,
First TransPennine Express, Grand Central, Greater Anglia,
Heathrow Express, London Midland, London Overground,
Merseyrail, Northern Rail, ScotRail, South West Trains,
Southeastern, Southern and Virgin Trains.

Network Rail publishes a national timetable which
contains details of rail services operated over the UK network
and sea ferry services which provide connections with
Ireland, the Isle of Man, the Isle of Wight, the Channel
Islands and some European destinations.

The national rail enquiries service offers information about
train times and fares for any part of the country, Transport for
London (TfL) provides London-specific travel information
for all modes of travel and Eurostar provides information for
international channel tunnel rail services:

NATIONAL RAIL ENQUIRIES
T 0845-748 4950 **W** www.nationalrail.co.uk
TRANSPORT FOR LONDON
T 0343-222 1234 **W** www.tfl.gov.uk
EUROSTAR
T 03432-186186 **W** www.eurostar.com

PASSENGER FOCUS AND LONDON TRAVELWATCH

Passenger Focus is the operating name of the Passengers'
Council, a single national consumer body for rail, which
is funded by the Department for Transport but whose
independence is guaranteed by an act of parliament. Under
the Passengers' Council (non-railway functions) Order
of February 2010, Passenger Focus also represents bus
passengers in England, outside London. Included in this
remit are local bus services and scheduled domestic coach
journeys.

Established in July 2000, London TravelWatch is the
operating name of the official watchdog organisation
representing the interests of transport users in and around
the capital. Officially known as the London Transport
Users' Committee, it is sponsored and funded by the London
Assembly and is independent of the transport operators.
London TravelWatch represents users of buses, the
Underground, river and rail services in and around London,
including Eurostar and Heathrow Express, Croydon
Tramlink and the Docklands Light Railway. The interests of
pedestrians, cyclists and motorists are also represented, as are
those of taxi users.

FREIGHT

On privatisation in 1996, British Rail's bulk freight
operations were sold to North and South Railways –
subsequently called English, Welsh and Scottish Railways
(EWS). In 2007, EWS was bought by Deutsche Bahn and in
January 2009 was re-named DB Schenker. The other major
companies in the rail freight sector are: Colas Rail, Direct
Rail Services, Freightliner and GB Railfreight (GBRf). In
2013–14 freight moved by rail amounted to 22.7 billion
tonne-kilometres, a 7.8 per cent increase from 2011–12.

NETWORK RAIL

Network Rail is responsible for the tracks, bridges, tunnels,
level crossings, viaducts and 19 main stations that form
Britain's rail network. In addition to providing the timetables
for the passenger and freight operators, Network Rail is also
responsible for all the signalling and electrical control

equipment needed to operate the rail network and for monitoring and reporting performance across the industry.

Network Rail is a private company run as a commercial business; it is directly accountable to its members and regulated by the ORR. The members have similar rights to those of shareholders in a public company except they do not receive dividends or share capital and thereby have no financial or economic interest in Network Rail. All of Network Rail's profits are reinvested into maintaining and upgrading the rail infrastructure.

ASSOCIATION OF TRAIN OPERATING COMPANIES, ATOC Ltd, 2nd Floor, 200 Aldersgate Street, London EC1A 4HD T 020-7841 8000 W www.atoc.org

LONDON TRAVELWATCH, Dexter House, 2 Royal Mint Court, London EC3N 4QN T 020-3176 2999 W www.londontravelwatch.org.uk

NETWORK RAIL, Kings Place, 90 York Way, London N1 9AG T 020-7557 8000 W www.networkrail.co.uk

OFFICE OF RAIL REGULATION, 1 Kemble Street, London WC2B 4AN T 020-7282 2000 W www.rail-reg.gov.uk

PASSENGER FOCUS, Freepost RTEH-XAGE-BYKZ, PO Box 5594, Southend-on-Sea SS1 9PZ T 0300-123 2350 W www.passengerfocus.org.uk

RAIL SAFETY
On 1 April 2006 responsibility for health and safety policy and enforcement on the railways transferred from the Health and Safety Executive to the Office of Rail Regulation (ORR).

In 2013–14 a total of 36 passengers, railway staff and other members of the public were fatally injured in all rail incidents (excluding suicides), compared with 48 in 2012–13.

ACCIDENTS ON RAILWAYS

	2012–13	2013–14
Rail incident fatalities	48	36
Passengers	4	4
Railway employees	2	3
Public	42	29
Rail incident major injuries	468	440
Passengers	312	270
Railway employees	114	126
Public	42	44

SUICIDES AND ATTEMPTED SUICIDES 2013–14

Fatalities	279
Major Injuries	54

Source: RSSB – Annual Safety Performance Report 2013–14

OTHER RAIL SYSTEMS
Responsibility for the London Underground passed from the government to the Mayor and Transport for London on 15 July 2003, with a public-private partnership already in place. Plans for a public-private partnership for London Underground were pushed through by the government in February 2002 despite opposition from the Mayor of London and a range of transport organisations. Under the PPP, long-term contracts with private companies were estimated to enable around £16bn to be invested in renewing and upgrading the London Underground's infrastructure over 15 years. In July 2007, Metronet, which was responsible for two of three PPP contracts, went into administration; TfL took over both contracts. Responsibility for stations, trains, operations, signalling and safety remains in the public sector. In 2013–14 there were 1,265 million passenger journeys on the London Underground.

In addition to Glasgow Subway, which is classified as an underground system (12.7 million passenger journeys in

2013–14), Britain has eight other light rail and tram systems: Blackpool Tramway, Croydon Tramlink, Docklands Light Railway (DLR), Manchester Metrolink, Midland Metro, Nottingham Express Transit (NET), Sheffield Supertram and Tyne and Wear Metro.

In 2013–14 there were 227 million passenger light rail and tram journeys in Great Britain; an increase of 2 per cent on 2012–13 figures.

THE CHANNEL TUNNEL
The earliest recorded scheme for a submarine transport connection between Britain and France was in 1802. Tunnelling began simultaneously on both sides of the Channel three times: in 1881, in the early 1970s, and on 1 December 1987, when construction workers bored the first of the three tunnels which form the Channel Tunnel. Engineers 'holed through' the first tunnel (the service tunnel) on 1 December 1990 and tunnelling was completed in June 1991. The tunnel was officially inaugurated by the Queen and President Mitterrand of France on 6 May 1994.

The submarine link comprises two rail tunnels, each carrying trains in one direction, which measure 7.6m (24.93ft) in diameter. Between them lies a smaller service tunnel, measuring 4.8m (15.75ft) in diameter. The service tunnel is linked to the rail tunnels by 130 cross-passages for maintenance and safety purposes. The tunnels are 50km (31 miles) long, 38km (24 miles) of which is under the seabed at an average depth of 40m (132ft). The rail terminals are situated at Folkestone and Calais, and the tunnels go underground at Shakespeare Cliff, Dover and Sangatte, west of Calais.

RAIL LINKS
The British Channel Tunnel Rail Link route runs from Folkestone to St Pancras station, London, with intermediate stations at Ashford and Ebbsfleet in Kent and more recently, Stratford International.

Construction of the rail link was financed by the private sector with a substantial government contribution. A private sector consortium, London and Continental Railways Ltd (LCR), comprising Union Railways and the UK operator of Eurostar, owns the rail link and was responsible for its design and construction. The rail link was constructed in two phases: phase one, from the Channel Tunnel to Fawkham Junction, Kent, began in October 1998 and opened to fare-paying passengers on 28 September 2003; phase two, from Southfleet Junction to St Pancras, was completed in November 2007.

There are direct services from the UK to Calais, Disneyland Paris, Lille and Paris in France and Brussels in Belgium. There are also direct services to Avignon in the south of France between July and September and during the winter months (December to April) to the French Alps. High-speed trains also run from Lille to the south of France.

Eurostar, the high-speed passenger train service, connects London with Paris in 2 hours 15 minutes, Brussels in 1 hour 51 minutes and Lille in 1 hour 20 minutes. There are Eurostar terminals at London St Pancras, Ashford and Ebbsfleet in Kent, Paris Gare Du Nord and Lille in France, and Brussels-South in Belgium.

ROADS

HIGHWAY AUTHORITIES
The powers and responsibilities of highway authorities in England and Wales are set out in the Highways Act 1980; for Scotland there is separate legislation.

Responsibility for motorways and other trunk roads in Great Britain rests in England with the Secretary of State for

Transport, in Scotland with the Scottish government, and in Wales with the Welsh government. The highway authority for non-trunk roads in England, Wales and Scotland is, in general, the local authority in whose area the roads lie. With the establishment of the Greater London Authority in July 2000, Transport for London became the highway authority for roads in London.

In Northern Ireland the Department for Regional Development is the statutory road authority responsible for public roads and their maintenance and construction; the Transport NI executive agency (formerly known as the Roads Service) carries out these functions on behalf of the department.

FINANCE

In England all aspects of trunk road and motorway funding are provided directly by the government to the Highways Agency, which operates, maintains and improves a network of motorways and trunk roads around 6,920km (4,300 miles) long, on behalf of the secretary of state. Since 2001 the length of the network that the Highways Agency is responsible for has been decreasing owing to a policy of de-trunking, which transfers responsibility for non-core roads to local authorities. For the financial year 2014–15 the Highways Agency's total budget, excluding depreciation, is £2,951m: £851m for maintenance, £1,137m for major schemes and the remainder for traffic management, technology improvements, other programmes and administration costs.

Government support for local authority capital expenditure on roads and other transport infrastructure is provided through grant and credit approvals as part of the Local Transport Plan (LTP). Local authorities bid for resources on the basis of a five-year programme built around delivering integrated transport strategies. As well as covering the structural maintenance of local roads and the construction of major new road schemes, LTP funding also includes smaller-scale safety and traffic management measures with associated improvements for public transport, cyclists and pedestrians.

Total expenditure by the Welsh government in 2013–14 to improve and maintain the motorway and trunk road network in Wales was £135.6m, a further £14.6m was allocated under the transport grant scheme (now closed to new schemes) and £24.5m was allocated for the delivery of regional transport plans, under which expenditure on local road schemes is determined. Total budgeted expenditure for the motorway and trunk road network in 2014–15 is £126.4m, with a further £23.5m allocated to regional transport plans.

Since 1 July 1999 all decisions on Scottish transport expenditure have been devolved to the Scottish government. Total expenditure on motorways and trunk roads in Scotland during 2013–14 was £711.8m (including depreciation and other annually managed expenditure charges). Planned expenditure for 2014–15 is £677.7m.

In Northern Ireland total expenditure by the Roads Service on all roads in 2013–14 was £186.4m, with £11.5m spent on trunk roads and motorways. Planned expenditure for 2014–15 is £140m, with £8.2m allocated for trunk roads and motorways.

The Transport Act 2000 gave English and Welsh local authorities (outside London) powers to introduce road-user charging or workplace parking levy schemes. The act requires that the net revenue raised is used to improve local transport services and facilities for at least ten years. The aim is to reduce congestion and encourage greater use of alternative modes of transport. Schemes developed by local authorities require government approval. The UK's first toll road, the M6 Toll, opened in December 2003 and runs for 43.5km (27 miles) around Birmingham from junction 3a to junction 11a on the M6.

Charging schemes in London are allowed under the 1999 Greater London Authority Act. The Central London Congestion Charge Scheme began on 17 February 2003 (see also Regional Government).

ROAD LENGTHS 2013
Miles

	England	Wales	Scotland	Great Britain
Major Roads	21,961	2,676	6,674	31,311
Motorways	1,891	88	284	2,262
Minor Roads	165,751	18,384	30,282	214,417
Total	187,712	21,061	36,956	245,728

Source: Department for Transport

BUSES

The majority of bus services outside London are provided on a commercial basis by private operators. Local authorities have powers to subsidise services where needs are not being met by a commercial service.

Since April 2008 men and women who have attained the state pension age and disabled people who qualify under the categories listed in the Transport Act 2000 have been able to travel for free on any local bus across England between 9.30am and 11pm Monday to Friday and all day on weekends and bank holidays. Local authorities recompense operators for the reduced fare revenue. The age of eligibility for concessionary travel currently stands at 60 but will increase in line with the state pension age, which is expected to reach 65 by 2018. A similar scheme operates in Wales and within London, although there is no time restriction. In Scotland, people aged 60 and over and disabled people have been able to travel for free on any local or long-distance bus since April 2006.

In London, Transport for London (TfL) has overall responsibility for setting routes, service standards and fares for the bus network. Almost all routes are competitively tendered to commercial operators.

In Northern Ireland, passenger transport services are provided by Ulsterbus and Metro (formerly Citybus), two wholly owned subsidiaries of the Northern Ireland Transport Holding Company. Along with Northern Ireland Railways, Ulsterbus and Metro operate under the brand name of Translink and are publicly owned. Ulsterbus is responsible for virtually all bus services in Northern Ireland except Belfast city services, which are operated by Metro. People living in Northern Ireland aged 65 and over can travel on buses and trains for free once they have obtained a Senior Citizen SmartPass from Translink.

LOCAL BUS PASSENGER JOURNEYS 2013–14

	No. of journeys (millions)
England	4,669
London	2,377
Scotland	425
Wales	109
Total	5,203

Source: Department for Transport

TAXIS AND PRIVATE HIRE VEHICLES

A taxi is a public transport vehicle with fewer than nine passenger seats, which is licensed to 'ply for hire'. This distinguishes taxis from private hire vehicles (PHVs) which must be booked in advance through an operator. In London, taxis and private hire vehicles are licensed by the Public Carriage Office (PCO), part of TfL. Outside London, local authorities are responsible for the licensing of taxis and private hire vehicles operational in their respective administrative areas. At the end of March 2013 there were 78,000 licensed taxis and 152,600 PHVs in England and Wales, of these 73,000 taxis and 148,600 PHVs were in England with around 31 per cent of both taxis and PHVs based in London.

ROAD TRAFFIC BY VEHICLE TYPE (GREAT BRITAIN) 2013

	Million vehicle km
All motor vehicles	488,800
Cars and taxis	383,200
Light goods vehicles	68,500
Heavy goods vehicles	25,200
Buses and coaches	4,500
Motorcycles	4,300
Pedal cycles	5,000

Source: Department for Transport

ROAD SAFETY

In May 2011, the government published *The Strategic Framework for Road Safety* which identified key indicators at national and local level intended to monitor the progress towards improving safety and decreasing the number of fatalities and seriously injured casualties on Great Britain's roads.

The key findings from the Department for Transport's 2013 annual road casuality report found that the number of people killed in road accidents reported to the police had decreased, by 2 per cent, from 1,754 in 2012 to 1,713 in 2013; the lowest figure since national records began in 1926. The total number of reported casualties in Great Britain (slight injuries, serious injuries and fatalities) decreased by 6 per cent, from 195,723 in 2012 to 183,670 in 2013. Total reported child casualities (0–15 years) continued to decrease, by 9 per cent in 2013 to 15,756, with the number of children killed or seriously injured also decreasing by 13 per cent to 1,980 in 2013.

ROAD ACCIDENT CASUALTIES 2013

	Killed	Serious	Slight	Total
Average for 2005–9	2,816	27,225	216,010	246,050
England	1,430	18,957	143,457	163,844
Wales	111	1,033	7,191	8,335
Scotland	172	1,667	9,652	11,491
Great Britain	1,713	21,657	160,300	183,670

Source: Department for Transport

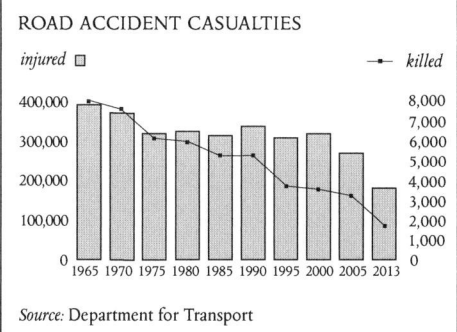

ROAD ACCIDENT CASUALTIES

injured ☐   —•— killed

Source: Department for Transport

DRIVING LICENCES

It is necessary to hold a valid full licence in order to drive unaccompanied on public roads in the UK. Learner drivers must obtain a provisional driving licence before starting to learn to drive and must then pass theory and practical tests to obtain a full driving licence.

There are separate tests for driving motorcycles, cars, passenger-carrying vehicles (PCVs) and large goods vehicles (LGVs). Drivers must hold full car entitlement before they can apply for PCV or LGV entitlements.

The Driver and Vehicle Licensing Agency (DVLA) ceased the issue of paper licences in March 2000, but those currently in circulation will remain valid until they expire or the details on them change. The photocard driving licence was introduced to comply with the second EC directive on driving licences. This requires a photograph of the driver to be included on all UK licences issued from July 2001. The photocard licence must be renewed every ten years, with fines of up to £1,000 for failure to do so.

To apply for a first photocard driving licence, individuals are required to complete the form *Application for a Driving Licence* (D1).

The minimum age for driving motor cars, light goods vehicles up to 3.5 tonnes and motorcycles is 17 (moped, 16). Since June 1997, drivers who collect six or more penalty points within two years of qualifying lose their licence and are required to take another test. Forms and leaflets are available from post offices and online (W www.gov.uk/dvlaforms or W www.gov.uk/government/organisations/driver-and-vehicle-licensing-agency).

The DVLA is responsible for issuing driving licences, registering and licensing vehicles, and collecting excise duty in Great Britain. Driver and Vehicle Licensing Northern Ireland (DVLNI), part of the Driver and Vehicle Agency (DVA), has similar responsibilities in Northern Ireland.

DRIVING LICENCE FEES

As at August 2014

Provisional licence	
Car, motorcycle or moped	£50.00
Bus or lorry	Free
After disqualification until passing re-test	Free
Changing a provisional licence to a full licence	Free
Renewal	
Renewing the photo on the licence (must be renewed every 10 years)	£20.00
At age 70 and over	Free
For medical reasons	Free
Bus or lorry entitlement	Free
After disqualification	£65.00
After disqualification for some drink driving offences*	£90.00
After revocation (under the New Drivers Act)	£50.00
Replacing a lost, stolen, defaced or destroyed licence	£20.00
Adding an entitlement to a full licence	Free
Removing expired endorsements	£20
Exchanging	
a paper licence for a photocard licence†	£20.00
a full Northern Ireland licence for a full GB licence	Free
a full GB licence for a full EU/EEA or other foreign licence (including Channel Islands and Isle of Man)‡	Free
a full EU/EEA or other foreign licence (including Channel Islands and Isle of Man) for a full GB licence	£50.00

Change of name or address (existing licence must be
    surrendered)†   Free
* For an alcohol-related offence where the DVLA need to arrange
medical enquiries
† If a paper licence is exchanged for a photocard at the same time as
name or address details are changed there is no charge
‡ If a GB licence was held previously

DRIVING TESTS

The Driver and Vehicle Standards Agency (DVSA) is
responsible for improving road safety in Great Britain by
setting standards for driving and motorcycling and making
sure drivers, vehicle operators and MOT garages understand
and follow roadworthiness standards. The agency also
provides a range of licensing, testing, education and
enforcement services.

DRIVING TESTS TAKEN AND PASSED
April 2013–March 2014

	Number Taken	Percentage Passed
Practical Test		
Car	1,477,585	47.1
Motorcycle Module 1	46,263	68.8
Motorcycle Module 2	43,475	70.0
LGV/PCV	57,309	54.4
Driver CPC*	15,380	87.3
Theory Test		
Car	1,541,896	51.6
Motorcycle	52,319	75.7
LGV/PCV		
Multiple choice	41,411	67.7
Hazard perception	37,500	79.8
Driver CPC*	25,652	59.4

LGV = Large goods vehicle; PCV = Passenger-carrying vehicle
* Driver Certificate of Professional Competence – legal requirement
for all professional bus, coach and lorry drivers
Source: DVSA

The theory and practical driving tests can be booked
online (W www.gov.uk/book-practical-driving-test) or by phone
(T 0300-200 1122).

DRIVING TEST FEES (WEEKDAY/EVENING* AND WEEKEND)
As at October 2014

Theory tests	
Car and motorcycle	£25.00
Bus and lorry	
Multiple choice	£28.00
Hazard perception	£12.00
Driver CPC	£24.00
Practical tests	
Car	£62.00/£75.00
Tractor and other specialist vehicles	£62.00/£75.00
Motorcycle	
Module 1 (off-road)	£15.50/£15.50
Module 2 (on-road)	£75.00/£88.50
Lorry and bus	£115.00/£141.00
Driver CPC	£55.00/£63.00
Car and trailer	£115.00/£141.00
Extended tests for disqualified drivers	
Car	£124.00/£150.00
Motorcycle	£150.00/£177.00
Module 1 (on-road)	

* After 4.30pm

VEHICLE LICENCES

Registration and first licensing of vehicles is through
local offices of the DVLA in Swansea. Local facilities for
relicensing are available at any post office which deals with
vehicle licensing. Applicants will need to take their vehicle
registration document (V5C) or, if this is not available, the
applicant must complete form V62. Forms are available at
post offices and online (W www.gov.uk/dvlaforms)

MOTOR VEHICLES LICENSED (GREAT BRITAIN)
As at 31 March 2014

	Thousands
All cars	29,372
Light goods vehicles	3,386
Motorcycles	1,218
Heavy goods vehicles	466
Buses and coaches	164
Other vehicles*	691
Total	35,297

* Includes rear diggers, lift trucks, rollers, ambulances, Hackney
Carriages, three-wheelers and agricultural vehicles
Source: Department for Transport

VEHICLE EXCISE DUTY

Details of the present duties chargeable on motor vehicles are
available at post offices and online (W www.gov.uk/overnment/
publications/rates-of-vehicle-tax-v149). The Vehicle Excise and
Registration Act 1994 provides *inter alia* that any vehicle
kept on a public road but not used on roads is chargeable to
excise duty as if it were in use. All non-commercial vehicles
constructed before 1 January 1973 are exempt from vehicle
excise duty. Any vehicle licensed on or after 31 January
1998, not in use and not kept on public roads must be
registered as SORN (Statutory Off Road Notification) to be
exempted from vehicle excise duty. From 1 January 2004 the
registered keeper of a vehicle remains responsible for taxing
a vehicle or making a SORN declaration until that liability
is formally transferred to a new keeper.

RATES OF DUTY *from 1 April 2014*

	6 months	12 months
Cars registered before 1 March 2001		
Under 1,549cc	£79.75	£145.00
Over 1,549cc	£126.50	£230.00
Light goods vehicles registered on or after 1 March 2001		
	£123.75	£225.00
Euro 4 light goods vehicles registered between 1 March 2003 and 31 December 2006	£77.00	£140.00
Euro 5 light goods vehicles registered between 1 January 2009 and 31 December 2010	£77.00	£140.00
Motorcycles (with or without sidecar)		
Not over 150cc	–	£17.00
151–400cc	–	£38.00
401–600cc	£31.90	£58.00
600cc+	£44.0	£80.00
Tricycles		
Not over 150cc	–	£17.00
All others	£44.00	£80.00

RATES OF DUTY *from 1 April 2014*
Cars registered on or after 1 March 2001 and first-year* rates

Band	CO_2	Petrol and Diesel Car			Alternative Fuel Car		
	Emissions (g/km)	6 months	12 months		6 months	12 months	
A	Up to 100	–	£0.00		–	£0.00	
B	101–110	–	£20.00		–	£10.00	
C	111–120	–	£30.00		–	£20.00	
D	121–130	£60.50	£110.00		£55.00	£100.00	
E	131–140	£71.50	£130.00		£66.00	£120.00	
F	141–150	£79.75	£145.00		£74.25	£135.00	
G	151–165	£99.00	£180.00		£93.50	£170.00	
H	166–175	£112.75	£205.00	(£290.00)	£107.25	£195.00	(£280.00)
I	176–185	£123.75	£225.00	(£345.00)	£118.25	£215.00	(£335.00)
J	186–200	£145.75	£265.00	(£485.00)	£140.25	£255.00	(£475.00)
K†	201–225	£156.75	£285.00	(£635.00)	£151.25	£275.00	(£625.00)
L	226–255	£266.75	£485.00	(£860.00)	£261.25	£475.00	(£850.00)
M	255+	£275.00	£500.00	(£1,090.00)	£269.50	£490.00	(£1,080.00)

* First-year rates (figures in parentheses) are payable for some vehicles' first tax disc taken out at first registration
† Includes cars that have a CO_2 emission figure over 225g/km but were registered before 23 March 2006

MOT TESTING

Cars, motorcycles, motor caravans, light goods and dual-purpose vehicles more than three years old must be covered by a current MOT test certificate. However, some vehicles (ie minibuses, ambulances and taxis) may require a certificate at one year old. All certificates must be renewed annually. Only MOT testing stations showing a blue sign with three triangles and an official 'MOT: Test: Fees and Appeals' poster may carry out an approved MOT. The MOT testing scheme is administered by the Driver and Vehicle Standards Agency (DVSA) on behalf of the Secretary of State for Transport.

A fee is payable to MOT testing stations. The current maximum fees are:

For cars, private hire and public service vehicles, motor caravans, dual purpose vehicles, ambulances and taxis (all up to eight passenger seats)	£54.85
For motorcycles	£29.65
For motorcycles with sidecar	£37.80
For three-wheeled vehicles (up to 450kg unladen weight)	£37.80
*Private passenger vehicles and ambulances with:	
9–12 passenger seats	£57.30 (£64.00)
13–16 passenger seats	£59.55 (£80.50)
16+ passenger seats	£80.65 (£124.50)
Goods vehicles (3,000–3,500kg)	£58.60

* Figures in parentheses include seatbelt installation check

SHIPPING AND PORTS

Sea trade has always played a central role in Britain's economy. By the 17th century Britain had built up a substantial merchant fleet and by the early 20th century it dominated the world shipping industry. Between 1997 and 2008, the size and tonnage of the UK-registered trading fleet saw substantial growth however between 2008 and 2013 this had begun to slow and decrease. By the end of 2013 the number of ships in the UK-flagged merchant fleet had increased by 30 per cent while gross tonnage had more than quadrupled since 1999. The UK-flagged merchant fleet now constitutes 0.9 per cent of the world merchant fleet in terms of vessels and 1.3 per cent in terms of gross tonnage.

Freight is carried by liner and bulk services, almost all scheduled liner services being containerised. About 95 per cent by weight of Britain's overseas trade is carried by sea; this amounts to 75 per cent of its total value. Passengers and vehicles are carried by roll-on, roll-off ferries, hovercraft, hydrofoils and high-speed catamarans. There were around 42 million ferry passengers in 2012, of whom 20 million travelled internationally.

Lloyd's of London provides the most comprehensive shipping intelligence service in the world. *Lloyd's Shipping Index,* published daily, lists some 25,000 ocean-going vessels and gives the latest known report of each.

PORTS

There are more than 650 ports in Great Britain for which statutory harbour powers have been granted. Of these 111 were commercially active in 2013. The largest ports in terms of freight tonnage in 2013 were Grimsby and Immingham (62 million tonnes), London (43 million tonnes), Milford Haven (41 million tonnes), Tees and Hartlepool (38 million tonnes), Southampton (36 million tonnes), Liverpool (31 million tonnes), Forth (26 million tonnes), Felixstowe (26 million tonnes) and Dover (25 million tonnes). Belfast (17 million tonnes) is the principal freight port in Northern Ireland.

Broadly speaking, ports are owned and operated by private companies, local authorities or self-owning bodies, known as trust ports. The largest operator is Associated British Ports which owns 21 ports. Port traffic results show that 503 million tonnes were handled by UK ports in 2013, remaining broadly stable compared to the previous year's figure of 501 million tonnes.

MARINE SAFETY

The Maritime and Coastguard Agency (MCA) is an executive agency of the Department for Transport responsible for implementing the government's maritime safety policy in the UK and works to prevent the loss of life on the coast and at sea.

HM Coastguard maintains a 24-hour search and rescue response and coordination capability for the whole of the UK coast and the internationally agreed search and rescue region. HM Coastguard is responsible for mobilising and organising resources in response to people in distress at sea, or at risk of injury or death on the UK's cliffs or shoreline.

The MCA also inspects and surveys ships to ensure that they are meeting UK and international safety rules, provides certification to seafarers, registers vessels and responds to pollution from shipping and offshore installations.

Locations hazardous to shipping in coastal waters are marked by lighthouses and other lights and buoys. The lighthouse authorities are the Corporation of Trinity House (for England, Wales and the Channel Islands), the Northern Lighthouse Board (for Scotland and the Isle of Man), and the Commissioners of Irish Lights (for Northern Ireland and the Republic of Ireland). Trinity House maintains 68 lighthouses, 10 light vessels/floats, nearly 436 buoys, 21 beacons, 52 radar beacons, eight DGPS (differential global positioning system) stations* and three AIS (automatic identification system) stations. The Northern Lighthouse Board maintains 205 lighthouses, 164 buoys, 26 beacons, 29 radar beacons, 35 AIS stations, four DGPS stations and one LORAN (long-range navigation) station; and Irish Lights looks after 72 lighthouses, 150 buoys, 29 beacons, 22 radar beacons, and three DGPS stations, with AIS in operation on 68 lighthouses/stations.

Harbour authorities are responsible for pilotage within their harbour areas; and the Ports Act 1991 provides for the transfer of lights and buoys to harbour authorities where these are used mainly for local navigation.

* DGPS is a satellite-based navigation system

UK-OWNED TRADING VESSELS
500 gross tons and over, as at end 2013

Type of vessel	No.	Gross tonnage
Tankers	119	4,832,000
Fully cellular container	105	5,389,000
Dry bulk carriers	88	4,115,000
Ro-Ro (passenger and cargo)	91	1,425,000
Passenger	33	1,741,000
Other general cargo	91	399,000
Specialised carriers	27	1,307,000
All vessels	554	19,209,000

Source: Department for Transport

UK SEA PASSENGER* MOVEMENTS 2012

Type of journey	No. of passenger movements
International	
Ro-Ro Passengers on short sea routes	19,680,000
Passengers on cruises beginning or ending at UK ports*	1,737,000
Passengers on long sea journeys	32,000
Total	21,449,000

* Passengers are included at both departure and arrival if their journeys begin and end at a UK seaport

Source: Department for Transport

UK SHIPPING FORECAST AREAS

Weather bulletins for shipping are broadcast daily on BBC Radio 4 at 00h 48m, 05h 20m, 12h 01m and 17h 54m. All transmissions are broadcast on long wave at 1515m (198kHz) and the 00h 48m and 05h 20m transmissions are also broadcast on FM. The bulletins consist of a gale warning summary, general synopsis, sea-area forecasts and coastal station reports. In addition, gale warnings are broadcast at the first available programme break after receipt. If this does not coincide with a news bulletin, the warning is repeated after the next news bulletin. Shipping forecasts and gale warnings are also available on the Met Office and BBC Weather websites.

KEY

Br	Bridlington
C	Channel Light-Vessel (automatic)
F	Fife Ness
G	Greenwich Light-Vessel (automatic)
J	Jersey
L	Lerwick
M	Malin Head
R	Ronaldsway
S	Sandettie Light-Vessel (automatic)
Sc	Scilly (automatic)
St	Stornoway
T	Tiree
V	Valentia

RELIGION IN THE UK

The 2011 census in England and Wales included a voluntary question on religion; 92.8 per cent of the population chose to answer the question. Christianity remained the largest religion, despite a decrease of 4 million people from the 2001 census, to 33.2 million adherents, or 59.3 per cent of the population. The second largest religious group were Muslims with 2.7 million people identifying themselves as such, an increase of 1.2 million since 2001. The number of people reporting that they had 'no religion' was 14.1 million, around a quarter of the population. Of those reporting that they had no religion, the majority identified themselves as white (93 per cent) and born in the UK (also 93 per cent); in terms of age, the largest demographic were those aged 20 to 24 (1.4 million or 10 per cent). More than 240,000 people listed 'other religion' on the census, which included, among many others, 176,632 Jedi Knights, 56,620 Pagans and 39,061 Spiritualists. Norwich remained the city with the highest proportion reporting no religion (42.5 per cent), while London was the most diverse region with the largest proportion of people classifying themselves as Buddhist, Hindu, Jewish and Muslim. Knowsley, in Merseyside, was the local authority with the highest proportion of Christians at 80.9 per cent, while Tower Hamlets in London had the highest population of Muslims at 34.5 per cent.

In Northern Ireland, the religion question was phrased differently; 738,033 (41 per cent) identified themselves as Roman Catholic, 752,555 (42 per cent) as 'Protestant and other Christian', 14,859 (0.8 per cent) belonged to an 'other religion' and 183,164 (10 per cent) stated they had no religion.

CENSUS 2011 RESULTS – RELIGION IN ENGLAND, WALES AND SCOTLAND*

	thousands	per cent
Christian	36,093	58.8
Buddhist	261	0.4
Hindu	833	1.4
Jewish	269	0.4
Muslim	2,783	4.5
Sikh	432	0.7
Other religion	256	0.4
All religions	40,927	66.6
No religion	16,038	26.1
Not stated	4,406	7.2
All no religion / not stated	20,444	33.3
TOTAL	61,371	100

* Figures from the 2011 census for Northern Ireland did not contain a full breakdown of each major religion
Source: Census 2011

INTER-CHURCH AND INTER-FAITH COOPERATION

The main umbrella body for the Christian churches in the UK is Churches Together in Britain and Ireland. There are also ecumenical bodies in each of the constituent countries of the UK: Churches Together in England, Action of Churches Together in Scotland, CYTUN (Churches Together in Wales), and the Irish Council of Churches. The Free Churches Group (formerly the Free Churches Council), which is closely associated with Churches Together in England, represents most of the free churches in England and Wales, and the Evangelical Alliance represents evangelical Christians.

The Inter Faith Network for the United Kingdom promotes cooperation between faiths, and the Council of Christians and Jews works to improve relations between the two religions. Churches Together in Britain and Ireland also has a commission on inter-faith relations.

ACTION OF CHURCHES TOGETHER IN SCOTLAND, Inglewood House, Alloa, Clackmannanshire FK10 2HU
T 01259-216980 W www.acts-scotland.org
General Secretary, Brother Stephen Smyth
CHURCHES TOGETHER IN BRITAIN AND IRELAND, 39 Ecclestone Square, London SW1V 1BX T 0845-680 6851
E info@ctbi.org.uk W www.ctbi.org.uk
General Secretary, Revd Bob Fyffe
CHURCHES TOGETHER IN ENGLAND, 27 Tavistock Square, London WC1H 9HH T 020-7529 8131
E office@cte.org.uk W www.cte.org.uk
General Secretary, Revd Dr David Cornick
COUNCIL OF CHRISTIANS AND JEWS, Godliman House, 21 Godliman Street, London EC4V 5BD T 020-7015 5160
E cjrelations@ccj.org.uk W www.ccj.org.uk
Chief Executive, Revd David Gifford
CYTUN (CHURCHES TOGETHER IN WALES), 58 Richmond Road, Cardiff CF24 3UR T 029-2046 4204
E post@cytun.org.uk W www.cytun.org.uk
Chief Executive, Revd Canon Aled Edwards, OBE
EVANGELICAL ALLIANCE, 176 Copenhagen Street, London N1 0ST T 020-7520 3830 E info@eauk.org
W www.eauk.org
General Director, Steve Clifford
FREE CHURCHES GROUP, 27 Tavistock Square, London WC1H 9HH T 020-7529 8131 E freechurch@cte.org.uk
W www.cte.org.uk
Secretary, Frank Kantor
INTERFAITH NETWORK FOR THE UK, 2 Grosvenor Gardens, London SW1W 0DH T 020-7730 0410
E ifnet@interfaith.org.uk W www.interfaith.org.uk
Director, Dr Harriet Crabtree
IRISH COUNCIL OF CHURCHES, Inter-Church Centre, 48 Elmwood Avenue, Belfast BT9 6AZ T 028-9066 3145
E info@irishchurches.org W www.irishchurches.org
Executive Officer, Mervyn McCullagh

RELIGIONS AND BELIEFS

BAHA'I FAITH

Baha'u'llah ('Glory of God'), the founder of the Baha'i faith, was born in Iran in 1817. He was imprisoned in 1852 for advocating the teachings of the Bab ('Gate'), a prophet who was martyred in 1850. Baha'u'llah was persecuted and sent into successive stages of exile, first to Baghdad – where in 1863 he announced that he was the 'promised one' foretold by the Bab – and then to Constantinople, Adrianople and eventually Acre, in present day Israel. He died in 1892 and was succeeded by his son, Abdu'l-Baha, as head of the Baha'i faith, under whose guidance the faith spread to Europe and North America. He was in turn succeeded by Shoghi Effendi, his grandson, who oversaw the establishment of the administrative order and the spread of the faith around the world until his death in 1957. The Universal House of Justice, an elected international governing council, was formed in 1963 in accordance with Baha'u'llah's teachings.

The Baha'i faith espouses the oneness of humanity and of religion and teaches that there is only one God, whose will has been revealed to mankind by a series of messengers, such as Zoroaster, Abraham, Moses, Buddha, Krishna, Christ, Muhammad, the Bab and Baha'u'llah, who were seen as the founders of separate religions, but whose common purpose was to bring God's message to mankind. The Baha'i faith attributes the differences in teachings between religions to humanity's changing needs. Baha'i teachings include that all races and both sexes are equal and deserving of equal opportunities and treatment, that education is a fundamental right and that extremes of wealth and poverty should be eliminated. In addition, the faith exhorts mankind to establish a world federal system to promote peace and unity.

In an effort to translate these principles into action, Baha'is have initiated an educational process across the world that seeks to raise the capacity of people of all ages and from all backgrounds to contribute towards the betterment of society. There is no clergy; each local community elects a local spiritual assembly to tend to its administrative needs. A national spiritual assembly is elected annually by locally elected delegates, and every five years the national spiritual assemblies meet together to elect the Universal House of Justice, the supreme international governing body of the Baha'i Faith. Worldwide there are over 13,000 local spiritual assemblies and more than 5 million members.

BAHA'I COMMUNITY OF THE UK, 27 Rutland Gate, London SW7 1PD T 020-7584 2566 E nsa@bahai.org.uk W www.bahai.org.uk
Director, Office of Public Affairs, Dr Kishan Manocha

BUDDHISM

Buddhism originated in what is now the Bihar area of northern India in the teachings of Siddhartha Gautama, who became the *Buddha* ('Enlightened One'). In the Thai or Suriyakati calendar the beginning of the Buddhist era is dated from the death of Buddha; the year 2015 is therefore 2558 by the Thai Buddhist reckoning.

Fundamental to Buddhism is the concept of rebirth, whereby each life carries with it the consequences of the conduct of earlier lives (known as the law of *karma)* and this cycle of death and rebirth is broken only when the state of *nirvana* has been reached. Buddhism steers a middle path between belief in personal continuity and the belief that death results in total extinction.

While doctrine does not have a pivotal position in Buddhism, a statement of four 'Noble Truths' is common to all its schools and varieties. These are: suffering is inescapable in even the most fortunate of existences; craving is the root cause of suffering; abandonment of the selfish mindset is the way to end suffering; and bodily and mental discipline, accompanied by the cultivation of wisdom and compassion, provides the spiritual path ('Noble Eightfold Path') to accomplish this. Buddhists deny the idea of a creator and prefer to emphasise the practical aspects of moral and spiritual development.

The schools of Buddhism can be broadly divided into three: *Theravada,* the generally monastic-led tradition practised in Sri Lanka and South East Asia; *Mahayana,* the philosophical and popular traditions of the Far East; and *Esoteric,* the Tantric-derived traditions found in Tibet and Mongolia and, to a lesser extent, China and Japan. The extensive Theravada scriptures are contained in the *Pali Canon,* which dates in its written form from the first century BC. Mahayana and Esoteric schools have Sanskrit-derived translations of these plus many more additional scriptures as well as exegetical material.

In the East the new and full moons and the lunar quarter days were (and to a certain extent, still are) significant in determining the religious calendar. Most private homes contain a shrine where offerings, worship and other spiritual practices (such as meditation, chanting or mantra recitation) take place on a daily basis. Buddhist festivals vary according to local traditions within the different schools and there is little uniformity – even in commemorating the birth, enlightenment and death of the Buddha.

There is no governing authority for Buddhism in the UK. Communities representing all schools of Buddhism operate independently. The Buddhist Society was established in 1924; it runs courses, lectures and meditation groups, and publishes books about Buddhism. The Network of Buddhist Organisations was founded in 1993 to promote fellowship and dialogue between Buddhist organisations and to facilitate cooperation in matters of common interest.

There are estimated to be at least 375 million Buddhists worldwide. Of the 248,000 Buddhists in England and Wales (according to the 2011 census), 72,000 are white British (the majority are converts), 49,000 Chinese, 93,000 'other Asian' and 36,000 are 'other ethnic'.

THE BUDDHIST SOCIETY, 58 Eccleston Square, London SW1V 1PH T 020-7834 5858 E info@thebuddhistsociety.org W www.thebuddhistsociety.org
LONDON BUDDHIST CENTRE, 51 Roman Road, London E2 0HU T 0845-458 4716 E info@lbc.org.uk W www.lbc.org.uk
THE NETWORK OF BUDDHIST ORGANISATIONS, PO Box 4147, Maidenhead SL60 1DN T 0845-345 8978 E secretary@nbo.org.uk W www.nbo.org.uk
THE OFFICE OF TIBET, Tibet House, 1 Culworth Street, London NW8 7AF T 020-7722 5378 E info@otlondon.org W www.tibet.com
Representative of HH the Dalai Lama, Thubten Samdup
SOKA GAKKAI INTERNATIONAL (UK), Taplow Court Grand Cultural Centre, Cliveden Road, Taplow, Berkshire SL6 0ER T 01628-773163 W www.sgi-uk.org

CHRISTIANITY

Christianity is a monotheistic faith based on the person and teachings of Jesus Christ, and all Christian denominations claim his authority. Central to its teaching is the concept of God and his son Jesus Christ, who was crucified and resurrected in order to enable mankind to attain salvation.

The Jewish scriptures predicted the coming of a *Messiah,* an 'anointed one', who would bring salvation. To Christians, Jesus of Nazareth, a Jewish rabbi (teacher) who was born in Palestine, was the promised Messiah. Jesus' birth, teachings, crucifixion and subsequent resurrection are recorded in the *Gospels,* which, together with other scriptures that summarise Christian belief, form the *New Testament.* This, together with the Hebrew scriptures – entitled the *Old Testament* by Christians – makes up the Bible, the sacred texts of Christianity.

Christians believe that sin distanced mankind from God, and that Jesus was the son of God, sent to redeem mankind from sin by his death. In addition, many believe that Jesus will return again at some future date, triumph over evil and establish a kingdom on earth, thus inaugurating a new age. The Gospel assures Christians that those who believe in Jesus and obey his teachings will be forgiven their sins and will be resurrected from the dead.

The Apostles were Jesus' first converts and are recognised by Christians as the founders of the Christian community. Early Christianity spread rapidly throughout the eastern provinces of the Roman Empire but was subjected to great persecution until AD 313, when Emperor Constantine's Edict of Toleration confirmed its right to exist. Christianity was established as the religion of the Roman Empire in AD 381.

Between AD 325 and 787 there were seven Oecumenical Councils at which bishops from the entire Christian world assembled to resolve various doctrinal disputes. The estrangement between East and West began after Constantine moved the centre of the Roman Empire from Rome to Constantinople, and it grew after the division of the Roman Empire into eastern and western halves. Linguistic and cultural differences between Greek East and Latin West served to encourage separate ecclesiastical developments which became pronounced in the tenth and early 11th centuries. Administration of the church was divided between five ancient patriarchates: Rome and all the West, Constantinople (the imperial city – the 'New Rome'), Jerusalem and all of Palestine, Antioch and all the East, and Alexandria and all of Africa. Of these, only Rome was in the Latin West and after the schism in 1054, Rome developed a structure of authority centralised on the Papacy, while the Orthodox East maintained the style of localised administration. Papal authority over the doctrine and jurisdiction of the church in Western Europe was unrivalled after the split with the Eastern Orthodox Church until the Protestant Reformation in the 16th century.

Christian practices vary widely between different Christian churches, but prayer, charity and giving (for the maintenance of the church buildings, for the work of the church, and to those in need) are common to all. In addition, certain days of observance, ie the *Sabbath, Easter* and *Christmas,* are celebrated by most Christians. The Orthodox, Roman Catholic and Anglican churches celebrate many more days of observance, based on saints and significant events in the life of Jesus. The belief in sacraments, physical signs believed to have been ordained by Jesus Christ to symbolise and convey spiritual gifts, varies greatly between Christian denominations; *baptism* and the *Eucharist* are practised by most Christians. Baptism, symbolising repentance and faith in Jesus, is an act marking entry into the Christian community; the Eucharist, the ritual re-enactment of the Last Supper, Jesus' final meal with his disciples, is also practised by most denominations. Other sacraments, such as anointing the sick, the laying on of hands to symbolise the passing on of the office of priesthood or to heal the sick, and speaking in tongues, where it is believed that the person is possessed by the Holy Spirit, are less common. In denominations where infant baptism is practised, confirmation (where the person confirms the commitments made on their behalf in infancy) is common. Matrimony and the ordination of priests are also widely believed to be sacraments. Many Protestants regard only baptism and the Eucharist to be sacraments; the Quakers and the Salvation Army reject the use of sacraments.

See Churches for contact details of the Church of England, the Roman Catholic Church and other Christian churches in the UK.

HINDUISM

Hinduism has no historical founder but had become highly developed in India by *c.*2500 BC. Its adherents originally called themselves Aryans; Muslim invaders first called the Aryans 'Hindus' (derived from 'Sindhu', the name of the river Indus) in the eighth century.

Most Hindus hold that *satya* (truthfulness), honesty, sincerity and devotion to God are essential for good living. They believe in one supreme spirit *(Brahman)*, and in the transmigration of *atman* (the soul). Most Hindus accept the doctrine of *karma* (consequences of actions), the concept of

samsara (successive lives) and the possibility of all atmans achieving *moksha* (liberation from samsara) through *jnana* (knowledge), *yoga* (meditation), *karma* (work or action) and *bhakti* (devotion).

Most Hindus offer worship to *murtis* (images of deities) representing different incarnations or aspects of Brahman, and follow their *dharma* (religious and social duty) according to the traditions of their *varna* (social class), *ashrama* (stage in life), *jaiti* (caste) and *kula* (family).

Hinduism's sacred texts are divided into *shruti* ('that which is heard'), including the *Vedas,* and *smriti* ('that which is remembered'), including the *Ramayana,* the *Mahabharata,* the *Puranas* (ancient myths), and the sacred law books. Most Hindus recognise the authority of the *Vedas,* the oldest holy books, and accept the philosophical teachings of the *Upanishads,* the *Vedanta Sutras* and the *Bhagavad-Gita.*

Hindus believe Brahman to be omniscient, omnipotent, limitless and all-pervading. Brahman is usually worshipped in its deity form. Brahma, Vishnu and Shiva are the most important deities or aspects of Brahman worshipped by Hindus; their respective consorts are Saraswati, Lakshmi and Durga or Parvati, also known as Shakti. There are believed to have been ten *avatars* (incarnations) of Vishnu, of whom the most important are Rama and Krishna. Other popular gods are Ganesha, Hanuman and Subrahmanyam. All Hindu gods are seen as aspects of the supreme spirit (Brahman), not as competing deities.

Orthodox Hindus revere all gods and goddesses equally, but there are many denominations, including the Hare-Krishna movement (ISKCon), the Arya Samaj and the Swaminarayan Hindu mission, in which worship is concentrated on one deity. The *guru* (spiritual teacher) is seen as the source of spiritual guidance.

Hinduism does not have a centrally trained and ordained priesthood. The pronouncements of the *shankaracharyas* (heads of monasteries) of Shringeri, Puri, Dwarka and Badrinath are heeded by the orthodox but may be ignored by the various sects.

The commonest form of worship is *puja,* in which water, flowers, food, fruit, incense and light are offered to the deity. Puja may be done either in a home shrine or a *mandir* (temple). Many British Hindus celebrate *samskars* (purification rites), to name a baby, for the sacred thread (an initiation ceremony), marriage and cremation.

The largest communities of Hindus in Britain are in Leicester, London, Birmingham and Bradford, and developed as a result of immigration from India, eastern Africa and Sri Lanka.

There are an estimated 800 million Hindus worldwide; there are around 817,000 adherents, according to the 2011 census in England and Wales, and around 135 temples in the UK.

ARYA SAMAJ LONDON, 69 Argyle Road, London W13 0LY
T 020-8991 1732 E aryasamajlondon@yahoo.co.uk
General Secretary, Amrit Lal Bhardwaj

BHARATIYA VIDYA BHAVAN, Institute of Indian Art and Culture, 4A Castletown Road, London W14 9HE
T 020-7381 3086/4608 E info@bhavan.net W www.bhavan.net
Executive Director, Dr M. N. Nandakumara

INTERNATIONAL SOCIETY FOR KRISHNA CONSCIOUSNESS (ISKCON), Bhaktivedanta Manor, Dharam Marg, Hilfield Lane, Aldenham, Watford, Herts WD25 8EZ T 01923-851000 E info@krishnatemple.com W www.krishnatemple.com
Temple President, Sruti Dharma Das

NATIONAL COUNCIL OF HINDU TEMPLES (UK), 1 Hans Close, Stoke, Coventry CV2 4WA T 0780-505 4776
E info@nchtuk.org W www.nchtuk.org
General Secretary, Dr Raj Pandit Sharma

SWAMINARAYAN HINDU MISSION (SHRI
SWAMINARAYAN MANDIR), 105–119 Brentfield Road,
London NW10 8LD T 020-8965 2651 E info@mandir.org
W www.mandir.org

HUMANISM

Humanism traces its roots back to ancient times, with
Chinese, Greek, Indian and Roman philosophers expressing
Humanist ideas some 2,500 years ago. Confucius, the
Chinese philosopher who lived c.500 BC, believed that
religious observances should be replaced with moral values
as the basis of social and political order and that 'the true
way' is based on reason and humanity. He also stressed the
importance of benevolence and respect for others, and
believed that the individual situation should be considered
rather than the global application of traditional rules.

Humanists believe that there is no God or other
supernatural being, that humans have only one life
(Humanists do not believe in an afterlife or reincarnation)
and that humans can live ethical and fulfilling lives without
religious beliefs through a moral code derived from a
shared history, personal experience and thought. There are
no sacred Humanist texts. Particular emphasis is placed on
science as the only reliable source of knowledge of the
universe. Many Humanists recognise a need for ceremonies
to mark important occasions in life and the British Humanist
Association has a network of celebrants who are trained and
accredited to conduct baby namings, weddings and funerals.
The British Humanist Association's campaigns for a secular
state (a state based on freedom of religious or non-religious
belief with no privileges for any particular set of beliefs)
are based on equality and human rights. The association
also campaigns for inclusive schools that meet the needs of
all parents and pupils, regardless of their religious or
non-religious beliefs. According to figures from the 2011
census, there are just over 15,000 Humanists in England and
Wales.

BRITISH HUMANIST ASSOCIATION, 39 Moreland Street,
London EC1V 8BB T 020-7324 3060 E info@humanism.org.uk
W www.humanism.org.uk
Chief Executive, Andrew Copson

ISLAM

Islam (which means 'peace arising from submission to the
will of Allah' in Arabic) is a monotheistic religion which was
taught in Arabia by the Prophet Muhammad, who was born
in Mecca (Al-Makkah) in 570 AD. Islam spread to Egypt,
north Africa, Spain and the borders of China in the century
following the Prophet's death, and is now the predominant
religion in Indonesia, the near and Middle East, northern and
parts of western Africa, Pakistan, Bangladesh, Malaysia and
some of the former Soviet republics. There are also large
Muslim communities in other countries.

For Muslims (adherents of Islam), there is one God (Allah),
who holds absolute power. Muslims believe that Allah's
commands were revealed to mankind through the prophets,
who include Abraham, Moses and Jesus, but that Allah's
message was gradually corrupted until revealed through the
angel Jibril (Gabriel)
over a period of 23 years. This last, incorruptible message is
said to have been recorded in the Qur'an (Koran), which
contains 114 divisions called surahs, each made up of ayahs of
various lengths, and is held to be the essence of all previous
scriptures. The Ahadith are the records of the Prophet
Muhammad's deeds and sayings (the Sunnah) as practised
and recounted by his immediate followers. A culture and a
system of law and theology gradually developed to form
a distinctive Islamic civilisation. Islam makes no distinction
between sacred and worldly affairs and provides rules for

every aspect of human life. The Shariah is the sacred law of
Islam based primarily upon prescriptions derived from the
Qur'an and the Sunnah of the Prophet.

The 'five pillars of Islam' are shahadah (a declaration of
faith in the oneness and supremacy of Allah and the
messengership of Muhammad); salat (formal prayer, to be
performed five times a day facing the Ka'bah (the most sacred
shrine in the holy city of Mecca)); zakat (welfare due, paid
annually on all savings at the rate of 2.5 per cent); sawm
(fasting during the month of Ramadan from dawn until
sunset); and hajj (pilgrimage to Mecca made once in a
lifetime if the believer is financially and physically able).
Some Muslims would add jihad as the sixth pillar (striving for
the cause of good and resistance to evil).

Two main groups developed among Muslims. Sunni
Muslims accept the legitimacy of Muhammad's first four
caliphs (successors as head of the Muslim community) and
of the authority of the Muslim community as a whole. About
90 per cent of Muslims are Sunni Muslims.

Shi'ites recognise only Muhammad's son-in-law Ali as his
rightful successor and the Imams (descendants of Ali, not to
be confused with imams, who are prayer leaders or religious
teachers) as the principal legitimate religious authority. The
largest group within Shi'ism is Twelver Shi'ism, which has
been the official school of law and theology in Iran since the
16th century; other subsects include the Ismailis, the Druze
and the Alawis, the latter two differing considerably from the
main body of Muslims. The Ibadis of Oman are neither Sunni
nor Shia, deriving from the strictly observant Khariji
(Seceders). There is no organised priesthood, but learned
men such as imams, ulama, and ayatollahs are accorded great
respect. The Sufis are the mystics of Islam. Mosques are
centres for worship and teaching and also for social and
welfare activities.

Islam was first recorded in western Europe in the eighth
century AD when 800 years of Muslim rule began in Spain.
Later, Islam spread to eastern Europe. More recently, Muslims
came to Europe from Africa, the Middle East and Asia in
the late 19th century. Both the Sunni and Shia traditions are
represented in Britain, but the majority of Muslims in Britain
adhere to Sunni Islam. Efforts to establish a representative
national body for Muslims in Britain resulted in the
founding, in 1997, of the Muslim Council of Britain. In
addition, there are many other Muslim organisations in the
UK. There are around 1.6 billion Muslims worldwide, with
around 2.8 million adherents in England, Wales and Scotland
and about 1,500 mosques in the UK.

IMAMS AND MOSQUES COUNCIL, 20–22 Creffield Road,
London W5 3RP T 020-8992 6636
E msraza@muslimcollege.ac.uk
Director, Moulana M. S. Raza
ISLAMIC CULTURAL CENTRE – THE LONDON
CENTRAL MOSQUE, 146 Park Road, London NW8 7RG
T 020-7725 2213 E info@iccuk.org W www.iccuk.org
Director, Dr Ahmad Al-Dubayan
MUSLIM WORLD LEAGUE LONDON, 46 Goodge Street,
London W1T 4LU T 020-7636 7568
Director, Dr Ahmad Makhoodom

JAINISM

Jainism traces its history to Vardhamana Jnatriputra, known
as Tirthankara Mahavira ('the Great Hero') whose traditional
dates were 599–527 BC. Jains believe he was the last of the
current era in a series of 24 Jinas (those who overcome all
passions and desires) or Tirthankaras (those who show a way
across the ocean of life) stretching back to remote antiquity.
Born to a noble family in north-eastern India (presently the
state of Bihar), he renounced the world for the life of
a wandering ascetic and after 12 years of austerity and

meditation he attained enlightenment. He then preached his message until, at the age of 72, he left the mortal world and achieved total liberation *(moksha)* from the cycle of death and rebirth.

Jains declare that the Hindu rituals of transferring merit are not acceptable as each living being is responsible for its own actions. They recognise some of the minor deities of the Hindu pantheon, but the supreme objects of worship are the Tirthankaras. The pious Jain does not ask favours from the Tirthankaras, but seeks to emulate their example in his or her own life.

Jains believe that the universe is eternal and self-subsisting, that there is no omnipotent creator God ruling it and the destiny of the individual is in his or her own hands. *Karma,* the fruit of past actions, is believed to determine the place of every living being and rebirth may be in the heavens, on earth as a human, an animal or other lower being, or in the hells. The ultimate goal of existence for Jains is *moksha,* a state of perfect knowledge and tranquillity for each individual soul, which can be achieved only by gaining enlightenment.

The Jainist path to liberation is defined by the three jewels: *Samyak Darshan* (right perception), *Samyak Jnana* (right knowledge) and *Samyak Charitra* (right conduct). Of the five fundamental precepts of the Jains, *Ahimsa* (non-injury to any form of being, in any mode: thought, speech or action) is the first and foremost, and was popularised by Gandhi as *Ahimsa paramo dharma* (non-violence is the supreme religion).

The largest population of Jains can be found in India but there are approximately 30,000 Jains in Britain, with sizeable communities in North America, East Africa, Australia and smaller groups in many other countries.

INSTITUTE OF JAINOLOGY, Unit 18, Silicon Business
Centre, 28 Wadsworth Road, Perivale, Greenford, Middx
UB6 7JZ T 020-8997 2300 E info@jainology.org
W www.jainology.org
Deputy Chair, Dr Harshad Sanghrajka

JUDAISM

Judaism is the oldest monotheistic faith. The primary text of Judaism is the Hebrew bible or *Tanakh,* which records how the descendants of Abraham were led by Moses out of their slavery in Egypt to Mount Sinai where God's law *(Torah)* was revealed to them as the chosen people. The *Talmud,* which consists of commentaries on the *Mishnah* (the first text of rabbinical Judaism), is also held to be authoritative, and may be divided into two main categories: the *halakah* (dealing with legal and ritual matters) and the *aggadah* (dealing with theological and ethical matters not directly concerned with the regulation of conduct). The *midrash* comprises rabbinic writings containing biblical interpretations in the spirit of the aggadah. The halakah has become a source of division: orthodox Jews regard Jewish law as derived from God and therefore unalterable; progressive Jews seek to interpret it in the light of contemporary considerations; and conservative Jews aim to maintain most of the traditional rituals but to allow changes in accordance with tradition. Reconstructionist Judaism, a 20th-century movement, regards Judaism as a culture rather than a theological system and accepts all forms of Jewish practice.

The family is the basic unit of Jewish ritual, with the synagogue playing an important role as the centre for public worship and religious study. A synagogue is led by a group of laymen who are elected to office. The Rabbi is primarily a teacher and spiritual guide. The *Sabbath* is the central religious observance. Most British Jews are descendants of either the *Ashkenazim* of central and eastern Europe or the *Sephardim* of Spain, Portugal and the Middle East.

The Chief Rabbi of the United Hebrew Congregations of the Commonwealth is appointed by a Chief Rabbinate Conference, and is the rabbinical authority of the mainstream Orthodox sector of the Ashkenazi Jewish community, the largest body of which is the United Synagogue. His formal ecclesiastical authority is not recognised by the Reform Synagogues of Great Britain (the largest progressive group), the Union of Liberal and Progressive Synagogues, the Spanish and Portuguese Jews' Congregation or the Assembly of Masorti Synagogues. He is, however, generally recognised both outside the Jewish community and within it as the public religious representative of the totality of British Jewry. The Chief Rabbi is President of the London *Beth Din* (Court of Judgment), a rabbinic court. The *Dayanim* (Judges) adjudicate in disputes or on matters of Jewish law and tradition; they also oversee dietary law administration, marriage, divorce and issues of personal status.

The Board of Deputies of British Jews, established in 1760, is the representative body of British Jewry. The basis of representation is through the election of deputies by synagogues and communal organisations. It protects and promotes the interests of British Jewry, acts as the central voice of the community and seeks to counter anti-Jewish discrimination and anti-Semitic activities.

There are approximately 13.5 million Jews worldwide; in the UK there are an estimated 269,000 adherents and over 400 synagogues.

OFFICE OF THE CHIEF RABBI, 305 Ballards Lane,
London N12 8GB T 020-8343 6301 E info@chiefrabbi.org
W www.chiefrabbi.org
Chief Rabbi, Ephraim Mirvis
BETH DIN (COURT OF THE CHIEF RABBI),
305 Ballards Lane, London N12 8GB T 020-8343 6270
E info@bethdin.org.uk W www.theus.org.uk
Registrar, David Frei
Dayanim, Yonason Abraham; Menachem Gelley
(Senior Dayan); Ivan Binstock; Shmuel Simons
ASSEMBLY OF MASORTI SYNAGOGUES, Alexander
House, 3 Shakespeare Road, London N3 1XE T 020-8349 6650
E enquiries@masorti.org.uk W www.masorti.org.uk
Executive Director, Michael Gluckman
BOARD OF DEPUTIES OF BRITISH JEWS,
6 Bloomsbury Square, London WC1A 2LP T 020-7543 5400
E info@bod.org.uk W www.bod.org.uk
Chief Executive, vacant
FEDERATION OF SYNAGOGUES, 65 Watford Way,
London NW4 3AQ T 020-8202 2263
E info@federationofsynagogues.com
W www.federationofsynagogues.com
President, Alan Finlay
Chief Executive, Dr Eli Kienwald
LIBERAL JUDAISM, The Montagu Centre, 21 Maple Street,
London W1T 4BE T 020-7580 1663 W www.liberaljudaism.org
Chief Executive, Rabbi Danny Rich
THE MOVEMENT FOR REFORM JUDAISM,
The Sternberg Centre for Judaism, 80 East End Road, London
N3 2SY T 020-8349 5640 E admin@reformjudaism.org.uk
W www.reformjudaism.org.uk
Chief Executive, Ben Rich
SPANISH AND PORTUGUESE JEWS' CONGREGATION,
2 Ashworth Road, London W9 1JY T 020-7289 2573
E admin@spsyn.org.uk W www.sandp.org.uk
Administrator, Rachel Menachem
UNION OF ORTHODOX HEBREW CONGREGATIONS,
140 Stamford Hill, London N16 6QT T 020-8802 6226
Executive Coordinator, Chanoch Kesselman
Secretary, Chayim Schneck
UNITED SYNAGOGUE HEAD OFFICE, Adler House,
735 High Road, London N12 0US T 020-8343 8989
E info@theus.org.uk W www.theus.org.uk
Chief Executive, Jeremy Jacobs

PAGANISM

Paganism draws on the ideas of the Celtic people of pre-Roman Europe and is closely linked to Druidism. The first historical record of Druidry comes from classical Greek and Roman writers of the third century BC, who noted the existence of Druids among a people called the Keltoi who inhabited central and southern Europe. The word druid may derive from the Indo-European 'dreo-vid', meaning 'one who knows the truth'. In practice it was probably understood to mean something like 'wise-one' or 'philosopher-priest'.

Paganism is a pantheistic nature-worshipping religion which incorporates beliefs and ritual practices from ancient times. Pagans place much emphasis on the natural world and the ongoing cycle of life and death is central to their beliefs. Most Pagans believe that they are part of nature and not separate from, or superior to it, and seek to live in a way that minimises harm to the natural environment (the word Pagan derives from the Latin *Paganus,* meaning 'rural'). Paganism strongly emphasises the equality of the sexes, with women playing a prominent role in the modern Pagan movement and goddess worship featuring in most ceremonies. Paganism cannot be defined by any principal beliefs because it is shaped by each individual's experiences.

The Pagan Federation was founded in 1971 to provide information on Paganism, campaigns on issues which affect Paganism and provides support to members of the Pagan community. Within the UK the Pagan Federation is divided into 13 districts each with a district manager, regional and local coordinators. Local meetings are called 'moots' and take place in private homes, pubs or coffee bars. The Pagan Federation publishes a quarterly journal, *Pagan Dawn,* formerly *The Wiccan* (founded in 1968). The federation also publishes other material, arranges members-only and public events and maintains personal contact by letter with individual members and the wider Pagan community. Regional gatherings and conferences are held throughout the year.

THE PAGAN FEDERATION, BM Box 7097, London
  WC1N 3XX **E** secretary@paganfederation.co.uk
  W www.paganfederation.co.uk
  President, Mike Stygal

SIKHISM

The Sikh religion dates from the birth of Guru Nanak in the Punjab in 1469. 'Guru' means teacher but in Sikh tradition has come to represent the divine presence of God giving inner spiritual guidance. Nanak's role as the human vessel of the divine guru was passed on to nine successors, the last of whom (Guru Gobind Singh) died in 1708. The immortal guru is now held to reside in the sacred scripture, *Guru Granth Sahib,* and so to be present in all Sikh gatherings.

Guru Nanak taught that there is one God and that different religions are like different roads leading to the same destination. He condemned religious conflict, ritualism and caste prejudices. The fifth Guru, Guru Arjan Dev, largely compiled the Sikh Holy scripture, a collection of hymns *(gurbani)* known as the *Adi Granth.* It includes the writings of the first five gurus and the ninth guru, and selected writings of Hindu and Muslim saints whose views are in accord with the gurus' teachings. Guru Arjan Dev also built the Golden Temple at Amritsar, the centre of Sikhism. The tenth guru, Guru Gobind Singh, passed on the guruship to the sacred scripture, Guru Granth Sahib, and founded the *Khalsa,* an order intended to fight against tyranny and injustice. Male initiates to the order added 'Singh' to their given names and women added 'Kaur'. Guru Gobind Singh also made the wearing of five symbols obligatory: *kaccha* (a special undergarment), *kara* (a steel bangle), *kirpan* (a small sword), *kesh* (long unshorn hair, and consequently the wearing of a

turban) and *kangha* (a comb). These practices are still compulsory for those Sikhs who are initiated into the Khalsa (the *Amritdharis*). Those who do not seek initiation are known as *Sehajdharis.*

There are no professional priests in Sikhism; anyone with a reasonable proficiency in the Punjabi language can conduct a service. Worship can be offered individually or communally, and in a private house or a *gurdwara* (temple). Sikhs are forbidden to eat meat prepared by ritual slaughter; they are also asked to abstain from smoking, alcohol and other intoxicants. Such abstention is compulsory for the Amritdharis.

There are about 24 million Sikhs worldwide and, according to the 2011 census, there are 432,000 adherents in England, Wales and Scotland. Every gurdwara manages its own affairs; there is no central body in the UK. The Sikh Missionary Society provides an information service.

SIKH MISSIONARY SOCIETY UK, 10 Featherstone Road,
  Southall, Middx UB2 5AA **T** 020-8574 1902
  E info@sikhmissionarysociety.org
  W www.sikhmissionarysociety.org
  Hon. General Secretary, Teja Singh Mangat

ZOROASTRIANISM

Zoroastrians are followers of the Iranian prophet Spitaman Zarathushtra (or Zoroaster in its hellenised form) who lived *c.*1200–1500 BC. Zoroastrians were persecuted in Iran following the Arab invasion of Persia in the seventh century AD and a group (who are known as Parsis) migrated to India in the ninth century AD to avoid harassment and persecution. Zarathushtra's words are recorded in 17 hymns called the *Gathas,* which, together with other scriptures, form the *Avesta.*

Zoroastrianism teaches that there is one God, *Ahura Mazda* ('Wise Lord'), and that all creation stems ultimately from God; the Gathas teach that human beings have free will, are responsible for their own actions and can choose between good and evil. It is believed that choosing *Asha* (truth or righteousness), with the aid of *Vohu Manah* (good mind), leads to happiness for the individual and society, whereas choosing evil leads to unhappiness and conflict. The *Gathas* also encourage hard work, good deeds and charitable acts. Zoroastrians believe that after death the immortal soul is judged by God, and is then sent to paradise or hell, where it will stay until the end of time to be resurrected for the final judgment.

In Zoroastrian places of worship, an urn containing fire is the central feature; the fire symbolises purity, light and truth and is a visible symbol of the *Fravashi* or *Farohar* (spirit), the presence of Ahura Mazda in every human being. Zoroastrians respect nature and much importance is attached to cultivating land and protecting air, earth and water.

The Zoroastrian Trust Funds of Europe is the main body for Zoroastrians in the UK. Founded in 1861 as the Religious Funds of the Zoroastrians of Europe, it disseminates information on the Zoroastrian faith, provides a place of worship and maintains separate burial grounds for Zoroastrians. It also holds religious and social functions and provides assistance to Zoroastrians as considered necessary, including the provision of loans and grants to students of Zoroastrianism, and participates in inter-faith educational activities.

There are approximately 150,000 Zoroastrians worldwide, of which around 4,000 reside in England and Wales, mainly in London and the South East.

ZOROASTRIAN TRUST FUNDS OF EUROPE, Zoroastrian
  Centre, 440 Alexandra Avenue, Harrow, Middx HA2 9TL
  T 020-8866 0765 **E** secretary@ztfe.com **W** www.ztfe.com
  President, Malcolm Deboo

CHURCHES

There are two established (ie state) churches in the UK: the Church of England and the Church of Scotland. There are no established churches in Wales or Northern Ireland, though the Church in Wales, the Scottish Episcopal Church and the Church of Ireland are members of the Anglican Communion.

CHURCH OF ENGLAND

The Church of England is divided into the two provinces of Canterbury and York, each under an archbishop. The two provinces are subdivided into 42 dioceses, the newest of which came into existence on 20 April 2014. The new diocese is known as West Yorkshire and the Dales – officially entitled the Diocese of Leeds – and was formed by the amalgamation of the former dioceses of Bradford, Ripon and Leeds and Wakefield.

Legislative provision for the Church of England is made by the General Synod, established in 1970. It also discusses and expresses opinion on any other matter of religious or public interest. The General Synod has 467 members in total, divided between three houses: the House of Bishops, the House of Clergy and the House of Laity. It is presided over jointly by the Archbishops of Canterbury and York and normally meets twice a year. The synod has the power, delegated by parliament, to frame statute law (known as a 'measure') on any matter concerning the Church of England. A measure must be laid before both houses of parliament, who may accept or reject it but cannot amend it. Once accepted the measure is submitted for royal assent and then has the full force of law. In addition to the General Synod, there are synods at diocesan level. The entire General Synod is re-elected once every five years. The ninth General Synod was inaugurated by the Queen on 23 November 2010.

The Archbishops' Council was established in January 1999. Its creation was the result of changes to the Church of England's national structure proposed in 1995 and subsequently approved by the synod and parliament. The council's purpose, set out in the National Institutions Measure 1998, is 'to coordinate, promote and further the work and mission of the Church of England'. It reports to the General Synod. The Archbishops' Council comprises the Archbishops of Canterbury and York, *ex officio,* the prolocutors elected by the convocations of Canterbury and York, the chair and vice-chair of the House of Laity, two bishops, two clergy and two lay persons elected by their respective houses of the General Synod, the Church Estates Commissioner, and up to six persons appointed jointly by the two archbishops.

There are also a number of national boards, councils and other bodies working on matters such as social responsibility, mission, Christian unity and education, which report to the General Synod through the Archbishops' Council.

GENERAL SYNOD OF THE CHURCH OF ENGLAND/ ARCHBISHOPS' COUNCIL, Church House, Great Smith Street, London SW1P 3NZ T 020-7898 1000
Secretary-General, William Fittall

THE ORDINATION AND CONSECRATION OF WOMEN
The canon making it possible for women to be ordained to the priesthood was promulgated in the General Synod in February 1994 and the first 32 women priests were ordained on 12 March 1994.

On 14 July 2014 the General Synod approved the Bishops and Priests (Consecration and Ordination of Women) Measure which makes provision for the consecration of women as bishops and for the continuation of provision for the ordination of women.

PORVOO DECLARATION
The Porvoo Declaration was approved by the General Synod of the Church of England in July 1995. Churches that approve the declaration regard baptised members of each other's churches as members of their own, and allow free interchange of episcopally ordained ministers within the rules of each church.

MEMBERSHIP AND MINISTRY
In 2012, 138,020 people were baptised, 55,750 people were married in parish churches, the Church of England had an electoral roll membership of 1.2 million, and each week an average 1.05 million people attended services. As at December 2012 there were over 15,861 churches and places of worship; 358 senior clergy (including bishops, archdeacons and cathedral clergy); 7,195 full-time parochial stipendiary clergy; 245 full-time non-parochial stipendiary clergy; 3,148 self-supporting ministers; 1,520 chaplains and other ministers; 262 lay workers and Church Army evangelists; 6,623 licensed readers and 2,777 readers with permission to officiate and active emeriti; and approximately 5,700 active retired ordained clergy.

	Full-time Equivalent Diocesan Clergy 2012		Electoral Roll Membership
	Male	Female	2012
Bath and Wells	144	53	35,200
Birmingham	115	48	16,900
Blackburn	148	20	32,800
*Bradford	69	18	10,800
Bristol	86	19	15,800
Canterbury	105	27	20,200
Carlisle	98	26	20,600
Chelmsford	265	89	47,300
Chester	168	56	46,000
Chichester	253	22	53,200
Coventry	99	18	17,300
Derby	104	45	17,500
Durham	132	33	21,700
Ely	81	46	19,000
Europe	110	14	11,000
Exeter	168	38	30,000
Gloucester	93	32	24,100
Guildford	136	34	30,000
Hereford	57	33	16,800
Leicester	95	41	17,400
Lichfield	241	51	45,000
Lincoln	112	35	24,600
Liverpool	150	56	28,600
London	450	80	68,600
Manchester	158	66	33,300
Newcastle	88	28	15,800
Norwich	145	37	18,000
Oxford	293	98	55,600
Peterborough	100	37	19,400
Portsmouth	76	22	17,000
*Ripon and Leeds	81	40	15,600

	Full-time Equivalent Diocesan Clergy 2012		Electoral Roll Membership
Rochester	158	42	29,800
St Albans	168	71	38,600
St Edmundsbury and			
Ipswich	94	39	22,200
Salisbury	142	50	40,300
	Male	Female	2012
Sheffield	107	38	18,000
Sodor and Man	13	2	2,300
Southwark	264	82	48,500
Southwell and Nottingham	92	43	19,300
Truro	73	21	15,100
*Wakefield	100	35	18,300
Winchester	137	33	38,200
Worcester	86	27	17,800
York	163	36	33,600
†Total	6,017	1,781	1,187,200

* Now part of the new Diocese of Yorkshire and the Dales (also known as the Diocese of Leeds)

† Figures are rounded to the nearest 10 and may not add up as a result.

STIPENDS*

	2014–15
Archbishop of Canterbury	£76,280
Archbishop of York	£65,370
Bishop of London	£59,920
Other diocesan bishops	£41,410
Suffragan bishops	£33,780
Assistant bishops (full-time)	£32,700
Deans	£33,780
Archdeacons (recommended)	£33,010
Residentiary canons	£26,140†
Incumbents and clergy of similar status	£24,210†

* For those appointed on or after 1 April 2004; transitional arrangements are in place for those appointed prior to this date
† Adjusted regionally to reflect variations in the cost of living

CANTERBURY
105TH ARCHBISHOP AND PRIMATE OF ALL ENGLAND
Most Revd and Rt. Hon. Justin Welby, *cons.* 2011, *apptd* 2013; Lambeth Palace, London SE1 7JU
Signs Justin Cantuar:

BISHOPS SUFFRAGAN
Dover, Rt. Revd Trevor Willmott, *cons.* 2002, *apptd* 2009; Upway, St Martin's Hill, Canterbury, Kent CT1 1PR
Ebbsfleet, Rt. Revd Jonathan Goodall, *cons.* 2013, *apptd* 2013; Hill House, Treetops, The Mount, Caversham, Reading RG4 7RE
Richborough, Rt. Revd Norman Banks, *cons.* 2011, *apptd* 2011; Parkside House, Abbey Mill Lane, St Albans AL3 4HE

*Temporarily reponsible for episcopal oversight of the Channel Islands in place of the Bishop of Winchester.

DEAN
Very Revd Robert Willis, *apptd* 2001

Organist, D. Flood, FRCO, *apptd* 1988

ARCHDEACONS
Ashford, Ven. Philip Down, *apptd* 2011
Canterbury, Ven. Sheila Watson, *apptd* 2007
Maidstone, Ven. Stephen Taylor, *apptd* 2011

Vicar-General of Province and Diocese, Chancellor Sheila Cameron, QC
Commissary-General, Morag Ellis, QC
Joint Registrars of the Province, Canon John Rees; Stephen Slack
Diocesan Registrar and Legal Adviser, Owen Carew Jones
Diocesan Secretary, Julian Hills, Diocesan House, Lady Wootton's Green, Canterbury CT1 1NQ T 01227-459401

YORK
97TH ARCHBISHOP AND PRIMATE OF ENGLAND
Most Revd and Rt. Hon. Dr John Sentamu, *cons.* 1996, *trans.* 2005; Bishopthorpe, York YO23 2GE
Signs Sentamu Ebor:

BISHOPS SUFFRAGAN
Hull, vacant
Selby, Rt. Revd John Thomson, *cons.* 2014, *apptd* 2014; 6 Pinfold Garth, Malton YO17 7XQ
Whitby, Rt. Revd Paul Fergson, *cons.* 2014, *apptd* 2014; 21 Thornton Road, Stainton TS8 9DS

PRINCIPAL EPISCOPAL VISITOR
Beverley, Rt. Revd Glyn Webster, *cons.* 2013, *apptd* 2013; Holy Trinity Rectory, Micklegate, York YO1 6LE

DEAN
Very Revd Vivienne Faull, *apptd* 2012

Director of Music, Robert Sharpe, *apptd* 2008

ARCHDEACONS
Cleveland, vacant
East Riding, vacant
York, Ven. Sarah Bullock, *apptd* 2013

Chancellor of the Diocese, His Hon. Judge Collier, QC, *apptd* 2006
Registrar and Legal Secretary, Caroline Mockford
Diocesan Secretary, Peter Warry, Diocesan House, Aviator Court, Clifton Moor, York YO30 4WJ T 01904-699500

LONDON *(CANTERBURY)*
132ND BISHOP
Rt. Revd and Rt. Hon. Richard Chartres, KCVO, *cons.* 1992, *apptd* 1995; The Old Deanery, Dean's Court, London EC4V 5AA
Signs Richard Londin:

AREA BISHOPS
Edmonton, Rt. Revd Peter Wheatley, *cons.* 1999, *apptd* 1999; 27 Thurlow Road, London NW3 5PP
Kensington, Rt. Revd Paul Williams, *cons.* 2009, *apptd* 2008; Dial House, Riverside, Twickenham, Middlesex TW1 3DT
Stepney, Rt. Revd Adrian Newman, *cons.* 2011, *apptd* 2011; 63 Coburn Road, London E3 2DB
Willesden, Rt. Revd Peter Broadbent, *cons.* 2001, *apptd* 2001; 173 Willesden Lane, London NW6 7YN

BISHOP SUFFRAGAN
Fulham, Rt. Revd Jonathan Baker, *cons.* 2011, *apptd* 2013; The Old Deanery, Dean's Court, London EC4V 5AA

DEAN OF ST PAUL'S
Very Revd Dr David Ison, PHD, *apptd* 2012

Director of Music, Andrew Carwood, *apptd* 2007

ARCHDEACONS
Charing Cross, Ven. Dr William Jacob, *apptd* 1996
Hackney, Ven. Rachel Treweek, *apptd* 2011

Hampstead, Ven. Luke Miller, *apptd* 2010
London, Ven. David Meara, *apptd* 2009
Middlesex, Ven. Stephan Welch, *apptd* 2006
Northolt, Ven. Duncan Green, *apptd* 2013

Chancellor, Nigel Seed, QC, *apptd* 2002
Registrar and Legal Secretary, Paul Morris
Diocesan Secretary, Andrew Brookes, London Diocesan House,
 36 Causton Street, London SW1P 4AU **T** 020-7932 1100

DURHAM *(YORK)*
74TH BISHOP
Rt. Revd Paul Butler, *cons.* 2004, *trans.* 2013; Auckland Castle,
 Bishop Auckland DL14 7NR
Signs Paul Dunelm:

BISHOP SUFFRAGAN
Jarrow, Rt. Revd Mark Bryant, *cons.* 2007, *apptd*
 2007; Bishop's House, 25 Ivy Lane, Low Fell, Gateshead
 NE9 6QD

DEAN
Very Revd Michael Sadgrove, *apptd* 2003

Organist, James Lancelot, FRCO, *apptd* 1985

ARCHDEACONS
Auckland, Ven. Nicholas Barker, *apptd* 2007
Durham, Ven. Ian Jagger, *apptd* 2006
Sunderland, Ven. Stuart Bain, *apptd* 2002

Chancellor, His Hon. Judge Bursell, QC, *apptd* 1989
Registrar and Legal Secretary, Hilary Monckton-Milnes
Diocesan Secretary, Andrew Thurston, Diocesan
 Office, Auckland Castle, Bishop Auckland DL14 7QJ
 T 01388-660010

WINCHESTER *(CANTERBURY)*
97TH BISHOP
Rt. Revd Tim Dakin, cons. 2012, *apptd* 2011; Wolvesey,
 Winchester SO23 9ND
Signs Tim Winton:

BISHOPS SUFFRAGAN
Basingstoke, vacant
Southampton, Rt. Revd Jonathan Frost, *cons.* 2010,
 apptd 2010; Bishop's House, St Mary's Church Close,
 Wessex Lane, Southampton SO18 2ST

DEANS
Dean of Winchester, Very Revd James Atwell, *apptd* 2005
Dean of Jersey (A Peculiar), Very Revd Robert Key, *apptd*
 2005
Dean of Guernsey (A Peculiar), Very Revd Paul Mellor,
 apptd 2003
Director of Music, Andrew Lumsden, *apptd* 2002

ARCHDEACONS
Bournemouth, Ven. Dr Peter Rouch, *apptd* 2011
Winchester, Ven. Michael Harley, *apptd* 2009

Chancellor, His Hon. Judge Clark, QC, *apptd* 1993
Registrar and Legal Secretary, Andrew Johnson
Diocesan Secretary, Andrew Robinson, Old Alresford Place,
 Alresford, Hants SO24 9DH **T** 01962-737300

BATH AND WELLS *(CANTERBURY)*
79TH BISHOP
Rt. Revd Peter Hancock, *cons.* 2010, *apptd* 2014; The Bishop's
 Palace, Wells, Somerset BA5 2PD
Signs Peter Bath & Wells

BISHOP SUFFRAGAN
Taunton, Rt. Revd Peter Maurice, *cons.* 2006, *apptd* 2006;
 The Palace, Wells BA5 2PD

DEAN
Very Revd John Clarke, *apptd* 2004

Organist, Matthew Owens, *apptd* 2005

ARCHDEACONS
Bath, Ven. Andrew Piggott, *apptd* 2005
Taunton, Ven. John Reed, *apptd* 1999
Wells, Ven. Nicola Sullivan, *apptd* 2006

Chancellor, Timothy Briden, *apptd* 1993
Registrar and Legal Secretary, Tim Berry
Diocesan Secretary, Nick May, The Old Deanery,
 St Andrew's Street, Wells, Somerset BA5 2UG
 T 01749-670777

BIRMINGHAM *(CANTERBURY)*
8TH BISHOP
Rt. Revd David Urquhart, *cons.* 2000, *apptd* 2006;
 Bishop's Croft, Old Church Road, Harborne,
 Birmingham B17 0BG
Signs David Birmingham:

BISHOP SUFFRAGAN
Aston, Rt. Revd Andrew Watson, *cons.* 2008, *apptd* 2008;
 1 Colmore Row, Birmingham B3 2BJ

DEAN
Very Revd Catherine Ogle, *apptd* 2010

Director of Music, Marcus Huxley, FRCO, *apptd* 1986

ARCHDEACONS
Aston, vacant
Birmingham, Ven. Hayward Osborne, *apptd* 2001

Chancellor, Mark Powell, QC, *apptd* 2012
Registrar and Legal Secretary, Hugh Carslake
Diocesan Secretary, Andrew Halstead, 1 Colmore Row,
 Birmingham B3 2BJ **T** 0121-426 0400

BLACKBURN *(YORK)*
9TH BISHOP
Rt. Revd Julian Henderson, *cons.* 2013, *apptd* 2013;
 Bishop's House, Ribchester Road, Blackburn BB1 9EF
Signs Julian Blackburn

BISHOPS SUFFRAGAN
Burnley, vacant
Lancaster, Rt. Revd Geoffrey Pearson, *cons.* 2006, *apptd*
 2006; The Vicarage, Whinney Brow Lane, Shireshead, Forton,
 Preston PR3 0AE

DEAN
Very Revd Christopher Armstrong, *apptd* 2001

Organist and Director of Music, Samuel Holden

ARCHDEACON
Blackburn, Ven. John Hawley, *apptd* 2002
Lancaster, Ven. Michael Everitt, *apptd* 2011

Chancellor, His Hon. Judge Bullimore, *apptd* 1990
Registrar and Legal Secretary, Stephen Crossley
Diocesan Secretary, Graeme Pollard, Diocesan Office,
 Cathedral Close, Blackburn BB1 5AA **T** 01254-503070

BRISTOL *(CANTERBURY)*
55TH BISHOP
Rt. Revd Michael Hill, *cons.* 1998, *apptd* 2003; 58A High
  Street, Winterbourne, Bristol BS36 1JQ
  Signs Michael Bristol

BISHOP SUFFRAGAN
Swindon, Rt. Revd Dr Lee Rayfield, *cons.* 2005, *apptd* 2005;
  Mark House, Field Rise, Swindon, Wiltshire SN1 4HP

DEAN
Very Revd David Hoyle, *apptd* 2010

Organist and Director of Music, Mark Lee, *apptd* 1998

ARCHDEACONS
Bristol, vacant
Malmesbury, Ven. Christine Froude, *apptd* 2011

Chancellor, The Worshipful Revd Justin Gau
Registrar and Legal Secretary, Tim Berry
Diocesan Secretary, Oliver Home, First Floor, Hillside House,
  1500 Parkway North, Stoke Gifford, Bristol BS34 8YU

CARLISLE *(YORK)*
67TH BISHOP
Rt. Revd James Newcome, *cons.* 2002, *apptd* 2009;
  Bishop's House, Ambleside Road, Keswick CA12 4DD
  Signs James Carliol

BISHOP SUFFRAGAN
Penrith, Rt. Revd Robert Freeman, *cons.* 2011, *apptd* 2011;
  Holm Croft, Castle Road, Kendal, Cumbria LA9 7AU

DEAN
Very Revd Mark Boyling, *apptd* 2004

Organist, Jeremy Suter, FRCO, *apptd* 1991

ARCHDEACONS
Carlisle, Ven. Kevin Roberts, *apptd* 2009
West Cumberland, Ven. Dr Richard Pratt, *apptd* 2009
Westmorland and Furness, Ven. Penny Driver, *apptd* 2012

Chancellor, Geoffrey Tattersall, QC, *apptd* 2003
Registrar and Legal Secretary, Jane Lowdon
Diocesan Secretary, Derek Hurton, Church House, West Walls,
  Carlisle CA3 8UE T 01228-522573

CHELMSFORD *(CANTERBURY)*
10TH BISHOP
Rt. Revd Stephen Cottrell, *cons.* 2004, *apptd* 2010;
  Bishopscourt, Main Road, Margaretting, Ingatestone,
  Essex CM4 0HD
  Signs Stephen Chelmsford

BISHOPS SUFFRAGAN
Barking, Rt. Revd Peter Hill, *cons.* 2014, *apptd* 2014;
  Barking Lodge, Verulam Avenue, London E17 8ES
Bradwell, Rt. Revd John Wraw, *cons.* 2012, *apptd* 2012;
  Bishop's House, Orsett Road, Horndon-on-the-Hill,
  Stanford-le-Hope, Essex SS17 8NS
Colchester, Rt. Revd Roger Morris, *cons.* 2014, *apptd* 2014;
  1 Fitzwalter Road, Colchester, Essex CO3 3SS

DEAN
Very Revd Peter Nicholas Henshall, *apptd* 2013

Director of Music, James Davey, *apptd* 2012

ARCHDEACONS
Barking, Ven. Dr john Perumbalath, *apptd* 2013
Chelmsford, Ven. David Lowman, *apptd* 2013

Colchester, Ven. Annette Cooper, *apptd* 2004
Harlow, Ven. Martin Webster, *apptd* 2009
Southend, Ven. Mina Smallman, *apptd* 2013
Stansted, Ven. Robin King, *apptd* 2013
West Ham, Ven. Elwin Cockett, *apptd* 2007

Chancellor, George Pulman, QC, *apptd* 2001
Registrar and Legal Secretary, Aiden Hargreaves-Smith
Chief Executive, John Ball, 53 New Street, Chelmsford,
  Essex CM1 1AT T 01245-294400

CHESTER *(YORK)*
40TH BISHOP
Rt. Revd Peter Forster, PHD, *cons.* 1996, *apptd* 1996;
  Bishop's House, Abbey Square, Chester CH1 2JD
  Signs Peter Cestr:

BISHOPS SUFFRAGAN
Birkenhead, Rt. Revd Keith Sinclair, *cons.* 2007, *apptd* 2007;
  Bishop's Lodge, 67 Bidston Road, Prenton CH43 6TR
Stockport, vacant

DEAN
Very Revd Dr Gordon McPhate, *apptd* 2002

Organist and Director of Music, Philip Rushforth, FRCO,
  apptd 2008

ARCHDEACONS
Chester, Ven. Dr Michael Gilbertson, *apptd* 2010
Macclesfield, Ven. Ian Bishop, *apptd* 2011

Chancellor, His Hon. Judge Turner, QC, *apptd* 1998
Registrar and Legal Secretary, Helen McFall
Diocesan Secretary, George Colville, Church House, 5500
  Daresbury Park, Daresbury, Warrington WA4 4GE
  T 01928-718834

CHICHESTER *(CANTERBURY)*
103RD BISHOP
Rt. Revd Dr Martin Warner, *cons.* 2010, *apptd* 2012;
  The Palace, Chichester PO19 1PY
  Signs Martin Cicestr:

BISHOPS SUFFRAGAN
Horsham, Rt. Revd Mark Sowerby, *cons.* 2009,
  apptd 2009; 21 Guildford Road, Horsham,
  W. Sussex RH12 1LU
Lewes, Rt. Revd Richard Jackson, *cons.* 2014, *apptd* 2014;
  c/o Church House, 211 New Church Road, Hove BN3 4ED

DEAN
Very Revd Nicholas Frayling, *apptd* 2002

Organist, Sarah Baldock, *apptd* 2007

ARCHDEACONS
Chichester, Ven. Douglas McKittrick, *apptd* 2002
Horsham, Ven. Roger Combes, *apptd* 2003
Lewes and Hastings, Ven. Philip Jones, *apptd* 2005

Chancellor, Prof. Mark Hill
Registrar and Legal Secretary, Matthew Chinery
Diocesan Secretary, Angela Sibson, OBE, Diocesan Church
  House, 211 New Church Road, Hove, E. Sussex BN3 4ED
  T 01273-421021

COVENTRY *(CANTERBURY)*
9TH BISHOP
Rt. Revd Dr Christopher Cocksworth, *cons.* 2008,
  apptd 2008; The Bishop's House, 23 Davenport Road,
  Coventry CV5 6PW
  Signs Christopher Coventry

BISHOP SUFFRAGAN
Warwick, Rt. Revd John Stroyan, *cons.* 2005, *apptd* 2005;
Warwick House, 139 Kenilworth Road, Coventry CV4 7AP

DEAN
Very Revd John Witcombe, *apptd* 2013

Director of Music, Mr Kerry Beaumont, *apptd* 2006

ARCHDEACONS
Coventry, Ven. John Green, CB, *apptd* 2013
Warwick, Ven. Morris Rodham, *apptd* 2010

Chancellor, Stephen Eyre, *apptd* 2009
Registrar and Legal Secretary, Mary Allanson
Diocesan Secretary, Simon Lloyd, Cathedral & Diocesan Offices,
   1 Hilltop, Coventry CV1 5AB T 024-7652 1200

DERBY *(CANTERBURY)*
7TH BISHOP
Rt. Revd Dr Alastair Redfern, *cons.* 1997, *apptd* 2005;
   The Bishop's House, 6 King Street, Duffield, Belper,
   Derbyshire DE56 4EU
   Signs Alastair Derby

BISHOP SUFFRAGAN
Repton, Rt. Revd Humphrey Southern, *cons.* 2007, *apptd*
   2007; Repton House, Lea, Matlock, Derbyshire DE4 5JP

DEAN
Very Revd Dr John Davies, *apptd* 2010

Organist, Peter Gould, *apptd* 1982

ARCHDEACONS
Chesterfield, Ven. Christine Wilson, *apptd* 2010
Derby, Ven. Dr Christopher Cunliffe, *apptd* 2006

Chancellor, His Hon. Judge Bullimore, *apptd* 1981
Registrar and Legal Secretary, Mrs Nadine Waldron
Diocesan Secretary, Maureen Cole, Derby Church House,
   Full Street, Derby DE1 3DR T 01332-388650

ELY *(CANTERBURY)*
69TH BISHOP
Rt. Revd Stephen Conway, *cons.* 2006, *apptd* 2011; The
   Bishop's House, Ely CB7 4DW
   Signs Stephen Ely

BISHOP SUFFRAGAN
Huntingdon, Rt. Revd David Thomson, DPHIL, *cons.* 2008,
   apptd 2008; 14 Lynn Road, Ely, Cambs CB6 1DA

DEAN
Very Revd Mark Bonney, *apptd* 2012

Director of Music, Paul Trepte, FRCO, *apptd* 1991

ARCHDEACONS
Cambridge, Ven. Alex Hughes, *apptd* 2014
Huntingdon and Wisbech, Ven. Hugh McCurdy,
   apptd 2005

Chancellor, His Hon. Judge Leonard, QC
Registrar, Howard Dellar
Diocesan Secretary, Paul Evans, Bishop Woodford House,
   Barton Road, Ely, Cambs CB7 4DX T 01353-652702

EXETER *(CANTERBURY)*
71ST BISHOP
Rt. Revd Robert Atwell, *cons.* 2008, *apptd* 2014; The Palace,
   Exeter EX1 1HY
   Signs Robert Exon:

BISHOPS SUFFRAGAN
Crediton, Rt. Revd Nick McKinnel, *cons.* 2012, *apptd* 2012;
   32 The Avenue, Tiverton, Devon EX16 4HW
Plymouth, vacant

DEAN
Very Revd Jonathan Draper, *apptd* 2012

Director of Music, Andrew Millington, *apptd* 1999

ARCHDEACONS
Barnstaple, vacant
Exeter, Ven. Christopher Futcher, *apptd* 2012
Plymouth, Ven. Ian Chandler, *apptd* 2010
Totnes, vacant

Chancellor, Hon. Sir Andrew McFarlane
Registrar and Legal Secretary, M. Follett
Diocesan Secretary, Mark Beedell, The Old Deanery,
   The Cloisters, Exeter EX1 1HS T 01392-272686

GIBRALTAR IN EUROPE *(CANTERBURY)*
4TH BISHOP
Rt. Revd Robert Innes, PHD, *cons.* 2014, *apptd* 2014;
   47, rue Capitaine Crespel-boite 49, 1050 Ixlles, Belgium

BISHOP SUFFRAGAN
In Europe, Rt. Revd David Hamid, *cons.* 2002, *apptd* 2002;
   14 Tufton Street, London SW1P 3QZ

Dean, Cathedral Church of the Holy Trinity, Gibraltar,
   Very Revd Dr John Paddock

Chancellor, Pro-Cathedral of St Paul, Valletta, Malta,
   Canon Simon Godfrey
Chancellor, Pro-Cathedral of the Holy Trinity, Brussels,
   Belgium, Canon Dr Robert Innes

ARCHDEACONS
Eastern, Ven. Patrick Curran
North-West Europe, Canon Meurig Williams *(acting)*
France, Ven. Ian Naylor
Gibraltar, Canon Geoffrey Johnston *(acting)*
Italy, Ven. Jonathan Boardman
Germany and Northern Europe, Ven. Peter Potter *(acting)*
Switzerland, Ven. Peter Potter

Chancellor, Mark Hill
Registrar and Legal Secretary, Aiden Hargreaves-Smith
Diocesan Secretary, Adrian Mumford, 14 Tufton Street,
   London SW1P 3QZ T 020-7898 1155

GLOUCESTER *(CANTERBURY)*
41ST BISHOP
vacant

BISHOP SUFFRAGAN
Tewkesbury, Rt. Revd Martyn Snow, *cons.* 2013, *apptd* 2013;
   2 College Green, Gloucester GL1 2LR

DEAN
Very Revd Stephen Lake, *apptd* 2011

Director of Music, Adrian Partington, *apptd* 2007

ARCHDEACONS
Cheltenham, Ven. Robert Springett, *apptd* 2010
Gloucester, Ven. Jackie Searle, *apptd* 2012

Chancellor and Vicar-General, June Rodgers, *apptd* 1990
Registrar and Legal Secretary, Jos Moule
Diocesan Secretary, Ben Preece Smith, Church House, College
   Green, Gloucester GL1 2LY T 01452-410022

GUILDFORD *(CANTERBURY)*
10TH BISHOP
vacant

BISHOP SUFFRAGAN
Dorking (Bishop Commissary during the Vacancy-in-See),
Rt. Revd Ian Brackley, *cons.* 1996, *apptd* 1995; Dayspring,
13 Pilgrims Way, Guildford GU4 8AD

DEAN
Very Revd Dianna Gwilliams, *apptd* 2013

Organist, Katherine Dienes-Williams, *apptd* 2007

ARCHDEACONS
Dorking, Ven. Paul Bryer, *apptd* 2014
Surrey, Ven. Stuart Beake, *apptd* 2005

Chancellor, Andrew Jordan
Registrars and Legal Secretaries, Lee Coley; Howard Dellar
Diocesan Secretary, Stephen Marriott, Diocesan House, Quarry
Street, Guildford GU1 3XG **T** 01483-790300

HEREFORD *(CANTERBURY)*
105TH BISHOP
Rt. Revd Richard Frith, *cons.* 1998, *apptd* 2014; Bishop's
House, The Palace, Hereford HR4 9BN
Signs Richard Hereford

BISHOP SUFFRAGAN
Ludlow, Rt. Revd Alistair Magowan, *cons.* 2009, *apptd* 2009;
Bishop's House, Corvedale Road, Craven Arms, Shropshire
SY7 9BT

DEAN
Very Revd Michael Tavinor, *apptd* 2002

Organist and Director of Music, Geraint Bowen, FRCO,
apptd 2001

ARCHDEACONS
Hereford, Ven. Paddy Benson, *apptd* 2011
Ludlow, Rt. Revd Alistair Magowan, *apptd* 2009

Chancellor, His Hon. Judge Kaye, QC
Registrar and Legal Secretary, Howard Dellar
Diocesan Secretary, John Clark, The Palace, Hereford HR4 9BL
T 01432-373300

LEICESTER *(CANTERBURY)*
6TH BISHOP
Rt. Revd Timothy Stevens, *cons.* 1995, *apptd* 1999;
Bishop's Lodge, 10 Springfield Road, Leicester LE2 3BD
Signs Timothy Leicester

ASSISTANT BISHOP
Rt. Revd Christopher Boyle, *cons.* 2000, *apptd* 2009;
St Martins House, 7 Peacock Lane, Leicester LE1 5PZ

DEAN
Very Revd David Monteith, *apptd* 2013

Director of Music, Dr Christopher Johns

ARCHDEACONS
Leicester, Ven. Timothy Stratford, *apptd* 2012
Loughborough, Ven. David Newman, *apptd* 2009

Chancellor, Mark Blackett-Ord
Registrar and Legal Secretary, Revd Trevor Kirkman
Diocesan Secretary, Carol Gibbons, St Martin's House, 7 Peacock
Lane, Leicester LE1 5PZ **T** 0116-261 5200

LICHFIELD *(CANTERBURY)*
98TH BISHOP
Rt. Revd Jonathan Gledhill, *cons.* 1996, *apptd* 2003;
Bishop's House, 22 The Close, Lichfield WS13 7LG
Signs Jonathan Lichfield

BISHOPS SUFFRAGAN
Shrewsbury, Rt. Revd Mark Rylands, *cons.* 2009, *apptd* 2009;
Athlone House, 66 London Road, Shrewsbury SY2 6PG
Stafford, Rt. Revd Geoffrey Annas, *cons.* 2010, *apptd* 2010;
Ash Garth, Broughton Crescent, Barlaston, Stoke-on-Trent
ST12 9DD
Wolverhampton, Rt. Revd Clive Gregory, *cons.* 2007,
apptd 2007; 61 Richmond Road, Wolverhampton WV3 9JH

DEAN
Very Revd Adrian Dorber, *apptd* 2005

Directors of Music, Ben and Cathy Lamb, *apptd* 2010
Organist, Martyn Rawles, *apptd* 2010

ARCHDEACONS
Lichfield, Ven. Simon Baker, *apptd* 2013
Salop, Ven. Paul Thomas, *apptd* 2011
Stoke-on-Trent, Ven. Matthew Parker, *apptd* 2013
Walsall, Ven. Christopher Sims, *apptd* 2009

Chancellor, Stephen Eyre, *apptd* 2012
Registrar and Legal Secretary, N. Blackie
Diocesan Secretary, Julie Jones, St Mary's House, The Close,
Lichfield, Staffs WS13 7LD **T** 01543-306030

LINCOLN *(CANTERBURY)*
72ND BISHOP
Rt. Revd Christopher Lowson, *cons.* 2011, *apptd* 2011;
Bishop's Office, The Old Palace, Minster Yard, Lincoln LN2 1PU
Signs Christopher Lincoln

BISHOPS SUFFRAGAN
Grantham, vacant
Grimsby, Rt. Revd Dr David Court, *cons.* 2014, *apptd* 2014;
The Old Palace, Minster Yard, Lincoln LN2 1PU

DEAN
Very Revd Philip Buckler, *apptd* 2007

Director of Music, Aric Prentice, *apptd* 2003

ARCHDEACONS
Boston, Ven. Dr Justine Allain Chapman, *apptd* 2013
Lincoln, Ven. Timothy Barker, *apptd* 2009
Stow and Lindsey, vacant

Chancellor, His Hon. Judge Bishop, QC, *apptd* 2007
Registrar and Legal Secretary, Caroline Mockford,
apptd 2008
Diocesan Secretary (interim), Revd Canon Richard Bowett,
Edward King House, Minster Yard, Lincoln LN2 1PU
T 01522-504050

LIVERPOOL *(YORK)*
8TH BISHOP
Rt. Revd Paul Bayes, *cons.* 2010, *apptd* 2014; Bishop's Lodge,
Woolton Park, Liverpool L25 6DT
Signs Paul Liverpool

BISHOP SUFFRAGAN
Warrington, Rt. Revd Richard Blackburn, *cons.* 2009,
apptd 2009; 34 Central Avenue, Eccleston Park,
Liverpool L34 2QP

DEAN
Very Revd Pete Wilcox, *apptd* 2012

Director of Music, David Poulter, *apptd* 2008

ARCHDEACONS
Liverpool, Ven. Richard Panter, *apptd* 2002
Warrington, Ven. Peter Bradley, *apptd* 2001

Chancellor, Hon. Sir Mark Hedley
Registrar and Legal Secretary, Howard Dellar
Diocesan Secretary, Mike Eastwood, St James House,
   20 St James Street, Liverpool L1 7BY **T** 0151-709 9722

MANCHESTER *(YORK)*
12TH BISHOP
Rt. Revd David Walker, *cons.* 2000 *apptd* 2013;
   Bishopscourt, Bury New Road, Manchester M7 4LE
   Signs David Manchester

BISHOPS SUFFRAGAN
Bolton, Rt. Revd Christopher Edmondson, *cons.* 2008,
   apptd 2008; Bishop's Lodge, Walkden Road, Worsley,
   Manchester M28 2WH
Middleton, Rt. Revd Mark Davies, *cons.* 2008, *apptd* 2008;
   The Hollies, Manchester Road, Rochdale OL11 3QY

DEAN
Very Revd Rogers Govender, *apptd* 2006

Organist, Christopher Stokes, *apptd* 1992

ARCHDEACONS
Bolton, Ven. David Bailey, *apptd* 2008
Manchester, Ven. Mark Ashcroft, *apptd* 2009
Rochdale, Ven. Cherry Vann, *apptd* 2008
Salford, Ven. David Sharples, *apptd* 2009

Chancellor, Geoffrey Tattersall, QC
Registrar and Legal Secretary, Jane Monks
Diocesan Secretary, Martin Miller, Diocesan Church House,
   90 Deansgate, Manchester M3 2GH **T** 0161-828 1400

NEWCASTLE *(YORK)*
12TH BISHOP
vacant

ASSISTANT BISHOP
Rt. Revd Frank White, *cons.* 2002, *apptd* 2010

DEAN
Very Revd Christopher C. Dalliston, *apptd* 2003

Director of Music, Michael Stoddart, *apptd* 2009

ARCHDEACONS
Lindisfarne, Ven. Dr Peter Robinson, *apptd* 2008
Northumberland, Ven. Geoffrey Miller, *apptd* 2004

Chancellor, Euan Duff, *apptd* 2013
Registrar and Legal Secretary, Jane Lowdon
Diocesan Secretary, Shane Waddle, Church House, St John's
   Terrace, North Shields NE29 6HS **T** 0191-270 4100

NORWICH *(CANTERBURY)*
71ST BISHOP
Rt. Revd Graham R. James, *cons.* 1993, *apptd* 2000;
   Bishop's House, Norwich NR3 1SB
   Signs Graham Norvic:

BISHOPS SUFFRAGAN
Lynn, Rt. Revd Jonathan Meyrick, *cons.* 2011, *apptd* 2011;
   The Old Vicarage, Castle Acre, King's Lynn PE32 2AA

Thetford, Rt. Revd Alan Winton, PHD, *cons.* 2009, *apptd*
   2009; The Red House, 53 Norwich Road, Stoke Holy Cross,
   Norwich NR14 8AB

DEAN
Very Revd Jane Hedges, *apptd* 2014

Master of Music, Ashley Grote, *apptd* 2012

ARCHDEACONS
Lynn, Ven. John Ashe, *apptd* 2009
Norfolk, Ven. Steven Betts, *apptd* 2012
Norwich, Ven. Jan McFarlane, *apptd* 2008

Chancellor, Ruth Arlow, *apptd* 2012
Registrar and Legal Secretary, Stuart Jones
Diocesan Secretary, Richard Butler, Diocesan House,
   109 Dereham Road, Easton, Norwich, Norfolk NR9 5ES
   T 01603-880853

OXFORD *(CANTERBURY)*
43RD BISHOP
vacant

AREA BISHOPS
Buckingham, Rt. Revd Dr Alan Wilson, *cons.* 2003,
   apptd 2003; Sheridan, Grimms Hill, Great Missenden,
   Bucks HP16 9BD
Dorchester, Rt. Revd Colin Fletcher, *cons.* 2000, *apptd* 2000;
   Arran House, Sandy Lane, Yarnton, Oxon OX5 1PB
Reading, Rt. Revd Andrew Proud, *cons.* 2011, *apptd* 2011;
   Bishop's House, Tidmarsh Lane, Tidmarsh, Reading RG8 8HA

DEAN OF CHRIST CHURCH
Very Revd Prof. Martyn Percy, *apptd* 2014

Organist, Dr Stephen Darlington, FRCO, *apptd* 1985

ARCHDEACONS
Berkshire, Ven. Olivia Graham, *apptd* 2013
Buckingham, Ven. Karen Gorham, *apptd* 2007
Oxford, Ven. Martin Gorick, *apptd* 2013

Chancellor, Revd Alex McGregor, *apptd* 2013
Registrar and Legal Secretary, Revd Canon John Rees
Diocesan Secretary, Rosemary Pearce, Diocesan Church House,
   North Hinksey, Oxford OX2 0NB **T** 01865-208202

PETERBOROUGH *(CANTERBURY)*
38TH BISHOP
Rt. Revd Donald Allister, *cons.* 2010, *apptd* 2009;
   Bishop's Lodging, The Palace, Peterborough PE1 1YA
   Signs Donald Petriburg:

BISHOP SUFFRAGAN
Brixworth, Rt. Revd John Holbrook, *cons.* 2011, *apptd* 2011;
   Orchard Acre, 11 North Street, Mears Ashby, Northants
   NN6 0DW

DEAN
Very Revd Charles Taylor, *apptd* 2007

Director of Music, Stephen Grahl, *apptd* 2014

ARCHDEACONS
Northampton, Ven. Richard Ormston, *apptd* 2014
Oakham, Ven. Gordon Steele, *apptd* 2012

Chancellor, David Pittaway, QC, *apptd* 2005
Registrar and Legal Secretary, Revd Raymond Hemingray
Diocesan Secretary, Andrew Roberts, Diocesan Office,
   The Palace, Peterborough PE1 1YB **T** 01733-887000

PORTSMOUTH *(CANTERBURY)*
9TH BISHOP
Rt. Revd Christopher Foster, *cons.* 2010, *apptd* 2010;
Bishopsgrove, 26 Osborn Road, Fareham, Hants PO16 7DQ
Signs Christopher Portsmouth

DEAN
Very Revd David Brindley, *apptd* 2002

Organist, David Price, *apptd* 1996

ARCHDEACONS
Isle of Wight, Ven. Peter Sutton, *apptd* 2012
Portsdown, Ven. Joanne Grenfell, *apptd* 2013
The Meon, Ven. Gavin Collins, *apptd* 2011

Chancellor, Philip Waller, CBE
Registrar and Legal Secretary, Hilary Tyler
Diocesan Secretary, Wendy Kennedy, Diocesan Offices, 1st Floor,
Peninsular House, Wharf Road, Portsmouth PO2 8HB
T 023-9289 9664

ROCHESTER *(CANTERBURY)*
107TH BISHOP
Rt. Revd James Langstaff, *cons.* 2004, *apptd* 2010;
Bishopscourt, 24 St Margaret's Street, Rochester ME1 1TS
Signs, James Roffen:

BISHOP SUFFRAGAN
Tonbridge, Rt. Revd Dr Brian Castle, *cons.* 2002,
apptd 2002; Bishop's Lodge, 48 St Botolph's Road,
Sevenoaks TN13 3AG

DEAN
Very Revd Dr Mark Beach, *apptd* 2012

Director of Music, Scott Farrell, *apptd* 2008

ARCHDEACONS
Bromley & Bexley, Ven. Dr Paul Wright, *apptd* 2003
Rochester, Ven. Simon Burton-Jones, *apptd* 2010
Tonbridge, Ven. Clive Mansell, *apptd* 2002

Chancellor, John Gallagher, *apptd* 2006
Registrar and Legal Secretary, Owen Carew-Jones
Diocesan Secretary, Geoff Marsh, St Nicholas Church,
Boley Hill, Rochester ME1 1SL T 01634-560000

ST ALBANS *(CANTERBURY)*
10TH BISHOP
Rt. Revd Dr Alan Smith, *cons.* 2001, *apptd* 2009, *trans.*
2009; Abbey Gate House, St Albans AL3 4HD
Signs Alan St Albans

BISHOPS SUFFRAGAN
Bedford, Rt. Revd Richard Atkinson, OBE, *cons.* 2012,
apptd 2012; Bishop's Lodge, Bedford Road, Cardington,
Bedford MK44 3SS
Hertford, vacant

DEAN
Very Revd Dr Jeffrey John, *apptd* 2004

Organist, Andrew Lucas, *apptd* 1998

ARCHDEACONS
Bedford, Ven. Paul Hughes, *apptd* 2004
Hertford, Ven. Dr Trevor Jones, *apptd* 1997
St Albans, Ven. Jonathan Smith, *apptd* 2008

Chancellor, Roger Kaye, *apptd* 2002
Registrar and Legal Secretary, Lee Coley

Diocesan Secretary, Susan Pope, Holywell Lodge, 41 Holywell Hill,
St Albans AL1 1HE T 01727-854532

ST EDMUNDSBURY AND IPSWICH
(CANTERBURY)
11TH BISHOP
vacant

BISHOP SUFFRAGAN
Dunwich, vacant

DEAN
Very Revd Frances Ward, *apptd* 2010

Director of Music, James Thomas, *apptd* 1997

ARCHDEACONS
Sudbury, Ven. Dr David Jenkins, *apptd* 2010
Suffolk, Ven. Ian Morgan, *apptd* 2012

Chancellor, David Etherington, QC
Registrar and Legal Secretary, James Hall
Diocesan Secretary, Nicholas Edgell, Diocesan Office,
St Nicholas Centre, 4 Cutler Street, Ipswich IP1 1UQ
T 01473-298500

SALISBURY *(CANTERBURY)*
78TH BISHOP
Rt. Revd Nicholas Holtam, *cons.* 2011, *apptd* 2011;
South Canonry, 71 The Close, Salisbury SP1 2ER
Signs Nicholas Sarum

BISHOPS SUFFRAGAN
Ramsbury, Rt. Revd Edward Condry, DPHIL, *cons.* 2012,
apptd 2012; Bishop's Office, Southbroom House, London
Road, Devizes SN10 1LT
Sherborne, Rt. Revd Graham Kings, PHD, *cons.* 2009,
apptd 2009; Sherborne Area Office, St Nicholas' Church
Centre, Wareham Road, Corfe Mullen BH21 3LE

DEAN
Very Revd June Osborne, *apptd* 2004

Organist, David Halls, *apptd* 2005

ARCHDEACONS
Dorset, Ven. Stephen Waine, *apptd* 2010
Sarum, Ven. Alan Jeans, *apptd* 2003
Sherborne, Ven. Paul Taylor, *apptd* 2004
Wilts, Ven. Ruth Worsley, *apptd* 2012

Chancellor, His Hon. Judge Wiggs, *apptd* 1997
Registrar and Legal Secretary, Andrew Johnson
Diocesan Secretary, Lucinda Herklots, Church House,
Crane Street, Salisbury SP1 2QB T 01722-411922

SHEFFIELD *(YORK)*
7TH BISHOP
Rt. Revd Steven Croft, PHD, *cons.* 2009, *apptd* 2008;
Bishopscroft, Snaithing Lane, Sheffield S10 3LG
Signs Steven Sheffield

BISHOP SUFFRAGAN
Doncaster, Rt. Revd Peter Burrows, *cons.* 2012, *apptd* 2011;
Doncaster House, Church Lane, Fishlake, Doncaster DN7 5JW

DEAN
Very Revd Peter Bradley, *apptd* 2003

Master of Music, Neil Taylor, *apptd* 1997

ARCHDEACONS
Doncaster, Ven. Steve Wilcockson, *apptd* 2012
Sheffield and Rotherham, Ven. Malcolm Chamberlain,
   apptd 2013

Chancellor, Prof. David McClean, *apptd* 1992
Registrar and Legal Secretary, Andrew Vidler
Diocesan Secretary, Malcolm Fair, Church House,
   95–99 Effingham Street, Rotherham S65 1BL T 01709-309100

SODOR AND MAN *(YORK)*
81ST BISHOP
Rt. Revd Robert Paterson, *cons.* 2008, *apptd* 2008;
   Thie yn Aspick, 4 The Falls, Douglas, Isle of Man IM4 4PZ
   Signs Robert Sodor as Mannin

ARCHDEACON OF MAN
Ven. Andrew Brown, *apptd* 2011
Vicar-General and Chancellor, Clare Faulds

Registrar, Kenneth Gumbley
Diocesan Secretary, Laura Stuart, Keeil Cottage, Clarum Road,
   Ballaragh, Lonan, Isle of Man IM4 7PL T 01624-861618

SOUTHWARK *(CANTERBURY)*
10TH BISHOP
Rt. Revd Christopher Chessun, *cons.* 2005, *apptd* 2011;
   Trinity House, 4 Chapel Court, Borough High Street, London
   SE1 1HW
   Signs Christopher Southwark

AREA BISHOPS
Croydon, Rt. Revd Jonathan Clark, *cons.* 2012, *apptd* 2012;
   St Matthew's House, 100 George Street, London CR0 1PE
Kingston upon Thames, Rt. Revd Dr Richard Cheetham,
   cons. 2002, *apptd* 2002 ; 620 Kingston Road, Raynes Park,
   London SW20 8DN
Woolwich, Rt. Revd Dr Michael Ipgrave, OBE, *cons.* 2012,
   apptd 2012; Trinity House, 4 Chapel Court, Borough High
   Street, London SE1 1HW

DEAN
Very Revd Andrew Nunn, *apptd* 2011

Organist, Peter Wright, FRCO, *apptd* 1989

ARCHDEACONS
Croydon, Ven. Christopher Skilton, *apptd* 2013
Lambeth, Ven. Simon Gates, *apptd* 2013
Lewisham & Greenwich, Ven. Alastair Cutting, *apptd* 2013
Reigate, Ven. Daniel Kajumba, *apptd* 2001
Southwark, Ven. Dr Jane Steen, *apptd* 2013
Wandsworth, Ven. Stephen Roberts, *apptd* 2005

Chancellor, Philip Petchey
Registrar and Legal Secretary, Paul Morris
Diocesan Secretary, Simon Parton, Trinity House, 4 Chapel Court,
   Borough High Street, London SE1 1HW T 020-7939 9400

SOUTHWELL AND NOTTINGHAM *(YORK)*
12TH BISHOP
vacant

BISHOP SUFFRAGAN
Sherwood, Rt. Revd Anthony Porter, *cons.* 2006, *apptd* 2006;
   Jubilee House, Westgate, Southwell NG25 0JH

DEAN
vacant

Organist, Paul Hale, *apptd* 1989

ARCHDEACONS
Newark, Ven. David Picken, *apptd* 2012
Nottingham, vacant

Chancellor, Linda Box, *apptd* 2005
Registrar and Legal Secretary, Amanda Redgate
Chief Executive, Nigel Spraggins, Jubilee House, Westgate,
   Southwell, Notts NG25 0JH T 01636-814331

TRURO *(CANTERBURY)*
15TH BISHOP
Rt. Revd Tim Thornton, *cons.* 2001, *apptd* 2008; Lis Escop,
   Truro TR3 6QQ
   Signs Tim Truro

BISHOP SUFFRAGAN
St Germans, Rt. Revd Christopher Goldsmith, DPHIL,
   cons. 2013, *apptd* 2013; Vounder, Tresillian, Truro TR2 4BW

DEAN
Very Revd Roger Bush, *apptd* 2012

Organist and Director of Music, Chris Gray, *apptd* 2008

ARCHDEACONS
Bodmin, Ven. Audrey Elkington, *apptd* 2011
Cornwall, Ven. Bill Stuart-White, *apptd* 2012

Chancellor, Timothy Briden, *apptd* 1998
Registrar and Legal Secretary, Martin Follett
Diocesan Secretary, Esther Pollard, Diocesan House, Kenwyn,
   Truro TR1 1JQ T 01872-274351

WEST YORKSHIRE AND THE DALES*
(YORK)
1ST BISHOP OF LEEDS*
Rt. Revd Nicholas Baines, *cons.* 2003, *apptd* 2014;
   Hollin House, Weetwood Avenue, Leeds LS16 5NG
   Signs Nicholas Leeds

AREA BISHOPS
Bradford, vacant
Huddersfield, vacant
Ripon, Rt. Revd James Bell, *cons.* 2004, *apptd* 2014;
   Thistledown, Main Street, Exelby, Bedale DL8 2HD
Wakefield, Rt. Revd Anthony Robinson, *cons.* 2002,
   apptd 2014; Pontefract House 181A Manygates Lane,
   Sandal, Wakefield WF2 7DR

DEANS
Bradford, Very Revd Jerry Lepine, *apptd* 2013
Ripon, Very Revd John Dobson, *apptd* 2014
Wakefield, Very Revd Jonathan Greener, *apptd* 2007

Directors of Music, Andrew Bryden (Ripon), *apptd* 2003;
   Thomas Moore (Wakefield), *apptd* 2010; Alexander
   Woodrow (Bradford), *apptd* 2012

ARCHDEACONS
Bradford, Ven. David Lee, *apptd* 2004
Halifax, Ven. Dr Anne Dawtry, *apptd* 2011
Leeds, Ven. Paul Hooper, *apptd* 2012
Richmond and Craven, Ven. Paul Slater, *apptd* 2005
Pontefract, Ven. Peter Townley, *apptd* 2008

Chancellor, vacant
Registrars and Legal Secretaries, vacant
Diocesan Secretary, John Tucket, Leeds Office, St Mary's Street,
   Leeds LS9 7DP T 0113-2000567

* The official name of the diocese is The Diocese of Leeds

WORCESTER *(CANTERBURY)*
113TH BISHOP
Rt. Revd Dr John Inge, *cons.* 2003, *apptd* 2007; The Bishop's Office, The Old Palace, Deansway, Worcester WR1 2JE
Signs John Wigorn

SUFFRAGAN BISHOP
Dudley, Rt. Revd Graham Usher, *cons.* 2014, *apptd* 2014; Bishop's Hosue, 60 Bishop's Walk, Cradley Heath, West Midlands B64 7RH

DEAN
Very Revd Peter Atkinson, *apptd* 2006

Organist, Dr Peter Nardone, *apptd* 2012

ARCHDEACONS
Dudley, Ven. Nikki Groarke, *apptd* 2014
Worcester, Ven. Robert Jones, *apptd* 2014

Chancellor, Charles Mynors, *apptd* 1999
Registrar and Legal Secretary, Michael Huskinson
Diocesan Secretary, Robert Higham, The Old Palace, Deansway, Worcester WR1 2JE **T** 01905-20537

ROYAL PECULIARS
WESTMINSTER
The Collegiate Church of St Peter
Dean, Very Revd Dr John Hall
Canon Steward, Ven. Jane Sinclair
Chapter Clerk, Receiver-General and Registrar, Sir Stephen Lamport, KCVO, Chapter Office, 20 Dean's Yard, London SW1P 3PA
Organist, James O'Donnell, *apptd* 1999
Legal Secretary, Christopher Vyse, *apptd* 2000

WINDSOR
The Queen's Free Chapel of St George within Her Castle of Windsor
Dean, Rt. Revd David Conner, KCVO, *apptd* 1998
Chapter Clerk, Charlotte Manley, LVO, OBE, *apptd* 2003; Chapter Office, The Cloisters, Windsor Castle, Windsor, Berks SL4 1NJ
Director of Music, James Vivian, *apptd* 2013

OTHER ANGLICAN CHURCHES

THE CHURCH IN WALES
The Anglican Church was the established church in Wales from the 16th century until 1920, when the estrangement of the majority of Welsh people from Anglicanism resulted in disestablishment. Since then the Church in Wales has been an autonomous province consisting of six sees. The bishops are elected by an electoral college comprising elected lay and clerical members, who also elect one of the diocesan bishops as Archbishop of Wales.

The legislative body of the Church in Wales is the Governing Body, which has 144 members divided between the three orders of bishops, clergy and laity. Its president is the Archbishop of Wales and it meets twice annually. Its decisions are binding upon all members of the church. The church's property and finances are the responsibility of the Representative Body. There are 56,396 members of the Church in Wales, with 487 stipendiary clergy and 899 parishes.

THE REPRESENTATIVE BODY OF THE CHURCH IN WALES, 39 Cathedral Road, Cardiff CF11 9XF
T 029-2034 8200 *Secretary,* John Shirley
12TH ARCHBISHOP OF WALES, Most Revd Dr Barry Morgan (Bishop of Llandaff), *elected* 2003
Signs Barry Cambrensis

BISHOPS
Bangor (81st), Rt. Revd Andrew John, *b.* 1964, *cons.* 2008, *elected* 2008; Ty'r Esgob, Bangor, Gwynedd LL57 2SS
Signs Andrew Bangor. *Stipendiary clergy,* 49
Llandaff (102nd), Most Revd Dr Barry Morgan (*also* Archbishop of Wales), *b.* 1947, *cons.* 1993, *trans.* 1999; Llys Esgob, The Cathedral Green, Llandaff, Cardiff CF5 2YE
Signs Barry Cambrensis. *Stipendiary clergy,* 109
Monmouth (10th), Rt. Revd Richard Pain, *b.* 1956, *cons.* 2013, *elected* 2013; Bishopstow, Stow Hill, Newport NP20 4EA *Signs* Richard Monmouth. *Stipendiary clergy,* 87
St Asaph (76th), Rt. Revd Gregory Cameron, *b.* 1959, *cons.* 2009, *elected* 2009; Esgobty, Upper Denbigh Road, St Asaph, Denbighshire LL17 0TW *Signs* Gregory Llanelwy. *Stipendiary clergy,* 100
St David's (128th), Rt. Revd (John) Wyn Evans, *b.* 1946, *cons.* 2008, *elected* 2008; Llys Esgob, Abergwili, Carmarthen SA31 2JG *Signs* Wyn St Davids. *Stipendiary clergy,* 98
Swansea and Brecon (9th), Rt. Revd John Davies, *b.* 1953, *cons.* 2008, *elected* 2008; Ely Tower, Castle Square, Brecon, Powys LD3 9DJ *Signs* John Swansea & Brecon. *Stipendiary clergy,* 71

The stipend for a diocesan bishop of the Church in Wales is £41,549 a year for 2014–15.

SCOTTISH EPISCOPAL CHURCH
The Scottish Episcopal Church was founded after the Act of Settlement (1690) established the presbyterian nature of the Church of Scotland. The Scottish Episcopal Church is a member of the worldwide Anglican Communion. The governing authority is the General Synod, an elected body of 140 members (70 from the clergy and 70 from the laity) which meets once a year. The bishop who convenes and presides at meetings of the General Synod is called the 'primus' and is elected by his fellow bishops.

There are 34,119 members of the Scottish Episcopal Church, seven bishops, 507 serving clergy and 306 churches and places of worship.

THE GENERAL SYNOD OF THE SCOTTISH EPISCOPAL CHURCH, 21 Grosvenor Crescent, Edinburgh EH12 5EE **T** 0131-225 6357 **W** www.scotland.anglican.org
Secretary-General, John Stuart
PRIMUS OF THE SCOTTISH EPISCOPAL CHURCH, Most Revd David Chillingworth (Bishop of St Andrews, Dunkeld and Dunblane), *elected* 2009

BISHOPS
Aberdeen and Orkney, Rt. Revd Dr Bob Gillies, *b.* 1951, *cons.* 2007, *elected* 2007. *Clergy,* 55
Argyll and the Isles, Rt. Revd Kevin Pearson, *b.* 1954, *cons.* 2011, *elected* 2010. *Clergy,* 28
Brechin, Rt. Revd Dr Nigel Peyton, *b.* 1951, *cons.* 2011, *elected* 2011. *Clergy,* 34
Edinburgh, Rt. Revd Dr John Armes, *b.* 1955, *cons.* 2012, *elected* 2012. *Clergy,* 163
Glasgow and Galloway, Rt. Revd Dr Gregor Duncan, *b.* 1950, *cons.* 2010, *elected* 2010. *Clergy,* 116
Moray, Ross and Caithness, Rt. Revd Mark Strange, *b.* 1961, *cons.* 2007, *elected* 2007. *Clergy,* 61
St Andrews, Dunkeld and Dunblane, Most Revd David Chillingworth, *b.* 1951, *cons.* 2005, *elected* 2005. *Clergy,* 78

The minimum stipend of a diocesan bishop of the Scottish Episcopal Church for 2014 is £36,315 (ie 1.5 times the standard clergy stipend of £24,210).

CHURCH OF IRELAND

The Anglican Church was the established church in Ireland from the 16th century but never secured the allegiance of the majority and was disestablished in 1871. The Church of Ireland is divided into the provinces of Armagh and Dublin, each under an archbishop. The provinces are subdivided into 12 dioceses.

The legislative body is the General Synod, which has 660 members in total, divided between the House of Bishops (12 members) and the House of Representatives (216 clergy and 432 laity). The Archbishop of Armagh is elected by the House of Bishops; other episcopal elections are made by an electoral college.

There are 383,186 members of the Church of Ireland, 248,821 in Northern Ireland and 134,365 in the Republic of Ireland. There are two archbishops, ten bishops and 436 stipendiary clergy.

CENTRAL OFFICE, Church of Ireland House, Church Avenue, Rathmines, Dublin 6 T (+353) (1) 497 8422

Chief Officer and Secretary of the Representative Church Body, Adrian Clements

PROVINCE OF ARMAGH

Archbishop of Armagh, Primate of all Ireland and Metropolitan, Most Revd Richard Clarke, PHD, *b.* 1949, *cons.* 1996, *trans.* 2012. *Clergy,* 38

BISHOPS

Clogher, Rt. Revd John McDowell, *b.* 1956, *cons.* 2011, *apptd* 2011. *Clergy,* 29

Connor, Rt. Revd Alan Abernethy, *b.* 1957, *cons.* 2007, *apptd* 2007. *Clergy,* 72

Derry and Raphoe, Rt. Revd Kenneth Good, *b.* 1952, *cons.* 2002, *apptd* 2002. *Clergy,* 43

Down and Dromore, Rt. Revd Harold Miller, *b.* 1950, *cons.* 1997, *apptd* 1997. *Clergy,* 77

Kilmore, Elphin and Ardagh, Rt. Revd Ferran Glenfield, *b.* 1954, *cons.* 2013, *apptd* 2013. *Clergy,* 18

Tuam, Killala and Achonry, Rt. Revd Patrick Rooke, *b.* 1955, *cons.* 2011, *apptd* 2011. *Clergy,* 8

PROVINCE OF DUBLIN

Archbishop of Dublin, Bishop of Glendalough, Primate of Ireland and Metropolitan, Most Revd Michael Jackson, PHD, DPHIL, *b.* 1956, *cons.* 2002, *trans.* 2011. *Clergy,* 61

BISHOPS

Cashel and Ossory, Rt. Revd Michael Burrows, *b.* 1961, *cons.* 2006, *apptd* 2006. *Clergy,* 33

Cork, Cloyne and Ross, Rt. Revd Paul Colton, PHD, *b.* 1960, *cons.* 1999, *apptd* 1999. *Clergy,* 24

Limerick and Killaloe, vacant. *Clergy,* 14

Meath and Kildare, Most Revd Patricia Storey, *b.* 1960, *cons.* 2013, *apptd* 2013. *Clergy,* 15

OVERSEAS

PRIMATES

Primate and Presiding Bishop of Aotearoa, New Zealand and Polynesia, Most Revd William Turei

Primate of Australia, Most Revd Phillip Aspinall

Primate of Brazil, Most Revd Francisco De Assis Da Silva

Archbishop of the Province of Burundi, Most Revd Bernard Ntahoturi

Archbishop and Primate of Canada, Most Revd Frederick Hiltz

Archbishop of the Province of Central Africa, Most Revd Albert Chama

Primate of the Central Region of America, Most Revd Armando Soria

Archbishop of the Province of Congo, Most Revd Henry Isingoma

Primate of the Province of Hong Kong Sheng Kung Hui, Most Revd Dr Paul Kwong

Archbishop of the Province of the Indian Ocean, Most Revd Ian Ernest

Primate of Japan (Nippon Sei Ko Kai), Most Revd Nathaniel Uematsu

President-Bishop of Jerusalem and the Middle East, Most Revd Dr Mouneer Anis

Archbishop of the Province of Kenya, Most Revd Eliud Wabukala

Archbishop of the Province of Korea, Most Revd Paul Kim

Archbishop of the Province of Melanesia, Most Revd David Vunagi

Archbishop of Mexico, Most Revd Francisco Moreno

Archbishop of the Province of Myanmar (Burma), Most Revd Stephen Oo

Archbishop of the Province of Nigeria, Most Revd Nicholas Okoh

Archbishop of Papua New Guinea, Rt. Revd Clyde Igara

Prime Bishop of the Philippines, Most Revd Edward Malecdan

Archbishop of the Province of Rwanda, Most Revd Onesphore Rwaje

Primate of the Province of South East Asia, Most Revd Bolly Lapok

Metropolitan of the Province of Southern Africa, Most Revd Thabo Makgoba

Presiding Bishop of the Southern Cone of America, Most Revd Hector Muñoz

Archbishop of the Province of the Sudan, Most Revd Daniel Yak

Archbishop of the Province of Tanzania, Most Revd Jacob Chimeledya

Archbishop of the Province of Uganda, Most Revd Stanley Ntagali

Presiding Bishop and Primate of the USA, Most Revd Katharine Schori

Archbishop of the Province of West Africa, Most Revd Dr Daniel Sarfo

Archbishop of the Province of the West Indies, Most Revd Dr John Holder

OTHER CHURCHES AND EXTRA-PROVINCIAL DIOCESES

Anglican Church of Bermuda, extra-provincial to Canterbury Bishop, Rt. Revd Nicholas Dill

Church of Ceylon, extra-provincial to Canterbury Bishop of Colombo, Rt. Revd Dhiloraj Canagasabey Bishop of Kurunagala, Rt. Revd Greg Francis

Episcopal Church of Cuba, Rt. Revd Griselda Del Carpio

Falkland Islands, extra-provincial to Canterbury Bishop, Rt. Revd Nigel Stock (Bishop to the Forces)

Lusitanian Church (Portuguese Episcopal Church), extra-provincial to Canterbury Bishop, Rt. Revd Jose Cabral

Reformed Episcopal Church of Spain, extra-provincial to Canterbury Bishop, Rt. Revd Carlos López-Lozano

MODERATION OF CHURCHES IN FULL COMMUNION WITH THE ANGLICAN COMMUNION

Church of Bangladesh, Most Revd Paul Sarkar

Church of North India, Most Revd Philip Marandih

Church of South India, Most Revd Govada Dyvasirvadam

Church of Pakistan, Most Revd Samuel Azariah

CHURCH OF SCOTLAND

The Church of Scotland is the national church of Scotland. The church is reformed in doctrine, and presbyterian in constitution; ie based on a hierarchy of courts of ministers and elders and, since 1990, of members of a diaconate. At local level the Kirk Session consists of the parish minister and ruling elders. At district level the presbyteries, of which there are 44 in Britain, consist of all the ministers in the district, one ruling elder from each congregation, and those members of the diaconate who qualify for membership. The General Assembly is the supreme authority, and is presided over by a Moderator chosen annually by the Assembly. The sovereign, if not present in person, is represented by a Lord High Commissioner who is appointed each year by the Crown.

The Church of Scotland has around 400,000 members and 800 parish ministers. The majority of parishes are in Scotland, but there are also churches in England, Europe and overseas.

Lord High Commissioner (2014–15), HRH the Earl of Wessex, KG, GCVO
Moderator of the General Assembly (2014–15), Rt. Revd John Chalmers
Acting Principal Clerk, Revd Dr George Whyte
Acting Depute Clerk, Revd George Cowie
Procurator, Laura Dunlop, QC
Law Agent and Solicitor of the Church, Janette Wilson
Parliamentary Officer, Chloe Clemmons
General Treasurer, Iain Grimmond
Secretary, Church and Society Council, Revd Ewan Aitken
CHURCH OFFICE, 121 George Street, Edinburgh EH2 4YN
T 0131-225 5722

PRESBYTERIES AND CLERKS

Aberdeen, Revd George Cowie; Revd John Ferguson
Abernethy, Catherine Buchan
Angus, Revd Mike Goss
Annandale and Eskdale, Revd Bryan Haston
Ardrossan, Alan Saunderson
Argyll, Ian MacLagan
Ayr, Revd Kenneth Elliott
Buchan, George Berstan
Caithness, Revd Ronald Johnstone
Dumbarton, Revd David Clark
Dumfries and Kirkcudbright, Revd William Hogg
Dundee, Revd James Wilson
Dunfermline, Revd Elizabeth Kenny
Dunkeld and Meigle, Revd John Russell
Duns, Helen Longmuir
Edinburgh, Revd Dr George Whyte
England, Revd Dr Pete Mills
Europe, Revd Jim Sharp
Falkirk, Revd Robert Allan
Glasgow, Very Revd William Hewitt
Gordon, Revd Euan Glen
Greenock and Paisley, Revd Dr Peter McEnhill
Hamilton, Revd Shaw Paterson
Inverness, Revd Reginald Campbell
Irvine and Kilmarnock, Steuart Dey
Jedburgh, Revd W. Frank Campbell
Kincardine and Deeside, Revd Hugh Conkey
Kirkcaldy, Revd Rosemary Frew
Lanark, Revd Helen Jamieson
Lewis, Revd Thomas Sinclair
Lochaber, Ella Gill
Lochcarron-Skye, Revd Allan Macarthur
Lothian, John McCulloch
Melrose and Peebles, Revd Victoria Linford
Moray, Revd Robert Anderson
Orkney, David Baker
Perth, Revd Alan Reid
Ross, Ronald Gunstone
St Andrews, Revd James Redpath
Shetland, Revd Charles Greig
Stirling, Revd Alex Millar
Sutherland, Mary Stobo
Uist, Wilson McKinlay
West Lothian, Revd Duncan Shaw
Wigtown and Stranraer, vacant

The stipends for ministers in the Church of Scotland in 2014 range from £25,607–£31,469, depending on length of service.

ROMAN CATHOLIC CHURCH

The Roman Catholic Church is a worldwide Christian church acknowledging as its head the Bishop of Rome, known as the Pope (father). Despite its widespread usage, 'Pope' is actually an unofficial term. The *Annuario Pontificio,* (Pontifical Yearbook) lists eight official titles: Bishop of Rome, Vicar of Jesus Christ, Successor of the Prince of the Apostles, Supreme Pontiff of the Universal Church, Primate of Italy, Archbishop and Metropolitan of the Roman Province, Sovereign of the State of the Vatican City and Servant of the Servants of God.

The Pope leads a communion of followers of Christ, who believe they continue His presence in the world as servants of faith, hope and love to all society. The Pope is held to be the successor of St Peter and thus invested with the power which was entrusted to St Peter by Jesus Christ. A direct line of succession is therefore claimed from the earliest Christian communities. With the fall of the Roman Empire the Pope also became an important political leader. His territory is now limited to the 0.44 sq. km (0.17 sq. miles) of the Vatican City State, created to provide some independence to the Pope from Italy and other nations. The episcopal jurisdiction of the Roman Catholic Church is called the Holy See.

The Pope exercises spiritual authority over the church with the advice and assistance of the Sacred College of Cardinals, the supreme council of the church. The number of cardinals was fixed at 70 by Pope Sixtus V in 1586 but has increased steadily since the pontificate of John XXIII. On 28 February 2013, the date of Pope Benedict XVI's resignation, there were 207 cardinals.

Following the death or resignation of the Pope, the members of the College of Cardinals under the age of 80 are called to the Vatican to elect a successor. They are known as cardinal electors and form an assembly called the conclave. The conclave, which comprised 115 cardinal electors when it convened in March 2013, conducts a secret ballot in complete seclusion to elect the next Pope. A two-thirds majority is necessary before the vote can be accepted as final. When a cardinal receives the necessary number of votes, the Dean of the Sacred College formally asks him if he will accept election and the name by which he wishes to be known. On his acceptance of the office of Supreme Pontiff, the conclave is dissolved and the first Cardinal Deacon announces the election to the assembled crowd in St Peter's Square.

The Pope has full legislative, judicial and administrative power over the whole Roman Catholic Church. He is aided in his administration by the curia, which is made up of a number of departments. The Secretariat of State is the central office for carrying out the Pope's instructions and is presided over by the Cardinal Secretary of State. It maintains relations with the departments of the curia, with the episcopate, with the representatives of the Holy See in various countries, governments and private persons. The congregations and pontifical councils are the Pope's ministries and include departments such as the Congregation for the Doctrine of Faith, whose field of competence concerns faith and morals; the Congregation for the Clergy and the Congregation for the Evangelisation of Peoples, the Pontifical Council for the Family and the Pontifical Council for the Promotion of Christian Unity.

The Holy See, composed of the Pope and those who help him in his mission for the church, is recognised by the Conventions of Vienna as an international moral body. Apostolic nuncios are the Pope's diplomatic representatives; in countries where no formal diplomatic relations exist between the Holy See and that country, the papal representative is known as an apostolic delegate.

According to the 2013 Pontifical Yearbook the number of Roman Catholics worldwide was 1,214 million in 2011; the number of bishops was 5,132 and there were 413,418 priests.

SUPREME PONTIFF
His Holiness Pope Francis (Jorge Mario Bergoglio), *born* Buenos Aires, Argentina, 17 December 1936; *ordained priest* 13 December 1969; *appointed Archbishop* (of Buenos Aires), 28 February 1998; *created Cardinal* 21 February 2001; *assumed pontificate* 13 March 2013

PONTIFF EMERITUS
His Holiness Pope Benedict XVI (Joseph Ratzinger), *born* Bavaria, Germany, 16 April 1927; *ordained priest* 29 June 1951; *appointed Archbishop* (of Munich), 24 March 1977; *created Cardinal* 27 June 1977; *assumed pontificate* 19 April 2005; *resigned pontificate* 28 February 2013

SECRETARIAT OF STATE
Secretary of State, His Eminence Cardinal Pietro Parolin
First Section (General Affairs), Most Revd Giovanni Angelo Becciu (Titular Archbishop of Roselle)
Second Section (Relations with Other States), Most Revd Dominique Mamberti (Titular Archbishop of Sagona)

BISHOPS' CONFERENCE
The Catholic Bishops' Conference of England and Wales is the permanent assembly of Catholic Bishops and Ordinaries in the two member countries. The membership of the Conference comprises the Archbishops, Bishops and Auxiliary Bishops of the 22 Dioceses within England and Wales, the Bishop of the Forces (Military Ordinariate), the Eparch of the Ukrainian Catholic Eparchy of the Holy Family of London (Great Britain), the Ordinary of the Personal Ordinariate of Our Lady of Walsingham, and the Apostolic Prefect of the Falkland Islands. The Conference is headed by a president and vice-president. There are six departments, each with an episcopal chair: Education and Formation, Christian Life and Worship, Christian Responsibility and Citizenship, Dialogue and Unity, Evangelisation and Catechesis, and International Affairs.

The Bishops' Conference Standing Committee is made up of two directly elected bishops in addition to the Metropolitan Archbishops and chairs from each of the above departments. The committee has general responsibility for continuity of policy between the plenary sessions of the conference, preparing the conference agenda and implementing its decisions.

The administration of the Bishops' Conference is funded by a levy on each diocese, according to income. A general secretariat in London coordinates and supervises the Bishops' Conference administration activities. There are also other agencies and consultative bodies affiliated to the conference.

The Bishops' Conference of Scotland is the permanently constituted assembly of the eight bishops of Scotland. The conference is headed by the president (Most Revd Philip Tartaglia, Archbishop of Glasgow). The conference establishes various agencies which perform advisory functions in relation to the conference. The more important of these agencies are called commissions; each one is headed by a bishop president who, with the other members of the commissions, are appointed by the conference.

The Irish Catholic Bishops' Conference (also known as the Irish Episcopal Conference) has as its president Cardinal Seán Brady of Armagh. Its membership comprises all the archbishops and bishops of Ireland. It appoints various commissions and agencies to assist with the work of the Catholic Church in Ireland.

The Catholic Church in the UK has over 900,000 mass attendees, 5,500 priests and 4,550 churches.

Bishops' Conferences secretariats:
ENGLAND AND WALES, 39 Eccleston Square, London SW1V 1BX T 020-7630 8220 E secretariat@cbcew.org.uk
W www.catholicchurch.org.uk
General Secretary, Mgr Marcus Stock
SCOTLAND, 64 Aitken Street, Airdrie ML6 6LT T 01236-764061
W www.bcos.org.uk
General Secretary, Mgr Hugh Bradley
IRELAND, Columba Centre, Maynooth, County Kildare T (+353) (1) 505 3000 E info@catholicbishops.ie
W www.catholicbishops.ie
Secretary, Most Revd Kieran O'Reilly (Bishop of Killaloe)
Executive Secretary, Mgr Gearóid Dullea

GREAT BRITAIN
APOSTOLIC NUNCIO TO GREAT BRITAIN
Most Revd Antonio Mennini, 54 Parkside, London SW19 5NE
T 020-8944 7189

ENGLAND AND WALES
THE MOST REVD ARCHBISHOPS
Westminster, Cardinal Vincent Nichols, *cons.* 1992, *apptd* 2009 *Archbishop Emeritus,* Cardinal Cormac Murphy-O'Connor, *cons.* 1977, *elevated* 2001 *Auxiliaries,* John Arnold, *cons.* 2006; John Sherrington, *cons* 2011; Nicholas Hudson, *cons.* 2014. *Clergy,* 318. *Archbishop's House,* Ambrosden Avenue, London SW1P 1QJ
T 020-7798 9033
Birmingham, Bernard Longley, *cons.* 2003, *apptd* 2009 *Auxiliaries,* William Kenney, *cons.* 1987; David McGough, *cons.* 2005; Robert Byrne, *cons.* 2014. *Clergy,* 430. *Archbishop's House,* 8 Shadwell Street, Birmingham B4 6EY
T 0121-236 9090
Cardiff, George Stack, *cons.* 2001, *apptd* 2011. *Clergy,* 47. *Archbishop's House,* 43 Cathedral Road, Cardiff CF11 9HD
T 029-2022 0411
Liverpool, Malcolm McMahon, *cons.* 2000, *apptd* 2014 *Auxiliary,* Thomas Williams, *cons.* 2003. *Clergy,* 407. *Liverpool Archdiocesan Centre for Evangelisation,* Croxteth Drive, Sefton Park, Liverpool L17 1AA T 0151-522 1000
Southwark, Peter Smith, *cons.* 1995, *apptd* 2010 *Auxiliaries,* Patrick Lynch, *cons.* 2006; Paul Hendricks, *cons.* 2006. *Clergy,* 433. *Archbishop's House,* 150 St George's Road, London SE1 6HX T 020-7928 2495

THE RT. REVD BISHOPS
Arundel and Brighton, Kieran Conry, *cons.* 2001, *apptd* 2001. *Clergy,* 96. *Bishop's House,* The Upper Drive, Hove, E. Sussex BN3 6NB T 01273-506387
Brentwood, Thomas McMahon, *cons.* 1980, *apptd* 1980. *Clergy,* 170. *Bishop's Office,* Cathedral House, Ingrave Road, Brentwood, Essex CM15 8AT T 01277-232266

Clifton, Declan Lang, *cons.* 2001, *apptd* 2001. *Clergy*, 153.
   Bishop's House, St Ambrose, North Road, Leigh Woods,
   Bristol BS8 3PW **T** 0117-973 3072
East Anglia, Alan Hopes, *cons.* 2003, *apptd* 2013. *Clergy*,
   129. *Diocesan Curia*, The White House, 21 Upgate,
   Poringland, Norwich NR14 7SH **T** 01508-492202
Hallam, Ralph Heskett, *cons.* 2010, *apptd* 2014. *Clergy*, 71.
   Bishop's House, 75 Norfolk Road, Sheffield S2 2SZ
   T 0114-278 7988
Hexham and Newcastle, Seamus Cunningham, *cons.* 2009,
   apptd 2009. *Clergy*, 164. *Bishop's House*, East Denton Hall,
   800 West Road, Newcastle upon Tyne NE5 2BJ
   T 0191-228 0003
Lancaster, Michael Campbell, *cons.* 2008, *apptd* 2009. *Clergy*,
   97. *Bishop's Office*, The Pastoral Centre, Balmoral Road,
   Lancaster LA1 3BT **T** 01524-596050
Leeds, vacant. *Clergy*, 193. *Diocesan Curia*, Hinsley Hall,
   62 Headingley Lane, Leeds LS6 2BX **T** 0113-261 8022
Menevia (Wales), Tom Burns, *cons.* 2002, *apptd* 2008.
   Clergy, 60. *Diocesan Office*, 27 Convent Street,
   Swansea SA1 2BX **T** 01792-644017
Middlesbrough, Terence Drainey, *cons.* 2008, *apptd* 2007.
   Clergy, 83. *Diocesan Curia*, 50ª The Avenue, Linthorpe,
   Middlesbrough TS5 6QT **T** 01642-850505
Northampton, Peter Doyle, *cons.* 2005, *apptd* 2005.
   Clergy, 116. *Bishop's House*, Marriott Street, Northampton
   NN2 6AW **T** 01604-715635
Nottingham, vacant. *Clergy*, 166. *Bishop's House*,
   27 Cavendish Road East, The Park, Nottingham NG7 1BB
   T 0115-947 4786
Plymouth, Mark O'Toole, *cons.* 2014, *apptd* 2013. *Clergy*, 50.
   Bishop's House, 31 Wyndham Street West, Plymouth PL1 5RZ
   T 01752-224414
Portsmouth, Philip Egan, *cons.* 2012, *apptd* 2012. *Clergy*,
   214. *Bishop's House*, Bishop Crispian Way, Portsmouth,
   Hants PO1 3HG **T** 023-9282 0894
Salford, Terence Brain, *cons.* 1991, *apptd* 1997. *Clergy*, 218.
   Diocesan Curia, Wardley Hall, Worsley, Manchester M28 2ND
   T 0161-794 2825
Shrewsbury, Mark Davies, *cons.* 2010, *apptd* 2010. *Clergy*
   119. *Diocesan Curia*, 2 Park Road South, Prenton, Wirral
   CH43 4UX **T** 0151-652 9855
Wrexham (Wales), Peter Brignall, *cons.* 2012, *apptd* 2012.
   Clergy, 16. *Bishop's House*, Sontley Road, Wrexham LL13 7EW
   T 01978-262726

SCOTLAND
THE MOST REVD ARCHBISHOPS
St Andrews and Edinburgh, Leo Cushley, *cons.* 2013,
   apptd 2013. *Archbishop Emeritus*, HE Cardinal Keith
   O'Brien, *cons.* 1985, *elevated* 2003. *Clergy*, 50.
   Archdiocesan Offices, 100 Strathearn Road, Edinburgh
   EH9 1BB **T** 0131-623 8911
Glasgow, Philip Tartaglia, *cons.* 2005, *elevated* 2012.
   Clergy, 198. *Diocesan Curia*, 196 Clyde Street, Glasgow
   G1 4JY **T** 0141-226 5898

THE RT. REVD BISHOPS
Aberdeen, Hugh Gilbert, *cons.* 2011, *apptd* 2011. *Clergy*, 47.
   Bishop's House, 3 Queen's Cross, Aberdeen AB15 4XU
   T 01224-319154
Argyll and the Isles, vacant. *Clergy*, 32. *Diocesan Office*, Bishop's
   House, Esplanade, Oban, Argyll PA34 5AB **T** 01631-567436
Dunkeld, Stephen Robson, *cons.* 2012, *apptd* 2013. *Clergy*,
   42. *Diocesan Curia*, 24–28 Lawside Road, Dundee DD3 6XY
   T 01382-225453
Galloway, John Cunningham, *cons.* 2004, *apptd* 2004.
   Clergy, 19. *Diocesan Office*, 8 Corsehill Road, Ayr KA7 2ST
   T 01292-266750

Motherwell, Joseph Toal, *cons.* 2008, *trans.* 2014.
   Clergy, 123. *Diocesan Curia*, Coursington Road, Motherwell
   ML1 1PP **T** 01698-269114
Paisley, John Keenan, *cons.* 2014, *apptd* 2014. *Clergy*, 75.
   Diocesan Curia, Cathedral Precincts, Incle Street, Paisley
   PA1 1HR **T** 0141-847 6131

BISHOPRIC OF THE FORCES
Rt. Revd Richard Moth, *cons.* 2009, *apptd* 2009.
   Administration, RC Bishopric of the Forces, Wellington House,
   St Omer Barracks, Thornhill Road, Aldershot, Hants GU11 2BG
   T 01252-348234

IRELAND
There is one hierarchy for the whole of Ireland. Several of
the dioceses have territory partly in the Republic of Ireland
and partly in Northern Ireland.

APOSTOLIC NUNCIO TO IRELAND
Most Revd Charles John Brown (Titular Archbishop of
   Aquileia), 183 Navan Road, Dublin 7 **T** (+353) (1) 838 0577

THE MOST REVD ARCHBISHOPS
Armagh, Cardinal Sean Brady (*also* Primate of all Ireland),
   cons. 1995, *apptd* 1996, *created Cardinal* 2007. *Coadjutor
   Archbishop*, Most Revd Eamon Martin, *cons.* 2013.
   Clergy, 156. *Bishop's Residence*, Ara Coeli, Cathedral Road,
   Armagh BT61 7QY **T** 028-3752 2045
Cashel and Emly, Dermot Clifford, *cons.* 1986, *apptd* 1988.
   Clergy, 83. *Archbishop's House*, Thurles, Co. Tipperary
   T (+353) (504) 21512
Dublin, Diarmuid Martin, *cons.* 1999, *apptd Coadjutor
   Archbishop* 2003, *succeeded as Archbishop* 2004.
   Archbishop Emeritus, HE Cardinal Desmond Connell,
   cons. 1988, *elevated* 2001. *Auxiliaries*, Eamonn Walsh,
   cons. 1990; Raymond Field, *cons.* 1997. *Clergy*, 397.
   Archbishop's House, Drumcondra, Dublin 9
   T (+353) (1) 837 9253
Tuam, Dr Michael Neary, *cons.* 1992, *apptd* 1995.
   Clergy, 110. *Archbishop's House*, Tuam, Co. Galway
   T (+353) (93) 24166

THE MOST REVD BISHOPS
Achonry, Brendan Kelly, *cons.* 2008, *apptd* 2007. *Clergy*, 50.
   Bishop's House, Edmondstown, Ballaghaderreen, Co.
   Roscommon **T** (+353) (94) 986 0021
Ardagh and Clonmacnois, Francis Duffy, *cons.* 2013,
   apptd 2013. *Clergy*, 60. *Diocesan Office*, St Michael's,
   Ballinalee Road, Longford, Co. Longford **T** (+353) (43) 46432
Clogher, Liam MacDaid, *cons.* 2010, *apptd* 2010. *Clergy*, 74.
   Bishop's House, Monaghan **T** (+353) (47) 81019
Clonfert, John Kirby, *cons.* 1988, *apptd* 1988. *Clergy*, 37.
   Bishop's House, Coorheen, Loughrea, Co. Galway
   T (+353) (91) 841560
Cloyne, William Crean, *cons.* 2013, *apptd* 2013. *Clergy*, 126.
   Diocesan Office, Cobh, Co. Cork **T** (+353) (21) 481 1430
Cork and Ross, John Buckley, *cons.* 1984, *apptd* 1998.
   Clergy, 133. *Diocesan Office*, Cork and Ross Offices,
   Redemption Road, Cork **T** (+353) (21) 430 1717
Derry, Donal McKeown, *cons.* 2001, *apptd* 2014. *Clergy*,
   108. *Bishop's House*, St Eugene's Cathedral, Derry BT48 9AP
   T 028-7126 2302
Down and Connor, Noel Treanor, *cons.* 2008, *apptd* 2008.
   cons. 1983. *Clergy*, 209. *Bishop's Residence*, Lisbreen,
   73 Somerton Road, Belfast, Co. Antrim BT15 4DE
   T 028-9077 6185
Dromore, John McAreavey, *cons.* 1999, *apptd* 1999.
   Clergy, 33. *Bishop's House*, 44 Armagh Road, Newry,
   Co. Down BT35 6PN **T** 028-3026 2444

Elphin, Kevin Doran, *cons.* 2014, *apptd* 2014. *Clergy,* 66.
  Bishop's House, St Mary's, Sligo T (+353) (71) 916 2670
Ferns, Denis Brennan, *cons.* 2006, *apptd* 2006. *Clergy,* 88.
  Bishop's House, Summerhill, Wexford T (+353) (53) 912 2177
Galway, Kilmacduagh and Kilfenora, Martin Drennan,
  cons. 1997, *apptd* 2005. *Clergy,* 57. *Diocesan Office,*
  The Cathedral, Galway T (+353) (91) 563566
Kerry, Ray Browne, *cons.* 2013, *apptd* 2013. *Clergy,* 88.
  Bishop's House, Killarney, Co. Kerry T (+353) (64) 663 1168
Kildare and Leighlin, Denis Nulty, *cons.* 2013,
  apptd 2013. *Clergy,* 72. *Bishop's House,* Carlow
  T (+353) (59) 917 6725
Killala, John Fleming, *cons.* 2002, *apptd* 2002. *Clergy,* 42.
  Bishop's House, Ballina, Co. Mayo T (+353) (96) 21518
Killaloe, Dr Kieran O'Reilly, *cons.* 2010, *apptd* 2010.
  Clergy, 97. *Diocesan Office,* Westbourne, Ennis, Co. Clare
  T (+353) (65) 682 8638
Kilmore, Leo O'Reilly, *cons.* 1997, *apptd* 1998. *Clergy,* 67.
  Bishop's House, Cullies, Co. Cavan T (+353) (49) 433 1496
Limerick, Brendan Leahy, *cons.* 2013, *apptd* 2013. *Clergy,*
  109. *Diocesan Office,* Social Service Centre, Henry Street,
  Limerick T (+353) (61) 315856
Meath, Michael Smith, *cons.* 1984, *apptd* 1990. *Clergy,* 120.
  Bishop's House, Dublin Road, Mullingar, Co. Westmeath
  T (+353) (44) 934 8841
Ossory, Séamus Freeman, *cons.* 2007, *apptd* 2007. *Clergy,* 81.
  Diocesan Office, James's Street, Kilkenny T (+353) (56) 776 2448
Raphoe, Dr Philip Boyce, *cons.* 1995, *apptd* 1995. *Clergy,* 80.
  Bishop's House, Ard Adhamhnáin, Letterkenny, Co. Donegal
  T (+353) (74) 912 1208
Waterford and Lismore, William Lee, *cons.* 1993, *apptd* 1993.
  Clergy, 114. *Bishop's House,* John's Hill, Waterford
  T (+353) (51) 874463

OTHER CHURCHES IN THE UK

ASSOCIATED PRESBYTERIAN CHURCHES OF SCOTLAND

The Associated Presbyterian Churches came into being in 1989 as a result of a division within the Free Presbyterian Church of Scotland. The Associated Presbyterian Churches is reformed and evangelistic in nature and emphasises the importance of doctrine based primarily on the Bible and secondly on the Westminster Confession of Faith. There are an estimated 500 members, 9 ministers and 14 congregations in Scotland. There are also congregations in Canada.
ASSOCIATED PRESBYTERIAN CHURCHES OF
  SCOTLAND, APC Manse, Polvinster Road, Oban PA34 5TN
  T 01631-567076 W www.apchurches.org
  Moderator of Presbytery, Hugh McKenzie
  Clerk of Presbytery, Revd Archibald McPhail

BAPTIST CHURCH

Baptists trace their origins to John Smyth, who in 1609 in Amsterdam reinstituted the baptism of conscious believers as the basis of the fellowship of a gathered church. Members of Smyth's church established the first Baptist church in England in 1612. They came to be known as 'General' Baptists and their theology was Arminian, whereas a later group of Calvinists who adopted the baptism of believers came to be known as 'Particular' Baptists. The two sections of the Baptists were united into one body, the Baptist Union of Great Britain and Ireland, in 1891. In 1988 the title was changed to the Baptist Union of Great Britain.

Baptists emphasise the complete autonomy of the local church, although individual churches are linked in various kinds of associations. There are international bodies (such as the Baptist World Alliance) and national bodies, but some Baptist churches belong to neither. However, in Great Britain the majority of churches and associations belong to the Baptist Union of Great Britain. There are also Baptist Unions in Wales, Scotland and Ireland, which are much smaller than the Baptist Union of Great Britain, and there is some overlap of membership.

There are currently around 135,000 members, 2,500 ministers and 2,084 churches associated with the Baptist Union of Great Britain. The Baptist Union of Great Britain is one of the founder members of the European Baptist Federation (1948) and the Baptist World Alliance (1905); the latter represents 42 million members worldwide.

In the Baptist Union of Wales (Undeb Bedyddwyr Cymru) there are 11,884 members, 101 pastors and 400 churches, including those in England.

In the Baptist Union of Scotland there are 11,500 members, 163 pastors and 167 churches.
BAPTIST UNION OF GREAT BRITAIN, Baptist House,
  PO Box 44, 129 Broadway, Didcot, Oxon OX11 8RT
  T 01235-517700 W www.baptist.org.uk
  President (2014–15), Revd Dr Christopher Ellis
  General Secretary, Revd Lynn Green
BAPTIST UNION OF WALES, Y Llwyfan, College Road,
  Carmarthen SA31 3EQ T 01267-245660
  E peter@bedyddwyrcymru.co.uk W www.buw.org.uk
  President of the English Assembly (2014–15), Revd Ifor
  Williams
  President of the Welsh Assembly (2014–15), Revd Eirian
  Wyn Lewis
  General Secretary of the Baptist Union of Wales, Revd Peter
  Thomas
BAPTIST UNION OF SCOTLAND, 48 Speirs Wharf, Glasgow
  G4 9TH T 0141-423 6169 E admin@scottishbaptist.org.uk
  General Director, Revd A. Donaldson

THE BRETHREN

The Brethren was founded in Dublin in 1827–8, basing itself on the structures and practices of the early church and rejecting denominationalism and clericalism. Many groups sprang up; the group at Plymouth became the best known, resulting in its designation by others as the 'Plymouth Brethren'. Early worship had a prescribed form but quickly assumed an unstructured, non-liturgical format.

There are services devoted to worship, usually involving the breaking of bread, and separate preaching meetings. There is no salaried ministry.

A theological dispute led in 1848 to schism between the Open Brethren and the Closed or Exclusive Brethren, each branch later suffering further divisions.

Open Brethren churches are run by appointed elders and are completely independent, but freely cooperate with each other. Exclusive Brethren churches believe in a universal fellowship between congregations. They do not have appointed elders, but use respected members of their congregation to perform certain administrative functions.

The Brethren are established throughout the UK, Ireland, Europe, India, Africa and Australasia. In the UK there are over 70,000 members, 1,250 assembly halls and over 200 full-time Bible teachers, evangelists and administrators. There are a number of publishing houses that publish Brethren-related literature. Chapter Two is the main supplier of such literature in the UK; it also has a Brethren history archive which is available for use by appointment.
CHAPTER TWO, Conduit Mews, London SE18 7AP
  T 020-8316 5389 E info@chaptertwobooks.org.uk
  W www.chaptertwobooks.org.uk

CONGREGATIONAL FEDERATION

The Congregational Federation was founded by members of Congregational churches in England and Wales who did not join the United Reformed Church in 1972. There are also churches in Scotland and France affiliated to the federation. The federation exists to encourage congregations of believers to worship in free assembly, but it has no authority over them and emphasises their right to independence and self-governance.

The federation has 7,240 members, 183 accredited ministers and 265 churches in England, Wales and Scotland.

CONGREGATIONAL FEDERATION, 6 Castle Gate, Nottingham NG1 7AS **T** 0115-911 1460 **E** admin@congregational.org.uk **W** www.congregational.org.uk
President of the Federation (2014–15), Revd Barbara Bridges
General Secretary, Revd M. Heaney

FELLOWSHIP OF INDEPENDENT EVANGELICAL CHURCHES

The Fellowship of Independent Evangelical Churches (FIEC) was founded by Revd E. J. Poole-Connor (1872–1962) in 1922. In 1923 the fellowship published its first register of non-denominational pastors, evangelists and congregations who had accepted the doctrinal basis for the fellowship.

Members of the fellowship have two primary convictions: firstly to defend the evangelical faith, and secondly that evangelicalism is the bond that unites the fellowship, rather than forms of worship or church government.

The FIEC exists to promote the welfare of non-denominational Bible churches and to give expression to the fundamental doctrines of evangelical Christianity. It supports individual churches by gathering and disseminating information and resources and advising churches on current theological, moral, social and practical issues.

There are currently 517 churches affiliated to the fellowship.

FELLOWSHIP OF INDEPENDENT EVANGELICAL CHURCHES, 39 The Point, Market Harborough, Leics LE16 7QU **T** 01858-434540 **E** admin@fiec.org.uk **W** www.fiec.org.uk
National Director, John Stevens

FREE CHURCH OF ENGLAND

The Free Church of England, otherwise called the Reformed Episcopal Church, is an independent episcopal church, constituted according to the historic faith, tradition and practice of the Church of England. Its roots lie in the 18th century, but it started to grow significantly from the 1840s onwards, as clergy and congregations joined it from the established church in protest against the Oxford Movement. The historic episcopate was conferred on the English church in 1876 through bishops of the Reformed Episcopal Church (which had broken away from the Protestant Episcopal Church in the USA in 1873). A branch of the Reformed Episcopal Church was founded in the UK and this merged with the Free Church of England in 1927 to create the present church. The Orders of the Free Church of England are recognised by the Church of England.

Worship is according to the *Book of Common Prayer* and some modern liturgy is permissable. Only men are ordained to the orders of deacon, presbyter and bishop.

The Free Church of England has 25 ministers, 21 congregations and around 900 members in England. There is one congregation in St Petersburg, Russia and three congregations and six missions in Brazil.

THE FREE CHURCH OF ENGLAND, 329 Wolverhampton Road West, Bentley, Walsall WV13 2RL **T** 01902-607335 **W** www.fcofe.org.uk
Bishop Primus, Rt. Revd Dr John Fenwick
General Secretary, Rt. Revd Paul Hunt

FREE CHURCH OF SCOTLAND

The Free Church of Scotland was formed in 1843 when over 400 ministers withdrew from the Church of Scotland as a result of interference in the internal affairs of the church by the civil authorities. In 1900, all but 26 ministers joined with others to form the United Free Church (most of which rejoined the Church of Scotland in 1929). In 1904 the remaining 26 ministers were recognised by the House of Lords as continuing the Free Church of Scotland.

The church maintains strict adherence to the Westminster Confession of Faith (1648) and accepts the Bible as the sole rule of faith and conduct. Its general assembly meets annually. It also has links with reformed churches overseas. The Free Church of Scotland has about 12,000 members, 90 ministers and 100 congregations.

FREE CHURCH OF SCOTLAND, 15 North Bank Street, The Mound, Edinburgh EH1 2LS **T** 0131-226 5286 **E** offices@freechurchofscotland.org.uk **W** www.freechurch.org
Chief Administrative Officer, Rod Morrison

FREE PRESBYTERIAN CHURCH OF SCOTLAND

The Free Presbyterian Church of Scotland was formed in 1893 by two ministers of the Free Church of Scotland who refused to accept a Declaratory Act passed by the Free Church General Assembly in 1892. The Free Presbyterian Church of Scotland is Calvinistic in doctrine and emphasises observance of the Sabbath. It adheres strictly to the Westminster Confession of Faith (1648).

The church has about 1,000 members in Scotland and about 4,000 in overseas congregations. It has 18 ministers and 40 churches in the UK.

FREE PRESBYTERIAN CHURCH OF SCOTLAND, 133 Woodlands Road, Glasgow G3 6LE **E** outreach@fpchurch.org.uk **W** www.fpchurch.org.uk
Moderator (2014–15), Revd Donald Macdonald
Clerk of the Synod, Revd John MacLeod

HOLY APOSTOLIC CATHOLIC ASSYRIAN CHURCH OF THE EAST

The Holy Apostolic Catholic Assyrian Church of the East traces its beginnings to the middle of the first century. It spread from Upper Mesopotamia throughout the territories of the Persian Empire. The Assyrian Church of the East became theologically separated from the rest of the Christian community following the Council of Ephesus in 431. The church is headed by the Catholicos Patriarch and is episcopal in government. The liturgical language is Syriac (Aramaic). The Assyrian Church of the East and the Roman Catholic Church agreed a common Christological declaration in 1994, and a process of dialogue between the Assyrian Church of the East and the Chaldean Catholic Church, which is in communion with Rome but shares the Syriac liturgy, was instituted in 1996.

The church has around 325,000 members in the Middle East, India, Russia, Europe, North America and Australasia. In Great Britain there is one parish, which is situated in London. The church in Great Britain forms part of the Diocese of Europe under HG Mar Odisho Oraham.

HOLY APOSTOLIC CATHOLIC ASSYRIAN CHURCH OF THE EAST, St Mary's Church, Westminster Road, Hanwell, London W7 3TU **T** 020-8567 1814

INDEPENDENT METHODIST CHURCHES

The Independent Methodist Churches were formed in 1805 and remained independent when the Methodist Church in Great Britain was formed in 1932. They are mainly concentrated in the industrial areas of the north of England.

The churches are Methodist in doctrine but their organisation is congregational. All the churches are members of the Independent Methodist Connexion of Churches. The controlling body of the Connexion is the Annual Meeting, to which churches send delegates. The Connexional President is elected every two years. Between annual meetings the affairs of the Connexion are handled by the Connexional Committee and departmental committees. Ministers are appointed by the churches and trained through the Connexion. The ministry is open to both men and women and is unpaid.

There are 1,600 members, 82 ministers and 78 churches in Great Britain.

INDEPENDENT METHODIST RESOURCE CENTRE,
The Resource Centre, Fleet Street, Wigan WN5 0DS
T 01942-223526 E resourcecentre@imcgb.org.uk
W www.imcgb.org.uk
President (2013–15), Ray Ursell
General Secretary, Brian Rowney

LUTHERAN CHURCH

Lutheranism is based on the teachings of Martin Luther, the German leader of the Protestant Reformation. The authority of the scriptures is held to be supreme over church tradition. The teachings of Lutheranism are explained in detail in 16th-century confessional writings, particularly the Augsburg Confession. Lutheranism is one of the largest Protestant denominations and it is particularly strong in northern Europe and the USA. Some Lutheran churches are episcopal, while others have a synodal form of organisation; unity is based on doctrine rather than structure. Most Lutheran churches are members of the Lutheran World Federation, based in Geneva.

Lutheran services in Great Britain are held in 15 languages to serve members of different nationalities. Services usually follow ancient liturgies. English-language congregations are members either of the Lutheran Church in Great Britain or of the Evangelical Lutheran Church of England. The Lutheran Church in Great Britain and other Lutheran churches in Britain are members of the Lutheran Council of Great Britain, which represents them and coordinates their common work.

There are around 70 million Lutherans worldwide, with around 180,000 members in Great Britain.

THE LUTHERAN COUNCIL OF GREAT BRITAIN,
30 Thanet Street, London WC1H 9QH T 020-7554 9753
E enquiries@lutheran.org.uk W www.lutheran.org.uk
Chair, Revd Torbjorn Holt

METHODIST CHURCH

The Methodist movement started in England in 1729 when the Revd John Wesley, an Anglican priest, and his brother Charles met with others in Oxford and resolved to conduct their lives by 'rule and method'. In 1739 the Wesleys began evangelistic preaching and the first Methodist chapel was founded in Bristol in the same year. In 1744 the first annual conference was held, at which the Articles of Religion were drawn up. Doctrinal emphases included repentance, faith, the assurance of salvation, social concern and the priesthood of all believers. After John Wesley's death in 1791 the Methodists withdrew from the established church to form the Methodist Church. Methodists gradually drifted into many groups, but in 1932 the Wesleyan Methodist Church, the United Methodist Church and the Primitive Methodist Church united to form the Methodist Church of Great Britain.

The governing body of the Methodist Church is the Conference. The Conference meets annually in June or July and consists of two parts: the ministerial and representative

sessions. The Methodist Church is structured as a 'Connexion' of churches, circuits and districts. The local churches in a defined area form a circuit, and a number of these circuits make up each of the 31 districts. There are around 80 million Methodists worldwide. In Great Britain there are nearly 230,000 members, 3,680 presbyters, 171 Deacons and 5,023 churches.

THE METHODIST CHURCH OF GREAT BRITAIN,
Methodist Church House, 25 Marylebone Road, London
NW1 5JR T 020-7486 5502
E helpdesk@methodistchurch.org.uk W www.methodist.org.uk
President of the Conference (2014–15), Revd Kenneth Howcroft
General Secretary and Secretary of the Conference, Revd Dr Martyn Atkins

THE METHODIST CHURCH IN IRELAND

The Methodist Church in Ireland is autonomous but has close links with British Methodism. It has a community roll of 50,879 members, 125 ministers, 279 lay preachers and 221 churches.

METHODIST CHURCH IN IRELAND,
1 Fountainville Avenue, Belfast BT9 6AN T 028-9032 4554
E secretary@irishmethodist.org W www.irishmethodist.org
President (2014–15), Revd Peter Murray
Secretary, Donald Ker

ORTHODOX CHURCHES

EASTERN ORTHODOX CHURCH

The Eastern (or Byzantine) Orthodox Church is a communion of self-governing Christian churches that recognises the honorary primacy of the Ecumenical Patriarch of Constantinople.

The position of Orthodox Christians is that the faith was fully defined during the period of the Oecumenical Councils. In doctrine it is strongly trinitarian, and stresses the mystery and importance of the sacraments. It is episcopal in government. The structure of the Orthodox Christian year differs from that of western churches.

Orthodox Christians throughout the world are estimated to number about 300 million; there are around 300,000 in the UK.

GREEK ORTHODOX CHURCH (PATRIARCHATE OF ANTIOCH)

The church is led by John X, Patriarch of Antioch, who was enthroned in February 2013. The UK forms part of the Archdiocese of the British Isles and Ireland. There are 15 parishes in the UK and the Republic of Ireland, including St George's Cathedral in London, and 27 clergy.

ANTIOCHIAN ORTHODOX DEANERY OF THE UK AND IRELAND, 29 Willis Road, Cale Green, Stockport, Cheshire SK3 8HQ T 0161-476 4847 E orthodox@.clara.net
W www.antiochian-orthodox.co.uk
Dean, Archpriest Fr. Gregory Hallam

GREEK ORTHODOX CHURCH (PATRIARCHATE OF CONSTANTINOPLE)

The presence of Greek Orthodox Christians in Britain dates back at least to 1677 when Archbishop Joseph Geogirenes of Samos fled from Turkish persecution and came to London. The present Greek cathedral in Moscow Road, Bayswater, was opened for public worship in 1879, and the Diocese of Thyateira and Great Britain was established in 1922. There are now 115 parishes and other communities (including two monasteries) in the UK, served by four bishops, 118 clergy, nine cathedrals and 106 parishes.

THE PATRIARCHATE OF CONSTANTINOPLE IN GREAT BRITAIN, Archdiocese of Thyateira and Great Britain, Thyateira House, 5 Craven Hill, London W2 3EN T 020-7723 4787 E mail@thyateira.org.uk W www.thyateira.org.uk
Archbishop, Gregorios of Thyateira and Great Britain

THE RUSSIAN ORTHODOX CHURCH (PATRIARCHATE OF MOSCOW)

The records of Russian Orthodox Church activities in Britain date from the visit to England of Tsar Peter I in the early 18th century. Clergy were sent from Russia to serve the chapel established to minister to the staff of the Imperial Russian Embassy in London.

In 2007, after an 80-year division, the Russian Orthodox Church Outside Russia agreed to become an autonomous part of the Russian Orthodox Church, Patriarchate of Moscow. The reunification agreement was signed by Patriarch Alexy II, 15th Patriarch of Moscow and All Russia and Metropolitan Laurus, leader of the Russian Orthodox Church Outside Russia on 17 May at a ceremony at Christ the Saviour Cathedral in Moscow. Patriarch Alexy II died on 5 December 2008. Metropolitan Kirill of Smolensk and Kaliningrad was enthroned as the 16th Patriarch of Moscow and All Russia on 1 February 2009, having been elected by a secret ballot of clergy on 27 January 2009.

The diocese of Sourozh is the diocese of the Russian Orthodox Church in Great Britain and Ireland and is led by Archbishop Elisey of Sourozh.

DIOCESE OF SOUROZH, Diocesan Office, Cathedral of the Dormition of the Mother of God and All Saints, 67 Ennismore Gardens, London SW7 1NH T 020-7584 0096 W www.sourozh.org
Diocesan Hierarch, Archbishop Elisey of Sourozh

SERBIAN ORTHODOX CHURCH (PATRIARCHATE OF SERBIA)

There are seven parishes in Great Britain and around 4,000 members. Great Britain is part of the Diocese of Great Britain and Scandinavia, which is led by Bishop Dositej. The church can be contacted via the church of St Sava in London.
SERBIAN ORTHODOX CHURCH IN GREAT BRITAIN, Church of Saint Sava, 89 Lancaster Road, London W11 1QQ T 020-7727 8367 E crkva@spclondon.org W www.spclondon.org
Archpriest, Very Revd Goran Spaic

OTHER NATIONALITIES

The Patriarchates of Romania and Bulgaria (Diocese of Western Europe) have memberships estimated at 20,000 and 2,000 respectively, while the Georgian Orthodox Church has around 500 members. The Belarusian (membership estimated at 2,400) and Latvian (membership of around 100) Orthodox churches are part of the Patriarchate of Constantinople.

ORIENTAL ORTHODOX CHURCHES

The term 'Oriental Orthodox Churches' is now generally used to describe a group of six ancient eastern churches (Armenian, Coptic, Eritrean, Ethiopian, Indian (Malankara) and Syrian) which rejected the Christological definition of the Council of Chalcedon (AD 451). There are around 50 million members worldwide of the Oriental Orthodox Churches and over 20,000 in the UK.

COUNCIL OF ORIENTAL ORTHODOX CHURCHES IN THE UK AND IRELAND, 264 Upper Fant Road, Maidstone, Kent ME16 8BX E fatherpeter@britishorthodox.org W www.orientalcounciluk.org
Secretary, Fr Peter Farrington

ARMENIAN ORTHODOX CHURCH (CATHOLICOSATE OF ETCHMIADZIN)

The Armenian Orthodox Church is led by HH Karekin II, Catholicos of All Armenians. The Rt. Revd Dr Vahan Hovhanessian is the Primate of the Armenian Church of the UK and Ireland and President of the Armenian Community and Church Council.
ARMENIAN CHURCH OF GREAT BRITAIN, The Armenian Vicarage, Iverna Gardens, London W8 6TP T 020-7937 0152 E information@armenianchurch.org.uk W www.armenianchurch.co.uk
Primate, Rt. Revd Bishop Dr Vahan Hovhanessian

COPTIC ORTHODOX CHURCH

The Coptic Orthodox Church is headed by Pope Tawadros II, who was appointed in November 2012. There are three dioceses in the UK: the Midlands, led by HG Bishop Missael; Ireland, Scotland and north-east England, led by HG Bishop Antony; and the Papal Diocese which is led by HG Bishop Angaelos and covers all the remaining parishes in the UK.
CATHEDRAL OF ST GEORGE AT THE COPTIC ORTHODOX CHURCH CENTRE, Shephalbury Manor, Broadhall Way, Stevenage, Herts SG2 8NP T 020-7993 9001 E admin@copticcentre.com W www.copticcentre.com
Bishop, HG Bishop Angaelos

BRITISH ORTHODOX CHURCH

The British Orthodox Church is canonically part of the Coptic Orthodox Patriarchate of Alexandria. As it ministers to British people, all of its services are in English.
THE BRITISH ORTHODOX CHURCH, 10 Heathwood Gardens, Charlton, London SE7 8EP T 020-8854 3090 E info@britishorthodox.org W www.britishorthodox.org
Metropolitan, Abba Seraphim

ERITREAN ORTHODOX TEWAHEDO CHURCH

The Eritrean Orthodox Church was granted independence in 1994 by Pope Shenouda III, following the declaration of Eritrea's independence from Ethiopia in 1993. In 2006, the Eritrean government removed the third patriarch, Abune Antonios, from office and imprisoned him; the government replaced him with Abune Dioskoros in 2007, although the Oriental Orthodox Churches continue to recognise Antonios as the rightful patriarch.
ERITREAN DIOCESE OFFICE (UK), 40 Raleigh Mews, Queen's Head Street, London N1 8NA E info@eritreanorthodoxchurch.org
Diocesan Bishop, HG Abune Makarios

INDIAN ORTHODOX CHURCH

The Indian Orthodox Church, also known as the Malankara Orthodox Church, traces its origins to the first century. The mother church of all the parishes in the UK and the Republic of Ireland is St Gregorios Church in London. The London parish has around 280 families as practising members.
INDIAN ORTHODOX CHURCH, St Gregorios Indian Orthodox Church, Cranfield Road, Brockley, London SE4 1UF T 020-8691 9456 E vicar@indian-orthodox.co.uk W www.indian-orthodox.co.uk
Diocesan Metropolitan, HG Dr Mathews Mar Thimothios
Vicar, Revd Fr Thomas P. John

SYRIAN ORTHODOX CHURCH

The Syrian (Syriac) Orthodox Church of Antioch is an Oriental Orthodox Church based in the Eastern Mediterranean. The Patriarchate Vicariate in the UK is represented by HE Archbishop Mor Athanasius Toma Dawood.

SYRIAN ORTHODOX CHURCH IN THE UK, St Thomas
Cathedral, 7–11 Armstrong Road, London W3 /JL
T 020-8749 5834 E enquiry-uk@syrianorthodoxchurch.net
W www.syrianorthodoxchurch.net
Archbishop, HE Mor Athanasius Toma Dawood

PENTECOSTAL CHURCHES

Pentecostalism is inspired by the descent of the Holy Spirit upon the apostles at Pentecost. The movement began in Los Angeles, USA, in 1906 and is characterised by baptism with the Holy Spirit, divine healing, speaking in tongues (glossolalia) and a literal interpretation of the scriptures.

The Pentecostal movement in Britain dates from 1907. Initially, groups of Pentecostalists were led by laymen and did not organise formally. However, in 1915 the Elim Foursquare Gospel Alliance (more commonly called the Elim Pentecostal Church) was founded in Ireland by George Jeffreys and currently has about 550 churches, 68,500 adherents and 650 accredited ministers. In 1924 about 70 independent assemblies formed a fellowship called Assemblies of God in Great Britain and Ireland, which now incorporates around 570 churches, around 75,000 adherents and 1,015 ministers.

The Apostolic Church grew out of the 1904–5 Christian revivals in South Wales and was established in 1916. The Apostolic Church has around 110 churches, 7,180 adherents and 115 ministers in the UK. The New Testament Church of God was established in England in 1953 and has over 125 congregations, nearly 30,000 members and over 300 ministers across England and Wales.

In recent years many aspects of Pentecostalism have been adopted by the growing charismatic movement within the Roman Catholic, Protestant and Eastern Orthodox churches. There are about 105 million Pentecostalists worldwide, with over 350,000 adherents in the UK.

THE APOSTOLIC CHURCH, PO Box 51298, London
SE11 9AJ T 020-7587 1802 E admin@apostolic-church.org
W www.apostolic-church.org
National Leader, Emmanuel Mbakwe
ASSEMBLIES OF GOD, National Ministry Centre, Mattersey,
Doncaster DN10 5HD T 017-7781 7663 E info@aog.org.uk
W www.aog.org.uk
National Leader, John Partington
THE ELIM PENTECOSTAL CHURCH, Elim International
Centre, De Walden Road, West Malvern, Worcestershire
WR14 4DF T 0345-302 6750 E info@elimhq.net
W www.elim.org.uk
General Superintendent, Revd John Glass
THE NEW TESTAMENT CHURCH OF GOD, National
Office, 3 Cheyne Walk, Northampton NN1 5PT
T 01604-824222 W www.ntcg.org.uk
Administrative Bishop, Donald Bolt

PRESBYTERIAN CHURCH IN IRELAND

Irish Presbyterianism traces its origins back to the Plantation of Ulster in 1606, when English and Scottish Protestants began to settle on the land confiscated from the Irish chieftains. The first presbytery was established in Ulster in 1642 by chaplains of a Scottish army that had been sent to crush a Catholic rebellion in 1641.

The Presbyterian Church in Ireland is reformed in doctrine and belongs to the World Alliance of Reformed Churches. Structurally, the 545 congregations are grouped in 19 presbyteries under the General Assembly. This body meets annually and is presided over by a moderator who is elected for one year. The ongoing work of the church is undertaken by 12 boards under which there are specialist committees.

There are over 240,000 members of Irish presbyterian churches in Ireland and Northern Ireland.

THE PRESBYTERIAN CHURCH IN IRELAND, Assembly
Buildings, 2–10 Fisherwick Place, Belfast BT1 6DW
T 028-9032 2284 E info@presbyterianireland.org
W www.presbyterianireland.org
Moderator (2014–15), Rt. Revd Dr Michael Barry
Clerk of Assembly and General Secretary, Revd Dr Donald
Watts

PRESBYTERIAN CHURCH OF WALES

The Presbyterian Church of Wales or Calvinistic Methodist Church of Wales is Calvinistic in doctrine and presbyterian in constitution. It was formed in 1811 when Welsh Calvinists severed the relationship with the established church by ordaining their own ministers. It secured its own confession of faith in 1823 and a Constitutional Deed in 1826, and since 1864 the General Assembly has met annually, presided over by a moderator elected for a year. The doctrine and constitutional structure of the Presbyterian Church of Wales was confirmed by act of parliament in 1931–2.

The Church has 25,000 members, 58 ministers and 653 congregations.

THE PRESBYTERIAN CHURCH OF WALES, Tabernacle
Chapel, 81 Merthyr Road, Whitchurch, Cardiff CF14 1DD
T 029-2062 7465 E swyddfa.office@ebcpcw.org.uk
W www.ebcpcw.org.uk
Moderator (2014–15), Revd Neil Kirkham
General Secretary, Revd Meirion Morris

RELIGIOUS SOCIETY OF FRIENDS (QUAKERS)

Quakerism is a religious denomination which was founded in the 17th century by George Fox and others in an attempt to revive what they saw as the original 'primitive Christianity'. The movement, at first called Friends of the Truth, started in the Midlands, Yorkshire and north-west England, but there are now Quakers all over the UK and in 36 countries around the world. The colony of Pennsylvania, founded by William Penn, was originally a Quaker settlement.

Quakers place an emphasis on the experience of God in daily life rather than on sacraments or religious occasions. There is no church calendar. Worship is largely silent and there are no appointed ministers; the responsibility for conducting a meeting is shared equally among those present. Religious tolerance and social reform have always been important to Quakers, together with a commitment to peace and non-violence in resolving disputes.

There are more than 23,000 'friends' or Quakers in Great Britain. There are around 475 places where Quaker meetings are held, many of them Quaker-owned Friends Meeting Houses. The Britain Yearly Meeting is the name given to the central organisation of Quakers in Britain.

THE RELIGIOUS SOCIETY OF FRIENDS (QUAKERS)
IN BRITAIN, Friends House, 173–177 Euston Road, London
NW1 2BJ T 020-7663 1000 E enquiries@quaker.org.uk
W www.quaker.org.uk
Recording Clerk, Paul Parker

SALVATION ARMY

The Salvation Army is an international Christian organisation working in 126 countries worldwide. As a church and registered charity, The Salvation Army is funded through donations from its members, the general public and, where appropriate, government grants.

The Salvation Army was founded by Methodists William and Catherine Booth, in the East End of London in 1865, and now has around 50,000 members and 1,500 Salvation Army Officers (full-time ministers) in the UK. There are over 800 local church and community centres, 62 residential support centres for homeless people, 15 care homes for older people and six substance-misuse centres. It also runs a clothing recycling programme, charity shops, foodbanks, a prison-visiting service and a family-tracing service. In 1878 it adopted a quasi-military command structure intended to inspire and regulate its endeavours and to reflect its view that the church was engaged in spiritual warfare.

UK TERRITORIAL HEADQUARTERS, 101 Newington Causeway, London SE1 6BN **T** 020-7367 4500
E info@salvationarmy.org.uk **W** www.salvationarmy.org.uk
UK Territorial Commanders, Commissioners Clive and Marianne Adams

SEVENTH-DAY ADVENTIST CHURCH
The Seventh-day Adventist Church is a worldwide Christian church marked by its observance of Saturday as the Sabbath and by its emphasis on the imminent second coming of Jesus Christ. Adventists summarise their faith in '28 fundamental beliefs'.

The church grew out of the Millerite movement in the USA during the mid-19th century and was formally established in 1863. The church has an ethnically and culturally diverse worldwide membership of over 17 million. In the UK and Ireland there are 34,048 members worshipping in around 300 churches and companies.

BRITISH UNION CONFERENCE OF SEVENTH-DAY ADVENTISTS, Stanborough Park, Watford WD25 9JZ
T 01923-672251 **E** info@adventist.org.uk
W www.adventist.org.uk
President, Pastor Ian Sweeney

THE (SWEDENBORGIAN) NEW CHURCH
The New Church is based on the teachings of the 18th-century Swedish scientist and theologian Emanuel Swedenborg (1688–1772), who believed that Jesus Christ appeared to him and instructed him to reveal the spiritual meaning of the Bible. He claimed to have visions of the spiritual world, including heaven and hell, and conversations with angels and spirits. He published several theological works, including descriptions of the spiritual world and a Bible commentary.

Swedenborgians believe that the second coming of Jesus Christ is taking place, being not an actual physical reappearance of Christ, but rather his return in spirit. It is also believed that concurrent with our life on earth is life in a parallel spiritual world, of which we are usually unconscious until death. There are around 30,000 Swedenborgians worldwide, with around 8,500 members, 19 churches and 13 ministers in the UK.

THE GENERAL CONFERENCE OF THE NEW CHURCH, Purley Chase Centre, Purley Chase Lane, Mancetter, Warwickshire CV9 2RQ **T** 01827-712370
E enquiries@generalconference.org.uk
W www.generalconference.org.uk
Company Secretary, Zoë Brooks

UNDEB YR ANNIBYNWYR CYMRAEG
Undeb Yr Annibynwyr Cymraeg (the Union of Welsh Independents) was formed in 1872 and is a voluntary association of Welsh Congregational churches and personal members. It is mainly Welsh-speaking. Congregationalism in Wales dates back to 1639 when the first Welsh Congregational church was opened in Gwent.

Member churches are traditionally congregationalist in organisation and Calvinistic in doctrine, although a wide range of interpretations are permitted. Each church has complete independence in the governance and administration of its affairs.

The Union has around 24,000 members, 80 ministers and 440 member churches.

UNDEB YR ANNIBYNWYR CYMRAEG, 5 Axis Court, Riverside Business Park, Swansea Vale, Swansea SA7 0AJ
T 01792-795888 **E** undeb@annibynwyr.org
W www.annibynwyr.org
President of the Union (2014–16), Revd Dr R. Alun Evans
General Secretary, Revd Dr Geraint Tudur

UNITED REFORMED CHURCH
The United Reformed Church (URC) was first formed by the union of most of the Congregational churches in England and Wales with the Presbyterian Church of England in 1972. It is Calvinistic in doctrine, and its followers form independent self-governing congregations bound under God by covenant, a principle laid down in the writings of Robert Browne (1550–1633). From the late 16th century the movement was driven underground by persecution, but the cause was defended at the Westminster Assembly in 1643 and the Savoy Declaration of 1658 laid down its principles. Congregational churches formed county associations for mutual support and in 1832 these associations merged to form the Congregational Union of England and Wales.

In the 1960s there was close cooperation locally and nationally between congregational and presbyterian churches. This led to union negotiations and a Scheme of Union, supported by an act of parliament in 1972. In 1981 a further unification took place, with the Reformed Association of Churches of Christ becoming part of the URC. In 2000 a third union took place, with the Congregational Union of Scotland. At its basis the URC reflects local church initiative and responsibility with a conciliar pattern of oversight.

The URC is divided into 13 synods, each with a synod moderator. There are around 1,500 churches which serve over 60,000 adults and around 42,000 children and young people. There are around 570 ministers in active service.

The General Assembly is the central body, and comprises around 400 representatives, mainly appointed by the synods, of which half are lay persons and half are ministers. Since 2010 the General Assembly has met biennially to elect two moderators (one lay and one ordained), who then become the public representatives of the URC.

UNITED REFORMED CHURCH, 86 Tavistock Place, London WC1H 9RT **T** 020-7916 2020 **E** urc@urc.org.uk
W www.urc.org.uk
Moderators of the General Assembly (2014–16), John Ellis; Revd David Grosch-Miller
General Secretary, Revd John Proctor

WESLEYAN REFORM UNION
The Wesleyan Reform Union was founded by Methodists who left or were expelled from Wesleyan Methodism in 1849 following a period of internal conflict. Its doctrine is conservative evangelical and its organisation is congregational, each church having complete independence in the government and administration of its affairs. The union has around 1,540 members, 20 ministers and 96 churches.

THE WESLEYAN REFORM UNION, Wesleyan Reform Church House, 123 Queen Street, Sheffield S1 2DU
T 0114-272 1938 **E** gen.sec@thewru.co.uk
W www.thewru.com
President (2014–15), George Philips
General Secretary, Revd Colin Braithwaite

NON-TRINITARIAN CHURCHES

CHRISTADELPHIAN
Christadelphians believe that the Bible is the word of God and that it reveals both God's dealings with mankind in the past and his plans for the future. These plans centre on the

work of Jesus Christ, who it is believed will return to Earth to establish God's kingdom. The Christadelphian group was founded in the USA in the 1830s by the Englishman, Dr John Thomas.

THE CHRISTADELPHIAN MAGAZINE AND
   PUBLISHING ASSOCIATION, 404 Shaftmoor Lane, Hall
   Green, Birmingham B28 8SZ T 0121-777 6328
   E enquiries@thechristadelphian.com
   W www.thechristadelphian.com

CHURCH OF CHRIST, SCIENTIST

The Church of Christ, Scientist was founded by Mary Baker Eddy in the USA in 1879 to 'reinstate primitive Christianity and its lost element of healing'. Christian Science teaches the need for spiritual regeneration and salvation from sin, but it is best known for its reliance on prayer alone in the healing of sickness. Adherents believe that such healing is the result of divine laws, or divine science, and is in direct line with that practised by Jesus Christ (revered, not as God, but as the son of God) and by the early Christian church.

The denomination consists of The First Church of Christ, Scientist, in Boston, Massachusetts, USA ('The Mother Church') and its branch churches in almost 80 countries worldwide. The Bible and Mary Baker Eddy's book, *Science and Health with Key to the Scriptures,* are used for daily spiritual guidance and healing by all members and are read at services. There are no clergy; those engaged in full-time healing are called Christian Science practitioners, of whom there are around 1,500 worldwide. The church also publishes *The Christian Science Monitor.*

No membership figures are available, since Mary Baker Eddy felt that numbers are no measure of spiritual vitality and ruled that such statistics should not be published. There are almost 2,000 branch churches worldwide, including over 100 in the UK.

CHRISTIAN SCIENCE COMMITTEE ON
   PUBLICATION, 90 Long Acre, London WC2E 9RZ
   T 020-8150 0245 E londoncs@csps.com
   W www.christianscience.co.uk
   District Manager for the UK and Ireland, Tony Lobl

CHURCH OF JESUS CHRIST OF LATTER-DAY SAINTS

The Church of Jesus Christ of Latter-day Saints (often referred to as 'the Mormon Church') was founded in New York State, USA, in 1830, and came to Britain in 1837. The oldest continuous congregation of the church is in Preston, Lancashire.

Mormons are Christians who claim to belong to the 'restored church' of Jesus Christ. They believe that true Christianity died when the last original apostle died, but that it was given back to the world by God and Jesus Christ through Joseph Smith, the church's founder and first president. They accept and use the Bible as scripture, but believe in continuing revelation from God; Mormons also use additional scriptures, including *The Book of Mormon: Another Testament of Jesus Christ.* The importance of the family is central to the church's beliefs and practices. Church members set aside Monday evenings as family home evenings when Christian family values are taught. Polygamy was formally discontinued in 1890.

The church has no paid ministry: local congregations are headed by a leader chosen from among their number. The world governing body, based in Utah, USA, is led by a president, believed to be the chosen prophet, and his two counsellors. There are 14.8 million members worldwide, with 188,426 members and 333 congregations in the UK.

THE CHURCH OF JESUS CHRIST OF LATTER-DAY
   SAINTS, UK Headquarters, 751 Warwick Road, Solihull,
   W. Midlands B91 3DQ T 0121-712 1161 W www.lds.org.uk

JEHOVAH'S WITNESSES

The movement now known as Jehovah's Witnesses grew from a Bible study group formed by Charles Taze Russell in 1872 in Pennsylvania, USA. In 1896 it adopted the name of the Watch Tower Bible and Tract Society, and in 1931 its members became known as Jehovah's Witnesses.

Jehovah's (God's) Witnesses believe in the Bible as the word of God, and consider it to be inspired and historically accurate. They take the scriptures literally, except where there are obvious indications that they are figurative or symbolic, and reject the doctrine of the Trinity. Witnesses also believe that all those approved of by Jehovah will have eternal life on a cleansed and beautified earth; only 144,000 will go to heaven to rule with Jesus Christ. They believe that the second coming of Christ began in 1914, that his thousand-year reign over the earth is imminent, and that armageddon (a final battle in which evil will be defeated) will precede Christ's rule of peace. Jehovah's Witnesses refuse to take part in military service and do not accept blood transfusions.

The eight-member world governing body is based in New York, USA. There is no paid ministry, but each congregation has elders assigned to look after various duties and every Witness takes part in the public ministry in their neighbourhood. There are 7.97 million Jehovah's Witnesses worldwide, with around 136,000 Witnesses in Great Britain organised into around 1,500 congregations.

BRITISH HEADQUARTERS, The Ridgeway, London
   NW7 1RN T 020-8906 2211 W www.jw.org

UNITARIAN AND FREE CHRISTIAN CHURCHES

Unitarianism has its historical roots in the Judaeo-Christian tradition but rejects the deity of Christ and the doctrine of the Trinity. It allows the individual to embrace insights from all of the world's faiths and philosophies, as there is no fixed creed. It is accepted that beliefs may evolve in the light of personal experience.

Unitarian communities first became established in Poland and Transylvania in the 16th century. The first avowedly Unitarian place of worship in the British Isles opened in London in 1774. The General Assembly of Unitarian and Free Christian Churches came into existence in 1928 as the result of the amalgamation of two earlier organisations.

There are around 3,400 Unitarians in Great Britain in 170 self-governing congregations and fellowship groups.

GENERAL ASSEMBLY OF UNITARIAN AND FREE
   CHRISTIAN CHURCHES, Essex Hall, 1–6 Essex Street,
   London WC2R 3HY T 020-7240 2384 E info@unitarian.org.uk
   W www.unitarian.org.uk
   President (2014–15), Marion Baker

COMMUNICATIONS

POSTAL SERVICES

Royal Mail was privatised on 15 October 2013 when it was listed on the London Stock Exchange. Royal Mail Holdings plc owns Royal Mail Group Ltd – which operates Royal Mail, Parcelforce Worldwide and General Logistics Systems (GLS) – and the Post Office Ltd.

Royal Mail is the sole provider of the 'universal service': postal products and associated minimum service standards that must be available to all addresses in the UK. In 2012–13 Royal Mail collected and delivered more than 1 billion parcels and 14 billion letters to 29 million addresses across the UK. The amount of mail sent on a daily basis decreased from around 63 million items in 2011–12 to 58 million items in 2012–13.

Following the passing of the Postal Services Act 2011, the Office of Communications (OFCOM) assumed regulatory responsibility for postal services. OFCOM's primary responsibility is to secure the provision of a universal postal service with regard to its financial sustainability.

ROYAL MAIL GROUP LTD, 100 Victoria Embankment, London EC4Y 0HQ T 0345-774 0740 W www.royalmailgroup.com

OFCOM, Riverside House, 2A Southwark Bridge Road, London SE1 9HA T 0300-123 3000 W www.ofcom.org.uk

PRICING IN PROPORTION

Since August 2006 Royal Mail has priced mail according to its size as well as its weight. The system is intended to reflect the fact that larger, bulkier items cost more to handle than smaller, lighter ones. There are four basic categories of correspondence:

LETTER: *Length* up to 240mm, *width* up to 165mm, *thickness* up to 5mm, *weight* up to 100g; eg most cards, postcards and bills

LARGE LETTER: *Length* up to 353mm, *width* up to 250mm, *thickness* up to 25mm, *weight* up to 750g; eg most A4 documents and magazines

SMALL PARCEL:

Wide option: Length up to 450mm, *width* up to 350mm, *thickness* up to 80mm, *weight* up to 2kg, eg books, clothes and gifts

Deep option: Length up to 350mm, *width* up to 250mm, *thickness* up to 160mm, *weight* up to 2kg, eg shoes, boots and gifts

MEDIUM PARCEL: *Length* up to 610mm, *width* up to 460mm, *thickness* up to 460mm, *weight* up to 20kg; eg gifts, shoes, heavy or bulky items

For rolled and cylinder shaped parcels, eg posters and prints, the length of the item plus twice the diameter must not exceed 104cm, with the greatest dimension being no more than 90cm. Rolled and cylinder shaped parcels which measure up to 450mm in length and 80mm in diameter and which do not exceed 2kg can be sent as small parcels. Items larger than those listed above can only be sent via Parcelforce Worldwide as large parcels.

INLAND POSTAL SERVICES

Following are details of a number of popular postal services along with prices correct as at June 2014. For a full list of prices *see* W www.royalmail.com

FIRST AND SECOND CLASS

Format	Maximum weight	First class	Second class*
Letter/postcard*	100g	£0.62	£0.53
Large letter	100g	£0.93	£0.73
	250g	£1.24	£1.17
	500g	£1.65	£1.48
	750g	£2.38	£2.01
Small parcel	1,000g	£3.20	£2.80
	2,000g	£5.45	£3.80
Medium parcel	1,000g	£5.65	£5.20
	2,000g	£8.90	£8.00
	5,000g	£15.85	£13.75
	10,000g	£21.90	£20.25
	20,000g	£33.40	£28.55

* First class post is normally delivered on the following working day and second class within three working days

LARGE PARCEL RATES*

Maximum weight	Lowest tariff
2kg	£9.99
5kg	£10.82
10kg	£13.67
15kg	£19.28
20kg	£23.76
25kg	£33.03
30kg	£36.48

* Up to 150cm long, with a combined length and width of less than 300cm and a maximum weight of 30 kg. The rate listed does not include VAT and is for delivery within two working days.

OVERSEAS POSTAL SERVICES

For charging purposes Royal Mail divides the world into four zones: UK, Europe, World Zone 1 and World Zone 2. A complete listing can be found at W www.royalmail.com/international-zones

Europe: Albania, Andorra, Armenia, Austria, Azerbaijan, Azores, Balearic Islands, Belarus, Belgium, Bosnia and Hercegovina, Bulgaria, Canary Islands, Corsica, Croatia, Cyprus, Czech Rep., Denmark, Estonia, Finland, France, Georgia, Germany, Gibraltar, Greece, Greenland, Hungary, Iceland, Ireland, Italy, Kazakhstan, Kosovo, Kyrgyzstan, Latvia, Liechtenstein, Lithuania, Luxembourg, Macedonia, Malta, Moldova, Monaco, Montenegro, Netherlands, Norway, Poland, Portugal, Romania, Russia, San Marino, Serbia, Slovakia, Slovenia, Spain, Sweden, Switzerland, Tajikistan, Turkey, Turkmenistan, Ukraine, Uzbekistan

World Zone 1: N. America, S. America, Africa, the Middle East, the Far East and S. E. Asia

World Zone 2: Australia, British Indian Ocean Territory, Fiji, French Polynesia, Kiribati, Laos, Macau, Nauru, New Caledonia, New Zealand, Palau, Papua New Guinea, Pitcairn Islands, Singapore, Solomon Islands, Tonga, Tuvalu, Samoa

INTERNATIONAL ECONOMY MAIL RATES*

Maximum weight	Standard tariff
Letters up to 100g†	
20g	£0.81
60g	£1.43
100g	£2.02
Small parcels up to 100g	£2.80
Letters, small parcels and printed papers over 100g	£3.65

plus an additional £1.45, for each 250g or part thereof, up to 2,000g‡

* Formerly Surface Mail
† Can only be sent by International Economy to destinations outside of Europe
‡ Up to 5,000g for printed papers

INTERNATIONAL STANDARD MAIL RATES*

Maximum weight	Standard tariff
EUROPE	
Letters up to 100g	
20g	£0.97
60g	£1.47
100g	2.35
Small parcels up to 100g	
100g	£3.20
Letters, small parcels and printed papers over 100g	
250g	£3.70

plus an additional £1.45, for each 250g or part thereof, up to 2,000g†

WORLD ZONE 1	
Letters up to 100g	
10g	£0.97
20g	£1.28
60g	£2.15
100g	£3.48
Small parcels up to 100g	
100g	£3.80
Letters, small parcels and printed papers over 100g	
250g	£4.75

plus an additional £2.70, for each 250g or part thereof, up to 2,000g†

WORLD ZONE 2	
Letters up to 100g	
10g	£0.97
20g	£1.28
60g	£2.15
100g	£3.48
Small parcels up to 100g	
100g	£4.00
Letters, small parcels and printed papers over 100g	
250g	£5.05

plus an additional £2.85, for each 250g or part thereof, up to 2,000g†

* Formerly Airmail
† Up to 5,000g for printed papers

SPECIAL DELIVERY SERVICES

INTERNATIONAL TRACKED AND SIGNED FOR SERVICES

There are various services available: International Tracked & Signed provides full end-to-end tracking, signature on delivery and online delivery confirmation; International Tracked provides tracking at five points after dispatch and online confirmation of delivery; and International Signed provides tracking in the UK plus a signature from the recipient. All Tracked and Signed For services deliver to Europe within 3–5 working days, and worldwide within 5–7 working days. Proof of posting and compensation up to £50 is provided as standard. Additional compensation up to £250 can be provided for an extra fee.

SAME DAY

A courier service which provides same day delivery of urgent items in most places in the UK. With collection within the hour of booking, satellite tracking, delivery confirmation and automatic compensation up to £2,500, and for an additional fee, up to £20,000, the service is charged for on a loaded mile basis T 0845-850 5522

SIGNED FOR

A service which offers proof of delivery including a signature from the receiver and compensation cover up to £50. The first class service is delivered the next working day and prices vary from £1.72 to £34.50 depending on the size and weight of the item. The second class service allows two to three working days for delivery with a charge of £1.63 to £29.65.

SPECIAL DELIVERY GUARANTEED

A guaranteed next working day delivery service by 9am or 1pm with a refund option guaranteed for late delivery. With many options available, Royal Mail offers a full list of prices online W www.royalmail.com/personal/uk-delivery/special-delivery

OTHER SERVICES

KEEPSAFE

Mail is held for up to two months while the addressee is away, and is delivered when the addressee returns. Prices start at £12.80 for 17 days up to £42.30 for 66 days.

PASSPORT CHECK & SEND

For a fee of £8.75 passport applications are checked to ensure they meet the requirements set by HM Passport Office and are dispatched by special delivery. For further information *see* W www.postoffice.co.uk

POST OFFICE BOX

A Post Office (PO) Box provides a short and memorable alternative address. Mail is held at a local delivery office until the addressee is ready to collect it, or delivered to a street address for an extra fee. Prices start at £142.90 for six months or £251.77 for a year.

POSTCODE FINDER

Customers can search an online database to find UK postcodes and addresses. For more information *see* Royal Mail's postcode finder W www.royalmail.com/postcode-finder

REDELIVERY

Customers can request a redelivery of an item for up to 18 days if it was unable to be delivered. A 48-hour notice period is required for redelivery or the item can be held at the recipient's local Post Office branch for a fee of £1.50 upon collection in addition to proof of identity and the original delivery notification card.

REDIRECTION

Customers may arrange the redirection of their mail via post, at the Post Office or online, subject to verification of their identity. The service is available for 0–3 months, 3–6 months or 6–12 months at varying prices depending on the location of delivery. A full price list is available at W www.royalmail.com/personal/receiving-mail/redirection

TRACK AND TRACE

An online service for customers to track the progress of items sent using any special delivery tracked and signed for service. It is accessible from W www.royalmail.com/track-trace

CONTACTS

Parcelforce Worldwide
    T 0844-800 4466 W www.parcelforce.com
Post Office enquiries T 0845-611 2970 W www.postoffice.co.uk
Postcode enquiry line T 0906-302 1222/ 0845-711 1222

TELECOMMUNICATIONS

Mobile network technology has improved dramatically since the launch in 1985 of the first-generation global system for mobile communications (GSM), which offered little or no data capability. In 1992 Vodafone launched a new GSM network, usually referred to as 2G or second generation, which used digital encoding and allowed voice and low-speed data communications. This technology was extended, via the enhanced data transfer rate of 2.5G, to 3G – a family of mobile standards that provide high bandwidth support to applications such as voice- and video-calling, high-speed data transfer, television streaming and full internet access. Most recently, a 4G superfast mobile spectrum was rolled out, which delivers speeds of up to 100 megabits per second (Mbps), allowing for faster download speeds on a range of devices.

FOURTH GENERATION (4G) AND WI-FI
In March 2011 OFCOM announced plans for the auction of additional spectrum (the airwaves on which all communications rely) to provide the necessary capacity for 4G technology in the UK. OFCOM originally aimed to begin the auction in early 2012, but following a consultation regarding the proposals in 2011, the auction did not take place until February 2013. The spectrum was auctioned in two bands – 800 MHz and 2.6 GHz – which lie within the 'sweetspot', the frequency in greatest demand. This combination of low and high frequencies provides the potential to cope with high demand of 4G services. The auction raised £2.34bn for HM Treasury, less than the £3.5bn that was forecast by the Office for Budget Responsibility, and considerably less than the 3G auction in 2000 which raised £22bn. The winning bidders for the distribution of 4G mobile broadband were Everything Everywhere (EE), Hutchison 3G UK (3), Niche Spectrum Ventures (a BT subsidiary), Telefonica (O2) and Vodafone.

4G coverage is expected to cover 98 per cent of the UK population indoors and above that when outdoors. The speeds offered by 4G are approximately five to ten times faster than 3G networks which allows for higher quality and faster streaming of media such as TV and films. The UK population in more rural areas that was often outside 3G coverage should also be able to access mobile broadband through the 4G spectrum.

EE was the first operator to launch 4G in late 2012 and by April 2013 the service was available in ten cities where the broadband speed was doubled to more than 20Mbps. O2 and Vodafone subsequently launched their 4G networks in late August 2013 while 3 began their service in December 2013. As at March 2014 EE, the largest network provider of 4G, had rolled out 4G coverage to around 180 towns and cities and by the end of 2014, forecasts 4G coverage for 98 per cent of the UK population.

The use of Wi-Fi (wireless networking) saw no change in 2013 as the UK remained second behind South Korea as the country with the highest number of public Wi-Fi locations. In the fourth quarter of 2013, the UK had 182,610 recognised hotspots, around 30,000 more locations than the

USA. Following the 2012 Olympic Games in London, there is Wi-Fi access at 130 London Underground stations, available for a fee in ticket halls, corridors and platforms. Additionally Wi-Fi is also available at 56 London Overground stations.

FIXED-LINE SERVICES
2012 saw a further decline in the number of fixed lines in the UK to 33.1 million connections from 33.3 million connections in 2011, following a trend which began in 2002. Business customers continued to gravitate towards the use of mobile phones, emails and voice over internet protocol (VoIP) services such as Skype, with a decline of 0.6 million (6.3 per cent) to 8.8 million in the number of business lines in 2012.

The decrease in the number of business lines was offset slightly by a small increase in the number of residential lines which rose by 0.5 million (2.0 per cent) to 24.4 million in 2012. The increase is most likely due to the necessity of UK households to have a fixed line in order to receive fixed broadband services. The average cost of a residential fixed broadband connection increased in 2012 to £16.35 (1.1 per cent) due to the take-up of superfast broadband services. In turn, the average headline speed increased by 4.5Mbps to 12.0Mbps, while users who invested in higher speed packages, including superfast services received a headline speed of up to 30Mbps or more. In the year to November 2012, the proportion of superfast fixed broadband connections increased from 5 to 13 per cent.

MOBILE COMMUNICATIONS
OFCOM reported that 92 per cent of adults in the UK own or use a mobile phone, while 51 per cent of adults own a smartphone. The volume of outgoing SMS messages in the fourth quarter of 2012 was 37.1 billion, 6.5 per cent less than the same quarter in 2011. The decline in text messaging is likely to be a result of the of the increasing number of smartphones being used for communication, with social media platforms and instant messaging services such as WhatsApp, often pre-installed, providing increased availability of alternatives to SMS. The total number of mobile connections continued to increase in 2012, by 1.3 per cent to 82.7 million. This figure is under half the annual average increase of 3.1 per cent recorded over the previous five years.

According to OFCOM's *Communications Market Report 2013* around half a million UK mobile subscribers have signed up to 4G services, representing 0.5 per cent of all UK mobile subscribers. An estimated 40.5 million mobile subscribers used their mobiles phones to access the internet

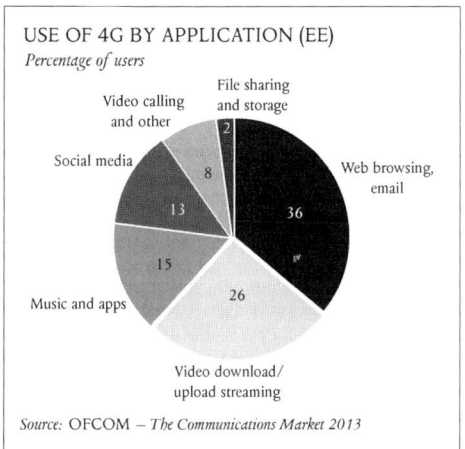

USE OF 4G BY APPLICATION (EE)
Percentage of users

Source: OFCOM – *The Communications Market 2013*

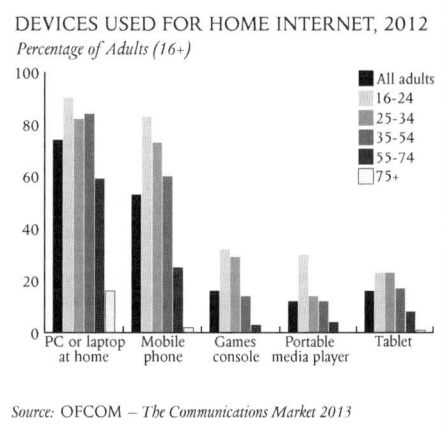

DEVICES USED FOR HOME INTERNET, 2012
Percentage of Adults (16+)

Source: OFCOM – *The Communications Market 2013*

in 2012, an increase of 14.5 million from 2010. Machine-to-machine (M2M) was a particularly large growth area for the mobile market in 2012, experiencing an increase of 1.1 million connections to 4.9 million by the end of the year. M2M includes cellular communications between machines as opposed to people, including smart electricity meters and office equipment.

MOBILE INTERNET USAGE

In February 2013, more than 30 per cent of web traffic came via mobile phones and tablets. In the 11-month period to February 2013, the proportion of web-page views from mobile phones almost tripled to 23 per cent while web-page views from tablets doubled to 8 per cent. Instant messaging similarly increased in popularity, with the total volume of instant messages sent in the UK increasing from 37 billion in 2011 to 57 billion in 2012, the equivalent of an increase from 49 to 75 messages per person per month.

HEALTH

In 1999 the Independent Expert Group on Mobile Phones (IEGMP) was established to examine the possible effects on health of mobile phones, base stations and transmitters. The main findings of the IEGMP's report *Mobile Phones and Health,* published in May 2000, were:
- exposure to radio frequency radiation below guideline levels did not cause adverse health effects to the general population
- the use of mobile phones by drivers of any vehicle can increase the chance of accidents
- the widespread use of mobile phones by children for non-essential calls should be discouraged because if there are unrecognised adverse health effects children may be more vulnerable
- there is no general risk to the health of people living near to base stations on the basis that exposures are expected to be much lower than guidelines set by the International Commission on Non-Ionising Radiation Protection

The government set up the Mobile Telecommunications Health and Research (MTHR) programme in 2001 to undertake independent research into the possible health risks from mobile telephone technology. The MTHR programme published its report in September 2007 concluding that, in the short term, neither mobile phones nor base stations have been found to be associated with any biological or adverse health effects. An international cohort study into the possible long-term health effects of mobile phone use was launched by the MTHR in April 2010. The study is known as COSMOS and aims to follow the health of 250,000 mobile phone users from five countries over 20 to 30 years. The full 2007 report and details of COSMOS can be found on the MTHR website (W www.mthr.org.uk).

A national measurement programme, to ensure that emissions from mobile phone base stations do not exceed the ICNIRP guideline levels, is overseen by OFCOM and annual audits of these levels can be found on the sitefinder part of its website. The Health Protection Agency (HPA), part of Public Health England from 1 April 2013, is responsible for providing information and advice in relation to the health effects of electromagnetic fields, including those emitted from mobile phones and base stations. In April 2012, the HPA's independent Advisory Group on Non-ionising Radiation published a report concluding that there was no convincing evidence that mobile phone technologies cause adverse effects on human health.

SAFETY WHILE DRIVING

Under legislation that came into effect in December 2003 it is illegal for drivers to use a hand-held mobile phone while driving. Since February 2007, under the Road Safety Act 2006, the fixed penalty for using a hand-held mobile device while driving is £100 and three penalty points. The same fixed penalty can also be issued to a driver for not having proper control of a vehicle while using a hands-free device. If the police or driver chooses to take the case to court rather than issue or accept a fixed penalty notice, the driver may be disqualified from driving in addition to a maximum fine of £1,000 for car drivers and £2,500 for drivers of buses, coaches or heavy goods vehicles. The only exceptions for using a mobile phone while driving are to call the emergency services, or when the driver is safely parked.

REGULATION

Under the Communications Act 2003, OFCOM is the independent regulator and competition authority for the UK communications industries, with responsibilities across television, radio, telecommunications and wireless communications services. Competition in the communications market is also regulated by the Office of Fair Trading, although OFCOM takes the lead in competition investigations in the UK market. The Competition Appeal Tribunal hears appeals against OFCOM's decisions, and price-related appeals are referred to the Competition Commission.

CONTACTS

OFCOM, Riverside House, 2A Southwark Bridge Road, London SE1 9HA T 020-7981 3040 W www.ofcom.org.uk

INTERNET

In 2013, 21 million households in Great Britain had internet access. This represented 83 per cent of households, up from 80 per cent in 2012. Of the households with internet access, 93 per cent used a fixed broadband connection, of which 42 per cent used a cable or fibre optic connection.

There was rapid growth in the use of tablet computers to access the internet, with 32 per cent of adults using a tablet to access the internet outside of the home or workplace in 2013, although 34 per cent of people still used a laptop to access the internet 'on the go'.

Over a three-year period between 2010–13, the number of adults who used a mobile phone to access the internet increased from 24 per cent to 53 per cent, with 94 per cent of those aged 16 to 24 reporting that they used their mobile phone to access the internet in 2013. The dramatic increase in these figures is predominantly due to the ownership of smartphones with enhanced technology to facilitate easier internet access.

In 2013, 53 per cent of 16 to 65 year olds used social networking sites such as Facebook and Twitter with 93 per cent of those aged 16 to 24 using these media platforms as a form of internet communication. For this age range, social networking has replaced sending emails as the most popular internet activity.

The youngest demographic represented, aged 16 to 24, were proportionally the largest users of many of the available internet activities, due to their familiarity with internet usage from an early age. This age group were most likely to engage in online activities including social networking, blogging, or downloading games, films or music. Those aged 25 to 34 engaged in more established activities such as personal banking and shopping – the latter saw an increased demand in Great Britain, with 72 per cent of adults buying goods or services online in 2013. A rise in internet shopping was also evident among those aged over 65, as nearly 36 per cent made purchases online, over twice as many as in 2008.

There were 4 million households with no internet access in 2013, the majority (59 per cent) stating they did not need it. One in five households said they did not have an internet connection due to a lack of computer skills, while other reasons included equipment and access costs. In 2012, 36 million adults accessed the internet daily, more than double the figure that did so in 2006.

TOP 10 BROADBAND SUBSCRIBERS BY COUNTRY

Country (2012 position)	2012
1. China (all territories) (1)	184,030,000
2. USA (2)	94,380,000
3. Japan (3)	34,860,000
4. Germany (4)	29,860,000
5. Russia (5)	24,120,000
6. France (6)	23,610,000
7. United Kingdom (7)	22,280,000
8. Brazil (9)	20,440,000
9. South Korea (8)	18,540,000
10. India (10)	15,210,000

Sources: Office for National Statistics – *Internet Access – Households and Individuals, 2013* (Crown Copyright); www.point-topic.com

GLOSSARY OF TERMS

The following is a list of selected internet terms. It is by no means exhaustive but is intended to cover those that the average computer user might encounter.

BANNER AD: An advertisement on a web page that links to a corresponding website when clicked.

BLOG: Short for 'web log' – an online personal journal that is frequently updated and intended to be read by the public. Blogs are kept by 'bloggers' and are commonly available as RSS feeds.

BOOKMARKS: A method of storing links or automatic pathways within web browsers which allow a user to quickly return to a webpage. Referred to as 'Favourites' in Internet Explorer.

BROWSER: Typically refers to a 'web browser' program that allows a computer user to view web page content on their computer, eg Firefox, Internet Explorer or Safari.

CLICK-THROUGH: The number of times a web user 'clicks through' a paid advertisement link to the corresponding website.

CLOUD COMPUTING: The use of IT resources as an on-demand service across a network; through cloud computing, software, advanced computation and archived information can be accessed remotely, without the user needing local dedicated hardware.

COOKIE: A piece of information placed on a user's hard disk by a web server. Cookies contain data about the user's activity on a website, and are returned to the server whenever a browser makes further requests. They are important for remembering information such as login and registration details, 'shopping cart' data, user preferences etc, and are often set to expire after a fixed period.

DOMAIN: A set of words or letters, separated by dots, used to identify an internet server, eg www.whitakers almanack.com, where 'www' denotes a web (http) server, 'whitakersalmanack' denotes the organisation name and 'com' denotes that the organisation is a company.

FIREWALL: A protection system designed to prevent unauthorised access to or from a private network.

FTP: File Transfer Protocol – a set of network rules enabling a user to exchange files with a remote server.

HACKER: A person who attempts to break or 'hack' into websites. Motives typically involve the desire to procure personal information such as addresses, passwords or credit card details. Hackers may also delete code or incorporate traces of malicious code to damage the functionality of a website.

HIT: A single request from a web browser for a single item from a web server. In order for a web browser to display a page that contains three graphics, four 'hits' would occur at the server: one for the HTML page and one for each of the three graphics. Therefore the number of hits on a website is not synonymous with the number of visitors.

HTML: HyperText Mark-up Language – a programming language used to denote or mark up how an internet page should be presented to a user from an HTTP server via a web browser.

HTTP: HyperText Transfer Protocol – an internet protocol whereby a web server sends web pages, images and files to a web browser.

HYPERLINK: A piece of specially coded text that users can click on to navigate to the web page, or element of a web page, associated with that link's code. Links are typically distinguished through the use of bold, underlined, or differently coloured text.

JAVA: A programming language used widely on the internet.

MALWARE: A combination of the words 'malicious' and 'software'. Malware is software designed with the intention of infiltrating a computer and damaging its system.

OPEN-SOURCE: Describes a computer program that has its source code (the instructions that make up a program) freely available for viewing and modification.

PAGERANK: A link analysis algorithm used by search engines that assigns a numerical value based on a website's relevance and reputation. In general, a site with a higher pagerank has more traffic than a site with a lower one.

PHISHING: The fraudulent practice of sending emails to acquire personal information by masquerading as a legitimate company.

PODCAST: A form of audio and video broadcasting using the internet. Although the word is a portmanteau of 'iPod' and broadcasting, podcasting does not require the use of an iPod. A podcaster creates a list of files and makes it available in the RSS 2.0 format. The list can then be obtained using podcast 'retriever' software which makes the files available to digital devices (including iPods); users may then listen or watch at their convenience.

RSS FEED: Rich Site Summary or RDF Site Summary or Real Simple Syndication – a commonly used protocol for syndication and sharing of content, originally developed to facilitate the syndication of news articles, now widely used to share the content of blogs.

SEO: Search engine optimisation – the process of optimising the content of a web page to ensure that it is indexed by search engines.

SERVER: A node on a network that provides service to the terminals on the network. These computers have higher hardware specifications, ie more resources and greater speed, in order to handle large amounts of data.

SOCIAL NETWORKING: The practice of using a web-hosted service such as Facebook or Twitter to upload and share content and build friendship networks.

SPAM: A term used for unsolicited, generally junk, email.

TRAFFIC: The number of visitors to a website.

TWITTER: An online microblogging service that allows users to stay connected through the exchange of 140-character posts, known as 'tweets'.

URL: Uniform Resource Locator – address of a file accessible on the internet, eg http://www.whitakersalmanack.com

USER-GENERATED CONTENT (UGC): Refers to various media content produced or primarily influenced by end-users, as opposed to traditional media producers such as licensed broadcasters and production companies. These forms of media include digital video, blogging, podcasting, mobile phone photography and wikis.

CONSERVATION AND HERITAGE

NATIONAL PARKS

© Natural England

The Environment Act 1995 replaced the existing national park boards and committees with free-standing national park authorities (NPAs). NPAs are the sole local planning authorities for their areas and as such influence land use and development, and deal with planning applications. NPAs are responsible for carrying out the statutory purposes of national parks stated above.

In pursuing these purposes they have a statutory duty to seek to foster the economic and social well-being of the communities within national parks. The NPAs publish management plans setting out overarching policies for their area and appoint their own officers and staff.

The Broads Authority was established under the Norfolk and Suffolk Broads Act 1988 and meets the requirement for the authority to have a navigation function in addition to a regard for the needs of agriculture, forestry and the economic and social interests of those who live or work in the Broads.

MEMBERSHIP
Membership of English NPAs comprises local authority appointees, members directly appointed by the Secretary of State for Environment, Food and Rural Affairs and members appointed by the secretary after consultation with local parishes. Under the Natural Environment and Rural Communities Act 2006 every district, county or unitary authority with land in a national park is entitled to appoint at least one member unless it chooses to opt out. The total number of local authority and parish members must exceed the number of national members.

Northumberland, Pembrokeshire Coast and Snowdonia NPAs have 18 members; Dartmoor has 19; Exmoor, the Lake District and North York Moors have 20; the Broads has 21; the New Forest and Yorkshire Dales have 22; Brecon Beacons 24; South Downs 27; and the Peak District 30.

In Wales, two-thirds of NPA members are appointed by the constituent local authorities and one-third by the Welsh government, advised by Natural Resources Wales.

FUNDING
Core funding for the English NPAs and the Broads Authority is provided by central government through the Department for Environment, Food and Rural Affairs (DEFRA). For 2014–15 a total of £45.6m was allocated between the authorities.

In Wales, national parks are funded by the Welsh government. Total revenue and capital funding for for 2014–15 amounted to £10.8m. The three NPAs in Wales receive further funding via a local authority levy.

All NPAs and the Broads Authority can take advantage of grants from other bodies including lottery and European grants.

The national parks (with date that designation was confirmed) are:

BRECON BEACONS (1957), Powys (66 per cent)/ Carmarthenshire/Rhondda, Cynon and Taff/Merthyr Tydfil/Blaenau Gwent/Monmouthshire, 1,347 sq. km/ 520 sq. miles – The park is centred on the Brecon Beacons mountain range, which includes the three highest mountains in southern Britain (Pen y Fan, Corn Du and Cribyn), but also includes the vallies of the rivers Usk and Wye, the Black Mountains to the east and the Black Mountain to the west. There are information centres at the visitor centre at Libanus (near Brecon), Abergavenny

ENGLAND AND WALES
There are nine national parks in England, and three in Wales. In addition, the Norfolk and Suffolk Broads are considered to have equivalent status to a national park. Under the provisions of the National Parks and Access to the Countryside Act 1949, as clarified by the Natural Environment and Rural Communities Act 2006, the two purposes of the national parks are to conserve and enhance the parks' natural beauty, wildlife and cultural heritage, and to promote opportunities for the understanding and enjoyment of the special qualities of national parks by the public. If there is a conflict between the two purposes, then conservation takes precedence.

Natural England is the statutory body that has the power to designate national parks in England, and Natural Resources Wales (formerly Countryside Council for Wales) is responsible for national parks in Wales. Designations in England are confirmed by the Secretary of State for Environment, Food and Rural Affairs and those in Wales by the Welsh government. The designation of a national park does not affect the ownership of the land or remove the rights of the local community. The majority of the land in the national parks is owned by private landowners (around 75 per cent) or by bodies such as the National Trust and the Forestry Commission. The national park authorities own only a small percentage of the land themselves.

and Llandovery, as well as the Waterfalls Centre in Pontneddfechan.

National Park Authority, Plas y Ffynnon, Cambrian Way, Brecon, Powys LD3 7HP **T** 01874-624437

W www.beacons-npa.gov.uk

Chief Executive, John Cook

BROADS (1989), Norfolk/Suffolk, 303 sq. km/117 sq. miles – The Broads are located between Norwich and Great Yarmouth on the flood plains of the six rivers flowing through the area to the sea. The area is one of fens, winding waterways, woodland and marsh. The 60 or so broads are man-made, and many are connected to the rivers by dykes, providing over 200km (125 miles) of navigable waterways. There are information centres at Hoveton, Whitlingham Country Park and Toad Hole Cottage at How Hill.

Broads Authority, Yare House, 62–64 Thorpe Road, Norwich NR1 1RY **T** 01603-610734 **W** www.broads-authority.gov.uk

Chief Executive, Dr John Packman

DARTMOOR (1951), Devon, 953 sq. km/368 sq. miles – The park consists of moorland and rocky granite tors, and is rich in prehistoric remains. There are visitor centres at Haytor, Princetown (main visitor centre) and Postbridge.

National Park Authority, Parke, Bovey Tracey, Devon TQ13 9JQ **T** 01626-832093 **E** hq@dartmoor.gov.uk

W www.dartmoor.gov.uk

Chief Executive, Kevin Bishop

EXMOOR (1954), Somerset (71 per cent)/Devon, 692 sq. km/267 sq. miles – Exmoor is a moorland plateau inhabited by wild Exmoor ponies and red deer. There are many ancient remains and burial mounds. There are national park centres at Dunster, Dulverton and Lynmouth.

National Park Authority, Exmoor House, Dulverton, Somerset TA22 9HL **T** 01398-323665 **E** info@exmoor-nationalpark.gov.uk

W www.exmoor-nationalpark.gov.uk

Chief Executive, Dr Nigel Stone

LAKE DISTRICT (1951), Cumbria, 2,292 sq. km/885 sq. miles – The Lake District includes England's highest mountains (Scafell Pike, Helvellyn and Skiddaw) but it is most famous for its glaciated lakes. There are national park information centres at Bowness-on-Windermere, Keswick, Ullswater and a visitor centre at Brockhole, Windermere.

National Park Authority, Murley Moss, Oxenholme Road, Kendal, Cumbria LA9 7RL **T** 01539-724555

E hq@lakedistrict.gov.uk **W** www.lakedistrict.gov.uk

Chief Executive, Richard Leafe

NEW FOREST (2005), Hampshire, 570 sq. km/220 sq. miles – The forest has been protected since 1079 when it was declared a royal hunting forest. The area consists of forest, ancient woodland, heathland, farmland, coastal saltmarsh and mudflats. Much of the forest is managed by the Forestry Commission, which provides several campsites. There is a visitor centre at Lyndhurst.

National Park Authority, Town Hall, Avenue Road, Lymington, Hants SO41 9ZG **T** 01590-646600

E enquiries@newforestnpa.gov.uk

W www.newforestnpa.gov.uk

Chief Executive, Alison Barnes

NORTH YORK MOORS (1952), North Yorkshire (96 per cent)/Redcar and Cleveland, 1,434 sq. km/554 sq. miles – The park consists of woodland, moorland and coast, and includes the Hambleton Hills and the Cleveland Way. There are visitor centres at Danby and Sutton Bank.

National Park Authority, The Old Vicarage, Bondgate, Helmsley, York YO62 5BP **T** 01439-772700

E general@northyorkmoors.org.uk

W www.northyorkmoors.org.uk

Chief Executive, Andy Wilson

NORTHUMBERLAND (1956), Northumberland, 1,049 sq. km/405 sq. miles – The park is an area of hill country, comprising open moorland, blanket bogs and very small patches of ancient woodland, stretching from Hadrian's Wall to the Scottish border. There is an information centre at Once Brewed, situated close to Hadrian's Wall.

National Park Authority, Eastburn, South Park, Hexham, Northumberland NE46 1BS **T** 01434-605555

E enquiries@nnpa.org.uk

W www.northumberlandnationalpark.org.uk

Chief Executive, Tony Gates

PEAK DISTRICT (1951), Derbyshire (64 per cent)/Staffordshire/South Yorkshire/Cheshire/West Yorkshire/Greater Manchester, 1,437 sq. km/555 sq. miles – The Peak District includes the gritstone moors of the 'Dark Peak' and the limestone dales of the 'White Peak'. There are information centres at Bakewell, Castleton, Edale and Upper Derwent.

National Park Authority, Aldern House, Baslow Road, Bakewell, Derbyshire DE45 1AE **T** 01629-816200

E customer.service@peakdistrict.gov.uk

W www.peakdistrict.gov.uk

Chief Executive, Jim Dixon

PEMBROKESHIRE COAST (1952 and 1995), Pembrokeshire, 621 sq. km/236 sq. miles – The park includes cliffs, moorland and a number of islands, including Skomer and Ramsey. There are information centres in Newport and Tenby and a gallery and visitor centre, Oriel y Parc, in St Davids. The park also manages Castell Henllys' Iron Age fort and Carew Castle and Tidal Mill.

National Park Authority, Llanion Park, Pembroke Dock, Pembrokeshire SA72 6DY **T** 0845-345 7275

E info@pembrokeshirecoast.org.uk

W www.pembrokeshirecoast.org.uk

Chief Executive, Tegryn Jones

SNOWDONIA/ERYRI (1951), Gwynedd/Conwy, 2,132 sq. km/823 sq. miles – Snowdonia, which takes its name from Snowdon – the highest peak in England and Wales – is an area of deep valleys and rugged mountains. There are information centres at Aberdyfi, Beddgelert, Betws y Coed, Dolgellau and Harlech.

National Park Authority, Penrhyndeudraeth, Gwynedd LL48 6LF **T** 01766-770274 **E** parc@snowdonia-npa.gov.uk

W www.snowdonia-npa.gov.uk

Chief Executive, Emyr Williams

THE SOUTH DOWNS (2010), West Sussex/Hampshire, 1,648 sq. km/636 sq. miles – The South Downs contains a diversity of natural habitats, including flower-studded chalk grassland, ancient woodland, flood meadow, lowland heath and rare chalk heathland. There are visitor centres at Beachy Head, Queen Elizabeth Country Park in Hampshire and Seven Sisters Country Park in East Sussex.

National Park Authority, North Street, Midhurst, W. Sussex GU29 9DH **T** 0300-303 1053 **W** www.southdowns.gov.uk

Chief Executive, Trevor Beattie

YORKSHIRE DALES (1954), North Yorkshire (88 per cent)/Cumbria, 1,762 sq. km/680 sq. miles – The Yorkshire Dales is composed primarily of limestone overlaid in places by millstone grit. The three peaks of Ingleborough, Whernside and Pen-y-ghent are within the park. There are information centres at Grassington, Hawes, Aysgarth Falls, Malham and Reeth.

National Park Authority, Yoredale, Bainbridge, Leyburn, N. Yorks DL8 3EL **T** 0300-456 0030

E info@yorkshiredales.org.uk

W www.yorkshiredales.org.uk

Chief Executive, David Butterworth

SCOTLAND

On 9 August 2000 the national parks (Scotland) bill received royal assent, giving parliament the ability to create national parks in Scotland. The first two Scottish national parks became operational in 2002 and 2003 respectively. The Act gives Scottish parks wider powers than in England and Wales, including statutory responsibilities for the local economy and rural communities. The board of the Cairngorms NPA comprises 19 members; seven appointed by the Scottish ministers, a further seven nominated to the board by the five local authorities in the park area and five locally elected members. The board of Loch Lomond and the Trossachs NPA comprises 17 members; six appointed by the Scottish ministers, a further six nominated by local authorities within the park boundaries and five elected via a postal ballot of the local electorate. In Scotland, the national parks are central government bodies and are wholly funded by the Scottish government. Funding for 2014–15 totals £12.9m.

CAIRNGORMS (2003), North-East Scotland, 4,528 sq. km/ 1,748 sq. miles – The Cairngorms national park is the largest in the UK, covering around 6 per cent of Scotland. It displays a vast collection of landforms, including five of the six highest mountains in the UK and contains 25 per cent of Britain's threatened species. The near natural woodlands contain remnants of the original ancient Caledonian pine forest. There are nine visitor centres within the park.
National Park Authority, 14 The Square, Grantown-on-Spey, Morayshire PH26 3HG **T** 01479-873535
E enquiries@cairngorms.co.uk **W** www.cairngorms.co.uk
Chief Executive, Grant Moir

LOCH LOMOND AND THE TROSSACHS (2002), Argyll and Bute/Perth and Kinross/Stirling/West Dunbartonshire, 1,865 sq. km/720 sq. miles – The park boundaries encompass lochs, rivers, forests, 21 mountains above 914m (3,000ft) including Ben More and a further 19 mountains between 762m (2,500ft) and 914m (3,000ft). There is a national park centre in Balmaha and a visitor centre in Inveruglas. There are also nine visitor centres administered by VisitScotland.
National Park Authority, Carrochan, Carrochan Road, Balloch G83 8EG **T** 01389-722600 **E** info@lochlomond-trossachs.org
W www.lochlomond-trossachs.org
Chief Executive, Fiona Logan

NORTHERN IRELAND

There is a power to designate national parks in Northern Ireland under the Nature Conservation and Amenity Lands Order (Northern Ireland) 1985, but there are currently no national parks in Northern Ireland.

AREAS OF OUTSTANDING NATURAL BEAUTY

ENGLAND AND WALES

Under the National Parks and Access to the Countryside Act 1949, provision was made for the designation of areas of outstanding natural beauty (AONBs). Natural England is responsible for AONBs in England and Natural Resources Wales for the Welsh AONBs. Designations in England are confirmed by the Secretary of State for Environment, Food and Rural Affairs and those in Wales by the National Assembly for Wales. The Countryside and Rights of Way (CROW) Act 2000 placed greater responsibility on local authorities to protect AONBs and made it a statutory duty for relevant authorities to produce a management plan for their AONB area. The CROW Act also provided for the creation of conservation boards for larger and more complex AONBs. The first two conservation boards for the Cotswolds and Chilterns AONBs were established in July 2004.

The primary objective of the AONB designation is to conserve and enhance the natural beauty of the area. Where an AONB has a conservation board, it has the additional purpose of increasing public understanding and enjoyment of the special qualities of the area; the board has greater weight should there be a conflict of interests between the two. In addition, the board is also required to foster the economic and social well-being of the local communities but without incurring significant expenditure in doing so. Overall responsibility for AONBs lies with the relevant local authorities or conservation board. To coordinate planning and management responsibilities between local authorities in whose area they fall, AONBs are overseen by a joint advisory committee (or similar body) which includes representatives from the local authorities, landowners, farmers, residents and conservation and recreation groups. Core funding for AONBs is provided by central government through DEFRA and Natural Resources Wales.

The 38 AONBs (with date designation confirmed) are:

ARNSIDE AND SILVERDALE (1972), Cumbria/ Lancashire, 75 sq. km/29 sq. miles
BLACKDOWN HILLS (1991), Devon/Somerset, 370 sq. km/143 sq. miles
CANNOCK CHASE (1958), Staffordshire, 68 sq. km/ 26 sq. miles
CHICHESTER HARBOUR (1964), Hampshire/West Sussex, 74 sq. km/29 sq. miles
CHILTERNS (1965; extended 1990), Bedfordshire/ Buckinghamshire/Herefordshire/Oxfordshire, 833 sq. km/322 sq. miles
CLWYDIAN RANGE AND DEE VALLEY (1985; extended 2011), Denbighshire/Flintshire, 389 sq. km/ 150 sq. miles
CORNWALL (1959; Camel Estuary 1983), 958 sq. km/ 370 sq. miles
COTSWOLDS (1966; extended 1990), Gloucestershire/ Oxfordshire/Warwickshire/Wiltshire/Worcestershire, 2,038 sq. km/787 sq. miles
CRANBORNE CHASE AND WEST WILTSHIRE DOWNS (1983), Dorset/Hampshire/Somerset/Wiltshire, 983 sq. km/380 sq. miles
DEDHAM VALE (1970; extended 1978, 1991), Essex/ Suffolk, 90 sq. km/35 sq. miles
DORSET (1959), Dorset/Somerset, 1,129 sq. km/436 sq. miles
EAST DEVON (1963), 268 sq. km/103 sq. miles
FOREST OF BOWLAND (1964), Lancashire/North Yorkshire, 802 sq. km/310 sq. miles
GOWER (1956), Swansea, 188 sq. km/73 sq. miles
HIGH WEALD (1983), East Sussex/Kent/Surrey/West Sussex, 1,460 sq. km/564 sq. miles
HOWARDIAN HILLS (1987), North Yorkshire, 204 sq. km/79 sq. miles
ISLE OF WIGHT (1963), 189 sq. km/73 sq. miles
ISLES OF SCILLY (1976), 16 sq. km/6 sq. miles
KENT DOWNS (1968), 878 sq. km/339 sq. miles
LINCOLNSHIRE WOLDS (1973), 558 sq. km/215 sq. miles
LLYN (1957), Gwynedd, 161 sq. km/62 sq. miles
MALVERN HILLS (1959), Gloucestershire/Worcestershire, 105 sq. km/41 sq. miles
MENDIP HILLS (1972; extended 1989), Somerset, 198 sq. km/76 sq. miles
NIDDERDALE (1994), North Yorkshire, 603 sq. km/ 233 sq. miles
NORFOLK COAST (1968), 451 sq. km/174 sq. miles

NORTH DEVON (1960), 171 sq. km/66 sq. miles
NORTH PENNINES (1988), Cumbria/Durham/North
  Yorkshire/Northumberland, 1,983 sq. km/766 sq. miles
NORTH WESSEX DOWNS (1972), Hampshire/
  Oxfordshire/Wiltshire, 1,730 sq. km/668 sq. miles
NORTHUMBERLAND COAST (1958), 135 sq. km/
  52 sq. miles
QUANTOCK HILLS (1957), Somerset, 99 sq. km/38 sq.
  miles
SHROPSHIRE HILLS (1959), 804 sq. km/310 sq. miles
SOLWAY COAST (1964), Cumbria, 115 sq. km/44 sq. miles
SOUTH DEVON (1960), 337 sq. km/130 sq. miles
SUFFOLK COAST AND HEATHS (1970), 403 sq. km/
  156 sq. miles
SURREY HILLS (1958), 419 sq. km/162 sq. miles
TAMAR VALLEY (1995), Cornwall/Devon, 195 sq. km/
  75 sq. miles
WYE VALLEY (1971), Gloucestershire/Herefordshire/
  Monmouthshire, 326 sq. km/126 sq. miles
YNYS MON (ISLE OF ANGLESEY) (1967), 221 sq. km/
  85 sq. miles

NORTHERN IRELAND
The Department of the Environment for Northern Ireland,
with advice from the Council for Nature Conservation and
the Countryside, designates AONBs in Northern Ireland.
At present there are eight and these cover a total area of 3,415
sq. km (1,318 sq. miles). Dates given are those of designation.

ANTRIM COAST AND GLENS (1988), Co. Antrim,
  725 sq. km/280 sq. miles
BINEVENAGH (2006), Co. Londonderry, 166 sq. km/
  64 sq. miles
CAUSEWAY COAST (1989), Co. Antrim, 42 sq. km/
  16 sq. miles
LAGAN VALLEY (1965), Co. Down, 39 sq. km/15 sq. miles
MOURNE (1986), Co. Down, 580 sq. km/224 sq. miles
RING OF GULLION (1991), Co. Armagh, 153 sq. km/
  59 sq. miles
SPERRIN (1968; extended 2008), Co. Tyrone/Co.
  Londonderry, 1,182 sq. km/456 sq. miles
STRANGFORD LOUGH AND LECALE (2010)*, Co.
  Down, 528 sq. km/204 sq. miles

*Strangford Lough (1972) and Lecale Coast (1967) merged in
2010

NATIONAL SCENIC AREAS

In Scotland, national scenic areas have a broadly equivalent
status to AONBs. Scottish Natural Heritage recognises areas
of national scenic significance. At the beginning of July 2014
there were 40, covering a land area of 1,021,600 hectares
(2,524,400 acres) and a marine area of 359,500 hectares
(888,300 acres).
  Development within national scenic areas is dealt with by
local authorities, who are required to consult Scottish Natural
Heritage concerning certain categories of development.
Disagreements between Scottish Natural Heritage and local
authorities are referred to the Scottish government. Land
management uses can also be modified in the interest of
scenic conservation.

ASSYNT-COIGACH, Highland, 90,200ha/222,884 acres
BEN NEVIS AND GLEN COE, Highland, 101,600ha/
  251,053 acres
CAIRNGORM MOUNTAINS, Highland/Aberdeenshire/
  Moray, 67,200ha/166,051 acres
CUILLIN HILLS, Highland, 21,900ha/54,115 acres
DEESIDE AND LOCHNAGAR, Aberdeenshire, 40,000ha/
  98,840 acres

DORNOCH FIRTH, Highland, 7,500ha/18,532 acres
EAST STEWARTRY COAST, Dumfries and Galloway,
  4,500ha/11,119 acres
EILDON AND LEADERFOOT, Borders, 3,600ha/
  8,896 acres
FLEET VALLEY, Dumfries and Galloway, 5,300ha/
  13,096 acres
GLEN AFFRIC, Highland, 19,300ha/47,690 acres
GLEN STRATHFARRAR, Highland, 3,800ha/9,390 acres
HOY AND WEST MAINLAND, Orkney Islands, 14,800ha/
  36,571 acres
JURA, Argyll and Bute, 21,800ha/53,868 acres
KINTAIL, Highland, 15,500ha/38,300 acres
KNAPDALE, Argyll and Bute, 19,800ha/48,926 acres
KNOYDART, Highland, 39,500ha/97,604 acres
KYLE OF TONGUE, Highland, 18,500ha/45,713 acres
KYLES OF BUTE, Argyll and Bute, 4,400ha/10,872 acres
LOCH LOMOND, Argyll and Bute, 27,400ha/67,705 acres
LOCH NA KEAL, Mull, Argyll and Bute, 12,700ha/
  31,382 acres
LOCH RANNOCH AND GLEN LYON, Perthshire and
  Kinross, 48,400ha/119,596 acres
LOCH SHIEL, Highland, 13,400ha/33,111 acres
LOCH TUMMEL, Perthshire and Kinross, 9,200ha/
  22,733 acres
LYNN OF LORN, Argyll and Bute, 4,800ha/11,861 acres
MORAR, MOIDART AND ARDNAMURCHAN, Highland,
  13,500ha/33,358 acres
NITH ESTUARY, Dumfries and Galloway, 9,300ha/
  22,980 acres
NORTH ARRAN, North Ayrshire, 23,800ha/58,810 acres
NORTH-WEST SUTHERLAND, Highland, 20,500ha/
  50,655 acres
RIVER EARN, Perthshire and Kinross, 3,000ha/7,413 acres
RIVER TAY, Perthshire and Kinross, 5,600ha/13,838 acres
ST KILDA, Eilean Siar (Western Isles), 900ha/2,224 acres
SCARBA, LUNGA AND THE GARVELLACHS, Argyll and
  Bute, 1,900ha/4,695 acres
SHETLAND, Shetland Isles, 11,600ha/28,664 acres
SMALL ISLANDS, Highland, 15,500ha/38,300 acres
SOUTH LEWIS, HARRIS AND NORTH UIST, Eilean Siar
  (Western Isles), 109,600ha/270,822 acres
SOUTH UIST MACHAIR, Eilean Siar (Western Isles),
  6,100ha/15,073 acres
THE TROSSACHS, Stirling, 4,600ha/11,367 acres
TROTTERNISH, Highland, 5,000ha/12,355 acres
UPPER TWEEDDALE, Borders, 10,500ha/25,945 acres
WESTER ROSS, Highland, 145,300ha/359,036 acres

THE NATIONAL FOREST

The National Forest is being planted across 518.5 sq. km
(200.2 sq. miles) of Derbyshire, Leicestershire and Staffordshire – 149ha were added in 2013–14. Almost 8.5 million
trees, of which 87 per cent are broadleaf species and 13 per
cent conifer, covering 6,931ha (17,127 acres) have been
planted. The aim is to eventually cover about one-third of the
designated area.
  The project was developed in 1992–5 by the Countryside
Commission and is now run by the National Forest
Company, which was established in April 1995. The
National Forest Company is responsible for the delivery of
the government-approved National Forest Strategy and is
sponsored by DEFRA. The grant-in-aid allocation for
2014–15 is £2.6m.
NATIONAL FOREST COMPANY, Bath Yard, Moira,
  Swadlincote, Derbyshire DE12 6BA T 01283-551211
  E enquiries@nationalforest.org W www.nationalforest.org
  Chief Executive, Sophie Churchill, OBE

SITES OF SPECIAL SCIENTIFIC INTEREST

Site of Special Scientific Interest (SSSI) is a legal notification applied to land in England, Scotland or Wales which Natural England (NE), Scottish Natural Heritage (SNH) or the Natural Resources Wales (NRW) identifies as being of special interest because of its flora, fauna, geological, geomorphological or physiographical features. In some cases, SSSIs are managed as nature reserves.

NE, SNH and NRW must notify the designation of an SSSI to the local planning authority, every owner/occupier of the land, and the environment secretary, the Scottish ministers or the National Assembly for Wales. Forestry and agricultural departments and a number of other interested parties are also formally notified.

Objections to the notification of an SSSI can be made and ultimately considered at a full meeting of the Council of NE or NRW. In Scotland an objection will be dealt with by the main board of SNH or an appropriate subgroup, depending on the nature of the objection.

The protection of these sites depends on the cooperation of individual landowners and occupiers. Owner/occupiers must consult NE, SNH or NRW and gain written consent before they can undertake certain listed activities on the site. Funds are available through management agreements and grants to assist owners and occupiers in conserving sites' interests. Sites can also be protected by management schemes, management notices and other enforcement mechanisms. As a last resort a site can be purchased.

The number and area of SSSIs in Britain as at May 2014 was:

	Number	Hectares	Acres
England	4,129	1,077,555	2,662,696
Scotland	1,425	1,022,260	2,526,060
Wales	1,064	268,552	663,606

NORTHERN IRELAND

In Northern Ireland 360 areas of special scientific interest (ASSIs) have been declared by the Department of the Environment for Northern Ireland.

NATIONAL NATURE RESERVES

National Nature Reserves are defined in the National Parks and Access to the Countryside Act 1949 as modified by the Natural Environment and Rural Communities Act 2006. National Nature Reserves may be managed solely for the purpose of conservation, or for both the purposes of conservation and recreation, providing this does not compromise the conservation purpose.

NE, SNH or NRW can declare as a national nature reserve land which is held and managed as a nature reserve under an agreement; land held and managed by NE, SNH or NRW; or land held and managed as a nature reserve by an approved body. NE, SNH or NRW can make by-laws to protect reserves from undesirable activities; these are subject to confirmation by the Secretary of State for Environment, Food and Rural Affairs, the National Assembly for Wales or the Scottish ministers.

The number and area of national nature reserves in Britain as at May 2014 was:

	Number	Hectares	Acres
England	224	94,400	233,267
Scotland	51	128,202	316,793
Wales	72	25,616	63,299

NORTHERN IRELAND

Nature reserves are established and managed by the Department of the Environment for Northern Ireland, with advice from the Council for Nature Conservation and the Countryside. Nature reserves are declared under the Nature Conservation and Amenity Lands (Northern Ireland) Order 1985; to date, 49 nature reserves have been declared.

LOCAL NATURE RESERVES

Local Nature Reserves are defined in the National Parks and Access to the Countryside Act 1949 (as amended by the Natural Environment and Rural Communities Act 2006) as land designated for the study and preservation of flora and fauna, or of geological or physiographical features. Local Nature Reserves also have a statutory obligation to provide opportunities for the enjoyment of nature or open air recreation, providing this does not compromise the conservation purpose of the reserve. Local authorities in England, Scotland and Wales have the power to acquire, declare and manage reserves in consultation with NE, SNH and NRW. There is similar legislation in Northern Ireland, where the consulting organisation is the Environment Agency.

Any organisation, such as water companies, educational trusts, local amenity groups and charitable nature conservation bodies, such as wildlife trusts, may manage local nature reserves, provided that a local authority has a legal interest in the land. This means that the local authority must either own it, lease it or have a management agreement with the landowner.

The number and area of designated local nature reserves in Britain as at May 2014 was:

	Number	Hectares	Acres
England	1,554	38,967	96,287
Scotland	70	10,706	26,455
Wales	82	5,860	14,480

There are 17 local nature reserves in Northern Ireland.

FOREST RESERVES

The Forestry Commission is the government department responsible for forestry policy throughout Great Britain. Forestry is a devolved matter, with the separate Forestry Commissions for England, Scotland and Wales reporting directly to their appropriate minister. The equivalent body in Northern Ireland is the Forest Service, an agency of the Department of Agriculture and Rural Development for Northern Ireland. The Forestry Commission in each country is led by a director who is also a member of the GB Board of Commissioners. As at March 2013, UK woodland certified by the Forestry Commission (including Forestry Commission-managed woodland) amounted to around 1,362,000ha (3,365,574 acres): 355,000ha (877,224 acres) in England, 139,000ha (343,476 acres) in Wales, 803,000ha (1,984,256 acres) in Scotland and 65,000ha (160,618 acres) in Northern Ireland. For more information, see W www.forestry.gov.uk

There are 34 forest nature reserves in Northern Ireland, covering 1,512 hectares (3,736 acres), designated and administered by the Forest Service. There are also 16 national nature reserves on Forest Service-owned property.

MARINE NATURE RESERVES

Marine protected areas provide protection for marine flora and fauna, and geological and physiographical features on land covered by tidal waters or parts of the sea in or adjacent to the UK. These areas also provide opportunities for study and research.

ENGLAND AND WALES

The Marine and Coastal Access Act 2009 created a new kind of statutory protection for marine protected areas in England and Wales, marine conservation zones (MCZs), which are designed to increase the protection of species and habitats deemed to be of national importance. The Secretary of State for Environment, Food and Rural Affairs and the National Assembly for Wales have the power to designate MCZs. Individual MCZs can have varying levels of protection: some include specific activities that are appropriately managed, while others prohibit all damaging and disturbing activities. The act converted the waters around Lundy Island, a former marine protected area, to MCZ status in 2010.

In 2009, Natural England and the Joint Nature Conservation Committee (JNCC) gave sea-users and stake-holders the ability to recommend potential MCZs to the UK government by establishing four regional projects. In September 2011, these projects recommended 127 MCZs, which were reviewed by Natural England and the JNCC. On 21 November 2013, the government announced the creation of 27 new MCZs, covering an area of around 9,700 sq. km, to protect wildlife including seahorses, coral reefs and oyster beds from dredging and bottom-trawling. In February 2014, DEFRA announced 37 new MCZs would be considered as potential candidates for consultation in 2015. The 27 MCZs (with date designation confirmed) are:

Inshore Sites
ALN ESTUARY (2013), Northumberland, 0.39 sq. km
BLACKWATER, CROUCH, ROACH AND COLNE
    ESTUARIES (2013), Essex, 284 sq. km
BEACHY HEAD WEST (2013), E. Sussex, 24 sq. km
CHESIL BEACH AND STENNIS LEDGES (2013), Dorset,
    37 sq. km
CUMBRIA COAST (2013), Cumbria, 18 sq. km
FOLKESTONE POMERANIA (2013), Kent, 34 sq. km
FYLDE (2013), Lancs, 260 sq. km
ISLES OF SCILLY (2013), 30 sq. km
KINGMERE (2013), Sussex, 47 sq. km
LUNDY (2010 and 2013), Bristol Channel, 31 sq. km
THE MANACLES (2013), Cornwall, 3.5 sq. km
MEDWAY ESTUARY (2013), Kent, 60 sq. km
PADSTOW BAY AND SURROUNDS (2013), Cornwall,
    90 sq. km
PAGHAM HARBOUR (2013), Sussex, 3 sq. km
POOLE ROCKS (2013), Dorset, 4 sq. km
SKERRIES BANK AND SURROUNDS (2013), Devon,
    250 sq. km
SOUTH DORSET (2013), 193 sq. km
TAMAR ESTUARY, Devon/Cornwall (2013), 15 sq. km
THANET COAST (2013), Kent, 64 sq. km
TORBAY (2013), Devon, 20 sq. km
UPPER FOWEY AND PONT PILL (2013), Cornwall,
    2 sq. km
WHITSAND AND LOOE BAY (2013), Cornwall, 52 sq. km

Offshore Sites
THE CANYONS (2013), Cornwall, 661 sq. km
EAST OF HAIG FRAS (2013), Cornwall, 400 sq. km
NORTH EAST OF FARNES DEEP (2013),
    Northumberland, 492 sq. km
SOUTH-WEST DEEPS (WEST) (2013), Cornwall,
    1,800 sq. km
SWALLOW SAND (2013), Northumberland, 4,746 sq. km

SCOTLAND

In July 2014, under the Marine (Scotland) Act 2010, the Scottish government designated 17 marine protected areas (MPAs) in Scottish inshore territorial waters (Clyde Sea Sill;

East Caithness Cliffs; Fetlar to Haroldswick; Loch Creran; Loch Sunart; Loch Sunart to the Sound of Jura; Loch Sween; Lochs Duich, Long and Alsh; Monarch Isles; Mousa to Boddam; Noss Head; Papa Westray; Small Isles; South Arran; Upper Loch Fyne and Loch Goil; Wester Ross; and Wyre and Rousay Sounds). A further 13, also in July 2014, were designated in offshore waters under the UK Marine and Coastal Access Act 2009. These are: Central Fladen; East of Gannet and Montrose Fields; Faroe–Shetland Sponge Belt; Firth of Forth Banks Complex; Geikie Slide and Hebridean Slope; Hatton–Rockall Basin; North-east Faroe Shetland Channel; North-west Orkney; Norwegian Sediment Boundary Plain; Rosemary Bank Seamount; Barra Fan and Hebrides Terrace Seamount; Turbot Bank; and West Shetland Shelf.

NORTHERN IRELAND

In Northern Ireland, marine nature reserves may be established under the Nature Conservation and Amenity Lands Order (Northern Ireland) 1985. Strangford Lough was designated a marine nature reserve in 1995.

INTERNATIONAL CONVENTIONS

The UK is party to a number of international conventions.

BERN CONVENTION

The 1979 Bern Convention on the Conservation of European Wildlife and Natural Habitats came into force in the UK in June 1982. Currently there are 51 contracting parties and a number of other states attend meetings as observers.

The aims are to conserve wild flora and fauna and their habitats, especially where this requires the cooperation of several countries, and to promote such cooperation. The convention imposes legal obligations on contracting parties, protecting over 500 wild plant species and more than 1,000 wild animal species.

All parties to the convention must promote national conservation policies and take account of the conservation of wild flora and fauna when setting planning and development policies. Reports on contracting parties' conservation policies must be submitted to the standing committee every four years.

SECRETARIAT OF THE BERN CONVENTION
    STANDING COMMITTEE, Council of Europe, Avenue
    de L'Europe, 67075 Strasbourg-Cedex, France
    W www.coe.int/bernconvention

BIOLOGICAL DIVERSITY

The UK ratified the Convention on Biological Diversity in June 1994. As at July 2014 there were 194 parties to the convention.

There are seven programmes addressing agricultural biodiversity, marine and coastal biodiversity and the biodiversity of inland waters, dry and sub-humid lands, islands, mountains and forests. On 29 January 2000 the Conference of the Parties adopted a supplementary agreement to the convention known as the Cartagena Protocol on Biosafety. The protocol seeks to protect biological diversity from potential risks that may be posed by introducing modified living organisms, resulting from biotechnology, into the environment. As at July 2014, 167 countries were party to the protocol; the UK joined on 17 February 2004. The Nagoya supplementary protocol was adopted in October 2010. It provides international rules and procedure on liability and redress for damage to biodiversity resulting from living modified organisms. As at July 2014, 92 countries have signed the protocol.

The UK Biodiversity Action Plan (UKBAP) is the UK government's response to the Convention on Biological Diversity and constitutes a record of UK biological resources and a detailed plan for their protection. The list of priority species and habitats under the UKBAP covers 1,150 species and 65 habitats. The UK Biodiversity Partnership Standing Committee guides and supports the UK Biodiversity Partnership in implementing UKBAP; it also coordinates between the four UK country groups which form the partnership and are responsible for implementing UKBAP at a national level. Information on UKBAP is available from the Joint Nature Conservation Committee (JNCC).

JNCC, Monkstone House, City Road, Peterborough PE1 1JY
T 01733-555948 W www.jncc.defra.gov.uk

BONN CONVENTION

The 1979 Convention on Conservation of Migratory Species of Wild Animals (also known as the CMS or Bonn Convention) came into force in the UK in October 1985. As at 1 July 2014, 120 countries were party to the convention.

It requires the protection of listed endangered migratory species and encourages international agreements covering these and other threatened species. International agreements can range from legally binding treaties to less formal memoranda of understanding.

Seven agreements have been concluded to date under the convention. They aim to conserve seals in the Wadden Sea; bat populations in Europe; small cetaceans of the Baltic, north-east Atlantic, Irish and North Seas; cetaceans of the Mediterranean Sea, Black Sea and contiguous Atlantic area; African-Eurasian migratory waterbirds; albatrosses and petrels; and gorillas and their habitats. A further 19 memorandums of understanding have been agreed for the Siberian crane, slender-billed curlew, marine turtles of the Atlantic coast of Africa, Indian Ocean and South East Asia, the middle-European population of the great bustard, bukhara deer, aquatic warbler, West-African populations of the African elephant, saiga antelope, cetaceans of the Pacific Islands, dugongs (large marine mammals), eastern-Atlantic populations of the Mediterranean monk seals, ruddy-headed goose, grassland birds of southern South America, birds of prey of Africa and Eurasia, small cetaceans and manatees of West Africa, sharks, huemuls (Andean deer) and high Andean flamingoes. In addition, there are three special species initiatives: the central Asian flyway, the central Asian mammals initiative and Sahelo–Saharan megafauna plan.

UNEP/CMS SECRETARIAT, Hermann-Ehlers-Str. 10, 53113 Bonn, Germany T (+49) (228) 815 2401 E secretariat@cms.int W www.cms.int

CITES

The 1973 Convention on International Trade in Endangered Species of Wild Fauna and Flora (CITES), which entered into force in 1975, is an agreement between governments to ensure that international trade in specimens of wild animals and plants does not threaten their survival. The convention came into force in the UK in October 1976 and there are currently 180 member countries. Countries party to the convention ban commercial international trade in an agreed list of endangered species and regulate and monitor trade in other species that might become endangered. The convention accords varying degrees of protection to more than 35,000 species of animals and plants whether they are traded as live specimens or as products derived from them, such as fur coats and dried herbs.

The Conference of the Parties to CITES meets every two to three years to review the convention's implementation. The Animal Health and Veterinary Laboratories Agency at the Department for Environment, Food and Rural Affairs carries out the government's responsibilities under CITES.

CITES is implemented in the EU through a series of EC regulations known as the Wildlife Trade Regulations.

CITES SECRETARIAT, International Environment House, 11 Chemin des Anémones, CH-1219 Châtelaine, Geneva, Switzerland T (+41) (22) 917 8139/40 E info@cites.org W www.cites.org

INTERNATIONAL CONVENTION FOR THE REGULATION OF WHALING

The International Convention for the Regulation of Whaling was signed in Washington DC in 1946 and currently has 89 member countries.

The measures in the convention provide for the complete protection of certain species; designate specified areas as whale sanctuaries; set limits on the numbers and size of whales which may be taken; prescribe open and closed seasons and areas for whaling; and prohibit the capture of suckling calves and female whales accompanied by calves. The International Whaling Commission meets annually to review and revise these measures.

THE INTERNATIONAL WHALING COMMISSION, The Red House, 135 Station Road, Impington, Cambridge, Cambridgeshire CB24 9NP T 01223-233 971 W www.iwc.int

OSPAR

The Convention for the Protection of the Marine Environment of the North-East Atlantic (the OSPAR Convention) was adopted in Paris, France in September 1992 and entered into force in March 1998. The OSPAR Convention replaced both the Oslo Convention (1972) and the Paris Convention (1974), with the intention of providing a comprehensive approach to addressing all sources of pollution which may affect the maritime area, and matters relating to the protection of the maritime environment. An annex on biodiversity and ecosystems was adopted in 1998 to cover non-polluting human activities that can adversely affect the sea.

Fifteen countries plus the European Union are party to convention; the UK ratified OSPAR in 1998. The OSPAR Commission makes decisions and recommendations and sets out actions to be taken by the contracting parties. The OSPAR Secretariat administers the work under the convention, coordinates the work of the contracting parties and runs the formal meeting schedule of OSPAR.

OSPAR SECRETARIAT, Victoria House, 37–63 Southampton Row, London WC1B 4DA T 020-7430 5200 E secretariat@ospar.org W www.ospar.org

RAMSAR CONVENTION

The 1971 Convention on Wetlands of National Importance, called the Ramsar Convention, is an inter-governmental treaty that provides for the conservation and sustainable use of wetlands and their resources. The Convention entered into force in the UK in 1976.

Governments that are contracting parties to the convention must designate wetlands for inclusion in the List of Wetlands of International Importance (the 'Ramsar List') and include wetland conservation considerations in their land-use planning. As at May 2014, the Convention's 168 contracting parties had designated 2,182 wetland sites, covering 208,546,927 hectares. The UK currently has 170 designated sites covering 1,278,930 hectares.

The contracting parties meet every three years to assess the progress of the convention. The next meeting will take place in Punta del Este, Uruguay in June 2015.

The UK has set targets under the Ramsar Strategic Plan, 2009–15. Progress towards these is monitored by the UK

Ramsar committee. The UK and the Republic of Ireland have established a formal protocol to ensure common monitoring standards for waterbirds in the two countries.
RAMSAR CONVENTION SECRETARIAT, Rue Mauverney 28, CH-1196 Gland, Switzerland **T** (+41) (22) 999 0170
E ramsar@ramsar.org **W** www.ramsar.org

UK LEGISLATION

The Wildlife and Countryside Act 1981 gives legal protection to a wide range of wild animals and plants. Every five years the statutory nature conservation agencies (Natural England, Natural Resources Wales and Scottish Natural Heritage), working jointly through the JNCC, are required to review schedules 5 (animals, other than birds) and 8 (plants) of the Wildlife and Countryside Act 1981. They make recommendations to the Secretary of State for Environment, Food and Rural Affairs, the National Assembly for Wales and the Scottish government for changes to these schedules. The most recent variations of schedules 5 and 8 for England came into effect on 1 October 2011, following the fifth quinquennial review. The sixth review is currently underway.

Under section 9 of the act it is an offence to kill, injure, take, possess or sell (whether alive or dead) any wild animal included in schedule 5 of the act and to disturb its place of shelter and protection or to destroy that place. However certain species listed on schedule 5 are protected against some, but not all, of these activities.

Under section 13 of the act it is illegal without a licence to pick, uproot, sell or destroy plants listed in schedule 8. Since January 2001, under the Countryside and Rights of Way Act 2000, persons found guilty of an offence under part 1 of the Wildlife and Countryside Act 1981 face a maximum penalty of up to £5,000 and/or up to a six-month custodial sentence per specimen.

BIRDS
The act lays down a close season for birds (listed on Schedule 2, part 1) from 1 February to 31 August inclusive, each year. Variations to these dates are made for:

Black grouse – 10 December to 20 August (10 December–1 September for Somerset, Devon and New Forest)
Capercaillie – 1 February to 30 September (England and Wales only)
Grey partridge – 1 February to 1 September
Pheasant – 1 February to 1 October
Ptarmigan and Red grouse – 10 December to 12 August
Red-legged partridge – 1 February to 1 September
Snipe – 1 February to 11 August
Woodcock – 1 February to 30 September (England and Wales); 1 February to 31 August (Scotland)
Birds listed on schedule 2, part 1 (below high water mark) (*see* below) – 21 February to 31 August
Wild duck and wild geese, in or over any area below the high-water mark of ordinary spring tides – 21 February to 31 August
Sundays and Christmas Day in Scotland, and Sundays for any area of England or Wales prescribed by the Secretary of State.

Birds listed on schedule 2, part 1, which may be killed or taken outside the close season are: capercaillie (England and Wales only); coot; certain wild duck (gadwall, goldeneye, mallard, Northern pintail, common pochard, Northern shoveler, teal, tufted duck, Eurasian wigeon); certain wild geese (Canada, greylag, pink-footed, white-fronted (in England and Wales only); golden plover; moorhen; snipe; and woodcock.

Section 16 of the 1981 act allows licences to be issued on either an individual or general basis, to allow the killing, taking and sale of certain birds for specified reasons such as public health and safety. All other wild birds are fully protected by law throughout the year.

ANIMALS PROTECTED BY SCHEDULE 5
Adder *(Vipera berus)*
Anemone, Ivell's Sea *(Edwardsia ivelli)*
Anemone, Starlet Sea *(Nematosella vectensis)*
Bat, Horseshoe, all species *(Rhinolophidae)*
Bat, Typical, all species *(Vespertilionidae)*
Beetle *(Hypebaeus flavipes)*
Beetle, Bembridge Water *(Paracymus aeneus)*
Beetle, Lesser Silver Water *(Hydrochara caraboides)*
Beetle, Mire Pill *(Curimopsis nigrita)*
Beetle, Moccas *(Hypebaeus flavipes)*
Beetle, Rainbow Leaf *(Chrysolina cerealis)*
Beetle, Spangled Water *(Graphoderus zonatus)*
Beetle, Stag *(Lucanus cervus)*
Beetle, Violet Click *(Limoniscus violaceus)*
Beetle, Water *(Paracymus aeneus)*
Burbot *(Lota lota)*
Butterfly, Adonis Blue *(Lysandra bellargus)*
Butterfly, Black Hairstreak *(Strymonidia pruni)*
Butterfly, Brown Hairstreak *(Thecla betulae)*
Butterfly, Chalkhill Blue *(Lysandra coridon)*
Butterfly, Chequered Skipper *(Carterocephalus palaemon)*
Butterfly, Duke of Burgundy Fritillary *(Hamearis lucina)*
Butterfly, Glanville Fritillary *(Melitaea cinxia)*
Butterfly, Heath Fritillary *(Mellicta athalia* or *Melitaea athalia)*
Butterfly, High Brown Fritillary *(Argynnis adippe)*
Butterfly, Large Blue *(Maculinea arion)*
Butterfly, Large Copper *(Lycaena dispar)*
Butterfly, Large Heath *(Coenonympha tullia)*
Butterfly, Large Tortoiseshell *(Nymphalis polychloros)*
Butterfly, Lulworth Skipper *(Thymelicus acteon)*
Butterfly, Marsh Fritillary *(Eurodryas aurinia)*
Butterfly, Mountain Ringlet *(Erebia epiphron)*
Butterfly, Northern Brown Argus *(Aricia artaxerxes)*
Butterfly, Pearl-bordered Fritillary *(Boloria euphrosyne)*
Butterfly, Purple Emperor *(Apatura iris)*
Butterfly, Silver Spotted Skipper *(Hesperia comma)*
Butterfly, Silver-studded Blue *(Plebejus argus)*
Butterfly, Small Blue *(Cupido minimus)*
Butterfly, Swallowtail *(Papilio machaon)*
Butterfly, White Letter Hairstreak *(Stymonida w-album)*
Butterfly, Wood White *(Leptidea sinapis)*
Cat, Wild *(Felis silvestris)*
Cicada, New Forest *(Cicadetta montana)*
Crayfish, Atlantic Stream *(Austropotamobius pallipes)*
Cricket, Field *(Gryllus campestris)*
Cricket, Mole *(Gryllotalpa gryllotalpa)*
Cricket, Wart-biter *(Decticus verrucivorus)*
Damselfly, Southern *(Coenagrion mercuriale)*
Dolphin, all species *(Cetacea)*
Dormouse *(Muscardinus avellanarius)*
Dragonfly, Norfolk Aeshna *(Aeshna isosceles)*
Frog, Common *(Rana temporaria)*
Frog, Pool, Northern Clade *(Pelophylax lessonae)*
Goby, Couch's *(Gobius couchii)*
Goby, Giant *(Gobius cobitis)*
Hatchet Shell, Northern *(Thyasira gouldi)*
Hydroid, Marine *(Clavopsella navis)*
Lagoon Snail, De Folin's *(Caecum armoricum)*
Lagoon Worm, Tentacled *(Alkmaria romijni)*
Leech, Medicinal *(Hirudo medicinalis)*
Lizard, Sand *(Lacerta agilis)*

Lizard, Viviparous *(Lacerta vivipara)*
Marten, Pine *(Martes martes)*
Moth, Barberry Carpet *(Pareulype berberata)*
Moth, Black-veined *(Siona lineata* or *Idaea lineata)*
Moth, Fiery Clearwing *(Bembecia chrysidiformis)*
Moth, Fisher's Estuarine *(Gortyna borelii)*
Moth, New Forest Burnet *(Zygaena viciae)*
Moth, Reddish Buff *(Acosmetia caliginosa)*
Moth, Slender Scotch Burnet *(Zygaena loti)*
Moth, Sussex Emerald *(Thalera fimbrialis)*
Moth, Talisker Burnet *(Zygaena lonicerae)*
Mussel, Fan *(Atrina fragilis)*
Mussel, Freshwater Pearl *(Margaritifera margaritifera)*
Newt, Great Crested (or Warty) *(Triturus cristatus)*
Newt, Palmate *(Triturus helveticus)*
Newt, Smooth *(Triturus vulgaris)*
Otter, Common *(Lutra lutra)*
Porpoise, all species *(Cetacea)*
Sandworm, Lagoon *(Armandia cirrhosa)*
Sea Fan, Pink *(Eunicella verrucosa)*
Sea Slug, Lagoon *(Tenellia adspersa)*
Sea-mat, Trembling *(Victorella pavida)*
Seahorse, Short Snouted (England only) *(Hippocampus hippocampus)*
Seahorse, Spiny (England only) *(Hippocampus guttulatus)*
Shad, Allis *(Alosa alosa)*
Shad, Twaite *(Alosa fallax)*
Shark, Angel (England only) *(Squatina squatina)*
Shark, Basking *(Cetorhinus maximus)*
Shrimp, Fairy *(Chirocephalus diaphanus)*
Shrimp, Lagoon Sand *(Gammarus insensibilis)*
Shrimp, Tadpole (Apus) *(Triops cancriformis)*
Skate, White *(Rostroraja alba)*
Slow-worm *(Anguis fragilis)*
Snail, Glutinous *(Myxas glutinosa)*
Snail, Roman (England only) *(Helix pomatia)*
Snail, Sandbowl *(Catinella arenaria)*
Snake, Grass *(Natrix natrix* or *Natrix helvetica)*
Snake, Smooth *(Coronella austriaca)*
Spider, Fen Raft *(Dolomedes plantarius)*
Spider, Ladybird *(Eresus niger)*
Squirrel, Red *(Sciurus vulgaris)*
Sturgeon *(Acipenser sturio)*
Toad, Common *(Bufo bufo)*
Toad, Natterjack *(Bufo calamita)*
Turtle, Flatback *(Cheloniidae / Natator Depressus)*
Turtle, Green Sea *(Chelonia mydas)*
Turtle, Hawksbill *(Eretmochelys imbricate)*
Turtle, Kemp's Ridley Sea *(Lepidochelys kempii)*
Turtle, Leatherback Sea *(Dermochelys coriacea)*
Turtle, Loggerhead Sea *(Caretta caretta)*
Turtle, Olive Ridley *(Lepidochelys olivacea)*
Vendace *(Coregonus albula)*
Vole, Water *(Arvicola terrestris)*
Walrus *(Odobenus rosmarus)*
Whale, all species *(Cetacea)*
Whitefish *(Coregonus lavaretus)*

PLANTS PROTECTED BY SCHEDULE 8
Adder's Tongue, Least *(Ophioglossum lusitanicum)*
Alison, Small *(Alyssum alyssoides)*
Anomodon, Long-leaved *(Anomodon longifolius)*
Beech-lichen, New Forest *(Enterographa elaborata)*
Blackwort *(Southbya nigrella)*
Bluebell *(Hyacinthoides non-scripta)*
Bolete, Royal *(Boletus regius)*
Broomrape, Bedstraw *(Orobanche caryophyllacea)*
Broomrape, Oxtongue *(Orobanche loricata)*
Broomrape, Thistle *(Orobanche reticulata)*

Cabbage, Lundy *(Rhynchosinapis wrightii)*
Calamint, Wood *(Calamintha sylvatica)*
Caloplaca, Snow *(Caloplaca nivalis)*
Catapyrenium, Tree *(Catapyrenium psoromoides)*
Catchfly, Alpine *(Lychnis alpina)*
Catillaria, Laurer's *(Catellaria laureri)*
Centaury, Slender *(Centaurium tenuiflorum)*
Cinquefoil, Rock *(Potentilla rupestris)*
Cladonia, Convoluted *(Cladonia convoluta)*
Cladonia, Upright Mountain *(Cladonia stricta)*
Clary, Meadow *(Salvia pratensis)*
Club-rush, Triangular *(Scirpus triquetrus)*
Colt's-foot, Purple *(Homogyne alpina)*
Cotoneaster, Wild *(Cotoneaster integerrimus)*
Cottongrass, Slender *(Eriophorum gracile)*
Cow-wheat, Field *(Melampyrum arvense)*
Crocus, Sand *(Romulea columnae)*
Crystalwort, Lizard *(Riccia bifurca)*
Cudweed, Broad-leaved *(Filago pyramidata)*
Cudweed, Jersey *(Gnaphalium luteoalbum)*
Cudweed, Red-tipped *(Filago lutescens)*
Cut-grass *(Leersia oryzoides)*
Diapensia *(Diapensia lapponica)*
Dock, Shore *(Rumex rupestris)*
Earwort, Marsh *(Jamesoniella undulifolia)*
Eryngo, Field *(Eryngium campestre)*
Fern, Dickie's Bladder *(Cystopteris dickieana)*
Fern, Killarney *(Trichomanes speciosum)*
Flapwort, Norfolk *(Leiocolea rutheana)*
Fleabane, Alpine *(Erigeron borealis)*
Fleabane, Small *(Pulicaria vulgaris)*
Fleawort, South Stack *(Tephroseris integrifolia ssp maritima)*
Frostwort, Pointed *(Gymnomitrion apiculatum)*
Fungus, Hedgehog *(Hericium erinaceum)*
Galingale, Brown *(Cyperus fuscus)*
Gentian, Alpine *(Gentiana nivalis)*
Gentian, Dune *(Gentianella uliginosa)*
Gentian, Early *(Gentianella anglica)*
Gentian, Fringed *(Gentianella ciliata)*
Gentian, Spring *(Gentiana verna)*
Germander, Cut-leaved *(Teucrium botrys)*
Germander, Water *(Teucrium scordium)*
Gladiolus, Wild *(Gladiolus illyricus)*
Goblin Lights *(Catolechia wahlenbergii)*
Goosefoot, Stinking *(Chenopodium vulvaria)*
Grass-poly *(Lythrum hyssopifolia)*
Grimmia, Blunt-leaved *(Grimmia unicolor)*
Gyalecta, Elm *(Gyalecta ulmi)*
Hare's-ear, Sickle-leaved *(Bupleurum falcatum)*
Hare's-ear, Small *(Bupleurum baldense)*
Hawk's-beard, Stinking *(Crepis foetida)*
Hawkweed, Northroe *(Hieracium northroense)*
Hawkweed, Shetland *(Hieracium zetlandicum)*
Hawkweed, Weak-leaved *(Hieracium attenuatifolium)*
Heath, Blue *(Phyllodoce caerulea)*
Helleborine, Red *(Cephalanthera rubra)*
Horsetail, Branched *(Equisetum ramosissimum)*
Hound's-tongue, Green *(Cynoglossum germanicum)*
Knawel, Perennial *(Scleranthus perennis)*
Knotgrass, Sea *(Polygonum maritimum)*
Lady's-slipper *(Cypripedium calceolus)*
Lecanora, Tarn *(Lecanora archariana)*
Lecidea, Copper *(Lecidea inops)*
Leek, Round-headed *(Allium sphaerocephalon)*
Lettuce, Least *(Lactuca saligna)*
Lichen, Arctic Kidney *(Nephroma arcticum)*
Lichen, Ciliate Strap *(Heterodermia leucomelos)*
Lichen, Coralloid Rosette *(Heterodermia propagulifera)*
Lichen, Ear-lobed Dog *(Peltigera lepidophora)*

Lichen, Forked Hair *(Bryoria furcellata)*
Lichen, Golden Hair *(Teloschistes flavicans)*
Lichen, Orange-fruited Elm *(Caloplaca luteoalba)*
Lichen, River Jelly *(Collema dichotomum)*
Lichen, Scaly Breck *(Squamarina lentigera)*
Lichen, Starry Breck *(Buellia asterella)*
Lily, Snowdon *(Lloydia serotina)*
Liverwort, Lindenberg's Leafy *(Adelanthus lindenbergianus)*
Lungwort, Tree *(Lobaria pulmonaria)*
Marsh-mallow, Rough *(Althaea hirsuta)*
Marshwort, Creeping *(Apium repens)*
Milk-parsley, Cambridge *(Selinum carvifolia)*
Moss *(Drepanocladius vernicosus)*
Moss, Alpine Copper *(Mielichoferia mielichoferi)*
Moss, Baltic Bog *(Sphagnum balticum)*
Moss, Blue Dew *(Saelania glaucescens)*
Moss, Blunt-leaved Bristle *(Orthotrichum obtusifolium)*
Moss, Bright Green Cave *(Cyclodictyon laetevirens)*
Moss, Cordate Beard *(Barbula cordata)*
Moss, Cornish Path *(Ditrichum cornubicum)*
Moss, Derbyshire Feather *(Thamnobryum angustifolium)*
Moss, Flamingo *(Desmatodon cernuus)*
Moss, Glaucous Beard *(Barbula glauca)*
Moss, Green Shield *(Buxbaumia viridis)*
Moss, Hair Silk *(Plagiothecium piliferum)*
Moss, Knothole *(Zygodon forsteri)*
Moss, Large Yellow Feather *(Scorpidium turgescens)*
Moss, Millimetre *(Micromitrium tenerum)*
Moss, Multi-fruited River *(Cryphaea lamyana)*
Moss, Nowell's Limestone *(Zygodon gracilis)*
Moss, Polar Feather *(Hygrohypnum polare)*
Moss, Rigid Apple *(Bartramia stricta)*
Moss, Round-leaved Feather *(Rhyncostegium rotundifolium)*
Moss, Schleicher's Thread *(Bryum schleicheri)*
Moss, Slender Green Feather *(Drepanocladus vernicosus)*
Moss, Triangular Pygmy *(Acaulon triquetrum)*
Moss, Vaucher's Feather *(Hypnum vaucheri)*
Mudwort, Welsh *(Limosella australis)*
Naiad, Holly-leaved *(Najas marina)*
Naiad, Slender *(Najas flexilis)*
Nail, Rock *(Calicium corynellum)*
Orache, Stalked *(Halimione pedunculata)*
Orchid, Early Spider *(Ophrys sphegodes)*
Orchid, Fen *(Liparis loeselii)*
Orchid, Ghost *(Epipogium aphyllum)*
Orchid, Lapland Marsh *(Dactylorhiza lapponica)*
Orchid, Late Spider *(Ophrys fuciflora)*
Orchid, Lizard *(Himantoglossum hircinum)*
Orchid, Military *(Orchis militaris)*
Orchid, Monkey *(Orchis simia)*
Pannaria, Caledonia *(Panneria ignobilis)*
Parmelia, New Forest *(Parmelia minarum)*
Parmentaria, Oil Stain *(Parmentaria chilensis)*
Pear, Plymouth *(Pyrus cordata)*
Penny-cress, Perfoliate *(Thlaspi perfoliatum)*
Pennyroyal *(Mentha pulegium)*
Pertusaria, Alpine Moss *(Pertusaria bryontha)*
Petalwort *(Petallophyllum ralfsi)*
Physcia, Southern Grey *(Physcia tribacioides)*
Pigmyweed *(Crassula aquatica)*
Pine, Ground *(Ajuga chamaepitys)*
Pink, Cheddar *(Dianthus gratianopolitanus)*
Pink, Childing *(Petroraghia nanteuilii)*
Pink, Deptford (England and Wales only) *(Dianthus armeria)*
Polypore, Oak *(Buglossoporus pulvinus)*
Pseudocyphellaria, Ragged *(Pseudocyphellaria lacerata)*
Psora, Rusty Alpine *(Psora rubiformis)*
Puffball, Sandy Stilt *(Battarraea phalloides)*
Ragwort, Fen *(Senecio paludosus)*

Ramping-fumitory, Martin's *(Fumaria martinii)*
Rampion, Spiked *(Phyteuma spicatum)*
Restharrow, Small *(Ononis reclinata)*
Rock-cress, Alpine *(Arabis alpina)*
Rock-cress, Bristol *(Arabis stricta)*
Rustwort, Western *(Marsupella profunda)*
Sandwort, Norwegian *(Arenaria norvegica)*
Sandwort, Teesdale *(Minuartia stricta)*
Saxifrage, Drooping *(Saxifraga cernua)*
Saxifrage, Tufted *(Saxifraga cespitosa)*
Saxifrage, Yellow Marsh *(Saxifrage hirulus)*
Solenopsora, Serpentine *(Solenopsora liparina)*
Solomon's-seal, Whorled *(Polygonatum verticillatum)*
Sow-thistle, Alpine *(Cicerbita alpina)*
Spearwort, Adder's-tongue *(Ranunculus ophioglossifolius)*
Speedwell, Fingered *(Veronica triphyllos)*
Speedwell, Spiked *(Veronica spicata)*
Spike-rush, Dwarf *(Eleocharis parvula)*
Star-of-Bethlehem, Early *(Gagea bohemica)*
Starfruit *(Damasonium alisma)*
Stonewort, Bearded *(Chara canescens)*
Stonewort, Foxtail *(Lamprothamnium papulosum)*
Strapwort *(Corrigiola litoralis)*
Sulphur-tresses, Alpine *(Alectoria ochroleuca)*
Turpswort *(Geocalyx graveolens)*
Violet, Fen *(Viola persicifolia)*
Viper's-grass *(Scorzonera humilis)*
Water-plantain, Floating *(Luronium natans)*
Water-plantain, Ribbon-leaved *(Alisma gramineum)*
Wood-sedge, Starved *(Carex depauperata)*
Woodsia, Alpine *(Woodsia alpina)*
Woodsia, Oblong *(Woodsia ilvenis)*
Wormwood, Field *(Artemisia campestris)*
Woundwort, Downy *(Stachys germanica)*
Woundwort, Limestone *(Stachys alpina)*
Yellow-rattle, Greater *(Rhinanthus serotinus)*

WORLD HERITAGE SITES

The Convention Concerning the Protection of the World Cultural and Natural Heritage was adopted by the United Nations Educational, Scientific and Cultural Organization (UNESCO) in 1972 and ratified by the UK in 1984. As at July 2014, 191 states were party to the convention. The convention provides for the identification, protection and conservation of cultural and natural sites of outstanding universal value.

Cultural sites may be:
• an extraordinary exponent of human creative genius
• sites representing architectural and technological innovation or cultural interchange
• sites of artistic, historic, aesthetic, archaeological, scientific, ethnologic or anthropologic value
• 'cultural landscapes', ie sites whose characteristics are marked by significant interactions between human populations and their natural environment
• exceptional examples of a traditional settlement or land- or sea-use, especially those threatened by irreversible changes.
• unique or exceptional examples of a cultural tradition or a civilisation either still present or extinct

Natural sites may be:
• those displaying critical periods of earth's history
• superlative examples of on-going ecological and biological processes in the evolution of ecosystems
• those exhibiting remarkable natural beauty and aesthetic significance or those where extraordinary natural phenomena are witnessed
• the habitat of threatened species and plants

Governments which are party to the convention nominate sites in their country for inclusion in the World Heritage List. Nominations are considered by the World Heritage Committee, an inter governmental committee composed of 21 representatives of the parties to the convention. The committee is advised by the International Council on Monuments and Sites (ICOMOS), the International Centre for the Study of the Preservation and Restoration of Cultural Property (ICCROM) and the International Union for the Conservation of Nature (IUCN). ICOMOS evaluates and reports on proposed cultural and mixed sites, ICCROM provides expert advice and training on how to conserve and restore cultural property and IUCN provides technical evaluations of natural heritage sites and reports on the state of conservation of listed sites. The Department for Culture, Media and Sport represents the UK government in matters relating to the convention.

A prerequisite for inclusion in the World Heritage List is the existence of an effective legal protection system in the country in which the site is situated and a detailed management plan to ensure the conservation of the site. Inclusion in the list does not confer any greater degree of protection on the site than that offered by the national protection framework.

If a site is considered to be in serious danger of decay or damage, the committee may add it to the World Heritage in Danger List. Sites on this list may benefit from particular attention or emergency measures to allay threats and allow them to retain their world heritage status, or in extreme cases of damage or neglect they may lose their world heritage status completely. As at July 2014, there were 45 sites on the World Heritage in Danger List.

Financial support for the conservation of sites on the World Heritage List is provided by the World Heritage Fund, administered by the World Heritage Committee. The fund's income is derived from compulsory and voluntary contributions from the states party to the convention and from private donations.

WORLD HERITAGE CENTRE, UNESCO, 7 Place de Fontenoy, 75352 Paris 07 SP, France **W** whc.unesco.org

DESIGNATED SITES

As at 1 July 2014, following the 38th session of the World Heritage Committee, 1,007 sites across 161 countries were inscribed on the World Heritage List. Of these, 25 are in the UK and three in British overseas territories; 23 are listed for their cultural significance (†), four for their natural significance (*) and one for both cultural and natural significance. The year in which sites were designated appears in the first set of parentheses. In 2005 Hadrian's Wall, a World Heritage Site in its own right since 1987, was joined by the upper German-Raetian Limes to form the first section of a trans-national world heritage site, Frontiers of the Roman Empire; in 2008 the Antonine Wall was inscribed by UNESCO, becoming a further part of this site. The number in the second set of parentheses denotes the position of each site on the map below.

UNITED KINGDOM

†Bath – the city (1987). (1)
†Blaenarvon industrial landscape, Wales (2000). (2)
†Blenheim Palace and Park, Oxfordshire (1987). (3)
†Canterbury Cathedral, St Augustine's Abbey, St Martin's Church, Kent (1988). (4)
†Castle and town walls of King Edward I, north Wales – Beaumaris, Caernarfon Castle, Conwy Castle, Harlech Castle (1986). (5)
†Cornwall and west Devon mining landscape (2006). (6)

†Derwent Valley Mills, Derbyshire (2001). (7)
*Dorset and east Devon coast (2001). (8)
†Durham Cathedral and Castle (1986). (9)
|Edinburgh old and new towns (1995). (10)
†Frontiers of the Roman Empire = Hadrian's Wall, northern England; Antonine Wall, central Scotland (1987, 2005, 2008). (11)
*Giant's Causeway and Causeway coast, Co. Antrim (1986). (12)
†Greenwich, London – maritime Greenwich, including the Royal Naval College, Old Royal Observatory, Queen's House, town centre (1997). (13)
†Heart of Neolithic Orkney (1999). (14)
†Ironbridge Gorge, Shropshire – the world's first iron bridge and other early industrial sites (1986). (15)
†Liverpool – six areas of the maritime mercantile city (2004). (16)
†New Lanark, South Lanarkshire, Scotland (2001). (17)
†Pontcysyllte Aqueduct and Canal, Wrexham, Wales (2009). (18)
†Royal Botanic Gardens, Kew (2003). (19)
†*St Kilda, Eilean Siar (Western Isles) (1986). (20)
†Saltaire, West Yorkshire (2001). (21)
†Stonehenge, Avebury and related megalithic sites, Wiltshire (1986). (22)
†Studley Royal Park, Fountains Abbey, St Mary's Church, N. Yorkshire (1986). (23)
†Tower of London (1988). (24)
†Westminster Abbey, Palace of Westminster, St Margaret's Church, London (1987). (25)

BRITISH OVERSEAS TERRITORIES

*Henderson Island, Pitcairn Islands, South Pacific Ocean (1988)
*Gough Island and Inaccessible Island (part of Tristan da Cunha), South Atlantic Ocean (1995)
†St George town and related fortifications, Bermuda (2000)

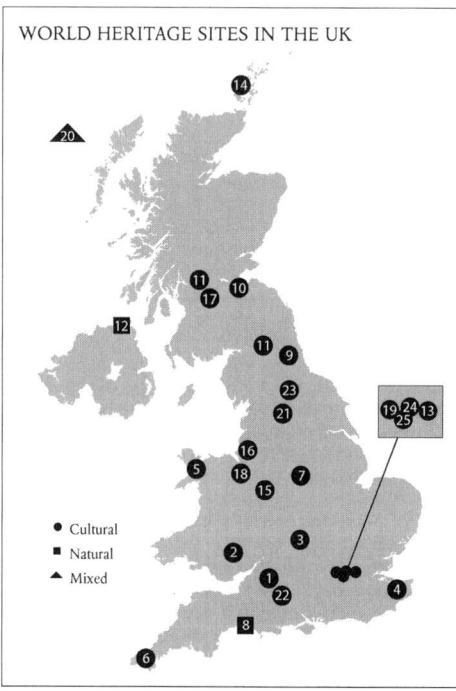

WORLD HERITAGE SITES IN THE UK

● Cultural
■ Natural
▲ Mixed

HISTORIC BUILDINGS AND MONUMENTS

ENGLAND

Under the Planning (Listed Buildings and Conservation Areas) Act 1990, the Secretary of State for Culture, Media and Sport has a statutory duty to approve lists of buildings or groups of buildings in England which are of special architectural or historic interest. In November 2009 responsibility for compiling the list of buildings was passed to English Heritage. Under the Ancient Monuments and Archaeological Areas Act 1979 as amended by the National Heritage Act 1983, the secretary of state is also responsible for compiling a schedule of ancient monuments. Decisions are taken on the advice of English Heritage. On 1 April 2005 responsibility for the administration of the listing system was transferred from the secretary of state to English Heritage. On 4 April 2011, English Heritage launched the National Heritage List for England, a searchable database of all nationally designated heritage assets (W http://list.english-heritage.org.uk).

LISTED BUILDINGS

Listed buildings are classified into Grade I, Grade II* and Grade II. There are 374,081 listed buildings in England, of which approximately 92 per cent are Grade II listed. Almost all pre-1700 buildings are listed, as are most buildings of 1700 to 1840. English Heritage carries out thematic surveys of particular types of buildings with a view to making recommendations for listing. The main purpose of listing is to ensure that care is taken in deciding the future of a building. No changes which affect the architectural or historic character of a listed building can be made without listed building consent (in addition to planning permission where relevant). Applications for consent are normally dealt with by the local planning authority, although English Heritage is always consulted about proposals affecting Grade I and Grade II* properties. It is a criminal offence to demolish a listed building, or alter it in such a way as to affect its character, without consent.

Area	No. of listed buildings
1. Devon	20,816
2. Greater London	19,272
3. Kent	17,680
4. Somerset (incl. Bath)	16,130
5. Essex	14,305
6. North Yorkshire	14,002
7. Cornwall	13,943
8. Suffolk	13,582
9. Hampshire (incl. Isle of Wight)	13,547
10. Gloucestershire	13,441

* *Source:* National Heritage List for England

SCHEDULED MONUMENTS

There are 19,717 scheduled monuments in England. All monuments proposed for scheduling are considered to be of national importance. Where buildings are both scheduled and listed, ancient monuments legislation takes precedence. The main purpose of scheduling a monument is to preserve it for the future and to protect it from damage, destruction or any unnecessary interference. Once a monument has been scheduled, scheduled monument consent is required before any works can be carried out. The scope of the control is more extensive and more detailed than that applied to listed

buildings, but certain minor works, as detailed in the Ancient Monuments (Class Consents) Order 1994, may be carried out without consent. It is a criminal offence to carry out unauthorised work to scheduled monuments.

WALES

Under the Planning (Listed Buildings and Conservation Areas) Act 1990 and the Ancient Monuments and Archaeological Areas Act 1979, the National Assembly for Wales is responsible for listing buildings and scheduling monuments in Wales on the advice of Cadw (the Welsh government's historic environment division) and the Royal Commission on the Ancient and Historical Monuments of Wales (RCAHMW). The criteria for evaluating buildings are similar to those in England and the same listing system is used. As at March 2014, there are 29,970 listed buildings and 4,181 scheduled monuments in Wales.

SCOTLAND

Under the Planning (Listed Buildings and Conservation Areas) (Scotland) Act 1997 and the Ancient Monuments and Archaeological Areas Act 1979, Scottish ministers are responsible for listing buildings and scheduling monuments in Scotland on the advice of Historic Scotland and the Royal Commission on the Ancient and Historical Monuments of Scotland (RCAHMS). The criteria for evaluating buildings are similar to those in England but an A, B, C(S) categorisation is used. As at March 2014 there were 47,554 listed buildings and 8,188 scheduled monuments in Scotland.

NORTHERN IRELAND

Under the Planning (Northern Ireland) Order 1991 and the Historic Monuments and Archaeological Objects (Northern Ireland) Order 1995, the Northern Ireland Environment Agency (part of the Department of the Environment of the Northern Ireland) is responsible for listing buildings and scheduling monuments. The Historic Buildings Council for Northern Ireland and the relevant district council must be consulted on listing proposals, and the Historic Monuments Council for Northern Ireland must be consulted on scheduling proposals. The criteria for evaluating buildings are similar to those in England but an A, B+, B1 and B2 categorisation is used. As at March 2014 there were around 8,621 listed buildings and 1,991 scheduled monuments in Northern Ireland.

ENGLAND

For more information on English Heritage properties, including those listed below, the official website is W www.english-heritage.org.uk
For more information on National Trust properties in England, including those listed below, the official website is W www.nationaltrust.org.uk
KEY
(EH) English Heritage property
(NT) National Trust property
* UNESCO World Heritage Site (*see also* World Heritage Sites)

A LA RONDE (NT), Exmouth, Devon EX8 5BD T 01395-265514
 Unique 16-sided house completed *c.*1796

ALNWICK CASTLE, Alnwick, Northumberland NE66 1NQ
T 01665-511100 W www.alnwickcastle.com
Seat of the Dukes of Northumberland since 1309; Italian
Renaissance-style interior; gardens with spectacular water
features

ALTHORP, Northants NN7 4HQ T 01604-770006
W www.althorp.com
Spencer family seat; permanent Diana, Princess of Wales
exhibition

ANGLESEY ABBEY (NT), Lode, Cambs CB25 9EJ
T 01223-810080
Jacobean house (c.1600) with gardens and a working
watermill (Lode Mill) on the site of a 12th-century priory;
fine furnishings and a unique clock collection

APSLEY HOUSE (EH), London W1J 7NT T 020-7499 5676
Built by Robert Adam 1771–8, home of the Dukes of
Wellington since 1817 and known as 'No. 1 London';
collection of fine and decorative arts

ARUNDEL CASTLE, Arundel, W. Sussex BN18 9AB
T 01903-882173 W www.arundelcastle.org
Castle dating from the Norman Conquest; seat of the
Dukes of Norfolk

AVEBURY (EH/NT), Wilts SN8 1RF T 01672-539250
Remains of stone circles constructed 4,000 years ago
enclosing part of the later village of Avebury

BANQUETING HOUSE, Whitehall, London SW1A 2ER
T 0844-482 7777 W www.hrp.org.uk
Designed by Inigo Jones in 1619; ceiling paintings by
Rubens; site of the execution of Charles I

BASILDON PARK (NT), Reading, Berks RG8 9NR
T 0118-984 3040
Palladian mansion built in 1776–83 by John Carr

BATTLE ABBEY (EH), Battle, E. Sussex TN33 0AD
T 01424-775705
Remains of the abbey founded by William the Conqueror
on the site of the Battle of Hastings

BEESTON CASTLE (EH), Cheshire CW6 9TX
T 01829-260464
Built in the 13th century by Ranulf, sixth Earl of Chester
on the site of an Iron Age hillfort

BELVOIR CASTLE, Grantham, Lincs NG32 1PE
T 01476-871002 W www.belvoircastle.com
Seat of the Dukes of Rutland; 19th-century Gothic-style
castle; notable art collection

BERKELEY CASTLE, Glos GL13 9BQ T 01453-810303
W www.berkeley-castle.com
Completed late 12th century; site of the murder of
Edward II (1327)

BIRDOSWALD FORT (EH), Brampton, Cumbria CA8 7DD
T 01697-747602
Stretch of Hadrian's Wall with Roman wall fort, turret and
milecastle

*BLENHEIM PALACE, Woodstock, Oxon OX20 1PP
T 01993-810530 W www.blenheimpalace.com
Seat of the Dukes of Marlborough and Winston
Churchill's birthplace; house designed by Vanbrugh;
landscaped parkland by Capability Brown

BLICKLING ESTATE (NT), Blickling, Norfolk NR11 6NF
T 01263-738030
Jacobean house with state rooms; extensive gardens,
temple and 18th-century orangery

BODIAM CASTLE (NT), Bodiam, E. Sussex TN32 5UA
T 01580-830196
Well-preserved medieval moated castle built in 1385

BOLSOVER CASTLE (EH), Bolsover, Derbys S44 6PR
T 01246-822844
17th-century castle on site of medieval fortress

BOSCOBEL HOUSE (EH), Bishops Wood, Shrops ST19 9AR
T 01902-850244

Timber-framed 17th-century hunting lodge; refuge of
fugitive Charles II from parliamentary troops

BOUGHTON HOUSE, Kettering, Northants NN14 1BJ
T 01536-515731 W www.boughtonhouse.org.uk
17th-century house with French-style additions; home of
the Dukes of Buccleuch and Queensbury

BOWOOD HOUSE, Calne, Wilts SN11 0LZ T 01249-812102
W www.bowood-house.co.uk
18th-century house in Capability Brown park, featuring
Robert Adam orangery and renowned pinetum and
arboretum

BUCKFAST ABBEY, Buckfastleigh, Devon TQ11 0EE
T 01364-645500 W www.buckfast.org.uk
Benedictine monastery on medieval foundations

BUCKINGHAM PALACE, London SW1A 1AA
T 020-7930 4832 W www.royalcollection.org.uk
Purchased by George III in 1761, and the Sovereign's
official London residence since 1837; 19 state rooms,
including the Throne Room, and Queen's Gallery

BUCKLAND ABBEY (NT), Yelverton, Devon PL20 6EY
T 01822-853607
13th-century Cistercian monastery; home of Sir Francis
Drake

BURGHLEY HOUSE, Stamford, Lincs PE9 3JY T 01780-752451
W www.burghley.co.uk
Late Elizabethan house built by William Cecil, first Lord
Burghley

CARISBROOKE CASTLE (EH), Newport, Isle of Wight
PO30 1XY T 01983-522107
W www.carisbrookecastlemuseum.org.uk
Norman castle; museum; prison of Charles I 1647–8

CARLISLE CASTLE (EH), Carlisle, Cumbria CA3 8UR
T 01228-591922
Medieval castle; prison of Mary Queen of Scots

CASTLE ACRE PRIORY (EH), King's Lynn, Norfolk PE32 2XD
T 01760-755394
Remains include 12th-century church and prior's
lodgings

CASTLE DROGO (NT), Drewsteignton, Devon EX6 6PB
T 01647-433306
Granite castle designed by Lutyens in 1911

CASTLE HOWARD, N. Yorks YO60 7DA T 01653-648333
W www.castlehoward.co.uk
Designed by Vanbrugh 1699–1726; mausoleum designed
by Hawksmoor

CASTLE RISING CASTLE (EH), King's Lynn, Norfolk
PE31 6AH T 01553-631330 W www.castlerising.co.uk
12th-century keep with gatehouse and bridge, surrounded
by 20 acres of defensive earthworks

CHARLES DARWIN'S HOUSE (DOWN HOUSE) (EH),
Downe, Kent BR6 7JT T 01689-859119
The family home where Darwin wrote *On the Origin of
Species*

CHARTWELL (NT), Westerham, Kent TN16 1PS
T 01732-868381
Home and studio of Sir Winston Churchill

CHATSWORTH, Bakewell, Derbys DE45 1PP T 01246-565300
W www.chatsworth.org
Tudor mansion set in magnificent parkland; seat of the
Dukes of Devonshire

CHESTERS ROMAN FORT (EH), Chollerford,
Northumberland NE46 4EU T 01434-681379
Roman cavalry fort built to guard Hadrian's Wall

CHYSAUSTER ANCIENT VILLAGE (EH), Penzance,
Cornwall TR20 8XA T 07831-757934
Remains of nearly 2,000-year-old Celtic settlement; eight
stone-walled homesteads

CLANDON PARK (NT), West Clandon, Guildford, Surrey
GU4 7RQ T 01483-222482 W www.clandonpark.co.uk

18th-century Palladian mansion and gardens, which contain a Maori meeting house, brought back from New Zealand in 1892

CLIFFORD'S TOWER (EH), York YO1 9SA T 01904-646940 W www.cliffordstower.com

13th-century keep built on a mound; remains of a castle built by William the Conqueror

CORBRIDGE ROMAN SITE (EH), Corbridge, Northumberland NE45 5NT T 01434-632349

Excavated central area of a Roman garrison town

CORFE CASTLE (NT), Wareham, Dorset BH20 5EZ T 01929-481294

Former royal castle dating from the 11th century and ruined during the English Civil War

CROFT CASTLE AND PARKLAND (NT), Yarpole, Herefordshire HR6 9PW T 01568-780246

17th-century quadrangular manor house with Georgian-Gothic interior; built close to ruin of pre-Conquest border castle

DEAL CASTLE (EH), Deal, Kent CT14 7BA T 01304-372762

Largest of the coastal defence forts built by Henry VIII; shaped like a rose with six inner and outer bastions

*DERWENT VALLEY MILLS, Belper, Derbyshire T 01629-536831

Series of 18th- and 19th-century cotton mills; birthplace of the modern factory

DOVER CASTLE (EH), Dover, Kent CT16 1HU T 01304-211067

Castle with Roman, Saxon and Norman features; tunnels used as wartime operations rooms

DR JOHNSON'S HOUSE, Gough Square, London EC4A 3DE T 020-7353 3745 W www.drjohnsonshouse.org

Home of Samuel Johnson 1748–59

DUNSTANBURGH CASTLE (EH/NT), Craster, nr Alnwick, Northumberland NE66 3TT T 01665-576231

14th-century castle ruins on a cliff with a substantial twin-towered gatehouse-keep

ELTHAM PALACE (EH), Eltham, London SE9 5QE T 02082-94 2577

Art Deco house next to remains of medieval palace once occupied by Henry VIII; moated gardens

FARLEIGH HUNGERFORD CASTLE (EH), Bath, Somerset BA2 7RS T 01225-754026

Late 14th-century castle with inner and outer courts; chapel with rare medieval wall paintings

FARNHAM CASTLE KEEP (EH), Farnham, Surrey GU9 0AG T 01252-721194 W www.farnhamcastle.com

Large 12th-century castle keep with motte and bailey wall

FISHBOURNE ROMAN PALACE, Fishbourne, Chichester, W. Sussex PO19 3QR T 01243-789859 W www.sussexpast.co.uk

Excavated Roman palace with largest collection of in-situ mosaics in Britain

*FOUNTAINS ABBEY (NT), nr Ripon, N. Yorks HG4 3DY T 01765-608888 W www.fountainsabbey.org.uk

Ruined Cistercian monastery and corn mill; site includes Studley Royal, a Georgian water garden and deer park

FRAMLINGHAM CASTLE (EH), Framlingham, Suffolk IP13 9BP T 01728-724189

Castle (c.1200) with high curtain walls enclosing an almshouse (1639); once the refuge of Mary Tudor

FURNESS ABBEY (EH), Barrow-in-Furness, Cumbria LA13 0PJ T 01229-823420

Remains of church and cloister buildings founded in 1123

GLASTONBURY ABBEY, Glastonbury, Somerset BA6 9EL T 01458-832267 W www.glastonburyabbey.com

12th-century abbey destroyed by fire in 1184 and later rebuilt; ruined in 1539 during dissolution of monasteries; site of an early Christian settlement

GOODRICH CASTLE (EH), Ross-on-Wye, Herefordshire HR9 6HY T 01600-890538

Remains of 12th- and 13th-century castle; contains a famous mortar that ruined the castle in 1646

GREENWICH, London SE10 9NF W www.visitgreenwich.org.uk

Former Royal Observatory (founded 1675) housing the time ball and zero meridian of longitude; the Queen's House, designed for Queen Anne, wife of James I, by Inigo Jones; Painted Hall and neoclassical Chapel (Old Royal Naval College)

GRIMES GRAVES (EH), Brandon, Norfolk IP26 5DE T 01842-810656

Neolithic flint mines; one shaft can be descended

GUILDHALL, London EC2V 7HH T 020-7606 3030 W www.guildhall.cityoflondon.gov.uk

Centre of civic government of the City built c.1441; facade built 1788–9

HADDON HALL, Bakewell, Derbys DE45 1LA T 01629-812855 W www.haddonhall.co.uk

Well-preserved 12th-century manor house

HAILES ABBEY (EH), Cheltenham, Glos GL54 5PB T 01242-602398

Ruins of a 13th-century Cistercian monastery

HAM HOUSE AND GARDEN (NT), Richmond-upon-Thames, Surrey TW10 7RS T 020-8940 1950

Stuart house with lavish interiors and formal gardens

HAMPTON COURT PALACE, East Molesey, Surrey KT8 9AU T 0844-482 7777 W www.hrp.org.uk

16th-century palace originally built for Cardinal Wolsey with 17th- and 18th-century additions by Wren; Royal Tennis Court and world-renowned maze

HARDWICK HALL (NT), Chesterfield, Derbys S44 5QJ T 01246-850430

Elizabethan house built for Bess of Hardwick

HARDY'S BIRTHPLACE (NT), Higher Bockhampton, Dorset DT2 8QJ T 01305-262366

Birthplace and home of Thomas Hardy

HAREWOOD HOUSE, Harewood, W. Yorks LS17 9LG T 0113-218 1010 W www.harewood.org

18th-century house designed by John Carr and Robert Adam; park by Capability Brown

HATFIELD HOUSE, Hatfield, Herts AL9 5NQ T 01707-287010 W www.hatfield-house.co.uk

Jacobean house built by Robert Cecil; features surviving wing of Royal Palace of Hatfield (c.1485), the childhood home of Elizabeth I

HELMSLEY CASTLE (EH), Helmsley, N. Yorks YO62 5AB T 01439-770442

12th-century keep and curtain wall with 16th-century buildings; spectacular earthwork defences

HEVER CASTLE, nr Edenbridge, Kent TN8 7NG T 01732-865224 W www.hevercastle.co.uk

13th-century double-moated castle; childhood home of Anne Boleyn

HIGH CROSS HOUSE (NT), nr Totnes, Devon TQ9 6ED T 01803-842382

Celebrated Modernist house containing original Bauhaus furniture

HOLKHAM HALL, Wells-next-the-Sea, Norfolk NR23 1AB T 01328-710227 W www.holkham.co.uk

Palladian mansion; notable fine art collection

HOUSESTEADS ROMAN FORT (EH), Hexham, Northumberland NE47 6NN T 01434-344363

Excavated Roman infantry fort on Hadrian's Wall with museum

*IRONBRIDGE GORGE, Ironbridge, Shropshire

Important Industrial Revolution site, featuring the world's first iron bridge

KEDLESTON HALL (NT), Derbys DE22 5JH T 01332-842191
Palladian mansion built 1759–65; complete Robert Adam
interiors; museum of Asian artefacts

KELMSCOTT MANOR, nr Lechlade, Glos GL7 3HJ
T 01367-252486 W www.kelmscottmanor.org.uk
Built c.1600; summer home of William Morris, with
products of Morris and Co.

KENILWORTH CASTLE (EH), Kenilworth, Warks CV8 1NE
T 01926-852078
Largest castle ruin in England; Norman keep with
13th-century outer walls

KENSINGTON PALACE, Kensington Gardens, London
W8 4PX T 0844-482 7777 W www.hrp.org.uk
Built in 1605 and enlarged by Wren; birthplace of
Queen Victoria; 'Victoria: love, duty and loss'
exhibition

KENWOOD HOUSE (EH), Hampstead Lane, London NW3 7JR
T 020-8348 1286
Neoclassical villa housing the Iveagh bequest of paintings
and furniture

KEW PALACE, Richmond-upon-Thames, Surrey TW9 3AB
T 0844-482 7777 W www.hrp.org.uk
Red-brick mansion (c.1631); includes Queen Charlotte's
Cottage, used by King George III and family as a
summerhouse

KINGSTON LACY (NT), Wimborne Minster, Dorset BH21 4EA
T 01202-883402
17th-century mansion with 19th-century alterations;
important art collection

KNEBWORTH HOUSE, Knebworth, Herts SG3 6PY
T 01438-812661 W www.knebworthhouse.com
Tudor manor house concealed by 19th-century Gothic
decoration; Lutyens gardens

KNOLE (NT), Sevenoaks, Kent TN15 0RP T 01732-462100
House built in 1456 set in 1,000-acre deer park;
fine art and furniture collection; birthplace of Vita
Sackville-West

LAMBETH PALACE, London SE1 7JU T 020-7898 1200
W www.archbishopofcanterbury.org
Official residence of the Archbishop of Canterbury since
the 13th century

LANERCOST PRIORY (EH), Brampton, Cumbria CA8 2HQ
T 01697-73030 W www.lanercostpriory.org.uk
The nave of the Augustinian priory's church, c.1166, is
still used; remains of other claustral buildings

LANHYDROCK (NT), Bodmin, Cornwall PL30 5AD
T 01208-265950
House dating from the 17th century; 50 rooms, including
kitchen and nursery

LEEDS CASTLE, nr Maidstone, Kent ME17 1PL
T 01622-765400 W www.leeds-castle.com
Castle dating from the 12th century, situated on two
islands in a lake; used as a royal palace by Henry VIII

LEVENS HALL, Kendal, Cumbria LA8 0PD T 01539-560321
W www.levenshall.co.uk
Elizabethan house with unique topiary garden (1694);
steam engine collection

LINCOLN CASTLE, Lincoln, Lincs LN1 3AA T 01522-782040
W www.lincolnshire.gov.uk
Built by William the Conqueror in 1068 on a Roman site;
one of only two double-motted castles in Britain

LINDISFARNE PRIORY (EH), Holy Island, Northumberland
TD15 2RX T 01289-389200
Founded in AD 635; re-established in the 12th century as
a Benedictine priory, now ruined

LITTLE MORETON HALL (NT), Congleton, Cheshire
CW12 4SD T 01260-272018
Iconic timber-framed moated Tudor manor house with
knot garden

LONGLEAT HOUSE, Warminster, Wilts BA12 7NW
T 01985-844400 W www.longleat.co.uk
Elizabethan house in Italian Renaissance style; Capability
Brown parkland with lakes; safari park

LULLINGSTONE ROMAN VILLA (EH), Eynsford, Kent
DA4 0JA T 01322-863467
Large villa occupied for much of the Roman period; fine
mosaics and unique Christian paintings

MIDDLEHAM CASTLE (EH), Middleham, N. Yorks DL8 4QG
T 01969-623899
12th-century keep within later fortifications; childhood
home of Richard III

MONTACUTE HOUSE (NT), Montacute, Somerset TA15 6XP
T 01935-823289
Elizabethan mansion with National Portrait Gallery
collection of portraits from the period

MOUNT GRACE PRIORY (EH), Northallerton, N. Yorks
DL6 3JG T 01609-883494
Carthusian priory with remains of monastic buildings

OLD SARUM (EH), Salisbury, Wilts SP1 3SD T 01722-335398
Iron Age hill fort enclosing remains of Norman castle and
cathedral

ORFORD CASTLE (EH), Orford, Suffolk IP12 2ND
T 01394-450472
Polygonal tower keep of c.1170 and remains of coastal
defence castle built by Henry II

OSBORNE HOUSE (EH), East Cowes, Isle of Wight PO32 6JX
T 01983-200022
Queen Victoria's seaside residence; built by Thomas Cubitt
in Italian Renaissance style; summer house, Swiss Cottage
and museum

OSTERLEY PARK (NT), Isleworth, Middx TW7 4RB
T 020-8232 5050 W www.osterleypark.org.uk
18th-century neoclassical mansion with Tudor stable
block

PENDENNIS CASTLE (EH), Falmouth, Cornwall TR11 4LP
T 01326-316594
Well-preserved 16th-century coastal defence castle

PENSHURST PLACE, Penshurst, Kent TN11 8DG
T 01892-870307 W www.penshurstplace.com
Medieval house featuring Baron's Hall (1341) and gardens
(1346); toy museum

PETWORTH HOUSE (NT), Petworth, W. Sussex GU28 0AE
T 01798-342207
Late 17th-century house set in Capability Brown
landscaped deer park; fine art collection

PEVENSEY CASTLE (EH), Pevensey, E. Sussex BN24 5LE
T 01323-762604
Walls of a fourth-century Roman fort; remains of an
11th-century castle

PEVERIL CASTLE (EH), Castleton, Derbys S33 8WQ
T 01433-620613
Remains of a 12th-century castle defended on two sides
by precipitous rocks

POLESDEN LACEY (NT), nr Dorking, Surrey RH5 6BD
T 01372-458203
Regency villa remodelled in the Edwardian era; fine
paintings and furnishings; walled rose garden

PORTCHESTER CASTLE (EH), Portchester, Hants PO16 9QW
T 02392-378291
Walls of a late Roman fort enclosing a Norman keep and
an Augustinian priory church

POWDERHAM CASTLE, Kenton, Devon EX6 8JQ
T 01626-890243 W www.powderham.co.uk
Medieval castle with 18th- and 19th-century alterations,
including James Wyatt music room

RABY CASTLE, Staindrop, Co. Durham DL2 3AH
T 01833-660202 W www.rabycastle.com
14th-century castle with walled gardens

RAGLEY HALL, Alcester, Warks B49 5NJ T 01789-762090
W www.ragleyhall.com
17th-century Palladian house with gardens and lake

RICHBOROUGH ROMAN FORT (EH), Richborough, Kent
CT13 9JW T 01304-612013
Remains of a Roman Saxon Shore fortress; landing-site of
the Claudian invasion in AD 43

RICHMOND CASTLE (EH), Richmond, N. Yorks DL10 4QW
T 01748-822493
12th-century keep with 11th-century curtain wall

RIEVAULX ABBEY (EH), nr Helmsley, N. Yorks YO62 5LB
T 01439-798228
Remains of a Cistercian abbey founded c.1132

ROCHESTER CASTLE (EH), Rochester, Kent ME1 1SW
T 01634-402276
11th-century castle partly on the Roman city wall, with a
well-preserved square keep of c.1127

ROCKINGHAM CASTLE, Market Harborough, Leics LE16 8TH
T 01536-770240 W www.rockinghamcastle.com
Built by William the Conqueror; formal gardens and
400-year-old 'elephant' hedge

ROMAN BATHS, Pump Room, Stall Street, Bath BA1 1LZ
T 01225-477785 W www.romanbaths.co.uk
Extensive remains of a Roman temple and bathing complex
which still flows with natural thermal water; museum

ROYAL PAVILION, Brighton BN1 1EE T 03000-290900
W www.brighton-hove-rpml.org.uk
Unique palace of George IV, in indo-gothic style with
chinoiserie interiors and Regency gardens

ST AUGUSTINE'S ABBEY (EH), Canterbury, Kent CT1 1PF
T 01227-378100
Remains of Benedictine monastery founded c.597

ST MAWES CASTLE (EH), St Mawes, Cornwall TR2 5DE
T 01326-270526
Coastal defence castle built by Henry VIII

ST MICHAEL'S MOUNT (NT), Marazion, Cornwall TR17 0HS
T 01736-710265 W www.stmichaelsmount.co.uk
12th-century church and castle with later additions,
situated on an iconic rocky island

*SALTAIRE, nr Shipley, W. Yorks
Victorian industrial village founded by mill owner Titus
Salt for his workers

SANDRINGHAM, Norfolk PE35 6EN T 01485-545400
W www.sandringhamestate.co.uk
The Queen's private residence; neo-Jacobean house built
in 1870 with gardens and country park

SCARBOROUGH CASTLE (EH), Scarborough, N. Yorks
YO11 1HY T 01723-372451
Remains of 12th-century keep and curtain walls

SHERBORNE CASTLE, Sherborne, Dorset DT9 5NR
T 01935-812072 W www.sherbornecastle.com
16th-century castle built by Sir Walter Raleigh set in
Capability Brown landscaped gardens

SHUGBOROUGH ESTATE (NT), Milford, Staffs ST17 0XB
T 0845-459 8900 W www.shugborough.org.uk
Late 17th century house in 18th-century park with
monuments, temples and pavilions in the Greek Revival
style; seat of the Earls of Lichfield

SKIPTON CASTLE, Skipton, N. Yorks BD23 1AW
T 01756-792442 W www.skiptoncastle.co.uk
Well-preserved D-shaped medieval castle with six round
towers and inner courtyard

SMALLHYTHE PLACE (NT), Tenterden, Kent TN30 7NG
T 01580-762334
Half-timbered 16th-century house

*STONEHENGE (EH), nr Amesbury, Wilts SP4 7DE
T 01722-343830
World-famous prehistoric monument comprising
concentric stone circles surrounded by a ditch and bank

STONOR PARK, Henley-on-Thames, Oxon RG9 6HF
T 01491-638587 W www.stonor.com
Medieval house with Georgian facade; refuge for Catholic
recusants after the Reformation

STOURHEAD (NT), Stourton, Wilts BA12 6QD
T 01747-842030
18th-century Palladian mansion with world-renowned
landscape gardens; King Alfred's Tower

STRATFIELD SAYE HOUSE, Hants RG7 2BT T 01256-882694
W www.stratfield-saye.co.uk
House built 1630–40; home of the Dukes of Wellington
since 1817

STRATFORD-UPON-AVON, Warks T 01789-204016
W www.shakespeare.org.uk
Shakespeare's Birthplace Trust with Shakespeare Centre;
Anne Hathaway's Cottage; Holy Trinity Church, where
Shakespeare is buried

SUDELEY CASTLE, Winchcombe, Glos GL54 5JD
T 01242-604244 W www.sudeleycastle.co.uk
Castle built in 1442; once owned by Richard III and
former home to Catherine Parr, sixth wife of Henry VIII;
restored in the 19th century

SULGRAVE MANOR, nr Banbury, Oxon OX17 2SD
T 01295-760205 W www.sulgravemanor.org.uk
Home of George Washington's family

SUTTON HOUSE (NT), Hackney, London E9 6JQ
T 020-8986 2264
Tudor house, built in 1535 by Sir Ralph Sadleir

SYON HOUSE, Brentford, Middx TW8 8JF T 020-8560 0882
W www.syonpark.co.uk
Built on the site of a former monastery; Robert Adam
interior; Capability Brown park

TINTAGEL CASTLE (EH), Tintagel, Cornwall PL34 0HE
T 01840-770328
13th-century cliff-top castle and 5th–6th-century Celtic
settlement; linked with Arthurian legend

TOWER OF LONDON, London EC3N 4AB T 0844-482 7777
W www.hrp.org.uk
Royal palace and fortress begun by William the Conqueror
in 1078; houses the Crown Jewels

TYNEMOUTH PRIORY AND CASTLE (EH), Tyne and Wear
NE30 4BZ T 0191-257 1090
Remains of a Benedictine priory, founded c.1090, moated
castle-towers, a gatehouse and keep on Saxon monastic site

UPPARK (NT), South Harting, W. Sussex GU31 5QR
T 01730-825415
17th-century house, restored after fire; Fetherstonhaugh
art collection; 18th-century dolls' house

WALMER CASTLE (EH), Walmer, Kent CT14 7LJ
T 01304-364288
One of Henry VIII's coastal defence castles, now the
residence of the Lord Warden of the Cinque Ports

WARKWORTH CASTLE (EH), Warkworth, Northumberland
NE65 0UJ T 01665-711423
14th-century keep amid earlier ruins, with hermitage
upstream

WHITBY ABBEY (EH), Whitby, N. Yorks YO22 4JT
T 01947-603568
Remains of Norman church on the site of a monastery
founded in AD 657

WILTON HOUSE, nr Salisbury, Wilts SP2 0BJ T 01722-746714
W www.wiltonhouse.com
17th-century house on the site of a Tudor house and
ninth-century nunnery; Palladian bridge

WINDSOR CASTLE, Windsor, Berks SL4 1NJ T 020-7766 7304
W www.royalcollection.org.uk
Official residence of the Queen; oldest royal residence still
in regular use; largest inhabited castle in the world. Also St
George's Chapel; Queen Mary's Dolls' House

WOBURN ABBEY, Woburn, Beds MK17 9WA T 01525-290333
W www.woburn.co.uk
Built on the site of a Cistercian abbey; seat of the Dukes of
Bedford; art collection; antiques centre
WROXETER ROMAN CITY (EH) nr Shrewsbury, Shropshire
SY5 6PH T 01743-761330
Second-century public baths and part of the forum of the
Roman town of *Viroconium*

WALES

For more information on Cadw properties, including those
listed below, the official website is W www.cadw.wales.gov.uk
For more information on National Trust properties in
Wales, including those listed below, the official website is
W www.nationaltrust.org.uk
KEY
(C) Property of Cadw: Welsh Historic Monuments
(NT) National Trust property
* UNESCO World Heritage Site (*see also* World Heritage
Sites)

*BEAUMARIS CASTLE (C), Anglesey LL58 8AP
T 01248-810361
Concentrically planned 13th-century castle, still virtually
intact
*BLAENAVON, Church Road, Blaenavon NP4 9AS
T 01495-742333
18th- and 19th-century industrial landscape associated
with coal and iron production
CAERLEON ROMAN BATHS AND AMPHITHEATRE (C),
Newport NP18 1AE T 01633-422518
Rare example of a legionary bath-house and late
first-century arena surrounded by bank for spectators
*CAERNARFON CASTLE (C), Gwynedd LL55 2AY
T 01286-677617
Huge fortress with polygonal towers built between 1283
and 1330, initially for King Edward I of England; setting
for the investiture of Prince Charles in 1969
CAERPHILLY CASTLE (C), Caerphilly CF83 1JD
T 029-2088 3143
Concentrically planned castle (*c.*1270) notable for its scale
and use of water defences
CARDIFF CASTLE, Cardiff CF10 3RB T 029-2087 8100
W www.cardiffcastle.com
Norman keep built on site of Roman fort; 'fairytale'
gothic-revival mansion added in the 19th century
CASTELL COCH (C), Tongwynlais, Cardiff CF15 7JS
T 029-2081 0101
'Fairytale'-style castle, rebuilt 1875–90 on medieval
foundations
CHEPSTOW CASTLE (C), Monmouthshire NP16 5EY
T 01291-624065
Rectangular keep amid extensive fortifications; developed
throughout the Middle Ages
*CONWY CASTLE (C), Gwynedd LL32 8AY
T 01492-592358
Built for Edward I in 1283–7 on narrow rocky outcrop;
features eight towers and two barbicans
CRICCIETH CASTLE (C), Gwynedd LL52 0DP
T 01766-522227
Native Welsh 13th-century castle, taken and altered by
Edward I and Edward II
DENBIGH CASTLE (C), Denbighshire LL16 3NB
T 01745-813385
Remains of the castle (begun 1282), including
triple-towered gatehouses
DYFFRYN GARDENS (NT), St Nicholas, Cardiff CF5 6SU
T 029-2059 3328

Edwardian gardens designed by Thomas Mawson,
overlooked by a grand Edwardian mansion
*HARLECH CASTLE (C), Gwynedd LL46 2YH
T 01766-780552
Well-preserved castle, constructed 1283–95, on an
outcrop above the former shoreline; withstood seven-year
siege 1461–8
PEMBROKE CASTLE, Pembrokeshire SA71 4LA
T 01646-684585 W www.pembroke-castle.co.uk
Castle founded in 1093; Great Tower built in late 12th
century; birthplace of King Henry VII
PENRHYN CASTLE (NT), Bangor, Gwynedd LL57 4HN
T 01248-353084
Neo-Norman castle built in the 19th century; railway and
dolls' museums; private art collection
*PONTCYSYLLTE AQUEDUCT AND CANAL, Trevor,
Wrexham T 01978-292015
Longest and highest aqueduct in Great Britain; designed
by Thomas Telford and finished in 1805
POWIS CASTLE (NT), Welshpool, Powys SY21 8RF
T 01938-551944
Medieval castle with interior in variety of styles;
17th-century gardens; Clive of India museum
RAGLAN CASTLE (C), Monmouthshire NP15 2BT
T 01291-690228
Remains of 15th-century castle with moated hexagonal
keep
ST DAVIDS BISHOP'S PALACE (C), Pembrokeshire SA62 6PE
T 01437-720517
Remains of residence of Bishops of St Davids built
1328–47
TINTERN ABBEY (C), nr Chepstow, Monmouthshire NP16 6SE
T 01291-689251
Remains of 13th-century church and conventual buildings
of a 12th-century Cistercian monastery
TRETOWER COURT AND CASTLE (C), nr Crickhowell,
Powys NP8 1RD T 01874-730279
Medieval manor house rebuilt in the 15th century, with
remains of 12th-century castle near by

SCOTLAND

For more information on Historic Scotland properties,
including those listed below, the official website is
W www.historic-scotland.gov.uk
For more information on National Trust for Scotland
properties, including those listed below, the official website is
W www.nts.org.uk
KEY
(HS) Historic Scotland property
(NTS) National Trust for Scotland property
* Part of the Heart of Neolithic Orkney UNESCO World
Heritage Site

ABBOTSFORD HOUSE, Melrose, Roxburghshire TD6 9BQ
T 01896-752043 W www.scottsabbotsford.co.uk
Home of Sir Walter Scott; features historic Scottish relics
and formal gardens
BALMORAL CASTLE, Ballater, Aberdeenshire AB35 5TB
T 01339-742534 W www.balmoralcastle.com
Baronial-style castle built for Victoria and Albert; the
Queen's private residence
BLACKHOUSE, ARNOL (HS), Lewis, Western Isles HS2 9DB
T 01851-710395
Traditional Lewis thatched house
BLAIR CASTLE, Blair Atholl, Perthshire PH18 5TL
T 01796-481207 W www.blair-castle.co.uk
Mid-18th-century mansion with 13th-century tower; seat
of the Dukes and Earls of Atholl

BOWHILL, Selkirk, Scottish Borders TD7 5ET **T** 01750-22204
  W www.bowhill.org
  Present house dates mainly from 1812; Seat of the Dukes
  of Buccleuch and Queensberry; fine collection of
  paintings
BROUGH OF BIRSAY (HS), Orkney KW17 2NH
  T 01856-841815
  Remains of Norse and Pictish village on the tidal island of
  Birsay
CAERLAVEROCK CASTLE (HS), Glencaple, Dumfries and
  Galloway DG1 4RU **T** 01387-770244
  Unique triangular 13th-century moated castle with
  classical Renaissance additions
CAIRNPAPPLE HILL (HS), Torphichen, West Lothian
  T 01506-634622
  Neolithic ceremonial site and Bronze Age burial chambers
CALANAIS STANDING STONES (HS), Lewis, Western Isles
  HS2 9DY **T** 01851-621422
  Standing stones in a cross-shaped setting, dating from
  between 2900 and 2600 BC
CATERTHUNS (BROWN AND WHITE) (HS), Menmuir,
  nr Brechin, Angus
  Two large Iron Age hill forts
CAWDOR CASTLE, Nairn, Moray IV12 5RD **T** 01667-404401
  W www.cawdorcastle.com
  14th-century keep with 15th- and 17th-century
  additions
CLAVA CAIRNS (HS), nr Inverness, Inverness-shire
  T 01667-460232
  Bronze Age cemetery complex of cairns and standing
  stones
CRATHES CASTLE (NTS), nr Banchory, Aberdeenshire
  AB31 5QJ **T** 08444-932166
  16th-century baronial castle in woodland, fields and
  gardens
CULZEAN CASTLE (NTS), Maybole, Ayrshire KA19 8LE
  T 08444-932149 **W** www.culzeanexperience.org
  18th-century Robert Adam castle with oval staircase and
  circular saloon
DRYBURGH ABBEY (HS), nr Melrose, Roxburghshire TD6 0RQ
  T 01835-822261
  12th-century abbey containing the tomb of Sir Walter
  Scott
DUNVEGAN CASTLE, Skye IV55 8WF **T** 01470-521206
  W www.dunvegancastle.com
  13th-century castle with later additions; home of the
  chiefs of the Clan MacLeod
EDINBURGH CASTLE (HS), EH1 2NG **T** 0131-225 9846
  W www.edinburghcastle.gov.uk
  Fortress perched on extinct volcano; includes the Scottish
  Crown Jewels, Scottish National War Memorial, Scottish
  United Services Museum
EDZELL CASTLE (HS), nr Brechin, Angus DD9 7UE
  T 01356-648631
  Ruined 16th-century tower house on medieval
  foundations; early 17th-century walled garden
EILEAN DONAN CASTLE, Dornie, Ross and Cromarty
  IV40 8DX **T** 01599-555202 **W** www.eileandonancastle.com
  13th-century castle situated at the meeting point of three
  sea lochs; Jacobite relics
ELGIN CATHEDRAL (HS), Moray IV30 1HU **T** 01343-547171
  13th-century cathedral and octagonal chapterhouse
FLOORS CASTLE, Kelso, Roxburghshire TD5 7SF
  T 01573-223333 **W** www.floorscastle.com
  Largest inhabited castle in Scotland; seat of the Dukes of
  Roxburghe; built in the 1720s by William Adam
FORT GEORGE (HS), Ardersier, Inverness-shire IV2 7TD
  T 01667-460232
  18th-century fort; still a working army barracks

GLAMIS CASTLE, Forfar, Angus DD8 1RJ **T** 01307-840393
  W www.glamis-castle.co.uk
  Seat of the Lyon family (later Earls of Strathmore and
  Kinghorne) since 1372; the setting for Shakespeare's
  Macbeth
GLASGOW CATHEDRAL (HS), Lanarkshire G4 0QZ
  T 0141-552 8198 **W** www.glasgowcathedral.org.uk
  Late 12th-century cathedral with vaulted crypt
GLENELG BROCHS (HS), Glenelg, Ross and Cromarty
  T 01667-460232
  Two broch towers (Dun Telve and Dun Troddan) with
  well-preserved structural features
HOPETOUN HOUSE, South Queensferry, West Lothian
  EH30 9SL **T** 0131-331 2451 **W** www.hopetoun.co.uk
  Designed by Sir William Bruce in 1699 and enlarged by
  William Adam 1721–48
HUNTLY CASTLE (HS), Aberdeenshire AB54 4SH
  T 01466-793191
  Ruin of a 16th- and 17th-century baronial residence
INVERARAY CASTLE, Argyll PA32 8XE **T** 01499-302203
  W www.inveraray-castle.com
  Gothic-style 18th-century castle designed by William
  Adam and Roger Morris; seat of the Dukes of Argyll
IONA ABBEY (HS), Iona, Inner Hebrides PA76 6SQ
  T 01681-700512
  Monastery founded by St Columba in AD 563
JARLSHOF (HS), Sumburgh Head, Shetland ZE3 9JN
  T 01950-460112
  Prehistoric settlement with later ninth-century Norse
  additions
JEDBURGH ABBEY (HS), Scottish Borders TD8 6JQ
  T 01835-863925
  Ruined Augustinian abbey founded *c.*1138
KISIMUL CASTLE (HS), Castlebay, Barra, Western Isles
  HS9 5UZ **T** 01871-810313
  Medieval island home of the Clan MacNeil
LINLITHGOW PALACE (HS), Kirkgate, Linlithgow, West
  Lothian EH49 7AL **T** 01506-842896
  Ruined royal palace, founded in 1424, set in park;
  birthplace of James V and Mary, Queen of Scots
*MAESHOWE (HS), Stenness, Orkney KW16 3HH
  T 01856-761606
  Neolithic chambered tomb with Viking runes
MEIGLE SCULPTURED STONES (HS), Meigle, Perthshire
  PH12 8SB **T** 01828-640612
  Twenty-six carved Pictish stones dating from the late
  8th to the late 10th centuries
MELROSE ABBEY (HS), Melrose, Roxburghshire TD6 9LG
  T 01896-822562
  Ruin of Cistercian abbey founded *c.*1136 by David I;
  museum of medieval objects
MOUSA BROCH (HS), Island of Mousa, Shetland
  T 01856-841815
  Finest surviving Iron Age broch tower
NEW ABBEY CORN MILL (HS), Dumfriesshire DG2 8BX
  T 01387-850260
  Working water-powered mill built in the late 18th century
*NEW LANARK, South Lanarkshire ML11 9DB
  T 01555-661 345
  18th-century village built around a cotton mill
PALACE OF HOLYROODHOUSE, Edinburgh EH8 8DX
  T 0131-556 5100 **W** www.royalcollection.org.uk
  The Queen's official Scottish residence; home to Mary,
  Queen of Scots; main part of the palace built 1671–9
  close to ruined 12th-century Augustinian abbey
*RING O' BRODGAR (HS), Stenness, Orkney
  T 01856-841815
  Neolithic circle of upright stones surrounded by circular
  ditch

ROSSLYN CHAPEL, Roslin, Midlothian EH25 9PU
T 0131-440 2159 W www.rosslynchapel.org.uk
Historic church built between 1446 and 1484 with
unique stone carvings

ST ANDREWS CASTLE AND CATHEDRAL (HS), Fife
KY16 9AR (castle); 9QL (cathedral) T 01334-477196 (castle);
01334-472563 (cathedral)
Ruins of 13th-century castle, the former residence of
bishops of St Andrews, and remains of the largest
cathedral in Scotland; museum

SCONE PALACE, Perth, Perthshire PH2 6BD
T 01738-552300
Georgian-Gothic house built 1802–12

*SKARA BRAE (HS), nr Stromness, Orkney KW16 3LR
T 01856-841815
Neolithic village with adjacent replica house

SMAILHOLM TOWER (HS), nr Kelso, Roxburghshire TD5 7PG
T 01573-460365
Well-preserved 15th-century tower-house

STIRLING CASTLE (HS), Stirlingshire FK8 1EJ
T 01786-450000 W www.stirlingcastle.gov.uk
Great Hall and gatehouse built for James IV c.1500; palace
built for James V in 1538; site of coronations including
Mary, Queen of Scots

*STONES OF STENNESS, Stenness, Orkney
T 01856 841815
Four surviving Neolithic standing stones and the uprights
of a three-stone dolmen

TANTALLON CASTLE (HS), North Berwick, East Lothian
EH39 5PN T 01620-892727
Ruined 14th-century curtain wall with towers

THREAVE CASTLE (HS), Castle Douglas, Kirkcudbrightshire
DG7 1TJ T 07711-223101
Ruined late 14th-century tower on an island; accessible
only by boat

URQUHART CASTLE (HS), Drumnadrochit, Inverness-shire
IV63 6XJ T 01456-450551
13th-century castle remains on the banks of Loch Ness

NORTHERN IRELAND

For the Northern Ireland Environment Agency, the official
website is W www.doeni.gov.uk/niea
For more information on National Trust properties in
Northern Ireland, including those listed below, the official
website is W www.nationaltrust.org.uk

KEY
(NIEA) Property in the care of the Northern Ireland
Environment Agency
(NT) National Trust property

CARRICKFERGUS CASTLE (NIEA), Carrickfergus, Co.
Antrim BT38 7BG T 028-9335 1273
Castle built in 1177 and taken by King John in 1210;
garrisoned until 1928

CASTLE COOLE (NT), Enniskillen, Co. Fermanagh BT74 6JY
T 028-6632 2690
18th-century neoclassical mansion in parkland; designed
by James Wyatt

CASTLE WARD (NT), Strangford, Co. Down BT30 7LS
T 028-4488 1204
18th-century house with Classical and Gothic facades

DEVENISH MONASTIC SITE (NIEA), nr Enniskillen, Co.
Fermanagh T 028-6862 1588
Island monastery founded in the sixth century by
St Molaise; church dating from 13th century

DOWNHILL DEMESNE AND HEZLETT HOUSE (NT),
Castlerock, Co. Londonderry BT51 4RP T 028-7084 8728
Ruins of 18th-century mansion and a 17th century
cottage in landscaped estate including Mussenden Temple

DUNLUCE CASTLE (NIEA), Bushmills, Co. Antrim BT57 8UY
T 028-2073 1938
Ruins of medieval stronghold of the McDonnells

FLORENCE COURT (NT), Enniskillen, Co. Fermanagh
BT92 1DB T 028-6634 8249
Mid-18th-century house with Rococo decoration

GREY ABBEY (NIEA), Greyabbey, Co. Down BT22 2NQ
T 028-9181 1491
Substantial remains of a Cistercian abbey founded in 1193
set in landscaped parkland

MOUNT STEWART (NT), Newtownards, Co. Down BT22 2AD
T 028-4278 8387
18th-century house; octagonal Temple of the Winds

NENDRUM MONASTIC SITE (NIEA), Mahee Island, Co.
Down T 028-9054 3037
Island monastery founded in the fifth century by St
Machaoi

PATTERSON'S SPADE MILL (NT), Templepatrick, Co. Antrim
BT39 0AP T 028-9443 3619
Last working water-driven spade mill in the UK

TULLY CASTLE (NIEA), Co. Fermanagh T 028-6862 1588
Fortified house and bawn built c.1619

MUSEUMS AND GALLERIES

There are approximately 2,500 museums and galleries in the UK. As of February 2014, 1,741 of these were fully accredited by Arts Council England. Accreditation indicates that the museum or gallery has an appropriate constitution, is soundly financed, has adequate collection management standards and public services and has access to professional curatorial advice. A further 106 museums and galleries have applied for, or are in the process of obtaining accreditation, and these applications are assessed by either Arts Council England; Museums, Archives and Libraries Wales (CyMAL); Museums Galleries Scotland or the Northern Ireland Museums Council.

The following is a selection of museums and art galleries in the UK. Opening hours and admission charges vary. Further information about museums and galleries in the UK is available from the Museums Association (W www.museumsassociation.org T 020-7566 7800).

W www.culture24.org includes a database of all the museums and galleries in the UK.

ENGLAND

* England's national museums and galleries, which receive funding from a government department, such as the DCMS or MoD. These institutions are deemed to have collections of national importance, and the government is able to call upon their staff for expert advice

ALTON
Jane Austen's House Museum, Chawton, Hants GU34 1SD
T 01420-83262 W www.jane-austens-house-museum.org.uk
17th-century house which tells the author's story
BARNARD CASTLE
The Bowes Museum, Co. Durham DL12 8NP T 01833-690606
W www.bowesmuseum.org.uk
Public gallery in a French châteaux style featuring archaeology, fashion and ceramics. Houses one of the largest collections of Spanish art in the country
BATH
American Museum, Claverton Manor BA2 7BD T 01225-460503
W www.americanmuseum.org
American decorative arts from the 17th to 20th centuries; American heritage exhibition
Fashion Museum, Bennett Street BA1 2QH T 01225-477789
W www.museumofcostume.co.uk
Fashion from the 17th century to the present day
Victoria Art Gallery, Bridge Street BA2 4AT T 01225-477233
W www.victoriagal.org.uk
European Old Masters and British art since the 15th century
BEAMISH
Beamish Museum, Co. Durham DH9 0RG T 0191-370 4000
W www.beamish.org.uk
Living working museum of a northern town during Georgian, Victorian and Edwardian times
BEAULIEU
National Motor Museum, Hants SO42 7ZN T 01590-612345
W www.beaulieu.co.uk
National motor museum within the New Forest national park
BIRMINGHAM
Aston Hall, Trinity Road B6 6JD T 0121-675 4722
W www.bmag.org.uk/aston-hall
Jacobean House containing paintings, furniture and tapestries from the 17th to 19th centuries

Barber Institute of Fine Arts, University of Birmingham, Edgbaston B15 2TS T 0121-414 7333 W www.barber.org.uk
Extensive coin collection; fine arts, including Old Masters
Birmingham Museum and Art Gallery, Chamberlain Square B3 3DH T 0121-303 1966 W www.bmag.org.uk
Includes notable collection of Pre-Raphaelite art
Museum of the Jewellery Quarter, Vyse Street, Hockley B18 6HA
T 0121-554 3598
W www.bmag.org.uk/museum-of-the-jewellery-quarter
Preserved jewellery workshop
Thinktank, Curzon Street B4 7XG T 0121-202 2222
W www.thinktank.ac
Science museum featuring over 200 hands-on displays and a Planetarium
BOURNEMOUTH
Russell-Cotes Art Gallery and Museum, East Cliff Promenade BH1 3AA T 01202-451858
W www.russell-cotes.bournemouth.gov.uk
Seaside villa housing 19th- and 20th-century art and sculptures from around the world
BOVINGTON
Tank Museum, Dorset BH20 6JG T 01929-405096
W www.tankmuseum.org
Collection of 200 tanks from their invention in 1915 to the modern conflict in Afghanistan
BRADFORD
Bradford Industrial Museum, Moorside Mills, Moorside Road, Eccleshill BD2 3HP T 01274-435900
W www.bradfordmuseums.org
Steam power, machinery and motor vehicle exhibits
Cartwright Hall Art Gallery, Lister Park BD9 4NS
T 01274-431212 W www.bradfordmuseums.org
British 19th- and 20th-century fine art, contemporary prints and south Asian art
National Media Museum, BD1 1NQ T 0844-856 3797
W www.nationalmediamuseum.org.uk
Photography, film and television interactive exhibits; features an IMAX cinema and the only permanent Cinerama screen in Europe
BRIGHTON
Booth Museum of Natural History, Dyke Road BN1 5AA
T 03000-290900
W www.brighton-hove-rpml.org.uk/museums/boothmuseum
Zoology, botany and geology collections; British birds in recreated habitats
Brighton Museum and Art Gallery, Royal Pavilion Gardens BN1 1EE T 03000-290900
W www.brighton-hove-rpml.org.uk/museums/brightonmuseum
Includes fine art and design, fashion, world art; Sussex history
BRISTOL
Arnolfini, Narrow Quay BS1 4QA T 0117-917 2300
W www.arnolfini.org.uk
Experimental contemporary visual arts, dance, performance, music; talks and workshops
Blaise Castle House Museum, Henbury Road BS10 7QS
T 0117-903 9818 W www.bristol.gov.uk/node/2869
18th-century mansion; social history collections
Bristol Museum and Art Gallery, Queen's Road BS8 1RL
T 0117-922 3571 W www.bristol.gov.uk/node/2904
Includes Victorian, Edwardian and French fine art; archaeology, local history and natural sciencies

M Shed, Prince's Wharf BS1 4RN **T** 0117-352 6600
   W www.mshed.org
   The story of Bristol's heritage of engineering, transport, music and industry

CAMBRIDGE

Fitzwilliam Museum, Trumpington Street CB2 1RB
   T 01223-332900 **W** www.fitzmuseum.cam.ac.uk
   Antiquities, fine and applied arts, clocks, ceramics, manuscripts, furniture, sculpture, coins and medals

*Imperial War Museum Duxford, Duxford CB22 4QR
   T 01223-835000 **W** duxford.iwm.org.uk
   Displays of military and civil aircraft, tanks and naval exhibits

Museum of Archaeology and Anthropology, Downing Street CB2 3DZ **T** 01223-333516 **W** www.maa.cam.ac.uk
   Global archaeological and anthropological collections; photography and modern art collections

Sedgwick Museum of Earth Sciences, Downing Street CB2 3EQ
   T 01223-333456 **W** www.sedgwickmuseum.org
   Extensive geological collection

University Museum of Zoology, Downing Street CB2 3EJ
   T 01223-336650 **W** www.museum.zoo.cam.ac.uk
   Extensive zoological collection

Whipple Museum of the History of Science, Free School Lane CB2 3RH **T** 01223-330906 **W** www.hps.cam.ac.uk/whipple
   Scientific instruments from the 14th century to the present

CARLISLE

Tullie House Museum and Art Gallery, Castle Street CA3 8TP
   T 01228-618718 **W** www.tulliehouse.co.uk
   Prehistoric archaeology, Hadrian's Wall; Viking and medieval Cumbria, and the social history of Carlisle

CHATHAM

The Historic Dockyard, ME4 4TE **T** 01634-823800
   W www.thedockyard.co.uk
   Maritime attractions including HMS *Cavalier*, the UK's last Second World War destroyer

Royal Engineers Museum, Prince Arthur Road, Gillingham ME4 4UG **T** 01634-822839 **W** www.re-museum.co.uk
   Regimental history, ethnography, decorative art and photography

CHELTENHAM

Art Gallery and Museum, Clarence Street GL50 3JT
   T 01242-237431 **W** www.cheltenhammuseum.org.uk
   Arts and crafts, local heroes, fine art and natural history

CHESTER

Grosvenor Museum, Grosvenor Street CH1 2DD **T** 01244-402033
   W www.grosvenormuseum.co.uk
   Roman collections, natural history, art, Chester silver, local history and costume

CHICHESTER

Weald and Downland Open Air Museum, Singleton PO18 0EU
   T 01243-811363 **W** www.wealddown.co.uk
   Rebuilt vernacular buildings from south-east England; includes medieval houses and a working watermill; craft demonstrations, Tudor kitchen and cooking

COLCHESTER

Colchester Castle Museum, Castle Park CO1 1TJ **T** 01206-282939
   W www.visitcolchester.com
   Largest Norman keep in Europe standing on foundations of the Roman Temple of Claudius

COVENTRY

Coventry Transport Museum, Hales Street CV1 1JD
   T 024-7623 4270 **W** www.transport-museum.com
   Extensive collection of motor vehicles and bicycles; land speed record-holding car; some redevelopment work until Spring 2015

Herbert Art Gallery and Museum, Jordan Well CV1 5QP
   T 024-7623 7521 **W** www.theherbert.org
   Local history, archaeology, industry and visual arts

DERBY

Derby Museum and Art Gallery, The Strand DE1 1BS
   T 01332-641901
   W www.derbymuseums.org/museumartgallery
   Includes paintings by Joseph Wright of Derby, origins of Derby and military history

Derby Silk Mill, Silk Mill Lane DE1 3AF **T** 01332-255308
   W wwww.derbymuseums.org/locations/the-silk-mill
   Built on the site of the world's first factory; wildlife gallery, fine art, Bonnie Prince Charlie Room

Pickford's House Museum, Friar Gate DE1 1DA **T** 01332-715181
   W www.derbymuseums.org/pickfords-house
   Georgian town house designed by architect Joseph Pickford; museum of Georgian life and costume

DEVIZES

Wiltshire Heritage Museum, Long Street SN10 1NS
   T 01380-727369 **W** www.wiltshireheritage.org.uk
   Natural and local history; art gallery; archaeological finds from prehistoric, Roman and Saxon sites

DORCHESTER

Dorset County Museum, High West Street DT1 1XA
   T 01305-262735 **W** www.dorsetcountymuseum.org
   Includes a collection of Thomas Hardy's manuscripts, books, notebooks and drawings; local history, geology and Roman mosaics

DOVER

Dover Museum, Market Square CT16 1PH **T** 01304-201066
   W www.dovermuseum.co.uk
   Contains the Dover Bronze Age Boat Gallery and archaeological finds from Bronze Age, Roman and Saxon sites

EXETER

Royal Albert Memorial Museum and Art Gallery, Queen Street EX4 3RX **T** 01392-265858 **W** www.rammuseum.org.uk
   Natural history; archaeology; worldwide fine and decorative art including Exeter silver

GATESHEAD

Baltic Centre for Contemporary Art, South Shore Road NE8 3BA
   T 0191-478 1810 **W** www.balticmill.com
   Contemporary art exhibitions and events

Shipley Art Gallery, Prince Consort Road NE8 4JB
   T 0191-477 1495 **W** www.twmuseums.org.uk/shipley
   Contemporary crafts

GAYDON

Heritage Motor Centre, Banbury Road, Warks CV35 0BJ
   T 01926-641188 **W** www.heritage-motor-centre.co.uk
   The world's largest collection of British cars with nearly 300 vehicles spanning the classic, vintage and veteran eras

GLOUCESTER

Gloucester Waterways Museum, Gloucester Docks GL1 2EH
   T 01452-318200
   W www.canalrivertrust.org.uk/gloucester-waterways-museum
   200-year history of Britain's canals and inland waterways

GOSPORT

Royal Navy Submarine Museum, Haslar Jetty Road, Hants PO12 2AS **T** 023-9251 0354 **W** www.submarine-museum.co.uk
   Underwater warfare exhibition, including submarines HMS *Alliance* and HMS *Holland 1* – the Royal Navy's first submarine

GRASMERE

Dove Cottage and the *Wordsworth Museum*, Cumbria LA22 9SH
   T 015394-35544 **W** www.wordsworth.org.uk
   William Wordsworth's manuscripts, home and garden

HOVE

Hove Museum and Art Gallery, New Church Road BN3 4AB
   T 03000-290900
   W www.brighton-hove-rpml.org.uk/museums/hovemuseum
   Toys, cinema, local history and fine art collections

HULL
Ferens Art Gallery, Queen Victoria Square HU1 3RA
T 01482-300300 W www.hullcc.gov.uk/ferens
European Old Masters, Victorian, Edwardian and
contemporary British art
Hull Maritime Museum, Queen Victoria Square HU1 3DX
T 01482-300300 W www.hullcc.gov.uk
Hull's maritime heritage including whaling, fishing,
navigation and merchant trade
HUNTINGDON
The Cromwell Museum, Grammar School Walk PE29 3LF
T 01480-375830
W www.cambridgeshire.gov.uk/leisure/museums/cromwell
Portraits and memorabilia relating to Oliver Cromwell
IPSWICH
Christchurch Mansion and *Wolsey Art Gallery*, Christchurch
Park IP4 2BE T 01473-433554 W www.cimuseums.org.uk
Tudor house with paintings by Gainsborough, Constable
and other Suffolk artists; furniture and 18th-century
ceramics; temporary exhibitions
KEIGHLEY
The Brontë Parsonage Museum, Haworth, W. Yorks BD22 8DR
T 01535-642323 W www.bronte.org.uk
The former home of the literary Brontë sisters
KESWICK
Pencil Museum, Southey Works CA12 5NG T 01768-773626
W www.pencilmuseum.co.uk
500-year history of the pencil; demonstration events and
workshops throughout the year
LEEDS
Armley Mills, Leeds Industrial Museum, Canal Road, Armley
LS12 2QF T 0113-263 7861 W www.leeds.gov.uk/armleymills
Once the world's largest woollen mill, now a museum for
textiles and Leeds' industrial heritage
Leeds Art Gallery, The Headrow LS1 3AA A 0113-247 8256
W www.leeds.gov.uk/artgallery
Includes English watercolours, sculpture, contemporary art
and prints from the region's artists
Royal Armouries Museum, Armouries Drive LS10 1LT
T 0113-220 1999 W www.royalarmouries.org
National collection of over 8,500 items of arms and
armour from BC to present over five galleries: War,
Tournament, Oriental, Self Defence and Hunting
LEICESTER
Jewry Wall Museum, St Nicholas Circle LE1 4LB T 0116-225 4971
W www.leicester.gov.uk
Archaeology; Roman Jewry Wall and baths; mosaics
New Walk Museum and Art Gallery, 53 New Walk LE1 7EA
T 0116-255 4900 W www.leicester.gov.uk
Natural and cultural history; ancient Egypt gallery;
European art and decorative arts
LINCOLN
The Collection, Danes Terrace LN2 1LP T 01522-782040
W www.thecollectionmuseum.com
Artefacts from the Stone Age to the Roman, Viking and
Medieval eras; adjacent art gallery; collections of
contemporary art and craft, sculpture, porcelain, clocks
and watches
Museum of Lincolnshire Life, Burton Road LN1 3LY
T 01522-782040
W www.lincolnshire.gov.uk/museumoflincolnshirelife
Social history; agricultural, industrial, military and
commercial exhibits
LIVERPOOL
International Slavery Museum, Albert Dock L3 4AX
T 0151-478 4499 W www.liverpoolmuseums.org.uk/ism
Explores historical and contemporary aspects of slavery
Lady Lever Art Gallery, Wirral CH62 5EQ T 0151-478 4136
W www.liverpoolmuseums.org.uk/ladylever
Paintings, furniture and porcelain

Merseyside Maritime Museum, Albert Dock L3 4AQ
T 0151-478 4499 W www.liverpoolmuseums.org.uk/maritime
Floating exhibits, working displays and craft
demonstrations; incorporates the *UK Border Agency
National Museum*
Museum of Liverpool, Pier Head L3 1DG T 0151-478 4545
W www.liverpoolmuseums.org.uk/mol
Explores the significance of the city's geography, history
and culture
Sudley House, Mossley Hill Road L18 8BX T 0151-478 4016
W www.liverpoolmuseums.org.uk/sudley
Late 18th- and 19th-century paintings in former
shipowner's home
Tate Liverpool, Albert Dock L3 4BB T 0151-1702 7400
W www.tate.org.uk/liverpool
20th-century paintings and sculpture
Walker Art Gallery, William Brown Street L3 8EL
T 0151-478 4199 W www.liverpoolmuseums.org.uk/walker
Paintings from the 14th century to the present day
World Museum Liverpool, William Brown Street L3 8EN
T 0151-478 4393 W www.liverpoolmuseums.org.uk/wml
Includes Egyptian mummies, weapons and classical
sculpture; planetarium, aquarium, vivarium and natural
history centre
LONDON: GALLERIES
Barbican Art Gallery, Barbican Centre, Silk Street EC2Y 8DS
T 020-7638 4141 W www.barbican.org.uk
Art, music, theatre, dance and film exhibitions
Courtauld Institute of Art Gallery, Somerset House, Strand
WC2R 0RN T 020-7848 2526 W www.courtauld.ac.uk
Impressionist and post-impressionist paintings
Dennis Severs' House, 18 Folgate Street E1 6BX T 020-7247013
W www.dennissevershouse.co.uk
Candlelit recreation of a Huguenot silk weaver's home
Dulwich Picture Gallery, Gallery Road SE21 7AD
T 020-8693 5254 W www.dulwichpicturegallery.org.uk
England's first public art gallery; designed by Sir John
Soane to house 17th- and 18th-century paintings
Estorick Collection of Modern Italian Art, Canonbury Square
N1 2AN T 020-7704 9522 W www.estorickcollection.com
Early 20th-century Italian drawings, paintings, sculptures
and etchings, with an emphasis on Futurism
Hayward Gallery, Belvedere Road SE1 8XX T 020-7960 4200
W www.southbankcentre.co.uk
Temporary exhibitions
National Gallery, Trafalgar Square WC2N 5DN
T 020-7747 2885 W www.nationalgallery.org.uk
Western painting from the 13th to 19th centuries; early
Renaissance collection in the Sainsbury Wing
Large collection of steam engines; reopened in 2014 after
refurbishment
National Portrait Gallery, St Martin's Place WC2H 0HE
T 020-7306 0055 W www.npg.org.uk
Portraits of eminent people in British history
Photographers' Gallery, Ramillies Street W1F 7LW
T 020-7087 9300 W www.thephotographersgallery.org.uk
Temporary exhibitions; permanent camera obscura
The Queen's Gallery, Buckingham Palace SW1A 1AA
T 020-7766 7300 W www.royalcollection.org.uk
Art from the Royal Collection
Royal Academy of Arts, Burlington House, Piccadilly W1J 0BD
T 020-7300 8000 W www.royalacademy.org.uk
British art since 1750 and temporary exhibitions; annual
Summer Exhibition
Saatchi Gallery, Duke of York's HQ, King's Road SW3 4RY
T 020-7823 2363 W www.saatchi-gallery.co.uk
Contemporary art including paintings, photographs,
sculpture and installations
Serpentine Gallery, Kensington Gardens W2 3XA
T 020-7402 6075 W www.serpentinegallery.org

Temporary exhibitions of British and international contemporary art

Tate Britain, Millbank SW1P 4RG T 020-7887 8888
W www.tate.org.uk/britain
British art from the 16th century to the present; international modern art

Tate Modern, Bankside SE1 9TG T 020-7887 8888
W www.tate.org.uk/modern
International modern art from 1900 to the present

Wallace Collection, Manchester Square W1U 3BN
T 020-7563 9500 W www.wallacecollection.org
Old Masters; French 18th-century paintings, furniture, armour, porcelain, clocks and sculpture

Whitechapel Art Gallery, Whitechapel High Street E1 7QX
T 020-7522 7888 W www.whitechapelgallery.org
Temporary exhibitions of modern art

LONDON: MUSEUMS

Bank of England Museum, Threadneedle Street EC2R 8AH
(entrance on Bartholomew Lane) T 020-7601 5545
W www.bankofengland.co.uk/museum
History of the Bank of England since 1694

British Museum, Great Russell Street WC1B 3DG
T 020-7323 8299 W www.britishmuseum.org
Collection of art and antiquities spanning 2 million years of human history; temporary exhibitions; houses the Elgin Marbles from the Parthenon

Brunel Museum, Rotherhithe SE16 4LF T 020-7231 3840
W www.brunel-museum.org.uk
Explores the engineering achievements of Isambard Kingdom Brunel and his father, Marc Brunel

Cartoon Museum, Little Russell Street WC1A 2HH
T 020-7580 8155 W www.cartoonmuseum.org
British cartoons, caricature and comic art from the 18th century to the present

Charles Dickens Museum, Doughty Street WC1N 2LX
T 020-7405 2127 W www.dickensmuseum.com
Dickens's home from 1837–9; manuscripts, personal items and paintings

Churchill War Rooms, King Charles Street SW1A 2AQ
T 020-7930 6961 W cwr.iwm.org.uk
Underground rooms used by Churchill and the government during the Second World War

Cutty Sark, King William Walk SE10 9HT T 020-8858 4422
W www.cuttysark.org.uk
The world's last remaining tea clipper; re-opened in April 2012 following extensive restoration

Design Museum, Shad Thames SE1 2YD T 020-7403 6933
W www.designmuseum.org
The development of design and the mass-production of consumer objects

Firepower, the Royal Artillery Museum, Royal Arsenal, Woolwich SE18 6ST T 020-8855 7755
W www.firepower.org.uk
The history and development of artillery over the last 700 years including the collections of the Royal Regiment of Artillery

Garden Museum, Lambeth Palace Road SE1 7LB T 020-7401 8865
W www.gardenmuseum.org.uk
History and development of gardens and gardening; temporary exhibitions, symposia and events

Geffrye Museum, Kingsland Road E2 8EA T 020-7739 9893
W www.geffrye-museum.org.uk
English urban domestic interiors from 1600 to the present day; also paintings, furniture, decorative arts, walled herb garden and period garden rooms

HMS Belfast, The Queen's Walk SE1 2JH T 020-7940 6300
W hmsbelfast.iwm.org.uk
Life and work on board a Second World War cruiser

Horniman Museum, London Road SE23 3PQ T 020-8699 1872
W www.horniman.ac.uk
Museum of anthropology, musical instruments and natural history; aquarium; reference library; gardens

Imperial War Museum, Lambeth Road SE1 6HZ
T 020-7416 5320 W www.iwm.org.uk
All aspects of the two World Wars and other military operations involving Britain and the Commonwealth since 1914

Jewish Museum, Albert Street NW1 7NB T 020-7284 7384
W www.jewishmuseum.org.uk
Jewish life, history, art and religion

London Metropolitan Archives, Northampton Road EC1R 0HB
T 020-7332 3820 W www.cityoflondon.gov.uk/lma
Material on the history of London and its people dating from 1067 to the present day

London Museum of Water and Steam, Green Dragon Lane TW8 0EN T 020-8568 4757 W www.waterandsteam.org.uk

London Transport Museum, Covent Garden Piazza WC2E 7BB
T 020-7379 6344 W www.ltmuseum.co.uk
Vehicles, photographs and graphic art relating to the history of transport in London

MCC Museum, Lord's Cricket Ground, St John's Wood NW8 8QN
T 020-7616 8595 W www.lords.org/mcc
Cricket exhibits including the Ashes, kits, paintings and W. G. Grace exhibit; guided tours by appointment

Museum of Childhood (V&A), Cambridge Heath Road E2 9PA
T 020-8983 5200 W www.museumofchildhood.org.uk
Toys, games and exhibits relating to the social history of childhood from the 17th century to the present

Museum of London, London Wall EC2Y 5HN T 020-7001 9844
W www.museumoflondon.org.uk
History of London from prehistoric times to the present day; Galleries of Modern London

Museum of London Docklands, West India Quay, Canary Wharf E14 4AL T 020-7001 9844
W www.museumoflondon.org.uk/docklands
Explores the story of London's river, port and people over 2,000 years; includes the London Sugar Slavery Gallery

National Archives Museum, Kew TW9 4DU T 020-8876 3444
W www.nationalarchives.gov.uk/museum
Displays treasures from the archives, including the Domesday Book and Magna Carta

National Army Museum, Royal Hospital Road SW3 4HT
T 020-7730 0717 W www.nam.ac.uk
Five-hundred-year history of the British soldier; exhibits include model of the Battle of Waterloo and recreated First World War trench

National Maritime Museum, Romney Road SE10 9NF
T 020-8858 4422
W www.rmg.co.uk/national-maritime-museum
Maritime history of Britain; collections include globes, clocks, telescopes and paintings; comprises the main building, the Royal Observatory and the Queen's House

Natural History Museum, Cromwell Road SW7 5BD
T 020-7942 5000 W www.nhm.ac.uk
Natural history collections and interactive Darwin Centre

Petrie Museum of Egyptian Archaeology, University College London, Malet Place WC1E 6BT T 020-7679 2884
W www.ucl.ac.uk/museums/petrie
Egyptian and Sudanese archaeology featuring around 80,000 objects

Royal Air Force Museum, Hendon NW9 5LL T 020-8205 2266
W www.rafmuseum.org.uk
Aviation from before the Wright brothers to the present

Royal Mews, Buckingham Palace SW1W 1QH T 020-7766 7302
W www.royalcollection.org.uk/visit/royalmews
State vehicles, including the Queen's gold state coach; home to the Queen's horses; guided tours

*Science Museum, Exhibition Road SW7 2DD T 0870 870 4868
   W www.sciencemuseum.org.uk
   Science, technology, industry and medicine exhibitions;
   children's interactive gallery; IMAX cinema
Shakespeare's Globe Exhibition, New Globe Walk, Bankside
   SE1 9DT T 020-7902 1400 W www.shakespearesglobe.com
   Recreation of Elizabethan theatre using 16th-century
   techniques; includes a tour of the theatre
*Sir John Soane's Museum, Lincoln's Inn Fields WC2A 3BP
   T 020-7405 2107 W www.soane.org
   Art and antiquities collected by Soane throughout his
   lifetime; authentic Georgian and Victorian interior
Tower Bridge Exhibition, SE1 2UP T 020-7403 3761
   W www.towerbridge.org.uk
   History of the bridge and display of Victorian steam
   machinery; panoramic views from walkways
*Victoria and Albert Museum, Cromwell Road SW7 2RL
   T 020-7942 2000 W www.vam.ac.uk
   Includes the National Art Library and the Gilbert
   Collection; fine and applied art and design; furniture,
   glass, textiles, theatre and dress collections; temporary
   exhibitions
Wellcome Collection, Euston Road NW1 2BE T 020-7611 2222
   W www.wellcomecollection.org
   Contemporary and historic exhibitions and collections
   including the Wellcome Library
Wimbledon Lawn Tennis Museum, Church Road SW19 5AE
   T 020-8944 1066 W www.wimbledon.com/museum
   Tennis trophies, fashion and memorabilia; view of Centre
   Court
MALTON
Eden Camp, N. Yorks YO17 6RT T 01653-697777
   W www.edencamp.co.uk
   Restored POW camp and Second World War memorabilia
MANCHESTER
Gallery of Costume, Platt Hall, Rusholme M14 5LL
   T 0161-245 7245 W www.manchestergalleries.org
   Exhibits from the 17th century to the present day
*Imperial War Museum North, Trafford Wharf Road M17 1TZ
   T 0161-836 4000 W www.iwm.org.uk/north
   History of war from the 20th century to the present
Manchester Art Gallery, Mosley Street M2 3JL T 0161-235 8888
   W www.manchestergalleries.org
   European fine and decorative art from the 17th to 20th
   centuries
Manchester Museum, Oxford Road M13 9PL T 0161-275 2648
   W www.museum.manchester.ac.uk
   Collections include decorative arts, natural history and
   zoology; three Ancient Worlds galleries
*Museum of Science and Industry, Liverpool Road, Castlefield
   M3 4FP T 0161-832 2244 W www.mosi.org.uk
   On site of world's oldest passenger railway station;
   galleries relating to space, energy, power, transport,
   aviation, textiles and social history
National Football Museum, Cathedral Gardens M4 3BG
   T 0161-605 8200 W www.nationalfootballmuseum.com
   Home to the FIFA, FA and Football League collections
   including the 1966 World Cup final ball
People's History Museum, Left Bank, Spinningfields M3 3ER
   T 0161-838 9190 W www.phm.org.uk
   History of British political and working life
Whitworth Art Gallery, Oxford Road M15 6ER T 0161-275 7450
   W www.whitworth.manchester.ac.uk
   Fine and modern art, wallpapers, prints, textiles and
   sculptures

MILTON KEYNES
Bletchley Park National Codes Centre, Bucks MK3 6EB
   T 01908-640404 W www.bletchleypark.org
   Home of British codebreaking during the Second World
   War; Enigma machine; computer museum and Alan Turing
   gallery
MONKWEARMOUTH
Monkwearmouth Station Museum, North Bridge Street,
   Sunderland SR5 1AP T 0191-567 7075
   W www.twmuseums.org.uk/monkwearmouth
   Victorian train station; interactive galleries
NEWCASTLE UPON TYNE
Discovery Museum, Blandford Square NE1 4JA T 0191-232 6789
   W www.twmuseums.org.uk/discovery
   Science and industry, local history, fashion; Tyneside's
   maritime history; digital jukebox of 2,000 film and TV
   titles from the BFI National Archive
Great North Museum: Hancock, Barras Bridge NE2 4PT
   T 0191-222 6765
   W www.twmuseums.org.uk/greatnorthmuseum
   Natural and ancient history; planetarium; Living Planet
   display incorporates live animal tanks and aquaria
Laing Art Gallery, New Bridge Street NE1 8AG T 0191-232 7734
   W www.twmuseums.org.uk/laing
   19th and 20th century art including local painters;
   ceramics, glass, Japanese decrotive arts and prints
NEWMARKET
National Horseracing Museum, High Street CB8 8JH
   T 01638-667333 W www.nhrm.co.uk
   The story of people and horses involved in racing;
   temporary exhibitions
NORTH SHIELDS
Stephenson Railway Museum, Middle Engine Lane NE29 8DX
   T 0191-200 7146 W www.twmuseums.org.uk/stephenson
   Locomotive engines and rolling stock
NOTTINGHAM
Museum of Nottingham Life, Brewhouse Yard, Castle Boulevard
   NG7 1FB T 0115-876 1400 W www.nottinghamcity.gov.uk
   Social history from the 17th to 20th centuries
Natural History Museum, Wollaton Hall, Wollaton NG8 2AE
   T 0115-876 3100 W www.nottinghamcity.gov.uk
   Geology, botany and zoology specimens housed in an
   Elizabethan mansion
Nottingham Castle and Art Gallery, Lenton Road NG1 6EL
   T 0115-876 1400
   W www.mynottingham.gov.uk/nottinghamcastle
   Paintings, ceramics, silver, glass and jewellery; history of
   Nottingham
OXFORD
Ashmolean Museum, Beaumont Street OX1 2PH T 01865-278002
   W www.ashmolean.org
   Art and archaeology including Egyptian, Minoan,
   Anglo-Saxon and Chinese exhibits; largest collection of
   Raphael drawings in the world
Modern Art Oxford, Pembroke Street OX1 1BP T 01865-722733
   W www.modernartoxford.org.uk
   Temporary exhibitions
Museum of the History of Science, Broad Street OX1 3AZ
   T 01865-277280 W www.mhs.ox.ac.uk
   Displays include early scientific instruments, chemical
   apparatus, clocks and watches
Oxford University Museum of Natural History, Parks Road
   OX1 3PW T 01865-272950 W www.oum.ox.ac.uk
   Entomology, geology, mineralogy and petrology, and
   zoology
Pitt Rivers Museum, South Parks Road OX1 3PP T 01865-270927
   W www.prm.ox.ac.uk
   Anthropological and archaeological artefacts

PLYMOUTH
City Museum and Art Gallery, Drake Circus PL4 8AJ
    T 01752-304774 W www.plymouthmuseum.gov.uk
    Local and natural history; ceramics; silver; Old Masters;
    world artefacts; temporary exhibitions
PORTSMOUTH
Charles Dickens Birthplace, Old Commercial Road PO1 4QL
    T 023-9282 1879 W www.charlesdickensbirthplace.co.uk
    Reproduction Regency house; Dickens memorabilia
D-Day Museum, Clarence Esplanade, Southsea PO5 3NT
    T 023-9282 7261 W www.ddaymuseum.co.uk
    Includes the Overlord embroidery
Portsmouth Historic Dockyard, HM Naval Base PO1 3LJ
    T 023-9283 9766 W www.historicdockyard.co.uk
    Incorporates the *National Museum of the Royal Navy*
    (PO1 3NH T 023-9272 7574 W www.nmrn.org.uk), *HMS*
    Victory – restoration work open to the public (PO1 3NH
    T 023-9283 9766 W www.hms-victory.com), *HMS Warrior*
    (PO1 3QX T 023-9277 8600 W www.hmswarrior.org), *Mary*
    Rose (PO1 3LX T 023-9281 2931 W www.maryrose.org) and
    Action Stations (PO1 3LJ T 023-9289 3338
    W www.actionstations.org)
    History of the Royal Navy and of the dockyard; warships
    and technology spanning 500 years
PRESTON
Harris Museum and Art Gallery, Market Square PR1 2PP
    T 01772-258248 W www.harrismuseum.org.uk
    British art since the 18th century; ceramics, glass, costume
    and local history; contemporary exhibitions
ST ALBANS
Verulamium Museum, St Michael's Street AL3 4SW
    T 01727-751814 W www.stalbansmuseums.org.uk
    Remains of Iron Age settlement and the third-largest city
    in Roman Britain; moving to a new site in 2017
ST IVES
Tate St Ives, Porthmeor Beach, Cornwall TR26 1TG
    T 01736-796226 W www.tate.org.uk/stives
    Modern art, much by artists associated with St Ives;
    includes the Barbara Hepworth Museum and Sculpture
    Garden; open after 2014 part closure
SALISBURY
Salisbury & South Wiltshire Museum, The Close SP1 2EN
    T 01722-332151 W www.salisburymuseum.org.uk
    Local history and archaeology; Stonehenge exhibits
SHEFFIELD
Graves Gallery, Surrey Street S1 1XZ T 0114-278 2600
    W www.museums-sheffield.org.uk
    Twentieth-century British art; European art spanning four
    centuries
Millennium Galleries, Arundel Gate S1 2PP T 0114-278 2600
    W www.museums-sheffield.org.uk
    Incorporates four different galleries: the Special
    Exhibition Gallery, the Craft and Design Gallery, the
    Metalwork Gallery and the Ruskin Gallery, which houses
    John Ruskin's collection of paintings, drawings, books and
    medieval manuscripts
Weston Park Museum, Western Bank S10 2TP T 0114-278 2600
    W www.museums-sheffield.org.uk
    World and local history; art and temporary exhibitions
SOUTHAMPTON
City Art Gallery, Commercial Road SO14 7LP T 023-8083 3007
    W www.southampton.gov.uk/art
    Western art from the Renaissance to the present
SeaCity Museum, Havelock Road SO14 7FY T 023-8083 3007
    W www.seacitymuseum.co.uk
    Opened in 2012, the museum tells the story of the city's
    maritime past and present

SOUTH SHIELDS
Arbeia Roman Fort, Baring Street NE33 2BB T 0191-456 1369
    W www.twmuseums.org.uk/arbeia
    Excavated ruins; reconstructions of original buildings
South Shields Museum and Art Gallery, Ocean Road NE33 2JA
    T 0191-456 8740 W www.twmuseums.org.uk/southshields
    South Tyneside history; interactive art gallery
STOKE-ON-TRENT
Etruria Industrial Museum, Lower Bedford Street ST4 7AF
    T 01782-233144 W www.stokemuseums.org.uk/eim
    Britain's sole surviving steam-powered potter's mill
Gladstone Pottery Museum, Uttoxeter Road, Longton ST3 1PQ
    T 01782-237777 W www.stokemuseums.org.uk/gpm
    The last complete Victorian pottery factory in Britain
Potteries Museum and Art Gallery, Bethesda Street ST1 3DW
    T 01782-232323 W www.stokemuseums.org.uk/pmag
    Pottery, china and porcelain collections and a Mark XVI
    Spitfire
The Wedgwood Museum, Barlaston ST12 9ER T 01782-371900
    W www.wedgwoodmuseum.org.uk
    The story of Josiah Wedgwood and the company he
    founded
SUNDERLAND
Sunderland Museum and Winter Gardens, Burdon Road SR1 1PP
    T 0191-553 2323 W www.twmuseums.org.uk/sunderland
    Fine and decorative art, local history and gardens
TELFORD
Ironbridge Gorge Museums, TF8 7DQ T 01952-433424
    W www.ironbridge.org.uk
    Ten museums including The Museum of the Gorge; The
    Iron Bridge and Tollhouse; Blists Hill (late Victorian
    working town); Brosely Pipeworks; Coalbrookdale
    Museum of Iron; Coalport China Museum; Jackfield Tile
    Museum; Tar Tunnel; Darby Houses
WAKEFIELD
Hepworth Wakefield, Gallery Walk WF1 5AW T 01924-247360
    W www.hepworthwakefield.org
    Historic and modern art; temporary exhibitions of
    contemporary art
National Coal Mining Museum for England, New Road, Overton
    WF4 4RH T 01924-848806 W www.ncm.org.uk
    Includes underground tours of one of Britain's oldest
    working mines
Yorkshire Sculpture Park, West Bretton WF4 4LG
    T 01924-832631 W www.ysp.co.uk
    Open-air sculpture gallery including works by Henry
    Moore, Barbara Hepworth and others in 500 acres of
    parkland
WEYBRIDGE
Brooklands Museum, Brooklands Road KT13 0QN
    T 01932-857381 W www.brooklandsmuseum.com
    Birthplace of British motorsport; world's first
    purpose-built motor racing circuit
WILMSLOW
Quarry Bank Mill and Styal Estate, Wilmslow SK9 4LA
    T 01625-527468 W www.quarrybankmill.org.uk
    Europe's most powerful working waterwheel owned by
    the National Trust illustrating history of cotton industry;
    costumed guides at restored Apprentice House
WINCHESTER
Winchester Science Centre and Planetarium, Telegraph Way,
    Hants SO21 1HZ T 01962-863791 W www.intech-uk.com
    Interactive science centre and planetarium
WORCESTER
City Art Gallery and Museum, Foregate Street WR1 1DT
    T 01905-25371
    W www.whub.org.uk/cms/museums-worcestershire/mag.aspx
    Includes the Regimental museum, 19th-century chemist
    shop and changing art exhibitions

Museum of Worcester Porcelain, Severn Street WR1 2ND
T 01905-21247 W www.worcesterporcelainmuseum.org.uk
Worcester porcelain from 1751 to the present day

WROUGHTON
Science Museum, Wilts SN4 9LT T 01793-846200
W www.sciencemuseum.org.uk/wroughton
Object stores closed to the public due to redevelopment
work; Library and Archive are open to the public by
appointment

YEOVIL
Fleet Air Arm Museum, RNAS Yeovilton, Somerset BA22 8HT
T 01935-840565 W www.fleetairarm.com
History of naval aviation; historic aircraft, including
Concorde 002

YORK
Beningbrough Hall, Beningbrough YO30 1DD T 01904-472027
W www.nationaltrust.org.uk/beningbrough-hall
18th-century house with portraits from the National
Portrait Gallery; parklands and gardens
JORVIK Viking Centre, Coppergate YO1 9WT T 01904-615505
W www.jorvik-viking-centre.co.uk
Reconstruction of Viking York based on archaeological
evidence
National Railway Museum, Leeman Road YO26 4XJ
T 0844-815 3139 W www.nrm.org.uk
Includes locomotives, rolling stock and carriages
York Art Gallery, Exhibition Square YO1 7EW
T 01904 687687 W www.yorkartgallery.org
600 years of British and European painting; ceramics
and sculpture; re-opens Easter 2015
York Castle Museum, Eye of York YO1 9RY T 01904-687687
W www.yorkcastlemuseum.org.uk
Includes Kirkgate, a reconstructed Victorian street;
costume and military collections
Yorkshire Museum, Museum Gardens YO1 7FR T 01904-687687
W www.yorkshiremuseum.org.uk
Yorkshire life from Roman to medieval times; geology and
biology; York observatory

WALES

* Members of National Museum Wales, a public body that receives
its funding through grant-in-aid from the Welsh Assembly

ABERYSTWYTH
Ceredigion Museum, Terrace Road SY23 2AQ T 01970-633088
W www.ceredigion.gov.uk
Local history, housed in a restored Edwardian theatre
Silver Mountain Experience, Ponterwyd SY23 3AB
T 01970-890620 W www.silvermountainexperience.co.uk
Tours of an 18th-century silver mine, with interactive
challenges and games for children

BLAENAFON
Big Pit National Coal Museum, Torfaen NP4 9XP
T 029-2057 3650 W www.museumwales.ac.uk/en/bigpit
Colliery with an underground tour and exhibitions of
modern mining equipment

BODELWYDDAN
Bodelwyddan Castle, Denbighshire LL18 5YA T 01745-584060
W www.bodelwyddan-castle.co.uk
Art gallery within an historic house; features temporary art
exhibits

CAERLEON
National Roman Legion Museum, NP18 1AE T 029-2057 3550
W www.museumwales.ac.uk/en/roman
Features the oldest recorded piece of writing in Wales;
pottery, Roman era gemstones

CARDIFF
National Museum Cardiff, Cathays Park CF10 3NP
T 029-2039 7951 W www.museumwales.ac.uk/en/cardiff
Houses Wales's national art, archaeology and natural
history collections
St Fagans: National History Museum, St Fagans CF5 6XB
T 029-2057 3500 W www.museumwales.ac.uk/en/stfagans
Open-air museum with re-erected buildings, agricultural
equipment and costume
TECHNIQUEST, Stuart Street CF10 5BW T 029-2047 5475
W www.techniquest.org
Interactive science exhibits, planetarium and science
theatre

CRICCIETH
Lloyd George Museum, Llanystumdwy LL52 0SH T 01766-522071
W www.gwynedd.gov.uk
Childhood home of David Lloyd George

DRE-FACH FELINDRE
National Wool Museum, Llandysul SA44 5UP T 029-2057 3070
W www.museumwales.ac.uk/en/wool
Exhibitions, a working woollen mill and craft workshops

LLANBERIS
National Slate Museum, Gwynedd LL55 4TY T 029-2057 3700
W www.museumwales.ac.uk/en/slate
Former slate quarry with original machinery and plant;
slate crafts demonstrations; working waterwheel

LLANDRINDOD WELLS
National Cycle Collection, Automobile Palace, Temple Street
LD1 5DL T 01597-825531 W www.cyclemuseum.org.uk
Approximately 250 bicycles on display, from 1819 to the
present

PRESTEIGNE
Judge's Lodging Museum, Broad Street LD8 2AD T 01544-260650
W www.judgeslodging.org.uk
Restored apartments, courtroom, cells and servants'
quarters

SWANSEA
National Waterfront Museum, Oystermouth Road SA1 3RD
T 029-2057 3600 W www.museumwales.ac.uk/en/swansea
Wales during the Industrial Revolution
Swansea Museum, Victoria Road SA1 1SN T 01792-653763
W www.swansea.gov.uk/swanseamuseum
Paintings, Egyptian artifacts, transport and nautical
collections; war time Swansea

TENBY
Tenby Museum and Art Gallery, Castle Hill SA70 7BP
T 01834-842809 W www.tenbymuseum.org.uk
Local archaeology, history, geology and art

SCOTLAND

* Members of National Museums of Scotland or National Galleries
of Scotland, which are non-departmental public bodies funded by,
and accountable to, the Scottish government

ABERDEEN
Aberdeen Art Gallery, Schoolhill AB10 1FQ T 01224-523700
W www.aagm.co.uk
Paintings, sculptures and graphics; temporary exhibitions
Aberdeen Maritime Museum, Shiprow AB11 5BY
T 01224-337700 W www.aagm.co.uk
Maritime history, including shipbuilding and North
Sea oil

AYR
Robert Burns Birthplace Museum, Murdoch's Lone, Alloway
KA7 4PQ T 0844-493 2601 W www.burnsmuseum.org.uk
Comprises Burns Cottage, birthplace of the poet, gardens
and a museum

EDINBURGH

Britannia, Leith EH6 6JJ **T** 0131-555 5566
W www.royalyachtbritannia.co.uk
Former royal yacht with royal barge and royal family picture gallery

City Art Centre, Market Street EH1 1DE **T** 0131-529 3993
W www.edinburghmuseums.org.uk
Rolling programme of exhibitions including historic and modern photography; contemporary art, design and architecture

Museum of Childhood, High Street EH1 1TG **T** 0131-529 4142
W www.edinburghmuseums.org.uk
Toys, games, clothes and exhibits relating to the social history of childhood

Museum of Edinburgh, Canongate, Royal Mile EH8 8DD
T 0131-529 4143 **W** www.edinburghmuseums.org.uk
Local history, silver, glass and Scottish pottery

*Museum of Flight, East Fortune Airfield, East Lothian EH39 5LF
T 0300-123 6789 **W** www.nms.ac.uk/flight
Aviation from the early 20th century to the present

*National Museum of Scotland, Chambers Street EH1 1JF
T 0300-123 6789 **W** www.nms.ac.uk/scotland
Scottish history; world cultures; natural world; art and design; science and technology

*National War Museum of Scotland, Edinburgh Castle EH1 2NG
T 0300-123 6789 **W** www.nms.ac.uk/war
Scotland's military history housed within Edinburgh Castle

*Scottish National Gallery, The Mound EH2 2EL
T 0131-624 6200 **W** www.nationalgalleries.org
Fine art from the early Renaissance to the end of the 19th century

*Scottish National Gallery of Modern Art, Belford Road EH4 3DR **T** 0131-624 6200 **W** www.nationalgalleries.org
Contemporary art featuring British, French and Russian collections; outdoor sculpture park

*Scottish National Portrait Gallery, Queen Street EH2 1JD
T 0131-624 6200 **W** www.nationalgalleries.org/portraitgallery
Portraits of eminent people in Scottish history; Photography Gallery; Victorian Library

The Writers' Museum, Lady Stair's Close EH1 2PA
T 0131-529 4901 **W** www.edinburghmuseums.org.uk
Exhibitions relating to Robert Burns, Sir Walter Scott and Robert Louis Stevenson

FORT WILLIAM

West Highland Museum, Cameron Square PH33 6AJ
T 01397-702169 **W** www.westhighlandmuseum.org.uk
Highland life; Victorian and Jacobite collections

GLASGOW

Burrell Collection, Pollokshaws Road G43 1AT **T** 0141-287 2550
W www.glasgowlife.org.uk/museums
Paintings by major artists; medieval art, Chinese and Islamic art

Gallery of Modern Art, Royal Exchange Square G1 3AH
T 0141-287 3050 **W** www.glasgowlife.org.uk/museums
Collection of contemporary Scottish and world art

Hunterian, University of Glasgow G12 8QQ **T** 0141-330 4221
W www.gla.ac.uk/hunterian
Rennie Mackintosh and Whistler collections; coins; Scottish paintings; Pacific ethnographic collection; archaeology; medicine

Kelvingrove Art Gallery & Museum, Argyle Street G3 8AG
T 0141-276 9599 **W** www.glasgowlife.org.uk/museums
Includes Old Masters; natural history; arms and armour

Museum of Piping, McPhater Street G4 0HW **T** 0141-353 0220
W www.thepipingcentre.co.uk
The history and origins of bagpiping

*Museum of Rural Life, Philipshill Road, East Kilbride G76 9HR
T 0300-123 6789 **W** www.nms.ac.uk/rural
History of rural life and work

People's Palace and Winter Gardens, Glasgow Green G40 1AT
T 0141-276 0795 **W** www.glasgowlife.org.uk/museums
Social history of Glasgow since 1750

Riverside Museum, 100 Pointhouse Place G3 8RS
T 0141-287 2720 **W** www.glasgowlife.org.uk/museums
Scotland's museum of transport and travel; the Tall Ship *Glenlee*, a Clyde-built sailing ship, is berthed alongside

St Mungo Museum of Religious Art and Life, Castle Street G4 0RH **T** 0141-276 1625
W www.glasgowlife.org.uk/museums
Exhibits detailing the world's major religions; oldest Zen garden in Britain

NORTHERN IRELAND

* Members of National Museums Northern Ireland, a non-departmental public body of the Northern Ireland Office

ARMAGH

*Armagh County Museum, The Mall East BT61 9BE
T 028-3752 3070 **W** www.nmni.com/acm
Local history; fine art; archaeology; crafts

BANGOR

North Down Museum, Town Hall BT20 4BT **T** 028-9127 1200
W www.northdownmuseum.com
Presents the history of North Down, including its early-Christian monastery and Plantation-era maps

BELFAST

Titanic Belfast, Queen's Road, Titanic Quarter BT3 9EP
T 028-9076 6386 **W** www.titanicbelfast.com
The story of RMS *Titanic* from her conception to demise; Shipyard ride and ocean exploration centre

*W5, Odyssey, Queen's Quay BT3 9QQ **T** 028-9046 7700
W www.w5online.co.uk
Interactive science and technology centre

HOLYWOOD

*Ulster Folk and Transport Museum, Cultra BT18 0EU
T 028-9042 8428 **W** www.nmni.com/uftm
Open-air museum with original buildings from Ulster town and rural life *c.*1900; indoor galleries including Irish rail and road transport

LONDONDERRY

The Tower Museum, Union Hall Place BT48 6LU
T 028-7137 2411
W www.derrycity.gov.uk/museums/tower-museum
Tells the story of Ireland through the history of Londonderry

NEWTOWNARDS

The Somme Heritage Centre, Bangor Road BT23 7PH
T 028-9182 3202 **W** www.irishsoldier.org/museum.htm
Commemorates the part played by Irish forces in the First World War

OMAGH

*Ulster American Folk Park, Castletown, Co. Tyrone BT78 5QU
T 028-8224 3292 **W** www.nmni.com/uafp
Open-air museum telling the story of Ulster's emigrants to America; restored or recreated dwellings and workshops; ship and dockside gallery

*Ulster Museum, Botanic Gardens BT9 5AB **T** 028-9044 0000
W www.nmni.com/um
Irish antiquities; natural and local history; fine and applied arts

SIGHTS OF LONDON

For historic buildings, museums and galleries in London, *see* the Historic Buildings and Monuments, and Museums and Galleries sections.

BRIDGES

The bridges over the Thames in London, from east to west, are:

Tower Bridge (268m/880ft by 18m/60ft), architect: Horace Jones, engineer: John Wolfe Barry, opened 1894

London Bridge (262m/860ft by 32m/105ft), original 13th-century stone bridge rebuilt and opened 1831 (engineer: John Rennie), reconstructed in Arizona when current London Bridge opened 1973 (architect: Lord Holford, engineer: Mott, Hay and Anderson)

Cannon Street Railway Bridge (261m/855ft), engineers: John Hawkshaw and John Wolfe Barry, originally named Alexandra Bridge, opened 1866; renovated 1979–82

Southwark Bridge (244m/800ft by 17m/56ft), engineer: John Rennie, originally named Queen Street Bridge, opened 1819; rebuilt 1912–21 (architect: Ernest George, engineer: Mott, Hay and Anderson)

Millennium Bridge (325m/1,066ft by 4m/13ft), architect: Foster and Partners, engineer: Ove Arup and Partners, opened 2000; reopened after modification 2002

Blackfriars Railway Bridge (284m/933ft), engineers: John Wolfe Barry and Henri Marc Brunel, orginally named St Paul's Railway Bridge, opened 1886

Blackfriars Bridge (294m/963ft by 32m/105ft), engineer: Robert Mylne, opened 1769; rebuilt 1869 (engineer: Joseph Cubitt); widened 1909

Waterloo Bridge (366m/1,200ft by 24m/80ft), engineer: John Rennie, opened 1817; rebuilt 1945 (architect: Sir Giles Gilbert Scott, engineer: Rendel, Palmer and Triton)

Golden Jubilee Bridges (325m/1,066ft by 4.7m/15ft), architect: Lifschutz Davidson, engineer: WSP Group, opened 2002; commonly known as the Hungerford Footbridges

Hungerford Railway Bridge (366m/1,200ft), engineer: Isambard Kingdom Brunel, suspension bridge opened 1845; present railway bridge opened 1864 (engineer: John Hawkshaw); widened in 1886

Westminster Bridge (228m/748ft by 26m/85ft), engineer: Charles Labelye, opened 1750; rebuilt 1862 (architect: Charles Barry, engineer: Thomas Page)

Lambeth Bridge (237m/776ft by 18m/60ft), engineer: Peter W. Barlow, original suspension bridge opened 1862; current structure opened 1932 (architect: Reginald Blomfield, engineer: George W. Humphreys)

Vauxhall Bridge (231m/759ft by 24m/80ft), engineer: James Walker, opened 1816; redesigned and opened 1906 (architect: William Edward Riley, engineers: Alexander Binnie and Maurice Fitzmaurice)

Grosvenor Railway Bridge (213m/699ft), engineer: John Fowler, opened 1860; rebuilt 1965; also known as the Victoria Railway Bridge

Chelsea Bridge (213m/699ft by 25m/83ft), original suspension bridge opened 1858 (engineer: Thomas Page); rebuilt 1937 (architects: George Topham Forrest and E. P. Wheeler, engineer: Rendel, Palmer and Triton)

Albert Bridge (216m/710ft by 12m/40ft), engineer: Rowland M. Ordish, opened 1873; restructured 1884 (engineer: Joseph Bazalgette); strengthened 1971–3

Battersea Bridge (204m/670ft by 17m/56ft), engineer: Henry Holland, opened 1771; rebuilt 1890 (engineer: Joseph Bazalgette)

Battersea Railway Bridge (204m/670ft), engineer: William Baker, opened 1863; also known as Cremorne Bridge

Wandsworth Bridge (189m/619ft by 18m/60ft), engineer: Julian Tolmé, opened 1873; rebuilt 1940 (architect: E. P. Wheeler, engineer: T. Pierson Frank)

Putney Railway Bridge (229m/750ft), engineers: W. H. Thomas and William Jacomb, opened 1889; also known as the Fulham Railway Bridge or the Iron Bridge – it has no official name

Putney Bridge (213m/699ft by 23m/74ft), architect: Jacob Ackworth, original wooden bridge opened 1729; current granite structure completed in 1886 (engineer: Joseph Bazalgette). The starting point of the Boat Race.

Hammersmith Bridge (210m/688ft by 10m/33ft), engineer: William Tierney Clarke; the first suspension bridge in London, originally built 1827; rebuilt 1887 (engineer: Joseph Bazalgette)

Barnes Railway Bridge (also footbridge, 110m/360ft), engineer: Joseph Locke, opened 1849; rebuilt 1895 (engineers: London and South Western Railway); the original structure stands unused

Chiswick Bridge (137m/450ft by 21m/70ft), architect: Herbert Baker, engineer: Alfred Dryland, opened 1933. The bridge marks the end point of the Boat Race.

Kew Railway Bridge (175m/575ft), engineer: W. R. Galbraith, opened 1869

Kew Bridge (110m/360ft by 17m/56ft), engineer: Robert Tunstall, original timber bridge built 1759; replaced by a Portland stone structure in 1789 (engineer: James Paine); current granite bridge renamed King Edward VII Bridge in 1903, but still known as Kew Bridge (engineers: John Wolfe Barry and Cuthbert Brereton)

Richmond Lock (91m/300ft by 11m/36ft), engineer: F. G. M. Stoney, lock and footbridge opened 1894

Twickenham Bridge (85m/280ft by 21m/70ft), architect: Maxwell Ayrton, engineer: Alfred Dryland, opened 1933

Richmond Railway Bridge (91m/300ft), engineer: Joseph Locke, opened 1848; rebuilt 1906–8 (engineer: J. W. Jacomb-Hood)

Richmond Bridge (85m/280ft by 10m/33ft), architect: James Paine, engineer: Kenton Couse, built 1777; widened 1939

Teddington Lock (198m/650ft), engineer: G. Pooley, two footbridges opened 1889; marks the end of the tidal reach of the Thames

Kingston Railway Bridge architects: J. E. Errington and W. R. Galbraith, engineer: Thomas Brassey, opened 1863

Kingston Bridge (116m/382ft), engineer: Edward Lapidge, built 1825–8; widened 1911–14 (engineers: Basil Mott and David Hay) and 1999–2001

Hampton Court Bridge, engineers: Samuel Stevens and Benjamin Ludgator, built 1753; replaced by iron bridge 1865; present bridge opened 1933 (architect: Edwin Lutyens, engineer: W. P. Robinson)

CEMETERIES

In 1832, in response to the overcrowding of burial grounds in London, the government authorised the establishment of seven non-denominational cemeteries that would encircle the city. These large cemeteries, known as the 'magnificent seven', were seen by many Victorian families as places in which to demonstrate their wealth and stature, and as a result there are some highly ornate graves and tombs.

THE MAGNIFICENT SEVEN

Abney Park, Stoke Newington, N16 (13ha/32 acres), established 1840; tomb of William and Catherine Booth, founders of the Salvation Army, and memorials to many nonconformists and dissenters

Brompton, Old Brompton Road, SW10 (16.5ha/40 acres), established 1840; graves of Sir Henry Cole, Emmeline Pankhurst, John Wisden

Highgate, Swains Lane, N6 (15ha/38 acres), established 1839; graves of Douglas Adams, George Eliot, Eric Hobsbawm, Michael Faraday, Karl Marx, Ralph Miliband and Christina Rossetti

Kensal Green, Harrow Road, W10 (29ha/72 acres), established 1833; tombs of Charles Babbage, Isambard Kingdom Brunel, Wilkie Collins, George Cruikshank, Tom Hood, Leigh Hunt, Harold Pinter, William Makepeace Thackeray, Anthony Trollope

Nunhead, Linden Grove, SE15 (21ha/52 acres), established 1840; closed in 1969, restored and opened for burials

Tower Hamlets, Southern Grove, E3 (11ha/27 acres), established 1841, 350,000 interments; bombed heavily during the Second World War and closed to burials in 1966; now a nature reserve

West Norwood Cemetery and Crematorium, Norwood High Street, SE27 (17ha/42 acres), established 1837; tombs of C. W. Alcock, Mrs Beeton, Sir Henry Tate and Joseph Whitaker *(Whitaker's Almanack)*

OTHER CEMETERIES

Bunhill Fields, City Road, EC1 (1.6ha/4 acres), 17th-century nonconformist burial ground containing the graves of William Blake, John Bunyan and Daniel Defoe

City of London Cemetery and Crematorium, Aldersbrook Road, E12 (81ha/200 acres), established 1856; grave of Bobby Moore

Golders Green Crematorium, Hoop Lane, NW11 (5ha/12 acres), established 1902; retains the ashes of Kingsley Amis, Lionel Bart, Enid Blyton, Marc Bolan, Sigmund Freud, Keith Moon, Ivor Novello, Bram Stoker and H. G. Wells

Hampstead, Fortune Green Road, NW6 (10.5ha/26 acres), established 1876; graves of Alan Coren, Kate Greenaway, Joseph Lister and Marie Lloyd

MARKETS

Billingsgate, Trafalgar Way, E14 (fish), a market site for over 1,000 years, with the Lower Thames Street site dating from 1876; moved to the Isle of Dogs in 1982; owned and run by the City of London Corporation

Borough, Southwark Street, SE1 (vegetables, fruit, meat, dairy, bread), established on present site in 1756; privately owned and run

Brick Lane, E1 (jewellery, vintage clothes, bric-a-brac, food), open Sunday

Brixton, SW9 (African-Caribbean food, music, clothing), open Monday to Saturday

Broadway, E8 (food, fashion, crafts), re-established in 2004, open Saturday

Camden Lock, NW1 (second-hand clothing, jewellery, alternative fashion, crafts), established in 1973

Columbia Road, E2 (flowers), dates from 19th century; became dedicated flower market in the 20th century

Covent Garden, WC2 (antiques, handicrafts, jewellery, clothing, food), originally a fruit and vegetable market (*see* New Covent Garden market); it has been trading in its current form since 1980

Grays, Davies Street, W1K (antiques), indoor market in listed building, established 1977

Greenwich, SE10 (crafts, fashion, food), market revived in the 1980s

Leadenhall, Gracechurch Street, EC3V (meat, poultry, cheese, clothing), site of market since 14th century; present hall built 1881; owned and run by the City of London Corporation

New Covent Garden, SW8 (wholesale vegetables, fruit, flowers), established in 1670 under a charter of Charles II; relocated from central London in 1974

New Spitalfields, E10 (vegetables, fruit), established 1682, modernised 1928, moved out of the City to Leyton in 1991

Old Spitalfields, E1 (arts, crafts, books, clothes, organic food, antiques), continues to trade on the original Spitalfields site on Commercial Street

Petticoat Lane, Middlesex Street, E1, a market has existed on the site for over 500 years, now a Sunday morning market selling almost anything

Portobello Road, W11, originally for herbs and horse-trading from 1870; became famous for antiques after the closure of the Caledonian Market in 1948

Smithfield, EC1 (meat, poultry), built 1866–8, refurbished 1993–4; the site of St Bartholomew's Fair from 12th to 19th century; owned and run by the City of London Corporation

MONUMENTS

CENOTAPH

Whitehall, SW1. The Cenotaph (from the Greek meaning 'empty tomb') was built to commemorate 'The Glorious Dead' and is a memorial to all ranks of the sea, land and air forces who gave their lives in the service of the Empire during the First World War. Designed by Sir Edwin Lutyens and constructed in plaster as a temporary memorial in 1919, it was replaced by a permanent structure of Portland stone and unveiled by George V on 11 November 1920, Armistice Day. An additional inscription was made in 1946 to commemorate those who gave their lives in the Second World War

FOURTH PLINTH

Trafalgar Square, WC2. The fourth plinth (1841) was designed for an equestrian statue that was never built due to lack of funds. From 1999 temporary works have been displayed on the plinth including *Ecce Homo* (Mark Wallinger), *Monument* (Rachel Whiteread), *Alison Lapper Pregnant* (Marc Quinn), *One & Other* (Antony Gormley) and *Nelson's Ship in a Bottle* (Yinka Shonibare). Since July 2013 *Hahn/Cock* (Katharina Fritsch), a 4.72m-high ultra-marine blue rendition of a domestic farmyard cockerel, has occupied the plinth. This will be followed by *Gift Horse* (Hans Haacke) in 2015.

LONDON MONUMENT

(Commonly called the Monument), Monument Street, EC3. Built to designs by Sir Christopher Wren and Robert Hooke between 1671 and 1677, the Monument commemorates the Great Fire of London, which broke out in Pudding Lane on 2 September 1666. The fluted Doric column is 36.6m (120ft) high, the moulded cylinder above the balcony supporting a flaming vase of gilt bronze is an additional 12.8m (42ft), and the column is based on a square plinth 12.2m (40ft) high (with fine carvings on the west face), making a total height of 61.6m (202ft) – the tallest isolated stone column in the world, with views of London from a gallery at the top (311 steps)

OTHER MONUMENTS
(sculptor's name in parentheses):
7 July Memorial (Carmody Groarke), Hyde Park
Viscount Alanbrooke (Roberts-Jones), Whitehall
Albert Memorial (Scott), Kensington Gore
Battle of Britain (Day), Victoria Embankment
Beatty (Wheeler), Trafalgar Square
Belgian Gratitude (setting by Blomfield, statue by Rousseau), Victoria Embankment
Boadicea (or *Boudicca*), *Queen of the Iceni* (Thornycroft), Westminster Bridge
Brunel (Marochetti), Victoria Embankment
Burghers of Calais (Rodin), Victoria Tower Gardens, Westminster
Burns (Steell), Embankment Gardens
Canada Memorial (Granche), Green Park
Carlyle (Boehm), Chelsea Embankment
Cavalry (Jones), Hyde Park
Edith Cavell (Frampton), St Martin's Place
Charles I (Le Sueur), Trafalgar Square
Charles II (Gibbons), Royal Hospital, Chelsea
Churchill (Roberts-Jones), Parliament Square
Cleopatra's Needle (20.9m/68.5ft high, *c.*1500 BC, erected in London in 1878; the sphinxes are Victorian), Thames Embankment
Clive (Tweed), King Charles Street
Captain Cook (Brock), The Mall
Oliver Cromwell (Thornycroft), outside Westminster Hall
Cunningham (Belsky), Trafalgar Square
Gen. Charles de Gaulle (Conner), Carlton Gardens
Diana, Princess of Wales Memorial Fountain (Gustafson Porter), Hyde Park
Disraeli, Earl of Beaconsfield (Raggi), Parliament Square
Lord Dowding (Winter), Strand
Duke of Cambridge (Jones), Whitehall
Duke of York (37.8m/124ft column, with statue by Westmacott), Carlton House Terrace
Edward VII (Mackennal), Waterloo Place
Elizabeth I (Kerwin, 1586, oldest outdoor statue in London; from Ludgate), Fleet Street
Eros (Shaftesbury Memorial) (Gilbert), Piccadilly Circus
Marechal/Marshall Foch (Mallisard, copy of one in Cassel, France), Grosvenor Gardens
Charles James Fox (Westmacott), Bloomsbury Square
Yuri Gagarin (Novikov, copy of Russian statue), The Mall
George III (Cotes Wyatt), Cockspur Street
George IV (Chantrey), Trafalgar Square
George V (Reid Dick and Scott), Old Palace Yard
George VI (McMillan), Carlton Gardens
Gladstone (Thornycroft), Strand
Guards' (Crimea; Bell), Waterloo Place
Guards Division (Ledward, figures, Bradshaw, cenotaph), Horse Guards' Parade
Haig (Hardiman), Whitehall
Sir Arthur (Bomber) Harris (Winter), Strand
Gen. Henry Havelock (Behnes), Trafalgar Square
International Brigades Memorial (Spanish Civil War) (Ian Walters), Jubilee Gardens, South Bank
Irving (Brock), north side of National Portrait Gallery
Isis (Gudgeon), Hyde Park
James II (Gibbons), Trafalgar Square
Jellicoe (McMillan), Trafalgar Square
Samuel Johnson (Fitzgerald), opposite St Clement Danes
Kitchener (Tweed), Horse Guards' Parade
Abraham Lincoln (Saint-Gaudens, copy of one in Chicago), Parliament Square
Mandela (Walters), Parliament Square
Milton (Montford), St Giles, Cripplegate
Mountbatten (Belsky), Foreign Office Green
Gen. Charles James Napier (Adams), Trafalgar Square

Nelson (Railton), Trafalgar Square, with Landseer's lions (cast from guns recovered from the wreck of the *Royal George*)
Florence Nightingale (Walker), Waterloo Place
Palmerston (Woolner), Parliament Square
Sir Keith Park (Johnson), Waterloo Place
Peel (Noble), Parliament Square
Pitt (Chantrey), Hanover Square
Portal (Nemon), Embankment Gardens
Prince Albert (Bacon), Holborn Circus
Queen Elizabeth Gate (Lund and Wynne), Hyde Park Corner
Queen Mother (Jackson), Carlton Gardens
Raleigh (McMillan), Greenwich
Richard I (Coeur de Lion) (Marochetti), Old Palace Yard
Roberts (Bates), Horse Guards' Parade
Franklin D. Roosevelt (Reid Dick), Grosvenor Square
Royal Air Force (Blomfield), Victoria Embankment
Royal Air Force Bomber Command Memorial (O'Connor), Green Park
Royal Artillery (Great War) (Jagger and Pearson), Hyde Park Corner
Royal Artillery (South Africa) (Colton), The Mall
Captain Scott (Lady Scott), Waterloo Place
Shackleton (Jagger), Kensington Gore
Shakespeare (Fontana, copy of one by Scheemakers in Westminster Abbey), Leicester Square
Smuts (Epstein), Parliament Square
Sullivan (Goscombe John), Victoria Embankment
Trenchard (McMillan), Victoria Embankment
Victoria Memorial (Webb and Brock), in front of Buckingham Palace
Raoul Wallenberg (Jackson), Great Cumberland Place
George Washington (Houdon copy), Trafalgar Square
Wellington (Boehm), Hyde Park Corner
Wellington (Chantrey), outside Royal Exchange
John Wesley (Adams Acton), City Road
Westminster School (Crimea) (Scott), Broad Sanctuary
William III (Bacon), St James's Square
Wolseley (Goscombe John), Horse Guards' Parade

PARKS, GARDENS AND OPEN SPACES

CITY OF LONDON CORPORATION OPEN SPACES
W www.cityoflondon.gov.uk
Ashtead Common (202ha/500 acres), Surrey
Burnham Beeches and *Fleet Wood* (220ha/540 acres), Bucks. Acquired by the City of London for the benefit of the public in 1880, Fleet Wood (26ha/65 acres) being presented in 1921
Coulsdon Common (51ha/127 acres), Surrey
Epping Forest (2,476ha/6,118 acres), Essex. Acquired by the City of London in 1878 and opened to the public in 1882. The Queen Elizabeth Hunting Lodge, built for Henry VIII in 1543, lies at the edge of the forest. The present forest is 19.3km (12 miles) long by around 3km (2 miles) wide, approximately one-tenth of its original area
*Epping Forest Buffer Land (718ha/1,774 acres), Waltham Abbey/Epping
Farthing Downs and New Hill (95ha/235 acres), Surrey
Hampstead Heath (275ha/680 acres), NW3. Including Golders Hill (15ha/36 acres) and Parliament Hill (110ha/271 acres)
Highgate Wood (28ha/70 acres), N6/N10
Kenley Common (56ha/139 acres), Surrey
Queen's Park (12ha/30 acres), NW6
Riddlesdown (43ha/104 acres), Surrey
Spring Park (20ha/50 acres), Kent
Stoke Common (80ha/198 acres), Bucks. Ownership was transferred to the City of London in 2007
West Ham Park (31ha/77 acres), E15

West Wickham Common (10ha/26 acres), Kent
Also over 150 smaller open spaces within the City of London, including *Finsbury Circus* and *St Dunstan-in-the-East*
* Includes Copped Hall Park, Woodredon Estate and Warlies Park

OTHER PARKS AND GARDENS
CHELSEA PHYSIC GARDEN, 66 Royal Hospital Road SW3 4HS T 020-7352 5646 W www.chelseaphysicgarden.co.uk
A garden of general botanical research and education, maintaining a wide range of rare and unusual plants; established in 1673 by the Society of Apothecaries
HAMPTON COURT PARK AND GARDENS (304ha/750 acres), Surrey KT8 9AU T 0844-482 7777 W www.hrp.org.uk
Also known as Home Park, the park lies beyond the palace's formal gardens. It contains a herd of deer and a 750-year-old oak tree from the original park
HOLLAND PARK (22ha/54 acres), Ilchester Place W8 T 020-7361 3000 W www.rbkc.gov.uk The largest park in the Royal Borough of Kensington and Chelsea, includes the Kyoto Garden
KEW, ROYAL BOTANIC GARDENS (120ha/300 acres), Richmond, Surrey TW9 3AB T 020-8332 5655 W www.kew.org
Founded in 1759 and declared a UNESCO World Heritage Site in 2003
THAMES BARRIER PARK (9ha/22acres), North Woolwich Road E16 2HP T 020-7476 3741 Opened in 2000, landscaped gardens with spectacular views of the Thames Barrier

ROYAL PARKS
W www.royalparks.org.uk
Bushy Park (450ha/1,099 acres), Middx. Adjoins Hampton Court; contains an avenue of horse-chestnuts enclosed in a fourfold avenue of limes planted by William III
Green Park (19ha/47 acres), W1. Between Piccadilly and St James's Park, with Constitution Hill leading to Hyde Park Corner
Greenwich Park (74ha/183 acres), SE10. Enclosed by Humphrey, Duke of Gloucester, and laid out by Charles II from the designs of Le Nôtre. On a hill in Greenwich Park is the Royal Observatory (founded 1675). Its buildings are now managed by the National Maritime Museum (T 020-8858 4422 W www.rmg.co.uk) and the earliest building is named Flamsteed House, after John Flamsteed (1646–1719), the first astronomer royal
Hyde Park (142ha/350 acres), W1/W2. From Park Lane to Kensington Gardens and incorporating the Serpentine lake, Apsley House, the Achilles Statue, Rotten Row and the Ladies' Mile; fine gateway at Hyde Park Corner. To the north-east is Marble Arch, originally erected by George IV at the entrance to Buckingham Palace and re-erected in the present position in 1851. At Hyde Park Corner stands Wellington Arch, built in 1825–7, it opened to the public in 2012 following major renovation
Kensington Gardens (111ha/275 acres), W2/W8. From the western boundary of Hyde Park to Kensington Palace; contains the Albert Memorial, Serpentine Gallery and Peter Pan statue
The Regent's Park and *Primrose Hill* (197ha/487 acres), NW1. From Marylebone Road to Primrose Hill surrounded by the Outer Circle; divided by the Broad Walk leading to the Zoological Gardens
Richmond Park (1,000ha/2,500 acres), Surrey. Designated a National Nature Reserve, a Site of Special Scientific Interest and a Special Area of Conservation
St James's Park (23ha/58 acres), SW1. From Whitehall to Buckingham Palace; ornamental lake of 4.9ha (12 acres); the Mall leads from Admiralty Arch to Buckingham Palace

PLACES OF HISTORICAL AND CULTURAL INTEREST

1 Canada Square
Canary Wharf E14 5AB T 020-7418 2000
W www.canarywharf.com
Also known as 'Canary Wharf', the steel and glass skyscraper is designed to sway 35cm in the strongest winds
20 Fenchurch Street
W www.20fenchurchstreet.co.uk
Designed by architect Rafael Viñoly the skyscraper was completed in March 2014 and is nicknamed the 'Walkie-Talkie' because of its shape. The top three floors include a large viewing platform and are open to the public
30 St Mary Axe
EC3A 8EP W www.30stmaryaxe.com
Completed in 2004 and commonly known as the 'Gherkin', each of the floors rotates five degrees from the one below
122 Leadenhall Street
EC3V 1LR W www.theleadenhallbuilding.com
The distinctive 225m (737ft) asymmetrical Leadenhall Building, designed by architects Rogers Stirk Harbour & Partners, was completed in 2014
Alexandra Palace
Alexandra Palace Way N22 7AY T 020-8365 2121
W www.alexandrapalace.com
The Victorian palace was severely damaged by fire in 1980 but was restored, and reopened in 1988. Alexandra Palace now provides modern facilities for exhibitions, conferences, banquets and leisure activities. There is a winter ice rink, a boating lake and a conservation area
Barbican Centre
Silk Street EC2Y 8DS T 020-7638 4141
W www.barbican.org.uk
Owned, funded and managed by the City of London Corporation, the Barbican Centre opened in 1982 and houses the Barbican Theatre, a studio theatre called The Pit and the Barbican Hall; it is also home to the London Symphony Orchestra. There are three cinemas, six conference rooms, two art galleries, a sculpture court, a lending library, trade and banqueting facilities and a conservatory
British Library
St Pancras, 96 Euston Road NW1 2DB T 0843-208 1144
W www.bl.uk
The largest building constructed in the UK in the 20th century with basements extending 24.5m underground. Holdings include the *Magna Carta,* the Gutenburg Bible, Shakespeare's First Folio, Beatles manuscripts and the first edition of *The Times* from 1788. Holds temporary exhibitions on a range of topics
Central Criminal Court
Old Bailey EC4M 7EH T 020-7248 3277
W www.cityoflondon.gov.uk
The highest criminal court in the UK, the 'Old Bailey' is located on the site of the old Newgate Prison. Trials held here have included those of Oscar Wilde, Dr Crippen and the Yorkshire Ripper. The courthouse has been rebuilt several times since 1674; Edward VII officially opened the current neo-baroque building in 1907
Charterhouse
Charterhouse Square EC1M 6AN T 020-7253 9503
W www.thecharterhouse.org
A Carthusian monastery from 1371 to 1538, purchased in 1611 by Thomas Sutton, who endowed it as a residence for aged men 'of gentle birth' and a school for poor scholars (removed to Godalming in 1872)

Downing Street

SW1 **W** www.number10.gov.uk

Number 10 Downing Street is the official town residence of the prime minister, number 11 of the Chancellor of the Exchequer and number 12 is the office of the government whips. The street was named after Sir George Downing, Bt., soldier and diplomat, who was MP for Morpeth 1660–84

George Inn

The George Inn Yard SE1 1NH **T** 020-7407 2056

W www.nationaltrust.org.uk/george-inn

The last galleried inn in London, built in 1677. Now owned by the National Trust and run as an ordinary public house

Horse Guards

Whitehall SW1

Archway and offices built about 1753. The changing of the guard takes place daily at 11am (10am on Sundays) and the inspection at 4pm. Only those with the Queen's permission may drive through the gates and archway into *Horse Guards Parade,* where the colour is 'trooped' on the Queen's official birthday

HOUSES OF PARLIAMENT **W** www.parliament.uk

House of Commons, Westminster SW1A 0AA **T** 020-7219 4272

House of Lords, Westminster SW1A 0PW **T** 020-7219 3107

The royal palace of Westminster, originally built by Edward the Confessor, was the normal meeting place of Parliament from about 1340. St Stephen's Chapel was used from about 1550 for the meetings of the House of Commons, which had previously been held in the Chapter House or Refectory of Westminster Abbey. The House of Lords met in an apartment of the royal palace. The fire of 1834 destroyed much of the palace, and the present Houses of Parliament were erected on the site from the designs of Sir Charles Barry and Augustus Welby Pugin between 1840 and 1867. The chamber of the House of Commons was destroyed by bombing in 1941, and a new chamber designed by Sir Giles Gilbert Scott was used for the first time in 1950. *Westminster Hall and the Crypt Chapel* was the only part of the old palace of Westminster to survive the fire of 1834. It was built by William II from 1097 to 1099 and altered by Richard II between 1394 and 1399. The hammerbeam roof of carved oak dates from 1396–8. The Hall was the scene of the trial of Charles I. *The Victoria Tower* of the House of Lords is 98.5m (323ft) high and *The Clock Tower* of the House of Commons is 96.3m (316ft) high and contains 'Big Ben', the hour bell said to be named after Sir Benjamin Hall, First Commissioner of Works when the original bell was cast in 1856. This bell, which weighed 16 tons 11 cwt, was found to be cracked in 1857. The present bell (13.5 tons) is a recasting of the original and was first brought into use in 1859. The dials of the clock are 7m (23ft) in diameter, the hands being 2.7m (9ft) and 4.3m (14ft) long (including balance piece).

During session, tours of the Houses of Parliament are only available to UK residents who have made advance arrangements through an MP or peer. Overseas visitors are no longer provided with permits to tour the Houses of Parliament during session, although they can tour on Saturdays and during the summer opening and attend debates for both houses in the Strangers' Galleries. During the summer recess, tickets for tours of the Houses of Parliament can be booked by telephone (**T** 0844-847 1672) or bought on site at the ticket office on Abingdon Green opposite Parliament and the Victoria Tower Gardens. The Strangers' Gallery of the House of Commons is open to the public when the house is sitting. To acquire tickets in advance, UK residents should write to their local MP and overseas visitors should apply to their embassy or high commission in the UK for a permit. If none of these arrangements has been made, visitors should join the public queue outside St Stephen's Entrance, where there is also a queue for entry to the House of Lords Gallery

INNS OF COURT

The Inns of Court are ancient unincorporated bodies of lawyers which for more than five centuries have had the power to call to the Bar those of their members who have qualified for the rank or degree of Barrister-at-Law. There are four Inns of Court as well as many lesser inns:

Lincoln's Inn, WC2A 3TL **T** 020-7405 1393

W www.lincolnsinn.org.uk

The most ancient of the inns with records dating back to 1422. The hall and library buildings are from 1845, although the library is first mentioned in 1474; the old hall (late 15th century) and the chapel were rebuilt *c.*1619–23

Inner Temple, King's Bench Walk EC4Y 7HL

T 020-7797 8250 **W** www.innertemple.org.uk

Middle Temple, Middle Temple Lane EC4Y 9BT

T 020-7427 4800 **W** www.middletemple.org.uk

Records for the Inner and Middle Temple date back to the beginning of the 16th century. The site was originally occupied by the Order of Knights Templar *c.*1160–1312. The two inns have separate halls thought to have been formed *c.*1350. The division between the two societies was formalised in 1732 with Temple Church and the Masters House remaining in common. The Inner Temple Garden is normally open to the public on weekdays between 12.30pm and 3pm

Temple Church, EC4Y 7BB

T 020-7353 8559 **W** www.templechurch.com

The nave forms one of five remaining round churches in England

Gray's Inn, South Square WC1R 5ET **T** 020-7458 7800

W www.graysinn.info

Founded early 14th century; hall 1556–8

No other 'Inns' are active, but there are remains of *Staple Inn,* a gabled front on Holborn (opposite Gray's Inn Road). *Clement's Inn* (near St Clement Danes Church), *Clifford's Inn,* Fleet Street, and *Thavies Inn,* Holborn Circus, are all rebuilt. *Serjeants' Inn,* Fleet Street, and another (demolished 1910) of the same name in Chancery Lane, were composed of Serjeants-at-Law, the last of whom died in 1922

Institute of Contemporary Arts

The Mall SW1Y 5AH **T** 020-7930 3647 **W** www.ica.org.uk

Exhibitions of modern art in the fields of film, theatre, new media and the visual arts

Lloyd's

Lime Street EC3M 7HA **T** 020-7327 1000 **W** www.lloyds.com

International insurance market which evolved during the 17th century from Lloyd's Coffee House. The present building was opened for business in May 1986, and houses the Lutine Bell. Underwriting is on three floors with a total area of 10,591 sq. m (114,000 sq. ft). The Lloyd's building is not open to the general public

London Central Mosque and the Islamic Cultural Centre

Park Road NW8 7RG **T** 020-7724 3363 **W** www.iccuk.org

The focus for London's Muslims; established in 1944 but not completed until 1977, the mosque can accommodate about 5,000 worshippers; guided tours are available

London Eye

South Bank SE1 7PB **T** 0870-990 8883 **W** www.londoneye.com

Opened in March 2000 as London's millennium landmark, this 137m (450ft) observation wheel is the tallest cantilevered observation wheel in the world. The wheel provides a 30 minute ride offering panoramic views of the capital

London Zoo
Regent's Park NW1 4RY T 0844-225 1826 W www.zsl.org

Madame Tussauds
Marylebone Road NW1 5LR T 0871-894 3000
W www.madametussauds.com
Waxwork exhibition

Mansion House
Cannon Street EC4N 8BH T 020-7626 2500
W www.cityoflondon.gov.uk
The official residence of the Lord Mayor. Built in the 18th century in the Palladian style. Open to groups by appointment only

Marlborough House
Pall Mall SW1Y 5HX T 020-7747 6500
W www.thecommonwealth.org
Built by Wren for the first Duke of Marlborough and completed in 1711, the house reverted to the Crown in 1835. In 1863 it became the London house of the Prince of Wales and was the London home of Queen Mary until her death in 1953. In 1959 Marlborough House was given by the Queen as the headquarters for the Commonwealth Secretariat and it was opened as such in 1965. The Queen's Chapel, Marlborough Gate, was begun in 1623 from the designs of Inigo Jones for the Infanta Maria of Spain, and completed for Queen Henrietta Maria. Marlborough House is not open to the public

Neasden Temple
BAPS Shri Swaminarayan Mandir, Brentfield Road, Neasden NW10 8LD T 020-8965 2651 W http://londonmandir.baps.org
The first and largest traditional Hindu Mandir outside of India; opened in 1995

Port of London
Port of London Authority, Royal Pier Road, Kent DA12 2BG
T 01474-562200 W www.pla.co.uk
The Port of London covers the tidal section of the river Thames from Teddington to the seaward limit (the outer Tongue buoy and the Sunk light vessel), a distance of 150km (93 miles). The governing body is the Port of London Authority (PLA). Cargo is handled at privately operated riverside terminals between Fulham and Canvey Island, including the enclosed dock at Tilbury, 40km (25 miles) below London Bridge. Passenger vessels and cruise liners can be handled at moorings at Greenwich, Tower Bridge and Tilbury

Queen Elizabeth Olympic Park
Stratford E20 T 0800-072 2110
W www.queenelizabetholympicpark.co.uk
Built for the London 2012 Olympic and Paralympic Games, the park, which included the Olympic Stadium, Velodrome and Aquatics Centre has been redeveloped to provide 227ha (560 acres) of parkland with play areas, outside arts and theatre spaces, waterways and wetlands. The north of the park, which includes the Copper Box Arena sport venue, re-opened to the public in 2013. The south of the park, which re-opened in April 2014, incorporates three venues for arts and sports events and the *ArcelorMittal Orbit,* designed by Sir Anish Kapoor and Cecil Balmond; it is the UK's tallest sculpture (114.5m/376ft) and has two accessible observation floors

Roman Remains
The city wall of Roman *Londinium* was largely rebuilt during the medieval period but sections may be seen near the White Tower in the Tower of London; at Tower Hill; at Coopers' Row; at All Hallows, London Wall, its vestry

being built on the remains of a semi-circular Roman bastion; at St Alphage, London Wall, showing a succession of building repairs from the Roman until the late medieval period; and at St Giles, Cripplegate. Sections of the great forum and basilica, more than 165 sq. m (1,776 sq. ft) have been encountered during excavations in the area of Leadenhall, Gracechurch Street and Lombard Street. Traces of Roman activity along the river include a massive riverside wall built in the late Roman period, and a succession of Roman timber quays along Lower and Upper Thames Street. Finds from these sites can be seen at the Museum of London.

Other major buildings are the amphitheatre at Guildhall, remains of bath-buildings in Upper and Lower Thames Street, and the temple of Mithras in Walbrook

Royal Albert Hall
Kensington Gore SW7 2AP T 0845-401 5045
W www.royalalberthall.com
The elliptical hall, one of the largest in the world, was completed in 1871; since 1941 it has been the venue each summer for the Promenade Concerts founded in 1895 by Sir Henry Wood. Other events include pop and classical music concerts, dance, opera, sporting events, conferences and banquets

Royal Courts of Justice
Strand WC2A 2LL T 020-7947 7726 W www.justice.gov.uk
Victorian Gothic building that is home to the high court. Visitors are free to watch proceedings

Royal Hospital, Chelsea
Royal Hospital Road SW3 4SR T 020-7881 5200
W www.chelsea-pensioners.co.uk
Founded by Charles II in 1682, and built by Wren; opened in 1692 for old and disabled soldiers. The extensive grounds include the former Ranelagh Gardens and are the venue for the Chelsea Flower Show each May

Royal Naval College
Greenwich SE10 9NN T 020-8269 4747 W www.ornc.org
The building was the Greenwich Hospital until 1869. It was built by Charles II, largely from designs by John Webb, and by Queen Mary II and William III, from designs by Wren. It stands on the site of an ancient abbey, a royal house and Greenwich Palace, which was constructed by Henry VII. Henry VIII, Mary I and Elizabeth I were born in the royal palace and Edward VI died there

Royal Opera House
Covent Garden WC2E 9DD T 020-7240 1200
W www.roh.org.uk
Home of The Royal Ballet (1931) and The Royal Opera (1946). The Royal Opera House is the third theatre to be built on the site, opening 1858; the first was opened in 1732

St James's Palace
Pall Mall SW1A 1BQ W www.royal.gov.uk
Built by Henry VIII, only the Gatehouse and Presence Chamber remain; later alterations were made by Wren and Kent. Representatives of foreign powers are still accredited 'to the Court of St James's'. *Clarence House* (1825), the official London residence of the Prince of Wales and his sons, stands within the St James's Palace estate

St Paul's Cathedral
St Paul's Churchyard EC4M 8AD T 020-7246 8350
W www.stpauls.co.uk
Built 1675–1710. The cross on the dome is 111m (365ft) above ground level, the inner cupola 66.4m (218ft) above the floor. 'Great Paul' in the south-west tower weighs nearly 17 tons. The organ by Father Smith (enlarged by Willis and rebuilt by Mander) is in a case carved by Grinling Gibbons, who also carved the choir stalls

Shakespeare's Globe

New Globe Walk SE1 9DT **T** 020-7902 1400
W www.shakespearesglobe.com

Reconstructed in 1997, the open-air playhouse is a unique resource for the works of William Shakespeare through perfomance and education; a new indoor replica Jacobean theatre staged its first public performance in January 2014

Shard

London Bridge SE1 **T** 020-7493 5311 **W** www.the-shard.com

Completed in May 2012, the skyscraper stands at 310m (1,016ft) and possesses a unique facade of 11,000 glass panels and a 360-degree viewing gallery

Somerset House

Strand WC2R 1LA **T** 020-7845 4600
W www.somersethouse.org.uk

The river facade (183m/600ft long) was built in 1776–1801 from the designs of Sir William Chambers; the eastern extension, which houses part of King's College, was built by Smirke in 1829–35. Somerset House was the property of Lord Protector Somerset, at whose attainder in 1552 the palace passed to the Crown, and it was a royal residence until 1692. Somerset House has recently undergone extensive renovation and is home to the Embankment Galleries and the Courtauld Gallery. Open-air concerts and ice-skating (Dec–Jan) are held in the courtyard

SOUTH BANK, SE1

Arts complex on the south bank of the river Thames which consists of:

BFI Southbank **T** 020-7928 3232 **W** www.bfi.org.uk

Opened in 1952 and administered by the British Film Institute, has four auditoria of varying capacities. Venue for the annual London Film Festival.

The *Royal Festival Hall* **T** 020-7960 4200
W www.southbankcentre.co.uk

Opened in 1951 for the Festival of Britain, adjacent are the *Queen Elizabeth Hall,* the *Purcell Room* and the *Hayward Gallery*

The *Royal National Theatre,* **T** 020-7452 3000
W www.nationaltheatre.org.uk

Opened in 1976; comprises the Olivier, the Lyttelton and Dorfman theatres. The Cottesloe Theatre closed in February 2013 and, following refurbishment reopened in 2014 as the Dorfman Theatre

Southwark Cathedral

London Bridge SE1 9DA **T** 020-7367 6700
W www.cathedral.southwark.anglican.org

Mainly 13th century, but the nave is largely rebuilt. The tomb of John Gower (1330–1408) is between the Bunyan and Chaucer memorial windows in the north aisle; Shakespeare's effigy, backed by a view of Southwark and the Globe Theatre, is in the south aisle; the tomb of Bishop Andrewes (*d.*1626) is near the screen. The Lady Chapel was the scene of the consistory courts of the reign of Mary (Gardiner and Bonner) and is still used as a consistory court. John Harvard, after whom Harvard University is named, was baptised here in 1607, and the chapel by the north choir aisle is his memorial chapel

Thames Embankments

Sir Joseph Bazalgette (1819–91) constructed the *Victoria Embankment,* on the north side from Westminster to Blackfriars for the Metropolitan Board of Works, 1864–70; (the seats, of which the supports of some are a kneeling camel, laden with spicery, and of others a winged sphinx, were presented by the Grocers' Company and by W. H. Smith, MP, in 1874); the *Albert Embankment,* on the south side from Westminster Bridge to Vauxhall, 1866–9, and the Chelsea Embankment, 1871–4. The total cost exceeded £2m. Bazalgette also inaugurated the London main drainage system, 1858–65. A medallion *(Flumini vincula posuit)* has been placed on a pier of the *Victoria Embankment* to commemorate the engineer

Thames Flood Barrier

W www.environment-agency.gov.uk

Officially opened in May 1984, though first used in February 1983, the barrier consists of ten rising sector gates which span approximately 520m from bank to bank of the Thames at Woolwich Reach. When not in use the gates lie horizontally, allowing shipping to navigate the river normally; when the barrier is closed, the gates turn through 90 degrees to stand vertically more than 50 feet above the river bed. The barrier took eight years to complete and can be raised within about 90 minutes

Trafalgar Tavern

Park Row, Greenwich SE10 9NW **T** 020-8858 2909
W www.trafalgartavern.co.uk

Regency-period riverside public house built in 1837. Charles Dickens and William Gladstone were patrons

Wembley Stadium

Wembley HA9 0WS **T** 0844-980 8001
W www.wembleystadium.com

The second largest stadium in Europe; hosts major sporting events and music concerts

Westminster Abbey

SW1P 3PA **T** 020-7222 5152 **W** www.westminster-abbey.org

Founded as a Benedictine monastery over 1,000 years ago, the church was rebuilt by Edward the Confessor in 1065 and again by Henry III in the 13th century. The abbey is the resting place for monarchs including Edward I, Henry III, Henry V, Henry VII, Elizabeth I, Mary I and Mary, Queen of Scots, and has been the setting of coronations since that of William the Conqueror in 1066. In Poets' Corner there are memorials to many literary figures, and many scientists and musicians are also remembered here. The grave of the Unknown Warrior is to be found in the nave

Westminster Cathedral

Francis Street SW1P 1QW **T** 020-7798 9055
W www.westminstercathedral.org.uk

Roman Catholic cathedral built 1895–1903 from the designs of John Francis Bentley. The campanile is 83m (273ft) high

Wimbledon All England Lawn Tennis Club

Church Road SW19 5AE **T** 020-8944 1066
W www.wimbledon.com

Venue for the Wimbledon Championships. Includes the Wimbledon Lawn Tennis Museum

HALLMARKS

Hallmarks are the symbols stamped on gold, silver, palladium or platinum articles to indicate that they have been tested at an official Assay Office and that they conform to one of the legal standards. The marking of gold and silver articles to identify the maker was instituted in England in 1363 under a statute of Edward III. In 1478 the Assay Office in Goldsmiths' Hall was established and all gold and silversmiths were required to bring their wares to be date-marked by the Hall, hence the term 'hallmarked'.

With certain exceptions, all gold, silver, palladium or platinum articles are required by law to be hallmarked before they are offered for sale. Current hallmarking requirements come under the UK Hallmarking Act 1973 and subsequent amendments. The act is built around the principle of description, where it is an offence for any person to apply to an unhallmarked article a description indicating that it is wholly or partly made of gold, silver, palladium or platinum. There is an exemption by weight: compulsory hallmarks are not needed on gold and palladium under 1g, silver under 7.78g and platinum under 0.5g. Also, some descriptions, such as rolled gold and gold plate, are permissible. The British Hallmarking Council is a statutory body created as a result of the Hallmarking Act. It ensures adequate provision for assaying and hallmarking, supervises the assay offices and ensures the enforcement of hallmarking legislation. The four assay offices at London, Birmingham, Sheffield and Edinburgh operate under the act.

BRITISH HALLMARKING COUNCIL Secretariat, 1 Colmore Square, Birmingham B4 6AA **T** 0870-763 1455
W www.gov.uk/government/organisations/british-hallmarking-council

COMPULSORY MARKS

Since January 1999 UK hallmarks have consisted of three compulsory symbols – the sponsor's mark, the millesimal fineness (purity) mark and the assay office mark. The distinction between UK and foreign articles has been removed, and more finenesses are now legal, reflecting the more common finenesses elsewhere in Europe.

SPONSOR'S MARK
Formerly known as the maker's mark, the sponsor's mark was instituted in England in 1363. Originally a device such as a bird or fleur-de-lis, now it consists of a combination of at least two initials (usually a shortened form of the manufacturer's name) and a shield design. The London Assay Office offers 45 standard shield designs but other designs are possible by arrangement.

MILLESIMAL FINENESS MARK
The millesimal fineness (purity) mark indicates the number of parts per thousand of pure metal in the alloy. The current finenesses allowed in the UK are:

Gold	999; 990; 916.6 (22 carat); 750 (18 carat); 585 (14 carat); 375 (9 carat)
Silver	999; 958.4 (Britannia); 925 (sterling); 800
Palladium	999; 950; 500
Platinum	999; 950; 900; 850

ASSAY OFFICE MARK
This mark identifies the particular assay office at which the article was tested and marked. The British assay offices are:

 LONDON, Goldsmiths' Hall, Gutter Lane, London EC2V 8AQ **T** 020-7606 8971 **W** www.thegoldsmiths.co.uk

 BIRMINGHAM, PO Box 151, Newhall Street, Birmingham B3 1SB **T** 0121-236 6951 **W** www.theassayoffice.co.uk

 SHEFFIELD, Guardians' Hall, Beulah Road, Hillsborough, Sheffield S6 2AN **T** 0114-231 2121 **W** www.assayoffice.co.uk

 EDINBURGH, Goldsmiths' Hall, 24 Broughton Street, Edinburgh EH1 3RH **T** 0131-556 1144 **W** www.edinburghassayoffice.co.uk

Assay offices formerly existed in other towns, eg Chester, Exeter, Glasgow, Newcastle, Norwich and York, each having its own distinguishing mark.

OPTIONAL MARKS

Since 1999 traditional pictorial marks such as a crown for gold, the Britannia for 958 silver, the lion passant for 925 silver (lion rampant in Scotland) and the orb for 950 platinum may be added voluntarily to the millesimal mark. In 2010 a pictorial mark for 950 palladium was introduced.

 Gold – a crown

 Sterling silver (Scotland)

 Britannia silver

 Platinum – an orb

 Sterling silver (England)

 Palladium – the Greek goddess Pallas Athene

OTHER MARKS

FOREIGN GOODS
Foreign goods imported into the UK are required to be hallmarked before sale, unless they already bear a convention mark (*see* below) or a hallmark struck by an independent assay office in the European Economic Area which is deemed to be equivalent to a UK hallmark.

The following are the assay office marks used for gold imported articles until the end of 1998. For silver and platinum the symbols remain the same but the shields differ in shape.

 London

 Sheffield

 Birmingham

 Edinburgh

CONVENTION HALLMARKS
The UK has been a signatory to the International Convention on Hallmarks since 1972. A convention hallmark struck by the UK assay offices is recognised by all member countries in the convention and, similarly, convention marks from member countries are legally recognised in the UK. There are currently 19 members of the hallmarking convention: Austria, Cyprus, Czech Republic, Denmark, Finland, Hungary, Ireland, Israel, Latvia, Lithuania, the

Netherlands, Norway, Poland, Portugal, Slovakia, Slovenia, Sweden, Switzerland, and the UK.

A convention hallmark comprises four marks: a sponsor's mark, a common control mark, a fineness mark, and an assay office mark.

Examples of common control marks (figures differ according to fineness, but the style of each mark remains the same for each article):

GOLD	SILVER	PALLADIUM	PLATINUM

COMMEMORATIVE MARKS

There are other marks to commemorate special events: the silver jubilee of King George V and Queen Mary in 1935, the coronation of Queen Elizabeth II in 1953, her silver jubilee in 1977, and her golden jubilee in 2002. During 1999 and 2000 there was a voluntary additional Millennium Mark. A mark to commemorate the Queen's diamond jubilee in 2012 was available from July 2011 to October 2012:

Diamond Jubilee Hallmark

DATE LETTER

The date letter shows the year in which an article was assayed and hallmarked. Each alphabetical cycle has a distinctive style of lettering or shape of shield. The date letters were different at the various assay offices and the particular office must be established from the assay office mark before reference is made to tables of date letters. Date letter marks became voluntary from 1 January 1999.

The table which follows shows one specimen shield and letter used by the London Assay Office on silver articles for each alphabetical cycle from 1498. The same letters are found on gold articles but the surrounding shield may differ. Until 1 January 1975 two calendar years are given for each specimen date letter as the letter changed annually in May on St Dunstan's Day (the patron saint of silversmiths). Since 1 January 1975, each date letter has indicated a calendar year from January to December and each office has used the same style of date letter and shield for all articles:

LONDON (GOLDSMITHS' HALL) DATE LETTERS FROM 1498

from	to		from	to
1498–9	1517–18		1756–7	1775–6
1518–19	1537–8		1776–7	1795–6
1538–9	1557–8		1796–7	1815–16
1558–9	1577–8		1816–17	1835–6
1578–9	1597–8		1836–7	1855–6
1598–9	1617–18		1856–7	1875–6
1618–19	1637–8		1876–7 (A to M square shield, N to Z as shown)	1895–6
1638–9	1657–8		1896–7	1915–16
1658–9	1677–8		1916–17	1935–6
1678–9	1696–7		1936–7	1955–6
1697 (from March, 1697 only)	1715–16		1956–7	1974
1716–17	1735–6		1975	1999
1736–7	1738–9		2000	
1739–40	1755–6			

BRITISH CURRENCY

The unit of currency is the pound sterling (£) of 100 pence. The decimal system was introduced on 15 February 1971.

COIN

Gold Coins	Bi-colour Coins‡
One hundred pounds £100*	Two pounds £2
Fifty pounds £50*	*Nickel-Brass Coins*
Twenty-five pounds £25*	Two pounds £2 (pre-1997)§
Ten pounds £10*	One pound £1
Five pounds £5	
Two pounds £2	*Cupro-Nickel Coins*
Sovereign £1	Crown £5 (since 1990)§
Half-sovereign 50p	50 pence 50p
	Crown 25p (pre-1990)§
Silver Coins	20 pence 20p
(Britannia coins)*	
Two pounds £2	*Nickel-plated Steel Coins ℂ*
One pound £1	10 pence 10p
50 pence 50p	5 pence 5p
Twenty pence 20p	
	Bronze Coins
Maundy Money†	2 pence 2p
Fourpence 4p	1 penny 1p
Threepence 3p	
Twopence 2p	*Copper-plated Steel Coins***
Penny 1p	2 pence 2p
	1 penny 1p

* Britannia coins: gold bullion introduced 1987; silver, 1997
† Ceremonial money given annually by the sovereign on Maundy Thursday to as many elderly men and women as there are years in the sovereign's age
‡ Cupro-nickel centre and nickel-brass outer ring
§ Commemorative coins; not intended for general circulation
ℂ Pre-2012 the 10p and 5p coins were struck in cupro-nickel
** Since September 1992, although in 1998 the 2p was struck in both copper-plated steel and bronze

GOLD COIN
Gold ceased to circulate during the First World War. Since then controls on buying, selling and holding gold coin have been imposed at various times but have subsequently been revoked. Under the Exchange Control (Gold Coins Exemption) Order 1979, gold coins may now be imported and exported without restriction, except gold coins which are more than 50 years old and valued at a sum in excess of £8,000; these cannot be exported without specific authorisation from the Department for Business, Innovation and Skills.

Value Added Taxation on the sale of gold coins was revoked in 2000.

SILVER COIN
Prior to 1920 silver coins were struck from sterling silver, an alloy of which 925 parts in 1,000 were silver. In 1920 the proportion of silver was reduced to 500 parts. Since 1947 all 'silver' coins, except Maundy money, have been struck from cupro-nickel, an alloy of 75 parts copper and 25 parts nickel, except for the 20p, composed of 84 parts copper, 16 parts nickel. Maundy coins continue to be struck from sterling silver.

BRONZE COIN
Bronze, introduced in 1860 to replace copper, is an alloy consisting mainly of copper with small amounts of zinc and tin. Bronze was replaced by copper-plated steel in September 1992 with the exception of 1998 when the 2p was made in both copper-plated steel and bronze.

LEGAL TENDER AND VALUE IN CIRCULATION
as at 31 March 2014

Denomination	Legal up to	Face value (£m est)
Gold*	any amount	–
£2	any amount	832
£1	any amount	1,553
50p	£10	474
20p	£10	553
10p	£5	163
5p	£5	192
2p	20p	131
1p	20p	113

* Dated 1838 onwards, if not below least current weight

£5 (Crown since 1990) and 25p (Crown pre-1990) up to £10 are also legal tender but are only redeemable at the Post Office.

The following coins have ceased to be legal tender:

Farthing	31 Dec 1960
Halfpenny (½d)	31 Jul 1969
Half-crown	31 Dec 1969
Threepence	31 Aug 1971
Penny (1d)	31 Aug 1971
Sixpence	30 Jun 1980
Halfpenny (½p)	31 Dec 1984
Old 5 pence	31 Dec 1990
Old 10 pence	30 Jun 1993
Old 50 pence	28 Feb 1998

The Channel Islands and the Isle of Man issue their own coinage, which is legal tender only in the island of issue.

COIN STANDARDS

	Metal	Standard weight (g)	Standard diameter (mm)
1p	bronze	3.56	20.3
1p	copper-plated steel	3.56	20.3
2p	bronze	7.13	25.9
2p	copper-plated steel	7.13	25.9
5p	nickel-plated steel	3.25	18.0
10p	nickel-plated steel	6.5	24.5
20p	cupro-nickel	5.0	21.4
25p Crown	cupro-nickel	28.28	38.6
50p	cupro-nickel	8.00	27.3
£1	nickel-brass	9.5	22.5
£2	nickel-brass	15.98	28.4
£2	cupro-nickel, nickel-brass	12.00	28.4
£5 Crown	cupro-nickel	28.28	38.6

The 'remedy' is the amount of variation from standard permitted in weight and fineness of coins when first issued from the Royal Mint.

THE TRIAL OF THE PYX

The Trial of the Pyx is the examination by a jury to ascertain that coins made by the Royal Mint, which have been set aside in the pyx (or box), are of the proper weight, diameter and composition required by law. The trial is held annually, presided over by the Queen's Remembrancer, with a jury of freemen of the Company of Goldsmiths.

BANKNOTES

Bank of England notes are issued in denominations of £5, £10, £20 and £50 for the amount of the fiduciary note issue, and are legal tender in England and Wales. No £1 notes have been issued since 1984 and in March 1998 the outstanding notes were written off in accordance with the provision of the Currency Act 1983.

The current E series of notes was introduced from June 1990, replacing the D series (see below). A new-style £20 note, the first in series F, was introduced in March 2007. A £50 note, the second in the F series, and the first banknote issued by the Bank of England to feature two portraits on the reverse, was issued in November 2011. The historical figures portrayed in these series are:

£5	May 2002–date	Elizabeth Fry
£5	Jun 1990–2003	George Stephenson*
£10	Nov 2000–date	Charles Darwin
£10	Apr 1992–2003	Charles Dickens*
£20	Mar 2007–date	Adam Smith
£20	Jun 1999–2010	Sir Edward Elgar*
£20	Jun 1991–2001	Michael Faraday*
£50	Nov 2011–date	Matthew Boulton and James Watt
£50	Apr 1994–2014	Sir John Houblon*

* These notes have been withdrawn from circulation

NOTE CIRCULATION

Note circulation is highest at the two peak spending periods of the year: around Christmas and during the summer holiday period.

The value of notes in circulation (£ million) at the end of February 2012 and 2013 was:

	2013	2014
£5	1,526	1,540
£10	7,234	7,182
£20	35,163	36,484
£50	10,323	11,025
Other notes*	3,776	3,967
Total	58,022	60,198

* Includes higher value notes used internally in the Bank of England, eg as cover for the note issues of banks in Scotland and Northern Ireland in excess of their permitted issue

LEGAL TENDER

Banknotes which are no longer legal tender are payable when presented at the head office of the Bank of England in London.

The white notes for £10, £20, £50, £100, £500 and £1,000, which were issued until April 1943, ceased to be legal tender in May 1945, and the white £5 note in March 1946.

The white £5 note issued between October 1945 and September 1956, the £5 notes issued between 1957 and 1963 (bearing a portrait of Britannia) and the first series to bear a portrait of the Queen, issued between 1963 and 1971, ceased to be legal tender in March 1961, June 1967 and September 1973 respectively.

The series of £1 notes issued during the years 1928 to 1960 and the 10 shilling notes issued from 1928 to 1961 (those without the royal portrait) ceased to be legal tender in May and October 1962 respectively. The £1 note first issued in March 1960 (bearing on the back a representation of Britannia) and the £10 note first issued in February 1964 (bearing a lion on the back), both bearing a portrait of the Queen on the front, ceased to be legal tender in June 1979. The £1 note first issued in 1978 ceased to be legal tender on 11 March 1988. The 10 shilling note was replaced by the 50p coin in October 1969, and ceased to be legal tender on 21 November 1970.

The D series of banknotes was introduced from 1970 and ceased to be legal tender from the dates shown below. The predominant identifying feature of each note was the portrayal on the back of a prominent figure from British history:

£1	Feb 1978–Mar 1988	Sir Isaac Newton
£5	Nov 1971–Nov 1991	Duke of Wellington
£10	Feb 1975–May 1994	Florence Nightingale
£20	Jul 1970–Mar 1993	William Shakespeare
£50	Mar 1981–Sep 1996	Sir Christopher Wren

The £1 coin was introduced on 21 April 1983 to replace the £1 note.

OTHER BANKNOTES

Scotland – Banknotes are issued by three Scottish banks. The Royal Bank of Scotland issues notes for £1, £5, £10, £20, £50 and £100. Bank of Scotland and the Clydesdale Bank issue notes for £5, £10, £20, £50 and £100. Scottish notes are not legal tender in the UK but they are an authorised currency.

Northern Ireland – Banknotes are issued by four banks in Northern Ireland. The Bank of Ireland and the Ulster Bank issue notes for £5, £10, £20, £50 and £100. The First Trust Bank issue notes for £10, £20, £50 and £100 and Danske Bank (formerly Northern Bank) issue notes for £10 and £20. Northern Ireland notes are not legal tender in the UK but in Northern Ireland they circulate widely and enjoy a status comparable to that of Bank of England notes.

Channel Islands – The States of Guernsey issues its own currency notes and coinage. The notes are for £1, £5, £10, £20 and £50, and the coins are for 1p, 2p, 5p, 10p, 20p, 50p, £1 and £2. The States of Jersey issues its own currency notes and coinage. The notes are for £1, £5, £10, £20, £50 and £100, and the coins are for 1p, 2p, 5p, 10p, 20p, 50p, £1 and £2.

The Isle of Man – The Isle of Man government issues notes for £1, £5, £10, £20 and £50. Although these notes are only legal tender in the Isle of Man, they are accepted at face value in branches of the clearing banks in the UK. The Isle of Man issues coins for 1p, 2p, 5p, 10p, 20p, 50p, £1, £2 and £5.

Although none of the series of notes specified above is legal tender in the UK, they are generally accepted by banks irrespective of their place of issue. At one time banks made a commission charge for handling Scottish and Irish notes but this was abolished some years ago.

BANK FAMILY TREE

Includes the major retail banks operating in the UK as at
April 2014. Financial results for these banks are given on
page 488. Building societies are only included in
instances where they demutualised to become a bank.

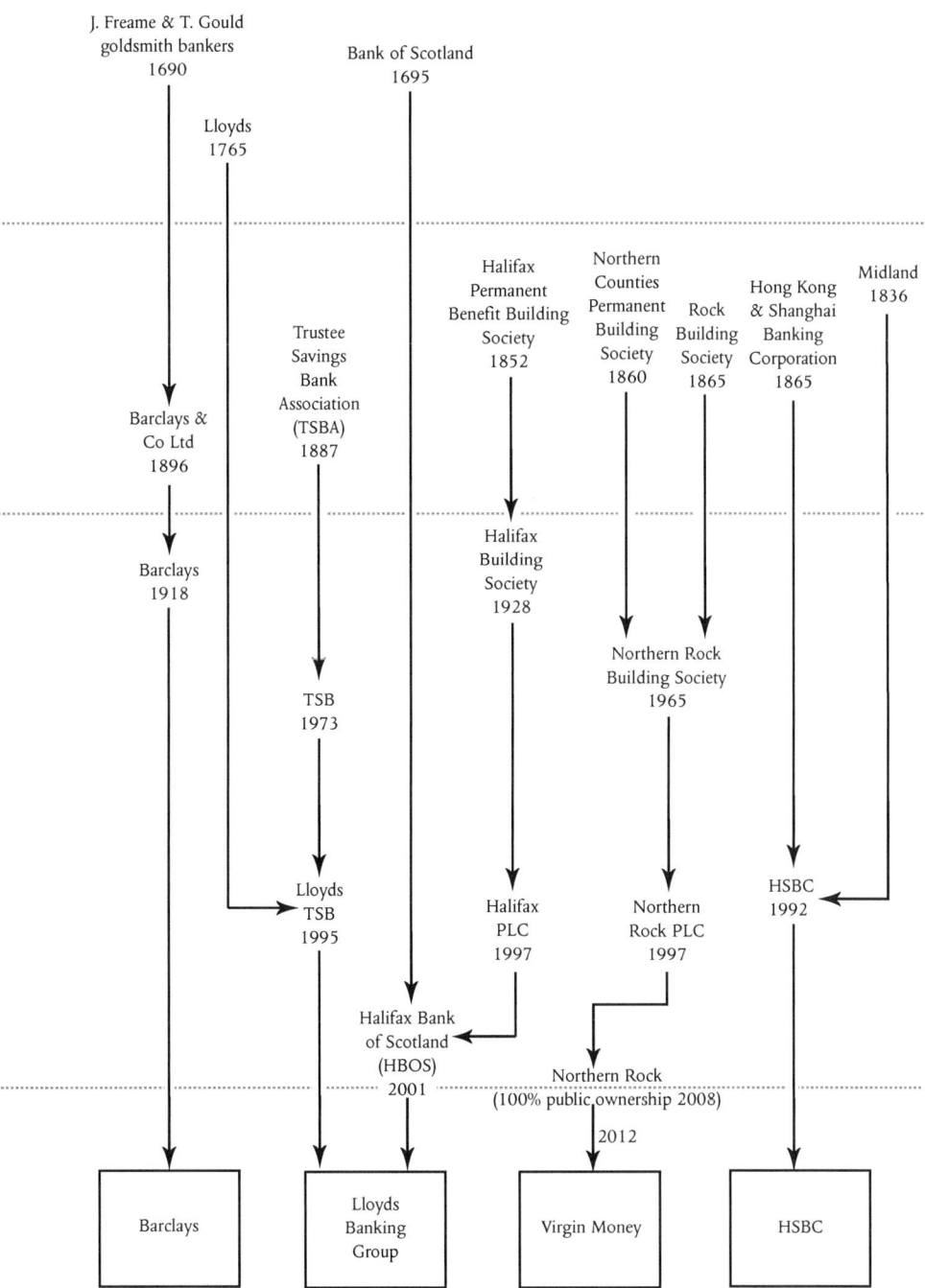

BANKING AND PERSONAL FINANCE

There are two main types of deposit-taking institutions: banks and building societies, although National Savings and Investments also provides savings products. Banks and building societies are regulated by the Prudential Regulation Authority, part of the Bank of England (*see* Financial Services Regulation), and National Savings and Investments is accountable to HM Treasury.

The main institutions within the British banking system are the Bank of England (the central bank), retail banks, investment banks and overseas banks. In its role as the central bank, the Bank of England acts as banker to the government and as a note-issuing authority; it also oversees the efficient functioning of payment and settlement systems.

Since May 1997, the Bank of England has had operational responsibility for monetary policy. At monthly meetings of its monetary policy committee the Bank sets the interest rate at which it will lend to the money markets.

OFFICIAL INTEREST RATES 2005–14

4 August 2005	4.50%
3 August 2006	4.75%
9 November 2006	5.00%
11 January 2007	5.25%
10 May 2007	5.50%
5 July 2007	5.75%
6 December 2007	5.50%
7 February 2008	5.25%
10 April 2008	5.00%
8 October 2008	4.50%
6 November 2008	3.00%
4 December 2008	2.00%
8 January 2009	1.50%
5 February 2009	1.00%
5 March 2009	0.50%

RETAIL BANKING

Retail banks offer a wide variety of financial services to individuals and companies, including current and deposit accounts, loan and overdraft facilities, credit and debit cards, investment services, pensions, insurance and mortgages. All banks offer telephone and internet banking facilities in addition to traditional branch services.

The Financial Ombudsman Service provides independent and impartial arbitration in disputes between banks and their customers (*see* Financial Services Regulation).

PAYMENT CLEARINGS

The UK Payments Administration (UKPA) is a trade body that brings together the organisations responsible for delivering payment services. It also provides information on payment issues such as card fraud, cheques, plastic cards, electronic payments and cash. The Payments Council sets strategy for UK payments to ensure they meet the needs of users, payment service providers and the wider economy. Membership of the Payments Council is open to any member of a payment scheme that is widely used or significant in the UK. As at April 2014 the Payments Council had 33 members, comprising banks, building societies, financial services providers and the Post Office.

There are four organisations, overseen by UKPA, that manage the majority of payment clearings in the UK:
- BACS is responsible for the schemes behind the clearing and settlement of automated payments including direct debit and BACS direct credit (W www.bacs.co.uk)
- CHAPS Clearing Company provides electronic same-day clearing and real-time settlement services for sterling payments (W www.chapsco.co.uk)
- The Cheque and Credit Clearing Company manages the cheque clearing system (W www.chequeandcredit.co.uk)
- The Faster Payments Service allows customers to make faster electronic payments, usually by phone or online banking (W www.fasterpayments.org.uk)

PAYMENTS COUNCIL/UKPA, 2 Thomas More Square, London E1W 1YN
T 020-3217 8200 W www.ukpayments.org.uk

GLOSSARY OF FINANCIAL TERMS

AER (ANNUAL EQUIVALENT RATE) – A notional rate quoted on savings and investment products which demonstrates the return on interest, when compounded and paid annually.

APR (ANNUAL PERCENTAGE RATE) – Calculates the total amount of interest payable over the whole term of a product (such as investment or loan), allowing consumers to compare rival products on a like-for-like basis. Companies offering loans, credit cards, mortgages or overdrafts are required by law to provide the APR rate. Where typical APR is shown, it refers to the company's typical borrower and so is given as a best example; rate and costs may vary depending on individual circumstances.

MAJOR RETAIL BANKS' FINANCIAL RESULTS 2013

Bank group	Profit/(loss) before taxation £ million	Profit/(loss) after taxation £ million	Total assets £ million
Banco Santander Group*	5,932	4,405	911,324
Barclays	2,868	1,297	1,312,267
Cooperative Bank	(586)	(748)	43,396
HSBC*	13,433	10,596	1,590,249
Lloyds Banking Group	415	(802)	847,030
RBS Group	(8,243)	(8,477)	1,027,878
Virgin Money Group	179	174	24,569

* Exchange rate as at May 2014 converting EUR and USD to GBP respectively

ANNUITY – A type of insurance policy that provides regular income in exchange for a lump sum. The annuity can be bought from a company other than the existing pension provider.

ASU – Accident, sickness and unemployment insurance taken out by a borrower to protect against being unable to work for these reasons. The policy will usually pay a percentage of the normal monthly mortgage repayment if the borrower is unable to work.

ATM (AUTOMATED TELLER MACHINES) – Commonly referred to as cash machines. Users can access their bank accounts using a card for simple transactions such as withdrawing money and viewing an account balance. Some banks and independent ATM deployers charge for transactions.

BANKER'S DRAFT – A cheque drawn on a bank against a cash deposit. Considered to be a secure way of receiving money in instances where a cheque could 'bounce' or where it is not desirable to receive cash.

BASE RATE – The interest rate set by the Bank of England at which it will lend to financial institutions. This acts as a benchmark for all other interest rates.

BASIS POINT – Unit of measure (usually one-hundredth of a percentage point) used to express movements in interest rates, foreign rates or bond yields.

BUY-TO-LET – The purchase of a residential property for the sole purpose of letting to a tenant. Not all lenders provide mortgage finance for this purpose. Buy-to-let lenders assess projected rental income (typical expectations are between 125 and 130 per cent of the monthly interest payment) in addition to, or instead of, the borrower's income. Buy-to-let mortgages are available as either interest only or repayment.

CAPITAL GAIN/LOSS – Increase/decrease in the value of a capital asset when it is sold or transferred compared to its initial worth.

CAPPED RATE MORTGAGE – The interest rate applied to a loan is guaranteed not to rise above a certain rate for a set period of time; the rate can therefore fall but will not rise above the capped rate. The level at which the cap is fixed is usually higher than for a fixed rate mortgage for a comparable period of time. The lender normally imposes early redemption penalties within the first few years.

CASH CARD – Issued by banks and building societies for withdrawing cash from ATMs.

CHARGE CARD – Charge cards, eg American Express and Diners Club, can be used in a similar way to credit cards but the debt must be settled in full each month.

CHIP AND PIN CARD – A credit/debit card which incorporates an embedded chip containing unique owner details. When used with a PIN, such cards offer greater security as they are less prone to fraud. Since 14 February 2006, most card transactions in the UK have required the use of a chip and pin card.

CREDIT CARD – Normally issued with a credit limit, credit cards can be used for purchases until the limit is reached. There is normally an interest-free period on the outstanding balance of up to 56 days. Charges can be avoided if the balance is paid off in full within the interest-free period. Alternatively part of the balance can be paid and in most cases there is a minimum amount set by the issuer (normally a percentage of the outstanding balance) which must be paid on a monthly basis. Some card issuers charge an annual fee and most issuers belong to at least one major credit card network, eg Mastercard or Visa.

CREDIT RATING – Overall credit worthiness of a borrower based on information from a credit reference agency, such as Experian or Equifax, which holds details of credit agreements, payment records, county court judgements etc for all adults in the UK. This information is supplied to lenders who use it in their credit scoring or underwriting systems to calculate the risk of granting a loan to an individual and the probability that it will be repaid. Each lender sets their own criteria for credit worthiness and may accept or reject a credit application based on an individual's credit rating.

CRITICAL ILLNESS COVER – Insurance that covers borrowers against critical illnesses such as stroke, heart attack or cancer and is designed to protect mortgage or other loan payments.

DEBIT CARD – Debit cards were introduced on a large scale in the UK in the mid-1980s, replacing cash and cheques to purchase goods and services. They can be used to withdraw cash from ATMs in the UK and abroad and may also function as a cheque guarantee card. Funds are automatically withdrawn from an individual's bank account after making a purchase and no interest is charged.

DIRECT DEBIT – An instruction from a customer to their bank, which authorises the payee to charge costs to the customer's bank account.

DISCOUNTED MORTGAGE – Discounted mortgages guarantee an interest rate set at a margin below the standard variable rate for a period of time. The discounted rate will move up or down with the standard variable rate, but the payment rate will retain the agreed differential below the standard variable rate. The lender normally imposes early redemption penalties within the first few years.

EARLY REDEMPTION PENALTY – *see* Redemption Penalty

ENDOWMENT MORTGAGE – Only the interest on a property loan is paid back to the lender each month as long as an endowment life insurance policy is taken out for an agreed amount of time, typically 25 years. When the policy matures the lender will take repayment of the money owed on the property loan and any surplus goes to the policyholder. If the endowment policy shows a shortfall on projected returns, the policy holder must make further provision to pay off the mortgage.

EQUITY – When applied to real estate, equity is the difference between the value of a property and the amount outstanding on any loan secured against it. Negative equity occurs when the loan is greater than the market value of the property.

FIXED RATE MORTGAGE – A repayment mortgage where the interest rate on the loan is fixed for a set amount of time, normally a period of between one and ten years. The interest rate does not vary with changes to the base rate resulting in the monthly mortgage payment remaining the same for the duration of the fixed period. The lender normally imposes early redemption penalties within the first few years.

ISA (INDIVIDUAL SAVINGS ACCOUNT) – A means by which investors can save (in a cash ISA) and invest (in a stocks and shares ISA) without paying any tax on the proceeds. There are limits on the amount that can be invested during any given tax year (*see* Taxation).

INTEREST ONLY MORTGAGE – Only interest is paid by the borrower and capital remains constant for the term of the loan. The onus is on the borrower to make provision to repay the capital at the end of the term. This is usually achieved through an investment vehicle such as an endowment policy or pension.

LOAN TO VALUE (LTV) – This is the ratio between the size of a mortgage loan sought and the mortgage lender's valuation. On a loan of £55,000, for example, on a property valued at £100,000 the loan to value is 55 per cent. This means that there is sufficient equity in the property for the lender to be reassured that if interest or capital repayments were stopped, it could sell the property and recoup the money owed. Fewer options are available to borrowers requiring high LTV.

LONDON INTERBANK OFFERED RATE (LIBOR) – Is the interest rate that London banks charge when lending to one another on the wholesale money market. LIBOR is set by supply and demand of money as banks lend to each other in order to balance their books on a daily basis.

MIG (MORTGAGE INDEMNITY GUARANTEE) – An insurance for the lender paid by the borrower on high LTV mortgages (typically more than 90 per cent). It is a policy designed to protect the lender against loss in the event of the borrower defaulting or ceasing to repay a mortgage and is usually paid as a one-off premium or can be added to the value of the loan. It offers no protection to the borrower. Not all lenders charge MIG premiums.

OVERDRAFT – An 'authorised' overdraft is an arrangement made between customer and bank allowing the balance of the customer's account to go below zero; interest is normally charged at an agreed rate and sometimes an arrangement fee is charged. If the negative balance exceeds the agreed terms or a prior arrangement for an overdraft facility has not been made (an 'unauthorised' overdraft) then additional penalty fees may be charged and higher interest rates may apply. Interest-free overdrafts are available for customers in certain circumstances, such as full-time higher education students and recent graduates.

PERSONAL PENSION PLAN (PPP) – Designed for the self-employed or those in non-pensionable employment. Contributions made to a PPP are exempt from tax and the retirement age may be selected at any time from age 50 to 75. Up to 25 per cent of the pension fund may be taken as a tax-free cash sum on retirement.

PHISHING – A fraudulent attempt to obtain bank account details and security codes through an email. The email purports to come from a *bona fide* bank or building society and attempts to steer the recipient, usually under the pretext that the banking institution is updating its security arrangements, to a website which requests personal details.

PIN (PERSONAL IDENTIFICATION NUMBER) – A PIN is issued alongside a cash card to allow the user to access a bank account via an ATM. PINs are also issued with smart, credit and debit cards and, since 14 February 2006, have been compulsory as a security measure in the majority of purchases.

PORTABLE MORTGAGE – A mortgage product that can be transferred to a different property in the event of a house move. Preferable where early redemption penalties are charged.

REDEMPTION PENALTY – A charge levied for paying off a loan, debt balance or mortgage before a date agreed with the lender.

REPAYMENT MORTGAGE – In contrast to the interest only mortgage, the monthly repayment includes an element of the capital sum borrowed in addition to the interest charged.

SELF-CERTIFICATION – Some lenders allow borrowers to self-certify their income. This type of scheme is useful to the self-employed who may not have accounts available or any other person who has difficulty proving their regular income.

SHARE – A share is a divided-up unit of the value of a company. If a company is worth £100m, and there are 50 million shares in issue, then each share is worth £2 (usually listed as pence). As the overall value of the company fluctuates so does the share price.

STANDING ORDER – An instruction made by the customer to their bank, which allows the transfer of a set amount to a payee at regular intervals.

UNIT TRUST – A 'pooled' fund of assets, usually shares, owned by a number of individuals. Managed by professional, authorised fund-management groups, unit trusts have traditionally delivered better returns than average cash deposits, but do rise and fall in value as their underlying investment varies in value.

VARIABLE RATE MORTGAGE – Repayment mortgages where the interest rate set by the lender increases or decreases in relation to the base interest rate which can result in fluctuating monthly repayments.

WITH-PROFITS – Usually applies to pensions, endowments, savings schemes or bonds. The intention is to smooth out the rises and falls in the stock market for the benefit of the investor. Actuaries working for the insurance company, or fund managers, hold back some profits in good years in order to make up the difference in years when shares perform badly.

FINANCIAL SERVICES REGULATION

Since April 2013 under the Financial Services and Markets Act 2000, as amended by the Financial Services Act (2012), the Financial Conduct Authority and the Prudential Regulation Authority have been responsible for financial regulation in the UK.

FINANCIAL CONDUCT AUTHORITY

The Financial Conduct Authority (FCA) is responsible for supervising the conduct of around 50,000 financial firms and for regulating the prudential standards of those firms not regulated by the Prudential Regulation authority. The FCA has three statutory objectives:

- to secure an appropriate degree of protection for consumers
- to protect and enhance the integrity of the UK financial system
- to promote effective market competition in the interests of consumers

ACCOUNTABILITY AND FUNDING

The FCA is accountable to HM Treasury and therefore to parliament, but is operationally independent of the government and is funded entirely by the firms which it regulates. The FCA is governed by a board appointed by HM Treasury, but day-to-day decisions and staff management are the responsibility of the executive committee.

The FCA's annual budget for 2014–15 is £452m.

THE FINANCIAL SERVICES REGISTER

The Financial Services Register lists financial services firms and individuals in the UK who are authorised by the FCA to do business and specifies which activity each firm or individual is regulated to undertake and what products or services each is approved to provide.

FINANCIAL CONDUCT AUTHORITY, 25 The North Colonnade, Canary Wharf, London E14 5HS T 020-7066 1000
W www.fca.org.uk
Chair, John Griffith-Jones
Chief Executive, Martin Wheatley

PRUDENTIAL REGULATION AUTHORITY

The Prudential Regulation Authority (PRA), part of the Bank of England, works alongside the FCA and is responsible for the prudential regulation and supervision of banks, building societies, credit unions, insurers and major investment firms. In total the PRA regulates around 1,700 financial firms.

The PRA has two statutory objectives: to promote the safety and soundness of these firms and, specifically for insurers, to contribute to the securing of an appropriate degree of protection for policyholders.

The PRA's board includes the Governor of the Bank of England, the Deputy Governor for Financial Stability, the Deputy Governor for Prudential Regulation (also the chief executive of the PRA) and the chief executive of the FCA and is accountable to parliament.

PRUDENTIAL REGULATION AUTHORITY, 20 Moorgate, London EC2R 6DA T 020-7601 4444 E enquiries@bankofengland.co.uk
W www.bankofengland.co.uk/pra
Chief Executive, Andrew Bailey

COMPENSATION

Created under the Financial Services and Markets Act (2000), the Financial Services Compensation Scheme (FSCS) is the UK's statutory fund of last resort for customers of authorised financial services firms. It provides compensation if a firm authorised by the FCA or PRA is unable, or likely to be unable, to pay claims against it. In general this is when a firm has stopped trading and has insufficient assets to meet claims, or is in insolvency. The FSCS covers deposits, insurance policies, insurance broking, investment business and mortgage advice and arranging. The FSCS is independent of the UK regulators (FCA and PRA), with separate staff and premises. However, the FCA and PRA appoint the directors. The chair's appointment (and removal) is subject to Treasury approval. The FSCS is funded by levies on authorised firms.

The Pension Protection Fund (PPF) is a statutory fund established under the Pensions Act 2004 and became operational on 6 April 2005. The fund was set up to pay compensation to members of eligible defined benefit pension schemes, where there is a qualifying insolvency event in relation to the employer and where there are insufficient assets in the pension scheme to cover PPF levels of compensation. Compulsory annual levies are charged on all eligible schemes to help fund the PPF, in addition to investment of PPF assets. The PPF is also responsible for the Fraud Compensation Fund – a fund that will provide compensation to occupational pension schemes that suffer a loss attributable to dishonesty.

FINANCIAL SERVICES COMPENSATION SCHEME, 10th Floor, Beaufort House, 15 St Botolph Street, London EC3A 7QU
T 020-7741 4100/0800-678 1100 W www.fscs.org.uk
Chair, Lawrence Churchill, CBE
Chief Executive, Mark Neale
PENSION PROTECTION FUND, Renaissance, 12 Dingwall Road, Croydon CR0 2NA T 0845-600 2541
E information@ppf.gsi.gov.uk
W www.pensionprotectionfund.org.uk
Chair, Lady Judge, CBE
Chief Executive, Alan Rubenstein

DESIGNATED PROFESSIONAL BODIES

Professional firms are exempt from requiring direct regulation by the FCA if they carry out only certain restricted activities that arise out of, or are complementary to, the provision of professional services, such as arranging the sale of shares on the instructions of executors or trustees, or providing services to small, private companies. These firms are, however, supervised by designated professional bodies (DPBs). There are a number of safeguards to protect consumers dealing with firms that do not require direct regulation. These arrangements include:

- the FCA's power to ban a specific firm from taking advantage of the exemption and to restrict the regulated activities permitted to the firms
- rules which require professional firms to ensure that their clients are aware that they are not authorised persons
- a requirement for the DPBs to supervise and regulate the firms and inform the FCA on how the professional firms carry on their regulated activities

See Professional Education section for contact details of the following DPBs:

Association of Chartered Certified Accountants
Council for Licensed Conveyancers
Institute of Actuaries
Institute of Chartered Accountants in England and Wales
Institute of Chartered Accountants in Ireland
Institute of Chartered Accountants of Scotland
Law Society of England and Wales
Law Society of Northern Ireland
Law Society of Scotland
Royal Institution of Chartered Surveyors

RECOGNISED INVESTMENT EXCHANGES

The FCA currently supervises seven recognised investment exchanges (RIEs) in the UK; recognition confers an exemption from the need to be authorised to carry out regulated activities in the UK. The RIEs are organised markets on which member firms can trade investments such as equities and derivatives. The RIEs are listed with their year of recognition in parentheses:

BATS TRADING (2013), 6th Floor 10 Lower Street, London EC3R 6AF T 020-7012 8900 W www.batstrading.co.uk
CME EUROPE LTD (2014), 1 New Change, London EC4M 9AF T 020-3379 3700 W www.cmegroup.com/europe
ICAP SECURITIES & DERIVATIVES EXCHANGE LTD (2007), 2 Broadgate, London EC2M 7UR T 020-7050 7650 W www.isdx.com
ICE FUTURES EUROPE (2001), 5th Floor Milton Gate, 60 Chiswell Street, London EC1Y 4SA T 020-7065 7700 W www.theice.com
LIFFE ADMINISTRATION AND MANAGEMENT (2001), Cannon Bridge House, 1 Cousin Lane, London EC4R 3XX T 020-7623 0444 W www.nyx.com
LONDON METAL EXCHANGE (2001), 56 Leadenhall Street, London EC3A 2BJ T 020-7264 5555 W www.lme.co.uk
LONDON STOCK EXCHANGE (2001), 10 Paternoster Square, London EC4M 7LS T 020-7797 1000 W www.londonstockexchange.com

RECOGNISED CLEARING HOUSES

The Bank of England is responsible for recognising and supervising recognised clearing houses (RCHs), which organise the settlement of transactions on recognised investment exchanges. There are currently four RCHs in the UK:

CME CLEARING EUROPE (2010), 1 New Change, London EC4M 9AF T 020-3379 3700 W www.cmeclearingeurope.co.uk
EUROCLEAR UK AND IRELAND (2001), 33 Cannon Street, London EC4M 5SB T 020-7849 0000 W www.crestco.co.uk
ICE CLEAR EUROPE (2008), 5th Floor, Milton Gate, 60 Chiswell Street, London EC1Y 4SA T 020-7265 3648 W www.theice.com/clear_europe
LCH (LONDON CLEARING HOUSE) CLEARNET (2001), Aldgate House, 33 Aldgate High Street, London EC3N 1EA T 020-7426 7000 W www.lchclearnet.com

OMBUDSMAN SCHEMES

The Financial Ombudsman Service was set up by the Financial Services and Markets Act 2000 to provide consumers with a free, independent service for resolving disputes with authorised financial firms. The Financial Ombudsman Service can consider complaints about most financial matters including: banking; credit cards and store cards; financial advice; hire purchase and pawnbroking; insurance; loans and credit; money transfer; mortgages; payday lending and debt collecting; payment protection insurance; pensions; savings and investments; stocks, shares, unit trusts and bonds.

Complainants must first complain to the firm involved. They do not have to accept the ombudsman's decision and are free to go to court if they wish, but if a decision is accepted, it is binding for both the complainant and the firm.

The Pensions Ombudsman can investigate and decide complaints and disputes regarding the way occupational and personal pension schemes are administered and managed. The Pensions Ombudsman is also the Ombudsman for the Pension Protection Fund (PPF) and the Financial Assistance Scheme (which offers help to those who were a member of an under-funded defined benefit pension scheme that started to wind-up in specific financial circumstances between 1 January 1997 and 5 April 2005).

FINANCIAL OMBUDSMAN SERVICE, South Quay Plaza, 183 Marsh Wall, London E14 9SR **Helpline** 0800-023 4567 T 020-7964 1000 E complaint.info@financial-ombudsman.org.uk W www.financial-ombudsman.org.uk
Interim Chief Executive and Chief Ombudsman, Tony Boorman
PENSIONS OMBUDSMAN, 11 Belgrave Road, London SW1V 1RB T 020-7630 2200 E enquiries@pensions-ombudsman.org.uk W www.pensions-ombudsman.org.uk
Pensions Ombudsman, Tony King
Deputy Pensions Ombudsman, Jane Irvine

PANEL ON TAKEOVERS AND MERGERS

The Panel on Takeovers and Mergers is an independent body, established in 1968, whose main functions are to issue and administer the City code and to ensure equality of treatment and opportunity for all shareholders in takeover bids and mergers. The panel's statutory functions are set out in the Companies Act 2006.

The panel comprises up to 35 members drawn from major financial and business institutions. The chair, deputy chair and up to 20 other members are nominated by the panel's own nomination committee. The remaining members are nominated by professional bodies representing the banking, insurance, investment, pension and accountancy industries, the Association for Financial Markets in Europe and the CBI.

PANEL ON TAKEOVERS AND MERGERS, 10 Paternoster Square, London EC4M 7DY T 020-7382 9026 W www.thetakeoverpanel.org.uk
Chair, Sir Gordon Langley

NATIONAL SAVINGS AND INVESTMENTS

NS&I (National Savings and Investments) is an executive agency of HM Treasury and one of the UK's largest financial providers, with almost 25 million customers and over £100bn invested. NS&I offers savings and investment products to personal savers and investors and the money is used to manage the national debt. When people invest in NS&I they are lending money to the government which pays them interest or prizes in return. All products are financially secure because they are guaranteed by HM Treasury.

TAX-FREE PRODUCTS

SAVINGS CERTIFICATES

Index-linked Saving Certificates
Otherwise known as inflation-beating savings, index-linked saving certificates are fixed rate investments that pay tax-free returns guaranteed to be above inflation. They are sold in limited issues with a minimum and maximum investment.

Fixed Interest Saving Certificates
Fixed interest saving certificates are fixed rate investments that pay tax-free returns. They are sold in limited issues with a minimum and maximum investment.

PREMIUM BONDS

Introduced in 1956, premium bonds enable savers to enter a regular draw for tax-free prizes, while retaining the right to get their money back. A sum equivalent to interest on each bond is put into a prize fund and distributed by monthly prize draws. The prizes are drawn by ERNIE (electronic random number indicator equipment) and are free of all UK income tax and capital gains tax. Two £1m jackpots are drawn each month in addition to other tax-free prizes ranging in value from £25 to £100,000.

Bonds are in units of £1, with a minimum purchase of £100, up to a maximum holding limit of £40,000 per person. Bonds become eligible for prizes once they have been held for one clear calendar month following the month of purchase. Each £1 unit can win only one prize per draw, but it will be awarded the highest for which it is drawn. Bonds remain eligible for prizes until they are repaid.

The scheme offers a facility to reinvest prize wins automatically. Upon completion of an automatic prize reinvestment mandate, holders receive new bonds which are immediately eligible for future prize draws. Bonds can only be held in the name of an individual and not by organisations.

CHILDREN'S BONDS

Children's bonus bonds were introduced in 1991. In September 2012 changes were made to the product; including a change in name to Children's Bonds, which reflects the way interest is paid. Any amount between £25 and £3,000 can be invested and interest is added at a fixed rate each year for five years. The minimum holding is £25 and the maximum holding is £3,000 per child per issue. They can be bought by parents, guardians and grandparents (including great grandparents) for any child under 16, but the investment must be managed by a parent or guardian. All returns are totally exempt from UK income tax.

INDIVIDUAL SAVINGS ACCOUNTS

Since April 1999 NS&I has offered cash individual savings accounts (ISAs). Its Direct ISA, launched in April 2006, can be opened and managed online and by telephone with a minimum investment of £1 and a maximum investment of £15,000 in the 2014–15 tax year. Interest for the Direct ISA is calculated daily and is free of tax.

OTHER PRODUCTS

GUARANTEED EQUITY BONDS

Guaranteed equity bonds are five-year investments where the returns are linked to the performance of the FTSE-100 index with a guarantee that the original capital invested will be returned even if the FTSE-100 index falls over the five years. They are sold in limited issues with a minimum investment of £1,000 and a maximum of £1m. The returns are subject to income tax on maturity, unless they are held in a self-invested pension plan (SIPP).

SAVINGS AND INVESTMENT ACCOUNTS

The direct saver account was launched in March 2010. Customers are able to invest between £1 and £2m per person. The account can be managed online or by telephone. Interest is paid without deduction of tax at source.

The investment account is a postal-only account which pays tiered rates of interest. It can be opened with a minimum balance of £20 and has a maximum limit of £1m. The interest is paid without deduction of tax at source.

INCOME BONDS

NS&I income bonds were introduced in 1982. They are suitable for those who want to receive regular monthly payments of interest while preserving the full cash value of their capital. The minimum holding for each investment is £500 and the maximum £1m per person. A variable rate of interest is calculated on a day-to-day basis and paid monthly. Interest is taxable but is paid without deduction of tax at source.

GUARANTEED INCOME BONDS

Guaranteed income bonds were introduced in February 2008 and changes were made to the product in September 2012. They are designed for those who want to receive regular monthly payments of interest while preserving the full cash value of their capital. There is a minimum and maximum holding per person, per issue. Joint investors can combine their allowance to invest up to double the maximum individual holding per issue. A fixed rate of interest is calculated on a day-to-day basis and paid monthly. Interest is taxable and tax is deducted at source. They are sold in limited issues.

GUARANTEED GROWTH BONDS

Guaranteed growth bonds were introduced in February 2008 and changes were made to the product in September 2012. As for Guaranteed income bonds, there is a minimum and maximum holding per person, per issue and joint investors can combine their allowance to invest up to double the maximum individual holding per issue. A fixed rate of interest is calculated on a day-to-day basis and is paid annually on the anniversary of the date of investment. Interest is taxable and tax is deducted at source. They are sold in limited issues.

FURTHER INFORMATION

Further information regarding products and their current availability can be obtained online (W www.nsandi.com) and by telephone (T 0500-007007).

THE NATIONAL DEBT

HISTORY

The early 1700s saw the meteoric rise of the banking and financial markets in Great Britain, with the emerging stock market revolving around government funds. The ability to raise money by means of creating debt through the issue of bills and bonds heralded the beginning of the national debt.

The war years of 1914–18 saw an increase in the national debt from £650m at the start of the war to £7,500m by 1919. The Treasury developed new expertise in foreign exchange, currency, credit and price control in order to manage the post-war economy. The slump of the 1930s necessitated the restructuring of the UK economy following the Second World War (the national debt stood at £21bn by its end) and the emphasis was placed on economic planning and financial relations.

The relatively high period of inflation in the 1970s and 1980s led to the rise of the national debt in nominal terms from £36bn in 1972 to £197bn in 1987 and then to £419bn in March 1998. Although in nominal terms the national debt has risen sharply in recent years, as a percentage of GDP it has decreased dramatically since the end of the Second World War, when it stood at 250 per cent of GDP (for current figures, *see* table below).

THE UK DEBT MANAGEMENT OFFICE

The decision in 1997 to transfer monetary policy to the Bank of England, while the Treasury retained control of fiscal policy, led to the creation of the UK Debt Management Office (DMO) as an executive agency of HM Treasury in April 1998. Initially the DMO was responsible only for the management of government marketable debt and for issuing gilts. In April 2000 responsibility for exchequer cash management and for issuing Treasury bills (short-dated securities with maturities of less than one year) was transferred from the Bank of England to the DMO. The national debt also includes the (non-marketable) liabilities of National Savings and Investments and other public sector and foreign currency debt.

In 2002 the operations of the long-standing statutory functions of the Public Works Loan Board, which lends capital to local authorities, and the Commissioners for the Reduction of the National Debt, which manages the investment portfolios of certain public funds, were integrated within the DMO (*see also* Government Departments).

UK PUBLIC SECTOR NET DEBT

	£ billion	per cent of GDP
2012–13 (outturn)	1,185	74.2
2013–14 (forecast)	1,258	74.5
2014–15 (forecast)	1,395	77.3

Source: HM Treasury: *Budget 2014* (Crown copyright)

THE LONDON STOCK EXCHANGE

The London Stock Exchange Group (LSEG) serves the needs of companies by providing facilities for raising capital. It also operates marketplaces for members to trade financial instruments, including equities, bonds and derivatives, on behalf of investors and institutions such as pension funds and insurers.

LSEG's key subsidiary companies are the London Stock Exchange, Borsa Italiana, MTS (an electronic platform for the trading of European government and corporate bonds), Turquoise (a trading platform for European equities) and FTSE (a global index provider).

Headquartered in London, with significant operations in Italy, France, North America and Sri Lanka, the group employs around 2,800 people.

HISTORY

The London Stock Exchange is one of the world's oldest stock exchanges, dating back more than 300 years to its origins in the coffee houses of 17th-century London. It was formally established as a membership organisation in 1801.

MAJOR DEVELOPMENTS

'BIG BANG'
In 1986 a package of reforms which are now known as 'Big Bang' transformed the London Stock Exchange and the City of London, liberalising the way in which banks and stock-broking firms operated and facilitating greater foreign investment. The London Stock Exchange ceased granting voting rights to individual members and became a private company. The 'Big Bang' also saw the start of a move towards fully electronic trading and the closure of the trading floor.

INTRODUCTION OF SETS
In October 1997, the Exchange introduced SETS, its electronic order book. The system enhanced the efficiency and transparency of trading on the Exchange, allowing trades to be executed automatically and anonymously rather than negotiated by telephone.

DEMUTUALISATION AND LISTING
The London Stock Exchange demutualised in 2000 and listed on its own main market in 2001.

MERGER WITH BORSA ITALIANA
In October 2007 the London Stock Exchange merged with the Italian stock exchange, Borsa Italiana, creating London Stock Exchange Group (LSEG).

DIVERSIFICATION
Since 2009 LSEG has diversified its business beyond the listing and trading of UK and Italian equities:

- In 2009 LSEG purchased Sri Lankan technology company MillenniumIT which provides technology to stock exchanges, brokerages and regulators around the world. It also supplies the trading technology to LSEG's own markets
- In 2010 LSEG acquired a majority stake in Turquoise, a platform facilitating the trading of stocks listed in 18 European countries and the USA
- In 2011 LSEG became the owner of FTSE, the international business which creates and manages over 200,000 financial indices
- In 2013 LSEG purchased a majority stake in LCH (London Clearing House) Clearnet (see also Financial Services Regulation, Recognised Clearing Houses)

UK EQUITY MARKETS

LSEG offers a range of listing options for companies, according to their size, history and requirements:

- The Main Market has the highest standards of regulation and disclosure obligations and is overseen by the UK Listing Authority (UKLA), a division of the Financial Conduct Authority (FCA). A Main Market listing enables established companies to raise capital, widen their investor base and have their shares traded alongside global peers. They are also eligible for inclusion in key indices, such as the FTSE 100 and the FTSE 250
- The Alternative Investment Market (AIM), established in June 1995, is specially designed to meet the needs of small and growing companies. It enables them to raise capital and broaden their investor base in a more flexible regulatory environment, while still being traded on an internationally recognised market. AIM companies retain an experienced Nominated Adviser (or 'Nomad') firm, which is responsible for ensuring the company's suitability for the market
- The Professional Securities Market (PSM), established in July 2005, allows companies to target professional investors only, on a market that offers greater flexibility in accounting standards
- The Specialist Fund Market (SFM), established in November 2007, is a market for highly specialised investment entities, such as hedge funds or private equity funds, that wish to target institutional investors only

As at April 2014 there were 2,461 companies quoted on LSEG's UK markets, with a combined value of £4,056,323m: 1,304 on the UK Main Market, 1,097 on the AIM, 39 on the PSM and 21 entities on the SFM.

LONDON STOCK EXCHANGE, 10 Paternoster Square, London EC4M 7LS **T** 020-7797 1000
W www.lseg.com
Chair, Chris Gibson-Smith, PHD
Chief Executive, Xavier Rolet

ECONOMIC STATISTICS

THE BUDGET (MARCH 2014)

GOVERNMENT EXPENDITURE

DEPARTMENTAL EXPENDITURE LIMITS £ billion

	Estimate 2013–14	Projection 2014–15	Projection 2015–16
Resource DEL			
Education	51.7	53.5	53.5
NHS (Health)	105.6	108.3	110.4
Transport	3.8	4.0	3.2
Business, Innovation and Skills	14.8	13.8	13.2
CLG Communities	2.0	2.5	1.1
CLG Local Government	16.6	13.8	12.1
Home Office	10.7	10.4	9.8
Justice	7.4	6.7	6.2
Law Officers' Departments	0.6	0.5	0.5
Defence	27.1	25.3	23.6
Foreign and Commonwealth Office	2.0	1.5	1.1
International Development	8.1	8.3	8.5
Energy and Climate Change	1.2	1.5	1.3
Environment, Food and Rural Affairs	1.8	1.8	1.6
Culture, Media and Sport	1.1	1.2	1.1
Work and Pensions	7.2	7.8	6.2
Scotland	25.5	25.8	25.8
Wales	13.9	13.7	13.7
Northern Ireland	9.7	9.7	9.7
Chancellor's departments	3.2	3.6	3.3
Cabinet Office	2.2	2.3	2.0
Independent bodies	1.5	1.9	1.6
Reserve	0.0	2.4	2.5
Special reserve	0.0	0.6	1.0
Adjustment for budget exchange	0.0	(2.2)	0.0
Spending commitments not yet in budgets	0.0	0.0	0.9
Allowance for shortfall	(2.4)	(0.8)	(1.0)
TOTAL RESOURCE DEL	315.4	317.9	312.9
Capital DEL			
Education	3.9	5.0	4.6
NHS (Health)	4.3	4.6	4.7
Transport	8.4	9.0	9.5
Business, Innovation and Skills	2.5	2.9	3.8
CLG Communities	3.8	5.1	3.4
CLG Local Government	0.0	0.0	0.0
Home Office	0.4	0.5	0.4
Justice	0.3	0.3	0.3
Law Officers' Departments	0.0	0.0	0.0
Defence	7.7	9.0	9.3
Foreign and Commonwealth Office	0.1	0.1	0.1
International Development	2.0	2.0	2.6
Energy and Climate Change	2.2	2.5	2.5
Environment, Food and Rural Affairs	0.5	0.6	0.5
Culture, Media and Sport	0.0	0.3	0.4
Work and Pensions	0.2	0.2	0.2
Scotland	2.9	2.9	3.0
Wales	1.3	1.4	1.5
Northern Ireland	1.0	1.0	1.1
Chancellor's departments	0.2	0.2	0.1
Cabinet Office	0.4	0.4	0.4
Independent bodies	0.1	0.1	0.1
Reserve	0.0	1.1	0.5
Special reserve	0.0	0.2	0.1
Adjustment for budget exchange	0.0	(2.0)	(0.7)
Adjustment for devolved administration borrowing	0.0	0.0	0.3
Spending commitments not yet in budgets	0.0	0.0	0.4
Allowance for shortfall	(1.1)	(1.8)	(2.0)
TOTAL CAPITAL DEL	41.1	45.9	47.0
TOTAL DEL	356.5	363.8	359.9

Source: HM Treasury – *Budget 2014* (Crown copyright)

TOTAL MANAGED EXPENDITURE £ billion

	Estimate 2013–14	Projection 2014–15	Projection 2015–16
Current Expenditure			
Resource Annually Managed Expenditure (AME)	326.2	341.6	356.3
Resource DELs	315.4	317.9	312.9
Ring-fenced depreciation	26.4	20.4	22.3
Capital Expenditure			
Capital AME	6.5	6.3	5.1
Capital DELs	41.1	45.9	47.0
TOTAL MANAGED EXPENDITURE	715.5	732.0	743.6
Total Managed Expenditure (% GDP)	43.5%	42.5%	41.6%

Source: HM Treasury – *Budget 2014* (Crown copyright)

GOVERNMENT RECEIPTS £ billion

	Outturn 2012–13	Forecast 2013–14	Forecast 2014–15
Income tax (gross of tax credits)[1]	152.3	155.6	166.5
Pay as you earn	132.0	135.5	140.2
Self assessment	20.6	20.9	27.2
Tax credits	(3.0)	(2.7)	(2.7)
National insurance contributions (NICs)	104.5	107.3	110.0
Value added tax	100.7	106.5	110.7
Corporation tax	40.4	40.1	41.4
Corporation tax credits	(0.9)	(1.0)	(0.9)
Petroleum revenue tax	1.7	1.1	1.2
Fuel duties	26.6	26.8	26.8
Business rates	26.3	26.6	26.9
Council tax	26.3	27.1	27.6
VAT refunds	13.8	13.9	14.1
Capital gains tax	3.9	3.9	5.4
Inheritance tax	3.1	3.5	3.9
Stamp duty land tax	6.9	9.5	12.7
Stamp taxes on shares	2.2	3.1	3.1
Tobacco duties	9.6	9.7	9.9
Spirits duties	3.0	3.0	3.0
Wine duties	3.5	3.7	3.9
Beer and cider duties	3.6	3.7	3.5
Air passenger duty	2.8	3.0	3.2
Insurance premium tax	3.0	3.1	3.2
Climate change levy	0.7	1.3	2.0
Other HMRC taxes[2]	5.9	6.5	6.7
Vehicle excise duties	6.0	6.1	5.9
Bank levy	1.6	2.3	2.7
Licence fee receipts	3.1	3.1	3.2
Enviromental levies	2.3	4.1	4.9

	Outturn 2012–13	Forecast 2013–14	Forecast 2014–15
Swiss capital tax	0.0	0.9	0.0
EU ETS Auction recipts	0.3	0.4	0.3
Other taxes	6.6	6.8	6.9
Total Taxes	556.8	579.1	606.0
Less own resources			
contribution to EU	(5.3)	(5.5)	(5.1)
Interest and dividends	14.4	19.0	19.3
Gross operating surplus	27.6	28.3	28.9
Other receipts	(0.2)	(1.0)	(1.0)
CURRENT RECEIPTS	593.4	619.8	648.1
UK oil and gas revenues[3]	6.1	4.7	3.7

[1] Income tax includes PAYE and Self Assessment receipts, and also includes tax on savings income and other minor income tax components
[2] Consists of landfill tax, aggregates levy, betting and gaming duties, and customs duties and levies
[3] Consists of offshore corporation tax and petroleum revenue tax
Source: HM Treasury – *Budget 2014* (Crown copyright)

TRADE

TRADE IN GOODS £ million

	Exports	Imports	Balance
2007	219,981	310,516	(90,535)
2008	251,565	345,826	(94,261)
2009	227,727	310,660	(82,933)
2010	265,243	363,828	(98,585)
2011	298,421	398,513	(100,092)
2012	300,457	409,157	(108,700)
2013	304,756	412,646	(107,890)

Source: ONS (Crown copyright)

BALANCE OF PAYMENTS, 2013

Current Account	*£ million*
Trade in goods and services	
Trade in goods	(107,890)
Trade in services	79,426
Total trade in goods and services	(28,464)
Income	
Compensation of employees	(326)
Investment income	(16,343)
Total income	(16,669)
Total current transfers	(27,628)
TOTAL (CURRENT BALANCE)	(72,761)

Source: ONS (Crown copyright)

UK EMPLOYMENT

DISTRIBUTION OF THE WORKFORCE

	Mar 2012	Mar 2014
Workforce jobs	31,929,000	33,051,000
HM forces	187,000	167,000
Self-employment jobs	4,108,000	4,529,000
Employees jobs	27,614,000	28,334,000
Government-supported trainees	21,000	21,000

Source: ONS – *Labour Market Statistics 2014* (Crown copyright)

EMPLOYED AND UNEMPLOYED BY GENDER
thousands

	Apr–Jun 2013		Apr–Jun 2014	
EMPLOYED	*Male*	*Female*	*Male*	*Female*
All aged 16+	15,914	13,863	16,379	14,218
UNEMPLOYED				
All aged 16+	1,445	1,070	1,151	926

Source: ONS – *Labour Market Statistics 2014* (Crown copyright)

UK GDP GROWTH (AT CURRENT MARKET PRICES)
volume % change on previous quarter

Source: ONS

DURATION OF UNEMPLOYMENT, APR–JUN 2014

All unemployed	2,077,000
Less than 6 months	1,006,000
6 months–1 year	333,000
1 year +	738,000 (35.5% of total)

Source: ONS – *Labour Market Statistics 2014* (Crown copyright)

MEDIAN EARNINGS, 2013

	All	Male	Female
Median gross annual earnings*			
(£, thousands)	27.0	29.3	23.6
Median gross weekly earnings *(£)*	416.50	508.00	327.50
Median hourly earnings, excluding			
overtime *(£)*	11.56	12.86	10.33

* Full-time
Source: ONS (Crown copyright)

LABOUR STOPPAGES BY DURATION, 2013

Under 5 days	102
5–10 days	9
11–20 days	2
21–30 days	0
31–50	0
50+	1
All stoppages	114

Source: ONS (Crown copyright)

LABOUR DISPUTES BY INDUSTRY, 2013

Industry Group	*Working Days Lost*
Manufacturing	7,100
Sewage, waste and water supply	1,800
Construction	4,300
Transport, storage, and communication	23,700
Financial, insurance and administration	5,900
Public administration and defence	180,200
Education	215,000
Human health and social work	3,900
Arts entertainment	1,600

Source: ONS (Crown copyright)

TRADE UNIONS

Year	No. of unions	Total membership
2010–11	176	7,328,905
2011–12	172	7,261,210
2012–13	166	7,197,415
2013–14	166	7,086,116

Source: Annual Report of the Certification Officer 2013–14

COST OF LIVING AND INFLATION RATES

The first cost of living index to be calculated took July 1914 as 100 and was based on the pattern of expenditure of working-class families in 1914. The cost of living index was superseded in 1947 by the general index of retail prices (RPI), although the older term is still popularly applied.

The Harmonised Index of Consumer Prices (HICP) was introduced in 1997 to enable comparisons within the European Union using an agreed methodology. In 2003 the National Statistician renamed the HICP the Consumer Prices Index (CPI) to reflect its role as the main target measure of inflation for macroeconomic purposes. In March 2013 CPIH, an additional index which includes owner-occupiers' housing costs, was introduced.

The RPI and indices based on it continue to be published alongside the CPI. Private-sector pensions and index-linked gilts continue to be calculated with reference to RPI or its derivatives.

CPI AND RPI

The CPI and RPI measure the changes month by month in the average level of prices of goods and services purchased by households in the UK. The indices are compiled using a selection of around 700 goods and services, and the prices charged for these items are collected at regular intervals at about 150 locations throughout the country. The Office for National Statistics (ONS) reviews the components of the indices once a year to reflect changes in consumer preferences and the establishment of new products. The table below shows changes made by the ONS to the CPI 'shopping basket' in 2014.

The CPI excludes a number of items that are included in the RPI, mainly related to housing, such as council tax, and a range of owner-occupier housing costs, such as mortgage payments. The CPI covers all private households, whereas the RPI excludes the top 4 per cent by income and pensioner households which derive at least three-quarters of their income from state benefits. The two indices use different methodologies to combine the prices of goods and services, which means that since 1996 the CPI inflation measure is less than the RPI inflation measure.

INFLATION RATE

The 12-monthly percentage change in the 'all items' index of the RPI or CPI is referred to as the rate of inflation. As the most familiar measure of inflation, the RPI is often referred to as the 'headline rate of inflation'. The CPI is the main measure of inflation for macroeconomic purposes and forms the basis of the government's inflation target, which is currently 2 per cent. The percentage change in prices between any two months/years can be obtained using this formula:

$$\frac{\text{Later date RPI/CPI} - \text{Earlier date RPI/CPI}}{\text{Earlier date RPI/CPI}} \times 100$$

CHANGES TO THE 'SHOPPING BASKET' OF GOODS AND SERVICES IN 2014

The table below shows changes to the CPI* basket of goods and services made by the ONS in 2014 in order to reflect changes in consumer preferences and the establishment of new products.

Goods and services group	Removed items	New items
Audio-visual equipment	DVD recorder	interchangeable lens digital camera
Catering services	take-away coffee	–
Clothing	–	men's clothing hire
Cultural services	DVD rental internet subscription	DVD rental/video-on-demand subscription services
Food	–	flavoured milk; fresh fruit snacking pot; honey
Footwear	–	canvas fashion shoe/trainer
Furniture & furnishings	hardwood flooring; tufted carpet	tufted carpet (100 per cent synthetic fibres); tufted carpet (minimum 80 per cent wool)
Gardens & pets	–	plant food; wild bird seed
Household maintenance	gardeners' fees	–
Maintenance of dwelling	wallpaper paste	–
Non-alcoholic beverages	–	mixer drink
Personal effects	–	fashion necklace
Social protection	after-school club charges	–
Vehicle maintenance	automatic drive-through car wash	car wash (manual or automatic)

* RPI goods and services are grouped together under different classifications

For example, to find the CPI rate of inflation for 2006, using the annual averages for 2005 and 2006:

$$\frac{102.3 - 100.0}{100.0} \times 100 = 2.3$$

From 14 February 2006 the reference year for the CPI was re-based to 2005=100 to improve price comparison clarity across the EU. None of the underlying data, from which the re-referenced series was calculated, was revised. Historical rates of change (such as annual inflation figures), calculated from the re-based rounded index levels, were revised due to the effect of rounding. The CPI rate of inflation figure given in the table below may differ by plus or minus 0.1 percentage points from the figure calculated by the above equation. The change of reference period and revision due to rounding does not apply to the RPI, which remains unchanged.

The RPI and CPI figures are published on either the second or third Tuesday of each month in an indices bulletin on the ONS website (W www.ons.gov.uk).

PURCHASING POWER OF THE POUND

Changes in the internal purchasing power of the pound may be defined as the 'inverse' of changes in the level of prices: when prices go up, the amount which can be purchased with a given sum of money goes down. To find the purchasing power of the pound in one month or year, given that it was 100p in a previous month or year, the calculation would be:

$$100p \times \frac{\text{Earlier month/year RPI}}{\text{Later month/year RPI}}$$

Thus, if the purchasing power of the pound is taken to be 100p in 1975, the comparable purchasing power in 2000 would be:

$$100p \times \frac{34.2}{170.3} = 20.1p$$

For longer term comparisons, it has been the practice to use an index which has been constructed by linking together the RPI for the period 1962 to date; an index derived from the consumers' expenditure deflator for the period from 1938 to 1962; and the pre-war 'cost of living' index for the period 1914 to 1938. This long-term index enables the internal purchasing power of the pound to be calculated for any year from 1914 onwards. It should be noted that these figures can only be approximate.

	Annual average RPI (1987 = 100)	Purchasing power of £ (1998 = 1.00)	Annual average CPI (2005 = 100)*	Annual average CPIH (2005=100)	Rate of inflation (RPI/CPI/CPIH)
1914	2.8	58.18			
1915	3.5	46.54			
1920	7.0	23.27			
1925	5.0	32.58			
1930	4.5	36.20			
1935	4.0	40.72			
1938	4.4	37.02			
There are no official figures for 1939–45					
1946	7.4	22.01			
1950	9.0	18.10			
1955	11.2	14.54			
1960	12.6	12.93			
1965	14.8	11.00			
1970	18.5	8.80			
1975	34.2	4.76			
1980	66.8	2.44	18.0		
1985	94.6	1.72	6.1		
1990	126.1	1.29	71.5		9.5/7.0
1995	149.1	1.09	86.0		3.5/2.6
1998	162.9	1.00	91.1		3.4/1.6
2000	170.3	0.96	93.1		3.0/0.8
2005	192.0	0.85	100.0	100.0	2.8/2.1
2006	198.1	0.82	102.3	102.3	3.2/2.3/2.3
2007	206.6	0.79	104.7	104.6	4.3/2.3/2.2
2008	214.8	0.76	108.5	108.1	4.0/3.6/3.4
2009	213.7	0.76	110.8	110.3	−0.5/2.2/2.0
2010	223.6	0.73	114.5	113.4	4.6/3.3/2.9
2011	235.2	0.69	119.6	118.0	5.2/4.5/4.1
2012	242.7	0.67	123.0	121.2	3.2/2.8/2.7
2013	250.1	0.65	126.1	124.1	3.0/2.6/2.4

* In accordance with an EU Commission regulation, all published CPI figures were re-based to 2005=100 with effect from 14 February 2006, replacing the 1996=100 series

INSURANCE

AUTHORISATION AND REGULATION OF INSURANCE COMPANIES

Under the Financial Services and Markets Act 2000, the Financial Services Authority (FSA) was the authorising, enforcement, supervisory and rule-making body of insurers. From 2005, its remit included insurance brokers and intermediaries. The FSA's role was to ensure that firms to which it granted authorisation satisfied the necessary financial criteria, that the senior management of the company were 'fit and proper persons' and that unauthorised firms were not permitted to trade.

In June 2010 the government announced its intention to replace the FSA with two successor bodies. In April 2013, under the Financial Services Act 2012, the prudential supervision of banks and insurers moved to a new operationally independent subsidiary of the Bank of England: the Prudential Regulation Authority (PRA). The FSA was renamed the Financial Conduct Authority (FCA) and now focuses on consumer protection and markets oversight. All life insurers, general insurers, reinsurers, insurance and reinsurance brokers, financial advisers and composite firms are statutorily regulated. See also Financial Services Regulation.

Firms wishing to effect or carry out contracts of insurance must apply for authorisation to do so. The PRA assesses applicant insurers from a prudential perspective, using the same framework that is employed for supervision of existing insurers. The FCA then assesses applicants from a conduct perspective. Although the PRA manages the authorisation process, an insurer will be granted authorisation only where both the FCA and the PRA are satisfied that an insurer meets the relevant requirements.

At the end of 2012 there were over 1,200 insurance organisations and friendly societies with authorisation from the FSA to transact one or more classes of insurance business in the UK. However, the single European insurance market, established in 1994, gave insurers authorised in any other European Union country automatic UK authorisation without further formality. This means a potential market of over 5,000 insurers.

COMPLAINTS

Disputes between consumers and financial businesses can be referred to the Financial Ombudsman Service (FOS). Consumers with a complaint about any form of money matter, including insurance, mortgages, savings and credit, must firstly take the matter to the highest level within the company. Thereafter, if it remains unresolved and it involves an amount below £150,000 (£100,000 for complaints received before 1 January 2012), it can be referred free of charge, to the FOS, which examines the facts of a complaint and delivers a decision binding on the provider (but not the consumer). Small businesses with a turnover of up to €2m (£1.7m) and fewer than ten employees also have access to the scheme. In 2012 the FOS handled around 2 million enquiries and around 508,000 complaints regarding financial services companies, twice as many as in 2011. See also Financial Services Regulation.

ASSOCIATION OF BRITISH INSURERS

Over 90 per cent of the domestic business of UK insurance companies is transacted by the 300 members of the Association of British Insurers (ABI). The ABI is a trade association which protects and promotes the interests of all its insurance company members. Only insurers authorised in the EU are eligible for membership. Brokers, intermediaries, financial advisers and claims handlers may not join ABI but may have their own trade associations.

ASSOCIATION OF BRITISH INSURERS (ABI)
51 Gresham Street, London EC2V 7HQ T 020-7600 3333
W www.abi.org.uk
Chair, Tidjane Thiam
Director-General, Otto Thoresen

BALANCE OF PAYMENTS

The financial services industry contributes 9.4 per cent to the UK's gross domestic product (GDP). In 2012 insurance sector net exports totalled £8.2bn.

WORLDWIDE MARKET

The UK insurance industry is the largest in Europe and currently the third largest in the world behind the USA and Japan. China has the fastest growing insurance market and is expected to become the third largest market by 2015.

Market	Premium income ($bn)	Percentage of total
USA	1,271	27.6
Japan	654	14.2
UK	311	6.1

TAKEOVERS AND MERGERS

For the third consecutive year predictions in the media of an increase in insurance takeover and merger activity proved unfounded. Companies seemed to be favouring organic growth rather than acquisitions. In fact, in 2013 the number of deals decreased by almost 50 per cent from 2012. There was some speculation that the Co-operative Group would sell its general insurance arm and Legal & General looked like the front runners. However the sale plan was shelved in January 2014.

In October and November 2013 speculation mounted about a takeover of Royal & Sun Alliance (RSA) following a profits warning, the ousting of the chief executive of their Irish operation and, in December, the resignation of the group's chief executive, Simon Lee. Almost all of the top ten composite insurers in the UK were tipped by the press to be lining up takeover bids but, in the event, the share price rallied and no bids were made.

INDUSTRY ISSUES

Since 2002 the European Commission (EC) has been formulating plans for Solvency II, which aims to establish an EU-wide set of requirements for capital adequacy and management standards, modernising and consolidating a large number of EU directives known as Solvency I which was established in the 1970s. The Solvency II directive was originally scheduled to come into force in 2012. In November 2013 the EC put forward a draft directive postponing the start date for Solvency II until 1 January 2016. This was the latest in a long line of delays and postponements, but at least sufficiently far into the future to offer the possibility that it may finally be implemented on this date.

It is estimated that by the time Solveny II is implemented most larger insurers will have spent up to £200m each on new technology, staff, training and systems in order to comply with the new regime.

GENERAL INSURANCE

The year 2013 began with the resumption of talks between the government and the insurance industry about the replacement for the Statement of Principles on Flood Insurance, which had been in place since 1953. This statement obliged insurers to offer flood cover to existing customers who had previously been flooded or who were at risk of flooding. It was due to expire on 31 July 2013 and, late in 2012, the ABI announced that they were seeking an alternative arrangement.

After intensive lobbying of backbench MPs and an appearance before the Environment, Food and Rural Affairs select committee, the ABI initially announced an extension of one month to the Statement of Principles, which gave the ABI and the government time to agree a Memorandum of Understanding on how to develop a new system called 'Flood Re', a not-for-profit industry scheme which would ensure flood insurance remains widely affordable and available. The aim is for Flood Re to begin in the summer of 2015; in the meantime, insurers have agreed to continue under the old Statement of Principles until the new system is operational. Flooding returned to the top of the agenda in winter 2013–14 when serious flooding again hit the UK at the end of December 2013 and continued until the end of February 2014. It is estimated that this period of flooding led to insurance payouts of around £6.5m a day.

Various aspects of motor insurance made the headlines during the year. Whiplash remained a major issue, with the first three months of 2014 seeing the Ministry of Justice consulting on reducing the number and cost of whiplash claims. Every day 1,500 people in the UK claim for a whiplash injury, with a total cost to insurers estimated to be around £2bn a year, and adding around £90 a year to each motor insurance premium. In the UK around 70 per cent of road accident personal injury claims are for whiplash, compared to 47 per cent in Germany, 32 per cent in Spain and just 3 per cent in France.

The cost of motor insurance has always been particularly high for drivers aged between 17 and 24, reflecting their higher accident rate. Young drivers account for 12 per cent of licence holders, but they are involved in 25 per cent of all road deaths and serious accidents. In March 2013 transport secretary Patrick McLoughlin announced that he would bring forward a green paper on reforming the way people are taught to drive, tested and monitored after passing their test. This was in response to a coalition of police, road safety officers, insurers and young people's groups who had called for a graduated driver licensing system.

The impact of the heavy flooding in December 2013 will largely be reflected in the 2014 claim statistics; until the final week of 2013, weather damage claims in 2013 were less than in 2012, mirroring the reduction in claims for theft, subsidence and business interruption. Among property insurance claims only fire damage saw a small – 5 per cent – increase in payouts.

LONDON INSURANCE MARKET

The London Insurance Market is a unique wholesale marketplace and a distinct, separate sector of the UK insurance and reinsurance industry. It is the world's leading market for internationally traded insurance and reinsurance, its business comprising mainly overseas non-life large and high-exposure risks. It is the only place in the world where all 20 of the world's largest insurance companies have an office. The market is centred on the square mile of the City of London, which provides the required financial, banking, legal and other support services. Around 56 per cent of London market business is transacted at Lloyd's of London, the remainder through insurance companies and protection and indemnity clubs. In 2012 the market had a written gross premium income of over £49bn. Around 200 Lloyd's brokers service the market.

The trade association for the international insurers and reinsurers writing primarily non-marine insurance and all classes of reinsurance business in the London market is the International Underwriting Association (IUA).

INTERNATIONAL UNDERWRITING ASSOCIATION,
London Underwriting Centre, 3 Minster Court, Mincing Lane, London EC3R 7DD T 020-7617 4444 W www.iua.co.uk
Chair, Malcolm Newman
Chief Executive, Dave Matcham

BRITISH INSURANCE COMPANIES

The following insurance company figures refer to members and certain non-members of the ABI.

CLAIMS STATISTICS *(£m)*

	2009	2010	2011	2012	2013
Theft	555	529	603	554	472
Fire	1,204	1,072	1,156	995	1,051
Weather	662	707	618	1,087	703
Domestic subsidence	161	171	158	114	101
Business interruption	131	180	161	161	100
Total	2,713	2,659	2,696	2,911	2,427

WORLDWIDE GENERAL BUSINESS TRADING RESULTS *(£m)*

	2011	2012
Net written premiums	48,019	46,810
Underwriting results	945	761
Investment income	3,435	2,822
Overall trading profit	4,379	3,583
Profit as percentage of premium income	9.1	7.7

NET PREMIUM INCOME BY SECTOR 2012 *(£m)*

	UK	Overseas
Motor	11,556	4,837
Non-motor	19,504	7,947
Marine, aviation and transport	1,187	495
Reinsurance	848	355
Total general business	33,095	13,634
Ordinary long-term	129,247	40,385
TOTAL	162,342	54,019

LLOYD'S OF LONDON

Lloyd's of London is an international market for almost all types of general insurance. Lloyd's currently has the capacity

WORLDWIDE GENERAL BUSINESS UNDERWRITING RESULTS (£m)

	2011			2012		
	UK	Overseas	Total	UK	Overseas	Total
Motor						
Premiums	12,039	5,041	17,080	11,556	4,837	16,393
Profit (loss)	(353)	244	(109)	(286)	191	(95)
Percentage of premiums	(2.9)	4.8	(0.6)	(2.5)	4.0	(0.6)
Non-motor						
Premiums	19,684	8,227	27,911	19,504	7,947	27,451
Profit (loss)	859	0	859	160	447	607
Percentage of premiums	4.4	–	3.1	0.8	5.6	2.2

to accept insurance premiums of around £24.9bn. Much of this business comes from outside the UK and makes a valuable contribution to the balance of payments.

A policy is underwritten at Lloyd's by a mixture of private and corporate members – the latter having been admitted for the first time in 1992. Specialist underwriters accept insurance risks at Lloyd's on behalf of members (referred to as 'Names') grouped in syndicates. There are currently 91 syndicates of varying sizes, each managed by one of the 56 underwriting agents approved by the Council of Lloyd's.

Members divide into three categories: corporate organisations, individuals who have no limit to their liability for losses, and those who have an agreed limit (known as NameCos).

Lloyd's is incorporated by an act of parliament (Lloyd's Acts 1871 onwards) and is governed by an 18-person council, made up of six working, six external and six nominated members. The structure immediately below this changed when, in 2002, Lloyd's members voted at an extraordinary general meeting to implement a new franchise system for the market with the aim of improving profitability. The first move was the introduction of a new governance structure, replacing the Lloyd's Market Board and the Lloyd's Regulatory Board with an 11-person Lloyd's Franchise Board. Four main committees report to this board.

The corporation is a non-profit making body chiefly financed by its members' subscriptions. It provides the premises, administrative staff and services enabling Lloyd's underwriting syndicates to conduct their business. It does not, however, assume corporate liability for the risks accepted by its members. Individual members are responsible to the full extent of their personal means for their underwriting affairs unless they have converted to limited liability companies.

Lloyd's syndicates have no direct contact with the public. All business is transacted through insurance brokers accredited by the Corporation of Lloyd's. In addition, non-Lloyd's brokers in the UK, when guaranteed by Lloyd's brokers, are able to deal directly with the Lloyd's motor syndicates, a facility that has made the Lloyd's market more accessible to the insuring public.

Under the Financial Services and Markets Act 2000, Lloyds is regulated by the FCA and the PRA. However, in situations where Lloyd's internal regulatory and compensation arrangements are more far-reaching – as for example with the Lloyd's Central Fund which safeguards claim payments to policyholders – the regulatory role is delegated to the Council of Lloyd's.

Lloyd's also provides the most comprehensive shipping intelligence service in the world. The shipping and other information received from Lloyd's agents, shipowners, news agencies and other sources throughout the world is collated and distributed to the media as well as to the maritime and commercial sectors in general. *Lloyd's List* is London's oldest daily newspaper and contains news of general commercial interest as well as shipping information. It has been

independent of Lloyd's since a management buy-out in 1992. *Lloyd's Shipping Index*, published weekly, lists some 23,000 ocean-going merchant vessels in alphabetical order and gives the latest known report of each.

DEVELOPMENTS IN 2013

In the annual report the chair of Lloyds described 2013 as 'an outstanding year' with profits reaching £3.2bn, an increase of 14 per cent on the 2012 figure of £2.8bn. Gross written premiums increased by 2.4 per cent to £26.1bn, with a 16.2 per cent return on capital. This was against a backdrop of low interest rates and investment returns.

The result reflected the low level of major claims. For example, 2013 was the first year since 1968 when no category 2 or above hurricanes were recorded and Lloyd's was not heavily exposed to the typhoon in the Philippines or the storms in the UK. The most costly event to the Lloyd's market was £120m for claims arising from flooding in Alberta, Canada.

Only the motor insurance account recorded a loss – £87m compared to a loss of £42m in 2012 – although a number of other accounts did report decreases in premium income.

LLOYD'S OF LONDON, 1 Lime Street, London EC3M 7HA

T 020-7327 1000 W www.lloyds.com

Chair, John Nelson
Chief Executive, Inga Beale

LLOYD'S MEMBERSHIP

	2012	2013
Individual	587	529
Corporate	1,576	1,623

LLOYD'S SEGMENTAL RESULTS 2013 (£m)

	Gross premiums written	Net earned premium	Result
Reinsurance	9,468	6,760	1,321
Casualty	4,850	3,826	47
Property	6,103	4,551	681
Marine	2,195	1,835	84
Motor	1,184	1,014	(87)
Energy	1,668	1,181	201
Aviation	562	485	90
Life	76	73	–
Total from syndicate operations	26,106	19,725	2,337

LIFE AND LONG-TERM INSURANCE AND PENSIONS

April 2013 saw the official beginning of the new regulatory system in which the Financial Services Authority (FSA) was replaced by the FCA and the PRA. Establishing a working relationship with this new 'twin peaks' regulatory system was a priority for many life and pension providers. The task was eased somewhat in March when the regulators agreed to allow companies 12 months, instead of six, to change all their documentation to reflect the new regime. It was estimated that complying with the original deadline could have cost companies up to £700,000 each.

October 2013 saw the first anniversary of the introduction of auto-enrolment into a workplace pension. It was estimated that 1.6 million people were auto-enrolled in the first year. Initially, only larger UK firms were obliged to set up a workplace pension for all of their UK workers aged between 22 and retirement age and earning over £10,000 per annum. An opt-out for individual employees is available, but figures from the Department for Work and Pensions suggest only 9 per cent of workers chose to do so.

The main problem for the financial services industry during the year under review was trying to attract savers at a time when the economic climate combined with historically low interest rates to make saving a far from attractive option. A survey conducted during 2013 found that the number of people making adequate provision for their retirement had decreased to 46 per cent from 51 per cent in 2011. The same survey also found that 81 per cent of people acknowledged that they needed to save more.

The Retail Distribution Review (RDR) was one of the last initiatives undertaken by the FSA. The changes proposed in the review came into force at the end of 2012 and introduced new standards for consumer advice on investment products and banned commission-based remuneration. At the end of 2013 the Personal Finance Society conducted a survey of consumers to gauge the public's views of the retail investment advice market: 55 per cent of the population had not sought professional financial advice on retail investments, pensions or retirement, but this had not materially changed with the introduction of the new RDR standards. Of those who had not sought advice, 38 per cent did not have the money to invest and 16 per cent thought they could not afford a professional financial adviser. Nearly a quarter said that they would rather self-advise using other sources of information, with the internet being the most popular choice.

The operating environment for UK life insurers remained challenging given the weak economic growth prospects and high level of household indebtedness, but there were some areas of growth, particularly in the annuity and protection lines.

PAYMENTS TO POLICYHOLDERS *(£m)*

	2011	2012
Payments to UK policyholders	154,927	166,131
Payments to overseas policyholders	21,206	30,034
Total	176,133	196,165

WORLDWIDE LONG-TERM PREMIUM INCOME *(£m)*

	2008	2009	2010	2011	2012
UK Life Insurance					
Regular Premium	8,179	7,917	7,453	6,557	5,773
Single Premium	27,599	11,958	11,531	9,092	8,407
Total	35,778	19,875	18,984	15,649	14,180
Individual Pensions					
Regular Premium	9,648	9,629	10,651	11,278	12,758
Single Premium	18,721	15,820	19,415	18,435	17,645
Total	28,369	25,449	30,066	29,713	30,403
Other Pensions					
Regular Premium	5,901	5,599	4,340	3,809	3,270
Single Premium	57,013	63,388	52,449	55,415	65,992
Total	62,914	68,987	56,789	59,224	69,262
Other (eg income protection, annuities)	3,956	4,111	3,734	3,376	3,956
TOTAL UK PREMIUM INCOME	131,017	118,422	109,573	107,962	117,801
Overseas Premium Income					
Regular Premium	10,425	11,506	12,012	11,744	12,049
Single Premium	26,318	29,038	29,843	27,295	28,315
Total	36,743	40,544	41,855	39,039	40,364
TOTAL WORLDWIDE PREMIUM INCOME	167,760	158,966	151,428	147,001	158,165

PRIVATE MEDICAL INSURANCE

	2009	2010	2011	2012	2013
Number of people covered *(thousand)*	5,938	5,841	5,668	5,611	5,143
Corporate	4,384	4,305	4,232	4,210	3,787
Personal	1,554	1,536	1,436	1,401	1,356
Gross Earned Premiums *(£m)*	3,444	3,614	3,548	3,625	3,597
Corporate	1,838	1,982	1,929	2,010	1,982
Personal	1,606	1,632	1,619	1,615	1,615
Gross Claims Incurred *(£m)*	2,679	2,858	2,727	2,770	2,674

NEW BUSINESS 2013 *(£m)*

New regular premiums		*New single premiums*	
Endowments	21	Investments and savings	4,427
Individual life	655	Individual life	168
Group schemes	375	Individual pension	6,894
Individual pension	3,170	Work-based pensions	7,360
Work-based pension	4,171	Trust-based pensions	23,822
Trust-based pension	1,482	Offshore business	4,085
UK-distributed offshore business	19	TOTAL SINGLE	46,756
TOTAL REGULAR	9,893		

TAXATION

The government raises money to pay for public services such as education, health and the social security system through tax. Each year the Chancellor of the Exchequer's budget sets out how much it will cost to provide these services and how much tax is therefore needed to pay for them. HM Revenue and Customs (HMRC) is the government department that collects it. There are several different types of tax. The varieties that individuals may have to pay include income tax payable on earnings, pensions, state benefits, savings and investments; capital gains tax (CGT) payable on the disposal of certain assets; inheritance tax (IHT) payable on estates upon death and certain lifetime gifts; stamp duty payable when purchasing property and shares; and value added tax (VAT) payable on goods and services, plus certain other duties such as fuel duty on petrol and excise duty on alcohol and tobacco. Government funds are also raised from companies and small businesses through corporation tax.

In early 2014 the government announced further funding and measures to tackle the 'tax gap'. This is the difference between the forecast tax revenues and the total actually collected by HMRC. Figures showed that the tax gap in the 2010–11 financial year was estimated to be £32bn; 6.7 per cent of the revenue forecast by HMRC. Of the £32bn, tax evasion and avoidance were thought to account for £9bn.

HMRC announced it would be taking swifter legal action against those who do not come forward and declare taxable income and would be allocating more resources to increase the pace and number of tax evasion cases being brought before the criminal and civil courts. Measures included establishing local task forces to specifically identify and deal with tax avoiders and the expansion of its Affluent Unit with the addition of 100 extra investigators and risk and intelligence staff to identify and deal with avoidance and evasion by the wealthiest individuals, particularly those who attempt to evade and avoid inheritance tax by the use of offshore trusts, bank accounts and other entities.

The government continued in its drive to simplify the UK tax system via the Office of Tax Simplification (OTS). Details of the OTS and its work can be found at: www.gov.uk/government/organisations/office-of-tax-simplification. The OTS welcomes views from individuals and can be contacted via email ots@ots.gsi.gov.uk

HELP AND INFORMATION ON TAXATION

For information and help on any aspect of personal taxation individuals may contact their local tax office or call the HMRC helpline (T 0300-200 3300).

HMRC closed its network of enquiry centres in the first half of 2014 because visitor numbers had dropped dramatically. To help the estimated 1.5 million customers identified as needing extra help to get their taxes and entitlements right, HMRC introduced a new service offering more in-depth support on the phone and a mobile advisory service if a face-to-face appointment is required.

The HMRC website (W www.hmrc.gov.uk) provides wide-ranging information online. All HMRC forms, leaflets and guides are listed on, and can be downloaded from, the website or ordered by telephone. A list of all HMRC telephone helplines and order lines is also on the website. Those most relevant to topics covered in this section on taxation are included at pertinent points throughout.

Information on taxation is also available on the government's public information website (W www.gov.uk).

INCOME TAX

Income tax is levied on different sorts of income. Not all types of income are taxable, however, and individuals are only taxed on their 'taxable income' above a certain level. Reliefs and allowances can also reduce or, in some cases, cancel out an individual's income tax bill.

An individual's taxable income is assessed each tax year, starting on 6 April and ending on 5 April the following year. The information below relates specifically to the year of assessment 2014–15, ending on 5 April 2015, and has only limited application to earlier years. Changes due to come into operation at a later date are briefly mentioned where information is available. Types of income that are taxable include:

- earnings from employment or self-employment
- most pensions income including state, company and personal pensions
- interest on most savings
- income (dividends) from shares
- income from property
- income received from a trust
- certain state benefits
- an individual's share of any joint income

There are certain sorts of income on which individuals never pay tax. These are ignored altogether when working out how much income tax an individual may need to pay. Types of income that are not taxable include:

- certain state benefits and tax credits such as child benefit, working tax credit, child tax credit, pension credit, attendance allowance, personal independence payment, housing benefit and maternity allowance
- winter fuel payments
- income from National Savings and Investments savings certificates
- interest, dividends and other income from various tax-free investments, notably individual savings accounts (ISAs)
- premium bond and national lottery prizes

PERSONAL ALLOWANCE

Every individual resident in the UK for tax purposes has a 'personal allowance'. This is the amount of taxable income that an individual can earn or receive each year tax-free. This tax year (2014–15) the basic personal allowance or tax-free amount is £10,000, an increase of £560 from the 2013–14 figure of £9,440. Individuals may be entitled to a higher personal allowance if they were born before 5 April 1948. As previously announced, the cash value of these date-of-birth related allowances will now be frozen until they eventually align with the basic personal allowance. The government's goal is to have a single personal allowance for all taxpayers regardless of age.

Income tax is only due on an individual's taxable income that is above his or her tax-free allowance. Husbands and wives are taxed separately, with each entitled to his or her personal allowance. Each spouse may obtain other allowances and reliefs where the required conditions are satisfied.

Up to and including the tax year 2012–13, the amount of an individual's personal allowance depended on their age and income in the tax year. Since 2013–14, the amount has depended on their date of birth and their total income received from all taxable sources for the tax year. There are three date-of-birth related levels of personal allowance – *see* table below.

If an individual born before 5 April 1948 has an income over the £27,000 'income limit' for age-related allowances but not more than £100,000, their age-related allowance reduces by half the amount (£1 for every £2) he or she has over the £27,000 limit, until the basic rate allowance for those born after 5 April 1948 is reached.

Since April 2010 all three levels of personal allowance have been subject to a single income limit of £100,000, meaning that the personal allowance is reduced for individuals with an 'adjusted net income' (*see* below) over £100,000. Those individuals with an 'adjusted net income' below or equal to the £100,000 limit are entitled to the full amount of personal allowance. However, where an individual's adjusted net income is above the £100,000 limit, their personal allowance is reduced by half the amount (£1 for every £2) they have over that limit, irrespective of their age or date of birth, until their personal allowance is reduced to nil.

'Adjusted net income' is the measure of an individual's income that is used for the calculation of the existing income-related reductions to personal allowances for those born between 6 April 1938 and 5 April 1948 and for those born before 6 April 1938. It is calculated in a series of steps. The starting point is 'net income', which is the total of the individual's income subject to income tax less specified deductions such as payments made gross to pension schemes. This net income is then reduced by the grossed-up amount of the individual's Gift Aid contributions to charities and the grossed-up amount of the individual's pension contributions that have received tax relief at source. The final step is to add back any relief for payments to trade unions or police organisations deducted in arriving at the individual's net income. The result is the individual's adjusted net income.

It was announced in the 2014 Budget that the basic personal allowance for people born after 5 April 1948 will increase by £500 to £10,500 in 2015–16.

It was also confirmed that from April 2015 married couples and civil partners, where neither partner is a higher rate taxpayer, will be eligible for a new transferable tax allowance worth up to £200. For a couple choosing to use the new allowance, one individual will be able to transfer £1,000 of their personal allowance to their spouse or civil partner, meaning that the higher earner will be able to earn £1,000 more before they start paying income tax. The spouse or civil partner receiving the transferred allowance will benefit from a reduced income tax liability of up to £200. The policy will benefit couples where one is a basic rate taxpayer and one has unused personal allowance. The claim will be made online and entitlement will be from the 2015–16 tax year. Couples will be entitled to the full benefit in their first year of marriage or civil partnership.

LEVELS OF PERSONAL ALLOWANCE FOR 2014–15

Date of birth	Personal allowance	Income limit
After 5 April 1948	£10,000	£100,000
Between 6 April 1938 and 5 April 1948	£10,500	£27,000
Before 6 April 1938	£10,660	£27,000

BLIND PERSON'S ALLOWANCE

If an individual is registered blind or is unable to perform any work for which eyesight is essential, he or she can claim blind person's allowance, an extra amount of tax-free income added to the personal allowance. In 2014–15 the blind person's allowance is £2,230. It is the same for everyone who can claim it, whatever his or her age or level of income. If an individual is married or in a civil partnership and cannot use all of his or her blind person's allowance because of insufficient income, the unused part of the allowance can be passed to the spouse or civil partner.

Other deductible allowances and reliefs that have the effect of reducing an income tax bill are available to taxpayers in certain circumstances and will be explained in more detail later in this section.

CALCULATING INCOME TAX DUE

Individuals' liability to pay income tax is determined by establishing their level of taxable income for the year. For married couples and civil partners, income must be allocated between the couple by reference to the individual who is beneficially entitled to that income. Where income arises from jointly held assets, it is normally apportioned equally between the partners. If, however, the beneficial interests in jointly held assets are not equal, in most cases couples can make a special declaration to have income apportioned by reference to the actual interests in that income.

To work out an individual's liability for tax, his or her taxable income must be allocated between three different types: earned income (excluding income from savings and dividends); income from savings; and company dividends from shares and other equity-based investments.

After the tax-free personal allowance plus any deductible allowances and reliefs have been taken into account, the amount of tax an individual pays is calculated using different tax rates and a series of tax bands. The tax band applies to an individual's income after tax allowances and any reliefs have been taken into account. Individuals are not taxed on all of their income.

For the tax year 2014–15, the basic rate of income tax is 20 per cent (20 pence in the pound) and the higher rate is 40 per cent (40 pence in the pound). The additional rate, applied from 2010–11, was reduced from 6 April 2013 from 50 per cent (50 pence in the pound) to 45 per cent (45 pence in the pound).

A 10 per cent starting rate is available for savings income only, with a limit of £2,880 for 2014–15. If an individual's taxable non-savings income is above £2,880, the 10 per cent savings rate is not applicable.

For 2014–15 the basic rate limit above which tax is payable at the higher rate of 40 per cent is £31,865 and the higher rate limit, above which tax is payable at the additional rate of 45 per cent, remains at £150,000.

INCOME TAX RATES (PER CENT) AND TAX BANDS FOR 2014–15

Band	Earned income	Band	Savings	Dividends
£0–£31,865	20%	£0–£2,880*	10%	10%
£31,865+	40%	£2,880–£31,865	20%	10%
£150,000+	45%	£31,865+	40%	32.5%
		£150,000+	45%	37.5%

* If an individual's taxable non-savings income is above £2,880 the 20 per cent tax band applies to savings income from £0–£31,865

The first calculation is applied to earned income which includes income from employment or self-employment, most pension income and rental income plus the value of a wide range of employee fringe benefits such as company cars, living accommodation and private medical insurance (for more information on fringe benefits, *see* later section on payment of income tax). In working out the amount of an individual's net taxable earnings, all expenses incurred 'wholly, exclusively and necessarily' in the performance of his or her work duties, together with the cost of business travel, may be deducted. Fees and subscriptions to certain professional bodies may also be deducted. Redundancy payments and other sums paid on the termination of an employment are assessable income, but the first £30,000 is normally tax-free provided the payment is not linked with the recipient's retirement or performance.

The first £31,865 of taxable income remaining after the tax-free allowance plus any deductible allowances and reliefs have been taken into account, is taxed at the basic rate of 20 per cent. Taxable income between £31,865 and £150,000 is taxed at the higher rate of 40 per cent. Taxable income above £150,000 is taxed at the additional rate of 45 per cent.

Savings and dividends income is added to an individual's other taxable income and taxed last. This means that tax on such sorts of income is based on an individual's highest income tax band.

SAVINGS INCOME
The second calculation is applied to any income from savings received by an individual. The appropriate rate at which it must be taxed is determined by adding income from savings to an individual's other taxable income, excluding dividends.

There is a 10 per cent starting rate for savings income only, with a limit of £2,880. If an individual's taxable non-savings income exceeds this limit, the 10 per cent savings rate is not applicable. Savings income above £2,880 and below the £31,865 basic rate limit is taxable at 20 per cent. Savings income between £31,865 and £150,000 is taxable at 40 per cent. Savings income over £150,000 is taxed at 45 per cent. If savings income falls on both sides of a tax band, the relevant amounts are taxed at the rates for each tax band.

Most savings income, such as interest paid on bank and building society accounts, already has tax at a rate of 20 per cent deducted from it 'at source' – that is, before it is paid out to individuals. This is confirmed by the entry 'net interest' on bank and building society statements.

Higher rate taxpayers whose income is sufficient to pay 40 or 45 per cent tax on their savings income must let their tax office know what savings income they have received so that the extra tax they owe can be collected.

Non-taxpayers – ie individuals, including most children, whose taxable income is less than their tax allowances – can register to have their savings interest paid 'gross' without any tax being deducted from it at source. To do this, they must complete form R85, available at all banks and building societies. Parents or guardians need to fill in this form on behalf of those under 16. For individuals who are unsure whether they qualify as non-taxpayers and, therefore, whether they are able to register to have their savings interest paid gross, HMRC offers an 'R85 checker' on its website (W www.hmrc.gov.uk/calcs/r85/).

Non-taxpayers who have already had tax deducted from their savings interest can claim it back from HMRC by filling in form R40. For help or information about registering to get interest paid tax-free or to claim tax back on savings interest, individuals may visit W www.hmrc.gov.uk/taxon/bank.htm or call a dedicated helpline on T 0300-200 3312.

It was announced in the 2014 Budget that from 6 April 2015 the starting rate of tax for savings income will be reduced from 10 per cent to nil and the maximum amount of taxable savings income that can be eligible for this starting rate will be increased from £2,880 to £5,000.

One of the effects of this change, when combined with changes to the tax-free personal allowance, is that savers will not be liable for tax on any interest they receive if their total taxable income for 2015–16 is less than £15,500. This figure will be £15,660 for those born before 6 April 1938.

The eligibility rules for completing a form R85 will also change from 6 April 2015 to enable more savers to register to receive interest payments without tax deducted. Currently an R85 can be completed by a saver whose total taxable income for the tax year will be below their tax-free personal allowance. From 6 April 2015, a saver whose total taxable income for the tax year will be below the total of their tax-free personal allowance *plus* the £5,000 starting rate limit for savings, will be able to register to have interest paid on their savings accounts without tax deducted using form R85.

DIVIDEND INCOME
The third and final income tax calculation is on UK dividends, which means income from shares in UK companies and other share-based investments including unit trusts and open-ended investment companies (OEICs).

Dividend tax rates differ from those on savings income. The rate that an individual pays on his or her dividends depends on the amount of his or her overall taxable income (after allowances). Dividend income at or below the £31,865 basic rate tax limit is taxable at 10 per cent, between £31,865 and £150,000 at 32.5 per cent, and above £150,000 at 37.5 per cent.

When dividends are paid, a voucher is sent that shows the dividend paid and the amount of associated 'tax credit'. Companies pay dividends out of profits on which they have already paid or are due to pay tax. The tax credit takes account of this and is available to the shareholder to offset against any income tax that may be due on their dividend income. The dividend paid represents 90 per cent of their dividend income. The remaining 10 per cent is made up of the tax credit. In other words the tax credit represents 10 per cent of the dividend income.

Individuals who pay tax at the basic rate have no tax to pay on their dividend income because the tax liability is 10 per cent – the same amount as the tax credit. Higher rate taxpayers pay a total of 32.5 per cent tax on dividend income above the £31,865 basic rate income tax limit, but because the first 10 per cent of the tax due on their dividend income is already covered by the tax credit, in practice they owe only 22.5 per cent. For the same reason, additional rate taxpayers who pay a total of 37.5 per cent on dividend income above the £150,000 additional rate tax limit, owe only 27.5 per cent in practice.

Non-taxpayers cannot claim the 10 per cent tax credit. This is because income tax has not been deducted from the dividends paid to them. The view is that they have simply been given a 10 per cent credit against any income tax due.

If there is significant change to an individual's savings or other income, whatever his or her current tax bracket, it is the individual's responsibility to contact the relevant tax office immediately, even if he or she does not normally complete a tax return. This enables the tax office to work out whether extra or less tax should be paid.

INDIVIDUAL SAVINGS ACCOUNTS
There is a small selection of savings and investment products that are tax-free. This means that there is no tax to pay on any income generated in the form of interest or dividends,

nor on any increase in the value of the capital invested. Their tax-efficient status has been granted by the government in order to give people an incentive to save more. For this reason there are usually limits and restrictions on the amount of money an individual may invest in such savings and investments. Individual savings accounts (ISAs) are the best known among tax-efficient savings and investments. They were introduced in 1999 to replace other similar schemes called PEPs and TESSAs. Individuals can use an ISA to save cash, or invest in stocks and shares.

To be eligible to invest in ISAs and receive all profits free of tax, individuals must be UK residents and be aged 18 or over (over 16 for cash ISAs). An ISA must be in an individual's name and cannot be held jointly with another person.

Major changes to ISAs were announced in the 2014 Budget to take effect from 1 July 2014.

Prior to 1 July 2014 the rules for ISA investment were as follows. For the 2014–15 tax year individuals could save up to £11,880 each tax year in an adult ISA and could invest in two separate ISAs each tax year: a cash ISA and a stocks and shares ISA (an umbrella term covering investments in unit trusts, company shares, bonds, investment-type life insurance etc). Up to £5,940 of an individual's ISA allowance could be saved in one cash ISA with one provider. The remainder of the £11,880 could be invested in one stocks and shares ISA with either the same or a different provider. Alternatively an individual could open a single stocks and shares ISA and invest the full £11,880 into it.

ISA savers had the option to transfer some or all of the money they had saved in previous tax years in cash ISAs to their stocks and shares ISA without affecting their annual ISA investment allowance. They could also choose to transfer all the money they had saved to date in a cash ISA in the current tax year to a stocks and shares ISA. However, the rules did not allow the reverse; that is, the transfer of monies saved in a stocks and shares ISA to a cash ISA.

On 1 July 2014 ISAs were reformed into a simpler product, labelled the 'New ISA' (NISA), by the government which said all existing ISAs would become NISAs.

The overall annual subscription limit for these accounts was increased to £15,000 for 2014–15 and individuals aged 18 or over can now hold any combination of cash or stocks and shares in a NISA. Individuals aged 16 to 18 also have a £15,000 allowance in the 2014–15 tax year but they are restricted to cash-only NISAs.

For the first time, NISA savers can choose to subscribe their full allowance to a cash account where previously only 50 per cent of the allowance could be saved in cash. Investors also now have the new right to transfer their investments from a stocks and shares to a cash account if they wish. There have also been consequential changes to the rules on the investments that can be held in a NISA, so that a wider range of securities, including certain retail bonds with less than five years before maturity, can be invested

Further details are available via HMRC's savings helpline (T 0845-604 1701).

DEDUCTIBLE ALLOWANCES AND RELIEF

Income taxpayers may be entitled to certain tax-deductible allowances and reliefs as well as their personal allowances. Examples include the married couple's allowance and maintenance payments relief, both of which are explained below. Unlike the tax-free allowances, these are not amounts of income that an individual can receive tax-free but amounts by which their tax bill can be reduced.

MARRIED COUPLE'S ALLOWANCE
A married couple's allowance (MCA) is available to taxpayers who are married or are in a civil partnership only where

one or other partner was born before 6 April 1935. Eligible couples can start to claim the MCA from the year of marriage or civil partnership registration.

The MCA is restricted to give relief at a fixed rate of 10 per cent, which means that – unlike the personal allowance – it is not income that can be received without paying tax. Instead, it reduces an individual's tax bill by up to a fixed amount calculated as 10 per cent of the amount of the allowance to which they are entitled.

In 2014–15, the MCA is £8,165 at 10 per cent, worth up to £816.50 off a couple's tax bill. The MCA is made up of two parts. There is a minimum amount (£3,140 in 2014–15) which will always be due. The remaining amount (£5,025 in 2014–15) can be reduced if the husband's income exceeds certain limits.

The husband will normally receive the allowance, but the couple can jointly decide which of them will get the minimum amount of the allowance. Alternatively, they can decide to have the minimum amount of the allowance split equally between them. They must inform their tax office of their decision before the start of the new tax year in which they want the decision to take effect. Once this is done, the change will apply until the couple decides to alter it. The remaining part of the allowance must go to the husband unless he lacks sufficient income to use it.

If an individual does not have enough income to use all of his or her share of the MCA, the tax office can transfer the unused part of it to his or her spouse or civil partner.

Like the personal allowance, the MCA can be gradually reduced at the rate of £1 of the allowance for every £2 of income above the income limit (£27,000 in 2014–15). The amount of MCA can only be affected by the husband's income, and it only starts to be affected if his personal allowance has already been reduced back to the basic level for people born after 5 April 1948. The wife's income never affects the amount of MCA. It does not matter whether all or part of the minimum amount of the allowance has been transferred to her. Whatever the level of the husband's income, the MCA can never be reduced below the minimum amount: in 2014–15 this is £3,140 at 10 per cent.

The same system of allowance allocation applies to civil partners based on the income of the highest earner.

MAINTENANCE PAYMENTS RELIEF
An allowance is available to reduce an individual's tax bill for maintenance payments he or she makes to his or her ex-spouse or former civil partner in certain circumstances. To be eligible one or other partner must have been born before 6 April 1935; the couple must be legally separated or divorced; the maintenance payments being made must be under a court order; and the payments must be for the maintenance of an ex spouse or former civil partner (provided he or she is not now remarried or in a new civil partnership) or for children who are under 21. For the tax year 2014–15, this allowance can reduce an individual's tax bill by:

- 10 per cent of £3,140 (maximum £314) – this applies where an individual makes maintenance payments of £3,140 or more a year
- 10 per cent of the amount the individual has actually paid – this applies where an individual makes maintenance payments of less than £3,140 a year

An individual cannot claim a tax reduction for any voluntary payments he or she makes for a child, ex-spouse or former civil partner. To claim maintenance payments relief, individuals should contact their tax office.

CHARITABLE DONATION

A number of charitable donations qualify for tax relief. Individuals can increase the value of regular or one-off charitable gifts of money, however small, by using the Gift Aid scheme that allows charities or community amateur sports clubs (CASCs) to reclaim 20 per cent basic rate tax relief on donations they receive.

The way the scheme works means that if a taxpayer gives £10 using Gift Aid, for example, the donation is worth £12.50 to the charity or CASC.

Individuals who pay 40 per cent higher rate income tax can claim back the difference between the 40 per cent and the 20 per cent basic rate of income tax on the total (gross) value of their donations. For example, a 40 per cent tax payer donates £100; the total value of this donation to the charity or CASC is £125, of which the individual can claim back 20 per cent (£25) for themselves. Similarly, those who pay 45 per cent additional rate income tax can claim back the difference between the 45 per cent and the 20 per cent basic rate on the total (gross) value of their donations. On a £100 donation, this means they can claim back £31.25.

In order to make a Gift Aid donation, individuals need to make a Gift Aid declaration. The charity or CASC will normally ask an individual to complete a simple form. One form can cover every gift made to the same charity or CASC for whatever period chosen, including both gifts made in the past and in the future. In April 2013 the government introduced a new scheme where charities are able to claim a Gift Aid-type tax refund on small, ad-hoc donations up to a total of £5,000 a year per charity, without the need for donors to fill in any forms at all. This means Gift Aid can be claimed on the contents of collecting tins, for example. If a charity collects the full £5,000, it will get £1,250 back.

Individuals can use Gift Aid provided the amount of income tax and/or capital gains tax they have paid in the tax year in which their donations are made is at least equal to the amount of basic rate tax the charity or CASC is reclaiming on their gifts. It is the responsibility of the individual to make sure this is the case. If an individual makes Gift Aid donations and has not paid sufficient tax, they may have to pay the shortfall to HMRC. The Gift Aid scheme is not suitable for non-taxpayers.

Individuals who complete a tax return and are due a tax refund can ask HMRC to treat all or part of it as a Gift Aid donation.

The government has announced that it is looking at options to improve the take-up of Gift Aid on donations through digital channels. It is consulting on a range of options including enabling donors to complete a single Gift Aid declaration to cover all their donations through a specific channel.

For employees or those in receipt of an occupational pension, a tax-efficient way of making regular donations to charities is to use the payroll giving scheme. It allows the donations to be paid from a salary or pension before income tax is deducted. This effectively reduces the cost of giving for donors, which may allow them to give more.

For example, it costs a basic-rate taxpayer only £8 in take-home pay to give £10 to charity from their pre-tax pay. Where a donor pays 40 per cent higher rate tax, that same £10 donation costs the taxpayer £6 and for donors who pay the additional 45 per cent rate tax, it costs £5.50.

Anyone who pays tax through the pay as you earn (PAYE) system (see Payment of Income Tax) can give to any charity of their choosing in this way, providing their employer or pension provider offers the payroll giving scheme. There is no limit to the amount individuals can donate.

A reduced rate of inheritance tax (IHT) applies where an individual, in their will, leaves 10 per cent or more of their net estate to charity. In such cases the current IHT 40 per cent rate is reduced to 36 per cent. The reduced rate applies where death occurred on or after 6 April 2012.

Details of tax-efficient charitable giving methods can be found at W www.hmrc.gov.uk/individuals/giving

TAX RELIEF ON PENSION CONTRIBUTIONS

Pensions are long-term investments designed to help ensure that people have enough income in retirement. The government encourages individuals to save towards a pension by offering tax relief on their contributions. Tax relief reduces an individual's tax bill or increases their pension fund.

The way tax relief is given on pension contributions depends on whether an individual pays into a company, public service or personal pension scheme.

For employees who pay into a company or public service pension scheme, most employers take the pension contributions from the employee's pay before deducting tax, which means that the individual – whether they pay income tax at the basic or higher rate – gets full tax relief straight away. Some employers, however, use the same method of paying pension contributions as that used by personal pension scheme payers described below.

Individuals who pay into a personal pension scheme make contributions from their net salary; that is, after tax has been deducted. For each pound that individuals contribute to their pension from net salary, the pension provider claims tax back from the government at the basic rate of 20 per cent and reinvests it on behalf of the individual into the scheme. In practice this means that for every £80 an individual pays into their pension, they receive £100 in their pension fund.

Higher rate taxpayers currently get 40 per cent tax relief on money they put into a pension. On contributions made from net salary, the first 20 per cent is claimed back from HMRC by the pension scheme in the same way as for a lower rate taxpayer. It is then up to individuals to claim back the other 20 per cent from their tax office, either when they fill in their annual tax return or by telephone or letter. In a similar fashion, individuals subject to the 45 per cent additional rate of income tax can get 45 per cent tax relief on their pension contributions.

Most providers of retirement annuities, which are a type of personal pension scheme set up before July 1988, do not offer a 'tax relief at source' scheme whereby they claim back tax at the basic rate, as is the case with more modern personal pensions. In such cases, contributing individuals need to claim the tax relief they are due through their tax return or by telephoning or writing to HMRC.

Non-taxpayers can still pay into a personal pension scheme and benefit from 20 per cent basic rate relief on the first £2,880 a year they contribute. In practice this means that the government tops up their £2,880 contribution to make it £3,600 which is the current universal pension allowance. Such pension contributions may be made on behalf of a non-taxpayer by another individual. An individual may, for example, contribute to a pension on behalf of a husband, wife, civil partner, child or grandchild. Tax relief will be added to their contribution at the basic rate, again on up to £2,880 a year benefiting the recipient, but their own tax bill will not be affected.

In any one tax year, individuals can get tax relief on pension contributions made into any number and type of registered pension schemes of 100 per cent of their annual earnings, irrespective of age, up to a maximum 'annual allowance'. For the tax year 2014–15 the annual allowance is £40,000 (reduced from £50,000 in 2013–14). Individuals pay tax at 40 per cent on any contributions they make above the annual allowance. Everyone now also has a 'lifetime allowance' (reduced from £1.5m in 2013–14 to £1.25m in

2014–15) which means taxpayers can save up to a total of £1.25m in their pension fund and still get tax relief at their highest income tax rate on all of their contributions.

A transitional 'fixed protection' regime is in place for individuals who may have been adversely affected by the reduction in the lifetime allowance.

For information on pensions and tax relief visit W www.gov.uk/browse/working. Another useful source of information and advice is The Pensions Advisory Service (TPAS), an independent voluntary organisation grant-aided by the Department for Work and Pensions at W www.pensionsadvisoryservice.org.uk; its Pensions Helpline is on T 0845-601 2923.

PAYMENT OF INCOME TAX
Employees have their income tax deducted from their wages throughout the year by their employer who sends it on to HMRC. Those in receipt of a company pension have their due tax deducted in the same way by their pension provider. This system of collecting income tax is known as 'pay as you earn' (PAYE).

BENEFITS IN KIND
The PAYE system is also used to collect tax on certain fringe benefits or 'benefits in kind' that employees or directors receive from their employer, but are not included in their salary. These include company cars, private medical insurance paid for by the employer or cheap or free loans from the employer. Some fringe benefits are tax-free, including employer-paid contributions into an employee's pension fund, cheap or free canteen meals, works buses, in-house sports facilities, reasonable relocation expenses, provision of a mobile phone and workplace nursery places provided for the children of employees. For taxable fringe benefits, tax is paid on the 'taxable value' of the benefit.

Employers submit returns for individual employees earning at or above the £8,500 per annum threshold (including the value of expenses and benefits) to the tax office on the form P11D, with details of any fringe benefits they have been given. For those earning less than the £8,500 threshold (part-time employees) a P9D form is submitted. Employees should get a copy of this form by 6 July following the end of the tax year and must enter the value of the fringe benefits they have received on their tax return for the relevant year, even if tax has already been paid on them under PAYE. Fringe benefits may be taxed under PAYE by being offset against personal tax allowances in an individual's PAYE code. Otherwise tax will be collected after the end of the tax year by the issue of an assessment on the fringe benefits.

SELF-ASSESSMENT
Individuals who are not on PAYE, notably the self-employed, need to complete a self-assessment tax return each year, in paper form or online at the HMRC website (W www.hmrc.gov.uk), and pay any income tax owed in twice-yearly instalments. Some individuals with more complex tax affairs such as those who earn money from rents or investments above a certain level may also need to fill out a self-assessment return, even if they are on PAYE. HMRC uses the figures supplied on the tax return to work out the individual's tax bill, or they can choose to work it out themselves. It is called 'self-assessment' because individuals are responsible for making sure the details they provide are correct.

Tax returns are usually sent out in early April, following the end of the tax year to which they apply. They may also go out at other times, for example if an individual wants to claim an allowance or repayment or to register for self-assessment for the first time.

Individuals with simple tax affairs may receive a short four-page return. Those with more complex affairs must fill out a full return that has 12 core pages plus extra pages, depending on the sorts of income received.

Central to the self-assessment system is the requirement for individuals to contact their tax office if they do not receive a self-assessment return but think they should or if their financial circumstances change. Individuals have six months from when the tax year ends to report any new income, for example. If an individual becomes self-employed, they have three months after the calendar month in which they began self-employed work to let HMRC know. This can be done by telephoning the helpline number for the newly self-employed on T 0300-200 3504.

TAX RETURN FILING AND PAYMENT DEADLINES
There are also key deadlines for filing (sending in) completed tax returns and paying the tax due. Failure to do so can incur penalties, interest charges and surcharges.

KEY FILING DATES FOR SELF-ASSESSMENT RETURNS

Date	Why the date is important
31 Oct*	Deadline for filing paper returns* for tax year ending the previous 5 April
30 Dec	Deadline for online filing where the amount owed for tax year ending the previous 5 April is less than £3,000 and the taxpayer wants HMRC to collect any tax due through their PAYE tax code
31 Jan†	Deadline for online filing of returns for tax year ending the previous 5 April

* Or three months from the date the return was requested if this was after 31 July
† Or three months from the date the return was requested if this was after 31 October

KEY SELF-ASSESSMENT PAYMENT DATES

Date	What payment is due?
31 Jan	Deadline for paying the balance of any tax owed – the 'balancing payment' – for the tax year ending the previous 5 April. It is also the date by which a taxpayer must make any first 'payment on account' (advance payment) for the current tax year. For example, on 31 January 2015 a taxpayer may have to pay both the balancing payment for the year 2014–15 and the first payment on account for 2015–16.
31 Jul	Deadline for making a second payment on account for the current tax year

LATE FILING AND PAYMENT PENALTIES
Late filing of tax returns incurs an automatic £100 penalty although individuals may appeal against the penalty if they have a reasonable excuse. For late filing of 2013–14 tax returns the following penalties also apply:

• Over three months late – £10 each day, up to a maximum of £900, in addition to the penalty above
• Over six months late – an additional £300 or 5 per cent of the tax due, whichever is the higher, in addition to the penalty above
• Over 12 months late – a further £300 or 5 per cent of the tax due, whichever is the higher. In serious cases HMRC reserve the right to ask for 100 per cent of the tax due instead. In both instances this is in addition to the penalty above

Late payment of tax owing for 2013–14 incurs the following penalties:

- Over 30 days – 5 per cent of the tax unpaid at that date
- Over six months – an additional 5 per cent of the tax unpaid at that date
- Over 12 months – a further 5 per cent of the tax unpaid at that date

Interest is due on all outstanding amounts, including any unpaid penalties, until payment is received in full.

TAX CREDITS

Child tax credit, working tax credit and the new universal credit are paid to qualifying individuals. Although the titles of these credits incorporates the word 'tax', they do not affect the amount of income tax payable or repayable. They are forms of social security benefits. *See* Social Welfare.

CAPITAL GAINS TAX

Capital gains tax (CGT) is a tax on the gain or profit that an individual makes when they sell, give away or otherwise dispose of an asset – that is, something they own such as shares, land or buildings. An individual potentially has to pay CGT on gains they make from any disposal of assets during a tax year. There is, however, a tax-free allowance and some additional reliefs that may reduce an individual's CGT bill. The following information relates to the tax year 2014–15 ending on 5 April 2015.

CGT is paid by individuals who are either resident or ordinarily resident in the UK for the tax year, executors or administrators – 'personal representatives' – responsible for a deceased person's financial affairs and trustees of a settlement. Non-residents are not usually liable to CGT unless they carry on a business in the UK through a branch or agency. However, the government has announced that from April 2015, a capital gains tax charge will be introduced on future gains made by non-residents disposing of UK residential property. Special CGT rules may apply to individuals who used to live and work in the UK but have since left the country.

CAPITAL GAINS CHARGEABLE TO CGT

Typically, individuals have made a gain if they sell an asset for more than they paid for it. It is the gain that is taxed, not the amount the individual receives for the asset. For example, a man buys shares for £1,000 and later sells them for £3,000. He has made a gain of £2,000 (£3,000 less £1,000). If someone gives an asset away, the gain will be based on the difference between what the asset was worth when originally acquired compared with its worth at the time of disposal. The same is true when an asset is sold for less than its full worth in order to give away part of the value. For example, a woman buys a property for £120,000 and three years later, when the property's market value has risen to £180,000, she gives it to her son. The son may pay nothing for the property or pay less than its true worth, eg £100,000. Either way, she has made a gain of £60,000 (£180,000 less £120,000).

If an individual disposes of an asset he or she received as a gift, the gain is worked out according to the market value of the asset when it was received. For example, a man gives his sister a painting worth £8,000. She pays nothing for it. Later she sells the painting for £10,000. For CGT purposes, she is treated as making a gain of £2,000 (£10,000 less £8,000). If an individual inherits an asset, the estate of the person who died does not pay CGT at the time. If the inheritor later disposes of the asset, the gain is worked out by looking at the market value at the time of the death. For example, a woman acquires some shares for £5,000 and leaves them to her niece when she dies. No CGT is payable at the time of death when the shares are worth £8,000. Later the niece sells the shares

for £10,000. She has made a gain of £2,000 (£10,000 less £8,000).

Individuals may also have to pay CGT if they dispose of part of an asset or exchange one asset for another. Similarly, CGT may be payable if an individual receives a capital sum of money from an asset without disposing of it, for example where he or she receives compensation when an asset is damaged.

Assets that may lead to a CGT charge when they are disposed of include:

- shares in a company
- units in a unit trust
- land and buildings (though not normally an individual's main home – *see* 'disposal of a home' section for details)
- higher value jewellery, paintings, antiques and other personal effects assets used in business such as goodwill

EXEMPT GAINS

Certain kinds of assets do not give rise to a chargeable gain when they are disposed of. Assets exempt from CGT include:

- an individual's private car
- an individual's main home, provided certain conditions are met
- tax-free investments such as assets held in an ISA
- UK government gilts or 'bonds'
- personal belongings including jewellery, paintings, antiques individually worth £6,000 or less
- cash in sterling or foreign currency held for an individual or his/her family's own personal use
- betting, lottery or pools winnings
- personal injury compensation

DISPOSAL OF A HOME: PRIVATE RESIDENCE RELIEF

When an individual sells their own home they automatically qualify for private residence relief which means they do not have to pay any CGT provided that:

- the property has been their only home or main residence since they bought it, and
- they have used it as their home and for no other purpose

Even if an individual has not lived in the property for all of the time that they owned it, they may still be entitled to the full relief.

Under the relief rules, the final 18 months of ownership are always treated as if the individual lived in the property even if they did not. This means that if an individual moves out of one home and into a new one, they have up to 18 months in which to sell their former home without incurring any CGT on the sale proceeds. This 'final period of exemption' was halved from 36 months to the current 18 months in April 2014.

Full relief is granted to individuals when they sell their home if they could not live in it for periods because they were working abroad. Full relief is also granted if an individual is prevented from living in the home for periods totalling a maximum of four years because their job requires them to work elsewhere in the UK. In both cases however, for the property to qualify for full relief, the general rule is that it must have been the individual's only or main home both before and after they worked away.

Individuals can also get full relief when they sell their home if they have lived away from it for reasons other than working away provided all of the following apply:

- they were not living away from the home for more than three years in total during the time they owned the property
- they were not entitled to private residence relief on any other property during that time
- the property was their only or main home both before and after they lived elsewhere

There are instances when individuals may not get the full amount of private residence relief when they sell their home. These include if:

- the garden or grounds, including the site of the house, are larger than 5,000 square metres
- any part of the home has been used exclusively for business purposes
- all or part of the home has been let out (or more than one lodger has been taken in at a time). The owner may, however, be entitled to another form of CGT relief – letting relief – instead
- the main reason the property was bought was to make a profit from a quick sale

If an individual lives in – not just owns – more than one property, they can 'nominate' which should be treated as their main home for private residence relief purposes. Married couples or those in a civil partnership must make such a nomination jointly as they are only entitled to private residence relief on one house between them.

It was announced in the 2014 Budget that, from April 2015, this ability to nominate which home should qualify for private residence relief will cease. Instead it will be decided on objective grounds which of an individual's two or more homes is indeed their main or primary residence.

Certain other kinds of disposal similarly do not give rise to a chargeable gain. For example, individuals who are married or in a civil partnership and who live together may sell or give assets to their spouse or civil partner without having to pay CGT. Individuals may not, however, give or sell assets cheaply to their children without having to consider CGT. There is no CGT to pay on assets given to a registered charity.

CALCULATING CGT

CGT is worked out for each tax year and is charged on the total of an individual's taxable gains after taking into account certain costs and reliefs that can reduce or defer chargeable gains, allowable losses made on assets to which CGT normally applies and an annual exempt (tax-free) amount that applies to every individual. If the total of an individual's net gains in a tax year is less than the annual exempt amount (AEA), the individual will not have to pay CGT. For the tax year 2014–15 the AEA is £11,000. The government has announced that the AEA will remain at £11,000 for 2015–16 and subsequent years. If an individual's net gains are more than the AEA, they pay CGT on the excess. Should any part of the exemption remain unused, this cannot be carried forward to a future year.

There are certain reliefs available that may eliminate, reduce or defer CGT. Some reliefs are available to many people while others are available only in special circumstances. Some reliefs are given automatically while others are given only if they are claimed. Some of the costs of buying, selling and improving assets may be deducted from total gains when working out an individual's chargeable gain.

RATES OF TAX

The net gains remaining, if any, calculated after subtracting the AEA, deducting costs and taking into account all CGT reliefs, incur liability to capital gains tax. Individuals pay CGT at a rate of 18 per cent on gains up to the unused amount of the basic rate income tax band (if any) and at 28 per cent on gains above that amount. The CGT rate charged to trustees and personal representatives is 28 per cent.

CGT for 2014–15 is due for payment in full on 31 January 2016. If payment is delayed, interest or surcharges may be imposed. A husband and wife or registered civil partners who live together are separately assessed for CGT. Each partner must independently calculate his or her gains and losses with each entitled to the AEA of £11,000 for 2014–15.

VALUATION OF ASSETS

The disposal proceeds – ie the amount received as consideration for the disposal of an asset – are the sum used to establish the gain or loss once certain allowable costs have been deducted. In most cases this is straightforward because the disposal proceeds are the amount actually received for disposing of the asset. This may include cash payable now or in the future and the value of any asset received in exchange for the asset disposed of. However, in certain circumstances, the disposal proceeds may not accurately reflect the value of the asset and the individual may be treated as disposing of an asset for an amount other than the actual amount (if any) that they received. This applies, in particular, where an asset is transferred as a gift or sold for a price known to be below market value. Disposal proceeds in such transactions are deemed to be equal to the market value of the asset at the time it was disposed of rather than the actual amount (if any) received for it.

Market value represents the price that an asset might reasonably be expected to fetch upon sale in the open market. In the case of unquoted shares or securities, it is to be assumed that the hypothetical purchaser in the open market would have available all the information that a prudent prospective purchaser of shares or securities might reasonably require if that person were proposing to purchase them from a willing vendor by private treaty and at arm's length. The market value of unquoted shares or securities will often be established following negotiations with the specialist HMRC Shares and Assets Valuation department. The valuation of land and interests in land in the UK is dealt with by the Valuation Office Agency. Special rules apply to determine the market value of shares quoted on the London Stock Exchange.

ALLOWABLE COSTS

When working out a chargeable gain, once the actual or notional disposal proceeds have been determined, certain allowable costs may be deducted. There is a general rule that no costs that could be taken into account when working out income or losses for income tax purposes may be deducted. Subject to this, allowable costs are:

- acquisition costs – the actual amount spent on acquiring the asset or, in certain circumstances, the equivalent market value
- incidental costs of acquiring the asset such as fees paid for professional advice, valuation costs, stamp duty and advertising costs to find a seller
- enhancement costs – incurred for the purpose of enhancing the value of the asset (not including normal maintenance and repair costs)
- expenditure on defending or establishing a person's rights over the asset
- incidental costs of disposing of the asset such as fees paid for professional advice, valuation costs, stamp duty and advertising costs to find a buyer

If an individual disposes of part of his or her interest in an asset, or part of a holding of shares of the same class in the same company, or part of a holding of units in the same unit trust, he or she can deduct part of the allowable costs of the asset or holding when working out the chargeable gain. Allowable costs may also be reduced by some reliefs.

ENTREPRENEURS' RELIEF

Entrepreneurs' Relief allows individuals in business and some trustees to claim relief on the first £10m of gains made on the disposal of any of the following: all or part of a business; the assets of a business after it has ceased; and shares in a company. The relief is available to taxpayers as individuals if they are in business, for example as a sole trader or as a partner in a trading business, or if they hold shares in their own personal trading company. This relief is not available for companies.

Depending on the type of disposal, certain qualifying conditions need to be met throughout a qualifying one-year period. For example, if an individual is selling all or part of their business, they must have owned the business during a one-year period that ends on the date of the disposal.

Where Entrepreneurs' Relief applies, qualifying gains liable to CGT are charged at 10 per cent. An individual can make claims for this relief on more than one occasion as long as the lifetime total of all their claims does not exceed £10m of gains qualifying for relief.

BUSINESS ASSET ROLL-OVER RELIEF

When certain types of business asset are sold or disposed of and the proceeds reinvested in new qualifying trading assets, business asset roll-over relief makes it possible to 'roll-over' or postpone the payment of any CGT that would normally be due. The gain is deducted from the base cost of the new asset and only becomes chargeable to CGT on the eventual disposal of that replacement asset unless a further roll-over situation then develops. Full relief is available if all the proceeds from the original asset are reinvested in the qualifying replacement asset.

For example, a trader sells a freehold office for £75,000 and makes a gain of £30,000. All of the proceeds are reinvested in a new freehold business premises costing £90,000. The trader can postpone the whole of the £30,000 gain made on the sale of the old office, as all of the proceeds have been reinvested. When the trader eventually sells the new business premises and the CGT bill becomes payable, the cost of the new premises will be treated as £60,000 (£90,000 less the £30,000 gain).

If only part of the proceeds from the disposal of an old asset is reinvested in a new one, it may still be possible to postpone paying tax on part of the gain until the eventual disposal of the new asset.

Relief is only available if the acquisition of the new asset takes place within a period between 12 months before, and 36 months after, the disposal of the old asset. However, HMRC may extend this time limit at their discretion where there is a clear intention to acquire a replacement asset. The most common types of business assets that qualify for roll-over relief are land, buildings occupied and used for the purposes of trade, and fixed plant and machinery. Assets used for the commercial letting of furnished holiday accommodation qualify if certain conditions are satisfied.

GIFTS HOLD-OVER RELIEF

The gift of an asset is treated as a disposal made for a consideration equal to market value, with a corresponding acquisition by the transferee at an identical value. In the case of gifts of business assets made by individuals and a limited range of trustees, a form of hold-over relief may be available.

This relief, which must be claimed, in effect enables liability for CGT to be deferred and passed to the person to whom the gift is made. Relief is limited to the transfer of certain assets including the following:

- gifts of assets used for the purposes of a business carried on by the donor or his or her personal company
- gifts of shares in trading companies that are not listed on a stock exchange
- gifts of shares or securities in the donor's personal trading company
- gifts of agricultural land and buildings that would qualify for inheritance tax agricultural property relief
- gifts that are chargeable transfers for inheritance tax purposes
- certain types of gifts that are specifically exempt from inheritance tax

Hold-over relief is automatically due on certain sorts of gifts including gifts to charities and community amateur sports clubs, and gifts of works of art where certain undertakings have been given. There are certain rules to prevent gifts hold-over relief being used for tax-avoidance purposes. For example, restrictions may apply where an individual gifts assets to trustees administering a trust in which the individual retains an interest or the assets transferred comprise a dwelling-house. Subject to these exceptions, the effect of a valid claim for hold-over relief is similar to that following a claim for roll-over relief on the disposal of business assets.

OTHER CGT RELIEFS

There are certain other CGT reliefs available on the disposal of property, shares and business assets. For detailed information on all CGT reliefs and for more general guidance on CGT, see the capital gains tax pages on the HMRC website (W www.hmrc.gov.uk/cgt).

REPORTING AND PAYING CGT

Individuals are responsible for telling HMRC about capital gains on which they have to pay tax. Individuals who receive a self-assessment tax return may report capital gains by filling in the capital gains supplementary pages – the return explains how to obtain these pages if needed.

Individuals who do not normally complete a tax return but who need to report capital gains or losses should contact their local tax office.

There is a time limit for claiming capital losses. The deadline is four years from 31 January after the end of the tax year in which the loss was made.

INHERITANCE TAX

Inheritance tax (IHT) is a tax on the value of a person's estate on death and on certain gifts made by an individual during his or her lifetime, usually payable within six months of death. Broadly speaking, a person's estate is everything he or she owned at the time of death including property, possessions, money and investments, less his or her debts. Not everyone pays IHT. It only applies if the taxable value of an estate is above the current IHT threshold. If an estate, including any assets held in trust and gifts made within seven years of death, is less than the threshold, no IHT will be due.

The nil-rate band for 2014–15 is £325,000.

A claim can be made to transfer any unused IHT nil-rate band on a person's death to the estate of their surviving spouse or civil partner. This applies where the IHT nil-rate band of the first deceased spouse or civil partner was not fully used in calculating the IHT liability of their estate.

When the surviving spouse or civil partner dies, the unused amount may be added to their own nil-rate band (*see* below for details).

IHT used to be something only very wealthy individuals needed to consider. This is no longer the case. The fact that the IHT threshold has not kept pace with house price inflation in recent years means that the estates of some 'ordinary' taxpayers, who would not consider themselves wealthy, are now liable for IHT purely because of the value of their home. However, there are a number of ways that individuals – while still alive – can legally reduce the IHT bill that will apply to their estates on death. Several valuable IHT exemptions are available (explained further below) which allow individuals to pass on assets during their lifetime or in their will without any IHT being due. Detailed information on IHT is available on the HMRC website (W www.hmrc.gov.uk/inheritancetax/index.htm). Further help is also available from the Probate and Inheritance Helpline (T 0300-123 1072).

DOMICILE

Liability to IHT depends on an individual's domicile at the time of any gift or on death. Domicile is a complex legal concept and what follows explains some of the main issues. An individual is domiciled in the country where he or she has a permanent home. Domicile is different from nationality or residence, and an individual can only have one domicile at any given time.

A 'domicile of origin' is normally acquired from the individual's father on birth, though this may not be the country in which he or she is born. For example, a child born in Germany while his or her father is working there, but whose permanent home is in the UK, will have the UK as his or her domicile of origin. Until a person legally changes his or her domicile, it will be the same as that of the person on whom they are legally dependent.

Individuals can legally acquire a new domicile – a 'domicile of choice' – from the age of 16 by leaving the current country of domicile and settling in another country and providing strong evidence of intention to live there permanently or indefinitely. Women who were married before 1974 acquired their husband's domicile and still retain it until they legally acquire a new domicile.

For IHT purposes, there is a concept of 'deemed domicile'. This means that even if a person is not domiciled in the UK under general law, he or she is treated as domiciled in the UK at the time of a transfer (ie at the time of a lifetime gift or on death) if he or she (a) was domiciled in the UK within the three years immediately before the transfer, or (b) was 'resident' in the UK in at least 17 of the 20 income tax years of assessment ending with the year in which a transfer is made. Where a person is domiciled, or treated as domiciled, in the UK at the time of a gift or on death, the location of assets is immaterial and full liability to IHT arises. A non-UK domiciled individual is also liable to IHT but only on chargeable property in the UK.

The assets of husband and wife and registered civil partners are not merged for IHT purposes, except that the IHT value of assets owned by one spouse or civil partner may be affected if the other also owns similar assets (eg shares in the same company or a share in their jointly owned house). Each spouse or partner is treated as a separate individual entitled to receive the benefit of his or her exemptions, reliefs and rates of tax.

IHT EXEMPTIONS

There are some important exemptions that allow individuals to legally pass assets on to others, both before and after their death – without being subject to IHT.

Exempt Beneficiaries
Assets can be given away to certain people and organisations without any IHT having to be paid. These gifts, which are exempt whether individuals make them during their lifetime or in their will, include gifts to:

• a husband, wife or civil partner, even if the couple is legally separated (but not if they are divorced or the civil partnership has dissolved). Note that gifts to an unmarried partner or a partner with whom the donor has not formed a civil partnership are not exempt
• a 'qualifying' charity established in the EU or another specified country
• some national institutions, including national museums, universities and the National Trust
• UK political parties

Annual Exemption
The first £3,000 of gifts made each tax year by each individual is exempt from IHT. If this exemption is not used, or not wholly used in any year, the balance may be carried forward to the following year only. A couple, therefore, may give away a total of £6,000 per tax year between them or £12,000 if they have not used their previous year's annual exemptions.

Wedding Gifts / Civil Partnership Ceremony Gifts
Some gifts are exempt from IHT because of the type of gift or reason for making it. Wedding or civil partnership ceremony gifts made to either of the couple are exempt from IHT up to certain amounts:

• gifts by a parent, £5,000
• gifts by a grandparent or other relative, £2,500
• gifts by anyone else, £1,000

The gift must be made on or shortly before the date of the wedding or civil partnership ceremony. If the ceremony is called off but the gift is made, this exemption will not apply.

Small Gifts
An individual can make small gifts, up to the value of £250, to any number of people in any one tax year without them being liable for IHT. However, a larger sum such as £500 cannot be given and exemption claimed for the first £250. In addition, this exemption cannot be used with any other exemption when giving to the same person. For example, a parent cannot combine a 'small gifts exemption' with a 'wedding/civil partnership ceremony gift exemption' to give a child £5,250 when he or she gets married or forms a civil partnership. Neither may an individual combine a 'small gifts exemption' with the 'annual exemption' to give someone £3,250. Note that it is possible to use the 'annual exemption' with any other exemption, such as the 'wedding/civil partnership ceremony gift exemption'. For example, if a child marries or forms a civil partnership, the parent can give him or her a total IHT-free gift of £8,000 by combining £5,000 under the wedding/civil partnership gift exemption and £3,000 under the annual exemption.

Normal Expenditure
Any gifts made out of individuals' after-tax income (not capital) are exempt from IHT if they are part of their normal expenditure and do not result in a fall in their standard of living. These can include regular payments to someone, such as an allowance or gifts for Christmas or a birthday and regular premiums paid on a life insurance policy for someone else.

Maintenance Gifts

An individual can make IHT-free maintenance payments to his or her spouse or registered civil partner, ex-spouse or former civil partner, relatives dependent because of old age or infirmity, and children (including adopted children and step-children) who are under 18 or in full-time education.

POTENTIALLY EXEMPT TRANSFERS

If an individual makes a gift to either another individual or certain types of trust and it is not covered by one of the above exemptions, it is known as a 'potentially exempt transfer' (PET). A PET is only free of IHT on two strict conditions: (a) the gift must be made at least seven years before the donor's death. If the donor does not survive seven years after making the gift, it will be liable for IHT and (b) the gift must be made as a true gift with no strings attached (technically known as a 'gift with reservation of benefit'). This means that the donor must give up all rights to the gift and stop benefiting from it in any way.

If a gift is made and the donor does retain some benefit from it then it will still count as part of his or her estate no matter how long he or she lives after making it. For example, a father could make a lifetime gift of his home to his child. However, HMRC would not accept this as a true gift if the father continued to live in the home (unless he paid his child a full commercial rent to do so) because he would be considered to still have a material interest in the gifted home. Its value, therefore, would still be liable for IHT.

In some circumstances a gift with strings attached might give rise to an income tax charge on the donor based on the value of the benefit he or she retains. In this case the donor can choose whether to pay the income tax or have the gift treated as a gift with reservation.

CHARGEABLE TRANSFERS

Any remaining lifetime gifts that are not (potentially or otherwise) exempt transfers are chargeable transfers or 'chargeable gifts', meaning that they incur liability to IHT. Chargeable transfers comprise mainly gifts to or from companies and gifts to particular types of trust. There is an immediate claim for IHT on chargeable gifts, and additional tax may be payable if the donor dies within seven years of making a chargeable gift.

DEATH

Immediately before the time of death an individual is deemed to make a transfer of value. This transfer will comprise the value of assets forming part of the deceased's estate after subtracting most liabilities. Any exempt transfers may be excluded such as transfers for the benefit of a surviving spouse or civil partner, and charities. Death may also trigger three additional liabilities:

- a PET made within the seven years before the death loses its potential status and becomes chargeable to IHT
- the value of gifts made with reservation may incur liability if any benefit was enjoyed within the seven years before the death
- additional tax may become payable for chargeable lifetime transfers made within the seven years before the death

The 'personal representative' (the person nominated to handle the affairs of the deceased person) arranges to value the estate and pay any IHT that is due. One or more personal representatives can be nominated in a person's will, in which case they are known as the 'executors'. If a person dies without leaving a will a court can nominate the personal representative, who is then known as the 'administrator'.

Valuing the deceased person's estate is one of the first things his or her personal representative needs to do. The representative will not normally be able to take over management of the estate (called 'applying for probate') until all or some of any IHT that is due has been paid.

VALUATIONS

When valuing a deceased person's estate all assets (property, possessions and money) owned at the time of death and certain assets given away during the seven years before death must be included. The valuation must accurately reflect what those assets would reasonably fetch in the open market at the date of death. The value of all of the assets that the deceased owned should include:

- his or her share of any assets owned jointly with someone else, for example a house owned with a partner
- any assets that are held in a trust, from which the deceased had the right to benefit
- any assets given away, but in which he or she kept an interest (gifts with reservation)
- PETs given away within the last seven years

Most estate assets can be valued quite easily, for example money in bank accounts or stocks and shares. In other instances the help of a professional valuer may be needed. Advice on how to value different assets including joint or trust assets is available at W www.hmrc.gov.uk. When valuing an estate, special relief is made available for certain assets. The two main reliefs are business relief and agricultural property relief, outlined below. Once all assets have been valued, the next step is to deduct from the total assets everything that the deceased person owed such as unpaid bills, outstanding mortgages and other loans plus their funeral expenses.

The value of all of the assets, less the deductible debts, is their estate. IHT is only payable on any value above £325,000 for the tax year 2014–15 at the current rate of 40 per cent.

A new reduced rate of IHT was introduced at the beginning of the 2012–13 tax year to encourage individuals to pledge part of their estate to charity on death. Where 10 per cent or more of a deceased's net estate (after deducting IHT exemptions, reliefs and the nil-rate band) is left to charity, the 40 per cent rate is reduced to 36 per cent.

RELIEF FOR SELECTED ASSETS

Agricultural Property

If an individual owns agricultural property and it is part of a working farm, it is possible to pass on some of this property free of IHT, either during that individual's lifetime or on their death. Agricultural property generally includes land or pasture used in the growing of crops or intensive rearing of animals for food consumption. It can also include farmhouses and farm cottages. The agricultural property can be owner-occupied or let. Relief is only due if the transferor has owned the property and it has been occupied for agricultural purposes for a minimum period.

The chargeable value transferred, either on a lifetime gift or on death, must be determined. This value may then be reduced by a percentage. Depending on the type of property, it will normally qualify for relief of 100 per cent.

Business Relief

Business relief is available on transfers of certain types of business and of business assets if they qualify as relevant business property and the transferor has owned them for a minimum period. The relief can be claimed for transfers made during the person's lifetime or on their death. Where the chargeable value transferred is attributable to relevant business property, the business relief reduces that value by a percentage of either 50 or 100 per cent, depending on the type of asset. Business relief may be claimed on relevant business property including property and buildings or assets such as unlisted shares or machinery.

It is a general requirement that the property must have been retained for a period of two years before the transfer or death, and restrictions may be necessary if the property has not been used wholly for business purposes. The same property cannot obtain both business property relief and the relief available for agricultural property.

CALCULATION OF TAX PAYABLE

The calculation of IHT payable adopts the use of a cumulative or 'running' total. Looking back seven years from the death the chargeable value of gifts in that period is added to the total value of the estate at death. The gifts will use up all or part of the inheritance tax threshold (the 'nil-rate band' above which IHT becomes payable) first.

Lifetime Chargeable Transfers
The value transferred by lifetime chargeable transfers must be added to the seven-year running total to calculate whether any IHT is due. If the nil-rate band is exceeded, tax will be imposed on the excess at the rate of 20 per cent. However, if the donor dies within a period of seven years from the date of the chargeable lifetime transfer, additional tax may be due. This is calculated by applying tax at the full rate of 40 per cent in substitution for the rate of 20 per cent previously used. The amount of tax is then reduced to a percentage by applying tapering relief. This percentage is governed by the number of years from the date of the lifetime gift to the date of death, as follows:

PERIOD OF YEARS BEFORE DEATH

Not more than 3	100%
More than 3 but not more than 4	80%
More than 4 but not more than 5	60%
More than 5 but not more than 6	40%
More than 6 but not more than 7	20%

Should this exercise produce liability greater than that previously paid at the 20 per cent rate on the lifetime transfer, additional tax, representing the difference, must be paid. Where the calculation shows an amount falling below tax paid on the lifetime transfer, no additional liability can arise nor will the shortfall become repayable.

Tapering relief is, of course, only available if the calculation discloses a liability to IHT. There is no liability if the lifetime transfer falls within the nil-rate band.

Potentially Exempt Transfers
Where a PET loses immunity from liability to IHT because the donor dies within seven years of making the transfer, the value transferred enters into the running total. Any liability to IHT will be calculated by applying the full rate of 40 per cent, reduced to the percentage governed by tapering relief if the original transfer occurred more than three years before death. Again, liability to IHT can only arise if the nil-rate band is exceeded.

Death
On death, IHT is due on the value of the deceased's estate plus the running total of gifts made in the seven years before death if they come to more than the nil-rate band. IHT is then charged at the full rate of 40 per cent on the amount in excess of the nil-rate band.

Settled Property and Trusts
Trusts are special legal arrangements that can be used by individuals to control how their assets are distributed to their beneficiaries and minimise their IHT liability. Complex rules apply to establish IHT liability on settled property which includes property held in trust, and individuals are advised to take expert legal advice when setting up trusts.

RATES OF TAX
There are four rates:

• a nil-rate
• a lifetime rate of 20 per cent
• a full rate of 40 per cent
• a reduced rate of 36 per cent applicable to taxable estates where 10 per cent of the net estate has been left to charity (*see* above)

The nil-rate band has been frozen at £325,000 since 2009–10 and will remain frozen at this rate until 2017–18. Any excess over this level is taxable at 20 per cent, 40 per cent or 36 per cent as the case may be.

TRANSFER OF NIL-RATE BAND
Transfers of property between spouses or civil partners are generally exempt from IHT. This means that someone who dies leaving some or all of their property to their spouse or civil partner may not have fully used up their nil-rate band. Under rules introduced in autumn 2007, any nil-rate band unused on the first death can be used when the surviving spouse or civil partner dies. A transfer of unused nil-rate band from a deceased spouse or civil partner (no matter what the date of their death) may be made to the estate of their surviving spouse or civil partner.

Where a valid claim to transfer unused nil-rate band is made, the nil-rate band that is available when the surviving spouse or civil partner dies is increased by the proportion of the nil-rate band unused on the first death. For example, if on the first death the chargeable estate is £150,000 and the nil-rate band is £300,000, 50 per cent of the nil-rate band would be unused. If the nil-rate band when the survivor dies is £325,000, then that would be increased by 50 per cent to £487,500. The amount of the nil-rate band that can be transferred does not depend on the value of the first spouse or civil partner's estate. Whatever proportion of the nil-rate band is unused on the first death is available for transfer to the survivor.

The amount of additional nil-rate band that can be accumulated by any one surviving spouse or civil partner is limited to the value of the nil-rate band in force at the time of their death. This may be relevant, for example, where a person dies having survived more than one spouse or civil partner.

Where these rules have effect, personal representatives do not have to claim for the unused nil-rate band to be transferred at the time of the first death. Any claims for transfer of unused nil-rate band amounts are made by the personal representatives of the estate of the second spouse or civil partner to die when they make an IHT return.

Detailed guidance on how to transfer the nil-rate band can be found on the HMRC website (W www.hmrc.gov.uk).

PAYMENT OF TAX
IHT is normally due six months after the end of the month in which the death occurs or the chargeable transaction takes place. This is referred to as the 'due date'. Tax on some assets such as business property, certain shares and securities and land and buildings (including the deceased person's home) can be deferred and paid in equal instalments over ten years, though interest will be charged in most cases. If IHT is due

on lifetime gifts and transfers, the person or transferee who received the gift or assets is normally liable to pay the IHT, though any IHT already paid at the time of a transfer into a trust or company will be taken into account. If tax owed is not paid by the due date, interest is charged on any unpaid IHT, no matter what caused the delay in payment.

It has been announced that HMRC will be investing in a new online service to support the administration of IHT. This will do away with the need to complete paper versions of forms and enable individuals to proceed with their application for probate and submit IHT accounts online. It is anticipated that the new online service will become available in 2016.

CORPORATION TAX

Corporation tax is a tax on a company's profits, including all its income and gains. This tax is payable by UK resident companies and by non-resident companies carrying on a trade in the UK through a permanent establishment. The following comments are confined to companies resident in the UK. The word 'company' is also used to include:

• members' clubs, societies and associations
• trade associations
• housing associations
• groups of individuals carrying on a business but not as a partnership (for example, cooperatives)

A company's taxable income is charged by reference to income or gains arising in its 'accounting period', which is normally 12 months long. In some circumstances accounting periods can be shorter than 12 months, but never longer. The accounting period is also normally the period for which a company's accounts are drawn up, but the two periods do not have to coincide.

If a company is liable to pay corporation tax on its profits, several things must be done. HMRC must be informed that the company exists and is liable for tax. A self-assessment company tax return plus full accounts and calculation of tax liability must be filed by the statutory filing date, normally 12 months after the end of the accounting period. Companies have to work out their own tax liability and have to pay their tax without prior assessment by HMRC. Records of all company expenditure and income must be kept in order to work out the tax liability correctly. Companies are liable to penalties if they fail to carry out these obligations.

A radically simpler way for small self-employed businesses, such as sole traders and partnerships, to calculate their tax was introduced with effect from the 2013–14 tax year. Such businesses with receipts of up to £81,000 are now able to work out their income on a cash basis and use simplified expenses rules, rather than having to follow the rules for larger businesses. Limited companies and limited liability partnerships can not use cash basis.

Extensive corporation tax information is available on the HMRC website (W www.hmrc.gov.uk/businesses) and companies may file their company tax returns online (W www.hmrc.gov.uk/ct/ct-online/file-return/online.htm).

RATE OF TAX
The rate of corporation tax is fixed for a financial year starting on 1 April and ending on the following 31 March. If a company's accounting period does not coincide with the financial year, its profits must be apportioned between the financial years and the tax rates for each financial year applied to those profits. The corporation tax liability is the total tax for both financial years.

The main rate of corporation tax for 2014–15 is 21 per cent, a decrease from 23 per cent in 2013–14. For North Sea oil and gas ringfence activities, the main rate of corporation tax is 30 per cent. The main rate of corporation tax applies when profits (including ringfence profits) are at a rate exceeding £1.5m, or where there is no claim to another rate, or where another rate does not apply.

It was announced in the 2013 Budget that the main rate of corporation tax will be reduced to 20 per cent for the financial year commencing 1 April 2015 at which time it will become unified with the small profits rate (*see* below).

SMALL PROFITS RATE
Where the profits of a company do not exceed stated limits, corporation tax becomes payable at the small profits rate (SPR).

The SPR for 2014–15 is 20 per cent and will remain at this rate for 2015–16, at which it will become unified with the main corporation tax rate. For North Sea oil and gas ringfence activities, the small profits rate is 19 per cent.

A company can make profits of up to £300,000 without losing the benefit of the small profits rate. If, however, its profits exceed £300,000 but fall below £1.5m, then marginal SPR relief applies to ease the transition. The effect of marginal relief is that the average rate of corporation tax imposed on all profits steadily increases from the lower small companies' rate of 20 per cent to the main rate of 21 per cent, with tax being imposed on profits in the margin at an increased rate. HMRC has produced an easy-to-use corporation tax marginal relief rate calculator (W www.hmrc.gov.uk/calcs/mrr.htm).

Where a change in the rate of tax is introduced and the accounting period of a company overlaps 31 March, profits must be apportioned to establish the appropriate rate for each part of those profits.

The lower limit of £300,000 and the upper limit of £1.5m apply to a period of 12 months and must be proportionately reduced for shorter periods. Some restriction in the SPR and the marginal rate may be necessary if there are two or more associated companies, namely companies under common control.

CORPORATION TAX ON PROFITS

£ per year	2013–14	2014–15
£0–£300,000	20%	20%
£300,001–£1,500,000	Marginal relief	Marginal relief
£1,500,001 or more	23%	21%

CAPITAL ALLOWANCES
Businesses can claim tax allowances, called capital allowances, on certain purchases or investments. This means that a proportion of these costs can be deducted from a business' taxable profits and reduce its tax bill. Capital allowances are currently available on plant and machinery, buildings, and research and development. The amount of the allowance depends on what is being claimed for.

Detailed information on capital allowances is available from the Enhanced Capital Allowances website (W www.etl.decc.gov.uk).

PAYMENT OF TAX
Corporation tax liabilities are normally due and payable in a single lump sum not later than nine months and one day after the end of the accounting period. For 'large' companies – those with profits over £1.5m which pay corporation tax at the main rate – there is a requirement to pay corporation tax in four quarterly instalments. Where a company is a member

of a group, the profits of the entire group must be merged to establish whether the company is 'large'.

HMRC runs a Business Payment Support Service (BPSS) which allows businesses facing temporary financial difficulties more time to pay their tax bills. Traders concerned about their ability to meet corporation tax, VAT or other payments owed to HMRC can call the Business Payment Support Line (T 0300-200 3835) seven days a week. This helpline is for new enquiries only, not for traders who have already been contacted by HMRC about an overdue payment. For details of the service visit W www.hmrc.gov.uk/payinghmrc/problems/bpps.htm

CAPITAL GAINS

Chargeable gains arising to a company are calculated in a manner similar to that used for individuals. However, companies are not entitled to the CGT annual exemption. Companies do not suffer CGT on chargeable gains but incur liability to corporation tax instead. Tax is due on the full chargeable gain of an accounting period after subtracting relief for any losses.

GROUPS OF COMPANIES

Each company within a group is separately charged to corporation tax on profits, gains and income. However, where one group member realises a loss for which special rules apply, other than a capital loss, a claim may be made to offset the deficiency against profits of some other member of the same group. The transfer of capital assets from one member of a group to a fellow member will usually incur no liability to tax on chargeable gains.

SPORTS CLUBS

Though corporation tax is payable by unincorporated associations including most sports clubs on their profits, a substantial exemption from liability to corporation tax is available to qualifying registered community amateur sports clubs (CASCs). Sports clubs that are registered as CASCs are exempt from liability to corporation tax on:

• profits from trading where the turnover of the trade is less than £30,000 in a 12-month period
• income from letting property where the gross rental income is less than £20,000 in a 12-month period
• bank and building society interest received
• chargeable gains
• any Gift Aid donations

All of the exemptions depend upon the club having been a registered CASC for the whole of the relevant accounting period and the income or gains being used only for qualifying purposes. If the club has only been a registered CASC for part of an accounting period the exemption amounts of £30,000 (for trading) and £20,000 (for income from property) are reduced proportionately. Only interest and gains received after the club is registered are exempted.

Charities are also generally exempt from corporation tax where they operate through a company structure.

VALUE ADDED TAX

Value added tax (VAT) is a tax on consumer expenditure charged when an individual buys goods and services in the European Union, including the UK. It is normally included in the sale price of goods and services and paid at the point of purchase. Each EU country has its own rate of VAT. From a business point of view, VAT is charged on most business transactions involving the supply of goods and services by a registered trader in the UK and Isle of Man. It is also charged on goods and some services imported from places outside the EU and on goods and some services coming into the UK from the other EU countries. VAT is administered by HMRC. A wide range of information on VAT, including VAT forms, is available online (W www.hmrc.gov.uk/vat/index.htm). HMRC also runs a VAT Enquiries helpline (T 0300-200 3700).

RATES OF TAX

There are three rates of VAT in the UK. The standard rate, payable on most goods and services in the UK, is 20 per cent.

The reduced rate – currently 5 per cent – is payable on certain goods and services including, for example, domestic fuel and power, children's car seats, women's sanitary products, contraceptive products, smoking cessation products and the installation of energy-saving materials such as wall insulation and solar panels.

A zero, or nil, rate applies to certain items including, for example, children's clothes, books, newspapers, most food and drink, and drugs and aids for disabled people. There are numerous exceptions to the zero-rated categories, however. While most food and drink is zero-rated, items including ice creams, chocolates, sweets, potato crisps and alcoholic drinks are not. Neither are drinks or items sold for consumption in a restaurant or cafe. Takeaway cold items such as sandwiches are zero-rated, while takeaway hot foods like fish and chips are not.

REGISTRATION

All traders, including professional persons and companies, must register for VAT if they are making 'taxable supplies' of a value exceeding stated limits. All goods and services that are VAT-rated are defined as 'taxable supplies' including zero-rated items which must be included when calculating the total value of a trader's taxable supplies – his or her 'taxable turnover'. The limits that govern mandatory registration are amended periodically.

An unregistered trader must register for VAT if:

• at the end of any month the total value of his or her taxable turnover (not just profit) for the past 12 months or less is more than the current VAT threshold of £81,000 – and
• at any time he or she has reasonable grounds to expect that his or her taxable turnover will be more than the current registration threshold of £81,000 in the next 30 days alone

To register for VAT, one or more forms must be completed and sent to HMRC within 30 days of any of the above. Basic VAT registration can currently be completed online (W https://online.hmrc.gov.uk/registration/). Traders who do not register at the correct time can be fined. Traders must charge VAT on their taxable supplies from the date they first need to be registered. Traders who only supply zero-rated goods may not have to register for VAT even if their taxable turnover goes above the registration threshold. However, a trader in this position must inform HMRC first and apply to be 'exempt from registration'. A trader whose taxable turnover does not reach the mandatory registration limit may choose to register for VAT voluntarily if what he or she does counts as a business for VAT purposes. This step may be thought advisable to recover input tax (see below) or to compete with other registered traders. Registered traders may submit an application for deregistration if their taxable turnover subsequently falls. An application for deregistration can be made if the taxable turnover for the year beginning on the application date is not expected to exceed £79,000.

INPUT TAX

Registered traders suffer input tax when buying in goods or services for the purposes of their business. It is the VAT that traders pay out to their suppliers on goods and services coming *in* to their business. Relief can usually be obtained for input tax suffered, either by setting that tax against output tax due or by repayment. Most items of input tax can be relieved in this manner. Where a registered trader makes both exempt supplies and taxable supplies to his customers or clients, there may be some restriction in the amount of input tax that can be recovered.

OUTPUT TAX
When making a taxable supply of goods or services, registered traders must account for output tax, if any, on the value of that supply. Output tax is the term used to describe the VAT on the goods and services that they supply or sell – the VAT on supplies going *out* of the business and collected from customers on each sale made. Usually the price charged by the registered trader will be increased by adding VAT, but failure to make the required addition will not remove liability to account for output tax. The liability to account for output tax, and also relief for input tax, may be affected where a trader is using a special secondhand goods scheme.

EXEMPT SUPPLIES
VAT is not chargeable on certain goods and services because the law deems them 'exempt' from VAT. These include the provision of burial and cremation facilities, insurance, loans of money, certain types of education and training and some property transactions. The granting of a lease to occupy land or the sale of land will usually comprise an exempt supply, for example, but there are numerous exceptions. Exempt supplies do not enter into the calculation of taxable turnover that governs liability to mandatory registration (*see* above). Such supplies made by a registered trader may, however, limit the amount of input tax that can be relieved. It is for this reason that the exemption may be useful.

COLLECTION OF TAX
Registered traders submit VAT returns for accounting periods usually of three months in duration, but arrangements can be made to submit returns on a monthly basis. Very large traders must account for tax on a monthly basis, but this does not affect the three-monthly return. The return will show both the output tax due for supplies made by the trader in the accounting period and also the input tax for which relief is claimed. If the output tax exceeds input tax the balance must be remitted with the VAT return. Where input tax suffered exceeds the output tax due, the registered trader may claim the excess from HMRC.

This basis for collecting tax explains the structure of VAT. Where supplies are made between registered traders the supplier will account for an amount of tax that will usually be identical to the tax recovered by the person to whom the supply is made. However, where the supply is made to a person who is not a registered trader there can be no recovery of input tax and it is on this person that the final burden of VAT eventually falls. Where goods are acquired by a UK trader from a supplier within the EU, the trader must also account for the tax due on acquisition. There are a number of simplified arrangements to make VAT accounting easier for businesses, particularly small businesses, and there is advice on the HMRC website about how to choose the most appropriate scheme for a business:

Cash Accounting
This scheme allows businesses to only pay VAT on the basis of payments received from their customers rather than on invoice dates or time of supply. It can therefore be useful for businesses with cash flow problems that cannot pay their VAT as a result. Businesses may use the cash accounting

scheme if taxable turnover is under £1.35m. There is no need to apply for the scheme – eligible businesses may start using it at the beginning of a new tax period. If a trader opts to use this scheme, he or she can do so until the taxable turnover reaches £1.6m.

Annual Accounting
If taxable turnover is under £1.35m a year, the trader may join the annual accounting scheme which allows them to make nine monthly or three quarterly instalments during the year based on an estimate of their total annual VAT bill. At the end of the year they submit a single return and any balance due. The advantages of this scheme for businesses are easier budgeting and cash flow planning because fixed payments are spread regularly throughout the year. Once a trader has joined the annual accounting scheme, membership may continue until the annual taxable turnover reaches £1.6m.

Flat Rate Scheme
This scheme allows small businesses with an annual taxable turnover of less than £150,000 to save on administration by paying VAT as a set flat percentage of their annual turnover instead of accounting internally for VAT on each individual 'in and out'. The percentage rate used is governed by the trade sector into which the business falls. The scheme can no longer be used once annual income exceeds £230,000.

Retail Schemes
There are special schemes that offer retailers an alternative if it is impractical for them to issue invoices for a large number of supplies direct to the public. These schemes include a provision to claim relief from VAT on bad debts where goods or services are supplied to a customer who does not pay for them.

VAT FACT SUMMARY
from 1 April 2014

Standard rate	20%
Reduced rate	5%
Registration (last 12 months or next 30 days)	£81,000
Deregistration (next 12 months under)	£79,000
Cash accounting scheme – up to	£1,350,000
Flat rate scheme – up to	£150,000
Annual accounting scheme – up to	£1,350,000

STAMP DUTY

For the majority of people, contact with stamp duty arises when they buy a property. Stamp duty is payable by the buyer as a way of raising revenue for the government based on the purchase price of a property, stocks and shares. This section aims to provide a broad overview of stamp duty as it may affect the average person.

STAMP DUTY LAND TAX
Stamp duty land tax was introduced on 1 December 2003 and covers the purchase of houses, flats and other land, buildings and certain leases in the UK.

Before 1 December 2003 property purchasers had to submit documents providing all details of the purchase to the Stamp Office for 'stamping'. The purchaser's solicitor or licensed conveyancer would then send the stamped documentation to the appropriate land registry to register ownership of the property. Under stamp duty land tax, purchasers do not have to send documents for stamping. Instead, a land transaction return form SDLT1, which contains all information regarding the purchase that is relevant to HMRC, is signed by the purchaser. Buyers of property are responsible for completing the land transaction return and payment of stamp duty, though the solicitor or licensed conveyancer acting for them in a land transaction will normally complete the relevant paperwork. Once HMRC has received the completed land transaction return and the payment of any stamp duty due, a certificate will be issued that enables a solicitor or licensed conveyancer to register the property in the new owner's name at the Land Registry.

The threshold for notification of residential property is currently £40,000. This means that taxpayers entering into a transaction involving residential or non-residential property where the chargeable consideration is less than £40,000 do not need to notify HMRC about the transaction.

RATES OF STAMP DUTY LAND TAX

Stamp duty is charged at different rates and has thresholds for different types of property and different values of transaction. The tax rate and payment threshold can vary according to whether the property is in residential or non-residential use and whether it is freehold or leasehold.

Below a certain threshold, currently £125,000, no stamp duty is payable on residential property purchases.

The following table shows the rates of stamp duty and payment thresholds that apply on residential property purchase prices during 2014–15:

Purchase price	Rate of tax (% of purchase price)
up to £125,000	0%
over £125,000 to £250,000	1%
over £250,000 to £500,000	3%
over £500,000 to £1,000,000	4%
over £1,000,000 to £2,000,000	5%
over £2,000,000	7%

When assessing how much stamp duty is payable, the entire purchase price must be taken into account so the relevant stamp duty rate is paid on the whole sum, not just on the amount over each tax threshold. For example, on a property bought for £250,000, 1 per cent (£2,500) is payable in stamp duty. On a property bought for £250,001, however, 3 per cent of the whole price (£7,500) is payable.

FIXTURES AND CHATTELS

As well as buying a property a purchaser may buy items inside the property. Some things inside a property are, in law, part of the land. These are called 'fixtures'. Examples are fitted kitchen units and bathroom suites. Because these fixtures are part of the land, any price paid for them must be taken into account for stamp duty purposes. Other things

inside a property are not part of the land. These are called 'chattels'. Examples are free-standing cookers, curtains and fitted carpets. The purchase of chattels is not chargeable to stamp duty. However, where both a property and chattels are purchased, the amount shown on the land transaction return as the purchase price of the property must be a 'just and reasonable' apportionment of the total amount paid. As with other entries on the form, the purchaser is responsible for the accuracy of this information. HMRC pays especial attention to residential property purchases just below stamp duty thresholds to prevent arrangements between buyer and seller to hand over cash so that the purchase price on paper looks lower, or where the buyer has paid an unreasonably high amount to buy chattels.

STAMP DUTY RESERVE TAX

Stamp duty or stamp duty reserve tax (SDRT) is payable at the rate of 0.5 per cent when shares are purchased. Stamp duty is payable when the shares are transferred using a stock transfer form, whereas SDRT is payable on 'paperless' share transactions where the shares are transferred electronically without using a stock transfer form. Most share transactions nowadays are paperless and settled by stockbrokers through CREST (the electronic settlement and registration system). SDRT therefore now accounts for the majority of taxation collected on share transactions effected through the London Stock Exchange.

The flat rate of 0.5 per cent is based on the amount paid for the shares, not what they are worth. If, for example, shares are bought for £2,000, £10 SDRT is payable, whatever the value of the shares themselves. If shares are transferred for free, no SDRT is payable.

A higher rate of 1.5 per cent is payable where shares are transferred into a 'depositary receipt scheme' or a 'clearance service'. These are special arrangements where the shares are held by a third party.

CREST automatically deducts the SDRT and sends it to HMRC. A stockbroker will settle up with CREST for the cost of the shares and the SDRT and then bill the purchaser for these and the broker's fees. If shares are not purchased through CREST, the stamp duty must be paid by the purchaser to HMRC.

UK stamp duty or SDRT is not payable on the purchase of foreign shares, though there may be foreign taxes to pay. SDRT is already accounted for in the price paid for units in unit trusts or shares in open-ended investment companies.

HELP AND INFORMATION

Further information on stamp duty land tax is available via the stamp taxes helpline on T 0300-200 3510 or the HMRC website (W www.hmrc.gov.uk), where a stamp duty calculator for both shares and land and property can be found.

LEGAL NOTES

These notes outline certain aspects of the law as they might affect the average person. They are intended only as a broad guideline and are by no means definitive. The law is constantly changing so expert advice should always be taken. In some cases, sources of further information are given in these notes.

It is always advisable to consult a solicitor without delay. Anyone who does not have a solicitor can contact the following for assistance in finding one: Citizens Advice (W www.citizensadvice.org.uk), the Community Legal Service (W www.gov.uk) or the Law Society of England and Wales. For assistance in Scotland, contact Citizens Advice Scotland (W www.cas.org.uk) or the Law Society of Scotland.

Legal aid schemes exist to make the help of a lawyer available to those who would not otherwise be able to afford one. Entitlement for most types of legal aid depends on an individual's means but a solicitor or Citizens Advice will be able to advise on this.

LAW SOCIETY OF ENGLAND AND WALES,
113 Chancery Lane, London WC2A 1PL T 020-7242 1222
W www.lawsociety.org.uk
LAW SOCIETY OF SCOTLAND, 26 Drumsheugh Gardens,
Edinburgh EH3 7YR T 0131-226 7411 W www.lawscot.org.uk

ABORTION

Abortion is governed by the Abortion Act 1967. Under its provisions, a legally induced abortion must be:
- performed by a registered medical practitioner
- carried out in an NHS hospital or other approved premises
- certified by two registered medical practitioners as justified on one or more of the following grounds:
  (a) that the pregnancy has not exceeded its 24th week and that the continuance of the pregnancy would involve risk, greater than if the pregnancy were terminated, of injury to the physical or mental health of the pregnant woman or any existing children of her family
  (b) that the termination is necessary to prevent grave permanent injury to the physical or mental health of the pregnant woman
  (c) that the continuance of the pregnancy would involve risk to the life of the pregnant woman, greater than if the pregnancy were terminated
  (d) that there is a substantial risk that if the child were born it would suffer from such physical or mental abnormalities as to be seriously handicapped.

In determining whether the continuance of a pregnancy would involve such risk of injury to health as is mentioned in grounds (a) or (b), account may be taken of the pregnant woman's actual or reasonably foreseeable environment.

The requirements relating to the opinion of two registered medical practitioners and to the performance of the abortion at an NHS hospital or other approved place cease to apply in circumstances where a registered medical practitioner is of the opinion, formed in good faith, that a termination is immediately necessary to save the life, or to prevent grave permanent injury to the physical or mental health, of the pregnant woman.

The Abortion Act 1967 does not apply to Northern Ireland, where abortion is not legal.

FAMILY PLANNING ASSOCIATION (UK), 50 Featherstone Street, London EC1Y 8QU T 020-7608 5240
W www.fpa.org.uk

BRITISH PREGNANCY ADVISORY SERVICE (BPAS),
20 Timothys Bridge Road, Stratford-upon-Avon CV37 9BF
T 0345-365 5050 W www.bpas.org

ADOPTION OF CHILDREN

The Adoption and Children Act 2002 reformed the framework for domestic and intercountry adoption in England and Wales and some parts of it extend to Scotland and Northern Ireland. The Children and Adoption Act 2006, recently amended by the Children and Families Act 2014, introduced further provisions for adoptions involving a foreign element.

WHO MAY APPLY FOR AN ADOPTION ORDER
A couple (whether married or two people living as partners in an enduring family relationship) may apply for an adoption order where both of them are over 21 or where one is only 18 but the natural parent and the other is 21. An adoption order may be made for one applicant where that person is 21 and: a) the court is satisfied that person is the partner of a parent of the person to be adopted; or b) they are not married and are not civil partners; or c) married or in a civil partnership but they are separated from their spouse or civil partner and living apart with the separation likely to be permanent; or d) their spouse/civil partner is either unable to be found, or their spouse/civil partner is incapable by reason of ill-health of making an application. There are certain qualifying conditions an applicant must meet eg residency in the British Isles.

ARRANGING AN ADOPTION
Adoptions may generally only be arranged by an adoption agency or by way of an order from the high court; breach of the restrictions on who may arrange an adoption would constitute a criminal offence. When deciding whether a child should be placed for adoption, the court or adoption agency must consider all the factors set out in the 'welfare checklist' – the paramount consideration being the child's welfare, throughout his or her life. These factors include the child's wishes, needs, age, sex, background and any harm which the child has suffered or is likely to suffer. At all times, the court or adoption agency must bear in mind that delay is likely to prejudice a child's welfare.

ADOPTION ORDER
Once an adoption has been arranged, a court order is necessary to make it legal; this may be obtained from the high court, county court or magistrates' court (including the family proceedings court). An adoption order may not be given unless the court is satisfied that the consent of the child's natural parents (or guardians) has been given correctly. Consent can be dispensed with on two grounds: where the parent or guardian cannot be found or is incapable of giving consent, or where the welfare of the child so demands.

An adoption order extinguishes the parental responsibility that a person other than the adopters (or adopter) has for the child. Where an order is made on the application of the partner of the parent, that parent keeps parental responsibility. Once adopted, the child has the same status as a child born to the adoptive parents, but may lose rights to the estates of those losing their parental responsibility.

REGISTRATION AND CERTIFICATES

All adoption orders made in England and Wales are required to be registered in the Adopted Children Register which also contains particulars of children adopted under registrable foreign adoptions. The General Register Office keeps this register from which certificates may be obtained in a similar way to birth certificates. The General Register Office also has equivalents in Scotland and Northern Ireland.

TRACING NATURAL PARENTS OR CHILDREN WHO HAVE BEEN ADOPTED

An adult adopted person may apply to the Registrar-General to obtain a certified copy of his/her birth certificate. Adoption agencies and adoption support agencies should provide services to adopted persons to assist them in obtaining information about their adoption and facilitate contact with their relatives. There is an Adoption Contact Register which provides a safe and confidential way for birth parents and other relatives to assure an adopted person that contact would be welcome. The BAAF (*see* below) can provide addresses of organisations which offer advice, information and counselling to adopted people, adoptive parents and people who have had their children adopted.

BRITISH ASSOCIATION FOR ADOPTION AND
   FOSTERING (BAAF), Saffron House, 6–10 Kirkby Street,
   London EC1N 8TS **T** 020-7421 2600 **W** www.baaf.org.uk

SCOTLAND

The relevant legislation is the Adoption and Children (Scotland) Act 2007 which came into force on 28 September 2009. In addition adoptions with a foreign element are governed by the Adoptions with a Foreign Element (Scotland) Regulations 2009. Pre-2009 adoptions are governed by Part IV of the Adoption (Scotland) Act 1978. The provisions of the 2007 act are similar to those described above. In Scotland, petitions for adoption are made to the sheriff court or the court of session.

BRITISH ASSOCIATION FOR ADOPTION AND
   FOSTERING (BAAF), BAAF Scottish Centre,
   113 Rose Street, Edinburgh EH2 3DT **T** 0131-226 9270

BIRTHS (REGISTRATION)

It is the duty of the parents of a child born in England or Wales to register the birth within 42 days of the date of birth at the register office in the district in which the baby was born. If it is inconvenient to go to the district where the birth took place, the information for the registration may be given to a registrar in another district, who will send your details to the appropriate register office. Failure to register the birth within 42 days without reasonable cause may leave the parents liable to a penalty. If a birth has not been registered within 12 months of its occurrence it is possible for the late registration of the birth to be authorised by the Registrar-General, provided certain requirements can be met.

Births that take place in England may only be registered in English, but births that take place in Wales may be registered bilingually in Welsh and English. In order to do this, the details must be given in Welsh and the registrar must be able to understand and write in Welsh.

If the parents of the child were married to each other at the time of the birth (or conception), either the mother or the father may register the birth. If the parents were not married to each other at the time of the child's birth (or conception), the father's particulars may be entered in the register only where he attends the register office with the mother and they sign the birth register together. Where an unmarried parent is unable to attend the register office, either parent may submit to the registrar a statutory declaration on Form 16 (or Form 16W for births which took place in Wales) acknowledging the father's paternity (this form may be obtained from any registrar in England or Wales or online at **W** www.gro.gov.uk); alternatively a parental responsibility agreement or appropriate court order may be produced to the registrar.

If the father's details are not included in the birth register, it may be possible to re-register the birth at a later date. If the parents do not register the birth of their child the following people may do so:

- the occupier of the house or hospital where the child was born
- a person who was present at the birth
- a person who is responsible for the child

Upon registration of the birth a short certificate is issued. It may be possible to register the birth while still at hospital. Hospitals will advise individually whether this is possible.

BIRTHS ABROAD

There are certain countries where birth registrations may be made for British citizens overseas (for more details on British citizenship *see* below). The British consul or high commission may register the births and issue certificates which are then sent to the General Register Office. If a birth is registered by the British consul or high commission, the registration would show the person's claim to British citizenship, British overseas territories citizenship or British overseas citizenship.

SCOTLAND

In Scotland the birth of a child must be registered within 21 days at the registration office of any registration district in Scotland.

If the child is born, either in or out of Scotland, on a ship, aircraft or land vehicle that ends its journey at any place in Scotland, the child, in most cases, will be registered as if born in that place.

CERTIFICATES OF BIRTHS, DEATHS OR MARRIAGES

Certificates of births, marriages and deaths that have taken place in England and Wales since 1837 can be obtained from the General Register Office (GRO).

Marriage or death certificates may also be obtained from the minister of the church in which the marriage or funeral took place. Any register office can advise about the best way to obtain certificates.

The fees for certificates are:

Online application:
- full certificate of birth, marriage, death or adoption, £9.25
- full certificate of birth, marriage, death or adoption with GRO reference supplied, £9.25

By postal/phone/fax application:
- full certificate of birth, marriage, death or adoption, £9.25
- full certificate of birth, marriage, death or adoption with GRO reference supplied, £9.25
- extra copies of the same birth, marriage or death certificate issued at the same time, £9.25

A priority service is available for an additional fee.

A complete set of the GRO indexes including births, deaths and marriages, civil partnerships, adoptions and provisional indexes for births and deaths from January 2011 to June 2012 are available at the British Library, City of Westminster Archives Centre, Manchester City Library, Newcastle City Library, Birmingham Central Library, Bridgend Reference and Information Library and Plymouth Central Library. Copies of GRO indexes may also be held at some libraries, family history societies, local records offices and The Church of Jesus Christ of Latter Day Saints family history centres. Some organisations may not hold a complete record of indexes and a small fee may be charged by some of them. GRO indexes are also available online.

The Society of Genealogists has many records of baptisms, marriages and deaths prior to 1837.

SCOTLAND

Certificates of births, deaths or marriages that have taken place in Scotland since 1855 can be obtained from the National Records of Scotland (formerly the General Register Office for Scotland) or from the appropriate local registrar.

Applicable fees – local registrar:
- each extract or abbreviated certificate of birth, death, marriage, civil partnership or adoption within a month of registration, £10.00
- each extract or abbreviated certificate of birth, death, marriage, civil partnership or adoption outwith a month of registration, £15.00

A priority service is available for an additional fee.

The National Records of Scotland also keeps the Register of Divorces (including decrees of declaration of nullity of marriage), and holds parish registers dating from before 1855.

Applicable fees – National Records of Scotland:
- personal application, or postal, telephone or fax order: £15.00

A priority service for a response within 24 hours is available for an additional fee of £15.00.

A search of birth, death and marriage records including records of Church of Scotland parishes and other statutory records can be done at the Scotland's People Centre. There are also indexes to some of the old parish registers death and burial records in the library at the centre and indexes and images of census records from 1841–1911 are available. The charges for such searches are as follows:
- full or part-day search pass, £15.00
- Quarterly search pass, £490.00
- annual search pass, £1,450.00

Online searching is also available. For more information, visit W www.scotlandspeople.gov.uk.

THE GENERAL REGISTER OFFICE, General Register Office, Certificate Services Section, PO Box 2, Southport PR8 2JD
T 0300-123 1837 W www.gro.gov.uk/gro/content/certificates

THE NATIONAL RECORDS OF SCOTLAND, New Register House, 3 West Register Street, Edinburgh EH1 3YT
T 0131-334 0380 W www.nrscotland.gov.uk

SCOTLAND'S PEOPLE CENTRE, General Register House, 2 Princes Street, Edinburgh EH1 3YY T 0131-314 4300
W www.scotlandspeoplehub.gov.uk

THE SOCIETY OF GENEALOGISTS, 14 Charterhouse Buildings, Goswell Road, London EC1M 7BA T 020-7251 8799
W www.sog.org.uk

BRITISH NATIONALITY

There are different types of British nationality status: British citizenship; British overseas citizenship; British national (overseas); British overseas territories citizenship; British protected persons; and British subjects. The most widely held of these is British citizenship. Everyone born in the UK before 1 January 1983 became a British citizen when the British Nationality Act 1981 came into force, with the exception of children born to certain diplomatic staff working in the UK at the time. Individuals born outside the UK before 1 January 1983 but who at that date were citizens of the UK and colonies and had a right of abode in the UK also became British citizens. British citizens have the right to live permanently in the UK and are free to leave and re-enter the UK at any time.

A person born on or after 1 January 1983 in the UK (including, for this purpose, the Channel Islands and the Isle of Man) is entitled to British citizenship if he/she falls into one of the following categories:
- he/she has a parent who is a British citizen
- he/she has a parent who is settled in the UK
- he/she is a newborn infant found abandoned in the UK
- his/her parents subsequently settle in the UK or become British citizens and an application is made before he/she is 18
- he/she lives in the UK for the first ten years of his/her life and is not absent for more than 90 days in each of those years
- he/she is adopted in the UK and one of the adopters is a British citizen
- the home secretary consents to his/her registration while he/she is a minor
- if he/she has always been stateless and lives in the UK for a period of five years before his/her 22nd birthday
- if he/she has been born on or after 13 January 2010 to a parent who is a member of the UK armed forces
- if he/she has been born on or after 13 January 2010 and a parent becomes a member of the UK armed forces, and an application is made before he/she is 18

A person born outside the UK may acquire British citizenship if he/she falls into one of the following categories:
- he/she has a parent who is a British citizen otherwise than by descent, eg a parent who was born in the UK
- he/she has a parent who is a British citizen serving the crown or a European community institution overseas and was recruited to that service in the UK (including qualifying territories for those born on or after 21 May 2002) or in the European Community (for services within an EU institution); or if the applicant himself/herself has at any time been in crown, or similar, service under the government of a British overseas territory
- if he/she has been born on or after 13 January 2010 to a parent who is a member of the UK armed forces serving outside the UK and qualifying territories, is of good character and (if he/she is a minor at the time of application) all parents then alive consent in signed writing
- the home secretary consents to his/her registration while he/she is a minor
- he/she is a British overseas territories citizen, a British overseas citizen, a British subject or a British protected person and has been lawfully resident in the UK for five years
- he/she is a British overseas territories citizen who acquired that citizenship from a connection with Gibraltar
- he/she is adopted or naturalised

Where parents are married, the status of either may confer citizenship on their child. Since July 2006, both parents are able to pass on nationality even if they are not married, provided that there is satisfactory evidence of paternity. For children born before July 2006, it must be shown that there is parental consent and that the child would have an automatic claim to citizenship or entitlement to registration had the parents been married. Where parents are not married, the status of the mother determines the child's citizenship.

Under the 1981 act, Commonwealth citizens and citizens of the Republic of Ireland were entitled to registration as British citizens before 1 January 1983. In 1983, citizens of the Falkland Islands were granted British citizenship.

Renunciation of British citizenship must be registered with the home secretary and will be revoked if no new citizenship or nationality is acquired within six months. If the renunciation was required in order to retain or acquire another citizenship or nationality, the citizenship may be reacquired only once. If the renunciation was for another reason, the home secretary may allow reacquisition more than once, depending on the circumstances. The secretary of state may deprive a person of a citizenship status if he or she is satisfied that the person has done anything seriously prejudicial to the vital interests of the UK, or a British overseas territory, unless making the order would have the effect of rendering such a person stateless. A person may also be deprived of a citizenship status which results from his registration or naturalisation if the secretary of state is satisfied that the registration or naturalisation was obtained by fraud, false representation or concealment of a material fact.

BRITISH DEPENDENT TERRITORIES CITIZENSHIP

Since 26 February 2002, this category of nationality no longer exists and has been replaced by British overseas territory citizenship.

If a person had this class of nationality only by reason of a connection to the territory of Hong Kong, they lost it automatically when Hong Kong was returned to the People's Republic of China. However, if after 30 June 1997, they had no other nationality and would have become stateless, or were born after 30 June 1997 and would have been born stateless (but had a parent who was a British national (overseas) or a British overseas citizen), they became a British overseas citizen.

BRITISH OVERSEAS CITIZENSHIP

Under the 1981 act, as amended by the British Overseas Territories Act 2002, this type of citizenship was conferred on any UK and colonies citizens who did not become either a British citizen or a British overseas territories citizen on 1 January 1983 and as such is now, for most purposes, only acquired by persons who would otherwise be stateless.

BRITISH OVERSEAS TERRITORIES CITIZENSHIP

This category of nationality replaced British dependent territories citizenship. Most commonly, this form of nationality is acquired where, after 31 December 1982, a person was a citizen of the UK and colonies and did not become a British citizen, and that person, and their parents or grandparents, were born, registered or naturalised in the specified British overseas territory. However, on 21 May 2002, people became British citizens if they had British overseas territories citizenship by connection with any British overseas territory, except for the sovereign base areas of Akrotiri and Dhekelia in Cyprus.

RESIDUAL CATEGORIES

British subjects, British protected persons and British nationals (overseas) may be entitled to registration as British citizens on completion of five years' legal residence in the UK.

Citizens of the Republic of Ireland who were also British subjects before 1 January 1949 can retain that status if they fulfil certain conditions.

EUROPEAN UNION CITIZENSHIP

British citizens (including Gibraltarians who are registered for this purpose) are also EU citizens and are entitled to travel freely to other EU countries to work, study, reside and set up a business. EU citizens have the same rights with respect to the UK.

NATURALISATION

Naturalisation is granted at the discretion of the home secretary. The basic requirements are lawful residence in the UK in the five years immediately preceding application (three years if the applicant is married to, or is the civil partner of a British citizen), good character, adequate knowledge of the English, Welsh or Scottish Gaelic language, passing the UK citizenship test and an intention to reside permanently in the UK.

STATUS OF ALIENS

Aliens, being persons without any of the above forms of British nationality, may not hold public office or vote in Britain and they may not own a British ship or aircraft. Citizens of the Republic of Ireland and Commonwealth citizens are not deemed to be aliens. Certain provisions of the Immigration and Asylum Act 1999 make provision about immigration and asylum and about procedures in connection with marriage by superintendent registrar's certificate.

CONSUMER LAW

SALE OF GOODS

A sale of goods contract is the most common type of contract. It is governed by the Sale of Goods Act 1979 (as amended by the Sale and Supply of Goods Act 1994). The act provides protection for buyers by implying terms into every sale of goods contract. These terms include:

- an implied term that the seller will pass good title to the buyer (unless it appears from the contract or is to be inferred from the circumstances that there is an intention that the seller should transfer only such title as he has)
- where the seller sells goods by reference to a description, an implied term that the goods will match that description and, where the sale is by sample and description, it will not be sufficient that the bulk of the goods correspond with the sample if the goods do not also correspond with the description
- where goods are sold by a business seller, an implied term that the goods will be of satisfactory quality ie they meet the standard that a reasonable person would regard as satisfactory, taking into account any description of the goods, the price, and all other relevant circumstances. The quality of the goods includes their state and condition, relevant aspects being whether they are fit for all the purposes for which such goods are commonly supplied, their appearance and finish, freedom from minor defects and their safety and durability. This term will not be implied, however, if a buyer has examined the goods (including in a sale by sample) and should have noticed the defect or if the seller specifically drew the buyer's attention to the defect
- where goods are sold by a business seller, an implied term that the goods are reasonably fit for any purpose made known to the seller by the buyer (either expressly or by implication), unless it is shown that the buyer does not rely on the seller's judgment, or it is not reasonable for him/her to do so
- where goods are sold by sample, implied terms that the bulk of the sample will correspond with the sample in quality, and that the goods are free from any defect rendering them unsatisfactory which would not have been apparent on a reasonable examination of the sample

Some of the above terms can be excluded from contracts by the seller. The seller's right to do this is, however, restricted by the Unfair Contract Terms Act 1977. The act offers more protection to a buyer who 'deals as a consumer' (that is where the seller is selling in the course of a business, the goods are of a type ordinarily bought for private use and the goods are bought by a buyer who is not a business buyer) and does not allow for the implied terms described above to be excluded. In a sale of second-hand goods by auction (at which individuals have the opportunity of attending the sale in person), a buyer does not deal as a consumer.

HIRE-PURCHASE AGREEMENTS

Terms similar to those implied in contracts of sales of goods are implied into contracts of hire-purchase, under the Supply of Goods (Implied Terms) Act 1973. The 1977 act limits the exclusion of these implied terms as before.

SUPPLY OF GOODS AND SERVICES

Under the Supply of Goods and Services Act 1982, similar terms are also implied in other types of contract under which ownership of goods passes, and contracts for the hire of goods (though not hire-purchase agreements). These types of contracts have additional implied terms:

- that the supplier will use reasonable care and skill in carrying out the service
- that the supplier will carry out the service in a reasonable time (unless the time has been agreed)
- that the supplier will make a reasonable charge (unless the charge has already been agreed)

The 1977 act limits the exclusion of these implied terms in a similar manner as before.

UNFAIR TERMS

The Unfair Terms in Consumer Contracts Regulations 1999 apply to contracts between business sellers (or suppliers of goods and services) and consumers. Where the terms have not been individually negotiated (ie where the terms were drafted in advance so that the consumer was unable to influence those terms), a term will be deemed unfair if it operates to the detriment of the consumer (ie causes a significant imbalance in the parties' rights and obligations arising under the contract). An unfair term does not bind the consumer but the contract may continue to bind the parties if it is capable of existing without the unfair term. The regulations contain a non-exhaustive list of terms that are regarded as potentially unfair. When a term does not fall into such a category, whether it will be regarded as fair or not will depend on many factors, including the nature of the goods or services, the surrounding circumstances (such as the bargaining strength of both parties) and the other terms in the contract. The recently introduced consumer rights bill (*see* below) will, if passed, replace the 1999 regulations.

CONSUMER PROTECTION

The Consumer Protection from Unfair Trading Regulations 2008 (CPRs) replaced much previous consumer protection regulation including the majority of the Trade Descriptions Act 1968. The CPRs prohibit 31 specific practices, including pyramid schemes. In addition the CPRs prohibit business sellers from making misleading actions and misleading omissions, which cause, or are likely to cause, the average consumer to take a different transactional decision. There is also a general duty not to trade unfairly. The CPRs were amended by the Consumer Protection (Amendment) Regulations 2014, which entered into force on 1 October 2014 and introduced a new direct civil right of redress for consumers against businesses for misleading and aggressive practices, as well as extending the CPRs to cover misleading and aggressive demands for payment.

Under the Consumer Protection Act 1987, producers of goods are liable for any injury, death or damage to any property exceeding £275 caused by a defect in their product (subject to certain defences).

Consumers are also afforded protection under the Consumer Contracts (Information, Cancellation and Additional Charges) Regulations 2013, which came into force on 13 June 2014.

A consumer rights bill, introduced to the House of Commons on 23 January 2014, will, if passed, amend much of the existing consumer legislation, including the Sale of Goods Act 1979, the Supply of Goods (Implied Terms) Act 1973 and the Supply of Goods and Services Act 1982.

CONSUMER CREDIT

In matters relating to the provision of credit (or the supply of goods on hire or hire-purchase), consumers are also protected by the Consumer Credit Act 1974 (as amended by the Consumer Credit Act 2006). The act was most recently amended by a number of statutory instruments made under the Financial Services and Markets Act 2000. These came into force on 1 April 2014 and represent a major overhaul of the consumer credit regime which was carried out in order to implement the recent EU Consumer Credit Directive. Under the new regime, responsibility for consumer credit regulation has been transferred from the Office of Fair Trading (OFT), which has ceased to exist, to the Financial Conduct Authority (FCA). Previously, a licence issued by the OFT was required in order to conduct a consumer credit, consumer hire or an ancillary credit business, subject to certain exemptions. The requirement to obtain a licence from the OFT has been replaced by the need to obtain authorisation from the FCA to carry out a consumer credit 'regulated' activity, likewise subject to certain exemptions. Provisions of the 1974 Act as amended include:

- in order for a creditor to enforce a regulated agreement, the agreement must comply with certain formalities and must be properly executed. An improperly executed regulated agreement is enforceable only on an order of the court. The debtor must also be given specified information by the creditor or his/her broker or agent during the negotiations which take place before the signing of the agreement. The agreement must also state certain information to ensure that the debtor or hirer is aware of the rights and duties conferred or imposed on him/her and the protection and remedies available to him/her under the act
- the right to withdraw from or cancel some contracts depending on the circumstances. For example, subject to certain exceptions, a borrower may withdraw from a regulated credit agreement within 14 days without giving any reason. The exceptions include agreements for credit exceeding £60,260 and agreements secured on land. The right to withdraw applies only to the credit agreement itself and not to goods or services purchased with it. The borrower must also repay the credit and any interest
- if the debtor is in breach of the agreement, the creditor must serve a default notice before taking any action such as repossessing the goods
- if the agreement is a hire-purchase or conditional sale agreement, the creditor cannot repossess the goods without a court order if the debtor has paid one third of the total price of the goods
- in agreements where the relationship between the creditor and the debtor is unfair to the debtor, the court may alter or set aside some of the terms of the agreement
- Where a credit reference agency has been used to check the debtor's financial standing, the creditor may be required to give the agency's name to the debtor, who is entitled to the see the agency's file. A fee of £2 is payable to the agency.

It is intended that the statutory basis of consumer credit regulation, under the 1974 Act, will be replaced by a rules-based approach under the new regime. The FCA will be reviewing the stautory framework over the next few years and will develop rule-based alternatives where possible.

SCOTLAND

The legislation governing the sale and supply of goods applies to Scotland as follows:
- the Sale of Goods Act 1979 applies with some modifications and it has been amended by the Sale and Supply of Goods Act 1994
- the Supply of Goods (Implied Terms) Act 1973 applies
- the Supply of Goods and Services Act 1982 does not extend to Scotland but some of its provisions were introduced by the Sale and Supply of Goods Act 1994
- only Parts II and III of the Unfair Contract Terms Act 1977 apply
- the Trade Descriptions Act 1968 applies with minor modifications
- the Consumer Credit Act 1974 applies
- the Consumer Credit Act 2006 applies
- the Consumer Protection Act 1987 applies
- the General Product Safety Regulations 2005 apply
- the Unfair Terms in Consumer Contracts Regulations 1999 apply
- the Unfair Terms in Consumer Contracts (Amendment) Regulations 2001 apply
- the Consumer Protection (Distance Selling) Regulations 2000 apply
- the Sale and Supply of Goods to Consumers Regulations 2002 apply
- the Consumer Protection from Unfair Trading Regulations 2008 apply

PROCEEDINGS AGAINST THE CROWN

Until 1947, proceedings against the Crown were generally possible only by a procedure known as a petition of right, which put the private litigant at a considerable disadvantage. The Crown Proceedings Act 1947 placed the Crown (not the sovereign in his/her private capacity, but as the embodiment of the state) largely in the same position as a private individual and made proceedings in the high court involving the Crown subject to the same rules as any other case. The act did not, however, extinguish or limit the Crown's prerogative or statutory powers, and it continued the immunity of HM ships and aircraft. It also left certain Crown privileges unaffected. The act largely abolished the special procedures which previously applied to civil proceedings by and against the Crown. Civil proceedings may be initiated against the appropriate government department or, if there is doubt regarding which is the appropriate department, against the attorney-general.

In Scotland proceedings against the Crown founded on breach of contract could be taken before the 1947 act and no special procedures applied. The Crown could, however, claim certain special pleas. The 1947 act applies in part to Scotland and brings the practice of the two countries as closely together as the different legal systems permit. As a result of the Scotland Act 1998, actions against government departments should be raised against the Lord Advocate or the advocate-general. Actions should be raised against the Lord Advocate where the department involved administers a devolved matter. Devolved matters include agriculture, education, housing, local government, health and justice. Actions should be raised against the advocate-general where the department is dealing with a reserved matter. Reserved matters include defence, foreign affairs and social security.

DEATHS

WHEN A DEATH OCCURS

If the death (including stillbirth) was expected, the doctor who attended the deceased during their final illness should be contacted. If the death was sudden or unexpected, the family doctor (if known) and police should be contacted. If the cause of death is quite clear, the doctor will provide:
- a medical certificate that shows the cause of death
- a formal notice that states that the doctor has signed the medical certificate and that explains how to get the death registered
- if the death was known to be caused by a natural illness but the doctor wishes to know more about the cause of death, he/she may ask the relatives for permission to carry out a post-mortem examination

In England and Wales a coroner is responsible for investigating deaths occurring:
- when there is no doctor who can issue a medical certificate of cause of death
- no doctor has treated the deceased during his or her last illness or when the doctor attending the patient did not see him or her within 14 days before death, or after death
- the death occurred during an operation or before recovery from the effect of an anaesthetic
- the death was sudden and unexplained or attended by suspicious circumstances
- the death might be due to an industrial injury or disease, or to accident, violence, neglect or abortion
- the death occurred in prison or in police custody

The doctor will write on the formal notice that the death has been referred to the coroner; if the post-mortem shows that death was due to natural causes, the coroner may issue a notification which gives the cause of death so that the death can be registered. If the cause of death was violent or unnatural, is still undetermined after a post-mortem, or took place in prison or police custody, the coroner must hold an inquest. The coroner must hold an inquest in these circumstances even if the death occurred abroad (and the body has been returned to England or Wales).

In Scotland the office of coroner does not exist. The local procurator fiscal inquires into sudden or suspicious deaths. A fatal accident inquiry will be held before the sheriff where the death has resulted from an accident during the course of the employment of the person who has died, or where the person who has died was in legal custody, or where the Lord Advocate deems it in the public interest that an inquiry be held.

REGISTERING A DEATH

In England and Wales the death must be registered by the registrar of births and deaths for the district in which it occurred. A death which occurs in Scotland can be registered in any registration district in Scotland. Information concerning a death can be given before any registrar of births and deaths in England and Wales. The registrar will pass the relevant details to the registrar for the district where the death occurred, who will then register the death.

In England and Wales the death must normally be registered within five days (unless the registrar says this period can be extended); in Scotland within eight days. If the death has been referred to the coroner/local procurator fiscal it cannot be registered until the registrar has received authority from the coroner/local procurator fiscal to do so. Failure to register a death involves a penalty in England and Wales and may lead to a court decree being granted by a sheriff in Scotland.

If the death occurred at a house or hospital, the death may be registered by:
- any relative of the deceased
- any person present at the death
- the occupier or any inmate of the house or hospital if he/she knew of the occurrence of the death
- any person making the funeral arrangements (but not the funeral director)

- an official from the hospital
- in Scotland, the deceased's executor or legal representative

For deaths that took place elsewhere, the death may be registered by:

- any relative of the deceased
- someone present at the death
- someone who found the body
- a person in charge of the body
- any person making the funeral arrangements

The majority of deaths are registered by a relative of the deceased. The registrar would normally allow one of the other listed persons to register the death only if there were no relatives available.

The person registering the death should take the medical certificate of the cause of death with them; it is also useful, though not essential, to take the deceased's birth and marriage/civil partnership certificates, NHS medical card, pension documentation and life assurance details. The details given to the registrar must be absolutely correct, otherwise it may be difficult to change them later. The person registering the death should check the entry carefully before it is signed. The registrar will issue a certificate for burial or cremation, and a certificate of registration of death (commonly known as a 'death certificate' which is issued for social security purposes if the deceased received a state pension or benefits) – both free of charge. A death certificate is a certified copy of the entry in the death register; copies can be provided on payment of a fee and may be required for the following purposes, in particular by the executor or administrator when sorting out the deceased's affairs:

- the will
- bank and building society accounts
- savings bank certificates and premium bonds
- insurance policies
- pension claims

If the death occurred abroad or on a foreign ship or aircraft, the death should be registered according to the local regulations of the relevant country and a death certificate should be obtained. In many countries the death can also be registered with the British consulate in that country and a record will be kept at the General Register Office. This avoids the expense of bringing the body back.

After 12 months (three months in Scotland) of death or the finding of a dead body, no death can be registered without the consent of the registrar-general.

BURIAL AND CREMATION

In most circumstances in England and Wales a certificate for burial or cremation must be obtained from the registrar before the burial or cremation can take place. If the death has been referred to the coroner, an order for burial or a certificate for cremation must be obtained. In Scotland a body may be buried (but not cremated) before the death is registered.

Funeral costs can normally be repaid out of the deceased's estate and will be given priority over any other claims. If the deceased has left a will it may contain directions concerning the funeral; however, these directions need not be followed by the executor.

The deceased's papers should also indicate whether a grave space had already been arranged. This information will be contained in a document known as a 'Deed of Grant'. Most town churchyards and many suburban churchyards are no longer open for burial because they are full. Most cemeteries are non-denominational and may be owned by local authorities or private companies; fees vary.

If the body is to be cremated, an application form, two cremation certificates (for which there is a charge) or a certificate for cremation if the death was referred to the coroner, and a certificate signed by the medical referee must be completed in addition to the certificate for burial or cremation (the form is not required if the coroner has issued a certificate for cremation). All the forms are available from the funeral director or crematorium. Most crematoria are run by local authorities; the fees usually include the medical referee's fee and the use of the chapel. Ashes may be scattered, buried in a churchyard or cemetery, or kept.

The registrar must be notified of the date, place and means of disposal of the body within 96 hours (England and Wales) or three days (Scotland).

If the death occurred abroad or on a foreign ship or aircraft, a local burial or cremation may be arranged. If the body is to be brought back to England or Wales, a death certificate from the relevant country or an authorisation for the removal of the body from the country of death from the coroner or relevant authority, together with a certificate of embalming, will be required. The British consulate can help to arrange this documentation. To arrange a funeral in England or Wales, an authenticated translation of a foreign death certificate or a death certificate issued in Scotland or Northern Ireland which must show the cause of death, is needed, together with a certificate of no liability to register from the registrar in England and Wales in whose sub-district it is intended to bury or cremate the body. If it is intended to cremate the body, a cremation order will be required from the Home Office or a certificate for cremation. If the body is to be cremated in Scotland, an order from the Scottish government Health Department must be obtained.

THE GENERAL REGISTER OFFICE, General Register Office, PO Box 2, Southport PR8 2JD **T** 0300-123 1837
W www.gro.gov.uk/gro/content/certificates
THE NATIONAL RECORDS OF SCOTLAND, New Register House, 3 West Register Street, Edinburgh EH1 3YT
T 0131-334 0380 **W** www.nrscotland.gov.uk

DIVORCE, DISSOLUTION AND RELATED MATTERS

Divorce is a legal process carried out by the civil courts to end a marriage, whilst dissolution is a similar process which ends a civil partnership. Divorce should be distinguished from judicial separation which is a court order confirming that the parties have separated but it does not legally dissolve the marriage/civil partnership. It is often applied for due to moral, religious or ethical grounds but it does allow for financial provision to be made as divorce does.

DIVORCE

The process for divorce begins with a petition and ends with what is known as a 'decree absolute' which dissolves the marriage.

The process begins with the lodging of a standard court form (known as an application for a matrimonial order) at any divorce county court or at the central family court in London. This must be accompanied by a court form outlining the current and proposed arrangements for any children of the family under 16 or between 16 and 18 and in full-time education.

An application for a matrimonial order for divorce may only be presented to the court after one year of marriage and it must be based on matters which occurred within that time. The spouse who lodges this document is known as the 'petitioner' throughout the divorce proceedings and the other spouse is the 'respondent'.

The issue of where the petitioner normally lives or the connections the parties have abroad may have to be considered by the court to determine whether a court has authority to deal with a particular divorce (whether the court has jurisdiction). These matters concern the law relating to domicile and habitual residence and can be complex. As of 21 June 2012, European Union regulation allows spouses of differing nationalities or residencies to choose which participating member state to file for divorce in. However, the UK and Ireland have elected not to participate and currently continue to apply their own national laws.

There is only one ground for divorce, namely that the marriage has broken down irretrievably. This ground must be 'proved' by one of the following facts:
- the respondent has committed adultery and the petitioner finds it intolerable to live with him/her
- the respondent has behaved in such a way that the petitioner cannot reasonably be expected to live with him/her
- the respondent has deserted the petitioner for a continuous period of at least two years
- the two spouses have lived apart for at least two years and the respondent agrees to a divorce
- the two spouses have lived apart for at least five years

If the court is satisfied that the petitioner has proved one of those facts then it must grant a decree nisi (see below) unless it is satisfied that the marriage has not broken down.

The procedure is more complex if the divorce is defended, although this is very rare.

DECREE NISI

If the judge is satisfied that the petitioner has proved the contents of the divorce petition, a date will be set for the pronouncement of the decree nisi in open court. The decree nisi is a preliminary decree of divorce which must be obtained but the marriage will not be legally dissolved until the decree absolute. Neither party needs to attend and all the proceedings up to this point are usually carried out on paper.

DECREE ABSOLUTE

The final step in the divorce procedure is to obtain a decree absolute which formally ends the marriage. The petitioner can apply for this six weeks and one day after the date of the decree nisi. If the petitioner does not apply the respondent can apply, but only after three months from the earliest date on which the petitioner could have applied.

A decree absolute will not normally be granted until the parties have agreed, or the court has dealt with, the parties' financial situation (see below for details of financial provision).

DISSOLUTION OF CIVIL PARTNERSHIPS

The legal process for dissolution of a civil partnership follows a model closely based on divorce. Irretrievable breakdown of the partnership is the sole ground for dissolution. The facts to be proved to establish this are the same as for divorce, with the exception of adultery which, due to its legal definition, can only apply to opposite sex couples. Adultery can, however, be used as an example of unreasonable behaviour.

FINANCIAL RELIEF ANCILLARY TO DIVORCE, NULLITY AND JUDICIAL SEPARATION

Following a petition for divorce, nullity or judicial separation, it is open to either spouse or former spouse to make a claim for financial provision provided they have not remarried. It is common practice for such an application to be made at the same time, or shortly after, a divorce petition has been issued. The courts have wide powers to make financial provision where a marriage breaks down. Orders can be made for:

- spousal maintenance (periodical payments) which can be capitalised into a lump sum
- lump sum payments
- adjustment or transfer of interests in property
- adjustment of interests in trusts and settlements
- orders relating to pensions

EXERCISE OF THE COURT'S POWERS TO ORDER FINANCIAL PROVISION

The court must exercise its powers so as to achieve an outcome which is fair between the parties, although it has a wide discretion in determining what is a fair financial outcome. It will consider the worldwide assets of both parties, whether liquid or illiquid. In exercising its discretion, the court has to consider a range of statutory factors including:

- the income, earning capacity, property and other financial resources which either party has or is likely to have in the foreseeable future
- the financial needs, obligations and responsibilities which each of the parties to the marriage has or is likely to have in the foreseeable future
- the standard of living enjoyed by the family
- the age of each party and the duration of the marriage
- any physical or mental disability of either party
- the contribution which each of the parties has made or is likely to make in the foreseeable future to the welfare of the family, including any contribution by looking after the home or caring for the family
- the conduct of parties
- loss of benefits

When considering the above factors, however, the court must give paramount consideration to the welfare of any child of the family.

The court has a wide discretion in considering these factors in order to achieve an outcome it considers to be fair. However, the court has emphasised that a 50:50 division of assets is frequently the correct result unless there are compelling reasons to the contrary. It is important to bear in mind that the House of Lords (now the supreme court) in White v White said that if each spouse contributed equally in their different sphere it does not matter in principle which of them earned the money and built up the assets. The contributions of the 'breadwinner' and 'homemaker' are considered equal.

In October 2010, the supreme court gave judgment in Radmacher v Granatino and made it clear that a person now entering into a pre-nuptial agreement will be considered to have intended to be held to that agreement. However, the court will still be able to decide as to whether the agreement is fair and whether it should govern all the financial results of divorce. The supreme court did not give clear guidelines on when a pre-nuptial agreement would be considered 'fair' and it is likely to depend on the facts of an individual case.

The Law Commission's Marital Property, Needs and Agreements project began in October 2009 and consultation papers were published in January 2011 and September 2012. The project examined the status and enforceability of agreements made between spouses or civil partners (or those contemplating marriage or civil partnership) concerning their property or finances and was completed in February 2014. The Law Commission proposed the introduction of 'qualifying nuptial agreements' which would be enforceable contracts allowing couples to make binding agreements concerning the financial consequences of divorce or dissolution. In order for an agreement to qualify, certain procedural safeguards would need to be met. Further, agreements could not be used by parties to contract out of meeting the financial needs of the other or of any children. The report is currently awaiting the government's response.

In *Miller v Miller* and *MacFarlane v MacFarlane*, the House of Lords said that fairness required the court to consider three strands:
- the needs of the parties going forwards
- compensation for any economic disparity between the parties (such as where one party has sacrificed their career to become a full-time parent)
- sharing

The court also has a duty to consider making an order which will settle once and for all the parties' financial responsibilities towards each other, known as a 'clean break'.

FINANCIAL PROVISION ON DISSOLUTION OF A CIVIL PARTNERSHIP

The Civil Partnership Act 2004 makes provisions for financial relief for civil partners generally and extends the same rights and responsibilities invoked by marriage. Again the court must consider a number of factors when exercising its discretion and must take into account all of the circumstances of the case while giving first consideration to the welfare of any child of the family who is under 18. The list of statutory factors the court must consider resemble those for marriage and it is likely that the interpretation of these factors will be based on the courts' interpretation of the factors relating to marriage.

COHABITING COUPLES

Rights of unmarried couples are not the same as for married couples. Agreements, whether express or inferred by conduct, often determine interest in money and property. Reliance upon inferences is problematic, therefore it is advisable to consider entering into a contract, or 'cohabitation agreement', which establishes how money and property should be divided in the event of a relationship breakdown.

This area of law is still developing. In July 2007, the Law Commission published its report to parliament, recommending a scheme to provide remedies for eligible candidates. The cohabitation bill was subsequently introduced to the House of Lords in December 2008 and in March 2009, a parallel bill, the cohabitation (no. 2) bill, was introduced to the Commons. On 6 September 2011, parliament announced that it had reviewed the Law Commission's report and would not be reforming co-habitation law in this term. The cohabitation rights bill 2013–14, which sought to introduce certain protections for cohabitees during their lifetime and on death, was introduced in October 2013 but will progress no further. In the meantime, cohabitation agreements continue to be governed by the general principles of contract law.

FINANCIAL PROVISION FOR CHILDREN

All parents are under a legal obligation to support their children financially and the parent who does not have day-to-day care of the child (the 'paying parent') pays child maintenance to the parent who does have main day-to-day care (the 'receiving parent'). In some cases, this person can be a grandparent or guardian.

Parents can arrange child maintenance themselves, ie a family-based arrangement, or through the Child Support Agency (CSA) or the Child Maintenance Service (CMS); together these organisations are known as the 'statutory child maintenance services'. When applying for the statutory maintenance service, the applicant will be told whether the CSA or CMS will manage their case, depending on the applicant's circumstances.

Statutory arrangements through the CSA or CMS include:
- 'Direct Pay' (known as 'Maintenance Direct' under a CSA arrangement) which enables parents to keep control of making and receiving payments. The statutory service works out the payment amounts for parents but will not be involved in other areas, such as collection and enforcement
- 'Collect and Pay' (known as the 'calculation and collection services' under a CSA arrangement) whereby the CSA or CMS calculates how much maintenance the paying parent owes. If payments aren't made on time, a range of enforcement actions can be taken

The CSA will only assess a maximum gross weekly income of the paying parent of £3,000. If the paying parent's net weekly income exceeds £3,000, the receiving parent can apply to the court for extra top-up maintenance. The CMS currently only takes applications if the paying and receiving parents have four or more children together and the CMS assesses the paying parent's gross annual income.

Within 72 hours of a payment being missed, the CMS will contact the paying parent to seek continuing payments. Where there is persistent non-payment, the CMS is able to take money directly from the paying parent, either from their earnings or bank account, or to take court action.

Provision is also made under Schedule 1 of the Children Act 1989 for unmarried parents to apply to the court for lump sum and property adjustment orders and, in limited circumstances, orders for child maintenance.

SCOTLAND

Although some provisions are similar to those for England and Wales, there is separate legislation for Scotland covering nullity of marriage, judicial separation, divorce and ancillary matters. The principal legislation in relation to family law in Scotland is the Family Law (Scotland) Act 1985. The Family Law (Scotland) Act 2006 came in to force on 4 May 2006, and introduced reforms to various aspects of Scottish family law. The following is confined to major points on which the law in Scotland differs from that of England and Wales.

An action for judicial separation or divorce may be raised in the court of session; it may also be raised in the sheriff court if either party was resident in the sheriffdom for 40 days immediately before the date of the action or for 40 days ending not more than 40 days before the date of the action and has no known residence in Scotland at that date. The fee for starting a divorce petition in the sheriff court is £141.

The grounds for raising an action of divorce in Scotland are set down in The Divorce (Scotland) Act 1976 and have been subject to reform in terms of the 2006 act. The current grounds for divorce are:
- the defender has committed adultery. When adultery is cited as proof that the marriage has broken down irretrievably, it is not necessary in Scotland to prove that it is also intolerable for the pursuer to live with the defender
- the defender's behaviour is such that the pursuer cannot reasonably be expected to cohabit with the defender
- there has been no cohabitation between the parties for one year prior to the raising of the action for divorce, and the defender consents to the granting of decree of divorce
- there has been no cohabitation between the parties for two years prior to the raising of the action for divorce
- an interim gender recognition certificate under the Gender Recognition Act 2004 has, after the date of marriage, been issued to either party to the marriage. Once the Marriage and Civil Partnership (Scotland) Act 2014 is in force, this ground of divorce will sometimes not be available where a full gender recognition certificate has been issued under the 2004 Act.

The previously available ground of desertion was abolished by the 2006 Act.

A simplified procedure for 'do-it-yourself divorce' was introduced in 1983 for certain divorces. If the action is based on one or two years' separation and will not be opposed or because a gender recognition certificate has been issued; there are no children under 16; no financial claims; there is no sign that the applicant's spouse is unable to manage his or her affairs through mental illness or handicap; and there are no other court proceedings underway which might result in the end of the marriage, the applicant can access the appropriate forms to enable him or her to proceed on the Scottish Courts website. The fee is £107 as at 1 April 2014, however the applicant may be exempt from paying the fee if they are in receipt of certain benefits; or if legal advice and assistance is being provided by a solicitor in terms of the Legal Aid (Scotland) Act 1986.

Where a divorce action has been raised, it may be put on hold for a variety of reasons. In all actions for divorce an extract decree, which brings the marriage to an end, will be made available 14 days after the divorce has been granted. Unlike in England, there is no decree nisi, only a final decree of divorce. Parties must ensure that all financial issues have been resolved prior to divorce, as it is not possible to seek further financial provision after divorce has been granted.

FINANCIAL PROVISION

In relation to financial provision on divorce, the first, and most important, principle is fair sharing of the matrimonial property. There is a presumption that fair share means an equal share of the matrimonial property, which can be departed from if justified by special circumstances. In terms of Scots law matrimonial property is defined as all property acquired by either spouse from the date of marriage up to the date of separation. Property acquired before the marriage is not deemed to be matrimonial unless it was acquired for use by the parties as a family home or as furniture for that home. Property acquired after the date of separation is not matrimonial property. Any property acquired by either of the parties by way of gift or inheritance during the marriage is excluded and does not form part of the matrimonial property.

When considering whether to make an award of financial provision a court shall also take account of any economic advantage derived by either party to the marriage as a result of contributions, financial or otherwise, by the other, and of any economic disadvantage suffered by either party for the benefit of the other party. The court must also ensure that the economic burden of caring for a child under the age of 16 is shared fairly between the parties.

A court can also consider making an order requiring one party to pay the other party a periodical allowance for a certain period of time following divorce. Such an order may be appropriate in cases where there is insufficient capital to effect a fair sharing of the matrimonial property. Orders for periodical allowance are uncommon, as courts will favour a 'clean break' where possible.

CHILDREN

The court has the power to award a residence order in respect of any children of the marriage or to make an order regulating the child's contact with the non-resident parent. The court will only make such orders if it is deemed better for the child to do so than to make no order at all, and the welfare of the children is of paramount importance. The fact that a spouse has caused the breakdown of the marriage does not in itself preclude him/her from being awarded residence.

NULLITY

An action for 'declaration of nullity' can be brought if someone with a legitimate interest is able to show that the marriage is void or voidable. The action can only be brought in the court of session. Although the grounds on which a marriage may be void or voidable are similar to those on

which a marriage can be declared invalid in England, there are some differences. Where a spouse is capable of sexual intercourse but refuses to consummate the marriage, this is not a ground for nullity in Scots law, though it could be a ground for divorce. Where a spouse was suffering from venereal disease at the time of marriage and the other spouse did not know, this is not a ground for nullity in Scots law, neither is the fact that a wife was pregnant by another man at the time of marriage without the knowledge of her husband.

COHABITING COUPLES

The law in Scotland now provides certain financial and property rights for cohabiting couples in terms of the Family Law (Scotland) Act 2006, or 'the 2006 Act'. The relevant 2006 Act provisions do not place cohabitants in Scotland on an equal footing with married couples or civil partners, but provide some rights for cohabitants in the event that the relationship is terminated by separation or death. The provisions relate to couples who cease to cohabit after 4 May 2006.

The legislation provides for a presumption that most contents of the home shared by the cohabitants are owned in equal shares. A former cohabitant can also seek financial provision on termination of the relationship in the form of a capital payment if they can successfully demonstrate that they have been financially disadvantaged, and that conversely the other cohabitant has been financially advantaged, as a consequence of contributions made (financial or otherwise). An order can also be made in respect of the economic burden of caring for a child of whom the cohabitants are the parents. Such a claim must be made no later than one year after the day on which the cohabitants cease to cohabit.

The 2006 Act also provides that a cohabitant may make a claim on their partner's estate in the event of that partner's death, providing that there is no will. A claim of this nature must be made no later than six months after the date of the partner's death.

THE CENTRAL FAMILY COURT, First Avenue House,
42–49 High Holborn, London WC1 6NP T 0207-421 8594
THE COURT OF SESSION, Parliament House,
Parliament Square, Edinburgh EH1 1RQ T 0131-225 2595
W www.scotcourts.gov.uk
THE CHILD SUPPORT AGENCY, T 0345-713 3133
W www.csa.gov.uk

EMPLOYMENT LAW

EMPLOYEES

A fundamental distinction in UK employment law is that drawn between an employee and someone who is self-employed. Further, there is an important, intermediate category introduced by legislation: 'workers' covers all employees but also catches others who do not have full employment status. An 'employee' is someone who has entered into or works under a contract of employment, while a 'worker' has entered into or works under a contract whereby he undertakes to do or perform personally any work or services for another party whose status is not that of a client or customer. Whether or not someone is an employee or a worker as opposed to being genuinely self-employed is an important and complex question, for it determines that person's statutory rights and protections. For certain purposes, such as protection against discrimination, protection extends to some genuinely self-employed people as well as workers and employees.

The greater the level of control that the employer has over the work carried out, the greater the depth of integration of the employee in the employer's business, and the closer the obligations to provide and perform work between the parties, the more likely it is that the parties will be employer and employee.

PAY AND CONDITIONS

The Employment Rights Act 1996 consolidated the statutory provisions relating to employees' rights. Employers must give each employee employed for one month or more a written statement containing the following information:

- names of employer and employee
- date when employment began and the date on which the employee's period of *continuous* employment began (taking into account any employment with a previous employer which counts towards that period)
- the scale, rate or other method of calculating remuneration and intervals at which it will be paid
- job title or description of job
- hours and the permitted place(s) of work and, where there are several such places, the address of the employer
- holiday entitlement and holiday pay
- provisions concerning incapacity for work due to sickness and injury, including provisions for sick pay
- details of pension scheme(s)
- length of notice the employee is obliged to give and entitled to receive in order to terminate the contract of employment
- length of notice period that employer and employee need to give to terminate employment
- if the employment is not intended to be permanent, the period for which it is expected to continue or, if it is for a fixed term, the end date of the contract
- details of any collective agreement (including the parties to the agreement) which directly affects the terms of employment
- details of disciplinary and grievance procedures (including the individual to whom a complaint should be made and the process of making that complaint)
- if the employee is to work outside the UK for more than one month, the period of such work and the currency in which payment is made and any additional remuneration or benefits payable to them
- a note stating whether a contracting-out certificate is in force

This must be given to the employee within two months of the start of their employment.

If the employer does not provide the written statement within two months (or a statement of any changes to these particulars within one month of the changes being made) then the employee can complain to an employment tribunal, which can specify the information that the employer should have given. When, in the context of an employee's successful tribunal claim, the employer is also found to have been in breach of the duty to provide the written statement at the time proceedings were commenced, the tribunal must award the employee two weeks' pay, and may award four weeks' pay, subject to the statutory cap, unless it would be unjust or inequitable to do so.

The Working Time Regulations 1998, the National Minimum Wage Act 1998, Employment Relations Act 1999, the Employment Act 2002 and the Employment Act 2008 now supplement the 1996 act.

FLEXIBLE WORKING

The Employment Act 2002 (and regulations made under it) gives employees who are responsible for the upbringing of a child, under the age of 17 (or under the age of 18 in the case of a disabled child), the right to apply for flexible working for the purpose of caring for that child. The right has been extended to carers of adults. Whether an employee has this right depends on both the employee and the child/adult

cared for meeting a number of criteria. If an application under the act is not dealt with in accordance with a prescribed procedure, or is rejected on other than specific grounds, the employee may complain to an employment tribunal.

SICK PAY

Employees absent from work through illness or injury are entitled to receive Statutory Sick Pay (SSP) from the employer from the fourth day of absence for a maximum period of 28 weeks in any three-year period.

MATERNITY AND PARENTAL RIGHTS

Under the Employment Relations Act 1999, the Employment Act 2002, the Maternity and Parental Leave Regulations 1999 (as amended in 2002 and 2006), the Paternity and Adoption Leave Regulations 2002 and 2003 and the Additional Paternity Leave Regulations 2010, both men and women are entitled to take leave when they become a parent (including by adoption). Women are protected from discrimination, detriment or dismissal by reason of their pregnancy or maternity, including discrimination by association and by perception. Men and adoptive parents are protected from suffering a detriment or dismissal for taking paternity, adoption or parental leave.

Any woman who needs to attend an antenatal appointment on the advice of a registered medical professional is entitled to paid leave from work to attend. All pregnant women are entitled to a maximum period of maternity leave of 52 weeks. This comprises 26 weeks' ordinary maternity leave, followed immediately by 26 weeks' additional maternity leave. A woman who takes ordinary maternity leave normally has the right to return to the job in which she was employed before her absence. If she takes additional maternity leave, she is entitled to return to the same job or, if that is not reasonably practicable, to another job that is suitable and appropriate for her to do. There is a two-week period of compulsory maternity leave, immediately following the birth of the child, wherein the employer is not permitted to allow the mother to work.

A woman will qualify for Statutory Maternity Pay (SMP), which is payable for up to 39 weeks, if she has been continuously employed for not less than 26 weeks prior to the 15th week before the expected week of childbirth. For further information *see* Social Welfare, Employer Payments.

Employees are entitled to adoption leave and adoption pay (at the same rates as SMP) subject to fulfilment of similar criteria to those in relation to maternity leave and pay, but note that there is a 26-week qualifying period for adoption leave. Where a couple is adopting a child, either one (but not both) of the parents may take adoption leave, and the other may take paternity leave.

Certain employees are entitled to paternity leave on the birth or adoption of a child. To be eligible, the employee must be the child's father, or the partner of the mother or adopter, and meet other conditions. These conditions are, firstly, that they must have been continuously employed for not less than 26 weeks prior to the 15th week before the expected week of childbirth (or, in the case of adoptions, 26 weeks ending with the week in which notification of the adoption match is given) and, secondly, that the employee must have or expect to have responsibility for the upbringing of the child. The employee may take either one week's leave, or two consecutive weeks' leave. This leave may be taken at any time between the date of the child's birth (or placement for adoption) and 56 days later. A statutory payment is available during this period.

For births and adoptions from 3 April 2011, an eligible employee has been able to take additional paternity leave at the end of the mother's or adopter's leave period provided the child is at least 20 weeks old or was placed for adoption at least 20 weeks previously. The maximum period of leave is 26 weeks and leave cannot extend beyond the child's first birthday.

For more information *see* Social Welfare, Employer Payments.

Any employee with one year's service who has, or expects to have, responsibility for a child may take parental leave to care for the child. Each parent is entitled to a total of 13 weeks parental leave for each of their children (or 18 weeks if the child is disabled). This leave must be taken (at the rate of no more than four weeks a year, and in blocks of whole weeks only) before the child's fifth birthday (18th birthday if the child is disabled) or before the fifth anniversary of the date of placement of an adopted child.

SUNDAY TRADING

The Sunday Trading Act 1994 allows shops to open on Sunday. The Employment Rights Act 1996 gives shop workers and betting workers the right not to be dismissed, selected for redundancy or to suffer any detriment (such as the denial of overtime, promotion or training) if they refuse to work on Sundays. This does not apply to those who, under their contracts, are employed to work on Sundays.

TERMINATION OF EMPLOYMENT

An employee may be dismissed without notice if guilty of gross misconduct but in other cases a period of notice must be given by the employer. The minimum periods of notice specified in the Employment Rights Act 1996 are:

- one week if the employee has been continuously employed for one month or more but for less than two years
- one week for each complete year of continuous employment, if the employee has been employed for two years or more, up to a maximum of 12 weeks' notice
- longer periods apply if these are specified in the contract of employment

If an employee is dismissed with less notice than he/she is entitled to by statute, or under their contract if longer, he/she will have a wrongful dismissal claim (unless the employer paid the employee in lieu of notice in accordance with a contractual provision entitling it to do so). This claim for wrongful dismissal can be brought by the employee either in the civil courts or the employment tribunal, but if brought in the tribunal the maximum amount that can be awarded is £25,000.

REDUNDANCY

An employee dismissed because of redundancy may be entitled to redundancy pay. This applies if:

- the employment commenced before 6 April 2012 and the employee has at least one year's continuous service or the employment commenced on or after 6 April 2012 and the employee has at least two years' continuous service
- the employee is dismissed by the employer (this can include cases of voluntary redundancy)

Redundancy can mean closure of the entire business, closure of a particular site of the business, or a reduction in the need for employees to carry out work of a particular kind.

An employee may not be entitled to a redundancy payment if offered a suitable alternative job by the same employer. The amount of statutory redundancy pay depends on the length of service, age, and their earnings, subject to a weekly maximum of (currently) £464. The maximum payment that can be awarded is £13,500. The redundancy payment is guaranteed by the government in cases where the employer becomes insolvent.

UNFAIR DISMISSAL

Complaints of unfair dismissal are dealt with by an employment tribunal. Any employee whose employment commenced before 6 April 2012 with at least one year's continuous service or any employee whose employment commenced on or after 6 April 2012 with at least two year's continuous service (subject to exceptions, including in relation to whistleblowers – *see* below) can make a complaint to the tribunal. At the tribunal, it is for the employee to show that the employer dismissed them either expressly or constructively and it is for the employer to prove that the dismissal was due to one or more potentially fair reasons: a statutory restriction preventing the continuation of the employee's contract; the employee's capability or qualifications for the job he/she was employed to do; the employee's conduct; redundancy; or some other substantial reason.

If the employer succeeds in showing this, the tribunal must then decide whether the employer acted reasonably in dismissing the employee for that reason. If the employee is found to have been unfairly dismissed, the tribunal can order that he/she be reinstated, re-engaged or compensated. Any person believing that they may have been unfairly dismissed should contact their local Citizens Advice bureau or seek legal advice. A claim must be brought within three months of the date of effective termination of employment.

The normal maximum compensatory award for unfair dismissal is £76,574 (as at April 2014). If the dismissal occurred after 6 April 2009 and the employer unreasonably failed to follow the ACAS Code of Practice on Disciplinary and Grievance Procedures in carrying out the dismissal, the tribunal may increase the employee's compensation by up to 25 per cent.

WHISTLEBLOWING

Under the whistleblowing legislation (Public Interest Disclosure Act 1998, which inserted provisions into the Employment Rights Act 1996) dismissal of an employee is automatically unfair if the reason or principal reason for the dismissal is that the employee has made a protected disclosure. The legislation also makes it unlawful to subject workers (a broad category that includes employees and certain other individuals, such as agency workers) who have made a protected disclosure to any detriment on the ground that they have done so.

For a disclosure to qualify for protection, the claimant must show that he or she has disclosed information, which in his or her reasonable belief tends to show one or more of the following six categories of wrongdoing: criminal offences; breach of any legal obligation; miscarriages of justice; danger to the health and safety of any individual; damage to the environment; or the deliberate concealing of information about any of the other categories. The malpractices can be past, present, prospective or merely alleged.

A qualifying disclosure will only be protected if the manner of the disclosure fulfils certain conditions, which varies according to the type of disclosure. With effect from 25 June 2013, there is no requirement for the disclosure to have been made in 'good faith', although where it appears to the tribunal that the protected disclosure was not made in good faith, the tribunal may reduce any compensatory award it makes by up to 25 per cent if it considers that it is just and equitable to do so in all the circumstances.

Any whistleblower claim in the employment tribunal must normally be brought within three months of the date of dismissal or other act leading to a detriment.

An individual does not need to have been working with the employer for any particular period of time to be able to bring such a claim and compensation is uncapped (and can include an amount for injury to feelings).

DISCRIMINATION

Discrimination in employment on the grounds of sex (including gender reassignment), sexual orientation, being pregnant or on maternity leave, race, colour, nationality, ethnic or national origins, religion or belief, marital or civil partnership status, age or disability is unlawful. Discrimination legislation generally covers direct discrimination, indirect discrimination, harassment and victimisation. Only in limited circumstances can such discrimination be justified (rendering it lawful).

An individual does not need to be employed for any particular period of time to be able to claim discrimination (discrimination can be alleged at the recruitment phase), and discrimination compensation is uncapped (and can include an amount for injury to feelings). These features distinguish the discrimination laws from, for example, the unfair dismissal laws.

The Equality Act 2010 was passed on 8 April 2010 and the main provisions came into force on 1 October 2010. The Act unifies several pieces of discrimination legislation, providing one definition of direct discrimination, indirect discrimination, harassment and victimisation. The Equality Act applies to those employed in Great Britain but not to employees in Northern Ireland or (subject to EC exceptions) to those who work mainly abroad, and provides that:

- it is unlawful to discriminate on the grounds of sex, gender reassignment or marital/civil partner status, being pregnant or on maternity leave, including discrimination by association and by perception. This covers all aspects of employment (including advertising for jobs), but there are some limited exceptions, such as where the essential nature of the job requires it to be given to someone of a particular sex, or where decency and privacy requires it. The act entitles men and women to equality of remuneration for equivalent work or work of the same value
- individuals have the right not to be discriminated against on the grounds of race, colour, nationality, or ethnic or national origins and this applies to all aspects of employment. Employers may also take lawful positive action, including in relation to recruitment and promotion
- discrimination against a disabled person in all aspects of employment is unlawful. This includes protecting carers from discrimination by association with the disabled persons that they look after. In certain circumstances, the employer may show that the less favourable treatment is justified and so does not constitute discrimination. The act also imposes a duty on employers to make 'reasonable adjustments' to the arrangements and physical features of the workplace if these place disabled people at a substantial disadvantage compared with those who are not disabled. The definition of a 'disabled person' is wide and includes people diagnosed with HIV, cancer and multiple sclerosis
- discrimination against a person on the grounds of religion or belief (or lack of belief) including discrimination by association and by perception, in all aspects of employment, is unlawful
- discrimination against an individual on the grounds of sexual orientation, including discrimination by association and by perception, in all aspects of employment, is unlawful
- age discrimination in the workplace is unlawful, and an employer may no longer dismiss an employee by reason of retirement once they have reached a certain age. However, it is lawful to discriminate because of age in relation to benefits based on length of service, redundancy pay, national minimum wage and insurance benefits.

The responsibility for monitoring equality in society rests with the Equality and Human Rights Commission.

In Northern Ireland similar provisions exist to those that were in force in Great Britain prior to the coming into force of the Equality Act but are contained in separate legislation (although the Disability Discrimination Act does extend to Northern Ireland).

In Northern Ireland there is one combined body working towards equality and eliminating discrimination, the Equality Commission for Northern Ireland.

WORKING TIME

The Working Time Regulations 1998 impose rules that limit working hours and provide for rest breaks and holidays. The regulations apply to workers and so cover not only employees but also other individuals who undertake to perform personally any work or services (eg freelancers). The regulations are complex and subject to various exceptions and qualifications but the basic provisions relating to adult day workers are as follows:

- No worker is permitted to work more than an average of 48 hours per week (unless they have made a genuine voluntary opt-out of this limit – it is not sufficient to make it a term of the contract that the worker opts out), and a worker is entitled to, but is not required to take, the following breaks:
- 11 consecutive hours' uninterrupted rest in every 24-hour period
- an uninterrupted rest period of 24 hours in each 7-day period or 48 hours in each fortnight (in addition to the daily rest period)
- 20 minutes' rest break provided that the working day is longer than 6 hours
- 5.6 weeks' paid annual leave (28 days full-time). This equates to 4 weeks plus public holidays

There are specific provisions relating to night work, young workers (ie those over school leaving age but under 18) and a variety of workers in specialised sectors (such as off-shore oil rig workers).

HUMAN RIGHTS

On 2 October 2000 the Human Rights Act 1998 came into force. This act incorporates the European Convention on Human Rights into the law of the UK. The main principles of the act are as follows:

- all legislation must be interpreted and given effect by the courts as compatible with the Convention so far as it is possible to do so. Before the second reading of a new bill the minister responsible for the bill must provide a statement regarding its compatibility with the Human Rights Act
- subordinate legislation (eg statutory instruments) which is incompatible with the Convention can be struck down by the courts
- primary legislation (eg an act of parliament) which is incompatible with the Convention cannot be struck down by a court, but the higher courts can make a declaration of incompatibility which is a signal to parliament to change the law
- all public authorities (including courts and tribunals) must not act in a way which is incompatible with the Convention
- individuals whose Convention rights have been infringed by a public authority may bring proceedings against that authority, but the act is not intended to create new rights as between individuals

The main human rights protected by the Convention are the right to life (article 2); protection from torture and inhuman or degrading treatment (article 3); protection from slavery or forced labour (article 4); the right to liberty and security of the person (article 5); the right to a fair trial (article 6); the right not to be subject to retrospective criminal offences (article 7); the right to respect for private and family life (article 8); freedom of thought, conscience and religion (article 9); freedom of expression (article 10); freedom of peaceful association and assembly (article 11); the right to marry and found a family (article 12); protection from discrimination (article 14); the right to property (article 1 protocol No.1); the right to education (article 2 protocol No.1); and the right to free elections (article 3 protocol No.1). Most of the Convention rights are subject to limitations which deem the breach of the right acceptable on the basis it is 'necessary in a democratic society'.

Human rights are also enshrined in the common law (of tort). Although this is of historical significance, the common law (for example the duty of confidentiality) remains especially important regarding violations of human rights that occur between private parties, where the Human Rights Act 1998 does not apply.

PARENTAL RESPONSIBILITY

The Children Act 1989 gives both the mother and father parental responsibility for the child if the parents are married to each other at the time of the child's birth. If the parents are not married, only the mother has parental responsibility. The father may acquire it in accordance with the provisions of section 4 of the Children Act 1989. He can do this in one of four ways: a) by being registered as the father on the child's birth certificate with the consent of the mother (only for fathers of children born after 1 December 2003, following changes to the Adoption and Children Act 2002); b) by applying to the court for a parental responsibility order; c) by entering into a parental responsibility agreement with the mother which must be in the prescribed form; or d) by obtaining a residence order from the court. Otherwise, a father can gain parental responsibility by marrying the mother of the child.

Where a child's parent, who has parental responsibility, marries or enters into a civil partnership with a person who is not the child's parent, the child's parent(s) with parental responsibility can agree for the step-parent to have parental responsibility, or the step-parent may acquire parental responsibility by order of the court (section 4A(1) Children Act 1989).

Where a child is adopted, parental responsibility will be given to the adopter of the child. However, before an order for adoption can be made, the court must be satisfied that every parent or guardian consents. The consent of a father without parental responsibility is not required, although adoption agencies and local authorities must be careful to establish, if possible, the identity of the father and satisfy themselves that any person claiming to be the father either has no intention to apply for parental responsibility or that if he did apply, the application would be likely to be refused.

In Scotland, the relevant legislation is the Children (Scotland) Act 1995, which gives the mother parental rights and responsibilities for her child whether or not she is married to the child's father. A father who is married to the mother, either at the time of the child's conception or subsequently, will also have automatic parental rights and responsibilities. Section 23 of the 2006 act provides that an unmarried father will obtain automatic parental responsibilities and rights if he is registered as the father on the child's birth certificate. For unmarried fathers who are not named on the birth certificate, or whose children were born before the 2006 act came into force, it is possible to acquire parental responsibilities and rights by applying to the court or by entering into a parental responsibilities and rights

agreement with the mother. The father of any child, regardless of parental rights, has a duty to aliment that child until he/she is 18 (or under 25 if the child is still at an educational establishment or training for employment or for a trade, profession or vocation).

LEGITIMATION

Under the Legitimacy Act 1976, an illegitimate person automatically becomes legitimate when his/her parents marry. This applies even where one of the parents was married to a third person at the time of the birth. In such cases it is necessary to re-register the birth of the child. In Scotland, the status of illegitimacy has been abolished by section 21 of the 2006 act. The Law Reform Act 1987 reformed the law so as to remove so far as possible the legal disadvantages of illegitimacy.

JURY SERVICE

In England and Wales, the law concerning juries is largely consolidated in the Juries Act 1974. In England and Wales, a person charged with a serious criminal offence is entitled to have their trial heard by a jury in a crown court, except in cases where there is a danger of jury tampering or where jury tampering has taken place.

In civil cases, there is a right to a jury in the Queen's Bench Division of the high court in cases where the person applying for a jury has been accused of fraud, as well as in cases of malicious prosecution or false imprisonment. The same applies to the county court. In all other cases in the Queen's Bench Division only the judge has discretion to order trial with a jury, though such an order is seldom made. In the chancery division of the high court a jury is never used. The same is true in the family division of the high court.

No right to a jury trial exists in Scotland, although more serious offences are heard before a jury. In England and Wales criminal cases and civil cases in the high court are generally heard by a jury of 12 members, but in the county court the jury is smaller, normally consisting of eight members. In the event that a juror is excused the trial can proceed so long as there are at least seven remaining jurors in the county court and nine in the case of the high court or crown court. At an inquest, there must be at least seven and no more than 11 members. In Scotland there are 12 members of a jury in a civil case in the court of session, and 15 in a criminal trial in the high court of justiciary. Jurors are normally asked to serve for ten working days, during which time they could sit on more than one case. Jurors selected for longer cases are expected to sit for the duration of the trial.

In England and Wales, every 'registered' parliamentary or local government elector between the ages of 18 and 70 who has lived in the UK (including, for this purpose, the Channel Islands and the Isle of Man) for any period of at least five years since reaching the age of 13 is qualified to serve on a jury unless he/she is 'mentally disordered' or disqualified. Those disqualified from jury service include:

- those who have at any time been sentenced by a court in the UK (including, for this purpose, the Channel Islands and the Isle of Man) to a term of imprisonment or youth custody of five years or more
- those who have been imprisoned for life, detained at Her Majesty's, or the Secretary of State's pleasure, detained for a period of at least five years, imprisoned or detained for public protection, or received an 'extended sentence' under the relevant provisions of the Criminal Justice Act 2003 or the Criminal Procedure (Scotland) Act 1995
- those who have within the previous ten years served any part of a sentence of imprisonment, youth custody or

detention, been detained in a young offenders' institution, received a suspended sentence of imprisonment or order for detention, or received a community order
• those who are on bail in criminal proceedings

The court has the discretion to excuse a juror from service, or defer the date of service, if the juror can show there is good reason why he/she should be excused from attending or good reason why his/her attendance should be deferred. It is an offence (punishable by a fine) to fail to attend when summoned, to serve knowing that you are disqualified from service, or to make false representations in an attempt to evade service. If a juror fails to turn up for service, or attends but cannot serve due to being under the influence of drink or drugs, this is punishable as contempt of court. Any party can object to any juror if he/she can show cause to the trial judge.

It may be appropriate for a judge to excuse a juror from a particular case if he is personally concerned in the facts of the particular case, or closely connected with a party to the proceedings or with a prospective witness. The judge may also discharge any juror who, from a mental or physical incapacity, temporary or permanent, or alternatively due to linguistic difficulties, cannot pay proper attention to the evidence.

An individual juror (or the entire jury) can be discharged if it is shown that they or any of their number have, among other things, separated from the rest of the jury without the leave of the court; talked to any person out of court who is not a member of the jury; determined the verdict of the trial by drawing lots; come to a compromise on the verdict; been drunk, or otherwise incapacitated, while carrying out their duties as a juror; exerted improper pressure on the other members of the jury (eg harassment or bullying); declined to take part in the jury's functions; displayed actual or apparent bias (eg racism, sexism or other discriminatory or deliberate hostility); or inadvertently possessed knowledge of the bad character of a party to the proceedings which has not been adduced as evidence in the proceedings. The factual situations that arise are many, and include falling asleep during the trial, asking friends on Facebook for help in making a decision, consulting an ouija board in the course of deliberations, making telephone calls after retirement, and lunching with a barrister not connected with the proceedings.

In England and Wales, the jury's verdict need not be unanimous. In criminal proceedings, and civil proceedings in the high court, the agreement of 10 jurors will suffice when there are not fewer than 11 people on the jury (or 9 in a jury of 10). In civil proceedings in the county court the agreement of seven or eight jurors will suffice. Where a majority verdict is given, the court must be satisfied that the jury had reasonable time to consider its verdict based on the nature and complexity of the case. In criminal proceedings this must be no less than two hours and ten minutes (allowing time for the jury to settle after retiring).

A juror is immune from prosecution or civil claim in respect of anything said or done by him or her in the discharge of their office. It is a contempt of court for a juror to disclose what happened in the jury room even after the trial is over. A juror may claim travelling expenses, a subsistence allowance and an allowance for other financial loss (eg loss of earnings or benefits, fees paid to carers or child-minders) up to a stated limit. For more information on jury service, visit W www.gov.uk/jury-service/overview

SCOTLAND

Qualification criteria for jury service in Scotland are similar to those in England and Wales, except that members of the judiciary are ineligible for ten years after ceasing to hold

their post, and others concerned with the administration of justice are only eligible for service five years after ceasing to hold office. Certain persons have the right to apply to be excused – full-time members of the medical, dental, nursing, veterinary and pharmaceutical professions, full-time members of the armed forces, ministers of religion, persons who have served on a jury within the previous five years, members of the Scottish parliament, members of the Scottish government, junior Scottish ministers and those aged 71 years or over. Those who are incapable by reason of a mental disorder may also be excused. Such an application will be accepted if the application is made within 7 days of the person being notified that they may have to serve. For civil trials there is an age limit of 65 years. Those convicted of a crime and sentenced to a period of imprisonment of 5 years or more are automatically disqualified. The maximum fine for a person serving on a jury while knowing himself/herself to be ineligible is £1,000. The maximum fine for failing to attend without good cause in criminal trials is also £1,000, however in civil proceedings the maximum fine is £200.

HER MAJESTY'S COURTS AND TRIBUNALS SERVICE,
102 Petty France, London SW1H 9AJ T 0845-456 8770
JURY CENTRAL SUMMONING BUREAU,
Freepost LON 19669, Pocock Street, London SE1 0YG
T 0845-803 8003 E jurysummoning@hmcts.gsi.gov.uk
SCOTTISH COURTS SERVICE, Saughton House,
Broomhouse Drive, Edinburgh EH11 3XD T 0131-444 3300
W www.scotcourts.gov.uk
THE CLERK OF JUSTICIARY, High Court of Justiciary,
Lawnmarket, Edinburgh EH2 2NS T 0131-240 6900

LANDLORD AND TENANT

RESIDENTIAL LETTINGS
The provisions outlined here apply only where the tenant lives in a separate dwelling from the landlord and where the dwelling is the tenant's only or main home. It does not apply to licensees such as lodgers, guests or service occupiers.

The 1996 Housing Act radically changed certain aspects of the legislation referred to below; in particular, the grant of assured and assured shorthold tenancies under the Housing Act 1988.

ASSURED SHORTHOLD TENANCIES
If a tenancy was granted on or after 15 January 1989 and before 28 February 1997, the tenant would have an assured tenancy unless the landlord served notice under section 20 in the prescribed form prior to the commencement of the tenancy, stating that the tenancy is to be an assured shorthold tenancy and the tenancy is for a minimum fixed term period of six months (see below). An assured tenancy gives that tenant greater security. The tenant could, for example, stay in possession of the dwelling for as long as the tenant observed the terms of the tenancy. The landlord cannot obtain possession from such a tenant unless the landlord can establish a specific ground for possession (set out in the Housing Act 1988) and obtains a court order. The rent payable is that agreed with the landlord at the start of the tenancy. The landlord has the right to increase the rent annually by serving a notice. If that happens the tenant can apply to have the rent fixed by the rent assessment committee of the local authority. The tenant or the landlord may request that the committee sets the rent in line with open market rents for that type of property.

Under the Housing Act 1996, all new lettings (below an annual rent threshold of £100,000 since October 2010) entered into on or after 28 February 1997 (for whatever term) will be assured shorthold tenancies unless the landlord serves a notice stating that the tenancy is not to be an assured shorthold tenancy. This means that the landlord is entitled to possession at the end of the tenancy provided he serves a notice under section 21 Housing Act 1988 and commences the proceedings in accordance with the correct procedure. The landlord must obtain a court order, however, to obtain possession if the tenant refuses to vacate at the end of the tenancy. If the tenancy is an assured shorthold tenancy, the court must grant the order. For both assured and assured shorthold tenancies, if the tenant is more than eight weeks in arrears, the landlord can serve notice and, if the tenant is still in arrears at the date of the hearing, the court must make an order for possession.

REGULATED TENANCIES
Before the Housing Act 1988 came into force on 15 January 1989 there were regulated tenancies; some are still in existence and are protected by the Rent Act 1977. Under this act it is possible for the landlord or the tenant to apply to the local rent officer to have a 'fair' rent registered. The fair rent is then the maximum rent payable.

SECURE TENANCIES
Secure tenancies are generally given to tenants of local authorities, housing associations (before 15 January 1989) and certain other bodies. This gives the tenant security of tenure unless the terms of the agreement are broken by the tenant and it is reasonable to make an order for possession. Those with secure tenancies may have the right to buy their property. In practice this right is generally only available to council tenants.

The Prevention of Social Housing Fraud Act came into force in October 2013. It creates criminal offences for unlawful sub-letting by secure and assured tenants of social housing.

AGRICULTURAL PROPERTY
Tenancies in agricultural properties are governed by the Agricultural Holdings Act 1986, the Agricultural Tenancies Act 1995 (both amended by the Regulatory Reform (Agricultural Tenancies) (England and Wales) Order 2006), the Tribunals, Courts and Enforcement Act 2007, the Legal Services Act 2007 and the Rent (Agriculture) Act 1976, which give similar protections to those described above, eg security of tenure, right to compensation for disturbance, etc. Similar provisions are applied to Scotland by the Agricultural Holdings (Scotland) Act 2003 for those leases entered into on or after 27 November 2003. The Agricultural Holdings (Scotland) Act 1991 continues to apply to those leases in Scotland entered into prior to this date and in certain other circumstances outlined by the 2003 act. However, one distinction to note between the 1991 act and the 2003 act is that those leases governed by the former have full security of tenure, subject to certain exceptions, whereas leases under the 2003 act are fixed term arrangements of various durations.

EVICTION
The Protection from Eviction Act 1977 (as amended by the Housing Act 1988 and Nationality, Immigration and Asylum Act 2002) sets out the procedure a landlord must follow in order to obtain possession of property. It is unlawful for a landlord to evict a tenant otherwise than in accordance with the law. For common law tenancies and for Rent Act tenants a notice to quit in the prescribed form giving 28 days notice is required. For secure and assured tenancies a notice seeking possession must be served. It is unlawful for the landlord to evict a person by putting their belongings on to the street, by changing the locks and so on. It is also unlawful for a landlord to harass a tenant in any way in order to persuade

him/her to give up the tenancy. The tenant may be able to obtain an injunction to restrain the actions of the landlord and get back into the property and be awarded damages.

LANDLORD RESPONSIBILITIES
Under the Landlord and Tenant Act 1985, where the term of the lease is less than seven years, the landlord is responsible for maintaining the structure and exterior of the property, for sanitation, for heating and hot water, and all installations for the supply of water, gas and electricity.

While the responsibility of maintaining the premises remains intact, since July 2012 landlords are no longer permitted to enter the rental premises for the purpose of viewing their state and condition. This power of entry was revoked by the Protection of Freedoms Act 2012.

LEASEHOLDERS
Strictly speaking, leaseholders have bought a long lease rather than a property and in certain limited circumstances the landlord can end the tenancy. Under the Leasehold Reform Act 1967 (as amended by the Housing Acts 1969, 1974, 1980 and 1985), leaseholders of houses may have the right to buy the freehold or to take an extended lease for a term of 50 years. This applies to leases where the term of the lease is over 21 years, at a low rent, and where the leaseholder has occupied the house as his/her only or main residence for the last two years, or for a total of two years over the last ten. The tenant must give the landlord written notice of his desire to acquire the freehold or extend the leasehold.

The Leasehold Reform, Housing and Urban Development Act came into force in 1993 and allows the leaseholders of flats in certain circumstances to buy the freehold of the building in which they live.

Responsibility for maintenance of the structure, exterior and interior of the building should be set out in the lease. Usually the upkeep of the interior of his/her part of the property is the responsibility of the leaseholder, and responsibility for the structure, exterior and common interior areas is shared between the freeholder and the leaseholder(s).

If leaseholders are dissatisfied with charges made in respect of lease extensions, they are entitled to have their situation evaluated by the Leasehold Valuation Tribunal.

The Commonhold and Leasehold Reform Act 2002 makes provision for the freehold estate in land to be registered as commonhold land and for the legal interest in the land to be vested in a 'commonhold association' ie a private limited company.

BUSINESS LETTINGS
The Landlord and Tenant Acts 1927 and 1954 (as amended) give security of tenure to the tenants of most business premises. The landlord can only evict the tenant on one of the grounds laid down in the 1954 act, and in some cases where the landlord repossesses the property the tenant may be entitled to compensation.

SCOTLAND
In Scotland assured and short assured tenancies exist for residential lettings entered into after 2 January 1989 and are similar to assured shorthold tenancies in England and Wales. The relevant legislation is the Housing (Scotland) Act 1988.

Most tenancies created before 2 January 1989 were regulated tenancies and the Rent (Scotland) Act 1984 still applies where these exist. The act defines, among other things, the circumstances in which a landlord can increase the rent when improvements are made to the property. The provisions of the Rent Act do not apply to tenancies where the landlord is the Crown, a local authority or a housing corporation.

The Antisocial Behaviour etc (Scotland) Act 2004 provides that all private landlords letting property in Scotland must register with the local authority in which the let property is situated, unless the landlord is a local authority, or a registered social landlord. Exceptions also apply to holiday lets, owner-occupied accommodation and agricultural holdings. The act applies to partnerships, trusts and companies as well as to individuals.

Tenancy Deposit Schemes (Scotland) Regulations 2011 require that a landlord must pay deposits taken from tenants into an approved scheme and ensure that the money is held by an approved scheme for the duration of the tenancy. Evidence of registration with the relevant local authority in terms of the 2004 Act must be provided when the deposit is paid over.

Landlords who provide an assured or short assured tenancy must provide new tenants with a tenant information pack. The Tenant Information Pack includes information on the Repairing Standard, and its provision satisfies the separate obligation of a landlord to provide a tenant with written information about the landlord's duty to repair and maintain in terms of the Housing (Scotland) Act 2006.

The Housing (Scotland) Acts of 1987 and 2001 relate to local authority and registered social landlord responsibilities for housing, the right to buy, and local authority secured tenancies. The provisions are broadly similar to England and Wales. The Housing (Scotland) Act 2010 is now in force. This reforms right-to-buy provisions, modernises social housing regulation, introduces the Scottish social housing charter and replaces the regulatory framework established by the 2001 act.

In Scotland, business premises are not controlled by statute to the same extent as in England and Wales, although the Tenancy of Shops (Scotland) Act 1949 gives some security to tenants of shops. Tenants of shops can apply to the sheriff, within 21 days of being served a notice to quit, for a renewal of tenancy if threatened with eviction. This application may be dismissed on various grounds including where the landlord has offered to sell the property to the tenant at an agreed price or, in the absence of agreement as to price, at a price fixed by a single arbiter appointed by the parties or the sheriff. The act extends to properties where the Crown or government departments are the landlords or the tenants.

Under the Leases Act 1449 the landlord's successors (either purchasers or creditors) are bound by the agreement made with any tenants so long as the following conditions are met:
• the lease, if for more than one year, must be in writing
• there must be a rent
• there must be a term of expiry
• the tenant must have entered into possession
• the subjects of the lease must be land
• the landlord, if owner, must be the proprietor with a recorded title, ie the title deeds recorded in the Register of Sasines or registered in the Land Register

On 28 November 2015 certain leases which were granted for more than 175 years and under which the rent does not exceed £100 a year, will convert to heritable titles. Therefore the tenants under these leases will become the owners of the property. Conversion of the lease will be automatic, provided certain conditions are met, unless the tenant opts out. It is possible for the landlord to claim compensation for their loss of income.

LEGAL AID

The Access to Justice Act 1999 transformed what used to be known as the Legal Aid system. The Legal Aid Board was replaced by the Legal Services Commission, which was responsible for the development and administration of two legal funding schemes in England and Wales, namely the Criminal Defence Service and the Community Legal Service. The Criminal Defence Service assisted people who were under police investigation or facing criminal charges. The Community Legal Service was designed to increase access to legal information and advice by involving a much wider network of funders and providers in giving publicly funded legal services. In Scotland, provision of legal aid is governed by the Legal Aid (Scotland) Act 1986, the Legal Profession and Legal Aid (Scotland) Act 2007 and the Scottish Civil Justice Council and Criminal Legal Assistance Act 2013, and administered by the Scottish Legal Aid Board.

Under the Legal Aid, Sentencing and Punishment of Offenders Act 2012, which came into force on 1 April 2013, the Legal Services Commission was abolished and replaced by the newly created Legal Aid Agency. The act has also limited the areas of law that fall within the scope of legal aid funding, especially those related to civil legal services. However, the act does include provisions for funding in exceptional cases, such as where failure to provide legal aid would result in a violation of an individual's human rights or where providing legal aid would serve a wider public interest. Further, the act allows for areas of law to be added or omitted from the scope of legal aid independently, without subsequent legislation.

LEGAL AID AGENCY, W www.justice.gov.uk/legal-aid

CIVIL LEGAL AID

From 1 January 2000, only organisations (such as solicitors or Citizens Advice) with a contract with the Legal Services Commission (now Legal Aid Agency) have been able to give initial help in any civil matter. Moreover, from that date decisions about funding were devolved from the Legal Services Commission to contracted organisations in relation to any level of publicly funded service in family and immigration cases. For other types of case, applications for public funding are made through a solicitor (or other contracted legal services providers) in much the same way as the former Legal Aid.

Under the civil funding scheme there are broadly six levels of service available:
• legal help
• help at court
• family help – either family help (lower) or family help (higher)
• legal representation – either investigative help or full representation
• family mediation
• such other services as authorised by specific orders

ELIGIBILITY
Eligibility for funding from the Legal Aid Agency depends broadly on five factors:
• the level of service sought (see above)
• whether the applicant qualifies financially
• the merits of the applicant's case
• a costs-benefits analysis (if the costs are likely to outweigh any benefit that might be gained from the proceedings, funding may be refused)
• whether there is any public interest in the case being litigated (ie whether the case has a wider public interest beyond that of the parties involved, eg a human rights case)

The limits on capital and income above which a person is not entitled to public funding vary with the type of service sought.

The Legal Aid, Sentencing and Punishment of Offenders Act 2012 has abolished capital passporting, meaning that all applicants are subject to the same capital test regardless of whether or not they are receiving benefits. The 2012 act also amended the merits criteria so that legal aid may be refused where the case is suitable for alternative funding, such as Conditional Fee Agreements.

CONTRIBUTIONS
Some of those who qualify for Legal Aid Agency funding will have to contribute towards their legal costs. Contributions must be paid by anyone who has a disposable income or disposable capital exceeding a prescribed amount. The rules relating to applicable contributions are complex and detailed information can be obtained from the Legal Aid Agency.

STATUTORY CHARGE
A statutory charge is made if a person keeps or gains money or property in a case for which they have received legal aid. This means that the amount paid by the Legal Aid Agency fund on their behalf is deducted from the amount that the person receives. This does not apply if the court has ordered that the costs be paid by the other party (unless the amount paid by the other party does not cover all of the costs). In certain circumstances, the Legal Aid Agency may waive or postpone payment.

CONTINGENCY OR CONDITIONAL FEES
This system was introduced by the Courts and Legal Services Act 1990. It can offer legal representation on a 'no win, no fee' basis. It provides an alternative form of assistance, especially for those cases which are ineligible for funding by the Legal Aid Agency. The main area for such work is in the field of personal injuries.

Not all solicitors offer such a scheme and different solicitors may well have different terms. The effect of the agreement is that solicitors may not make any charges, or may waive some of their charges, until the case is concluded successfully. If a case is won then the losing party will usually have to pay towards costs, with the winning party contributing around one third.

SCOTLAND
Civil legal aid is available for cases in the following:
- the sheriff courts
- the court of session
- the supreme court
- the lands valuation appeal court
- the Scottish land court
- the Lands Tribunal for Scotland
- the Employment Appeal Tribunals
- the Proscribed Organisations Appeal Commission
- certain appeals before the Social Security Commissioners

Civil legal aid is not available for election petitions, small claims, simplified divorce procedures or petitions by a debtor for his own sequestration. In defamation actions additional criteria must be met in order for legal aid to be available.

Eligibility for civil legal aid is assessed in a similar way to that in England and Wales, though the financial limits differ in some respects. A person shall be eligible for civil legal aid if their disposable income does not exceed £26,239 a year. A person may be refused civil aid if their disposable capital exceeds £13,017 and it appears to the Legal Aid board that they can afford to pay without legal aid. Additionally:
- if disposable capital is between £7,853 and £13,017, the applicant will be required to pay a contribution which will be equal to the difference between £7,853 and their disposable capital

- if disposable income is between £3,522 and £11,540, a contribution of one third of the difference between £3,522 and the disposable income may be payable
- if disposable income is between £11,541 and £15,743, one third of the difference between £3,522 and £11,540 plus half the difference between £11,541 and the disposable income may be payable
- if disposable income is between £15,744 and £26,239, a contribution of the following: one third of the difference between £3,522 and £11,540, plus half the difference between £11,541 and £15,743, plus all the remaining disposable income between £15,744 and £26,239 – will be payable

CRIMINAL LEGAL AID
The Legal Aid Agency provides defendants facing criminal charges with free legal representation if they pass a merits test and a means test.

Criminal legal aid covers the cost of preparing a case and legal representation in criminal proceedings. It is also available for appeals against verdicts or sentences in magistrates' courts, the crown court or the court of appeal. It is not available for bringing a private prosecution in a criminal court.

If granted criminal legal aid, either the person may choose their own solicitor or the court will assign one. Contributions to the legal costs may be required. The rules relating to applicable contributions are complex and detailed information can be obtained from the Legal Aid Agency.

DUTY SOLICITORS
The Legal Aid, Sentencing and Punishment of Offenders Act 2012 also provides for free initial advice and initial assistance to anyone questioned by the police (whether under arrest or helping the police with their enquiries). No means test or contributions are required for this.

SCOTLAND
Legal advice and assistance operates in a similar way in Scotland. A person is eligible:
- if disposable income does not exceed £245 a week. If disposable income is between £105 and £245 a week, contributions are payable
- if disposable capital does not exceed £1,716 (if the person has dependent relatives, the savings allowance is higher)
- if receiving income support or income-related job seeker's allowance they qualify automatically provided their disposable capital is not over the limit

The procedure for application for criminal legal aid depends on the circumstances of each case. In solemn cases (more serious cases, such as murder) heard before a jury, a person is automatically entitled to criminal legal aid until they are given bail or placed in custody. Thereafter, it is for the court to decide whether to grant legal aid. The court will do this if the person accused cannot meet the expenses of the case without undue hardship on him or his dependants. In less serious cases the procedure depends on whether the person is in custody:
- anyone taken into custody has the right to free legal aid from the duty solicitor up to and including the first court appearance
- if the person is not in custody and wishes to plead guilty, they are not entitled to criminal legal aid but may be entitled to legal advice and assistance, including assistance by way of representation

However, regardless of whether the person is in custody if they wish to plead not guilty, they can apply for criminal legal aid. This must be done within 14 days of the first court appearance at which they made the plea

The criteria used to assess whether or not criminal legal aid should be granted is similar to the criteria for England and Wales. When meeting with your solicitor, take evidence of your financial position such as details of savings, bank statements, pay slips, pension book or benefits book.

Under the current provisions of the Scottish Civil Justice Council and Criminal Legal Assistance Act 2013, a person in receipt of criminal legal aid or criminal assistance by way of representation, will be required, in most circumstances, to make contributions where their weekly disposable income is £82 or above or if their disposable capital is £750 or more. The Scottish government has delayed the implementation of these provisions and no timetable has yet been proposed.

THE SCOTTISH LEGAL AID BOARD, 44 Drumsheugh Gardens, Edinburgh EH3 7SW T 0131-226 7061
W www.slab.org.uk

MARRIAGE

Any two persons may marry provided that:
- they are at least 16 years old on the day of the marriage (in England and Wales persons under the age of 18 must generally obtain the consent of their parents or guardian; if consent is refused an appeal may be made to the high court, the county court or a court of summary jurisdiction)
- they are not related to one another in a way which would prevent their marrying
- they are unmarried (a person who has already been married must produce documentary evidence that the previous marriage has been ended by death, divorce or annulment)
- they are capable of understanding the nature of a marriage ceremony and of consenting to marriage

It is now lawful for same sex couples to marry by way of civil or religious ceremony following the passing of the Marriage (Same Sex Couples) Act 2013, which came into force in March 2014. In addition, an existing marriage will now be able to continue where one or both parties change their legal gender and both parties wish to remain married. The Act also makes provision for civil partners to convert their civil partnership into a marriage if they wish to do so.

The parties should check the marriage will be recognised as valid in their home country if either is not a British citizen.

DEGREES OF RELATIONSHIP

A marriage between persons within the prohibited degrees of consanguinity, affinity or adoption is void.

A man may not marry his mother, daughter, grandmother, granddaughter, sister, aunt, niece, adoptive mother, former adoptive mother, adopted daughter or former adopted daughter.

A woman may not marry her father, son, grandfather, grandson, brother, uncle, nephew, adoptive father, former adoptive father, adopted son or former adopted son. Under the Marriage (Prohibited Degrees of Relationship) Act 1986, some exceptions to the law permit a man or a woman to marry certain step-relatives or in-laws.

In addition to the above, a person may not marry a child of their former civil partner, a child of a former spouse, the former civil partner of a grandparent, the former civil partner of a parent, the former spouse of a grandparent, the former spouse of a parent, the grandchild of a former civil partner or the grandchild of a former spouse, unless the only reason they cannot marry is the affinity mentioned above and both persons are over 21 and the younger party has not at any time before attaining the age of 18 been a child of the family in relation to the other party. All references to brothers/sisters include half-brothers/sisters.

ENGLAND AND WALES
TYPES OF MARRIAGE CEREMONY

It is possible to marry by either religious or civil ceremony. However, same-sex marriages can only take place in a religious building if the relevant religious organisation has elected to conduct same-sex marriages and the minister agrees. A religious ceremony can take place at a church or chapel of the Church of England or the Church in Wales, or at any other place of worship which has been formally registered by the Registrar-General.

A civil ceremony can take place at a register office, a registered building or any other premises approved by the local authority.

An application for an approved premises licence must be made by the owners or trustees of the building concerned; it cannot be made by the prospective marriage couple. Approved premises must be regularly open to the public so that the marriage can be witnessed; the venue must be deemed to be a permanent and immovable structure. Open-air ceremonies are prohibited.

Non-Anglican marriages may also be solemnised following the issue of a Registrar-General's licence in unregistered premises where one of the parties is seriously ill, is not expected to recover, and cannot be moved to registered premises. Detained and housebound persons may be married at their place of residence.

MARRIAGE IN THE CHURCH OF ENGLAND OR THE CHURCH IN WALES
Marriage by banns

The marriage can take place in a parish in which one of the parties lives, or in a church in another parish if it is the usual place of worship of either or both of the parties. New regulations introduced in October 2008 also allow marriages to take place in a parish where one of the parties was baptised or prepared for confirmation (but not if combined rite); a parish where one of the parties lived or attended worship for six months or more; a parish where one of the parents of either of the parties lived for six months or more; a parish where one of the parents of either of the parties has attended public worship for six months or more in the child's lifetime; or a parish where the parents or grandparents of either of the parties were married. The banns (ie the announcement of the marriage ceremony) must be called in the parish in which the marriage is to take place on three Sundays before the day of the ceremony; if either or both of the parties lives in a different parish the banns must also be called there. After three months the banns are no longer valid. The minister will not perform the marriage unless satisfied that the banns have been properly called.

Marriage by common licence

The vicar who is to conduct the marriage will arrange for a common licence to be issued by the diocesan bishop; this dispenses with the necessity for banns. One of the parties must have lived in the parish for 15 days immediately before the issuing of the licence or must usually worship at the church. Eligibility requirements vary from diocese to diocese, but it is not normally required that the parties should have been baptised. The licence is valid for three months.

Marriage by special licence

A special licence is granted by the Archbishop of Canterbury in special circumstances for the marriage to take place at any place, with or without previous residence in the parish, or at any time. It is usually required that at least one of the parties has been baptised. The special licence will expire after three months. Application must be made to the registrar of the Faculty Office: 1 The Sanctuary, London SW1P 3JT T 020-72225381.

Marriage by certificate

The marriage can be conducted on the authority of the superintendent registrar's certificate, provided that the vicar's consent is obtained (the vicar is not obliged to accept the certificate). One of the parties must live in the parish or must usually worship at the church.

MARRIAGE BY OTHER RELIGIOUS CEREMONY

One of the parties must normally live in the registration district where the marriage is to take place. If the building where the parties wish to be married has not been registered, the couple can still have a religious ceremony there, but will also need to have a separate civil ceremony for the marriage to be valid. If the building is registered, in addition to giving notice to the superintendent registrar it may also be necessary to book a registrar, or authorised person to be present at the ceremony.

CIVIL MARRIAGE

A marriage may be solemnised at any register office, registered building or approved premises in England and Wales, without either of the parties being resident in the same district. The superintendent registrar of the district should be contacted, and, if the marriage is to take place at approved premises, the necessary arrangements at the venue must also be made.

NOTICE OF MARRIAGE

Unless it is to take place by banns or under common or special licence in the Church of England or the Church in Wales, a notice of the marriage must be given in person to the superintendent registrar. Notice of marriage may be given in the following ways:

- by certificate. Both parties must have lived in a registration district in England or Wales for at least seven days immediately before giving notice personally at the local register office. If they live in different registration districts, notice must be given in both districts by the respective party in person. The marriage can take place in any register office or other approved premises in England and Wales no sooner than 16 days after notice has been given, when the superintendent registrar issues a certificate
- by licence. One of the parties must have lived in a registration district in England or Wales for at least 15 days before giving notice at the register office; the other party need only be a resident of, or be physically in, England and Wales on the day notice is given

A notice of marriage is valid for 12 months, unless it is for the marriage of a detained or housebound person, when it will usually only be accepted within three months of publication. Notice for marriages taking place within the Church of England or Church of Wales are also only valid for three months following publication. It should be possible to make an advance (provisional) booking 12 months before the ceremony. In this case it is still necessary to give formal notice three months before the marriage. When giving notice of the marriage it is necessary to produce official proof, if relevant, that any previous marriage has ended in divorce or death by producing a decree absolute or death certificate; it is also necessary to provide proof of age, identity and nationality for each of the parties, for example, with a passport. If either party is under 18 years old, evidence of consent by their parent or guardian is required. There are special procedures for those wishing to get married in the UK that are subject to immigration control; the register office will be able to advise on these.

SOLEMNISATION OF THE MARRIAGE

On the day of the wedding there must be at least two other people present who are prepared to act as witnesses and sign the marriage register. A registrar of marriages must be present at a marriage in a register office or at approved premises, but an authorised person may act in the capacity of registrar in a registered building.

If the marriage takes place at approved premises, the room must be separate from any other activity on the premises at the time of the ceremony, and no food or drink can be sold or consumed in the room during the ceremony or for one hour beforehand.

The marriage must be solemnised with open doors. At some time during the ceremony the parties must make a declaration that they know of no legal impediment to the marriage and they must also say the contracting words; the declaratory and contracting words may vary according to the form of service. A civil marriage cannot contain any religious aspects, but it may be possible for non-religious music and/or readings to be included. It may also be possible to embellish the marriage vows taken by the couple.

CIVIL FEES

Notice and registration of Marriage at a Register Office

By superintendent registrar's certificate, £35 per person for the notice of the marriage (which is not refundable if the marriage does not in fact take place) and £45 for the registration of the marriage.

Marriage at a Register Office/Approved Premises

Fees for marriage at a register office are set by the local authority responsible. An additional fee will also be payable for the superintendent registrar's and registrar's attendance at the marriage on an approved premises. This is also set locally by the local authority responsible. A further charge is likely to be made by the owners of the building for the use of the premises. For marriages taking place in a religious building other than the Church of England or Church of Wales, an additional fee of £84 is payable for the registrar's attendance at the marriage unless an 'Authorised Person' appointed by the trustees of the building has agreed to register the marriage. Additional fees may be charged by the trustees of the building for the wedding and by the person who performs the ceremony.

ECCLESIASTICAL FEES

(Church of England and Church in Wales)

Marriage by banns

For publication of banns, £21*

For certificate of banns issued at time of publication, £13.00*

For marriage service, £392*

For marriage certificate at registration if required £4†

* These fees are revised from 1 January each calendar year. Some may not apply to the Church in Wales

† This fee is revised from 1 April each calendar year

SCOTLAND

REGULAR MARRIAGES

A regular marriage is one which is celebrated by a minister of religion or authorised registrar or other celebrant. Each of the parties must complete a marriage notice form and return it to the district registrar for the area in which they are to be married, irrespective of where they live, within the three month period prior to the date of the marriage and not later than 15 days prior to that date. The district registrar must then enter the date of receipt and certain details in a marriage book kept for this purpose, and must also enter the names of the parties and the proposed date of marriage in a list which is displayed in a conspicuous place at the registration office until the date of the marriage has passed. All persons wishing to enter into a regular marriage in Scotland must follow the same preliminary procedure regardless of whether they intend to have a religious or civil ceremony. Before the marriage ceremony takes place any person may submit an objection in writing to the district registrar.

A marriage schedule, which is prepared by the registrar, will be issued to one or both of the parties in person up to seven days before a religious marriage; for a civil marriage the schedule will be available at the ceremony. The schedule must be handed to the celebrant before the ceremony starts and it must be signed immediately after the wedding. For religious marriages the schedule must be sent within three days by the parties to the district registrar who must register the marriage as soon as possible thereafter. In civil marriages, the district registrar must register the marriage as soon as possible.

The authority to conduct a religious marriage is deemed to be vested in the authorised celebrant rather than the building in which it takes place; open-air religious ceremonies are therefore permissible in Scotland.

From 10 June 2002 it has been possible, under the Marriage (Scotland) Act 2002, for venues or couples to apply to the local council for a licence to allow a civil ceremony to take place at a venue other than a registration office. To obtain further information, a venue or couple should contact the district registrar in the area they wish to marry. A list of licensed venues is also available on the National Records of Scotland website.

MARRIAGE BY COHABITATION WITH HABIT AND REPUTE

Prior to the enactment of the Family Law (Scotland) Act 2006, if two people had lived together constantly as husband and wife and were generally held to be such by the neighbourhood and among their friends and relations, a presumption could arise from which marriage could be inferred. Before such a marriage could be registered, however, a decree of declarator of marriage had to be obtained from the court of session. Section 3 of the 2006 act provides that it will no longer be possible for a marriage to be constituted by cohabitation with habit and repute, but it will still be possible for couples whose period of cohabitation began before commencement of the 2006 act to seek a declarator under the old rule of law.

SAME-SEX MARRIAGES

On 12 March 2014 the Scottish government passed the Marriage and Civil Partnership (Scotland) Act 2014. This legislation will permit same-sex couples to get married, either in a civil ceremony or a 'religious or belief' ceremony where the religious or belief body has opted-in to solemnising same-sex marriage. Also, certain same-sex couples who have entered into a civil partnership will have the option under the Act to change their civil partnership to a marriage.

It will still be possible for same-sex couples to enter into a civil partnership and this may be a 'religious or belief' civil partnership if the religious or belief body has agreed to perform these.

It is expected that the majority of the provisions of this Act will have come into force by the end of 2014.

CIVIL FEES

The fee for submitting a notice of marriage to the district registrar is £30.00 per person. Solemnisation of a civil marriage costs £55.00, while the extract of the entry in the register of marriages attracts a fee of £10.00. The costs of religious marriage ceremonies can vary.

THE GENERAL REGISTER OFFICE, PO Box 2,
Southport PR8 2JD T 0845-603 7788
W www.gro.gov.uk/gro/content/certificates

THE NATIONAL RECORDS OF SCOTLAND,
New Register House, 2 Princes Street, Edinburgh EH1 3YY
T 0131-314 0380 W www.nrsscotland.gov.uk

TOWN AND COUNTRY PLANNING

The planning system can help to protect the environment and assist individuals in assessing their land rights. There are a number of acts governing the development of land and buildings in England and Wales and advice should always be sought from Citizens Advice or the local planning authority before undertaking building works on any land or property. If development takes place which requires planning permission without permission being given, enforcement action may take place and the situation may need to be rectified. Planning law in Scotland is similar but certain Scotland-specific legislation applies so advice should always be sought.

PLANNING PERMISSION

Planning permission is needed if the work involves:
- making a material change in use, such as dividing off part of the house or garden so that it can be used as a separate home or dividing off part of the house for commercial use, eg for a workshop
- going against the terms of the original planning permission, eg there may be a restriction on fences in front gardens on an open-plan estate
- building, engineering or mining, except for the permitted developments below
- new or wider access to a main road
- additions or extensions to flats or maisonettes
- work which might obstruct the view of road users

Planning permission is not needed to carry out internal alterations or work which does not affect the external appearance of the building, and are not works for making good war damage or works begun after 5 December 1968 for the alteration of a building by providing additional space in it underground.

Under regulations which came into effect on 1 October 2008, there are certain types of development for which the Secretary of State for the Environment, Food and Rural Affairs has granted general permissions (permitted development rights). These include house extensions and additions, outbuildings and garages, other ancillary garden buildings such as swimming pools or ponds, and laying patios, paths or driveways for domestic use. All developments are subject to a number of conditions.

Before carrying out any of the above permitted developments you should contact your local planning authority to find out whether the general permission has been modified in your area. For more information, visit W www.planningportal.gov.uk

OTHER RESTRICTIONS

It may be necessary to obtain other types of permissions before carrying out any development. These permissions are separate from planning permission and apply regardless of whether or not planning permission is needed, eg:
- building regulations will probably apply if a new building is to be erected, if an existing one is to be altered or extended, or if the work involves building over a drain or sewer. The building control department of the local authority will advise on this
- any alterations to a listed building or the grounds of a listed building must be approved by the local authority. Listing will include not only the main building but everything in the curtilage of the building

- local authority approval is necessary if a building (or, in some circumstances, gates, walls, fences or railings) in a conservation area is to be demolished; each local authority keeps a register of all local buildings that are in conservation areas
- a council order is required if your proposed development would obstruct a public path which crosses your property, and you should discuss any such proposals with the council at an early stage
- many trees are protected by tree preservation orders and must not be pruned or taken down without local authority consent
- bats and many other species are protected, and Natural England, Natural Resources Wales or Scottish Natural Heritage must be notified before any work is carried out that will affect the habitat of protected species, eg timber treatment, renovation or extensions of lofts
- developments in areas with special designations, such as National Parks, Areas of Outstanding Natural Beauty, National Scenic Areas or in the Norfolk or Suffolk Broads, are subject to greater restrictions. The local planning authority will advise or refer enquirers to the relevant authority

There may also be restrictions contained in the title to the property which require you to get someone else's agreement before carrying out certain developments, and which should be considered when works are planned.

VOTERS' QUALIFICATIONS

Those entitled to vote at parliamentary, and local government elections are those who, at the date of taking the poll, are:
- on the electoral roll
- aged 18 years or older
- British citizens, Commonwealth citizens or citizens of the Irish Republic who are resident in the UK
- those who suffer from no other legal bar to voting (eg prisoners). It should be noted that there is some uncertainty regarding the future of the legal bar on prisoners' voting following a decision taken by the European Court of Human Rights
- in Northern Ireland electors must have been resident in Northern Ireland during the whole of the three-month period prior to the relevant date
- citizens of any EU member state may vote in local elections if they meet the criteria listed above (save for the nationality requirements)

British citizens resident abroad are entitled to vote, provided they have been registered to vote in the UK within the last 15 years, as overseas electors in domestic parliamentary elections in the constituency in which they were last resident if they are on the electoral roll of the relevant constituency. Members of the armed forces and their spouses or civil partners, Crown servants and employees of the British Council who are overseas, along with their spouses and civil partners, are entitled to vote regardless of how long they have been abroad. British citizens who had never been registered as an elector in the UK are not eligible to register as an overseas voter unless they left the UK before they were 18, providing they left the country no more than 15 years ago. Overseas electors may opt to vote by proxy or by postal vote. Overseas voters may not vote in local government elections.

The main categories of people who are not entitled to vote at general elections are:
- sitting peers in the House of Lords
- convicted persons detained in pursuance of their sentences (though remand prisoners, unconvicted prisoners and civil prisoners can vote if on the electoral register). This is currently subject to review, as detailed above
- those convicted within the previous five years of corrupt or illegal election practices
- EU citizens (who may only vote in EU and local government elections)

Under the Representation of the Peoples Act 2000, several new groups of people are permitted to vote for the first time. These include: people who live on barges; people in mental health hospitals (other than those with criminal convictions) and homeless people who have made a 'declaration of local connection'.

REGISTERING TO VOTE

Voters must be entered on an electoral register. The Electoral Registration Officer (ERO) for each council area is responsible for preparing and publishing the register for his area by 1 December each year. Names may be added to the register to reflect changes in people's circumstances as they occur and each month during December to August, the ERO publishes a list of alterations to the published register.

A registration form is sent to all households in the autumn of each year and the householder or 'head of household' decides who to register. The householder is required to provide details of all occupants who are eligible to vote, including ones who will reach their 18th birthday in the year covered by the register. On 10 May 2012, the government introduced the electoral registration and administration bill, which received royal assent on 31 January 2013. The act replaced household registration with individual voter registration. Individuals will also be asked for identifying information such as date of birth and national insurance number. The act also introduced a number of changes relating to electoral administration and the conduct of elections. Anyone failing to supply information to the ERO when requested, or supplying false information, may be fined by up to £1,000. Application forms and more information are available from the Electoral Commission (W www.aboutmyvote.co.uk).

VOTING

Voting is not compulsory in the UK. Those who wish to vote do so in person at the allotted polling station. Postal votes are now available to anyone on request and you do not need to give a reason for using a postal vote.

A proxy (whereby the voter nominates someone to vote in person on their behalf) can be appointed to act in a specific election, for a specified period of time or indefinitely. For the appointment of an indefinite or long-term proxy, the voter needs to specify physical employment, study reasons or a disability to explain why they are making an application. With proxy votes where a particular election is specified, the voter needs to provide details of the circumstances by which they cannot reasonably be expected to go to the polling station. Applications for a proxy are normally available up to six working days before an election, but should the voter fall ill on election day, it is possible to appoint a proxy up until polling day.

Further information can be obtained from the local authority's ERO in England and Wales or the electoral registration office in Scotland, or the Chief Electoral Officer in Northern Ireland.

WILLS

A will is used to appoint executors (who will administer the estate), give directions as to the disposal of the body, appoint guardians for children and determine how and to whom property is to be passed. A well-drafted will can operate to reduce the level of inheritance tax which the estate pays. It is best to have a will drawn up by a solicitor, but if a solicitor

is not employed the following points must be taken into account:
- if possible the will must not be prepared on behalf of another person by someone who is to benefit from it or who is a close relative of a major beneficiary
- the language used must be clear and unambiguous and it is better to avoid the use of legal terms where the same thing can be expressed in plain language
- it is better to rewrite the whole document if a mistake is made. If necessary, alterations can be made by striking through the words with a pen, and the signature or initials of the testator and the witnesses must be put in the margin opposite the alteration. No alteration of any kind should be made after the will has been executed
- if the person later wishes to change the will or part of it, it is better to write a new will revoking the old. The use of codicils (documents written as supplements or containing modifications to the will) should be left to a solicitor
- the will should be typed or printed, or if handwritten be legible and preferably in ink

The form of a will varies to suit different cases – a solicitor will be able to advise as to wording, however, 'DIY' will-writing kits can be purchased from good stationery shops and many banks offer a will-writing service.

LAPSED LEGATEES

If a person who has been left property in a will dies before the person who made the will, the gift fails and will pass to the person entitled to everything not otherwise disposed of (the residuary estate).

If the person left the residuary estate dies before the person who made the will, their share will pass to the closest relative(s) of the testator under the intestacy rules. It is always better to draw up a new will if a beneficiary predeceases the person who made the will.

EXECUTORS

It is usual to appoint two executors, although one is sufficient. No more than four persons can deal with the estate of the person who has died. The name and address of each executor should be given in full (the addresses are not essential but including them adds clarity to the document). Executors should be 18 years of age or over. An executor may be a beneficiary of the will.

WITNESSES

A person who is a beneficiary of a will, or the spouse or civil partner of a beneficiary at the time the will is signed, must not act as a witness or else he/she will be unable to take his/her gift except in some limited circumstances. Husband and wife can both act as witnesses provided neither benefits from the will.

It is better that a person does not act as an executor and as a witness, as he/she can take no benefit under a will to which he/she is witness. The identity of the witnesses should be made as explicit as possible.

EXECUTION OF A WILL

The person making the will should sign his/her name in the presence of the two witnesses. It is advisable to sign at the foot of the document, so as to avoid uncertainty about the testator's intention. The witnesses must then sign their names while the person making the will looks on. If this procedure is not adhered to, the will may be considered invalid. There are certain exceptional circumstances where these rules are relaxed, eg where the person may be too ill to sign.

CAPACITY TO MAKE A WILL

Anyone aged 18 or over can make a will. However, if there is any suspicion that the person making the will is not, through reasons of infirmity or age, fully in command of his/her faculties, it is advisable to arrange for a medical practitioner to examine the person making the will at the time it is to be executed (to verify his/her mental capacity and to record that medical opinion in writing), and to ask the examining practitioner to act as a witness. If a person is not mentally able to make a will, the court may do this for him/her by virtue of the Mental Capacity Act 2005.

REVOCATION

A will may be revoked or cancelled in a number of ways:
- a later will revokes an earlier one if it says so; otherwise the earlier will is by implication revoked by the later one to the extent that it contradicts or repeats the earlier one
- a will is revoked if the physical document on which it is written is destroyed by the person whose will it is. There must be an intention to revoke the will and an act of destruction. It may not be sufficient to obliterate the will with a pen
- a will is revoked by the testator making a written declaration to this effect executed in the same way as a will
- a will is also revoked when the person marries or forms a civil partnership, unless it is clear from the will that the person intended the will to stand after that particular marriage or civil partnership
- where a marriage or civil partnership ends in divorce or dissolution or is annulled or declared void, gifts to the spouse or civil partner and the appointment of the spouse or civil partner as executor fail unless the will says that this is not to happen. A former spouse or civil partner is treated as having predeceased the testator. A separation does not change the effect of a married person or civil partner's will.

PROBATE AND LETTERS OF ADMINISTRATION

Probate is granted to the executors named in a will and once granted, the executors are obliged to carry out the instructions of the will. Letters of administration are granted where no executor is named in a will or is willing or able to act or where there is no will or no valid will; this gives a person, often the next of kin, similar powers and duties to those of an executor.

Applications for probate or for letters of administration can be made to the Principal Registry of the Family Division, to a district probate registry or to a probate sub-registry. Applicants will need the following documents: the Probate Application Form; the original will and codicils (if any); a certificate of death; oath for executors or administrators; and the appropriate tax form (an 'IHT 205' if no inheritance tax is owed; otherwise an 'IHT 400' and 'IHT 421'), in addition to a cheque for the relevant probate fee. Certain property, up to the value of £5,000, may be disposed of without a grant of probate or letters of administration, as can assets that do not pass under the will such as jointly owned assets which pass automatically on the death of one of the joint holders to the survivor.

WHERE TO FIND A PROVED WILL

Since 1858 wills which have been proved, that is wills on which probate or letters of administration have been granted, must have been proved at the Principal Registry of the Family Division or at a district probate registry. The Lord Chancellor has power to direct where the original documents are kept but most are filed where they were proved and may be inspected there and a copy obtained. The Principal Registry also holds copies of all wills proved at district probate registries and these may be inspected at First Avenue House, High Holborn, London. An index of all grants, both of probate and of letters of administration, is compiled by the

Principal Registry and may be seen either at the Principal Registry or at a district probate registry.

It is also possible to discover when a grant of probate or letters of administration is issued by requesting a standing search. In response to a request and for a small fee, a district probate registry will supply the names and addresses of executors or administrators and the registry in which the grant was made, of any grant in the estate of a specified person made in the previous 12 months or following six months. This is useful for creditors of the deceased and for applicants who may be beneficiaries to a will but who have lost contact with the deceased.

INTESTACY

Intestacy occurs when someone dies without leaving a will or leaves a will which is invalid or which does not take effect for some reason. Intestacy can be partial, for instance, if there is a will which disposes of some but not all of the testator's property. In such cases the person's estate (property, possessions, other assets following the payment of debts) passes to certain members of the family. If a will has been written that disposes of only part of a person's property, these rules apply to the part which is undisposed of.

Some types of property do not follow the intestacy rules, for example, property held as joint tenants, insurance policies taken out for specified individuals or assigned into trust during the testator's lifetime and death benefits under a pension scheme.

Following a lengthy review by the Law Commission, the intestacy rules changed on 1 October 2014.

If the person (intestate) leaves a spouse or a civil partner who survives for 28 days and children (legitimate, illegitimate and adopted children and other descendants), the estate is divided as follows:
- if the estate is worth more than £250,000, the spouse or civil partner takes the 'personal chattels' (household articles, including cars, but nothing used for business purposes), £250,000 and half of the rest of the estate absolutely
- the rest of the estate goes to the children*

If the intestate leaves a spouse or civil partner who survives for 28 days but no children, the spouse or civil partner will take the estate in its entirety, regardless of its value.

If there is no surviving spouse or civil partner, the estate is distributed among those who survive the intestate as follows (these provisions remained unchanged at 1 October 2014):
- to surviving children*, but if none to
- parents (equally, if both alive), but if none to
- brothers and sisters of the whole blood* (including issue of deceased ones), but if none to
- brothers and sisters of the half blood* (including issue of deceased ones), but if none to
- grandparents (equally, if more than one), but if none to
- aunts and uncles of the whole blood*, but if none to
- aunts and uncles of the half blood*, but if none to
- the Crown, Duchy of Lancaster or the Duke of Cornwall *(bona vacantia)*

* To inherit, a member of these groups must survive the intestate and attain the age of 18, or marry under that age. If they die under the age of 18 (unless married under that age), their share goes to others, if any, in the same group. If any member of these groups predeceases the intestate leaving children, their share is divided equally among their children.

In England and Wales the provisions of the Inheritance (Provision for Family and Dependants) Act 1975 may allow other people to claim provision from the deceased's assets. This act also applies to cases where a will has been made and allows a person to apply to the court if they feel that the will or rules of intestacy (or both) do not make adequate provision for them. The court can order payment from the deceased's assets or the transfer of property from them if the applicant's claim is accepted. The application must be made within six months of the grant of probate or letters of administration and the following people can make an application:
- the spouse or civil partner
- a former spouse or civil partner who has not remarried or formed a subsequent civil partnership
- a child of the deceased
- someone treated as a child of the deceased's family where the deceased stood in the role of a parent to the applicant
- someone maintained by the deceased
- someone who has cohabited for two years before the death in the same household as the deceased and as the husband or wife or civil partner of the deceased

SCOTLAND

In Scotland any person over 12 and of sound mind can make a will. The person making the will can only freely dispose of the heritage and what is known as the 'dead's part' of the estate because:
- the spouse or civil partner has the right to inherit one-third of the moveable estate if there are children or other descendants, and one-half of it if there are not
- children are entitled to one-third of the moveable estate if there is a surviving spouse or civil partner, and one-half of it if there is not

The remaining portion of the moveable estate is the dead's part, and legacies and bequests are payable from this. Debts are payable out of the whole estate before any division.

From August 1995, wills no longer needed to be 'holographed' and it is now only necessary to have one witness. The person making the will still needs to sign each page. It is better that the will is not witnessed by a beneficiary although the attestation would still be sound and the beneficiary would not have to relinquish the gift.

Subsequent marriage or civil partnership does not revoke a will but the birth of a child who is not provided for may do so. A will may be revoked by a subsequent will, either expressly or by implication, but in so far as the two can be read together both have effect. If a subsequent will is revoked, the earlier will may be revived provided it wasn't physically destroyed.

Wills may be registered in the sheriff court Books of the Sheriffdom in which the deceased lived or in the Books of Council and Session at the Registers of Scotland.

CONFIRMATION

Confirmation (the Scottish equivalent of probate) is obtained in the sheriff court of the sheriffdom in which the deceased was domiciled at the time of death. Executors are either 'nominate' (named by the deceased in the will) or 'dative' (appointed by the court in cases where no executor is named in a will or in cases of intestacy). Applicants for confirmation must first provide an inventory of the deceased's estate and a schedule of debts, with an affidavit. In estates under £36,000 gross, confirmation can be obtained under a simplified procedure at reduced fees, with no need for a solicitor. The local sheriff clerk's office can provide assistance.

PRINCIPAL REGISTRY (FAMILY DIVISION),
First Avenue House, 42–49 High Holborn, London WC1 6NP
T 020-7947 6000

REGISTERS OF SCOTLAND, Meadowbank House,
153 London Road, Edinburgh EH8 7AU T 0845-607 0161

INTESTACY

The rules of distribution are contained in the Succession (Scotland) Act 1964 and are extended to include civil partners by the Civil Partnership Act 2004.

A surviving spouse or civil partner is entitled to 'prior rights'. Once the provisions of the Marriage and Civil Partnership Act 2014 come into force references to people who are or were married are to be read as referring to both opposite and same-sex marriage. Prior rights mean that if certain conditions are met the spouse or civil partner has the right to inherit:

- the matrimonial or family home up to a value of £473,000, or one matrimonial or family home if there is more than one, or, in certain circumstances, the value of the home
- the furnishings and contents of that home, up to the value of £29,000
- a cash sum of £50,000 if the deceased left children or other descendants, or £89,000 if not

These figures are increased from time to time by regulations.

Once prior rights have been satisfied legal rights are settled. Legal rights are:

- *Jus relicti(ae) and rights under the section 131 of the Civil Partnership Act 2004* – the right of a surviving spouse or civil partner to one-half of the net moveable estate, after satisfaction of prior rights, if there are no surviving children; if there are surviving children, the spouse or civil partner is entitled to one-third of the net moveable estate
- *Legitim and rights under the section 131 of the Civil Partnership Act 2004* – the right of surviving children to one-half of the net moveable estate if there is no surviving spouse or civil partner; if there is a surviving spouse or civil partner, the children are entitled to one-third of the net moveable estate after the satisfaction of prior rights

Once prior and legal rights have been satisfied, the remaining estate will be distributed in the following order:

- to descendants
- if no descendants, then to collaterals (ie brothers and sisters) and parents with each being entitled to half of the estate, or if only either parents or collaterals survive, the whole of the estate
- surviving spouse or civil partner
- if no collaterals, parents, spouse or civil partner, then to ascendants collaterals (ie aunts and uncles), and so on in an ascending scale
- if all lines of succession fail, the estate passes to the Crown

Relatives of the whole blood are preferred to relatives of the half blood. Also the right of representation, ie the right of the issue of a person who would have succeeded if he/she had survived the intestate applies.

The Family Law (Scotland) Act 2006 makes provision to allow an unmarried cohabitant to make a financial claim against the estate of a cohabitant who dies intestate. In general a claim must be made within six months of the deceased's death. The court must take into account certain factors when considering such a claim. If the claim is successful the court has the power to order payment of a capital sum and transfer of property.

INTELLECTUAL PROPERTY

Intellectual property is a broad term covering a number of legal rights provided by the government to help people protect their creative works and encourage further innovation. By using these legal rights people can own the things they create and control the way in which others use their innovations. Intellectual property owners can take legal action to stop others using their intellectual property, they can license their intellectual property to others or they can sell it on. Different types of intellectual property utilise different forms of protection including copyright, designs, patents and trade marks, which are all covered below in more detail.

CHANGES TO INTELLECTUAL PROPERTY LAW
• The Enterprise and Regulatory Reform Act 2013 increases the period of time within which copyright protection can be claimed for mass produced artistic works ie paintings, diagrams, photographs, sculptures etc. The protection period now extends up until 70 years from the death of the artist, bringing the rules surrounding mass produced artistic works in line with general UK copyright laws and European practice. The act also makes it possible to license 'orphan art' ie art for which the author cannot be identified
• The UK Patent Box scheme went live in April 2013 allowing corporations to claim a reduced 10 per cent tax rate on profits derived from any products that incorporate patents
• The Patents Act 1977 has been updated to include an exemption for clinical and research trials. This allows trials to be performed using technology patented by others without the risk of being liable for patent infringement, bringing the UK in line with other European countries
• The intellectual property bill passed through its third and final House of Commons reading, and received royal assent on 14 May 2014. The bill implements changes in response to the 2011 Hargreaves review and includes new powers to enable the UK to implement the Unitary Patent Court agreement. This is considered a major step towards implementation of a single patent process to cover protection in almost all EU countries

COPYRIGHT

Copyright protects all original literary, dramatic, musical and artistic works, as well as sound and film recordings and broadcasts. Among the works covered by copyright are novels, computer programs, newspaper articles, sculptures, technical drawings, websites, maps and photographs. Under copyright the creators of these works can control the various ways in which their material may be exploited, the rights broadly covering copying, adapting, issuing (including renting and lending) copies to the public, performing in public, and broadcasting the material. The transfer of copyright works to formats accessible to visually impaired persons without infringement of copyright was enacted in 2002.

Copyright protection in the UK is automatic and there is no official registration system. The creator of a work can help to protect it by including the copyright symbol ©, the name of the copyright owner, and the year in which the work was created. In addition, steps can be taken by the work's creator to provide evidence that he/she had the work at a particular time (eg by depositing a copy with a bank or solicitor). The main legislation is the Copyright, Designs and Patents Act 1988 (as amended). As a result of an EU directive effective from January 1996, the term of copyright protection for literary, dramatic, musical (including song lyrics and musical compositions) and artistic works lasts for 70 years after the death of the creator. For film, copyright lasts for 70 years after the director, authors of the screenplay and dialogue, or the composer of any music specially created for the film have all died. Sound recordings are protected for 50 years after their publication (or their first performance if they are not published), and broadcasts for 50 years from the end of the year in which the broadcast/transmission was made. The typographical arrangement of published editions remains under copyright protection for 25 years from the end of the year in which the particular edition was published.

The main international treaties protecting copyright are the Berne Convention for the Protection of Literary and Artistic Works (administered by the World Intellectual Property Organisation (WIPO)), the Rome Convention for the Protection of Performers, Producers of Phonograms and Broadcasting Organisations (administered by the United Nations Educational, Scientific and Cultural Organization (UNESCO), the International Labour Organization and WIPO), the Geneva Phonograms Convention (administered by WIPO), and the Universal Copyright Convention (developed by UNESCO); the UK is a signatory to these conventions. Copyright material created by UK nationals or residents is protected in the countries that have signed one of the above-named conventions by the national law of that country. A list of participating countries may be obtained from the UK Intellectual Property Office. The World Trade Organisation's Trade-Related Aspects of Intellectual Property Rights (TRIPS) agreement, signed in 1995, may also provide copyright protection abroad.

Two treaties which strengthen and update international standards of protection, particularly in relation to new technologies, were agreed in December 1996: the WIPO Copyright Treaty, and the WIPO Performances and Phonograms Treaty. In May 2001 the European Union passed a new directive (which in 2003 became law in the UK) aimed at harmonising copyright law throughout the EU to take account of the internet and other technologies. More information can be found online (W www.ipo.gov.uk).

LICENSING
Use of copyright material without seeking permission in each instance may be permitted under 'blanket' licences available from national copyright licensing agencies. The International Federation of Reproduction Rights Organisations facilitates agreements between its member licensing agencies and on behalf of its members with organisations such as WIPO, UNESCO, the European Union and the Council of Europe. More information can be found online (W www.ifrro.org).

DESIGN PROTECTION

Design protection covers the outward appearance of an article and in the UK takes two forms: registered design and design right, which are not mutually exclusive. Registered design protects the aesthetic appearance of an article, including shape, configuration, pattern or ornament; artistic works such as sculptures are excluded, being generally protected by copyright. To achieve design protection the owner of the design must apply to the Intellectual Property Office. In order to qualify for protection, a design must be new and materially different from earlier UK published designs. Initial registration lasts for five years and can be extended in five-year increments to a maximum of 25 years.

The current legislation is the Registered Designs Act 1949 which has been amended several times, most recently by the Regulatory Reform Order 2006.

UK applicants wishing to protect their designs in the EU can do so by applying for a Registered Community Design with the Office for Harmonisation in the Internal Market. Outside the EU separate applications must be made in each country in which protection is sought.

Design right is an automatic right which applies to the shape or configuration of articles and does not require registration. Unlike registered design, two-dimensional designs do not qualify for protection but designs of electronic circuits are protected by design right. Designs must be original and non-commonplace. The term of design right is ten years from first marketing of the design, or 15 years after the creation of the design, whichever is earlier. This right is effective only in the UK. After five years anyone is entitled to apply for a licence of right, which allows others to make and sell products copying the design. The current legislation is Part 3 of the Copyright, Designs and Patents Act 1988.

PATENTS

A patent is a document issued by the UK Intellectual Property Office relating to an invention. It gives the proprietor the right for a limited period to stop others from making, using, importing or selling the invention without the inventor's permission. In return the patentee pays a fee to cover the costs of processing the patent and publicly discloses details of the invention.

To qualify for a patent an invention must be new, must be functional or technical, must exhibit an inventive step, and must be capable of industrial application. The patent is valid for a maximum of 20 years from the date on which the application was filed, subject to payment of annual fees from the end of the fifth year.

The UK Intellectual Property Office, established in 1852, is responsible for ensuring that all stages of an application comply with the Patents Act 1977, and that the invention meets the criteria for a patent.

WIPO is responsible for administering many of the international conventions on intellectual property. The Patent Cooperation Treaty allows inventors to file a single application for patent rights in some or all of the contracting states. This application is searched by an International Searching Authority to confirm the invention is novel and that the same concept has not already been made publicly available. The application and search report are then published by the International Bureau of WIPO. It may also be the subject of an (optional) international preliminary examination. Applicants must then deal directly with the patent offices in the countries where they are seeking patent rights. The European Patent Convention allows inventors to obtain patent rights in all the contracting states by filing a single application with the European Patent Office. More information can be found online (W www.ipo.gov.uk).

RESEARCH DISCLOSURES

Research disclosures are publicly disclosed details of inventions. Once published, an invention is considered no longer novel and becomes 'prior art'. Publishing a disclosure is significantly cheaper than applying for a patent; however, unlike a patent, it does not entitle the author to exclusive rights to use or license the invention. Instead, research disclosures are primarily published to ensure the inventor the freedom to use the invention. This works because publishing legally prevents other parties from patenting the disclosed innovation and in the UK, patent law dictates that by disclosing details of an invention, even the inventor relinquishes their right to a patent.

In theory, publishing details of an invention anywhere should be enough to constitute a research disclosure. However, to be effective, a research disclosure needs to be published in a location which patent examiners will include in their prior art searches. To ensure global legal precedent it must be included in a publication with a recognised date stamp and made publicly available throughout the world.

Research Disclosure, established in 1960 and operated by Questel Ireland Ltd, is the primary publisher of research disclosures. It is the only disclosure service recognised by the Patent Cooperation Treaty as a mandatory search resource which must be consulted by the international search authorities. More information can be found online (W www.researchdisclosure.com).

TRADE MARKS

Trade marks are a means of identification, enabling traders to make their goods and services readily distinguishable from those supplied by others. Trade marks can take the form of words, a logo or a combination of both. Registration prevents other traders using the same or similar trade marks for similar products or services.

In the UK trade marks are registered at the UK Intellectual Property Office. In order to qualify for registration a trade mark must be capable of distinguishing its proprietor's goods or services from those of other undertakings; it should be non-deceptive, should not describe the goods and services or any characteristics of them, should not be contrary to law or morality and should not be similar or identical to any earlier trade marks for the same or similar goods or services. The owner of a registered trade mark may include an ® symbol next to it, and must renew their registration every ten years to keep it in force. The relevant current legislation is the Trade Marks Act 1994 (as amended).

It is possible to obtain an international trade mark registration, effective in 91 countries, under the Madrid system for the international registration of marks, to which the UK is party. British companies can obtain international trade mark registration in those countries party to the system through a single application to WIPO.

EU trade mark regulation is administered by the Office for Harmonisation in the Internal Market (Trade Marks and Designs) in Alicante, Spain. The office registers Community trade marks, which are valid throughout the European Union. The registration of trade marks in individual member states continues in parallel with EU trade mark standards.

DOMAIN NAMES
An internet domain name (eg www.bloomsbury.com) has to be registered separately from a trade mark, and this can be done through a number of registrars which charge varying rates and compete for business. For each top-level domain name (eg .uk .com), there is a central registry to store the unique internet names and addresses using that suffix. A list of accredited registrars can be found online (W www.icann.org).

CONTACTS

COPYRIGHT LICENSING AGENCY LTD, Saffron House, 6–10 Kirby Street, London EC1N 8TS T 020-7400 3100 W www.cla.co.uk

EUROPEAN PATENT OFFICE, 80298 Munich, Germany T (+49) 89 2399-0 W www.epo.org

INTELLECTUAL PROPERTY OFFICE, Concept House, Cardiff Road, Newport NP10 8QQ T 0300-300 2000 W www.ipo.gov.uk

WORLD INTELLECTUAL PROPERTY ORGANIZATION, 34 chemin des Colombettes, CH-1211 Geneva 20, Switzerland T (+41) 22 338 9111 W www.wipo.int

THE MEDIA

CROSS-MEDIA OWNERSHIP

The rules surrounding cross-media ownership were overhauled as part of the 2003 Communications Act. The act simplified and relaxed existing rules to encourage dispersion of ownership and new market entry while preventing the most influential media in any community being controlled by too narrow a range of interests. However, transfers and mergers are not solely subject to examination on competition grounds by the competition authorities. The Secretary of State for Culture, Media and Sport has a broad remit to decide if a transaction is permissible and can intervene on public interest grounds (relating both to newspapers and cross-media criteria, if broadcasting interests are also involved); the Secretary of State for Business, Innovation and Skills may also intervene in a media merger if it raises public interest considerations. The Office of Communications (OFCOM) has an advisory role in this context. Government and parliamentary assurances were given that any intervention into local newspaper transfers would be rare and exceptional. Following a request from the Secretary of State for Culture, Media and Sport in June 2010 for a removal of all restrictions from the ownership of local media, OFCOM recommended the liberalisation of local cross-media regulations to enable a single owner to control newspapers, a TV licence and radio stations in one area.

REGULATION

OFCOM is the regulator for the communication industries in the UK and has responsibility for television, radio, telecommunications and wireless communications services. OFCOM is required to report annually to parliament and exists to further the interests of consumers by balancing choice and competition with the duty to foster plurality; protect viewers and listeners and promote cultural diversity in the media; and to ensure full and fair competition between communications providers.

OFFICE OF COMMUNICATIONS (OFCOM)
Riverside House, 2A Southwark Bridge Road, London SE1 9HA
T 020-7981 3000 W www.ofcom.org.uk
Chief Executive, Ed Richards

COMPLAINTS

Under the Communications Act 2003 OFCOM's licensees are obliged to adhere to the provisions of its codes (including advertising, programme standards, fairness, privacy and sponsorship). Complainants should contact the broadcaster in the first instance (details can be found on OFCOM's website); however, if the complainant wishes the complaint to be considered by OFCOM, it will do so. Complaints should be made within a reasonable time, as broadcasters are only required to keep recordings for the following periods: radio, 42 days; television, 90 days; and cable and satellite, 60 days. OFCOM can fine a broadcaster, revoke a licence or take programmes off the air. Since November 2004 complaints relating to individual advertisements on TV or radio have been dealt with by the Advertising Standards Authority.

ADVERTISING STANDARDS AUTHORITY
Mid City Place, 71 High Holborn, London WC1V 6QT
T 020-7492 2222 W www.asa.org.uk
Chief Executive, Guy Parker

TELEVISION

There are six major television broadcasters operating in the UK. Four of these – the BBC, ITV, Channel 4 and Channel 5 – launched as free-to-air analogue terrestrial networks. BSkyB and Virgin Media Television provide satellite television services.

Beginning as a radio station in 1922, the BBC is the oldest broadcaster in the world. The corporation began a London-only television service from Alexandra Palace in 1936 and achieved nationwide coverage 15 years later. A second station, BBC Two, was launched in 1964. The BBC's other free-to-air channels available in the UK comprise BBC Three, BBC Four, BBC One HD, BBC Two HD, BBC News, BBC Parliament and the children's channels, CBeebies and CBBC. BBC's iPlayer service was launched Christmas Day 2007 and allows users to view and listen to programmes from the last seven days instantly, stream live television and download programmes on to a computer or mobile device for up to 30 days. An integrated service for radio was launched in June 2008. In 2009, iPlayer was extended to more than 20 devices, including mobile phones and games consoles, and an HD service was launched. The BBC services are funded by the licence fee. The corporation also has a commercial arm, BBC Worldwide, which was formed in 1994 and exists to maximise the value of the BBC's programme and publishing assets for the benefit of the licence payer. Its businesses include international programming distribution, magazines, other licensed products, live events and media monitoring.

The ITV (Independent Television) network began broadcasting in 1955 on Channel 3 in the London area, under the Television Act 1954 which made provision for commercial television in the UK. The ITV network originally comprised a number of independent licensees, the majority of which have now merged to form ITV plc. The network generates funds through broadcasting television advertisements. The ITV network channels now include ITV2, ITV3, ITV4, ITVBe and CiTV. ITV Player, similar to iPlayer, was launched December 2008. ITV Network Centre is wholly owned by the ITV companies and undertakes commissioning and scheduling of programmes shown across the ITV network and, as with the other terrestrial channels, 25 per cent of programmes must come from independent producers.

Channel 4 and S4C (Sianel Pedwar Cymru – Channel Four Wales) were launched in 1982 to provide programmes with a distinctive character that appeal to interests not catered for by ITV. The broadcaster has a remit to be innovative, experimental and distinctive. Although publicly owned, Channel 4 receives no public funding and is financed predominantly through advertising, but unlike ITV, Channel 4 is not shareholder-owned. It has expanded to create the stations E4, More4, Film4, 4Music and, in July 2012, catchup channel 4seven. 4oD is Channel 4's online service which enables viewers to download and revisit programmes from the last 30 days as well as access an older archive of footage. In September 2014, Channel 4 announced 4oD would be replaced by a new online hub called All4, which would be introduced in 2015. S4/C, the Welsh language public service broadcaster, received annual funding from the Department for Culture, Media and Sport (DCMS), which was reduced substantially from £101m in 2010 to £7m in 2014–15. Amid funding concerns for the future of S4C, it was agreed that the BBC would fund most of S4C's activities from the licence fee, contributing £76m in 2014–15. S4C will remain independent and be entitled to receive UK government funding and generate its own revenue. The on-demand service is called S4C Clic.

Channel 5 began broadcasting in 1997. It was rebranded Five in 2002 but reverted to its original name, Channel 5, after the station was acquired by Northern & Shell in July 2010. Digital stations 5USA and 5* (formerly Five Life, then Fiver) were launched in October 2006. Demand Five is an online service, launched in June 2008, where viewers can watch and download content from the last 30 days.

BSkyB was formed after the merger in 1990 of Sky Television and British Sky Broadcasting. 21st Century Fox has a 39.14 per cent controlling stake in the company, which operates a satellite television service and has around 40 television channels, including Sky One and the Sky Sports and Sky Movies ranges. Sky Digital was launched on 1 October 1998. Its key selling points were the improvement in sound and picture quality and an increased number of channels, some of which were exclusive to Sky Digital. In 2001, Sky Digitial was rebranded to just 'Sky'. With the 2005 acquisition of Easynet, an internet access provider and network operator, BSkyB now offers voice over IP (VoIP) telephony, video on demand and internet-based TV. With a free box, Sky+ and Sky+ HD customers are able to pause and rewind live TV and record favourite programmes both at home or with a compatible device while on the move. In July 2010 BSkyB acquired Virgin Media Television, including its portfolio of channels such as Bravo and Challenge. On 25 July 2014 it was announced BSkyB would pay 21st Century Fox £4.9bn to buy out Sky Italia and a 57 per cent interest in Sky Deutschland. The transaction will give BSkyB 20 million pay-TV customers across Europe. As at 30 June 2013, there were 10.5 million Sky customers in the UK.

In February 2011, a new version of OFCOM's Broadcasting Code came into force, permitting product placement for the first time in UK-produced television programmes. A large 'P' logo designed by OFCOM and broadcasters is displayed at the beginning and end of each programme containing product placement. The first instance of product placement occurred on 28 February 2011.

THE TELEVISION LICENCE

In the UK and its dependencies, a television licence is required to receive any publicly broadcast television service, regardless of its source, including commercial, satellite and cable programming. A TV licence registered to a home address allows the viewer to watch television on laptops, tablets and mobile phones outside the place of residence. If a viewer only watches catch-up TV, not live TV, using services such as BBC iPlayer, and this is the only means by which the viewer watches broadcasts, a television licence is not required.

The TV licence is classified as a tax, therefore non-payment is a criminal offence. A fine of up to £1,000 can be imposed on those successfully prosecuted. The TV licence is issued on behalf of the BBC as the licensing authority under the Communications Act 2003. In 2013–14 income from licence fees totalled £3.7bn, an £16.4m increase on 2012–13. A six-year licence fee settlement was agreed in 2010 which froze the annual colour television licence fee at £145.50 until 2017. A black and white licence costs £49. Concessions are available for the elderly and people with disabilities. Further details can be found at
W www.tvlicensing.co.uk/information

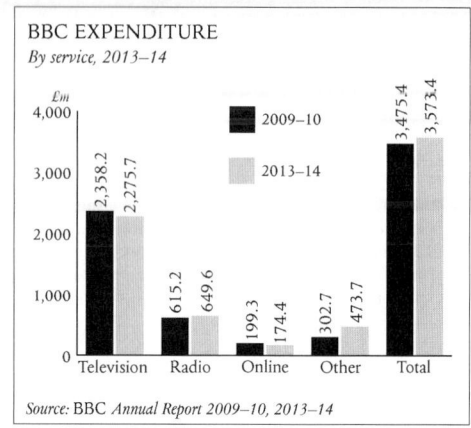

BBC EXPENDITURE
By service, 2013–14

Source: BBC *Annual Report 2009–10, 2013–14*

DIGITAL TELEVISION

The Broadcasting Act 1996 provided for the licensing of 20 or more digital terrestrial television (DTT) channels (on six frequency channels or 'multiplexes'). The first digital services went on air in autumn 1998.

In June 2002, following the collapse of ITV Digital, the digital terrestrial television licence was awarded to a consortium made up of the BBC, BSkyB and transmitter company Crown Castle by the Independent Television Commission. Freeview was launched on 30 October 2002: it now offers around 70 digital channels and 30 radio stations and requires the one-off purchase of a set-top box, but is subsequently free of charge with no subscription. In Autumn 2005 ITV and Channel 4 officially became shareholders, each taking a 20 per cent stake. As at July 2014, more than 19 million homes use Freeview on at least one set, amounting to around 75 per cent of UK households. Freeview additionally offers the UK's top six channels in HD, with a further seven channels, including BBC News and Aljazeera, available to 70 per cent of UK homes since June 2014. There is an additional Freeview+ service which works in a similar fashion to Sky+.

As at July 2014, 98.5 per cent of British homes had access to digital TV. In 2013, combined digital channels amounted to a 46.8 per cent share of viewing, comparable to a 21 per cent share for BBC and 16.3 per cent for ITV and ITV+1.

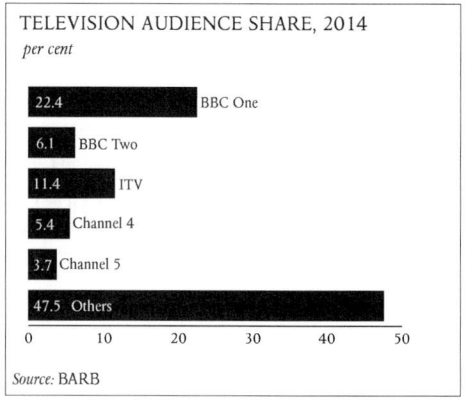

TELEVISION AUDIENCE SHARE, 2014
per cent

22.4	BBC One
6.1	BBC Two
11.4	ITV
5.4	Channel 4
3.7	Channel 5
47.5	Others

Source: BARB

RECENT DEVELOPMENTS

The internet has now firmly established itself as an alternative to live and programmed TV, particularly for those aged 16 to 34. Since the launch of 4oD in 2006 and

BBC iPlayer in 2007, there has been a noticeable shift in the way viewers can watch their favourite programmes. Technological advancements have also contributed to this new phenomenon; one in three people in the UK uses a tablet, nearly 75 per cent of UK homes have access to superfast broadband and the number of public Wi-Fi spots reached 32,000 in 2013. There is now a much bigger emphasis on catch-up, on-demand and streaming services than previously, with 3 billion requests on iPlayer in 2013, up 33 per cent on 2012. Tablet requests alone increased by 104 per cent and downloads of the iPlayer mobile app reached 20 million, although PCs were still the biggest platform for iPlayer requests. Streaming services such as Netflix have experienced a surge in popularity, with subscribers able to stream programmes through computers, mobiles, tablets and games consoles on up to four devices at a time for a monthly subscription fee. Netflix also commissions and distributes its own programmes, available exclusively to their subscribers, contributing to their popularity; as at August 2013, Netflix had an estimated 1.5 million subscribers in the UK. Furthermore, the BBC has outlined a move towards exclusive content and programmes on the iPlayer for 2014, while also announcing plans (subject to approval from the BBC Trust) to move BBC Three to an online service on the iPlayer from autumn 2015 (and thereby cease broadcasting on Freeview and satellite). These transitions indicate that online catch-up and streaming services are now becoming competitive TV destinations in their own right.

Set-top boxes have also adapted to this viewing shift. YouView, in partnership with BBC, ITV, Channel Four, Channel Five, BT, Talk Talk and Arqiva, launched in July 2012. Subscribers are able to watch programmes (including on-demand), pause and rewind live TV and listen to digital radio via a hybrid set-top box connected to broadband. Originally envisaged as free-to-air, it has drawn criticism for tying customers into broadband services and subscriptions with BT and Talk Talk, with the one-off payment for the YouView box more expensive than the Freeview box. In June 2014, Freeview announced plans for a Freeview Connect service, which would provide catch-up services including iPlayer and 4oD as standard on smart TVs with broadband connections. It is seen as a free alternative to YouView, whereby viewers would still require a broadband connection but would not be tied to a specific provider. BBC, ITV and Channel Four announced they will substantially decrease their investment in YouView and instead invest a total of around £100m in the development of Freeview Connect.

Despite the rise in the popularity of tablets, traditional TV sets are still the most popular way to watch television. HD TV provides more vibrant colours and greater detail and picture clarity, along with improved sound quality. An HD television screen uses 1,280 by 720 pixels up to 1,920 by 1,080 pixels. HD Ready TVs operate at 720p while full HD TVs tend to operate on 1080p or 1080i; the differences between these three settings are down to the number of lines in the resolution and the type of scanning technology. 'HD Ready' simply means the TV will only operate a higher definition once plugged into a decoder, whereas full HD has this built in. Up to 13 channels are available in HD through Freeview. In 2013, the average screen size in the UK was 34.5 inches wide, indicating a trend towards bigger screens. Sales of Smart TVs, which can access apps, browse the internet and stream video, reached nearly 1.5 million in 2013 – a 211 per cent increase since 2011.

In April 2010, Samsung released the first consumer 3D TV; in the same month Sky launched the UK's first dedicated 3D channel. Several sporting events have been broadcast in 3D including the Wimbledon Championships. The BBC began a two-year 3D trial in 2011 but announced in July 2013 it would suspend 3D programming for an indefinite period of time due to a lack of public appetite for the technology. Of the estimated 1.5 million 3D TV sets in the UK, just 5 per cent used 3D to watch the Queen's Christmas Speech 2013.

In September 2012 OFCOM awarded its first local TV licences after announcing plans to broadcast 19 channels in total. In November 2013 Estuary TV, based in Grimsby, was the first to be launched. The government has backed the local TV initiative and the channels broadcast on channel 8 on Freeview in England and Northern Ireland and channel 26 in Scotland and Wales.

CONTACTS

THE BRITISH BROADCASTING CORPORATION
BBC Broadcasting House Portland Place, London W1A 1AA
W www.bbc.co.uk
BBC North, Media City UK, Salford Quays, Manchester M50 2BH
Chair, Rona Fairhead
Director-General, Tony Hall
BBC Worldwide, 201 Wood Lane, London W12 7TQ
W www.bbcworldwide.com

INDEPENDENT TELEVISION NETWORK
ITV Network Centre, 200 Gray's Inn Road, London WC1X 8HF
T 020-7156 6000 **W** www.itv.com
Chair, Archie Norman

INDEPENDENT TELEVISION NETWORK REGIONS
Anglia (eastern England) **W** www.itv.com/anglia
Border (Borders and the Isle of Man) **W** www.itv.com/border
Calendar (Yorkshire) **W** www.itv.com/calendar
Central (east, west and south Midlands) **W** www.itv.com/central
Channel (Channel Islands) **W** www.channelonline.tv
Granada (north-west England) **W** www.itv.com/granada
London **W** www.itv.com/london
Meridian (south and south-east England)
   W www.itv.com/meridian
STV (Scotland) **W** www.stv.tv
Tyne Tees (north-east England) **W** www.itv.com/tynetees
Ulster (Northern Ireland) **W** www.u.tv
Wales **W** www.itv.com/wales
West **W** www.itv.com/west

OTHER TELEVISION COMPANIES
Channel 4 Television, 124 Horseferry Road, London SW1P 2TX
   T 020-7396 4444 **W** www.channel4.com
Channel 5 Broadcasting Ltd, 10 Lower Thames Street,
   London EC3R 6EN **T** 020-8612 7700 **W** www.channel5.com
Independent Television News (ITN), 200 Gray's Inn Road,
   London WC1X 8XZ **T** 020-7833 3000 **W** www.itn.co.uk
   Provides news programming for ITV and Channel 4.
Sianel Pedwar Cymru (S4/C), Parc Ty Glas, Llanishen,
   Cardiff CF14 5DU **T** 0870-600 4141 **W** www.s4c.co.uk

DIRECT BROADCASTING BY SATELLITE TELEVISION
British Sky Broadcasting Group PLC, Grant Way, Isleworth,
   Isleworth TW7 5QD **T** 020-7705 3000 **W** www.sky.com
Chair, Nicholas Ferguson, CBE

RADIO

UK domestic radio services are broadcast across three wavebands: FM, medium wave and long wave (used by BBC Radio 4). In the UK the FM waveband extends in frequency from 87.5MHz to 108MHz and the medium waveband from 531kHz to 1602kHz. A number of radio stations are broadcast in both analogue and digital as well as a growing number in digital alone. As at June 2013, the BBC Radio network controlled around 53.3 per cent of the listening market (*see* BBC Radio section), and the independent sector (*see* Independent Radio section) 43.2 per cent. As at June 2014, a listener tunes into an average of 21.4 hours of radio per week.

ESTIMATED AUDIENCE SHARE

	Apr–Jun 2012	Apr–Jun 2013	Percentage Apr–Jun 2014
BBC Radio 1	8.3	6.8	6.8
BBC Radio 2	16.1	17.2	17.7
BBC Radio 3	1.1	1.2	1.0
BBC Radio 4	12.1	12.1	11.6
BBC Radio Five Live	4.5	4.1	4.1
Five Live Sports Extra	0.4	0.3	0.3
BBC 6 Music	1.1	1.5	1.6
BBC Asian Network UK	0.3	0.3	0.3
1Xtra	0.6	0.5	0.5
BBC Local/Regional	8.1	8.3	7.7
BBC World Service	0.6	0.6	0.7
All BBC	54.3	53.9	53.3
All independent	43.3	43.7	43.2
All national independent	12.7	13.3	12.9
All local independent	30.5	30.4	30.3
Other	2.5	2.4	3.5

Source: RAJAR

DIGITAL RADIO

DAB (digital audio broadcasting) allows more services to be broadcast to a higher technical quality and provides the data facility for text and pictures. It was developed in a collaborative research project under the pan-European Eureka 147 initiative and has been adopted as a world standard by the International Telecommunication Union for new digital radio systems. The frequencies allocated for terrestrial digital radio in the UK are 174 to 239MHz. Additional spectrum (in the 'L-Band' range: 1452–1478MHz) was introduced in 2007.

Digital radio is available through digital radio sets, car radios, online, on games consoles and on mobile devices such as phones and tablets. An alternative method is to listen to digital radio through television sets via Freeview, cable or satellite.

The listening share via all digital platforms at the end of June 2014 was 36.8 per cent, the same as in June 2013. DAB accounts for 65 per cent of total digital listening, 17 per cent is online and 13 per cent on digital TV (DTV). In June 2009 the government published the white paper *Digital Britain*, which recommended that most services carried on the national and local DAB multiplexes should cease broadcasting on analogue radio by 2015, though this date is now no longer deemed feasible. Ultra-local radio, consisting of small independent and community stations, would continue to broadcast on FM. There are two criteria that must be met for digital migration to occur:

• at least 50 per cent of radio listening is digital
• national DAB coverage is comparable to FM coverage, and local DAB reaches 90 per cent of the population and all major roads

LICENSING

The Broadcasting Act 1996 provided for the licensing of digital radio services (on multiplexes, where a number of stations share one frequency to transmit their services). To allocate the multiplexes, OFCOM advertises licences for which interested parties can bid. Once the licence has been awarded, the new owner seeks out services to broadcast on the multiplex. The BBC has a separate national multiplex for its services. There are local multiplexes around the country, each broadcasting an average of seven services, plus the local BBC station.

INNOVATIONS

The internet offers a number of advantages compared to other digital platforms such as DAB including higher sound quality, a greater range of channel availability and flexibility

in listening opportunity. Listeners can tune in to the majority of radio stations live on the internet or listen again online generally up to seven days after broadcast. DAB radio does not allow the same interactivity: the data is only able to travel one-way from broadcaster to listener whereas the internet allows a two-way flow of information.

Increase in WiFi hotspots also means listening to radio, podcasts and catch-up programmes is easy to do through tablets and mobile phones; 22 per cent of adults claim to listen to the radio via a mobile phone or tablet at least once a month, while the percentage for those aged 15 to 24 is noticeably higher at 36 per cent. The increase in music streaming services and radio-related apps has had a major effect on music discovery and sharing. In the UK in 2013–14 the number of streams a week averaged 260 million. Since 6 July 2014 the UK Official Charts Company has included streaming services in its compilation, with 100 streams the equivalent to one purchase.

Since 2005 most radio stations offer all or part of their programmes as downloadable files, known as podcasts, to listen to on computers, mobiles or tablets.. Podcasting technology allows listeners to subscribe in order to receive automatically the latest episodes of regularly transmitted programmes as soon as they become available.

The relationship between radio stations and their audiences is also undergoing change. The quantity and availability of music on the internet has led to the creation of shows dedicated entirely to music sent in by listeners. Another new development in internet-based radio has been personalised radio stations, such as last.fm and Spotify. Last.fm 'recommends' songs based on the favourite artists and previous choices of the user. Spotify, available as an app on most smart phones and tablets as well as online, allows listeners access to the track, artist or genre of their choice, or to share and create playlists. It has seen steady growth in popularity since its launch in 2008, with over 10 million paying subscribers and over 40 million active users globally (as at May 2014). Spotify 'learns as you listen' and makes associated recommendations based on user choices. SoundCloud, founded in 2007, is an innovative 'sound platform' which enables users to upload their own music and recordings to share privately or publicly. Artists who upload their music are given a URL, allowing their music to be embedded anywhere, making it easier to share through social media platforms such as Twitter and Facebook. Users can also create their own playlists and link them to social media platforms. Radioplayer (W www.radioplayer.co.uk), a not-for-profit company backed by the BBC, Global Radio, Bauer Media and RadioCentre, allows audiences to listen to live and catch-up radio from one place. There are around 330 stations available and a 'recommended' service which offers station suggestions depending on location, what is trending and the type of music the user likes. Radioplayer launched as a mobile app in 2012 (as at February 2014, there were over 1 million users) and a tablet app in 2013. Through the tablet app, users sample an average of 4.6 stations a week in comparison with just 2.1 for analogue users.

BBC RADIO

BBC Radio broadcasts network services to the UK, Isle of Man and the Channel Islands, with over 35 million listeners each week. There is also a tier of national services in Wales, Scotland and Northern Ireland and around 40 local radio stations in England and the Channel Islands. In Wales and Scotland there are also dedicated language services in Welsh and Gaelic respectively. The frequency allocated for digital BBC broadcasts is 225.648MHz.

BBC Radio, Broadcasting House, Portland Place, London
W1A 1AA **W** www.bbc.co.uk/radio

BBC NETWORK RADIO STATIONS

Radio 1 (contemporary pop music and entertainment news) – 24 hours a day, *Frequencies:* 97–99 FM and digital

Radio 2 (popular music, entertainment, comedy and the arts) – 24 hours a day, *Frequencies:* 88–91 FM and digital

Radio 3 (classical music, classic drama, documentaries and features) – 24 hours a day, *Frequencies:* 90–93 FM and digital

Radio 4 (news, documentaries, drama, entertainment and cricket on long wave in season) – 5.20am–1am daily, with BBC World Service overnight, *Frequencies:* 92–95 FM/103–105 FM and 198 LW and digital

Radio Five Live (news and sport) – 24 hours a day, *Frequencies:* 909/693 MW and digital

Five Live Sports Extra (live sport) – schedule varies, digital only

6 Music (contemporary and classic pop and rock music) – 24 hours a day, digital only

Asian Network (news, music and sport) – 5am–1am, with Radio Five Live overnight, *Frequencies:* various MW frequencies in Midlands and digital

1Xtra (urban music: drum & bass, garage, hip hop, R&B) – 24 hours a day, digital only

BBC NATIONAL RADIO STATIONS

Radio Cymru (Welsh-language), *Frequencies:* 92–105 FM and digital

Radio Foyle, Frequencies: 93.1 FM and 792 MW and digital

Radio nan Gaidheal (Gaelic service), *Frequencies:* 103–105 FM and digital

Radio Scotland, Frequencies: 92–95 FM and 810 MW and digital. Local programmes for Orkney, Shetland and Highlands and Islands

Radio Ulster, Frequencies: 1341 MW and 92–95 FM and digital. Local programmes on Radio Foyle

Radio Wales, Frequencies: 657/882 MW and 93–104 FM and digital

BBC WORLD SERVICE

The BBC World Service broadcasts to an estimated weekly audience of 1.3 million people in the UK and 191.4 million worldwide, in 28 languages including English, and is now available in around 150 capital cities. It no longer broadcasts in Dutch, French for Europe, German, Hebrew, Italian, Japanese or Malay because it was found that most speakers of these languages preferred to listen to the English broadcasts. In 2006 services in ten languages (Bulgarian, Croatian, Czech, Greek, Hungarian, Kazakh, Polish, Slovak, Slovene and Thai) were terminated to provide funding for a new Arabic television channel, which was launched in March 2008. In August 2008 the BBC's Romanian World Service broadcasts were discontinued after 68 years. In January 2011 the BBC announced five more language services would be terminated: Albanian, Caribbean English, Macedonian, Portuguese for Africa and Serbian. The BBC World Service website offers interactive news services in 32 languages including English, Arabic, Chinese, Hindi, Persian, Portuguese for Brazil, Russian, Spanish and Urdu with audiostreaming available.

LANGUAGES
Arabic, Azeri, Bangla, Burmese, Chinese, English, French, Hausa, Hindi, Indonesian, Kinyarwanda, Kirundi, Kyrgyz, Nepali, Pashto, Persian, Portuguese, Russian, Sinhala, Somali, Spanish, Swahili, Tamil, Turkish, Ukrainian, Urdu, Uzbek and Vietnamese.

UK frequencies: digital; overnight on BBC Radio 4.
BBC Learning English teaches English worldwide through radio, television and a wide range of published and online courses.

BBC Media Action is a registered charity established in 1999 by BBC World Service, known as the BBC World Service Trust until December 2011. It promotes development through the innovative use of the media in the developing world.

BBC Monitoring tracks the global media for the latest news reports emerging around the world.

BBC WORLD SERVICE, 1st Floor Brock House, 19 Langham Street, London W1A 1AA **W** www.bbc.co.uk/worldservice

INDEPENDENT RADIO

Until 1973, the BBC had a legal monopoly on radio broadcasting in the UK. During this time, the corporation's only competition came from pirate stations located abroad, such as Radio Luxembourg. Christopher Chataway, Minister for Post and Telecommunications, changed this by creating the first licences for commercial radio stations. The Independent Broadcasting Authority (IBA) awarded the first of these licences to the London Broadcasting Company (LBC) to provide London's news and information service. LBC was followed by Capital Radio, to offer the city's entertainment service, Radio Clyde in Glasgow and BRMB in Birmingham.

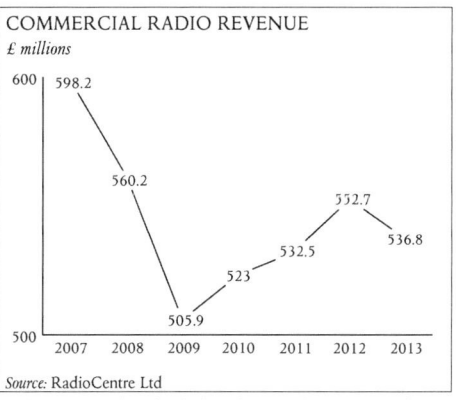

COMMERCIAL RADIO REVENUE
£ millions

598.2 (2007)
560.2 (2008)
505.9 (2009)
523 (2010)
532.5 (2011)
552.7 (2012)
536.8 (2013)

Source: RadioCentre Ltd

The IBA was dissolved when the Broadcasting Act of 1990 de-regulated broadcasting, to be succeeded by the less rigid Radio Authority (RA). The RA began advertising new licences for the development of independent radio in January 1991. It awarded national and local radio, satellite and cable services licences, and long-term restricted service licences for stations serving non-commercial establishments such as hospitals and universities. The first national commercial digital multiplex licence was awarded in October 1998 and a number of local digital multiplex licences followed. At the end of 2003 the RA was replaced by OFCOM, which now carries out the licensing administration.

RadioCentre was formed in July 2006 as a result of the merger between the Radio Advertising Bureau (RAB) and the Commercial Radio Companies Association (CRCA), the former non-profit trade body for commercial radio companies in the UK, to operate essentially as a union for commercial radio stations. According to the 2011 Commercial Radio Audit, it is possible to listen to 95 per cent of independent radio stations online, while 150 commercial stations can be listened to on DAB radios. There are currently 296 licenced stations associated with RadioCentre.

RadioCentre, 6th Floor, 55 New Oxford Street, London WC1A 1BS **T** 020-7010 0600 **W** www.radiocentre.org
Chief Executive, Siobhan Kenny

THE PRESS

The newspaper and periodical press in the UK is large and diverse, catering for a wide variety of views and interests. There is no state control or censorship of the press; however, it is subject to the laws on publication.

The press is not state-subsidised and receives few tax concessions. The income of most newspapers and periodicals is derived largely from sales and from advertising. Advertising revenue from national and regional newspapers decreased from £2.2bn in 2013 (15.3 per cent of the media advertising market share) to £2.1bn in 2014 (13.8 per cent of the market share).

SELF-REGULATION

The Press Complaints Commission (PCC) was founded by the newspaper and magazine industry in January 1991 to replace the Press Council (established in 1953). It is a voluntary, non-statutory body set up to operate the press's self-regulation system following the Calcutt report in 1990 on privacy and related matters, when the industry feared that failure to regulate itself might lead to statutory regulation of the press. The performance of the PCC was reviewed in February 2010 by the Culture, Media and Sport Select Committee, which concluded in favour of continuing self-regulation. In July 2010 an independent review into the commission's governance made 75 recommendations for enhancing the system of press self-regulation.

In November 2012, responding to the publication of Lord Justice Leveson's Report (see below), Lord Hunt, chair of the PCC, reiterated a commitment to moving forward as swiftly as possible to a new regulatory body. As a result, the UK newspaper and magazine industry agreed to construct a new regulatory system, compliant with Lord Justice Leveson's recommendations. In accordance with the Leveson principles, the Independent Press Standards Organisation (IPSO), was created to replace the PCC and commenced operations in September 2014.

LEVESON INQUIRY

The Leveson Inquiry, established under the Inquiries Act 2005, was announced by the prime minister on 13 July 2011 to investigate the role of press and police in the *News of the World* phone-hacking scandal. Lord Justice Leveson was appointed as chair of the inquiry. The hearings began on 14 November 2011 and ended on 24 July 2012 following the testimonies of 650 witnesses.

The Leveson Report was published in late November 2012 and featured several broad and complex recommendations as to how the press should be regulated. The report generally recommended that the press should continue to be self-regulated, with the government allowed no direct power over what is published, and that a new press standards body, with a new code of conduct, should be established by legislation in order to ensure regulation is independent and effective. Lord Justice Leveson concluded that this arrangement should give the public confidence that their complaints would be dealt with seriously and ensure the press would be protected from interference.

In March 2013, the three main political parties decided that an independent regulator with powers to demand prominent corrections and apologies from UK news publishers and the ability to impose fines of up to £1m would be established by royal charter. In response, the Newspaper Society, which represents national and local titles, announced it rejected 'state-sponsored' regulation and would apply for its own royal charter to establish a new system. At the time of going to press no further decisions on a new regulator had been reached.

NEWSPAPERS

Newspapers are mostly financially independent of any political party, though most adopt a political stance in their editorial comments, usually reflecting proprietorial influence. Ownership of the national and regional daily newspapers is concentrated in the hands of large corporations whose interests cover publishing and communications, although *The Guardian* and *The Observer* are owned by the Scott Trust, formed in 1936 to protect the financial and editorial independence of *The Guardian* in perpetuity. The rules on cross-media ownership, as amended by the Broadcasting Act 1996, which limited the extent to which newspaper organisations may become involved in broadcasting, have been relaxed by the Communications Act 2003: newspapers with over a 20 per cent share of national circulation may own national and/or local radio licences.

In October 2010, *The Independent* launched a concise newspaper, *i*, the first new daily newspaper since 1986. In July 2011, *News of the World* was closed by its parent company, News International, following accusations of phone-hacking. In February 2012 News International printed the first edition of *The Sun on Sunday*, a Sunday format of the daily tabloid paper *The Sun*. There are 14 daily and Sunday national papers and several hundred local papers that are published daily, weekly or twice-weekly. Scotland, Wales and Northern Ireland all have at least one daily and one Sunday national paper.

UK CIRCULATION

National Daily Newspapers	June 2013	June 2014	% +/−
The Sun	2,243,903	2,033,606	−9.37
Daily Mail	1,806,569	1,673,580	−7.36
Daily Mirror	1,038,753	958,675	−7.71
The Daily Telegraph	547,106	514,591	−5.94
Daily Express	522,264	479,703	−8.15
Daily Star	540,849	466,934	−13.67
The Times	390,941	393,531	+0.33
i	303,009	286,357	−5.5
Financial Times	258,488	220,532	−14.68
Daily Record	252,626	213,895	−15.33
The Guardian	187,000	185,312	−0.9
The Independent	73,060	63,506	−13.08

National Sunday Newspapers	June 2013	June 2014	% +/−
The Sun on Sunday	1,875,220	1,635,068	−12.81
The Mail on Sunday	1,638,049	1,528,562	−6.68
Sunday Mirror	1,037,542	922,941	−11.09
The Sunday Times	840,201	815,760	−2.91
Sunday Express	455,901	418,131	−8.28
The Sunday Telegraph	422,590	406,200	−3.88
The Sunday People	415,075	369,312	−11.03
Daily Star Sunday	335,864	294,944	−12.18
Sunday Mail	284,051	237,636	−16.34
Sunday Post	244,257	216,694	−11.28
The Observer	212,376	207,005	−2.53
The Independent on Sunday	111,986	100,102	−10.61

Source: Audit Bureau of Circulations Ltd

Newspapers are usually published in either broadsheet or smaller, tabloid format. The 'quality' daily papers – ie those providing detailed coverage of a wide range of public matters – have traditionally been broadsheets, the more populist newspapers tabloid. In 2004 this correlation between format and content was redefined when two traditionally broadsheet newspapers, *The Times* and *The Independent*, switched to tabloid-sized editions, while *The Guardian* launched a 'Berliner' format in September 2005. In October 2005 *The Independent on Sunday* became the first Sunday broadsheet to be published in the tabloid (or 'compact') size, and *The Observer*, like its daily counterpart *The Guardian*, began publishing in the Berliner format in January 2006.

NEWSPAPERS ONLINE

The demand to read news instantly and while on the move has increased the popularity of newspaper websites. Most newspapers now operate their own websites in line with their print editions, often including the same material as seen in daily printed editions but can also include video and audio features. Many articles and columns additionally have the option of reader contributions and debate. Certain newspapers charge a subscription fee to access their websites but the majority are free to browse.

NATIONAL PRESS WEBSITE DAILY AVERAGE BROWSERS

National Press Website	June 2013	June 2014	% +/−
MailOnline	8,111,988	10,912,083	34.52
theguardian.com	4,884,043	5,718,502	17.09
Telegraph	2,733,136	3,901,515	42.75
Mirror Group Nationals	1,440,082	2,680,547	86.14
The Independent	1,099,561	1,856,894	68.88
express.co.uk	–	705,976	–
dailystar.co.uk	–	524,986	–

Source: Audit Bureau of Circulations Ltd

NATIONAL DAILY NEWSPAPERS

DAILY EXPRESS
Northern & Shell Building, 10 Lower Thames Street, London EC3R 6EN T 020-8612 7000 W www.express.co.uk
Editor, Hugh Whittow

DAILY MAIL
Northcliffe House, 2 Derry Street, London W8 5TT
T 020-7938 6000 W www.dailymail.co.uk
Editor, Paul Dacre

DAILY MIRROR
1 Canada Square, Canary Wharf, London E14 5AP
T 020-7293 3000 W www.mirror.co.uk
Editor, Lloyd Embley

DAILY RECORD
1 Central Quay, Glasgow G3 8DA T 0141-309 3000
W www.dailyrecord.co.uk
Editor, Allan Rennie

DAILY STAR
Northern & Shell Building, 10 Lower Thames Street, London EC3R 6EN T 020-8612 7000 W www.dailystar.co.uk
Editor, Dawn Neesom

THE DAILY TELEGRAPH
111 Buckingham Palace Road, London SW1W 0DT
T 020-7931 2000 W www.telegraph.co.uk
Editor, Ian MacGregor

FINANCIAL TIMES
1 Southwark Bridge, London SE1 9HL T 020-7873 3000
W www.ft.com
Editor, Lionel Barber

THE GUARDIAN
King's Place, 90 York Way, London N1 9GU T 020-3353 2000
W www.theguardian.com
Editor, Alan Rusbridger

THE HERALD
200 Renfield Street, Glasgow G2 3QB T 0141-302 7000
W www.heraldscotland.com
Editor, Magnus Llewellin

THE INDEPENDENT *AND* i
Northcliffe House, 2 Derry Street, London W8 5HF
T 020-7005 2000 W www.independent.co.uk
Editor, Amol Rajan and Oliver Duff

THE SCOTSMAN
152 Morrison Street, Edinburgh EH3 8EB T 0131-620 8620
W www.scotsman.com
Editor, Ian Stewart

THE SUN
3 Thomas More Square, London E98 1XY T 020-7782 4000
W www.thesun.co.uk
Editor, David Dinsmore

THE TIMES
1 Pennington Street, London E98 1TT T 020-7782 5000
W www.thetimes.co.uk
Editor, John Witherow

WEEKLY NEWSPAPERS

DAILY STAR SUNDAY
Northern and Shell Building, 10 Lower Thames Street, London EC3R 6EN T 020-8612 7000 W www.dailystar.co.uk/sunday
Editor, Peter Carbery

INDEPENDENT ON SUNDAY
Northcliffe House, 2 Derry Street, London W8 5TT
T 020-7005 2000 W www.independent.co.uk
Editor, Lisa Markwell

MAIL ON SUNDAY
2 Derry Street, London W8 HFT T 020-7938 6000
W www.mailonsunday.co.uk
Editor, Geordie Greig

THE OBSERVER
Kings Place, 90 York Way, London N1 9GU T 020-3353 2000
W www.observer.theguardian.com
Editor, John Mulholland

THE PEOPLE
1 Canada Square, Canary Wharf, London E14 5AP
T 020-7293 3000 W www.people.co.uk
Editor, James Scott

SCOTLAND ON SUNDAY
Barclay House, 108 Holyrood Road, Edinburgh EH8 8AS
T 0131-620 8620 W www.scotlandonsunday.com
Editor, Ian Stewart

THE SUN ON SUNDAY
3 Thomas More Square, London E98 1XY T 020-7782 4000
W www.thesun.co.uk
Editor, Victoria Newton

SUNDAY EXPRESS
Northern & Shell Building, 10 Lower Thames Street, London EC4R 6EN T 020-8612 7000 W www.sundayexpress.co.uk
Editor, Martin Townsend

SUNDAY HERALD
200 Renfield Street, Glasgow G2 3QB T 0141-302 7000
W www.sundayherald.com
Editor, Richard Walker

SUNDAY MAIL
1 Central Quay, Glasgow G3 8DA T 0141-309 3000
W www.sundaymail.com
Editor, Allan Rennie

SUNDAY MIRROR
1 Canada Square, Canary Wharf, London E14 5AP
T 020-7293 3000 W www.sundaymirror.co.uk
Editor, Lloyd Embley

SUNDAY POST
144 Port Dundas Road, Glasgow G4 0HZ T 0141-332 9933
W www.sundaypost.com
Editor, Donald Martin

SUNDAY TELEGRAPH
111 Buckingham Palace Road, London SW1W 0DT
　T 020-7931 2000 W www.telegraph.co.uk
　Editor, Ian MacGregor
THE SUNDAY TIMES
3 Thomas More Square, London E98 1XY T 020-7782 5000
　W www.thesundaytimes.co.uk
　Editor, Martin Ivens

REGIONAL DAILY NEWSPAPERS
EAST ANGLIA
CAMBRIDGE NEWS
Winship Road, Milton, Cambs. CB24 6PP T 01223-434434
　W www.cambridge-news.co.uk
　Editor, Paul Brackley
EAST ANGLIAN DAILY TIMES
Lower Brook Street, Ipswich IP4 1AN T 01473-230023
　W www.eadt.co.uk
　Editor, Terry Hunt
EASTERN DAILY PRESS
Prospect House, Rouen Road, Norwich NR1 1RE T 01603-628311
　W www.edp24.co.uk
　Editor, Nigel Pickover
IPSWICH STAR
Lower Brook Street, Ipswich, Suffolk IP4 1AN T 01473-230023
　W www.ipswichstar.co.uk
　Editor, Terry Hunt
NORWICH EVENING NEWS
Prospect House, Rouen Road, Norwich NR1 1RE T 01603-628311
　W www.eveningnews24.co.uk
　Editor, Nigel Pickover

EAST MIDLANDS
BURTON MAIL
65–68 High Street, Burton upon Trent DE14 1LE T 01283-512345
　W www.burtonmail.co.uk
　Editor, Kevin Booth
DERBY TELEGRAPH
Northcliffe House, Meadow Road, Derby DE1 2BH
　T 01332-291111 W www.derbytelegraph.co.uk
　Editor, Neil White
THE LEICESTER MERCURY
St George Street, Leicester LE1 9FQ T 0116-251 2512
　W www.leicestermercury.co.uk
　Editor, Richard Bettsworth
LINCOLNSHIRE ECHO
Witham Wharf, Brayford Wharf East, Lincoln LN5 7HY
　T 01522-820000 W www.lincolnshireecho.co.uk
　Editor, Mel West
NORTHAMPTON CHRONICLE & ECHO
Albert House, Victoria Street, Northants NN1 3NR
　T 01604-467000 W www.northamptonchron.co.uk
　Editor, David Summers
NOTTINGHAM POST
City Gate, Tollhouse Hill, Notts NG1 5FS T 0115-948 2000
　W www.nottinghampost.com
　Editor, Mike Sassi

LONDON
EVENING STANDARD
Northcliffe House, 2 Derry Street, London W8 5TT
　T 020-3367 7000 W www.standard.co.uk
　Editor, Sarah Sands
METRO
Northcliffe House, 2 Derry Street, London W8 5TT
　T 020-3615 3480 W www.metro.co.uk
　Editor, Kenny Campbell

NORTH EAST
EVENING CHRONICLE
Groat Market, Newcastle upon Tyne NE1 1ED T 0191-232 7500
　W www.chroniclelive.co.uk
　Editor, Darren Thwaites
EVENING GAZETTE
Borough Road, Middlesbrough TS1 3AZ T 01642-245401
　W www.gazettelive.co.uk
　Editor, Chris Styles
HARTLEPOOL MAIL
New Clarence House, Wesley Square, Hartlepool TS24 8BX
　T 01429-239333 W www.hartlepoolmail.co.uk
　Editor, Joy Yates
THE JOURNAL
Groat Market, Newcastle upon Tyne NE1 1ED T 0191-201 6491
　W www.thejournal.co.uk
　Editor, Brian Aitken
THE NORTHERN ECHO
PO Box 14, Priestgate, Darlington, Co. Durham DL1 1NF
　T 01325-381313 W www.thenorthernecho.co.uk
　Editor, Peter Barron
THE SHIELDS GAZETTE
Chapter Row, South Shields, Tyne & Wear NE33 1BL
　T 0191-427 4800 W www.shieldsgazette.com
　Editor, Joy Yates
THE SUNDAY SUN
Groat Market, Newcastle upon Tyne NE1 1ED T 0191-232 7500
　W www.sundaysun.co.uk
　Editor, Matt McKenzie
SUNDERLAND ECHO
Echo House, Pennywell, Sunderland SR4 9ER T 0191-501 5800
　W www.sunderlandecho.com
　Editor, John Szymanski

NORTH WEST
THE BLACKPOOL GAZETTE
Avroe House, Avroe Crescent, Blackpool FY4 2DP
　T 01253-400888 W www.blackpoolgazette.co.uk
　Editor, Jon Rhodes
THE BOLTON NEWS
The Wellsprings, Victoria Square, Bolton BL1 1AR T 01204-522345
　W www.theboltonnews.co.uk
　Editor, Ian Savage
CARLISLE NEWS AND STAR
Newspaper House, Dalston Road, Carlisle CA2 5UA
　T 01228-612600 W www.newsandstar.co.uk
　Editor, David Helliwell
LANCASHIRE EVENING POST
Oliver's Place, Preston PR2 9ZA T 01772-254841
　W www.lep.co.uk
　Editor, Gillian Gray
LANCASHIRE TELEGRAPH
1 High Street, Newspaper House, Blackburn, Lancs. BB1 1HT
　T 01254 678678 W www.lancashiretelegraph.co.uk
　Editor, Kevin Young
LIVERPOOL ECHO
PO Box 48, Old Hall Street, Liverpool L69 3EB T 0151-227 2000
　W www.liverpoolecho.co.uk
　Editor, Alastair Machray
MANCHESTER EVENING NEWS
Mitchell Henry House, Hollinwood Avenue,
　Chadderton OL9 8EF T 0161-832 7200
　W www.manchestereveningnews.co.uk
　Editor, Rob Irvine
NORTH-WEST EVENING MAIL
Abbey Road, Barrow-in-Furness, Cumbria LA14 5QS
　T 01229-840100 W www.nwemail.co.uk
　Editor, Jonathan Lee

OLDHAM EVENING CHRONICLE
PO Box 47, 172 Union Street, Oldham, Lancs. OL1 1EQ
 T 0161-633 2121 W www.oldham-chronicle.co.uk
 Editor, Dave Whaley

SOUTH EAST
THE ARGUS
Argus House, Crowhurst Road, Hollingbury, Brighton BN1 8AR
 T 01273-544544 W www.theargus.co.uk
 Editor, Michael Beard
ECHO
Newspaper House, Chester Hall Lane, Basildon, Essex SS14 3BL
 T 01268-522792 W www.echo-news.co.uk
 Editor, Colin Channon
MEDWAY MESSENGER
Medway House, Ginsbury Close, Sir Thomas Longley Road,
 Medway City Estate, Strood, Kent ME2 4DU T 01634-227800
 W www.kentonline.co.uk/medway
 Editor, Bob Bounds
THE NEWS, PORTSMOUTH
1000 Lakeside, North Harbour, Portsmouth PO6 3EN
 T 023-9266 4488 W www.portsmouth.co.uk
 Editor, Mark Waldron
OXFORD MAIL
Osney Mead, Oxford OX2 0EJ T 01865-425262
 W www.oxfordmail.co.uk
 Editor, Simon O'Neill
READING EVENING POST
8 Tessa Road, Reading, Berks. RG1 8NS T 0118-918 3000
 W www.getreading.co.uk
 Editor, Andy Murrill
THE SOUTHERN DAILY ECHO
Newspaper House, Test Lane, Redbridge, Southampton SO16 9JX
 T 023-8042 4777 W www.dailyecho.co.uk
 Editor, Ian Murray

SOUTH WEST
BRISTOL POST
Temple Way, Bristol BS2 0BY T 0117-934 3000
 W www.bristolpost.co.uk
 Editor, Mike Norton
DAILY ECHO
Richmond Hill, Bournemouth BH2 6HH T 01202-554601
 W www.bournemouthecho.co.uk
 Editor, Toby Granville
DORSET ECHO
Fleet House, Hampshire Road, Weymouth, Dorset DT4 9XD
 T 01305-830930 W www.dorsetecho.co.uk
 Editor, Toby Granville
EXETER EXPRESS & ECHO
Heron Road, Sowton, Exeter EX2 7NF T 01392-442220
 W www.exeterexpressandecho.co.uk
 Editor, Jon-Paul Hedge
GLOUCESTER CITIZEN
6–8 The Oxebode, Gloucester GL1 2RZ T 01242-278000
 W www.gloucestercitizen.co.uk
 Editor, Jenny Eastwood
GLOUCESTERSHIRE ECHO
St James's Square, Cheltenham GL50 3PR T 01242-278000
 W www.gloucestershireecho.co.uk
 Editor, Kevan Blackadder
THE HERALD
3rd Floor, Millbay Road, Plymouth PL1 3LF T 01752-293000
 W www.plymouthherald.co.uk
 Editor, Paul Burton
SUNDAY INDEPENDENT
Sunday Independent Ltd, Tindle Suite, Webbs House, Cornwall
 PL14 6AH T 01579-342174 W www.sundayindependent.co.uk
 Editor, John Noble

SWINDON ADVERTISER
100 Victoria Road, Old Town, Swindon SN1 3BE T 01793-528144
 W www.swindonadvertiser.co.uk
 Editor, Gary Lawrence
TORQUAY HERALD EXPRESS
Barton Hill Road, Torquay, Devon TQ2 8JN T 01803-676000
 W www.torquayheraldexpress.co.uk
 Editor, Jim Parker
WESTERN DAILY PRESS
Temple Way, Bristol BS99 7HD T 0117-934 3000
 W www.westerndailypress.co.uk
 Editor, Tim Dixon
THE WESTERN MORNING NEWS
3rd Floor, Millbay Road, Plymouth PL1 3LF T 01752-293000
 W www.westernmorningnews.co.uk
 Editor, Bill Martin

WEST MIDLANDS
BIRMINGHAM MAIL
6th Floor, Fort Dunlop, Fort Parkway, Birmingham B24 9FF
 T 0121-234 5536 W www.birminghammail.co.uk
 Editor, David Brookes
THE BIRMINGHAM POST
6th Floor, Fort Dunlop, Fort Parkway, Birmingham B24 9FF
 T 0121-236 3366 W www.birminghampost.co.uk
 Editor, Stacey Barnfield
COVENTRY TELEGRAPH
Corporation Street, Coventry CV1 1FP T 024-7663 3633
 W www.coventrytelegraph.net
 Editor, Alun Thorne
EXPRESS & STAR
51–53 Queen Street, Wolverhampton WV1 1ES T 01902-313131
 W www.expressandstar.com
 Editor, Keith Harrison
THE SENTINEL
Sentinel House, Bethesda Street, Stoke-on-Trent ST1 3GN
 T 01782-864100 W www.stokesentinel.co.uk
 Editor, Richard Bowyer
SHROPSHIRE STAR
Waterloo Road, Ketley, Telford TF1 5HU T 01952-242424
 W www.shropshirestar.com
 Editor, Martin Wright
WORCESTER NEWS
Berrows House, Hylton Road, Worcester WR2 5JX
 T 01905-748200 W www.worcesternews.co.uk
 Editor, Peter John

YORKSHIRE AND HUMBERSIDE
GRIMSBY TELEGRAPH
80 Cleethorpe Road, Grimsby, Lincs DN31 3EH T 01472-360360
 W www.grimsbytelegraph.co.uk
 Editor, Michelle Lalor
HALIFAX COURIER
PO Box 19, King Cross Street, Halifax HX1 2SF T 01422-260200
 W www.halifaxcourier.co.uk
 Editor, John Kenealy
THE HUDDERSFIELD DAILY EXAMINER
Pennine Business Park, Longbow Close, Bradley Road, Huddersfield
 HD2 1GQ T 01484-430000 W www.examiner.co.uk
 Editor, Roy Wright
HULL DAILY MAIL
Blundell's Corner, Beverley Road, Hull HU3 1XS T 01482-327111
 W www.hulldailymail.co.uk
 Editor, Neil Hodgkinson
THE PRESS
PO Box 29, 76–86 Walmgate, York YO1 9YN T 01904-567131
 W www.yorkpress.co.uk
 Editor, Steve Hughes

SCARBOROUGH NEWS
17–23 Aberdeen Walk, Scarborough, N. Yorks YO11 1BB
   T 01723-363636 W www.thescarboroughnews.co.uk
   Editor, Ed Asquith
SHEFFIELD STAR
York Street, Sheffield S1 1PU T 0114-276 7676
   W www.thestar.co.uk
   Editor, James Mitchinson
TELEGRAPH & ARGUS
Hall Ings, Bradford BD1 1JR T 01274-729511
   W www.telegraphandargus.co.uk
   Editor, Perry Austin-Clarke
YORKSHIRE EVENING POST
26 Whitehall Road, Leeds LS12 1BE T 0113-243 2701
   W www.yorkshireeveningpost.co.uk
   Editor, Jeremy Clifford
YORKSHIRE POST
26 Whitehall Road, Leeds LS12 1BE T 0113-243 2701
   W www.yorkshirepost.co.uk
   Editor, Jeremy Clifford

SCOTLAND
THE COURIER
80 Kingsway East, Dundee DD4 8SL T 01382-223131
   W www.thecourier.co.uk
   Editor, Richard Neville
DUNDEE EVENING TELEGRAPH
80 Kingsway East, Dundee DD4 8SL T 01382-575331
   W www.eveningtelegraph.co.uk
   Editor, Richard Prest
EVENING EXPRESS
Aberdeen Journals Ltd, Lang Stracht, Mastrick, Aberdeen
   AB15 6DF T 01224-691212 W www.eveningexpress.co.uk
   Editor, Alan McCabe
EVENING NEWS
Barclay House, 108 Holyrood Road, Edinburgh EH8 8AS
   T 0131-620 8620 W www.edinburghnews.scotsman.com
   Editor, Frank O'Donnell
GLASGOW EVENING TIMES
200 Renfield Street, Glasgow G2 3QB T 0141-302 7000
   W www.eveningtimes.co.uk
   Editor, Tony Carlin
INVERNESS COURIER
New Century House, Stadium Road, Inverness IV1 1FF
   T 01463-233059 W www.inverness-courier.co.uk
   Editor, Robert Taylor
PAISLEY DAILY EXPRESS
1 Central Quay, Glasgow G3 8DA T 0141-887 7911
   W www.paisleydailyexpress.co.uk
   Editor, John Hutcheson
THE PRESS AND JOURNAL
Lang Stracht, Aberdeen AB15 6DF T 01224-690222
   W www.pressandjournal.co.uk
   Editor, Damian Bates

WALES
THE LEADER
Mold Business Park, Mold, Flintshire CH7 1XY T 01352-707707
   W www.leaderlive.co.uk
   Editor, Barrie Jones
SOUTH WALES ARGUS
Cardiff Road, Maesglas, Newport NP20 3QN T 01633-810000
   W www.southwalesargus.co.uk
   Editor, Kevin Ward
SOUTH WALES ECHO
6 Park Street, Cardiff CF10 1XR T 029-2024 3630
   W www.walesonline.co.uk
   Editor, Tim Gordon

SOUTH WALES EVENING POST
Urban Village, High Street, Swansea SA1 1NW T 01792-545500
   W www.southwales-eveningpost.co.uk
   Editor, Jonathan Roberts
WESTERN MAIL
6 Park Street, Cardiff CF10 1XR T 029-2024 3630
   W www.walesonline.co.uk
   Editor, Alan Edmunds

NORTHERN IRELAND
BELFAST TELEGRAPH
124–144 Royal Avenue, Belfast BT1 1DN T 028-9026 4000
   W www.belfasttelegraph.co.uk
   Editor, Mike Gilson
IRISH NEWS
113–117 Donegall Street, Belfast BT1 2GE T 028-9032 2226
   W www.irishnews.com
   Editor, Noel Doran
NEWS LETTER
Ground Floor, Metro Building, 6–9 Donegall Sq. South,
   Belfast BT1 5JA T 028-9089 7700 W www.newsletter.co.uk
   Editor, Rankin Armstrong
SUNDAY LIFE
124–144 Royal Avenue, Belfast BT1 1EB T 028-9026 4000
   W www.sundaylife.co.uk
   Editor, Martin Breen

CHANNEL ISLANDS
GUERNSEY PRESS AND STAR
PO Box 57, Braye Road, Vale, Guernsey GY1 3BW
   T 01481-240240 W www.guernseypress.com
   Editor, Richard Digard
JERSEY EVENING POST
Guiton House, Five Oaks, St Saviour, Jersey JE4 8XQ
   T 01534-611611 W www.jerseyeveningpost.com
   Editor, Andy Sibcy

PERIODICALS

ART
AESTHETICA
PO Box 371, York YO23 1WL T 01904-629137
   W www.aestheticamagazine.com
   Editor, Cherie Federico
APOLLO
22 Old Queen Street, London SW1H 9HP T 020-7961 0150
   W www.apollo-magazine.com
   Editor, Thomas Marks
ART MONTHLY
28 Charing Cross Road, London WC2H 0DB T 020-7240 0389
   W www.artmonthly.co.uk
   Editor, Patricia Bickers
ARTREVIEW
1 Honduras Street, London EC1Y 0TH T 020-7490 8138
   W www.artreview.com
   Editor, Mark Rappolt
TATE ETC.
Tate, Millbank, London SW1P 4RG T 020-7887 8724
   W www.tate.org.uk
   Editor, Simon Grant

BUSINESS AND FINANCE
THE ECONOMIST
25 St James's Street, London SW1A 1HG T 020-7830 7000
   W www.economist.com
   Editor, John Micklethwait
MANAGEMENT TODAY
Haymarket, Teddington Studios, Broom Road, Teddington
   TW11 9BE T 01604-828702 W www.managementtoday.co.uk
   Editor, Matthew Gwyther

MARKETING WEEK
79 Wells Street, London W1T 3QN **T** 020-7292 3711
  W www.marketingweek.co.uk
  Editor, Ruth Mortimer
MONEYWEEK
8th Floor, Friars Bridge Court, 41-45 Blackfriars Road, London
SE1 8NZ **T** 020-7633 3780 **W** www.moneyweek.com
  Editor, Merryn Somerset Webb
PUBLIC FINANCE
17 Britton Street, London EC1M 5TP **T** 020-8950 9117
  W www.publicfinance.co.uk
  Editor, Mike Thatcher

CELEBRITY
CLOSER
Endeavour House, 189 Shaftesbury Avenue, London WC2H 8JG
  T 020-7859 8463 **W** www.closeronline.co.uk
  Editor, Lisa Burrow
HEAT
Endeavour House, 189 Shaftesbury Avenue, London WC2H 8JG
  T 020-7437 9011 **W** www.heatworld.com
  Editor, Lucie Cave
HELLO!
Wellington House, 69–71 Upper Ground, London SE1 9PQ
  T 020-7667 8901 **W** www.hellomagazine.com
  Editor, Rosie Nixon
OK!
10 Lower Thames Street, London EC3R 6EN **T** 020-8612 7000
  W www.ok.co.uk
  Editor, Kirsty Tyler

CHILDREN'S AND FAMILY
THE BEANO
185 Fleet Street, London EC4A 2HS **W** www.beano.com
  Editor, Craig Graham
MOTHER & BABY
Endeavour House, 189 Shaftesbury Avenue, London WC2H 8JG
  T 020-7437 9011 **W** www.motherandbaby.co.uk
  Editor, Claire Irvin
YOUR CAT
BPG Stamford Ltd, 1-6 Buckminster Yard, Main Street,
  Buckminster, Grantham, Lincs NG33 5SA **T** 0844-848-8257
  W www.yourcat.co.uk
  Editor, Sue Parslow
YOUR DOG
BPG Stamford Ltd, 1-6 Buckminster Yard, Main Street,
  Buckminster, Grantham, Lincs NG33 5SA **T** 0844-848 8257
  W www.yourdog.co.uk
  Editor, Sarah Wright
YOUR HORSE
Media House, Peterborough Business Park, Lynch Wood,
  Peterborough PE2 6EA **T** 01733-468000
  W www.yourhorse.co.uk
  Editor, Imogen Johnson

CLASSICAL AND OPERA MUSIC
BBC MUSIC
Immediate Media Company Bristol Ltd, Tower House,
  Fairfax Street, Bristol BS1 3BN **T** 0117-927 9009
  W www.classical-music.com
  Editor, Oliver Condy
CLASSICAL MUSIC
Rhinegold House, 20 Rugby Street, London WC1N 3QZ
  T 020-7333 1729 **W** www.classicalmusicmagazine.org
  Editor, Kimon Daltas
GRAMOPHONE
Haymarket, Teddington Studios, Broom Road, Teddington,
  Middlesex TW11 9BE **T** 020-8267 5000
  W www.gramophone.co.uk
  Editor, Martin Cullingford

OPERA
36 Black Lion Lane, London W6 9BE **T** 020-8563 8893
  W www.opera.co.uk
  Editor, John Allison

COMPUTERS AND TECHNOLOGY
ANDROID
Imagine Publishing, Richmond House, 33 Richmond Hill,
  Bournemouth BH2 6EZ **T** 01202-586200
  W www.littlegreenrobot.co.uk
  Deputy Editor, Jack Parsons
EDGE
Future Publishing Ltd, 2 Balcombe Street, London NW1 6NW
  T 01225-442244 **W** www.edge-online.com
  Editor, Tony Mott
MACFORMAT
Future Publishing Ltd, 2 Balcombe Street, London NW1 6NW
  T 01225-442244 **W** www.macformat.techradar.com
  Editor, Christopher Phin
PC PRO
Dennis Technology, 30 Cleveland Street, London W1T 4JD
  T 020-7907 6000 **W** www.pcpro.co.uk
  Editor, Tim Danton
STUFF
Haymarket, Teddington Studios, Broom Road, Teddington,
  Middlesex TW11 9BE **T** 020-8267 5036 **W** www.stuff.tv
  Editor, Will Findlater
T3
Future Publishing, 2 Balcombe Street, London NW1 6NW
  T 020-7042 4000 **W** www.t3.com
  Editor, Kieran Alger
WEB USER
Dennis Publishing, 30 Cleveland Street, London W1T 4JD
  T 020-7907 6000 **W** www.webuser.co.uk
  Editor, Daniel Booth
WIRED
Condé Nast, Vogue House, Hanover Square, London W1S 1JU
  T 0844-848 5202 **W** www.wired.co.uk
  Editor, Scott Dadich

CRAFT
CARDMAKING & PAPERCRAFT
Immediate Media, Tower House, Fairfax Street, Bristol BS1 3BN
  T 0117-933 8081 **W** www.cardmakingandpapercraft.com
  Editor, Kirstie Sleight
SIMPLY KNITTING
Future Publishing Ltd, 30 Monmouth Street, Bath BA1 2BW
  T 01225-442244 **W** simplyknitting.co.uk
  Editor, Kirstie McLeod
THE WORLD OF CROSS STITCHING
Immediate Media, Tower House, Fairfax Street, Bristol BS1 3BN
  T 0117-314 8351 **W** www.cross-stitching.com
  Editor, Ruth Southorn

ENTERTAINMENT
EMPIRE
Endeavour House, 189 Shaftesbury Avenue, London WC2H 8JG
  T 020-7437 9011 **W** www.empireonline.com
  Editor, Mark Dinning
RADIO TIMES
Vineyard House, 44 Brook Green, London W6 7BT
  T 020-7150 5800 **W** www.radiotimes.com
  Editor, Ben Preston
SIGHT & SOUND
3rd Floor Chancery Exchange, 10 Furnival Street, London
  EC4A 1AB **T** 020-8955 7070 **W** www.bfi.org.uk/sightandsound
  Editor, Nick James

TIME OUT
4th Floor, 125 Shaftesbury Avenue, London WC2H 8AD
  T 020-7813 3000 W www.timeout.com
  Editor, Caroline McGinn
TOTAL FILM
2 Balcombe Street, London NW1 6NW T 020-7042 4000
  W www.totalfilm.com
  Editor, Jane Crowther

FASHION AND BEAUTY
COSMOPOLITAN
Hearst Magazines, 33 Broadwick Street, London W1F 0DQ
  T 020-7439 5000 W www.cosmopolitan.co.uk
  Editor, Louise Court
ELLE
Hearst Magazines, 72 Broadwick Street, London W1F 9EP
  T 020-7150 7000 W www.elleuk.com
  Editor, Lorraine Candy
GLAMOUR
Condé Nast, Vogue House, Hanover Square, London W1S 1JU
  T 020-7499 9080 W www.glamourmagazine.co.uk
  Editor, Cindi Leive
GRAZIA
Endeavour House, 189 Shaftesbury Avenue, London WC2H 8JG
  T 0845-601 1356 W www.graziadaily.co.uk
  Editor, Angela Buttolph
HARPER'S BAZAAR
Hearst Magazines, 72 Broadwick Street, London W1F 9EP
  T 0844-848 5203 W www.harpersbazaar.co.uk
  Editor, Justine Picardie
MARIE CLAIRE
Blue Fin Building, 110 Southwark Street, London SE1 4SU
  T 020-3148 5000 W www.marieclaire.co.uk
  Editor, Trish Halpin
VOGUE
Condé Nast, Vogue House, Hanover Square, London W1S 1JU
  T 0844-848 5202 W www.vogue.co.uk
  Editor, Alexandra Shulman

FOOD AND DRINK
FOOD AND TRAVEL
Suite 51, The Business Centre, Ingate Place, London SW8 3NS
  T 020-7501 0511 W www.foodandtravel.com
  Editor, Renate Ruge
GOOD FOOD
44 Vineyard House, Brook Green, London W6 7BT
  T 020-7150 5022 W www.bbcgoodfood.com
  Editor, Gillian Carter
JAMIE
800 Guillat Avenue, Kent Science Park, Sittingbourne ME9 8GU
  T 0844-249 0478 W www.jamieoliver.com/magazine
  Editor, Andy Harris
OLIVE
Vineyard House, 44 Brook Green, London W6 7BT
  T 020-7150 5024 W www.olivemagazine.com
  Editor, Christine Hayes
WHISKY
St Faiths House, Mountergate, Norwich NR1 1PY T 01603-633 808
  W www.whiskymag.com
  Editor, Rob Allanson

GENERAL INTEREST
BBC HISTORY
Tower House, Fairfax Street, Bristol BS1 3BN T 0117-927 9009
  W www.historyextra.com
  Editor, Rob Attar
BOOKSELLER
Crowne House, 56-58 Southwark Street, London SE1 1UN
  T 01604-251040 W www.thebookseller.com
  Editor, Philip Jones

HISTORY TODAY
25 Bedford Avenue, London WC1B 3AT T 020-3219 7810
  W www.historytoday.com
  Editor, Paul Lay
LITERARY REVIEW
44 Lexington Street, London W1F OLW T 020-7437 9392
  W www.literaryreview.co.uk
  Editor, Nancy Sladek
NEW STATESMAN
John Carpenter House, 7 Carmelite Street, Blackfriars, London
  EC4Y 0AN T 020-7936 6400 W www.newstatesman.com
  Editor, Jason Cowley
PRIVATE EYE
6 Carlisle Street, London W1D 3BN T 020-7437 4017
  W www.private-eye.co.uk
  Editor, Ian Hislop
PROSPECT
25 Sackville Street, London W1S 3HQ T 020-7255 1281
  W www.prospectmagazine.co.uk
  Editor, Bronwen Maddox
RAILWAY
Mortons Media Ltd, Horncastle, Lincs LN9 6JR T 01507-529529
  W www.railwaymagazine.co.uk
  Editor, Nick Pigott
READER'S DIGEST
PO Box 7853, Ringwood BH24 9FH T 0844-332 4994
  W www.readersdigest.co.uk
  Editor, Catherine Haughney
SAGA
Saga Publishing Ltd, Enbrook Park, Folkestone, Kent CT20 3SE
  T 01303-771111 W www.saga.co.uk
  Editor, Katy Bravery
THE SPECTATOR
22 Old Queen Street, London SW1H 9HP T 020-7961 0200
  W www.spectator.co.uk
  Editor, Fraser Nelson
TLS (THE TIMES LITERARY SUPPLEMENT)
1 London Bridge Street, London SE1 9GF T 020-7782 5000
  W www.the-tls.co.uk
  Editor, Peter Stothard
THE WEEK
30 Cleveland Street, London W1T 4JD T 020-7907 6000
  W www.theweek.co.uk
  Editor, Holden Frith
WHO DO YOU THINK YOU ARE?
Tower House, Fairfax Street, Bristol BS1 3BN T 0117-314 7400
  W www.whodoyouthinkyouaremagazine.com
  Editor, Sarah Williams

HEALTH AND FITNESS
HEALTH & FITNESS
30 Cleveland Street, London W1T 4JD T 020-7907 6000
  W www.womensfitness.co.uk
  Editor, Mary Comber
MEN'S FITNESS
Dennis Publishing, 30 Cleveland Street, London W1T 4JD
  T 020-7907 6000 W www.mensfitness.co.uk
  Editor, Max Anderton
MEN'S HEALTH
Hearst Magazines, 72 Broadwick Street, London W1F 9EP
  T 01858-438851 W www.menshealth.co.uk
  Editor, Toby Wiseman
RUNNER'S WORLD
33 Broadwick Street, London W1F 9EP T 020-7339 4409
  W www.runnersworld.co.uk
  Editor, David Wiley
WEIGHT WATCHERS
Millennium House, Ludlow Road, Maidenhead, Berkshire SL6 2SL
  T 07900-494 736 W www.weightwatchers.co.uk
  Editor, Julie Lee

WOMEN'S FITNESS
30 Cleveland Street, London W1T 4JD **T** 020-7907 6000
  W www.womensfitness.co.uk
  Editor, Joanna Knight

HOBBIES AND GAMES
AIRFIX MODEL WORLD
Key Publishing Ltd, PO Box 100, Stamford PE9 1XQ
  T 01780-755131 **W** www.airfixmodelworld.com
  Editor, Chris Clifford
ANGLING TIMES
Bauer Consumer Media Ltd, 1 Lincoln Court, Lincoln Road,
  Peterborough PE1 2RF **T** 01733-395097
  W www.gofishing.co.uk
  Editor, Steve Fitzpatrick
BRITISH RAILWAY MODELLING
Warners Group Publications, The Maltings, West Street,
  Bourne, Lincs PE10 9PH **T** 01778-391000
  W www.model-railways-live.co.uk
  Editor, Ben Jones
CHESS
Chess & Bridge Ltd, 44 Baker Street, London W1U 7RT
  T 020-7486 7015 **W** www.chess.co.uk
  Editor, John Saunders
COIN NEWS
Token Publishing Ltd, Orchard House, Duchy Road, Heathpark,
  Honiton, Devon EX14 1YD **T** 01404-46972
  W www.tokenpublishing.com
  Editor, John Mussell
HORNBY
Key Publishing Ltd, PO Box 100, Stamford PE9 1XQ
  T 01780-755131 **W** www.hornbymagazine.com
  Editor, Mike Wild

HOME AND GARDEN
GARDENERS' WORLD
Immediate Media, 5th Floor, Vineyard House, 44 Brook Green,
  London W6 7BT **T** 020-7150 5700
  W www.gardenersworld.com
  Editor, Lucy Hall
GOOD HOUSEKEEPING
Hearst Magazines, 72 Broadwick Street, London W1F 9EP
  T 020-7439 5000 **W** www.goodhousekeeping.co.uk
  Editor, Jane Francisco
HOUSE & GARDEN
Condé Nast Publications, Vogue House, Hanover Square,
  London W1S 1JU **T** 020-7499 9080
  W www.houseandgarden.co.uk
  Editor, Susan Crew
LIVING ETC
IPC Media, Blue Fin Building, 110 Southwark Street, London
  SE1 0SU **T** 020-3148 7443
  W www.housetohome.co.uk/livingetc
  Editor, Suzanne Imre

MEN'S LIFESTYLE
ATTITUDE
Vitality Publishing Ltd, 3rd Floor, 207 Old Street, London EC1V 9NR
  T 020-7608 6300 **W** www.attitude.co.uk
  Editor, Matthew Todd
ESQUIRE
Hearst Magazines, 72 Broadwick Street, London W1F 9EP
  T 020-7439 5000 **W** www.esquire.co.uk
  Editor, Alex Bilmes
FHM
Endeavour House, 189 Shaftesbury Avenue, London WC2H 8JG
  T 020-7295 8534 **W** www.fhm.com
  Editor, Joe Barnes

GAY TIMES
Millivres Prowler Group, Spectrum House, 32-34 Gordon House
  Road, London NW5 1LP **T** 020-7424 7400
  W www.gaytimes.co.uk
  Editor, Darren Scott
GQ
Vogue House, 1 Hanover Square, London W1S 1JU
  T 020-7499 9080 **W** www.gq-magazine.co.uk
  Editor, Dylan Jones
LOADED
Clarenden House, Shenley Road, Borehamwood, Herts WD6 1AG
  T 020-7580 6419 **W** www.loaded.co.uk
  Editor, Aaron Tinney

MOTORING
BIKE
Bauer Media, Media House, Lynchwood, Peterborough PE2 6EA
  T 01733-468000 **W** www.bikemagazine.co.uk
  Editor, Brice Minnigh
CARAVAN
Warners Group Publications, The Maltings, West Street, Bourne,
  Lincs PE10 9PH **T** 01778-392450
  W www.outandaboutlive.co.uk
  Editor, John Sootheran
F1 RACING
Haymarket, Teddington Studios, Broom Road, Teddington
  TW11 9BE **T** 020-8267 5806 **W** www.f1racing.co.uk
  Editor, Anthony Rowlinson
OCTANE
Dennis Publishing Ltd, 30 Cleveland Street, London W1T 4JD
  T 020-7907 6000 **W** www.classicandperformancecar.com
  Editor, David Lillywhite
PRACTICAL CARAVAN
Haymarket, Teddington Studios, Teddington Lock, Broom Road,
  Teddington TW11 9BE **T** 020-8267 5629
  W www.practicalcaravan.com
  Editor, Nigel Donnelly
TOP GEAR
Energy Centre, Media Centre, 201 Wood Lane, London W12 7TQ
  T 020-8433 3598 **W** www.topgear.com
  Editor, Charlie Turner

PHOTOGRAPHY
AMATEUR PHOTOGRAPHER
Blue Fin Building, 110 Southwark Street, London SE1 0SU
  T 020-3148 4138 **W** www.amateurphotographer.co.uk
  Editor, Nigel Atherton
DIGITAL PHOTOGRAPHER
Imagine Publishing, Richmond House, 33 Richmond Hill,
  Bournemouth BH2 6EZ **T** 01202-586200
  W www.dphotographer.co.uk
  Editor, Amy Squibb
PHOTOGRAPHY MONTHLY
Archant House, Oriel Road, Cheltenham GL50 1BB
  T 01242-211080 **W** www.photographymonthly.com
  Editor, Jeff Meyer
PROFESSIONAL PHOTOGRAPHER
Archant House, Oriel Road, Cheltenham GL50 1BB
  T 0844-848 5232 **W** www.professionalphotographer.co.uk
  Editor, Adam Scorey

POPULAR MUSIC
CLASH
194 Hercules Road, London SE1 7LD **T** 020-7628 2312
  W www.clashmusic.com
  Editor, Simon Harper
CLASSIC ROCK
Prospect Business Centre, 3 Stanley Boulevard, Blantyre G72 0BN
  T 01604-251040 **W** www.classicrockmagazine.com
  Editor, Scott Rowley

DIY
Arch 462, Kingsland Viaduct, 83 Rivington Street, London
EC2A 3AY **W** www.diymag.com
Editor, Stephen Ackroyd
GUITARIST
Future Publishing Ltd, Beauford Court, 30 Monmouth Street, Bath
BA1 2BW **T** 01225-442244 **W** www.musicradar.com/guitarist
Editor, Mick Taylor
KERRANG!
Bauer Media, Media House, Lynchwood, Peterborough PE2 6EA
T 01733-468000 **W** www.kerrang.com
Editor, James McMahon
MOJO
Endeavour House, 189 Shaftesbury Avenue, London WC2H 8JG
T 020-7208 3443 **W** www.mojo4music.com
Editor, Phil Alexander
NME
9th Floor, Blue Fin Building, 110 Southwark Street, London
SE1 0SU **T** 0845-676 7778 **W** www.nme.com
Editor, Mike Williams
Q
Endeavour House, 189 Shaftesbury Avenue, London WC2H 8JG
T 020-7295 5000 **W** www.qthemusic.com
Editor, Jane Johnson
UNCUT
Blue Fin Building, 110 Southwark Street, London SE1 0SU
T 020-3148 5000 **W** www.uncut.co.uk
Editor, John Mulvey

SCIENCE AND NATURE
BBC WILDLIFE
4th Floor, Tower House, Fairfax Street, Bristol BS1 3BN
T 0117-314 7366 **W** www.discoverwildlife.com
Editor, Matt Swaine
BIRD WATCHING
Bauer Media, Media House, Lynch Wood, Peterborough PE2 6EA
T 01733-468000 **W** www.birdwatching.co.uk
Editor, Matthew Merritt
COUNTRYFILE
9th Floor, Tower House, Fairfax Street, Bristol BS1 3BN
T 0117-927 9009 **W** www.countryfile.com
Editor, Fergus Collins
FOCUS
Bristol Magazines Ltd, Tower House, Fairfax Street, Bristol BS1 3BN
T 0117-314 7388 **W** www.sciencefocus.com
Editor, Graham Southorn
HOW IT WORKS
Imagine Publishing Ltd, Richmond House, 33 Richmond Hill,
Bournemouth BH2 6EZ **T** 01202-586200
W www.howitworksdaily.com
Editor, Dave Farfield
NEW SCIENTIST
Lacon House, 84 Theobalds Road, London WC1X 8NS
T 020-7611 1206 **W** www.newscientist.com
Editor, Sumit Paul-Choudhury
SKY AT NIGHT
Immediate Media Company Bristol Ltd, Tower House, Fairfax
Street, Bristol BS1 3BN **T** 0844 844 0254
W www.skyatnightmagazine.com
Editor, Chris Bramley

SPORT
ALL OUT CRICKET
TriNorth Ltd, Unit 3.40 Canterbury Court, 1–3 Brixton Road,
London SW9 6DE **T** 020-3176 0187 **W** www.alloutcricket.com
Editor, Phil Walker
BOXING MONTHLY
Topwave Ltd, 40 Morpeth Road, London E9 7LD **T** 020-8986 4141
W www.boxing-monthly.co.uk
Editor, vacant

COUNTRY WALKING
Bauer Media, 1 Lincoln Court, Lincoln Road, Peterborough
PE1 2RF **T** 01733-468205 **W** www.livefortheoutdoors.com
Editor, Mark Sutcliffe
THE CRICKETER
The Cricketer Publishing Ltd, 70 Great Portland Street,
London W1W 7UW **T** 020-7460 5200 **W** www.thecricketer-
magazine.com
Editor, Andrew Miller
FOURFOURTWO
Haymarket, Teddington Studios, Broom Road, Teddington,
Middlesex TW11 9BE **T** 020-8267 5661
W www.fourfourtwo.com
Editor, David Hall
GOLF MONTHLY
9th Floor, Blue Fin Building, 110 Southwark Street, London
SE1 0SU **T** 020-3148 4527 **W** www.golf-monthly.co.uk
Editor, Michael Harris
HORSE & HOUND
Blue Fin Building, 110 Southwark Street, London SE1 0SU
T 020-3148 4562 **W** www.horseandhound.co.uk
Editor, Sarah Jenkins
MATCH
Media House, Lynchwood, Peterborough PE2 6EA
T 01733-468008 **W** www.matchmag.co.uk
Editor, James Bandy
RUGBY WORLD
Blue Fin Building, 110 Southwark Street, London SE1 0SU
T 0844-848 0848 **W** www.rugbyworld.com
Editor, Owain Jones
SPORT
Third Floor, Courtyard Building, 11 Curtain Road, London
EC2A 3LT **T** 020-7959 7942 **W** www.sport-magazine.co.uk
Editor, Simon Caney
SUPERBIKE
Blaze Publishing, Lawrence House, Morrell Street,
Leamington Spa CV37 5SZ **T** 020-8873 4454
W www.superbike.co.uk
Editor, John Hogan
TENNISHEAD
PO Box 70948, London SW19 9GL **T** 020-8408 7148
W www.tennishead.net
Editor, Lee Goodall
WORLD SOCCER
Blue Fin Building, 110 Southwark Street, London SE1 0SU
T 020-3148 4817 **W** www.worldsoccer.com
Editor, Gavin Hamilton

TRAVEL
CONDÉ NAST TRAVELLER
Vogue House, Hanover Square, London W1S 1JU
T 0844-848 2851 **W** www.cntraveller.com
Editor, Melinda Stevens
FRANCE
Archant House, 3 Oriel Road, Cheltenham GL50 1BB
T 01242-216050 **W** www.completefrance.com
Editor, Carolyn Boyd
LIVING FRANCE
Archant House, 3 Oriel Road, Cheltenham GL50 1BB
T 01242-216050 **W** www.completefrance.com
Editor, Andy Duncan
LONELY PLANET
Media Centre (GH0S), 201 Wood Lane, London W12 7TQ
T 020-8433 1333 **W** www.lonelyplanet.com
Editor, Peter Grunert
NATIONAL GEOGRAPHIC TRAVELLER
Absolute Publishing Ltd, 197-199 City Road, London EC1V 1JN
T 020-7253 9906 **W** www.natgeotraveller.co.uk
Editor, Pat Riddell

TRADE AND PROFESSIONAL BODIES

The following is a list of employers' and trade associations and other professional bodies in the UK. It does not represent a comprehensive list. For further professional bodies *see* Professional Education.

ASSOCIATIONS

ABTA – THE TRAVEL ASSOCIATION, 30 Park Street, London SE1 9EQ T 020-3117 0500 E abta@abta.co.uk
W www.abta.com
Chief Executive, Mark Tanzer

ADVERTISING ASSOCIATION, 7th Floor North, Artillery House, 11–19 Artillery Row, London SW1P 1RT T 020-7340 1100
E aa@adassoc.org.uk W www.adassoc.org.uk
Chief Executive, Tim Lefroy

AEROSPACE DEFENCE SECURITY, Salamanca Square, 9 Albert Embankment, London SE1 7SP T 020-7091 4500
E enquiries@adsgroup.org.uk W www.adsgroup.org.uk
Chief Executive, Paul Everitt

AGRICULTURAL ENGINEERS ASSOCIATION, Samuelson House, 62 Forder Way, Hampton, Peterborough PE7 8JB
T 08456-448748 E ab@aea.uk.com W www.aea.uk.com
Chief Executive, Roger Lane-Nott, CB, FCMI

ASBESTOS REMOVAL CONTRACTORS ASSOCIATION, Unit 1, Stretton Business Park 2, Brunel Drive, Stretton DE13 0BY T 01283-566467 E info@arca.org.uk
W www.arca.org.uk
Chief Executive, Steve Sadley

ASSOCIATION FOR CONSULTANCY AND ENGINEERING, Alliance House, 12 Caxton Street, London SW1H 0QL T 020-7222 6557 E consult@acenet.co.uk
W www.acenet.co.uk
Chief Executive, Nelson Ogunshakin, OBE

ASSOCIATION OF ACCOUNTING TECHNICIANS, 140 Aldersgate Street, London EC1A 4HY T 020-7397 3000
E aat@aat.org.uk W www.aat.org.uk
Chief Executive, Mark Farrar

ASSOCIATION OF ANAESTHETISTS OF GREAT BRITAIN AND IRELAND, 21 Portland Place, London W1B 1PY T 020-7631 1650 E info@aagbi.org
W www.aagbi.org
President, Dr William Harrop-Griffiths

ASSOCIATION OF BRITISH INSURERS, 51 Gresham Street, London EC2V 7HQ T 020-7600 3333 E info@abi.org.uk
W www.abi.org.uk
Director-General, Otto Thoresen

ASSOCIATION OF BUSINESS RECOVERY PROFESSIONALS, 8th Floor, 120 Aldersgate Street, London EC1A 4JQ T 020-7566 4200 E association@r3.org.uk
W www.r3.org.uk
Chief Executive, Graham Rumney

ASSOCIATION OF CONSULTING SCIENTISTS, 5 Willow Heights, Cradley Heath B64 7PL T 0121-602 3515
E secretary@consultingscientists.co.uk
W www.consultsci.uku.co.uk
Secretary, Dr Stuart Guy

ASSOCIATION OF CONVENIENCE STORES LTD, Federation House, 17 Farnborough Street, Farnborough GU14 8AG T 01252-515001 E acs@acs.org.uk
W www.acs.org.uk
Chief Executive, James Lowman

ASSOCIATION OF CORPORATE TREASURERS, 51 Moorgate, London EC2R 6BH T 020-7847 2540
E enquiries@treasurers.org W www.treasurers.org
Chief Executive, Colin Tyler

ASSOCIATION OF DRAINAGE AUTHORITIES, 6 Electric Parade, Surbiton KT6 5NT T 020-8399 7350
E admin@ada.org.uk W www.ada.org.uk
Chief Executive, Jean Venables, CBE FRENG

BOOKSELLERS ASSOCIATION, 6 Bell Yard, London WC2A 2JR T 020-7421 4640 E mail@booksellers.org.uk
W www.booksellers.org.uk
Chief Executive, T. E. Godfray

BPI (BRITISH RECORDED MUSIC INDUSTRY), Riverside Building, County Hall, Westminster Bridge Road, London SE1 7JA T 020-7803 1300 E general@bpi.co.uk
W www.bpi.co.uk
Chief Executive, Geoff Taylor

BRITISH ANTIQUE DEALERS' ASSOCIATION, 20 Rutland Gate, London SW7 1BD T 020-7589 4128
E info@bada.org W www.bada.org
Director-General, Mark Dodgson

BRITISH ASSOCIATION OF SOCIAL WORKERS, 16 Kent Street, Birmingham B5 6RD T 0121-622 3911
E online@basw.co.uk W www.basw.co.uk
Chief Executive, Bridget Robb

BRITISH BANKERS' ASSOCIATION, Pinners Hall, 105–108 Old Broad Street, London EC2N 1EX
T 020-7216 8800 E info@bba.org.uk W www.bba.org.uk
Chief Executive, Anthony Browne

BRITISH BEER & PUB ASSOCIATION, Ground Floor, Brewers' Hall, Aldermanbury Square, London EC2V 7HR
T 020-7627 9191 E contact@beerandpub.com
W www.beerandpub.com
Chief Executive, Brigid Simmonds, OBE

BRITISH CHAMBERS OF COMMERCE, 65 Petty France, London SW1H 9EU T 020-7654 5800
W www.britishchambers.org.uk
Director-General, John Longworth

BRITISH ELECTROTECHNICAL AND ALLIED MANUFACTURERS ASSOCIATION (BEAMA), Westminster Tower, 3 Albert Embankment, London SE1 7SL
T 020-7793 3000 E info@beama.org.uk W www.beama.org.uk
Chief Executive, Dr Howard Porter

BRITISH HOROLOGICAL INSTITUTE, Upton Hall, Upton, Newark NG23 5TE T 01636-813795
E clocks@bhi.co.uk W www.bhi.co.uk
Chief Executive, Dudley Giles

BRITISH HOSPITALITY ASSOCIATION, Queens House, 55–56 Lincoln's Inn Fields, London WC2A 3BH
T 020-7404 7744 E bha@bha.org.uk W www.bha.org.uk
Chief Executive, Ms Ufi Ibrahim

BRITISH INSTITUTE OF PROFESSIONAL PHOTOGRAPHY, The Coach House, The Firs, High Street, Whitchurch, Aylesbury HP22 4SJ T 01296-642020
E info@bipp.com W www.bipp.com
Chief Executive, Chris Harper

BRITISH INSURANCE BROKERS' ASSOCIATION, 8th Floor, John Stow House, 18 Bevis Marks, London EC3A 7JB T 0870-950 1790 E enquiries@biba.org.uk
W www.biba.org.uk
Chief Executive, Steve White

BRITISH MARINE FEDERATION, Marine House, Thorpe Lea Road, Egham TW20 8BF T 01784-473377
E info@britishmarine.co.uk W www.britishmarine.co.uk
Chief Executive, Howard Pridding

BRITISH MEDICAL ASSOCIATION, BMA House, Tavistock Square, London WC1H 9JP T 020-7387 4499
W www.bma.org.uk
Chief Executive (interim), Keith Ward

BRITISH OFFICE SUPPLIES AND SERVICES (BOSS) FEDERATION, c/o British Printing Industries Federation, 2 Villiers Court, Meriden Business Park, Copse Drive, Coventry CV5 9RN **T** 01676-526030 **E** info@bossfederation.co.uk **W** www.bossfederation.co.uk
Chief Executive, Michael Gardner

BRITISH PLASTICS FEDERATION, 6 Bath Place, Rivington Street, London EC2A 3JE **T** 020-7457 5000 **E** reception@bpf.co.uk **W** www.bpf.co.uk
Director-General, Peter Davis, OBE

BRITISH PORTS ASSOCIATION, 1st Floor, 30 Park Street, London SE1 9EQ **T** 020-7260 1780 **E** info@britishports.org.uk **W** www.britishports.org.uk
Director, David Whitehead

BRITISH PRINTING INDUSTRIES FEDERATION, 2 Villiers Court, Meriden Business Park, Copse Drive, Coventry CV5 9RN **T** 01676-526030 **W** www.britishprint.com
Chief Executive, Kathy Woodward

BRITISH PROPERTY FEDERATION, 5th Floor, St Albans House, 57–59 Haymarket, London SW1Y 4QX **T** 020-7828 0111 **E** info@bpf.org.uk **W** www.bpf.org.uk
Chief Executive, Liz Peace

BRITISH RETAIL CONSORTIUM, 21 Dartmouth Street, London SW1H 9BP **T** 020-7854 8900 **E** info@brc.org.uk **W** www.brc.org.uk
Director-General, Helen Dickinson

BRITISH TYRE MANUFACTURERS' ASSOCIATION LTD, 5 Berewyk Hall Court, White Colne, Colchester CO6 2QD **T** 01787-226995 **E** mail@btmauk.com **W** www.btmauk.com
Chief Executive, Graham Willson

BUILDING SOCIETIES ASSOCIATION, York House, 23 Kingsway, London WC2B 6UJ **T** 020-7520 5900 **E** simon.rex@bsa.org.uk **W** www.bsa.org.uk
Chief Executive, Robin Fieth

CHARTERED ASSOCIATION OF BUILDING ENGINEERS, Lutyens House, Billing Brook Road, Weston Favell, Northampton NN3 8NW **T** 01604-404121 **E** building.engineers@cbuild.com **W** www.cbuilde.com
Chief Executive, Dr John Hooper

CHARTERED INSTITUTE OF ENVIRONMENTAL HEALTH, Chadwick Court, 15 Hatfields, London SE1 8DJ **T** 020-7928 6006 **E** information@cieh.org **W** www.cieh.org
Chief Executive, Graham Jukes

CHARTERED INSTITUTE OF JOURNALISTS, 2 Dock Offices, Surrey Quays Road, London SE16 2XU **T** 020-7252 1187 **E** memberservices@cioj.co.uk **W** www.cioj.co.uk
General Secretary, Dominic Cooper

CHARTERED INSTITUTE OF PURCHASING AND SUPPLY, Easton House, Church Street, Easton on the Hill, Stamford PE9 3NZ **T** 01780-756777 **W** www.cips.org
Chief Executive, David Noble

CHARTERED INSTITUTE OF TAXATION, 1st Floor Artillery House, 11–19 Artillery Row, London SW1P 1RT **T** 020-7340 0550 **W** www.tax.org.uk
Chief Executive, Peter Fanning

CHARTERED INSURANCE INSTITUTE, 42–48 High Road, South Woodford, London E18 2JP **T** 020-8989 8464 **E** customer.serv@cii.co.uk **W** www.cii.co.uk
Chief Executive, Dr Alexander Scott

CHARTERED MANAGEMENT INSTITUTE, Management House, Cottingham Road, Corby NN17 1TT **T** 01536-204222 **E** enquiries@managers.org.uk **W** www.managers.org.uk
Chief Executive, Anne Francke

CHARTERED QUALITY INSTITUTE, 2nd Floor North, Chancery Exchange, 10 Furnival Street, London EC4A 1AB **T** 020-7245 6722 **E** info@thecqi.org **W** www.thecqi.org
Chief Executive, Simon Feary

CHEMICAL INDUSTRIES ASSOCIATION, Kings Buildings, Smith Square, London SW1P 3JJ **T** 020-7834 3399 **E** enquiries@cia.org.uk **W** www.cia.org.uk
Chief Executive, Steve Elliott

CONFEDERATION OF PAPER INDUSTRIES, 1 Rivenhall Road, Swindon SN5 7BD **T** 01793-889600 **E** cpi@paper.org.uk **W** www.paper.org.uk
Director-General, David Workman

CONFEDERATION OF PASSENGER TRANSPORT UK, Drury House, 34–43 Russell Street, London WC2B 5HA **T** 020-7240 3131 **W** www.cpt-uk.org
Chief Executive, Simon Posner

CONSTRUCTION PRODUCTS ASSOCIATION, 26 Store Street, London WC1E 7BT **T** 020-7323 3770 **W** www.constructionproducts.org.uk
Chief Executive, Diana Montgomery

DAIRY UK, 93 Baker Street, London W1U 6QQ **T** 020-7486 7244 **E** info@dairyuk.org **W** www.dairyuk.org
Chief Executive, Dr Judith Bryans

EEF, THE MANUFACTURERS' ORGANISATION, Broadway House, Tothill Street, London SW1H 9NQ **T** 020-7222 7777 **E** enquiries@eef.org.uk **W** www.eef.org.uk
Chief Executive, Terry Scuoler

ENERGY UK, Charles House, 5–11 Regent Street, London SW1Y 4LR **T** 020-7930 9390 **W** www.energy-uk.org.uk
Chief Executive, Angela Knight, CBE

FEDERATION OF BAKERS, 6 Catherine Street, London WC2B 5JW **T** 020-7420 7190 **E** info@bakersfederation.org.uk **W** www.bakersfederation.org.uk
Director, Gordon Polson

FEDERATION OF MASTER BUILDERS, David Croft House, 25 Ely Place, London EC1N 6TD **T** 020-7025 2900 **W** www.fmb.org.uk
Chief Executive, Brian Berry

FEDERATION OF SPORTS AND PLAY ASSOCIATIONS, Federation House, Stoneleigh Park, CV8 2RF **T** 024-7641 4999 **E** info@sportsandplay.com **W** www.sportsandplay.com
Managing Director, Jane Montgomery

FINANCE AND LEASING ASSOCIATION, 2nd Floor, Imperial House, 15–19 Kingsway, London WC2B 6UN **T** 020-7836 6511 **E** info@fla.org.uk **W** www.fla.org.uk
Director-General, Stephen Sklaroff

FOOD AND DRINK FEDERATION, 6 Catherine Street, London WC2B 5JJ **T** 020-7836 2460 **W** www.fdf.org.uk
Director-General, Melanie Leech

FREIGHT TRANSPORT ASSOCIATION LTD, Hermes House, St John's Road, Tunbridge Wells TN4 9UZ **T** 01892-526171 **E** enquiries@fta.co.uk **W** www.fta.co.uk
Chief Executive, Theo de Pencier

GLASGOW CHAMBER OF COMMERCE, 30 George Square, Glasgow G2 1EQ **T** 0141-204 2121 **E** chamber@glasgowchamberofcommerce.com **W** www.glasgowchamberofcommerce.com
Chief Executive, Stuart Patrick

INSTITUTE FOR ARCHAEOLOGISTS, Miller Building, University of Reading, RG6 6AB **T** 0118-378 6446 **E** admin@archaeologists.net **W** www.archaeologists.net
Hon. Chair, Jan Wills

INSTITUTE OF BREWING & DISTILLING, 33 Clarges Street, London W1J 7EE **T** 020-7499 8144 **E** enquiries@ibd.org.uk **W** www.ibd.org.uk
Executive Director, Simon Jackson

INSTITUTE OF BRITISH ORGAN BUILDING, 13 Ryefields, Thurston, Bury St Edmunds IP31 3TD **T** 01359-233433 **E** administrator@ibo.co.uk **W** www.ibo.co.uk
President, Dr Christopher Batchelor

INSTITUTE OF CHARTERED FORESTERS, 59 George Street, Edinburgh EH2 2JG **T** 0131-240 1425 **E** icf@charteredforesters.org **W** www.charteredforesters.org
Executive Director, Shireen Chambers, FRSA

INSTITUTE OF CHARTERED SECRETARIES AND
ADMINISTRATORS, Saffron House, 6–10 Kirby Street,
London EC1N 8TS T 020-7580 4741 E info@icsa.org.uk
W www.icsa.org.uk
Chief Executive, Simon Osborne

INSTITUTE OF CHARTERED SHIPBROKERS,
85 Gracechurch Street, London EC3V 0AA T 020-7623 1111
E enquiries@ics.org.uk W www.ics.org.uk
Director, Julie Lithgow

INSTITUTE OF DIRECTORS, 116 Pall Mall, London
SW1Y 5ED T 020-7766 8866 E enquiries@iod.com
W www.iod.com
Director-General, Simon Walker

INSTITUTE OF EXPORT, Export House, Minerva Business
Park, Lynch Wood, Peterborough PE2 6FT T 01733-404400
W www.export.org.uk
Director General, Lesley Batchelor

INSTITUTE OF FINANCIAL ACCOUNTANTS,
Burford House, 44 London Road, Sevenoaks TN13 1AS
T 01732-458080 E mail@ifa.org.uk W www.ifa.org.uk
Chief Executive, David Woodgate

INSTITUTE OF HEALTHCARE MANAGEMENT,
John Snow House, 59 Mansell Street, London E1 8AN
T 020-7265 7321 E enquiries@ihm.org.uk W www.ihm.org.uk
Chief Executive, Shirley Cramer, CBE

INSTITUTE OF HOSPITALITY, Trinity Court, 34 West Street,
Sutton, Surrey SM1 1SH T 020-8661 4900
E info@instituteofhospitality.org
W www.instituteofhospitality.org
Chief Executive, Peter Ducker

INSTITUTE OF INTERNAL COMMUNICATION,
Woodlands Business Park, Breckland MK14 6EY
T 01908-313755 E enquiries@ioic.org.uk W www.ioic.org.uk
Chief Executive, Steve Doswell

INSTITUTE OF MANAGEMENT SERVICES, Brooke House,
24 Dam Street, Lichfield WS13 6AA T 01543-266909
E admin@ims-stowe.fsnet.co.uk W www.ims-productivity.com
Chair, Dr Andrew Muir

INSTITUTE OF QUARRYING, McPherson House,
8A Regan Way, Chetwynd Business Park, Chilwell,
Nottingham NG9 6RZ T 0115-972 9995 E mail@quarrying.org
W www.quarrying.org
Executive Director, Phil James

INSTITUTE OF THE MOTOR INDUSTRY, Fanshaws,
Brickendon, Hertford SG13 8PQ T 01992-511521
E comms@theimi.org.uk W www.theimi.org.uk
Chief Executive, Steve Nash

INSTITUTION OF OCCUPATIONAL SAFETY AND
HEALTH, The Grange, Highfield Drive, Wigston LE18 1NN
T 0116-257 3100 E techinfo@iosh.co.uk W www.iosh.co.uk
Chief Executive, Jan Chmiel

IP FEDERATION, 5th Floor, 63–66 Hatton Garden, London
EC1N 8LE T 020-7242 3923 E admin@ipfederation.com
W www.ipfederation.org
President, Dr Bobby Mukherjee

MAGISTRATES' ASSOCIATION, 28 Fitzroy Square, London
W1T 6DD T 020-7387 2353
E information@magistrates-association.org.uk
W www.magistrates-association.org.uk
Chief Executive, Chris Brace

MANAGEMENT CONSULTANCIES ASSOCIATION,
5th Floor, 36–38 Cornhill, London EC3V 3NG T 020-7645 9750
E info@mca.org.uk W www.mca.org.uk
Chief Executive, Alan Leaman, OBE

MASTER LOCKSMITHS ASSOCIATION, 5D Great
Central Way, Wood Halse, Daventry, Northants NN11 3PZ
T 01327-262 255 E enquiries@locksmiths.co.uk
W www.locksmiths.co.uk
Director of Business Development, Steffan George

NATIONAL ASSOCIATION OF BRITISH MARKET
AUTHORITIES, The Guildhall, Oswestry, Shrops SY11 1PZ
T 01691-680713 E nabma@nabma.com W www.nabma.com
Chief Executive, Graham Wilson, OBE

NATIONAL ASSOCIATION OF ESTATE AGENTS,
Arbon House, 6 Tournament Court, Edgehill Drive, Warwick
CV34 6LG T 0844-387 0555 W www.naea.co.uk
President, Simon Gerrard

NATIONAL CATTLE ASSOCIATION (DAIRY), Brick House,
Risbury, Leominster HR6 0NQ T 01568-760632
E timbrigstocke@hotmail.com
Executive Secretary, Tim Brigstocke, MBE

NATIONAL FARMERS' UNION (NFU), Agriculture House,
Stoneleigh Park, Stoneleigh CV8 2LZ T 024-7669 6969
W www.nfuonline.com
Director General, Andy Robertson

NATIONAL FEDERATION OF RETAIL NEWSAGENTS,
Yeoman House, Sekforde Street, London EC1R 0HF
T 020-7253 4225 E service@nfrnonline.com
W www.nfrnonline.com
Chief Executive, Paul Baxter

NATIONAL LANDLORDS ASSOCIATION, 22–26 Albert
Embankment, London SE1 7TJ T 020-7840 8900
E info@landlords.org.uk W www.landlords.org.uk
Chief Executive, Richard Lambert

NATIONAL MARKET TRADERS FEDERATION,
Hampton House, Hawshaw Lane, Hoyland, Barnsley S74 0HA
T 01226-749021 E genoffice@nmtf.co.uk W www.nmtf.co.uk
Chief Executive, Joe Harrison

NATIONAL PHARMACY ASSOCIATION, 38–42 St Peter's
Street, St Albans, Herts AL1 3NP T 01727-858687
E npa@npa.co.uk W www.npa.co.uk
Chief Executive, Michael Holden

NEWSPAPER SOCIETY, 292 Vauxhall Bridge Road,
London SW1V 1AE T 020-7963 7480
E ns@newspapersoc.org.uk W www.newspapersoc.org.uk
Director, David Newell

OIL AND GAS UK, 6th Floor East, Portland House,
Bressenden Place, London SW1E 5BH T 020-7802 2400
E info@oilandgasuk.co.uk W www.oilandgasuk.co.uk
Chief Executive, Malcolm Webb

PROPERTY CARE ASSOCIATION, 11 Ramsay Court,
Kingfisher Way, Hinchingbrooke Business Park, Huntingdon
PE29 6FY T 0844-375 4301 E pca@property-care.org
W www.property-care.org
Chief Executive, Stephen Hodgson

PUBLISHERS ASSOCIATION, 29B Montague Street,
London WC1B 5BW T 020-7691 9191
E mail@publishers.org.uk W www.publishers.org.uk
Chief Executive, Richard Mollet

RADIOCENTRE, 6th Floor, 55 New Oxford Street,
London WC1A 1BS T 020-7010 0600 E info@radiocentre.org
W www.radiocentre.org
Chief Executive, Siobhan Kenny

ROAD HAULAGE ASSOCIATION LTD, Roadway House,
Bretton PE3 8DD T 01733-261131 W www.rha.uk.net
Chief Executive, Geoff Dunning

ROYAL ASSOCIATION OF BRITISH DAIRY FARMERS,
Dairy House, Unit 31, Abbey Park, Stareton, Kenilworth
CV8 2LY T 0845-458 2711 E office@rabdf.co.uk
W www.rabdf.co.uk
Chief Executive, Nick Everington

ROYAL FACULTY OF PROCURATORS IN GLASGOW,
12 Nelson Mandela Place, Glasgow G2 1BT T 0141-332 3593
E library@rfpg.org W www.rfpg.org
Chief Executive, John McKenzie

SHELLFISH ASSOCIATION OF GREAT BRITAIN,
Fishmongers' Hall, London Bridge, London EC4R 9EL
T 020-7283 8305 W www.shellfish.org.uk
Director, David Jarrad

SOCIETY OF LOCAL AUTHORITY CHIEF
EXECUTIVES AND SENIOR MANAGERS (SOLACE),
Hope House, 45 Great Peter Street, London SW1P 3LT
T 0845 652 4010 E hope.house@solace.org.uk
W www.solace.org.uk
Directors, Graeme McDonald; Debbie Wood
SOCIETY OF MOTOR MANUFACTURERS AND
TRADERS LTD, 71 Great Peter Street, London SW1P 2BN
T 020-7235 7000 E membership@smmt.co.uk
W www.smmt.co.uk
Chief Executive, Mike Hawes
TIMBER TRADE FEDERATION, The Building Centre,
26 Store Street, London WC1E 7BT T 020-3205 0067
W www.ttf.co.uk
Chief Executive, John White
TRADING STANDARDS INSTITUTE, 1 Sylvan Court,
Sylvan Way, Southfields Business Park, Basildon SS15 6TH
T 0845-608 9400 E institute@tsi.org.uk
W www.tradingstandards.gov.uk
Chief Executive, Leon Livermore
UK CHAMBER OF SHIPPING, 30 Park Street, London
SE1 9EQ T 020-7417 2800 E query@ukchamberofshipping.com
W www.ukchamberofshipping.com
Chief Executive, Guy Platten
UK FASHION AND TEXTILE ASSOCIATION,
3 Queen Square, London WC1N 3AR T 020-7843 9460
E info@ukft.org W www.ukft.org
Chief Executive, John Miln
UK LEATHER FEDERATION, Leather Trade House,
Kings Park Road, Moulton Park, Northampton NN3 6JD
T 01604-679955 E info@uklf.org W www.ukleather.org
Director, Dr Kerry Senior
UK PETROLEUM INDUSTRY ASSOCIATION LTD,
Quality House, Quality Court, Chancery Lane, London
WC2A 1HP T 020-7269 7600 E info@UKPIA.com
W www.ukpia.com
Director-General, Chris Hunt
ULSTER FARMERS' UNION, 475 Antrim Road, Belfast
BT15 3DA T 028-9037 0222 E info@ufuhq.com
W www.ufuni.org
Chief Executive, Clarke Black

WINE AND SPIRIT TRADE ASSOCIATION, International
Wine and Spirit Centre, 39–45 Bermondsey Street, London
SE1 3XF T 020-7089 3877 E info@wsta.co.uk
W www.wsta.co.uk
Chief Executive, Miles Beale

CBI

Cannon Place, 78 Cannon Street, London EC4N 6HN
T 020-7379 7400 E enquiries@cbi.org.uk W www.cbi.org.uk

The CBI was founded in 1965 and is an independent
non-party political body financed by industry and commerce.
It works with the UK government, international legislators
and policymakers to help UK businesses compete effectively.
It is the recognised spokesman for the business viewpoint
and is consulted as such by the government.

The CBI speaks for some 240,000 businesses that
together employ approximately one-third of the private
sector workforce. Member companies, which decide all
policy positions, include 80 of the FTSE 100 index, some
200,000 small- and medium-size firms, more than 20,000
manufacturers and over 150 sectoral associations.

The CBI board is chaired by the president and meets
around five times a year. It is assisted by 10 expert standing
committees which advise on the main aspects of policy.
There are 12 regional councils and offices, covering the
administrative regions of England, Wales, Scotland and
Northern Ireland. There are also offices in Beijing, Brussels,
New Delhi and Washington DC.

Director-General, John Cridland, CBE

WALES: 2 Caspian Point, Caspian Way, Cardiff Bay, Cardiff
CF10 4DQ T 029-2097 7600
Regional Director, Emma Watkins
SCOTLAND: 16 Robertson Street, Glasgow G2 8DS
T 0141-222 2184
Regional Director, Iain McMillan
NORTHERN IRELAND: 2nd Floor, Hamilton House, 3 Joy
Street, Belfast BT2 8LE T 028-9010 1100
Regional Director, Nigel Smyth

TRADE UNIONS

A trade union is an organisation of workers formed (historically) for the purpose of collective bargaining over pay and working conditions. Today, trade unions may also provide legal and financial advice, sickness benefits and education facilities to their members. Legally any employee has the right to join a trade union, but not all employers recognise all or any trade unions. Conversely an employee also has the right not to join a trade union, in particular since the practice of a 'closed shop' system, where all employees have to join the employer's preferred union, is no longer permitted. Below is a list of key dates in the development of the British trade unionist movement.

2011: More than 250,000 people attend a TUC-organised rally in central London in protest against public spending cuts

1999: The Employment Relations Act introduces the statutory right to trade union recognition where supported by a majority of the workforce

1980: Trade union membership peaks at 13 million

1946: Repeal of the 1927 act allows civil service unions to affiliate to the TUC

1906: The Trade Disputes Act declares that unions are not to be held liable for damages caused by industrial action

1868: The first meeting of the Trades Union Congress (TUC) takes place

1824: The Combination Acts are repealed but subsequently replaced by the Combination Act 1825; this allows trade unions but severely restricts their activity and influence

1799–1800: The Combination Acts make it illegal for workers to join together and press employers for shorter hours or increased pay

2005: Number of work days lost to industrial disputes at lowest point on record; women outnumber men among trade union members for the first time

1984–5: The National Union of Mineworkers goes on strike in protest at the proposed closure of pits and is defeated by the Conservative government

1978–9: The Winter of Discontent; widespread strikes take place. The Conservative Party regains power and introduces legislation to restrict trade unions

1927: The Trade Disputes and Trade Unions Act is passed in response to the General Strike (1926), when 3 million unionists stopped work for ten days. General or sympathetic strikes are outlawed, and civil servants are banned from joining unions affiliated to the TUC

1871: The Trade Union Act recognises unions as legal entities, and as such they are entitled to legal protection

1819: The so-called Six Acts are passed by government, including the gagging of radical newspapers and prevention of large meetings

2000
1950
1900
1850
1800

THE CENTRAL ARBITRATION COMMITTEE

22nd Floor, Euston Tower, 286 Euston Road, London NW1 3JJ
T 020-7904 2300 E enquiries@cac.gov.uk W www.cac.gov.uk

The Central Arbitration Committee's main role is concerned with requests for trade union recognition and de-recognition under the statutory procedures of Schedule A1 of the Employment Rights Act 1999. It also determines disclosure of information complaints under the Trade Union and Labour Relations (Consolidation) Act 1992, considers applications and complaints under the Information and Consultation Regulations 2004, and performs a similar role in relation to European works councils, companies, cooperative societies and cross-border mergers.

Chair, Sir Michael Burton
Chief Executive, Simon Gouldstone

TRADES UNION CONGRESS (TUC)

Congress House, 23–28 Great Russell Street, London WC1B 3LS
T 020-7636 4030
E info@tuc.org.uk W www.tuc.org.uk

The Trades Union Congress (TUC), founded in 1868, is an independent association of trade unions. The TUC promotes the rights and welfare of those in work and helps the unemployed. The TUC brings Britain's unions together to draw up common polices; lobbies the government to implement policies that will benefit people at work; campaigns on economic and social issues; represents working people on public bodies, in the European Union and at the UN employment body – the International Labour Organisation; carries out research on employment-related issues; runs training and education programmes for union representatives; helps unions to develop new services for their members and negotiate with each other; and builds links with other trade union bodies worldwide.

The governing body of the TUC is the annual congress which sets policy. Between congresses, business is conducted by a 56-member general council, which meets every two months to oversee the TUC's work programme and sanction new policy initiatives. Each year, at its first post-congress meeting, the general council appoints an executive committee and the TUC president for that congress year. The executive committee meets monthly to implement and develop policy, manage TUC financial affairs and deal with any urgent business. The president chairs general council and executive meetings and is consulted by the General Secretary on all major issues.

There are 54 affiliated unions, with a total membership of around 6.2 million.
President (2014–15), Leslie Manasseh
General Secretary, Frances O'Grady

SCOTTISH TRADES UNION CONGRESS (STUC)
333 Woodlands Road, Glasgow G3 6NG **T** 0141-337 8100
E info@stuc.org.uk **W** www.stuc.org.uk

The congress was formed in 1897 and acts as a national centre for the trade union movement in Scotland. The STUC promotes the rights to welfare of those in work and helps the unemployed. It helps its member unions to promote membership in new areas and industries, and campaigns for rights at work for all employees, including part-time and temporary workers, whether union members or not. It also makes representations to government and employers. In April 2014 it consisted of 37 affiliated unions, with a membership of more than 625,000, and 20 trade union councils.

The annual congress in April elects a 36-member general council on the basis of six sections.
President, June Minnery
General Secretary, Grahame Smith

WALES TUC
Transport House, 1 Cathedral Road, Cardiff CF11 9SD
T 029-2034 7010
E wtuc@tuc.org.uk **W** www.tuc.org.uk/wales

The Wales TUC was established in 1974 to ensure that the role of the TUC was effectively undertaken in Wales. Its structure reflects the four economic regions of Wales and matches the regional committee areas of the National Assembly of Wales. The regional committees oversee the implementation of Wales TUC policy and campaigns in the relevant regions, and liaise with local government, training organisations and regional economic development bodies. The Wales TUC seeks to reduce unemployment, increase the levels of skill and pay, and eliminate discrimination.

The governing body of Wales TUC is the conference, which meets annually in May and elects a general council (usually of around 50 people) that oversees the work of the TUC throughout the year.

There are around 50 affiliated unions representing around 500,000 workers.
President, David Evans
General Secretary, Martin Mansfield

TUC-AFFILIATED UNIONS

As at April 2014
ACCORD, Simmons House, 46 Old Bath Road, Charvil RG10 9QR **T** 0118-934 1808 **E** info@accordhq.org
W www.accord-myunion.org
General Secretary, Ged Nichols *Membership:* 26,028

ADVANCE, 2nd Floor, 16–17 High Street, Tring HP23 5AH
T 01442-891122 **E** info@advance-union.org
W www.advance-union.org
General Secretary, Linda Rolph *Membership:* 7,452
AEGIS THE UNION, AEGON UK plc, Lochside Crescent, Edinburgh Park, Edinburgh EH12 9SE **T** 0131-549 5665
E members@aegistheunion.co.uk **W** www.aegistheunion.co.uk
General Secretary, Brian Linn *Membership:* 1,254
AEP (ASSOCIATION OF EDUCATIONAL PSYCHOLOGISTS), Unit 4, The Riverside Centre, Frankland Lane, Durham DH1 5TA **T** 0191-384 9512
E enquiries@aep.org.uk **W** www.aep.org.uk
General Secretary, Kate Fallon *Membership:* 3,317
AFA (ASSOCIATION OF FLIGHT ATTENDANTS), Council 7, United Airlines Cargo Centre, Shoreham Road East, Heathrow Airport, Hounslow TW6 3UA **T** 0208-276 6723
E afalhr@unitedafa.org **W** www.afacwa.org
President, Anthony King *Membership:* 500
ASLEF (ASSOCIATED SOCIETY OF LOCOMOTIVE ENGINEERS AND FIREMEN), 75–77 St John Street, Clerkenwell, London EC1M 4NN **T** 020-7324 2400
E info@aslef.org.uk **W** www.aslef.org.uk
General Secretary, Mick Whelan *Membership:* 18,000
ATL (ASSOCIATION OF TEACHERS AND LECTURERS), 7 Northumberland Street, London WC2N 5RD
T 020-7930 6441 **E** info@atl.org.uk **W** www.atl.org.uk
General Secretary, Dr Mary Bousted
Membership: 127,936
BACM-TEAM (BRITISH ASSOCIATION OF COLLIERY MANAGEMENT – TECHNICAL, ENERGY AND ADMINISTRATIVE MANAGEMENT), Edwinstowe House, High Street, Edwinstowe NG21 9PR
T 01623-821510 **E** enquiries@bacmteam.org.uk
W www.bacmteam.org.uk
General Secretary, Patrick Carragher *Membership:* 2,093
BALPA (BRITISH AIRLINE PILOTS ASSOCIATION), BALPA House, 5 Heathrow Boulevard, 278 Bath Road, West Drayton UB7 0DQ **T** 020-8476 4000
E balpa@balpa.org **W** www.balpa.org
General Secretary, Jim McAuslan *Membership:* 7,900
BDA (BRITISH DIETETIC ASSOCIATION), 5th Floor, Charles House, 148–149 Great Charles Street, Queensway, Birmingham B3 3HT **T** 0121-200 8080
E info@bda.uk.com **W** www.bda.uk.com
Chief Executive, Andy Burman *Membership:* 7,064
BECTU (BROADCASTING, ENTERTAINMENT, CINEMATOGRAPH AND THEATRE UNION), 373–377 Clapham Road, London SW9 9BT **T** 020-7346 0900
E info@bectu.org.uk **W** www.bectu.org.uk
General Secretary, Gerry Morrissey *Membership:* 23,406
BFAWU (BAKERS, FOOD AND ALLIED WORKERS' UNION), Stanborough House, Great North Road, Stanborough, Welwyn Garden City AL8 7TA **T** 01707-260150
E info@bfawu.org **W** www.bfawu.org
General Secretary, Ronnie Draper *Membership:* 20,371
BIOS (BRITISH AND IRISH ORTHOPTIC SOCIETY), Salisbury House, Station Road, Ely, Cambridge CB1 2LA
T 01353-665541 **E** bios@orthoptics.org.uk
W www.orthoptics.org.uk
Chair, Lesley-Anne Baxter *Membership:* 926
BSU (BRITANNIA STAFF UNION), Court Lodge, Leonard Street, Leek ST13 5JP **T** 01538-399627
E bsu@themail.co.uk **W** www.britanniasu.org.uk
General Secretary, John Stoddard *Membership:* 2,802
COMMUNITY, 67–68 Long Acre, London WC2E 9FA
T 0800-389 6332 **E** info@community-tu.org
W www.community-tu.org
General Secretary, Roy Rickhuss *Membership:* 50,012

CSP (CHARTERED SOCIETY OF PHYSIOTHERAPY),
14 Bedford Row, London WC1R 4ED T 020-7306 6666
E enquiries@csp.org.uk W www.csp.org.uk
Chief Executive, Karen Middleton, CBE
Membership: 52,000

CWU (COMMUNICATION WORKERS UNION),
150 The Broadway, Wimbledon, London SW19 1RX
T 020-8971 7200 E info@cwu.org W www.cwu.org
General Secretary, W. Hayes *Membership:* 201,875

EIS (EDUCATIONAL INSTITUTE OF SCOTLAND),
46 Moray Place, Edinburgh EH3 6BH T 0131-225 6244
E enquiries@eis.org.uk W www.eis.org.uk
General Secretary, Larry Flanagan *Membership:* 55,000

EQUITY, Guild House, Upper St Martin's Lane, London
WC2H 9EG T 020-7379 6000 E info@equity.org.uk
W www.equity.org.uk
General Secretary, Christine Payne *Membership:* 38,000

FBU (FIRE BRIGADES UNION), Bradley House,
68 Coombe Road, Kingston upon Thames KT2 7AE
T 020-8541 1765 E office@fbu.org.uk W www.fbu.org.uk
General Secretary, Matt Wrack *Membership:* 41,270

FDA, 8 Leake Street, London SE1 7NN T 020-7401 5555
E info@fda.org.uk W www.fda.org.uk
General Secretary, Dave Penman *Membership:* 18,000

GMB, 22 Stephenson Way, London NW1 2HD
T 020-7391 6700 E info@gmb.org.uk W www.gmb.org.uk
General Secretary, Paul Kenny *Membership:* 626,000

HCSA (HOSPITAL CONSULTANTS' AND
SPECIALISTS' ASSOCIATION), 1 Kingsclere Road,
Overton, Basingstoke RG25 3JA T 01256-771777
E conspec@hcsa.com W www.hcsa.com
Chief Executive, Eddie Saville *Membership:* 3,245

MU (MUSICIANS' UNION), 60–62 Clapham Road,
London SW9 0JJ T 020-7582 5566 E info@theMU.org
W www.musiciansunion.org.uk
General Secretary, John F. Smith *Membership:* 30,446

NACO (NATIONAL ASSOCIATION OF COOPERATIVE
OFFICIALS), 6A Clarendon Place, Hyde SK14 2QZ
T 0161-351 7900 E info@naco.coop W www.naco.coop
General Secretary, Neil Buist *Membership:* 1,866

NACODS (NATIONAL ASSOCIATION OF COLLIERY
OVERMEN, DEPUTIES AND SHOTFIRERS),
Wadsworth House, 130–132 Doncaster Road, Barnsley S70 1TP
T 01226-203743 E natnacods@googlemail.com
W www.nacods.org.uk
General Secretary, Rowland Soar *Membership:* 226

NAPO (TRADE UNION AND PROFESSIONAL
ASSOCIATION FOR FAMILY COURT AND
PROBATION STAFF), 4 Chivalry Road, London SW11 1HT
T 020-7223 4887 E info@napo.org.uk
W www.napo.org.uk
General Secretary, Ian Lawrence *Membership:* 8,700

NASS (NATIONAL ASSOCIATION OF STABLE
STAFF), The New Astley Club, Fred Archer Way,
Newmarket CB8 8NT T 01638 663411 E office@naoss.co.uk
W www.naoss.co.uk
Chief Executive, George McGrath *Membership:* 1,782

NASUWT (NATIONAL ASSOCIATION OF
SCHOOLMASTERS/UNION OF WOMEN
TEACHERS), Hillscourt Education Centre, Rose Hill, Rednal,
Birmingham B45 8RS T 0121-453 6150
E nasuwt@mail.nasuwt.org.uk W www.nasuwt.org.uk
General Secretary, Ms Chris Keates
Membership: 294,230

NAUTILUS INTERNATIONAL, 1–2 The Shrubberies,
George Lane, South Woodford, London E18 1BD
T 020-8989 6677 E enquiries@nautilusint.org
W www.nautilusint.org
General Secretary, Mark Dickinson *Membership:* 15,865

NGSU (NATIONWIDE GROUP STAFF UNION),
Middleton Farmhouse, 37 Main Road, Middleton Cheney
OX17 2QT T 01295-710767 E ngsu@ngsu.org.uk
W www.ngsu.co.uk
General Secretary, Tim Poil *Membership:* 11,628

NUJ (NATIONAL UNION OF JOURNALISTS),
Headland House, 308–312 Gray's Inn Road, London WC1X 8DP
T 020-7843 3700 E info@nuj.org.uk W www.nuj.org.uk
General Secretary, Michelle Stanistreet
Membership: 30,000

NUM (NATIONAL UNION OF MINEWORKERS),
Miners' Offices, 2 Huddersfield Road, Barnsley S70 2LS
T 01226-215555 E chris.kitchen@num.org.uk
W www.num.org.uk
National Secretary, Chris Kitchen *Membership:* 1,853

NUT (NATIONAL UNION OF TEACHERS),
Hamilton House, Mabledon Place, London WC1H 9BD
T 020-7388 6191 E enquiries@nut.org.uk
W www.teachers.org.uk
General Secretary, Christine Blower
Membership: 387,610

PCS (PUBLIC AND COMMERCIAL SERVICES UNION),
160 Falcon Road, London SW11 2LN T 020-7924 2727
W www.pcs.org.uk
General Secretary, Mark Serwotka *Membership:* 262,819

PFA (PROFESSIONAL FOOTBALLERS' ASSOCIATION),
20 Oxford Court, Bishopsgate, Manchester M2 3WQ
T 0161-236 0575 E info@thepfa.co.uk W www.thepfa.com
Chief Executive, Gordon Taylor, OBE
Membership: 4,500

POA (PROFESSIONAL TRADE UNION FOR PRISON,
CORRECTIONAL AND SECURE PSYCHIATRIC
WORKERS), Cronin House, 245 Church Street, London
N9 9HW T 020-8803 0255 E general@poauk.org.uk
W www.poauk.org.uk
General Secretary, Steve Gillan *Membership:* 31,266

PROSPECT, New Prospect House, 8 Leake Street, London
SE1 7NN T 020-7902 6600 E enquiries@prospect.org.uk
W www.prospect.org.uk
General Secretary, Mike Clancy *Membership:* 118,620

RMT (NATIONAL UNION OF RAIL, MARITIME AND
TRANSPORT WORKERS), Unity House, 39 Chalton Street,
London NW1 1JD T 020-7387 4771 E info@rmt.org.uk
W www.rmt.org.uk
Acting General Secretary, Mick Cash *Membership:* 80,305

SCP (SOCIETY OF CHIROPODISTS AND
PODIATRISTS), 1 Fellmonger's Path, Tower Bridge Road,
London SE1 3LY T 0845-450 3720 E enq@scpod.org
W www.scpod.org
General Secretary, Joanna Brown *Membership:* 9,246

SOR (SOCIETY OF RADIOGRAPHERS), 207 Providence
Square, Mill Street, London SE1 2EW T 020-7740 7200
E info@sor.org W www.sor.org
Chief Executive, Richard Evans *Membership:* 27,500

STAFF UNION WEST BROMWICH BUILDING
SOCIETY, 374 High Street, West Bromwich B70 8LR
T 0870-220 7720 E StaffUnion@westbrom.co.uk
General Secretary, Julie Holton *Membership:* 543

SURGE (SKIPTON UNION REPRESENTING GROUP
EMPLOYEES), The Bailey, Harrogate Road,
Skipton BD23 1DN T 01756-705826
E contact.SURGE@skiptonunion.co.uk
W www.skiptonunion.co.uk
General Secretary, Brian McDaid *Membership:* 1,302

TSSA (TRANSPORT SALARIED STAFFS'
ASSOCIATION), Walkden House, 10 Melton Street,
London NW1 2EJ T 020-7387 2101 E enquiries@tssa.org.uk
W www.tssa.org.uk
General Secretary, Manuel Cortes *Membership:* 22,762

UCAC (UNDEB CENEDLAETHOL ATHRAWON CYMRU) (NATIONAL UNION OF THE TEACHERS OF WALES), Prif Swyddfa UCAC, Ffordd Penglais, Aberystwyth SY23 2EU T 01970-639950
E ucac@athrawon.com W www.athrawon.com
General Secretary, Elaine Edwards *Membership:* 3,874
UCATT (UNION OF CONSTRUCTION, ALLIED TRADES AND TECHNICIANS), UCATT House, 177 Abbeville Road, London SW4 9RL T 020-7622 2442
E info@ucatt.org.uk W www.ucatt.org.uk
General Secretary, Steve Murphy *Membership:* 84,377
UCU (UNIVERSITY AND COLLEGE UNION), Carlow Street, London NW1 7LH T 020-7756 2500
E hq@ucu.org.uk W www.ucu.org.uk
General Secretary, Sally Hunt *Membership:* around 120,000
UNISON, 130 Euston Road, London NW1 2AY
T 0800-085 7857 W www.unison.org.uk
General Secretary, Dave Prentis *Membership:* 1,301,500
UNITE, 128 Theobald's Road, London WC1X 8TN
T 020-7611 2500 W www.unitetheunion.org
General Secretary, Len McCluskey *Membership:* 1,319,413
UNITY, Hillcrest House, Garth Street, Hanley, Stoke-on-Trent ST1 2AB T 01782-272755
E harryhockaday@unitytheunion.org.uk
W www.unitytheunion.org.uk
General Secretary, Harry Hockaday *Membership:* 3,940
URTU (UNITED ROAD TRANSPORT UNION), Almond House, Oak Green, Stanley Green Business Park, Cheadle Hulme SK8 6QL T 0800-526639 E info@urtu.com
W www.urtu.com
General Secretary, Robert Monks *Membership:* 12,250
USDAW (UNION OF SHOP, DISTRIBUTIVE AND ALLIED WORKERS), 188 Wilmslow Road, Manchester M14 6LJ T 0161-224 2804 E enquiries@usdaw.org.uk
W www.usdaw.org.uk
General Secretary, John Hannett *Membership:* 433,071
WGGB (WRITERS' GUILD OF GREAT BRITAIN), 40 Rosebery Avenue, London EC1R 4RX T 020-7833 0777
E admin@writersguild.org.uk W www.writersguild.org.uk
General Secretary, Bernie Corbett *Membership:* 1,075
YISA (YORKSHIRE INDEPENDENT STAFF ASSOCIATION), c/o Yorkshire Building Society, Yorkshire House, Yorkshire Drive, Rooley Lane, Bradford BD5 8LJ
T 01274-472629 E ahgrota@ybs.co.uk
General Secretary, Ania Grota *Membership:* 1,727

NON-AFFILIATED UNIONS

As at April 2014
ASCL (ASSOCIATION OF SCHOOL AND COLLEGE LEADERS), 130 Regent Road, Leicester LE1 7PG
T 0116-299 1122 E info@ascl.org.uk W www.ascl.org.uk
General Secretary, Brian Lightman
Membership: 18,000
BDA (BRITISH DENTAL ASSOCIATION), 64 Wimpole Street, London W1G 8YS T 020-7935 0875
E enquiries@bda.org W www.bda.org
Chief Executive, Peter Ward *Membership:* 20,120
CIOJ (CHARTERED INSTITUTE OF JOURNALISTS), 2 Dock Offices, Surrey Quays Road, London SE16 2XU
T 020-7252 1187 E memberservices@cioj.co.uk
W www.cioj.co.uk
General Secretary, Dominic Cooper
Membership: around 2,000
NAHT (NATIONAL ASSOCIATION OF HEAD TEACHERS), 1 Heath Square, Boltro Road, Haywards Heath RH16 1BL T 01444-472472 E info@naht.org.uk
W www.naht.org.uk
General Secretary, Russell Hobby *Membership:* 27,993
NSEAD (NATIONAL SOCIETY FOR EDUCATION IN ART AND DESIGN), 3 Mason's Wharf, Potley Lane, Corsham SN13 9FY T 01225-810134 E info@nsead.org
W www.nsead.org
General Secretary, Mrs Lesley Butterworth
Membership: around 2,000
RCM (ROYAL COLLEGE OF MIDWIVES), 15 Mansfield Street, London W1G 9NH T 030-0303 0444 E info@rcm.org.uk
W www.rcm.org.uk
General Secretary, Prof. Cathy Warwick, CBE
Membership: 42,000
SOCIETY OF AUTHORS, 84 Drayton Gardens, London SW10 9SB T 020-7373 6642 E info@societyofauthors.org
W www.societyofauthors.org
Chief Executive, Nicola Solomon
Membership: around 9,000
SSTA (SCOTTISH SECONDARY TEACHERS' ASSOCIATION), West End House, 14 West End Place, Edinburgh EH11 2ED T 0131-313 7300 E info@ssta.org.uk
W www.ssta.org.uk
General Secretary (acting), Alan McKenzie
Membership: around 8,500

SPORTS BODIES

SPORTS COUNCILS

SPORT AND RECREATION ALLIANCE,
Burwood House, 14 Caxton Street, London SW1H 0QT
T 020-7976 3933 E info@sportandrecreation.org.uk
W www.sportandrecreation.org.uk
Acting Chief Executive, Sallie Barker

SPORT ENGLAND, 1st Floor, 21 Bloomsbury Street,
London WC1B 3HF T 0845-850 8508
E info@sportengland.org W www.sportengland.org
Chief Executive, Jennie Price

SPORT NORTHERN IRELAND, House of Sport,
2A Upper Malone Road, Belfast BT9 5LA T 028-9038 1222
E info@sportni.net W www.sportni.net
Chair, Brian Henning

SPORTSCOTLAND, Doges, Templeton on the Green,
62 Templeton Street, Glasgow G40 1DA T 0141-534 6500
E website@sportscotland.org.uk W www.sportscotland.org.uk
Chief Executive, Stewart Harris

SPORT WALES, Sophia Gardens, Cardiff CF11 9SW
T 0300-300 3111 E info@sportwales.org.uk
W www.sportwales.org.uk
Chief Executive, Sarah Powell

UK SPORT, 40 Bernard Street, London WC1N 1ST
T 020-7211 5100 E info@uksport.gov.uk
W www.uksport.gov.uk
Chief Executive, Liz Nicholl, OBE

AMERICAN FOOTBALL

BRITISH AMERICAN FOOTBALL ASSOCIATION,
West House, Hedley on the Hill, Stocksfield NE43 7SW
T 01661-843179 E bafachairman@gmail.com
W www.britishamericanfootball.org
Chair, Charles Macnamara

ANGLING

ANGLING TRUST, Eastwood House, 6 Rainbow Street,
Leominster, Herefordshire HR6 8DQ T 0844-770 0616
E admin@anglingtrust.net W www.anglingtrust.net
Chief Executive, Mark Lloyd

ARCHERY

ARCHERY GB, Lilleshall National Sports Centre,
Newport TF10 9AT T 01952-677888
E enquiries@archerygb.org W www.archerygb.org
Chief Executive, David Sherratt

ASSOCIATION FOOTBALL

FOOTBALL ASSOCIATION, Wembley Stadium,
PO Box 1966, SW1P 9EQ T 0844-980 8200 E info@thefa.com
W www.thefa.com
Chair, Greg Dyke

FOOTBALL ASSOCIATION OF WALES, 11–12 Neptune
Court, Vanguard Way, Cardiff CF24 5PJ T 029-2043 5830
E info@faw.org.uk W www.faw.org.uk
Chief Executive, Jonathan Ford

FOOTBALL LEAGUE, Edward VII Quay, Navigation Way,
Preston PR2 2YF T 0844-463 1888
E enquiries@football-league.co.uk
W www.football-league.co.uk
Chief Executive, Shaun Harvey

IRISH FOOTBALL ASSOCIATION, 20 Windsor Avenue,
Belfast BT9 6EG T 028-9066 9458 E info@irishfa.com
W www.irishfa.com
Chief Executive, Patrick Nelson

PREMIER LEAGUE, 30 Gloucester Place, London W1U 8PL
T 020-7864 9000 E info@premierleague.com
W www.premierleague.com
Chief Executive, Richard Scudamore

SCOTTISH FOOTBALL ASSOCIATION, Hampden Park,
Glasgow G42 9AY T 0141-616 6000 E info@scottishfa.co.uk
W www.scottishfa.co.uk
Chief Executive, Stewart Regan

SCOTTISH PROFESSIONAL FOOTBALL LEAGUE,
The National Stadium, Hampden Park, Glasgow G42 9EB
T 0141-620 4160 E info@spfl.co.uk W www.spfl.co.uk
Chief Executive, Neil Doncaster

ATHLETICS

ATHLETICS NORTHERN IRELAND, Athletics House,
Old Coach Road, Belfast BT9 5PR T 028-9060 2707
E info@athleticsni.org W www.athleticsni.org
General Secretary, John Allen

SCOTTISH ATHLETICS, Caledonia House, South Gyle,
Edinburgh EH12 9DQ T 0131-539 7320
E admin@scottishathletics.org.uk
W www.scottishathletics.org.uk
Chief Executive, Nigel Holl

UK ATHLETICS, Athletics House, Alexander Stadium, Perry
Barr, Birmingham B42 2BE T 0121-713 8400
W www.britishathletics.org.uk
Chief Executive, Niels de Vos

WELSH ATHLETICS, Cardiff International Sports Stadium,
Leckwith Road, Cardiff CF11 8AZ T 029-2064 4870
E office@welshathletics.org W www.welshathletics.org
Chief Executive, Matt Newman

BADMINTON

BADMINTON ENGLAND, National Badminton Centre,
Bradwell Road, Milton Keynes MK8 9LA T 01908-268400
E enquiries@badmintonengland.co.uk
W www.badmintonengland.co.uk
Chief Executive, Adrian Christy

BADMINTON SCOTLAND, Cockburn Centre,
40 Bogmoor Place, Glasgow G51 4TQ T 0141-445 1218
E enquiries@badmintonscotland.org.uk
W www.badmintonscotland.org.uk
Chief Executive, Anne Smillie

BADMINTON WALES, Sport Wales National Centre,
Sophia Gardens, Cardiff CF11 9SW T 0300-300 3124
E wbu@badmintonwales.net W www.badmintonwales.net
Chief Executive, Eddie O'Neill

BASEBALL

BASEBALLSOFTBALL UK, Ariel House,
74A Charlotte Street, London W1T 4QJ T 020-7453 7055
W www.baseballsoftballuk.com
Chief Executive, Jenny Fromer

BASKETBALL

BASKETBALL SCOTLAND, Caledonia House, South Gyle,
Edinburgh EH12 9DQ T 0131-317 7260
E enquiries@basketball-scotland.com
W www.basketballscotland.co.uk
Chief Executive, Kevin Pringle

ENGLAND BASKETBALL, Unit 2, 1 Arena Court, Sheffield
S9 2LF T 0114-284 1060 E info@englandbasketball.co.uk
W www.englandbasketball.co.uk
Chief Executive, Huw Morgan

BILLIARDS AND SNOOKER

WORLD SNOOKER, 75 Whiteladies Road, Clifton,
Bristol BS8 2NT T 0117-317 8200 E info@worldsnooker.com
W www.worldsnooker.com
Chair, Jason Ferguson

BOBSLEIGH

BRITISH BOBSLEIGH AND SKELETON ASSOCIATION,
Sports Training Village, University of Bath, Bath BA2 7AY
T 01225-383696 E office@britishskeleton.co.uk
W www.britishskeleton.co.uk
Chair, Lord Clifton Wrottesley

BOWLS

BOWLS ENGLAND, Riverside House, Milverton Hill,
Royal Leamington Spa CV32 5HZ T 01926-334609
E enquiries@bowlsengland.com W www.bowlsengland.com
Chief Executive, Tony Allcock, MBE
BRITISH ISLES BOWLS COUNCIL, 12/1 Oxgangs Avenue,
Edinburgh EH13 9JB T 01314-455838
E bibcsecretary@aol.co.uk W www.britishislesbowls.com
Hon. Secretary, Duncan McLaren
ENGLISH INDOOR BOWLING ASSOCIATION,
David Cornwell House, Bowling Green, Melton Mowbray
LE13 0FA T 01664-481900 E enquiries@eiba.co.uk
W www.eiba.co.uk
Chief Executive, Peter Thompson

BOXING

AMATEUR BOXING ASSOCIATION OF ENGLAND,
English Institute of Sport, Coleridge Road, Sheffield S9 5DA
T 0114-223 5654 W www.abae.co.uk
Chief Executive, Mark Abberley
BRITISH BOXING BOARD OF CONTROL, 14 North Road,
Cardiff CF10 3DY T 029-2036 7000 E admin@bbbofc.com
W www.bbbofc.com
General Secretary, Robert Smith

CANOEING

BRITISH CANOE UNION, National Water Sport Centre,
Adbolton Lane, Nottingham NG12 2LU T 0845-370 9500
E info@bcu.org.uk W www.bcu.org.uk
Secretary, Paul Owen

CHESS

ENGLISH CHESS FEDERATION, The Watch Oak,
Chain Lane, Battle TN33 0YD T 01424-775222
E office@englishchess.org.uk W www.englishchess.org.uk
Chief Executive, Phil Ehr

CRICKET

ENGLAND AND WALES CRICKET BOARD,
Lord's Cricket Ground, London NW8 8QZ T 020-7432 1200
E feedback@ecb.co.uk W www.ecb.co.uk
Chief Executive, David Collier
MCC, Lord's Cricket Ground, St John's Wood, London NW8 8QN
T 020-7616 8500 E reception@mcc.org.uk W www.lords.org
Chief Executive, Derek Brewer

CROQUET

CROQUET ASSOCIATION, Old Bath Road, Cheltenham
GL53 7DF T 01242-242318 E caoffice@croquet.org.uk
W www.croquet.org.uk
President, Quiller Barrett

CURLING

BRITISH CURLING, Cairnie House, Ingliston EH28 8NB
T 0131-333 3003 E info@britishcurling.com
W www.britishcurling.org.uk
Chief Operating Officer, Bruce Crawford

ROYAL CALEDONIAN CURLING CLUB, Cairnie House,
Ingliston, Newbridge EH28 8NB T 0131-333 3003
E office@royalcaledoniancurlingclub.org
W www.royalcaledoniancurlingclub.org
Chief Executive, Bruce Crawford

CYCLING

BRITISH CYCLING FEDERATION, Stuart Street,
Manchester M11 4DQ T 0161-274 2000
E info@britishcycling.org.uk W www.britishcycling.org.uk
Chief Executive, Ian Drake

DARTS

BRITISH DARTS ORGANISATION, Unit 4, Glan-y-Llyn
Industrial Estate, Taffs Well, Cardiff CF15 7JD T 02920-811815
E britishdartsorg@btconnect.com W www.bdodarts.com
Director, Wayne Williams

EQUESTRIANISM

BRITISH EQUESTRIAN FEDERATION, Abbey Park,
Kenilworth CV8 2RH T 02476-698871 E info@bef.co.uk
W www.bef.co.uk
Chief Executive, Andrew Finding, OBE
BRITISH EVENTING, Abbey Park, Kenilworth CV8 2RN
T 0845-262 3344 E info@britisheventing.com
W www.britisheventing.com
Chief Executive, Mike Etherington-Smith

ETON FIVES

ETON FIVES ASSOCIATION, 45 Sandhills Crescent,
Hillfield, Solihull B91 3UE T 07833-600230
E efa@etonfives.co.uk W www.fivesonline.net
Chair, Peter Worth

FENCING

BRITISH FENCING, 1 Baron's Gate, 33 Rothschild Road,
London W4 5HT T 020-8742 3032
E headoffice@britishfencing.com W www.britishfencing.com
Chief Executive, Georgina Usher

GLIDING

BRITISH GLIDING ASSOCIATION, 8 Merus Court,
Meridian Business Park, Leicester LE19 1RJ T 0116-289 2956
E office@gliding.co.uk W www.gliding.co.uk
Chief Executive, Pete Stratten

GOLF

ENGLAND GOLF, The National Golf Centre, Woodhall Spa
LN10 6PU T 01526-354500 E info@englandgolf.org
W www.englandgolf.org
Chief Executive, David Joy
LADIES' GOLF UNION, The Scores, St Andrews KY16 9AT
T 01334-475811 E info@lgu.org W www.lgu.org
Chief Executive, Shona Malcolm
THE ROYAL AND ANCIENT GOLF CLUB, Golf Place,
St Andrews KY16 9JD T 01334-460000
E thesecretary@randagc.org W www.randa.org
Chief Executive, Peter Dawson

GYMNASTICS

BRITISH GYMNASTICS, Ford Hall, Lilleshall National Sports
Centre, Newport TF10 9NB T 0845-129 7129
E information@british-gymnastics.org
W www.british-gymnastics.org
Chief Executive, Jane Allen

HANDBALL

BRITISH HANDBALL ASSOCIATION, Henwood House,
Henwood, Ashford TN24 8DH T 01233-878099
E office@britishhandball.com W www.britishhandball.com
Chair, John Brewer

HOCKEY

ENGLAND HOCKEY, Bisham Abbey National Sports Centre,
Marlow SL7 1RR **T** 01628-897500
E info@englandhockey.co.uk **W** www.englandhockey.co.uk
Chief Executive, Sally Munday

SCOTTISH HOCKEY UNION, Glasgow National Hockey
Centre, 8 King's Drive, Glasgow G40 1HB **T** 0141-550 5999
W www.scottish-hockey.org.uk
Chief Executive, David Sweetman

WELSH HOCKEY UNION, Sport Wales National Centre,
Sophie Gardens, Cardiff CF11 9SW **T** 029-2033 4909
E info@hockeywales.org.uk **W** www.hockeywales.org.uk
Chief Executive, Helen Bushell

HORSERACING

BRITISH HORSERACING AUTHORITY,
75 High Holborn, London WC1V 6LS **T** 020-7152 0000
E info@britishhorseracing.com **W** www.britishhorseracing.com
Chief Executive, Paul Bittar

THE JOCKEY CLUB, 75 High Holborn, London WC1V 6LS
T 020-7611 1800 **E** info@thejockeyclub.co.uk
W www.thejockeyclub.co.uk
Chief Executive, Simon Bazalgette

ICE SKATING

NATIONAL ICE SKATING ASSOCIATION OF THE UK,
Grains Building, High Cross Street, Hockley, Nottingham
NG1 3AX **T** 0115-988 8060 **E** info@iceskating.org.uk
W www.iceskating.org.uk
Chief Executive, Nick Sellwood

LACROSSE

ENGLISH LACROSSE ASSOCIATION, PO Box 116,
Manchester M11 0AX **T** 0843-658 5006
E info@englishlacrosse.co.uk **W** www.englishlacrosse.co.uk
Chief Executive, Mark Coups

LAWN TENNIS

LAWN TENNIS ASSOCIATION, National Tennis Centre,
100 Priory Lane, London SW15 5JQ **T** 020-8487 7000
E info@lta.org.uk **W** www.lta.org.uk
Chief Executive, Michael Downey

MARTIAL ARTS

BRITISH JUDO ASSOCIATION, Suite B, Loughborough
Technology Centre, Epinal Way, Loughborough LE11 3GE
T 01509-631670 **E** bja@britishjudo.org.uk
W www.britishjudo.org.uk
Chief Executive, Andrew Scoular

BRITISH JU JITSU ASSOCIATION, 5 Avenue Parade,
Accrington BB5 6PN **T** 07850-317553 **E** bjjagb@icloud.com
W www.bjjagb.com
Chair, Martin Dixon

BRITISH TAEKWONDO COUNCIL, TKD Centre,
192 High Street, West Drayton UB7 7PE **T** 01895-459949
E admin@tkdcouncil.com **W** www.tkdcouncil.com
Chair, D. Oliver

MODERN PENTATHLON

PENTATHLON GB, Wessex House, University of Bath,
Claverton Down, Bath BA2 7AY **T** 01225-386808
E admin@pentathlongb.org **W** www.pentathlongb.org
Chief Executive, Jon Austin

MOTOR SPORTS

AUTO-CYCLE UNION, ACU House, Wood Street,
Rugby CV21 2YX **T** 01788-566400 **E** admin@acu.org.uk
W www.acu.org.uk
General Secretary, Gary Thompson, MBE

MOTOR SPORTS ASSOCIATION, Motor Sports House,
Riverside Park, Colnbrook SL3 0HG **T** 01753-765000
W www.msauk.org
Chief Executive, Rob Jones

SCOTTISH AUTO CYCLE UNION, 28 West Main Street,
Uphall EH52 5DW **T** 01506-858354 **E** office@sacu.co.uk
W www.sacu.co.uk
President, Ian Barnes

MOUNTAINEERING

BRITISH MOUNTAINEERING COUNCIL,
The Old Church, 177–179 Burton Road, Manchester M20 2BB
T 0161-445 6111 **E** office@thebmc.co.uk
W www.thebmc.co.uk
Chief Executive, Dave Turnbull

MULTI-SPORTS BODIES

BRITISH OLYMPIC ASSOCIATION, 60 Charlotte Street,
London W1T 2NU **T** 020-7842 5700 **E** boa@boa.org.uk
W www.teamgb.com
Chief Executive, Bill Sweeney

BRITISH PARALYMPIC ASSOCIATION, 60 Charlotte
Street, London W1T 2NU **T** 020-7842 5789
E info@paralympics.org.uk **W** www.paralympics.org.uk
Chief Executive, Tim Hollingsworth

BRITISH UNIVERSITIES AND COLLEGES SPORT,
20–24 Kings Bench Street, London SE1 0QX
T 020-7633 5080 **W** www.bucs.org.uk
Chief Executive, Karen Rothery

COMMONWEALTH GAMES ENGLAND,
307–308 High Holborn, National Sports Centre,
London WC1V 7LL **T** 020-7831 3444
E info@weareengland.org **W** www.weareengland.org
Chief Executive, Adam Paker

COMMONWEALTH GAMES FEDERATION, 2nd Floor,
138 Piccadilly, London W1J 7NR **T** 020-7491 8801
E info@thecgf.com **W** www.thecgf.com
Chief Executive, Mike Hooper

ENGLISH FEDERATION OF DISABILITY SPORT,
Loughborough University, 3 Oakwood Drive,
Loughborough LE11 3QF **T** 01509-227750 **W** www.efds.co.uk
Chief Executive, Barry Horne

NETBALL

ENGLAND NETBALL, Netball House, 1–12 Old Park Road,
Hitchin SG5 2JR **T** 01462-442344 **E** info@englandnetball.co.uk
W www.englandnetball.co.uk
Chief Executive, Paul Clark

NETBALL NI, City of Lisburn Racquets Club, Belfast Road,
Lisburn BT27 4AF **T** 028-9266 8412 **W** www.netballni.org
Hon. President, Lorraine Lindsay

NETBALL SCOTLAND, Emirates Arena, 1000 London Road,
Glasgow G40 3HY **T** 0141-428 3460
E membership@netballscotland.com
W www.netballscotland.com
Chief Executive, Maggie Murray

WELSH NETBALL ASSOCIATION, Sport Wales National
Centre, Sophia Gardens, Cardiff CF11 9SW **T** 0845-045 4302
E welshnetball@welshnetball.com **W** www.welshnetball.co.uk
Chief Executive, Mike Watson

ORIENTEERING

BRITISH ORIENTEERING, 8A Stancliffe House,
Whitworth Road, Darley Dale, Matlock DE4 2HJ
T 01629-734042 **E** info@britishorienteering.org.uk
W www.britishorienteering.org.uk
Chief Executive, Mike Hamilton

POLO

THE HURLINGHAM POLO ASSOCIATION,
Manor Farm, Little Coxwell, Faringdon SN7 7LW
T 01367-242020 E enquiries@hpa-polo.co.uk
W www.hpa-polo.co.uk
Chief Executive, David Woodd

RACKETS AND REAL TENNIS

TENNIS AND RACKETS ASSOCIATION,
c/o The Queen's Club, Palliser Road, London W14 9EQ
T 020-7835 6937 E office@tennisandrackets.com
W www.tennisandrackets.com
Chief Executive, C. S. Davies

ROWING

BRITISH ROWING, 6 Lower Mall, Hammersmith, London
W6 9DJ T 020-8237 6700 E info@gbrowningteam.org.uk
W www.britishrowing.org
Acting Chief Executive, Neil Chugani
HENLEY ROYAL REGATTA, Regatta Headquarters,
Henley-on-Thames RG9 2LY T 01491-572153
W www.hrr.co.uk
Secretary, D. G. M. Grist

RUGBY LEAGUE

BRITISH AMATEUR RUGBY LEAGUE ASSOCIATION,
West Yorkshire House, 4 New North Parade, Huddersfield
HD1 5JP T 01484-599113 E info@barla.org.uk
W www.barla.org.uk
Chair, Sue Taylor
RUGBY FOOTBALL LEAGUE, Red Hall, Red Hall Lane,
Leeds LS17 8NB T 0844-477 7113 E enquiries@rfl.uk.com
W www.therfl.co.uk
Chief Executive, Nigel Wood

RUGBY UNION

IRISH RUGBY FOOTBALL UNION, 10–12 Lansdowne Road,
Ballsbridge, Dublin 4 T (+353) 1647 3800 E info@irishrugby.ie
W www.irishrugby.ie
Chief Executive, Philip Browne
RUGBY FOOTBALL UNION, Rugby House, Twickenham
Stadium, 200 Whitton Road, Twickenham TW2 7BA
T 0871-222 2120 E enquiries@therfu.com W www.rfu.com
Chief Executive, Ian Ritchie
RUGBY FOOTBALL UNION FOR WOMEN, Rugby House,
Twickenham Stadium, 200 Whitton Road, Twickenham,
TW2 7BA T 0871-222 2120 E enquiries@therfu.com
W www.rfu.com
Managing Director, Rosie Williams
SCOTTISH RUGBY UNION, Murrayfield, Edinburgh EH12 5PJ
T 0131-346 5000 E feedback@sru.org.uk
W www.scottishrugby.org
Chief Executive, Mark Dodson
SCOTTISH WOMEN'S RUGBY UNION, Scottish Rugby
Union, Murrayfield, Edinburgh EH12 5PJ T 0131-346 5000
W www.scottishrugby.org
Chief Executive, Mark Dodson
WELSH RUGBY UNION, Millennium Stadium,
Westgate Street, Cardiff CF10 1NS T 0844-249 1999
E info@wru.co.uk W www.wru.co.uk
Chief Executive, Roger Lewis

SHOOTING

BRITISH SHOOTING, 40 Bernard Street, London WC1N 1ST
T 020-7211 5189 E admin@britishshooting.org.uk
W www.britishshooting.org.uk
Chief Executive, Hamish McInnes

CLAY PIGEON SHOOTING ASSOCIATION,
Edmonton House, National Shooting Centre, Brookwood,
Woking GU24 0NP T 01483-485400 E info@cpsa.co.uk
W www.cpsa.co.uk
Chief Executive, Nick Fellows
NATIONAL RIFLE ASSOCIATION, Bisley, Brookwood,
GU24 0PB T 01483-797777 E info@nra.org.uk
W www.nra.org.uk
Chief Executive, Andrew Mercer
NATIONAL SMALL-BORE RIFLE ASSOCIATION,
Lord Roberts Centre, Bisley Camp, Brookwood, Woking
GU24 0NP T 01483-485505 W www.nsra.co.uk
Chair, Robert Newman

SNOWBOARDING

BRITISH SKI AND SNOWBOARD, 60 Charlotte Street,
London W1T 2NU T 020-7842 5764 W www.teambss.org.uk
Chief Executive, Dave Edwards

SPEEDWAY

BRITISH SPEEDWAY, ACU Headquarters, Wood Street,
Rugby CV21 2YX T 01788-560648 E office@speedwaygb.co
W www.speedwaygb.co
Chair, Alex Harkess

SQUASH

ENGLAND SQUASH AND RACKETBALL,
National Squash Centre, Sportcity, Manchester M11 3FF
T 0161-231 4499
E enquiries@englandsquashandracketball.com
W www.englandsquashandracketball.com
Acting Chief Executive, Susan Meadows
SCOTTISH SQUASH AND RACKETBALL LIMITED,
Caledonia House, 1 Redheughs Rigg, South Gyle,
Edinburgh EH12 9DQ T 0131-625 4425
E info@scottishsquash.org W www.scottishsquash.org
Chief Executive, John Dunlop
WALES SQUASH AND RACKETBALL, Sport Wales National
Centre, Sophia Close, Cardiff CF11 9SW T 0845-045 0902
W www.walessquashandracketball.co.uk
Chair, Phil Brailey

SUB-AQUA

BRITISH SUB-AQUA CLUB, Telford's Quay, South Pier Road,
Ellesmere Port CH65 4FL T 0151-350 6200 E info@bsac.com
W www.bsac.com
Chief Executive, Mary Tetley

SWIMMING

AMATEUR SWIMMING ASSOCIATION, Pavilion 3,
Sport Park, 3 Oakwood Drive, Loughborough LE11 3QF
T 01509-618700 E customerservices@swimming.org
W www.swimming.org
Chief Executive, D. Sparkes, OBE
SCOTTISH SWIMMING, National Swimming Academy,
University of Stirling, Stirling FK9 4LA T 01786-466520
E info@scottishswimming.com W www.scottishswimming.com
Chief Executive, Forbes Dunlop
SWIM WALES, WNPS, Sketty Lane, Swansea SA2 8QG
T 01792-513636 W www.swimwales.org
Chief Executive, Robert James

TABLE TENNIS

ENGLISH TABLE TENNIS ASSOCIATION, Norfolk House,
88 Saxon Gate West, Milton Keynes MK9 2DL T 01908-208860
E admin@etta.co.uk W www.etta.co.uk
Chief Executive, Sara Sutcliffe

TABLE TENNIS ASSOCIATION OF WALES, 8 Petit Close,
Cefn-y-Bedd, Wrexham LL12 9YE **T** 01978-760791
E admin@ttaw.co.uk **W** www.ttaw.co.uk
Chair, Bernard Carter
TABLE TENNIS SCOTLAND, Caledonia House, South Gyle,
Edinburgh FH12 9DQ **T** 0131-317 8077
W www.tabletennisscotland.com
Chair, Terry McLernon

TRIATHLON
BRITISH TRIATHLON, PO Box 25, Loughborough LE11 3WX
T 01509-226161 **E** info@britishtriathlon.org
W www.britishtriathlon.org
Chief Executive, Zara Hyde Peters, OBE

VOLLEYBALL
ENGLISH VOLLEYBALL ASSOCIATION, SportPark,
Loughborough University, 3 Oakwood Drive, Loughborough
LE11 3QF **T** 01509-227722 **E** info@volleyballengland.org
W www.volleyballengland.org
Chief Executive, Lisa Wainwright
NORTHERN IRELAND VOLLEYBALL ASSOCIATION,
University of Ulster, Shore Road, Newtownabbey BT37 0QB
T 028-9036 6373 **E** mark@nivb.com **W** www.nivb.com
General Secretary, Peter Lundy
SCOTTISH VOLLEYBALL ASSOCIATION,
48 The Pleasance, Edinburgh EH8 9TJ **T** 0131-556 4633
W www.scottishvolleyball.org
Chief Executive, Margaret Ann Fleming
VOLLEYBALL WALES, 13 Beckgrove Close, Pengam Green,
Cardiff CF24 2SE **T** 029-2041 6537 **E** mail@volleyballwales.org
W www.volleyballwales.org
Chair, Yvonne Saker

WALKING
RACE WALKING ASSOCIATION, Hufflers, Heard's Lane,
Shenfield, Brentwood CM15 0SF **T** 01277-220687
E racewalkingassociation@btinternet.com
W www.racewalkingassociation.org.uk
Hon. General Secretary, Peter Cassidy

WATER SKIING
BRITISH WATER SKI AND WAKEBOARD, The Forum,
Hanworth Lane, Chertsey KT16 9JX **T** 01932-560007
E info@bwsf.co.uk **W** www.bwsw.org.uk
Chief Executive, Patrick Donovan

WEIGHTLIFTING
BRITISH WEIGHT LIFTING, Belmont House,
20 Wood Lane, Leeds LS6 2AE **T** 0113-224 9402
E enquiries@britishweightlifting.org
W www.britishweightlifting.org
Chief Executive, Ashley Metcalfe

WRESTLING
BRITISH WRESTLING ASSOCIATION,
12 Westwood Lane, Chesterfield S43 1PA
T 01246-236443 **E** admin@britishwrestling.org
W www.britishwrestling.org
Chief Executive, Colin Nicholson

YACHTING
ROYAL YACHTING ASSOCIATION, RYA House,
Ensign Way, Hamble, Southampton SO31 4YA
T 023-8060 4100 **W** www.rya.org.uk
Chief Executive, Sarah Treseder

CLUBS

Originally called gentlemen's clubs, these organisations are permanent institutions with a fixed clubhouse, which usually includes restaurants, bars, a library and overnight accommodation. Members are fee-paying and typically vetted for their suitability.

Gentlemen's clubs were created for males of the English upper class and grew out of the 17th-century fashion for coffee houses which enjoyed enormous popularity, despite opposition from Charles II, who believed they encouraged the spreading of royal disaffection. The first of the London clubs – White's – was founded in 1693 by Francesco Bianco in St James's Street, in the area that quickly became known as 'clubland'. Membership to the first of the clubs was a matter of hereditary privilege or special favour, a deliberately exclusionary measure which prompted an enormous growth in the number of clubs throughout the 19th century, fed by a burgeoning and aspirational middle class.

At the turn of the 20th century, there were more than 200 gentlemen's clubs in London alone, half of which had been founded since 1870. Inevitably, this level of competition could not be sustained, particularly given the number of men killed in two world wars. Financial restrictions necessitated greater provision for women and the relaxation of the social qualifications needed for membership. Nevertheless, waiting lists still exist for the leading clubs and a recommendation from at least one current member is almost always required to join.

ARMY AND NAVY CLUB (1837), 36 Pall Mall, London SW1Y 5JN T 020-7930 9721 E secretary@therag.co.uk
W www.armynavyclub.co.uk
Chief Executive and Secretary, Ayres de Souza
Former member: The Duke of Wellington
ARTS CLUB (1863), 40 Dover Street, London W1S 4NP
T 020-7499 8581 E reservations@theartsclub.co.uk
W www.theartsclub.co.uk
Secretary, Rémy Lysé
Former members: Charles Dickens, Algernon Charles Swinburne, Ivan Turgenev
ATHENAEUM (1824), 107 Pall Mall, London SW1Y 5ER
T 020-7930 4843 E library@hellenist.org.uk
W www.athenaeumclub.co.uk
Secretary, J. H. Ford
Former members: Matthew Arnold, Michael Faraday, Anthony Trollope
ATHENAEUM (1797), Church Alley, Liverpool L1 3DD
T 0151-709 7770 E reception@theathenaeum.org.uk
W www.theathenaeum.org.uk
Honorary Secretary, David Honour
Former members: William H. Duncan, William Roscoe
AUTHORS' CLUB (1891), c/o Black's, 67 Dean Street, London W1D 4QH T 020-7287 3381
E mbarnard@authorsclub.co.uk W www.authorsclub.co.uk
Honorary Secretary, Margaret Barnard
Former members: Arthur Conan Doyle, Graham Greene, Thomas Hardy, HG Wells, Oscar Wilde
*BEEFSTEAK CLUB (1876), 9 Irving Street, London WC2H 7AH T 020-7930 5722 E office@thebeefsteakclub.co.uk
Secretary, Maria Hibbert
Former members: John Betjeman, Rudyard Kipling, Harold Macmillan
*BOODLE'S (1762), 28 St James's Street, London SW1A 1HJ
T 020-7930 7166 E secretary@boodles.org
Secretary, Andrew Phillips
Former members: Winston Churchill, Ian Fleming

*BROOKS'S (1764), St James's Street, London SW1A 1LN
T 020-7493 4411 E secretary@brooksclub.org
Secretary, Graham Snell
Former members: Edward Gibbon, Roy Jenkins, William Pitt
*BUCK'S CLUB (1919), 18 Clifford Street, London W1S 3RF
T 020-7734 2337 E secretary@bucksclub.co.uk
Secretary, Maj. Rupert Lendrum
CALEDONIAN CLUB (1891), 9 Halkin Street, London SW1X 7DR T 020-7235 5162 E admin@caledonianclub.com
W www.caledonianclub.com
Secretary, Ian Campbell
CANNING CLUB (1910), 4 St James's Square, London SW1Y 4JU T 020-7827 5768 E canningclub@theinandout.co.uk
Secretary, Sarah Sinclair
CARLTON CLUB (1832), 69 St James's Street, London SW1A 1PJ T 020-7493 1164 E info@carltonclub.co.uk
W www.carltonclub.co.uk
Secretary, Jonathan Orr Ewing
Former members: Stanley Baldwin, Benjamin Disraeli, Harold Macmillan, John Major, Margaret Thatcher
CAVALRY AND GUARDS CLUB (1890), 127 Piccadilly, London W1J 7PX T 020-7499 1261 E secretary@cavgds.co.uk
W www.cavgds.co.uk
Secretary, David J Cowdery
Former member: Lawrence Oates
CHELSEA ARTS CLUB (1891), 143 Old Church Street, London SW3 6EB T 020-7376 3311
E office@chelseaartsclub.com W www.chelseaartsclub.com
Secretary, Geoffrey Matthews
CITY LIVERY CLUB (1914), Bell Wharf Lane, Upper Thames Street, London EC4R 3TB T 020-7248 0620
E clerk@cityliveryclub.com W www.cityliveryclub.com
Hon. Secretary, Dr Trevor Brignall
CITY OF LONDON CLUB (1832), 19 Old Broad Street, London EC2N 1DS T 020-7588 7991
E secretary@cityoflondonclub.com
W www.cityoflondonclub.com
Secretary, Ian Faul
Former members: Robert Peel, Duke of Wellington
CITY UNIVERSITY CLUB (1895), 50 Cornhill, London EC3V 3PD
T 020-7626 8571 E secretary@cityuniversityclub.co.uk
W www.cityuniversityclub.co.uk
Secretary, MaryAnne Salisbury
*EAST INDIA CLUB (1849), 16 St James's Square, London SW1Y 4LH T 020-7930 1000 E secretary@eastindiaclub.co.uk
W www.eastindiaclub.co.uk
Secretary, A. Bray
FARMERS CLUB (1842), 3 Whitehall Court, London SW1A 2EL
T 020-7930 3557 E reception@thefarmersclub.com
W www.thefarmersclub.com
Secretary, Air Cdre Stephen Skinner
FOX CLUB (2003), 46 Clarges Street, London W1J 7ER
T 020-7495 3656 E essi@foxclublondon.com
W www.foxclublondon.com
General Manager, Bethan Seaton
*GARRICK CLUB (1831), 15 Garrick Street, London WC2E 9AY T 020-7379 6478 E office@garrickclub.co.uk
W www.garrickclub.co.uk
Secretary, Olaf Born
Former members: Charles Dickens, Henry Irving, William Thackeray
GROUCHO CLUB (1985), 45 Dean Street, London W1D 4QB
T 020-7439 4685 E reception@thegrouchoclub.com
W www.thegrouchoclub.com
Manager, Bernie Katz

HURLINGHAM CLUB (1869), Ranelagh Gardens, London
SW6 3PR T 020-7610 7400
E membership@hurlinghamclub.org.uk
W www.hurlinghamclub.org.uk
Chief Executive, Rear-Adm. Niall Kilgour, CB
Former member: King Edward VII
IN & OUT (NAVAL AND MILITARY CLUB) (1862),
4 St James's Square, London SW1Y 4JU T 020-7827 5757
E club@theinandout.co.uk W www.theinandout.co.uk
Secretary, Lt. Col. Christopher Hogan
Former member: Robert Falcon Scott
LANSDOWNE CLUB (1935), 9 Fitzmaurice Place, London
W1J 5JD T 020-7629 7200 E secretary@LansdowneClub.com
W www.lansdowneclub.com
General Manager, Chris Pickup
LONDON PRESS CLUB (1882), 7–10 Adam Street,
The Strand, London WC2N 6AA T 020-7520 9082
E info@londonpressclub.co.uk W www.londonpressclub.co.uk
Secretary, Peter Durrant
Former members: Lord Astor, Lord Rothermere,
Edgar Wallace
NATIONAL LIBERAL CLUB (1882), Whitehall Place, London
SW1A 2HE T 020-7930 9871 E secretary@nlc.org.uk
W www.nlc.org.uk
Secretary, Simon Roberts
Former members: Winston Churchill, William Gladstone,
Ramsay MacDonald, George Bernard Shaw, H. G. Wells
NEW CAVENDISH CLUB (1920), 44 Great Cumberland
Place, London W1H 7BS T 020-7723 0391
E info@newcavendishclub.co.uk
W www.newcavendishclub.co.uk
Club Manager, Alex Maitland
Former member: Lady Bonham-Carter
NEW CLUB (1874), 2 Montpellier Parade, Cheltenham
GL50 1UD T 01242-541121 E secretary@thenewclub.co.uk
W www.thenewclub.co.uk
Hon. Secretary, Peter Walsh
NEW CLUB (1787), 86 Princes Street, Edinburgh EH2 2BB
T 0131-226 4881 E info@newclub.co.uk
W www.newclub.co.uk
Secretary, Col. A. P. W. Campbell
Former members: Alec Douglas-Home, Walter Scott
NORFOLK CLUB (1770), 17 Upper King Street, Norwich
NR3 1RB T 01603-626767
E generalmanager@thenorfolkclub.co.uk
W www.thenorfolkclub.co.uk
General Manager, George A. Wortley
NORTHERN COUNTIES CLUB (1829), 11 Hood Street,
Newcastle upon Tyne NE1 6LH T 0191-232 2744
E secretary@northerncountiesclub.co.uk
W www.northerncountiesclub.co.uk
General Manager, David Devennie
ORIENTAL CLUB (1824), Stratford House, Stratford Place,
London W1C 1ES T 020-7629 5126 E sec@orientalclub.org.uk
W www.orientalclub.org.uk
Secretary, M. Rivett
Former member: The Duke of Wellington
OXFORD AND CAMBRIDGE CLUB (1830), 71 Pall Mall,
London SW1Y 5HD T 020-7930 5151 E club@oandc.uk.com
W www.oxfordandcambridgeclub.co.uk
Secretary, Alistair E. Telfer
Former members: Clement Attlee, William Gladstone,
Duke of Wellington
PORTLAND CLUB (1816), 69 Brook Street, London W1Y 4ER
T 020-7499 1523 E theportlandclub@aol.com
W www.portlandclub.org
Secretary, John Burns, CBE
*PRATT'S CLUB (1841), 14 Park Place, London SW1A 1LP
T 020-7493 0397 E secretary@prattsclub.org
Secretary, Lt. Col. O. R. StJ. Breakwell, MBE
Former member: Winston Churchill

REFORM CLUB (1836), 104–105 Pall Mall, London
SW1Y 5EW T 020-7930 9374 E generaloffice@reformclub.com
W www.reformclub.com
Secretary, Crispin Morton
Former members: Isambard Kingdom Brunel, Guy Burgess,
Arthur Conan Doyle, Henry James, David Lloyd George
ROYAL AIR FORCE CLUB (1918), 128 Piccadilly, London
W1J 7PY T 020-7399 1000 E admin@rafclub.org.uk
W www.rafclub.org.uk
Secretary, P. N. Owen
ROYAL AUTOMOBILE CLUB (1897), 89 Pall Mall, London
SW1Y 5HS T 020-7930 2345
E members@royalautomobileclub.co.uk
W www.royalautomobileclub.co.uk
Secretary, Miles Wade, CBE
Former members: Winston Churchill, Rudyard Kipling,
Charles Rolls
*ROYAL NORTHERN & UNIVERSITY CLUB (1854),
9 Albyn Place, Aberdeen AB10 1YE T 01224-583292
E secretary@rnuc.org.uk W www.rnuc.org.uk
Manager, Chris Morrish
ROYAL OVER-SEAS LEAGUE (1910), Over-Seas House,
Park Place, St James's Street, London SW1A 1LR
T 020-7408 0214 E info@rosl.org.uk W www.rosl.org.uk
Director-General, Maj.-Gen. Roddy Porter, MBE
*SAVILE CLUB (1868), 69 Brook Street, London W1K 4ER
T 020-7629 5462 W www.savileclub.co.uk
Secretary, Julian Malone-Lee
Former members: Max Beerbohm, Thomas Hardy,
Robert Louis Stevenson
SCOTTISH ARTS CLUB (1872), 24 Rutland Square,
Edinburgh EH1 2BW T 0131-229 8157
E manager@scottishartsclub.co.uk
W www.scottishartsclub.co.uk
President, Diana Allen
SLOANE CLUB (1976), Lower Sloane Street, London
SW1W 8BS T 020-7730 9131 E reservations@sloaneclub.co.uk
W www.sloaneclub.co.uk
Membership Secretary, Fran Bremner
*TRAVELLERS CLUB (1819), 106 Pall Mall, London
SW1Y 5EP T 020-7930 8688
E secretary@thetravellersclub.org.uk
W www.thetravellersclub.org.uk
Secretary, David Broadhead
Former members: Arthur Balfour, Alec Douglas-Home,
Anthony Powell
TURF CLUB (1868), 5 Carlton House Terrace, London
SW1Y 5AQ T 020-7930 8555 E mail@turfclub.co.uk
Secretary, Col. A. J. E. Malcolm, OBE
ULSTER REFORM CLUB (1885), 4 Royal Avenue, Belfast
BT1 1DA T 028-9032 3411 E info@ulsterreformclub.com
W www.ulsterreformclub.com
Chief Executive, A. W. Graham
†UNIVERSITY WOMEN'S CLUB (1883), 2 Audley Square,
London W1K 1DB T 020-7499 2268 E uwc@uwc-london.com
W www.universitywomensclub.com
Hon. Sec., Monica Sasso
*VINCENT'S (1863), 1A King Edward Street, Oxford OX1 4HS
T 01865-722984 E bursar@vincents.org W www.vincents.org
Bursar, Stephen Eeley
Former members: Roger Bannister, King Edward VIII
WESTERN CLUB (1825), 32 Royal Exchange Square,
Glasgow G1 3AB T 0141-221 2016
E secretary@westernclub.co.uk W www.westernclub.co.uk
Secretary, Douglas H. Gifford
*WHITE'S (1693), 37–38 St James's Street, London SW1A 1JG
T 020-7493 6671
Secretary, D. A. Anderson
Former members: Beau Brummel, Evelyn Waugh

* Men only   † Women only

CHARITIES AND SOCIETIES

The following is a selection of charities, societies and non-profit organisations in the UK and does not represent a comprehensive list. For professional and employment-related organisations, *see* Professional Education and Trade and Professional Bodies.

ABBEYFIELD SOCIETY (1956), Abbeyfield House,
53 Victoria Street, St Albans AL1 3UW T 01727-857536
E post@abbeyfield.com W www.abbeyfield.com
Chief Executive, Paul Allen

ACE CULTURAL TOURS (1958), Babraham, Cambridge
CB22 3AP T 01223-835055 E ace@aceculturaltours.co.uk
W www.aceculturaltours.co.uk
General Secretary, Paul Barnes

ACTIONAID (1972), 33–39 Bowling Green Lane, London
EC1R 0BJ T 020-3122 0561 E mail@actionaid.org.uk
W www.actionaid.org.uk
Chief Executive, Richard Miller

ACTION FOR BLIND PEOPLE (1857), 53 Sandgate Street,
London SE15 1LE T 020-7635 4800 E helpline@rnib.org.uk
W www.actionforblindpeople.org.uk
Chief Executive, Miriam Martin

ACTION FOR CHILDREN (1869), 3 The Boulevard,
Watford WD18 8AG T 0300-123 2112
E ask.us@actionforchildren.org.uk
W www.actionforchildren.org.uk
Chief Executive, Clare Tickell, DBE

ACTION MEDICAL RESEARCH (1952), Vincent House,
Horsham RH12 2DP T 01403-210406 E info@action.org.uk
W www.action.org.uk
Chief Executive, Julie Buckler

ACTION ON HEARING LOSS (1911), 19–23 Featherstone
Street, London EC1Y 8SL T 0808-808 0123,
Textphone 0808-808 9000 E informationline@rnid.org.uk
W www.rnid.org.uk
Chief Executive, Paul Breckell

ACTORS' BENEVOLENT FUND (1882), 6 Adam Street,
London WC2N 6AD T 020-7836 6378 E office@abf.org.uk
W www.actorsbenevolentfund.co.uk
General Secretary, Willie Bicket

ACTORS' CHILDREN'S TRUST (1896), 58 Bloomsbury
Street, London WC1B 3QT T 020-7636 7868
E robert@tactactors.org W www.tactactors.org
General Secretary, Robert Ashby

ADAM SMITH INSTITUTE (1977), 23 Great Smith Street,
London SW1P 3BL T 020-7222 4995 W www.adamsmith.org
Director, Dr Eamonn Butler

ADDACTION (1967), 67–69 Cowcross Street, London
EC1M 6PU T 020-7251 5860 E info@addaction.org.uk
W www.addaction.org.uk
Chief Executive, Simon Antrobus

ADVERTISING STANDARDS AUTHORITY (1962),
Mid City Place, 71 High Holborn, London WC1V 6QT
T 020-7492 2222 W www.asa.org.uk
Chief Executive, Guy Parker

AFASIC (1968), 1st Floor, Olive House, 20 Bowling Green Lane,
London EC1R 0BD T 020-7490 9410 E info@afasic.org.uk
W www.afasic.org.uk
Chief Executive, Linda Lascelles

AGE CYMRU (2010), Ty John Pathy, 13–14 Neptune Court,
Vanguard Way, Cardiff CF24 5PJ T 029-2043 1555
E enquiries@agecymru.org.uk W www.agecymru.org.uk
Chief Executive, Robert Taylor

AGE SCOTLAND (1943), Causewayside House, 160
Causewayside, Edinburgh EH9 1PR T 0845-833 0200
E info@agescotland.org.uk W www.agescotland.org.uk
Chief Executive, Brian Sloan

AGE UK (2010), Tavis House, 1–6 Tavistock Square, London
WC1H 9NA T 0800-169 6565 E contact@ageuk.org.uk
W www.ageuk.org.uk
Chief Executive, Tom Wright, CBE

ALCOHOLICS ANONYMOUS (1947), PO Box 1,
10 Toft Green, York YO1 7NJ T 01904-644026,
Helpline 0845-769 7555 E help@alcoholics-anonymous.org.uk
W www.alcoholics-anonymous.org.uk
General Secretary, Roger Booth

ALEXANDRA ROSE CHARITIES (1912), 5 Mead Lane,
Farnham GU9 7DY T 01252-726171
E enquiries@alexandrarose.org.uk
W www.alexandrarosecharities.org.uk
National Director, Margaret Stock

ALZHEIMER'S SOCIETY (1979), Devon House, 58 St
Katharine's Way, London E1W 1LB T 020-7423 3500
E enquiries@alzheimers.org.uk W www.alzheimers.org.uk
Chief Executive, Jeremy Hughes

AMBITION (1925), 371 Kennington Lane, London SE11 5QY
T 020-7793 0787 E info@ambitionuk.org
W www.ambitionuk.org
Chief Executive, Helen Marshall

AMNESTY INTERNATIONAL UK (1961), The Human
Rights Action Centre, 17–25 New Inn Yard, London EC2A 3EA
T 020-7033 1777 E sct@amnesty.org.uk
W www.amnesty.org.uk
UK Director, Kate Allen

AMREF UK (1957), 15–18 White Lion Street, London N1 9PD
T 020-7269 5520 E info@amrefuk.org W www.amrefuk.org
Chief Executive, Samara Hammond

ANCIENT MONUMENTS SOCIETY (1924),
St Ann's Vestry Hall, 2 Church Entry, London EC4V 5HB
T 020-7236 3934 E office@ancientmonumentssociety.org.uk
W www.ancientmonumentssociety.org.uk
Secretary, M. J. Saunders, MBE

ANGLO-BELGIAN SOCIETY (1982), 5 Hartley Close,
Bickley BR1 2TP T 020-8467 8442
E secretary@anglo-belgiansoc.co.uk
W www.anglo-belgiansoc.co.uk
Chair, David Colvin, CMG

ANGLO-DANISH SOCIETY (1924), 43 Maresfield Gardens,
London NW3 5TF T 020-7794 8781
E info@anglo-danishsociety.org.uk
W www.anglo-danishsociety.org.uk
Chair, Simon Freeman

ANGLO-NORSE SOCIETY (1918), 25 Belgrave Square,
London SW1X 8QD T 020-8452 4843
E secretariat@anglo-norse.org.uk W www.anglo-norse.org.uk
Chair, Sir Richard Dales, KCVO, CMG

ANIMAL CONCERN (1876), PO Box 5178, Dumbarton
G82 5YJ T 01389-841639 E animals@jfrobins.force9.co.uk
W www.animalconcern.org
Secretary, John F. Robins

ANIMAL HEALTH TRUST (1942), Lanwades Park, Kentford,
Newmarket CB8 7UU T 01638-751000 E info@aht.org.uk
W www.aht.org.uk
Chief Executive, Dr Mark Vaudin

ANTHONY NOLAN (1974), 2–3 Heathgate Place,
75–87 Agincourt Road, London NW3 2NU T 0303-303 0303
E info@anthonynolan.org W www.anthonynolan.org
Chief Executive, Henny Braund

ANTHROPOSOPHICAL SOCIETY IN GREAT BRITAIN (1923), Rudolf Steiner House, 35 Park Road, London NW1 6XT
T 020-7723 4400 E rsh-office@anth.org.uk
W www.rsh.anth.org.uk
General Secretary, Philip Martyn

ANTI-SLAVERY INTERNATIONAL (1839), Thomas Clarkson House, The Stableyard, Broomgrove Road, London SW9 9TL T 020-7501 8920 E info@antislavery.org
W www.antislavery.org
Director, Aidan McQuade

ARCHITECTS BENEVOLENT SOCIETY (1850), 43 Portland Place, London W1B 1QH T 020-7580 2823
E help@absnet.org.uk W www.absnet.org.uk
CEO, Robert Ball

ARCHITECTURAL HERITAGE FUND (1976), 15 Whitehall, London SW1A 2DD T 020-7925 0199
E ahf@ahfund.org.uk W www.ahfund.org.uk
Chief Executive, Ian Lush

ARLIS/UK AND IRELAND (1969), The National Art Library, Word & Image Department, Victoria & Albert Museum, Cromwell Road, London SW7 2RL T 020-7942 2317
E arlis@vam.ac.uk W www.arlis.org.uk
Chair, Chris Fowler

ART FUND (1903), 2 Granary Square, King's Cross, London N1C 4BH T 020-7225 4800 W www.artfund.org
Director, Dr Stephen Deuchar

ARTHRITIS CARE (1947), Linen Court, 10 East Road, London N1 6AD T 020-7380 6500 E info@arthritiscare.org.uk
W www.arthritiscare.org.uk
Chief Executive, Judi Rhys

ASSOCIATION FOR LANGUAGE LEARNING (1990), University of Leicester, University Road, Leicester LE1 7RH
T 0116-229 7602 E info@all-languages.org.uk
W www.all-languages.org.uk
Director, Linda Parker

ASSOCIATION FOR SCIENCE EDUCATION (1901), College Lane, Hatfield AL10 9AA T 01707-283000
E info@ase.org.uk W www.ase.org.uk
Chief Executive, Shaun Reason

ASSOCIATION FOR THE PROTECTION OF RURAL SCOTLAND (1926), 3rd Floor, Gladstone's Land, 483 Lawnmarket, Edinburgh EH1 2NT T 0131-225 7012
E info@ruralscotland.org W www.ruralscotland.btck.co.uk
Director, John Mayhew

ASSOCIATION OF FINANCIAL MUTUALS (1995), 7 Castle Hill, Caistor, LN7 6QL T 0844-879 7863
E martin@financialmutuals.org W www.financialmutuals.org
Chief Executive, Martin Shaw

ASSOCIATION OF GENEALOGISTS AND RESEARCHERS IN ARCHIVES (1968), 43 Bowes Wood, New Ash Green DA3 8QL E info@agra.org.uk
W www.agra.org.uk
Chair, Ian Marson

ASSOCIATION OF ROYAL NAVY OFFICERS (1920), 70 Porchester Terrace, London W2 3TP T 020-7402 5231
E asec@arno.org.uk W www.arno.org.uk
Director, Cdr Mike Goldthorpe

ASSOCIATION OF SPEAKERS CLUBS (1971), 40 Brougham Street, Greenock PA16 8AH T 01475-806214
E national.secretary@the-asc.org.uk W www.the-asc.org.uk
National President, Graham McLachlan

ASTHMA UK (1927), 18 Mansell Street, London E1 8AA
T 020-7786 4900 E info@asthma.org.uk
W www.asthma.org.uk
Chief Executive, Kay Boycott

AUDIT BUREAU OF CIRCULATIONS LTD (1931), Saxon House, 211 High Street, Berkhamsted HP4 1AD
T 01442-870800 E info@abc.org.uk W www.abc.org.uk
Chair, Sally Cartwright, OBE

AUTISM INITIATIVES (1971), 7 Chesterfield Road, Liverpool L23 9XL T 0151-330 9500
E headoffice@autisminitiatives.org W www.autisminitiatives.org
Chair, Brian Williams

AUTOMOBILE ASSOCIATION (1905), Lambert House, Stockport Road, Cheadle SK8 2DY T 0800-085 2721
E customer.services@theaa.com W www.theaa.com
Chief Executive, Chris Jansen

BALTIC EXCHANGE (1744), 38 St Mary Axe, London EC3A 8BH T 020-7283 9300 E enquiries@balticexchange.com
W www.balticexchange.com
Chief Executive, Jeremy Penn

BALTIC EXCHANGE CHARITABLE SOCIETY (1978), 20 St Dunstans Hill, London EC3R 8HL T 020-7283 6090
E enquiries@balticexchange.com W www.balticexchange.com
Secretary, R. J. M. Butler

BARNARDO'S (1866), Tanners Lane, Barkingside, Ilford IG6 1QG T 020-8550 8822 W www.barnardos.org.uk
Chief Executive, Javed Khan

BARRISTERS' BENEVOLENT ASSOCIATION (1873), 14 Gray's Inn Square, London WC1R 5JP T 020-7242 4761
E enquiries@the-bba.com W www.the-bba.com
Chair, Terence Mowschenson, QC

BBC MEDIA ACTION (1999), Media Centre, Wood Lane, London W12 7TQ T 020-8743 8000 E media.action@bbc.co.uk
W www.bbc.co.uk/mediaaction
Executive Director, Caroline Nursey

BCS, THE CHARTERED INSTITUTE FOR IT (1957), 1st Floor, Block D, North Star House, North Star Avenue SN2 1FA T 01793-417417 W www.bcs.org
Chief Executive, David Clarke

BEAT (1989), Wensum House, 103 Prince of Wales Road, Norwich NR1 1DW T 0300-123 3355, **Helpline** 0845-634 1414, **Youthline** 0845-634 7650 E info@b-eat.co.uk
W www.b-eat.co.uk
Chief Executive, Susan Ringwood

BEVIN BOY VETERANS (1989), 23 Great Cranford Street, Poundbury, Dorchester DT1 3SQ T 01305-261269
E warwicktaylor@btinternet.com
W www.theforgottenconscript.co.uk
President, Warwick Taylor, MBE

BIBLE SOCIETY (1804), Stonehill Green, Westlea, Swindon SN5 7DG T 01793-418222 E contactus@biblesociety.org.uk
W www.biblesociety.org.uk
President, Rt. Revd Richard Chartres, KCVO, PC

BIBLIOGRAPHICAL SOCIETY (1892), c/o University of London, Institute of English Studies, Senate House, Malet Street, London WC1E 7HU T 020-7862 8679
E secretary@bibsoc.org.uk W www.bibsoc.org.uk
Hon. Secretary, Margaret Ford

BIPOLAR UK (1983), 11 Belgrave Road, London SW1V 1RB
T 020-7931 6480 E info@bipolaruk.org.uk
W www.bipolaruk.org.uk
Chief Executive, Suzanne Hudson

BIRMINGHAM AND WARWICKSHIRE ARCHAEOLOGICAL SOCIETY (1870), c/o Birmingham and Midland Institute, 9 Margaret Street, Birmingham B3 3BS
W www.birminghamandwarwickshirearchaeological society.co.uk
President, Dr Della Hooke

BLISS (1979), Chapter House, London SE1 3JW
T 020-7378 1122, **Helpline** 0500-618140
E information@bliss.org.uk W www.bliss.org.uk
Chief Executive, Andy Cole

BLUE CROSS (1897), Shilton Road, Burford OX18 4PF
T 030-079 0990 E info@bluecross.org.uk
W www.bluecross.org.uk
Chief Executive, Kim Hamilton

BOOK AID INTERNATIONAL (1954), 39–41 Coldharbour
Lane, London SE5 9NR **T** 020-7733 3577 **E** info@bookaid.org
W www.bookaid.org
Director, Alison Hubert

BOOK TRADE CHARITY (BTBS) (1037), The Foyle Centre,
The Retreat, Kings Langley WD4 8LT **T** 01923-263128
E david@booktradecharity.org **W** www.booktradecharity.org
Chief Executive, David Hicks

BOOKTRUST (1926), Book House, 45 East Hill,
London SW18 2QZ **T** 020-8516 2977
E query@booktrust.org.uk **W** www.booktrust.org.uk
Chief Executive, Viv Bird

BOTANICAL SOCIETY OF BRITAIN AND IRELAND
(1836), 57 Walton Road, Shirehampton, Bristol BS11 9TA
E info@bsbi.org.uk **W** www.bsbi.org.uk
President, Ian Denholm

BOTANICAL SOCIETY OF SCOTLAND (1836),
c/o Royal Botanic Garden Edinburgh, 20A Inverleith Row,
Edinburgh EH3 5LR **T** 0131-552 7171
W www.botanical-society-scotland.org.uk
Hon. General Secretary, Dr B. A. Harvie

BOYS' BRIGADE (1883), Felden Lodge, Felden,
Hemel Hempstead HP3 0BL **T** 01442-231681
E enquiries@boys-brigade.org.uk **W** www.boys-brigade.org.uk
Brigade Secretary, Steve Dickinson

BRISTOL AND GLOUCESTERSHIRE
ARCHAEOLOGICAL SOCIETY (1876), Stonehatch,
Oakridge Lynch, Stroud GL6 7NR **T** 01285-760460
E john@loosleyj.freeserve.co.uk **W** www.bgas.org.uk
Hon. General Secretary, John Loosley

BRITISH ACADEMY OF FORENSIC SCIENCES (1960),
Franklin-Wilkins Building, 150 Stamford Street, King's College
London, London SE1 9NH **T** 020-7848 4130
E denise.syndercombe-court@kcl.ac.uk **W** www.bafs.org.uk
Secretary-General, Dr Denise Syndercombe Court

BRITISH ASSOCIATION FOR EARLY CHILDHOOD
EDUCATION (1923), 136 Cavell Street, London E1 2JA
T 020-7539 5400 **E** office@early-education.org.uk
W www.early-education.org.uk
Chief Executive, Megan Pacey

BRITISH ASSOCIATION FOR LOCAL HISTORY (1982),
PO Box 6549, Somersal Herbert DE6 5WH **T** 01283-585947
E mail@balh.co.uk **W** www.balh.co.uk
Business Manager, Annmarie Jones

BRITISH ASTRONOMICAL ASSOCIATION (1890),
Burlington House, Piccadilly, London W1J 0DU
T 020-7734 4145 **W** www.britastro.org
President, Prof. Bill Leatherbarrow

BRITISH BEEKEEPERS' ASSOCIATION (1874),
National Beekeeping Centre, Stoneleigh Park, Kenilworth
CV8 2LG **T** 0871-811 2282 **E** bbka@britishbeekeepers.com
W www.bbka.org.uk
General Secretary, Jane Moseley

BRITISH BOARD OF FILM CLASSIFICATION (1912),
3 Soho Square, London W1D 3HD **T** 020-7440 1570
E feedback@bbfc.co.uk **W** www.bbfc.co.uk
Director, David Cooke

BRITISH CATTLE BREEDERS CLUB (1946), Lake Villa,
Bradworthy, Holsworthy, Devon EX22 7SQ **T** 01409-241579
E lesley.lewin@cattlebreeders.org.uk
W www.cattlebreeders.org.uk
Chair, Neil Darwent

BRITISH COPYRIGHT COUNCIL (1965),
29–33 Berners Street, London W1T 3AB **T** 01986-788122
E britishcopyright@ **W** www.britishcopyright.org
Chief Executive, Janet Ibbotson

BRITISH DEAF ASSOCIATION (1890), 18 Leather Lane,
London EC1N 7SU **T** 020-7697 4140 **E** bda@bda.org.uk
W www.bda.org.uk
Chief Executive, David Buxton

BRITISH DRIVING SOCIETY LTD (1957), 83 New Road,
Helmingham, Stowmarket IP14 6EA **T** 01473-892001
E email@britishdrivingsociety.co.uk
W www.britishdrivingsociety.co.uk
President, John Parker

BRITISH ECOLOGICAL SOCIETY (1913),
Charles Darwin House, 12 Roger Street, London WC1N 2JU
T 020-7685 2500 **E** info@britishecologicalsociety.org
W www.britishecologicalsociety.org
Executive Director, Dr Hazel Norman

BRITISH FALSE MEMORY SOCIETY (1993),
Bradford on Avon BA15 1NF **T** 01225-868682
E bfms@bfms.org.uk **W** www.bfms.org.uk
Director, Madeline Greenhalgh

BRITISH HEALTH CARE ASSOCIATION (1930),
PO Box 6752, Elgin IV30 9BN **T** 01343-830148
E info@bhca.org.uk **W** www.bhca.org.uk
National Secretary, Liz Price

BRITISH HEART FOUNDATION (1961),
Greater London House, 180 Hampstead Road,
London NW1 7AW **T** 020-7554 0000 **W** www.bhf.org.uk
Chief Executive, Simon Gillespie

BRITISH HEDGEHOG PRESERVATION SOCIETY
(1982), Hedgehog House, Dhustone, Ludlow SY8 3PL
T 01584-890801 **E** info@britishhedgehogs.org.uk
W www.britishhedgehogs.org.uk
Chief Executive, Fay Vass

BRITISH HERPETOLOGICAL SOCIETY (1947),
11 Strathmore Place, Montrose DD10 8LQ **T** 01674-671676
E info@thebhs.org **W** www.thebhs.org
President, Prof. Trevor J. C. Beebee

BRITISH HORSE SOCIETY (1947), Abbey Park,
Stareton, Kenilworth CV8 2XZ **T** 024-7684 0500
E enquiry@bhs.org.uk **W** www.bhs.org.uk
Chief Executive, Lynn Petersen

BRITISH INSTITUTE IN EASTERN AFRICA (1959),
10 Carlton House Terrace, London SW1Y 5AH
T 020-7969 5201 **E** biea@britac.ac.uk **W** www.biea.ac.uk
Director, Dr Joost Fontein

BRITISH INTERPLANETARY SOCIETY (1933),
27–29 South Lambeth Road, London SW8 1SZ
T 020-7735 3160 **E** info@bis-space.com
W www.bis-space.com
Executive Secretary, Suszann Parry

BRITISH-ISRAEL-WORLD FEDERATION (1919),
121 Low Etherley, Bishop Auckland, Co. Durham DL14 0HA
T 01388-834395 **E** admin@britishisrael.co.uk
W www.britishisrael.co.uk
President, M. A. Clark

BRITISH LUNG FOUNDATION (1985), 73–75 Goswell
Road, London EC1V 7ER **T** 020-7688 5555 **W** www.blf.org.uk
Chief Executive, Dr Penny Woods

BRITISH MENSA LTD (1946), St John's House, St John's
Square, Wolverhampton WV2 4AH **T** 01902-772771
E enquiries@mensa.org.uk **W** www.mensa.org.uk
Chief Executive, John Stevenage

BRITISH MUSIC HALL SOCIETY (1963), 45 Mayflower
Road, Park Street, St Albans AL2 2QN **T** 01727-768878
W www.music-hall-society.com
President, Roy Hudd, OBE

BRITISH NATURALISTS' ASSOCIATION (1905),
BM 8129, London WC1N 3XX **E** info@bna-naturalists.org
W www.bna-naturalists.org
National Secretary, Mo Norrington

BRITISH NUTRITION FOUNDATION (1967), 6th Floor,
Imperial House, 15–19 Kingsway, London WC2B 6UN
T 020-7557 7930 **E** postbox@nutrition.org.uk
W www.nutrition.org.uk
Director-General, Prof. Judith Buttriss, PHD

BRITISH ORNITHOLOGISTS' UNION (1858),
PO Box 417, Peterborough PE7 3FX T 01733-844820
E bou@bou.org.uk W www.bou.org.uk
Senior Administrator, S. P. Dudley

BRITISH PHARMACOLOGICAL SOCIETY (1931),
16 Angel Gate, City Road, London EC1V 2PT T 020-7239 0171
E info@bps.ac.uk W www.bps.ac.uk
Chief Executive, Jonathan Brüün

BRITISH PIG ASSOCIATION (1884), Trumpington Mews,
40B High Street, Trumpington, Cambridge CB2 9LS
T 01223-845100 E bpa@britishpigs.org
W www.britishpigs.org.uk
Chief Executive, Marcus Bates

BRITISH RED CROSS (1870), 44 Moorfields, London
EC2Y 9AL T 0844-871 1111, **Textphone** 020-7562 2000
E information@redcross.org.uk W www.redcross.org.uk
Chief Executive, Sir Nicholas Young

BRITISH SCIENCE ASSOCIATION (1831), Wellcome
Wolfson Building, 165 Queen's Gate, London SW7 5HD
T 0870-770 7101 E info@britishscienceassociation.org
W www.britishscienceassociation.org
Chief Executive, Imran Khan

BRITISH SUNDIAL SOCIETY (1989), c/o The Royal
Astronomical Society, Burlington House, London W1J 0BQ
T 01233-712550 E secretary@sundialsoc.org.uk
W www.sundialsoc.org.uk
Chairman, Dr Frank King

BRITISH TRUST FOR ORNITHOLOGY (1933),
The Nunnery, Thetford IP24 2PU T 01842-750050
E info@bto.org W www.bto.org
Director, Dr Andy Clements

BUCKINGHAMSHIRE ARCHAEOLOGICAL SOCIETY
(1847), County Museum, Church Street,
Aylesbury HP20 2QP T 01296 397200
E bucksas@buckscc.gov.uk W www.bucksas.org.uk
Hon. Secretary, Michael Ghirelli

BUSINESS AND PROFESSIONAL WOMEN UK LTD
(1938), 74 Fairfield Rise, Billericay CM12 9NU T 01277-623867
E hq@bpwuk.co.uk W www.bpwuk.co.uk
President, Elizabeth Burden

CALOUSTE GULBENKIAN FOUNDATION (1956),
50 Hoxton Square, Hoxton, London N1 6PB T 020-7012 1400
E info@gulbenkian.org.uk W www.gulbenkian.org.uk
Director, Andrew Barnett

CAMPAIGN FOR FREEDOM OF INFORMATION
(1984), Unit 109, Davina House, 137–149 Goswell Road,
London EC1V 7ET T 020-7390 3958
E admin@cfoi.demon.co.uk W www.cfoi.org.uk
Director, Maurice Frankel

CAMPAIGN FOR NUCLEAR DISARMAMENT (1958),
162 Holloway Road, London N7 8DQ T 020-7700 2393
E enquiries@cnduk.org W www.cnduk.org
General Secretary, Kate Hudson

CAMPAIGN FOR THE PROTECTION OF RURAL
WALES (1928), Ty Gwyn, 31 High Street,
Welshpool SY21 7YD T 01938-552525
E info@cprwmail.org.uk W www.cprw.org.uk
Director, Peter Ogden

CANCER RESEARCH UK (2002), Angel Building,
407 St John Street, London EC1V 4AD T 020-7242 0200
W www.cancerresearchuk.org
Chief Executive, Harpal Kumar

CARERS TRUST (2012), 32–36 Loman Street,
London SE1 0EH T 0844-800 4361 E info@carers.org
W www.carers.org
Chief Executive, Thea Stein

CARERS UK (1965), 20 Great Dover Street, London SE1 4LX
T 020-7378 4999 W www.carersuk.org
Chief Executive, Helena Herklots

CARNEGIE UNITED KINGDOM TRUST (1913),
Andrew Carnegie House, Pittencrieff Street,
Dunfermline KY12 8AW T 01383-721445
E info@carnegieuk.org W www.carnegieuktrust.org.uk
Chief Executive, Martyn Evans

CATHOLIC UNION OF GREAT BRITAIN (1872),
St Maximillian Kolbe House, 63 Jeddo Road, London W12 9EE
T 020-8749 1321 E administrator@catholicunion.org
W www.catholicunion.org
President, Lord Brennan, QC

CAVELL NURSES' TRUST (1917), Grosvenor House,
Prospect Hill, Worcestershire, B97 4DL T 01527-595999
E admin@cavellnursestrust.org W www.cavellnursestrust.org
Chief Executive, Kate Tompkins

CENTREPOINT (1969), Central House,
25 Camperdown Street, London E1 8DZ T 0845-466 3400
W www.centrepoint.org.uk
Chief Executive, Seyi Obakin

CHATHAM HOUSE (1920), Chatham House,
10 St James's Square, London SW1Y 4LE T 020-7957 5700
E contact@chathamhouse.org.uk
W www.chathamhouse.org.uk
Director, Dr Robin Niblett

CHILD POVERTY ACTION GROUP (1965),
94 White Lion Street, London N1 9PF T 020-7837 7979
E info@cpag.org.uk W www.cpag.org.uk
Chief Executive, Alison Garnham

CHILDREN 1ST (1884), 83 Whitehouse Loan,
Edinburgh EH9 1AT T 0131-446 2300
E info@children1st.org.uk W www.children1st.org.uk
Chief Executive, Anne Houston

CHILDREN'S SOCIETY (1881), Edward Rudolf House,
Margery Street, London WC1X 0JL T 020-7841 4400
E supportercare@childrenssociety.org.uk
W www.childrenssociety.org.uk
Chief Executive, Matthew Reed

CHURCH BUILDINGS COUNCIL (1921), Church House,
Great Smith Street, London SW1P 3NZ T 020-7898 1000
E churchcare@churchofengland.org W www.churchcare.co.uk
Secretary, Janet Gough

CHURCH MONUMENTS SOCIETY (1979), Moor View,
Exbourne EX20 3SA T 01837-851483
E churchmonuments@aol.com
W www.churchmonumentssociety.org
Hon. Secretary, Barbara Tomlinson

CHURCHILL CENTRE UK (1968), Churchill College,
Storey's Way, Cambridge CB3 0DS T 01223-336190
E tcc.membership@chu.cam.ac.uk
W www.winstonchurchill.org
Executive Director, Allen Packwood

CHURCHILL SOCIETY – LONDON (1990), Ivy House,
18 Grove Lane, Ipswich IP4 1NR T 01473-413533
E dutysecretary@churchill-society-london.org.uk
W www.churchill-society-london.org.uk
General Secretary, J. H. Rogers

CITIZENS ADVICE (1939), 3rd Floor North, 200 Aldersgate,
London EC1A 4HD T 030-0023 1999
W www.citizensadvice.org.uk
Chief Executive, Gillian Guy

CITY BUSINESS LIBRARY (1970), City Business Library,
Aldermanbury, London EC2V 7HH T 020-7332 1812
E cbl@cityoflondon.gov.uk
W www.cityoflondon.gov.uk/citybusinesslibrary
Head of City Business Library, Goretti Considine

CITY OF COVENTRY FREEMEN'S GUILD (1946),
111 Hall Green Road, Coventry CV6 7BT
W www.coventryfreemensguild.wordpress.com
Hon. Clerk, Jim Parry

CLASSICAL ASSOCIATION (1903), Park House,
15–23 Greenhill Crescent, Watford WD18 8PH
T 01923 239 300 E office@classicalassociation.org
W www.classicalassociation.org
Secretary, Claire Davenport

COMBAT STRESS (1919), Tyrwhitt House, Oaklawn Road,
Leatherhead KT22 0BX T 01372-587000
E contactus@combatstress.org.uk W www.combatstress.org.uk
Chief Executive, Cdre Andrew Cameron

COMMUNITY INTEGRATED CARE (1988), Old Market
Court, Miners Way, Widnes WA8 7SP T 0151 420 3637
E information@c-i-c.co.uk W www.c-i-c.co.uk
Chief Executive, Neil Matthewman

CONCERN WORLDWIDE (1968), 13–14 Calico House,
Clove Hitch Quay, London SW11 3TN T 020-7801 1850
W www.concern.net
Chief Executive, Dominic MacSorley

CONTEMPORARY APPLIED ARTS (1948),
89 Southwark Street, London SE1 0HX T 020 7620 0086
E sales@caa.org.uk W www.caa.org.uk
Director, Clare Maddison

CO-OPERATIVE PARTY (1917), 77 Weston Street,
London SE1 3SD T 020-7367 4150 E mail@party.coop
W www.party.coop
General Secretary, Karin Christiansen

CORONERS' SOCIETY OF ENGLAND AND WALES
(1846), HM Coroner's Court, St George's Hall,
St George's Place, Liverpool L1 1JJ T 0151-225 5060
W www.coronersociety.org.uk
Hon. Secretary, André Joseph Anthony Rebello, OBE

CORPORATION OF THE CHURCH HOUSE (1888),
Church House, Great Smith Street, London SW1P 3AZ
T 020-7898 1316 E info@churchhouse.org.uk
W www.churchhouse.org.uk
Secretary, Christopher Palmer, CBE

COUNCIL FOR AWARDS OF ROYAL AGRICULTURAL
SOCIETIES (1970), Springvale, Orchard Close,
Shaldon, TQ14 0HF T 01626-873159
E ejwibberley@btinternet.com
Hon. Secretary, Prof. John Wibberley

COUNCIL FOR BRITISH ARCHAEOLOGY (1944),
St Mary's House, 66 Bootham, York YO30 7BZ
T 01904-671417 W www.archaeologyuk.org
Director, Dr Mike Heyworth, MBE

COUNCIL OF CHRISTIANS AND JEWS (1942),
Godliman House, 21 Godliman Street, London EC4V 5BD
T 020-7015 5160 E cjrelations@ccj.org.uk W www.ccj.org.uk
Chief Executive, David Gifford

COUNCIL OF UNIVERSITY CLASSICAL
DEPARTMENTS (1972), School of Classics, University of
St Andrews, St Andrews, Fife KY16 9AL T 01334-462600
E gdw2@st-andrews.ac.uk W www.rhul.ac.uk/classics/cucd
Chair, Prof. G. Woolf

COUNTRY LAND & BUSINESS ASSOCIATION (1907),
16 Belgrave Square, London SW1X 8PQ T 020-7235 0511
E mail@cla.org.uk W www.cla.org.uk
President, Harry Cotterell

COUNTRYSIDE ALLIANCE (1997), Old Town Hall, 367
Kennington Road, London SE11 4PT T 020-7840 9200
W www.countryside-alliance.org.uk
Executive Chair, Barney White-Spunner

CPRE (CAMPAIGN TO PROTECT RURAL ENGLAND)
(1926), 5–11 Lavington Street, London SE1 0NZ
T 020-7981 2800 E info@cpre.org.uk W www.cpre.org.uk
Chief Executive, Shaun Spiers

CRISIS UK (1967), 66 Commercial Street, London E1 6LT
T 0300-636 1967 E enquiries@crisis.org.uk
W www.crisis.org.uk
Chief Executive, Leslie Morphy, OBE

CROHN'S AND COLITIS UK (1979), 4 Beaumont House,
Sutton Road, St Albans AL1 5HH T 01727-830038
E info@chronsandcolitis.org.uk W www.chronsandcolitis.org.uk
Chief Executive, David Barker

CUMBERLAND AND WESTMORLAND ANTIQUARIAN
AND ARCHAEOLOGICAL SOCIETY (1866),
Westlands, Westbourne Drive, Lancaster LA1 5AH
T 01524-67523 E info@cwaas.org.uk W www.cwaas.org.uk
General Secretary, Marion E. M. McClintock

CYSTIC FIBROSIS TRUST (1964), 11 London Road,
Bromley BR1 1BY T 020-8464 7211
W www.cysticfibrosis.org.uk
Chief Executive, Ed Owen

DAY ONE CHRISTIAN MINISTRIES (1831),
Ryelands Road, Leominster HR6 8NZ T 01568-613740
E sales@dayone.co.uk W www.dayone.co.uk
Managing Director, Mark Roberts

DEMOS (1994), Third Floor, Magdalen House, 136 Tooley Street,
London SE1 2TU T 0845-458 5949 E hello@demos.co.uk
W www.demos.co.uk
Chair, Philip Collins

DESIGN AND TECHNOLOGY ASSOCIATION (1989),
16 Wellesbourne House, Walton Road, Wellesbourne CV35 9JB
T 01789-470007 E info@data.org.uk W www.data.org.uk
Chief Executive, Richard Green

DEVON ARCHAEOLOGICAL SOCIETY (1929), Royal
Albert Memorial Museum, Queen Street, Exeter EX4 3RX
E dashonsec@devonarchaeologicalsociety.org.uk
W www.devonarchaeologicalsociety.org.uk
Hon. Secretary, Amanda Eversett

DIABETES UK (1934), Macleod House, 10 Parkway,
London NW1 7AA T 034-5123 2399 E info@diabetes.org.uk
W www.diabetes.org.uk
Chief Executive, Barbara Young

DISABILITY RIGHTS UK (1977), Ground Floor,
49–51 East Road, London N1 6AH T 020-7250 8181
E enquiries@disabilityrightsuk.org W www.disabilityrightsuk.org
Chief Executive, Liz Sayce

DITCHLEY FOUNDATION (1958), Ditchley Park, Enstone,
Chipping Norton OX7 4ER T 01608-677346
E info@ditchley.co.uk W www.ditchley.co.uk
Director, Sir John Holmes, GCVO, KBE, CMG

DOWN'S SYNDROME ASSOCIATION (1970),
Langdon Down Centre, 2A Langdon Park,
Teddington TW11 9PS T 0333-121 2300
E info@downs-syndrome.org.uk
W www.downs-syndrome.org.uk
Chief Executive, Carol Boys

DUKE OF EDINBURGH'S AWARD (1956), Gulliver House,
Madeira Walk, Windsor SL4 1EU T 01753-727400
E info@dofe.org W www.dofe.org
Chief Executive, Peter Westgarth

DYSLEXIA ACTION (2006), Dyslexia Action House,
10 High Street, Egham TW20 9EA T 0300-3038357
E info@dyslexiaaction.org.uk W www.dyslexiaaction.org.uk
Chief Executive, Kevin Geeson

EAST OF ENGLAND AGRICULTURAL SOCIETY (1797),
East of England Showground, Peterborough PE2 6XE
T 01733-234451 E info@eastofengland.org.uk
W www.eastofengland.org.uk
Chief Executive, Jeremy Staples

EDINBURGH CHAMBER OF COMMERCE (1785),
Chamber Business Centre, 40 George Street, Edinburgh
EH2 2LE T 0131-221 2999 W www.edinburghchamber.co.uk
Chief Executive, David Birrell

EGYPT EXPLORATION SOCIETY (1882),
3 Doughty Mews, London WC1N 2PG T 020-7242 1880
E contact@ees.ac.uk W www.ees.ac.uk
Director, Chris Naunton

ELECTORAL REFORM SOCIETY (1884),
2–6 Boundary Row, London SE1 8HP T 020-7928 1622
E ers@electoral-reform.org.uk W www.electoral-reform.org.uk
Chief Executive, Katie Ghose

ELGAR SOCIETY (1951), 6 Carriage Close, St Johns,
Worcester WR2 6AE T 01905-339371 E vice.chair@elgar.org
W www.elgar.org
Hon. Secretary, Helen Petchey

ELIZABETH FINN CARE (1897), Hythe House, 200
Shepherds Bush Road, London W6 7NL T 020-8834 9200
E info@elizabethfinn.org.uk W www.elizabethfinn.org.uk
Chief Executive, Maj.-Gen. Matthew Sykes, CVO

EMERGENCY PLANNING SOCIETY (1993), The
Hawkhills, Easingwold, York YO61 3EG T 0845-600 9587
E info@the-eps.org W www.the-eps.org
Chair, Helen Hinds

ENABLE SCOTLAND (1954), Inspire House, 3 Renshaw Place,
Eurocentral, Glasgow ML1 4UF T 01698 737031
E enable@enable.org.uk W www.enable.org.uk
Chief Executive, Peter Scott

ENERGY INSTITUTE (2003), 61 New Cavendish Street,
London W1G 7AR T 020-7467 7100 E info@energyinst.org
W www.energyinst.org
Chief Executive, Louise Kingham, OBE

ENGLISH ASSOCIATION (1906), University of Leicester,
University Road, Leicester LE1 7RH T 0116-229 7622
E engassoc@le.ac.uk W www.le.ac.uk/engassoc
Chief Executive, Helen Lucas

ENGLISH CHESS FEDERATION (1904), The Watch Oak,
Chain Lane, Battle TN33 0YD T 01424-775222
E office@englishchess.org.uk W www.englishchess.org.uk
Chief Executive, Phil Ehr

ENGLISH FOLK DANCE AND SONG SOCIETY (1932),
Cecil Sharp House, 2 Regent's Park Road, London NW1 7AY
T 020-7485 2206 E info@efdss.org W www.efdss.org
Chief Executive, Katy Spicer

ENGLISH SPELLING SOCIETY (1908), 71 Stoneleigh
Avenue, Earlsdon, Coventry CV5 6DA T 024-7671 2119
E enquiries@spellingsociety.org W www.spellingsociety.org
Chairman, Stephen Linstead

EPILEPSY ACTION (1950), New Anstey House,
Gate Way Drive, Yeadon, Leeds LS19 7XY T 0113-210 8800,
Helpline 0808-800 5050 E epilepsy@epilepsy.org.uk
W www.epilepsy.org.uk
Chief Executive, Philip Lee

EPILEPSY SOCIETY (1892), Chesham Lane,
Chalfont St Peter SL9 0RJ T 01494-601300,
Helpline 01494-601400 W www.epilepsysociety.org.uk
Chief Executive, Angela Geer

ESPERANTO ASSOCIATION OF BRITAIN (1976),
Esperanto House, Station Road, Barlaston, Stoke-on-Trent
ST12 9DE T 0845-230 1887 E eab@esperanto.org.uk
W www.esperanto.org.uk
President, Paul Gubbins

EVANGELICAL LIBRARY Units 5 & 6 Gateway Mews,
Ring Way, Bounds Green, London N11 2UT T 020-8362 0868
E elenquire@gmail.com W www.evangelical-library.org.uk
Librarian, S. J. Taylor

FABIAN SOCIETY (1884), 61 Petty France, London SW1H 9EU
T 020-7227 4900 E info@fabian-society.org.uk
W www.fabians.org.uk
General Secretary, Andrew Harrop

FACULTY OF ROYAL DESIGNERS FOR INDUSTRY
(1936), RSA, 8 John Adam Street, London WC2N 6EZ
T 020-7930 5115 E general@rsa.org.uk W www.thersa.org
Chief Executive, Matthew Taylor

FAIR ISLE BIRD OBSERVATORY TRUST (1948),
Fair Isle Bird Observatory, Fair Isle ZE2 9JU T 01595-760258
E fibo@btconnect.com W www.fairislebirdobs.co.uk
Warden, Andrew Parnaby

FAMILY ACTION (1869), 501–505 Kingsland Road,
London E8 4AU T 020-7254 6251 W www.family-action.org.uk
Chief Executive, David Holmes

FAUNA & FLORA INTERNATIONAL (1903), Jupiter House,
Station Road, Cambridge CB1 2JD T 01223-571000
E info@fauna-flora.org W www.fauna-flora.org
Chief Executive, Mark Rose

FEDERATION OF BRITISH ARTISTS (1961),
17 Carlton House Terrace, London SW1Y 5BD T 020-7930 6844
E info@mallgalleries.com W www.mallgalleries.org.uk
Director, Lewis McNaught

FEDERATION OF FAMILY HISTORY SOCIETIES (1974),
PO Box 8857, Lutterworth LE17 9BJ T 01455-203133
E info@ffhs.org.uk W www.ffhs.org.uk
Administrator, Philippa McCray

FEDERATION OF SMALL BUSINESSES (1974),
Sir Frank Whittle Way, Blackpool Business Park,
Blackpool, Lancashire FY4 2FE T 020-7592 8100
E press@fsb.org.uk W www.fsb.org.uk
Honorary National Chairman, John Allan

FIELDS IN TRUST (1925), 2nd Floor, 15 Crinan Street,
London N1 9SQ T 020-7427 2110 E info@fieldsintrust.org
W www.fieldsintrust.org
Chief Executive, Helen Griffiths

FIELD STUDIES COUNCIL (1943), Preston Montford,
Montford Bridge, Shrewsbury SY4 1HW T 0845-345 4071
E enquiries@field-studies-council.org
W www.field-studies-council.org
Chief Executive, Rob Lucas

FIGHT FOR SIGHT (1965), 5th Floor, 9–13 Fenchurch
Buildings, Fenchurch Street, London EC3M 5HR
T 020-7264 3900 E info@fightforsight.org.uk
W www.fightforsight.org.uk
Chief Executive, Michele Acton

FIRE FIGHTERS CHARITY (1943), Level 6, Belvedere,
Basing View, Basingstoke RG21 4HG T 01256-366566
E info@firefighterscharity.org.uk
W www.firefighterscharity.org.uk
Chief Executive, John Parry

FLEET AIR ARM OFFICERS' ASSOCIATION (1957),
4 St James's Square, London SW1Y 4JU T 020-7930 7722
E admin@fleetairarmoa.org W www.fleetairarmoa.org
President, Vice-Adm. Sir Adrian Johns, KCB, CBE

FOREIGN PRESS ASSOCIATION IN LONDON (1888),
Award House, 7–11 Matthew Street, London SW1P 2JT
T 020-3727 4319 W www.fpalondon.org
Director, Christopher Wyld

FORENSIC SCIENCE SOCIETY (1959), Clarke House,
18A Mount Parade, Harrogate HG1 1BX T 01423-506068
E info@csofs.org W www.forensic-science-society.org.uk
Chief Executive, Dr Anya Hunt

FRANCO-BRITISH SOCIETY (1924), 3 Dovedale Studios,
465 Battersea Park Road, London SW11 4LR
E execsec@francobritishsociety.org.uk
W www.francobritishsociety.org.uk
Executive Secretary, Kate Brayn

FRIENDS OF CATHEDRAL MUSIC (1956), 27 Old
Gloucester Street, London WC1N 3XX T 0845-644 3721
E info@fcm.org.uk W www.fcm.org.uk
Secretary, Roger Bishton

FRIENDS OF FRIENDLESS CHURCHES (1957),
St Ann's Vestry Hall, 2 Church Entry, London EC4V 5HB
T 020-7236 3934 E office@friendsoffriendlesschurches.org.uk
W www.friendsoffriendlesschurches.org.uk
Director, Matthew Saunders, MBE

FRIENDS OF THE BODLEIAN (1925), Bodleian Library,
Broad Street, Oxford OX1 3BG T 01865-277234
E fob@bodleian.ox.ac.uk
W www.bodleian.ox.ac.uk/bodley/friends
Chair, Prof. Richard McCabe

FRIENDS OF THE EARTH SCOTLAND (1978),
Thorn House, 5 Rose Street, Edinburgh EH2 2PR
T 0131-243 2700 E info@foe-scotland.org.uk
W www.foe-scotland.org.uk
Chief Executive, Dr Richard Dixon

FRIENDS OF THE NATIONAL LIBRARIES (1931),
c/o Department of Manuscripts, The British Library,
96 Euston Road, London NW1 2DB T 020-7412 7559
W www.friendsofnationallibraries.org.uk
Chair, Lord Egremont, FRSL

FURNITURE HISTORY SOCIETY (1964), 1 Mercedes
Cottages, St John's Road, Haywards Heath RH16 4EH
T 01444-413845 E furniturehistorysociety@hotmail.com
W www.furniturehistorysociety.org
President, Sir Nicholas Goodison

GALLIPOLI ASSOCIATION (1969), Box 630 Wey House,
15 Church Street, Weybridge KT138NA T 01344-626523
E webmaster@gallipoli-association.org
W www.gallipoli-association.org
Hon. Secretary, J. C. Watson Smith

GAME AND WILDLIFE CONSERVATION TRUST (1969),
Burgate Manor, Fordingbridge SP6 1EF T 01425-652381
E info@gwct.org.uk W www.gwct.org.uk
Chief Executive, Teresa Dent

GARDEN HISTORY SOCIETY (1965), 70 Cowcross Street,
London EC1M 6EJ T 020-7608 2409
E enquiries@gardenhistorysociety.org
W www.gardenhistorysociety.org
Chair, Dominic Cole

GEMMOLOGICAL ASSOCIATION OF GREAT BRITAIN
(1931), 21 Ely Place, London EC1N 6TD T 020-7404 3334
E information@gem-a.com W www.gem-a.com
Chief Executive, James Riley, FGA, DGA

GENERAL MEDICAL COUNCIL (1858), 3 Hardman Street,
Manchester M3 3AW T 0161-923 6602 E gmc@gmc-uk.org
W www.gmc-uk.org
Chief Executive, Niall Dickson

GENERAL OPTICAL COUNCIL (1958), 41 Harley Street,
London W1G 8DJ T 020-7580 3898 E goc@optical.org
W www.optical.org
Chief Executive/Registrar, Samantha Peters

GEOGRAPHICAL ASSOCIATION (1893), 160 Solly Street,
Sheffield S1 4BF T 0114-296 0088 E info@geography.org.uk
W www.geography.org.uk
Chief Executive, Alan Kinder

GEOLOGICAL SOCIETY OF LONDON (1807), Burlington
House, Piccadilly, London W1J 0BG T 020-7434 9944
E enquiries@geolsoc.org.uk W www.geolsoc.org.uk
Executive Secretary, E. Nickless

GEOLOGISTS' ASSOCIATION (1858), Burlington House,
Piccadilly, London W1J 0DU T 020-7434 9298
E sarah@geologistsassociation.org.uk
W www.geologistsassociation.org.uk
Executive Secretary, Sarah Stafford

GIRLGUIDING UK (1910), 17–19 Buckingham Palace Road,
London SW1W 0PT T 020-7834 6242 E info@girlguiding.org.uk
W www.girlguiding.org.uk
Chief Guide, Gill Slocombe

GIRLS' BRIGADE ENGLAND AND WALES (1965),
Cliff College, Calver, Hope Valley S32 3XG T 01246-582322
E gbco@girlsbrigadeew.org.uk W www.girlsb.org.uk
National Director, Ruth Gilson

GLADSTONE'S LIBRARY (1894), Church Lane,
Hawarden CH5 3DF T 01244-532350 E enquiries@gladlib.org
W www.gladstoneslibrary.org
Warden & Chief Librarian, Revd Peter Francis

GREEK INSTITUTE (1969), 29 Onslow Gardens,
London N21 1DY T 020-8360 7968 E info@greekinstitute.co.uk
W www.greekinstitute.co.uk
Director, Dr K. Tofallis

GREENPEACE UK (1979), Canonbury Villas, London N1 2PN
T 020-7865 8100 E info.uk@greenpeace.org
W www.greenpeace.org.uk
Executive Director, John Sauven

GUIDE DOGS (1934), Hillfields, Burghfield Common,
Reading RG7 3YG T 0118-983 5555
E guidedogs@guidedogs.org.uk W www.guidedogs.org.uk
Chief Executive, Richard Leaman

GUILD OF FREEMEN OF THE CITY OF LONDON
(1908), 4 Dowgate Hill, London EC4R 2SH T 020-8541 1435
E clerk@guild-freemen-london.co.uk
W www.guild-freemen-london.co.uk
Clerk to the Guild, Brig. M. I. Keun

GUILD OF GLASS ENGRAVERS (1975), Compton Drive,
Kingswinford, West Midlands DY6 9NS T 07834-549925
E enquiries@gge.org.uk W www.gge.org.uk
President, Tracey Sheppard

GURKHA WELFARE TRUST (1969), PO Box 2170,
22 Queen Street, Salisbury SP2 2EX T 01722-323955
E staffassistant@gwt.org.uk W www.gwt.org.uk
Director, William Shuttlewood, OBE

GUY'S AND ST THOMAS' CHARITY (1553), Second Floor,
Francis House, 9 King's Head Yard, London SE1 1NA
T 020-7089 4550 E info@gsttcharity.org.uk
W www.gsttcharity.org.uk
Chief Executive, Peter Hewitt

HAKLUYT SOCIETY (1846), c/o Map Library,
The British Library, 96 Euston Road, London NW1 2DB
T 01428-641850 E office@hakluyt.com W www.hakluyt.com
President, Capt. M. K. Barritt, RN

HALIFAX ANTIQUARIAN SOCIETY (1900),
115 Siddal Lane, Halifax HX3 9JS T 01422-823966
E halifaxantiquarian@gmail.com W www.halifaxhistory.org.uk
Hon. Secretary, Anne Kirker

HANSARD SOCIETY (1944), 5th Floor, 9 King Street,
London EC2V 8EA T 020-7710 6070
E contact@hansardsociety.org.uk
W www.hansardsociety.org.uk
Chief Executive, Fiona Booth

HARVEIAN SOCIETY OF LONDON (1831), Lettsom
House, 11 Chandos Street, London W1G 9EB T 020-7580 1043
E harveiansoclondon@btconnect.com
W www.harveiansocietyoflondon.btck.co.uk
Executive Secretary, Cdr R. C. Ireland, MBE

HAWICK ARCHAEOLOGICAL SOCIETY (1856),
8 Melgund Place, Hawick TD9 9HY T 01450-376220
E info@airchieoliver.co.uk W www.airchieoliver.co.uk
Hon. Secretary, Gerald M. Graham

HEARING LINK (1947), 27–28 The Waterfront,
Eastbourne BN23 5UZ T 0300-111 1113
E enquiries@hearinglink.org W www.hearinglink.org
Chief Executive, Dr Lorraine Gailey

HERALDRY SOCIETY (1947), 53 Hitchin Street, Baldock
SG76AQ T 01462892062 E memsec@theheraldrysociety.com
W www.theheraldrysociety.com
Hon. Secretary, John Tunesi of Liongam

HISPANIC AND LUSO BRAZILIAN COUNCIL (1943),
Canning House, 14/15 Belgrave Square, London SW1X 8PS
T 020-7811 5600 E enquiries@canninghouse.org
W www.canninghouse.org
Chief Executive, Robert Capurro

HONOURABLE SOCIETY OF CYMMRODORION
(1751), PO Box 55178, London N12 2AY T 01582-832971
E secretary@cymmrodorion W www.cymmrodorion.org
Hon. Secretary, Peter Jeffreys

HOUSING JUSTICE (2003), 256 Bermondsey Street,
London SE1 3UJ T 020-3544 8094
E info@housingjustice.org.uk W www.housingjustice.org.uk
Chief Executive, Alison Gelder

HR SOCIETY LTD (1970), 4 Durnford Close, Chilbolton SO20 6AP **T** 07909-515 126 **E** gemma@hrsociety.co.uk **W** www.hrsociety.co.uk
President, Angela O'Connor

IFS SCHOOL OF FINANCE (1879), 8th Floor, Peninsular House, 36 Monument Street, London, EC3R 8LJ **T** 01227-818609 **E** customerservices@ifslearning.ac.uk **W** www.ifslearning.ac.uk
Principal, Gavin Shreeve

INCORPORATED COUNCIL OF LAW REPORTING FOR ENGLAND AND WALES (1865), Megarry House, 119 Chancery Lane, London WC2A 1PP **T** 020-7242 6471 **E** enquiries@iclr.co.uk **W** www.iclr.co.uk
Chief Executive, Kevin Laws

INCORPORATED SOCIETY OF MUSICIANS (1882), 4–5 Inverness Mews, London W2 3JQ **T** 020-7221 3499 **E** membership@ism.org **W** www.ism.org
Chief Executive, Deborah Annetts

INDEPENDENT AGE (1863), 6 Avonmore Road, London W14 8RL **T** 020-7605 4200 **E** charity@independentage.org.uk **W** www.independentage.org
Chief Executive, Janet Morrison

INDUSTRY AND PARLIAMENT TRUST (1977), Suite 101, 3 Whitehall Court, London SW1A 2EL **T** 020-7839 9400 **E** industryandparliamenttrust@ipt.org.uk **W** www.ipt.org.uk
Chief Executive, Nick Maher

INSTITUTE OF CANCER RESEARCH (1909), 123 Old Brompton Road, London SW7 3RP **T** 020-7352 8133 **W** www.icr.ac.uk
Chief Executive, Prof. Alan Ashworth

INSTITUTE OF HEALTH PROMOTION AND EDUCATION (1962), School of Dentistry, University of Manchester, Coupland 3, Oxford Road, Manchester M13 9PL **T** 0161-275 6610 **E** honsec@ihpe.org.uk **W** www.ihpe.org.uk
Hon. Secretary, Kathy Lewis

INSTITUTE OF HERALDIC AND GENEALOGICAL STUDIES (1961), 79–82 Northgate, Canterbury CT1 1BA **T** 01227-768664 **E** ihgs@ihgs.ac.uk **W** www.ihgs.ac.uk
Principal, Dr Richard Baker

INSTITUTE OF MATHEMATICS AND ITS APPLICATIONS (1964), Catherine Richards House, 16 Nelson Street, Southend-on-Sea SS1 1EF **T** 01702-354020 **E** post@ima.org.uk **W** www.ima.org.uk
Executive Director, David Youdan

INSTITUTE OF PHYSICS AND ENGINEERING IN MEDICINE (1997), Fairmount House, 230 Tadcaster Road, York YO24 1ES **T** 01904-610821 **E** office@ipem.ac.uk **W** www.ipem.ac.uk
Chief Executive, Rosemary Cook, CBE

INSTITUTION OF ENGINEERING AND TECHNOLOGY (1871), Michael Faraday House, Six Hills Way, Stevenage SG1 2AY **T** 01438-313311 **E** postmaster@theiet.org **W** www.theiet.org
Chief Executive & Secretary, Nigel Fine

INTERCONTINENTAL CHURCH SOCIETY (1823), Unit 11, Ensign Business Centre, Westwood Way, Westwood Business Park, Coventry CV4 8JA **T** 024-7646 3940 **E** enquiries@ics-uk.org **W** www.ics-uk.org
Mission Director, Revd Richard Bromley

INTERNATIONAL AFRICAN INSTITUTE (1926), SOAS, Thornhaugh Street, Russell Square, London WC1H 0XG **T** 020-7898 4420 **E** iai@soas.ac.uk **W** www.internationalafricaninstitute.org
Hon. Director, Prof. Philip Burnham

INTERNATIONAL INSTITUTE FOR CONSERVATION OF HISTORIC AND ARTISTIC WORKS (1950), 3 Birdcage Walk, London SW1H 9JJ **T** 020-7799 5500 **E** iic@iiconservation.org **W** www.iiconservation.org
Secretary-General, Josephine Kirby Atkinson

INTERNATIONAL TREE FOUNDATION (1924), 2 Lancaster Close, Stevenage SG1 4RX **T** 01293-227065 **W** www.internationaltreefoundation.org
Director, Andy Egan

INTERSERVE (1852), 5–6 Walker Avenue, Wolverton Hill MK12 5TW **T** 01908-552700 **E** info@interserve.org.uk **W** www.interserve.org.uk
National Director, Steve Bell

IRAN SOCIETY (1911), 25 Eccleston Place, London SW1W 9NF **T** 020-7235 5122 **E** info@iransociety.org **W** www.iransociety.org
President, Sir Richard Dalton, KCMG

ISLE OF WIGHT NATURAL HISTORY AND ARCHAEOLOGICAL SOCIETY (1919), Unit 16, Prospect Business Centre, Prospect Road, Cowes PO31 7AD **T** 01983-282596 **E** iwnhas@btconnect.com **W** www.iwnhas.org
President, Mrs D. Backhouse Fry

JACQUELINE DU PRÉ MUSIC BUILDING (1995), St Hilda's College, Oxford OX4 1DY **T** 01865-286660 **E** jdp@st-hildas.ox.ac.uk **W** www.st-hildas.ox.ac.uk/jdp
Manager, Joel Baldwin

JAPAN SOCIETY (1891), 13/14 Cornwall Terrace, London NW1 4QP **T** 020-7935 0475 **W** www.japansociety.org.uk
Chief Executive, Heidi Potter

JERUSALEM AND THE MIDDLE EAST CHURCH ASSOCIATION (1929), 1 Hart House, The Hart, Farnham GU9 7HJ **T** 01252-726994 **E** secretary@jmeca.eclipse.co.uk **W** www.jmeca.org.uk
Chair, John Clark

KENT ARCHAEOLOGICAL SOCIETY (1857), Maidstone Museum, St Faiths Street, Maidstone ME14 1LH **T** 07792-601328 **E** secretary@kentarchaeology.org.uk **W** www.kentarchaeology.org.uk
Hon. General Secretary, Dr P. Stutchbury

KING'S FUND (1897), 11–13 Cavendish Square, London W1G 0AN **T** 020-7307 2400 **E** enquiry@kingsfund.org.uk **W** www.kingsfund.org.uk
Chief Executive, Chris Ham

KIPLING SOCIETY (1927), 31 Brookside, Billericay, Essex CM11 1DT **T** 077-1432 6532 **E** john.lambert1@btinternet.com **W** www.kipling.org.uk
Hon. Secretary, John Lambert

LCIA (LONDON COURT OF INTERNATIONAL ARBITRATION) (1892), 70 Fleet Street, London EC4Y 1EU **T** 020-7936 6200 **E** lcia@lcia.org **W** www.lcia.org
Director-General, Adrian Winstanley

LEPROSY MISSION, ENGLAND, WALES, THE CHANNEL ISLANDS AND THE ISLE OF MAN (1874), Goldhay Way, Orton Goldhay, Peterborough PE2 5GZ **T** 01733-370505 **E** post@tlmew.org.uk **W** www.leprosymission.org.uk
National Director, Peter A. Walker

LEUKAEMIA AND LYMPHOMA RESEARCH (1960), 39–40 Eagle Street, London WC1R 4TH **T** 020-7504 2200 **E** info@beatingbloodcancers.org.uk **W** www.leukaemialymphomaresearch.org.uk
Chief Executive, Cathy Gilman

LIONS CLUBS INTERNATIONAL (BRITISH ISLES AND IRELAND) (1950), 257 Alcester Road South, Kings Heath, Birmingham B14 6DT **T** 0845-833 9502 **E** enquiries@lionsclubs.co **W** www.lionsclubc.co
Office Manager, Brigitte Waterfield

LISTENING BOOKS (1959), 12 Lant Street, London SE1 1QH **T** 020-7407 9417 **E** info@listening-books.org.uk **W** www.listening-books.org.uk
Director, Bill Dee

LOCAL GOVERNMENT ASSOCIATION (1997),
Local Government House, Smith Square, London SW1P 3HZ
T 020-7664 3000 **E** info@local.gov.uk **W** www.local.gov.uk
Chief Executive, Carolyn Downs

LONDON AND MIDDLESEX ARCHAEOLOGICAL
SOCIETY (1855), c/o Museum of London, 150 London Wall,
London EC2Y 5HN **T** 020-7410 2228 **W** www.lamas.org.uk
Hon. Secretary, Karen Thomas

LONDON CATALYST (1873), 45 Westminster Bridge Road,
London SE1 7JB **T** 020-7021 4204
E london.catalyst@peabody.org.uk
W www.londoncatalyst.org.uk
Director, Victor Willmott

LONDON COUNCILS (2000), 59½ Southwark Street,
London SE1 0AL **T** 020-7934 9999
E info@londoncouncils.gov.uk **W** www.londoncouncils.gov.uk
Chief Executive, John O'Brien

LONDON LIBRARY (1841), 14 St James's Square,
London SW1Y 4LG **T** 020-7930 7705
E reception@londonlibrary.co.uk **W** www.londonlibrary.co.uk
Librarian, Inez Lynn

LONDON SOCIETY (1912), Mortimer Wheeler House,
46 Eagle Wharf Road, London N1 7ED **T** 020-7253 9400
E info@londonsociety.org.uk **W** www.londonsociety.org.uk
Chair, Peter Murray

LULLABY TRUST (1971), 11 Belgrave Road, London
SW1V 1RB **T** 020-7802 3200 **E** office@lullabytrust.org.uk
W www.lullabytrust.co.uk
Chief Executive, Francine Bates

MACMILLAN CANCER SUPPORT (1911), 89 Albert
Embankment, London SE1 7UQ **T** 020-7840 7840
W www.macmillan.org.uk
Chief Executive, Ciarán Devane

MANORIAL SOCIETY OF GREAT BRITAIN (1906),
104 Kennington Road, London SE11 6RE **T** 020-7735 6633
E manorial@msgb.co.uk **W** www.msgb.co.uk
Chair, Robert Smith

MARIE CURIE CANCER CARE (1948), 89 Albert
Embankment, London SE1 7TP **T** 0800-716146
E supporter.services@mariecurie.org.uk
W www.mariecurie.org.uk
Chief Executive, Dr Jane Collins

MARINE BIOLOGICAL ASSOCIATION OF THE UK
(1884), Citadel Hill, Plymouth PL1 2BP **T** 01752-633207
E sec@mba.ac.uk **W** www.mba.ac.uk
President, Sir Geoffrey Holland, KCB

MATHEMATICAL ASSOCIATION (1871),
259 London Road, Leicester LE2 3BE **T** 0116-221 0013
E office@m-a.org.uk **W** www.m-a.org.uk
President, Peter Ransom

ME ASSOCIATION (1976), 7 Apollo Office Court,
Radclive Road, Gawcott MK18 4DF **T** 0844-576 5326
E meconnect@meassociation.org.uk
W www.meassociation.org.uk
Chair, Neil Riley

MEDICAL WOMEN'S FEDERATION (1917),
Tavistock House North, Tavistock Square, London WC1H 9HX
T 020-7387 7765 **E** admin.mwf@btconnect.com
W www.medicalwomensfederation.org.uk
President, Dr Sally Davies

MENCAP (ROYAL MENCAP SOCIETY) (1946),
123 Golden Lane, London EC1Y 0RT **T** 020-7454 0454
E information@mencap.org.uk **W** www.mencap.org.uk
Chief Executive, Jan Tregelles

MENTAL HEALTH FOUNDATION (1972), Colechurch
House, 1 London Bridge Walk, London SE1 2SX **T** 020-7803
1100 **E** mhf@mentalhealth.org.uk
W www.mentalhealth.org.uk
Chief Executive, Jenny Edwards, CBE

MHA (1943), Epworth House, 3 Stuart Street, Derby DE1 2EQ
T 01332-296200 **E** enquiries@mha.org.uk **W** www.mha.org.uk
Chief Executive, Adrian Bagg

MIGRAINE ACTION ASSOCIATION (1958), 27 East
Street, LE1 6NB **T** 0116-275 8317 **E** info@migraine.org.uk
W www.migraine.org.uk
Chairman, Michael Wakefield

MILITARY HISTORICAL SOCIETY (1948),
National Army Museum, Royal Hospital Road,
London SW3 4HT **T** 01252-621056
E mhsqm.mt@btinternet.com
W www.themilitaryhistoricalsociety.co.uk
Chair, Clive Elderton, CBE

MIND (NATIONAL ASSOCIATION FOR MENTAL
HEALTH) (1946), 15–19 Broadway, London E15 4BQ
T 020-8519 2122, Infoline 0300-123 3393
E contact@mind.org.uk **W** www.mind.org.uk
Chief Executive, Paul Farmer

MINERALOGICAL SOCIETY (1876), 12 Baylis Mews,
Amyand Park Road, Twickenham TW1 3HQ **T** 020-8891 6600
E info@minersoc.org **W** www.minersoc.org
Executive Director, Kevin Murphy

MISSING PEOPLE (1993), 284 Upper Richmond Road West,
London SW14 7JE **T** 020-8392 4590
E info@missingpeople.org.uk **W** www.missingpeople.org.uk
Chief Executive, Jo Youle

MISSION TO SEAFARERS (1856), St Michael Paternoster
Royal, College Hill, London EC4R 2RL **T** 020-7248 5202
E info@missiontoseafarers.org **W** www.missiontoseafarers.org
Secretary General, Revd Andrew Wright

MULTIPLE SCLEROSIS SOCIETY (1953),
MS National Centre, 372 Edgware Road, London NW2 6ND
T 020-8438 0700 **W** www.mssociety.org.uk
Chief Executive, Michelle Mitchell

MUSEUMS ASSOCIATION (1889), 42 Clerkenwell Close,
London EC1R 0AZ **T** 020-7566 7800
E www.museumsassociation.org
Director, vacant

MUSICIANS BENEVOLENT FUND (1921),
7–11 Britannia Street, London WC1X 9JS **T** 020-7239 9100
E info@helpmusicians.org.uk **W** www.helpmusicians.org.uk
Chief Executive, David Sulkin, OBE

NABS (1916), 6th Floor, 388 Oxford Street, London W1C 1JT
T 020-7290 7070 **E** nabs@nabs.org.uk **W** www.nabs.org.uk
Chief Executive, Zoe Osmond

NACRO, THE CRIME REDUCTION CHARITY (1966),
Park Place, 10–12 Lawn Lane, London SW8 1UD
T 020-7840 7200 **E** debbie.mcintosh@nacro.org.uk
W www.nacro.org.uk
Chief Executive, Jacob Tas

NATIONAL BENEVOLENT CHARITY (1812),
Peter Herve House, Eccles Court, Tetbury GL8 8EH
T 01666-505500 **E** office@thenbc.org.uk
W www.thenbc.org.uk
Chief Executive, Paul Rossi

NATIONAL CAMPAIGN FOR COURTESY (1986),
Egmont House, 240 Tolworth Rise South, Surbiton,
Surrey KT5 9NB **T** 020-8330 3707
E peter.foot1@btinternet.com
W www.campaignforcourtesy.org.uk
Chair, Peter G. Foot

NATIONAL FEDERATION OF WOMEN'S INSTITUTES
(1915), 104 New Kings Road, London SW6 4LY
T 020-7371 9300 **W** www.thewi.org.uk
General Secretary, Jana Osborne

NATIONAL FOUNDATION FOR EDUCATIONAL
RESEARCH IN ENGLAND AND WALES (1946),
The Mere, Upton Park, Slough SL1 2DQ **T** 01753-574123
E enquiries@nfer.ac.uk **W** www.nfer.ac.uk
Chief Executive, Carole Willis

NATIONAL GARDENS SCHEME CHARITABLE TRUST (1927), Hatchlands Park, East Clandon, Guildford GU4 7RT **T** 01483-211535 **E** ngs@ngs.org.uk **W** www.ngs.org.uk *Chief Executive,* George Plumptre

NATIONAL HEALTH SERVICE CONFEDERATION (1997), 50 Broadway, London SW1H 0DB **T** 020-7799 6666 **E** enquiries@nhsconfed.org **W** www.nhsconfed.org *Chief Executive,* Rob Webster

NATIONAL OPERATIC AND DRAMATIC ASSOCIATION (1899), 15 The Metro Centre, Peterborough PE2 7UH **T** 01733-374790 **E** info@noda.org.uk **W** www.noda.org.uk *Chief Executive,* Tony Gibbs

NATIONAL TRUST (1895), Heelis, Kemble Drive, Swindon SN2 2NA **T** 0844-800 1895 **E** enquiries@thenationaltrust.org.uk **W** www.nationaltrust.org.uk *Director-General,* Dame Helen Ghosh

NATIONAL TRUST FOR SCOTLAND (1931), Hermiston Quay, 5 Cultins Road, Edinburgh EH11 4DF **T** 0844-493 2100 **E** information@nts.org.uk **W** www.nts.org.uk *Chief Executive,* Kate Mavor

NATIONAL UNION OF STUDENTS (NUS) (1922), Macadam House, 275 Gray's Inn Road, London WC1X 8QB **T** 0845-521 0262 **W** www.nus.org.uk *President,* Toni Pearce

NATIONAL WOMEN'S REGISTER (1966), 23 Vulcan House, Vulcan Road North, Norwich NR6 6AQ **T** 0845-450 0287 **E** office@nwr.org.uk **W** www.nwr.org.uk *Chair of Trustees,* Pam McKee

NAT (NATIONAL AIDS TRUST) (1987), New City Cloisters, 196 Old Street, London EC1V 9FR **T** 020-7814 6767 **E** info@nat.org.uk **W** www.nat.org.uk *Interim Chief Executive,* Susie Parsons

NAVY RECORDS SOCIETY (1893), c/o Pangbourne College, Pangbourne, Berks RG8 8LA **T** 01189-744789 **E** honsec@navyrecords.org.uk **W** www.navyrecords.org.uk *Hon. Secretary,* Robin Brodhurst

NEWCOMEN SOCIETY (1920), The Science Museum, London SW7 2DD **T** 020-7371 4445 **E** office@newcomen.com **W** www.newcomen.com *President,* Geoff Wallis

NSPCC (1884), Weston House, 42 Curtain Road, London EC2A 3NH **T** 0808-800 5000 **E** help@nspcc.org.uk **W** www.nspcc.org.uk *Chief Executive,* Peter Wanless

NUCLEAR INSTITUTE (1962), CK International House, 1–6 Yarmouth Place, London W1J 7BU **T** 020-3475 4701 **W** www.nuclearinst.com *Executive Secretary,* Elaine Boyes

NUFFIELD FOUNDATION (1943), 28 Bedford Square, London WC1B 3JS **T** 020-7631 0566 **E** info@nuffieldfoundation.org **W** www.nuffieldfoundation.org *Director,* Sharon Witherspoon, MBE

NUFFIELD TRUST (1940), 59 New Cavendish Street, London W1G 7LP **T** 020-7631 8450 **E** info@nuffieldtrust.org.uk **W** www.nuffieldtrust.org.uk *Chief Executive,* Nigel Edwards

OPEN-AIR MISSION (1853), 4 Harrier Court, Woodside Road, Slip End, Luton LU1 4DQ **T** 01582-841141 **E** oamission@btinternet.com **W** www.oamission.com *General Secretary,* Andy Banton

OPEN SPACES SOCIETY (1865), 25A Bell Street, Henley-on-Thames RG9 2BA **T** 01491-573535 **E** hq@oss.org.uk **W** www.oss.org.uk *General Secretary,* Kate Ashbrook

ORDER OF SAINT LAZARUS OF JERUSALEM (1098), Centre for Evangelisation, Croxteth Drive, Sefton Park L17 1AA **E** grand-secretary@oslj.org **W** www.oslj.org *Delegate,* Aaron Kiely

ORDERS AND MEDALS RESEARCH SOCIETY (1942), PO Box 6195, Royal Leamington Spa CV31 9JU **T** 01926-312176 **E** generalsecretary@omrs.org **W** www.omrs.org *General Secretary,* Dahlia Harrison, OMRS

OVERSEAS DEVELOPMENT INSTITUTE (1960), 203 Blackfriars Road, London SE1 8NJ **T** 020-7922 0300 **E** odi@odi.org.uk **W** www.odi.org.uk *Executive Director,* Kevin Watkins

OVERSEAS SERVICE PENSIONERS' ASSOCIATION (1960), 138 High Street, Tonbridge TN9 1AX **T** 01732-363836 **E** mail@ospa.org.uk **W** www.ospa.org.uk *Secretary and Treasurer,* D. F. B. Le Breton, CBE

OXFAM GREAT BRITAIN (1942), Oxfam House, John Smith Drive, Cowley, Oxford OX4 2JY **T** 0300-200 1292 **E** enquiries@oxfam.org.uk **W** www.oxfam.org.uk *Chief Executive,* Max Goldring

PARKINSON'S UK (1969), 215 Vauxhall Bridge Road, London SW1V 1EJ **T** 020-7931 8080 **E** hello@parkinsons.org.uk **W** www.parkinsons.org.uk *Chief Executive,* Steve Ford

PARLIAMENTARY AND SCIENTIFIC COMMITTEE (1939), 3 Birdcage Walk, Westminster, London SW1H 9JJ **T** 020-7222 7085 **E** secretariat@pandsctte.demon.co.uk **W** www.scienceinparliament.org.uk *Executive Secretary,* Prof. Alan Malcolm

PEABODY TRUST (1862), Minster Court, 45 Westminster Bridge Road, London SE1 7JB **T** 020-7021 4444 **E** peabody.direct@peabody.org.uk **W** www.peabody.org.uk *Chief Executive,* Stephen Howlett

PERENNIAL (1839), 115–117 Kingston Road, Leatherhead KT22 7SU **T** 0845-230 1839 **E** info@perennial.org.uk **W** www.perennial.org.uk *Chief Executive,* Richard Capewell

POETRY SOCIETY (1909), 22 Betterton Street, London WC2H 9BX **T** 020-7420 9880 **E** info@poetrysociety.org.uk **W** www.poetrysociety.org.uk *Director,* Judith Palmer

PRINCE'S TRUST (1976), 9 Eldon Street, London EC2M 7LS **T** 020-7543 1234 **E** webinfops@princes-trust.org.uk **W** www.princes-trust.org.uk *Chief Executive,* Martina Milburn, CBE

PRISONERS ABROAD (1978), 89–93 Fonthill Road, London N4 3JH **T** 020-7561 6820 **E** info@prisonersabroad.org.uk **W** www.prisonersabroad.org.uk *Chief Executive,* Pauline Crowe

PROSTATE CANCER UK (1996), Fourth Floor, The Counting House, 53 Tooley Street, London SE1 2QN **T** 020-3310 7000 **E** info@prostatecanceruk.org **W** www.prostatecanceruk.org *Chief Executive,* Owen Sharp

QUEEN ELIZABETH'S FOUNDATION FOR DISABLED PEOPLE (1934), Leatherhead Court, Woodlands Road, Leatherhead KT22 0BN **T** 01372-841100 **E** info@qef.org.uk **W** www.qef.org.uk *Chief Executive,* Jonathan Powell

QUEEN'S NURSING INSTITUTE (1887), 1A Henrietta Place, London W1G 0LZ **T** 020-7549 1400 **E** mail@qni.org.uk **W** www.qni.org.uk *Director,* Dr Crystal Oldman

QUEEN VICTORIA CLERGY FUND (1897), Church House, Great Smith Street, London SW1P 3AZ **T** 020-7898 1000 **E** info@churchhouse.org.uk *Chief Executive,* Christopher Palmer, CBE

REFUGEE COUNCIL (1951), PO Box 68614, London E15 9DQ **T** 020-7346 6700 **E** info@refugeecouncil.org.uk **W** www.refugeecouncil.org.uk *Chief Executive,* Maurice Wren

REGULAR FORCES EMPLOYMENT ASSOCIATION LTD (1885), 1st Floor, Mountbarrow House, 6–20 Elizabeth Street, London SW1W 9RB T 01212-360058 E adminrfea@rtp.org.uk W www.rfea.org.uk
Chief Executive, Brig. Stephen Gledhill

RETHINK (1972), 89 Albert Embankment, London SE1 7TP T 0300-5000 927 E info@rethink.org W www.rethink.org
Acting Chief Executive, Mark Winstanley

RICHARD III SOCIETY (1924), 23 Ash Rise, Halstead, Essex CO9 1RD T 01787-472512 E secretaries@richardiii.net W www.richardiii.net
Chair, Dr P. T. Stone

RNIB NATIONAL LIBRARY SERVICE (1868), PO Box 173, Peterborough PE2 6WS T 0303-123 9999 E helpline@rnib.org.uk W www.rnib.org.uk/reading
Chief Executive, Lesley-Anne Alexander, CBE

ROYAL AERONAUTICAL SOCIETY (1866), 4 Hamilton Place, London W1J 7BQ T 020-7670 4300 E raes@aerosociety.com W www.aerosociety.com
Chief Executive, Simon Luxmoore

ROYAL AGRICULTURAL SOCIETY OF THE COMMONWEALTH (1957), c/o Royal Highland Centre, Ingliston, Edinburgh EH28 8NF T 0131-335 6200 E info@therasc.com W www.therasc.com
Hon. Secretary, Michael Lambert

ROYAL AIR FORCES ASSOCIATION (1943), 117½ Loughborough Road, Leicester LE4 5ND T 0116-266 5224 E enquiries@rafa.org.uk W www.rafa.org.uk
Secretary General, Nick Bunting

ROYAL ASSOCIATION FOR DEAF PEOPLE (1841), Century House South, North Station Road, Colchester CO1 1RE T 0845-688 2525 E info@royaldeaf.org.uk W www.royaldeaf.org.uk
Chief Executive, Dr Jan Sheldon

ROYAL ASTRONOMICAL SOCIETY (1820), Burlington House, Piccadilly, London W1J 0BQ T 020-7734 4582 E info@ras.org.uk W www.ras.org.uk
Executive Secretary, Pamela Mortimer

ROYAL BRITISH LEGION (1921), 199 Borough High Street, London SE1 1AA T 0808-802 8080 E info@britishlegion.org.uk W www.britishlegion.org.uk
Director-General, Chris Simpkins

ROYAL BRITISH LEGION SCOTLAND (1921), New Haig House, Logie Green Road, Edinburgh EH7 4HQ E ceo@rblscotland.org W www.rblscotland.org
Chief Executive, Kevin Gray, MD

ROYAL CHORAL SOCIETY (1872), Studio 9, 92 Lots Road, London SW10 0QD T 020-7376 3718 E administrator@royalchoralsociety.co.uk W www.royalchoralsociety.co.uk
Administrator, Janet Jalfon

ROYAL HISTORICAL SOCIETY (1868), University College London, Gower Street, London WC1E 6BT T 020-7387 7532 E royalhistsoc@ucl.ac.uk W www.royalhistoricalsociety.org
Executive Secretary, Dr S E Carr, PHD

ROYAL HORTICULTURAL SOCIETY (1804), 80 Vincent Square, London SW1P 2PE T 0845-260 5000 W www.rhs.org.uk
Director-General, Sue Biggs

ROYAL HUMANE SOCIETY (1774), 50/51 Temple Chambers, 3–7 Temple Avenue, London EC4Y 0HP T 020-7936 2942 E info@royalhumanesociety.org.uk W www.royalhumanesociety.org.uk
Secretary, Dick Wilkinson, TD

ROYAL INSTITUTE OF NAVIGATION (1947), 1 Kensington Gore, London SW7 2AT T 020-7591 3130 E admin@rin.org.uk W www.rin.org.uk
Director, Capt. P. Chapman-Andrews, LVO, MBE, RN

ROYAL INSTITUTE OF OIL PAINTERS (1882), 17 Carlton House Terrace, London SW1Y 5BD T 020-7930 6844 E enquiries@theroi.org.uk W www.theroi.co.uk
President, Ian Cryer

ROYAL INSTITUTE OF PAINTERS IN WATER COLOURS (1831), 17 Carlton House Terrace, London SW1Y 5BD T 020-7930 6844 E info@mallgalleries.com W www.royalinstituteofpaintersinwatercolours.org
President, Ronald Maddox

ROYAL INSTITUTION OF GREAT BRITAIN (1799), 21 Albemarle Street, London W1S 4BS T 020-7409 2992 E ri@ri.ac.uk W www.rigb.org
Chief Executive, Chris Rofe

ROYAL LIFE SAVING SOCIETY UK (1891), River House, High Street, Broom B50 4HN T 01789-773994 E info@rlss.org.uk W www.rlss.org.uk
President, P. Moyes

ROYAL LONDON SOCIETY FOR THE BLIND (1838), Victoria Charity Centre, 11 Belgrave Road, London SW1V 1RB T 020-7808 6170 W www.rlsb.org.uk
Chief Executive, Dr Tom Pey

ROYAL MUSICAL ASSOCIATION (1874), c/o Sayers Butterworth LLP, 3rd Floor, 12 Gough Square, London EC4A 3DW T 0161-861 7542 E exec@rma.ac.uk W www.rma.ac.uk
President, Prof. Mark Everist

ROYAL NATIONAL LIFEBOAT INSTITUTION (1824), West Quay Road, Poole BH15 1HZ T 0845-122 6999 W www.rnli.org
Chief Executive, Paul Boissier, CB MA

ROYAL NAVAL BENEVOLENT TRUST (1922), Castaway House, 311 Twyford Avenue, Portsmouth PO2 8RN T 023-9269 0112 E rnbt@rnbt.org.uk W www.rnbt.org.uk
Chief Executive, Cdr. Stephen Farrington, QGM, RN

ROYAL PHILATELIC SOCIETY LONDON (1869), 41 Devonshire Place, London W1G 6JY T 020-7486 1044 E secretary@rpsl.org.uk W www.rpsl.org.uk
President, Christopher King

ROYAL PHILHARMONIC SOCIETY (1813), 10 Stratford Place, London W1C 1BA T 020-7491 8110 E web@royalphilharmonicsociety.org.uk W www.royalphilharmonicsociety.org.uk
Executive Director, Rosemary Johnson

ROYAL PHOTOGRAPHIC SOCIETY (1853), Fenton House, 122 Wells Road, Bath BA2 3AH T 01225-325733 E reception@rps.org W www.rps.org
Director-General, Dr Michael Pritchard

ROYAL SCHOOL OF CHURCH MUSIC (1927), 19 The Close, Salisbury SP1 2EB T 01722-424848 E enquiries@rscm.com W www.rscm.com
Director, Andrew Reid

ROYAL SCHOOL OF NEEDLEWORK (1872), Apartment 12A, Hampton Court Palace KT8 9AU T 020-3166 6932 E enquiries@royal-needlework.org.uk W www.royal-needlework.org.uk
Chief Executive, Dr Susan Kay-Williams

ROYAL SOCIETY FOR THE PREVENTION OF CRUELTY TO ANIMALS (1824), Wilberforce Way, Southwater, Horsham RH13 9RS T 0300-123 0100 W www.rspca.org.uk
Chief Executive, vacant

ROYAL SOCIETY FOR THE PROTECTION OF BIRDS (1889), The Lodge, Sandy SG19 2DL T 01767-680551 W www.rspb.org.uk
Chief Executive, Mike Clarke

ROYAL SOCIETY OF CHEMISTRY (1841), Burlington House, Piccadilly, London W1V 0BA T 020-7437 8656 E rsc@rsc.org W www.rsc.org
Chief Executive, Dr Robert Parker

ROYAL SOCIETY OF MARINE ARTISTS (1939),
17 Carlton House Terrace, London SW1Y 5BD **T** 020-7930 6844
E info@rsma-web.co.uk **W** www.rsma-web.co.uk
President, David Howell

ROYAL SOCIETY OF MUSICIANS OF GREAT BRITAIN
(1738), 10 Stratford Place, London W1C 1BA
T 020-7629 6137 **E** enquiries@royalsocietyofmusicians.co.uk
W www.royalsocietyofmusicians.co.uk
Secretary, Charlotte Penton-Smith

ROYAL SOCIETY OF PORTRAIT PAINTERS (1891),
17 Carlton House Terrace, London SW1Y 5BD **T** 020-7930 6844
E enquiries@therp.co.uk **W** www.therp.co.uk
President, Alastair Adams

ROYAL SOCIETY OF TROPICAL MEDICINE AND
HYGIENE (1907), Northumberland House,
303–306 High Holborn, London WC1V 7JZ **T** 020-7405 2628
E info@rstmh.org **W** www.rstmh.org
Chief Executive, Gerri McHugh

ROYAL STAR AND GARTER HOMES FOR DISABLED
EX-SERVICE MEN AND WOMEN (1916),
15 Castle Mews, Hampton TW12 2NP **T** 020-8481 7676
E general.enquiries@starandgarter.org
W www.starandgarter.org
Chief Executive, Mike Barter

ROYAL THEATRICAL FUND (1839), 11 Garrick Street,
London WC2E 9AR **T** 020-7836 3322 **E** admin@trtf.com
W www.trtf.com
President, Robert Lindsay

RSABI (1897), The Rural Centre, West Mains of Ingliston,
Newbridge, Edinburgh EH28 8LT **T** 0131-472 4166
W www.rsabi.org.uk
Chief Executive, Nina Clancy

ST JOHN AMBULANCE (1877), 27 St John's Lane,
London EC1M 4BU **T** 0870-010 4950 **W** www.sja.org.uk
Chief Executive, Sue Killen

SAMARITANS (1953), The Upper Mill, Kingston Road,
Ewell KT17 2AF **T** 020-8394 8300, **Helpline** 0845-790 9090
E admin@samaritans.org **W** www.samaritans.org
Chief Executive, Catherine Johnstone

SANE (1986), 1st Floor, Cityside House, 40 Adler Street,
London E1 1EE **T** 020-7375 1002, **Helpline** 0845-767 8000
E info@sane.org.uk **W** www.sane.org.uk
Chief Executive, Ms M. Wallace, MBE

SAVE THE CHILDREN (1919), 1 St John's Lane,
London EC1M 4AR **T** 020-7012 6400
E supporter.care@savethechildren.org.uk
W www.savethechildren.org.uk
Chief Executive, Justin Forsyth

SCHOOL LIBRARY ASSOCIATION (1937), 1 Pine Court,
Kembrey Park, Swindon SN2 8AD **T** 01793-530166
E info@sla.org.uk **W** www.sla.org.uk
Chief Executive, Mrs T. Adams

SCOPE (1952), 6 Market Road, London N7 9PW
T 020-7619 7100, **Helpline** 0808-800 3333
E supportercare@scope.org.uk **W** www.scope.org.uk
Chief Executive, Richard Hawkes

SCOTTISH ASSOCIATION FOR MARINE SCIENCE
(1884), Scottish Marine Institute, Oban, Argyll PA37 1QA
T 01631-559000 **E** info@sams.ac.uk **W** www.sams.ac.uk
Director, Prof. Laurence Mee

SCOTTISH COUNCIL FOR VOLUNTARY
ORGANISATIONS (1943), Mansfield Traquair Centre,
15 Mansfield Place, Edinburgh EH3 6BB **T** 0131-474 8000
E enquiries@scvo.org.uk **W** www.scvo.org.uk
Chief Executive, M. Sime

SCOTTISH LAND AND ESTATES (1906), Stuart House,
Eskmills Business Park, Musselburgh EH21 7PB
T 0131-653 5400 **E** info@scottishlandandestates.co.uk
W www.scottishlandandestates.co.uk
Chief Executive, Douglas McAdam

SCOTTISH NATIONAL WAR MEMORIAL (1927),
The Castle, Edinburgh EH1 2YT **T** 0131-226 7393
E info@snwm.org **W** www.snwm.org
Secretary to the Trustees, Lt.-Col. R. J. Binks

SCOTTISH SOCIETY FOR THE PROTECTION OF
WILD BIRDS (1927), 2 Lochside View, Edinburgh Park
EH12 9DH **T** 0131-3174100
Director, Stuart Housden, OBE

SCOTTISH WILDLIFE TRUST (1964), Harbourside House,
110 Commercial Street, Edinburgh EH6 6NF **T** 0131-312 7765
E enquiries@scottishwildlifetrust.org.uk
W www.scottishwildlifetrust.org.uk
Chief Executive, Jonathan Hughes

SCOUT ASSOCIATION (1907), Gilwell Park,
Chingford, London E4 7QW **T** 020-8443 7100
E info.centre@scouts.org.uk **W** www.scouts.org.uk
Chief Executive, Derek Twine

SELDEN SOCIETY (1887), School of Law, Queen Mary,
Mile End Road, London E1 4NS **T** 020-7882 3968
E selden-society@qmul.ac.uk
W www.selden-society.qmul.ac.uk
Secretary, V. Tunkel

SENSE (THE NATIONAL DEAFBLIND AND RUBELLA
ASSOCIATION) (1955), 101 Pentonville Road,
London N1 9LG **T** 020-7520 0999 **E** info@sense.org.uk
W www.sense.org.uk
Chief Executive, Gill Morbey, OBE

SHELTER (NATIONAL CAMPAIGN FOR HOMELESS
PEOPLE) (1966), 88 Old Street, London EC1V 9HU
T 0300-330 1234, **Helpline** 0808-800 4444
E info@shelter.org.uk **W** www.shelter.org.uk
Chief Executive, Campbell Robb

SOCIETY FOR NAUTICAL RESEARCH (1910),
The Lodge, The Drive, Hellingly, Hailsham BN27 4EP
T 01482-465183 **E** honsec@snr.org.uk **W** www.snr.org.uk
Hon. Secretary, Dr Byrne Mcleod

SOCIETY FOR THE PROMOTION OF ROMAN
STUDIES (1910), Senate House, Malet Street,
London WC1E 7HU **T** 020-7862 8727
E office@romansociety.org **W** www.romansociety.org
Secretary, Dr Fiona Haarer

SOCIETY FOR THE PROTECTION OF ANCIENT
BUILDINGS (1877), 37 Spital Square, London E1 6DY
T 020-7377 1644 **E** info@spab.org.uk **W** www.spab.org.uk
Director, Matthew Slocombe

SOCIETY OF ANTIQUARIES OF LONDON (1707),
Burlington House, Piccadilly, London W1J 0BE
T 020-7479 7080 **E** admin@sal.org.uk **W** www.sal.org.uk
General-Secretary, John S. C. Lewis, FSA

SOCIETY OF ANTIQUARIES OF NEWCASTLE UPON
TYNE (1813), Great North Museum: Hancock, Barras Bridge,
Newcastle upon Tyne NE2 4PT **T** 0191-231 2700
E admin@newcastle-antiquaries.org.uk
W www.newcastle-antiquaries.org.uk
President, Derek Cutts

SOCIETY OF BIOLOGY (2009), Charles Darwin House,
12 Roger Street, London WC1N 2JU **T** 020-7685 2550
E info@societyofbiology.org **W** www.societyofbiology.org
Chief Executive, Dr Mark Downs

SOCIETY OF EDITORS (1999), University Centre,
Granta Place, Mill Lane, Cambridge CB2 1RU
T 01223-304080 **E** office@societyofeditors.org
W www.societyofeditors.co.uk
Executive Director, Bob Satchwell

SOCIETY OF INDEXERS (1957), Woodbourn Business
Centre, 10 Jessell Street, Sheffield S9 3HY **T** 0114-244 9561
E admin@indexers.org.uk **W** www.indexers.org.uk
Chair, Adele Furbank

SOCIETY OF SCRIBES AND ILLUMINATORS (1921),
6 Queen Square, London WC1N 3AT T 0121 244 8006
E scribe@calligraphyonline.org W www.calligraphyonline.org
Chair, Angela Dalleywater
SOCIETY OF SOLICITORS IN THE SUPREME
COURT OF SCOTLAND (1784), SSC Library,
Parliament House, 11 Parliament Square, Edinburgh EH1 1RF
T 0131-225 6268 E enquiries@sclibrary.co.uk
W www.ssclibrary.co.uk
Secretary, I. L. S. Balfour
SOCIETY OF WOMEN ARTISTS (1855),
Larchlands, Daisybank Road, Cheltenham GL53 9QQ
T 07528-477002 E rebeccacottonswa@gmail.com
W www.society-women-artists.org.uk
Executive Secretary, Rebecca Cotton
SOIL ASSOCIATION (1946), South Plaza,
Marlborough Street, Bristol BS1 3NX T 0117-314 5000
W www.soilassociation.org
Chief Executive, Helen Browning, OBE
SOUTH AMERICAN MISSION SOCIETY IRELAND
(1844), 1 Irwin Crescent, Lurgan BT66 7EZ
T 028-3831 0144 E info@samsukireland.com
W www.samsireland.com
Mission Director, Bishop Ken Clarke
SPURGEONS (1867), 74 Wellingborough Road,
Rushden NN10 9TY T 01933-412412 E info@spurgeons.org
W www.spurgeons.org
Chief Executive, Tim Jeffery
SUSTRANS (1977), 2 Cathedral Square, College Green,
Bristol BS1 5DD T 0117-926 8893 E info@sustrans.org.uk
W www.sustrans.org.uk
Chief Executive, Malcolm Shepherd
TEACHER SUPPORT NETWORK (1877),
40A Drayton Park, London N5 1EW T 020-7697 2750,
Helpline 0800-056 2561 E support@teachersupport.info
W www.teachersupport.info
Chief Executive, Julian Stanley
TERRENCE HIGGINS TRUST (1982),
314–320 Gray's Inn Road, London WC1X 8DP
T 020-7812 1600 E info@tht.org.uk W www.tht.org.uk
Chief Executive, Dr Rosemary Gillespie
THEATRES TRUST (1976), 22 Charing Cross Road,
London WC2H 0QL T 020-7836 8591
E info@theatrestrust.org.uk W www.theatrestrust.org.uk
Director, Mhora Samuel
TOWN AND COUNTRY PLANNING ASSOCIATION
(1899), 17 Carlton House Terrace, London SW1Y 5AS
T 020-7930 8903 W www.tcpa.org.uk E tcpa@tcpa.org.uk
Chief Executive, Kate Henderson
TREE COUNCIL (1974), 71 Newcomen Street,
London SE1 1YT T 020-7407 9992 E info@treecouncil.org.uk
W www.treecouncil.org.uk
Director-General, Pauline Buchanan Black
UK YOUTH (1911), First Floor Millbank Tower,
21–24 Millbank, London SW1P 4QP T 0203-137 3810
E info@ukyouth.org W www.ukyouth.org
Interim Chief Executive, Dominic Cotton
UNITED GRAND LODGE OF ENGLAND (1717),
Freemasons' Hall, Great Queen Street, London WC2B 5AZ
T 020-7831 9811 E enquiries@ugle.org.uk
W www.ugle.org.uk
Grand Master, HRH the Duke of Kent, KG, GCMG,
GCVO
UNITED NATIONS ASSOCIATION OF GREAT BRITAIN
AND NORTHERN IRELAND (1945), 3 Whitehall Court,
London SW1A 2EL T 020-7766 3454 E info@una.org.uk
W www.una.org.uk
Executive Director, Natalie Samarasinghe

UNITED REFORMED CHURCH HISTORY SOCIETY
(1972), Westminster College, Madingley Road,
Cambridge CB3 0AA T 01223-330620 F hw271@cum.ac.uk
Hon. Secretary, Mrs M. Thompson
UNIVERSITIES UK (2000), Woburn House,
20 Tavistock Square, London WC1H 9HQ T 020-7419 4111
E info@universitiesuk.ac.uk W www.universitiesuk.ac.uk
Chief Executive, Nicola Dandridge
VEGETARIAN SOCIETY OF THE UNITED KINGDOM
LTD (1847), Parkdale, Dunham Road, Altrincham,
Cheshire WA14 4QG T 0161-925 2000 E info@vegsoc.org
W www.vegsoc.org
Chief Executive, Lynne Elliot
VERNACULAR ARCHITECTURE GROUP (1952),
Sunnyfield, 3 Church Row, RedwickNewport, NP26 3DE
T 01633-889019 E lindajhall@googlemail.com
W www.vag.org.uk
President, Martin Cherry
VICTORIAN SOCIETY (1958), 1 Priory Gardens,
Bedford Park, London W4 1TT T 020-8994 1019
E admin@victoriansociety.org.uk
W www.victoriansociety.org.uk
Director, Christopher Costelloe
WAR WIDOWS ASSOCIATION OF GREAT BRITAIN
(1971), 199 Borough High Street, SE1 1AA T 0845-241 2189
E info@warwidows.org.uk W www.warwidows.org.uk
Chair, Irene Wills
WESTMINSTER FOUNDATION FOR DEMOCRACY
(1992), Artillery House, 11–19 Artillery Row,
London SW1P 1RT T 020-7799 1311 W www.wfd.org
Acting Chief Executive, Paul Naismith
WOMEN'S ENGINEERING SOCIETY (1919),
c/o The IET, Michael Faraday House, Six Hills Way,
Stevenage SG1 2AY T 01438-765506 E info@wes.org.uk
W www.wes.org.uk
Company Secretary, Milada Williams
WOMEN'S ROYAL NAVAL SERVICE BENEVOLENT
TRUST (1941), 311 Twyford Avenue, Portsmouth PO2 8RN
T 023-9265 5301 E generalsecretary@wrnsbt.org.uk
W www.wrnsbt.org.uk
General Secretary, Sarah Ayton
WOODLAND TRUST (1972), Kempton Way, Grantham
NG31 6LL T 01476-581111 E england@woodlandtrust.org.uk
W www.woodlandtrust.org.uk
Chief Executive, Beccy Speight
WORCESTERSHIRE ARCHAEOLOGICAL SOCIETY
(1854), 26 Albert Park Road, Malvern WR14 1HN
T 01684 565190
E secretary@worcestershirearchaeologicalsociety.org.uk
W www.worcestershirearchaeologicalsociety.org.uk
Hon. Secretary, Dr J. W. Dunleavey
YMCA (1844), 29–35 Farringdon Road, London EC1M 3JF
T 020-7186 9500 E enquiries@ymca.org.uk
W www.ymca.org.uk
Chief Executive, Denise Hatton
YORKSHIRE ARCHAEOLOGICAL SOCIETY (1863),
Claremont, 23 Clarendon Road, Leeds LS2 9NZ
T 0113-245 7910 E yas.secretary@googlemail.com
W www.yas.org.uk
General Secretary, Paul White
YOUTH HOSTELS ASSOCIATION (ENGLAND &
WALES) (1930), Trevelyan House, Dimple Road,
Matlock DE4 3YH T 01629-592600
E customerservices@yha.org.uk W www.yha.org.uk
Chief Executive, Caroline White
ZOOLOGICAL SOCIETY OF LONDON (1826),
Regent's Park, London NW1 4RY T 0844-225 1826
W www.zsl.org
President, Prof. Sir Patrick Bateson, FRS

THE WORLD

THE WORLD IN FIGURES

THE EARTH

The shape of the Earth is that of an oblate spheroid or solid of revolution whose meridian sections are ellipses, while the sections at right angles are circles.

DIMENSIONS
Equatorial diameter = 12,742.01km (7,917.51 miles)
Polar diameter = 12,713.50km (7,899.80 miles)
Equatorial circumference = 40,030.20km
(24,873.6 miles)
Polar circumference = 40,007.86km (24,859.73 miles)
Mass = 5,972,190,000,000,000,000,000,000kg
$(5.972 \times 10^{24}kg)$

The equatorial circumference is divided into 360 degrees of longitude, which is measured in degrees, minutes and seconds east or west of the Greenwich (or 'prime') meridian (0°) to 180°; the meridian 180° E coinciding with 180° W. This was internationally ratified in 1884.

Distance north and south of the equator is measured in degrees, minutes and seconds of latitude. The equator is 0°, the North Pole is 90°N. and the South Pole is 90°S. The tropics lie at 23° 27′ N. (tropic of cancer) and 23° 27′ S. (tropic of capricorn). The Arctic Circle lies at 66° 33′ N. and the Antarctic Circle at 66° 33′ S. (Note the tropics and the Arctic and Antarctic circles are affected by the slow decrease in obliquity of the ecliptic, of about 0.47 arcseconds per year. The effect of this is that the Arctic and Antarctic circles are currently moving towards their respective poles by about 14m per annum, while the tropics move towards the equator by the same amount.)

AREA ETC
The surface area of the Earth is 510,064,472km² (196,936,994 miles²), of which the water area is 70.92 per cent and the land area is 29.08 per cent.

The radial velocity on the Earth's surface at the equator is 1,669.79km per hour (1,037.56mph). The Earth's mean velocity in its orbit around the Sun is 107,218km per hour (66,622mph). The Earth's mean distance from the Sun is 149,598,262km (92,956,050 miles).

OCEANS

LARGEST BY AREA
	km²	miles²
Pacific	165,250,000	63,800,000
Atlantic	82,440,000	31,830,000
Indian	73,440,000	28,360,000
Southern	20,327,000	7,848,300
Arctic	14,090,000	5,440,000

The equator divides the Pacific into the North and South Pacific and the Atlantic into the North and South Atlantic. In 2000 the International Hydrographic Organisation approved the description of the 20,327,000km² (7,848,300 miles²) of circum-Antarctic waters up to 60°S. as the Southern Ocean.

GREATEST KNOWN OCEAN DEPTHS
Greatest depth	Location	metres	feet
Mariana Trench*	Pacific	10,911	35,798
Puerto Rico Trench	Atlantic	8,380	27,493
Diamantina Trench	Indian	8,047	26,401
South Sandwich Trench	Southern	7,235	23,737
Molloy Deep	Arctic	5,607	18,397

* On 23 January 1960, Jacques Piccard (Switzerland) and Don Walsh (USA) descended in the bathyscaphe *Trieste* to the floor of the Mariana Trench, a depth later calculated as 10,916m (35,814ft). The current depth was calculated by the Japanese remote-controlled probe *Kaiko* on 24 March 1995. On 1 June 2009, sonar mapping of the Challenger Deep in the Mariana Trench by the US oceanographic research vessel *Kilo Moana* indicated a possible depth of 10,971m (35,994ft).

SEAS

LARGEST BY AREA
	km²	miles²
South China	3,685,000	1,423,000
Caribbean	2,753,000	1,063,000
Mediterranean	2,509,900	969,100
Bering	2,304,000	890,000
Okhotsk	1,582,000	611,000
Gulf of Mexico	1,550,000	600,000
Japan	978,000	377,600
Hudson Bay	819,000	316,000
Andaman	798,000	308,000
East China	750,000	290,000
North Sea	570,000	220,000
Red Sea	453,000	174,900
Black Sea	422,000	163,000

GREATEST KNOWN SEA DEPTHS
Greatest depth	metres	feet
Caribbean (Cayman Trench)	7,686	25,216
Philippine Sea (Ryukyu Trench)	7,507	24,629
Mediterranean (Calypso Deep)	5,267	17,280
Gulf of Mexico (Sigsbee Deep)	5,203	17,070
South China	5,016	16,457
Andaman	4,400	14,500
Bering (Bowers Basin)	4,097	13,442
Japan	3,742	12,276
Okhotsk	3,372	11,063
Red Sea	3,040	9,974
Black Sea	2,212	7,257
North Sea	700	2,300

THE CONTINENTS

There are generally considered to be seven continents: Africa, North America, South America, Antarctica, Asia, Australia and Europe. Europe and Asia are sometimes considered a single continent: Eurasia, and North and South America are sometimes referred to together as the Americas.

AFRICA is surrounded by sea except for the narrow isthmus of Suez in the north-east, through which was cut the Suez Canal (opened 17 November 1869). Its extreme longitudes are 17° 20′ W. at Cabo Verde, Senegal, and 51° 24′ E. at Raas Xaafunn, Somalia. The extreme latitudes are 37° 20′ N. at Cape Blanc, Tunisia, and 34° 50′ S. at Cape

Agulhas, South Africa, about 7,081km (4,400 miles) apart. The equator passes across Gabon, Republic of the Congo, Uganda, Kenya and Somalia in the middle of the continent.

NORTH AMERICA, including Mexico, is surrounded by ocean except in the south, where the isthmian states of Central America link North America with South America. Its extreme longitudes are 168° 5′ W. at Cape Prince of Wales, Alaska, and 55° 40′ W. at Cape Charles, Newfoundland. The extreme continental latitudes are the tip of the Boothia peninsula, NW Territories, Canada (71° 51′ N.) and 14° 22′ N. in southern Mexico near La Victoria, Guatemala.

SOUTH AMERICA lies mostly in the southern hemisphere, the equator passing across Ecuador, Colombia and Brazil in the north of the continent. It is surrounded by ocean except where it is joined to Central America in the north by the narrow isthmus through which was cut the Panama Canal (opened 15 August 1914). Its extreme longitudes are 34° 47′ W. at Cape Branco in Brazil and 81° 20′ W. at Punta Pariña, Peru. The extreme continental latitudes are 12° 25′ N. at Punta Gallinas, Colombia, and 53° 54′ S. at the southernmost tip of Peninsula de Brunswick, Chile. Cape Horn, on Cape Island, Chile, lies in 55° 59′ S.

ANTARCTICA lies almost entirely within the Antarctic Circle (66° 33′ S.) and is the largest of the world's glaciated areas. Ninety-eight per cent of the continent is permanently covered in ice. The ice amounts to some 29 million km³ (7 million miles³) and represents more than 70 per cent of the world's fresh water. The ice sheet is on average 2.45km (1.5 miles) thick; if it were to melt, the world's seas would rise by more than 60m (197ft). The environment is too hostile for unsupported human habitation.

ASIA is the largest continent and occupies 29.6 per cent of the world's land surface. The extreme longitudes are 26° 05′ E. at Baba Buran, Turkey, and 169° 40′ W. at Mys Dezhneva, Russia, a distance of about 9,656km (6,000 miles). Its extreme northern latitude is 77° 45′ N. at Mys Chelyuskin, Russia, and it extends over 8,046km (5,000 miles) south to Tanjong Piai, Malaysia.

AUSTRALIA is the smallest of the continents and lies in the southern hemisphere. It is entirely surrounded by ocean. Its extreme longitudes are 113° 11′ E. at Steep Point, Western Australia, and 153° 11′ E. at Cape Byron, New South Wales. The extreme latitudes are 10° 42′ S. at Cape York, Queensland, and 39°S. at South East Point, Tasmania. Australia, together with New Zealand (Australasia), Papua New Guinea and the Pacific Islands, comprises Oceania.

EUROPE, including European Russia, is the smallest continent in the northern hemisphere. Its extreme latitudes are 71° 11′ N. at Nord Kapp in Norway, and 36° 23′ N. at Akra Tainaron (Matapas) in southern Greece, a distance of about 3,862km (2,400 miles). Its breadth from Cabo Carvoeiro in Portugal (9° 34′ W.) in the west to the Kara River, north of the Urals (66° 30′ E.) in the east is about 5,310km (3,300 miles). The division between Europe and Asia is generally regarded as the watershed of the Ural Mountains; down the Ural river to Atyrau, Kazakhstan; across the Caspian Sea to Apsheronskiy Poluostrov, near Baku; along the watershed of the Caucasus Mountains to Anapa and then across the Black Sea to the Bosporus in Turkey; across the Sea of Marmara to Canakkale Bogazi (Dardanelles).

Continent	Area	
	km²	miles²
Asia	44,614,000	17,226,000
Africa	30,365,000	11,724,000
North America	24,230,000	9,355,000
South America	17,814,000	6,878,000
Antarctica	14,200,000	5,500,000
Europe*	9,699,000	3,745,000
Australia	7,702,501	2,973,952

* Includes 5,571,000km² (2,151,000 miles²) of former USSR territory, including the Baltic states, Belarus, Moldova, Ukraine and the part of Russia west of the Ural Mountains and Kazakhstan west of the Ural river. European Turkey (24,378km²/9,412 miles²) comprises territory to the west and north of the Bosporus and the Dardanelles

GLACIATED AREAS

It is estimated that around 14,800,000km² (5,712,800 miles²) or 10 per cent of the world's land surface is permanently covered with ice. Glacial retreat and thinning occurs where glaciers melt faster than they are created. The phenomenon has been observed since the mid-19th century but has accelerated since about 1980 as a result of global warming. It is most notable in the Antarctic: a 2005 report by the American Association for the Advancement of Science indicated that 87 per cent of the continent's 244 marine glaciers have retreated over the past 50 years. The largest glacier is the 515km (320 miles) long Lambert-Fisher Ice Passage, Mac Robertson Land, Eastern Antarctica.

Location	Area	
	km²	miles²
South Polar regions	13,829,000	5,340,000
North Polar regions (incl. Greenland)	1,965,000	758,500

LARGEST ISLANDS

Island and ocean	Area	
	km²	miles²
Greenland (Kalaallit Nunaat), Arctic	2,166,086	836,330
New Guinea, Pacific	785,753	303,381
Borneo, Pacific	743,330	287,000
Madagascar, Indian	587,041	226,657
Baffin Island, Arctic	507,451	195,928
Sumatra, Indian	473,606	182,860
Honshu, Pacific	227,898	87,992
Great Britain, Atlantic	218,077	84,200
Victoria Island, Arctic	217,291	83,896
Ellesmere Island, Arctic	196,236	75,767

LARGEST DESERTS

Desert and location	Area (approx)	
	km²	miles²
Antarctica	14,200,000	5,500,000
Sahara, N. Africa	8,600,000	3,320,000
Arabian, Middle East	2,330,000	900,000
Gobi, Mongolia/China	1,300,000	500,000
Kalahari, Botswana/Namibia/ S. Africa	930,000	360,000
Patagonian, Argentina/Chile	670,000	260,000
Great Victoria, Australia	424,400	163,900
Syrian, Middle East	518,000	200,000

Desert and location	Area (approx)	
	km²	miles²
Great Basin, USA	492,000	190,000
Chihuahuan, USA/Mexico	450,000	175,000

DEEPEST DEPRESSIONS

Depression and location	Maximum depth below sea level	
	metres	feet
Dead Sea, Jordan/Israel	413	1,354
Lake Assal, Djibouti	157	515
Turfan Depression, Sinkiang, China	155	508
Qattara Depression, Egypt	133	435
Batyr Depression, Kazakhstan	130	425
Kobar Sink, Ethiopia	116	381
Death Valley, California, USA	86	282
Salton Sea, California, USA	69	227
Caspian Depression, Russia/Kazakhstan	27	90

The world's largest exposed depression is the Caspian Depression covering the hinterland of the northern third of the Caspian Sea, which is itself 27m (90ft) below sea level.

Western Antarctica and central Greenland largely comprise crypto-depressions under ice burdens. The Antarctic Bentley subglacial trench has a bedrock 2,538m (8,326ft) below sea level. In Greenland (lat. 73° N., long. 39° W.) the bedrock is 365m (1,197ft) below sea level.

Around 26 per cent of the area of the Netherlands lies marginally below sea level, an area of more than 10,000km² (3,860 miles²).

CAVES

DEEPEST CAVES

The world's deepest cave was discovered in January 2001 by a team of Ukrainian cave explorers in the Arabikskaya system in the western Caucasus mountains of Georgia. It is a branch of the Voronya or 'Crow's Cave'.

Cave system/location	Depth	
	metres	feet
Krubera (Voronya), Georgia	2,191	7,188
Illyuzia-Mezhonnogo-Snezhnaya, Georgia	1,753	5,751
Lamprechtsofen Vogelschacht, Austria	1,632	5,354
Gouffre Mirolda, France	1,626	5,335
Réseau Jean Bernard, France	1,602	5,256
Torca del Cerro del Cuevon/Torca de las Saxifragas, Spain	1,589	5,213
Sarma, Georgia	1,543	5,062
Shakta Vyacheslav, Georgia	1,508	4,947
Sima de la Cornisa (Torca Magali), Spain	1,507	4,944
Cehi 2, Slovenia	1,502	4,928
Sistema Cheve (Cuicateco), Mexico	1,484	4,868
Sistema Huautla, Mexico	1,475	4,839

LONGEST CAVE SYSTEMS

Cave system/location	Total known length	
	km	miles
Mammoth Cave System, Kentucky, USA	643.7	400
Jewel Cave, South Dakota, USA	241.6	150
Optymistychna, Ukraine	232.0	144
Wind Cave, South Dakota, USA	218.4	136
Sistema Sac Actun, Mexico (submerged, but dry)	217.4	135
Lechuguilla Cave, New Mexico, USA	209.6	130
Hölloch, Switzerland	195.9	122
Fisher Ridge System, Kentucky, USA	183.6	114
Sistema Ox Bel Ha, Mexico (submerged)	182.2	113
Gua Air Jernih, Malaysia	175.7	109
Siebenhengste-hohgant, Switzerland	156.0	97
Schoenbergsystem, Austria	130.2	81

LONGEST MOUNTAIN RANGES

Range and location	Length	
	km	miles
Cordillera de Los Andes, South America	8,900	5,500
Rocky Mountains, North America	4,800	3,000
Great Dividing Range, Australia	3,700	2,300
Transantarctic Mountains, Antarctica	3,200	2,000
West Sumatran-Javan Range, Indonesia	2,900	1,800
Serra do Mar, Brazil	2,600	1,600
Himalaya, Central Asia	2,500	1,550
Tien Shan, Central Asia	2,400	1,500
Central New Guinea Range, New Guinea	2,010	1,250

HIGHEST MOUNTAINS

Mountain (first ascent)	Height	
	metres	feet
Mt Everest* [Qomolangma] (29 May 1953)	8,848	29,028
K2 [Qogir]† (31 July 1954)	8,611	28,251
Kangchenjunga (25 May 1955)	8,586	28,169
Lhotse (18 May 1956)	8,501	27,890
Makalu (15 May 1955)	8,463	27,766
Cho Oyu (19 October 1954)	8,201	26,906
Dhaulagiri I (13 May 1960)	8,167	26,795
Manaslu I [Kutang I] (9 May 1956)	8,163	26,781
Nanga Parbat [Diamir] (3 July 1953)	8,126	26,660
Annapurna I (3 June 1950)	8,091	26,545

* Named after Sir George Everest (1790–1866), Surveyor-General of India 1830–43, in 1863. He pronounced his name 'Eve-rest'.

† Formerly named after Col. Henry Haversham Godwin-Austen (1834–1923), who worked on the Trigonometrical Survey of India, which established the heights of the Himalayan peaks, including Everest

The culminating summits in the other major mountain ranges are:

Mountain, by range or country	Height	
	metres	feet
Victory Peak [Pik Pobedy], Tien Shan	7,439	24,406
Mt Aconcagua, Cordillera de Los Andes	6,959	22,831
Mt McKinley (S. Peak), Alaska Range	6,194	20,320
Kilimanjaro (Kibo), Tanzania	5,895	19,340
Hkakabo Razi, Myanmar	5,881	19,296
Mt Elbrus, (W. Peak), Caucasus	5,642	18,510
Citlaltépetl [Orizaba], Mexico	5,610	18,406
Jaya Peak, Central New Guinea Range	5,030	16,500
Vinson Massif, Antarctica	4,892	16,050
Mt Blanc, Alps	4,807	15,771

HIGHEST ACTIVE VOLCANOES

Although it displays fumarolic activity, emitting steam and gas, no major eruption has ever been observed of the world's highest volcano and second highest peak in the western hemisphere, the 6,893m (22,615ft) Ojos del Salado, in the Andes on the

Argentina/Chile border. For comparison, Eyjafjallajokull, the Icelandic volcano which erupted in 2010 causing air transport chaos, has an elevation of 1,666m (5,466ft).

The volcanoes listed below include only those that have had activity recorded since 1960.

Volcano and location (most recent activity)	Height	
	metres	feet
San Pedro, Andes, Chile (1960)	6,145	20,161
Aracar, Andes, Argentina (1993)	6,082	19,954
Volcan Guallatiri, Andes, Chile (1960)	6,071	19,918
Tupungatito, Andes, Chile (1987)	6,000	19,685
Sabancaya, Andes, Peru (2003)	5,967	19,577
San José, Andes, Argentina/Chile (1960)	5,856	19,213
Lascar, Andes, Chile (2007)	5,591	18,346
Popocatepetl, Mexico (2010)	5,426	17,802
Nevado del Ruiz, Colombia (1991)	5,321	17,457
Sangay, Andes, Ecuador (2010)	5,230	17,159
Irruputuncu, Chile (1995)	5,163	16,939
Tungurahua, Ecuador (2010)	5,023	16,479
Kliochevskoi, Kamchatka peninsula, Russia (2010)	4,835	15,863

LAKES

LARGEST LAKES

The areas of some of the lakes listed are subject to seasonal variation. The most voluminous lakes are the Caspian Sea (saline) with 78,200km³ (18,800 miles³) and Baikal (fresh water) with 23,000km³ (5,518 miles³). Baikal is also the world's deepest lake (see below). It is estimated that it contains as much water as the entire Great Lakes system in North America – more than 20 per cent of the world's fresh water and some 90 per cent of all the fresh water in Russia.

The Aral was once the fifth largest in the world, with an area of 68,000km² (26,255 miles²), but since the 1960s many of its feeder rivers have been diverted for irrigation, as a result of which its area shrank to 17,160km² (6,626 miles²). Its salinity was almost three times that of seawater, and pollution led to the extinction of many aquatic species. Since the construction of the Kok-Aral dam (2005), water levels are rising again, especially in the north.

Lake and location	Area		Length	
	km²	miles²	km	miles
Caspian Sea, Iran/ Azerbaijan/Russia/ Turkmenistan/ Kazakhstan	386,400	149,200	1,200	750
Michigan–Huron, USA/Canada*	117,610	45,300	1,010	627
Superior, Canada/USA	82,100	31,700	563	350
Victoria, Uganda/ Tanzania/Kenya	69,484	26,828	337	210
Tanganyika, Dem. Rep. of Congo/Tanzania/ Zambia/Burundi	32,900	12,700	660	410
Baikal, Russia	31,500	12,200	636	395
Great Bear, Canada	31,328	12,096	320	200
Malawi [Nyasa], Tanzania/Malawi/ Mozambique	29,604	11,430	584	363
Great Slave, Canada	28,568	11,030	480	298
Erie, Canada/USA	25,670	9,910	388	241

* Lakes Michigan and Huron may be regarded as lobes of the same lake. The Michigan lobe has an area of 57,750km² (22,300 miles²) and the Huron lobe an area of 59,570km² (23,000 miles²)

UNITED KINGDOM (BY COUNTRY)

Lake and location	Area		Length	
	km²	miles²	km	miles
Lough Neagh, Northern Ireland	396.00	153.00	28.90	18.00
Loch Lomond, Scotland	71.12	27.46	36.44	22.64
Windermere, England	14.74	5.69	16.90	10.50
Lake Vyrnwy, Wales (artificial)	4.53	1.75	7.56	4.70
Llyn Tegid [Bala], Wales	4.38	1.69	5.80	3.65

LARGEST MANMADE LAKES

Dam/lake* (year of completion)	Volume	
	km³	miles³
Nalubaale dam [Owen Falls], Uganda/Kenya/Tanzania (1954)	204.80	49.13
Kariba, Zimbabwe/Zambia (1959)	180.60	43.33
Bratsk, Russia (1967)	169.27	40.61
Nasser, Egypt (1970)	168.90	40.52
Volta, Ghana (1965)	153.00	36.71
Manicouagan [Daniel Johnson dam], Canada (1968)	141.85	34.03
Guri [Raul Leoni], Venezuela (1986)	138.00	33.11
Krasnoyarskoye, Russia (1967)	73.30	17.58
Wadi-Tatar, Iraq (1967)	72.80	17.46
Williston (W. A. C. Bennett dam), Canada (1967)	70.31	16.87

* Formed as a result of dam construction
The UK's largest reservoir is Kielder Water, Northumberland (1982) with a volume of 0.2km³ (0.048 miles³)

DEEPEST LAKES

Lake and location	Greatest depth	
	metres	feet
Baikal, Russia	1,637	5,371
Tanganyika, Burundi/Tanzania/Dem. Rep. of Congo/Zambia	1,436	4,710
Caspian Sea, Azerbaijan/Iran/ Kazakhstan/Russia/Turkmenistan	1,025	3,363
O'Higgins [San Martin], Chile/Argentina	836	2,743
Malawi [Nyasa], Malawi/Mozambique/ Tanzania	704	2,310
Ysyk, Kyrgyzstan	668	2,192
Great Slave, Canada	614	2,015
Quesnel, Canada	610	2,001
Crater, Oregon, USA	592	1,943
Matano, South Sulawesi, Indonesia	590	1,936
Buenos Aires [General Carrera], Argentina/Chile	586	1,923
Hornindalsvastnet, Norway	514	1,686
Sarez, Tajikistan	505	1,657
Toba, Sumatra, Indonesia	505	1,657
Argentino, Argentina	500	1,640
Tahoe, California/Nevada, USA	500	1,640

Loch Morar, Highland, Scotland is the UK's deepest lake at 310m (1,017ft).

LONGEST RIVERS

River, source–outflow	Length	
	km	miles
Nile [Bahr-el-Nil], R. Luvironza, Burundi–E. Mediterranean Sea	6,650	4,132
Amazon [Amazonas], Lago Villafro, Peru–S. Atlantic Ocean	6,448	4,007

River, source–outflow	Length	
	km	miles
Yangtze [Chang Jiang], Kunlun Mts, W. China–Yellow Sea	6,300	3,915
Mississippi-Missouri-Red Rock, Montana–Gulf of Mexico	5,971	3,710
Yenisey-Selenga, W. Mongolia–Kara Sea	5,539	3,442
Huang He [Yellow River], Bayan Har Shan range, Central China–Yellow Sea	5,464	3,395
Ob-Irtysh, W. Mongolia–Kara Sea	5,410	3,362
Congo [Zambia], R. Lualaba, Dem. Rep. of Congo-Zambia–S. Atlantic Ocean	4,665	2,900
Amur-Argun, R. Argun, Khingan Mts, N. China–Sea of Okhotsk	4,416	2,744
Lena, R. Kirenga, W. of Lake Baikal–Laptev Sea, Arctic Ocean	4,400	2,734

BRITISH ISLES

River, source–outflow	Length	
	km	miles
Shannon, Co. Cavan, Rep. of Ireland–Atlantic Ocean	372	231
Severn, Powys, Wales–Bristol Channel	354	220
Thames, Gloucestershire, England–North Sea	330	205
Tay, Perthshire, Scotland–North Sea	193	120
Clyde, Lanarkshire, Scotland–Firth of Clyde	170	106
Tweed, Scottish Borders–North Sea	155	96.5
Bann (Upper and Lower), Co. Down, N. Ireland–Atlantic Ocean	129	80

WATERFALLS

GREATEST BY HEIGHT

Waterfall, river and location	Total drop		Greatest single leap	
	metres	feet	metres	feet
Angel, Carrao Auyan Tepui, Venezuela	979	3,212	807	2,648
Tugela, Tugela, S. Africa (5 leaps)	947	3,110	411	1,350
Ramnefjellsfossen, Jostedal Glacier, Norway	800	2,625	600	1,970
Mongefossen, Monge, Norway	773	2,535	–	–
Gocta, Cocahuayco, Peru	771	2,531	–	–
Mutarazi, Mutarazi, Zimbabwe	762	2,499	479	1,572
Yosemite, Yosemite Creek, USA	740	2,425	436	1,430
Ostre Mardola Foss, Mardals, Norway*	655	2,149	296	974
Tyssestrengene, Tysso, Norway*	646	2,120	289	948
Kukenaam, Arabopo, Venezuela	610	2,000	–	–

* Volume much affected by hydroelectric harnessing

POPULATIONS

MOST POPULOUS COUNTRIES IN THE WORLD

Country	Population*	Area (sq. km)	World Comparison
China	1,355,692,576	9,596,961	4
India	1,236,344,631	3,287,263	7
USA	318,892,103	9,826,675	3
Indonesia	253,609,643	1,904,569	15
Brazil	202,656,788	8,514,877	5
Pakistan	196,174,380	796,095	36
Nigeria	177,155,754	923,768	32
Bangladesh	166,280,712	143,998	95
Russia	142,470,272	17,098,242	1
Japan	127,103,388	377,915	62

*July 2014 estimate

POPULATION GROWTH RATE

Top 10		Bottom 10	
Country	Growth Rate (%)	Country	Growth Rate (%)
Lebanon	9.37	Syria	−9.73
Zimbabwe	4.36	Moldova	−1.02
South Sudan	4.12	Bulgaria	−0.83
Jordan	3.86	Estonia	−0.68
Qatar	3.58	Ukraine	−0.64
Malawi	3.33	Latvia	−0.62
Niger	3.28	Montenegro	−0.49
Burundi	3.28	South Africa	−0.48
Uganda	3.24	Serbia	−0.46
Libya	3.08	Fed. States of Micronesia	−0.42

DAMS

TALLEST DAMS

Dam and location (year of completion)	Height	
	metres	feet
Jinping-I, China (2014)	305	1,001
Nurek, Tajikistan (1980)	300	984
Xiaowan, China (2010)	292	958
Dibang, India (2017*)	288	945
Grande Dixence, Switzerland (1961)	285	935
Xiluodu, China (2014)	278	912
Inguri, Georgia (1980)	272	892
Vajont, Italy (1961)†	262	859
Nuozhadu, China (2013)	262	858
Manuel Moreno Torres, Mexico (1981)	261	856

* Scheduled completion date
† Disused

TALLEST

All heights are in accordance with the Council on Tall Buildings and Urban Habitat's regulations, which measure from the ground level of the main entrance to the architectural tip of the building and include spires but not antennae, signage or flag poles.

INHABITED BUILDINGS

Building and location (year of completion)	Height	
	metres	feet
Burj Khalifa, Dubai, UAE (2010)	828	2,717
Shanghai Tower, Shanghai, China (2015*)	632	2,073
Abraj Al-Bait, Mecca, Saudi Arabia (2012)	601	1,972
One World Trade Center, New York, USA (2014)	541	1,776
Taipei 101, Taipei, Taiwan (2004)	508	1,667
Shanghai World Finance Centre, Shanghai, China (2008)	492	1,614

Building and location (year of completion)

	Height	
	metres	feet
International Commerce Centre, Hong Kong, China (2010)	484	1,588
Petronas Towers I and II, Kuala Lumpur, Malaysia (1998)	452	1,482
Zifeng Tower, Nanjing, China (2010)	450	1,476
KK100, Shenzhen, China (2011)	442	1,450
Willis Tower, Chicago, USA (1974)†	442	1,450
Guangzhou International Finance Centre, China (2010)	439	1,440
Trump International Hotel and Tower, Chicago, USA (2009)	423	1,389
Jin Mao Tower, Shanghai, China (1999)	421	1,380
Princess Tower, Dubai, UAE (2012)	413	1,356
Al Hamra Tower, Kuwait (2011)	412	1,354
Two International Finance Centre, Hong Kong, China (2003)	412	1,354

* Scheduled completion date
† With TV antennae, 520m (1,707ft)

STRUCTURES

Structure and location (year of completion)

Tokyo Skytree, Tokyo, Japan (2012)	634	2,080
KVLY (formerly KTHI)-TV Mast, North Dakota (guyed), USA (1963)*	629	2,063
Canton, Guangzhou, China (2010)	600	1,968
CN Tower, Toronto, Canada (1976)	553	1,815
Ostankino Tower, Moscow, Russia (1967)	540	1,774

* The USA has numerous other guyed TV towers above 600m (1,969ft)

TWIN TOWERS

Structure and location (year of completion)

	Floors	Height	
		metres	feet
Petronas Towers, Kuala Lumpur, Malaysia (1998)	88	452	1,483
Emirates Park Towers, Dubai, UAE (2012)	82	355	1,166
SPG Globel Twin Towers, Suzhou, China (2010)	54	282	925
The Cullinan, Hong Kong, China (2008)	68	270	886
Al Kazim Towers, Dubai, UAE (2008)	53	265	869
Grand Gateway, Shanghai, China (2005)	54	262	859
Dual Towers, Manama, Bahrain (2007)	53	260	853
The Imperial, Mumbai, India (2009)	60	256	840
Al Fattan Towers, Dubai, UAE (2006)	51	245	804
Abraj Al Bait Towers, Mecca, Saudi Arabia (2012)	42	240	787

Destroyed 2001

World Trade Center One, New York City, USA (1972)	110	417	1,368
World Trade Center Two, New York City, USA (1973)	110	415	1,362

CHURCHES

Structure and location (year of completion)

	Height	
	metres	feet
Sagrada Família, Barcelona, Spain (2026*)	170	560
Ulm Cathedral, Ulm, Germany (1890)	162	530
Our Lady of Peace Basilica, Yamoussoukro, Côte d'Ivoire (1990)	158	518
Cologne Cathedral, Cologne, Germany (1880)	157	515
Notre-Dame Cathedral, Rouen, France (1876)	151	495
St Nicholas Church, Hamburg, Germany (1874)	148	485
Notre-Dame Cathedral, Strasbourg, France (1439)	144	472
Queen of Peace Shrine and Basilica, Lichen, Poland (2004)	140	459
Basilica of St Peter, Rome, Italy (1626)	138	452
St Stephen's Cathedral, Vienna, Austria (1433)	137	448

* Scheduled completion date, the 100th anniversary of the death of its architect, Antoni Gaudí; open for worship following its consecration by Pope Benedict XVI in 2010

The Chicago Methodist Temple, Chicago, USA (completed 1924) is 173m (568ft) high, but is sited atop a 25-storey, 100m (328ft) building. Salisbury Cathedral (1521), at 123m (404ft), is the UK's tallest religious building. St Paul's Cathedral, London, and Liverpool Anglican Cathedral are the only others in the UK over 100m (328ft) tall. At 94m (309ft) the Church of St Walburge, Preston, Lancashire is the tallest church in Britain that is not a cathedral.

TALLEST STRUCTURES – A CHRONOLOGY

Structure and location	Year	Height	
		metres	feet
Djoser's Step Pyramid, Saqqara, Egypt	c.2650 BC	62	204
Pyramid of Meidum, Egypt	c.2600 BC	92	302
Snefru's Bent Pyramid, Dahshur, Egypt	c.2600 BC	102	336
Red Pyramid, Dahshur, Egypt	c.2590 BC	104	341
Great Pyramid, Giza, Egypt*	c.2580 BC	147	481
Liuhe (Six Harmonies) Pagoda, Hangzhou, China†	AD 970	150	492
Lincoln Cathedral, Lincoln, England‡	1311–1400	160	525
St Paul's Cathedral, London, England§	1315	149	489
St Mary's Church, Stralsund, Germany	1384–1478	151	495
St Olaf's Church, Tallinn, Estonia₵	1438–1519	159	522
Notre-Dame Cathedral, Strasbourg, France	1439	142	466
St Nicholas Church, Hamburg, Germany	1874	147	482
Notre-Dame Cathedral, Rouen, France	1876	151	495
Cologne Cathedral, Cologne, Germany	1880	157	515
Washington Monument, Washington DC, USA	1884	169	555
Eiffel Tower, Paris, France	1889	300	984
Chrysler Building, New York, USA	1930	319	1,046
Empire State Building, New York, USA	1931	381	1,250
KWTV Mast, Oklahoma City, USA	1954	481	1,577
KOBR-TV Tower, Caprock, USA	1960	490	1,608
KFVS TV Mast, Egypt Mills, USA	1960	511	1,677

Structure and location	Year	Height	
		metres	feet
KVLY (formerly KTHI)-TV Mast, Blanchard, USA	1963	629	2,063
Warszawa Radio Mast, Konstantynow, Poland**	1974	646	2,120
Burj Khalifa, Dubai, UAE	2010	828	2,717

* Later reduced through loss of topstone to 137m (449ft)
† Destroyed in 1121
‡ Destroyed in 1549
§ Destroyed in 1561
℃ Spire burned down in 1625; renovated in 1931 to present height of 123m (403ft)
** Collapsed in 1991 during renovation

BRIDGES

The longest stretch of bridging of any kind is the Danyang–Kunshan Grand Bridge (2010) in China at 164km (102 miles). The 'floating' bridging at Evergreen Point, Seattle, Washington, USA (1963), is 3,839m (12,596ft) long, of which 2,310m (7,578ft) floats.

LONGEST SUSPENSION SPANS

Bridge and location (year of completion)	Length	
	metres	feet
Akashi-Kaikyo, Japan (1998)	1,991	6,532
Xihoumen, China (2009)	1,650	5,413
Great Belt Bridge, Denmark (1998)	1,624	5,328
Yi Sun-sin, South Korea (2012)	1,545	5,069
Runyang, China (2005)	1,490	4,888
Nanjing Fourth Yangtze, China (2012)	1,418	4,652
Humber, England (1981)	1,410	4,626
Jiangyin, China (1999)	1,385	4,544
Tsing Ma, Hong Kong, China (1997)	1,377	4,518
Hardanger, Norway (2013)	1,310	4,298

LONGEST CANTILEVER SPANS

Bridge and location (year of completion)	Length	
	metres	feet
Pont de Québec, St Lawrence, Canada (1917)	548.6	1,800
Firth of Forth, Scotland (two spans of 1,710ft each) (1890)	521.2	1,710
Minato, Japan (1974)	510.0	1,673
Commodore Barry, New Jersey/Pennsylvania, USA (1974)	501.1	1,644
Crescent City Connection, Louisiana, USA (I 1958, II 1988)	480.0	1,575
Howrah, India (1943)	457.2	1,500
Veterans Memorial, Louisiana, USA (1995)	445.0	1,460
San Francisco Oakland Bay, California, USA (1936)	426.7	1,400
Horace Wilkinson, Louisiana, USA (1968)	376.0	1,235
Tappan Zee, New York, USA (1955)	369.0	1,212

LONGEST STEEL ARCH SPANS

Bridge and location (year of completion)	Length	
	metres	feet
Sheikh Rashid bin Saeed Crossing, Dubai, UAE (2015*)	667.0	2,188
Chaotianmen, China (2009)	552.0	1,811
Lupu, China (2003)	550.0	1,804
New River Gorge, West Virginia, USA (1977)	518.0	1,700
Bayonne [Kill van Kull], New Jersey/New York, USA (1931)	510.0	1,675
Sydney Harbour, Australia (1932)	502.9	1,650
Yongjiang, China (2011)	464.0	1,522
Chenab, India (2017*)	460.0	1,509
Wushan, China (2005)	460.0	1,509
Mingzhou, China (2011)	450.0	1,476

* Scheduled completion date

LONGEST SHIP CANALS

Canal	Length		Min. depth	
	km	miles	metres	feet
White Sea–Baltic [formerly Stalin] (1933), of which canalised river 51.5km (32 miles)	227	141.00	5.0	16.5
Rhine–Main–Danube, Germany (1992)	171	106.25	4.0	13.1
*Suez (1869), links Red and Mediterranean Seas	162	100.60	12.9	42.3
V. I. Lenin Volga–Don, Russia (1952), links Black and Caspian Seas	100	62.20	3.6	11.8
Kiel (or North Sea), Germany (1895), links North and Baltic Seas	98	60.90	11.0	37.0
Alphonse XIII, Spain (1926), gives Seville access to Atlantic Ocean	85	53.00	7.6	25.0
Panama (1914), links Pacific Ocean and Caribbean Sea; lake chain, 78.9km (49 miles) dug	82	50.71	13.0	43.0
*Houston, USA (1940), links inland city with Gulf of Mexico	81	50.50	11.0	36.0
Danube–Black Sea, Romania (1984)	64.4	40.02	7.0	23.0
Manchester Ship, UK (1894), links city with Irish Channel	58	36.00	8.5	28.0

* Has no locks

The first section of China's Grand Canal, running 1,782km (1,107 miles) from Beijing to Hangzhou, was opened in AD 610 and completed in 1283. Today it is limited to 2,000-tonne vessels.

The St Lawrence Seaway comprises the Beauharnois, Welland and Welland Bypass and Seaway 54–59 canals, and allows access to Duluth, Minnesota, USA via the Great Lakes from the Atlantic end of Canada's Gulf of St Lawrence, a distance of 3,769km (2,342 miles). The St Lawrence Canal, completed in 1959, is 293km (182 miles) long.

AIR DISTANCES

	London (LHR)	Paris (CDG)	Madrid (MAD)	Rome (FCO)	Moscow (DME)	Dubai (DXB)	New York (JFK)	Delhi (DEL)	Beijing (PEK)	Los Angeles (LAX)	Durban (DUR)	Bangkok (BKK)	Tokyo (HND)	Hong Kong (HKG)	Singapore (SIN)	Buenos Aires (BHI)	Sydney (SYD)
London (LHR)		216 / 348km	773 / 1,244km	899 / 1,446km	1,587 / 2,553km	3,421 / 5,505km	3,452 / 5,554km	4,191 / 6,744km	5,081 / 8,175km	5,457 / 8,780km	5,904 / 9,499km	5,959 / 9,588km	5,975 / 9,614km	5,996 / 9,647km	6,767 / 10,888km	7,241 / 11,651km	10,575 / 17,016km
Paris (CDG)	216 / 348km		660 / 1,063km	685 / 1,102km	1,547 / 2,489km	3,260 / 5,245km	3,635 / 5,849km	4,088 / 6,578km	5,103 / 8,211km	5,671 / 9,124km	5,692 / 9,159km	5,879 / 9,459km	6,047 / 9,730km	5,971 / 9,607km	6,668 / 10,729km	7,220 / 11,617km	10,529 / 16,941km
Madrid (MAD)	773 / 1,244km	660 / 1,063km		829 / 1,334km	2,140 / 3,444km	3,517 / 5,659km	3,589 / 5,775km	4,518 / 7,269km	5,734 / 9,226km	5,846 / 9,406km	5,312 / 8,546km	6,343 / 10,206km	6,706 / 10,790km	6,541 / 10,524km	7,079 / 11,390km	6,589 / 10,602km	10,986 / 17,676km
Rome (FCO)	899 / 1,446km	685 / 1,102km	829 / 1,334km		1,491 / 2,398km	2,703 / 4,349km	4,278 / 6,884km	3,694 / 5,944km	5,076 / 8,167km	6,356 / 10,226km	5,059 / 8,140km	5,523 / 8,886km	6,162 / 9,915km	5,779 / 9,298km	6,250 / 10,057km	7,252 / 11,668km	10,157 / 16,342km
Moscow (DME)	1,587 / 2,553km	1,547 / 2,489km	2,140 / 3,444km	1,491 / 2,398km		2,262 / 3,639km	4,702 / 7,566km	2,679 / 4,311km	3,605 / 5,800km	6,122 / 9,851km	5,868 / 9,441km	4,388 / 7,060km	4,672 / 7,518km	4,424 / 7,118km	5,218 / 8,396km	8,720 / 14,031km	8,992 / 14,468km
Dubai (DXB)	3,421 / 5,505km	3,260 / 5,245km	3,517 / 5,659km	2,703 / 4,349km	2,262 / 3,639km		6,850 / 11,022km	1,359 / 2,187km	3,639 / 5,855km	8,340 / 13,420km	4,102 / 6,600km	3,051 / 4,909km	4,941 / 7,949km	3,685 / 5,929km	3,634 / 5,847km	8,733 / 14,051km	7,482 / 12,039km
New York (JFK)	3,452 / 5,554km	3,635 / 5,849km	3,589 / 5,775km	4,278 / 6,884km	4,702 / 7,566km	6,850 / 11,022km		7,319 / 11,777km	6,839 / 11,004km	2,475 / 3,983km	8,249 / 13,273km	8,678 / 13,963km	6,774 / 10,899km	8,074 / 12,990km	9,539 / 15,349km	5,511 / 8,868km	9,952 / 16,013km
Delhi (DEL)	4,191 / 6,744km	4,088 / 6,578km	4,518 / 7,269km	3,694 / 5,944km	2,679 / 4,311km	1,359 / 2,187km	7,319 / 11,777km		2,371 / 3,815km	8,015 / 12,896km	5,024 / 8,083km	1,831 / 2,947km	3,649 / 5,871km	2,332 / 3,752km	2,580 / 4,152km	10,017 / 16,117km	6,477 / 10,422km
Beijing (PEK)	5,081 / 8,175km	5,103 / 8,211km	5,734 / 9,226km	5,076 / 8,167km	3,605 / 5,800km	3,639 / 5,855km	6,839 / 11,004km	2,371 / 3,815km		6,252 / 10,059km	7,276 / 11,707km	2,057 / 3,309km	1,303 / 2,097km	1,235 / 1,987km	2,781 / 4,474km	12,321 / 19,825km	5,553 / 8,934km
Los Angeles (LAX)	5,457 / 8,780km	5,671 / 9,124km	5,846 / 9,406km	6,356 / 10,226km	6,122 / 9,851km	8,340 / 13,420km	2,475 / 3,983km	8,015 / 12,896km	6,252 / 10,059km		10,635 / 17,111km	8,271 / 13,308km	5,489 / 8,831km	7,261 / 11,684km	8,772 / 14,114km	6,164 / 9,918km	7,490 / 12,051km
Durban (DUR)	5,904 / 9,499km	5,692 / 9,159km	5,312 / 8,546km	5,059 / 8,140km	5,868 / 9,441km	4,102 / 6,600km	8,249 / 13,273km	5,024 / 8,083km	7,276 / 11,707km	10,635 / 17,111km		5,511 / 8,868km	8,353 / 13,440km	6,560 / 10,555km	5,244 / 8,438km	5,147 / 8,282km	6,571 / 10,573km
Bangkok (BKK)	5,959 / 9,588km	5,879 / 9,459km	6,343 / 10,206km	5,523 / 8,886km	4,388 / 7,060km	3,051 / 4,909km	8,678 / 13,963km	1,831 / 2,947km	2,057 / 3,309km	8,271 / 13,308km	5,511 / 8,868km		2,853 / 4,590km	1,049 / 1,688km	877 / 1,411km	10,420 / 16,766km	4,663 / 7,503km
Tokyo (HND)	5,975 / 9,614km	6,047 / 9,730km	6,706 / 10,790km	6,162 / 9,915km	4,672 / 7,518km	4,941 / 7,949km	6,774 / 10,899km	3,649 / 5,871km	1,303 / 2,097km	5,489 / 8,831km	8,353 / 13,440km	2,853 / 4,590km		1,805 / 2,904km	3,289 / 5,292km	11,217 / 18,048km	4,838 / 7,785km
Hong Kong (HKG)	5,996 / 9,647km	5,971 / 9,607km	6,541 / 10,524km	5,779 / 9,298km	4,424 / 7,118km	3,685 / 5,929km	8,074 / 12,990km	2,332 / 3,752km	1,235 / 1,987km	7,261 / 11,684km	6,560 / 10,555km	1,049 / 1,688km	1,805 / 2,904km		1,588 / 2,555km	11,278 / 18,147km	4,582 / 7,372km
Singapore (SIN)	6,767 / 10,888km	6,668 / 10,729km	7,079 / 11,390km	6,250 / 10,057km	5,218 / 8,396km	3,634 / 5,847km	9,539 / 15,349km	2,580 / 4,152km	2,781 / 4,474km	8,772 / 14,114km	5,244 / 8,438km	877 / 1,411km	3,289 / 5,292km	1,588 / 2,555km		9,717 / 15,634km	3,908 / 6,288km
Buenos Aires (BHI)	7,241 / 11,651km	7,220 / 11,617km	6,589 / 10,602km	7,252 / 11,668km	8,720 / 14,031km	8,733 / 14,051km	5,511 / 8,868km	10,017 / 16,117km	12,321 / 19,825km	6,164 / 9,918km	5,147 / 8,282km	10,420 / 16,766km	11,217 / 18,048km	11,278 / 18,147km	9,717 / 15,634km		6,996 / 11,257km
Sydney (SYD)	10,575 / 17,016km	10,529 / 16,941km	10,986 / 17,676km	10,157 / 16,342km	8,992 / 14,468km	7,482 / 12,039km	9,952 / 16,013km	6,477 / 10,422km	5,553 / 8,934km	7,490 / 12,051km	6,571 / 10,573km	4,663 / 7,503km	4,838 / 7,785km	4,582 / 7,372km	3,908 / 6,288km	6,996 / 11,257km	

Figures are in miles, and represent the great circle distance (the shortest distance between two points on the surface of the earth)

TRAVEL OVERSEAS

PASSPORT REGULATIONS

Application forms for UK passports can be obtained from Her Majesty's Passport Office's telephone advice line or website, regional passport offices, or from main post offices.

HM PASSPORT OFFICE
T 0300-222 0000
W www.gov.uk/government/organisations/hm-passport-office

REGIONAL OFFICES

- Law Society House, 90–106 Victoria Street, Belfast BT1 3GN
- Millburngate House, Durham DH97 1PA
- 3 Northgate, 96 Milton Street, Cowcaddens, Glasgow G4 0BT
- 101 Old Hall Street, Liverpool L3 9BD
- Globe House, 89 Eccleston Square, London SW1V 1PN
- Nexus House, Mission Court, Newport NP20 2DW
- Aragon Court, Northminster Road, Peterborough PE1 1QG

The passport offices are open Monday to Saturday on an appointment-only basis (appointments should be arranged by calling the central telephone number listed above). For an additional fee, passport offices provide either a premium one-day service (not available for a first adult or child passport, extending a limited passport, replacing a lost, stolen or damaged passport or for complex amendments) or a one-week fast track service (except for first adult passports).

Standard postal applications take at least three weeks to be processed. The completed application form should be posted, with the appropriate supporting documents and fee, to the regional passport office indicated on the addressed envelope which is provided with each application form. Accompanying cheques should be made payable to 'Her Majesty's Passport Office', or to 'Post Office Ltd' when using the Check & Send service. For online applications, the completed online form will be printed out by the applicant, signed and posted to the Passport Office. After the paper copy has been received, online applications are returned within three weeks.

Applications can also be submitted through Check & Send outlets at selected main post offices, who, for a small handling charge of £8.75, will forward the application form to the relevant regional passport office after having checked that it has been completed correctly and has the appropriate documents attached. These applications take a minimum of two weeks (first adult passport applications may take six weeks including a passport interview).

A passport cannot be issued or extended on behalf of a person already abroad; such persons should apply to the nearest local embassy, British High Commission or Consulate.

UK passports are granted to British citizens, British nationals (overseas), British overseas territories citizens, British overseas citizens, British subjects and British protected persons, and are generally available for travel to all countries. The possession of a passport does not exempt the holder from compliance with any immigration regulations in force in British or foreign countries, or from the necessity of obtaining a visa where required (see below for a list of countries for which UK citizens do not require a visa).

Biometric passports were introduced in 2006. The design and security features, including a chip containing the biometrics (the facial image and biographical data of the holder), render the passport more secure against forgery and aid border controls.

ADULTS

A passport granted to a person over 16 will normally be valid for ten years. Thereafter, or if at any time the passport contains no further space for visas, a new passport must be obtained.

British nationals born on or before 2 September 1929 are eligible for a free standard passport.

CHILDREN

Since 5 October 1998 all children under the age of 16 are required to have their own passport. This is primarily to help prevent child abductions. The passports are initially valid for five years, but can be renewed for a further five years at the end of this period.

COUNTERSIGNATURES

A countersignature is needed if the application is for a first passport, to replace a lost, stolen or damaged passport, or to renew a passport for a child aged 11 or under. A countersignature is also needed for renewals if the applicant's appearance has significantly changed and the photograph in their previous passport is unrecognisable. The signatory must be willing to enter their own passport number on to the form. The list of acceptable countersignatories includes: MP; justice of the peace; minister of religion; a professionally qualified person (eg doctor, engineer, lawyer, teacher); bank officer; military officer; airline pilot; police officer; or a person of similar standing who has known the applicant for at least two years, who lives in the UK and who holds a British or Irish passport. A relative or partner, someone living at the same address as the applicant, or an employee of HM Passport Office must not countersign the application.

PHOTOGRAPHS

Two identical, unmounted, recent colour photographs of the applicant must be sent. These photographs should measure 45mm by 35mm, be printed on plain white photographic paper and should be taken full face against a plain cream or light grey background. The photo must show the applicant's full face, looking straight at the camera, with a neutral expression and with their mouth closed. If a countersignature is required for the application, the person who countersigned the form should also certify one photograph as a true likeness of the applicant.

DOCUMENTATION

In addition to two photographs, the applicant's current or previous British passport, and other documents in support of the statements made in the application, must be produced at the time of applying. Details of which documents are required are set out in the notes accompanying the application form.

If the passport applicant is a British national by naturalisation or registration, the certificate proving this must be produced with the application, unless the applicant holds a previous British passport issued after registration or naturalisation.

INTERVIEWS

Interviews for adults applying for their first passport (not including those who held their own passport as a child) were introduced on 1 June 2007 to combat passport fraud and forgery. After applying for a passport, applicants will be sent a letter asking them to book an interview at one of the offices in the UK. Interviews last for approximately 30 minutes and applicants are asked to confirm facts about themselves that someone attempting to steal their identity would not know. HM Passport Office recommends that new applicants now allow six weeks to receive their passport. There is no one-week fast-track service for first adult passports.

48-PAGE PASSPORTS

The 48-page 'jumbo' passport is intended to meet the needs of frequent travellers who fill standard passports well before the validity has expired. It is valid for ten years but is not available for children.

PASSPORT FEES*	
Adult passport†	£72.50
Child passport†	£46.00
48-page passport	£85.50
People born on or before 2 Sep 1929	Free

* Standard postal applications only. Applications made at UK regional offices have a higher fee

† New passports and renewal or amendment of a passport are priced at the same rate

HEALTH ADVICE

The NHS Choices website provides health advice for those travelling abroad, including information on immunisations and reciprocal health agreements with other countries. *See* W www.nhs.uk/livewell/travelhealth

See also National Health Service, Health Advice and Medical Treatment Abroad.

VISA REQUIREMENTS

The countries listed below do not require British citizens to hold a valid visa or tourist card before arrival on short visits. For longer visits – or for countries not listed – it is advisable to check specific visa requirements with the appropriate embassy before making final travel arrangements (*see* Countries of the World section for foreign embassy contact details or W www.gov.uk/browse/abroad).

All EU member states and their overseas territories (*see* The European Union) except Ascension Island and Tristan da Cunha; Albania, Andorra, Antigua and Barbuda, Argentina, Armenia, Bahamas, Barbados, Belize, Bolivia, Bosnia and Hercegovina, Botswana, Brazil, Brunei, Canada, Chile, Colombia, Costa Rica, Dominica, Ecuador, El Salvador, Fiji, Gambia, Georgia, Grenada, Guatemala, Guyana, Haiti, Honduras*, Hong Kong, Iceland, Israel, Jamaica, Japan, Kiribati, Kosovo, Republic of Korea (South Korea), Lesotho*, Liechtenstein, Macau, Macedonia, Malawi*, Malaysia, Maldives*, Mauritius, Mexico*, Micronesia (Federated States of)*, Moldova, Monaco, Montenegro, Morocco, Namibia, New Zealand, Nicaragua, Norway, Palau, Panama, Paraguay, Peru, Qatar*, Rwanda, Samoa, San Marino, Seychelles, Singapore, South Africa, St Kitts and Nevis, St Lucia, St Vincent and the Grenadines, Swaziland, Switzerland, Taiwan, Tonga, Trinidad and Tobago, Tunisia, Tuvalu, Ukraine, United Arab Emirates*, Uruguay, USA†, Vanuatu, Venezuela‡, Western Sahara.

* Upon entry to these countries a visa or tourist card will be issued at no extra charge

† Those travelling to the USA under the Visa Waiver Programme must provide details online (the Electronic System for Travel Authorisation) at least 72 hours in advance of travel

‡ Only applicable when arriving by air, those arriving at overland crossings or by sea should arrange documentation in advance

The following countries bar entry to travellers with HIV or AIDS:

Brunei, Iraq, Jordan, Papua New Guinea, Qatar, Russian Federation, Singapore, Solomon Islands, Sudan, UAE, Yemen.

Residents of the following countries must hold a valid visa for every entry to the UK:

Afghanistan, Albania, Algeria, Angola, Armenia, Azerbaijan, Bahrain, Bangladesh, Belarus, Benin, Bhutan, Bolivia, Bosnia and Hercegovina, Burkina Faso, Burundi, Cabo Verde, Cambodia, Cameroon, Central African Republic, Chad, China, Colombia, Comoros, Dem. Rep. of Congo, Rep. of Congo, Côte d'Ivoire, Cuba, Djibouti, Dominican Republic, Ecuador, Egypt, Equatorial Guinea, Eritrea, Ethiopia, Fiji, Gabon, Gambia, Georgia, Ghana, Guinea, Guinea-Bissau, Guyana, Haiti, India, Indonesia, Iran, Iraq, Jamaica, Jordan, Kazakhstan, Kenya, Dem. People's Republic of Korea (North Korea), Kosovo, Kuwait, Kyrgyzstan, Laos, Lebanon, Lesotho, Liberia, Libya, Macedonia, Madagascar, Malawi, Mali, Mauritania, Moldova, Mongolia, Montenegro, Morocco, Mozambique, Myanmar, Nepal, Niger, Nigeria, Oman*, Pakistan, Palestinian Authority, Peru, Philippines, Qatar*, Russian Federation, Rwanda, Sao Tome and Príncipe, Saudi Arabia, Senegal, Serbia, Sierra Leone, Somalia, South Africa, South Sudan, Sri Lanka, Sudan, Suriname, Swaziland, Syria, Taiwan†, Tajikistan, Tanzania, Thailand, Togo, Tunisia, Turkey, Turkmenistan, Uganda, Ukraine, United Arab Emirates*, Uzbekistan, Venezuela, Vietnam, Yemen, Zambia, Zimbabwe.

* An electronic visa waiver should be obtained online prior to travel

† Passports containing personal ID numbers do not require visas

BAGGAGE RESTRICTIONS

Individual airlines may set their own limits for hand luggage sizes, and travellers should check these before arriving at the airport: oversized baggage may have to be checked in as hold luggage, which often incurs a fee. Since January 2008, some airports have allowed passengers to take more than one item into the aircraft cabin. Other airports in the UK still have a one-bag restriction in place, and individual airlines may operate their own policies.

Passengers are allowed to carry small amounts of liquids as cabin luggage. These must be in containers not greater than 100ml, and placed in a single, transparent resealable bag which must not exceed 1 litre in capacity. Liquids are classified as drinks, make-up such as mascara or lipstick, sprays, pastes and gels. Medicines that are larger than 100ml must be accompanied by relevant documentation, such as a doctor's letter, and prior approval should be sought from the airline and departure airport. Liquid baby food or milk can be taken on board but may have to be tasted by the adult. One lighter is permitted as cabin luggage; this must be carried in the clear bag or separately for the duration of the flight and not placed in the main hand luggage bag.

Sharp items must not be carried in hand luggage; any essential items should be placed in a bag in the hold. Prohibited sharp items include knives, large scissors, razor blades, cutlery, tools, hiking poles and hypodermic needles. Other prohibited items include ammunition, chemical and toxic substances, work tools, sporting equipment, fireworks, party poppers and non-safety matches.

Electrical equipment such as laptops, MP3 players, mobile phones and cameras are allowed in hand luggage but they must be removed and screened seperately prior to boarding. Some electronic equipment is prohibited from use at certain times during a flight.

The amount passengers can check-in to the hold is determined by each airline. The airline will usually set a 'free baggage allowance' according to the number of items and the weight of each item; if this is exceeded there is normally an excess charge. *See* W www.gov.uk/hand-luggage-restrictions/overview for more information on baggage restrictions.

THE EUROPEAN UNION

MEMBER STATE	ACCESSION DATE	POPULATION*	COUNCIL VOTES	EP SEATS†
Austria	1 Jan 1995	8,223,062	10	18
Belgium	1 Jan 1958	10,449,361	12	21
Bulgaria	1 Jan 2007	6,924,716	10	17
Croatia	1 July 2013	4,470,534	7	11
Cyprus	1 May 2004	1,172,458	4	6
Czech Republic	1 May 2004	10,627,448	12	21
Denmark	1 Jan 1973	5,569,077	7	13
Estonia	1 May 2004	1,257,921	4	6
Finland	1 Jan 1995	5,268,799	7	13
France	1 Jan 1958	66,259,012	29	74
Germany	1 Jan 1958	80,996,685	29	96
Greece	1 Jan 1981	10,775,557	12	21
Hungary	1 May 2004	9,919,128	12	21
Ireland	1 Jan 1973	4,832,765	7	11
Italy	1 Jan 1958	61,680,122	29	73
Latvia	1 May 2004	2,165,165	4	8
Lithuania	1 May 2004	3,505,738	7	11
Luxembourg	1 Jan 1958	520,672	4	6
Malta	1 May 2004	412,655	3	6
The Netherlands	1 Jan 1958	16,877,351	13	26
Poland	1 May 2004	38,346,279	27	51
Portugal	1 Jan 1986	10,813,834	12	21
Romania	1 Jan 2007	21,729,871	14	32
Slovakia	1 May 2004	5,443,583	7	13
Slovenia	1 May 2004	1,988,292	4	8
Spain	1 Jan 1986	47,737,941	27	54
Sweden	1 Jan 1995	9,723,809	10	20
United Kingdom	1 Jan 1973	63,742,977	29	73

* July 2014 estimate

† Under the Lisbon Treaty the total number of MEPs was set at 751 from the 2014 election onwards

Sources: CIA World Factbook; www.europa.eu

Treaty of Rome establishes the European Economic Community (EEC) and the European Atomic Energy Authority (EURATOM) — 1957

UK joins the European Community — 1967

European Monetary System comes into operation; first direct elections to European parliament — 1979

European Economic Area agreement comes into operation — 1994

Ten more countries become members of the EU — 2004

Lisbon Treaty enters into force — 2009

1951 · 1962 · 1967 · 1973 · 1991 · 1993 · 1997 · 1999 · 2000 · 2007 · 2013

European Coal and Steel Community (ECSC) formed

Common Agricultural Policy agreed

EEC, ECSC and EURATOM merge to form the European Communities

Maastricht Treaty agreed

European Union (EU) established

Amsterdam Treaty agreed

Treaty of Nice agreed

Bulgaria and Romania join the EU

Croatia joins the EU

LEGISLATION

The core of the European Union (EU) policy-making process is a dialogue between the European Commission (EC), which initiates and implements policy, and the Council of the European Union and the European parliament, which take policy decisions.

The original legislative process is known as the consultation procedure. The commission drafts a proposal which it submits to the council and to the parliament. The council then consults the Economic and Social Committee, the parliament and the Committee of the Regions; the parliament may request that amendments are made. With or without these amendments, the proposal is then adopted by the council and becomes law. The consultation procedure now only applies to cases not specifically subject to one of the other procedures.

The Single European Act introduced the assent procedure (now the consent procedure), whereby an absolute majority of the parliament must vote to approve laws in certain fields before they are passed. Issues covered by the procedure include uniform procedure for elections, some international agreements, violation of human rights and the accession of new member states.

The Maastricht Treaty introduced the co-decision procedure as an extension of the cooperation procedure; if, after the parliament's second reading of a proposal, the council and parliament fail to agree, a conciliation committee of the two will aim to reach a compromise. If a compromise is not reached, the parliament can reject the legislation by the vote of an absolute majority of its members. The Amsterdam Treaty extended the co-decision procedure to all areas covered by qualified majority voting, with the exception of measures related to the European Monetary Union.

The Lisbon Treaty extended the use of the co-decision procedure to several new fields, and renamed it the ordinary legislative procedure. The treaty strengthens the role of the European parliament so that it is involved in almost all new legislation. The changes give the European parliament equal powers in areas such as legal immigration, crime prevention and police cooperation. As a result of the Lisbon Treaty, the Council of the European Union must now vote in public on any new legislation, and if one-third of national parliaments disagree with a proposal then it can be sent back to be reviewed.

The council, commission and parliament can issue the following legislation:

- regulations, which are binding in their entirety and directly applicable to all member states; they do not need to be incorporated into national law to come into effect
- directives, which are less specific, binding as to the result to be achieved but leaving the method of implementation open to member states; a directive thus has no force until it is incorporated into national law
- decisions, which are also binding but are addressed solely to one or more member states or individuals in a member state
- recommendations or opinions, which are merely persuasive.

The council and parliament also have certain budgetary powers and determine all expenditure together. The final decision on whether the budget should be adopted or rejected lies with the parliament.

The European Central Bank (ECB) has legislative powers within its field of competence. The commission also has limited legislative powers, where it has been delegated the power to implement or revise legislation by the council.

SCHENGEN AGREEMENT

The Schengen agreement was signed by France, Germany, Belgium, Luxembourg and the Netherlands in 1985. The agreement committed the five states to abolishing internal border controls, erecting external frontiers against illegal immigrants, drug traffickers, terrorists and organised crime, and it implemented the Schengen Information System which enables national border control, customs and police authorities from Schengen member states to share and access data on specific individuals, such as a person who may have been involved in a serious crime, or vehicles, documents or objects which may have been stolen, lost or misappropriated. The second-generation Schengen Information System (SIS II) entered into operation in April 2013. SIS II has improved functionalities such as new types of alerts and the potential to enter biometrics. It also contains copies of European arrest warrants, facilitating the detention of persons wanted for arrest, surrender or extradition.

Subsequently signed by Portugal and Spain, the agreement was ratified by the seven signatory states and entered into force in March 1995 with the removal of internal frontier, passport, customs and immigration controls. Austria and Italy became full members of the agreement in 1997; Greece in 2000; and Denmark, Finland and Sweden in 2001. The Czech Republic, Estonia, Hungary, Latvia, Lithuania, Malta, Poland, Slovakia and Slovenia joined in 2007. Although not members of the EU, Iceland and Norway joined the agreement in 2001 and Switzerland in 2008. The European Council granted Liechtenstein membership in 2011. There is no date set for Bulgaria, Croatia, Cyprus or Romania to join. The UK and the Republic of Ireland have not signed the agreement and are only partial participants, since their border controls have been maintained.

The Schengen agreement originated as an intergovernmental agreement but was adopted by the EU following the signing of the Amsterdam Treaty.

MAASTRICHT TREATY

Agreed in Maastricht, the Netherlands, in 1991, the treaty came into effect in November 1993 following ratification by the member states. Three pillars formed its basis:

- the European Community (removing Economic from its name) with its established institutions and decision-making processes
- a common foreign and security policy charged with providing a forum for member states and EU institutions to consult on foreign affairs

- cooperation in justice and home affairs, with the Council of the European Union coordinating policies on asylum, immigration, conditions of entry, cross-border crime, drug trafficking and terrorism

The treaty established a common European citizenship for nationals of all member states and introduced the principle of subsidiarity, whereby decisions are taken at the most appropriate level (national, regional or local). It extended European Community competency into the areas of environmental and industrial policies, consumer affairs, health, and education and training, and extended qualified majority voting in the Council of the European Union to some areas which had previously required a unanimous vote. The powers of the European parliament over the budget and over the EC were also enhanced, and a co-decision procedure enabled the parliament to override decisions made by the council in certain policy areas. A separate protocol to the Maastricht Treaty on social policy was agreed by 11 states and was incorporated into the Amsterdam Treaty in 1997 following adoption by the UK.

AMSTERDAM TREATY

The treaties of Rome and Maastricht were amended through the Amsterdam Treaty, which was signed in 1997 and came into effect on 1 May 1999. It extended the scope of qualified majority voting and the powers of the European parliament. It also included a formal commitment to fundamental human rights, gave additional powers to the European Court of Justice and provided for the reform of common foreign and security policy.

LISBON TREATY

The Lisbon Treaty was drawn up to replace the original European constitution, which was rejected in referendums in France and the Netherlands in 2005. It amends, rather than replaces, existing EU and European Community treaties. Ireland, the only country to hold a referendum on the Lisbon Treaty, voted against ratification in 2008. It held a second referendum in October 2009 in which 67 per cent voted in favour, and – as a result of all EU countries approving the treaty – it came into force on 1 December 2009.

The Lisbon Treaty granted 'legal personality' (the right under international law to adopt laws and treaties) to the EU. The three pillars created by the Maastricht Treaty (*see* above) merged to make the EU a single legal entity, replacing the European Community. The Lisbon Treaty introduced a number of changes to the EU: a new president was appointed to the European Council for a two-and-a-half year term to replace the previous system of a six-month rotating presidency (this still exists in a reduced capacity for the Council of the European Union). The position of High Representative of the Union for Foreign Affairs and Security Policy was created, to enhance the EU's relations with other countries. The European parliament was strengthened and given more legislative and budgetary powers, and the number of MEPs was set at 751 from the 2014 election onwards. The system of qualified majority voting was extended to new policy areas and since 2014 has been based on a double majority of member states and people; a decision must be agreed by 55 per cent of member states representing at least 65 per cent of the EU population. The treaty establishes the principle of 'mutual recognition', whereby each member state acknowledges that legal decisions by other member states are valid; the UK has an opt-out clause with regard to some policies, such as external borders, asylum and immigration.

ENLARGEMENT AND EXTERNAL RELATIONS

The procedure for accession to the EU is laid down in the Treaty of Rome; states must be stable European democracies governed by the rule of law with free-market economies. A membership application is studied by the EC, which produces an 'opinion'. If the opinion is positive, negotiations may be opened leading to an accession treaty that must be approved by all member state governments and parliaments, the European parliament, and the applicant state's government and parliament.

Cyprus, the Czech Republic, Estonia, Hungary, Latvia, Lithuania, Malta, Poland, Slovakia and Slovenia became full members of the EU on 1 May 2004. Bulgaria and Romania joined the EU on 1 January 2007, and Croatia on 1 July 2013. The European Council recalled the offer of an accession partnership to Turkey in 2002 following the commission's conclusion that Turkey did not yet fully meet the required political criteria. However, at its December 2004 meeting in Brussels, the council decided that Turkey sufficiently met the Copenhagen political criteria, and accession negotiations began in October 2005.

Montenegro was granted candidate status in December 2005 and accession negotiations began on 29 June 2012. Macedonia was granted candidate status in December 2005, but accession negotiations have not yet begun. Iceland applied for membership in July 2009 and accession negotiations started in June 2010 but were put on hold by the Icelandic government in May 2013. Serbia applied for membership in December 2009 and accession negotiations commenced in January 2014. There are currently three potential candidates for membership of the EU: Albania, Bosnia and Hercegovina, and Kosovo. Of these countries, only Albania has applied for membership.

The EU has several types of agreements with other European and non-European states. Association agreements (AAs), which must be ratified by all EU member states, can include commitments to reforming the country's trade, human rights, economy or political system in exchange for financial assistance or trade agreements. Partnership and cooperation agreements (PCAs) are legal frameworks, based on respect for democratic principles and human rights, setting out the political, economic and trade relationship between the EU and its partner countries. Each PCA is a ten-year bilateral treaty signed and ratified by the EU and the individual state. After the ten-year period expires the agreements are automatically renewed annually unless one of the parties objects. Agreements have been implemented (date when PCA entered into force in parentheses) with Russia (1997), Moldova and Ukraine (1998), Armenia, Azerbaijan, Georgia, Kazakhstan, Kyrgyzstan and Uzbekistan (1999), Tajikistan (2010) and Indonesia (2014). In 2003 the PCA council summit strengthened EU cooperation with the Russian Federation by establishing a permanent partnership council (PPC). Negotiations for a new agreement to replace and update the existing PCA between the EU and Russia began in 2008 but have not been concluded.

Trade and cooperation agreements are intended to foster trade and economic relations, and include a commitment to respect the human rights and democratic principles of both parties. The EC has negotiated around 120 agreements worldwide.

The European neighbourhood policy was developed in 2004 and applies to the enlarged EU's immediate neighbours. It aims to strengthen stability and security through economic integration and deeper political relationships based on a mutual commitment to common values (democracy, human rights, rule of law, good governance and market economy).

A stabilisation and association agreement (SAA) – which is tailored to the western Balkan states – provides the contractual framework for relations to enable accession to the EU. Candidate or potential candidate countries with SAAs in force are Macedonia (2004), Albania (2009), Montenegro (2010) and Serbia (2013). An SAA agreement was signed by Bosnia and Hercegovina in June 2008 which will enter into force following ratification, and in October 2013 SAA negotiations began between the EU and Kosovo.

TREATY OF NICE
The Treaty of Nice was signed in 2001 and came into effect in 2003. It enabled the EU to accommodate up to 13 new member states, and extended qualified majority voting to 30 further articles of the treaties that previously required unanimity. The weighting of votes in the European Council was altered from 1 January 2005 for the new member states. To obtain a qualified majority, a decision requires a specified number of votes (to be reviewed following each accession); the decision has to be approved by a majority of member states and represent at least 62 per cent of the total population of the EU. The treaty also set the number of MEPs that both existing and new member states would have following enlargement.

The Maastricht Treaty established the right of groups of member states to work together without requiring the participation of all members (enhanced cooperation); the Treaty of Nice removed the right of individual member states to veto the launch of enhanced cooperation.

ECONOMY

BUDGET OF THE EUROPEAN UNION
The principles of funding the European Union budget (formerly known as the European Community budget) were established by the Treaty of Rome and remain, with modifications, to this day. There is a legally binding limit on the overall level of resources (known as 'own resources') that the EU can raise from its member states; this limit is defined as a percentage of gross national income (GNI). Budget revenue and expenditure must balance, and there is therefore no deficit financing. The 'own resources' decision, which came into effect in 1975 and has been regularly updated, states that there are four sources of funding under which each member state makes contributions: duties charged on agricultural imports into the EU from non-member states; customs duties on imports from non-member states; contributions based on member states' shares of a notional EU-harmonised VAT base; and contributions based on member states' shares of total GNI. The latter is the budget-balancing item and covers the difference between total expenditure and the revenue from the other three sources. On 3 July 2013 the European parliament voted in favour of a budget for 2014–20; the budget was officially adopted following a vote on the legislation in November 2013. The overall budget for the seven-year period is €960bn in commitments and €908bn in payments (at 2011 prices).

The EU's multiannual financial framework (MFF) for 2014–20 is 3.5 per cent less than the commitment appropriations under the MFF 2007–13 and 3.7 per cent less than the payment appropriations for the same period. In line with the political priorities of the EU, a strong emphasis was put on expenditure aimed at boosting growth and creating jobs, with an increase of 37 per cent over the 2007–13 model dedicated to 'competitiveness for growth and jobs'.

EU BUDGET 2014

	CA	PA
Smart and inclusive growth*	63,986.3	62,392.8
Sustainable growth: natural resources	59,267.2	56,458.9
Security and citizenship	2,172.0	1,677.0
Global Europe	8,325.0	6,191.2
Administration	8,405.1	8,406.0
Compensations	28.6	28.6
Special Instruments	456.2	350.0
Total	€142,640.5m	€135,504.6m

(1 euro = £0.82 as at 10 May 2014)
* Includes 'competitiveness for growth and jobs' and 'economic, social and territorial cohesion'
CA: commitment appropriations (maximum value of commitments to pay future bills)
PA: payment appropriations (actual amounts to pay for previous commitments)
Source: www.ec.europa.eu

SINGLE MARKET
Even after the removal of tariffs and quotas between member states in the 1970s and 1980s, the European Community was still separated into a number of national markets by a series of non-tariff barriers. It was to overcome these internal barriers to trade that the concept of the single market was developed. The measures to be undertaken were codified in the commission's 1985 white paper on completing the internal market.

The white paper included articles removing obstacles distorting the internal market: the elimination of frontier controls; the mutual recognition of professional qualifications; the harmonisation of product specifications, largely by the mutual recognition of national standards; open tendering for public procurement contracts; the free movement of capital; the harmonisation of VAT and excise duties; and the reduction of state aid to particular industries. The Single European Act (SEA) aided the completion of the single market by changing the legislative process within the European Community, particularly with the introduction of qualified majority voting in the Council of the European Union for some policy areas, and the introduction of the assent procedure in the European parliament. The Single European Act also extended European Community competence into the fields of technology, the environment, regional policy, monetary policy and external policy. The single market came into effect on 1 January 1993, though full implementation of the elimination of frontier controls and the harmonisation of taxes have been repeatedly delayed. A fundamental review of the single market was completed in 2007, which resulted in an operational set of initiatives intended to modernise single market policy. Following the abolition of the European Community in 2009 as a result of the Lisbon Treaty, the single market policy now applies to the EU.

EUROPEAN ECONOMIC AREA
The single market programme spurred European non-member states to open negotiations with the European Community on preferential access for their goods, services, labour and capital to the single market. Principal among these states were European Free Trade Association (EFTA) members, who opened negotiations on extending the single market to EFTA by the formation of the European Economic Area (EEA), encompassing all 19 European Community and EFTA states. Agreement was reached in 1992, but the operation of the EEA was delayed by its rejection in a Swiss

referendum, necessitating an additional protocol agreed by the remaining 18 states. The EEA came into effect in 1994 after ratification by 17 member states (Liechtenstein joined in 1995 after adapting its customs union with Switzerland).

Austria, Finland and Sweden joined the EU on 1 January 1995, leaving only Iceland, Liechtenstein and Norway as the non-EU EEA members. Under the EEA agreement, the three states are to adopt the EU's *acquis communautaire*, apart from in the fields of agriculture, fisheries, and coal and steel.

The EEA is controlled by regular ministerial meetings and by a joint EU-EFTA committee which extends relevant EU legislation to EEA states. Apart from single market measures, there is cooperation in several areas, including education, civil protection, research and development, consumer policy and tourism. An EFTA court has been established in Luxembourg and an EFTA surveillance authority in Brussels to supervise the implementation of the EEA Agreement.

The EEA Enlargement Agreement came into force on 1 May 2004, which allowed the simultaneous expansion of both the EU and the EEA without disruption of the internal market. A similar process took place to ensure that Bulgaria and Romania could become contracting parties to the EEA upon joining the EU in 2007 and Croatia in 2013.

EUROPEAN MONETARY SYSTEM AND THE SINGLE CURRENCY

The European Monetary System (EMS) began operation in March 1979 with three main purposes. The first was to establish monetary stability in Europe, initially in exchange rates between European Community member state currencies through the Exchange Rate Mechanism (ERM), and in the longer term as part of a wider stabilisation process, overcoming inflation and budget and trade deficits. The second purpose was to overcome the constraints resulting from the interdependence of European Community economies, and the third was to aid the long-term process of European monetary integration.

The Maastricht Treaty set in motion timetables for achieving economic and monetary union (EMU) and a single currency (the euro). In May 1998, 11 member states were judged to fulfil or be close to fulfilling the necessary convergence criteria for participation in the first stage of EMU: Austria, Belgium, Finland, France, Germany, Ireland, Italy, Luxembourg, the Netherlands, Portugal and Spain. The criteria were that:

- the budget deficit should be 3 per cent or less of gross domestic product (GDP)
- total national debt must not exceed 60 per cent of GDP
- inflation should be no more than 1.5 per cent above the average rate of the three best-performing economies in the EU
- long-term interest rates should be no more than 2 per cent above the average of the three best-performing economies in the EU in the previous 12 months
- applicants must have been members of the ERM for two years without having realigned or devalued their currency.

Under the terms of a stability and growth pact agreed in December 1996 and revised in 2005, penalties may be imposed on EMU members with high budget deficits. Governments with deficits exceeding 3 per cent of GDP will receive a warning and will be obliged to pay up to 0.5 per cent of their GDP into a fund after ten months. This will become a fine if the budget deficit is not rectified within two years. A member state with negative growth will be allowed to apply for an exemption from the fine by referring to a number of relevant factors outlined in the pact.

As a result of the global economic downturn, by May 2010, 24 out of 27 countries in the EU had a deficit exceeding 3 per cent of GDP. The EC revised its existing recommendations in November 2009 and proposed extended deadlines for each country to correct its budget deficit. In the case of the UK, a deadline of 2014–15 was proposed, the longest deadline given to any of the EMU nations.

On 1 January 1999 the 11 qualifying member states adopted the euro at irrevocably fixed exchange rates, the European Central Bank (ECB) took charge of the single monetary policy, and the euro replaced the ECU (an artificial currency adopted by European Community member states in 1979 as an internal accounting unit for the EMS) on a one-for-one basis.

Subsequent member states who have fulfilled the criteria for participation and adopted the euro include Greece on 1 January 2001, Slovenia on 1 January 2007, Cyprus and Malta on 1 January 2008, Slovakia on 1 January 2009, Estonia on 1 January 2011 and Latvia on 1 January 2014. Referendums on the adoption of the euro have been held in Denmark and Sweden, but participation was rejected. In June 2003 the UK announced that the euro would not be adopted at present on the grounds that the country was not economically ready to join the single currency, though a future joining of the eurozone was not ruled out.

The euro is now the legal currency in the 18 participating states and is used by around 334 million people. Euro notes and coins were introduced on 1 January 2002 and circulated alongside national currencies for a period of up to two months, after which time national notes and coins ceased to be legal tender.

The ECB meets twice a month in Frankfurt to set the following month's monetary policy applicable to the countries participating in the euro. Its governing council has 24 member: the six members of the ECB's executive board and the 18 governors of the national central banks of the participating states.

THE EURO CRISIS

Early in 2010, Greece's soaring budget deficit and the escalating cost of servicing the country's debt brought it to the verge of economic meltdown. In May 2010 a rescue package totalling €110bn (£95bn) was agreed following negotiations with the EC, the IMF and the ECB. In February 2012, the EC, IMF and ECB agreed to provide a second bailout package worth €130bn (£110bn). On 11 November 2012, facing a default by the end of November, the Greek parliament passed a new austerity package worth €18.8bn (£15.9bn), including labour market reforms raising the retirement age to 67 from 65 and cuts to pensions of between 5 and 15 per cent.

In November 2010 the near collapse of the banking system in Ireland led to the approval of an €85bn (£72bn) rescue package by the EU and the IMF. In April 2011 Portugal became the third country to request financial assistance from the EU after rising borrowing costs left the government unable to pay its debts, and in May 2011 European finance ministers finalised the terms of a three-year bailout agreement worth €78bn (£69bn).

In December 2011 an amendment to the Lisbon Treaty was agreed between 25 of the 27 EU countries (the Czech Republic and the UK abstained) in order to tackle the crisis. The amendment, a new fiscal pact which made it more difficult for individual countries to break budget deficit rules, was signed at the end of January 2012.

Shortly after interest rates on Spain's ten-year bonds reached 7 per cent, the Spanish government requested a eurozone rescue loan of around €100bn (£77bn) on 10 June 2012. Eurozone finance ministers approved the loan on the same day. On 25 June, Cyprus became the fifth eurozone member to ask for financial assistance, citing significant exposure to the crippled Greek economy. A €10bn support package was agreed on 25 March 2013 and the first €2bn (£1.7bn) instalment arrived in May.

On 14 August 2013, the European economic commissioner announced that the eurozone had returned to growth – 0.3 per cent in the three months to June 2013 – following 18 months in a double-dip recession. However, the commissioner warned against complacency, due to Europe's job crisis and the large disparity in economic performance between different countries in the eurozone.

COMMON AGRICULTURAL POLICY

The Common Agricultural Policy (CAP) was established to increase agricultural production, provide a fair standard of living for farmers and ensure the availability of food at reasonable prices. This aim was achieved by a number of mechanisms, including import levies, intervention purchase and export subsidies.

These measures stimulated production but also placed increasing demands on the budget, which was exacerbated by the increase in EC members and yields enlarged by technological innovation; the CAP now accounts for over 40 per cent of EU expenditure. To surmount these problems reforms were agreed in 1984, 1988, 1992, 1997, 1999, 2003, 2008 and 2013.

REFORMS

The 1984 reforms created the system of co-responsibility levies: farm payments to the EC by volume of product sold. This system was supplemented by national quotas for particular products, such as milk. The 1988 reforms emphasised 'set-aside', whereby farmers are given direct grants to take land out of production as a means of reducing surpluses. The set-aside reforms were extended in 1993 for another five years and to every farm in the EC. The 1999 reforms further reduced surpluses of cereals, beef and milk by cutting the intervention prices by up to 20 per cent and compensating producers by making area payments. Under the reforms, CAP rules were also simplified, eliminating inconsistencies between policies.

In 2003, EU farm ministers adopted a fundamental reform of the CAP, which included the following provisions:

• a single farm payment for EU farmers, independent of production (begun in 2005)
• payment to be linked to meeting environmental, food safety, animal and plant health and animal welfare standards, and the requirement to keep all farmland in good condition
• a strengthened rural development policy with more EU money to help farmers meet EU production standards (begun in 2005)
• a reduction in direct payments for bigger farms
• a mechanism for financial discipline to ensure that the farm budget fixed until 2013 is not exceeded

The ten EU members that joined in 2004 were also given access to a special €5.8bn (£3.9bn) three-year funding package. The 2007–13 EU budget stipulated that no extra money would be made available to pay farm subsidies to Bulgaria and Romania.

A CAP 'health check' was carried out in 2008 and resulted in proposals intended to further modernise and streamline EU agricultural policy, and to allow farmers to follow market signals by breaking the link between direct payments and production. These include abolishing the requirement for farmers to leave 10 per cent of their arable land fallow, a gradual increase in milk quotas before their abolition in 2015 and a general reduction in market intervention.

On 13 March 2013, MEPs voted to adopt a controversial package of legislation, including approving both the extension of quotas and the rural development programme that involves shared financing with national governments. The stated aim of the CAP reform was to strengthen the competitiveness and sustainability of agriculture and maintain its presence in all regions, to guarantee European citizens healthy and quality food production, and to preserve the environment and develop rural areas. On 26 June 2013, a political agreement on the CAP 2014–20 reforms was reached between the European Commission, parliament and council, and on 16 December 2013, the council of EU agriculture ministers formally adopted the four basic regulations for the reformed CAP in addition to the transition rules for 2014. On 1 March 2014, the EC adopted the first package of delegated acts.

INSTITUTIONS

EUROPEAN PARLIAMENT
E eplondon@europarl.europa.eu W www.europarl.europa.eu; www.europarl.org.uk

The European parliament (EP) originated as the common assembly of the ECSC, acquiring its present name in 1962. The parliament now comprises 751 seats representing citizens of the 28 countries in the EU. Members (MEPs), initially appointed from the membership of national parliaments, have been directly elected at five-year intervals since 1979. Elections to the parliament are held on differing bases throughout the EU; British MEPs have been elected by a regional list system of proportional representation since June 1999. The most recent elections were held in May 2014.

MEPs serve on committees which scrutinise draft EU legislation and the activities of the EC. A minimum of 12 plenary sessions a year are held in Strasbourg and six additional shorter plenary sessions a year are held in Brussels; committees meet in Brussels, and the secretariat's headquarters is in Luxembourg.

The influence of the EP has gradually expanded within the EU since the Single European Act 1985, which introduced the cooperation procedure; the Maastricht Treaty, which extended the cooperation procedure and introduced the co-decision (now ordinary legislative) procedure (see Legislation); the Amsterdam Treaty, which effectively extended the ordinary legislative procedure to all areas except economic and monetary union, and taxation; and the Lisbon Treaty, which gave the parliament legislative powers comparable with the Council of the European Union. The EP has general powers of supervision over the EC, and powers of consultation and co-decision with the Council of the European Union; it votes to approve a newly appointed commission and can dismiss it at any time by a two-thirds majority. Under the Maastricht Treaty it has the right to be consulted on the appointment of the new commission, and can also veto its appointment. Under the Lisbon Treaty, the parliament elects the president of the commission on the proposal of the European Council. The EP has an equal right to decide on budgetary matters as the Council of the European Union, and they work together to approve and adopt the entire annual budget. In accordance with the Maastricht Treaty, the EP appoints the European Ombudsman to provide citizens with redress against maladministration by EU institutions.

The EP's organisation is deliberately biased in favour of multinational political groupings; recognition of a political grouping in the parliament entitles it to offices, funding, representation on committees and influence in debates and legislation. A political group must be composed of a minimum of 25 MEPs elected in at least seven member states. For a list of UK MEPs, *see* European Parliament section.

PARLIAMENT, allée du Printemps, F-67070 Strasbourg Cedex, France
E epstrasbourg@europarl.europa.eu
Wiertzstraat 60, B-1047 Brussels, Belgium
E parlamentarium@europarleuropa.eu

SECRETARIAT, Centre Européen, Plateau du Kirchberg, BP 1601, L-2929 Luxembourg
T (+352) 43001
President, Martin Schulz (Germany)

OMBUDSMAN, 1 avenue du Président Robert Schuman, CS 30403, F-67001 Strasbourg Cedex, France
W www.ombudsman.europa.eu
Ombudsman, Emily O'Reilly (Ireland)

EUROPEAN PARLIAMENT UK OFFICE

Europe House, 32 Smith Square, London SW1P 3EU
E eplondon@europarl.europa.eu W www.europarl.org.uk

EUROPEAN PARLIAMENT OFFICE IN SCOTLAND

The Tun, 4 Jackson's Entry, Holyrood Road, Edinburgh EH8 8PJ
E epedinburgh@europarl.europa.eu W www.europarl.org.uk

COUNCIL OF THE EUROPEAN UNION

Wetstraat 175, rue de la Loi, B-1048 Brussels, Belgium
W www.consilium.europa.eu

The Council of the European Union (Council of Ministers) is the main decision-making body of the EU, and formally comprises the ministers of the member states. Depending on the issue on the agenda, each country will be represented by the minister responsible for that subject. It passes laws, usually legislating jointly with the European parliament; coordinates the broad economic policies of the member states; approves the EU's budget jointly with the European parliament; defines and implements the EU's common foreign and security policy; concludes agreements between the EU and other states or international organisations; and coordinates the actions of member states and adopts measures in the area of police and judicial cooperation.

Council decisions are taken using one of three methods: by qualified majority vote, by a simple majority, or by unanimity. The treaties define which one of the three methods should be used in each subject area. Unanimity votes are taken on sensitive issues such as taxation and defence, but the qualified majority vote (QMV) is now used for the majority of council decisions. Under the provisions of the Lisbon Treaty, a new system of QMV began on 1 November 2014 although, until 31 March 2017, any member state may request that a decision be taken in accordance with the old QMV rules outlined below. Under the new system a qualified majority is achieved if:

- at least 55 per cent of member states approve (72 per cent where the council does not act on a proposal from the commission) *and*
- these member states represent at least 65 per cent of the EU's population

This system therefore assigns a vote to each member state while taking account of their demographic weight.

Under the old QMV system, member states had weighted votes in the council loosely proportional to their relative population sizes (*see* introductory table), with a total of 345 votes. Under this system a qualified majority was reached if a majority of member states approved (in some cases a two-thirds majority) *and* a minimum of 255 votes was cast in favour of the proposal (ie 73.9 per cent of the total). In addition, a member state could ask for confirmation that the votes in favour represented at least 62 per cent of the total

population of the EU. If this was found not to be the case, the decision was not adopted.

The presidency of the Council of the European Union is held in rotation for six-month periods, setting the agenda for and chairing council meetings in all policy areas except foreign affairs. The holders of the presidency for the years 2014–15 are:

2014 Jan–Jun, Greece	2015 Jan–Jun, Latvia
2014 Jul–Dec, Italy	2015 Jul–Dec, Luxembourg

In the area of foreign affairs, council meetings are chaired by the High Representative of the Union for Foreign Affairs and Security Policy.
High Representative of the Union for Foreign Affairs and Security Policy, Federica Mogherini (Italy)

GENERAL SECRETARIAT OF THE COUNCIL OF THE EUROPEAN UNION

Wetstraat 175, rue de la Loi, B-1048 Brussels, Belgium
W www.consilium.europa.eu
Secretary-General of the Council of the European Union, Uwe Corsepius (Germany)

EUROPEAN COUNCIL

The European Council, formed in 1974, was given formal recognition by the Single European Act in 1987; on 1 December 2009, under the Lisbon Treaty it has become a fully fledged institution of the EU with a permanent president. It normally meets four times a year, unless a special meeting is convened by the president, and comprises the heads of state or government of each EU member state and the president of the EC. Meetings are chaired by the president of the council.

The primary function of the European Council is to give political guidance in all areas of EU activity at both European and national levels. The European Council can issue declarations and resolutions expressing the opinions of the heads of state and governments, but its decisions are not legally binding.
President of the European Council, Donald Tusk (Poland)

EUROPEAN COMMISSION

Wetstraat 200, rue de la Loi, B-1049 Brussels, Belgium

The European Commission (EC) consists of 28 commissioners, one per member state. The members of the commission are appointed for five-year renewable terms by the agreement of the member states; the terms run concurrently with the terms of the European parliament. The president and the other commissioners are nominated by the governments of the member states, and, under the terms of the Lisbon Treaty, the appointments are approved by the European parliament. The commissioners pledge sole allegiance to the EU. The commission initiates and implements EU legislation and is the guardian of the EU treaties. It is the exponent of community-wide interests rather than the national preoccupations of the council. Each commissioner is supported by advisers and oversees the departments assigned to them, known as directorates-general and services.

President Jean-Claude Juncker was elected for a first mandate by the European parliament on 15 July 2014. He received 422 votes from a total of 729 and he took office in November 2014.

The commission has a total staff of around 33,000 permanent civil servants and temporary agents.
COMMISSIONERS *as at November 2014*
President, Jean-Claude Juncker (Luxembourg)
First Vice-President, Better Regulation, Inter-Institutional Relations, the Rule of Law and the Charter of Fundamental Rights, Frans Timmermans (Netherlands)

Vice-President, High Representative of the Union for Foreign Affairs and Security Policy, Federica Mogherini (Italy)
Vice-President, Budget and Human Resources, Kristalina Georgieva (Bulgaria)
Vice-President, Digital Single Market, Andrus Ansip (Estonia)
Vice-President, Energy Union, Alenka Bratusek (Slovenia)
Vice-President, Euro and Social Dialogue, Valdis Dombrovskis (Latvia)
Vice-President, Jobs, Growth, Investment and Competitiveness, Jyrki Katainen (Finland)
Transport and Space, Maros Sefcovic (Slovakia)
Digital Economy and Society, Gunther Oettinger (Germany)
European Neighbourhood Policy and Enlargement Negotiations, Johannes Hahn (Austria)
Trade, Cecilia Malmstrom (Sweden)
International Cooperation and Development, Neven Mimica (Croatia)
Climate Action and Energy, Miguel Arias Canete (Spain)
Environment, Maritime Affairs and Fisheries, Karmenu Vella (Malta)
Health and Food Safety, Vytenis Andriukaitis (Lithuania)
Migration and Home Affairs, Dimitris Avramopoulos (Greece)
Employment, Social Affairs, Skills and Labour Mobility, Marianne Thyssen (Belgium)
Economic and Financial Affairs, Taxation and Customs, Pierre Moscovici (France)
Humanitarian Aid and Crisis Management, Christos Stylianides (Cyprus)
Agriculture and Rural Development, Phil Hogan (Ireland)
Financial Stability, Financial Services and Capital Markets Union, Jonathan Hill (UK)
Internal Market, Industry, Entrepreneurship and SMEs, Elzbieta Bienkowska (Poland)
Justice, Consumers and Gender Equality, Vera Jourova (Czech Republic)
Education, Culture, Youth and Citizenship, Tibor Navracsics (Hungary)
Regional Policy, Corina Cretu (Romania)
Competition, Margrethe Vestager (Denmark)
Research, Innovation and Science, Carlos Moedas (Portugal)

EC REPRESENTATION OFFICES

UK, Europe House, 32 Smith Square, London SW1P 3EU
　T 020-7973 1992
WALES, 2 Caspian Point, Caspian Way, Cardiff CF10 4QQ
　T 029-2089 5020
SCOTLAND, 9 Alva Street, Edinburgh EH2 4PH
　T 0131-225 2058
NORTHERN IRELAND, 74–76 Dublin Road, Belfast BT2 7HP
　T 028-9024 0708

UK PERMANENT REPRESENTATIVE TO THE EU

10 Ave d'Auderghem, Oudergemselaan, 1040 Brussels, Belgium
T (+32) 2287 8211 W http://ukeu.fco.gov.uk
　UK Permanent Representative to the EU, Ivan Rogers, *apptd* 2013

COURT OF JUSTICE OF THE EUROPEAN UNION

Palais de la Cour de Justice, boulevard Konrad Adenauer, Kirchberg, L-2925 Luxembourg
W www.curia.europa.eu

The Lisbon Treaty gave a new framework to the EU court system. The court of justice of the European Union is now composed of three courts: the court of justice, the general court and the civil service tribunal.

COURT OF JUSTICE

Palais de la Cour de Justice, boulevard Konrad Adenauer, Kirchberg, L-2925 Luxembourg

The court of justice exists to safeguard the law in the interpretation and application of EU treaties, to decide on the legality of EU legislation, and to determine infringements of the treaties. Cases may be brought to it directly by the member states and EU institutions. Questions on EU law may be referred to the court of justice by national courts. The decisions of the court are directly binding in the member states. The court's powers were extended by the Maastricht Treaty, allowing it to impose fines on member states who breach EU law. The court comprises 28 judges – one from each member state – and nine advocates-general. These positions are appointed for renewable six-year terms by the member governments.
President, Vassilios Skouris (Greece)

GENERAL COURT

Palais de la Cour de Justice, boulevard Konrad Adenauer, Kirchberg, L-2925 Luxembourg

Established under powers conferred by the Single European Act, the general court (known as the Court of First Instance until 1 December 2009) has jurisdiction to hear and determine direct actions brought by natural persons (ie human beings) or legal persons (ie an entity with a legal personality, such as a company, association etc) against any of the institutions, bodies, agencies or offices of the EU, except those cases reserved for the court of justice. Additionally, the general court hears actions seeking compensation for damage caused by the institutions of the EU or their staff. It also has jurisdiction to hear actions brought by member states against the EC and actions relating to community trade marks. The court is composed of 28 judges, one from each member state, appointed for renewable six-year terms by the individual national governments.
President, Marc Jaeger (Luxembourg)

CIVIL SERVICE TRIBUNAL

35A avenue J. F. Kennedy, L-1855 Luxembourg

Established in 2005, the civil service tribunal has jurisdiction to hear disputes between civil servants and the EU in matters such as pay, disciplinary measures and accidents at work. It does not deal with disputes between national governments and their employees. There are seven judges, appointed for renewable six-year terms.
President, Sean Van Raepenbusch (Belgium)

EUROPEAN COURT OF AUDITORS

12 rue Alcide de Gasperi, L-1615 Luxembourg
E eca-info@eca.europa.eu W www.eca.europa.eu

The European Court of Auditors, established in 1977, examines the accounts of all revenue and expenditure of the EU. It evaluates whether all revenue has been received and all expenditure incurred in a lawful and regular manner and in accordance with the principles of sound financial management. The court issues an annual report and a statement of assurance as to the reliability of the accounts and the legality and regularity of the underlying transactions. It also publishes special reports on specific topics and delivers opinions on financial matters. The court has one member from each member state, appointed for a renewable six-year term by the Council of the European Union following consultation with the European parliament.
President, Vitor Caldeira (Portugal)

FINANCIAL BODIES

EUROPEAN CENTRAL BANK

Kaiserstrasse 29, D-60311 Frankfurt am Main, Germany
E info@ecb.europa.eu W www.ecb.europa.eu

The ECB, which superseded the European Monetary Institute, became fully operational on 1 January 1999 and defines and implements the single monetary policy for the euro area. The ECB's main task is to maintain the euro's purchasing power and price stability in the 18 EU countries that have introduced the currency since 1999. Its decision-making bodies are the executive board, the governing council and the general council. The executive board consists of the president, the vice-president and four other members. All members are appointed by the governments of the states participating in the single currency, at the level of heads of state and government. The governing council, the main decision-making body of the ECB, comprises the six members of the executive board and the governors of the national central banks of the 18 euro area states. The general council comprises the president and vice-president and the 28 governors of the national central banks of all the member states of the EU, the other members of the executive board being entitled to participate but not to vote. The ECB is independent of national governments and of all other EU institutions.
President, Mario Draghi (Italy)
Vice-President, Vitor Constancio (Portugal)

EUROPEAN INVESTMENT BANK

100 boulevard Konrad Adenauer, L-2950 Luxembourg
E info@eib.org W www.eib.org

The European Investment Bank (EIB) was set up in 1958 under the terms of the Treaty of Rome and is the financing arm of the EU. The EIB's main activity is to provide long-term loans in support of investments undertaken by private or public promoters, for projects furthering European integration.

The EIB also operates outside the EU, in support of EU development and cooperation policies in partner countries including the enlargement area of Europe (both candidate and potential candidate countries), the Mediterranean, Russia and the southern Caucasus, Africa, the Caribbean, the Pacific, Asia and Latin America.

The EIB assesses and selects the projects it finances independently and usually only finances up to 50 per cent of the total cost of a project.

The bank is not dependent on the EU budget, and raises its own resources on the capital markets. It is the biggest supranational bond issuer and lender in the world with an AAA credit rating. In 2013 it raised €72.0bn (£57.2bn) and lent a total of €71.7bn (£56.9bn), of which €64.0bn (£50.8bn) was lent within the EU.

The shareholders of the EIB are the 28 member states, whose ministers of economy and finance constitute its board of governors. This body lays down general directives on the credit policy of the bank and appoints members to the board of directors. The board of directors consists of 28 members nominated by the member states, and one by the European Commission. It takes decisions on the granting and raising of loans and the fixing of interest rates. The management committee, composed of the bank's president and eight vice-presidents and also appointed by the board of governors, is responsible for the day-to-day operations of the bank.
President, Werner Hoyer (Germany)

ADVISORY BODIES

COMMITTEE OF THE REGIONS

Bâtiment Jacques Delors, rue Belliard 99–101, B-1040 Brussels, Belgium
W www.cor.europa.eu

The Committee of the Regions (CoR) was established in 1994 and is the political assembly which provides local and regional authorities with a voice within the EU. The Lisbon Treaty obliges the EC, the Council of the European Union and the European parliament to consult the CoR whenever new legislative proposals are made in areas which have repercussions at regional or local level. The CoR then issues opinions on these proposals for EU laws, and also has the right to comment on any amendments to proposed legislation by MEPs. The CoR has the right to challenge new EU laws in the European court of justice if it believes it has not been correctly consulted by the commission, parliament or council or for any infringement of the subsidiarity principle.

The committee has 353 full members; the proportion of members from each of the 28 member states of the EU approximately reflects the size of the individual country's population. Committee members are proposed by the member states to the Council of the European Union, which appoints them for a five-year renewable term of office. Members must hold a regional or local authority electoral mandate or be politically accountable to an elected assembly. They participate in the work of six specialist commissions which are responsible for drafting the CoR's opinions and resolutions on a wide range of topics.
President, Ramón Luis Valcárcel Siso (Spain)
Secretary-General (interim), Daniel Janssens (Belgium)

EUROPEAN ECONOMIC AND SOCIAL COMMITTEE

rue Belliard 99, B-1040 Brussels, Belgium W www.eesc.europa.eu

The European Economic and Social Committee (EESC) is a consultative body of the EU. It comprises 353 members drawn from economic and social interest groups in Europe; these members are appointed by the governments of the 28 member states for a five-year renewable term. The last renewal occurred in October 2010 for the 2010–15 mandate. The EESC is divided into three groups: employers, workers, and other interest groups such as consumers, farmers and the self-employed. Every two-and-a-half years the EESC elects a bureau made up of 40 members, including a president and two vice-presidents chosen from each of the three groups in rotation. The EESC issues opinions on draft EU legislation, which are forwarded to the commission, council and parliament. The EESC's competencies have increased as a result of revisions to the Treaty of Rome, and the Lisbon Treaty strengthens the committee's role.
President, Henri Malosse (France)
Secretary-General, Luis Planas Puchades (Spain)

AGENCIES

EUROPEAN ENVIRONMENT AGENCY

Kongens Nytorv 6, DK-1050 Copenhagen K, Denmark
T (+45) 3336 7100 W www.eea.europa.eu

The European Environment Agency (EEA) aims to support sustainable development and to help achieve significant and measurable improvement in Europe's environment through the provision of information to policy-making agents and the public. The EEA has been operational since 1994, and now has 33 member countries. It is an EU body but is open to non-EU countries that share its objectives. The management board consists of representatives of the member countries, two representatives of the EC and two representatives designated by the European parliament.

Chair, Dr Karsten Sach (Germany)

EUROPEAN JUDICIAL COOPERATION UNIT (EUROJUST)

Maanweg 174, 2516 AB The Hague, The Netherlands
E info@eurojust.europa.eu W www.eurojust.europa.eu

The European Union's Judicial Cooperation Unit (Eurojust) was established in 2002 with the aim of developing Europe-wide cooperation in cases involving serious crime committed across more than one member state's jurisdiction. Eurojust also facilitates the provision of international mutual legal assistance and helps to implement extradition requests. It is a key interlocutor with the European parliament, the Council of the European Union and the EC.

The college of Eurojust is composed of 28 national members, one nominated by each member state. These members are experienced prosecutors, judges or police officers.

President of the College, Michèle Coninsx (Belgium)

EUROPEAN POLICE OFFICE (EUROPOL)

Eisenhowelaan 73, 2517 KK The Hague, The Netherlands
W www.europol.europa.eu

The European Police Office (Europol) came into being on 1 October 1998 and assumed its full powers on 1 July 1999. It superseded the Europol Drugs Unit and exists to improve police cooperation between member states and to combat terrorism, illicit traffic in drugs and other serious forms of organised international crime. It is ultimately responsible to the Council of the European Union. Each member state has a national unit to liaise with Europol, and the units send at least one liaison officer to represent its interests at Europol headquarters. Europol employs around 800 staff at its headquarters and handles around 9,000 cases a year. It works closely with law enforcement agencies in the 28 EU member states and non-EU partner states, including Australia, the USA and Canada.

On 11 January 2013, the European Cybercrime Centre (EC3), located at Europol headquarters, was launched to combat illegal online activities carried out by organised crime groups.

Director, Rob Wainwright (UK)

EUROPEAN PARLIAMENT POLITICAL GROUPINGS

as at June 2014

	EPP	S&D	ALDE	Greens/EFA	ECR	GUE/NGL	EFD	NA	Others	Total
Austria	5	5	1	3	–	–	–	4	–	18
Belgium	4	4	6	2	4	–	–	1	–	21
Bulgaria	7	4	4	–	2	–	–	–	–	17
Croatia	5	2	2	1	1	–	–	–	–	11
Cyprus	2	2	–	–	–	2	–	–	–	6
Czech Republic	7	4	4	–	2	3	1	–	–	21
Denmark	1	3	3	1	4	1	–	–	–	13
Estonia	1	1	3	1	–	–	–	–	–	6
Finland	3	2	4	1	2	1	–	–	–	13
France	20	13	7	6	–	4	1	23	–	74
Germany	34	27	4	13	8	8	–	–	2	96
Greece	5	4	–	–	1	6	–	2	3	21
Hungary	12	4	–	2	–	–	–	3	–	21
Ireland	4	1	1	–	1	4	–	–	–	11
Italy	17	31	–	–	–	3	17	5	–	73
Latvia	4	1	–	1	1	–	1	–	–	8
Lithuania	2	2	3	1	1	–	2	–	–	11
Luxembourg	3	1	1	1	–	–	–	–	–	6
Malta	3	3	–	–	–	–	–	–	–	6
The Netherlands	5	3	7	2	2	3	–	4	–	26
Poland	23	5	–	–	19	–	–	–	4	51
Portugal	7	8	2	–	–	4	–	–	–	21
Romania	15	16	1	–	–	–	–	–	–	32
Slovakia	6	4	1	–	2	–	–	–	–	13
Slovenia	5	1	1	1	–	–	–	–	–	8
Spain	17	14	8	4	–	11	–	–	–	54
Sweden	4	6	3	4	–	1	2	–	–	20
UK	–	20	1	6	20	1	24	1	–	73
Total	221	191	67	50	70	52	48	43	9	751

EPP – European People's Party (Christian Democrats)
W www.eppgroup.eu
S&D – Progressive Alliance of Socialists and Democrats in the European Parliament
W www.socialistsanddemocrats.eu
ALDE – Alliance of Liberals and Democrats for Europe
W www.alde.eu
Greens/EFA – Greens/European Free Alliance
W www.greens-efa.eu

ECR – European Conservatives and Reformists
W www.ecrgroup.eu
GUE/NGL – European United Left/Nordic Green Left
W www.guengl.eu
EFD – Europe of Freedom and Democracy Group
W www.efdgroup.eu
NA – non-attached

INTERNATIONAL ORGANISATIONS

International organisations are intergovernmental organisations, whose membership can only include either sovereign states or other international organisations. They are subject to international law and are capable of entering into agreements among themselves or with states. They do not include private non-governmental organisations with an international scope. International organisations are usually established by a treaty providing them with legal recognition, which distinguishes them from collections of states such as the G8.

AFRICAN UNION
PO Box 3243, Addis Ababa, Ethiopia
T (+251) (1) 1551 7700 E webmaster@africa-union.org
W www.au.int

The African Union (AU) was launched in 2002 as a successor to the amalgamated Organisation of African Unity (OAU) and the African Economic Community. It currently has 54 members, representing every African country except Morocco. Morocco left the OAU in 1984 in protest at the admission of Saharan Arab Democratic Republic (representing Western Sahara). The AU aims to further African unity, solidarity and democracy, to coordinate political, economic, social and defence policies, and to intervene in regional conflicts on a humanitarian basis.

Chief AU governing organs include the assembly of heads of state or government, the ultimate decision-making body; the executive council, composed of foreign ministers from member states and which advises the assembly; the African Commission, which is the AU secretariat and consists of one chair, one deputy chair and eight commissioners, each with a separate portfolio, who elect a chair to a four-year term; the peace and security council, modelled on that of the UN and capable of military intervention; and the pan-African parliament, established in 2004 to advise heads of state.

Substantial budgetary arrears due to delays in the payment of national contributions have presented the AU with difficulties in achieving its objectives. Currently the AU has a joint peace keeping force with the United Nations (UNAMID) that has been deployed in the Darfur region of Sudan since 2007 (*see also* United Nations, Peacekeeping Forces). The AU mission in Somalia, AMISOM, was mandated in 2007 by the AU peace and security council and, as at June 2014, had deployed 21,586 military personnel and 540 police officers to the country.
Chair, Dr Nkosazana Dlamini Zuma (South Africa)

ANDEAN COMMUNITY
General Secretariat, Paseo de la República 3895, esq. Aramburú, San Isidro, Lima 27, Peru
T (+51) (1) 710 6400 E contacto@comunidadandina.org
W www.comunidadandina.org

The Andean Community (CAN), known as the Andean Pact until 1996, began operating formally on 21 November 1969 when its commission was established. It comprises four member states – Bolivia, Colombia, Ecuador and Peru – and the organisations and institutions of the Andean Integration System (AIS). Argentina, Brazil, Chile, Paraguay and Uruguay are associated states.

The community's objectives are to facilitate economic growth, create jobs and facilitate regional integration towards the goal of a Latin American common market. It also aims to reduce the inequalities in development between member states. It pursues its objectives through a programme of trade liberalisation, a common external tariff, the relaxation of border controls, coordination between national legislatures and the promotion of industrial, agricultural and technological development. The community also promotes democratic practices, respect for human rights and environmental sustainability. Additionally, CAN supports cultural integration by providing media platforms for sharing documentaries, news and other cultural programming.

The general secretariat of the Andean Community is its executive body, responsible for administration and dispute resolution. The general secretariat operates under the direction of the secretary-general, who is elected by the Andean council of foreign ministers (ACFM). It can propose decisions or suggestions to the ACFM; it also manages the integration process, ensures that community commitments are fulfilled and maintains relations with the member countries and the executive bodies of other international organisations.

The Andean presidential council is the highest-level body of the AIS and comprises the presidents of the member states. Its responsibilities include setting new policies, evaluating the integration process and communicating with other bodies. The chairmanship is rotated among the members of the council each calendar year.

Since 2005, a policy of free flow of persons has enabled citizens to travel, work and study throughout the area without a visa.
Secretary-General, Adalid Contreras Baspineiro (Bolivia)

ARAB MAGHREB UNION
73 rue Tensift, Agdal, Rabat, Morocco
T (+212) (5) 376 81371 E sg.uma@maghrebarabe.org
W www.maghrebarabe.org

The Treaty establishing the Arab Maghreb Union (AMU) was signed on 17 February 1989 by the heads of state of the five member states: Algeria, Libya, Mauritania, Morocco and Tunisia. The AMU aims to strengthen ties between the member countries by developing agriculture and commerce, working towards a customs union and economic common market.

Decisions must be unanimous and are made by a council of heads of state, which is briefed by a council of foreign affairs ministers. The council of heads of state has not assembled since 1994 because of a dispute over the status of Western Sahara. A consultative assembly – consisting of 30 representatives from each member state – is based in Algiers; the secretariat is in Rabat; and the court of justice, with two judges from each country, operates in Nouakchott, Mauritania.
Secretary-General, Habib Ben Yahia (Tunisia)

ARCTIC COUNCIL
Framsenteret, N-9296 Tromso, Norway
T (+47) 7775 0140 E acs@arctic-council.org
W www.arctic-council.org

The Arctic Council was founded in 1996 in Ottawa, Canada, and is a regional forum for socio-economic development and scientific research within the Arctic region, with particular emphasis on environmental conservation and sustainable developments. It comprises eight states: Canada, Denmark (including Greenland and the Faroe Islands), Finland,

Iceland, Norway, Russia, Sweden and the USA. A further six organisations representing indigenous peoples are granted permanent participatory status and include the Saami Council, Inuit Circumpolar Conference and the Arctic Athabaskan Council. 12 states (China, France, Germany, India, Italy, Japan, the Netherlands, Poland, Singapore, South Korea, Spain and the UK) have observer status.

Decisions within the Arctic Council are made at biennial ministerial meetings attended by foreign ministers or designates of the member states. The chairmanship of the council and secretariat also rotate on a biennial basis. Between these meetings, the operation of the council is administered by the Committee of Senior Arctic Officials, which meets biannually.

Arctic Council initiatives are carried out by six working groups, each focusing on specific issues such as the monitoring and prevention of pollution; climate change; biodiversity; and public health.

Chair 2013–15, Leona Aglukkaq (Canada)

ASIA COOPERATION DIALOGUE
E acd@mfa.go.th W www.acddialogue.com

The Asia Cooperation Dialogue (ACD) was initiated by the former prime minister of Thailand, Thaksin Shinawatra, and inaugurated in June 2002. It currently has 33 members, with Morocco granted development partner status.

Its purpose is to provide a continent-wide forum to assist development in countries in Asia, with the ultimate goal of creating a consolidated Asian trade community to enhance competitiveness in the global market and to reduce poverty. It aims to achieve these objectives through promoting interdependence among Asian countries, improving quality of life and expanding the continent's trade and financial markets.

Representatives from each of the member states (typically foreign ministers) meet annually to discuss ACD developments, issues of regional cooperation and methods of enhancing Asian unity. In addition, ministers also meet during the annual UN general assembly to discuss the implementation of policy and a common approach to international issues.

ASIAN-AFRICAN LEGAL CONSULTATIVE ORGANISATION
29 C, Rizal Marg, Diplomatic Enclave, Chanakyapuri, New Delhi 110021, India
T (+91) (11) 2419 7000 E mail@aalco.int W www.aalco.int

The Asian-African Legal Consultative Organisation (AALCO), founded as a result of the Bandung Conference of 1955, was previously known as both the Asian Legal Consultative Committee and the Asian-African Legal Consultative Committee before its name was changed again in 2001. It was initially established as a non-permanent committee for a five-year term which was repeatedly extended until 1981, when it was granted permanent status. It has 47 member states.

The functions of the AALCO include serving as an advisory body to its member states in the field of international law, operating as a forum for common concerns among its members and making recommendations to governments and other international organisations.

Representatives from member states meet for the annual session which is hosted on a rotational basis and is attended by members of government, observers from other organisations and members of the International Court of Justice and International Law Commission.

The secretariat is located in New Delhi and is responsible for the day-to-day functioning of the organisation. It is headed by a secretary-general, who is elected to a four-year term. Other infrastructure includes four regional arbitration centres, located in Egypt, Iran, Malaysia and Nigeria.
Secretary-General, Dr Rahmat Mohamad (Malaysia)

ASIAN DEVELOPMENT BANK
6 ADB Avenue, Mandaluyong City 1550, The Philippines
T (+63) 632 4444 W www.adb.org

The Asian Development Bank (ADB), founded in 1966, is a multilateral financial institution dedicated to reducing poverty in Asia and the Pacific. It has 67 member countries from across the world. The ADB extends loans, equity investments and technical assistance to governments and public and private enterprises in its member countries, and promotes the investment of public and private capital for development. The bank's programmes prioritise economic growth, human development, good governance, environmental protection, private sector growth and regional cooperation.

The ADB is controlled by its board of governors, which meets annually and consists of a representative from each of the member states. It elects and delegates its powers to a board of directors which is responsible for administration and policy review.

The ADB raises funds through members' contributions and issuing bonds on the world's capital markets. In 2013, support given by the ADB in the form of both loans and direct investment totalled US$10,600m (£6,625m).
President, Takehiko Nakao (Japan)

ASIA-PACIFIC ECONOMIC COOPERATION
35 Heng Mui Keng Terrace, Singapore 119616
T (+65) 6891 9600 E info@apec.org W www.apec.org

Asia-Pacific Economic Cooperation (APEC) is an economic forum for Pacific Rim countries to discuss regional economy, cooperation, trade and investment. APEC was founded in 1989 in response to the growing interdependence among Asia-Pacific economies. The 1994 Declaration of Common Resolve envisaged free and open trade between member states with industrialised economies by 2010, extending to members with developing economies by 2020. At the 2013 summit in Bali, Indonesia APEC leaders issued the Bali declaration in which they committed to increased regional economic integration, sustainable and equitable economic growth and regional resource security. Its 21 members define and fund work programmes for APEC's four committees, 15 working groups and other special task groups.

APEC's chairmanship rotates annually among member states and the chair is responsible for hosting the annual leaders' meeting, as well as meetings of foreign affairs and trade ministers. The permanent secretariat, based in Singapore, is responsible for implementing policy, and is headed by an executive director selected by member states to serve a three-year term.
Executive Director, Dr Alan Bollard (New Zealand)

ASSOCIATION OF SOUTH-EAST ASIAN NATIONS
Jalan Sisingamangaraja 70a, Jakarta 12110, Indonesia
T (+62) (21) 726 2991/724 3372 E public@aseansec.org
W www.asean.org

The Association of South-East Asian Nations (ASEAN) is a geo-political and economic organisation formed in 1967 with the aim of accelerating economic growth, social progress and cultural development, and ensuring regional stability. It currently has ten member states.

The ASEAN summit, a biannual meeting of the heads of government, is the organisation's highest authority. The biannual ASEAN foreign ministers' meeting (ASEAN

Coordinating Council) is responsible for preparing summit meetings, implementing their policies, and coordinating ASEAN's activities. The ASEAN economic ministers meet annually to coordinate economic policy.

An ASEAN free trade area was implemented in 2003, while a common preferential tariff was introduced in 1993. At the ASEAN summit in 1995, a South East Asia nuclear-weapon-free zone was declared. In December 2008 a new charter came into force which gave ASEAN legal status and a new institutional framework, committed it to the promotion of democracy, and provided for the establishment of the intergovernmental commission on human rights.

The secretary-general of ASEAN is appointed by rotation and can initiate, advise on, coordinate and implement ASEAN activities. In addition to the ASEAN secretariat based in Jakarta, each member state has a national secretariat in its foreign ministry which organises and implements activities at a national level.

Secretary-General, Le Luong Minh (Vietnam)

BALTIC ASSEMBLY

Citadeles Street 2–616, Riga, LV-1010, Latvia
T (+371) 6722 5178 E baltasam@baltasam.org
W www.baltasam.org

Established in November 1991, the Baltic Assembly (BA) is an international organisation for cooperation between the parliaments of Estonia, Latvia and Lithuania. Each member state appoints between 12 and 16 parliamentarians to the assembly, including a chair and vice-chair of the national delegation. The political allegiances of the appointees reflect party proportions in each of the domestic parliaments. The BA holds an annual session in each of the member states in rotation. Several permanent and *ad hoc* committees also meet at least three times a year. The Baltic council of ministers, which comprises the heads of government and ministers of the member states, meets with the BA once a year and promotes intergovernmental and regional cooperation between the Baltic states; the joint sessions are known as the Baltic council.

President, Laine Randjarv (Estonia, 2014)

CAB INTERNATIONAL

Nosworthy Way, Wallingford, Oxon OX10 8DE
T 01491-832111 E enquiries@cabi.org W www.cabi.org

Founded in 1910, CAB International (CABI) (formerly the Commonwealth Agricultural Bureau) is a non-profit organisation that provides scientific expertise to assist sustainable development and environmental protection. The organisation consists of 42 countries, five British overseas territories and one associate member (Netherlands); each is represented on both the executive council, which meets biannually, and the review conference, held every five years to appraise policy and set future goals. A governing board provides guidance on policy issues.

CABI has three divisions: publishing, development projects and research, and microbial services. Each division undertakes research and provides consultancy aimed at raising agricultural productivity, conserving biological resources, protecting the environment and controlling disease. Any country is eligible to apply for membership.

Chief Executive Officer, Dr Trevor Nicholls (UK)

CARIBBEAN COMMUNITY

PO Box 10827, Turkeyen, Greater Georgetown, Guyana
T (+592) 222 0001/0075 E registry@caricom.org
W www.caricom.org

The Caribbean Community (CARICOM) was established as the Caribbean Community and Common Market in 1973 with the signing of the Treaty of Chaguaramas. The objectives of CARICOM is to improve member states' working and living standards, boost employment levels, promote economic development and competitiveness, coordinate foreign and economic policies and enhance cooperation in the delivery of services such as health and education.

The supreme organ is the Conference of Heads of Government, which determines policy and resolves conflict. The Community Council of Ministers consists of ministers of government assigned to CARICOM affairs and is responsible for economic and strategic planning. The principal administrative arm is the secretariat, based in Guyana. The Bureau of the Conference of Heads of Government is the executive body; it comprises the chair of the conference, the outgoing chair and the secretary-general, who are all authorised to initiate proposals and to secure the implementation of decisions. In addition, there are five ministerial councils dealing with trade and economic development, foreign and community relations, human and social development, finance and planning, and national security and law enforcement.

There are 15 member states of CARICOM plus five associate members, 13 of which are party to the Revised Treaty of Chaguaramas, which established the Caribbean Community including the CARICOM single market and economy (CSME) in 2006.

Secretary-General, Irwin LaRocque (Dominica)

THE COMMONWEALTH

The Commonwealth is a voluntary association of 53 sovereign and independent states together with their associated states and dependencies. All of the states were formerly parts of the British Empire or League of Nations (later the UN) mandated territories, except for Mozambique and Rwanda which were admitted because of their history of cooperation with neighbouring Commonwealth nations.

The status and relationship of member nations were first defined by the inter-imperial relations committee of the 1926 Imperial Conference, when the six existing dominions (Australia, Canada, the Irish Free State, Newfoundland, New Zealand and South Africa) were described as 'autonomous communities within the British Empire, equal in status, in no way subordinate one to another in any aspect of their domestic or external affairs, though united by a common allegiance to the Crown and freely associated as members of the British Commonwealth of Nations'. This formula was given legal substance by the statute of Westminster in 1931.

This concept of a group of countries owing allegiance to a single crown changed in 1949 when India became a republic. India's continued membership of the Commonwealth was agreed by the other members on the basis of its 'acceptance of the monarch as the symbol of the free association of its independent member nations and as such the head of the Commonwealth'. This enabled subsequent new republics to join the association. Member nations agreed at the time of the accession of Queen Elizabeth II to recognise Her Majesty as the new head of the Commonwealth. However, the position is not vested in the British Crown.

THE MODERN COMMONWEALTH

As the UK's former colonies joined, after India and Pakistan in 1947, the Commonwealth was transformed into a multiracial association of equal nations, increasingly focused on promoting development and racial equality. South Africa withdrew in 1961 when it became clear that its reapplication for membership on becoming a republic would be rejected over its policy of apartheid.

The new goals of advocating democracy, the rule of law, good government and social justice were enshrined in the Harare Commonwealth Declaration (1991), which formed the basis of new membership guidelines agreed in Cyprus in 1993. Following the adoption of measures at the New Zealand summit in 1995 against serious or persistent violations of these principles, Nigeria was suspended in 1995 and Sierra Leone was suspended in 1997 for anti-democratic behaviour. Sierra Leone's suspension was revoked the following year when a legitimate government was returned to power. Similarly, Nigeria's suspension was lifted in 1999, the day a newly elected civilian president took office. The Edinburgh Commonwealth Economic Declaration (1997) established a set of economic principles for the Commonwealth, promoting economic growth while protecting smaller member states from the negative effects of globalisation. Zimbabwe was suspended from the councils of the Commonwealth in March 2002, and in 2003 the Zimbabwean government officially confirmed its departure from the association. Following the bloodless coup led by General Pervez Musharraf in 1999, Pakistan faced its first suspension from the Commonwealth. It was readmitted in 2004 only to be suspended again in 2007 after the imposition of emergency rule. The suspension was lifted after successful democratic elections in February 2008. Fiji's Commonwealth membership was suspended in September 2009 after its military government refused to commit to elections in 2010.

MEMBERSHIP
Membership of the Commonwealth involves acceptance of the association's basic principles and is subject to the approval of existing members. There are 53 members at present, of which 16 have Queen Elizabeth II as head of state, 32 are republics and five have national monarchies. (The date of joining the Commonwealth is shown in parentheses.)

*Antigua and Barbuda (1981)
*Australia (1931)
*The Bahamas (1973)
Bangladesh (1972)
*Barbados (1966)
*Belize (1981)
Botswana (1966)
Brunei (1984)
Cameroon (1995)
*Canada (1931)
Cyprus (1961)
Dominica (1978)
†Fiji (1970)
Ghana (1957)
*Grenada (1974)
Guyana (1966)
India (1947)
*Jamaica (1962)
Kenya (1963)
Kiribati (1979)
Lesotho (1966)
Malawi (1964)
Malaysia (1957)
Maldives (1982)
Malta (1964)
Mauritius (1968)
Mozambique (1995)

Namibia (1990)
Nauru (1968)
*New Zealand (1931)
Nigeria (1960)
Pakistan (1947)
*Papua New Guinea (1975)
Rwanda (2009)
*St Kitts and Nevis (1983)
*St Lucia (1979)
*St Vincent and the
    Grenadines (1979)
Samoa (1970)
Seychelles (1976)
Sierra Leone (1961)
Singapore (1965)
*Solomon Islands (1978)
South Africa (1931)
Sri Lanka (1948)
Swaziland (1968)
Tanzania (1961)
Tonga (1970)
Trinidad and Tobago (1962)
*Tuvalu (1978)
Uganda (1962)
*United Kingdom
Vanuatu (1980)
Zambia (1964)

* Realms of Queen Elizabeth II
† Currently suspended from the Commonwealth

COUNTRIES THAT HAVE LEFT THE COMMONWEALTH
Republic of Ireland (1949)
South Africa (1961, rejoined 1994)
Pakistan (1972, rejoined 1989; suspended 1999, suspension lifted 2004; suspended 2007, suspension lifted 2008)
Zimbabwe (2003)
The Gambia (2013)

In each of the realms where Queen Elizabeth II is head of state (except for the UK), she is personally represented by a governor-general, who holds in all essential respects the same position in relation to the administration of public affairs in the realm as is held by Her Majesty in the UK. The governor-general is appointed by the Queen on the advice of the government of the state concerned.

INTERGOVERNMENTAL AND OTHER LINKS
The main forum for consultation is the Commonwealth Heads of Government Meetings, held biennially to discuss international developments and to consider cooperation among members. Decisions are reached by consensus and the views of the meeting are set out in a communiqué. There are also annual meetings of finance ministers and frequent meetings of ministers and officials in other fields, such as education, health, gender and youth affairs. Inter-governmental links are complemented by the activities of some 80 Commonwealth non-governmental organisations linking professionals, sportsmen and sportswomen, and interest groups. The Commonwealth Games take place every four years.

COMMONWEALTH SECRETARIAT
The Commonwealth has a secretariat, established in 1965 in London, which is funded by member governments. This is the main agency for multilateral communication between member governments on issues relating to the Commonwealth as a whole. It promotes consultation and cooperation, disseminates information on matters of common concern, organises meetings including the biennial summits, coordinates Commonwealth activities and provides technical assistance for economic and social development through the Commonwealth fund for technical cooperation.

The Commonwealth Foundation was established by Commonwealth governments in 1965 as an autonomous body with a board of governors representing Common-wealth governments that fund the foundation. It promotes and funds exchanges and other activities aimed at strengthening the skills and effectiveness of professionals and non-governmental organisations. It also promotes culture, rural development, social welfare, human rights and gender equality.

COMMONWEALTH SECRETARIAT, Marlborough House, Pall Mall, London SW1Y 5HX T 020-7747 6500
E info@commonwealth.int W www.thecommonwealth.org
Secretary-General, Kamalesh Sharma (India)
COMMONWEALTH FOUNDATION, Marlborough House, Pall Mall, London SW1Y 5HY T 020-7930 3783
E foundation@commonwealth.int
W www.commonwealthfoundation.com
Chair, Anand Satyanand (New Zealand)
COMMONWEALTH EDUCATION TRUST, New Zealand House, 80 Haymarket, London SW1Y 4TE T 020-7024 9822
E info@cet1886.org W www.cet1886.org

COMMONWEALTH OF INDEPENDENT STATES

Ulitsa Kirova 17, Minsk 220030, Belarus
T (+375) (17) 222 35 17 E cr@cis.minsk.by W www.cis.minsk.by

The Commonwealth of Independent States (CIS) is a multilateral grouping of 11 former Soviet republics. It was formed in 1991 and its charter was signed by ten states in 1993–4. The CIS acts as a coordinating mechanism for foreign, defence and economic policies and as a forum for addressing problems common to former members of the USSR. These matters are addressed in more than 70 inter-state, intergovernmental coordinating and consultative statutory bodies.

The two supreme CIS organs are the council of heads of state, which meets twice a year, and the council of heads of government. The executive committee, based in Minsk and Moscow, provides administrative support. There are also numerous ministerial, parliamentary, economic and security councils.

On becoming members of the CIS, the member states agreed to recognise their existing borders, respect one another's territorial integrity and reject the use of military force or coercion to settle disputes. A treaty on collective security was signed in 1992 by six states, and a joint peacemaking force, to intervene in CIS conflicts, was agreed upon by nine states. Russia concluded bilateral and multilateral agreements with other CIS states under the supervision of the council of heads of collective security (established 1993). These agreements became the Collective Security Treaty, enabling Russia to station troops in eight of the CIS states, and giving Russian forces *de facto* control of virtually all of the former USSR's external borders. Only Ukraine and Moldova remained outside the defence cooperation framework and did not sign the treaty. In 1999, Azerbaijan, Georgia and Uzbekistan withdrew from the treaty and formed a new defensive (GUAM) with Moldova and Ukraine. Georgia withdrew from the organisation entirely in August 2009, following the country's war with Russia in 2008. In May 2014, Ukraine announced that it would begin the process of withdrawing from the CIS.

In 1991, 11 republics signed a treaty forming an economic community. Members agreed to refrain from economic actions that would damage each other and to coordinate economic and monetary policies. A coordinating consultative committee, an economic arbitration court and an inter-state bank were established. Members also affirmed the principles of private ownership, free enterprise and competition as the basis for economic recovery.

The 11 CIS members who signed the Establishment of an Economic Union Treaty in September 1993 committed themselves to a common economic space with free movement of goods, services, capital and labour. Belarus, Kazakhstan, Kyrgyzstan and Russia signed a treaty on the establishment of a customs union in 1996; the treaty was later signed by Tajikistan. In 2000 the presidents of the five countries approved a treaty establishing the Eurasian Economic Community, and in 2010 Russia, Belarus and Kazakhstan formed a customs union. In April 2011 the economic council approved a draft agreement for the development of a free trade zone that would include all of the CIS member states: the agreement was signed by the CIS states with the exception of Azerbaijan, Uzbekistan and Turkmenistan in October 2011. On 1 January 2012 the customs union of Russia, Belarus and Kazakhstan transformed into a single economic space (SES), a higher form of economic integration, ensuring freedom of movement of goods, services, capital, labour, and equal treatment of economic entities within the three countries. Belarus assumed the presidency of the Commonwealth on 1 January 2013.
Executive Secretary, Sergey Lebedev (Russia)

COOPERATION COUNCIL FOR THE ARAB STATES OF THE GULF

PO Box 7153, Riyadh 11–462, Saudi Arabia
T (+966) (1) 482 7777 W www.gcc-sg.org

The Cooperation Council for the Arab States of the Gulf, or Gulf Cooperation Council (GCC), was established on 25 May 1981. Its main objectives are increasing coordination and integration, harmonising economic, commercial, educational and social policies and promoting scientific and technical innovation among its member states. It established a common market in 2008, and set up a customs union in 2003 which is yet to be fully enforced. The GCC has six members: Oman, the United Arab Emirates, Bahrain, Kuwait, Qatar and Saudi Arabia

The highest authority of the GCC is the supreme council, whose presidency rotates among members' heads of states. It holds one regular session every year, but extraordinary sessions may be convened if necessary.

The ministerial council, which ordinarily meets every three months, consists of the foreign ministers of the member states or other delegated ministers. It is authorised to propose policies and recommendations.
Secretary-General, Abdul Latif bin Rashid Al Zayani (Bahrain)

COUNCIL OF EUROPE

Avenue de l'Europe, F-67075 Strasbourg-Cedex, France
T (+33) (3) 8841 2000 W www.coe.int

The Council of Europe was founded in 1949. Its aim is to achieve greater unity between its members, to safeguard their European heritage and to facilitate their progress in economic, social, cultural, educational, scientific, legal and administrative matters, and to further pluralist democracy, human rights and fundamental freedoms. It has 47 member states, including the 28 members of the European Union.

The organs are the committee of ministers, consisting of the foreign ministers of member countries, and the parliamentary assembly of 318 members (and 318 substitutes), elected or chosen by the national parliaments of member countries in proportion to the relative strength of political parties.

The committee of ministers is the executive organ. The majority of its conclusions take the form of international agreements (known as European conventions) or recommendations to governments. Decisions of the ministers may also be embodied in partial agreements to which a limited number of member governments are party.

One of the principal achievements of the Council of Europe is the European Convention on Human Rights (1950), which entered into force on 3 September 1953, and under which the European Court of Human Rights was established in 1959. The court oversees the implementation of the convention in the member states. It sits in chambers of seven judges or, exceptionally, as a grand chamber of 17 judges. Litigants must exhaust legal processes in their own country prior to bringing cases before the court.

Among other conventions and agreements are the European Convention for the Prevention of Torture, the European Social Charter, the Framework Convention for the protection of national minorities, the Istanbul Convention which combats violence against women, the Lanzarote Convention to protect children against sexual abuse and the Convention on Cyber Crime

In 1990 the Venice Commission, an independent legal

advisory body, was set up to assist in developing legislative, administrative and constitutional reforms in both European and non-European countries; it currently has 59 member states, one associate member, five observers and three states with special status.

Non-member states take part in certain Council of Europe activities, such as educational, cultural and sports activities on a regular or *ad hoc* basis.

The council's ordinary budget for 2014 totals €404m (£334m).

Secretary-General, Thorbjorn Jagland (Norway)

COUNCIL OF THE BALTIC SEA STATES
PO Box 2010, Slussplan 9, SE-103 11 Stockholm, Sweden
T (+46) 8440 1920 E cbss@cbss.org W www.cbss.org

The Council of the Baltic Sea States was established in 1992 with the aim of creating a regional forum to increase cooperation and coordination among the states that border on the Baltic Sea. The organisation focuses mainly on the environment, economic development, energy, education and culture, civil security and humanitarian issues. It currently has 12 members (11 countries and the European Commission) while a further ten countries (including the UK and the USA) hold observer status.

The council consists of the foreign ministers of each member state and a member of the European Commission. Chairmanship of the council rotates on an annual basis, and the annual session is held in the country currently in the chair. The foreign minister of the presiding country is responsible for coordinating activities between the sessions. Since 1998 a permanent international secretariat has been established in Stockholm, Sweden. Since 2012, the council is the lead partner in the EU Strategy for the Baltic Sea Region: the first comprehensive EU strategy to target a 'macro region'. The flagship strategy aims to mobilise all relevant EU funding and policies and coordinate the actions of the EU, EU countries, regions, pan-Baltic organisations, financing institutions and non-governmental bodies to promote a more balanced development of the Baltic Sea region.

Chair, Estonia (2014–15)

ECONOMIC COMMUNITY OF WEST AFRICAN STATES
101 Yakubu Gowon Crescent, Asokoro District, PMB 401,
Abuja, Nigeria
T (+234) (9) 314 76479 E info@ecowas.int W www.ecowas.int

The Economic Community of West African States (ECOWAS) was founded in 1975 and came into operation in 1977. It aims to promote the economic, social and cultural development of West Africa through mutual cooperation, and to prevent and control regional conflicts.

The supreme authority of ECOWAS is vested in the annual summit of heads of government of all 15 member states. A council of ministers meets biannually to monitor the organisation and make recommendations to the summit. Since restructuring in 2007, ECOWAS has been managed by a commission, headed by the president. The ECOWAS parliament was inaugurated in November 2000 and judges for the court of justice were appointed in January 2001. Chad currently holds observer status.

Five member states of ECOWAS (The Gambia, Ghana, Guinea, Nigeria and Sierra Leone) plan to introduce the eco as a single common currency in 2015. Eight other states currently use the CFA franc – it is planned eventually to amalgamate the two currencies. An ECOWAS travel certificate is issued allowing free movement within the community, and nine countries have a common passport.

An ECOWAS peacekeeping force has been involved in attempts to restore peace in Liberia (1990–6), Sierra Leone (1997–9) and in Guinea-Bissau (1998–9). In December 2010 the Côte d'Ivoire was suspended from ECOWAS following the failure of its *de facto* president, Laurent Gbagbo, to step down after a presidential election; the country was reinstated the following year following Mr Gbagbo's arrest. In March 2011 both Guinea and Niger were reinstated to the organisation; their memberships had been suspended for failure to hold satisfactory democratic elections in 2009. ECOWAS suspended Mali in March 2012 and, a few weeks later, in April, Guinea-Bissau, demanding the immediate restoration of constitutional order in both states following military coups in both countries.

President, Kadré Désiré Ouédraogo (Burkina Faso)

EUROPEAN BANK FOR RECONSTRUCTION AND DEVELOPMENT
One Exchange Square, London EC2A 2JN
T 020-7338 6000 W www.ebrd.com

Since its establishment in 1991 the European Bank for Reconstruction and Development (EBRD) has become the largest financial investor in a region that stretches from central Europe and the Western Balkans to central Asia. Since 2011 the Bank – owned by 64 countries, the EU and the European Investment Bank – has been laying the foundations for the expansion of its operations to the southern and eastern Mediterranean region.

The main forms of EBRD financing are loans, equity investments and guarantees. EBRD's charter stipulates that at least 60 per cent of lending must go to the private sector, reflecting its particular interest in strengthening the financial sector and to promoting small and medium-sized businesses. It works in cooperation with national governments, private companies and international organisations such as the OECD, the IMF, the World Bank and the UN specialised agencies. The EBRD is also able to borrow on world capital markets.

The EBRD's highest authority is the board of governors; each member appoints one governor and one alternate. The governors delegate most powers to a 23-member board of directors; the directors are responsible for the EBRD's operations and budget, and are elected by the governors for three-year terms. The governors also elect the president of the board of directors, who acts as the bank's president for a four-year term.

The EBRD sustained a business volume of €8.5bn (£6.8bn) in 2013 and its portfolio of investments increased slightly from €37.5bn (£30bn) at the end of 2012 to €37.8bn (£30.3bn) at the end of 2013.

President, Sir Suma Chakrabarti (India)

EUROPEAN FREE TRADE ASSOCIATION
9–11 rue de Varembé, CH-1211 Geneva 20, Switzerland
T (+41) (22) 332 2600 E mail.gva@efta.int W www.efta.int

The European Free Trade Association (EFTA) was founded in 1960 on the premise of free trade as a means of achieving growth and prosperity among its member states as well as promoting closer economic cooperation between the Western European countries. The immediate aim of the Association was to provide a framework for the liberalisation of trade in goods among its member states.

EFTA was founded by seven countries: Austria, Denmark, Norway, Portugal, Sweden, Switzerland and the UK. Finland joined in 1961, Iceland in 1970 and Liechtenstein in 1991. In 1973, the UK and Denmark left EFTA to join the European Community. They were followed by Portugal in 1986 and by Austria, Finland and Sweden in 1995. Today the EFTA member states are Iceland, Liechtenstein, Norway and Switzerland.

The Agreement on the European Economic Area (EEA) was signed in 1992 and entered into force in January 1994. The agreement brings together the 27 EU (European Union) member states and the three EEA EFTA states – Iceland, Liechtenstein and Norway – in a single market, referred to as the 'internal market'. Switzerland is not a member of the EEA, but has a series of bilateral agreements with the EU. The secretariat in Brussels provides support for the mangement of the EEA agreement, including the preparation of new legislation.

Currently, the EFTA states have free trade agreements with the following partners: Albania; Bosnia and Hercegovina; Canada; Central American States (Costa Rica and Panama); Chile; Colombia; Egypt; the Cooperation Council for Arab States of the Gulf; Hong Kong, China; Israel; Jordan; the Rep. of Korea; Lebanon; Macedonia; Mexico; Montenegro; Morocco; the Palestinian Authority; Peru; Serbia; Singapore; Southern African Customs Union; Tunisia; Turkey; and Ukraine. Negotiations on free trade agreements are ongoing with Algeria; Central American States (Guatemala and Honduras); India; Indonesia; Malaysia; the customs union of Russia, Belarus and Kazakhstan; Thailand; and Vietnam.

The EFTA Council is the highest governing body in the EFTA. Member states usually meet eight times a year at ambassadorial level in Geneva.

Secretary-General, Kristinn Arnason (Iceland)

EUROPEAN ORGANISATION FOR NUCLEAR RESEARCH (CERN)
CH-1211 Geneva 23, Switzerland
T (+41) (22) 767 8484 E cern.reception@cern.ch W www.cern.ch

The convention establishing the European Organisation for Nuclear Research (CERN) came into force in 1954. CERN promotes European collaboration in high-energy physics with scientific goals and no military implication. It has 21 member states, one candidate for accession, one associate member state in the pre-stage to membership, and seven members with observer status, including the European Commission and UNESCO.

The council, which is the highest policy-making body, comprises two delegates from each member state and is chaired by the president, who is elected by the council in session. The council also appoints a director-general, who is responsible for the internal organisation of CERN. The director-general heads a workforce of approximately 2,400, including physicists, craftsmen, technicians and administrative staff. At present more than 10,000 scientists use CERN's facilities.

Tim Berners-Lee developed the World Wide Web while working at CERN in 1989, and in 2008 CERN completed construction work on the Large Hadron Collider, the world's largest and most powerful particle accelerator.

Director-General, Dr Rolf-Dieter Heuer (Germany)

EUROPEAN SPACE AGENCY
8–10 rue Mario Nikis, 75738 Paris Cedex 15, France
T (+33) (1) 5369 7654 E contactesa@esa.int W www.esa.int

The European Space Agency (ESA) was created in 1975 by the merger of the European Space Research Organisation and the European Launcher Development Organisation. Its aims include the advancement of space research and technology and the implementation of European space policy. ESA has 20 member states and one cooperating state, with seven other nations participating in the Plan for European Cooperating States. ESA's mandatory activities

are funded by contributions from all member states and calculated in accordance with each country's gross national income. In 2014, ESA's budget amounted to €4,102m (£3,287m).

The agency is directed by a council composed of the representatives of its member states; its chief officer is the director-general who is elected by the council every four years. ESA has liaison offices in Belgium (for the EU), the USA and Russia, while a launch base is stationed in French Guiana.

Director-General, Jean-Jacques Dordain (France)

EUROPEAN UNION
See European Union section

FOOD AND AGRICULTURE ORGANISATION OF THE UNITED NATIONS
Viale delle Terme di Caracalla, 00153 Rome, Italy
T (+39) (06) 57051 E fao-hq@fao.org W www.fao.org

The Food and Agriculture Organisation (FAO) is a specialised UN agency, established in 1945. It assists rural populations by raising levels of nutrition and living standards, and by encouraging greater efficiency in food production and distribution. It analyses and publishes information on agriculture and natural resources. The FAO also advises governments on national agricultural policy and planning through its investment centre and collaboration with the World Bank and other financial institutions. The FAO's field programme covers a range of activities, including strengthening crop yields, rural development and livestock heath and productivity.

The FAO's priorities are sustainable agriculture, rural development and food security. The organisation monitors potential famine areas, channels emergency aid from governments and other agencies, assists in rehabilitation and responds to urgent or unforeseen requests for technical assistance.

The FAO has 195 members (194 states plus the European Union), and two associate members (the Faroe Islands and Tokelau). It is governed by a biennial conference of its members which sets a programme and budget. The budget for 2014–15 is US$2,400m (£1,414m), funded by member countries in proportion to their gross national income. The FAO is also funded by donor governments and other institutions.

The conference elects a director-general and a 49-member council which governs between conferences. The regular and field programmes are administered by a secretariat, headed by the director-general. Five regional, ten sub-regional and 74 national offices help administer the field programme.

Director-General, Jose Graziano da Silva (Brazil)

INTERNATIONAL ATOMIC ENERGY AGENCY
PO Box 100, Wagramer Strasse 5, A-1400 Vienna, Austria
T (+43) (1) 26000 E official.mail@iaea.org W www.iaea.org

The International Atomic Energy Agency (IAEA) was established in 1957. It is an intergovernmental organisation that reports to, but is not a specialised agency of, the UN.

The IAEA aims to enhance the contribution of atomic energy to peace, health and prosperity. It does not advocate the use of atomic energy for military purposes. It establishes atomic energy safety standards and offers services to its member states to upgrade safety and security measures for their nuclear installations and material, and for radioactive sources, material and waste. It is the focal point for international conventions on the early notification of a nuclear accident, accident assistance, civil liability for nuclear damage, physical protection of nuclear material and the safety of spent fuel and radioactive waste management. The IAEA also encourages research and training in nuclear power. It is additionally charged with drawing up safeguards and verifying their enforcement in accordance with several international nuclear weapons treaties.

The IAEA has 162 members that meet annually in a general conference. The conference decides policy, a programme and a budget – €349.8m (£280.9m) in 2014 – as well as electing a director-general and a 35-member board of governors. The board meets five times a year to review and formulate policy, address budgetary concerns and consider applications for membership. Project and policy changes are implemented by the secretariat.

Director-General, Yukiya Amano (Japan)

INTERNATIONAL CIVIL AVIATION ORGANISATION

999 University Street, Montréal, Québec, Canada H3C 5H7
T (+1) (514) 954 8219 E icaohq@icao.int W www.icao.int

The International Civil Aviation Organisation (ICAO) was founded with the signing of the Chicago Convention on International Civil Aviation in 1944 and became a specialised agency of the UN in 1947. It sets international technical standards and regulations for aviation safety, security and efficiency, as well as environmental protection.

ICAO has 191 members and is governed by an assembly, which convenes triennially. A council of 36 members is elected, which represents leading air transport nations as well as less developed countries. The council elects the president, appoints the secretary-general and supervises the organisation through subsidiary committees, serviced by a secretariat.

President of the Council, Dr Olumuyiwa Bernard Aliu (Nigeria)

INTERNATIONAL CRIMINAL POLICE ORGANISATION (INTERPOL)

200 Quai Charles de Gaulle, F-69006 Lyon, France
W www.interpol.int

Interpol was set up in 1923 to establish an international criminal records office and to harmonise extradition procedures. In 2013, the organisation comprised 190 member countries. Interpol's aims are to promote cooperation between criminal police authorities and to support government agencies concerned with combating crime, while respecting national sovereignty. It is financed largely by annual contributions from the governments of the member countries and supplementary funding from private and commercial sources.

Interpol policy is formulated by the general assembly which meets annually and is composed of delegates appointed by the member countries. The 13-member executive committee is elected by the general assembly from the member countries' delegates and is chaired by the president, who serves a four-year term of office. The permanent administrative organ is the general secretariat, headed by the secretary-general, who is appointed by the general assembly.

The UK Interpol National Central Bureau is operated by the National Crime Agency (NCA).

Secretary-General, Ronald Noble (USA)

INTERNATIONAL ENERGY AGENCY

9 rue de la Fédération, F-75739 Paris Cedex 15, France
T (+33) (1) 4057 6500/01 E info@iea.org W www.iea.org

The International Energy Agency (IEA), founded in 1974, is an autonomous agency within the framework of the Organisation for Economic Cooperation and Development

(OECD). The IEA's objectives include the improvement of energy cooperation worldwide, development of alternative energy sources and the promotion of relations between oil-producing and oil-consuming countries. The IEA also maintains an emergency system to alleviate the effects of severe oil supply disruptions.

The main decision-making body is the governing board, composed of senior energy officials from member countries. The IEA secretariat, with a staff of energy experts, carries out the work of the governing board and its subordinate bodies. The executive director is appointed by the board. The IEA has 29 member states; the European Commission also participates in its work.

Executive Director, Maria van der Hoeven (The Netherlands)

INTERNATIONAL FRANCOPHONE ORGANISATION

Cabinet du Secrétaire général, 19–21 avenue Bosquet, 75007 Paris, France
T (+33) (1) 4437 3300 W www.francophonie.org

The International Francophone Organisation *(International Organisation of La Francophonie* – IOF) is an inter-governmental organisation founded in 1970 by 21 French-speaking countries. Its 77 member states and governments, 57 members and 20 observers, together represent over 890 million people; 220 million of which speak French regularly, with varying degrees of fluency. The IOF organises political activities and actions multilateral cooperation that benefits French-speaking populations. It represents its member states internationally, promotes French language and francophone cultural industries with the aim of preventing conflict and promoting development.

The conference of heads of state and government of countries with French as a common language – also known as La Francophonie summit – takes place biennially. Other institutions include the permanent ministerial conference and the permanent council.

Secretary-General, Abdou Diouf (Senegal)

INTERNATIONAL FUND FOR AGRICULTURAL DEVELOPMENT

44 Via Paolo di Dono, 00142 Rome, Italy
T (+39) (06) 54591 E ifad@ifad.org W www.ifad.org

The International Fund for Agricultural Development (IFAD) began operations as a UN specialised agency in 1977. It develops and finances agricultural and rural projects in developing countries and aims to promote employment and additional income for poor farmers, reduce malnutrition and improve food security systems.

IFAD has 173 member states divided into three lists: List A (primarily OECD countries), List B (primarily OPEC countries), and List C (developing countries) which is subdivided into C1 (Africa), C2 (Europe, Asia and the Pacific) and C3 (Latin America and the Caribbean). All powers are vested in a governing council of all member states, which meets annually. It elects an executive board which is composed of 18 members and 18 alternate members and chaired by the president of IFAD. The president serves a four-year term that can be renewed once.

President, Kanayo F. Nwanze (Nigeria)

INTERNATIONAL HYDROGRAPHIC ORGANISATION

4 Quai Antoine 1er, B.P. 445, 98011, Monaco
T (+377) 9310 8100 E info@iho.int W www.iho.int

The International Hydrographic Organisation (IHO) began operating in 1921 with 19 member states and headquarters

in the Principality of Monaco. In 1970 its name was changed from the International Hydrographic Bureau. The IHO is an intergovernmental organisation that has a purely consultative role and aims to support safety in international navigation, set policy for marine conservation and improve coordination between national hydrographic institutions. The IHO has a membership of 82 states that meet at five-yearly conferences to set policy, approve budget, review progress and adopt programmes of work. Each member is represented at these conferences by their most senior hydrographer. All member states have an opportunity to initiate new proposals for IHO consideration. Outside of its membership, the IHO acts to promote hydrography and facilitate the exchange of technology with developing countries. It is also the source that defines the boundaries between seas and oceans.
President, Robert Ward (Australia)

INTERNATIONAL LABOUR ORGANISATION
4 route des Morillons, CH-1211, Genève 22, Switzerland
T (+41) (22) 799 6111 E ilo@ilo.org W www.ilo.org

The International Labour Organisation (ILO) was established in 1919 as an autonomous body of the League of Nations and became the UN's first specialised agency in 1946. The ILO aims to promote employment, improve working conditions, extend social protection and promote dialogue between government, workers' and employers' organisations.

It sets minimum international labour standards through the drafting of international conventions. Member countries are obliged to submit these to their domestic authorities for ratification, and thus undertake to bring their domestic legislation in line with the conventions. Members must report to the ILO periodically on how these regulations are being implemented. The ILO is also a principal resource centre for information, analysis and guidance on labour and employment.

The ILO has 185 member states and is composed of the International Labour Conference, the governing body and the International Labour Office. The conference of members meets annually and is attended by national delegations. It adopts international labour conventions and recommendations, provides a forum for discussion of economic and social issues and approves the ILO's programme and budget.

The 56-member governing body is composed of 28 government, 14 worker and 14 employer members and acts as the ILO's executive council. It convenes triannually. Ten governments, including the UK, hold permanent seats on the governing body because of their industrial importance. There are also various regional conferences and advisory committees. The ILO acts as a secretariat and as a centre for operations, publishing and research.
Director-General, Guy Ryder (UK)

INTERNATIONAL MARITIME ORGANISATION
4 Albert Embankment, London SE1 7SR
T 020-7735 7611 E info@imo.org W www.imo.org

Originally named the Inter-Governmental Maritime Consultative Organisation, the International Maritime Organisation (IMO) was established as a UN specialised agency in 1948. Owing to delays in treaty ratification it did not commence operations until 1958.

The IMO fosters intergovernmental cooperation in technical matters relating to international shipping, particularly regarding safety and security at sea, efficiency in navigation and protecting the marine environment from pollution caused by shipping. The IMO is responsible for convening maritime conferences and drafting marine conventions. It also provides technical aid to countries wishing to develop their activities at sea.

In 2014, the IMO had 170 members and three associate members. It is governed by an assembly comprising delegates of all its members. It meets biennially to formulate policy, set a budget (£64.3m for 2014–15), to vote on specific recommendations on pollution, maritime safety and security, and to elect the council. The council, which meets twice a year, fulfils the functions of the assembly between sessions and appoints a secretary-general. It consists of 40 members: ten from the world's largest shipping nations, ten from the nations most dependent on seaborne trade and 20 other members to ensure a fair geographical representation. The IMO acts as the secretariat for the London Convention (1972) and its 1996 protocol which regulates the disposal of land-generated waste at sea.
Secretary-General, Koji Sekimizu (Japan)

INTERNATIONAL MONETARY FUND
700 19th Street NW, Washington DC 20431, USA
T (+1) (202) 623 7000 E publicaffairs@imf.org W www.imf.org

The International Monetary Fund (IMF) was established at the UN Monetary and Financial Conference at Bretton Woods, New Hampshire, in 1944. Its articles of agreement entered into force in 1945 and it began operations in 1947.

The IMF exists to promote international monetary cooperation and the expansion of world trade to ensure international economic stability. It advises members on their economic and financial policies; promotes policy coordination among the major industrial countries; gives technical assistance in central banking, balance of payments accounting, taxation and other financial matters; and provides loans to states with weak economies. The IMF serves as a forum for members to discuss monetary policy issues and seeks the balanced growth of international trade. It has 188 members; Tuvalu joined in June 2010 and South Sudan in April 2012.

Upon joining the IMF, a member is assigned a quota based on that member's relative standing in the world economy and its balance of payments. The quota determines the maximum size of the member's capital subscription to the fund, access to IMF resources, voting power and share in the allocation of special drawing rights (SDRs). Quotas are reviewed every five years and adjusted accordingly. After the 13th general review in 2008 the IMF board of governors adopted a reform package which would grant *ad hoc* quota increases to 54 countries found to be under-represented, and allocate triple the number of basic votes to all members. These reforms became effective in March 2011. In December 2010 the board of governors approved recommendations of the 14th general review – namely the doubling of all available quotas, a shift in 6 per cent of quotas from over-to under-represented countries, and an overall realignment in quota shares to reflect emerging markets and developing countries (EDMCs). Under these reforms, China will become the third largest member country and three further EDMCs (Brazil, India and Russia) will be among the top ten shareholders. These reforms will become effective upon their acceptance by three-fifths of members having 85 per cent of total voting power.

The SDR (special drawing rights), the reserve currency created by the IMF in 1969, is calculated daily on a basket of usable currencies and is the IMF's unit of account; as at 31 July 2014, 1 SDR equalled US$1.53 (£0.91). SDRs are allocated at intervals to supplement members' reserves and thereby improve international financial liquidity. Total quotas currently stand at SDR238.1bn.

The IMF is not a bank and does not lend money; it provides temporary financial assistance by selling a member's SDRs or other members' currencies in exchange for the member's own currency. The member can then use the purchased currency to alleviate its balance of payments difficulties. IMF financial resources derive primarily from members' capital subscriptions, which are proportionally related to their quotas. In addition, the IMF is authorised to borrow from official lenders. It may also draw on a line of credit from 38 member countries and institutions under the new arrangements to borrow (NAB). Once activated, NAB can provide supplementary resources of up to SDR370bn to the IMF. In limited cases the IMF can also access a potential amount totalling SDR17bn from 11 countries under the so-called general arrangements to borrow (GAB).

Benign market conditions between 2004 and 2008 prompted many countries to start repaying their outstanding loans and demand for the fund's resources dropped dramatically; however, in 2008 the IMF increased its lending in response to the global financial crisis. In March 2009 the IMF announced a number of reforms to its lending framework, intended to provide greater speed and flexibility in lending arrangements, double access limits on loans and more closely tailor the conditionality of loans to fit the recipient state's needs and strengths. In February 2010 a defined poverty line (a gross national income of $1,135 per capita) was introduced under which countries would qualify to access low-cost concessional loans under the poverty reduction and growth trust. On 31 July 2014 total outstanding IMF credits amounted to SDR88.1bn, or US$135bn (£79.9bn).

The IMF supports long-term efforts at economic reform and transformation as well as medium-term programmes under the extended fund facility, which runs for three to four years and is aimed at overcoming balance of payments difficulties stemming from macroeconomic and structural problems. Typically, measures are introduced to reform taxation and the financial sector, to privatise state-owned enterprises and to make labour markets more flexible.

The IMF is headed by a board of governors, comprising one representative and one alternate representative of each member state, which meets annually. The governors delegate powers to 24 executive directors, who are appointed or elected by member countries. The executive directors operate the fund on a daily basis under a managing director, whom they elect.

Managing Director, Christine Lagarde (France)

INTERNATIONAL ORGANISATION FOR MIGRATION

17 Route des Morillons, CH-1211 Geneva 19, Switzerland
T (+41) 22717 9111 E hq@iom.int W www.iom.int

The International Organisation for Migration (IOM) was founded in 1951 to resettle European displaced persons and refugees. During the 1960s and 1970s the IOM developed links with the United Nations High Commissioner for Refugees and began a programme of assistance and reintegration outside of Europe.

The role of the IOM is to help ensure the orderly and humane management of migration; its remit includes migration health services, international migration law, counter-trafficking measures, emergency and post-crisis management and assisted voluntary returns. It employs more than 8,400 staff and is present in over 480 field locations. There are 156 member states.

Internally, the IOM is led by a director-general who is elected for a five-year term. The director-general's office has the constitutional authority to manage the organisation,

carry out the activities within its mandate and develop current policies, procedures and strategies. The office of the inspector-general (OIG) incorporates the functions of evaluation, internal audit and assessment of projects.
Director-General, William Lacy Swing (USA)

INTERNATIONAL RED CROSS AND RED CRESCENT MOVEMENT

PO Box 303, CH-1211 Geneva 19, Switzerland
T (+41) 2273 04222 W www.icrc.org

The International Red Cross and Red Crescent Movement is composed of three elements – the International Committee of the Red Cross, the International Federation of Red Cross and Red Crescent Societies, and the National Red Cross and Red Crescent Societies.

The International Committee of the Red Cross (ICRC), the organisation's founding body, was formed in 1863. It aims to protect and assist victims of armed conflict. It also seeks to ensure the application of the Geneva Conventions regarding prisoners of war and detainees.

The International Federation of Red Cross and Red Crescent Societies (IFRC) was founded in 1919 to assist the humanitarian activities of national societies, coordinate their relief operations for victims of natural disasters and care for refugees outside areas of conflict. There are Red Cross and Red Crescent societies in 189 countries and it has more than 60 field delegations internationally.

The international conference of the Red Cross and Red Crescent meets every four years, bringing together delegates of the ICRC, the International Federation and the national societies, as well as representatives of all 194 states party to the Geneva Conventions.
President of the IFRC, Tadateru Konoe (Japan)

INTERNATIONAL TELECOMMUNICATION UNION

Place des Nations, CH-1211 Geneva 20, Switzerland
T (+41) (22) 730 5111 E itumail@itu.int W www.itu.int

The International Telecommunication Union (ITU) was founded in Paris in 1865 as the International Telegraph Union and became a UN specialised agency in 1947.

ITU is an intergovernmental organisation for the development of telecommunications and the harmonisation of national telecommunication policies. It comprises 193 member states, more than 700 sector members and associates who represent public and private organisations involved in telecommunications. Its mission is to promote the development of information and communication technologies and to offer assistance to developing countries.

For nearly 150 years, ITU has coordinated the shared global use of the radio spectrum, promoted international cooperation in assigning satellite orbits, worked to improve communication infrastructure in the developing world and established the worldwide standards for the interconnection of a vast range of communications systems: from broadband networks to new-generation wireless technologies, aeronautical and maritime navigation, radio astronomy, satellite-based meteorology and converging fixed-line and mobile telephone, internet and broadcasting technologies.
Secretary-General, Dr Hamadoun Touré (Mali)

INTERNATIONAL TRADE UNION CONFEDERATION

Boulevard du Roi Albert II, 5 B 1, B-1210 Brussels, Belgium
T (+32) (2) 224 0211 E info@ituc-csi.org W www.ituc-csi.org

The International Trade Union Confederation (ITUC) was created in 2006 by the merger between the International

Confederation of Free Trade Unions (ICFTU), the World Confederation of Labour (WCL) and other independent unions. Through public and industrial advocacy work it seeks to assert and defend the rights and interests of workers, and to foster international cooperation between trade unions. In November 2013 the ITUC represented 176 million workers in 161 countries and territories and had 325 national affiliates.

The congress, the supreme authority of the ITUC, meets once every four years to review and propose policy and to elect the 78-member general council. Council members are elected according to population-weighted geographical regions, with six seats reserved for nomination by the women's committee, and two by the youth committee. The council, and the general secretary elected at each congress, govern the organisation. It also elects a 25-member executive bureau from among its members which deals with urgent issues and those delegated to it by the council; it also makes decisions on finances and formulates the annual budget for council approval.

The ITUC has regional organisations for Asia-Pacific (ITUC-AP), Africa (ITUC-AF), the Americas (TUCA) and Europe (the pan-European regional council, or PERC). It also cooperates closely with the Global Union Federations, the Trade Union Advisory Committee to the Organisation for Economic Cooperation and Development (OECD), the European Trade Union Confederation, the International Labour Organisation, a number of other UN specialised agencies and national and regional unions and organisations.
General Secretary, Sharan Burrow (Australia)

INTERNATIONAL WHALING COMMISSION

The Red House, 135 Station Road, Impington, Cambridge
CB24 9NP
T 01223-233971 W www.iwc.int

The International Whaling Commission (IWC) was set up under the International Convention for the Regulation of Whaling, signed in Washington DC in 1946. It has 88 member states. The purpose of the IWC is to provide for the conservation of whale stocks, enabling the development of the whaling industry. The organisation reviews and revises the schedule to the convention that decrees the complete protection of certain species, sets limits for when and where whaling can take place, coordinates and funds whale research and publishes and promotes scientific studies.

The IWC has four main committees, responsible for scientific, technical, conservation and finance matters. There are further sub-committees and working groups concerned with aboriginal subsistence whaling, infractions, small cetaceans, whalewatching, whale-killing methods and animal welfare issues.
Executive Secretary, Simon Brockington (UK)

LATIN UNION

204 rue de Vaugirard, 75015 Paris, France
T (+33) (1) 4549 6060 E ulsg@unilat.org W www.unilat.org

The Latin Union is an international organisation whose member states use a Romance language. It was created in 1954 with the signing of a constituent agreement in Madrid and has existed as a functioning institution since 1983. The aims of the organisation are to protect, project and promote the common heritage and to unify identities of the Latin and Latin-influenced world. It has 36 member states and four members with observer status.

The senior body of the organisation, the congress, consists of representatives from each of the member states and meets every two years. It is responsible for approving the budget and setting the agenda for the Union's activities.

The executive council is made up of representatives from 12 member states who are elected for a four-year term by congress, as is the secretary-general who is responsible for the implementation of policy through the general secretariat.

The official languages of the Latin Union are Catalan, French, Italian, Portuguese, Castillian (Spanish) and Romanian, although Catalan and Romanian are not used as working languages.
Secretary-General, José Luis Ballester Dicenta (Spain)

LEAGUE OF ARAB STATES

Al-Tahrir Square, PO Box 11642, Cairo, Egypt
T (+20) (2) 2575 0511 W www.lasportal.org

The League of Arab States was founded in 1945 to protect the independence and sovereignty of its member states, supervise the affairs and interests of Arab countries and promote coordination among them. The organisation has 22 members, including Palestine. The League itself has observer status at the United Nations.

The heads of member states meet annually at the Arab League summit, while foreign ministers convene every six months as part of the Arab League council. Member states participate in various specialised agencies which develop specific areas of cooperation between Arab states. These include the Arab Monetary Fund; the Arab Satellite Communications Organisation; the Arab Academy for Science, Technology and Maritime Transport; the Arab Bank for Economic Development in Africa; the Arab League Educational, Cultural and Scientific Organisation; and the Council of Arab Economic Unity.
Secretary-General, Nabil El Araby (Egypt)

MERCOSUR

Luis Piera 1992, Piso 1, 11200-Montevideo, Uruguay
T (+598) (2) 412 9024 W www.mercosur.int

MERCOSUR (the Southern Common Market) was created by the Treaty of Asunción, signed by Argentina, Brazil, Paraguay and Uruguay on 26 March 1991. Venezuela signed an adhesion protocol in 2006 and became a full member in 2012. Bolivia, which has been an associate member since 1997, began the process of becoming a full member in December 2012; as a member in the process of incorporation Boliva is active in MERCOSUR and has right of word but not the right to vote. Four other countries (Chile, Colombia, Ecuador and Peru) have associate member status. Guyana and Suriname are in the process of becoming associate members.

The Common Market Council (CMC) is the highest-level agency of MERCOSUR, with authority to formulate policy and enforce member states' compliance with the Treaty of Asunción. The CMC comprises ministers of foreign affairs and economic ministers of the member states; it meets at least once a year.

The Common Market Group is the executive body of MERCOSUR and is coordinated by the foreign ministries of the member states. Its function is to implement decisions made by the CMC and resolve disputes, and if necessary, establish subgroups to work on particular issues. Other bodies include a joint parliamentary committee, a trade commission and a socio-economic advisory forum. The presidency of MERCOSUR rotates between member states every six months.

In 2005, Argentina, Brazil, Paraguay and Uruguay became associate members of the Andean Community, reciprocating MERCOSUR's action to grant associate membership to all Andean Community nations. In December 2005, the Colombian president ratified a free trade agreement (FTA) with MERCOSUR giving Colombian products preferential access to MERCOSUR countries. MERCOSUR signed an

FTA with Israel in December 2007, the bloc's first such agreement outside Latin America. An FTA with Egypt was signed in August 2010 and ratified in July 2014. After stalling in 2004, negotiations with the EU over a possible FTA were relaunched in May 2010.

Presidency, Argentina (Jul–Dec 2014)

NORDIC COUNCIL

Ved Stranden 18, 1061 Copenhagen K, Denmark
T (+45) 3396 0400 E nordisk-rad@norden.org W www.norden.org

The Nordic Council was established in March 1952 as an advisory body on economic and social cooperation, comprising parliamentary delegates from Denmark, Iceland, Norway and Sweden. It was subsequently joined by Finland (1955), and representatives from the Faroes (1970), the Aland Islands (1970) and Greenland (1984).

Cooperation is regulated by the Helsinki Treaty, signed in 1962. This was amended in 1971 to create a Nordic council of ministers, which discusses all matters except defence and foreign affairs. Decisions of the council of ministers, which are taken by consensus, are binding, although if ratification by member parliaments is required, decisions only become effective following parliamentary approval. The council of ministers is advised by the Nordic Council, to which it reports annually. There are ministers for Nordic cooperation in every member government.

The Nordic Council comprises 87 voting delegates nominated from member parliaments and numerous non-voting government representatives. It meets at least once a year in plenary sessions. The full council chooses a 13-member presidium, which conducts business between sessions. A secretariat, headed by a secretary-general, provides administrative support. The presidency of the Nordic Council rotates between the five countries, and the presiding country always hosts the annual council session.

President, Karin Astrom (Sweden, 2014)

NORTH AMERICAN FREE TRADE AGREEMENT

NAFTA SECRETARIAT, CANADIAN SECTION,
    111 Sussex Drive, 5th Floor, Ottawa, Ontario K1N 1J1, Canada
    T (+1) (343) 203 4274 E canada@nafta-sec-alena.org
NAFTA SECRETARIAT, MEXICAN SECTION, Blvd. Adolfo
    López Mateos 3025, 2o Piso, Col. Héroes de Padierna, C.P.
    10700, Mexico, D.F.
    T (+52) (55) 5629 9630 E naftamexico@nafta-sec-alena.org
NAFTA SECRETARIAT, US SECTION, Room 2061,
    14th Street and Constitution Avenue, NW, Washington DC,
    20230, USA
    T (+1) (202) 482 5438 E usa@nafta-sec-alena.org
    W www.nafta-sec-alena.org

The leaders of Canada, Mexico and the USA signed the North American Free Trade Agreement (NAFTA) on 17 December 1992 in their respective capitals; it came into force in January 1994 after being ratified by the legislatures of the three member states.

NAFTA aims to eliminate barriers to trade in goods and services, promote fair competition within the free trade area, protect and enforce intellectual property rights and create a framework for further cooperation. To achieve these aims, import tariffs, quotas and limits on cross-border investment have been removed.

The NAFTA secretariat is composed of Canadian, Mexican and US sections. It is responsible for administering the dispute-settlement provisions of the agreement, providing assistance to the Free Trade Commission and support for various committees and working groups, and facilitating the operation of the agreement.

NORTH ATLANTIC TREATY ORGANISATION

Bvld Leopold III, Brussels B-1110, Belgium
T (+32) (2) 707 4111 E natodoc@hq.nato.int W www.nato.int

The North Atlantic Treaty Organisation (NATO) is a political and military alliance designed to provide common security for its members through cooperation and consultation in political, military and economic as well as scientific and other non-military fields.

The North Atlantic Treaty (Treaty of Washington) was signed in 1949 by Belgium, Canada, Denmark, France, Iceland, Italy, Luxembourg, the Netherlands, Norway, Portugal, the UK and the USA. Greece and Turkey acceded to the treaty in 1952, the Federal Republic of Germany in 1955 (the reunited Germany acceded in October 1990), Spain in 1982, and the Czech Republic, Hungary and Poland in 1999. Bulgaria, Estonia, Latvia, Lithuania, Romania, Slovakia and Slovenia signed membership protocols in March 2003 and officially joined NATO in March 2004. Albania and Croatia became official members in April 2009, having signed membership accords in September 2008.

STRUCTURE

The North Atlantic council (NAC), chaired by the secretary-general, is the highest authority of the alliance and is composed of permanent representatives of the 28 member countries. It meets weekly, but also holds meetings at higher levels involving foreign and defence ministers and heads of government. The permanent representatives (ambassadors) head national delegations of advisers and experts. The nuclear planning group (NPG) is composed of all member countries, with the exception of France, and meets at ministerial level at least once a year. The NATO secretary-general chairs the council and the NPG. Much of the NAC policy is prepared and drafted by the senior political committee, a group of deputy permanent representatives and policy advisers.

The senior military authority in NATO, which advises the council, is the military committee, composed of the chief of defence staffs of each member country except Iceland, which has no military forces and is represented by a civilian. The military committee, which is assisted by an integrated international military staff, also meets in permanent session with permanent military representatives and is responsible for making recommendations to the council on measures considered necessary for the common defence of the NATO area and for supplying guidance on military matters to the NATO strategic commanders. The chair of the military committee, elected for a period of two to three years, represents the committee on the council.

The alliance's military command structure is divided between two functional strategic commands: Allied Command Operations (ACO) is responsible for all NATO military operations, whereas Allied Command Transformation (ACT) is charged with training and restructuring NATO military forces and capabilities. The headquarters of ACO is at the Supreme Headquarters of the Allied Powers Europe (SHAPE) at Mons, Belgium, and comes under the command of the Supreme Allied Commander Europe (SACEUR). The headquarters of ACT is at Norfolk, Virginia, USA, and is under the command of the Supreme Allied Commander Transformation (SACT). There is also a regional planning group for Canada and the USA. At the Lisbon summit in November 2010, NATO leaders approved a plan to streamline the ACO while maintaining its military capability; the plans will result in a reduction of personnel within the military command structure from 13,000 to 8,800 and is expected to be fully implemented by the end of 2015.

POST COLD WAR DEVELOPMENTS

The Euro-Atlantic partnership council (EAPC) was established in 1997 to develop closer security links with Eastern European and former Soviet states. Replacing the North Atlantic cooperation council (NACC) as the first institutional framework for cooperation between NATO member countries and former adversaries from Central and Eastern Europe, the EAPC focuses on defence planning, defence industry conversion, defence management and force structuring. Its membership comprises the 28 NATO members and Armenia, Austria, Azerbaijan, Belarus, Bosnia and Hercegovina, Finland, Georgia, Ireland, Kazakhstan, Kyrgyzstan, Macedonia, Malta, Moldova, Montenegro, Russia, Serbia, Sweden, Switzerland, Tajikistan, Turkmenistan, Ukraine and Uzbekistan. The EAPC provides the multilateral, political framework for the partnership for peace programme (PFP). The PFP is the basis for practical, bilateral security cooperation between NATO and all partner countries in the fields of defence planning and budgeting, military exercises and civil emergency operations. It also works to improve the interoperability between the forces of partner and member countries to enable them to undertake joint operations and has provided the context for cooperation by many of the partner countries in NATO-led peacekeeping and peace-support operations in Bosnia and Hercegovina, Kosovo and Afghanistan.

NATO and Russia committed themselves to helping build a stable and secure partnership based on mutual interest when they signed the 1997 Founding Act on mutual relations, cooperation and security, which provided for the creation of a NATO-Russia permanent joint council (PJC). In 2002 it was replaced by the NATO-Russia council (NRC). The NRC usually meets every month at ambassadorial level and twice each year at ministerial level to address issues of joint concern such as terrorist threats and the narcotics trade, and to pursue bilateral programmes in defence reform, search and rescue, and civil emergency planning. Since April 2014, following Russia's military intervention in Ukraine, NATO has suspended all practical cooperation with Russia, including the NRC, save for high level communications at ambassadorial level and above. NATO previously suspended formal NRC meetings and cooperation with Russia in response to Russia's military action in Georgia in 2008.

The establishment of the NATO-Ukraine commission (NUC) in 1997 committed both parties to developing their relationship under a programme of consultation and co-operation on political and security issues. The NATO-Georgia commission (NGC), created in 2008, is pursuing political dialogue between NATO and Georgia, and helping to supervise Georgia's progress towards membership of NATO. The NGC is also co-ordinating support to help the country recover from the summer 2008 conflict.

NATO's Mediterranean dialogue, launched in 1994, aims to improve trust and understanding of NATO's goals and objectives among the countries of the southern Mediterranean area: Algeria, Egypt, Israel, Jordan, Mauritania, Morocco and Tunisia. At its summit meeting in 2004, the alliance launched the Istanbul cooperation initiative (ICI), promoting practical cooperation with the Gulf cooperation council (GCC) and other interested countries in the Middle East. To date Bahrain, Qatar, Kuwait and the United Arab Emirates have joined the ICI.

The development of a European security and defence identity, which would strengthen NATO's European pillar, was agreed at the 1999 NATO summit meeting in Washington. Subsequent developments have served to strengthen cooperation between NATO and the European Union and to establish a strategic partnership.

At the 2002 Prague summit, further measures to improve defence capabilities were taken on the basis of a new capabilities commitment, in which member countries agreed to specific targets and time frames for improvements. A military concept for defence against terrorism was also agreed, and additional initiatives taken in the areas of nuclear, biological and chemical weapons defence and protection against cyber attacks. The NATO response force, a rapid-reaction unit comprising land, sea and air special forces, was officially launched at the Prague summit and became fully operational in 2006. The Lisbon summit in 2010 saw the publication of NATO's strategic concept, a statement of core principles that emphasized the importance of international cooperation in defence, security and crisis management, with particular reference to strengthening NATO's relationships with the EU and UN.

AFGHANISTAN

From January 2001, following the establishment of the Afghan Transitional Authority, an international security assistance force (ISAF) was created on the basis of a UN mandate to provide the security required to allow infrastructure reconstruction and create a stable democratic government. In 2002, NATO began providing support for ISAF at the request of the lead nations and, in August 2003, assumed full responsibility for the leadership of ISAF. In accordance with an October 2003 UN security council mandate, ISAF gradually extended its authority from the capital, Kabul, to assume responsibility for the security, reconstruction and development of the entire country in October 2006. The gradual transition of security responsibility from ISAF to the Afghan national security forces commenced in 2010 and is scheduled to be fully completed by the end of 2014. To aid a successful transition of responsibility, ISAF oversees provincial reconstruction teams, which provide security for aid workers and help with reconstruction work across the country; it also provides training and mentoring for the Afghan National Army and the Afghan National Police. NATO officials have pledged their continuing commitment to the region after troops are withdrawn in December 2014.

KOSOVO

NATO has been leading a peace-support operation in Kosovo since June 1999 in support of wider international efforts to build peace and stability in the area. Just under 5,000 troops from the NATO-led Kosovo Force (KFOR), provided by 31 countries, are currently deployed in the region.

TURKEY

In December 2012, the Turkish government requested support for its air defence system in the wake of the escalating conflict in Syria. The request was prompted by several incidents of cross-border fire and resulting civilian casualties. Germany, The Netherlands and the USA agreed to provide patriot air defence systems for purely defensive deployment in Adana, Gaziantep and Kahramanmaras. All defence systems have been operational under NATO command and control since February 2013.

AFRICA

NATO counter-piracy operations were active between October and December 2008, and again between March and July 2009, in response to the growing threat presented by piracy in the Horn of Africa region. Currently, Operation Ocean Shield – approved by the North Atlantic council in August 2009 and extended until the end of 2016 – is focused on at-sea operations, but also offers assistance to regional states in developing their capacity to combat piracy.

Since 2007 NATO has provided specialist support to the African Union in their ongoing deployment to Somalia (AMISOM) and is also assisting in the establishment of a continental on-call security force (African Standby Force) which is expected to reach its full operational capability by 2015.

Secretary-General and Chair of the North Atlantic Council, of the DPC and of the NPG, Anders Fogh Rasmussen (Denmark)

ORGANISATION FOR ECONOMIC COOPERATION AND DEVELOPMENT

2 rue André Pascal, 75775 Paris Cedex 16, France
T (+33) (1) 4524 8200 E webmaster@oecd.org W www.oecd.org

The Organisation for Economic Cooperation and Development (OECD) was formed in 1961 to replace the Organisation for European Economic Cooperation. It is the instrument for international cooperation among industrialised member countries on economic and social policies. Its objectives are to assist its member governments in creating policies designed to achieve high, sustained economic growth and maintain financial stability, to contribute to world trade on a multilateral basis and to stimulate members' aid to developing countries. The OECD has 34 member countries, most of which have developed, high-income economies. The European Commission is involved in the work of the OECD but is not a member of the organisation.

The council is the supreme body of the organisation. It is composed of one representative for each member country plus one representative of the European Commission and meets at permanent representative level under the chairmanship of the secretary-general, and at ministerial level (usually once a year) under the chair of a minister. Decisions and recommendations are adopted by consensus. Most of the OECD's work is undertaken by around 250 specialised committees and working parties. These are serviced by an international secretariat headed by a secretary-general.

In 2010 Chile, Estonia, Israel and Slovenia acceded to the OECD; the Russian Federation is a candidate for accession. The organisation has links to many other non-member states and in 2007 launched a programme of enhanced engagement with Brazil, China, India, Indonesia and South Africa. The funding of the OECD is divided according to a member state's economy and population size; the USA, the largest contributor, supplies almost 22 per cent of the organisation's budget.

Secretary-General, Angel Gurría (Mexico)

ORGANISATION FOR SECURITY AND COOPERATION IN EUROPE

6 Wallnerstrasse, 1010 Vienna, Austria
T (+43) (1) 514360 E info@osce.org W www.osce.org

The Organisation for Security and Cooperation in Europe (OSCE) was launched in 1975 as the Conference on Security and Cooperation in Europe (CSCE) under the Helsinki Final Act. This established agreements between NATO members, Warsaw Pact members, and neutral and non-aligned European countries covering security, cooperation and human rights. It was renamed in 1995.

The Charter of Paris for a New Europe, signed in November 1990, committed members to support multiparty democracy, free-market economics, the rule of law and human rights. The signatories also agreed to regular meetings of heads of government, ministers and officials. The first CSCE summit was held in Helsinki in July 1992, at which the Helsinki Document was adopted. This declared

the CSCE to be a regional organisation under the UN charter and defined the structures of the organisation.

Three structures have been established: the ministerial council, which comprises the foreign ministers of participating states and meets at least once a year; the permanent council, which is the main regular body for political consulation, meeting weekly in Vienna; and the forum for security cooperation, also meeting weekly. The chairmanship of the OSCE rotates annually and the post of chair-in-office is held by the foreign minister of a participating state.

The OSCE is also underpinned by four permanent institutions: a secretariat (Vienna); an office for democratic institutions and human rights (Warsaw), which is charged with furthering human rights, democracy and the rule of law; an office of the high commissioner on national minorities (The Hague), which identifies ethnic tensions that might endanger peace and promotes their resolution; and a representative on freedom of the media (Vienna), which is responsible for assisting governments in the furthering of free, independent and pluralistic media.

The OSCE has 15 field operations in Europe, the Caucasus and Central Asia. Since 1996, the OSCE has observed more than 150 elections and supervised all elections in Bosnia and Hercegovina between 1996 and 2000 and in Kosovo between 2000 and 2004. In 1999, the charter on European security committed the OSCE to cooperating with other organisations and institutions concerned with the promotion of security within the OSCE area. The OSCE has 57 participating states and in 2014 its budget was €142.3m (£112.6m).

Chair, Didier Burkhalter (Switzerland, 2014)

ORGANISATION OF AMERICAN STATES

17th Street and Constitution Avenue, NW, Washington DC 20006–4499, USA
T (+1) (202) 370 5000 W www.oas.org

Originally founded in 1890 for largely commercial purposes, the Organisation of American States (OAS) adopted its present name and charter in 1948. The charter entered into force in 1951 and was amended in 1970, 1988, 1996 and 1997. OAS has 35 member states, though the membership of Honduras was suspended in July 2009 following a coup against President Jose Zelaya; its suspension was lifted in June 2011. The European Union and 69 non-American states have permanent observer status.

The OAS aims to strengthen the peace and security of the Americas; to promote and consolidate representative democracy; to prevent or resolve any political, judicial or economic issues which may arise among member states; to promote their economic, social and cultural development; and to achieve an effective limitation of conventional weapons.

Policy is determined by the annual general assembly, the organisation's supreme authority, which elects the secretary-general for a five-year term. The meeting of consultation of ministers of foreign affairs considers urgent problems on an *ad hoc* basis. The permanent council, comprising one ambassador from each member state, implements the policies approved by the general assembly, acts as an intermediary in cases of disputes arising between states and oversees the general secretariat, the main administrative body. The inter-American council for integral development was created in 1996 by the ratification of the protocol of Managua to promote sustainable development and eliminate poverty.

Secretary-General, José Miguel Insulza (Chile)

ORGANISATION OF ARAB PETROLEUM EXPORTING COUNTRIES

PO Box 20501, Safat 13066, Kuwait

T (+965) 2495 9000 E oapec@oapecorg.org W www.oapecorg.org

The Organisation of Arab Petroleum Exporting Countries (OAPEC) was founded in 1968. Its objectives are to promote cooperation in economic activities, unite efforts to ensure the flow of oil to consumer markets and create a favourable climate for capital investment and the development of the petroleum industry. OAPEC has 11 member states, although Tunisia's membership has been inactive since 1986.

The ministerial council is composed of oil ministers from the member countries and meets twice a year to determine policy and approve the budgets and accounts of the general secretariat and the judicial tribunal. The judicial tribunal is composed of between seven and 11 judges who rule on disputes between member countries and between countries and oil companies. The executive organ of OAPEC is the general secretariat.

The active members are Algeria, Bahrain, Egypt, Iraq, Kuwait, Libya, Qatar, Saudi Arabia, Syria and the United Arab Emirates.

Secretary-General, Abbas Ali Naqi (Kuwait)

ORGANISATION OF THE BLACK SEA ECONOMIC COOPERATION

Sakip Sabanci Caddesi, Musir Fuad Pasa Yalisi, Eski Tersane, 34467-Emirgan, Istanbul, Turkey

T (+90) (212) 229 6330/6335 E info@bsec-organization.org W www.bsec-organization.org

The Black Sea Economic Cooperation (BSEC) resulted from the Istanbul Summit Declaration and the adoption of the Bosphorus statement on 25 June 1992; it acquired a permanent secretariat in 1994. A charter was inaugurated to found the Organisation of the Black Sea Economic Cooperation in May 1999 following the Yalta Summit of the heads of state or government in June 1998. It has 12 member states.

The organisation aims to promote closer political and economic cooperation between the countries in the Black Sea region and to foster greater security, foreign investment and good governance.

The council of the ministers of foreign affairs is the highest decision-making authority; it elects the organisation's secretary-general and meets twice-yearly. The meetings rotate among the member states and the chair is the foreign minister of the state in which the meeting is held. There is also a committee of senior officials, and a number of working groups which deal with specific areas of cooperation. BSEC has a permanent secretariat based in Istanbul.

Secretary-General, Victor Tvircun (Moldova)

ORGANISATION OF THE ISLAMIC CONFERENCE

PO Box 178, Jeddah 21411, Saudi Arabia

T (+966) (2) 651 5222 W www.oic-oci.org

The Organisation of the Islamic Conference (OIC) was established in 1969 with the purpose of promoting solidarity and cooperation between its member states. It also has the specific aims of supporting the formation of a Palestinian state, coordinating the views of member states in international forums such as the UN, and improving cooperation in the fields of economics, culture and science.

The OIC has three main bodies: the Islamic summit, the organisation's supreme authority composed of the heads of member states, which meets triennially; the annual conference of foreign ministers; and the general secretariat, which implements policy and is headed by a secretary-general elected by the conference of foreign ministers for a once-renewable five-year term.

In addition to this structure, the OIC has several subsidiary bodies, institutions and standing committees. These include the Islamic Solidarity Fund, to aid Islamic institutions in member countries; the Islamic Development Bank, to finance development projects in member states and the Islamic Educational, Scientific and Cultural Organisation.

Since 1991, the OIC has spoken out in protest of violence against Muslims in India, the Occupied Territories and Bosnia-Hercegovina. From 1993 to 1995 the OIC coordinated the offering of troops to the UN by Muslim states to protect Muslim areas of Bosnia-Hercegovina.

The organisation has 57 members (27 states in Africa; 24 in the Middle East, central and South East Asia plus the Palestinian Authority; three in Europe, and two in South America) and five observer states.

Secretary-General, Iyad Ameen Madani (Saudi Arabia)

ORGANISATION OF THE PETROLEUM EXPORTING COUNTRIES

Helferstorferstrasse 17, A-1010 Vienna, Austria

T (+43) (1) 2111 20 W www.opec.org

The Organisation of the Petroleum Exporting Countries (OPEC) was created in 1960 as a permanent intergovernmental organisation with the principal aims of unifying and coordinating the petroleum policies of its 12 member countries, and stabilising prices and supply in international oil markets.

The supreme authority is the conference of ministers, which generally comprises the oil and energy ministers of the member countries. The conference meets in formal session twice a year to discuss oil policy, energy and administrative matters. The board of governors implements conference resolutions and oversees the running of the OPEC secretariat located in Vienna, Austria.

According to OPEC's annual statistical review, OPEC's 12 member countries held 81 per cent of the world's crude oil reserves at the end of 2013, and that year accounted for 43.4 per cent of the world's oil production.

Secretary-General, Abdalla Salem El-Badri (Libya)

PACIFIC ISLANDS FORUM

Secretariat, Private Mail Bag, Suva, Fiji

T (+679) 331 2600 E info@forumsec.org W www.forumsec.org

The Pacific Islands Forum (PIF), formerly the South Pacific Forum, was established in 1971 and represents heads of governments of 16 independent and self-governing Pacific island countries. It aims to foster cooperation between its governments and to represent the interests of the region in international organisations. The PIF meets annually, after which a dialogue is conducted at ministerial level with 14 forum partner states and the European Union.

The PIF secretariat is governed by the forum officials committee (FOC), composed of senior figures from each member country. It comprises divisions dealing with development and economic policy, trade and investment, political and international affairs and services, and is responsible for implementing the forum's decisions.

In 2006, French Polynesia and New Caledonia became associate members. Tokelau, Wallis and Futuna, Guam, American Samoa, the Commonwealth, the Asia Development Bank, Commonwealth of the Northern Marianas, Western and Central Pacific Fisheries Commission, the ACP Group, the United Nations and the World Bank currently hold observer status, with Timor–Leste as a special observer.

Fiji's membership was suspended in May 2009 over the failure of its military government to commit to a timeframe for a return to democratic government.

Secretary-General, Tuiloma Neroni Slade (Samoa)

PARTNERS IN POPULATION AND DEVELOPMENT

IPH Building, Mohakhali, Dhaka-1212, Bangladesh
T (+88) (2) 988 1882 E partners@ppdsec.org
W www.partners-popdev.org

Partners in Population and Development (PPD) is an intergovernmental organisation launched at the UN International Conference on Population and Development in Cairo in 1994. It has 25 member states. PPD is dedicated to forming partnerships between and among individuals, organisations and the governments of developing countries. It provides a platform for its members to share successful experiences in education, migration, sexual health and combating infant mortality.

PPD is controlled by a board of directors consisting of ministers or other high-ranking officials in the field of population and development from member countries. The responsibilities of the board include setting policy, promoting cooperation among members and providing advice to the secretariat. The secretariat is based in Dhaka, Bangladesh, and is mandated to serve as the administrative centre of the organisation. It ensures policies are implemented and identifies new areas for collaboration. PPD also has an international programme advisory committee consisting of specialists who advise the board and secretariat on current trends in population, development and reproductive health.

PPD is a permanent observer at the United Nations.

Chair, Harsh Vardhan (India)

SECRETARIAT OF THE PACIFIC COMMUNITY

BP D5, Nouméa, 98848, New Caledonia
T (+687) 262 000 E spc@spc.int W www.spc.int

The Secretariat of the Pacific Community (SPC) (formerly the South Pacific Commission) was established in 1947 by Australia, France, the Netherlands, New Zealand, the UK and the USA with the aim of promoting the economic and social stability of the islands in the region. The community now numbers 26 member states and territories: the four remaining founder states (the Netherlands and the UK have withdrawn) and the other 22 states and territories of Melanesia, Micronesia and Polynesia.

The SPC is a technical assistance agency with programmes in marine and land development and health and social policy. The governing body is the conference of the Pacific community, which meets every two years.

Director-General, Dr Colin Tukuitonga (Niue)

SHANGHAI COOPERATION ORGANISATION

7 Ritan Road, Chaoyang District, 100600 Beijing, China
T (+86) (10) 6532 9807 E sco@sectsco.org W www.sectsco.org

The Shanghai Cooperation Organisation (SCO) is a permanent intergovernmental organisation. It was established in 1996 as the Shanghai Five, when China, Kazakhstan, Kyrgyzstan, Russia and Tajikistan signed an agreement on cooperating to resolve disputes along the former Sino-Soviet border. It was renamed in 2001 when Uzbekistan became an official member.

The main principle of the SCO is strengthening cooperation among member states across a range of fields, including politics, economics, science, culture, energy, transport, environmental protection and tourism.

The heads of state council is the organisation's supreme body and meets annually to formulate SCO policy. The heads of government council also holds annual meetings to discuss cooperation strategies and approve budgets. The SCO has two permanent bodies: a secretariat based in Beijing and a regional anti-terrorist structure in Tashkent. The secretary-general and the director of the executive committee are appointed by the council of heads of state for a period of three years.

Secretary-General, Dmitry F. Mezentsev (Russia)

SOUTH ASIAN ASSOCIATION FOR REGIONAL COOPERATION

PO Box 4222, Tridevi Marg, Kathmandu, Nepal
T (+977) (1) 422 1785/ 6350 E saarc@saarc-sec.org
W www.saarc-sec.org

The South Asian Association for Regional Cooperation (SAARC) was established in 1985 by Bangladesh, Bhutan, India, the Maldives, Nepal, Pakistan and Sri Lanka; Afghanistan was admitted as its eighth member in 2007. Its primary objective is the acceleration of economic and social development in member states through collective action in agreed areas of cooperation. These include agricultural development, climate change, science and technology, health, education and communications.

A SAARC preferential trading arrangement, designed to reduce tariffs on trade between SAARC member states, was signed in 1993 and entered into force in 1995. The South Asian free trade area (SAFTA) was agreed in 2004 and came into effect in 2006, with the aim of greatly reducing trade tarriffs by the end of 2016.

The highest authority rests with the heads of state or government of each member state. The council of ministers, which meets twice a year, is made up of the foreign ministers of the member states and is responsible for formulating policy. The standing committee is composed of the foreign secretaries of the member states and monitors and coordinates SAARC programmes; it meets as often as is necessary. Technical committees are assigned to individual areas of SAARC's activities. Its secretariat monitors, facilitates and promotes SAARC's activities and serves as a channel of communication between the association and other regional and intergovernmental institutions.

In 2005, as the only country in South Asia not to be a member of SAARC, Iran declared its wish to join and has since become an observer member, along with seven other states and the European Union.

Secretary-General, Arjun Bahadur Thapa (Nepal)

SOUTHERN AFRICAN DEVELOPMENT COMMUNITY

Plot No. 54385, Private Bag 0095, Gaborone, Botswana
T (+267) 395 1863 E registry@sadc.int W www.sadc.int

The Southern African Development Community (SADC) was formed in 1992 by the members of its predecessor, the Southern African Development Coordination Conference. The latter was founded in 1980 to harmonise economic development among southern Africa's 'majority ruled' countries and reduce their dependence on then apartheid South Africa. The SADC now comprises 15 countries, including South Africa. Madagascar's membership was reactivated in January 2014 after years of suspension following a coup in March 2009.

The SADC aims to evolve common political values, promote economic growth, regional security, sustainable development and the interdependence of member states. An annual summit attended by members' heads of state is the SADC's supreme authority, and its policies are implemented by a secretariat.

Executive Secretary, Stergomena Lawrence Tax (Tanzania)

UNITED NATIONS

Block C2, 7th Floor, rue de la Loi 155, Brussels 1040, Belgium
T +32 02788 8484 W www.un.org

The United Nations (UN) is an intergovernmental organisation dedicated, through signature of the UN charter, to the maintenance of international peace and security and the solution of economic, social and political problems through international cooperation.

The UN was founded as a successor to the League of Nations and inherited many of its procedures and institutions. The name United Nations was first used in the Washington Declaration of 1942 to describe the 26 states that had allied to fight the Axis powers. The UN charter developed from discussions at the Moscow conference of the foreign ministers of China, the Soviet Union, the UK and the USA in 1943. Further progress was made at Dumbarton Oaks, Washington, in 1944 during talks involving the same states. The role of the security council was formulated at the Yalta conference in 1945. The charter was formally drawn up by 50 allied nations at the San Francisco conference between April and June 1945, when it was signed. Following ratification, the UN came into effect on 24 October 1945, which is celebrated annually as United Nations Day. The UN flag is light blue with the UN emblem centred in white.

The principal organs of the UN are the general assembly, the security council, the economic and social council, the secretariat and the international court of justice. The economic and social council is an auxiliary, charged with assisting and advising the general assembly, security council and member states, and coordinating the economic and social aspects of the work of UN agencies and commissions. The official languages used are Arabic, Chinese, English, French, Russian and Spanish; the working languages of the secretariat and the international court of justice are English and French.

MEMBERSHIP

Membership is open to all countries that accept the charter and its principle of peaceful co-existence. New members are admitted by the general assembly on the recommendation of the security council. The original membership of 51 states has grown to 193 (*see* below).

Members of the UN

Afghanistan	Croatia	Japan	Nepal
Albania	Cuba*	Jordan	The Netherlands*
Algeria	Cyprus	Kazakhstan	New Zealand*
Andorra	Czech Republic	Kenya	Nicaragua*
Angola	Denmark*	Kiribati	Niger
Antigua and Barbuda	Djibouti	Korea, Dem. People's	Nigeria
Argentina*	Dominica	Rep. of	Norway*
Armenia	Dominican Republic*	Korea, Rep. of	Oman
Australia*	Ecuador*	Kuwait	Pakistan
Austria	Egypt*	Kyrgyzstan	Palau
Azerbaijan	El Salvador*	Laos	Panama*
Bahamas	Equatorial Guinea	Latvia	Papua New Guinea
Bahrain	Eritrea	Lebanon*	Paraguay*
Bangladesh	Estonia	Lesotho	Peru*
Barbados	Ethiopia*	Liberia*	The Philippines*
Belarus*	Fiji	Libya	Poland*
Belgium*	Finland	Liechtenstein	Portugal
Belize	France*	Lithuania	Qatar
Benin	FYR Macedonia	Luxembourg*	Romania
Bhutan	Gabon	Macedonia, Former	Russian Federation*
Bolivia*	The Gambia	Yugoslav Republic of	Rwanda
Bosnia and Hercegovina	Georgia	Madagascar	St Kitts and Nevis
Botswana	Germany	Malawi	St Lucia
Brazil*	Ghana	Malaysia	St Vincent and the
Brunei	Greece*	Maldives	Grenadines
Bulgaria	Grenada	Mali	Samoa
Burkina Faso	Guatemala*	Malta	San Marino
Burundi	Guinea	Marshall Islands	São Tomé and Princpe
Cabo Verde	Guinea-Bissau	Mauritania	Saudi Arabia*
Cambodia	Guyana	Mauritius	Senegal
Cameroon	Haiti*	Mexico*	Serbia
Canada*	Honduras*	Micronesia, Federated	Seychelles
Central African Republic	Hungary	States of	Sierra Leone
Chad	Iceland	Moldova	Singapore
Chile*	India*	Monaco	Slovakia
China*	Indonesia	Mongolia	Slovenia
Colombia*	Iran*	Montenegro	Solomon Islands
Comoros	Iraq*	Morocco	Somalia
Congo, Dem. Rep of the	Ireland	Mozambique	South Africa*
Congo, Republic of the	Israel	Myanmar	South Sudan
Costa Rica*	Italy	Namibia	Spain
Côte d'Ivoire	Jamaica	Nauru	Sri Lanka

Sudan	Thailand	Tuvalu	Vanuatu
Suriname	Timor-Leste	Uganda	Venezuela*
Swaziland	Togo	Ukraine*	Vietnam
Sweden	Tonga	United Arab Emirates	Yemen
Switzerland	Trinidad and Tobago	United Kingdom*	Zambia
Syria*	Tunisia	United States of America*	Zimbabwe
Tajikistan	Turkey*	Uruguay*	
Tanzania	Turkmenistan	Uzbekistan	

* Original member (ie from 1945). Czechoslovakia, Yugoslavia and the USSR were all original members until their dissolution.

OBSERVERS
Permanent observer status is held by the Holy See. The Palestinian Authority has special observer status.

THE GENERAL ASSEMBLY
UN Plaza, New York, NY 10017, USA

The general assembly is the main deliberative organ of the UN. It consists of all members, each entitled to five representatives but having only one vote. The annual session begins on the third Tuesday of September, when the president is elected, and usually continues until mid-December. Special sessions are held on specific issues and emergency special sessions can be called within 24 hours.

The assembly is empowered to discuss any matter within the scope of the charter – except when it is under consideration by the security council – and to make recommendations. Under the peace resolution, adopted in 1950, the assembly may also take action to maintain international peace and security when the security council fails to do so because of a lack of unanimity of its permanent members. Important decisions (such as those on peace and security, the election of officers, the budget, etc) need a two-thirds majority. Others need a simple majority. The assembly has effective power only over the internal operations of the UN itself; external recommendations are not legally binding.

The work of the general assembly is divided among a number of committees, on each of which every member has the right to be represented. Subjects include human rights, the use of torture, peacekeeping, assistance to developing countries and discrimination. In addition, the general assembly appoints *ad hoc* committees to consider more specific issues. All committees consider items referred to them by the assembly and recommend draft resolutions to its plenary meeting.

The assembly is assisted by a number of functional committees. The general committee coordinates its proceedings and operations, while the credentials committee verifies the representatives.
President of the General Assembly, John W. Ashe (Antigua and Barbuda)

SPECIALISED BODIES
The assembly has created a large number of specialised bodies, some of which are supervised jointly with the economic and social council. They are supported by UN and voluntary contributions from governments, non-governmental organisations and individuals. These organisations include:

CONFERENCE ON DISARMAMENT
Palais des Nations, CH-1211 Geneva 10, Switzerland

The Conference on Disarmament (CD) was established in 1979 as the international community's multilateral disarmament negotiating forum. Originally comprising 40 member states, the CD has expanded to 65 members. The Non-Proliferation of Nuclear Weapons Treaty entered into force on 5 March 1970 and has so far been ratified by 190 states. A chemical weapons convention was agreed in Paris in 1993 and came into force in April 1997 after being ratified by 87 countries. Currently 184 states participate in the convention, which bans the use, production, stockpiling and transfer of all chemical weapons. A convention prohibiting the use of cluster munitions, agreed in Dublin in 2008 and currently ratified by 84 states, entered into force on 1 August 2010.

UNITED NATIONS CHILDREN'S FUND (UNICEF)
3 UN Plaza, New York, NY 10017, USA T (+1) 212 326 7000
W www.unicef.org
UNICEF House, 30A Great Sutton St, London EC1V 0DU
T 020-7490 2388

Established in 1946 to assist children and mothers in the immediate post-war period, UNICEF now concentrates on developing countries. It provides primary healthcare and health education, and conducts programmes in oral hydration, immunisation against common diseases, HIV/AIDS treatment and prevention and child growth monitoring. It also works to provide children with equal access to quality education.

UNITED NATIONS DEVELOPMENT PROGRAMME (UNDP)
1 UN Plaza, New York, NY 10017, USA T (+1) 212 906 5000
W www.undp.org

Established in 1965 from the merger of the UN expanded programme of technical assistance and the UN special fund, UNDP is the central funding agency for economic and social development projects around the world. Much of its annual expenditure is channelled through UN specialised agencies, governments and non-governmental organisations.

UNITED NATIONS HIGH COMMISSIONER FOR REFUGEES (UNHCR)
Case Postale 2500, CH-1211 Geneva 2 Depot, Switzerland
T (+41) 22 739 8111 W www.unhcr.org

Established in 1950 to protect the rights and interests of refugees, UNHCR organises emergency relief and longer-term solutions, such as voluntary repatriation, local integration or resettlement. UNHCR is also mandated to assist stateless people.

UNITED NATIONS RELIEF AND WORKS AGENCY FOR PALESTINE REFUGEES IN THE NEAR EAST (UNRWA)
HQ Gaza, PO Box 371, Gaza City
T (+972) 8 288 7701 W www.unrwa.org

The UNRWA was established in 1949 to bring relief to the Palestinians displaced by the Arab-Israeli conflict. The UN general assembly has repeatedly voted every three years to extend its mandate, most recently until June 2017.

UNITED NATIONS HUMAN RIGHTS COUNCIL (UNHRC)
Palais des Nations, CH-1211 Geneva 10, Switzerland
T (+41) (22) 917 9220 E infodesk@ohchr.org W www.ohchr.org

The UNHRC is a 47-member council, established in 2006, replacing the United Nations Commission on Human Rights (UNCHR). The UNHRC has a mandate to promote (and prevent violations of) human rights by engaging in dialogue with governments and international organisations. It is also responsible for the coordination of all UN human rights activities and reports to, and is directly elected by, the general assembly.

THE SECURITY COUNCIL
UN Plaza, New York, NY 10017, USA
W www.un.org/en/sc

The security council is the senior arm of the UN and has the primary responsibility for maintaining world peace and security. It consists of 15 members, each with one representative and one vote. There are five permanent members – China, France, Russia, the UK and the USA – and ten non-permanent members. Each of the non-permanent members is elected for a two-year term by a two-thirds majority of the general assembly and is ineligible for immediate re-election. Five of the elective seats are allocated to Africa and Asia, one to eastern Europe, two to Latin America and two to western Europe and remaining countries. Decisions on procedural matters require affirmative votes from at least nine of the 15 members. Other matters require the same, but must include the affirmative votes of the permanent members; they thus have a right of veto. The abstention of a permanent member does not constitute a veto. The presidency rotates each month by state in (English) alphabetical order. Parties in a dispute, other non-members and individuals can be invited to participate in security council debates but are not permitted to vote.

The security council is empowered to settle or adjudicate in disputes or situations which threaten international peace and security. It can adopt political, economic and military measures to achieve this end. Any matter considered to be a threat to or breach of the peace or an act of aggression can be brought to the security council's attention by any member state or by the secretary-general. The charter envisaged members placing at the disposal of the security council armed forces and other facilities which would be coordinated by the military staff committee, composed of military representatives of the five permanent members. The security council is also supported by a committee of experts, to advise on procedural and technical matters, and a committee on admission of new members.

Owing to superpower disunity, the security council has rarely played the decisive role set out in the charter; the military staff committee was effectively suspended from 1948 until 1990, when a meeting was convened during the Gulf crisis on the formation and control of UN-supervised armed forces. In 1992, heads of government laid plans to transform the UN in light of the changed post-Cold War world. The secretary-general produced *An Agenda for Peace,* a report which centred on the establishment of a UN army composed of national contingents on permanent standby, as envisaged at the time of the UN's formation. However, enthusiasm for UN intervention waned during the rest of the decade after a problematic mission in Somalia during which 42 UN personnel were killed. The security council has since been criticised for its failure to intervene in subsequent conflicts, including the genocide in Rwanda and the ongoing situation in Darfur. More recently it has applied sanctions to Iran, North Korea, the Pakistani militant group Lashkar-e-Taiba, and figures within Libya and the Côte d'Ivoire.

The security council also has the power to elect judges to the international court of justice and to recommend to the general assembly the election of a secretary-general.

PEACEKEEPING FORCES
The security council has established a number of peace-keeping forces since its foundation, comprising contingents provided mainly by neutral and non-aligned UN members. As at 30 June 2014, current operations were:

Continent	UN Code	Year implemented	Personnel deployed
Africa			
Western Sahara	MINURSO	1991	508
Liberia	UNMIL	2003	7,651
Côte d'Ivoire	UNOCI	2004	9,717
Darfur, Sudan	UNAMID	2007	21,888
Dem. Rep. of the Congo	MONUSCO	2010	25,665
South Sudan	UNMISS	2011	12,955
Sudan	UNISFA	2011	4,284
Mali	MINUSMA	2013	10,217
Central African Rep.	MINUSCA	2014	782
The Americas			
Haiti	MINUSTAH	2004	9,193
Asia			
India and Pakistan	UNMOGIP	1949	109
Europe			
Cyprus	UNFICYP	1964	1,067
Kosovo	UNMIK	1999	366
Middle East	UNTSO	1948	379
Syria	UNDOF	1974	1,406
Lebanon	UNIFIL	1978	11,176

TOP FIVE CONTRIBUTORS TO UN PEACEKEEPING MISSIONS (*as at* 31 July 2014)	
Country	*Number of Troops*
Bangladesh	8,430
India	8,129
Ethiopia	7,806
Pakistan	7,205
Nepal	5,104

Source: www.un.org/en/peacekeeping

INTERNATIONAL CRIMINAL TRIBUNAL FOR THE FORMER YUGOSLAVIA
Churchillplein 1, 2517 JW The Hague, The Netherlands
T (+31) 7051 28752 W www.icty.org

In February 1993, the security council voted to establish the International Criminal Tribunal for the Former Yugoslavia (ICTY), a war crimes tribunal to hear cases covering breaches of the Geneva Conventions and crimes against humanity during the Balkans conflict of the 1990s. In December 2010 the UN security council approved the creation of the International Residual Mechanism for Criminal Tribunals (IRMCT), which took over the functions of the ICTY on 1 July 2013 and can not raise new indictments. The IRMCT will oversee the completion of the ICTY and ICTR (*see* below) by December 2014.
President, Theodor Meron (USA)

INTERNATIONAL CRIMINAL TRIBUNAL FOR RWANDA
Churchillplein 1, 2517 JW The Hague, The Netherlands
T (+31) 7051 25027 E ictr-press@un.org W www.unictr.org

Following serious violations of humanitarian law in Rwanda, the UN security council created the International Criminal Tribunal for Rwanda on 8 November 1994 in order to contribute to the process of national reconciliation and the maintenance of peace in the region. Its remit was to prosecute persons responsible for genocide and other serious international humanitarian law violations committed in the territory of Rwanda between 1 January 1994 and 31 December 1994, and by Rwandan citizens in the territory of neighbouring states during the same period. The IRMCT (*see* above) took over the functions of the ICTR on 1 July 2012 and can not raise new indictments.

President, Vagn Joensen (Denmark)

THE ECONOMIC AND SOCIAL COUNCIL
UN Plaza, New York, NY 10017, USA
E ecosocinfo@un.org W www.un.org/ecosoc

The economic and social council is responsible under the general assembly for the economic and social work of the UN and for the coordination of the activities of the 14 specialised agencies and other UN bodies. It makes reports and recommendations on economic, social, cultural, educational, health and related matters, often in consultation with non-governmental organisations, passing the reports to the general assembly and other UN bodies. It also drafts conventions for submission to the assembly and calls conferences on matters within its remit.

The council consists of 54 members, who are elected by the general assembly for overlapping three-year terms. Each member has one vote and can be immediately re-elected. The council elects a president and four vice-presidents each year: this five-member bureau proposes the council's agenda, draws up a programme of work and organises the substantive session. This session is held each July, and decisions are reached by a simple majority vote of those present.

The council has established a number of functional commissions and standing committees on particular issues. These include commissions on social development, sustainable development, population and development, the status of women, crime prevention and criminal justice, narcotic drugs, and science and technology for development, as well as five regional economic commissions.

President, Martin Sajdik (Austria)

THE SECRETARIAT
UN Plaza, New York, NY 10017, USA

The secretariat services the other principle UN organs and administers their programmes and policies. It is headed by a secretary-general elected by a majority vote of the general assembly on the recommendation of the security council. He is assisted by some 43,000 staff worldwide. The secretary-general is charged with bringing to the attention of the security council any matter which he considers poses a threat to international peace and security. He may also bring other matters to the attention of the general assembly and other UN bodies and may be entrusted by them with additional duties. As chief administrator to the UN, the secretary-general is present in person or via representatives at all meetings of the other five main organs of the UN. He may also act as a mediator in disputes between member states.

The power and influence of the secretary-general has been determined largely by the character of the office-holder and by the state of relations between the superpowers. The improvement of these relations since the mid-1980s has increased the effectiveness of the UN, particularly in its attempts to intervene in international disputes. Good collaboration betweeen the Secretary-General and superpowers helped to end the Iran-Iraq War and sponsored peace in Central America. Following Iraq's invasion of Kuwait in 1990, the UN took its first collective security action since the Korean War. Conflicts in Cyprus, Timor–Leste, Libya, Nigeria and Western Sahara were successfully prevented from escalating or spreading during the administration of Kofi Annan. However, the UN was heavily criticised for its failure to act in the Rwandan genocide of 1994 and its inability to halt the conflict in Darfur, while the invasion of Iraq by the USA and UK in 2003 without a UN mandate, illegal under the organisation's charter, seriously undermined its authority.

Secretary-General, Ban Ki-moon (South Korea)
Deputy Secretary General, Jan Eliasson (Sweden)

FORMER SECRETARIES-GENERAL	
1946–52	Trygve Lie (Norway)
1953–61	Dag Hammarskjöld (Sweden)
1961–71	U Thant (Myanmar)
1972–81	Kurt Waldheim (Austria)
1982–91	Javier Pérez de Cuéllar (Peru)
1992–96	Boutros Boutros-Ghali (Egypt)
1997–2006	Kofi Annan (Ghana)

UK MISSION TO THE UN
1 Dag Hammarskjold Plaza, 885 Second Avenue, New York, NY 10017, USA
T (+1) (212) 745 9200 E uk@un.int W www.ukun.fco.gov.uk
Permanent Representative to the UN and Representative on the Security Council, HE Sir Mark Lyall Grant, *apptd* 2009

UK MISSION TO THE UN AND OTHER INTERNATIONAL ORGANISATIONS IN GENEVA
58 Avenue Louis Casai, 1216 Cointrin GE Geneva, Switzerland
T (+41) (22) 918 2300 E geneva_un@fco.gov.uk
Permanent UK Representative, HE Karen Pierce, CMG, *apptd* 2012

UK MISSION TO THE UN IN VIENNA
Jaurèsgasse 12, A-1030 Vienna, Austria
T (+43) (1) 716 130 E ukmis.vienna@fco.gov.uk
W ukinaustria.fco.gov.uk
Permanent UK Representative, HE Susan le Jeune d'Allegeershecque CMG, *apptd* 2012

REGIONAL UN INFORMATION CENTRE
Block C2, Level 7, 155 rue de la Loi, Brussels 1040, Belgium
T (+32) 2788 8484 E info@unric.org W www.unric.org

THE INTERNATIONAL COURT OF JUSTICE
Peace Palace, Carnegieplein 2, 2517 KJ, The Hague, The Netherlands
T (+31) (70) 302 2323 W www.icj-cij.org

The international court of justice is the principal judicial organ of the UN, and its statute is an integral part of the UN charter; all members of the UN are *ipso facto* parties to it. The court is composed of 15 judges, elected by both the general assembly and the security council for nine-year terms, which are renewable. Judges may deliberate over cases in which their country is involved. If no judge on the bench is from a country that is a party to a dispute under consideration, that party may designate a judge to participate *ad hoc* in that particular deliberation. If any party to a case fails to adhere to the judgment of the court, the other party may have recourse to the security council.

President, Peter Tomka (Slovakia)
Vice-President, Bernardo Sepúlveda-Amor (Mexico)
Judges, Antonio A. Cancado Trindade (Brazil); Xue Hanqin (China); Ronny Abraham (France); Dalveer Bhandari (India); Giorgio Gaja (Italy); Hisashi Owada (Japan); Mohamed Bennouna (Morocco); Kenneth Keith (New Zealand); Leonid Skotnikov (Russia); Abdulqawi Ahmed Yusuf (Somalia); Julia Sebutinde (Uganda); Christopher Greenwood (UK); Joan Donoghue (USA)

UNITED NATIONS EDUCATIONAL, SCIENTIFIC AND CULTURAL ORGANISATION

7 place de Fontenoy, F-75352 Paris, France
T (+33) (01) 4568 1000 W www.unesco.org

The United Nations Educational, Scientific and Cultural Organisation (UNESCO) was established in 1945. It promotes collaboration among its member states in education, science, culture and communication. It aims to promote a universal respect for human rights, justice and the rule of law, without distinction of race, sex, language or religion, in accordance with the UN charter.

UNESCO runs a number of programmes to improve education and extend access to it. It provides assistance to ensure the free flow of information and its wider dissemination without any barriers to freedom of expression, to safeguard cultural heritages and encourage sustainable development. It fosters research and study in the social and environmental sciences. The UNESCO world heritage list, decided upon by a 21-member committee of state representatives, includes 1007 cultural and natural sites of 'outstanding universal value'.

UNESCO has 195 member states and nine associate members. The general conference, consisting of representatives of all the members, meets biennially to decide the programme and the budget. It elects the 58-member executive board, which supervises operations, and appoints a director-general who heads a secretariat responsible for carrying out the organisation's programmes. In most member states national commissions liaise with UNESCO to execute its policies.

Director-General, Irina Bokova (Bulgaria)

UNITED NATIONS INDUSTRIAL DEVELOPMENT ORGANISATION

Vienna International Centre, Wagramerstrasse 5, PO Box 300, A-1400 Vienna, Austria
T (+43) (1) 260 260 E unido@unido.org W www.unido.org

The United Nations Industrial Development Organisation (UNIDO) was established in 1966 by the UN general assembly to act as the central coordinating body for industrial activities within the UN. It became a UN specialised agency in 1979. UNIDO aims to help countries with developing and transitional economies by increasing the productivity and competitiveness of their agricultural, technological and energy industries.

UNIDO has 171 members. It is funded by regular and operational budgets, together with contributions for technical cooperation activities. The regular budget is derived from member states' contributions. Technical co-operation is funded mainly through voluntary contributions from donor countries and institutions and by inter-governmental and non-governmental organisations. A general conference of all the members meets biennially to discuss strategy and policy, approve the budget – €176.5m (£140m) for the biennium 2014–15 – and elect the director-general. The industrial development board is composed of representatives from 52 member states and reviews the work programme and the budget, which is prepared by the programme and budget committee of 27 member states.

Director-General, Li Yong (China)

UNIVERSAL POSTAL UNION

4 Weltpoststrasse, CH-3000 Bern 15, Switzerland
T (+41) (31) 350 3111 E info@upu.int W www.upu.int

The Universal Postal Union (UPU) was established by the Treaty of Bern 1874, taking effect from 1875, and became a UN specialised agency in 1948. The UPU exists to form and regulate a single postal territory of all member countries for the reciprocal exchange of correspondence without discrimination. With a total of 192 members, it also assists and advises on the improvement of postal services.

The universal postal congress is the UPU's supreme authority and meets every four years. The council of administration meets annually to supervise the union's work between congresses, to investigate regulatory developments and policy issues, to approve the budget and to examine proposed treaty changes. The consultative committee was set up in 2004 to further the interests of the wider postal sector. It brings together representative bodies of customers, service providers, manufacturers and suppliers, and provides a forum for dialogue between postal industry stakeholders. The three UPU bodies are served by the international bureau, a secretariat headed by a director-general.

Funding is provided by members according to a scale of contributions drawn up by the congress. The council of administration sets the budget which amounts to approximately SFr37m (£25.8m) a year.

Director-General, Bishar Abdirahman Hussein (Kenya)

UNREPRESENTED NATIONS AND PEOPLES ORGANISATION

Laan van Meerdervoort 70, 2517 AN, The Hague, The Netherlands
T (+31) (0) 70 364 6504 E unpo@unpo.org W www.unpo.org

The Unrepresented Nations and Peoples Organisation (UNPO) was founded in 1991 to offer an international forum for occupied nations, indigenous peoples and national minorities who are not represented in other international organisations.

The UNPO does not aim to represent these nations and peoples, but rather to assist and empower them to represent themselves more effectively, and provides professional services and facilities as well as education and training in the fields of diplomacy, international and human rights law, democratic processes, institution building, conflict management and resolution, and environmental protection.

Participation is open to all nations and peoples who are inadequately represented at the UN and who declare allegiance to five principles relating to the right of self-determination of all peoples: human rights, democracy, tolerance, non-violence and respect for the rights of minorities. Applicants must show that they constitute a nation or people and that the organisation applying for membership is representative of that nation or people.

As at August 2014, UNPO had 46 full members.
General Secretary, Marino Busdachin (Italy)

WORLD BANK GROUP

1818 H Street NW, Washington DC 20433, USA
T (+1) (202) 473 1000 W www.worldbank.org

The World Bank Group was founded in 1944 from the consolidation of five major development organisations and is one of the world's largest sources of development assistance. It has 188 member states. Originally directed towards post-war reconstruction in Europe, the bank subsequently turned towards assisting less-developed countries worldwide, and in 2013 provided US$52.6bn (£31.4bn) for 12,097 projects across the developing world. It works with government agencies, non-governmental organisations and the private sector to formulate assistance strategies. Its local offices implement the bank's programme in each country.

The World Bank is owned by the governments of member countries and its capital is subscribed by its members. It finances its lending primarily from borrowing in world capital markets, and derives a substantial contribution to its resources from its retained earnings and the repayment of loans.

The World Bank Group consists of two institutions and three affiliates. The International Bank for Reconstruction and Development (IBRD) provides loans and development assistance to middle-income countries and credit-worthy poorer countries (total loans for 2013 US$15.3bn (£9.12bn)). The International Development Association (IDA) performs the same function as the IBRD but primarily to less-developed countries and on terms that bear less heavily on their balance of payments than IBRD loans (total loans for 2013 US$16.3bn (£9.72bn)).

The three affiliates are the International Finance Corporation (IFC), which has 184 members and promotes private sector investment in developing countries by mobilising domestic and foreign capital; the Multilateral Investment Guarantee Agency (MIGA), which has 180 members and promotes foreign direct investment in developing states by insuring investors against political risk and helping member countries to improve their investment climates; and the International Centre for Settlement of Investment Disputes, which has 150 full members (known as contracting states) and provides facilities for resolving disputes between foreign investors and their host countries.

The IBRD, IDA and the affiliates are financially and legally distinct but share headquarters. The IBRD is headed by a board of governors, which meets annually and consists of one governor and one alternate governor appointed by each member country; most IBRD governors also serve on the separate boards of the IDA, IFC and MIGA. Twenty-five executive directors exercise all powers of the World Bank (except those reserved to the board of governors). The president, elected by the board of executive directors, conducts the business of the bank, assisted by an international staff. Membership in both the IFC and the IDA is open to all IBRD countries. The IDA is administered by the same staff as the bank; the IFC has its own personnel but can draw on the IBRD for administrative and other support. All share the same president.

President, Jim Yong Kim (USA)

WORLD CUSTOMS ORGANISATION

30 rue de Marché, B-1210, Brussels, Belgium
T (+32) 2209 9211 W www.wcoomd.org

Established in 1952 as the Customs Cooperation Council, the World Customs Organisation (WCO) is an independent intergovernmental organisation whose primary mission is to enhance the effectiveness and efficiency of customs administrations worldwide. It is the only international body specialised in customs matters, and is recognised as the voice of the global customs community and a centre of customs expertise.

Comprising 179 member customs administrations that process approximately 98 per cent of international trade, the WCO is governed by a council which meets annually and in which each member has one vote. The council is supported by a policy commission, a finance committee, an audit committee, various technical committees, and a permanent secretariat charged with implementing council decisions.

Secretary-General, Kunio Mikuriya (Japan)

WORLD HEALTH ORGANISATION

Avenue Appia 20, 1211 Geneva 27, Switzerland
T (+41) (22) 791 2111 W www.who.int

The UN International Health Conference, held in 1946, established the World Health Organisation (WHO) as a UN specialised agency, with effect from 1948. It is dedicated

to attaining the highest possible level of health for all. It collaborates with member governments, UN agencies and other bodies to improve health standards, control communicable diseases and promote all aspects of family and environmental health. It seeks to raise the standards of health teaching and training, and promotes research through collaboration with research centres worldwide.

WHO has 194 members and is governed by an annual assembly of members. This sets policy, approves the budget, appoints a director-general and adopts health conventions and regulations. It also elects 34 member states to designate one expert each to serve on the executive board. The board sets the assembly's agenda and implements its policies, suggests initiatives, and is empowered to deal with emergencies. A secretariat, headed by the director-general, supervises the activities of six regional offices.

Director-General, Dr Margaret Chan (China)

WORLD INTELLECTUAL PROPERTY ORGANISATION

34 chemin des Colombettes, CH-1211, Geneva 20, Switzerland
T (+41) (22) 338 9111 W www.wipo.int

The World Intellectual Property Organisation (WIPO) was established in Stockholm in 1967 by the signing of the WIPO Convention, which entered into force in 1970. WIPO administers 26 treaties that deal with different legal and administrative aspects of intellectual property, notably the Paris Convention for the protection of industrial property and the Bern Convention for the protection of literary and artistic works. WIPO became a UN specialised agency in 1974.

Intellectual property falls into two main branches: industrial property (inventions, trademarks, industrial designs and geographical indications) and copyright (literary, musical, photographic, audiovisual and artistic works, etc). WIPO helps ensure that creative intellectual activity is rewarded, and facilitates technology transfer, particularly to developing countries.

WIPO's mission is to promote the protection of intellectual property rights worldwide. The organisation's activities fall into three broad categories: the progressive development of international intellectual property law, assistance to developing countries, and the provision of services which facilitate the process of obtaining intellectual property rights in multiple countries.

WIPO had 187 members as at August 2014. The biennial session of the general assembly, the conference and the coordination committee set policy, a programme and a budget. A separate agency, the International Union for the Protection of New Varieties of Plants (UPOV), established by convention in 1961, is linked to WIPO and has 72 members.

Director-General, Francis Gurry (Australia)

WORLD METEOROLOGICAL ORGANISATION

7 bis, avenue de la Paix, PO Box 2300, CH-1211 Geneva 2, Switzerland
T (+41) (22) 730 8111 W www.wmo.int

The World Meteorological Organisation (WMO) was established in 1950 and became a UN specialised agency in 1951, succeeding the International Meteorological Organisation founded in 1873. It facilitates cooperation in the establishment of networks for making, processing and exchanging meteorological, climatological, hydrological and geophysical observations. It also fosters collaboration between meteorological and hydrological services, and furthers the application of meteorology to aviation, shipping, environment, water problems, agriculture and the mitigation of natural disasters.

In August 2014, the WMO had 185 member states and six member territories. Six regional associations are responsible for the coordination of activities within their own regions. There are also eight technical commissions, which study meteorological and hydrological problems, establish methodology and procedures, and make recommendations to the executive council and the congress. The supreme authority is the world meteorological congress, which meets every four years to determine general policy and set the budget (SFr276m (£180m) proposed for 2012–15). It also elects 31 members of the 37-member executive council which supervises the implementation of congress decisions, initiates studies and makes recommendations on matters requiring international action. The secretariat is headed by a secretary-general, appointed by the congress.
Secretary-General, Michel Jarraud (France)

WORLD TOURISM ORGANISATION
Capitán Haya 42, 28020 Madrid, Spain
T (+34) 9156 78100 E omt@unwto.org W www2.unwto.org

The World Tourism Organisation (UNWTO) was officially launched in 1975 to act as an executing agency of the United Nations Development Programme. Primarily concerned with developing public and private sector partnerships, the UNWTO also promotes the global code of ethics for tourism, a framework of policy aimed at tour operators, governments, labour organisations and travellers. There are 156 member states and six associate member states.

The general assembly is the principal gathering of the UNWTO and meets every two years in order to approve policy and budget. Every four years, the assembly elects a secretary-general. The executive council is UNWTO's governing board and meets at least twice a year to ensure the organisation adheres to policy and budget. It is composed of 32 members of the general assembly. As host country of UNWTO's headquarters, Spain has a permanent seat on the executive council.
Secretary-General, Taleb Rifai (Jordan)

WORLD TRADE ORGANISATION
Centre William Rappard, 154 rue de Lausanne, CH-1211 Geneva 21, Switzerland
T (+41) (22) 739 5111 E enquiries@wto.org W www.wto.org

The World Trade Organisation was established on 1 January 1995 as the successor to the General Agreement on Tariffs and Trade (GATT).

The GATT was dedicated to the expansion of non-discriminatory international trade and progressively extended free trade via 'rounds' of multilateral negotiations. The final act of the comprehensive Uruguay round of negotiations was signed by trade ministers from the 123 GATT negotiating states and the EU in Marrakesh, Morocco, in 1994. New talks on agriculture and services began in 2000 and were incorporated into a broader agenda launched at the 2001 ministerial conference in Doha, Qatar.

The WTO is the legal and institutional foundation of the multilateral trading system. It provides the contractual obligations determining how governments frame and implement trade policy, and provides the forum for the debate, negotiation and adjudication of trade issues. The WTO's principal aims are to liberalise world trade and place it on a secure basis; it seeks to achieve this through the combination of an agreed set of trade rules and market-access agreements and further trade liberalisation negotiations. The WTO also administers and implements multilateral agreements in fields such as agriculture, industrial goods, services, government procurement, rules of origin and intellectual property.

The highest authority of the WTO is the ministerial conference composed of all members, which usually meets once every two years. The general council meets as required and acts on behalf of the ministerial conference in regard to the regular working of the WTO. The general council also convenes in two particular forms: as the dispute-settlement body, dealing with disagreements between members arising from WTO agreements or commitments; and as the trade policy review body, conducting regular reviews of the trade policies of members. A secretariat of 640 staff, headed by a director-general, services WTO bodies and provides trade performance and trade policy analysis.

As of August 2014, the WTO has 160 members and 24 observer governments. The most recent member – Yemen – joined the WTO in 2014. The WTO budget for 2014 is SFr197.2m (£129.2m), with members' contributions calculated on the basis of their share of international trade. The official languages of the WTO are English, French and Spanish.
Director-General, Robert Azevedo (Brazil)

COUNTRIES OF THE WORLD A–Z

DEFINITIONS AND ABBREVIATIONS

est = estimate
IDD = International direct dialling
(m) = male; (f) = female

AIRPORTS – figures reference airports with paved runways only, unless otherwise specified
BIRTH RATE – figures are per 1,000 population
CORRUPTION PERCEPTIONS INDEX (CPI) SCORE – the perception of the degree of public sector corruption as seen by business people and country analysts; ranging from 0 (highly corrupt) to 100 (very clean). Overall position given in parentheses © Transparency International
DEATH PENALTY:
Retained (not used) – countries that retain the death penalty for ordinary crimes such as murder but can be considered to have abolished it in practice
Retained for certain crimes – countries whose laws provide for the death penalty only for exceptional crimes ('Last used' = date of last execution)
Retained – countries that retain the death penalty for ordinary crimes
GROSS ENROLMENT RATIO – the ratio of total enrolment, regardless of age, to the total population of the relevant age group expressed as a percentage; this figure can be above 100 per cent where, for example, a greater number of children are attending classes designed for six-year-olds than there are six-year-olds in the country, owing to some children starting school late or skipping a year
GROSS NATIONAL INCOME (GNI) – the total income earned by a country's residents; the second figure is GNI divided by the population to give a per capita figure
HIV/AIDS ADULT PREVALENCE – estimate of the percentage of the total adult population (aged 15–49) infected with HIV/AIDS
INFANT MORTALITY RATE – averages for male and female infants under one year old and per 1,000 live births
LIFE EXPECTANCY – averages, at birth, for males and females
LITERACY (ADULT) – the World Bank defines literacy as the percentage of the population aged 15 and above that can read and write a short statement on their everyday life. Where the World Bank figure is not available the statistic provided is that given by the government of that country. This figure is not always comparable due to differing definitions of what constitutes adult literacy.
MILITARY EXPENDITURE – figures are the most recent available at constant 2011 prices and exchange rates
MORTALITY RATE – figures are per 1,000 population. This indicator is significantly affected by age distribution, and most countries will eventually show a rise in the overall death rate, in spite of continued decline in mortality at all ages, as declining fertility results in an ageing population
POPULATION BELOW POVERTY LINE – although strict definitions of poverty vary considerably between nations, this figure most commonly represents the percentage of the adult population whose income is less than US$1 per day
TOTAL EXTERNAL DEBT – the total public and private debt owed to non-residents repayable in foreign currency, goods or services
WORLD PRESS FREEDOM INDEX (WPFI) SCORE – the perception of press freedom based on assessments carried out by journalists and human rights activists; two scores ranging

between 0 (low censorship) and 100 (high censorship) are given. The first is based on six criteria – pluralism, media independence, environment and self-censorship, legislative framework, transparency, and infrastructure – the second score measures the treatment of journalists. The overall position is given in parentheses. © Reporters Without Borders

AFGHANISTAN

Jomhuri-ye Eslami-ye Afghanestan – Islamic Republic of Afghanistan

Area – 652,230 sq. km
Capital – Kabul; population, 4,065,871 (2012 est)
Major cities – Herat, Jalalabad, Kandahar, Mazar-e-Sharif
Currency – Afghani (Af) of 100 puls
Population – 31,108,077 rising at 2.25 per cent a year (2013 est); Pashtun (42 per cent), Tajik (27 per cent), Hazara (9 per cent), Uzbek (9 per cent), Aimak (4 per cent), Turkmen (3 per cent), Baloch (2 per cent) (est)
Religion – Muslim (Sunni 80 per cent, Shia 19 per cent) (est); Islam is the state religion
Language – Dari (a dialect of Persian), Pashto (both official), Uzbek, Turkmen
Population density – 45 per sq. km (2011 est)
Urban population – 23.8 per cent (2012 est)
Median age (years) – 17.9 (2013 est)
National anthem – 'Milli Surud' ['National Anthem']
National day – 19 August (Independence Day)
Death penalty – Retained
CPI score – 8 (175)

CLIMATE AND TERRAIN
Mountains, chief among which are the Hindu Kush, cover three-quarters of the country, with plains in the north and south-west. Elevation extremes range from 7,485m (Noshak, a peak in the Hindu Kush) to 258m (Amu Dar'ya). There are three great river basins: the Amu Dar'ya (Oxus), Helmand and Kabul. Natural hazards are flooding, drought and earthquakes. Average annual rainfall is around 247mm per year. Temperatures in Afghanistan average 3°C in January and 28.9°C in July.

POLITICS
Under the 2004 constitution, the executive president, who is directly elected for a five-year term, appoints the government, subject to the approval of the lower house of the legislature. The bicameral National Assembly, the *Jirga*, comprises the House of the People *(Wolesi Jirga)*, the lower house, and the House of Elders *(Meshrano Jirga)*. The House of the People has 249 members directly elected for a five-year term; ten seats

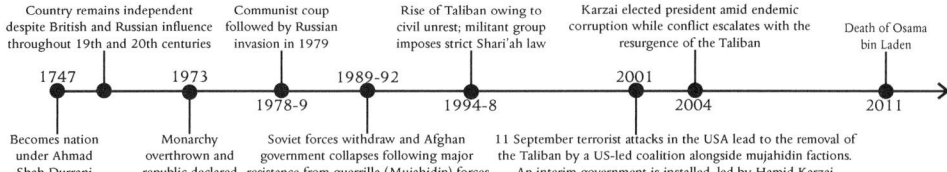

Country remains independent despite British and Russian influence throughout 19th and 20th centuries

Communist coup followed by Russian invasion in 1979

Rise of Taliban owing to civil unrest; militant group imposes strict Shari'ah law

Karzai elected president amid endemic corruption while conflict escalates with the resurgence of the Taliban

Death of Osama bin Laden

1747   1973   1989–92   2001   2011
1978–9   1994–8   2004

Becomes nation under Ahmad Shah Durrani

Monarchy overthrown and republic declared

Soviet forces withdraw and Afghan government collapses following major resistance from guerrilla (Mujahidin) forces

11 September terrorist attacks in the USA lead to the removal of the Taliban by a US-led coalition alongside mujahidin factions. An interim government is installed, led by Hamid Karzai

are reserved for the Kuchi ethnic group and at least 65 seats for women. The House of Elders has 102 members: 34 elected by provincial councils for a three-year term, 34 elected by district councils for a four-year term, and 34 appointed by the president for a five-year term. Political parties have not been legally recognised since the 2005 parliamentary elections and candidates must run as independents.

Hamid Karzai was elected president in 2004, and was re-elected in 2009; the first round of voting was marred by widespread electoral fraud. President Karzai took control of the Electoral Complaints Commission in February 2010, causing international concern about the management of the 2010 legislative elections. These were postponed from May to September 2010 and took place amid Taliban violence and widespread fraud. Karzai announced he would step down when his second term concluded in 2014, after NATO handed control to the Afghan state. Following the disputed June 2014 presidential elections, it was declared on 21 September that Ashraf Ghani would become President, ending moonths of political deadlock.

HEAD OF STATE
President, Hamid Karzai, *elected* 9 October 2004, *sworn in* 7 December 2004, *re-elected* 2009
First Vice-President, Mohammad Younus Qanooni
Vice-President, Karim Khalili

SELECTED GOVERNMENT MEMBERS *as at September 2014*
Defence, Gen. Bismillah Khan Mohammadi
Finance, Omar Zakhilwal
Foreign Affairs, Zarar Ahmad Moqbel

EMBASSY OF THE ISLAMIC REPUBLIC OF AFGHANISTAN
31 Princes Gate, London SW7 1QQ
T 020-7589 8891 E consulate@afganistanembassy.org.uk
Ambassador Extraordinary and Plenipotentiary, HE Dr Mohammad Daud Yaar, *apptd* 2012

BRITISH EMBASSY
PO Box 334, 15th Street, Roundabout Wazir Akbar Khan, Kabul
T (+93) (0) 700 102 000 E britishembassy.kabul@fco.gov.uk
W www.gov.uk/government/world/afghanistan
Ambassador Extraordinary and Plenipotentiary, HE Richard Stagg, KCMG, *apptd* 2013

DEFENCE
NATO's International Security Assistance Force has approximately 100,330 troops in Afghanistan.

Aged 16–49, 2010 est	Males	Females
Available for military service	7,056,339	6,653,419
Fit for military service	4,050,222	3,797,087

Military expenditure – US$1,333m (2013)

ECONOMY AND TRADE
The economy, devastated by over 30 years of conflict, has improved significantly since 2001. Economic growth has

been sustained over the decade despite drought in 2006–7 and the global downturn in 2008, although security problems, weak governance, poor infrastructure and corruption continue to hamper reconstruction. Poverty is being reduced through substantial civilian aid donations, including an additional US$16bn (£10.5bn) pledged in July 2012. Eradication of the opium trade (which constitutes about 60 per cent of the economy) and exploration for oil and gas in the north are two major long-term policy objectives.

Nearly 80 per cent of the workforce is engaged in agriculture, both subsistence and commercial, which accounts for some 20 per cent of GDP. The main agricultural products are opium, wheat, fruit, nuts, wool, meat, sheepskins and lambskins. Natural gas, coal, copper and gemstones are extracted. The main trading partners are the USA, Pakistan and India. Principal exports are agricultural products, handwoven carpets and gemstones. Imports are chiefly machinery and other capital goods, food, textiles and petroleum products.

GNI – US$20,524m; US$680 per capita (2012)
Annual average growth of GDP – 3.1 per cent (2013 est)
Inflation rate – 6.8 per cent (2012 est)
Population below poverty line – 36 per cent (2008–9 est)
Unemployment – 35 per cent (2008 est)
Total external debt – US$1,280m (2010–11 est)

BALANCE OF PAYMENTS
Trade – US$6,906m deficit (2010)
Current Account – US$798m surplus (2012)

Trade with UK	2012	2013
Imports from UK	£103,970,476	£66,275,962
Exports to UK	£3,615,129	£2,362,667

COMMUNICATIONS
Airports – 23; two international, including Kabul and Kandahar
Waterways – The Amu Dar'ya river makes up most of the 1,200km of inland waterways; the main river ports are Kheyrabad and Shir Khan
Roadways – Much of the road system is in disrepair, although major highways between Kabul, Kandahar and Herat have been reconstructed; there are 12,350km of paved roadways
Telecommunications – 13,500 fixed lines and 18 million mobile subscriptions (2012); there were 1 million internet users in 2009
Internet code and IDD – af; 93 (from UK), 44 (to UK)
Major broadcasters – The principal and state-owned broadcaster is Radio-TV Afghanistan
Press – There are nine daily newspapers including the privately owned *Hasht-e Sobh*
WPFI score – 37,07 (128)

EDUCATION AND HEALTH
Education is free and nominally compulsory, elementary schools having been established in most centres.
Literacy rate – 28.0 per cent (2008 est)
Gross enrolment ratio (percentage of relevant age group) – primary 97 per cent; secondary 52 per cent; tertiary 4 per cent (2011 est)

Health expenditure (per capita) – US$56 (2011)
Hospital beds (per 1,000 people) – 0.4 (2004–10)
Life expectancy (years) – 50.11 (2013 est)
Mortality rate – 14.35 (2013 est)
Birth rate – 39.05 (2013 est)
Infant mortality rate – 119.41 (2013 est)

ALBANIA

Republika e Shqiperise – Republic of Albania

Area – 28,748 sq. km
Capital – Tirana; population, 419,000 (2011 est)
Major towns – Durres, Elbasan, Shkoder, Vlore
Currency – Lek (Lk) of 100 qindarka
Population – 3,011,405 rising at 0.29 per cent a year (2013 est); Albanian (82.6 per cent), Greek (0.9 per cent) (est)
Religion – Muslim 58.8 per cent (Sunni, and Bektashi form of Shia Sufism), Christian 16.8 per cent (Albanian Orthodox and Roman Catholic) (est). Religious observance was banned in 1967; private religious practice has been permitted since 1990
Language – Albanian (official), Greek, Vlach, Romani, Slavic dialects
Population density – 115 per sq. km (2011)
Urban population – 54.5 per cent (2012 est)
Median age (years) – 31.2 (2013 est)
National anthem – 'Himni i Flamurit' ['Hymn to the Flag']
National day – 28 November (Independence Day)
Death penalty – Abolished for all crimes (since 2007)
CPI score – 31 (116)

CLIMATE AND TERRAIN
About two-thirds of the country is mountainous, and 36 per cent is covered by forest. Elevation extremes range from 2,764m (Maja e Korabit, a peak on the Macedonian border) to 0m (Adriatic Sea). The climate is Mediterranean on the coast and continental in the interior. The average daily temperature in Tirana ranges between 6°C in January and 24°C in July.

POLITICS
Under the 1998 constitution, the president is elected by the legislature for a five-year term, renewable once. The unicameral legislature, the People's Assembly, has 140 members directly elected for four-year terms. The president appoints the prime minister, who must be approved by the People's Assembly. The assembly elects the council of ministers.

Bujar Nishani, of the Democratic Party (PD), was elected president in 2012 in the fourth round of voting. Legislative elections were held in June 2013 and won by the Alliance for a European Albania, a coalition led by the Socialist Party of Albania (PS), who secured a landslide victory against the incumbent PD, taking a total of 84 seats to their 56.

HEAD OF STATE
President, Bujar Nishani, *elected* 11 June 2012, *took office* 24 July 2012

SELECTED GOVERNMENT MEMBERS *as at February 2014*
Prime Minister, Edi Rama
Deputy Prime Minister, Niko Peleshi
Defence, Mimi Kodheli
Finance, Shkelgim Cani

EMBASSY OF THE REPUBLIC OF ALBANIA
33 St George's Drive, London SW1V 4DG
T 020-7828 8897 E embassy.london@mfa.gov.al
W www.albanianembassy.co.uk
Ambassador Extraordinary and Plenipotentiary, HE Mal Berisha, *apptd* 2013

BRITISH EMBASSY
Rruga Skenderbeg 12, Tirana
T (+355) (4) 223 4973 E enquiries.tirana@fco.gov.uk
W www.gov.uk/government/world/albania
Ambassador Extraordinary and Plenipotentiary, Nicholas Cannon, OBE, *apptd* 2012

DEFENCE
The Albanian Armed Forces (AAF) is a joint force.

Aged 16–49, 2010 est	*Males*	*Females*
Available for military service	731,111	780,216
Fit for military service	622,379	660,715

Military expenditure – US$168m (2012)*

* Does not include spending on paramilitary forces

ECONOMY AND TRADE
Albania is one of the poorest countries in Europe, although liberalisation measures have resulted in gradual growth since 2004, and inflation is under control. The economy is still heavily dependent on overseas aid, primarily from the EU, and remittances from expatriate workers, worth about 9 per cent of GDP, although these have suffered in the wake of the global financial crisis. Infrastructure and energy supply inadequacies, organised crime and corruption have deterred foreign investment, and tackling these are government priorities. The government is taking steps to improve the sub-standard national road and rail networks, and a new thermal power plant and improved transmission lines from neighbouring countries should relieve energy shortages.

Declares independence after first Balkan war — 1468
Italian followed by German occupation — 1925-8
Elections result in a communist-controlled assembly aligned with the USSR; republic declared — 1944
— 1961
Following moves towards westernisation, Communists lose power in first democratic elections — 1997-9
Becomes member of NATO

Ottoman rule — 1912
Declared republic and monarchy formed — 1939-43
Liberated by communist partisans led by Enver Hoxha — 1945-6
Aligns with China and pursues isolationist policy until Hoxha's death in 1985 — 1992
Faltering investment schemes force a change in government. Influx of some 480,000 refugees fleeing ethnic cleansing in Kosovo — 2009

Agriculture accounts for 47.8 per cent of employment but only 18 per cent of GDP. The main crops are wheat, corn, vegetables, fruit, sugar beet and livestock products. The principal industries are food processing, perfumes and cosmetic products, textiles and clothing, timber, oil, cement, chemicals, mining (base metals) and hydro-electric power.

Trade is mainly with Italy, Spain, Greece and China. Exports include textiles and footwear, asphalt, metals and metal ores, crude oil, tobacco, fruit and vegetables. Imports include machinery and equipment, foodstuffs, textiles and chemicals.

GNI – US$12,483m; US$4,030 per capita (2012)
Annual average growth of GDP – 1.7 per cent (2013 est)
Inflation rate – 2 per cent (2013 est)
Population below poverty line – 12.5 per cent (2008 est)
Unemployment – 12.9 per cent (2013 est)
Total external debt – US$6,108m (2013 est)
Imports – US$4,882m (2012)
Exports – US$1,968m (2012)

BALANCE OF PAYMENTS
Trade – US$2,914m deficit (2012)
Current Account – US$1,513m deficit (2012)

Trade with UK	2012	2013
Imports from UK	£21,242,679	£19,284,249
Exports to UK	£1,875,188	£9,766,564

COMMUNICATIONS
Airport – There is an international airport in Tirana
Roadways and railways – 18,000km; 339km
Telecommunications – 312,000 fixed lines and 3.5 million mobile subscriptions (2012); there were 1.3 million internet users in 2009
Internet code and IDD – al; 355 (from UK), 44 (to UK)
Major broadcasters – Albanian Radio and TV (RTSh)
WPFI score – 29,92 (85)

EDUCATION AND HEALTH
Literacy rate – 97 per cent (2011 est)
Gross enrolment ratio (percentage of relevant age group) – primary 110 per cent; secondary 78 per cent (2010 est)
Health expenditure (per capita) – US$255 (2009)
Hospital beds (per 1,000 people) – 2.4 (2011)
Life expectancy (years) – 77.77 (2013 est)
Mortality rate – 6.36 (2013 est)
Birth rate – 12.57 (2013 est)
Infant mortality rate – 13.65 (2013 est)

ALGERIA

Al-Jumhuriyah al-Jaza'iriyah ad Dimuqratiyah ash Sha'biyah – People's Democratic Republic of Algeria

Area – 2,381,741 sq. km
Capital – Algiers (El Djazair, Al Jaza'ir); population, 2,920,325 (2012 est)
Major cities – Annaba, Blida, Constantine (Qacentina), Oran (Wahran)
Currency – Algerian dinar (DA) of 100 centimes
Population – 38,087,812 rising at 1.9 per cent a year (2013 est); Arab-Berber (99 per cent est)
Religion – Muslim (Sunni 99 per cent), Christian and Jewish (less than 1 per cent) (est)
Language – Arabic (official), French, Berber dialects
Population density – 16 per sq. km (2011)
Urban population – 73.8 per cent (2012 est)
Median age (years) – 27 (2013 est)
National anthem – 'Kassaman' ['We Pledge']
National day – 1 November (Revolution Day)
Death penalty – Retained (last used 1993)
CPI score – 36 (94)

CLIMATE AND TERRAIN
Algeria, the largest country in Africa, is dominated by the Sahara desert, which covers more than 80 per cent of its territory. Elevation extremes range from 3,003m (Mt Tahat) to −40m (Chott Melrhir, a salt lake). The mountains are subject to earthquakes, and to flooding during the rainy season (November–March). The temperate northern coastal areas receive the greatest and most frequent rainfall, whereas the interior plateaux are drier and experience cold winters and hot summers.

POLITICS
Algeria's 1976 constitution was amended in 1989 to reintroduce political pluralism, and was revised in 2008, most notably to remove the limit on presidential terms. The president is directly elected for a five-year term, which may be renewed. The bicameral *Barlaman* comprises the National People's Assembly, the lower house, and the National Council. The assembly has 389 members, directly elected for a five-year term. The National Council has 144 members; 48 are appointed by the president, and 96 are indirectly elected for a six-year term by electoral colleges formed by local councils; half of these elected members are re-elected every three years. Although Algeria is no longer a one-party state, parties based on religion or on race, language, gender or region are banned under the constitution.

In the 2012 legislative election, the ruling National Liberation Front-led coalition won the most seats and retained control in both houses; former minister for water resources, Abdelmalek Sellal, became prime minister in September 2012, replacing Ahmed Ouyahia. In April 2014, President Bouteflika was re-elected for a fourth term despite not campaigning due to ill health. The elections were widely boycotted by secular and Islamist opposition parties.

HEAD OF STATE
President, Defence, Abdelaziz Bouteflika, *elected* 15 April 1999, *re-elected* 2004, 2009, 2014

SELECTED GOVERMENT MEMBERS *as at April 2014*
Interim Prime Minister, Youcef Yousfi
Finance, Karim Djoudi
Foreign Affairs, Ramtane Lamamra

ALGERIAN EMBASSY
54 Holland Park, London W11 3RS
T 020-7221 7800 E info@algerianembassy.org.uk
W www.algerianembassy.org.uk
Ambassador Extraordinary and Plenipotentiary, HE Amar Abba, *apptd* 2010

Conquered by the Ottoman Empire — *c.*600

Gains independence following guerrilla war with socialist *Front de Libération Nationale* — 1830

Elected president Abdelaziz Bouteflika's 'civil concord' with Islamists approved by referendum — 1989–92

Second amnesty between militants approved but broken by bombings carried out by a group aligning itself with al-Qaida — 2005

2011

*c.*1525 — A Berber-populated Roman province, Algeria is conquered by Arabs and converted to Islam

1962 — Annexed by France

1999 — A ban on the Islamic Salvation Front triggers civil unrest and a state of emergency

2006 — Agreement reached with Berber-populated Kabylie for increased investment in the region and greater recognition of the Berber language

Major demonstrations cause government to cut food prices and lift the 19-year state of emergency

BRITISH EMBASSY
3 Chemin Capitaine Hocine Slimane, Hydra, Algiers
T (+213) (770) 085 000 E britishembassy.algiers@fco.gov.uk
W www.gov.uk/government/world/algeria
Ambassador Extraordinary and Plenipotentiary, HE Martyn Roper, *apptd* 2010

DEFENCE

Aged 16–49, 2010 est	Males	Females
Available for military service	10,273,129	10,114,552
Fit for military service	8,622,897	8,626,222

Military expenditure – US$9,902m (2013)
Conscription – 19–30 years of age; 18 months

ECONOMY AND TRADE
Recent economic reforms and the initiation of a privatisation programme in 1997, combined with high oil prices, resulted in trade surpluses, record foreign exchange reserves and the reduction of foreign debt for Algeria, but diversification away from the energy sector and development of the financial system is slow because of difficulty in attracting foreign investment. A wave of economic protests at the start of 2011 prompted the government to offer more than US$23bn (£14.5bn) in public grants and retroactive benefit increases.

Algeria has substantial oil and gas reserves and the hydrocarbon industry accounts for 30 per cent of GDP, nearly 60 per cent of government revenue and over 95 per cent of export earnings. Services provide 29.6 per cent of GDP, industry 61 per cent and agriculture 9.5 per cent. Industries other than oil and gas production and processing include mining, electrical goods, food processing and light industries.

Algeria's main trading partners are the USA, France, Italy, other EU countries and China. The chief imports are capital goods, foodstuffs and consumer goods.
GNI – US$203,594m; US$5,020 per capita (2012)
Annual average growth of GDP – 3.1 per cent (2013 est)
Inflation rate – 3.9 per cent (2013 est)
Population below poverty line – 23 per cent (2006 est)
Unemployment – 10.3 per cent (2013 est)
Total external debt – US$5,278m (2013 est)
Imports – US$50,369m (2012)
Exports – US$72,862m (2012)

BALANCE OF PAYMENTS
Trade – US$22,493m surplus (2012)
Current Account – US$12,290m surplus (2012)

Trade with UK	2012	2013
Imports from UK	£363,004,958	£529,997,028
Exports to UK	£2,062,861,191	£3,310,758,321

COMMUNICATIONS
Airports and waterways – 12, including Algiers and Constantine; major ports are at Algiers and Bejaia
Roadways and railways – 113,655km; 3,973km

Telecommunications – 3.2 million fixed lines and 37.69 million mobile subscriptions (2012); there were 4.7 million internet users in 2009
Internet code and IDD – dz; 213 (from UK), 44 (to UK)
Major broadcaster – Enterprise Nationale de Télévision (ENTV)
WPFI score – 36,26 (121)

EDUCATION AND HEALTH
Literacy rate – 72.6 per cent (2010 est)
Gross enrolment ratio (percentage of relevant age group) – primary 115 per cent; secondary 98 per cent; tertiary 30 per cent (2011 est)
Health expenditure (per capita) – US$225 (2011)
Life expectancy (years) – 76.18 (2012 est)
Mortality rate – 4.31 (2013 est)
Birth rate – 24.25 (2013 est)
Infant mortality rate – 22.57 (2013 est)

ANDORRA

Principat d'Andorra – Principality of Andorra

Area – 468 sq. km
Capital – Andorra la Vella; population, 23,000 (2011 est)
Major cities – Encamp, Escaldes-Engordany, Sant Julià de Lòria
Currency – Euro (€) of 100 cents
Population – 85,293 rising at 0.22 per cent a year (2013 est); Spanish (43 per cent), Andorran (33 per cent), Portuguese (11 per cent), French (7 per cent) (est)
Religion – Christian (predominantly Roman Catholic)
Language – Catalan (official), French, Spanish (Castilian), Portuguese
Population density – 166 per sq. km (2011)
Urban population – 86.7 per cent (2012 est)
Median age (years) – 41.8 (2013 est)
National anthem – 'El Gran Carlemany' ['The Great Charlemagne']
National day – 8 September (Our Lady of Meritxell Day)
Death penalty – Abolished for all crimes (since 1990)
Life expectancy (years) – 82.58 (2013 est)
Mortality rate – 6.67 (2013 est)
Birth rate – 8.88 (2013 est)
Infant mortality rate – 3.73 (2013 est)

CLIMATE AND TERRAIN

Andorra is a country of dramatic mountains interspersed by narrow valleys; over a third of the country is forested. Elevation extremes range from 2,946m (Pic de Coma Pedrosa) and 840m (Riu Runer). The climate is alpine, with heavy snowfall in winter and warm summers. Average temperature ranges from −1.4°C in January to 14.1°C in July.

HISTORY AND POLITICS

Liberated from Moorish rule by Charlemagne in 803, Andorra is a neutral principality that was formed by a *paréage* (a type of feudal treaty) in 1278 and since then has owed dual allegiance to two co-princes, the Spanish Bishop of Urgell and the head of state of France. Andorra became an independent democratic parliamentary co-principality in 1993. The country subsequently formalised its links with the EU, and joined the UN and the Council of Europe.

Andorra has a unicameral legislature, the General Council of the Valleys *(Consell General de las Valls)*, whose 28 members are directly elected for a four-year term by proportional representation. The council appoints the president of the executive council, who nominates government members.

Under the 1993 constitution, the heads of state are two co-princes, the President of France and the Bishop of Urgel, Spain. They are represented in Andorra by the permanent delegates (the Spanish vicar-general of the diocese of Urgel and the French prefect of the Pyrénées Orientales department), but their powers now relate solely to relations with France and Spain. The constitution established an independent judiciary and allows Andorra to conduct its own foreign policy, while its people may now join political parties and trade unions.

In the April 2011 legislative election, the opposition Democrats for Andorra party won 21 seats and formed a government, securing an overall majority in the parliament.

HEADS OF STATE
The President of France, François Hollande
The Bishop of Urgell, Joan Enric Vives i Sicilia
Permanent French Delegate, Sylvie Hubac
Permanent Episcopal Delegate, Josep Maria Mauri i Prior

SELECTED GOVERNMENT MEMBERS *as at February 2014*
President of the Executive Council, Culture, Antoni Martí
Economy and Territory, Jordi Alcobé
Foreign Affairs, Gilbert Saboya
Interior and Justice, Marc Vila

BRITISH CONSULATE-GENERAL
Ambassador, HE Simon Manley, CMG, *apptd* 2013, resident at Madrid, Spain

ECONOMY AND TRADE

The economy is largely based on tourism, banking and commerce, which together account for over 75 per cent of GDP. A recent drop in tourism, caused by the economic downturn in neighbouring countries, contributed to a dip in GDP and a deterioration in public finances, forcing the government to implement several austerity measures. Other activities include manufacturing tobacco products, forestry, furniture-making and sheep-farming.
GNI – US$3,712m; US$41,750 per capita (2008)
Annual average growth of GDP −1.6 per cent (2012 est)
Inflation rate – 1.1 per cent (2012 est)
Unemployment – 4 per cent (2012 est)
Imports – US$1,396m (2012)
Exports – US$68m (2012)

BALANCE OF PAYMENTS
Trade – US$1,327m deficit (2012)

Trade with UK	2012	2013
Imports from UK	£9,080,090	£8,833,612
Exports to UK	£298,067	£178,651

COMMUNICATIONS

Roadways – 320km
Telecommunications – 39,000 fixed lines and 65,000 mobile subscriptions (2012); there were 67,100 internet users in 2009
Internet code and IDD – ad; 376 (from UK), 44 (to UK)
Press – Major newspapers include *Diari d'Andorra* and *El Periodic*
WPFI score – 6,82 (5)

ANGOLA

Republica de Angola – Republic of Angola

Area – 1,246,700 sq. km; includes the exclave of Cabinda
Capital – Luanda; population, 5,288,806 (2012 est)
Major cities – Benguela, Huambo, Lubango
Currency – Kwanza (Kzrl) of 100 centimos
Population – 18,565,269 rising at 2.78 per cent a year (2013 est); Ovimbundu (37 per cent), Kimbundu (25 per cent), Bakongo (13 per cent), Mestizo (2 per cent), other African, including Lunda-Chokwe and Ngangela (22 per cent) (est)
Religion – Indigenous beliefs 47 per cent, Christian (Roman Catholic 38 per cent, Protestant 15 per cent) (est)
Language – Portuguese (official), Bantu
Population density – 16 per sq. km (2011)
Urban population – 60 per cent (2012 est)
Median age (years) – 17.7 (2013 est)
National anthem – 'Angola Avante' ['Forward Angola']
National day – 11 November (Independence Day)
Death penalty – Abolished for all crimes (since 1992)
CPI score – 23 (153)
Literacy rate – 70 per cent (2011 est)
Gross enrolment ratio (percentage of relevant age group) – primary 140 per cent; secondary 32 per cent; tertiary 7 per cent (2011 est)
Health expenditure (per capita) – US$186 (2011)
Hospital beds (per 1,000 people) – 0.8 (2004–9)
Life expectancy (years) – 54.95 (2013 est)
Mortality rate – 11.86 (2013 est)
Birth rate – 39.16 (2013 est)
Infant mortality rate – 81.75 (2013 est)
HIV/AIDS adult prevalence – 2.3 per cent (2012 est)

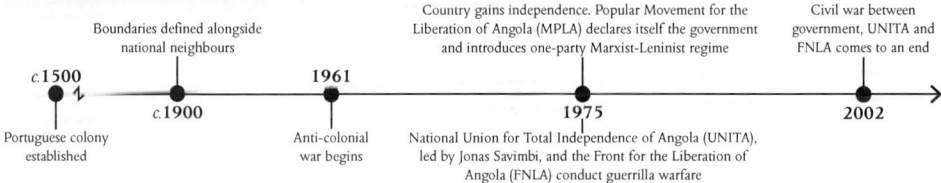

Boundaries defined alongside national neighbours — *c.*1500 ⚓ — *c.*1900 — 1961

Country gains independence. Popular Movement for the Liberation of Angola (MPLA) declares itself the government and introduces one-party Marxist-Leninist regime — 1975

Civil war between government, UNITA and FNLA comes to an end — 2002

Portuguese colony established

Anti-colonial war begins

National Union for Total Independence of Angola (UNITA), led by Jonas Savimbi, and the Front for the Liberation of Angola (FNLA) conduct guerrilla warfare

CLIMATE AND TERRAIN
The land rises from a narrow coastal plain to a vast interior plateau, with desert to the south. The highest point of elevation is 2,620m (Morro do Moco) and the lowest is 0m (Atlantic Ocean). The climate is tropical in the north – with a cool, dry season from April to September and a hot, rainy season from October to March – and sub-tropical in the south and along the coast to Luanda.

POLITICS
Under the 2010 constitution, the president is the head of the party with the largest number of seats in the legislature. The unicameral National Assembly has 223 members, elected by proportional representation for a five-year term.

Political pluralism was introduced under the 1991 peace agreement and multiparty elections were held in 1992, though the National Union for Total Independence of Angola (UNITA) refused to accept the results. The first legislative elections since 1992, held in 2008, were won by the People's Movement for the Liberation of Angola (MPLA); it retained its majority in the 2012 legislative election, with 175 seats to UNITA's 32. The new constitution introduced in 2010 ended direct election of the president, created the office of vice-president and abolished the post of prime minister; as leader of the MPLA, Jose Eduardo dos Santos remained president following the 2012 legislative election.

HEAD OF STATE
President, Jose Eduardo dos Santos, *took office* 21 September 1979, *re-elected* 30 September 1992, 2008, 2012
Vice-President, Manuel Domingos Vicente

SELECTED GOVERNMENT MEMBERS *as at February 2014*
Defence, Candido Pereira dos Santos Van-Dunem
Finance, Armando Manuel
Foreign Affairs, George Rebelo Pinto Chicoti
Interior, Angelo de Barros Veiga Tavares

EMBASSY OF THE REPUBLIC OF ANGOLA
22 Dorset Street, London W1U 6QY
T 020-7299 9850 E embassy@angola.org.uk
W www.angola.org.uk
Ambassador Extraordinary and Plenipotentiary, HE Miguel Gaspar Fernandes Neto, *apptd* 2012

BRITISH EMBASSY
Rua 17 de Setembro 4, Luanda
T (+244) (22) 233 4583 E postmaster.luand@fco.gov.uk
W www.gov.uk/government/world/angola
Ambassador Extraordinary and Plenipotentiary, HE John Dennis, *apptd* 2014

SECESSION
In the oil-rich northern exclave of Cabinda, separatists have conducted a low-level guerrilla war since the mid-1970s. The government has been unable to end the fighting either through negotiation or by military means. A ceasefire and peace agreement reached in 2006 has not been observed by all parties.

DEFENCE

Aged 16–49, 2010 est	*Males*	*Females*
Available for military service	3,062,438	2,964,262
Fit for military service	1,546,781	1,492,308

Military expenditure – US$5,208m (2012)
Conscription – 20–45 years of age, male only; 2 years

ECONOMY AND TRADE
The economy is still recovering from decades of corruption, mismanagement and civil war, but liberalisation and stabilisation are being achieved. Post-war increases in oil, diamond and agricultural production have driven strong economic growth, although the economy contracted in 2009 as the global downturn reduced demand for exports. The extractive industries and infrastructure projects have attracted foreign investment despite the corruption and stifling bureaucracy that have deterred investors in other sectors.

Angola, especially Cabinda, is rich in natural resources. The main industries involve extracting and processing oil (oil production and related activities account for around 85 per cent of GDP), diamonds, metals and other minerals, forestry, fishing, food processing and the manufacture of cement, metal products, tobacco products and textiles, and ship repair. Angola has large areas of good farmland, but the prevalence of unexploded landmines has reduced the area under cultivation and forced many areas back to subsistence agriculture, although coffee, sisal and cotton are produced for export. Despite rising production, the country still imports half of its food.

The main trading partners are China, the USA, India and Portugal. The principal exports are crude oil, diamonds, refined petroleum products, coffee, sisal, fish, timber and cotton. The main imports are machinery and electrical equipment, vehicles and spare parts, medicines, food, textiles and military goods.
GNI – US$102,612m; US$4,580 per capita (2012)
Annual average growth of GDP – 5.6 per cent (2013 est)
Inflation rate – 8.9 per cent (2013 est)
Population below poverty line – 40.5 per cent (2006 est)
Total external debt – US$22,710m (2013 est)
Imports – US$23,717m (2012)
Exports – US$70,088m (2012)

BALANCE OF PAYMENTS
Trade – US$46,371m surplus (2012)
Current Account – US$10,636m surplus (2012)

Trade with UK	2012	2013
Imports from UK	£401,526,513	£548,232,630
Exports to UK	£804,544,924	£660,427,462

COMMUNICATIONS
Airports and waterways – 31; main ports include Cabinda, Luanda, Lobito and Namibe
Roadways and railways – 51,429km; 2,764km
Telecommunications – 303,000 fixed lines and 9.8 million mobile subscriptions (2012); there were 606,700 internet users in 2009

Internet code and IDD – ao; 244 (from UK), 44 (to UK)
WPFI score – 36,50 (124)

ANTIGUA AND BARBUDA

Antigua and Barbuda

Area – 442.6 sq. km; Antigua 280 sq. km; Barbuda 161 sq. km; Redonda 1.6 sq. km
Capital – St John's; population, 27,000 (2011 est)
Currency – East Caribbean dollar (EC$) of 100 cents
Population – 90,156; rising at 1.26 per cent a year (2013 est)
Religion – Christian (Protestant 76.4 per cent, Roman Catholic 10.4 per cent, other Christian 1.7 per cent) (est)
Language – English (official)
Population density – 200 per sq. km (2011)
Urban population – 29.8 per cent (2012 est)
Median age (years) – 30.8 (2013 est)
National anthem – 'Fair Antigua, We Salute Thee'
National day – 1 November (Independence Day)
Death penalty – Retained
Literacy rate – 99 per cent (2011 est)
Gross enrolment ratio (percentage of relevant age group) – primary 101 per cent; secondary 106 per cent; tertiary 14 per cent (2011 est)
Life expectancy (years) – 75.91 (2013 est)
Mortality rate – 5.7 (2013 est)
Birth rate – 16.07 (2013 est)
Infant mortality rate – 13.72 (2013 est)

CLIMATE AND TERRAIN
Unlike most other Leeward Islands, Antigua has few high hills and little forest cover. Its elevation extremes range from 402m (Boggy Peak) to 0m (Caribbean Sea). Barbuda, 48km north of Antigua, is a flat coral island with a large lagoon. Both islands are tropical, but drier than most of the West Indies. They lie within the hurricane belt and are subject to tropical storms and hurricanes between August and October.

HISTORY AND POLITICS
Prehistoric settlers were succeeded by the Arawaks, then the Caribs. Although the islands were discovered by Columbus in 1493, the European (English) settlement of Antigua began only in 1632. Barbuda was colonised from Antigua in 1661. Administered as part of the Leeward Islands Federation from 1871 to 1956, it became internally self-governing in 1967 and fully independent on 1 November 1981.
The head of state is Queen Elizabeth II, represented by the governor-general. The bicameral parliament comprises a senate of 17 members, appointed by the governor-general on the advice of the prime minister and opposition leader, and a House of Representatives of 17 directly elected members; both chambers serve a five-year term.

The Antigua Labour Party defeated The United Progressive Party in the 2014 legislative elections.
Governor-General, HE Dr Rodney Williams, *apptd* 2014

SELECTED GOVERNMENT MEMBERS *as at September 2014*
Prime Minister, Gaston Browne
Minister of Foreign Affairs, Charles Fernardez
Tourism, Asot Michael

HIGH COMMISSION FOR ANTIGUA AND BARBUDA
2nd Floor, 45 Crawford Place, London W1H 4LP
T 020-7258 0070 W www.antigua-barbuda.com
High Commissioner, HE Dr Carl Roberts, CMG, *apptd* 2004

BRITISH HIGH COMMISSION
High Commissioner, HE Victoria Glynis Dean, *apptd* 2013, resident at Bridgetown, Barbados

DEFENCE

Aged 16–49, 2010 est	Males	Females
Available for military service	21,141	24,056
Fit for military service	17,676	19,960

Military expenditure – not available

ECONOMY AND TRADE
The economy is largely based on tourism and related services (contributing nearly 60 per cent of GDP), with light manufacturing (bedding, handicrafts, electronic components) for export, and agriculture (livestock, sea island cotton, market gardening, fishing) for local consumption. Economic growth and fiscal reform between 2004 7 enabled the government to reduce public debt. However, from 2008, a severe decline in tourism caused by the global economic downturn and the collapse of Alan Stanford's Antigua-based financial group (which included Antigua's major financial institution) hit the economy badly and public debt is rising again.
GNI – US$1,092m; US$12,480 per capita (2012)
Annual average growth of GDP – 1.7 per cent (2013 est)
Inflation rate – 3 per cent (2013 est)
Total external debt – US$441.2m (2012 est)
Imports – US$535m (2012)
Exports – US$29m (2012)

BALANCE OF PAYMENTS
Trade – US$506m deficit (2012)
Current Account – US$167m deficit (2012)

Trade with UK	2012	2013
Imports from UK	£8,684,598	£13,698,715
Exports to UK	£3,416,072	£5,496,973

COMMUNICATIONS
Airports and waterways – Two; the main port is at St John's
Roadways – 1,170km
Telecommunications – 35,000 fixed lines and 179,800 mobile subscriptions (2012); there were 65,000 internet users in 2009
Internet code and IDD – ag; 1 268 (from UK), 011 44 (to UK)
Major broadcasters – The Antigua Labour Party and the Bird family owns or controls many of the country's television and radio stations. Antigua's first independent radio station, Observer Radio, began broadcasting in 2001
WPFI score – 20,81 (36)

ARGENTINA

República Argentina – Argentine Republic

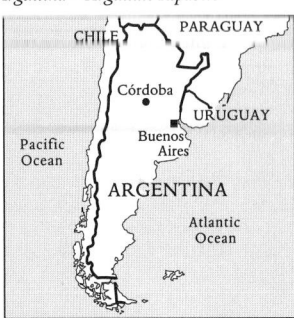

Area – 2,780,400 sq. km
Capital – Buenos Aires; population, 13,223,565 (2012 est)
Major cities – Córdoba, La Plata, Mar del Plata, Mendoza,
   Rosario, Salta, San Miguel de Tucumán, Santa Fé
Currency – Peso of 100 centavos
Population – 42,610,981 rising at 0.98 per cent a year
   (2013 est)
Religion – Christian (Roman Catholic 92 per cent, Protestant
   2 per cent), Jewish (2 per cent) (est)
Language – Spanish (official), Italian, English, German,
   French
Population density – 15 per sq. km (2011)
Urban population – 92.7 per cent (2012 est)
Median age (years) – 31 (2013 est)
National anthem – 'Marcha de la Patria' ['March of the
   Fatherland']
National day – 25 May (Revolution Day)
Death penalty – Abolished for all crimes (since 2008)
CPI score – 34 (106)

CLIMATE AND TERRAIN
The Andes mountain range runs the full length of the
country, along its western border with Chile, and the area is
prone to earthquakes. East of the Andes, the north is mostly
subtropical rainforest, the centre contains the vast grasslands
of the pampas, and the southern Patagonian plateau is arid
and desolate, with glaciers in the far south. The highest point
of elevation is 6,960m (Cerro Aconcagua) and the lowest
is −105m (Laguna del Carbon). Temperatures range from
subtropical in the north to subantarctic in the south. In
Buenos Aires average temperatures are between 25°C in
January and 11°C in July.

POLITICS
Following constitutional amendments agreed in 1994, the
executive president is directly elected for a four-year term,
renewable once. The bicameral National Congress consists of
a 72-member senate (three members for each province and
three for Buenos Aires) and a 257-member Chamber of
Deputies. Deputies are directly elected for a four-year term,
with half of the seats renewable every two years. Senators are
directly elected for a six-year term, with one-third of seats
renewable every two years.

The Argentine Republic is a federation of 23 provinces,
each with an elected governor and legislature, plus the
federal district of Buenos Aires, which has an elected mayor
and autonomous government.

The 2011 presidential election was won in the first round
by Cristina Fernández de Kirchner, who gained re-election
with 54 per cent of the overall vote. The Front for Victory
(FpV), the pro-presidential wing of the internally divided
Judicialist Party, a Peronist grouping, regained control of
both houses of the legislature, previously lost in the 2009
mid-term legislative elections. October 2013 legislative
elections saw the FpV and its allies retain control of both
houses despite a slight drop in the number of seats, blamed in
part on a lack of active campaigning by Kirchner who was
recovering from recent brain surgery.

HEAD OF STATE
President, Cristina Fernández de Kirchner, *sworn in*
   10 December 2007, *re-elected* 10 December 2011
Vice-President, Amado Boudou

SELECTED GOVERNMENT MEMBERS *as at*
February 2014
Cabinet Chief, Jorge Capitanich
Defence, Agustin Rossi
Economy, Axel Kicillof
Foreign Relations, Héctor Timerman
Interior, Anibal Randazzo

EMBASSY OF THE ARGENTINE REPUBLIC
65 Brook Street, London W1K 4AH
T 020-7318 1300 E info@argentine-embassy-uk.org
W www.argentine-embassy-uk.org
Ambassador Extraordinary and Plenipotentiary, HE Alicia
   Castro, *apptd* 2012

BRITISH EMBASSY
Dr Luis Agote 2412, 1425 Buenos Aires
T (+54) (11) 4808 2200
W www.gov.uk/government/world/argentina
Ambassador Extraordinary and Plenipotentiary, HE John
   Freeman, *apptd* 2012

DEFENCE

Aged 16–49, 2010 est	Males	Females
Available for military service	10,038,967	9,959,134
Fit for military service	8,458,362	8,414,460

Military expenditure – US$4,929m (2013 est)

ECONOMY AND TRADE
The economy recovered rapidly from the economic collapse
of 2001–2, experiencing strong growth from 2003.
Argentina restructured its defaulted debt in 2005 and repaid
its IMF loan in 2006. Inflation rose sharply in 2007–8
and remains high, pushing up prices, despite a recession
in 2008–9 caused by the global downturn. A shortfall in
energy supplies remains a problem as does the vast depletion
of hard currency reserves and the continuing devaluation of

Ruled by Spain | Military coup; government under military rule | Perón overthrown triggering political instability | María Perón overthrown by military junta during which 8,000 people are allegedly murdered | Submits to the UN a formal claim to an area of South Atlantic Ocean governed by Britain

1515 — 1600 — 1816 — 1943 — 1946 — 1955 — 1973 — 1976 — 1982-3 — 2009

Discovered by Juan Díaz de Solís and colonised by the Spanish | Independence declared | Juan Perón becomes president, establishing an authoritarian regime | Juan Perón recalled from exile, but dies soon after becoming president for second time. Succeeded by María ('Isabelita') Perón | Failure to annex Falkland Islands discredits junta. Civilian rule restored the peso, which in January 2014 saw its sharpest one-day fall against the dollar since the 2002 crisis.

The country is rich in natural resources, particularly lead, zinc, tin, copper, iron ore, manganese, uranium, oil and coal. The fertile pampas supports a strong and export-orientated agricultural sector; the main crops are cereals, oil-bearing seeds, fruit, tea, tobacco and livestock products, especially beef, mutton and wool.

The main industrial activities are food processing (meat-packing, flour-milling, sugar-refining, wine production) and the production of motor vehicles, consumer durables, textiles, chemicals, petrochemicals, printing, metallurgy and steel.

The main trading partners are Brazil, China and the USA. The principal exports include soya beans and derivatives, petroleum and gas, motor vehicles and cereals. The major imports are machinery, motor vehicles, petroleum and natural gas, organic chemicals and plastics.

GNI – US$435,223m; US$9,740 per capita (2011)
Annual average growth of GDP – 3.5 per cent (2013 est)
Inflation rate – 20.8 per cent (2013 est)
Population below poverty line – 30 per cent (2010 est)
Unemployment – 7.5 per cent (2013 est)
Total external debt – US$111,500m (2013 est)
Imports – US$68,507m (2012)
Exports – US$75,219m (2012)

BALANCE OF PAYMENTS
Trade – US$6,711m surplus (2012)
Current Account – US$278m deficit (2012)

Trade with UK	2012	2013
Imports from UK	£354,544,465	£343,382,547
Exports to UK	£608,719,924	£619,267,587

COMMUNICATIONS
Airports and waterways – 161, major airports include Buenos Aires, Córdoba, Salta and Rio Gallegos; 11,000km of waterways
Roadways and railways – There are 231,374km of roadways (69,412km surfaced and 734km motorway) and 36,966km of railways
Telecommunications – 10 million fixed lines and 58.6 million mobile subscriptions (2012); there were 13.69 million internet subscribers in 2009
Internet code and IDD – ar; 54 (from UK), 44 (to UK)
Major broadcasters – Telefe, America, Canal 9, Canal 13 stations are all privately owned
Press – there are over 150 daily newspapers, including seven major dailies published in Buenos Aires
WPFI score – 25,27 (55)

EDUCATION AND HEALTH
Education is compulsory until the age of 14.
Literacy rate – 98 per cent (2011 est)
Gross enrolment ratio (percentage of relevant age group) – primary 118 per cent; secondary 90 per cent; tertiary 75 per cent (2011 est)
Health expenditure (per capita) – US$892 (2011)
Hospital beds (per 1,000 people) – 4.5 (2004–11)
Life expectancy (years) – 77.32 (2013 est)
Mortality rate – 7.35 (2013 est)
Birth rate – 17.12 (2013 est)
Infant mortality rate – 10.24 (2013 est)

ARGENTINE ANTARCTIC TERRITORY

The Argentine Antarctic Territory consists of the Antarctic Peninsula and a triangular section extending to the South Pole, defined as the area between 25°W and 74°W and 60°S. This overlaps with both Britain's and Chile's claimed areas (*see also* The North and South Poles). Administratively, the territory is a department of the province of Tierra del Fuego, Antarctica and South Atlantic Islands. The population varies seasonally between approximately 150 and 660 people, all of whom are scientific researchers and their dependants.

ARMENIA

Hayastani Hanrapetut'yun – Republic of Armenia

Area – 29,743 sq. km
Capital – Yerevan; population, 1,114,582 (2012 est)
Major cities – Gyumri, Vanadzor
Currency – Dram of 100 luma
Population – 3,064,267 rising at 0.14 per cent a year (2013 est); Armenian (98.1 per cent), Yezidi (1.1 per cent) (2011). The Armenian diaspora numbers at least 4,700,000
Religion – Christian (Armenian Apostolic 92.6 per cent, other Christian 3.4 per cent) (est). The kingdom of Armenia was the first state to adopt Christianity as its official religion, in AD 301
Language – Armenian, Kurdish
Population density – 104 per sq. km (2011)
Urban population – 64.1 per cent (2012 est)
Median age (years) – 32.9 (2013 est)
National anthem – 'Mer Hayrenik' ['Our Fatherland']
National day – 21 September (Independence Day)
Death penalty – Abolished for all crimes (since 2003)
CPI score – 36 (94)

CLIMATE AND TERRAIN
Landlocked Armenia is situated in the south-western part of the Caucasus region. It lies at a high altitude and consists of vast plateaux surrounded by mountain ranges. The elevation extremes range from 4,090m (Mt Aragats) to 400m (Debed river). The climate is continental, with hot summers, cold winters and low rainfall. Armenia experiences occasional droughts and severe earthquakes.

POLITICS
The 1995 constitution was amended by referendum in 2005. The president is directly elected for a five-year term, renewable only once. The unicameral National Assembly (*Azgayin Joghov*) has 131 members who are directly elected for a five-year term.

In the 2012 legislative election, the Republican Party of Armenia (RPA) remained the largest party in the legislature, with 69 seats, and its leader, Serzh Sargsyan, continued in office at the head of a four-party coalition government. Sargsyan was re-elected in the 2013 presidential election in the first round with 52.8 per cent of the vote.

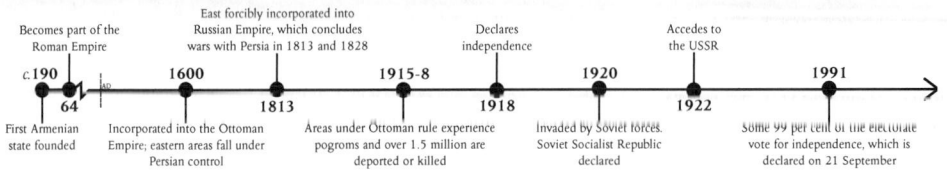

Becomes part of the Roman Empire		East forcibly incorporated into Russian Empire, which concludes wars with Persia in 1813 and 1828		Declares independence		Accedes to the USSR	
c.190	1600		1915-8		1920		1991
64		1813		1918		1922	
First Armenian state founded	Incorporated into the Ottoman Empire; eastern areas fall under Persian control		Areas under Ottoman rule experience pogroms and over 1.5 million are deported or killed		Invaded by Soviet forces. Soviet Socialist Republic declared		Some 99 per cent of the electorate vote for independence, which is declared on 21 September

HEAD OF STATE

President, Serzh Sargsyan, *elected* 19 February 2008, *re-elected* 13 February 2013

SELECTED GOVERNMENT MEMBERS *as at February 2014*

Prime Minister, Tigran Sargsyan
Deputy Prime Minister, Armen Gevorgyan
Defence, Seyran Ohanyan
Economy, Vahram Avanesyan

EMBASSY OF THE REPUBLIC OF ARMENIA

25A Cheniston Gardens, London W8 6TG
T 020-7938 5435 E armembassyuk@mfa.am
W http://uk.mfa.am/en
Ambassador Extraordinary and Plenipotentiary, HE Dr Armen Sarkissian, *apptd* 2013

BRITISH EMBASSY

34 Baghramyan Avenue, Yerevan 0019
T (+374) (10) 264 301 E Enquiries.Yerevan@fco.gov.uk
W www.gov.uk/government/world/armenia
Ambassador Extraordinary and Plenipotentiary, HE Jonathan Aves and HE Katherine Leach, *apptd* 2012

FOREIGN RELATIONS

There is a longstanding dispute with Azerbaijan over the predominantly Armenian-populated Azeri region of Nagorny-Karabakh; Armenia claims this territory as historically native land arbitrarily granted to Soviet Azerbaijan by Stalin in 1921–2. The territory's government voted to transfer to Armenia in 1988 but this was rejected by the USSR. When the USSR collapsed in 1991, the territory declared independence. Azeri attempts to reassert control were met with resistance which escalated into a war that lasted from 1992 until a ceasefire was agreed between Armenia, Azerbaijan and Nagorny-Karabakh in 1994. By this time, Nagorno-Karabakh forces, supported by Armenia, had captured all of Nagorny-Karabakh, all Azeri territory that separated Nagorny-Karabakh from Armenia and all mountainous Azeri territory around the enclave. Talks mediated by the Organisation for Security and Cooperation in Europe failed to make any progress towards a peaceful resolution until 2008, when Armenia and Azerbaijan agreed to intensify efforts, although recent years have seen stalled negotiations and regular ceasefire breaches – including some serious incidents in 2010–11.

DEFENCE

Russia maintains around 5,000 army personnel in Armenia, and in 2010 its lease on a military base was extended to 2044.

Aged 16–49, 2010 est	Males	Females
Available for military service	805,847	854,296
Fit for military service	644,372	717,272

Military expenditure – US$428m (2013 est)
Conscription – 18–27 years of age; 2 years

ECONOMY AND TRADE

The economy experienced a severe decline following the break-up of the USSR in 1991, adding to existing problems arising from the 1988 earthquake and subsequently exacerbated by the Nagorny-Karabakh conflict and the consequent trade embargos imposed by Azerbaijan and Turkey, both of which are still in place. Economic liberalisation from 1994 brought sustained high growth and falls in inflation and poverty levels until the global economic crisis. This triggered a severe recession in 2009, largely owing to declines in construction and remittances, despite loans from Russia and international institutions; a recovery began in 2010 and strengthened significantly in 2011, before dipping in 2012 following sharp currency depreciation and high unemployment rates.

The agricultural sector produces fruit, vegetables and livestock as cash crops, and grain; it contributes 20.5 per cent of GDP and employs 44.2 per cent of the workforce. There are large mineral deposits, including iron and copper ore and non-ferrous metals. Industry, which contributes 37 per cent of GDP, is diversified and most small- and medium-sized enterprises are now privatised. The main activities are diamond-processing, the production of industrial machinery, vehicles and parts, textiles and clothing, chemicals, instruments, microelectronics, jewellery, software development and food processing.

The main trading partners are Russia, EU countries, Iran, other former Soviet bloc states, China and the USA. Principal exports are pig iron, copper, non-ferrous metals, diamonds, mineral products, food and energy. The main imports are natural gas, petrol, tobacco products, foodstuffs and diamonds.
GNI – US$10,430m; US$3,3,720 per capita (2012)
Annual average growth of GDP – 4.6 per cent (2013 est)
Inflation rate – 6.2 per cent (2013 est)
Population below poverty line – 35.8 per cent (2010 est)
Unemployment – 17.3 per cent (2012 est)
Total external debt – US$7,839m (2013 est)
Imports – US$4,267m (2012)
Exports – US$1,428m (2012)

BALANCE OF PAYMENTS

Trade – US$2,839m deficit (2012)
Current Account – US$1,115m deficit (2012)

Trade with UK	2012	2013
Imports from UK	£15,482,317	£19,450,400
Exports to UK	£481,632	£2,321,823

COMMUNICATIONS

Airports – Ten
Roadways and railways – 7,705km; 869km
Telecommunications – 584,000 fixed lines and 3.22 million mobile subscriptions (2012); there were 208,200 internet users in 2009
Internet code and IDD – am; 374 (from UK), 44 (to UK)
Major broadcasters – Public TV of Armenia (state-run) and Armenia TV (commercial), alongside 40 private television stations
WPFI score – 29,07 (78)

EDUCATION AND HEALTH

State education is free and compulsory for all children aged seven to 14. Senior secondary school may be attended from the ages of 14 to 16.

Literacy rate – 100 per cent (2011 est)
Gross enrolment ratio (percentage of relevant age group) – primary 102 per cent; secondary 96 per cent; tertiary 51 per cent (2011 est)
Health expenditure (per capita) – US$142 (2011)
Hospital beds (per 1,000 people) – 4 (2011)
Life expectancy (years) – 73.75 (2013 est)
Mortality rate – 8.51 (2013 est)
Birth rate – 12.86 (2013 est)
Infant mortality rate – 17.59 (2013 est)

AUSTRALIA

Commonwealth of Australia

Area – 7,691,951 sq. km (excluding overseas territories)
Capital – Canberra; population, 399,000 (2011 est)
Major cities – Adelaide, Brisbane, Melbourne, Perth, Sydney
Currency – Australian dollar ($A) of 100 cents
Population – 22,262,501 rising at 1.11 per cent a year (2013 est)
Religion – Christian (Protestant 28.8 per cent, Roman Catholic 25.3 per cent, Buddhist 2.5 per cent, Muslim 2.2 per cent, Hindu 1.3 per cent (est)
Language – English, Mandarin, Italian, Arabic, Aboriginal languages
Population density – 3 per sq. km (2011)
Urban population – 89.4 per cent (2012 est)
Median age (years) – 38.1 (2013 est)
National anthem – 'Advance Australia Fair'
National day – 26 January (Australia Day)
Death penalty – Abolished for all crimes (since 1985)
CPI score – 81 (9)

CLIMATE AND TERRAIN

The majority of Australia is a plateau, with hills, low mountain ranges and sparsely populated deserts in the interior, and tropical wetlands and rainforest in the north-east. Mountain ranges running down the east coast are the source of the Murray and Darling river systems, which flow across the densely populated fertile plain in the south-east. Off the north-east coast is the Great Barrier Reef, the world's largest coral reef. Elevation ranges from 2,229m (Mt Kosciuszko) to −15m (Lake Eyre). The climate is arid or semi-arid in the interior, tropical in the north and temperate in the south and east.

POLITICS

Under the 1901 constitution, the Commonwealth of Australia is a federation of six states. The constitution defines the powers of the federal government, and residuary legislative power remains with the states.

The head of state is Queen Elizabeth II, represented by the governor-general, who is appointed on the advice of the Australian prime minister. The bicameral parliament consists of the senate and the House of Representatives. The constitution provides that the number of members of the House of Representatives shall be proportionate to the population of each state, with a minimum of five members for each state, and that the number of senators shall be, as nearly as is practicable, half the number of representatives. There are currently 150 members, including two members for the Northern Territory and two for the Australian Capital Territory; they are directly elected for a three-year term. There are 76 senators; each state returns 12 senators, who are directly elected for a six-year term, with half retiring every third year. The Australian Capital Territory and the Northern Territory each return two senators, who are directly elected for a three-year term.

Each of the six states has its own constitution, executive, legislature and judicature. Executive authority is vested in a governor (appointed by the Crown), assisted by a council of ministers or executive council headed by a state premier. There are ten territories, and three – the Australian Capital Territory, Northern Territory and Norfolk Island – have limited self-government, with an executive authority headed by an administrator (appointed by the governor-general), and legislative assembly led by a chief minister. The other territories are directly administered by the federal government.

The Liberal–National Coalition, led by Tony Abbott of the Liberal Party of Australia, defeated the incumbent Australian Labor Party (ALP) in the September 2013 federal elections, winning a significant overall majority in the House of Representatives, but not in the Senate. Abbott promised to repeal controversial taxes on carbon emissions and mining,

STATES AND TERRITORIES

	Area (sq. km)	Population (2013 est)	Capital	Premier (2013)
Australian Capital Territory (ACT)	2,358	383,400	Canberra	Katy Gallagher†
New South Wales (NSW)	800,642	7,407,700	Sydney	Barry O'Farrell
Northern Territory (NT)	1,349,129	239,500	Darwin*	Adam Giles†
Queensland (Qld)	1,730,648	4,658,600	Brisbane	Campbell Newman
South Australia (SA)	983,482	1,670,800	Adelaide	Jay Weatherill
Tasmania (Tas.)	68,401	513,000	Hobart	Lara Giddings
Victoria (Vic.)	227,416	5,737,600	Melbourne	Dennis Napthine
Western Australia (WA)	2,529,875	2,517,200	Perth	Colin Barnett

* Seat of administration   † Chief Minister

and immediately introduced a tougher policy against asylum-seekers. His victory ended seven years of government by the ALP and followed a divisive leadership battle within the party that saw deputy prime minister Julia Gillard challenge Kevin Rudd and become Australia's first female prime minister in June 2010 and then relinquish the premiership back to him exactly three years later, following plummeting opinion polls.

Governor-General, Quentin Bryce, *apptd* 2008

SELECTED GOVERNMENT MEMBERS *as at February 2014*
Prime Minister, Tony Abbott
Deputy Prime Minister, Infrastructure and Regional Development, Warren Truss
Defence, David Johnston

AUSTRALIAN HIGH COMMISSION
Australia House, Strand, London WC2B 4LA
T 020-7379 4334 W www.uk.embassy.gov.au
High Commissioner, HE Mike Rann, LVO, *apptd* 2012

BRITISH HIGH COMMISSION
Commonwealth Avenue, Yarralumla, Canberra, ACT 2600
T (+61) (2) 6270 6666 E canberra.enquiries@fconet.fco.gov.uk
W www.gov.uk/government/world/australia
High Commissioner, HE Paul Madden, *apptd* 2011

DEFENCE

Aged 16–49, 2010 est	Males	Females
Available for military service	5,316,464	5,116,722
Fit for military service	4,411,958	4,239,985

Military expenditure – US$24,638m (2013)

ECONOMY AND TRADE
Australia has a highly diversified and internationally competitive market economy that saw sustained strong growth from the early 1990s until 2008. It weathered the global downturn better than most developed countries, avoiding recession through a government fiscal stimulus package and low interest rates. Recent problems have been climate related, with floods, droughts and extensive bush fires all affecting agriculture, mining and infrastructure. The service sector contributes 68.9 per cent of GDP and employs 75 per cent of the workforce, industry accounts for 27.2 per cent of GDP and 21.1 per cent of labour, and agriculture contributes 3.9 per cent of GDP and employs 3.6 per cent of the workforce.

The diversity of Australia's climate and soil conditions means that a wide range of crops can be grown, although most are confined to specific regions. Scant or erratic rainfall, limited scope for irrigation and unsuitable soils or topography have restricted intensive agriculture, although wheat is a major export and sugar cane and fruit are important crops. Cattle and sheep ranching is widespread, providing meat, meat derivatives, wool and dairy products.

Significant natural resources include bauxite, coal, copper, diamonds, gold, iron ore, lead, mineral salts, nickel, silver, tin, tungsten, uranium, zinc, oil and natural gas. The main industrial activities are mining, the production of industrial and transport equipment, chemicals and steel, and food processing. Production and processing of hydrocarbons are expected to increase once the oil and gas fields in the Timor Sea begin full production.

Over the past 20 years, the focus of Australia's trade, like its foreign policy, has shifted from Europe to Asia and the Pacific region. It is a leading member of the Asia-Pacific Economic Cooperation forum, and a free-trade agreement (FTA) between Australia and the Association of Southeast Asian Nations (ASEAN) countries entered into force in 2010; it is also negotiating for FTAs with China, Japan, India, South Korea and Malaysia. Major trading partners include China, Japan, South Korea, India, Thailand, Singapore and Germany. The chief exports are coal, iron ore, gold, meat, wool, alumina, wheat, machinery and transport equipment. The main imports are machinery and transport equipment, computers, office and telecoms equipment, crude oil and petroleum products.
GNI – US$1,476,339m; US$59,360 per capita (2012)
Annual average growth of GDP – 2.5 per cent (2013 est)
Inflation rate – 2.4 per cent (2013 est)
Unemployment – 5.7 per cent (2013 est)
Total external debt – US$1,506,000m (2013 est)
Imports – US$260,939m (2012)
Exports – US$256,664m (2012)

BALANCE OF PAYMENTS
Trade – US$4,275m deficit (2012)
Current Account – US$64,002m deficit (2012)

Trade with UK	2012	2013
Imports from UK	£4,423,904,169	£4,050,387,789
Exports to UK	£2,367,992,249	£2,147,361,027

COMMUNICATIONS
Airports – 349; there are international airports in each of the eight territories
Waterways – 2,000km; major ports in all of the state capitals except Hobart
Roadways and railways – 823,217km; 38,455km
Telecommunications – 10.47 million fixed lines and 24.4 million mobile subscriptions (2012); there were 15.81 million internet subscribers in 2009
Internet country code and IDD – au; 61 (from UK), 11 41 (to UK)
Major broadcasters – The Australian Broadcasting Corporation (ABC) and Special Broadcasting Service (SBS); other major television networks include Australia Network and Foxtel (owned by News Corporation)
Press – Four major media groups – including Rupert Murdoch's News Corporation – own 80 per cent of newspaper titles; major publications include *The Sydney Morning Herald, The Australian* and *The Daily Telegraph*
WPFI score – 16,91 (28)

EDUCATION AND HEALTH

Education is administered by each state and territory, and is compulsory between the ages of five and 17.

Gross enrolment ratio (percentage of relevant age group) –
   primary 104 per cent; secondary 133 per cent; tertiary
   83 per cent (2011 est)
Health expenditure (per capita) – US$5,939 (2011)
Hospital beds (per 1,000 people) – 3.9 (2010)
Life expectancy (years) – 81.98 (2013 est)
Mortality rate – 7.01 (2013 est)
Birth rate – 12.23 (2013 est)
Infant mortality rate – 4.49 (2013 est)

EXTERNAL TERRITORIES

Most of the territories are administered by the federal government through the Department of Regional Australia, Regional Development and Local Government; the Australian Antarctic Territory and the Territory of Heard Island and McDonald Islands are administered through the Australian Antarctic Division of the Department of Sustainability, Environment, Water, Population and Communities.

ASHMORE AND CARTIER ISLANDS

The Ashmore Islands (comprising Middle, East and West Islands) and Cartier Island are situated in the Indian Ocean 320km off Australia's north-west coast. The islands became an Australian territory in 1933. A nature reserve was established on Ashmore Reef in 1983 and a marine reserve around Cartier Island in 2000.

THE AUSTRALIAN ANTARCTIC TERRITORY

The Australian Antarctic Territory was established in 1933 and is 5,896,500 sq. km. It comprises all the islands and territories, other than Adélie Land, that are situated south of latitude 60°S. and lying between 160°E. longitude and 45°E. longitude. (*See also* The North and South Poles.)

CHRISTMAS ISLAND

Area – 135 sq. km
Population – 1,513 rising at 1.12 per cent a year (2013 est)

Christmas Island is situated in the Indian Ocean about 1,565km north-west of Northwest Cape in Western Australia. The island was annexed by Britain in 1888. Sovereignty was transferred to Australia in 1958. The Shire of Christmas Island (SOCI) is responsible for local government services on the island; its council has nine members directly elected for a four-year term. The main activities are phosphate mining, tourism and the government sector.
Administrator, Jon Stanhope, *apptd* 2012

COCOS (KEELING) ISLANDS

Area – 14 sq. km
Population – 596 (2013 est)

The Cocos (Keeling) Islands are two separate atolls (North Keeling Island and, 24km to the south, the main atoll) comprising 27 small coral islands, situated in the Indian Ocean, about 2,950km north-west of Perth. The two inhabited islands of the southern atoll are West Island and Home Island, where around 80 per cent of the population lives, including most of the Cocos Malay community.

The islands were declared a British possession in 1857. In 1886 Queen Victoria granted all land in the islands to George Clunies-Ross and his heirs, who established coconut plantations worked by imported Malay labour. Sovereignty was transferred to Australia in 1955, and the government purchased the Clunies-Ross land and property in 1978, 1984 and 1993. The land is held in trust for the residents, with the local government body, the Shire of the Cocos (Keeling) Islands, as trustee. In 1984 the Cocos community, in a UN-supervised Act of Self-Determination, voted to integrate with Australia. The seven-member Shire Council of Cocos (Keeling) Islands is responsible for local government services. The public sector is the main employer and there is a little tourism; coconuts are the only cash crop.
Administrator, Jon Stanhope, *apptd* 2012

CORAL SEA ISLANDS TERRITORY

The Coral Sea Islands Territory lies east of Queensland between the Great Barrier Reef and longitude 156° 06'E., and between latitudes 12°S. and 24°S. It comprises scattered islands, spread over a sea area of 780,000 sq. km. There is a manned meteorological station on Willis Island but otherwise the islands are uninhabited. Established in 1969, the territory is now a nature reserve, administered jointly by the Department of Sustainability, Environment, Water, Population and Communities and the Department of Agriculture, Fisheries and Forestry.

HEARD ISLAND AND MCDONALD ISLANDS

The Territory of Heard Island and the McDonald Islands, about 4,100km south-west of Perth, comprises all the islands and rocks lying between 52° 30' and 53° 30' S. latitude and 72° and 74° 30' E. longitude. The subantarctic islands, which have active volcanoes, were discovered in the 1850s and sovereignty was transferred from Britain to Australia in 1947. The islands are now part of a marine reserve established in 2002.

JERVIS BAY TERRITORY

Area – 73 sq. km
Population – 377 (2011 census)

The territory consists of 65 sq. km of land on the southern shore of Jervis Bay, 8 sq. km of marine waters and Bowen Island (0.5 sq. km), and lies about 200km south of Sydney. Originally part of New South Wales, the territory was acquired by the federal government in 1915 to provide Canberra with access to the sea. Much of the land and water now comprises Booderee National Park, leased from the Wreck Bay Aboriginal Community who since the 1980s have been granted 90 per cent of the land. The main economic activity is tourism.

NORFOLK ISLAND

Area – 36 sq. km
Population – 2,196 rising at 0.01 per cent a year (2013 est)
Seat of government – Kingston
National day – 8 June (Bounty Day)

Discovered by Captain Cook in 1774, Norfolk Island is situated in the South Pacific Ocean, about 1,600km north-east of Sydney. In 1856, 194 descendants of the *Bounty* mutineers accepted an invitation to leave Pitcairn and settle on Norfolk Island, which had served as a penal colony.

The island became a territory in 1914 and has been internally self-governing since 1979. The nine-member legislative assembly is directly elected for a three-year term, and elects the five-member executive council. This advises the Administrator, who represents the federal government. The economy is dependent on tourism; other economic activities include the sale of postage stamps and pine and palm seeds, livestock-rearing and agriculture.
Administrator, Neil Pope, *apptd* 2012

AUSTRIA

Republik Österreich – Republic of Austria

Area – 83,871 sq. km
Capital – Vienna (Wien); population, 1,727,857 (2012 est)
Major cities – Graz, Innsbruck, Klagenfurt, Linz, Salzburg
Currency – Euro (€) of 100 cents
Population – 8,221,646 rising at 0.02 per cent a year (2013 est); Austrian (91.1 per cent), former Yugoslav (4 per cent), Turkish (1.6 per cent) (2001 est)
Religion – Christian (Roman Catholic 66 per cent, Protestant 4 per cent, Eastern Orthodox 2 per cent), Muslim 4 per cent (est)
Language – German (official), Croatian and Hungarian (official in Burgenland), Slovene (official in Carinthia), Turkish, Serbian
Population density – 102 per sq. km (2011)
Urban population – 67.9 per cent (2012 est)
Median age (years) – 43.9 (2013 est)
National anthem – 'Land der Berge, Land am Strome' ['Land of Mountains, Land on the River']
National day – 26 October (date law of neutrality passed, 1955)
Death penalty – Abolished for all crimes (since 1968)
CPI score – 69 (26)

CLIMATE AND TERRAIN

The north and east of the country feature rolling hills in the river Danube basin, while the west and south contain the eastern Alps, which cover nearly two-thirds of the country. The highest point of elevation is 3,798m (Grossglockner) and the lowest is 115m (Neusiedler See). The climate is continental in the lowlands, and alpine in the mountains, with average temperatures in Vienna ranging from 1°C in January to 22°C in July.

POLITICS

Under the 1955 constitution, the federal president is directly elected for a six-year term, renewable once. There is a bicameral legislature, the *Parlament*, consisting of the National Council *(Nationalrat)*, which has 183 members directly elected for a four-year term, and the Federal Council *(Bundesrat)*, which has 62 members elected for terms of five to six years by the provincial assemblies. Some powers may only be exercised by both houses acting together as the Federal Assembly *(Bundesversammlung)*. The executive is headed by the federal chancellor, who is appointed by the president.

The 2004 presidential election was won by Heinz Fischer of the Social Democrats (SPÖ), who was re-elected in 2010. Following the 2013 legislative election, the SPÖ and the Austrian People's Party (ÖVP) remained the largest parties but both lost ground to the right-wing Freedom Party of Austria (FPÖ); the SPÖ–ÖVP coalition continued under SPÖ leader, Werner Faymann.

HEAD OF STATE
Federal President, Heinz Fischer, *took office* 8 July 2004, *re-elected* 2010

SELECTED GOVERNMENT MEMBERS *as at February 2014*
Chancellor, Werner Faymann
Vice-Chancellor, Finance, Michael Spindelegger
Defence, Sports, Gerald Klug

EMBASSY OF AUSTRIA
18 Belgrave Mews West, London SW1X 8HU
T 020-7344 3250 E london-ob@bmeia.gv.at
W www.bmeia.gv.at/london
Ambassador Extraordinary and Plenipotentiary, HE Dr Emil Brix, *apptd* 2010

BRITISH EMBASSY
Jaurèsgasse 12, 1030 Vienna
T (+43) (1) 716 130 E viennaconsularenquiries@fco.gov.uk
W www.gov.uk/government/world/austria
Ambassador Extraordinary and Plenipotentiary, HE Susan le Jeune d'Allegeershecque, *apptd* 2011

FEDERAL STRUCTURE
There are nine provinces *(Bundesländer)*: Burgenland, Carinthia, Lower Austria, Salzburg, Styria, Tyrol, Upper Austria, Vienna and Vorarlberg. Each has its own assembly and government.

DEFENCE

Aged 16–49, 2010 est	*Males*	*Females*
Available for military service	1,941,110	1,910,434
Fit for military service	1,579,862	1,554,130

Military expenditure – US$3,230m (2013)
Conscription – 18–35 years of age, male only; 6 months

ECONOMY AND TRADE

Austria has a well-developed market economy which is closely linked to other EU states. Its strong commercial links with central, eastern and south-eastern Europe, an attraction for foreign investors in the past, increased its vulnerability in the global economic downturn, and its financial sector required state support. The economy went into recession in 2008 but started to recover throughout 2010 and 2011

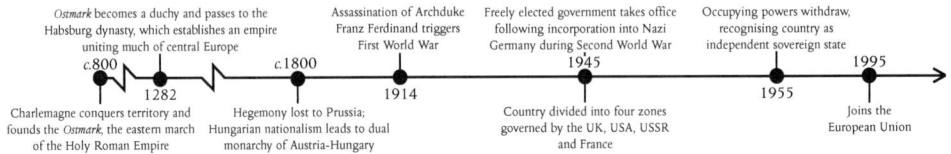

Ostmark becomes a duchy and passes to the Habsburg dynasty, which establishes an empire uniting much of central Europe
*c.*800

Charlemagne conquers territory and founds the Ostmark, the eastern march of the Holy Roman Empire
1282

Hegemony lost to Prussia; Hungarian nationalism leads to dual monarchy of Austria-Hungary
*c.*1800

Assassination of Archduke Franz Ferdinand triggers First World War
1914

Freely elected government takes office following incorporation into Nazi Germany during Second World War
1945

Country divided into four zones governed by the UK, USA, USSR and France
1955

Occupying powers withdraw, recognising country as independent sovereign state
1995

Joins the European Union

before contracting in 2012; the Austrian parliament agreed an austerity budget in March 2012 that aims to bring the public finances into balance by 2016.

The services sector contributes most to GDP (69.8 per cent in 2012), followed by industry (28.6 per cent) and the small but highly developed agricultural sector (1.6 per cent). The main industries include tourism, construction, manufacturing of machinery, vehicles and parts, food processing, timber and wood processing, production of metals and metal goods, chemicals, paper and cardboard, and communications equipment.

Austria's main trading partners are Germany, France, Italy and Switzerland. Principal exports include the goods produced by the main industries, iron and steel, and textiles. The main imports are machinery and equipment, vehicles, chemical products, metal goods, oil and oil products, and foodstuffs.

GNI – US$392,272m; US$47,660 per capita (2012)
Annual average growth of GDP – 0.4 per cent (2013 est)
Inflation rate – 2.1 per cent (2013 est)
Population below poverty line – 6.2 per cent (2012 est)
Unemployment – 4.9 per cent (2013 est)
Total external debt – US$812,000m (2012 est)
Imports – US$169,657m (2012)
Exports – US$158,821m (2012)

BALANCE OF PAYMENTS
Trade – US$10,836m deficit (2012)
Current Account – US$7,026 surplus (2012)

Trade with UK	2012	2013
Imports from UK	£1,514,459,505	£1,648,265,431
Exports to UK	£2,600,581,861	£2,622,650,678

COMMUNICATIONS
Airports – 24; principal airports include Vienna, Salzburg and Innsbruck
Waterways – 358km of navigable waterways; considerable trade through Danube ports (Vienna, Krems, Enns, Linz)
Roadways and railways – 124,508km; 6,399km
Telecommunications – 3.34 million fixed lines and 13.59 million mobile subscriptions (2012); there were 6.14 million internet subscribers in 2009
Internet code and IDD – at; 43 (from UK), 44 (to UK)
Major broadcasters – Österreichischer Rundfunk (ÖRF) and ATV
Press – There are five main daily titles: *Die Presse, Kronen Zeitung, Wiener Zeitung, Der Standard* and *Der Kurier*
WPFI score – 10,01 (12)

EDUCATION AND HEALTH
Education is free and compulsory from six to 15.
Gross enrolment ratio (percentage of relevant age group) – primary 100 per cent; secondary 98 per cent; tertiary 71 per cent (2011 est)
Health expenditure (per capita) – US$5,280 (2011)
Hospital beds (per 1,000 people) – 7.6 (2010)
Life expectancy (years) – 80.04 (2013 est)
Mortality rate – 10.31 (2013 est)
Birth rate – 8.73 (2013 est)
Infant mortality rate – 4.21 (2013 est)

AZERBAIJAN

Azarbaycan Respublikasi – Republic of Azerbaijan

Area – 86,600 sq. km
Capital – Baku (Baki); population, 2,016,118 (2012 est)
Major cities – Ganca, Sumqayit
Currency – New Manat of 100 gopik
Population – 9,590,159 rising at 1.01 per cent a year (2013 est); Azeri (91.6 per cent), Lezgian (2 per cent), Russian (1.3 per cent), Armenian (1.3 per cent), Talysh (1.3 per cent) (2009). There are more Azeris in Iran than in Azerbaijan. Almost all of the Armenian population lives in the Nagorny-Karabakh enclave
Religion – Muslim 93.4 per cent (Shia 65 per cent, Sunni 35 per cent) (est)
Language – Azeri (official), Lezgi, Russian, Armenian
Population density – 111 per sq. km (2011)
Urban population – 53.9 per cent (2012 est)
Median age (years) – 29.8 years (2013 est)
National anthem – 'Azerbaijan Marsi' ['March of Azerbaijan']
National day – 28 May (founding of the republic, 1918)
Death penalty – Abolished for all crimes (since 1998)
CPI score – 28 (127)

CLIMATE AND TERRAIN
Azerbaijan lies on the western shore of the Caspian Sea, in the eastern part of the Caucasus region. It includes the exclave of Nakhichevana, separated from it by Armenia. The north-east of Azerbaijan rises to the south-eastern end of the main Great Caucasus mountain range; to the country's south-west lie the lower Caucasus hills, and in its south-eastern corner the spurs of the Talysh Ridge. Central Azerbaijan lies in a low plain irrigated by the river Kura and the lower reaches of its tributary the Araks. Elevation ranges from 4,485m (Bazarduzu Dagi) to −28m (Caspian Sea). Climate and landscape vary greatly, but rainfall is generally low.

POLITICS
The 1995 constitution was amended in 2002 and 2009, when the limit on presidential terms was amended to two terms (2002) and then abolished (2009). The executive president is directly elected for a five-year term, which is renewable. The unicameral National Assembly *(Milli Majlis)* has 125 members directly elected for a five-year term. The president appoints the prime minister and the cabinet.

Ilham Aliyev was re-elected for a third term in 2013. In the 2010 legislative election, the New Azerbaijan Party, which is aligned with President Aliyev, increased its number of seats, achieving an overall majority. For dispute with Armenia over the Nagorny-Karabakh region *see* Armenia, Foreign Relations.

HEAD OF STATE
President, Ilham Aliyev, *sworn in* 31 October 2003, *re-elected* 2008, 2013

Invaded by Muslim Arabs c.100

c.600 — Turkic Azeri people form an independent state

Divided into the Russian north and the Persian, and subsequently Iranian, south c.1500

1828 — Invaded by Persia

1920 — Newly formed Azerbaijani republic overthrown by Soviet Red Army invasion

Accedes to the USSR

1922

Declares independence from Soviet Union 1990

1991 — Azeri Popular Front takes power from the local Communist Party

1993 — Former communist leader Heydar Aliyev becomes president and is re-elected in 1998

Heydar Aliyev's son Ilham is elected president

2003

SELECTED GOVERNMENT MEMBERS *as at February 2014*
Prime Minister, Artur Rasizade
First Deputy Prime Minister, Yagub Abdulla Eyyubov
Deputy Prime Ministers, Ismat Abbasov, Ali Ahmadov, Elchin Efendiyev; Ali Hasanov; Abid Sharifov
Defence, Col.-Gen. Zakir Hasanov

EMBASSY OF THE REPUBLIC OF AZERBAIJAN
4 Kensington Court, London W8 5DL
T 020-7938 3412 E london@mission.mfa.gov.az
W www.azembassy.org.uk
Ambassador Extraordinary and Plenipotentiary, HE Fakhraddin Gurbanov, *apptd* 2007

BRITISH EMBASSY
45 Khagani Street, Baku AZ 1010
T (+994) (12) 437 7878 E generalenquiries.baku@fco.gov.uk
W www.gov.uk/government/world/azerbaijan
Ambassador Extraordinary and Plenipotentiary, HE Irfan Siddiq, OBE, *apptd* 2013

DEFENCE

Aged 16–49, 2010 est	*Males*	*Females*
Available for military service	2,354,249	2,334,632
Fit for military service	1,773,993	1,964,012

Military expenditure – US$3,264m (2013)
Conscription – 18–35 years of age, male only; 18 months, or 12 months for university graduates

ECONOMY AND TRADE

Despite high economic growth in recent years, Azerbaijan's transition from a command to a market economy is slow. This has been exacerbated by its failure to attract foreign investment in sectors other than energy, widespread corruption and systemic inefficiencies. The economy is dominated by oil and natural gas extraction and related industries, centred in Baku and Sumqayit, and exploited through co-production deals with foreign companies. Oil pipelines (1,424km) link the Azeri oilfields to Black Sea ports in Russia, Georgia and Turkey. The economy avoided recession in the global economic downturn, but contracted owing to the fall in world oil prices, and transfers from the State Oil Fund were needed to make up the 2009 budget shortfall.

Although agriculture contributes only 6.2 per cent of GDP, it employs nearly 40 per cent of the workforce. The main crops are cotton, cereals, rice, fruit, vegetables, tea, tobacco and livestock. Industry, which contributes 64.3 per cent of GDP, produces oil, natural gas, petroleum products, oilfield equipment, steel, iron ore, cement, chemicals, petrochemicals and textiles.

Russia and other former Soviet republics are increasingly being replaced as trade partners by Turkey, India, the USA and various European countries. Oil and gas constitute around 90 per cent of exports, which also include machinery, cotton and foodstuffs. Principal imports are machinery and equipment, oil products, foodstuffs, metals and chemicals.
GNI – US$61,226m; US$6,220 per capita (2012)
Annual average growth of GDP – 3.5 per cent (2013 est)

Inflation rate – 2.4 per cent (2013 est)
Population below poverty line – 6 per cent (2012 est)
Unemployment – 6 per cent (2013 est)
Total external debt – US$9,552m (2013 est)
Imports – US$9,653m (2012)
Exports – US$23,908m (2012)

BALANCE OF PAYMENTS
Trade – US$14,255m surplus (2012)
Current Account – US$14,958m surplus (2012)

Trade with UK	2012	2013
Imports from UK	£508,687,864	£372,701,933
Exports to UK	£660,733,689	£228,258,472

COMMUNICATIONS

Airports – 30; international airports at Baku, Ganca, Nakhichevan and Lankaran
Waterways – The Baku International Sea Trade port provides links to Turkmenistan and other trade and passenger routes
Roadways and railways – 52,942km; 2,918km
Telecommunications – 1.73 million fixed lines and 10.12 million mobile telephone subscriptions (2012); there were 2.42 million internet users in 2009
Internet code and IDD – az; 994 (from UK), 44 (to UK)
Major broadcasters – AzTV (state-run), iTV and ANS TV
Press – Three major daily newspapers: the *Azadliq* and *Ekho* and the government-comissioned *Azarbaycan*
WPFI score – 52,87 (160)

EDUCATION AND HEALTH

Education up to university level is free.
Literacy rate – 99.5 per cent (2008 est)
Gross enrolment ratio (percentage of relevant age group) – primary 96 per cent; secondary 100 per cent; tertiary 20 per cent (2011 est)
Health expenditure (per capita) – US$357 (2011)
Hospital beds (per 1,000 people) – 4.6 (2011)
Life expectancy (years) – 71.61 (2013 est)
Mortality rate – 7.11 (2013 est)
Birth rate – 17.17 (2013 est)
Infant mortality rate – 27.69 (2013 est)

THE BAHAMAS

Commonwealth of the Bahamas

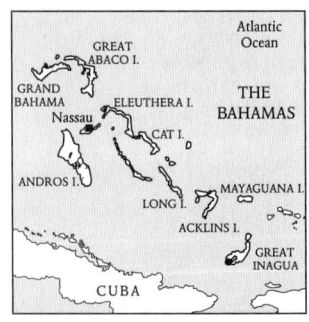

Area – 13,880 sq. km
Capital – Nassau, on New Providence; population, 254,000 (2011 est)
Major city – Freeport, on Grand Bahama
Currency – Bahamian dollar (B$) of 100 cents
Population – 319,031 rising at 0.89 per cent a year (2013 est)
Religion – Christian (Protestant 69.9 per cent, Roman Catholic 12 per cent, other 13 per cent) (est)
Language – English (official), Creole
Population density – 37 per sq. km (2011)
Urban population – 84.5 per cent (2012 est)
Median age (years) – 30.8 (2013 est)
National anthem – 'March on, Bahamaland'
National day – 10 July (Independence Day)
Death penalty – Retained (last used 2000)
CPI score – 71 (22)
Life expectancy (years) – 71.69 (2013 est)
Mortality rate – 6.96 (2013 est)
Birth rate – 15.81 (2013 est)
Infant mortality rate – 12.89 (2013 est)
HIV/AIDS adult prevalence – 3.3 per cent (2012 est)

CLIMATE AND TERRAIN
The Bahamas consist of more than 700 islands and 2,400 cays, all low-lying. The highest point is 63m (Mt Alvernia, on Cat Island) and the lowest 0m (Atlantic Ocean). The principal islands include: Abaco Islands, Acklins, Andros, Berry Islands, Bimini, Cat Island, Crooked Island, Eleuthera, Exuma, Grand Bahama, Great Inagua, Harbour Island, Long Island, Mayaguana, New Providence, Ragged Island, Rum Cay, San Salvador and Spanish Wells. The 14 major islands are inhabited, as are a few of the smaller islands. The climate is semitropical. The hurricane season is June to November.

HISTORY AND POLITICS
The islands were discovered by Columbus in 1492, settled by the British from the 17th century and became a crown colony in 1717. The Bahamas became internally self-governing in 1964 and gained independence on 10 July 1973.
The Progressive Liberal Party (PLP) held power for 25 years until the Free National Movement (FNM) won an absolute majority in the 1992 general election. Power has subsequently alternated between the two parties. The PLP regained its majority in the 2012 legislative election, winning 29 of the 38 seats.
The head of state is Queen Elizabeth II, who is represented by a governor-general. The bicameral parliament has a senate of 16 appointed members and a House of Assembly of 41 members; both chambers serve a five-year term.
Governor-General, HE Sir Arthur Foulkes, *apptd* 2010

SELECTED GOVERNMENT MEMBERS *as at February 2014*
Prime Minister, Perry Christie
Deputy Prime Minister, Philip Davies
National Security, Bernard Nottage

HIGH COMMISSION OF THE COMMONWEALTH OF THE BAHAMAS
10 Chesterfield Street, London W1J 5JL
T 020-7408 4488 E information@bahamashclondon.net
W www.bahamashclondon.net
High Commissioner, HE Eldred Edison Bethel, *apptd* 2012

BRITISH HIGH COMMISSION
High Commissioner, Howard Drake, *apptd* 2010, resident in Kingston, Jamaica

DEFENCE

Aged 16–49, 2010 est	Males	Females
Available for military service	85,568	–
Fit for military service	63,429	64,645

Military expenditure – US$68.9 million (2013)

ECONOMY AND TRADE
The economy is dominated by tourism and offshore financial services, which together contribute over 90 per cent of GDP. A tightening of financial regulations in 2000 caused a number of international businesses to relocate elsewhere, and visitor numbers from the USA (over 75 per cent of all visitors) have declined since 2006. The effects of the global downturn have caused the economy to contract further, although the decline was diminished as tourism and investment returned in 2011.
Manufacturing and agriculture account for 10 per cent of GDP and employment. Agriculture centres mainly on fresh vegetables, fruit, meat and eggs. Mineral reserves produce aragonite and salt for export. Other industries include cement, rum, pharmaceuticals and steel pipe production, and the provision of oil trans-shipment services.
The main trading partners are the USA, Singapore, South Korea, India and China. The chief exports are mineral products and salt, animal products, fruit and vegetables, and polystyrene products. Imports are chiefly machinery and transport equipment, manufactured articles, chemicals, fuel, foodstuffs and livestock.
GNI – US$7,599m; US$20,600 per capita (2012)
Annual average growth of GDP – 1.9 per cent (2013 est)
Inflation rate – 1.8 per cent (2013 est)
Population below poverty line – 9.3 per cent (2004 est)
Unemployment – 14 per cent (2012 est)
Total external debt – US$17,560m (2013 est)
Imports – US$3,647m (2012)
Exports – US$828m (2012)

BALANCE OF PAYMENTS
Trade – US$2,819m deficit (2012)
Current Account – US$1,150m deficit (2012)

Trade with UK	2012	2013
Imports from UK	£38,446,708	£15,899,753
Exports to UK	£12,418,838	£4,317,450

COMMUNICATIONS
Airports – 24; international airports are operated from Andros, Chubb Cay, Eleuthera, Exuma, Grand Bahama and New Providence
Waterways – The main ports are Nassau (New Providence), Freeport and South Riding Point (Grand Bahama); the Bahamas is a major ship registry, and 1,063 of the 1,160 ships registered in 2010 were foreign-owned
Roadways – 2,700km, of which 1,620km are paved
Telecommunications – 137,000 fixed lines (2011) and 254,000 mobile phone subscriptions (2012); there were 115,800 internet users in 2009
Internet code and IDD – bs; 1 242 (from UK), 011 44 (to UK)
Press – The government-owned ZNS-TV is the country's principal television broadcaster; daily newspapers include *The Nassau Guardian, The Tribune* and *The Freeport News*

BAHRAIN

Mamlakat al-Bahrayn – Kingdom of Bahrain

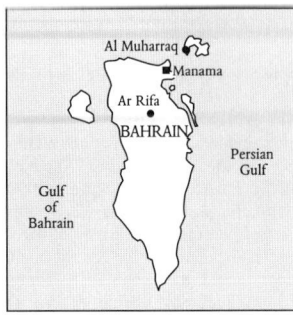

Area – 760 sq. km
Capital – Manama; population, 262,000 (2011 est)
Major towns – Al Muharraq, Ar Rifa, Madinat Hamad
Currency – Bahraini dinar (BD) of 1,000 fils
Population – 1,281,332 (including 235,108 non-nationals) rising at 2.57 per cent a year (2013 est); the non-Bahraini population includes large numbers of Europeans and South Asians
Religion – Muslim 99.8 per cent (est); Islam is the state religion
Language – Arabic (official), English, Farsi, Urdu
Population density – 1,701 per sq. km (2011)
Urban population – 88.7 per cent (2012 est)
Median age (years) – 31.4 (2013 est)
National anthem – 'Bahrainona' ['Our Bahrain']
National day – 16 December (date of independence from British protection, 1971)
Death penalty – Retained
CPI score – 48 (57)
Literacy rate – 95 per cent (2010 est)
Life expectancy (years) – 78.43 (2013 est)
Mortality rate – 2.65 (2013 est)
Birth rate – 14.16 (2013 est)
Infant mortality rate – 9.93 (2013 est)

CLIMATE AND TERRAIN

Bahrain consists of an archipelago of 36 low-lying islands situated approximately halfway down the Persian Gulf, some 32km off the east coast of Saudi Arabia. The largest of these, Bahrain Island, is about 48km long and 16km wide at its broadest. Elevation extremes range from 122m (Jabal ad Dukhan) to 0m at sea level. The climate is arid, hot and humid, with average maximum temperatures ranging from 19°C to 37°C.

HISTORY AND POLITICS

Bahrain was ruled by Persia (Iran) from 1602 until it was ousted in 1783 by the al-Khalifa family, who remain in power. The emirate was a British protectorate from 1820 until 1971, when it became independent. In 1975 the legislature was suspended and the emir assumed virtually absolute power after clashes between Sunni and Shia factions. Moves to return to democratic rule were made in response to civil agitation in the 1990s, until Sheikh Hamad succeeded to the throne and initiated the transition to a constitutional monarchy. The 2002 constitution established Bahrain as a kingdom and a constitutional monarchy, and legalised elections. There has been ongoing agitation for further democratisation, particularly by the Shia majority against the predominantly Sunni authorities.

In February 2011 this flared up into mass demonstrations that were repressed brutally by the government from March, when martial law was declared and the Pearl monument, the focal point of the demonstrations in Manama, was demolished. A report into the unrest, commissioned by Sheikh Hamad, was released in November 2011 and confirmed the practice of torture and infringements of human rights; in response, the ruler vowed to 'learn lessons' from the unrest and promised to reform the country's laws to make them compatible with international standards. Despite national talks beginning in February 2013 and the appointment of the moderate Sheikh Salman bin Hamad al-Khalifa as First Deputy Prime Minister in March of that year, there has yet to be a resolution to the unrest.

In the 2010 legislative election, the radical Shia group al-Wefaq remained the largest bloc, with 18 seats. A number of ministers resigned in spring 2011 in protest against the treatment of demonstrators. A by-election was held in September 2011 after al-Wefaq withdrew from the National Assembly; the seats were taken by independent candidates following low voter turnout.

Under the 2002 constitution, the country is a hereditary constitutional monarchy with the king as head of state. The king appoints the cabinet. The bicameral National Assembly consists of a lower house, the Council of Representatives, and an upper house, the Consultative Council. The lower house has 40 members directly elected for a four-year term, and the upper house has 40 members appointed by the king for a four-year term. The 2002 constitution granted women the right to vote and to stand for election.

HEAD OF STATE
HH The King of Bahrain, Sheikh Hamad bin Isa al-Khalifa, KCMG, *Commander-in-Chief of the Armed Forces, succeeded as emir* 6 March 1999, *proclaimed king* 14 February 2002
Crown Prince, First Deputy Prime Minister, Chair of the Economic Development Board, Sheikh Salman bin Hamad al-Khalifa

SELECTED GOVERNMENT MEMBERS *as at May 2013*
Prime Minister, HH Sheikh Khalifa bin Salman al-Khalifa
Deputy Prime Ministers, Sheikh Mohammed bin Mubarak al-Khalifa; Sheikh Ali bin Khalifa al-Khalifa; Jawad bin Salem al-Oraied; Sheikh Khalid bin Abdullah al-Khalifa
Foreign Affairs, Sheikh Khalid bin Ahmed bin Mohammed al-Khalifa
Defence, Sheikh Mohammad bin Abdullah al-Khalifa
Finance, Sheikh Ahmed bin Mohammed al-Khalifa

EMBASSY OF THE KINGDOM OF BAHRAIN
30 Belgrave Square, London SW1X 8QB
T 020-7201 9170 E information@bahrainembassy.co.uk
W www.bahrainembassy.co.uk
Ambassador Extraordinary and Plenipotentiary, HE Alice Thomas Samaan, *apptd* 2011

BRITISH EMBASSY
PO Box 114, 21 Government Avenue, Manama 306
T (+973) 1757 4100 W www.gov.uk/government/world/bahrain
Ambassador Extraordinary and Plenipotentiary, HE Iain Lindsay, OBE, *apptd* 2011

DEFENCE

Aged 16–49, 2010 est	Males	Females
Available for military service	508,863	290,801
Fit for military service	423,757	245,302

Military expenditure – US$1,172m (2012)

ECONOMY AND TRADE

Bahrain was one of the first Gulf states to discover oil, in the 1930s, but reserves and production are lower than in neighbouring countries. It has diversified its economy, developing particularly as a regional financial and business centre, and as a tourist destination. Petroleum production and refining still accounts for an estimated 11 per cent of GDP, 70 per cent of government revenue and 60 per cent of total exports. Other industries include petrochemicals, aluminium smelting, and shipbuilding and repair. Bahrain's main trading partners are Saudi Arabia, the EU, Far Eastern countries and the USA, with whom a Free Trade Agreement is in place.

GNI – US$20,572m; US$15,920 per capita (2010)
Annual average growth of GDP – 4.4 per cent (2013 est)
Inflation rate – 3.1 per cent (2013 est)
Unemployment – 15 per cent (2005 est)
Total external debt – US$28,820m (2013 est)
Imports – US$14,900m (2012)
Exports – US$20,500m (2012)

BALANCE OF PAYMENTS
Trade – US$5,600m surplus (2012)
Current Account – US$2,221m surplus (2012)

Trade with UK	2012	2013
Imports from UK	£286,810,588	£269,824,984
Exports to UK	£253,708,663	£173,351,287

COMMUNICATIONS

Airports – Four; Bahrain International Airport is a major air traffic centre in the Gulf
Waterways – The main ports are Khalifa bin Salman and Mina Salman
Roadways – There are 3,392km of paved roadways; the four main islands are connected by causeways, and a 25km causeway links Bahrain Island to Saudi Arabia
Telecommunications – 290,000 main lines and 2.125 million mobile phone subscriptions (2012); there were 419,500 internet users in 2009
Internet code and IDD – bh; 973 (from UK), 44 (to UK)
Major broadcasters – State-run Bahrain Radio and Television Corporation operates five terrestrial TV networks. Bahrain is set to host the Saudi-financed Al-Arab satellite news TV channel
Press – Major daily newspapers include *Akhbar al-Khaleej*, *Al-Ayam* and *Al-Wasat*
WPFI score – 58,26 (163)

BANGLADESH

Gana Prajatantri Bangladesh – People's Republic of Bangladesh

Area – 143,998 sq. km
Capital – Dhaka; population, 15,431,777 (2012 est)
Major cities – Chittagong, Gazipur, Khulna, Narayanganj
Currency – Taka (Tk) of 100 paisa
Population – 163,654,860 rising at 1.59 per cent a year (2013 est); Bengali (98 per cent) (1998 est)
Religion – Muslim 89.5 per cent (the vast majority are Sunni), Hindu 9.6 per cent (est); Islam is the state religion
Language – Bengali (official), English
Population density – 1,174 per sq. km (2011)
Urban population – 28.9 per cent (2012 est)
Median age (years) – 23.9 (2013 est)
National anthem – 'Amar Shonar Bangla' ['My Golden Bengal']
National day – 26 March (Independence Day)
Death penalty – Retained
CPI score – 27 (136)

CLIMATE AND TERRAIN

Although hilly in the south-east and north-east, over 75 per cent of the country is less than 3m above sea-level, situated on the alluvial plain and delta of the Ganges (Padma)–Brahmaputra (Jamuna)–Meghna river system, which empties into the Bay of Bengal, the largest estuarine delta in the world. The highest elevation is 1,230m (Keokradong) and the lowest 0m at the Indian Ocean. The climate is tropical, with a monsoon season (June–September) during which heavy rainfall causes flooding in around one-third of the country each year; annual average rainfall is up to 2,339mm.

HISTORY AND POLITICS

Bangladesh consists of what was the eastern part of Bengal province and the Sylhet district of Assam province in British India. On independence in 1947, these territories acceded to Pakistan, forming the province of East Bengal (renamed East Pakistan in 1955). Tensions between East and West Pakistan (separated by over 1,600km) caused the East to secede in 1971. After months of civil war, and following the intervention of India, Bangladesh achieved independence from Pakistan on 16 December 1971.

Since independence, Bangladesh has experienced periods of political instability, with a number of coups and attempted coups, the assassinations of President Mujibar Rahman (1975) and President Zia (1981), and periods of government under martial law (1975–8, 1982–6) or a state of emergency (1987–8, 2007–8).

Parliamentary government has remained in place since 1991, despite occasional boycotts of parliament. Governments have been formed, or coalition governments led, by one of the two main parties: the Bangladesh Nationalist Party (BNP), led by Khaleda Zia (widow of President Zia), in 1991–6 and 2001–6; and the Awami League, led by Sheikh Hasina Wajed (daughter of President Mujibar Rahman), in 1996–2001 and since January 2009.

The run-up to legislative elections in January 2014 was marred by widespread, violent protests throughout the country after the BNP's Khaleda Zia declared a boycott of the election in response to Sheikh Hasina's refusal to hand over to a neutral caretaker government – a constitutional requirement overturned in 2011 – for the duration of the proceedings. The boycott resulted in a default win and overwhelming majority for the Awami League, with the party gaining 234 seats to the BNP's 34. Following the death of Zillur Rahman in March 2013, Abdul Hamid was elected president unopposed.

During 2013 the recently established Bangladesh International Crimes Tribunal tried a number of prominent figures for crimes against humanity during the 1971 independence war; five senior members of the Jamaat-e-Islami party were sentenced to death, alongside Salahuddin Quader Chowdhury, a BNP MP. These sentences came amid increasingly violent protests and concerns that the tribunal does not meet international standards.

The head of state is the president, elected by the legislature for a five-year term. The unicameral parliament, *Jatiya Sangsad*, has 345 members directly elected for a five-year term; under a 2004 constitutional amendment, 45 seats are reserved for women. The president appoints the prime minister, and the cabinet on the advice of the prime minister.

HEAD OF STATE
President, Abdul Hamid, *elected* 22 April 2013

SELECTED GOVERNMENT MEMBERS *as at March 2014*
Prime Minister, Defence, Sheikh Hasina Wajed
Finance, Abu Maal Abdul Muhith
Law, Justice and Parliamentary Affairs, Anisul Haque

HIGH COMMISSION FOR THE PEOPLE'S REPUBLIC OF BANGLADESH
28 Queen's Gate, London SW7 5JA
T 020-7584 0081 E info@bhclondon.org.uk
W www.bhclondon.org.uk
High Commissioner, vacant

BRITISH HIGH COMMISSION
PO Box 6079, United Nations Road, Baridhara, Dhaka 1212
T (+880) (2) 882 2705 E consular.bangladesh@fco.gov.uk
W www.gov.uk/government/world/bangladesh
High Commissioner, vacant

DEFENCE

Aged 16–49, 2010 est	Males	Females
Available for military service	36,520,491	–
Fit for military service	30,486,086	35,616,093

Military expenditure – US$1,636m (2012)

ECONOMY AND TRADE
Bangladesh is a poor country, highly dependent on foreign aid. Nearly a third of the population lives below the poverty line. Many migrate to the Gulf states and South East Asia to find work, and their remittances and garment manufacturing are the mainstay of the economy. These have fuelled the steady growth of 5.8 per cent a year since the mid-1990s, which has continued throughout the global downturn. However, inefficient state-owned enterprises, slow implementation of economic reforms, corruption and unreliable power supplies are obstacles to greater growth.

The service and industrial sectors account for 53.9 per cent and 28.9 per cent of GDP respectively. Although the smallest contributor to GDP (17.2 per cent), agriculture is the primary occupation of 45 per cent of the workforce. The chief industries are based on processing agricultural and fisheries products such as cotton, jute, tea, sugar, fish and seafood, the manufacture of textiles, garments, newsprint, cement and fertiliser, and light engineering. Most exports are to the USA and EU countries; imports come mainly from China, India and other Asian countries.
GNI – US$127,672m; US$840 per capita (2012)
Annual average growth of GDP – 5.8 per cent (2013 est)
Inflation rate – 7.6 per cent (2013 est)

Population below poverty line – 31.5 per cent (2010 est)
Unemployment – 5 per cent (2013 est)
Total external debt – US$30,690m (2013 est)
Imports – US$34,133m (2012)
Exports – US$25,133m (2012)

BALANCE OF PAYMENTS
Trade – US$9,020m deficit (2012)
Current Account – US$1,337m deficit (2011)

Trade with UK	2012	2013
Imports from UK	£103,773,822	£140,821,633
Exports to UK	£1,692,738,329	£1,796,616,521

COMMUNICATIONS
Airports – 16, including international airports at Dhaka, Cittagong and Sylhet
Waterways – Principal seaports are Chittagong and Mongla, and there are smaller ports in Chalna and Khulna; the 8,370km of waterways are a key element of the transport infrastructure, although reduced to 5,200km in dry season
Roadways and railways – There are 21,269km of roadways (1,063km surfaced) and 2,622km of railways
Telecommunications – 962,000 fixed lines (2012) and 97.18 million mobile phone subscriptions (2011); there were 617,300 internet users in 2009
Internet country code and IDD – bd; 880 (from UK), 44 (to UK)
Major broadcasters – The government-run Bangladesh Television and Radio Bangladesh are the principal channels; private broadcasters include ATN Bangla, Channel i and NTV
Press – Major newspapers include English-language dailies *The Daily Star*, *The New Nation* and *The Independent*
WPFI score – 42,58 (146)

EDUCATION AND HEALTH
Education is compulsory and free for children aged 6 to 10, but drop-out rates are high.
Literacy rate – 58 per cent (2011 est)
Gross enrolment ratio (percentage of relevant age group) – primary 114 per cent; secondary 51 per cent; tertiary 13 per cent (2011 est)
Health expenditure (per capita) – US$27 (2011)
Hospital beds (per 1,000 people) – 0.6 (2011)
Life expectancy (years) – 70.36 (2013 est)
Mortality rate – 5.67 (2013 est)
Birth rate – 22.07 (2013 est)
Infant mortality rate – 47.3 (2013 est)

BARBADOS

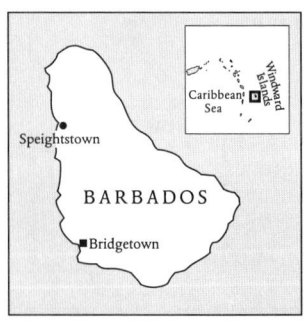

Area – 430 sq. km
Capital – Bridgetown, in the parish of St Michael;
    population, 122,000 (2011 est)
Currency – Barbados dollar (BD$) of 100 cents
Population – 288,725 rising at 0.34 per cent a year
    (2013 est)
Religion – Christian 75.5 per cent (Protestant 66.3 per cent,
    of which the largest denomination is Anglican),
    Rastafarian 1 per cent (est)
Language – English (official), Bajan
Population density – 655 per sq. km (2011)
Urban population – 44.9 per cent (2012)
Median age (years) – 37.3 (2013 est)
National anthem – 'In Plenty and in Time of Need'
National day – 30 November (Independence Day)
Death penalty – Retained (last used 1984)
CPI score – 15 (75)

CLIMATE AND TERRAIN

Barbados is the most easterly of the Caribbean islands. The land rises gently to central highlands, and elevation extremes range from 336m (Mt Hillaby) to 0m (Atlantic Ocean). The climate is tropical with a wet season from July to November, when the island is subject to occasional hurricanes.

HISTORY AND POLITICS

Early settlers were succeeded by the Arawaks and then the Caribs. The island was uninhabited when settled by the English in 1627 and was a crown colony from 1652, achieving self-government in 1961. It became an independent state on 30 November 1966.

Since independence, power has alternated between the two main political parties, the Barbados Labour Party (BLP) and the Democratic Labour Party (DLP). In the 2008 general election the DLP defeated the BLP and took office under David Thompson. He died in October 2010 and was succeeded as prime minister by his deputy, Freundel Stuart. In February 2013, the DLP and Stuart narrowly retained power, winning 16 of the 30 seats in the parliamentary elections.

The head of state is Queen Elizabeth II, represented by the governor-general. The bicameral parliament consists of a senate of 21 appointed members and a House of Assembly of 30 directly elected members; both chambers serve a five-year term.

There are 11 administrative areas (parishes): Christ Church, St Andrew, St George, St James, St John, St Joseph, St Lucy, St Michael, St Peter, St Philip and St Thomas.

Governor-General, HE Sir Elliott Belgrave, GCMG, *apptd* June 2012

SELECTED GOVERNMENT MEMBERS *as at February 2014*
Prime Minister, Freundel Stuart
Attorney-General, Home Affairs, Adriel Brathwaite
Finance, Christopher Sinckler
Foreign Affairs, Maxine McClean

BARBADOS HIGH COMMISSION
1 Great Russell Street, London WC1B 3ND
T 020-7631 4975 E london@foreign.gov.bb
High Commissioner, HE Hugh Arthur, *apptd* 2008

BRITISH HIGH COMMISSION
PO Box 676, Lower Collymore Rock, Bridgetown
T (+1) (246) 430 7800 E ukinbarbados@fco.gov.uk
W www.gov.uk/government/world/barbados
High Commissioner, HE Victoria Dean, *apptd* 2013

DEFENCE

Aged 16–49, 2010 est	Males	Females
Available for military service	73,820	73,835
Fit for military service	58,125	58,016

Military expenditure – US$20.9m (2013)

ECONOMY AND TRADE

Historically, Barbados' chief products were sugar, rum and molasses. Since independence, tourism, offshore finance and information services, and light industry have become more significant. The global economic downturn affected tourism in particular, causing the economy to contract in 2009. By 2013 Barbados' public debt-to-GDP ratio had risen to 90.5 per cent.

The main trading partners are Trinidad and Tobago, the USA and Jamaica. Chief exports are manufactured goods, sugar and molasses, rum, other food and beverages, chemicals and electronic components.

GNI – US$4,093m; US$15,080 per capita (2012)
Annual average growth of GDP – −0.8 per cent (2013 est)
Inflation rate – 2.1 per cent (2013 est)
Unemployment – 11.4 per cent (2013 est)
Total external debt – US$4,490m (2012 est)
Imports – US$1,806m (2012)
Exports – US$570m (2012)

BALANCE OF PAYMENTS
Trade – US$1,236m deficit (2012)
Current Account – US$426m deficit (2012)

Trade with UK	2012	2013
Imports from UK	£38,076,102	£42,721,556
Exports to UK	£20,867,613	£11,026,618

COMMUNICATIONS

Airports – The Grantley Adams International near Bridgetown is the only international airport on the island
Waterways – Bridgetown, the only port of entry, has a deep-water harbour
Roadways – There are 1,600km of roadways, all of which are surfaced
Telecommunications – 144,000 fixed lines and 347,000 mobile phone subscriptions (2012); there were 188,000 internet users in 2008
Internet country code and IDD – bb; 1 246 (from UK), 011 44 (to UK)
Major broadcasters – Caribbean Broadcasting Corporation, which also operates MCTV, a multi-channel and pay TV service
Press – Major newspapers include *The Barbados Advocate* and *The Nation*

EDUCATION AND HEALTH

Education is free in government schools at primary (ages four to 11), secondary (ages 11 to 18) and tertiary levels, and is compulsory until the age of 16.
Literacy rate – 99.7 per cent (2004 est)
Gross enrolment ratio (percentage of relevant age group) –
    primary 105 per cent; secondary 105 per cent; tertiary
    61 per cent (2011 est)
Hospital beds (per 1,000 people) – 6.6
Life expectancy (years) – 74.75 (2013 est)
Mortality rate – 8.4 (2013 est)
Birth rate – 12.1 (2013 est)
Infant mortality rate – 11.13 (2013 est)
HIV/AIDS adult prevalence – 0.9 per cent (2012 est)

BELARUS

Respublika Byelarus' – Republic of Belarus

Area – 207,600 sq. km
Capital – Minsk (the administrative centre of the CIS);
   population, 1,879,065 (2012 est)
Major cities – Brest, Homyel, Hrodna, Mahilyow, Vitsyebsk
Currency – Belarusian rouble (Br) of 100 kopeks
Population – 9,625,888 falling at 0.18 per cent a year
   (2013 est); Belarusian (83.7 per cent), Russian (8.3 per
   cent), Polish (3.1 per cent), Ukrainian (1.7 per cent)
   (2009)
Religion – Christian (Belarusian Orthodox 80 per cent,
   Roman Catholic 10 per cent) (est)
Language – Belarusian, Russian (both official), Polish,
   Ukrainian
Population density – 47 per sq. km (2011)
Urban population – 75.5 per cent (2012 est)
Median age (years) – 39.2 (2013 est)
National anthem – 'My Belarusy' ['We, the Belarusians']
National day – 3 July (Independence Day)
Death penalty – Retained
CPI score – 29 (123)

CLIMATE AND TERRAIN
Much of Belarus is a plain, with many lakes, swamps and
marshes, and forest cover is around 43 per cent. Its main
rivers are the upper reaches of the Dnieper, the Nyoman and
the Western Dvina. Elevation extremes range from 346m
(Dzyarzhynskaya Hara) to 90m (Nyoman river). The climate
is continental, with cold winters and warm, humid summers.

HISTORY AND POLITICS
In the 13th century the area was absorbed into the grand
duchy of Lithuania, which entered into the Polish
Commonwealth from the 16th until the 18th centuries.
Following the partitions of Poland in the late 18th century it
became part of the expanding Russian Empire. It was the site
of fierce fighting during the First World War, but its brief
period of independence in 1918 ended, after a war over the
territory, in partition between Poland and the USSR. The
Polish territory was largely regained by the USSR after the
Second World War, which devastated Belarus; over a quarter
of the population was killed.
   Belarus declared its independence from the USSR after a
failed coup in Moscow in 1991. Stanislav Shuskevich
became Belarusian leader at the head of a coalition of
communists and democrats, but he was forced to resign in
1994. He was replaced by Gen. Mecheslav Grib, who
pursued closer political, economic and trade relations with
Russia.
   Alexander Lukashenko was elected to the newly created
post of president in 1994. Since coming to power, President

Lukashenko has opposed privatisation and economic
liberalisation (precipitating economic collapse), subverted
political processes and repressed opposition and the media,
creating a virtual dictatorship. Elections since 2000 have
been condemned as neither free nor fair by opposition
groups and international observers. The EU and USA have
imposed sanctions several times because of the regime's
poor human rights record and obstructiveness towards
international election monitors. In the 2010 presidential
election, President Lukashenko was returned with 79.7
per cent of the vote. In the 2010 legislative elections, all the
seats were won by the president's supporters. The result
prompted mass protests and arrests amid claims the election
had been rigged. In September, opposition parties boycotted
the parliamentary elections, asserting the elections were
undemocratic.
   Under the 1994 constitution, the president is directly
elected for a five-year term; this was renewable only once
until a 2004 constitutional amendment removed the two-
term limit. The legislature is the bicameral National Assembly,
comprising a 110-member House of Representatives (lower
chamber), directly elected for a four-year term, and a Council
of the Republic, with 56 members elected by regional *soviets*
(councils) and eight members appointed by the president, for
a four-year term.
   The president may appoint half the members of the
constitutional court and the electoral commission.

HEAD OF STATE
President, Alexander Lukashenko, *elected* 10 July 1994,
   re-elected 2001, 2006, 2010

SELECTED GOVERNMENT MEMBERS *as at May 2013*
Prime Minister, Mikhail Myasnikovich
First Deputy Prime Minister, Vladimir Semashko
Deputy Prime Ministers, Anatoly Kalinin; Mikhail Rusyy;
   Piotr Prokopovich, Anatoly Tozik
Foreign Affairs, Vladimir Makey

EMBASSY OF THE REPUBLIC OF BELARUS
6 Kensington Court, London W8 5DL
T 020-7937 3288 E uk.london@mfa.gov.by
W http://uk.mfa.gov.by/en
Ambassador Extraordinary and Plenipotentiary, HE Sergei
   Aleinik, *apptd* 2013

BRITISH EMBASSY
37 Karl Marx Street, 220030 Minsk
T (+375) (172) 298 200 E ukin.belarus@fconet.fco.gov.uk
W www.gov.uk/government/world/belarus
Ambassador Extraordinary and Plenipotentiary, HE Bruce
   Bucknell, *apptd* 2012

FOREIGN RELATIONS
Belarus was a founder member of the Commonwealth of
Independent States (CIS) in 1991. President Lukashenko,
who opposed the break-up of the Soviet Union, has sought
closer relations with Russia. In 1997 a treaty was signed with
Russia providing for closer political and economic
integration, and in 1999 the two countries signed a treaty
that committed them to becoming a confederal state.
However, there has been little progress towards integration,
and Russia has increasingly condemned Belarus's poor
economic development; relations have also been strained
over energy supplies and transshipment fees. In 2011 Belarus
formed an economic union with Kazakhstan and Russia,
removing tariffs and customs control along their shared
borders.

DEFENCE

Aged 16–49, 2010 est	Males	Females
Available for military service	2,401,785	2,429,653
Fit for military service	1,693,626	2,012,401

Military expenditure – US$921m (2013)
Conscription – 18–27 years of age; 12–18 months, dependent on level of education

ECONOMY AND TRADE

Although prosperous under the Soviet regime, the country experienced a dramatic decline after independence and over a quarter of the population now lives below the poverty line. Since 1994 President Lukashenko has resisted structural reform of the economy and reimposed state control of prices and currency exchange rates. Some privatised businesses have been renationalised, and the small private sector is subject to pressure and intervention by the state, circumstances that continue to discourage foreign investment. The drop in revenue and the global downturn pushed the economy into recession in 2009, leading to a devaluation of the rouble. The country is highly dependent on Russia for its energy needs, and economic growth in recent years was largely based on the re-export at market prices of heavily discounted oil and natural gas from Russia. This revenue stream has been reduced by sharp increases in oil and gas prices from 2007 (increasing to world prices by 2011), although the establishment of a new economic union with Kazakhstan and Russia in 2011 removed all Belarusian oil duties and increased the country's GDP to around 5 per cent. In June 2011 Belarus asked the IMF and Russia for large bailout loans in the wake of a balance of payments crisis. Russian economic dominance over Belarus further increased in November 2011 in a deal which agreed the sale of oil to Belarus at a discount of 60 per cent below other European states in exchange for Russian ownership of Belarusian oil pipeline firm Beltransgaz, and again in January 2013 when a US$2 billion loan was announced.

The main economic activities are oil-refining and the manufacture of heavy machinery and equipment, vehicles, domestic appliances, chemicals and textiles. These commodities, along with oil, mineral products, metals and foodstuffs, constitute the main exports and the main imports. The main trading partner is Russia.

GNI – US$61,750m; US$6,530 per capita (2012)
Average annual growth of GDP – 2.1 per cent (2013 est)
Inflation rate – 19 per cent (2013 est)
Population below poverty line – 27.1 per cent (2003 est)
Unemployment – 1 per cent (2009 est)
Total external debt – US$1,204m (2013 est)
Imports – US$46,404m (2012)
Exports – US$46,060m (2012)

BALANCE OF PAYMENTS
Trade – US$344m deficit (2012)
Current Account – US$1,688m deficit (2012)

Trade with UK	2012	2013
Imports from UK	£123,018,406	£92,845,271
Exports to UK	£87,266,369	£73,977,076

COMMUNICATIONS

Airports – 33, including an international airport in Minsk plus six other major domestic airports
Waterways – Belarus has an extensive 2,500km canal and river system, but its use is limited by shallowness or remoteness

Roadways and railways – 86,392km; 5,537km
Telecommunications – 4.41 million fixed lines and 10.67 million mobile phone subscriptions (2012); there were 2.64 million internet users in 2009
Internet code and IDD – by; 375 (from UK), 810 44 (to UK)
Major broadcasters – Belarussian TV and Belarussian Radio are the principal television and radio broadcasters; other television broadcasters include Nationwide TV and the Polish-based Belsat
Press – Major newspapers include *Sovetskaya Belorussiya* (Russian-language daily) and *Zvyazda* (Belarussian-language daily)
WPFI score – 47,82 (157)

EDUCATION AND HEALTH

Education is compulsory between the ages of six and 15.
Literacy rate – 99.6 per cent (2010 est)
Gross enrolment ratio (percentage of relevant age group) – primary 101 per cent; secondary 106 per cent; tertiary 86 per cent (2011 est)
Health expenditure (per capita) – US$307 (2011)
Hospital beds (per 1,000 people) – 11.1 (2009–11)
Life expectancy (years) – 71.81 (2013 est)
Mortality rate – 13.68 (2013 est)
Birth rate – 10.99 (2013 est)
Infant mortality rate – 3.67 (2013 est)

BELGIUM

Koninkrijk Belgie / Royaume de Belgique / Königreich Belgien – Kingdom of Belgium

Area – 30,528 sq. km
Capital – Brussels; population, 1,924,236 (2012 est)
Major cities – Antwerp, Bruges, Charleroi, Ghent, Liège
Currency – Euro (€) of 100 cents
Population – 10,444,268 rising at 0.05 per cent a year (2013 est); Fleming (58 per cent), Walloon (31 per cent) (est)
Religion – Christian (Roman Catholic 75 per cent, other, including Protestant, 25 per cent) (est)
Language – Dutch (Flemish), French, German (all official)
Population density – 365 per sq. km (2011)
Urban population – 97.5 per cent (2012 est)
Median age (years) – 42.8 (2013 est)
National anthem – 'La Brabançonne' ['The Song of Brabant']
National day – 21 July (Accession of King Leopold I, 1831)
Death penalty – Abolished for all crimes (since 1996)
CPI score – 75 (15)

CLIMATE AND TERRAIN

There are two distinct regions: the west is generally low-lying and fertile, while in the east the forested hills of the Ardennes are more rugged with poorer soil. Elevation extremes range from 694m (Signal de Botrange) to 0m

Part of the Roman Empire until second century c.200BC | Absorbed by the duchy of Burgundy | Area conquered and ruled by Revolutionary France 1477 | Revolution leads to the declaration of independence and, in 1831, a constitutional monarchy 1814 | Establishment of regional assemblies owing to inter-communal disputes between the Flemings and the Walloons 1914-44 1989 | Joins the Eurozone 2002

Invaded by Germanic tribes and becomes part of the Frankish Empire 1385 | Under the rule of the Spanish, then Austrian, Habsburgs 1794 | Unites with the Netherlands following the collapse of the Napoleonic regime 1830 | Invasion and occupation by Germany during both world wars 1980 | Adopts a federal constitution 2002

on the North Sea coast. The polders near the coast, which are protected against floods by dykes, cover an area of around 500 sq. km. Average temperatures range from 1.6°C in January to 16.5°C in July.

POLITICS
Belgium is a constitutional monarchy with a hereditary monarch as head of state. Amendments to the constitution since 1968 have devolved power to the regions. The national government retains competence only in foreign and defence policies, the national budget and monetary policy, social security, and the judicial, legal and penal systems. The bicameral legislature, the Federal Chambers, consists of a senate and a Chamber of Representatives. The latter has 150 members, directly elected by proportional representation for a four-year term. From 2014, the Senate has 60 members indirectly elected by Parliament and the regions.

There are three language communities: Flemish, Francophone and Germanophone. Each community has its own assembly, which elects the community government. At this level, Flanders is covered by the Flemish community assembly; most of Wallonia is covered by the Francophone community assembly, and areas of Wallonia lying in the German-speaking communities of Eupen and Malmédy are covered by the Germanophone community assembly; Brussels is covered by a joint community commission of the Flemish and Francophone community assemblies.

At regional level, Belgium is divided into the three regions of Brussels, Flanders and Wallonia. Each region has its own directly elected assembly and government.

The ten provinces of Belgium are: Antwerp, East Flanders, Flemish Brabant, Hainaut, Liège, Limburg, Luxembourg, Namur, Walloon Brabant and West Flanders. In addition, 589 communes form the lowest level of local government.

In July 2013, Crown Prince Philippe was sworn in as Belgium's seventh king following the abdication after nearly 20 years on the throne of his 79-year-old father, King Albert, due to ill health. In the May 2014 legislative elections, the New Flemish Alliance emerged as the lagest party, as it had done in the 2010 elections, and was nominated to form a ruling coalition. Ongoing negotiations delayed the formation of a new government and Elio Di Rupo of the Socialist Party remained acting prime minster, depsite his resignation on 26 May. Regional elecctions took place simulataneously.

Minister-President of the Brussels Capital Government, Rudi Vervoort

Minister-President of the Flemish Community and Flemish Region, Geert Bourgeois

Minister-President of the French Community and Walloon Region, Paul Magnette

Minister-President of the German-speaking Community, Oliver Paasch

HEAD OF STATE
HM The King of the Belgians, King Philippe, *born* 15 April 1960; *acceded* 21 July 2013

Heir, HRH Princess Elisabeth, *born* 25 October 2001

SELECTED GOVERNMENT MEMBERS *as at February 2014*
Prime Minister, Elio Di Rupo

Deputy Prime Ministers, Alexander De Croo *(Pensions);* Koen Geens *(Finance);* Didier Reynders *(Foreign Affairs);* Joëlle Milquet *(Interior);* Laurette Onkelinx *(Social Affairs and Public Health);* Johan Vande Lanotte *(Economy)*

EMBASSY OF BELGIUM
17 Grosvenor Crescent, London SW1X 7EE
T 020-7470 3700 E london@diplobel.fed.be
W www.diplomatie.be/london
Ambassador Extraordinary and Plenipotentiary, HE Guy Trouveroy, *apptd* 2014

BRITISH EMBASSY
Avenue d'Auderghem 10, Oudergemlaan, 1040 Brussels
T (+32) (2) 287 6211 E public.brussels@fco.gov.uk
W www.gov.uk/government/world/belgium
Ambassador Extraordinary and Plenipotentiary, HE Jonathan Brenton, *apptd* 2010

DEFENCE
The headquarters of NATO, and of its Supreme Headquarters Allied Powers Europe, are in Belgium.

Aged 16–49, 2010 est	Males	Females
Available for military service	2,359,232	2,291,689
Fit for military service	1,934,957	1,877,268

Military expenditure – US$5,287m (2013)

ECONOMY AND TRADE
Belgium has a free-market economy with highly diversified industrial and commercial sectors. With few natural resources, industry is based largely on processing imported raw materials for export. This makes the economy dependent on the state of world markets; public debt remains close to 100 per cent of GDP. The banking sector was severely affected by the international banking crisis and government bailouts, although the deficit has since been reduced to around 3 per cent of GDP. Despite a rise in unemployment from 7.2 to 8.8 per cent, 2013 saw an overall growth figure of 0.1 per cent for the economy.

Principal industries are engineering and metal products, vehicle assembly, transport equipment, scientific instruments, food processing and beverages, chemicals, base metals, textiles, glass, petroleum and diamonds. Industry accounts for 22.6 per cent of GDP and 25 per cent of employment. There is a large service sector, partly owing to the location in Brussels of EU institutions, NATO headquarters and a number of other international organisations. The service sector accounts for 76.6 per cent of GDP. There is a small agricultural sector (0.8 per cent of GDP).

Around three-quarters of trade is with other EU states, especially Germany, France and the Netherlands. External trade statistics relate to Luxembourg as well as Belgium, as the two countries formed an economic union in 1921.

GNI – US$484,576m; US$44,660 per capita (2012)
Annual average growth of GDP – 0.1 per cent (2013 est)
Inflation rate – 1.3 per cent (2013 est)
Population below poverty line – 15.2 per cent (2007 est)
Unemployment – 8.8 per cent (2013 est)

Total external debt – US$1,424,000m (2012 est)
Imports – US$439,492m (2012)
Exports – US$446,637m (2012)

BALANCE OF PAYMENTS
Trade – US$7,145m surplus (2012)
Current Account – US$9,734m deficit (2012)

Trade with UK	2012	2013
Imports from UK	£13,991,744,438	£13,622,087,228
Exports to UK	£18,164,406,650	£19,925,517,706

COMMUNICATIONS
Airports – 26; the main airports are at Antwerp, Brussels, Liège and Ostend-Bruges
Waterways – There are 2,043km of inland waterways, of which 1,528km are in regular commercial use; ship canals and the Meuse (Maas), Sambre and Schelde rivers form an integral part of the network. The major inland ports are located in Brussels, Ghent and Antwerp
Roadways – There are 154,012km of roadways, including 1,756km of motorways
Railways – The rail system is run by Belgian National Railways and, at 3,233km, the network is one of the densest in the world
Telecommunications – 4.631 million main lines and 12.88 million mobile phone subscriptions (2012); there were 8.113 million internet users in 2009
Internet code and IDD – be; 32 (from UK), 44 (to UK)
Major broadcasters – Television broadcasters include French-language RTBF and Dutch-language VRT
Press – Major newspapers include Dutch-language daily Het Nieuwsblad and French-language daily Le Soir
WPFI score – 12,80 (23)

EDUCATION AND HEALTH
Nursery schools provide free education for children from two-and-a-half to six years of age. The official school-leaving age is 18.
Gross enrolment ratio (percentage of relevant age group) – primary 104 per cent; secondary 106 per cent; tertiary 69 per cent (2011 est)
Health expenditure (per capita) – US$4,962 (2011)
Hospital beds (per 1,000 people) – 6.5 (2011)
Life expectancy (years) – 79.78 (2013 est)
Mortality rate – 10.7 (2013 est)
Birth rate – 10 (2013 est)
Infant mortality rate – 4.23 (2013 est)

BELIZE

MEXICO
Belize City
Turneffe Is.
Belmopan
BELIZE
Gulf of Honduras
GUATEMALA
HONDURAS

Area – 22,966 sq. km
Capital – Belmopan; population, 14,000 (2011 est)
Major towns – Belize City (the former capital), Orange Walk, San Ignacio
Currency – Belize dollar (BZ$) of 100 cents; the Belize dollar is tied to the US dollar
Population – 334,297 rising at 1.97 per cent a year (2013 est); mestizo (48.7 per cent), Creole (24.9 per cent), Maya (10.6 per cent), Garifuna (6.1 per cent) (2000)
Religion – Christian 71.8 per cent (of which Roman Catholic 39.3 per cent) (est)
Language – English (official), Spanish, Creole, Mayan dialects, Garifuna, German
Population density – 14 per sq. km (2011)
Urban population – 44.5 per cent (2012 est)
Median age (years) – 21.5 (2013 est)
National anthem – 'Land of the Free'
National day – 21 September (Independence Day)
Death penalty – Retained

CLIMATE AND TERRAIN
Belize comprises a large coastal plain, swamps in the north, fertile land in the south, and the Maya Mountains in the south-west. The highest point of elevation is 1,160m (Doyle's Delight), the lowest is 0m (Caribbean Sea). Part of the Mesoamerican barrier reef system, the western hemisphere's longest, runs nearly the entire length of the coastline. The climate is subtropical but is cooled by trade winds. The hurricane season is from May to November.

HISTORY AND POLITICS
Numerous ruins in the area indicate that Belize was heavily populated by the Maya. The first British settlement was established in 1638 but was subject to repeated attacks by the Spanish, who claimed sovereignty until their defeat by the British navy and settlers in 1798. In 1862 the settlement was given colonial status as British Honduras. The colony became self-governing in 1964. In 1973 it was renamed Belize and it was granted independence on 21 September 1981.

Since independence, power has alternated between the two main political parties, the People's United Party (PUP) and the United Democratic Party (UDP). The UDP lost seats to PUP in the 2012 legislative elections, but retained its overall majority under prime minister Dean Barrow.

Under the 1981 constitution, the head of state is Queen Elizabeth II, represented by a governor-general. There is a bicameral National Assembly, comprising a House of Representatives with 31 members directly elected for a five-year term, and a senate of 13 members appointed by the governor-general, including six on the advice of the prime minister, three on the advice of the opposition leader, and three representing various sectors of society; a referendum in 2008 approved the reform of the senate into an elected chamber effective from the next elections. The prime minister is appointed by the governor-general and is responsible to the legislature.
Governor-General, HE Sir Colville Young, GCMG, apptd 17 November 1993

SELECTED GOVERNMENT MEMBERS as at February 2014
Prime Minister, Finance, Dean Barrow
Deputy Prime Minister, Gaspar Vega
Foreign Affairs, Wilfred Elrington

BELIZE HIGH COMMISSION
3rd Floor, 45 Crawford Place, London W1H 4LP
T 020-7723 3603 E bzhc-lon@btconnect.com
W www.belizehighcommission.com
High Commissioner, HE Perla Maria Perdomo, apptd 2012

BRITISH HIGH COMMISSION
PO Box 91, Belmopan
T (+501) 822 2981 E brithicom@btl.net
W www.gov.uk/government/world/belize
High Commissioner, HE Peter Hughes, OBE, *apptd* 2013

FOREIGN RELATIONS
There is a longstanding territorial dispute with Guatemala, which claims the southern part of Belize. Following years of negotiations, both countries were due to hold simultaneous referenda in October 2013 as to whether the dispute should be presented to the International Court of Justice, but the referenda were later suspended and are due to be carried out in 2014.

DEFENCE

Aged 16–49, 2010 est	Males	Females
Available for military service	81,284	79,185
Fit for military service	59,431	57,221

Military expenditure – US$16.25m (2013)

ECONOMY AND TRADE
The economy grew steadily from 1999 to 2007, bolstered from 2006 by commercial exploitation of oil reserves. It contracted sharply in 2009 owing to the global downturn, natural disasters and the drop in international oil prices but started to recover in 2010. From 2010–2 the economy grew at a rate of 2 per cent per year and then by 2.5 per cent in 2013. In January 2013 the government announced the restructure of its US$544m commercial external debt, or 'superbond', on which it defaulted in 2012. Over a third of the population lives below the poverty line.

The services sector has grown as tourism has developed, and accounts for around 64 per cent of GDP; industry contributes around 23 per cent, and agriculture and fisheries around 13 per cent. The main industries apart from tourism are garment manufacturing, food processing, construction and oil production. The chief trading partners are the USA, the UK and Mexico. The major exports are sugar, bananas, citrus fruits and juice, garments, shrimp, fish products, molasses, timber and crude oil. Imports are primarily machinery and transport equipment, manufactured goods, fuel, chemicals, pharmaceuticals, food, beverages and tobacco.
GNI – US$1,444m; US$4,490 per capita (2011)
Annual average growth of GDP – 2.5 per cent (2013 est)
Inflation rate – 1.3 per cent (2013 est)
Population below poverty line – 41 per cent (2013 est)
Unemployment – 15.5 per cent (2012 est)
Total external debt – US$1,048m (2013 est)
Imports – US$882m (2012)
Exports – US$340m (2012)

BALANCE OF PAYMENTS
Trade – US$541m deficit (2012)
Current Account – US$35m deficit (2012)

Trade with UK	2012	2013
Imports from UK	£10,817,272	£8,618,556
Exports to UK	£73,740,363	£72,223,351

COMMUNICATIONS
Airports – Six, including the international airport at Belize City
Waterways – Although there are 825km of waterways, these are only accessible by small craft
Roadways – There are 2,870km of roadways, 488km of which are surfaced

Telecommunications – 25,400 fixed lines and 164,200 mobile phone subscriptions (2012); there were 36,000 internet users in 2009
Internet code and IDD – bz; 501 (from UK), 44 (to UK)
Major broadcasters – Commercial channels 5 and 7
WPFI score – 29 (17,05)

EDUCATION AND HEALTH
Education is free and compulsory for eight years.
Literacy rate – 75.1 per cent (2008 est)
Gross enrolment ratio (percentage of relevant age group) – primary 119 per cent; secondary 81 per cent; tertiary 23 per cent (2011 est)
Hospital beds (per 1,000 people) – 1.1
Life expectancy (years) – 68.4 (2013 est)
Mortality rate – 5.93 (2013 est)
Birth rate – 25.58 (2013 est)
Infant mortality rate – 20.82 (2013 est)
HIV/AIDS adult prevalence rate – 1.4 per cent (2012 est)

BENIN

République du Bénin – Republic of Benin

Area – 112,622 sq. km
Capital – Porto Novo; population, 314,000 (2011 est); Cotonou, the seat of government, population, 924,000 (2011 est)
Major cities – Abomey-Calavi, Bohicon, Djougou, Parakou
Currency – Franc CFA of 100 centimes
Population – 9,877,292 rising at 2.84 per cent a year (2013 est); Fon (39.2 per cent), Adja (15.2 per cent), Yoruba (12.3 per cent), Bariba (9.2 per cent), Peulh (7 per cent), Ottamari (6.1 per cent), Yoa-Lokpa (4 per cent), Dendi (2.5 per cent) (2002)
Religion – Christian 43 per cent (Roman Catholic 27 per cent, Protestant 10.4 per cent), Muslim 24 per cent (predominantly Sunni), Vodun (voodoo) 17 per cent, other indigenous religions 6 per cent. Many Christians and Muslims also practise voodoo, which originated in this region of Africa, or other indigenous religions
Language – French (official), Fon, Yoruba and other African languages
Population density – 87 per sq. km (2011)
Urban population – 45.6 per cent (2012 est)
Median age (years) – 17.6 (2013 est)
National anthem – 'L'Aube Nouvelle' ['The Dawn of a New Day']
National day – 1 August (Independence Day)
Death penalty – Abolished for all crimes (since 2012)
CPI score – 36 (94)
Literacy rate – 42.4 per cent (2010 est)
Gross enrolment ratio (percentage of relevant age group) – primary 119 per cent; secondary 48 per cent; tertiary 12 per cent (2011 est)

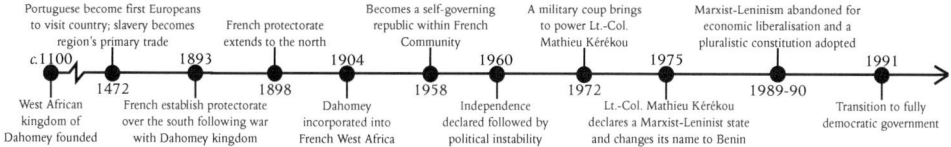

Portuguese become first Europeans to visit country; slavery becomes region's primary trade c.1100

French protectorate extends to the north 1893

Becomes a self-governing republic within French Community 1904

A military coup brings to power Lt.-Col. Mathieu Kérékou 1960

Marxist-Leninism abandoned for economic liberalisation and a pluralistic constitution adopted 1975

1991

West African kingdom of Dahomey founded 1472

French establish protectorate over the south following war with Dahomey kingdom 1898

Dahomey incorporated into French West Africa 1958

Independence declared followed by political instability 1972

Lt.-Col. Mathieu Kérékou declares a Marxist-Leninist state and changes its name to Benin 1989–90

Transition to fully democratic government

Health expenditure (per capita) – US$37 (2011)
Hospital beds (per 1,000 people) – 0.5 (2010)
Life expectancy (years) – 60.67 (2013 est)
Mortality rate – 8.59 (2013 est)
Birth rate – 37.02 (2013 est)
Infant mortality rate – 58.54 (2013 est)
HIV/AIDS adult prevalence – 1.1 per cent (2012 est)

CLIMATE AND TERRAIN
Benin has a short coastline of 121km on the Gulf of Guinea, but extends northwards inland for over 700km. The coast is a sandbar backed by lagoons that are fed by rivers. The land rises to a central plateau with the Atacora massif in the north-west, and falls to plains in the Niger basin in the north-east. Elevation extremes range from 658m (Mt Sokbaro) to 0m (Atlantic Ocean) at the lowest. The climate is tropical in the south and semi-arid in the north.

POLITICS
Under the 1990 constitution, the executive president is directly elected for a five-year term, renewable only once. The unicameral National Assembly has 83 members, directly elected for a four-year term. The president appoints and chairs the council of ministers.

The 2006 presidential election was won in the second round by Thomas Yayi Boni, an independent candidate, and he was re-elected in March 2011. In the 2011 legislative election, the Cauri Forces for an Emerging Benin, which supports the president, remained the largest group in the National Assembly, winning 41 seats. In August 2013 the president removed the post of prime minister from the cabinet.

HEAD OF STATE
President and Head of the Armed Forces, Thomas Yayi Boni, *elected* 19 March 2006, *re-elected* 2011

SELECTED GOVERNMENT MEMBERS *as at February 2014*
Foreign Affairs, Nassirou Arifari Bako
Defence, Dénis Ali Yérima
Economy, Finance, Jonas Aliou Gbian
Interior, Security, François Houéssou

EMBASSY OF THE REPUBLIC OF BENIN
87 Avenue Victor Hugo, 75116 Paris, France
T (+33) 1 4500 9882 E ambassade.benin@gofornet.com
Ambassador Extraordinary and Plenipotentiary, HE Albert Agossou, *apptd* 2009

BRITISH HIGH COMMISSION
HE Peter Jones, *apptd* 2011, resident at Accra, Ghana

DEFENCE

Aged 16–49, 2010 est	Males	Females
Available for military service	2,095,373	2,038,351
Fit for military service	1,385,065	1,400,045

Military expenditure – US$82m (2013)
Conscription – 18–35 years of age; 18 months (selective)

ECONOMY AND TRADE
Although the economy is underdeveloped and still burdened by foreign debt, Benin has benefited from increased competitiveness and debt reduction or relief since its economic restructuring commenced. Privatisation of industries, including utilities, began in 2001 and economic growth has been steady since 2000. However, this has been outweighed by rapid population growth, and over a third of the population remains below the poverty line. Despite the global recession, the level of economic growth (4 per cent) was roughly the same in 2012 as it was before the economic crisis. The economy is based on agriculture, particularly cotton production, and re-export trade with neighbouring countries; customs receipts provide about half of government revenue, but much of the re-export trade operates outside the official economy and is unrecorded.

Agriculture is mostly at subsistence level and contributes 31.6 per cent to GDP, declining recently as industry (12.9 per cent) and services (55.6 per cent) have developed. The main cash crops are cotton, cashew nuts, shea butter, palm products and seafood, and the principal industrial activities are textiles and food processing. The main trading partners are China (25 per cent of exports; 37.2 per cent of imports) and India, to which textiles and some of the cash crops are exported. The principal imports are food, capital goods and fuel.

GNI – US$7,511m; US$750 per capita (2012)
Annual average growth of GDP – 5 per cent (2013 est)
Inflation rate – 2.4 per cent (2013 est)
Population below poverty line – 37.4 per cent (2007 est)
Total external debt – US$1,236m (2013 est)
Imports – US$2,200m (2012)
Exports – US$1,400m (2012)

BALANCE OF PAYMENTS
Trade – US$800m deficit (2012)
Current Account – US$574m deficit (2010)

Trade with UK	2012	2013
Imports from UK	£64,247,720	£70.180,970
Exports to UK	£54,913	£60,618

COMMUNICATIONS
Airports and waterways – One, serving Cotonou, which is also the major seaport
Roadways and railways – 16,000km; 438km
Telecommunications – 156,700 fixed lines and 8.408 million mobile telephones in use (2012); there were 200,100 internet users in 2009
Internet code and IDD – bj; 229 (from UK), 44 (to UK)
Major broadcasters – The state runs a television channel and a radio network, and there are a handful of other commercial TV broadcasters; major broadcasters include Television Nationale and Golfe TV
Press – There are over 50 internet news sites, newspapers and periodicals, including six daily newspapers, five of which are privately owned
WPFI score – 28,83 (75)

BHUTAN

Druk Gyalkhap – Kingdom of Bhutan

Area – 38,394 sq. km
Capital – Thimphu; population, 99,000 (2011 est)
Major towns – Geylegphug, Phuentsholing, Wangdue
   Phodrang
Currency – Ngultrum (Nu) of 100 chetrum (Indian currency
   is also legal tender)
Population – 725,296 rising at 1.15 per cent a year (2013 est);
   Ngalop (Bhote) (50 per cent), ethnic Nepalese (35 per
   cent), indigenous or migrant tribes (15 per cent) (est)
Religion – Lamaistic Buddhist 75.3 per cent, Hindu 22.1 per
   cent (est)
Language – Dzongkha (official), Sharchhopka, Lhotshamkha
Population density – 19 per sq. km (2011)
Urban population – 36.4 per cent (2012 est)
Median age (years) – 25.7 (2013 est)
National anthem – 'Druk Tsendhen' ['The Thunder Dragon
   Kingdom']
National day – 17 December (inauguration of first hereditary
   monarch, 1907)
Death penalty – Abolished for all crimes (since 2004)
CPI score – 63 (31)
Literacy rate – 52.8 per cent (2010 est)
Gross enrolment ratio (percentage of relevant age group) –
   primary 112 per cent; secondary 70 per cent; tertiary
   9 per cent (2011 est)
Life expectancy (years) – 68.44 (2013 est)
Mortality rate – 6.88 (2013 est)
Birth rate – 18.43 (2013 est)
Infant mortality rate – 39.97 (2013 est)

CLIMATE AND TERRAIN

Bhutan is crossed by numerous rivers, and most of the
population and cultivated land is found in the deep, fertile
valleys of the highlands. There is a mountainous northern
region that is infertile and sparsely populated, central
highlands, and densely forested foothills in the south, which
are mainly inhabited by Nepalese settlers and indigenous
tribespeople. Extremes of elevation range from 7,570m
(Gangkar Puensum) to 97m (Drangme Chhu). The climate is
determined by altitude, varying from subtropical in the south
to alpine in the north. There is heavy annual rainfall of up to
1,000mm in the central valleys and 5,000mm in the south,
which experiences monsoons from June to September.

HISTORY AND POLITICS

Bhutan's external relations were under the guidance of
Britain from the 19th century until 1947, and of India from
1947 until 2007; a 2007 revision of the friendship treaty
between the two countries left Bhutan free to manage its
external relations without India's advice.
   Although the country has opened up since the 1970s,
the monarchy has taken measures to preserve its indigenous
culture and the environment, including the compulsory
wearing of national dress and restrictions on tourism. The
emphasis on the majority culture has caused tension with the
sizeable Nepali minority. Many were denied citizenship in
the 1990s and obliged to leave, which resulted in over
100,000 becoming refugees in Nepal, where most remain,
living in refugee camps.
   Bhutan's transition from an absolute monarchy to a
democracy began in the 1950s, with the establishment of
an elected legislature in 1953, and the transfer of powers
from the king to the legislature in 1969 and 1989. The 2008
constitution formally established Bhutan as a parliamentary
democracy with a constitutional monarchy, and provided for
universal suffrage. King Jigme Singye Wangchuk abdicated
in 2006 in favour of the Crown Prince.
   In July 2013, elections to the National Assembly resulted
in an unexpected win for the People's Democratic Party
(PDP), who overtook the ruling Bhutan Peace and Prosperity
Party (DPT) with a total of 32 seats to the DPT's 15.
Tshering Tobgay, leader of the PDP, was appointed prime
minister and formed a government.
   Under the 2008 constitution, the head of state is a
hereditary constitutional monarch, who must retire at the
age of 65 and who may be required to abdicate by a two-
thirds majority of the legislature. The bicameral parliament
comprises a National Assembly with 47 directly elected
members and a National Council with 25 members: 20
directly elected and five appointed by the king. Both
chambers serve a fixed five-year term. The cabinet is
appointed by the king on the recommendation of the prime
minister, who may serve two parliamentary terms. In April
2013 a new National Council was elected.

HEAD OF STATE
HM The King of Bhutan, Jigme Khesar Namgyal Wangchuk,
   born 21 February 1980, *acceded* 14 December 2006,
   crowned 6 November 2008

SELECTED GOVERNMENT MEMBERS *as at
February 2014*
Prime Minister, Tshering Tobgay
Finance, Namgay Dorji
Foreign Affairs, Rinzin Dorje
Home and Cultural Affairs, Damcho Dorji

HONORARY CONSULATE
2 Windacres, Warren Road, Guildford GU1 2HG
T 01483-538189 E mrutland@aol.com
Honorary Consul, Michael R. Rutland

BRITISH DEPUTY HIGH COMMISSION
British Deputy High Commissioner, Scott Furssedonn-Wood,
   apptd 2013 resident at Kolkata, India

ECONOMY AND TRADE
The economy is being cautiously modernised but is still
based on agriculture (13.8 per cent of GDP in 2013) in what
is largely a self-sufficient rural society. Industry (41.2
per cent of GDP) is on a small scale, and the growing
services sector (45 per cent of GDP) is mostly the result of
increased tourism. Agriculture and animal husbandry, much
at subsistence level, engage over 43 per cent of the
workforce, although the mountainous terrain and heavy
forest cover limit the area under cultivation. The principal
food crops are rice, cereals, vegetables and fruit, especially
oranges. Industries include forestry, mining (limestone,
gypsum, dolomite, graphite, coal), cement and calcium
carbide production, food processing, distilling, hydro-electric
power generation and tourism.

The main trading partner is India, which also provides most of Bhutan's development funding. The principal exports are electricity (to India), ferrosilicon, cement, calcium carbide, copper wire, manganese and vegetable oil. The main imports are fuel and lubricants, passenger vehicles, machinery and parts, fabrics and rice.

GNI – US$1,675m; US$2,420 per capita (2012)
Annual average growth of GDP – 5.8 per cent (2013 est)
Inflation rate – 11 per cent (2013 est)
Population below poverty line – 23.2 per cent (2008 est)
Unemployment – 4 per cent (2009 est)
Total external debt – US$1,275m (2011 est)
Imports – US$1,020m (2012)
Exports – US$590m (2012)

BALANCE OF PAYMENTS
Trade – US$430m deficit (2012)
Current Account – US$67m deficit (2010)

Trade with UK	2012	2013
Imports from UK	£610,619	£1,341,698
Exports to UK	£59,568	£35,711

COMMUNICATIONS
Airports – Two, including an international airport in Paro
Roadways – 8,050km, of which 4,991km are surfaced
Telecommunications – 27,000 fixed lines and 560,000 mobile subscriptions (2012); there were 50,000 internet users in 2009
Internet code and IDD – bt; 975 (from UK), 44 (to UK)
Major broadcasters – Fear that outside influences would undermine Bhutanese culture meant that radio broadcasting began only in 1973, and television broadcasting and internet access in 1999; radio and television services are provided by the state owned Bhutan Broadcasting Services (BBS)
Press – The country's first daily newspaper, *Bhutan Today*, privately owned and published in English, was launched in 2008
WPFI score – 30,73 (92)

BOLIVIA

Estado Plurinacional de Bolivia – Plurinational State of Bolivia

Area – 1,098,581 sq. km
Capital – La Paz, the seat of government; population, 1,715,000 (2011 est); Sucre, the legal capital and seat of the judiciary; population, 307,000 (2011 est)
Major cities – Cochabamba, El Alto, Oruro, Santa Cruz, Sucre
Currency – Boliviano ($b) of 100 centavos
Population – 10,461,053 rising at 1.63 per cent a year (2013 est); Quechua (30 per cent), mestizo (30 per cent), Aymara (25 per cent) (est)

Religion – Christian (Roman Catholic 95 per cent, Protestant 5 per cent) (est)
Language – Spanish, 36 indigenous languages (all official); Quechua and Aymara are the main indigenous languages
Population density – 10 per sq. km (2011)
Urban population – 67.2 per cent (2012 est)
Median age (years) – 23.1 (2013 est)
National anthem – 'Himno Nacional de Bolivia' ['National Anthem of Bolivia']
National day – 6 August (Independence Day)
Death penalty – Abolished for all crimes (since 2013)
CPI score – 34 (106)

CLIMATE AND TERRAIN
Landlocked Bolivia's main topographical feature is its great central plateau, the Altiplano. Over 800km in length and at an average altitude of 3,750m above sea level, this plateau lies between two great chains of the Andes that traverse the country from north to south. Lake Titicaca, shared with Peru, lies on the Altiplano. Elevation extremes range from 6,542m (Nevado Sajama) to 90m (Rio Paraguay). The low-lying north and eastern plains are drained by the principal rivers, the Beni, Itenez, Madre de Dios and Mamoré. The climate varies dramatically between regions: on the lowlands of the Amazon basin, temperatures average around 25°C; above 500m on the Altiplano, conditions are subpolar. The south is prone to droughts. The wet season is October to April.

POLITICS
The 1967 constitution was revised in 1994 and 2009. It provides for an executive president who is directly elected for a five-year term, which may be renewed once. The bicameral Plurinational Legislative Assembly, or National Congress, consists of a 36-member Chamber of Senators and a 130-member Chamber of Deputies; members of both chambers are directly elected for a five-year term.

President Morales, leader of the Movement Towards Socialism (MAS), took office in 2006 after winning the 2005 presidential elections, and was re-elected in 2009. After the 2005 legislative elections, the MAS had an outright majority in the lower chamber of the legislature but the Social and Democratic Power party was the largest party in the upper chamber. The MAS won a majority in both chambers in the 2009 legislative elections.

HEAD OF STATE
President, Juan Evo Morales Ayma, *elected* 18 December 2005, *sworn in* 22 January 2006, *re-elected* 2009
President of the Senate, Vice-President, Alvaro Garcia Linera

SELECTED GOVERNMENT MEMBERS *as at February 2014*
Defence, Ruben Saavedra Soto
Economy and Public Finance, Luis Alberto Arce Catacora
Foreign Affairs, David Choquehuanca Cespedes

BOLIVIAN EMBASSY
106 Eaton Square, London SW1W 9AD
T 020-7235 4248 E embol@bolivianembassy.co.uk
W www.bolivianembassy.co.uk
Ambassador Extraordinary and Plenipotentiary, HE Roberto Calzadilla, *apptd* 2014

BRITISH EMBASSY
PO Box 694, Avenida Arce 2732, La Paz
T (+591) (2) 243 3424 E BELaPaz@fco.gov.uk
W www.gov.uk/government/world/bolivia
Ambassador Extraordinary and Plenipotentiary, HE Ross Denny, *apptd* 2011

Conquered by the Spanish — c.1450

Assimilated into the Inca Empire — 1323

Gained independence after a war of liberation led by Simón Bolívar — 1825

Ruled by military juntas — 1936-52

Ruled by military juntas — 1964-82

Austerity measures introduced to curb rising inflation and attract foreign investment widen social divisions and create civil unrest — 1983

Former coca growers' leader, Evo Morales, elected first indigenous president. He renationalises the energy industry and reduces restrictions on coca cultivation — 2006

Morales seeks to give greater political power to the indigenous population through constitutional changes; he wins a recall referendum and presses ahead with a draft constitution — 2008

DEFENCE

Aged 16–49, 2010 est	Males	Females
Available for military service	2,472,490	2,535,768
Fit for military service	1,762,260	2,013,281

Military expenditure – US$404m (2013)
Conscription – 18–49 years of age; 12 months

ECONOMY AND TRADE

The country is one of the most underdeveloped and least affluent in South America, although steady growth since the 1990s has lowered the proportion of the population living below the poverty line to less than half. Economic growth slowed in the 2000s owing to lower commodity prices and political instability, and the economy contracted in 2009 because of the global downturn, recovering strongly in 2010 as commodity prices rose. The renationalised energy industry is the mainstay of the economy. The nationalisation of Spanish-owned electricity company REE, three Spanish-owned airports and Glencore's tin and zinc mine between 2012 and 2013 sparked controversy and speculation that future foreign investment will decline.

Mining (principally for zinc, tin and gold) and smelting, natural gas and oil production, agriculture and textiles are the principal industries. Industry contributes 38.5 per cent of GDP, agriculture 9.2 per cent and services 52.3 per cent.

The main trading partners are Brazil, the USA, Argentina and Chile. Principal exports are natural gas, soya beans and soya products, crude oil, zinc ore and tin. The main imports are petroleum products, plastics, paper, aircraft and aircraft parts, processed food, vehicles and insecticides.

GNI – US$25,405m; US$2,220 per capita (2012)
Annual average growth of GDP – 6.5 per cent (2013 est)
Inflation rate – 5.9 per cent (2013 est)
Population below poverty line – 49.6 per cent (2010 est)
Unemployment – 7.4 per cent (2013 est)
Total external debt – US$7,429m (2013 est)
Imports – US$8,109m (2012)
Exports – US$10,312m (2012)

BALANCE OF PAYMENTS
Trade – US$2,203m surplus (2012)
Current Account – US$2,127m surplus (2012)

Trade with UK	2012	2013
Imports from UK	£22,143,343	£23,241,330
Exports to UK	£15,253,246	£15,953,636

COMMUNICATIONS

Airports – 21, including four international airports serving the major cities
Waterways – There are 10,000km of commercially navigable waterways, with an inland port on the river Paraguay at the border with Brazil; Bolivia has free port privileges at seaports in Argentina, Brazil, Chile and Paraguay, and a lease on a free-trade zone at the Peruvian port of Ilo
Roadways – 80,488km, of which 11,993km are surfaced
Railways – The 3,652km of railways form an eastern network and an Andean network

Telecommunications – 880,600 fixed lines and 9.494 million mobile subscriptions (2012); there were 1.103 million internet users in 2009
Internet code and IDD – bo; 591 (from UK), 10/11/12/13 44 (to UK; depends on area and/or carrier)
Major broadcasters – Television broadcasters include the government-run Bolivia TV and the commercial ATB, Red and Unitel broadcasters; Radio Panamericana and the state-run RadioPatria Nueva are some of the country's major radio broadcasters
Press – There are six national daily newspapers, including *La Razon, El Deber* and *El Mundo*
WPFI score – 31,04 (94)

EDUCATION AND HEALTH

Elementary education is free and officially, though often not in practice, compulsory from the ages of six to 13.
Literacy rate – 91.2 per cent (2010 est)
Gross enrolment ratio (percentage of relevant age group) – primary 94 per cent; secondary 77 per cent (2011 est)
Health expenditure (per capita) – US$118 (2011)
Hospital beds (per 1,000 people) – 1.1 (2009–11)
Life expectancy (years) – 68.22 (2013 est)
Mortality rate – 6.67 (2013 est)
Birth rate – 23.77 (2013 est)
Infant mortality rate – 39.76 (2013 est)

BOSNIA AND HERCEGOVINA

Bosna i Hercegovina – Bosnia and Hercegovina

Area – 51,197 sq. km
Capital – Sarajevo; population, 389,000 (2011 est)
Major towns – Banja Luka, Bijeljina, Mostar, Tuzla, Zenica
Currency – Convertible mark (KM) of 100 fenings
Population – 3,875,723 falling at 0.1 per cent a year (2013 est); Bosniak (48 per cent), Serb (37.1 per cent), Croat (14.3 per cent) (2000 est)
Religion – Muslim 40 per cent (predominantly Sunni), Christian (Serb Orthodox 31 per cent, Roman Catholic 15 per cent) (est)
Language – Bosnian, Croatian, Serbian (all official)
Population density – 75 per sq. km (2011)
Urban population – 48.8 per cent (2012 est)
Median age (years) – 40.4 (2013 est)

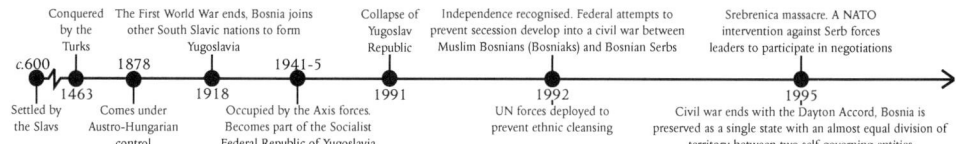

Conquered by the Turks — The First World War ends, Bosnia joins other South Slavic nations to form Yugoslavia — Collapse of Yugoslav Republic — Independence recognised. Federal attempts to prevent secession develop into a civil war between Muslim Bosnians (Bosniaks) and Bosnian Serbs — Srebrenica massacre. A NATO intervention against Serb forces leaders to participate in negotiations

c.600 — 1878 — 1941-5

1463 — 1918 — 1991 — 1992 — 1995

Settled by the Slavs — Comes under Austro-Hungarian control — Occupied by the Axis forces. Becomes part of the Socialist Federal Republic of Yugoslavia — UN forces deployed to prevent ethnic cleansing — Civil war ends with the Dayton Accord, Bosnia is preserved as a single state with an almost equal division of territory between two self-governing entities

National anthem – 'Drzavna Himna Bosne i Hercegovine' ['National Anthem of Bosnia and Hercegovina']
National day – 25 November (formation of the anti-fascist resistance council, 1943)
Death penalty – Abolished for all crimes (since 2001)
CPI score – 42 (72)
Literacy rate – 98 per cent (2011 est)
Gross enrolment ratio (percentage of relevant age group) – primary 88 per cent; secondary 90 per cent; tertiary 35.9 per cent (2010 est)
Health expenditure (per capita) – US$493 (2011)
Hospital beds (per 1,000 people) – 3.5 (2010)
Life expectancy (years) – 76.12 (2013 est)
Mortality rate – 9.53 (2013 est)
Birth rate – 8.92 (2013 est)
Infant mortality rate – 5.97 (2013 est)

CLIMATE AND TERRAIN

The mountainous centre of the country is split by deep valleys, while the north is lower-lying, falling to the basin of the river Sava, which forms the northern border with Croatia. The Dinaric Alps lie along the western border. The highest point of elevation is 2,386m (Maglic), the lowest point is 0m (Adriatic Sea). Average temperatures in Sarajevo range from −1°C in January to 19°C in July.

POLITICS

Under the Dayton Peace Accord, the Bosnian republican (national) government is responsible for foreign affairs, currency, citizenship and immigration. The head of state is a collective presidency comprising a representative from each of the three main ethnic groups, all directly elected for a four-year term; the chair of the presidency rotates among its members every eight months. Legislative authority is vested in the bicameral Parliamentary Assembly, comprising a House of Peoples and a House of Representatives. Both houses have four-year terms. The House of Peoples has 15 members – ten from the Federation and five from the Republika Srpska – who are appointed from the House of Representatives. The House of Representatives has 42 members who are directly elected to the two constituent chambers: the Chamber of Deputies of the Federation, which has 28 members, and the Chamber of Deputies of the Republika Srpska, which has 14 members.

In the Bosniak–Croat Federation, the president and vice-president are elected by the Bosniak and Croat members of the House of Peoples for a four-year term; a second vice-president is elected to represent the Serb population. There is a bicameral Assembly comprising a 58-member House of Peoples elected on an ethnic basis and a House of Representatives with 98 directly elected members.

In the Republika Srpska, the president is directly elected for a four-year term. There is a unicameral People's Assembly with 83 members directly elected for a four-year term.

There is a national council of ministers and each of the entities also has its own executive. All appointments to the executives are in consultation with the UN High Representative, who has the power of veto.

The latest legislative elections were held in October 2010. In the federal legislature, the Bosniak-dominated Social Democratic Party (SDP) and the Serb-dominated Party of

Independent Social Democrats (SNSD) won an equal number of seats, eventually leading to the formation of a coalition government led by Vjekoslav Bevanda, the Bosnian-Croat leader of the Croatian Democratic Union at the end of 2011. The SDP won a narrow majority in the Bosniak–Croat legislature and formed a coalition government under Nermin Niksic. In the Republika Srpska, the SNSD retained its majority and formed a new coalition government under Aleksandar Dzombic.

In the presidential elections in October 2010, Nebojsa Radmanovic (Serb) and Zeljko Komsic (Croat) were re-elected to the collective federal presidency and Bakir Izetbegovic was elected as the Bosniak member. Milorad Dodik, previously the prime minister, was elected president of Republika Srpska. The presidential election in the Bosniak–Croat Federation in March 2011 was won by Zivko Budimir.

REPUBLIC OF BOSNIA AND HERCEGOVINA
HEADS OF STATE
Presidency Members, Nebojsa Radmanovic *(Serb),* Zeljko Komsic *(Croat),* Bakir Izetbegovic *(Bosniak)*

SELECTED GOVERNMENT MEMBERS *as at February 2014*
Chair of the Council of Ministers, Vjekoslav Bevanda
Defence, Zekerijah Osmic
Finance, Nikola Spiric
Foreign Affairs, Zlatko Lagumdzija

FEDERATION OF BOSNIA AND HERCEGOVINA
President, Zivko Budimir
Vice-Presidents, Mirsad Kebo; Svetozar Pudaric

SELECTED GOVERNMENT MEMBERS *as at February 2014*
Prime Minister, Nermin Niksic
Deputy Prime Ministers, Jerko Ivankovic-Lijanovic; Desnica Radivojevic
Interior, Predrag Kurtes

REPUBLIKA SRPSKA
President, Milorad Dodik
Vice-Presidents, Enes Suljkanovic; Emil Vlajki

SELECTED GOVERNMENT MEMBERS *as at February 2014*
Prime Minister, Zeljka Cvijanovic
Finance, Zoran Tegeltija
Interior, Radislav Jovicic

OFFICE OF THE UN HIGH REPRESENTATIVE/EU SPECIAL REPRESENTATIVE
UN High Representative, Dr Valentin Inzko, *apptd* 2009
EU Special Representative, Peter Sorensen, *apptd* 2011

EMBASSY OF BOSNIA AND HERCEGOVINA
5–7 Lexham Gardens, London W8 5JJ
T 020-7373 0867 E embassy@bhembassy.co.uk
W www.bhembassy.co.uk
Ambassador Extraordinary and Plenipotentiary, HE Mustafa Mujezinovic, *apptd* 2012

BRITISH EMBASSY
39a Hamdije Cemerlica, 71000 Sarajevo
T (+387) (0) 33 282 200 E britemb@bih.net.ba
W www.gov.uk/government/world/bosnia-and-herzegovina
Ambassador Extraordinary and Plenipotentiary, HE Edward
Ferguson, *apptd* 2014

DEFENCE
A reform process completed in 2006 united the separate armies of the Republika Sprska and the Federation of Bosnia and Hercegovina into a single entity.

Aged 16–49, 2010 est	Males	Females
Available for military service	1,180,829	1,143,919
Fit for military service	968,242	937,327

Military expenditure – US$204m (2013)*

* Does not include spending on paramilitary forces

ECONOMY AND TRADE
When the civil war broke out, the structure of the economy – dominated by state-owned industries, mainly of a military nature – still reflected the central planning of the communist era. Since the war, growth has been largely generated by reconstruction, funded by external aid, but the private sector is increasingly significant. Economic restructuring, such as privatisation, has been slow and uneven, although the financial sector is now largely privatised and stable. The difficulties inherent in tackling problems such as the large public sector, large deficits and high unemployment are exacerbated by the duplication of administrative functions and reluctant cooperation between the different national and local political and administrative entities. There is a large unofficial economy, but undeclared activity has declined since the introduction of VAT in 2006. Since the global economic crisis GDP has been sluggish and government spending accounts for about half of GDP. In October 2012 the IMF agreed a new stand-by arrangement with Bosnia and Hercegovina to ease fiscal problems brought about by social spending and the global downturn.

Most agricultural products are for domestic consumption and foodstuffs also have to be imported. The main industrial activities include mining (metals, minerals and coal), production of steel, textiles, tobacco products, wooden furniture, ammunition and domestic appliances, assembly of vehicles, tanks and aircraft, and oil refining. The country produces enough hydroelectric power for its needs and exports electricity. The main trading partners are Croatia, Slovenia, Germany, Austria and Italy. Principal exports are metals, clothing and wood products, and the main imports are machinery and equipment, chemicals, fuels and foodstuffs.

GNI – US$17,953m; US$4,750 per capita (2012)
Annual average growth of GDP – 0.5 per cent (2013 est)
Inflation rate – 0.4 per cent (2013 est)
Population below poverty line – 18.6 per cent (2007 est)
Unemployment – 44.1 per cent (2012 est)
Total external debt – US$11,140m (2013 est)
Imports – US$10,014m (2012)
Exports – US$5,187m (2012)

BALANCE OF PAYMENTS
Trade – US$4,827m deficit (2012)
Current Account – US$1,636m deficit (2012)

Trade with UK	2012	2013
Imports from UK	£22,606,127	£21,261,849
Exports to UK	£11,413,314	£22,244,549

COMMUNICATIONS
Airports – Seven, including international airports in Sarajevo, Banja Luka, Mostar and Tuzla
Waterways – Although the country has 20km of coastline on the Adriatic Sea, there are no seaports
Roadways and railways – 22,926km, including 4,652km of motorways; 601km
Telecommunications – 878,000 fixed lines and 3.35 million mobile subscriptions (2012); there were 1.422 million internet users in 2009
Internet code and IDD – ba; 387 (from UK), 44 (to UK)
Major broadcasters – More than 200 commercial TV stations are on the air in Bosnia, although their development has been disrupted by a weak advertising market. There is a national broadcaster, BHTV1, which operates alongside two separate-entity broadcasters; major radio broadcasters include the Bosniak-Croat Radio FBiH and the Bosnian Serb station RTRS
Press – There are five major newspapers, including *Oslobodjenje* and *Dnevni Avaz*
WPFI score – 26,86 (66)

BOTSWANA

Republic of Botswana

Area – 581,730 sq. km
Capital – Gaborone; population, 202,000 (2011 est)
Major cities – Francistown, Maun, Molepolole
Currency – Pula (P) of 100 thebe
Population – 2,127,825 rising at 1.35 per cent a year (2013 est); Tswana (79 per cent), Kalanga (11 per cent), Basarwa (3 per cent) (est)
Religion – Christian 71.6 per cent (predominantly Protestant), Badimo 6 per cent (est)
Language – English (official), Setswana, Kalanga, Sekgalagadi
Population density – 4 per sq. km (2011)
Urban population – 62.3 per cent (2012 est)
Median age (years) – 22.7 (2013 est)
National anthem – 'Fatshe Leno La Rona' ['Blessed Be This Noble Land']
National day – 30 September (Botswana Day)
Death penalty – Retained
CPI score – 64 (30)

CLIMATE AND TERRAIN
Botswana lies on an undulating plateau and is covered by the Kalahari desert in the south and west. To the east, streams run into the Marico, Notwani and Limpopo rivers. In the north lies a flat region comprising the Makgadikgadi salt pans and the swampland of the Okavango delta. Elevation extremes range from 1,489m (Tsodilo Hills) to 513m (junction of the Limpopo and Shashe rivers). The climate is

subtropical in the north, arid in the south and west, and more temperate in the east, which has regular rain. Average temperatures range from 14°C in July to 26°C in January.

HISTORY AND POLITICS

The Tswana people were predominant in the area from the 17th century. In 1885, at the request of indigenous chiefs fearing invasion by the Boers, Britain formally took control of Bechuanaland, and the northern part of the territory was declared the Bechuanaland Protectorate, while land to the south of the Molopo river became British Bechuanaland, which was later incorporated into the Cape Colony and eventually South Africa. In 1964, the Bechuanaland Protectorate became self-governing, and on 30 September 1966 it became an independent republic under the name Botswana. Since independence, Botswana has been stable and relatively prosperous owing to the diamond mining industry. There is a high level of HIV/AIDS among the population, and although an advanced treatment programme in place since 2001 is reducing the level of infection, the country faces serious demographic and social problems.

President Festus Mogae stood down in 2008, having completed two terms of office, and was succeeded by the vice-president, Lt.-Gen. Ian Khama, son of the country's first president. The 2009 legislative election was won by the Botswana Democratic Party (BDP), with 45 seats. President Khama, of the BDP, was elected president two days later.

Under the 1966 constitution, the executive president is elected by the legislature for a five-year term, renewable once. He appoints the vice-president and the cabinet. The unicameral National Assembly has 57 members directly elected for a five-year term, plus a variable number of members (currently four) nominated by the president and elected by the assembly. A 15-member House of Chiefs advises on tribal matters and constitutional changes.

HEAD OF STATE
President, Lt.-Gen. (retd) Ian Khama, *sworn in* 1 April 2008, *elected* 18 October 2009
Vice-President, Ponatshego Kedikilwe

SELECTED GOVERNMENT MEMBERS *as at February 2014*
Finance and Development Planning, Kenneth Matambo
Foreign Affairs, Phandu Skelemani
Defence, Dikgakgamatso Seretse

BOTSWANA HIGH COMMISSION
6 Stratford Place, London W1C 1AY
T 020-7499 0031 E bohico@govbw.com
High Commissioner, HE Roy Blackbeard, *apptd* 1998

BRITISH HIGH COMMISSION
Plot 1079-1084, Main Mall, off Queens Road, Gaborone
T (+267) 395 2841 E bhc@botsnet.bw
W www.gov.uk/government/world/botswana
High Commissioner, HE Nicholas Pyle OBE, MBE *apptd* 2013

DEFENCE

Aged 16–49, 2010 est	Males	Females
Available for military service	557,647	531,095
Fit for military service	340,949	302,332

Military expenditure – US$319m (2013)

ECONOMY AND TRADE

Botswana has been relatively prosperous since independence because of its mining industry, political stability and sound economic management. Despite this, about 30 per cent of the population lives below the poverty line. Longer-term problems are the impact of the high levels of HIV/AIDS among the workforce and the levelling off of diamond production, which usually accounts for 70 to 80 per cent of export earnings; diamond exports declined owing to the global downturn, causing the economy to contract sharply in 2009. The government has sought to reduce the economy's dependence on the diamond industry by diversifying. However, in 2012 a major diamond company signed a ten-year deal to move a division from London to Gaborone. Safari tourism and financial services have grown in recent years, and the services sector now contributes 62.4 per cent of GDP. The industrial sector contributes 35.7 per cent of GDP, mainly from mining diamonds, copper, nickel, salt, soda ash, potash, coal, iron ore and silver. Agriculture is mostly pastoral and accounts for 1.9 per cent of GDP.

The main trading partners are EU, southern African countries and Israel. Principal exports are diamonds, copper, nickel, soda ash, meat and textiles. The main imports are foodstuffs, machinery, electrical goods, transport equipment, textiles, fuel and petroleum products.

GNI – US$14,463m; US$7,650 per capita (2012)
Annual average growth of GDP – 3.9 per cent (2013 est)
Inflation rate – 6.1 per cent (2013 est)
Population below poverty line – 30.3 per cent (2003 est)
Unemployment – 17.8 per cent (2009 est)
Total external debt – US$2,416m (2013 est)
Imports – US$8,046m (2012)
Exports – US$5,987m (2012)

BALANCE OF PAYMENTS
Trade – US$2,058m deficit (2012)
Current Account – US$1,041m deficit (2009)

Trade with UK	2012	2013
Imports from UK	£834,831,579	£668,442,149
Exports to UK	£1,812,677,945	£2,352,809,830

COMMUNICATIONS

Airports – Ten, including the international airport in Gaborone
Roadways – 17,916km, of which 6,116km are paved
Railways – The only railway is the 888km line from Zimbabwe to South Africa, which passes through eastern Botswana
Telecommunications – 160,500 fixed lines and 3.08 million mobile subscriptions (2012); there were 120,000 internet users in 2009
Internet code and IDD – bw; 267 (from UK), 44 (to UK)
Major broadcasters – State-run television broadcaster Botswana TV was established in 2000 and a private station is hosted by eBotswana; state-run Radio Botswana operates a commercial FM station from Gaborone, while other stations such as Yarona FM operate a private service
Press – Major daily newspapers include the *Daily News* and the privately owned *Mmegi*
WPFI score – 22,91 (41)

EDUCATION AND HEALTH

Botswana does not have a compulsory education policy, although many children receive 12 years of education (seven years of primary education, three years of junior secondary and two years of senior secondary). In 2006 fees were reintroduced for state secondary schools, which had been free of charge for over 20 years.

Literacy rate – 85 per cent (2011 est)
Gross enrolment ratio (percentage of relevant age group) –
primary 108 per cent; secondary 80 per cent (2011 est)
Health expenditure (per capita) – US$432 (2011)
Hospital beds (per 1,000 people) – 1.8 (2010)
Life expectancy (years) – 54.47 (2013 est)
Mortality rate – 12.91 (2013 est)
Birth rate – 21.69 (2012 est)
Infant mortality rate – 9.9 (2013 est)
HIV/AIDS adult prevalence – 23 per cent (2012)

BRAZIL

Republica Federativa do Brasil – Federative Republic of Brazil

Area – 8,514,877 sq. km
Capital – Brasilia; population, 3,813,000 (2011 est)
Major cities – Belo Horizonte, Fortaleza, Porto Alegre, Recife,
Rio de Janeiro (the former capital), Salvador, Sao Paulo
Currency – Real (R$) of 100 centavos
Population – 201,009,622 rising at 0.83 per cent a year
(2013 est)
Religion – Christian (Roman Catholic 64.6 per cent,
Protestant 22.2 per cent), Spiritist 2.2 per cent (est)
Language – Portuguese (official), Spanish, German, Italian,
Japanese, English, Amerindian languages
Population density – 23 per sq. km (2011)
Urban population – 84.9 per cent (2012 est)
Median age (years) – 30.3 (2013 est)
National anthem – 'Hino Nacional Brasileiro' ['Brazilian
National Anthem']
National day – 7 September (Independence Day)
Death penalty – Retained for certain crimes (last used 1855)
CPI score – 42 (72)

CLIMATE AND TERRAIN
Brazil has six distinct topographical areas: the Amazon basin
(north and west of the country), the Parana-Paraguay river
basin (south; the Parana drains the Pantanal, the world's
largest freshwater wetland), the Guiana Highlands (north of
the Amazon), the Mato Grosso plateau (centre), the Brazilian
Highlands (south of the Amazon) and the coastal strip.
Elevation extremes range from 2,994m (Pico da Neblina) to
0m (Atlantic Ocean). Brazil has the world's largest rainforest,
as well as large expanses of savannah *(cerrado)*. The climate is

mostly tropical, with the equator passing through the north
and the Tropic of Capricorn through the south-east. The
Amazon basin sees annual rainfall of up to 2,300mm a year
and there is no dry season. The north-east is the driest area of
the country and can experience long periods of drought. The
southern states have a seasonal temperate climate.

POLITICS
The Federative Republic of Brazil is composed of the Federal
District of Brasilia, in which the capital lies, and 26 states:
Acre, Alagoas, Amapa, Amazonas, Bahia, Ceara, Espirito
Santo, Goias, Maranhao, Mato Grosso, Mato Grosso do Sul,
Minas Gerais, Para, Paraiba, Parana, Pernambuco, Piaui, Rio
de Janeiro, Rio Grande do Norte, Rio Grande do Sul,
Rondonia, Roraima, Santa Catarina, Sao Paulo, Sergipe and
Tocantins. Each state has its own governor and legislative
assembly.

Under the 1988 constitution (amended in 1997), the
executive president is directly elected for a four-year term,
which is renewable once. The National Congress consists of
an 81-member federal senate (three senators per state,
directly elected for an eight-year term) and a 513-member
Chamber of Deputies which is directly elected every four
years; the number of deputies per state depends upon the
state's population.

Dilma Rousseff of the Workers' Party (PT) was elected in
2010, becoming Brazil's first female president. In the 2010
legislative election, the PBSM alliance led by the PT and the
Brazilian Democratic Movement Party (PMDB) won a
majority in both houses of Congress. President Rousseff
appointed a coalition government dominated by the PT and
including the PMDB, five other parties and independents; her
government was dogged by corruption allegations throughout 2011 and early 2012, and growing social discontent and
protests over the costs of the 2014 football World Cup.

HEAD OF STATE
President, Dilma Rousseff, *sworn in* 1 January 2011
Vice-President, Michel Temer

SELECTED GOVERNMENT MEMBERS *as at*
February 2014
Attorney-General, Luis Inacio Lucena Adams
Defence, Celso Amorim
Finance, Guido Mantega
Foreign Affairs, Luiz Alberto Figueiredo Machado

EMBASSY OF BRAZIL
14/16 Cockspur Street, London SW1Y 5BL
T 020-7747 4500 E info.london@itamaraty.gov.br
W www.brazil.org.uk
Ambassador Extraordinary and Plenipotentiary, HE Roberto
Jaguaribe, *apptd* 2010

BRITISH EMBASSY
Setor de Embaixadas Sul, Quadra 801, Lote 8, CEP 70408-900,
Brasilia DF
T (+55) (61) 3329 2300 W www.gov.uk/government/world/brazil
Ambassador Extraordinary and Plenipotentiary, HE Alex Ellis,
CMG, *apptd* 2013

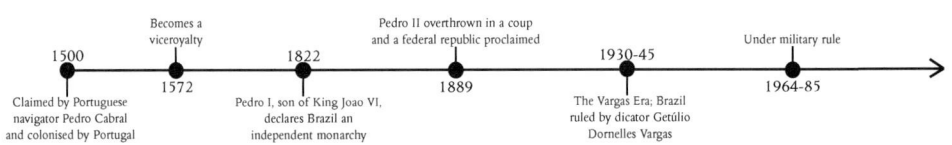

DEFENCE

Aged 16–49, 2010 est	Males	Females
Available for military service	53,350,703	53,433,918
Fit for military service	38,993,989	44,841,661

Military expenditure – US$36,165m (2013)
Conscription – 18–45 years of age; 9–12 months

ECONOMY AND TRADE

Historically subject to boom and bust cycles, the economy was stabilised by reforms in the 1990s. Tight fiscal management, IMF programmes, a growth in output and an expanding export base have produced steady growth since 2003, although poverty is still widespread. Brazil's economy is based on well-developed agriculture, mining, manufacturing and service sectors, and in 2011, became the seventh largest economy in the world, ahead of the UK. Brazil's high interest rates have proved appealing to foreign investors, allowing the currency to increase in value, however this has had a damaging effect on competitiveness in Brazilian manufacturing; the government has intervened in exchange markets, raising taxes on foreign capital.

The country is rich in mineral deposits, including iron ore (haematite), bauxite, gold, manganese, nickel, platinum and uranium. It produces oil, gas and hydroelectricity, and is close to self-sufficiency in oil. Brazil is the world's largest producer of coffee; the other main agricultural products are soya beans, wheat, rice, maize, sugar cane, cocoa, citrus fruit and beef. The expansion of agriculture and forestry threaten the rainforest, although recent governments' attempts to prevent further depredations by loggers and farmers have slowed the rate of deforestation considerably. Tourism is a growing industry. In 2013, services generated 68.1 per cent of GDP, industry 26.4 per cent and agriculture 5.5 per cent.

Brazil's main trading partners are the USA, China, Argentina and Germany. Principal exports are transport equipment, iron ore, soya beans, footwear, coffee and vehicles. The main imports are machinery, electrical and transport equipment, chemical products, oil, vehicle parts and electronics.

GNI – US$2,217,452m; US$11,630 per capita (2012)
Annual average growth of GDP – 2.5 per cent (2013 est)
Inflation rate – 6.2 per cent (2013 est)
Population below poverty line – 21.4 per cent (2009 est)
Unemployment – 5.7 per cent (2013 est)
Total external debt – US$475,900m (2012 est)
Imports – US$2228,377m (2012)
Exports – US$242,580m (2012)

BALANCE OF PAYMENTS
Trade – US$14,203m surplus (2012)
Current Account – US$54,229m deficit (2012)

Trade with UK	2012	2013
Imports from UK	£2,582,360,854	£2,583,718,597
Exports to UK	£2,466,586,799	£2,497,242,996

COMMUNICATIONS

Airports – 698; international flights operate to the major cities
Waterways – In remote regions, transport is primarily by air or water, utilising the 50,000km of navigable waterways
Roadways – 1,580,964km; the Trans-Amazonian Highway connects the Amazon region with the rest of the country, although it is mostly unpaved and often becomes impassable in the rainy season

Railways – 28,538km
Telecommunications – 44.3 million fixed lines and 248.324 million mobile subscriptions (2012); there were 75.98 million internet users in 2009
Internet code and IDD – br; 55 (from UK), 14/15/21/23/31 44 (to UK, varies depending on area and/or carrier)
Major broadcasters – Domestic conglomerates – most notably Globo – dominate the market and run television and radio networks, newspapers and subscription television stations
Press – There are six major daily newspapers, including *O Dia, O Correio Brazilinese* and *Jornal do Brasil*
WPFI score – 34.03 (111)

EDUCATION AND HEALTH

Public education is free at all levels, and is compulsory between the ages of seven and 14.
Literacy rate – 90.3 per cent (2010 est)
Gross enrolment ratio (percentage of relevant age group) – primary 127 per cent; secondary 101 per cent; tertiary 36.1 per cent (2011 est)
Health expenditure (per capita) – US$1,121 (2011)
Hospital beds (per 1,000 people) – 2.3 (2011)
Life expectancy (years) – 73.02 (2013 est)
Mortality rate – 6.51 (2013 est)
Birth rate – 14.97 (2013 est)
Infant mortality rate – 19.83 (2012 est)

BRUNEI

Negara Brunei Darussalam – Brunei Darussalam

Area – 5,765 sq. km
Capital – Bandar Seri Begawan; population, 241,000 (2011 est)
Major towns – Kampong Ayer, Kuala Belait, Seria
Currency – Brunei dollar (B$) of 100 sen (fully interchangeable with Singapore currency)
Population – 415,717 rising at 1.67 per cent a year (2013 est); Malay (65.7 per cent), Chinese (10.3 per cent), indigenous (3.4 per cent) (2011 est)
Religion – Muslim 78.8 per cent (predominantly Sunni), Christian 8.7 per cent, Buddhist 7.8 per cent (est); Islam is the state religion
Language – Malay (official), English, Chinese languages
Population density – 77 per sq. km (2011)
Urban population – 76.4 per cent (2012 est)
Median age (years) – 29 (2013 est)
National anthem – 'Allah Peliharakan Sultan' ['God Bless the Sultan']
National day – 23 February (date of independence from British protection, 1984)
Death penalty – Retained (no known use since 1957)
CPI score – 60 (38)

CLIMATE AND TERRAIN

The country lies on the north-west coast of the island of Borneo. It is surrounded and divided in two by the Malaysian state of Sarawak. The terrain is estimated to be around 70 per cent rainforest, with extensive mangrove swamps along the coastal plain. There are mountains on the border with Sarawak. Elevation extremes range from 1,850m (Bukit Pagon) to 0m (South China Sea). The climate is tropical, with high humidity, and an annual average daily temperature of 27°C.

HISTORY AND POLITICS

Formerly a powerful Muslim sultanate that controlled Borneo and parts of the Philippines, Brunei was reduced to its present size by the mid-19th century and came under British protection in 1889. It chose to remain a British dependency in 1963 rather than joining the Federation of Malaysia. Internally self-governing from 1959, Brunei gained full independence on 1 January 1984.

In 1962 the legislative election was annulled after it was won by a party that sought to remove the sultan; a state of emergency was declared and the sultan has ruled by decree ever since. A ministerial system of government was introduced in 1984. Some political liberalisation and modernisation has taken place since 2004, when the legislature was reconvened after 20 years.

Parts of the 1959 constitution have been suspended since the state of emergency began in 1962. Supreme executive authority is vested in the sultan, a hereditary monarch who presides over and is advised by a privy council, a religious council and the council of cabinet ministers. The legislative council was reconvened in 2004 with 21 members appointed by the sultan; it has passed constitutional amendments to increase its size to 45 members, 15 of whom will be directly elected. No date has been set for an election.

HEAD OF STATE

HM The Sultan of Brunei, Prime Minister, Defence, Finance, HM Hassanal Bolkiah, GCB, *acceded 5 October* 1967, *crowned* 1 August 1968
HM Crown Prince, Senior Minister in the Prime Minister's Office, Prince Al-Muhtadee Billah

SELECTED GOVERNMENT MEMBERS *as at February 2014*
Home Affairs, Pehin Dato Ustaz Badaruddin bin Pengarah Othman
Foreign Affairs, Prince Mohamed Bolkiah

BRUNEI DARUSSALAM HIGH COMMISSION
19–20 Belgrave Square, London SW1X 8PG
T 020-7581 0521 E info@bdhcl.co.uk
High Commissioner, HE Dato Paduka Mohd Aziyan Abdullah, *apptd* 2010

BRITISH HIGH COMMISSION
2.01, 2nd Floor, Block D, Kompleks Yayasan Sultan Haji Hassanal Bolkiah, Jalan Pretty, PO Box 2197
T (+673) (2) 222 231 E ukinbrunei@fco.gov.uk
W www.gov.uk/government/world/brunei
High Commissioner, David Campbell, *apptd* 2013

DEFENCE

Aged 16–49, 2010 est	Males	Females
Available for military service	112,688	117,536
Fit for military service	95,141	99,386

Military expenditure – US$402m (2013)

ECONOMY AND TRADE

The economy is based on the production of oil and natural gas and the income from overseas investments. Royalties and taxes from these operations form the bulk of government revenue and have enabled the construction of free health, education and welfare services; Brunei's GDP per capita is one of the highest in Asia, however, oil and gas reserves, which make up 60 per cent of GDP are declining and Brunei is now trying to diversify its economy, developing financial services and tourism. A new monetary authority was established in January 2011 with a view to develop and monitor the country's growing financial institutions.

Agriculture accounts for 0.7 per cent of GDP, industry 70.9 per cent and services 28.4 per cent. The main trading partners are Japan, Singapore, Indonesia, South Korea and the UK. Principal exports are crude oil, natural gas and clothing. The main imports are machinery and transport equipment, manufactured goods, food (over 80 per cent of domestic requirements are imported) and chemicals.
GNI – US$10,784m; US$31,590 per capita (2009)
Annual average growth of GDP – 1.4 per cent (2013 est)
Inflation rate – 1 per cent (2013 est)
Unemployment – 2.6 per cent (2011 est)
Imports – US$3,365m (2010)
Exports – US$9,172m (2010)

BALANCE OF PAYMENTS
Trade – US$6,448m surplus (2010)
Current Account – US$5,294m surplus (2011)

Trade with UK	2012	2013
Imports from UK	£49,910,416	£75,907,491
Exports to UK	£56,307,333	£51,967,370

COMMUNICATIONS

Airports and waterways – There is one international airport; the largest port is at Muara and the 209km of internal waterways are navigable only by shallow craft
Roadways – 3,029km
Telecommunications – 70,933 fixed lines and 469,700 mobile subscriptions (2012); there were 319,000 internet users in 2009
Internet code and IDD – bn; 673 (from UK), 44 (to UK)
Major broadcasters – The only broadcast media organisation, Radio Television Brunei (RTB), is state-owned; it broadcasts in Malay and English
WPFI score – 35,45 (117)

EDUCATION AND HEALTH

All levels of education are free but not compulsory, most children receive a minimum of 12 years of schooling.
Literacy rate – 95 per cent (2011 est)
Gross enrolment ratio (percentage of relevant age group) – primary 98 per cent; secondary 103 per cent; tertiary 20 per cent (2011 est)
Hospital beds (per 1,000 people) 2.8 (est)
Life expectancy (years) – 76.57 (2013 est)
Mortality rate – 3.43 (2013 est)
Birth rate – 17.63 (2013 est)
Infant mortality rate – 10.81 (2013 est)

BULGARIA

Republika Balgariya – Republic of Bulgaria

Area – 110,879 sq. km
Capital – Sofia; population, 1,203,939 (2012 est)
Major cities – Burgas, Plovdiv, Varna
Currency – Lev of 100 stotinki
Population – 6,981,642 falling at 0.81 per cent a year (2013 est); Bulgarian (76.9 per cent), Turkish (8 per cent), Roma (4.4 per cent) (2011)
Religion – Eastern Orthodox 59.4 per cent, Muslim 7.8 per cent (predominantly Sunni) (est)
Language – Bulgarian (official), Turkish, Romani
Population density – 68 per sq. km (2011)
Urban population – 73.7 per cent (2012 est)
Median age (years) – 42.3 (2013 est)
National anthem – 'Mila Rodino' ['Dear Motherland']
National day – 3 March (Liberation Day)
Death penalty – Abolished for all crimes (since 1998)
CPI score – 41 (77)

CLIMATE AND TERRAIN

The Balkan Mountains cross the country from west to east, averaging 2,000m in height, and the Rhodope Mountains in the south-west climb to almost 3,000m. Elevation extremes range from 2,925m (Musala) to 0m (Black Sea). The lowland plains of the north and south-east are in the basins of the main rivers: the Danube in the north, which forms much of the border with Romania, and the Maritsa, which divides the Balkan and Rhodope ranges. The climate is temperate, with cold, damp winters and hot, dry summers. Average temperatures in Sofia range from −1°C in January to 20°C in July.

POLITICS

Under the 1991 constitution, the president is directly elected for a five-year term, renewable once. The head of government is the prime minister, who is appointed by the president, and is usually the leader of the largest party in the legislature. There is a unicameral National Assembly of 240 members who are directly elected for a four-year term.

In the 2009 legislative election, the new centre-right party Citizens for European Development of Bulgaria (GERB) won the most seats, but without an overall majority, and formed a minority government with support from small right-wing parties. Rosen Plevneliev of the GERB won the 2011 presidential election, picking up 40 per cent of the vote; he was inaugurated on 21 January 2012.

Following clashes between anti-austerity protesters and police in February 2013 Prime Minister Boiko Borisov and his government resigned; Marin Raikov was appointed as caretaker prime minister in March and replaced by Plamen Oresharski on 23 May. A parliamentary election was held in May 2013 in which the centre-right Gerb party won 97 seats, beating the socialist party by 12 seats, but falling short of the majority needed to form a government.

HEAD OF STATE
President, Rosen Plevneliev, *elected* 30 October 2011
Vice-President, Margarita Popova

SELECTED GOVERNMENT MEMBERS *as at February 2014*
Prime Minister, Plamen Oresharski
Deputy Prime Ministers, Zinaida Zlatanova, Tsvetlin Yovchev, Daniela Bobeva
Defence, Angel Naydenov
Finance, Peter Tchobanov

EMBASSY OF THE REPUBLIC OF BULGARIA
186–188 Queen's Gate, London SW7 5HL
T 020-7584 9400 E info@bulgarianembassy.org.uk
W www.bulgarianembassy-london.org
Ambassador Extraordinary and Plenipotentiary, HE Konstantin Stefanov Dimitrov, *apptd* 2012

BRITISH EMBASSY
9 Moskovska Street, Sofia 1000
T (+359) (2) 933 9222 E britishembassysofia@fco.gov.uk
W www.gov.uk/government/world/bulgaria
Ambassador Extraordinary and Plenipotentiary, HE Jonathan Allen, *apptd* 2011

DEFENCE

Aged 16–49, 2010 est	*Males*	*Females*
Available for military service	1,637,470	1,621,352
Fit for military service	1,320,955	1,337,616

Military expenditure – US$841m (2013)

ECONOMY AND TRADE

The government adopted radical economic reforms in 1996 and the economy achieved stability and attracted significant foreign investment, although administrative corruption, a weak judiciary and organised crime remain potential deterrents. Despite steady economic growth in 2004–8 and responsible fiscal management, the economy contracted in the global economic downturn as industrial production and exports declined. Recovery has been slow with growth at 0.5 per cent in 2013.

Natural resources include copper, lead, zinc, other minerals, coal and timber. Fertile arable land produces vegetables, fruit, tobacco, wine, wheat, barley, sunflowers and livestock. Agriculture employs 7.1 per cent of the workforce and accounts for 6.7 per cent of GDP. Industries include energy generation, food processing, beverages, tobacco, machinery and equipment, base metals, chemicals, mining and oil refining. Tourism is growing, with a 5.8 per cent increase in visitors reported for 2013.

The main trading partners are EU countries, Russia and Turkey. Principal exports are clothing and footwear, iron and steel, machinery and equipment, and fuels. The main imports are predominantly machinery and raw materials for the industrial sector.

GNI – US$49,100m; US$6,840 per capita (2012)
Annual average growth of GDP – 0.5 per cent (2013 est)
Inflation rate – 1.5 per cent (2013 est)
Population below poverty line – 21.8 per cent (2008 est)
Unemployment – 11.6 per cent (2013 est)
Total external debt – US$37,850m (2013 est)
Imports – US$32,712m (2012)
Exports – US$26,670m (2012)

BALANCE OF PAYMENTS
Trade – US$6,042m deficit (2012)
Current Account – US$471m deficit (2012)

Trade with UK	2012	2013
Imports from UK	£302,669,524	£389,430,877
Exports to UK	£291,977,683	£366,053,756

COMMUNICATIONS
Airports and waterways – 57, the main airports are at Sofia, Plovdiv, Burgas and Varna; the main ports are Burgas and Varni on the Black Sea, and there are 470km of waterways
Roadways and railways – 19,512km of roadways, including 458km of motorways; 4,125km of railways
Telecommunications – 2.253 million fixed lines and 10.78 million mobile telephone subscriptions (2012); there were 3.395 million internet users in 2009
Internet code and IDD – bg; 359 (from UK), 44 (to UK)
Major broadcasters – Public service broadcasters Bulgarian National Radio and Bulgarian National Television share the market with a vigorous commercial sector that provides national and regional broadcasting
Press – There are seven major daily newspapers, including *Dnevnik, Trud* and *24 Chasa*
WPFI score – 31,42 (100)

EDUCATION AND HEALTH
Education is free and compulsory from seven to 16 years.
Literacy rate – 98 per cent (2011 est)
Gross enrolment ratio (percentage of relevant age group) –
    primary 101 per cent; secondary 93 per cent; tertiary 60 per cent (2011 est)
Health expenditure (per capita) – US$522 (2011)
Hospital beds (per 1,000 people) – 6.5 (2010)
Life expectancy (years) – 74.08 (2013 est)
Mortality rate – 14.31 (2013 est)
Birth rate – 9.07 (2013 est)
Infant mortality rate – 15.6 (2013 est)

BURKINA FASO

Area – 274,200 sq. km
Capital – Ouagadougou; population, 2,188,504 (2012 est)
Major city – Bobo-Dioulasso
Currency – Franc CFA of 100 centimes
Population – 17,812,961 rising at 3.06 per cent a year (2013 est); 63 ethnic groups, of which Mossi (40 per cent) (est) is the largest
Religion – Muslim 60.5 per cent (predominantly Sunni), Christian (Roman Catholic 19 per cent, Protestant denominations 4.2 per cent)
Language – French (official), various African languages (spoken by 90 per cent of the population)
Population density – 58 per sq. km (2011)
Urban population – 27.4 per cent (2012 est)
Median age (years) – 17 (2013 est)
National anthem – 'Une Seule Nuit' ['One Single Night']
National day – 11 December (Republic Day)
Death penalty – Retained (last used 1988)
CPI score – 38 (83)

CLIMATE AND TERRAIN
The landlocked state occupies a plateau dissected by the White, Black and Red Volta rivers. There are tropical savannahs in the south and the north is semi-desert. Elevation extremes range from 749m (Tena Kourou) to 200m (Mouhoun, or Black Volta, river). The climate is tropical, with a wet season from May to September; there are recurring droughts. Average temperatures in Ouagadougou range from 24°C to 32°C.

HISTORY AND POLITICS
Burkina Faso (Upper Volta until 1983) was part of the Mossi Empire in the 18th and 19th centuries. It was administered as part of other French colonies between 1932 and 1947, and in 1958 it became autonomous within the French Community; independence was achieved on 5 August 1960.

In the three decades after independence there was a succession of military regimes; the last military coup, in 1987, brought to power Capt. Blaise Compaoré. Military rule ended in 1991 when a new constitution was adopted and multiparty elections were held in 1992. Despite the constitutional restriction on the number of terms that a president may serve, President Compaoré was re-elected for a fourth term in 2010. The 2007 legislative election was won by the governing Congress for Democracy and Progress (CDP) with a large overall majority. The government was dissolved in April 2011 following protests over food prices and an army mutiny, and a new government was appointed. The CDP comfortably won the parliamentary election of December 2012.

The 1991 constitution was amended in 2000 to reduce the presidential term from seven years. The president is directly elected for a five-year term, renewable once, although this limit has been ignored by President Compaoré. The unicameral National Assembly has 111 deputies, who are directly elected for a five-year term. Executive power is vested jointly in the president and the council of ministers, both responsible to the legislature.

HEAD OF STATE
President, Minister for Defence, Capt. Blaise Compaoré, assumed office 1987, elected 1991, re-elected 1998, 2005, 2010

SELECTED GOVERNMENT MEMBERS *as at February 2014*
Prime Minister, Luc Adolphe Tiao
Economy and Finance, Lucien Marie Noël Bembamba
Foreign Affairs, Yipènè Djibril Bassolé

EMBASSY OF THE REPUBLIC OF BURKINA FASO
16 Place Guy d'Arezzo, 1180 Brussels, Belgium
T (00) (+32) (2) 345 9912 E ambassade.burkina@skynet.be
W www.ambassadeduburkina.be
Ambassador Extraordinary and Plenipotentiary, HE Frédéric
Assomption Korsaga, *apptd* 2013

BRITISH AMBASSADOR
HE Peter Jones, *apptd* 2011, resident at Accra, Ghana

DEFENCE

Aged 16–49, 2010 est	Males	Females
Available for military service	3,735,735	–
Fit for military service	2,366,168	2,367,673

Military expenditure – US$161m (2013)

ECONOMY AND TRADE
The country is one of the poorest in the world, with around 90 per cent of the population engaged in subsistence agriculture and animal husbandry, which are vulnerable to periodic droughts. The economy is heavily dependent on cotton and gold exports and therefore also exposed to the vagaries of global price fluctuations. Civil war in neighbouring Côte d'Ivoire harmed trade by cutting off transport routes, and caused many expatriate Burkinabes to return home, adding to the unemployment problem and depriving the economy of their remittances. During 2013, unrest in Mali caused similar problems and a number of public protests were held about socio-economic issues, the government reduced income taxes and price controls to alleviate discontent.

Agriculture contributes 33.6 per cent of GDP; the main product apart from cotton is livestock. Although there are few natural resources, a growing quantity of gold is mined and exploration for other minerals has begun. The processing of cotton and other agricultural products, gold mining and the manufacturing of beverages, soap, cigarettes and textiles are the main industries, contributing 23.6 per cent to GDP. Services account for 42.8 per cent of GDP.

The main export markets are China, Turkey and Belgium. Principal exports are cotton, livestock and gold. The chief import providers are Côte d'Ivoire and France, supplying capital goods, foodstuffs and fuel.
GNI – US$10,453m; US$670 per capita (2012)
Annual average growth of GDP – 6.5 per cent (2013 est)
Inflation rate – 2.1 per cent (2013 est)
Population below poverty line – 46.7 per cent (2009 est)
Unemployment – 77 per cent (2004 est)
Total external debt – US$2,863m (2013 est)
Imports – US$3,420m (2012)
Exports – US$2,183m (2012)

BALANCE OF PAYMENTS
Trade – US$1,237m deficit (2012)
Current Account – US$123m deficit (2011)

Trade with UK	2012	2013
Imports from UK	£12,692,103	£13,090,484
Exports to UK	£76,624	£351,725

COMMUNICATIONS
Airports – Two; the main international airport is at Ouagadougou
Roadways and railways – 15,272km; 622km
Telecommunications– 141,400 fixed lines and 9.98 million mobile subscriptions (2012); there were 178,100 internet users in 2009

Internet code and IDD – bf; 226 (to UK), 44 (from UK)
Major broadcasters – Radio is the most popular medium with the state-run Radio Burkina the largest broadcaster; state-run Television Nationale du Burkina is one of the largest television broadcasters
WPFI score – 24,45 (52)

EDUCATION AND HEALTH
Education is nominally compulsory from ages six to 16 but the prohibitive cost of school supplies and a lack of resources prevent many children from attending.
Literacy rate – 28.7 per cent (2010)
Gross enrolment ratio (percentage of relevant age group) – primary 82 per cent; secondary 24 per cent; tertiary 4 per cent (2011 est)
Health expenditure (per capita) – US$37 (2011)
Hospital beds (per 1,000 people) – 0.4 (2010)
Life expectancy (years) – 54.43 (2013 est)
Mortality rate – 12.21 (2013 est)
Birth rate – 42.81 (2012 est)
Infant mortality rate – 78.3 (2013 est)
HIV/AIDS adult prevalence – 1 per cent (2012 est)

BURUNDI

Republika y'u Burundi/République du Burundi – Republic of Burundi

Area – 27,830 sq. km
Capital – Bujumbura; population, 605,000 (2011 est)
Major towns – Bubanza, Gitega, Muyinga, Ngozi
Currency – Burundi franc (FBu) of 100 centimes
Population – 10,8395,931 rising at 3.28 per cent a year (2014 est); Hutu (85 per cent), Tutsi (14 per cent), Twa (1 per cent) (est)
Religion – Christian (Roman Catholic 62.1 per cent, Protestant denominations 23.9 per cent), Muslim 2.5 per cent
Language – Kirundi, French (both official), Swahili
Population density – 372 per sq. km (2011)
Urban population – 11.2 per cent (2012 est)
Median age (years) – 16.9 (2013 est)
National anthem – 'Burundi Bwacu' ['Our Burundi']
National day – 1 July (Independence Day)
Death penalty – Abolished for all crimes (since 2009)
CPI score – 21 (157)
Literacy rate – 67.2 per cent (2010 est)
Gross enrolment ratio (percentage of relevant age group) – primary 139 per cent; secondary 26 per cent; tertiary 3 per cent (2011 est)
Health expenditure (per capita) – US$23 (2011)
Hospital beds (per 1,000 people) – 1.9 (2011)
Life expectancy (years) – 59.69 (2013 est)
Mortality rate – 9.12 (2013 est)

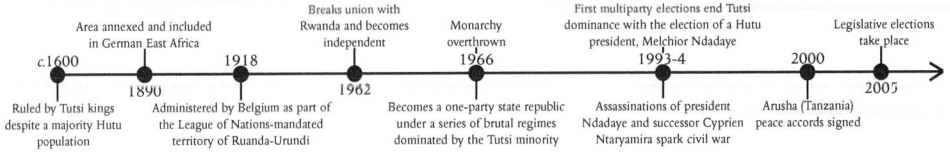

Area annexed and included in German East Africa

Breaks union with Rwanda and becomes independent

Monarchy overthrown

First multiparty elections end Tutsi dominance with the election of a Hutu president, Melchior Ndadaye

Legislative elections take place

c.1600 — 1918 — 1966 — 1993-4 — 2000

1890 — 1962 — 2005

Ruled by Tutsi kings despite a majority Hutu population

Administered by Belgium as part of the League of Nations-mandated territory of Ruanda-Urundi

Becomes a one-party state republic under a series of brutal regimes dominated by the Tutsi minority

Assassinations of president Ndadaye and successor Cyprien Ntaryamira spark civil war

Arusha (Tanzania) peace accords signed

Birth rate – 40.04 (2012 est)
Infant mortality rate – 58.86 (2013 est)
HIV / AIDS adult prevalence – 1.3 per cent (2012 est)

CLIMATE AND TERRAIN
Burundi lies across the Nile–Congo watershed in central Africa. A hilly interior rises from an average altitude of 1,700m to the country's highest point at 2,670m (Heha) and falls to a plateau in the east. The river Ruzizi forms part of the north-western border with the Democratic Republic of the Congo, along with Lake Tanganyika (the lowest elevation in the country at 772m) in the south-west. The climate is equatorial, moderated by altitude; the average temperature in the lower regions is 29°C, and in the higher regions is 20°C. There are two rainy seasons: February to April and October to December.

POLITICS
Under the 2005 constitution, the executive president is directly elected for a five-year term, renewable once. The bicameral *Parlement* comprises the National Assembly and the senate; members of both serve a five-year term. The National Assembly has 100 directly elected members, three co-opted members from the Twa ethnic group, and up to 21 members (currently 15) co-opted to ensure a 60 per cent Hutu and 40 per cent Tutsi split and that 30 per cent of the total are women. The senate has 49 members: 34 directly elected members (one Hutu and one Tutsi from each province); three co-opted Twa members; all former presidents; and enough women to make the number of women senators up to 30 per cent of the total. The constitution also specifies the proportion of Hutu, Tutsi and female members of the council of ministers.

Pierre Nkurunziza of the National Council for the Defence of Democracy–Forces for the Defence of Democracy (CNDD-FDD), a Hutu party, was elected president by the newly elected legislature in 2005. He was re-elected unopposed in the country's first direct presidential election in June 2010, after opposition candidates boycotted the poll in protest at the alleged rigging of local elections held the previous month. Most opposition parties also boycotted the legislative elections in July 2010, in which the CNDD-FDD retained large majorities in both chambers. Anti-government rebel forces remain in Burundi; in November 2012 the Murundi People's Front Abatabazi became the sixth group to attack government forces across the border from the Democratic Republic of Congo.

HEAD OF STATE
President, Pierre Nkurunziza, *sworn in* 26 August 2005, *re-elected* 2010
First Vice-President, Therence Sinunguruza
Second Vice-President, Gervais Rufyikiri

SELECTED GOVERNMENT MEMBERS *as at February 2014*
Defence, Maj.-Gen. Pontien Gaciyubwenge
Finance, Tabu Abdallah Manirakiza
Interior, Edouard Nduwimana

EMBASSY OF THE REPUBLIC OF BURUNDI
Uganda House, 2nd Floor, 58-59 Trafalgar Square, London WC2N 5DX

T 020-7930 4958 E info@burundiembassy.org.uk
W www.burundiembassy.org.uk
Ambassador Extraordinary and Plenipotentiary, vacant

BRITISH AMBASSADOR
HE William Gelling, OBE, *apptd* 2014, resident at Kigali, Rwanda

DEFENCE

Aged 16–49, 2010 est	*Males*	*Females*
Available for military service	2,182,327	2,202,125
Fit for military service	1,398,769	1,481,417

Military expenditure – US$57.8m (2013)

ECONOMY AND TRADE
Economic activity has increased since the civil war ended, but reform and reconstruction are hampered by a lack of administrative capacity, a poorly educated workforce, corruption and poor law enforcement. Agriculture is the mainstay of the economy, contributing 34.4 per cent of GDP. Subsistence agriculture has contracted recently owing to continued insecurity, population growth and soil erosion. Exports of coffee and tea account for around 90 per cent of foreign exchange earnings, leaving the economy vulnerable to the effects of global price fluctuations and weather conditions. Industry is relatively small-scale and employs around 2.3 per cent of the workforce but contributes 18.4 per cent of GDP. The main activities are light manufacturing, food processing, the assembly of imported components and public sector construction. Highly dependent on the international community, 53.5 per cent of Burundi's national income is provided by foreign aid.

Most trade is with Switzerland, Belgium, Saudi Arabia, the UK and China, but it is constrained by the poor transport infrastructure and landlocked location. The main exports are coffee, tea, sugar, cotton and hides. The principal imports are capital goods, petroleum products and food.
GNI – US$2,463m; US$240 per capita (2012)
Annual average growth of GDP – 4.5 per cent (2013 est)
Inflation rate – 9.3 per cent (2013 est)
Population below poverty line – 68 per cent (2008 est)
Total external debt – US$677,200m (2013 est)
Imports – US$751m (2012)
Exports – US$132m (2012)

BALANCE OF PAYMENTS
Trade – US$619m deficit (2012)
Current Account – US$323m deficit (2011)

Trade with UK	2012	2013
Imports from UK	£3,731,258	£2,119,724
Exports to UK	£77,322	£68,492

COMMUNICATIONS
Airports and waterways – Bujumbura has the only airport with a surfaced runway and the only port, while movement around Lake Tanganyika is by water
Roadways – A limited road network of 12,322km, only 1,286km of which is paved, is concentrated around Bujumbura

Railways – There are no railways at present but the East African railways master plan, a project designed to expand the rail network in this region of Africa, is in its planning stage
Telecommunications – 17,400 fixed lines and 2.247 million mobile subscriptions (2012); there were 157,800 internet users in 2009
Internet code and IDD – bi; 257 (from UK), 44 (to UK)
Major broadcasters – The government-controlled Radio Télévision Nationale du Burundi (RTNB) runs the main national television and radio stations
Press – The only regularly published newspaper is the government-owned *Le Renouveau*
WPFI score – 40,50 (142)

CABO VERDE

Republica de Cabo Verde – Republic of Cabo Verde

Area – 4,033 sq. km; comprises the Windward Islands (Sao Vicente, Santa Luzia, Santo Antao, Sao Nicolau, Boa Vista and Sal) and Leeward Islands (Brava, Fogo, Maio and Sao Tiago)
Capital – Praia, on Sao Tiago; population, 132,000 (2011 est)
Major town – Mindelo
Currency – Escudo Caboverdiano ($) of 100 centavos
Population – 531,046 rising at 1.41 per cent a year (2013 est)
Religion – Christian (Roman Catholic 77.3 per cent, Protestant 3.7 per cent), Muslim 1.8 per cent (est)
Language – Portuguese (official), Creole
Population density – 122 per sq. km (2011)
Urban population – 63.4 per cent (2012 est)
Median age (years) – 23.5 (2013 est)
National anthem – 'Cantico da Liberdade' ['Song of Freedom']
National day – 5 July (Independence Day)
Death penalty – Abolished for all crimes (since 1981)
CPI score – 58 (41)
Literacy rate – 85 per cent (2011 est)
Gross enrolment ratio (percentage of relevant age group) – primary 112 per cent; secondary 90 per cent; tertiary 21 per cent (2011 est)
Life expectancy (years) – 71.28 (2013 est)
Mortality rate – 6.22 (2013 est)
Birth rate – 20.96 (2013 est)
Infant mortality rate – 25.13 (2013 est)

CLIMATE AND TERRAIN
The archipelago of ten islands of volcanic origin lies 600km off the west African coast. Elevation extremes range from 2,829m (Mt Fogo, an active volcano on Fogo island) to 0m (Atlantic Ocean). The climate is hot and dry, with periodic droughts.

HISTORY AND POLITICS
The islands were first discovered and colonised *c.*1460 by Portugal. Administered with Portuguese Guinea until 1879, they became an overseas province in 1951. The country achieved independence on 5 July 1975 after a campaign by the African Party for the Independence of Guinea Bissau and Cape Verde (PAIGC).

The republic was a one-party state under the African Party for the Independence of Cape Verde (PAICV) until 1990. Multiparty elections in 1991 were won by the opposition Movement for Democracy (MPD), and the MPD candidate was elected president. The 2001 legislative elections returned the PAICV to power and the party retained its overall majority in the 2006 and 2011 legislative elections. MPD leader Jorge Fonseca won the 2011 presidential election, taking office in September of that year.

Under the 1992 constitution, the president is directly elected for a five-year term. There is a unicameral National Assembly with 72 members directly elected for a five-year term. The prime minister appoints the council of ministers.

HEAD OF STATE
President, Jorge Fonseca, *elected* 21 August 2011

SELECTED GOVERNMENT MEMBERS *as at February 2014*
Prime Minister, Jose Maria Neves
Deputy Prime Minister, Cristina Lopes de Almeida Fontes Lima
Finance and Planning, Cristina Duarte
Foreign Relations, Jorge Borges
Defence, Jorge Tolentino

EMBASSY OF THE REPUBLIC OF CABO VERDE
Avenue Jeanne 29, 1050 Brussels, Belgium
T (+32) (2) 643 6270
Ambassador Extraordinary and Plenipotentiary, vacant

BRITISH AMBASSADOR
HE John Marshall, *apptd* 2011, resident at Dakar, Senegal

DEFENCE

Aged 16–49, 2010 est	Males	Females
Available for military service	132,087	136,956
Fit for military service	106,864	117,518

Military expenditure – US$9.3m (2013)
Conscription – 18–35 years of age; 24 months (selective)

ECONOMY AND TRADE
The islands have few natural resources, little fresh water and are subject to periods of prolonged drought. A well-managed economy has produced steady growth, and further reforms are intended to attract foreign investment to aid diversification and development of the private sector. Despite becoming a member of the World Trade Organisation in 2008, a large trade deficit leaves the government dependent on foreign aid and remittances; owing to large-scale emigration the expatriate population is larger than the resident one, and remittances are equivalent to over 20 per cent of GDP. The service sector dominates, with commerce, tourism, transport and public services accounting for 71.9 per cent of GDP. Industry contributes 18.8 per cent and agriculture 9.3 per cent; fishing resources are not fully exploited. The main industries are the production of food, beverages, garments and footwear, fishing and fish processing, salt mining and ship repair.

The main trading partners are Portugal, Spain and the Netherlands. Exports are fuel, footwear, garments, fish and

hides. Imports include foodstuffs (over 80 per cent of food is imported), industrial products, transport equipment and fuel.
GNI – US$1,857m; US$3830 per capita (2012)
Annual average growth of GDP – 1.5 per cent (2013 est)
Inflation rate – 1.9 per cent (2013 est)
Population below poverty line – 30 per cent (2000 est)
Total external debt – US$1,328m (2013 est)
Imports – US$766m (2012)
Exports – US$53m (2012)

BALANCE OF PAYMENTS
Trade – US$713m deficit (2012)
Current Account – US$201m deficit (2012)

Trade with UK	2012	2013
Imports from UK	£3,331,964	£13,234,597
Exports to UK	£317,863	£391,947

COMMUNICATIONS
Airports and waterways – Nine, including airports at Praia and on Sal; the main ports are Praia and Mindelo
Roadways – 1,350km, 932km of which are surfaced
Telecommunications – 70,200 fixed lines and 425,300 mobile subscriptions (2012); there were 150,000 internet users in 2009
Internet code and IDD – cv; 238 (from UK), 44 (to UK)
Major broadcasters – Radio and television services are operated by Radiotelevisao Caboverdiana
WPFI Score – 14,32 (24)

CAMBODIA

Preahreacheanachakr Kampuchea – Kingdom of Cambodia

Area – 181,035 sq. km
Capital – Phnom Penh; population, 1,652,995 (2012 est)
Major towns – Battambang, Siem Reap, Poipet
Currency – Riel of 100 sen; the US dollar is widely used
Population – 15,205,539 rising at 1.67 per cent a year (2013 est); Khmer (90 per cent), Vietnamese (5 per cent), Chinese (1 per cent) (est)
Religion – Buddhist (Theravada) 96.9 per cent, Muslim 1.9 per cent (predominantly Sunni) (est)
Language – Khmer (official), French, English
Population density – 83 per sq. km (2011)

Urban population – 20.1 per cent (2012 est)
Median age (years) – 23.7 (2013 est)
National anthem – 'Nokoreach' ['Royal Kingdom']
National day – 9 November (Independence Day)
Death penalty – Abolished for all crimes (since 1989)
CPI score – 20 (160)
Literacy rate – 77.6 per cent (2010 est)
Gross enrolment ratio (percentage of relevant age group) – primary 127 per cent; secondary 46 per cent (2011 est)
Health expenditure (per capita) – US$51 (2011)
Hospital beds (per 1,000 people) – 0.7 (2011)
Life expectancy (years) – 63.41 (2013 est)
Mortality rate – 7.88 (2013 est)
Birth rate – 24.88 (2013 est)
Infant mortality rate – 52.7 (2013 est)

CLIMATE AND TERRAIN
Cambodia is a mostly flat country, apart from the Cardamom Mountains in the south-west and the uplands of the north-east. The fertile central plains are drained by rivers that run into Tonle Sap, the largest lake in South East Asia, and into the Mekong river, which flows through the country from north to south. The highest point of elevation is 1,810m (Phnum Aoral) while the lowest is 0m (Gulf of Thailand). The climate is tropical, with a monsoon season from May to November.

POLITICS
Under the 1993 constitution, Cambodia is a pluralist liberal democracy with a hereditary constitutional monarchy. The monarch is chosen from eligible royal males by a Council of the Throne elected by parliament. Executive power rests with the government, which is responsible to parliament. The bicameral parliament comprises the National Assembly, which has 123 members directly elected for a five-year term, and the senate, which has 61 members, 57 of whom are elected for a six-year term by the National Assembly and commune councils, with two members appointed by the king and two appointed by the National Assembly.

King Sihanouk abdicated in 2004 and was succeeded by his son, Prince Norodom Sihamoni. In the 2013 election the Cambodian People's Party won 68 seats in the National Assembly – losing the large majority that, in the 2008 elections, had allowed them to form a government without a coalition for the first time. Prime Minister Hun Sen, who has been in office since 1985, was sworn in for a further five-year term in September 2013.

HEAD OF STATE
HM The King of Cambodia, Norodom Sihamoni, *crowned* 29 October 2004
President of the National Assembly, Heng Samrin

SELECTED GOVERNMENT MEMBERS *as at February 2014*
Prime Minister, Hun Sen
Deputy Prime Ministers, Gen. Tea Banh *(Defence);* Keat Chhon; Hor Namhong *(Foreign Affairs);* Sar Kheng *(Interior);* Sok An; Yim Chhai Ly; Ben Chhin; Men Sam An; Ke Kim Yan

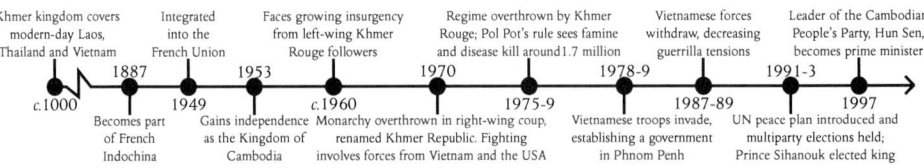

Khmer kingdom covers modern-day Laos, Thailand and Vietnam	Integrated into the French Union	Faces growing insurgency from left-wing Khmer Rouge followers	Regime overthrown by Khmer Rouge; Pol Pot's rule sees famine and disease kill around 1.7 million	Vietnamese forces withdraw, decreasing guerrilla tensions	Leader of the Cambodian People's Party, Hun Sen, becomes prime minister
	1887	1953	1970	1978-9	1991-3
c.1000	1949	c.1960	1975-9	1987-89	1997
	Becomes part of French Indochina	Gains independence as the Kingdom of Cambodia	Monarchy overthrown in right-wing coup, renamed Khmer Republic. Fighting involves forces from Vietnam and the USA	Vietnamese troops invade, establishing a government in Phnom Penh	UN peace plan introduced and multiparty elections held; Prince Sihanouk elected king

ROYAL EMBASSY OF CAMBODIA
64 Brondesbury Park, London NW6 7AT
T 020-8451 7850 E cambodianembassy@btconnect.com
W www.cambodianembassy.org.uk
Ambassador Extraordinary and Plenipotentiary, HE Nambora
Hor, *apptd* 2004

BRITISH EMBASSY
27–29 Street 75, Sangat Srah Chak, Khan Daun Penh, Phnom Penh
12201
T (+855) (0) 23 427 124
W www.gov.uk/government/world/cambodia
Ambassador Extraordinary and Plenipotentiary, HE William
Longhurst, *apptd* 2014

SECURITY PROBLEMS
The Khmer Rouge continued to fight a guerrilla war until
1996, when it was weakened by internal divisions. Pol Pot
was tried by the Khmer Rouge in 1997 and died in captivity
in 1998. The remaining Khmer Rouge soldiers surrendered
in 1999. A UN-backed tribunal was established in 2007 to
try former leaders of the Khmer Rouge regime for atrocities
committed during its rule.

Relations with Thailand deteriorated after 2008 because
of a long-running dispute over the border in the area of the
Preah Vihear temple, with sporadic exchanges of fire and
occasional fighting between the two countries' forces. In
November 2013 the ICJ ruled that Thailand must withdraw
its troops from the temple and granted most of the territory
to Cambodia.

DEFENCE

Aged 16–49, 2010 est	Males	Females
Available for military service	3,883,724	4,003,585
Fit for military service	2,638,167	2,965,328

Military expenditure – US$228m (2013)

ECONOMY AND TRADE
Since 1999 the government has made progress with
economic reform and development but the country remains
very poor. The demographic imbalance (over half the
population is under 25), lack of education and skills, deeply
ingrained corruption and an absence of basic infrastructure
also pose serious problems. Economic growth has been
driven by the expansion of garment manufacturing,
construction, agriculture and tourism, and mining is
attracting foreign investment, but the benefits are largely
limited to urban areas. The discovery of oil and gas deposits
in territorial waters promises additional revenue once
exploitation begins, however, more than half of the
government's budget comes from donor assistance.

The service sector contributes 40.7 per cent of GDP,
agriculture 34.8 per cent and industry 24.5 per cent.
Agriculture engages 55.8 per cent of the workforce; the main
crops are rice, rubber, maize, vegetables, cashew nuts and
tapioca. The main industrial activities are tourism, garment
and textiles manufacturing, processing of agricultural and
forestry products, fishing, and mining gemstones. The main
trading partners are the USA (32.6 per cent of exports),
Thailand (27.1 per cent of imports), Vietnam, the UK and
China.
GNI – US$13,326m; US$880 per capita (2012)
Annual average growth of GDP – 7 per cent (2013 est)
Inflation rate – 3.2 per cent (2013 est)
Population below poverty line – 20 per cent (2012 est)
Unemployment – 0 per cent (2011 est)
Total external debt – US$4,912m (2013 est)

Imports – US$11,000m (2012)
Exports – US$8,200m (2012)

BALANCE OF PAYMENTS
Trade – US$2,800m deficit (2012)
Current Account – US$1,233m deficit (2010)

Trade with UK	2012	2013
Imports from UK	£10,806,497	£17,782,635
Exports to UK	£483,652,148	£589,391,949

COMMUNICATIONS
Airports – Six, the main airports are at Phnom Penh, Siem
Reap and Sihanoukville
Waterways – There are 3,700km of navigable waterways,
mostly on the Mekong river, and ships of up to 2,500 tonnes
can sail as far as Phnom Penh all year round
Roadways and railways – There are 39,619km of roadways, of
which 2,492km are surfaced and 690km of railways
Telecommunications – 584,000 fixed lines and 19.1 million
mobile phone subscriptions (2012); there were 78,500
internet users in 2009
Internet code and IDD – kh; 855 (from UK), 1 44 (to UK)
Major broadcasters – There are seven TV broadcasters, six of
which are either jointly owned or private; there are roughly
50 radio broadcasters, of which one is state-owned. Much of
the press is pro-government and English language
WPFI score – 40,97 (144)

CAMEROON

République du Cameroun – Republic of Cameroon

Area – 475,440 sq. km
Capital – Yaoundé; population, 2,432,000 (2011 est)
Major cities – Bafoussam, Bamenda, Douala, Garoua
Currency – Franc CFA of 100 centimes
Population – 22,534,532 rising at 2.04 per cent a year
(2013 est); Cameroon Highlanders (31 per cent),
Equatorial Bantu (19 per cent), Kirdi (11 per cent), Fulani
(10 per cent), Northwestern Bantu (8 per cent), Eastern
Nigritic (7 per cent) (est)
Religion – Christian 40 per cent, indigenous beliefs 40 per
cent, Muslim 20 per cent (est)
Language – English, French (both official), about 24 African
languages
Population density – 45 per sq. km (2011)
Urban population – 52.7 per cent (2012 est)
Median age (years) – 19.7 (2013 est)
National anthem – 'O Cameroun, Berceau de nos Ancetres'
['O Cameroon, Cradle of Our Forefathers']
National day – 20 May (Republic Day)
Death penalty – Retained (last used 1997)
CPI score – 25 (144)

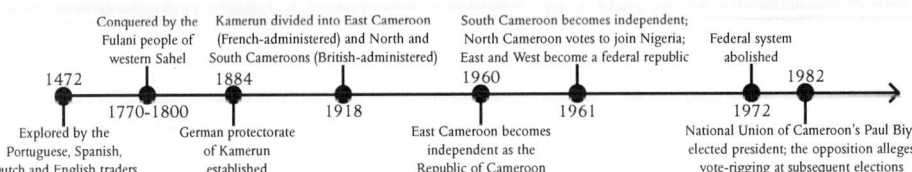

Conquered by the Fulani people of western Sahel

1472

Explored by the Portuguese, Spanish, Dutch and English traders

1770–1800

German protectorate of Kamerun established

1884

Kamerun divided into East Cameroon (French-administered) and North and South Cameroons (British-administered)

1918

East Cameroon becomes independent as the Republic of Cameroon

1960

South Cameroon becomes independent; North Cameroon votes to join Nigeria; East and West become a federal republic

1961

Federal system abolished

1972

National Union of Cameroon's Paul Biya elected president; the opposition alleges vote-rigging at subsequent elections

1982

Literacy rate – 71 per cent (2010 est)
Gross enrolment ratio (percentage of relevant age group) – primary 106 per cent; secondary 47 per cent; tertiary 12 per cent (2011 est)
Health expenditure (per capita) – US$68 (2011)
Hospital beds (per 1,000 people) – 1.3 (2010)
Life expectancy (years) – 55.02 (2013 est)
Mortality rate – 11.51 (2013 est)
Birth rate – 31.93 (2013 est)
Infant mortality rate – 58.51 (2013 est)
HIV/AIDS adult prevalence – 5.3 per cent (2009 est)

CLIMATE AND TERRAIN

There are three main geographic zones: desert plains and savannah in the north (the Lake Chad basin), mountains and plateaux in the central region and tropical rainforests in the south and east. Elevation extremes range from 4,095m (Fako on Mt Cameroon, an active volcano) to 0m (Atlantic Ocean). The climate varies from tropical in the south to arid in the north. There is a wet season from April to September in the north, while there is low rain from March to June and heavy rain from September to November in the south.

POLITICS

The 1972 constitution was amended in 1990 to enable a return to multiparty rule, in 1996 to extend the presidential term and to provide for the establishment of a second legislative chamber (yet to be implemented), and in 2008 to remove the limit on the number of presidential terms.

The president is directly elected for a seven-year term and appoints the prime minister and cabinet. The unicameral National Assembly has 180 members, directly elected for a five-year term.

In the 2013 legislative election, the Cameroon People's Democratic Movement (RDPC) retained its overwhelming majority in the legislature, winning 148 of the available 180 seats. Incumbent president Paul Biya retained the presidency in 2011, picking up 78 per cent of the vote.

HEAD OF STATE
President, Paul Biya, *took power* 6 November 1982, *elected* 14 January 1984, *re-elected* 1988, 1992, 1997, 2004, 2011

SELECTED GOVERNMENT MEMBERS *as at February 2014*
Prime Minister, Philemon Yang
Deputy Prime Minister, Amadou Ali
Economy, Emmanuel Nganou Djoumessi
Foreign Affairs, Pierre Mbonjo

HIGH COMMISSION FOR THE REPUBLIC OF CAMEROON
84 Holland Park, London W11 3SB
T 020-7727 0771 E info@cameroonhighcommission.co.uk
W www.cameroonhighcommission.co.uk
High Commissioner, HE Nkwelle Ekaney, *apptd* 2008

BRITISH HIGH COMMISSION
PO Box 547, Avenue Winston Churchill, Yaoundé
T (+237) 2222 0796 E bhc.yaounde@fco.gov.uk
W www.gov.uk/government/world/cameroon
High Commissioner, HE Brian Olley, *apptd* 2013

DEFENCE

Aged 16–49, 2010 est	Males	Females
Available for military service	4,667,251	4,548,909
Fit for military service	2,794,998	2,718,110

Military expenditure – US$390m (2013)

ECONOMY AND TRADE

Political stability and natural resources such as oil and timber have enabled agricultural, industrial and infrastructure development, although the economy is vulnerable to commodity price fluctuations and so contracted briefly in the global downturn. Cameroon also has a large and top-heavy public sector and endemic corruption, and recent IMF funding and debt relief have been conditional on progress towards privatisation and greater financial transparency.

Industry contributes 27.3 per cent to GDP, agriculture 20.6 per cent and services 52.1 per cent. Around 70 per cent of the workforce is engaged in agriculture. The main industrial activity is oil production and refining. Revenue is also earned from the oil pipeline passing through the country from Chad. Despite starting several large-scale energy projects, Cameroon struggles to appeal to foreign investors due to the structure of its public sector and corruption.

The main trading partners are EU countries, China, Nigeria, India and the USA. Principal exports are crude oil and petroleum products, timber, cocoa, aluminium, coffee and cotton. Imports are chiefly machinery, electrical and transport equipment, fuel and food.

GNI – US$24,876m; US$1,170 per capita (2011 est)
Annual average growth of GDP – 4.6 per cent (2013 est)
Inflation rate – 2.6 per cent (2013 est)
Population below poverty line – 48 per cent (2000 est)
Total external debt – US$3,455m (2013 est)
Imports – US$7,101m (2012)
Exports – US$4,500m (2012)

BALANCE OF PAYMENTS
Trade – US$2,602m deficit (2012)
Current Account – US$677m deficit (2010)

Trade with UK	2012	2013
Imports from UK	£56,919,205	£65,709,955
Exports to UK	£133,442,970	£99,709,343

COMMUNICATIONS

Airports – 11; the main airports are at Douala, Garoua and Yaoundé
Waterways – The main seaports are at Douala and the Limboh terminal. The river Benue is navigable up to Garoua in the rainy season
Roadways and railways – The 51,350km of roadways include 4,108km of surfaced roads linking the main population centres; a rail network of 1,245km links the coast with the capital and the central highlands
Telecommunications – There are 737,400 fixed lines and 13.1 million mobile subscriptions (2012); there were 749,600 internet users in 2009
Internet code and IDD – cm; 237 (from UK), 44 (to UK)

Major broadcasters – The state-run Cameroon Radio-Television Corporation (CRTV) held a monopoly on broadcast media until liberalisation in 2000 allowed commercial television and radio stations to be established; other major broadcasters include Canal 2 and Radio Siantou

Press – Major newspapers include the privately owned *Le Messager* and the state-owned *Cameroon Tribune*

WPFI score – 38,13 (131)

CANADA

Area – 9,984,670 sq. km

Capital – Ottawa; population, 1,208,000 (2011 est)

Major cities – Calgary, Edmonton, Hamilton, Montréal, Québec, Toronto, Vancouver, Winnipeg

Currency – Canadian dollar (C$) of 100 cents

Population – 35,158,300 rising at 0.77 per cent a year (2013 est)

Religion – Christian (Catholic 40.5 per cent, Protestant 20.3 per cent, other 6.3 per cent), Muslim 3.2 per cent, Hindu 1.5 per cent, Sikh 1.4 per cent, Buddhist 1.1 per cent, Jewish 1 per cent (est)

Language – English, French (both official)

Population density – 4 per sq. km (2011)

Urban population – 80.8 per cent (2012 est)

Median age (years) – 41.5 (2013 est)

National anthem – 'O Canada'

National day – 1 July (Canada Day)

Death penalty – Abolished for all crimes (since 1998)

CPI score – 81 (9)

CLIMATE AND TERRAIN

The six main geographic divisions of Canada are: the Appalachian–Acadian region; the Canadian Shield, which comprises more than half the country; the St Lawrence–Great Lakes lowland; the interior plains; the Cordilleran region; and the Arctic archipelago, which lies under continuous permafrost. The most southerly point is Middle Island in Lake Erie. Elevation extremes range from 5,959m (Mt Logan) to 0m (Atlantic Ocean). The climate varies from temperate in the south to subarctic and arctic in the north. The east and centre experience greater extremes than in corresponding latitudes in Europe, but the climate is milder in the south-western part of the prairie region and the southern parts of the Pacific slope. The tornado season is April to September, peaking in June and early July in southern Ontario, Alberta and Québec, Saskatchewan and Manitoba through to Thunder Bay. The interior of British Columbia and western New Brunswick are also tornado zones.

POLITICS

Under the 1982 constitution, the head of state is Queen Elizabeth II, represented by a governor-general appointed on the advice of the Canadian prime minister.

The bicameral parliament consists of a senate and a House of Commons. The senate comprises 105 members, who serve until the age of 75, appointed by the governor-general on the recommendation of the prime minister; seats are assigned on a regional basis. A reform bill introduced in 2011 proposed nine-year non-renewable terms for senators. The House of Commons has 308 members, directly elected for a four-year term. Representation is proportional to the population of each province. Each province is largely self-governing, with its own lieutenant-governor and unicameral legislative assembly. The territories are administered by the federal government.

A parliamentary vote of no confidence ended 12 years of Liberal government in 2005. In snap general elections in 2006 and 2008, the Conservative Party won the most seats, but not a majority, and formed minority governments under Stephen Harper. His government won a snap general election in May 2011, increasing its seats to achieve an overall majority.

GOVERNOR-GENERAL
Governor-General, HE David Johnston, *apptd* 2010

SELECTED GOVERNMENT MEMBERS *as at March 2014*
Prime Minister, Stephen Harper
Defence, Robert Douglas Nicholson
Finance, Joe Oliver
Foreign Affairs, John Baird

CANADIAN HIGH COMMISSION
Macdonald House, 1 Grosvenor Square, London W1K 4AB
T 020-7258 6600 W www.unitedkingdom.gc.ca
High Commissioner, HE Gordon Campbell, *apptd* 2011

BRITISH HIGH COMMISSION
80 Elgin Street, Ottawa, Ontario K1P 5K7
T (+1) (613) 237 1530 E ukincanada@fco.gov.uk
W www.gov.uk/government/world/canada
High Commissioner, HE Howard Drake, OBE, *apptd* 2013

DEFENCE

The Canadian armed forces are unified and organised into three functional commands: land force command, maritime command and air command.

Aged 16–49, 2010 est	Males	Females
Available for military service	8,031,266	7,755,550
Fit for military service	6,633,472	6,389,669

Military expenditure – US$18,704m (2013)

FEDERAL STRUCTURE

Provinces or Territories (with official contractions)	Population (2013)	Area (sq. km)	Capital	Premier
Alberta (AB)	4,025,400	640,081	Edmonton	Alison Redford
British Columbia (BC)	4,587,000	922,509	Victoria	Christy Clark
Manitoba (MB)	1,265,000	552,329	Winnipeg	Greg Selinger
New Brunswick (NB)	756,100	71,377	Fredericton	David Alward
Newfoundland and Labrador (NL)	526,700	370,510	St John's	Tom Marshall
Northwest Territories (NT)	43,500	1,143,793	Yellowknife	Bob McLeod*
Nova Scotia (NS)	940,800	52,939	Halifax	Stephen McNeil
Nunavut (NU)	35,600	1,877,787	Iqaluit	Peter Taptuna*
Ontario (ON)	13,538,000	908,607	Toronto	Kathleen Wynne
Prince Edward Island (PE)	145,200	5,685	Charlottetown	Robert Ghiz
Québec (QC)	8,155,300	1,356,547	Québec City	Pauline Marois
Saskatchewan (SK)	1,108,300	588,239	Regina	Brad Wall
Yukon Territory (YT)	36,700	474,712	Whitehorse	Darrell Pasloski*

* Territorial government leader

ECONOMY AND TRADE

Canada has a highly developed, industrialised and diversified market economy, which was transformed from a predominantly rural to an industrial economy in the second half of the 20th century by the growth of mining, manufacturing and services. Tight management of government finances resulted in balanced budgets from the late 1990s until 2007, and free-trade agreements with the USA in 1989 and 1994 (NAFTA) stimulated trade. The economy went into recession in 2008 owing to the global downturn, although the financial sector proved more stable than that of many other major economies; recovery began in 2010 and marginal growth was achieved in 2011, 2012 and 2013.

Canada's wealth of natural resources make it the world's largest exporter of timber, pulp and newsprint (over half the land is tree-covered), and it is one of the world's largest exporters of minerals, particularly uranium (of which it is the world's second largest single producer) and diamonds. About 5 per cent of the land area is farmed, of which 4.6 per cent is under cultivation, mostly in the prairie region of western Canada. The country is one of the world's leading food producers, particularly of wheat, barley, oilseed, tobacco, fruit, vegetables and dairy products. The fishing industry is also significant but has declined in recent years because of restrictions introduced to protect stocks after decades of overfishing. Oil, natural gas and hydroelectricity production is high enough for Canada to be a net exporter of energy; oil production, in particular, has become a significant economic driver, and Canada's oil reserves are ranked third in the world behind Saudi Arabia and Venezuela. The government has plans to develop the oil and gas-rich Arctic area but the assertion of its sovereignty has attracted criticism from other Arctic countries and is complicated by the lack of international agreement on countries' territorial claims.

In 2013, the services sector contributed 69.9 per cent of GDP, industry 28.4 per cent and agriculture 1.7 per cent.

The USA is Canada's main trading partner, taking 74.5 per cent of exports and providing 50.6 per cent of imports. The main exports are motor vehicles and parts, industrial machinery, aircraft, telecommunications equipment, chemicals, plastics, fertilisers, forestry products, energy products (including crude oil, natural gas and electricity) and aluminium.

GNI – US$1,821,424m; US$50,970 per capita (2012)
Annual average growth of GDP – 1.6 per cent (2013 est)
Inflation rate – 1 per cent (2013 est)
Unemployment – 7.1 per cent (2013 est)
Total external debt – US$1,331,000m (2012 est)
Imports – US$462,423m (2012)
Exports – US$454,833m (2012)

BALANCE OF PAYMENTS
Trade – US$7,591m deficit (2012)
Current Account – US$62,266m deficit (2012)

Trade with UK	2012	2013
Imports from UK	£4,363,368,206	£4,236,148,644
Exports to UK	£5,835,241,282	£5,752,593,117

COMMUNICATIONS

Airports – There are 523 paved airports and airstrips, of which 26 serve major cities
Waterways – There are 636km of waterways and over 300 ports, the most significant of which are Vancouver and Prince Rupert on the Pacific coast and Montréal, Halifax, Port Cartier, Sept-Iles/Pointe Noire, Saint John and Québec in the east. Most deep-water ports are open all year, and Churchill, on Hudson's Bay, is ice-free for longer periods as a result of climate change. In addition, the Great Lakes/ St Lawrence Seaway system, the world's longest inland waterway for ocean-going shipping, provides access to the North American interior
Roadways and railways – There are 1,042,300km of roadways, including 17,000km of motorways; the 46,552km railway network transports over 340 million tonnes of freight each year
Telecommunications – There are 18.01 million fixed lines and 26.263 million mobile telephones subscriptions (2012); there were 26.96 million internet users in 2009
Internet code and IDD – ca; 1 (from UK), 011 44 (to UK)
Major broadcasters – The public broadcaster, the Canadian Broadcasting Corporation (CBC), transmits programmes in English and French, and provides services for indigenous peoples in the north of the country. Société Radio-Canada is the French-language public broadcasting service
Press – Major newspapers include *The Toronto Sun, National Post* and *Le Journal de Montreal*
WPFI score – 10,99 (18)

EDUCATION AND HEALTH

Education is compulsory from ages six to 16 (18 in Ontario and New Brunswick).

Gross enrolment ratio (percentage of relevant age group) – primary 99 per cent; secondary 102 per cent (2011 est)
Health expenditure (per capita) – US$5,630 (2011)
Hospital beds (per 1,000 people) – 3.2 (2010)
Life expectancy (years) – 81.57 (2013 est)
Mortality rate – 8.2 (2013 est)
Birth rate – 10.28 (2013 est)
Infant mortality rate – 4.78 (2013 est)

CENTRAL AFRICAN REPUBLIC

République Centrafricaine – Central African Republic

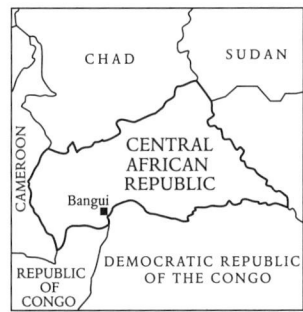

Area – 622,984 sq. km
Capital – Bangui; population, 740,000 (2011 est)
Major cities – Berbérati, Bimbo, Carnot
Currency – Franc CFA of 100 centimes
Population – 5,166,510 rising at 2.14 per cent a year
  (2013 est); Baya (33 per cent), Banda (27 per cent),
  Mandja (13 per cent), Sara (10 per cent), Mboum
  (7 per cent), M'Baka (4 per cent), Yakoma (4 per cent) (est)
Religion – Christian (Protestant denominations 25 per cent,
  Roman Catholic 25 per cent), Muslim 15 per cent (est).
  Some also practise animism, although these beliefs are
  often integrated into Christian and Muslim worship
Language – French (official), Sangho, other African languages
Population density – 7 per sq. km (2011)
Urban population – 39.3 per cent (2012 est)
Median age (years) – 19.3 (2013 est)
National anthem – 'La Renaissance' ['The Rebirth']
National day – 1 December (Republic Day)
Death penalty – Retained (last used 1981)
CPI score – 25 (144)
Literacy rate – 57 per cent (2011 est)
Gross enrolment ratio (percentage of relevant age group) –
  primary 94 per cent; secondary 18 per cent; tertiary
  3 per cent (2011 est)
Health expenditure (per capita) – US$18 (2011)
Hospital beds (per 1,000 people) – 1 (2011)
Life expectancy (years) – 50.9 (2013 est)
Mortality rate – 14.42 (2013 est)
Birth rate – 35.8 (2013 est)
Infant mortality rate – 95.04 (2013 est)
HIV / AIDS adult prevalence – 4.7 per cent (2009 est)

CLIMATE AND TERRAIN

This landlocked state lies on a plateau between the Chad and Congo river basins, with mostly savannah in the north and rainforest in the south. The main river is the Oubangui, which is the lowest point of elevation (335m). The highest point is Mt Ngaoui (1,420m). The climate is tropical, with a wet season in the north from May to September and in the south from May to October. The north can experience average temperatures of up to 34°C between January and April, and the humidity can be extreme. The south has a more equatorial climate with temperatures in the southernmost city of Nola averaging 24.6°C.

POLITICS

Under the 2004 constitution, the president is elected for a five-year term, renewable once. The unicameral National Assembly has 105 members, directly elected for a five-year term. The prime minister is appointed by the president and appoints the ministers.

Legislative elections in January and March 2011 were won by the Kwa Na Kwa (KNK) coalition, a group loyal to President Francois Bozizé. In March 2013 President Bozizé, who initially seized power in 2003 and won presidential elections in 2005 and 2011, fled the country after the New Seleka rebel coalition took the capital by force; the rebel leader Michel Djotodia suspended the constitution and dissolved parliament. Djotodia held power until January 2014 when he was forced to resign after his failure to stop widespread sectarian violence between Seleka and Christian militias. On 20 January Catherine Samba-Panza was elected interim president. Interim governments were formed on 25 January and again on 22 August.

HEAD OF STATE
Interim President, Catherine Samba-Panza *took office*
  January 2014

SELECTED GOVERNMENT MEMBERS *as at*
September 2014
Interim Prime Minister, Mahamat Kamoun
Defence, Aristide So Kambi
Finance, Bernard Bouhandele
Foreign Affairs, Toussaint Kongo Doudou

EMBASSY OF THE CENTRAL AFRICAN REPUBLIC
30 Rue des Perchamps, 75016 Paris, France
(+33) (1) 4224 4256
Ambassador Extraordinary and Plenipotentiary, HE Jean
  Willybiro Sako, *apptd* 2009

BRITISH AMBASSADOR
HE Brian Olley, *apptd* 2013, resident at Yaoundé, Cameroon

DEFENCE

Aged 16–49, 2010 est	Males	Females
Available for military service	1,149,856	1,145,897
Fit for military service	655,875	661,308

Military expenditure – US$54.8m (2010)
Conscription – 18 years of age; 24 months (selective)

ECONOMY AND TRADE

The economy is largely undeveloped owing to decades of instability and misrule. Development is still hindered by political factionalism, a landlocked position and poor transport infrastructure, an unskilled workforce, massively unequal income distribution, and corruption. The country is

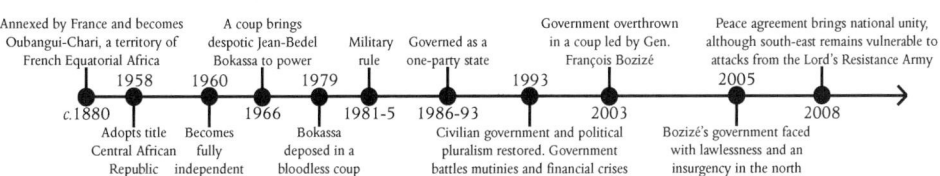

Annexed by France and becomes
Oubangui-Chari, a territory of
French Equatorial Africa
  1958

A coup brings
despotic Jean-Bedel
Bokassa to power
  1960

Military
rule

Governed as a
one-party state

Government overthrown
in a coup led by Gen.
François Bozizé
  1993

Peace agreement brings national unity,
although south-east remains vulnerable to
attacks from the Lord's Resistance Army
  2005

*c.*1880 ●

1966
Adopts title
Central African
Republic

Becomes
fully
independent

1979

1981-5
Bokassa
deposed in a
bloodless coup

1986-93
Civilian government and political
pluralism restored. Government
battles mutinies and financial crises

2003
Bozizé's government faced
with lawlessness and an
insurgency in the north

2008

dependent on international aid and the amount received only partially meets humanitarian needs. Sectarian fighting in 2013 displaced over one million people, resulting in an 11 per cent decline in industrial growth and a 14.5 per cent drop in GDP growth – a significant change from the positive 4.5 per cent recorded the year before.

Natural resources include diamonds, gold, uranium and timber; diamond and gold mining, and forestry are among the main industrial activities but the economy still depends mostly on agriculture, which accounts for over 56 per cent of GDP. Most production is at subsistence level but cotton, coffee and tobacco form the main exports along with diamonds and timber. The main imports are food, textiles, fuels and machinery. Trade is mainly with Belgium, the Netherlands, France and China.

GNI – US$2,183m; US$510 per capita (2012)
Annual average growth of GDP – −14.5 per cent (2013 est)
Inflation rate – 7 per cent (2013 est)
Total external debt – US$634.2m (2013 est)
Imports – US$276m (2012)
Exports – US$112m (2012)

BALANCE OF PAYMENTS
Trade – US$163m deficit (2012)
Current Account – US$122m deficit (2012)

Trade with UK	2012	2013
Imports from UK	£301,470	£659,685
Exports to UK	£24,874	£214,270

COMMUNICATIONS
Airports – Two, the principal airport is at Bangui
Waterways – There are 2,800km of waterways, mostly on the Oubangui and Sangha rivers, that are navigable all year and are important passenger and freight transport routes
Roadways – 20,278km
Telecommunications – There are 5,600 fixed lines and 1.07 million mobile telephone subcriptions (2012); there were 22,600 internet users in 2009
Internet code and IDD – cf; 236 (from UK), 44 (to UK)
Major broadcasters – Only state-run radio and television stations have a national reach; the major broadcasters include Télévision Centrafricaine and privately owned Tropic RTV
Press – There are five privately owned daily newspapers, including *Le Citoyen*, *Le Confident* and *L'Hirondelle*, and one state-owned bi-weekly newspaper, *Centrafique-Presse*
WPFI score – 33,13 (109)

CHAD

République du Tchad / Jumhuriyat Tshad – Republic of Chad

Area – 1,284,000 sq. km
Capital – N'Djamena; population, 873,338 (2012 est)

Major cities – Abéché, Moundou, Sarh
Currency – Franc CFA of 100 centimes
Population – 11,193,452 rising at 1.95 per cent a year (2013 est); the population is made up of around 200 ethnic groups of which Sara, Mayo-Kebbi, Kanem-Bornou, Ouaddai, Hadjarai and Arab are the largest
Religion – Muslim 53.1 per cent, Christian (Catholic 20.1 per cent, Protestant 14.2 per cent), Animist 7.3 per cent
Language – French, Arabic (both official), Sara (in the south)
Population density – 10 per sq. km (2011)
Urban population – 21.9 per cent (2012 est)
Median age (years) – 17 (2013 est)
National anthem – 'La Tchadienne' ['People of Chad']
National day – 11 August (Independence Day)
Death penalty – Retained
CPI score – 19 (163)
Literacy rate – 35 per cent (2011 est)
Gross enrolment ratio (percentage of relevant age group) – primary 91 per cent; secondary 23 per cent; tertiary 2 per cent (2011 est)
Health expenditure (per capita) – US$35 (2011)
Life expectancy (years) – 49.07 (2013 est)
Mortality rate – 14.85 (2013 est)
Birth rate – 37.99 (2013 est)
Infant mortality rate – 91.94 (2013 est)
HIV / AIDS adult prevalence – 2.7 per cent (2012 est)

CLIMATE AND TERRAIN
The population is concentrated in the fertile lowlands of the south, away from the arid central and northern desert areas. The highest point of elevation is 3,415m (Emi Koussi) and the lowest is 160m (the Djourab depression). The climate is desert in the north and tropical in the south, with a wet season from July to September.

HISTORY AND POLITICS
Chad was colonised by France from the 1890s, becoming part of French Equatorial Africa. It became self-governing after the Second World War and independent on 11 August 1960. A one-party state was declared in 1963 by the president, a southerner, which in 1965 prompted a rebellion in the north against a perceived pro-southern bias in the government. Regional and ethnic tensions, most notably between the Muslim Arab north and the Christian and animist African south, underlie the series of rebellions and coups that have made the country politically unstable since independence. Chad's instability was exacerbated from the 1970s to the 1990s by Libya's support for some rebels and its annexation of territory in northern Chad, and since 2004 by the overspill of the Darfur conflict in Sudan.

Idriss Déby seized power in 1990 after leading a rebellion in eastern Chad, and initiated a transition to democracy. A new constitution was introduced in 1996, and the first multiparty elections were held.

Déby won the first multiparty presidential election in 1996 and was re-elected in 2001, 2006 and 2011, despite doubts over the integrity of the polls. The 2011 legislative election was won by Déby's Patriotic Salvation Movement (MPS) and its allies, with 133 seats.

The 1996 constitution was amended in 2005 to remove the limit on the number of terms a president may serve. The president is directly elected for a five-year term. The unicameral National Assembly of 188 members is directly elected for a four-year term. The prime minister is appointed by the president.

HEAD OF STATE
President, Idriss Déby, *took power* December 1990, *elected* 3 July 1996, *re-elected* 2001, 2006, 2011

SELECTED GOVERNMENT MEMBERS *as at February 2014*
Prime Minister, Kalzeubet Pahimi Deubet
Economy, Mariam Mahamat Nour
Finance, Bédoumra Kordjé
Foreign Affairs, Moussa Faki Mahamat
Defence, Benaindo Tatola

EMBASSY OF THE REPUBLIC OF CHAD
Boulevard Lambermont 52, 1030 Brussels, Belgium
T (+32) (2) 215 1975 W www.ambassadedutchad.be
Ambassador Extraordinary and Plenipotentiary, HE Ousmane Matar Breme, *apptd* 2013

BRITISH AMBASSADOR
HE Brian Olley, *apptd* 2013, resident at Yaoundé, Cameroon

INSURGENCIES
The series of insurgencies over the decades since independence means that no government has ever controlled the whole of the country. Rebel offensives reached the capital in 2006 and 2008 before being repulsed. In 2009, eight rebel groups united to form the Union of Resistance Forces alliance.

From 2004, the east and south-east were further destabilised by the overspill of fighting from Sudan's Darfur region, with some militias mounting cross-border incursions to attack the estimated 250,000 Sudanese refugees in Chad. The EU/UN mission deployed in 2008 to protect Sudanese refugees in Chad was withdrawn in 2010, and relations with Sudan have now been normalised and the border reopened. An estimated 185,000 Chadians have also been displaced by the incursions, the insurgencies and Chadian ethnic violence. In 2012, the leader of rebel group FPR (Popular Front for Recovery), Abdel Kader Baba Ladde, surrendered to military forces in the Central African Republic and returned to Chad. In 2013, following a coup in the Central African Republic, a regional summit in Chad agreed that neighbouring countries should send troops to restore security to the region.

DEFENCE

Aged 16–49, 2010 est	Males	Females
Available for military service	2,090,244	2,441,321
Fit for military service	1,183,242	1,395,811

Military expenditure – US$242m (2011 est)
Conscription – 20 years of age, male only; 36 months (women are subject to 12 months of service at age 21)

ECONOMY AND TRADE
Economic development has been limited by political instability, corruption, the landlocked location and poor transport infrastructure. About 80 per cent of the workforce is occupied in subsistence agriculture, herding and fishing, which contributes over 46 per cent of GDP, and the remaining 20 per cent are practically all employed in services, which contribute 43.8 per cent of GDP. The main focus of development, funded by foreign investment and international aid, is the exploitation of oil deposits in the Doba basin in the south, which came into production in 2003; the oil is exported via a pipeline through Cameroon, and a refinery is under construction. Other industries include processing cotton (the main industry before oil) and other agricultural products, and light manufacturing. Industry generates 9.9 per cent of GDP. In 2013 the economy suffered from the costs of repatriating Chadians escaping violence in South Sudan and the Central African Republic.

Chad's main trading partners are the USA (81.9 per cent of exports), France, China and Cameroon. Principal exports are oil, cattle, cotton and gum arabic. The main imports are machinery and transport equipment, industrial goods, food and textiles.
GNI – US$9,751m; US$770 per capita (2012)
Annual average growth of GDP – 3.9 per cent (2013 est)
Inflation rate – 4.5 per cent (2013 est)
Population below poverty line – 80 per cent (2001 est)
Total external debt – US$1,828m (2013 est)
Imports – US$2,600m (2012)
Exports – US$3,901m (2012)

BALANCE OF PAYMENTS
Trade – US$1,301m surplus (2012)
Current Account – US$956m deficit (2010)

Trade with UK	2012	2013
Imports from UK	£7,528,360	£11,154,871
Exports to UK	£172,933	£407,048

COMMUNICATIONS
Airports and waterways – Nine, the principal airport is at N'Djamena; the Chari and Legone rivers are navigable only in the wet season
Roadways – Of the 40,000km of roads, only 206km are surfaced
Telecommunications – There are 29,900 fixed lines and 4.2 million mobile subscriptions (2012); there were 168,100 internet users in 2009
Internet code and IDD – td; 235 (from UK), 15 44 (to UK)
Major broadcasters – The only television station, Télé-Tchad, is state-owned and its coverage favours the government; Radiodiffusion Nationale Tchadienne is the state-controlled radio station
Press – Le Progres is the country's only daily newspaper; there are four other privately owned weeklies, including N'Djamena Hebdo and Le Temps
WPFI score – 40,22 (139)

CHILE

República de Chile – Republic of Chile

Area – 756,102 sq. km
Capital – Santiago; population, 6,079,500 (2012 est)
Major cities – Antofagasta, Concepción, Puente Alto, San Bernardo, Temuco, Valparaíso, Viña del Mar
Currency – Chilean peso ($) of 100 centavos
Population – 17,216,945 rising at 0.86 per cent a year (2013 est)
Religion – Christian (Roman Catholic 66.7 per cent, Protestant 16.4 per cent) (est)
Language – Spanish (official), Mapudungun, English, other indigenous languages

Population density – 23 per sq. km (2011)
Urban population – 89.4 per cent (2012 est)
Median age (years) – 33 (2013 est)
National anthem – 'Himno Nacional de Chile' ['National Anthem of Chile']
National day – 18 September (Independence Day)
Death penalty – Retained for certain crimes (last used 1985)
CPI score – 71 (22)

CLIMATE AND TERRAIN
Chile extends over 4,600km from the arid north around Arica to Cape Horn, with an average breadth of 180km. The Atacama desert lies in the north. In the central zone there is a fertile valley between the Andes and the low coastal range of mountains, with a Mediterranean climate; two-thirds of the population live here. Chilean Patagonia, in the south, extends into subantarctic terrain, with glaciers and icefields; the climate is cool with high precipitation. Elevation extremes range from 6,880m (Nevado Ojos del Salado) to 0m (Pacific Ocean). Its Pacific island possessions include the Juan Fernández group and Easter Island, and the Chilean Antarctic Territory covers the Antarctic peninsula and an area of the landmass that extends from 53°W. to 90°W. along a latitude of 60°S.

HISTORY AND POLITICS
Chile was conquered in the 16th century by the Spanish, who subjugated the indigenous population. It remained under Spanish rule until 1810, when the first autonomous government was established. Independence was achieved in 1818 after a revolutionary war.

A military coup in 1973 overthrew the Marxist president Salvador Allende. General Augusto Pinochet, the coup leader, assumed the presidency and retained the office until elections were held in 1989, beginning the transition to full democracy. Between 1998 and his death in 2006, a number of unsuccessful attempts were made to bring Gen. Pinochet to trial for human rights atrocities committed during his time in office.

In the 2013 legislative elections, the centre-left New Majority coalition won 67 seats, 18 more than the incumbent Alliance for Chile, in the lower chamber, and 21 of the 38 seats in the senate. Michelle Bachelet, the former president and the candidate of the Socialist Party of Chile (part of the New Majority), won the 2013 presidential election.

The 1981 constitution was amended in 1989 and 2005. The executive president is directly elected for a four-year term that is not renewable. The bicameral National Congress comprises a senate of 38 members elected for an eight-year term (half renewed every four years) and a Chamber of Deputies of 118 members directly elected for a four-year term.

HEAD OF STATE
President, Michelle Bachelet, *elected* 10 January 2014, *sworn in* 11 March 2014

SELECTED GOVERNMENT MEMBERS *as at March 2014*
Defence, Jorge Burgos Varela
Economy, Luis Felipe Céspedes
Finance, Alberto Arenas de Mesa
Interior, Rodrigo Peñailillo Briceño

EMBASSY OF CHILE
37–41 Old Queen Street, London SW1H 9JA
T 020-7222 2361 E embachile@embachile.co.uk
W www.chileabroad.gov.cl/reino-unido
Ambassador Extraordinary and Plenipotentiary, HE Tomás E. Müller Sproat, *apptd* 2010

BRITISH EMBASSY
Avda. El Bosque Norte 0125, Las Condes, Santiago
T (+56) (2) 370 4100 E embsan@britemb.cl
W www.gov.uk/government/world/chile
Ambassador Extraordinary and Plenipotentiary, HE Fiona Clouder, *apptd* 2014

DEFENCE

Aged 16–49, 2010 est	*Males*	*Females*
Available for military service	4,324,732	4,251,954
Fit for military service	3,621,475	3,561,099

Military expenditure – US$5,309m (2013)

ECONOMY AND TRADE
Economic reforms in the late 1970s and the 1980s and sound financial management have made Chile one of the most successful economies in Latin America; in 2010 it became the first South American country to join the OECD. Growth is based on high copper prices, a strong export base and growing domestic demand. Although the economy contracted slightly in 2009 owing to the global downturn, it began to recover later that year and GDP has grown at over five per cent every year since. In 2012, foreign investment reached a record US$28.2 billion, a 63 per cent increase on the previous record in 2011.

Chile is the world's largest producer of copper, and the world's only commercial producer of nitrate of soda (Chile saltpetre) from natural resources. The chief industries are mining, forestry, fishing, food and fish processing, and winemaking.

The main trading partners are the USA, China, Brazil, Argentina and Japan. Principal exports are copper, fruit, fish products, paper and pulp, chemicals and wine. The main imports are petrol and petroleum products, chemicals, electrical and telecommunications equipment, industrial machinery, vehicles and natural gas.

GNI – US$257,127m; US$14,310 per capita (2012)
Annual average growth of GDP – 4.4 per cent (2013 est)
Inflation rate – 1.7 per cent (2013 est)
Population below poverty line – 15.1 per cent (2009 est)
Unemployment – 6 per cent (2013 est)
Total external debt – US$119,000m (2013 est)
Imports – US$79,080m (2012)
Exports – US$79,712m (2012)

BALANCE OF PAYMENTS
Trade – US$632m surplus (2012)
Current Account – US$9,081m deficit (2012)

Trade with UK	*2012*	*2013*
Imports from UK	£648,879,262	£1,076,832,437
Exports to UK	£565,006,691	£610,752,462

COMMUNICATIONS
Airports and waterways – 90, the principal airport is at Santiago; the main ports are Arica, Antofagasta, Coquimbo, San Antonio, Talcahuano and Valparaíso
Roadways and railways – 77,764km of roadways, of which 18,119km are surfaced; 7,082km of railways
Telecommunications – 3.276 million fixed lines and 24.13 million mobile subscriptions (2012); there were around 7 million internet users in 2009
Internet code and IDD – cl; 56 (from UK), 44 (to UK)
Major broadcasters – The National Television of Chile is state-owned but not under direct government control; Radio Cooperativa is a news-based private network which broadcasts alongside numerous other private radio stations

Press – Major newspaper publications include *El Mercurio,* a conservative daily, and *La Nación,* a government-owned daily
WPFI score – 25,80 (58)

EDUCATION AND HEALTH

Education is free and compulsory from ages six to 17, although the education system has suffered from under-investment and mismanagement resulting in ongoing student protests.
Literacy rate – 98.6 per cent (2010 est)
Gross enrolment ratio (percentage of relevant age group) – primary 102 per cent; secondary 90 per cent; tertiary 71 per cent (2011 est)
Health expenditure (per capita) – US$1,075 (2011)
Hospital beds (per 1,000 people) – 2 (2010)
Life expectancy (years) – 78.27 (2013 est)
Mortality rate – 5.86 (2013 est)
Birth rate – 14.12 (2013 est)
Infant mortality rate – 7.19 (2013 est)

CHINA

Zhonghua Renmin Gongheguo – *People's Republic of China*

Area – 9,596,961 sq. km
Capital – Beijing; population, 15,594,000 (2012 est)
Major cities – Chengdu, Chongqing, Dongguan, Foshan, Guangzhou, Nanjing, Shanghai, Shenyang, Shenzhen, Tianjin, Wuhan, Xi'an
Currency – Renminbi (RMB) or yuan (Y) of ten jiao or 100 fen
Population – 1,349,585,838 rising at 0.46 per cent a year (2013 est); Han Chinese (91.56 per cent), around 55 ethnic minorities (8.5 per cent) (2000)
Religion – officially atheist, but permits four state-registered religions: Buddhism, Taoism, Islam, and Catholic and Protestant Christianity. It is difficult to estimate numbers, as many congregations worship in private; Mahayana Buddhism and Taoism are the predominant faiths but Christianity is growing rapidly
Language – Mandarin (official), Cantonese, Shanghainese, Fuzhou, Xiang, Gan, Taiwanese; common speech, or *putonghua* (often referred to as Mandarin), is based on the northern dialect and is promoted throughout the country
Population density – 144 per sq. km (2011)

Urban population – 51.9 per cent (2012 est)
Median age (years) – 36.3 (2013 est)
National anthem – 'Yiyongjun Jinxingqu' ['The March of the Volunteers']
National day – 1 October (Founding of People's Republic)
Death penalty – Retained
CPI score – 40 (80)

CLIMATE AND TERRAIN

China is twice the size of western Europe and contains a vast range of landscapes and climates. The highest mountains are on the Tibetan plateau, in the west of the country, where the highest elevation is 8,850m (Mt Everest). To the north of the Tibetan plateau, the land drops to the arid, semi-desert steppes bisected by the Tian Shan mountains; the country's lowest elevation is −154m at Turpan Pendi. The southern plains and east coast have the most fertile land, irrigated by the Huang He (Yellow), Chang Jiang (Yangtze) and Xi Jiang (West) rivers, and are the most heavily populated areas.

There are seven climate zones. The north-east has cold winters, fierce winds, warm and humid summers and erratic rainfall. The mountainous south-west has mild winters and warm summers. Inner Mongolia has cold winters and hot summers. Central China has warm and humid summers with occasional tropical cyclones. South China is partly tropical with heavy rainfall. The high Tibet plateau is subject to harsh winters. Xinjiang and the west have a desert climate, with cold winters and little rain.

POLITICS

The Communist Party of China is the dominant political party, and all elements of the political system are subordinate to it. A party congress is held every five years and elects the Politburo and its standing committee. This standing committee is the policy- and decision-making body and the *de facto* government.

Under the 1982 constitution, the National People's Congress (NPC) is the highest organ of state power. It has 2,987 members, indirectly elected for a five-year term, and holds only one full session a year; between sessions, its work is delegated to its standing committee. The congress elects the premier and, on his nomination, the State Council. The head of state is the president, also elected by the congress, who serves a five-year term, renewable once.

Deputies to people's congresses at the primary level are directly elected by the voters from a list of approved candidates. These congresses elect the deputies to the congress at the next highest level. Deputies to the NPC are elected by the provincial and municipal people's congresses, and by the armed forces.

Local government is conducted through people's governments at provincial/municipal, prefecture/city, county/district, township and village levels. There are 22 provinces (Taiwan is claimed as a 23rd province), four municipalities directly under the central government, five autonomous regions, and two special administrative areas; provinces may contain autonomous counties or towns for ethnic minorities.

In 2012 Xi Jinping took over as General Secretary of the Communist Party of China, becoming president in 2013. He stated that he aimed to make corruption-free governance

Last emperor of the Qing dynasty abdicates. Revolution spreads	Japan occupies Manchuria and other areas	Internal disagreements result in Japan's occupation of most northern and coastal areas	CCP victors of civil war. The party inaugurates the People's Republic of China and the KMT goes into exile in Taiwan		Pro-democracy demonstrations, centred on Tiananmen Square in Beijing, lead to the deaths of over 3,000 protestors

2000 · 1927 · 1934-5 · 1945 · 1958-61 · 1966-70 · 2003

1912 · 1932 · 1939 · 1946-9 · 1989

Ruled by imperial dynasties · The KMT forms a government in Nanjing · The Chinese Communist Party breaks and retreats in the 'Long March' · Japanese occupation ended by the Allies. CCP seizes control over territory · Millions die from famine after Mao Zedong's 'Great Leap Forward'; an attempt to industrialise rural areas · Cultural Revolution · Hu Jintao is elected president and economic growth key elements of his administration, the former of which has resulted in several high-profile purges of senior officials.

HEAD OF STATE
President, Xi Jinping, *elected* 14 March 2013
Vice-President, Li Yuanchao

STATE COUNCIL *as at February 2014*
Premier, Li Keqiang
Vice-Premiers, Zhang Gaoli; Ma Kai; Liu Yandong; Wang Yang
State Councillors, Yang Jiechi; Yang Jing; Guo Shengkun; Wang Yong; Chang Wanquan

SELECTED GOVERNMENT MEMBERS *as at February 2014*
Civil Affairs, Li Liguo
Finance, Lou Jiwei
Foreign Affairs, Wang Yi

EMBASSY OF THE PEOPLE'S REPUBLIC OF CHINA
49–51 Portland Place, London W1B 1JL
T 020-7299 4049 W www.chinese-embassy.org.uk
Ambassador Extraordinary and Plenipotentiary, HE Liu Xiaoming, *apptd* 2010

BRITISH EMBASSY
11 Guang Hua Lu, Jian Guo Men Wai, Beijing 100600
T (+86) 0(10) 5192 4000 E consular.beijing@fco.gov.uk
W www.gov.uk/government/world/china
Ambassador, HE Sir Sebastian Wood, KCMG, *apptd* 2010

HUMAN RIGHTS
Liberalisation has allowed ordinary people greater personal choice: they can now travel freely, for example, or change professions. However, freedom of expression, religion and association are still tightly controlled, and the regime firmly suppresses dissent by ethnic minorities or other groups that it perceives as a threat to its authority. This has led to moves against separatists from the Uygur Muslim minority group in Xinjiang Autonomous Region since the 1990s, the banning of the Falun Gong spiritual movement in 1999 and the violent suppression of demonstrations in Tibet in 2008. Religious gatherings that have not been approved by the state-sanctioned religious bodies are broken up by the authorities and their leaders harassed; despite this, all religions are experiencing a revival throughout China, and underground Protestant churches in particular are growing rapidly. In 2011 the arrest of artist Ai Weiwei, a prominent critic of the Chinese government, sparked international controversy.

DEFENCE
All three military arms are part of the People's Liberation Army (PLA).

Aged 16–49, 2010 est	Males	Females
Available for military service	385,821,101	363,789,674
Fit for military service	318,265,016	300,323,611

Military expenditure – US$171,381m (2013)
Conscription – 18–24 years of age; 24 months (selective)

ECONOMY AND TRADE
Liberalisation since the 1980s has transformed the economy, developing a more autonomous state sector, a rapidly growing private sector and a leading presence in global trade and investment. A massive industrial base and transport infrastructure have been constructed, especially in the coastal regions, and the economy has become a free market in all but name, with several stock markets and Shanghai's emergence as a financial centre. China attracts considerable foreign investment and has become a major investor overseas. GDP has grown more than ten-fold since 1978, and China's economy is now the second-largest in the world after the US.

Although some 250 million people who migrated to urban areas have been lifted out of poverty in the past two decades, the effects of the rapid transformation have been unevenly distributed. In 2012 it was reported China's city dwellers outnumber China's rural population for the first time; there are wide income differences between urban and rural areas, poor healthcare provision, lack of access to public services for migrant workers, rampant official corruption and environmental degradation of land, water and air. The government is also keen to increase domestic consumption (a priority of the 2011–16 five-year plan), and so reduce the economy's reliance on exports for growth, especially as foreign demand slowed in 2008 and plummeted in 2009 owing to the global economic downturn. Nevertheless, China remains the world's largest exporter.

China's expansion boosted its need for oil and coal, met initially by imports but increasingly by domestic production. However, to achieve its aim of reducing environmental degradation, China is looking more to nuclear power (although nuclear approval has been suspended indefinitely owing to safety concerns following the Fukushima Daiichi plant disaster in Japan) and alternative energy generation, such as hydroelectric power from the Three Gorges Dam.

Although rural areas have seen few benefits from the economic transformation and are suffering the effects of rural depopulation and pollution, agriculture remains important; it contributes 9.7 per cent of GDP but employs 34.8 per cent of the workforce. The main crops are rice, cereals, vegetables, peanuts, tea, fruit, cotton and oilseed crops. Livestock is raised in large numbers. Silk farming is one of the oldest industries. Cotton, woollen and silk textiles are manufactured in large quantities.

The highly diversified industrial sector, encompassing heavy industry, manufacturing and construction, contributes 45.3 per cent of GDP and employs 29.5 per cent of the workforce. The services sector accounts for 45 per cent of GDP and 35.7 per cent of employment. Tourism is now a major industry.

Exports include machinery, electrical equipment, data processing equipment, garments, textiles, iron and steel, and optical and medical equipment. The principal imports are electrical and other machinery, oil and mineral fuels, optical and medical equipment, metal ores, plastics and organic chemicals. The main trading partners are the USA, Hong Kong, Japan, South Korea and Australia, although trade with Latin America and Africa is growing.

GNI – US$8,184,963m; US$5,720 per capita (2012)
Annual average growth of GDP – 7.6 per cent (2013 est)
Inflation rate – 2.6 per cent (2013 est)
Population below poverty line – 13.4 per cent (2011 est)
Unemployment – 6.4 per cent (2013 est)
Total external debt – US$784,800m (2013 est)
Imports – US$1,817,780m (2012)
Exports – US$2,048,940m (2012)

BALANCE OF PAYMENTS
Trade – US$231,160m surplus (2012)
Current Account – US$193,139m surplus (2012)

Trade with UK	2012	2013
Imports from UK	£9,892,397,758	£11,584,076,894
Exports to UK	£30,021,348,271	£31,576,127,681

COMMUNICATIONS

Airports – There are 463 airports and airfields and several national air carriers

Waterways – The main seaports are Shanghai and Dalian in the north, and Guangzhou in the south; there are 110,000km of navigable waterways, Nanjing is the largest river port, and the Huang He (Yellow), Chang Jiang (Yangtze) and Xi Jiang (West) are the most significant river routes

Roadways – The 4,106,387km road network allows access to all towns and villages, and the major cities are linked by 84,946km of modern highways

Railways – The rail system has 86,000km of track, although only 36,000km is electrified; extension of the Qinghai–Tibet railway has opened up the remote western province

Telecommunications – 278.86 million fixed lines and 1.1 billion mobile subscriptions (2012); there were 618 million internet users in 2013

Internet code and IDD – cn; 86 (from UK), 44 (to UK)

Major broadcasters – The Communist Party maintains a firm grip on the media and the internet. Television is the most popular medium in a huge media industry; state-run stations offer around 2,100 channels, and in 2013 over 210m households had cable subscription services

Press – Every city has its own newspaper, as well as a local Communist Party publication; approximately 2,000 newspapers are published every week

WPFI score – 72,91 (175)

EDUCATION AND HEALTH

Primary education lasts six years and secondary education six years (three years in junior middle school and three optional years in senior middle school).

Literacy rate – 95 per cent (2010 est)

Gross enrolment ratio (percentage of relevant age group) – primary 128 per cent; secondary 87 per cent; tertiary 24 per cent (2011 est)

Health expenditure (per capita) – US$278 (2011)

Hospital beds (per 1,000 people) – 3.8 (2011)

Life expectancy (years) – 74.99 (2013 est)

Mortality rate – 7.31 (2013 est)

Birth rate – 12.25 (2013 est)

Infant mortality rate – 15.2 (2013 est)

TIBET

Area – 1,199,164 sq. km

Population – 3,002,166 (2011 est)

Capital – Lhasa

Tibet is a plateau, seldom lower than 3,000m, in south-west China. It forms the frontier with India (boundary imperfectly demarcated), from which it is separated by the Himalayas from Kashmir to Myanmar; Nepal and Bhutan also border it to the south. The Indus, Brahmaputra, Mekong and Yangtze rivers all rise on the Tibet plateau.

Tibet was under Mongol rule almost continuously from the 13th to the 17th centuries. Chinese control grew from the 18th century and direct rule began in 1910, but with the collapse of the Chinese Empire in 1911, Tibet declared its independence and the Dalai Lama ruled undisturbed until Communist rule was established in China. In 1950 Chinese Communist forces invaded Tibet, and in 1951 the Tibetan authorities signed a treaty agreeing joint Chinese–Tibetan rule. A series of revolts against Chinese rule culminated in a 1959 uprising in the capital, which was crushed following several days of fighting after which military rule was imposed. The Dalai Lama fled to India where he and his followers were granted political asylum and established a government in exile. Tibet became an Autonomous Region

of China in 1965. Martial law was declared in Tibet in 1989.

The Panchen Lama, the second-highest Lama, remained in Lhasa after 1959; when he died in 1989, China rejected the Dalai Lama's choice of successor and enthroned its own candidate. Subsequent appointments have been handled in a similar manner. Despite occasional talks between the Chinese government and representatives of the Dalai Lama, relations remain poor. In March 2011, the Dalai Lama announced his intention to withdraw from political life, transferring leadership to Lobsang Sangay, prime minister of the Tibetan parliament. In September 2012 his title was amended to political leader (*Sikyong*).

Another source of tension is the large number of Chinese migrants who have settled in Tibet since the 1970s, a development that the Tibetan government-in-exile regards as an attempt to eradicate the culture of the Tibetan people. Chinese now considerably outnumber Tibetans and have benefited disproportionately from the economic development of recent years.

Peaceful anti-Chinese demonstrations in Tibet increased in early 2008 as the imminence of the Beijing Olympics put China's human rights record under greater international scrutiny. The violence of the Chinese crackdown was condemned worldwide, and pro-Tibet activists abroad disrupted the Olympic torch relay in several countries. Resistance and unrest continue: in 2009, in a show of passive resistance, farmers in Tibet and neighbouring provinces refused to till the fields or plant crops; in 2011, demonstrations sparked by the self-immolation of a Tibetan monk in the Sechuan province led to hundreds of arrests. More than 100 other self-immolations were reported over the course of the next two years.

SPECIAL ADMINISTRATIVE REGIONS

HONG KONG

Xianggang Tebie Xingzhengqu – Hong Kong Special Administrative Region

Area – 1,104 sq. km

Currency – Hong Kong dollar (HK$) of 100 cents

Population – 7,112,688 rising at 0.41 per cent a year (2014 est)

Population density – 6,787 per sq. km (2011)

Flag – Red, with a white bauhinia flower of five petals each containing a red star

National day – 1 July (Establishment Day)

Death penalty – Abolished for all crimes (since 2003)

CPI score – 75 (15)

CLIMATE AND TERRAIN

Hong Kong consists of Hong Kong Island, Kowloon and the New Territories (on a peninsula of the mainland in Guangdong province) and over 260 islands, including Lantau Island. Hong Kong Island is about 18km long and 3–8km wide. It is separated from the mainland by a narrow strait. The highest point is Tai Mo Shan (958m). The climate is subtropical, with hot, wet summers and cool, dry winters. Mean monthly temperatures range from 16°C to 29°C. Tropical cyclones occur between May and November, and over 75 per cent of the average annual rainfall of 2,180mm falls between May and September.

HISTORY AND POLITICS

Hong Kong developed as a major regional trading port because of its location on the main Far Eastern trade routes. Hong Kong Island was first occupied by Britain in 1841 and formally ceded to Britain in 1842. Kowloon was acquired in 1860, and the New Territories by a 99-year lease signed in 1898.

In 1984, the UK and China agreed that China would resume sovereignty over Hong Kong in 1997, and on 1 July 1997, Hong Kong became a Special Administrative Region (SAR) of the People's Republic of China. The 1984 joint declaration and the Basic Law (1990) guarantee that the SAR's social and economic systems will remain unchanged for 50 years and grant it a high degree of autonomy.

Although the Basic Law provides for the development of democratic processes, political reform has been slow, prompting frequent demonstrations to demand full democracy or to oppose measures perceived to be repressive. In 2007 the Chinese government said that the chief executive could be directly elected from 2017 and the legislature members from 2020.

The Basic Law, approved in 1990, has served as Hong Kong's constitution since 1997. Its government is headed by the chief executive, who is elected by a 1200-member electoral committee and serves a five-year term. The chief executive is aided by an executive council consisting of 15 principal officials, who are the heads of administrative departments, and 14 non-official members. The legislative council consists of 70 members, 35 directly elected by geographic constituencies, and 30 elected by functional, occupation-based constituencies; they serve a four-year term.

Leung Chun-ying was elected chief executive in March 2012, replacing Donald Tsang, who served two terms between 2005 and 2012. In the 2012 legislative elections, pro-China parties won 43 seats while pro-democracy parties won 27.

Chief Executive, Leung Chun-ying, *elected* 25 March 2012, *sworn in* 1 July 2012

SELECTED GOVERNMENT MEMBERS *as at March 2014*
Chief Secretary for Administration, Carrie Lam Cheng Yuet-ngor
Financial Secretary, John Tsang Chun-wah
Secretary for Justice, Rimsky Yuen Kwok-keung

BRITISH CONSULATE-GENERAL
PO Box 528, 1 Supreme Court Road, Central Hong Kong
T (+852) 2901 3000 E hongkong.consular@fco.gov.uk
W www.gov.uk/government/world/hong-kong
Consul-General, Caroline Wilson, *apptd* 2012

ECONOMY AND TRADE
The economy has moved away from manufacturing (which has mostly relocated to mainland China) and is now service-based, with a high reliance on international trade and re-exports. It has developed into a regional corporate and banking centre, and has benefited in recent years from closer integration with China through increased trade, tourism and financial links. Although badly affected by the global economic downturn in 2008–9, and vulnerable to future volatility, the strength of the Chinese economy helped it to recover quickly.

The economy is dominated by the service sector, which accounted for 93 per cent of GDP in 2013. The main contributors to this are tourism, financial services and shipping. Industry contributes 6.9 per cent of GDP. Principal products are textiles, clothing, electronics, plastics, toys, clocks and watches.

The principal export markets are China (57.7 per cent), the USA and Japan. China is also Hong Kong's principal supplier of imported goods (44.5 per cent).

GNI – US$268,865m; US$36,560 per capita (2012)
Annual average growth of GDP – 3 per cent (2013 est)
Inflation rate – 4.3 per cent (2013 est)
Unemployment – 3.1 per cent (2013 est)
Imports – US$504,405m (2012)
Exports – US$442,799m (2012)

BALANCE OF PAYMENTS
Trade – US$61,606m deficit (2012)
Current Account – US$12,908m surplus (2011)

Trade with UK	2012	2013
Imports from UK	£5,037,428,889	£5,256,336,801
Exports to UK	£7,062,651,870	£6,972,668,817

COMMUNICATIONS
Airports – There are two airports, one accommodating international flights
Waterways – Hong Kong has one of the world's finest natural harbours, and is the third-busiest container port in the world
Roadways – 2,090km (2012)
Telecommunications – 4.346 million fixed lines and 16.403 million mobile subscriptions (2012); there were 4.873 million internet users in 2009
Internet code and IDD – hk; 852 (from UK), 1 44 (to UK)
WPFI score – 26,55 (61)

EDUCATION AND HEALTH
Education is free and compulsory for children up to age 15.
Gross enrolment ratio (percentage of age group) – primary 98 per cent; secondary 86 per cent; tertiary 60 per cent (2011 est)
Life expectancy (years) – 82.78 (2014 est)
Mortality rate – 6.93 (2014 est)
Birth rate – 9.38 (2014 est)
Infant mortality rate – 2.73 (2014 est)

MACAU (AOMEN)
Aomen Tebie Xingzhengqu – Macau Special Administrative Region

Area – 28.2 sq. km
Currency – Pataca (MOP$) of 100 avos
Population – 587,914 rising at 0.83 per cent a year (2014 est)
Population density – 19,510 per sq. km (2011)
Flag – Green, with a white lotus flower above a white stylised bridge and water, under a large gold five-point star and four gold stars in crescent
National day – 20 December (Establishment Day)
Internet code and IDD – mo; 853 (from UK), 44 (to UK)

CLIMATE AND TERRAIN
Macau consists of the Macau peninsula and the islands of Coloane and Taipa. It is situated at the western side of the mouth of the Pearl river, bordering Guangdong province in south-east China. It is 64km from Hong Kong. Its area has nearly doubled since the 19th century due to land reclamation. The highest point is Coloane Alto (172m). The climate is subtropical.

HISTORY AND POLITICS
The first Portuguese ship arrived at Macau in 1513 and trade with China commenced in 1553. Macau became a Portuguese colony in 1557; China recognised Portugal's sovereignty over Macau by treaty in 1887. An agreement to transfer the administration of Macau to China was signed in 1987, and Macau became the Macau Special Administrative Region (MSAR) of China on 20 December 1999. Fernando Chui was elected unopposed as chief executive in 2009, and the most recent legislative election was held in September 2009.

The Basic Law (1993) has served as Macao's constitution since 1999. The chief executive is elected by a 300-member election committee and serves a five-year term of office, which may be renewed once. The chief executive is assisted by the ten-member executive council. The legislative assembly has 29 members, who serve for four years; 12 are directly elected in geographic constituencies, ten are indirectly elected in functional constituencies and seven are appointed by the chief executive.

Chief Executive, Fernando Chui Sai On, *elected* July 2009, *sworn in* 20 December 2009

SELECTED GOVERNMENT MEMBERS *as at March 2014*
Economy and Finance, Francis Tam Pak Yuen
Secretary for Administration and Justice, Florinda da Rosa Silva Chan

CONSUL-GENERAL
Caroline Wilson, *apptd* 2012, resident at Hong Kong

ECONOMY AND TRADE
The economy is based on tourism and gambling, which have grown rapidly since 2001, and garment and textile manufacturing, which is in decline. Visitors totalled 29.3 million in 2013, the majority coming from mainland China, where gambling is illegal. The service sector contributes about 93.5 per cent of GDP and industry 6.5 per cent. The principal products and exports are clothing, textiles, footwear, toys, electronics, machinery and parts. The main trading partners are Hong Kong, China – with whom a Comprehensive Economic Partnership Agreement was signed in 2013 – and the USA.
GNI – US$31,809m; US$55,720 per capita (2011)
Annual average growth of GDP – 10 per cent (2012 est)
Inflation rate – 5.4 per cent (2013 est)
Unemployment – 1.9 per cent (2012 est)
Imports – US$8,877m (2012)
Exports – US$1,021m (2012)

BALANCE OF PAYMENTS
Trade – US$67,856m deficit (2012)
Current Account – US$6,238m surplus (2009)

Trade with UK	2012	2013
Imports from UK	£50,612,011	£64,996,812
Exports to UK	£18,508,812	£17,463,801

COLOMBIA

República de Colombia – Republic of Colombia

Area – 1,138,910 sq. km
Capital – Bogotá; population, 8,955,776 (2012 est)
Major cities – Barranquilla, Cali, Cartagena, Medellín
Currency – Colombian peso ($) of 100 centavos
Population – 45,745,783 rising at 1.1 per cent a year (2013 est)

Religion – Christian (predominantly Roman Catholic) (est)
Language – Spanish (official)
Population density – 42 per sq. km (2011)
Urban population – 75.6 per cent (2012 est)
Median age (years) – 28.6 (2013 est)
National anthem – 'Himno Nacional de la República de Colombia' ['National Anthem of the Republic of Colombia']
National day – 20 July (Independence Day)
Death penalty – Abolished for all crimes (since 1910)
CPI score – 36 (94)

CLIMATE AND TERRAIN
The western, central and eastern ranges of the Andes run from the south-west to north-east of Colombia, separating the arid north-eastern peninsula and the tropical coastal regions in the north and west from the densely forested south-eastern lowlands and the vast tablelands in the east. This last region, having a temperate climate, is the most densely populated part of the country. Elevation extremes range from 5,775m (Pico Cristobal Colon) to 0m (Pacific Ocean). The principal rivers are the Magdalena, which flows into the Caribbean; the Guaviare and Meta, tributaries of the Orinocco; and the Caquetá and Putumayo, which drain into the Amazon basin. The predominantly tropical climate is moderated by altitude in the interior.

HISTORY AND POLITICS
Spanish settlement of the region began in 1525, and Colombia was ruled as part of a vice-royalty until 1810, when independence was declared. In 1819, Simón Bolivar established the Republic of Gran Colombia, consisting of the territories now known as Colombia, Panama, Venezuela and Ecuador, after finally defeating the Spanish. In 1829–30 Venezuela and Ecuador withdrew, and in 1831 the remaining territories formed a separate state, which adopted the name of Colombia in 1866; Panama seceded in 1903.

Power alternated between the Conservative and Liberal parties from the mid-19th century. In 1949, a civil war broke out which lasted until 1957, when the Conservative and Liberal parties formed a coalition government known as the National Front. This arrangement continued until 1974 and was revived in 1978 in an attempt to maintain the rule of law in the face of violence by drugs cartels, a left-wing insurgency and counter-attacks by right-wing paramilitaries. Despite foreign assistance and increased military spending, drug trafficking continues to be widespread, although less of a threat to civil order than hitherto, but the government has been unable to suppress or reach a negotiated settlement with insurgents' leaders despite sporadic peace talks.

In the 2014 legislative elections, parties that supported President Calderón won the majority of seats in both chambers. The 2014 presidential election was won by President Calderón after a second round of voting.

Under the 1991 constitution, amended in 2005, the executive president is directly elected for a four-year term, which is renewable once. The bicameral congress comprises the 166-member House of Representatives, and the 102-member senate. All members are directly elected for a four-year term. Two senate seats are reserved for representatives of indigenous people.

HEAD OF STATE
President, Juan Manuel Santos Calderón, *elected* 20 June 2010, *sworn in* 7 August 2010 *re-elected* June 2014, *sworn in* in 8 August
Vice-President, German Vargas Lleras

SELECTED GOVERNMENT MEMBERS *as at February 2014*
Defence, Juan Carlos Pinzon
Finance, Mauricio Cardenas Santa Maria
Foreign Affairs, Maria Angela Holguin
Justice, Alfonso Gomez Mendez

EMBASSY OF COLOMBIA
3 Hans Crescent, London SW1X 0LN
T 020-7589 9177 E elondres@cancilleria.gov.co
W www.colombianembassy.co.uk
Ambassador Extraordinary and Plenipotentiary, HE Nestor
  Osorio, *apptd* 2014

BRITISH EMBASSY
Carrera 9, No 76–49, Piso 8, Edificio ING Barings, Bogotá D.C.
T (+57) (1) 326 8300 E embajadabritanica.bogota@fco.gov.uk
W www.gov.uk/government/world/colombia
Ambassador Extraordinary and Plenipotentiary, HE Lindsay
  Croisdale-Appleby, *apptd* 2013

INSURGENCIES
Colombia has been dogged by violence since the 1960s,
initially from insurgency by left-wing guerrilla groups,
mainly the Revolutionary Armed Forces of Colombia
(FARC) and the National Liberation Army (ELN), countered
by right-wing paramilitaries affiliated with the United
Self-Defence Forces of Colombia (AUC), which was
suspected of having links with the security forces. In the
1980s, lawlessness increased with the rise of drug-producing
and drug-trafficking cartels. The guerrillas and paramilitaries
became involved in these and other crimes, including
kidnapping, and often act to protect these sources of funding
as much as to further their political aims.

Action against the insurgents and drug cartels since 2002
has extended state control to the extent that the government
now has a presence in every municipality. Talks with the
AUC from 2004 led to demobilisation of most units in 2006,
and in November 2012, FARC rebels declared a two-month
ceasefire and began talks; unrest continued but in January
2014 President Santos announced a peace treaty would be
signed within a year.

Neighbouring countries are affected by the overspill
from the violence in Colombia, and cross-border incursions
by Colombian forces in pursuit of the FARC, ELN or
AUC have affected relations with both Ecuador and
Venezuela in recent years. Venezuela also strongly opposes
the USA's military presence in Colombia to counter
drug-trafficking.

DEFENCE

Aged 16–49, 2010 est	Males	Females
Available for military service	11,692,647	11,727,625
Fit for military service	9,150,400	9,861,760

Military expenditure – US$12,465m (2013)
Conscription – 18–24 years of age; 18 months

ECONOMY AND TRADE
An improving security situation, economic liberalisation and
international investment aided economic growth from 2002
to 2008. Although the economy contracted in 2009 owing
to the global downturn, it recovered strongly and real GDP
has grown at a rate of over 4 per cent for the past three years.
The government has encouraged diversification to reduce
dependence on a limited range of commodities and markets,
and this has led to the growth of new export-orientated

industries (particularly textiles, clothing and footwear), and a
broader range of export markets.

Services account for around 55.6 per cent of GDP,
industry 37.8 per cent and agriculture 6.6 per cent. Coal,
oil, natural gas and hydroelectricity resources are exploited,
and coal accounts for about 88 per cent of mining output;
iron ore, nickel, gold, emeralds, copper and other minerals
account for the remainder. Major cash crops are coffee,
bananas and cut flowers. Cattle are raised in large numbers,
and forestry is also important.

The principal trading partners are the USA, China, Mexico
and the EU. Main exports are oil, coffee, coal, nickel,
emeralds, garments, bananas and cut flowers. Imports include
industrial and transport equipment, consumer goods,
chemicals, paper products and fuels.

GNI – US$353,678m; US$7,020 per capita (2012)
Annual average growth of GDP – 4.2 per cent (2013 est)
Inflation rate – 2.2 per cent (2013 est)
Population below poverty line – 32.7 per cent (2012 est)
Unemployment – 9.7 per cent (2013 est)
Total external debt – US$85,830m (2013 est)
Imports – US$58,633m (2012)
Exports – US$59,573m (2012)

BALANCE OF PAYMENTS
Trade – US$941m surplus (2012)
Current Account – US$11,846m deficit (2012)

Trade with UK	2012	2013
Imports from UK	£302,896,140	£338,028,885
Exports to UK	£888,030,827	£781,087,651

COMMUNICATIONS
Airports – 121, the principal airports are at Bogotá,
Barranquilla and Cali
Waterways – 18,300km of navigable waterways; the main
seaports are Barranquilla and Cartagena on the Caribbean
Sea and Buenaventura on the Pacific coast
Roadways and railways – 141,374km; 874km
Telecommunications – 6.29 million fixed lines and 49.07
million mobile subscriptions (2012); there were 22.54
million internet users in 2009
Internet code and IDD – co; 57 (from UK), 5/7/9 44 (to UK)
Major broadcasters – The state-run Senal Columbia is one of
the largest television broadcasters in the country; Caracol
runs several radio networks across the country alongside the
state-run Radio Nacional de Columbia
Press – There are seven major daily newspapers, including
El Tiempo and *El Nuevo Siglo*
WPFI score – 36,68 (126)

EDUCATION AND HEALTH
Elementary education is free and compulsory from age 6
to 15. Health care is provided through a mixture of
contributory and subsidised health schemes by both the
private and the public sector.
Literacy rate – 94 per cent (2011 est)
Gross enrolment ratio (percentage of relevant age group) –
  primary 111 per cent; secondary 97 per cent; tertiary
  43 per cent (2011 est)
Health expenditure (per capita) – US$432 (2011)
Hospital beds (per 1,000 people) – 1.4 (2011)
Life expectancy (years) – 75.02 (2013 est)
Mortality rate – 5.33 (2013 est)
Birth rate – 16.98 (2013 est)
Infant mortality rate – 15.46 (2013 est)

THE COMOROS

Udzima wa Komori/Jumhuriyat al-Qamar al-Muttahidah/ Union des Comores – Union of the Comoros

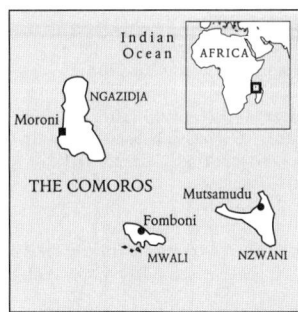

Area – 1,862 sq. km (excluding Mayotte). The Comoros includes the islands of Ngazidja (formerly Grande Comore), Nzwani (Anjouan), Mwali (Moheli) and certain islets in the Indian Ocean. Mayotte, the easternmost island of the archipelago, is a French dependency

Capital – Moroni, on Ngazidja; population, 54,000 (2011 est)

Major towns – Domoni, Fomboni, Mutsamudu

Currency – Comoran franc (KMF) of 100 centimes. The Franc CFA of 100 centimes is also used

Population – 752,288 rising at 1.97 per cent a year (2013 est)

Religion – Muslim (Sunni 99 per cent) (est); Islam is the state religion

Language – Arabic, French (both official), Shikomoro (a blend of Swahili and Arabic)

Population density 376 per sq. km (2011)

Urban population – 28.1 per cent (2012 est)

Median age (years) – 19 (2013 est)

National anthem – 'Udzima wa ya Masiwa' ['The Union of the Great Islands']

National day – 6 July (Independence Day)

Death penalty – Retained

CPI score – 28 (127)

Literacy rate – 76 per cent (2011 est)

Gross enrolment ratio (percentage of relevant age group) – primary 106 per cent; secondary 73 per cent; tertiary 10 per cent (2011 est)

Life expectancy (years) – 63.12 (2013 est)

Mortality rate – 7.97 (2013 est)

Birth rate – 30.26 (2013 est)

Infant mortality rate – 67.12 (2013 est)

HIV/AIDS adult prevalence – 2.1 per cent (2012 est)

CLIMATE AND TERRAIN
Located in the Mozambique Channel between Africa and Madagascar, Njazidja, Nzwani and Mwali are mountainous volcanic islands in the Comoros archipelago. The highest point is Karthala (2,360m) on Njazidja, an active volcano that last erupted in 2007, and the lowest is 0m (Indian Ocean). The climate is tropical, with a hot, rainy season from October to April; the islands are prone to cyclones during the rainy season.

HISTORY AND POLITICS
The islands were settled by a variety of peoples before becoming part of the trading empire of the Shirazis of Persia, who established sultanates in the 15th to 16th centuries. In 1886, France established protectorates over the islands, making them a colony in 1912. They achieved internal self-government in 1961. In a 1974 referendum, the

residents of three of the main islands voted in favour of independence, which was declared on 6 July 1975; Mayotte voted to remain part of France.

The republic experienced about 18 coups or attempted coups between 1975 and 1999. Nzwani and Mwali seceded in 1997 but, after a coup in 1999, the military took control of all the islands' governments and reunited the state. Talks on the secessionist crisis produced a new constitution, introducing a federal structure with greater autonomy for the individual islands. Another constitutional crisis arose in June 2007 when the incumbent president of Nzwani, Mohamed Bacar, refused to stand down and then held elections which he claimed to have won. The federal government declared the elections null and void, and in March 2008 federal troops, supported by African Union forces, ousted Bacar.

Elections to the union parliament and the islands' legislatures were held in December 2009; in the union elections, supporters of President Sambi won 20 of the 24 seats. The federal president and island governors were elected in December 2010 and took office in May 2011; the federal presidency election was won by Ikililou Dhoinine, of Mwali.

The 2002 constitution created a federal structure. Constitutional amendments approved in 2009 downgraded the islands' presidents to governors, ended the rotation of the federal presidency among the islands, and harmonised presidential and legislative terms by extending those of the president and governors.

Under the amended constitution, the union president is elected for a five-year term. The executive president appoints the union ministers. The unicameral Assembly of the Union has 33 members; three are appointed by each of the three island parliaments and 24 are directly elected for a five-year term.

Each island has its own governor and legislative assembly, and each governor may appoint eight ministers to form a government. Governors serve a five-year term. The islands' governments deal with local issues; foreign affairs, finance, defence, judicial and religious matters remain the responsibility of the union government. There are still areas of dispute, principally over security, budget control and customs revenue.

HEAD OF STATE
President of the Union, Ikililou Dhoinine, *elected* 26 December 2010, *sworn in* 26 May 2011

SELECTED GOVERNMENT MEMBERS *as at February 2014*
Vice-Presidents, Nourdine Bourhane; Fouad Ben Mohadji; Mohamed Ali Soilihi *(Finance, Economy)*
Foreign Relations, Elarif Said Hassane
Interior, Housseine Hassan Ibrahim

BRITISH AMBASSADOR
HE Nick Leake, *apptd* 2010, resident at Port Louis, Mauritius

ECONOMY AND TRADE
The Comoros is very poor and heavily dependent on foreign aid and technical assistance. It has few natural resources, an uneducated workforce and poor transport infrastructure. Although continuing political tensions hinder government attempts to reform and develop the economy and social welfare provision, progress is sufficient to attract further international aid and debt relief. Unemployment is high and remittances from 150,000 Comorans living abroad are a valuable contribution to the economy. In December 2012 the IMF and World Bank supported US$176 million in debt relief for the Comoros, allowing a 59 per cent decrease in future external debt over a period of 40 years. Agriculture, fishing and forestry account for 51 per cent of GDP and

employ around 80 per cent of the population; service industries account for about 39 per cent and the manufacturing industry 10 per cent. The main industries are fishing, tourism and perfume distillation. The main trading partners are the Netherlands, France, Pakistan and Singapore. Principal exports are vanilla, perfume essence, copra and cloves; coconuts, bananas and cassava are also cultivated.

GNI – US$595,354m; US$840 per capita (2012)
Annual average growth of GDP – 3.5 per cent (2013 est)
Inflation rate – 2.5 per cent (2013 est)
Population below poverty line – 60 per cent (2002 est)
Total external debt – US$142,900m (2013 est)
Imports – US$300m (2012)
Exports – US$25m (2012)

BALANCE OF PAYMENTS
Trade – US$275m deficit (2012)
Current Account – US$23m deficit (2012)

Trade with UK	2012	2013
Imports from UK	£560,837	£381,037
Exports to UK	£1,045,174	£147,115

COMMUNICATIONS
Airports and waterways – Four, the main international airport is based on Moroni; the principal ports are based at Moroni and Mutsamudu
Roadways – 880km
Telecommunications – 24,000 fixed lines and 250,000 mobile subscriptions (2012); there were 24,300 internet users in 2009
Internet code and IDD – km; 269 (from UK), 44 (to UK)
Major broadcasters – National radio and television broadcasting is provided by state-run networks, and some island governments run radio and television stations
Press – Several weekly papers are published; the leading title is the state-owned *Al-Watwan*
WPFI score – 24,52 (53)

DEMOCRATIC REPUBLIC OF THE CONGO

République Démocratique du Congo – Democratic Republic of the Congo

Area – 2,344,858 sq. km
Capital – Kinshasa; population, 9,490,647 (2012 est)
Major cities – Bukavu, Kananga, Kisangani, Kolwezi, Likasi, Lubumbashi, Mbuji-Mayi
Currency – Congolese franc (FC) of 100 centimes
Population – 75,507,308 rising at 2.54 per cent a year (2013 est). The population is composed of over 200 ethnic groups, including Bantu, Hamitic, Nilotic, Sudanese and Pygmoid; the four largest tribes, Mongo, Luba, Kongo

(all Bantu) and Mangbtu-Azande (Hamitic), make up around 45 per cent of the population
Religion – Christian (Roman Catholic 50 per cent, Protestant 20 per cent), Kimbanguist 10 per cent, Muslim 10 per cent (est)
Language – French (official), Lingala, Kingwana (a Swahili dialect), Kikongo, Tshiluba
Population density – 28 per sq. km (2011)
Urban population – 34.8 per cent (2012 est)
Median age (years) – 17.7 (2013 est)
National anthem – 'Debout Congolais' ['Stand Up, Congolese']
National day – 30 June (Independence Day)
Death penalty – Retained
CPI score – 22 (154)
Literacy rate – 66.8 per cent (2010 est)
Gross enrolment ratio (percentage of relevant age group) – primary 105 per cent; secondary 43 per cent; tertiary 8 per cent (2011 est)
Health expenditure (per capita) – US$20 (2011)
Life expectancy (years) – 56.14 (2013 est)
Mortality rate – 10.54 (2013 est)
Birth rate – 36.34 (2013 est)
Infant mortality rate – 74.87 (2013 est)
HIV/AIDS adult prevalence – 1.1 per cent (2012 est)

CLIMATE AND TERRAIN
Africa's second-largest country lies on the equator, most of it in the basin of the river Congo and its principal tributaries, the Lualaba and the Kasai. A chain of mountains and lakes (Albert, Edward, Kivu and Tanganyika) runs along the eastern border. Elevation extremes range from 5,110m (Mt Ngaliema, also known as Mt Stanley) to 0m (Atlantic Ocean). The climate is tropical, though cooler in the eastern and southern highlands. There are different climatic cycles either side of the equator, which passes through the north of the country, with a wet season in the north from April to November and in the south from October to May.

POLITICS
Under the 2006 constitution, the executive president is directly elected for a five-year term, renewable once. The bicameral *Parlement* consists of the National Assembly, which has 500 members directly elected for a five-year term, and the senate, which has 108 members elected by the provincial assemblies to serve a five-year term, plus former elected presidents, who are senators for life.

Joseph Kabila succeeded his father Laurent (assassinated in 2001) as president. After a period of transitional government, a new constitution came into effect in 2006 and presidential and legislative elections were held. The presidential election was won in the second round by Joseph Kabila, who went on to win re-election in November 2011, picking up nearly 49 per cent of the vote; his People's Party for Reconstruction and Development lost a large number of seats in the 2011 legislative election. Some 17 seats in the lower house were investigated by the supreme court following allegations of fraud and errors during the election. Elections to the senate were last made in 2007 and have since been postponed until 2014.

HEAD OF STATE
President, Maj.-Gen. Joseph Kabila, *sworn in* 26 January 2001, *sworn in as president of the transitional government* 7 April 2003, *elected* 29 October 2006, *re-elected* 2011

SELECTED GOVERNMENT MEMBERS *as at February 2014*
Prime Minister, Augustin Matata Ponyo Mapon
Deputy Prime Ministers, Alexandre Luba Ntambo; Daniel Mokoko Samba

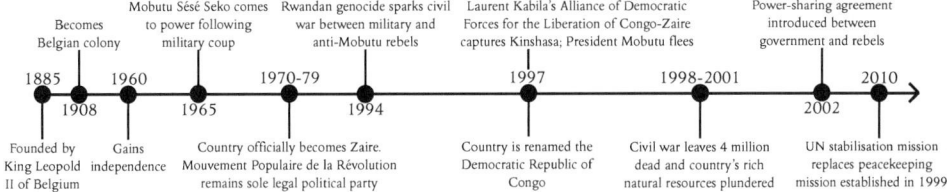

	Mobutu Sésé Seko comes	Rwandan genocide sparks civil	Laurent Kabila's Alliance of Democratic	Power-sharing agreement
Becomes	to power following	war between military and	Forces for the Liberation of Congo-Zaire	introduced between
Belgian colony	military coup	anti-Mobutu rebels	captures Kinshasa; President Mobutu flees	government and rebels

| 1885 | 1960 | 1970-79 | 1997 | 1998-2001 | 2010 |
| 1908 | 1965 | 1994 | | 2002 | |

Founded by	Gains	Country officially becomes Zaire.	Country is renamed the	Civil war leaves 4 million	UN stabilisation mission
King Leopold	independence	Mouvement Populaire de la Révolution	Democratic Republic of	dead and country's rich	replaces peacekeeping
II of Belgium		remains sole legal political party	Congo	natural resources plundered	mission established in 1999

Economy, Jean-Paul Nemayato Begepole
Foreign Affairs, Raymond Tshibanda

EMBASSY OF THE DEMOCRATIC REPUBLIC OF THE CONGO
45–49 Great Portland Street, London W1W 7LD
T 020-7580 3931 **E** info@ambardc-londres.gouv.cd
W http://ambardc-londres.gouv.cd
Ambassador Extraordinary and Plenipotentiary, HE Barnabé
Kikaya Bin Karubi, *apptd* 2009

BRITISH EMBASSY
83 Avenue du Roi Baudouin, Gombe, Kinshasa
T (+243) 81 556 6200 **E** ambassade.britannique@fco.gov.uk
W www.gov.uk/government/world/democratic-republic-of-congo
Ambassador Extraordinary and Plenipotentiary, HE Diane
Corner, *apptd* 2013

DEFENCE

Aged 16–49, 2010 est	Males	Females
Available for military service	15,980,106	–
Fit for military service	10,168,258	10,331,693

Military expenditure – US$402m (2013)

ECONOMY AND TRADE
A decade of civil war left the country with huge external debt, little infrastructure, widespread corruption and an environment that discourages foreign investment. Improved stability since 2003 has allowed some economic growth, although the global downturn caused the economy to contract in 2008–9. Growth returned in 2010–11, and government reforms, international aid and debt relief are helping the economy in its continuing recovery. In 2012 the Democratic Republic of the Congo updated its business law to comply with the Organisation for the Harmonisation of Business Law in Africa (OHADA).

The country has great potential wealth in the form of immense natural resources, including copper, cobalt, diamonds, gold, silver, uranium, other minerals, coal, oil, timber and hydroelectric power; mining is the largest source of export income. Agriculture contributes 44.3 per cent of GDP, the services sector 34 per cent and industry 21.7 per cent. Apart from mining and mineral processing, the main industrial activities are the production of textiles, plastics, footwear, cigarettes, metal products, processed food, beverages, timber and cement, and ship repair. Oil deposits are exploited off the Congo estuary, and hydroelectric schemes on the river Congo supply power to the major cities.

The main trading partners are China, South Africa, Belgium, Zambia and Zimbabwe. Principal exports are diamonds, gold, copper, cobalt, wood products, crude oil and coffee. The main imports are foodstuffs, industrial machinery, transport equipment and fuels.

GNI – US$16,061m; US$230 per capita (2012)
Annual average growth of GDP – 6.2 per cent (2013 est)
Inflation rate – 7.1 per cent (2013 est)

Population below poverty line – 71 per cent (2006 est)
Total external debt – US$6,874m (2013 est)
Imports – US$6,100m (2012)
Exports – US$6,300m (2012)

BALANCE OF PAYMENTS
Trade – US$200m surplus (2012)
Current Account – US$2,212m deficit (2012)

Trade with UK	2012	2013
Imports from UK	£24,854,768	£33,247,902
Exports to UK	£3,817,226	£2,947,661

COMMUNICATIONS
Airport – 26, the principal airports being at Kinshasa, Kananga, Goma, Gemena and Mbandaka
Waterways – The river Congo and its main tributaries provide 15,000km of waterways, with the principal ports in Banana, Boma and Matadi
Roadways and railways – There are about 153,497km of roadways, of which 2,794km are surfaced; the 4,007km rail system links the interior to the rivers and to the great lakes in the east
Telecommunications – 58,200 fixed lines in use and 19.487 million mobile subscriptions (2012); there were 290,000 internet users in 2008
Internet code and IDD – cd; 243 (from UK), 44 (to UK)
Major broadcasters – The state-controlled Radio-Télévision Nationale Congolaise (RTNC) and La Voix du Congo have the greatest influence and broadcast reach
Press – Around 15 newspapers are published regularly in Kinshasa
WPFI score – 44,64 (151)

REPUBLIC OF THE CONGO

République du Congo – Republic of the Congo

Area – 342,000 sq. km
Capital – Brazzaville; population, 1,389,782 (2012 est)
Major cities – Loubomo, Pointe-Noire
Currency – Franc CFA of 100 centimes
Population – 4,574,099 rising at 2.86 per cent a year
(2013 est); Kongo (48 per cent), Sangha (20 per cent),

Teke (17 per cent) and M'Bochi (12 per cent) (est) are the largest of the 15 main Bantu groups
Religion – Christian (Roman Catholic 33.1 per cent, Awakening Churches 22.3 per cent, Protestant 19.9 per cent), Muslim 1.6 per cent, Kimbanguist 1.5 per cent (est)
Language – French (official), Lingala, Monokutuba, Kikongo
Population density – 12 per sq. km (2011)
Urban population – 64.1 per cent (2012 est)
Median age (years) – 17.1 (2013 est)
National anthem – 'La Congolaise' ['The Congolese']
National day – 15 August (Independence Day)
Death penalty – Retained (last used 1982)
CPI score – 22 (154)

CLIMATE AND TERRAIN
The republic, which lies on the equator, is covered by grassland, mangrove and dense rainforest. The land rises from the narrow Atlantic coastal plain to a central plateau; in the north and east it falls to the northern part of the basin of the river Congo, which forms part of the border with the Democratic Republic of the Congo, and to the valleys of the Sangha and Alima rivers in the north. Elevation extremes range from 903m (Mt Berongou) to 0m (Atlantic Ocean). The climate is tropical. The average temperature in Brazzaville is 25°C and humidity is high. Outside the main dry season between June and September, the country is prone to flooding.

HISTORY AND POLITICS
The first European visitors to the area were the Portuguese, who established slave trading in the 16th century. The French established a colonial presence in the area in the 1880s and, as Middle Congo, it was part of French Equatorial Africa from 1910. It became independent as the Republic of the Congo on 17 August 1960.

One-party socialism was introduced in 1964; the Congolese Labour Party (PCT) was set up shortly after a military coup in 1968 and continued to rule until 1990, when Marxism was renounced and, after popular pressure, the PCT abandoned its monopoly of power. Elections in 1993 left the PCT a minority party, and the power shift destabilised the country, with factional fighting after the 1993 election, a civil war between 1997 and 1999 following Denis Sassou-Nguesso's deposition of the elected president, and a renewed insurgency by opponents of the PCT over the manipulation of the 2002 elections. A peace accord ended the insurgency in 2003 but the peace remains fragile and remnants of the rebel militias are still active in the south of the country, where many have turned to banditry.

Sassou-Nguesso was elected president in 2002, and was re-elected in 2009; the legitimacy of both victories was suspect after the barring or withdrawal of opponents, fraud and other irregularities. In the 2012 legislative election the PCT expanded upon its large majority, taking 89 of the 139 seats available.

Under the 2002 constitution, parties organised on regional, ethnic or religious lines are banned. The executive president is directly elected for a seven-year term, renewable once, and appoints the cabinet. The bicameral *Parlement* comprises the National Assembly, with 137 members directly elected for a five-year term, and the senate, which has 72 members indirectly elected for a six-year term, half of the members retiring every three years.

HEAD OF STATE
President, Denis Sassou-Nguesso, *took power* October 1997, *elected* 10 March 2002, *re-elected* 2009

SELECTED GOVERNMENT MEMBERS *as at February 2014*
Defence, Charles Richard Mondjo
Economy, Finance and Planning, Gilbert Ondongo
Foreign Affairs, Basile Ikouébé

EMBASSY OF THE REPUBLIC OF THE CONGO
37 bis Rue Paul Valéry, 75116 Paris, France
T (+33) (1) 4500 6057
Ambassador Extraordinary and Plenipotentiary, HE Henri Lopes, *apptd* 1999

BRITISH AMBASSADOR
HE Diane Corner, *apptd* 2013, resident at Kinshasa, DR of the Congo

DEFENCE

Aged 16–49, 2010 est	Males	Females
Available for military service	928,664	914,265
Fit for military service	577,944	566,587

Military expenditure – US$142m (2010)

ECONOMY AND TRADE
A decade of civil conflict left the country with a high external debt, a devastated infrastructure and widespread poverty. Since 2003 the government has made efforts to address these problems and has benefited from debt relief in 2006, 2007 and 2010.

Oil production is the backbone of the economy, making it vulnerable to market slumps, however the recent recovery in oil prices has boosted GDP. Mining (particularly of diamonds), forestry, brewing, agricultural processing and cement production are the other main industries; new projects, notably the mining of iron ore, are expected to add around $1 billion to annual revenue. Industry accounts for 73.9 per cent of GDP, services for 22.9 per cent and agriculture, which is mostly at subsistence level, for 3.3 per cent.

The main trading partners are China, the USA and France. Principal exports are oil, timber, plywood, sugar, cocoa, coffee and diamonds. Imports are mainly capital equipment, construction materials and foodstuffs.
GNI – US$10,831m; US$2,550 per capita (2012)
Annual average growth of GDP – 5.8 per cent (2013 est)
Inflation rate – 1.7 per cent (2013 est)
Population below poverty line – 46.5 per cent (2011 est)
Unemployment – 53 per cent (2012 est)
Total external debt – US$3,274m (2013 est)
Imports – US$5,200m (2012)
Exports – US$10,999m (2012)

BALANCE OF PAYMENTS
Trade – US$5,799m surplus (2012)
Current Account – US$177m deficit (2008 est)

Trade with UK	2012	2013
Imports from UK	£52,272,102	£64,859,649
Exports to UK	£94,270,816	£222,360,453

COMMUNICATIONS
Airports – Eight, including an international airport at Brazzaville
Waterways – Pointe-Noire is the main seaport and also the centre of the offshore oil industry. Brazzaville is the main river port, lying on the river Congo which, with the river Oubangui, provides 1,120km of commercially navigable waterways

Roadways and railways – 17,289km of roadways, 864km of which are surfaced; 886km of railways
Telecommunications – 14,900 fixed lines and 4.283 million mobile subscriptions (2012); there were 245,200 internet users in 2009
Internet code and IDD – cg; 242 (from UK), 44 (to UK)
Major broadcasters – TV Congo is the only television station and is controlled by the state. Two government radio stations, Radio Congo and Radio Brazzaville, exist alongside commercial and community stations
Press – Five privately owned newspapers are regularly published in Brazzaville, the centre of the country's print media
WPFI score – 29,44 (82)

EDUCATION AND HEALTH
Schooling is free and compulsory between ages six and 16.
Literacy rate – 81.1 per cent (2008 est)
Gross enrolment ratio (percentage of relevant age group) – primary 112 per cent; secondary 54 per cent; tertiary 9 per cent (2011 est)
Health expenditure (per capita) – US$87 (2011)
Hospital beds (per 1,000 people) – 1.6 (2004–9)
Life expectancy (years) – 55.6 (2013 est)
Mortality rate – 11.03 (2013 est)
Birth rate – 39.63 (2013 est)
Infant mortality rate – 72.45 (2013 est)
HIV/AIDS adult prevalence – 2.8 per cent (2012 est)

COSTA RICA

República de Costa Rica – Republic of Costa Rica

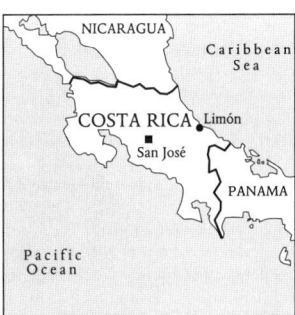

Area – 51,100 sq. km
Capital – San José; population, 1,545,735 (2012 est)
Major towns – Alajuela, Liberia, Limón, Paraíso, San Francisco
Currency – Costa Rican colón of 100 céntimos
Population – 4,695,942 rising at 1.27 per cent a year (2013 est)
Religion – Christian (Roman Catholic 70 per cent, Evangelical Protestant 17 per cent) (est)
Language – Spanish (official), English
Population density – 93 per sq. km (2011)
Urban population – 65.1 per cent (2012 est)
Median age (years) – 29.6 (2013 est)
National anthem – 'Noble Patria, Tu Hermosa Bandera' ['Noble Fatherland, Your Beautiful Flag']
National day – 15 September (Independence Day)
Death penalty – Abolished for all crimes (since 1877)
CPI score – 49 (53)
Literacy rate – 96 per cent (2011 est)
Gross enrolment ratio (percentage of relevant age group) –

primary 107 per cent; secondary 101 per cent; tertiary 43 per cent (2011 est)
Health expenditure (per capita) – US$943 (2011)
Hospital beds (per 1,000 people) – 1.2 (2011)
Life expectancy (years) – 78.06 (2013 est)
Mortality rate – 4.44 (2013 est)
Birth rate – 16.25 (2013 est)
Infant mortality rate – 8.95 (2013 est)

CLIMATE AND TERRAIN
The Cordillera de Guanacaste (north-west), Cordillera de Talamanca and Cordillera Central (south-east) form a chain of volcanic mountain ranges that traverse the country from north to south. A central valley lies between the ranges, and the land slopes to plains on the Pacific and Caribbean coasts. Elevation extremes range from 3,810m (Cerro Chirripó Grande) to 0m (Pacific Ocean). The climate is tropical, with an average annual temperature of 24.7°C, and a wet season from May to November. The area is subject to occasional earthquakes, hurricanes, flooding and landslides.

HISTORY AND POLITICS
Visited by Columbus in 1502, Costa Rica was colonised by the Spanish from the 1560s and remained under Spanish rule until Central America gained its independence in 1821. Costa Rica was part of a Central American federation of former Spanish provinces from 1823 until its secession in 1838. Political unrest in the mid-20th century led to a brief civil war in 1948, after which the army was abolished and replaced with a national guard. Subsequently power alternated between the two main political parties, the National Liberation Party (PLN) and the Social Christian Unity Party (PUSC), but in recent years the scandal-ridden PUSC has lost ground to emerging new parties.

In the 2014 legislative elections, the PLN remained the largest party despite losing seats for the second consecutive election. The simultaneous presidential election was won by the Citizen's Action Party candidate Luis Guillermo Solís.

Under the 1949 constitution, the executive president is directly elected for a four-year term. The unicameral legislative assembly has 57 members directly elected for a four-year term.

HEAD OF STATE
President, Luis Guillermo Solís, *elected* 7 April 2014, *sworn in* 8 May 2010
First Vice President, Helios Venegas
Second Vice President, And Chacón

SELECTED GOVERNMENT MEMBERS *as at September 2014*
Economy, Welmer Ramos
Finance, Helios Venegas
Foreign Affairs, Manuel Gonzalez

EMBASSY OF COSTA RICA
14 Lancaster Gate, London W2 3LH
T 020-7706 8844 E embassy@costaricanembassy.co.uk
Ambassador Extraordinary and Plenipotentiary, HE Pilar Saborio de Rocafort, *apptd* 2007

BRITISH EMBASSY
Apartado 815–1007, Edificio Centro Colón (11th Floor), San José 1007
T (+506) 2258 2025 E ukin.costarica@fco.gov.uk
W www.gov.uk/government/world/costa-rica
Ambassadors Extraordinary and Plenipotentiary, HE Sharon Campbell, *apptd* 2011

DEFENCE

Aged 16–49, 2010 est	Males	Females
Available for military service	1,255,798	1,230,202
Fit for military service	1,058,419	1,037,053

ECONOMY AND TRADE

Sixty years of political stability have allowed steady economic growth, the creation of a social welfare system and a reduction in poverty to less than 25 per cent of the population, though the social benefit system is becoming increasingly strained due to restrictions on government spending and increased immigration. Although the economy contracted in 2008 owing to the global downturn, the impact of this on government spending was tempered by reductions in the internal and external debt since 2006; the economy grew by approximately 4.5 per cent from 2010–12.

Tourism is the largest single industry, and with one-third of the country now national parkland or nature reserve, eco-tourism is on the increase. Services account for about 72.5 per cent of GDP while the manufacturing industry accounts for 21.3 per cent, the principal products being microprocessors, foodstuffs, medical equipment, textiles, clothing, construction materials, fertiliser and plastic goods. The agricultural sector contributes 6.2 per cent of GDP; the principal products are tropical fruit, coffee, ornamental plants, sugar, rice, vegetables, meat and timber.

The main trading partners are the USA, China, the Netherlands and Mexico. The chief exports are tropical fruit, coffee, plants, sugar, beef, seafood, electrical components and medical equipment. The chief imports are raw materials, consumer goods, capital equipment, petrol and construction materials.

GNI – US$42,271m; US$8,820 per capita (2012)
Annual average growth of GDP – 3.5 per cent (2013 est)
Inflation rate – 5.6 per cent (2013 est)
Population below poverty line – 24.8 per cent (2011 est)
Unemployment – 7.9 per cent (2013 est)
Total external debt – US$15,100m (2013 est)
Imports – US$17,513m (2012)
Exports – US$11,151m (2012)

BALANCE OF PAYMENTS
Trade – US$6,362m deficit (2012)
Current Account – US$2,382m deficit (2012)

Trade with UK	2012	2013
Imports from UK	£49,018,992	£52,971,301
Exports to UK	£176,975,173	£182,484,662

COMMUNICATIONS

Airports and waterways – 47, the principal airports are at San José and Limón; the chief seaports are Limón on the Atlantic coast, and Puntarenas and de Caldera on the Pacific coast
Roadways and railways – There are 39,018km of roadways, 10,133km of which are surfaced, and 278km of railways, none of which is in use
Telecommunications – 1.018 million fixed lines and 6.151 million mobile subscriptions (2012); there were 1.485 million internet users in 2009
Internet code and IDD – cr; 506 (from UK), 44 (to UK)
WPFI score – 12,23 (21)

CÔTE D'IVOIRE

République de Côte d'Ivoire – the Ivory Coast

Area – 322,463 sq. km
Capital – Yamoussoukro (since 1983); population, 966,000 (2011 est); slow progress in transferring functions means that the former capital, Abidjan (population, 4,288,000; 2011 est), remains the seat of government at present
Major cities – Abidjan, Bouaké, Daloa, Korhogo
Currency – Franc CFA of 100 centimes
Population – 22,400,835 rising at 2 per cent a year (2012 est); over 60 ethnic groups, including the Akan (42.1 per cent), Voltaiques or Gur (17.6 per cent), Northern Mandes (16.5 per cent), Krous (11 per cent), Southern Mandes (10 per cent) (est)
Religion – Muslim 38.6 per cent, Christian 32.8 per cent, indigenous religions 11.9 per cent (est); many Christians and Muslims incorporate indigenous beliefs into their worship
Language – French (official), around 60 native dialects of which Dioula is the most widely spoken
Population density – 61 per sq. km (2011)
Urban population – 52 per cent (2012 est)
Median age (years) – 20 (2013 est)
National anthem – 'L'Abidjanaise' ['Song of Abidjan']
National day – 7 August (Independence Day)
Death penalty – Abolished for all crimes (since 2000)
CPI score – 27 (136)
Literacy rate – 57 per cent (2011 est)
Gross enrolment ratio (percentage of relevant age group) – primary 90 per cent; secondary 27 per cent; tertiary 8 per cent (2011 est)
Health expenditure (per capita) – US$79 (2011)
Hospital beds (per 1,000 people) – 0.4 (2004–9)
Life expectancy (years) – 57.66 (2013 est)
Mortality rate – 9.8 (2013 est)
Birth rate – 29.83 (2013 est)
Infant mortality rate – 61.66 (2013 est)
HIV/AIDS adult prevalence – 3.2 per cent (2012 est)

CLIMATE AND TERRAIN

The land rises from a coastal plain to a large interior plateau with mountains in the north and west. Coastal lagoons give way to tropical rainforest in the centre and savannah in the north; deforestation means that the area of savannah is increasing. The country is dissected by the Sassandra, Bandama and Komoé rivers, the first two forming large central lakes. Elevation extremes range from 1,752m (Mt Nimba) to 0m (Gulf of Guinea). The climate is tropical in the south and semi-arid in the north. The south has two rainy seasons (May to July, October to November) and the north has one (June to September). The average annual temperature is 26°C.

Area comes under French influence	Gains independence as a one-party state under Felix Houphoët-Boigny		Factional violence mars the presidential election won by Laurent Gbagbo	Civil war ends. Country divided into government-controlled south and rebel-held north		President Gbagbo and Alassane Ouattara both claim victory in presidential election	

1460-1600	1889-93	1990	1993	2002	2007	2011
1842	1960	2000	2003	2010

| First Europeans introduce the ivory and slave trades | Côte d'Ivoire becomes French protectorate and colony | Multiparty system introduced | Death of President Houphoët-Boigny | Country plunged into civil war after reconciliation talks break down | Government of national unity formed; rebel leader Guillaume Soro becomes prime minister | Ouattara's militia takes control of country and captures Gbagbo |

POLITICS

Since the turn of the century Côte d'Ivoire has seen increased civil unrest and ethnic tensions. Following an election in 2010 the incumbent president Laurent Gbagbo refused to concede to the internationally acknowledged victor, Alassane Ouattara; following a four-month stalemate Ouattara took office by force. In the 2011 parliamentary elections, President Ouattara and his allies obtained a majority, however in 2012 Ouattara sacked his government in a row over changes in marriage laws.

Under the 2000 constitution, the executive president is directly elected for a five-year term, renewable once. The president appoints the prime minister and the other ministers, who are nominated by the prime minister. The unicameral National Assembly has 225 members, directly elected for a five-year term.

HEAD OF STATE

President, Alassane Ouattara, *elected* 28 November 2010, *sworn in* 6 May 2011

SELECTED GOVERNMENT MEMBERS *as at February 2014*

Prime Minister, Finance and Economy, Daniel Kablan Duncan
Foreign Affairs, Charles Koffi Diby
Interior, Hamed Bakayoko

EMBASSY OF THE REPUBLIC OF CÔTE D'IVOIRE

2 Upper Belgrave Street, London SW1X 8BJ
T 020-7235 6991
Ambassador Extraordinary and Plenipotentiary, HE Claude Stanislaus Bouah-Kamon, *apptd* 2011

BRITISH EMBASSY

Cocody, Quartier Ambassades, Rue l'Impasse du Belier, Abidjan 01
T (+225) 2244 2669 E uk_abidjan@yahoo.fr
W www.gov.uk/government/world/cote-d-ivoire
Ambassador Extraordinary and Plenipotentiary, HE Simon Tonge, *apptd* 2012

DEFENCE

Aged 16–49, 2010 est	Males	Females
Available for military service	5,247,522	5,047,901
Fit for military service	3,360,087	3,196,033

Military expenditure – US$435m (2012 est)

ECONOMY AND TRADE

The country was one of the most prosperous in the region, attracting large numbers of migrant workers from neighbouring countries, until the political turbulence of the late 1990s caused many to return home. The civil war particularly damaged the economy in the cotton-growing north, although recovery is beginning, and continuing political instability has hampered diversification away from agriculture, which makes the economy vulnerable to price fluctuations in its key exports. However, since 2006, revenue from oil, gas and refined products has outstripped earnings from cocoa, and offshore exploration for other deposits continues. Post-election conflict in 2011 caused a severe downturn in the economy, however there has since been some recovery and in 2012 the IMF and World Bank granted US$4.4bn in debt relief.

Services account for 52.4 per cent of GDP, agriculture for 26.3 per cent and industry for 21.3 per cent. Agriculture employs around 68 per cent of the workforce, producing cocoa (of which Côte d'Ivoire is the world's largest producer and exporter), coffee, cotton, bananas, pineapples and palm oil for export. The principal industries are food processing, forestry, oil refining, vehicle assembly, gold mining, textiles, fishing and the production of oil, natural gas and hydroelectric power; the country is a net exporter of electricity. The main trading partners are Nigeria, France, other EU and west African states, and the USA.

GNI – US$23,682m; US$1,220 per capita (2012)
Annual average growth of GDP – 8 per cent (2013 est)
Inflation rate – 2.9 per cent (2013 est)
Population below poverty line – 42 per cent (2006 est)
Total external debt – US$8,959m (2013 est)
Imports – US$9,774m (2012)
Exports – US$10,861m (2012)

BALANCE OF PAYMENTS

Trade – US$1,087m surplus (2012)
Current Account – US$1,699m surplus (2009)

Trade	2012	2013
Imports from UK	£84,084,941	£74,262,411
Exports to UK	£156,871,086	£125,906,878

COMMUNICATIONS

Airports – Seven, the principal international airport being at Abidjan
Waterways – There are 980km of navigable rivers, canals and lagoons; the main seaports are Abidjan and San Pedro
Roadways and railways – Côte d'Ivoire has 81,996km of roadways, 6,502km of which are surfaced, and 660km of railways
Telecommunications – 268,000 fixed lines and 19.827 million mobile telephone subscriptions (2012); there were 967,300 internet users in 2009
Internet code and IDD – ci; 225 (from UK), 44 (to UK)
Major broadcasters – The state broadcaster, Radiodiffusion Télévision Ivoirienne (RTI), operates two national radio stations and two television channels
Press – Nine newspapers are published daily, including the state-owned *Fraternité Matin* and the privately owned *Le Nouveau Reveil*
WPFI score – 31,63 (101)

CROATIA

Republika Hrvatska – Republic of Croatia

Area – 56,594 sq. km
Capital – Zagreb; population, 686,000 (2011 est)
Major cities – Zadar, Osijek, Rijeka (Fiume), Split
Currency – Kuna of 100 lipa
Population – 4,475,611 falling at 0.11 per cent a year
  (2013 est); Croat (90.4 per cent), Serb (4.4 per cent)
  (2011)
Religion – Christian (Roman Catholic 86.3 per cent, Serbian
  Orthodox 4.4 per cent), Muslim 1.5 per cent (est)
Language – Croatian (official), Serbian
Population density – 76 per sq. km (2011)
Urban population – 58.1 per cent (2012 est)
Median age (years) – 41.8 (2013 est)
National anthem – 'Lijepa Nasa Domovino' ['Our Beautiful
  Homeland']
National day – 8 October (Independence Day)
Death penalty – Abolished for all crimes (since 1990)
CPI score – 48 (57)

CLIMATE AND TERRAIN

There are three major geographic areas: the plains of the
Pannonian region in the north, the central mountain belt,
and the Adriatic coast region of Istria and Dalmatia, which
has 1,185 islands and islets and 1,777km of coastline.
Elevation extremes range from 1,831m (Dinara) to 0m
(Adriatic Sea). The climate varies significantly between the
Dalmatian coast, where the winters are mild and the summers
hot, and inland areas, which have colder temperatures and
rain in the summer. Average temperatures in Zagreb range
from 3°C in January to 21°C in July and August.

POLITICS

The 1990 constitution was amended in 2000 to increase
the powers of the legislature, making the presidency a
largely ceremonial role, and in 2001 to abolish the upper
house of the legislature. The head of state is a president,
who is directly elected for a five-year term. The legislature,
the Croatian Assembly, has one chamber, the House of
Representatives, which has 151 members directly elected for
a four-year term. The prime minister is appointed by the
legislature and appoints the cabinet.

The 2010 presidential election was won by Ivo Josipovic,
who picked up 20 per cent more votes than the nearest
competitor (Milan Bandic) in the second round of voting. In
the 2011 legislative election, a coalition consisting of the
Social Democratic Party of Croatia (SDP), the Croatian
People's Party and two smaller parties (the Kukuriku
coalition) overtook the Croatian Democratic Union to secure
an overall majority in the parliament. SDP leader Zoran
Milanovic was named prime minister in December 2011 and
set about forming a government based on the Kukuriku
coalition. Croatia became a member of the EU in July 2013.

HEAD OF STATE
President, Ivo Josipovic, *elected* 10 January 2010, *sworn in*
  18 February 2010

SELECTED GOVERNMENT MEMBERS *as at*
February 2014
Prime Minister, Zoran Milanovic
First Deputy Prime Minister, Foreign Affairs, Vesna Pusic
Deputy Prime Ministers, Branko Grcic; Neven Mimica;
  Milanka Opacic
Defence, Ante Kotromanovic
Finance, Slavko Linic

EMBASSY OF THE REPUBLIC OF CROATIA
21 Conway Street, London W1T 6BN
T 020-7387 2022 E croemb.london@mvep.hr
W http://uk.mvep.hr
Ambassador Extraordinary and Plenipotentiary, HE Dr Ivan
  Grdesic, *apptd* 2012

BRITISH EMBASSY
Ivana Lucica 4, 10000 Zagreb
T (+385) 600 9100 E british.embassyzagreb@fco.gov.uk
W www.gov.uk/government/world/croatia
Ambassador, HE David Slinn, *apptd* 2012

DEFENCE

Aged 16–49, 2010 est	Males	Females
Available for military service	1,016,234	1,017,355
Fit for military service	770,710	839,732

Military expenditure – US$959m (2012)

ECONOMY AND TRADE

As part of Yugoslavia, Croatia was a prosperous and
industrialised area, but the conflict in 1991–5 damaged its
infrastructure, large areas of farmland, industrial productivity
and the tourist industry. From 2000 to 2007 there was
steady economic growth, led by a recovery in tourism,
banking and public investment. However, a growing trade
deficit, high unemployment, the size of the public sector and
the economy's over-reliance on tourism are longer-term
problems that left the economy vulnerable in the global
economic downturn in 2008. Greater financial restrictions
and stricter tax collection have been used to combat a second
recession, which began in 2012. The country joined the EU

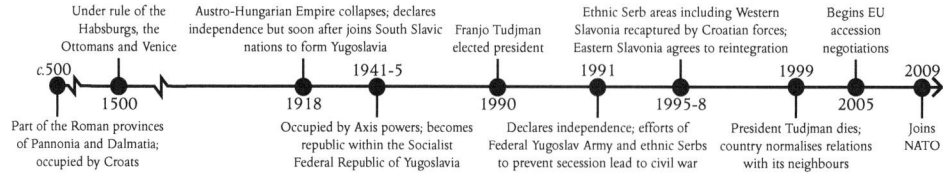

	Under rule of the Habsburgs, the Ottomans and Venice	Austro-Hungarian Empire collapses; declares independence but soon after joins South Slavic nations to form Yugoslavia	Franjo Tudjman elected president	Ethnic Serb areas including Western Slavonia recaptured by Croatian forces; Eastern Slavonia agrees to reintegration	Begins EU accession negotiations	
c.500				1991	1999	2009
1500		1918	1990	1995-8	2005	
Part of the Roman provinces of Pannonia and Dalmatia; occupied by Croats		Occupied by Axis powers; becomes republic within the Socialist Federal Republic of Yugoslavia	Declares independence; efforts of Federal Yugoslav Army and ethnic Serbs to prevent secession lead to civil war	President Tudjman dies; country normalises relations with its neighbours	Joins NATO	

in 2013 but does not yet qualify to join the Economic and Monetary Union.

The service sector accounts for 69.2 per cent of GDP, industry for 25.8 per cent and agriculture for 5 per cent. Tourism is a major contributor to GDP. Industry produces chemicals and plastics, machine tools, metals and metal products, electronics, wood products, construction materials and textiles, and includes food processing, shipbuilding and oil refining. Agricultural production includes cereals, pulses, fruit and vegetables, livestock and dairy products. Most trade is with EU and neighbouring countries.

GNI – US$57,081m; US$13,490 per capita (2012)
Annual average growth of GDP – –0.6 per cent (2013 est)
Inflation rate – 3 per cent (2013 est)
Population below poverty line – 21.1 per cent (2011 est)
Unemployment – 20.5 per cent (2013 est)
Total external debt – US$63,300m (2013 est)
Imports – US$20,762m (2012)
Exports – US$12,347m (2012)

BALANCE OF PAYMENTS
Trade – US$8,415m deficit (2012)
Current Account – US$4m surplus (2012)

Trade with UK	2012	2013
Imports from UK	£144,667,303	£65,277,062
Exports to UK	£83,431,830	£74,005,870

COMMUNICATIONS
Airports and waterways – 24; there are 785km of inland waterways and frequent ferry services to the many Adriatic islands
Roadways and railways – 29,410km of roadways, including 1,254km of motorways; 2,722km of railways
Telecommunications – 1 64 million fixed lines and 4.97 million mobile subscriptions (2012); there were 2.234 million internet users in 2009
Internet code and IDD – hr; 385 (from UK), 44 (to UK)
Major broadcasters – Croatian Radio-Television (HRT) is the national state-owned public service broadcaster
Press – There are three main news publications: *Vecernji List* (daily), *Jutarnji List* (daily) and *Nacional* (weekly)
WPFI score – 26,82 (65)

EDUCATION AND HEALTH
Education is free and compulsory for all children from ages six to 15.
Literacy rate – 99 per cent (2011 est)
Gross enrolment ratio (percentage of relevant age group) – primary 94 per cent; secondary 98 per cent; tertiary 59 per cent (2011 est)
Health expenditure (per capita) – US$1,138 (2011)
Hospital beds (per 1,000 people) – 6 (2011)
Life expectancy (years) – 76.2 (2013 est)
Mortality rate – 12.06 (2013 est)
Birth rate – 9.53 (2013 est)
Infant mortality rate – 5.96 (2013 est)

CUBA

República de Cuba – Republic of Cuba

Area – 110,860 sq. km
Capital – Havana; population, 2,113,366 (2012 est)
Major cities – Camagüey, Guantánamo, Holguín, Santa Clara, Santiago de Cuba
Currency – Cuban peso ($) of 100 centavos
Population – 11,061,886 falling at 0.13 per cent a year (2013 est)
Religion – Christian (Roman Catholic 60 per cent, Protestant 5 per cent) (est); many practise Santería (African religions syncretised with Christianity). Religious activity is tightly controlled; house churches must be state-registered
Language – Spanish (official)
Population density – 106 per sq. km (2011)
Urban population – 75.1 per cent (2012 est)
Median age (years) – 39.5 (2013 est)
National anthem – 'El Himno de Bayamo' ['The Anthem of Bayamo']
National day – 1 January (Triumph of the Revolution)
Death penalty – Retained
CPI score – 46 (63)

CLIMATE AND TERRAIN
The largest island in the Caribbean, Cuba is part of an archipelago that also includes Isla de la Juventud and around 1,600 other islets and cays. The island of Cuba has three mountainous ranges running from east to west. Elevation extremes range from 2,005m (Pico Turquino) to 0m (Caribbean Sea). The climate is subtropical, with an average annual temperature of 25°C.

POLITICS
The Communist Party of Cuba (PCC) is the only authorised political party. The 1976 constitution was amended in 1991 to allow direct election of the National Assembly by secret ballot, and in 2002 to enshrine socialism in the constitution. The president is elected by the legislature for a five-year term. The unicameral National Assembly of the People's Power has 614 members directly elected for a five-year term; all candidates are approved by the PCC and stand unopposed. Between its sessions, the assembly is represented by the Council of State, whose members are elected by the assembly.

Fidel Castro, who had been president since 1959, announced in February 2008 that he would not accept another term in office due to ill health. His brother, Raúl Castro, who had been acting president since July 2006, was elected head of state and head of government later that month by the National Assembly; he was re-elected in February 2013 and announced that he would step down at the end of his second term.

				Communist state established,	Collapse of the USSR; Cuban government
	Settled by	Becomes independent; USA		allied with USSR; USA begins	introduces rationing and relaxes state
	Spanish	retains naval bases on the island		economic and trade embargo	controls on economic activity

1492   1898   1959   1962   2008
          1600   1902   1961   1991

Visited by	War of independence won;	Dictator Gen. Fulgencio	Cuban missile crisis; the USA and	Fidel Castro steps down as
Columbus	Spain cedes Cuba to the USA	Batista overthrown by	USSR almost engage in nuclear conflict	president owing to ill-health; he
		Fidel Castro	due to missile site construction on Cuba	is replaced by his brother Raúl

HEAD OF STATE
President of Council of State and Council of Ministers, Gen. Raúl Castro Ruz, *elected* 24 February 2008, *re-elected* February 2013
First Vice-President of Council of State, Miguel Diaz-Canel Bermudez

SELECTED GOVERNMENT MEMBERS *as at February 2014*
Vice Presidents of Council of Ministers, Gen. Antonio Enrique Lusson Batlle; Marino Murillo Jorge; Ramiro Valdes Menendez; Adel Izquierdo Rodriguez; Ricardo Cabrisas Ruiz; Ulises Rosales del Toro, Jose Ramon Machado Ventura
Finance and Prices, Lina Pedraza Rodriguez
Foreign Relations, Bruno Rodriguez Parrilla

EMBASSY OF THE REPUBLIC OF CUBA
167 High Holborn, London WC1 6PA
T 020-7240 2488 E secembajador@uk.embacuba.cu
W www.cubadiplomatica.cu/reinounido
Ambassador Extraordinary and Plenipotentiary, HE Esther G. Armenteros Cárdenas, *apptd* 2010

BRITISH EMBASSY
Calle 34, No 702, Miramar, Playa, Havana
T (+53) (0) 7214 2200 E embrit@enet.cu
W www.gov.uk/government/world/cuba
Ambassador Extraordinary and Plenipotentiary, HE Timothy Cole, *apptd* 2012

DEFENCE

Aged 16–49, 2010 est	Males	Females
Available for military service	2,998,201	2,919,107
Fit for military service	2,446,131	2,375,590

Military expenditure – US$98.9m (2011)
Conscription – 17–28 years of age; 24 months for men and women

ECONOMY AND TRADE
After the revolution virtually all land and industrial and commercial enterprises were nationalised. With the collapse of communism in Europe in 1989–91, the economy deteriorated sharply, necessitating rationing of energy, food and consumer goods, and obliging the government to introduce reforms. Since 1993, liberalisation has gradually opened up the economy to limited private enterprise and foreign ownership of property and business enterprises, and introduced price rises for some goods and services and income tax. The reforms resulted in steady growth, in particular stimulating tourism and the oil and mining industries, but the standard of living for most Cubans is still below the pre-1991 level. Further economic difficulties arising from the global economic downturn, which precipitated a marked fall in tourism and nickel prices, led to a further easing of restrictions on private enterprise in 2010 and plans to reduce public sector employment.

The first Cuban Communist Party Congress in 13 years was held in 2011, approving extensive economic changes to the state model as well as various changes in lifestyle options for Cubans, such as greater opportunities for self-employment.

Agriculture contributes 3.8 per cent of GDP and employs around 19.7 per cent of the workforce. Industrial activities include sugar refining, oil production, tobacco processing, construction, nickel mining and production of steel, cement, agricultural machinery and pharmaceuticals. Industry contributes 22.3 per cent of GDP, and the service sector 73.9 per cent. The state sector employs 72.3 per cent of the workforce.

The main trading partners are China, Canada, Venezuela and Spain; Venezuela provides oil on preferential terms. Principal exports are sugar, nickel, tobacco, fish, medical products, citrus fruits and coffee. The main imports are oil, food, machinery and equipment, and chemicals.
GNI – US$67,240m; US$5,890 per capita (2011)
Annual average growth of GDP – 3.1 per cent (2012 est)
Inflation rate – 6 per cent (2013 est)
Unemployment – 4.3 per cent (2013 est)
Total external debt – US$23,440m (2013 est)

BALANCE OF PAYMENTS
Trade – US$6,573m deficit (2010)

Trade with UK	2012	2013
Imports from UK	£26,362,791	£24,092,004
Exports to UK	£35,608,187	£114,169,535

COMMUNICATIONS
Airports – 64; the main international airport is at Havana
Waterways – There are 240km of navigable waterways; the main ports are Havana, Cienfuegos and Matanzas
Roadways and railways – There are 60,858km of roadways, 29,820km of which are surfaced and 8,203km of railways, 4,533km of which are used exclusively by sugar plantations
Telecommunications – 1.217 million fixed line users and 1.682 million mobile subscriptions (2012); there were 1.6 million internet users in 2009
Internet code and IDD – cu; 53 (from UK), 44 (to UK)
Major broadcasters – The main television stations are Cubavision and Portal de la TV Cubana. The main radio stations are Radio Rebelde and Radio Reloj; Radio-TV Marti, a US government-backed station, transmits from Florida
Press – The official Communist Party newspaper is *Granma*
WPFI score – 70,92 (170)

EDUCATION AND HEALTH
Education is free of charge and compulsory between ages six and 15. Health care is free.
Literacy rate – 100 per cent (2011 est)
Gross enrolment ratio (percentage of relevant age group) – primary 101 per cent; secondary 90 per cent; tertiary 80 per cent (2011 est)
Health expenditure (per capita) – US$606 (2011)
Hospital beds (per 1,000 people) – 5.1 (2011)
Life expectancy (years) – 78.05 (2013 est)
Mortality rate – 7.58 (2013 est)
Birth rate – 9.92 (2013 est)
Infant mortality rate – 4.76 (2013 est)

CYPRUS

Kypriaki Dimokratia / Kibris Cumhuriyeti – Republic of Cyprus

Area – 9,251 sq. km, of which 3,355 sq. km are in the Turkish Cypriot-administered area
Capital – Nicosia, population, 253,000 (2011 est)
Major cities – Larnaca, Limassol, Strovolos (south of the partition); Famagusta, Kyrenia (north)
Currency – Euro (€) of 100 cents (south), Turkish lira (north)
Population – 1,155,403 rising at 1.52 per cent a year (2013 est); Greek (77 per cent), Turkish (18 per cent) (2001 est)
Religion – Christian (Greek Orthodox 95 per cent) south of the partition; Muslim 98 per cent (mainly Sunni) in the north
Language – Greek, Turkish (both official), English
Population density – 121 per sq. km (2011)
Urban population – 70.7 per cent (2012 est)
Median age (years) – 35.4 (2013 est)
National anthem – 'Imnos eis tin Eleutherian' ['Hymn to Freedom']
National day – 1 October (Independence Day); Turkish Cypriots celebrate on 15 November
Death penalty – Abolished for all crimes (since 2002)
CPI score – 63 (31)
Literacy rate – 99 per cent (2011 est)
Life expectancy (years) – 78.17 (2013 est)
Mortality rate – 6.52 (2013 est)
Birth rate – 11.45 (2013 est)
Infant mortality rate – 8.82 (2013 est)

CLIMATE AND TERRAIN
Cyprus is the third-largest island in the Mediterranean. It has two mountain ranges, the Pentadaktylos along the north coast, and the Troodos in the centre and west. Plains lie between the two ranges and on parts of the south coast. Elevation extremes range from 1,951m (Mt Olympus, Troodos range) to 0m (Mediterranean Sea). The climate is Mediterranean, with very warm summers.

POLITICS
The 1960 constitution provides for power-sharing between the Greek and Turkish Cypriots but some of these provisions have been in abeyance since 1963, when the Turkish

Cypriots withdrew from the power-sharing arrangements. The executive president is directly elected for a five-year term. The unicameral legislature, the House of Representatives, has 80 members, directly elected for a five-year term; elections to the 24 seats reserved for Turkish Cypriots have not taken place since 1963.

Legislative elections held in May 2011 resulted in gains for the Progressive Party of the Working People (AKEL) and the opposition Democratic Rally (DISY) party; AKEL maintained its majority in the House of Representatives through a coalition with the Democratic Party (DIKO), although a munitions blast in the south of the country in July 2011 forced a major cabinet reshuffle and the resignation of key coalition members. DISY's Nicos Anastasiades was elected president in February 2013.

HEAD OF STATE
President, Nikos Anastasiades, *elected* 24 February 2013, *sworn in* 28 February 2013

SELECTED GOVERNMENT MEMBERS *as at February 2014*
Defence, Fotis Fotiou
Finance, Charis Georgiadis
Foreign Affairs, Ioannis Kasoulidis

HIGH COMMISSION FOR THE REPUBLIC OF CYPRUS
13 St James's Square, London SW1Y 4LB
T 020-7321 4100 E cyphclondon@btconnect.com
High Commissioner, HE Euripides L. Evriviades, *apptd* 2013

BRITISH HIGH COMMISSION
PO Box 21978, Alexander Pallis Street, 1587 Nicosia
T (+357) 2286 1100 E brithc.2@cytanet.com.cy
W www.gov.uk/government/world/cyprus
High Commissioner, HE Matthew Kidd, apptd 2010

BRITISH SOVEREIGN BASE AREAS
The Sovereign Base Areas (SBAs) of Akrotiri and Dhekelia are those parts of Cyprus that remained under British sovereignty and jurisdiction after independence, and have the status of a UK overseas territory. They are around 254 sq. km in size. There are approximately 15,700 residents: 7,700 Cypriots, and 8,000 military and UK-based civilian personnel and their dependants.
Administrator of the British Sovereign Base Areas, Major-General Richard J. Cripwell, *apptd* 2013

TURKISH REPUBLIC OF NORTHERN CYPRUS

In 1974, a Greece-backed coup against the Cypriot government led Turkey, fearing the coup was a precursor to the union of Cyprus with Greece, to invade northern Cyprus and occupy over a third of the island. The following year, a Turkish Federated State of Cyprus was declared, and in 1983 a declaration of statehood was issued which purported to establish the Turkish Republic of Northern Cyprus. The declaration was condemned by the UN security council and

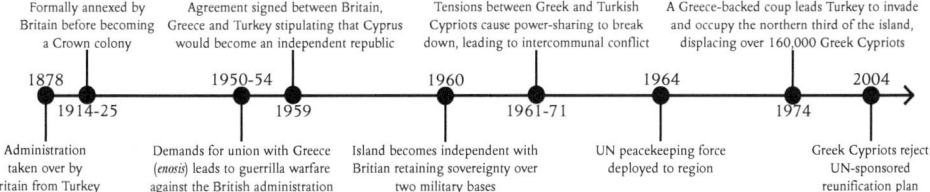

Formally annexed by Britain before becoming a Crown colony	Agreement signed between Britain, Greece and Turkey stipulating that Cyprus would become an independent republic	Tensions between Greek and Turkish Cypriots cause power-sharing to break down, leading to intercommunal conflict	A Greece-backed coup leads Turkey to invade and occupy the northern third of the island, displacing over 160,000 Greek Cypriots
1878	1950-54	1960	1964	2004
1914-25	1959	1961-71	1974	
Administration taken over by Britain from Turkey	Demands for union with Greece (*enosis*) leads to guerrilla warfare against the British administration	Island becomes independent with Britian retaining sovereignty over two military bases	UN peacekeeping force deployed to region	Greek Cypriots reject UN-sponsored reunification plan

only Turkey has recognised the republic. A constitution was adopted in 1985, and elections have been held at regular intervals since.

Reunification talks were unsuccessful in the 1980s and 1990s, and although Turkish Cypriots approved a UN-sponsored reunification plan put to simultaneous referendums in 2004, it was rejected by Greek Cypriots. Since 2004, the EU has given aid to the area to promote and ease reunification, and UN-facilitated talks began in 2008.

The 2009 legislative election was won by the National Unity Party, which favours unification with Turkey. Dervis Eroglu won the 2010 presidential election, replacing Mehmet Ali Talat.

DE FACTO HEAD OF STATE
President, Dervis Eroglu, *elected* 18 April 2010, *sworn in* 23 April 2010
Prime Minister, Ozkan Yorgancioglu

DEFENCE
A military airfield in Paphos provides a base for Greek military aircraft, as Cyprus does not possess its own air force.

Aged 16–49, 2010 est	Males	Females
Available for military service	327,875	287,891
Fit for military service	275,842	239,862
(All Greek Cypriot National Guard)		

Military expenditure – US$461m (2013)
Conscription – 18–50 years of age, Greek Cypriot males only; 25 months

ECONOMY AND TRADE
The Greek Cypriot economy is dominated by the service sector, which accounted for 81.7 per cent of GDP in 2013; this was derived mainly from tourism and financial services. Tourism represents a major part of the total GDP, making the economy vulnerable to fluctuations; reduced visitor numbers due to the global economic downturn contributed to the economy entering recession in 2009 and registering no growth in 2011. Shipping services are also important; about 20 per cent of the world's shipping is Cypriot-registered. Industry contributes 15.9 per cent of GDP and agriculture 2.4 per cent. The main products for export are citrus fruits, potatoes, pharmaceuticals, cement and garments. Imports are primarily consumer goods, fuel and lubricants, machinery and transport equipment. Over half of trade is with other EU countries.

Between 2009 and 2013, the economy contracted by a total of 8.2 per cent following a banking crisis triggered by excessive exposure to the damaged Greek economy. In 2013 Cyprus received a $13bn (£7.6bn) economic bailout from the European Commission, the European Central Bank and the International Monetary Fund ('the Troika'). Conditions included the privatisation of state-owned enterprises and the downsizing and restructuring of the banking sector. While the most recent Troika review in May 2014 indicated that Cyprus was meeting economic targets, positive growth is not expected until 2015.

The Turkish Cypriot economy suffers from a small domestic market, international isolation and a bloated public sector. It is heavily dependent on financial support from the Turkish government. Services accounted for about 69.1 per cent of GDP in 2006, industry for 22.5 per cent and agriculture for 8.6 per cent. The main products for export are citrus fruits, dairy products, potatoes and textiles. The main imports are vehicles, fuel, cigarettes, food, minerals, chemicals and machinery. The tourist industry is small because the only international transport links are via Turkey.
GNI – US$22,079m; US$26,110 per capita (2012)
Annual average growth of GDP – –8.7 per cent (2013 est)

Inflation rate – 0.2 per cent (2013 est)
Unemployment – 17.4 per cent (2013 est)
Total external debt – US$95,280m (2013 est)
Imports – US$7,381m (2012)
Exports – US$1,829m (2012)

BALANCE OF PAYMENTS
Trade – US$5,552m deficit (2012)
Current Account – US$1,565m deficit (2012)

Trade with UK	2012	2013
Imports from UK	£470,662,054	£462,351,202
Exports to UK	£152,957,692	£181,114,836

COMMUNICATIONS
Airports and waterways – Larnaca and Paphos (Greek area); flight connections to Turkish area are via Turkey; principal ports are Limassol, Larnaca and Vasilikos (Greek area), and Famagusta and Kyrenia (Turkish area)
Roadways – The road network (13,006km in the Greek part of the island and 7,000km in the Turkish part) serves the main population centres
Telecommunications – 405,000 (Greek area) and 86,228 (Turkish area) fixed lines and 1.09 million (Greek area) and 147,522 (Turkish area) mobile subscriptions (2011); there were 433,900 internet users in 2009
Internet code and IDD – cy; 357 (from UK), 44 (to UK)
Major broadcasters – The state-run Cyprus Broadcasting Corporation competes with a number of privately owned television and radio stations; the Turkish north operates its own services
Press – Major newspapers include *Cyprus Mail* (English-language daily), *Politis* (Greek-language daily) and *Kibris Gazete* (Turkish language)
WPFI score – 14,45 (25) (Greek area), 29,54 (83) (Turkish area)

CZECH REPUBLIC

Ceska Republika – Czech Republic

Area – 78,867 sq. km
Capital – Prague (Praha); population, 1,163,742 (2012 est)
Major cities – Brno (Brünn), Ostrava, Plzen (Pilsen)
Currency – Koruna (Kc) of 100 haleru
Population – 10,609,762 falling at 0.15 per cent a year (2013 est); Czech (64.3 per cent), Moravian (5 per cent), Slovak (1.4 per cent) (2011)
Religion – Christian (Roman Catholic 10.4 per cent, Protestant 1.1 per cent) (est)
Language – Czech (official), Slovak
Population density – 136 per sq. km (2011)
Urban population – 73.4 per cent (2012 est)
Median age (years) – 41.4 (2013 est)

Collapse of Austro-Hungarian Empire; creation of Czechoslovakia, an amalgamation of Bohemia, Moravia, Slovakia and Ruthenia

Liberated by Soviet and US forces

The Communist Party embarks on a reform programme (the Prague Spring) which is abandoned after Gustav Husak becomes leader

The Communist Party is defeated in first free elections

Joins NATO

Joins the EU

1526 — 1939 — 1948 — 1989 — 1992

1918 — 1945 — 1968-9 — 1990 — 1999 — 2004

Medieval kingdom of Bohemia comes under rule of the Habsburg dynasty

German forces invade Czech lands; Slovakia becomes a puppet state

Soviets take power in a coup

The Communist Party forced to concede its monopoly on power following mass protests

Leaders of the Czech and Slovak republics agree to dissolve the federation and form two sovereign states

National anthem – 'Kde Domov Muj?' ['Where is My Homeland?']
National day – 28 October (Founding Day)
Death penalty – Abolished for all crimes (since 1990)
CPI score – 48 (57)

CLIMATE AND TERRAIN
The landlocked republic is composed of Bohemia (the west and centre) and Moravia (the east). Bohemia contains the fertile plains of the river Elbe and the surrounding low mountains, while the hilly region of Moravia extends towards the basin of the river Danube. Roughly a third of the country is covered by forest. Elevation extremes range from 1,602m (Snezka) to 115m (river Elbe). The climate is continental, with warm, humid summers and cold, dry winters. The average temperature in Prague ranges from −1°C in January to 17°C in July and August.

POLITICS
The 1992 constitution provided for the separation of the Czech Republic and Slovakia; federal laws remain in place unless superseded by Czech ones. The president is elected by popular vote for a five-year term, renewable once; prior to 2012 the president was elected by a joint session of both chambers of the legislature. The bicameral *Parlament* comprises a 200-member Chamber of Deputies, directly elected for a four-year term, and an 81-member senate directly elected for a six-year term, one-third being elected every two years. The council of ministers is appointed by the president on the recommendation of the prime minister.

Early legislative elections in October 2013 gave a combined majority to three centre-left parties – the Czech Social Democratic Party (CSSD), the Christian Democratic Union/Czech People's Party (KDU–CSL) and the Action of Dissatisfied Citizens (ANO) – which formed a coalition government under CSSD chairman Bohuslav Sobotka. The incumbent Civic Democratic Party (ODS) lost more than two-thirds of its seats. Partial senate elections in autumn 2012 saw the CSSD increase its majority from one seat to two. Milos Zeman was elected president in January 2013.

HEAD OF STATE
President, Milos Zeman, *elected* 25 January 2013, *sworn in* 8 March 2013

SELECTED GOVERNMENT MEMBERS *as at February 2014*
Prime Minister, Bohuslav Sobotka
First Deputy Prime Minister, Finance, Andrej Babis
Defence, Martin Stropnicky
Foreign Affairs, Lubomir Zaoralek

EMBASSY OF THE CZECH REPUBLIC
26 Kensington Palace Gardens, London W8 4QY
T 020-7243 1115 E london@embassy.mzv.cz
W www.mzv.cz/london
Ambassador Extraordinary and Plenipotentiary, HE Michael Zantovsky, *apptd* 2009

BRITISH EMBASSY
Thunovska 14, 11800 Prague 1
T (+420) (2) 5740 2111 E ukinczechrepublic@fco.gov.uk
W www.gov.uk/government/world/czech-republic
Ambassador Extraordinary and Plenipotentiary, HE Jan Thompson, OBE, *apptd* 2013

DEFENCE

Aged 16–49, 2010 est	Males	Females
Available for military service	2,506,826	2,407,634
Fit for military service	2,072,267	1,988,839

Military expenditure – US$2,259m (2013)

ECONOMY AND TRADE
Economic reforms and accession to the EU have produced a stable and successful market economy, as well as contributing to steady growth by expanding export markets and encouraging foreign investment. The global economic downturn caused the economy to contract in 2009, largely because of a reduced demand for the country's major exports. A slow recovery began in late 2009 and continued through 2011, however the economy went into recession in 2012 due to a lack of external demand and the government's austerity measures.

Services account for 58.2 per cent of GDP, industry for 39.6 per cent and agriculture for 2.2 per cent. The principal agricultural products are cereal crops, sugar beet and potatoes; the timber industry is also important. The country has been industrialised since the 19th century, and motor vehicles, metals, machinery, glass and armaments are major products. Electricity is also exported. The principal trading partners are EU countries – especially Germany – and China and Russia.

GNI – US$181,892m; US$18,120 per capita (2012)
Annual average growth of GDP – −0.4 per cent (2013 est)
Inflation rate – 1.6 per cent (2013 est)
Population below poverty line – 9 per cent (2010 est)
Unemployment – 7.6 per cent (2013 est)
Total external debt – US$103,200m (2013 est)
Imports – US$141,515m (2012)
Exports – US$157,167m (2012)

BALANCE OF PAYMENTS
Trade – US$15,652m surplus (2012)
Current Account – US$4,727m deficit (2012)

Trade with UK	2012	2013
Imports from UK	£1,714,691,770	£1,875,452,017
Exports to UK	£4,413,875,308	£4,553,307,635

COMMUNICATIONS
Airports and waterways – There are 41 airports, with the principal airport at Prague; the 664km of waterways include the Elbe, Vltava and Oder rivers

Roadways and railways – Extensive road (130,671km) and rail (9,469km) networks link the main population centres
Telecommunications = 2.1 million fixed lines and 12.97 million mobile subscriptions (2012), there were 6.681 million internet users in 2009
Internet code and IDD – cz; 420 (from UK), 44 (to UK)
Major broadcasters – The public broadcaster Ceska Televize (CT) runs two networks and a 24-hour news channel alongside two major private television stations; Czech public radio, Cesky Rozhlas (CRo), operates three national networks and local services
Press – There are four major daily newspaper: *Lidove Noviny, Mlada Fronta Dnes, Pravo* and *Blesk*
WPFI score – 10,07 (13)

EDUCATION AND HEALTH

Education is free and compulsory for all children from the age of six to 15.
Gross enrolment ratio (percentage of relevant age group) –
  primary 102 per cent; secondary 96 per cent; tertiary
  65 per cent (2011 est)
Health expenditure (per capita) – US$1,507 (2011)
Hospital beds (per 1,000 people) – 7 (2010)
Life expectancy (years) – 77.56 (2013 est)
Mortality rate – 11.01 (2013 est)
Birth rate – 8.55 (2013 est)
Infant mortality rate – 3.67 (2013 est)

DENMARK

Kongeriget Danmark – Kingdom of Denmark

Area – 43,094 sq. km (excluding the Faroe Islands and
  Greenland)
Capital – Copenhagen; population, 1,206,895 (2012 est)
Major cities – Aalborg, Aarhus, Esbjerg, Odense
Currency – Danish krone (DKr) of 100 ore
Population – 5,5696,077 rising at 0.22 per cent a year
  (2014 est)
Religion – Christian (Lutheran 80 per cent, Roman Catholic
  1 per cent), Muslim 4 per cent (est); the Evangelical
  Lutheran Church is the state church
Language – Danish (official), Faroese, Greenlandic, German;
  English is widely spoken as a second language
Population density – 131 per sq. km (2011)
Urban population – 87.1 per cent (2012)
Median age (years) – 41.6 (2014 est)
National anthem – 'Det er et Yndigt Land' ['There is a Lovely
  Land']
National day – 5 June (Constitution Day)
Death penalty – Abolished for all crimes (since 1978)
CPI score – 91 (1)

CLIMATE AND TERRAIN

Denmark consists of most of the Jutland peninsula and 406 islands, mainly in the Baltic Sea or among the northern Frisian Islands in the North Sea. The largest islands are Sjaelland (Zealand), Fyn, Lolland, Faister and Bornholm It is a low-lying country, indented by fjords on its east coast and with lagoons and sand dunes along the west coast; Lim Fjord nearly bisects the north of Jutland. Elevation extremes range from 171m (Mollehoj) to −7m (Lammefjord). The climate is temperate, with cold winters and warm summers. Average temperatures range from 0.5°C in January to 16°C in July.

HISTORY AND POLITICS

The Danes were at the forefront of Viking expansionism from the eighth century. Denmark was unified in the tenth century and was the centre of a short-lived empire, also including Norway and England, created by Cnut (Canute) in the 11th century. The Union of Kalmar (1397) brought Norway and Sweden (including Finland) under Danish rule. Danish power waned during the 16th century, enabling Sweden to re-establish its independence in 1523, and Norway was ceded to Sweden under the Treaty of Kiel in 1814. Denmark was neutral during the First World War, but in the Second World War it was invaded and occupied by Germany until May 1945.

Denmark joined the European Community in 1973. In a 2000 referendum, it rejected adopting the euro.

In the 2011 legislative election, the Liberal Party remained the largest party in parliament, but a surge of support for the Red Bloc (a political alliance consisting of centre-left parties including the Social Democrats) gave them an overall majority with 97 seats. Helle Thorning-Schmidt, leader of the Social Democrats, formed a coalition with other member parties of the Red Bloc, and took office in October 2011.

The country is a constitutional monarchy, with a hereditary monarch as head of state. The head of government is the prime minister, who appoints the cabinet. The unicameral legislature, the *Folketing*, has 179 members, including two for the Faeroes and two for Greenland; members are elected for a four-year term by proportional representation.

HEAD OF STATE
HM The Queen of Denmark, Queen Margrethe II, KG, *born*
  16 April 1940, *acceded* 14 January 1972
Heir, HRH Crown Prince Frederik, *born* 26 May 1968

SELECTED GOVERNMENT MEMBERS *as at April 2014*
Prime Minister, Helle Thorning-Schmidt
Deputy Prime Minister, Magrethe Vestager
Defence, Nicolai Wammen
Finance, Bjarne Corydon

ROYAL DANISH EMBASSY
55 Sloane Street, London SW1X 9SR
T 020-7333 0200 **E** lonamb@um.dk
W www.storbrittanien.um.dk
Ambassador Extraordinary and Plenipotentiary, HE Claus
  Grube, *apptd* 2013

BRITISH EMBASSY
Kastelsvej 36–40, 2100 Copenhagen
T (+45) 3544 5200 **E** enquiry.copenhagen@fco.gov.uk
W www.gov.uk/government/world/denmark
Ambassador Extraordinary and Plenipotentiary, Vivien Life,
  apptd 2012

DEFENCE

Aged 16–49, 2010 est	Males	Females
Available for military service	1,236,337	1,224,182
Fit for military service	1,014,560	1,003,921

Military expenditure – US$4,614m (2013)
Conscription – 18 years of age; 4–12 months

ECONOMY AND TRADE

Denmark has a diversified and industrialised market economy with a high dependence on exports. It is a net exporter of food and energy (oil and natural gas). Slowing growth from 2007 and then the global downturn pushed the economy into recession in 2009; a modest recovery began in 2010 but the economy re-entered a technical recession at the beginning of 2011, with unemployment averaging 6 per cent from 2010–13. The service sector contributes 76.8 per cent of GDP, industry 22.7 per cent and the highly efficient agricultural sector 1.5 per cent. Metals, pharmaceuticals, shipping and renewable energy are key industries.

The main trading partners are other EU countries, especially Germany and Sweden. Principal exports are machinery and instruments, meat and meat products, dairy products, fish, pharmaceuticals, furniture and windmills. The main imports are machinery and equipment, industrial raw materials and semi-manufactures, chemicals, grain and foodstuffs, and consumer goods.

GNI – US$324,263m; US$59,850 per capita (2012)
Annual average growth of GDP – 0.1 per cent (2013 est)
Inflation rate – 0.8 per cent (2013 est)
Population below poverty line – 13.4 per cent (2011)
Unemployment – 6 per cent (2013 est)
Total external debt – US$586,700m (2012)
Imports – US$92,300m (2012)
Exports   US$106,127m (2012)

BALANCE OF PAYMENTS
Trade – US$13,827m surplus (2012)
Current Account – US$17,541m surplus (2012)

Trade with UK	2012	2013
Imports from UK	£2,753,245,221	£2,752,490,775
Exports to UK	£5,812,040,151	£5,312,744,650

COMMUNICATIONS

Airports and waterways – The principal airports are at Copenhagen, Aarhus, Aalborg and near Vejle; the main ports are Aarhus, Odense, Copenhagen, Aalborg and Esbjerg
Roadways and railways – There are 73,929km of roadways, including 1,143km of motorways and 2,667km of railways, of which 640km are electrified
Telecommunications – 2.431 million fixed lines and 6.6 million mobile subscriptions (2012); there were 4.75 million internet users in 2009
Internet code and IDD – dk; 45 (from UK), 44 (to UK)
Major broadcasters – The public broadcaster is Danmarks Radio, which operates two television networks, and national and regional radio stations
Press – There are six major daily newspapers, including *Morgenavisen Jyllands-Posten*, *Berlingske Tidende* and *Ekstra Bladet*
WPFI score – 7,43 (7)

EDUCATION AND HEALTH

Education is free and compulsory for nine years.
Gross enrolment ratio (percentage of relevant age group) –
primary 100 per cent; secondary 120 per cent; tertiary 74 per cent (2011)

Health expenditure (per capita) – US$6,648 (2011)
Hospital beds (per 1,000 people) – 3.5 (2010)
Life expectancy (years) – 79.09 (2014 est)
Mortality rate – 10.23 (2014 est)
Birth rate – 10.22 (2014 est)
Infant mortality rate – 4.1 (2014 est)

THE FAROE ISLANDS

Area – 1,393 sq. km
Capital – Torshavn; population, 12,333 (2011 est)
Population – 49,947 at 0.49 per cent per year (2014 est)
National day – 29 July (Olaifest)
Internet code and IDD – fo; 298 (from UK), 44 (to UK)

The Faroe (Sheep) Islands are a group of 18 rugged islands (17 inhabited) and a few islets in the North Atlantic Ocean, between the Shetland Islands and Iceland. First settled in the ninth century, the islands were a Norwegian province and, with Norway, came under Danish rule in the 14th century. Since 1948 the Faeroes have been self-governing and are not part of the EU.

The sovereign is represented in the islands by a high commissioner, and the islands elect two representatives to the Danish legislature. The Faroese government *(Landsstyri)* is responsible for internal affairs. The parliament *(Loegting)* has 33 members, elected for a four-year term. In the 2011 election, the Union Party overtook the Republican Party to become the largest party in parliament; the incumbent prime minister Kaj Leo Johannesen continued to head a coalition government comprising the Union Party, the Social Democrats and the People's Party.
Prime Minister, Kaj Leo Johannesen

ECONOMY AND TRADE

The economy has grown steadily in recent years, although it slowed during the global downturn. It remains highly dependent on fishing and fish processing; fish and fish products account for 95 per cent of exports. Offshore oil discoveries raise the possibility of future diversification and less dependence on Danish government subsidies.

BALANCE OF PAYMENTS
Trade – US$44m (2010)
Current Account – US$7m deficit (2003)

Trade with UK	2012	2013
Imports from UK	£12,604,708	£10,982,989
Exports to UK	£137,547,726	£206,976,990

BRITISH CONSULATE
P/F Damfar, PO Box 1154, Niels Finsengota 5, FR-110 Torshavn
T (+298) 35 00 77
Honorary Consul, Joannes Hansen

GREENLAND (KALAALLIT NUNAAT)

Area – 2,166,086 sq. km
Capital – Nuuk (Godthab); population, 15,000 (2009)
Population – 57,728 rising at 0.02 per cent per year (2014 est)
National day – 21 June (longest day)
Internet code and IDD – gl; 299 (from UK), 44 (to UK)

Greenland, the world's largest island, lies between the Atlantic and Arctic oceans, to the east of Canada and to the west of Iceland. Most of Greenland is within the Arctic Circle, with permafrost covering about 80 per cent of the island, although this ice cap is beginning to melt (*see* North and South Poles). Elevation extremes range from 3,700m (Gunnbjorn) to 0m (Atlantic Ocean).

Greenland was first discovered by small groups of hunters and nomadic groups who migrated from Canada c.500 BC. In the late tenth century Icelanders established settlements along the south-eastern coast, but these colonies had died out by the 16th century. Danish colonisation began in the 18th century. Greenland was integrated into Denmark in 1953 and was granted internal autonomy in 1979; greater autonomy was granted in 2009. Greenland negotiated its withdrawal from the EU, without discontinuing relations with Denmark, and left in 1985. The USA maintains air bases on the island.

The sovereign is represented by a high commissioner, and Greenland elects two representatives to the Danish legislature. The Greenlandic government *(Landsstyri)* is elected by the parliament *(Landsting),* which has 31 members, elected for a four-year term. In the 2009 election to the *Landsting,* the Siumut (Forward) party, in power since the 1970s, was defeated by the Inuit Ataqatigiit (Brotherhood of the People) party, which won 14 seats. In March 2013 the Siumut party won over 40 per cent of the popular vote, making Aleqa Hammond the country's first female prime minister.
Prime Minister, Aleqa Hammond

ECONOMY AND TRADE
The economy is dependent on Danish subsidies (56 per cent of government revenue) and fishing; fish and fish products comprise 89 per cent of exports. Natural resources include zinc, iron ore, lead, coal, molybdenum, gold, platinum and uranium, some of which are mined. Mineral exploration and mining operations are being extended as the ice cap shrinks. This is also benefiting offshore oil exploration, and global warming is extending the growing season. Tourism is being encouraged.

Trade with UK	2012	2013
Imports from UK	£1,823,801	£4,463,405
Exports to UK	£27,064,161	£1,476,999

DJIBOUTI

Jumhuriyat Jibuti / République de Djibouti – Republic of Djibouti

Area – 23,200 sq. km
Capital – Djibouti; population, 496,000 (2011 est)
Currency – Djibouti franc (DJF) of 100 centimes
Population – 810,179, (2014 est) rising at 2.23 per cent a year (2014 est); Somali (Issa) 60 per cent, Afar 35 per cent (est)
Religion – Muslim 94 per cent, Christian 6 per cent
Language – French, Arabic (both official), Somali, Afar
Population density – 37 per sq. km (2011)
Urban population – 77.1 per cent (2012)
Median age (years) – 22.8 (2014 est)
National anthem – 'Djibouti'
National day – 27 June (Independence Day)
Death penalty – Abolished for all crimes (since 1995)
CPI score – 36 (94)
Life expectancy (years) – 62.4 (2014 est)
Mortality rate – 7.84 (2014 est)
Birth rate – 24.08 (2014 est)
Infant mortality rate – 50.2 (2014 est)
HIV / AIDS adult prevalence – 1.2 per cent (2012 est)

CLIMATE AND TERRAIN
Djibouti is situated on the strait linking the Gulf of Aden with the Red Sea, close to busy shipping lanes. The coastal plain is separated from an inland plateau by the central mountains. Elevation extremes range from 2,028m (Moussa Ali) to −155m (Lake Assal). Although the climate is semi-arid with a hot season between April and October, occasional heavy rains can cause flash floods. The country is also prone to cyclones, drought and earthquakes.

POLITICS
Under the 1992 constitution, amended in 2010, the president is directly elected for a five-year term, renewable without limit. The president appoints the council of ministers. The unicameral National Assembly has 65 members, directly elected for a five-year term. The 2010 constitutional amendments provided for the establishment of a senate.

In the 2008 legislative elections, which were boycotted by the opposition, the Union for a Presidential Majority (UMP) – an alliance of the RPP, FRUD and two other parties supporting President Guelleh – retained all 65 seats in the legislature. The 2011 presidential election was boycotted by the opposition and President Guelleh won a third term in office. Though opposition parties took part in the February 2013 parliamentary elections, the ruling party took 49 of 65 seats; the Union of National Salvation issued a statement claiming the vote was rigged.

HEAD OF STATE
President, Ismail Omar Guelleh, *elected* 9 April 1999, *re-elected* 2005, 2011

SELECTED GOVERNMENT MEMBERS *as at April 2014*
Prime Minister, Mohamed Kamil Abdoulkader
Defence, Hassan Darar Houffaneh
Economy and Finance, Ilyas Moussa Dawaleh
Foreign Affairs, Mahamoud Ali Youssouf
Interior, Hassan Omar

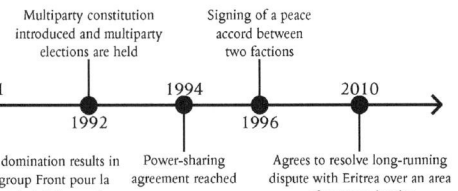

EMBASSY OF THE REPUBLIC OF DJIBOUTI
26 Rue Emile Ménier, 75116 Paris, France
T (+33) (1) 4727 4922 E webmaster@amb-djibouti.org
Ambassador Extraordinary and Plenipotentiary, HE Rachad
   Farah, *apptd* 2005

BRITISH AMBASSADOR
HE Greg Dorey, *apptd* 2011, resident at Addis Ababa,
   Ethiopia

DEFENCE

Aged 16–49, 2010 est	Males	Females
Available for military service	170,386	221,411
Fit for military service	114,557	154,173

Military expenditure – US$40m (2008)

ECONOMY AND TRADE
A barren country with few natural resources and little
industry, Djibouti's chief asset is its location on major
shipping lanes. It is a transit port for neighbouring
landlocked countries (especially Ethiopia, 70 per cent of
whose trade passes through Djibouti), an international
trans-shipment and refuelling centre, and a military base for
US and EU forces because of its strategic position. The
country is dependent on foreign aid, has a very high level
of unemployment and has to import nearly all its food. The
service sector accounts for 79.7 per cent of GDP, industry for
17.3 per cent and agriculture for 3 per cent.
   The main trading partners are Ethiopia (which takes 70 per
cent of exports), Saudi Arabia, India and China. Principal
exports are re-exports, hides and skins, and coffee (in transit).
The main imports are food, beverages, transport equipment,
chemicals and petroleum products.
GNI – US$1,120m; US$1,270 per capita (2009)
Annual average growth of GDP – 5 per cent (2013 est)
Inflation rate – 2.5 per cent (2013 est)
Population below poverty line – 18.8 per cent (2012 est)
Unemployment – 59 per cent (2007 est)
Total external debt – US$821,600m (2013 est)
Imports – US$580m (2012)
Exports – US$95m (2012)

BALANCE OF PAYMENTS
Trade – US$485m deficit (2012)
Current Account – US$175m deficit (2011)

Trade with UK	2012	2013
Imports from UK	£28,169,237	£6,748,776
Exports to UK	£1,071,924	£1,424,752

COMMUNICATIONS
Airports and waterways – The main port and principal airport
are located in Djibouti
Roadways and railways – Of the 3,065km of roads, 1,226km
are surfaced, the 100km Djibouti section of the Addis
Ababa–Djibouti railway is controlled by both Djibouti and
Ethiopia but is largely inoperable
Telecommunications – 18,000 fixed lines and 209,000 mobile
telephones in use (2012); there were 25,900 internet users in
2009
Internet code and IDD – dj; 253 (from UK), 44 (to UK)
Major broadcasters – The main newspaper, *La Nation,* and the
national radio and television stations, operated by
Radiodiffusion-Télévision de Djibouti, are government-
owned; *Le Renouveau* is published by the opposition Party
for Democratic Renewal
WPFI score – 70,34 (169)

DOMINICA

Commonwealth of Dominica

Area – 751 sq. km
Capital – Roseau; population, 14,000 (20011 est)
Currency – East Caribbean dollar (EC$) of 100 cents
Population – 73,449 rising at 0.22 per cent a year (2014 est)
Religion – Christian (Roman Catholic 61 per cent,
   Pentecostal 6 per cent, Seventh-day Adventist 6 per cent,
   Baptist 4 per cent, Methodist 4 per cent) (est)
Language – English (official), Creole
Population density – 95 per sq. km (2011)
Urban population – 67.2 per cent (2012 est)
Median age (years) – 32.1 (2014 est)
National anthem – 'Isle of Beauty, Isle of Splendour'
National day – 3 November (Independence Day)
Death penalty – Retained
CPI score – 58 (41)
Life expectancy (years) – 78.59 (2014 est)
Mortality rate – 7.94 (2014 est)
Birth rate – 15.53 (2014 est)
Infant mortality rate – 11.61 (2014 est)

CLIMATE AND TERRAIN
Dominica, the most northerly of the Windward Islands, is
46km long and 25km wide, with a mountainous and
forested centre. Its peaks include volcanic craters, one of
which contains Boiling Lake, the world's second-largest
thermally active lake. Elevation extremes range from 1,447m
(Morne Diablotins) to 0m (Caribbean Sea). The climate is
tropical, with an average temperature of 25°C. The island is
located within the hurricane zone.

HISTORY AND POLITICS
Dominica was discovered by Columbus in 1493, when it was
a stronghold of the Caribs, the sole inhabitants of the island
until the French founded settlements in the 18th century. It
was ceded to the British in 1763 but passed back and forth
between France and Britain until 1805, after which British
possession was unchallenged. From 1871 until the 1960s
Dominica was administered by Britain as part of various
federations of West Indian islands. Internal self-government
from 1967 was followed on 3 November 1978 by
independence as a republic.
   The Dominica Labour Party (DLP) won the legislative
election in 2009 and continued in government. Charles
Savarin was elected president in 2013; the main opposition
United Workers Party boycotted this election, claiming the
process was unconstitutional.
   Under the 1978 constitution, the president is elected by
the legislature for a five-year term, renewable once. The
unicameral House of Assembly has 30 members, 21 directly
elected, and nine appointed senators; all members serve a
five-year term.

HEAD OF STATE
President, Charles Savarin, *elected* 2013

SELECTED GOVERNMENT MEMBERS *as at April 2014*
Prime Minister, Finance, Foreign Affairs, National Security,
   Roosevelt Skerrit
Attorney-General, Levi Peter

OFFICE OF THE HIGH COMMISSIONER FOR THE
COMMONWEALTH OF DOMINICA
1 Collingham Gardens, London SW5 0HW
T 020-7370 5194 E info@dominicahighcommission.co.uk
W www.dominicahighcommission.co.uk
High Commissioner, Francine Baron, *apptd* 2012

BRITISH HIGH COMMISSIONER
HE Victoria Dean, *apptd* 2013, resident at Bridgetown,
   Barbados

ECONOMY AND TRADE
The economy, traditionally dependent on banana exports,
struggled in the early 2000s as EU preferential access for the
fruit was phased out; the industry also suffered serious
hurricane damage in 2007. Economic restructuring from
2003 led to steady growth, with an emphasis on
eco-agriculture and eco-tourism, until the global downturn
caused the economy to contract in 2009, picking up only
slightly in 2011 and 2012. Diversification into offshore
financial services, medical education and light industry is also
being encouraged, and exploitation of geothermal energy,
fishing and forestry resources is planned.

Agriculture is the principal occupation, employing 40 per
cent of the workforce but producing only 15.7 per cent of
GDP. Services contribute 68.7 per cent of GDP and industry
15.6 per cent. The main trading partners are Japan, the USA,
other Caribbean countries and China. Principal exports are
bananas, soap, bay oil, vegetables and citrus fruits. The main
imports are manufactured goods, machinery and equipment,
food and chemicals.
GNI – US$462m; US$6,440 per capita (2012)
Annual average growth of GDP – 1.1 per cent (2013 est)
Inflation rate – 1.8 per cent (2013 est)
Total external debt – US$274,900m (2013)
Imports – US$195m (2012)
Exports – US$34m (2012)

BALANCE OF PAYMENTS
Trade – US$161m deficit (2012)
Current Account – US$55m deficit (2012)

Trade with UK	2012	2013
Imports from UK	£5,388,442	£5,570,890
Exports to UK	£1,892,109	£1,426,787

COMMUNICATIONS
Airports and waterways – The principal airports are Melville
Hall on the north-east tip of the island and Canefield, just
outside Roseau; the main seaports are located at Portsmouth
and Roseau
Roadways – 762km
Telecommunications – 14,600 fixed lines and 109,300 mobile
subscriptions (2012); there were 28,000 internet users in
2009
Internet code and IDD – dm; 1 767 (from UK), 011 44
(to UK)
Major broadcasters – There is no national television on the
island, but cable television provider Marpim Telecom and
Broadcasting covers parts of the island

DOMINICAN REPUBLIC

República Dominicana – Dominican Republic

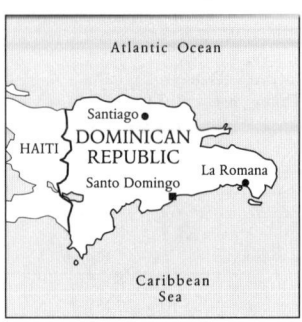

Area – 48,670 sq. km
Capital – Santo Domingo; population, 2,263,145 (2012 est)
Major cities – La Romana, San Pedro de Macorís, Santiago de
   los Caballeros, Los Alcarrizos
Currency – Dominican Republic peso (RD$) of 100 centavos
Population – 10,349,741, rising at 1.25 per cent a year
   (2014 est)
Religion – Christian (Roman Catholic) 95 per cent, other
   5 per cent
Language – Spanish (official)
Population density – 210 per sq. km (2011)
Urban population – 70.3 per cent (2012 est)
Median age (years) – 27.1 (2014 est)
National anthem – 'Quisqueyanos Valientes' ['Valiant
   Quisqueyans']
National day – 27 February (Independence Day)
Death penalty – Abolished for all crimes (since 1966)
CPI score – 29 (123)
Literacy rate – 90 per cent (2011)
Gross enrolment ratio (percentage of relevant age group) –
   primary 105 per cent; secondary 75 per cent (2011)
Health expenditure (per capita) – US$296 (2011)
Hospital beds (per 1,000 people) – 1.7 (2011)
Life expectancy (years) – 77.8 (2014 est)
Mortality rate – 4.5 (2014 est)
Birth rate – 18.97 (2014 est)
Infant mortality rate – 19.63 (2014 est)

CLIMATE AND TERRAIN
The republic forms the eastern two-thirds of the island
of Hispaniola and is crossed from the north-west to the
south-east by the Cordillera Central mountain range, which
has a number of peaks over 3,000m. Elevation extremes
range from 3,175m (Pico Duarte) to −46m (Lake Enriquillo).
The climate is maritime tropical, with an average temperature
of 24.8°C.

HISTORY AND POLITICS
The island was discovered by Columbus in 1492, and a
Spanish colony was established in 1496. The eastern
province of Santo Domingo remained under Spanish rule
after the partition of Hispaniola in 1697, but was ceded to
France in 1795. It was restored to Spain in 1809, but
rebelled in 1821 and achieved independence briefly before
being annexed by Haiti in 1822. Haitian rule ended in
1844 when independence was declared as the Dominican
Republic, although the country was voluntarily under
Spanish rule again from 1861 to 1865. A long dictatorship
at the end of the 19th century was followed by revolution
and bankruptcy, which led to occupation by US forces from
1916 until 1924. A military coup in 1930 established the

dictatorship of Gen. Rafael Trujillo, whose corrupt rule continued until his assassination in 1961. After a period of political instability, a new constitution was adopted in 1966 and democracy was restored.

The 2012 presidential election was won by Danilo Medina of the Dominican Liberation Party (PLD); he replaced outgoing president Leonel Fernández (president 1996–2000 and 2004–12). In legislative elections held in May 2010 the ruling PLD increased its majority in both houses.

Under the 2010 constitution, the executive president is directly elected for a four-year term, which is not renewable. The bicameral National Congress comprises the Chamber of Deputies, which has 183 members, and the senate, with 32 members, one for each province and one for Santo Domingo. Both chambers are directly elected for a four-year term, but the current members will serve until 2016 so that presidential and legislative elections can be held simultaneously.

HEAD OF STATE

President, Danilo Medina, *elected* 2012, *sworn in* August 2012
Vice-President, Margarita Cedeno de Fernández

SELECTED GOVERNMENT MEMBERS *as at April 2014*

Armed Forces, Adm. Sigfrido Aramis Pared Perez
Finance, Simon Lizardo Mezquita
Foreign Affairs, Carlos Morales
Interior, Jose Ramon Fadul

EMBASSY OF THE DOMINICAN REPUBLIC

139 Inverness Terrace, London W2 6JF
T 020-7727 7091 E info@dominicanembassy.org.uk
W www.dominicanembassy.org.uk
Ambassador Extraordinary and Plenipotentiary, HE Federico Alberto Cuello Camilo, *apptd* 2011

BRITISH EMBASSY

Edificio Corominas Pepín, 7th–8th Floor, Ave 27 de Febrero No 233, Santo Domingo
T (+1) (829) 472 7111 E brit.emb.sadom@codetel.net.do
W www.gov.uk/government/world/dominican-republic
Ambassador Extraordinary and Plenipotentiary, HE Steven Fisher, *apptd* 2009

DEFENCE

Aged 16–49, 2010 est	Males	Females
Available for military service	2,580,083	2,464,698
Fit for military service	2,188,358	2,090,180

Military expenditure – US$374m (2013)

ECONOMY AND TRADE

In recent years, tourism and the free trade zones have overtaken agriculture as the mainstay of the economy, and services now account for 64.9 per cent of GDP. Industry accounts for 29.9 per cent of GDP, agriculture for 6 per cent. The main crops are sugar, coffee, cotton, cocoa, tobacco, rice, vegetables and bananas, and the main industrial activities are tourism, sugar processing, mining and the production of textiles, cement and tobacco products. Remittances from expatriate workers represent nearly 10 per cent of GDP but, like tourism, were affected by the global economic downturn. The economy rebounded in 2010–11, but unemployment and fluctuations in nickel prices remain problematic.

The main trading partner is the USA, which takes 43.3 per cent of exports and provides 47 per cent of imports. Principal exports are ferro-nickel, sugar, gold, silver, coffee, cocoa, tobacco, meats and consumer goods. The chief imports are foodstuffs, fuel, cotton and fabrics, chemicals and pharmaceuticals.

GNI – US$56,834m; US$5,470 per capita (2012)
Annual average growth of GDP – 2 per cent (2013 est)
Inflation rate – 5 per cent (2013 est)
Population below poverty line – 34.4. per cent (2010 est)
Unemployment – 15 per cent (2013 est)
Total external debt – US$18,010m (2013 est)
Imports – US$14,939m (2012)
Exports – US$4,129m (2012)

BALANCE OF PAYMENTS
Trade – US$10,810m deficit (2012)
Current Account – US$4,037m deficit (2012)

Trade with UK	2012	2013
Imports from UK	£74,141,690	£74,138,343
Exports to UK	£137,798,945	£135,487,885

COMMUNICATIONS

Airports and waterways – 16, the principal airport is at Santo Domingo; Santo Domingo, Rio Haina and Caucedo are the main seaports
Roadways and railways – There are 19,705km of roadways, 9,872km of which are surfaced, and 142km of railways
Telecommunications – 1.044 million fixed lines and 8.77 million mobile subscriptions (2011); there were 2.7 million internet users in 2009
Internet code and IDD – do; 1 809/829 (from UK), 011 44 (to UK)
Major broadcasters – The state-owned broadcaster is Corporacion Estatal de Radio y Television (CERTV)
Press – Five main daily newspapers published in Spanish
WPFI score – 27,17 (68)

ECUADOR

República del Ecuador – Republic of Ecuador

Area – 283,561 sq. km
Capital – Quito; population, 1,622,000 (2011 est)
Major cities – Cuenca, Guayaquil, Machala, Manta, Santo Domingo de los Colorados
Currency – US dollar (US$) of 100 cents
Population – 15,654,411 rising at 1.37 per cent a year (2014 est)
Religion – Christian (Roman Catholic) 95 per cent, other 5 per cent
Language – Spanish (official), Quechua, other Amerindian languages
Population density – 61 per sq. km (2011)
Urban population – 68 per cent (2012 est)
Median age (years) – 26.7 (2014 est)
National anthem – 'Salve, Oh Patria' ['We Salute You, Our Homeland']

National day – 10 August (Independence Day)
Death penalty – Abolished for all crimes (since 1906)
CPI score – 35 (102)

CLIMATE AND TERRAIN

The Andes run north to south through the centre of Ecuador, dividing the coastal plain in the west from the low-lying rainforest in the east, and between two local Andean chains lie the central highlands. Elevation extremes range from 6,267m (Chimborazo) to 0m (Pacific Ocean). Other Andean peaks include Cotopaxi (5,896m) and Cayambe (5,790m) in the Eastern Cordillera. Ecuador is located in an earthquake zone and five of its volcanoes have erupted since 2000 – most recently Tungurahua in April 2014. The country has four different climatic zones and is one of the most biodiverse countries on earth; its territory includes the Galápagos Islands in the Pacific Ocean. The average temperature in Quito is 14°C.

HISTORY AND POLITICS

The kingdom of the Caras, around Quito, was conquered by the Incas in the 15th century. After the Spanish defeated the Incas in Peru, Ecuador was conquered in 1534 and added to the Spanish viceroyalty of Peru. Independence from Spain was achieved in a revolutionary war that culminated in the battle of Mt Pichincha (1822). Ecuador then formed part of Gran Colombia with Colombia, Panama and Venezuela, but left this union to become a fully independent state in 1830. After independence, the country experienced periods of political instability interspersed with dictatorships and military rule. Democratic rule under civilian government was restored in 1979.

The exploitation of oil reserves funded economic and social transformation from the 1970s onwards but also caused rapid inflation and increased foreign debt. In recent years, these problems have worsened because of economic recession, leading to strikes and demonstrations. The most notable of these were by indigenous people, who have benefited least from the oil boom but been hardest hit by the economic downturn. Civil unrest forced three presidents from office between 1997 and 2003.

Presidential and legislative elections were held in 2009 after a new constitution was approved by a national referendum in 2008, and in 2013 President Correa was elected for a third term – and his second four-year term – while his party, the left-wing PAIS Alliance, won 52 per cent of the legislative vote.

The 2008 constitution provides for an executive president who is directly elected for a four-year term, renewable once. The unicameral National Assembly has 137 members elected on a party-list proportional representation basis for a four-year term. The republic is divided into 24 provinces.

HEAD OF STATE

President, Rafael Correa, *took office* 15 January 2007, *re-elected* April 2009, February 2013
Vice-President, Lenin Moreno

SELECTED GOVERNMENT MEMBERS *as at April 2014*
Finance, Fausto Herrera Nicolalde
Foreign Affairs, Ricardo Patino
National Defence, Maria Fernanda Espinosa

EMBASSY OF ECUADOR
Flat 3B, 3 Hans Crescent, London SW1X 0LS
T 020-7584 1367 E eecugranbretania@mmrree.gov.ec
W www.consuladoecuador.org.uk
Ambassador Extraordinary and Plenipotentiary, HE Juan Eduardo Falconi Puig, *apptd* 2013

BRITISH EMBASSY
PO Box 17-17-830, Citiplaza Building, Av. Naciones Unidas y Republica de El Salvador, Piso 14, Quito
T (+593) (2) 2970 800 E britembq@interactive.net.ec
W www.gov.uk/government/world/ecuador
Ambassador Extraordinary and Plenipotentiary, HE Patrick Mullee, *apptd* 2012

DEFENCE

Aged 16–49, 2010 est	*Males*	*Females*
Available for military service	3,728,906	3,844,918
Fit for military service	2,834,213	3,269,535

Military expenditure – US$2,596m (2013)
Conscription – 18 years of age; 12 months (selective), currently suspended

ECONOMY AND TRADE

Structural reforms in 2000, including the adoption of the US dollar, in response to the severe economic crisis of 1999 paved the way for strong growth from 2002 to 2006. Growth has slowed since owing to the uncertainty created by windfall taxes imposed on foreign oil companies, a fall in oil production since 2007, the government defaulting on 30 per cent of public external debt in 2008, and the cancellation of a number of bilateral investment treaties in 2009. The global downturn further reduced oil revenue, remittances from expatriate workers (who number nearly one million) and export earnings, although the economy started to recover and recorded 4 per cent growth in 2013.

Oil is Ecuador's principal export, accounting for over half of export earnings and a third of government revenue in recent years. After oil, agriculture, fishing and forestry are the most important activities, providing products both for export and for the food- and wood-processing industries. The main exports are oil, bananas, cut flowers, fish, cacao, coffee, hemp and timber. The main imports are industrial materials, fuels and lubricants, and consumer goods. Principal trading partners are the USA and China; in 2012 Ecuador completed a trade agreement with China which saw US$9 billion worth of oil exchanged for cash and loans.

GNI – US$82,734m; US$5,170 per capita (2012)
Annual average growth of GDP – 4 per cent (2013 est)
Inflation rate – 2.6 per cent (2013 est)
Population below poverty line – 27.3 per cent (2012 est)
Unemployment – 4.9 per cent (2013 est)
Total external debt – US$19,910m (2013)
Imports – US$25,304m (2012)
Exports – US$23,765m (2012)

BALANCE OF PAYMENTS
Trade – US$1,539m deficit (2012)
Current Account – US$157m deficit (2012)

Trade with UK	2012	2013
Imports from UK	£292,150,847	£248,074,961
Exports to UK	£147,774,535	£149,492,754

COMMUNICATIONS

Airports and waterways – 104, with international flights operating to Quito and Guayaquil; the main ports are Guayaquil and Esmeraldas
Roadways and railways – There are 43,670km of roadways, 6,472km of which are surfaced, and 965km of railways
Telecommunications – 2.31 million fixed lines and 16.46 million mobile subscriptions (2012); there were 3.352 million internet users in 2009

Internet code and IDD – ec; 593 (from UK), 44 (to UK)
Major broadcasters – Six private television broadcasters dominate broadcasting, including TC Television and Ecuavisa
Press – Six newspapers are published daily, including *El Comercio, El Tiempo* and the Guayaquil-based daily *El Universo*
WPFI – 31,16 (95)

EDUCATION AND HEALTH

Elementary education is free and compulsory until age 14.
Literacy rate – 92 per cent (2011 est)
Gross enrolment ratio (percentage of relevant age group) – primary 115 per cent; secondary 85 per cent (2011 est)
Health expenditure (per capita) – US$332 (2011)
Hospital beds (per 1,000 people) – 1.6 (2010)
Life expectancy (years) – 76.36 (2014 est)
Mortality rate – 5.04 (2014 est)
Birth rate – 18.87 (2014 est)
Infant mortality rate – 17.93 (2014 est)

GALÁPAGOS ISLANDS

The Galápagos (Giant Tortoise) Islands, about 960km from the mainland, were annexed by Ecuador in 1832. The 12 large and several hundred smaller islands lie on the equator, and most form part of a national park where unique marine birds, iguanas and the giant tortoises are conserved. This wildlife provided naturalist Charles Darwin (1809–82) with inspiration and research material for his theory of evolution by natural selection, expounded in *On the Origin of Species* (1859). The islands were declared a UNESCO World Heritage site in 1978.

EGYPT

Jumhuriyat Misr al-Arabiyah – Arab Republic of Egypt

Area – 1,001,450 sq. km
Capital – Cairo; population, 11,231,385 (2012 est); stands on the Nile about 22km from the head of the delta
Major cities – Alexandria (founded 332 BC by Alexander the Great; the capital for over 1,000 years), Giza, Port Said, Shubra al-Khema, Suez

Currency – Egyptian pound (£E) of 100 piastres
Population – 86,895,099 rising at 1.84 per cent a year (2014 est); Egyptian (including Berber and Bedouin) 99.6 per cent (2006)
Religion – Muslim 90 per cent (almost all Sunni), Christian 10 per cent (mostly Coptic) (est)
Language – Arabic (official), English, French
Population density – 80 per sq. km (2011)
Urban population – 43.6 per cent (2012 est)
Median age (years) – 25.1 (2014 est)
National anthem – 'Biladi, Biladi, Biladi' ['My Homeland, My Homeland, My Homeland']
National day – 23 July (Revolution Day)
Death penalty – Retained
CPI score – 51,89(159)

CLIMATE AND TERRAIN

There are four broad regions: the Western Desert, which covers nearly two-thirds of the country to the west of the Nile valley; the Eastern Desert, which lies between the Nile and the mountains along the Red Sea coast; the fertile Nile valley and delta, where most of the population lives; and the Sinai peninsula, where a coastal plain on the Mediterranean rises to mountains in the south. The deserts are arid plateaux, with depressions in the Western Desert whose springs irrigate oases, while the Eastern Desert is dissected by wadis (dry watercourses). Elevation extremes range from 2,629m (Mt Catherine, Sinai) to −133m (Qattara depression). The country has a desert climate, with hot, dry summers and mild winters. Temperatures increase further south, and rainfall increases nearer the coast. Average daily temperatures in Cairo range from 13°C to 28°C.

POLITICS

The 1971 constitution was suspended after President Mubarak's resignation in 2011 and substantial changes to it were approved by referendum in March 2011. Following the ousting of President Mursi, a new constitution was approved in January 2014 which provides the army with greater political powers, established Sharia as the basis of the country's laws and provides for an executive president who is directly elected for a four-year term, which is renewable once.

Under the 2014 constitution the legislature is bicameral. The lower chamber, the House of Representatives, has 350 members, directly elected for a five-year term and has the right to propose a referendum on the president's rule. The upper chamber, the Senate, has at least 150 members: three-quarters elected and a quarter appointed by the president.

The first legislative election since President Mubarak's departure from office was held in November 2011 and saw the Freedom and Justice Party (FJP, founded by the Muslim Brotherhood) win the most seats in the former unicameral People's Assembly but fail to win a majority. The People's Assembly was suspended in July 2013 and legislative elections under the new 2014 constitution were held in July 2014.

In the first presidential election in the country's history, FJP candidate Mohammed Mursi narrowly defeated the National Democratic Party candidate Ahmed Shafiq and was inaugurated on 30 June 2012. Following mass demonstrations, Mohammed Mursi was deposed by the army in July 2013. In 2014, amid boycotts from opposition parties and claims that rivals had been intimidated, Independent candidate and Commander-in-Chief of the Egyptian armed forces Abdel al-Sisi won the subsequent presidential election with 90 per cent of the vote.

HEAD OF STATE
President, Abdel Fattah Al-Sisi, *elected* 29 May 2014, *sworn in,* 8 June 2014
Minister of Defence, Sedki Sobhil

SELECTED GOVERNMENT MEMBERS *as at August 2014*
Prime Minister, Ibrahim Mehleb
Finance, Hany Qadry
Foreign Affairs, Sameh Shokri
Interior, Mohamed Ibrahim Moustafa

EMBASSY OF THE ARAB REPUBLIC OF EGYPT
26 South Street, London W1K 1DW
T 020-7499 3304 E eg.emb_london@mfa.gov.eg
W www.egyptembassyuk.org
Ambassador Extraordinary and Plenipotentiary, HE Ashraf Elkholy, *apptd* 2012

BRITISH EMBASSY
7 Ahmed Ragheb Street, Garden City, Cairo
T (+20) (2) 2791 6000 E info@britishembassy.org.eg
W www.gov.uk/government/world/egypt
Ambassador Extraordinary and Plenipotentiary, HE John Casson, *apptd* 2014

DEFENCE

Aged 16–49, 2010 est	Males	Females
Available for military service	21,012,199	20,145,021
Fit for military service	18,060,543	17,244,838

Military expenditure – US$4,303m (2013)
Conscription – 18–30 years of age, male only; 18–36 months

ECONOMY AND TRADE
Economic liberalisation in recent years has attracted foreign investment and promoted exports, producing strong growth in GDP, but political uncertainty significantly reduced government revenues in 2012, and Egypt's attempts to obtain a multi-billion dollar loan from the IMF in 2012–13 failed. The country's budget deficit has concerned the IMF, though this is expected to fall to 8.7 per cent in 2014 from 13.3 percent in 2013. In 2011 and 2012, the government drew down foreign exchange reserves by 50 per cent. Although the dams on the Nile have expanded the area of land under cultivation, other factors, such as population growth, put a greater strain on resources. 22 per cent of the population lives below the poverty line.

The services sector contributes 48 per cent to GDP and employs 47 per cent of the workforce. Tourism is the largest component of this sector (visitor numbers have increased by over 50 per cent since the late 1990s), along with Suez Canal revenues and expatriate remittances. Industry accounts for 37.5 per cent of GDP and 24 per cent of employment, but despite increasing industrialisation, agriculture still employs 29 per cent of the workforce, contributing 14.5 per cent of GDP. Egypt is a net importer of foodstuffs, especially grain,

and a food security programme has been set up with the aim of achieving self-sufficiency.

The main cash crop is cotton, of which Egypt is one of the world's main producers. Other important crops are rice, maize, wheat, vegetables, fruit and livestock. Industry is centred on oil and gas extraction, processing hydrocarbons, cotton and other agricultural products, producing textiles, chemicals and pharmaceuticals. Oil is the backbone of the economy and helps, alongside considerable reserves of natural gas and the hydroelectric power produced by the Aswan and High dams, to make Egypt self-sufficient in energy.

The main trading partners are the USA, Italy, China and Germany. Principal exports are crude oil and petroleum products, cotton, textiles, metal products, chemicals and processed food. The main imports are machinery and equipment, foodstuffs, chemicals, wood products and fuels.
GNI – US$256,346m; US$2,980 per capita (2012)
Annual average growth of GDP – 1.8 per cent (2013 est)
Inflation rate – 9 per cent (2013 est)
Population below poverty line – 22 per cent (2008 est)
Unemployment – 13.4 per cent (2013 est)
Total external debt – US$48,760m (2013)
Imports – US$65,774m (2012)
Exports – US$29,409m (2012)

BALANCE OF PAYMENTS
Trade – US$36,365m deficit (2012)
Current Account – US$7,928m deficit (2012)

Trade with UK	2012	2013
Imports from UK	£920,606,649	£909,352,126
Exports to UK	£623,983,886	£769,162,704

COMMUNICATIONS
Airports – 72; the principal airports are at Cairo, Sharm el-Sheikh, Luxor, Alexandria and Hurghada
Waterways – Egypt has 3,500km of waterways, including the River Nile and Lake Nasser, the Alexandria–Cairo waterway, numerous small canals in the Nile delta and the Suez Canal (opened 1869; closed 1967–75); the main seaports are Alexandria, Damietta and Port Said on the Mediterranean Sea and Suez on the Red Sea
Roadways and railways – A road network of 126,742km and a rail network of 5,083km link the Nile valley and delta with the main development areas east and west of the river, but there are few routes in the interior
Telecommunications – 8.56 million fixed lines and 96.8 million mobile subscriptions (2013); there were 20.136 million internet users in 2009
Internet code and IDD – eg; 20 (from UK), 44 (to UK)
Major broadcasters – Two state-run national television channels and six regional channels compete with the country's thriving satellite television industry, which is watched throughout the Arab-speaking world
Press – Four major newspapers are published daily, including *Al-Ahram,* the oldest newspaper in the Arab world
WPFI score – 51,89 (159)

EDUCATION AND HEALTH
Education is free between the ages of six and 15.
Literacy rate – 74 per cent (2012 est)
Gross enrolment ratio (percentage of relevant age group) – primary 109 per cent; secondary 76 per cent; tertiary 29 per cent (2011 est)
Health expenditure (per capita) – US$137 (2011)
Hospital beds (per 1,000 people) – 1.7 (2010)
Life expectancy (years) – 73.45 (2014 est)
Mortality rate – 4.77 (2014 est)

Birth rate – 23.35 (2014 est)
Infant mortality rate – 22.41 (2014 est)

EL SALVADOR

República de El Salvador – *Republic of El Salvador*

Area – 21,041 sq. km
Capital – San Salvador; population, 1,605,000 (2011)
Major cities – San Miguel, Santa Ana, Soyapango
Currency – US dollar (US$) of 100 cents
Population – 6,125,512 (2014 est) rising at 0.27 per cent a
   year (2014 est)
Religion – Christian (Roman Catholic 57 per cent,
   Protestant 21 per cent)
Language – Spanish (official), Nahua
Population density – 302 per sq. km (2011)
Urban population – 65.3 per cent (2012 est)
Median age (years) – 25.6 (2014 est)
National anthem – 'Himno Nacional de El Salvador'
   ['National Anthem of El Salvador']
National day – 15 September (Independence Day)
Death penalty – Retained for certain crimes (last used 1973)
CPI score – 38 (83)

CLIMATE AND TERRAIN

El Salvador is mountainous, with narrow coastal plains and
a central plateau. Many of its peaks are volcanoes; most are
extinct, but Ilamatepec (or Santa Ana) erupted in 2005.
There are also numerous volcanic lakes. Elevation extremes
range from 2,730m (Cerro El Pital) to 0m (Pacific Ocean).
The climate is tropical on the coast but more temperate at
higher altitudes. The average annual temperature in San
Salvador is 24°C. Earthquakes and volcanic activity are
common, and the country is also susceptible to hurricanes
and tropical storms.

HISTORY AND POLITICS

El Salvador was part of the Aztec kingdom conquered in
1524 by Pedro de Alvarado, and formed part of the Spanish
viceroyalty of Guatemala until 1821. It was part of a Central
American federation of former Spanish provinces from 1823
until the federation's dissolution in 1838, becoming fully
independent in 1840.

There was political unrest in the 1970s, and guerrilla
activity by the left-wing Farabundo Martí National
Liberation Front (FMLN), which intensified from 1977 amid
reports of human rights abuses by government troops and
right-wing death squads. Decades of military rule ended in
1979, but elections in 1982 were boycotted by left-wing
parties and the right-wing National Republican Alliance
(ARENA) took office. The civil war between the FMLN and
the US-backed government lasted throughout the 1980s,

until a UN-sponsored peace agreement was signed in 1992.
The FMLN was recognised as a political party, and it won
a few seats in the 1994 election, steadily increasing its share
of the vote in subsequent elections.

ARENA regained its position as the largest party in
parliament in the 2012 legislative elections, although
without a majority. In March 2014 the FMLN candidate and
former guerrilla fighter Salvador Sanchez Ceren was elected
president, defeating his ARENA opponent Norman Quijano
by less than 1 per cent of the vote following an electoral
recount.

Under the 1983 constitution, the executive president is
directly elected for a five-year term, which is not renewable.
The unicameral legislative assembly has 84 members, who
are directly elected for a three-year term. The president
appoints the Council of State. The country is divided into
14 departments.

HEAD OF STATE
President, Salvador Sanchez Ceren, *elected* 13 March, *took*
   office 1 June
Vice-President, Osacar Ortiz

SELECTED GOVERNMENT MEMBERS *as at August 2014*
Defence, David Payes
Economy, Tharsis Lopez
Foreign Affairs, Hugo Martinez

EMBASSY OF EL SALVADOR
8 Dorset Square, 1st & 2nd Floors, London NW1 6PU
T 020-7224 9800 E embajadalondres@rree.gob.sv
Ambassador Extraordinary and Plenipotentiary, HE Werner
   Matías Romero, *apptd* 2009

BRITISH EMBASSY
Edificio Torre Futura, 14th Floor, Colonia Escalon, San Salvador
T (+503) 2511 5757 E britishembassy.elsalvador@fco.gov.uk
W www.gov.uk/government/world/el-salvador
Ambassador Extraordiniary and Plenipotentiary, vacant

DEFENCE

Aged 16–49, 2010 est	Males	Females
Available for military service	1,449,214	1,611,248
Fit for military service	1,079,038	1,373,368

Military expenditure – US$257m (2013 est)
Conscription – 18 years of age; 12 months (selective)

ECONOMY AND TRADE

The country is one of the most industrialised in Central
America and has the region's third-largest economy despite
being its smallest country and having few natural resources.
Recovery after the civil war was set back by a series of natural
disasters, but the economy has been transformed from
a mainly agricultural to a service-based economy with a
growing manufacturing sector. Government diversification
efforts have promoted textile production, international port
services and tourism. Even so, the value of expatriates'
remittances accounted for 17 per of GDP in 2013, and
over 36.5 per cent of the population live below the
poverty line. The economy contracted in 2009, with both
exports and remittances adversely affected by the global
downturn, and slowed even further from 2010–12. In
September 2013, El Salvador was awarded US$277 million
by US government agency the Millennium Challenge
Corporation with the aim of stimulating economic growth
and reducing poverty.

Services, through tourism, commerce and financial services, contribute 60.1 per cent of GDP. Industry contributes 29.5 per cent of GDP, mostly through assembly for re-export, food processing, beverages, oil, chemicals, fertiliser, textiles, furniture and light metals. Agriculture contributes 10.3 per cent to GDP and employs 21 per cent of the workforce. The principal agricultural products are coffee, sugar, maize, rice, beans, oilseed, cotton, sorghum, beef and dairy products.

The main trading partners are the USA and other Central American states. Principal exports are offshore assembly products, coffee, sugar, textiles, garments, gold, ethanol, chemicals and electricity. The chief imports are raw materials, consumer goods, capital goods, fuels, foodstuffs, oil and electricity.

GNI – US$22,931m; US$3,590 per capita (2012)
Annual average growth of GDP – 1.6 per cent (2013 est)
Inflation rate – 0.9 per cent (2013 est)
Population below poverty line – 36.5 per cent (2010 est)
Unemployment – 6.3 per cent (2013 est)
Total external debt – US$14,440m (2013)
Imports – US$10,207m (2012)
Exports – US$5,340m (2012)

BALANCE OF PAYMENTS
Trade – US$4,929m deficit (2012)
Current Account – US$1,255m deficit (2012)

Trade with UK	2012	2013
Imports from UK	£14,710,525	£14,233,503
Exports to UK	£12,437,357	13,714,884

COMMUNICATIONS
Airports and waterways – Five; the principal ports are Cutuco and Acajutla, and ports in Honduras and Guatemala are also used
Roadways and railways – There are 6,918km of roadways, of which 3,247km are surfaced; the 283km rail network has not been in operation since 2005 due to lack of maintenance
Telecommunications – 1.06 million fixed lines and 8.65 million mobile subscriptions (2012); there were 746,000 internet users in 2009
Internet code and IDD – sv; 503 (from UK), 44 (to UK)
Major broadcasters – Broadcasting is dominated by private operators, including Teledos and Canal Cuatro; there are hundreds of radio broadcasters, including the state-run Radio Nacional de El Salvador
Press – There are four main daily newspapers: *La Prensa Grafica*, *El Mundo*, *El Diario de Hoy* and *El Diario Co Latino*
WPFI score – 21,57 (38)

EDUCATION AND HEALTH
Primary education is state-run, compulsory and free.
Literacy rate – 84 per cent (2011 est)
Gross enrolment ratio (percentage of relevant age group) – primary 114 per cent; secondary 67 per cent; tertiary 25 per cent (2011 est)
Health expenditure (per capita) – US$251 (2011)
Hospital beds (per 1,000 people) – 1 (2011)
Life expectancy (years) – 74.18 (2014 est)
Mortality rate – 5.67 (2014 est)
Birth rate – 16.79 (2014 est)
Infant mortality rate – 18.44 (2014 est)

EQUATORIAL GUINEA

República de Guinea Ecuatorial/République de Guinée Equatoriale – Republic of Equatorial Guinea

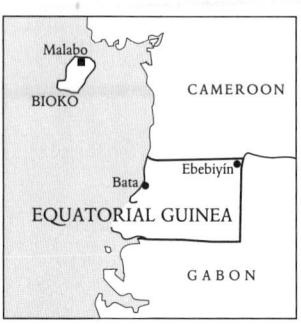

Area – 28,051 sq. km
Capital – Malabo, on Bioko; population, 137,000 (2011 est)
Major towns – Bata, the principal town and port of Río Muni; Ebebiyín
Currency – Central African CFA franc of 100 centimes
Population – 722,254 (2014 est) rising at 2.54 per cent a year (2014 est); predominantly Fang; indigenous Bubi now a minority on Bioko
Religion – Christian (Roman Catholic 87 per cent, other denominations 6 per cent), traditional indigenous religions 5 per cent (est); many Catholics also follow traditional beliefs
Language – Spanish, French (both official), Fang, Bubi
Population density – 26 per sq. km (2011)
Urban population – 39.6 per cent (2012)
Median age (years) – 19.4 (2014 est)
National anthem – 'Caminemos pisando las sendas de nuestra inmensa felicidad' ['Let Us Tread the Path of our Immense Happiness']
National day – 12 October (Independence Day)
Death penalty – Retained
CPI score – 20 (163)
Literacy rate – 94 per cent (2011 est)
Life expectancy (years) – 63.49 (2014 est)
Mortality rate – 8.39 (2014 est)
Birth rate – 33.83 (2014 est)
Infant mortality rate – 71.128 (2014 est)
HIV/AIDS adult prevalence – 6.2 per cent (2012 est)

CLIMATE AND TERRAIN
The country consists of several islands off the Cameroon coast and a small area on the mainland, Río Muni, where 80 per cent of the population lives. The islands, of which Bioko is the largest, are of volcanic origin. The mainland rises from a narrow coastal plain to a mountainous interior plateau, and is covered in dense vegetation. Elevation extremes range from 3,008m (Pico Basile) to 0m (Atlantic Ocean). The climate is tropical, with a rainy season from July to January on Bioko, and from April to May and October to December on the mainland.

HISTORY AND POLITICS
The island of Fernando Po (Bioko) was claimed by the Portuguese in 1494 and held until 1777, when it was ceded to Spain. The mainland territory of Río Muni came under Spanish rule in 1844, and the two territories became one colony, subsequently known as Spanish Guinea, in 1904. The colony became autonomous in 1963, and independent in 1968 under its present name.

The first president, Francisco Macías Nguema, established a one-party state in 1970. His brutal regime was overthrown in 1979 in a military coup led by his nephew, Col. Obiang Nguema. A military regime was established after the coup, and only presidential nominees were allowed to stand in the 1983 and 1988 elections. Constitutional amendments were introduced in 1991 to allow multiparty elections, but President Nguema and the Democratic Party of Equatorial Guinea (PDGE) have retained power since 1992; most elections have been boycotted by the opposition parties because of election irregularities and intimidation. The regime has been accused of human rights abuses and the suppression of political opposition, and in 2003 opposition leaders set up a 'government-in-exile' in Spain. There is also a separatist movement on Bioko.

In the 2008 legislative election, the PDGE retained its overwhelming majority in parliament. President Nguema won the 2009 presidential election with 95 per cent of the vote.

The 1991 constitution introduced a multiparty system. The president is directly elected for a seven-year term; constitutional amendments approved by referendum in November 2011 introduced a two-term limit. Constitutional amendments in 2012 created a bicameral system with a lower chamber, the House of Deputies, with 100 members, and an upper chamber, the Senate, containing 55 elected officials and 15 presidential appointments.

HEAD OF STATE
President, Brig.-Gen. Teodoro Obiang Nguema Mbasogo, took power August 1979, *re-elected* 1989, 1996, 2002, 2009

SELECTED GOVERNMENT MEMBERS *as at April 2014*
Prime Minister, Ignacio Milam Tang
Defence, Gen. Antonio Mba Nguema Mikwe
Economy, Conrado Okenve Ndoho
Foreign Affairs, Agapito Mba Mokuy

EMBASSY OF THE REPUBLIC OF EQUATORIAL GUINEA
13 Park Place, St James' London SW1A 1LP
T 020-7499 6867 E embarege-londres@embarege-londres.org
Ambassador Extraordinary and Plenipotentiary, HE Mari-Cruz Evuna Andeme, *apptd* 2012

BRITISH HIGH COMMISSION
Higher Commissioner, HE Andrew Pocock, *apptd 2012, resident at Abjua, Nigeria*

DEFENCE

Aged 16–49, 2010 est	Males	Females
Available for military service	151,147	150,345
Fit for military service	113,277	115,320

Military expenditure – US$429m (2009)
Conscription – 18 years of age; 24 months, although conscription is rarely enforced

ECONOMY AND TRADE
Large oil and natural gas deposits discovered off Bioko in the 1990s have transformed the economy, which has grown dramatically since production began in 1996. Despite contracting in 2009–10 during the global downturn, the economy recovered quickly in 2011–12 due to higher oil prices and investments in public infrastructure. The country has the reputation of being one of the most corrupt in the world; oil exploitation has not benefited much of the population as most businesses are owned by government officials or their families. Despite the oil revenues, the country has a large external debt.

Industry contributes 87.3 per cent of GDP, services 8.1 per cent and agriculture 4.6 per cent. The oil-driven growth in the GDP masks stagnation in other sectors; agriculture, once the mainstay of the economy, has declined to subsistence level owing to neglect and lack of investment. The main crops are coffee, cocoa, rice, fruit, nuts, livestock and timber. Industrial activities other than oil and natural gas production include fishing and timber processing.

The main trading partners are the USA, China and Japan. Principal exports are petroleum and timber. The main imports are oil industry and other industrial equipment.
GNI – US$11,051m; US$13,560 per capita (2012)
Annual average growth of GDP – –1.5 per cent (2013 est)
Inflation rate – 6 per cent (2013 est)
Total external debt – US$2,104m (2013 est)
Imports – US$5,517m (2012)
Exports – US$14,252m (2012)

BALANCE OF PAYMENTS
Trade – US$8,735m surplus (2012)
Current Account – US$2,227m deficit (2012 est)

Trade with UK	2012	2013
Imports from UK	£59,212,991	£48,436,012
Exports to UK	£47,242,208	£1,094,072,743

COMMUNICATIONS
Airports – The principal airport is based in Malabo
Roadways – 2,880km
Telecommunications – 14,900 fixed lines (2012) and 501,000 mobile subscriptions (2012); there were 14,400 internet users in 2009
Internet code and IDD – gq; 240 (from UK), 44 (to UK)
Broadcasters and press – Television and radio broadcasts are state-controlled; the main newspaper, *Ebano,* is state-owned and there are very few private publications
WPFI score – 67,95 (168)

ERITREA

Hagere Ertra – State of Eritrea

Area – 117,600 sq. km
Capital – Asmara; population, 649,000 (2009 est)
Major towns – Assab, Keren, Massawa
Currency – Nakfa (Nfk) of 100 cents
Population – 6,380,803 rising at 2.3 per cent a year (2014 est); Tigrinya (55 per cent), Tigre (30 per cent), Saho (4 per cent), Kunama (2 per cent), Rashaida (2 per cent), Bilen (2 per cent) (2010 est)

Religion – Muslim (Sunni) 50 per cent, Christian 40 per cent (Eritrean Orthodox 24 per cent, Roman Catholic 10 per cent), animist 2 per cent; only Christians of the Eritrean Orthodox, Catholic and Lutheran churches, and Muslims may meet freely

Language – Arabic, English, Tigrinya (all official), Tigre, Afar, Kunama

Population density – 59 per sq. km (2011)

Urban population – 21.8 per cent (2012 est)

Median age (years) – 19.1 (2014 est)

National anthem – 'Ertra, Ertra, Ertra' ['Eritrea, Eritrea, Eritrea']

National day – 24 May (Independence Day)

Death penalty – Retained (last used 1989)

CPI score – 20 (160)

Literacy rate – 69 per cent (2011 est)

Gross enrolment ratio (percentage of relevant age group) – primary 42 per cent; secondary 29 per cent; tertiary 2 per cent (2011 est)

Health expenditure (per capita) – US$14 (2011)

Hospital beds (per 1,000 people) – 0.7 (2011)

Life expectancy (years) – 63.51 (2014 est)

Mortality rate – 7.65 (2014 est)

Birth rate – 30.69 (2014 est)

Infant mortality rate – 38.44 (2014 est)

HIV/AIDS adult prevalence – 0.7 per cent (2012 est)

CLIMATE AND TERRAIN

The northern end of the Ethiopian Highlands extends into central Eritrea, where the average altitude is over 2,000m. The mountains fall in the west to a plateau, which then rises to the hills on the Sudanese border. To the east of the mountains, the land falls to the narrow coastal plain. The coastal strip extending to the Djibouti border is low-lying, while the border with Ethiopia runs along the edge of the Danakil desert. Elevation extremes range from 3,018m (Soira) to −75m (Danakil depression). The climate varies according to altitude, with temperatures averaging 17°C in the mountains, which are also wetter, and 30°C on the arid coastal plain.

HISTORY AND POLITICS

Part of the Axum empire from the first century AD, the area came under the control of the Ottoman Empire in the mid-16th century. It was occupied by Italy in the late 19th century and was the base for Italy's 1936 invasion of Abyssinia (now Ethiopia). After the Italian defeat in North Africa in 1941, Eritrea became a British protectorate until 15 September 1952, when a federation with Ethiopia was established by the UN. In 1962, Ethiopia annexed Eritrea outright.

The Eritrean Liberation Front (ELF) fought a guerrilla war for independence from 1961, and the Eritrean People's Liberation Front (EPLF) – a breakaway faction of the ELF – emerged in the 1970s, becoming the dominant rebel group in the 1980s. The EPLF joined with Ethiopian resistance groups to fight the Mengistu regime, which was overthrown in 1991. The EPLF secured the whole of Eritrea and formed an autonomous provisional government. The new Ethiopian government agreed to an Eritrean referendum on independence, held in April 1993, which recorded a 99.89 per cent vote in favour. Independence was declared on 24 May 1993.

Following independence, a transitional government for a four-year period was formed under Isaias Afewerki, and the EPLF became the ruling political party, renaming itself the People's Front for Democracy and Justice (PFDJ) in 1994. The post-independence regime has become increasingly authoritarian, and since 2001 has dealt harshly with anyone openly critical of the government. Although a new constitution was adopted in 1997, no presidential election has taken place since independence, and legislative elections have been postponed indefinitely.

Few of the provisions outlined in the 1997 constitution have been enacted and no presidential or legislative elections have been held, so the transitional president, state council (cabinet) and legislature remain in place. Under the constitution, the president is elected for a five-year term by the legislature, and the 150-member unicameral National Assembly is directly elected for a four-year term. The People's Front for Democracy and Justice (PFDJ) is the only legal political party.

HEAD OF STATE

President, Chairman of the State Council and of the National Assembly, Isaias Afewerki, *elected by the National Assembly* 22 May 1993

SELECTED GOVERNMENT MEMBERS *as at April 2014*
Defence, Gen. Sebhat Ephrem
Finance, Berhane Abrehe
Foreign Affairs, Osman Saleh

EMBASSY OF THE STATE OF ERITREA
96 White Lion Street, London N1 9PF
T 020-7713 0096 E eriemba@eriembauk.com
Ambassador Extraordinary and Plenipotentiary, HE Tesfamicael Gerahtu Ogbaghiorghis, *apptd* 2007

BRITISH EMBASSY
PO Box 5584, 66–68 Mariam Ghimbi Street, Asmara
T (+291) (1) 120 145 W www.gov.uk/government/world/eritrea
Ambassador Extraordinary and Plenipotentiary, HE Dr Amanda Susannah Tansfield, *apptd* 2011

FOREIGN RELATIONS

Since independence, Eritrea has been involved in disputes with Yemen, Ethiopia and Djibouti over territory, while Sudan has accused Eritrea of supporting rebels in eastern Sudan. The dispute with Yemen was over the Hanish and Mohabaka islands in the Red Sea; possession was divided between Yemen and Eritrea by international arbitration.

There has been fighting with Ethiopia in disputes over border territory, especially in the Tigray region, since 1998. Though usually sporadic, fighting escalated in 1999–2000 into a war that left thousands of people dead. An independent boundary commission defined the international border between the two countries in 2002, but both countries have failed to abide by the original demarcation or a revised ruling in 2006, and Ethiopia rejected the 2007 virtual demarcation. The UN peacekeeping mission deployed in 2000 was withdrawn in 2008, largely owing to the obstructiveness of the Eritrean government.

Fighting broke out on the part of the border disputed with Djibouti in 2008 after alleged incursions by Eritrean troops. Eritrea has repulsed international efforts to monitor a withdrawal or negotiate a settlement but agreed to seek a peaceful settlement in 2010.

Following border disputes in early 2011, Ethiopia announced that it would support Eritrean rebels fighting President Afewerki.

In July 2011, a UN report accused Eritrea of planning to attack an African Union Summit in Ethiopia; owing to Eritrea's alleged support for Islamist insurgents in Somalia, the UN further tightened sanctions in December 2011. In March 2012 Ethiopia attacked three millitary camps in Eritrea, claiming the country was supporting Ethiopian rebels who mounted attacks on western tourists.

DEFENCE

Aged 16–49, 2010 est	Males	Females
Available for military service	1,350,446	1,362,575
Fit for military service	896,096	953,757

Military expenditure – US$522 (2003 est)
Conscription – 18–40 years of age; 16 months

ECONOMY AND TRADE
Over 30 years of conflict left the country's economy devastated, and the restrictive policies of the post-independent regime have hampered recovery. The command economy has concentrated business ownership in military and party hands. Agricultural output is restricted by lack of labour owing to the failure to demobilise the large army, the conflict with Ethiopia and the frequent droughts and ensuing famines. Nevertheless, agriculture and herding are the means of subsistence of around 80 per cent of the population, but food production is insufficient and emergency food aid is needed for two-thirds of the people. The industrial sector has contracted since trade with Ethiopia halted in 1998, and the principal ports have suffered from the loss of this transit trade.

Mineral reserves include zinc, potash, gold, copper and possibly oil; these are not fully exploited at present, although mining production began in 2010. Industries include food processing, beverages, clothing and textiles, salt, cement and light manufacturing. The opening of a free trade zone at Massawa in 2008 may boost revenues, which are heavily dependent on remittances from expatriates.

The main trade partners are India, Italy, Saudi Arabia, China and Sudan. Principal exports are livestock, sorghum, textiles, food and light manufactures. The main imports are machinery, petroleum products, food and manufactured goods.
GNI – US$3,063m; US$450 per capita (2012)
Annual average growth of GDP – 7 per cent (2013 est)
Inflation rate – 13 per cent (2013 est)
Population below poverty line – 50 per cent (2004 est)
Total external debt – US$1,094m (2013 est)

BALANCE OF PAYMENTS
Trade – US$418m deficit (2010)
Current Account – US$72m surplus (2012 est)

Trade with UK	2012	2013
Imports from UK	£5,259,902	£7,133,569
Exports to UK	£171,863	£168,383

COMMUNICATIONS
Airports and waterways – Four, with the main international airport at Asmara; the principal seaports are at Assab and Massawa
Roadways and railways – There are 4,101km of roadways, of which 874km are surfaced, and 306km of railways, which link Massawa to Sudan via Asmara
Telecommunications – There are 60,000 fixed lines and 305,300 mobile subscriptions (2012); there were 200,000 internet users in 2009
Internet code and IDD – er; 291 (from UK), 44 (to UK)
Media – Eritrea is the only country in Africa without any privately owned media; Eri TV is the state-run broadcaster and *Hadas Eritrea* and *Eritrea Profile* are the government-owned newspaper publications
WPFI score – 84,83 (180)

ESTONIA

Eesti Vabariik – Republic of Estonia

Area – 45,228 sq. km
Capital – Tallinn; population, 399,000 (2009 est)
Major towns – Kohtla-Jarve, Narva, Parnu, Tartu
Currency – Euro (€) of 100 cents
Population – 1,257,921 falling at 0.68 per cent a year (2014 est); Estonian (68.7 per cent), Russian (24.8 per cent), Ukrainian (1.7 per cent), Belarusian (1 per cent), Finn (0.6 per cent) (2008)
Religion – Christian (Lutheran 10 per cent, Orthodox 16 per cent) (est)
Language – Estonian (official), Russian
Population density – 32 per sq. km (2011)
Urban population – 69.5 per cent (2012 est)
Median age (years) – 41.2 (2014 est)
National anthem – 'Mu Isamaa, Mu Onn Ja Room' ['My Fatherland, My Joy and Delight']
National day – 24 February (Independence Day)
Death penalty – Abolished for all crimes (since 1998)
CPI score – 68 (28)

CLIMATE AND TERRAIN
The country is mostly a plain of lakes, marshes and forests, with a range of low hills in the south-east. Elevation extremes range from 318m (Suur Munamagi) to 0m (Baltic Sea). Part of the border with Russia runs through the large Lake Peipsi. The climate is maritime, with average temperatures ranging from −5°C in February to 16.7°C in July.

HISTORY AND POLITICS
The area came under Swedish control between 1561 and 1629, and was ceded to the Russian Empire in 1721. An Estonian nationalist movement developed in the late 19th century and fought against occupying German forces during the First World War. Estonia declared its independence in February 1918 and defended it against Soviet forces until 1920, when independence was recognised by the USSR. However, the USSR annexed Estonia in 1940, and the country was subsequently occupied by German forces when they invaded the USSR in 1941. In 1944 the USSR expelled the Germans and reannexed the country, beginning a process of 'Sovietisation'.

There was a resurgence of nationalist sentiment in the 1980s, and in 1989 the Estonian Supreme Soviet declared the republic to be sovereign and its 1940 annexation by the USSR to be illegal. In 1990, the Communist Party's monopoly on power was abolished and, following multiparty elections in which pro-independence candidates won the majority of seats, a period of transition to independence was inaugurated, culminating in its declaration on 20 August 1991. The last Russian troops withdrew in 1994. Since independence, Estonia has pursued pro-Western policies. It joined NATO and the EU in 2004.

In 2011 Toomas Hendrik Ilves was re-elected president by an electoral assembly. In the 2011 legislative election, the Reform Party (ER), the main partner in the coalition government since 2005, remained the largest party and formed a coalition with the Union of Pro Patria and Res Publica (IRL). In February 2014 long-serving prime minster Andrus Ansip stood down, allowing for change in the ER leadership before legislative elections on 16 March 2015.

Under the 1992 constitution, the president is elected for a five-year term by the legislature by a two-thirds majority or, if no candidate receives this majority after three rounds of voting, by an electoral assembly composed of the legislature members and 266 local government representatives. The unicameral legislature, the *Riigikogu*, has 101 members, directly elected for a four-year term. The prime minister is appointed by the president and nominates the government.

HEAD OF STATE
President, Toomas Hendrik Ilves, *elected by electoral assembly* 23 September 2006, *sworn in* 9 October 2006, *re-elected* 2011

SELECTED GOVERNMENT MEMBERS *as at April 2014*
Prime Minister, Taavi Roivas
Defence, Sven Mikser
Finance, Jurgen Ligi
Foreign Affairs, Urmas Paet
Internal Affairs, Hanno Pevkur

EMBASSY OF THE REPUBLIC OF ESTONIA
16 Hyde Park Gate, London SW7 5DG
T 020-7589 3428 E london@mfa.ee W www.estonia.gov.uk
Ambassador Extraordinary and Plenipotentiary, HE Aino Lepik von Wiren, *apptd* 2010

BRITISH EMBASSY
Wismari 6, Tallinn 10136
T (+372) 667 4700 E infotallinn@fco.gov.uk
W www.gov.uk/government/world/estonia
Ambassador Extraordinary and Plenipotentiary, HE Christopher Holtby OBE, *apptd* 2012

DEFENCE

Aged16–49, 2010 est	Males	Females
Available for military service	291,801	302,696
Fit for military service	210,854	251,185

Military expenditure – US$467m (2013)
Conscription – 18–27 years of age; 8–11 months, depending on education

ECONOMY AND TRADE
Economic reforms and restructuring since 1992 have resulted in a market economy, the growth of which was boosted by the country's accession to the EU in 2004. Estonia entered recession in 2008 after an investment and consumption slump and a drop in demand for exports. Prudent financial management has enabled the economy to recover slowly, and it met the accession criteria for the eurozone, which Estonia joined in January 2011; it has since garnered one of the highest GDP growth rates in Europe. Before the unrest in Ukraine, the economy was expected to grow by 2 per cent in 2014.

Agriculture engages 4.2 per cent of the workforce and accounts for 3.9 per cent of GDP, the main products being cereals, vegetables, livestock, dairy products and fish. Industry accounts for 20.2 per cent of employment and 30 per cent of GDP, concentrating on engineering, electronics, wood and wood products, textiles, information technology and telecommunications; electronics and telecommunications are particularly strong. The services sector accounts for 75.6 per cent of employment and 66.2 per cent of GDP.

The main trading partners are other EU countries, particularly Finland, Sweden and Russia. Principal exports are machinery and electrical equipment, wood and wood products, metals, furniture, vehicles and parts, food products and textiles. The main imports are machinery and electrical equipment, fuels, foodstuffs, plastics and textiles. Estonia remains dependent on Russian natural gas supplies.

GNI – US$21,322m; US$16,150 per capita (2012)
Annual average growth of GDP – 1.5 per cent (2013 est)
Inflation rate – 3.4 per cent (2013 est)
Population below poverty line – 17.5 per cent (2010)
Unemployment – 10.9 per cent (2013 est)
Total external debt – US$26,740m (2013 est)
Imports – US$17,796m (2012)
Exports – US$16,083m (2012)

BALANCE OF PAYMENTS
Trade – US$1713m deficit (2012)
Current Account – US$399m deficit (2012)

Trade with UK	2012	2013
Imports from UK	£280,304,797	£321,294,139
Exports to UK	£201,327,663	£147,908,618

COMMUNICATIONS
Airports and waterways – 13; with the principal international airport in Tallinn; there are 335km of year-round navigable waterways, and the main seaports are at Talinn, Parnu Reid and Haapsalu Jahtklubi
Roadways and railways – 58,412km; 1,196km
Telecommunications – 448,200 fixed lines and 2.07 million mobile subscriptions (2012); there were 971,700 internet users in 2009
Internet code and IDD – ee; 372 (from UK), 44 (to UK)
Major broadcasters – Public broadcasters Eesti Televisioon and Eesti Radio compete with private-sector, usually Swedish- or Norwegian-owned broadcasters
Press – Major newspapers include *Postimees* and *Eesti Paevaleht*
WPFI score – 9,63 (11)

EDUCATION AND HEALTH
Primary and secondary level education is compulsory between the ages of seven and 15.
Literacy rate – 99 per cent (2011 est)
Gross enrolment ratio (percentage of relevant age group) – primary 98 per cent; secondary 109 per cent; tertiary 72 per cent (2011 est)
Health expenditure (per capita) – US$987 (2011)
Hospital beds (per 1,000 people) – 5.3 (2010)
Life expectancy (years) – 74.07 (2014 est)
Mortality rate – 13.69 (2014 est)
Birth rate – 10.29 (2014 est)
Infant mortality rate – 6.7 (2014 est)
HIV/AIDS adult prevalence – 1.2 per cent (2012 est)

ETHIOPIA

Ityop'iya Federalawi Demokrasiyawi Ripeblik – Federal Democratic Republic of Ethiopia

Area – 1,104,300 sq. km
Capital – Addis Ababa; population, 3,081,472 (2012 est)
Major cities – Bahir Dar, Dese, Dire Dawa, Gonder, Mek'ele, Nazret
Currency – Birr (EB) of 100 cents
Population – 96,633,458 rising at 2.89 per cent a year (2014 est); Oromo (34.5 per cent), Amhara (26.9 per cent), Somali (6.2 per cent), Tigray (6.1 per cent), Sidama (4 per cent), Guragie (2.5 per cent), Welaita (2.3 per cent) (2007)
Religion – Christian 63 per cent (Ethiopian Orthodox 44 per cent, Protestant 19 per cent), Muslim 34 per cent (mostly Sunni) (est)
Language – Amharic, English, Arabic (all official), Oromo Tigrinya, Somali, Guaragigna, Sidamo
Population density – 89 per sq. km (2011)
Urban population – 17.2 per cent (2012 est)
Median age (years) – 17.6 (2014 est)
National anthem – 'Wodefit Gesgeshi Widd Innat Ityopp'ya' ['March Forward, Dear Mother Ethiopia']
National day – 28 May (defeat of Mengistu government, 1991)
Death penalty – Retained
CPI score – 33 (111)

CLIMATE AND TERRAIN

Ethiopia is dominated by a central plateau, rising to the mountains of the Ethiopian Highlands, which are divided by the Great Rift Valley. The western mountains are the source of the Blue Nile. The land drops to desert plains in the east (Ogaden) and north-east (Danakil desert). Elevation extremes range from 4,533m (Ras Dejen) to −125m (Danakil depression). There is a tropical monsoon climate, with variations according to altitude. The wet season is from April to September.

POLITICS

The 1994 constitution provides for a federal government responsible for foreign affairs, defence and economic policy,

and nine ethnically based states. The president is elected by both houses of the legislature for a six-year term, renewable once. The prime minister is appointed by the lower chamber of the legislature and appoints the government. The Federal Parliamentary Assembly is bicameral. The lower chamber, the House of People's Representatives, has 547 members, directly elected for a five-year term. The House of the Federation has 110 members, elected for a five-year term by the government councils of the nine states in the federation. These regional administrations have considerable autonomy and the right to secede.

In the 2010 legislative election, the Ethiopian People's Revolutionary Democratic Front won an overwhelming majority of seats; observers considered the polls flawed and opposition leaders called for a re-run, alleging government intimidation. In 2012 Prime Minister Meles Zenawi died and was succeeded by Deputy Prime Minister Hailemariam Desalegn; Mulatu Teshome was elected president in 2013.

HEAD OF STATE
President, Mulatu Teshome, *elected* 7 October 2013

SELECTED GOVERNMENT MEMBERS *as at April 2014*
Prime Minister, Hailemariam Desalegn
Deputy Prime Minister, Finance, Debretsion Gebremichael *(Finance);* Aster Mamo; Demeke Mekonnen

EMBASSY OF THE FEDERAL DEMOCRATIC REPUBLIC OF ETHIOPIA
17 Prince's Gate, London SW7 1PZ
T 020-7589 7212 E info@ethioembassy.org.uk
W www.ethioembassy.org.uk
Ambassador Extraordinary and Plenipotentiary, HE Berhanu Kebede, *apptd* 2006

BRITISH EMBASSY
PO Box 858, Comoros Street, Addis Ababa
T (+251) (11) 661 2354
W www.gov.uk/government/world/ethiopia
Ambassador Extraordinary and Plenipotentiary, HE Greg Dorey, *apptd* 2008

FOREIGN RELATIONS
There has been fighting with Eritrea in disputes over border territory, especially in Tigray, since 1998. Though usually sporadic, fighting escalated in 1999–2000 into a war in which thousands of people died. An independent boundary commission defined the international border between the two countries in 2002 but both countries have failed to abide by the original demarcation or a revised ruling in 2006, and Ethiopia rejected a 2007 virtual demarcation. In 2011 Ethiopia announced it would support rebels seeking to oust Eritrea's President Afewerki.

Ethiopia intervened in Somalia in 2006 in support of the Somali transitional government. It formally withdrew its forces in January 2009, in accordance with a 2008 peace agreement between the Somali government and rebels. In

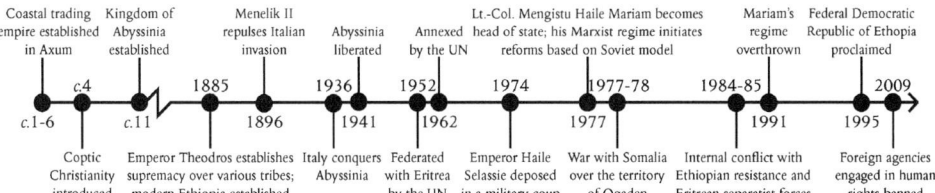

Coastal trading empire established in Axum	Kingdom of Abyssinia established	Menelik II repulses Italian invasion	Abyssinia liberated	Annexed by the UN	Lt.-Col. Mengistu Haile Mariam becomes head of state; his Marxist regime initiates reforms based on Soviet model	Mariam's regime overthrown	Federal Democratic Republic of Ethopia proclaimed
c.4	1885	1936	1952	1974	1977-78	1984-85	2009
c.1-6	c.11	1896	1941	1962	1977	1991	1995
Coptic Christianity introduced	Emperor Theodros establishes supremacy over various tribes; modern Ethiopia established	Italy conquers Abyssinia	Federated with Eritrea by the UN	Emperor Haile Selassie deposed in a military coup	War with Somalia over the territory of Ogaden	Internal conflict with Ethiopian resistance and Eritrean separatist forces	Foreign agencies engaged in human rights banned

January 2014, 4,000 Ethiopian troops reinforced African Union soldiers fighting the al-Qaeda-aligned al-Shabab group in northern Somalia.

DEFENCE

Aged 16–49, 2010 est	Males	Females
Available for military service	19,067,499	19,726,816
Fit for military service	11,868,084	12,889,260

Military expenditure – US$315m (2013)

ECONOMY AND TRADE

The economy is highly dependent on agriculture, and therefore reliant on the rains; recurring droughts led to famine conditions in 1984–5, 1992, 1997, 2000, 2002, 2009 and 2011. In 2004, the government began to move more than two million people from the drought-stricken and overworked highlands to the east of the country, claiming that this would be a long-term solution to food shortages, but food aid is still required at times of drought. Although most foreign debt was cancelled in 2005 and economic growth has been steady, emergency IMF funding was needed to cushion the country from the effects of the global downturn.

Agriculture and herding account for 47 per cent of GDP, and 85 per cent of the population is dependent upon the land for a living. The main crops are cereals, pulses, coffee, oilseed, cotton, sugar, potatoes, qat (or khat, a flowering plant chewed for its stimulant properties), cut flowers, livestock products and fish. Natural resources, including gold, platinum, copper, potash, oil and natural gas, are largely unexploited; most industrial activity involves the processing of agricultural products, gold mining and metalworking, and textiles. Work continues on the Grand Ethiopian Renaissance Dam on the Nile, which is intended to generate electricity for domestic consumption and export, and is due to be completed in 2017, despite claims from the Egyptian government the new dam could threaten Egypt's water supply.

The main trade partners are China, Saudi Arabia, the USA, Germany and Belgium. Principal exports are coffee, qat, gold, leather products, livestock and oilseeds. The main imports are food, livestock, petroleum and petroleum products, chemicals, machinery, vehicles, cereals and textiles.

GNI – US$41,511m; US$380 per capita (2012)
Annual average growth of GDP – 7 per cent (2013 est)
Inflation rate – 8.4 per cent (2013 est)
Population below poverty line – 39 per cent (2012 est)
Total external debt – US$11,990m (2013 est)
Imports – US$11,980m (2012)
Exports – US$2,995m (2012)

BALANCE OF PAYMENTS
Trade – US$8,985m deficit (2012)
Current Account – US$2,800m deficit (2012)

Trade with UK	2012	2013
Imports from UK	£103,426,722	£98,714,598
Exports to UK	£86,313,382	£69,968,579

COMMUNICATIONS

Airports and waterways – 17; this landlocked country uses ports in Djibouti city and Berbera in Somalia
Roadways and railways – There are 44,359km of roads, 6,064km of which are surfaced; the only railway line links Addis Ababa and Djibouti over 681km but is largely inoperable
Telecommunications – 797,500 fixed lines and 20.524 million mobile subscriptions (2012); there were 447,300 internet users in 2009

Internet country code and IDD – et; 251 (from UK), 44 (to UK)
Major broadcasters – The state-owned Ethiopian Television and Radio Ethiopia operate national and regional stations
Press – The number of privately owned newspapers has increased in recent years: *Addis Zemen* and *Ethiopian Herald* are the state-owned dailies, *The Daily Monitor* and *Addis Admass* are privately owned publications
WPFI score – 40,58 (143)

EDUCATION AND HEALTH

Non-compulsory elementary and secondary education is provided by government schools in the major population centres; there are also mission schools.

Literacy rate – 39 per cent (2008 est)
Gross enrolment ratio (percentage of relevant age group) – primary 95 per cent; secondary 36 per cent; tertiary 8 per cent (2011 est)
Health expenditure (per capita) – US$17 (2011)
Hospital beds (per 1,000 people) – 6.3 (2011)
Life expectancy (years) – 60.75 (2014 est)
Mortality rate – 8.52 (2014 est)
Birth rate – 37.66 (2014 est)
Infant mortality rate – 55.7 (2014 est)
HIV / AIDS adult prevalence – 1.3 per cent (2012 est)

FIJI

Matanitu ko Viti – Republic of the Fiji Islands

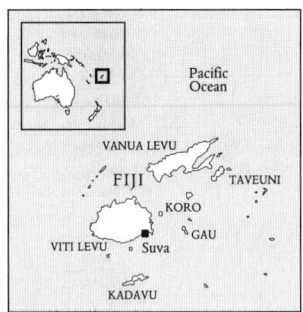

Area – 18,274 sq. km
Capital – Suva, on Viti Levu; population, 174,000 (2009 est)
Major towns – Lautoka, Nasinu, Nausori
Currency – Fijian dollar (F$) of 100 cents
Population – 903,207 rising at 0.7 per cent a year (2014 est); Fijian (57.3 per cent), Indian (37.6 per cent), Rotuman (1.2 per cent) (2007)
Religion – Christian 65 per cent (predominantly Methodist), Hindu 28 per cent, Muslim 6 per cent (predominantly Sunni) (est)
Language – English, Fijian, Fijian Hindustani (all official)
Population density – 48 per sq. km (2011)
Urban population – 52.6 per cent (2012 est)
Median age (years) – 27.9 (2014 est)
National anthem – 'Meda Dau Doka' ['God Bless Fiji']
National day – Second Monday of October (Independence Day)
Death penalty – Retained for certain crimes (last used 1964)
Life expectancy (years) – 72.15 (2014 est)
Mortality rate – 6 (2014 est)
Birth rate – 19.86 (2014 est)

Infant mortality rate – 10.2 (2014 est)
Gross enrolment ratio (percentage of relevant age group) –
   primary 105 per cent; secondary 90 per cent (2011 est);
   tertiary 62 per cent (2011 est)

CLIMATE AND TERRAIN

Fiji comprises a group of about 330 islands (around 110 are permanently inhabited) and over 500 islets in the South Pacific, about 1,770km north of New Zealand. The group extends 480km from east to west and 480km north to south. The International Date Line has been diverted to the east of the island group. The largest islands are Viti Levu and Vanua Levu. The terrain is mountainous and volcanic, with tropical rainforest and grassland, and most islands are surrounded by coral reefs. Elevation extremes range from 1,324m (Tomanivi, on Viti Levu) to 0m (Pacific Ocean). Fiji has a tropical maritime climate with high humidity and an average annual temperature of 24.7°C.

HISTORY AND POLITICS

The islands were settled by Melanesian peoples. European contact began with the visit of the Dutch explorer Abel Tasman in 1643; later visitors included Captain Cook in 1774. The islands became a British colony in 1874, and sugar plantations, employing more than 60,000 indentured Indian labourers, were established. Fiji became independent as a constitutional monarchy on 10 October 1970, and became a republic after the 1987 coups.

The growing size and political strength of the ethnic Indian population caused political instability in the late 1980s. There were two coups in 1987 and one in 2000 as indigenous Fijians attempted to reassert their political dominance and entrench this in the constitution. A fourth coup occurred in 2006 over the government's proposed amnesty for those involved in the 2000 coup.

Since the 2006 coup a military regime headed by the coup leader, Commodore 'Frank' Bainimarama, has held power. Although President Iloilo was reinstated in 2007, when Bainimarama became prime minister, the regime has become increasingly authoritarian. In response to a court of appeal ruling in April 2009 stating that the military government was illegal, President Iloilo suspended the constitution, dismissed the judiciary, reappointed Bainimarama as interim prime minister and declared a state of emergency.

President Iloilo retired in 2009 and was replaced by the vice-president, Ratu Epeli Nailatikau.

Political instability and failure to hold elections caused Fiji to be suspended from the Commonwealth of Nations from of May 2009. Instability also caused Fiji to be suspended from the Commonwealth between 1987 and 1997, and from 2000 to 2001. The first legislative elections in eight years were hield on 17 September 2014.

In September 2013, Fiji's fourth constitution was signed into law by President Nailatikau, the first to abolish race-based electoral rolls and seat quotas. It vests sole legislative authority in the single-chamber, 50-seat Parliament, which is due to convene following 2014 elections.

HEAD OF STATE

President, Ratu Epeli Nailatikau, *sworn in* 5 November 2009

SELECTED GOVERNMENT MEMBERS *as at*
April 2014
Prime Minister, Finance, Commodore Voreqe ('Frank')
   Bainimarama
Attorney-General, Aiyaz Sayed-Khaiyum
Defence (acting), Joketani Cokanasiga
Foreign Affairs, Ratu Inoke Kubuabola

HIGH COMMISSION OF THE REPUBLIC OF FIJI
34 Hyde Park Gate, London SW7 5DN
T 020-7584 3661 E mail@fijihighcommission.org.uk
W www.fijihighcommission.org.uk
High Commissioner, HE Solo Mara, *apptd* 2011

BRITISH HIGH COMMISSION
PO Box 1355, Victoria House, 47 Gladstone Road, Suva
T (+679) 322 9100 E publicdiplomacy@fco.gov.uk
W www.gov.uk/government/world/fiji
High Commissioner, HE Roderick Drummond, *apptd* 2013

DEFENCE

Aged 16–49, 2010 est	*Males*	*Females*
Available for military service	233,240	222,587
Fit for military service	183,730	188,325

Military expenditure – US$52.2m (2012)

ECONOMY AND TRADE

Fiji has abundant natural resources and one of the more developed economies in the region. However, the economy suffered after the 1987 coups because of the mass emigration of Indian Fijians, and is now contracting owing to structural problems, inefficiency and continuing political instability. Tourism, the mainstay of the economy, has declined since the most recent coup in 2006; in addition, remittances from expatriate Fijians have decreased significantly, and development aid has largely been reduced or suspended until the interim government moves to restore democracy.

Agriculture, much of it at subsistence level, accounts for 11.7 per cent of GDP and employs 70 per cent of the workforce. The principal cash crop is sugar cane, but revenue has been affected by cuts in EU subsidies. The other main agricultural products are coconuts, cassava, rice, sweet potatoes, bananas, livestock and fish. The main industries are tourism, sugar processing, garment manufacturing, copra production, gold and silver mining, forestry and small cottage industries. The main trade partners are Australia, Singapore, New Zealand, the USA and the UK. Principal exports are sugar, garments, gold, timber, fish, molasses and coconut oil. The chief imports are manufactured goods, machinery and transport equipment, petroleum products, food and chemicals.

GNI – US$3,755m; US$4,110 per capita (2012)
Annual average growth of GDP – 3 per cent (2013 est)
Inflation rate – 3 per cent (2013)
Total external debt – US$779,900m (2013 est)
Imports – US$2,450m (2012)
Exports – US$940m (2012)

BALANCE OF PAYMENTS
Trade – US$1,510m deficit (2012)
Current Account – US$56m deficit (2012)

Trade with UK	*2012*	*2013*
Imports from UK	£4,573,230	£7,959,645
Exports to UK	£34,299,984	£49,975,047

COMMUNICATIONS

Airports and waterways – Four, including international airports at Suva and Nadi; the main seaports are Suva and Lautoka
Roadways and railways – There are 3,440km of roadways, 1,686 km of which are surfaced, and 597km of railway track, principally used by the sugar industry

Telecommunications – 88,400 fixed lines and 858,800 mobile subscriptions (2012); there were 114,200 internet users in 2009
Internet code and IDD – fj; 679 (from UK), 44 (to UK)
Major broadcasters – There are two main television networks: national Fiji TV Ltd and the commercial Mai TV
Press – Fiji's privately owned newspapers are published in English, Fijian and Hindi
WPFI score – 32,57 (107)

FINLAND

Suomen tasavalta / Republiken Finland – Republic of Finland

Area – 338,145 sq. km
Capital – Helsinki (Helsingfors); population, 1,134,022 (2012 est)
Major cities – Espoo (Esbo), Oulu (Uleaborg), Tampere (Tammerfors), Turku (Aabo), Vantaa (Vanda)
Currency – Euro (€) of 100 cents
Population – 5,268,799 rising at 0.05 per cent a year (2014 est); Finnish (93.4 per cent), Swedish (5.6 per cent), Sami (0.1 per cent) (2006)
Religion – Christian (Lutheran 79 per cent, Orthodox 1 per cent), none 19 per cent
Language – Finnish, Swedish (both official)
Population density – 18 per sq. km (2011)
Urban population – 83.8 per cent (2012 est)
Median age (years) – 43.2 (2014 est)
National anthem – 'Maamme' / 'Vart Land' ['Our Land']
National day – 6 December (Independence Day)
Death penalty – Abolished for all crimes (since 1972)
CPI score – 90 (1)

CLIMATE AND TERRAIN
Much of the centre of the country is a glaciated plateau of forests and lakes, with low hills along the eastern border with Russia and in the far north. Forests cover around 70 per cent of the country, including those of the coastal peatlands in the south-west. There are over 60,000 lakes, with an average depth of 7m. Elevation extremes range from 1,328m (Haltiatunturi, or Halti) to 0m (Baltic Sea). A quarter of the country lies north of the Arctic Circle; temperatures there can range from −13°C in January to 13°C in July. Average temperatures in Helsinki range from −6°C in February to 16°C in July.
Owing to isostatic uplift (the rise of land mass no longer depressed by the weight of glaciers), the surface area of Finland is growing by around 7 sq. km a year.

HISTORY AND POLITICS
Finland was part of the Swedish Empire from the 12th century until it was ceded to Russia in 1809, when it became an autonomous grand duchy of the Russian Empire. After the Russian Revolution in 1917, Finland declared its independence. An attempted coup by Finnish Bolsheviks led to a short civil war that ended in their defeat in 1918, and in 1919 a republic was established. It resisted the 1939 invasion by the USSR but was defeated in 1940 and forced to cede territory; in the hope of recovering this territory it joined Germany's attack on the USSR in 1941. After agreeing an armistice with the USSR in 1944, Finland concluded a peace treaty in 1947 that conceded further territory to the USSR and obliged it to pay reparations. A Soviet-Finnish cooperation treaty in 1948 forced Finland to demilitarise its Soviet border and to adopt a stance of neutrality; these terms lasted until the demise of the USSR in 1991.
Finland joined the EU in 1995 and the European Monetary Union in 1998.
The results of the legislative election in April 2011 were inconclusive, with the four leading parties winning similar numbers of seats. After two months of negotiations, a six-party coalition government, comprising the National Coalition Party (KOK), the Social Democratic Party (SDP) and four smaller parties, took office under the SDP leader Jyrki Katainen. KOK candidate Sauli Niinisto won the 2012 presidential election, picking up 37 per cent of the overall vote. In April 2014, Jyrki Katainen stood down as Prime minister and was replaced by alexander Stubb of the KOK. New legislative elections are due in April 2015.
Under the 2000 constitution, the president is directly elected for a six-year term. There is a unicameral legislature, the *Eduskunta,* with 200 members directly elected for a four-year term. The prime minister is elected by the *Eduskunta* and appointed by the president.

HEAD OF STATE
President, Sauli Niinisto, *elected* 5 February 2012, *inaugurated* 1 March 2012

SELECTED GOVERNMENT MEMBERS *as at September 2014*
Prime Minister, Alexander Stubb
Deputy Prime Minister, Finance, Antti Rinne
Defence, Carl Haglund
Foreign Affairs, Erkki Tuomioja
Interior, Paivi Rasanen

EMBASSY OF FINLAND
38 Chesham Place, London SW1X 8HW
T 020-7838 6200 E sanomat.lon@formin.fi
W www.finemb.org.uk
Ambassador Extraordinary and Plenipotentiary, HE Pekka Huhtaniemi, *apptd* 2010

BRITISH EMBASSY
Itainen Puistotie 17, 00140 Helsinki
T (+358) (9) 2286 5100 E info.helsinki@fco.gov.uk
W www.gov.uk/government/world/finland
Ambassador Extraordinary and Plenipotentiary, HE Sarah Price, *apptd* 2014

DEFENCE

Aged 16–49, 2010 est	Males	Females
Available for military service	1,155,368	1,106,193
Fit for military service	955,151	912,983

Military expenditure – US$3,244m (2013)
Conscription – 18 years of age, male only; 6–12 months

ECONOMY AND TRADE

The country has a highly industrialised market economy which has thrived as a result of its telecommunications and electronics industries, particularly the manufacture of mobile phones, as well as its traditional timber and metals industries. The drop in exports and domestic demand due to the global economic downturn pushed the economy into recession in 2009, but there was economic growth in 2010–11. The economy is particularly vulnerable to fluctuations in trade with Russia, both its own trade (Russia is its leading supplier of imports and a major export market) and foreign trade, for which Finland is a major transit point.

The main trade partners are Russia, Germany and Sweden. Principal exports are electrical and optical equipment, machinery, transport equipment, paper and pulp, chemicals, base metals and timber. The main imports are foodstuffs (especially grain), petroleum and petroleum products, chemicals, transport equipment, iron and steel, machinery, textile yarn and fabrics, and components for manufactured goods. Finland is a net importer of energy.

GNI – US$247,239m; US$46,490 per capita (2012)
Annual average growth of GDP – –0.6 per cent (2013 est)
Inflation rate – 2.2 per cent (2013 est)
Unemployment – 8.1 per cent (2013 est)
Total external debt – US$586,900m (2013)
Imports – US$76,558m (2012)
Exports – US$73,114m (2012)

BALANCE OF PAYMENTS
Trade – US$3,444m deficit (2012)
Current Account – US$4,404m deficit (2012)

Trade with UK	2012	2013
Imports from UK	£1,503,150,757	£1,515,421,200
Exports to UK	£2,141,362,710	£2,501,663,520

COMMUNICATIONS

Airports and waterways – The principal airports are at Helsinki, Turku and Tampere; the main seaports are Helsinki, Kotka, Rauma and Turku
Roadways and railways – The 78,000km road network and 5,944km rail network are concentrated in the southern half of the country, where most of the population and industry are located
Telecommunications – 890,000 fixed lines (2012) and 9.32 million mobile telephone subscriptions (2009); there were 4.393 million internet users in 2009
Internet code and IDD – fi; 358 (from UK), 44 (to UK)
Major broadcasters – There are both commercial and state-owned broadcasters; the state broadcaster, Yleisradio Oy (YLE), is funded by licence fees and provides radio and television services in Swedish and Finnish, with radio in Sami (Lappish)
Press – Newspapers appear in both Finnish and Swedish; major publications include *Helsingin Sanomat, Hufvudstadsbladet* and the English-language *Helsinki Times*
WPFI score – 6,4 (1)

EDUCATION AND HEALTH

Basic education is free and compulsory for children from seven to 16 years.
Gross enrolment ratio (percentage of relevant age group) –
   primary 99 per cent; secondary 107 per cent; tertiary 96 per cent (2011 est)
Health expenditure (per capita) – US$4,325 (2011)
Hospital beds (per 1,000 people) – 5.9 (2010)
Life expectancy (years) – 79.69 (2014 est)
Mortality rate – 10.51 (2014 est)

Birth rate – 10.35 (2014 est)
Infant mortality rate – 3.36 (2014 est)

FRANCE

République française – French Republic

Area – 551,500 sq. km (excluding overseas territories)
Capital – Paris; population, 10,623,407 (2012 est)
Major cities – Bordeaux, Lille, Lyon, Marseille, Montpellier, Nantes, Nice, Reims, Rennes, Strasbourg, Toulouse. The chief towns of Corsica are Ajaccio and Bastia
Currency – Euro (€) of 100 cents
Population – 66,259,012 (excluding overseas territories), rising at 0.45 per cent a year (2014 est)
Religion – Christian (Roman Catholic 83–88 per cent, Protestant 2 per cent, Muslim 5–10 per cent, Jewish 1 per cent, Buddhist 1 per cent (est)
Language – French (official)
Population density – 119 per sq. km (2011) (excluding overseas territories)
Urban population – 86.4 per cent (2012 est)
Median age (years) – 40.9 (2014 est)
National anthem – 'La Marseillaise' ['Song of Marseille']
National day – 14 July (Fête de la Fédération/Fête Nationale)
Death penalty – Abolished for all crimes (since 1981)
CPI score – 71 (22)

CLIMATE AND TERRAIN

The north and west consist of flat plains, particularly in the basins of the Somme, Seine, Loire and Garonne rivers, with some low hills. The centre of the south is occupied by the Massif Central plateau, which is divided by the valley of the Rhone and Soane rivers from the mountains – the French Alps, the Jura and the Vosges – on the eastern border. The Pyrenees range lies along the southern border with Spain. Elevation extremes range from 4,807m (Mt Blanc, Alps) to −2m (Rhône delta). The climate is generally temperate, though the south has a Mediterranean climate and the east a continental climate.

POLITICS

Under the 1958 constitution, the head of state is a president directly elected for a five-year term, which is renewable once. The legislature, the *Parlement*, consists of the National Assembly and the senate. The National Assembly has 577 deputies, 555 for metropolitan France and 22 for the overseas departments and territories; members are directly elected for a five-year term. The senate has been enlarged gradually over the past decade; since the September 2011 elections there are 348 senators (328 for metropolitan France and the overseas departments, eight for overseas collectivities and territories, and 12 for French nationals abroad) elected

Remains province of Gaul until Frankish invasion	Civil war hinders attempt to establish European power	Republic declared; King Louis XVI executed	Second Republic declared after the congress of Vienna briefly restores monarchy	Third Republic declared	North occupied by Germany during the Second World War, with a pro-German government in the south	Joins European Monetary Union		

*c.*100 — 843 — 1789 — 1804-14 — 1852 — 1914-18 — 1946-62 — 2005-8

*c.*500-600 — 1562-98 — 1792 — 1848 — 1870-71 — 1940-44 — 1999

Conquered by the Romans	*Francia Occidentalis* becomes the basis of modern France	*Ancien régime* overthrown by French Revolution	Republic overthrown by Napoléon Bonaparte, who establishes the French Empire	Napoléon III declares second French Empire	Victorious in the First World War	Fourth Republic collapses in 1958; colonies granted independence	Population rejects EU constitution; country signs Lisbon Treaty

by an electoral college to serve a six-year term, with half elected every three years.

The prime minister is nominated by the National Assembly and appointed by the president, as is the council of ministers. They are responsible to the legislature, but as the executive is constitutionally separate from the legislature, ministers may not sit in the legislature and must hand over their seats to a substitute.

The constitution was amended in 2003 to pave the way for the devolution to the 22 metropolitan regions and 96 metropolitan departments of powers over economic development, transport, tourism, culture and further education.

The 2012 presidential election was won in the second round by Socialist Party (PS) candidate François Hollande. In the 2012 legislative elections, the Socialist Party won an overall majority, defeating Nicolas Sarkozy's Union for a Popular Movement party by 86 seats. Following poor local election results for the PS, Manuel Valls replaced Jean-Marc Ayrault as prime minister on 1 April 2014 and instigated a major cabinet reshuffle.

HEAD OF STATE
President of the French Republic, François Hollande, *elected* 6 May 2012

SELECTED GOVERNMENT MEMBERS *as at May 2014*
Prime Minister, Manuel Valls
Defence, Jean-Yves Le Drian
Finance, Michel Sapin
Foreign Affairs, Laurent Fabius

EMBASSY OF FRANCE
58 Knightsbridge, London SW1X 7JT
T 020-7073 1000 E presse.londres-amba@diplomatie.gouv.fr
W www.ambafrance-uk.org
Ambassador Extraordinary and Plenipotentiary, HE Bernard Emié, *apptd* 2011

BRITISH EMBASSY
35 rue du Faubourg St Honoré, 75383 Paris Cédex 08
T (+33) (1) 4451 3100 W www.gov.uk/government/world/france
Ambassador Extraordinary and Plenipotentiary, HE Sir Peter Ricketts, GCMG, *apptd* 2012

INSURGENCIES
Corsican separatists have pursued a campaign of bombings and shootings since the 1970s apart from a ceasefire in 2003–5 observed by the main separatist faction. The French government's proposals to combine the island's two departments and to give the Corsican regional parliament greater autonomy were narrowly rejected in a 2003 referendum.

DEFENCE

Aged 16–49, 2010 est	Males	Females
Available for military service	14,563,662	14,238,434
Fit for military service	12,025,341	11,721,827

Military expenditure – US$62,272m (2013)

ECONOMY AND TRADE

The economy is in transition from extensive government ownership and intervention to a more liberal and market-oriented form with many large, state-run companies becoming privatised; reform was initiated in response to poor economic growth and high unemployment. Implementation has been slow because of the constraints of eurozone membership, and strong resistance to the government's plans for privatisation and reform of labour, pensions and welfare. François Hollande's government advocates pro-growth economic policies and the implementation of new banking reforms, as well as the introduction of a new top bracket income tax.

Over one-third of the land area of metropolitan France is utilised for agricultural production and a further quarter is covered by forests. Viniculture is extensive, although France has lost market share to other countries in recent years. Cognac, liqueurs and cider are also produced. Other important agricultural products include cereals, sugar beet, potatoes, beef, dairy products and fish. Agriculture employs 3.8 per cent of the workforce and contributes 1.9 per cent of GDP.

Oil is produced from fields in the Landes area, but France is a net importer of crude oil, for processing by its oil-refining industry. Natural gas is produced in the foothills of the Pyrenees.

Industry contributes 18.7 per cent of GDP, employing 24.3 per cent of the workforce. The sector is highly diversified and includes the production of machinery, iron, steel, aluminium, chemicals, vehicles, aircraft, electronic goods, textiles and processed food. The service sector contributes 79.4 per cent of GDP and employs 71.8 per cent of the workforce. Tourism is an important contributor to GDP: France is the most-visited country in the world.

The main trading partners are other EU countries, especially Germany. Principal exports are machinery, vehicles, aircraft, plastics, chemicals, pharmaceutical products, iron and steel, and beverages. The main imports are raw materials for industry (eg crude oil, chemicals, plastics), machinery, vehicles and aircraft.

GNI – US$2,657,720m; US$41,750 per capita (2012)
Annual average growth of GDP – 0.2 per cent (2013 est)
Inflation rate – 1.1 per cent (2013 est)
Population below poverty line – 7.8 per cent (2010)
Unemployment – 10.5 per cent (2013 est)
Total external debt – US$5,371,000m (2011)
Imports – US$665,457m (2012)
Exports – US$557,258m (2012)

BALANCE OF PAYMENTS
Trade – US$108,199m deficit (2012)
Current Account – US$57,142m deficit (2012)

Trade with UK	2012	2013
Imports from UK	£22,084,940,646	£22,486,212,890
Exports to UK	£23,451,150,220	£24,759,241,557

COMMUNICATIONS

Airports – 294; there are two international airports serving Paris, and many regional airports capable of accepting international flights

Waterways – The principal seaports are Marseille on the Mediterranean Sea, Bordeaux and Nantes on the Atlantic coast, and Le Havre, Calais and Dunkirk on the Channel coast; there are 8,501km of navigable inland waterways, 1,621km navigable by large vessels, and Paris, Rouen and Strasbourg are significant river ports. The French mercantile marine consisted in 2011 of 162 ships of 1,000 gross tonnage or over, 151 of which are registered overseas
Roadways and railways – There are 1,028,446 km of roadways, including 11,416km of motorways, and 29,640km of railways
Telecommunications – 39.29 million fixed lines and 62.28 million mobile subscriptions (2012); there were 44.63 million internet users in 2009
Internet code and IDD – fr; 33 (from UK), 44 (to UK)
Major broadcasters – TV5 is an international French-language television channel co-financed by Belgium, Canada, France and Switzerland. The main domestic channel, TF1, was privatised in 1987. A global news channel, France 24, was launched in 2006 and broadcasts in French, English and Arabic
Press – France has over 100 daily newspapers, including *Le Monde*, *Le Figaro* and *Libération*
WPFI score – 21,89 (39)

EDUCATION AND HEALTH

Education is compulsory and free between the ages of six and 16. There are three types of *lycée* – *général, technique* and *professionel* – and each leads to its own *baccalauréat* qualification. Specialist schools are numerous.
Gross enrolment ratio (percentage of relevant age group) –
   primary 108 per cent; secondary 110 per cent; tertiary 57 per cent (2011 est)
Health expenditure (per capita) – US$4,952 (2011)
Hospital beds (per 1,000 people) – 6.6 (2010)
Life expectancy (years) – 81.66 (2014 est)
Mortality rate – 9.06 (2014 est)
Birth rate – 12.49 (2014 est)
Infant mortality rate – 3.31 (2014 est)

OVERSEAS DEPARTMENTS/REGIONS

French Guiana, Guadeloupe, Martinique and Réunion have had departmental status since 1946. They were given regional status with greater powers of self-government and elected assemblies in 1982, and were redesignated as Overseas Regions in 2003. Their regional and departmental status is identical to that of regions and departments of metropolitan France, and they can choose to replace these with a single structure by merging their regional and departmental assemblies. The French government is represented by a *prefect* in each. In referendums in 2010, French Guiana and Martinique rejected proposals for granting greater autonomy to their local governments.

FRENCH GUIANA
Area – 83,534 sq. km
Capital – Cayenne; population, 56,002 (2010 est)
Population – 237,200 (2011 est)

Situated on the north-eastern coast of South America, French Guiana is flanked by Suriname to the west and by Brazil to the south and east. Under the administration of French Guiana are the Îles du Salut group of islands (St Joseph, Île Royal and Île du Diable). The European Space Agency rocket launch site is situated at Kourou and accounts for 25 per cent of GDP. Fishing, forestry and mining are the main activities,

and the economy is dependent on government subsidies. The main exports are timber, shrimp and gold. Tourism is restricted by the lack of infrastructure, as much of the interior is only accessible by river.
Prefect, Éric Spitz, *apptd* 2013

GUADELOUPE
Area – 1,705 sq. km
Capital – Basse-Terre; population, 12,145 (2010 est), on Guadeloupe
Population – 463,000 (2011)

The Guadeloupe archipelago consists of a number of islands in the Leeward Islands group in the West Indies, including Guadeloupe (or Basse-Terre), Grande-Terre, Marie-Galante, La Désirade and the Îles des Saintes. The main towns are Les Abymes, Pointe-à-Pitre (Grande-Terre) and Grand Bourg (Marie-Galante). The main industries are tourism, agriculture, sugar refining and rum distilling. Bananas, sugar, rum and vanilla are the main exports.
Prefect, Marcelle Pierrot, *apptd* 2013

MARTINIQUE
Area – 1,100 sq. km
Capital – Fort-de-France; population, 88,623 (2010 est)
Population – 407,000 (2008)

An island in the Windward Islands group in the West Indies, Martinique lies between Dominica in the north and St Lucia in the south. It is dominated by Mt Pelée (1,397m), an active volcano that last erupted in 1902. Tourism is a major industry. The main exports are bananas, rum and petroleum products.
Prefect, Laurent Prévost, *apptd* 2011

MAYOTTE
Area – 374 sq. km
Capital – Mamoudzou; population, 53,022 (2007 est)
Population – 223,765 (2009 est)

Part of the Comoros archipelago, Mayotte remained a French dependency when the other three islands became independent as the Comoros Republic in 1975. It became a *collectivité territoriale* in 1976, and an overseas department/ region in 2011. The main products are vanilla, ylang-ylang (perfume essence), coffee, copra, lobster and shrimp. The economy is dependent on French subsidies.
Prefect, Jacques Witkowski, *apptd* 2013

RÉUNION
Area – 2,507 sq. km
Capital – St-Denis; population, 140,906 (2009 est)
Population – 821,168 (2009 est)

A French possession since 1638, Réunion lies in the Indian Ocean, about 650km east of Madagascar and 180km south-west of Mauritius. The main industries are tourism and sugar and rum production.
Prefect, Jean-Luc Marx, *apptd* 2012

TERRITORIAL COLLECTIVITIES

Overseas *collectivités* are administrative divisions with a degree of autonomy but without the status of a similar administrative division in metropolitan France; each has its own laws and an elected assembly and president. The French government is represented by a *prefect* or high commissioner in each. Constitutional changes in 2003 redesignated most of the former overseas territories as *collectivités;* New Caledonia is treated in this category because this is its *de facto* status at present, but its official designation depends upon the outcome of independence referendums to be held between 2014 and 2018.

FRENCH POLYNESIA
Area – 4,167 sq. km
Capital – Papeete, on Tahiti; population, 133,000 (2009 est)
Population – 280,026 rising at 0.97 per cent a year
(2014 est)

French Polynesia consists of over 118 volcanic or coral islands and atolls in the South Pacific. There are five archipelagos: the Society Islands (Windward Islands group includes Tahiti, Moorea, Makatea, Mehetia, Tetiaroa, Tubuai Manu; Leeward Islands group includes Huahine, Raiatea, Tahaa, Bora-Bora, Maupiti); the Tuamotu Islands (Rangiroa, Hao, Turéia etc); the Gambier Islands (Mangareva etc); the Tubuai Islands (Rimatara, Rurutu, Tubuai, Raivavae, Rapa etc); and the Marquesas Islands (Nuku-Hiva, Hiva-Oa, Fatu-Hiva, Tahuata, Ua Huka etc). Some of the atolls were used by France for testing nuclear weapons between 1966 and 1996. The main industries are tourism, pearl-farming, deep-sea fishing, coconut products and vanilla production.
High Commissioner, Jean-Pierre Laflaquiere, *apptd* 2012

NEW CALEDONIA
Area – 18,575 sq. km
Capital – Nouméa; population, 144,000 (2009 est)
Population – 267,840 rising at 1.42 per cent a year
(2014 est)

New Caledonia is a large island in the western Pacific, 1,120km off the eastern coast of Australia. Its dependencies are the Isle of Pines, the Loyalty Islands (Mahé, Lifou, Urea, etc), the Bélep Archipelago, the Chesterfield Islands, the Huon Islands and Walpole. New Caledonia was discovered in 1774 and annexed by France in 1853. Agitation for independence from the 1980s ended with the Nouméa accord in 1998, under which an increasing degree of autonomy will be transferred to the territory up to 2018, with a referendum on independence to be held between 2014 and 2018. The territory is divided into three provinces, each with a provincial assembly; these combine to form the territorial assembly.

A quarter of the world's nickel deposits are found in the territory, and nickel mining and smelting are the main industries, along with tourism and fishing. Ferronickel, nickel ore and fish are the main exports. About 20 per cent of food has to be imported.
High Commissioner, Jean-Jacques Brot, *apptd* 2013

ST BARTHÉLEMY
Area – 21 sq. km
Capital – Gustavia
Population – 7,267 (2013 est)

The island lies in the Caribbean Sea about 240km north-west of Guadeloupe. It was settled by the French from 1648. France sold the island to Sweden in 1784 but bought it back again in 1878 and it was under the administration of Guadeloupe until 2007, when it became a *collectivité territoriale.* The economy is based on luxury tourism and duty-free commerce in luxury goods. Freshwater sources are limited, so all food and energy and most manufactured goods are imported.
Prefect, Philippe Chopin, *apptd* 2011

ST MARTIN
Area – 54.4 sq. km
Capital – Marigot
Population – 31,530 (2014 est)

The territory occupies the northern part of the island of St Martin, 250km to the north-west of Guadeloupe; the southern part (Sint Maarten) is a territory of the Netherlands. The island was claimed for Spain by Columbus in 1493 but the Spanish relinquished it in 1648 to the Dutch and French, who divided the island between them. The French part was administered from Guadeloupe until it was made a *collectivité territoriale* in 2007. The economy is dependent on tourism, which employs 85 per cent of the workforce. Nearly all food, energy and manufactured goods are imported.
Prefect, Philippe Chopin, *apptd* 2011

ST PIERRE AND MIQUELON
Area – 242 sq. km
Capital – St-Pierre; population, 5,000 (2009 est)
Population – 5,716 falling at 1.02 per cent a year (2014 est)

These two small groups of eight islands off the south coast of Newfoundland became a *collectivité territoriale* in 1985. The main industry of fishing and servicing fishing fleets has declined in step with the decline in cod stocks, and fish farming, crab fishing and agriculture are being developed. Tourism is of growing importance, but the economy is dependent on government subsidies.
Prefect, Patrice Latron, *apptd* 2011

WALLIS AND FUTUNA ISLANDS
Area – 142 sq. km
Capital – Mata-Utu, on Uvea, the main island of the Wallis
group; population, 1,112 (2009 est)
Population – 15,561 rising at 0.33 per cent a year (2014 est)

The two groups of islands (the Wallis Archipelago and the Îles de Horne) lie in the South Pacific, north-east of Fiji. They became a French protectorate from the 1840s and were administered from New Caledonia until 1961. The main products are copra, vegetables, bananas, livestock products, fish and timber.
Administrator, Michel Jeanjean, *apptd* 2010

OVERSEAS TERRITORIES

TERRITORY OF THE FRENCH SOUTHERN AND ANTARCTIC LANDS
Created in 1955 from former Réunion dependencies, the territory comprises the islands of Amsterdam (55 sq. km) and St Paul (7 sq. km), the Kerguelen Islands (7,215 sq. km) and Crozet Islands (352 sq. km) archipelagos, Adélie Land (about 500,000 sq. km) in the Antarctic continent and, since 2007, the islands of Bassas da India (80 sq. km), Europa (28 sq. km), les Glorieuses (5 sq. km), Juan de Nova (4.4 sq. km) and Tromelin (1 sq. km). The population consists only of staff of the meteorological and scientific research stations.
Administrator, Pascal Bolot, *apptd* 2012

THE FRENCH COMMUNITY OF STATES
The 1958 constitution envisaged the establishment of a French Community of States. A number of former French colonies in Africa have seceded from the community but for all practical purposes continue to enjoy the same close links with France as do those that remain formal members. Most former French African colonies are closely linked to France by financial, technical and economic agreements.

GABON

République Gabonaise – Gabonese Republic

Area – 267,667 sq. km
Capital – Libreville; population, 619,000 (2009 est)
Major towns – Franceville (Masuku), Moanda, Oyem,
   Port-Gentil
Currency – Central African CFA franc of 100 centimes
Population – 1,672,597 rising at 1.94 per cent a year
   (2014 est); over 40 predominantly Bantu tribes, of which
   the Fang, Bapounou, Nzebi and Obamba are the largest
   tribal groupings
Religion – Christian 55–75 per cent, Muslim less than 1 per
   cent; many people combine elements of Christian and
   indigenous beliefs
Language – French (official), Fang, Myene, Nzebi, Bapounou,
   Bandjabi
Population density – 6 per sq. km (2011)
Urban population – 86.5 per cent (2012 est)
Median age (years) – 18.6 (2014 est)
National anthem – 'La Concorde' ['The Concord']
National day – 17 August (Independence Day)
Death penalty – Abolished for all crimes (since 2010)
CPI score – 34 (106)
Literacy rate – 89 per cent (2011 est)
Health expenditure (per capita) – US$358 (2011)
Hospital beds (per 1,000 people) – 6.3 (2010)
Life expectancy (years) – 52.06 (2014 est)
Mortality rate – 13.13 (2014 est)
Birth rate – 34.64 (2014 est)
Infant mortality rate – 47.03 (2014 est)
HIV/AIDS adult prevalence – 4 per cent (2012 est)

CLIMATE AND TERRAIN

The country lies on the equator. It rises from a narrow coastal plain to a hilly interior; approximately 85 per cent of the land is rainforest, with savannah in the east and south, although by 2006 as much as half of the country's forest was being leased for timber. In 2002, 10 per cent of the country was designated as national park. Elevation extremes range from 1,575m (Mt Iboundji) to 0m (Atlantic Ocean). The climate is tropical, with an average temperature of 24.7°C. There are two wet seasons each year, from January to June and September to December.

HISTORY AND POLITICS

The first Europeans to visit the region were the Portuguese in the 15th century; Dutch, French and English traders arrived soon after. Sovereignty was signed over to the French in 1839 by a local Mpongwe ruler. In 1849, slaves freed by the French formed a settlement which they called Libreville, now the capital. The country was occupied by the French in 1885 and became part of French Equatorial Africa in 1910. Gabon

became autonomous within the French Community in 1958 and gained independence on 17 August 1960.

Omar Bongo succeeded to the presidency in 1967 after the death of the first president, and in 1968 he established a one-party state with the *Parti Démocratique Gabonais* (PDG) as the only party. By the late 1980s, the deteriorating economy was provoking unrest and demands for greater democracy, and in 1991 a multiparty system was reintroduced.

Under the multiparty system, the PDG has remained in power (amid allegations of electoral fraud) although it has included opposition party members in coalition governments since 1994. The PDG and its coalition partners retained the majority in the 2011 legislative election, which was boycotted by the main opposition party. President Bongo was re-elected for a sixth term of office in 2005; he died in June 2009, and was succeeded by his son, Ali-Ben Bongo, who was elected president in August 2009 amid allegations of vote-rigging. In January 2014 Daniel Ona Ondo replaced Raymond Ndong Sima as prime minister, with Sima having been in office since February 2012.

The 1991 constitution, amended in 1995, 1997 and 2003, provides for a president who is directly elected for a seven-year term; since 2003, there has been no limit on the number of terms a president may serve. The president appoints the prime minister, who then appoints the council of ministers. There is a bicameral *Parlement*, comprising the 120-member National Assembly (111 directly elected and nine appointed by the president, all for a five-year term) and the senate, which has 102 members elected for a six-year term by municipal and regional councillors.

HEAD OF STATE
President, Ali-Ben Bongo, *elected* 30 August 2009, *sworn in*
   16 October 2009

SELECTED GOVERNMENT MEMBERS *as at April 2014*
Prime Minister, Daniel Ona Ondo
Defence, Ernest Mpouho Epigat
Economy, Jean Christophe Akagha Mba
Foreign Affairs, Emmanuel Issozet Ngondet
Interior, Guy-Bertrand Mapangou

EMBASSY OF THE GABONESE REPUBLIC
27 Elvaston Place, London SW7 5NL
T 020-7823 9986 W www.gabonembassyuk.org
Ambassador Extraordinary and Plenipotentiary, Omer Piankali,
   apptd 2009

BRITISH HIGH COMMISSION
HE Brian Olley, *apptd* 2013, resident at Yaoundé, Cameroon

DEFENCE

Aged 16–49, 2010 est	*Males*	*Females*
Available for military service	350,640	351,718
Fit for military service	202,404	195,389

Military expenditure – US$263m (2013)

ECONOMY AND TRADE

Gabon is one of the most prosperous countries in Africa, largely owing to its small population and abundance of oil and mineral resources. The economy is heavily dependent on oil (which contributes over 50 per cent of GDP) and other mineral resources, including manganese and uranium, and timber, but the government is investing in diversification to reduce vulnerability to fluctuating commodity prices and the gradual decline in oil production as reserves become exhausted. Despite the country's wealth, a large proportion of the population remains poor, and weak fiscal management has resulted in a high foreign debt which has had to be rescheduled several times. GDP grew by 6 per cent between 2010 and 2013.

Industry contributes 63.9 per cent of GDP and employs 15 per cent of the workforce, mainly in oil and mineral extraction, oil refining, chemicals, ship repair, textiles, and processing agricultural and forestry products. Agriculture is largely at subsistence level, employing 60 per cent of the workforce but contributing only 4.2 per cent of GDP. It is restricted by the forest cover and lack of suitable land. The main products include cocoa, coffee, sugar, palm oil, rubber, cattle, timber and fish.

The main trading partners are France, Japan, the USA and China. Principal exports are crude oil (70 per cent), timber, manganese and uranium. The main imports are machinery and equipment, food, chemicals and construction materials.
GNI – US$16,428m; US$10,040 per capita (2012)
Annual average growth of GDP – 6.6 per cent (2013 est)
Inflation rate – 1.2 per cent (2013 est)
Unemployment – 21 per cent (2006 est)
Total external debt – US$3,433m (2013 est)
Imports – US$3,630m (2012)
Exports – US$9,662m (2012)

BALANCE OF PAYMENTS
Trade – US$6,032m surplus (2012)
Current Account – US$2,434m surplus (2012 est)

Trade with UK	2012	2013
Imports from UK	£52,786,832	£59,624,588
Exports to UK	£8,309,529	£82,028,156

COMMUNICATIONS
Airports and waterways – 14, including international airports in Libreville and Port-Gentil; there are 1,600km of navigable waterways and the principal seaport is in Port-Gentil
Roadways and railways – 9,170km; 649km
Telecommunications – 17,000 fixed lines and 2.93 million mobile subscriptions (2012); there were 98,800 internet users in 2009
Internet code and IDD – ga; 241 (from UK), 44 (to UK)
Media – The state-controlled broadcaster, Radiodiffusion-Télévision Gabonaise, operates two television channels and two radio networks; the only daily newspaper, *L'Union*, is also government-run; Africa No1, a pan-African radio broadcaster, is based in Gabon

THE GAMBIA

Republic of The Gambia

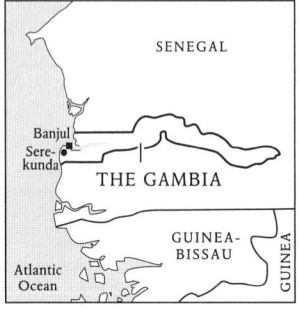

Area – 11,295 sq. km
Capital – Banjul; population, 436,000 (2009 est)
Major towns – Bakau, Brikama, Farafenni, Serekunda
Currency – Dalasi (D) of 100 butut
Population – 1,925,527 rising at 2.23 per cent a year (2014 est); Mandinka (42 per cent), Fulani (18 per cent), Wolof (16 per cent), Jola (10 per cent), Serahuli (Soninke) (9 per cent) (2003)
Religion – Sunni Muslim 90 per cent (majority Malikite Sufi), Christian 8 per cent (predominantly Roman Catholic), animist 2 per cent (est)
Language – English (official), Mandinka, Wolof, Fula
Population density – 171 per sq. km (2011)
Urban population – 57.9 per cent (2012 est)
Median age (years) – 20.2 (2014 est)
National anthem – 'For The Gambia Our Homeland'
National day – 18 February (Independence Day)
Death penalty – Retained
CPI score – 28 (127)

CLIMATE AND TERRAIN
The Gambia consists of a narrow strip of land along the river Gambia, mostly comprising the basin and flood plain of the river, flanked by savannah and low hills. Elevation extremes range from 53m to 0m (Atlantic Ocean). The climate is tropical, with a wet season from June to November.

HISTORY AND POLITICS
The Gambia river basin was part of an area dominated from the 10th to 16th centuries by the Mali and Songhai kingdoms. The Portuguese reached the river Gambia in 1447 and, followed later by other European merchants, established trading posts along the river. In 1816 a British garrison was stationed on an island at the river mouth; this became the capital of a small British colony, and a crown colony in 1843. The boundaries of the country were agreed by France and Britain in 1889; British territory would extend 10km from the upper river on either bank. The Gambia became independent on 18 February 1965 and a republic in 1970. The country withdrew from the Commonwealth in 2013, describing the organisation as 'neo-colonialist'.

The post-independence prime minister, Sir Dawda Jawara, was president from 1970 until 1994, when he was over-thrown in a military coup. The coup leader, Lt. (later Col.) Yahya Jammeh, assumed the presidency and a civilian-military government was formed to govern in conjunction with the ruling military council. Civilian government was restored after elections in 1996 and 1997 following the approval of a new constitution. Jammeh was elected president and his Alliance for Patriotic Reorientation and Construction (APRC) won an overall majority of the legislative seats. Jammeh and the APRC have won all subsequent elections; the opposition and media are subject to harassment and detention without charge.

In the 2011 presidential election, Jammeh was re-elected with 71 per cent of the vote. The 2012 legislative election was won by the APRC, with 43 of the 48 elected seats.

Under the 1997 constitution, the executive president is directly elected for a five-year term; there is no limit on re-election. The unicameral National Assembly has 53 members, of whom 48 are directly elected and five are appointed by the president, for a five-year term.

HEAD OF STATE
President, Defence, Agriculture, Col. Yahya Jammeh, *took power* July 1994, *elected* September 1996, *re-elected* 2001, 2006, 2012
Vice-President, Women's Affairs, Ajaratou Isatou Njie-Saidy

SELECTED GOVERNMENT MEMBERS *as at April 2014*
Finance and Economic Affairs, Kebba Touray
Foreign Affairs, Mamour Alieu Jagne
Interior, Ousman Sonko
Justice, Attorney-General, Fatima Singhateh

EMBASSY OF THE GAMBIA
92 Ledbury Road, London W11 2AH
T 020-7229 8066 E info@gambiaembassy.org.uk
W www.gambiaembassy.org.uk
Ambassador Extraordinary and Plenipotentiary, HE Elizabeth
    Ya Eli Harding, *apptd* 2013

BRITISH HIGH COMMISSION
PO Box 507, 48 Atlantic Road, Fajara, Banjul
T (+220) 449 5133 E ukinthegambia@fco.gov.uk
W www.gov.uk/government/world/gambia
High Commissioner, HE Colin Crorkin MBE, *apptd* 2014

DEFENCE

Aged 16–49, 2010 est	*Males*	*Females*
Available for military service	423,306	438,641
Fit for military service	315,176	347,017

Military expenditure – US$4.6m (2007 est)

ECONOMY AND TRADE

The country has limited natural resources and agricultural land. Historically, the mainstay of the economy was re-export trade with neighbouring countries, but this has declined since the late 1990s, owing to the vagaries of government policies and trade and transport disputes with Senegal. There are high levels of public and foreign debt and the country is dependent on financial and technical aid from foreign donors. Remittances from Gambians working abroad and tourism are vital revenue sources. In 2012 a drop in tourism led to a decline in GDP.

The services sector employs only 6 per cent of the workforce but contributes 59.5 per cent of GDP, largely owing to the growing tourism and banking sectors. About 75 per cent of the population is dependent on subsistence agriculture, which contributes 19.7 per cent of GDP. The chief product, peanuts, is also the main export and the basis of the main industrial activity, leaving the economy vulnerable to market fluctuations and the weather. Industry contributes 12.6 per cent to GDP, chiefly through processing peanuts, fish and hides, assembling agricultural machinery, metalworking, woodworking and the production of beverages and clothing.

The main trade partners are China, India, Brazil, EU countries and Senegal. Principal exports are peanut products, fish, cotton lint and palm kernels. The main imports are foodstuffs, manufactures, fuel, machinery and transport equipment.

GNI – US$874m; US$510 per capita (2012)
Annual average growth of GDP – −6.4 per cent (2013 est)
Inflation rate – 6 per cent (2013 est)
Total external debt – US$517.7m (2013 est)
Imports – US$349m (2012)
Exports – US$15m (2010)

BALANCE OF PAYMENTS
Trade – US$286m deficit (2010)
Current Account – US$140m deficit (2011)

Trade with UK	*2012*	*2013*
Imports from UK	£37,688,985	£29,481,129
Exports to UK	£3,812,331	£2,053,862

COMMUNICATIONS

Airports and waterways – There is an international airport at Banjul; there are 390km of navigable waterways on the River Gambia
Roadways – 3,740km
Telecommunications – 64,200 fixed lines and 1.526 million mobile subscriptions (2012); there were 130,100 internet users in 2009
Internet code and IDD – gm; 220 (from UK), 44 (to UK)
Major broadcasters – The state operates the only national television station, although there is also a private satellite channel. State-run Radio Gambia produces carefully controlled news broadcasts, which are relayed by private radio stations
Press – Major publications include the *Daily Observer, The Daily News* and *The Point*
WPFI score – 46,42 (155)

EDUCATION AND HEALTH

Education is compulsory between the ages of seven and 12.
Gross enrolment ratio (percentage of relevant age group) – primary 82 per cent; secondary 57 per cent (2011 est)
Health expenditure (per capita) – US$27 (2011)
Hospital beds (per 1,000 people) – 1.1 (2011)
Life expectancy (years) – 64.36 (2014 est)
Mortality rate – 7.26 (2014 est)
Birth rate – 31.75 (2014 est)
Infant mortality rate – 65.74 (2014 est)
HIV/AIDS adult prevalence – 1.3 per cent (2012 est)

GEORGIA

Sak'art'velo – Georgia

Area – 69,700 sq. km
Capital – Tbilisi; population, 1,128,537 (2012 est)
Major cities – Batumi, Kutaisi, Poti, Rustavi, Zugdidi
Currency – Lari of 100 tetri
Population – 4,935,880 falling at 0.11 per cent a year (2014 est); Georgian (83.8 per cent), Azeri (6.5 per cent), Armenian (5.7 per cent), Russian (1.5 per cent) (2002)
Religion – Christian 89 per cent (Orthodox 84 per cent, Armenian–Gregorian 4 per cent, Catholic 1 per cent), Muslim 10 per cent (est)
Language – Georgian (official), Russian, Armenian, Azeri, Abkhaz (official in Abkhazia)
Population density – 7 per sq. km (2012)
Urban population – 52.9 per cent (2012 est)
Median age (years) – 37.7 (2014 est)
National anthem – 'Tavisupleba' ['Freedom']
National day – 26 May (Independence Day, 1918)
Death penalty – Abolished for all crimes (since 1997)
CPI score – 49 (55)
Literacy rate – 100 per cent (2010 est)

Converted to Christianity — c.100

Invaded by Moguls — c.1000

Ottoman and Persian empires compete for influence — 1500–1700

Absorbed into Russian Empire — 1801–4

Russia invades; Georgia joins USSR as part of the Transcaucasian Soviet Socialist Republic — 1917

Independent nationalist government comes to power — 1921–22

Communist Party's monopoly on power abolished — 1936

Country becomes separate republic — 1990

Declares independence from USSR — 1991

Authoritarian president Zviad Gamsakhurdia overthrown; an uprising forces the country to join Commonwealth of Independent States (COIS) — 1992–93

Leaves COIS to join the EU-initiated Eastern Partnership — 2009

Kingdom of Georgia comes under Roman influence — c.400

Independence established following domination by Persian, Arabs and Turks — 1236

Gross enrolment ratio (percentage of relevant age group) – primary 107 per cent; secondary 87 per cent; tertiary 30 per cent (2011 est)
Health expenditure (per capita) – US$328 (2011)
Hospital beds (per 1,000 people) – 2.9 (2011)
Life expectancy (years) – 75.72 (2014 est)
Mortality rate – 10.77 (2014 est)
Birth rate – 12.93 (2014 est)
Infant mortality rate – 16.68 (2014 est)

CLIMATE AND TERRAIN
Georgia lies in the western part of the Caucasus region, on the eastern shore of the Black Sea. It is mountainous, with the Great Caucasus mountain range along the northern border with Russia, and the Lesser Caucasus in the south. These are divided by the Kolkhida lowland in the west and the Mtkvari (Kura) river basin in the east, between which runs the valley of the Mtkvari river. Elevation extremes range from 5,201m (Mt Shkhara) to 0m (Black Sea). The climate is almost tropical in summer, while cold winters affect both the mountains and valleys. Average temperatures range from 4.7°C in January to 22.8°C in August.

POLITICS
The 1995 constitution provides for a federal republic with a unicameral legislature, to become bicameral 'following the creation of appropriate conditions'. It was amended in 2010 to transfer some of the president's powers to the legislature and prime minister. The president is directly elected for a five-year term, renewable once. The unicameral parliament has 150 members, 75 elected in single-member constituencies and 75 by proportional representation, who serve for a five-year term.

In November 2013 Irakli Garibashvili of the Georgian Dream party replaced Bidzina Ivanishvili as the country's prime minister, becoming the world's youngest elected leader at the time, aged 31. The October 2013 presidential election was won by ally Giorgi Margvelashvili, marking an end to a decade in power for outgoing President Mikheil Saakashvili.

HEAD OF STATE
President, Giorgi Margvelashvili, *sworn in* 17 November 2014

SELECTED GOVERNMENT MEMBERS *as at April 2014*
Prime Minister, Irakli Garibashvili
First Deputy Prime Minister, Giorgi Kvirikashvili
Deputy Prime Minister, Kakha Kaladze
Defence, Irakli Alasania
Finance, Nodar Khaduri

EMBASSY OF GEORGIA
4 Russell Gardens, London W14 8EZ
T 020-7348 1941 E embassy@geoemb.plus.com
W www.uk.mfa.gov.ge
Ambassador Extraordinary and Plenipotentiary, vacant

BRITISH EMBASSY
51 Krtsanisi Street, 0114 Tbilisi
T (+995) (32) 227 47 47
W www.gov.uk/government/world/georgia

Ambassador Extraordinary and Plenipotentiary, HE Alexandra Hall Hall *apptd* 2013

SECESSION
Fears that Georgian independence would deprive them of their own autonomy led to unilateral declarations of independence by the central region of South Ossetia (1991) and the north-western region of Abkhazia (1992) followed by a year of conflict in both separatist areas. In August 2008, clashes between Georgian troops and South Ossetian separatists escalated into a brief war between Georgia and Russia, in which Georgian forces were expelled from South Ossetia and Abkhazia. Russia has not fully complied with an EU-brokered ceasefire, maintaining a military presence in the areas and a 'buffer zone' around them; only Russia, Venezuela, Nicaragua and Nauru recognise their unilateral declarations of independence. In both regions the economy and infrastructure are in ruins and the secessionists are dependent on Russia, which has stepped up its economic support.

Relations between Georgia and Ajaria, a semi-autonomous region in the south-west and a key trade hub, deteriorated briefly in 2004 when Aslan Abashidze, Ajaria's leader since 1991, refused to recognise the authority of the newly elected President Saakashvili, and accused Georgia of planning to invade Ajaria. Public demonstrations against Abashidze forced him to resign. The Georgian parliament granted the Ajarian assembly powers over local affairs but the Georgian president retains the power to nominate the region's head of government and to dissolve its government and assembly.

DEFENCE

Aged 16–49, 2010 est	*Males*	*Females*
Available for military service	1,080,840	1,122,031
Fit for military service	893,003	931,683

Military expenditure – US$442m (2014 est)
Conscription – 18–34 years of age; 18 months

ECONOMY AND TRADE
The economy grew rapidly from 2003, making good progress towards recovery following the near-collapse of the 1990s. Reform of the tax system nearly quadrupled government revenue, while added impetus in privatisation and anti-corruption programmes attracted foreign investment. However, the economy slowed in 2008 following the war with Russia and contracted in 2009 as the global economic downturn affected the regional economy and led to a decline in foreign investment and expatriates' remittances. The fuel crises in 2005–6 prompted the renovation of hydroelectric power plants and the repair of a pipeline from Azerbaijan; the country now meets the majority of its energy needs. The government is also looking to diversify its export markets since Russia lifted an embargo on key exports in 2012, and it hopes Georgia's position as a transit state for oil and gas pipelines and for trade between central Asia and Europe will stimulate economic growth.

Agriculture employs 55.6 per cent of the workforce and generates 8.5 per cent of GDP, with a concentration on grapes for winemaking, tea, citrus fruits and hazelnuts. Industry, which contributes 21.6 per cent of GDP, produces steel, aircraft, machine tools, electrical appliances, manganese, copper, chemicals, wood products and wine.

The main trading partners are Turkey, Azerbaijan and Armenia. Principal exports are scrap metal, wine, mineral water, mineral ores, vehicles, fruit and nuts. The main imports are fuels, vehicles, machinery and parts, food (especially grain) and pharmaceuticals.

GNI – US$15,641m; US$3,270 per capita (2012)
Annual average growth of GDP – 2.5 per cent (2013 est)
Inflation rate – −0.5 per cent (2013 est)
Population below poverty line – 9.2 per cent (2010)
Unemployment – 15 per cent (2012 est)
Total external debt – US$11,740m (2013)
Imports – US$7,842m (2012)
Exports – US$2,377m (2012)

BALANCE OF PAYMENTS
Trade – US$5,465m deficit (2012)
Current Account – US$1,817m deficit (2012)

Trade with UK	2012	2013
Imports from UK	£55,962,709	£47,278,641
Exports to UK	£82,635,483	£34,177,186

COMMUNICATIONS
Airports – 18, including an international terminal in Tbilisi
Roadways and railways – 19,109km; 1,612km
Telecommunications – 1.276 million fixed lines and 4.7 million mobile subscriptions (2012); there were 1.3 million internet users in 2009
Internet code and IDD – ge; 995 (from UK), 810 44 with no extra zeros (to UK)
Major broadcasters – Government-funded Georgian Public Broadcasting provides television and radio services
WPFI score – 29,78 (84)

GERMANY

Bundesrepublik Deutschland – Federal Republic of Germany

Area – 357,022 sq. km
Capital – Berlin; population, 3,469,979 (2012 est)

Major cities – Bremen, Cologne, Dortmund, Dresden, Düsseldorf, Essen, Frankfurt, Hamburg, Hannover, Leipzig, Munich, Nuremberg, Stuttgart
Currency – Euro (€) of 100 cents
Population – 80,996,685 falling at 0.18 per cent a year (2014 est); German (91.5 per cent), Turkish (2.4 per cent) (est)
Religion – Protestant 34 per cent, Roman Catholic 34 per cent, Muslim 4 per cent, unaffiliated or other 29 per cent
Language – German (official)
Population density – 235 per sq. km (2011)
Urban population – 74.1 per cent (2012 est)
Median age (years) – 46.1 (2014 est)
National anthem – 'Das Deutschlandlied' ['The Song of Germany']
National day – 3 October (Unity Day)
Death penalty – Abolished for all crimes (since 1949 in FRG and 1987 in GDR)
CPI score – 78 (12)

CLIMATE AND TERRAIN
The north of the country is low-lying, rising in the centre to uplands and Alpine foothills, then to the Bavarian Alps in the south. Elevation extremes range from 2,963m (Zugspitze, Bavaria) to −3.54m (Neuendorf bei Wilster). The Rhine, Weser and Elbe rivers flow from the south to the North Sea, the Oder and Neisse rivers flow north to the Baltic Sea, and the Danube flows east from its source in the south of the country to the Austrian border. Nearly a third of the land is covered by forest or woodland. The climate is temperate, with average temperatures in Berlin ranging from −1°C in January to 18°C in July.

POLITICS
The Basic Law was adopted in 1949 as the constitution of West Germany; at unification in 1990, Berlin and the five reformed *Länder* (states) of East Germany acceded to the Federal Republic. The president is elected for a five-year term by the *Bundesversammlung,* an electoral college comprising the members of the *Bundestag* (*see* below) and an equal number of representatives elected by the state legislatures. The bicameral legislature comprises a lower house, the Federal Assembly *(Bundestag),* with 631 members elected by a mixed constituency and proportional representation system for a four-year term. The Federal Council *(Bundesrat)* has 69 members appointed by the governments of the *Länder* in proportion to their populations; their term of office is determined by their *Land's* constitution. The head of government is the chancellor, who is proposed by the president and elected by the *Bundestag.*

Angela Merkel, leader of the Christian Democratic Union of Germany and the Christian Social Union of Bavaria (CDU/CSU), became Germany's first female chancellor in 2005 at the head of a CDU/CSU and Social Democratic Party (SPD), governing without the latter following re-election in 2009. In 2013 the CDU again formed a 'grand coalition' with the SPD after the CDU fell five seats short of claiming a historic majority in the *Bundestag* with 41.5 per cent of the vote. Independent candidate Joachim Gauck won

843		1866		1918	1933	1945		1999
	1806		1871	1929		1939	1989-90	

German Confederation replaces Holy Roman Empire — 843

Second German Empire formed; King of Prussia proclaimed emperor — 1866

World economic crisis precipitates the rise of the National Socialist movement led by Adolf Hitler — 1918

Germany invades Poland, beginning the Second World War — 1933

Communist GDR government collapses; Berlin declared capital of unified Germany — 1945

Treaty of Verdun establishes eastern part of Charlemagne's Frankish empire, the foundations of modern Germany — 1806

German Confederation dissolved, replaced by Prussian-dominated North German Federation — 1871

Abdication of Prussian emperor after defeat in First World War; Germany made a republic — 1929

Hitler becomes Chancellor — 1939

Germany surrenders to the Allied forces — 1989-90

Germany joins Eurozone — 1999

732   Countries of the World

the 2012 presidential election, picking up 991 votes; he replaced Christian Wulf following the president's resignation amid allegations of corruption.

HEAD OF STATE
Federal President, Joachim Gauck, *elected and sworn in* 23 March 2012

SELECTED GOVERNMENT MEMBERS *as at April 2014*
Federal Chancellor, Angela Merkel
Defence, Ursula von der Leyen
Finance, Wolfgang Schäuble
Foreign Affairs, Frank-Walter Steinmeier

EMBASSY OF THE FEDERAL REPUBLIC OF GERMANY
23 Belgrave Square, London SW1X 8PZ
T 020-7824 1300 W www.london.diplo.de
Ambassador Extraordinary and Plenipotentiary, HE Peter Ammon, *apptd* May 2014

BRITISH EMBASSY
Wilhelmstrasse 70, 10117 Berlin
T (+49) (30) 204 570 W www.gov.uk/government/world/germany
Ambassador Extraordinary and Plenipotentiary, HE Sir Simon McDonald, KCMG, *apptd* 2010

FEDERAL STRUCTURE
Germany is a federal republic composed of 16 states *(Länder)* (ten from the former Federal Republic of Germany (FRG), five from the former German Democratic Republic (GDR), and Berlin). Each *Land* has its own directly elected legislature and government led by a minister-president (prime minister) or equivalent. The 1949 Basic Law vests executive power in the *Länder* governments except in those areas reserved for the federal government.

State (Capital, where name differs)	Population (millions) (2011 est)
Baden-Württemberg (Stuttgart)	10.78
Bavaria (Munich)	12.5
Berlin	3.5
Brandenburg (Potsdam)	2.49
Bremen	0.6
Hamburg	1.79
Hesse (Wiesbaden)	6
Lower Saxony (Hannover)	7.9
Mecklenburg-West Pomerania (Schwerin)	1.6
North Rhine-Westphalia (Düsseldorf)	17.8
Rhineland-Palitanate (Mainz)	3.9
Saarland (Saarbrücken)	1.0
Saxony (Dresden)	4.1
Saxony-Anhalt (Magdeburg)	2.3
Schleswig-Holstein (Kiel)	2.8
Thuringia (Erfurt)	2.2

DEFENCE

Aged 16–49, 2010 est	Males	Females
Available for military service	18,529,299	17,888,543
Fit for military service	15,027,866	14,510,527

Military expenditure – US$49,297m (2013)

ECONOMY AND TRADE
Germany has the world's fifth largest economy and the largest in Europe, but decades of strong economic performance gave way in the 1990s to a severe recession, largely an aftermath of reunification and of macroeconomic stagnation. Although the economy as a whole began to grow again in 2006, in the east it remains weak despite costly modernisation and integration measures. However, the revival was largely export-led and a decline in demand due to the global economic downturn caused a recession in 2008–9. The government's economic stimulus measures pushed the budget deficit slightly beyond the eurozone's 3 per cent threshold in 2010, although it remained at 1.7 per cent in 2011. The country achieved a budget surplus of 0.1 per cent in 2012.

The country has a modern, diverse, highly industrialised and technologically advanced market economy. The services sector contributes 69 per cent of GDP, industry 30.1 per cent and agriculture 0.8 per cent. The industrial sector is among the world's largest producers of iron, steel, coal, cement, chemicals, machinery, vehicles, machine tools, electronics, food and beverages, ships and textiles. Germany depends on imports to meet its oil and natural gas needs, but it remains a net exporter of electricity; in the wake of Japan's Fukushima crisis in March 2011, the German government revoked a decision to extend the life of the country's 17 nuclear power stations (which supply about 23 per cent of its electricity). All stations are expected to close by 2022.

The main trading partners are the Netherlands, France, the USA and China. Machinery, vehicles, chemicals, metals and manufactures, foodstuffs and textiles are the principal imports and exports.

GNI – US$3,509,989m; US$44,260 per capita (2012)
Annual average growth of GDP – 0.5 per cent (2013 est)
Inflation rate – 1.6 per cent (2013 est)
Unemployment – 5.3 per cent (2013 est)
Total external debt – US$5,717,000m (2012)
Imports – US$1,164,626m (2012)
Exports – US$1,408,370m (2012)

BALANCE OF PAYMENTS
Trade – US$243,744m surplus (2012)
Current Account – US$238,493m surplus (2012)

Trade with UK	2012	2013
Imports from UK	£32,744,637,661	£30,743,572,549
Exports to UK	£51,949,379,655	£55,319,941,012

COMMUNICATIONS
Airports – 318; the busiest airport is at Frankfurt, other major airports include Berlin, Munich and Bonn
Waterways – Around 20 per cent of domestic freight is carried on 7,467km of inland waterways. The Rhine and the Danube are linked by the Rhine-Maine-Danube canal, creating a through route from the North Sea to the Black Sea. The Kiel canal links the North Sea and the Baltic Sea. The main river ports are Duisburg, Frankfurt, Karlsruhe and Mainz; the main seaports are Hamburg, Bremen, Bremerhaven, Lübeck, Rostock and Wilhemshaven
Roadways and railways – There is an extensive 645,000km road network, including 12,800km of motorways; there are 41,981km of railways
Telecommunications – 50.7 million fixed lines and 107.7 million mobile subscriptions (2011); there were 65.13 million internet users in 2009
Internet code and IDD – de; 49 (from UK), 44 (to UK)
Major broadcasters – National and regional public television competes with a large private sector, with about 90 per cent of households having access to cable or satellite stations; broadcasters include ARD (which operates Das Erste, the main national public TV channel) and ZDF
Press – Major newspapers include *Frankfurter Allgemeine Zeitung* and *Süddeustche Zeitung*
WPFI score – 10,23 (14)

EDUCATION AND HEALTH

Education is free and compulsory between the ages of six and 18.

The largest universities are in Munich, Berlin, Hamburg, Bonn, Frankfurt and Cologne. Germany's oldest university is Heidelberg, founded in 1386.

Gross enrolment ratio (percentage of relevant age group) – primary 101 per cent; secondary 102 per cent (2011 est); tertiary 57 per cent (est 2011)

Health expenditure (per capita) – US$4,875 (2011)

Hospital beds (per 1,000 people) – 8.3 (2010)

Life expectancy (years) – 80.44 (2014 est)

Mortality rate – 11.29 (2014 est)

Birth rate – 8.42 (2014 est)

Infant mortality rate – 3.46 (2014 est)

GHANA

Republic of Ghana

Area – 238,533 sq. km

Capital – Accra; population, 2,491,555 (2012 est)

Major cities – Kumasi, Sekondi-Takoradi, Tamale

Currency – Cedi of 100 pesewas

Population – 25,758,108 rising at 2.19 per cent a year (2014 est); Akan (47.5 per cent), Mole-Dagbon (16.6 per cent), Ewe (13.9 per cent), Ga-Dangme (7.4 per cent), Gurma (5.7 per cent), Guan (3.7 per cent), Grusi (2.5 per cent) (2010)

Religion – Christian 71 per cent, Muslim 18 per cent (predominantly Sunni), indigenous and other religions 11 per cent (est)

Language – English (official), Asante, Ewe, Fante, Boron, Dagomba, Dangme, Dagarte, Akyem, Ga, Akuapem

Population density – 109 per sq. km (2011)

Urban population – 52.6 per cent (2012 est)

Median age (years) – 20.8 (2014 est)

National anthem – 'God Bless Our Homeland Ghana'

National day – 6 March (Independence Day)

Death penalty – Retained (last used 1993)

CPI score – 46 (63)

CLIMATE AND TERRAIN

Ghana consists mostly of plains dissected by the Volta river basin and the great central Lake Volta, rising to the Ashanti plateau in the west. There is dense rainforest in the south and west and forested hills in the north, with savannah in the east and far north. Elevation extremes range from 885m (Mt Afadjato) to 0m (Atlantic Ocean). The climate is tropical but with cooler temperatures on the south-east coast, and less rainfall in the south-east and north. Average temperatures range between 24.9°C and 28.4°C.

HISTORY AND POLITICS

First reached by Europeans in the 15th century, after which it became a centre for gold and slave trading, the constituent parts of Ghana came under British administration at various times. The original Gold Coast colony was constituted in 1874 and Ashanti and the Northern Territories Protectorate in 1901. Trans-Volta-Togoland, part of the former German colony of Togo, was mandated to Britain by the League of Nations after the First World War and was integrated with the Gold Coast colony in 1956 following a plebiscite. The colony became independent as Ghana on 6 March 1957. It was proclaimed a republic in 1960.

Ghana became a one-party state in 1964 and from 1966 experienced long periods of military rule (1966–9, 1972–9, 1981–91) interspersed with short-lived civilian governments (1969–72, 1979–81). Flt. Lt. Jerry Rawlings, who had ousted the military regime in 1979 and deposed the civilian government in 1981, was elected president in 1992 when the country returned to multiparty politics after a referendum approved a new constitution.

Since the mid-1990s there have been intermittent clashes over land ownership between ethnic groups in the north; a state of emergency was in place there for two years after the last major outbreak of ethnic violence in 2002.

In the 2008 elections, John Atta Mills, the candidate of the National Democratic Congress (NDC), was elected president, and the NDC became the largest party in the legislature, winning half the seats. Vice-president John Dramani Mahama took over the presidency following the death of John Atta Mills in July 2012. In December 2012 Mahama was re-elected as president, and the NDC retained their majority in legislative elections.

Under the 1993 constitution, the executive president is directly elected for a four-year term, renewable once. The president appoints members of the council of ministers subject to approval by the legislature. The unicameral parliament has 230 members who are directly elected for a four-year term.

HEAD OF STATE
President, John Dramani Mahama, *apptd* 24 July 2012

SELECTED GOVERNMENT MEMBERS *as at April 2014*
Defence, Mark Woyongo
Finance, Seth Terkper
Foreign Affairs, Hannah Tetteh
Interior, Kwesi Ahwoi

OFFICE OF THE HIGH COMMISSION FOR GHANA
13 Belgrave Square, London SW1X 8PN
T 020-7201 5900 W www.ghanahighcommissionuk.com
High Commissioner, HE Victor Emmanuel Smith, *apptd* 2014

BRITISH HIGH COMMISSION
PO Box 296, Osu Link, off Gamel Abdul Nasser Avenue, Accra
T (+233) (302) 213 250 E high.commission.accra@fco.gov.uk
W www.gov.uk/government/world/ghana
High Commissioner, HE Peter Jones, *apptd* 2011

DEFENCE

Aged 16–49, 2010 est	*Males*	*Females*
Available for military service	6,268,191	6,194,339
Fit for military service	4,136,406	4,220,761

Military expenditure – US$272m (2013 est)

ECONOMY AND TRADE
Ghana has abundant natural resources, but high foreign debt and budget and trade deficits make it dependent on international financial and technical aid to fund its economic and social development programmes. It has benefited from tighter government management of the economy since 2001, and from debt relief in 2002 and 2006. Ghana was recategorised as a lower middle-income country in 2010.

The sale of gold and cocoa helped create an estimated GDP growth of 6.5 per cent in 2013. Agriculture, mostly at subsistence level, forms the basis of the economy, along with forestry and fishing. The sector employs 56 per cent of the workforce and generates 21.5 per cent of GDP. The main cash crops are cocoa, timber and tuna. Industry employs 15 per cent of the workforce and contributes 28.7 per cent of GDP, mainly from mining (gold, manganese, bauxite, diamonds), forestry, light manufacturing, aluminium smelting, food processing and shipbuilding. Services employ 29 per cent and account for 49.8 per cent of GDP. Hydroelectric power is generated at dams on Lake Volta and is transmitted to most of Ghana, and to Togo and Benin. Oil was discovered offshore in 2007 and production began in 2010. More oil projects are planned and the country is believed to have reserves totalling 700 million barrels.

The main export markets are EU countries, Ukraine and Malaysia. Principal exports are gold, oil, cocoa, timber, tuna, metals, minerals and diamonds. Imports are provided mainly by China, Nigeria, the USA, Singapore and the EU. The main imports are capital equipment, fuel and foodstuffs.

GNI – US$38,564m; US$1,550 per capita (2012)
Annual average growth of GDP – 7.9 per cent (2013 est)
Inflation rate – 11 per cent (2013 est)
Population below poverty line – 28.5 per cent (2007 est)
Total external debt – US$14,680m (2013 est)
Imports – US$17,965m (2012)
Exports – US$11,976m (2012)

BALANCE OF PAYMENTS
Trade – US$5,989m deficit (2012)
Current Account – US$3,541m deficit (2011)

Trade with UK	2012	2013
Imports from UK	£516,411,070	£393,966,646
Exports to UK	£219,940,122	£289,183,080

COMMUNICATIONS
Airports and waterways – Seven, including an international terminal in Accra; there are 1,293km of navigable waterways
Roadways and railways – 109,515km; 947km
Telecommunications – 285,000 fixed lines and 25.62 million mobile subscriptions (2012); there were 1.29 million internet users in 2009
Internet code and IDD – gh; 233 (from UK), 44 (to UK)
WPFI score – 16,29 (27)

EDUCATION AND HEALTH
The government provides ten years of compulsory basic education for all children free of charge. Ghana has one of Africa's oldest universities, at Legon in Accra (established in 1948).

Literacy rate – 71 per cent (2010 est)
Gross enrolment ratio (percentage of relevant age group) – primary 107 per cent; secondary 57 per cent; tertiary 12 per cent (2011 est)
Health expenditure (per capita) – US$75 (2011)
Hospital beds (per 1,000 people) – 0.9 (2011)
Life expectancy (years) – 65.75 (2014 est)
Mortality rate – 7.37 (2014 est)
Birth rate – 31.4 (2014 est)

Infant mortality rate – 38.52 (2014 est)
HIV/AIDS adult prevalence – 1.4 per cent (2012 est)

GREECE

Elliniki Dhimokratia – Hellenic Republic

Area – 131,957 sq. km
Capital – Athens; population, 3,267,193 (2012 est)
Major cities – Iraklion (Heraklion) on Crete, Larisa, Patrai (Patras), Piraeus, Thessaloniki (Salonika)
Currency – Euro (€) of 100 cents
Population – 10,775,557 rising at 0.01 per cent a year (2014 est)
Religion – Christian (Greek Orthodox 98 per cent) (est)
Language – Greek (official)
Population density – 88 per sq. km (2011)
Urban population – 61.7 per cent (2012 est)
Median age (years) – 43.5 (2014 est)
National anthem – 'Ymnos eis tin Eleutherian' ['Hymn to Freedom']
National day – 25 March (Independence Day)
Death penalty – Abolished for all crimes (since 2004)
CPI score – 40 (80)

CLIMATE AND TERRAIN
The main areas of Greece are: Macedonia, Thrace, Epirus, Thessaly, Continental Greece, the Peloponnese and Attica on the mainland and the island of Crete. The main island groups are the Sporades, the Dodecanese or Southern Sporades and the Cyclades in the Aegean Sea, and the Ionian islands, including Corfu, to the west of the mainland. Low-lying coastal areas rise to a hilly or mountainous interior on the mainland and the islands. The Pindos mountains form a spine down the centre of the mainland, continuing down the Peloponnese, which is divided from the mainland by the Gulf of Corinth, the largest of the gulfs and bays indenting the coast. Elevation extremes range from 2,917m (Mt Olympus) to 0m (Mediterranean Sea). The climate is temperate; the coastline and islands have a Mediterranean climate but the weather is cooler at higher altitudes. The average temperature in Athens ranges from 8.7°C in January to 25.9°C in July.

POLITICS
Under the 1975 constitution, the head of state is the president, elected by the legislature for a five-year term, renewable once. The unicameral legislature, the *Vouli*, has 300 members directly elected for a four-year term.

Karolos Papoulias was elected president in 2005, and was re-elected in 2010. A legislative election was held in October 2009, nearly two years early, and Panhellenic Socialist Movement (PASOK) returned to government after winning an outright majority of seats. In 2010 the PASOK government pushed through unpopular austerity measures to

Conquered by the Romans	Turks overthrown in a war of independence	Occupied by Germany during Second World War	Right-wing faction of the army seizes power and establishes military regime (Greek Colonels); the king goes into exile	Joins the European Community
c.400	c.1450	1829	1944-49	1974	2001
146	1821-7	1941-44	1967	1981
Conquered by Philip II of Macedon	Conquered by the Turks	Establishment of Greek kingdom	Civil war between monarchist and communist groups	Democratic rule restored; monarchy rejected and Greece becomes a republic	Greece adopts the euro

address the severe financial crisis, and agreed a three-year programme of economic reforms with the IMF and other EU countries. Prime minister George Papandreou tendered his resignation in November 2011 in order to enable a government of national unity to pass controversial austerity measures in parliament; he was replaced by economist Lucas Papademos, who subsequently resigned in preparation for the country's legislative elections in 2012. The New Democracy party (ND) won the most seats in the 2012 legislative elections but was unable to form a coalition government; the party increased its number of seats in the subsequent election and ND leader Antonis Samaras was sworn into office on 20 June 2012. On 21 June 2013, the Democratic Left (DIMAR) quit the ruling coalition in protest at the planned closure of the Hellenic Broadcasting Company, leaving the government with a slim majority of three in the *Vouli*.

HEAD OF STATE
President of the Hellenic Republic, Karolos Papoulias, *elected* 8 February 2005, *sworn in* 12 March 2005, *re-elected* 2010

SELECTED GOVERNMENT MEMBERS *as at April 2014*
Prime Minister, Antonis Samaras
Finance, Yannis Stournaras
Foreign Affairs, Evangelos Venizelos
Interior, Yannis Michelakis

EMBASSY OF GREECE
1A Holland Park, London W11 3TP
T 020-7229 3850 E political@greekembassy.org.uk
W www.mfa.gr/uk
Ambassador Extraordinary and Plenipotentiary, HE
  Konstantinos Bikas, *apptd* 2012

BRITISH EMBASSY
1 Ploutarchou Street, 106 75 Athens
T (+30) (210) 727 2600 E information.athens@fco.gov.uk
W www.gov.uk/government/world/greece
Ambassador Extraordinary and Plenipotentiary, HE John
  Kittmer, *apptd* 2013

DEFENCE

Aged 16–49, 2010 est	Males	Females
Available for military service	2,485,389	2,469,854
Fit for military service	2,032,378	2,016,552

Military expenditure – US$6,177m (2013)
Conscription – 19–45 years of age, male only; 12 months

ECONOMY AND TRADE
Greece has a large public sector which currently accounts for 40 per cent of GDP, although several state enterprises are being privatised as part of the government's economic reforms. It experienced rapid economic growth in the final quarter of the 20th century, owing largely to increased tourism and its accession to the European Community. But in the 2000s, high government spending, low fiscal revenue and recession contributed to a growing budget deficit, which soared to over 15 per cent of GDP in 2009 and left the country particularly vulnerable in the global economic downturn. The New Democracy government's persistent failure to address the public finances crisis contributed to Greece's international debt rating being downgraded in late 2009, amid fears of an imminent default on its debt. The PASOK government's austerity measures, and financial assistance from the IMF and other EU countries, saw the budget deficit reduced to 9 per cent of GDP in 2011 but unemployment rose by over 5 per cent causing many economists to doubt the effectiveness of the government's fiscal policies.

Against a backdrop of protests, in spring 2012 the government agreed new austerity measures and a 'debt swap' deal with private-sector lenders – all conditions of an EU bailout. Eurozone finance ministers and the IMF agreed to release an instalment of the bailout loan in December 2012. Further austerity measures were agreed in April 2013 in order to pave the way for more bailout funds. By the end of 2013, investor confidence began to show signs of returning as a result of an improved macroeconomic outlook.

The service sector employs 65.1 per cent of the workforce and generates 80.5 per cent of GDP; much of this is derived from tourism, which accounts for about 18 per cent of GDP, and shipping. Greece is a net importer of energy, including oil for refining and re-export. Industrial activities, which contribute 16 per cent of GDP, include food and tobacco processing, textiles, chemicals, metal products, mining and petroleum production. Despite substantial industrialisation in the 20th century, agriculture still employs 12.4 per cent of the workforce, contributing 3.5 per cent of GDP. The most important agricultural products are cereals, vegetables, fruit, tobacco, beef and dairy products.

The main trading partners are Turkey, Russia and Italy and China. Principal exports are food and drink, manufactured goods, petroleum products, chemicals and textiles. The main imports are machinery, transport equipment, fuels and chemicals.

GNI – US$250,328m; US$23,260 per capita (2012)
Annual average growth of GDP – −4.2 per cent (2013 est)
Inflation rate – −0.8 per cent (2013 est)
Population below poverty line – 20 per cent (2009 est)
Unemployment – 27.9 per cent (2013 est)
Total external debt – US$568,700m (2012)
Imports – US$63,380m (2012)
Exports – US$35,485m (2012)

BALANCE OF PAYMENTS
Trade – US$27,895m deficit (2012)
Current Account – US$8,396m deficit (2012)

Trade with UK	2012	2013
Imports from UK	£843,000,708	£920,464,250
Exports to UK	£6673,552,419	£722,927,888

COMMUNICATIONS

Airports – 68; the largest of which are at Athens, Thessaloniki, Iraklion (Crete) and Corfu town (Corfu)
Waterways – The main seaports are Piraeus, Thessaloniki and Patrai on the mainland, and Iraklion on Crete. An extensive ferry system connects the islands to one another and to the mainland. The 6km Corinth canal across the Corinth isthmus shortens the sea journey by 325km
Roadways and railways – There are 116,960km of roads, including 948km of motorways; 2,548km of railways are state-owned (with the exception of the Athens–Piraeus Electric Railway) but the loss-making state-controlled rail network operator TrainOSE is being privatised
Telecommunications – 5.46 million fixed lines and 13.35 million mobile subscriptions (2012); there were 4.97 million internet users in 2009
Internet code and IDD – gr; 30 (from UK), 44 (to UK)
Major broadcasters – ERT operates a number of regional and cultural channels; private broadcasters include Mega TV and ANT 1
Press – There are three major daily news publications: *Eleftherotypia*, *Ta Nea* and *Kathimerini*
WPFI score – 31,33 (99)

EDUCATION AND HEALTH

Education is free and compulsory between the ages of six and 14, and is maintained by state grants.
Literacy rate – 97 per cent (2011 est)
Gross enrolment ratio (percentage of relevant age group) –
    primary 103 per cent; secondary 111 per cent (2011 est)
Health expenditure (per capita) – US$2,864 (2011)
Hospital beds (per 1,000 people) – 4.9 (2009)
Life expectancy (years) – 80.3 (2014 est)
Mortality rate – 11 (2014 est)
Birth rate – 8.8 (2014 est)
Infant mortality rate – 4.78 (2014 est)

GRENADA

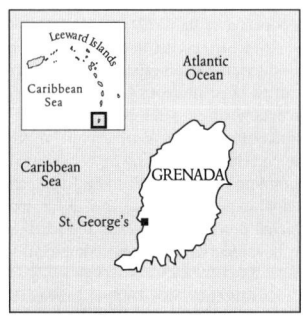

Area – 344 sq. km
Capital – St George's; population, 40,400 (2009 est)
Currency – East Caribbean dollar (EC$) of 100 cents
Population – 110,152 rising at 0.5 per cent a year (2014 est)
Religion – Christian (Roman Catholic 53 per cent, Anglican 14 per cent, other Protestant 33 per cent)
Language – English (official), Creole (small minority)
Population density – 309 per sq. km (2011)
Urban population – 39.5 per cent (2012 est)
Median age (years) – 29.9 (2014 est)
National anthem – 'Hail Grenada'
National day – 7 February (Independence Day)
Death penalty – Retained (last used 1978)

Literacy rate – 97.3 per cent (2008 est)
Gross enrolment ratio (percentage of relevant age group) –
    primary 103 per cent; secondary 108 per cent (2011 est);
    tertiary 53 per cent (2011 est)
Life expectancy (years) – 73.8 (2014 est)
Mortality rate – 8.04 (2013 est)
Birth rate – 16.3 (2014 est)
Infant mortality rate – 10.5 (2014 est)

CLIMATE AND TERRAIN

The most southerly of the Windward Islands, Grenada comprises three islands: Grenada (the largest at 18km in length and 34km in width), Carriacou and Petite Martinique. Elevation extremes range from 840m (Mt St Catherine) to 0m (Caribbean Sea). The climate is subtropical, with the wettest weather from July to November. Grenada lies in a hurricane zone.

HISTORY AND POLITICS

Discovered by Columbus in 1498 and named Concepción, Grenada was colonised from the mid-17th century by the French, who subdued the native Caribs; the island was ceded to Britain in 1763. It became a crown colony in 1877, a self-governing associated state in 1967 and an independent nation on 7 February 1974.

The government was overthrown in 1979 by the New Jewel Movement led by Maurice Bishop, and the People's Revolutionary Government (PRG) was set up with Bishop as prime minister. In 1983, disagreements within the PRG led to the deposition and execution of Bishop, whose government was replaced by a revolutionary military council. These events prompted the intervention of Caribbean and US forces. After a period of interim government, democracy was restored and a general election held in 1984. Since the restoration of democracy, power has alternated between the New National Party (NNP) and the National Democratic Congress (NDC).

In 2013 the NNP won all 15 seats in parliamentary elections; Keith Mitchell returned as prime minister.

Under the 1974 constitution, reinstated in 1984, the head of state is Queen Elizabeth II, represented locally by a governor-general. The bicameral parliament consists of the House of Representatives, with 15 directly elected members, and a senate with 13 appointed members, ten of whom are appointed by the government and three by the opposition; both chambers serve a five-year term.
Governor-General, HE Cécile La Grenade, GCMG, OBE
    apptd 2013

SELECTED GOVERNMENT MEMBERS *as at May 2013*
Prime Minister, Finance, Energy, Keith Mitchell
Foreign Affairs, Nickolas Steele

HIGH COMMISSION FOR GRENADA
The Chapel, Archel Road, London W14 9QH
T 020-7385 4415 E office@grenada-highcommission.co.uk
W www.grenadahclon.co.uk
High Commissioner, HE Joslyn Raphael Whiteman, *apptd* 2013

BRITISH HIGH COMMISSIONER
HE Victoria Dean, *apptd* 2013, resident at Bridgetown, Barbados

ECONOMY AND TRADE

The economy has grown considerably in recent decades owing to diversification into tourism, offshore financial services and other service industries. Tourism and agriculture have recovered from severe hurricane damage in 2004 and 2005, but reconstruction has burdened the country with considerable debt, and the global downturn's effect on tourism and remittances caused the economy to contract in 2009 and stagnate in 2010–12.

Agriculture now employs only 11 per cent of the workforce and produces 5.6 per cent of GDP. Industry consists of processing agricultural products, textile manufacturing, light assembly operations and construction, and contributes 15.8 per cent of GDP. The service sector, including tourism and offshore financial services, accounts for 69 per cent of employment and 78.5 per cent of GDP.

The main trading partners are Trinidad and Tobago (44.3 per cent of imports), the USA and other Caribbean states. Principal exports are bananas, cocoa, nutmeg, fruit, vegetables, clothing and mace. Imports include food, manufactured goods, machinery, chemicals and fuels.
GNI – US$725m; US$7,220 per capita (2012)
Annual average growth of GDP – 0.8 per cent (2013 est)
Inflation rate – 2.4 per cent (2013 est)
Total external debt – US$538m (2010)
Imports – US$336m (2012)
Exports – US$35m (2012)

BALANCE OF PAYMENTS
Trade – US$301m deficit (2012)
Current Account – US$196m deficit (2012)

Trade with UK	2012	2013
Imports from UK	£5,278,519	£5,687,830
Exports to UK	£302,669	£417,866

COMMUNICATIONS
Airports and waterways – The main airport and port are based at Saint George's
Roadways – 1,127km
Telecommunications – 28,500 fixed lines and 128,000 mobile subscriptions (2012); there were 25,000 internet users in 2009
Internet code and IDD – gd; 1 473 (from UK), 011 44 (to UK)
Major broadcasters and press – The Grenada Broadcasting Network is jointly owned by the government and the Caribbean Communications Network; there are no daily newspapers but several weeklies, including *Grenada Today* and *The Grenada Informer*

GUATEMALA

República de Guatemala – Republic of Guatemala

Area – 108,889 sq. km
Capital – Guatemala City; population, 1,169,633 (2012 est)
Major cities – Mixco, Quezaltenango, Villa Nueva
Currency – Quetzal (Q) of 100 centavos

Population – 14,647,083 rising at 1.86 per cent a year (2014 est); mestizo and European (59.4 per cent), Mayan (40.3 per cent), indigenous non-Mayan (0.2 per cent) (2001)
Religion – Christian (Roman Catholic 65 per cent, Evangelical Protestant 43 per cent) (est)
Language – Spanish, 23 Amerindian languages (all official)
Population density – 137 per sq. km (2011)
Urban population – 50.2 per cent (2012 est)
Median age (years) – 21 (2014 est)
National anthem – 'Himno Nacional de Guatemala' ['National Anthem of Guatemala']
National day – 15 September (Independence Day)
Death penalty – Retained
CPI score – 29 (123)

CLIMATE AND TERRAIN
Narrow tropical plains on both the north (Caribbean) and south (Pacific) coasts rise to a mountainous interior in the centre and south. The mountains fall in the north to lowlands covered in tropical jungle. Elevation extremes range from 4,211m (Tajumulco volcano) to 0m (Pacific Ocean). There are 37 volcanoes, three active, in the central plateau. The climate is tropical but is cooler in the highlands. The wet season runs from May to September, when mudslides and hurricanes can occur. There are also frequent minor earth tremors and some earthquakes.

HISTORY AND POLITICS
Mayan and Aztec civilisations flourished in the area until the Spanish conquest in 1523–4, after which the area became a Spanish colony. It gained independence in 1821, and formed part of a Central American federation of former Spanish provinces from 1823 to 1839. After independence, the country was ruled by a series of dictatorships and military regimes, interspersed with periods of democratic government. In 1960 a civil war between military governments, right-wing vigilantes and left-wing guerrillas began, lasting 36 years and during which over 200,000 people died or disappeared.

In 1996 the democratically elected civilian government concluded a peace agreement with the left-wing Guatemalan Revolutionary National Unity guerrillas that ended the civil war and began a reduction in the size and political influence of the army. In 1999, an independent commission found that 93 per cent of human rights abuses during the war had been instigated by the security forces, and in 2000 and 2004 the state formally admitted guilt in several human rights cases, paying damages to the victims. At present, only a small number of the military personnel found to be responsible for the atrocities have been prosecuted.

In the 2011 legislative election, the Patriotic Party (PP) won the most seats, but without an overall majority. The 2011 presidential election was won in the second round by the PP candidate Gen. Otto Perez Molina.

Under the 1986 constitution, the executive president is directly elected for a four-year term, which is not renewable. He or she is responsible to the congress and appoints the cabinet. The unicameral Congress of the Republic has 158 members, who are directly elected for a four-year term.

HEAD OF STATE
President, Gen. Otto Perez Molina, *elected* 4 November 2011, *sworn in* 14 January 2012
Vice-President, Roxanna Baldetti

SELECTED GOVERNMENT MEMBERS *as at May 2014*
Defence, Ulises Noe Anzuetto Giron
Economy, Sergio de la Torre
Foreign Relations, Luis Fernando Carrera Castro

EMBASSY OF GUATEMALA
13 Fawcett Street, London SW10 9HN
T 020-73513042 E inglaterra@minex.gob.gt
Ambassador Extraordinary and Plenipotentiary, HE Acisclo
Valladares Molina, *apptd* 2010

BRITISH EMBASSY
Edificio Torre Internacional, Nivel 11, 16 Calle 0-55, Zona 10,
Guatemala City
T (+502) 2380 7300 E embassy@intelnett.com
W www.gov.uk/government/world/guatemala
Ambassador Extraordinary and Plenipotentiary, HE Sarah
Dickson, *apptd* 2012

DEFENCE

Aged 16–49, 2010 est	Males	Females
Available for military service	3,165,870	3,371,217
Fit for military service	2,590,843	2,926,544

Military expenditure – US$241m (2013)
Conscription – 18–50 years of age, male only; 12–24 months
(selective)

ECONOMY AND TRADE

IMF funding and foreign aid have underpinned the
government's economic reforms and stabilisation programmes, but the trade deficit, poor infrastructure, security
problems and high levels of corruption still deter foreign
investment. The country suffers from a huge imbalance in
wealth, and over half the population lives below the poverty
line. Remittances from expatriates, equivalent to nearly
10 per cent of GDP, are vital to the economy, which began
to recover from the global downturn in 2010–11.

Half of the population is dependent on agriculture, which
contributes 13.5 per cent of GDP and accounts for a high
proportion of exports. Industry accounts for 22.8 per cent
of GDP, and the services sector, which includes tourism, for
62.7 per cent of GDP.

The main trading partners are the USA, El Salvador,
Honduras and Mexico. The principal exports are coffee,
sugar, petroleum, garments, bananas, other fruit, vegetables
and cardamom. The chief imports are fuels, machinery and
transport equipment, construction materials, grain, fertilisers
and electricity.
GNI – US$48,862m; US$3,120 per capita (2012)
Annual average growth of GDP – 3.3 per cent (2013 est)
Inflation rate – 4.4 per cent (2013 est)
Population below poverty line – 54 per cent (2011 est)
Unemployment – 4.1 per cent (2011 est)
Total external debt – US$17,670m (2013 est)
Imports – US$14,873m (2012)
Exports – US$7,139m (2012)

BALANCE OF PAYMENTS
Trade – US$7,734m deficit (2012)
Current Account – US$1,599m deficit (2011)

Trade with UK	2012	2013
Imports from UK	£31,085,166	£31,229,824
Exports to UK	£41,578,936	£53,287,767

COMMUNICATIONS

Airports – 16; the principal international airport is based in
Guatemala City
Waterways – There are 990km of navigable waterways, of
which only 260km are navigable all year round; the main

seaports are at Quetzal on the Pacific Ocean and Santo
Tomas de Castilla on the Gulf of Honduras
Roadways and railways – 11,501km; 332km
Telecommunications – 1.744 million fixed lines and 20.787
million mobile subscriptions (2012); there were 2.279
million internet users in 2009
Internet code and IDD – gt; 502 (from UK), 44 (to UK)
Major broadcasters – Private broadcasters dominate the
media; four national television stations, including Canal 3,
share the same owner
Press – There are four main daily newspapers, including
Prensa Libre and *elPeriodico*
WPFI score – 36,61 (125)

EDUCATION AND HEALTH

There are nine years of compulsory education.
Literacy rate – 76 per cent (2011 est)
Gross enrolment ratio (percentage of relevant age group) –
primary 114 per cent; secondary 65 per cent (2011 est)
Health expenditure (per capita) – US$214 (2011)
Hospital beds (per 1,000 people) – 0.7 (2011)
Life expectancy (years) – 71.74 (2014 est)
Mortality rate – 4.82 (2014 est)
Birth rate – 25.46 (2014 est)
Infant mortality rate – 23.51 (2014 est)

GUINEA

République de Guinée – Republic of Guinea

Area – 245,857 sq. km
Capital – Conakry; population, 1,780,606 (2012 est)
Major cities – Guéckédou, Kankan, Nzérékoré
Currency – Guinea franc of 100 centimes
Population – 11,474,383 rising at 2.63 per cent a year
(2014 est); Fulani (40 per cent), Malinke (30 per cent),
Susu (20 per cent) (est)
Religion – Muslim 85 per cent (predominantly Sunni),
Christian 8 per cent, traditional indigenous religions
7 per cent (est); some combine Islam or Christianity with
indigenous beliefs
Language – French (official), Eastern Maninkakan, Guinea
Kpelle, Northern Kissi, Pular, Susu, Toma
Population density – 45 per sq. km (2011)
Urban population – 35.9 per cent (2012 est)
Median age (years) – 18.7 (2014 est)
National anthem – 'Liberté' ['Freedom']
National day – 2 October (Independence Day)
Death penalty – Retained
CPI score – 24 (150)
Literacy rate – 25 per cent (2010 est)
Gross enrolment ratio (percentage of relevant age group) –
primary 89 per cent; secondary 38 per cent; tertiary
10 per cent (2011 est)

Portuguese establish ivory and slave trade; north-east areas part of the Mali Empire — *c.1200*

Country renamed French Guinea — *1849*

Becomes part of French West Africa — *1958*

Death of Touré; successor Lansana Conté introduces greater economic liberalisation — *1984*

Civil wars in neighbouring countries cause an influx of refugees, leading to strikes and violent protests — *1991*

A massacre of pro-democracy demonstrators ends in Sékouba Konaté becoming acting president — *2008*

Susi kingdoms established — *c.1500*

French establish protectorate over coastal areas — *1891*

Becomes independent under President Ahmed Sekou Touré, who establishes a one-party state — *1904*

Conté introduces a multiparty election system and is successful in all subsequent elections amid allegations of electoral fraud — *2006-8*

Military junta seizes power the day after Conté's death — *2008*

The first presidential elections take place under power-sharing government — *2009-10*

Health expenditure (per capita) – US$30 (2011)
Hospital beds (per 1,000 people) – 0.3 (2011)
Life expectancy (years) – 59.6 (2014 est)
Mortality rate – 9.69 (2014 est)
Birth rate – 36.02 (2014 est)
Infant mortality rate – 55.24 (2014 est)
HIV/AIDS adult prevalence – 1.7 per cent (2012 est)

CLIMATE AND TERRAIN
Guinea has a flat coastal plain that rises to the hilly Fouta Djallon plateau in the north-west, where the Gambia and Senegal rivers rise. East of the plateau is the central savannah, the source of the Niger river, with rainforest in the south-east. Elevation extremes range from 1,752m (Mt Nimba) to 0m (Atlantic Ocean). The climate is tropical, with a wet season from April to November; the average daily temperature in Conakry is 27°C.

POLITICS
Under the 2010 constitution, the executive president is directly elected for a five-year term, renewable once. The unicameral National Assembly has 114 members, who are directly elected for a five-year term. The president appoints the council of ministers.

The presidential election in 2010, the first democratic election since independence, was won by Alpha Condé; the second round of voting was delayed by allegations of fraud in the first round, and his victory sparked off several weeks of intercommunal violence. Delayed 2013 legislative elections resulted in Alpha Condé's ruling Rally of the Guinean People party (RPG) winning 53 seats and forming a coalition with smaller parties. The opposition Union of Democratic Forces in Guinea declared the result invalid and violent demonstrations occurred in the capital, Conakry.

HEAD OF STATE
President, Defence, Alpha Condé, *elected* 7 November 2010, *sworn in* 21 December

SELECTED GOVERNMENT MEMBERS *as at May 2013*
Prime Minister, Mohamed Said Fofana
Economy and Finance, Mohamed Diaré
Foreign Affairs, François Fall
Security, Madifing Diané

EMBASSY OF THE REPUBLIC OF GUINEA
258 Belsize Road, London NW6 4BT
T 020-7316 1861 E office@ambaguinee-london.co.uk
Ambassador Extraordinary and Plenipotentiary, Paul Goa Zoumanigui, *apptd* 2013

BRITISH EMBASSY
Villa 1, Residence 2000, Corniche Sud Conakry
T (+224) 6335 5329 E britembconakry@hotmail.com
W www.gov.uk/government/world/guinea
Ambassador Extraordinary and Plenipotentiary, HE Graham Styles, *apptd* 2011

DEFENCE

Aged 16–49, 2010 est	Males	Females
Available for military service	2,359,203	2,329,784
Fit for military service	1,493,991	1,535,418

Military expenditure – US$103m (2004)
Conscription – 18–25 years of age; 18 months

ECONOMY AND TRADE
Although Guinea is the second largest producer of bauxite in the world and despite an abundance of natural resources, decades of mismanagement and corruption have left the economy undeveloped, and nearly half the population live below the poverty line. There is a large foreign debt, and budget and trade deficits, aggravated by the suspension of foreign aid following the 2008 coup. Aid was resumed in 2012 following democratic elections in 2010.

Mining is, however, attracting foreign investment and a new mining code introduced in September 2011 includes provisions to combat corruption. Agriculture, much of it at subsistence level, employs 76 per cent of the population and contributes 22.9 per cent of GDP. Industry accounts for 46.5 per cent of GDP, mostly through mining and the processing of minerals and agricultural produce.

The main trading partners are India, China and EU countries, especially Spain. Principal exports are bauxite, alumina, gold, diamonds, coffee, fish and other agricultural products. The main imports are petroleum products, metals, machinery, transport equipment, textiles, grain and other foodstuffs.
GNI – US$5,202m; US$440 per capita (2012)
Annual average growth of GDP – 2.9 per cent (2013 est)
Inflation rate – 11.9 per cent (2013 est)
Population below poverty line – 55.2 per cent (2012 est)
Total external debt – US$2,584m (2012 est)
Imports – US$2,300m (2012)
Exports – US$1,400m (2012)

BALANCE OF PAYMENTS
Trade – US$900m deficit (2012)
Current Account – US$1,918m deficit (2012)

Trade with UK	2012	2013
Imports from UK	£96,865,138	£160,667,613
Exports to UK	£10,982,296	£1,657,367

COMMUNICATIONS
Airports – Four with surfaced runways; the principal airport is at Conakry
Waterways – The major seaports are Conakry and Kamsar; there are 1,300km of waterways
Roadways and railways – 44,348km of roadways, only 10 per cent of which are surfaced, and 1,185km of railways
Telecommunications – 18,000 fixed lines and 4.781 million mobile telephone lines in use (2011); there were 95,000 internet users in 2009
Internet code and IDD – gn; 224 (from UK), 44 (to UK)
Major broadcasters – Radiodiffusion-Télévision Guinéenne is the principal, state-run broadcaster
Press – Horoya is the main government-owned daily
WPFI score – 31,67(102)

GUINEA-BISSAU

Republica da Guine-Bissau – Republic of Guinea-Bissau

Area – 36,125 sq. km
Capital – Bissau; population, 302,000 (2009 est)
Currency – West African CFA franc of 100 centimes
Population – 1,693,398 rising at 1.93 per cent a year
   (2014 est); Balanta (30 per cent), Fulani (20 per cent),
   Manjaca (14 per cent), Mandinga (13 per cent), Papel
   (7 per cent) (est)
Religion – Muslim 50 per cent, indigenous beliefs 40 per
   cent, Christian 10 per cent
Language – Portuguese (official), Creole
Population density – 58 per sq. km (2011)
Urban population – 44.6 per cent (2012 est)
Median age (years) – 19.8 (2014 est)
National anthem – 'Esta e a Nossa Patria Bem Amada' ['This
   is Our Beloved Country']
National day – 24 September (Independence Day)
Death penalty – Abolished for all crimes (since 1993)
CPI score – 19 (163)
Literacy rate – 55 per cent (2011 est)
Gross enrolment ratio (percentage of relevant age group) –
   primary 116 per cent (2011 est)
Health expenditure (per capita) – US$37 (2011)
Hospital beds (per 1,000 people) – 1.0 (2009)
Life expectancy (years) – 49.87 (2014 est)
Mortality rate – 14.54 (2014 est)
Birth rate – 33.83 (2014 est)
Infant mortality rate – 90.92 (2014 est)
HIV/AIDS adult prevalence – 3.9 per cent (2012 est)

CLIMATE AND TERRAIN
Guinea-Bissau has a low coastal plain that rises to savannah
in the east. The coast is heavily indented and covered with
mangrove swamps. Elevation extremes range from 300m
(in the north-east) to 0m (Atlantic Ocean). The climate is
tropical, with a wet season from July to September.

HISTORY AND POLITICS
A part of the ancient African empire of Mali, Guinea-Bissau
was once the kingdom of Gabu, which became independent
of the empire in 1546 and survived until 1867. In 1446,
Portuguese traders discovered the coast and established slave
trading there, subsequently administering Guinea-Bissau
with the Cape Verde islands; it became a separate colony in
1879. After a guerrilla war led by the left-wing African Party
for the Independence of Guinea and Cape Verde (PAIGC),
Guinea-Bissau declared independence unilaterally in 1973
and Portugal recognised this in 1974.

After independence Guinea-Bissau became a one-party
socialist state under the PAIGC, led by Luis Cabral. He was
deposed in 1980, in a military coup led by General Joao

Vieira, and the country was under military rule until 1994.
A multiparty system was introduced in 1991 after popular
agitation, but the following 15 years saw a short civil war
(1998–9) and two more military coups (1999, 2003);
democratic government was restored in 2004–5.

The 2008 legislative election was won by the PAIGC,
which formed a government in January 2009. The PAIGC
candidate, Malam Bacai Sanha, was elected president in July
2009, but became seriously ill and died on 9 January 2012;
he was temporarily replaced by Speaker of the National
Assembly Raimundo Pereira. A military coup in April 2012
detained Pereira and the presidential front-runner, outgoing
prime minister Carlos Gomes Jr; Guinea-Bissau has since
been ruled by a Transitional National Council, headed by
Manuel Serifo Nhamadjo, a former parliamentary speaker.
The April 2014 legislative election was won by the PAIGC,
whose candidate, Jose Mario Vaz, was elected president in
May 2014.

Under the 1999 constitution, the executive president is
directly elected for a five-year term, which is renewable once.
The president appoints the council of ministers. The
unicameral National People's Assembly has 102 members,
who are directly elected for a four-year term.

HEAD OF STATE
President, Jose Mario Vaz, *elected* 20 May 2014, *sworn in*
   23 June 2014

SELECTED GOVERNMENT MEMBERS *as at August 2014*
Prime Minister, Domingos Simoes
Economy, Geraldo Martins
Foreign Affairs, Mario Lopes Da Rosa

EMBASSY OF THE REPUBLIC OF GUINEA-BISSAU
94 Rue St Lazare, 75009 Paris, France
T (+33) (1) 4874 3639
Ambassador Extraordinary and Plenipotentiary, vacant

BRITISH CONSULATE
Ambassador Extraordinary and Plenipotentiary, HE Robert
   Marshall, *apptd* 2011, resident in Dakar, Senegal

DEFENCE

Aged 16–49, 2010 est	Males	Females
Available for military service	370,790	372,171
Fit for military service	205,460	212,277

Military expenditure – US$16.6m (2012)
Conscription – 18–25 years of age (selective)

ECONOMY AND TRADE
The economy is in a poor state owing to decades of
mismanagement and corruption, the devastating effects of
the 1998–9 civil war and ongoing political instability. There
is massive foreign debt and the country is heavily dependent
on foreign aid.

Although Guinea-Bissau has mineral resources, including
oil, the high cost of exploiting these inhibits development
and the economy is based almost exclusively on agriculture
and fishing; drug trafficking is the most lucrative industry in
the country. The agricultural sector employs 82 per cent
of the population and contributes 58 per cent of GDP. The
small industrial sector generates 13.5 per cent of GDP,
mainly through processing agricultural products and beer,
and soft drink production.

The main trading partners are India (56.5 per cent of
exports) and Nigeria. Principal exports include fish, cashew

nuts, peanuts, palm kernels and timber. The main imports are foodstuffs, machinery and transport equipment, and fuels. Agricultural exports have fallen following disruption caused by the March 2012 coup.
GNI – US$821m; US$510 per capita (2012)
Annual average growth of GDP – 3.5 per cent (2013 est)
Inflation rate – 1.9 per cent (2013 est)
Imports – US$250m (2012)
Exports – US$100m (2010)

BALANCE OF PAYMENTS
Trade – US$250m surplus (2012)
Current Account – US$11m deficit (2011)

Trade with UK	2012	2013
Imports from UK	£361,793	£614,135
Exports to UK	£110,828	£11,930

COMMUNICATIONS
Airports – Two; the principal airport is at Bissau
Waterways – The main rivers are navigable for part of their lengths, and shallow-draught craft can access much of the interior via creeks and inlets; Bissau is the main seaport
Roadways – There are 3,455km of roadways, of which 965km are surfaced
Telecommunications – 5,000 fixed lines and 1.1 million mobile subscriptions (2012); there were 37,100 internet users in 2009
Internet code and IDD – gw; 245 (from UK), 44 (to UK)
Major broadcasters – The state-run Radio Televisao de Guinea-Bissau is the main broadcaster
Press – Major newspapers include state-run weekly *No Pintcha* and the privately run *Gazeta de Noticias*
WPFI score – 30,05 (86)

GUYANA

Cooperative Republic of Guyana

Area – 214,969 sq. km
Capital – Georgetown; population, 132,000 (2009 est)
Major towns – Linden, New Amsterdam
Currency – Guyana dollar (G$) of 100 cents
Population – 735,554 falling at 0.11 per cent a year (2014 est); Indo-Guyanese 43.5 per cent, Afro-Guyanese 30.2 per cent, mixed 16.7 per cent, Amerindian 9.1 per cent (2002)
Religion – Protestant 31 per cent, Hindu 28 per cent, Roman Catholic 8 per cent
Language – English (official), Amerindian dialects, Creole, Caribbean Hindustani (a dialect of Hindi), Urdu
Population density – 4 per sq. km (2011)
Urban population – 28.4 per cent (2012 est)

Median age (years) – 25 (2014 est)
National anthem – 'Dear Land of Guyana, of Rivers and Plains'
National day – 23 February (Republic Day)
Death penalty – Retained
CPI score – 27 (136)
Gross enrolment ratio (percentage of relevant age group) – primary 80 per cent; secondary 105 per cent; tertiary 12 per cent (2011 est)
Life expectancy (years) – 67.81 (2014 est)
Mortality rate – 7.3 (2014 est)
Birth rate – 15.9 (2014 est)
Infant mortality rate – 33.56 (2014 est)
HIV/AIDS adult prevalence – 1.3 per cent (2012 est)

CLIMATE AND TERRAIN
The land rises from a narrow coastal plain to forested highlands in the west and savannah on the southern border; about 90 per cent of the population lives on the coastal plain, which constitutes 5 per cent of the land area. Around 79 per cent of the country is covered by rainforest. Elevation extremes range from 2,835m (Mt Roraima) to 0m (Atlantic Ocean). The climate is tropical, with an average daily temperature in Georgetown of 26°C, and two wet seasons, from April to July and from November to January.

HISTORY AND POLITICS
Carib and Arawak peoples inhabited the coastal region of Guyana when Dutch merchants founded the first European settlement in the late 16th century. Guyana became an important producer of sugar, grown on plantations worked first by African slaves and then, after the abolition of slavery in 1834, by indentured labourers, mostly from India. Several areas were ceded to Britain in 1815, and consolidated as British Guiana in 1831. The country became independent, as Guyana, on 26 May 1966, and became a republic in 1970.

Guyana's first political party, the People's Progressive Party (PPP), split along ethnic lines in the 1950s; the PPP continued as a predominantly Indian party under Cheddi Jagan, while those of African descent formed the People's National Congress (PNC), led by Forbes Burnham. Burnham dominated political life after independence, first as prime minister (1966–80) and then as executive president until his death in 1985. Under his autocratic rule, politics became characterised by suspect elections and a disregard for civil liberties and human rights. The PPP's electoral victory in 1992 ended the PNC's monopoly of power but persistent ethnic tensions continue to destabilise politics.

Bharrat Jagdeo of the PPP, interim president from 1999 to 2001, was elected president in 2001. His presidency has seen attempts to encourage joint action between the government and the private sector, and reconciliation between the PPP and Guyana's other political parties.

The 2011 legislative election was won by the PPP, securing its fifth consecutive term of office but without an overall majority; Donald Ramotar (PPP) won the 2011 presidential election, replacing president Bharrat Jagdeo (also PPP).

Under the 1980 constitution, the executive president is nominated by the majority party in the legislature after each legislative election, and serves a five-year term, renewable once. The unicameral National Assembly has 65 members, of whom 53 are elected by proportional representation and 12 are regional representatives; they serve a five-year term.

HEAD OF STATE
President, Donald Ramotar, *elected* 28 November 2011, *sworn in* 3 December 2011

SELECTED GOVERNMENT MEMBERS *as at April 2014*
Prime Minister, Samuel Hinds
Finance, Ashni Kumar Singh
Foreign Affairs, Carolyn Rodrigues-Burkett
Home Affairs, Clement Rohee

HIGH COMMISSION FOR GUYANA
3 Palace Court, Bayswater Road, London W2 4LP
T 020-7229 7684 E info@guyanahclondon.co.uk
W www.guyanahclondon.co.uk
High Commissioner, HE Laleshwar Singh, *apptd* 1993

BRITISH HIGH COMMISSION
PO Box 10849, 44 Main Street, Georgetown
T (+1592) 226 5881 E bhcguyana@networksgy.com
W www.gov.uk/government/world/guyana
High Commissioner, HE Andrew Ayre, *apptd* 2011

DEFENCE

Aged 16–49, 2010 est	Males	Females
Available for military service	189,840	–
Fit for military service	133,239	147,719

Military expenditure – US$31.2m (2013)

ECONOMY AND TRADE

The economy grew from 2001 to 2008 owing to expansion in agriculture and mining, the cancellation of over one-third of Guyana's external debt, and increases in foreign direct investment and remittances from expatriate workers. Following contraction in 2009 due to the global downturn and lower commodity prices, recovery began in 2010. In the longer term, poor infrastructure and skills shortages inhibit growth, especially attempts to develop tourism.

Agriculture accounts for 20.7 per cent of GDP and provides the raw materials for the major industries of sugar processing and rice milling. Non-agricultural activities include bauxite and gold mining, forestry, fishing and textile manufacturing; industry accounts for 38.5 per cent of GDP.

The main trading partners are the USA, Trinidad and Tobago, Canada and the UK. Principal exports include sugar, gold, bauxite, alumina, rice, shrimp, molasses, rum and timber. The main imports are manufactured goods, machinery, fuel and food.

GNI – US$2,849m; US$3,410 per capita (2012)
Annual average growth of GDP – 5.3 per cent (2013 est)
Inflation rate – 3.9 per cent (2013 est)
Unemployment – 11 per cent (2007 est)
Total external debt – US$1,846m (2011)
Imports – US$1,997m (2012)
Exports – US$1,393m (2012)

BALANCE OF PAYMENTS
Trade – US$603m deficit (2012)
Current Account – US$337m deficit (2011)

Trade with UK	2012	2013
Imports from UK	£28,001,059	£26,356,049
Exports to UK	£76,121,777	£70,055,879

COMMUNICATIONS

Airports and waterways – 11; 330km of navigable waterways (principally the Berbice, Demerara and Essequibo rivers) form the main arteries of communication
Roadways – There are 7,970km of roads, of which 590km are surfaced

Telecommunications – 154,200 fixed lines and 547,000 mobile subscriptions (2011); there were 189,600 internet users in 2009
Internet code and IDD – gy, 592 (from UK), 1 44 (to UK)
Major broadcasters – The state-owned National Communications Network operates national television and radio networks
Press – There are three major daily newspapers: the government-owned *Guyana Chronicle, Stabroek News* and *Kaieteur News*
WPFI score – 27,08 (67)

HAITI

République d'Haïti / Repiblik d'Ayiti – Republic of Haiti

Area – 27,750 sq. km
Capital – Port-au-Prince; population, 2,272,735 (2012 est)
Major cities – Cap-Haïtien, Gonaïves, Pétionville
Currency – Gourde of 100 centimes
Population – 9,996,731 rising at 1.08 per cent a year (2014 est)
Religion – Christian (Roman Catholic 80 per cent, Baptist 10 per cent, Pentecostal 4 per cent, Seventh-day Adventist 1 per cent); many Christians also practise Voodoo, recognised as an official religion in 2003
Language – French, Creole (both official)
Population density – 364 per sq. km (2011)
Urban population – 54.8 per cent (2012 est)
Median age (years) – 22.2 (2014 est)
National anthem – 'La Dessalinienne' ['Song of Dessalines']
National day – 1 January (Independence Day)
Death penalty – Abolished for all crimes (since 1987)
CPI score – 19 (163)
Literacy rate – 48.7 per cent (2011 est)
Health expenditure (per capita) – US$58 (2011)
Hospital beds (per 1,000 people) – 1.3 (2007)
Life expectancy (years) – 63.18 (2014 est)
Mortality rate – 7.91 (2014 est)
Birth rate – 22.83 (2014 est)
Infant mortality rate – 49.43 (2014 est)
HIV/AIDS adult prevalence – 2.1 per cent (2012 est)

CLIMATE AND TERRAIN

The country occupies the western third of the island of Hispaniola. The terrain is mountainous, with coastal plains and a large central plateau. Elevation extremes range from 2,680m (Chaîne de la Selle) to 0m (Caribbean Sea). The climate is tropical, and semi-arid where the eastern mountains block the trade winds, with two wet seasons (April–June, August–November) and a hurricane season from June to November.

Western part of Hispaniola ceded to France and named Saint-Domingue, becoming the richest French colony | Republic of Haiti founded; it is world's first black republic and, after the USA, the oldest republic in the western hemisphere | Sovereign rule restored | Jean-Bertrand Aristide wins presidential election | Armed rebellion ousts Aristide; an interim government is sworn in and a UN-led stabilisation force is deployed

c.1490 — 1791 — 1915 — 1956-85 — 1994 — 2010

1697 — 1804 — 1934 — 1990 — 2004

Hispaniola visited by Columbus and colonised by the Spanish | Slave rebellion expels French from the northen region; a long war between freed slaves and colonists begins | Ongoing political disorder leads to USA occupation | Duvalier family dictatorial rule | Aristide restored to power after 1991 military coup | Earthquake leaves 230,000 dead and 1.2 million homeless

POLITICS

Under the 1987 constitution, the president is directly elected for a five-year term that may not be renewed immediately. The bicameral National Assembly comprises a lower house, the Chamber of Deputies, with 99 members directly elected for a four-year term, and the senate, with 30 members directly elected for a six-year term; one-third of the senators are elected every two years. The president appoints the prime minister, who must be approved by the legislature.

The presidential and legislative elections due in 2010 were postponed because of the earthquake. The presidential election was won in the second round of voting in March 2011 by Michel Martelly of the Repons Peyizan party. The Inite party won a majority in both the National Assembly and Chamber of Deputies in a legislative election dogged by allegations of irregularities. In April 2014, Prime Minister Laurent Lamothe announced a major cabinet reshuffle before delayed legislative elections in October 2014, with one third of the seats in the legislature due to be contested. Elections for the legislature have been overdue since 2012.

HEAD OF STATE
President, Michel Martelly, *elected* 20 March 2011, *sworn in* 14 May 2011

SELECTED GOVERNMENT MEMBERS *as at May 2014*
Prime Minister, Laurent Lamothe
Economy and Finance, Marie-Carmelle Jean-Marie
Interior, Réginald Delva

EMBASSY OF THE REPUBLIC OF HAITI
14 Cavendish Place, London W1G 9DJ
T 020-7637 8985
Ambassador Extraordinary and Plenipotentiary, vacant

BRITISH AMBASSADOR
HE Steven Fisher, *apptd* 2009, resident at Santo Domingo, Dominican Republic

ECONOMY AND TRADE

The country is the poorest in the western hemisphere, with most of the population living below the poverty line and over half in abject poverty. Its economy, damaged by years of political instability, violence and corruption as well as the natural disasters to which it is vulnerable, experienced moderate growth from 2005 and Haiti had its foreign debt written off in 2009 and 2010. But the 2010 earthquake reversed these gains, devastating the infrastructure and continuing the government's complete dependence on foreign aid. While there was some economic recovery in 2011, hurricanes in 2012 provided a further setback; GDP grew by 2.8 per cent in 2012 and 3.4 per cent in 2013. Remittances from the estimated one in six Haitians who live abroad, principally in the USA, are the main source of foreign revenue, worth nearly 20 per cent of GDP. Two-fifths of the population depend on agriculture – predominantly small-scale subsistence farming – which contributes 24.1 per cent of GDP. Industrial activities include production of textiles and garments, sugar refining, flour milling and assembly of goods, especially vehicle parts, for re-export.

The main trading partners are the USA and Dominican Republic. Principal exports are garments (three-quarters of exports), manufactured goods, essential oils, cocoa, mangoes and coffee. The main imports are food, manufactured goods, machinery and transport equipment, fuels and raw materials.
GNI – US$7,911m; US$760 per capita (2012)
Annual average growth of GDP – 3.4 per cent (2013 est)
Inflation rate – 6.3 per cent (2013 est)
Population below poverty line – 80 per cent (2003 est)
Total external debt – US$1,118m (2013 est)
Imports – US$3,170m (2012)
Exports – US$814m (2012)

BALANCE OF PAYMENTS
Trade – US$2,356m deficit (2012)
Current Account – US$359m deficit (2012)

Trade with UK	2012	2013
Imports from UK	£11,226,814	£9,069,554
Exports to UK	£2,897,273	£3,302,530

COMMUNICATIONS

Airports and waterways – Four; the international airports and main ports are at Port-au-Prince and Cap-Haitien
Roadways – Fewer than a quarter of the country's 4,266km of highways are surfaced
Telecommunications – 50,000 fixed lines (2010) and 6.095 million mobile subscriptions (2012); there were 1 million internet users in 2009
Internet code and IDD – ht; 509 (from UK), 44 (to UK)
Major broadcasters – The government-owned Television Nationale d'Haiti broadcasts in Creole, French and Spanish
Press – There are two daily newspapers, *Le Matin* and *Le Nouvelliste*
WPFI score – 23,53 (47)

HONDURAS

República de Honduras – Republic of Honduras

Area – 112,090 sq. km
Capital – Tegucigalpa; population, 1,086,952 (2012 est)
Major cities – Choloma, La Ceiba, El Progreso, San Pedro Sula
Currency – Lempira of 100 centavos

Population – 8,598,561 rising at 1.74 per cent a year (2014 est); mainly mestizo, with Amerindian and black minorities
Religion – Christian (Roman Catholic 97 per cent, Protestant 3 per cent)
Language – Spanish (official), Amerindian dialects
Population density – 70 per sq. km (2011)
Urban population – 52.7 per cent (2012 est)
Median age (years) – 21.9 (2014 est)
National anthem – 'Himno Nacional de Honduras' ['National Anthem of Honduras']
National day – 15 September (Independence Day)
Death penalty – Abolished for all crimes (since 1956)
CPI score – 26 (140)

CLIMATE AND TERRAIN

Honduras has a mountainous interior, falling to narrow coastal plains. Elevation extremes range from 2,870m (Cerro Las Minas) to 0m (Caribbean Sea). The climate is subtropical in the lowlands and temperate in the mountains. The average temperature in Tegucigalpa is 22°C.

HISTORY AND POLITICS

Honduras was home to part of the Mayan civilisation between the fourth and ninth centuries AD. Christopher Columbus first set foot on the American mainland at Trujillo in Honduras in 1502, but it was 1525 before Spanish colonisation began. In 1821, the country gained independence from Spain, and it was part of a Central American federation of former Spanish colonies from 1823 until it became fully independent in 1839. Thereafter the country underwent periods of political instability interspersed with military rule until 1982, when a civilian government took office. During the civil wars in Nicaragua and El Salvador, Honduras acted as a base for US forces and anti-Sandinista Contras, and there was a marked decline in its respect for human rights. The end of the civil wars led to a decline in the power of the army, which was brought under civilian control in 1999, but there are still very high levels of violent crime. In 2011 congress voted to allow troops to take on police responsibilities in an attempt to curb the high murder rate.

In November 2013, Juan Orlando Hernández of the National Party was declared the winner of the presidential election, winning 36 per cent of votes cast amid allegations of fraud.

Under the 1982 constitution, the executive president is directly elected for a four-year term, which is not renewable, and appoints the government. The unicameral National Congress has 128 members, directly elected for a four-year term.

HEAD OF STATE
President, Juan Orlando Hernández, *elected* 24 November 2013, *took office* 27 January 2014
Vice-President, Ricardo Antonio Alvarez Arias

SELECTED GOVERNMENT MEMBERS *as at April 2014*
Defence, Samuel Reyes Rendon
Finance, Wilfredo Cerrato
Foreign Relations, Mireya Aguero de Corrales

EMBASSY OF HONDURAS
115 Gloucester Place, London W1U 6JT
T 020-7486 4880 E hondurasuk@lineone.net
Ambassador Extraordinary and Plenipotentiary, HE Ivan Romero-Martinez, *apptd* 2008

BRITISH AMBASSADOR
HE Sarah Dickson, *apptd* 2012, resident at Guatemala City, Guatemala

DEFENCE

Aged 16–49, 2010 est	*Males*	*Females*
Available for military service	2,045,914	1,991,418
Fit for military service	1,525,578	1,539,688

Military expenditure – US$223m (2013)

ECONOMY AND TRADE

The country has a huge imbalance in wealth and high levels of corruption and violent crime, often connected with drug-trafficking. Economic activity is heavily dependent on the USA; a drop in exports and remittances due to the global economic downturn contributed to the economy's contraction in 2009. In October 2012 the country secured IMF support, which renewed multilateral confidence and attracted interest from foreign investors. Remittances from expatriate workers are equivalent to one-fifth of GDP. Economic difficulties lead to government workers and suppliers going without pay in the winter of 2012.

Although still dependent on agriculture, fishing and forestry, whose products form the basis of industrial activity and are the main exports, the economy is gradually diversifying into offshore assembly for re-export and tourism. Agriculture employs 39.2 per cent of the workforce and contributes 14 per cent of GDP. Industry accounts for 28.2 per cent of GDP and 20.9 per cent of employment, and the services sector for 57.8 per cent of GDP and 39.8 per cent of employment.

The main trading partner is the USA, which takes 34.5 per cent of exports and provides 44.3 per cent of imports. Principal exports are garments, coffee, shrimp, wire harnessing, cigars, bananas, gold, palm oil, fruit, lobster and timber. The main imports are machinery and transport equipment, industrial raw materials, chemical products, fuels and foodstuffs.

GNI – US$17,129m; US$2,120 per capita (2012)
Annual average growth of GDP – 2.8 per cent (2013 est)
Inflation rate – 5.2 per cent (2013 est)
Unemployment – 4.5 per cent (2013 est)
Population below poverty line – 60 per cent (2010)
Total external debt – US$6,173m (2013 est)
Imports – US$9,464m (2012)
Exports – US$4,427m (2012)

BALANCE OF PAYMENTS
Trade – US$5,037m deficit (2012)
Current Account – US$1,587m deficit (2012)

Trade with UK	*2012*	*2013*
Imports from UK	£10,194,311	£11,812,365
Exports to UK	£52,111,295	£63,810,030

COMMUNICATIONS

Airports – 13; the principal airports are at Tegucigalpa, La Ceiba and San Pedro Sula
Waterways – Honduras has ports on its Caribbean (Puerto Castilla, Puerto Cortes, Tela) and Pacific (San Lorenzo) coasts, and 465km of navigable waterways (mostly by small boats)
Roadways and railways – There are 14,742km of roadways, 3,367km of which are surfaced, and 44km of railways
Telecommunications – 610,000 fixed lines and 7.37 million mobile subscriptions (2012); there were 731,700 internet users in 2009
Internet code and IDD – hn; 504 (from UK), 44 (to UK)
Major broadcasters – Televicentro operates several channels throughout the country; CBC Canal 6, Vica TV and Sotel Canal 11 are all private broadcasters

Press – There are four private daily newspapers, including *El Heraldo* and *La Prensa*
WPFI score – 37,14 (129)

EDUCATION AND HEALTH

Primary and secondary education is free of charge and primary education is compulsory between the ages of six and 11.
Literacy rate – 85 per cent (2011 est)
Gross enrolment ratio (percentage of relevant age group) – primary 114 per cent; secondary 74 per cent (2011 est); tertiary 21 per cent (2011 est)
Health expenditure (per capita) – US$193 (2011)
Hospital beds (per 1,000 people) – 0.7 (2011)
Life expectancy (years) – 70.91 (2014 est)
Mortality rate – 5.13 (2014 est)
Birth rate – 23.66 (2014 est)
Infant mortality rate – 18.72 (2014 est)

HUNGARY

Magyarorszag – Republic of Hungary

Area – 93,028 sq. km
Capital – Budapest; population, 1,708,552 (2012 est)
Major cities – Debrecen, Gyor, Miskolc, Pecs, Szeged
Currency – Forint of 100 filler
Population – 9,919,128 falling at 0.21 per cent a year (2014 est); Hungarian (92.3 per cent), Roma (1.9 per cent) (2001). There are also smaller groups of ethnic Germans, Serbs, Romanians and Slovaks
Religion – Christian (Roman Catholic 37 per cent, Protestant 14 per cent), Jewish (less than 1 per cent) (est)
Language – Hungarian (official)
Population density – 110 per sq. km (2011)
Urban population – 69.9 per cent (2012 est)
Median age (years) – 41.1 (2014 est)
National anthem – 'Himnusz' ['Hymn']
National day – 20 August (St Stephen's Day)
Death penalty – Abolished for all crimes (since 1990)
CPI score – 54 (47)

CLIMATE AND TERRAIN

Hungary lies mostly on the vast plain created by the Danube and Tisza rivers, with hills and mountains along the northern border. Elevation extremes range from 1,014m (Mt Kekes) to 78m (river Tisza). Lake Balaton lies in the west. Average temperatures range from −0.7°C in January to 20.5°C in July.

POLITICS

The 1949 constitution was superseded in 2012 by a new constitution approved by the legislature in April 2011. Parliament has since acted to limit the powers of the constitutional court following clashes, notably on electoral law. The president is elected by the legislature for a five-year term, renewable once; under the new constitution, he or she nominates the prime minister who is then elected by parliament. The unicameral National Assembly has 199 members directly elected for a four-year term.

The 2010 legislative election was won by the opposition Fidesz and Christian Democratic People's Party bloc with an overwhelming majority, and it formed a government under Viktor Orban (prime minister 1998–2002), who was re-elected in 2014. The 2010 presidential election was won outright at the first vote by Pal Schmitt of the Fidesz party, who subsequently resigned from office in April 2012 after admitting he had plagiarised much of his doctoral thesis; the Fidesz party elected Janos Ader as Schmitt's replacement in a vote that was boycotted by the opposition Socialist party.

HEAD OF STATE

President, Janos Ader, *elected* 2 May 2012, *sworn in* 10 May 2012

SELECTED GOVERNMENT MEMBERS *as at May 2014*

Prime Minister, Viktor Orban
Deputy Prime Ministers, Tibor Navracsics; Zsolt Semjen
Defence, Csaba Hende
Economy, Mihaly Varga
Foreign Affairs, Janos Martonyi

EMBASSY OF THE REPUBLIC OF HUNGARY

35 Eaton Place, London SW1X 8BY
T 020-7201 3440 E mission.lon@mfa.gov.hu
W www.mfa.gov.hu/emb/london
Ambassador Extraordinary and Plenipotentiary, HE Janos Csak, *apptd* 2011

BRITISH EMBASSY

Harmincad Utca 6, 1051 Budapest
T (+36) (1) 266 2888 E info@britemb.hu
W www.gov.uk/government/world/hungary
Ambassador Extraordinary and Plenipotentiary, HE Jonathan Knott, *apptd* 2012

DEFENCE

Aged 16–49, 2010 est	*Males*	*Females*
Available for military service	2,349,948	2,290,568
Fit for military service	1,902,639	1,897,378

Military expenditure – US$1,245m (2013)

Most of kingdom conquered by Ottoman Turks | Dual monarchy created between Austrian and Hungarian crowns; period of economic success | Austro-Hungarian Empire defeated in the First World War | Joins Axis powers in Second World War | Opens border with Austria, indirectly triggering the fall of communism throughout eastern Europe; communist rule ends soon after

c.1000   1699   1920   1944   1949   1999   2004
1526   1867   1918   1941   1989

Settled by Magyar tribes, becomes a Christian kingdom under St Stephen | Turks expelled by Habsburgs; country becomes a province in dynasty's central European empire | Becomes a kingdom with Admiral Horthy as regent | Horthy deposed after seeking armistice with USSR | Becomes a communist state aligned with the Soviet Union | Joins NATO | Joins the EU

ECONOMY AND TRADE

Hungary made a successful transition to a market economy after 1989, attracting high levels of foreign direct investment, and over 80 per cent of GDP is now generated by the private sector. This strong economic growth started to slow in 2006–7, partly as a result of a government austerity programme intended to reduce the budget deficit and public debt. The global economic downturn left Hungary struggling to service both state and private debt in the face of rising interest rates and falling export demand, and the government had to obtain international assistance in 2008. While the economy achieved growth in 2011 the government had to seek further international financial assistance at the end of the year; however, controversial new central bank reforms in Hungary led to a breakdown in talks with lenders. By 2013 Hungary had cut its deficit to under 3 per cent of GDP, allowing the country to exit the EU's Excessive Deficit Procedure.

Nearly half the land is under cultivation, but agriculture accounts for only 3.4 per cent of GDP; the main crops are cereals, sunflower seeds, vegetables, livestock and dairy products. Industry contributes 28 per cent of GDP; the main activities include mining, metallurgy, food processing, and the production of construction materials, textiles, chemicals (especially pharmaceuticals) and motor vehicles. The main trading partners are Germany, Austria, Russia and China. Machinery and manufactured goods account for 84.7 per cent of exports and 79.7 per cent of imports. The country is a net importer of fuels and electricity.

GNI – US$117,509m; US$12,380 per capita (2012)
Annual average growth of GDP – 0.2 per cent (2013 est)
Inflation rate – 1.9 per cent (2013 est)
Unemployment – 10.5 per cent (2013 est)
Population below poverty line – 14 per cent (2012)
Total external debt – US$170,300m (2013 est)
Imports – US$94,282m (2012)
Exports – US$103,047m (2012)

BALANCE OF PAYMENTS
Trade – US$8,765m surplus (2012)
Current Account – US$2,192m surplus (2012 est)

Trade with UK	2012	2013
Imports from UK	£1,071,189,795	£1,209,799,227
Exports to UK	£2,615,299,668	£2,582,081,879

COMMUNICATIONS

Airports and waterways – 20, with the principal airport at Budapest; there are 1,622km of permanently navigable waterways, mainly on the river Danube, which has several major river ports and harbours including Budapest
Roadways and railways – There are 199,567km of roadways, 76,075km of which are surfaced, and 8,057km of railways (including a cross-border line to Austria jointly managed by the two countries)
Telecommunications – 2.96 million fixed lines and 11.58 million mobile subscriptions (2012); there were 6.176 million internet users in 2009
Internet code and IDD – hu; 36 (from UK), 44 (to UK)
Major broadcasters – Magyar Televizio operates two public channels alongside private channels TV2 and RTL Klub; Duna TV operates satellite channels for Hungarian minorities living in neighbouring states
Press – There are four daily newspapers, including *Nepszabadsag* and *Magyar Hirlap*
WPFI score – 26,73 (64)

EDUCATION AND HEALTH

Hungarians have ten years of compulsory education until age 16; a further two years at secondary level is optional.
Literacy rate – 99 per cent (2011 est)
Gross enrolment ratio (percentage of relevant age group) – primary 101 per cent; secondary 101 per cent; tertiary 60 per cent (2011 est)
Health expenditure (per capita) – US$1,085 (2011)
Hospital beds (per 1,000 people) – 7.2 (2010)
Life expectancy (years) – 75.64 (2014 est)
Mortality rate – 12.72 (2014 est)
Birth rate – 9.26 (2014 est)
Infant mortality rate – 5.09 (2014 est)

ICELAND

Lydveldid Island – Republic of Iceland

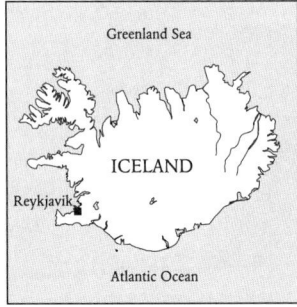

Area – 103,000 sq. km
Capital – Reykjavik; population, 198,000 (2009 est)
Major towns – Hafnarfjordur, Kopavogur
Currency – Icelandic kronur (Kr) of 100 aurar
Population – 317,351 rising at 0.65 per cent a year (2014 est)
Religion – Christian (Lutheran 76 per cent, Roman Catholic 3 per cent) (est)
Language – Icelandic (official), English, German
Population density – 3 per sq. km (2011)
Urban population – 93.8 per cent (2012 est)
Median age (years) – 36.4 (2014 est)
National anthem – 'Lofsongur' ['Hymn']
National day – 17 June (Independence Day)
Death penalty – Abolished for all crimes (since 1928)
CPI score – 78 (12)
Military expenditure – US$17.4m (2012)
Gross enrolment ratio (percentage of relevant age group) – primary 99 per cent; secondary 109 per cent; tertiary 81 per cent (2011 est)
Life expectancy (years) – 81.22 (2014 est)
Mortality rate – 7.13 (2014 est)
Birth rate – 13.09 (2014 est)
Infant mortality rate – 3.15 (2014 est)

CLIMATE AND TERRAIN

Iceland is a volcanic island in the North Atlantic Ocean, to the east of Greenland and to the west of Norway, and its northernmost point reaches the Arctic Circle. Some parts of the coastline have narrow strips of low-lying land, others are sheer cliffs. An inland plateau of glaciers, lakes and lava fields covers most of the interior, with mountainous areas in the north and at the four glaciers in the centre and south. Elevation extremes range from 2,110m (Hvannadalshnukur, on the Oraefajokull volcano) to 0m (North Atlantic Ocean). There are geysers and hot springs owing to the numerous active volcanoes, which can create new islands, such as Surtsey in 1963; the volcano under the Eyjafjallajokull glacier has been active since March 2010. It is estimated that over the past 500 years, Iceland has emitted one-third of the earth's total lava flow. The climate is influenced by the Gulf Stream; average temperatures range from −1.1°C in January to 9.8°C in July.

HISTORY AND POLITICS

The first major settlement occurred from around AD 870 onwards, as turmoil in Scandinavia drove migrants to seek new homelands. Iceland hosted a flourishing Viking culture in the ninth and tenth centuries, becoming a fully Christian country in 1000. Iceland recognised Norwegian sovereignty in 1263 and, with Norway, came under Danish rule in 1397. When Norway was ceded to Sweden in 1814, Iceland remained Danish territory, achieving autonomy in domestic affairs in 1874. Although it became an independent state with the same sovereign as Denmark in 1918, Copenhagen continued to control its foreign policy and defence. The treaty of union with Denmark expired in 1943, while Denmark was under German occupation, and in a referendum Icelanders voted to become a fully independent republic, proclaimed on 17 June 1944.

The country's dependence on the fishing industry has led occasionally to fraught foreign relations. The introduction and extensions of an exclusive fishing limit around Iceland in 1958, 1972 and 1975 caused the so-called 'Cod War' disputes with the UK.

Post-independence politics was dominated by the conservative Independence Party (SSF) until January 2009, when the country's economic crisis forced the government first to call an early election, then to resign with immediate effect. Incumbent president Olafur Ragnar Grimsson was re-elected for a fifth term in June 2012. The Progressive and Independence parties won the April 2013 parliamentary elections with 19 seats each and formed a coalition government in May; the new Eurosceptic government has indicated it will seek to withdraw from EU membership talks.

Under the 1944 constitution, the head of state is the president, who is directly elected for a four-year term, which is renewable. The unicameral legislature, the *Althing*, has 63 members, who are directly elected for a four-year term. Founded in AD 930, the *Althing* is the world's oldest functioning parliament.

HEAD OF STATE
President, Olafur Ragnar Grimsson, *elected* 29 June 1996, *re-elected* 2000, 2004, 2008, 2012

SELECTED GOVERNMENT MEMBERS *as at April 2014*
Prime Minister, Sigmundur Gunnlaugsson
Finance, Bjarni Benediktsson
Foreign Affairs, Gunnar Bragi Sveinsson

EMBASSY OF ICELAND
2A Hans Street, London SW1X 0JE
T 020-7259 3999 E emb.london@mfa.is W www.iceland.is/uk
Ambassador Extraordinary and Plenipotentiary, HE Benedikt Jonsson, *apptd* 2009

BRITISH EMBASSY
Laufasvegur 31, 101 Reykjavík
T (+354) 550 5100 E info@britishembassy.is
W www.gov.uk/government/world/iceland
Ambassador Extraordinary and Plenipotentiary and Consul-General, HE Stuart Gill, *apptd* 2012

ECONOMY AND TRADE

Iceland has a market economy with an extensive welfare system. While it remains heavily dependent on the fishing industry, which accounts for more than 12 per cent of GDP and 40 per cent of export earnings, there has been recent diversification into aluminium smelting, ferrosilicon production, software production, biotechnology and tourism, encouraged by the plentiful supply of geothermal power. A major area of diversification was into banking, but aggressive expansion in the 2000s led to over-exposure in foreign markets. In the 2008 global financial crisis, the three largest banks collapsed and the government required over US$10bn in loans to stabilise its currency and financial system. The economy contracted sharply, causing widespread unemployment and rapid inflation, and has been in recession since 2009; GDP, however, rose steadily in 2011 and 2012 and the country has begun compensation payments to international claimants of failed Icelandic banks. In January 2013 Iceland awarded licences for oil and gas exploration and production in the waters off its north-east coast to Faroe Petroleum and Valiant Petroleum; Norway took a 25 per cent stake in both. EU accession negotiations started in 2010 but were suspended in 2013 amid concerns about loss of control of the fishing industry and the Eurozone's ongoing financial troubles.

The main trading partners are the Netherlands, Norway and the USA. Principal exports are fish and fish products, aluminium, animal products, ferrosilicon and diatomite. The main imports are machinery, petroleum products, foodstuffs and textiles.

GNI – US$12,077m; US$38,330 per capita (2012)
Annual average growth of GDP – 1.9 per cent (2013 est)
Inflation rate – 3.9 per cent (2013 est)
Unemployment – 4.56 per cent (2012 est)
Total external debt – US$102,000m (2012 est)
Imports – US$4,772m (2012)
Exports – US$5,064m (2012)

BALANCE OF PAYMENTS
Trade – US$292m surplus (2012)
Current Account – US$668m deficit (2012)

Trade with UK	2012	2013
Imports from UK	£200,799,719	£193,548,618
Exports to UK	£376,967,684	£386,486,772

COMMUNICATIONS

Airports – Seven, with the principal airports at Keflavik, near Reykjavik, in the south, and Akureyri in the north
Roadways – Although the country has 12,890km of roads, about two-thirds are unsurfaced
Telecommunications – 189,000 fixed lines and 346,000 mobile subscriptions (2012); there were 301,600 internet users in 2009
Internet code and IDD – is; 354 (from UK), 44 (to UK)
Major broadcasters – Icelandic National Broadcasting Service operates radio and television services across the country
Press – There are three major daily newspapers: *Frettabladid, Morgunbladid* and *DV*
WPFI score – 8,50 (8)

INDIA

Bharatiya Ganarajya – Republic of India

Area – 3,287,263 sq. km
Capital – New Delhi; population, 22,968,412 (2012 est)
Major cities – Ahmadabad, Bengaluru (Bangalore), Chennai
   (Madras), Hyderabad, Jaipur, Kanpur, Kolkata (Calcutta),
   Mumbai (Bombay), Pune, Surat
Currency – Indian rupee (Rs) of 100 paise
Population – 1,236,344,361 rising at 1.25 per cent a year
   (2014 est); Indo-Aryan (72 per cent), Dravidian (25 per
   cent) (2000 est)
Religion – Hindu 80 per cent, Muslim 13 per cent (Sunni
   85 per cent, Shia 15 per cent), Christian 2 per cent, Sikh
   2 per cent (est)
Language – Hindi (official national language), English,
   Assamese, Bengali, Bodo, Dogri, Gujarati, Kannada,
   Kashmiri, Konkani, Maithili, Malayalam, Manipuri,
   Marathi, Nepali, Oriya, Punjabi, Sanskrit, Santhali, Sindhi,
   Tamil, Telugu, Urdu (all official)
Population density – 411 per sq. km (2011)
Urban population – 31.6 per cent (2012 est)
Median age (years) – 27 (2014 est)
National anthem – 'Jana Gana Mana' ['Thou Art the Ruler of
   the Minds of all People']
National day – 26 January (Republic Day)
Death penalty – Retained
CPI score – 36 (94)

CLIMATE AND TERRAIN

India has three well-defined regions: the mountain range of
the Himalayas, the Indo-Gangetic plain and the southern
peninsula. The Himalayas along the northern border reach
8,598m (Kanchenjunga), then drop to the northern plains
formed by the basins of the Indus, Ganges and Brahmaputra
rivers before rising to low hills running east to west that
mark the division with the southern Deccan peninsula. The
peninsula has narrow coastal plains rising to a central
plateau, with the Western Ghats and Eastern Ghats ranges of
hills lying along the west and east coasts respectively. The
Thar Desert lies in the north-west. The climate varies from
tropical in the south to temperate in the north. It is
influenced by the south-west monsoon; the main rainy
season is June to October. During the drier season from
December to May, the weather is cooler until February and
then becomes increasingly hot until the monsoon breaks.
The average temperature in New Delhi ranges from 13.8°C
in January to 34°C in June.

POLITICS

Under the 1950 constitution, the president is elected for a
five-year term by an electoral college consisting of members
of both chambers of the legislature. The president appoints
the prime minister, who is responsible to the legislature. The
vice-president, who is elected by both chambers for a
five-year term, is *ex-officio* chair of the upper chamber. The
legislature, the *Sansad,* consists of two chambers. The upper
chamber, the Council of States *(Rajya Sabha),* has up to 250
members, who serve a six-year term; up to 238 members are
elected by the state legislative assemblies as individual terms
expire, and the rest are nominated by the president. The
House of the People *(Lok Sabha)* has 545 members; 543 are
directly elected for a five-year term, and two representatives
of the Anglo-Indian community are nominated by the
president.

There are 28 states and seven union territories (including
the national capital territory). Each state has its own
executive, comprising a governor, who is appointed by the
president for a five-year term, and a council of ministers. All
states have a legislative assembly, and some also have a
legislative council, elected directly for a maximum period of
five years. The states have considerable autonomy, although
the union government controls such matters as foreign
policy, defence and external trade. The union territories
are administered, except where otherwise provided by
parliament, by a lieutenant-governor or an administrator
appointed by the president.

The 2012 presidential election was won by Pranab
Mukherjee. In the legislative elections held in May 2014
the Bharatiya Janata Party (BJP) won a landslide victory
against the incumbent India National Congress (INC) and
its coalition partners, establishing India's first majority
government since 1984 with 282 seats in the *Lok Sabha.* The
2014 legislative election saw the largest turnout in history
with 551 million votes cast.

HEAD OF STATE
President, Pranab Mukherjee, *elected* 19 July 2012, *took office*
   25 July 2012
Vice-President, Hamid Ansari

SELECTED GOVERNMENT MEMBERS *as at June 2014*
Prime Minister, Narendra Modi
Finance, Defence, Arun Jaitley
Home Affairs, Raj Nath Singh

OFFICE OF THE HIGH COMMISSIONER FOR INDIA
India House, Aldwych, London WC2B 4NA
T 020-7836 8484
E pnihci@compuserve.comadministration@hcilondon.in
W www.hcilondon.in
High Commissioner, HE Ranjan Mathai, *apptd* 2013

BRITISH HIGH COMMISSION
Shantipath, Chanakyapuri, New Delhi 110021
T (+91) (11) 2419 2100 E postmaster.newdelhi@fco.gov.uk
W www.gov.uk/government/world/india
High Commissioner, Sir James Bevan, KCMG, *apptd* 2011

FOREIGN RELATIONS
Since partition, sovereignty over the predominantly Muslim state of Jammu and Kashmir has been disputed by India and Pakistan. A short war in 1947–8 resulted in the state being partitioned between the two countries; its status remains unresolved, despite further outbreaks of war in 1965 and 1971, low-level conflict for control of the Siachen glacier since 1985 and occasional increases in military exchanges, most recently in 1999–2002 and 2003. Tension was exacerbated by Pakistan's support of the Muslim insurgency in the Indian part of the state, which began in the late 1980s and has included terrorist attacks in Indian cities, and by both countries' acquisition of nuclear weapons. Moves towards a peaceful settlement began in 2003, when diplomatic missions were reopened and the resumption of transport links was initiated. Formal diplomatic talks began in 2004 and have achieved several accords intended to reduce tension between the two countries, although the status of Kashmir has yet to be addressed. Talks were temporarily suspended by the Indian government after the 2008 terrorist attacks on Mumbai, but resumed in 2010.

In the Sino-Indian war in 1962, India lost territory to China. In addition, China claims Arunachal Pradesh and does not recognise Indian sovereignty over Sikkim. Talks between India and China in 2003 resulted in India's formal recognition of the Tibetan Autonomous Region as a part of China and a cross-border trade agreement on Sikkim.

DEFENCE

Aged 16–49, 2010 est	Males	Females
Available for military service	319,129,420	296,071,637
Fit for military service	249,531,562	240,039,958

Military expenditure – US$49,091m (2013)

ECONOMY AND TRADE
The economy was closed for several decades after independence, with high import tariffs and limits on foreign investment intended to stimulate domestic growth. Since 1991, economic liberalisation and increased foreign investment have generated rapid expansion, with GDP growing by an average of 7 per cent a year since 1997. Following a brief contraction in 2008–9 during the global economic downturn, growth exceeded 8 per cent in 2010, but slowed to a ten-year low in 2013 due to the economy performing poorly in a number of key areas.

India's large skilled workforce has enabled it to develop knowledge-based industries and become a global centre for manufacturing and services. Other areas of growth are pharmaceuticals, tourism and the provision of services to the burgeoning urban middle class. The service sector now accounts for 66.1 per cent of GDP and industry for 17 per cent, employing 31 per cent and 20 per cent of the workforce respectively.

Although about 1 per cent of the population has been lifted out of poverty each year since 1997, rural areas have benefited disproportionately little from the economic growth. Since 2004 the government has initiated schemes intended to reduce rural poverty, which has been exacerbated by prolonged drought in some areas and the effects of the Indian Ocean tsunami of 2004. Agriculture, forestry and fishing support 49 per cent of the population and contribute 16.9 per cent of GDP. The main food crops are rice, cereals (principally wheat) and pulses. The major cash crops include cotton, jute, tea and sugar cane. Agriculture and forestry are threatened by deforestation, soil erosion, over-grazing and desertification.

Despite recent advances, the economy faces a number of problems, chief among which is population growth. Economic constraints on continued growth include underinvestment in infrastructure, shortfalls in energy generation, excessive regulation and corruption.

The main trading partners are the USA, the UAE and China. Principal exports include petroleum products, precious stones, machinery, iron and steel, chemicals, vehicles and garments. Its main imports are crude oil, precious stones, machinery, fertiliser, iron and steel, and chemicals.

GNI – US$1,887,143m; US$1,580 per capita (2012)
Annual average growth of GDP – 3.8 per cent (2013 est)
Inflation rate – 9.6 per cent (2013 est)
Population below poverty line – 29.8 per cent (2010 est)
Unemployment – 8.8 per cent (2013 est)
Total external debt – US$412,200m (2013 est)
Imports – US$490,005m (2012)
Exports – US$296,889m (2012)

BALANCE OF PAYMENTS
Trade – US$193,116m deficit (2012)
Current Account – US$88,163m deficit (2012)

Trade with UK	2012	2013
Imports from UK	£4,553,846,961	£5,051,555,200
Exports to UK	£5,993,495,663	£6,182,222,618

COMMUNICATIONS
Airports – There are 253 airports and airfields, principally at Delhi, Mumbai, Chennai and Kolkata
Waterways – The chief seaports are Mumbai, Kolkata, Haldia, Chennai, Cochin, Visakhapatnam, Mangalore and Tuticorin; there are 340 ships of over 1,000 tonnes in the merchant fleet. There are 485km of canals and the great rivers provide around 5,200km of navigable waterways
Roadways and railways – 4,689,842km; 63,974km
Telecommunications – 31.08 million fixed lines and 893.862 million mobile subscriptions (2012); there were 61.338 million internet users in 2009
Internet code and IDD – in; 91 (from UK), 44 (to UK)
Major broadcasters – The public-owned Doordarshan network operates several national, regional and local services, and All India Radio is the country's largest radio broadcaster
Press – Eight major daily newspapers make up a lively press sector; these include *The Times of India, The Hindu* and *India Today*
WPFI score – 40,34 (140)

EDUCATION AND HEALTH
Education is free and became compulsory for children aged six to 14 years in April 2010.
Literacy rate – 62.8 per cent (2010 est)
Gross enrolment ratio (percentage of relevant age group) –
    primary 113 per cent; secondary 69 per cent (2011 est);
    tertiary 23 per cent (2011 est)
Health expenditure (per capita) – US$59 (2011)
Hospital beds (per 1,000 people) – 0.9 (2004–9)
Life expectancy (years) – 67.8 (2014 est)
Mortality rate – 7.35 (2014 est)
Birth rate – 19.89 (2014 est)
Infant mortality rate – 43.19 (2014 est)

INDONESIA

Republik Indonesia – Republic of Indonesia

Area – 1,904,569 sq. km

Capital – Jakarta; population, 9,400,428 (2012 est)

Major cities – Bandung, Bekasi, Depok, Makasar, Medan, Palembang, Semarang, Surabaya, Tangerang

Currency – Rupiah (Rp) of 100 sen

Population – 253,609,643 rising at 0.95 per cent a year (2014 est); Javanese (40.6 per cent), Sundanese (15 per cent), Madurese (3.3 per cent), Minangkabau (2.7 per cent), Betawi (2.4 per cent), Bugis (2.4 per cent), Banten (2 per cent), Banjar (1.7 per cent) (2000)

Religion – Muslim 87 per cent (predominantly Sunni), Christian 7 per cent, Hindu 2 per cent (est)

Language – Bahasa Indonesia (official), English, Dutch, Javanese, over 580 languages and dialects

Population density – 135 per sq. km (2011)

Urban population – 51.5 per cent (2012 est)

Median age (years) – 29.2 (2014 est)

National anthem – 'Indonesia Raya' ['Great Indonesia']

National day – 17 August (Independence Day)

Death penalty – Retained

CPI score – 32 (114)

Literacy rate – 93 per cent (2011 est)

Gross enrolment ratio (percentage of relevant age group) – primary 109 per cent; secondary 81 per cent; tertiary 27 per cent (2011 est)

Health expenditure (per capita) – US$95 (2011)

Life expectancy (years) – 72.17 (2014 est)

Mortality rate – 6.34 (2014 est)

Birth rate – 17.04 (2014 est)

Infant mortality rate – 25.16 (2014 est)

CLIMATE AND TERRAIN

Indonesia is an archipelago of over 17,500 islands, of which about 6,000 are inhabited. They include the islands of Sumatra, Java, Madura, Bali, Lombok, Sumbawa, Sumba, Flores, the Riouw-Lingga archipelago, Bangka and Billiton, part of the island of Borneo (Kalimantan), Sulawesi (formerly Celebes), the Maluku (formerly Moluccas) archipelago and others comprising the provinces of East and West Nusa Tenggara, and the western halves of the islands of New Guinea (Papua; formerly Irian Jaya) and Timor. Many of the islands have narrow coastal plains with hilly or mountainous interiors, and around half of the country is covered by tropical rainforest. Elevation extremes range from 4,884m (Puncak Jaya, in Papua) to 0m (Indian Ocean). The climate is tropical; the average temperature is 26.3°C and rainfall peaks in January and February, and is lowest in August.

The country is located near to an intersection of tectonic plates, making it susceptible to seismic activity such as earthquakes and volcanic eruptions; in January 2014 the eruption of Mt Kelud caused mass evacuations in East Java. Indonesia's weather patterns are being affected by climate change.

HISTORY AND POLITICS

Hindu and Buddhist kingdoms existed in some parts of the Indonesian islands until the 14th century. Islam was introduced in the 13th century and spread over the next three centuries. Trading by the Portuguese began in the 16th century, but the Portuguese were displaced by the Dutch who, lured by the rich spice trade, came to dominate Indonesia by the early 20th century. Opposition to Dutch rule grew in the 1920s and the Japanese occupation of Indonesia during the Second World War strengthened nationalism, leading to a declaration of independence after liberation in 1945. This was not recognised by the Dutch, but after four years of guerrilla warfare they granted independence to the Netherlands Indies in 1949. Irian Jaya (now Papua) was annexed in 1963. Timor–Leste was invaded and annexed in 1975 but gained its independence in 2002.

Achmed Soekarno, the foremost proponent of self-rule since the 1920s, became president in 1949 but was deposed in 1966 in a military coup suppressed by General Suharto, who subsequently became president. Suharto remained in power until 1998 when, amid economic and social upheaval, he was succeeded by his deputy B. J. Habibie. Habibie was defeated in 1999 by Abdurrahman Wahid, in the first democratic elections for 44 years. President Wahid was impeached for alleged financial corruption and in 2001 the legislature appointed Megawati Soekarnoputri (daughter of Achmed Soekarno) to replace him.

The April 2014 legislative elections were won by the ruling Democratic Party and the July 2014 presidential election by their candidate, Joko Widodo. The results were subsequently challenged by his opponent Prabowo Subianto who alleged that widespread electoral fraud had taken place. In August, the constitutional court rejected the claims, allowing Widodo to form a cabinet in October 2014.

The 1959 constitution was amended in 2001 to provide for the establishment of the upper chamber of the legislature, and in 2002 to provide for the direct election of the president and the abolition of parliamentary seats reserved for the armed forces.

The executive president is directly elected for a five-year term, renewable once, and appoints the cabinet. The bicameral People's Consultative Assembly comprises the House of Representatives, which has 560 members directly elected for a five-year term, and the House of Representatives of the Regions, which has 132 members, four for each province, directly elected on a non-partisan basis for a five-year term.

HEAD OF STATE
President elect, Joko Widodo, *elected* 22 July 2014

SELECTED GOVERNMENT MEMBERS *as at May 2014*
Defence, Purnomo Yusgiantoro
Finance, Muhammed Chatib Basri
Foreign Affairs, Marty Muliana Natalegawa

EMBASSY OF THE REPUBLIC OF INDONESIA
38 Grosvenor Square, London W1K 2HW
T 020-7499 7661 E kbri@btconnect.com
W www.gov.uk/government/world/indonesia
Ambassador Extraordinary and Plenipotentiary, HE Teuku Mohammad Hamzah Thayeb, *apptd* 2012

BRITISH EMBASSY
Jalan M. H. Thamrin 75, Jakarta 10310
T (+62) (21) 2356 5200 W http://ukinindonesia.fco.gov.uk
Ambassador Extraordinary and Plenipotentiary, HE Mark Canning, CMG, *apptd* 2011

INSURGENCIES
Separatist movements developed in several parts of Indonesia after independence, including Maluku, which fought an unsuccessful separatist war in the 1950s; Irian Jaya (now Papua), which was granted greater autonomy in 2002, although separatist agitation continues; Timor–Leste, from its annexation in 1975 until independence in 2002; and Aceh province in Sumatra, which was granted a degree of autonomy in 2005.

Since the fall of Suharto in 1998, tensions between different ethnic and religious groups have surfaced, and there has been intercommunal violence in Kalimantan (1996–7, 1999, 2001), Sulawesi (1998–2000, 2001, 2005) and Maluku (1999–2002, 2004).

At least two Muslim extremist groups are based in Indonesia and claim links with al-Qaida. They have been held responsible for bombings in Bali in 2002 and 2005, and Jakarta in 2003, 2004 and 2009.

DEFENCE

Aged 16–49, 2010 est	Males	Females
Available for military service	65,847,171	63,228,017
Fit for military service	54,264,299	53,274,361

Military expenditure – US$8,356m (2013)
Conscription – 18–45 years of age; 24 months (selective)

ECONOMY AND TRADE
The economy struggled from the late 1990s until recent years, hit in succession by the Asian financial crisis, the political turmoil following the fall of Suharto, a downturn in tourism following the Bali bombings and a number of natural disasters since 2004. President Yudhoyono's government introduced significant economic reforms which reduced debt, unemployment and inflation, and boosted growth in 2004–8. Although growth slowed in 2008, government stimulus measures countered the effect of the global downturn in 2009 and by 2011 Indonesia's credit rating was raised to investment grade due mainly to its low rates of inflation and small current account surplus. Poverty, poor infrastructure, corruption, a complex regulatory regime and inequitable resource distribution among Indonesia's regions continue to present problems.

Natural resources include oil, tin, natural gas, nickel, timber, bauxite, copper, coal, gold and silver. However, a lack of investment in prospecting for new sources has led to a decline in oil production and Indonesia has been a net importer since 2004. The exploitation and processing of mineral assets, production of textiles, clothing, cement, fertilisers, plywood and rubber, and tourism are the main industrial activities; industry accounts for 46.6 per cent of GDP and services 39.1 per cent, employing 22.2 per cent and 47.9 per cent of the workforce respectively. Agriculture contributes only 14.3 per cent of GDP but employs 38.9 per cent of the workforce. The main crops are rice, cassava, peanuts, rubber, cocoa, coffee, palm oil, copra and livestock products.

The main trading partners are Singapore, Japan, China, the USA, South Korea and other Pacific Rim nations. Principal exports are oil and natural gas, electrical appliances, plywood, textiles and rubber. The main imports are machinery and equipment, chemicals, fuel and foodstuffs.

GNI – US$852,561m; US$3,420 per capita (2012)
Annual average growth of GDP – 5.3 per cent (2013 est)
Inflation rate – 7.7 per cent (2013 est)
Population below poverty line – 12 per cent (2013)
Unemployment – 6.6 per cent (2013 est)
Total external debt – US$223,800m (2013 est)
Imports – US$190,992m (2012)
Exports – US$188,516m (2012)

BALANCE OF PAYMENTS
Trade – US$2,476m deficit (2012)
Current Account – US$24,074m decifit (2012)

Trade with UK	2012	2013
Imports from UK	£633,167,151	£692,488,946
Exports to UK	£1,232,595,862	£1,202,763,902

COMMUNICATIONS
Airports – 186; each of the main islands has a major airport, with most capable of accepting international flights
Waterways – There are nine major ports, usually the chief towns of the major islands, and the merchant fleet contains 1,340 ships of over 1,000 tonnes
Roadways and railways – 496,607km; 5,042km
Telecommunications – 38.62 million fixed lines and 249.8 million mobile subscriptions (2011); there were 20 million internet users in 2009
Internet code and IDD – id; 62 (from UK), 1 44/ 8 44 (to UK)
Major broadcasters – Radio and Televisi Republik Indonesia, the country's principal broadcaster, operates six television and two radio networks
Press – The Jakarta Post and The Jakarta Globe dominate a competitive market that includes eight other dailies
WPFI score – 38,15 (132)

IRAN

Jomhuri-ye Eslami-ye Iran – Islamic Republic of Iran

Area – 1,648,195 sq. km
Capital – Tehran; population, 7,368,347 (2012 est)
Major cities – Ahvaz, Esfahan, Karaj, Mashhad, Qom, Shiraz, Tabriz
Currency – Iranian rial of 100 dinar
Population – 80,840,713 rising at 1.22 per cent a year (2014 est); Persian (61 per cent), Azeri (16 per cent), , Kurdish (10 per cent), Lur (6 per cent), Arab (2 per cent), Baloch (2 per cent), Turkmen (2 per cent) (est)
Religion – Muslim (official) 99 per cent (Shia 90–95 per cent, Sunni 5–10 per cent) (est); small Zoroastrian, Jewish, Christian and Baha'i minorities
Language – Persian (official), Turkic, Kurdish, Luri, Balochi, Arabic, Turkish
Population density – 46 per sq. km (2011)
Urban population – 69.2 per cent (2012 est)
Median age (years) – 28.3 (2014 est)
National anthem – 'Sorud-e Melli-e Jomhouri-ye Eslami-ye Iran' ['Anthem of the Islamic Republic of Iran']
National day – 1 April (Republic Day)
Death penalty – Retained
CPI score – 25 (144)

CLIMATE AND TERRAIN

Apart from narrow coastal plains on the Gulf coasts and the shores of the Caspian Sea, the interior is a plateau consisting of barren desert in the centre and east. This is enclosed by high mountains in the west and north, with smaller ranges on the eastern border and the southern coast. Elevation extremes range from 5,671m (Kuh-e Damavand) to −28m (Caspian Sea). Earthquakes are frequent. The climate is arid or semi-arid in the interior, and subtropical on the Caspian shores. Average temperatures in Tehran are 1°C in January and 31°C in July.

POLITICS

Under the 1979 constitution, overall authority rests with the spiritual leader of the republic, who is appointed for life by the Assembly of Experts; this consists of 83 clerics who are directly elected and decide religious and spiritual matters.

The executive president is directly elected for a four-year term, renewable once. Ministers are nominated by the president but must be approved by the legislature. The unicameral Consultative Council *(Majlis al-Shoura)* has 290 members who are directly elected for a four-year term on a non-party basis; five seats are reserved for religious minorities. Laws passed by the legislature must be approved by the Council of Guardians of the Constitution, six theologians appointed by the spiritual leader and six jurists nominated by the judiciary and approved by the legislature; it also has a supervisory role in elections. In 1997, the Constitutional Surveillance Council, a five-member body, was established to supervise the proper application of constitutional laws.

Mahmoud Ahmadinejad won the presendential elections in 2005 and 2009. The results of the 2009 election were challenged by the other candidates, who alleged electoral fraud. Following massive protest rallies, the Council of Guardians confirmed Ahmadinejad's victory and ruled out an annulment; further popular protests were suppressed. After the protests in summer 2009, Ahmadinejad's government ruthlessly suppressed the opposition (the Green Movement) and purged liberals from official positions. Conservative candidates retained the majority of seats in the *Majlis* in the 2012 legislative election. In the 15 June 2013 presidential elections, moderate candidate Hassan Rouhani defeated the conservative mayor of Tehran Mohammed Baqer Qaliaf, gaining 50 per cent of the vote.

Spiritual Leader of the Islamic Republic and C.-in-C. of Armed Forces, Ayatollah Seyed Ali Khamenei, *appointed* June 1989
President, Hassan Rouhani, *elected* 15 June 2013
First Vice-President, Es'haq Jahangiri

SELECTED GOVERNMENT MEMBERS *as at April 2014*
Defence, Hossein Dehqan
Economic Affairs and Finance, Ali Tayebnia
Foreign Affairs, Mohammad Javad Zarif

EMBASSY OF THE ISLAMIC REPUBLIC OF IRAN
16 Prince's Gate, London SW7 1PT
T 020-7225 3000 W london.mfa.ir
Ambassador Extraordinary and Plenipotentiary, vacant

BRITISH EMBASSY
The Swedish Embassy and embassies of EU countries offer limited consular assistance to British citizens; Swedish Embassy, 27 Nastaran Street, Boostan Avenue, Tehran
T (+98) (21) 2371 2200
E ambassaden.teheran@foreign.ministry.se

FOREIGN RELATIONS
Between 1980 and 1988, Iran was engaged in a bitter war with Iraq over the Shatt-al-Arab waterway. Iran remained neutral in the Gulf War (1991) and the Iraq War (2003), but it has been accused since of subverting reconstruction in Iraq by arming Shia insurgents.

Since the 1978 revolution, Iran's relations with the West, and especially the USA and the UK, have been strained. It has not cooperated with international efforts to achieve peace in the Middle East, and has long been suspected of sponsoring terrorism by Islamic fundamentalists, especially in Lebanon and Palestine, and now is believed to be supplying arms to the Taliban.

Since 2002 international relations have deteriorated further because of concerns over Iran's nuclear and ballistic missile programmes, especially its acquisition of the ability to enrich uranium. Iran insists that this is for power generation and is not a precursor to developing nuclear weapons, but refuses to halt the programme or cooperate with the International Atomic Energy Agency. The UN has passed six resolutions since 2006 calling on Iran to suspend uranium enrichment and reprocessing and to comply with its IAEA obligations and responsibilities; four of the resolutions imposed or extended sanctions on trade and travel. In an escalation of the nuclear row, the EU imposed an oil embargo on Iran in January 2012, after the country reportedly began to enrich uranium at its underground plant in Fordo. Following an attack on the British embassy in November 2011, economic sanctions were strengthened, and Britain closed its embassy in Tehran and expelled all Iranian diplomats from London. President Rouhani's election was expected to improve Iran's relations with the West following the tension characterised by the previous regime.

DEFENCE

Aged 16–49, 2010 est	Males	Females
Available for military service	23,619,215	22,628,341
Fit for military service	20,149,222	19,417,275

Military expenditure – US$9,573m (2012)*
Conscription – 18 years of age, male only; 18 months

* Figure does not include paramilitary spending

ECONOMY AND TRADE
Iran was one of the best-performing economies in the Middle East owing to its vast reserves of oil and natural gas, but its performance has been deteriorating; the predominantly state-controlled economy is inefficient, with little diversification and only a limited, small-scale private sector. Unemployment and underemployment are serious problems, and there is a flourishing unofficial economy. Falling oil prices in 2008–10 and UN sanctions since 2008 have exacerbated Iran's economic problems; international sanctions in January 2013 caused a substantial reduction in Iran's oil revenue and depreciated the currency by 20 per cent. The election of the reformer Hassan Ruhani has coincided with a strengthened national currency and an increase in the value of the Tehran stock exchange.

Oil and gas extraction and processing dominate the economy, but other industries include petrochemicals, textiles, construction materials, food processing, metal fabrication and armaments. Agricultural production includes wheat, rice, other grains, sugar beet and sugar cane, fruit, nuts, cotton, dairy products, wool and caviar.

The main trading partners are China, the UAE, Turkey, South Korea and Japan. Principal exports are petroleum (80 per cent), chemical and petrochemical products, fruit and nuts, and carpets. The main imports are industrial raw materials and intermediate goods, capital goods, foodstuffs, consumer goods and technical services.

GNI – US$328,593m; US$4,520 per capita (2009)
Annual average growth of GDP – –1.5 per cent (2013 est)
Inflation rate – 42.3 per cent (2013 est)

Population below poverty line – 18.7 per cent (2007 est)
Unemployment – 16 per cent (2013 government est)
Total external debt – US$15,640m (2013 est)
Imports – US$56,500m (2012)
Exports – US$955,500m (2012)

BALANCE OF PAYMENTS
Trade – US$39,000m surplus (2012)
Current Account – US$59,382m surplus (2012)

Trade with UK	2012	2013
Imports from UK	£100,335,806	£79,691,990
Exports to UK	£116,747,364	£31,911,854

COMMUNICATIONS
Airports and waterways – 140, the principal airports are at Tehran and Shiraz; Iran's seaports include Asaluyeh, Bushehr and Abadan on the Persian Gulf and Bandar Abbas on the Strait of Hormuz
Roadways and railways – There are 198,866 km of roadways, including 1,948km of motorways, and 8,442km of railways
Telecommunications – 28.76 million fixed lines and 58.16 million mobile subscriptions (2012); there were 8.214 million internet users in 2009
Internet code and IDD – ir; 98 (from UK), 44 (to UK)
Major broadcasters – The state-run IRIB network operates national and international networks in an industry dominated by satellite channels
Press – Major newspapers include the English-language daily *Tehran Times* and the conservative daily *Kayhan*
WPFI score – 72,29 (173)

EDUCATION AND HEALTH
Primary education, between age six and 14, is compulsory and free.
Literacy rate – 85 per cent (2010 est)
Gross enrolment ratio (percentage of relevant age group) – primary 106 per cent; secondary 84 per cent (2011 est); tertiary 49 per cent (2011 est)
Health expenditure (per capita) – US$346 (2011)
Hospital beds (per 1,000 people) – 1.7 (2009)
Life expectancy (years) – 70.89 (2014 est)
Mortality rate – 5.94 (2014 est)
Birth rate – 18.23 (2014 est)
Infant mortality rate – 39 (2014 est)

IRAQ

Jumhuriyat al-Iraq – Republic of Iraq

Area – 438,317 sq. km
Capital – Baghdad; population, 6,175,540 (2012 est)
Major cities – Arbil, Basra, Kirkuk, Mosul, Najaf, Sulaymaniyah

Currency – Iraqi dinar (NID) of 1,000 fils
Population – 32,585,692 rising at 2.23 per cent a year
(2014 est); Arab (75–80 per cent), Kurdish (15–20 per
cent) (est)
Religion – Muslim (official) 97 per cent (of which Shia
60–65 per cent, Sunni 32–37 per cent), Christian 0.8 per
cent (predominantly Chaldean Catholic) (est)
Language – Arabic (official), Kurdish (official in Kurdish
Autonomous Region), Turkoman, Assyrian, Armenian
Population density – 73 per sq. km (2011 est)
Urban population – 66.4 per cent (2012 est)
Median age (years) – 21.5 (2014 est)
National anthem – 'Mawtini' ['My Homeland']
National day – 14 July (Republic Day)
Death penalty – Retained
CPI score – 16 (171)

CLIMATE AND TERRAIN
The north-west and south of Iraq consist of an almost barren
desert plain. The area between the Euphrates and Tigris
rivers, which run across the country from north-west to
south-east, is fertile, irrigated and heavily cultivated. The
rivers run through marshland to their outflow in the Persian
Gulf, on which Iraq has a 58km coastline. In the north-east
the land rises to the Kurdistan mountains. Elevation extremes
range from 3,611m to 0m (Persian Gulf). The climate is
mostly desert, though colder and wetter in the mountains.
Average temperatures in Baghdad range from 8°C in January
to 34°C in July.

POLITICS
Under the 2005 constitution, the president is elected by
the legislature for a four-year term, renewable once. The
president nominates the prime minister, subject to the
approval of the legislature. The unicameral Council of
Representatives (Majlis al-Nuwab) has 325 members, of
whom 82 must be women and 15 from minorities; members
are directly elected for a four-year term.

In the March 2010 legislative elections, the Iraqi National
Movement (al-Iraqiya) bloc led by former prime minister
Iyad Allawi won the most seats. After several months of
negotiations, the al-Iraqiya, SL and Kurdistan Alliance (KA)
blocs agreed to form a coalition government under Nouri
al-Maliki, and this was sworn in on 21 December. Jalal
Talabani, the Kurdish president of the interim government
in 2005 and re-elected to the office in 2006, was re-elected
for a second term in November 2010. In the April 2014
legislative elections al-Malili's coalition remained the largest
political grouping and Fouad Moussoum was elected
president in July. However, the military victories of the
Islamic State in the north of the country (see Events) resulted
in al-Maliki's resignation as prime minister on 14 August in
favour of Haider al-Abadi. On 8 September, an inclusive
unitary government was formed with the aim of tackling the
threat of IS (see Events).

HEAD OF STATE
President, Fouad Massoum, elected 24 July 2014
Vice-Presidents, Ivad Allawi; Nouri Al-Maliki; Osamu Al-
Nujaifi

SELECTED GOVERNMENT MEMBERS as at August 2014
Prime Minister, Haider al-Abadi
Finance, Roj Shawis
Foreign Affairs, Ibrahim Al-Jaafari

EMBASSY OF THE REPUBLIC OF IRAQ
3 Elvaston Place, London SW7 5QH
T 020-7594 0180 W www.iraqembassy.org.uk
Ambassador Extraordinary and Plenipotentiary, HE Faik Ferik
Abdileziz Nerweyi, apptd 2013

BRITISH EMBASSY
International Zone, Baghdad
T (+964) 790 192 6280 E baghdad.consularenquiries@fco.gov.uk
W www.gov.uk/government/world/iraq
Ambassador Extraordinary and Plenipotentiary, HE Simon
Collis, apptd 2012

INTERNAL UNREST
There are about 4 million Kurds in north-east Iraq, in
areas adjoining the predominantly Kurdish areas in Iran
and Turkey. Iraq's Kurdish nationalists have demanded an
autonomous homeland, Kurdistan, since the 1960s, and
turned to militant tactics in the 1970s. Their demands were
opposed by Saddam Hussein's regime with great brutality.
An uprising after the Gulf War (1991) was suppressed by
Iraqi troops, prompting the creation of UN safe havens which
enabled the Kurds to set up a semi-autonomous region in the
north. An air exclusion zone was also established, but there
was further conflict with Iraqi forces and between the two
main Kurdish parties in the 1990s. During the war in 2003,
Kurdish fighters fought alongside US troops in the north,
taking control of the northern cities and establishing an
administration in the area, which is now autonomous. The
boundary of the autonomous area has yet to be defined,
and its precise location will decide control of Kirkuk and
of oilfields in the region; this issue is the cause of tension
between the central and regional governments, and of some
intercommunal violence between Arabs and Kurds in the
area.

The Shias in southern Iraq also rebelled after the Gulf
War and were brutally suppressed. The UN established an air
exclusion zone over southern Iraq in 1992 to protect the
population, but persecution continued until 2003.

After May 2003, there was insurgent activity throughout
the country, particularly in the Baghdad area, the predominantly Sunni-populated towns in the centre and west
of the country, and in and around Mosul. Initially the targets
were foreign troops, Iraqi military and police, and foreign aid
and reconstruction workers, but from early 2005 the attacks
became increasingly sectarian in nature. The level of violence
has dropped since 2007 because of the US military 'surge', a
ceasefire by one of the main militias, the Mahdi Army, from
August 2007, and a key Sunni militia, the Awakening
movement, turning against al-Qaida. There was an upsurge
of violence in 2008 as the government mounted offensives
against militias in Basra, Mosul and parts of Baghdad, and
another upsurge in 2009–10 in the run-up to the legislative

election and in the months following its inconclusive result. The approximate number of deaths as at December 2010 was: Iraqi civilians 99,000–108,000; US troops 4,400; and other coalition troops 318. Sectarian violence has continued following the withdrawal of coalition troops; in 2012 Shia areas were targeted with numerous bomb and gun attacks. In 2013 a series of deadly bomb attacks marked the ten-year anniversary of the US-led invasion.

DEFENCE

Aged 16–49, 2010 est	Males	Females
Available for military service	7,767,329	7,461,766
Fit for military service	6,591,185	6,421,717

Military expenditure – US$7,251m (2013)

ECONOMY AND TRADE

The economy suffered three decades of state intervention, mismanagement, corruption, militarisation, war and international sanctions as well as the looting, insurgency and sabotage that followed the 2003 Allied invasion. With the improvement in the security situation, economic activity has increased, the institutions required to implement economic policy are being put in place and a debt reduction programme has been arranged. However, regulatory restrictions, inadequate infrastructure and corruption hamper economic development, and unemployment remains high (16 per cent).

Oil is the main resource and export, and production has returned to pre-2003 levels, providing more than 80 per cent of foreign exchange earnings. In 2012 oil exports hit a 30-year high, reaching 2.6 million barrels per day Other industries include chemicals, textiles, construction materials, food processing and metal fabrication.

The main trading partners are Turkey (25.3 per cent of imports), India (22.5 per cent of exports), China and Syria. Principal exports are crude oil (84 per cent), other crude materials, food and livestock. The main imports are food, medicine and manufactured goods.

GNI – US$213,115m; US$5,870 per capita (2012)
Annual average growth of GDP – 3.7 per cent (2013 est)
Inflation rate – 2 per cent (2013 est)
Population below poverty line – 25 per cent (2008 est)
Total external debt – US$59,490m (2013 est)

BALANCE OF PAYMENTS
Trade – US$19,077m surplus (2010)
Current Account – US$14,890m surplus (2012 est)

Trade with UK	2012	2013
Imports from UK	£285,016,506	£407,091,596
Exports to UK	£2,938,758	£4,091,504

COMMUNICATIONS

Airports and waterways – 72, the main international airport is at Baghdad; the 5,279km of waterways are primarily on the Tigris and Euphrates rivers
Roadways and railways – 59,623km; 2,370 km
Telecommunications – 1.87 million fixed lines and 26.76 million mobile subscriptions (2012); there were 325,900 internet users in 2009
Internet code and IDD – iq; 964 (from UK), 44 (to UK)
Major broadcasters – State-run services include Al-Iraqiya (TV) and Republic of Iraq Radio; there are several private radio and television broadasters
Press – There are more than 100 newspapers and periodicals,

many with an ethnic or religious affiliation; publications include the state-run *Al-Sabah* and private *Al-Mada*
WPFI score – 45,44 (153)

EDUCATION AND HEALTH

Since 2003 the country's education system has been reviewed and over 2,500 schools have been refurbished. Primary education is compulsory.
Literacy rate – 78 per cent (2011 est)
Health expenditure (per capita) – US$332 (2011)
Hospital beds (per 1,000 people) – 1.3 (2010)
Life expectancy (years) – 71.42 (2014 est)
Mortality rate – 4.57 (2014 est)
Birth rate – 26.85 (2014 est)
Infant mortality rate – 37.53 (2014 est)

IRELAND

Eire – Ireland

Area – 70,273 sq. km
Capital – Dublin *(Baile Atha Cliath)*; population, 1,130,186 (2012 est)
Major cities – Cork (Corcaigh), Galway (Gaillimh), Limerick (Liumneach), Swords (Sord Cholm Cille), Waterford (Port Lairge)
Currency – Euro (€) of 100 cents
Population – 4,832,765 rising at 1.2 per cent a year (2014 est)
Religion – Christian (Roman Catholic 84 per cent, Anglican 3 per cent), Muslim 1 per cent (est)
Language – English, Irish (Gaelic) (both official)
Population density – 66 per sq. km (2011)
Urban population – 62.5 per cent (2012 est)
Median age (years) – 35.7 (2014 est)
National anthem – 'Amhran na bhFiann' ['The Soldier's Song']
National day – 17 March (St Patrick's Day)
Death penalty – Abolished for all crimes (since 1990)
CPI score – 72 (21)

CLIMATE AND TERRAIN

The greatest length of the island of Ireland is 486km, from Torr Head in the north-east to Mizen Head in the south-west, and the greatest breadth is 280km, from Dundrum Bay in the east to Annagh Head in the west. Northern Ireland, in the north-east, is part of the UK. The republic has a central plain broken by hills and numerous lakes and bogs. It is surrounded by low mountains, including the Wicklow, Knockmealdown, Galty and Boggeragh mountains, and drained by the principal river, the Shannon (386km), which flows into the Atlantic Ocean. On the north coast of Achill Island (Co. Mayo) are the highest cliffs in the British Isles, 609m above sea level. Elevation extremes range from 1,041m (Carrauntoohil, Co. Kerry) to 0m (Irish Sea).

Introduction of Christianity — c.300
c.800–900 — Henry II of England declares himself Lord of Ireland
Widespread support for the royalists in the English Civil War prompts Oliver Cromwell to invade — c.1500-1600
1690
Irish nationalists gain a majority in parliament and declare independence — 1800
Irish Free State declares independence — 1919–23
Ireland becomes a republic — 1993
Good Friday agreement — 1999

c.400 — Settled by the Celts
1171 — Viking raiders establish settlements
1650 — Henry VIII declared King of Ireland. The Plantation of Ulster begins.
Battle of the Boyne
1918 — Abolition of the Irish parliament; Act of the Union unites Ireland and Britain
1937 — Anglo-Irish War concludes in Irish Free State Treaty; opposition leads to civil war
1948 — Downing Street declaration
1998 — Joins the eurozone

POLITICS

Under the 1937 constitution, the president *(Uachtaran na Eireann)* is directly elected for a seven-year term, renewable once. The bicameral National Parliament *(Oireachtas)* consists of the House of Representatives *(Dail Eireann)* and the senate *(Seanad Eireann)*. The *Dail* has 166 members, elected for a five-year term by proportional representation. The *Seanad* has 60 members, who serve a five-year term; of these, 11 are nominated by the prime minister *(Taoiseach)* and 49 are elected, six by the universities and 43 from panels of candidates representing various sectoral interests.

The *Taoiseach* is appointed by the president on the nomination of the *Dail,* while other members of the government are appointed by the president on the nomination of the *Taoiseach* with the previous approval of the *Dail.* The *Taoiseach* appoints a member of the government to be the deputy prime minister *(Tanaiste).*

The 1997 presidential election was won by Mary McAleese, and she was confirmed in office unopposed in 2004. The coalition government of the Fianna Fail, Progressive Democrats and Green Party lost the early election called in February 2011 because of the country's economic crisis. The opposition Fine Gail (FG) won the most seats but without a majority, and formed a coalition government with the Labour Party; the FG leader Enda Kenny was elected prime minister. Labour Party candidate Michael D. Higgins won the 2011 presidential election, picking up over half of the total vote.

HEAD OF STATE

President, Michael D. Higgins, *elected* 27 October 2011, *confirmed in office* 11 November 2011

SELECTED GOVERNMENT MEMBERS *as at May 2014*
Taoiseach (Prime Minister), Enda Kenny
Tanaiste (Deputy PM), Foreign Affairs, Charles Flanagan
Defence, Paul Kehoe
Finance, Michael Noonan

EMBASSY OF IRELAND
17 Grosvenor Place, London SW1X 7HR
T 020-7235 2171 W www.embassyofireland.co.uk
Ambassador Extraordinary and Plenipotentiary, HE Daniel Mulhall, *apptd* 2013

BRITISH EMBASSY
29 Merrion Road, Ballsbridge, Dublin 4
T (+353) (1) 205 3700 W www.gov.uk/government/world/ireland
Ambassador Extraordinary and Plenipotentiary, HE Dominick Chilcott, CMG, *apptd* 2012

DEFENCE

Aged 16–49, 2010 est	Males	Females
Available for military service	1,179,125	1,163,728
Fit for military service	977,631	965,900

Military expenditure – US$1,220m (2013)

ECONOMY AND TRADE

Since the 1980s Ireland's economy has been transformed from a mainly agricultural to a modern, export-led economy that experienced strong growth from the mid-1990s. But an over-inflated property sector and high levels of personal debt left the economy exposed in the 2008 global financial crisis, causing it to go into a deep recession which put severe pressure on the financial system and government finances. Stabilisation of the financial system pushed the budget deficit to nearly 32 per cent of GDP in 2010, despite austerity budgets in 2009 and 2010, and in November 2010 the government agreed loan packages with the IMF and EU to avoid defaulting on its sovereign debt. Since Enda Kenny took office in March 2011, austerity measures have increased in order to reach Ireland's EU-IMF deficit targets; Ireland achieved growth of 1.4 per cent in 2011 and in 2012 the budget deficit was cut to 8.5 per cent of GDP. Towards the end of 2013, Ireland exited its EU-IMF bailout program after meeting deficit reduction targets and reducing banking debt.

Agriculture now accounts for 1.6 per cent of GDP and 5 per cent of employment; services contribute 70.4 per cent and industry 28 per cent of GDP, and the sectors account for 76 per cent and 19 per cent of employment respectively. Major industries include mining, pharmaceuticals, chemicals, computer hardware and software, food and drink production, and tourism. Although the Kinsale gas field off the south coast meets some of Ireland's gas needs, and hydroelectric power is generated from the Shannon barrage and other schemes, the country is a net importer of energy.

The main trading partners are the UK, other EU countries and the USA. Principal exports are machinery, computers, chemicals, pharmaceuticals, livestock and livestock products. The main imports are data processing equipment, other machinery, chemicals, petroleum and petroleum products, textiles and clothing.

GNI – US$172,106m; US$39,110 per capita (2012)
Annual average growth of GDP – 0.6 per cent (2013 est)
Inflation rate – 0.6 per cent (2013 est)
Population below poverty line – 5.5 per cent (2009 est)
Unemployment – 13.5 per cent (2013 est)
Total external debt – US$2,164,000m (2012)
Imports – US$63,228m (2012)
Exports – US$117,770m (2012)

BALANCE OF PAYMENTS
Trade – US$54,542m surplus (2012)
Current Account – US$9,325m surplus (2012)

Trade with UK	2012	2013
Imports from UK	£16,894,272,940	£12,751,935,568
Exports to UK	£18,112,696,605	£11,907,153,947

COMMUNICATIONS

Airports – The principal airport is at Dublin, with others at Shannon, Waterford, Cork, Killarney, Galway and Knock
Waterways – There are 956km of waterways, although these are used only by leisure craft; the main ports are Cork, Dun Laoghaire, Galway, Limerick and Waterford

Roadways and railways – 96,036km; 3,237km
Telecommunications – 2.007 million fixed lines and 4.906 million mobile subscriptions (2012); there were 3.04 million internet users in 2009
Internet code and IDD – ie; 353 (from UK), 44 or 048 for Northern Ireland (to UK)
Major broadcasters – The main radio and television broadcaster is the state-run Raidio Telefís Eireann (RTE), whose competitors include a handful of Irish commercial stations and British terrestrial and satellite services
Press – There are three national newspapers: the *Irish Times, Irish Independent* and *Irish Examiner*
WPFI score – 10,87 (16)

EDUCATION AND HEALTH

Primary education is directed by the state and education is compulsory until age 16.
Gross enrolment ratio (percentage of relevant age group) – primary 105 per cent; secondary 118 per cent; tertiary 73 per cent (2011 est)
Health expenditure (per capita) – US$4,542 (2011)
Hospital beds (per 1,000 people) – 3.2 (2010)
Life expectancy (years) – 80.56 (2014 est)
Mortality rate – 6.45 (2014 est)
Birth rate – 15.18 (2014 est)
Infant mortality rate – 3.74 (2014 est)

ISRAEL AND PALESTINIAN TERRITORIES

Medinat Yisra'el / Dawlat Isra'il – State of Israel

Area – 20,770 sq. km (includes Jerusalem and the Golan Heights)
Capital – The legislature and most government departments are in Jerusalem; population 768,000 (2009). A resolution proclaiming Jerusalem as the capital of Israel was adopted by the *Knesset* in 1950. It is not, however, recognised as the capital by the UN because East Jerusalem is part of the Occupied Territories captured in 1967; the UN and international law consider Tel Aviv (population, 3.22 million) to be the capital
Major cities – Haifa, Rishon Le'Zion
Currency – New Israeli Shekel (NIS) of 100 agora

Population – 7,821,850 rising at 1.46 per cent a year (2014 est); includes about 531,129 (est) settlers in the occupied areas. Since independence, Israel has had a policy of granting an immigration visa to every Jew who expresses a desire to settle in the country; between 1948 and 2009, over 3 million immigrants entered Israel from over 100 different countries
Religion – Jewish 75 per cent, Muslim 17 per cent (predominantly Sunni, Druze 2 per cent), Christian 2 per cent (predominantly Eastern Orthodox) (est)
Language – Hebrew, Arabic (both official), English
Population density – 359 per sq. km (2011)
Urban population – 91.9 per cent (2012 est)
Median age (years) – 29.9 (2014 est)
National anthem – 'Hatikvah' ['The Hope']
National day – Fifth day of Jewish month of Iyar (anniversary of Independence Day, 1948)
Death penalty – Retained for certain crimes (last used 1962)
CPI score – 61 (36)

CLIMATE AND TERRAIN

Israel comprises the partly forested hill country of Galilee and parts of Judea and Samaria, the coastal plain from the Gaza Strip to north of Acre (including the plain of Esdraelon running from Haifa Bay to the south-east); the Negev, a triangular rocky desert in the south; and parts of the Jordan valley, including the Hula region, Lake Tiberias and the south-western part of the Dead Sea. Elevation extremes range from 1,208m (Har Meron) to −408m (Dead Sea), which is the Earth's deepest depression. The climate is temperate, with hotter, drier conditions in the south and east. Average temperatures range from 11.2°C in January to 26.5°C in August.

POLITICS

Israel has no written constitution; most constitutional provision is set out in the basic law on government. The head of state is the president, elected by the legislature for a seven-year term, which is not renewable. The unicameral *Knesset* has 120 members elected by proportional representation for a four-year term. The prime minister is responsible to the *Knesset,* and appoints the cabinet, subject to the approval of the *Knesset.*
In the January 2013 parliamentary elections the Likud party won 31 seats and prime minister Benjamin Netanyahu formed a coalition government with centre party Yesh Atid (19 seats) as a main coalition partner, as well as the Jewish Home (12 seats) and Hatnuah (6 seats) parties. The 2014 Presidential election was won by Reuven Rivlin.

HEAD OF STATE
President, Reuven Rivlin, *elected* 10 June, *sworn in* 27 July 2014

SELECTED GOVERNMENT MEMBERS *as at May 2014*
Prime Minister, Benjamin Netanyahu
Defence, Moshe Ya'alon
Finance, Yair Lapid
Interior, Gideon Sa'ar

EMBASSY OF ISRAEL
2 Palace Green, London W8 4QB
T 020-7957 9500 E info@london.mfa.gov.il
W http://london.mfa.gov.il
Ambassador Extraordinary and Plenipotentiary, HE Daniel
Taub, *apptd* 2011

BRITISH EMBASSY
192 Hayarkon Street, Tel Aviv 6340502
T (+972) (3) 725 1222 E webmaster.telaviv@fco.gov.uk
W www.gov.uk/government/world/israel
Ambassador Extraordinary and Plenipotentiary, HE Matthew
Gould, MBE, *apptd* 2010

DEFENCE

Aged 16–49, 2010 est	Males	Females
Available for military service	1,797,960	1,713,230
Fit for military service	1,517,510	1,446,132

Military expenditure – US$16,019 (2013 est)
Conscription – 18 years of age (Jews and Druze only;
Christians, Circassians and Muslims may volunteer);
21–48 months

ECONOMY AND TRADE
Israel has a technically advanced market economy, having
developed its agriculture and industry intensively since the
1970s despite limited natural resources. After a short
recession in the early 2000s, structural reforms and tighter
fiscal control were implemented, resulting in steady growth
from 2003 to 2007, increased foreign investment and a
rising demand for exports. Despite the high level of external
debt, the economy proved resilient in the global downturn,
although it contracted slightly in 2008–9. Its debt and
deficits are covered by foreign aid and loans; the USA is the
main source of economic and military aid and is Israel's main
creditor, owed about half of its external debt. Israel's income
inequality and poverty rates are among the highest of any
developed nation.

Israel has developed a strong technology sector, central
to which are the aviation, electronics, biotechnology,
communications and software industries. Other important
industries include timber and paper, mineral and metal
products, cement, chemicals, plastics, textiles, diamond
cutting and tourism, which is reviving. The country is also an
important producer of citrus fruits, vegetables, cotton, beef,
poultry and dairy products. Service industries account for
66.4 per cent of GDP, industry for 31.2 per cent and
agriculture for 2.5 per cent.

The main trading partners are the USA (28.8 per cent of
exports), Hong Kong, EU states and China. Principal exports
are high-technology machinery and equipment, software,
cut diamonds, agricultural products, chemicals, textiles
and clothing. The main imports are raw materials, military
equipment, investment goods, rough diamonds, fuels, grain
and consumer goods.
GNI – US$236,682m; US$28,380 per capita (2011)
Annual average growth of GDP – 3.8 per cent (2013 est)
Inflation rate – 1.7 per cent (2013 est)

Population below poverty line – 21 per cent (2012)
Unemployment – 6.8 per cent (2013 est)
Total external debt – US$96,300m (2013)
Imports – US$75,392m (2012)
Exports – US$63,191m (2012)

BALANCE OF PAYMENTS
Trade – US$12,201m deficit (2012)
Current Account – US$850m surplus (2012)

Trade with UK	2012	2013
Imports from UK	£1,489,671,206	£1,381,374,511
Exports to UK	£2,329,946,558	£1,870,651,181

COMMUNICATIONS
Airports and waterways – 28, with the chief international
airport Ben Gurion, between Tel Aviv and Jerusalem; the
chief seaports are Haifa and Ashdod on the Mediterranean,
and Eilat on the Red Sea
Roadways and railways – There are 18,566km of roadways,
including 449km of motorway, and Israel State Railways
operates a network of 975km
Telecommunications – 3.594 million fixed lines and 9.225
million mobile subscriptions (2012); there were 4.525
million internet users in 2009
Internet code and IDD – il; 972 (from UK),
44/012/013/014 (to UK)
Major broadcasters – The Israel Broadcasting Authority
operates public television and radio services across the
country
Press – There are five main daily newspapers, including *Yediot
Aharonot, Ha'aretz* and *Jerusalem Post*
WPFI score – 31,19 (96)

EDUCATION AND HEALTH
Education is compulsory between the ages of five and 16 and
is free.
Gross enrolment ratio (percentage of relevant age group) –
primary 104 per cent; secondary 102 per cent; tertiary
62 per cent (2011 est)
Health expenditure (per capita) – US$2,426 (2011)
Hospital beds (per 1,000 people) – 3.4 (2011)
Life expectancy (years) – 81.28 (2014 est)
Mortality rate – 5.54 (2014 est)
Birth rate – 18.44 (2014 est)
Infant mortality rate – 3.98 (2014 est)

PALESTINIAN AUTONOMOUS AREAS

Area – The total area is 6,231 sq. km. The area which is fully
autonomous is 412 sq. km, of which the Gaza Strip is 360
sq. km and the Jericho enclave 60 sq. km
Capital – Although Palestinians claim East Jerusalem as their
capital, the administrative capital was established in 1994
in Gaza City; population, 479,400 (2005 est); since 2007
the president and transitional government have been
located in Ramallah, on the West Bank; population,
69,479 (2009 est)

Frustration at occupation leads to popular uprising	Creation of the Palestinian National Authority (PNA)	Oslo Accords talks break down; second uprising begins	Death of PNA president Yasser Arafat; talks with Israel resume but are hindered by violence of Palestinian extremists	Victory in the legislative election for the anti-Israeli party Hamas	Confrontation leads to military invasion from Israel
1967	1993	1995	2003	2005	2007
1987	1994	2000-2	2004	2006	2008-9
Gaza Strip and West Bank under Israeli occupation	Signing of Oslo Accords	Six West Bank towns and Hebron returned to PNA	UN 'road map' peace plan proposed	Establishment of autonomous Palestinian state; presidential election won by Fatah candidate Mahmoud Abbas	Conflict between Hamas and Fatah movements; Abbas declares state of emergency and dissolves government

Major towns – Jabalia, Khan Yunis, Rafah in the Gaza Strip; Hebron, Jericho, Nablus and Ramallah on the West Bank
Population – 4,4,000 (2010)
Religion – Muslim 98 per cent (Sunni); small Jewish and Christian minorities (est)
Flag – Three horizontal stripes of black, white, green with a red triangle based on the hoist (the PLO flag)
National anthem – 'Fidai, Fidai' ['Freedom Fighter, Freedom Fighter']
Death penalty – Retained
Literacy rate – 94.9 per cent (2010 est)

POLITICS

The Interim Agreement of 1995 invested the Palestinian Authority with executive, legislative and judicial authority, but not sovereignty, in the autonomous areas.

The executive president is directly elected for a five-year term. The unicameral Palestinian Legislative Council *(Majlis al-Tashri'i)* has one seat reserved for the president and 132 seats for members elected from party lists for a five-year term. The president appoints the prime minister, who appoints the council of ministers, which must be approved by the legislature. In August 2013 Rami Hamdallah was appointed prime minister having served briefly in office in June 2013.

SELECTED GOVERNMENT MEMBERS *as at May 2014*
President, Mahmoud Abbas, *elected* 9 January 2005
Prime Minister, Rami Hamdallah
Foreign Affairs, Riyad Najib Abd-al-Rahman al-Maliki
Interior, Sa'id Abu Ali

PALESTINIAN GENERAL DELEGATION
5 Galena Road, London W6 0LT
T 020-8563 0008 W www.palestinianmissionuk.com
General Delegate, Prof. Manuel Hassassian

BRITISH CONSULATE-GENERAL
PO Box 19690, 19 Nashashibi Street, Sheikh Jarrah Quarter, East Jerusalem 97200
T (+972) (2) 541 4100 W www.gov.uk/government/world/the-occupied-palestinian-territories
Consul-General, Alastair McPhail, CMG OBE, *apptd* 2014

ECONOMY AND TRADE

The *intifada,* and Israeli security restrictions in response to it, have damaged infrastructure and severely constrained economic activity in the Palestinian areas and external trade since 2000. Incomes had dropped and poverty risen sharply even before 2006, when the policies of the new Hamas government led to an embargo by international funding providers, and Israel stopped remitting customs dues collected on behalf of the Palestinian Authority. Emergency aid, provided through channels that bypass the Hamas government, was resumed in late 2006. The effects were and remain most severe in Gaza, where the population is dependent on food aid. On the West Bank, some Israeli restrictions have been eased since 2007, and the president's economic and structural reforms since 2008, underpinned by foreign aid donors, have stimulated economic development.

Most economic activity consists of small family businesses engaged in farming, quarrying and small-scale manufacturing of construction materials and textiles, metal goods, handicrafts and agricultural processing. The main exports are stone, fruit, olives, vegetables and flowers, and the main trading partners are Israel, Jordan and Egypt.
Inflation rate – 3.5 per cent (2012 est)

Population below poverty line – West Bank 18.3 per cent (2010 est); Gaza Strip 38 per cent (2010 est)
Imports – US$4,492m (2011)
Exports – US$759m (2011)

BALANCE OF PAYMENTS
Trade – US$3,733m deficit (2011)

Trade with UK	2012	2013
Imports from UK	£1,489,671,206	£1,381,374,511
Exports to UK	£2,329,946,558	£1,870,651,181

ITALY

Repubblica Italiana – Italian Republic

Area – 301,340 sq. km
Capital – Rome; population, 3,370,705 (2012 est)
Major cities – Bari, Bologna, Florence, Genoa, Milan, Naples, Turin, Venice, Verona. The chief towns of Sicily and Sardinia are Palermo and Cagliari respectively
Currency – Euro (€) of 100 cents
Population – 61,680,122 rising at 0.3 per cent a year (2014 est)
Religion – Christian (Roman Catholic 80 per cent) (est); unaffiliated 20 per cent
Language – Italian (official), German, French, Slovene
Population density – 206 per sq. km (2011)
Urban population – 68.5 per cent (2012)
Median age (years) – 44.5 (2014 est)
National anthem – 'Il Canto degli Italiani' ['The Song of the Italians']
National day – 2 June (Republic Day)
Death penalty – Abolished for all crimes (since 1994)
CPI score – 43 (69)

CLIMATE AND TERRAIN

Italy consists of a peninsula, the islands of Sicily, Sardinia, Elba and about 70 smaller islands. The smaller islands include Pantelleria, the Pelagian islands, the Aeolian islands, Capri, the Flegrean islands, the Pontine archipelago, the Tremiti islands and the Tuscan archipelago. Most of the islands are mountainous.

The peninsula is also largely mountainous, but between the spine of the Apennines and the eastern coastline are two large fertile plains: Emilia-Romagna in the north and Apulia in the south. Italy is divided from France and Switzerland by the Alps, and from Austria and Slovenia by both the Alps and the Dolomites. Three volcanoes, Vesuvius, Etna and Stromboli, are still active. Elevation extremes range from 4,748m (Mt Bianco di Courmayeur) to 0m (Mediterranean Sea). At the foot of the Alps lie the great lakes of Como, Maggiore and Garda. The chief rivers are the Po (651km)

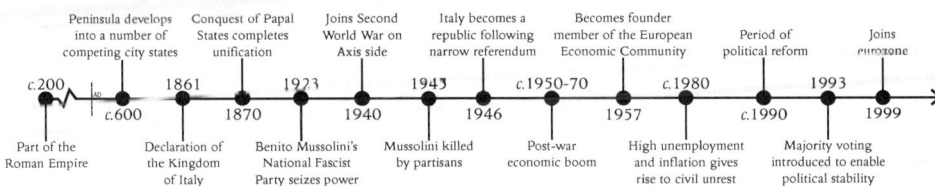

Timeline top							
Peninsula develops into a number of competing city states	Conquest of Papal States completes unification	Joins Second World War on Axis side	Italy becomes a republic following narrow referendum	Becomes founder member of the European Economic Community		Period of political reform	Joins eurozone

c.200   AD   1861   1923   1943   c.1950-70   c.1980   1993
     c.600   1870   1940   1946   1957   c.1990   1999

| Part of the Roman Empire | Declaration of the Kingdom of Italy | Benito Mussolini's National Fascist Party seizes power | Mussolini killed by partisans | Post-war economic boom | High unemployment and inflation gives rise to civil unrest | Majority voting introduced to enable political stability |

and the Adige, flowing through the northern plain to the Adriatic Sea, and the Arno (Florentine plain) and the Tiber (flowing through Rome to Ostia), which flow to the west coast. The climate is Mediterranean, with warm dry summers and mild winters.

POLITICS

The 1948 constitution has been amended several times, notably in 2001 to provide for greater autonomy for the 20 regions in tax, education and environment matters. The president, who must be over 50 years of age, is elected for a seven-year term by an electoral college consisting of both chambers of the legislature and 58 regional representatives. The bicameral *Parlamento* comprises a 630-member Chamber of Deputies and a senate with 315 members directly elected on a regional basis and a variable number of life senators, who are past presidents and senators appointed by incumbent presidents. Elected members of both chambers serve a five-year term.

Having been elected the leader of the Democratic Party (PD) in December 2013, Matteo Renzi succeeded Enrico Letta as prime minister in February 2014, becoming the third prime minster in a row not to be directly elected by the Italian people. His PD-led coalition government was sworn in on 22 February. On 20 April 2013, 87-year-old Georgio Napolitano was re-elected president.

HEAD OF STATE

President, Giorgio Napolitano, *elected* 11 May 2006, *took office* 15 May 2006, *re-elected* 20 April 2013

SELECTED GOVERNMENT MEMBERS *as at April 2014*
Prime Minister, Matteo Renzi
Defence, Roberta Pinotti
Foreign Affairs, Federica Mogherini
Interior, Angelino Alfano

ITALIAN EMBASSY
14 Three Kings Yard, Davies Street, London W1K 4EH
T 020-7312 2200 E ambasciata.londra@esteri.it
W www.amblondra.esteri.it
Ambassador Extraordinary and Plenipotentiary, HE Pasquale
   Terracciano, *apptd* 2013

BRITISH EMBASSY
Via XX Settembre 80A, 00187 Rome
T (+39) (06) 4220 0001 W www.gov.uk/government/world/italy
Ambassador Extraordinary and Plenipotentiary, HE
   Christopher Prentice, CMG, *apptd* 2011

DEFENCE

Aged 16–49, 2010 est	Males	Females
Available for military service	13,865,688	14,003,755
Fit for military service	11,247,446	11,348,695

Military expenditure – US$32,663m (2013)

ECONOMY AND TRADE

Economically, Italy is divided between a prosperous and industrially developed north and a largely agricultural and welfare-dependent south that has high unemployment levels. There is a large unofficial economy that is estimated to be worth 17 per cent of GDP, but measures to tackle this and wider structural reforms have made slow progress because of political opposition and sluggish economic performance. The growth rate has been low in recent years, and the global economic downturn caused a recession in 2008–9. A large budget deficit and public debt of over 126 per cent of GDP in 2012 helped cause growth to reach −1.8 per cent in 2013. Unemployment reached 12.4 per cent, with youth unemployment increasing to 40 per cent.

Tourism is the largest industry. Other major industries include precision machinery, iron and steel, chemicals, food processing, textiles, motor vehicles, fashion clothing, footwear, ceramics and electrical goods. The services sector contributes 73.5 per cent of GDP, industry 24.4 per cent and agriculture 2 per cent. The main trading partners are other EU states, especially Germany and France. Principal exports are the products of the main industries, plus food, beverages, minerals and non-ferrous metals. The main imports are engineering and energy products, industrial raw materials and transport equipment.

GNI – US$2,001,518m; US$33,860 per capita (2012)
Annual average growth of GDP – −1.8 per cent (2013 est)
Inflation rate – 1.2 per cent (2013 est)
Unemployment – 12.4 per cent (2013 est)
Total external debt – US$2,604,000m (2012 est)
Imports – US$489,096m (2012)
Exports – US$501,534m (2012)

BALANCE OF PAYMENTS
Trade – US$12,438m surplus (2012)
Current Account – US$14,881m deficit (2012)

Trade with UK	2012	2013
Imports from UK	£7,920,727,839	£8,384,815,182
Exports to UK	£14,396,627,100	£15,135,142,901

COMMUNICATIONS

Airports and waterways – 98, including major airports at Rome, Milan, Naples and Venice, Palermo and Catania (Sicily), and Cagliari (Sardinia); the main seaports are Naples, Genoa, Livorno, Trieste, Venice, Palermo and Catania
Roadways – A 6,700km network of motorways *(autostrade)* covers the country but there are 487,700km of roads in total
Railways – There are 20,255km of railways; the main railway system is run by the state-owned *Ferrovia dello Stato.* In 2001, Italy and France agreed plans to build a 52km rail tunnel through the Alps as part of a high-speed rail link between Turin and Lyon; as of May 2014 it has not been completed
Telecommunications – 21.656 million fixed lines and 97.225 million mobile subscriptions (2012); there were 29.24 million internet users in 2009
Internet code and IDD – it; 39 (from UK), 44 (to UK)
Major broadcasters – Rai is Italy's public radio and television broadcaster and competes with a number of private television broadcasters, the leading one being Mediaset, part of the media empire of former prime minister Silvio Berlusconi
Press – The press is highly regionalised, although there are

five national dailies, including *La Stampa* and *La Repubblica*
WPFI score – 23,75 (49)

EDUCATION AND HEALTH

Education is free and compulsory between the ages of six
and 16.
Literacy rate – 99 per cent (2011 est)
Gross enrolment ratio (percentage of relevant age group) –
    primary 100 per cent; secondary 101 per cent; tertiary
    64 per cent (2011 est)
Health expenditure (per capita) – US$3,436 (2011)
Hospital beds (per 1,000 people) – 3.5 (2010)
Life expectancy (years) – 82.03 (2014 est)
Mortality rate – 10.1 (2014 est)
Birth rate – 8.84 (2014 est)
Infant mortality rate – 3.31 (2014 est)

JAMAICA

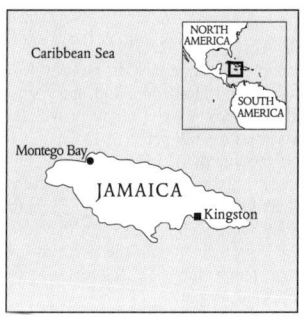

Area – 10,991 sq. km
Capital – Kingston; population, 580,000 (2009)
Major towns – Montego Bay, Portmore, Spanish Town
Currency – Jamaican dollar (J$) of 100 cents
Population – 2,930,050 rising at 0.69 per cent a year
    (2014 est)
Religion – Christian (Protestant 64 per cent, Roman Catholic
    2 per cent), Rastafarian 1 per cent (est)
Language – English (official), Jamaican patois
Population density – 250 per sq. km (2011)
Urban population – 52.1 per cent (2012)
Median age (years) – 24.9 (2014 est)
National anthem – 'Jamaica, Land We Love'
National day – 6 August (Independence Day)
Death penalty – Retained (last used 1988)
CPI score – 38 (83)

CLIMATE AND TERRAIN

An island in the Caribbean Sea, south of Cuba and west of
Hispaniola, Jamaica is mostly mountainous and forested,
with a narrow coastal plain. Elevation extremes range from
2,256m (Blue Mountain Peak) to 0m (Caribbean Sea). The
climate is tropical, although more temperate inland. The
average temperature in Jamaica is 25.4°C.

HISTORY AND POLITICS

Jamaica was visited by Columbus in 1494 and settled by the
Spanish from 1509. Captured by the British in 1655, it
became a crown colony in 1865. Jamaica became internally
self-governing in 1959 and independent in 1962.

Post-independence politics has been dominated by the
conservative Jamaican Labour Party (JLP) and social-
democratic People's National Party (PNP). Relations
between the two parties, often fraught, degenerated in the
1970s into violence that marred elections and political life

for some years. Despite the current political stability, there is
still widespread lawlessness, which now is often connected to
drug-trafficking.

In the 2011 legislative election, the PNP, narrowly
defeated by the JLP in the previous election, won a two-
thirds majority, picking up 42 of the 63 seats. The PNP
formed a government under Portia Simpson Miller.

Under the 1962 constitution, the head of state is Queen
Elizabeth II, represented locally by a governor-general.
The bicameral parliament consists of the House of
Representatives, with 63 directly elected members, and the
senate of 21 appointed members, 13 nominated by the prime
minister and eight by the leader of the opposition; both
chambers serve five-year terms. The prime minister is the
leader of the majority party in the elected chamber.
Governor-General, HE Patrick Allen, GCMG, *apptd* 2009

SELECTED GOVERNMENT MEMBERS *as at May 2014*
Prime Minister, Defence, Portia Simpson Miller
Finance, Peter Phillips
Minister of Foreign Affairs and Foreign Trade, Arnold
    Nicholson
National Security, Peter Bunting

JAMAICAN HIGH COMMISSION
1–2 Prince Consort Road, London SW7 2BZ
T 020-7823 9911 E jamhigh@jhcuk.com W www.jhcuk.org
High Commissioner, HE Aloun Ndombet-Assamba, *apptd*
2012

BRITISH HIGH COMMISSION
PO Box 575, 28 Trafalgar Road, Kingston 10
T (+1) (876) 936 0700 E ppa.kingston@fco.gov.uk
W www.gov.uk/government/world/jamaica
High Commissioner, HE David Fitton, *apptd* 20132

DEFENCE

Aged 16–49, 2010 est	Males	Females
Available for military service	726,263	742,958
Fit for military service	590,673	596,414

Military expenditure – US$121m (2013)

ECONOMY AND TRADE

The economy is weak owing to high interest rates, increased
foreign competition, high unemployment, growing internal
and external debt, and hurricane and storm damage in 2004,
2007 and 2008. Jamaica depends on foreign aid and
remittances from expatriates; remittances were worth nearly
20 per cent of GDP but declined to about 15 per cent after
the global downturn began. This hit the economy badly, and
IMF support was needed in 2010. Economic growth is
hindered by the high level of violent crime, corruption a
debt-to-GDP ratio of 125 per cent. Tourism, accounting for
5 per cent of GDP, remains strong, though the bauxite/
alumina industry (the main industry after tourism) suffered in
the downturn.

The economy is dominated by the service sector, which
makes up 64.1 per cent of GDP; industry accounts for 29.4
per cent, and agriculture for 6.5 per cent. Industries include
alumina and bauxite extraction, processing agricultural
produce and light manufacturing.

The main trading partners are the USA, Trinidad and
Tobago, Canada, Venezuela and the UK. Principal exports
are alumina, bauxite, sugar, bananas, rum, coffee, yams,
beverages, chemicals and clothing. The main imports are
food, consumer goods, industrial supplies, fuel, and parts and
accessories for capital goods.

GNI – US$14,321m; US$5,120 per capita (2012)
Annual average growth of GDP – 0.4 per cent (2013 est)
Inflation rate – 9.4 per cent (2013 est)
Population below poverty line – 16.5 per cent (2009 est)
Unemployment – 16.3 per cent (2013 est)
Total external debt – US$13,820m (2013 est)
Imports – US$6,485m (2012)
Exports – US$1,709m (2012)

BALANCE OF PAYMENTS
Trade – US$4,776m deficit (2012)
Current Account – US$1,916m deficit (2012)

Trade with UK	2012	2013
Imports from UK	£46,413,031	£42,999,759
Exports to UK	£29,794,424	£57,750,311

COMMUNICATIONS
Airports and waterways – The principal airports are at Kingston and Montego Bay; there are several harbours, Kingston being the main seaport
Roadways and railways – The island has 22,121km of roadways; the rail network is no longer in use
Telecommunications – 265,000 fixed lines and 2.665 million mobile telephone subscriptions (2011); there were 1.58 million internet users in 2009
Internet code and IDD – jm; 1 876 (from UK), 011 44 (to UK)
Major broadcasters – The state broadcaster was privatised in 1997 and now operates as Television Jamaica Ltd
Press – There are three main daily newspapers: *The Jamaica Gleaner*, *The Jamaica Star* and the *Jamaica Observer*
WPFI score – 10,9 (17)

EDUCATION AND HEALTH
In 2010 the Inter-American Development Bank provided US$45m in funding to enable the government to make improvements to the education system and expand compulsory schooling from age 16 to 18.
Literacy rate – 87 per cent (2011 est)
Gross enrolment ratio (percentage of relevant age group) – primary 89 per cent; secondary 93 per cent; tertiary 26 per cent (2011 est)
Health expenditure (per capita) – US$270 (2011)
Hospital beds (per 1,000 people) – 1.8 (2010)
Life expectancy (years) – 73.48 (2014 est)
Mortality rate – 6.67 (2014 est)
Birth rate – 18.14 (2014 est)
Infant mortality rate – 13.69 (2014 est)
HIV/AIDS adult prevalence – 1.7 per cent (2012 est)

JAPAN

Nihon-koku/Nippon-koku – Japan

Area – 377,915 sq. km
Capital – Tokyo; population, 36,897,716 (2012 est)
Major cities – Fukuoka, Hiroshima, Kawasaki, Kobe, Kyoto (the ancient capital), Nagoya, Osaka, Saitama, Sapporo, Yokohama
Currency – Yen of 100 sen
Population – 127,103,388 falling at 0.13 per cent a year (2014 est)
Religion – Shinto 83.9 per cent, Buddhist 71.4 per cent, Christian 2 per cent (est); much of the population adheres to more than one religion, most commonly combining Shinto and Buddhist beliefs
Language – Japanese (official)
Population density – 351 per sq. km (2011)
Urban population – 91.9 per cent (2012)
Median age (years) – 46.1 (2014 est)
National anthem – 'Kimigayo' ['His Majesty's Reign']
National day – 23 December (Birthday of Emperor Akihito)
Death penalty – Retained
CPI score – 74 (18)

CLIMATE AND TERRAIN
Japan consists of four large islands: Honshu (or Mainland), Shikoku, Kyushu and Hokkaido, and many smaller islands. Typically, the islands have coastal plains and wooded, mountainous interiors; 67 per cent of Japan's land area is forested. The mountains running across the mainland from the Sea of Japan to the Pacific Ocean include a number of volcanoes, mainly extinct or dormant. Elevation extremes range from 3,776m (Mt Fuji) to –4m (Hachiro-gata). The climate varies from temperate in the north to tropical in the south. Average temperatures in Tokyo range from 5°C in January to 27°C in August.

The islands are located at the intersection of three tectonic plates and are prone to seismic activity; 20 per cent of the world's major earthquakes occur in this area. A magnitude-9 earthquake and the ensuing tsunami devastated the north-east of Honshu in March 2011.

POLITICS
The 1947 constitution established Japan as a constitutional monarchy with a hereditary emperor as head of state. The bicameral Diet comprises the House of Representatives (the lower house) and the House of Councillors. The House of Representatives has 480 members directly elected for a four-year term, including 180 by proportional representation. The House of Councillors has 242 members, including 96 elected by proportional representation, who serve six-year terms, with half elected every three years; unlike the lower house, it cannot be dissolved by the prime minister. The prime minister is formally elected by the House of Representatives and appoints the cabinet.

The Liberal Democrat Party (LDP) has dominated post-war politics, holding power continuously from 1955 to 1993, and then – usually as the main party in coalition governments – from 1994 to 2009. In 2010, it regained control of the upper house of the legislature from the Democratic Party of Japan (DPJ); prime minister and leader of the DPJ-led coalition, Naoto Kan, subsequently resigned from office in August 2011, and was replaced by former finance minister Yoshihiko Noda. In December 2012 the LDP returned to power, taking 294 seats in the parliamentary election while the DPJ won only 57; Shinzo Abe once again took the position of prime minister.

HEAD OF STATE
HIM The Emperor of Japan, Akihito, *born* 23 December 1933, *succeeded* 8 January 1989, *enthroned* 12 November 1990

Period of conflict between samurai families and successive dynasties of shoguns	Imperial control re-established	First Sino-Japanese War	Annexation of Korea	Enters into Second World War alongside Germany and Italy	Surrenders after atomic bombing of Hiroshima and Nagasaki	Independence restored

c.600   AD   1852-54   1889   1904-5   1931   1941-42   1945-52
c.1100-1800   1868   1894-95   1910   1941   1945   1952

Centralised state established	Commodore Perry visits Japan, precipitating first trade with the west	Adopts Western-style constitution	Defeated Russia in the Russo-Japanese War	Invasion of China	Japanese attack on the US naval base Pearl Harbour brings USA into the war	Allied occupation introduces political, social and economic reforms

Heir, HRH Crown Prince Naruhito Hironomiya, *born* 23 February 1960

SELECTED GOVERNMENT MEMBERS *as at April 2014*
Prime Minister, Shinzo Abe
Defence, Itsunori Onodera
Finance, Taro Aso
Foreign Affairs, Fumio Kishida

EMBASSY OF JAPAN
101–104 Piccadilly, London W1J 7JT
T 020-7465 6500 E info@ld.mofa.go.jp
W www.uk.emb-japan.go.jp
Ambassador Extraordinary and Plenipotentiary, HE Keiichi Hayashi, *apptd* 2011

BRITISH EMBASSY
No. 1 Ichiban-cho, Chiyoda-ku, Tokyo 102–8381
T (+81) (3) 5211 1100 W www.gov.uk/government/world/japan
Ambassador Extraordinary and Plenipotentiary, HE Tim Hitchens, *apptd* 2012

DEFENCE

The constitution prohibits the maintenance of armed forces, although internal security forces were created in the 1950s and their mission was extended in 1954 to include the defence of Japan against aggression. In the 1990s, legislation was passed permitting limited participation by the armed forces in UN peacekeeping missions and allowing them to enter foreign conflicts in order to rescue Japanese nationals. A revision to the USA–Japan defence cooperation guidelines agreed in 1997 permits Japan to play a supporting role in US military operations in areas surrounding Japan; Japanese troops were also deployed in Iraq to assist with post-war reconstruction between 2003 and 2006.

Aged 16–49, 2010 est	*Males*	*Females*
Available for military service	27,301,443	26,307,003
Fit for military service	22,390,431	21,540,322

Military expenditure – US$59,431m (2013)

ECONOMY AND TRADE

Japan has the fourth-largest economy in the world after the USA, China and India. Its rapid post-war economic growth, based largely on car and consumer electronics manufacturing, experienced a marked contraction from 1990. Exacerbated by the 1997 Asian economic crisis, the recession lasted 14 years, causing unprecedented levels of bankruptcy, unemployment and homelessness and a huge public debt (estimated at 230 per cent of GDP in 2013). Reforms introduced from 2001, particularly to the corporate and public sectors, improved economic growth from 2002 to 2007, but the economy went into recession again in 2008 owing to the global downturn. Government stimulus packages and an increase in global demand spurred the start of a recovery from late 2009. Following the 2011 earthquake and tsunami there was a drop in production; the economy has largely recovered in the following two years, but was less complete in the Tohoku region.

High-technology industries remain the mainstay of the economy, producing vehicles, electronic equipment, machine tools, steel and other metals, ships, chemicals, textiles and processed food. Financial services is also a major sector, supplying a global market. Agriculture is constrained by the mountainous terrain but intensive cultivation produces high yields, and there is a large fishing industry. The service sector contributes 73.2 per cent of GDP, industry 25.6 per cent and agriculture 1.1 per cent.

The main trading partners are China, the USA, other Pacific Rim countries and the Gulf states. Principal exports include transport equipment, motor vehicles, semiconductors, electrical machinery and chemicals. The main imports are machinery and equipment, fuels, foodstuffs, chemicals, textiles and raw materials.

GNI – US$6,150,131m; US$47,880 per capita (2012)
Annual average growth of GDP – 2 per cent (2013 est)
Inflation rate – 0.2 per cent (2013 est)
Unemployment – 4.1 per cent (2013 est)
Total external debt – US$3,017,000m (2012)
Imports – US$885,609m (2012)
Exports – US$798,620m (2012)

BALANCE OF PAYMENTS
Trade – US$86,989m deficit (2012)
Current Account – US$60,446m surplus (2012)

Trade with UK	2012	2013
Imports from UK	£4,578,902,640	£4,469,798,408
Exports to UK	£8,161,866,647	£7,210,702,369

COMMUNICATIONS

Airports – 142; the principal airports include Haneda (Tokyo), Narita, Kansai and Chubu
Waterways – Japan has a large merchant fleet, with 684 ships of over 1,000 tonnes in 2011; the main seaports are Tokyo, Osaka, Nagoya, Yokohama, Kobe and Kawasaki
Roadways and railways – There are 1,210,251km of roadways, including 7,803km of motorways, and 27,182km of railways
Telecommunications – 64.27 million fixed lines and 138.36 million mobile subscriptions (2011); there were 99.18 million internet users in 2009
Internet code and IDD – jp; 81 (from UK), 1 44/010 44/41 44/61 44 (to UK)
Major broadcasters – A public broadcaster, NHK, provides radio and television services; satellite and cable television is widespread and digital broadcasting is expanding
Press – Around 80 per cent of the population reads a daily newspaper, creating huge markets for publications such as *Asahi Shimbun* and English-language title *The Japan Times*
WPFI score – 26,02 (59)

EDUCATION AND HEALTH

Elementary education is free and compulsory at elementary level (six-year course) and lower secondary (three-year course).
Gross enrolment ratio (percentage of relevant age group) –
    primary 103 per cent; secondary 102 per cent; tertiary
    60 per cent (2011 est)

Health expenditure (per capita) – US$3,958 (2010)
Hospital beds (per 1,000 people) – 13.7 (2009)
Life expectancy (years) – 84.46 (2014 est)
Mortality rate – 9.38 (2014 est)
Birth rate – 8.07 (2014 est)
Infant mortality rate – 2.13 (2014 est)

JORDAN

Al-Mamlakah al-Urduniyah al-Hashimiyah – Hashemite Kingdom of Jordan

Area – 89,342 sq. km
Capital – Amman; population, 1,141,029 (2012 est)
Major cities – Aqaba, Az Zarqa, Irbid
Currency – Jordanian dinar (JD) of 10 dirhams
Population – 7,930,491 rising at 3.86 per cent a year
   (2014 est); Arab (98 per cent), Armenian (1 per cent),
   Circassian (1 per cent) (est)
Religion – Muslim (Sunni) 97 per cent, Christian 2 per cent
   (est)
Language – Arabic (official), English
Population density – 70 per sq. km (2011)
Urban population – 83 per cent (2012 est)
Median age (years) – 21.8 (2014 est)
National anthem – 'As-Salam al-Malaki al-Urdoni' ['The
   Royal Anthem of Jordan']
National day – 25 May (Independence Day)
Death penalty – Retained
CPI score – 45 (66)

CLIMATE AND TERRAIN
Most of the country is a desert plateau, with the valley of
the River Jordan and the Dead Sea in the west marking the
border with Israel. The Jordan Valley and its extension from
the Dead Sea to the Gulf of Aqaba are part of the Great
Rift Valley in Africa. The only hills lie in the south, along
the edge of the Great Rift Valley, although there is a hilly
outcrop in the centre of the desert. Elevation extremes range
from 1,854m (Jabal Umm ad Dami) to −408m (Dead Sea).
The climate is arid, but with a rainy season in the west from
November to April. Summers are very hot, and temperatures
in the capital, Amman, have been known to reach 41°C.
Winters can be cold, with frost and snow on the plateau.

POLITICS
The 1952 constitution provides for a monarchy with a
hereditary king as head of state. The bicameral National
Assembly comprises a House of Deputies and a senate or
House of Notables. The House of Deputies has 120
members, directly elected for a four-year term; 12 seats are
now reserved for women. The senate has 55 members, who
are appointed by the king for a four-year term. The king
appoints the prime minister, who chooses the council of
ministers.

The legislature was dissolved halfway through its term in
November 2009. After the legislative election in November
2010, over 85 per cent of seats were won by pro-government
candidates; the announcement of this result led to rioting.
Since January 2011, Jordan has experienced demonstrations
similar to those elsewhere in the Arab world, with protestors
demanding political reform, lower food prices and measures
to tackle unemployment. This led to the king dismissing the
government in February 2011 and to the appointment
of four prime ministers in 14 months. In October 2012
Abdullah Ensour was appointed prime minister and
reappointed to the post in March 2013.

HEAD OF STATE
HM The King of Jordan, Abdullah II, *born* 30 January 1962,
   succeeded 7 February 1999
Crown Prince, Hamzeh ibn al-Hussein, *born* 29 March 1982

SELECTED GOVERNMENT MEMBERS *as at May 2014*
Prime Minister, Defence, Abdullah Ensour
Finance, Umayya Toukan
Foreign Affairs, Nasser Judah
Interior, Hussein Majali

EMBASSY OF THE HASHEMITE KINGDOM OF
JORDAN
6 Upper Phillimore Gardens, London W8 7HA
T 020-7937 3685 E london@fm.gov.jo
W www.jordanembassy.org.uk
Ambassador Extraordinary and Plenipotentiary, HE Mazen
   Kemel Homoud, *apptd* 2011

BRITISH EMBASSY
PO Box 87, Abdoun, Amman 11118
T (+962) (6) 590 9200 E amman.enquiries@fco.gov.uk
W www.gov.uk/government/world/jordan
Ambassador Extraordinary and Plenipotentiary, HE Peter
Millett, *apptd* 2011

DEFENCE

Aged 16–49, 2010 est	Males	Females
Available for military service	1,674,260	1,611,315
Fit for military service	1,439,192	1,384,500

Military expenditure – US$1,078m (2013)

ECONOMY AND TRADE
Jordan's economic development has been hindered by its lack
of natural resources, influxes of refugees from the West Bank

Previously part of the Roman and Byzantine empires, then under Arab control	Emirate of Transjordan created under a League of Nations Mandate	Seizes part of the West Bank during the first Arab-Israeli war	Recognises Palestinian Liberation Organisation as sole representative of Palestinians in the Occupied Territories	Ban on political parties lifted	Formally renounces sovereignty over West Bank and East Jerusalem
c.1600–1918	1946	1967	1986	1989	1994
c.700	1921	1948	1974	1992	1999
	Becomes part of the Ottoman Empire	Mandate ends; Transjordan becomes independent as the Hashemite Kingdom of Jordan	West Bank recaptured by Israel during Six-Day War, refugees forced into Jordan	Severs links with PLO	Riots force political and economic reforms	Signs peace agreement with Israel

in 1967, Iraq since 2003, and Syria since 2013, and the impact of conflict on its trade with Israel and Iraq. High levels of poverty, unemployment and government debt are long-term problems. Since 1999, King Abdullah has implemented economic reforms, and these measures have increased productivity and exports, begun to attract foreign direct investment, and won agreement to debt rescheduling from international donors. Even so, the economy is still dependent on foreign aid, of which the USA is the largest provider, and in 2011 the government agreed two economic relief packages to improve the living conditions for the middle and poor classes. In 2012 Jordan entered into a US$2.1 billion, multiple-year IMF stand-by arrangement.

Jordan has no oil reserves of its own and few water resources. Shale reserves and renewable energy sources are being explored by the government. Since 2003, several Gulf states have temporarily extended aid to Jordan in order to compensate for the loss of its usual oil supplies from Iraq. The country also imports natural gas, but aims to become a net exporter of electricity via its national grid's links with those of Syria and Egypt. It is currently considering nuclear power generation to ensure an adequate future supply. Jordan has also begun joint ventures with Israel and Syria to guarantee water supplies.

The service sector, including tourism, accounts for 67 per cent of GDP. Industry generates 29.9 per cent, from activities that include garment manufacturing, fertilisers, potash and phosphate mining, pharmaceuticals, oil refining, cement, inorganic chemicals and light manufacturing. Agriculture, which accounts for 3.2 per cent of GDP, produces citrus and stone fruits, tomatoes, cucumbers, olives, sheep, poultry and dairy products.

The main trade partners are the USA, Iraq, India, China and Saudi Arabia. Principal exports are clothing, fertilisers, potash, phosphates, vegetables and pharmaceuticals. The main imports are crude oil, machinery, transport equipment, iron and cereals.

GNI – US$30,709m; US$4,670 per capita (2012)
Annual average growth of GDP – 3.3 per cent (2013 est)
Inflation rate – 5.9 per cent (2013 est)
Unemployment – 14 per cent (2013 est)
Total external debt – US$22,040m (2013 est)
Imports – US$20,691 (2012)
Exports – US$7,926m (2012)

BALANCE OF PAYMENTS
Trade – US$12,765m deficit (2012)
Current Account – US$5,640m deficit (2012)

Trade with UK	2012	2013
Imports from UK	£232,285,248	£233,665,424
Exports to UK	£31,582,031	£26,889,601

COMMUNICATIONS
Airports – 16; the largest airports are at Amman and Aqaba
Waterways – Amman is linked to Jordan's seaport at Aqaba, the Saudi Arabian port of Jeddah and the Syrian and Iraqi capitals by roads which are of considerable importance in the overland trade of the Middle East
Roadways and railways – 7,203km; 507km
Telecommunications – 435,000 fixed lines and 8.984 million mobile subscriptions (2012); there were 1.64 million internet users in 2009
Internet code and IDD – jo; 962 (from UK), 44 (to UK)
Major broadcasters – Jordan Radio and Television, the state-run broadcaster, operates three terrestrial television channels and a satellite channel as well as radio services in Arabic, English and French

Press – Major daily newspapers include *Ad Dustour, Al Ra'y* and *Al Ghadd*
WPFI score – 40,42 (141)

EDUCATION AND HEALTH
Literacy rate – 96 per cent (2011 est)
Gross enrolment ratio (percentage of relevant age group) – primary 99 per cent; secondary 89 per cent; tertiary 40 per cent (2011 est)
Health expenditure (per capita) – US$392 (2011; includes contributions from the UN Relief and Works Agency for Palestinian refugees)
Hospital beds (per 1,000 people) – 1.8 (2010)
Life expectancy (years) – 74.1 (2014 est)
Mortality rate – 3.8 (2014 est)
Birth rate – 25.23 (2014 est)
Infant mortality rate – 15.73 (2014 est)

KAZAKHSTAN

Qazaqstan Respublikasy – Republic of Kazakhstan

Area – 2,724,900 sq. km
Capital – Astana (previously known as Akmola and Tselinograd); population, 650,000 (2009)
Major cities – Almaty (the former capital), Oskemen, Pavlodar, Qaraghandy, Semey, Shymkent, Taraz
Currency – Tenge of 100 tiyn
Population – 17,948,816 rising at 1.17 per cent a year (2014 est); Kazakh (63.1 per cent), Russian (23.7 per cent), Uzbek (2.8 per cent), Ukrainian (2.1 per cent), Uygur (1.4 per cent), Tatar (1.3 per cent), German (1.1 per cent) (2009). The Russian population is concentrated in the north of the country, where it forms a significant majority, and in Almaty
Religion – Muslim 70 per cent (predominantly Sunni), Christian 26 per cent (mostly Russian Orthodox) (est)
Language – Kazakh, Russian (both official)
Population density – 6 per sq. km (2011)
Urban population – 53.5 per cent (2012 est)
Median age (years) – 29.7 (2014 est)
National anthem – 'Menin Qazaqstanym' ['My Kazakhstan']
National day – 16 December (Independence Day)
Death penalty – Retained for certain crimes
CPI score – 26 (140)
Literacy rate – 100 per cent (2010 est)
Gross enrolment ratio (percentage of relevant age group) – primary 105 per cent; secondary 97 per cent; tertiary 42 per cent (2011 est)
Health expenditure (per capita) – US$455 (2011)
Hospital beds (per 1,000 people) – 7.6 (2009)
Life expectancy (years) – 70.24 (2014 est)
Mortality rate – 8.31 (2014 est)

Birth rate – 19.61 (2014 est)
Infant mortality rate – 21.61 (2014 est)

CLIMATE AND TERRAIN

Kazakhstan stretches from the basin of the river Volga and the Caspian Sea in the west to the Altai and Tien Shan mountains in the east. The terrain consists of arid steppes and semi-deserts, flat in the west, hilly in the east and mountainous in the south-east. Elevation extremes range from 6,995m (Khan Tangiri Shyngy) to −132m (Vpadina Kaundy). The country contains the northern part of the Aral Sea in the south-west, and Lake Balkhash and Lake Zaysan in the east. The Aral Sea has suffered significant pollution and desertification since the 1960s, creating the Aralkum desert. The climate is continental, and while arid in much of the country, it can be Siberian in the north. Average yearly temperatures in Astana range from −16°C in January to 20°C in July.

HISTORY AND POLITICS

Kazakhstan was inhabited by nomadic tribes before being invaded by Genghis Khan and incorporated into his empire in 1218. After this empire disintegrated, feudal towns emerged based on large oases and the nomadic tribes formed federations led by khans. The towns affiliated in the late 15th century and established a Kazakh state which engaged in almost continuous warfare with the marauding khanates on its southern border. After turning to Russia for protection in the 1730s, the Kazakh khanates were formally incorporated into the Russian Empire in the early 19th century.

The 1917 Bolshevik revolution in Russia was followed by civil war in Kazakhstan, which became an autonomous republic within the USSR in 1920 and a full union republic in 1936. Kazakhstan suffered severely under Stalin's policies of agricultural collectivisation and 'sedentarisation', which forced nomadic tribes to become farmers; around 1.5 million people died of famine or disease. Later Soviet rule saw the country used as a test site for nuclear weapons.

Growing nationalism in the 1980s and a reformist leader led to economic and cultural reforms in 1989 and a declaration of sovereignty in 1990. Kazakhstan declared its independence in December 1991, and became a founding member of the Commonwealth of Independent States. It entered an economic, social and military union with Kyrgyzstan and Uzbekistan in 1994, and an economic and military pact with Russia in 1995, when it achieved nuclear-free status. It agreed in 2009 to form a customs union with Belarus and Russia from 2011.

Nursultan Nazarbayev, the reformist communist leader of 1989, became head of state in 1990 and was re-elected in 1991, 1999, 2005 and 2011; the April 2011 election, in which he received 95 per cent of the vote, was criticised by international observers. A 2007 constitutional reform allows him to serve for an unlimited number of terms.

In 2006, three pro-government parties merged with Nazarbayev's Fatherland Republican Party (Otan), which subsequently changed its name to Nur-Otan. Nur-Otan won every seat in the lower legislative chamber in the 2007 legislative elections and retained 83 seats in the 2012 elections, but opposition parties Democratic Party of Kazakhstan and Communist People's Party of Kazakhstan picked up the remaining 15 seats. In April 2014 Karim Massimov became prime minister for the second time replacing Serik Akhmetov.

The president is directly elected; in 2007 the constitution was amended to reduce the presidential term from seven to five years, renewable once, although President Nazarbayev is exempt from this restriction. The bicameral parliament is composed of the assembly *(Majlis)* and the senate. The assembly has 107 members, 98 directly elected on a single constituency basis and nine seats reserved for ethnic groups; all serve a five-year term. The senate has 47 members, of whom 32 are indirectly elected and 15 are appointed for a six-year term, with half elected every three years. The president appoints the prime minister and other senior ministers.

HEAD OF STATE

President, Nursultan Nazarbayev, *elected* 1 December 1991, *confirmed in office by referendum* 1995, *re-elected* 1999, 2005, 2011

SELECTED GOVERNMENT MEMBERS *as at April 2014*

Prime Minister, Karim Massimov
First Deputy Prime Minister, Bakytzhan Sagintayev
Defence, Serik Akhmetov
Foreign Affairs, Yerlan Idrisov
Internal Affairs, Kalmukhanbet Kasymov

EMBASSY OF THE REPUBLIC OF KAZAKHSTAN

125 Pall Mall, London SW1Y 5EA
T 020-7925 1757 E london@mfa.kz W www.kazembassy.org.uk
Ambassador Extraordinary and Plenipotentiary, HE Kairat Abusseitov, *apptd* 2008

BRITISH EMBASSY

62 Kosmonavtov Street, Astana
T (+7) (717) 255 6200 E ukinkz@fco.gov.uk
W www.gov.uk/government/world/kazakhstan
Ambassador Extraordinary and Plenipotentiary, HE Dr Carolyn Browne, *apptd* 2013

DEFENCE

The CIS Mutual Defence Treaty of 1993, to which Kazakhstan is a signatory, retains a common air defence force, and Kazakh forces also take part in the CIS peacekeeping force on the Tajikistan–Afghanistan border. An agreement signed with Russia in 1995 provides for eventual reunification of the two states' armed forces. By 1996, all nuclear warheads had been returned to Russia, although Kazakhstan retained 48 SS-18 intercontinental ballistic missiles. Kazakhstan participates in the NATO partnership for peace programme.

Aged 16–24, 2010 est	*Males*	*Females*
Available for military service	4,163,629	4,179,051
Fit for military service	2,909,999	3,528,169

Military expenditure – US$2,599m (2012)
Conscription – 18 years of age; 24 months

ECONOMY AND TRADE

Economic reforms and privatisation in the 1990s enabled GDP to grow by at least 8 per cent a year from 2002 to 2007, although lower commodity prices and banking sector problems caused the economy to contract briefly in 2008–9. Growth has largely been achieved through exploitation of vast oil and natural gas reserves, particularly since the opening of export pipelines to Black Sea ports (in 2001) and China (2005), and Kazakhstan's use of the Azerbaijan–Turkey pipeline (from 2008); the country is also part of a four-country consortium developing another pipeline to China. As a result of the boom, the government has eliminated the budget deficit, but it is also trying to stimulate growth in other industries to reduce dependency on oil. In 2010 the country joined the Belarus-Kazakhstan-Russia Customs Union to increase foreign investment and improve trade relationships. Despite these revenues and reforms, poverty remains widespread.

Other mineral resources are considerable and there is a significant mining industry exploiting coal, iron ore, manganese, chrome, lead, zinc, copper, titanium, bauxite, silver, gold, phosphate and uranium deposits. A large and well-developed agricultural sector produces grain, wool, cotton and livestock as cash crops. The main industries are mineral extraction and processing and machine-building, especially agricultural machinery and electric motors. Services contribute 56.9 per cent of GDP, industry 37.9 per cent and agriculture 5.2 per cent, although agriculture employs 25.8 per cent of the workforce.

The main trading partners are China, Russia, Ukraine and EU states. Principal exports are oil and oil products, ferrous metals, chemicals, machinery, grain, wool, meat and coal. The main imports are machinery and equipment, metal products and foodstuffs. In May 2014 Kazakhstan founded the Eurasian Economic Union (EaEU); a customs union with Russia and Belarus. The union will be formally established on 1 January 2015.

GNI – US$175,469m; US$9,780 per capita (2012)
Annual average growth of GDP – 5 per cent (2013 est)
Inflation rate – 5.8 per cent (2013 est)
Population below poverty line – 5.3 per cent (2011 est)
Unemployment – 5.3 per cent (2013 est)
Total external debt – US$131,300m (2013 est)
Imports – US$35,307m (2012)
Exports – US$88,575m (2012)

BALANCE OF PAYMENTS
Trade – US$53,268m surplus (2012)
Current Account – US$7,716m surplus (2012)

Trade with UK	2012	2013
Imports from UK	£513,474,381	£514,523,283
Exports to UK	£601,484,008	£458,253,307

COMMUNICATIONS
Airports – 63; the largest airports are at Astana, Almaty and Atyrau
Waterways – There are important ports on the Caspian and Aral seas which permit international trade, while the Syr Darya and Irtysh rivers provide 4,000km of navigable waterways
Roadways and railways – 97,418km; 15,333km
Telecommunications – 4.34 million fixed lines and 28.731 million mobile subscriptions (2012); there were 5.299 million internet users in 2009
Internet code and IDD – kz; 7 (from UK), 810 44 (to UK)
Major broadcasters – There are 250 television and radio stations according to official statistics; the influential Khabar Agency, founded by the president's eldest daughter, Dariga Nazarbayeva, operates channels in both Russian and Kazakh
Press – Major newspapers include the government-backed Russian-language *Kazakhstanskaya Pravda* and the Kazakh-language *Egemen Kazakhstan*
WPFI score – 54,94 (161)

KENYA

Jamhuri ya Kenya – Republic of Kenya

Area – 580,367 sq. km
Capital – Nairobi; population, 3,825,710 (2012 est)
Major cities – Eldoret, Kisumu, Mombasa, Nakuru
Currency – Kenyan shilling (Ksh) of 100 cents
Population – 45,010,056 rising at 2.11 per cent a year (2014 est); Kikuyu (22 per cent), Luhya (14 per cent), Luo (13 per cent), Kalenjin (12 per cent), Kamba (11 per cent), Kisii (6 per cent), Meru (6 per cent) (2009)
Religion – Christian 82 per cent (Protestant 47 per cent, Roman Catholic 23 per cent, other 12 per cent), Muslim 11 per cent
Language – English, Swahili (both official), indigenous languages
Population density – 74 per sq. km (2011)
Urban population – 24.4 per cent (2012 est)
Median age (years) – 19.1 (2014 est)
National anthem – 'Ee Mungu Nguvu Yetu' ['Oh God of All Creation']
National day – 12 December (Independence Day)
Death penalty – Retained (last used 1987)
CPI score – 27 (136)

CLIMATE AND TERRAIN
The coastal plain and semi-desert plains in the east rise to mountainous highlands in the centre and west that are divided by the Great Rift Valley. Elevation extremes range from 5,199m (Mt Kenya) to 0m (Indian Ocean). The country includes part of Lake Victoria in the south-west and most of Lake Turkana (Rudolph) in the north. Kenya is an equatorial country; the climate is tropical on the coast and arid in the interior, tempered by altitude. The average temperature is 20.8°C.

HISTORY AND POLITICS
Fossils of early hominids found in the Lake Turkana region suggest that the area was inhabited some 2.6 million years ago. Arabs and Persians settled on the Kenyan coast from the eighth century AD. The Portuguese gained control of coastal areas in the 16th century but Arab overlordship was reasserted in the 18th century.

European exploration of the interior began in the 19th century and in 1895, Kenya became part of Britain's East African Protectorate, becoming a colony in 1920. Demands for internal self-government by white settlers were rejected in 1923, but from 1944 a nationalist group, the Kenya African Union (KAU), was founded to campaign for African rights. The Mau Mau rebellion of 1952–6, intended to drive white settlers from African tribal lands, resulted in a state of emergency that lasted until 1960, when preparations for majority African rule began. Kenya became independent in 1963, and a republic in 1964. President Jomo Kenyatta's death in 1978 brought Daniel arap Moi to power, and he remained president until 2002, when he was barred from standing for re-election.

Kenya was a one-party state ruled by the Kenya African National Union (KANU) between 1964 and 1991. A multiparty system was reintroduced after violent agitation and international pressure in the early 1990s but KANU maintained its grip on power until the 2002 elections, which were won by the National Rainbow Coalition (NARC). Despite the NARC's anti-corruption electoral platform, once in government it made little headway against endemic corruption, and government ministers were implicated in corruption scandals in 2005 and 2006. It is estimated that up to US$1,000m (£650m) of official funds were misappropriated in 2002–7.

After decades of stability, intercommunal violence and conflict over land and water rights have become more frequent since the 1990s, exacerbated by a rural food crisis since 2004 following persistent drought and crop failures.

The 2007 legislative elections were won by the Orange Democratic Movement (ODM), led by Raila Odinga. The announcement that President Kibaki had won the simultaneous presidential election triggered weeks of serious rioting; this developed into ethnic violence that left over 1,000 dead and 600,000 displaced. After international mediation, a power-sharing agreement was signed in February 2008; under this, Kibaki remained president and the post of prime minister was created for Raila Odinga, although this post was abolished in 2013.

In March 2013 Uhuru Kenyatta, the son of Kenya's first president, was elected president with 50.5 per cent of the vote; his Jubilee coalition became the largest bloc in both houses in the legislative elections. In October 2014 Uhuru Kenyatta is due to face International Criminal Court charges relating to 2007's post-election violence.

In recent years Kenya has suffered a number of terrorist attacks linked to Islamism, with the Somalian group Al-Shabaab attacking US, Israeli and Kenyan targets within the country. In September 2013, Al Shabaab gunmen killed at least 62 people in the Westgate shopping mall attack.

The president is directly elected for a five-year term, renewable once. The bicameral parliament as defined in the 2010 constitution was first elected in 2013; members of both houses serve five-year terms. The lower chamber, the National Assembly, was increased to 350 members, of whom 290 are directly elected; 47 seats are reserved for women, directly elected from each county, 12 members are nominated pro rata by political parties to represent special interests including youth, persons with disabilities and workers, and the speaker is a member ex officio. The new upper chamber, the Senate, has 68 members: 47 are directly elected from each county, 16 seats are reserved for women, nominated pro rata by political parties, four members are nominated to represent youth and persons with disabilities; the speaker is a member ex officio.

HEAD OF STATE
President, C-in-C of the Armed Forces, Uhuru Kenyatta, *elected* 4 March 2013, *took office* 9 April 2013
Deputy President, William Ruto

SELECTED GOVERNMENT MEMBERS *as at April 2014*
Defence, Raychelle Omamo
Foreign Affairs, Amina Mohammed

KENYA HIGH COMMISSION
45 Portland Place, London W1B 1AS
T 020-7636 2371 E info@kenyahighcom.org.uk
W www.kenyahighcom.org.uk
High Commissioner, HE Ephraim Ngare, *apptd* 2009

BRITISH HIGH COMMISSION
PO Box 30465, Upper Hill Road, 00100 Nairobi
T (1254) (20) 284 4000 W www.gov.uk/government/world/kenya
Interim High Commissioner, HE Christian Turner, *apptd* 2012

DEFENCE

Aged 16–49, 2010 est	Males	Females
Available for military service	9,768,140	9,466,257
Fit for military service	6,361,268	6,106,870

Military expenditure – US$724m (2013)

ECONOMY AND TRADE

Kenya acts as a regional trade and finance hub for its landlocked neighbours. However, its own economy is weak owing to endemic corruption, low commodity prices, low investor confidence and the frequent suspension of international aid because of successive governments' failure to tackle corruption. These problems are exacerbated by occasional severe droughts, and in 2008–9 the economy contracted owing to post-election violence and the global downturn, which reduced tourism, exports and expatriates' remittances. There are high budget and trade deficits, a huge foreign debt, 40 per cent unemployment and extreme poverty, with 50 per cent of the population living below the poverty line.

The country is overwhelmingly agricultural, with 75 per cent of the population engaged in agricultural and horticultural production; this sector contributes 24.2 per cent of GDP. The world's third largest producer of tea, Kenya also grows coffee, maize, wheat, sugar cane, fruit and vegetables. Natural resources include gold, limestone, soda ash, salt, rubies, garnets and hydroelectric power, which makes it self-sufficient in energy.

The industrial sector has grown over the past two decades, developing a manufacturing base in consumer goods (such as textiles) and agricultural products (such as dehydrated vegetables), as well as oil refining, commercial ship repair and the production of steel, aluminium, lead and cement. Tourism is an important source of income, though it is threatened by terrorism. Industry contributes 17.4 per cent to GDP and the service sector 53.3 per cent.

The main export markets are the UK, the Netherlands, Uganda, Tanzania, the USA and Pakistan, while imports come mainly from India, China, the UAE and South Africa. Principal exports are tea, horticultural products, coffee, petroleum products, fish and cement. The main imports are machinery and transport equipment, petroleum products, vehicles, iron and steel, resins and plastics.

GNI – US$40,526m; US$860 per capita (2012)
Annual average growth of GDP – 5.1 per cent (2013 est)
Inflation rate – 5.8 per cent (2013 est)
Unemployment – 40 per cent (2008 est)
Total external debt – US$11,960m (2013 est)
Imports – US$16,298m (2012)
Exports – US$6,130m (2012)

BALANCE OF PAYMENTS
Trade – US$10,169m deficit (2012)
Current Account – US$3,785m deficit (2012)

Trade with UK	2012	2013
Imports from UK	£385,859,779	£438,958,819
Exports to UK	£335,294,689	£361,375,394

COMMUNICATIONS

Airports – 16; the largest airports are at Nairobi, Mombasa and Eldoret

Roadways and railways – There are 160,878km of roadways; the Kenya Railways Corporation operates 2,066km of railways
Telecommunications – 251,600 fixed lines and 30.732 million mobile subscriptions (2012); there were 3.996 million internet users in 2009
Internet code and IDD – ke; 254 (from UK), 0 44 (to UK)
Major broadcasters – The state-run Kenya Broadcasting Corporation (KBC) competes with a range of commercial television and radio stations
Press – There are three main daily newspapers representing a range of political views; two are published in English and one in Swahili
WPFI score – 30,7 (90)

EDUCATION AND HEALTH
The state provides eight years of free primary education.
Literacy rate – 87.4 per cent (2010 est)
Gross enrolment ratio (percentage of relevant age group) – primary 112 per cent; secondary 60 per cent; tertiary 4 per cent (2011 est)
Health expenditure (per capita) – US$36 (2011)
Hospital beds (per 1,000 people) – 1.4 (2010)
Life expectancy (years) – 63.52 (2014 est)
Mortality rate – 7 (2014 est)
Birth rate – 28.27 (2014 est)
Infant mortality rate – 40.71 (2014 est)
HIV/AIDS adult prevalence – 6.1 per cent (2012 est)

KIRIBATI

Republic of Kiribati

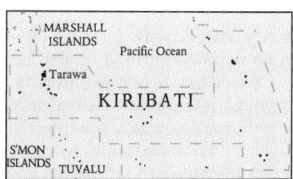

Area – 811 sq. km
Capital – Tarawa, on Bairiki; population, 43,000 (2009 est)
Currency – Australian dollar ($A) of 100 cents
Population – 104,488 rising at 1.18 per cent a year (2014 est); Micronesian (99.2 per cent), mixed (9.7 per cent) (2000)
Religion – Christian (Roman Catholic 56 per cent, Presbyterian 34, per cent Mormon 5 per cent), Baha'i 3 per cent (est)
Language – English, Kiribati (Gilbertese) (both official)
Population density – 123 per sq. km (2011)
Urban population – 44 per cent (2012 est)
Median age (years) – 23.6 (2014 est)
National anthem – 'Teirake Kaini Kiribati' ['Stand up, Kiribati']
National day – 12 July (Independence Day)
Death penalty – Abolished for all crimes (since 1979)
Gross enrolment ratio (percentage of relevant age group) – primary 116 per cent; secondary 86 per cent (2011 est)
Life expectancy (years) – 65.47 (2014 est)
Mortality rate – 7.18 (2014 est)
Birth rate – 21.85 (2014 est)
Infant mortality rate – 35.37 (2014 est)

CLIMATE AND TERRAIN
Kiribati (pronounced Kiri-bas) comprises 32 atolls and one island. About 20 are inhabited: Banaba island; the Kiribati (Gilbert) group (17); the Rawaki (Phoenix) Islands (8); and some of the Line Islands (11), including Kiritimati (Christmas Island). They are situated in the southern central Pacific Ocean, crossed by the Equator; the area was also crossed by the international date line until 1995, when the government unilaterally moved the date line eastwards so that the whole country shared the same day. Few of the atolls are more than 800m wide or more than 3m high, making the country particularly vulnerable to rising sea levels. The highest point is 81m (on Banaba) and the lowest is 0m (Pacific Ocean). The climate is tropical.

HISTORY AND POLITICS
The islands were settled by Austronesian-speaking peoples in the first millennium BC and Samoans, Fijians and Tongans migrated there in the 11th to 14th centuries. British settlers arrived in the islands in the early 19th century. In 1892, the Gilbert (Kiribati) and Ellice (Tuvalu) islands were proclaimed a British protectorate and in 1916 became a British colony which subsequently incorporated the Line Islands and Phoenix Islands. During the Second World War, Banaba and the Gilbert islands were occupied by the Japanese and were the scene of fierce fighting between Japanese and US troops. Some of the Line Islands were used for British nuclear weapons tests in the 1950s and 1960s. In 1975, the territories separated and the Gilbert, Phoenix and Line Islands became independent as the Republic of Kiribati in 1979.

Open-cast phosphate mining left Banaba unfit for human habitation and the population was evacuated in 1945, to be relocated to a northern island of Fiji. Overcrowding and lack of infrastructure have caused more general environmental degradation, especially in urban areas. However, the main problem is the rise in the sea level due to global warming; salination is already contaminating water supplies and agricultural land, causing villages to be relocated, and Kiribati is expected to be the first state to lose territory. The government is seeking permanent refugee status for its citizens in neighbouring countries.

Independent members gained the most number of seats in the 2011 legislative elections, picking up 17 of the 44 seats available; the Pillars of Truth group and United Coalition Party won 15 and 11 seats respectively. The incumbent president, Anote Tong, was re-elected for a third term in the 2012 presidential election.

Under the 1979 constitution, the executive president is directly elected for a four-year term, with a maximum of three terms; presidential candidates are selected by and from members of the legislature. The unicameral legislature, the House of Assembly, has 46 members: 44 members directly elected for a four-year term, an appointed representative of the Banaban community in Fiji and the attorney-general. There are no formal political parties, but since the 1980s some associations of politicians formed for elections have proved durable enough to be given names.

HEAD OF STATE
President, Foreign Affairs, Anote Tong, *elected* 4 July 2003, *sworn in* 6 July 2003, *re-elected* 2007, 2012
Vice-President, Teima Onorio

SELECTED GOVERNMENT MEMBERS *as at May 2014*
Commerce, Industry and Co-Operatives, Pinto Kaita
Finance and Economic Development, Tim Murdoch

KIRIBATI HONORARY CONSUL
The Great House, Llanddewi Rhydderich, Monmouthshire NP7 9UY
Honorary Consul, Michael Walsh

BRITISH HIGH COMMISSIONER
HE Roderick Drummond, *apptd* 2013, resident at Suva, Fiji

ECONOMY AND TRADE

Since the phosphate deposits on Banaba ran out in 1979, the economy has been weak, dependent on coconuts, fish and tourism (over 20 per cent of GDP) as the main economic activities; development is hampered by remoteness, poor transport connections and the lack of funding, infrastructure and skills. Additional revenue comes from international aid (over 20 per cent of GDP, mainly from Australia), the sale of fishing licences, remittances from expatriates and monies from the trust fund established with phosphate mining revenues. A financial sector is being developed. The main trading partners are Pacific Rim countries. The principal exports are copra (62 per cent), coconuts, seaweed and fish. The principal imports are foodstuffs, machinery and transport equipment, manufactured goods and fuel.

GNI – US$258m; US$2,520 per capita (2012)
Annual average growth of GDP – 2.9 per cent (2013)
Inflation rate – 0.2 per cent (2007 est)
Imports – US$100m (2012)
Exports – US$10m (2012)

BALANCE OF PAYMENTS
Trade – US$90m deficit (2012)
Current Account – US$30m deficit (2009)

Trade with UK	2012	2013
Imports from UK	£71,393	£132,736
Exports to UK	£20,524	£22,224

COMMUNICATIONS

Airports and waterways – Four, with the main international airport on Tarawa, while another on Kiritimati operates regular services to Fiji and Hawaii; the main seaport is Betio, on Tarawa
Roadways – 670km
Telecommunications – 9,000 fixed lines and 16,000 mobile subscriptions (2012); there were 7,800 internet users in 2009
Internet code and IDD – ki; 686 (from UK), 44 (to UK)
Media – The government-run newspaper and radio stations offer a diverse range of views; *Te Uekera* is the principal weekly newspaper

DEMOCRATIC PEOPLE'S REPUBLIC OF KOREA

Choson-minjujuui-inmin-konghwaguk – *Democratic People's Republic of Korea*

Area – 120,538 sq. km
Capital – Pyongyang; population, 2,843,000 (2011)

Major cities – Chongjin, Hamhung, Hungnam, Nampo
Currency – North Korean won of 100 chon
Population – 24,851,627 rising at 0.53 per cent a year (2014 est)
Religion – Religious activity is almost non-existent outside government-sponsored religious groups, although many believers are thought to worship in private. Historically, the main religions were Buddhism and Confucianism; Buddhism, Christianity and Chondo (a syncretic religion) are officially recognised
Language – Korean (official)
Population density – 205 per sq. km (2011)
Urban population – 60.4 per cent (2012 est)
Median age (years) – 33.4 (2014 est)
National anthem – 'Aegukka' ['The Patriotic Song']
National day – 9 September (Founding of the Democratic People's Republic of Korea, 1948)
Death penalty – Retained
CPI score – 8 (175)
Health expenditure (per capita) – $22 (2007)
Life expectancy (years) – 69.81 (2014 est)
Mortality rate – 9.18 (2014 est)
Birth rate – 14.51 (2014 est)
Infant mortality rate – 24.5 (2014 est)

CLIMATE AND TERRAIN

The republic occupies the northern half of the Korean peninsula. The land rises from coastal plains in the west to mountains and hills that occupy 80 per cent of the land area. Elevation extremes range from 2,744m (Paektu-san) to 0m (Sea of Japan). The climate is temperate, though more extreme than in South Korea. Average temperatures in Pyongyang range from −6°C in January to 24°C in July and August.

HISTORY AND POLITICS

After the Korean war ended in 1953, Kim Il-sung continued the process of Soviet-style reform begun in 1946. He also developed *Juche* (self-reliance), an ideology demanding total economic independence. North Korea pursued an isolationist foreign policy for several decades, only signing a mutual assistance treaty with China in 1961 and improving relations with the USSR in 1985. It established diplomatic contacts with South Korea and Japan in 1990, raising hopes that it was abandoning its isolationism, but it remains a secretive, closed country under rigid state control.

Kim Il-sung died in 1994. His son Kim Jong-il became chairman of the National Defence Commission, designated as the highest post of the state, and general secretary of the Korean Workers' Party in 1997. The most recent elections to the Supreme People's Assembly took place in April 2009, and the assembly re-elected Kim Jong-il to his post. In September 2010 the Korean Workers' Party congress (the first for 44 years) renewed the top party leadership; Kim Jong-il's third son, Kim Jong-un, was appointed to senior political and military posts, before ascending to supreme leader following the death of Kim Jong-il in December 2012. In December 2013 Kim Jong-un's uncle Chang Song-thaek, a senior political figure within North Korea, was executed in a move seen by observers as an attempt to consolidate Kim's regime.

The communist Korean Workers' Party, founded in 1946 by Kim Il-sung, is the only permitted political party. However, political control and leadership is maintained by the cult of personality created by Kim Il-sung and continued by his successors Kim Jong-il and Kim Jong-un.

The 1972 constitution was amended in 1998 to designate leading state posts; it made Kim Il-sung the Eternal President and the chairmanship of the National Defence Commission

Yi dynasty; rise of   Divided along the 38th parallel by   Unification defied by North Korea (NK);   Both sides agree need for peace
Koryo   Confucianism; becomes   occupying armies of liberation: US troops   South Korea (SK) declares independence,   treaty; armistice tested by
dynasty   a vassal of China   in south and Soviet troops in north   triggering invasion from NK   sinking of SK ship by NK forces

1876-
1910
668   1948   1953
          935   1395-   1950   2007-10
                       c.1900   1945

Independent kingdoms   Japan annexes   Republic of Korea founded; Democratic   A UN/US force   Armistice signed;
and city states united by   country and   People's Republic of Korea established   intervenes; China enters   demilitarised border
Buddhist Silla dynasty   forces trade route   along with a Supreme People's Soviet   war in support of NK   zone established

(NDC), held by Kim Jong-il, the highest post in the state, while providing that the chairman of the Presidium of the Supreme People's Assembly would represent the state on formal occasions. A further amendment in 2009 named the NDC chairman as the 'supreme leader of the state'; it also removed all references to communism, and established the *songun* principle of military responsibility for all internal affairs.

There is a unicameral legislature, the Supreme People's Assembly, which has 687 members directly elected from a single list of candidates for a five-year term. The assembly elects a presidium and the premier, appointing the government on the recommendation of the premier. The Central People's Committee, which is also elected by the assembly, directs the administrative council (government), which implements the policy formulated by the committee.

HEAD OF STATE
Eternal President, Kim Il-sung (deceased)
Eternal General Secretary, Kim Jong-il (deceased)
Supreme Leader, Kim Jong-un
President of the Presidium of the Supreme People's Assembly,
   Kim Yong-nam

SELECTED GOVERNMENT MEMBERS *as at May 2014*
Premier, Pak Pong Ju
Deputy Premiers, Ri Chol-man; Jon Sung-hun; Kim In-sik;
   Ri Mu-yong; Kang Nung-su; Kim Yong-jin; Kang Sok-ju
Finance, Chow Kwang-jin
Foreign Affairs, Ri Su-yong

EMBASSY OF THE DEMOCRATIC PEOPLE'S
REPUBLIC OF KOREA
73 Gunnersbury Avenue, London W5 4LP
T 020-8992 4965 E
prkinfo@yahoo.com
Ambassador Extraordinary and Plenipotentiary, HE Hak Bong
   Hyon, *apptd* 2012

BRITISH EMBASSY
Munsu Dong compound, Pyongyang
T (+850) (2) 381 7980
W www.gov.uk/government/world/north-korea
Ambassador Extraordinary and Plenipotentiary, HE Michael
   Gifford, *apptd* 2012

INTERNATIONAL RELATIONS
The D.P.R.K's relations with other countries have been erratic over the past 20 years, largely owing to its nuclear ambitions and international reaction to these. It first agreed to freeze its nuclear development programme in return for fuel and development aid in 1994, only to restart the programme in 2002, claiming that other parties to the agreement had reneged on it. This pattern has been repeated several times, with the regime using the discontinuation of its nuclear and missile development programmes to bargain for aid from international agencies and regional powers. Six-nation talks to resolve the nuclear issues began in 2003 after North Korea withdrew from the Nuclear Non-

proliferation Treaty, but North Korea has never fully complied with any of the agreements concluded at the talks. The consequent suspension of aid by other nations, and UN censure and sanctions after North Korea test-fired ballistic missiles and nuclear devices in 2006, 2009, 2012 and 2013 have been interpreted as acts of aggression by North Korea and met with a bellicose response from the regime.

DEFENCE

Aged 16–49, 2010 est	*Males*	*Females*
Available for military service	6,515,279	6,418,693
Fit for military service	4,836,567	5,230,137

Conscription – 18 years of age (presumed)

ECONOMY AND TRADE
Although North Korea is rich in natural resources and had developed a heavy industry base in the first half of the 20th century, the economy is stagnant after decades of mismanagement, underinvestment, low export levels and the diversion of resources to military expenditure. Its long decline was compounded by the loss of Soviet support from 1991.

A series of natural disasters in the 1990s caused severe famine, obliging the government to request international aid. It is estimated that 3 million people have died since the 1990s as a result of the acute food shortages, which continue despite international food and fuel aid.

A redenomination of North Korea's currency in 2009 wiped out many people's savings, disrupted the nascent private sector, triggered rapid inflation and was met with unprecedented public protests that lasted some weeks. The country continues to develop special economic zones with China, however, and in 2012 expressed willingness to permit a construction of a gas pipeline that would carry Russian gas to the Republic of Korea.

Industrial output is centred on mining, steel, chemicals and machine building, but antiquated machinery and fuel shortages have limited output to a fraction of pre-1990 levels. Agriculture is in an equally parlous state, as collective farming, lack of arable land and chronic shortages of fertilisers and agricultural machinery prevent the country from producing enough to feed its population. It has been dependent on massive amounts of food aid since the mid-1990s to avert a repeat of the 1995 famine, but chronic malnutrition is widespread. A relaxation of restrictions on private farming and markets in 2003 was partially rescinded in 2005 and a centralised rationing system was reinstated. South Korean assistance in developing infrastructure, industry, the Kaesong Industrial Zone and tourism has been limited by North Korea's restrictions, and was reduced or suspended when South Korea imposed sanctions on the North in 2010.

The main trading partners are China and South Korea. Principal exports are minerals, metallurgical products, armaments, textiles, and agricultural and fish products. The main imports are petroleum, coal, machinery and equipment, textiles and grain.

Annual average growth of GDP – 1.3 per cent (2011 est)

Trade with UK	2012	2013
Imports from UK	£333,826	£557,274
Exports to UK	£1,333,663	£3,744,599

COMMUNICATIONS

Airports and waterways – There are 39 airports, the largest of which is at Pyongyang. There are some 2,250km of waterways but these are navigable only by small craft; the main seaports are Chongjin, Nampo and Wonsan
Roadways and railways – There are 104,983km of roadways, although few are surfaced, and 3,381km of railways
Telecommunications – 1.18 million fixed lines and 1.7 million mobile subscriptions (2012)
Internet code and IDD – kp; 850 (from UK), 44 (to UK)
Media – There are no independent media outlets in North Korea; all television, radios and national newspapers are government organs
WPFI score – 81,96 (179)

REPUBLIC OF KOREA

Taehan-min'guk – Republic of Korea

Area – 99,720 sq. km
Capital – Seoul; population, 9,768,874 (2012 est)
Major cities – Busan, Changwon, Daegu, Daejon, Gwangju, Incheon, Suwon, Urusan
Currency – South Korean won of 100 jeon
Population – 49,039,986 rising at 0.16 per cent a year (2014 est)
Religion – Buddhist 24 per cent (predominantly the Jogye order of the Seon (Zen) school), Christian (Protestant 24 per cent, Roman Catholic 8 per cent), none 43 per cent (est)
Language – Korean (official), English
Population density – 513 per sq. km (2011)
Urban population – 83.5 per cent (2012 est)
Median age (years) – 40.2 (2014 est)
National anthem – 'Aegukka' ['The Patriotic Song']
National day – 15 August (Liberation Day)
Death penalty – Retained (last used 1997)
CPI score – 56 (45)

CLIMATE AND TERRAIN

The country occupies the southern part of the mountainous Korean peninsula, with highlands and mountains accounting for around 70 per cent of the land area. Elevation extremes range from 1,950m (Halla-san) to 0m (Sea of Japan). The climate is temperate, although winters are very cold for the latitude. Average temperatures in Seoul range from −2°C in January to 25°C in August. The rainy season lasts from June to September.

HISTORY AND POLITICS

From 1948, South Korea experienced over 40 years of mostly authoritarian, often military, rule and great industrial development. Syngman Rhee, president from 1948, resigned in 1960 in the face of popular protests at corruption and electoral fraud. A military coup in 1961 brought General Park Chung-hee to power and he instigated a programme of industrial development; by the time of his assassination in 1979, Korea was a leading shipbuilding nation and producer of electronic goods.

Following riots against the interim government, General Chun Do-hwan assumed power in 1980 after martial law was declared. Pro-democracy agitation in the mid-1980s led to constitutional changes in 1987 and the first multi-party legislative elections in 1988, but despite the anti-corruption campaign of the new democratically elected president Roh Tae-woo, politics continued to be plagued by allegations of corruption and fraud, and was subject to military influence. The first civilian president and the first wholly civilian government since 1961 were appointed in 1993.

The 2007 presidential election was won by Lee Myung-bak, the Grand National Party (GNP) candidate. Lee Myung-bak's government reversed the 'sunshine policy' of greater political contact with the north in 2008; it imposed sanctions on North Korea in 2010, blaming the north for the sinking of one of its warships in March 2010. In the 2012 legislative election, the New Frontier Party, formerly known as the GNP, won a small overall majority in the National Assembly. In December 2012 Park Geun-hye was elected South Korea's first female president and assumed office in February 2013. In June 2014, it was announced that Prime minister Chung Hong-won would retain his poisition, despite previously resigning after the *Sewol* ferry disaster (*see* Events).

A new constitution was adopted when the Sixth Republic was inaugurated in 1988. Under this, the president is directly elected for a five-year term, which is not renewable. The president appoints the prime minister with the approval of the legislature, and members of the state council (cabinet) on the recommendation of the prime minister. The president is also empowered to take wide-ranging measures in an emergency, including the declaration of martial law, but must obtain the agreement of the legislature. The unicameral National Assembly has 300 members who are directly elected for a four-year term.

HEAD OF STATE
President, Park Geun-hye, *elected* 19 December 2012, *sworn in* 25 February 2013

SELECTED GOVERNMENT MEMBERS *as at September 2014*
Prime Minister, Chung Hong-Won
Defence, Gen. Han Min-Koo
Finance, Choi Kyung-Hwan
Foreign Affairs, Yun Byung-se

EMBASSY OF THE REPUBLIC OF KOREA
60 Buckingham Gate, London SW1E 6AJ
T 020-7227 5500 E koreanembinuk@mofat.go.kr
W www.gbr.mofat.go.kr
Ambassador Extraordinary and Plenipotentiary, HE Sungnam Lim, *apptd* 2013

BRITISH EMBASSY
Sejong-daero 19-gil 24, Jung-gu, Seoul 100-120
T (+82) (2) 3210 5500 E enquiry.seoul@fco.gov.uk
W https://www.gov.uk/government/world/south-korea
Ambassador Extraordinary and Plenipotentiary, HE Scott Wightman, CMG, *apptd* 2011

DEFENCE

Aged 16–49, 2010 est	Males	Females
Available for military service	13,185,794	12,423,496
Fit for military service	10,864,566	10,168,709

Military expenditure – US$32,352m (2013)
Conscription – 20–30 years of age; 21–24 months (selective)

ECONOMY AND TRADE

Industrialisation from the 1960s transformed South Korea from a predominantly agrarian country into one of the Asian 'miracle' economies by the 1980s. Initially based on shipbuilding and electrical goods, production shifted towards electronics and IT goods in the 1980s. By 1997 South Korea was the world's eleventh-largest economy, with an annual GDP growth rate of 8 per cent. However, the dominating conglomerates *(chaebols)* were experiencing difficulties which, exacerbated by the Asian financial crisis in 1997, caused a number to collapse in the late 1990s and the economy to contract sharply. Corporate and financial reforms were introduced and GDP growth resumed from the early 2000s. Slow growth in Europe, the US and China reduced South Korean growth in 2012 and 2013. Long-term challenges include an ageing population, reliance on a small number of large companies and a dependence on exports.

Services contribute 58.2 per cent to GDP, industry 39.2 per cent and agriculture 2.6 per cent. Major manufacturing industries include electronics, telecommunications, motor vehicles, chemicals, shipbuilding and steel. Tourism is of growing importance.

The main trading partners are China, Japan and the USA (the US-South Korea Trade Agreement was first signed in 2007 and ratified in 2011). Principal exports are semi-conductors, telecommunications equipment, motor vehicles, computers, steel, ships and petrochemicals. The main imports are machinery, electronics and electronic equipment, oil, steel, transport equipment, organic chemicals and plastics.
GNI – US$1,135,889m; US$22,670 per capita (2012)
Annual average growth of GDP – 2.8 per cent (2013 est)
Inflation rate – 1.1 per cent (2013 est)
Population below poverty line – 16 per cent (2009 est)
Unemployment – 3.2 per cent (2013 est)
Total external debt – US$430,900m (2013 est)
Imports – US$519,565m (2012)
Exports – US$547,879m (2012)

BALANCE OF PAYMENTS
Trade – US$28,310m surplus (2012)
Current Account – US$43,139m surplus (2012)

Trade with UK	2012	2013
Imports from UK	£4,571,743,881	£4,827,221,291
Exports to UK	£3,134,474,111	£3,264,365,313

COMMUNICATIONS

Airports and waterways – 71, including international airports at Seoul (Kimpo), Kimhae (near Busan), Daegu, Cheju city and Incheon; Busan, Incheon and Pohang are the major ports, although development and operations at Incheon are hampered by tidal variations of 9–10m
Roadways and railways – There are 104,983km of roadways, of which 3,779km are motorways, and 3,381km of railway in commercial operation, of which 1,843km are electrified
Telecommunications – 30.1 million fixed lines and 53.625 million mobile telephone subscriptions (2012); there were 39.4 million internet users in 2009

Internet code and IDD – kr; 82 (from UK), 1 44/2 44 (to UK)
Major broadcasters – Korea has a number of public radio and television broadcasters, including Korea Broadcasting System (KBS) and Munhwa Broadcasting Corporation (MBC), as well as a diversified commercial sector
Press – Major newspapers include *Korea Daily* and English-language daily *Korea Herald*
WPFI score – 25,66 (57)

EDUCATION AND HEALTH

Primary education is free and compulsory for nine years from the age of six.
Gross enrolment ratio (percentage of relevant age group) – primary 104 per cent; secondary 97 per cent; tertiary 101 per cent (2011 est)
Health expenditure (per capita) – US$1,616 (2011)
Hospital beds (per 1,000 people) – 10.3 (2009)
Life expectancy (years) – 79.8 (2014 est)
Mortality rate – 6.63 (2014 est)
Birth rate – 8.26 (2014 est)
Infant mortality rate – 3.93 (2014 est)

KOSOVO

Republika e Kosoves – Republic of Kosovo

Area – 10,887 sq. km
Capital – Pristina; population, 500,000 (2009 est)
Major towns – Mitrovica, Pec, Prizren
Currency – Euro (€) of 100 cents; the Serbian dinar is also in circulation
Population – 1,859,203 (2014 est); Albanian (92 per cent), Serb, Bosniak, Turk, Ashkali, Egyptian, Roma and Gorani (8 per cent) (2008)
Religion – Muslim, Christian (Serbian Orthodox, Roman Catholic, Protestant)
Language – Albanian, Serbian (both official), Bosnian, Turkish, Romani
Population density – 165 per sq. km (2011)
Median age (years) – 27.8 (2014 est)
National anthem – 'Europe'
National day – 17 February (Independence Day)
CPI score – 33 (111)

CLIMATE AND TERRAIN

Kosovo has a hilly central region which divides plains in the east and west. Mountains lie along the borders with Albania, Macedonia and Montenegro, and along much of the border with Serbia. Elevation extremes range from 2,656m (Gjeravica) to 297m (Drini i Bardhe river). The main rivers are the Drini i Bardhe in the west and the Iberi in the north. The climate is continental.

Serbia regains control after First Balkan War; becomes province of Serbia, then part of Yugoslavia — 1389

Stripped of its autonomy by Serbian government and Albanian majority; gradually excluded from public life — 1945

Insurgency by the Kosovan Liberation Army provokes Serbian military reprisals — 1991

NATO intervention; Serbia signs peace plan and withdraws forces — 1998

International Court of Justice rules declaration legal; it is accepted by UN but refused by Serbia — 2008

1913 — Battle of Kosovo; Serbian principalities become part of the Ottoman Empire

1989 — Becomes an autonomous republic within Serbia

c.1995 — Vote of independence declared illegal by Serbian government

1999 — Serbia begins systematic ethnic cleansing of country

2010 — Kosovan government declares independence; it goes unrecognised by the UN

POLITICS

Under the 2008 constitution, the president is elected by the legislature for a five-year term and can be re-elected once. The unicameral legislature, the Assembly of Kosovo, has 120 members, elected for a four-year term; 100 seats have directly elected members, ten seats are reserved for Serbs and ten for other minorities. The majority party or coalition nominates the prime minister, who is appointed by the president. Both the prime minister and the government must be approved by the legislature.

In the June 2014 legislative elections, the ruling Democratic Party of Kosovo won the most seats but failed to form a new coalition government as of September. Behgjet Pacolli was elected president unopposed in February 2011, but the constitutional court declared the election unconstitutional; Atifete Jahjaga was elected president in April 2011.

HEAD OF STATE
President, Atifete Jahjaga, *elected* 7 April 2011

SELECTED GOVERNMENT MEMBERS *as at May 2014*
Prime Minister, Hashim Thaci
First Deputy Prime Minister, Behgjet Pacolli
Finance, Besim Beqaj
Foreign Affairs, Enver Hoxhaj

EMBASSY OF THE REPUBLIC OF KOSOVO
100 Pall Mall, London SW1Y 5NQ
T 020-7659 6140 E embassy.uk@ks-gov.net
W kosovoembassy.org.uk
Ambassador Extraordinary and Plenipotentiary, HE Lirim Greicevci, *apptd* 2012

BRITISH EMBASSY
Ismail Qemali 6, Arberi, Dragodan, Pristina
T (+381) 3825 4700 E britishembassy.pristina@fco.gov.uk
W www.gov.uk/government/world/kosovo
Ambassador Extraordinary and Plenipotentiary, HE Ian Cameron Cliff, OBE, *apptd* 2011

ECONOMY AND TRADE

Under UN administration Kosovo began the transition to a market economy, and over half of state-owned businesses have been privatised. However, income levels are the lowest in Europe, and the economy is dependent on international and foreign aid and the remittances of expatriates, worth about 10 per cent and 14 per cent of GDP respectively. Agriculture is close to subsistence level and inefficient; industrial output has declined because of insufficient investment and an unemployment level of over 45 per cent encourages emigration. International agencies and foreign governments are working with the Kosovan government to stimulate economic growth, attract investment and reduce unemployment

Kosovo joined the Central Europe Free Trade Area (CEFTA) in 2006, and its members are the main markets for exports of minerals and processed metal products, scrap metals, leather goods, machinery and appliances. Imports of foodstuffs, wood, fuels, chemicals, machinery and electrical equipment come mainly from EU and neighbouring countries. In 2011 Serbia and Bosnia resumed trade with Kosovo, while a free trade agreement was signed with Turkey in 2013. The country continues to negotiate trade liberalisation with the EU.

GNI – US$6,401m; US$3,600 per capita (2012)
Annual average growth of GDP – 2.6 (2013 est)
Inflation rate – 8.3 per cent (2011 est)
Population below poverty line – 30 per cent (2010 est)
Unemployment – 45.3 per cent (2011 est)

BALANCE OF PAYMENTS
Current Account – US$917m deficit (2011)

Trade with UK	2012	2013
Imports from UK	£5,995,200	£3,639,089
Exports to UK	£929,374	£718,185

COMMUNICATIONS

Airports – Four; the principal international terminal is at Pristina
Roadways and railways – 1,843km; 430km
Telecommunications – 106,300 fixed lines (2006) and 562,900 mobile telephone subscriptions (2007)
Internet code and IDD – kv; 381 (from UK), 44 (to UK)
Media – Kosovo Radio-Television is the country's main broadcaster and there are six daily newspapers selling to a limited readership
WPFI score – 29,29 (80)

KUWAIT

Dawlat al-Kuwayt – State of Kuwait

Area – 17,818 sq. km
Capital – Kuwait City (al-Kuwayt); population, 2,436,985 (2012 est)
Currency – Kuwaiti dinar (KD) of 1,000 fils
Population – 2,742,711 rising at 1.7 per cent a year (2014 est); Kuwaiti (45 per cent), other Arab (35 per cent), South Asian (9 per cent), Iranian (4 per cent) (est)

Religion – Muslim (official) (Sunni 77 per cent, the remainder predominantly Shia) (est); Christian, Hindu and Parsi minorities, mostly expatriates
Language – Arabic (official), English
Population density – 175 per sq. km (2011)
Urban population – 98.3 per cent (2012 est)
Median age (years) – 28.9 (2014 est)
National anthem – 'Al-Nasheed al-Watani' ['National Anthem']
National day – 25 February
Death penalty – Retained
CPI score – 44 (66)

CLIMATE AND TERRAIN
Kuwait is an almost entirely flat desert plain, with elevation extremes ranging from 306m to 0m (Persian Gulf). Its territory includes the island of Bubiyan and others at the head of the Persian Gulf. The climate is arid, with little rainfall but high levels of humidity. Average temperatures range from 12°C in January to 36°C in July.

HISTORY AND POLITICS
The area was under the nominal control of the Ottoman Empire from the late 16th century, but in 1756 an autonomous sheikhdom was founded that has been ruled by the al-Sabah family ever since. Kuwait entered into a treaty of friendship with Britain in 1899, in order to protect itself from Ottoman and Saudi domination, and it became a British protectorate in 1914. The borders with Saudi Arabia and Iraq were agreed between 1922 and 1933. Full independence was achieved in 1961, although Britain retained a military presence in the country until 1971.

An attempted Iraqi invasion shortly after independence in 1961 was discouraged by British troops in the Gulf. However, in August 1990 Iraq invaded and occupied Kuwait, proclaiming it a province of Iraq. In 1991, a short military campaign by a US-led alliance expelled the Iraqi forces, although there were further Iraqi incursions in 1993 before Iraq renounced its claim and recognised the new UN-demarcated border in 1994. Extensive damage was caused to the country's infrastructure and environment during the Iraqi occupation and the liberation campaign, and reconstruction was a priority throughout the 1990s. In 2003, Kuwait was a base for forces involved in the Iraq War, and it remains an important transit route for military and civilian traffic into and out of Iraq.

In recent years, there have been clashes between security forces and militant Islamists, some of whom are alleged to have links to al-Qaida.

Although Kuwait was the first Arab country in the Gulf to have an elected legislature, this was suspended from 1977–81, 1986–92, and in 1999, 2012 and 2013. The political system is subject to instability, with electoral boycotts by Islamist and liberal parties common; two elections were held in 12 months in 2008–9 owing to the legislature's efforts to subject the government to parliamentary scrutiny. Pro-reform demonstrations took place in spring 2011, forcing Sheikh Nasser al-Muhammad al-Ahmed al-Sabeh's government to resign from office; the cabinet was replaced by a new government headed by Sheikh Jaber Mubarak al-Hamad al-Sabeh who retained power until the next election. The 2012 legislative election saw Islamists retain the largest bloc in the National Assembly, after which Sheikh Jaber was reappointed prime minster.

The 1962 constitution was amended in 2005 to extend the franchise to women. The head of state is the emir, chosen from among the ruling family. He exercises executive power through the council of ministers; in 2003, the post of prime minister was separated from the role of heir to the throne for the first time. The unicameral National Assembly has 50 members directly elected for a four-year term. There are no political parties.

The country is divided into six governorates: Capital, Hawalli, al-Ahmadi, al-Jahrah, al-Farwaniya and Mubarak al-Kabeer.

HEAD OF STATE
HH The Emir of Kuwait, Sheikh Sabah al-Ahmad al-Jaber al-Sabah, *born* 1929, *acceded* 29 January 2006
Crown Prince, HH Sheikh Nawaf al-Ahmad al-Jaber al-Sabah

SELECTED GOVERNMENT MEMBERS *as at May 2014*
Prime Minister, Sheikh Jaber Mubarak al-Hamad al-Sabah
First Deputy Prime Minister, Interior, Sheikh Ahmad Hamoud al-Jaber al-Sabah
Deputy Prime Minister, Defence, Sheikh Ahmad Khalid al-Hamad al-Sabah
Deputy Prime Minister, Foreign Affairs, Sheikh Sabah Khaled al-Hamad al-Sabah

EMBASSY OF THE STATE OF KUWAIT
2 Albert Gate, London SW1X 7JU
T 020-7590 3400 E kuwait@dircon.co.uk
Ambassador Extraordinary and Plenipotentiary, HE Khaled al-Duwaisan, GCVO, *apptd* 1993

BRITISH EMBASSY
PO Box 2, Arabian Gulf Street, Safat 13001
T (+965) 2259 4320 W www.gov.uk/government/world/kuwait
Ambassador Extraordinary and Plenipotentiary, HE Frank Baker, OBE, *apptd* 2010

DEFENCE

Aged 16–49, 2010 est	*Males*	*Females*
Available for military service	1,002,480	616,958
Fit for military service	840,912	523,206

Military expenditure – US$5,644m (2013)

ECONOMY AND TRADE
Oil was discovered in 1938 and the development of the oil industry after 1945 transformed the country from one of the poorest in the world to one of the richest. Petroleum accounts for 95 per cent of export revenues and 95 per cent of government income. Income from foreign reserves and investment is also high, cushioning the economy from the effects of dependency on oil. Economic reform is slow owing to the tensions between the government and legislature; a diversification fund worth US$130 billion was established in 2010, though much of this money has yet to be spent.

The climate and terrain limit agriculture and, with the exception of fish, all food is imported; the primary sector contributes only 0.3 per cent of GDP. Services account for 50.6 per cent of GDP and industry for 49.1 per cent. Apart from the oil and petrochemical industries, activities include the production of cement and construction materials, shipbuilding and repair, water desalination and food processing.

The main export markets are South Korea, India, Japan, China and the USA, and the main sources of imports are the USA, China, Saudi Arabia and South Korea. Principal exports are oil and refined products, and fertilisers. The main imports are food, construction materials, vehicles and vehicle parts, and clothing.

GNI – US$132,166m (2010); US$44,100 per capita (2010)
Annual average growth of GDP – 2.3 per cent (2013 est)

Inflation rate – 2.8 per cent (2013 est)
Unemployment – 3.4 per cent (2011 est)
Total external debt – US$34,410m (2013 est)
Imports – US$25,881m (2012)
Exports – US$118,546m (2012)

BALANCE OF PAYMENTS
Trade – US$92,666m surplus (2012)
Current Account – US$79,768m surplus (2012)

Trade with UK	2012	2013
Imports from UK	£578,774,976	£531,106,548
Exports to UK	£1,457,245,485	£1,647,186,395

COMMUNICATIONS
Airports and waterways – Four, with an international airport at Kuwait City; the main seaports are Ash Shu'aybah and Ash Shuwaykh
Roadways – There are 6,608 km of roadways, most of which are surfaced
Telecommunications – 510,000 fixed lines and 5.526 million mobile subscriptions; there were 1.1 million internet users in 2009
Internet code and IDD – kw; 965 (from UK), 44 (to UK)
Major broadcasters – State-run radio and television broadcasters compete with commercial stations; satellite television is also widely watched
WPFI score – 30,71 (91)

EDUCATION AND HEALTH
Education is free and compulsory from six to 14 years.
Literacy rate – 93.9 per cent (2010 est)
Gross enrolment ratio (percentage of relevant age group) –
    primary 106 per cent; secondary 101 per cent (2011 est)
Health expenditure (per capita) – US$1,500 (2011)
Hospital beds (per 1,000 people) – 2 (2009)
Life expectancy (years) – 77.64 (2014 est)
Mortality rate – 2.16 (2014 est)
Birth rate – 20.26 (2013 est)
Infant mortality rate – 7.51 (2014 est)

KYRGYZSTAN

Kyrgyz Respublikasy – Kyrgyz Republic

Area – 199,951 sq. km
Capital – Bishkek; population, 882,797 (2012 est)
Major city – Osh
Currency – Som of 100 tyiyn
Population – 5,604,212 rising at 1.04 per cent a year (2014 est); Kyrgyz (64.7 per cent), Uzbek (13.6 per cent), Russian (12.5 per cent), Dungan (1 per cent), Ukrainian (1 per cent), Uygur (1 per cent) (est)

Religion – Muslim 75 per cent (predominantly Sunni), Christian (Russian Orthodox) 20 per cent, other 5 per cent
Language – Kyrgyz, Russian (both official), Uzbek, Dungun
Population density – 29 per sq. km (2011)
Urban population – 35.4 per cent (2012)
Median age (years) – 25.7 (2014 est)
National anthem – 'Kyrgyz Respublikasynyn Mamlekettik Gimni' ['National Anthem of the Kyrgyz Republic']
National day – 31 August (Independence Day)
Death penalty – Abolished for all crimes (since 2007)
CPI score – 24 (150)
Literacy rate – 99 per cent (2010 est)
Gross enrolment ratio (percentage of relevant age group) –
    primary 101 per cent; secondary 88 per cent; tertiary 41 per cent (2011 est)
Health expenditure (per capita) – US$71 (2011)
Hospital beds (per 1,000 people) – 4.8 (2011)
Life expectancy (years) – 70.06 (2014 est)
Mortality rate – 6.74 (2014 est)
Birth rate – 23.33 (2014 est)
Infant mortality rate – 28.71 (2014 est)

CLIMATE AND TERRAIN
Kyrgyzstan is a landlocked and mountainous country lying in the Tien Shan mountain range, with the Pamir mountains in the extreme south. Elevations range from 7,439m (Jengish Chokusu) to 132m (Kara-Darya), though most of the country lies at over 1,000m. The principal rivers are the Naryn and the Chu, and the vast Issyk-Kul lake lies in the north-east. The climate is continental but with temperatures and humidity moderated by the altitude; typical temperatures in Bishkek range from −2.6°C in January to 24.9°C in July. Rainfall is low for the altitude, owing to Kyrgyzstan's distance from the sea and the rain-shadow effect of the Himalayan and Pamir ranges.

HISTORY AND POLITICS
After centuries of Turkic, Mongol and Chinese rule, the Kyrgyz became part of the Russian Empire in the 1860s and 1870s. After the October 1917 revolution in Russia, the area became part of the Turkestan autonomous republic within the USSR until 1924, when the Kirgiz Autonomous Region was formed. Soviet rule brought land reforms in the 1920s that resulted in the settlement of many of the nomadic Kyrgyz. Kyrgyzstan became an autonomous republic in 1926 and a constituent republic of the USSR in 1936.

Reform in the USSR in the 1980s provoked an upsurge in nationalism in Kyrgyzstan and agitation for independence. Following the attempted coup in Moscow in 1991, Kyrgyzstan became an independent republic and joined the Commonwealth of Independent States.

Since independence, there has been tension between the Kyrgyz and ethnic Uzbeks, concentrated around Osh, and between the Kyrgyz and Dungans (ethnic Chinese) near Bishkek. There have also been clashes between security forces and militant Islamists, active near the border with Tajikistan.

Askar Akayev, a pro-reform Communist, was president from 1990 until he was deposed in March 2005 in a popular uprising over alleged electoral fraud; the uprising was also fuelled by years of unrest over the dire economic situation, corruption, nepotism and crime. The opposition leader Kurmanbek Bakiyev was elected president in July 2005 and re-elected in 2009, but forced from office in April 2010 after attempts to suppress anti-government demonstrations left over 80 protesters dead.

An interim government was formed, but intercommunal violence between Kyrgyz and Uzbeks erupted in June 2010, spreading to Jalalabad; a referendum held in the same month approved a draft constitution granting greater powers to parliament at the expense of the president.

The 2010 legislative election was indecisive: the four main parties won roughly the same number of seats each. Two, the Social Democratic Party (SDPK) and Respublika, formed a coalition government with the Homeland party and took office in December. Former prime minister and SDPK leader Almazbek Atambayev won the 2011 presidential election, taking over from interim president Roza Otunbayeva. In March 2014, the government of Prime Minister Zhantoro Satybaldiyev resigned following allegations of corruption; reformist politician Joomart Otorbaev was elected to the premiership vote by a majority of the legislature.

Under the 2010 constitution, the president will be directly elected for a six-year term, which is not renewable. The unicameral Supreme Council has 120 members directly elected for a five-year term. The largest party in the legislature nominates the prime minister, and the president appoints the cabinet; the appointments are subject to the approval of the Supreme Council.

HEAD OF STATE
President, Almazbek Atambayev, *sworn in* 1 December 2011

SELECTED GOVERNMENT MEMBERS *as at May 2014*
Prime Minister, Joomart Otorbaev
First Vice-Prime Minister, Tayirbek Sarpashev
Foreign Affairs, Erlan Abdyldayev
Internal Affairs, Abdylda Suranchiyev

EMBASSY OF THE KYRGYZ REPUBLIC
Ascot House, 119 Crawford Street, London W1U 6BJ
T 020-7935 1462 E mail@kyrgyz embassy.org.uk
W www.kyrgyz-embassy.org.uk
Ambassador Extraordinary and Plenipotentiary, vacant

BRITISH EMBASSY
21 Erkindik Boulevard, Office 404, Bishkek, 720040, Kyrgyzstan
T (+996) 312 303 637 E ukinkyrgyzrepublic@fco.gov.uk
W www.gov.uk/government/world/kyrgyzstan
Ambassador Extraordinary and Plenipotentiary, HE Judith Margaret Farnworth, *apptd* 2011

DEFENCE

Aged 16–49, 2010 est	Males	Females
Available for military service	1,456,881	1,470,317
Fit for military service	1,119,224	1,257,263

Military expenditure – US$221m (2013)
Conscription – 18–27 years of age, male only; 12 months

ECONOMY AND TRADE
Economic reforms in the early 1990s caused severe hardship, and although productivity and exports have grown since the late 1990s, poverty is widespread and unemployment high, particularly in the south. The economy, which is heavily dependent on gold exports, contracted in 2009 owing to the global downturn, and production and trade were reduced further by the political violence and disruption of 2010. Despite such damage to the infrastructure, the economy grew 1 per cent in 2013 increasing to 17.4 per cent in 2013. The government, with international support, is pursuing poverty-reduction and economic-growth programmes, but the greater foreign direct investment that these require may be deterred by political volatility, lack of transparency and the high level of organised crime. Kyrgyzstan has expressed interest in joining the customs union between Russia, Belarus and Kazakhstan.

The economy is predominantly agrarian, with agriculture accounting for 20.8 per cent of GDP and employing 48 per cent of the workforce. There are deposits of gold, uranium, mercury and natural gas. Apart from mining, industry consists of hydroelectric power generation and light manufacturing, contributing 34.4 per cent of GDP; services contribute 44.8 per cent.

The main trading partners are China, Russia, the UAE, Kazakhstan and Uzbekistan. Principal exports are cotton, wool, meat, tobacco, gold, mercury, uranium, natural gas, hydroelectric power, machinery and shoes. The main imports are oil, gas, machinery and equipment, chemicals and foodstuffs.

GNI – US$6,085m; US$990 per capita (2012)
Annual average growth of GDP – 7.4 per cent (2013 est)
Inflation rate – 6.8 per cent (2013 est)
Population below poverty line – 33.7 per cent (2011 est)
Unemployment – 8.6 per cent (2011)
Total external debt – US$3,859m (2013)
Imports – US$5,374m (2012)
Exports – US$1,894m (2012)

BALANCE OF PAYMENTS
Trade – US$3,480m deficit (2012)
Current Account – US$991m deficit (2012)

Trade with UK	2012	2013
Imports from UK	£12,352,007	£3,021,349
Exports to UK	£1,219,180	£556,661

COMMUNICATIONS
Airports and waterways – 18, with an international airport outside Bishkek; there are 600km of waterways
Roadways and railways – 34,000km; 470km
Telecommunications – 489,000 fixed lines and 6.8 million mobile subscriptions (2011); there were 2.195 million internet users in 2009
Internet code and IDD – kg; 996 (from UK), 44 (to UK)
Media – Kyrgyz National TV and Radio Broadcasting Corporation runs various networks alongside a number of private broadcasters
WPFI score – 31,24 (97)

LAOS

Sathalanalat Paxathipatai Paxaxon Lao – Lao People's Democratic Republic

Area – 236,800 sq. km
Capital – Vientiane; population, 905,852 2009)
Major towns – Luang Prabang, Pakse, Savannakhet

Currency – Kip (K) of 100 att
Population – 6,803,699 rising at 1.59 per cent a year
 (2014 est); there are (officially) 47 ethnic groups,
 including Lao (55 per cent), Khmou (11 per cent), Hmong
 (8 per cent) (2005)
Religion – Buddhist 67 per cent (predominantly Theravada),
 Christian 1.5 per cent; most of the remainder practise
 animist beliefs
Language – Lao (official), French, English, ethnic languages
Population density – 28 per sq. km (2011)
Urban population – 35.4 per cent (2012 est)
Median age (years) – 22 (2014 est)
National anthem – 'Pheng Xat Lao' ['Hymn of the Lao
 People']
National day – 2 December (Republic Day)
Death penalty – Retained (last used 1989)
CPI score – 26 (140)
Literacy rate – 72.7 per cent (2010 est)
Gross enrolment ratio (percentage of age group) – primary
 123 per cent; secondary 47 per cent; tertiary 17 per cent
 (2012 est)
Health expenditure (per capita) – US$37 (2011)
Hospital beds (per 1,000 people) – 0.7 (2010)
Life expectancy (years) – 63.51 (2014 est)
Mortality rate – 7.74 (2014 est)
Birth rate – 24.76 (2014 est)
Infant mortality rate – 54.53 (2014 est)

CLIMATE AND TERRAIN
Laos is mostly mountainous, the land rising from the
Mekong river basin in the west to mountains in the north
and east. Elevation extremes range from 2,817m (Phou Bia)
to 70m (Mekong river). Much of the land is covered by
rainforest. The climate is tropical, with a wet season from
May to October, during which humidity levels are very high.
Average temperatures in Vientiane range from 22°C in
January and December to 29°C in April.

HISTORY AND POLITICS
From the ninth to the 13th centuries, Laos was part of the
Khmer Empire centred on Angkor in Cambodia. Small
principalities developed from the 12th century and were
united in the 14th century into the Lao kingdom of Lan
Xang ('the land of a million elephants'), which dominated
until 1713, when it split into the separate kingdoms of
Luang Prabang, Vientiane and Champassac, which became
tributaries of Siam (Thailand) in the late 18th century and
then a protectorate of France from 1893.

Japanese occupation during the Second World War
inspired a Lao nationalist movement, which proclaimed
independence in 1945, but the French regained control
of the country in 1946. Independence as a constitutional
monarchy was granted in 1953, but much of the following
20 years was spent in civil war between the Communist
Pathet Lao movement, backed first by China and then
by North Vietnam, and royalists, who attracted US and
Thai support from the early 1960s. A ceasefire in 1973
partitioned the country between the two sides, but in 1975
the Pathet Lao seized power in the rest of the country and
proclaimed a republic, introducing a one-party state and
initiating socialist policies. Greater economic liberalisation
was introduced from the mid-1980s, and the first legislative
elections since 1975 were held in 1989.

Ethnic Hmong minority groups have maintained a
low-level insurgency against the communist regime since
1975. In 2000 and 2004, Laos suffered serious civil
disturbances, including bombings and armed attacks on
buses. These were variously attributed to Hmong insurgents
and anti-government groups based abroad.

In the 2011 legislative election, Lao People's
Revolutionary Party (LPRP) candidates won all but four
of the seats, the remaining seats being taken by approved
independent candidates. The legislature re-elected
Choummaly Sayasone as president in June 2011 and
approved a reshuffled council of ministers. In May 2014 a
plane crash in northern Laos killed the Defence Minister and
a Deputy Prime Minister, along with other government
officials.

Under the 1991 constitution, the head of state is a
president elected by the legislature for a five-year term. The
unicameral National Assembly has 132 members, who are
party-approved candidates directly elected for a five-year
term. The LPRP is the only legal political party, although it
has given approval to non-partisan candidates for legislative
seats. Party congresses are held every five years.

HEAD OF STATE
President, Lt.-Gen. Choummaly Sayasone, *elected* 8 June
 2006, *re-elected* 2011
Vice-President, Bounnhang Vorachit

SELECTED GOVERNMENT MEMBERS *as at June 2014*
Prime Minister, Thongsing Thammavong
Deputy Prime Ministers, Maj.-Gen. Asang Laoly; Somsavat
 Lengsavad; Maj.-Gen. Sengnouane Xayalath *(Defence,
 acting)*; Thongloun Sisoulith *(Foreign Affairs)*

EMBASSY OF THE LAO PEOPLE'S DEMOCRATIC
REPUBLIC
74 Avenue Raymond-Poincaré, 75116 Paris, France
T (+33) (1) 4553 0298 E ambalaoparis@wanadoo.fr
Ambassador Extraordinary and Plenipotentiary, Boungnalith
 Southichak *apptd* 2014

BRITISH EMBASSY
Rue J. Nehru, Phonexay, Saysettha District, Vientiane
T (+856) 030 770 0000 E britishembassy.vientiane@fco.gov.uk
W www.gov.uk/government/world/organisations/british-embassy-
vientiane
Ambassador Extraordinary and Plenipotentiary, HE
 Philip Malone, *apptd* 2012

DEFENCE

Aged 16–49, 2010 est	Males	Females
Available for military service	1,574,362	1,607,856
Fit for military service	1,111,629	1,190,035

Military expenditure – US$19.1m (2012 est)
Conscription – 18 years of age; 18 months

ECONOMY AND TRADE
Economic liberalisation and a measure of private enterprise
were introduced from 1986, producing growth averaging
6 per cent a year since 1988, except during the 1997 Asian
financial crisis. Recent economic growth has been driven
by foreign investment in dam and transport construction
projects, hydroelectric power and mining. Laos' growth
exceeded 7 per cent a year from 2008 to 2012, however, the
country remains very poor, with only a rudimentary
infrastructure, and is dependent on international aid and
investment; a stock market began trading in January 2011 to
encourage further inward investment. Laos was admitted
to the World Trade Organisation in 2012. A financial crisis
was created in 2013 by public sector wage increases and
fiscal mismanagement.

Subsistence agriculture, principally rice, accounts for 24.8
per cent of GDP and about 73.1 per cent of employment.

Deposits of copper, tin, gold and gypsum are exploited, as is the abundance of timber in the rainforests. Other activities include food processing, manufacture of garments and cement, and tourism. A hydro-electric dam on the Mekong river exports electricity to Thailand.

The main trading partners are Thailand (34 per cent of exports; 62.1 per cent of imports), Vietnam and China. Principal exports are timber products, coffee, electricity, tin, copper and gold. The main imports are machinery and equipment, vehicles, fuel and consumer goods.
GNI – US$8,794m; US$1,270 per capita (2012)
Annual average growth of GDP – 8.3 per cent (2013 est)
Inflation rate – 6.5 per cent (2013 est)
Population below poverty line – 26 per cent (2010 est)
Unemployment – 2.5 per cent (2009 est)
Total external debt – US$6,690m (2013 est)
Imports – US$2,700m (2012)
Exports – US$2,4006m (2012)

BALANCE OF PAYMENTS
Trade – US$300m deficit (2012)
Current Account – US$1,262m deficit (2011)

Trade with UK	2012	2013
Imports from UK	£3,465,115	£4,522,940
Exports to UK	£40,941,934	£43,869,089

COMMUNICATIONS
Airports and waterways – Eight, with the largest airports at Vientiane and Luang Prabang; there are around 4,600km of navigable waterways, principally on the Mekong and its tributaries, although some are not passable in the dry season
Roadways and railways – There are 39,568km of roadways, mostly unpaved; the Friendship Bridge over the Mekong river connects with Thailand, and links up road routes from Singapore to China. A rail track across the bridge links the Thai and Laotian rail systems
Telecommunications – 112,000 fixed lines (2012) and 6.492 million mobile subscriptions (2011); there were 300,000 internet users in 2009
Internet code and IDD – la; 856 (from UK), 44 (to UK)
Major broadcasters – The state-run Lao National TV is the country's principal broadcaster
Press – There are three state-run news publications, including the *Vientiane Mai*
WPFI score – 71,22 (171)

LATVIA

Latvijas Republika – Republic of Latvia

Area – 64,589 sq. km
Capital – Riga; population, 711,000 (2009)
Major cities – Daugavpils, Jelgava, Liepaja
Currency – Euro (€) of 100 cents
Population – 2,165,165 falling at 0.62 per cent a year (2014 est); Latvian (61.1 per cent), Russian (26.2 per cent), Belarusian (3.5 per cent), Ukrainian (2.3 per cent), Polish (2.2 per cent), Lithuanian (1.3 per cent) (2013 est)
Religion – Christian (Lutheran 19.6 per cent, Orthodox 15.3 per cent, other 0.4 per cent), unspecified 63.7 per cent (est)
Language – Latvian (official), Russian
Population density – 33 per sq. km (2011)
Urban population – 67.7 per cent (2012 est)
Median age (years) – 41 (2014 est)
National anthem – 'Dievs, Sveti Latviju' ['God Bless Latvia']
National day – 18 November (Independence Day)
Death penalty – Abolished for all crimes (since 2012)
CPI score – 53 (49)

CLIMATE AND TERRAIN
Latvia is a flat, low-lying country on the eastern shore of the Baltic Sea, with low hills and many lakes in the south-east. Elevation extremes range from 312m (Gaizinkalns) to 0m (Baltic Sea). The climate is temperate, and average temperatures in Riga range from −3°C in January and February to 17°C in July.

HISTORY AND POLITICS
Conquered and Christianised in the 13th century by the Teutonic Knights, Latvia was successively under Polish, Lithuanian and Swedish rule in the 16th and 17th centuries until it was incorporated into the Russian Empire in 1721. Under partial German occupation during the First World War, it declared its independence in 1918 and successfully defended this against the Bolsheviks in 1918–20. A dictatorship was established in 1934 following a period of political instability and economic depression. The USSR invaded and annexed Latvia in 1940, and regained control in 1944 after ousting the German forces that had invaded in 1941. Latvia suffered huge civilian losses during the Second World War, including the destruction of its large Jewish community. Many more Latvians died after the war in purges and deportations ordered by Stalin.

Agitation by nationalist groups grew from the mid-1980s. In May 1990 the legislature declared independence. The last Russian troops left in 1994 but a large Russian minority remains and there are intercommunal tensions. Latvia joined NATO and the EU in 2004.

In the 2011 legislative election, the pro-Russian Harmony Centre party won a small majority of seats. In January 2014 Laimdota Straujuna was appointed prime minister following the resignation of Valdis Dombrovskis. Andris Berzins was elected president in June 2011 after his nomination by five members of the Green and Farmers' Union (ZZS).

The 1922 constitution was restored in 1993. The head of state is a president, who is elected by the legislature for a four-year term which may be renewed once. The president appoints the prime minister, who appoints the cabinet subject to approval by the legislature. The unicameral *Saeima* has 100 deputies who are directly elected for a four-year term. The next general election will take place in October 2014.

HEAD OF STATE
President, Andris Berzins, *elected* 2 June 2011, *sworn in* 8 July 2011

SELECTED GOVERNMENT MEMBERS *as at June 2014*
Prime Minister, Laimdota Straujuna
Defence, Raimonds Vejonis
Finance, Andris Vilks
Foreign Affairs, Edgars Rinkevics

EMBASSY OF THE REPUBLIC OF LATVIA
45 Nottingham Place, London W1U 5LY
T 020-7312 0041 E embassy.uk@mfa.gov.lv
W www.mfa.gov.lv/london
Ambassador Extraordinary and Plenipotentiary, HE
   Andris Teikmanis, *apptd* 2013

BRITISH EMBASSY
5 J. Alunana Street, Riga LV1010
T (+371) 6777 4700 E britishembassy.riga@fco.gov.uk
W www.gov.uk/government/world/latvia
Ambassador Extraordinary and Plenipotentiary, HE
   Sarah Cowley, *apptd* 2013

DEFENCE

Aged 16–49, 2010 est	Males	Females
Available for military service	546,090	540,810
Fit for military service	401,691	447,638

Military expenditure – US$307m (2013)

ECONOMY AND TRADE
The country made the transition from a planned to a market economy in the decade after independence, although a few large enterprises remain in state ownership. The economy grew rapidly from 2004 to 2007, but was severely affected by the global economic downturn because of its large current account deficit and private-sector debt. The economy contracted by 20 per cent in 2008–9 and was slow to return to growth. The IMF, the World Bank and the EU provided aid in 2008–9 to avoid devaluation of the lat in return for a 40 per cent cut in public spending. The IMF programme was successfully concluded in December 2011 and the country posted a reduction in its fiscal deficit of 4 per cent of GDP at the end of the year.

The economy has shifted towards service industries since independence. Services, especially transit services and banking, is the largest sector, contributing 69.4 per cent of GDP. Industry contributes 25.7 per cent of GDP and includes food processing and the manufacture of processed wood products, textiles, processed metals, pharmaceuticals, rail transport vehicles, synthetic fibres and electronics. The agricultural sector accounts for 4.9 per cent of GDP, employs 8.8 per cent of the workforce and specialises in rearing livestock, dairy farming and crops including grain, rapeseed, potatoes and other vegetables.

The main trading partners are other EU states and Russia, with exports contributing nearly a third of GDP. Principal exports are food products, timber and wood products, metals, machinery and equipment, and textiles. The main imports are machinery and equipment, consumer goods, chemicals, fuel and vehicles.
GNI – US$28,387m; US$14,120 per capita (2012)
Annual average growth of GDP – 4 per cent (2013 est)
Inflation rate – 0.2 per cent (2013 est)
Unemployment – 9.8 per cent (2012 est)
Total external debt – US$39,870m (2013 est)
Imports – US$16,077m (2012)
Exports – US$12,679m (2012)

BALANCE OF PAYMENTS
Trade – US$3,399m deficit (2012)
Current Account – US$476m deficit (2012)

Trade with UK	2012	2013
Imports from UK	£249,444,058	£368,959,099
Exports to UK	£349,943,453	£505,250,886

COMMUNICATIONS
Airports and waterways – There are 18 airports with the largest at Riga, Ventspils and Liepaja; there are major ports at Riga and Ventspils
Roadways and railways – 72,440km; 2,239km
Telecommunications – 501,000 fixed lines and 2.31 million mobile subscriptions (2012); there were 1.504 million internet users in 2009
Internet code and IDD – lv; 371 (from UK), 44 (to UK)
Media – There are around 140 newspapers in circulation, including many in Russian; television and radio output is provided by public service broadcaster Latvian Television and a number of commercial stations
WPFI score – 21,1 (37)

EDUCATION AND HEALTH
Education is compulsory from the age of seven until 16 years, after which there is the option for a further three years of either secondary or vocational study.
Literacy rate – 100 per cent (2011 est)
Gross enrolment ratio (percentage of relevant age group) – primary 105 per cent; secondary 99 per cent; tertiary 67 per cent (2012 est)
Health expenditure (per capita) – US$841 (2011)
Hospital beds (per 1,000 people) – 5.3 (2010)
Life expectancy (years) – 73.44 (2014 est)
Mortality rate – 13.6 (2014 est)
Birth rate – 9.79 (2014 est)
Infant mortality rate – 7.91 (2014 est)

LEBANON

Al-Jumhuriyah al-Lubnaniyah – Lebanese Republic

Area – 10,400 sq. km
Capital – Beirut (Bayrut); population, 1,983,057 (2012)
Major cities – Sidon, Tripoli (Tarabulus)
Currency – Lebanese pound (L£) of 100 piastres
Population – 5,882,562 rising at 9.37 per cent a year (2014 est); Arab (95 per cent), Armenian (4 per cent) (est)
Religion – Muslim 54 per cent (27 per cent Sunni, 27 per cent Shia), Christian 40.5 per cent (includes 21 per cent Maronite Catholic), Druze 5.6 per cent, small numbers of Jews, Baha'is, Buddhists, Hindus and Mormons
Language – Arabic (official), French, English, Armenian
Population density – 428 per sq. km (2011)
Urban population – 87.4 per cent (2012 est)
Median age (years) – 29.3 (2014 est)
National anthem – 'Kulluna lil-watan' ['All of us, for our country']
National day – 22 November (Independence Day)
Death penalty – Retained
CPI score – 28 (127)

Comes under Roman rule | Area contested during Crusades | Becomes French mandated territory | Achieves independence | Country close to partition as rival political and religious factions seek control | Israel withdraws forces; Hezbollah continues to control south | Hezbollah captures Israeli soldiers; sparks conflict with Israel

c.500 — c.600–1000 — c.1500 — 1975 — 1991-92 — 2005 — 2014

c.100 — c.1100–1300 — 1920 — 1943 — 1985 — 2000 — 2006

Part of the Phoenician Empire | Muslims introduce Islam; Druze faith develops | Part of Ottoman Empire | Civil war between Christian and Muslim militias; conflict draws in neighbouring countries | Fragile peace achieved; democratic elections take place | Huge protest rallies bring down pro-Syrian government | 1 million Syrian refugees officialy registered as living in Lebanon

CLIMATE AND TERRAIN

A narrow plain along the Mediterranean Sea coast is backed by the Lebanon Mountains, along which the Anti-Lebanon range runs parallel, forming the border with Syria. Between the two ranges lies the fertile Bekaa valley, the northern extremity of Africa's Great Rift Valley. Elevations range from 3,088m (Qurnat as Sawda') to 0m (Mediterranean Sea). The climate is Mediterranean, although the mountains usually receive snow in winter. Average temperatures in Beirut are 12°C in January and 26°C in July and August.

POLITICS

The constitution dates from 1926 but has been heavily amended, most significantly in 1943, when the National Covenant set out the division of power between the religious communities, and in 1990 to incorporate the provisions of the Ta'if accord. By convention, the presidency is held by a Maronite Christian, the prime minister is a Sunni Muslim and the speaker is a Shia Muslim.

The president is elected by the legislature for a six-year term, which is not renewable. The unicameral National Assembly has 128 members, directly elected for a four-year term; seats are divided equally between Christians and Muslims, whose quotas are subdivided by confession according to the distribution formalised in the 2008 election law. The prime minister is appointed by the president following consultation with the legislature.

In May 2008, a neutral candidate, General Michel Suleiman, the head of the armed forces, was elected president. After months of negotiation following the 2009 legislative election, the '14 March' leader Saad Hariri formed a national unity government which took office in November 2009. This government collapsed in January 2011 with the withdrawal of pro-Syria parties, and Najib Mikati was elected prime minister-designate later that month. In April 2013 Sunni politician Tamam Salam was nominated prime minister and charged with forming a new government. In May 2014, Michel Suleiman's presidential team ended; political deadlock prevented a new appointment. The 2014 legislative elections have been delayed until November.

HEAD OF STATE
President, vacant

SELECTED GOVERNMENT MEMBERS *as at September 2014*
Prime Minister, Tamam Salam
Deputy Prime Minister, Defence, Samir Mokbel
Finance, Ali Hassan Khali

EMBASSY OF LEBANON
15 Palace Garden Mews, London W8 4RA
T 020-7229 7265 W www.lebaneseembassyuk.org
Ambassador Extraordinary and Plenipotentiary, HE
    Inaam Osseiran, *apptd* 2008

BRITISH EMBASSY
PO Box 11–471, Serail Hill, Beirut Central District, Beirut
T (+961) (1) 960 800 W www.gov.uk/government/world/lebanon

Ambassador Extraordinary and Plenipotentiary, HE
    Tom Fletcher, CMG, *apptd* 2011

DEFENCE

Aged 16–49, 2010 est	Males	Females
Available for military service	1,081,016	1,115,349
Fit for military service	920,825	941,806

Military expenditure – US$1,709m (2013 est)

ECONOMY AND TRADE

The civil war seriously damaged Lebanon's economy and infrastructure, as well as its role as an entrepôt and financial services centre for the region. Reconstruction was almost complete when the Israeli attacks in 2006 caused an estimated US$3.6bn (£2.1bn) of infrastructure damage. Recovery was hindered by internal instability, which also postponed the introduction of the economic reforms that were a condition of international funding for reconstruction. Economic growth began anew in 2008 but slowed to less than 2 per cent from 2011 to 2013 due to the war in neighbouring Syria.

The service sector contributes 75.4 per cent of GDP, largely through banking and tourism, which are the two main economic activities. Industry accounts for 20 per cent, through food processing, wine production and the manufacture of jewellery, cement, textiles, mineral and chemical products, timber and furniture, oil refining and metal fabrication. Agriculture contributes 4.6 per cent of GDP, producing fruit, vegetables, tobacco and livestock.

The main export markets are South Africa, Switzerland, Saudi Arabia and the UAE, while imports come mainly from the USA, Italy, China and France. Principal exports include jewellery, base metals, chemicals, consumer goods, fruit, vegetables, tobacco and construction materials. The main imports are petroleum products, cars, medicines, clothing, meat, livestock and consumer goods.

GNI – US$42,321m; US$9,190 per capita (2012)
Annual average growth of GDP – 1.5 per cent (2013 est)
Inflation rate – 5 per cent (2013 est)
Unemployment – 9.2 per cent (2007 est)
Total external debt – US$26,740m (2013 est)
Imports – US$21,945m (2012)
Exports – US$5,615m (2010)

BALANCE OF PAYMENTS
Trade – US$16,330m deficit (2012)
Current Account – US$4,853m deficit (2011)

Trade with UK	2012	2013
Imports from UK	£421,406,131	£500,791,887
Exports to UK	£55,028,459	£36,279,279

COMMUNICATIONS

Airports and waterways – There are five airports, including the international airport at Beirut; the principal seaports are Beirut and Tripoli

Roadways and railways – 6,970km; 401km
Telecommunications – 878,000 fixed lines and 4 million mobile subscriptions (2012); there were 1 million internet users in 2009
Internet code and IDD – lb; 961 (from UK), 44 (to UK)
Major broadcasters – Tele-Liban is the state-run broadcaster and competes with several commercial stations, including pro-Hezbollah al-Manar TV and the market-leading Lebanese Broadcasting Corporation and Future TV
Press – There are a number of daily newspapers, including French- and English-language publications
WPFI score – 31,89 (106)

EDUCATION AND HEALTH
There are nine years of compulsory education.
Literacy rate – 89.6 per cent (2010 est)
Gross enrolment ratio (percentage of relevant age group) – primary 107 per cent; secondary 74 per cent; tertiary 46 per cent (2012 est)
Health expenditure (per capita) – US$622 (2011)
Hospital beds (per 1,000 people) – 3.5 (2009)
Life expectancy (years) – 77.22 (2014 est)
Mortality rate – 4.95 (2014 est)
Birth rate – 14.8 (2014 est)
Infant mortality rate – 7.98 (2014 est)

LESOTHO

Kingdom of Lesotho

Area – 30,355 sq. km
Capital – Maseru; population, 220,000 (2009)
Currency – Loti (M) of 100 lisente; the South African rand is also legal tender
Population – 1,942,008 rising at 0.34 per cent a year (2014 est); Sotho (99.7 per cent) (est)
Religion – Christian 80 per cent, indigenous beliefs 20 per cent
Language – English, Sesotho (both official), Zulu, Xhosa
Population density – 67 per sq. km (2011)
Urban population – 28.3 per cent (2012 est)
Median age (years) – 23.6 (2014 est)
National anthem – 'Lesotho Fatse la Bontata Rona' ['Lesotho, Land of Our Fathers']
National day – 4 October (Independence Day)
Death penalty – Retained
CPI score – 49 (55)
Military expenditure – US$56.4m (2013)

CLIMATE AND TERRAIN
Lesotho consists of a highland plateau with mountains in the east. The lower land in the west contains most of the arable land and 70 per cent of the population. Elevation

extremes range from 3,482m (Thabana Ntlenyana) to 1,400m (the junction of the Orange and Makhaleng rivers). As 80 per cent of the country lies above 1,800m, the climate is temperate, with snow in the highlands in winter. Temperatures in Maseru (1,528m altitude) average 19°C in January and 7°C in June and July.

HISTORY AND POLITICS
The area was organised into a single territory by Moshoeshoe the Great from the 1820s as the Sotho people came under pressure from both the expanding Zulu nation and the Boers. In 1868, after fighting two wars with the Boers, Moshoeshoe sought protection from the British government, and Basutoland became first a British territory (1868) and then a crown colony (1884).

The country gained independence in 1966 as the kingdom of Lesotho, under Moshoeshoe II and with Chief Lebua Jonathan as prime minister. The post-independence period has been one of political instability, with a number of coups, mutinies and periods of civil unrest. Chief Jonathan was overthrown in a military coup in 1986; military rule ended with multiparty elections in 1993 and democratic rule was restored in 1994. The 1998 elections were also followed by severe disturbances, which were quelled by an intervention force from neighbouring countries. King Moshoeshoe II, deposed in 1990, was reinstated in 1995 but died in 1996; he was succeeded by King Letsie III, who had been king during his father's exile.

In the 2012 legislative election, the Democratic Congress party won the largest number of seats but did not gain a majority; Motsoahae Tom Thabane was appointed prime minister. In August 2014, an attempted military coup caused Thabane to flee to South Africa, although his government officially remained in place. In September, the South African government advised it would not intervene militarily.

Under the 1993 constitution, subsequently amended, the head of state is a hereditary monarch, with ceremonial duties but no executive or legislative powers. The bicameral parliament comprises the National Assembly, with 120 members elected for a five-year term, one-third by proportional representation, and the senate, whose 33 members comprise 22 principal chiefs and 11 members nominated by the king. The prime minister is the leader of the majority party in the legislature and appoints the council of ministers.

HEAD OF STATE
HM The King of Lesotho, King Letsie III, *acceded* 7 February 1996, *crowned* 31 October 1997

SELECTED GOVERNMENT MEMBERS *as at September 2014*
Prime Minister, Motsoahae Tom Thabane
Deputy Prime Minister, Mothetjoa Metsing
Finance, Leketekete Ketso

HIGH COMMISSION OF THE KINGDOM OF LESOTHO
7 Chesham Place, London SW1X 8HN
T 020-7235 5686 E lhc@lesotholondon.org.uk
W www.lesotholondon.org.uk
High Commissioner, HE Felleng Mamakeka Makeka, *apptd* 2013

BRITISH HIGH COMMISSION
High Commissioner, HE Judith Macgregor, CMG, LVO *apptd* 2013, resident at Pretoria (Tshwane), South Africa

ECONOMY AND TRADE

The country is one of the poorest in the world, with 49 per cent of the population living below the poverty line. With few natural resources apart from water, the main sources of government revenue are customs dues from the South African customs union and, since 1998, the export of water and electricity to South Africa from the hydroelectric facilities created by the Lesotho Highlands Water Project. The economic situation worsened in the early 2000s with the severe droughts since 2001 and the declining demand for mineworkers in South Africa.

This decline has been partially compensated for by the resumption of diamond mining in 2003, and the development of a small manufacturing base processing agricultural products, producing textiles and assembling garments, and of tourism, especially in the highlands. Even so, around a quarter of the population is unemployed. Lesotho's economy recovered well from the global economic crisis in 2008–9 with growth averaging nearly 5 per cent per year since 2010. The economy is heavily reliant on government consumption, which accounts for 39 per cent of the economy, and remittances supplied by migrants to South Africa.

Subsistence agriculture is the major employer and engages 86 per cent of the population, although productivity has declined in recent years because of drought, soil erosion and loss of labour due to HIV/AIDS; nearly a quarter of the workforce is infected with the disease.

Principal exports are clothing, footwear, road vehicles, wool and mohair, food and livestock. The main imports are food, construction materials, vehicles, machinery, medicines and petroleum products.

GNI – US$2,751m; US$1,380 per capita (2012)
Annual average growth of GDP – 4.1 per cent (2013 est)
Inflation rate – 5 per cent (2013 est)
Unemployment – 25 per cent (2008)
Total external debt – US$794m (2011 est)
Imports – US$2,591m (2011)
Exports – US$1,099m (2012)

BALANCE OF PAYMENTS
Trade – US$1,422m deficit (2011)
Current Account – US$555m deficit (2011)

Trade with UK	2012	2013
Imports from UK	£1,093,260	£927,403
Exports to UK	£112,349	£76,024

COMMUNICATIONS

Airports – There are three airports; the international airport is at Maseru
Roadways – Of the 5,940km of roads, 1,069km are surfaced
Telecommunications – 43,100 fixed lines and 1.312 million mobile subscriptions (2012); there were 76,800 internet users in 2009
Internet code and IDD – ls; 266 (from UK), 44 (to UK)
Broadcasters – Radio is the most important medium, although only the state-run Radio Lesotho has national coverage; Lesotho Television, also state run, is the only television station, but South African broadcasts can be received
WPFI score – 28,36 (74)

EDUCATION AND HEALTH

Literacy rate – 76 per cent (2009)
Gross enrolment ratio (percentage of relevant age group) – primary 111 per cent; secondary 53 per cent; tertiary 11 per cent (2012 est)

Health expenditure (per capita) – US$141 (2011)
Hospital beds (per 1,000 people) – 1.3 (2004–9)
Life expectancy (years) – 52.65 (2014 est)
Mortality rate – 14.91 (2014 est)
Birth rate – 25.92 (2014 est)
Infant mortality rate – 50.48 (2014 est)
HIV/AIDS adult prevalence – 23.1 per cent (2012 est)

LIBERIA

Republic of Liberia

Area – 111,369 sq. km
Capital – Monrovia; population, 755,518 (2012 est)
Currency – Liberian dollar (L$) of 100 cents
Population – 4,092,310 rising at 2.52 per cent a year (2014 est); Kpelle (20.3 per cent), Bassa (13.4 per cent), Grebo (10 per cent), Gio (8 per cent), Mano (7.9 per cent), Kru (6 per cent), Loma (5.1 per cent), Kissi (4.8 per cent), Gola (4.4 per cent) (2008)
Religion – Christian 85.6 per cent, Muslim 12.2 per cent, traditional/other 0.8 per cent
Language – English (official), about 20 ethnic languages
Population density – 42 per sq. km (2011)
Urban population – 48.5 per cent (2012)
Median age (years) – 17.9 (2014 est)
National anthem – 'All Hail, Liberia, Hail!'
National day – 26 July (Independence Day)
Death penalty – Retained (last used 2000)
CPI score – 38 (83)
Military expenditure – US$13.3m (2013)
Literacy rate – 60.8 per cent (2010 est)
Gross enrolment ratio (percentage of relevant age group) – primary 102 per cent (2012 est)
Health expenditure (per capita) – US$55 (2011)
Hospital beds (per 1,000 people) – 0.8 (2010)
Life expectancy (years) – 58.21 (2014 est)
Mortality rate – 9.9 (2014 est)
Birth rate – 35.07 (2014 est)
Infant mortality rate – 69.19 (2014 est)
HIV/AIDS adult prevalence – 0.9 per cent (2012 est)

CLIMATE AND TERRAIN

Liberia lies on the west African coast, just north of the equator. There are forested highlands and grassy plateaux in the interior and swampy plains on the coast, where several rivers enter the ocean. Elevation extremes range from 1,380m (Mt Wuteve) to 0m (Atlantic Ocean). The climate is tropical, with very high rainfall.

HISTORY AND POLITICS

The land was purchased by the American Colonisation Society in 1821 and turned into a settlement for liberated black slaves from the USA, gaining recognition as an independent state in 1847.

In the first century of statehood, politics was dominated by the True Whig Party of the Americo-Liberian minority. Political stability ended in 1980 when a coup installed a military government under Samuel Doe. When civilian rule was restored in 1985, Doe became president, but his regime's arbitrary, corrupt rule combined with an economic collapse led to a revolt in 1989 by Charles Taylor's National Patriotic Forces of Liberia (NPFL) and the Armed Forces of Liberia (AFL). The country descended into a civil war that, apart from a respite in 1996–9, lasted until 2003. Around 250,000 people were killed and thousands were displaced. Following mediation by a number of African and European countries, all factions in the conflict signed a peace agreement in 2003 and a UN peacekeeping force was deployed. The disarming of militias was completed in 2005, and a truth and reconciliation commission was set up in 2006 and reported in 2009. In 2012 Taylor was found guilty of war crimes and sentenced to 50 years in jail to be served in a British prison.

After a period of transitional government, presidential and legislative elections were held in late 2005. In the legislative election, the Congress for Democratic Change (CDC) won the most seats but without an overall majority. The Unity Party leader Ellen Johnson Sirleaf was elected president in the second round of voting and took office in January 2006, nominating a new government that included members of two smaller parties and some independents. Sirleaf regained the presidential nomination in the 2011 election, picking up 43.9 per cent of the overall vote. The Unity Party gained the most votes in the 2011 legislative election, but fell short of an overall majority.

Under the 1986 constitution, the head of state is an executive president who is directly elected for a six-year term, renewable once. There is a bicameral National Assembly, consisting of the House of Representatives, with 64 members directly elected for a six-year term, and a senate, with 30 members (two from each of the 15 counties) normally elected for a nine-year term, although half of the current senate will serve for only six years. The president appoints the cabinet, which must be approved by the legislature.

HEAD OF STATE
President, Ellen Johnson Sirleaf, *elected* 2005,
    re-elected 2011
Vice-President, Joseph N. Boakai

SELECTED GOVERNMENT MEMBERS, *as at June 2014*
Defence, Brownie Samukai
Finance, Amara Konneh
Foreign Affairs, Augustine Ngafuan

EMBASSY OF THE REPUBLIC OF LIBERIA
23 Fitzroy Square, London W1 6EW
T 020-7388 5489 E info.liberiaembassy@gmail.com
W www.embassyofliberia.org.uk
Ambassador Extraordinary and Plenipotentiary, HE
    Rudolf von Ballmoos, *apptd* 2014

BRITISH AMBASSADOR
Leone Compound, 12th Street Beach-side, Sinkor, Monrovia
T (+231) (0)77530320 E ukemb.liberia@gmail.com
W www.gov.uk/government/world/libera
Ambassador Extraordinary and Plenipotentiary, HE
    Fergus Cochrane-Dyet, *apptd* 2013

ECONOMY AND TRADE

The civil war devastated an economy already weakened by government mismanagement and corruption, and drove those with expertise and capital into exile. Since the war ended, foreign aid has been received to finance reconstruction, conditional on the adoption of anti-corruption measures, and economic activity has revived. Growth since 2006 has been driven by donor aid and exports, particularly of rubber and, since UN sanctions were lifted in 2006 and 2007 respectively, timber and diamonds. The country also benefited from substantial debt relief in 2010, and in 2011 the African Development Bank approved a grant of US$48 million to support economic governance and competitiveness. Liberia's economy grew by 8.1 per cent in 2013, led by iron ore exports, and is set to grow by a similar amount in 2014 and 2015.

Agriculture was the main economic activity during the civil war but its contribution to GDP and its share of the labour market has declined as the industrial and service sectors have revived. Industry centres on the processing of rubber and palm oil, forestry and mining (diamonds and iron ore).

The main export markets are EU countries, South Africa and USA, while imports come mainly from South Korea, Singapore, Japan and China. Principal exports are rubber, timber, iron, diamonds, cocoa and coffee. The main imports are fuels, chemicals, machinery, transport equipment, manufactured goods and foodstuffs.

GNI – US$1,581m; US$370 per capita (2012)
Annual average growth of GDP – 8.1 per cent (2013 est)
Inflation rate – 5.2 per cent (2013 est)
Total external debt – US$438.1m (2013 est)
Import – US$814m (2011)
Export – US$459m (2012)

BALANCE OF PAYMENTS
Trade – US$447m deficit (2011)
Current Account – US$583m deficit (2012)

Trade with UK	2012	2013
Imports from UK	£19,123,993	£16,634,203
Exports to UK	£2,092,134	£3,018,623

COMMUNICATIONS

Airports and waterways – There are two international airports, Robertsfield and Spriggs Payne, in Monrovia; the main seaports are Monrovia and Buchanan, and there is a merchant fleet of 2,771 ships of over 1,000 tonnes, including 2,581 foreign-owned ships registered in Liberia
Roadways and railways – There are 10,600km of roadways; owing to war damage, little of the 429km of railway track is operational, although reconstruction is underway
Telecommunications – 3,200 fixed lines (2011) and 2.394 million mobile subscriptions (2012); there were 20,000 internet users in 2009
Internet code and IDD – lr; 231 (from UK), 44 (to UK)
Major broadcasters – Media are largely privately owned, although the state-run Liberian Broadcasting System operates Radio Liberia; television broadcasters include Clar TV and Power TV
Press – There are two major daily newspapers, *The Inquirer* and *The New Dawn,* both privately owned
WPFI score – 30,65 (89)

LIBYA

Dawlat Libya – State of Libya

Area – 1,759,540 sq. km
Capital – Tripoli (Tarabulus); population, 1,137,684 (2012)
Major cities – al-Hums, az-Zawiyah, Benghazi, Misratah, Tarhunah, Zuwarah
Currency – Libyan dinar (LD) of 1,000 dirhams
Population – 6,244,174 rising at 3.08 per cent a year (2014 est); Arab–Berber (97 per cent), with some Tuareg in the south-west
Religion – Muslim 96.6 per cent (vast majority Sunni), Christian 2.7 per cent, other 0.5 per cent
Language – Arabic (official), Italian, English
Population density – 3 per sq. km (2011)
Urban population – 77.9 per cent (2012 est)
Median age (years) – 27.5 (2014 est)
National anthem – 'Libya, Libya, Libya'
National day – 23 October (Liberation Day)
Death penalty – Retained
CPI score – 15 (172)

CLIMATE AND TERRAIN

Apart from hills on the north-west and north-east coasts and in the far south, the country is made up of plains and plateaux, with some depressions; 90 per cent is desert or semi-desert. Elevation extremes range from 2,267m (Bikku Bitti) to −47m (Sabkhat Ghuzayyil). The climate is Mediterranean on the coast, and arid desert in the interior. Average temperatures in Tripoli range from 12°C in January to 28°C in August.

POLITICS

Following the overthrow of the 'Leader of the Revolution', Col. Muammar al-Gaddafi, the National Transitional Council (NTC) set out plans for a 'political democratic regime to be based upon the political multitude and multi-party system'.

In July 2012 the General National Congress was elected and power was handed over from the transitional government in August; the congress elected Mohammed Magarief as its interim head of state. In October 2012, prime minister-elect Mustafa Abu Shagur failed in two attempts to gain parliamentary approval for his government; the national congress elected Ali Zidan prime minister in his place and in November 2012 a new government was sworn in. In May 2014 businessman Ahmed Maiteg was elected prime minister but stood down one month later, when the Supreme Court ruled his election unconstitutional. On 4 August 2014, the House of Representatives replaced the General National Congress as the legislative body. On 5 August Akila Issa, the president of the new legislative body replaced Nouri Abusahmen, former head of the General National Congress, as head of state. Abdullah al-Thinni was appointed Libya's acting prime minister in place of Ahmed Maiteg on 9 June. Al-Thinni had previously served as interim prime minister between 11 March and 25 May 2014. Continuing political chaos saw the former legislative body – the General National Congress – appoint their own prime minister, Islamist Omar al-Hassi, on 25 August, resulting in two rival governments.

HEAD OF STATE
Chair of the House of Representatives, Akila Issa

SELECTED GOVERNMENT MEMBERS *as at August 2014*
Prime Minister, Abdullah al-Thinni
First Deputy Prime Minister, Sadiq Abdulkarim Abdulrahman Karim
Second Deputy Prime Minister, vacant
Third Deputy Prime Minister, Abdussalam al-Mehdi al-Qadi
Economy, Souhail Abu Sheikha

EMBASSY OF LIBYA
15 Knightsbridge, London SW1X 7LY
T 020-7201 8280 W www.libyanembassy.org
Ambassador Extraordinary and Plenipotentiary, HE Mahmud Nacua, *apptd* 2012

BRITISH EMBASSY
24th Floor, Tripoli Towers, Tripoli
T (+218) (21) 335 1084 E tripoliconsular@fco.gov.uk
W www.gov.uk/government/world/libya
Ambassador Extraordinary and Plenipotentiary, HE Michael Aron, *apptd* 2013

DEFENCE

Aged 16–49, 2010 est	*Males*	*Females*
Available for military service	1,775,078	1,714,194
Fit for military service	1,511,144	1,458,934

Military expenditure – US$2,903m (2012 est)
Conscription duration – 12–24 months (selective)

ECONOMY AND TRADE

Normalisation of international relations stimulated economic liberalisation and the start of a slow transition towards a more market-orientated economy, as well as attracting more foreign direct investment.

The state-controlled oil industry dominates the economy, accounting for 95 per cent of export earnings and about 65 per cent of GDP and 80 per cent of government revenue;

Tripolitania, Cyrenaica and Phazzania become provinces of the Roman Empire	Part of the Ottoman Empire	Scene of heavy fighting during Second World War	Discovery of oil introduces wealth and social discord	Gaddafi's brand of Islamic socialism leads to support of international terrorism	UN sanctions introduced after government refuses to release two men suspected of bombing an aircraft over Lockerbie, Scotland

c.600 — 1911 — 1951 — 1969 — 2011
c.100 — c.1550 — 1940-45 — 1959 — c.1980 — 1992

| Comes under Arab control; Islam introduced | Conquered and colonised by Italy | Gains independence through UN resolution | King deposed by Col. Muammar al-Gaddafi | Protests begin against Gaddafi regime; National Transitional Council (NTC) set up by rebels; Gaddafi killed; liberation of country declared |

as the population is small, this gives the country one of the highest per capita GDPs in Africa, although the benefits are not felt by much of the population. The considerable oil and natural gas reserves are relatively undeveloped, and further exploration has been licensed in recent years in auctions open to foreign companies. The end of unilateral US sanctions in 2006 dramatically increased foreign investment in the energy and banking sectors. Attempts to diversify the economy have led to expansion of the service and construction sectors within the past five years, which together account for around 60 per cent of GDP, to include the production of petrochemicals, iron, steel and aluminium in addition to food processing. Owing to the terrain and climate, agriculture is a small sector, contributing only 2 per cent of GDP with 80 per cent of food imported.

The main trading partners are Italy, Germany, other EU countries and China. Principal exports are crude oil, refined petroleum products, natural gas and chemicals. The main imports are machinery, semi-finished goods, food, transport equipment and consumer products.

GNI – US$61,985m; US$12,930 per capita (2009)
Annual average growth of GDP – –5.1 per cent (2013 est)
Inflation rate – 3.2 per cent (2013 est)
Population below poverty line – 7.4 per cent (2005 est)
Unemployment – 30 per cent (2004 est)
Total external debt – US$6,319m (2013 est)
Imports – US$10,506m (2010)
Exports – US$46,016m (2010)

BALANCE OF PAYMENTS
Trade – US$35,510m surplus (2010)
Current Account – US$14,578m surplus (2010)

Trade with UK	2012	2013
Imports from UK	£187,209,169	£269,201,178
Exports to UK	£1,646,703,131	£1,242,219,542

COMMUNICATIONS
Airports and waterways – There are 68 airports; the principal airports are at Tripoli, Benghazi and Sebha, while the main seaports are Benghazi, Tripoli and Tubruq
Roadways – There are 100,024km of roadways, of which 57,214km are paved
Telecommunications – 814,000 million fixed lines and 9.59 million mobile subscriptions (2012); there were 353,900 internet users in 2009
Internet code and IDD – ly; 218 (from UK), 44 (to UK)
Major broadcasters – Launched in April 2011 following the uprising, Libyan Radio and TV (LRT) has been joined by more than 20, mainly privately owned, TV and radio stations
Press – Since the removal of Gaddafi, Benghazi has emerged as a publishing hub, distributing dailies such as *February* and *New Quryna*
WPFI score – 39,84 (137)

EDUCATION AND HEALTH
There are six years of primary education and six of secondary, nine of which are compulsory.
Literacy rate – 90 per cent (2011 est)
Health expenditure (per capita) – US$398 (2011)
Hospital beds (per 1,000 people) – 3.7 (2009)
Life expectancy (years) – 76.04 (2014 est)
Mortality rate – 3.57 (2014 est)
Birth rate – 18.4 (2014 est)
Infant mortality rate – 11.87 (2014 est)

LIECHTENSTEIN

Fürstentum Liechtenstein – Principality of Liechtenstein

Area – 160 sq. km
Capital – Vaduz; population, 5,000 (2009)
Major town – Schaan
Currency – Swiss franc of 100 rappen (or centimes)
Population – 37,313 rising at 0.82 per cent a year (2014 est)
Religion – Christian (Roman Catholic 75.9 per cent, Protestant Reformed 6.5 per cent, Lutheran 1.3 per cent, Muslim 5.4 per cent, other 9.8 per cent
Language – German (official); Alemannic is the the main dialect
Population density – 227 per sq. km (2011)
Median age (years) – 42.4 (2014 est)
National anthem – 'Oben am Jungen Rhein' ['Up Above the Young Rhine']
National day – 15 August (Feast of the Assumption)
Death penalty – Abolished for all crimes (since 1987)
Gross enrolment ratio (percentage of relevant age group) – primary 105 per cent; secondary 111 per cent; tertiary 44 per cent (2012 est)
Life expectancy (years) – 81.68 (2014 est)
Mortality rate – 7.02 (2014 est)
Birth rate – 10.53 (2014 est)
Infant mortality rate – 4.33 (2014 est)

CLIMATE AND TERRAIN
Liechtenstein is a small, mountainous landlocked principality in the Alps. The land falls in the west, in the valley of the river Rhine, which forms the western border. Elevation extremes range from 2,599m (Grauspitz) to 430m (Ruggeller Riet). The climate is continental, with heavy snowfall in winter; average temperatures in Vaduz range from 2.3°C in January to 18.8°C in August.

HISTORY AND POLITICS
Although there was a sovereign state within the present boundaries from the 14th century, the present state of Liechtenstein was formed from the lordships of Schellenberg and Vaduz in 1719. Part of the Holy Roman Empire, the principality became a member of the Confederation of the Rhine that succeeded the Empire in 1806, and then of the German Confederation from 1815 until 1866. It was the only German principality to remain outside the German Empire formed in 1871. The country abolished its armed forces and declared permanent neutrality in 1868. This was maintained in world wars.

Economic decline in the years following the First World War led Liechtenstein to adopt the Swiss currency in 1921 and to enter into a Swiss customs union in 1923. The country became extremely prosperous as an international finance centre after the Second World War. Since 2000 it has tightened its laws to prevent money laundering, and since

2008 it has started to meet international financial transparency standards.

Governments in the 20th and 21st centuries have been formed by the two main parties, the northern-based Progressive Citizens' Party (FBP) and the southern-based Fatherland Union (VU). Usually they have formed a coalition government, although the FBP formed a single-party government from 2001 to 2005. However, the government's power is limited by that of the monarchy, whose powers over the government and judiciary were increased by a 2003 referendum. Prince Hans Adam II remains head of state but in 2004 he handed over day-to-day responsibility for government to his son, Prince Alois.

The VU won an overall majority in the 2009 election. The coalition government formed with the FBP in 2005 continued, although the premiership passed from the FBP to the VU's Klaus Tschütscher. After the February 2013 legislative elections the FBP formed a coalition with the VU as the junior party.

Under the 1921 constitution, Liechtenstein is a constitutional monarchy, with the hereditary prince as head of state. The unicameral legislature, the *Landtag*, has 25 members directly elected for a four-year term. The cabinet is appointed by the prince on the advice of the *Landtag* and consists of the head of government and four ministers.

HEAD OF STATE

HSH *The Prince of Liechtenstein,* Hans Adam II, *born* 14 February 1945, *succeeded* 13 November 1989
Heir, HSH Prince Alois, *born* 11 June 1968

SELECTED GOVERNMENT MEMBERS *as at June 2014*
Head of Government, Finance, Adrian Hasler
Deputy Head of Government, Home Affairs, Justice, Economy,
    Thomas Zwiefelhofer
Foreign Affairs, Aurelia Frick

BRITISH AMBASSADOR

HE David Moran, CMG, MVO, resident at Bern, Switzerland

ECONOMY AND TRADE

Liechtenstein has a prosperous, highly industrialised and diversified economy. Its mainstay is the financial services sector, which, with other service industries such as tourism, employs over half of the workforce. A light industrial base produces electronics, metal manufactures, dental products, ceramics, pharmaceuticals, food products, precision and optical instruments, and employs 37 per cent of the workforce. Over half the workforce commutes daily from Austria, Switzerland and Germany.

Liechtenstein became a member of the European Free Trade Association in 1991, and of the European Economic Area in 1995. After completing 12 bilateral information-sharing agreements in 2009, Liechtenstein was removed from the OECD's 'grey list' of countries that have not implemented the organisation's model tax convention. In 2011 Liechtenstein joined the Schengen area. Most of its trade is with EU countries and Switzerland. The principal exports are its industrial products. The main imports are agricultural products, industrial raw materials, energy, machinery, metal goods, textiles, foodstuffs and vehicles.
GNI – US$4,816m; US$136,770 per capita (2009)
Annual average growth of GDP – 0.5 per cent (2009 est)
Inflation rate – −0.7 per cent (2012)
Unemployment – 2.5 per cent (2011)

Trade with UK	2012	2013
Imports from UK	£11,169,375	£5,238,276
Exports to UK	£3,721,467	£4,227,166

COMMUNICATIONS

Transport – Liechtenstein has no airports and only 380km of roads, 28km of waterways and 9km of rail track, which is part of the Austrian system connecting Austria and Switzerland
Telecommunications – 20,000 fixed lines and 38,000 mobile subscriptions (2012); there were 23,000 internet users in 2009
Internet code and IDD – li; 423 (from UK), 44 (to UK)
Media – The country has a very small media sector; its citizens rely on foreign broadcasters for most television and radio services. News publications include *Liechtensteiner Vaterland* and *Liechtensteiner Volksblatt*

LITHUANIA

Lietuvos Respublika – Republic of Lithuania

Area – 65,300 sq. km
Capital – Vilnius; population, 546,000 (2009)
Major cities – Kaunas, Klaipeda, Siauliai
Currency – Litas of 100 centas, pegged to the euro
Population – 3,505,738 falling at 0.29 per cent a year (2014 est); Lithuanian (84.1 per cent), Polish (6.6 per cent), Russian (5.8 per cent), Belarusian (1.2 per cent) (2011 est)
Religion – Christian (Roman Catholic 77.2 per cent, Orthodox 4.1 per cent), none 6.1 per cent
Language – Lithuanian (official), Russian, Polish
Population density – 48 per sq. km (2011)
Urban population – 67.2 per cent (2012)
Median age (years) – 41.2 (2014 est)
National anthem – 'Tautiska Giesme' ['National Song']
National day – 16 February (Independence Day)
Death penalty – Abolished for all crimes (since 1998)
CPI score – 57 (43)

CLIMATE AND TERRAIN

Lithuania is a low-lying country with low hills in the west and south-east. It contains around 6,000 lakes and lagoons – over 2,800 of them sizeable – mostly lying in the east, although the Courland lagoon on the west coast is a major feature. Elevation extremes range from 294m (Aukstojas Hill) to 0m (Baltic Sea). The climate is mainly continental, and average temperatures range from −4.1°C in January to 16.7°C in July.

HISTORY AND POLITICS

Lithuania became a nation in the 13th century. It remained pagan for far longer than the rest of Europe, only becoming fully Christian in the 15th century when the Samogitians and the Aukstaitiai, the two main ethnic groups in the region, were converted. In the 14th century, a grand duchy was formed that stretched from the Baltic to the Black Sea and eastwards almost as far as Moscow. It confederated with Poland in the 16th century, before coming under Russian rule in 1795. The country joined Poland in rebelling against Russian domination twice in the 19th century.

Occupied by Germany during the First World War, Lithuania declared its independence in 1918 and successfully defended its autonomy against the Bolsheviks in 1918–19. However, the province and city of Vilnius were occupied by the newly independent Poland from 1920 until 1939. The USSR invaded and annexed Lithuania in 1940, but the country revolted in 1941 and briefly established its own government before being invaded and occupied by the Germans in their 1941 offensive against the USSR. Around 210,000 Lithuanians, mainly Jews, were killed during the German occupation. Soviet troops ousted the Germans in 1944 and re-established Soviet control, against which Lithuanians carried on a guerrilla war until 1952.

Growing nationalist sentiment led to the formation of the pro-democracy *Sajudis* ('The Movement') in 1988 to campaign for greater autonomy. A unilateral declaration of independence in 1990 was blocked by the USSR but following the failed coup in Moscow in 1991, Lithuania declared its independence a second time, and this was internationally recognised. The last Russian troops left the country in 1993. Lithuania joined NATO and the EU in 2004.

In the 2012 legislative elections, the Social Democratic Party of Lithuania became the largest party but remained short of a majority. Its leader, Algirdas Butkevicius, became prime minister at the head of a four-party coalition government. Dalia Grybauskaite was re-elected in the 2014 presidential election.

Under the 1992 constitution, the head of state is a president, who is directly elected for a five-year term, renewable once. The unicameral *Seimas* has 141 members who are directly elected for a four-year term; 71 members are elected in first-past-the-post constituencies and 70 by proportional representation. The prime minister is appointed by the president with the approval of the *Seimas,* and ministers are appointed upon the recommendation of the prime minister.

HEAD OF STATE

President, Dalia Grybauskaite, *elected* 17 May 2009, *sworn in* 12 July 2009, *re-elected* 25 May 2014, *sworn in* 12 July 2014

SELECTED GOVERNMENT MEMBERS *as at June 2014*
Prime Minister, Algirdas Butkevicius
Defence, Juozas Olekas
Foreign Affairs, Linas Antanas Linkevicius
Interior, Dailis Alfonsas Barakauskas

EMBASSY OF THE REPUBLIC OF LITHUANIA
Lithuania House, 2 Bessborough Gardens SW1V 2JE
T 020-7592 2840 E amb.uk@urm.lt
W www.lithuanianembassy.co.uk/
Ambassador Extraordinary and Plenipotentiary, HE
   Asta Skaisgiryte Liauskiene, *apptd* 2012

BRITISH EMBASSY
2 Antakalnio, Vilnius 10308
T (+370) (5) 246 2900
W www.gov.uk/government/world/lithuania
Ambassador Extraordinary and Plenipotentiary, HE
   David Hunt, *apptd* 2011

DEFENCE

Aged 16–49, 2010 est	Males	Females
Available for military service	890,074	875,780
Fit for military service	669,111	724,803

Military expenditure – US$357m (2013 est)
Conscription – 18 years of age; 12 months

ECONOMY AND TRADE

Lithuania's transition to a market economy is nearly complete, with the private sector now accounting for about 80 per cent GDP. The transition initially caused a recession, but the economy recovered and grew steadily from 2004 to 2008 before being plunged into a deep recession, along with the other Baltic states, by the global economic downturn. Drastic government cuts in public spending and the halving of imports in 2009 restored the current account deficit, which had soared to 15 per cent of GDP in 2007–8, to a surplus. GDP grew 1.3 per cent in 2010 before jumping to 5.8 per cent in 2011, making the country one of the fastest growing economies in the EU. Despite high unemployment, successive governments dramatically increased the minimum wage in 2011 and 2013. Foreign investment and export markets are being developed, and Lithuania has recently began to reform its energy networks to reduce its dependence on Russian output. The country aims to join the eurozone by 2015.

The economy is diverse, and industries include metal-cutting machine tools, electric motors, domestic appliances, oil refining, shipbuilding, furniture making, textiles and amber extraction and jewellery making. Industry contributes 28.3 per cent to GDP, services 68 per cent and agriculture 3.7 per cent.

The main trading partners are Russia and other EU countries. Principal exports are mineral products, machinery and equipment, chemicals, textiles, foodstuffs and plastics. The main imports are mineral products, machinery, transport equipment, chemicals, textiles, clothing and metals.

GNI – US$40,930m; US$13,830 per capita (2012)
Annual average growth of GDP – 3.4 per cent (2013 est)
Inflation rate – 1.2 per cent (2013 est)
Population below poverty line – 4 per cent (2008)
Unemployment – 12.4 per cent (2013 est)
Total external debt – US$29,550m (2012 est)
Imports – US$31,992m (2012)
Exports – US$29,625m (2012)

BALANCE OF PAYMENTS
Trade – US$2,367m deficit (2012)
Current Account – US$230m deficit (2012)

Trade with UK	2012	2013
Imports from UK	£368,253,347	£324,137,567
Exports to UK	£826,861,220	£887,318,069

COMMUNICATIONS

Airports and waterways – There are 22 airports, with the largest at Vilnius, Kaunas and Palanga; the main seaport is at Klaipeda
Roadways and railways – There are 84,166km of roadways, and a railway system of 1,767km linking the major towns with Vilnius and Klaipeda
Telecommunications – 667,300 fixed lines and 5 million mobile subscriptions (2012); there were 1.96 million internet users in 2009
Internet code and IDD – lt; 370 (from UK), 44 (to UK)

Media – Lithuanian Radio and Television operates several networks, in competition with a number of thriving commercial stations. There are ten major national newspapers available, in Lithuanian, Russian, Polish and English
WPFI score – 19,2 (32

EDUCATION AND HEALTH

Education is free and compulsory from seven to 16 years, with the system comprising primary school (four years), lower secondary school (six years) and upper secondary education (two years).
Literacy rate – 100 per cent (2011 est)
Gross enrolment ratio (percentage of relevant age group) – primary 99 per cent; secondary 107 per cent; tertiary 77 per cent (2012 est)
Health expenditure (per capita) – US$875 (2011)
Hospital beds (per 1,000 people) – 6.8 (2010)
Life expectancy (years) – 75.98 (2014 est)
Mortality rate – 11.55 (2014 est)
Birth rate – 9.36 (2014 est)
Infant mortality rate – 6 (2014 est)

LUXEMBOURG

Groussherzogtom Lëtzebuerg / Grand-Duché de Luxembourg / Großherzogtum Luxembourg – Grand Duchy of Luxembourg

Area – 2,586 sq. km
Capital – Luxembourg; population, 90,000 (2009)
Major towns – Esch-sur-Alzette, Dudelange
Currency – Euro (€) of 100 cents
Population – 520,672 rising at 1.12 per cent a year (2014 est); Luxembourger (63.1 per cent), Portuguese (13.3 per cent), French (4.5 per cent), Italian (4.3 per cent), German (2.3 per cent), other EU 7.3 per cent (2000)
Religion – Christian (Roman Catholic 68.8 per cent, Protestant 1.8 per cent), Muslim 2.2 per cent (est)
Language – Luxembourgish, French, German (all official)
Population density – 200 per sq. km (2011)
Urban population – 85.7 per cent (2012 est)
Median age (years) – 39.6 (2014 est)
National anthem – 'Ons Heemecht' ['Our Homeland']
National day – 23 June (official birthday of Grand Duchess Charlotte)
Death penalty – Abolished for all crimes (since 1979)
CPI score – 80 (11)
Military expenditure – US$306m (2013 est)
Gross enrolment ratio (percentage of relevant age group) – primary 97 per cent; secondary 101 per cent; tertiary 18 per cent (2012 est)
Health expenditure (per capita) – US$8,798 (2011)
Life expectancy (years) – 80.01 (2014 est)

Mortality rate – 8.53 (2014 est)
Birth rate – 11.75 (2014 est)
Infant mortality rate – 4.28 (2014 est)

CLIMATE AND TERRAIN

Luxembourg has the forested plateau of the Ardennes in the north, forming part of the Natural Germano-Luxembourg Park which extends east into Germany. The south of the country is mainly fertile farmland, and in the east is the wine-growing region of the Moselle valley. Elevation extremes range from 559m (Buurgplaatz) to 133m (Moselle river). The climate is modified continental, and average temperatures in Luxembourg city range from 1°C in February to 17°C in July and August.

HISTORY AND POLITICS

The area was part of the Roman Empire and then became part of the Frankish Empire in the fifth century AD. It became autonomous within the Holy Roman Empire under Siegfried, Count of Ardennes, and was given the status of a duchy in 1354. Controlled by a succession of European powers after 1437 (when the House of Luxembourg died out), it was made a grand duchy under Dutch rule after the Napoleonic wars. Much of Luxembourg joined the Belgians in their revolt against the Netherlands in 1830; in 1838 the western, French-speaking region was assigned to Belgium, and the remainder became an independent grand duchy in 1839. The Treaty of London in 1867 confirmed its independence and neutrality. Occupation by Germany in both world wars prompted Luxembourg to give up its neutrality and it was a founding member of NATO in 1949.

Luxembourg entered into economic union with Belgium in 1921 and joined the Benelux economic union in 1948. It was a founder member of the EEC in 1958 and joined the eurozone in 1999.

Following a snap election in October 2013, the Democratic Party (DP) formed a small majority in the legislature. The elections were called after prime minister Jean-Claude Juncker of the Christian Social Party (CSV) stood down following revelations that his administration failed to prevent corruption within the security services.

Under the 1868 constitution, the head of state is a hereditary grand duke, whose role is now largely ceremonial. The unicameral legislature, the Chamber of Deputies, has 60 members directly elected for a five-year term. There is also a Council of State, which has 21 members nominated by the grand duke; this acts as the supreme administrative tribunal and has some legislative functions. The prime minister is appointed by the grand duke on the basis of the election results and appoints the cabinet.

HEAD OF STATE
HRH The Grand Duke of Luxembourg, Grand Duke Henri, *born* 16 April 1955; *succeeded* 7 October 2000
Heir, HRH Prince Guillaume, *born* 11 November 1981

SELECTED GOVERNMENT MEMBERS *as at June 2014*
Prime Minister, Xavier Bettel
Deputy Prime Minister, Defence, Etienne Schneider
Finance, Pierre Gramegna
Interior, Dan Kersch

EMBASSY OF LUXEMBOURG
27 Wilton Crescent, London SW1X 8SD
T 020-7235 6961 E londres.amb@mae.etat.lu
W http://londres.mae.lu
Ambassador Extraordinary and Plenipotentiary, HE Patrick Jean-Marie Engelberg, *apptd* 2013

BRITISH EMBASSY
5 Boulevard Joseph II, L-1840, Luxembourg
T (+352) 229 864 W www.gov.uk/government/world/luxembourg
Ambassador Extraordinary and Plenipotentiary, HE Hon.
Alice Walpole, *apptd* 2011

ECONOMY AND TRADE

The economy is stable, with steady growth, low unemployment and low inflation providing an exceptionally high standard of living and the highest GDP per capita in the eurozone. The government offset the contraction in the economy in 2008–9 with economic stimulus measures, which led to a budget deficit in 2009 but growth resumed in 2010. The budget was cut to 1.1 per cent in 2011 and 0.9 per cent in 2012. Banking and financial services are the dominant sector, contributing 27 per cent of GDP, but have come under EU pressure to reform practices said to encourage tax evasion by foreign citizens. Steel production used to dominate the industrial sector, but this has diversified to include IT, telecommunications, freight transport, food processing, chemicals, metal products and engineering. Tourism accounts for 6.5 per cent of GDP. The small agricultural sector consists mainly of family-owned farms. Services account for 86.4 per cent of GDP, industry for 13.3 per cent and agriculture for 0.3 per cent. Around 60 per cent of the workforce commutes daily from France, Belgium and Germany.

The main trading partners are other EU countries and the US. Principal exports are the products of industrial activities. The main imports are minerals, metals, foodstuffs and quality consumer goods.

GNI – US$37,597m; US$71,620 per capita (2012)
Annual average growth of GDP – 0.5 per cent (2013 est)
Inflation rate – 2 per cent (2013 est)
Unemployment – 4.9 per cent (2013 est)
Total external debt – US$2,935,000m (2013 est)
Imports – US$24,181m (2012)
Exports – US$13,990m (2012)

BALANCE OF PAYMENTS
Trade – US$10,192m deficit (2011)
Current Account – US$3,265m surplus (2012)

Trade with UK	2012	2013
Imports from UK	£218,694,730	£231,707,413
Exports to UK	£651,965,311	£355,210,808

COMMUNICATIONS

Transport – Luxembourg has one airport with paved runways, there are 2,899km of roads (including 152km of motorways), and 275km of railways; the Moselle river provides 37km of navigable waterway
Telecommunications – 266,700 fixed lines and 761,300 mobile subscriptions (2012); there were 424,500 internet users in 2009
Internet code and IDD – lu; 352 (from UK), 44 (to UK)
Media – Luxembourg is the headquarters of the Société Européenne des Satellites (SES), which operates Europe's largest satellite operation; RTL Tele Letzebuerg is the country's principal domestic network and popular national dailies include *Luxemburger Wort* and *Tageblatt*
WPFI score – 6,7 (4)

MACEDONIA

Republika Makedonija – *Republic of Macedonia*

Area – 25,713 sq. km
Capital – Skopje; population, 480,000 (2009)
Major city – Bitola, Kumanovo
Currency – Denar of 100 deni
Population – 2,091,719 rising at 0.21 per cent a year (2014 est); Macedonian (64.2 per cent), Albanian (25.2 per cent), Turkish (3.9 per cent), Roma (2.7 per cent), Serb (1.8 per cent) (2002)
Religion – Christian (Orthodox 65 per cent), Muslim 33 per cent (est)
Language – Macedonian, Albanian (both official), Turkish, Romani, Serbian (each official in different regions)
Population density – 83 per sq. km (2011)
Urban population – 59 per cent (2010)
Median age (years) – 36.8 (2014 est)
National anthem – 'Denes Nad Makedonija' ['Today Over Macedonia']
National day – 8 September (Independence Day)
Death penalty – Abolished for all crimes (since 1991)
CPI score – 44 (67)
Literacy rate – 97 per cent (2011 est)
Gross enrolment ratio (percentage of relevant age group) – primary 90 per cent; secondary 82 per cent; tertiary 41 per cent (2012 est)
Health expenditure (per capita) – US$334 (2011)
Hospital beds (per 1,000 people) – 4.6 (2010)
Life expectancy (years) – 75.8 (2014 est)
Mortality rate – 9.04 (2014 est)
Birth rate – 11.64 (2014 est)
Infant mortality rate – 7.9 (2014 est)

CLIMATE AND TERRAIN

The landlocked country is a mountainous plateau divided by deep river valleys and basins, including the valleys of the Vardar river and its tributaries. Elevation extremes range from 2,764m (Golem Korab) to 50m (Vardar river). Lakes Ohrid and Prespa straddle the border with Albania, and Lake Doiran the border with Greece. The climate is continental, with average temperatures in Skopje ranging from 1°C in December to 22°C in July and August.

HISTORY AND POLITICS

The area of present-day Macedonia was part of the ancient Macedonian kingdom, which also included northern Greece and south-west Bulgaria, in the fourth century BC. Macedonia became a province of the Roman Empire in the second century BC, coming under the control of the Byzantine Empire from the fourth century AD. Slav peoples settled the area in the seventh century and mixed with the Greek, Illyrian, Thracian, Scythian and Turkish peoples.

From the ninth to the 14th centuries the area was under the rule successively of the Bulgars, Byzantium and the Serbs, and became part of the Ottoman Empire in the late 14th century. Following the Balkan wars of 1912 and 1913 the region was divided between Bulgaria, Serbia and Greece. After the First World War, the Serbian part was awarded to the newly created state that became Yugoslavia. During the Second World War, this area was occupied by Bulgaria from 1941 to 1944, and after liberation became a republic within the communist Federal Republic of Yugoslavia.

Nationalist sentiment grew throughout the 1980s, and in 1991 Macedonia declared its independence, which Yugoslavia recognised in 1992. International recognition was initially delayed by Greece's objections to the republic's name (Greece claims that its region of Macedonia is the only one entitled to the name), but the country joined the UN in 1993 as the Former Yugoslav Republic of Macedonia; Greece recognised it under this name and lifted its trade blockade in 1995, but in 2008 blocked the republic's membership of NATO.

Throughout the 1990s there was tension and sporadic violence with the large ethnic Albanian minority, aggrieved at their lack of civil rights. Instability in neighbouring Kosovo spilled over into Macedonia in 2001, sparking a two-month uprising by ethnic Albanian separatists. Peace talks facilitated by international bodies resulted in the Ohrid framework agreement, giving Albanians greater recognition within Macedonia and making Albanian an official language.

The 2009 presidential election was won in the second round by the VMRO-DPMNE candidate, Gjorge Ivanov. President Ivanor was re-elected in July 2014. In the legislative election in June 2011, the governing Better Macedonia alliance, led by the VMRO-DPMNE, remained the largest bloc; despite tensions between the VMRO-DPMNE and coalition partner the Democratic Union for Integration (BDI), Prime Minister Nikola Gruevski formed another coalition government with the BDI after elections in April 2014.

The 1991 constitution was amended in 2001 to incorporate provisions of the Ohrid agreement relating to ethnic Albanian rights, and several times since, most notably in 2004 to give ethnic Albanians greater local autonomy in areas where they predominate.

The head of state is a president, who is directly elected for a five-year term. The unicameral legislature, the *Sobranie,* has 123 members directly elected for a four-year term. The prime minister is appointed by the president. Government ministers are elected by the assembly but are not members of it.

HEAD OF STATE

President, Gjorge Ivanov, *elected* 5 April 2009, *sworn in* 12 May 2009, *re-elected* 2 July 2014

SELECTED GOVERNMENT MEMBERS *as at June 2014*

Prime Minister, Nikola Gruevski
Deputy Prime Ministers, Vladimir Pesevski *(Economy);* Zoran Stavrevski *(Finance);* Musa Xhaferi
Foreign Affairs, Nikola Poposki
Interior, Gordana Jankulovska

EMBASSY OF THE REPUBLIC OF MACEDONIA

Suites 2.1/2.2, Buckingham Court, 75–83 Buckingham Gate, London SW1E 6PE
T 020-7976 0535 E london@mfa.gov.mk
W www.missions.gov.mk/london
Ambassador Extraordinary and Plenipotentiary, HE Jovan Donev, *apptd* 2013

BRITISH EMBASSY

Todor Aleksandrov 165, Skopje 1000
T (+389) (2) 329 9299 E consular.skopje@fco.gov.uk
W www.gov.uk/government/world/macedonia
Ambassador Extraordinary and Plenipotentiary, HE Christopher Yvon, *apptd* 2010

DEFENCE

Aged 16–49, 2010 est	*Males*	*Females*
Available for military service	532,196	511,964
Fit for military service	443,843	426,251

Military expenditure – US$125m (2013)

ECONOMY AND TRADE

Macedonia was the least developed republic in the former Yugoslavia before 1991, and economic growth was initially hindered by the trade embargo by Greece (1993–5) and the 2001 ethnic Albanian uprising. Economic growth was steady from 2003 to 2008, although the economy contracted briefly in 2009 owing to the global downturn. Unemployment remains high at around 30 per cent, although official figures may be overstated because of the size of the grey economy, estimated to be between 20 and 45 per cent of GDP. The country remains poor, with 30.4 per cent of the population living below the poverty line. Small GDP growth was achieved in 2013, although the budget deficit increased by 4.2 per cent of GDP in the same year.

Services produce 62.3 per cent of GDP, industry 27.5 per cent and agriculture 10.2 per cent. Food processing and winemaking are major industries, along with textiles, chemicals, iron, steel, cement, energy and pharmaceuticals. The main trading partners are Germany, the UK, Greece, Bulgaria, and other Balkan and EU states. Principal exports are food, wine, tobacco, textiles, manufactured goods, iron and steel. The main imports are machinery and equipment, cars, chemicals, fuels and food.

GNI – US$9,372m; US$4,620 per capita (2012)
Annual average growth of GDP – 2.2 per cent (2013 est)
Inflation rate – 3.1 per cent (2013 est)
Population below poverty line – 30.4 per cent (2011)
Unemployment – 30 per cent (2013 est)
Total external debt – US$6,278m (2013 est)
Imports – US$6,511m (2012)
Exports – US$4,002m (2012)

BALANCE OF PAYMENTS

Trade – US$2,509m deficit (2012)
Current Account – US$317m deficit (2012)

Trade with UK	*2012*	*2013*
Imports from UK	£324,456,313	£421,932,512
Exports to UK	£35,072,856	£46,727,859

COMMUNICATIONS

Airports – The principal airports are at Skopje and Ohrid, and there are a further six airports around the country
Roadways and railways – There are 14,038km of roadways, and 699km of railways, of which 234km are electrified
Telecommunications – 407,900 fixed lines and 2.235 million mobile subscriptions (2012); there were 1.06 million internet users in 2009
Internet code and IDD – mk; 389 (from UK), 44 (to UK)
Media – There are 12 major daily and weekly press publications, including the partially government-owned *Nova Makedonija*
WPFI score – 36,43 (123)

MADAGASCAR

Repoblikan'i Madagasikara / République de Madagascar –
Republic of Madagascar

Area – 587,041 sq. km
Capital – Antananarivo; population, 2,013,679 (2012)
Major cities – Antsirabe, Fianarantsoa, Mahajanga, Toamasina
Currency – Ariary (MGA) of five iraimbilanja
Population – 23,201,926 rising at 2.62 per cent a year
    (2014 est); the people are of mixed Malayo-Indonesian,
    Arab and African origin. There are sizeable French,
    Chinese and Indian communities
Religion – Indigenous beliefs 52 per cent, Christian 41 per
    cent, Muslim 7 per cent
Language – Malagasy, French, English (all official)
Population density – 37 per sq. km (2011)
Urban population – 33.2 per cent (2012 est)
Median age (years) – 19.2 (2014 est)
National anthem – 'Ry Tanindrazanay malala ô' ['Oh, Beloved
    Land of our Ancestors']
National day – 26 June (Independence Day)
Death penalty – Retained (no known use since 1958)
CPI score – 28 (127)

CLIMATE AND TERRAIN

Madagascar, the fourth-largest island in the world, lies
386km off the south-east coast of Africa, from which it is
separated by the Mozambique Channel. Coastal plains rise to
a central plateau and mountains indented with river valleys.
Elevation extremes range from 2,876m (Maromokotro) to
0m (Indian Ocean).

The climate is tropical on the coast, temperate in the
interior and arid in the south. Average temperatures in
Antananarivo range from 15°C in July to 21°C from
December to March. Madagascar is subject to tropical
cyclones, which cause flooding and wind damage,
particularly on the coast.

HISTORY AND POLITICS

The island was settled by peoples from South East Asia and
East Africa from around the first century AD. Although first
visited by Europeans c.1500, local kingdoms ruled until the
early 19th century, when the Merina kingdom conquered
the island. France made the island a protectorate in 1895
after the last indigenous resistance was defeated. During the
Second World War, the British invaded in order to replace
the pro-Vichy government with a Free French government.
At the end of the war Madagascar was returned to France,
which suppressed a nationalist uprising in 1947–8.
Nationalist agitation continued throughout the 1950s and
resulted in independence in 1960.

The military took control in 1972 following civil
disturbances, and in 1975 martial law was imposed after a
coup. A Marxist one-party state was created with Lt-Cdr

Didier Ratsiraka as president. Marxism was abandoned
in 1980 and a new constitution introduced parliamentary
democracy in 1992.

Didier Ratsiraka was defeated in the 1993 presidential
elections but returned to office in 1997 after winning the
1996 election. He refused to accept his defeat in the 2001
presidential election and the six-month struggle between his
supporters and those of Marc Ravalomanana, the successful
candidate, brought the country close to civil war until, in
July 2002, Ratsiraka went into exile and his supporters
surrendered. President Ravalomanana was re-elected in 2006
and his I Love Madagascar party (TIM) retained its large
majority in the 2007 legislative election.

A power struggle between President Ravalomanana and
opposition leader Andry Rajoelina began in December 2008.
Following an army mutiny and Ravalomanana's resignation,
Rajoelina assumed power in March 2009 with the backing
of the military and the high court, but the takeover provoked
continued demonstrations and widespread international
condemnation. Although the four main political parties
agreed transitional government arrangements in late 2009,
disputes between the four have created political deadlock. A
referendum approved a new constitution in November 2010
The first round of delayed presidential elections took place in
October 2013, followed by a second round accompanied by
parliamentary elections in December.

Under the 2010 constitution, the president is directly
elected and serves a five-year term, renewable once; the
minimum age requirement for presidential candidates was
lowered in 2010. The legislature is bicameral, comprising the
National Assembly, which has 127 members directly elected
for a four-year term, and the senate, which has 100 members,
of whom two-thirds are appointed by the regional assemblies
and one-third by the president; they serve a four-year term.
The 258-member Congress of Transition and 65-member
Higher Transition Council set up under 2009 agreements
remain in office until elections give effect to the 2010
constitution.

HEAD OF STATE
President, Hery Rajaonarimampianina, *took office* 25 January
    2014

SELECTED GOVERNMENT MEMBERS *as at June 2014*
Prime Minister, Roger Kolo
Finance, Jean Razafindravonona
Foreign Affairs, Arisoa Lala Razafitrimo

EMBASSY OF THE REPUBLIC OF MADAGASCAR
Avenue de Tervuren 276,1150 Brussels, Belgium
T (+32) (0) 2770 1726 E info@madagascar-embassy.eu
W www.madagascar-embassy.eu
Ambassador Extraordinary and Plenipotentiary, HE
    Jeannot Rakotomalal, *apptd* 2007

BRITISH EMBASSY
Tour Zital, Ravoninahitriniarivo Street, Antananarivo 101
T (+261) (20) 223 3053 E BEAntananarivo@moov.mg
W www.gov.uk/government/world/madagascar
Ambassador Extraordinary and Plenipotentiary, HE
    Timothy Smart, *apptd* 2012

DEFENCE

Aged 16–49, 2010 est	*Males*	*Females*
Available for military service	4,900,729	4,909,061
Fit for military service	3,390,071	3,682,180

Military expenditure – US$52.8m (2013)

ECONOMY AND TRADE

Economic liberalisation and privatisation since the mid-1990s have resulted in slow but steady growth, although the political disturbances in 2002 and 2009–10, and cyclone devastation in 2000 and 2004, have been serious setbacks. President Ravalomanana's reforms and anti-corruption measures attracted increased international aid, and in 2004 half of the country's foreign debt was written off, but aid has been suspended and investment and government spending have slowed since 2009. Fifty per cent of the population live below the poverty line and unemployment remains high.

Agriculture, fishing and forestry are the mainstays of the economy, accounting for 27.3 per cent of GDP and employing 80 per cent of the workforce. The main cash crops include coffee, vanilla, fish, sugar cane, cocoa, cloves and pepper. The industrial sector contributes 16.4 per cent of GDP, through mining (chromite, graphite, sapphires), processing meat, fish and other agricultural products, manufacturing (textiles, paper, cement, chemicals), car assembly and oil refining. Tourism is of growing importance .

The main trading partners are France, the USA, China and Singapore. Principal exports are agricultural products, textiles, chromite and petroleum products. The main imports are capital goods, petroleum, consumer goods and food.

GNI – US$9,685m; US$430 per capita (2012)
Annual average growth of GDP – 2.2 per cent (2013 est)
Inflation rate – 8.8 per cent (2013 est)
Population below poverty line – 50 per cent (2004 est)
Total external debt – US$3,361m (2013 est)
Imports – US$3,053m (2012)
Exports – US$1,499m (2012)

BALANCE OF PAYMENTS
Trade – US$1,554m deficit (2012)
Current Account – US$680m deficit (2011)

Trade with UK	2012	2013
Imports from UK	£12,314,426	£12,157,525
Exports to UK	£22,484,866	£24,935,245

COMMUNICATIONS

Airports and waterways – There are 28 airports with the largest at Antananarivo and Mahajanga; there are 432km of navigable waterways
Roadways and railways – 34,476km; 854km
Telecommunications – 143,700 fixed lines and 8.56 million mobile subscriptions (2012); there were 319,900 internet users in 2009
Internet code and IDD – mg; 261 (from UK), 44 (to UK)
Media – State-owned Television Malagasy is the principal broadcaster; there are four main daily newspapers, all privately owned
WPFI score – 29,38 (81)

EDUCATION AND HEALTH

Education is free and compulsory for nine years, but attendance is variable.
Literacy rate – 64 per cent (2009)
Gross enrolment ratio (percentage of relevant age group) –
    primary 145 per cent; secondary 38 per cent; tertiary 4 per cent (2012 est)
Health expenditure (per capita) – US$19 (2011)
Hospital beds (per 1,000 people) – 0.2 (2010)
Life expectancy (years) – 65.2 (2014 est)
Mortality rate – 6.95 (2014 est)
Birth rate – 33.12 (2014 est)
Infant mortality rate – 44.88 (2014 est)

MALAWI

Dziko la Malawi – Republic of Malawi

Area – 118,484 sq. km
Capital – Lilongwe; population, 821,000 (2009 est)
Major cities – Blantyre, the commercial and industrial centre; Mzuzu; Zomba, the former capital
Currency – Kwacha (K) of 100 tambala
Population – 17,377,468 rising at 3.33 per cent a year (2014 est); about nine ethnic groups, of which the largest are Chewa (32.6 per cent), Lomwe (17.6 per cent), Yao (13.5 per cent) and Angoni (Nguni) (11.5 per cent) (est)
Religion – Christian 82.6 per cent, Muslim 13 per cent, none 2.5 per cent, other 1.9 per cent
Language – Chichewa, English (both official), Chinyanja, Chiyao, Chitumbuka
Population density – 164 per sq. km (2011)
Urban population – 15.8 per cent (2012 est)
Median age (years) – 16.3 (2014 est)
National anthem – 'Mulungu dalitsa Malawi' ['Oh God Bless Malawi']
National day – 6 July (Independence Day)
Death penalty – Retained (last used 1992)
CPI score – 37 (91)

CLIMATE AND TERRAIN

The landlocked state lies along the western and southern shores of Lake Malawi (Nyasa). The northern and central regions are plateaux with rolling terrain, while the south is mainly hills and mountains. Elevation extremes range from 3,002m (Sapitwa) to 37m (junction of Shire river and Mozambique border). The climate is subtropical, with a wet season from November to April; average temperatures in Lilongwe range from 14°C in July to 23°C in November.

HISTORY AND POLITICS

Until contact was made with European missionaries in the 19th century, Malawi was dominated by a succession of powerful tribes that included the Maravi, the Yao and the Nguni. The missionaries campaigned for official intervention to end the east-coast slave trade, which had begun in the early 19th century, and in 1891 Britain established the Nyasaland and District Protectorate over the area. Renamed the British Central Africa Protectorate in 1893, it became the British colony of Nyasaland in 1907. The country was joined with Northern and Southern Rhodesia (now Zambia and Zimbabwe) between 1953 and 1963. It became independent, as Malawi, in 1964, with Dr Hastings Banda as prime minister.

In 1966, the country became a one-party state ruled by the Malawi Congress Party (MCP) and Dr Banda became president, declaring himself president for life in 1971. In the early 1990s, increasing pro-democracy agitation and international pressure forced Banda to introduce multiparty democracy in 1994.

In the 2004 legislative election, the MCP became the largest party with 60 seats, but without an overall majority. The simultaneous presidential election was won by the United Democratic Front (UDF) candidate Bingu wa Mutharika, who appointed a coalition government made up of the UDF and smaller parties.

In 2005, President Mutharika resigned from the UDF over the hostility of the party and his predecessor, Bakili Muluzi, to his anti-corruption campaign and founded a new party, the Democratic Progressive Party (DPP). The DPP returned to power in the May 2014 legislative elections. Opposition parties claimed widespread electoral fraud had taken place, but the results were upheld by Malawi's electoral commission on 30 May. Peter Mutharika was elected president. The 2009 legislative election was won by the DPP and President Mutharika was re-elected; Joyce Banda was appointed interim president following Mutharika's death in April 2012.

Under the 1995 constitution, the executive president is directly elected for a five-year term, renewable once. The unicameral National Assembly consists of 193 members, who are directly elected for a five-year term.

HEAD OF STATE
President, Peter Mutharika *elected* 30 May 2014
Vice-President, Saulos Chilima

SELECTED GOVERNMENT MEMBERS *as at June 2014*
Finance, Goodall Gonwe
Foreign Affairs, George Chaponda
Home Affairs, Paul Chibingu

HIGH COMMISSION OF THE REPUBLIC OF MALAWI
36 John Street, London WC1N 2AT
T 020-7421 6010 E malawihighcommission@btconnect.com
W www.malawihighcommission.co.uk
High Commissioner, Bernard Sande, *apptd* 2012

BRITISH HIGH COMMISSION
PO Box 30042, Lingadzi House, Lilongwe 3
T (+265) (1) 772 400 E bhclilongwe@fco.gov.uk
W www.gov.uk/government/world/malawi
High Commissioner, HE Michael Nevin, *apptd* 2012

DEFENCE

Aged16–49, 2010 est	Males	Females
Available for military service	3,514,809	–
Fit for military service	2,132,909	2,043,925

Military expenditure – US$76.8m (2013 est)

ECONOMY AND TRADE
Malawi is one of the poorest countries in Africa. It has few natural resources and its agricultural land is under pressure because of population growth. It also experienced years of mismanagement under earlier governments, and corruption remains a problem despite the government's determination to eliminate it. These factors, high HIV/AIDS rates and the vulnerability of agricultural production to both drought and severe flooding, make the country heavily dependent on food and economic aid from international agencies and donor nations, although international aid was suspended in January 2014 after US$100m (£60m) was allegedly stolen from government funds. Around 40 per cent of Malawi's budget is donor-funded. Debt relief and tighter fiscal control reduced public debt from over 200 per cent of GDP to 36.8 per cent by 2011.

The economy is primarily agricultural, with 90 per cent of the workforce engaged in agriculture, which accounts for 29.4 per cent of GDP and 90 per cent of export revenue. Tobacco is the most important cash crop, providing 53 per cent of export earnings, along with tea, sugar, cotton, coffee and peanuts. The main industrial activities are agricultural processing, sawmill products, cement and consumer goods, now supplemented by mining uranium, of which exports began in 2009.

The main export markets are India, Germany, South Africa, Russia and Zimbabwe; imports come mainly from South Africa (31 per cent), Zambia, India and China. Apart from tobacco and other agricultural products, wood products and clothing are principal exports. The main imports are food, fuels, semi-manufactures, consumer goods and transport equipment.

GNI – US$4,139m; US$320 per capita (2012)
Annual average growth of GDP – 5 per cent (2013 est)
Inflation rate – 26.9 per cent (2013 est)
Population below poverty line – 50 per cent (2004)
Total external debt – US$1,556m (2013 est)
Imports – US$2,213m (2012)
Exports – US$1,226m (2012)

BALANCE OF PAYMENTS
Trade – US$9870m deficit (2012)
Current Account – US$185m deficit (2012)

Trade with UK	2012	2013
Imports from UK	£19,086,492	£15,329,055
Exports to UK	£15,837,772	£22,244,361

COMMUNICATIONS
Airports and waterways – The main airports are at Blantyre and Lilongwe, with five smaller airports around the country; there are 700km of navigable waterways on Lake Malawi (Nyasa) and the Shire river
Roadways and railways – There are 15,450km of roadways, of which 6,951km are surfaced, and 797km of railways, including a line linking the Zambian town of Chipata to the Indian Ocean coast at Nacala in Mozambique
Telecommunications – 227,300 fixed lines and 4.42 million mobile subscriptions (2012); there were 716,400 internet users in 2009
Internet code and IDD – mw; 265 (from UK), 44 (to UK)
Media – There are two national daily newspapers; radio is the main source of information, provided by the state-run Malawi Broadcasting Corporation and a number of private stations
WPFI score – 28,29 (73)

EDUCATION AND HEALTH
The government is responsible for primary and secondary schools, technical education and primary teacher training.
Literacy rate – 61 per cent (2010 est)
Gross enrolment ratio (percentage of relevant age group) – primary 141 per cent; secondary 34 per cent (2012 est)
Health expenditure (per capita) – US$31 (2011)
Hospital beds (per 1,000 people) – 1.3 (2011)
Life expectancy (years) – 59.99 (2014 est)
Mortality rate – 8.74 (2014 est)
Birth rate – 41.8 (2014 est)
Infant mortality rate – 48.0198 (2014 est)
HIV/AIDS adult prevalence – 10.8 per cent (2012 est)

MALAYSIA

Area – 329,847 sq. km
Capital – Kuala Lumpur; population, 1,576,080 (2012);
  Putrajaya is the administrative capital
Major cities – Ampang Jaya, Ipoh, Johor Bahru, Klang, Kota
  Kinabalu, Kuantan, Kuching, Petaling Jaya, Shah Alam
Currency – Malaysian ringgit (RM) of 100 sen; also known as
  Malaysian dollar
Population – 30,073,353 rising at 1.47 per cent a year
  (2014 est); Malay (50.4 per cent), Chinese (23.7 per cent),
  indigenous (11 per cent), Indian (7.1 per cent) (2004 est)
Religion – Muslim 61.3 per cent, Buddhist 19.8 per cent,
  Christian 9.2 per cent, Hindu 6.3 per cent, Chinese
  traditional religions 1.3 per cent
Language – Bahasa Malaysia (Malay) (official), English,
  Cantonese, Mandarin, Tamil, Telugu, Malayalam, Punjabi,
  Thai, Iban, Kadazan
Population density – 88 per sq. km (2011)
Urban population – 73.5 per cent (2012 est)
Median age (years) – 27.7 (2014 est)
National anthem – 'Negaraku' ['My Country']
National day – 31 August (Independence Day)
Death penalty – Retained
CPI score – 50 (53)

CLIMATE AND TERRAIN

Malaysia comprises the 11 states of peninsular Malaya plus
the states of Sabah and Sarawak on the island of Borneo. The
Malay peninsula, which extends from the isthmus of Kra to
the Singapore Strait, is a plain with two highland areas in
the north. The Malaysian part of Borneo is mostly high
plateau, rising to mountains in western Sabah and eastern
Sarawak, while Sarawak also has lower-lying land along
the coast and in the Rajang valley; both states are densely
forested. Elevation extremes range from 4,100m (Gunung
Kinabalu, Sabah) to 0m (Indian Ocean). The climate is
tropical, experiencing the south-west monsoon from May to
September and the north-east monsoon from November
to March. The average temperature in Kuala Lumpur is 27°C.

POLITICS

The federal *Parlimen* has two houses, the House of
Representatives and the senate. The former is the lower house
and has 222 members, directly elected for a five-year term.
The senate has 70 members who serve a three-year term; the
legislative assembly of each state elects two members, and
44 are nominated by the head of state.

Each of the 13 states has its own constitution, which
must not be inconsistent with the federal constitution. The
Malay rulers are either chosen or succeed to their position
in accordance with the custom of their particular state; in
other states of Malaysia, choice of the head of state is at the
discretion of the *Yang di-Pertuan Agong* after consultation

with the chief minister of the state. The ruler or governor acts
on the advice of an executive council appointed on the
advice of the chief minister and a single-chamber legislative
assembly. The legislative assemblies are elected on the same
basis as the lower chamber of the federal legislature.

The *Barisan Nasional* coalition won the 2008 legislative
election, but with a majority reduced from 198 to 140 seats
after a significant swing to the opposition parties. Abdullah
Ahmed Badawi, prime minister since 2003, stood down in
2009 and was replaced as leader of UMNO and prime
minister by his deputy, Najib Tun Abdul Razak.

The 1957 constitution provides for a federal government
and a degree of autonomy for the state governments. The
supreme head of state (Abdul Halim al-Marhum Badlishah) is
elected by the nine hereditary rulers of the peninsular states
from among their number and serves a five-year term.

HEAD OF STATE
Supreme Head of State, HM Tuanku Abdul Halim al-Marhum
  Badlishah, *sworn in* 13 December 2011
Deputy Head of State, HM Sultan Muhammad V

SELECTED GOVERNMENT MEMBERS *as at June 2014*
Prime Minister, Finance, Najib Tun Abdul Razak
Deputy Prime Minister, Muhyiddin bin Mohamed Yassin
Defence, Hishammuddin bin Tun Hussein
Foreign Affairs, Anifah Aman

MALAYSIAN HIGH COMMISSION
45 Belgrave Square, London SW1X 8QT
T 020-7235 8033 E mwlon@btconnect.com
W www.jimlondon.net
High Commissioner, HE Dato' Ahmad Rasidi Hazizi, *apptd*
  2014

BRITISH HIGH COMMISSION
PO Box 11030, 185 Jalan Ampang, 50450 Kuala Lumpur
T (+60) (3) 2170 2200 E consular.kualalumpur@fco.gov.uk
W www.gov.uk/government/world/malaysia
High Commissioner, HE Simon Featherstone, *apptd* 2010

DEFENCE

Aged 16–49, 2010 est	Males	Females
Available for military service	7,501,518	7,315,999
Fit for military service	6,247,306	6,175,274

Military expenditure – US$4,809m (2013)

ECONOMY AND TRADE

The economy has grown vigorously since the 1970s,
transforming the country into a diversified emerging
economy. The government's goal is to achieve developed
nation status by 2020. To this end, it has encouraged

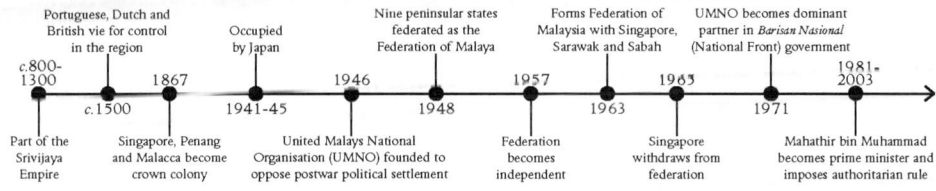

investment in high-technology industries, medical technology and pharmaceuticals, and growth as a regional financial hub, especially for Islamic finance. Growth has largely been driven by manufacturing, and oil and gas exports.

The agricultural sector produces the raw materials for its highly developed industries. Industrial production includes rubber manufacturing, palm oil processing, pharmaceuticals, medical technology, electronics, tin mining and smelting, and logging and timber processing; in addition, oil is produced in Sabah and Sarawak, and refined in Sarawak. Tourism is a major industry. The services sector contributes 48.1 per cent of GDP, industry 40.6 per cent and agriculture 11.2 per cent.

The main trading partners are China, Singapore, Japan, the USA and other South East Asian countries. Principal exports are electronic equipment, petroleum and liquefied natural gas, timber and wood products, palm oil, rubber, textiles and chemicals. The main imports are electronics, machinery, petroleum products, plastics, vehicles, iron and steel products, and chemicals.

GNI – US$293,358m; US$9,820 per capita (2012)
Annual average growth of GDP – 4.7 per cent (2013 est)
Inflation rate – 2.2 per cent (2013 est)
Unemployment – 3.1 per cent (2013 est)
Total external debt – US$100,100m (2013 est)
Imports – US$196,615m (2012)
Exports – US$227,391m (2012)

BALANCE OF PAYMENTS
Trade – US$30,776m surplus (2012)
Current Account – US$18,566m surplus (2012)

Trade with UK	2012	2013
Imports from UK	£1,481,680,654	£1,568,793,497
Exports to UK	£1,725.975,149	£1,684,623,665

COMMUNICATIONS

Airports – There are 39 airports; the main international airports are at Kuala Lumpur, Kota Kinabalu, Kuching and Penang
Waterways – There are six main seaports in peninsular Malaysia, plus Kota Kinabalu (Sabah) and Kuching (Sarawak), and a merchant fleet of 315 ships of more than 1,000 tonnes; there are 7,200km of navigable waterways
Roadways and railways – 116,1691km; 1,849km
Telecommunications – 4.589 million fixed lines and 41.325 million mobile subscriptions (2012); there were 15.355 million internet users in 2009
Internet country code and IDD – my; 60 (from UK), 44 (to UK)
Major broadcasters – The state-run Radio Television Malaysia provides services in competition with commercial operators, which broadcast in Malay, Tamil, Chinese and English
Press – The four main national daily newspapers are in English: *The Star, The Sun, New Straits Times* and *The Malay Mail*
WPFI score – 42,73 (147)

EDUCATION AND HEALTH

There are six years of compulsory education.
Literacy rate – 93 per cent (2010 est)
Gross enrolment ratio (percentage of relevant age group) – secondary 67 per cent; tertiary 36 per cent (2012 est)
Health expenditure (per capita) – US$346 (2011)
Hospital beds (per 1,000 people) – 1.8 (2011)
Life expectancy (years) – 74.52 (2014 est)
Mortality rate – 5 (2014 est)
Birth rate – 20.06 (2014 est)
Infant mortality rate – 13.69 (2014 est)

MALDIVES

Dhivehi Raajjeyge Jumhooriyyaa – Republic of Maldives

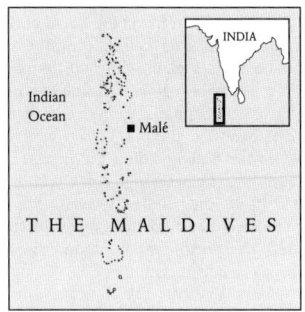

Area – 298 sq. km
Capital – Malé; population, 120,000 (2009 est)
Currency – Rufiyaa of 100 laarees
Population – 393,595 falling at 0.09 per cent a year (2014 est)
Religion – Sunni Muslim; public practice of other religions is illegal
Language – Dhivehi (official), English
Population density – 1,107 per sq. km (2011)
Urban population – 42.3 per cent (2012 est)
Median age (years) – 27.1 (2014 est)
National anthem – 'Gaumii Salaam' ['National Salute']
National day – 26 July (Independence Day)
Death penalty – Retained (no known use since 1952)
Literacy rate – 98.4 per cent (2010 est)
Life expectancy (years) – 75.15 (2014 est)
Mortality rate – 3.84 (2014 est)
Birth rate – 15.59 (2014 est)
Infant mortality rate – 24.59 (2014 est)

CLIMATE AND TERRAIN

The republic is an archipelago of atolls in the Indian Ocean, 643km to the south-west of Sri Lanka. There are about 1,190 coral islands grouped into 26 clusters of atolls, about 200 of which are inhabited. The islands are all flat and low-lying; none is more than 2.4m above sea level, making them vulnerable to rising sea levels caused by climate change.

The climate is tropical, affected by the dry north-east monsoon (January–March) and the wet south-west monsoon (May–November).

HISTORY AND POLITICS

The Maldives were an independent sultanate from the mid-12th century. The sultan was overthrown by the Portuguese in 1558 but they were driven out in 1573 and the sultanate was re-established. In 1645, the islands became a dependency of Ceylon, which was under Dutch and then British rule. In 1887 they became an internally self-governing British protectorate. Independence was achieved in 1965, and in 1968 the Maldives became a republic under President Ibrahim Nasir.

The autocratic Nasir retired in 1978 and was succeeded by Maumoon Abdul Gayoom. His 30-year tenure, although equally autocratic, maintained political stability and economic development. However, unprecedented violence during anti-government demonstrations in 2003 and 2004 led to the legalising of political parties in 2005.

In the first multi-party legislative elections in 2009, the People's Party, led by Maumoon Abdul Gayoom, won only two more seats than the Maldivian Democratic Party (MDP) but through alliances with smaller parties secured control of the legislature. In the presidential elections of November 2013 Abdulla Gayoom of the Gayoom Progressive Party of Maldives (PPM) and half brother of former dictator Maumoon Gayoom, defeated Mohamed Nasheed, the country's first democratically elected president from 2008–12. The March 2014 legislative elections were won by the PPM.

Under the 2008 constitution, the executive president is directly elected for a five-year term, renewable once. The unicameral People's Assembly *(Majlis)* has 77 members, who are directly elected for a five-year term.

HEAD OF STATE
President, Abdulla Yameen Abdul Gayoom, *sworn in* 17 November 2013
Vice-President, Mohamed Jameel Ahmed

SELECTED GOVERNMENT MEMBERS *as at June 2014*
Defence, Mohamed Nazim
Finance, Abdula Jihad
Foreign Affairs, Dunya Maumoon

HIGH COMMISSION OF THE REPUBLIC OF MALDIVES
22 Nottingham Place, London W1U 5NJ
T 020-7224 2135 E info@maldiveshighcommission.org
W www.maldiveshighcommission.org
High Commissioner (acting), Ahmed Shiaan

BRITISH HIGH COMMISSIONER
HE John Rankin, *apptd* 2011, resident at Colombo, Sri Lanka

ECONOMY AND TRADE

Political stability and economic liberalisation have produced steady economic growth since the 1980s, except in 2005 owing to the devastation caused by the 2004 tsunami, and 2009, when tourist numbers and exports fell owing to the global economic downturn. Balance of payments difficulties forced the government to seek IMF standby funding in 2009; after the first two disbursements the IMF halted further funds due to the Maldives' growing budget deficit. The economy is heavily dependent on tourism, which accounts for 30 per cent of GDP and 60 per cent of foreign exchange receipts. A business profit tax and tourism-related taxes introduced in 2011 have provided a boost in revenue.

Agriculture and manufacturing are constrained by a shortage of cultivable land and domestic labour, so most food is imported. Industry is concentrated on clothing manufacture, fish processing, boat-building and handicrafts, contributing 17 per cent to GDP.

The main export markets are France, Singapore and the UAE. The only significant export is fish. Imports include petroleum products, ships, food and clothing, and are provided mainly by Singapore, the UAE, India and Malaysia.
GNI – US$1,883m; US$5,750 per capita (2012)
Annual average growth of GDP – 3.5 per cent (2013 est)
Inflation rate – 5.1 per cent (2012 est)
Population below poverty line – 16 per cent (2008)
Unemployment – 28 per cent (2012 est)
Total external debt – US$890.8m (2013 est)
Imports – US$1,554m (2012)
Exports – US$162m (2012)

BALANCE OF PAYMENTS
Trade – US$1,393m deficit (2012)
Current Account – US$221m deficit (2009)

Trade with UK	2012	2013
Imports from UK	£7,911,374	£8,291,086
Exports to UK	£14,154,580	£10,659,512

COMMUNICATIONS

Transport – The country has seven airports, two of which handle international traffic; the main port is Malé and there are 88km of roads
Telecommunications – 23,140 fixed lines and 560,000 mobile subscriptions (2012); there were 86,400 internet users in 2009
Internet code and IDD – mv; 960 (from UK), to UK (44)
Media – The state-run Maldives National Broadcasting Corporation operates the main television and radio stations
WPFI score – 33,11 (108)

MALI

République de Mali – Republic of Mali

Area – 1,240,192 sq. km
Capital – Bamako; population, 1,847,191 (2012)
Major cities – Kayes, Mopti, Ségou, Sikasso, Koutiala, Timbuktu
Currency – Franc CFA of 100 centimes
Population – 16,455,903 rising at 3 per cent a year (2014 est); Mandé (50 per cent), Fulani (17 per cent), Voltaic (12 per cent), Tuareg and Moor (10 per cent), Songhai (6 per cent) (est); about 10 per cent are nomadic

Religion – Muslim 94.8 per cent, Christian 2.4 per cent,
   Animist 2 per cent
Language – French (official), Bambara, other African
   languages
Population density – 12 per sq. km (2011)
Urban population – 35.6 per cent (2012 est)
Median age (years) – 16 (2014 est)
National anthem – 'Pour l'Afrique et Pour Toi, Mali' ['For
   Africa and For You, Mali']
National day – 22 September (Independence Day)
Death penalty – Retained (last used 1980)
CPI score – 28 (127)

CLIMATE AND TERRAIN

The west African state is mainly savannah in the south and
desert plains in the north, with some hills in the north-east;
over 60 per cent is desert or semi-desert. The centre is
drained by the Niger river and the south-west by the Senegal
river. Elevation extremes range from 1,155m (Hombori
Tondo) to 23m (Senegal river). The climate is subtropical
in the south with a rainy season from June to November,
and arid in the north. Average temperatures in Bamako
range from 25°C in January and December to 32°C in
April.

HISTORY AND POLITICS

Mali was successively part of the empire of the Malinke
people from the 13th to 15th centuries, and of the Songhai
Empire in the 15th to 16th centuries. With the fall of the
Songhai Empire, it was divided between the Tuareg and
the Fulani and Bambara kingdoms, and then the Tukolor
and Samori kingdoms. It was conquered by the French in
1880–95 and became a French colony. In 1959, it formed
the Federation of Mali with Senegal before becoming a
separate independent state in 1960 under a one-party
socialist regime.

In 1968, a military coup led by Lt. Moussa Traoré resulted
in 23 years of oppressive military rule. Traoré was ousted as
president in 1991 in a military coup led by Gen. Amadou
Toumani Touré. Multiparty elections were held in 1992,
returning the country to civilian government.

A degree of decentralisation was introduced in 1999,
partly in response to rebellions in the north by the Tuareg
over land and cultural rights. Another rebellion in 2006 by
Tuareg seeking greater autonomy for their region was settled
within a few months, but a more militant faction carried
on an insurrection from 2007 to 2009, when the rebels
disarmed and returned to negotiations. In May 2014 Tuareg
separatists occupied the northern towns Menaka, Agelhok,
Anefis and Tessalit.

Amadou Toumani Touré, standing as an independent
candidate, won the 2002 presidential elections, and was
re-elected in 2007. In the 2007 legislative elections, the
Alliance for Democracy in Mali (ADEMA), which had
dominated government coalitions since 1992, won the
largest number of seats, and the three-party Alliance for
Democracy and Progress coalition (of which ADEMA is a
part) retained its overall majority. A military coup overthrew Touré's government in March 2012, claiming that
the government had not supported the country's army
against the advancing Tuareg-led rebellion. Cissé Mariam
Kaidama Sidibé, the country's first female prime minister,
was arrested shortly after the coup. In the subsequent 2013
presidential elections, former prime minister Ibrahim
Boubacar Keita comfortably defeated rival candidate
Soumaila Cissé.

Under the 1992 constitution, the president is directly
elected for a five-year term, which is renewable once. The
unicameral National Assembly has 160 members, 147
directly elected for a maximum of two terms and 13 to
represent Malians abroad; all serve a five-year term. The
president appoints the prime minister, who appoints the
cabinet.

HEAD OF STATE

President, Ibrahim Boubacar Keita, *apptd* 4 September 2014

SELECTED GOVERNMENT MEMBERS *as at June 2014*
Prime Minister, Moussa Mara
Economy and Finance, Bouaré Fily Sissoko
Foreign Affairs, Abdoulaye Diop

EMBASSY OF THE REPUBLIC OF MALI
Avenue Molière 487, 1050 Brussels, Belgium
T (+32) (2) 345 7432 E info@amba-mali.be W www.amba-mali.be
Ambassador Extraordinary and Plenipotentiary, HE Ibrahim
   Bocar Ba, *apptd* 2003

BRITISH AMBASSADOR
Immeuble Semega, Route de Koulikoro, Hippodrome, BP 2069,
Bamako
T (+223) 2021 3412 W www.gov.uk/government/world/mali
Ambassador Extraordinary and Plenipotentiary, HE Joanne
   Adamson, *apptd* 2014

DEFENCE

Aged 16–49, 2010 est	Males	Females
Available for military service	2,848,412	2,981,106
Fit for military service	1,825,779	1,968,563

Military expenditure – US$153m (2013)
Conscription – 18 years; 24 months (selective)

ECONOMY AND TRADE

Mali is one of the world's poorest countries, with over 30 per
cent of the population living below the poverty line.
Economic reform since the mid-1990s has produced steady
growth, but Mali is heavily dependent on foreign aid and
remittances from expatriates. A huge foreign debt has been
reduced to a more manageable size by debt cancellation and
rescheduling.

The economy is based primarily on subsistence farming
and animal husbandry, which contribute 38.5 per cent
of GDP and occupy 80 per cent of the population. Gold,
phosphate and iron-ore mining, and cotton and food
processing are the main activities in Mali's industrial sector,
which accounts for 24.4 per cent of GDP. Export of
hydro-electric power is expected to contribute to future
earnings.

The main export markets are China and South Korea;
imports come mainly from Senegal, France and the Ivory
Coast. Principal exports are cotton, gold and livestock. The
main imports are fuel, machinery and equipment,
construction materials, foodstuffs and textiles.

GNI – US$9,087m; US$660 per capita (2012)
Annual average growth of GDP – –4.8 per cent (2013 est)
Inflation rate – 0.1 per cent (2013 est)
Population below poverty line – 36.1 per cent (2005 est)
Unemployment – 30 per cent (2004 est)
Total external debt – US$3,349m (2013)
Imports – US$2,940m (2012)
Exports – US$2,163m (2012)

BALANCE OF PAYMENTS
Trade – US$776m deficit (2012)
Current Account – US$645m deficit (2011)

Trade with UK	2012	2013
Imports from UK	£9,792,905	£10,122,395
Exports to UK	£410,030	£274,247

COMMUNICATIONS

Airports and waterways – There are eight airports, with the largest at Bamako; the main port is Koulikoro on the Niger river

Roadways and railways – 22,474 km; 593km

Telecommunications – 112,000 fixed lines and 14.613 million mobile subscriptions (2012); there were 249,800 internet users in 2009

Internet code and IDD – ml; 223 (from UK), 44 (to UK)

Major broadcasters – Office de la Radiodiffusion Télévision du Mali operates a number of radio and television channels in French and local vernacular languages

Press – There are five main daily newspapers, including *L'Essor,* the state-owned national daily

WPFI score – 36,29 (122)

EDUCATION AND HEALTH

There are nine years of free, compulsory education beginning at age seven.

Literacy rate – 33 per cent (2011 est)

Gross enrolment ratio (percentage of relevant age group) – primary 88 per cent; secondary 51 per cent; tertiary 7 per cent (2012 est)

Health expenditure (per capita) – US$45 (2011)

Hospital beds (per 1,000 people) – 0.1 (2010)

Life expectancy (years) – 54.95 (2014 est)

Mortality rate – 13.22 (2014 est)

Birth rate – 45.53 (2014 est)

Infant mortality rate – 104.34 (2014 est)

HIV/AIDS adult prevalence – 0.9 per cent (2012 est)

MALTA

Repubblika ta' Malta – Republic of Malta

Area – 316 sq. km

Capital – Valletta; population, 199,000 (2009)

Major towns – Birkirkara, Mosta, Qormi, Saint Paul's Bay (San Pawl il-Bahar)

Currency – Euro (€) of 100 cents

Population – 412,655 rising at 0.33 per cent a year (2014 est)

Religion – Christian (Roman Catholic 98 per cent)

Language – Maltese, English (both official)

Population density – 1,302 per sq. km (2011)

Urban population – 95 per cent (2012 est)

Median age (years) – 40.9 (2014 est)

National anthem – 'L-Innu Malti' ['Hymn of Malta']

National day – 21 September (Independence Day)

Death penalty – Abolished for all crimes (since 2000)

CPI score – 56 (45)

Life expectancy (years) – 80.11 (2014 est)

Mortality rate – 8.96 (2014 est)

Birth rate – 10.24 (2014 est)

Infant mortality rate – 3.59 (2014 est)

CLIMATE AND TERRAIN

Malta is an archipelago of six islands in the Mediterranean Sea; Malta, Gozo and Comino are the largest. The island of Malta has a coastal plain in the north-east, rising to low hills in the south-west. Elevation extremes range from 253m (Ta'Dmejrek) to 0m (Mediterranean Sea). Average temperatures in Valletta range from 12°C in January and February to 26°C in August.

HISTORY AND POLITICS

The islands were ruled successively by the Phoenicians, Greeks, Carthaginians, Romans, Arabs, Spanish and the Sovereign Military Order of Malta (known as the Knights of St John), which held them from 1530 until a French invasion in 1798. Liberated from French rule with British naval support in 1800, the island of Malta became a British colony in 1814, and was developed into a substantial naval base and dockyard. Malta was strategically important in both world wars, but particularly the second, when it was blockaded and subjected to aerial bombardment for five months. Its resistance led to the people of Malta being awarded the George Cross, the UK's highest award for civilian bravery, in 1942.

Malta gained its independence in 1964 and became a republic in 1974. In the 1970s it developed close links with communist and Arab states, but more pro-European and pro-US policies were adopted after the election of the Nationalist Party in 1987. Malta became a member of the EU in 2004, and adopted the euro in 2008. Since joining the EU, Malta has experienced a marked increase in illegal immigration from northern Africa.

In March 2013 the Labour Party returned to power after winning 39 seats in legislative elections and in April 2014 the party's Marie-Louise Coleiro Preca was confirmed as president.

Under the 1974 constitution, the president is elected by the legislature for a five-year term, renewable once. The unicameral legislature, the House of Representatives, has 69 members directly elected for a five-year term; if a party wins the majority of votes in a general election without winning a majority of seats, new seats are created until that party holds a majority of one seat. The prime minister is appointed by the president and nominates the other ministers.

HEAD OF STATE
President, Marie-Louise Coleiro Preca, *elected* 1 April 2014, *took office* 4 April 2014

SELECTED GOVERNMENT MEMBERS *as at June 2014*
Prime Minister, Dr Joseph Muscat
Economy, Dr Christian Cardona
Finance, Edward Scicluna
Foreign Affairs, George Vella
Home Affairs, Dr Emanuel Mallia

MALTA HIGH COMMISSION
Malta House, 36–38 Piccadilly, London W1J 0LE
T 020-7292 4800 E maltahighcommission.london@gov.mt
W www.foreign.gov.mt/uk
High Commissioner, HE Norman Hamilton, *apptd* 2013

BRITISH HIGH COMMISSION
Whitehall Mansions, Ta' Xbiex Seafront, Ta' Xbiex XBX 1026
T (+356) 2323 0000 E bhcvalletta@fco.gov.uk
W www.gov.uk/government/world/malta
High Commissioner HE Rob Luke, *apptd 2012*

DEFENCE

Aged 16–49, 2010 est	Males	Females
Available for military service	95,499	90,919
Fit for military service	79,645	75,684

Military expenditure – US$59.7m (2013)

ECONOMY AND TRADE

The mainstay of the economy for over a century was the dockyard, and shipbuilding and ship repairs remain significant industries, but since the 1980s Malta has developed into a tourist destination, financial services centre and freight trans-shipment point. Tourism is now the main source of income, followed by foreign trade and manufacturing, especially of electronics and pharmaceuticals. All were adversely affected by the global downturn in 2009, and new fiscal measures contributed further to a deterioration in public finances in 2011. An excessive deficit procedure against Malta was opened by the EU in 2013, despite a previous procedure being lifted in 2012. The service sector accounts for 73.3 per cent of GDP, industry for 25.3 per cent and agriculture for 1.4 per cent.

The main trading partners are other EU states. Principal exports are electrical machinery, mechanical appliances, fish and shellfish, pharmaceuticals and printed material. The main imports are mineral fuels and oil, machinery, aircraft and other transport equipment, semi-manufactured goods, food, beverages and tobacco.

GNI – US$8,113m; US$19,760 per capita (2012)
Annual average growth of GDP – 1.1 per cent (2013 est)
Inflation rate – 1.7 per cent (2013 est)
Unemployment – 6.4 per cent (2013)
Total external debt – US$46,220m (2013 est)
Imports – US$7,909m (2012)
Exports – US$5,684m (2012)

BALANCE OF PAYMENTS
Trade – US$2,226m deficit (2012)
Current Account – US$95m surplus (2012)

Trade with UK	2012	2013
Imports from UK	£393,576.364	£436,130,985
Exports to UK	£129,501,119	£107,878,740

COMMUNICATIONS

Airports and waterways – The international airport is at Luqa, south-west of Valletta; the main ports are Marsaxlokk (Malta's freeport) and Valletta, and there is a large merchant fleet of 1,650 ships of over 1,000 tonnes
Roadways – 3,096km
Telecommunications – 229,700 fixed lines and 539,500 mobile subscriptions (2012); there were 240,600 internet users in 2009
Internet code and IDD – mt; 356 (from UK), 44 (to UK)
Media – There are public-service radio and television broadcasters, as well as a thriving private sector
WPFI score – 23,84 (51)

EDUCATION

Education is free at all levels and compulsory between the ages of five and 16.

Literacy rate – 92.4 per cent (2010 est)
Gross enrolment ratio (percentage of relevant age group) – primary 96 per cent; secondary 95 per cent; tertiary 39 per cent (2012 est)

MARSHALL ISLANDS

Republic of the Marshall Islands

Area – 181 sq. km (plus 11,673 sq. km of lagoon waters)
Capital – Majuro; population, 30,000 (2009 est)
Major towns – Ebeye, Rita
Currency – US dollar (US$) of 100 cents
Population – 70,983 rising at 1.72 per cent a year (2014 est); mainly Micronesian. About 70 per cent of the population lives on Majuro and Kwajalein
Religion – Christian (Protestant 80.6 per cent, Roman Catholic 8.4 per cent, other 8.5 per cent)
Language – Marshallese, English (both official)
Population density – 292 per sq. km (2011)
Urban population – 72.2 per cent (2012 est)
Median age (years) – 22.5 (2014 est)
National anthem – 'Forever Marshall Islands'
National day – 1 May (Constitution Day)
Death penalty – Abolished for all crimes (since 1986)
Life expectancy (years) – 72.58 (2014 est)
Mortality rate – 4.24 (2014 est)
Birth rate – 26.36 (2014 est)
Infant mortality rate – 21.39 (2014 est)

CLIMATE AND TERRAIN

The republic consists of two chains of 29 atolls, five islands and over 1,000 islets in the western Pacific Ocean. All of the islands are low-lying (the highest point is 10m) and vulnerable to rising sea levels, which could submerge them by the mid-21st century. The climate is tropical, with a wet season from June to November.

HISTORY AND POLITICS

The Marshall Islands were first claimed by Spain in 1592 but were left largely undisturbed. Subsequently they were seized by Germany and formally became a protectorate in 1886. Japan took control of the islands in 1914 on behalf of the Allied powers and administered them from 1920 until 1944, when they were captured by US forces. In 1947 the islands became part of the UN Trust Territory of the Pacific Islands, administered by the USA. Between 1946 and 1958, US nuclear weapons were tested on Bikini and Enewetak atolls. Enewetak has been partially decontaminated but Bikini is uninhabitable; the USA paid compensation to the test victims in the 1980s but the government is seeking further compensation to cover the medical care of radiation victims and rectify environmental damage.

The islands became internally self-governing in 1979, and US administration ended in 1986, when a compact of free association between the Republic of the Marshall Islands and the USA came into effect. Under this agreement, the USA recognised the republic as a sovereign and independent state but retained responsibility for external security and defence as well as giving financial help. UN trust territory status was terminated in 1990 and full independence was granted in December 1990. A renegotiated compact with the USA was signed in 2003. The USA retains control of the Kwajalein atoll, where it has a military base and missile tracking station.

There were no formal political parties in the 2011 legislative elections, with all 33 members of the chamber standing as independents. Christopher Loeak was elected

United Kingdom & Ireland

Shetland Islands

Lerwick

60°N

10°W   5°W   0°   60°N

Fair Isle

A T L A N T I C   O C E A N

Orkney Islands

Kirkwall

Cape Wrath   Pentland Firth
                    Thurso Duncansby Head
                    Wick

Lewis
Stornoway

Outer Hebrides

Harris

N. Uist

S. Uist

Ullapool

Dingwall
Dornoch

Moray Firth
Elgin   Fraserburgh
                         Peterhead

North West Highlands

Inverness

Loch Ness

Spey

Cairngorms
Ben Macdhui
1309

Aberdeen

Stonehaven

N O R T H

Skye
Kyle of Lochalsh

Mallaig

Fort William

Ben Nevis
1343

S C O T L A N D

Grampian Mts.

S e a

Mull
Oban

Perth

Dundee
St. Andrews

Fife Ness

Islay

Loch Lomond

Stirling
Greenock Dunfermline
         Falkirk
Paisley Glasgow

Kirkcaldy
Firth of Forth
Edinburgh

Berwick-upon-Tweed

Kintyre
Arran

Kilmarnock

Peebles Galashiels

Southern Uplands

Jedburgh

Tweed

Alnwick

Ayr

Malin Head

Bloody Foreland

Londonderry

Coleraine

Stranraer

Dumfries

Cheviot Hills

Blyth

55°N

Malinmore Head

Donegal

Ballymena Larne

N O R T H E R N
I R E L A N D

Omagh

Strabane

Lough Neagh

Belfast
Bangor

Wigtown Kirkcudbright

Carlisle

Solway Firth

Tyne

Consett

Newcastle upon Tyne

Durham Sunderland

Hartlepool

55°N

Donegal Bay

Sligo

Enniskillen

Lough Erne

Lurgan Armagh
Portadown

Downpatrick
Strangford Lough

Newry

Mourne Mts.

Workington

Keswick
Lake District

Penrith

Darlington

Middlesbrough

Scarborough

Ballina
L. Conn

Carrick on Shannon

Cavan

Dundalk

Kendal

Barrow-in-Furness

Lancaster

Windermere

Harrogate

York

Bridlington

R E P U B L I C

Roscommon

Longford

Navan

Clew Bay

Castlebar

L. Mask

Mullingar

Isle of Man
Douglas

Blackpool

Preston

Bradford

Leeds

Kingston upon Hull

Spurn Head

Clifden

Athlone

Tullamore

Lough Derg Port Laoise

Dublin

Liverpool

Manchester

Sheffield

Grimsby

Galway Bay

L. Corrib

O F

Kildare

Dún Laoghaire

Birkenhead

Peak District

Chesterfield

Lincoln

Boston

The Wash

Skegness

Cromer

Milltown Malbay

Ennis

Carlow

Wicklow Mts.

Anglesey
Holyhead

Llandudno

Chester

Crewe

Stoke-on-Trent

Nottingham

Grantham

Kings Lynn

Norfolk Broads

Great Yarmouth

I R E L A N D

Kilkenny

Wicklow

Caernarfon

Snowdon
1085

Wrexham

Derby

Leicester

Peterborough

Norwich

Waveney

Kilrush

Tipperary

Clonmel

Enniscorthy

Cardigan Bay

Dolgellau

Shrewsbury

E N G L A N D

Limerick

Mallow

Waterford

Suir

Wexford

Rosslare

Montgomery

Aberystwyth

Wolverhampton

Birmingham

Coventry

Rugby

Northampton

Bedford

Cambridge

Ipswich

Harwich
The Naze

Dingle

Tralee

Killarney

Youghal

Dungarvan
Mine Head

Fishguard

Llandrindod Wells

Worcester

Gloucester

Luton

Colchester

Valentia

Kenmare

Bantry

Cork

St. David's Head

Milford Haven

Carmarthen

W A L E S

Teifi
Towy
Wye

Ebbw Vale

Cotswolds

Oxford

Swindon

Reading

Chiltern Hills

LONDON

Thames

Southend-on-Sea

Margate

Cape Clear

Llanelli

Swansea
Port Talbot

Newport

Cardiff

Bristol

Bath

Avon

Salisbury Plain

Guildford

Winchester

Canterbury

Maidstone

The Weald

Dover
Strait of Dover

Folkestone

Calais

Bristol Channel

Hartland Point

Barnstaple

Exmoor

Taunton

Salisbury

Southampton

Isle of Wight

Portsmouth

Brighton

Hastings

Boulogne

Le Touquet

0   25   50   75   100 Miles

0   50   100   150 Kms

Bude

Dartmoor

Exe

Exeter

Yeovil

Poole

Bournemouth

Weymouth
Portland Bill

Torquay

English

Abbeville

Dieppe

50°N

Bodmin

Tavistock

Start Point

C h a n n e l

50°N

Penzance
Land's End

Plymouth

Truro
Falmouth

FRANCE

Lizard Point

Isles of Scilly

Alderney

Cherbourg

Baie de la Seine

Le Havre

Rouen

Conical Orthomorphic Projection

Guernsey

Sark

Jersey

Caen

Collines de Normandie

Seine

© Oxford Cartographers, 97835
+44 (0)1993 705 394
E & OE

10°W   5°W   0°

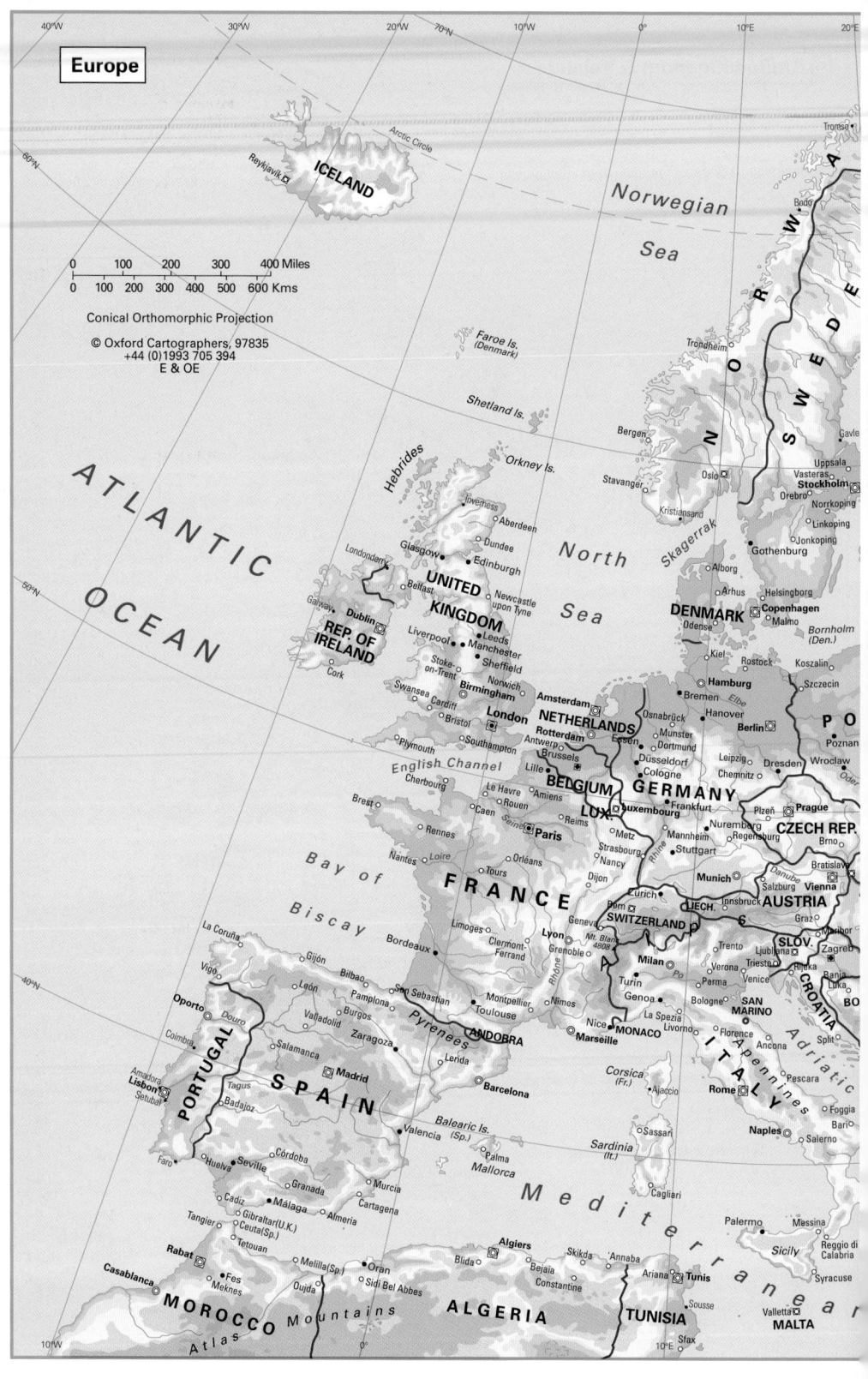

Europe

40°W 30°W 20°W 10°W 0° 10°E 20°E

70°N

60°N

50°N

40°N

ICELAND
Reykjavík

Arctic Circle

Norwegian Sea

N O R W A Y

Tromsö
Bodö

S W E D E N

0 100 200 300 400 Miles
0 100 200 300 400 500 600 Kms

Conical Orthomorphic Projection

© Oxford Cartographers, 97835
+44 (0)1993 705 394
E & OE

Faroe Is.
(Denmark)

Shetland Is.

Trondheim

Bergen
Stavanger
Kristiansand

Oslo
Gävle
Uppsala
Västerås
Stockholm
Örebro
Norrköping
Linköping
Jönköping
Gothenburg

Hebrides
Orkney Is.
Inverness
Aberdeen
Dundee
Glasgow Edinburgh
Newcastle
upon Tyne

North Sea

Skagerrak

Ålborg
Århus
Helsingborg
DENMARK Copenhagen
Odense Malmö
Kiel Bornholm
(Den.)

A T L A N T I C

O C E A N

Londonderry
Belfast
Galway **Dublin**
**REP. OF
IRELAND**
Cork

**UNITED
KINGDOM**
Leeds
Liverpool Manchester
Sheffield
Stoke-
on-Trent
Norwich
Swansea Cardiff Birmingham
Bristol
Plymouth Southampton

Rostock Koszalin
Hamburg Szczecin
Bremen Elbe
Osnabrück Hanover Berlin P O
Münster Poznań
Amsterdam Dortmund Leipzig Dresden Wrocław
NETHERLANDS Essen Düsseldorf Cologne Chemnitz Oder
Rotterdam **GERMANY** Plzeň **Prague**
Antwerp Frankfurt Nuremberg **CZECH REP.** Brno
BELGIUM Brussels Regensburg Bratislav
Lille **LUX.** Luxembourg Mannheim Stuttgart Danube
Metz Strasbourg Munich Salzburg **Vienna**

English Channel
Cherbourg
Le Havre Amiens
Brest Caen Rouen Reims
Rennes Seine **Paris**
Nantes Loire Orléans
Tours
Limoges
La Coruña Bordeaux
Clermont-
Ferrand Lyon
Gijón Grenoble
Mt.Blanc
4808

Bergen

B a y   o f

B i s c a y

F R A N C E

Dijon
Nancy Zürich
Bern **LIECH.** Innsbruck **AUSTRIA**
Graz
SWITZERLAND Maribor
Geneva **SLOV.** Zagreb
Milan Trento Banja
Turin Verona Triest Luka
Genoa Po Venice
Parma **CROATIA** **BO**
Bologne **SAN** Split
MARINO Florence Ancona
Nice **MONACO** La Spezia Livorno
Marseille Pescara Adriatic

Oporto
Coimbra
Vigo
La Coruña
León
PORTUGAL
Amadora
Lisbon
Setúbal
Badajoz

Bilbao
San Sebastián
Pamplona
Burgos Pyrenees
Valladolid Zaragoza Lérida **ANDORRA**
Madrid **Barcelona**

Douro
Tagus
Salamanca
SPAIN
Córdoba
Faro Huelva Seville
Granada Murcia
Cádiz Málaga Almería
Gibraltar(U.K.) Cartagena
Ceuta(Sp.)
Tangier Melilla(Sp.) Oran
Tetouan
Rabat Sidi Bel Abbès
Casablanca Fes Oujda
Meknes
MOROCCO *M o u n t a i n s*
Atlas

Montpellier
Toulouse
Nîmes

Valencia
Balearic Is.
(Sp.)
Palma
Mallorca

Corsica
(Fr.)
Ajaccio

Sassari

Sardinia
(It.)

Cagliari

Rome Apennines
Foggia
Naples Bari
Salerno

I T A L Y

M e d i t e r r a n e a n

Palermo Messina
Reggio di
Calabria
Sicily Syracuse

Algiers Blida Skikda Annaba
Bejaia Ariana Tunis
Constantine Sousse
ALGERIA **TUNISIA**
Valletta Sfax
MALTA

10°E

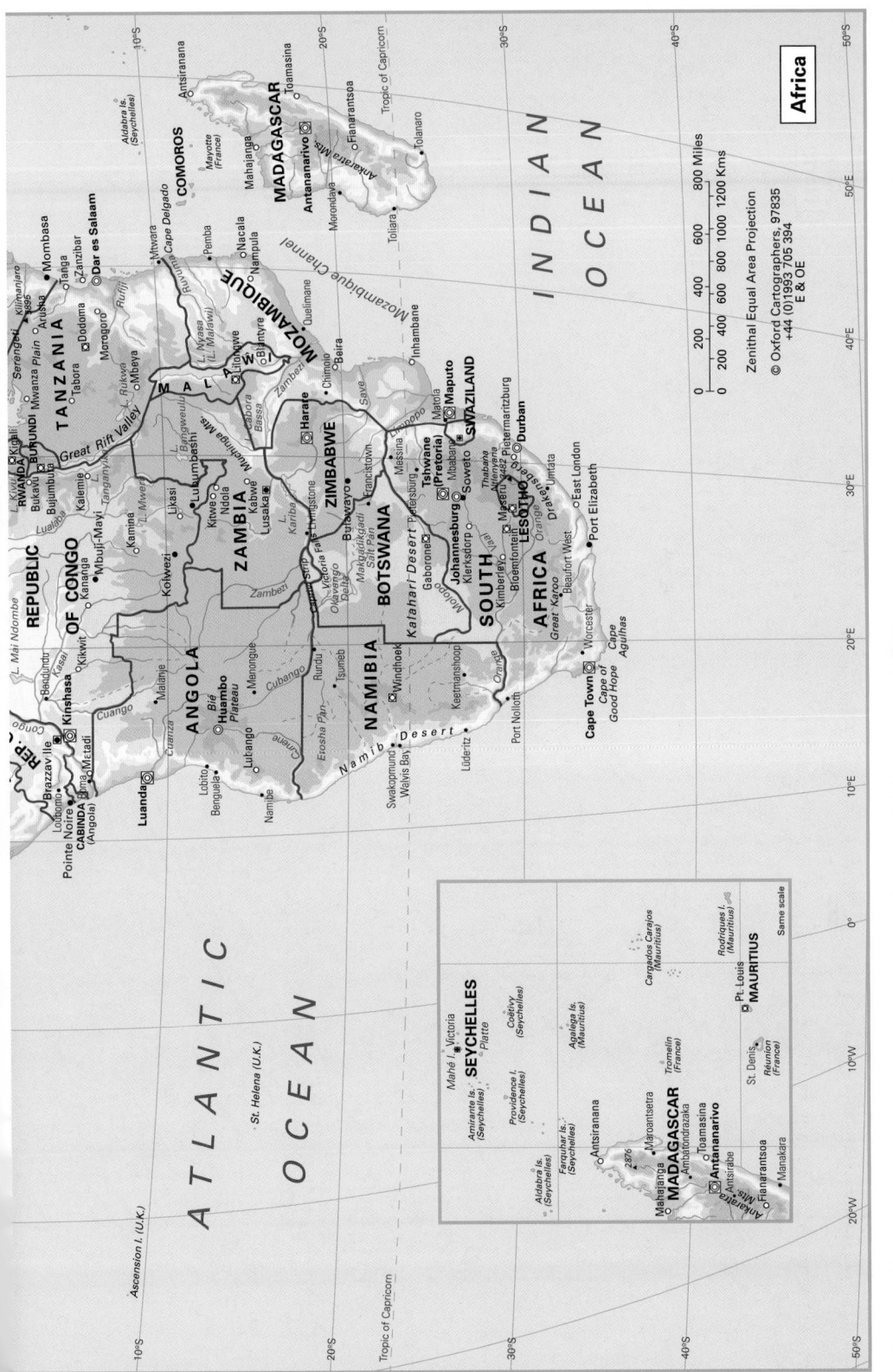

Africa

ATLANTIC OCEAN

INDIAN OCEAN

Ascension I. (U.K.)

St. Helena (U.K.)

REP. OF
CONGO
Brazzaville
Kinshasa
Matadi
Boma
Pointe Noire
CABINDA
(Angola)
Loubomo
L. Mai Ndombe
Bandundu
Kwilu
Kikwit
Kananga
Mbuji-Mayi
Kamina
Lualaba
L. Mweru
Lubumbashi
Likasi
Kolwezi
Luena
Malanje
Cuango

ANGOLA
Luanda
Lobito
Benguela
Namibe
Cuanza
Bié
Huambo
Plateau
Lutango
Menongue
Cubango
Cunene
Rundu
Tsumeb
Etosha
Pan

NAMIBIA
Windhoek
Okavango
Delta
Menongue

REPUBLIC
OF CONGO

RWANDA
BURUNDI
Kigali
Bukavu
Bujumbura
Kisangani
Kivu

TANZANIA
Kilimanjaro
Arusha 5895
Mwanza Plain
Serengeti
Kalemie
L. Tanganyika
Kigoma
Tabora
Dodoma
Morogoro
Rufiji
Great Rift Valley
Mbeya
Kagera

Mombasa
Tanga
Zanzibar
Dar es Salaam

COMOROS
Mayotte
(France)
Cape Delgado
Mtwara
Ruvuma
Pemba

ZAMBIA
Kabwe
Lusaka
Kitwe
Ndola
L. Bangweulu
Mpika
Muchinga Mts.
L. Mweru
Zambezi
Victoria Falls
Livingstone
L. Kariba
Kariba

MALAWI
L. Nyasa
(L. Malawi)
Lilongwe
Blantyre
Zomba
Cabora
Bassa

MOZAMBIQUE
Nacala
Nampula
Quelimane
Chimoio
Beira
Inhambane
Maputo
Matola
Limpopo
Save
Mozambique Channel

ZIMBABWE
Harare
Bulawayo
Francistown
Masvingo

BOTSWANA
Gaborone
Kalahari Desert
Makgadikgadi
Salt Pan
Molopo
Ghanzi

SOUTH AFRICA
Johannesburg
Tshwane
(Pretoria)
Soweto
Mbabane
SWAZILAND
Maseru
LESOTHO
Klerksdorp
Kimberley
Bloemfontein
Thabana
Ntlenyana 3482
Drakensberg
Bhisho
Mthatha
East London
Port Elizabeth
Beaufort West
Great Karoo
Worcester
Cape Town
Cape of
Good Hope
Cape
Agulhas
Port Nolloth
Lüderitz
Keetmanshoop
Orange
Upington
Mafikeng
Pietersburg
Messina
Witbank
Durban
Pietermaritzburg
Namib Desert
Swakopmund
Walvis Bay

MADAGASCAR
Antsiranana
Mahajanga
Antananarivo
Toamasina
Fianarantsoa
Ankaratra Mts.
Toliara
Morondava
Antalaha
Tôlanaro
Aldabra Is.
(Seychelles)

Tropic of Capricorn
Tropic of Capricorn

Oxford Cartographers, 97835
+44 (0)1993 705 394
E & OE
Zenithal Equal Area Projection

0 200 400 600 800 1000 1200 Kms
0   200   400   600   800 Miles

SEYCHELLES
Mahé
Victoria
Platte
Coëtivy
(Seychelles)
Amirante Is.
(Seychelles)
Providence I.
(Seychelles)
Farquhar Is.
(Seychelles)
Aldabra Is.
(Seychelles)
Agalega Is.
(Mauritius)
Tromelin
(France)
Cargados Carajos
(Mauritius)
Rodrigues I.
(Mauritius)
Pt. Louis
MAURITIUS
St. Denis
Réunion
(France)

MADAGASCAR
Antsiranana
Maroantsetra
Mahajanga
Ambatondrazaka
Ambanja
2876
Antananarivo
Toamasina
Antsirabe
Fianarantsoa
Manakara
Ankaratra Mts.

Same scale

North America

South America

NORTH ATLANTIC OCEAN

Caribbean Sea

CUBA
Camagüey
Cayman Is. (U.K.)   Santiago de Cuba   Guantanamo
Kingston   JAMAICA   HAITI   DOMINICAN REP.
Port-au-Prince   Santo Domingo
Turks & Caicos Islands (U.K.)
San Juan
Puerto Rico (USA)
ANTIGUA & BARBUDA
Guadeloupe (Fr.)
DOMINICA
Martinique (Fr.)
ST. LUCIA
BARBADOS
GRENADA

HONDURAS
NICARAGUA
Lake Nicaragua
Limón
COSTA RICA
PANAMA
Colón
San Miguelito
Panama City
Gulf of Panama
Neth. Antilles
Lesser Antilles
Windward Is.
TRINIDAD & TOBAGO
Port of Spain

Barranquilla
Cartagena
Maracaibo
Caracas
Barquisimeto
L. Maracaibo
Bucaramanga
Cúcuta
Mérida
Orinoco
Ciudad Guayana
Ciudad Bolívar
Georgetown
Paramaribo
Cayenne
French Guiana

VENEZUELA
Manizales
Medellín
Bogotá
Cali
Buenaventura
COLOMBIA
Llanos
Guaviare
GUYANA
SURINAME
Guiana Highlands

Tumaco
Quito
ECUADOR
Cotopaxi 5896
Chimborazo 6310
Guayaquil
Cuenca
Equator

Sullana
Chiclayo
Cajamarca
Trujillo
Chimbote
Iquitos
Leticia
Negro
Amazon
Manaus
Santarém
Marajó I.
Belém
São Luís
Fernando de Noronha (Brazil)

Japurá
Amazon
Madeira
Juruá
Purus
Selvas
Cruzeiro do Sul
Pucallpa
Río Branco
Porto Velho
Tapajós
Xingu
Tocantins
São Francisco
Bacabal
Teresina
Mossoró
Floriano
Juazeiro do Norte
Campina Grande
Natal
João Pessoa
Recife

Marañón
Ucayali
Huánuco
Callao
Lima
Huancayo
Cuzco
PERU
Trinidad
BOLIVIA
La Paz
El Alto
Oruro
L. Poopó
Potosí
Sucre
Cochabamba
Santa Cruz
Mato Grosso
Cuiabá
Corumbá
Brazilian Plateau
Barreiras
Feira de Santana
Ilhéus
Salvador
Aracaju
Maceió
Paulo Afonso

Serra dos Parecis
Goiânia
Brasília
Brazilian Highlands
Uberlândia
Uberaba
Montes Claros
Governador Valadares
Caratinga
Vitória

Arequipa
Puno
Titicaca
Mollendo
Arica
Iquique
Antofagasta
Tarija
Campo Grande
Ribeirão Preto
Belo Horizonte
Marília
Campinas
São Paulo
Santos
Campos
Rio de Janeiro
Tropic of Capricorn

San Félix (Chile)
San Ambrosio (Chile)
SOUTH PACIFIC OCEAN
San Salvador de Jujuy
Salta
Tucumán
Gran Chaco
PARAGUAY
Asunción
Ciudad del Este
Formosa
Sorocaba
Londrina
Cascavel
Curitiba
Florianópolis

Copiapó
Catamarca
La Rioja
Santiago del Estero
Resistencia
Corrientes
Posadas
Santa Maria
Passo Fundo
Porto Alegre
Pelotas
Paraná
Uruguay
Tacuarembó

La Serena
San Juan
Córdoba
Santa Fé
Paraná
ARGENTINA
Cerro Aconcagua 6960
Mendoza
San Luis
Rosario
Paysandú
Durazno
URUGUAY
Montevideo

Viña del Mar
Valparaíso
Santiago
Rancagua
Puente Alto
Talca
Pampas
Bahía Blanca
Río de la Plata
Buenos Aires
La Plata
Mar del Plata

Concepción
Chillán
Colorado
Neuquén
Negro
Viedma

Temuco
Valdivia
Osorno
Puerto Montt
Chiloé Island
Trelew
Valdés Peninsula

Taitao Peninsula
Comodoro Rivadavia
G. of S. George
Deseado

PACIFIC OCEAN
SOUTH ATLANTIC OCEAN

Punta Arenas
Ushuaia
Río Gallegos
Magellan Strait
Tierra del Fuego
Cape Horn
Stanley
Falkland Islands (U.K.)
South Georgia (U.K.)
South Shetland Islands (U.K.)
South Orkney Islands (U.K.)
South Sandwich Islands (U.K.)

Oblique Mercator Projection

© Oxford Cartographers, 97835
+44 (0)1993 705 394
E & OE

0 200 400 600 Miles
0 200 400 600 800 1000 Kms

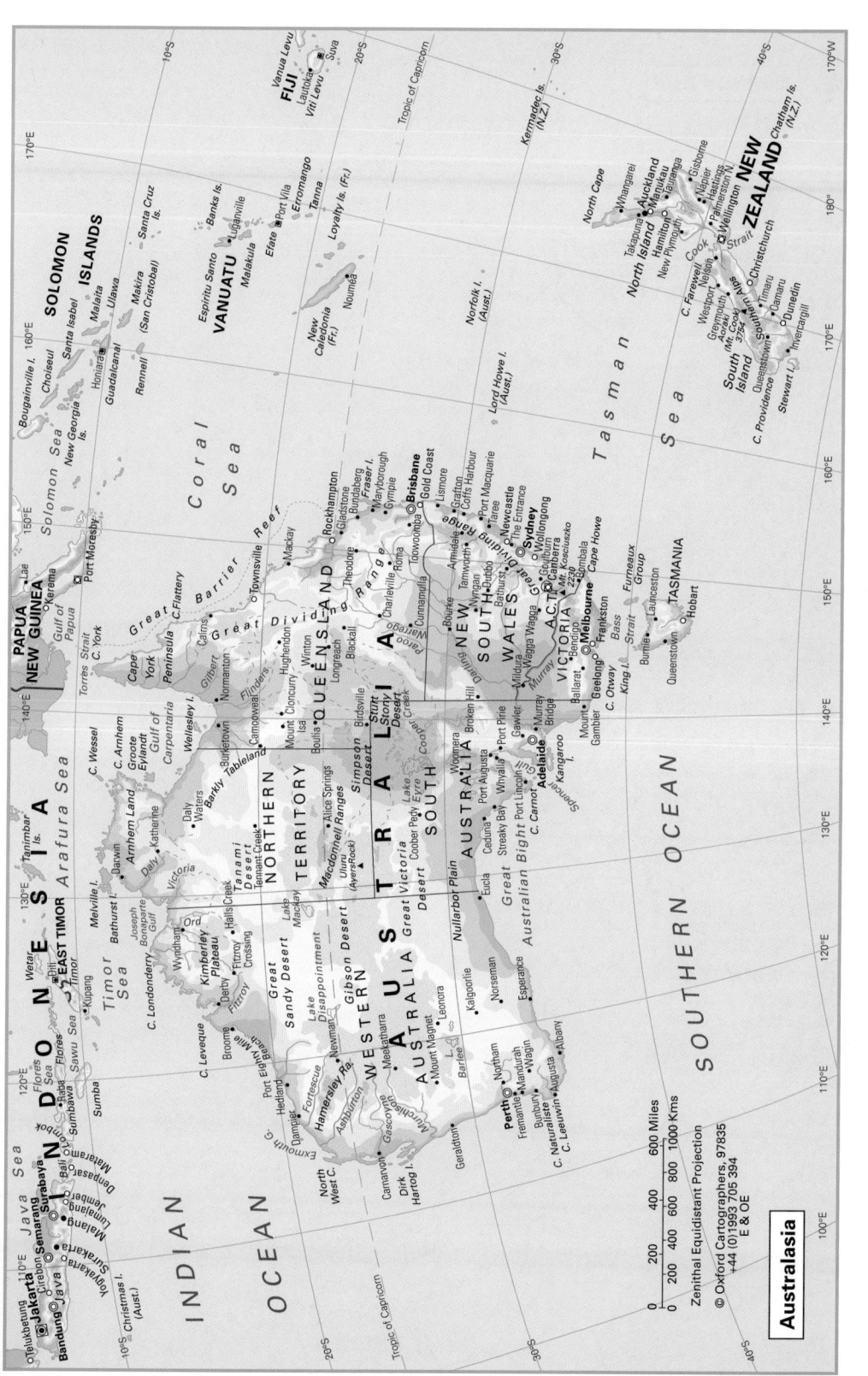

INDONESIA

Java Sea
Telukbetung
Bandung
Jakarta
Cirebon Semarang
Surabaya
Yogyakarta Surakarta
Malang Jember
Lumajang
Madura
Java
Bali
Denpasar
Mataram
Lombok
Bima
Sumbawa
Sumba
Kupang
EAST TIMOR
Wetar
Tanimbar Is.
Flores
Maumere
Ende
Sawu Sea
Flores Sea
Banda Sea

Christmas I. (Aust.)

INDIAN

OCEAN

PAPUA
NEW GUINEA

Lae
Yeremu
Port Moresby
Gulf of Papua

SOLOMON
ISLANDS

Bougainville I.
Buka
Choiseul
New Georgia Is.
Santa Isabel
Malaita
Ulawa
Makira (San Cristobal)
Honiara
Guadalcanal
Rennell
Solomon Sea

VANUATU

Banks Is.
Espiritu Santo
Malekula
Luganville
Efate Port Vila
Erromango
Tanna
Santa Cruz Is.

FIJI
Vanua Levu
Viti Levu
Lautoka
Suva

Coral Sea

New Caledonia (Fr.)
Nouméa
Loyalty Is. (Fr.)

Lord Howe I. (Aust.)

Norfolk I. (Aust.)

Kermadec Is. (N.Z.)

Arafura Sea
C. Wessel
C. Arnhem
Arnhem Land
Groote Eylandt
Gulf of Carpentaria
Wellesley I.
C. York
Cape York Peninsula
Torres Strait

NEW ZEALAND

North Cape
Whangarei
Takapuna Auckland
Manukau
Hamilton Tauranga
New Plymouth
Napier
Hastings
Palmerston N.
North Island
Cook Strait
Wellington
Nelson
Westport
Greymouth
Christchurch
Ashburton
Southern Alps
Mt. Cook 3764
Timaru
Oamaru
South Island
Queenstown
Dunedin
Invercargill
Stewart I.
C. Providence
C. Farewell

Tasman Sea

Melville I.
Bathurst I.
Darwin
Katherine
Daly Waters
C. Londonderry
Wyndham
Kimberley Plateau
Halls Creek
Derby
Fitzroy
Broome
C. Leveque
Port Hedland
Dampier
North West C.

Joseph Bonaparte Gulf
Ord
Victoria
Daly
Tanami Desert
Tennant Creek
Barkly Tableland
NORTHERN TERRITORY
Alice Springs
Macdonnell Ranges
Uluru (Ayers Rock)
Simpson Desert
Lake Mackay
Lake Amadeus

QUEENSLAND
Normanton
Burketown
Gilbert
Flinders
Cloncurry
Mount Isa
Camooweal
Boulia
Winton
Hughenden
Birdsville
Cooktown
Cairns
C. Flattery
Townsville
Mackay
Rockhampton
Gladstone
Bundaberg
Maryborough
Gympie
Fraser I.
Gold Coast
Brisbane
Toowoomba
Roma
Theodore
Charleville
Blackall
Longreach
Barcaldine
Warrego
Paroo
Bourke
Cunnamulla
Narran

Great Barrier Reef

Great Dividing Range

WESTERN AUSTRALIA

Great Sandy Desert
Lake Disappointment
Gibson Desert
Great Victoria Desert
Nullarbor Plain
Hamersley Ra.
Newman
Meekatharra
Mount Magnet
Leonora
Kalgoorlie
Norseman
Esperance
Carnarvon
Gascoyne
Murchison
Geraldton
Northam
Perth
Fremantle
Mandurah
Bunbury
Busselton
Albany
C. Leeuwin
C. Naturaliste
Wagin
Dirk Hartog I.
Exmouth G.
Ashburton
Fortescue
Bartle Frere
Meekatharra

SOUTH AUSTRALIA

Woomera
Coober Pedy
Lake Eyre
Tarcoola
Lake Torrens
Lake Gairdner
Ceduna
Streaky Bay
Whyalla
Port Augusta
Port Pirie
Port Lincoln
C. Carnot
Adelaide
Gawler
Kangaroo I.
Great Australian Bight
Eucla
Spencer Gulf

NEW SOUTH WALES
Broken Hill
Mildura
Wilcannia
Cobar
Dubbo
Nyngan
Wagga Wagga
Deniliquin
Darling
Lachlan
Murrumbidgee
Griffith
Bathurst
Armidale
Tamworth
Grafton
Lismore
Coffs Harbour
Port Macquarie
Taree
Newcastle
The Entrance
Sydney
Wollongong
A.C.T.
Canberra
Mt. Kosciuszko 2230
Cooma
Bombala
Cape Howe
Goulburn

VICTORIA
Murray
Bendigo
Ballarat
Geelong
Melbourne
Frankston
Mount Gambier
C. Otway
Bass Strait
King I.
Furneaux Group
Burnie
Launceston
TASMANIA
Queenstown
Hobart

Cook Strait
Stewart

SOUTHERN OCEAN

Tropic of Capricorn

Zenithal Equidistant Projection

© Oxford Cartographers, 97835
+44 (0)1993 705 394
E & OE

0   200   400   600 Miles
0 200 400 600 800 1000 Kms

Australasia

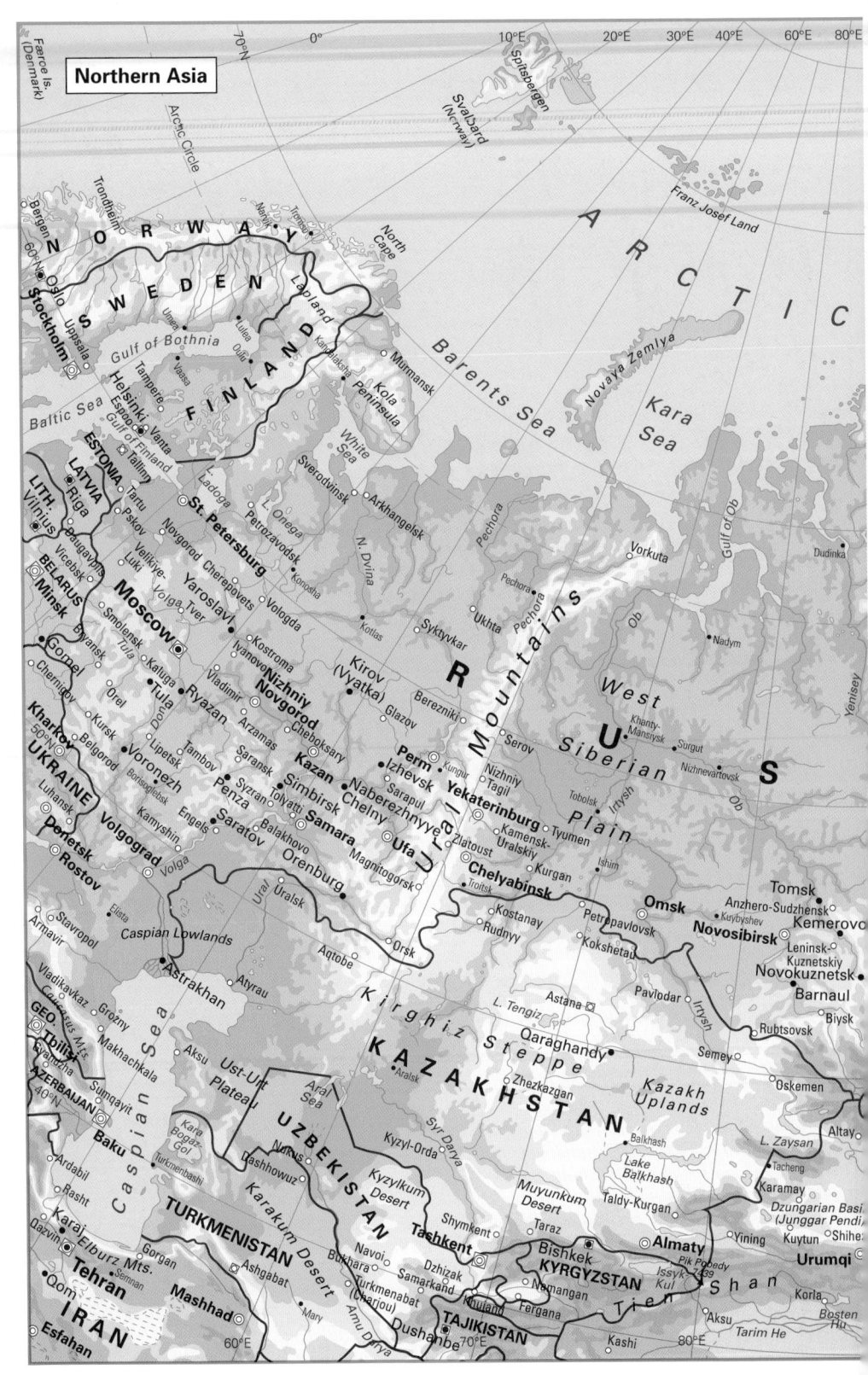

Northern Asia

Faroe Is. (Denmark)

Svalbard (Norway)

Spitsbergen

Franz Josef Land

A R C T I C

Barents Sea

Novaya Zemlya

Kara Sea

Gulf of Ob

Arctic Circle

N O R W A Y

Trondheim

Bergen
Oslo
Stockholm

S W E D E N

Trondheim
Tromsø

North Cape

Murmansk

Kola Peninsula

Umeå

F I N L A N D

Lapland

Kandalaksha

White Sea

Vorkuta

Dudinka

Nadym

Tampere

Gulf of Bothnia

Luleå

Oulu

Vaasa

Arkhangelsk

N. Dvina

Ob

Yenisey

Baltic Sea

Helsinki
Espoo
Vantaa

Gulf of Finland

ESTONIA

LATVIA

LITH.

Vilnius

BELARUS

Minsk

Tallinn

Tartu

Pskov

Vitebsk

Riga

St. Petersburg

Ladoga

Petrozavodsk

L. Onega

Sverodvinsk

Vologda

Kotlas

Syktyvkar

Berezniki

Ukhta

Pechora

Pechora

U r a l

M o u n t a i n s

Serov

Khanty-Mansiysk

Surgut

Nizhnevartovsk

W e s t

S i b e r i a n

P l a i n

R U S

Moscow

Smolensk
Bryansk

Velikiye Luki

Novgorod
Cherepovets

Yaroslavl

Tver

Ivanovo
Kostroma

Nizhniy Novgorod

Kirov (Vyatka)

Glazov

Perm

Izhevsk

Kungur

Sarapul

Yekaterinburg

Nizhniy Tagil

Tyumen

Tobolsk

Ishim

Irtysh

Ob

Tomsk

Omsk

Novosibirsk

Anzhero-Sudzhensk

Kemerovo

Leninsk-Kuznetskiy

Novokuznetsk

Barnaul

Biysk

UKRAINE

Kharkov

Chernigov

Gomel

Tula
Kaluga

Orel

Kursk

Belgorod

Lipetsk

Tambov

Voronezh

Ryazan

Vladimir

Cheboksary

Arzamas

Saransk

Penza

Simbirsk

Kazan

Naberezhnyye Chelny

Samara

Tolyatti

Ufa

Zlatoust

Uralskiy

Kamensk-
Uralskiy

Kurgan

Troitsk

Chelyabinsk

Kostanay

Rudnyy

Petropavlovsk

Orsk

Kokshetau

Pavlodar

Semey

Rubtsovsk

Oskemen

Altay

L. Zaysan

Tacheng

Karamay

Dzungarian Basin (Junggar Pendi)

Kuytun

Shihe-

Yining

Urumqi

Korla

Kashi

Bosten Hu

Tarim He

Aksu

Tien Shan

Pik Pobedy 7439

Issyk Kul

KYRGYZSTAN

Bishkek

Almaty

Taldy-Kurgan

Lake Balkhash

Balkhash

Kazakh Uplands

Zhezkazgan

Qaraghandy

Astana

L. Tengiz

K A Z A K H S T A N

Kirghiz Steppe

Aqtobe

Uralsk

Ural

Atyrau

Caspian Lowlands

Elista

Aral Sea

Aralsk

Ust-Urt Plateau

Kyzyl-Orda

Syr Darya

Shymkent

Taraz

Muyunkum Desert

Muyunkum

Donetsk

Rostov

Luhansk

Stavropol

Armavir

Astrakhan

Makhachkala

Grozny

Vladikavkaz

Caucasus Mts.

GEO.

Tbilisi

Kutaisi

Rustavi

AZERBAIJAN

Baku

Sumqayit

C a s p i a n S e a

Kara Bogaz Gol

Turkmenbashi

TURKMENISTAN

Dashhowuz

Nukus

UZBEKISTAN

Kyzylkum Desert

Navoi

Bukhara

Dzhizak

Samarkand

Tashkent

Khujand

Namangan

Fergana

TAJIKISTAN

Dushanbe

Karakum Desert

Ashgabat

Turkmenabat (Charjou)

Amu Darya

Mary

IRAN

Tehran

Qom

Esfahan

Mashhad

Gorgan

German

Elburz Mts.

Rasht

Ardabil

Qazvin

Karaj

Kyandzha

ARMENIA

Volgograd

Volga

Saratov

Engels

Balakhovo

Borisoglebsk

Kamyshin

Magnitogorsk

Orenburg

Syzran

100°E 120°E 140°E 150°E 160°E 170°E 180°

0   100   200   300   400   500 Miles
0 100 200 300 400 500 600 700 800 Kms
Conical Orthomorphic Projection

© Oxford Cartographers, 97835
+44 (0)1993 705 394
E & OE

Bering
Sea

Wrangel I.

Anadyr Range

Arctic Circle

Pevek   70°N   Anadyr

Severnaya
Zemlya

New Siberia Is.

East Siberian
Sea

Koryak
Range

O C E A N

Lyakhov
Is.

Laptev
Sea

Indigirka

Kolyma

Kolyma Mts.

Taymyr Pen.

Tiksi

Cherskogo Range

L. Taymyr

Olenek

Yana

Verkhoyansk

Range

Sea of
Okhotsk

Norilsk

Central

Lena

Okhotsk

Dzhugdzhur Range

Sakhalin

Lower Tunguska

Siberian

Vilyuy

Yakutsk

Aldan

Komsomolsk
Na-Amure

Alexandrovsk
Sakhalinskiy

50°N

Plateau

Olekminsk

Lensk

A

Angara

Lena

Neryungri

Stanovoy Mts.

Amur

Khabarovsk

Sikhote-Alin Mts.

Lesosibirsk

S

I

Tynda

Skovorodino

Achinsk   Kansk   Tayshek
Krasnoyarsk

Bratsk

Ust
Ilimsk

Ust-Kut

Severobaikalsk

Skovorodino

Belogorsk

Birobidzhan

Yichun

Shuangyashan

Quitaihe

Abakan

Sayan Mts.

Tulup

Usolye-
Sibirskoye-
Angarsk

Lake Baikal

Yablonovyy Mts.

Bei'an

Blagoveshchensk

Hegang

Jiamusi

Mudanjiang

Ussuriysk

Kyzyl

Irkutsk

Chita

Sretensk

Hailar

Da Hinggan Ling

Qiqihar

Harbin

Jilin

Vladivostok

Yanji

Chongjin

Hovsgol
Nuur

Ulan-
Ude

Manzhouli

Ulanhot

Daqing

Baicheng

Uvs Nuur

Daman

Ondorhaan

Changchun

Liaoyuan

Fushun

Altai Range

Hangayan Mts.

Ulaanbaatar

Tongliao

Siping

DEM. PEOPLE'S
REP. OF KOREA

Hovd

Altay

MONGOLIA

Saynshand

Chifeng

Shenyang

Anshan

Pyongyang

Fuxin

Turpan
rpan Depression

Hami

Gobi Desert

INNER MONGOLIA

Jining

Zhang-
jiakou

Jinzhou

Chengde

Seoul

Baotou

Hohhot

Beijing

Tangshan

Dalian

Inchon

REP. OF
KOREA

Linhe

Huang He (Yellow)

Datong

(Peking)

Tianjin

Yantai

Weihai

Kwangju

Lop Nur

Baoding

Cangzhou Bo Hai

Korea
Bay

90°E

Turpan

Wuhai

Shizuishan

C   H   I   N   A

Taiyuan

Yuci

Dezhou

Shijiazhuang

Handan

Jinan

Zibo

Weifang

Qingdao

Yellow
Sea

100°E   110°E   120°E

25°E   30°E   40°E   45°E   50°E   55°E   •Aqtobe   60°E   65°

ROMANIA   •Odesa   UKRAINE   •Mariupol   •Rostov   •Volgograd   KAZA
45°N   ◎Bucharest   •Kherson   Simferopol   •Krasnodar   •Emba   Kirghiz

BULGARIA   •Varna   Constanta   Sea of Azov   Kerch   Stravropol   •Astrakhan   Caspian Lowlands   •Atyrau   •Aralsk

Plovdiv•   •Burgas   Sudak   •Novorossiysk   Armavir   •Elista

•Edirne   Black Sea   Tuapse•   •Maykop   RUSSIA
Istanbul   Bosporus   Ereğli   Zonguldak   Sinop•   •Sochi   Caucasus Mts.   •Cherkessk   •Aksu   Ust-Urt Pateau   Aral Sea   •Kyzyl-Orda

40°N   Bursa   Bakirkoy   •Karabuk   Sukhumi   Abkhazia   Elbruz   Grozny•   Vladikavkaz• •Makhachkala   UZBEKISTAN
Balikesir•   Kocaeli   Sakarya   Corum   •Ordu   Batumi•   S. Ossetia   •Derbent   •Nukus   Kyzylkum Desert
•Manisa   Eskisehir   Ankara   Trabzon   GEORGIA   •Dashhowuz   •Urgench
İzmir◎   Uşak   Kirikkale   Pontine Mountains   ◎Tbilisi   Kara-Bogaz-Gol   Bukhara•
•Aydin   Yozgat   •Sivas   ARMENIA   AZERBAIJAN   Turkmenbashi•   Nebitdag•   Karakum Desert   Amu Darya
•Denizli   TURKEY   •Kayseri   Mt. Ararat 5123 ▲   •Yerevan   •Sumqayit   TURKMENISTAN   Mary•   •Ashgabat
Antalya•   Konya◎   •Erzurum   L. Van   AZER.   •Baku   Turkmenabat (Charjou)   Bujnurd•
35°N   Taurus Mts.   •Elazig   Van•   Khvoy•   Araks   •Neyshabur   Paropamisus
CYPRUS   Nicosia   •Adana   Kahramanmaras   •Diyarbakir   Batman•   •Marand   ◎Mashhad
Limassol◎   Icel   Hatay   •Osmaniye   Şanlıurfa   •Tabriz   •Ardabil   •Rasht   •Gonbad   Sabzevar•   •Meymaneh
•Latakia   •Gaziantep   Damishli   L. Urmia   •Zanjan   •Qazvin   Elburz Mts. Damavand   Gorgan•   •Herat
Mediterranean Sea   Aleppo◎   •Raqqah   •Orumiyeh   Maragheh•   ▲5671   •Emamrud   AFGHA
•Alexandria   Tripoli   Hama•   •Mosul   Sanandaj•   •Karaj   •Tehran   •Semnan
LEBANON   Homs•   Dayr az Zawr•   •Arbil   Bakhtaran (Kermanshah)•   •Qom   Dasht-e Kavir   •Birjand   Farah•
Beirut◎   SYRIA   •Sulaymaniyah   •Hamadan   I R A N
Haifa•   Zahle•   Orbid•   Tigris   Boroujerd•   •Kashan   •Yazd
30°N   Tel Aviv•   •Damascus   •Kazimiyah   •Esfahan   Dasht-e Lut   •Zabol
ISRAEL   Jerusalem◎   Syrian Desert   •Baghdad   •Hilla   •Arak   Kerman•   •Zahedan
•GAZA   •Amman   •Karbala   Khorramabad•   Dezful•   BALOCH
Cairo◎   •Az Zarqa   JORDAN   •Najaf   Euphrates   •Ahvaz   Zagros Mts.   •Rafsanjan   •Bam   Nok Kundi•
El Giza   Dead Sea   IRAQ   •Amarah   Abadan•   •Sirjan   •Siahan M
Ismailiya   Suez   Elat   •Aqaba   Nasiriyah•   Basra•   The Gulf   •Borazjan   •Jahrom   •Jiroft   Makran
EGYPT   Sinai   Sharm al Sheikh•   Nafud   Jobra• KUWAIT   •Kuwait   •Bushehr   •Shiraz   Bandar Abbas•   •Chabahar   •Gwadar
25°N   El Minya   •Tabuk   Ha'il•   Dhahran•   Dammam•   Hajjiabad•   •Khasab
•Asyut   •Al Wajh   •Buraidah   BAHRAIN   •Manama   Ras al Khaimah•   OMAN   •Turbat
•Qena   Hurghada•   S A U D I   Hoful•   QATAR   Sharjah•   Gulf of Oman
•Luxor   Medina•   Najd   Riyadh◎   •Doha   Dubai•   •Sohar   •Muscat
Kom Ombo   •Yanbu   Hasa   Abu Dhabi•   •Al Ain   Sumail•
Aswan•   Tropic of Cancer   •Harad   UNITED ARAB EMIRATES   Nizwa•   •Ibra   •Sur
Lake Nasser   Halaib•   Jeddah◎   Mecca•   A R A B I A   Ar Rustaq•   •Masirah
20°N   Nubian Desert   •Taif   Asir   Rub'al Khali   O M A N   Masirah
Port Sudan•   Red Sea   •Abha   •Masirah
SUDAN   Attbara•   Farasan Is.   Najran•   Dhufar   A r a b
•Ed Damer   •Jizan   Sa'dah•   Hajjar•   •Halaaniyat Is.   S e
15°N   ERITREA   Kassala•   Dahlak Arch.   •Salalah
•Agordat   Massawa•   Sana'a•   Hadhramaut
Gedaref•   Asmara◎   Dhamar•   •Mukalla
▲Ras Dashen 4620   •Assab   Y E M E N.   •Ibb
•Gonder   L. Tana   Hudaida   •Taiz
Bahir Dar•   Gulf of Aden   Socotra (Yemen)
10°N   Blue Nile   DJIBOUTI◎   •Aden   Cape Caseyr
ETHIOPIA   Djibouti•   •Boosaaso   0   100   200   300   400 miles
Addis Ababa◎   Dire Dawa•   •Berbera   0 100 200 300 400 500 600 kms
•Nazret   Harer•   Burao•   Conical Orthomorphic Projection
•Jima   Ethiopian Highlands   Hargeysa•   SOMALIA   © Oxford Cartographers, 97835
•Awasa   •Garoowe   +44 (0)1993 705 394
5°N   Ogaden   E & OE
Shebele   I N D I A
KENYA   Junba
40°E   45°E   50°E   55°E   60°E   65

Middle East & South Asia

Pacific

World Physical

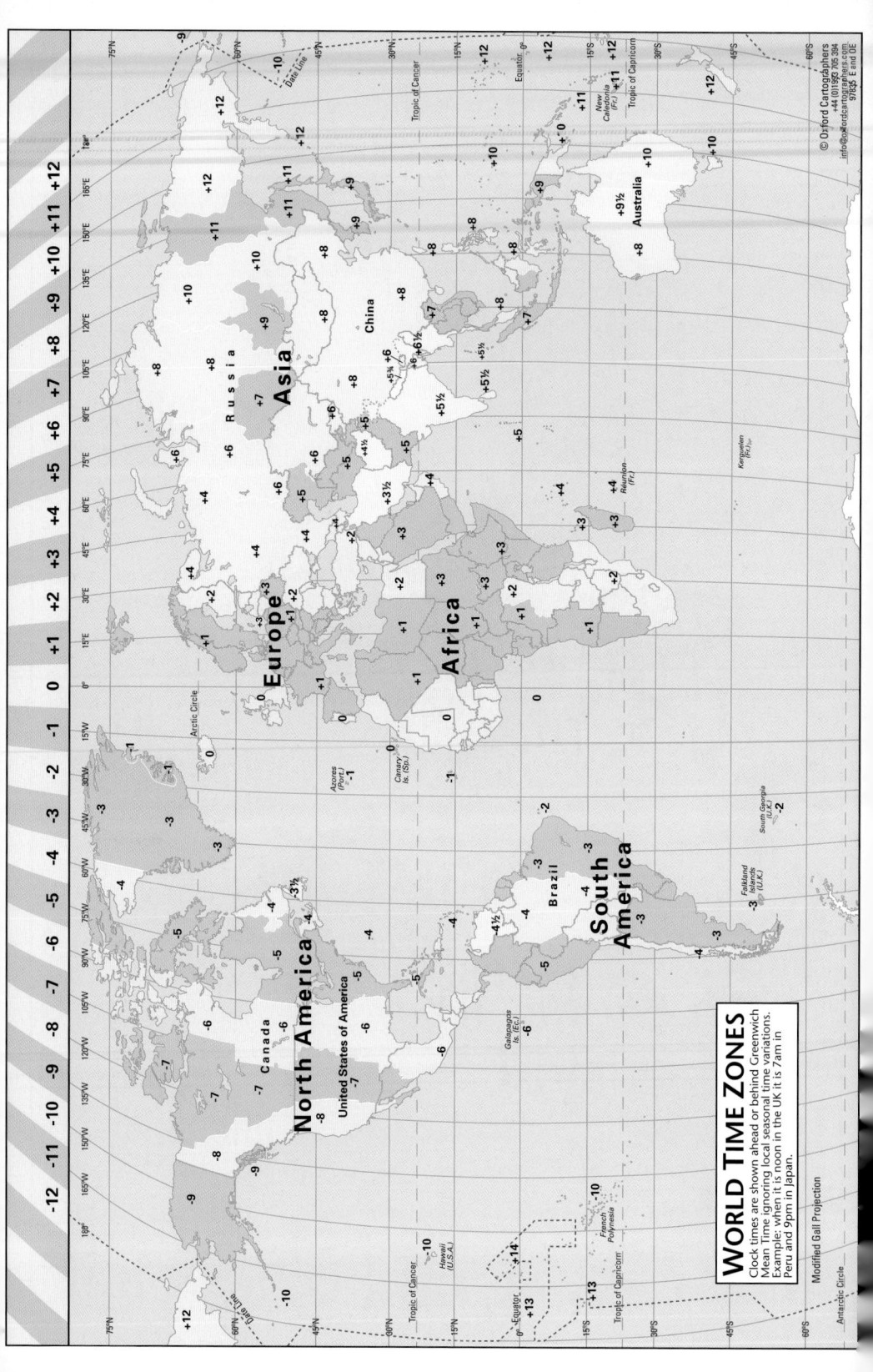

WORLD TIME ZONES

Clock times are shown ahead or behind Greenwich Mean Time ignoring local seasonal time variations.
Example: when it is noon in the UK it is 7am in Peru and 9pm in Japan.

Modified Gall Projection

© Oxford Cartographers
+44 (0)1993 705384
info@oxfordcartographers.com
9781 E and OE

FLAGS OF THE WORLD

The following four pages show the national flag of each country, as it is used for international purposes. In some cases this means that the state flag is shown. Where this is the case the country name is marked (†).

AFGHANISTAN

ALBANIA

ALGERIA

ANDORRA

ANGOLA

ANTIGUA AND BARBUDA

ARGENTINA

ARMENIA

AUSTRALIA

AUSTRIA

AZERBAIJAN

THE BAHAMAS

BAHRAIN

BANGLADESH

BARBADOS

BELARUS

BELGIUM

BELIZE

BENIN

BHUTAN

BOLIVIA†

BOSNIA AND HERCEGOVINA

BOTSWANA

BRAZIL

BRUNEI

BULGARIA

BURKINA FASO

BURUNDI

CAMBODIA

CAMEROON

CANADA

CAPE VERDE

CENTRAL AFRICAN REPUBLIC

CHAD

CHILE

CHINA

COLOMBIA

THE COMOROS

DEM. REPUBLIC OF THE CONGO

REPUBLIC OF THE CONGO

COSTA RICA

CÔTE D'IVOIRE

CROATIA

CUBA

CYPRUS

CZECH REPUBLIC

DENMARK

DJIBOUTI

DOMINICA

DOMINICAN REPUBLIC

EAST TIMOR

ECUADOR

EGYPT

EL SALVADOR

EQUATORIAL GUINEA

ERITREA

ESTONIA

ETHIOPIA

FIJI

FINLAND

FRANCE

GABON

THE GAMBIA

GEORGIA

GERMANY

GHANA

GREECE

GRENADA

GUATEMALA

GUINEA

GUINEA-BISSAU

GUYANA

HAITI†

HONDURAS

HUNGARY

ICELAND

INDIA

INDONESIA

IRAN

IRAQ

IRELAND

ISRAEL

ITALY

JAMAICA

JAPAN

JORDAN

KAZAKHSTAN

KENYA

KIRIBATI

DEM. PEOPLE'S REPUBLIC OF KOREA

REPUBLIC OF KOREA

KOSOVO

KUWAIT

KYRGYZSTAN

LAOS

LATVIA

LEBANON

LESOTHO

LIBERIA

LIBYA

LIECHTENSTEIN

 LITHUANIA

 LUXEMBOURG

 MACEDONIA

 MADAGASCAR

 MALAWI

 MALAYSIA

 MALDIVES

 MALI

 MALTA

 MARSHALL ISLANDS

 MAURITANIA

 MAURITIUS

 MEXICO

 FEDERATED STATES OF MICRONESIA

 MOLDOVA

 MONACO

 MONGOLIA

 MONTENEGRO

 MOROCCO

 MOZAMBIQUE

 MYANMAR

 NAMIBIA

 NAURU

 NEPAL

 THE NETHERLANDS

 NEW ZEALAND

 NICARAGUA

 NIGER

 NIGERIA

 NORWAY

 OMAN

 PAKISTAN

 PALAU

 PANAMA

 PAPUA NEW GUINEA

 PARAGUAY

 PERU

 THE PHILIPPINES

 POLAND

 PORTUGAL

 QATAR

 ROMANIA

 RUSSIAN FEDERATION

 RWANDA

ST CHRISTOPHER AND NEVIS

ST LUCIA

ST VINCENT AND THE GRENADINES

SAMOA

SAN MARINO†

SAO TOME AND
PRINCIPE

SAUDI ARABIA

SENEGAL

SERBIA†

SEYCHELLES

SIERRA LEONE

SINGAPORE

SLOVAKIA

SLOVENIA

SOLOMON ISLANDS

SOMALIA

SOUTH AFRICA

SOUTH SUDAN

SPAIN

SRI LANKA

SUDAN

SURINAME

SWAZILAND

SWEDEN

SWITZERLAND

SYRIA

TAIWAN

TAJIKISTAN

TANZANIA

THAILAND

TOGO

TONGA

TRINIDAD AND
TOBAGO

TUNISIA

TURKEY

TURKMENISTAN

TUVALU

UGANDA

UKRAINE

UNITED ARAB
EMIRATES

UNITED KINGDOM

UNITED STATES OF
AMERICA

URUGUAY

UZBEKISTAN

VANUATU

VATICAN CITY
STATE

VENEZUELA

VIETNAM

YEMEN

ZAMBIA

ZIMBABWE

2014 EUROPEAN PARLIAMENT ELECTIONS

The elections to the European Parliament took place across the European Union from 22 to 25 May 2014.

The European People's Party remained the largest faction in the new parliament but lost ground to the Progressive Alliance of Socialists and Democrats.

The turnout for the election was 42.54%.

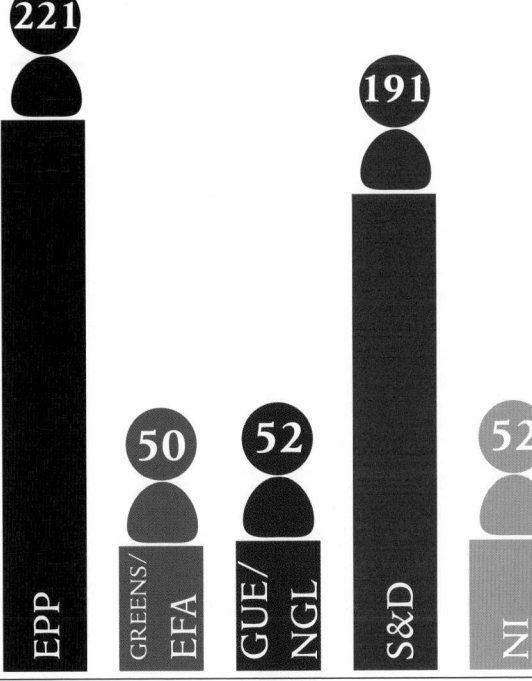

ALDE	Alliance of Liberals and Democrats for Europe	
ECR	European Conservatives and Reformists	
EFDD	Europe of Freedom and Direct Democracy Group	
EPP	Group of the European People's Party (Christian Democrats)	

Greens/EFA	European Free Alliance
GUE/NGL	European United Left/ Nordic Green Left
S&D	Group of the Progressive Alliance of Socialists and Democrats in the European Parliament
NI	Non-attached members

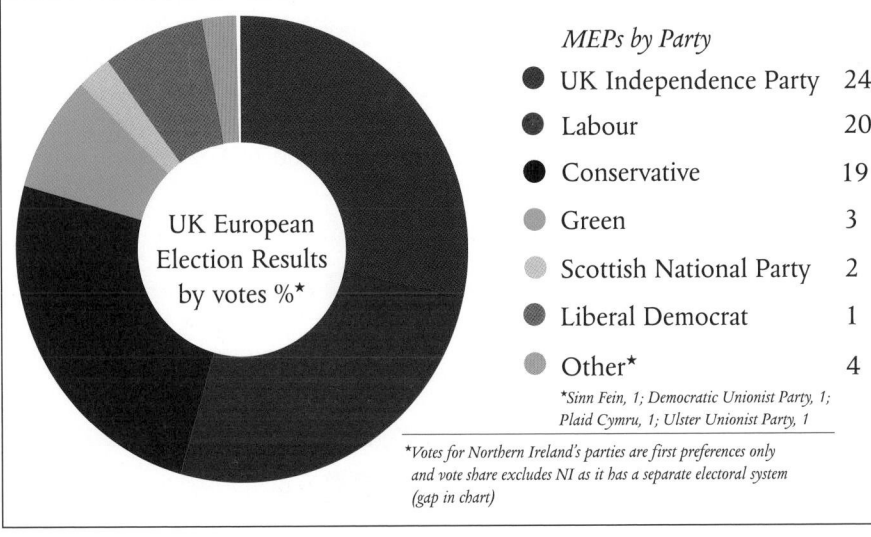

UK European Election Results by votes %*

MEPs by Party

●	UK Independence Party	24
●	Labour	20
●	Conservative	19
●	Green	3
●	Scottish National Party	2
●	Liberal Democrat	1
●	Other*	4

*Sinn Fein, 1; Democratic Unionist Party, 1; Plaid Cymru, 1; Ulster Unionist Party, 1

*Votes for Northern Ireland's parties are first preferences only and vote share excludes NI as it has a separate electoral system (gap in chart)

MILITARY AND POLICE
CONTRIBUTIONS TO THE UN

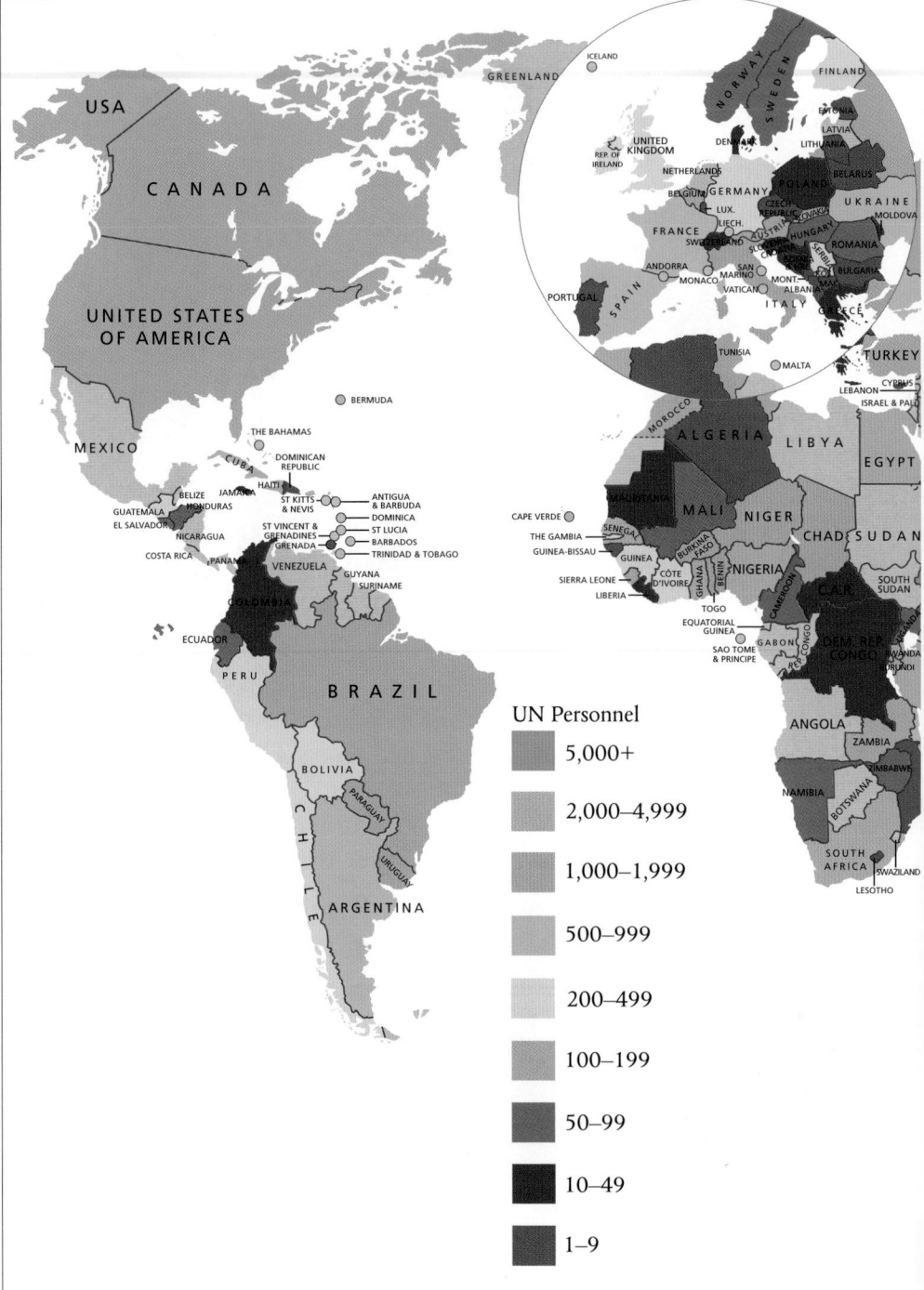

ICELAND
GREENLAND

ICELAND

NORWAY
SWEDEN
FINLAND

ESTONIA
LATVIA
UNITED KINGDOM
REP. OF IRELAND
DENMARK
LITHUANIA

NETHERLANDS
BELARUS
BELGIUM
GERMANY
POLAND
LUX.
CZECH REPUBLIC
UKRAINE
LIECH.
SLOVAKIA
MOLDOVA
FRANCE
SWITZERLAND
AUSTRIA
HUNGARY
ROMANIA
ANDORRA
SAN MARINO
SLOVENIA
CROATIA
SERBIA
BULGARIA
MONACO
VATICAN
MONT.
ALBANIA
MAC.
PORTUGAL
SPAIN
ITALY
GREECE
TURKEY

TUNISIA
MALTA
CYPRUS
LEBANON
ISRAEL & PAL.

USA

CANADA

UNITED STATES
OF AMERICA

BERMUDA

THE BAHAMAS

MEXICO

CUBA
DOMINICAN REPUBLIC
HAITI
JAMAICA
BELIZE
HONDURAS
GUATEMALA
EL SALVADOR
NICARAGUA
COSTA RICA
PANAMA

ST KITTS
& NEVIS
ST VINCENT &
GRENADINES
GRENADA

ANTIGUA
& BARBUDA
DOMINICA
ST LUCIA
BARBADOS
TRINIDAD & TOBAGO

VENEZUELA

COLOMBIA

GUYANA
SURINAME

ECUADOR

PERU

BRAZIL

BOLIVIA

PARAGUAY

URUGUAY

ARGENTINA

CHILE

CAPE VERDE

THE GAMBIA
GUINEA-BISSAU

SIERRA LEONE
LIBERIA

MOROCCO

ALGERIA
LIBYA
EGYPT

MAURITANIA
MALI
NIGER

SENEGAL
BURKINA FASO
GUINEA
CÔTE D'IVOIRE
GHANA
BENIN
NIGERIA
CHAD
SUDAN

TOGO
CAMEROON
C.A.R.
SOUTH SUDAN

EQUATORIAL GUINEA
GABON
REP. CONGO
DEM. REP. CONGO
RWANDA
BURUNDI
SAO TOME
& PRINCIPE

ANGOLA
ZAMBIA
ZIMBABWE
NAMIBIA
BOTSWANA

SOUTH AFRICA
SWAZILAND
LESOTHO

UN Personnel

5,000+

2,000–4,999

1,000–1,999

500–999

200–499

100–199

50–99

10–49

1–9

United Nations Peacekeeping Forces help countries torn by conflict create the conditions for lasting peace. The peacekeeping forces comprise civilian, police and military personnel.

123 countries contributed military and police personnel with a total workforce of 96,824 according to the UN report of 31 July 2014.

The five highest contributing countries were:

1. Bangladesh, 8,430
2. India, 8,129
3. Ethiopia, 7,806
4. Pakistan, 7,205
5. Nepal, 5,104

GOVERNMENT DEPARTMENTAL BUDGETS 2014–15

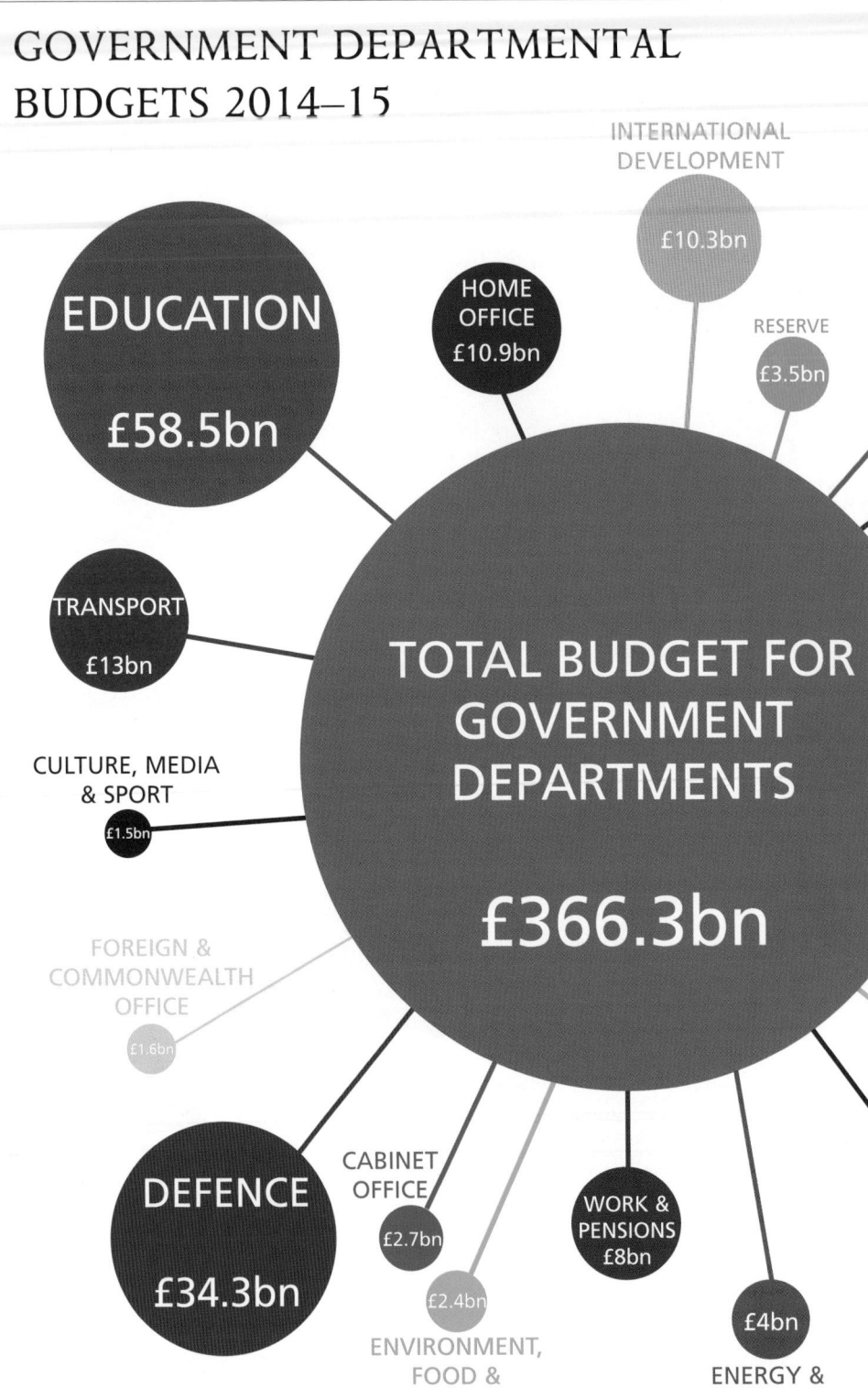

INTERNATIONAL DEVELOPMENT
£10.3bn

EDUCATION £58.5bn

HOME OFFICE £10.9bn

RESERVE £3.5bn

TRANSPORT £13bn

TOTAL BUDGET FOR GOVERNMENT DEPARTMENTS £366.3bn

CULTURE, MEDIA & SPORT £1.5bn

FOREIGN & COMMONWEALTH OFFICE £1.6bn

DEFENCE £34.3bn

CABINET OFFICE £2.7bn

£2.4bn

ENVIRONMENT, FOOD & RURAL AFFAIRS

WORK & PENSIONS £8bn

£4bn

ENERGY & CLIMATE CHANGE

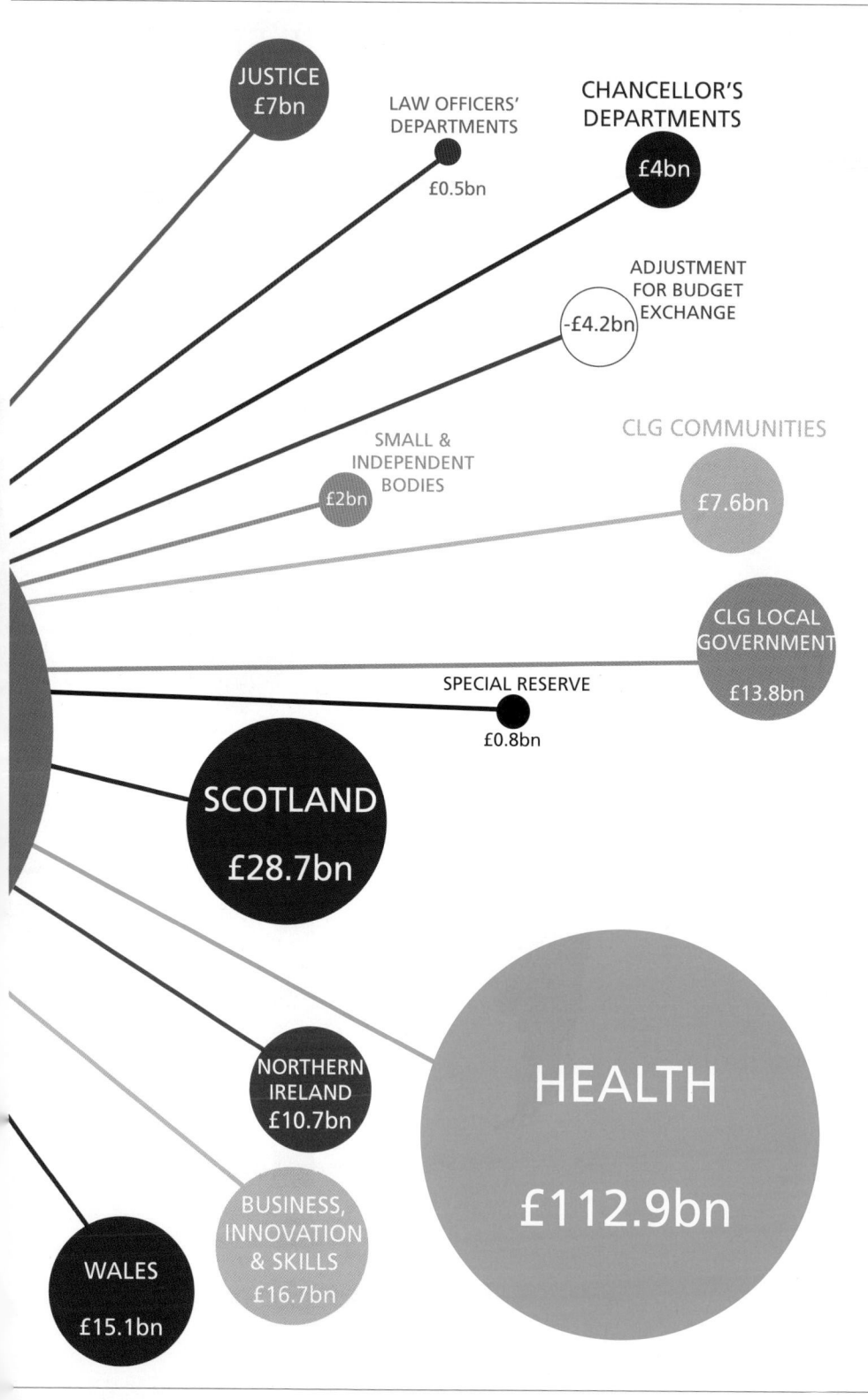

JUSTICE
£7bn

LAW OFFICERS'
DEPARTMENTS
£0.5bn

CHANCELLOR'S
DEPARTMENTS
£4bn

ADJUSTMENT
FOR BUDGET
EXCHANGE
-£4.2bn

CLG COMMUNITIES
£7.6bn

SMALL &
INDEPENDENT
BODIES
£2bn

CLG LOCAL
GOVERNMENT
£13.8bn

SPECIAL RESERVE
£0.8bn

SCOTLAND
£28.7bn

HEALTH
£112.9bn

NORTHERN
IRELAND
£10.7bn

BUSINESS,
INNOVATION
& SKILLS
£16.7bn

WALES
£15.1bn

UNESCO WORLD HERITAGE SITES

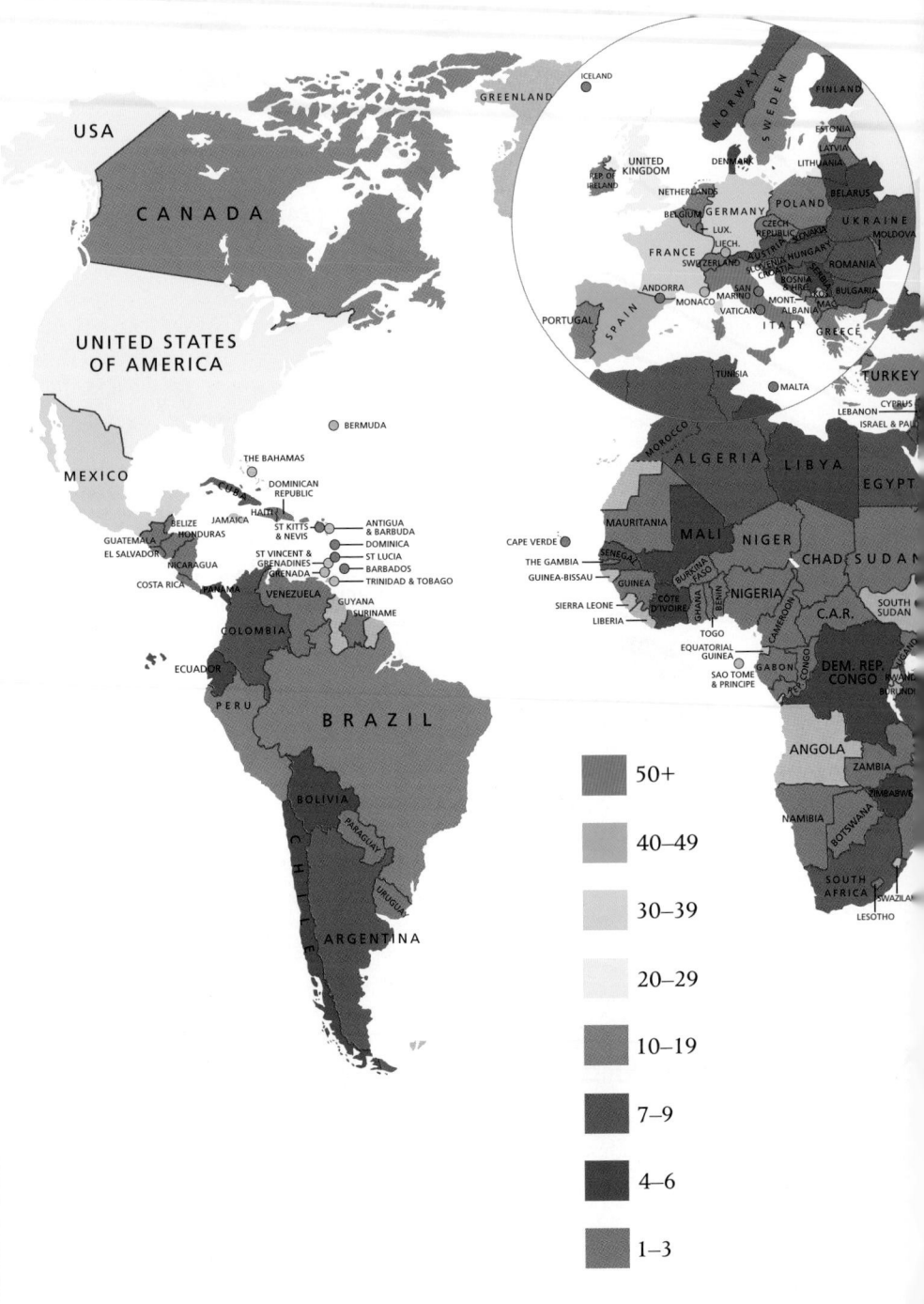

50+

40–49

30–39

20–29

10–19

7–9

4–6

1–3

RUSSIAN FEDERATION

KAZAKHSTAN

MONGOLIA

GEORGIA
UZBEKISTAN
KYRGYZSTAN
TURKMENISTAN
TAJIKISTAN
AFGHANISTAN

CHINA

D.P.R. KOREA
REP. KOREA

JAPAN

IRAN
IRAQ
KUWAIT
JORDAN
SAUDI ARABIA
BAHRAIN
QATAR
UAE
PAKISTAN
NEPAL
BHUTAN
BANGLADESH

INDIA

MYANMAR
LAOS

TAIWAN

SYRIA

ERITREA
YEMEN
OMAN

DJIBOUTI

ETHIOPIA

SOMALIA

KENYA

SRI LANKA

MALDIVES

THAILAND
VIETNAM
CAMBODIA

THE PHILIPPINES

MARSHALL ISLANDS

BRUNEI
MALAYSIA
SINGAPORE

PALAU

MICRONESIA

SEYCHELLES

INDONESIA

PAPUA NEW GUINEA

KIRIBATI

NAURU

TANZANIA

THE COMOROS

EAST TIMOR

SOLOMON ISLANDS

TUVALU

SAMOA

MALAWI
MOZAMBIQUE

MADAGASCAR

MAURITIUS

VANUATU

FIJI

TONGA

AUSTRALIA

NEW ZEALAND

The Unesco World Heritage List comprises 1,007 sites (as at 2014) around the world, of which 779 are cultural, 197 are natural and 31 are mixed properties. Each site is designated as being of outstanding universal value to humanity and is to be protected for future generations.

The list include sites such as the Pyramids of Egypt, the Grand Canyon in USA, the Acropolis in Greece and the Tower of London in the UK. Italy has the most sites on the list, ranging from Mount Etna to Venice.

WOMEN IN POWER

USA

CANADA

GREENLAND

ICELAND

UNITED STATES
OF AMERICA

BERMUDA

THE BAHAMAS

MEXICO

DOMINICAN
REPUBLIC

BELIZE   JAMAICA   HAITI
GUATEMALA   HONDURAS
EL SALVADOR   ST KITTS
NICARAGUA   & NEVIS
COSTA RICA   PANAMA   ST VINCENT &
                          GRENADINES
              VENEZUELA   GRENADA

ANTIGUA
& BARBUDA
DOMINICA
ST LUCIA
BARBADOS
TRINIDAD & TOBAGO

GUYANA
SURINAME

COLOMBIA

ECUADOR

PERU

BOLIVIA

PARAGUAY

CHILE

URUGUAY

ARGENTINA

BRAZIL

NORWAY   SWEDEN   FINLAND

DENMARK

ESTONIA
LATVIA
LITHUANIA

REP. OF
IRELAND

NETHERLANDS

UNITED
KINGDOM

BELGIUM   GERMANY
         LUX.   CZECH
         LIECH.   REPUBLIC
FRANCE   SWITZERLAND
                  AUSTRIA
ANDORRA   SAN   SLOVENIA
           MARINO   CROATIA
MONACO   VATICAN   BOSNIA

BELARUS

POLAND

UKRAINE
MOLDOVA

SLOVAKIA
HUNGARY
ROMANIA

PORTUGAL   SPAIN

TUNISIA

SERBIA   BULGARIA
MONT.   MAC.
ALBANIA
ITALY   GREECE

MALTA

TURKEY

CYPRUS
LEBANON
ISRAEL & PAL.

MOROCCO

ALGERIA   LIBYA

EGYPT

MAURITANIA

CAPE VERDE

THE GAMBIA
GUINEA-BISSAU

SIERRA LEONE
LIBERIA

MALI   NIGER

SENEGAL

GUINEA

CÔTE
D'IVOIRE

GHANA

BURKINA
FASO

BENIN

TOGO

NIGERIA

CHAD   SUDAN

CAMEROON

EQUATORIAL
GUINEA

SAO TOME
& PRINCIPE

GABON   REP. CONGO

C.A.R.

SOUTH
SUDAN

DEM. REP.
CONGO

RWANDA
BURUNDI

ANGOLA

ZAMBIA

NAMIBIA

BOTSWANA

ZIMBABWE

SOUTH
AFRICA

SWAZILAND

LESOTHO

RUSSIAN FEDERATION

KAZAKHSTAN

MONGOLIA

GEORGIA
AZERBAIJAN
ARMENIA
UZBEKISTAN
KYRGYZSTAN
TURKMENISTAN
TAJIKISTAN

CHINA

D.P.R.
KOREA

REP.
KOREA

SYRIA
IRAQ
JORDAN
IRAN
KUWAIT
AFGHANISTAN

PAKISTAN

NEPAL
BHUTAN

TAIWAN

SAUDI
ARABIA
BAHRAIN
QATAR
UAE

OMAN

INDIA

BANGLADESH

MYANMAR
LAOS

ERITREA
YEMEN

DJIBOUTI

ETHIOPIA

SOMALIA

KENYA

SRI LANKA

MALDIVES

SEYCHELLES

TANZANIA

THE
COMOROS

MALAWI
MOZAMBIQUE

MADAGASCAR

MAURITIUS

VIETNAM

THAILAND

CAMBODIA

THE
PHILIPPINES

BRUNEI

MALAYSIA

SINGAPORE

INDONESIA

PALAU

MICRONESIA

MARSHALL ISLANDS

KIRIBATI

NAURU

PAPUA
NEW
GUINEA

SOLOMON ISLANDS

EAST
TIMOR

VANUATU

TUVALU

SAMOA

FIJI

TONGA

AUSTRALIA

NEW
ZEALAND

No Female Leader

Female Head of State

Female Head of Government

Female Head of State and Government

SALARIES OF THE UNITED KINGDOM IN 2014

Position	Salary
Metropolitan Police Commissioner	£260,088
Chief of the Defence Staff	£249,934
President of the Supreme Court	£218,470
Prime Minister*	£142,500
Scottish First Minister*	£142,257
Speaker of the House of Commons	£142,162
Cabinet Minister (Commons)*	£134,565
Wales First Minister*	£132,427
Northern Ireland First Minister	£120,000
MEP	£78,444
GP	£68,826
MP	£67,060
Dentist	£59,788
MSP	£58,097
Nurse	£44,642
Police Sergeant	£38,780
Teacher (Inner London)	£36,360
Second Lieutenant	£25,220

*Includes MP/MSP/AM salary

This chart represents the salaries of key figures in the political, judicial, health and public sector jobs in the UK. Most salaries have a range. Where this is the case, the median salary for that post has been given.

president in the 2012 presidential election, beating the incumbent Jurelang Zedkaia by ten votes.

Under the 1979 constitution, the executive president is elected by the legislature from among its members to serve a four-year term. The unicameral legislature, the *Nitijela,* has 33 members, directly elected for a four-year term. There are no formal political parties, although groupings of like-minded independents have emerged in recent years. There is also a 12-member Council of Chiefs *(Iroij)* which has a consultative and advisory role.

HEAD OF STATE
President, Christopher Loeak, *elected* 4 January 2012,
   sworn in 12 January 2012

SELECTED GOVERNMENT MEMBERS *as at June 2013*
Finance, Jack Ading
Foreign Affairs, Tony A. de Brum
Internal Affairs, David Kabua

BRITISH AMBASSADOR
HE Asif Ahmad, *apptd* 2013, resident at Manila, the Philippines

ECONOMY AND TRADE
The islands have few natural resources, apart from possible seabed mineral deposits, and the economy is dependent on aid from the USA, supplemented by ship registration fees and the sale of fishing licences. Most islanders live by subsistence farming and fishing, with coconuts, breadfruit and fish the main commercial crops. A small-scale industrial sector produces copra and handicrafts and processes tuna. Tourism is being encouraged but has declined recently which, with a similar decline in fishing licence sales, has limited economic growth. The government is the largest employer. The main trading partners are Japan, the USA, New Zealand, Australia, China and Taiwan. Principal exports are copra and coconut products, handicrafts and fish. Main imports include food and fuel.
GNI – US$219m; US$4,040 per capita (2012)
Annual average growth of GDP – 2.3 per cent (2013 est)
Inflation rate – 12.9 per cent (2008 est)
Unemployment – 36 per cent (2006 est)
Total external debt – US$87m (2008 est)

Trade with UK	2012	2013
Imports from UK	£355,607	£913,160
Exports to UK	£8,189,409	£2,636,317

COMMUNICATIONS
Airports and waterways – There are four airports throughout the islands; Majuro is the main airport as well as the main port, with a merchant fleet of 1,593 ships of over 1,000 tonnes, 1,468 of which are foreign-owned
Roadways – There are 2,028km of surfaced roads
Telecommunications – 4,400 fixed lines and 3,800 mobile subscriptions (2010); there were 2,200 internet users in 2009
Internet code and IDD – mh; 692 (from UK), 011 44 (to UK)
Media – MBC TV is the state-run broadcaster; the English and Marshallese-language *Marshall Islands Journal* is published on a weekly basis

MAURITANIA

Al-Jumhuriyah al-Islamiyah al-Muritaniyah – Islamic Republic of Mauritania

Area – 1,030,700 sq. km
Capital – Nouakchott; population, 709,000 (2009)
Major towns – Kaedi, Kiffa, Nouadhibou, Rosso, Zuwarat
Currency – Ouguiya (UM) of 5 khoums
Population – 3,516,806 rising at 2.26 per cent a year (2014 est)
Religion – Muslim 100 per cent (almost entirely Sunni) (est)
Language – Arabic (official), Pulaar, Soninke, Wolof, French
Population density – 4 per sq. km (2011)
Urban population – 41.7 per cent (2012 est)
Median age (years) – 19.9 (2014 est)
National anthem – 'National Anthem of Mauritania'
National day – 28 November (Independence Day)
Death penalty – Retained (last used 1987)
CPI score – 30 (119)
Literacy rate – 59 per cent (2011 est)
Gross enrolment ratio (percentage of relevant age group) – primary 97 per cent; secondary 27 per cent; tertiary 5 per cent (2012 est)
Health expenditure (per capita) – US$58 (2011)
Hospital beds (per 1,000 people) – 0.4 (2004–9)
Life expectancy (years) – 62.28 (2014 est)
Mortality rate – 8.35 (2014 est)
Birth rate – 31.83 (2014 est)
Infant mortality rate – 56.04 (2014 est)

CLIMATE AND TERRAIN
About 60 per cent of the country is covered by the plains of the Sahara Desert, with some hills in the centre. The terrain is arid, apart from in the Senegal river valley on the southern border; most of the population lives there or on the coast at Nouakchott and Nouadhibou. Elevation extremes range from Kediet Ijill (915m) to −5m (Sebkhet Te-n-Dghamcha). There is a desert climate; the north of the country is virtually rainless, while the south receives some unreliable rainfall between June and October. Humidity can be high in the wet season, especially on the coast. Average temperatures in Nouakchott range from 21°C in January to 30°C in September.

HISTORY AND POLITICS
Eastern Mauritania was part of the Ghana Empire and then the Muslim Almoravid and Almohad empires from the 11th to the 13th century. The area became part of the French West Africa protectorate in 1903 and then a colony in 1920. The country became independent as the Islamic Republic of Mauritania on 28 November 1960.

Mauritania has experienced several military coups and periods of military rule since independence. The 1984 coup brought to power Col. Maaouya ould Sid Ahmed Taya, who restored civilian rule in 1992 with multi-party elections in which he was elected president. President Taya was deposed in a military coup in 2005 and after a period of transitional government, elections were held in late 2006 and early 2007.

The 2007 presidential election was won by Sidi ould Cheikh Abdallahi who was subsequently overthrown in a military coup after attempting to sack four military leaders. Democracy was restored with the 2009 presidential election, which was won by General Mohamed ould Abdelaziz, who had led the 2008 coup, but the 2011 legislative elections were postponed. In December 2013 Abdelaziz's Union for the Republic party won a majority in the first legislative elections since 2006, although the polls were widely boycotted by opposition parties. President Abdelaziz was elected for a further five-year term on 30 June 2014

The 1991 constitution was amended in 2007 to reduce the term of the president, who is directly elected, to five years, renewable once. The bicameral legislature comprises the National Assembly (the lower house) and the senate. The National Assembly has 95 members who are directly elected for a five-year term. The senate has 56 members (including three representing Mauritanians abroad), who are indirectly elected for a six-year term; one-third is elected every two years.

HEAD OF STATE

President, Gen. Mohamed ould Abdelaziz, *elected* 18 July 2009, *sworn in* 5 August 2009, *re-elected* 30 June 2014

SELECTED GOVERNMENT MEMBERS *as at August 2014*
Prime Minister, Yahya ould Hademine
Finance, Thiam Dioumbar
Foreign Affairs, Ahmed ould Teguedi
Interior, Mohamed oula Salem

EMBASSY OF THE ISLAMIC REPUBLIC OF MAURITANIA
Carlyle House, 235 Vauxhall Bridge Road, London SW1V 1EJ
T 020-7233 6158 E info@mauritanianembassy.org.uk
W www.mauritanianembassy.org.uk
Chargé d'Affaires, Mohamed Yahya Ould Sidi Haiba,

BRITISH AMBASSADOR
HE Clive Alderton, *apptd* 2012, resident at Rabat, Morocco

DEFENCE

Aged 16–49, 2010 est	Males	Females
Available for military service	718,713	804,622
Fit for military service	480,042	581,473

Military expenditure – US$145m (2013)
Conscription duration – 24 months

ECONOMY AND TRADE
Mauritania is one of the poorer countries in the region, with 40 per cent of the population living below the poverty line and unemployment at 30 per cent. Past economic mismanagement and droughts created a huge foreign debt, although the country has benefited from debt cancellation since 2000. The economy grew at around 5 per cent a year in 2011–12.

Natural resources include iron ore, copper, gold, gypsum, oil (off-shore production began in 2006) and rich fishing waters, although the latter are threatened by over-exploitation. Agriculture and animal husbandry, mainly at subsistence level, are the mainstay of the economy, accounting for 16.9 per cent of GDP and engaging 50

per cent of the population. The main industries are fish processing, oil production and refining, and mining.

The main trading partners are China, EU countries and the USA. Principal exports are iron ore, fish and fish products, gold, copper and oil. The main imports are machinery, petroleum products, capital goods, food and consumer goods.

GNI – US$4,066m; US$1,110 per capita (2012)
Annual average growth of GDP – 6.4 per cent (2013 est)
Inflation rate – 4.6 per cent (2013 est)
Population below poverty line – 40 per cent (2004 est)
Unemployment – 30 per cent (2008 est)
External debt – $3,233m (2013 est)

BALANCE OF PAYMENTS
Trade – US$347m deficit (2012)
Current Account – US$350m deficit (2009)

Trade with UK	2012	2013
Imports from UK	£43,704,892	£55,898,171
Exports to UK	£971,846	£5,390,177

COMMUNICATIONS
Transport – There are nine airports; the main seaports are Nouakchott and Nouadhibou; there are 10,628km of roadways and 728km of railways
Telecommunications – 65,100 fixed lines and 4.024 million mobile subscriptions (2012); there were 75,000 internet users in 2009
Internet code and IDD – mr; 222 (from UK), 44 (to UK)
Media – Télévision de Mauritanie broadcasts in Arabic and French alongside numerous privately owned daily newspapers
WPFI score – 26,53 (60)

MAURITIUS

Republic of Mauritius

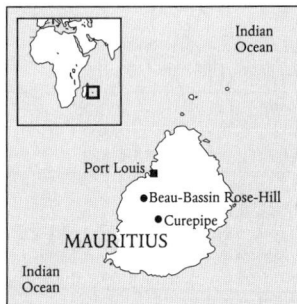

Area – 2,040 sq. km (includes Rodrigues and other islands)
Capital – Port Louis; population, 149,000 (2009)
Major towns – Beau-Bassin Rose-Hill, Curepipe, Quatre Bornes, Vacoas-Phoenix
Currency – Mauritius rupee of 100 cents
Population – 1,331,155 rising at 0.66 per cent a year (2014 est); Indo-Mauritian (68 per cent), Creole (27 per cent), Sino-Mauritian (3 per cent), Franco-Mauritian (2 per cent) (est)
Religion – Hindu 48.5 per cent, Christian (Roman Catholic) 26.3 per cent, Muslim 17.3 per cent
Language – English (official), Creole, French, Bhojpuri
Population density – 634 per sq. km (2011)
Urban population – 41.8 per cent (2012 est)

Median age (years) – 33.9 (2014 est)
National anthem – 'Motherland'
National day – 12 March (Independence Day)
Death penalty – Abolished for all crimes (since 1995)
CPI score – 52 (52)

CLIMATE AND TERRAIN

The republic is an island group in the Indian Ocean, approximately 885km east of Madagascar. The volcanic island of Mauritius rises from narrow coastal plains to a central plateau ringed by mountains. Elevation extremes range from 828m (Mt Piton) to 0m (Indian Ocean). The island of Rodrigues, formerly a dependency but now part of Mauritius, is about 563km east of Mauritius, with an area of 109 sq. km; the population is 37,922 (2011). The islands of Agalega and St Brandon are dependencies of Mauritius; their total population is about 350 (2011).

There is a tropical climate, modified by south-east trade winds, and little variation in temperature throughout the year. The cyclone season (December–April) brings rain but cyclones usually miss the islands.

HISTORY AND POLITICS

The islands were first visited in the tenth century, but were settled only after 1638 by the Dutch, who introduced sugar cane cultivation; the colonists withdrew in 1710. A decade later they were replaced by the French, who established plantations that were worked by African slaves. In 1814 Mauritius was ceded to the British, who had occupied it in 1810. The British abolished slavery in 1834 and imported indentured Indian and Chinese labourers to work on the plantations. Independence was achieved on 12 March 1968 and the state became a republic in 1992.

The Militant Socialist Movement (MSM) under Sir Aneerood Jugnauth held power from 1983 until 1995, and then returned to power in 2000 in coalition with the Mauritian Militant Movement (MMM). Jugnauth stood down as party leader and prime minister in 2003; he was elected president later that year and again in 2008. The MSM-MMM coalition lost the 2005 election to the opposition Socialist Alliance, which included the Mauritius Labour Party (MPT) led by Navinchandra Ramgoolam, who became prime minister. The MPT-led Alliance of the Future, now also including the MSM, won the 2010 legislative election. President Jugnauth resigned from office in March 2012 following disagreements with prime minister Ramgoolam; in July 2012 Rajkeswur Purryag was elected president.

The 1968 constitution was amended in 1992 to introduce a republican form of government, and in 2001 to give the island of Rodrigues a degree of autonomy.

The president is elected by the legislature for a five-year term, renewable once. The unicameral National Assembly has 62 elected members (including two representing Rodrigues) and eight appointed members, all of whom serve a five-year term; the electoral commission allocates the appointed seats on a 'best loser' basis to give more equitable representation to ethnic minorities. The prime minister is the leader of the majority party in the legislature.

Rodrigues has had an 18-member regional assembly, a chief commissioner and a chief executive since 2002.

HEAD OF STATE

President , Rajkeswur Purryag, *elected* 20 July 2014

SELECTED GOVERNMENT MEMBERS *as at June 2013*
Prime Minister, Defence, Interior, Navinchandra Ramgoolam
Deputy Prime Minister, Ahmed Rashid Beebeejaun
Foreign Affairs, Arvin Boolell

MAURITIUS HIGH COMMISSION
32–33 Elvaston Place, London SW7 5NW
T 020-7581 0294 E londonmhc@btinternet.com
W london.mauritius.gov.mu
High Commissioner, HE Abhimanu Kundasamy, *apptd* 2005

BRITISH HIGH COMMISSION
PO Box 1063, Les Cascades Building, Edith Cavell Street, Port Louis
T (+230) 202 9400 E bhc@intnet.mu
W www.gov.uk/government/world/mauritius
High Commissioner, HE Nick Leake, *apptd* 2010

DEFENCE

Aged 16–49, 2010 est	*Males*	*Females*
Available for military service	343,628	–
Fit for military service	280,596	283,317

Military expenditure – US$23.7m (2013)

ECONOMY AND TRADE

Since independence Mauritius has developed from an economy dependent on agriculture to one with prospering tourist, manufacturing (primarily of textiles and garments) and financial sectors. Although sugar remains an important commodity (sugar cane is grown on 90 per cent of cultivated land and produces 15 per cent of export earnings), both the sugar and textile industries are beginning to decline. Diversification into fish processing, information and communications technology, banking, hospitality and property development is being encouraged. The services sector accounts for 73.4 per cent of GDP, industry for 22 per cent and agriculture for 4.5 per cent.

The main trading partners are France, the UK and India. Principal exports are clothing, textiles, sugar, cut flowers, molasses and fish. The main imports are manufactured goods, capital equipment, food, fuels and chemicals.
GNI – US$10,597m; US$8,570 per capita (2012)
Annual average growth of GDP – 3.4 per cent (2013 est)
Inflation rate – 3.5 per cent (2013 est)
Population below poverty line – 8 per cent (2012 est)
Unemployment – 8.3 per cent (2013 est)
Total external debt – US$2,894m (2013 est)
Imports – US$5,354m (2012)
Exports – US$2,673m (2012)

BALANCE OF PAYMENTS
Trade – US$2,681m deficit (2012)
Current Account – US$1,171m deficit (2012)

Trade with UK	*2012*	*2013*
Imports from UK	£63,396,020	£62,683,581
Exports to UK	£254,175,379	£263,818,908

COMMUNICATIONS
Airports and waterways – The international airport and the main port are at Port Louis
Roadways – 2,149km
Telecommunications – 349,100 fixed lines and 1.485 million mobile subscriptions (2012); there were 290,000 internet users in 2009
Internet code and IDD – mu; 230 (from UK), 44 (to UK)
Media – The state-owned Mauritius Broadcasting Corporation runs television and radio services funded through advertising and a licence fee
WPFI score – 27,69 (70)

EDUCATION AND HEALTH

Twelve years of education are free and compulsory.
Literacy rate – 89 per cent (2011 est)
Gross enrolment ratio (percentage of relevant age group) –
   primary 108 per cent; secondary 96 per cent; tertiary
   40 per cent (2012 est)
Health expenditure (per capita) – US$510 (2011)
Hospital beds (per 1,000 people) – 3.4 (2011)
Life expectancy (years) – 75.17 (2014 est)
Mortality rate – 6.85 (2014 est)
Birth rate – 13.46 (2014 est)
Infant mortality rate – 10.59 (2014 est)
HIV/AIDS adult prevalence – 1.2 per cent (2012 est)

MEXICO

Estados Unidos Mexicanos – United Mexican States

Area – 1,964,375 sq. km
Capital – Mexico City; population, 19,728,695 (2012)
Major cities – Ciudad Juárez, Ecatepec, Guadalajara, León,
   Monterrey, Puebla, Tijuana
Currency – Peso of 100 centavos
Population – 120,286,655 rising at 1.21 per cent a year
   (2014 est)
Religion – Christian (Roman Catholic 82.7 per cent,
   Protestant 7 per cent), none 4.7 per cent
Language – Spanish (official) indigenous languages including
   dialects of Mayan and Nahuatl
Population density – 61 per sq. km (2011)
Urban population – 78.4 per cent (2012 est)
Median age (years) – 27.3 (2014 est)
National anthem – 'Himno Nacional Mexicano' ['Mexican
   National Anthem']
National day – 16 September (Independence Day)
Death penalty – Abolished for all crimes (since 2005)
CPI score – 34 (106)

CLIMATE AND TERRAIN

The Rio Grande river forms the eastern part of the border
with the USA. South of this, coastal plains rise to a central
plateau which lies between two spines of high mountains, the
Western and the Eastern Sierra Madre, running from the
north-west to south-east. The mountains include volcanoes
such as Popocatepetl, and in the south are covered with
dense jungle. The Yucatán peninsula in the south-east is
low-lying, and marshy on the coast. The narrow Baja
California peninsula, separated from the rest of the country
by the Gulf of California, has a range of hills running along
it. Elevation extremes range from 5,700m (Volcan Pico de
Orizaba) to –10m (Laguna Salada). The north has a desert
climate, while the south is tropical. The average temperature
ranges from 16.2°C in January to 23.8°C in June.

POLITICS

Under the 1917 constitution, the federal republic consists
of 31 states and the federal capital. The head of state is an
executive president, directly elected for a single six-year term.
The bicameral legislature is the Congress of the Union: the
lower house, the Chamber of Deputies, has 500 members,
directly elected for a three-year term, and the senate has 128
members, directly elected for a six-year term. The president
appoints the cabinet.

Each of the states has its own constitution and is
administered by a governor, elected for a six-year term, and
a state chamber of deputies, elected for a three-year term.

The Institutional Revolutionary Party's (PRI) political
dominance ended at the 1997 election, when it lost its
absolute majority in the lower house of the legislature,
although it continued in government until 2000 and was
again in power from 2003 until 2006. The 2006 presidential
election was won by Felipe Calderón of the Partido Accion
Nacional (PAN); Lopez Obrador, Calderón's closest rival,
refused to accept the result, alleging voting irregularities.
Lopez Obrador also stood in the 2012 presidential election,
eventually losing to PRI's Enrique Pena Nieto in another
election marred by accusations of voting irregularities. PRI
became the largest party in the Chamber of Deputies in the
2012 legislative election, picking up 93 more seats than
nearest rival PAN.

HEAD OF STATE
President, Enrique Pena Nieto, *elected* 1 July 2012, *sworn in*
   1 December 2012

SELECTED GOVERNMENT MEMBERS *as at June 2014*
Defence, Gen. Salvador Cienfuegos Zepeda
Economy, Ildefonso Guajardo
Foreign Affairs, José Antonio Meade
Interior, Miguel Angel Osorio Chong

EMBASSY OF MEXICO
16 St George Street, London W1S 1FD
T 020-7499 8586 E mexuk@sre.gob.mx
W www.sre.gob.mx/reinounido
Ambassador Extraordinary and Plenipotentiary, HE Diego
   Gómez Pickering, *apptd* 2013

BRITISH EMBASSY
Río Lerma 71, Col. Cuauhtémoc, 06500 Mexico City
T (+52) (55) 1670 3200 E ukinmexico@fco.gov.uk
W www.gov.uk/government/world/mexico
Ambassador Extraordinary and Plenipotentiary, HE Duncan
   Taylor CBE, *apptd* 2013

DEFENCE

Aged 16–49, 2010 est	Males	Females
Available for military service	28,815,506	30,363,558
Fit for military service	23,239,866	25,642,549

Military expenditure – US$7,471m (2013)
Conscription – 18 years; 12 months

ECONOMY AND TRADE

Mexico had a relatively closed economy until the mid-1980s,
but increased trade and domestic liberalisation in the 1990s
stimulated economic growth and development, particularly
in the industrial sector. However, although it has free trade
agreements with over 50 countries, covering 90 per cent of
its trade, its economy is still closely tied to that of the USA
and experienced a deep recession in 2009 as the global
downturn affected its main export market. Despite posting
positive growth in 2010 and 2011, Mexico remains a poor

| | Protracted revolt; independence declared | War of Reform; a Conservative vs. Liberal civil war | Ruled by dictator Poifirio Díaz; overthrown in revolution | Oil-fuelled economic boom | Pro-indigenous Zapatista National Liberation Front (EZLN) leads revolution in south |
| Aztec rule begins | | | | | |

c.1200-900 AD
1519-21
1836-48
1862-67
1929
1982
2006

c.1200
1810-21
1857-61
1876-1911
c.1970
1994-95

| Occupied by various civilisations, including Olmecs, Zapotecs and Mayans | Conquered for Spain by Hernán Cortés | Wars with USA lead to loss of territory | Interest payments on foreign debt suspended; war with Britain, France and Spain ensues | National Revolutionary Party founded; dominant until 1997 | Serious financial crisis; Mexico defaults on debt | Mexican Drug War begins |

country. In November 2012 former president Felipe Calderón signed a comprehensive labour reform into law.

Agriculture is diverse and productive; major crops include maize, wheat, soya beans, rice, beans, cotton, coffee, fruit, tomatoes, beef, poultry and dairy products. Agriculture accounts for 3.6 per cent of GDP and 13.4 per cent of employment. The main industries include production of food, beverages, tobacco, chemicals, iron and steel, textiles, clothing, motor vehicles, consumer durables, oil production, mining and tourism. Tourism is now the fourth-largest revenue earner. The services sector accounts for 59.8 per cent of GDP and industry for 36.6 per cent.

The main trading partner is the USA (78 per cent of exports; 49.7 per cent of imports). Canada is the other main export market, and China and South Korea the other main source of imports. Principal exports include manufactured goods, oil and oil products, silver, fruit, vegetables, coffee and cotton. The main imports include metal-working machines, steel mill products, agricultural machinery, electrical equipment, car parts for assembly, vehicle repair parts, aircraft and aircraft parts.

GNI – US$1,157,952m; US$9,640 per capita (2012)
Annual average growth of GDP – 1.2 per cent (2013 est)
Inflation rate – 4 per cent (2013 est)
Population below poverty line – 52.3 per cent (2012)
Unemployment – 4.9 per cent (2013 est)
Total external debt – US$354,900m (2013 est)
Imports – US$370,746m (2012)
Exports – US$370,889m (2012)

BALANCE OF PAYMENTS
Trade – US$143m surplus (2012)
Current Account – US$14,184m deficit (2012)

Trade with UK	2012	2013
Imports from UK	£951,838,614	£1,070,756,842
Exports to UK	£1,055,540,715	£757,597,085

COMMUNICATIONS

Airports – The main international airport is at Mexico City, with 242 others around the country
Waterways – Veracruz, Tampico and Coatzacoalcos are the chief seaports on the east coast, and Guaymas, Mazatlán, Lázaro Cárdenas and Salina Cruz on the Pacific; there are 2,900km of navigable rivers and coastal canals
Roadways and railways – There are 377,660km of roadways, of which 137,544km are surfaced, and 17,166km of railways; the Baluarte bridge, the highest cable-stayed bridge in the world, opened in 2012 and stretches 1,124m across the Durango-Mazatlán motorway in the north
Telecommunications – 20.22 million fixed lines and 100.79 million mobile subscriptions (2012); there were 31.02 million internet users in 2009
Internet code and IDD – mx; 52 (from UK), 44 (to UK)
Major broadcasters – The Televisa group used to dominate broadcasting but now competes with other television channels and a huge number of independent radio stations
Press – There are six national daily newspapers, representing a variety of political opinions
WPFI score – 45,04 (152)

EDUCATION AND HEALTH

Education is compulsory in Mexico for ten years from age six, although attainment varies among states.
Literacy rate – 94 per cent (2011 est)
Gross enrolment ratio (percentage of relevant age group) – primary 104 per cent; secondary 84 per cent; tertiary 28 per cent (2012 est)
Health expenditure (per capita) – US$620 (2011)
Hospital beds (per 1,000 people) – 1.7 (2010)
Life expectancy (years) – 75.43 (2014 est)
Mortality rate – 5.24 (2014 est)
Birth rate – 19.02 (2014 est)
Infant mortality rate – 12.58 (2014 est)

FEDERATED STATES OF MICRONESIA

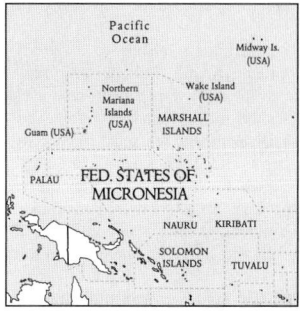

Area – 702 sq. km
Capital – Palikir, on Pohnpei; population, 7,000 (2009)
Major town – Weno, Kolonia
Currency – US dollar (US$) of 100 cents
Population – 105,681 falling at 0.42 per cent a year (2014 est); Chuukese (48.8 per cent), Pohnpeian (24.2 per cent), Kosraen (6.2 per cent), Yapese (5.2 per cent), Yap outer islands (4.5 per cent), Polynesian (1.5 per cent) (2000)
Religion – Christian (Roman Catholic 54.7 per cent, Protestant 41.1 per cent, Mormon 1.5 per cent)
Language – English (official), Chuukese, Pohnpeian, Yapese, Ulithian, Woleaian, Nukuoro, Kapingamarangi
Population density – 159 per sq. km (2011)
Urban population – 22.7 per cent (2012 est)
Median age (years) – 23.8 (2014 est)
National anthem – 'Patriots of Micronesia'
Death penalty – Abolished for all crimes (since 1986)
National day – 10 May (Constitution Day)
Life expectancy (years) – 72.35 (2014 est)
Mortality rate – 4.25 (2014 est)
Birth rate – 20.97 (2014 est)
Infant mortality rate – 21.93 (2014 est)

CLIMATE AND TERRAIN

The republic consists of four major island groups totalling over 600 mountainous volcanic islands and low-lying atolls, extending over 2,900 sq. km of the western Pacific Ocean.

Elevation extremes range from 791m (Dolohmwar) to 0m (Pacific Ocean). The climate is tropical, with only slight seasonal variations in temperatures; there is a stormy season between July and November. The islands are vulnerable to the effects of global warming, particularly an increase in the frequency and intensity of cyclones in the region.

HISTORY AND POLITICS
Inhabited since around 4,000 BC by migrants from the Philippines and Indonesia, Micronesia experienced contact with Europeans from the 1520s, and the islands were colonised by Spain from the 16th century. German encroachment in the 1870s and 1880s was resisted until 1899, when Germany purchased the islands from Spain. The islands were occupied by Japan on behalf of the Allies during the First World War, and administered as a League of Nations mandated territory by Japan from 1920 until the Japanese defeat in the Second World War. In 1947 the islands became part of the UN Trust Territory of the Pacific, administered by the USA.

A constitution was adopted in 1979 and the islands became independent in 1986 under a compact of free association with the USA, by which the USA retains responsibility for defence and provides substantial financial aid; a renegotiated agreement came into force in 2004. The UN trusteeship was formally terminated in 1990.

Emmanuel ('Manny') Mori was elected president in 2007, and re-elected in May 2011 following the legislative election in March.

The 1979 constitution established a federal republic of four states: Chuuk, Kosrae, Pohnpei and Yap. The federal head of state is an executive president, who is elected by the federal legislature for a four-year term. The unicameral congress has 14 members, ten senators directly elected for a two-year term and four senators 'at large' (one from each state) elected for a four-year term; the president and vice-president must be selected from among the 'at large' senators. The federal cabinet is appointed by the president and approved by the congress. There are no formal political parties.

Each state has its own constitution, legislature and government.

HEAD OF STATE
President, Emmanuel Mori, *elected* 11 May 2007, *re-elected* 2011
Vice-President, Alik L. Alik

SELECTED GOVERNMENT MEMBERS *as at June 2014*
Attorney-General, Maketo Robert
Finance, Finley S. Perman
Foreign Affairs, Lorin S. Robert

BRITISH AMBASSADOR
HE Asif Ahmad, *apptd* 2013, resident at Manila, the Philippines

ECONOMY AND TRADE
Micronesia has few natural resources apart from phosphate, which is not exploited, and is highly dependent on aid from the USA, which constitutes over a quarter of GDP. The main economic activities are subsistence farming and fishing, which account for 14 per cent of GDP, but both are threatened by climate change and over-fishing. The islands' remoteness and lack of facilities has constrained the development of tourism, the main industry; other industries include construction, fish processing, specialised aquaculture and handicrafts. Two-thirds of the workforce is employed by

the government. The main trading partners are the USA and Japan. Principal exports are fish, garments, bananas and black pepper. The main imports are food, manufactured goods and machinery.

GNI – US$343m; US$3,230 per capita (2012)
Annual average growth of GDP – 0.6 per cent (2013 est)
Inflation rate – 3.4 per cent (2011)
Total external debt – US$60.8m (2005 est)

Trade with UK	2012	2013
Imports from UK	£89,784	£32,263
Exports to UK	£4,950	£27,036

COMMUNICATIONS
Transport – There are six airports, including major airports on the four main islands; the main seaports are Colonia (Yap), Kolonia (Pohnpei), Lele and Moen; there are 240km of roadways, 42km of which are paved
Telecommunications – 8,400 fixed lines and 27,600 mobile subscriptions; there were 17,000 internet users in 2010
Internet code and IDD – fm; 691 (from UK), 011 44 (to UK)
Media – The federal government produces a fortnightly information bulletin and state governments produce weekly news publications; the majority of television programming is imported

MOLDOVA

Republica Moldova – Republic of Moldova

Area – 33,851 sq. km
Capital – Chisinau; population, 650,043 (2009 est)
Major towns – Balti, Tighina, Tiraspol
Currency – Moldovan leu (plural lei) of 100 bani
Population – 3,583,288 falling at 1.02 per cent a year (2014 est); Moldovan/Romanian (78.2 per cent), Ukrainian (8.4 per cent), Russian (5.8 per cent), Gagauz (4.4 per cent), Bulgarian (1.9 per cent) (2004)
Religion – Christian (Orthodox 93.3 per cent)
Language – Moldovan (official; linguistically identical to Romanian), Russian, Gagauz
Population density – 124 per sq. km (2012)
Urban population – 48.4 per cent (2012 est)
Median age (years) – 35.7 (2014 est)
National anthem – 'Limba Noastra' ['Our Language']
National day – 27 August (Independence Day)
Death penalty – Abolished for all crimes (since 1995)
CPI score – 35 (102)

CLIMATE AND TERRAIN
The landlocked country consists of rolling steppe lying mostly between the Prut and Dniester rivers. Elevation extremes range from 430m (Dealul Balanesti) at the highest

		Area returned to USSR;		Joins Commonwealth of
Becomes part of a larger	Bessarabia granted	becomes the Moldavian	Recaptured	Independent States
Moldovan kingdom	to Russia	Soviet Socialist Republic	by USSR	following collapse of USSR

1500–1800

| 106 | | | 1918 | | 1941 | | 1990 | | 1994 |

| 1350 | | 1812 | | 1940 | | 1944 | | 1991 | |

Part of the Roman	Territory contested	Becomes province of	Area retaken	Parliament asserts its	Referendum
province of Dacia	by Ottoman and	Romania following	by Romania	political and economic	endorses
(known as Bessarabia)	Russian empires	Russian Revolution		sovereignty	independence

point to 2m (river Dniester) at the lowest. The climate is continental, and average temperatures in Chisinau range from −2°C in January to 20°C in July and August.

POLITICS
The 1997 constitution was amended in 2000 to increase the powers of the legislature and the executive. The head of state is a president who is elected by the legislature by a three-fifths majority for a four-year term, renewable once. The unicameral legislature, the *Parlamentul,* has 101 members, who are directly elected for a four-year term. The prime minister and government are nominated by the president.

The governments in the first decade after independence were made up of moderate reformists, but there was a resurgence in support for the Communist Party of Moldova (PCM), which won the majority of seats in the 1998, 2001, 2005, 2009 (April and July) and 2010 legislative elections, forming the government from 2005 to 2009. Although the PCM won most seats in the legislative election in November 2010, the four-party pro-Western coalition government continued in office; neither bloc was able to elect its candidate as president, but the leader of the Democratic Party of Moldova was elected as speaker and as acting president. The presidential stalemate was broken in March 2012 after independent candidate Nicolae Timofti picked up 62 of 101 parliamentary votes in an election boycotted by the PCM.

HEAD OF STATE
President, Nicolae Timofti, *took office* 23 March 2012

SELECTED GOVERNMENT MEMBERS *as at June 2013*
Prime Minister, Iurie Leanca
Deputy Prime Ministers, Valeriu Lazar *(Economy);* Natalia Gherman *(Foreign Affairs);* Eugen Carpov; Tatiana Poting
Defence, Igor Panfile
Finance, Veaceslav Negruta

EMBASSY OF THE REPUBLIC OF MOLDOVA
5 Dolphin Square, Edensor Road, London W4 2ST
T 020-8995 6818 E embassy.london@mfa.md
W www.britania.mfa.gov.md
Ambassador Extraordinary and Plenipotentiary, HE Iulian Frunatsu, *apptd* 2011

BRITISH EMBASSY
18 Nicolae Iorga Str., Chisinau MD-2012
T (+373) 222 225902 E enquiries.chisinau@fco.gov.uk
W www.gov.uk/government/world/moldova
Ambassador Extraordinary and Plenipotentiary, HE Philip Batson, *apptd* 2013

SECESSION
Moldovan nationalism in the late 1980s and possible reunification with Romania alarmed the republic's Russian and Ukrainian ethnic minorities in the Transdniestria region (east of the Dniester) and the Gagauz (Turkish-speaking Christians) in the south-west. Both areas declared

independence unilaterally in 1990, though this was not recognised. The regions were granted a special status by the 1994 constitution, and the Gagauz have since exercised a degree of autonomy over their political, economic and cultural affairs.

In response to the Russian takeover of Crimea, in March 2014 President Timofti warned Russia against trying to annex Transdniestria while also calling on the EU to fast-track Moldova's entry into the organisation in order to deter invasion.

DEFENCE

Aged 16–49, 2010 est	*Males*	*Females*
Available for military service	1,143,440	1,156,958
Fit for military service	875,224	969,903

Military expenditure – US$23.9m (2013)*
Conscription duration – 12 months

* Figure does not include paramilitary spending

ECONOMY AND TRADE
Moldova is one of the poorest countries in Europe, despite moves towards a market economy since independence. With few natural resources and most industry lying in the breakaway Transdniestria region, the economy is dependent on agriculture and remittances from expatriate workers. Following the global downturn, the economy recovered in 2011, posting growth of around 6 per cent, but remains susceptible to political uncertainty, increasing fuel prices and a weak investment market. EU integration has yielded generally positive results, with the economy growing 8.9 per cent in 2013, though Moldova is highly dependent on Russia for its energy supply.

The agricultural sector accounts for 13.8 per cent of GDP. Principal crops include vegetables, fruit, wine, grain, sugar beet, sunflower seed, tobacco, beef and milk. Major industrial activities include food processing and production of sugar, vegetable oil, agricultural machinery, foundry equipment, domestic appliances, footwear and textiles. Industry accounts for 19.9 per cent of GDP and services for 66.2 per cent.

The main trading partners are Russia, Romania and Italy. Principal exports are foodstuffs, textiles and machinery. The main imports are mineral products and fuel, machinery and equipment, chemicals and textiles.
GNI – US$7,818m; US$2,070 per capita (2012)
Annual average growth of GDP – 4 per cent (2013 est)
Inflation rate – 4.2 per cent (2013 est)
Population below poverty line – 29.8 per cent (2011)
Unemployment – 5.8 per cent (2013 est)
Total external debt – US$6,008m (2013)
Imports – US$5,2132m (2012)
Exports – US$2,162m (2012)

BALANCE OF PAYMENTS
Trade – US$3,051m deficit (2011)
Current Account – US$449m deficit (2010)

Trade with UK	2012	2013
Imports from UK	£40,650,149	£44,760,375
Exports to UK	£43,273,334	£48,598,071

COMMUNICATIONS

Airports and waterways – There are five airports, including the principal airport at Chisinau; there are 558km of navigable waterways on the Prut, Dniester and Danube rivers
Roadways and railways – 9,352km; 1,190km
Telecommunications – 1.206 million fixed lines and 4.08 million mobile subscriptions (2012); there were 1.333 million internet users in 2009
Internet code and IDD – md; 373 (from UK), 44 (to UK)
Media – Public network Moldova One broadcasts nationally alongside Russian and Romanian broadcasters; newspapers are published in both Moldovan *(Timpul* and *Moldova Suverana)* and Russian *(Kommersant Moldoviy* and *Nezavisimaya Moldova)*
WPFI score – 25,35 (56)

EDUCATION AND HEALTH

Literacy rate – 99 per cent (2011 est)
Gross enrolment ratio (percentage of relevant age group) – primary 94 per cent; secondary 75 per cent; tertiary 38 per cent (2012 est)
Health expenditure (per capita) – US$224 (2011)
Hospital beds (per 1,000 people) – 6.2 (2011)
Life expectancy (years) – 70.12 (2014 est)
Mortality rate – 12.6 (2014 est)
Birth rate – 12.21 (2014 est)
Infant mortality rate – 12.93 (2014 est)

MONACO

Principauté de Monaco – Principality of Monaco

Area – 2 sq. km
Capital – Monaco
Major town – Monte Carlo
Currency – Euro (€) of 100 cents
Population – 30,508 growing at 0.06 per cent a year (2014 est); French (47 per cent), Monegasque (16 per cent), Italian (16 per cent) (est)
Religion – Christian (Roman Catholic 90 per cent)
Language – French (official), English, Italian, Monegasque
Population density – 18,631 per sq. km (2011)
Urban population – 100 per cent (2012)
Median age (years) – 51.1 (2014 est)
National anthem – "Hymne Monegasque' ['Hymn of Monaco']
National day – 19 November (St Rainier's Day)
Death penalty – Abolished for all crimes (since 1962)
Life expectancy (years) – 89.57 (2014 est)
Mortality rate – 9.01 (2014 est)

Birth rate – 6.72 (2014 est)
Infant mortality rate – 1.81 (2014 est)

CLIMATE AND TERRAIN

Monaco lies on 4km of steep, rugged coastline. It has been expanded by 0.3 sq. km with land reclaimed from the sea by infilling. Elevation extremes range from 140m (Mt Agel) to 0m (Mediterranean Sea). The climate is Mediterranean, with average temperatures ranging from 7.2°C in February to 22.8°C in August and September.

HISTORY AND POLITICS

Monaco has been ruled by the Grimaldi family since the 13th century. Monarchical France recognised Monaco's independence in the 15th century, but Revolutionary France annexed it in 1793. Although the prince was restored to power in 1814, Monaco did not regain its independence until 1861. It was occupied by the Italians and subsequently by the Germans in the Second World War. The principality's foreign relations and security have been aligned to those of France since 1861 by various treaties; the terms were changed in 2005 to allow Monaco greater control over its foreign relations and internal administration.

The 1962 constitution was amended in 2002 to allow the throne to pass through the female line in the absence of male heirs. Legislative power is held jointly by the prince and a 24-member National Council, which is directly elected for a five-year term. Executive power is exercised by the prince and a six-member Council of Government, headed by a minister of state who is nominated by the prince and approved by the French government. The judicial code is based on that of France.

Michel Roger replaced Jean-Paul Proust as head of the government in March 2010. In the 2013 legislative election, the Horizon Monaco Party won 20 seats, an overwhelming majority, in the legislature.

HEAD OF STATE
HSH The Prince of Monaco, Prince Albert II (Alexandre Louis Pierre), *born* 14 March 1958, *succeeded* 6 April 2005
Heir, HSH Princess Caroline von Hannover, *born* 23 January 1957

SELECTED GOVERNMENT MEMBERS *as at July 2014*
Minister of State, Michel Roger
Finance and Economy, Jean Castellini
Foreign Affairs, José Badia
Interior, Paul Masseron

EMBASSY OF THE PRINCIPALITY OF MONACO
7 Upper Grosvenor Street, London W1K 2LX
T 020-7318 1083 E embassy.uk@gouv.mc
W www.monaco-embassy-uk.gouv.mc
Ambassador Extraordinary and Plenipotentiary, Evelyne Genta, *apptd* 2010

BRITISH HONORARY CONSULATE
Contact British Consulate Marseille, 24 Avenue du Prado, 13006 Marseille
T (+33) (0) 4 9115 7210

ECONOMY AND TRADE

The economy has diversified away from its historic dependence on tourism and gambling, and over half its revenue now comes from financial services, retail, real estate, construction and light industry (chemicals, pharmaceuticals, cosmetics, medical devices, plastics, electronics).

As the state collects no taxes from individuals and little from businesses, it has become a tax haven for wealthy expatriates and foreign companies. The state retains monopolies in a number of sectors, including tobacco, the telephone network and the postal service. Since 1963 Monaco has been in a customs union with France, and through this it participates in the EU market. Over half its trade is with EU countries, particularly Italy.

GNI – US$6,075m; US$167,021 per capita (2011)
Unemployment – 0 per cent (2005 est)

COMMUNICATIONS
Transport – The nearest international airport is the Cote d'Azur airport in Nice, France; the installation of a large floating jetty in 2002 doubled the port of Monaco's capacity to handle cruise ships; there are 77km of roads and a single railway station, Monaco-Monte Carlo
Telecommunications – 44,500 fixed lines and 33,200 mobile subscriptions (2012); there were 23,000 internet users in 2009
Internet code and IDD – mc; 377 (from UK), 44 (to UK)
Media – Monaco has one television station and the principality's news is covered by the French press

MONGOLIA

Mongol Uls – *Mongolia*

Area – 1,564,116 sq. km
Capital – Ulaanbaatar; population, 999,688 (2012 est)
Major towns – Darhan, Erdenet
Currency – Tugrik of 100 mongo
Population – 2,953,190 rising at 1.37 per cent a year (2014 est); Khalkh (81.9 per cent), Kazak (3.8 per cent), Dorvod (2.7 per cent) and several others (2010 est)
Religion – Buddhist 53 per cent, none 38.6 per cent, Muslim 3 per cent, Shamanist 2.9 per cent, Christian 2.2 per cent
Language – Khalkha Mongol (official), Turkic, Russian
Population density – 2 per sq. km (2011)
Urban population – 69.5 per cent (2012 est)
Median age (years) – 27.1 (2014 est)
National anthem – 'Mongol ulsiin toriin duulal' ['National Anthem of Mongolia']
National day – 11 July (Revolution Day)
Death penalty – Abolished for all crimes (since 2012)
CPI score – 38 (83)
Literacy rate – 97 per cent (2011 est)

Gross enrolment ratio (percentage of relevant age group) – primary 117 per cent; secondary 103 per cent; tertiary 61 per cent (2012 est)
Health expenditure (per capita) – US$161 (2011)
Hospital beds (per 1,000 people) – 6.8 (2011)
Life expectancy (years) – 68.98 (2014 est)
Mortality rate – 6.38 (2014 est)
Birth rate – 20.88 (2014 est)
Infant mortality rate – 23.15 (2014 est)

CLIMATE AND TERRAIN
The eastern part of Mongolia lies on a semi-desert plateau, with steppes rising to the Mongolian Altai and Hangai mountain ranges in the west. The Gobi desert covers the southern third of the country. Elevation extremes range from 4,374m (Nayramadlin Orgil) to 560m (Hoh Nuur). The country has long, cold winters, which quickly turn into short and warm summers. The wet season runs from June to September. Average temperatures range from −20.8°C in January to 16.9°C in July.

POLITICS
The 1992 constitution was amended in 2000 to give the president the right to dissolve the legislature if it is unable to reach agreement on appointing a prime minister. The president is directly elected for a four-year term, which is renewable. The unicameral State Great Hural has 76 members who are directly elected for a four-year term. The prime minister is elected by the legislature and appoints the cabinet.

In the 2012 legislative election the Democratic Party (DP) overtook the incumbent Mongolian People's Revolutionary Party (MPRP) but failed to pick up an overall majority. The DP formed a coalition with the MPRP and Norov Altankhuyag was named prime minister in July 2012. The 2013 presidential election was won by the incumbent, Tsakhiagiin Elbegdorj (prime minister 1998, 2006–8).

HEAD OF STATE
President, Tsakhiagiin Elbegdorj, *elected* 24 May 2009, *re-elected* 26 June 2013

SELECTED GOVERNMENT MEMBERS *as at June 2014*
Prime Minister, Norov Altankhuyag
Deputy Prime Minister, D. Terbishdagva
Defence, Dashdemberel Bat-Erdene
Justice and Internal Affairs, K.H. Temuujin

EMBASSY OF MONGOLIA
7–8 Kensington Court, London W8 5DL
T 020-7937 0150 **E** office@embassyofmongolia.co.uk
W www.embassyofmongolia.co.uk
Ambassador Extraordinary and Plenipotentiary, HE Narkhuu Tulgu, *apptd* 2013

BRITISH EMBASSY
Peace Avenue 30, Bayanzurkh District, Ulaanbaatar 13381
T (+976) (11) 458 133 **E** britemb@mongol.net
W www.gov.uk/government/world/mongolia
Ambassador Extraordinary and Plenipotentiary, HE Christopher Stuart, *apptd* 2012

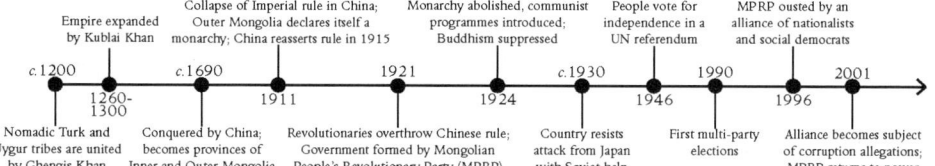

DEFENCE

Aged 16–49, 2010 est	Males	Females
Available for military service	898,546	891,192
Fit for military service	726,199	756,628

Military expenditure – US$107m (2012 est)
Conscription duration – 12 months

ECONOMY AND TRADE

The economy suffered during the transition to a market economy but recovered to show strong growth in recent years. This had faltered before the global downturn began; in 2008 declining commodity prices and export demand and soaring inflation caused difficulties that forced the government to seek an IMF loan in spring 2009. Mongolia has attracted foreign investment, particularly in mining, agricultural processing and infrastructure, but administrative corruption, dependency on imported energy supplies (mostly from Russia) and the vulnerability of the agrarian sector to climate extremes continue to hinder growth.

Deposits of copper, coal, molybdenum, fluorspar, tin, tungsten, uranium, gold and oil are being exploited; copper and gold sales are major drivers of recent economic growth (up 12.3 per cent in 2012 and 11.8 per cent in 2013). The agrarian sector, which makes up 16.5 per cent of GDP, engages 33 per cent of the workforce in agriculture and herding. The main products are grains, vegetables, forage crops, sheep, goats and other livestock. The main industries are construction, mining, processing animal products, and the production of oil, food and beverages, cashmere and natural yarns.

The main export market is China (89 per cent); the main import providers are China (37.5 per cent) and Russia (25.6 per cent). Principal exports are copper, clothing, livestock, animal products, cashmere, wool, hides, fluorspar, metals and coal. The main imports are machinery and equipment, fuels, cars, foodstuffs, industrial consumer goods, chemicals and construction materials.

GNI – US$9,592m; US$3,160 per capita (2012)
Annual average growth of GDP – 11.8 per cent (2013)
Inflation rate – 8.2 per cent (2013 est)
Population below poverty line – 29.8 per cent (2011)
Unemployment – 9 per cent (2011)
Total external debt – US$4,954m (2013 est)
Imports – US$6,739m (2012)
Exports – US$4,385m (2012)

BALANCE OF PAYMENTS
Trade – US$2,354m deficit (2012)
Current Account – US$3,362m deficit (2012)

Trade with UK	2012	2013
Imports from UK	£11,083,607	£20,752,773
Exports to UK	£5,964,051	£7,274,020

COMMUNICATIONS

Airports and waterways – The main airport is at Ulaanbaatar; there are 29 other airports around the country; the 580km of waterways are navigable in the summer months although Lake Hovsgol near the Russian border is the only waterway in commercial operation
Roadways and railways – 49,249km; 1,908km
Telecommunications – 176,700 fixed lines and 3.375 million mobile subscriptions (2012); there were 330,000 internet users in 2009
Internet code and IDD – mn; 976 (from UK), 1 44 (to UK)
Major broadcasters – Mongolian National Broadcaster is the state-owned national broadcaster

Press – There are 16 daily newspapers, including *Onoodor,* which has the biggest circulation, and *Unen* (Truth), the organ of the MPRP and the country's oldest newspaper
WPFI score – 30,3 (88)

MONTENEGRO

Crna Gora – Montenegro

Area – 13,812 sq. km
Capital – Podgorica; population, 144,000 (2009 est)
Major cities – Cetinje (historic and cultural capital), Niksic, Pljevlja
Currency – Euro (€) of 100 cents
Population – 650,036 falling at 0.49 per cent a year (2014 est); Montenegrin (45 per cent), Serbian (28.7 per cent), Bosniak (8.7 per cent), Albanian (4.9 per cent) (2011)
Religion – Christian (Orthodox 72 per cent, Roman Catholic 3.4 per cent), Muslim 19 per cent
Language – Montenegrin (a version of Serbo-Croat) (official), Serbian, Bosnian, Albanian, Croatian
Population density – 46 per sq. km (2011)
Urban population – 63.5 per cent (2012 est)
Median age (years) – 39.2 (2014 est)
National anthem – 'Oj, Svijetla Majska Zoro' ['O, Bright Dawn of May']
National day – 13 July (Statehood Day)
Death penalty – Abolished for all crimes (since 2002)
CPI score – 44 (67)
Mortality rate – 9.3 (2014 est)
Birth rate – 10.59 (2014 est)

CLIMATE AND TERRAIN

The terrain is mountainous in the north and centre of the country, intersected by deep canyons and river valleys, and falls to a narrow plain on the highly indented Adriatic coast. About 40 per cent of the country is forested. Elevation extremes range from 2,522m (Bobotov Kuk) to 0m (Adriatic Sea). The main rivers are the Piva (Drina), the Tara and the Lim. Lake Skadarsko straddles the border with Albania. The climate is Mediterranean on the coast, but more continental inland. Average temperatures in Podgorica range from 5°C in January to 26°C in July.

HISTORY AND POLITICS

The area was part of the Roman province of Illyria, and then was settled by Slavs in the seventh century. In the late 12th century it was incorporated into the medieval kingdom of Serbia and so became part of the Ottoman Empire after Serbia's defeat by the Turks in 1389. When Serbia became independent in 1878, Montenegro followed and remained an independent monarchy until the end of the First World War. In 1918, Montenegro joined with Serbia and the former Austro-Hungarian provinces of Slovenia, Croatia and Bosnia-Hercegovina to form the Kingdom of Serbs, Croats and Slovenes, which was renamed Yugoslavia in 1929. Yugoslavia was occupied by Axis forces in 1941, and after liberation it reformed as a communist federal republic in 1945. When the federation disintegrated in 1991, Serbia and Montenegro formed the Federal Republic of Yugoslavia, declared on 27 April 1992.

Montenegro's desire for independence led in 2002 to an EU-brokered agreement between the leaders of Serbia, Montenegro and the Federal Republic of Yugoslavia that restructured the republic into a union of two semi-independent states, named Serbia and Montenegro, with effect from March 2003. The agreement provided for the two republics to hold referendums on whether to retain or end the union after a minimum of three years. In a referendum held in Montenegro on 21 May 2006, 55.5 per cent voted in favour of independence, which was declared on 3 June and acknowledged by Serbia on 5 June. Montenegro joined the UN in June 2006, and formally applied for EU membership in 2008.

In the 2012 legislative election, the Coalition for a European Montenegro again won the most seats but failed to retain an overall majority. In December 2012 Milo Djukanovic became prime minister for the seventh time. In the 2013 presidential election, President Vujanovic was re-elected with 51.2 per cent of the vote.

Under the 2007 constitution, the president is directly elected for a five-year term, which is renewable once. The unicameral Assembly of the Republic of Montenegro has 81 members directly elected for a four-year term; five members are elected from the ethnic Albanian community. The prime minister appoints the cabinet, subject to the approval of the assembly.

HEAD OF STATE

President, Filip Vujanovic, *elected* 11 May 2003, *re-elected* 6 April 2008, 7 April 2013

SELECTED GOVERNMENT MEMBERS *as at June 2014*
Prime Minister, Milo Djukanovic
Deputy Prime Ministers, Igor Luksic (*Foreign Affairs*); Dusko Markovic; Vujica Lazovic; Rafet Husovic
Defence, Milica Pejanovic Djurisic
Finance, Radoje Zugic

EMBASSY OF MONTENEGRO
18 Callcott Street, London W8 7SU
T 020-7727 6007 E unitedkingdom@mfa.gov.me
Ambassador Extraordinary and Plenipotentiary, HE Ljubisa Stankovic, *apptd* 2011

BRITISH EMBASSY
Ulcinjska 8, Gorica C, 81000 Podgorica
T (+382) (20) 618 010 E podgorica@fco.gov.uk
W /www.gov.uk/government/world/montenegro
Ambassador Extraordinary and Plenipotentiary, HE Ian Whitting, *apptd* 2013

DEFENCE

Aged 16–49, 2010 est	Males	Females
Available for military service	–	–
Fit for military service	149,159	131,823

Military expenditure – US$68.3m (2013)

ECONOMY AND TRADE

Montenegro achieved fiscal autonomy from the Yugoslav federation in the 1990s. However, it faced the same problems as Serbia – slow growth, foreign debt, lack of foreign investment, high unemployment, corruption and organised crime – as well as having more limited health and education facilities, and a poor administrative capacity. Since independence, it has pursued international integration, prioritising in particular its bid for EU membership; negotiations for membership began in June 2012. It has privatised its aluminium industry and financial sector, and is attracting direct foreign investment in its growing tourism industry. The economy contracted sharply during the global downturn, leading to tax increases in 2012 and a freeze on pensions and salary increases for government workers in 2013.

The main agricultural products are tobacco, fruit and vegetables. Major industrial activities include production of steel, aluminium and consumer goods, processing of agricultural products and tourism. The main trading partners are EU and other Balkan countries.

GNI – US$4,445m; US$7,220 per capita (2012)
Annual average growth of GDP – 1.5 per cent (2013 est)
Inflation rate – 4 per cent (2012)
Population below poverty line – 6.6 per cent (2010 est)
Unemployment – 19.1 per cent (2012 est)
Total external debt – US$1,700m (2012)

BALANCE OF PAYMENTS
Current Account – US$756m deficit (2012)

Trade with UK	2012	2013
Imports from UK	£13,095,093	£15,701,513
Exports to UK	£3,744,910	£3,364,783

COMMUNICATIONS

Airports and waterways – There are five airports, including international airports at Podgorica and Tivat; the major seaport is located at Bar
Roadways and railways – There are 7,763 km of roadways and 250km of railway track linking the Adriatic port of Bar with Belgrade, via Podgorica
Telecommunications – 163,000 fixed lines and 1.13 million mobile subscriptions (2012); there were 280,000 internet users in 2009
Internet code and IDD – me; 382 (from UK), 44 (to UK)
Major broadcasters – The state-funded TV Montenegro operates two networks and a satellite channel
Press – There are four main daily newspapers: *Vijesti, Pobjeda, Republika* and *Dan*
WPFI score – 34,78 (114)

MOROCCO

Al-Mamlakah al-Maghribiyah – Kingdom of Morocco

Area – 446,550 sq. km
Capital – Rabat; population, 1,770,000 (2009 est)
Major cities – Agadir, Casablanca, Fez, Marrakesh, Meknes, Tangier
Currency – Dirham (DH) of 100 centimes
Population – 32,987,206 rising at 1.02 per cent a year (2014 est); Arab–Berber (99 per cent) (est)
Religion – Muslim 99 per cent (predominantly Sunni)
Language – Arabic (official), French, Berber dialects
Population density – 72 per sq. km (2011)
Urban population – 57.4 per cent (2012 est)
Median age (years) – 28.1 (2014 est)
National anthem – 'Hymne Chérifien' ['Hymn of the Sharif']
National day – 30 July (Throne Day)
Death penalty – Retained (last used 1993)
CPI score – 37 (91)

CLIMATE AND TERRAIN

Fertile coastal plains in the west rise to a mountainous centre, with ranges, including the Atlas range, running north-east to south-west. The Rif mountains lie along the northern, Mediterranean coast. Elevation extremes range from 4,165m (Jebel Toubkal) to −55m (Sebkha Tah). The climate is Mediterranean, becoming more extreme in the interior. Average temperatures range from 11.1°C in January to 24.7°C in August, although summer temperatures in the desert can reach over 40°C.

HISTORY AND POLITICS

From the tenth century BC, the northern coast was settled by the Phoenicians. Morocco was part of the Roman Empire from the first century AD until it was invaded by first the Vandals and then the Visigoths in the fifth and sixth centuries. Arab conquest of the area began in the seventh century but Morocco was independent from about the ninth century, successfully resisting inclusion in the Ottoman Empire in the 16th century. The current Alawite dynasty was founded in the mid-17th century. Morocco remained isolated until the mid-19th century, when the country opened up to European trade. The subsequent growth in Spanish and French influence resulted in its partition into two protectorates from 1912. In the Second World War, Morocco was a base for the Allied offensives that drove German forces out of North Africa.

Nationalist campaigning for independence began in the 1940s. French and Spanish forces withdrew in 1956, leaving Morocco independent under Sultan Mohammed V, who adopted the title of king in 1957; the coastal towns of Ceuta and Melilla remain under Spanish control. King Hassan II, who ruled from 1961 to 1999, annexed the mineral-rich Western Sahara region in 1975.

Since the accession of King Mohammed VI in 1999, Morocco has been moving away from absolute monarchy, increasing civil liberties and addressing human rights issues. Pro-reform demonstrations in spring 2011 led to a referendum in July in which an overwhelming majority voted in favour of constitutional changes that would make the prime minister, rather than the king, the head of government.

In the 2011 legislative election the Justice and Development Party (PJD) became the largest party in the House of Representatives, but its leader Abdelilah Benkirane's government collapsed when one of three other parties withdrew from the coalition in April 2013; further resignations from the newly formed government followed in July.

The head of state is a hereditary constitutional monarch. The king appoints the prime minister, who appoints the members of the council of ministers. There is a bicameral legislature; the lower house, the House of Representatives (*Majlis al-Nuwab*) has 395 members who are directly elected

for a five-year term. The House of Councillors (*Majlis al-Mustasharin*) has 270 members, elected by local councils, professional organisations and the 'salaried classes'; one-third of its members is elected every three years, to serve a nine-year term

HEAD OF STATE

HM The King of Morocco, King Mohammed VI (Sidi Mohammed Ben Hassan), *born* 21 August 1963, *acceded* 23 July 1999, *crowned* 30 July 1999
Heir, HRH Crown Prince Moulay Hassan, *born* 2003

SELECTED GOVERNMENT MEMBERS *as at June 2014*
Prime Minister, Abdelilah Benkirane
Economy and Finance, Mohamed Boussaid
Foreign Affairs, Salaheddine Mezouar
Interior, Mohamed Hassad

EMBASSY OF THE KINGDOM OF MOROCCO
49 Queen's Gate Gardens, London SW7 5NE
T 020-7581 5001 E ambalondres@maec.gov.ma
W www.moroccanembassylondon.org.uk
Ambassador Extraordinary and Plenipotentiary,
  HH Princess Lalla Joumala Aaoui, *apptd* 2009

BRITISH EMBASSY
28 Avenue SAR Sidi Mohammed, Souissi 10105 (BP45), Rabat
T (+212) (0) 537 633 333 E rabat.consular@fco.gov.uk
W www.gov.uk/government/world/morocco
Ambassador Extraordinary and Plenipotentiary, HE
  Clive Alderton, *apptd* 2012

DEFENCE

Aged 16–49, 2010 est	Males	Females
Available for military service	8,252,682	8,691,419
Fit for military service	7,026,016	7,377,045

Military expenditure – US$4,077m (2013)
Conscription duration – 18 months

ECONOMY AND TRADE

Economic liberalisation since 1999 has attracted foreign direct investment, and the industrial and service sectors are being developed. Despite steady growth, Morocco remains a poor country, with unemployment at around 9 per cent, and in 2005 the king launched a poverty-alleviation programme. The remittances of expatriate workers are crucial to the domestic economy but these, along with tourism and export demand, declined in 2008–9 owing to the global downturn; recovery is slow because of dependence on the sluggish European market and, more recently, the increasing prices in the fuel and food markets. Unemployment, poverty and illiteracy remain high in rural areas.

The large agrarian sector generates 15.1 per cent of GDP and engages 44.6 per cent of the workforce, producing cereals, citrus fruits, vegetables, wine, olives and livestock. It faces environmental problems such as desertification and soil erosion. Another major sector is the exploitation of mineral reserves, especially phosphate. Other industries include food processing, textiles, leather goods, construction and tourism. Industry accounts for 31.7 per cent of GDP and services for 53.2 per cent.

The main trading partners are EU countries, especially France and Spain. Principal exports are clothing, textiles, electrical components, inorganic chemicals, transistors, crude minerals, fertilisers, petroleum products, fruit and vegetables. The main imports are crude petroleum, fabrics, telecommunications equipment, wheat, gas and electricity.

GNI – US$93,084m; US$2,960 per capita (2012; includes Western Sahara)
Annual average growth of GDP – 5.1 per cent (2013 est)
Inflation rate – 2.5 per cent (2013 est)
Population below poverty line – 15 per cent (2007 est)
Unemployment – 9.5 per cent (2013 est)
Total external debt – US$36,510m (2013 est)
Imports – US$43,290m (2012)
Exports – US$21,291m (2012)

BALANCE OF PAYMENTS
Trade – US$21,999m deficit (2012)
Current Account – US$9,570m deficit (2012)

Trade with UK	2012	2013
Imports from UK	£605,208,097	£447,872,298
Exports to UK	£453,180,896	£505,809,249

COMMUNICATIONS
Airports and waterways – The principal airports are at Rabat, Agadir, Casablanca and Marrakesh; the main ports are Tangier, Casablanca and Agadir, on the Atlantic coast
Roadways and railways – There are 58,395km of roadways, with a 41,116km network of surfaced roads connecting the main towns, and 2,067km of railways
Telecommunications – 3.28 million fixed lines and 39.02 million mobile subscriptions (2012); there were 13.213 million internet users in 2009
Internet code and IDD – ma; 212 (from UK), 44 (to UK)
Major broadcasters – The government owns Radio-Télévision Marocaine and has a stake in 2M, the other main television network
Press – There are a number of daily newspapers, including the semi-offical *Le Matin*
WPFI score – 39,72 (136)

EDUCATION AND HEALTH
Education is compulsory between the ages of six and 15.
Literacy rate – 67 per cent (2011 est)
Gross enrolment ratio (percentage of relevant age group) – primary 116 per cent; secondary 69 per cent; tertiary 16 per cent (2012 est)
Health expenditure (per capita) – US$186 (2011)
Hospital beds (per 1,000 people) – 1.1 (2009)
Life expectancy (years) – 76.51 (2014 est)
Mortality rate – 4.79 (2014 est)
Birth rate – 18.47 (2014 est)
Infant mortality rate – 24.52 (2014 est)

WESTERN SAHARA

Al-Jumhuriyya al-'Arabiyya as-Sahrawiyya ad-Dimuqratiyya – Sahrawi Arab Democratic Republic
Area – 266,000 sq. km. Neighbours: Morocco (north), Algeria (north-east), Mauritania (east and south)
Administrative centre – El-Aaiun (Laayoune); population, 237,000 (2011 est)
Population – 538,811 rising at 2.96 per cent a year (2013 est)
Religion – Muslim (99 per cent) (est)
Language – Hassaniyya Arabic, Moroccan Arabic
Flag – Three horizontal stripes of black, white and green with a red crescent and a five-pointed star in the centre and a red triangle based on the hoist

Western Sahara came under Spanish rule in 1884, and became a province in 1934. Following Spain's withdrawal in 1976, Morocco and Mauritania annexed the territory and divided it between them. The Polisario Front declared the Western Sahara's independence as the Sahrawi Arab Democratic Republic in 1976, and began a guerrilla war to win the territory, setting up a government in exile. In 1979, Mauritania withdrew from its part of the territory, which was annexed by Morocco.

A ceasefire was established in 1991 following both sides' agreement in 1988 to UN proposals for a peace settlement, which included holding a referendum on the future status of Western Sahara. But the precise terms of the referendum have proved a sticking point and an impasse was reached that has still not been overcome, despite further negotiations in 2001–4; Polisario agreed to a referendum offering the options of independence, semi-autonomy or integration for Western Sahara, but Morocco is only prepared to accept semi-autonomy or integration. Talks have taken place intermittently since 2007 but have made no progress.

MOZAMBIQUE

Republica de Mocambique – Republic of Mozambique

Area – 799,380 sq. km
Capital – Maputo; population, 1,788,333 (2012)
Major cities – Beira, Chimoio, Matola, Nampula
Currency – New metical (MT) of 100 centavos
Population – 24,692,144 rising at 2.45 per cent a year (2014 est)
Religion – Christian (Roman Catholic 28.4 per cent, Zionist Christian 15.5 per cent, Protestant 12.2 per cent), none 18.7 per cent, Muslim 17.9 per cent
Language – Portuguese (official), Emakhuwa, Xichangana, Elomwe, Cisena, Echuwabo
Population density – 31 per sq. km (2011)
Urban population – 31.4 per cent (2012)
Median age (years) – 16.9 (2014)
National anthem – 'Patria Amada' ['Beloved Fatherland']
National day – 25 June (Independence Day)
Death penalty – Abolished for all crimes (since 1990)
CPI score – 30 (119)
Literacy rate – 56.1 per cent (2010 est)
Gross enrolment ratio (percentage of relevant age group) – primary 105 per cent; secondary 26 per cent (2012 est)
Health expenditure (per capita) – US$35 (2011)
Hospital beds (per 1,000 people) – 0.7 (2011)
Life expectancy (years) – 52.6 (2014 est)
Mortality rate – 12.34 (2014 est)
Birth rate – 38.83 (2014 est)
Infant mortality rate – 72.42 (2014 est)
HIV/AIDS adult prevalence – 11.1per cent (2012 est)

CLIMATE AND TERRAIN
Coastal plains rise to plateaux in the centre and west, with mountains on the western borders. Elevation extremes range

from 2,436m (Mt Binga) to 0m (Indian Ocean). A number of rivers run from the western highlands to the Indian Ocean coast, including the Zambezi, Limpopo, Save and Ruvuma. The climate is tropical, with average temperatures in Maputo ranging from 19°C in July to 27°C in January and February.

HISTORY AND POLITICS

Between the first and fourth centuries Mozambique was settled by Bantu peoples. Trade with India and the Arabian peninsula grew and migrants from both these regions settled in the coastal areas. From the 16th century the Portuguese established settlements on the coast and along the Zambezi, trading in gold, ivory, spices and slaves, and in the late 19th century they succeeded in conquering the interior. The area was administered as part of Portuguese India from 1751, becoming a separate colony in the late 19th century and an overseas province of Portugal in 1951. Concessions to private companies that had operated as de facto rulers over much of the country were ended in 1930.

The Frente de Libertacao de Mocambique (Frelimo) was founded in 1962 to fight for independence, and a ten-year guerrilla war against Portuguese forces began in 1964. Independence was achieved in 1975, when a one-party socialist republic was set up. Opposition to this was led from 1977 by the Resistencia Nacional de Mocambique (Renamo) and a brutal civil war broke out that lasted until 1992. Mozambique joined the Commonwealth in 1995; although it had never been under British rule, it has close relationships and a shared experience with its neighbours, all former British colonies. Reconstruction of the economy and infrastructure progressed quickly after the civil war, although a series of natural catastrophes since 2000 have been major setbacks. Additional problems are the large number of remaining landmines, and the high number of people living with HIV/AIDS.

In 1990 Frelimo abandoned Marxist-Leninism and ended one-party rule, introducing a multiparty system. The first elections under the new constitution were held in 1994 and won by Frelimo. Frelimo retained power in the 1999, 2004 and 2009 elections, prompting allegations of vote-rigging by Renamo, though monitors believe that any irregularities were minor. In the 2009 elections President Guebuza, of Frelimo, was re-elected, and Frelimo retained its overall majority in the legislature.

Under the 2004 constitution, the executive president is directly elected for a five-year term, renewable once. The unicameral Assembly of the Republic has 250 members, who are directly elected for a five-year term. The president appoints the prime minister and the council of ministers. The next presidential election is scheduled for 15 October 2014.

HEAD OF STATE
President, Armando Guebuza, elected 22 December 2004, sworn in 2 February 2005, re-elected 2009

SELECTED GOVERNMENT MEMBERS as at June 2014
Prime Minister, Alberto Clementino Vaquina
Finance, Manuel Chang
Foreign Affairs, Oldemiro Julio Marques Baloi
Interior, Ricardo Alberto Mondlane

HIGH COMMISSION FOR THE REPUBLIC OF MOZAMBIQUE
21 Fitzroy Square, London W1T 6EL
T 020-7383 3800 E sectorconsular@mozambiquehc.co.uk
W www.mozambiquehighcommission.org.uk
High Commissioner, HE Carlos Dos Santos, apptd 2011

BRITISH HIGH COMMISSION
PO Box 55, Av. Vladimir I Lenine 310, Maputo
T (+258) (21) 356 000 E maputo.consularenquiries@fco.gov.uk
W www.gov.uk/government/world/mozambique
High Commissioner, HE Joanna Kuenssberg, apptd 2014

DEFENCE

Aged 16–49, 2010 est	Males	Females
Available for military service	4,613,367	–
Fit for military service	2,677,473	2,941,073

Military expenditure – US$106m (2010)
Conscription – Men and women aged 18 to 35; 24 months (selective)

ECONOMY AND TRADE

Political stability and economic liberalisation have attracted foreign direct investment and donor support, and achieved economic growth despite setbacks from devastating flooding (2000, 2001, 2007, 2008, 2010), droughts (2002, 2003, 2009, 2010) and an earthquake (2006). But the country remains dependent on foreign aid with over half of the population living below the poverty line. The huge foreign debt has been reduced to a more manageable size by debt cancellation and rescheduling, but there is a substantial ongoing trade imbalance. Despite these problems, the economy grew by 7.4 per cent in 2012 and 7 per cent in 2013.

Agriculture and forestry are the mainstay of the economy, accounting for 28.7 per cent of GDP and engaging about 81 per cent of the workforce; shellfish, cashew nuts, cotton, sugar, citrus fruits and timber are important exports. There are considerable oil, gas, mineral and hydroelectric power resources, which are increasingly being exploited. Industries include aluminium extraction and smelting, food processing, production of beverages, chemicals, petroleum products and textiles. There are plans to expand titanium extraction and processing, and garment-manufacturing. Industry generates 24.9 per cent of GDP and services 46.4 per cent.

The main trading partners are South Africa, Belgium and China. The country also benefits from trade with its landlocked neighbours. Principal exports are aluminium, agricultural products, timber and electricity. The main imports are machinery, vehicles, fuel, chemicals, metal products, foodstuffs and textiles.

GNI – US$14,203m; US$510 per capita (2012)
Annual average growth of GDP – 7 per cent (2013 est)
Inflation rate – 4.4 per cent (2013 est)
Population below poverty line – 52 per cent (2009 est)
Total external debt – US$6,276m (2013 est)
Imports – US$6,800m (2012)
Exports – US$4,100m (2012)

BALANCE OF PAYMENTS
Trade – US$2,700m deficit (2012)
Current Account – US$3,059m deficit (2011)

Trade with UK	2012	2013
Imports from UK	£68,327,988	£45,250,709
Exports to UK	£63,462,228	£105,159,563

COMMUNICATIONS

Airports and waterways – The principal airports are at Maputo and Beira, with 21 other airports around the country; the main seaports are Maputo, Beira and Nacala, which also handle trade for neighbouring countries
Roadways and railways – Of the 30,331km of roadways, 6,303km are surfaced; there are 4,787km of railways

Telecommunications – 88,100 fixed lines and 8.12 million mobile subscriptions (2012); there were 613,600 internet users in 2009
Internet code and IDD – mz; 258 (from UK), 44 (to UK)
Major broadcasters – Radio is the principal news medium for most people, with services provided by the state broadcaster; state and privately owned television services, including Portuguese and Brazilian channels, compete for a mainly urban audience
Press – Noticias is the country's main daily and is partially owned by the government
WPFI score – 29,26 (79)

MYANMAR

Pyidaungzu Myanma Naingngandaw – Republic of the Union of Myanmar

Area – 676,578 sq. km
Capital – Naypyitaw; population, 992,000 (2009 est)
Major cities – Bago, Mandalay, Mawlamyine (Moulmein), Pathein (Bassein), Yangon (Rangoon)
Currency – Kyat (K) of 100 pyas
Population – 55,746,253 rising at 1.03 per cent a year (2014 est); Burman (68 per cent), Shan (9 per cent), Karen (7 per cent), Rakhine (4 per cent), Chinese (3 per cent), Indian (2 per cent), Mon (2 per cent) (est)
Religion – Buddhist 89 per cent, Christian 4 per cent (Baptist 3 per cent, Roman Catholic 1 per cent), Muslim 4 per cent
Language – Burmese (official), numerous ethnic languages
Population density – 80 per sq. km (2011)
Urban population – 33.2 per cent (2012 est)
Median age (years) – 27.6 (2013 est)
National anthem – 'Kaba Ma Kyei' ['Till the End of the World, Myanmar']
National day – 4 January (Independence Day)
Death penalty – Retained (last used the 1980s)
CPI score – 21 (157)

CLIMATE AND TERRAIN
Central lowlands are ringed by mountains in the west, north (part of the foothills of the Himalayas) and east. The eastern range extends down the Kra isthmus that Myanmar shares with Thailand, forming a natural border. Elevation extremes in Myanmar range from 5,881m (Hkakabo Razi) to 0m (Andaman Sea). The lowlands are drained by the Irrawaddy river and its chief tributary, the Chindwin, and the eastern mountains by the Salween. The Irrawaddy has a large delta on the Andaman coast. The climate is tropical, with a wet season from May to September. Average temperatures in Mandalay, representative of the interior lowlands, range from 20°C in January to 31°C in April and May, although temperatures in the interior can reach 44°C in May.

POLITICS
Under the 2010 constitution, the head of state is a president elected by the legislature for a five-year term, renewable once. The president is also head of government and appoints ministers with the approval of the legislature. The bicameral People's Assembly comprises the 440-member House of Representatives, the lower chamber, and the 224-member House of Nationalities. In each chamber, 25 per cent of seats are reserved for the military and the rest are directly elected; both chambers serve a five-year term. Constitutional changes require approval by a 75 per cent majority.

In preparation for legislative elections in late 2010, several electoral laws were introduced in March 2010; these excluded many political activists, such as Aung San Suu Kyi, from participation in the elections, set restrictive conditions for party registration, and tightly regulated campaigning and funding; the National League for Democracy (NLD) announced a boycott of the elections. Several members of the government resigned their military commissions to contest the elections as civilians, registering a new political party, the Union Solidarity and Development Party (USDP).

In November 2010, the USDP won 259 of the seats in the lower chamber and 129 of the seats in the upper chamber in elections that opposition groups claimed were fraudulent and were condemned internationally as a sham. The new legislature convened in January 2011, electing prime minister Thein Sein as president in February 2011. A new, nominally civilian government was sworn in on 30 March, and the dissolution of the State Peace and Development Council was announced. In April 2012, the NLD, led by Aung San Suu Kyi, contested 44 of the 46 seats in the lower house by-elections, winning 43 of them.

HEAD OF STATE
President, Chair of National Defence and Security Council,
Lt.-Gen. (retd) Thein Sein
Vice-Presidents, Mauk Kham; Adm. (retd) Nyan Tun

SELECTED GOVERNMENT MEMBERS *as at June 2014*
Defence, Vice Senior Gen. Wai Lwin
Foreign Affairs, Gen. (retd) Wunna Maung Lwin
Home Affairs, Lt.-Gen. Ko Ko

EMBASSY OF THE UNION OF MYANMAR
19A Charles Street, London W1J 5DX
T 020-7499 4340
E ambassadoroffice@myanmarembassylondon.com
W www.myanmarembassylondon.com
Ambassador Extraordinary and Plenipotentiary, HE Kyaw Zwar Minn, *apptd* 2013

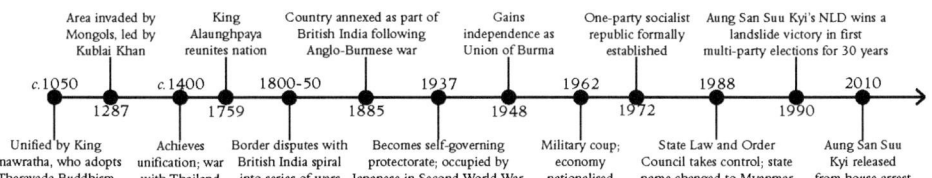

BRITISH EMBASSY
PO Box 638, 80 Strand Road, Yangon
T (+95) (1) 370 865 E be.rangoon@fco.gov.uk
W www.gov.uk/government/world/burma
Ambassador Extraordinary and Plenipotentiary, HE
    Andrew Patrick, *apptd* 2013

INSURGENCIES

Since independence in 1948 there have been various insurgencies, mostly by ethnic groups. These have included the Kachin, Kayin (Karen), Karenni, Wa, Shan, Mon, Arakan Chin and Kokang ethnic minorities. Since 1992, 18 ethnic groups have signed ceasefire agreements; the government is accused of breaking four of these since the November 2010 election. Some groups have achieved a degree of autonomy in their region; others have splintered, creating intra-ethnic tension. The country's ethnic minorities are believed to bear the brunt of the government's human rights abuses, with the Muslim Rohingya of western Burma considered one of the most oppressed peoples in the world; military offensives against insurgents have displaced over half a million people.

DEFENCE

Aged 16–49, 2010 est	*Males*	*Females*
Available for military service	14,747,845	14,710,871
Fit for military service	10,451,515	11,181,537

ECONOMY AND TRADE

Myanmar has fertile soil and an abundance of natural resources such as natural gas (it is Asia's largest exporter), timber (it is the world's largest exporter of teak), precious gems (jade, pearls, rubies and sapphires) and oil, but the economy is characterised by mismanagement and corruption. The country became increasingly poverty-stricken under military rule and 32.7 per cent of the population lives below the poverty line. The economy suffers from unpredictable policies, market distortions and inadequate commercial, transport and energy infrastructure. The regime's repressiveness lost it development aid, and attracted economic and trade sanctions, although foreign direct investment grew from US$1.9b (£1.12b) in 2011 to US$2.7b (£1.59b) in 2012. There is a large grey economy and considerable unofficial cross-border trade. In 2012 the US eased a wide range of economic restrictions following reforms implemented by president Thein Sein.

Agriculture is the dominant economic activity, accounting for 38 per cent of GDP and engaging 70 per cent of the workforce; the most important export crops are rice, pulses, beans and fish. The main industries are forestry, mining and oil and gas extraction, and these have attracted some foreign investment; manufacturing and services are struggling, and the then growing tourist industry declined dramatically after the violent suppression of demonstrations in 2007. Industry contributes 20.3 per cent of GDP and services 41.7 per cent.

The main trading partners are Thailand (40.7 per cent of exports; 20.2 per cent of imports), China (36.9 per cent of imports), Singapore and India. Principal exports are natural gas, wood products, agricultural produce, clothing and gems. The main imports are fabric, petroleum products, fertiliser, plastics, machinery, transport equipment, construction materials, crude oil and food.

Annual average growth of GDP – 6.8 per cent (2013 est)
Inflation rate – 5.7 per cent (2013 est)
Population below poverty line – 32.7 per cent (2007 est)
Unemployment – 5.2 per cent (2013 est)
Total external debt – US$5,379m (2013 est)
Imports – US$9,109m (2011)
Exports – US$9,2380m (2011)

BALANCE OF PAYMENTS

Trade – US$221m surplus (2011)
Current Account – US$1,338m deficit (2011)

Trade with UK	*2012*	*2013*
Imports from UK	£6,040,007	£12,862,636
Exports to UK	£36,876,749	£44,900,710

COMMUNICATIONS

Airports and waterways – The main airports are at Yangon and Mandalay; the 12,800km of navigable waterways include the Irrawaddy and Chindwin rivers, and the chief seaports are Yangon (Rangoon), Mawlamyine (Moulmein) and Akyab (Sittwe)
Roadways and railways – 34,377km of roadways and 5,031km of railways
Telecommunications – 556,000 fixed lines and 5.44 mobile subscriptions (2011); there were 110,000 internet users in 2009
Internet code and IDD – mm; 95 (from UK), 44 (to UK)
Major broadcasters – Democratic Voice of Burma, an opposition radio station broadcasting via short-wave from Norway, and foreign services such as the BBC and Voice of America, are key sources of information for the population; TV Myanmar is the state-run national broadcaster
Press – There are four national newspapers, all of which are tightly controlled by the government; *Kyehmon* is the principal state-run daily
WPFI score – 41,43 (145)

EDUCATION AND HEALTH

Literacy rate – 93 per cent (2011 est)
Gross enrolment ratio (percentage of relevant age group) – primary 114 per cent; secondary 50 per cent (2012 est)
Health expenditure (per capita) – US$23 (2011)
Hospital beds (per 1,000 people) – 0.6 (2004–9)
Life expectancy (years) – 65.6 (2013 est)
Mortality rate – 8.05 (2013 est)
Birth rate – 18.89 (2013 est)
Infant mortality rate – 46.31 (2013 est)

NAMIBIA

Republic of Namibia

Area – 824,292 sq. km
Capital – Windhoek; population, 342,000 (2009)
Major towns – Rundu, Walvis Bay, Oshakati
Currency – Namibian dollar of 100 cents, at parity with
    South African rand
Population – 2,198,406 rising at 0.67 per cent a year
    (2014 est); Ovambo (50 per cent), Kavangos (9 per cent),
    Herero (7 per cent), Damara (7 per cent), Nama (5 per

cent), Caprivian (4 per cent), San (Bushmen) (3 per cent), Baster (2 per cent) (est)

Religion – Christian 80 to 90 per cent (at least 50 per cent Lutheran), indigenous beliefs 10 to 20 per cent

Language – English (official), Afrikaans (lingua franca), German, Oshiwambo, Herero, Nama, other indigenous languages

Population density – 3 per sq. km (2011)

Urban population – 39 per cent (2012 est)

Median age (years) – 22.8 (2014 est)

National anthem – 'Namibia, Land of the Brave'

National day – 21 March (Independence Day)

Death penalty – Abolished for all crimes (since 1990)

CPI score – 48 (57)

Literacy rate – 88.8 per cent (2010 est)

Gross enrolment ratio (percentage of relevant age group) – primary 109 per cent (2012 est); tertiary 9 per cent (2011 est)

Health expenditure (per capita) – US$283 (2011)

Hospital beds (per 1,000 people) – 2.7 (2009)

Life expectancy (years) – 51.85 (2014 est)

Mortality rate – 13.6 (2014 est)

Birth rate – 20.28 (2014 est)

Infant mortality rate – 45.64 (2014 est)

HIV/AIDS adult prevalence – 13.3 per cent (2012 est)

CLIMATE AND TERRAIN

The Namib desert runs along the Atlantic coast and is separated by a line of hills and high veldt from the Kalahari desert in the interior. Elevation extremes range from 2,606m (Konigstein) to 0m (Atlantic Ocean). Major rivers include the Orange, which forms the southern border with South Africa, and the Zambezi, which runs through the Caprivi Strip in the extreme north-east of the country. The climate is arid in the west and semi-arid in the centre and north-east; rainfall is sparse and droughts are frequent. The coast is cooler and frequently foggy. Average temperatures in Windhoek range from 13°C in June and July to 25°C from November to January.

HISTORY AND POLITICS

Pre-colonial Namibia was inhabited by San and then by Bantu tribes. It was annexed by Germany in 1884 and named South West Africa. Indigenous uprisings against colonial settlement in the early 20th century were brutally suppressed, with some tribes suffering severe losses; the Herero and Nama were nearly wiped out. The territory was occupied by South Africa on behalf of the Allies in 1915 and after the First World War it became a League of Nations mandated territory, administered by South Africa.

The arrangement continued under the UN after the Second World War, but South Africa exceeded its mandate by effectively annexing the country, extending representation in the South African parliament to the white population in 1949, and applying apartheid in 1966. These actions were taken despite the UN's refusal to permit the country's incorporation into South Africa in 1946 and its termination of the mandate in 1966. In 1968, the UN changed the country's name to Namibia, and the South West Africa People's Organisation (SWAPO), which had campaigned for racial equality and independence since 1960, began a guerrilla war against South Africa.

South Africa's peace talks with Angola in 1988 led to agreement on independence for Namibia, and this was achieved on 21 March 1990; South Africa's Walvis Bay enclave was returned to Namibia in 1994.

The country has enjoyed stability since independence, apart from a brief period of secessionist violence in the Caprivi Strip in the late 1990s. In recent years there has been agitation for an acceleration of land reform, and the government programme moved from voluntary sales to expropriation of white-owned farms in 2005. The country's main problems arise from the demographic, economic and social impact of the high level of HIV/AIDS infection among the population.

SWAPO has been the dominant party since independence, holding the presidency and commanding a parliamentary majority without interruption. The 2004 presidential election was won by Hifikepunye Pohamba, who was re-elected in November 2009. In the 2009 legislative elections, SWAPO retained its majority in both legislative chambers. Despite SWAPO's dominance, elections in Namibia have been categorised as free by international observers and the country's media is thought to be one of the freest in Africa.

Under the 1990 constitution, the executive president is directly elected for a five-year term, renewable once. There is a bicameral parliament consisting of a National Assembly, with 72 members directly elected for a five-year term and up to six additional non-voting members appointed by the president, and a National Council, whose 26 members are elected by the regional councils from among their own members for a six-year term; the latter's main function is to review and consider legislation from the lower chamber. The president appoints the prime minister and the other ministers. The next parliamentary elections are due to be held in November 2014.

HEAD OF STATE

President, Hifikepunye Pohamba, *elected* 16 November 2004, *sworn in* 21 March 2005, *re-elected* 2009

SELECTED GOVERNMENT MEMBERS *as at June 2014*

Prime Minister, Hage Geingob

Deputy Prime Minister, Marco Hausiku

Defence, Nahas Gideon Angula

Finance, Saara Kuugongelwa-Amathila

HIGH COMMISSION FOR THE REPUBLIC OF NAMIBIA

6 Chandos Street, London W1G 9LU

T 020-7636 6244 E info@namibiahc.org.uk

W www.namibiahc.org.uk

High Commissioner, HE Steve Vemunavi Katjiuanjo, *apptd* 2013

BRITISH HIGH COMMISSION

PO Box 22202, 116 Robert Mugabe Avenue, Windhoek

T (+264) (61) 274 800 E general.windhoek@fco.gov.uk

W www.gov.uk/government/world/namibia

High Commissioner, HE Marianne Young, *apptd* 2011

DEFENCE

Aged 16–49, 2010 est	Males	Females
Available for military service	568,231	–
Fit for military service	351,431	311,513

Military expenditure – US$465m (2013)

ECONOMY AND TRADE

Namibia is a poor country, where about 55.8 per cent of the population live on US$2 a day. Its arid terrain limits agriculture, but the emphasis on environmental protection (enshrined in the constitution) is helping the development of tourism. The country has rich mineral deposits; extraction of these is the main industrial activity and minerals account for over 50 per cent of foreign exchange earnings. This leaves the economy vulnerable to global price fluctuations, and the government is encouraging foreign investment to help diversification. Other industries process the products of the farming and fisheries sectors. Agriculture operates mostly at subsistence level, accounting for 7.7 per cent of GDP.

The main trading partners are South Africa, the UK, Angola, Spain, Japan and China. Principal exports are diamonds, copper, gold, zinc, lead, uranium, cattle, processed fish and skins. The main imports are foodstuffs (particularly grain), petroleum products and fuel, machinery and equipment, and chemicals.

GNI – US$12,715m; US$5,610 per capita (2012)
Annual average growth of GDP – 4.4 per cent (2013 est)
Inflation rate – 5.5 per cent (2013 est)
Population below poverty line – 55.8 per cent (2005 est)
Unemployment – 51.2 per cent (2008 est)
Total external debt – US$4,31m (2013 est)
Imports – US$6,733m (2012)
Exports – US$4,090m (2012)

BALANCE OF PAYMENTS
Trade – US$2,643m deficit (2012)
Current Account – US$99m deficit (2009)

Trade with UK	2012	2013
Imports from UK	£143,489,176	£55,174,571
Exports to UK	£273,209,584	£77,346,165

COMMUNICATIONS
Airports and waterways – The main airports are at Windhoek and Odangwa, with 17 smaller airports around the country; the two main seaports are Walvis Bay and Luderitz
Roadways and railways – 44,138km; 2,626km
Telecommunications – 171,000 fixed lines and 2.435 million mobile subscriptions (2012); there were 127,500 internet users in 2009
Internet code and IDD – na; 264 (from UK), 44 (to UK)
Media – There are seven major newspapers, published in English, German, Afrikaans and Oshiwambo; the principal broadcaster is the state-administered Namibian Broadcasting Corporation
WPFI score – 12,50 (22)

NAURU

Republic of Nauru

Area – 21 sq. km
Capital – Yaren District (unofficial)
Currency – Australian dollar (A$) of 100 cents
Population – 9,488 rising at 0.56 per cent a year (2014 est);

Nauruan (58 per cent), other Pacific Islander (26 per cent), Chinese (8 per cent), European (8 per cent) (est)
Religion – Christian (Protestant 60.4 per cent, Roman Catholic 33 per cent)
Language – Nauruan (official), English
Urban population – 100 per cent (2012)
Median age (years) – 253 (2014 est)
National anthem – 'Nauru Bwiema' ('Song of Nauru')
National day – 31 January (Independence Day)
Death penalty – Retained (last used 1968)
Life expectancy (years) – 66.4 (2014 est)
Mortality rate – 5.9 (2014 est)
Birth rate – 25.61 (2014 est)
Infant mortality rate – 8.21 (2014 est)

CLIMATE AND TERRAIN
Nauru is a low-lying island in the southern Pacific Ocean, 42km south of the equator and 4,000km north-east of Sydney, Australia. There is a fertile coastal plain but about 60 per cent of the land area consists of the central plateau, formed of phosphate, which has been extensively mined. The plateau rim is the highest point, at 61m; the lowest is 0m at sea level. The climate is tropical, with a rainy season from November to February.

HISTORY AND POLITICS
Nauru was first settled by Polynesian and Melanesian groups. The first Europeans to visit the island were British whalers in 1798, and by 1888 Nauru was annexed by Germany. At the outbreak of the First World War, Nauru was occupied by Australia, which continued to administer the island under a League of Nations mandate from 1920. The island was occupied by the Japanese in 1942–3, but in 1947 UN trusteeship status superseded the mandate and Nauru continued to be administered by Australia until it became independent on 31 January 1968. A detention centre, established in partnership with Australia to house asylum seekers headed towards that country, has attracted controversy for its allegedly harsh conditions.

A financial crisis in 2003 caused some political instability, though a more stable period during Ludwig Scotty's second presidency (2004–7) saw the introduction of austerity measures and public sector reform. Scotty lost a vote of confidence in December 2007 and was replaced by Marcus Stephen. President Stephen resigned in 2011 amid allegations of corruption and was replaced first by Frederick Pitcherr and then former transport minister Sprent Dabwido; Baron Waqa won the 2013 presidential election. A third of the MPs elected in the 2013 legislative elections were new to parliament.

Under the 1968 constitution, the executive president is elected by the legislature from among its members for a three-year term. The unicameral parliament has 18 members, who are directly elected for a three-year term. The president appoints the cabinet. Although there are active political parties, most parliamentary candidates stand as independents.

HEAD OF STATE
President, Foreign Affairs, Baron Waqa, *elected* 11 June 2013

SELECTED GOVERNMENT MEMBERS *as at June 2014*
Finance, Justice, David Adeang
Commerce, Industry and Environment, Aaron Cook

HONORARY CONSULATE
Romshed Courtyard, Underriver, Sevenoaks, Kent TN15 0SD
T 01732-746061 E nauru@weald.co.uk
Honorary Consul, Martin Weston

BRITISH HIGH COMMISSIONER
HE Roderick Drummond, *apptd* 2013, resident at Suva, Fiji

ECONOMY AND TRADE

Phosphate is the only resource and its extraction is the sole industry, but reserves will be exhausted in 30 years. Profits derived from the mining industry were invested in trust funds to provide for the post-mining future, but heavy spending from the funds has left the country virtually bankrupt, causing it to default on loans and have assets seized in 2004. The economy is dependent on international aid (principally from Australia) and revenue from the sale of fishing licences, but diversification efforts include offshore banking and small-scale tourism.

The main trading partners are Australia and New Zealand. The only export is phosphate. All food, fuel, manufactured goods, machinery and construction materials are imported.

Unemployment – 90 per cent (2004 est)
Total external debt – US$33.3m (2004 est)

Trade with UK	2012	2013
Imports from UK	£81,066	£132,149
Exports to UK	£5,207,932	£121,502

COMMUNICATIONS

Transport – The island has one international airport and 24km of roadways
Telecommunications – 1,900 fixed lines (2009) and 6,800 mobile phone subscriptions (2012)
Internet code and IDD – nr; 674 (from UK), 44 (to UK)
Media – The government-owned Nauru Television is the island's principal broadcaster; there are no daily newspapers

NEPAL

Sanghiya Loktantrik Ganatantra Nepal – Federal Democratic Republic of Nepal

Area – 147,181 sq. km
Capital – Kathmandu; population, 1,135,970 (2012)
Major cities – Biratnagar, Lalitpur, Pokhara, Lumbini
Currency – Nepalese rupee (Rs) of 100 paisa
Population – 30,986,975 rising at 1.82 per cent a year (2014 est); Chhettri (16.6 per cent), Brahman-Hill (12.2 per cent), Magar (7.1 per cent), Tharu (6.6 per cent), Tamang (5.5 per cent), Newar (5 per cent), Kami (3.9 per cent), Yadav (3.9 per cent) (2001)
Religion – Hindu 81.3 per cent, Buddhist 9 per cent, Muslim 4.4 per cent, Kirant 3 per cent (practised by a large proportion of Nepal's Kirati population)
Language – Nepali (official), English, Maithali, Bhojpuri, Tharu, Tamang, Newar, Magar, Awadhi
Population density – 189 per sq. km (2011)

Urban population – 17.3 per cent (2012 est)
Median age (years) – 22.9 (2014 est)
National anthem – 'Sayaun Thunga Phool Ka' ['Hundreds of Flowers']
National day - 29 May (Republic Day)
Death penalty – Abolished for all crimes (since 1997)
CPI score – 31 (116)

CLIMATE AND TERRAIN

The north of Nepal lies in the Himalayas, with the snowline at about 4,880m. The terrain descends from the mountains through a hilly central region with fertile valleys to the southern plains, the Terai, that lie in the valley of the Ganges. Elevation extremes range from 8,850m (Mt Everest) to 70m (Kanchan Kalan). The climate varies from subtropical in the south to much cooler with severe winters in the north. Average temperatures in Kathmandu range from 10°C in January to 23°C from June to August. The rainy season lasts from June to September.

HISTORY AND POLITICS

Modern Nepal was formed from a number of small states that were conquered and unified in the 18th century by the Gurkha ruler Prithvi Naryan Shah. After war with the British in 1815–16, Nepal became a British-dependent buffer state; its independence was formally recognised in 1923.

Power was seized by Jung Bahdur in 1846. He assumed the title Rana and his family became hereditary chief ministers, reducing the monarchy to a purely ceremonial role and keeping the country isolated. In 1950–1, the Ranas were overthrown and the monarchy was restored to power. Apart from 1959–60, when a parliamentary system of government was in place, the kings ruled as absolute monarchs until 1990, when a new constitution was introduced that made the country a constitutional monarchy and multiparty parliamentary democracy.

However, factionalism led to frequent changes of government, causing political and social instability, which was exacerbated from 1996 by a Maoist insurgency led by the Nepal Communist Party. The insurgency began in the west and spread quickly. By 2006 the insurgents controlled 80 per cent of the country.

King Gyanendra's assumption of direct rule in 2005 led politicians to ally themselves with the Maoists to achieve the restoration of democracy, and in April 2006 the king reinstated the legislature after three months of violent pro-democracy protests. In November 2006 a peace accord was signed, an interim legislature established in January 2007 and a multiparty government took office in April.

Elections to the constituent assembly took place in April 2008; the Communist Party of Nepal–Maoists (CPN-M) won the most seats and abolished the monarchy on 28 May 2008. The assembly elected Ram Baran Yadav of the Nepali Congress party as the country's first president in July. In legislative elections in November 2013, the Nepali Congress party became the largest party, winning 105 of the 240 seats allocated by the first past the post system and 91 of the 335 allocated by proportional representation. Congress leader Sushil Koirala was then elected prime minister by parliament.

The 2007 interim constitution is in force until a new constitution is drafted by the constituent assembly and is approved. The monarchy was abolished in May 2008 and the country declared a republic. The head of state is the president, who was elected by the constituent assembly. The legislature consists of 575 directly elected members and 26 appointed by the council of ministers. Prime minister Koirala has said his government will draft a new constitution by the end of 2014.

The prime minister is appointed by consensus among the political parties or elected by a two-thirds majority of the assembly. The council of ministers is responsible to the legislature.

HEAD OF STATE
President, Ram Baran Yadav, *elected* 21 July 2008, *sworn in* 23 July 2008
Vice-President, Paramananda Jha

SELECTED GOVERNMENT MEMBERS *as at June 2014*
Prime Minister, *Defence,* Sushil Koirala
Foreign Affairs, Mahendra Bahadur Pande
Finance, Ram Sharan Mahat

EMBASSY OF NEPAL
12A Kensington Palace Gardens, London W8 4QU
T 020-7229 1594 E eon@nepembassy.org.uk
W www.nepembassy.org.uk
Ambassador Extraordinary and Plenipotentiary, vacant

BRITISH EMBASSY
PO Box 106, Lainchaur, Kathmandu
T (+977) (1) 441 0583 E bekathmandu@fco.gov.uk
W www.gov.uk/government/world/nepal
Ambassador Extraordinary and Plenipotentiary, HE Andrew James Sparkes, CMG, *apptd* 2013

DEFENCE

Aged 16–49, 2010 est	Males	Females
Available for military service	6,941,152	7,618,397
Fit for military service	5,260,878	5,947,512

Military expenditure – US$272m (2013)*

* Figure does not include paramilitary spending

ECONOMY AND TRADE
The country is one of the poorest in Asia, and the economy is dependent on foreign aid and trade with India. Tourism and hydroelectric power have potential for development, although this might compound growing environmental problems.

Agriculture is the main economic sector, generating 36.8 per cent of GDP and engaging about 75 per cent of the workforce; principal crops are pulses, rice, maize, wheat, sugar cane, jute, root crops, milk and meat. Industries other than tourism include carpets, textiles, cigarettes, cement and bricks, and the processing of rice, jute, sugar and oilseed. Industry accounts for 15.5 per cent of GDP and services for 48.7 per cent.

The main export market is India (93.9 per cent); the main import providers are India (79.4 per cent) and South Korea. Principal exports are clothing, pulses, carpets, textiles, juice, pashmina and jute goods. The main imports are petroleum products, machinery, gold, electrical goods and medicine.
GNI – US$19,145m; US$700 per capita (2012)
Annual average growth of GDP – 3.6 per cent (2013 est)
Inflation rate – 9.6 per cent (2013 est)
Population below poverty line – 25.2 per cent (2011)
Unemployment – 46 per cent (2008 est)
Total external debt – US$3,956m (2012)
Imports – US$6,499m (2012)
Exports – US$960m (2012)

BALANCE OF PAYMENTS
Trade – US$5,539m deficit (2012)
Current Account – US$181m deficit (2012)

Trade with UK	2012	2013
Imports from UK	£8,720,933	£8,1121,76
Exports to UK	£13,785,475	£16,205,634

COMMUNICATIONS
Airports – The principal airport is at Kathmandu, and there are 11 smaller airports around the country
Roadways and railways – 10,844km; 59km
Telecommunications – 834,000 fixed lines and 18.148 million mobile subscriptions (2013); there were 577,800 internet users in 2009
Internet code and IDD – np; 977 (from UK), 44 (to UK)
Major broadcasters – The state-run Nepal Television Corporation operates various channels across the country alongside numerous private operators
Press – The semi-official *The Kathmandu Post* and *The Rising Nepal* have the widest circulations of the dailies
WPFI score – 36,16 (120)

EDUCATION AND HEALTH
Literacy rate – 57 per cent (2011 est)
Health expenditure (per capita) – US$33 (2011)
Hospital beds (per 1,000 people) – 5.0 (2004–9)
Life expectancy (years) – 67.19 (2014 est)
Mortality rate – 6.62 (2014 est)
Birth rate – 21.07 (2014 est)
Infant mortality rate – 40.43 (2014 est)

THE NETHERLANDS

Koninkrijk der Nederlanden – Kingdom of the Netherlands

Area – 41,543 sq. km
Capital – Amsterdam; population, 1,059,658 (2012 est)
Seat of government – The Hague (Den Haag or, in full, 's-Gravenhage), population 629,000 (2009 est)
Major cities – Almere, Eindhoven, Rotterdam, Tilburg, Utrecht, Haarlem
Currency – Euro (€) of 100 cents
Population – 16,877,351 rising at 0.42 per cent a year (2014 est); Dutch (80.7 per cent), Indonesian (2.4 per cent), Turkish (2.2 per cent), Surinamese (2 per cent), Moroccan (2 per cent) (2008 est)
Religion – Christian (Roman Catholic 28 per cent, Protestant 19 per cent – includes Dutch Reformed 9 per cent, Protestant Church of The Netherlands 7 per cent, Calvinist 3 per cent), Muslim 5 per cent
Language – Dutch, Frisian (both official); English is widely spoken
Population density – 495 per sq. km (2011)
Urban population – 83.6 per cent (2012 est)
Median age (years) – 42.1 (2014 est)

Timeline (top labels):
- **c.700** – Part of the Frankish Empire and subsequently Middle Francia
- **c.1400** – Independent 'states' come under the rule of the Duke of Burgundy
- **1477** – 'States' come under rule of Spanish Habsburgs
- **1579** – Northern provinces, led by William of Orange, rebel against Spanish rule
- **1586** – War ends; seven northern provinces form Union of Utrecht
- **1581** – United Provinces declare independence
- **c.1600** – Golden age; world leaders in trade, art and science
- **1795** – Comes under French revolutionary rule
- **1815** – Southern and northern areas reunite; King William I becomes *Stadtholder*
- **1830** – Southern provinces secede to form Belgium
- **1867** – Duchy of Luxembourg made an independent state
- **1940-45** – Invaded and occupied by Germany
- **1948** – Forms Benelux Economic Union
- **1958** – Founder member of European Economic Community (EEC)
- **1999** – Joins eurozone

National anthem – 'Het Wilhelmus' ['The William']
National day – 30 April (Queen's Day)
Death penalty – Abolished for all crimes (since 1982)
CPI score – 83 (8)

CLIMATE AND TERRAIN

The Netherlands is a low-lying country; about a quarter is below sea level, making it susceptible to flooding despite the coastal defences and a network of dykes and canals. Its land area has been extended over the centuries by land reclamation (polders), found especially in the west around the huge freshwater lake of Yssel, created in the 1930s by damming the Zuider Zee. The country is crossed by three major European rivers, the Rhine, Maas (Meuse) and Scheldt, whose estuaries are in the south-west. Mount Scenery (862m), on the Caribbean island of Saba, is considered the highest point of the Kingdom of the Netherlands. Elevation extremes in the Netherlands itself range from 322m (Vaalserberg) to −7m (Zuidplaspolder). The climate is temperate, with average temperatures in Amsterdam ranging from 3°C in January to 16°C in July and August.

POLITICS

Under the 1983 constitution, the head of state is a hereditary constitutional monarch. The States-General *(Staten-Generaal)* consists of the First Chamber *(Eerste Kamer)* of 75 members, elected for a four-year term by the Provincial States; and the Second Chamber *(Tweede Kamer)* of 150 members, directly elected for a four-year term. The head of government is the prime minister, who is responsible to the legislature.

Although it is a stable democracy, one party has rarely commanded a sufficient parliamentary majority to govern alone in the post-war period; governments have usually been coalitions of two or more parties. In the September 2012 elections the VVD led by Mark Rutte retained its position as the largest party in the second chamber; since 2011 the VVD has been the largest party in the first chamber. In April 2013, Queen Beatrix abdicated in favour of Willem-Alexander, her eldest son.

HEAD OF STATE

HM The King of the Netherlands, King Willem-Alexander, *born* 27 April 1967; *succeeded* 30 April 2013
Heiress, HRH Princess Catharina-Amalia, *born* 7 December 2003

SELECTED GOVERNMENT MEMBERS *as at June 2014*

Prime Minister, Mark Rutte
Deputy Prime Minister, Lodewijk Asscher
Defence, Jeanine Hennis-Plasschaert
Foreign Affairs, Frans Timmermans

ROYAL NETHERLANDS EMBASSY

38 Hyde Park Gate, London SW7 5DP
T 020-7590 3200 E lon@minbuza.nl
W www.dutchembassyuk.org
Ambassador Extraordinary and Plenipotentiary, HE Laetitia van den Assum, *apptd* 2012

BRITISH EMBASSY

Lange Voorhout 10, The Hague, 2514 ED
T (+31) (70) 427 0427 E ukinnl@fco.gov.uk
W www.gov.uk/government/world/netherlands
Ambassador Extraordinary and Plenipotentiary, HE Sir Geoffrey Adams, *apptd* 2013

DEFENCE

Aged 16–49, 2010 est	Males	Females
Available for military service	3,911,098	3,817,031
Fit for military service	3,201,328	3,122,889

Military expenditure – US$10,258m (2013)

ECONOMY AND TRADE

The Netherlands has a highly industrialised and diversified market economy, and is a major European transportation hub. The economy depends heavily on foreign trade and financial services, and contracted sharply in 2009 as exports fell by almost 25 per cent in the global economic downturn. The government nationalised two banks to stabilise the financial sector and introduced stimulus measures, creating a budget deficit; the implementation of new fiscal measures in early 2011, however, reduced the budget deficit, which remained at 3.8 per cent of GDP by the end of the year. In 2013 the budget deficit decreased to 3.3 per cent of GDP, although unemployment rates and government spending remains high.

The highly mechanised agricultural sector employs only 2.3 per cent of the workforce but output supplies the food processing industries and the export as well as the domestic market. Flower bulbs and cut flowers are a major contributor to this sector, as is the fishing industry. The industrial sector contributes 25.4 per cent of GDP; major industries include food processing, and the manufacture of metal and engineering products, electrical machinery and equipment, chemicals, oil refining, construction and micro-electronics. The service industries represent 72.1 per cent of the economy. Other EU countries, China and Russia account for most overseas trade. Principal exports are machinery and equipment, chemicals, fuels and foodstuffs. The main imports are machinery and transport equipment, chemicals, fuels, foodstuffs and clothing.

GNI – US$777,825m; US$47,970 per capita (2012)
Annual average growth of GDP – −1.3 per cent (2013 est)
Inflation rate – 2.8 per cent (2013 est)
Population below poverty line – 10.5 per cent (2005)
Unemployment – 6.8 per cent (2013 est)
Total external debt – US$2,504,000m (2012 est)
Imports – US$501,163m (2012)
Exports – US$554,699m (2012)

BALANCE OF PAYMENTS

Trade – US$53,536m surplus (2012)
Current Account – US$77,839m surplus (2012)

Trade with UK	2012	2013
Imports from UK	£23,986,591,325	£23,896,428,937
Exports to UK	£31,194,775,370	33,956,909,810

COMMUNICATIONS

Airports – The principal airports are at Amsterdam, Rotterdam, Eindhoven and Maastricht, with a further 19 airports around the country

Waterways – The main seaport is Rotterdam, although there are a number of other ports on river estuaries or linked to the coast by the canals; 6,237km of inland waterways are navigable by ships of up to 50 tonnes. The large merchant fleet includes 744 ships of over 1,000 tonnes

Roadways and railways – There are 139,295km of roads and 3,013km of railways, of which 2,195km are electrified

Telecommunications – 7.086 million fixed lines and 19.643 million mobile subscriptions (2012); there were 14.872 million internet users in 2009

Internet code and IDD – nl; 31 (from UK), 44 (to UK)

Major broadcasters – A competitive broadcasting sector includes Nederlandse Omroep Stichting (NOS), which oversees the country's broadcasting

Press – There are seven national daily newspapers, including *Algemeen Dagblad, NRC Handelsblad* and *De Telegraaf*

WPFI score – 6,46 (2)

EDUCATION AND HEALTH

Education is free and compulsory for 13 years.

Gross enrolment ratio (percentage of relevant age group) – primary 108 per cent; secondary 128 per cent; tertiary 76 per cent (2012 est)

Health expenditure (per capita) – US$5,995 (2011)

Hospital beds (per 1,000 people) – 4.7 (2009)

Life expectancy (years) – 81.12 (2014 est)

Mortality rate – 8.57 (2014 est)

Birth rate – 10.83 (2014 est)

Infant mortality rate – 3.66 (2014 est)

OVERSEAS TERRITORIES

The Kingdom of the Netherlands consists of four autonomous elements: the Netherlands (European and Caribbean Netherlands), Aruba, Curacao and St Maarten; the latter two were part of the Netherlands Antilles until its dissolution on 10 October 2010. The other three islands of the Netherlands Antilles, the 'Caribbean Netherlands', comprising Bonaire, St Eustatius and Saba, are now autonomous special municipalities of the Netherlands.

ARUBA

Area – 180 sq. km

Capital – Oranjestad; population, 37,000 (2011)

Major town – Sint Nicolaas

Currency – Aruban florin of 100 cents

Population – 110,663 rising at 1.39 per cent a year (2013 est)

Language – Dutch (official), Papiamento, Spanish, English

National Day – 18 March (Flag Day)

The Caribbean island was colonised by the Dutch in the 17th century. It was part of the Netherlands Antilles until 1986, when it became a separate, autonomous territory. The Dutch government is responsible for external affairs and represented by a resident governor. Internal government is in the hands of the prime minister and council of ministers, who are responsible to the 21-member unicameral legislature (*Staten*), directly elected for a four-year term.

The principal economic activities are tourism and offshore financial services.

Governor, Fredis Refunjol, *apptd* 2004

Prime Minister, Mike Eman, *elected* 2009

CURACAO

Area – 444 sq. km

Capital – Willemstad; population, 146,836 (2013 est)

Currency – Caribbean guilder of 100 cents

Population – 146,836 (2013 est)

Language – Dutch (official), Papiamento, English, Spanish

The island was colonised by the Dutch in the 17th century and was part of the Netherlands Antilles from 1954 until 10 October 2010, when it became a separate, autonomous territory. The Dutch government is responsible for external affairs and represented by a resident governor. Internal affairs are in the hands of a prime minister and council of ministers, who are responsible to the 21-member unicameral legislature (*Staten*), which serves a four-year term.

The principal economic activities are tourism, oil refining and offshore financial services.

Acting Governor, Adele ven der Pluijm-Vrede, *apptd* 2012

Prime Minister, Daniel Hodge, *elected* 2012

ST MAARTEN

Area – 34 sq. km

Capital – Philipsburg

Currency – Caribbean guilder of 100 cents

Population – 39,689 (2013)

Language – Dutch, English (official), Spanish, Creole

The territory forms the southern part of the island of St Martin in the Caribbean; the north is French territory. Possession of the island was disputed between the Dutch and the Spanish until 1648, when the Spanish relinquished it to the Dutch and French, who divided it between them. The Dutch territory was part of the Netherlands Antilles from 1954 until 10 October 2010, when it became a separate, autonomous territory. The Dutch government is responsible for external affairs and represented by a governor. Internal affairs are in the hands of a prime minister and council of ministers, who are responsible to the 15-member unicameral legislature *(Staten),* which serves a four-year term.

The principal economic activities are tourism and sugar production.

Governor, Eugene Holiday, *apptd* 2010

Prime Minister, Sarah Westcott-Williams, *apptd* 2010

NEW ZEALAND

Aotearoa – *New Zealand*

Area – 267,710 sq. km (includes outlying islands)

Capital – Wellington; population, 391,000 (2009)

Major cities – Auckland, Christchurch, Dunedin, Hamilton, Manakau, North Shore, Tauranga, Waitakere

Currency – New Zealand dollar (NZ$) of 100 cents

Population – 4,401,916 rising at 0.83 per cent a year (2014 est); European (71.2 per cent), Maori (14.1 per cent), Asian (11.3 per cent), Pacific Islander (7.6 per cent) (2013)
Religion – Christian (Protestant 22.8 per cent, Roman Catholic 11.6 per cent, Anglican 10.8 per cent), Hindu 2.1 per cent
Language – English, Maori (both official)
Population density – 17 per sq. km (2011)
Urban population – 86.3 per cent (2012 est)
Median age (years) – 37.6 (2014 est)
National anthem – 'God Defend New Zealand'/'God Save the Queen'
National day – 6 February (Waitangi Day)
Death penalty – Abolished for all crimes (since 1989)
CPI score – 91 (1)

CLIMATE AND TERRAIN

New Zealand consists of North Island, South Island and neighbouring coastal islands such as Stewart Island, and outlying islands that include the Chatham, Kermadec, Three Kings, Bounty, Antipodes, Snares, Auckland and Campbell groups in the South Pacific Ocean. The two larger islands, North Island and South Island, are separated by the relatively narrow Cook Strait. The island groups are much smaller and more widely dispersed.

Much of the North and South Islands is mountainous. The North Island mountains include several volcanoes, three of which are active. The principal range is the Southern Alps, extending the entire length of the South Island to the west of the Canterbury Plains. There are geysers and hot springs in the Rotorua district and glaciers in the Southern Alps. Elevation extremes range from 3,754m (Aoraki/Mt Cook) to 0m (Pacific Ocean). The climate is temperate, though with marked regional variations; average temperatures in Christchurch (South Island) range from 5.8°C in July to 17.2°C in January. The country is subject to seismic activity; a major earthquake devastated Christchurch in February 2011.

HISTORY AND POLITICS

Settled by Polynesian tribes, the ancestors of the Maori, from about the tenth century, New Zealand was sighted by the Dutch navigator Abel Tasman in 1642 but he did not land. The British explorer James Cook surveyed the coastline in 1769, the year in which the islands were claimed by the British. The Maori accepted British sovereignty in 1840, under the Treaty of Waitangi, in return for land rights and the rights of British subjects. Large-scale European immigration and the 1860s gold rush led to encroachment by settlers and 'land wars' with the Maori in 1860 and 1872; Maori resistance was defeated but concessions such as parliamentary representation were won. A tribunal was set up in 1975 to consider grievances caused by breaches of the Waitangi Treaty, and in the 1990s the Maori were compensated for land lost to European settlers.

New Zealand was administered as part of Britain's New South Wales colony until 1841, when it became a separate colony. In 1907 it was granted dominion status; in 1931 the Statute of Westminster tacitly acknowledged its independence, which was formally confirmed in 1947.

New Zealand forces took part in the Boer War, both world wars, the Korean War and the Vietnam War. Since the UK's entry into the EEC in 1973, the focus of New Zealand's foreign and trade policies has shifted to Asia and the Pacific region.

Post-war politics has been dominated by the National Party and the Labour Party, either forming governments on their own or in coalition with smaller parties; coalitions have been the norm since a proportional representation voting system was introduced in 1993. In the 2011 legislative election, the National Party won the most seats but failed to gain a majority. The 2014 legislative elections were won by the New Zealand National Party.

There is no written constitution. The head of state is Queen Elizabeth II, represented by the governor-general, who is appointed on the advice of the New Zealand government. The unicameral House of Representatives currently has 122 members (usually 120), elected for a three-year term; there are 70 members from single-member constituencies, which include seven Maori constituencies, and 52 (usually 50) allocated from party lists; if a party wins a significantly larger proportion of constituency seats relative to their party list vote, this can result in an 'overhang' of extra seats. The prime minister and cabinet are appointed by the governor-general on the advice of the legislature. New legislative elections were due to be held on 20 September 2014.

GOVERNOR-GENERAL
Governor-General, HE Lt.-Gen. Sir Jerry Mateparae, *sworn in* August 2011

SELECTED GOVERNMENT MEMBERS *as at September 2014*
Prime Minister, John Key
Deputy Prime Minister, Finance, Bill English
Defence, Jonathan Coleman
Internal Affairs, Peter Dunne

NEW ZEALAND HIGH COMMISSION
New Zealand House, 80 Haymarket, London SW1Y 4TQ
T 020-7930 8422 E email@newzealandhc.org.uk
W www.nzembassy.com/uk
High Commissioner, HE Sir Lockwood Smith, *apptd* 2013

BRITISH HIGH COMMISSION
44 Hill Street, Thorndon, Wellington 6011
T (+64) (4) 924 2888 E consularmail.wellington@fco.gov.uk
W www.gov.uk/government/world/new-zealand
High Commissioner, HE Jonathan Sinclair, *apptd* 2014

DEFENCE

With Australia and the USA, New Zealand formed the ANZUS Pacific Security Treaty in 1951, but its non-nuclear military policy led to disagreements with the USA and France in 1985, and in 1986 the USA suspended its ANZUS obligations towards New Zealand.

Aged 16–49, 2010 est	*Males*	*Females*
Available for military service	1,019,798	1,003,429
Fit for military service	843,526	828,779

Military expenditure – US$1,732m (2013)

ECONOMY AND TRADE

Since the 1980s industrial and service sectors have superseded the large, efficient agricultural sector. Growth has been driven by trade, particularly in agricultural products, but various factors had pushed the economy into recession in 2008 before the global downturn. Government stimulus measures were introduced to cushion the effects of the recession in 2009, after which a fragile recovery began. Growth of about 2 per cent was achieved in 2010–13.

The agricultural sector contributes 5 per cent of GDP and employs 7 per cent of the workforce. The main products are dairy products, meat, cereals, pulses, fruit, vegetables, wool and fish. The major industries are food processing, wood and paper products, textiles, machinery, transport equipment, financial services, mining, and tourism, which is overtaking agriculture as the main source of foreign exchange revenue. Non-metallic minerals such as coal, limestone and dolomite are heavily exploited, and gold and iron production is economically important. Natural gas deposits in offshore and onshore fields are used for electricity generation, though a significant amount of the country's energy is derived from sustainable sources such as hydroelectric power. Industry contributes 25.5 per cent of GDP and services 69.5 per cent.

The main trading partners are Australia, China, the USA and Japan. Principal exports are dairy products, meat, wood, wood products, fish and machinery. The main imports are machinery and equipment, vehicles and aircraft, petroleum, electronics, textiles and plastics.

GNI – US$154,294m; US$30,640 per capita (2011)
Annual average growth of GDP – 2.5 per cent (2013 est)
Inflation rate – 1.3 per cent (2013 est)
Unemployment – 6.4 per cent (2013 est)
Total external debt – US$81,360m (2013 est)
Imports – US$37,818m (2012)
Exports – US$37,383m (2012)

BALANCE OF PAYMENTS
Trade – US$435m deficit (2012)
Current Account – US$8,507m deficit (2012)

Trade with UK	2012*	2013**
Imports from UK	£569,937,672	£601,067,549
Exports to UK	£861,459,695	£845,900,198

* Includes Tokelau, Cook Islands and Niue
** Includes Cook Islands and Niue

COMMUNICATIONS
Airports and waterways – The principal airports are at Auckland, Wellington (North Island), Christchurch and Dunedin (South Island) and there are 39 smaller airports around the country; Tauranga, Christchurch, New Plymouth, Auckland and Napier are the main seaports
Roadways and railways – There are 94,160km of roadways, of which 62,759 km are surfaced, and 4,128km of railways
Telecommunications – 1.88 million fixed lines and 4.82 million mobile subscriptions (2012); there were 3.4 million internet users in 2009
Internet code and IDD – nz; 64 (from UK), 44 (to UK)
Major broadcasters – The state-owned Television New Zealand competes with two other private networks; Niu FM is the national government-funded station for the Pacific island communities
Press – The Auckland-based *New Zealand Herald* has the largest circulation, alongside Wellington-based *Dominion Post* and Christchurch-based *The Press*
WPFI score – 8,55 (9)

EDUCATION AND HEALTH
Education is free of charge and compulsory between the ages of 5 and 16.
Gross enrolment ratio (percentage of relevant age group) – primary 100 per cent; secondary 120 per cent; tertiary 81 per cent (2012)
Health expenditure (per capita) – US$3,666 (2011)
Hospital beds (per 1,000 people) – 2.3 (2011)
Life expectancy (years) – 80.93 (2014 est)
Mortality rate – 7.3 (2014 est)

Birth rate – 13.4 (2014 est)
Infant mortality rate – 4.59 (2014 est)

TERRITORIES

TOKELAU
Area – 12 sq. km
Population – 1,337 (2014 est)

Tokelau consists of three atolls, Fakaofo, Nukunonu and Atafu, in the southern Pacific Ocean. Formerly part of Britain's Gilbert and Ellice Islands colony, Tokelau was transferred to New Zealand administration in 1926 and proclaimed part of New Zealand in 1949.

The territory is self-administering, but has rejected greater autonomy in two referendums (2006 and 2007). The Council for the Ongoing Government (cabinet) comprises three *Faipule* (village leaders) and three *Pulenuku* (village mayors), one from each atoll; the position of *Ulu-o-Tokelau* (leader) is rotated among the three *Faipule* members annually. The *General Fono,* which has 20 members elected for a three-year term, has legislative powers. Each atoll has a *Taupulega* (council of elders).

The economy is dependent on New Zealand budgetary aid, with some revenue derived from remittances and the sale of fishing rights, stamps, coins and the use of its internet suffix. The main activities are subsistence farming, copra production and handicrafts. In 2011 Tokelau changed its position within the international dateline in order to improve trade links with Australia and New Zealand.
Administrator, Jonathan Kings, *apptd* 2011

THE ROSS DEPENDENCY
New Zealand has administrative responsibility for the Ross Dependency. This is defined as all the Antarctic islands and territories between 160° E. and 150° W. longitude which are situated south of the 60° S. parallel, including Edward VII Land and portions of Victoria Land (*see also* The North and South Poles).

ASSOCIATED STATES

COOK ISLANDS
Area – 236 sq. km
Population – 10,134 (2013 est)
Capital – Avarua, on Rarotonga

The Cook Islands consist of 15 volcanic islands and coral atolls in the southern Pacific Ocean. A former British protectorate, since 1965 the islands have been self-governing in free association with New Zealand.

Queen Elizabeth II has a representative on the islands, and the New Zealand government is represented by a high commissioner. There is a 24-member legislative assembly, and the House of Ariki, made up of 15 traditional leaders who advise on traditional matters. Executive power is exercised by a prime minister and a cabinet responsible to the legislature.

The main economic activities are tourism, agriculture (especially tropical fruits), fruit processing, fishing, garment manufacturing, handicrafts and pearl-farming; black pearls are the main export.
HM Representative, Sir Frederick Goodwin, KBE, *apptd* 2001
Prime Minister, Henry Puna *apptd* 2010

NIUE
Area – 260 sq. km
Population – 1,190(2013 est)
Capital – Alofi; population, 547 (2009 est)

Although part of the Cook Islands group, Niue was administered separately after 1903. Since 1974 the island has been self-governing in free association with New Zealand.

A New Zealand high commissioner represents both the Queen and the New Zealand government. There is a 20-member legislative assembly; executive power is exercised by a prime minister and a three-member cabinet drawn from the assembly's members.

The principal economic activities are agriculture, fishing, tourism, handicrafts, food processing and the sale of postage stamps and the use of its internet suffix.

New Zealand High Commissioner, Ross Ardern, *apptd* 2014
Premier, Toke Talagi

NICARAGUA

República de Nicaragua – Republic of Nicaragua

Area – 130,370 sq. km
Capital – Managua; population, 967,708 (2012)
Major cities – Chinandega, Estelí, León, Masaya, Tipitapa
Currency – Córdoba (C$) of 100 centavos
Population – 5,848,641 rising at 1.02 per cent a year (2014 est)
Religion – Christian (Roman Catholic 58.5 per cent, Protestant 23.2 per cent), none 15.7 per cent
Language – Spanish (official), English, Miskito
Population density – 49 per sq. km (2011)
Urban population – 57.8 per cent (2012 est)
Median age (years) – 24.2 (2014 est)
National anthem – 'Salve a ti, Nicaragua' ['Hail to Thee, Nicaragua']
National day – 15 September (Independence Day)
Death penalty – Abolished for all crimes (since 1979)
CPI score – 28 (127)

CLIMATE AND TERRAIN
The narrow Pacific coastal plain is broken by active volcanoes and lakes Managua and Nicaragua. A mountainous central region separates it from the broad Atlantic coastal plain, which constitutes 60 per cent of the country and is covered by tropical rainforest. Elevation extremes range from 2,438m (Mogoton) to 0m (Pacific Ocean). The climate is generally tropical on the plains but cooler at altitude; the average temperature in Managua is 27°C. The country is subject to frequent earthquakes.

HISTORY AND POLITICS
Nicaragua was originally populated by tribes related to the Aztec, Maya and other indigenous people. Fossilised footprints, the oldest in South America, indicate a human presence in Nicaragua dating back 6,000 years. Spanish colonisation began in 1523 but in the 17th and 18th centuries the British were the dominant presence on the Caribbean coast, with the Spanish controlling the Pacific plain. Independence from Spain was achieved in 1821 and the area was initially incorporated into Mexico. In 1823 it became part of a Central American federation of former Spanish provinces but seceded and became fully independent in 1838. British control of the Caribbean coast was ceded to Nicaragua in 1860.

In 1893, General José Santos Zelaya established a dictatorship that lasted until 1909, when he was overthrown by US troops. General Anastasio Somoza established a dictatorship in 1938 and ruled until his assassination in 1956, when he was succeeded as president by his sons Luis (1956–67) and Anastasio (1967–79). After 44 years in power, the family was overthrown in 1979 in a popular revolt led by the Frente Sandinista de Liberacíon Nacional (FSLN), popularly known as the Sandinistas.

The Sandinistas' socialist government redistributed land and promoted education and health services, but was opposed by US-backed right-wing guerrillas (the Contras). The civil war lasted from 1982 until 1990 (although there was a ceasefire from 1988), when the Sandinistas were unexpectedly defeated in elections by a coalition of opposition parties.

From 1990 to 2006, governments were liberal or liberal-dominated coalitions, keeping the FSLN from power even though it was often the largest party in the legislature. However, in the 2006 presidential and legislative elections, the FSLN candidate, Daniel Ortega (president 1984–90), was elected president and the FSLN became the largest party in the assembly. Ortega was re-elected in the 2011 presidential election, picking up over 62 per cent of the vote; his FSLN party won an outright majority in the country's legislative election, also in 2011.

In 2009 the Supreme Court lifted the ban on a president serving two consecutive terms and in January 2014 the National Assembly eliminated constitutional term limits for the presidency altogether, potentially allowing President Ortega to run for re-election in 2016. Opposition parties have labeled the chages undemocratic. The executive president is directly elected for a five-year term, which may be renewed only once. The unicameral National Assembly has 90 members directly elected for a five-year term; unsuccessful presidential and vice-presidential candidates may be awarded a seat if they receive more than the average percentage of the vote in each electoral district. The cabinet is appointed by the president.

HEAD OF STATE
President, Daniel Ortega, *re-elected* 6 November 2011, *sworn in* 11 January 2012
Vice-President, Moises Omar Halleslevens

SELECTED GOVERNMENT MEMBERS *as at June 2013*
Defence, Martha Elena Ruiz
Finance, Ivan Acosta Montalvan
Foreign Affairs, Samuel Santos Lopez
Interior, Ana Isabel Morales Mazún

EMBASSY OF NICARAGUA
Suite 31, Vicarage House, 58–60 Kensington Church Street, London W8 4DP
T 020-7938 2373
Ambassador Extraordinary and Plenipotentiary, HE Carlos Argüello-Gomez, *apptd* 2010

BRITISH AMBASSADOR
Ambassador Extraordinary and Plenipotentiary, HE Sharon Campbell, resident at San José, Costa Rica

DEFENCE

Aged 16–49, 2010 est	Males	Females
Available for military service	1,452,107	1,552,698
Fit for military service	1,227,757	1,335,653

Military expenditure – US$81.3m (2013)
Conscription duration – 18–36 months (voluntary)

ECONOMY AND TRADE

Progress towards economic recovery and reconstruction after the civil war has been slow and the country remains the poorest in Central America. The economy contracted in 2009 as the global downturn reduced key commodity prices, export demand and remittances (worth almost 15 per cent of GDP). Although almost 80 per cent of debt was cancelled in 2004 and 2006, the government is dependent on foreign aid and 42.5 per cent of the population lives below the poverty line. The economy grew 4.6 per cent in 2013, despite a 33 per cent decline in coffee export revenues due to fungus which infected crops

Agriculture is the mainstay of the economy, accounting for 17.1 per cent of GDP and 31 per cent of employment. The main commercial crops are coffee, beef, shellfish, tobacco, sugar and peanuts. Industry includes food and timber processing, mining, the manufacture of chemicals, machinery, metal products, textiles, clothing and footwear, oil refining and tourism. Industry contributes 25.5 per cent of GDP and services 57.5 per cent.

The main trading partners are the USA and other central and south American countries. Principal exports are the main commercial crops and gold. The main imports are consumer goods, machinery and equipment, raw materials and petroleum products.

GNI – US$10,215m; US$1,650 per capita (2012)
Annual average growth of GDP – 4.2 per cent (2013 est)
Inflation rate – 7.4 per cent (2012 est)
Population below poverty line – 42.5 per cent (2009)
Unemployment – 7.2 per cent (2013 est)
Total external debt – US$8,160m (2013 est)
Imports – US$5,847m (2012)
Exports – US$2,644m (2012)

BALANCE OF PAYMENTS
Trade – US$3,204m deficit (2012)
Current Account – US$1,354m deficit (2012)

Trade with UK	2012	2013
Imports from UK	£5,580,968	£6,092,469
Exports to UK	£26,778,835	£23,157,424

COMMUNICATIONS

Airports – The main airport is at Managua, and there are a further 11 airports around the country
Waterways – The chief ports are Corinto (Pacific) and Bluefields and El Bluff (Caribbean); there are 2,220km of inland waterways, mostly on lakes Managua and Nicaragua
Roadways – There are 23,897km of roadways; the Inter-American Highway runs between Nicaragua's Honduran and Costa Rican borders, and the Inter-Oceanic Highway runs from Corinto on the Pacific coast via Managua to Rama, where there is a natural waterway to Bluefields on the Caribbean
Telecommunications – 320,000 fixed lines and 5.346 million mobile subscriptions (2012); there were 199,800 internet users in 2009

Internet code and IDD – ni; 505 (from UK), 44 (to UK)
Major broadcasters – There are several commercial television and radio broadcasters, including Nicavision Canal 12 and Radio Mundial
Press – *La Pensa* and *El Nuevo Diario* are the country's two principal daily newspapers
WPFI score – 27,70 (71)

EDUCATION AND HEALTH
Literacy rate – 78 per cent (2010 est)
Gross enrolment ratio (percentage of relevant age group) – primary 117 per cent; secondary 69 per cent (2012 est)
Health expenditure (per capita) – US$125 (2011)
Hospital beds (per 1,000 people) – 1.1 (2011)
Life expectancy (years) – 72.72 (2014 est)
Mortality rate – 5.07 (2014 est)
Birth rate – 18.41 (2014 est)
Infant mortality rate – 20.36 (2014 est)

NIGER

République du Niger – Republic of Niger

Area – 1,267,000 sq. km
Capital – Niamey; population, 1,141,372 (2012)
Major cities – Agadez, Maradi, Zinder
Currency – Franc CFA of 100 centimes
Population – 17,466,172 rising at 3.28 per cent a year (2014 est); Hausa (55.4 per cent), Djerma (21 per cent), Tuareg (9.3 per cent), Fulani (8.5 per cent), Kanouri Manga (4.7 per cent) (2001)
Religion – Muslim 80 per cent, other (includes indigenous beliefs and Christian) 20 per cent
Language – French (official), Arabic, Hausa, Djerma
Population density – 13 per sq. km (2011)
Urban population – 18.1 per cent (2012 est)
Median age (years) – 15.1 (2014 est)
National anthem – 'La Nigérienne' ['The Nigerian']
National day – 18 December (Republic Day)
Death penalty – Retained (no known use since 1976)
CPI score – 34 (106)
Literacy rate – 28.7 per cent (2010 est)
Gross enrolment ratio (percentage of relevant age group) – primary 85 per cent; secondary 44 per cent (2012 est); tertiary 1.5 per cent (2011 est)
Health expenditure (per capita) – US$20 (2011)
Hospital beds (per 1,000 people) – 0.3 (2004–9)
Life expectancy (years) – 54.74 (2014 est)
Mortality rate – 12.73 (2014 est)
Birth rate – 46.12 (2014 est)
Infant mortality rate – 86.27 (2014 est)

CLIMATE AND TERRAIN

Niger is mostly desert, with low hills in the north and savannah in the south. Elevation extremes range from 2,022m (Mt Idoukal-n-Taghes/Bagzane) to 200m (Niger River). The Niger valley in the south-west is the only well-watered area. There is a desert climate, except in the extreme south which is sub-tropical. Average temperatures in Niamey range from 24°C in January to 33°C in April and May.

HISTORY AND POLITICS

The area was divided between several kingdoms formed by different tribes (Tuareg, Songhai, Hausa, Fulani) from the tenth to 19th centuries. French colonial expansion from the 1880s brought the whole area under its control in 1898 and in 1904 it became part of French West Africa. The country became autonomous in 1958 and achieved full independence in 1960.

The first president introduced a one-party regime, which continued under the military government installed after a coup in 1974. Following popular agitation, civilian government was reintroduced in 1989, other parties were legalised in 1990, and multi-party elections held in 1993. This political liberalisation was reversed following a military coup in 1996 led by Brig. Ibrahim Barre Mainassara. He was assassinated in 1999 by the military, who restored political pluralism.

From 1990 there was a rebellion in the north by Tuareg seeking greater social equality and political representation. Peace agreements with rebel groups in 1995 and 1997 brought calm until 2007, when a new rebel group emerged, seeking greater autonomy and access to mining revenue; this group signed a ceasefire with the government in 2009.

After seeking to increase his powers in 2009, President Mamadou Tandja (first elected in 1999) was deposed in February 2010 by the military. A referendum on a new constitution was held in October 2010, and presidential and legislative elections were held in January 2011. The Nigerien Party for Democracy and Socialism (PNDS-Tarayya) won the most seats, but without a majority; in August 2013 a unity government was declared under prime minister Brigi Rafini. The PNDS-Tarayya leader Mamadou Issoufou was elected president in the second round of voting in March 2011.

The 2010 constitution reduced the president's powers and restored the limit on presidential terms. The executive president is directly elected for a five-year term, renewable once. The unicameral National Assembly has 113 members directly elected for a five-year term. The prime minister is appointed by the president.

HEAD OF STATE

President, Mahamadou Issoufou, *elected* 12 March 2011, *took office* 7 April 2011

SELECTED GOVERNMENT MEMBERS *as at June 2014*
Prime Minister, Brigi Rafini
Finance, Gilles Bayet
Foreign Affairs, Bazoum Mohamed
Interior, Massaoudou Hassoumi

EMBASSY OF THE REPUBLIC OF NIGER
154 rue de Longchamp, 75116 Paris, France
T (+33) (1) 4504 8060 **W** www.ambassadeniger-fr.org
Ambassador Extraordinary and Plenipotentiary, HE
   Abderahamane Assane Mayaki,

BRITISH AMBASSADOR
HE Joanne Adamson, *apptd* 2014, resident at Bamako, Mali

DEFENCE

Aged 16–49, 2010 est	Males	Females
Available for military service	3,329,184	3,267,669
Fit for military service	2,194,570	2,219,416

Military expenditure – US$75.2m (2012)
Conscription duration – 24 months (selective)

ECONOMY AND TRADE

Niger is one of the poorest countries in the world, with 63 per cent of the population living below the poverty line. Economic progress has been hampered by political instability, recurrent droughts (most recently in 2009–10), desertification, over-grazing and rapid population growth, leaving the country dependent on foreign aid, which makes up over half of government revenue. Its huge foreign debt burden was much reduced by debt relief and cancellation in 2000 and 2005. Niger has large reserves of oil and has produced and refined oil since 2012; exports are expected to grow to 2016.

The mainstay of the economy is currently subsistence agriculture and herding, which accounts for 35.2 per cent of GDP and engages 90 per cent of the population; the main cash crops are cowpeas, cotton, vegetables, cereals and livestock. The most significant export is uranium, making the economy vulnerable to fluctuations in global prices; efforts are being made to diversify into exploitation of other mineral resources, including gold and oil. The other industries include processing agricultural products and manufacturing cement, bricks, soap, textiles and chemicals. Industry contributes 14.2 per cent of GDP and services 50.6 per cent.

The main trading partners are Nigeria (40.3 per cent of exports), the USA and France. Principal exports are uranium ore, livestock, cowpeas and onions. The main imports are foodstuffs, machinery, vehicles and parts, petroleum and cereals.

GNI – US$6,656m; US$390 per capita (2012)
Annual average growth of GDP – 6.2 per cent (2012 est)
Inflation rate – 1.9 per cent (2013 est)
Total external debt – US$1,556m (2013 est)
Imports – US$1,814m (2011)
Exports – US$903m (2011)

BALANCE OF PAYMENTS
Trade – US$910m deficit (2011)
Current Account – US$1,144m deficit (2010)

Trade with UK	2012	2013
Imports from UK	£1,773,847	£6,603,887
Exports to UK	£2,556,982	£44,371

COMMUNICATIONS

Airports and waterways – The principal airport is at Niamey and there are a further nine airports; the river Niger is navigable between September and March for 300km from Niamey to the Benin frontier
Roadways – Of the 18,949km of roadways, only 3,912km are surfaced
Telecommunications – 100,500 fixed lines and 5.4 million mobile subscriptions (2012); there were 115,900 internet users in 2009
Internet code and IDD – ne; 227 (from UK), 44 (to UK)
Media – Tele-Sahel is the country's principal broadcaster; there are two major newspapers, consisting of the state-run *Le Sahel* and the weekly *Le Republican*
WPFI score – 23,59 (48)

NIGERIA

Federal Republic of Nigeria

Area – 923,768 sq. km
Capital – Abuja (since 1991); population, 1,857,000 (2009)
Major cities – Aba, Benin City, Ibadan, Ilorin, Kaduna, Kano,
    Lagos (the former capital), Port Harcourt, Warri, Zaria
Currency – Naira (N) of 100 kobo
Population – 177,155,754 rising at 2.47 per cent a year
    (2014 est); Hausa and Fulani (29 per cent), Yoruba (21 per
    cent), Igbo (18 per cent), Ijaw (10 per cent), Kanuri
    (4 per cent), Ibibio (3.5 per cent), Tiv (2.5 per cent) (est)
Religion – Muslim 50 per cent, Christian 40 per cent,
    indigenous beliefs 10 per cent
Language – English (official), Hausa, Yoruba, Igbo, Fula, over
    500 other languages
Population density – 180 per sq. km (2011)
Urban population – 50.3 per cent (2012 est)
Median age (years) – 18.2 (2014 est)
National anthem – 'Arise O Compatriots, Nigeria's Call Obey'
National day – 1 October (Independence Day)
Death penalty – Retained
CPI score – 25 (144)

CLIMATE AND TERRAIN

The north is arid savannah and semi-desert plains, which rise
to central hills and plateaux. There are mountains along the
south-eastern border, but the south is generally low-lying
and covered in tropical rainforest, with mangrove swamps
along the coast and hills in the south-east. Elevation
extremes range from 2,419m (Chappal Waddi) to 0m
(Atlantic Ocean). The river Niger flows across the country
from the north-west to the south coast, where it forms a
broad delta on the Gulf of Guinea. The climate is equatorial
in the south, tropical in the centre and arid in the north. The
north has one rainy season (June to September), while the
south has two (March–July, September–October); the average
temperature in Lagos is 27°C.

POLITICS

The country is a federal democratic republic. Under the 1999
constitution, the executive president is directly elected for a

four-year term, renewable once. The president appoints the
federal executive council, which must be approved by the
senate. The bicameral National Assembly comprises the
360-member House of Representatives and the 109-member
senate, both elected for a four-year term.

The People's Democratic Party (PDP) has dominated
politics since 1999, and retained its majority in both
legislative chambers in the 2007 and 2011 elections.
President Goodluck Jonathan, elected as vice-president in
2007, succeeded to the presidency after the death of
President Yar'Adua in May 2010, and was elected president
in the first round of voting in April 2011.

HEAD OF STATE
President, Goodluck Jonathan, *sworn in* 6 May 2010, *elected*
    16 April 2011
Vice-President, Namadi Sambo

SELECTED GOVERNMENT MEMBERS *as at June 2013*
Finance, Ngozi Okonjo-Iweala
Foreign Affairs, Aminu Wali
Internal Affairs, Patrick Abba Moro

HIGH COMMISSION FOR THE FEDERAL REPUBLIC
OF NIGERIA
Nigeria House, 9 Northumberland Avenue, London WC2N 5BX
T 020-7839 1244 E hc@nigeriahc.org.uk
W www.nigeriahc.org.uk
High Commissioner, HE Dr Dalhatu Sarki Tafida, *apptd* 2008

BRITISH HIGH COMMISSION
19 Torrens Close, Mississippi, Maitama, Abuja
T (+234) (9) 462 2200 E information.abuja@fco.gov.uk
W www.gov.uk/government/world/nigeria
High Commissioner, HE Andrew Pocock, *apptd* 2012

FEDERAL STRUCTURE
The federal republic is divided into 36 states and the Federal
Capital Territory: Abia, Adamawa, Akwa Ibom, Anambra,
Bauchi, Bayelsa, Benue, Borno, Cross River, Delta, Ebonyi,
Edo, Ekiti, Enugu, Gombe, Imo, Jigawa, Kaduna, Kano,
Katsina, Kebbi, Kogi, Kwara, Lagos, Nassarawa, Niger, Ogun,
Ondo, Osun, Oyo, Plateau, Rivers, Sokoto, Taraba, Yobe and
Zamfara. Each state has an elected governor and legislature.

DEFENCE

Aged 16–49, 2010 est	*Males*	*Females*
Available for military service	37,087,711	35,232,127
Fit for military service	20,839,976	19,867,683

Military expenditure – US$1,995m (2013)

ECONOMY AND TRADE

In April 2014 a statistical 'revaluation' of the economy by the
Nigerian government increased the size of the Nigerian
economy by 89 per cent overnight, Nigeria has now emerged

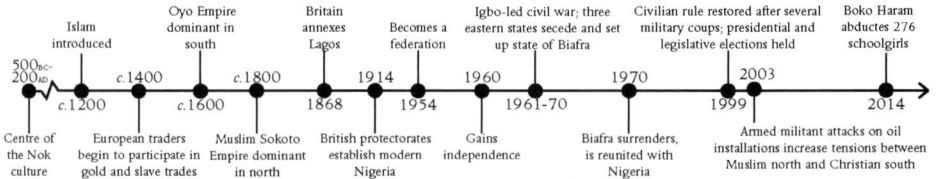

as Africa's largest economy, with 2013 GDP estimated at US$ 502bn (£296bn). The country is the leading sub-Saharan oil producer, enjoying an oil boom in the 1970s and recently benefiting again from high oil prices. However, mismanagement and corruption mean the majority of the population has yet to derive much benefit, and 70 per cent live below the poverty line. Past governments also failed to diversify the economy away from its dependence on oil, which accounts for 80 per cent of government revenue and 95 per cent of foreign exchange earnings. However, since 2008 economic reforms have been introduced to improve fiscal and monetary management, curb inflation and address regional agitation for wider distribution of oil revenues. Factors such as security and inadequate infrastructure remain obstacles to growth, but infrastructure improvements are a priority, especially in electricity supply and roads. Recent high oil revenues and debt relief or cancellation have freed Nigeria from much of its large foreign debt.

The mainstay of the economy is agriculture, mostly at subsistence level, which generates 30.9 per cent of GDP and engages 70 per cent of the labour force. The main crops include cocoa, peanuts, cotton, palm oil, maize, rice, sorghum, millet and rubber. However, agricultural output has failed to keep pace with rapid population growth, changing Nigeria from a net food exporter to a food importer. Industrial activities include oil and natural gas production, mining (coal, tin, columbite), processing agricultural products, textiles, cement and other construction materials and footwear. Industry contributes 43 per cent of GDP and services 26 per cent.

The main trading partners are the USA (16.8 per cent of exports), China, India, Brazil and the EU. Principal exports are oil and oil products, cocoa and rubber. The main imports are machinery, chemicals, transport equipment, manufactured goods, food and live animals.

GNI – US$241,297m; US$1,440 per capita (2012)
Annual average growth of GDP – 6.2 per cent (2013 est)
Inflation rate – 8.7 per cent (2013 est)
Population below poverty line – 70 per cent (2010 est)
Unemployment – 23.9 per cent (2011 est)
Total external debt – US$15,730m (2013 est)
Imports – US$51,000m (2012)
Exports – US$114,000m (2012)

BALANCE OF PAYMENTS
Trade – US$63,000m surplus (2012)
Current Account – US$20,443m surplus (2012)

Trade with UK	2012	2013
Imports from UK	£1,591,914,258	£1,550,030,461
Exports to UK	£3,955,015,314	£3,135,052,281

COMMUNICATIONS
Airports and waterways – There are 40 airports, including the principal airports at Lagos, Abuja, Kano and Port Harcourt; there are 8,600km of waterways, mostly on the Niger and Benue rivers; the main seaports are Lagos, Port Harcourt, Warri and Calabar
Roadways and railways – There are 193,200km of roadways; the Nigerian railway network, which is controlled by the Nigerian Railway Corporation, has 3,505km of track
Telecommunications – 418,200 fixed lines and 112.78 million mobile subscriptions (2012); there were 43.99 million internet users in 2009
Internet code and IDD – ng; 234 (from UK), 9 44 (to UK)
Major broadcasters – The state-run Nigerian Television Authority reaches nearly half of the population

Press – *The Guardian* is one of the most influential news publications in the country; the government-backed *New Nigerian* prints separate editions in Lagos and Kaduna
WPFI score – 34,24 (112)

EDUCATION AND HEALTH
Literacy rate – 61.3 per cent (2010 est)
Gross enrolment ratio (percentage of relevant age group) – primary 85 per cent; secondary 44 per cent (2012 est)
Health expenditure (per capita) – US$80 (2011)
Hospital beds (per 1,000 people) – 0.5 (2004–9)
Life expectancy (years) – 52.62 (2014 est)
Mortality rate – 13.16 (2014 est)
Birth rate – 38.03 (2014 est)
Infant mortality rate – 74.09 (2014 est)
HIV/AIDS adult prevalence – 3.1 per cent (2012 est)

NORWAY

Kongeriket Norge – Kingdom of Norway

Area – 386,224 sq. km, of which Svalbard and Jan Mayen have a combined area of 62,422 sq. km
Capital – Oslo; population, 875,000 (2009)
Major cities – Bergen, Stavanger, Trondheim
Currency – Krone of 100 ore
Population – 5,147,792 rising at 1.19 per cent per year (2014 est)
Religion – Christian (Lutheran 82.1 per cent, other 3.9 per cent), Muslim 2.3 per cent
Language – Bokmal and Nynorsk Norwegian (both official), Finnish, Sami (official in six municipalities)
Population density – 16 per sq. km (2011)
Urban population – 79.7 per cent (2012 est)
Median age (years) – 39.1 (2014 est)
National anthem – 'Ja, Vi Elsker Dette Landet' ['Yes, We Love This Country']
National day – 17 May (Constitution Day)
Death penalty – Abolished for all crimes (since 1979)
CPI score – 86 (5)

CLIMATE AND TERRAIN
The terrain is mostly mountainous, with elevated, barren plateaux separated by deep, narrow valleys; the north is arctic tundra. The coastline is deeply indented with numerous fjords and fringed with thousands of rocky islands and islets; Geirangerfjord and Naeroyfjord are UNESCO World Heritage Sites. Elevation extremes range from 2,469m (Galdhopiggen) to 0m (Norwegian Sea).

Nearly half of the country lies north of the Arctic Circle, and at North Cape the sun does not appear to set between about 14 May and 29 July, causing the phenomenon known as the midnight sun; conversely, there is no apparent sunrise from about 18 November to 24 January. The climate is temperate on the coast but colder and wetter inland; average temperatures in Oslo range from −3°C in January and February to 17°C in July, but winter temperatures in parts of the north can drop to −40°C.

HISTORY AND POLITICS

Norway became a unified country under the rule of King Harald Fairhair in c.900 but dissolved after his death and was reunified by Olav II in c.1016–28. Canute brought Norway under Danish rule in 1028 but the throne reverted on his death to Magnus I. When the royal house died out in the 14th century, the Danish monarch was the nearest heir and in 1397 Norway, Denmark and Sweden were united under a single monarch in the Kalmar Union. Sweden seceded from the union in 1523, but Norway continued to be ruled by the Danish crown until 1814, when it was ceded to Sweden.

Although internal self-government was established in 1814, growing tension over constraints on the Norwegian government led to the union being dissolved, and Norway became independent in 1905. The first king of the newly independent country was a Danish prince, who took the throne as King Haakon VII.

The country was neutral in the First World War, but in the Second World War Norway was invaded and occupied by Germany from 1940 until 1945. Norway joined NATO in 1949 and was a founder member of the European Free Trade Association in 1960. Membership of the EU was rejected in referendums in 1972 and 1994.

After 1945, governments pursued policies of economic planning and an extensive welfare state. The Labour Party dominated politics from the 1930s to the early 1980s, governing either on its own or in coalition with smaller parties. It was returned to power in 2005. In September 2013 the Conservative Party formed a minority government with the right-wing Progress Party, despite the Labour Party remaining the largest single party in the legislature.

Norway is a constitutional monarchy with a hereditary monarch as head of state. Under the 1814 constitution, the unicameral *Storting* has 169 members who are directly elected for a four-year term; a 2007 constitutional amendment abolished a bicameral division within the *Storting*, which took effect from the 2009 election. The prime minister, who is responsible to parliament, appoints the cabinet.

HEAD OF STATE

HM *The King of Norway,* King Harald V, KG, GCVO, *born* 21 February 1937; *succeeded* 17 January 1991
Heir, HRH Crown Prince Haakon Magnus, *born* 20 July 1973

SELECTED GOVERNMENT MEMBERS *as at June 2014*
Prime Minister, Erna Solberg
Defence, Ine Marie Eriksen Soreide
Finance, Siv Jensen
Foreign Affairs, Borge Brende

ROYAL NORWEGIAN EMBASSY
25 Belgrave Square, London SW1X 8QD
T 020-7591 5500 E emb.london@mfa.no W www.norway.org.uk
Ambassador Extraordinary and Plenipotentiary, HE Kim Traavik, *apptd* 2010

BRITISH EMBASSY
Thomas Heftyes Gate 8, 0244 Oslo
T (+47) 2313 2700 E britemb@online.no
W www.gov.uk/government/world/norway

Ambassador Extraordinary and Plenipotentiary, HE Jane Owen, *apptd* 2010

DEFENCE

Aged 16–49, 2010 est	Males	Females
Available for military service	1,079,043	1,051,210
Fit for military service	888,761	865,697

Military expenditure – US$7,398m (2013)
Conscription – men aged 19 to 35; 12 months

ECONOMY AND TRADE

Norway's prosperity depends primarily upon oil and gas extraction, which accounts for nearly half of exports, and its fisheries. Oil production is declining, but exploration for oil and gas in the Barents Sea, and other areas that are becoming more accessible as the Arctic ice cap retreats, is ongoing. Norway has planned for the time when reserves are exhausted by investing revenue from this sector in the world's largest sovereign wealth fund, valued at over $830 billion in January 2014. The state retains a majority share in key enterprises, including the oil industry.

The nature of the terrain restricts agriculture, which generates 1.2 per cent of GDP. The main industries apart from oil and gas are fishing, forestry, food processing, shipbuilding, pulp and paper products, metals, chemicals, mining and textiles. Shipping freight services are also significant, with Norwegian companies controlling 4.5 per cent of the world's shipping fleet by tonnage. Industry contributes 42.3 per cent of GDP and services 56.5 per cent.

The main trading partners are the UK (25.6 per cent of exports), other EU countries, the USA and China. Principal exports are oil and petroleum products, machinery and equipment, metals, chemicals, ships and fish. The main imports are machinery and equipment, chemicals, metals and foodstuffs.

GNI – US$509,710m; US$98,860 per capita (2012)
Annual average growth of GDP – 1.6 per cent (2013 est)
Inflation rate – 1.9 per cent (2013 est)
Unemployment – 3.6 per cent (2013 est)
Total external debt – US$720,600m (2013)
Imports – US$87,316m (2012)
Exports – US$161,026m (2012)

BALANCE OF PAYMENTS
Trade – US$73,710m surplus (2012)
Current Account – US$70,817m surplus (2012)

Trade with UK	2012	2013
Imports from UK	£3,639,323,376	£3,458,623,471
Exports to UK	£21,566,002,754	£16,773,732,408

COMMUNICATIONS

Airports and waterways – There are 67 airports, including the principal airports at Oslo, Bergen, Stavanger and Trondheim; the main ports are Oslo, Bergen, Kristiansand, Tonsberg, Stavanger and Narvik, and there is a large merchant fleet, with 585 ships of over 1,000 tonnes registered in Norway and 974 registered abroad
Roadways and railways – 93,870km; 4,237km
Telecommunications – 1.465 million fixed lines and 5.732 million mobile subscriptions (2011); there were 4.431 million internet users in 2009
Major broadcasters – The public broadcaster NRK operates radio and television channels, in competition with a number of commercial rivals

Press – VG has the largest circulation amongst the country's daily news publications; other newspapers include *The Norway Post* and *Dagbladet*
WPFI score – 6,52 (3)

EDUCATION AND HEALTH
Education from six to 16 is free and compulsory in the basic schools, and free from 16 to 19 years.
Gross enrolment ratio (percentage of relevant age group) –
primary 99 per cent; secondary 113 per cent; tertiary 73 per cent (2012 est)
Health expenditure (per capita) – US$8,987 (2011)
Hospital beds (per 1,000 people) – 3.3 (2010)
Life expectancy (years) – 81.6 (2014 est)
Mortality rate – 8.19 (2014 est)
Birth rate – 12.09 (2014 est)
Infant mortality rate – 2.48 (2014 est)

TERRITORIES

SVALBARD
Area – 62,045 sq. km
Population – 1,921 (2013 est); Norwegian 55.4 per cent, Russian and Ukrainian 44.3 per cent

The Svalbard archipelago consists of Spitsbergen, North East Land, the Wiche Islands, Barents Island, Edge Island, Prince Charles Foreland, Hope Island and Bear Island. It lies north of the Arctic Circle, and glaciers and snow cover around 60 per cent of the area, although the west coast is ice-free for about half the year. Some 65 per cent of the Svalbard archipelago is protected to ensure biodiversity; there are seven national parks, six large nature reserves, 15 bird sanctuaries and one geotopic protected area. A global seed repository has been established on Spitsbergen. Norway's sovereignty was recognised by treaty in 1920 but the other signatories were granted equal rights to exploit mineral deposits, although this right is now only exercised by Russia. The territory is administered by a governor, who is responsible to the Ministry of Justice and Police. The main economic activities are coal mining, tourism, and research and education.

JAN MAYEN ISLAND
Area – 377 sq. km
Population – The only residents are the staff of the radio and meteorological stations

The island is barren, volcanic and partially covered by glaciers, with no exploitable natural resources. It lies in the North Atlantic Ocean about 950 km west of Norway and is home to the Beerenberg volcano, the northernmost active volcano on earth. It was annexed by Norway in 1922 and integrated into the kingdom in 1930; since 1995 it has been administered by the governor of Nordland county.

NORWEGIAN ANTARCTIC TERRITORY
The Norwegian Antarctic Territory consists of Queen Maud Land, Bouvet Island and Peter the First Island. Claimed in 1938, Queen Maud Land is a sector of the Antarctic continent which extends from 45° E. to 20° E. Peter the First Island was formally claimed in 1931 and is the only claimed area covered under the Antarctic Treaty that is not part of the main land mass. Bouvet Island was claimed in 1930 (*see also* The North and South Poles).

OMAN

Saltanat Uman – Sultanate of Oman

Area – 309,500 sq. km
Capital – Muscat (Masqat); population, 634,000 (2009)
Major cities – Ibri, Salalah, Suhar, as-Suwayq
Currency – Omani Rial (OR) of 1,000 baisas
Population – 3,219,775 rising at 2.06 per cent a year (2014 est)
Religion – Muslim 85.9 per cent (majority are Ibadhi, lesser numbers of Sunni and Shia), Christian 6.5 per cent, Hindu 5.5 per cent
Language – Arabic (official), English, Baluchi, Urdu
Population density – 10 per sq. km (2011)
Urban population – 73.7 per cent (2012 est)
Median age (years) – 24.9 (2014 est)
National anthem – 'Nashid as-Salaam as-Sultani' ['The Sultan's Anthem']
National day – 18 November (Birthday of Sultan Qaboos, 1940)
Death penalty – Retained
CPI score – 47 (61)

CLIMATE AND TERRAIN
Oman lies at the south-eastern corner of the Arabian peninsula and includes territory at the tip of the Musandam peninsula, which is separated from the rest of the country by the UAE. There are mountains in the north and the south-west of the country, divided by high desert plateau; over 80 per cent of the country is desert. The plateau descends to a fertile plain on the Arabian Sea coast. Elevation extremes range from 2,980m (Jabal Shams) to 0m (Arabian Sea). The climate is arid, with high temperatures and humidity throughout the year; temperatures are lower on the coast, but the high humidity often makes coastal areas the most inhospitable. Average temperatures in Muscat range from 21°C in January to 35°C in June.

HISTORY AND POLITICS
Oman began to build an empire in the Middle East from the eighth century AD and remained largely unchallenged until the arrival in 1506 of the Portuguese, who were ousted in 1650. An independent sultanate was established in 1749 by the founder of the dynasty that still rules the country. By the early 19th century, Omani rule extended to the east African coast and parts of Persia and Balochistan (in modern Pakistan). The kingdom came under British influence from the late 19th century until 1951.

The country was divided from 1913, with religious leaders in control of the interior and the sultan of the coastal regions. The interior's attempts to assert its independence led to clashes in the 1950s, but by 1959 the sultan had established control over the whole country. An insurrection in the south by left-wing rebels supported by South Yemen began in 1965 and was defeated with British military assistance in 1975. The discovery and subsequent exploitation of oil in the mid-1960s led to the steady economic transformation of Oman, and in 1970 the sultan was overthrown in a bloodless coup by his son, Sultan Qaboos bin Said al-Said, who initiated a modernisation programme.

The country is still essentially an absolute monarchy, although a degree of political liberalisation has occurred in the past 20 years and the 1996 Basic Statute sets out the development of the political and legal systems; the first direct election to the consultative council was held in 2000 and the first by universal adult suffrage in 2003. In the 2011 election, all the candidates contesting the 84 seats were independents. Pro-reform demonstrations occurred prior to the October 2011 elections.

In 1996 the sultan issued a Basic Statute that is in effect a constitution; it established a succession mechanism, codified the system of government and set up a bicameral legislature. At present, legislation is proposed by the sultan and passed by decree. The sultan is advised by the bicameral Council of Oman, comprising the Consultative Council *(Majlis al-Shura)*, which has 84 members directly elected for a four-year term, and the Council of State *(Majlis al-Dawlah)*, which has 59 members appointed by the sultan for a four-year term. The Consultative Council has the right to review legislation, question ministers and make policy proposals. The Council of State is intended to facilitate 'constructive cooperation between the government and the citizens'. There are no political parties.

HEAD OF STATE

HM The Sultan of Oman, Prime Minister, Sultan Qaboos bin Said al-Said, *succeeded following a coup,* 23 July 1970

SELECTED GOVERNMENT MEMBERS *as at June 2014*
Deputy Prime Minister, Fahd bin Mamud al-Said
Defence, Badr bin Saud bin Hareb al-Busaidi
Foreign Affairs, Yusuf bin Alawi bin Abdullah
Interior, Sayyid Hamoud bin Faisal al-Busaidi

EMBASSY OF THE SULTANATE OF OMAN

167 Queen's Gate, London SW7 5HE
T 020-7225 0001 W www.omanembassy.org.uk
Ambassador Extraordinary and Plenipotentiary, HE Abdul Aziz al-Hinai, *apptd* 2009

BRITISH EMBASSY

PO Box 185, Mina al-Fahal, 116 Muscat
T (+968) (24) 609 000 E enquiries.muscat@fco.gov.uk
W www.gov.uk/government/world/oman
Ambassador Extraordinary and Plenipotentiary, HE Jamie Bowden, *apptd* 2011

DEFENCE

Aged 16–49, 2010 est	Males	Females
Available for military service	985,957	737,812
Fit for military service	837,886	642,427

Military expenditure – US$8,738m (2013)

ECONOMY AND TRADE

Although its production is more modest than other Gulf states, oil and gas are the mainstay of Oman's economy. Oil reserves are dwindling and development plans centre on diversification, industrialisation and privatisation, with the aim of reducing the oil sector's contribution to GDP to 9 per

cent by 2020. Industrial development is focused on natural gas production, metal manufacturing, petrochemicals and trans-shipment ports, with plans also to develop tourism and communication technology industries. Improved training, especially in IT and business skills, is intended to enable the local population to replace expatriate workers. The global economic crisis has slowed development.

Agriculture and fishing account for 1 per cent of GDP, producing dates, limes, bananas, alfalfa and vegetables as well as fish. The main industries apart from oil and natural gas extraction are oil refining, liquefied natural gas production, construction and production of cement, copper, steel, chemicals and optic fibre. Industry accounts for 64.4 per cent of GDP and services for 34.6 per cent.

The main trading partners are the UAE, China, Japan and South Korea. Principal exports are petroleum, re-exports, fish, metals and textiles. The main imports are machinery, transport equipment, manufactured goods, food and livestock.

GNI – US$54,687m; US$19,110 per capita (2010)
Annual average growth of GDP – 5.1 per cent (2013 est)
Inflation rate – 1.6 per cent (2013 est)
Unemployment – 15 per cent (2004 est)
Total external debt – US$10,840m (2013 est)
Imports – US$29,447m (2012)
Exports – US$53,174m (2012)

BALANCE OF PAYMENTS
Trade – US$23,727m surplus (2012)
Current Account – US$10,723m surplus (2011)

Trade with UK	2012	2013
Imports from UK	£450,847,671	£555,314,819
Exports to UK	£119,654,679	£115,665,054

COMMUNICATIONS

Airports and waterways – The main airports are at Muscat and Salalah; the main ports are Salalah and Port Qaboos at Mutrah, which has eight deepwater berths
Roadways – There are 60,240km of roadways, of which 29,685km are surfaced
Telecommunications – 305,000 fixed lines and 5.278 million mobile telephone subscriptions (2012); there were 1.465 million internet users in 2009
Internet code and IDD – om; 968 (from UK), 44 (to UK)
Media – Oman TV is the state-run national news network; *Al-Watan* and the *Oman Daily* are the principal daily newspapers
WPFI score – 38,83 (134)

EDUCATION AND HEALTH

Literacy rate – 87 per cent (2010 est)
Gross enrolment ratio (percentage of relevant age group) – primary 109 per cent; secondary 94 per cent; tertiary 28 per cent (2012 est)
Health expenditure (per capita) – US$598 (2011)
Hospital beds (per 1,000 people) – 1.8 (2009)
Life expectancy (years) – 74.97 (2014 est)
Mortality rate – 3.38 (2014 est)
Birth rate – 24.47 (2014 est)
Infant mortality rate – 14 (2014 est)

PAKISTAN

Jamhuryat Islami Pakistan – Islamic Republic of Pakistan

Area – 796,095 sq. km
Capital – Islamabad; population, 832,000 (2009 est)
Major cities – Faisalabad, Gujranwala, Hyderabad, Karachi, Lahore, Multan, Peshawar, Quetta, Rawalpindi
Currency – Pakistan rupee of 100 paisa
Population – 196,174,380 rising at 1.49 per cent a year (2014 est); Punjabi (44.7 per cent), Pashtun (15.4 per cent), Sindhi (14.1 per cent), Sariaki (8.4 per cent), Muhajirs (7.6 per cent), Balochi (3.6 per cent) (est)
Religion – Muslim 96.4 per cent (predominantly Sunni), other (includes Christian and Hindu) 3.6 per cent; Islam is the state religion
Language – English, Urdu (both official), Balochi, Brahui, Burushaski, Hindko, Punjabi, Pashto, Sindhi, Siraiki
Population density – 229 per sq. km (2011)
Urban population – 36.5 per cent (2012 est)
Median age (years) – 22.6 (2014 est)
National anthem – 'Qaumi Tarana' ['The Sacred Land']
National day – 23 March (Republic Day)
Death penalty – Retained
CPI score – 28 (127)

CLIMATE AND TERRAIN

The arid Thar desert in the east gives way to the fertile Indus valley in the centre of the country. The terrain then rises to the Makran, Kirthar and Sulaiman mountain ranges in the west and the Karakoram and Himalayan ranges in the north. Elevation extremes range from 8,611m (K2) to 0m (Indian Ocean). The climate varies greatly across the country. For most areas, the rainy season runs from July to September and is accompanied by very high humidity. Average temperatures in Lahore range from 13°C in January to 33°C in June. Pakistan is prone to earthquakes, the most recent in 2005 and 2008, and flooding; following heavy monsoon rains in 2010 the entire length of the Indus valley was flooded, displacing millions of people.

POLITICS

Pakistan is a federal republic. The 1973 constitution has been suspended and restored several times, amended in 1985, 2002 and 2003, and in 2010 was reinstated in its original form, returning some of the president's powers to the prime minister.

The president is elected by the legislature for a five-year term. The parliament *(Majlis as-Shura)* comprises a lower house, the National Assembly and the senate. The National Assembly has 342 members, of whom 60 are women and ten are elected by non-Muslim minorities; members serve a five-year term. The senate has 104 members, 92 elected by provincial assemblies, eight chosen by tribal agencies and four elected by the National Assembly; they serve a six-year term, with half elected every three years. The prime minister is nominated by and is responsible to the legislature.

There are four provinces: Balochistan, Khyber Pukhtoonkhwa (formerly North-West Frontier Province), Punjab and Sindh. Each has a provincial assembly and government. In addition, there are the Federally Administered Tribal Areas and the Islamabad Capital Territory.

The legislative elections originally scheduled for January 2008 were postponed to February after the assassination of Benazir Bhutto in December 2007. The two main opposition parties, Bhutto's Pakistan People's Party (PPP) and the Pakistan Muslim League–Nawaz Sharif (PML-N), won the most seats and formed a coalition government with two smaller parties; the PML-N withdrew from the coalition government in August 2008. The presidential election in July 2013 was won by Mamnoon Hussain, the first instance in Pakistan's history in which one elected civilian president was replaced by another. In the May 2013 legislative elections, the Pakistani Muslim League won the most seats but without a majority. However, 50 of the 70 reserved seats were assigned to PML supporters, giving the PML a majority in the chamber. Nawaz Sharif was elected prime minister in June 2013.

HEAD OF STATE
President, Mamnoon Hussain, *elected* 30 July 2013, *sworn in* 9 September 2013

SELECTED GOVERNMENT MEMBERS *as at June 2014*
Prime Minister, Defence, Nawaz Sharif
Finance, Muhammad Ishaq Dar
Foreign Affairs, Sartaj Aziz

HIGH COMMISSION FOR THE ISLAMIC REPUBLIC OF PAKISTAN
34–36 Lowndes Square, London SW1X 9JN
T 020-7664 9204 W www.phclondon.org
High Commissioner (acting), HE Mohamed Imran Mirza, *apptd* 2013

BRITISH HIGH COMMISSION
PO Box 1122, Diplomatic Enclave, Ramna 5, Islamabad
T (+92) (51) 201 2000 E consularenquiries.karachi@fco.gov.uk
W www.gov.uk/government/world/pakistan
High Commissioner, HE Philip Barton, *apptd* 2014

INSURGENCIES
Balochistan, Punjab and Sindh provinces have all been affected since the 1980s by conflict between Shia and Sunni

fundamentalists. Balochistan and, since the early 1990s, Sindh (especially Karachi) have experienced violence by armed militants seeking greater autonomy for each province.

Civil order has always been harder to maintain in the North-West Frontier Province and the federally administered tribal areas than in the rest of the country. These areas became havens for the Taliban and al-Qaida fleeing Afghanistan after 2001 and for like-minded Pakistani militants, who became entrenched along the Afghan border, radicalising and destabilising increasingly wide areas. Government military and security forces are struggling to maintain control in over half of these areas. The government conceded the imposition of Shariah law in the Swat valley as part of a cease-fire agreement with the Taliban in early 2009, but when the Taliban attempted to extend their influence further into the country, the army began a counter-insurgency offensive to retake the area in April 2009, subsequently moving against the Taliban in other strongholds such as South Waziristan. These offensives led to an increase in militants' attacks in the major cities, while by 2010 the Taliban began to reassert its influence in some of the areas cleared by the army offensives in 2009. Islamist attacks continue to be carried out against civilian targets; in March 2014 peace talks with the Taliban resumed in Waziristan.

FOREIGN RELATIONS

Since partition, sovereignty over the predominantly Muslim state of Jammu and Kashmir has been disputed between Pakistan and India. A short war in 1947–8 resulted in the state being partitioned between the two countries; its status remains unresolved, despite further outbreaks of war in 1965 and 1971, low-level conflict for control of the Siachen glacier since 1985 and occasional increases in military exchanges, most recently in 1999–2002 and 2003. Tension was exacerbated by Pakistan's support of the Muslim insurgency in the Indian part of the state, which began in the 1980s, and by both countries' acquisition of nuclear weapons. Moves towards a peaceful settlement began in 2003, when diplomatic missions were reopened and the resumption of transport links was initiated. Formal diplomatic talks began in 2004 and have achieved several accords intended to reduce tension between the two countries, although the status of Kashmir has yet to be addressed. Talks were temporarily suspended by the Indian government after the Mumbai terrorist attacks in 2008, but resumed in 2010.

DEFENCE

Aged 16–49, 2010 est	Males	Females
Available for military service	48,453,305	44,898,096
Fit for military service	37,945,440	37,381,549

Military expenditure – US$7,637m (2013)*

* Figure does not include paramilitary spending

ECONOMY AND TRADE

Decades of political instability, inefficiency, corruption and high military expenditure have left Pakistan an underdeveloped country, averaging poor economic growth of 3.5 per cent between 2008 and 2015. In the 2000s economic reforms, international aid and greater foreign investment produced steady growth of 5–8 per cent a year until 2008, notably in the industrial and service sectors, and reduced poverty levels by 10 per cent between 2001 and 2007. However, slower growth in 2008 caused budget and fiscal deficits that forced Pakistan to seek IMF assistance;

inflation, already a persistent problem, rose to 12 per cent in 2011, declining to 10 per cent in 2012. These problems have been exacerbated by the 2010 floods, which left millions homeless, destroyed crops and damaged infrastructure. A large proportion of the country's labour force works abroad, especially in the Middle East, providing valuable remittances but also causing use of child labour within Pakistan. The Pakistani rupee has depreciated more than 40 per cent since 2007 due to political and economic instability.

Agriculture employs 45.1 per cent of the workforce, producing cotton, wheat, rice, sugar cane, vegetables, milk, meat and eggs, and contributes 25.3 per cent of GDP. Significant manufacturing industries include textiles and clothing, food processing, pharmaceuticals, construction materials, paper products, fertiliser and seafood. Industry accounts for 21.6 per cent of GDP and services for 53.1 per cent.

The main trading partners are the UAE, the USA, China, Saudi Arabia and Afghanistan. Principal exports are textiles (clothing, bed linen, cotton cloth and yarn), rice, leather goods, sports goods, chemicals, carpets and rugs. The main imports are petroleum, machinery, plastics, transport equipment, edible oils, paper, iron, steel and tea.

GNI – US$236,749m; US$1,260 per capita (2012)
Annual average growth of GDP – 3.6 per cent (2013 est)
Inflation rate – 7.7 per cent (2013 est)
Population below poverty line – 24 per cent (2005–6 est)
Unemployment – 6.6 per cent (2013 est)
Total external debt – US$52,430m (2013 est)
Imports – US$42,920m (2012)
Exports – US$22,807m (2012)

BALANCE OF PAYMENTS

Trade – US$20,114m deficit (2012)
Current Account – US$214m surplus (2011)

Trade with UK	2012	2013
Imports from UK	£530,086,647	£471,560,151
Exports to UK	£809,567,975	£916,338,032

COMMUNICATIONS

Airports and waterways – The principal airports are at Karachi, Islamabad, Lahore, Peshawar and Sialkot, and 1048 other airports; the main seaports are Karachi and Port Muhammad bin Qasim, and there is a deepwater port at Gwadar
Roadways and railways – 262,256km; 7,791
Telecommunications – 5.803 million fixed lines and 125 million mobile subscriptions (2012); there were 20.431 million internet users in 2009
Internet code and IDD – pk; 92 (from UK), 44 (to UK)
Media – There are eight national daily newspapers, and the state-owned broadcaster, Pakistan Television Corporation Ltd, competes with around 50 private channels
WPFI score – 51,46 (158)

EDUCATION AND HEALTH

Education is free to upper secondary level.
Literacy rate – 55 per cent (2009)
Gross enrolment ratio (percentage of relevant age group) – primary 93 per cent; secondary 37 per cent; tertiary 10 per cent (2012 est)
Health expenditure (per capita) – US$30 (2011)
Hospital beds (per 1,000 people) – 0.6 (2010)
Life expectancy (years) – 67.05 (2014 est)
Mortality rate – 6.58 (2014 est)
Birth rate – 23.19 (2014 est)
Infant mortality rate – 57.48 (2014 est)

PALAU

Beluu er a Belau – Republic of Palau

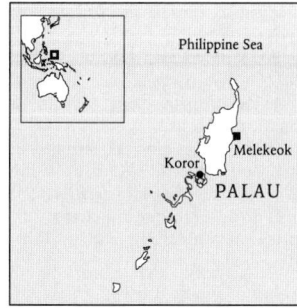

Area – 459 sq. km
Capital – Melekeok, on Babeldaob; population, 566 (2009 est)
Major town – Koror
Currency – US dollar (US$) of 100 cents
Population – 21,186 rising at 0.37 per cent a year (2014 est); Palauan (69.9 per cent), Filipino (15.3 per cent), Chinese (4.9 per cent) (2000)
Religion – Christian (Roman Catholic 49.4 per cent, Protestant 30.9 per cent), Modekngei 8.7 per cent (indigenous to Palau; combines Animism and Christianity)
Language – Palauan (official in most islands), English (official in all islands), Tobi, Sonsoralese, Angaur (official in respective islands), Japanese (official in Angaur), Filipino, Chinese
Population density – 45 per sq. km (2011)
Urban population – 85.1 per cent (2012 est)
Median age (years) – 33 (2014 est)
National anthem – 'Belau rekid' ['Our Palau']
National day – 9 July (Constitution Day)
Death penalty – Abolished for all crimes (since 1994)
Life expectancy (years) – 72.6 (2014 est)
Mortality rate – 7.93 (2014 est)
Birth rate – 10.95 (2014 est)
Infant mortality rate – 11.46 (2014 est)

CLIMATE AND TERRAIN

The republic consists of six island groups in the western Pacific Ocean; these comprise eight large islands and over 300 smaller islands or islets that are either volcanic and mountainous or coral and low-lying. Elevation extremes range from 242m (Mt Ngerchelchuus) to 0m (Pacific Ocean). The climate is tropical, with a wet season from May to November. The average temperature is 27.2°C.

HISTORY AND POLITICS

Palau has been inhabited since the first millennium BC. In the 19th century, Spain and Germany vied for possession until 1889, when Spain sold the islands to Germany, which exploited the phosphate deposits and developed coconut plantations. Japan occupied the islands on behalf of the Allies in 1914 and administered them after the First World War under a League of Nations mandate. Japanese forces were ousted by US troops during the Second World War.

In 1947 the islands became part of the UN Trust Territory of the Pacific, administered by the USA. In 1982 a compact of free association was signed with the USA under which the USA retained responsibility for defence and foreign policy in return for providing economic aid; the compact was ratified in 1993 and entered into force when Palau became independent on 1 October 1994.

The latest presidential and legislative elections were held in 2012; Tommy Remengesau Jr was elected president.

Under the 1981 constitution, the executive president is directly elected for a four-year term, renewable once. The president appoints the cabinet. The bicameral National Congress comprises the House of Delegates, which has 16 members (one from each state), and the 13-member senate; members of both chambers stand for election as independents, and serve a four-year term. A council of indigenous chiefs, composed of the paramount chief from each of the 16 states, acts as an advisory body to the president on matters concerning traditional law and customs.

Each of the 16 constituent states has its own governor and legislature.

HEAD OF STATE
President, Tommy Remengesau Jr, *elected* 6 November 2012, *inaugurated* 17 January 2013
Vice-President, Finance, Antonio Bells

SELECTED GOVERNMENT MEMBERS *as at June 2014*
Finance, Elbuchel Sadang
Minister of State, Billy Kuartei

BRITISH AMBASSADOR
HE Asif Ahmad, *apptd* 2013, resident at Manila, the Philippines

ECONOMY AND TRADE

The economy is reliant on economic aid from the USA and the government is keen to diversify. Tourism is now the main industry, catering for over 80,000 people a year, but the government is limiting development to protect the environment. The other main industries are handicrafts, construction and garment manufacturing. Subsistence agriculture and fishing remain important, engaging 20 per cent of the workforce and producing crops such as coconuts, copra, cassava and sweet potatoes as well as fish. Revenue is also derived from the sale of licences to foreign fishing fleets.

The main trading partners are the USA, Japan, Taiwan, Singapore and South Korea. Principal exports are shellfish, tuna, copra and clothing. The main imports are machinery and equipment, fuels, metals and foodstuffs.

GNI – US$205m; US$9,860 per capita (2012)
Annual average growth of GDP – 3.5 per cent (2013 est)
Inflation rate – 2.3 per cent (2011 est)
Unemployment – 4.2 per cent (2005 est)

Trade with UK	2012	2013
Imports from UK	£64,003	£44,792
Exports to UK	£5,221	£11,270

COMMUNICATIONS

Airports and waterways – There are three airports, on Koror, Peleliu and Angaur, which receive international flights from Guam, Japan, the Philippines and Taiwan; Koror is also the main seaport
Roadways – 61km
Telecommunications – 7,300 fixed lines and 17,150 mobile subscriptions (2012)
Internet code and IDD – pw; 680 (from UK), 011 44 (to UK)

PANAMA

República de Panamá – Republic of Panama

Area – 75,420 sq. km
Capital – Panama City; population, 1,440,480 (2012)
Major cities – Colón, Davíd, San Miguelito
Currency – Balboa of 100 centésimos; at parity with the US
   dollar, which is used as paper currency. Both Panamanian
   and US coins are used
Population – 3,608,431 rising at 1.35 per cent a year
   (2014 est)
Religion – Christian (Roman Catholic 85 per cent, Protestant
   15 per cent) (est)
Language – Spanish (official), English
Population density – 50 per sq. km (2011)
Urban population – 75.9 per cent (2012 est)
Median age (years) – 28.3 (2014 est)
National anthem – 'Himno Istmeño' ['Hymn of the Isthmus']
National day – 3 November (Independence Day)
Death penalty – Abolished for all crimes (since 1922)
CPI score – 35 (102)

CLIMATE AND TERRAIN
Panama lies on the isthmus connecting North and South
America. A mountain range runs along the centre, falling
to coastal plains on both coasts. There is dense tropical
rainforest in the east. Elevation extremes range from 3,475m
(Volcan Baru) to 0m (Pacific Ocean). The climate is tropical,
with a prolonged wet season from May to January. The
average temperature is 26°C.

HISTORY AND POLITICS
Panama was visited by Spanish explorers from 1502, and
in 1519 became part of the Viceroyalty of New Andalucia,
later New Grenada. When it gained its independence
from Spain in 1821, Panama joined the confederacy of Gran
Colombia (comprising Colombia, Venezuela, Ecuador, Peru
and Bolivia). The confederacy split up in 1830 and Panama
became part of Colombia until 1903, when it achieved its
independence.
   In the 1880s, the French attempted to construct a canal
across Panama to link the Atlantic and Pacific oceans. In
1903 the USA bought the rights to build the canal, which
was completed in 1914 and opened in 1919. The USA was
also given control of the canal and land to either side of it,
known as the Canal Zone, in perpetuity but, under a 1977
agreement, sovereignty over the Canal Zone was transferred
to Panama on 31 December 1999.
   Panama was under the military rule of General Omar
Torrijos from 1968 until his death in 1981. In 1983, General
Manuel Noriega seized power and instigated a period of
military rule, supported by the USA until 1987. An internal

coup to unseat Noriega was unsuccessful in 1988, but in
1989 US forces invaded and deposed him. Noriega
surrendered in 1990 and was tried and sentenced in the USA
on drug-trafficking and money-laundering charges in 1992.
He was extradited to Panama in 2011 to serve a further
20 years in prison.
   The May 2014 presidential election was won by Juan
Carlos Varela of the *Panameñista* party. In the simultaneous
legislative election the four-party Alliance for Change
coalition won the most seats.
   Under the 1972 constitution, as amended in 1983, the
executive president is directly elected for a five-year term,
which is not renewable. The unicameral National Assembly
has 71 members, who are directly elected for a five-year
term. The president, who is responsible to the legislature,
appoints the cabinet.

HEAD OF STATE
President, Juan Carlos Varela, *elected* 4 May 2014, *sworn in*
   1 July 2014
First Vice-President, Foreign Affairs, Isabel St Malo de
   Aluarado

SELECTED GOVERNMENT MEMBERS *as at June 2014*
Economy and Finance, Dulcidio de la Guardia
Interior, Milton Henríquez

EMBASSY OF PANAMA
40 Hertford Street, London W1J 7SH
T 020-7493 4646 W www.panamaconsul.co.uk
Ambassador Extraordinary and Plenipotentiary, HE Ana
   Delgado, *apptd* 2011

BRITISH EMBASSY
PO Box 0816–07946, Torre MMG, Calle 53, Marbella, Panama City
T (+507) 297 6550 W www.gov.uk/government/world/panama
Ambassador Extraordinary and Plenipotentiary, HE Dr Ian
   Collard, *apptd* 2013

DEFENCE

Aged 16–49, 2010 est	*Males*	*Females*
Available for military service	890,006	–
Fit for military service	731,254	728,329

ECONOMY AND TRADE
The economy is based on a large service sector and has
experienced steady growth in recent years, although this
slowed in 2009 because of the global economic downturn.
However, the distribution of wealth is uneven: over
one-quarter of the population lives below the poverty line,
although unemployment has reduced significantly from 12
per cent to 4.4 per cent of the labour force in 2012. The
economy has grown quickly since 2009, expanding by
7.5 per cent in 2013 and by over 10 per cent in 2011 and
2012.
   The service sector accounts for 78.4 per cent of GDP,
derived from the operation of the Panama Canal and the
Colón free trade zone, financial services, container ports,
ship registry and tourism. Enlargement of the canal to
take more and larger vessels is scheduled for completion
in 2015. Industry, which contributes 17.9 per cent of
GDP, includes construction, brewing, sugar refining and the
manufacture of cement and other construction materials.
Agriculture, which accounts for 3.7 per cent of GDP, is
centred on bananas, rice, maize, coffee, sugar cane,
vegetables, livestock and shrimp.

The main trading partners are Japan, the USA, Singapore, South Korea, EU countries and China. Principal exports are gold, bananas, shrimp, sugar, iron and steel waste and fruit. The main imports are fuel products, medicines, vehicles, iron and steel rods, and mobile phones.

GNI – US$33,596m; US$8,510 per capita (2012)
Annual average growth of GDP – 7.5 per cent (2013 est)
Inflation rate – 4.1 per cent (2013 est)
Population below poverty line – 26 per cent (2012 est)
Unemployment – 4.5 per cent (2013 est)
Total external debt – US$15,220m (2013 est)
Imports – US$12,633m (2012)
Exports – US$785m (2011)

BALANCE OF PAYMENTS
Trade – US$10,556m deficit (2012)
Current Account – US$3,267m deficit (2012)

Trade with UK	2012	2013
Imports from UK	£193,600,286	£184,917,422
Exports to UK	£31,039,353	£42,082,523

COMMUNICATIONS
Airports – There are 57 airports; the principal airport is at Panama City
Waterways – The Panama Canal connects the Pacific and Atlantic oceans. Each year the canal handles about 5 per cent of world trade and over 40 per cent of trade between Asia and the east coast of the USA. The chief ports are Colón, Cristóbal and Balboa, at either end of the canal. Because of its role as a ship registry, there were 6,413 Panamanian- and 5,162 foreign-owned ships of over 1,000 tonnes registered under its flag in 2011
Roadways and railways – 15,137km; 76km
Telecommunications – 640,000 fixed lines and 6.77 million mobile subscriptions (2012); there were 959,800 internet users in 2009
Internet code and IDD – pa; 507 (from UK), 44 (to UK)
Media – Broadcasting is dominated by the private sector, and there are several television networks and about 100 radio stations. *La Prensa, Panama News* and *El Siglo* are among the leading newspapers
WPFI score – 30,20 (87)

EDUCATION AND HEALTH
There are nine years of compulsory education.
Literacy rate – 94 per cent (2010 est)
Gross enrolment ratio (percentage of relevant age group) – primary 100 per cent; secondary 84 per cent; tertiary 42 per cent (2012 est)
Health expenditure (per capita) – US$703 (2011)
Hospital beds (per 1,000 people) – 2.4 (2010)
Life expectancy (years) – 78.3 (2014 est)
Mortality rate – 4.77 (2014 est)
Birth rate – 18.61 (2014 est)
Infant mortality rate – 10.7 (2014 est)

PAPUA NEW GUINEA

Gau Hedinarai ai Papua-Matamata Guinea – Independent State of Papua New Guinea

Area – 462,840 sq. km
Capital – Port Moresby; population, 314,000 (2009 est)
Major town – Arawa, Lae
Currency – Kina (K) of 100 toea
Population – 6,552,730 rising at 1.84 per cent a year (2014 est)
Religion – Christian (Protestant 69.4 per cent, Roman Catholic 27 per cent), indigenous beliefs and other 3.3 per cent
Language – English, Tok Pisin, Hiri Motu (all official), Motu; 836 indigenous languages are spoken, representing over 12 per cent of the world total
Population density – 15 per sq. km (2011)
Urban population – 12.5 per cent (2012 est)
Median age (years) – 22.4 (2014 est)
National anthem – 'O Arise, All You Sons'
National day – 16 September (Independence Day)
Death penalty – Retained (last used 1950)
CPI score – 25 (144)

CLIMATE AND TERRAIN
Papua New Guinea lies in the south-western Pacific Ocean and consists of the eastern half of the island of New Guinea, the islands of Bougainville, New Britain and New Ireland, the Admiralty Islands, the D'Entrecasteaux Islands and the Louisiade archipelago. A range of densely forested mountains runs across the centre of the Papuan part of New Guinea, descending to coastal plains and swamps, and coral reefs. Elevation extremes range from 4,509m (Mt Wilhelm) to 0m (Pacific Ocean). There are a number of active volcanoes and the country is subject to frequent eruptions and earthquakes. Over 50 per cent of the country is forested, and 20 per cent is permanently or seasonally flooded. The climate is tropical and subject to the north-west monsoon (December–March) and south-east monsoon (May–October).

POLITICS
The 1975 constitution was amended in 1998 to grant greater autonomy to Bougainville, and in March 2010 to expand the maximum number of cabinet ministers from 28 to 31. The head of state is Queen Elizabeth II, represented by a governor-general who is elected by the legislature for a six-year term. The unicameral National Parliament has 109 members, 20 from provincial electorates and the remainder from open electorates, who are directly elected for a five-year term. The prime minister is nominated by the legislature and appointed by the governor-general.

Factionalism and shifting alliances have caused political instability since independence, and a proportional representation element was introduced into the voting system

Dutch incorporate the western part of the island into the Dutch East Indies — South-eastern New Guinea annexed by a British protectorate — British protectorate placed under Australian administration — Occupied by Japan — Becomes self-governing — Gains independence — Peace agreement brings autonomy

c.1500   1884-6   1899   1920-42   1945   1989-98

1828   1888   1906   1942-45   1973   1975   2001

Portuguese and Spanish navigators visit area — Britain and Germany divide the east of the island — North-east becomes a German colony — Both German and British territories administered by Australia — Territories combine as a UN trust territory and administered by Australia — Separatism on Bougainville island leads to years of conflict

in 2007 to try to increase the stability of governments. Following the 2007 legislative election, the National Alliance Party (NAP) leader Sir Michael Somare was elected prime minister for the fourth time, forming a new coalition government. Somare was convicted of financial irregularities in March 2011 and suspended for 14 days; former transport minister Peter O'Neill was elected as prime minister in August 2011. Legislative elections in 2012 saw the People's National Congress Party (PNC) gain the most seats but without a majority; following this, O'Neill announced that he would lead the government.

Governor-General, HE Sir Michael Ogio, GCMG, CBE *sworn in* 25 February 2012

SELECTED GOVERNMENT MEMBERS *as at June 2014*
Prime Minister, Peter O'Neill
Deputy Prime Minister, Leo Dion
Foreign Affairs, Rimbink Pato

PAPUA NEW GUINEA HIGH COMMISSION
3rd Floor, 14 Waterloo Place, London SW1Y 4AR
T 020-7930 0922 E info@pnghighcomm.org.uk
W www.pnghighcomm.org.uk
High Commissioner, HE Winnie Kiap, *apptd* 2011

BRITISH HIGH COMMISSION
Sec 411 Lot 1 & 2, Kiroki Street, Waigani, National Capital District, Port Moresby
T (+675) 325 1677 E uk.inpng@fco.gov.uk
W www.gov.uk/government/world/papua-new-guinea
High Commissioner, HE Jacqueline Barson, MBE, *apptd* 2010

DEFENCE

Aged 16–49, 2010 est	Males	Females
Available for military service	1,568,210	1,478,965
Fit for military service	1,130,951	1,137,753

Military expenditure – US$77m (2013)

ECONOMY AND TRADE

Political instability, corruption, a weak economy and high unemployment and crime levels had brought the country to the brink of economic and social collapse in 2004. The economy has grown since, achieving 12 years of continuous growth as of 2014, owing to higher commodity prices and tight control of the national budget but the country does remain poor and underdeveloped. Foreign investment in oil and liquid natural gas extraction since 2004 has boosted economic growth; the export of liquefied natural gas to Asian economies began in March 2014.

About 85 per cent of the population practises subsistence farming, including some tribes in the interior so isolated that their economy is unmonetised. Mineral deposits, including copper, gold, silver, nickel, oil and natural gas, are abundant and constitute the main sources of revenue, although exploitation is forced to overcome difficult terrain and poor infrastructure. This has been addressed by the government, which passed legislation in 2011 for an offshore sovereign wealth fund to manage government surpluses from mineral, oil and natural gas projects. The main industries are mining, oil extraction and refining, forestry, processing of agricultural and forestry products, construction and tourism. Industry contributes 38.5 per cent of GDP and services 33.6 per cent.

The main trading partners are Australia, Singapore and Japan. Principal exports are oil, gold, copper ore, logs, palm oil, coffee, cocoa and shellfish. The main imports are machinery and transport equipment, manufactured goods, food, fuels and chemicals.

GNI – US$15,023m; US$1,790 per capita (2012)
Annual average growth of GDP – 5.4 per cent (2013 est)
Inflation rate – 3.8 per cent (2013 est)
Population below poverty line – 37 per cent (2002 est)
Unemployment – 1.9 per cent (2008 est)
Total external debt – US$13,610m (2013 est)
Imports – US$5,500m (2012)
Exports – US$6,128m (2012)

BALANCE OF PAYMENTS
Trade – US$628m surplus (2012)
Current Account – US$2,283m deficit (2011)

Trade with UK	2012	2013
Imports from UK	£45,145,561	£48,935,941
Exports to UK	£112,869,272	£120,962,404

COMMUNICATIONS

Airports and waterways – 21, the principal airports being at Port Moresby, Lae and Rabaul; there are 11,000km of navigable waterways
Roadways – 9,349km
Telecommunications – 139,000 fixed lines and 2.709 million mobile subscriptions (2012); there were 125,000 internet users in 2009
Internet code and IDD – pg; 675 (from UK), 44 (to UK)
Major broadcasters – Commercial channel EMTV broadcasts alongside the state-run National Television Service
Press – The are two foreign-owned daily newspapers, *The National* and *The Post-Courier*
WPFI score – 23,46 (44)

EDUCATION AND HEALTH

Literacy rate – 62 per cent (2011 est)
Health expenditure (per capita) – US$79 (2011)
Life expectancy (years) – 66.85 (2014 est)
Mortality rate – 6.53 (2014 est)
Birth rate – 24.89 (2014 est)
Infant mortality rate – 39.67 (2014 est)
HIV/AIDS adult prevalence rate – 0.5 per cent (2012 est)

PARAGUAY

República del Paraguay – Republic of Paraguay

Area – 406,752 sq. km
Capital – Asunción; population, 2,131,402 (2012)
Major cities – Ciudad del Este, Lambaré, Limpio, San Lorenzo
Currency – Guaraní (Gs) of 100 céntimos
Population – 6,703,860 rising at 1.19 per cent a year (2014 est)
Religion – Christian (Roman Catholic 89.6 per cent, Protestant 6.2 per cent)
Language – Spanish, Guaraní (both official)
Population density – 17 per sq. km (2011)
Urban population – 62.5 per cent (2012)
Median age (years) – 26.8 (2014 est)
National anthem – 'Paraguayos, República o Muerte' ['Paraguayans, the Republic or Death']
National day – 15 May (Independence Day)
Death penalty – Abolished for all crimes (since 1992)
CPI score – 24 (150)

CLIMATE AND TERRAIN

The country is divided by the river Paraguay into two distinct regions. The area east of the Paraguay is a fertile, grassy plateau where most of the population lives. The area to the west, the Gran Chaco, consists of a grassy and occasionally marshy plain that extends into neighbouring countries. Elevation extremes range from 842m (Cerro Pero) to 46m (the junction of the Paraguay and Paraná rivers). The climate varies from subtropical to temperate, with higher rainfall in the east and semi-arid conditions in the west. Average temperatures in Asunción range from 18°C in June and July to 27°C in January and February.

HISTORY AND POLITICS

Spanish colonisation of Paraguay began in the early 16th century and Asunción was founded in 1537. Paraguay became independent from Spain in 1811 under the dictator José Gaspar Rodriguez de Francia, who ruled until his death in 1840. His successors instigated a period of reform and modernisation which ended in 1865–70 with the catastrophic War of the Triple Alliance against Brazil, Uruguay and Argentina over access to the sea. The war resulted in the loss of over half the population as well as 150,000 sq.km of territory, and initiated a period of political instability that lasted until 1912. In the Chaco War of 1932–5, Paraguay gained territory in the west from Bolivia in a conflict that killed 100,000 people.

Political instability and conflict in the late 1940s ended with a coup in 1954 in which General Alfredo Stroessner seized power. His rule was autocratic and increasingly repressive, marked by corruption and human rights abuses. He was ousted in a coup in 1989 that paved the way for free multiparty elections to the presidency and legislature in 1993. These were won by the National Republican Association-Colorado Party (ANR-PC) and its presidential candidate, and the ANR-PC won all subsequent elections until 2008. Instability has prevailed since the 1990s, however, with the assassination of a vice-president, an attempted coup, widespread corruption and the growth of drug-trafficking, money-laundering and organised crime.

The 2008 presidential election was won by Fernando Lugo of the Patriotic Alliance for Change coalition (APC), the first president from outside the ANR-PC in 61 years; Lugo, however, was removed from office by impeachment of the senate in June 2012 for failing to manage fatal clashes over land evictions. He was replaced by vice-president Federico Franco. In the 2013 presidential and legislative elections, Horacio Cartes of the ANR-PC was elected president while the ANR-RC remained the largest party in both chambers.

Under the 1992 constitution, the executive president is directly elected for a five-year term, which is not renewable. The bicameral Congress consists of a 45-member senate and an 80-member Chamber of Deputies, both directly elected for a five-year term. The president, who is responsible to the legislature, appoints the council of ministers.

HEAD OF STATE
President elect, Horacio Cartes, *elected* 22 April 2013
Vice-President elect, Juan Afara Marques

SELECTED GOVERNMENT MEMBERS *as at June 2014*
Defence, Bernardino Soto Estiqarribia
Foreign Affairs, Eladio Loizaga
Interior, Francisco de Vargas

EMBASSY OF THE REPUBLIC OF PARAGUAY
3rd Floor, 344 Kensington High Street, London W14 8NS
T 020-7610 4180 E consular@paraguayembassy.co.uk
W www.paraguayembassy.co.uk
Ambassador Extraordinary and Plenipotentiary, HE Miguel Solano López, *apptd* 2009

BRITISH EMBASSY
Edificio Citicenter, Piso 5, Av. Mariscal López y Cruz del Chaco, Asunción T (595) (21) 328 5507
E BE-Asuncion.Enquiries@fco.gov.uk
W www.gov.uk/government/world/paraguay
Ambassador Extraordinary and Plenipotentiary, HE Dr Jeremy Hobbs, *apptd* 2013

DEFENCE

Aged 16–49, 2010 est	Males	Females
Available for military service	1,678,335	1,675,352
Fit for military service	1,409,859	1,433,037

Military expenditure – US$458m (2013)
Conscription – 18 years of age; 12 – 24 months (selective)

ECONOMY AND TRADE

Paraguay's economy features a large informal sector and benefits from the proceeds of re-exporting to neighbouring countries. The economy started to slow in 2008, when drought reduced production of key exports, and went into recession in 2009, when the global downturn reduced export demand and commodity prices. Although growth resumed in 2010, in the longer term it is hampered by political instability, corruption, national and foreign debt, inadequate infrastructure and high crime levels. Strong export growth saw the economy grow by 12 per cent in 2013 despite a contraction in 2012. About one third of the population lives below the poverty line, although this rate is higher in the cities because of migration from the countryside of families made landless by the commercialisation of agriculture and forest clearances.

The country has few mineral resources although exploration for oil and gas is under way. The economy is largely agricultural, much of it at subsistence level. Agricultural production, which accounts for 20.4 per cent of GDP and engages 26.5 per cent of the workforce, is centred on cotton, sugar cane, soya beans, maize, wheat, tobacco, cassava, fruit, vegetables and livestock products. The main industries are sugar refining, forestry, manufacturing (cement, textiles, beverages, wood products, steel) and hydro-electric power generation. Industry accounts for 17.7 per cent of GDP and services for 61.9 per cent.

The main trading partners are Brazil, China, Argentina, Uruguay and Chile. Principal exports are soya beans, feed, cotton, meat, edible oils, electricity, timber and leather. The main imports are road vehicles, consumer goods, tobacco and petroleum products.

GNI – US$24,143m; US$3,400 per capita (2012)
Annual average growth of GDP – 12 per cent (2013 est)
Inflation rate – 2.3 per cent (2013 est)
Population below poverty line – 34.7 per cent (2010 est)
Unemployment – 6.6 per cent (2013 est)
Total external debt – US$7,013m (2013 est)
Imports – US$11,502m (2012)
Exports – US$7,282m (2012)

BALANCE OF PAYMENTS
Trade – US$4,220m deficit (2012)
Current Account – US$98m surplus (2012)

Trade with UK	2012	2013
Imports from UK	£31,914,564	£35,505,812
Exports to UK	£4,680,371	£6,752,015

COMMUNICATIONS
Airports and waterways – 15, including the principal airport at Asunción; and around 3,100km of navigable waterways around the country
Roadways and railways – There are 32,059km of roadways and a small railway system of around 36km
Telecommunications – 376,000 fixed lines and 6.79 million mobile subscriptions (2012); there were 1.105 million internet users in 2009
Internet code and IDD – py; 595 (from UK), 44 (to UK)
Media – The majority of the media is privately owned; principal newspapers include *ABC Color* and *La Nación*
WPFI score – 31,81 (105)

EDUCATION AND HEALTH
Basic education is free and compulsory for nine years.
Literacy rate – 94 per cent (2010 est)
Gross enrolment ratio (percentage of relevant age group) – primary 95 per cent; secondary 70 per cent; tertiary 51 per cent (2012 est)
Health expenditure (per capita) – US$352 (2011)
Hospital beds (per 1,000 people) – 1.3 (2011)
Life expectancy (years) – 76.8 (2014 est)
Mortality rate – 4.64 (2014 est)
Birth rate – 16.66 (2014 est)
Infant mortality rate – 20.75 (2014 est)

PERU

República del Perú – Republic of Peru

Area – 1,285,216 sq. km
Capital – Lima; population (including Callao), 9,259,967 (2012)
Major cities – Arequipa, Chiclayo, Cusco, Iquitos, Piura, Trujillo
Currency – New sol of 100 centimos
Population – 30,147,935 rising at 0.99 per cent a year (2014 est)
Religion – Christian (Roman Catholic 81.3 per cent, Protestant 12.5 per cent)
Language – Spanish, Quechua, Aymara (all official), other Amerindian languages
Population density – 23 per sq. km (2011)
Urban population – 77.6 per cent (2012)
Median age (years) – 27 (2014 est)
National anthem – 'Himno Nacional del Perú' ['National Anthem of Peru']
National day – 28 July (Independence Day)
Death penalty – Retained for certain crimes (last used 1979)
CPI score – 38 (83)

CLIMATE AND TERRAIN
Peru has three main regions: the Costa, the coastal desert plain west of the Andes; the Sierra (mountain range) of the Andes, which runs parallel to the Pacific coast; and the Montaña (or Selva), a vast area of jungle stretching from the eastern foothills of the Andes to the country's eastern and north-eastern borders. Elevation extremes range from 6,768m (Nevado Huascaran) to 0m (Pacific Ocean). The climate is arid in the west, temperate in the mountains and tropical in the east. Occasionally, due to the El Niño weather system, the northern districts experience a period of higher temperatures accompanied by torrential rain. The average temperature in Lima is 20°C.

HISTORY AND POLITICS
The Inca Empire centred on Cuzco superseded earlier civilisations in Peru and flourished from the 13th to the 15th century, when the empire reached its zenith before falling to Spanish conquistadores led by Francisco Pizarro in 1532–3. The territory formed the Viceroyalty of Peru and its gold and silver mines made Peru the principal source of wealth in Spain's American empire. After 1810, Peru became the centre of Spanish colonial government as its other colonies rebelled. Although Peru declared its independence in 1821, this was achieved only with the final defeat of Spanish forces in 1824.

Peru entered into several border disputes with its neighbours in the 19th and 20th centuries, including the Pacific War (1879–83) in which it lost three southern coastal provinces to Chile. A border dispute with Ecuador was renewed in 1981, leading to a short, inconclusive war in 1995, but was resolved in 1998 following adjudication. A border dispute with Chile ended in 1999 with the implementation of accords first agreed in 1929.

Following independence, Peru alternated between periods of military dictatorship and democratic rule. Two left-wing insurgencies, by the Maoist *Sendero Luminoso* (Shining Path) and the *Movimento Revolucionario Tupac Amaru* (MRTA), began in the 1980s. The activities of the *Sendero Luminoso* in particular destabilised the government and the economy; the conflict caused about 69,000 deaths and saw human rights abuses by both the security forces and the guerrillas. By the late 1990s both insurgencies had been overcome, although a few Maoists remain active. The conflict has left a legacy of criminal violence, much of it related to drug production and trafficking.

Alberto Fujimori, elected president in 1990 on a platform of economic reform, subverted democratic institutions in Peru during his decade in power, suspending the legislature for three years, sacking judges and imposing order through an 'emergency national reconstruction government'. He fled to Japan in 2000 to escape corruption charges, but was extradited and convicted in 2007 of abuse of power and in 2009 of human rights abuses.

In the 2011 legislative election, the Peru Wins alliance gained the most seats but without a majority. The presidential election was won in the second round in June 2011 by the Peruvian Nationalist Party candidate Ollanta Humala.

Under the 1993 constitution, the executive president is directly elected for a five-year term, renewable once. The unicameral legislature, the Congress of the Republic, has 130 members, directly elected for a five-year term. The president, who is responsible to the legislature, appoints the council of ministers.

HEAD OF STATE
President, Ollanta Humala, *elected* 5 June 2011, *sworn in* 28 July 2011
First Vice-President, Marisol Espinoza

SELECTED GOVERNMENT MEMBERS *as at July 2014*
President of Council of Ministers, Rene Diaz
Defence, Pedro Cateriano
Economy and Finance, Luis Castilla Rubio
Foreign Affairs, Eda Rivas

EMBASSY OF PERU
52 Sloane Street, London SW1X 9SP
T 020-7235 1917 E postmaster@peruembassy-uk.com
W www.peruembassy-uk.com
Ambassador Extraordinary and Plenipotentiary, HE Julio Munoz-Deacon

BRITISH EMBASSY
Torre Parque Mar (Piso 22), Avenida José Larco 1301, Lima
T (+51) (1) 617 3000 E belima@fco.gov.uk
W www.gov.uk/government/world/peru
Ambassador Extraordinary and Plenipotentiary, HE James Dauris, *apptd* 2010

DEFENCE

Aged 16–49, 2010 est	Males	Females
Available for military service	7,385,588	7,727,623
Fit for military service	5,788,629	6,565,097

Military expenditure – US$2,638m (2013)

ECONOMY AND TRADE
The Peruvian economy has been growing by an average of 5.6 per cent for the past five years, driven by exports of silver, copper, agricultural produce and fish. Tourism has also driven growth. Poverty remains widespread, but the benefits of economic growth are starting to be felt in the poorer regions and the poverty rate has declined by 23 per cent since 2002. The dependence on metal exports and imported foodstuffs makes the economy vulnerable to fluctuations in world prices and the economy slowed during the 2009 recession

Mineral resources, including copper, gold, silver, zinc, oil and natural gas, are abundant, and extracting and refining these is the mainstay of the economy. Other industries include steel and metal fabrication, fishing and fish processing, textiles and clothes manufacture and food processing. Agriculture is centred on asparagus, coffee, cocoa, cotton, sugar cane, rice, cereals, vegetables, fruit, coca, medicinal plants, meat and dairy products. Services contribute 56.3 per cent to GDP, industry 37.5 per cent and agriculture 6.2 per cent.

The main trading partners are the USA, China, Canada, Japan, Spain and other South American countries. Principal exports are copper, gold, zinc, tin, crude oil and petroleum products, natural gas, coffee, vegetables and fruit. The main imports are oil and petroleum products, chemicals, plastics, machinery, vehicles, telecommunications equipment, iron and steel, and food.

GNI – US$191,089m; US$6,060 per capita (2012)
Annual average growth of GDP – 5.1 per cent (2013 est)
Inflation rate – 2.9 per cent (2013 est)
Population below poverty line – 25.8 per cent (2012 est)
Unemployment – 3.6 per cent (2013 est)
Total external debt – US$50,150m (2013 est)
Imports – US$41,089m (2012)
Exports – US$45,600m (2012)

BALANCE OF PAYMENTS
Trade – US$4,510m surplus (2012)
Current Account – US$7,135m deficit (2012)

Trade with UK	2012	2013
Imports from UK	£164,079,991	£167,711,466
Exports to UK	£218,959,126	£225,093,890

COMMUNICATIONS
Airports and waterways – There are 59 airports, including the international airport at Lima; there are 8,808km of inland waterways, and the main seaports are Callao and Matarani
Roadways and railways – There are 140,672km of roadways, including sections of the east-west Andean Highway, linking the Pacific and Atlantic coasts, and the north–south Pan-American Highway running along the Pacific coast; the state-run railways have 1,907km of track
Telecommunications – 3.42 million fixed lines and 29.4 million mobile subscriptions (2012); there were 9.16 million internet users in 2009
Internet code and IDD – pe; 51 (from UK), 44 (to UK)
Media – The state-owned Television Nacional de Peru broadcasts alongside a number of commercial television channels; daily newspapers include *El Bocón* and *La República*
WPFI score – 31,70 (104)

EDUCATION AND HEALTH
Education is free and compulsory for 11 years.
Literacy rate – 89.6 per cent (2010 est)
Gross enrolment ratio (percentage of relevant age group) – primary 100 per cent; secondary 86 per cent (2012 est)

Health expenditure (per capita) – US$289 (2011)
Hospital beds (per 1,000 people) – 1.5 (2011)
Life expectancy (years) – 73.23 (2014 est)
Mortality rate – 5.99 (2014 est)
Birth rate – 18.57 (2014 est)
Infant mortality rate – 20.21 (2014 est)

THE PHILIPPINES

Republika ng Pilipinas – Republic of the Philippines

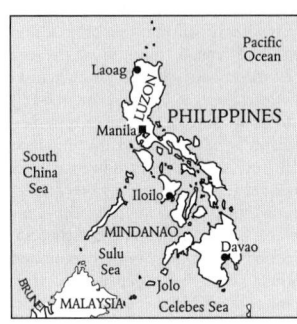

Area – 300,000 sq. km
Capital – Manila; population (Metro Manila, including
   Quezon City), 11,997,401 (2012)
Major cities – Bacolod, Cagayan de Oro, Cebu, Davao,
   General Santos (Dadiangas), Iloilo, Zamboanga
Currency – Philippine peso (P) of 100 centavos
Population – 107,668,231 rising at 1.81 per cent a year
   (2014 est); Tagalog (28.1 per cent), Cebuano (13.1 per
   cent), Ilocano (9 per cent), Bisaya (7.6 per cent),
   Hiligaynon Ilonggo (7.5 per cent), Bikol (6 per cent),
   Waray (3.4 per cent) (2000)
Religion – Christian (Roman Catholic 82.9 per cent,
   Evangelical 2.8 per cent), Muslim 5 per cent
Language – Filipino, English (both official), Tagalog,
   Cebuano, Ilocano, Hiligaynon, Bicol, Waray, Pampango,
   Pangasinan
Population density – 319 per sq. km (2011)
Urban population – 49.1 per cent (2012)
Median age (years) – 23.5 (2014 est)
National anthem – 'Lupang Hinirang' ['Chosen Land']
National day – 12 June (Independence Day)
Death penalty – Abolished for all crimes (since 2006)
CPI score – 36 (94)

CLIMATE AND TERRAIN
The Philippines comprises over 7,100 islands in the western
Pacific Ocean. The principal islands are Luzon, Mindanao,
Mindoro, Samar, Negros, Palawan, Panay and Leyte; other
groups include the Sulu islands, Babuyanes and Batanes,
Calamian and Kalayaan islands. The islands mostly have
mountainous interiors and narrow coastal plains. The
mountain ranges are volcanic, and some volcanoes are still
active. Elevation extremes range from 2,954m (Mt Apo) to
0m (Philippine Sea). The climate is tropical; the average
temperature in Manila is 27°C, and relative humidity is high.
The country is affected by the monsoons, which cause the
rainy season between July and October. During this period
the country is also susceptible to typhoons, which frequently
cause widespread damage and loss of life.

HISTORY AND POLITICS
The Philippine islands were settled first by Malays, then by
Chinese, Indonesian and Arab traders. Islam was introduced

in the 14th century and became the dominant religion in
the south. The islands were discovered by Spain and then
settled from 1565 by the Spanish, who introduced
Roman Catholicism. Colonial rule lasted until 1898, when
Spain ceded the colony to the USA following the
Spanish-American War. The country became internally
self-governing in 1935, was occupied by Japan from 1942 to
1944, and achieved independence from the USA in 1946.
   Ferdinand Marcos was elected president in 1965,
imposing martial law in 1972. His regime became
increasingly repressive, corrupt and violent, and when he
falsified election results in 1986 to prevent Corazon Aquino
from taking office as president, a popular uprising forced him
to flee the country. Aquino survived political unrest and ten
attempted military coups to introduce a new constitution and
entrench democratic politics.
   Fidel Ramos, Aquino's successor in 1992, built on her
work, raised the country's international profile and instigated
peace talks with insurgents (*see* below). Joseph Estrada,
elected president in 1998, was overthrown in 2001 in a
popular uprising; his term was completed by vice-president
Gloria Arroyo. President Arroyo retained the presidency in
the 2004 presidential election, but her popularity plummeted
and her anti-corruption measures and economic reforms
were undermined by corruption scandals and impeachment
attempts.
   The 2010 presidential election was won by Benigno
('Noynoy') Aquino III, son of former president Corazon
Aquino. In the May 2013 legislative elections, the Liberal
Party (LP) won the most seats in the house of representatives
but without a majority.
   Under the 1987 constitution, the executive president is
directly elected for a six-year term, which is not renewable.
There is a bicameral Congress. The lower house, the House
of Representatives, has up to 250 directly elected members,
plus 20 per cent are appointed from party and minority
group lists; all serve a three-year term. The senate has 24
members directly elected for a six-year term, with half
re-elected every three years.
   The Autonomous Region of Muslim Mindanao comprises
the provinces of Lanao del Sur and Maguindanao on
Mindanao and the island provinces of Sulu, Tawi-Tawi
and Basilan. It has a 24-member regional assembly and a
governor.

HEAD OF STATE
President, Benigno ('Noynoy') Aquino III, *elected* 10 May
   2010, *sworn in* 30 June 2010
Vice-President, Jejomar Binay

SELECTED GOVERNMENT MEMBERS *as at June 2014*
Defence, Voltaire Gazmin
Finance, Cesar Purisima
Foreign Affairs, Albert del Rosario
Trade and Industry, Gregory Domingo

EMBASSY OF THE REPUBLIC OF THE PHILIPPINES
6–8 Suffolk Street, London SW1Y 4HG
T 020-7451 1780 E embassy@philemb.co.uk
W http://philembassy-uk.org
Ambassador Extraordinary and Plenipotentiary, HE Enrique
   Manalo, *apptd* 2011

BRITISH EMBASSY
120 Upper McKinley Road, McKinley Hill, Taguig City 1634, Manila
T (+63) (2) 858 2200 E ukinthephilippines@fco.gov.uk
W www.gov.uk/government/world/philippines
Ambassador Extraordinary and Plenipotentiary, HE Asif
   Ahmad, *apptd* 2013

INSURGENCIES

A communist insurgency by the New People's Army (NPA) began in the late 1960s. The NPA is based in Mindanao but has groups in rural areas throughout the country. Peace talks between the government and the NPA's political front, the National Democratic Front, stalled in 2004 but were resumed in early 2011.

There has been a Muslim (Moro) insurgency in the southern islands, particularly Mindanao, since the 1970s. The Moro National Liberation Front (MNLF) concluded a peace agreement with the government in 1996 that ended its insurgency and established the Autonomous Region of Muslim Mindanao (ARMM). The Moro Islamic Liberation Front (MILF) agreed a ceasefire with the government in 2003, but negotiations over a Muslim 'homeland' broke down in 2008; a resumption of violence in 2009 displaced over 300,000 people until another ceasefire was agreed and peace talks resumed in late 2009. Talks broke-down in October 2011, however, after air strikes on MILF areas in Zamboanga left 35 people dead.

The radical Muslim separatist group Abu Sayyaf, based on Jolo and Basilan, is viewed as a terrorist organisation and the government refuses to negotiate with it. It has links with Jamaah Islamiyah, the group responsible for the Bali bombings, and possibly with al-Qaida. Since 2001 it has carried out a series of violent kidnappings and bombings, but military operations since 2006 have depleted its numbers and its leadership.

DEFENCE

Aged 16–49, 2010 est	Males	Females
Available for military service	25,614,135	25,035,061
Fit for military service	20,142,940	21,427,792

Military expenditure – US$3,208m (2013 est)

ECONOMY AND TRADE

The economy has survived the 2009 recession better than other Asian economies thanks to low dependence on exports, robust domestic consumption and remittances from four- to five-million overseas workers. Despite this, poverty has increased as economic expansion struggles to offset the high rate of population growth, and nearly a quarter of the population lives below the poverty line. The government announced a stimulus effort after growth slowed significantly in 2011. In 2012 the Philippines saw growth of 6.8 per cent, in 2012 and 2013

Major industries include electronics assembly, manufacture of clothing, footwear, pharmaceuticals, chemicals and wood products, food processing, oil refining and fishing. The large agricultural sector employs 32 per cent of the workforce, producing sugar cane, coconuts, rice, maize, tropical fruits and livestock products. Agriculture accounts for 11.2 per cent of GDP, industry for 31.6 per cent and services for 57.2 per cent.

The main trading partners are the USA, Japan, China, Singapore and other Asian states. Principal exports are semiconductors and electronic products, clothing, copper products, petroleum products, coconut oil and fruit. The main imports are electronic products, fuels, machinery and transport equipment, iron and steel, fabrics, grains, chemicals and plastics.

GNI – US$252,549m; US$2,500 per capita (2012)
Annual average growth of GDP – 6.8 per cent (2013 est)
Inflation rate – 2.8 per cent (2013 est)
Population below poverty line – 26.5 per cent (2009 est)
Unemployment – 7.4 per cent (2013 est)

Total external debt – US$72,810m (2013 est)
Imports – US$65,845m (2012)
Exports – US$52,071m (2012)

BALANCE OF PAYMENTS
Trade – US$13,773m deficit (2012)
Current Account – US$7,177m surplus (2012)

Trade with UK	2012	2013
Imports from UK	£332,569,766	£374,262443
Exports to UK	£432,279,429	£383,595,978

COMMUNICATIONS

Airports and waterways – There are 89 airports; the main ports are Manila (Luzon), Cebu, Davao, Subic Bay, Batangas and Iloilo, and there are 3,219km of waterways
Roadways and railways – There are 213,151km of roadways and Philippine National Railway operates 995km of railways
Telecommunications – 3.939 million fixed lines and 103 million mobile subscriptions (2012); there were 8.28 million internet users in 2009
Internet code and IDD – ph; 63 (from UK), 44 (to UK)
Major broadcasters – The government-owned People's Television network competes with three commercial broadcasters and over 600 radio stations
Press – There are four main national newspapers, including the *Daily Tribune* and *Malaya*
WPFI score – 43,69 (149)

EDUCATION AND HEALTH

There are seven years of free and compulsory primary education, followed by three years of free but non-compulsory secondary education.
Literacy rate – 95.4 per cent (2010 est)
Gross enrolment ratio (percentage of relevant age group) – primary 106 per cent; secondary 85 per cent; tertiary 28.9 per cent (2011 est)
Health expenditure (per capita) – US$97 (2011)
Hospital beds (per 1,000 people) – 1 (2011)
Life expectancy (years) – 72.48 (2014 est)
Mortality rate – 4.92 (2014 est)
Birth rate – 24.24 (2014 est)
Infant mortality rate – 17.64 (2014 est)

POLAND

Rzeczpospolita Polska – Republic of Poland

Area – 312,685 sq. km
Capital – Warsaw; population, 1,716,647 (2021)
Major cities – Bydgoszcz, Gdansk, Katowice, Krakow, Lodz, Lublin, Poznan, Szczecin, Wroclaw

c.800　　1772-95　　　　　1918　　　　1944-5　　1947　　　　1981　　　　2004

　　1386　　　1814-5　　　1939　　　1945　　　1980　　　1989

Currency – Zloty of 100 groszy
Population – 38,346,279 falling at 0.11 per cent a year (2014 est)
Religion – Christian (Roman Catholic 87.2 per cent, Orthodox 1.3 per cent, Protestant 0.4 per cent)
Language – Polish (official)
Population density – 127 per sq. km (2011)
Urban population – 60.8 per cent (2012 est)
Median age (years) – 39.5 (2014 est)
National anthem – 'Mazurek Dabrowskiego' ['Dabrowski's Mazurka']
National day – 3 May (Constitution Day)
Death penalty – Abolished for all crimes (since 1997)
CPI score – 60 (38)

CLIMATE AND TERRAIN

Poland lies mostly in a great plain crossed by the Oder, Neisse and Vistula rivers. The land rises to the Carpathian, Tatra and Sudeten mountains along the southern border. Elevation extremes range from 2,499m (Rysy) to −2m (Raczki Elblaskie). The climate is continental, and average temperatures in Warsaw range from −1°C in January to 17°C in July and August.

POLITICS

Under the 1997 constitution, the head of state is the president, who is directly elected for a five-year term, renewable once. The president nominates the prime minister and has the right to be consulted over the appointment of the foreign, defence and interior ministers. The National Assembly is bicameral; the lower house, the Diet *(Sejm)*, has 460 members elected by proportional representation for a four-year term. The senate has 100 members elected on a provincial basis for a four-year term.

Bronislaw Komorowski of The Civil Platform (PO), was elected president in July 2014. In 2014, the PO remained the largest party in both houses after legislation elections. Prime Minister Donald Tusk stood down in September 2014, Ewa Kopacz replaced him on 15 September. A new government was expected to be formed on 22 September.

HEAD OF STATE

President, Bronislaw Komorowski, *elected* 4 July 2010, *sworn in* 6 August 2010

SELECTED GOVERNMENT MEMBERS *as at June 2014*
Prime Minister, Donald Tusk
Deputy Prime Minister, Economy, Janusz Piechocinski
Finance, Mateusz Szczurek
Defence, Tomasz Siemoniak

EMBASSY OF THE REPUBLIC OF POLAND
47 Portland Place, London W1B 1JH
T 020-7291 3520 **E** london@msz.gov.pl
W http://london.polemb.net
Ambassador Extraordinary and Plenipotentiary, HE Witold Sobków, *apptd* 2012

BRITISH EMBASSY
ul. Kawalerii 12, 00-468 Warsaw
T (+48) (22) 311 0000 **E** info@britishembassy.pl
W www.gov.uk/government/world/poland
Ambassador Extraordinary and Plenipotentiary, HE Robin Barnett, CMG, *apptd* 2011

DEFENCE
Military expenditure – US$9,431m (2013)

Aged 16–49, 2010 est	Males	Females
Available for military service	9,531,855	9,298,593
Fit for military service	7,817,556	7,766,361

ECONOMY AND TRADE
Poland's successful transition to a market economy in the 1990s came at the cost of high levels of public debt, unemployment and inflation, which were reduced by subsequent governments. The economy has grown steadily since 1992 and particularly since accession to the EU in 2004, avoiding recession in 2008–9. Further economic development is hindered by inefficiency, rigidity and low-level corruption, although the Tusk government is committed to further privatisation and restructuring public finances. Economic problems in the eurozone caused growth to slow in 2012 and 2013, and unemployment remains high at 10.3 per cent.

Poland has vast mineral resources, especially coal, and nearly half its area is fertile arable land. The large agricultural sector has been modernised but remains inefficient; it employs 12.9 per cent of the workforce but contributes only 4 per cent of GDP. The agricultural products are vegetables, fruit, wheat, meat, eggs and dairy products. The main industries are machine-building, iron and steel production, coal-mining, chemicals, shipbuilding, food processing, glass, beverages and textiles. Industry accounts for 33.3 per cent of GDP.

The main trading partners are other EU countries (especially Germany) and Russia. Principal exports include machinery and vehicles, manufactured and semi-manufactured goods, food and livestock. The main imports are machinery and vehicles, semi-manufactured goods, chemicals, minerals, fuels and lubricants.

GNI – US$467,868m; US$12,660 per capita (2012)
Annual average growth of GDP – 1.3 per cent (2013 est)
Inflation rate – 1 per cent (2013 est)
Population below poverty line – 10.6 per cent (2008 est)
Unemployment – 13.5 per cent (2013 est)
Total external debt – US$365,200m (2013 est)
Imports – US$196,199m (2012)
Exports – US$183,524m (2012)

BALANCE OF PAYMENTS
Trade – US$12,675m deficit (2012)
Current Account – US$17,169m deficit (2012)

Trade with UK	2012	2013
Imports from UK	£3,378,229,092	£3,641,781,897
Exports to UK	£7,364,884,925	£7,722,951,881

COMMUNICATIONS

Airports and waterways – The principal airports are at Warsaw, Krakow, Katowice and Wroclaw, and there are 83 smaller aiports; the principal seaports are Gdansk, Gdynia, Swinoujscie and Szczecin, and there are 3,997km of navigable rivers and canals

Roadways and railways – 423,997km; 19,428km

Telecommunications – 6.125 million fixed lines and 50.84 million mobile subscriptions (2012); there were 22.45 million internet users in 2009

Internet code and IDD – pl; 48 (from UK), 44 (to UK)

Major broadcasters – State-owned television (TVP) still has the largest national audience share for its output, although there are competitive commercial and subscription services

Press – *Gazeta Wyborcza* and *Fakt* are the principal mass-circulation dailies

WPFI score – 11,03 (19)

EDUCATION AND HEALTH

Elementary education (ages seven to 15) is free and compulsory. Secondary education is also free, but optional.

Literacy rate – 100 per cent (2011 est)

Gross enrolment ratio (percentage of relevant age group) – primary 101 per cent; secondary 98 per cent; tertiary 73 per cent (2012 est)

Health expenditure (per capita) – US$899 (2011)

Hospital beds (per 1,000 people) – 6.6 (2010)

Life expectancy (years) – 76.65 (2014 est)

Mortality rate – 10.37 (2014 est)

Birth rate – 9.77 (2014 est)

Infant mortality rate – 6.19 (2014 est)

PORTUGAL

República Portuguesa – *Portuguese Republic*

Area – 92,090 sq. km

Capital – Lisbon; population, 2,856,916 (2012)

Major cities – Coimbra, Oporto

Currency – Euro (€) of 100 cents

Population – 10,813,834 rising at 0.12 per cent a year (2014 est)

Religion – Christian (Roman Catholic 81 per cent, other 3.3 per cent)

Language – Portuguese, Mirandese (both official)

Population density – 115 per sq. km (2011)

Urban population – 61.6 per cent (2012)

Median age (years) – 41.1 (2014 est)

National anthem – 'A Portuguesa' ['The Portuguese']

National day – 10 June (Portugal Day)

Death penalty – Abolished for all crimes (since 1976)

CPI score – 62 (33)

CLIMATE AND TERRAIN

The terrain is mountainous north of the river Tagus, with rolling hills and plains in the south. Elevation extremes range from 2,351m (Ponta do Pico, Azores) to 0m (Atlantic Ocean). Forests of pine, cork oak and eucalyptus cover about 38 per cent of the country. The climate is temperate, with average temperatures in Lisbon ranging from 11.3°C in January to 23°C in August.

HISTORY AND POLITICS

Part of the Roman Empire from the second century BC, the country was overrun by Vandals and Visigoths in the fifth century AD. The Visigoths were ousted by Muslims from north Africa in the eighth century, but Christian reconquest began in the tenth century and an independent Christian kingdom was established in the 12th century.

Portuguese navigators led the 15th-century European age of exploration and the country soon became a major commercial and colonial power, its empire expanding to include Brazil, parts of China and large areas of Africa. In 1807 Portugal was invaded by Napoleonic France and then became the base from which Allied forces liberated Portugal and Spain in the Peninsular War. The 19th century was politically turbulent, with power struggles between conservative and liberal politicians and between different factions of the royal family. In 1910 an armed uprising in Lisbon drove King Manuel II into exile and a republic was declared.

A period of political instability ensued until the military intervened in 1926. The constitution of 1933 gave formal expression to the authoritarian *Estado Novo* (New State) introduced by Dr Antonio Salazar, prime minister from 1932 until 1968. Marcello Caetano succeeded Salazar in 1968 but the regime's failure to liberalise at home or to conclude wars in the African colonies resulted in the government's overthrow in a military coup in 1974. Great political turmoil followed in 1974–5, a period in which most of the country's colonies gained their independence. Elections in 1976 stabilised the situation and full civilian government was restored in 1982. Portugal joined the EEC in 1986 and adopted the euro in 2002.

The 2006 presidential election was won by the Social Democrat candidate Anibal Cavaco Silva (prime minister 1985–95), and he was re-elected in January 2011. The Socialist Party government, in power since 2005 but as a minority government since the 2009 election, resigned after its austerity programme was defeated in March 2011. In the legislative election in June, the Social Democratic Party (PSD) won the most seats but not an overall majority, and formed a coalition with the Democratic and Social Centre-People's Party and independents under the PSD leader Pedro Passos Coelho.

Under the 1976 constitution, amended in 1982 and 1989, the head of state is a president who is directly elected for a five-year term, renewable once. The unicameral Assembly of the Republic has 230 members, directly elected by proportional representation for a four-year term. The prime minister, appointed by the president, is usually the leader of the largest party in the assembly.

HEAD OF STATE

President of the Republic, Anibal Cavaco Silva, *elected* 22 January 2006, *sworn in* 9 March 2006, *re-elected* 2011

SELECTED GOVERNMENT MEMBERS *as at June 2014*

Prime Minister, Pedro Passos Coelho

Interior, Miguel Macedo

Finance, Maria Luis Albuquerque

EMBASSY OF PORTUGAL
11 Belgrave Square, London SW1X 8PP
T 020-7235 5331 E londres@mne.pt
W www.portuguese-embassy.co.uk
Ambassador Extraordinary and Plenipotentiary, HE Joao de Vallera, *apptd* 2011

BRITISH EMBASSY
Rua de Sao Bernardo 33, 1249-082 Lisbon
T (+351) (21) 392 4000 E ppa.lisbon@fco.gov.uk
W www.gov.uk/government/world/portugal
Ambassador Extraordinary and Plenipotentiary, HE Kirsty Hayes, *apptd* 2014

DEFENCE

Aged 16–49, 2010 est	Males	Females
Available for military service	2,566,264	2,458,297
Fit for military service	2,103,080	2,018,004

Military expenditure – US$4,842m (2013)

ECONOMY AND TRADE

Portugal's economy was transformed after it joined the EU in 1986 into a diversified and increasingly service-based economy. The rapid growth of the 1990s slowed in 2001–8, and the global downturn pushed the economy into recession in 2009. Despite government austerity measures, a budget deficit treble the eurozone limit led to the country's credit rating being downgraded in 2010 amid concerns about the country's ability to service its sovereign debt; in April 2011 the government obtained EU financial support. GDP fell in 2012 and 2013, as the government cut spending and increased tax to comply with the conditions of an EU-IMF financial rescue package. Unemployment remains high at 16.8 per cent, with unemployment among the under-25s reaching 36.5 per cent.

Around 12 per cent of the workforce is engaged in agriculture, contributing 2.6 per cent of GDP. The chief products are grain, fruit and vegetables, livestock, fish, dairy products and timber and cork from the forests. The main industries are tourism, manufacturing (textiles, footwear, cork, pulp and paper, chemicals, motor vehicle components), metalworking, winemaking, oil refining, and shipbuilding and repair. Natural resources are being exploited to generate electricity from hydroelectric and solar sources to reduce dependence on imported fuel and energy. Industry accounts for 22.2 per cent of GDP and services for 75.2 per cent.

The main trading partners are other EU countries, particularly Spain and Angola. Principal exports are agricultural products, food, wine, oil products, wood products, other industrial products, machinery and tools. The main imports include agricultural products, chemicals, vehicles, optical and precision instruments, computer and IT components.

GNI – US$207,098m; US$20,620 per capita (2012)
Annual average growth of GDP – –1.8 per cent (2013 est)
Inflation rate – 0.4 per cent (2013 est)
Population below poverty line – 18 per cent (2006)
Unemployment – 16.8 per cent (2013 est)
Total external debt – US$508,300m (2013)
Imports – US$72,306m (2012)
Exports – US$58,255m (2012)

BALANCE OF PAYMENTS
Trade – US$14,051m deficit (2012)
Current Account – US$3,289m deficit (2012)

Trade with UK	2012	2013
Imports from UK	£1,341,845,362	£1,327,514,130
Exports to UK	£1,739,201,933	£1,908,487,023

COMMUNICATIONS

Airports and waterways – There are 43 airports, including international airports at Lisbon, Oporto, Faro, Santa Maria (Azores) and Funchal (Madeira); the main ports are Aveiro, Figueira da Foz, Leixoes, Lisbon, Setubal and Sines
Roadways and railways – 82,900km; 3,319km
Telecommunications – 4.558 million fixed lines and 12.3121 million mobile subscriptions (2012); there were 5.168 million internet users in 2009
Internet code and IDD – pt; 351 (from UK), 44 (to UK)
Major broadcasters – The monopoly of the public broadcaster RTP ended in 1992, and commercial stations now dominate the market
Press – Principal national newspapers include the daily titles *Diario de Noticias, Correio da Manha* and *Jornal de Noticias*
WPFI score – 17,73 (30)

EDUCATION AND HEALTH

Education is free and compulsory for nine years from the age of six. The university at Coimbra was founded in 1290.
Literacy rate – 95 per cent (2011 est)
Gross enrolment ratio (percentage of relevant age group) – primary 114 per cent; secondary 107 per cent; tertiary 62.2 per cent (2011 est)
Health expenditure (per capita) – US$2,311 (2011)
Hospital beds (per 1,000 people) – 3.4 (2010)
Life expectancy (years) – 79.01 (2014 est)
Mortality rate – 10.97 (2013 est)
Birth rate – 9.42 (2014 est)
Infant mortality rate – 4.48 (2014 est)

AUTONOMOUS REGIONS

Madeira and the Azores are both autonomous regions, each with its own locally elected assembly and government.
MADEIRA is a group of islands in the Atlantic Ocean about 990km south-west of Lisbon, and consists of Madeira, Porto Santo and three uninhabited islands. Total area is 801 sq. km; population, 267,938 (2011 est). Funchal on Madeira, the largest island, is the capital.
THE AZORES is an archipelago of nine islands in the Atlantic Ocean 1,400–1,800km west of Lisbon, and consists of Flores, Corvo, Terceira, Sao Jorge, Pico, Faial, Graciosa, Sao Miguel and Santa Maria. Total area is 2,322 sq. km; population, 246,102 (2011 est). Ponta Delgada, on Sao Miguel, is the capital.

QATAR

Dawlat Qatar – State of Qatar

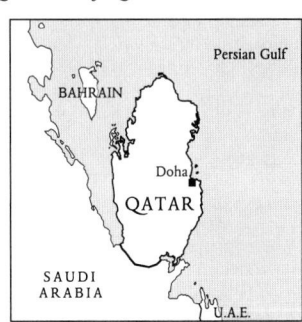

Area – 11,586 sq. km
Capital – Doha; population, 427,000 (2009)
Major cities – Ar Rayyan, al-Wakrah
Currency – Qatar riyal of 100 dirhams
Population – 2,123,160 rising at 3.58 per cent a year
(2014 est); Arab (40 per cent), Indian (18 per cent),
Pakistani (18 per cent), Iranian (10 per cent) (est)
Religion – Muslim 77.5 per cent (predominantly Sunni),
Christian 8.5 per cent, other 14 per cent
Language – Arabic (official), English
Population density – 165 per sq. km (2011)
Urban population – 98.9 per cent (2012 est)
Median age (years) – 32.6 (2014 est)
National anthem – 'As-Salam al-Amiri' ['Peace to the Amir']
National day – 18 December
Death penalty – Retained
CPI score – 68 (28)
Literacy rate – 96 per cent (2011)
Life expectancy (years) – 78.38 (2014 est)
Mortality rate – 1.53 (2014 est)
Birth rate – 9.95 (2014 est)
Infant mortality rate – 6.42 (2014 est)

CLIMATE AND TERRAIN

Qatar occupies a peninsula in the Persian Gulf and is mostly a low-lying desert plain, with sand dunes in the south. Elevation extremes range from 103m (Qurayn Abu al-Bawl) to 0m (Persian Gulf). The country has a desert climate, with low rainfall and average temperatures ranging from 17.2°C in January to 34.7°C in July. Humidity along the coast often reaches 90 per cent in summer.

HISTORY AND POLITICS

Towns on the Qatari coast developed into important trading centres from the 18th century. Persian rule of the area ended in the mid-18th century and after a period of conflict, the peninsula became a dependency of Bahrain in the 1850s. A revolt against Bahraini rule in the 1860s was suppressed, but Britain intervened in 1867, recognising the dependency as a separate entity. Nominally under the rule of the Ottoman Empire from 1871 until the outbreak of the First World War, Qatar became a British protectorate in 1916, when the al-Thani family was recognised as the ruling house. It became independent in 1971.

In 1972 Sheikh Ahmad was overthrown by the crown prince and prime minister, Sheikh Khalifa. Sheikh Khalifa was overthrown in 1995 by his son and heir, Sheikh Hamad, who has since introduced liberal reforms. Municipal elections, the first democratic polls since independence, were held in 1999. A referendum in 2003 approved a new constitution, which came into force in 2005. Elections to the partially elected consultative council established by the constitution have yet to take place. In June 2013 Sheikh Tamim bin Hamad al-Thani took over as emir after his father abdicated.

A new constitution came into force in 2005. The head of state is a hereditary absolute monarch, the amir. There is no legislature at present, although the 2005 constitution provides for a legislative council with 45 members, 30 directly elected and 15 appointed by the amir, and this will have legislative powers. At present there is an advisory council with 35 members appointed by the amir. There are no political parties. Women have been permitted to vote and stand for election since 1999.

HEAD OF STATE

HH Amir of Qatar, Defence, Sheikh Tamim bin Hamad al-Thani, *assumed power* 25 June 1913
Crown Prince, Vacant

SELECTED GOVERNMENT MEMBERS *as at June 2014*
Prime Minister, Interior, HH Sheikh Abdullah bin Nasser bin Khalifa al-Thani
Deputy Prime Minister, Ahmed bin Abdullah bin Zaid al-Mahmoud
Finance, Ali Sherif al-Emadi
Economy and Trade, Ahmed bin Jassim bin Mohamed al-Thani

EMBASSY OF THE STATE OF QATAR
1 South Audley Street, London W1K 1NB
T 020-7493 2200 W www.qatarembassy.info
Ambassador Extraordinary and Plenipotentiary, HE Khalid Rashid al-Hamoudi al-Mansouri, *apptd* 2005

BRITISH EMBASSY
West Bay, PO Box 3, Off Wahda Street near Rainbow Roundabout, Doha
T (+974) 4496 2000 E embassy.qatar@fco.gov.uk
W www.gov.uk/government/world/qatar
Ambassador Extraordinary and Plenipotentiary, Michael O'Neill, *apptd* 2012

DEFENCE

Aged 16–49, 2010 est	Males	Females
Available for military service	389,487	165,572
Fit for military service	321,974	140,176

Military expenditure – US$1,913m (2010)

ECONOMY AND TRADE

The economy is based largely on the production of oil and gas, which account for more than 50 per cent of GDP, about 85 per cent of export earnings and 70 per cent of government revenues, and have made Qatar the world's highest per-capita income country. The state-owned Qatar General Petroleum Corporation controls the industry, and is responsible for oil production onshore and offshore. There has been substantial foreign investment in exploitation of Qatar's large gasfields, and the country is now the world's leading exporter of liquefied natural gas.

Other industries include oil refining, production of ammonia, fertilisers, petrochemicals, steel and cement, and ship repairing. Industry contributes 72.2 per cent of GDP and services 27.7 per cent.

The main export markets are Japan, South Korea and India; the chief sources of imports are EU states, the USA, UAE, Saudi Arabia, China and Japan. Principal exports are liquefied natural gas, petroleum products, fertilisers and steel. The main imports are machinery and transport equipment, food and chemicals.

Annual average growth of GDP – 5.5 per cent (2013 est)
Inflation rate – 3.1 per cent (2013 est)
Unemployment – 0.3 per cent (2013 est)
Total external debt – US$149,400m (2013 est)
Imports – US$36,000m (2012)
Exports – US$128,500m (2012)

BALANCE OF PAYMENTS
Trade – US$92,500m surplus (2012)
Current Account – US$62,335m surplus (2012)

Trade with UK	2012	2013
Imports from UK	£1,308,892,622	£1,467,245,767
Exports to UK	£3,019,508,685	£2,565,142,282

COMMUNICATIONS
Airports and waterways – Doha is the principal airport and also the main seaport
Roadways – 9,830km
Telecommunications – 327,000 fixed lines and 2.6 million mobile subscriptions (2012); there were 563,800 internet users in 2009
Internet code and IDD – qa; 974 (from UK), 44 (to UK)
Media – Domestic television and radio are exclusively state-run; al-Jazeera is the principal broadcaster and one of the largest broadcasters in the Middle East
WPFI score – 34,32 (113)

ROMANIA

Area – 238,391 sq. km
Capital – Bucharest; population, 1,938,245 (2012)
Major cities – Brasov, Cluj-Napoca, Constanta, Craiova, Galati, Iasi, Timisoara
Currency – New leu (plural lei) of 100 bani
Population – 21,729,871 falling at 0.29 per cent a year (2014 est); Romanian (83.4 per cent), Hungarian (6.1 per cent), Roma (3.1 per cent) (2011); small minority of Sasi (Transylvanian Saxons)
Religion – Christian (Orthodox 81.9 per cent, Protestant 6.4 per cent, Roman Catholic 4.3 per cent)
Language – Romanian (official), Hungarian, Romani
Population density – 93 per sq. km (2011)
Urban population – 52.8 per cent (2012 est)
Median age (years) – 39.8 (2014 est)
National anthem – 'Desteapta-te, Romane' ['Awake Thee, Romanian']
National day – 1 December (Unification Day)
Death penalty – Abolished for all crimes (since 1989)
CPI score – 43 (69)

CLIMATE AND TERRAIN
The Carpathian mountain range runs south from the Ukrainian border into the centre of the country and then turns west (the Transylvanian Alps) and north. The mountains enclose the central Transylvanian plateau and divide it from the southern Wallachian plain, part of the basin of the river Danube, which runs along most of the southern border, and the eastern Moldavian plateau, through which the river Siret flows, and the Black Sea coast. The mountains are thickly forested. Elevation extremes range from 2,544m (Moldoveanu) to 0m (Black Sea). The climate is continental, with average temperatures in Bucharest ranging from −1°C in January to 22°C in July.

POLITICS
The 1991 constitution was amended in 2003 to bring it into line with EU requirements. The president is directly elected for a five-year term, renewable once. The bicameral parliament comprises the Chamber of Deputies with 412 seats, of which 18 are reserved for ethnic minorities, and the senate with 176 seats. Both houses are directly elected for a four-year term by proportional representation. The prime minister is appointed by the president.

In the December 2012 legislative elections, the four-party Social Liberal Union won a significant majority in both chambers; the leader of the PSD (Social Democratic Party), Victor Ponta, was reappointed following the December 2012 elections.

HEAD OF STATE
President of the Republic, Traian Basescu, *elected* 12 December 2004, *re-elected* 2009

SELECTED GOVERNMENT MEMBERS *as at July 2014*
Prime Minister, Victor Ponta
Vice Prime Minister, Interior, Gabriel Oprea
Defence, Mircea Dusa
Finance, Ioana-Maria Petrescu

EMBASSY OF ROMANIA
Arundel House, 4 Palace Green, London W8 4QD
T 020-7937 9666 E londra@mae.ro W http://www.londra.mae.ro
Ambassador Extraordinary and Plenipotentiary, HE Dr Ion Jinga, *apptd* 2008

BRITISH EMBASSY
24 Strada Jules Michelet, 010463 Bucharest
T (+40) (21) 201 7200 E Press.Bucharest@fco.gov.uk
W www.gov.uk/government/world/romania
Ambassador Extraordinary and Plenipotentiary, HE Martin Harris, *apptd* 2010

DEFENCE
Under an agreement signed in 2005, the USA is allowed to use military bases in Romania.

Aged 16–49, 2010 est	Males	Females
Available for military service	5,601,234	5,428,939
Fit for military service	4,550,409	4,507,880

Military expenditure – US$2,548m (2013)

ECONOMY AND TRADE

Transition to a market economy made sluggish progress until 2000, accelerating after 2004 in order to meet the requirements for EU accession. Although the economy grew steadily from 2000 to 2008, it was from a low base and poverty remains high. The economy contracted sharply in 2009 owing to the global downturn, and the government sought IMF and EU funding in spring 2009, but political volatility in late 2009 delayed the implementation of measures to address the economic problems. Following austerity measures the economy returned to positive growth in 2011; economic growth increased from 0.6 per cent in 2012 to 3.5 per cent in 2013, driven by strong industrial exports and a fecund agricultural harvest. Inflation fell to a historic low of 1.6 per cent in December 2013, with the financial deficit also substantially reduced in this period.

Agriculture remains inefficient, employing 29 per cent of the workforce but contributing only 6.4 per cent of GDP. The principal crops are grains, sugar beet, sunflower seeds, vegetables and livestock products. Vines and fruit are grown, and extensive forests support an important timber industry. There are reserves of natural gas and oil, but Romania is a net importer of fossil fuels, although it exports electricity. Mineral deposits, including coal, iron ore, bauxite, chromium and uranium support a mining industry. Other industries include manufacturing, electrical and light machinery and car assembly, metallurgy, food processing and oil refining.

The main trading partners are EU states (especially Italy and Germany), Turkey and China. Principal exports include machinery and equipment, textiles, footwear, metals and metal products, minerals and fuels, chemicals and agricultural products. The main imports are machines and equipment, fuels, minerals, chemicals, textiles, base metals and agricultural products.

GNI – US$191,032m; US$8,820 per capita (2012)
Annual average growth of GDP 2 per cent (2013 est)
Inflation rate – 4.1 per cent (2013 est)
Population below poverty line – 22.2 per cent (2011 est)
Unemployment – 4.8 per cent (2013 est)
Total external debt – US$130,400m (2013 est)
Imports – US$70,260m (2012)
Exports – US$57,904m (2012)

BALANCE OF PAYMENTS

Trade – US$12,355m deficit (2012)
Current Account – US$6,625m deficit (2012)

Trade with UK	2012	2013
Imports from UK	£939,918,717	£930,145,403
Exports to UK	£1,309,434,962	£1,439,047,624

COMMUNICATIONS

Airports and waterways – The main airports are at Bucharest and Timisoara; the main ports are Braila, Constanta, Galati and Tulcea, with 1,599km of navigable waterways on the river Danube and its tributaries and 132km of canals
Roadways and railways – There are 84,185km of surfaced roadways, of which 337km are motorway, and 10,777km of railways, over one-third of which are electrified
Telecommunications – 4.68 million fixed lines and 22.7 million mobile subscriptions (2012); there were 7.79 million internet users in 2009
Internet code and IDD – ro; 40 (from UK), 44 (to UK)
Major broadcasters – The state-owned Televiziunea (TVR) is the country's principal broadcaster
Press – There are several daily newspapers, including *Adevarul*, and *Libertatea*
WPFI score – 23,48 (45)

EDUCATION AND HEALTH

Primary and secondary education is free and compulsory for ten years.
Literacy rate – 98 per cent (2011 est)
Gross enrolment ratio (percentage of relevant age group) – primary 96 per cent; secondary 95 per cent; tertiary 63.8 per cent (2011 est)
Health expenditure (per capita) – US$500 (2011)
Hospital beds (per 1,000 people) – 6.3 (2010)
Life expectancy (years) – 74.69 (2014 est)
Mortality rate – 11.88 (2014 est)
Birth rate – 9.27 (2014 est)
Infant mortality rate – 10.16 (2014 est)

RUSSIA

Rossiyskaya Federatsiya – Russian Federation

Area – 17,098,242 sq. km. Includes the Kaliningrad exclave, between Lithuania and Poland. Neighbours: Norway, Finland, Estonia, Latvia, Belarus, Ukraine (west), Georgia, Azerbaijan, Kazakhstan, China, Mongolia, North Korea (south)
Capital – Moscow; population, 10,596,734 (2012). Founded in around 1147, it became the centre of the rising Moscow principality and in the 15th century the capital of the whole of Russia (Muscovy). In 1703 Peter the Great transferred the capital to St Petersburg, but Moscow became the capital again in 1918
Major cities – Chelyabinsk, Kazan, Nizhniy Novgorod (Gorky 1932–90), Novosibirsk (Novonikolayevsk until 1926), Omsk, Perm, Rostov, St Petersburg (Petrograd 1914–24; Leningrad 1924–91), Samara (Kuibyshev 1935–90), Ufa, Volgograd (Stalingrad 1925–61), Yekaterinburg (Sverdlovsk 1924–91)
Currency – Rouble of 100 kopeks
Population – 142,470,272 falling at 0.03 per cent a year (2014 est); Russian (77.7 per cent), Tatar (3.7 per cent), Ukrainian (1.4 per cent), Bashkir (1.1 per cent), Chuvash (1.1 per cent), and a further 150 nationalities (2010)
Religion – Christian (Russian Orthodox 41 per cent, other 5.8 per cent), Muslim 6.5 per cent; other groups include Buddhists, Hindus and Jews
Language – Russian (official); many minority languages
Population density – 9 per sq. km (2011)
Urban population – 74 per cent (2012 est)
Median age (years) – 38.9 (2014 est)
National anthem – 'Gosudarstvenny Gimn Rossiyskoy Federatsii' ['State Anthem of the Russian Federation']
National day – 12 June (Russia Day)
Death penalty – Retained (last used 1999)
CPI score – 28 (127)

CLIMATE AND TERRAIN

Russia includes the easternmost areas of Europe and the whole of northern Asia. It lies mostly on plains which extend eastwards to the Ural mountains and then from the Urals to the Yenesei river. To the east of the Yenesei are plateaus, with lowlands in northern Siberia. Mountainous areas lie along the southern borders, in eastern Siberia and the Kamchatka peninsula. The terrain varies from the tundra of the Arctic region, through the taiga (the largest zone) of the north and centre, to the grassy plains (steppe) between the forests and the mountains. Elevation extremes range from 5,633m (Mt Elbrus, Caucasus) to −28m (Caspian Sea). Russia has the longest Arctic coastline in the world (over 27,000km); it also has Baltic, Black Sea and Pacific coastlines.

The most important rivers are the Volga, the Northern Dvina, the Neva, the Don and the Kuban in the European part, and in the Asiatic part the Ob, the Irtysh, the Yenisei, the Lena, the Amur and, further north, the Khatanga, Olenek, Yana, Indigirka and Kolyma. Lake Baikal in eastern Siberia is the deepest lake in the world. Part of the Caspian Sea lies within Russia.

The climate is mostly continental, but varies with latitude and terrain from arctic conditions in the north to subtropical in the far east and on the Black Sea coast. Average temperatures in Moscow range from −8°C in January to 17°C in July. Rainfall is low to moderate in most of the country.

POLITICS

The 1993 constitution introduced multiparty democracy and enshrines various human rights and civil liberties; amendments in 2008 extended the terms of office for the presidency and the State Duma from the 2012 elections. The head of state is a president, who is directly elected for a six-year term, renewable once consecutively. The bicameral Federal Assembly comprises the State Duma (lower house) of 450 members, all elected by proportional representation for a five-year term, and the Council of the Federation, which has 166 members (two from each member of the federation), appointed for terms of varying lengths. The president appoints the chairman of the council of ministers (prime minister), subject to the approval of the legislature, but is also entitled to chair sessions of the council.

In the 2011 legislative elections, the pro-Vladimir Putin United Russia party retained its overall majority in the *Duma* but with a reduced majority. Putin (elected president between 2000–8) also retained the presidency in March 2012, picking up 63.6 per cent of the overall vote in a highly controversial presidential election. He was inaugurated as president in May 2012 and duly appointed former president Dmitry Medvedev to be chair of the Council of Ministers.

HEAD OF STATE
President, Vladimir Putin, *elected* 4 March 2012, *took office* 7 May 2012

SELECTED GOVERNMENT MEMBERS *as at June 2014*
Chair of the Council of Ministers, Dmitry Medvedev
First Deputy Chair, Igor Shuvalov

Deputy Chairs, Aleksandr Khloponin; Dmitry Rogozin; Dmitry Kozak; Arkady Dvorkovich; Olga Golodets; Yury Trutnev

EMBASSY OF THE RUSSIAN FEDERATION
6–7 Kensington Palace Gardens, London W8 4QP
T 020-7229 6412 E info@rusemb.org.uk W www.rusemb.org.uk
Ambassador Extraordinary and Plenipotentiary, HE Alexander Yakovenko, *apptd* 2011

BRITISH EMBASSY
Smolenskaya Naberezhnaya 10, 121099 Moscow
T (+7) (495) 956 7200 E ukinrussia@fco.gov.uk
W www.gov.uk/government/world/russia
Ambassador Extraordinary and Plenipotentiary, HE Tim Barrow, CMG, LVO, MBE, *apptd* 2011

INSURGENCIES
Chechnya occupies an area that is strategically important to Russia because routes from central Russia to the Black Sea and Caspian Sea, and oil and gas pipelines from neighbouring countries, pass through it. The republic declared itself independent in 1991 but its attempts to assert its independence led to two wars with the federal government. The first of these, in 1994–6, resulted in the signing of the Khasavyurt accords. After the peace broke down and Russia invaded Chechnya again in 1999, President Putin refused negotiations and imposed direct rule from Moscow in 2000. Rebels continued with terrorist attacks, although these have decreased since 2007. Russia announced the end of counter-terrorism operations in Chechnya in 2009, but has had to reinstate these in some areas where rebels remain active.

The conflict in Chechnya has destabilised the whole of the northern Caucasus, especially Ingushetia and Dagestan, where violence has increased in recent years. The violence has also affected other parts of Russia, where extremists linked to Chechen separatists have carried out suicide bombings and attacks such as the Moscow theatre siege in 2002, the Beslan school siege in 2004 and the bombing of Moscow's metro system in 2010.

FEDERAL STRUCTURE
Following the break-up of the USSR in 1991, a new federal treaty was signed in 1992 between the central government

and the autonomous republics of the Russian Federation. Tatarstan and Bashkortostan signed the treaty in 1994 after securing considerable legislative and economic autonomy.

The Russian Federation comprises 46 *oblasti* (regions), 9 *krai* (autonomous territories), 21 *respubliki* (autonomous republics), 4 *okrugi* (autonomous areas), two cities with federal status (Moscow and St Petersburg) and one autonomous Jewish *oblast*, Yevrey. The *oblasti* are Amur, Arkhangelsk, Astrakhan, Belgorod, Bryansk, Chelyabinsk, Irkutsk, Ivanovo, Kaliningrad, Kaluga, Kemerovo, Kirov, Kostroma, Kurgan, Kursk, Leningrad, Lipetsk, Magadan, Moscow, Murmansk, Nizhny Novgorod, Novgorod, Novosibirsk, Omsk, Orenburg, Orel, Penza, Pskov, Rostov, Ryazan, Sakhalin, Samara, Saratov, Smolensk, Sverdlovsk, Tambov, Tomsk, Tula, Tver, Tyumen, Ulyanovsk, Vladimir, Volgograd, Vologda, Voronezh and Yaroslavl. The *krai* are Altai, Kamchatka, Khabarovsk, Krasnodar, Krasnoyarsk, Perm, Primorski, Stavropol and Zabaykalsk. The *respubliki* are Adygeia, Altai, Bashkortostan, Buryatia, Chechnya, Chuvashia, Dagestan, Ingushetia, Kabardino-Balkaria, Kalmykiya, Karachayevo-Cherkessia, Karelia, Khakassia, Komi, Mari-El, Mordovia, North Ossetia, Sakha, Tatarstan, Tuva and Udmurtia. The *okrugi* are Chukotka, Khanty-Mansi, Nenets and Yamalo-Nenets.

DEFENCE

Since the demise of the USSR, Russia's armed forces have been considerably reduced and major army reform is ongoing.

The CIS Collective Security Treaty enables Russia to station troops in Armenia, Belarus, Kazakhstan, Kyrgyzstan and Tajikistan. The Black Sea fleet was divided between Russian and Ukraine under an agreement signed in 1997. In April 2010, the Strategic Arms Reduction Treaty (START) was renewed by president Medvedev and US president Obama; the bilateral treaty, originally drafted in 1991, is an agreement between the two states to continue to significantly reduce the number of operational strategic nuclear weapons.

Aged 16–49, 2010 est	Males	Females
Available for military service	34,132,156	34,985,115
Fit for military service	20,431,035	26,381,518

Military expenditure – US$84,864m (2013 est)
Conscription duration – 12 months

ECONOMY AND TRADE

Under the Soviet regime, an essentially agrarian economy in 1917 was transformed by the early 1960s into the second-greatest industrial power in the world. However, by the early 1970s the concentration of resources on the military-industrial complex had caused stagnation in the civilian economy. Economic reforms were introduced by President Gorbachev, including the legalisation of small private businesses, the reduction of state control over the economy, and denationalisation and privatisation. Mass privatisation of state industries began in 1992, and 80 per cent of the economy had been privatised by 1996. The largest and most economically significant industries, oil and gas, were partially renationalised from 2004.

The transition to a market economy caused severe economic crises in 1993 and 1998, but from 1999 to 2008 the economy sustained growth averaging 7 per cent a year. Political and economic uncertainties, corruption, excessive red tape and a lack of trust in institutions continue to inhibit growth however. Other problems include the economy's vulnerability to fluctuations in global prices of key commodities and a dilapidated infrastructure. Some of these factors exacerbated the impact on Russia of the global financial crisis in autumn 2008, when a sharp fall in oil prices coincided with turmoil in the banking system and a 70 per cent drop in the stock market. Despite US$200bn in government aid to the financial sector, credit problems, a severe drop in production and rising unemployment caused a sharp contraction in the economy until late 2009, before high oil prices boosted economic growth in 2011–12. Russia joined the World Trade Organisation in 2012, providing greater access to foreign markets. Russia's involvement in the Ukraine crisis is expected to reduce growth to 0 per cent in 2014. Growth forecasts through to 2030 have been revised down to an estimate of 2.5 per cent growth per year.

Russia has some of the world's richest natural resources, especially mineral deposits and timber. The recent growth in the economy is founded on the exploitation and export of its oil and natural gas reserves. Russia is now the world's leading oil producer (surpassing Saudi Arabia in 2011) and exporter of hydrocarbons, and the leading supplier to European countries and China, a position that has led the country into disputes with some of its neighbours; Ukraine, Georgia, Lithuania, Czech Republic, Armenia, Azerbaijan, Poland and Belarus have all had gas or oil supplies cut for short periods during price negotiations. Economic diversification, especially into high technology sectors, is a government priority.

Mining (coal, iron ore, aluminium and other non-ferrous metals) and oil and natural gas extraction are concentrated in the region south of Moscow, the Volga valley, the northern Caucasus, the Urals, Siberia and the far east and north. Russia is also keen to exploit the shrinking of the Arctic ice-cap to prospect for previously inaccessible deposits under the Arctic Sea. The main industries are extracting and processing oil, gas and minerals, forestry, all forms of machine building (including transport, communications, agricultural, construction, and power generating and transmitting equipment), defence industries, shipbuilding, medical and scientific instruments, consumer durables, textiles and food processing

The vast area and the great variety in climatic conditions are reflected in the structure of agriculture. In the far north, only reindeer breeding, hunting and fishing are possible; further south, forestry is combined with grain growing. In the southern half of the forest zone and in the adjacent forest-steppe zone, the acreage under grain crops is larger and agriculture more complex. The southern part of the Western Siberian plain is an important grain-growing and stock-breeding area. In the extreme south, cotton is cultivated. Vine, tobacco and other southern crops are grown on the Black Sea shore of the Caucasus.

The service sector is the largest, accounting for 58.3 per cent of GDP and employing 62.5 per cent of the workforce; industry contributes 37.5 per cent of GDP and employs 27.8 per cent; and agriculture accounts for 4.2 per cent of GDP and 9.7 per cent of employment.

Russia's main trading partners are EU countries (especially Germany), China and Ukraine. Principal exports are oil and petroleum products, natural gas, metals, timber and wood products, chemicals, manufactured goods, military vehicles and defence equipment. The main imports are machinery, vehicles, pharmaceutical products, plastics, semi-finished metal products, meat, fruits and nuts, optical and medical equipment, iron and steel.

GNI – US$1,947,554m; US$12,700 per capita (2012)
Annual average growth of GDP – 1.3 per cent (2013 est)
Inflation rate – 6.8 per cent (2013 est)

Population below poverty line – 11 per cent (2013)
Unemployment – 5.8 per cent (2013 est)
Total external debt – US$714,200m (2013 est)
Imports – US$314,150m (2012)
Exports – US$525,383m (2012)

BALANCE OF PAYMENTS
Trade – US$211,233m surplus (2012)
Current Account – US$74,799m surplus (2012)

Trade with UK	2012	2013
Imports from UK	£5,516,379,535	£5,181,636,167
Exports to UK	£8,403,872,771	£6,910,744,739

COMMUNICATIONS

Airports – There are 594 airports; the principal international airports are at Moscow, St Petersburg and Novosibirsk
Waterways – Major ports include Kaliningrad on the Baltic Sea and Novorossiysk on the Black Sea. Two of the three northern ports, St Petersburg and Arkhangelsk, are icebound during winter; only Murmansk is accessible. There is a large merchant fleet of 1,143 ships of 1,000 tonnes and over, with a further 439 ships registered in other countries. There are 102,000km of waterways, supplemented by a 72,000km system of canals which provides a through route between the White Sea and Baltic Sea in the north and the Black Sea, Caspian Sea and the Sea of Azov in the south
Roadways – There are 1,283,387km of roadways, 927,721km of which are surfaced
Railways – The railways are state-run, with 87,157km of the network used for passenger transport plus 30,000km by industry
Telecommunications – 42.9 million fixed lines and 261.9 million mobile subscriptions (2011); there were 40.85 million internet users in 2009
Internet code and IDD – ru; 7 (from UK), 810 44 (to UK)
Major broadcasters – Broadcasting is dominated by the Russian State Television and Radio Broadcasting Company (VGTRK) and stations part-owned by the government or whose owners have close ties to it
Press – There are over 400 major newspapers printed every week, including mass-circulation dailies Komsomolskaya Pravda and Moskovsky Komsomolets
WPFI score – 42,78 (148)

EDUCATION AND HEALTH

There are 11 years of compulsory education: nine at basic school level and a further two at senior secondary level.
Literacy rate – 100 per cent (2010 est)
Gross enrolment ratio (percentage of relevant age group) –
    primary 99 per cent; secondary 89 per cent; tertiary
    75.9 per cent (2011 est)
Health expenditure (per capita) – US$807 (2011)
Hospital beds (per 1,000 people) – 9.7 (2004–9)
Life expectancy (years) – 70.16 (2014 est)
Mortality rate – 13.83 (2014 est)
Birth rate – 11.87 (2014 est)
Infant mortality rate – 7.08 (2014 est)
HIV/AIDS adult prevalence – 1 per cent (2009 est)

RWANDA

Republika y'u Rwanda / République du Rwanda – Republic of Rwanda

Area – 26,338 sq. km
Capital – Kigali; population, 1,146,016 (2012)
Major towns – Butare, Gisenyi, Gitarama, Ruhengeri
Currency – Rwanda franc of 100 centimes
Population – 12,337,272 rising at 2.63 per cent a year
    (2014 est); Hutu (84 per cent), Tutsi (15 per cent), Twa
    (1 per cent) (est)
Religion – Christian (Roman Catholic 49.5 per cent,
    Protestant 39.4 per cent, other 4.5 per cent)
Language – Kinyarwanda, French, English (all official),
    Swahili
Population density – 452 per sq. km (2011)
Urban population – 19.4 per cent (2012 est)
Median age (years) – 18.7 (2014 est)
National anthem – 'Rwanda Nziza' ['Beautiful Rwanda']
National day – 1 July (Independence Day)
Death penalty – Abolished for all crimes (since 2007)
CPI score – 53 (49)
Literacy rate – 66 per cent (2010 est)
Gross enrolment ratio (percentage of relevant age group) –
    primary 143 per cent; secondary 32 per cent (2010 est);
    tertiary 5.5 per cent (2009 est)
Health expenditure (per capita) – US$63 (2011)
Hospital beds (per 1,000 people) – 1.6 (2004–9)
Life expectancy (years) – 59.26 (2014 est)
Mortality rate – 9.18 (2014 est)
Birth rate – 34.61 (2014 est)
Infant mortality rate – 59.59 (2014 est)
HIV/AIDS adult prevalence – 2.9 per cent (2012 est)

CLIMATE AND TERRAIN

Landlocked Rwanda's terrain is mostly savannah uplands and mountains, including the volcanic Virunga range in the north-west. Elevation extremes range from 4,519m (Volcan Karisimbi) to 950m (Rusizi River). Rwanda's western border runs through Lake Kivu. The climate is temperate, with a wet season from October to May. The average daily temperature in Rwanda is 19.6°C.

HISTORY AND POLITICS

The Rwandan Patriotic Front (FPR) won the 2003 legislative elections and retained an overall majority in the 2008 election, continuing in government in coalition with six other parties and a number of independent members. The FPR leader Paul Kagame was elected president in 2003, and re-elected in 2010, before gaining election to the senate in September 2011; he was succeeded by former minister of education Pierre Damien Habumuremyi in October 2011.

Under the 2003 constitution, the president is directly elected for a seven-year term, renewable once. The bicameral

Tutsi migrants become dominant and establish a kingdom — c.900
Occupied then mandated by Belgium — 1899
Becomes republic — 1959
Repeated invasions by armed Tutsi exiles — 1962
Tutsi exiles form Rwandan Patriotic Front (FPR) — 1973
FPR invades country, beginning cycle of rebel uprisings — 1993
Habyarimana assassinated, mass genocide of Tutsi minority — 2009

c.1300–1450 — Settled by Hutu peoples
1914–18 — Part of German East Africa
1961 — Hutu population rebel and overthrow Tutsi king
c.1960–70 — Independence achieved under a Hutu president
1985 — Hutu president overthrown in coup led by Maj.-Gen. Juvenal Habyarimana; dictatorship established
1990 — Arusha Peace Accords signed
1994 — FPR forces establish unified government
Joins Commonwealth

parliament consists of the Chamber of Deputies (the lower house) and the senate. The Chamber of Deputies has 80 members, of whom 53 are directly elected, 24 are women members elected by the provinces, two represent youth organisations and one represents organisations of disabled people; all serve a five-year term. The senate has 26 members indirectly elected for an eight-year term. Political parties are barred from organising on an ethnic, regional or religious basis.

In 2006 the 12 provinces were replaced by five provinces: North, East, South, West and Kigali, with the aim of creating more ethnically diverse administrative areas.

HEAD OF STATE

President, Maj.-Gen. Paul Kagame, *appointed* 17 April 2000, *sworn in* 22 April 2000, *elected* 25 August 2003, *re-elected* 2010

SELECTED GOVERNMENT MEMBERS *as at July 2014*
Prime Minister, Pierre Damien Habumuremyi
Defence, Gen. James Kabarebe
Finance and Economic Planning, Claver Gatete
Foreign Affairs, Louise Mushikiwabo

HIGH COMMISSION OF THE REPUBLIC OF RWANDA
120–122 Seymour Place, London W1H 1NR
T 020-7224 9832 E uk@rwandahc.org W www.rwandahc.org
High Commissioner, Williams Nkurunziza, *apptd* 2013

BRITISH HIGH COMMISSION
Parcelle No. 1131, Blvd de l'Umuganda, Kacyira-Sud, BP 576 Kigali
T (+250) 252 556 000 E BHC.Kigali@fco.gov.uk
W www.gov.uk/government/world/rwanda
High Commissioner, HE William Gelling, OBE, *apptd* 2014

DEFENCE

Aged 16–49, 2010 est	Males	Females
Available for military service	2,625,917	2,608,110
Fit for military service	1,685,066	1,749,580

Military expenditure – US$79.1m (2013)

ECONOMY AND TRADE

Rwanda is the most densely populated country in Africa, with few natural resources and minimal industry. Nearly half the population lives below the poverty line and economic growth, especially in food production, struggles to keep up with population growth. It is dependent on international aid but the demands of its high foreign debt have been reduced by debt relief. Regional instability, inadequate transport links with other countries and energy shortages hamper development, although electricity supply is expected to become more reliable when methane from Lake Kivu starts to be tapped.

Around 90 per cent of the population is engaged in agriculture, which is mainly at subsistence level and contributes 31.9 per cent of GDP. The main industries are mining, processing agricultural products, small-scale manufacturing and tourism, which is now the main foreign exchange earner.

The main trading partners are Kenya, Uganda and the Democratic Republic of the Congo. The main exports are coffee, tea, hides and tin ore. The principal imports are foodstuffs, machinery and equipment, steel, petroleum products and construction materials.

GNI – US$7,029m; US$600 per capita (2012)
Annual average growth of GDP – 7.5 per cent (2013 est)
Inflation rate – 5.9 per cent (2013 est)
Total external debt – US$1,656m (2013 est)
Imports – US$1,999m (2012)
Exports – US$470m (2012)

BALANCE OF PAYMENTS
Trade – US$1,529m deficit (2012)
Current Account – US$813m deficit (20132)

Trade with UK	2012	2013
Imports from UK	£13,074,729	£9,776,267
Exports to UK	£2,682,123	£7,099,414

COMMUNICATIONS

Airports and waterways – The principal airport is at Kigali; Lake Kivu is navigable by shallow boats, and provides access to the Democratic Republic of the Congo
Roadways – The main internal transport system is the 4,700km road network, which links with those of neighbouring countries to provide access to Kenyan and Tanzanian ports
Telecommunications – 44,400 fixed lines and 5.69 million mobile subscriptions (2012); there were 450,000 internet users in 2009
Internet code and IDD – rw; 250 (from UK), 44 (to UK)
Media – The state-run Radio Rwanda has the largest audience; major newspapers include *The New Times* and *Rwanda Herald*
WPFI score – 56,57 (162)

ST KITTS AND NEVIS

Federation of St Christopher and Nevis (Federation of St Kitts and Nevis)

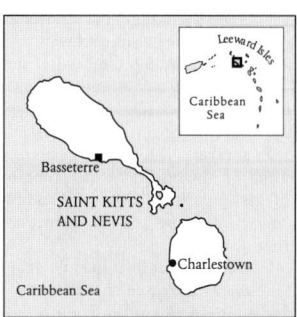

Area – 261 sq. km
Capital – Basseterre; population, 12,000 (2011)
Major town – Charlestown, the chief town of Nevis
Currency – East Caribbean dollar (EC$) of 100 cents
Population – 51,538 rising at 0.78 per cent a year
  (2014 est)
Religion – Christian (Anglican 50 per cent, Roman Catholic
  25 per cent) (est)
Language – English (official)
Population density – 204 per sq. km (2011)
Urban population – 32 per cent (2012 est)
Median age (years) – 33.5 (2014 est)
National anthem – 'Oh Land of Beauty!'
National day – 19 September (Independence Day)
Death penalty – Retained (last used 2008)
Life expectancy (years) – 75.29 (2014 est)
Mortality rate – 7.08 (2014 est)
Birth rate – 13.64 (2014)
Infant mortality rate – 8.98 (2014 est)

CLIMATE AND TERRAIN
The volcanic islands of St Kitts (St Christopher) (168 sq. km)
and Nevis (93 sq. km) are part of the Leeward group in the
eastern Caribbean Sea. The centre of St Kitts is forest-clad
and mountainous, with the Great Salt Pond occupying the
tip of its southern peninsula; elevation extremes range from
1,156m (Mt Liamuiga) to 0m (Caribbean Sea). Nevis,
separated from the southern tip of St Kitts by a strait 3km
wide, is dominated by Nevis Peak (985m). The climate is
tropical, moderated by north-east trade winds, and a wet
season occurs from May to September. The islands are in the
hurricane belt.

HISTORY AND POLITICS
The islands were inhabited by Carib, or Kalinago, people
when discovered in 1493 by Christopher Columbus, who
gave St Christopher its name. Colonisation by the British
began in 1623–4, when St Kitts became the first British
colony in the West Indies, and French settlement began
shortly after. The island was held jointly from 1628 to 1713,
although there were skirmishes between the British and
French settlers in the 17th century; France dropped its claims
after 1783. Nevis was settled by the British from 1628. The
two islands were part of the Leeward Islands colony from
1871 to 1956, and then of the West Indies Federation from
1958 to 1962. They achieved internal self-government in
1967 and became independent in September 1983.

A separatist movement was formed on Nevis in 1970. A
referendum on the issue in 1998 resulted in a 61.8 per cent
vote in favour of secession, which fell short of the two-thirds
majority required.

The Labour Party, which has been in power since 1995,
retained its overall majority in the 2010 legislative election,
and began its fourth term of office under Denzil Douglas. In
Nevis's 2013 assembly election, the Concerned Citizens'
Movement won three of the five elected seats.

Under the 1983 constitution, the head of state is Queen
Elizabeth II, represented by a governor-general appointed on
the advice of the prime minister. The unicameral National
Assembly has 15 members: 11 directly elected for a five-
year term, a speaker, and three appointed by the
governor-general on the advice of the prime minister and
the leader of the opposition. The prime minister, who is
responsible to the legislature, and the cabinet are appointed
by the governor-general.

Nevis is responsible for its own internal affairs. It has an
eight-member Nevis Island assembly and is governed by the
Nevis Island administration, headed by the premier.

Governor-General, HE Sir Edmund Lawrence, GCMG, OBE,
  apptd 2013

SELECTED GOVERNMENT MEMBERS *as at July 2014*
Prime Minister, Finance, Rt. Hon. Denzil Douglas
Deputy Prime Minister, Earl Asim Martin
Foreign Affairs, National Security, Patrice Nisbett

HIGH COMMISSION FOR ST KITTS AND NEVIS
10 Kensington Court, London W8 5DL
T 020-7937 9718 E info@sknhc.co.uk W www.stkittsnevisuk.com/
High Commissioner, HE Kevin Isaac, apptd 2011

BRITISH HIGH COMMISSIONER
HE Victoria Dean, apptd 2013, resident at Bridgetown,
  Barbados

ECONOMY AND TRADE
The sugar industry was the mainstay of the economy for over
300 years but was closed down in 2005 after decades of
operating at a loss. Tourism (the chief source of foreign
exchange revenue), offshore financial services and
manufacturing, especially distilling, food processing,
clothing and electronics, are being developed. Services now
account for 75.1 per cent of GDP, industry for 23.1 per cent
and agriculture for 1.8 per cent. The economy of Nevis relies
on farming, but a sea-island cotton industry is being
developed for export. The economy is restricted by one
of the world's highest public debt burdens (estimated at
83 per cent of GDP in 2013) and the country remains
vulnerable to costly damage from natural disasters and shifts
in tourism demand.

The main trading partners are the USA, and Trinidad and
Tobago. Principal exports are machinery, food, electronic
equipment, beverages and tobacco. The main imports are
machinery, manufactured goods, food and fuels.
GNI – US$735m; US$13,610 per capita (2012)
Annual average growth of GDP – 1.9 per cent (2013 est)
Inflation rate – 2.2 per cent (2013 est)
Total external debt – US$158.9m (2013 est)

BALANCE OF PAYMENTS
Trade – US$176m deficit (2012)
Current Account – US$99m deficit (2012)

Trade with UK	2012	2013
Imports from UK	£7,507,417	£4,172,003
Exports to UK	£190,158	£137,498

COMMUNICATIONS
Airports – There are two airports; that on St Kitts can take
most large jet aircraft
Waterways – Basseterre is a port of registry and has
deep-water harbour facilities; there are regular ferries
between Basseterre and Charlestown
Roadways and railways – The islands have 383km of
roadways, of which 163km are surfaced, and 50km
of narrow-gauge railways on St Kitts
Telecommunications – 20,000 fixed lines and 84,000 mobile
subscriptions (2012); there were 17,000 internet users in
2009
Internet code and IDD – kn; 1 869 (from UK), 011 44
(to UK)
Media – The government-owned broadcaster ZIZ operates
national television and radio networks; *The Sun* is the sole
daily newspaper

ST LUCIA

Area – 616 sq. km
Capital – Castries; population, 21,000 (2011)
Currency – East Caribbean dollar (EC$) of 100 cents
Population – 163,362 rising at 0.35 per cent a year
  (2014 est)
Religion – Christian (Roman Catholic 61.5 per cent,
  Seventh-day Adventists 10.4 per cent, Pentecostals 8.9
  per cent, Baptists 2.2 per cent), Rastafarian 1.9 per cent
  (est)
Language – English (official), French patois
Population density – 204 per sq. km (2011)
Urban population – 16.8 per cent (2012 est)
Median age (years) – 32.9 (2014 est)
National anthem – 'Sons and Daughters of Saint Lucia'
National day – 22 February (Independence Day)
Death penalty – Retained
CPI score – 71 (22)
Life expectancy (years) – 77.41 (2014 est)
Mortality rate 7.32 (2014 est)
Birth rate – 13.94 (2014 est)
Infant mortality rate – 11.75 (2014 est)

CLIMATE AND TERRAIN

St Lucia is the second-largest island in the Windward group.
The interior is mountainous and densely forested, with
elevation extremes ranging from 950m (Mt Gimie) to 0m
(Caribbean Sea). The area around the volcanic peaks of Gros
Piton and Petit Piton is a UNESCO World Heritage Site. The
climate is tropical, moderated by trade winds and with a wet
season from July to November. The island is in the hurricane
belt.

HISTORY AND POLITICS

The original Arawak settlers were superseded by Caribs
by AD 800. The island was sighted by Columbus in 1502
and European settlement began in the 1550s. Control was
disputed between France and Britain from the mid-17th
century until 1814, when the island was ceded to Britain.
It achieved internal self-government in 1967 and became
independent in 1979. Violent crime and a gang culture
have grown in recent years, largely as a result of
drug-trafficking.

The St Lucia Labour Party (SLP) won the 2011 legislative
election, defeating the incumbent United Workers' Party;
SLP leader Kenny Anthony was sworn into office in
November 2011.

Under the 1979 constitution, the head of state is Queen
Elizabeth II, represented by a governor-general appointed on
the advice of the prime minister. The bicameral parliament
consists of the house of assembly and the senate. The senate
has 11 members, six nominated by the government, three
by the opposition and two by the governor-general. The

House of Assembly has 17 elected members and an
appointed speaker who serve a five-year term. The prime
minister, who is responsible to the legislature, and the cabinet
are appointed by the governor-general.
Governor-General, HE Dame Pearlette Louisy, *apptd* 1997

SELECTED GOVERNMENT MEMBERS *as at July 2014*
Prime Minister, Finance, Economy, Kenny Anthony
Home Affairs, Victor Lacobiniere
Foreign Affairs, Alva Baptiste

HIGH COMMISSION FOR ST LUCIA
1 Collingham Gardens, London SW5 0HW
T 020-7370 7123 E enquiries@stluciahcuk.org
W www.stluciahcuk.org
High Commissioner, HE Ernest Hilaire, *apptd* 2012

BRITISH HIGH COMMISSIONER
HE Victoria Dean, *apptd* 2013, resident at Bridgetown,
  Barbados

ECONOMY AND TRADE

The economy was dependent on bananas, but has diversified
since preferential access to EU markets ended in 1999.
Tourism and offshore financial services have been developed,
and the manufacturing sector is the most diverse in the
Caribbean, processing agricultural products, assembling
electronic components and producing clothing, beverages
and corrugated cardboard boxes. Tourism now accounts for
65 per cent of GDP, industry for 17.4 per cent and
agriculture for 3.1 per cent. The economy contracted in
the global downturn as tourist numbers fell.

The main trading partners are Brazil, the USA and Peru.
Principal exports are bananas, clothing, cocoa, vegetables,
fruit and coconut oil. The main imports are food,
manufactured goods, machinery and transport equipment,
chemicals and fuels.
GNI – US$1,2224m; US$6,890 per capita (2012)
Annual average growth of GDP – 0.2 per cent (2013 est)
Inflation rate – 5.3 per cent (2013 est)
Unemployment – 20 per cent (2003 est)
Total external debt – US$446.4m (2013 est)
Imports – US$683m (2012)
Exports – US$156m (2012)

BALANCE OF PAYMENTS
Trade – US$527m deficit (2012)
Current Account – US$191m deficit (2012)

Trade with UK	2012	2013
Imports from UK	£14,466,359	£14,272,546
Exports to UK	£7,677,446	£7,726,163

COMMUNICATIONS

Airports and waterways – There are two airports in Castries
and Vieux Fort; Castries also has a deep-water harbour
Roadways – 1,210km
Telecommunications – 36,800 fixed lines and 227,000 mobile
subscriptions (2012); there were 142,900 internet users in
2009
Internet code and IDD – lc; 1-758 (from UK), 011 44 (to UK)
Media – Television and radio services are privately owned
and the island has two main newspapers, *The Star* and
The Voice

ST VINCENT AND THE GRENADINES

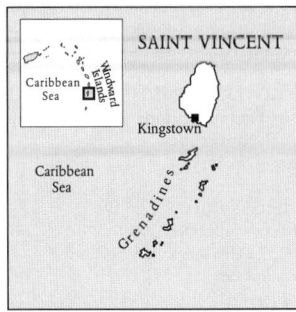

Area – 389 sq. km
Capital – Kingstown; population, 31,000 (2011)
Currency – East Caribbean dollar (EC $) of 100 cents
Population – 102,918 falling at 0.29 per cent a year
(2014 est)
Religion – Christian (Anglican 47 per cent, Methodist
28 per cent and Roman Catholic 13 per cent), Baha'i,
Rastafarian
Language – English (official), French patois
Population density – 280 per sq. km (2011)
Urban population – 49.7 per cent (2012)
Median age (years) – 31.9 (2014)
National anthem – 'St Vincent, Land So Beautiful'
National day – 27 October (Independence Day)
Death penalty – Retained
CPI score – 62 (33)
Life expectancy (years) – 74.86 (2014 est)
Mortality rate – 7.12 (2014 est)
Birth rate – 13.85 (2014 est)
Infant mortality rate – 13.07 (2014 est)
Death penalty – Retained

CLIMATE AND TERRAIN
The state, which lies in the Windward group, consists of St
Vincent and the 32 small islands and cays of the northern
Grenadines, a chain stretching 64km across the eastern
Caribbean Sea between St Vincent and Grenada. St Vincent
itself is a mountainous and densely forested volcanic island.
The Grenadines, of which the largest are Bequia, Canouan,
Mayreau, Mustique and Union Island, are low-lying coral
islands. Elevation extremes range from 1,234m (La Soufrière
volcano, St Vincent) to 0m (Caribbean Sea). The climate is
tropical, with a rainy season from May to November. The
islands lie in the hurricane belt.

HISTORY AND POLITICS
Settled successively by the Ciboney people, the Arawaks
and the Caribs, St Vincent was sighted by Christopher
Columbus in 1498. Although granted by Charles I to the
Earl of Carlisle in 1627, control was disputed between the
British and the French until the islands were ceded to Britain
in 1783. A Black Carib uprising in 1795–7 resulted in
thousands of Black Caribs being deported. Internal
self-government was granted in 1969, and independence as
St Vincent and the Grenadines was achieved in 1979.

An early election in 2001 was won decisively by the
opposition Unity Labour Party (ULP), which was returned
for a second term in 2005 and narrowly retained its majority
at the 2010 election. A referendum in 2009 rejected a draft
constitution which proposed to replace the monarchy with a
republic.

Under the 1979 constitution, the head of state is Queen
Elizabeth II, represented by a governor-general appointed on
the advice of the prime minister. The unicameral House of
Assembly has 21 members: 15 directly elected for a five-year
term and six senators appointed by the governor-general
(four on the advice of the government and two on the advice
of the opposition). The prime minister, who is responsible to
the legislature, and the cabinet are appointed by the
governor-general.
Governor-General, Sir Frederick Ballantyne, GCMG,
apptd 2002

SELECTED GOVERNMENT MEMBERS *as at July 2014*
Prime Minister, Finance, National Security, Ralph Gonsalves
Deputy Prime Minister, Girlyn Miguel

HIGH COMMISSION FOR ST VINCENT AND THE
GRENADINES
10 Kensington Court, London W8 5DL
T 020-7565 2874 E info@svghighcom.co.uk W
www.svghighcom.co.uk
High Commissioner, HE Cenio E. Lewis, apptd 2001

BRITISH HIGH COMMISSIONER
HE Victoria Dean, apptd 2013, resident at Bridgetown,
Barbados

ECONOMY AND TRADE
Tourism (the development of which has been hampered by
drug-related crime), manufacturing and offshore banking
services have all expanded, although the economy contracted
in 2009 owing to the global downturn and the economy is
expected to grow weakly in 2014. Services now account
for 74.4 per cent of GDP, industry for 20.3 per cent and
agriculture for 5.4 per cent. Floods and mudslides caused by
heavy rainfall in 2013 resulted in US$112m worth of
damage.

The main export markets are Trinidad and Tobago, and
St. Lucia. Imports come mostly from Singapore, Trinidad
and Tobago, and the USA. Principal exports are bananas,
vegetables, starch and tennis racquets. The main imports are
foodstuffs, machinery and equipment, chemicals, fertilisers,
minerals and fuel.
GNI – US$700m; US$6,400 per capita (2012)
Annual average growth of GDP – 1.3 per cent (2013 est)
Inflation rate – 2.8 per cent (2013 est)
Total external debt – US$255.3m (2013 est)
Imports – US$357m (2012)
Exports – US$44m (2012)

BALANCE OF PAYMENTS
Trade – US$314m deficit (2012)
Current Account – US$216m deficit (2012)

Trade with UK	2012	2013
Imports from UK	£8,772,084	£14,048,947
Exports to UK	£905,832	£807,865

COMMUNICATIONS
Airports and waterways – There are five airports; although
none can accommodate international flights at present, an
international airport is under construction and scheduled for
completion in late 2014. The main harbour is at Kingstown
Roadways – 829km
Telecommunications – 19,400 fixed lines and 135,500 mobile
subscriptions (2012); there were 76,000 internet users in
2009
Internet code and IDD – vc; 1 784 (from UK), 011 44 (to UK)

Media – Television broadcasting is operated by the St Vincent and the Grenadines Broadcasting Corporation; there is one daily newspaper, *The Herald,* and several other weekly titles

SAMOA

Malo Sa'oloto Tuto'atasi o Samoa – Independent State of Samoa

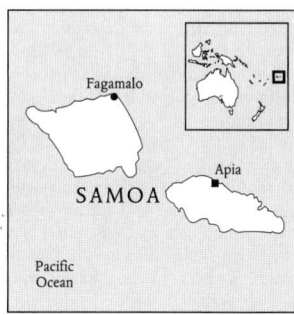

Area – 2,831 sq. km
Capital – Apia, on Upolu; population, 37,000 (2011)
Currency – Tala (S$) of 100 sene
Population – 196,628 rising at 0.59 per cent a year (2014 est); Samoan (Polynesian) (92.6 per cent) (2006); the population also includes Euronesians, Chinese and Europeans
Religion – Christian (Congregational 31.8 per cent, Roman Catholic 19.4 per cent, Mormon 15.2 per cent, Methodist 13.7 per cent, Assemblies of God 8 per cent, Seventh-day Adventist 3.9 per cent) (2011)
Language – Samoan (official), English
Population density – 66 per sq. km (2011)
Urban population – 19.6 per cent (2012)
Median age (years) – 23.1 (2014 est)
National anthem – 'The Banner of Freedom'
National day – 1 June (Independence Day)
Death penalty – Abolished for all crimes (since 2004)
Literacy rate – 99 per cent (2011 est)
Life expectancy (years) – 73.21 (2014 est)
Mortality rate – 5.32 (2014 est)
Birth rate – 21.29 (2014 est)
Infant mortality rate – 20.5 (2014 est)

CLIMATE AND TERRAIN

Samoa consists of the islands of Savai'i, Upolu, Apolima, Manono, Fanuatapu, Namua, Nu'utele, Nu'ulua and Nu'usafe'e in the south Pacific Ocean. All the islands are volcanic in origin, with narrow coastal plains and mountainous, densely forested interiors. Elevation extremes range from 1,857m (Mauga Silisili, Savai'i) to 0m (Pacific Ocean). The climate is tropical, with a wet season from November to April; the average temperature is 25.7°C. The islands are vulnerable to cyclones and tsunamis.

HISTORY AND POLITICS

Inhabited since c.1000 BC, Samoa was visited by European traders, explorers and missionaries from the 18th century. Germany, the UK and the USA disputed control of the islands until 1899, when the nine western islands (Western Samoa) became a German colony and the eastern islands American Samoa. Western Samoa was occupied by New Zealand on the outbreak of the First World War and became a mandated territory administered by New Zealand from 1920. Internal self-government was granted in 1959, and

Western Samoa became independent on 1 June 1962. The state was treated as a member country of the Commonwealth until its formal admission in 1970. In 1997 the state dropped 'Western' from its name.

Former prime minister Tuiatua Tupua Tamasese Efi was elected head of state in June 2007 and re-elected unopposed in July 2012. The Human Rights Protection Party, which has been in power since 1981, remained the largest party in the legislature after the March 2011 election; it won 28 seats, the Tautua Samoa Party won 13 seats and independents won eight.

Under the 1962 constitution, the head of state is elected and has functions analogous to those of a constitutional monarch. Initially an office held for life, the monarch is now elected by the legislature for a five-year term. The unicameral legislative assembly *(Fono)* has 49 members elected for a five-year term; only members of the *Matai* (elected clan leaders) may stand for election. The prime minister is appointed by the monarch on the recommendation of the legislature and appoints the cabinet.

HEAD OF STATE
Head of State, Tuiatua Tupua Tamasese Efi, *elected* 16 June 2007, *re-elected* 20 July 2012

SELECTED GOVERNMENT MEMBERS *as at July 2014*
Prime Minister, Finance, Foreign Affairs, Tuilaepa Sailele Malielegaoi
Deputy Prime Minister, Fonotoe Nuafesili Pierre Lauofo

EMBASSY OF SAMOA
20 avenue de l'Oree, 1000 Brussels, Belgium
T (+32) (2) 660 8454 E samoaembassy@skynet.be
W www.samoaembassybelgium.com
High Commissioner, HE Dr Fatumanava Pa'olelei Luteru, *apptd* 2013

BRITISH HIGH COMMISSIONER
HE Victoria Treadell, CMG, MVO, *apptd* 2010, resident at Wellington, New Zealand

ECONOMY AND TRADE

The economy is underdeveloped but has grown steadily in the past decade, diversifying away from its traditional dependence on fishing, agriculture, remittances from migrant workers and international aid. Economic strengths include a flexible labour market, stable external debt and low inflation. Agriculture and fishing generates 10.2 per cent of GDP, employing about two-thirds of the labour force and supplying about 90 per cent of exports. Manufacturing is branching out from small-scale processing of agricultural products into light manufacturing (particularly of motor vehicle components), and offshore financial services are being developed. Tourism has grown rapidly and accounts for about 25 per cent of GDP. The economy has contracted since 2008, as remittances and tourism fell during the global downturn; a tsunami in 2009 and a tropical cyclone in 2012 caused severe damage.

The main trading partners are American Samoa, Australia, New Zealand, Singapore and Fiji. Principal exports are fish, coconut oil and cream, copra, taro, vehicle parts, garments and beer. The main imports are machinery and equipment, industrial supplies and foodstuffs.
GNI – US$647m; US$3,260 per capita (2012)
Annual average growth of GDP – 0.1 per cent (2013 est)
Inflation rate – 2.7 per cent (2013 est)
Total external debt – US$368.3m (2011 est)
Imports – US$308m (2012)
Exports – US$34m (2012)

BALANCE OF PAYMENTS
Trade – US$274m deficit (2012)
Current Account – US$68m deficit (2012)

Trade with UK	2012	2013
Imports from UK	£1,276,962	£176,423
Exports to UK	£318,739	£258,650

COMMUNICATIONS

Airports and waterways – There is one international airport on Upolu; the southern island also contains the harbours of Apia and Mulifanua, and Salelologa, the harbour of Savai'i
Roadways – 2,337km
Telecommunications – 35,300 fixed lines and 167,400 mobile subscriptions (2010); there were 9,000 internet users in 2009
Internet code and IDD – ws; 685 (from UK), 044 (to UK)
Media – The state-run Samoa Broadcasting Corporation operates broadcasting networks; there are two daily newspapers
WPFI score – 22,02 (40)

SAN MARINO

Repubblica di San Marino – *Republic of San Marino*

Area – 61 sq. km
Capital – San Marino; population, 4,389 (2009 est)
Currency – Euro (€) of 100 cents
Population – 32,742 rising at 0.87 per cent a year (2014 est)
Religion – Christian (Roman Catholic 97 per cent) (est)
Language – Italian (official)
Population density – 517 per sq. km (2011)
Urban population – 94.1 per cent (2012)
Median age (years) – 43.6 (2014 est)
National anthem – 'Inno Nazionale della Repubblica' ['National Anthem of the Republic']
National day – 3 September (Republic Day)
Death penalty – Abolished for all crimes (since 1865)
Life expectancy (years) – 83.18 (2014 est)
Mortality rate – 8.31 (2014 est)
Birth rate – 8.7 (2014 est)
Infant mortality rate – 4.52 (2014 est)

CLIMATE AND TERRAIN

A landlocked enclave in central Italy, the republic lies in the foothills of the Apennines, 20km from the Adriatic Sea. Elevation extremes range from 755m (Mt Titano) to 55m (Torrente Ausa). The climate is Mediterranean, with an average annual rainfall of 836mm.

HISTORY AND POLITICS

The republic is said to have been founded in the fourth century by a Christian stonecutter seeking refuge from religious persecution. By the 12th century a self-governing commune was established, and a parliamentary constitution was adopted in 1600. The republic resisted papal claims and those of neighbouring dukedoms from the 15th to 18th centuries, and the papacy recognised its independence in 1631. In 1862 it signed a treaty with the newly united kingdom of Italy which recognised its integrity and sovereignty and accorded it the protection of Italy. San Marino became a member of the UN in 1992. A 2013 poll supported moves to join the EU, but the number of voters did not exceed the minimum 32 per cent of the electorate needed to enact the measure.

A coalition led by the Christian Democratic Party (PDCS) retained its majority in the November 2012 election.

The 1600 constitution has been amended several times. The joint heads of state are two captains-regent who are elected at six-monthly intervals (March and September) by the legislature, taking office the month after the election. Executive power is vested in the captains-regent and the Congress of State (cabinet), which is also elected by the legislature. The unicameral legislature, the Great and General Council, has 60 members, who are directly elected for a five-year term.

HEADS OF STATE
Captains-Regent, Valeria Ciavatta; Luca Beccari

SELECTED GOVERNMENT MEMBERS *as at July 2013*
Finance, Claudio Felici
Foreign Affairs, Pasquale Valentini
Internal Affairs, Giancarlo Venturini

EMBASSY OF THE REPUBLIC OF SAN MARINO
c/o Department of Foreign Affairs, Palazzo Begni – Contrado Ormerelli, 47890 San Marino
T 378 (0549) 88 2229 E dipartimentoaffariesteri@pa.sm
Ambassador Extraordinary and Plenipotentiary, HE Federica Bigi, *apptd* 2013

BRITISH AMBASSADOR
HE Christopher Prentice, CMG, *apptd* 2011, resident at Rome, Italy

ECONOMY AND TRADE

Tourism and banking are the basis of the economy, and the service sector contributes 60.7 per cent of GDP. In 2009, investment outflows following Italy's tax amnesty, a money-laundering scandal at its largest bank and the global downturn contributed to a deep recession and growing budget deficit. The government is working to improve standards of financial transparency.

The principal agricultural products are grains, grapes, olives, cheeses and hides. The main industries, apart from tourism and banking, are quarrying, forestry, winemaking and the manufacture of clothing, electronics and ceramics. Sales of postage stamps and coins also generate significant revenue. San Marino is in a customs union with the EU.
GNI – US$1,681m; US$50,400 per capita (2008)
Annual average growth of GDP – −3.5 per cent (2013 est)
Inflation rate – 2.8 per cent (2012 est)
Unemployment – 7 per cent (2012 est)

Trade with UK	2012	2013
Imports from UK	£3,138,234	£6,796,306
Exports to UK	£4,743,880	£2,796,436

COMMUNICATIONS
Roadways – 292km
Telecommunications – 18,700 fixed lines and 36,500 mobile subscriptions (2012); there were 17,000 internet users in 2009
Internet code and IDD – sm; 378 (from UK), 44 (to UK)
Media – Broadcasting services are state-run; the two daily newspapers are *La Tribuna Sammarinese* and *San Marino Oggi*

SAO TOME AND PRINCIPE

Republica Democratica de Sao Tome e Principe – Democratic Republic of Sao Tome and Principe

Area – 964 sq. km
Capital – Sao Tome; population, 64,000 (2011)
Currency – Dobra of 100 centimos
Population – 190,428 rising at 1.89 per cent a year (2014 est)
Religion – Christian (Roman Catholic 55.7 per cent, Adventist 4.1 per cent)
Language – Portuguese (official), Creole dialects
Population density – 191 per sq. km (2011)
Urban population – 63.4 per cent (2012)
Median age (years) – 17.8 (2014 est)
National anthem – 'Independencia total' ['Total Independence']
National day – 12 July (Independence Day)
Death penalty – Abolished for all crimes (since 1990)
CPI score – 42 (72)
Literacy rate – 89.2 per cent (2010 est)
Life expectancy (years) – 64.22 (2014 est)
Mortality rate – 7.45 (2014 est)
Birth rate – 35.12 (2014 est)
Infant mortality rate – 49.16 (2014 est)

CLIMATE AND TERRAIN
The republic consists of the islands of Sao Tome, Principe and several uninhabited islets off the west coast of Africa. The islands, which are volcanic in origin, are mountainous and thickly forested. Elevation extremes range from 2,024m (Pico de Sao Tome) to 0m (Atlantic Ocean). The climate is tropical, with a wet season from October to May. The average temperature is 25.2°C.

HISTORY AND POLITICS
The uninhabited islands were discovered by the Portuguese between 1469 and 1472, and settlement began in 1493. Agitation against Portuguese rule began in the late 1950s. The islands gained independence from Portugal in 1975 and became a one-party state under the rule of the Movement for the Liberation of Sao Tome and Principe (MLSTP). Close links with the communist bloc were scaled down in the 1980s as the economy deteriorated, and in 1990 the MLSTP abandoned Marxism and introduced political pluralism and economic liberalisation. The first multiparty elections were held in 1991. Democracy has brought a degree of political instability, and tensions have been heightened recently by disagreements over the exploitation of offshore oil reserves.

In the 2010 legislative election, the opposition Independent Democratic Action (ADI) party became the largest party in the legislature, but without a majority, and formed a government with a number of independent members under the ADI leader Patrice Trovoada. Manuel Pinto da Costa, the country's first post-independence president and former leader of the MLSTP, won the 2011 presidential election as an independent candidate.

Under the 1990 constitution, the president is directly elected for a five-year term, renewable once. The unicameral National Assembly has 55 members, directly elected for a four-year term. The prime minister is appointed by the president and nominates the cabinet.

Since 1995 Principe has been internally self-governing, with an eight-member regional council.

HEAD OF STATE
President, Manuel Pinto da Costa, *elected* 7 August 2011, *sworn in* 3 September 2011

SELECTED GOVERNMENT MEMBERS *as at July 2014*
Prime Minister, Gabriel Arcanjo Ferreira da Costa
Defence, Oscar Aguiar Sacramento e Sousa
Finance, Helio Silva Vaz d'Almeida
Foreign Affairs, Natália Pedro da Costa Umbelina Neto

EMBASSY OF SAO TOME AND PRINCIPE
175 avenue de Tervuren, 1150 Brussels, Belgium
T (+32) (2) 734 8966 E ambassade@saotomeprincipe.be
Ambassador Extraordinary and Plenipotentiary, vacant

BRITISH AMBASSADOR
HE John Dennis, *apptd* 2014, resident at Luanda, Angola

ECONOMY AND TRADE
The economy has benefited from cancellation of about 90 per cent of the country's external debt over the past decade. It is largely dependent on cocoa, but tourism is being encouraged in an attempt to diversify. A major economic shift will begin with the start of oil production from offshore reserves in the Gulf of Guinea. The fields are being developed jointly with Nigeria, and Sao Tome and Principe will receive 40 per cent of the revenue. Most of the population is engaged in subsistence farming and fishing.

The principal export markets are the Netherlands (33.3 per cent) and Belgium (21.8 per cent), and the main source of imports is Portugal (63.8 per cent). Principal exports are cocoa (80 per cent), copra, coffee and palm oil. The main imports are machinery and electrical equipment, foodstuffs and petroleum products.
GNI – US$261m; US$1,310 per capita (2012)
Annual average growth of GDP – 4.5 per cent (2013 est)
Inflation rate – 8.7 per cent (2013 est)
Population below poverty line – 66.2 per cent (2009 est)
Total external debt – US$406.8m (2013 est)

BALANCE OF PAYMENTS
Trade – US$129m deficit (2012)
Current Account – US$56m deficit (2012)

Trade with UK	2012	2013
Imports from UK	£304,262	£380,503
Exports to UK	£40,692	£1,135,977

COMMUNICATIONS

Airports and waterways – There are two airports; and the ports are Santo Antonio, on Principe, and Sao Tome

Roadways – There are 320km of roads, 218km of which are surfaced but in poor condition

Telecommunications – 8,000 fixed lines and 122,000 mobile subscriptions (2012); there were 26,700 internet users in 2009

Internet code and IDD – st; 239 (from UK), 44 (to UK)

Media – Televisao Saotomense is the state-run national broadcaster

SAUDI ARABIA

Al-Mamlakah al-Arabiyah as Suudiyah – Kingdom of Saudi Arabia

Area – 2,149,690 sq. km

Capital – Riyadh; population, 5,073,993 (2012)

Major cities – Dammam, Jeddah, Mecca, Medina, Tabuk, At Taif

Currency – Saudi riyal (SR) of 100 halalas

Population – 27,345,986 rising at 1.49 per cent a year (2014 est); includes some 5,576,076 non-nationals (2013 est)

Religion – Muslim (Sunni 85–90 per cent, predominantly Wahhabi; Shia 10–15 per cent) (est); public practice of other religions is forbidden

Language – Arabic (official)

Population density – 13 per sq. km (2011)

Urban population – 82.5 per cent (2012)

Median age (years) – 26.4 (2014)

National anthem – 'As-Salaam al Malaki' ['The Royal Salute']

National day – 23 September (Unification Day)

Death penalty – Retained

CPI score – 44 (63)

CLIMATE AND TERRAIN

Saudi Arabia comprises about 80 per cent of the Arabian peninsula. The Hejaz region (north-west) runs along the northern Red Sea coast to the Asir and contains the holy cities of Mecca and Medina. The mountainous Asir (south-west) and the coastal plain of the Tihama lie along the southern Red Sea coast from the Hejaz to the border with Yemen. The Nejd plateau extends over the centre, including the Nafud and Dahna deserts. The Hasa (east) is low-lying and largely desert. The Empty Quarter (south) is the world's largest sand desert. Elevation extremes range from 3,133m (Jabal Sawda) to 0m (Persian Gulf). There is a desert climate, with extremes of temperature in the interior; coastal areas are more temperate but extremely humid. Average temperatures in Riyadh range from 14°C in January to 36°C in July.

HISTORY AND POLITICS

The Arabian peninsula was the birthplace of the Muslim faith in the seventh century and the base from which the religion and four Islamic Caliphates, the Rashidun, Umayyad, Abbasid and Fatimid, emerged. When the Fatimid empire declined in the 12th century, Arabia became isolated and internally divided. The rise of the al-Saud family began in the 18th century, when it united the Nejd in support of the Wahhabi religious movement. The modern state was the culmination of a 30-year campaign by Abd-al Aziz al-Saud (often known as Ibn Saud) to unite the four tribal regions of the Hejaz, Asir, Najd and Hasa; the Kingdom of Saudi Arabia was proclaimed on 23 September 1932.

The ruling family preserved stability for many years by suppressing dissent and resisting calls for greater democracy, with some of its actions raising international concerns over human rights abuses. Since 2003 demand for political reform has grown and become more militant. In 2005, the country's first nationwide elections were held for half the seats on municipal councils, with voting by universal male suffrage.

King Abdullah acceded to the throne after the death of his half-brother King Fahd in 2005.

There is no written constitution; constitutional practice is provided for by articles of government based on the Qur'an and the teachings and sayings of the Prophet Muhammad *(Sunnah)* and issued by royal decree.

Saudi Arabia is a hereditary monarchy. The king is head of government and appoints the council of ministers (established in 1953), whose term of office was fixed in 1993 at four years.

There is no legislature; the Consultative Council *(Majlis-al-Shura)* debates policy, proposes legislation in certain areas and makes recommendations to the king. The council's 150 members are appointed by the king and serve a four-year term. Its decisions are taken by majority vote. There are no political parties.

Each of the 13 provinces has a governor appointed by the king and a council of prominent local citizens to advise the governor on local government, budgetary and planning issues.

HEAD OF STATE

The King of Saudi Arabia, Custodian of the Two Holy Mosques, Prime Minister, King Abdullah bin Abdul Aziz al-Saud, *born* 1923, *succeeded* 2 August 2005

HRH Crown Prince, Deputy Prime Minister, Defence, Prince Salman bin Abdul Aziz al-Saud

SELECTED GOVERNMENT MEMBERS *as at July 2014*

Finance, Ibrahim bin Abdul Aziz al-Assaf

Foreign Affairs, HRH Prince Saud al-Faisal bin Abdul Aziz al-Saud

Economy, Mohammed bin Sulaiman bin Mohammed al-Jasser

ROYAL EMBASSY OF SAUDI ARABIA
30 Charles Street, London W1J 5DZ
T 020-7917 3000 E ukemb@mofa.gov.sa
W www.saudiembassy.org.uk
Ambassador Extraordinary and Plenipotentiary, HE HRH Prince Mohamed bin Nawaf bin Abdul Aziz al-Saud, *apptd* 2005

BRITISH EMBASSY
PO Box 94351, Diplomatic Quarter, Riyadh 11693
T (+966) (0) 11 4819 100 E consular.riyadh@fco.gov.uk
W www.gov.uk/government/world/saudi-arabia
Ambassador Extraordinary and Plenipotentiary, HE Sir John Jenkins, *apptd* 2012

DEFENCE

Aged 16–49, 2010 est	Males	Females
Available for military service	8,644,522	6,601,985
Fit for military service	7,365,624	5,677,819

Military expenditure – US$62,760m (2013)

ECONOMY AND TRADE

The economy is based on oil extraction and processing, but since 1970 the government has used five-year development plans to encourage diversification, and the non-oil sector now accounts for 45 per cent of GDP. The 2010–14 development plan aims to increase natural gas production and to promote the growth of small- and medium-sized businesses, partly through further privatisation; it also partially opened the Saudi stock market to foreign investors, and between 2010 and 2014 intends to spend over $373bn on social development and infrastructure projects on six 'economic cities' across the country.

Oil extraction since the 1940s has brought great wealth. Saudi Arabia has the second-largest proven reserves of oil in the world (about 16 per cent of the world total) and the fifth-largest reserves of recoverable gas. The oil and gas industry contributes around 45 per cent of GDP and about 80 per cent of government revenue.

The main industries, apart from oil extraction and refining, include production of petrochemicals, ammonia, industrial gases, caustic soda, cement, fertiliser, plastics and metals, commercial ship and aircraft repair and construction. Industry accounts for 62.5 per cent of GDP and the service sector for 35.5 per cent. Agriculture contributes 2 per cent but is limited by the terrain, although productivity has been increased by extensive irrigation, desalination and the use of aquifers. The main products are grains, fruit, meat and dairy.

The main trading partners are China, the USA, Japan and South Korea. Oil and petroleum products constitute 90 per cent of exports. The principal imports are machinery and equipment, foodstuffs, chemicals, motor vehicles and textiles.

GNI – US$679,175m; US$21,2100 per capita (2011)
Annual average growth of GDP – 3.6 per cent (2013 est)
Inflation rate – 3.7 per cent (2013 est)
Unemployment – 10.5 per cent (males only) (2013 est)
Total external debt – US$149,4m (2013 est)
Imports – US$155,595m (2012)
Exports – US$386,000m (2012)

BALANCE OF PAYMENTS
Trade – US$230,405m surplus (2012)
Current Account – US$164,693m surplus (2012)

Trade with UK	2012	2013
Imports from UK	£3,258,551,378	£4,213,980,981
Exports to UK	£1,749,746,159	£2,618,632,244

COMMUNICATIONS

Airports – There are 82 airports; the three international airports are at Riyadh, Jeddah (serving Mecca) and Dammam
Waterways – The main cargo ports are Jeddah on the Red Sea coast and Dammam on the Gulf coast; the main oil port (the world's largest) is Ras Tanura
Roadways and railways – The road network totals 221,372km, including a 3,891km motorway system, and 1,378km of railways, operated by the state-run Saudi Railway Organisation
Telecommunications – 4.8 million fixed lines and 53 million mobile subscriptions (2012); there were 9.774 million internet users in 2009
Internet code and IDD – sa; 966 (from UK), 44 (to UK)

Major broadcasters – Television and radio networks are operated by the state-run Broadcasting Service of Saudi Arabia
Press – There are around seven daily newspapers, including *al-Watan* and the English-language *Arab News*
WPFI score – 58,3 (164)

EDUCATION AND HEALTH

With the exception of a few schools for expatriate children, all schools are segregated and supervised by the government.
Literacy rate – 87 per cent (2011 est)
Gross enrolment ratio (percentage of relevant age group) – primary 103 per cent; secondary 114 per cent; tertiary 51 per cent (2012 est)
Health expenditure (per capita) – US$758 (2011)
Hospital beds (per 1,000 people) – 2.2 (2009)
Life expectancy (years) – 74.82 (2014 est)
Mortality rate – 3.32 (2014 est)
Birth rate – 18.78 (2014 est)
Infant mortality rate – 14.58 (2014 est)

SENEGAL

République du Sénégal – Republic of Senegal

Area – 196,722 sq. km
Capital – Dakar; population, 3,037,146 (2012)
Major cities – Kaolack, Mbour, Saint-Louis, Thiès, Touba, Ziguinchor
Currency – Franc CFA of 100 centimes
Population – 13,635,927 rising at 2.48 per cent a year (2014 est); Wolof (43.3 per cent), Pular (23.8 per cent), Serer (14.7 per cent), Jola (3.7 per cent), Mandinka (3 per cent), Soninke (1.1 per cent), European and Lebanese (1 per cent) (est)
Religion – Muslim 94 per cent, Christian 5 per cent (est). Most incorporate indigenous beliefs into their worship
Language – French (official), Wolof, Fula, Jola, Mandinka
Population density – 69 per sq. km (2011)
Urban population – 42.8 per cent (2012 est)
Median age (years) – 18.4 (2014 est)
National anthem – 'Pincez Tous vos Koras, Frappez les Balafons' ['All Pluck Your Koras, Strike the Balafons']
National day – 4 April (Independence Day)
Death penalty – Abolished for all crimes (since 2004)
CPI score – 41 (77)

CLIMATE AND TERRAIN

The terrain is generally low and rolling, with plains rising to hills in the south-east. There is desert in the north, savannah in the centre and tropical forest in the south. Elevation extremes range from 581m (near Nepen Diakha) to 0m (Atlantic Ocean). There are three rivers: the Senegal on the northern border; and the Gambia and the Casamance in the south. The climate is tropical, with a wet season from June to September; the average temperature in Dakar is 24°C.

HISTORY AND POLITICS

Senegal was part of the Mali Empire in the 14th to 15th centuries. The first European visitors were the Portuguese in 1445. The French established a fort at Saint-Louis in 1659 and European traders exported slaves, ivory, gold and other commodities from there in the 17th and 18th centuries. The interior was colonised by the French in the mid-19th century and the territory became part of French West Africa in 1902. It became an autonomous state in 1958 and achieved independence as part of the Federation of Mali in June 1960, seceding to form the Republic of Senegal in August 1960. From 1966 to 1978, the country was a one-party state under the rule of the Senegalese Progressive Union (UPS), which changed its name to the Socialist Party (PS) in 1976.

In the early 1980s a separatist insurgency led by the Movement of Democratic Forces of Casamance (MFDC) began in the impoverished Casamance region south of the river Gambia. Splits and leadership changes among the separatists have prevented the implementation of peace agreements in 2001 and 2004, and clashes continue between government troops and rebels.

The Socialist Party's 40 years of political domination ended in 2000 with the election of Abdoulaye Wade, leader of the Senegalese Democratic Party (PDS), as president. President Wade lost the 2012 presidential election to the Alliance for the Republic–Yakaar leader Macky Sall, who picked up 65 per cent of the overall vote in the second round. A new prime minister and cabinet were appointed by the president on 1 September 2013.

The 2001 constitution was amended in 2007 to re-establish the senate as the upper chamber of a bicameral legislature, but this was abolished in 2012 by the National Assembly. The National Assembly has 150 members, directly elected for a five-year term; 90 are elected by majority in single member constituencies and 60 are elected by proportional representation. The president is directly elected for a seven-year term, renewable once; the president appoints the prime minister, who nominates the other ministers.

HEAD OF STATE
President, Macky Sall, *elected* 18 March 2012, *sworn in* 2 April 2012

SELECTED GOVERNMENT MEMBERS *as at July 2014*
Prime Minister, Aminata Toure
Finance and Economy, Amadou Ba
Interior, Abdoulaye Daouda Diallo
Foreign Affairs, Mankeur Ndiaye

EMBASSY OF THE REPUBLIC OF SENEGAL
39 Marloes Road, London W8 6LA
T 020-7938 4048
Ambassador Extraordinary and Plenipotentiary, HE Abdou Sourang, *apptd* 2007

BRITISH EMBASSY
PO Box 6025, 20 rue du Docteur Guillet, Dakar
T (+221) 823 7392 E dakar.consularenquiries@fco.gov.uk
W www.gov.uk/government/world/senegal
Ambassador Extraordinary and Plenipotentiary, HE John Marshall, *apptd* 2011

DEFENCE

Aged 16–49, 2010 est	Males	Females
Available for military service	2,699,196	3,018,565
Fit for military service	1,788,493	2,133,370

Military expenditure – US$242m (2013)*
Conscription duration – 24 months (selective)

* Figure does not include paramilitary spending

ECONOMY AND TRADE

Despite steady growth since the mid-1990s and the cancellation of two-thirds of its foreign debt in recent years, Senegal remains poor; 54 per cent of the population live below the poverty line and 48 per cent are unemployed, which has encouraged migration to Europe. The country is heavily dependent on foreign aid and remittances from expatriate workers, but infrastructure projects and the development of the textiles, information technology, telecommunications services and tourism industries are government priorities.

Agriculture and fishing are the mainstays of the economy, engaging 77.5 per cent of the workforce and contributing 14.9 per cent of GDP. The main industries are food and fish processing, mining (phosphate, iron, zircon, gold), oil refining, the production of fertiliser and construction materials, ship construction and tourism. Industry accounts for 22.7 per cent of GDP and services for 62.4 per cent.

The main trading partners are Mali, France, other EU countries, India and China. The principal exports are fish, groundnuts, petroleum products, phosphates and cotton. Principal imports are food, beverages, capital goods and fuels.
GNI – US$13,865m; US$1,030 per capita (2012)
Annual average growth of GDP – 4 per cent (2013 est)
Inflation rate – 0.8 per cent (2013 est)
Unemployment – 48 per cent (2007 est)
Total external debt – US$4,375m (2013 est)
Imports – US$5,883m (2012)
Exports – US$2,382m (2012)

BALANCE OF PAYMENTS
Trade – US$3,501m deficit (2012)
Current Account – US$1,139m deficit (2012)

Trade with UK	2012	2013
Imports from UK	£937,728,407	£319,993,639
Exports to UK	£28,640,859	£27,840,390

COMMUNICATIONS

Airports and waterways – Dakar is the main port and the location of the principal airport; seaport facilities are being modernised and there are 1,000km of navigable waterways, mainly on the Senegal, Saloum and Casamance rivers
Roadways and railways – 14,008km; 906km
Telecommunications – 338,200 fixed lines and 11.47 million mobile subscriptions (2012); there were 1.82 million internet users in 2009
Internet code and IDD – sn; 221 (from UK), 44 (to UK)
Major broadcasters – State-run Radiodiffusion Television Senegalaise operates the only free television channels and the main national and regional radio networks
Press – There are five daily newspapers, including the state-owned daily *Le Soleil*
WPFI score – 26,68 (62)

EDUCATION AND HEALTH

Literacy rate – 50 per cent (2009)
Gross enrolment ratio (percentage of relevant age group) – primary 84 per cent; secondary 41 per cent; tertiary 8 per cent (2012 est)
Health expenditure (per capita) – US$67 (2011)
Hospital beds (per 1,000 people) – 0.3 (2004–9)
Life expectancy (years) – 60.95 (2014 est)
Mortality rate – 8.65 (2014 est)
Birth rate – 35.09 (2014 est)
Infant mortality rate – 52.72 (2014 est)

SERBIA

Republika Srbija – Republic of Serbia

Area – 77,474 sq. km
Capital – Belgrade; population, 1,122,240 (2012)
Major cities – Kragujevac, Nis, Novi Sad
Currency – Serbian dinar of 100 paras
Population – 7,209,764 falling at 0.46 per year
   (2014 est); Serb (83.3 per cent), Hungarian (3.5 per
   cent), Romany (2.1 per cent), Bosniak (2 per cent)
   (2011 est)
Religion – Christian (Serbian Orthodox 84.6 per cent,
   Roman Catholic 5 per cent, Protestant 1 per cent),
   Muslim 3.1 per cent (est)
Language – Serbian (official), Hungarian, Romanian, Slovak,
   Ukrainian, Croatian (all official in different regions),
   Bosnian, Romani
Population density – 83 per sq. km (2011)
Urban population – 56.7 per cent (2012 est)
Median age (years) – 41.9 (2014 est)
National anthem – 'Boze Pravde' ['God of Justice']
National day – 15 February (Constitution Day)
Death penalty – Abolished for all crimes (since 2002)
CPI score – 42 (72)
Literacy rate – 98 per cent (2011 est)
Gross enrolment ratio (percentage of relevant age group) –
   primary 96 per cent; secondary 91 per cent; tertiary
   49.1 per cent (2011 est)
Health expenditure (per capita) – US$622 (2011)
Hospital beds (per 1,000 people) – 5.4 (2009)
Life expectancy (years) – 75.02 (2014 est)
Mortality rate – 13.71 (2014 est)
Birth rate – 9.13 (2014 est)
Infant mortality rate – 6.16 (2014 est)

CLIMATE AND TERRAIN

The landlocked country is mountainous in the south, while
the north is dominated by the low-lying plains of the
Danube and its major tributaries, the Sava, the Tisa and the
Morava. Its highest point is 2,169m (Midzor) and its lowest
is 35m (the confluence of the Danube and Timok rivers).
The climate is continental; average temperatures in Belgrade
range from 1.4°C in January to 23°C in July.

POLITICS

Under the 2006 constitution, the president is directly elected
for a five-year term, renewable once. The unicameral
National Assembly has 250 members, directly elected for a
four-year term. The prime minister is appointed by the
president.

   Boris Tadic, leader of the Democratic Party (DS), was
elected president in 2004 and re-elected in 2008 but lost the
2012 presidential election to Tomislav Nikolic, leader of the
Serbian Progressive Party (SNS). The SNS-led coalition won
a majority in the 2014 legislative election, but required
support from a bloc led by the Socialist Party of Serbia (SPS)
to govern.

HEAD OF STATE
President, Tomislav Nikolic, *elected* 20 May 2012, *took office*
   31 May 2012

SELECTED GOVERNMENT MEMBERS *as at July 2014*
Prime Minister, Interior, Aleksandar Vucic
First Deputy Prime Minister, Foreign Affairs, Ivica Dacic
Finance and Economy, Lazar Krstic

EMBASSY OF THE REPUBLIC OF SERBIA
28 Belgrave Square, London SW1X 8QB
T 020-7235 9049 E london@serbianembassy.org.uk
W www.serbianembassy.org.uk
Ambassador Extraordinary and Plenipotentiary, Ognjen
   Pribicevic, *apptd* 2014

BRITISH EMBASSY
Resavska 46, 11000 Belgrade
T (+381) (11) 306 0900 E belgrade.PPD@fco.gov.uk
W www.gov.uk/government/world/serbia
Ambassador Extraordinary and Plenipotentiary, HE Michael
   Davenport, LVO, *apptd* 2011

DEFENCE

Aged 16–49, 2010 est	Males	Females
Available for military service	–	–
Fit for military service	1,395,426	1,356,415

Military expenditure – US$919m (2013)
Conscription – abolished in 2010

ECONOMY AND TRADE

Economic mismanagement, UN sanctions in the 1990s along
with damage to infrastructure and industry from NATO
bombing in 1999 reduced the economy to about 50 per cent
of its 1990 size by 1999. Since 2000, governments have
pursued economic reforms and international reintegration,
obtained international support for economic restructuring,
rescheduled payments and received debt relief on much of
its foreign debt. Progress has been intermittent, but most
of the economy is now privatised.

   Economic growth averaged 6 per cent until 2008, but the
economy was severely affected by the global downturn,
which brought credit constraints, a fall in foreign investment

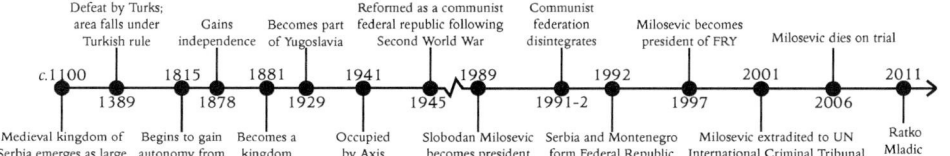

Defeat by Turks; area falls under Turkish rule	Gains independence	Becomes part of Yugoslavia	Reformed as a communist federal republic following Second World War	Communist federation disintegrates	Milosevic becomes president of FRY	Milosevic dies on trial
c.1100	1815	1881	1941	1989	1992	2001	2011
1389	1878	1929	1945	1991-2	1997	2006	
Medieval kingdom of Serbia emerges as large state in Balkans	Begins to gain autonomy from Ottoman Empire	Becomes a kingdom	Occupied by Axis powers	Slobodan Milosevic becomes president	Serbia and Montenegro form Federal Republic of Yugoslavia (FRY)	Milosevic extradited to UN International Criminal Tribunal after violent 'ethnic cleansing'	Ratko Mladic arrested

and manufacturing output, a sharp drop in export demand and reduced remittances from expatriate workers. The economy dropped by 1.7 per cent in 2012 before achieving growth of 2 per cent in 2013. The government sought external fiscal support in 2008 and signed a stand-by agreement with the IMF in 2011–12 which was frozen after the country's 2012 budget deviated from the programme framework. A decision on EU membership, which was submitted in 2009, has made some progress; Serbia attained candidate status in March 2012.

Agriculture accounts for 7.9 per cent of GDP and employs 23.9 per cent of the workforce. The main agricultural products are wheat, maize, sugar beet, sunflowers, fruit, meat and milk. Industry includes food processing and production of base metals, furniture, machinery, chemicals, sugar, tyres, clothing and pharmaceuticals. Industry contributes 31.8 per cent of GDP and services 60.3 per cent.

The main trading partners are Russia, the EU and neighbouring states. Principal exports are iron and steel, rubber, clothing, wheat, fruit, vegetables and non-ferrous metals.
GNI – US$36,318m; US$5,280 per capita (2012)
Annual average growth of GDP – 2 per cent (2013 est)
Inflation rate – 8.2 per cent (2013 est)
Population below poverty line – 24.6 per cent (2012 est)
Unemployment – 27.7 per cent (2013 est)
Total external debt – US$35,110m (2013 est)

BALANCE OF PAYMENTS
Trade – US$7,579m deficit (2012)
Current Account – US$4,058m deficit (2012)

Trade with UK	2012	2013
Imports from UK	£119,532,956	£136,587,458
Exports to UK	£82,947,838	£114,650,122

COMMUNICATIONS
Airports and waterways – The main international airport is at Belgrade; there are 587km of navigable waterways, and principal ports include Belgrade and Novi Sad on the Danube
Roadways and railways – 44,248km; 3,809km
Telecommunications – 2.977 million fixed lines and 9.138 million mobile subscriptions (2012); there were 4.11 million internet users in 2009
Internet code and IDD – rs; 381 (from UK), 44 (to UK)
Major broadcasters – The state-funded national broadcaster RTS aims to develop into a public service, and state-funded local and regional media outlets are to be privatised
Press – Newspapers include dailies *Danas, Blik,* and *Politika*
WPFI score – 25,05 (54)

SEYCHELLES

République des Seychelles / Repiblik Sesel – Republic of Seychelles

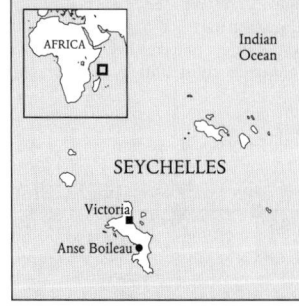

Area – 455 sq. km
Capital – Victoria, on Mahé; population, 27,000 (2011)
Currency – Seychelles rupee of 100 cents
Population – 91,650 rising at 0.87 per cent a year (2014 est)
Religion – Christian (Roman Catholic 76.2 per cent, Anglican 6.1 per cent), Hindu 2.4 per cent (2011)
Language – Seychellois Creole, English, French (all official)
Population density – 190 per sq. km (2011)
Urban population – 54 per cent (2012 est)
Median age (years) – 33.9 (2014 est)
National anthem – 'Koste Seselwa' ['Seychellois Unite']
National day – 18 June (Constitution Day)
Death penalty – Abolished for all crimes (since 1993)
CPI score – 54 (47)
Literacy rate – 92 per cent (2011 est)
Life expectancy (years) – 74.25 (2014 est)
Mortality rate – 6.90 (2014 est)
Birth rate – 14.54 (2014 est)
Infant mortality rate – 10.77 (2014 est)

CLIMATE AND TERRAIN
Seychelles consists of 115 islands spread over 643,737 sq. km of the south-west Indian Ocean, north of Madagascar. There is a relatively compact granitic group of 32 islands, with high hills and mountains, of which Mahé is the largest and most populated (about 90 per cent of the population lives on Mahé), and an outlying coralline group, for the most part only slightly above sea-level. Elevation extremes range from 905m (Morne Seychellois) to 0m (Indian Ocean). The climate is tropical, with an average temperature of 26.7°C, and a wet season from November to March.

HISTORY AND POLITICS
The uninhabited islands were proclaimed French territory in 1756, but settlement of the Mahé group began only in 1770. The group was a dependency of Mauritius, and was ceded to Britain with Mauritius in 1814. In 1903 these islands, together with the coralline group, were formed into a colony separate from Mauritius. On 29 June 1976, the islands became an independent republic.

Following a coup d'état in 1977, when France-Albert René became president, Seychelles became a one-party state ruled by the Seychelles People's Progressive Front (SPPF) in 1979. Opposition parties were permitted from 1991 and in 1993 President René reintroduced a multiparty constitution. Power has remained with the SPPF under the pluralist system, although opposition parties are beginning to achieve a greater share of the vote.

President René stepped down in mid-term in 2004 and the rest of his term was served by the vice-president, James Michel, who was elected president in 2006 and re-elected in May 2011. In the 2011 legislative election, the People's Party (formerly SPPF) retained its overall majority.

Under the 1993 constitution, the executive president is directly elected for a five-year term, with a maximum of three consecutive terms. The unicameral National Assembly has up to 34 members: 25 directly elected by constituencies and up to nine allocated by proportional representation; members serve a five-year term. The council of ministers is appointed by the president.

HEAD OF STATE
President, Defence, James Michel, *assumed office* 14 April 2004, *elected* July 2006, *re-elected* 2011
Vice-President, Danny Faure

SELECTED GOVERNMENT MEMBERS *as at July 2014*
Foreign Affairs, Jean-Paul Adam
Internal Affairs, Joel Morgan

SEYCHELLES HIGH COMMISSION
4th Floor, 111 Baker Street, London W1U 6RR
T 020-7935 7770 E consulate@seychelles-gov.net
W www.seychelles-gov.net
High Commissioner, Marie-Pierre Lloyd

BRITISH HIGH COMMISSION
PO Box 161, Oliaji Trade Centre, Victoria, Mahé
T (+248) 283 666 E bhcvictoria@fco.gov.uk
W www.gov.uk/government/world/seychelles
High Commissioner, HE Lindsay Skoll, *apptd* 2012

DEFENCE

Aged 16–49, 2010 est	Males	Females
Available for military service	26,257	23,996
Fit for military service	20,231	19,891

Military expenditure – US$11.3m (2013)

ECONOMY AND TRADE
Seychelles prospered after independence owing to the development of tuna fishing and tourism, which employs about 30 per cent of the workforce and provides over 70 per cent of hard currency earnings. The economy struggled in 2008–9 owing to external debt, high deficits, food and oil price rises and a reduction in foreign exchange earnings after tourism declined in the global economic downturn, but recovered in 2010–11. By 2013 the IMF declared that Seychelles had a successful market-based economy with full employment and a fiscal surplus

Agriculture, small-scale manufacturing and offshore financial services are being developed to diversify the economy. Apart from fishing and tourism, the main industries involve processing fish, coconuts and vanilla, producing coir rope, furniture and beverages, boat-building and printing.

The main trading partners are EU countries, Saudi Arabia and Japan. The principal exports are canned tuna, frozen fish, cinnamon bark, copra and re-exports of petroleum products. The principal imports are machinery and equipment, foodstuffs, petroleum products and chemicals.
GNI – US$1,087m; US$12,260 per capita (2012)
Annual average growth of GDP – 3.3 per cent (2013 est)
Inflation rate – 4.3 per cent (2013 est)
Unemployment – 2 per cent (2006 est)
Total external debt – US$1,719m (2013 est)
Imports – US$800m (2012)
Exports – US$496m (2012)

BALANCE OF PAYMENTS
Trade – US$303m deficit (2012)
Current Account – US$224m deficit (2012)

Trade with UK	2012	2013
Imports from UK	£20,568,521	£19,605,972
Exports to UK	£48,116,655	£74,458,419

COMMUNICATIONS
Airports and waterways – The principal airport is at Mahé; the main port is Victoria, and ferries run regularly between Mahé, Praslin and La Digue
Roadways – There are 508km of roads
Telecommunications – 28,900 fixed lines and 138,300 mobile subscriptions (2012); there were 32,000 internet users in 2008
Media – The state-run Seychelles Broadcasting Corporation operates various channels across the country; *Seychelles Nation* is the main government-owned daily newspaper
WPFI score – 31,68 (103)

SIERRA LEONE
Republic of Sierra Leone

Area – 71,740 sq. km
Capital – Freetown; population, 955,353 (2012)
Major towns – Bo, Kenema
Currency – Leone (Le) of 100 cents
Population – 5,743,725 rising at 2.33 per cent a year (2014 est); 20 ethnic groups, of which the largest are the Temne (35 per cent), Mende (31 per cent), Limba (8 per cent) and Kono (5 per cent) (2008)
Religion – Muslim 60 per cent, Christian 10 per cent, indigenous 30 per cent (est)
Language – English (official), Krio (Creole; lingua franca), Mende (in the south), Temne (in the north)
Population density – 82 per sq. km (2011)
Urban population – 39.6 per cent (2012 est)
Median age (years) – 19 (2014 est)
National anthem – 'High We Exalt Thee, Realm of the Free'
National day – 27 April (Independence Day)
Death penalty Retained (last used 1998)
CPI score – 30 (119)

CLIMATE AND TERRAIN
The land rises from mangrove swamps along the coast, to low-lying wooded country, and then to a mountainous plateau in the east. Elevation extremes range from 1,948m (Loma Mansa) to 0m (Atlantic Ocean). The climate is tropical, with a rainy season from May to November; rainfall peaks in July and August, and is particularly heavy on the coast. The average temperature is 26.1°C.

HISTORY AND POLITICS
Coastal trading posts were established by the Portuguese in the 15th century and the British in the 17th century. In 1787 British philanthropists and abolitionists established a settlement for repatriated former slaves from Britain and its colonies on the Freetown peninsula. In 1808 the settlement was declared a crown colony and became the main base in west Africa for enforcing the 1807 Act outlawing the slave trade. In 1896 a protectorate was declared over the hinterland. The Freetown colony and the protectorate were united in 1951, and in 1961 Sierra Leone became independent.

The country became a republic in 1971 and a one-party state in 1978. Transition to a multiparty democracy began in 1991 but was aborted by a military coup in 1992. Civilian rule was restored with the 1996 elections. Another coup in May 1997 was short-lived, and the government was reinstated in March 1998 with the assistance of Economic Community of West African States (ECOWAS) troops.

The transition to multiparty and civilian rule was complicated by the civil war with the Revolutionary United Front (RUF), which began in 1991. Fighting continued until 2001, when a lasting ceasefire was agreed, and the war was declared over in 2002. An estimated 50,000 people were killed, 30,000 mutilated and a third of the population displaced between 1991 and 2002. A truth and reconciliation commission and a UN-supported war crimes tribunal were set up in 2002.

The 2012 presidential election was won by the incumbent, Ernest Bai Koroma, of the All People's Congress (APC). The APC won a majority of seats in the simultaneous legislative election, defeating the Sierra Leone People's Party.

Under the 1991 constitution, the executive president is directly elected for a five-year term, renewable once. The unicameral parliament has 124 members: 112 directly elected for a five-year term and 12 indirectly elected to represent the 12 provincial districts. The president, who is responsible to the legislature, appoints and chairs the cabinet.

HEAD OF STATE
President, Ernest Bai Koroma, *elected* 18 September 2007, *re-elected* 17 November 2012
Vice-President, Samuel Sam-Sumana

SELECTED GOVERNMENT MEMBERS *as at July 2014*
Defence, Alfredo Conteh
Finance, Kaifala Marah
Foreign Affairs, Samura Kamara
Internal Affairs, Joseph Dauda

SIERRA LEONE HIGH COMMISSION
41 Eagle Street, London WC1R 4TL
T 020-7404 0140 E info@slhc-uk.org.uk W www.slhc-uk.org.uk
High Commissioner, HE Edward Turay, *apptd* 2010

BRITISH HIGH COMMISSION
6 Spur Road, Freetown
T (+232) (0) 76 541 386 E freetown.general.enquiries@fco.gov.uk
W www.gov.uk/government/world/sierra-leone
High Commissioner, HE Peter West, *apptd* 2013

DEFENCE

Aged 16–49, 2010 est	Males	Females
Available for military service	1,183,093	–
Fit for military service	731,898	838,032

Military expenditure – US$24.2m (2013)

ECONOMY AND TRADE
The country was devastated by a decade of civil war, and unemployment increased with the demobilisation of former combatants. Economic activity has grown since the end of the war but the country remains extremely poor, dependent on foreign aid and expatriates' remittances. It benefited from having around 90 per cent of its foreign debt written off in 2006.

There are significant mineral deposits and agricultural and fishery resources, although the lack of infrastructure hampers development. Diamonds account for about half of export earnings, but 47.9 per cent of GDP is generated by agriculture, much of which is at subsistence level. Industry consists mainly of mining (diamonds, rutile, bauxite), processing agricultural products, light manufacturing for the domestic market, oil refining and ship repair. Exploitation of offshore oil reserves boosted growth to 20 per cent in 2012.

The main export market is China (51.1 per cent), followed by Belgium and Japan; the chief import suppliers are China, India and South Africa. Principal exports are diamonds, rutile, cocoa, coffee and fish. The main imports are foodstuffs, machinery and equipment, fuels and lubricants, and chemicals.

GNI – US$3,796m; US$580 per capita (2012)
Annual average growth of GDP – 13.3 per cent (2013 est)
Inflation rate – 11.16 per cent (2013 est)
Population below poverty line – 52.9 per cent (2011)
Total external debt – US$1,331m (2013 est)
Imports – US$521m (2009)
Exports – US$233m (2009)

BALANCE OF PAYMENTS
Trade – US$300m deficit (2010)
Current Account – US$1,389m deficit (2012)

Trade with UK	2012	2013
Imports from UK	£67,688,894	£72,495,390
Exports to UK	£8,028,875	£13,595,671

COMMUNICATIONS
Airports and waterways – There is an international airport at Freetown; Freetown, which has one of the world's largest natural harbours, is the main port and there are smaller ports at Pepel and Sherbro
Roadways and railways – The railway system was phased out in 1974, but an extensive 11,300km road network has been developed since
Telecommunications – 18,000 fixed lines (2010) and 2.21 million mobile subscriptions (2012); there were 14,900 internet users in 2009
Internet code and IDD – sl; 232 (from UK), 44 (to UK)
Media – The Sierra Leone Broadcasting Corporation was formed in 2010 and is the country's principal broadcaster; newspapers include *Awoko* and the *Standard Times*
WPFI score – 28,23 (72)

EDUCATION AND HEALTH
The public University of Sierra Leone incorporates several campuses in Freetown, and Njala University was established in Bo in 2005; there are a number of other technical and teacher-training institutes throughout the country.
Literacy rate – 43 per cent (2011 est)
Health expenditure (per capita) – US$69 (2011 est)
Hospital beds (per 1,000 people) – 0.4 (2004–9)
Life expectancy (years) – 57.39 (2014 est)
Mortality rate – 11.03 (2014 est)
Birth rate – 37.4 (2014 est)
Infant mortality rate – 73.29 (2014 est)
HIV/AIDS adult prevalence – 1.5 per cent (2012 est)

SINGAPORE

Xinjiapo   Gongheguo/Republik   Singapura/Cinkappur
Kutiyaracu – Republic of Singapore

Area – 697 sq. km
Capital – Singapore
Currency – Singapore dollar (S$) of 100 cents
Population – 5,567,301 rising at 1.92 per cent a year
 (2014 est); Chinese (74.2 per cent), Malay (13.3 per cent),
 Indian (9.2 per cent) (2013 est)
Religion – Buddhist 33.9 per cent, Muslim 14.3 per cent,
 Taoist 11.3 per cent, Christian (Roman Catholic 7.1
 per cent, other Christian 11 per cent) (2010 est)
Language – Mandarin, English, Malay, Tamil (all official),
 Hokkien, Cantonese, Teochew
Population density – 7,405 per sq. km (2011)
Urban population – 100 per cent (2012 est)
Median age (years) – 33.8 (2014 est)
National anthem – 'Majulah Singapura' ['Onward, Singapore']
National day – 9 August (Independence, 1965)
Death penalty – Retained
CPI score – 86 (5)
Literacy rate – 96 per cent (2010)
Health expenditure (per capita) – US$2,286 (2011)
Hospital beds (per 1,000 people) – 2.7 (2011)
Life expectancy (years) – 84.38 (2014 est)
Mortality rate – 3.42 (2014 est)
Birth rate – 8.1 (2014 est)
Infant mortality rate – 2.53 (2014 est)

CLIMATE AND TERRAIN

Singapore consists of the island of Singapore and 63 islets situated off the southern extremity of the Malay peninsula, from which it is separated by the Straits of Johor. The land rises from the shore to a low, undulating central plateau. Elevation extremes range from 166m (Bukit Timah) to 0m (Singapore Strait). The state is just north of the Equator and the climate is tropical, subject to monsoons in June to September and December to March. The average temperature is 26.5°C, and there is frequent rain and high humidity.

HISTORY AND POLITICS

Singapore, a trading site since the 13th century, was established as a British trading post by Sir Stamford Raffles in 1819 and was ceded to Britain in perpetuity in 1824. In 1826 it was incorporated with Penang and Malacca to form the Straits Settlements and they became a crown colony in 1867. Singapore became the commercial and financial hub of South East Asia in the 19th century, and the principal British military base in the Far East in the 1920s. In 1942, during the Second World War, it fell to Japanese forces. Liberated in 1945, it became a separate colony in 1946, and internal self-government was introduced in 1959. It became part of the Federation of Malaysia in 1963, before withdrawing to become an independent sovereign state in 1965.

Although Singapore is a multiparty state, the People's Action Party (PAP) has dominated politics since 1959; opposition candidates were elected to parliament for the first time in 1981.

Independent candidate Tony Tan was elected president in August 2011, replacing PAP's Sellapan rama Nathan. In the 2011 general election, the PAP retained its large majority with 81 seats, but opposition parties won an unprecedented six seats. Lee Hsien Loong, the son of Lee Kuan Yew, continued in office as prime minister, a post he has held since 2004.

The 1959 constitution was amended in 1965 to end the affiliation with Malaysia and make Singapore a republic, and in 1991 to make the presidency directly elected. The president is directly elected for a six-year term, which is renewable. The president appoints the prime minister and, on his advice, the members of the cabinet. There is a unicameral parliament with 87 directly elected members and up to nine extra members from opposition parties (NCMPs) (currently three), depending on their share of the vote; all members serve a five-year term. Up to nine members can also be nominated by the government for a two-year term (NMPs) to bring the opposition numbers up to 18.

HEAD OF STATE

President, Tony Tan, *took office* 1 September 2011

SELECTED GOVERNMENT MEMBERS *as at July 2014*
Prime Minister, Lee Hsien Loong
Deputy Prime Minister, Home Affairs, Rear-Adm. Teo Chee
 Hean
Foreign Affairs, Kasiviswanathan Shanmugam
Finance, Tharman Shanmugaratnam

HIGH COMMISSION FOR THE REPUBLIC OF SINGAPORE
9 Wilton Crescent, London SW1X 8SP
T 020-7235 8315 E singhc_lon@sgmfa.gov.sg
W www.mfa.gov.sg/london
High Commissioner, HE Thambynathan Jasudasen, *apptd*
 2011

BRITISH HIGH COMMISSION
100 Tanglin Road, Singapore 247919
T (+65) 6424 4200 E consular.singapore@fco.gov.uk
W www.gov.uk/government/world/organisations/british-high-
commission-singapore
High Commissioner, HE Antony Phillipson, *apptd* 2011

DEFENCE

Aged 16–49, 2010 est	*Males*	*Females*
Available for military service	1,255,902	–
Fit for military service	1,018,839	1,087,134

Military expenditure – US$9,077m (2013)
Conscription duration – 24 months

ECONOMY AND TRADE

Historically based on trade in raw materials from surrounding countries and on entrepôt trade in finished products, the economy industrialised rapidly after independence and diversified, becoming a regional financial and technology centre and a tourist destination. Economic growth has rarely flagged since 1965; although the global economic downturn pushed the economy into recession in 2008, it recovered strongly in 2010, rebounding 14.8 per cent due to a renewed export market, but growth slowed to 1.9 per cent in 2012 and 4.1 per cent in 2013.

Agriculture is limited and contributes little to GDP. Industries include manufacturing (especially consumer electronics, information technology products, biomedical sciences, pharmaceuticals and chemicals), engineering, oil refining, rubber processing, food processing and ship repair; industry contributes 29.4 per cent of GDP. The service sector (financial and business services, entrepot trade, tourism) accounts for 70.6 per cent of GDP and employs 80.1 per cent of the workforce.

The main trading partners are Malaysia, China, Indonesia, the USA and Hong Kong. Principal exports are machinery and equipment (especially electronic), consumer goods, pharmaceuticals and other chemicals and mineral fuels. The main imports are machinery and equipment, mineral fuels, chemicals, food and consumer goods.

GNI – US$271,585m; US$47,210 per capita (2012)
Annual average growth of GDP – 3.5 per cent (2013 est)
Inflation rate – 2.4 per cent (2013 est)
Unemployment – 2.1 per cent (2013 est)

Total external debt – US$1,174,000m (2013 est)
Imports – US$379,723m (2012)
Exports – US$408,393m (2012)

BALANCE OF PAYMENTS
Trade – US$28,670m surplus (2012)
Current Account – US$51,437m surplus (2012)

Trade with UK	2012	2013
Imports from UK	£4,241,679,1662	£4,118,440,102
Exports to UK	£3,632,695,292	£2,642,266,680

COMMUNICATIONS
Airports and waterways – Singapore is one of the busiest seaports in the world, although there is a high risk of piracy in the South China Sea; it has a large merchant fleet of 1,599 ships of over 1,000 tonnes, with 344 registered in other countries, while 966 foreign-owned ships are registered in Singapore. There is one international airport, at Changi
Roadways and railways – There are 3,425km of roadways and an extensive light rail system on the island
Telecommunications – 1.99 million fixed lines and 8.063 million mobile subscriptions (2012); there were 3.235 million internet users in 2009
Internet code and IDD – sg; 65 (from UK), 1/2/8 44 (to UK)
Major broadcasters – Broadcasting is dominated by MediaCorp, owned by a state investment agency
Press – Singapore Press Holdings, which has close links to the ruling party, has a virtual monopoly on the newspaper industry, and publishes 17 newspapers
WPFI score – 44,29 (150)

SLOVAKIA

Slovenska Republika – Slovak Republic

Area – 49,035 sq. km
Capital – Bratislava; population, 434,000 (2011)
Major city – Kosice
Currency – Euro (€) of 100 cents
Population – 5,443,583 rising at 0.03 per cent a year (2014 est); Slovak (80.7 per cent), Hungarian (8.5 per cent), Roma (2 per cent) (2011 est)
Religion – Christian (Roman Catholic 62 per cent, Protestant 8.2 per cent), none 13.4 (2011)

Language – Slovak (official), Hungarian, Romani, Ukrainian
Population density – 112 per sq. km (2011)
Urban population – 54.7 per cent (2012 est)
Median age (years) – 39.2 (2014 est)
National anthem – 'Nad Tatrou sa blýska' ['Lightning Over the Tatras']
National day – 1 September (Constitution Day)
Death penalty – Abolished for all crimes (since 1990)
CPI score – 47 (61)
Gross enrolment ratio (percentage of relevant age group) – primary 102 per cent; secondary 89 per cent; tertiary 54.2 per cent (2011 est)
Health expenditure (per capita) – US$1,534 (2011)
Hospital beds (per 1,000 people) – 6.4 (2010)
Life expectancy (years) – 76.69 (2014 est)
Mortality rate – 9.70 (2014 est)
Birth rate – 10.01 (2014 est)
Infant mortality rate – 5.35 (2014 est)

CLIMATE AND TERRAIN
Slovakia is landlocked and mountainous, lying in the western Carpathian range which includes the Tatra and Beskid mountains to the north. The mountains fall to plains in the south-east and south-west; the latter is the plain of the river Danube and its tributary the Vah, which rises in the Tatras. Elevation extremes range from 2,655m (Gerlachovsky stit) to 94m (Bodrog river). The climate is temperate, with warm humid summers and cold dry winters. Average temperatures in Bratislava range from1°C in January to 20°C in July.

POLITICS
The 1993 constitution has been amended several times, most recently in 1999 to allow direct elections to the presidency. The president is directly elected for a five-year term, renewable once. The unicameral National Council has 150 members, who are directly elected for a four-year term by proportional representation. The prime minister, who is appointed by the president, nominates the cabinet.

The 2014 presidential election was won by Andrej Kiska. Direction-Social Democracy (Smer-SD) remained the largest party after the 2010 legislative election, but four centre-right parties held a majority of seats and formed a coalition government. Smer-SD won the 2012 legislative election, gaining an overall majority and forming a government under Robert Fico.

HEAD OF STATE
President, Andrej Kiska, *elected* 29 March 2014

SELECTED GOVERNMENT MEMBERS *as at July 2014*
Prime Minister, Robert Fico
Defence, Martin Glvac
Foreign Affairs, Miroslav Lajcak
Interior, Robert Kalinak

EMBASSY OF THE SLOVAK REPUBLIC
25 Kensington Palace Gardens, London W8 4QY
T 020-7313 6470 E emb.london@mzv.sk
W www.slovakembassy.co.uk
Ambassador Extraordinary and Plenipotentiary, Miroslav Wlachovsky, *apptd* 2011

BRITISH EMBASSY
Panska 16, Bratislava 811 01
T (+421) (2) 5998 2000 E bebra@internet.sk
W www.gov.uk/government/world/slovakia
Ambassador Extraordinary and Plenipotentiary, HE Susannah Montgomery, *apptd* 2011

DEFENCE

Aged 16–49, 2010 est	Males	Females
Available for military service	1,405,310	1,369,897
Fit for military service	1,156,113	1,139,380

Military expenditure – US$988m (2013)
Conscription – suspended for peacetime in 2006

ECONOMY AND TRADE

Slovakia has nearly completed the transition from a centrally planned to a free-market economy, following structural reforms and privatisation begun after 1998. As a result, foreign investment has risen, especially in the vehicle and electronics industries, and GDP grew steadily in 2000–8. The economy contracted in 2009 because of the global economic downturn, recovering in 2010. In 2012 a number of pro-growth economic reforms were scaled back to shore up government finances. Corruption and slow dispute resolution remain key factors reducing economic growth.

Natural resources include brown coal and lignite, natural gas, oil, iron ore, copper and manganese. Major industries include production of metal and metal products, food and beverages, fuel and energy (electricity, gas, coke, oil and nuclear), chemicals and synthetic fibres, machinery, paper and printing, ceramics, transport vehicles, textiles and electrical and optical equipment. Industry accounts for 30.8 per cent of GDP, services 47 per cent and agriculture 3.1 per cent.

The main trading partners are other EU countries (especially Germany and the Czech Republic) and Russia. Principal exports are machinery and electrical equipment, vehicles, base metals, chemicals, minerals and plastics. The main imports are machinery and transport equipment, mineral products, vehicles, base metals, chemicals and plastics.

GNI – US$89,695m; US$17,180 per capita (2012)
Annual average growth of GDP – 0.8 per cent (2013 est)
Inflation rate – 1.7 per cent (2013 est)
Unemployment – 14.4 per cent (2013 est)
Total external debt – US$68,440m (2012 est)
Imports – US$79,077m (2012)
Exports – US$79,882m (2012)

BALANCE OF PAYMENTS
Trade – US$805m surplus (2012)
Current Account – US$2,076m surplus (2012)

Trade with UK	2012	2013
Imports from UK	£514,256,893	£464,275,221
Exports to UK	£1,565,023,657	£1,804,545,017

COMMUNICATIONS

Airports and waterways – The principal airport is at Bratislava and the main Danube ports are Bratislava and Komarno
Roadways and railways – There are 43,916km of roadways, including 417km of motorways, and 3,622km of railways
Telecommunications – 975,000 fixed lines and 6.095 million mobile subscriptions (2012); there were 4.063 million internet users in 2009
Internet code and IDD – sk; 421 (from UK), 44 (to UK)
Major broadcasters – The public broadcasters, Slovak TV and

Slovak Radio, operate national networks in competition with private companies
Press – The major daily newspapers, including *Pravda* and *Sme*, are all privately owned
WPFI score – 11,39 (20)

SLOVENIA

Republika Slovenija – Republic of Slovenia

Area – 20,273 sq. km
Capital – Ljubljana; population, 273,000 (2011)
Major city – Maribor
Currency – Euro (€) of 100 cents
Population – 1,988,292 falling at 0.23 per cent a year (2014 est); Slovene (83.1 per cent), Serb (2 per cent), Croat (1.8 per cent), Bosniak (1.1 per cent) (2002)
Religion – Christian (Roman Catholic 57.8 per cent, Orthodox 2.3 per cent), Muslim 2.4 per cent (2002)
Language – Slovene (official), Serbo-Croat; Hungarian and Italian are also official in designated municipalities
Population density – 102 per sq. km (2011)
Urban population – 49.8 per cent (2012)
Median age (years) – 43.5 (2014 est)
National anthem – 'Zdravljica' ['A Toast']
National day – 25 June (Statehood Day)
Death penalty – Abolished for all crimes (since 1989)
CPI score – 57 (43)

CLIMATE AND TERRAIN

The Alps cover 42 per cent of the country, towards the north, and the south lies on the high Karst plateau. The only low-lying areas are the Pannonian plain in the east and north-east, and the short (47km) narrow coastal belt on the Adriatic Sea. Elevation extremes range from 2,864m (Triglav) to 0m (Adriatic Sea). The climate is continental in most of the country but Mediterranean on the coast. Average temperatures in Ljubljana range from −1°C in January to 19°C in July.

POLITICS

Under the 1991 constitution, the president is directly elected for a five-year term. The unicameral National Assembly has 90 members directly elected for a four-year term. The National Council, which has 40 members indirectly elected for a five-year term, has an advisory role. The prime minister, who is nominated by the president and elected by the legislature, appoints the cabinet.

The November 2012 presidential election was won by Borut Pahor of the Social Democrats (SD), defeating the incumbent, Danilo Turk. The centre-left party of Miro Cerar (SMC) became the largest party after the 2014 legislative elections.

HEAD OF STATE

President, Borut Pahor, *elected* 2 December 2012; *sworn in* 22 December 2012

SELECTED GOVERNMENT MEMBERS *as at September 2014*

Prime Minister, Miro Cevat
Defence, Janko Veber
Foreign Affairs, Karl Erjavec

EMBASSY OF THE REPUBLIC OF SLOVENIA

10 Little College Street, London SW1P 3SH
T 020-7222 5700 E vlo@gov.si W http://london.embassy.si
Ambassador Extraordinary and Plenipotentiary, vacant

BRITISH EMBASSY

4th Floor, Trg Republike 3, 1000 Ljubljana
T (+386) (1) 200 3910 E info@british-embassy.si
W www.gov.uk/government/world/slovenia
Ambassador Extraordinary and Plenipotentiary, HE Sophie Honey, *apptd* 2013

DEFENCE

Aged 16–49, 2010 est	Males	Females
Available for military service	477,592	464,301
Fit for military service	392,075	380,077

Military expenditure – US$544m (2013)

ECONOMY AND TRADE

Always the most prosperous republic of the former Yugoslavia, Slovenia's transition to a market economy was smoothed by good infrastructure and a well-educated workforce. Much of the economy remains in state ownership and taxes are high, deterring foreign investment and inhibiting its international competitiveness. The economy contracted sharply in 2009 owing to the global downturn; 2014 is expected to see the economy contract by 1 per cent, resulting in a third consecutive year of recession. Unemployment has steadily risen, reaching 13.1 per cent in 2013.

Industry contributes 35 per cent of GDP, the service sector 62.8 per cent and agriculture 2.2 per cent. The main agricultural products are potatoes, hops, wheat, sugar beet, maize, grapes and livestock. Industries include mining and mineral processing (iron ore, aluminium, lead, zinc), electronics (including for military purposes), vehicles, electric power equipment, wood products, textiles, chemicals and machine tools.

The main trading partners are other EU countries (particularly Germany and Italy) and Austria. Principal exports are manufactured goods, machinery and transport equipment, chemicals and food. These items, along with fuels and lubricants, are also the main imports.

GNI – US$44,900m; US$22,800 per capita (2012)
Annual average growth of GDP – −2.6 per cent (2013 est)
Inflation rate – 2.1 per cent (2013 est)
Population below the poverty line – 13.6 per cent (2011 est)
Unemployment – 12.4 per cent (2013 est)
Total external debt – US$53,900m (2012 est)
Imports – US$28,392m (2012)
Exports – US$27,080m (2012)

BALANCE OF PAYMENTS

Trade – US$1,312m deficit (2012)
Current Account – US$203m surplus (2011)

Trade with UK	2012	2013
Imports from UK	£210,506,703	£203,266,291
Exports to UK	£332,907,136	£315,392,513

COMMUNICATIONS

Airports and waterways – The international airports are at Ljubljana, Maribor and Portoroz; Koper is the main port
Roadways and railways 38,985km, 1,228km
Telecommunications – 825,000 fixed lines and 2.216 million mobile subscriptions (2012); there were 1.298 million internet users in 2009
Internet code and IDD – si; 386 (from UK), 44 (to UK)
Media – The television market is mainly shared between the public service, RTV Slovenia, and private stations; daily newspapers include *Dnevnik* and *Slovenske Novice*
WPFI score – 20,38 (34)

EDUCATION AND HEALTH

Education is free and compulsory between the ages of six and 15.
Literacy rate – 100 per cent (2011)
Gross enrolment ratio (percentage of relevant age group) – primary 99 per cent; secondary 98 per cent; tertiary 86 per cent (2012 est)
Health expenditure (per capita) – US$2,218 (2011)
Hospital beds (per 1,000 people) – 4.6 (2010)
Life expectancy (years) – 77.83 (2014 est)
Mortality rate – 11.25 (2014 est)
Birth rate – 8.54 (2014 est)
Infant mortality rate – 4.04 (2014 est)

SOLOMON ISLANDS

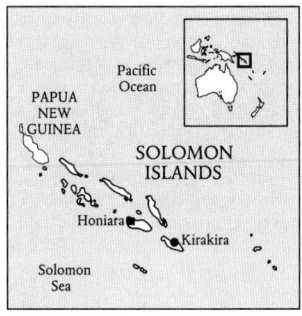

Area – 28,896 sq. km
Capital – Honiara, on Guadalcanal; population, 68,000 (2011)
Currency – Solomon Islands dollar (SI$) of 100 cents
Population – 609,883 rising at 2.07 per cent a year (2014 est); Melanesian (95.3 per cent), Polynesian (3.1 per cent), Micronesian (1.2 per cent) (2009 est)
Religion – Christian (Church of Melanesia 31.9 per cent, Roman Catholic 19.6 per cent, Evangelical 17.1 per cent, Seventh-day Adventist 11.7 per cent) (est)
Language – English (official), Melanesian Pidgin (lingua franca); around 120 indigenous languages exist
Population density – 19 per sq. km (2010)
Urban population – 20.9 per cent (2012)
Median age (years) – 21.6 (2014 est)
National anthem – 'God Save Our Solomon Islands'
National day – 7 July (Independence Day)
Death penalty – Abolished for all crimes (since 1966)
Life expectancy (years) – 74.89 (2014 est)
Mortality rate – 3.86 (2014 est)
Birth rate – 26.33 (2014 est)
Infant mortality rate – 16.17 (2014 est)

CLIMATE AND TERRAIN

Forming a scattered archipelago of mountainous islands and low-lying coral atolls in the south-west Pacific Ocean, the

Solomon Islands stretch about 1,448km in a south-easterly direction from the Shortland Islands to the Santa Cruz islands. The six biggest islands are Choiseul, New Georgia, Santa Isabel, Guadalcanal, Malaita and Makira (San Cristobal). They are characterised by thickly forested mountain ranges intersected by deep, narrow valleys. Elevation extremes range from 2,310m (Mt Popomanaseu) to 0m (Pacific Ocean). The climate is tropical, with little variation in temperature, and a wet season between November and April. The islands are prone to seismic activity and tsunamis.

HISTORY AND POLITICS
The islands were colonised by Austronesian people 30,000 years ago. Spanish explorers reached the islands in 1568 and the area continued to be visited by Europeans intermittently for about 300 years. Following the arrival of missionaries and traders, Britain declared a protectorate in 1893 over the southern islands; the northern islands were ceded to Britain by Germany in 1899. After the Second World War, campaigns began for self-government, which was achieved in 1976; independence followed in 1978.

Ethnic tension on Guadalcanal between the indigenous Isatabus and migrants from the island of Malaita escalated from 1998 into conflict between militant factions. Despite a fragile peace following a ceasefire agreement signed in October 2000, and elections in 2001, lawlessness and corruption pervaded the country. In June 2003 the government requested assistance from neighbouring countries. An Australian-led regional assistance mission restored public order and disarmed the militias by late 2003, and has since worked to restore stable government and revive the economy.

In the August 2010 legislative election, independents won over the half the seats, but the largest party was the Solomon Islands Democratic Party (SIDP), with 14 seats. The SIDP leader, Danny Philip, was elected prime minister and appointed a government which included a number of members of the previous administration; after numerous ministerial dismissals, however, Philip resigned from government in November 2011, ahead of a vote of no confidence. He was replaced by former finance minister Gordon Darcy Lilo.

Under the 1978 constitution, the Solomon Islands is a constitutional monarchy. The head of state is Queen Elizabeth II, represented by a governor-general, who is chosen by the legislature. The unicameral National Parliament has 50 members who are directly elected for a four-year term. The prime minister is elected by the legislature from among its members, and nominates the cabinet, which is formally appointed by the governor-general.
Governor-General, Frank Kabui, *apptd* 2009

SELECTED GOVERNMENT MEMBERS *as at July 2014*
Prime Minister, Gordon Darcy Lilo
Deputy Prime Minister, Home Affairs, Manasseh Maelanga
Finance, Rick Hou
Foreign Affairs, Clay Forau Soalaoi

HIGH COMMISSION FOR THE SOLOMON ISLANDS
17 Avenue Edouard Lacombe, 1040 Brussels, Belgium
T (+32) (2) 732 7085 **E** siembassy@compuserve.com
High Commissioner, HE Joseph Ma'ahanua, *apptd* 2006

BRITISH HIGH COMMISSION
PO Box 676, Tanuli Ridge, Honiara
T (+677) 21705 **E** bhc@solomon.com.sb
W www.gov.uk/government/world/solomon-islands
High Commissioner, HE Dominic Meiklejohn, *apptd* 2012

ECONOMY AND TRADE
The civil unrest of 1998–2003 left the country virtually bankrupt but the restoration of law and order enabled the economy to recover until its modest but steady growth was curtailed by the global downturn and natural disasters in 2009 and 2010. The country's greater dependency since 2003 on foreign aid, principally from Australia, increased as the downturn reduced government revenues.

Agriculture, much at subsistence level, is the largest economic sector, accounting for 50 per cent of GDP and engaging 75 per cent of the population. Abundant mineral resources are largely undeveloped, although there are plans to reopen a major gold mine. The main industries are fishing, mining, forestry and processing agricultural products; industry contributes 10.6 per cent of GDP.

The main trade partners are China, Australia and Singapore. Principal exports are timber, fish, copra, palm oil and cocoa. The main imports are food, machinery and equipment, manufactured goods, fuels and chemicals.
GNI – US$699m; US$1,130 per capita (2012)
Annual average growth of GDP – 4 per cent (2013 est)
Inflation rate – 2.6 per cent (2012 est)
Total external debt – US$255.5m (2011)
Imports – US$300m (2010)
Exports – US$221m (2010)

BALANCE OF PAYMENTS
Trade – US$30m deficit (2012)
Current Account – US$1m deficit (2012)

Trade with UK	2011	2012
Imports from UK	£720,180	£480,988
Exports to UK	£2,950,270	£28,212

COMMUNICATIONS
Airports and waterways – Air Niugini flies from Papua New Guinea to Honiara; the main ports are Honiara and Viru
Roadways – 1,390km
Telecommunications – 8,060 fixed lines and 302,100 mobile subscriptions (2012); there were 10,000 internet users in 2009
Internet code and IDD – sb; 677 (from UK), 44 (to UK)
Media – The Solomon Islands Broadcasting Corporation (SIBC) operates public radio services and One Television provides television programmes; the press consists of one daily, two weekly and two monthly newspapers

SOMALIA

Jamhuuriyada Demuqraadiga Soomaaliyeed – Somalia

British protectorate | Two protectorates | One-party | Siad Barre regime toppled; civil war | Federal government, with
First contact | established in the | merge to form United | socialist regime | continues between rival 'warlords'; | support from Ethiopian forces,
with Europe | north | Republic of Somalia | established | central government demolished | attempts to assert authority

1889-
c.700   1869   1905   1969   1988   2004   2008
c.1500   1887   1960   1979   1991   2007-9

Arab settlers | Opening of Suez | Italian protectorate | Armed forces seize control | Opposition to | Two years of peace talks | Alliance against Ethiopian
begin to | Canal increases | established in the | in a coup led by Maj.-Gen. | governments leads | establish a transitional legislature | presence in country agrees
introduce Islam | interest in area | south | Muhammad Siad Barre | to civil war | and appointment of president | ceasefire with government

Area – 637,657 sq. km
Capital – Mogadishu; population, 1,610,576 (2012)
Major cities – Baidoa, Berbera, Burao, Hargeisa, Kismayu
Currency – Somali shilling of 100 cents; other currencies are
  also in circulation
Population – 10,428,043 (2013 est) rising at 1.75 per cent
  a year (2014 est)
Religion – Muslim (predominantly Sunni, including Sunni
  forms of Sufism)
Language – Somali (official), Arabic, Italian, English
Population density – 16 per sq. km (2011)
Urban population – 38.2 per cent (2012 est)
Median age (years) – 17.7 (2014 est)
National anthem – 'Qolobaa Calankeed' ['Praise the
  Homeland']
National day – 1 July (Foundation Day)
Death penalty – Retained
CPI score – 8 (175)
Life expectancy (years) – 51.58 (2014 est)
Mortality rate – 13.91 (2014 est)
Birth rate – 40.87 (2014 est)
Infant mortality rate – 100.14 (2014 est)

CLIMATE AND TERRAIN
The country is mostly an arid and flat or undulating plateau,
rising to hills in the north. Elevation extremes range from
2,416m (Shimbiris) to 0m (Indian Ocean). The climate is
tropical, influenced by the north-east and south-west
monsoons. Rainfall is greater in the south than the north,
but is low and irregular throughout the country, leading to
frequent droughts. The average temperature in Mogadishu is
27°C.

POLITICS
Hassan Sheikh Mohamud took office immediately following
his presidential election victory in September 2012.
Legislative elections could not be held in 2012 due to a lack
of security; initial members of the parliament were chosen
by 135 clan elders, themselves selected by the outgoing
constituent assembly. Nominees were approved for 215 of
the seats and were sworn into office on 21 August. A new
prime minister and cabinet were appointed by the president
on 12 December 2013.
   Under the 2012 provisional constitution the president is
elected by the legislature for a four-year term. The president
appoints the prime minister, who names the cabinet. The
bicameral parliament has 225 directly elected members in
the House of the People, who serve a four-year term; the
Upper House has a maximum of 54 members, serving a
four-year term and directly elected from the 18 regions of
Somalia.

HEAD OF STATE
President, Hassan Sheikh Mohamud, *elected* 10 September
  2012 *sworn in* 16 September 2012

SELECTED GOVERNMENT MEMBERS *as at July 2014*
Prime Minister, Abdiweli Sheikh Ahmed
Deputy Prime Minister, Ridwaan Hirsi Mohamed

Finance, Hussein Abdi Halane
Defence, Mohamed Sheikh Hassan Hamud
Foreign Affairs, Abdirahman Ducaale Bayle

SOMALI EMBASSY
Moran House, Suite 9, 449 High Road, Neasden, London NW10 2JJ
T 07852-280959 E somaliembassyuk@gmail.com
W http://www.uk.somaligov.net/
Ambassador Extraordinary and Plenipotentiary, HE Abdullahi
  Mohamed Ali Sanbaloshe, *apptd 2013*

BRITISH AMBASSADOR
Ambassador Extraordinary and Plenipotentiary, HE Neil
  Wigan, *apptd 2013,* based at Nairobi, Kenya

DEFENCE

Aged 16–49, 2010 est	Males	Females
Available for military service	2,260,175	2,159,293
Fit for military service	1,331,894	1,357,051

ECONOMY AND TRADE
The lack of central government before 2012 prevented
broad-based economic development or assistance from
international donors. Natural resources are not exploited and
industry is virtually non-existent, but the lack of regulation
led to a thriving and relatively sophisticated entrepreneurial
economy, especially in livestock, remittance/money transfer
services (in the absence of a banking sector) and
telecommunications. Infrastructure has been developed by
commercial concerns, with businesses building small airfields
and using natural harbours for overseas trade, and the three
main telecommunications companies jointly funding internet
infrastructure.
   Agriculture, primarily livestock-raising by nomads or
semi-nomads, is the most important economic sector. It
accounts for about 59.3 per cent of GDP and over half of
export earnings, but is vulnerable to drought.
   The main export markets are the UAE and Yemen; imports
come mainly from Djibouti. Principal exports are livestock,
bananas, hides, fish, charcoal and scrap metal. The main
imports are manufactured goods, petroleum products,
foodstuffs, construction materials and qat.
Annual average growth of GDP – 2.6 per cent (2010 est)
Total external debt – US$3,050m (2011 est)

BALANCE OF PAYMENTS

Trade with UK	2012	2013
Imports from UK	£7,882,370	£10,742,217
Exports to UK	£21,317	£404,574

COMMUNICATIONS
Airports and waterways – The international airports are at
Mogadishu and Hargeisa; the main ports are Mogadishu,
Kismayu and Merca in the south, and Berbera in the north.
Piracy and armed robbery against ships in the Gulf of Aden
and Indian Ocean are rife; despite a significant drop in 2012,

the number of attacks still accounted for one quarter of the global total in 2012

Roadways – There are 22,100km of roadways, 2,608km of which are surfaced

Telecommunications – 100,000 fixed lines and 658,000 mobile subscriptions (2012); there were 106,000 internet users in 2009

Internet code and IDD – so; 252 (from UK), 44 (to UK)

Media – There is one state operated TV station and two private broadcasters, with a number of radio stations operating on a regional basis; there are various Mogadishu-based newspapers and an English-language weekly, *Somaliland Times*, but journalists are routinely threatened

WPFI score – 73,19 (176)

SOUTH AFRICA

Republic of South Africa

Area – 1,219,090 sq. km

Capital – The seat of government is Pretoria (Tshwane): population, 1,501,000; the seat of the legislature is Cape Town: population, 3.353; and the seat of the judiciary is Bloemfontein: population, 468,000 (2011 est)

Major cities – Durban, Johannesburg, Port Elizabeth

Currency – Rand (R) of 100 cents

Population – 48,375,645 falling at 0.48 per cent a year (2014 est)

Religion – Christian 80 per cent (Zionist Christian 11.1 per cent, Charismatic 8.2 per cent, Roman Catholic 7.1 per cent, other 36 per cent), none 15.1 per cent.

Language – Afrikaans, English, isiNdebele, isiXhosa, isiZulu, Sepedi, Sesotho, Setswana, siSwati, Tshivenda, Xitsonga (all official); the most widely spoken are isiZulu, isiXhosa and Afrikaans, but English is the lingua franca

Population density – 42 per sq. km (2011)

Urban population – 62.4 per cent (2012 est)

Median age (years) – 25.7 (2014 est)

National anthems – 'Nkosi Sikelel' iAfrika' ['God Bless Africa'], incorporating 'Die Stem van Suid Afrika' ['The Call of South Africa']

National day – 27 April (Freedom Day)

Death penalty – Abolished for all crimes (since 1997)

CPI score – 42 (72)

CLIMATE AND TERRAIN

South Africa occupies the southernmost part of the African continent, with the exception of Lesotho and Swaziland. Its territory includes Prince Edward and Marion Islands, 1,920km to the south-east of Cape Town. The narrow coastal plain is separated by a mountainous escarpment, including the Drakensberg range, from a high inland plateau (the Great Karoo and the Highveld), an area of semi-arid scrubland in the west merging into grasslands or savannah in the centre and east. Elevation extremes range from 3,408m (Njesuthi) to 0m (Atlantic Ocean). The main rivers are the Orange and the Limpopo and their tributaries. The country lies at the convergence of the Atlantic and Indian oceans, and the climate is influenced by the cold Benguela current along the west coast and the warm Agulhas current along the east, as well as by the altitude of the interior. These influences cause cooler, drier conditions in the west and almost subtropical warmth and rainfall in the east. Average temperatures in Pretoria (Tshwane) range from 12°C in June and July to 23°C in January and February.

POLITICS

Under the 1997 constitution, the executive president is elected by the National Assembly for a five-year term, renewable once. The president, who is responsible to the legislature, appoints the cabinet. The bicameral parliament consists of the National Assembly, the lower house, and the National Council of Provinces. The National Assembly has 400 members directly elected by proportional representation for a five-year term. The National Council of Provinces has 90 members, ten for each province, selected by the provincial legislatures for a five-year term.

South Africa is divided into nine provinces: Eastern Cape, Free State, Gauteng, KwaZulu-Natal, Limpopo, Mpumalanga, Northern Cape, North-West, and Western Cape. Each province has its own premier, legislature and constitution.

The ANC has won all the legislative elections since 1994, but is increasingly racked by internal tensions and tainted by corruption allegations. In the May 2014 legislative elections, the ANC received 62.2 per cent of the vote and Jacob Zuma of the ANC was elected president for the second time.

HEAD OF STATE

President, Jacob Zuma, *elected* 6 May 2009, *sworn in* 9 May 2009, *re-elected* 21 May 2014, *sworn in* 24 May 2014

Deputy President, Cyril Ramaphosa

SELECTED GOVERNMENT MEMBERS *as at July 2014*

Defence, Nosiviwe Noluthando Mapisa-Nqakula

Finance, Nhlanhla Nene

Home Affairs, Malusi Knowledge Nkanyezi Gigaba

SOUTH AFRICAN HIGH COMMISSION

South Africa House, Trafalgar Square, London WC2N 5DP

T 020-7451 7299 W www.southafricahouseuk.com

High Commissioner, HE Obed Mlaba *apptd* 2014

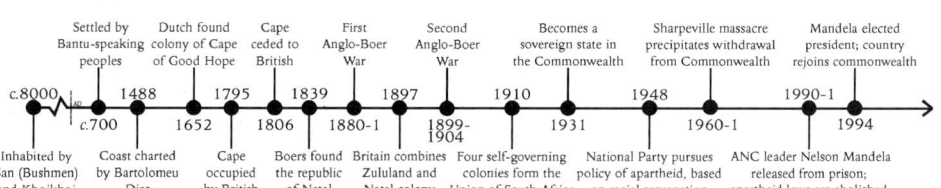

BRITISH HIGH COMMISSION
255 Hill Street, Arcadia 0028, Pretoria (Tshwane)
T (+27) (12) 421 7500
E pta.assistanceforbritishnationals@fco.gov.uk
W www.gov.uk/government/world/south-africa
High Commissioner, HE Judith Macgregor, CMG, LVO *apptd*
    2013

DEFENCE
The South African National Defence Force (SANDF) was
created in 1994 from the merger of the South African
Defence Forces (SADF), the Umkhonto we Sizwe (MK)
armed wing of the ANC, the Azanian People's Liberation
Army (APLA) of the Pan Africanist Congress of Azania,
and the defence forces of the four former 'independent'
homelands.

Aged 16–49, 2010 est	Males	Females
Available for military service	13,439,781	12,473,641
Fit for military service	7,617,063	6,476,264

Military expenditure – US$4,894m (2013)

ECONOMY AND TRADE
The economy varies between the sophisticated and
well-developed, based on manufacturing, mining and
financial services; the living eked out by the very poor,
mostly through subsistence agriculture; and a large informal
sector. Growth was strong until 2008, when the global
economic downturn caused a contraction in the economy
from which recovery is slowly being made, with 2 per cent
growth achieved in 2014. State-owned enterprises are being
used to create jobs and raise incomes. However, unemployment remains high at 24.9 per cent and 31.3 per cent of
the population live below the poverty line. Productivity and
trade are constrained by outdated infrastructure in some
sectors; power cuts have been frequent since 2007 because of
the unreliability of the electricity supply. Large-scale strike
action affected a number of industries in 2014 (*see* Events of
the year).

Agriculture, forestry and fishing account for 2.6 per cent of
GDP and employ 9 per cent of the workforce. Principal crops
are maize, wheat, sugar cane, fruit and vegetables. Livestock
farming, cotton and viticulture are also widespread.

The largest industry is mining; South Africa is the world's
largest producer of gold, platinum and chromium, as well as
producing diamonds, manganese, coal, copper, iron ore,
tin, uranium and titanium. Other industries include car
assembly, metalworking, food processing, ship repair and
production of machinery, textiles, iron and steel, chemicals
and fertiliser; manufacturing is concentrated most heavily
around Johannesburg, Pretoria (Tshwane) and the major
ports. Tourism is a significant industry, and South Africa
is a major transit point for its landlocked neighbours.
Industry contributes 26 per cent of GDP and services 65
per cent.

Fossil-fuel based electricity generation is being
supplemented by nuclear power; one nuclear power station is
in operation and others are planned. Water resources are
inadequate to meet demand, so water is imported from the
highlands of Lesotho.

The main trading partners are China, Germany, the USA
and Saudi Arabia. Principal exports are gold, diamonds,
platinum, other metals and minerals, and machinery and
equipment. Principal imports are machinery and equipment,
chemicals, petroleum products, scientific instruments and
foodstuffs.

GNI – US$375,785m; US$7,610 per capita (2012)
Annual average growth of GDP – 2 per cent (2013 est)

Inflation rate – 5.8 per cent (2013 est)
Unemployment – 24.9 per cent (2013 est)
Total external debt – US$139,000m (2013 est)
Imports – US$101,413m (2012)
Exports – US$87,367m (2012)

BALANCE OF PAYMENTS
Trade – US$14,047m deficit (2012)
Current Account – US$13,620m deficit (2011)

Trade with UK	2012	2013
Imports from UK	£2,588,529,547	£2,408,087,730
Exports to UK	£3,176,234,152	£2,468,786,865

COMMUNICATIONS
Airports and waterways – 144 airports, with international
airports at Johannesburg, Durban and Cape Town; Durban
is the largest seaport, while other major ports are Cape Town,
Port Elizabeth, East London, Saldanha, Mossel Bay and
Richards Bay
Roadways and railways – There are 364,131km of roadways
and 20,192km of railways, including the high-speed
Gautrain which links Johannesburg's main international
airport and Pretoria
Telecommunications – 4.03 million fixed lines and 68.4
million mobile subscriptions (2012); there were 4.42 million
internet users in 2009
Internet code and IDD – za; 27 (from UK), 44 (to UK)
Major broadcasters – The South African Broadcasting
Corporation (SABC) is the country's major, state-owned
television and radio broadcaster
Press – *The Star* is Johannesburg's oldest daily newspaper,
while the *Sunday Times* is the longest running weekly title;
Beeld is a popular Afrikaans daily title
WPFI score – 23,19 (42)

EDUCATION AND HEALTH
Education is compulsory between the ages of seven and 15.
Literacy rate – 93 per cent (2011 est)
Gross enrolment ratio (percentage of relevant age group) –
    primary 102 per cent; secondary 102 per cent (2012 est)
Health expenditure (per capita) – US$689 (2011)
Hospital beds (per 1,000 people) – 2.8 (2004–9)
Life expectancy (years) – 49.56 (2014 est)
Mortality rate – 17.49 (2014 est)
Birth rate – 18.94 (2014 est)
Infant mortality rate – 41.61 (2014 est)
HIV/AIDS adult prevalence – 17.9 per cent (2012 est)

SOUTH SUDAN

The Republic of South Sudan

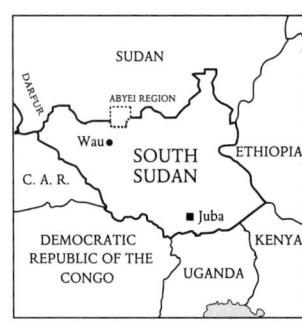

Area – 644,329 sq. km
Capital – Juba; population, 269,000 (2011 est)
Major cities – Malakal, Wau
Currency – South Sudanese pound (SSDP) of 100 piastres
Population – 11,562,695 (2014 est); Dinka (35.8 per cent),
(Nuer 15.6 per cent) (2011 est)
Religion – Christian, animist (many animists also follow
Christian practices)
Language – English (official), Arabic, indigenous languages
Urban population – 18.2 per cent (2012)
Median age (years) – 16.8 (2014 est)
National anthem – 'South Sudan Oyee!' ['Hooray!']
National day – 9 July (Independence day)
Literacy rate – 27 per cent (2009)
Infant mortality rate – 68.16 (2014 est)

CLIMATE AND TERRAIN
The White Nile, flowing north out of the uplands of central
Africa, is the principal feature of the country, and formed part
of the Sudd, a vast swamp of more than 100,000 sq. km.
Divided by the river, the terrain rises from the plains on
the northern border to wet southern highlands along the
Kenya–Uganda divide to a maximum height of 3,187m
(Mt Kinyeti). The climate is hot with seasonal rainfall and the
average annual temperature in Juba is 27°C.

HISTORY AND POLITICS
The history of the area is largely unrecorded until the early
19th century, as natural barriers prevented the invasions and
occupations affecting northern Sudan. In the 19th century,
Egypt attempted to extend its influence in the region but
the south was only joined with the north with the arrival
of the British in the late 19th century, becoming part of a
joint Anglo-Egyptian condominium from 1899. Following
the independence of Sudan in 1955, tensions between the
dominant Arab, Muslim north and the black African,
Christian and animist south led to civil war from 1955 to
1972, and again in 1983. A peace process began in
2000 and the parties to it – the government, the Sudan
People's Liberation Army/Movement (SPLA/M) and the
southern National Democratic Alliance – finalised a peace
agreement in 2004. Under this, the southern parties
joined a national unity government, a largely autonomous
administration was set up in the south in October 2005 and
a referendum on independence for the south was held after
six years.

In the referendum in January 2011, the south voted
overwhelmingly to separate from the north. In the run-up to
independence on 9 July, disputes led to a deteriorating
security situation in border areas, particularly over control of
the oil-rich territory of Abyei. A separate referendum in
Abyei on whether to join northern or southern Sudan has
been postponed indefinitely because of the conflict, while
South Kurdufan and Blue Nile states are to hold 'popular
consultations' on their status.

In December 2013, fighting broke out between political
factions after the finance minster was dismissed following
corruption allegations in July. Thousands of people, including
civilians, were killed and over a million people had been
displaced by April 2014. Ceasefire agreements signed in
January, May and June 2014 were broken by one or both
sides.

The transitional constitution came into force at
independence and will remain in force until a permanent
constitution is adopted. It provides for the current president
of the government of South Sudan to become president of
the independent republic, and for the National Legislative
Assembly (comprising 170 members of the former South
Sudan Legislative Assembly, plus 96 South Sudanese former

members of the National Assembly to the Republic of Sudan;
both these groups were directly elected in 2010) and the
Council of States (comprising 20 former South Sudan
members of the Council of States of the Republic of Sudan,
plus 30 representatives appointed by the president). The
president and the legislature will serve a four-year term.

HEAD OF STATE
President, Salva Kiir Mayardit, *sworn in under draft constitution*
9 July 2011
Vice-President, James Wani Igga

SELECTED GOVERNMENT MINISTERS *as at July* 2013
Foreign Affairs, Barnaba Marial Benjamin
Internal Affairs, Aleu Ayeny Aleu

EMBASSY OF THE REPUBLIC OF SOUTH SUDAN
16 Upper Woburn Place, London WC1H 0BS
T 020-3741 8083 E info@embrss.org.uk W www.embrss.org.uk
Ambassador Extraordinary and Plenipotentiary, Sabit Abbe
Alley, *apptd* 2013

BRITISH EMBASSY
EU Compound, Kololo Road, Thom Ping, Juba
T (+211) (0) 912 323 712 E ukin.southsudan@fco.gov.uk
W www.gov.uk/government/world/south-sudan
Ambassador Extraordinary and Plenipotentiary, HE Ian
Hughes, *apptd* 2013

ECONOMY AND TRADE
The troubled South Sudan economy, hindered by decades of
civil war with the north, is based on subsistence agriculture
which provides a living for the majority of the population.
Poverty is widespread, with over half the population
living below the poverty line, and a lack of industry
and infrastructure has forced the reliance on imports of
goods and services from the north. The government derives
98 per cent of its budget from oil revenues. The country
faces tough economical challenges and has received more
than US$4bn in foreign aid since 2005, mainly from the
UK, the Netherlands, the USA and Norway. The South
Sudanese government issued its own currency following
independence; annual inflation rose to 79 per cent in May
2012 before falling dramatically to 1.7 per cent in 2013.
A reduction in oil exports in 2013 led to reduced growth
forecasts in 2014. The country consists of one of the richest
agricultural areas in Africa with fertile soils and excellent
water supplies

Subsistence crops include maize, rice millet, wheat,
sugarcane, papayas, bananas and peanuts.
GNI – US$9,272m, US$790 per capita (2012 est)
Annual average growth of GDP – US$10,620m (2012 est)
Population below the poverty line – 51 per cent (2010 est)
Imports – US$4,160m (2010)
Exports – US$8,229m (2010)

COMMUNICATIONS
Airports – There are three airports including an international
terminal in Juba
Roadways and railways – There are 7,000km of roadways and
248km of railway (2014), although much of the road and
rail network is in disrepair
Internet code and IDD – ss; 211 (from UK), 44 (to UK)
Media – The country's fledgling media network faces
political, social and logistical challenges; the government-run
Southern Sudan TV and Radio is the country's sole network,
while *The Juba Post*, *The Citizen* and *Sudan Mirror* are all
privately owned newspapers
WPFI score – 36,05 (119)

SPAIN

Reino de España – Kingdom of Spain

Area – 505,370 sq. km
Capital – Madrid; population, 6,017,954 (2012)
Major cities – Barcelona, Bilbao, Las Palmas (Gran Canaria), Málaga, Murcia, Palma (Majorca), Seville, Valencia, Zaragoza
Currency – Euro (€) of 100 cents
Population – 47,737,941 rising at 0.81 per cent a year (2014 est)
Religion – Christian (Roman Catholic 94 per cent) (est)
Language – Castilian (Spanish) (official), Catalan, Galician, Basque (all are official in certain regions)
Population density – 93 per sq. km (2011)
Urban population – 77.6 per cent (2012)
Median age (years) – 41.6 (2014 est)
National anthem – 'La Marcha Real' ['The Royal March']
National day – 12 October
Death penalty – Abolished for all crimes (since 1995)
CPI score – 59 (40)

CLIMATE AND TERRAIN

Spain occupies over 80 per cent of the Iberian peninsula, and includes two archipelagos and territories on or just off the Moroccan coast. The interior consists of an elevated plateau surrounded and traversed by mountain ranges: the Pyrenees on the border with France, the Cantabrian Mountains (north-west), the Sierra de Guadarrama, Sierra Morena, Montes de Toledo (centre) and the Sierra Nevada (south). Elevation extremes range from 3,718m (Pico de Teide, Tenerife, Canary Islands) to 0m (Mediterranean Sea). The principal rivers are the Duero, the Tajo (Tagus), the Guadiana, the Guadalquivir, the Ebro and the Miño. The climate is Mediterranean in the southern and eastern coastal areas, and temperate further inland and at altitude. Average temperatures in Madrid range from 5.4°C in January to 24.5°C in July.

POLITICS

The 1978 constitution has been amended at various times to devolve powers to the 19 autonomous regions. The head of state is a hereditary constitutional monarch. There is a bicameral legislature, the *Cortes Generales*, comprising a 350-member Congress of Deputies directly elected for a four-year term, and a senate with 264 members, 208 directly elected and 56 appointed by the assemblies of the autonomous regions, for a four-year term.

There are 19 autonomous regions: Andalucia, Aragón, Asturias, Balearic Islands, the Basque Country, Canary Islands, Cantabria, Castilla-La Mancha, Castilla y León, Catalonia, Ceuta, Extremadura, Galicia, La Rioja, Madrid, Melilla, Murcia, Navarra and Valencia. Each has its own elected legislature and government. In 2006 a referendum endorsed the *Cortes'* approval of greater autonomy for Catalonia.

In the 2011 early legislative elections the Popular Party (PP) won an overall majority in both houses. Mariano Rajoy, leader of the PP, was appointed prime minister in December 2011, replacing José Luis Rodríguez Zapatero.

HEAD OF STATE
HM The King of Spain, King Felipe VI de Borbon y Grecia, *born* 30 January 1968, *acceded to the throne* 19 June 2014
Heir, HRH The Princess of the Asturias (Leonor de Borbon y Ortiz), *born* 31 October 2005

SELECTED GOVERNMENT MEMBERS *as at July 2014*
Prime Minister, Mariano Rajoy
Vice President, Soraya Saenz de Santamaria
Foreign Affairs, Jose Manuel Garcia-Margallo
Interior, Jorge Fernandez Diaz
Defence, Pedro Morenes Eulate

EMBASSY OF SPAIN
39 Chesham Place, London SW1X 8SB
T 020-7235 5555 emb.londres@maec.es
W www.mae.es/embajadas/londres/es
Ambassador Extraordinary and Plenipotentiary, HE Federico Trillo-Figueroa Martinez Conde, *apptd* 2012

BRITISH EMBASSY
Torre Espacio, Paseo de la Castellana 259D, 28046 Madrid
T (+34) (91) 714 6300 E info.consulate@fco.gov.uk
W www.gov.uk/government/world/spain
Ambassador Extraordinary and Plenipotentiary, HE Simon Manley, CMG, *apptd* 2013

INSURGENCIES
The Basque separatist organisation ETA (*Euzkadi ta Azkatasuna* – Basque Nation and Liberty), formed in 1959, began a terrorist campaign of bombings, shootings and kidnappings in 1961 in an attempt to gain independence for the Basque country. ETA rejected regional autonomy for the Basque country in 1979 as insufficient and continued its campaign, but was greatly weakened in the early 1990s by increased cooperation between Spanish security forces and their European counterparts. ETA announced a permanent ceasefire in January 2011.

DEFENCE

Aged 16–49, 2010 est	Males	Females
Available for military service	11,759,557	11,204,688
Fit for military service	9,603,939	9,116,928

Military expenditure – US$12,822m (2013)

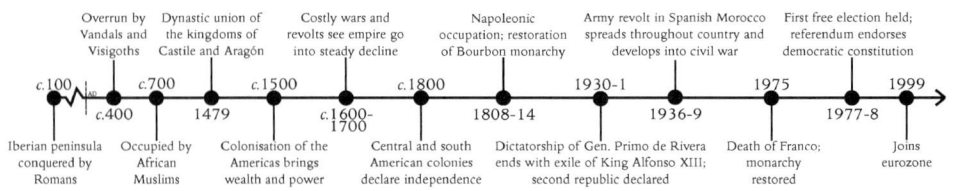

Overrun by Vandals and Visigoths	Dynastic union of the kingdoms of Castile and Aragón	Costly wars and revolts see empire go into steady decline		Napoleonic occupation; restoration of Bourbon monarchy	Army revolt in Spanish Morocco spreads throughout country and develops into civil war	First free election held; referendum endorses democratic constitution
c.100	c.700	c.1500	c.1800	1930-1	1975	1999
c.400	1479	c.1600-1700	1808-14	1936-9	1977-8	
Iberian peninsula conquered by Romans	Occupied by African Muslims	Colonisation of the Americas brings wealth and power	Central and south American colonies declare independence	Dictatorship of Gen. Primo de Rivera ends with exile of King Alfonso XIII; second republic declared	Death of Franco; monarchy restored	Joins eurozone

ECONOMY AND TRADE

Economic protectionism and isolation held back economic development until the mid-20th century, but the economy improved from the 1950s with industrialisation and the development of tourism. The mixed capitalist economy showed above-average growth, stimulated by liberalisation, privatisation and deregulation, from the mid-1990s until 2007. In 2008 it entered a severe recession because of the global economic downturn. This pushed unemployment to 26 per cent in 2012 (from 8 per cent in 2007).

The downturn in construction and the property market left many banks struggling in 2010, and rising public-sector debt led to Spain's international credit rating being downgraded; the government introduced austerity measures in response but concern continues over the impact on the eurozone of Spain's sovereign debt.

Public debt continues to rise – from 60.1 per cent of GDP in 2010 to 93.4 per cent in 2013 – but rising labour productivity, decreasing labour costs and falling inflation have increased foreign investor interest. The government shored up struggling banks exposed to Spain's depressed domestic construction and real estate sectors by completing an EU-funded restructuring and recapitalisation programme in December 2013.

The generally fertile country produces grains, vegetables, olives, sugar beets, citrus and other fruits, meat and dairy products. Viticulture is widespread. Spain also has one of Europe's largest fishing industries. The agricultural sector contributes 3.1 per cent of GDP and employs 4.2 per cent of the workforce. Abundant mineral resources include coal, iron ore, copper, zinc, lead, uranium and tungsten. Metal extraction and the manufacture of metal products, including steel, are major industries. A diverse industrial sector includes manufacturing (principally textiles, clothing, footwear, beverages, chemicals, cars, machine tools, clay products, pharmaceuticals and medical equipment), food processing, shipbuilding and tourism. Industry accounts for 26 per cent of GDP and the service sector for 70.8 per cent.

The main trading partners are other EU countries, especially France and Germany. Principal exports include machinery, vehicles, foodstuffs, pharmaceuticals, medicines and other consumer goods. The main imports are machinery and equipment, fuels, chemicals, semi-finished goods, foodstuffs, consumer goods, and measuring and medical control instruments.

GNI – US$1,307,562m; US$29,620 per capita (2012)
Annual average growth of GDP – −1.3 per cent (2013 est)
Inflation rate – 1.8 per cent (2013 est)
Population below the poverty line – 21.1 per cent (2012)
Unemployment – 26.3 per cent (2013 est)
Total external debt – US$2,278,000m (2012 est)
Imports – US$325,836m (2012)
Exports – US$286,219m (2012)

BALANCE OF PAYMENTS
Trade – US$39,618m deficit (2012)
Current Account – US$14,821m deficit (2012)

Trade with UK	2012	2013
Imports from UK	£8,265,571,061	£8,441,425,792
Exports to UK	£10,401,668,678	£11,936,351,453

COMMUNICATIONS

Airports – Of the 99 airports, the principal terminals are at Madrid, Barcelona, Alicante, Málaga, Valencia and Bilbao
Waterways – The main ports are Algeciras, Alicante, Barcelona, Bilbao, Cádiz, Santander and Valencia, and Las Palmas in the Canary Islands; there are also 1,000km of navigable inland waterways

Roadways and railways – 683,175km; 15,293km
Telecommunications – 19.22 million fixed lines and 50.663 million mobile subscriptions (2012); there were 28.12 million internet users in 2009
Internet code and IDD – es; 34 (from UK), 44 (to UK)
Major broadcasters – Public radio and television services are run by Radio Television Espanola (RTVE), which is funded by advertising and state subsidies
Press – Popular newspaper titles include *El Mundo, ABC, El País* and *El Periodico de Catalunya.*
WPFI score – 20,63 (35)

EDUCATION AND HEALTH

Education is free from age six to 18, and compulsory to the age of 16.
Literacy rate – 98 per cent (2010)
Gross enrolment ratio (percentage of relevant age group) – primary 103 per cent; secondary 131 per cent; tertiary 83 per cent (2012 est)
Health expenditure (per capita) – US$3,027 (2011)
Hospital beds (per 1,000 people) – 3.2 (2010)
Life expectancy (years) – 81.47 (2014 est)
Mortality rate – 9.00 (2014 est)
Birth rate – 9.88 (2014 est)
Infant mortality rate – 3.33 (2014 est)

ISLANDS AND ENCLAVES

THE BALEARIC ISLES form an archipelago off the east coast of Spain. There are four large islands (Majorca/Mallorca, Minorca, Ibiza and Formentera) and seven smaller ones (Aire, Aucanada, Botafoch, Cabrera, Dragonera, Pinto and El Rey). Area 4,992 sq. km; population 1,111,674 (2013 est). The archipelago forms a province of Spain. The capital is Palma, on Majorca.

THE CANARY ISLANDS are an archipelago in the Atlantic off the African coast, consisting of seven islands and six islets. Area 7,447 sq. km; population 2,118,679 (2013 est). The Canary Islands form two provinces of Spain: Las Palmas, comprising Gran Canaria, Lanzarote, Fuerteventura and six islets, with the seat of administration at Las Palmas, in Gran Canaria; and Santa Cruz de Tenerife, comprising Tenerife, La Palma, La Gomera and El Hierro, with the seat of administration at Santa Cruz, in Tenerife.

ISLA DE FAISANES an uninhabited Franco-Spanish condominium, at the mouth of the Bidassoa in La Higuera bay.

CEUTA is a fortified post on the Moroccan coast, opposite Gibraltar. Area 19 sq. km; population 84,180 (2013 est). Ceuta is an autonomous city of Spain.

MELILLA is a town on a rocky promontory of the Moroccan coast, connected with the mainland by a narrow isthmus. Area 13 sq. km; population 83,679 (2013 est). Melilla is an autonomous city of Spain.

OVERSEAS TERRITORIES

The following territories, which are Spanish settlements on the Moroccan seaboard, come under direct Spanish administration. They are uninhabited other than by military personnel.

PENON DE ALHUCEMAS is a bay including six islands.

PENON DE LA GOMERA (or Peñón de Velez) is a fortified rocky islet.

THE CHAFFARINAS (or Zaffarines) is a group of three islands near the Algerian frontier.

SRI LANKA

Shri Lamka Prajatantrika Samajaya di Janarajaya/Ilankai Jananayaka Choshalichak Kutiyarachu – *Democratic Socialist Republic of Sri Lanka*

Area – 65,610 sq. km
Capital – Colombo; population, 681,000 (2009), Sri Jayewardenepura Kotte; population, 123,090 (2009 est) is the administrative capital
Major cities – Dehiwala-Mount Lavinia, Jaffna, Kalmunai, Kandy, Moratuwa, Negombo, Trincomalee, Vavuniya
Currency – Sri Lankan rupee of 100 cents
Population – 21,866,445 rising at 0.86 per cent a year (2014 est); Sinhalese (73.8 per cent), Sri Lankan Moor (7.2 per cent), Indian Tamil (4.6 per cent), Sri Lankan Tamil (3.9 per cent) (2001 est; excludes predominantly Tamil areas then held by rebels)
Religion – Buddhist 69.1 per cent (predominantly Theravada), Muslim 7.6, Hindu 7.1 per cent, Christian 6.2 per cent (predominantly Roman Catholic) (est)
Language – Sinhala (official), Tamil, English
Population density – 333 per sq. km (2011)
Urban population – 15.2 per cent (2012)
Median age (years) – 31.8 (2014 est)
National anthem – 'Sri Lanka Matha' ['Mother Sri Lanka']
National day – 4 February (Independence Day)
Death penalty – Retained (last used 1976)
CPI score – 37 (91)
Literacy rate – 91 per cent (2010 est)
Gross enrolment ratio (percentage of relevant age group) – primary 99 per cent (2011 est)
Health expenditure (per capita) – US$97 (2011)
Hospital beds (per 1,000 people) – 3.1 (2004–9)
Life expectancy (years) – 76.35 (2014 est)
Mortality rate – 6.06 (2014 est)
Birth rate – 16.24 (2014 est)
Infant mortality rate – 9.02 (2014 est)

CLIMATE AND TERRAIN

Sri Lanka (formerly Ceylon) is an island in the Indian Ocean, separated from India by the narrow Palk Strait. The land is low-lying in the north and along the coasts, rising to a central massif with hills and mountains in the south and centre. Forests, jungle and scrub cover the greater part of the island. In areas over 600m above sea level, grasslands *(patanas* or *talawas)* are found. Elevation extremes range from 2,524m (Pidurutalagala) to 0m (Indian Ocean). The climate is tropical with little seasonal variation in conditions and humidity, which often reaches around 90 per cent. The island experiences the south-west monsoon from May to September and the north-east monsoon from October to January.

HISTORY AND POLITICS

The 1978 constitution was amended in 1983 to ban parties advocating separatism, in 1987 to create provincial councils, and in 2010 to remove the limit on presidential terms. The executive president is directly elected for a six-year term, which may be renewed. The unicameral parliament has 225 members directly elected by proportional representation for a six-year term. The president appoints the prime minister and cabinet.

Elected councils were set up in the nine provinces in 1987 in an attempt to defuse ethnic tensions. The Northern and Eastern provinces were merged into one from 1988 to 2006.

The 2005 presidential election was won by the Sri Lanka Freedom Party (SLFP) leader Mahinda Rajapaksa, and he was re-elected in an early election in January 2010. The legislative election in April 2010 was won by the SLFP-led United People's Freedom Alliance, with an increased majority.

HEAD OF STATE
President, Defence, Finance, Mahinda Rajapaksa, *elected* 17 November 2005, *re-elected* 2010

SELECTED GOVERNMENT MEMBERS *as at July 2014*
Prime Minister, Dissanayake Jayaratne
Home Affairs, John Seneviratne
Foreign Affairs, G. L. Peiris

HIGH COMMISSION OF THE DEMOCRATIC SOCIALIST REPUBLIC OF SRI LANKA
13 Hyde Park Gardens, London W2 2LU
T 020-7262 1841 E mail@slhc-london.co.uk
W http://www.srilankahighcommission.co.uk
High Commissioner, HE Chrisantha Nonis, *apptd* 2011

BRITISH HIGH COMMISSION
389 Bauddhaloka Mawatha, Colombo 7
T (+94) (11) 539 0639 E bhctrade@slt.lk
W www.gov.uk/government/world/sri-lanka
High Commissioner, HE John Rankin, *apptd* 2011

DEFENCE

Aged 16–49, 2010 est	*Males*	*Females*
Available for military service	5,342,147	5,466,409
Fit for military service	4,177,432	4,574,833

Military expenditure – US$1,854m (2013)

ECONOMY AND TRADE

Despite the 26-year civil war and the 2004 Indian Ocean tsunami, which destroyed tourist resorts and the fishing industry, the economy saw sustained growth throughout the 2000s. The 2008–9 global downturn affected productivity only slightly, but high government debt and budget deficits obliged the government to seek an IMF loan, which in turn resulted in two years of strong growth. From 2010–11 Sri Lanka achieved 8 per cent growth, however, this dropped to 6 per cent in 2012. The once predominantly agricultural economy has become increasingly industrialised and diversified, with service industries such as tourism now making the greatest contribution to GDP. Remittances from expatriate workers are also economically significant. Government debt of around 80 per cent of GDP is among the highest of developing nations, while a large trade deficit remains a concern.

Agriculture still accounts for 10.6 per cent of GDP and over 31.8 per cent of employment. The main crops are rice, sugar cane, grains, pulses, oilseed, spices, vegetables, fruit, tea, rubber, coconuts, livestock products and fish. Manufacturing is based on processing the main cash crops of rubber, tea, coconuts, tobacco and other commodities, and production of textiles, clothing, beverages and cement; other industries include oil refining and mining gemstones. Service industries such as telecommunications, banking and insurance, information technology services and tourism are also important. The service sector accounts for 57 per cent of GDP and industry for 32.4 per cent.

The main trading partners are India, the USA, China, the UK and Singapore. Principal exports are textiles and clothing, tea, rubber manufactures, spices, diamonds, emeralds, rubies, coconut products and fish. The main imports are oil, textile fabrics, machinery, transport equipment, building materials, mineral products and foodstuffs.

GNI – US$58,259m; US$2,920 per capita (2012)
Annual average growth of GDP – 6.3 per cent (2013 est)
Inflation rate – 6.8 per cent (2013 est)
Population below poverty line – 8.9 per cent (2010 est)
Unemployment – 5.1 per cent (2013 est)
Total external debt – US$27,530m (2013 est)
Imports – US$19,086m (2012)
Exports – US$9,480m (2012)

BALANCE OF PAYMENTS
Trade – US$9,606m deficit (2012)
Current Account – US$4,615m deficit (2011)

Trade with UK	2012	2013
Imports from UK	£145,740,480	£166,534,377
Exports to UK	£907,376,261	£848,550,394

COMMUNICATIONS
Airports and waterways – The principal airport is Bandaranaike International, to the north of the capital; Colombo is the main port although the first phase of a deep-water container port opened in 2010 at Hambantota
Roadways and railways – 114,093km; 1,449km
Telecommunications – 2.796 million fixed lines and 19.553 million subscriptions (2012); there were 1.78 million internet users in 2009
Internet code and IDD – lk; 94 (from UK), 44 (to UK)
Media – The state-owned Sri Lanka Rupavahini Corporation operates three major channels; there are eight daily newspapers, published in Sinhala, Tamil and English
WPFI score – 59,13 (165)

SUDAN

Jumhuriyat as-Sudan – *Republic of the Sudan*

Area – 1,861,484 sq. km
Capital – Khartoum; population, 5,502,174 (2012)

Major cities – Kassala, Kusti, Nyala, El Obeid, Port Sudan
Currency – Sudanese pound (SDP) of 100 piastres
Population – 35,482,233 rising at 1.78 per cent a year (2014 est); Arab and Nubian peoples
Religion – Muslim 96 per cent (predominantly Sunni), Christian 3 per cent, indigenous beliefs less than 1 per cent (est)
Language – Arabic, English (both official), Nubian, Ta Bedawie
Population density – 20 per sq. km (2011)
Urban population – 33.3 per cent (2012 est)
Median age (years) – 19.1 (2014 est)
National anthem – 'Nahnu Jund Allah Jund Al-Watan' ['We Are the Army of God and of Our Land']
National day – 1 January (Independence Day)
Death penalty – Retained
CPI score – 11 (174)

CLIMATE AND TERRAIN
Sudan is predominantly desert; the Libyan Desert in the west is separated from the rocky Nubian Desert in the east by the fertile valley of the Nile and its tributaries. There are mountains in the west and the south, and along the Red Sea coast. Elevation extremes range from 3,071m (Jabal Marrah) to 0m (Red Sea). The climate is arid on the desert plains, tropical in the south, and cooler at altitude. There is a rainy season from April to October. Average temperatures in Khartoum range from 23°C in January to 34°C in May and June.

POLITICS
Under the 2005 constitution, the executive president is directly elected for a five-year term, renewable once. The bicameral National Legislature comprises a National Assembly with 354 members, including 88 seats reserved for women, directly elected for a five-year term, and a Council of States of 32 members, two members from each state. The president appoints the cabinet.

The first multiparty presidential and legislative elections for 24 years were held in 2010. President al-Bashir was re-elected as national president and his National Congress Party won an overall majority nationally amid allegations of vote-rigging and intimidation.

HEAD OF STATE
President, Prime Minister, Field Marshal Omar al-Bashir, *seized power* 1989, *elected* 1996, *re-elected* 2000, *sworn in under new constitution* 9 July 2005, *re-elected* 2010
First Vice-President, Bakri Hassan Salih

SELECTED GOVERNMENT MEMBERS *as at July 2014*
Defence, Lt.-Gen. Abdel-Rahim Hussein
Finance, Badr al-Din Mahmoud Abbas
Foreign Affairs, Ali Ahmed Karti
Interior, Ismat Abdul-Rahman Zain al-Abdin

EMBASSY OF THE REPUBLIC OF THE SUDAN
3 Cleveland Row, London SW1A 1DD
T 020-7839 8080 E admin@sudanembassy.co.uk
W www.sudan-embassy.co.uk
Ambassador Extraordinary and Plenipotentiary, Abdullahi Hamad Ali Alazreg, *apptd* 2001

BRITISH EMBASSY
PO Box 801, Off Sharia Al Baladiya, Khartoum East
T (+249) (1) 8377 7105 E consular.khartoum@fco.gov.uk
W www.gov.uk/government/world/sudan
Ambassador Extraordinary and Plenipotentiary, Peter Tibber, *apptd* 2011

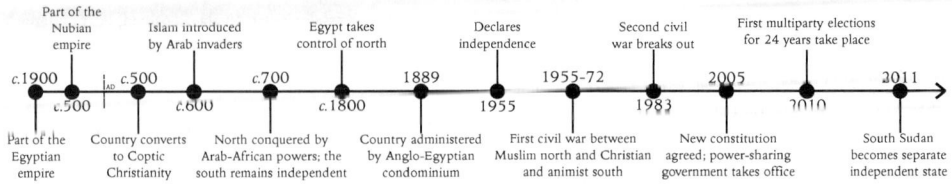

| Part of the Nubian empire | Islam introduced by Arab invaders | Egypt takes control of north | Declares independence | Second civil war breaks out | First multiparty elections for 24 years take place |

*c.*1900 |AD *c.*500 *c.*700 1889 1955-72 2005 2011
  *c.*500 *c.*600 *c.*1800 1955 1983 2010

| Part of the Egyptian empire | Country converts to Coptic Christianity | North conquered by Arab-African powers; the south remains independent | Country administered by Anglo-Egyptian condominium | First civil war between Muslim north and Christian and animist south | New constitution agreed; power-sharing government takes office | South Sudan becomes separate independent state |

INSURGENCIES

In the western region of Darfur, tension between nomadic Arab livestock herders and black African farmers over land and grazing rights led to a rise in intercommunal violence in the 1990s. Between 2002 and 2009 black African rebels protesting at marginalisation were ruthlessly suppressed by government forces, often operating through Arab militia *(Janjaweed)* which carried out mass executions and forcible depopulation. The government resisted international pressure to disarm the militias, and obstructed the deployment of peacekeeping troops and the work of aid agencies inside Darfur.

Incursions into neighbouring countries to attack refugees there destabilised the region. Two of the main rebel groups signed peace agreements with the government, one in 2006 and the other in 2009, although violence by smaller rebel groups and banditry continues. An estimated 300,000 have died from violence, starvation or disease since 2003, and 2.7 million people have been internally displaced or become refugees in Chad and the Central African Republic. The International Criminal Court issued a warrant for the arrest of President al-Bashir for war crimes and crimes against humanity in 2009, and for genocide in 2010.

DEFENCE

Aged 16–49, 2010 est	Males	Females
Available for military service	10,433,973	10,411,443
Fit for military service	6,475,530	6,840,885

Military expenditure – US$2,3768m (2006 est)
Conscription duration – 12–24 months

ECONOMY AND TRADE

Since 1997 Sudan has worked with the IMF to implement economic reforms which, despite the country's political instability and vulnerability to drought, have stabilised the economy. In 1999 Sudan began exporting oil, and increases in oil and agricultural production, light industry and exports have resulted in steady growth in GDP in recent years. However, three quarters of its former oilfields are now controlled by South Sudan.

Agriculture, much at subsistence level, provides employment for around 80 per cent of the workforce and contributes 27.6 per cent of GDP. Mechanised and traditional agriculture is practised in areas with sufficient rainfall and irrigation. The principal crops include cotton, groundnuts, sorghum, millet, wheat, sugar cane, tropical fruits and livestock. The country exports 75 to 80 per cent of the world's gum arabic. Industry consists of oil extraction and refining, cotton ginning, manufacture of textiles, cement, edible oils, sugar, soap, shoes, pharmaceuticals, armaments and vehicle assembly. Industry contributes 33.6 per cent of GDP and services 39 per cent.

The main trading partners are the UAE, Macau and India. Principal exports are oil and petroleum products, cotton, sesame, livestock, groundnuts, gum arabic and sugar. The main imports are foodstuffs, manufactured goods, refinery and transport equipment, medicines, chemicals, textiles and wheat.

GNI – US$56,347m; US$1,500 per capita (2012)
Annual average growth of GDP – 3.9 per cent (2013 est)
Inflation rate – 25 per cent (2013 est)
Population below poverty line – 46.5 per cent (2009 est)
Unemployment – 20 per cent (2012 est)
Total external debt – US$40,920m (2013 est)
Imports – US$9,100m (2012)
Exports – US$9,694m (2011)

BALANCE OF PAYMENTS

Trade – US$463m surplus (2011)
Current Account – US$290m deficit (2011)

Trade with UK	2012	2013
Imports from UK	£138,535,364	£99,702,261
Exports to UK	£6,746,130	£10,016,576

COMMUNICATIONS

Airports and waterways – There are 16 airports, with the principal terminal at Khartoum; there are 4,068km of navigable waterways, including 1,723km on the White and Blue Nile rivers
Roadways and railways – 11,900km; 5,978km
Telecommunications – 425,000 fixed lines and 27.659 million mobile subscriptions (2012); there were 4.2 million internet users in 2008
Internet and IDD – sd; 249 (from UK), 44 (to UK)
Media – The government-run Sudan National Broadcasting Corporation operates two channels across the country; there are four daily newspapers, including the privately owned *Al-Ra'y al-Amm*
WPFI score – 71,88 (172)

EDUCATION AND HEALTH

Education is free of charge for most children, and compulsory for eight years; six years of primary education is followed by at least two years of secondary education.
Literacy rate – 72 per cent (2011 est)
Gross enrolment ratio (percentage of relevant age group) –
primary 73 per cent; secondary 39 per cent (2011 est)
Health expenditure (per capita) – US$104 (2011)
Hospital beds (per 1,000 people) – 0.7 (2009)
Life expectancy (years) – 63.32 (2014 est)
Mortality rate – 7.87 (2014 est)
Birth rate – 30.01 (2014 est)
Infant mortality rate – 52.86 (2014 est)
HIV/AIDS adult prevalence – 1.1 per cent (2009 est)

SURINAME

Republiek Suriname – Republic of Suriname

Area – 163,820 sq. km
Capital – Paramaribo; population, 278,000 (2011)
Major towns – Lelydorp, Nieuw Nickerie
Currency – Suriname dollar of 100 cents
Population – 573,311 rising at 1.12 per cent a year
  (2014 est); Hindustani (37 per cent), Creole (31 per cent),
  Javanese (15 per cent), Maroons (10 per cent), Amerindian
  (2 per cent), Chinese (2 per cent) (est)
Religion – Hindu 27.4 per cent, Christian (Protestant,
  predominantly Moravian, 25.2 per cent, Roman
  Catholic 22.8 per cent), Muslim 19.6 per cent, indigenous
  5 per cent
Language – Dutch (official), English, Surinamese (Sranang
  Tongo), Caribbean Hindustani (a dialect of Hindi),
  Javanese
Population density – 3 per sq. km (2011)
Urban population – 70.1 per cent (2012 est)
Median age (years) – 28.6 (2014 est)
National anthem – 'God zij met ons Suriname' ['God Be With
  Our Suriname']
National day – 25 November (Independence Day)
Death penalty – Retained (last used 1982)
CPI score – 36 (94)
Literacy rate – 95 per cent (2010 est)
Life expectancy (years) – 71.69 (2014 est)
Mortality rate – 6.13 (2014 est)
Birth rate – 16.73 (2014 est)
Infant mortality rate – 27.07 (2014 est)
HIV / AIDS adult prevalence – 1.1 per cent (2012 est)

CLIMATE AND TERRAIN

The narrow, swampy coastal plain is home to about 90
per cent of the population. From the coastal belt, the land
rises to a hilly interior covered by tropical rainforest and
savannah; the rainforest contains a great diversity of flora and
fauna. Elevation extremes range from 1,230m (Juliana Top)
to −2m (coastal plain). The land is drained by several rivers,
some of which have been dammed to create large artificial
lakes used to generate hydro-electric power. The climate is
tropical, moderated by the north-east trade winds. There are
two wet seasons, from April to August and November to
February.

HISTORY AND POLITICS

Originally settled by Arawak and Carib peoples, the area was
visited by Spanish explorers in 1593. Early European
settlements failed, until a British colony was founded in
1651. The colony was ceded to the Dutch in 1667. Dutch
rule was interrupted by British occupation during the
French Revolutionary and Napoleonic wars, but was restored
in 1816. The colony, known as Dutch Guiana, became

autonomous in 1954, and achieved independence in 1975
as Suriname. At independence, about 40 per cent of the
population emigrated to the Netherlands.

The early years of independence were politically unstable,
with a period of military rule under Desi Bouterse following
a coup in 1980. Democratic, civilian rule was restored with
elections in 1987, but the military overthrew the government
in 1990 in a coup engineered by Bouterse. Democratic
elections in 1991 were won by the New Front for
Democracy and Development alliance, led by Ronald
Venetiaan, who became president. President Venetiaan
introduced an unpopular austerity programme, which
improved the economy but lost him the 1996 election.

Ronald Venetiaan was elected president again in 2000,
and again introduced an austerity programme to tackle
dire economic conditions; he was re-elected in 2005. After
the 2010 legislative election, the Mega Combination bloc,
dominated by Desi Bouterse's National Democratic Party,
held the most seats in the legislature, and agreed with the A
Combination bloc to form a coalition government. Desi
Bouterse was subsequently elected president by parliament.

Under the 1987 constitution, the executive president is
elected for a five-year term by a two-thirds majority in the
legislature or, if the required majority cannot be achieved, by
a specially convened United People's Assembly including
district and local council representatives. The vice-president
is elected in the same way. The unicameral National
Assembly has 51 members directly elected for a five-year
term. The council of ministers is appointed by the president
and chaired by the vice-president.

HEAD OF STATE
President, Desi Bouterse, *elected* 19 July 2010, *sworn in*
  12 August 2010
Vice-President, Robert Ameerali

SELECTED GOVERNMENT MEMBERS *as at July 2014*
Defence, Lamuré Latour
Finance, vacant
Foreign Affairs, Winston Lackin
Internal Affairs, Soewarto Moestadja

HONORARY CONSULATE OF THE REPUBLIC OF
SURINAME
89 Pier House, 31 Cheyne Walk, London SW3 5HG
T 07768-196 326 E ajethu@honoraryconsul.info
W www.honoraryconsul.info
Honorary consul, Amwedhkar Jethu

BRITISH AMBASSADOR
HE Andrew Ayre, *apptd* 2011, resident at Georgetown,
  Guyana

DEFENCE

Aged 16–49, 2010 est	*Males*	*Females*
Available for military service	134,218	134,439
Fit for military service	109,445	112,538

ECONOMY AND TRADE

Former president Venetiaan introduced policies that
contained rampant inflation and other economic problems,
and produced steady growth for a few years before the global
downturn, which caused the economy to contract owing to
reduced global prices for key commodities. The mainstays of
the economy are mining, especially bauxite and gold, and oil
and alumina production; these account for 85 per cent of
exports and 25 per cent of government revenue, making the

economy vulnerable to global price fluctuations. Bauxite reserves are declining, but oil production is increasing from existing offshore fields and onshore exploration has begun. Other industries include forestry, food processing and fishing. Industry accounts for 36.6 per cent of GDP and services for 54.5 per cent. Agriculture employs only 8 per cent of the population but produces 8.9 per cent of GDP.

The main trading partners are the USA, the UAE, Belgium and the Netherlands. Principal exports are alumina, gold, crude oil, timber, fish and shrimps, rice and bananas. The main imports are capital equipment, petroleum, foodstuffs, cotton and consumer goods.

GNI – US$4,818m; US$8,680 per capita (2012)
Annual average growth of GDP – 4.7 per cent (2013 est)
Inflation rate – 4.2 per cent (2013 est)
Unemployment – 9 per cent (2008 est)
Total external debt – US$860m (2013 est)
Imports – US$1,755m (2012)
Exports – US$2,525m (2012)

BALANCE OF PAYMENTS
Trade – US$769m surplus (2012)
Current Account – US$251m surplus (2011)

Trade with UK	2012	2013
Imports from UK	£12,871,386	£15,724,645
Exports to UK	£442,890	£655,563

COMMUNICATIONS

Airports and waterways – The principal airport and seaport is at Paramaribo
Roadways – 4,304km
Telecommunications – 83,000 fixed lines and 977,000 mobile subscriptions (2012); there were 163,000 internet users in 2009
Internet code and IDD – sr; 597 (from UK), 44 (to UK)
Media – There are two government-owned television broadcasters and the two daily newspapers, *De West* and *De Ware Tijd,* are privately owned
WPFI score – 18,2 (31)

SWAZILAND

Umbuso weSwatini – Kingdom of Swaziland

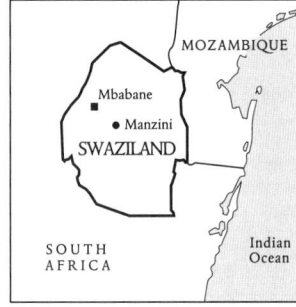

Area – 17,364 sq. km
Capital – Mbabane; population, 66,000 (2011). Lobamba is the legislative capital
Major town – Manzini
Currency – Lilangeni (E; plural *Emalangeni*) of 100 cents; the Lilangeni has a par value with the South African rand, which is also in circulation
Population – 1,419,623 rising at 1.14 per cent a year (2014 est)

Religion – Christian (Zionist 40 per cent, Roman Catholic 20 per cent), Muslim 10 per cent
Language – English, siSwati (both official)
Population density – 70 per sq. km (2011)
Urban population – 21.2 per cent (2012 est)
Median age (years) – 21 (2014 est)
National anthem – 'Nkulunkulu Mnikati wetibusiso temaSwati' ['Oh God, Bestower of Blessings on the Swazi']
National day – 6 September (Independence Day)
Death penalty – Retained (last used 1983)
CPI score – 39 (82)
Literacy rate – 88 per cent (2011 est)
Gross enrolment ratio (percentage of relevant age group) – primary 116 per cent; secondary 58 per cent (2011 est)
Health expenditure (per capita) – US$265 (2011)
Hospital beds (per 1,000 people) – 2.1 (2011)
Life expectancy (years) – 50.54 (2014 est)
Mortality rate – 13.75 (2014 est)
Birth rate – 25.18 (2014 est)
Infant mortality rate – 54.82 (2014 est)
HIV/AIDS adult prevalence – 26.5 per cent (2012 est)

CLIMATE AND TERRAIN

The main regions of the landlocked country are: the densely forested and mountainous Highveld along the western border, with an average altitude of 1,219m; the Middleveld, a mixed farming area which averages about 609m in altitude, and the Lowveld, which was mainly scrubland until the introduction of sugar cane plantations, in the centre; and the Lubombo ridge, along the eastern edge of the Lowveld. Elevation extremes range from 1,862m (Emlembe) to 21m (Great Usutu river). Four rivers, the Komati, Usutu, Mbuluzi and Ngwavuma, flow from west to east.

The climate varies; the Highveld is humid and temperate, the Middleveld and Lubombo are subtropical, and the Lowveld is tropical and semi-arid. Average temperatures in Mbabane, in the Highveld, range from 15.5°C in August to 22.2°C in March.

HISTORY AND POLITICS

The Swazi people are believed to have arrived in the area in the 16th century, and by the mid-17th century had developed a strong kingdom three times the size of the present country. This became a protectorate of the Boer republic of the Transvaal in 1884, and subsequently of Britain. The Kingdom of Swaziland became independent in 1968.

In 1973 King Sobhuza II suspended the constitution, banned political parties and assumed absolute power. The parliamentary system was replaced by traditional tribal communities *(tinkhundla).* Sobhuza II died in 1982, and was succeeded by a son who was a minor. The regency between 1982 and 1986 led to power struggles within the royal family, but the real power passed to the Dlamini clan, which continues to dominate the government.

Demands for democratisation of the constitution have grown over the past 20 years, with the campaigning of political movements and trade unions supported by popular demonstrations, general strikes and blockades of the border with South Africa.

Swaziland has the highest levels of HIV/AIDS infection in the world, and as a consequence faces serious demographic, economic and social problems.

The 2005 constitution retains the executive powers of the king; it appears to permit political parties while maintaining the ban on their members standing for election. The head of state is a hereditary king who is effectively an absolute monarch who rules by decree. There is a bicameral parliament comprising a 30-member senate and a 65-member House of Assembly; members of both serve a five-year term. Each of the country's 55 administrative districts *(tinkhundla)* directly elects one member to the House of Assembly and the king appoints ten members; there is also a provision for four female members to be regionally elected if the total percentage of women is less than 30 per cent. The members of the House of Assembly elect ten of their own number to the senate and a further 20 senators are appointed by the king.

HEAD OF STATE
HM *The King of Swaziland,* King Mswati III, *crowned* 25 April 1986

SELECTED GOVERNMENT MEMBERS *as at July 2014*
Prime Minister, Barnabas Sibusiso Dlamini
Deputy Prime Minister, Paul Dlamin
Finance, Martin Dlamini
Foreign Affairs, Mgwagwa Gamedze

KINGDOM OF SWAZILAND HIGH COMMISSION
20 Buckingham Gate, London SW1E 6LB
T 020-7630 6611 **E** enquiries@swaziland.org.uk
High Commissioner, HE Dumsile Sukati, *apptd* 2011

BRITISH HIGH COMMISSIONER
HE Judith Macgregor, CMG, LVO, *apptd* 2013, resident at Pretoria (Tshwane), South Africa

ECONOMY AND TRADE
The country is very poor, with 63 per cent of the population living below the poverty line. Customs dues from the South African Customs Union and remittances from expatriates working in South Africa are a vital supplement to the domestic economy; customs revenue dropped sharply in the global downturn and the government applied for international financial assistance. Overgrazing, soil depletion, drought and floods are potential future problems.

Subsistence agriculture occupies about 70 per cent of the population and contributes 7.6 per cent of GDP. Sugar cane, cotton, citrus fruits and pineapples are the main cash crops and the basis of industries producing sugar, canned fruit and soft drink concentrates. Coal mining has become less important since the 1980s with diversification into manufacturing such products as textiles, clothing, wood pulp and refrigerators. Industry contributes 47.8 per cent of GDP and services 44.6 per cent.

South Africa accounts for about 60 per cent of exports and over 90 per cent of imports. Principal exports are the products of agriculture and manufacturing. The main imports are vehicles, machinery, transport equipment, foodstuffs, petroleum products and chemicals.
GNI – US$3,454m; US$2,860 per capita (2012)
Annual average growth of GDP – 0 per cent (2013 est)
Inflation rate – 6.1 per cent (2013 est)
Population below poverty line – 63 per cent (2009)
Unemployment – 40 per cent (2006 est)
Total external debt – US$609.5m (2013 est)
Imports – US$1,946m (2012)
Exports – US$1,897m (2012)

BALANCE OF PAYMENTS
Trade – US$49m deficit (2012)
Current Account – US$388m deficit (2010)

Trade with UK	2012	2013
Imports from UK	£2,387,945	£2,459,735
Exports to UK	£5,126,222	£5,897,800

COMMUNICATIONS
Airports – There is an international airport at Manzini, which is expected to be replaced by the new Mswati III International Airport
Roadways and railways – There are 3,594km of roads and 301km of railway connecting with the Mozambique port of Maputo and the South African railway to Richards Bay and Durban
Telecommunications – 48,600 fixed lines and 805,000 mobile subscriptions (2012); there were 90,100 internet users in 2009
Internet code and IDD – sz; 268 (from UK), 44 (to UK)
Media – The state-run Swaziland Television Authority runs various channels across the country; daily newspapers include *The Times of Swaziland* and *The Swazi Observer*
WPFI score – 46,76 (156)

SWEDEN

Konungariket Sverige – Kingdom of Sweden

Area – 450,295 sq. km
Capital – Stockholm; population, 1,296,521 (2012)
Major cities – Gothenburg, Malmo, Uppsala
Currency – Swedish krona of 100 ore
Population – 9,723,809 rising at 0.79 per cent a year (2014 est)
Religion – Christian (Lutheran 87 per cent) (est)
Language – Swedish (official), Finnish, Sami dialects
Population density – 23 per sq. km (2011)
Urban population – 85.4 per cent (2012 est)
Median age (years) – 41.2 (2014 est)
National anthem – 'Du Gamla, Du Fria' ['Thou Ancient, Thou Freeborn']
National day – 6 June (Flag Day)
Death penalty – Abolished for all crimes (since 1972)
CPI score – 89 (3)

CLIMATE AND TERRAIN
The terrain is mostly flat or rolling lowlands in the south and along the east coast, with mountains in the west. Elevation extremes range from 2,111m (Kebnekaise) to −2.4m (reclaimed bay of Lake Hammarsjon). There are many lakes, including Vanern, Vattern, Malaren and Hjalmaren in the south, and over 20,000 islands off the coast near Stockholm. The climate is temperate in the south and subarctic in the north; average temperatures in Stockholm range from −3°C in February to 17°C in July.

POLITICS
Sweden is a hereditary constitutional monarchy. The 1975 constitution was amended in 1979 to vest the succession in the monarch's eldest child irrespective of sex. The unicameral legislature, the *Riksdag,* has 349 members directly elected by proportional representation for a four-year term. The prime minister appoints the council of ministers.

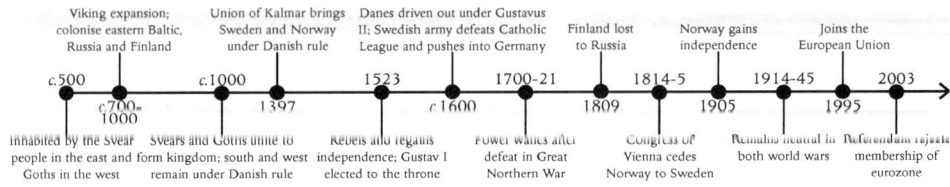

Viking expansion; colonise eastern Baltic, Russia and Finland — Union of Kalmar brings Sweden and Norway under Danish rule — Danes driven out under Gustavus II; Swedish army defeats Catholic League and pushes into Germany — Finland lost to Russia — Norway gains independence — Joins the European Union

c.500   c.1000   1523   1700–21   1814–5   1914–45   2003

c.700–1000   1397   c.1600   1809   1905   1995

Inhabited by the Svear people in the east and Goths in the west — Svears and Goths unite to form kingdom; south and west remain under Danish rule — Rebels and regains independence; Gustav I elected to the throne — Power wanes after defeat in Great Northern War — Congress of Vienna cedes Norway to Sweden — Remains neutral in both world wars — Referendum rejects membership of eurozone

Legislative elections in 2014 saw the Social Democrats win the most seats. Coalition negotiations proved difficult and the Alliance for Sweden coalition remained in government during early September.

Sweden is divided into 21 counties *(lan)* and 290 municipalities *(kommun)*.

HEAD OF STATE

HM The King of Sweden, King Carl XVI Gustaf, KG, *born* 30 April 1946, *succeeded* 15 September 1973
Heir, HRH Crown Princess Victoria Ingrid Alice Desiree, Duchess of Vastergotland, *born* 14 July 1977

SELECTED GOVERNMENT MEMBERS *as at September 2014*
Prime Minister, Fredrik Reinfeldt
Deputy Prime Minister, Jan Bjorklund
Defence, Karin Enstrom
Finance, Anders Borg

EMBASSY OF SWEDEN

11 Montagu Place, London W1H 2AL
T 020-7917 6400 E ambassaden.london@foreign.ministry.se
W www.swedenabroad.com/london
Ambassador Extraordinary and Plenipotentiary, HE Nicola Clase, *apptd* 2010

BRITISH EMBASSY

PO Box 27819, Skarpogatan 6–8, 115 93 Stockholm
T (+46) (8) 671 3000 E info@britishembassy.se
W www.gov.uk/government/world/sweden
Ambassador Extraordinary and Plenipotentiary, HE Paul Johnston, *apptd* 2011

DEFENCE

Sweden has a policy of non-alignment in peace and neutrality in war, and has declined to become a member of NATO.

Aged 16–49, 2010 est	Males	Females
Available for military service	2,065,691	1,996,764
Fit for military service	1,709,055	1,650,432

Military expenditure – US$6,469m (2013)
Conscription – Abolished in practice as of 2009; retained for emergencies

ECONOMY AND TRADE

Sweden developed from an agricultural to an industrial economy in the early 20th century. The prosperity that had funded the generous welfare state after 1946 ended in the early 1990s, when Sweden experienced a deep recession. It recovered to experience strong growth before briefly entering recession again in 2008–9 as a result of the global downturn. Despite improving results for the banking sector, growth slowed from 1 per cent in 2012 to 0.9 percent in 2013 due to the poor performance of the eurozone

The main export-orientated industries are engineering and high-tech manufacturing, mining and forestry. Mineral resources include iron ore, copper lead, zinc, sulphur, granite, marble, precious and heavy metals (the latter not exploited) and extensive deposits of low-grade uranium ore. The engineering sector provides 50 per cent of output and exports, particularly specialised machinery and systems such as electrical and electronic equipment and armaments, and motor vehicles and aircraft; other industries produce pharmaceuticals, plastics and chemicals.

Agriculture contributes 2 per cent of GDP, industry 31.3 per cent and services 66.8 per cent.

The main trading partners are other EU states, Norway and Russia. Principal exports include machinery, vehicles, paper products, pulp and wood, iron and steel products, and chemicals. The main imports are machinery, oil and petroleum products, chemicals, vehicles, iron and steel, foodstuffs and clothing.

GNI – US$535,523m; US$55,970 per capita (2012)
Annual average growth of GDP – 0.9 per cent (2013 est)
Inflation rate – 0 per cent (2013 est)
Unemployment – 8.1 per cent (2013 est)
Total external debt – US$1,039,000m (2012)
Imports – US$163,815m (2012)
Exports – US$172,712m (2012)

BALANCE OF PAYMENTS
Trade – US$8,896m surplus (2012)
Current Account – US$31,306m surplus (2012)

Trade with UK	2012	2013
Imports from UK	£164,707,832	£449,401,401
Exports to UK	£2,484,012,648	£2,350,113,400

COMMUNICATIONS

Airports and waterways – The principal airports are at Stockholm, Gothenburg, Lulea, Malmo and Umea; the main ports are Gothenburg, Helsingborg, Malmo and Stockholm
Roadways and railways – 579,564km; 11,633km
Telecommunications – 4.321 million fixed lines and 11.643 million mobile subscriptions (2012); there were 8.4 million internet users in 2009
Internet code and IDD – se; 46 (from UK), 44 (to UK)
Major broadcasters – Public television is run by Sveriges Television (SVT)
Press – There are four Stockholm-based daily newspapers, plus one based in Gothenburg and one in Malmo
WPFI score – 8,98 (10)

EDUCATION AND HEALTH

The state education system provides nine years of free and compulsory schooling from the age of seven to 16 in the comprehensive elementary schools.
Gross enrolment ratio (percentage of relevant age group) – primary 101 per cent; secondary 97 per cent; tertiary 74 per cent (2012 est)
Health expenditure (per capita) – US$5,331 (2011)
Life expectancy (years) – 81.89 (2014 est)
Mortality rate – 9.45 (2014 est)
Birth rate – 11.92 (2014 est)
Infant mortality rate – 2.6 (2014 est)

SWITZERLAND

Schweizerische   Eidgenossenschaft / Confédération   suisse /
Confederazione   Svizzera / Confederaziun   svizra   –   Swiss
Confederation

Area – 41,277 sq. km
Capital – Bern; population, 353,000 (2011)
Major cities – Basel, Geneva, Lausanne, Zurich
Currency – Swiss franc of 100 rappen (or centimes)
Population – 8,061,516 rising at 0.78 per cent a year
    (2014 est); German (65 per cent), French (18 per cent),
    Italian (10 per cent), Romansch (1 per cent) (est)
Religion – Christian (Roman Catholic 38.2 per cent,
    Protestant 26.9 per cent), Muslim 4.95 per cent (majority
    Sunni), none 21.4 (2012)
Language – German, French, Italian, Romansch (all official),
    Albanian, English, Portuguese, Serbo-Croatian, Spanish
Population density – 198 per sq. km (2011)
Urban population – 73.8 per cent (2012)
Median age (years) – 42 (2014)
National anthem – 'Schweizerpsalm'/'Cantique
    suisse'/'Salmo svizzero'/'Psalm svizzer' ['Swiss Psalm']
National day – 1 August (Confederation Day)
Death penalty – Abolished for all crimes (since 1992)
CPI score – 85 (7)

CLIMATE AND TERRAIN

Switzerland is the most mountainous country in Europe.
The central plateau of hills, plains and over 1,500 lakes is
enclosed by mountains. The Jura mountains lie in the north-
west and the Alps, which cover two-thirds of the country,
occupy the south and east. Elevation extremes range from
4,634m (Dufourspitze, Alps) to 195m (Lake Maggiore).
Lakes Neuchâtel, Lucerne and Zurich lie wholly within the
country, but Lake Maggiore is shared with Italy, Lake Geneva
with France and Lake Constance with Germany and Austria.
The Rhine, Rhône and Inn rivers all rise in the Alps. The
climate is temperate, with conditions that vary with altitude.
Average temperatures in Zurich range from 0.3°C in January
to 18.6°C in July.

HISTORY AND POLITICS

The area was conquered by the Romans in 58 BC and then
overrun by Germanic tribes in the fourth century AD. It was a
province of the medieval Holy Roman Empire from 1033.
The Swiss confederation began in 1291 as a defensive
alliance of three cantons to protect their autonomy, and
expanded during the following centuries, becoming
independent of the Habsburgs in the 14th century. Its
independence was recognised by the Treaty of Westphalia
in 1648. French revolutionary forces captured Switzerland in
1789 and named it the Helvetic Republic. Independence was
restored in 1814, and the congress of Vienna (1815) joined
Geneva, Neuchatel and Valais to the confederation and

recognised the country's perpetual neutrality in international
affairs. A new constitution was adopted in 1848 which
replaced the loose confederation of cantons with a federal
state and enhanced the powers of the central government.

Many policy decisions are submitted to national
referendums. Although the federal government has pursued a
policy of gradual integration with the EU and applied for
membership in 1992, referendums have rejected membership
of the European Economic Area (1992), approved bilateral
trade agreements with the EU (2000), and rejected EU
membership (2001).

Proportional representation, introduced in 1919, resulted
in coalition governments throughout the 20th and into the
21st century. Apart from a 12-month period in 2007–8,
since 1959 the federal government has been a coalition
of four parties: the Swiss People's Party (SVP), the Social
Democratic Party, the Christian Democratic People's Party
and the Radical Democratic Party. The SVP, in coalition with
the Democratic Centre Union, remained the largest party in
the National Council in the 2011 legislative election. In
2014 Dieder Burkhalter of the Free Democratic Party was
elected president.

Under the 1998 constitution, the head of state is a
president elected annually (along with the vice-president) for
a one-year term by the federal legislature from the members
of the Federal Council; consecutive terms may not be served.
The bicameral legislature, the Federal Assembly, has two
chambers: the National Council has 200 members, directly
elected for a four-year term; the Council of States has 46
members (two from each canton and one from each
half-canton) directly elected within each canton for a
four-year term.

Executive power is in the hands of a Federal Council of
seven members, elected for a four-year term by the Federal
Assembly after every legislative election. The Federal Council
is chaired by the president. Not more than one person from
the same canton may be elected a member of the Council;
however, there is a tradition that Italian- and French-
speaking areas should between them be represented on the
council by at least two members.

Any citizen able to obtain 100,000 voters' signatures in
support of holding a referendum on a given issue can initiate
a national referendum. A referendum to restrict immigration
from the EU passed in 2014, receiving 50.3 per cent of the
vote.

SELECTED GOVERNMENT MEMBERS *as at July 2014*
President of the Swiss Confederation, Didier Burkhalter
Vice-President, Simonetta Sommaruga
Finance, Eveline Widmer-Schlumpf
Interior, Alain Berset

EMBASSY OF SWITZERLAND
16–18 Montagu Place, London W1H 2BQ
T 020-7616 6000 E lon.vertretung@eda.admin.ch
W www.eda.admin.ch/london
Ambassador Extraordinary and Plenipotentiary, HE Dominik
    Furgler, *apptd* 2013

BRITISH EMBASSY
Thunstrasse 50, 3005 Bern
T (+41) (31) 359 7700 E info.berne@fco.gsi.gov.uk
W www.gov.uk/government/world/switzerland
Ambassador Extraordinary and Plenipotentiary, HE David
    Moran, *apptd* 2014

CONFEDERAL STRUCTURE
There are 23 cantons, three of which are subdivided, making
20 cantons and six half-cantons, or 26 in all. Each canton

and half-canton has its own government and a substantial degree of autonomy. The main language in 19 of the cantons is German; in six others it is French and one Italian.

DEFENCE

Aged 16–49, 2010 est	Males	Females
Available for military service	1,828,043	1,786,552
Fit for military service	1,493,509	1,459,450

Military expenditure – US$5,321m (2013)*
Conscription duration – 18 weeks mandatory training, then intermittent three-week refresher courses

* Figure des not include paramilitary spending

ECONOMY AND TRADE

Switzerland has a prosperous and stable market economy with low unemployment and a highly skilled labour force. Its prosperity is based on banking, financial services and export-orientated industrial manufacturing. The economy went into recession in 2009 owing to slower export demand and the impact on the banking sector during the 2008 global financial crisis; the largest bank required government support. Growth remained slow at 2 per cent in 2013 due to the poor performance of the eurozone and the strength of the Swiss Franc, which helped make exports less competitive. Although not an EU member, Switzerland has brought many practices in line with the EU to maintain competitiveness, and it is currently adopting OECD standards on tax administration and transparency.

Agriculture is practised in the mountain valleys and the central plateau, where grains, fruits and vegetables are grown. Dairy farming and stock-raising are also important. The industrial sector is noted for precision, electrical and mechanical engineering, pharmaceuticals, chemicals, telecommunications, food processing and packaging, and graphics. Banking, insurance and tourism are the major service industries. Agriculture contributes 0.7 per cent of GDP, industry 26.8 per cent and services 72.5 per cent.

The main trading partners are EU countries (especially Germany) and the USA. Principal exports are machinery, chemicals, metals, watches and agricultural products. The main imports are machinery, chemicals, vehicles, metals, agricultural products and textiles.
GNI – US$652,638m; US$80,970 per capita (2012)
Annual average growth of GDP – 1.7 per cent (2013 est)
Inflation rate – −0.4 per cent (2013 est)
Population below poverty line – 7.9 per cent (2010 est)
Unemployment – 2.9 per cent (2013 est)
Total external debt – US$1,544,000m (2012)
Imports – US$188,618m (2012)
Exports – US$213,982m (2012)

BALANCE OF PAYMENTS
Trade – US$25,364m surplus (2012)
Current Account – US$70,756m surplus (2012)

Trade with UK	2012	2013
Imports from UK	£6,513,109,658	£5,682,364,616
Exports to UK	£9,010,201,911	£7,785,296,550

COMMUNICATIONS

Airports and waterways – The principal airports are at Zurich, Basel, Bern and Geneva; the Rhine carries commercial shipping on the 65km stretch from Basel-Rheinfelden and Schaffhausen-Bodensee, and there are 12 navigable lakes
Roadways and railways – There are 71,464km of roadways, including 1,790km of motorways, and 4,876km of railways
Telecommunications – 4.382 million fixed lines and 10.46 million mobile subscriptions (2012); there were 6.152 million internet users in 2009
Internet code and IDD – ch; 41 (from UK), 44 (to UK)
Major broadcasters – The public-service Swiss Broadcasting Corporation (SRG/SSR), which is funded mainly through licence fees, dominates broadcasting
Press – Newspapers tend to be regional, reflecting linguistic divisions: there are two German-language dailies based in Zurich, two French-language dailies in Geneva and an Italian-language daily in Lugano
WPFI score – 10,47 (15)

EDUCATION AND HEALTH

Education is controlled by cantonal and communal authorities and is free and compulsory from ages seven to 16.
Gross enrolment ratio (percentage of relevant age group) – primary 103 per cent; secondary 96 per cent; tertiary 54 per cent (2012 est)
Health expenditure (per capita) – US$9,121 (2011)
Hospital beds (per 1,000 people) – 5.0 (2010)
Life expectancy (years) – 82.39 (2014 est)
Mortality rate – 8.10 (2014 est)
Birth rate – 10.48 (2014 est)
Infant mortality rate – 3.73 (2014 est)

SYRIA

Al-Jumhuriyah al-Arabiyah asSuriyah – Syrian Arab Republic

Area – 185,180 sq. km
Capital – Damascus; population, 3,277,787 (2012)
Major cities – Aleppo (Halab), Hama (Hamah), Homs (Hims), Latakia (al-Ladhiqiyah)
Currency – Syrian pound (S£) of 100 piastres
Population – 17,951,639 falling at 9.73 per cent a year (2014 est)
Religion – Muslim (Sunni 74 per cent, other 13 per cent, including Alawite, Ismaili), Christian 10 per cent (est) (of which Greek Orthodox is the largest denomination), Druze 3 per cent
Language – Arabic (official), Kurdish, Armenian, Aramaic, Circassian, French
Population density – 120 per sq. km (2011)
Urban population – 56.5 per cent (2012 est)
Median age (years) – 23.3 (2014 est)
National anthem – 'Homat el Diyar' ['Guardians of the Homeland']
National day – 17 April (Independence Day)
Death penalty – Retained
CPI score – 17 (168)

CLIMATE AND TERRAIN

There is a narrow coastal plain and ranges of mountains in the west, and the fertile basin of the river Euphrates in the north-east. The centre and south of the interior consist of semi-arid and desert plateaux. Elevation extremes range from 2,814m (Mt Hermon) to −200m (unnamed location near Lake Tiberias). There is a desert climate in much of the country, moderated by altitude in the mountains, and a Mediterranean climate on the coast. Average temperatures in Damascus range from 6°C in January to 26°C in July and August.

HISTORY AND POLITICS

In March 2011, protests against the ruling Asad regime broke out in a number of cities, including Damascus and Deraa. In May the army was used to restore order in a number of towns. Many soldiers and commanders unwilling to use force against civilians broke away from the government, forming the Free Syrian Army, which began fighting against the administration. Mounting civilian casualties escalated the conflict, leading to the involvement of a number of different anti-Asad groups, including the Kurdish People's Protection Units (YPG) operating in the north-east of the country, Islamist groups and Hezbollah fighters from neighbouring Lebanon.

Following a chemical attack on the town of Ghouta by the Syrian air force in August 2013, the Syrian government came under sustained international pressure to abandon its stockpile of chemical weapons. In April 2014, 92.5 per cent of the country's chemical weapons were confirmed to have been removed or destroyed by UN observers.

The conflict has created a humanitarian disaster, with millions of Syrians fleeing the country. Remaining civilians face acute shortages of food, medical supplies and other necessities.

In February 2012, a new constitution providing for multiparty elections was approved via a referendum. The majority of countries refused to recognise the outcome of the poll; exceptions included Russia and China.

HEAD OF STATE

President, Lt.-Gen. Bashar al-Assad, *elected* 27 June 2000, *confirmed by referendum* 10 July 2000, *re-elected* 2007, 2014

Vice-Presidents, Farouk al-Shara; Najah al-Attar

SELECTED GOVERNMENT MEMBERS *as at July 2014*
Prime Minister, Wael Nader al-Halaqi
Defence, Gen. Fahad Jassim al-Freij
Finance, Ismail Ismail
Foreign Affairs, Walid al-Muallem

EMBASSY OF THE SYRIAN ARAB REPUBLIC

8 Belgrave Square, London SW1X 8PH
T 020-7245 9012 W www.syremb.com
Ambassador Extraordinary and Plenipotentiary, vacant

DEFENCE

Aged 16–49, 2010 est	Males	Females
Available for military service	5,889,837	5,660,751
Fit for military service	5,055,510	4,884,151

Military expenditure – US$2,495m (2011)
Conscription duration – 18 months

ECONOMY AND TRADE

The economy is state-controlled and predominantly state-owned, although unrest and international sanctions have slowed economic growth. Conflict-related problems include infrastructure damage, reduced domestic consumption, decreased production and sharply rising inflation. The continuing violence has left approximately 11 million Syrians needing international aid.

Oil and agriculture account for nearly half of GDP, but other activities, such as financial services, telecommunications, tourism and non-oil industry and trade, are becoming increasingly important. Gas is produced for domestic use, and phosphate is mined and processed; other non-oil industry includes the manufacture of textiles, processed food, beverages, tobacco and cement, and car assembly. Agriculture contributes 17.6 per cent of GDP, industry 22.2 per cent and services 60.2 per cent.

The main export markets are Iraq, Saudi Arabia, Kuwait and the UAE; imports come chiefly from Saudi Arabia, the UAE, Iran and China. Principal exports are crude oil, minerals, petroleum products, fruit and vegetables, cotton fibre, textiles, clothing, meat, livestock and wheat. The main imports are machinery and transport equipment, electric power machinery, food and livestock, metals and metal products, chemicals, plastics, yarn and paper.

GNI – US$70,501m; US$2,610 per capita (2010)
Annual average growth of GDP – −2.3 per cent (2011 est)
Inflation rate – 59.1 per cent (2013 est)
Population below poverty line – 11.9 per cent (2006 est)
Unemployment – 17.8 per cent (2013 est)
Total external debt – US$9,796m (2013 est)
Imports – US$16,400m (2011)
Exports – US$10,700m (2011)

BALANCE OF PAYMENTS

Trade – US$5,700m deficit (2011)
Current Account – US$1,584m deficit (2009)

Trade with UK	2012	2013
Imports from UK	£2,640,474	£16,863,847
Exports to UK	£9,109,584	£3,038,069

COMMUNICATIONS

Airports and waterways – The principal airports are at Aleppo and Damascus; the main port is Latakia
Roadways and railways – 69,873km; 2,052km
Telecommunications – 4.425 million fixed lines and 12.928 million mobile subscriptions (2012); there were 4.469 million internet users in 2009
Internet code and IDD – sy; 963 (from UK), 44 (to UK)
Major broadcasters – The state-run Syrian TV operates domestic and satellite networks
Press – The government-owned *Al-Baath* and *Al-Thawra* newspapers are published on a daily basis
WPFI score – 77,04 (177)

EDUCATION AND HEALTH

Education is under state control. Elementary education is free at state schools and is compulsory from the age of seven.

Literacy rate – 84 per cent (2011 est)
Gross enrolment ratio (percentage of relevant age group) – primary 122 per cent; secondary 74 per cent (2012 est)
Health expenditure (per capita) – US$101 (2011)
Hospital beds (per 1,000 people) – 1.5 (2010)
Life expectancy (years) – 68.41 (2014 est)
Mortality rate – 6.51 (2014 est)
Birth rate – 22.76 (2014 est)
Infant mortality rate – 15.79 (2014 est)

TAIWAN

T'ai-wan – *Taiwan (Republic of China)*

Area – 35,980 sq. km
Capital – Taipei; population, 2,646,474 (2001 est)
Major cities – Kaohsiung, Taichung, Tainan
Currency – New Taiwan dollar (NT$) of 100 cents
Population – 23,359,928 rising at 0.25 per cent a year (2014 est); Taiwanese 84 per cent, Mainland Chinese 14 per cent, indigenous 2 per cent (est)
Religion – Mixture of Buddhist and Taoist 93 per cent, Christian 4.5 per cent; many also practise Chinese folk beliefs
Language – Mandarin (official), Taiwanese (Min-Nan), Hakka dialects
Population density – 618 per sq. km (2001)
Median age (years) – 39.2 (2014 est)
National anthem – 'San Min Chu I' ['Three Principles of the People']
National day – 10 October (Republic Day)
Death penalty – Retained (last used 2011)
CPI score – 61 (36)
Life expectancy (years) – 79.84 (2014 est)
Mortality rate – 6.97 (2014 est)
Birth rate – 8.55 (2014 est)
Infant mortality rate – 4.49 (2014 est)

CLIMATE AND TERRAIN

The island of Taiwan (formerly Formosa) lies 145km east of the Chinese mainland. Mountains run the length of the island, covering over half the terrain, with lowlands in the west. Elevation extremes range from 3,952m (Yu Shan) to 0m (South China Sea). Taiwan shares the tropical monsoon climate of southern China, with large seasonal variations in temperature, dry winters and wet summers. The typhoon season lasts from May to November, with particularly high humidity between July and September. Average temperatures in Taipei range from 16°C in January and February and 29°C in July and August.
    Territories include the Penghu (Pescadores) islands (80.47 sq. km), some 56km west of Taiwan, as well as Kinmen (Quemoy) (109 sq. km) and Matsu (7 sq. km), which are only a few kilometres from mainland China.

HISTORY AND POLITICS

Originally settled by Austronesian people 8,000 years ago, Chinese colonists arrived on the island from around the 12th century. The island was annexed by China in the 17th century, and ceded to Japan in 1895 at the end of the Sino-Japanese War. It was returned to China after Japan's defeat in the Second World War. The Kuomintang (KMT) government, led by Gen. Chiang Kai-shek, withdrew to Taiwan in 1949 after being defeated by the communists in mainland China. The territory remained under Chiang Kai-shek's presidency until his death in 1975. He was succeeded as president by his son, Gen. Chiang Ching-kuo, who ruled until his death in 1988. Martial law was lifted in 1987 after 38 years. In 1991 the Taiwanese government declared an end to the state of war with China, officially recognising the People's Republic of China for the first time, and ended emergency measures that had frozen political life in Taiwan since 1949.
    Democratisation of the authoritarian one-party state began in the 1980s and led to the first multiparty elections in 1992. The 'Senior Parliamentarians' who had retained their seats since being elected on the mainland in 1948 were forcibly retired in 1991–2. From this point, power shifted away from the mainlanders to the native Taiwanese, and 50 years of KMT rule ended when the Democratic Progressive Party (DPP), which favours self-determination, won the presidency in 2000 and the 2001 legislative election.
    The DPP retained the presidency and continued in government after the 2004 elections. However, in the 2008 elections the KMT returned to power, and the KMT candidate, Ma Ying-jeou, was elected president. The KMT retained its majority in the 2012 legislative election and Ma Ying-jeou gained re-election, picking up over 51 per cent of the vote.
    Most nations acknowledge the position of the Chinese government that Taiwan is a province of the People's Republic of China, and as a result Taiwan has formal diplomatic relations with only 22 countries and no seat at the UN. China has sanctioned the use of force to prevent Taiwan declaring itself independent.
    Contacts between Taiwan and China began in the 1980s and have led to a gradual relaxation of restrictions on direct economic, trade and transport links, and on travel and tourism. Since the KMT returned to power in 2008, Taiwan has sought greater economic cooperation and integration with China.
    The 1947 constitution (which originally applied to the whole of China) has been amended a number of times since 1991. In 2004 an amendment provided for future proposed constitutional changes to be put to a referendum instead of the National Assembly (formerly the upper house of the legislature), which was disbanded under 2005 provisions that also reduced the number of legislative seats with effect from the 2008 election.
    The president is directly elected for a four-year term, renewable once. The unicameral Legislative Yuan has 113 members: 73 directly elected, 34 elected proportionately by party and six elected by indigenous peoples in two constituencies; all serve a four-year term. The president appoints the premier and, on the premier's advice, the cabinet.

HEAD OF STATE
President, Ma Ying-jeou, *elected* 22 March 2008, *re-elected* 14 January 2012
Vice-President, Wu Den-yih

SELECTED GOVERNMENT MEMBERS *as at July 2013*
Premier, Jiang Yi-huah
Defence, Yen Ming
Economy, Chang Chia-juch
Foreign Affairs, David Lin Yung-lo

DEFENCE

Aged 16–49, 2010 est	Males	Females
Available for military service	6,183,567	6,006,676
Fit for military service	5,074,173	4,951,088

Military expenditure – US$10,288m (2013)
Conscription duration – 24 months

ECONOMY AND TRADE

Since the 1950s Taiwan has transformed itself from a mainly agricultural country into a highly developed industrial economy. This transition was driven by exports. There has been a gradual shift away from state domination of the economy, with a reduction in government influence on investment and foreign trade, and privatisation in the financial and industrial sectors. Taiwan's export markets suffered severely in the global economic downturn and the economy contracted sharply in 2008–9; despite a strong recovery in 2010, growth fell to 1.3 per cent in 2012 and rose slowly to 2.2 per cent in 2013 due to weak global demand.

Only a quarter of the land area is suitable for agriculture but the soil is very fertile, producing rice, corn, vegetables, fruit, tea, flowers, meat and dairy products. The industrial base includes electronics, communications and information technology products, oil refining, armaments, chemicals, textiles, iron and steel, machinery, cement, food processing, vehicles, consumer goods, pharmaceuticals and fishing. Agriculture contributes 2 per cent of GDP, industry 29.4 per cent and services 68.6 per cent.

The main trading partners are China (27.1 per cent of exports), Japan (17.6 per cent of imports), the USA and Hong Kong. Principal exports are electronic and computer equipment, flat panels, machinery, metals, textiles, plastics, chemicals and precision instruments. The main imports are electronic and electrical equipment, machinery, crude oil and precision instruments.

Average annual growth of GDP – 2.2 per cent (2013 est)
Inflation rate – 1.1 per cent (2013 est)
Population below poverty line – 1.5 per cent (2012 est)
Unemployment – 4.1 per cent (2013 est)
Total external debt – US$146,800m (2013 est)
Imports – US$251,500m (2010)
Exports – US$274,600m (2010)

BALANCE OF PAYMENTS
Trade – US$23,100m surplus (2010)
Current Account – US$49,923m surplus (2012)

Trade with UK	2012	2013
Imports from UK	£1,077,317,760	£1,159,561,939
Exports to UK	£3,779,811,250	3,429,146,990

COMMUNICATIONS

Airports and waterways – There are international airports at Taoyuan (near Taipei), Kaohsiung and Taichung; the main ports are Keelung, Kaohsiung and Taichung
Roadways and railways – 41,475km; 1,580km
Telecommunications – 15.998 million fixed lines and 29.455 million mobile subscriptions (2012); there were 16.15 million internet users in 2009
Internet code and IDD – tw; 886 (from UK), 2 44 (to UK)

Media – The government runs a non-profit public broadcaster, Public Television Service, alongside various commercial companies; there are six daily newspapers, including the *United Daily News* and the *China Times*
WPFI score – 23,82 (50)

TAJIKISTAN

Jumhurii Tojikiston – Republic of Tajikistan

Area – 143,100 sq. km
Capital – Dushanbe; population, 739,000 (2011)
Major towns – Khujand, Kulob
Currency – Somoni of 100 dirams
Population – 8,051,512 rising at 1.75 per cent a year (2014 est); Tajik (79.9 per cent), Uzbek (15.3 per cent), Russian (1.1 per cent), Kyrgyz (1.1 per cent) (2000)
Religion – Muslim (Sunni 85 per cent, Shia 5 per cent) (est)
Language – Tajik (official), Russian
Population density – 56 per sq. km (2011)
Urban population – 26.5 per cent (2012 est)
Median age (years) – 23.5 (2014 est)
National anthem – 'Surudi Milli' ['National Anthem']
National day – 9 September (Independence Day)
Death penalty – Retained (last used 2004)
CPI score – 22 (154)
Literacy rate – 100 per cent (2011 est)
Gross enrolment ratio (percentage of relevant age group) – primary 102 per cent; secondary 87 per cent; tertiary 19.7 per cent (2011 est)
Health expenditure (per capita) – US$54 (2011)
Hospital beds (per 1,000 people) – 5.5 (2011)
Life expectancy (years) – 67.06 (2014 est)
Mortality rate – 6.28 (2014 est)
Birth rate – 24.99 (2014 est)
Infant mortality rate – 35.03 (2014 est)

CLIMATE AND TERRAIN

Tajikistan is mountainous, with the Pamir highlands in the east and the high ridges of the Pamir-Altai ranges in the centre. More than half of the country lies above 3,000m. Elevation extremes range from 7,495m (Qullai Ismoili Somoni) to 300m (Syr Darya river). The main rivers are the Syr Darya, flowing through the Fergana valley in the north, and the Amu Darya and its tributaries in the west and south. Most of the population lives on the fertile plains formed by these rivers. The climate is continental; average temperatures range from −2.2°C in January to 24.1°C in July.

HISTORY AND POLITICS

The area that is now Tajikistan was first settled by Iranian peoples 3,000 years ago and was conquered by Alexander the Great in the fourth century BC, remaining under Greek and Greco-Persian rule for 200 years until the kingdom of Kushan was established throughout the Bactria region.

Tajikistan was invaded by Muslim Arabs in the eighth century AD, and Islam was the prevalent religion by the time of the Samanid Persian conquest in the ninth century. From the ninth to the 16th century, the region was ruled by a succession of Turkic, Mongol and Uzbek states. In 1868, the northern part was subsumed within the Russian Empire, while the south was annexed by the Bukhara khanate. At the time of the Russian revolution in 1917 the Central Asian territories attempted to establish their independence, but Bolshevik power was consolidated in the north by April 1918, and in the rest of Tajikistan by 1920. In 1924 the Tajikistan Autonomous Soviet Socialist Republic was formed as part of the Uzbek Republic, before Tajikistan was given full republican status within the USSR in 1929.

Tajikistan declared its independence on 9 September 1991. In 1992, anti-government demonstrations escalated into a five-year civil war between government forces and Islamic and pro-democracy groups. A peace accord signed in 1997 was implemented by 2000. Political assassinations and bombings occurred after the end of the civil war, but the level of violence has dropped since 2002.

Former communists have dominated politics since 1991 and power is concentrated in the president's hands. Opposition parties are weak and face harassment; a number of opposition leaders have been arrested on criminal charges, moves that their supporters claim are politically motivated.

President Rakhmon has served as head of state since 1992, and was re-elected for a fourth term in 2013. The 2010 legislative elections were won by the incumbent (former communist) People's Democratic Party of Tajikistan (HDKT) with an overwhelming majority, although international observers considered the polls flawed. A comprehensive cabinet reshuffle was initiated by president Rakhmon in December 2013.

The 1994 constitution was amended in 1999 and 2003, following referendums, to introduce changes to the presidential term of office and the legislative structure. The executive president is directly elected for a single seven-year term, although the 2003 amendment permits the current incumbent to stand for two further terms. The bicameral parliament consists of the Assembly of Representatives *(Majlisi Namoyandogan)*, which has 63 members directly elected for a five-year term, and the National Assembly *(Majlisi Milli)*, which has 33 members, 25 elected by five regional assemblies and eight appointed by the president, to serve a five-year term. Administratively, Tajikistan is divided into two provinces and the Gorno-Badakhshan autonomous region.

HEAD OF STATE

President, Emomali Rakhmon, *elected by Supreme Soviet* 19 November 1992, *elected* 6 November 1994, *re-elected* 1999, 2006, 2013

SELECTED GOVERNMENT MEMBERS *as at July 2014*

Prime Minister, Kohir Rasulzoda
First Deputy Prime Minister, Davlatali Saidov
Deputy Prime Ministers, Murodali Alimardon; Marhabo Jabbarova; Azim Ibrohim
Defence, Mirzo Sherali

EMBASSY OF THE REPUBLIC OF TAJIKISTAN

Grove House, 26-28 Hammersmith Grove, London W6 7BA
T 020-8834 1003 E info@tajembassy.org.uk
W www.tajembassy.org.uk
Ambassador Extraordinary and Plenipotentiary, HE Erkin Kasymov, *apptd* 2008

BRITISH EMBASSY

65 Mirzo Tursunzoda Street, Dushanbe 734002
T (+992) 372 42221 E dushanbe.reception@fco.gov.uk
W www.gov.uk/government/world/tajikistan
Ambassador Extraordinary and Plenipotentiary, HE Robin Ord-Smith, *apptd* 2012

DEFENCE

Aged 16–49, 2010 est	*Males*	*Females*
Available for military service	2,012,790	2,020,618
Fit for military service	1,490,267	1,675,083

Conscription duration – 24 months

ECONOMY AND TRADE

Since the civil war, there has been steady economic growth but the economy remains fragile owing to the inconsistent implementation of structural reforms, corruption, poor industrial and transport infrastructure, energy shortages and high foreign debt. The country has benefited from debt cancellation, and is receiving substantial aid, primarily to develop industrial and transport infrastructure. However, 35.6 per cent of the population lives below the poverty line and many are dependent on remittances. The global downturn reduced the value of remittances and export commodity prices in 2009.

Agriculture accounts for 21.1 per cent of GDP but 46.5 per cent of employment. Cattle-raising and cotton-growing predominate; other crops are grain, fruit, grapes and vegetables. Abundant mineral deposits are not fully exploited. Industry consists of aluminium and hydro-electric power production, mining (zinc and lead) and production of cement and vegetable oil. The sector contributes 23.2 per cent of GDP and employs 10.7 per cent of the workforce. The services sector contributes the most to GDP at 55.7 per cent and employs 41.2 per cent of the workforce.

The main trading partners are China, Turkey and Russia. Principal exports are aluminium, electricity, cotton, fruit, vegetable oil and textiles. The main imports are petroleum products, aluminium oxide, machinery and equipment, and foodstuffs.

GNI – US$6,925m; US$860 per capita (2012)
Annual average growth of GDP – 6.8 per cent (2013 est)
Inflation rate – 5.6 per cent (2013 est)
Population below poverty line – 39.6 per cent (2012 est)
Unemployment – 2.5 per cent (2012 est)
Total external debt – US$3,595m (2013 est)

BALANCE OF PAYMENTS

Trade – US$2,421m deficit (2012)
Current Account – US$307m surplus (2011)

Trade with UK	*2012*	*2013*
Imports from UK	£2,215,605	£2,377,308
Exports to UK	£173,294	£993,417

COMMUNICATIONS

Airports and waterways – The main airport is at Dushanbe, and there are 17 other airports around the country; 200km of the river Vakhsh is navigable
Roadways and railways – 27,767km; 680km
Telecommunications – 393,000 fixed lines and 6.528 million mobile subscriptions (2012); there were 700,000 internet users in 2009
Internet code and IDD – tj; 992 (from UK), 810 44 (to UK)
Media – The state-run Tajik TV operates various channels across the country; major newspapers include the government-owned *Jumhuriyat* and the privately owned *Neru-i Sukhan*
WPFI score – 34,86 (115)

TANZANIA

Jamhuri ya Muungano wa Tanzania – United Republic of Tanzania

Area – 947,300 sq. km
Capital – Dodoma; population, 3,651,452 (2012 est)
Major cities – Arusha, Dar es Salaam, Mbeya, Mwanza, Zanzibar
Currency – Tanzanian shilling of 100 cents
Population – 49,639,138 rising at 2.8 per cent a year (2014 est); over 130 African ethnic groups on the mainland; Arab, African and mixed race on Zanzibar
Religion – mainland: Christian 30 per cent, Muslim 35 per cent, indigenous 35 per cent; Zanzibar: Muslim 99 per cent (2010 est)
Language – Swahili, English (both official), Arabic (especially on Zanzibar)
Population density – 52 per sq. km (2011)
Urban population – 27.2 per cent (2012 est)
Median age (years) – 17.4 (2014 est)
National anthem – 'Mungu ibariki Afrika' ['God Bless Africa']
National day – 26 April (Union Day)
Death penalty – Retained (last used 1995)
CPI score – 33 (111)

CLIMATE AND TERRAIN

Tanzania comprises the former Tanganyika, on the mainland of east Africa, and the islands of Zanzibar, Pemba and Mafia. Most of the country lies on the central African plateau, from which rise mountains that run across the centre of the country from north-east to south-west. Peaks include Mt Kilimanjaro (5,895m), the highest point on the continent of Africa; the lowest point is 0m (Indian Ocean). Large areas of lakes Victoria, Tanganyika and Malawi (Nyasa) lie on the northern and western borders, and there are smaller lakes in the north-east and south-west. The Serengeti National Park covers an area of 9,656 sq. km in the north of the country. The climate is tropical, modified by altitude, with a rainy season from November to April except in coastal regions, which get most rain between March and May; rainfall is sporadic in the interior but more reliable and heavier on the coast.

POLITICS

The 1977 constitution was amended in 1992 to introduce multiparty elections, and in 2000 to allow the president to nominate up to ten members of parliament. The executive president is directly elected for a five-year term, renewable once. The president is always from Tanganyika and the vice-president is always from Zanzibar. The unicameral National Assembly *(Bunge)* has 357 members: 239 directly elected, 102 seats reserved for women, ten appointed by the president (including five women), five chosen by Zanzibar's legislature, and the speaker. All serve a five-year term. The *Bunge* enacts laws that apply to the whole of Tanzania and laws that apply only to the mainland; laws that apply specifically to Zanzibar are enacted by the island's own legislature, the 81-member House of Representatives. Zanzibar also has its own directly elected president (who is a member of the Union government) and legislature.

In the 2010 national elections, Jakaya Kikwete was re-elected president, and the Revolutionary Party of Tanzania (CCM) retained its overwhelming majority in the legislature. In Zanzibar's simultaneous 2010 presidential and legislative elections, the CCM candidate Ali Mohamed Shein was elected president, and the CCM retained a narrow majority in the legislature.

HEAD OF STATE

President of the United Republic, Jakaya Kikwete, *elected* 14 December 2005, *took office* 21 December 2005, *re-elected* 2010
Vice-President, Mohammed Gharib Bilal
President of Zanzibar, Ali Mohamed Shein

SELECTED GOVERNMENT MEMBERS *as at July 2013*
Prime Minister, Mizengo Pinda
Defence, Hussein Mwiny
Finance, Mary Nagu

HIGH COMMISSION FOR THE UNITED REPUBLIC OF TANZANIA

3 Stratford Place, London W1C 1AS
T 020-7569 1470 E tanzarep@tanzania-online.gov.uk
W www.tanzania-online.gov.uk
High Commissioner, HE Peter Kallaghe, *apptd* 2010

BRITISH HIGH COMMISSION

PO Box 9200, Umoja House, Garden Avenue, Dar es Salaam
T (+255) (22) 229 0000 E bhc.dar@fco.gov.uk
W www.gov.uk/government/world/tanzania
High Commissioner, HE Dianna Patricia Melrose, *apptd* 2013

DEFENCE

Aged 16–49, 2010 est	Males	Females
Available for military service	9,985,445	–
Fit for military service	5,860,339	5,882,279

Military expenditure – US$308m (2013 est)

ECONOMY AND TRADE

State control has been dismantled gradually since the mid-1980s. Liberalisation and modernisation policies, supported by the World Bank, IMF and aid donors, have increased private-sector growth and investment. However, 36 per cent of the population still lives below the poverty line. The high price of gold and an increase in production saw the economy grow by 6 to 7 per cent from 2009 to 2013.

Agriculture is the mainstay of the economy, accounting for 27.6 per cent of GDP, about 80 per cent of employment and 85 per cent of exports. It provides coffee, tea, cotton, pyrethrum, cashew nuts, grains, fruit and vegetables as well as the raw materials for industries producing sugar, beer, cigarettes and sisal twine. Zanzibar and Pemba produce cloves and clove oil, and coconuts and their derivatives. Increased output of minerals (chiefly diamonds, gold and iron) has driven recent economic growth, and salt, soda ash, cement, petroleum products, footwear, clothing, wood products and fertiliser are also produced. Tourism is a major source of revenue, especially for Zanzibar. Industry accounts for 25 per cent of GDP and services for 47.4 per cent.

The main trading partners are China, India, the UAE and Kenya. Principal exports are gold, coffee, cashew nuts, manufactures (especially clothing) and cotton. The main imports are consumer goods, machinery and transport equipment, industrial raw materials and crude oil.

GNI – US$27,983m; US$570 per capita (2012; mainland Tanzania only)
Annual average growth of GDP – 7 per cent (2013 est)
Inflation rate – 7.8 per cent (2013 est)
Total external debt – US$13,8200m (2013 est)
Imports – US$11,266m (2012)
Exports – US$5,075m (2012)

BALANCE OF PAYMENTS
Trade – US$6,191m deficit (2012)
Current Account – US$2,131m deficit (2010)

Trade with UK	2012	2013
Imports from UK	£175,309,629	£170,936,596
Exports to UK	£44,209,299	£41,791,304

COMMUNICATIONS

Airports – The principal international airports are at Dar es Salaam, Kilimanjaro and Zanzibar
Waterways – The three great lakes (Tanganyika, Victoria and Nyasa) are the principal trade routes with neighbouring countries; the main seaports are Dar es Salaam, Tanga, Mtwara, Zanzibar, Mkoani and Wete (Pemba)
Roadways and railways – 86,472km; 3,689km
Telecommunications – 161,100 fixed lines (2011) and 27.22 million mobile subscriptions (2012); there were 678,000 internet users in 2009
Internet code and IDD – tz; 255 (from UK), 44 (to UK)
Major broadcasters – The state-run Tanzania Broadcasting Corporation is one of the most popular broadcasters, alongside the privately owned Independent Media
Press – The government-owned *Daily News* is the country's oldest daily newspaper
WPFI score – 27,3 (69)

EDUCATION AND HEALTH

Education is compulsory for seven years.
Literacy rate – 68 per cent (2010 est)
Gross enrolment ratio (percentage of relevant age group) – primary 93 per cent; secondary 35 per cent (2012 est)
Health expenditure (per capita) – US$37 (2011)
Hospital beds (per 1,000 people) – 0.7 (2010)

Life expectancy (years) – 61.24 (2014 est)
Mortality rate – 8.20 (2014 est)
Birth rate – 36.82 (2014 est)
Infant mortality rate – 43.74 (2014 est)
HIV / AIDS adult prevalence – 5.1 per cent (2012 est)

THAILAND

Ratcha Anachak Thai – Kingdom of Thailand

Area – 513,120 sq. km
Capital – Bangkok (Krung Thep); population, 7,135,267 (2012)
Major cities – Chon Buri, Nonthaburi, Samut Prakan, Udon Thani
Currency – Baht of 100 satang
Population – 67,741,401 rising at 0.35 per cent a year (2014 est); Thai (95.9 per cent), Burmese (2 per cent) (2010 est)
Religion – Buddhist 93.6 per cent (predominantly Theravada), Muslim 4.9 per cent (predominantly Sunni)
Language – Thai (official), English, Burmese
Population density – 130 per sq. km (2011)
Urban population – 34.4 per cent (2012 est)
Median age (years) – 36.2 (2014 est)
National anthem – 'Phleng Chat' ['National Song']
National day – 5 December (Birthday of the King)
Death penalty – Retained (last used 2009)
CPI score – 35 (102)

CLIMATE AND TERRAIN

Thailand is divided geographically into four regions: the north is mountainous and forested; to the north-east is the semi-arid Korat plateau; the centre is a fertile plain lying in the Chao Phraya basin; and the south is the narrow, mountainous isthmus of Kra. Extremes of elevation range from 2,576m (Doi Inthanon) to 0m (Gulf of Thailand). The principal rivers are the Chao Phraya and its tributaries in the central plains and the Mekong on the north and eastern borders. The climate is tropical, with a monsoon season from June to October and high humidity.

POLITICS

On 22 May 2014, the Royal Thai Armed Forces conducted a millitary coup after months of political tension between the ruling Pheu Thai Party and the opposition People's Democratic Reform Committee. Following the successful corruption proceedings filed against prime minister Yingluck and her subsequent removal from office on 7 May, martial law was declared by the military on 20 May before a new millitary government styled the National Council for Peace and Order was established. A number of politicians from across the political spectrum have been arrested. Largely peaceful anti-coup protests have taken place.

	Reunification of country under first king of the present Chakri dynasty	Revolution; becomes a constitutional monarchy with parliamentary government	Under military control	Military coup ousts Prime Minister Thaksin Shinawatra	PPP dissolved following mass protests against electoral fraud; replaced by coalition led by Democratic Party	
Isolationist policy adopted						

c.1200   c.1700   c.1875   1941–5   1992   2007   2014
    1699   1782   1932   2006   2008
         c.1945–91

| Thai nation founded | Invaded by Burma | Thailand (Siam) opens up trade with Europe; only country in the region to avoid colonisation by European power | Occupied by Japan | Mass demonstrations force power from military government | Democracy restored; Thaksin-affiliated People Power Party (PPP) wins elections | Prime Minister Yingluck resigns; military seize power |

Thailand is a constitutional monarchy with a hereditary monarch as head of state. The 2007 constitution has been suspended by the millitary and the senate has been dissolved.

HEAD OF STATE
HM The King of Thailand, King Bhumibol Adulyadej (Rama IX), *born* 5 December 1927, *succeeded* 9 June 1946
Heir, HRH Crown Prince Maha Vajiralongkorn, *born* 28 July 1952

SELECTED GOVERNMENT MEMBERS *as at September 2014*
Prime Minister, Cdr-in-Chief Gen. Prayuth Chan-ocha
Deputy Prime Ministers, Youngyuth Yutthamong, Pridiyathon Devakula, Thanasak Patimaprakorn *(Foreign Affairs, Finance, Defence); Finance* Sommal Phasi

ROYAL THAI EMBASSY
29–30 Queen's Gate, London SW7 5JB
T 020-7589 2944 E csinfo@thaiembassyuk.org.uk
W www.thaiembassyuk.org.uk
Ambassador Extraordinary and Plenipotentiary, HE Pasan Teparak, *apptd* 2012

BRITISH EMBASSY
14 Wireless Road, Bangkok 10330
T (+66) (0) 2 305 8333 E info.bangkok@fco.gov.uk
W www.gov.uk/government/world/thailand
Ambassador Extraordinary and Plenipotentiary, HE Mark Kent, *apptd* 2012

INSURGENCY
The Muslim minority is concentrated in the isthmus of Kra. A separatist campaign in the region began in the 1970s but died down in the 1980s. Violence resumed in 2004 and has since claimed over 3,000 lives.

FOREIGN RELATIONS
Sovereignty over border territory around the Hindu temple complex at Preah Vihear has been disputed with Cambodia for over a century. Although the temple complex was awarded to Cambodia in 1962, the status of adjacent territory remains unsettled. Tensions increased in 2008, when Cambodia had the temple listed as a UNESCO World Heritage Site, and there has been frequent sporadic fighting in the area between the countries' troops. Despite talks between the Cambodian and Thai prime ministers in 2011, a resolution to the dispute has failed to materialise.

DEFENCE

Aged 16–49, 2010 est	Males	Females
Available for military service	17,689,921	17,754,795
Fit for military service	13,308,372	14,182,567

Military expenditure – US$5,622m (2013)
Conscription duration – 24 months

ECONOMY AND TRADE
Thailand was transformed from an agricultural to an export-orientated industrial economy in the last quarter of the 20th century, sustaining steady growth after its quick recovery from the 1997 economic crisis. The 2008 global economic downturn caused the export-dependent economy to contract sharply, and flooding in October and November 2011 reduced growth to only 0.1 per cent in 2011; growth increased to 5.5 per cent in 2012, however, as the industrial sector recovered and the private sector improved. The Thai government is currently implementing tax reforms and a new minimum wage of 300 baht (US$10) per day.

The agricultural sector generates 12.1 per cent of GDP and employs 38.2 per cent of the workforce. The main crops are rice, cassava, rubber, maize, sugar cane, coconuts and soya beans. In recent years fishing and livestock production have grown in importance. There are reserves of natural gas, lignite, tin, tungsten and lead.

The main industry is tourism, which has been the chief foreign exchange earner since the 1980s. Other industries include textiles and clothing, agricultural processing, beverages, tobacco, cement, mining and light manufacturing (jewellery, electrical appliances, computers and parts), furniture, plastics and cars and vehicle parts. Industry contributes 43.6 per cent of GDP and services 48.2 per cent.

The main trading partners are Japan, China, the USA and the UAE. Principal exports are textiles and footwear, fish products, rice, rubber, jewellery, cars, computers and electrical appliances. The main imports are capital goods, intermediate goods and raw materials, consumer goods and fuels.

GNI – US$351,389m; US$5,210 per capita (2012)
Annual average growth of GDP – 3.1 per cent (2013 est)
Inflation rate – 2.2 per cent (2013 est)
Population below poverty line – 13.2 per cent (2011 est)
Unemployment – 0.8 per cent (2013 est)
Total external debt – US$86,100m (2013 est)
Imports – US$250,238m (2012)
Exports – US$228,175m (2012)

BALANCE OF PAYMENTS
Trade – US$22,062m surplus (2012)
Current Account – US$169m surplus (2012)

Trade with UK	2012	2013
Imports from UK	£1,881,541,646	£1,832,619,968
Exports to UK	£2,513,489,724	£2,598,596,681

COMMUNICATIONS
Airports and waterways – Bangkok is the main international airport and the main seaports are located in Bangkok and Sattahip; there are also 3,701km of inland waterways
Roadways and railways – 180,053km; 4,071km
Telecommunications – 6.391 million fixed lines and 84.075 million mobile subscriptions (2012); there were 17.48 million internet users in 2009
Internet and IDD – th; 66 (from UK), 1 44 (to UK)
Media – Newspapers are largely privately run, with popular titles including *Bangkok Post* and *Thairath*; chief broadcasters include the government-owned Thai TV3 and the military-owned TV5
WPFI score – 37,94 (130)

EDUCATION AND HEALTH

Primary and lower secondary education is compulsory and free, and upper secondary education is free in government schools.

Literacy rate – 93.5 per cent (2012 est)
Gross enrolment ratio (percentage of relevant age group) – primary 91 per cent (2011 est); secondary 87 per cent; tertiary 51 per cent (2012 est)
Health expenditure (per capita) – US$202 (2011)
Life expectancy (years) – 74.18 (2014 est)
Mortality rate – 7.72 (2014 est)
Birth rate – 11.26 (2014 est)
Infant mortality rate – 9.86 (2014 est)
HIV/AIDS adult prevalence – 1.1 per cent (2012 est)

TIMOR–LESTE

Republika Demokratika Timor Lorosa'e / Republica Democratica de Timor-Leste – Democratic Republic of Timor-Leste

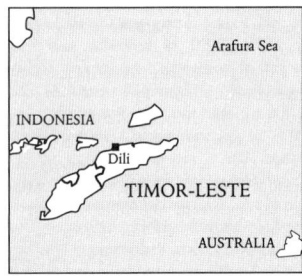

Area – 14,874 sq. km. Includes the enclave of Oecussi
Capital – Dili; population, 166,000 (2009)
Major towns – Baucau, Los Palos, Maliana, Pantemakassar (Oecussi), Same
Currency – US dollar (US$) of 100 cents
Population – 1,201,542 rising at 2.44 per cent a year (2014 est)
Religion – Christian (Roman Catholic 96.8 per cent, Protestant 2.2 per cent, Muslim 0.3 per cent (est)
Language – Tetum, Portuguese (both official), Indonesian, English, around 16 indigenous languages
Population density – 79 per sq. km (2011)
Urban population – 28.7 per cent (2012 est)
Median age (years) – 18.5 (2014 est)
National anthem – 'Patria' ['Fatherland']
National day – 28 November (Independence Day)
Death penalty – Abolished for all crimes (since 1999)
CPI score – 30 (119)
Literacy rate – 58 per cent (2010 est)
Gross enrolment ratio (percentage of relevant age group) – primary 117 per cent; secondary 56 per cent; tertiary 16.7 per cent (2011 est)
Health expenditure (per capita) – US$46 (2011)
Life expectancy (years) – 67.39 (2014 est)
Mortality rate – 6.18 (2014 est)

Birth rate – 34.48 (2014 est)
Infant mortality rate – 38.79 (2014 est)

CLIMATE AND TERRAIN

The republic comprises the eastern half of the island of Timor, plus the enclave of Oecussi, which lies on the northern coast, separated from the rest of the country by the Indonesian province of West Timor. The island, about 296km long and 72km wide, lies at the eastern end of the Malay archipelago and is the largest of the Lesser Sunda Islands. The interior is covered in forests and mountains. Elevation extremes range from 2,963m (Mt Tatamailau) to 0m (Timor Sea). The climate is tropical.

POLITICS

The 2002 constitution established a parliamentary democracy. The president is directly elected for a five-year term, renewable once. The unicameral National Parliament has 65 members, directly elected for a five-year term. The council of ministers is nominated by the prime minister, who is appointed by the president.

The 2012 presidential election was won in the second round by Jose Maria Vasconcelos. In the 2012 legislative election, the National Congress for Timorese Reconstruction party, led by former guerrilla leader Xanana Gusmao, won over 36 per cent of the vote but failed to claim an overall majority.

HEAD OF STATE
President, Jose Maria Vasconcelos, *elected* 16 April 2012, *took office* 30 May 2012

SELECTED GOVERNMENT MEMBERS *as at August 2014*
Prime Minister, Xanana Gusmao
Deputy Prime Minister, Fernando Lasama
Finance, Emilia Pires
Foreign Affairs, José Luís Guterres

BRITISH EMBASSY
Ambassador Extraordinary and Plenipotentiary, HE Mark Canning, *apptd* 2011, resident at Jakarta, Indonesia

ECONOMY AND TRADE

An internationally funded programme in 2002–5 achieved substantial reconstruction of the infrastructure destroyed in the 1999 post-referendum violence, but the civil unrest of 2006 caused further damage and disrupted economic activity. Economic growth since independence is largely owing to the exploitation of offshore oil and gas deposits, which has boosted government revenue but has had little impact on unemployment levels; there are no domestic production facilities so oil and gas are piped to Australia for processing. High levels of poverty and unemployment, weak civil administration, a low skills base and inadequate infrastructure all hinder development, although in late 2011 parliament passed an ambitious infrastructure-focused budget which would allow the government to borrow for the first time in ten years. Oil revenues have caused the economy to grow by 8.3 per cent in 2012 and 8.1 per cent in 2013.

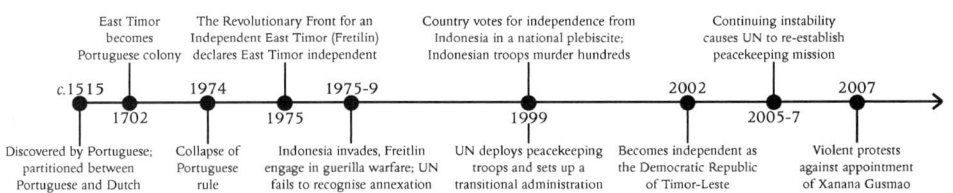

Industry contributes 81.6 per cent of GDP, services 15.8 per cent, and agriculture 2.6 per cent, although it engages 64 per cent of the population. The main commercial crops are coffee, timber, rice, maize, vegetables, tropical fruits and vanilla. The main trading partners are Australia, Indonesia and EU countries. Principal exports are coffee, oil, natural gas, sandalwood and marble. The main imports are food, fuels and machinery.

GNI – US$4,852m; US$3,620 per capita (2012)
Annual average growth of GDP – 8.1 per cent (2013 est)
Inflation rate – 4.5 per cent (2013 est)
Population below poverty line – 41 per cent (2009 est)
Unemployment – 18.4 per cent (2010 est)

BALANCE OF PAYMENTS
Current Account – US$2,340m surplus (2011)

Trade with UK	2012	2013
Imports from UK	£243,820	£198,686
Exports to UK	£116,884	£52,857

COMMUNICATIONS
Airports and waterways – The international airport and seaport are at Dili
Roadways – There are 6,040 of roads, including one major road linking the main townships on the northern coast
Telecommunications – 3,000 fixed lines and 621,200 mobile subscriptions (2012); there were 2,100 internet users in 2009
Internet code and IDD – tl; 670 (from UK), 44 (to UK)
Media – Televisao de Timor-Leste is the main public-owned broadcaster; there are three daily newspapers, including the *Timor Post*
WPFI score – 29,04 (77)

TOGO

République togolaise – Togolese Republic

Area – 56,785 sq. km
Capital – Lomé; population, 1,815,938 (2012)
Major cities – Atakpamé, Kara, Sokodé
Currency – Franc CFA of 100 centimes
Population – 7,351,374 rising at 2.71 per cent a year (2014 est); 37 tribes, largest of which are Ewe, Mina and Kabre.
Religion – Indigenous beliefs 51 per cent, Christian 29 per cent, Muslim 20 per cent
Language – French (official), Ewe, Mina (in the south), Kabye, Dagomba (in the north)
Population density – 119 per sq. km (2011)
Urban population – 38.5 per cent (2012 est)
Median age (years) – 19.6 (2014 est)

National anthem – 'Salut à toi, pays de nos aïeux' ['Hail to Thee, Land of Our Forefathers']
National day – 27 April (Independence Day)
Death penalty – Abolished for all crimes (since 2009)
CPI score – 29 (123)
Literacy rate – 60 per cent (2011 est)
Gross enrolment ratio (percentage of relevant age group) – primary 140 per cent; secondary 46 per cent; (2011 est)
Health expenditure (per capita) – US$45 (2011)
Hospital beds (per 1,000 people) – 0.7 (2011)
Life expectancy (years) – 64.06 (2014 est)
Mortality rate – 7.43(2014 est)
Birth rate – 34.52 (2014 est)
Infant mortality rate – 46.73 (2014 est)
HIV/AIDS adult prevalence – 2.9 per cent (2012 est)

CLIMATE AND TERRAIN
From hills in the centre of the country, the terrain declines to savannah in the north and in the south to a plateau that leads to a coastal plain with marshes and lagoons. Elevation extremes range from 986m (Mt Agou) to 0m (Atlantic Ocean). The climate in the south is tropical with two wet seasons (March to July and September to November). In the north it is semi-arid with one wet season (May to September). The average temperature in Lomé is 27°C.

HISTORY AND POLITICS
Germany established a protectorate, Togoland, over the area in 1884, and this was occupied on the outbreak of the First World War by Britain and France. The country was divided between Britain and France as a League of Nations mandate after the war and the mandate was renewed by the UN in 1946. In 1957, following a plebiscite, British Togoland integrated with Ghana when it became independent. French Togoland achieved independence as the Republic of Togo in 1960.

There was a military coup in 1963 led by Gnassingbé Eyadéma, who installed a civilian president. In 1967 Eyadéma overthrew the government and became president himself, introducing a one-party state under his *Rassemblement du peuple togolais* (RPT). Violent demonstrations in 1990 forced the government to introduce a multiparty constitution in 1992. Eyadéma and the RPT were returned to power in the first multiparty elections in 1993 and in two subsequent elections. The regime continued its brutal suppression of the opposition, particularly before and after elections.

After President Eyadéma's death in February 2005, the military attempted to install his son, Faure Gnassingbé, as president but this attracted domestic and international condemnation. Gnassingbé resigned as acting president, only to be elected to the presidency in April 2005. Following reconciliation talks in 2006, the government and opposition leaders signed an accord providing for the participation of opposition parties in a transitional government, and a national unity government was appointed until a legislative election was held in 2007. The election, was nevertheless won by the RPT; the 2013 election was won by President Gnassingbé's UNIR (Union for the Republic) party following the RPT's dissolution.

Under the 1992 constitution, the president is directly elected for a five-year term. The unicameral National Assembly has 81 members, who are directly elected for a five-year term. The prime minister is appointed by the president and appoints the cabinet in consultation with the president.

HEAD OF STATE
President, Defence, Faure Gnassingbé, *elected* 24 April 2005, *sworn in* 4 May 2005, *re-elected* 2010

SELECTED GOVERNMENT MEMBERS *as at July 2014*
Prime Minister, Kwesi Séléagodji Ahoomey-Zunu
Economy and Finance, Adji Otheth Ayassor
Foreign Affairs, Robert Dussey

EMBASSY OF THE REPUBLIC OF TOGO
8 rue Alfred Roll, 75017 Paris, France
T (+33) (1) 4380 1213
Ambassador Extraordinary and Plenipotentiary, HE Calixte
Batossie Madjoulba, *apptd* 2011

BRITISH AMBASSADOR
HE Peter Jones, *apptd* 2011, resident at Accra, Ghana

DEFENCE

Aged 16–49, 2010 est	Males	Females
Available for military service	1,577,572	1,589,715
Fit for military service	1,104,536	1,158,061

Military expenditure – US$59m (2011 est)
Conscription duration – 24 months (selective)

ECONOMY AND TRADE

Progress on economic reform, intended to attract foreign investment and balance the budget, is slow, lacking impetus on privatisation and financial transparency. Resumption of aid to Togo, mostly suspended in the 1990s because of its human rights record, has increased since the 2007 election, and the country had 95 per cent of its external debt written off in 2010. Growth is hampered by declining productivity and underinvestment.

The economy is predominantly based on agriculture, accounting for 27.6 per cent of GDP, engaging 65 per cent of the workforce and providing most of the country's exports as well as the raw materials for industry. Industrial activity centres on phosphate mining, agricultural processing and manufacture of cement, handicrafts, textiles and beverages. Industry accounts for 33.7 per cent of GDP and 5 per cent of employment. The service sector accounts for 38.7 per cent of GDP and employs 30 per cent of the workforce.

The main export markets are India, Lebanon, Burkina Faso and Benin; imports come mainly from China (40.4 per cent) and EU states. Principal exports are re-exports, cotton, phosphates, coffee and cocoa. The main imports are machinery and equipment, foodstuffs and petroleum products.

GNI – US$3,331m; US$500 per capita (2012)
Annual average growth of GDP – 5.5 per cent (2013 est)
Inflation rate – 2.2 per cent (2013 est)
Total external debt – US$719m (2013 est)
Imports – US$1,793m (2012)
Exports – US$997m (2012)

BALANCE OF PAYMENTS
Trade – US$796m deficit (2012)
Current Account – US$212m deficit (2010)

Trade with UK	2012	2013
Imports from UK	£282,749,165	£90,972,300
Exports to UK	£448,026	£1,169,165

COMMUNICATIONS

Airports – The principal airport is at Lomé
Roadways and railways – 11,652km; 568km
Telecommunications – 225,000 fixed lines in use and 3.518 million mobile subscriptions (2012); there were 356,300 internet users in 2009

Internet code and IDD – tg; 228 (from UK), 44 (to UK)
Media – Télévision Togolaise is the principal, state-run broadcaster; daily newspapers include *Togo-Presse* and *Liberté*
WPFI score – 29 (76)

TONGA

Pule'anga Tonga – Kingdom of Tonga

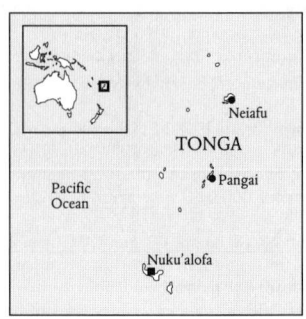

Area – 747 sq. km
Capital – Nuku'alofa, on Tongatapu; population, 25,000 (2011 est)
Currency – Pa'anga (T$) of 100 seniti
Population – 106,440 rising at 0.09 per cent a year (2014 est)
Religion – Christian (Free Wesleyan 37.3 per cent, Mormon 16.8 per cent, Roman Catholic 15.6 per cent, Free Church 11.4 per cent) (2006)
Language – English, Tongan (both official)
Population density – 145 per sq. km (2011)
Urban population – 23.5 per cent (2012 est)
Median age (years) – 22 (2014 est)
National anthem – 'Koe Fasi Oe Tu'i Oe Otu Tonga' ['Song of the King of the Tonga Islands']
National day – 4 June (Emancipation Day)
Death penalty – Retained (last used 1982)
Literacy rate – 99 per cent (2011 est)
Life expectancy (years) – 75.82 (2014 est)
Mortality rate – 4.86 (2014 est)
Birth rate – 23.55 (2014 est)
Infant mortality rate – 12.36 (2014 est)

CLIMATE AND TERRAIN

Tonga comprises over 170 islands in three groups, situated in the south Pacific Ocean some 724km east-south-east of Fiji. Most of the islands are of coral formation, but some are volcanic (Tofua, Kao and Niuafo'ou or 'Tin Can' Island). Elevation extremes range from 1,033m (on Kao Island) to 0m (Pacific Ocean). The climate is tropical, moderated by trade winds, with an average temperature of 24.8°C.

HISTORY AND POLITICS

The islands were settled by Polynesians from *c.*1000 AD. They were visited by European explorers from the 17th century. The country was reunited in 1845 after a civil war, and a modern constitution adopted in 1875. Tonga became a British protectorate in 1900, and regained full independence on 4 June 1970.

A pro-democracy movement began in 1992 and gathered momentum throughout the 1990s, with the first political party being established in 1994. Following consultation on political and constitutional reform in 2005 and negotiations in 2007, a commission reported in 2009, recommending reducing the monarchy to a ceremonial role and introducing a popularly elected legislature. These constitutional changes took effect with the 2010 legislative election.

In the 2010 legislative election, the Democratic Party of the Friendly Islands (DPFI), a breakaway faction of the pro-reform Human Rights and Democracy Movement, won 12 of the popularly elected seats, and independents the remaining five. The legislature elected a noble, Tu'ivakano, as prime minister.

The 1875 constitution was amended in 2003 to give greater powers to the king; the present king relinquished some of his executive powers in 2008 and most of the remainder in 2010, when new constitutional arrangements came into effect. The head of state is a hereditary monarch whose role is now largely ceremonial. The unicameral Legislative Assembly *(Fale Alea)* has 26 members: nine hereditary nobles elected by their peers, and 17 popularly elected representatives who serve a three-year term. The 14-member privy council acts as a cabinet. The prime minister is elected by the legislature.

HEAD OF STATE
HM The King of Tonga, King Tupou VI, *born* 12 July 1959, *acceded* 18 March 2012

SELECTED GOVERNMENT MEMBERS *as at July 2014*
Prime Minister, Foreign Affairs, Lord Tu'ivakano
Deputy Prime Minister, Samiu Vaipulu
Finance, 'Aisake Valu Eke

TONGA HIGH COMMISSION
36 Molyneux Street, London W1H 6AB
T 020-7724 5828 E
office@tongahighcom.co.uk
Acting High Commissioner, HE Sione Sonata Tupou, *apptd* 2012

BRITISH HIGH COMMISSIONER
HE Roderick Drummond, resident at Suva, Fiji, *apptd* 2013

ECONOMY AND TRADE

There are few natural resources and the country is dependent on foreign aid and remittances from Tongans working abroad. The government is encouraging the development of a private sector and committing increased funds towards education and health. Unemployment is high at 13 per cent and most severe among the young.

The main economic activities are agriculture, fishing and tourism, which is the second-largest source of foreign exchange revenue after remittances. The main crops are squashes, coconuts, bananas, vanilla beans, cocoa, coffee, ginger and black pepper. Fish is an important staple food. A small light industry sector processes agricultural produce.

The main export markets are South Korea, the USA and New Zealand; imports come chiefly from Fiji and New Zealand. Principal exports are squashes, fish, vanilla beans and root crops. The main imports are foodstuffs, machinery and transport equipment, fuels and chemicals.
GNI – US$4485m; US$4,220 per capita (2012)
Annual average growth of GDP – 1 per cent (2013 est)
Inflation rate – 2 per cent (2013 est)
Population below poverty line – 24 per cent (FY2003/2004 est)
Unemployment – 13 per cent (2004 est)
Total external debt – US$215.8m (2013 est)
Imports – US$199m (2012)
Exports – US$14m (2012)

BALANCE OF PAYMENTS
Trade – US$185m deficit (2012)
Current Account – US$29m deficit (2012)

Trade with UK	2012	2013
Imports from UK	£777,038	£144,526
Exports to UK	£123,099	£24,685

COMMUNICATIONS

Airports and waterways – There is one airport; the principal port is Nuku'alofa
Roadways – 680km
Telecommunications – There are 30,000 main telephone lines in use (2012), 56,000 mobile telephone lines subscriptions (2012); there were 8,400 internet users in 2009
Internet code and IDD – to; 676 (from UK), 44 (to UK)
Media – The weekly newspaper, *Tonga Chronicle,* and the Tonga Broadcasting Commission, which operates television and radio stations, are both state-run

TRINIDAD AND TOBAGO

Republic of Trinidad and Tobago

Area – 5,128 sq. km
Capital – Port of Spain, on Trinidad; population, 66,000 (2011)
Major towns – Chaguanas, San Fernando, Scarborough (Tobago)
Currency – Trinidad and Tobago dollar (T$) of 100 cents
Population – 1,223,916 falling at 0.11 per cent a year (2014 est)
Religion – Christian (Protestant 32.1 per cent, Roman Catholic 21.6 per cent, other 20.5 per cent), Hindu 18.2 per cent, Muslim 5 per cent, Jehovah's Witnesses 1.5 per cent
Language – English (official), Caribbean Hindustani (a dialect of Hindi), French, Spanish, Chinese
Population density – 260 per sq. km (2011)
Urban population – 14 per cent (2012 est)
Median age (years) – 34.4 (2014 est)
National anthem – 'Forged from the Love of Liberty'
National day – 31 August (Independence Day)
Death penalty – Retained (last used 1999)
CPI score – 38 (83)

CLIMATE AND TERRAIN

Trinidad, the most southerly of the West Indian islands, lies 11km off the north coast of Venezuela. The island is mostly flat, with low mountains, the Northern Range, across almost its entire northern width and some low hills in the centre. Elevation extremes range from 940m (Mt Aripo) to 0m (Caribbean Sea). Pitch Lake, on the south-west coast, is the world's largest natural source of asphalt.

Tobago lies 30km north-east of Trinidad. The island has a range of hills, Main Ridge, running along its length; the highest point is 549m. Several islands, mainly, Chacachacare,

Huevos, Monos and Gaspar Grande, lie west of Corozal Point, the north-west extremity of Trinidad.

The climate is tropical, with a wet season from June to December. Temperatures are constant all year round.

HISTORY AND POLITICS

Trinidad is believed to be the oldest site of human habitation in the Caribbean archipelago, with excavated human remains dating back 7,200 years. The islands were home to a number of indigenous peoples, including the Nepuyo, Yaio and Caribs.

Trinidad and Tobago were discovered by Columbus in 1498. Trinidad was colonised in 1532 by Spain, capitulated to the British in 1797, and was ceded to Britain in 1802. Tobago was colonised by the Dutch from the 1630s but subsequently changed hands numerous times until it was ceded to Britain by France in 1814. The two islands were amalgamated into a single British colony in 1889. Internal self-government was granted in 1959 and independence was attained in 1962; the country became a republic in 1976.

The People's National Movement (PNM) has dominated post-independence politics, only out of office in 1986–91, 1995–2001, and since May 2010. The PNM won the 2009 election for the Tobago legislature, but lost the early general election in 2010 to the People's Partnership coalition, which took office under Kamla Persad-Bissessar, the country's first female prime minister. President Richards, first elected in 2003, was declared re-elected in 2008, when he was the only candidate for the presidency. President Richards was succeeded by the independent candidate Anthony Carmona; Carmona was declared elected president unopposed in February 2013.

Under the 1976 constitution, the president is elected for a five-year term by an electoral college consisting of both houses of the legislature. The bicameral parliament comprises the House of Representatives and the senate. The former has 41 members directly elected for a five-year term. The senate has 31 members, of whom 16 are appointed on the advice of the prime minister, six on the advice of the leader of the opposition and nine at the discretion of the president, to serve a five-year term.

Since 1980 Tobago has had internal self-government through its House of Assembly, which has 15 members, 12 directly elected and four appointed, who serve a four-year term.

HEAD OF STATE
President, Anthony Carmona, *elected* 15 February 2013, *took office* 18 March 2013

SELECTED GOVERNMENT MEMBERS *as at July 2014*
Prime Minister, Kamla Persad-Bissessar
Attorney-General, Anand Ramlogan
Finance, Larry Howai
Foreign Affairs, Winston Dookeran

HIGH COMMISSIONER OF THE REPUBLIC OF TRINIDAD AND TOBAGO
42 Belgrave Square, London SW1X 8NT
T 020-7245 9351 W www.tthighcommission.co.uk
High Commissioner, HE Garvin Nicholas, *apptd* 2011

BRITISH HIGH COMMISSION
PO Box 778, 19 St Clair Avenue, St Clair, Port of Spain
T (+868) 350 0444
W www.gov.uk/government/world/trinidad-and-tobago
High Commissioner, HE Arthur Snell, *apptd* 2011

DEFENCE

All aged 16–49, 2010 est	Males	Females
Available for military service	341,764	317,899
Fit for military service	269,824	261,735

ECONOMY AND TRADE

The country is the most prosperous in the Caribbean, owing largely to its oil and natural gas reserves, but the government has encouraged diversification into petrochemicals, aluminium, plastics, financial services and tourism to reduce its dependence on the energy sector. After years of steady growth, the economy contracted briefly in 2009 as export demand and oil prices fell. Crime and bureaucracy deter greater foreign investment.

The agricultural sector is small, accounting for 0.3 per cent of GDP; the main products are cocoa, rice, citrus fruits, coffee, vegetables and poultry. Apart from oil and gas extraction and processing, the main industries are tourism, food processing, production of chemicals, steel products, cement, beverages and cotton textiles.

The main trading partners are the USA (42.1 per cent of exports; 33.1 per cent of imports), Colombia, Argentina and Chile. Principal exports are oil and petroleum products, liquefied natural gas, chemicals, steel products, beverages, cereals and cereal products, sugar, cocoa, coffee, citrus fruits, vegetables and flowers. The main imports are fuels, lubricants, machinery, transport equipment, manufactured goods, food, chemicals and livestock.

GNI – US$20,080m; US$14,710 per capita (2012)
Annual average growth of GDP – 1.6 per cent (2013 est)
Inflation rate – 5.4 per cent (2013 est)
Population below poverty line – 17 per cent (2007 est)
Unemployment – 5.9 per cent (2013 est)
Total external debt – US$4,823m (2013 est)
Imports – US$9,400m (2012)
Exports – US$13,100m (2012)

BALANCE OF PAYMENTS
Trade – US$3,700m surplus (2012)
Current Account – US$2,670m surplus (2012)

Trade with UK	2012	2013
Imports from UK	£114,410,464	£128,434,980
Exports to UK	£74,506,535	£114,997,445

COMMUNICATIONS

Airports and waterways – The international airport is at Port of Spain on Trinidad, and Tobago is served by Crown Point airport; the three main ports are Scarborough (Tobago), Port of Spain and Point Lisas
Roadways – 8,320km
Telecommunications – 287,000 fixed lines and 1.884 million mobile subscriptions (2012); there were 593,000 internet users in 2009
Internet code and IDD – tt; 1 868 (from (UK), 011 44 (to UK)
Media – The privately run TV6 dominates television broadcasting and *Newsday* and *Trinidad Guardian* are popular newspapers

EDUCATION AND HEALTH

Education is free at all state-owned and government-assisted denominational schools, and at certain faculties at the University of the West Indies.
Literacy rate – 99 per cent (2011 est)
Gross enrolment ratio (percentage of relevant age group) – primary 106 per cent (2012 est); secondary 90 per cent (2011 est)

Health expenditure (per capita) – US$956 (2011)
Hospital beds (per 1,000 people) – 2.1 (2010)
Life expectancy (years) – 72.29 (2014 est)
Mortality rate – 8.48 (2014 est)
Birth rate – 13.8 (2014 est)
Infant mortality rate – 24.82 (2014 est)
HIV/AIDS adult prevalence – 1.6 per cent (2012 est)

TUNISIA

Al-Jumhuriyah at-Tunisiyah – Tunisian Republic

Area – 163,610 sq. km
Capital – Tunis; population, 790,000 (2011)
Major cities – Sfax, Sousse
Currency – Tunisian dinar of 1,000 millimes
Population – 10,937,521 rising at 0.92 per cent a year
    (2014 est)
Religion – Muslim 99.1 per cent (predominantly Sunni) (est);
    small minorities of Christians and Jews. Sunni Islam is the
    official religion
Language – Arabic (official), French, Berber
Population density – 69 per sq. km (2011)
Urban population – 66.5 per cent (2012 est)
Median age (years) – 31.4 (2014 est)
National anthem – 'Humat al-Hima' ['Defenders of the
    Homeland']
National day – 20 March (Independence Day)
Death penalty – Retained (last used 1991)
CPI score – 41 (77)

CLIMATE AND TERRAIN

A central plain rises to mountains in the north, and in the semi-arid south merges into the Sahara desert. There are salt lakes in the west. Elevation extremes range from 1,544m (Jebel ech Chambi) to −17m (Shatt al Gharsah). The northern and coastal regions have a Mediterranean climate, while there is a desert climate in the south. Average temperatures in Tunis range from 11°C in January to 27°C in August.

HISTORY AND POLITICS

The area was ruled successively by the Phoenicians, Carthaginians, Romans, Byzantines and Arabs before becoming a largely autonomous part of the Ottoman Empire in the 16th century. In the 19th century French influence grew and it was formally declared a French protectorate in 1883. It was briefly occupied by Germany during the Second World War (1942–3), and became independent as a monarchy under the bey in 1956. In 1957 the bey was deposed and the country became a republic under one-party rule with Habib Bourguiba as president.

Multiparty legislative elections were held in 1981, but the ruling party, the Constitutional Democratic Rally (RCD),

retained its grip on power until 2011. Although proclaimed president for life in 1975, President Bourguiba was deposed in 1987 on the grounds of senility by the prime minister Zine el-Abidine Ben Ali. Ben Ali was subsequently elected president in unopposed elections in 1989 and 1994, and in multiparty elections in 1999, 2004 and 2009.

Ben Ali's authoritarian regime maintained tight constraints on the political opposition, with electoral laws and media access weighted in favour of the RCD. However, nationwide protests over unemployment and political restrictions from December 2010 forced Ben Ali to leave office and flee the country in January 2011, and the RCD was dissolved by the courts in March 2011. Moncef Marzouki was elected interim president by the new Constituent Assembly in December 2011; his nomination followed legislative elections in which the former opposition party En-Nahda won the most seats but not an overall majority. Attempts to implement some Islamic reforms by the moderate Islamist government resulted in protests by supporters of secularism and more violent demonstrations from Salafi Islamists. In July 2013, the assassination of the Arab nationalist politician Mohamed Brahmi caused a general strike and calls for the government to resign. An interim government was created in December 2013, with new electoral laws to govern legislative and presidential elections approved in May 2014. Legislative elections will take place in October 2014.

The new constitution was implemented on 26 January 2014. The legislature, the Assembly of People's Representatives (Majlis Nuwab al-Shab), is unicameral and directly elected for a five-year term. It has 217 seats, 18 of which are reserved for Tunisians abroad.

HEAD OF STATE
Interim President, Moncef Marzouki, took office 12 December
    2011

SELECTED GOVERNMENT MEMBERS as at July 2014
Prime Minister (Interim), Mehdi Jomaa
Defence, Ghazi Jeribi
Finance, Hakim Ben Hammouda
Foreign Affairs, Mongi Hamdi

EMBASSY OF TUNISIA
29 Prince's Gate, London SW7 1QG
T 020-7584 8117 E london@tunisianembassy.co.uk
W http://www.at-londres.diplomatie.gov.tn/
Ambassador Extraordinary and Plenipotentiary, HE Nabil
    Ammar, apptd 2012

BRITISH EMBASSY
Rue du Lac Windermere, Les Berges du Lac, 1053 Tunis
T (+216) (71) 108 700 E britishembassytunis@fco.gov.uk
W www.gov.uk/government/world/tunisia
Ambassador Extraordinary and Plenipotentiary, HE Hamish
    Cowell, apptd 2013

DEFENCE

Aged 16–49, 2010 est	Males	Females
Available for military service	2,846,572	2,952,180
Fit for military service	2,397,716	2,484,097

Military expenditure – US$978m (2013)
Conscription duration – 12 months (selective)

ECONOMY AND TRADE

The economy is diverse and an increasing proportion is in private ownership, with further liberalisation planned.

Growth was steady from the late 1990s until 2008, although the economy contracted in 2009 as export demand dropped.

A focus on political problems in 2012 and 2013 led to a neglect of the economy that resulted in several downgrades of Tunisia's credit rating. Present economic problems include budget and current account deficits, high unemployment, and economic disparities between the more developed coastal region and the impoverished interior.

Agriculture and fisheries account for 8.6 per cent of GDP; the main products are olives, grain, tomatoes, citrus fruits, sugar beets, dates, almonds, meat and dairy products. The main industries are oil production, mining (principally phosphates and iron ore), tourism, processing agricultural products and manufacture of textiles, footwear and beverages.

The main trading partners are EU countries, especially France and Italy. Principal exports are clothing, semi-finished goods and textiles, agricultural products, mechanical goods, phosphates and chemicals, hydrocarbons and electrical equipment. The main imports are textiles, machinery and equipment, hydrocarbons, chemicals and foodstuffs.

GNI – US$43,638m; US$4,150 per capita (2012)
Annual average growth of GDP – 2.8 per cent (2013 est)
Inflation rate – 6.1 per cent (2013 est)
Population below poverty line – 15.5 per cent (2010 est)
Unemployment – 17.2 per cent (2013 est)
Total external debt – US$26,950m (2013 est)
Imports – US$24,447m (2012)
Exports – US$17,008m (2012)

BALANCE OF PAYMENTS
Trade – US$7,439m deficit (2012)
Current Account – US$3,674m deficit (2012)

Trade with UK	2012	2013
Imports from UK	£159,051,813	£160,165,273
Exports to UK	£345,707,275	£448,309,844

COMMUNICATIONS
Airports and waterways – The principal airports are at Tunis, Monastir and Djerba, and the main ports include Bizerte, Sfax and Rades
Roadways and railways – 19,418km; 2,165km
Telecommunications – 1.105 million fixed lines and 12.84 million mobile subscriptions (2012); there were 3.5 million internet users in 2009
Internet code and IDD – tn; 216 (from UK), 44 (to UK)
Major broadcasters – National Tunisian TV operates two national TV channels
Press – There are five daily newspapers, including *La Presse* and *Esshafa*
WPFI score – 38,69 (133)

EDUCATION AND HEALTH
There are 11 years of free and compulsory education.
Literacy rate – 79 per cent (2010 est)
Gross enrolment ratio (percentage of relevant age group) – primary 110 per cent; secondary 91 per cent; tertiary 35 per cent (2012 est)
Health expenditure (per capita) – US$267 (2011)
Hospital beds (per 1,000 people) – 2.1 (2010)
Life expectancy (years) – 75.68 (2014 est)
Mortality rate – 5.94 (2014 est)
Birth rate – 16.9 (2014 est)
Infant mortality rate – 23.19 (2014 est)

TURKEY

Turkiye Cumhuriyeti – Republic of Turkey

Area – 783,562 sq. km
Capital – Ankara (Angora), in Asia; population, 4,194,000 (2011)
Major cities – Adana, Antalya, Bursa, Gaziantep, Istanbul, Izmir, Konya
Currency – Turkish lira (TL) of 100 kurus
Population – 81,619,392 rising at 1.12 per cent a year (2014 est); Turkish (70–75 per cent), Kurdish (18 per cent) (2008 est)
Religion – Muslim (predominantly Sunni) 99.8 per cent (est)
Language – Turkish (official), Kurdish, Dimli, Azeri, Kabardian
Population density – 95 per sq. km (2011)
Urban population – 72.5 per cent (2012 est)
Median age (years) – 29.6 (2014 est)
National anthem – 'Istiklal Marsi' ['The Independence March']
National day – 29 October (Republic Day)
Death penalty – Abolished for all crimes (since 2004)
CPI score – 50 (53)

CLIMATE AND TERRAIN
Turkey in Europe consists of the relatively low-lying area of Eastern Thrace, including the cities of Istanbul and Edirne, and is separated from Asia by the Bosporus at Istanbul and by the Sea of Marmara and the Dardanelles (a strait about 64km in length, with a width varying from 1.6km to 6.4km).

Turkey in Asia comprises the whole of Asia Minor or Anatolia. Western Anatolia consists of a high central plateau with narrow coastal plains fringed by mountains in the north and south. Eastern Anatolia is mountainous, the land falling to a plateau between the mountains and the Syrian border. Elevation extremes range from 5,166m (Mt Ararat) to 0m (Mediterranean Sea). The Euphrates and Tigris rivers rise in the eastern mountains, which also contain many lakes, including Lake Van. Anatolia is prone to earthquakes.

The climate is temperate, but more extreme in the interior. Average temperatures in Ankara range from −2°C in January to 20°C in July and August.

HISTORY AND POLITICS
The 1982 constitution has been amended several times, mostly recently in 2010; the 2010 amendments increase parliamentary control over the judiciary and the military. The current president was elected by the legislature for a single seven-year term; from 2014, the president will be directly elected for a four-year term, renewable once. The unicameral Turkish Grand National Assembly has 550

| | Ottoman Empire dissolved and much of | Joins Allies in Second | Civil unrest precipitates military | Further military intervention is tempered by constitutional and economic reforms; | |
| Ottoman Empire founded | its territory is partitioned | World War | intervention | becomes a candidate for EU membership | EU accession process begins |

c.1000   c.1600   1923   1952   1980   2002

c.1200   1918   1945   1971   1997-9   2005

| Asia Minor comes under Turkish rule | Steady decline of Ottoman Empire begins | Sultanate abolished and Turkey is proclaimed a republic; Gazi Mustafa Kemal is elected president | Joins NATO | Military intervention to restore civil stability | Recep Tayyip Erdogan of the Islamic-based Justice and Development Party is elected prime minister; tension grows between secularists and Islamists |

members who were directly elected for a four-year term. The prime minister is appointed by the president and appoints the cabinet.

Tension between secularists and Islamists has grown in recent years, particularly since the Islamic-based Justice and Development Party (AKP), led by Recep Tayyip Erdogan, came to power in 2002. Secularists' concerns about the AKP's agenda caused a four-month political crisis in 2007, preventing the election of a new president and leading outgoing President Sezer to refuse approval of constitutional amendments. The impasse was ended by early legislative elections in July 2007, in which the AKP won a greatly increased majority. In August the AKP candidate, Abdullah Gul, was elected president in the third round of voting. The AKP retained its overall majority in the legislative election in June 2011. In August 2014, incumbent prime minister Recep Erdogan won the first direct election for a president, necessitating the selection of a new prime minister and a cabinet reshuffle.

HEAD OF STATE
President, Recep Tayyip Erdogan, *elected* 10 August 2014, *sworn in* 28 August 2014

SELECTED GOVERNMENT MEMBERS *as at August 2014*
Prime Minister, Ahmet Davutoglu
Deputy Prime Ministers, Besir Atalay; Ali Babacan; Bulent Arinc; Emrullah Isler
Finance, Mehmet Simsek
Foreign Affairs, Disisleri Bakani

EMBASSY OF THE REPUBLIC OF TURKEY
43 Belgrave Square, London SW1X 8PA
T 020-7393 0202 E turkemb.london@mfa.gov.tr
W www.londra.be.mfa.gov.tr
Ambassador Extraordinary and Plenipotentiary, HE Abdurrahman Bilgic, *apptd* 2014

BRITISH EMBASSY
Sehit Ersan Caddesi 46/A, Cankaya, Ankara
T (+90) (312) 455 3344 E info.officer@fco.gov.uk
W www.gov.uk/government/world/turkey
Ambassador Extraordinary and Plenipotentiary, HE Richard Moore, *apptd* 2014

INSURGENCIES
Turkey's 12 million Kurds are the majority population in the south-east of the country, and have sought greater political and cultural rights for many years. The Kurdistan Workers' Party (PKK) has fought a guerrilla war for an ethnic homeland in the south-east since 1984 and has been blamed for bombings in other parts of Turkey. Conflict on the Turkey–Iraq border has caused tension in relations with Iraq, especially in 2008 after Turkish military incursions into the autonomous Kurdish area in northern Iraq, where PKK fighters have taken refuge. The government started to seek a political solution to the violence in 2009, introducing measures to increase Kurdish language rights and reduce the

military presence in the south-east. Iran and Turkey agreed in October 2011 to work together to defeat Kurdish militants.

Following a statement requesting a ceasefire by jailed PKK leader Abdullah Ocalan, Kurdish fighters led by Murat Karayilan agreed to withdraw from Turkey in May 2013.

DEFENCE

Aged 16–49, 2010 est	Males	Females
Available for military service	21,079,077	20,558,696
Fit for military service	17,664,510	17,340,816

Military expenditure – US$18,682m (2013)
Conscription duration – 6–15 months

ECONOMY AND TRADE
The economy combines modern industry and commerce with a traditional agriculture sector. The private sector is growing steadily following large-scale privatisations of basic industry, banking, transport and communications. Financial and fiscal reforms from 2002 achieved growth averaging over 5 per cent a year from 2005 to 2007, although large current account and trade deficits remain. Growth dropped to 2.2 per cent in 2012, but recovered to 3.8 per cent in 2013.

The agricultural sector accounts for 8.9 per cent of GDP and employs 25.5 per cent of the workforce. The principal crops are tobacco, cotton, grain, olives, sugar beets, pulses, nuts, citrus and other fruits, and livestock products. A diverse industrial sector is dominated by textiles and clothing (which employ one-third of the industrial workforce), food processing, vehicle assembly, electronics, mining, iron and steel, oil, construction, timber and paper. Turkey is also a destination and a transit route for oil and gas from central Asian countries. Tourism is a major industry and source of foreign revenue. Industry contributes 27.3 per cent of GDP and services 63.8 per cent.

The main trading partners are EU countries (especially Germany), Russia, China and Iraq. Principal exports are clothing, foodstuffs, textiles, metal manufactures and transport equipment. The main imports are machinery, chemicals, semi-finished manufactures, fuels and transport equipment.
GNI – US$782,278m; US$10,830 per capita (2012)
Annual average growth of GDP – 3.8 per cent (2013 est)
Inflation rate – 7.6 per cent (2013 est)
Population below poverty line – 16.9 per cent (2010 est)
Unemployment – 9.3 per cent (2013 est)
Total external debt – US$359,500m (2013)
Imports – US$236,545m (2012)
Exports – US$152,462m (2012)

BALANCE OF PAYMENTS
Trade – US$84,083m deficit (2012)
Current Account – US$47,750m deficit (2012)

Trade with UK	2012	2013
Imports from UK	£3,507,323,275	£3,833,480,458
Exports to UK	£5,669,037,918	£5,945,611,145

COMMUNICATIONS

Airports and waterways – The principal airports are at Istanbul and Ankara, and the main ports are at Istanbul (Europe) and Izmir (Asia)

Roadways and railways – 385,748km; 12,008km

Telecommunications – 15.86 million fixed lines and 67.68 million mobile subscriptions (2012); there were 27.23 million internet users in 2009

Internet code and IDD – tr; 90 (from UK), 44 (to UK)

Major broadcasters – Turkey has one state television and radio broadcaster, TRT, over 300 private television channels and more than 1,000 private radio stations

Press – There are around 40 national daily newspapers, including *Hurriyet*, *Milliyet* and *Cumhuriyet*

WPFI score – 45,87 (154)

EDUCATION AND HEALTH

Education is free and compulsory from the ages of six to 14.

Literacy rate – 94 per cent (2011 est)

Gross enrolment ratio (percentage of relevant age group) – primary 102 per cent; secondary 89 per cent; tertiary 61 per cent (2012 est)

Health expenditure (per capita) – US$696 (2011)

Hospital beds (per 1,000 people) – 2.5 (2010)

Life expectancy (years) – 73.29 (2014 est)

Mortality rate – 6.12 (2014 est)

Birth rate – 16.86 (2014 est)

Infant mortality rate – 21.43 (2014 est)

TURKMENISTAN

Area – 488,100 sq. km

Capital – Ashgabat; population, 683,000 (2011)

Major cities – Dashoguz, Turkmenabat

Currency – Manat of 100 tennesi

Population – 5,171,943 rising at 1.14 per cent a year (2014 est); Turkmen (85 per cent), Uzbek (5 per cent), Russian (4 per cent) (2003 est)

Religion – Muslim 89 per cent (majority Sunni), Christian 9 per cent (mainly Eastern Orthodox) (est)

Language – Turkmen (official), Russian, Uzbek

Population density – 11 per sq. km (2011)

Urban population – 49 per cent (2012 est)

Median age (years) – 26.6 (2014 est)

National anthem – 'Garassyz, Bitarap, Turkmenistanyn Dowlet Gimni' ['National Anthem of Independent Neutral Turkmenistan']

National day – 27 October (Independence Day, 1991)

Death penalty – Abolished for all crimes (since 1999)

CPI score – 17 (168)

Literacy rate – 100 per cent (2011 est)

Health expenditure (per capita) – US$129 (2011)

Hospital beds (per 1,000 people) – 4.1 (2011)

Life expectancy (years) – 69.47 (2014 est)

Mortality rate – 6.16 (2014 est)

Birth rate – 19.46 (2014 est)

Infant mortality rate – 38.13 (2014 est)

CLIMATE AND TERRAIN

Over 80 per cent of the country is taken up by the Kara Kum (Black Sands) desert. There are mountains in the south and along the Iranian border, and areas below sea level along the edges of the Caspian Sea. Elevation extremes range from 3,139m (Gora Ayribaba) to −81m (Lake Akchanaya, although Lake Sarygamysh sometimes has a lower elevation because of fluctuations in its water level). There is a subtropical desert climate. Average temperatures in Ashgabat range from 3.5°C in January to 31.3°C in July.

HISTORY AND POLITICS

Turkmenistan was conquered successively by the Persians, Greeks (under Alexander the Great), Parthians, Arabs and Mongols from the sixth century BC. From the early 19th century Turkmenistan was gradually incorporated into the Russian Empire. A Turkmen revolt against Russian rule in 1916 brought a period of autonomy until 1921, when Soviet control over Turkmenistan was established and it became an Autonomous Soviet Socialist Republic. Turkmenistan became a full republic of the USSR in 1925. It declared its independence from the USSR on 27 October 1991.

Saparmurat Niyazov became leader of the Turkmen Communist Party in 1985, and was elected president in 1990, becoming president for life in 2004. His autocratic regime, through harassment and authoritarianism, prevented the development of any effective political opposition or press freedom, rejecting political pluralism in favour of a cult of personality. After President Niyazov's death in 2006, Gurbanguly Berdimuhammedov was elected president, and was re-elected with an overwhelming majority in the 2012 presidential election. He is introducing reforms, but the country remains in effect a one-party state under an authoritarian regime.

The Democratic Party of Turkmenistan (DP), the renamed Communist Party, is currently the only legal political party, although the president said in 2010 that other political parties might be registered. The DP held all the seats in the legislature after the 2008 elections.

A new constitution was adopted in 2008 which encouraged multiparty politics and economic liberalisation, abolished the People's Council and increased the powers of the enlarged legislature. The executive president is directly elected for a five-year term. The unicameral parliament *(Majlis)* has 125 members directly elected for a five-year term.

The country is divided into five provinces (Ahal, Balkan, Dashhowuz, Lebap and Mary) and the city of Ashgabat.

HEAD OF STATE

President, Chair of the Council of Ministers, Gurbanguly Berdimuhammedov, *elected* 14 February 2007, *re-elected* 2012

SELECTED GOVERNMENT MEMBERS *as at July 2014*

First Deputy Chair, Foreign Affairs, Rashid Meredov

Defence, Begench Gundogdiyev

Finance, Dovletgeldy Sadykov

EMBASSY OF TURKMENISTAN

131 Holland Park Avenue, London W11 4UT

T 020-7255 1071 E tkm-embassy-uk@btconnect.com

W www.turkmenembassy.org.uk

Ambassador Extraordinary and Plenipotentiary, HE Yazmurad N. Seryayev, *apptd* 2003

BRITISH EMBASSY
Third Floor Office Building, Four Points Ak Altin Hotel, 744001
Ashgabat
T (+993) (12) 363 462 E beasb@online.tm
W www.gov.uk/government/world/turkmenistan
Ambassador Extraordinary and Plenipotentiary, Sanjay
    Wadvani, *appointed* 2013

DEFENCE

Aged 16–49, 2010 est	Males	Females
Available for military service	1,380,794	1,387,211
Fit for military service	1,066,649	1,185,538

Conscription duration – 12–24 months

ECONOMY AND TRADE

Turkmenistan has large reserves of natural gas and some oil, but exports were restricted by a lack of export routes until 2009–10, when existing pipelines to Russia and Iran were supplemented by a new gas pipeline to China and a second pipeline to Iran; a trans-Caucasian route to European markets is also under exploration. However, government misuse of the revenues from these commodities means little has been done to alleviate the widespread poverty or reduce the high unemployment rate of 60 per cent. Attempts to privatise the primarily state-run and inefficient economy have been made since 2012, but implementation has been slow.

Agriculture is intensive around the irrigated oases, with half the irrigated land used to grow cotton. Agriculture accounts for 7.2 per cent of GDP and 48.2 per cent of employment; grain and livestock are the other main products. The principal industries are gas and oil production, petroleum products, textiles (including silk) and food processing. Industry contributes 24.4 per cent of GDP.

The main trading partners are China, Turkey, Russia, Ukraine, the UAE and the EU. Principal exports are gas, crude oil, petrochemicals, textiles and cotton fibre. The main imports are machinery and equipment, chemicals and foodstuffs.
GNI – US$30,628m; US$4,800 per capita (2012)
Annual average growth of GDP – 12.2 per cent (2013 est)
Inflation rate – 9 per cent (2013 est)
Population below poverty line – 30 per cent (2004 est)
Unemployment – 60 per cent (2004 est)
Total external debt – US$428.9m (2012 est)

BALANCE OF PAYMENTS
Trade – US$120m surplus (2003)
Current Account – US$15m surplus (2012)

Trade with UK	2012	2013
Imports from UK	£106,404,033	£146,302,316
Exports to UK	£129,179,996	£111,516,601

COMMUNICATIONS

Airports and waterways – The main airport is at Ashgabat; there are two important waterways, the Amu Darya river in the north-east and the Niyazov (formerly Kara Kum) canal, and the main port is Turkmenbashi, on the Caspian Sea
Roadways and railways – There are 58,592km of roads, 47,577km of which are surfaced, and 2,980km of railways
Telecommunications – 575,000 fixed lines and 3.953 million mobile subscriptions (2012); there were 80,400 internet users in 2009
Internet code and IDD – tm; 993 (from UK), 810 44 (to UK)
Media – The country's major broadcaster is Turkmen TV; there are numerous news publications, including the Russian-language *Neytralnyy Turkmenistan* and the Turkmen-language *Turkmenistan*
WPFI score – 80,81 (178)

TUVALU

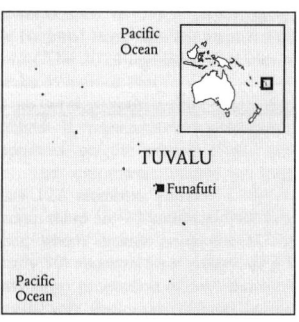

Area – 26 sq. km
Capital – Funafuti; population, 5,000 (2011 est)
Currency – The Australian dollar (A$) of 100 cents is legal tender; in addition there are Tuvalu dollar and cent coins in circulation
Population – 10,782 rising at 0.8 per cent a year (2014 est); Polynesian (96 per cent), Micronesian (4 per cent) (est)
Religion – Christian (Church of Tuvalu 97 per cent, Seventh-day Adventist 1.4 per cent), Baha'i 1 per cent (est)
Language – English, Tuvaluan (both official), Samoan, Kiribati (on Nui)
Population density – 328 per sq. km (2011)
Urban population – 51 per cent (2012 est)
Median age (years) – 24.9 (2014 est)
National anthem – 'Tuvalu mo te Atua' ['Tuvalu for the Almighty']
National day – 1 October (Independence Day)
Death penalty – Abolished for all crimes (since 1978)
Life expectancy (years) – 65.81 (2014 est)
Mortality rate – 8.90 (2014 est)
Birth rate – 23.74 (2014 est)
Infant mortality rate – 31.69 (2014 est)

CLIMATE AND TERRAIN

Tuvalu comprises nine low-lying coral islands and atolls in the south-west Pacific Ocean. The highest elevation is 5m and the lowest is 0m (Pacific Ocean). The climate is tropical, with an average temperature of 27.3°C all year round.

HISTORY AND POLITICS

The islands were settled by Polynesians from Tonga 2,000 years ago. Europeans arrived in the 18th century and, as the Ellice Islands, Tuvalu came under the control of the British in 1877. They formed part of the Gilbert and Ellice Islands protectorate (later a colony) from 1892, but were granted separate status from the Gilbert Islands in 1975. The islands became independent as Tuvalu on 1 October 1978. The country is seriously affected by rising sea levels, which are threatening its economic viability.

There are no political parties; allegiances are influenced by personal and island loyalties. Although politically stable as a democracy, there are frequent changes in government as support in parliament shifts. In August 2013, the government of Willy Telavi lost a vote of no confidence, ending the administration, and Enele Sopoaga was elected prime minister by parliament.

Under the 1978 constitution, Tuvalu is a constitutional monarchy with Queen Elizabeth II as head of state, represented by a governor-general who is appointed on the advice of the prime minister. The unicameral legislature, the Parliament of Tuvalu, has 15 members who are directly elected for a four-year term. The prime minister is elected by the legislature from among its members, and appoints the cabinet, who must be members of parliament. Local government services are provided by elected island councils.

Governor-General, HE Sir Iakoba Italeli, GCMG

SELECTED GOVERNMENT MEMBERS *as at July 2014*
Prime Minister, Enele Sopoaga
Finance, Maatia Toafa
Foreign Affairs, Taukelina Finikaso

HONORARY CONSULATE OF TUVALU
Tuvalu House, 230 Worple Road, London SW20 8RH
T 020-8879 0985 E tuvaluconsulate@netscape.net
Honorary Consul, Dr Iftikhar A. Ayaz

BRITISH HIGH COMMISSIONER
HE Roderick Drummond, *apptd* 2013, resident at Suva, Fiji

ECONOMY AND TRADE
The main economic activities are subsistence agriculture and fishing, although agricultural productivity is threatened by the increasing salinity of the soil as the sea level rises; the only cash crop is coconuts. Tourism is limited by the state's remoteness. Most employment is in the public sector or abroad, often as merchant seamen; many families rely on remittances from expatriate workers. The government receives substantial annual income from a trust fund set up in 1987, and raises revenue through the sale of fishing licences, postage stamps and coins, and the leasing of its telephone code and internet suffix.

The main trading partners are Japan, the USA, New Zealand and Australia. The only exports are copra and fish. The main imports are food, livestock, fuels, machinery and manufactured goods.
Annual average growth of GDP – 1.1 per cent (2013 est)
Inflation rate – 3.8 per cent (2006 est)

BALANCE OF PAYMENTS
Trade – US$16m deficit (2007)

Trade with UK	2012	2013
Imports from UK	–	–
Exports to UK	£118,300	£49,542

COMMUNICATIONS
Airports and waterways – Funafuti has an airfield, from which a regular service operates to Fiji and Kiribati, and it is also the main port
Roadways – 8km
Telecommunications – 1,450 fixed lines and 2,800 mobile subscriptions (2012); there were 4,200 internet users in 2008
Internet code and IDD – tv; 688 (from UK), 44 (to UK)
Media – The state-owned Tuvalu Media Corporation publishes a fortnightly newspaper and runs Radio Tuvalu, the main information source for islanders

UGANDA

Republic of Uganda

Area – 241,038 sq. km
Capital – Kampala; population, 1,736,808 (2012)
Major towns – Entebbe, Gulu, Lira
Currency – Uganda shilling of 100 cents
Population – 35,918,915 rising at 3.24 per cent a year (2014 est); Baganda (16.9 per cent), Banyakole (9.5 per cent), Basoga (8.4 per cent), Bakiga (6.9 per cent), Iteso (6.4 per cent), Langi (6.1 per cent), Acholi (4.7 per cent), Bagisu (4.6 per cent), Lugbara (4.2 per cent), Bunyoro (2.7 per cent); other 29.6 per cent (2002)
Religion – Christian 83.9 per cent (Roman Catholic 41.9 per cent, Anglican 35.9 per cent, Pentecostal 4.6 per cent), Muslim 12.1 per cent (predominantly Sunni) (est); indigenous beliefs are often blended into or observed alongside Christianity or Islam
Language – English (official), Luganda, Swahili, Arabic
Population density – 176 per sq. km (2011)
Urban population – 16 per cent (2012 est)
Median age (years) – 15.5 (2014 est)
National anthem – 'O Uganda, Land of Beauty'
National day – 9 October (Independence Day)
Death penalty – Retained
CPI score – 26 (140)

CLIMATE AND TERRAIN
Uganda lies on a high plateau with mountain ranges in the west, south-west and north-east. Elevation extremes range from 5,110m (Mt Stanley) to 621m (Lake Albert). Nearly 20 per cent of the country is covered by lakes, rivers and wetlands, and it contains about half of lakes Victoria, Edward and Albert (Mobuto), as well as lakes Kyoga, Kwania, George and Bisina (formerly Salisbury) and the course of the Nile from its outlet from Lake Victoria to the South Sudan border at Nimule. The climate is tropical, moderated by the altitude. There are two rainy seasons (March–May, October–December) in the south; the north is drier, semi-arid in places, with a single, longer rainy season.

HISTORY AND POLITICS
Indigenous people had formed several kingdoms in the area by the 14th century. External contact began in the early 19th century with Arab traders and then European explorers. A British protectorate was established over the kingdom of Buganda in 1894 and gradually extended to other territory by 1914. Uganda became independent on 9 October 1962 as a federation of the kingdoms of Ankole, Buganda, Bunyoro, Busoga and Toro.

In 1963 Uganda was proclaimed a federal republic but in 1966 prime minister Milton Obote overthrew the president, ended the federal status and became executive president. In 1971 President Obote was deposed in an army coup led by

Maj.-Gen. Idi Amin, who proclaimed himself head of state. His brutal dictatorship was overthrown in 1979 with military assistance from Tanzania.

Milton Obote was re-elected president in 1980 but political instability and human rights abuses continued. He was ousted by a military coup in 1985 amid a civil war with the rebel National Resistance Army (NRA) led by Yoweri Museveni. A military council was installed but the NRA captured Kampala in January 1986, securing control of the rest of the country in the following few months. Museveni began a process of reconstruction which resulted in Uganda becoming relatively peaceful and stable, and restored a degree of prosperity.

Museveni's 'Movement' system of government, under which political parties were allowed to exist but not to contest elections, was in place from 1986 until a 2005 referendum resulted in a return to multiparty politics. In multiparty elections held in February and March 2011, President Museveni was re-elected for a fourth term in the first round of the presidential election, and the National Resistance Movement retained its majority in parliament.

The Lord's Resistance Army (LRA), whose aims have never been specified, began a low-level insurgency in northern Uganda in the late 1980s. Its activities have spread into north-eastern Congo (where most of the LRA is now located), southern Sudan, the Central African Republic and Kenya, despite offensives against LRA bases by Ugandan, Sudanese and Congolese forces since 2008. In Uganda, thousands have been massacred or mutilated, an estimated 20,000 children abducted to serve in its forces, and 1.7 million people displaced into camps.

Terrorist attacks by Islamic extremists have begun in recent years. Some were carried out by Somalian Islamists, as African Union peacekeepers (predominantly Ugandan) have prevented them establishing complete control of the Somalian capital, but other attacks were the work of the Allied Democratic Forces, based in the Democratic Republic of Congo, which seeks to create an Islamic state in Uganda.

The 1995 constitution was amended in 2005 to allow multiparty elections. The president is directly elected for a five-year term; the two-term limit was abolished in 2005. The unicameral parliament has 238 directly elected members and 137 (including 112 women) elected indirectly to represent particular groups; all serve a five-year term. The prime minister is appointed by the president, subject to the approval of parliament.

HEAD OF STATE
President, Yoweri Museveni, *sworn in* 29 January 1986, *elected* 9 May 1996, *re-elected* 2001, 2006, 2011
Vice-President, Edward Kiwanuka Sekandi

SELECTED GOVERNMENT MEMBERS *as at July 2014*
Prime Minister, Amama Mbabazi
Deputy Prime Ministers, Henry Muganwa Kajura; Gen. Moses Ali
Defence, Crispus W. C. B. Kiyonga
Finance, Maria Kiwanuka

UGANDA HIGH COMMISSION
Uganda House, 58–59 Trafalgar Square, London WC2N 5DX
T 020-7839 5783 E info@ugandahighcommission.co.uk
W www.ugandahighcommission.co.uk
High Commissioner, HE Joyce Kikafunda, *apptd* 2013

BRITISH HIGH COMMISSION
PO Box 7070, 4 Windsor Loop, Kampala
T (+256) (31) 231 2000 E bhcinfo@starcom.co.ug
W www.gov.uk/government/world/uganda
High Commissioner, HE Alison Blackburne, *apptd* 2012

DEFENCE

Aged 16–49, 2010 est	Males	Females
Available for military service	7,249,271	7,025,439
Fit for military service	4,313,068	4,200,901

Military expenditure – US$398m (2013)

ECONOMY AND TRADE
Economic reforms adopted since 1986 have produced steady economic growth, which was only slightly affected by the global downturn. However, there has been little industrialisation, so the economy is vulnerable to fluctuations in global commodity prices, especially that of coffee, its main export. Uganda's debt burden has been reduced by debt relief since 2000 but it is still dependent on foreign aid. Rising commodity prices in 2011 led to protests across the country and instability in Sudan remains a problem for the Ugandan economy.

Agriculture is the most important economic sector, contributing 23.1 per cent of GDP and engaging about 82 per cent of the workforce. The principal crops are coffee, tea, cotton, tobacco, cassava, potatoes, maize, millet, pulses, cut flowers and livestock products. Industrial activity centres on production of sugar, tobacco, cotton textiles, cement and steel, brewing and fishing. Tourism is growing, and oil has been discovered but is not yet being exploited.

The main export markets are neighbouring countries, the UAE and Rwanda; imports come chiefly from Kenya, the UAE, China and India. Principal exports are coffee, fish and fish products, tea, cotton, cut flowers, horticultural products and gold. Electricity is exported to Kenya, Tanzania and Rwanda. The main imports are capital equipment, vehicles, petroleum, medical supplies and cereals.
GNI – US$16,760m; US$440 per capita (2012)
Annual average growth of GDP – 5.6 per cent (2013 est)
Inflation rate – 6.2 per cent (2013 est)
Total external debt – US$5,223m (2013 est)
Imports – US$5,230m (2012)
Exports – US$2,861m (2012)

BALANCE OF PAYMENTS
Trade – US$2,369m deficit (2012)
Current Account – US$2,224m deficit (2012)

Trade with UK	2012	2013
Imports from UK	£63,481,259	£49,106,773
Exports to UK	£14,047,424	£16,710,183

COMMUNICATIONS
Airports and waterways – There is an international airport at Entebbe; some of the lakes and parts of the river Nile provide navigable routes internally
Roadways and railways – 20,000km; 1,244km
Telecommunications – 315,000 fixed lines and 16.355 million mobile subscriptions (2012); there were 3.2 million internet users in 2009
Internet code and IDD – ug; 256 (from UK), 0 44 (to UK)
Media – UBC is the main public-run broadcaster; major newspapers include the state-owned *New Vision*
WPFI score – 33,29 (110)

EDUCATION AND HEALTH
Education is a joint undertaking by the government, local authorities and voluntary agencies.
Literacy rate – 73 per cent (2010 est)
Gross enrolment ratio (percentage of relevant age group) – primary 110 per cent (2012 est); secondary 28 per cent (2011 est); tertiary 9 per cent (2012 est)

Health expenditure (per capita) – US$42 (2011)
Hospital beds (per 1,000 people) – 0.5 (2010)
Life expectancy (years) – 54.46 (2014 est)
Mortality rate – 10.26 (2014 est)
Birth rate – 44.17 (2014 est)
Infant mortality rate – 60.82 (2014 est)
HIV/AIDS adult prevalence – 7.2 per cent (2012 est)

UKRAINE

Ukrayina – Ukraine

Area – 603,550 sq. km
Capital – Kiev (Kyiv); population, 2,850,205 (2012)
Major cities – Dnipropetrovsk, Donetsk, Kharkiv, L'viv,
    Odesa, Zaporizhzhya
Currency – Hryvnia of 100 kopiykas
Population – 44,291,413 falling at 0.64 per cent a year
    (2014 est); Ukrainian (77.8 per cent), Russian (17.3
    per cent); small Belarusian, Moldovan, Crimean Tatar,
    Bulgarian, Romanian, Polish, Hungarian and Greek
    minorities (2001)
Religion – Christian (Ukrainian Orthodox 68 per cent,
    Greek Catholic 8–10 per cent, Protestant 1.9 per cent),
    Muslim 0.9 per cent (est)
Language – Ukrainian (official), Russian
Population density – 79 per sq. km (2011)
Urban population – 69.1 per cent (2012 est)
Median age (years) – 40.6 (2014 est)
National anthem – 'Shche ne vmerla, Ukrainy' ['Ukraine's
    Glory Has Not Perished']
National day – 24 August (Independence Day)
Death penalty – Abolished for all crimes (since 1999)
CPI score – 25 (144)

CLIMATE AND TERRAIN
Much of the country lies in a plain (steppe), with the
Carpathian mountains in the west and mountains in the
south of the Crimean peninsula. Elevation extremes range
from 2,061m (Hora Hoverla) to 0m (Black Sea). The main
rivers are the Dnieper, which runs through the centre of the
country, the Dniester in the west, the Southern Buh and
the Northern Donets (a tributary of the Don). The climate
is continental, and Mediterranean in the southern Crimea.

Average temperatures in Kiev range from –6°C in January to
18°C in July.

POLITICS
The 1996 constitution was amended in 2004 to transfer
some powers from the president to the legislature *(Verkhovna
Rada)*; the constitutional court returned these powers to the
president in late 2010 although in February 2014 the 2004
constitutional amendments were reinstated. The president is
directly elected for a five-year term. The unicameral Supreme
Council has 450 members, who are directly elected for
a five-year term. The prime minister is appointed by the
president, subject to the legislature's approval.

Following the decision of Viktor Yanukovych's government to abandon plans for an association agreement with
the EU in November 2013, tens of thousands of pro-EU
demonstrators protested in Kiev and other cities. The
widespread and sometimes violent demonstrations, which
left at least 77 protestors dead in Kiev, resulted in President
Yanukovych leaving Ukraine and seeking asylum in Russia,
causing opposition parties to form an interim government.

The speaker of the parliament, Oleksandr Turchynov,
was appointed interim president on 22 February 2014. A
national unity government was subsequently established,
with Arseniy Yatsenyuk of the Fatherland party sworn in as
prime minister on 26 February. A cabinet was selected by
Yatsenyuk on 27 February and in May 2014, Petro
Poroshenko was elected president with 54.7 per cent of the
vote. While voting in the east of the country was disrupted
by violence, the results were recognised by the international
community, including by Russia.

Yatsenyuk resigned on 25 July 2014 citing frustration
at parliament's failure to pass legislation to increase army
financing and regulate the country's energy situation,
sparking legislative elections.

HEAD OF STATE
President, Petro Poroshenko, *elected* 25 May 2014, *sworn in*
    7 June 2014

SELECTED GOVERNMENT MEMBERS *as at July 2014*
Prime Minister (caretaker), Arseniy Yatsenyuk
First Deputy Prime Minister, Vitaliy Yarema
Deputy Prime Ministers, Oleksandr Sych; Volodymyr
    Hroisman
Finance, Oleksandr Shlapak

EMBASSY OF UKRAINE
60 Holland Park, London W11 3SJ
T 020-7727 6312 E emb_gb@mfa.gov.ua W www.ukremb.org.uk
Ambassador Extraordinary and Plenipotentiary, HE Volodymyr
    Khandogiy, *apptd* 2010

BRITISH EMBASSY
Desyatynna 9, Kiev 01025
T (+380) (44) 490 3660 E ukembinf@gmail.com
W www.gov.uk/government/world/ukraine
Ambassador Extraordinary and Plenipotentiary, HE Simon
    Smith, *apptd* 2012

Area invaded by Tatar-Mongols	Part of the Polish-Lithuanian Commonwealth	West becomes part of the Habsburg empire	Civil war partitions country between USSR and Poland	German occupation begins	Crimea transferred from Russia to Ukraine	Declares independence from USSR
c.800	c.1300	1685	1918	1922	1944	1986	2014
c.1200	c.1500	1795	1921	1941	1954	1991
Slavic state formed on the river Dnieper with its capital at Kiev	Comes under Lithuanian rule	Eastern rebellion; area becomes part of Russia	Reunified Ukraine declares independence	Country becomes constituent republic of USSR	Red Army forces out German troops	Chernobyl nuclear disaster kills at least 10,000 people	Crimea annexed by Russia; separatist violence in the east.

FOREIGN RELATIONS

Following the disintegration of the USSR in 1991, relations between Ukraine and Russia were strained by disputes over the Black Sea fleet and the status of Crimea, a self-administered republic within the Ukraine which had been part of Russia until 1954; these disputes often came to a head when Russia suspended gas supplies to Ukraine. However, in February 2014 armed pro-Russian groups seized government buildings in Crimea. In March, Russian forces helped pro-Russian separatists seize power, with the Crimea formally annexed by the Russian government on the 18 March 2014 after a controversial independence vote in the Crimean parliament. Ukraine and a majority of UN member states do not accept the status of Crimea and Sevastopol as federal subjects of the Russian Federation.

From April, pro-Russian groups in the east of the Ukraine seized government buildings and were initially supported by the Russian government. Two self-proclaimed pro-Russian states were established in the east of the country: the Donetsk People's Republic and the Luhansk People's Republic. Independence referendums were held on 11 May in both territories, with adminstrators claiming very large wins for supporters of independence. Both republics merged on 24 May to form The Federal State of Novorossiya. The breakaway states have not been recognised by Russia, Ukraine or the wider international community.

By June at least 270 people had been killed as these groups clashed with the Ukrainian military. While political tensions eased when the Russian government advised it would be pulling troops away from the Ukrainian border, violence between the Ukrainian army and separatist militias continued to occur, despite a number of brief ceasefires. A Ukraine–European Union Association Agreement was formalised by the incoming government on 27 June 2014.

Tensions were reignited by the downing of Malaysian Airlines flight MH17 on 17 July 2014, apparently by pro-Russian separatists. On 5 September, a ceasefire was agreed between the government and separatists.

DEFENCE

Aged 16–49, 2010 est	Males	Females
Available for military service	10,984,394	11,260,000
Fit for military service	6,893,551	8,792,504

Military expenditure – US$5,327m (2013)
Conscription duration – 12–18 months

ECONOMY AND TRADE

The first decade of independence was characterised by economic mismanagement and opposition to economic restructuring. When reform began in the late 1990s, it brought economic growth, with rises in output and exports and a reduction in inflation. However, slow progress has been a drag on the economy, leaving it vulnerable to external factors such as the global economic downturn; the economy contracted severely in 2009 and is now smaller than it was after independence in 1992. Economic growth slowed in 2012 amid allegations the Yanukovych regime misappro-priated billions of dollars during its time in power. The economy is heavily indebted and will receive up to US$18bn from the IMF over a number of years. After incurring debts worth US$1.9bn with state-run Russian energy firm Gazprom, Russia ended its practice of supplying Ukraine with subsidised fossil fuels, greatly increasing domestic prices. The conflict in the east of the country is expected to do significant harm to the economy.

The agricultural sector is large and productive, with over half the land under cultivation. The main crops are grain, sugar beet, sunflower seeds and vegetables; stock-raising and dairy-farming are also important. Agriculture accounts for 9.9 per cent of GDP and 5.6 per cent of employment. There are large deposits of coal, iron ore and other minerals. The main industrial activities are mining and metal processing, manufacture of machinery and transport equipment and chemicals, electricity generation and food processing, especially sugar. Ukraine imports three-quarters of its oil and gas, principally from Russia; supplies have been suspended on occasions due to price disputes.

The main trading partners are Russia (25.6 per cent of exports; 32.4 per cent of imports), China, Germany and Turkey. Principal exports are ferrous and non-ferrous metals (especially steel), fuel and petroleum products, chemicals, machinery and transport equipment, and foodstuffs. The main imports are energy (primarily gas), machinery and equipment, and chemicals.

GNI – US$173,344m; US$3,500 per capita (2012)
Annual average growth of GDP – 0.4 per cent (2013 est)
Inflation rate – 0.7 per cent (2013 est)
Population below poverty line – 24.1 per cent (2010)
Unemployment – 8 per cent (2013 est)
Total external debt – US$138,300m (2013 est)
Imports – US$84,658m (2012)
Exports – US$68,810m (2012)

BALANCE OF PAYMENTS
Trade – US$15,848m deficit (2012)
Current Account – US$14,761m deficit (2012)

Trade with UK	2012	2013
Imports from UK	£581,013,719	£553,000,330
Exports to UK	£315,263,308	£379,463,268

COMMUNICATIONS

Airports and waterways – The principal airports are at Kiev and Odesa; the main seaports are Mariupol on the Sea of Azov, and Kherson, Mykolayiv, Odesa and Sevastopol on the Black Sea
Roadways and railways – 169,694km; 21,619km
Telecommunications – 12.182 million fixed lines and 59.344 million mobile subscriptions (2012); there were 7.77 million internet users in 2009
Internet code and IDD – ua; 380 (from UK), 44 (to UK)
Major broadcasters – The National TV Company of Ukraine operates the popular UT1, UT2, and UT3 channels
Press – Major titles include *Fakty i Kommentarii, Silski Visti* and *Segodnya*
WPFI score – 36,93 (127)

EDUCATION AND HEALTH

Literacy rate – 100 per cent (2011)
Gross enrolment ratio (percentage of relevant age group) – primary 106 per cent; secondary 98 per cent; tertiary 80 per cent (2012 est)
Health expenditure (per capita) – US$263 (2011)
Hospital beds (per 1,000 people) – 8.7 (2009)
Life expectancy (years) – 69.14 (2014 est)
Mortality rate – 15.72 (2014 est)
Birth rate – 9.41 (2014 est)
Infant mortality rate – 8.1 (2014 est)
HIV/AIDS adult prevalence – 0.9 per cent (2012 est)

UNITED ARAB EMIRATES

Al-Imarat al-Arabiyah al-Muttahidah – United Arab Emirates

Area – 83,600 sq. km
Capital – Abu Dhabi; population, 942,000 (2011)
Major cities – Ajman, al-Ain, Dubai, Sharjah
Currency – UAE dirham (Dh) of 100 fils
Population – 5,628,805 rising at 2.71 per cent a year
(2014 est); Emirati (19 per cent), other Arab and Iranian
(23 per cent), South Asian (50 per cent) (2005 est)
Religion – Muslim 76 per cent, Christian 9 per cent,
other (primarily Hindu and Buddhist) 15 per cent
(2005 est)
Language – Arabic (official), Persian, English, Hindi, Urdu
Population density – 107 per sq. km (2011)
Urban population – 84.7 per cent (2012 est)
Median age (years) – 30.3 (2014 est)
National anthem – 'Ishy Bilady' ['Long Live My Homeland']
National day – 2 December (Independence Day, 1971)
Death penalty – Retained
CPI score – 68 (26)

CLIMATE AND TERRAIN
The United Arab Emirates (UAE) is situated in the south-east
of the Arabian peninsula. Six of the emirates lie on the shore
of the Gulf, between the Musandam peninsula in the east and
the Qatar peninsula in the west, while the seventh, Fujairah,
lies on the Gulf of Oman. A flat coastal plain merges into the
desert of the interior, and there are mountains in the east.
Elevation extremes range from 1,527m (Jabal Yibir) to 0m
(Persian Gulf). There is a desert climate, although it is cooler
in the mountains, with high humidity on the coast. Average
temperatures in Dubai range from 18.5°C in January to
34.2°C in July and August.

HISTORY AND POLITICS
The United Arab Emirates (formerly the Trucial States) is
composed of seven emirates. Six of these came together as an
independent state on 2 December 1971 when they ended
their individual special treaty relationships with the British
government, and they were joined by Ras al-Khaimah on
10 February 1972. On independence, the union government
assumed full responsibility for all internal and external affairs
apart from those internal matters that remain the prerogative
of the individual emirates.

Sheikh Zayed of Abu Dhabi was president from
independence until his death in 2004. He was succeeded as
Sultan of Abu Dhabi by his son, Sheikh Khalifa, who was
also elected president of the UAE. The first national elections
were held in 2006, when half the members of the Federal
National Council (FNC) were elected by a small electoral
college of 6,600 voters. The size of the electoral college
increased significantly, to 129,274 voters (women comprised

just under half of this total), in the most recent legislative
election held in September 2011.

The 1971 provisional constitution, approved in 1996, was
amended in 2008 to convert the Federal National Council
from a consultative into a legislative body and to extend its
original two-year term to 2011. Overall authority lies with
the Supreme Council, comprising the hereditary rulers of the
seven emirates, each of whom also governs in his own
territory. The president and vice-president are elected every
five years by the Supreme Council from among its members.
The president appoints the prime minister and the council of
ministers. The unicameral Federal National Council has 40
members, eight members each from Abu Dhabi and Dubai,
six each from Sharjah and Ras al-Khaimah and four each
for Fujairah, Umm al-Qaiwain and Ajman; half are elected by
an electoral college and half are appointed by the rulers of
each emirate.

HEAD OF STATE
President, HH Sheikh Khalifa bin Zayed al-Nahyan *(Abu
Dhabi), elected* 3 November 2004, *re-elected* 2009
Vice-President, Prime Minister, Defence, HH Sheikh
Mohammed bin Rashid al-Maktoum *(Dubai)*

SELECTED GOVERNMENT MEMBERS *as at July 2014*
Deputy Prime Ministers, Lt.-Gen. Sheikh Saif bin Zayed
al-Nahyan *(Interior);* Sheikh Mansour bin Zayed
al-Nahyan
Finance, HH Sheikh Hamdan bin Rashid al-Maktoum
Foreign Affairs, Sheikh Abdullah bin Zayed al-Nahyan

EMBASSY OF THE UNITED ARAB EMIRATES
30 Prince's Gate, London SW7 1PT
T 020-7581 1281 E informationuk@mofa.gov.ae
W www.uae-embassy.ae/uk
Ambassador Extraordinary and Plenipotentiary, HE Abdul
Rahman Ghanim al-Mutaiwee, *apptd* 2009

BRITISH EMBASSY
PO Box 248, Khalid bin al-Waleed Street (Street 22), Abu Dhabi
T (+971) (2) 610 1100 E consular.UAE@fco.gov.uk
W www.gov.uk/government/world/united-arab-emirates
Ambassador Extraordinary and Plenipotentiary, HE Philip
Parham, *apptd* 2014

FEDERAL STRUCTURE
The emirates are: Abu Dhabi, Ajman, Dubai, Fujairah, Ras
al-Khaimah, Sharjah and Umm al-Qaiwain. Each emirate has
its own government, judicial system and penal code. Abu
Dhabi has an executive council chaired by the crown prince.

DEFENCE

Aged 16–49, 2010 est	Males	Females
Available for military service	2,676,928	981,649
Fit for military service	2,229,366	842,759

Military expenditure – US$18,898m (2012)

ECONOMY AND TRADE
Exploitation of the territories' oil reserves began in the
1960s and transformed the UAE from poor rural
principalities into modern states with a high standard of
living. Oil and gas production dominate the economy,
although diversification means that output now accounts for
25 per cent of GDP. The economy is also dependent on
foreign workers, but the government aims to increase
opportunities for its citizens through improved education

and expansion of the private sector. The economy was badly hit by the global downturn, particularly in Dubai, which was heavily exposed when property prices crashed; its debt crisis has been alleviated by loans from federal and Abu Dhabi institutions.

Agriculture is limited by the terrain but the area under cultivation has been extended by irrigation and water desalination projects. The main products are dates, vegetables, watermelons, poultry, eggs and dairy products. Non-hydrocarbon industries include fishing, aluminium, cement, petrochemicals, fertilisers, commercial ship repair, construction materials, handicrafts, textiles, boat-building, financial services and tourism. Several free-trade zones are attracting foreign investment.

The main export markets are Japan, India and Iran; imports come chiefly from India, China, the USA and Germany. Principal exports are crude oil (45 per cent), natural gas, re-exports, dried fish and dates. The main imports are machinery and transport equipment, chemicals and food.

GNI – US$360,245m; US$35,770 per capita (2011)
Annual average growth of GDP – 4 per cent (2013 est)
Inflation rate – 1.3 per cent (2013 est)
Population below poverty line – 19.5 per cent (2003)
Total external debt – US$167,900m (2013 est)
Imports – US$220,000m (2012)
Exports – US$300,000m (2012)

BALANCE OF PAYMENTS
Trade – US$80,000m surplus (2012)
Current Account – US$66,553m surplus (2012)

Trade with UK	2012	2013
Imports from UK	£5,161,062,865	£5,833,571,558
Exports to UK	£2,193,742,145	£2,528,510,100

COMMUNICATIONS
Airports and waterways – There is an international airport in every emirate except Ajman, and significant ports in Jebel Ali, Khor Fakkan, Mina Zayed, Mina Rashid, Mina Saqr and Mina Khalid
Roadways – 4,080km
Telecommunications – 1.967 million fixed lines and 13.775 million mobile subscriptions (2012); there were 3.45 million internet users in 2009
Internet code and IDD – ae; 971 (from UK), 44 (to UK)
Media – MBC operates two major channels across the Emirates; major newspapers include *al-Bayan* and *Gulf News*
WPFI score – 36,03 (118)

EDUCATION AND HEALTH
Education is free in state schools and compulsory from ages six to 14.
Literacy rate – 90 per cent (2010 est)
Health expenditure (per capita) – US$1,640 (2011)
Hospital beds (per 1,000 people) – 1.9 (2008)
Life expectancy (years) – 77.09 (2014 est)
Mortality rate – 1.99 (2014 est)
Birth rate – 15.54 (2014 est)
Infant mortality rate – 10.92 (2014 est)

UNITED KINGDOM

United Kingdom of Great Britain and Northern Ireland

Area – 243,610 sq. km
Capital – London; population, 8,658,155 (2012)
Major cities – Belfast, Birmingham, Cardiff, Edinburgh, Glasgow, Leeds, Liverpool, Manchester
Currency – Pound sterling (£) of 100 pence
Population – 63,742,977 rising at 0.54 per cent a year (2014 est)
Religion – Christian 59.5 per cent, Muslim 4.4 per cent, Hindu 1.3 per cent, none 25.7 per cent (est); small Jewish, Sikh and Buddhist minorities
Language – English, Welsh, Lowland Scots, Scottish Gaelic, Irish
Population density – 259 per sq. km (2011)
Urban population – 79.7 per cent (2012 est)
Median age (years) – 40.4 (2014 est)
National anthem – 'God Save the Queen'
Death penalty – Abolished for all crimes (since 1998)
CPI score – 76 (14)

CLIMATE AND TERRAIN
The terrain of Great Britain is higher in the north and west, with low mountains and rugged hills in Scotland, northern England and Wales; the land declines towards the south and east, with its lowest points in the south-east. Northern Ireland is more low-lying, with low mountains in the north and east. The heavily indented coastline varies in height between high cliffs and sea level. Elevation extremes range from 1,343m (Ben Nevis, Scotland) to –4m (the Fens, eastern England). Although Scotland contains numerous large lochs and northern England includes an area known as the Lake District, the largest freshwater lake is Lough Neagh in Northern Ireland. The main rivers are the Thames, the Severn and the Trent in England and Wales, and the Tay in Scotland. The climate is temperate and extremes are rare, but the convergence of Atlantic, Arctic and European weather systems produces unusually changeable weather conditions. Average temperatures in London range from 4.3°C in January to 17.3°C in July.

POLITICS
There is no written constitution. The head of state is a hereditary constitutional monarch. The bicameral parliament consists of the House of Commons, the lower house, and the House of Lords. The House of Commons has 650 seats, directly elected for a five-year term. The House of Lords is appointed and numbers vary; in September 2014 it had 778 members, comprising 26 archbishops and bishops of the Church of England, 665 life peers and 87 hereditary peers. The prime minister is the leader of the majority party or coalition in the House of Commons.

Powers over certain internal matters were devolved in 1999 to Scotland, Wales and Northern Ireland, each of which has

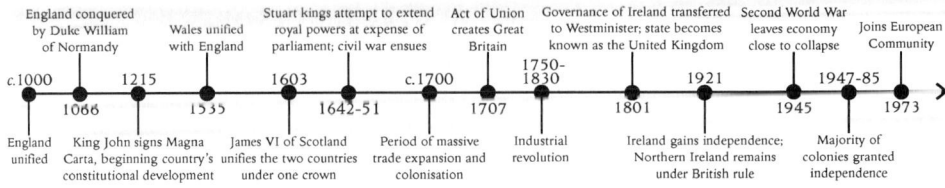

England conquered by Duke William of Normandy — c.1000
England unified — 1066
King John signs Magna Carta, beginning country's constitutional development — 1215
Wales unified with England — 1535
Stuart kings attempt to extend royal powers at expense of parliament; civil war ensues — 1603
James VI of Scotland unifies the two countries under one crown — 1642–51
Act of Union creates Great Britain — c.1700
Period of massive trade expansion and colonisation — 1707
Governance of Ireland transferred to Westminister; state becomes known as the United Kingdom — 1750–1830
Industrial revolution — 1801
Second World War leaves economy close to collapse — 1921
Ireland gains independence; Northern Ireland remains under British rule — 1945
Joins European Community — 1947–85
Majority of colonies granted independence — 1973

its own legislature and government; devolution was suspended in Northern Ireland several times between 2000 and 2007 owing to the breakdown of power-sharing arrangements.

The Labour government elected in 1945 pursued socialist economic and welfare policies, nationalising key industries, setting up the National Health Service and expanding the social security system. Economic decline continued until the 1980s, when it was reversed by the Conservative government led by Margaret Thatcher, the country's first woman prime minister. Her administration privatised nationalised industries, opened up welfare services to market forces and reduced the role of local government, polarising politics and public opinion. She also established a close relationship with the USA that was supportive of its foreign policy. This has been continued by her successors, most recently in the support for the US 'war on terror' and the deployment of British forces in Afghanistan since 2001, Iraq from 2003 to 2009, and in Libyan air space in 2011.

At the 2010 legislative election, the Conservative party won the most seats but without an outright majority. After negotiations with the Liberal Democrat party, a coalition government was formed under the Conservative leader, David Cameron, with the Liberal Democrat leader, Nick Clegg, as deputy prime minister.

HEAD OF STATE

HM The Queen of the United Kingdom of Great Britain and Northern Ireland, Queen Elizabeth II, *born* 21 April 1926; *succeeded* 6 February 1952; *crowned* 2 June 1953
Heir, HRH The Prince of Wales (Prince Charles Philip Arthur George), *born* 14 November 1948

SELECTED GOVERNMENT MEMBERS *as at September 2014*

Prime Minister, First Lord of the Treasury, Civil Service, David Cameron
Deputy Prime Minister, Nick Clegg
Chancellor of the Exchequer, George Osborne
Defence, Michael Fallon
Foreign and Commonwealth Affairs, Philip Hammond
Home Affairs, Theresa May
Justice, Lord Chancellor, Chris Grayling

DEFENCE

Aged 16–49, 2010 est	Males	Females
Available for military service	14,856,917	14,307,316
Fit for military service	12,255,452	11,779,679

Military expenditure – US$56,231m (2013)

ECONOMY AND TRADE

The UK has a highly developed and technologically advanced economy that is now dominated by services and trade. It was the first industrialised nation, developing an economy in the 19th century based on heavy industry, mass manufacturing and global trade. It became less predominant as industrialisation spread to other countries, and the demands of the Second World War caused a postwar industrial decline that left the economy less efficient than many of its competitors and increasingly undercut by

cheaper production in the developing world. In the 1980s, privatisation of state industries and constraints on public spending improved government finances, and primary industrial activities were increasingly replaced by service industries. After emerging from recession in the early 1990s, the economy experienced its longest-recorded period of expansion, outperforming the rest of the EU states, until 2008. The global economic downturn, tight credit and the end of the property boom caused the economy to go into recession from early 2008 until late 2009 and again at the start of 2012. The banking sector in particular was badly affected by the global financial crisis in 2008 and government intervention was necessary to stabilise the financial system, including nationalising or part-nationalising major banks. These measures left the government with a massive public-sector debt to service, and the new coalition government announced tight constraints on public spending from 2010. In 2013 GDP grew by 1.4 per cent accelerating unexpectedly due to an increase in consumer spending and a buoyant housing market. The budget deficit has fallen but remains high at nearly 7 per cent. Public debt has continued to increase.

The service sector, especially banking, insurance and business services, electronics, telecommunications and tourism, now contributes 78.9 per cent of GDP and employs 80.4 per cent of the workforce. Agriculture is intensive, highly mechanised and efficient, employing 1.4 per cent of the workforce, although contributing only 0.7 per cent of GDP. The UK has large but declining reserves of oil, gas and coal, and the country became a net importer of energy in 2005. Other industrial output is mostly of manufactured goods, including machine tools, electrical power equipment, automation and transport equipment, aircraft, ships, motor vehicles and parts, electronics and communications equipment, metals, chemicals, paper and paper products, food processing, textiles, clothing and other consumer goods.

The main trading partners are other EU countries, the USA and China. The principal exports are manufactured goods, fuels, chemicals, food, beverages and tobacco. The main imports are manufactured goods, machinery, fuels and foodstuffs.

GNI – US$2,464,325m; US$38,670 per capita (2012)
Annual average growth of GDP – 41.4 per cent (2013 est)
Inflation rate – 2.7 per cent (2013)
Population below poverty line – 14 per cent (2006 est)
Unemployment – 7.7 per cent (2013 est)
Total external debt – US$9,457,000m (2012)
Imports – US$648,677m (2012)
Exports – US$476,294m (2012)

BALANCE OF PAYMENTS

Trade – US$172,383m deficit (2012)
Current Account – US$93,866m deficit (2012)

COMMUNICATIONS

Airports – There are 271 licensed civil airports, of which Heathrow (the world's fifth busiest international airport), Gatwick, Stansted and Manchester handle the highest volume of passengers
Waterways – Traditionally a seafaring nation, the UK has a large merchant navy, with 504 ships of over 1,000 tonnes

registered in the UK and 308 ships registered overseas. The main ports are at Grimsby and Immingham, London, Milford Haven, Southampton, Tees and Hartlepool, Liverpool, Felixstowe, Forth, Dover and Belfast

Roadways – There are 394,428km of roadways, including 3,617km of motorways

Railways – The 16,454km of rail network is operated by 23 rail companies

Telecommunications – 33.01 million fixed lines and 82.109 million mobile subscriptions (2012); there were 51.44 million internet users in 2009

Major broadcasters – The British Broadcasting Corporation is a public service broadcaster and provides radio and television programmes, in competition with several commercial radio and television stations, including cable and satellite services

Press – The lively and occasionally controversial newspaper press publishes around ten newspapers daily, including *The Times*, *The Guardian* and *The Sun*

WPFI score – 19,93 (33)

EDUCATION AND HEALTH

Full-time education is compulsory between the ages of five and 16 in Wales and Scotland and four and 16 in Northern Ireland. In England full-time education is compulsory betwen the age of five until the end of the academic year of the pupil's 17th birthday.

Gross enrolment ratio (percentage of relevant age group) – primary 107 per cent; secondary 97 per cent; tertiary 61 per cent (2012 est)

Health expenditure (per capita) – US$3,609 (2011)

Hospital beds (per 1,000 people) – 3.0 (2010)

Life expectancy (years) – 80.42 (2014 est)

Mortality rate – 9.34 (2014 est)

Birth rate – 12.22 (2014 est)

Infant mortality rate – 4.44 (2014 est)

OVERSEAS TERRITORIES

See pp 931–939

UNITED STATES OF AMERICA

Area – 9,826,675 sq. km

Capital – Washington, District of Columbia; population, 4,705,000 (2011)

Major cities – Boston, Chicago, Dallas, Houston, Los Angeles, New York, Philadelphia, Phoenix, San Antonio, San Diego, San Francisco, San José

Currency – US dollar (US$) of 100 cents

Population – 318,892,103 rising at 0.77 per cent a year (2014 est); white 79.9 per cent, black 12.8 per cent, Asian 4.4 per cent, Amerindian and Alaskan native 0.97 per cent, native Hawaiian and other Pacific islander 0.18 per cent; Hispanic 15.1 per cent (persons of Hispanic origin may be of any race or ethnic group) (2007 est)

Religion – Christian (Protestant 51.3 per cent, Roman Catholic 23.9, Mormon 1.7 per cent), Jewish 1.7 per cent, Buddhist 0.7 per cent, Muslim 0.6 per cent (est)

Language – English, Spanish, Hawaiian (official in Hawaii)

Population density – 34 per sq. km (2011)

Urban population – 82.6 per cent (2012 est)

Median age (years) – 37.6 (2014 est)

National anthem – 'The Star-Spangled Banner'

National day – 4 July (Independence Day)

Death penalty – Abolished in 18 states, District of Columbia and US insular territories

CPI score – 73 (19)

CLIMATE AND TERRAIN

The coastline has a length of about 3,329km on the Atlantic Ocean, 12,268km on the Pacific, 1,705km on the Arctic, and 2,624km on the Gulf of Mexico. The principal river is the Mississippi-Missouri-Red (5,970km long), traversing the whole country from Montana to its mouth in the Gulf of Mexico. The Rocky Mountains range runs the length of the western portion of the country. West of this, bordering the Pacific coast, the Cascade Mountains and Sierra Nevada form the outer edge of a high tableland, consisting partly of stony and sandy desert and partly of grazing land and forested mountains, and including the Great Salt Lake, which extends to the Rocky Mountains. A vast central plain lies between the Rockies and the hills and low mountains of the eastern states, where large forests still exist, remnants of the forests which formerly extended over the entire Atlantic slope. Elevation extremes range from 6,194m (Mt McKinley, Alaska) to −86m (Death Valley, California). The climate varies with latitude but is mostly temperate, with semi-arid conditions on the great plains and arid in the south-west. Average temperatures in Washington DC range from 1.6°C in January to 25.7°C in July.

Two states are detached: Alaska and Hawaii. Alaska occupies the north-western extremity of North America, separated from the rest of the USA by the Canadian province of British Columbia. The terrain is arctic tundra with mountain ranges, and the climate is arctic. The state of Hawaii is a chain of about 20 mountainous volcanic islands in the north Pacific Ocean, of which the chief islands are Hawaii, Maui, Oahu, Kauai and Molokai. The climate is tropical.

The Pacific coast and Hawaii are prone to seismic activity. The Atlantic and Gulf of Mexico coasts frequently experience hurricanes.

POLITICS

By the constitution of 17 September 1787 (which has been amended 15 times, most recently in 1992), the government

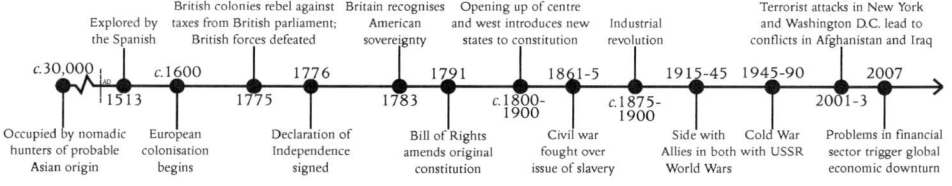

of the USA is entrusted to three separate authorities: the federal executive (the president and cabinet), the legislature (Congress, which consists of a senate and a House of Representatives) and the judicature. The president is indirectly elected by an electoral college to serve a four-year term, and may serve a maximum of two consecutive terms. If a president dies in office, the vice-president serves the remainder of his term. The president appoints the cabinet officers and all the chief officials, subject to confirmation by the senate. He makes recommendations of a general nature to Congress, and when laws are passed, he may return them to Congress with a veto. But, if a measure so vetoed is again passed by both houses by a two-thirds majority in each house, it becomes law, notwithstanding the objection of the president.

Each of the 50 states has its own executive, legislature and judiciary. In theory, they are sovereign, but in practice their autonomy is increasingly circumscribed.

PRESIDENTIAL ELECTIONS
Candidates for the presidency must be at least 35 years of age and a native citizen of the USA. The electoral college for each state is directly elected by universal adult suffrage in the November preceding the January in which the presidential term expires. The number of members of the electoral college is equal to the whole number of senators and representatives to which the state is entitled in the national congress. The electoral college for each state meets in its state in December and each member votes for a presidential candidate by ballot. The ballots are sent to Washington, and opened on 6 January by the president of the senate in the presence of Congress. The candidate who has received a majority of the whole number of electoral votes cast is declared president for the ensuing term. If no one has a majority, then from the highest on the list (not exceeding three) the House of Representatives elects a president, the votes being taken by states, the representation from each state having one vote. A presidential term begins at noon on 20 January.

The 2008 presidential election was won by the Democrat candidate Barack Obama, the first African-American to hold the office; he was re-elected in November 2012. In the 2012 legislative elections the Republican party retained its majority in the House of Representatives with 234 seats to 201 while the Democrats maintained a slight majority in the senate. The next legislative election will be held in November 2014.

HEAD OF STATE
President, Barack Obama, *elected* 2008, *sworn in* 20 January 2009, *re-elected* 6 November 2012, *sworn in* 20 January 2013
Vice-President, Joseph Biden
SELECTED GOVERNMENT MEMBERS *as at July 2014*
Defence, Chuck Hagel
Interior, Sally Jewel
Treasury, Jack Lew
Secretary for Homeland Security, Jeh Johnson
Secretary of State, John Kerry

THE CONGRESS
Legislative power is vested in the bicameral Congress, comprising the senate and the House of Representatives. The senate has 100 members, two from each state, elected for a six-year term, with one-third elected every two years. The House of Representatives has 435 members directly elected in each state for a two-year term; a resident commissioner from Puerto Rico and a delegate each from American Samoa, the District of Columbia, Guam, the Northern Mariana Islands and the Virgin Islands serve as non-voting members of the house.

Members of the 113th congress were elected on 6 November 2012 and sworn into office on 3 January 2013. As at July 2013, the 113th congress is constituted as follows:
Senate: Democrats 53; Republicans 45; Independent 2
House of Representatives: Republicans 234; Democrats 199; vacancies 2
President of the Senate, The Vice-President
Senate majority leader, Harry Reid *(D), Nevada*
Speaker of the House of Representatives, John Boehner *(R), Ohio*
House majority leader, Kevin McCarthy *(R), California*

THE JUDICATURE
The federal judiciary consists of three sets of federal courts: the Supreme Court at Washington, DC, consisting of a Chief Justice and eight Associate Justices; the US court of appeals, consisting of 179 circuit judges within 12 regional circuits and one federal circuit; and the 94 US district courts served by 678 district court judges.

THE SUPREME COURT
US Supreme Court Building, Washington DC 20543
Chief Justice, John Roberts, *apptd* 2005

UNITED STATES EMBASSY
24 Grosvenor Square, London W1A 1AE
T 020-7499 9000 W http://london.usembassy.gov
Ambassador Extraordinary and Plenipotentiary, HE Matthew Barzun, *apptd* 2013

BRITISH EMBASSY
3100 Massachusetts Avenue NW, Washington DC 20008
T (+1) (202) 588 6500 E washi@fco.gov.uk
W www.gov.uk/government/world/usa k
Ambassador Extraordinary and Plenipotentiary, Sir Peter Westmacott, KCMG, LVO, *apptd* 2012

DEFENCE
Each military department is separately organised and functions under the direction, authority and control of the Secretary of Defence (except the Coast Guard, which is part of the Department of Homeland Security created in 2002). The air force has primary responsibility for the Department of Defence space development programmes and projects.

Aged 16–49, 2010 est	Males	Females
Available for military service	73,270,043	71,941,969
Fit for military service	60,620,143	59,401,941

Military expenditure – US$618,681m (2013)

ECONOMY AND TRADE
The USA is one of the world's leading industrial nations, with a sophisticated market economy that saw huge growth during the 20th century. Economic development was due in part to the mechanisation of the agrarian economy, the expansion of the transport infrastructure and large amounts of relatively cheap migrant labour; more recently it has been driven by rapid advances in technology. In the late 20th century, the economy shifted emphasis from industry to services, and government involvement in the economy was steadily reduced. Until 2008, the economy experienced steady growth, with low unemployment and inflation, although there were large budget and trade deficits, high levels of personal debt and an increasingly uneven distribution of wealth.

THE STATES OF THE UNION

The USA is a federal republic consisting of 50 states and the federal District of Columbia, and also of organised territories. Of the present 50 states, 13 are original states, seven were admitted without previous organisation as territories, and 30 were admitted after such organisation.

§ The 13 original states

(D) Democratic Party; (I) Independent; (R) Republican Party

State (date and order of admission)	Area sq. km	Population*	Capital	Governor (end of term in office)
Alabama (AL) (1819, 22)	135,767	4,833,722	Montgomery	Robert Bentley (R), Jan. 2015
Alaska (AK) (1959, 49)	1,723,337	735,132	Juneau	Sean Parnell (R), Dec. 2014
Arizona (AZ) (1912, 48)	295,234	6,626,624	Phoenix	Jan Brewer (R), Jan. 2015
Arkansas (AR) (1836, 25)	137,732	2,959,373	Little Rock	Mike Beebe (D), Jan. 2015
California (CA) (1850, 31)	423,967	38,332,521	Sacramento	Jerry Brown (D), Jan. 2015
Colorado (CO) (1876, 38)	269,601	5,268,367	Denver	John Hickenlooper (D), Jan. 2015
Connecticut (CT) § (1788, 5)	14,357	3,596,080	Hartford	Dan Malloy (D), Jan. 2015
Delaware (DE) § (1787, 1)	6,446	925,749	Dover	Jack Markell (D), Jan. 2017
Florida (FL) (1845, 27)	170,312	19,552,860	Tallahassee	Rick Scott (R), Jan. 2015
Georgia (GA) § (1788, 4)	153,910	9,992,167	Atlanta	Nathan Deal (R), Jan. 2015
Hawaii (HI) (1959, 50)	28,313	1,404,054	Honolulu	Neil Abercrombie (D), Dec. 2014
Idaho (ID) (1890, 43)	216,443	1,612,136	Boise	C. L. (Butch) Otter (R), Jan. 2015
Illinois (IL) (1818, 21)	149,995	12,882,135	Springfield	Patrick Quinn III (D), Jan. 2015
Indiana (IN) (1816, 19)	94,326	6,570,902	Indianapolis	Mike Pence (R), Jan. 2017
Iowa (IA) (1846, 29)	145,746	3,090,416	Des Moines	Terry Branstad (R), Jan. 2015
Kansas (KS) (1861, 34)	213,100	2,893,957	Topeka	Sam Brownback (R), Jan. 2015
Kentucky (KY) (1792, 15)	104,656	4,395,295	Frankfort	Steve Beshear (D), Dec. 2015
Louisiana (LA) (1812, 18)	135,659	4,625,470	Baton Rouge	Bobby Jindal (R), Jan. 2016
Maine (ME) (1820, 23)	91,633	1,328,302	Augusta	Paul LePage (R), Jan. 2015
Maryland (MD) § (1788, 7)	32,131	5,928,814	Annapolis	Martin O'Malley (D), Jan. 2015
Massachusetts (MA) § (1788, 6)	27,336	6,692,824	Boston	Deval Patrick (D), Jan. 2015
Michigan (MI) (1837, 26)	250,487	9,895,622	Lansing	Rick Snyder (R), Jan. 2015
Minnesota (MN) (1858, 32)	225,163	5,420,380	St Paul	Mark Dayton (D), Jan. 2015
Mississippi (MS) (1817, 20)	125,438	2,991,207	Jackson	Phil Bryant (R), Jan. 2016
Missouri (MO) (1821, 24)	180,540	6,044,171	Jefferson City	Jeremiah (Jay) Nixon (D), Jan. 2017
Montana (MT) (1889, 41)	380,831	1,015,165	Helena	Steve Bullock (D), Jan. 2017
Nebraska (NE) (1867, 37)	200,330	1,868,516	Lincoln	Dave Heineman (R), Jan. 2015
Nevada (NV) (1864, 36)	286,380	2,790,136	Carson City	Brian Sandoval (R), Jan. 2015
New Hampshire (NH) § (1788, 9)	24,214	1,323,459	Concord	Maggie Hassan (D), Jan. 2015
New Jersey (NJ) § (1787, 3)	22,591	8,899,339	Trenton	Chris Christie (R), Jan. 2018
New Mexico (NM) (1912, 47)	314,917	2,085,287	Santa Fé	Susana Martinez (R), Jan. 2015
New York (NY) § (1788, 11)	141,297	19,651,127	Albany	Andrew Cuomo (D), Jan. 2015
North Carolina (NC) § (1789, 12)	139,391	9,848,060	Raleigh	Pat McCrory (D), Jan. 2017
North Dakota (ND) (1889, 39)	183,108	723,393	Bismarck	Jack Dalrymple (R), Dec. 2016
Ohio (OH) (1803, 17)	116,098	11,570,808	Columbus	John Kasich (R), Jan. 2015
Oklahoma (OK) (1907, 46)	181,037	3,850,568	Oklahoma City	Mary Fallin (R), Jan. 2015
Oregon (OR) (1859, 33)	254,799	3,930,065	Salem	John Kitzhaber (D), Jan. 2015
Pennsylvania (PA) § (1787, 2)	119,280	12,773,801	Harrisburg	Tom Corbett (R), Jan. 2015
Rhode Island (RI) § (1790, 13)	4,001	1,051,511	Providence	Lincoln Chafee (I), Jan. 2015
South Carolina (SC) § (1788, 8)	82,933	4,774,839	Columbia	Nikki R. Haley (R), Jan. 2015
South Dakota (SD) (1889, 40)	199,729	844,877	Pierre	Dennis Daugaard (R), Jan. 2015
Tennessee (TN) (1796, 16)	109,153	6,495,978	Nashville	Bill Haslam (R), Jan. 2015
Texas (TX) (1845, 28)	695,662	26,448,193	Austin	Rick Perry (R), Jan. 2015
Utah (UT) (1896, 45)	219,882	2,900,872	Salt Lake City	Gary Herbert (R), Jan 2017
Vermont (VT) (1791, 14)	24,906	626,630	Montpelier	Peter Shumlin (D), Jan. 2015
Virginia (VA) § (1788, 10)	110,787	8,260,405	Richmond	Terry McAuliffe (D), Nov. 2018
Washington (WA) (1889, 42)	184,661	6,971,406	Olympia	Jay Inslee (D), Nov. 2017
West Virginia (WV) (1863, 35)	62,756	1,854,304	Charleston	Earl Ray Tomblin (D), Nov. 2017
Wisconsin (WI) (1848, 30)	169,635	5,742,713	Madison	Scott Walker (R), Jan. 2015
Wyoming (WY) (1890, 44)	253,335	582,658	Cheyenne	Matthew (Matt) Mead (R), Jan. 2015
Dist. of Columbia (DC) (1791)	177	646,449	—	Vincent Gray (D), Jan. 2015 (Mayor)

OUTLYING TERRITORIES AND POSSESSIONS

American Samoa	199	54,719	Pago Pago	Lolo Matalasi Moliga (I), Jan. 2017
Guam	544	161,001	Hagatna	Eddie Calvo (R), Jan. 2015
Northern Mariana Islands	464	51,483	Saipan	Eloy Inos (C), Jan. 2015
Puerto Rico	13,790	3,620,897	San Juan	Alejandro Garcia Padilla (R), Jan. 2017
US Virgin Islands	346	104,170	Charlotte Amalie	John de Jongh Jr (D), Jan. 2015

*States 2012 estimate; outlying territories 2012 estimate

The US sub-prime mortgage crisis in 2007 triggered a global economic downturn, and falling property prices and tight credit pushed the domestic economy into recession by mid 2008. Following the failure of several investment banks, Congress passed a US$700bn relief programme to stabilise the financial markets in October 2008, and in spring 2009 a US$787bn fiscal stimulus package and a record US$3.6 trillion budget for 2010 were approved. Despite these measures, the economy still experienced the collapse of key industries (such as vehicle manufacturing), and rising unemployment and inflation before growth restarted in late 2009 after the USA's longest and deepest recession since the 1930s; the budget and trade deficits remain very high. The USA's triple 'A' credit rating was reduced in August 2011 following a deficit reduction plan passed by Congress.

Agriculture is a major industry in the USA; principal crops are wheat, maize, other grains, fruit, vegetables, cotton, meat and dairy products. Agriculture, fishing and forestry contribute 1.1 per cent of GDP and employ 0.7 per cent of the workforce.

Mining and extraction are important to the economy. Large quantities of coal, iron ore, phosphate rock, copper, zinc and lead are mined. About one-third of the country's oil requirements are supplied by domestic production, principally from fields in the Gulf of Mexico. Natural gas is also produced. Despite its domestic oil and natural gas resources and its electricity generating capacity, the USA is a net importer of energy.

The industrial sector is highly diversified and technologically advanced. The main manufacturing industries produce steel, vehicles, aircraft and aerospace equipment, telecommunications equipment, chemicals, electronic equipment and consumer goods, and process food. Industry contributes 19.5 per cent of GDP and services account for 79.4 per cent of GDP.

The main trading partners are Canada, China, Mexico, Japan and Germany. Principal exports are capital goods (chiefly transistors, aircraft, vehicle parts, computers, telecommunications equipment), industrial supplies (e.g. organic chemicals), consumer goods (cars, medicines) and agricultural produce (soya beans, fruit, maize). The main imports are industrial goods (especially crude oil), consumer goods (cars, clothing, medicines, furniture, toys), capital goods (computers, telecommunications equipment, vehicle parts, office machines, electric power machinery) and agricultural products.

GNI – US$16,515m; US$52,340 per capita (2012)
Annual average growth of GDP – 1.6 per cent (2013 est)
Inflation rate – 1.5 per cent (2013 est)
Population below poverty line – 15.1 per cent (2010 est)
Unemployment – 7.3 per cent (2013 est)
Total external debt – US$15,680,000m (2012)
Imports – US$2,335,540m (2012)
Exports – US$1,545,710m (2012)

BALANCE OF PAYMENTS
Trade – US$789,830m deficit (2012)
Current Account – US$440,417m deficit (2012)

Trade with UK	2012	2013
Imports from UK	£40,344,477,021	£39,739,569,296
Exports to UK	£31,454,052,147	£30,983,052,981

COMMUNICATIONS
Airports – There are 5,054 airports; nearly 200 are capable of handling international flights, the rest cater for the high domestic demand

Waterways – The main seaports are at Baton Rouge, Corpus Christi, Hampton Roads, Houston, Long Beach, Los Angeles, Miami, New Orleans, New York, Oaklands, Plaquemines, Port Canaveral, Port Everglades, Savannah, Seattle, Tampa and Texas City
Roadways – There are 6,586,610km of roadways, including 75,238km of motorways
Railways – There are 224,792km of railways
Telecommunications – 139 million fixed lines and 310 million mobile subscriptions (2012); there were 245 million internet users in 2009
Internet code and IDD – us; 1 (from UK), 011 44 (to UK)
Major broadcasters – The major television networks are ABC, CBS, NBC, CNN, Fox, MTV, HBO and the Public Broadcasting System, which serves around 350 local member stations and is partially funded by the government and by private grants
Press – There are more than 1,500 daily newspapers, including *The Wall Street Journal, USA Today, The Washington Post* and *The New York Times*
WPFI score – 23,49 (46)

EDUCATION AND HEALTH
All the states have compulsory school attendance laws. In general, children are obliged to attend school from seven to 16 years of age.
Gross enrolment ratio (percentage of relevant age group) – primary 98 per cent; secondary 94 per cent; tertiary 95per cent (2012 est)
Health expenditure (per capita) – US$8,608 (2011)
Hospital beds (per 1,000 people) – 3.0 (2010)
Life expectancy (years) – 79.56 (2014 est)
Mortality rate – 8.15 (2014 est)
Birth rate – 13.42 (2014 est)
Infant mortality rate – 6.17 (2014 est)

US TERRITORIES ETC

US insular areas are territories that are not part of one of the 50 US states or a federal district. The US Department of the Interior's Office of Insular Affairs has jurisdiction over American Samoa, Guam, the Northern Mariana Islands, the US Virgin Islands, part of Palmyra Atoll (4 sq. km) and Wake Atoll (6.4 sq. km), the latter shared with the US army's Space and Strategic Defence Command. The US Fish and Wildlife Service has jurisdiction over Baker Island (1.5 sq. km), Howland Island (2.5 sq. km), Jarvis Island (4.2 sq. km), Johnston Atoll (2.5 sq. km, shared with the Defence Threat Reduction Agency), Midway Atoll (5.2 sq. km), Navassa Island (7.8 sq. km), Kingman Reef and part of Palmyra Atoll. The Aleutian Islands (17,666 sq. km) form part of the Alaskan archipelago.

AMERICAN SAMOA
Territory of American Samoa
Area – 199 sq. km
Capital – Pago Pago
Population – 54,719 rising at 0.9 per cent per year (2013 est)
National day – 17 April (Flag Day)

American Samoa consists of the islands of Tutuila, Aunu'u, Ofu, Olosega, Ta'u, Rose Island and Swains Island. The islands were discovered by Europeans in the 18th century and the USA took possession in 1900. Those born in American Samoa are US non-citizen nationals, although some have acquired citizenship through service in the US armed forces or other naturalisation procedures. American Samoa is represented in Congress by a non-voting delegate, who is directly elected for a two-year term. Under the 1966 constitution, American Samoa has a measure of self-government, with certain powers reserved to the US Secretary of the Interior. The governor and deputy governor are directly elected for a four-year term. The bicameral legislative assembly comprises a 21-member House of Representatives (one appointed member and 20 members directly elected for a two-year term) and an 18-seat senate with members elected from among the traditional chiefs for a four-year term. Tuna fishing and canning are the principal economic activities.

Governor, Lolo Matalasi Moliga (I)

GUAM
Guahan – Territory of Guam
Area – 544 sq. km
Capital – Hagatna (also known as Agana); population, 153,000 (2009 est)
Population – 161,001 rising at 0.44 per cent per year (2014 est); Chamorro (37.3 per cent), Filipino (26.3 per cent), white (7.1 per cent). The official languages are Chamorro (a language of the Malayo-Polynesian family with admixtures of Spanish) and English; most Chamorro residents are bilingual
National day – first Monday in March (Discovery Day)

Guam is the largest of the Mariana Islands, in the north Pacific Ocean. A Spanish colony for centuries, it was ceded to the USA in 1898 after the Spanish–American War. Guam was occupied by the Japanese in 1941 but was recaptured by US forces in 1944. Any person born in Guam is a US citizen. Guam is represented in Congress by a non-voting delegate, who is directly elected for a two-year term. Under the Organic Act of Guam 1950, Guam has statutory powers of self-government. The governor and lieutenant-governor are directly elected for a four-year term. The 15-member unicameral legislature is directly elected every two years. The main sources of revenue are tourism (particularly from Japan) and US military spending; the military installation is one of the most strategically important US bases in the Pacific.

Governor, Eddie Calvo (R)

Trade with UK	2012	2013
Imports from UK	£3,121,726	£1,849,855
Exports to UK	£64,805	£240,639

NORTHERN MARIANA ISLANDS
Commonwealth of the Northern Mariana Islands
Area – 464 sq. km
Seat of government – Saipan
Population – 51,483 rising at 1.13 per cent per year (2014 est)
National day – 8 January (Commonwealth Day)

The USA administered the Northern Mariana Islands, a group of 14 islands in the north-west Pacific Ocean, as part of a UN trusteeship until the trusteeship agreement was terminated in 1986, when the islands became a commonwealth under US sovereignty. Those resident in 1976 or subsequently born in the islands are US citizens. The islands are represented in Congress by a non-voting representative, who is directly elected for a two-year term. Under the 1978 constitution, the islands are self-governing. The governor and lieutenant-governor are directly elected for a four-year term. The bicameral legislature comprises a 20-member House of Representatives and a nine-member senate; members are directly elected, representatives for two

years and senators for four years. Tourism and manufacturing, especially of clothing, are the main industries.

Governor, Eloy Inos (C)

PUERTO RICO
Commonwealth of Puerto Rico
Area – 13,790 sq. km
Capital – San Juan; population, 2.475 m (2011). Other major towns are: Bayamón, Carolina, Ponce]
Population – 3,620,897 falling at –0.65 per cent per year (2014 est); most people are of Spanish descent. The official languages are Spanish and English
National day – 25 July (Constitution Day)

Puerto Rico (Rich Port) is an island of the Greater Antilles group in the Caribbean Sea and was discovered in 1493 by Columbus. It was a Spanish possession until 1898, when it was ceded to the USA after the Spanish–American War. Residents have been US citizens since 1917, and Puerto Rico is represented in Congress by a non-voting resident commissioner, who is directly elected for a four-year term. Under its 1952 constitution, Puerto Rico is a self-governing commonwealth. The governor is directly elected for a four-year term. The bicameral legislative assembly consists of a 31-member senate and a 53-member House of Representatives, whose members serve four-year terms. Tourism, pharmaceuticals, electronics, clothing and food processing are the main economic activities.

Governor, Alejandro Garcia Padilla (R)

THE UNITED STATES VIRGIN ISLANDS
Area – 1,910 sq. km
Capital – Charlotte Amalie, on St Thomas; population, 60,000 (2011 est)
Population – 104,170 falling at –0.56 per cent per year (2013 est)
National day – 31 March (Transfer Day)

There are three main islands, St Thomas, St Croix and St John, and about 50 small islets or cays. These constituted the Danish part of the Virgin Islands from the 17th century until purchased by the USA in 1917. Those born in the US Virgin Islands are US nationals. The Virgin Islands are represented in Congress by a non-voting representative, who is directly elected for a two-year term. Under the provisions of the Revised Organic Act of 1954, the islands have powers of self-government. The governor and lieutenant-governor are directly elected for a four-year term. The unicameral senate has 15 members directly elected for a two-year term. Tourism, oil refining and manufacturing are the main industries.

Governor, John de Jongh Jr (D)

URUGUAY

República Oriental del Uruguay – Oriental Republic of Uruguay

Area – 176,215 sq. km
Capital – Montevideo; population, 1,638,617 (2012)
Major towns – Ciudad de la Costa, Salto
Currency – Uruguayan peso of 100 centésimos
Population – 3,332,972 rising at 0.26 per cent a year (2014 est)
Religion – Christian 81 per cent (Roman Catholic 47.1 per cent) (2006)
Language – Spanish (official), Portunol or Brazilero (Portuguese-Spanish mix used along the northern border)
Population density – 19 per sq. km (2011)
Urban population – 92.6 per cent (2012 est)
Median age (years) – 34.3 (2014 est)
National anthem – 'Himno Nacional' ['National Anthem']
National day – 25 August (Independence Day)
Death penalty – Abolished for all crimes (since 1907)
CPI score – 73 (19)

CLIMATE AND TERRAIN

The country consists mainly of undulating grassy plains, with low hills. Elevation extremes range from 514m (Cerro Catedral) to 0m (Atlantic Ocean). The principal river is the Rio Negro (with its tributary, the Yi), flowing from north-east to south-west into the Rio Uruguay; damming of the Negro has created a reservoir that is the largest artificial lake in South America. The climate is warm temperate, with occasional cold and strong winds. Average temperatures in Montevideo range from 10°C in July to 22°C in January.

HISTORY AND POLITICS

The hostility of the indigenous Charrúa Amerindians when the Rio de la Plata was first explored by the Spanish in 1516 discouraged colonisation until the 17th century. Although initially settled by the Portuguese, the *Banda Oriental,* as the territory lying on the eastern bank of the river Uruguay was then called, was disputed between the Portuguese and the Spanish until the late 18th century and then between Brazil and Argentina after Spanish rule was overthrown. Uruguay's independence was recognised in 1828 and a republic was inaugurated in 1830. In the mid-19th century there was a power struggle between the conservatives *(Blancos)* and liberals *(Colorados)* which descended into civil war. From 1904 until the 1960s the country experienced political stability and prosperity.

The period from 1962 to 1973 saw economic decline and turmoil caused by the Marxist Tupamaros guerrillas. They were crushed by a military dictatorship that held power from 1973 until 1985, when a return to civilian rule was agreed after violent anti-government protests at the regime's repressive rule and the deteriorating economy.

The Colorado and National *(Blanco)* parties now both occupy the centre ground, but their dominance of politics has been eroded by left-wing parties such as New Space and coalitions such as the Progressive Encounter-Broad Front (EP-FA). The EP-FA won outright majorities in both legislative chambers in the 2004 and the 2009 elections. The 2009 presidential election was won by the EP-FA candidate José Mujica, and he appointed an EP-FA-led coalition government.

Under the 1997 constitution, the executive president is directly elected for a five-year term, which is not renewable. The president, who appoints the council of ministers, is responsible to the legislature. The bicameral general assembly consists of a Chamber of Representatives, with 99 members directly elected for a five-year term, and the Chamber of Senators, which has 31 members, 30 directly elected for a five-year term and the vice-president as an *ex officio* member.

The republic is divided into 19 departments, each with an elected governor and legislature.

HEAD OF STATE
President, José Mujica, *elected* 29 November 2009, *took office* 1 March 2010
Vice-President, Danilo Astori

SELECTED GOVERNMENT MEMBERS *as at July 2014*
Defence, Eleuterio Fernandez Huidobro
Economy and Finance, Mario Bergara
Foreign Affairs, Luis Almagro
Interior, Eduardo Bonomi

EMBASSY OF URUGUAY
150 Brompton Road, London SW3 1HX
T 020-7937 4170 E emburuguay@emburuguay.org.uk
Ambassador Extraordinary and Plenipotentiary, HE Julio Moreira Moran, *apptd* 2009

BRITISH EMBASSY
PO Box 16024, Calle Marco Bruto 1073, 11300 Montevideo
T (+598) (2) 622 3630 E ukinuruguay@adinet.com.uy
W www.gov.uk/government/world/uruguay
Ambassador Extraordinary and Plenipotentiary, HE Ben Lyster-Binns, *apptd* 2012

DEFENCE

Aged 16–49, 2010 est	*Males*	*Females*
Available for military service	771,159	780,932
Fit for military service	649,025	654,903

Military expenditure – US$942m (2013)

ECONOMY AND TRADE

After years of steady growth, Uruguay suffered a severe recession from 1998, largely owing to the economic problems of Brazil and Argentina, its main export markets and sources of tourists. It reduced many to poverty in what had previously been a moderately prosperous society, and nearly a fifth of households remained below the poverty line in 2010. The recession culminated in a banking crisis in 2002; IMF loans, the rescheduling of foreign debt repayments and the government's emergency measures achieved a recovery and the economy grew strongly from 2004 to 2008. The 2008 global downturn slowed economic growth in 2009, but Uruguay avoided recession, mainly through increased public expenditure. Uruguay achieved growth of 8.9 per cent in 2010, but this dropped to 3.9 per cent by 2013.

Ranching and livestock products (beef, mutton, wool) have been the mainstay of the economy since the mid-19th century, generating the prosperity that enabled Uruguay to develop an extensive welfare system in the early 20th century, although dependence on these products leaves the economy vulnerable to price fluctuations. Other crops include rice, grains, soya beans, citrus fruits, wine grapes, linseed and sunflower seed. Agricultural produce is the basis of the food processing and beverage industries. Other industries include fishing, forestry and the manufacture of electrical machinery, transport equipment, petroleum products, textiles and chemicals. Exploited minerals include clinker, dolomite, marble and granite. Tourism and offshore financial services also contribute substantially to revenue. Agriculture contributes 7.5 per cent of GDP, industry 21.5 per cent and services 71 per cent.

The main trading partners are China, Brazil, Argentina, and the USA. Principal exports are meat, soya beans, cellulose, rice, wheat, timber, dairy products and wool. The main imports are crude and refined oil, vehicles and vehicle parts, mobile phones and insecticide.

GNI – US$48,456m; US$13,580 per capita (2012)
Annual average growth of GDP – 3.5 per cent (2013 est)
Inflation rate – 8.3 per cent (2013 est)
Unemployment – 6.5 per cent (2013 est)
Total external debt – US$17,610m (2013 est)
Imports – US$10,642m (2012)
Exports – US$8,601m (2012)

BALANCE OF PAYMENTS
Trade – US$2,041m deficit (2012)
Current Account – US$1,369m deficit (2011)

Trade with UK	2012	2013
Imports from UK	£106,949,571	£157,755,339
Exports to UK	£113,681,381	£90,880,018

COMMUNICATIONS
Airports and waterways – There are 11 airports, including an international airport near Montevideo; there are 1,600km of navigable waterways, mainly on the Uruguay and Negro rivers, and the main ports are located in Montevideo, Colonia, Fray Bentos and Paysandú
Roadways and railways – 77,732km; 1,641km
Telecommunications – 1.01 fixed lines in use and 5 million mobile subscriptions (2011); there were 1.41 million internet users in 2009
Internet code and IDD – uy; 598 (from UK), 44 (to UK)
Major broadcasters – State-run television and radio are operated by SODRE, the official broadcasting service
Press – Major daily newspapers include El Pais, El Observador and El Telegrafo
WPFI score – 16,08 (26)

EDUCATION AND HEALTH
Primary and secondary education is compulsory and free, and technical and trade schools and evening courses for adult education are state-run.
Literacy rate – 98 per cent (2010 est)
Gross enrolment ratio (percentage of relevant age group) – primary 112 per cent; secondary 90 per cent; tertiary 63 per cent (2012 est)
Health expenditure (per capita) – US$1,105 (2011)
Hospital beds (per 1,000 people) – 3 (2011)
Life expectancy (years) – 76.81 (2014 est)
Mortality rate – 9.48 (2014 est)
Birth rate – 13.18 (2014 est)
Infant mortality rate – 8.97 (2014 est)

UZBEKISTAN

O'zbekiston Respublikasi – Republic of Uzbekistan

Area – 447,400 sq. km
Capital – Tashkent; population, 2,230,749 (2012)

Major cities – Andijan, Bukhara, Karsi, Namangan, Nukus, Samarkand
Currency – Som of 100 tiyins
Population – 28,929,716 rising at 0.93 per cent a year (2014 est); Uzbek (80 per cent), Russian (5.5 per cent), Tajik (5 per cent), Kazakh (3 per cent), Karakalpak (2.5 per cent), Tatar (1.5 per cent) (est)
Religion – Muslim 88 per cent (predominantly Sunni), Eastern Orthodox 9 per cent (est)
Language – Uzbek (official), Russian, Tajik
Population density – 69 per sq. km (2011)
Urban population – 36.2 per cent (2012 est)
Median age (years) – 27.1 (2014 est)
National anthem – 'O'zbekiston Respublikasining Davlat Madhiyasi' ['National Anthem of the Republic of Uzbekistan']
National day – 1 September (Independence Day, 1991)
Death penalty – Abolished for all crimes (since 2008)
CPI score – 17 (168)

CLIMATE AND TERRAIN
Landlocked Uzbekistan has four regions: the Ustyurt plateau and Amu Darya delta in the west; the Kyzyl Kum desert east of the Aral Sea; the Tien Shan and Pamir mountains in the east and south-east; and the fertile Fergana valley in the east, crossed by the Syr Darya river. Elevation extremes range from 4,301m (Adelunga Toghi) to −12m (Sariqarnish Kuli). The country includes the southern part of the Aral Sea. There is a semi-arid desert climate, although it is colder in the mountains. Average temperatures in Tashkent range from 1.9°C in January to 27.8°C in July.

HISTORY AND POLITICS
Settlements in the south developed as important transit points on the ancient 'Silk Road' in the first century BC. Bukhara and Samarkand became two of the most important cultural and academic centres in the Islamic world after the religion was introduced in the eighth century. In the 13th century the area became part of the Mongol Empire, with Samarkand as its capital during the reign of Amir Timur (Tamerlane). As the empire declined, independent principalities emerged. The three khanates in what is now Uzbekistan, Khiva, Kokand and Bukhara, were annexed by the Russian Empire in the second half of the 19th century. In 1917 a Bolshevik revolution broke out in Tashkent and by 1921 all of Uzbekistan had been absorbed into the USSR. Under Soviet rule a massive land irrigation programme was implemented to allow the cultivation of cotton, but this also led to the drying up of the Aral Sea.

Uzbekistan declared its independence from the USSR on 1 September 1991 but post-independence political life has been dominated by the former communists. The main opposition parties, Erk (Freedom) and Birlik (Unity), were banned in 1992 and have since become inactive; other forms of opposition are suppressed and the government has been accused of human rights abuses, including the systematic use of torture. The former communist leader Islam Karimov, who came to power in 1990, was elected president in 1991 and has retained the presidency since, in unopposed elections or through the extension of his term of office in referendums. He was re-elected in 2007 for a third term, despite the constitutional restriction to two terms.

All legislative elections since independence have been won by the People's Democratic Party (the former Communist Party) or its allies. After the latest legislative election in December 2009 and January 2010, the largest party in the legislative chamber was the pro-Karimov Liberal Democratic Party; opposition parties were barred from contesting the election. Most elections have been reported by observers to be neither free nor fair and have attracted international criticism.

The Islamic Movement of Uzbekistan (IMU), founded in 1996, has carried out armed attacks and bombings sporadically since 1999, but has little support. However, its activities have provided the government with an excuse to curtail human rights and suppress political opposition and protests, such as those in Andijan in 2005, when over 180 protesters were killed by troops.

The 1992 constitution was amended in 2002 to create a bicameral legislature and extend the president's term of office, and in 2011 to make the prime minister responsible to the legislature. The president is directly elected; his term of office was five years, renewable only once, but was extended to seven years. The legislature, the Supreme Assembly, became bicameral after the 2004–5 elections. The Legislative Chamber has 150 members, 135 directly elected and 15 members of the Ecological Movement of Uzbekistan. The senate has 101 members, 16 appointed by the president, 84 elected by regional deputies to represent the regions and the capital, and President Karimov. Members of both houses serve a five-year term. The president appoints the cabinet, which is chaired by the prime minister.

The country is divided into 12 provinces, the autonomous republic of Karakalpakstan, and the city of Tashkent.

HEAD OF STATE
President, Islam Karimov, *elected* 29 December 1991, *elected by referendum for a five-year term* 1995, *re-elected* 2000, 2007

SELECTED GOVERNMENT MEMBERS *as at July 2014*
Prime Minister, Shavkat Mirziyoev
First Deputy Prime Minister, Finance, Rustam Azimov
Deputy Prime Ministers, Elmira Basitkhanova; Gulomjon Ibragimov; Adham Ikromov; Ulugbek Rozukulov; Batir Zakirov

EMBASSY OF THE REPUBLIC OF UZBEKISTAN
41 Holland Park, London W11 3RP
T 020-7229 7679 E info@uzbekembassy.org
W www.uzbekembassy.org
Ambassador Extraordinary and Plenipotentiary, HE Otabek Akbarov, *apptd* 2007

BRITISH EMBASSY
Ul. Gulyamova 67, Tashkent 100000
T (+998) (71) 120 1500 E ukin.uzbekistan@fco.gov.uk
W www.gov.uk/government/world/uzbekistan
Ambassador Extraordinary and Plenipotentiary, HE Christopher George Edgar, OBE, *apptd* 2012

DEFENCE

Aged 16–49, 2010 est	Males	Females
Available for military service	7,887,292	7,886,459
Fit for military service	6,566,118	6,745,818

Conscription duration – 12 months

ECONOMY AND TRADE
The economy remains centrally planned and control has increased in some areas, stifling economic activity. Economic growth and living standards are among the worst in the former Soviet republics, with over a quarter of the population living below the poverty line. The 2008 global downturn had little impact owing to the country's relative economic isolation.

The economy is based on intensive agricultural production, particularly of cotton, made possible by extensive irrigation schemes. Vegetables, fruit, grain and livestock are also produced. The main industries are textile manufacture, food processing, machine building, metallurgy, mining (especially for gold), oil and natural gas production and chemicals. Oil and gas exports offer potential for greater economic growth and have attracted foreign interest, notably from Russia and China, but exploitation is hampered by a lack of modern oil pipelines and basic infrastructure. Agriculture contributes 19.1 per cent of GDP, industry 32.2 per cent and services 48.7 per cent.

The main trading partners are Russia, China, Kazakhstan and South Korea. Principal exports are oil and natural gas, cotton, gold, mineral fertilisers, metals, textiles, food products, machinery and motor vehicles. The main imports are machinery and equipment, foodstuffs, chemicals and metals.

GNI – US$53,028m; US$1,720 per capita (2012)
Annual average growth of GDP – 7 per cent (2013 est)
Inflation rate – 10.1 per cent (2013 est)
Population below poverty line – 17 per cent (2011 est)
Unemployment – 4.9 per cent (2013 est)
Total external debt – US$8,733m (2013 est)

BALANCE OF PAYMENTS
Trade – US$3,301m surplus (2011)
Current Account – US$367m surplus (2012)

Trade with UK	2012	2013
Imports from UK	£44,092,460	£42,170,101
Exports to UK	£17,730,806	£13,625,606

COMMUNICATIONS
Airports and waterways – The principal airport is at Tashkent and the country has 1,100km of waterways
Roadways and railways – 86,496km; 4,230km
Telecommunications – 1.963 million fixed lines and 20.274 million mobile subscriptions (2012); there were 4.689 million internet users in 2009
Media – The National Television and Radio Company includes flagship network Ozbekistan; major newspapers include *Khalq Sozi* and Russian-language daily *Narodnoye Slovo*
WPFI score – 61,01 (166)

EDUCATION AND HEALTH
Literacy rate – 99 per cent (2011 est)
Gross enrolment ratio (percentage of relevant age group) – primary 93 per cent; secondary 105 per cent; tertiary 9 per cent (2012 est)
Health expenditure (per capita) – US$88 (2011)
Hospital beds (per 1,000 people) – 4.5 (2010)
Life expectancy (years) – 73.29 (2014 est)
Mortality rate – 5.29 (2014 est)
Birth rate – 17.02 (2014 est)
Infant mortality rate – 19.84 (2014 est)

VANUATU

Ripablik blong Vanuatu/République de Vanuatu – Republic of Vanuatu

Area – 12,189 sq. km
Capital – Port Vila, on Efaté; population, 47,000 (2011 est)
Major town – Luganville, on Espiritu Santo
Currency – Vatu
Population – 266,937 rising at 2.01 per cent a year (2014 est); 98.5 per cent are Melanesian, the rest being mostly Micronesian, Polynesian and European (est)
Religion – Christian 82.4 per cent (Presbyterian 27.9 per cent, Anglican 15.1 per cent, Roman Catholic 12.4 per cent, Seventh-day Adventist 12.5 per cent) (est)
Language – English, French, Bislama (all official); over 100 local languages exist
Population density – 20 per sq. km (2011)
Urban population – 25.2 per cent (2012 est)
Median age (years) – 21.1 (2014 est)
National anthem – 'Yumi, Yumi, Yumi' ['We, We, We']
National day – 30 July (Independence Day)
Death penalty – Abolished for all crimes (since 1980)
Literacy rate – 83 per cent (2011 est)
Life expectancy (years) – 72.72 (2014 est)
Mortality rate – 4.14 (2014 est)
Birth rate – 25.69 (2014 est)
Infant mortality rate – 16.41 (2014 est)

CLIMATE AND TERRAIN
Situated in the south Pacific Ocean, Vanuatu comprises 13 large and some 70 small islands, of either coral or volcanic origin, including the Banks Islands and Torres Islands in the north. The principal islands are Vanua Lava, Espiritu Santo, Maewo, Pentecost, Ambae, Malekula, Ambrym, Epi, Efaté, Erromango, Tanna and Aneityum. Most islands are mountainous and covered with dense rainforest. Elevation extremes range from 1,877m (Tabwemasana) to 0m (Pacific Ocean). The climate varies from tropical in the north of the archipelago to subtropical in the south, and all the islands experience cyclones.

HISTORY AND POLITICS
Some of the islands of Vanuatu have been inhabited for over 4,000 years. Europeans first visited in the early 17th century, and Captain Cook named the islands the New Hebrides in 1774. In the 19th century, the British and the French established plantations, and from 1906 jointly administered the islands as the Condominium of the New Hebrides. This became independent as the Republic of Vanuatu in 1980.

The 2009 presidential election was won by Iolu Abil in the third round of voting. Governments are formed by frequently shifting coalitions of various parties. In the 2012 legislative election the Vanuaaka Pati was the largest party in parliament, however prime minister Sato Kilman resigned in March 2013 before a vote of confidence; Moana Carcasses Kalosil was then elected to replace him. In May 2014 Joe Natuman was elected prime minister by parliament following a vote of no confidence in the Kalosil government.

Under the 1980 constitution, the head of state is a president who is elected for a five-year term by an electoral college consisting of the members of the legislature and the presidents of the six provincial governments. The unicameral parliament has 52 members, directly elected for a four-year term. The prime minister is elected by parliament from among its members, and appoints the council of ministers. The National Council of Chiefs advises on matters of custom.

HEAD OF STATE
President, Iolu Abil, *elected* 2 September 2009

SELECTED GOVERNMENT MEMBERS *as at July 2014*
Prime Minister, Joe Natuman
Deputy Prime Minister, Ham Lini
Finance, Maki Simelum
Internal Affairs, Charlot Tabimasmas

BRITISH HIGH COMMISSIONER
HE Dominic Meiklejohn, *apptd* 2012, resident at Honiara, Solomon Islands

ECONOMY AND TRADE
The economy is based on small-scale agriculture and fishing; 65 per cent of the population is employed on plantations or in subsistence agriculture. Subsistence crops include yams, taro, fruit and vegetables; the principal cash crops are coconuts, cocoa and coffee. Cattle are kept on the plantations. There is a small light industrial sector producing frozen food and fish and canned meat, and processing wood. Eco-tourism and offshore financial services are of growing importance. Australia and New Zealand supply revenue via aid and tourism.

The main export markets are Thailand (59.9 per cent) and Côte d'Ivoire; imports come chiefly from China, Singapore, the USA and Japan. Principal exports are copra, beef, cocoa, timber, kava and coffee. The main imports are machinery and equipment, foodstuffs and fuels.

GNI – US$748m; US$3,000 per capita (2012)
Annual average growth of GDP – 3.3 per cent (2013 est)
Inflation rate – 1.9 per cent (2013 est)
Total external debt – US$307.7m (2011 est)
Imports – US$312m (2011)
Exports – US$69m (2011)

BALANCE OF PAYMENTS
Trade – US$241m deficit (2012)
Current Account – US$50m deficit (2012)

Trade with UK	2012	2013
Imports from UK	£683,209	£339,966
Exports to UK	£619,509	£459,377

COMMUNICATIONS
Airports and waterways – The main international airport is at Port Vila and the main ports are located in Forari, Port Vila and Santo
Roadways – 1,070km
Telecommunications – 5,800 main fixed lines and 137,000 mobile subscriptions (2012); there were 17,000 internet users in 2009
Media – Vanuatu Broadcasting and Television Corporation operates Television Blong Vanuatu

VATICAN CITY STATE

Status Civitatis Vaticanae or Sancta Sedes/stato Della Città del Vaticano or Santa Sede – State of the Vatican city or the Holy See

Area – 0.44 sq. km (enclave only)
Capital – Vatican City
Currency – Euro (€) of 100 cents
Population – 839 (2013 est)
Religion – Christian (Roman Catholic)
Language – Latin (official), Italian, French
National anthem – 'Inno e Marcia Pontificale' ['Pontifical Anthem and March']
National day – 13 March (election of Pope Francis, 2013)
Death penalty – Abolished for all crimes (since 1969)

HISTORY AND POLITICS

The Vatican City State is an independent sovereign state that consists of an enclave within the city of Rome and extraterritorial areas including offices and basilicas in Rome, the pope's summer residence and the location of Vatican Radio's transmitter. The Holy See, which comprises the pope and the departments that carry out the government of the Roman Catholic Church worldwide, has sovereign authority over the Vatican City State's territory, providing its government and diplomatic representation overseas.

The head of the Roman Catholic Church became a temporal ruler in the eighth century, holding territory in central Italy. The Papal States were annexed in 1860 by the newly unified kingdom of Italy, and Rome was captured by Italian troops in 1870–1, when the pope withdrew into the Vatican palace. In the Lateran treaties (1929), Italy recognised the pope's sovereignty over the city of the Vatican, and declared the state to be neutral and inviolable territory. The Vatican City State has special observer status at the United Nations.

The pope, the Sovereign Pontiff, is the head of state of the Vatican City, which is governed as an absolute monarchy. He is elected for life by a conclave consisting of those members of the Sacred College of Cardinals who are under the age of 80. Administration of the state is carried out by the Pontifical Commission and the Secretariat of State, which are appointed by the pope. All Vatican officials vacate their offices on the death of a pope. Pope Benedict XVI confirmed in office the president of the Pontifical Commission and the members of the Secretariat of State after his election. Pope Benedict XVI resigned in February 2013 and was succeeded by Pope Francis.

Sovereign Pontiff, His Holiness Pope Francis (Jorge Mario Bergoglio), *born* 17 December 1936, *elected* 13 March 2013, *inaugurated* 19 March 2013

SECRETARIAT OF STATE *as at July 2013*
Secretary of State, Cardinal Pietro Parolin
Substitute for General Affairs, Archbishop Giovanni Becciu

Secretary for Relations with States, Archbishop Dominique Mamberti

PONTIFICAL COMMISSION
President, Archbishop Giuseppe Bertello

APOSTOLIC NUNCIATURE
54 Parkside, London SW19 5NE
T 020-8944 7189
Apostolic Nuncio, HE Archbishop Antonio Mennini, *apptd* 2011

BRITISH EMBASSY TO THE HOLY SEE
Via XX Settembre 80/A, 00187 Rome
T (+39) (6) 4220 4000 E holysee@fco.gov.uk
W www.gov.uk/government/world/holy-see
Ambassador Extraordinary and Plenipotentiary, HE Nigel Baker, OBE, MVO, *apptd* 2011

ECONOMY

The Vatican City budget is separate from that of the Holy See. The City's revenue is generated by museum admission charges and the sale of postage stamps, coins, medals, souvenirs and publications. The Holy See derives its income from investments, property, global banking and financial services and donations from Roman Catholics worldwide. Pope Francis has begun the process of reforming the Vatican Bank following a number of scandals (*see* Events of the year). The annual collections known as Peter's Pence are used for charitable and overseas aid work and disaster relief.

VENEZUELA

República Bolivariana de Venezuela – Bolivarian Republic of Venezuela

Area – 912,050 sq. km
Capital – Caracas; population, 3,171,898 (2012)
Major cities – Barquisimeto, Ciudad Guayana, Maracaibo, Valencia
Currency – Bolívar fuerte (Bs. F) of 100 céntimos
Population – 28,868,486 rising at 1.42 per cent a year (2014 est)
Religion – Christian (Roman Catholic 96 per cent) (est)
Language – Spanish (official), several indigenous languages
Population density – 33 per sq. km (2011)
Urban population – 93.7 per cent (2012 est)
Median age (years) – 26.9 (2014 est)
National anthem – 'Gloria al Bravo Pueblo' ['Glory to the Brave People']
National day – 5 July (Independence Day)
Death penalty – Abolished for all crimes (since 1863)
CPI score – 20 (160)

CLIMATE AND TERRAIN

The Andean mountains, of which the main range is the Sierra Nevada de Mérida, run across the north-west of the country, separating the northern coast from the central plains *(llanos)*. The Guiana Highlands occupy the south-east of the country. Elevation extremes range from 5,007m (Pico Bolivar) to 0m (Caribbean Sea). The Orinoco flows across the centre of the country to its delta on the Atlantic coast. Its upper waters are united with those of the Rio Negro (a Brazilian tributary of the Amazon) by a natural river or canal, known as the Brazo Casiquiare. The coastal lowlands contain many lagoons and lakes, including Lake Maracaibo (area 13,351 sq. km), the largest lake in South America. The climate varies from tropical to alpine, depending on altitude, and most areas experience a wet season from May to November. The average temperature in Caracas is 23°C.

HISTORY AND POLITICS

Columbus landed on the coast in 1498, and the first Spanish settlement was established at Cumaná in 1520. Venezuela became part of the Viceroyalty of New Granada in the early 18th century. There were several revolts against Spanish colonial rule, and a declaration of independence in 1811 was followed by several years of struggle until troops led by Simón Bolivar defeated the Spanish at the battle of Carabobo in 1821. Venezuela became part of Gran Colombia (with Colombia, Ecuador and Panama), and then an independent republic in 1830 under the first of a series of *caudillos* (military leaders). The first truly democratic elections were held in 1947 but the government was overthrown by the military within months. An enduring civilian democracy was established in 1958.

Oil revenues supported a buoyant economy in the 1970s but a price collapse in the mid-1980s led to economic difficulties and widespread poverty, causing social unrest and a number of attempted coups. After he came to power in 1998, President Hugo Chávez's economic and social reforms, and his authoritarian style polarised domestic opinion, provoking strikes and demonstrations, an attempted military coup in 2002 and a recall referendum in 2004, which he won.

President Chávez was re-elected in 2006. Despite re-election in October 2012, President Chávez was too ill to be re-inaugurated and died on 5 March 2013. Nicolas Maduro, also of the United Socialist Party of Venezuela (PSUV), was elected to succeed him in April 2013. In the 2010 legislative election, the PSUV and its allies won an overall majority, but lost its two-thirds majority (needed to change the constitution) as opposition parties won 67 seats. A number of large and frequently violent protests have occurred since the beginning of 2014. *See* Events of the year.

Under the 1999 constitution, the executive president is directly elected for a six-year term; the limit on the number of successive terms was abolished in 2009. The unicameral National Assembly has 165 members, 162 directly elected and three representing indigenous people, who serve a five-year term. The president appoints the vice-president and the council of ministers.

The country is divided into 23 states, one capital district and one federal dependency composed of 11 island groups (72 individual islands). The states have considerable autonomy and each has its own legislature and elected governor.

HEAD OF STATE

President, Nicolas Maduro, *elected* 14 April 2013, *sworn in* 19 April 2013

Executive Vice-President, Jorge Arreaza

SELECTED GOVERNMENT MEMBERS *as at July 2013*

Defence, Rear Adm. Carmen Teresa Melendez Maniglia
Finance, Rodolfo Marco Torres
Interior and Justice, Gen. Miguel Rodriguez Torres

EMBASSY OF THE BOLIVARIAN REPUBLIC OF VENEZUELA

1 Cromwell Road, London SW7 2HW
T 020-7584 4206 E info@venezlon.co.uk
W www.embavenez-uk.org
Ambassador Extraordinary and Plenipotentiary, vacant

BRITISH EMBASSY

Edificio Torre la Castellana, Piso 11, Avenida la Principal de la Castellana, Caracas 1601
T (+58) (212) 263 8411 E ukinvenezuela@fco.gov.uk
W www.gov.uk/government/world/venezuela
Ambassador Extraordinary and Plenipotentiary, HE Catherine Nettleton, *apptd* 2010

DEFENCE

Aged 16–49, 2010 est	Males	Females
Available for military service	7,013,854	7,165,661
Fit for military service	5,614,743	6,074,834

Military expenditure – US$4,487m (2013)
Conscription duration – 30 months (selective)

ECONOMY AND TRADE

Much of industry is state-owned, and since President Chávez came to power an increasing proportion of the private sector, some foreign-owned, has been nationalised, including oil, electricity, financial, steel, construction and agribusiness companies. Laws passed in December 2010 aimed to increase government control of the economy, which is struggling because of imbalances, high inflation and electricity shortages after a severe drought in 2009–10 left hydroelectric plants inoperable. Inflation is an increasing problem, rising 20 per cent in 2012 and 56 per cent in 2013.

Oil and gas are the mainstays of the economy, providing over 95 per cent of exports and over 45 per cent of government revenue, but heavy dependence on them makes the economy vulnerable to global price fluctuations. The economy went into recession in 2009 owing to lower prices and the global downturn. The government struggled with housing and electricity crises alongside food shortages throughout 2013.

Other major industries are mining (coal, iron ore, bauxite, gold), production of construction materials, textiles, steel and aluminium, food processing and vehicle assembly. Industry contributes 35.5 per cent of GDP and services 60.8 per cent.

Agriculture comprises large-scale commercial farms and subsistence farming. Land distribution is uneven, but redistribution of land to the rural poor, breaking up larger estates, has begun. Agricultural products include maize, sorghum, sugar cane, rice, bananas, vegetables and coffee. There is an extensive beef and dairy farming industry. Agriculture provides 3.7 per cent of GDP and engages 7.3 per cent of the workforce.

The main trading partners are the USA (39.1 per cent of exports; 31.7 per cent of imports), Colombia, China and India. Principal exports are oil, bauxite and aluminium, minerals, chemicals, agricultural products and basic manufactures. The main imports are agricultural products, raw materials, machinery, transport equipment and construction materials.

GNI – US$371,238m; US$12,460 per capita (2012)
Annual average growth of GDP – 1.6 per cent (2013 est)
Inflation rate – 56.2 per cent (2013 est)
Population below poverty line – 31.6 per cent (2011 est)
Unemployment – 7.9 per cent (2013 est)
Total external debt – US$74,870m (2013 est)
Imports – US$60,000m (2012)
Exports – US$97,340m (2012)

BALANCE OF PAYMENTS
Trade – US$37,340m surplus (2012)
Current Account – US$11,016m surplus (2012)

Trade with UK	2012	2013
Imports from UK	£372,449,824	£290,068,639
Exports to UK	£454,182,664	£245,384,422

COMMUNICATIONS
Airports and waterways – There are 127 airports, the principal terminals being at Caracas and Maracaibo; the main ports are Maracaibo, Puerto Cabello and Caracas-La Guaira
Roadways and railways – 96,155km; 806km
Telecommunications – 7.65 million fixed lines in use and 30.52 million mobile subscriptions (2012); there were 8.918 million internet users in 2009
Internet code and IDD – ve; 58 (from UK), 44 (to UK)
Major broadcasters – Radio Caracas Television had its terrestrial licence terminated in 2007; other networks include the government-run Venezolana de Television
Press – There are six daily newspapers, including *El Mundo* and *El Nacional*
WPFI score – 35,37 (116)

EDUCATION AND HEALTH
There are nine years of compulsory education.
Literacy rate – 96 per cent (2009 est)
Gross enrolment ratio (percentage of relevant age group) –
   primary 102 per cent; secondary 85 per cent (2012 est);
   tertiary 78.1 per cent (2011 est)
Health expenditure (per capita) – US$555 (2011)
Hospital beds (per 1,000 people) – 0.9 (2011)
Life expectancy (years) – 74.39 (2014 est)
Mortality rate – 5.27 (2014 est)
Birth rate – 19.42 (2014 est)
Infant mortality rate – 19.33 (2014 est)

VIETNAM

Cong Hoa Xa Hoi Chu Nghia Viet Nam – Socialist Republic of Vietnam

Area – 331,210 sq. km
Capital – Hanoi; population, 2,955,000 (2011)

Major cities – Bien Hoa, Da Nang, Haiphong, Ho Chi Minh City (Saigon)
Currency – Dong of 10 ho or 100 xu
Population – 93,421,835 rising at 1 per cent a year (2014 est); Kinh (85.7 per cent), Tay (1.9 per cent), Thai (1.8 per cent), Muong (1.5 per cent), Khmer (1.5 per cent), Hmong (1.2 per cent), Nung (1.1 per cent) (2009)
Religion – Buddhist 9.3 per cent, Christian (Roman Catholic, 6.7 per cent, Protestant 0.5 per cent), Hoa Hao 1.5 per cent, Cao Dai 1.1 per cent, none 80.8 per cent. Cao Dai is a syncretistic religion that combines elements of several faiths. Hoa Hao is a branch of Buddhism
Language – Vietnamese (official), English, French, Chinese, Khmer; Mon-Khmer and Malayo-Polynesian are spoken in mountain areas
Population density – 283 per sq. km (2011)
Urban population – 31.7 per cent (2012 est)
Median age (years) – 29.2 (2014 est)
National anthem – 'Tien Quan Ca' ['Army March']
National day – 2 September (Independence Day)
Death penalty – Retained
CPI score – 31 (116)

CLIMATE AND TERRAIN
The country is mostly mountainous, apart from the densely populated fertile plains around the deltas of the Hong (Red River) in the north and the Mekong in the south. Elevation extremes range from 3,144m (Fan Si Pan) to 0m (South China Sea). The climate is tropical and affected by the monsoon cycle. The wet season lasts from May to September, although the coast, being affected by typhoons and tropical storms, receives most rain between September and January.

POLITICS
The 1992 constitution was amended in 2001 to allow small-scale capitalism greater freedom. The president is elected by the legislature to serve a five-year term. The unicameral National Assembly *(Quoc-Hoi)* has 500 members, who are directly elected for a five-year term. The head of government is the prime minister, who is responsible to the National Assembly, which appoints the council of ministers. However, effective power lies with the Communist Party of Vietnam. Its highest executive body is the Central Committee, elected by the national party congress held every five years. The politburo and the secretariat of the central committee, which exercise the real power, are elected at the party congress.

After the 2006 Communist Party Congress, the president and prime minister resigned to allow a younger leadership to be appointed; Nguyen Minh Triet was elected president to complete his predecessor's term of office, and he appointed Nguyen Tan Dung as prime minister. Both were re-elected to their posts in 2007, but the former lost the 2011 presidential race to Truong Tan Sang. In the May 2011 legislative election, the Communist Party and its allies held all the seats apart from four won by independent candidates.

HEAD OF STATE
President, Truong Tan Sang, *elected* 25 July 2011
Vice-President, Nguyen Thi Doan

SELECTED GOVERNMENT MEMBERS *as at July 2014*
Prime Minister, Nguyen Tan Dung
Deputy Prime Ministers, Hoang Trung Hai; Nguyen Xuan Phuc; Vu Duc Dam; Pham Binh Minh *(Foreign Affairs)*
Finance, Dinh Tien Dung
Internal Affairs, Nguyen Thai Binh

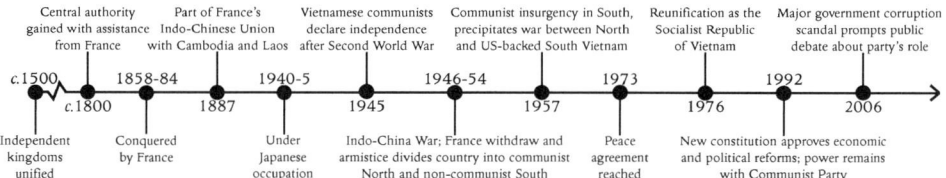

| c.1500 | 1858-84 | 1940-5 | 1946-54 | 1973 | 1992 |
| c.1800 | 1887 | 1945 | 1957 | 1976 | 2006 |

Central authority gained with assistance from France — Part of France's Indo-Chinese Union with Cambodia and Laos — Vietnamese communists declare independence after Second World War — Communist insurgency in South, precipitates war between North and US-backed South Vietnam — Reunification as the Socialist Republic of Vietnam — Major government corruption scandal prompts public debate about party's role

Independent kingdoms unified — Conquered by France — Under Japanese occupation — Indo-China War; France withdraw and armistice divides country into communist North and non-communist South — Peace agreement reached — New constitution approves economic and political reforms; power remains with Communist Party

EMBASSY OF THE SOCIALIST REPUBLIC OF VIETNAM
12–14 Victoria Road, London W8 5RD
T 020-7937 1912 E consular@vietnamembassy.org.uk
W www.vietnamembassy.org.uk
Ambassador Extraordinary and Plenipotentiary, HE Vu Quang
  Minh, *apptd* 2011

BRITISH EMBASSY
Central Building, 31 Hai Ba Trung, Hanoi
T (+84) (4) 3936 0500 E consularenquiries.vietnam@fco.gov.uk
W www.gov.uk/government/world/vietnam
Ambassador Extraordinary and Plenipotentiary, HE Dr Antony
  Stokes, LVO, *apptd* 2010

DEFENCE

Aged 16–49, 2010 est	Males	Females
Available for military service	25,649,738	24,995,692
Fit for military service	20,405,847	21,098,102

Military expenditure – US$3,205m (2013 est)
Conscription duration – 18–24 months

ECONOMY AND TRADE
The economy struggled for a decade after 1975 owing to the devastation of war and the imposition of a centrally planned economy. Since economic liberalisation and international integration were adopted in 1986, the economy has grown substantially, albeit from a low base, and export-driven industries are being developed. Poverty was reduced by over 40 per cent between 1993 and 2007, although more remote rural areas have yet to benefit. The global downturn reduced economic growth in 2008–9, and in early 2012 the government introduced a three-fold economic reform programme, proposing a restructuring of the banking sector, public spending and state-owned enterprises.

Agriculture's contribution is gradually shrinking, but still accounts for 19.3 per cent of GDP and employs 48 per cent of the workforce. The main industries are food processing, clothing and footwear, machine building, coal mining, steel, cement, chemical fertiliser, glass, tyres and paper, and oil and gas production from large offshore reserves. Industry now contributes 38.5 per cent of GDP and services 42.2 per cent.

The main trading partners are China, Japan, South Korea and the USA. Principal exports are clothing, footwear, fish and seafood, crude oil, electronics, wood products, rice and machinery. The main imports are machinery and equipment, petroleum products, steel products, raw materials, electronics, plastics and vehicles.

GNI – US$148,961m; US$1,270 per capita (2012)
Annual average growth of GDP – 5.3 per cent (2013 est)
Inflation rate – 6.8 per cent (2013 est)
Population below poverty line – 11.3 per cent (2012 est)
Unemployment – 1.3 per cent (2013 est)
Total external debt – US$68,380m (2013 est)
Imports – US$115,101m (2012)
Exports – US$115,458m (2012)

BALANCE OF PAYMENTS
Trade – US$357m surplus (2012)
Current Account – US$233m surplus (2011)

Trade with UK	2012	2013
Imports from UK	£292,168,081	£304,181,668
Exports to UK	£2,456,460,661	£2,895,918,023

COMMUNICATIONS
Airports and waterways – The principal airports and ports are at Ho Chi Minh City, Hanoi and Da Nang
Roadways and railways – 206,633km; 2,632km
Telecommunications – 10.191 million fixed lines and 134.066 million mobile subscriptions (2012); there were 23.382 million internet users in 2009
Internet code and IDD – vn; 84 (from UK), 44 (to UK)
Major broadcasters – VTV is the state-run broadcaster
Press – There are over a hundred different newspapers and magazines, including *Nhan Dan*, the Communist Party daily, and the English-language *Vietnam Economic Times*
WPFI score – 72,36 (174)

EDUCATION AND HEALTH
Literacy rate – 93 per cent (2011 est)
Gross enrolment ratio (percentage of relevant age group) –
  primary 105 per cent (2012 per cent); secondary 77
  per cent (2011 per cent); tertiary 25 per cent (2012 est)
Health expenditure (per capita) – US$95 (2011)
Hospital beds (per 1,000 people) – 2.2 (2010)
Life expectancy (years) – 72.91 (2014 est)
Mortality rate – 5.93 (2014 est)
Birth rate – 16.26 (2014 est)
Infant mortality rate – 18.99 (2014 est)

YEMEN

Al-Jumhuriyah al-Yamaniyah – Republic of Yemen

Area – 527,968 sq. km
Capital – Sana'a; population, 2,573,763 (2012)
Major cities – Aden (the former capital of South Yemen),
  Hudaida (al-Hudaydah), Ibb, Mukulla, Taiz

Achieves some independence; Ottomans regain control — North Yemen becomes independent kingdom under the rule of the Hamid al-Din dynasty — Armed rebellion against British rule in Aden begins — Unification; Republic of Yemen declared — Civil war between former northern and southern elites

c.1500   1839   1962   1967   2004-10
c.1600-1870   1918   1963   1990   1994

Part of the Ottoman Empire — Aden comes under British rule — Revolution overthrows monarchy; Yemen Arab Republic declared — British troops withdraw; power seized by National Liberation Front repressive communist regime established in the People's Republic of South Yemen — Fighting in north-west as government attempt to suppress al-Houthis insurgency

Currency – Riyal of 100 fils
Population – 26,052,966 rising at 2.72 per cent a year (2014 est)
Religion – Muslim (Sunni 65 per cent, Shia 35 per cent) (est)
Language – Arabic (official)
Population density – 44 per sq. km (2011)
Urban population – 32.9 per cent (2012 est)
Median age (years) – 18.6 (2014 est)
National anthem – 'United Republic'
National day – 22 May (Unification Day)
Death penalty – Retained
CPI score – 18 (167)

CLIMATE AND TERRAIN

A mountainous region in the west and south divides the desert plains of the interior from the narrow coastal plains. Elevation extremes range from 3,760m (Jabal an Nabi Shu'ayb) to 0m (Arabian Sea). There is a desert climate, which is particularly harsh in the east, but moderated in the western mountains by the monsoon. The coast experiences high humidity and the average temperature in Aden is 29°C.

The islands of Perim and Kamaran in the Red Sea, and Suqutra in the Gulf of Aden, are Yemeni territory. The border with Saudi Arabia, except for the north-west corner, is unclear and is being delineated following an agreement between the two countries.

POLITICS

The president announced in March 2011 the drafting of a new constitution transferring powers from the presidency to the legislature. Under the 1991 constitution, the president is directly elected for a seven-year term, renewable once. The unicameral House of Representatives *(Majlis al-Nowab)* has 301 members directly elected for a six-year term. In addition, there is an advisory Shura council, whose 111 members are appointed by the president. The prime minister is appointed by the president.

In the 2003 legislative election, the ruling General People's Congress (GPC) won 238 seats and formed a coalition government with the Yemeni Alliance for Reform (YAR or al-Islah). The legislative election due in 2009 was postponed pending constitutional reform. Lt.-Gen. Ali Abdullah Saleh, president of North Yemen from 1978 and president of the united country since 1990, faced sustained popular protests from early 2011 demanding his resignation and greater democracy. Saleh announced that he would not stand for re-election in 2013 but refused to leave office early despite international mediation attempts and the defection of senior military and political figures. Saleh was forced to resign in December 2011 and formally ceded power after he was granted immunity from prosecution. Former vice-president Abd-Rabbu Mansour Hadi was elected transitional president in the 2012 elections; elections were planned for 2014 under a new constitution.

HEAD OF STATE

President, Gen. Abd-Rabbu Mansour Hadi, *elected* 21 February 2012

SELECTED GOVERNMENT MEMBERS *as at July 2014*
Prime Minister, Mohammed Salem Basindwa
Defence, Mohammad Nasser Ahmed
Foreign Affairs, Jamal Abdullah al-Sallal

EMBASSY OF THE REPUBLIC OF YEMEN
57 Cromwell Road, London SW7 2ED
T 020-7584 6607 E yemen.embassy@btconnect.com
Ambassador Extraordinary and Plenipotentiary, HE Abdulla Ali al-Radhi, *apptd* 2010

BRITISH EMBASSY
PO Box 1287, 938 Thaher Himiyar Street, East Ring Road (opposite Mövenpick Hotel), Sana'a
T (+967) (1) 308 114 E britishembassysanaa@fco.gov.uk
W www.gov.uk/government/world/yemen
Ambassador Extraordinary and Plenipotentiary, HE Jane Marriott, *apptd* 2013

DEFENCE

Aged 16–49, 2010 est	*Males*	*Females*
Available for military service	5,652,256	5,387,160
Fit for military service	4,056,944	4,116,895

Military expenditure – US$1,511m (2008)
Conscription duration – 24 months

ECONOMY AND TRADE

Despite its oil industry, the mainstay of the economy, Yemen is one of the poorest countries in the Arab world. The government began an IMF restructuring programme in 2006 that aims to diversify the economy and attract foreign investment. Implementation has been hampered by popular protests, security problems internally and from piracy in nearby waters, corruption and rapid population growth. Falling oil prices nearly halved the government's revenue in 2009, although Yemen also benefited from its first exports of liquefied natural gas. Civil unrest in 2011 caused the economy to contract by 11 per cent.

Agriculture is largely of a subsistence nature, and, with herding and fishing, engages the majority of the population, contributing 7.7 per cent of GDP. Apart from oil and natural gas extraction and oil refining, industry consists of small-scale manufacturing of cotton textiles, leather goods, handicrafts, aluminium products and cement, food processing and ship repair.

The main trading partners are China, India, the UAE and Thailand. Principal exports are crude oil, coffee, dried and salted fish, and liquefied natural gas. The main imports are food, livestock, machinery and equipment, and chemicals.
GNI – US$33,649m; US$1,070 per capita (2012)
Annual average growth of GDP – 3.8 per cent (2013 est)
Inflation rate – 11.8 per cent (2013 est)
Population below poverty line – 45.2 per cent (2003)
Unemployment – 45.2 per cent (2003 est)
Total external debt – US$7,806m (2013 est)
Imports – US$11,975m (2012)
Exports – US$8,500m (2012)

BALANCE OF PAYMENTS
Trade – US$3,475m deficit (2012)
Current Account – US$3,29m deficit (2012)

Trade with UK	2012	2013
Imports from UK	£81,127,910	£101,644,713
Exports to UK	£20,248,256	£579,75,042

COMMUNICATIONS
Airports and waterways – Principal airports are at Sana'a and Aden and the main ports are at Aden, al-Hudaydah and al-Mukalla
Roadways – 71,300km
Telecommunications – 1.1 million fixed lines and 13.9 million mobile subscriptions (2012); there were 2.349 million internet users in 2009
Internet code and IDD – ye; 967 (from UK), 44 (to UK)
Media – Republic of Yemen Television is the state-run broadcaster and there are four main newspapers: *al-Thawra, Yemen Times, Yemen Observer* and *Al-Ayyam.*
WPFI score – 67,26 (167)

EDUCATION AND HEALTH
Literacy rate – 65 per cent (2011 est)
Gross enrolment ratio (percentage of relevant age group) – primary 97 per cent; secondary 47 per cent (2012 est)
Health expenditure (per capita) – US$88 (2011)
Hospital beds (per 1,000 people) – 0.7 (2010)
Life expectancy (years) – 64.83 (2014 est)
Mortality rate – 6.45 (2014 est)
Birth rate – 31.02 (2014 est)
Infant mortality rate – 50.41 (2014 est)

ZAMBIA

Republic of Zambia

Area – 752,618 sq. km
Capital – Lusaka; population, 1,531,101 (2012)
Major cities – Kitwe, Ndola
Currency – Kwacha (K) of 100 ngwee
Population – 14,638,505 rising at 2.88 per cent a year (2014 est); over 70 ethnic groups, of which the Lozi, Bemba, Ngoni, Tonga, Luvale and Kaonde are the largest
Religion – Christian (Protestant 75.3 per cent, Roman Catholic 20.2 per cent) (est)
Language – English (official), Bembe, Kaonde, Lozi, Lunda, Luvale, Nyanja, Tonga (national), over 70 other local languages
Population density – 18 per sq. km (2011)
Urban population – 39.6 per cent (2012 est)
Median age (years) – 16.7 (2014 est)
National anthem – 'Stand and Sing of Zambia, Proud and Free'
National day – 24 October (Independence Day)
Death penalty – Retained (last used 1997)

CPI score – 38 (83)
Literacy rate – 71.2 per cent (2010 est)
Gross enrolment ratio (percentage of relevant age group) – primary 115 per cent (2011 est)
Health expenditure (per capita) – US$87 (2011)
Hospital beds (per 1,000 people) – 2 (2010)
Life expectancy (years) – 51.83 (2014 est)
Mortality rate – 12.92 (2014 est)
Birth rate – 42.46 (2014 est)
Infant mortality rate – 66.62 (2014 est)
HIV/AIDS adult prevalence – 12.7 per cent (2012 est)

CLIMATE AND TERRAIN
Landlocked Zambia lies on a forested plateau cut through by river valleys and with higher land in the north and north-east. Elevation extremes range from 2,301m (in the Mafinga Hills) to 329m (Zambezi river). The Zambezi and its tributaries are the main rivers. Lake Bangweulu and parts of Lakes Tanganyika, Mweru and Kariba lie within its boundaries. The climate is tropical, moderated by altitude, with a rainy season from October to April.

HISTORY AND POLITICS
Most of the ethnic groups in Zambia migrated there between the 16th and the 18th centuries. Portuguese explorers arrived in the late 18th century and, with Arab traders, began slave-trading in the 19th century. The area came under British administration in 1889, was named Northern Rhodesia in 1911 and became a British protectorate in 1924. It was part of the Central African Federation with South Rhodesia (Zimbabwe) and Nyasaland (Malawi) from 1953 to 1963, when the federation was dissolved and Northern Rhodesia achieved internal self-government. It became an independent republic in 1964 under the name of Zambia.

Kenneth Kaunda of the United National Independence Party (UNIP) became president at independence and remained in power until 1991. Zambia was a one-party state ruled by the UNIP from 1972 until 1990, when pressure from opposition groups led to a new constitution, under which multiparty legislative and presidential elections were held in 1991.

Serious food shortages have occurred in recent years owing to floods and drought, leading to appeals for international food aid in 2001 and 2005. The country also faces serious demographic, economic and social problems because of high levels of HIV/AIDS infection.

The Patriotic Front (PF) won the 2011 legislative election, gaining enough seats for a small majority in the National Assembly. The PF's leader, Michael Sata, won the 2011 presidential election, defeating incumbent president and Movement for Multiparty Democracy (MMD) leader Rupiah Banda. A number of cabinet reshuffles have been instigated by the president from 2012 onwards.

Under the 1991 constitution, the executive president is directly elected for a five-year term, renewable once. The unicameral National Assembly has 158 members: 150 directly elected, up to eight nominated by the president, and a speaker; all serve a five-year term. The president appoints the cabinet. A new constitution is under debate, although it is unclear when it will be adopted.

HEAD OF STATE
President, Michael Sata, *elected* 20 September 2011, *sworn in* 23 September 2011
Vice-President, Guy Scott

SELECTED GOVERNMENT MEMBERS *as at July 2014*
Home Affairs, Ngosa Simbyakula
Foreign Affairs, Harry Kalaba
Finance, Alexander Chikwanda

HIGH COMMISSION FOR THE REPUBLIC OF ZAMBIA
Zambia House, 2 Palace Gate, London W8 5NG
T 020-7589 6655 E info@zambiahc.org.uk
W www.zambiahc.org.uk
High Commissioner, HE Paul Lumbi, apptd 2013

BRITISH HIGH COMMISSION
PO Box 5005, 5210 Independence Avenue, 15101 Ridgeway,
Lusaka
T (+260) (21) 1423 2001251 133
E lusakageneralenquiries@fco.gov.uk
W www.gov.uk/government/world/zambia
High Commissioner, HE James Thornton, apptd 2012

DEFENCE

Aged 16–49, 2010 est	Males	Females
Available for military service	3,041,069	2,948,291
Fit for military service	1,745,656	1,688,670

Military expenditure – US$367m (2013)

ECONOMY AND TRADE

The transition since the 1990s from a state-controlled to a free-market economy has improved productivity, especially in the now-privatised copper industry. The economy grew in 2010 due to high copper prices and a good maize crop harvest. It is also driven in particular by mining, hydro-electric power generation, construction and tourism. Poverty remains a problem in the country, with 60.5 per cent of the population below the poverty line.

Copper is the main source of foreign earnings and increased demand in recent years for electronics has spurred investment and greater output, although weakening global copper prices caused a rapid depreciation of the kwacha in 2014. However, 85 per cent of the workforce remains engaged in agriculture, mostly at subsistence level, which accounts for 19.8 per cent of GDP. The main industries are copper and cobalt mining and processing, construction, food processing, beverages, chemicals, textiles, fertiliser and horticulture.

The main trading partners are China and South Africa. Principal exports are copper, cobalt, electricity, tobacco, cut flowers and cotton. The main imports are machinery, transport equipment, petroleum products, electricity, fertiliser, foodstuffs and clothing.

GNI – US$19,542m; US$1,060 per capita (2012)
Annual average growth of GDP – 6 per cent (2013 est)
Inflation rate – 7.1 per cent (2013 est)
Total external debt – US$5,985m (2013 est)
Imports – US$8,000m (2012)
Exports – US$8,550m (2012)

BALANCE OF PAYMENTS
Trade – US$550m surplus (2012)
Current Account – US$10m surplus (2012)

Trade with UK	2012	2013
Imports from UK	£89,170,219	£88,176,187
Exports to UK	£32,063,560	£37,495,337

COMMUNICATIONS

Airports and waterways – There are eight airports and 2,250km of navigable waterways on Lake Tanganyika and the Zambezi and Luapula rivers
Roadways and railways – 67,671km; 2,922km
Telecommunications – 82,500 fixed lines and 10.525 million mobile subscriptions (2012); there were 816,200 internet users in 2009

Internet code and IDD – zm; 260 (from UK), 44 (to UK)
Media – The state-run Zambia National Broadcasting Association broadcasts alongside private companies

ZIMBABWE

Republic of Zimbabwe

Area – 390,757 sq. km
Capital – Harare; population, 1,699,882 (2012)
Major cities – Bulawayo, Chitungwiza, Gweru, Mutare
Currency – Zimbabwe dollar (Z$) of 100 cents; circulation suspended April 2009; US dollar, South African rand and other currencies in use
Population – 13,771,721 rising at 4.36 per cent a year (2013 est); Shona (82 per cent), Ndebele (14 per cent) (est)
Religion – Syncretic (part Christian, part indigenous belifs) 50 per cent, Christian 25 per cent cent, indigenous beliefs 24 per cent
Language – English (official), Shona, Ndebele, numerous tribal dialects
Population density – 35 per sq. km (2011)
Urban population – 39.1 per cent (2012 est)
Median age (years) – 20.2 (2014 est)
National anthem – 'Simudzai Mureza wedu WeZimbabwe' ['Blessed be the Land of Zimbabwe']
National day – 18 April (Independence Day)
Death penalty – Retained
CPI score – 21 (157)

CLIMATE AND TERRAIN

Zimbabwe lies mainly on a high plateau with a central high veld and mountains in the east. Elevation extremes range from 2,592m (Inyangani) to 162m (confluence of the Runde and Save rivers). The climate is tropical, moderated by altitude, with a wet season from November to March. Average temperatures in Harare range from 15°C in June and July to 22°C in November.

POLITICS

Under the 2013 constitution, the term of the executive president was reduced from six years to five and is renewable once, however this does not apply retrospectively to the incumbent, Robert Mugabe. The bicameral parliament comprises the National Assembly and the senate. The former has 210 members directly elected for a five-year term plus 60 seats reserved for women. The senate has 80 members, who serve a five-year term: 62 elected (including six from each of the eight provinces) and 18 traditional chiefs.

The country is divided into eight provinces and two cities (Bulawayo and Harare) with provincial status. The provinces are: Manicaland, Mashonaland Central, Mashonaland East, Mashonaland West, Masvingo, Matabeleland North, Matabeleland South and Midlands.

Ndebele people occupy area of south; frequent disputes with northern Mashonaland

Becomes self-governing colony

Opposition to black majority rule leads to unilateral declaration of independence (UDI) by white-dominated government

Becomes independent as the Republic of Zimbabwe

Appropriation of white-owned farms begins

ZANU-PF loses majority to Movement for Democratic Change

18,000ᴮᶜ
1800ᴬᴰ   1898   1953–63   1979   1987   2008
c.1800   1923   1965   1980   2000

Ruled by a succession of Shona kingdoms

Becomes British protectorate of Southern Rhodesia

Part of the Central African Federation

Government forced to negotiate with guerilla African nationalists; UDI terminated

Zimbabwe African National Union-Patriotic Front's (ZANU-PF) Robert Mugabe becomes prime minister and president

Mugabe conducts campaign of violence and wins uncontested second round

An internationally brokered power-sharing arrangement was agreed between ZANU-PF and the MDC in September 2008 and January 2009, although negotiations over the composition of the cabinet were not completed until February 2009, when Morgan Tsvangirai was sworn in as prime minister at the head of a national unity government. The 2013 presidential election was won by Robert Mugabe with 61.1 per cent of the vote; ZANU-PF won the legislative election. The office of prime minister was abolished under the 2013 constitution.

HEAD OF STATE
President, Robert Mugabe, *elected* 30 December 1987, *re-elected* 1990, 1996, 2002, 2008, 2013
Vice-President, Joyce Mujuru

SELECTED GOVERNMENT MEMBERS *as at July 2014*
Defence, Sydney Sekeramyi
Finance, Patrick Chinamasa
Foreign Affairs, Simbarashe Mumbengegwi

EMBASSY OF THE REPUBLIC OF ZIMBABWE
Zimbabwe House, 429 Strand, London WC2R 0JR
T 020-7836 7755 **E** zimlondon@yahoo.co.uk
W www.zimlondon.gov.zw
Ambassador Extraordinary and Plenipotentiary, HE Gabriel Mharadze Machinga, *apptd* 2005

BRITISH EMBASSY
PO Box 4490, 3 Norfolk Road, Mount Pleasant, Harare
T (+263) (4) 8585 5200 **E** ukinfo.harare@fco.gov.uk
W www.gov.uk/government/world/zimbabwe
Ambassador Extraordinary and Plenipotentiary, HE Deborah Bronnert, CMG, *apptd* 2011

DEFENCE

Aged 16–49, 2010 est	Males	Females
Available for military service	2,616,051	2,868,376
Fit for military service	1,528,166	1,646,041

Military expenditure – US$334m (2013)

ECONOMY AND TRADE
Poor governance, and in particular the seizure of almost all the white-owned commercial farms, caused a rapid contraction in the agriculture-based economy in the decade from the late 1990s; agricultural output and GDP halved, international aid was suspended because of the government's outstanding arrears on past loans, and the migration of professional and skilled labour and high levels of HIV/AIDS infection depleted the workforce. After the national unity government took office, hyperinflation was stemmed by adopting the US dollar in 2009 and the economy has grown rapidly, but unemployment remains high. Poverty and dependence on food aid is widespread.

Agriculture accounts for 20.1 per cent of GDP and engages two-thirds of the workforce. The most important crops are cotton and tobacco for export and maize for domestic consumption. Other crops include wheat, coffee, sugar cane, peanuts and livestock.

The mining sector is important to the economy as a foreign exchange earner. Almost all mineral production is exported. Gold is the most important product; others are coal, platinum, copper, nickel, tin, diamonds, iron ore and other metal and non-metal ores. Mining is now the largest industrial activity and supports a ferro-alloy industry and a steel works. Manufacturing, traditionally highly dependent on the agricultural sector for raw materials, produces wood products, cement, chemicals, fertiliser, clothing, footwear, foodstuffs and beverages; output has dropped in some industries because of transport difficulties and power rationing. Industry generates 25.4 per cent of GDP and services 54.5 per cent.

The main trading partners are South Africa, China the Democratic Republic of Congo and Botswana. Principal exports are platinum, cotton, tobacco, gold, ferro-alloys, textiles and clothing. The main imports are machinery and transport equipment, other manufactures, chemicals, fuels and food.

GNI – US$9,420m; US$660 per capita (2012)
Annual average growth of GDP – 3.2 per cent (2013 est)
Inflation rate – 8.5 per cent (2013 est)
Population below poverty line – 72.3 per cent (2011)
Unemployment – 95 per cent (2009 est)
Total external debt – US$8,445m (2013 est)
Imports – US$4,400m (2012)
Exports – US$3,800m (2012)

BALANCE OF PAYMENTS
Trade – US$600m deficit (2012)
Current Account – US$1,913m deficit (2010)

Trade with UK	2012	2013
Imports from UK	£60,234,779	£52,120,383
Exports to UK	£11,690,260,477	£11,728,706,680

COMMUNICATIONS
Airports – The main airports are at Harare and Bulawayo, ther are 179 other airports and airfields
Roadways and railways – 97,267km; 3,427km
Telecommunications – 301,600 fixed lines and 12.614 million mobile subscriptions (2012); there were 1.423 million internet users in 2009
Internet code and IDD – zw; 263 (from UK), 44 (to UK)
Media – The Zimbabwe Broadcasting Corporation operates the only TV and radio stations; there are three daily newspapers, including the government-owned *The Herald*
WPFI score – 39,19 (135)

EDUCATION AND HEALTH
Education is compulsory at primary level, and the language of instruction is English.
Literacy rate – 84 per cent (2011 est)
Gross enrolment ratio (percentage of relevant age group) – tertiary 6 per cent (2012 est)
Hospital beds (per 1,000 people) – 1.7 (2011)
Life expectancy (years) – 55.68 (2014 est)
Mortality rate – 10.62 (2014 est)
Birth rate – 32.47 (2014 est)
Infant mortality rate – 26.55 (2014 est)
HIV/AIDS adult prevalence – 14.7 per cent (2012 est)

THE NORTH AND SOUTH POLES

THE ARCTIC

The Arctic is the region around the Earth's north pole; it includes the ice-covered Arctic Ocean, parts of Canada, the USA, Greenland, Iceland, Finland, Norway, Sweden and Russia. The area is commonly defined as lying north of the line of latitude known as the Arctic Circle (running at 66° 33′ N.) or inside the 10°C July isotherm.

The climate is harsh, particularly during winter (October–March) when the Arctic receives little sunlight; the average monthly temperature in December, January and February is around −10 to −15°C, but on individual nights may fall as low as −60°C over the larger land masses. In summer, conditions are often damp and foggy although there is daylight for 24 hours a day. The average monthly temperature in high summer ranges from just above zero over permanent ice to 15°C in continental areas. The Arctic is rarely as cold as the Antarctic since there is water, not land, underneath the Arctic ice. The water is warmer than the air above it, causing heat to rise and moderate the cold.

The polar bear is the region's apex predator. Other native species include varieties of caribou, lemming, wolf, hare and fox; many bird species also migrate to tundra areas in summer. Until recently, vegetation was limited to Arctic tundra, a biome consisting of around 1,700 species of low-lying shrubs, grasses, sedges, lichens and mosses. However, this tundra is slowly being replaced with flora typical of more southern locations, such as trees and evergreen shrubs. In 2013, a comprehensive study of these changes, the Arctic Biodiversity Assessment (www.arcticbiodiversity.is), concluded that climate change and the effects of collective industrial development were degrading arctic biodiversity.

ARCTIC SEA ROUTES

In 1906 Norwegian explorer Roald Amundsen first successfully navigated the Northwest passage, but the shallow waterways he encountered ensured that the route held little commercial potential until recently. Similarly, the Northern Sea route (formerly the Northeast passage) linking the Atlantic and Pacific oceans around Russia's Arctic coast, was first navigated by Finnish-Swedish explorer Adolf Erik Nordenskjold in 1878–9, but thereafter only icebreakers and Russian submarines regularly traversed it.

In summer 2007, the Northwest passage was declared open and ice-free for the first time since records began in late 1978; the first commercial ship travelled through it in September 2008. In August 2008 the Northwest passage and the Northern Sea route were open simultaneously for the first time, making the Arctic circumnavigable. Two German cargo vessels became the first to navigate the Northern Sea route in September 2009 and in August 2012 *The World* became the largest passenger ship to navigate the Northwest Passage, following Amundsen's route.

CLIMATE CHANGE

The extent of ice in the Arctic has become a key measure of global climate change. The rate at which the ice melts grows exponentially: whereas the white ice reflects sunlight back into space, the darker seas absorb its heat, and the rising sea temperature melts the surrounding ice. The extent of sea ice roughly doubles between summer and winter, typically reaching its greatest extent in March and retreating to its lowest point in September. In September 2013 the minimum ice extent was recorded as 5.1 million km² (1.97 million miles²); 1.69 million km² (653,000 miles²) above the record minimum extent, which occurred in September 2012, and 1.6 million km² (620,000 miles²) below the 1979 to 2000 average minimum. Since 2010, estimates of sea ice thickness and volume have been obtained via the European Space Agency's CryoSat satellite. In October 2013 CryoSat measured approximately 9,000km³ (2,200 miles³) of sea ice, around 50 per cent higher than in autumn 2012. Around 90 per cent of the increase in volume between the two years was due to the retention of thick multiyear ice. However, it is estimated that in the early 1980s, October ice volume was around 20,000km³ (4,800 miles³).

NATURAL RESOURCES

The Arctic's receding ice presents opportunities for national governments to lay claim to a wealth of hydrocarbon and mineral deposits. In 2008 the US Geological Survey estimated that 20 per cent of the world's undiscovered oil and gas reserves – as much as 90 billion barrels of oil, 44 billion barrels of natural gas liquids and 1,670 trillion cubic feet of natural gas – are located within the Arctic Circle. Under the 1982 UN Convention on the Law of the Sea, no state owns the pole or the ocean surrounding it: the five countries that border the Arctic Ocean – Canada, Denmark, Norway, Russia and the USA (a non-signatory) – are limited to an economic zone of 200 nautical miles from their coastline, unless able to prove that their continental shelf extends beyond that limit. In August 2007, Russia planted a flag in the seabed below the pole, on the Lomonosov Ridge which spans much of the Arctic, and which Russia claims is an extension of the Eurasian continent and therefore part of its territory. However, Canadian and Danish geologists assert that Lomonosov is an extension of the North American continent, and therefore falls under their jurisdiction. In May 2008 politicians from the five countries bordering the Arctic Ocean attended a summit in Ilulissat, Greenland in an attempt to ease the territorial tensions in the region, to seek clarification regarding oil and environmental regulation and to block any attempt to establish an international legal regime to govern the Arctic Ocean.

THE ANTARCTIC

The Antarctic is generally defined as the area lying within the Antarctic Convergence, the zone where cold northward-flowing Antarctic sea water sinks below warmer southward-flowing water. This zone fluctuates unevenly between the latitudes of 48° S. and 61° S., typically extending further north in the Atlantic Ocean than in the Pacific. The continent itself lies almost entirely within the Antarctic Circle; it has an area of around 14 million km², 98 per cent of which is permanently ice-covered. The average thickness of the grounded ice is 2,034m, but it exceeds 4,700m in places; it amounts to some 25.4 million km³, and represents around 90 per cent of the world's fresh water and 91 per cent of the world's glacier ice. Much of the sea freezes in winter, forming fast ice which breaks free of the coast in summer and drifts north as pack ice.

CLIMATE AND TERRAIN

Antarctica is the highest, coldest and driest continent on Earth, with average coastal temperatures ranging from just above freezing in the summer (December–February) to

−20°C in winter. Conditions on the interior plateau are more severe, with katabatic (gravity-driven) winds and frequent cyclonic storms pushing average winter temperatures down to −65°C. The Vostok research station holds the record for the lowest surface temperature recorded on Earth at −89.2°C. Elevation extremes range from 4,897m (Vinson Massif) at the highest point to −2,540m (Bentley Subglacial Trench) at the lowest. The Transantarctic mountains bisect the continent north–south, dividing the west Antarctic ice-sheet – an ice-filled marine basin – from the significantly larger and more elevated east sheet. With average precipitation of just 140mm a year, Antarctica is considered a desert.

CLIMATE CHANGE

While the recent decline in levels of ice in the Arctic has been clear and visible, concurrent changes in the Antarctic have been more complex. Despite reports of a recent thickening of the interior of the east ice-sheet due to increased snowfall, studies of data produced by NASA's Grace satellite indicate that the Antarctic ice-sheet as a whole has declined by more than 100km^3 (24 miles^3) a year since 2002, the majority of that loss having taken place in the west Antarctic.

The British Antarctic Survey has found that the west coast of the Antarctic Peninsula has become one of the fastest-warming areas on the planet, with annual mean temperatures rising by around 3°C over the past 50 years. In 2009, a group of British geophysicists found that the retreat of the Pine Island Glacier in the Western Antarctic had quadrupled between 1995 and 2006. Curiously, the temperatures recorded by the Amundsen-Scott station at the South Pole actually show a recent cooling, as do some studies of east Antarctica as a whole. The precise cause of this is unknown, but scientists have proposed that the warming of the seas in the surrounding ocean has produced more precipitation, which cools the area when it falls as snow. Greater snowfall has also been associated with an expansion of Antarctica's sea ice. The snow's additional weight appears to push existing sea ice deeper into the water, causing more of it to freeze. However, this expansion is neither uniform nor universally accepted, and a number of other studies cite a long-term and continuing decline in Antarctic sea ice since at least the 1950s.

HISTORY AND DISCOVERY

The idea of Antarctica is much older than proof of the continent's existence. The notion of *Terra Australis*, a vast southern continent which counterbalanced the northern lands of Europe, Asia and North Africa, originated with Aristotle, and was depicted on a world map as early as 1531. The supposed size of this land was gradually amended over the course of 16th-century exploration and further corrected after James Cook's circumnavigation of the globe in 1774. His journey from New Zealand to the Cape of Good Hope (via Tierra del Fuego), travelling at a high southern latitude (between 53° and 60°), confirmed that any land mass must be confined to the polar region.

The date of the first sighting of Antarctica is unclear. In 1820 three separate expeditions, from the UK, the USA and Russia, each claimed to have seen the continent within days of each other, and the argument has never been settled. The golden age of Antarctic exploration was prompted by the discovery of the magnetic North Pole in 1831, but it was not until the beginning of the 20th century that real progress was made. James Clark Ross was the first to identify the approximate location of the South Pole, but was unable to reach it. British explorers Robert Scott in 1901–4 and Ernest Shackleton in 1907–9 got closer, but it was not until Norwegian adventurer Roald Amundsen pioneered a new route, through the Axel Heiberg Glacier, that the pole was reached in December 1911. Scott's second attempt was also successful, but he arrived a month later and perished with his team on the return journey.

FLORA AND FAUNA

The only land animals to survive on the Antarctic continent are tiny invertebrates, including microscopic mites, lice, ticks, nematodes, rotifers and tardigrades. The largest land animal is the *Belgica antarctica*, a flightless midge just 2–6mm in size. The snow petrel, one of only three birds that breed exclusively in Antarctica, has been spotted at the South Pole. Large numbers of seals, penguins and other seabirds go ashore to breed in the summer; the emperor penguin is the only species that breeds ashore throughout the winter. Four species of albatross breed in South Georgia during the summer, but their numbers are in serious decline owing to the effects of longline fishing in the Southern Ocean region. Recent climate change has also affected the continent's wildlife, with the number of Adelie penguins falling significantly, as open-water species such as the chinstrap and gentoo penguins invade its Antarctic Peninsula habitat to take advantage of the warming temperatures.

By contrast, the Antarctic seas abound with life; recent expeditions identified over 700 previously unknown species. Krill, which congregates in large schools, is crucial to the ecosystem and provides a diet for migratory whales (including killer, humpback and blue whales), a number of species of seal, penguin, albatross and other smaller birds. Each of these species is threatened by a substantial fall in recorded levels of krill since the 1970s, thought to be caused by a reduction in the sea ice which shields its larvae from predators during winter. In 2010 a group of research bodies completed the Census of Antarctic Marine Life, an inventory of over 16,000 marine species compiled from 19 expeditions; scientists estimate that 39–58 per cent of the Antarctic's marine species are yet to be described.

With almost all of the Antarctic continent permanently covered in ice, only a small number of flowering plants, ferns and club mosses survive. Most of these are found on the sub-Antarctic islands, while only two species (a grass and a pearlwort) extend south of 60° S. Antarctic vegetation is dominated by lichens and mosses, with a few liverworts, algae and fungi surviving in the cracks and pore spaces of sandstone and granite rocks.

ANTARCTIC LAW

The Antarctic Treaty was signed on 1 December 1959 when 12 states (Argentina, Australia, Belgium, Chile, France, Japan, New Zealand, Norway, South Africa, the Soviet Union, the UK and the USA) pledged to promote scientific and technical cooperation unhampered by politics. The signatories agreed to establish free use of the Antarctic continent for peaceful scientific purposes; freeze all territorial claims and disputes in the Antarctic; ban all military activities in the area; and prohibit nuclear explosions and the disposal of radioactive waste. The Antarctic Treaty was defined as covering areas south of latitude 60° S., excluding the high seas but including the ice shelves, and came into force in 1961. The treaty provides that any member of the UN can accede to it; it has since been signed by a further 38 states. In 1998 an extension to the treaty came into effect, placing a 50-year ban on mining, oil exploration and mineral extraction in Antarctica, and stipulating that all tourists, explorers and expeditions now require permission to enter the Antarctic from a relevant national authority. However, in recent years the region's coastal states have asserted often conflicting claims to oil- and gas-rich territory on the Antarctic seabed. Under the terms of the UN Convention on the Law of the Sea, each nation's sovereignty over its continental shelf extends up to 350 nautical miles beyond its territorial coasts; the UN Commission on the Limits of the Continental Shelf is examining evidence submitted in support of these claims.

SCIENTIFIC RESEARCH
There are 20 nations with permanently manned research stations in Antarctica:

Country	Number of research stations
Argentina	6
Chile	5
Russian Federation	5
Australia	3
USA	3
China	2
France	2
UK	2

Brazil, Germany, India, Italy (shared with France), Japan, New Zealand, Norway, Poland, South Africa, South Korea, Ukraine and Uruguay each have a single station. Brazil's Comandante Ferraz research station was partially destroyed by fire in February 2012; reconstruction began in 2014 and is scheduled to be completed by March 2015.

POPULATION AND TOURISM
Antarctica has no indigenous inhabitants, although the continent maintains a population of tourists, scientists and research workers which peaks in the summer months at over 4,400.

Antarctic tourism is a growth industry. The first *Lonely Planet* guide to Antarctica was published in 1996, and ship-borne cruises typically depart from Argentina, Chile and the Falkland Islands. The continent has also become a popular venue for extreme sports enthusiasts: it is now possible to sky-dive, ski, ride a motorbike and fly a helicopter across the continent, and the Vinson Massif and other peaks have become desirable destinations for mountaineers. The huts built by Scott and Shackleton are also popular attractions. In 1991 the International Association of Antarctica Tour Operators (IAATO) was founded with the objective of providing a self-regulating code of conduct for all operators to follow, but membership is voluntary, and fears remain regarding tourism-related environmental damage. IAATO recorded 6,704 tourists in the 1992–3 summer season, rising to more than 46,000 in 2007–8 and dipping to 34,354 in 2012–13.

THE BRITISH ANTARCTIC SURVEY
The British Antarctic Survey (BAS) is part of the Natural Environment Research Council and carries out the majority of Britain's scientific research in Antarctica. Over 400 staff are employed by BAS and the organisation supports five research stations, four of which are staffed throughout the winter months (two in South Georgia and two in Antarctica). *See* the BAS website (W www.antarctica.ac.uk) for further information.

UK OVERSEAS TERRITORIES

ANGUILLA

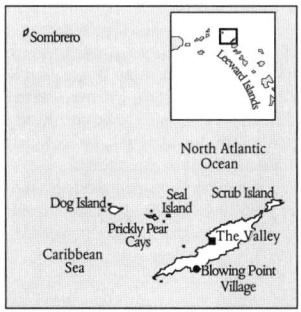

Area – 91 sq. km
Capital – The Valley; population, 2,000 (2011 est)
Currency – East Caribbean dollar (EC$) of 100 cents
Population – 15,754 rising at 2.11 per cent a year (2013 est)
Religion – Christian (Protestant 83 per cent, Roman Catholic 6 per cent) (est)
Language – English (official)
Population density – 150 per sq. km (2005 est)
Flag – British blue ensign with the coat of arms and three dolphins in the fly
National day – 30 May (Anguilla Day)
Life expectancy (years) – 81.09 (2013 est)
Mortality rate – 4.44 (2013 est)
Birth rate – 12.82 (2013 est)
Infant mortality rate – 3.42 (2013 est)

CLIMATE AND TERRAIN
Anguilla is a flat coralline island in the eastern Caribbean and one of the most northerly of the Leeward Islands. Elevation extremes range from 65m (Crocus Hill) to 0m (Caribbean Sea). The climate is tropical, modified by north-east trade winds, with temperatures ranging from 25°C to 30°C throughout the year.

HISTORY AND POLITICS
Anguilla has been a British colony since 1650. For much of its history it was linked administratively with St Kitts, but three months after the Associated State of Saint Christopher (St Kitts)-Nevis-Anguilla came into being in 1967, the Anguillans repudiated government from St Kitts. Final separation from St Kitts and Nevis was effected in December 1980 and Anguilla reverted to a British dependency.

The 1982 constitution (amended in 1990) provides for a governor, an executive council comprising four of the elected assembly members and two *ex-officio* members (the attorney-general and deputy governor), and a 12-member House of Assembly, consisting of a speaker, seven elected members, two nominated members and two *ex-officio* members (the attorney-general and deputy governor). The 2010 general election was won by the Anguilla United Movement with four seats.

Governor, Christina Scott, *apptd* 2013
Chief Minister, Hon. Hubert Hughes

ECONOMY
The main economic activity is tourism, which has stimulated construction. Offshore financial services, lobster fishing and expatriates' remittances are also important. Export earnings are mainly from sales of fish, lobsters, livestock, salt, concrete blocks and rum.
Imports – US$150m (2012)
Exports – US$8m (2012)

BALANCE OF PAYMENTS
Trade – US$142m deficit (2012)
Current Account – US$102.4m deficit (2011 est)

Trade with UK	2012	2013
Imports from UK	£501,016	£1,602,879
Exports to UK	£38,951	£81,862

COMMUNICATIONS
The 175km road network is gradually expanding but less than half is paved. The main ports are Blowing Point ferry terminal and Clayton J. Lloyd (formerly Wallblake) airport, near The Valley.

BERMUDA

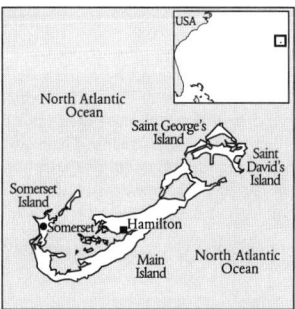

Area – 54 sq. km
Capital – Hamilton, on Main Island; population, 11,000 (2011 est)
Currency – Bermudan dollar of 100 cents
Population – 69,467 rising at 0.55 per cent a year (2013 est)
Religion – Christian (Protestant 49 per cent, Roman Catholic 15 per cent) (est)
Language – English (official), Portuguese
Population density – 1,291 per sq. km (2011 est)
Flag – British red ensign with the coat of the arms in the fly
National day – 24 May (Bermuda Day)
Life expectancy (years) – 80.93 (2013 est)
Mortality rate – 7.9 (2013 est)
Birth rate – 11.39 (2013 est)
Infant mortality rate – 2.47 (2013 est)
GNI – US$6,852m; US$104,590 per capita (2012)

CLIMATE AND TERRAIN
Bermuda is a group of over 130 small islands, of which about 20 are inhabited, in the North Atlantic Ocean. All the islands are volcanic in origin, with hilly interiors, surrounded by

coral reefs. Elevation extremes range from 76m (Town Hill) to 0m (Atlantic Ocean). The climate is subtropical, regulated by the Gulf Stream, with an average temperature of 22°C.

HISTORY AND POLITICS

Bermuda was discovered by the Spanish in 1503 but colonised by the British from the early 17th century, becoming a colony in 1684. Independence from the UK was rejected in a 1995 referendum.

Internal self-government was introduced in 1968. The governor is responsible for external affairs, defence, internal security and the police, although administrative matters for the police service have been delegated to the minister of labour, home affairs and public safety. The cabinet comprises the premier and six elected assembly members. The legislature consists of the senate of 11 appointed members and the House of Assembly with 36 members elected for a five-year term. At the 2012 election, opposition party One Bermuda Alliance won 19 of the 36 available seats, ousting the ruling Progressive Labour Party for the first time in 14 years; the Alliance party's leader, Craig Cannonier, was sworn in as premier in December 2012.

Governor, HE George Fergusson, *apptd* 2012
Premier, Hon. Craig Cannonier

ECONOMY

The economy is based on offshore financial services for international business (especially re-insurance), and tourism. Other activities include light manufacturing (re-exports of pharmaceuticals are the main export) and construction.

Trade with UK	2012	2013
Imports from UK	£98,921,526	£69,184,547
Exports to UK	£1,667,172	£15,957,716

COMMUNICATIONS

The main islands are connected by a series of bridges and causeways. There are 447km of roads, all of which are paved but only around half of which are public, and one airport, near Ferry Reach on St David's Island. The main ports are at Hamilton, Freeport and St George. The telephone system is extensive, and mobile telephone distribution is widespread.

BRITISH ANTARCTIC TERRITORY

See also The North and South Poles

Area – 1,709,400 sq. km. This area is overlapped by territorial claims from Chile and Argentina. However, no claims are recognised internationally under the Antarctic Treaty of 1961
Population – There is no indigenous population. The British Antarctic Survey maintains two permanently staffed research stations, at Halley and Rothera; one part-time (summer-only) station at Signy (South Orkney Islands); and two summer-only logistics facilities, at Fossil Bluff (Alexander Island) and Sky Blu (Eastern Ellsworth Land). Several other countries maintain research stations in the territory
Flag – British white ensign, without the cross of St George, with the territory's coat of arms in the fly

CLIMATE AND TERRAIN

The British Antarctic Territory (BAT) consists of the areas south of 60°S. latitude, between longitudes 20°W. and 80°W. The territory includes the South Orkney Islands, the South Shetland Islands, the mountainous Antarctic Peninsula and all adjacent islands, and the land mass extending to the

South Pole. The highest point of the territory is 3,184m (Mt Jackson).

Only around 0.7 per cent of the territory remains ice-free, and the permanent ice-sheet that covers the remainder is, in places, nearly 5km thick. The climate is polar desert with very little precipitation, and the annual average temperature at the South Pole is −49°C.

HISTORY AND POLITICS

Britain made its first territorial claim to part of the Antarctic in 1908. Since 1943, a permanent presence has been maintained, which became the British Antarctic Survey (BAS) in 1962. In the same year, the territory, originally a Dependency of the Falkland Islands, became a UK overseas territory in its own right, although it continued to be administered from the Falkland Islands until 1989 when the role of Comissioner of the British Antarctic Territory was created.

The BAT is administered by the Foreign and Commonwealth Office, and has a full suite of laws, legal and postal administrations. All activities are governed by the Antarctic Treaty of 1961, which has the objectives of keeping Antarctica demilitarised and promoting international scientific cooperation. The territory is self-financing from income-tax revenue and the sale of postage stamps and coins.

GOVERNMENT OF THE BRITISH ANTARCTIC TERRITORY

Polar Regions Department, Overseas Territories Directorate, Room WH 2.308, King Charles Street, London SW1A 2AH
T 020-7008 1639 E polarregions@fco.gov.uk
Commissioner (non-resident), Dr Peter Hayes, *apptd* 2012
Administrator, Henry Burgess

BRITISH INDIAN OCEAN TERRITORY

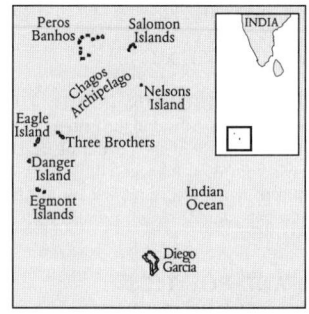

Area – 54,400 sq. km, of which 60 sq. km is land
Currency – US dollar (US$) of 100 cents
Population – No indigenous population now lives in the archipelago; around 4,000 military personnel and civilian contract employees (2004 est) are based at the joint UK–US naval support facility on Diego Garcia
Flag – Divided horizontally into blue and white wavy stripes, with the Union Flag in the canton and a crowned palm tree over all in the fly

CLIMATE AND TERRAIN

The British Indian Ocean Territory (BIOT) comprises the Chagos Archipelago of 55 islands in six main groups, situated on the Great Chagos Bank in the Indian Ocean. The largest and most southerly of the islands is Diego Garcia, a sand cay with an area of about 44 sq. km. The main island groups are Peros Banhos (29 islands with a total land area of 6.5 sq. km) and Salomon (11 islands with a total land area of 3.2 sq. km).

The flat and low terrain rarely rises more than 2m above sea-level, being only 15m at its highest point. The climate is hot and humid, although moderated by trade winds.

HISTORY AND POLITICS

The Chagos Archipelago, originally colonised by the French, was one of the dependencies of Mauritius ceded to Britain in 1814 and was administered from Mauritius until 1965, when the BIOT was established. The islands of Farquhar, Desroches and Aldabra became part of the Seychelles when it became independent in 1976. Since the 1980s, successive Mauritian governments have claimed sovereignty over the remaining Chagos islands, arguing that they were annexed illegally.

Diego Garcia is used as a joint naval support facility by Britain and the USA. The islands' former inhabitants were forcibly relocated between 1967 and 1973 to allow for the construction of the naval base, most being resettled in Mauritius and the Seychelles. Since the 1990s they have taken legal action to obtain the right to return to and settle in the islands. In 2006, the Chagossians won a High Court case allowing them to return to the archipelago, but not to Diego Garcia. The House of Lords overturned this ruling on appeal in 2008; a case before the European Court of Human Rights was ruled inadmissible in December 2012 as the islanders had previously accepted financial compensation. The British government unilaterally, and controversially, declared the Chagos Archipelago a marine-protected area in April 2010.

Commissioner (non-resident), Dr Peter Hayes, *apptd* 2012
Administrator (non-resident), John McManus, *apptd* 2011

BRITISH VIRGIN ISLANDS

Area – 151 sq. km
Capital – Road Town, on Tortola; population, 10,000 (2011 est)
Currency – US dollar (US$) of 100 cents
Population – 31,912 rising at 2.4 per cent a year (2013 est)
Religion – Christian (Protestant 84 per cent, Roman Catholic 10 per cent) (est)
Language – English (official)
Population density – 156 per sq. km (2011)
Flag – British blue ensign with the coat of arms in the fly
National day – 1 July (Territory Day)
Life expectancy (years) – 78.12 (2013 est)
Mortality rate – 4.89 (2013 est)
Birth rate – 10.78 (2013 est)
Infant mortality rate – 13.93 (2013 est)

CLIMATE AND TERRAIN

The easternmost part of the Virgin Islands archipelago in the Caribbean Sea, the British Virgin Islands comprise Tortola,

Anegada, Virgin Gorda, Jost Van Dyke and about 40 islets and cays; 16 of the islands are inhabited. Apart from Anegada, which is flat, the British Virgin Islands are hilly with coral reefs offshore. The highest point of elevation is 521m (Mt Sage, on Tortola). The climate is sub-tropical, with little variation in temperature, which typically ranges between 25°C in January and 27°C in July. The hurricane season is from June to November.

HISTORY AND POLITICS

Initially settled by Arawak Indians, the islands were named by Christopher Columbus in 1493 and colonised by the Dutch in the early 17th century. Annexed by the British in 1672, the islands were part of the Leeward Islands colony from 1872 to 1960. After a period of direct rule, a measure of self-government was introduced by the 1977 constitution and extended in 2000.

Under the 2007 constitution, the governor, appointed by the crown, retains responsibility for defence, security, external affairs and the civil service. The executive council comprises the premier, four other elected Assembly members and the attorney-general. The House of Assembly consists of a speaker, one *ex-officio* member (the attorney-general) and 13 members elected for a four-year term.

The 2011 election was won by the opposition National Democratic Party with nine seats.

Governor, HE Boyd McCleary, CMG, CVO, *apptd* 2010
Premier, Hon. Orlando Smith, OBE

ECONOMY

The main industries are tourism, which generates about 45 per cent of GDP, and offshore financial services. Other industries include construction and light manufacturing. The major exports are rum, fresh fish, fruit, livestock, gravel and sand. Chief imports are building materials, cars, foodstuffs and machinery.

Trade with UK	2012	2013
Imports from UK	£15,998,223	£59,697,254
Exports to UK	£9,892,068	£47,438,592

COMMUNICATIONS

The principal airport is on Beef Island, linked by bridge to Tortola, and there are also airfields on Anegada and Virgin Gorda. Road Harbour, at Road Town, is the main port, and ferry services connect the main islands. Many of the 200km of roads are steep and narrow.

CAYMAN ISLANDS

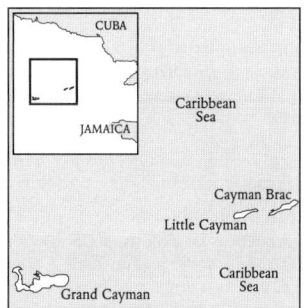

Area – 264 sq. km
Capital – George Town, on Grand Cayman; population, 30,202 (2011 est)

Currency – Cayman Islands dollar (CI$) of 100 cents
Population – 53,737 rising at 2.19 per cent a year (2013 est)
Religion – Christian (Protestant 68 per cent, Roman Catholic
13 per cent) (est)
Language – English (official), Spanish
Population density – 236 per sq. km (2011 est)
Flag – British blue ensign with the coat of arms in the fly
National day – first Monday in July (Constitution Day)
Life expectancy (years) – 80.91 (2013 est)
Mortality rate – 5.3 (2013 est)
Birth rate – 12.17 (2013 est)
Infant mortality rate – 6.35 (2013 est)
Annual average growth of GDP – 1.1 per cent (2008)

CLIMATE AND TERRAIN
The Cayman Islands comprise Grand Cayman, Cayman Brac
and Little Cayman. Situated about 240km south of Cuba,
the low-lying islands are divided from Jamaica, 268km to the
south-east, by the Cayman Trench, the deepest part of the
Caribbean Sea. The average temperature is 27°C. Hurricane
season is from July to November.

HISTORY AND POLITICS
The territory derives its name from the Carib word *caymanas*
(crocodile). The islands were ceded to Britain by Spain in
1670, and permanent settlement began in the 1730s. A
dependency of Jamaica from 1863, the islands came under
direct rule after 1962, and a measure of self-government was
granted in 1972.

The 1972 constitution (revised in 1994 and 2009) provides
for a governor, a legislative assembly and a cabinet. The
governor is responsible for the police, civil service, internal
security, defence, external affairs, and chairs the cabinet.
The cabinet comprises two appointed official members
(the deputy governor and attorney-general) and five of the
assembly's elected members. The Legislative Assembly has
15 members elected for a four-year term and the two
appointed official members of the cabinet, as well as a speaker.
Governor, HE Helen Kilpatrick, CB, *apptd* 2013
Leader of Government Business, Hon. Alden McLaughlin,
MBE

CAYMAN ISLANDS GOVERNMENT OFFICE
6 Arlington Street, London SW1A 1RE **T** 020-7491 7772
W www.gov.ky

ECONOMY
The mainstays of the economy are offshore financial services
(largely owing to the absence of direct taxation) and tourism.
Government revenue is derived from fees and duties.
Imports – US$910m (2012)
Exports – US$20m (2012)

BALANCE OF PAYMENTS
Trade – US$891m deficit (2012)

Trade with UK	2012	2013
Imports from UK	£21,042,953	£30,560,253
Exports to UK	£24,567,500	£103,567,552

COMMUNICATIONS
The islands are served by airports at George Town and on
Cayman Brac and by an airfield on Little Cayman. George
Town is the main port. There are 785km of surfaced roads.

FALKLAND ISLANDS

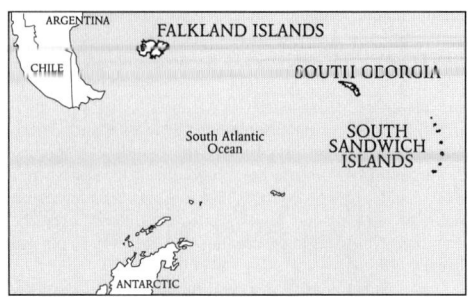

Area – 12,173 sq. km
Capital – Stanley, on E. Falkland; population, 2,120 (2012
est)
Currency – Falkland Island pound of 100 pence
Population – 2,931 static at 0 per cent a year (2012 est)
Religion – Christian 67 per cent, other 1 per cent (est)
Language – English
Flag – British blue ensign with coat of arms centred in the fly
National day – 14 June (Liberation Day)

CLIMATE AND TERRAIN
The Falkland Islands consist of East Falkland (6,759 sq. km),
West Falkland (5,413 sq. km) and around 700 small islands.
Elevation extremes range from 705m (Mt Usbourne) to 0m
(Atlantic Ocean). Temperatures range from −5°C in July to
24°C in January with an average annual temperature of
around 5.6°C, and annual rainfall is low (around 625mm
per year).

HISTORY AND POLITICS
The Falkland Islands have a long history of occupation by
European countries, including France, Spain and the UK,
which claimed sovereignty in 1765 and established its first
settlement in 1766.

In 1820 the Falklands were claimed for the newly
independent Argentina and a settlement was founded in
1826 but this was destroyed by the USA in 1831. In 1833
occupation was resumed by the British, and the islands were
permanently colonised. Argentina continued to claim
sovereignty over the islands (known to them as *las Islas
Malvinas)*, and invaded the islands on 2 April 1982. A
British naval and military task force recaptured the islands on
14 June 1982. A small naval and military garrison remains in
the islands. Argentina has reasserted its claims of sovereignty
since 2007, and political tensions with the UK remain
high. In a referendum in March 2013, the islanders voted
overwhelmingly to remain a UK overseas territory; on a
turnout of more than 90 per cent, 1,513 votes were cast in
favour, with three against.

Under the 2009 constitution, the governor chairs an
executive council consisting of three of the elected members
of the legislative assembly and two *ex-officio* members, the
chief executive and the financial secretary. The legislative
assembly consists of eight members elected for a four-year
term, the same two *ex-officio* members and a speaker. The last
election was held in 2013. There are no political parties and
all members sit as independents.
Governor, HE Colin Roberts, CVO, *apptd* 2014
Chief Executive, Keith Padgett, *apptd* 2012

FALKLAND ISLANDS GOVERNMENT OFFICE
Falkland House, 14 Broadway, London SW1H 0BH
T 020-7222 2542 **W** www.falklands.gov.fk

ECONOMY

Since the establishment of a conservation and managed fishing zone around the islands in 1987, the economy has been transformed, with revenue from fishing and related activities overtaking sheep-farming as the main industry. Fishing licence fees now provide about half of government revenue, making the islands self-supporting in all but defence costs, although there has been concern since 2005 about the effect of overfishing on fish stocks. Tourism, especially wildlife tourism, has grown rapidly, with over 61,000 people visiting each year. Fish, meat, wool and hides are the principal exports. Chief imports are fuel, food and drink, construction materials and clothing.

There are believed to be substantial reserves of oil and gas offshore and the Falkland Islands government has licensed exploration for exploitable sites; a British exploration firm announced plans to commence oil production in 2016.

Trade with UK	2012	2013
Imports from UK	£61,537,584	£52,063,585
Exports to UK	£17,693,555	£24,219,240

COMMUNICATIONS

There is an international airport at Mt Pleasant, served by military flights to the UK and by commercial flights to Chile. The main port is Stanley Harbour and a regular shipping service operates to the UK. The road network is gradually expanding but only roads in and around Stanley are paved, and most longer internal journeys are by light aircraft. International telecommunications are possible through a satellite link, and the majority of households have internet access.

GIBRALTAR

Area – 6.5 sq. km
Capital – Gibraltar
Currency – Gibraltar pound of 100 pence
Population – 29,111 rising at 0.26 per cent a year (2013 est)
Religion – Christian (Roman Catholic 78 per cent, other
  10 per cent), Muslim 4 per cent, Jewish 2 per cent,
  Hindu 2 per cent (est)
Language – English (official), Spanish, Italian, Portuguese
Population density – 4,616 per sq. km (2012 est)
Flag – White with a red stripe along the lower edge; over all a
  red castle with a key hanging from its gateway
National day – 10 September
Life expectancy (years) – 78.98 (2013 est)
Mortality rate – 8.28 (2013 est)
Birth rate – 14.19 (2013 est)
Infant mortality rate – 6.42 (2013 est)

CLIMATE AND TERRAIN

Gibraltar is a rocky promontory, 426m at its highest point, that juts southwards from the south-east coast of Spain, with which it is connected by a low isthmus. It is about 32km from the coast of Africa, across the Strait of Gibraltar.

HISTORY AND POLITICS

Gibraltar was captured in 1704, during the War of the Spanish Succession, by a combined Dutch and English force, and was ceded to Britain in the Treaty of Utrecht (1713).

Spanish claims to the territory were a source of tension for many years, but after the overwhelming rejection of a joint sovereignty arrangement in a referendum in 2002, Spain moderated its attitude and the previously bilateral Anglo-Spanish talks about the territory became tripartite with the inclusion of Gibraltar from 2006.

Gibraltar is part of the EU (with the UK government responsible for enforcing EU directives affecting Gibraltar), but is not a full member and is exempt from the common policies on customs, commerce, agriculture, fisheries and VAT. Gibraltarians have voted in EU elections since 2004.

The 1969 constitution made provision for self-government in respect of certain domestic matters, but full internal autonomy came into effect with the 2006 constitution. This limited the governor's responsibilities to external affairs, defence, internal security and public service. The House of Assembly was restyled the Gibraltar Parliament, and may determine its own size; at present, it consists of an appointed speaker and 17 members elected for a four-year term. The government is formed by the chief minister (who is the leader of the majority party) and ministers from among the elected members of parliament.

The 2011 elections were won by the incumbent Gibraltar Social Democrats with ten seats.

Governor, HE Vice-Admiral Sir Adrian Johns KBE, CBE,
  apptd 2009
Chief Minister, Hon. Fabian Picardo

GOVERNMENT OF GIBRALTAR
150 Strand, London WC2R 1JA **T** 020-7836 0777
W www.gibraltar.gov.uk

ECONOMY

The economy is dominated by tourism (especially retail for day visitors), offshore financial services and shipping, and these three sectors account for about 85 per cent of GDP. Diversification efforts have encouraged telecommunications in particular and Gibraltar has become a centre for internet businesses, especially internet gaming. A shift from a pre-dominantly public-sector to a private-sector economy has occurred in recent years, although government spending still has a significant impact on the local economy. The chief sources of government revenue are port dues, the rent of the Crown Estate in the town, and duties on consumer items (although value added tax is not applied in the territory).
Imports – US$640m (2012)
Exports – US$253m (2012)

BALANCE OF PAYMENTS
Trade – US$388m deficit (2012)

Trade with UK	2012	2013
Imports from UK	£555,209,268	£516,052,200
Exports to UK	£97,348,044	£5,737,634

COMMUNICATIONS

Gibraltar has one international airport. The 29km road network is all surfaced; road links to Spain reopened in the

1980s. The port services the large shipping industry, cruise liners and a regular ferry service to Tangiers (Morocco).

MONTSERRAT

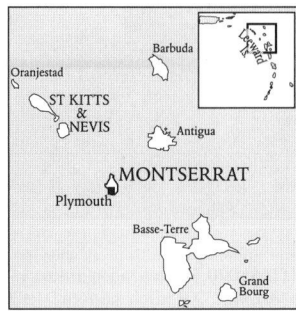

Area – 102 sq. km
Capital – Plymouth (abandoned 1997); the seat of government is now at Brades, in the north, population, 449 (2011 est); a new capital is under construction at nearby Little Bay
Currency – East Caribbean dollar (EC$) of 100 cents
Population – 5,189 rising at 0.48 per cent a year (2013 est)
Religion – Christian
Language – English (official)
Population density – 55 per sq. km (2005 est)
Flag – British blue ensign with the coat of arms in the fly
National day – Second Saturday in June (birthday of Queen Elizabeth II)
Life expectancy (years) – 73.65 (2013 est)
Mortality rate – 6.55 (2013 est)
Birth rate – 11.37 (2013 est)
Infant mortality rate – 14.16 (2013 est)

CLIMATE AND TERRAIN
Montserrat is a mountainous volcanic island in the Leeward group in the Caribbean Sea. Its lowest point of elevation is 0m (Caribbean Sea); its highest point was 914m (Chances Peak), although a lava dome in a crater in the Soufrière Hills volcano is estimated to be over 930m. Volcanic activity since 1995 has left over half of the island devastated by lava flows and ash. The climate is tropical and the average temperature is 27°C.

HISTORY AND POLITICS
Discovered by Columbus in 1493, Montserrat became a British colony in 1632. It was fought over by the French and British throughout the 17th and 18th centuries, before being finally restored to Britain in 1783.

Continual volcanic activity by the Soufrière Hills volcano between 1995 and 2014 has left over half of the island uninhabitable, and prompted the migration of two-thirds of the population in the late 1990s. A 'special vulnerable area' to which access is restricted, covers two-thirds of the island and two maritime exclusion zones extend between 2km and 4km offshore.

The 1990 constitution was amended in 1999 after more than half of the constituencies were made uninhabitable by volcanic activity. Following modernisation talks, a new constitution came into force in September 2011, which established a new National Advisory Council to enhance democracy and governance. Under the new constitution, the cabinet is chaired by the governor and comprises the premier and three other elected members and two *ex-officio* members

(the attorney-general and the financial secretary). The legislative assembly consists of nine members elected for a five-year term and two *ex-officio* members. In the 2009 general election the Movement for Change and Prosperity won the most seats.

Governor, HE Adrian Davis, *appd* 2011
Chief Minister, Hon. Reuben Meade

GOVERNMENT OF MONTSERRAT
180–186 Kings Cross Road, London WC1X 9DE T 020-7520 2622

ECONOMY
Continuing volcanic activity has restricted economic activity to the northern third of the island and considerably impacted the agricultural sector. Activity includes mining and quarrying, construction (mostly public sector), financial and professional services, and tourism. In January 2013 the EU granted a £33.4m aid package to bolster recovery. Communications improved with the opening of Gerald's Airport in the north in 2005, allowing regular commercial air services to resume. There are port facilities at Little Bay, and a ferry service to and from Antigua was reintroduced in December 2009.
Imports – US$35m (2012)
Exports – US$2m (2012)

BALANCE OF PAYMENTS
Trade – US$34m deficit (2012)

Trade with UK	2012	2013
Imports from UK	£420,544	£7,072,672
Exports to UK	£63,392	£103,258

PITCAIRN ISLANDS

Pitcairn, Henderson, Ducie and Oeno Islands
Area – 47 sq. km
Capital – Adamstown, on Pitcairn Island
Currency – New Zealand dollar (NZ$) of 100 cents
Population – 48 (2012 est)
Religion – Christian (Seventh-day Adventist)
Language – English, Pitkern (both official)
Flag – British blue ensign with the coat of arms in the fly
National day – 23 January (Bounty Day)

CLIMATE AND TERRAIN
Pitcairn is the chief of a group of rugged islands situated in the South Pacific Ocean. The other main islands of the group are Henderson, lying 168km north-east of Pitcairn; Oeno, lying 120km north-west; and Ducie, lying 470km east. These are uninhabited. Henderson Island is a UNESCO World Heritage Site. The climate is tropical with an average temperature of 20°C.

HISTORY AND POLITICS
Pitcairn was settled in 1790 by mutineers from the *Bounty* and their Tahitian companions. It became a British settlement under the British Settlements Act 1887.

Under the 2010 constitutional arrangements, the islands are administered by the governor (usually the British High Commissioner to New Zealand), in consultation with the island council, which manages internal affairs. The commissioner liaises between the governor and the council. The island council comprises ten members: the governor; two members appointed by the governor; one member appointed by the council itself; and six, including the mayor, who are elected. The mayor is elected every three years; elections for other council members are held every year in December.

Governor (non-resident), HE Victoria Treadell, CMG, MVO, apptd 2010 *(British High Commissioner to New Zealand)*
Mayor, Mike Warren

ECONOMY
The islanders live by subsistence fishing and horticulture, and the sale of honey and handicrafts, although tourism is being promoted. Apart from small fees charged for licences there are no taxes and government revenue is derived almost solely from the sale of postage stamps and .pn internet domain names, and income from investments. Since financial reserves became exhausted a few years ago the islands have received budgetary aid from the UK.

Trade with UK	2012	2013
Imports from UK	£233,301	£351,598
Exports to UK	£138,207	£98,654

COMMUNICATIONS
There is no airfield and the only means of access is by sea; cruise and container ships stop irregularly but a regular shipping supply route to French Polynesia was established in 2006. There are 6.4km of dirt roads on the islands. A telephone system and internet access have been introduced in recent years.

ST HELENA, ASCENSION AND TRISTAN DA CUNHA

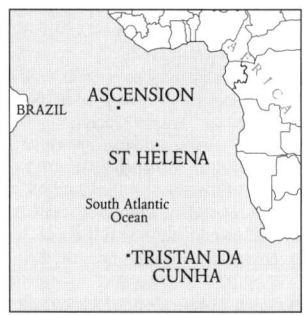

BRAZIL

ASCENSION

ST HELENA

South Atlantic
Ocean

·TRISTAN DA
CUNHA

Population – 7,754 rising at 0.3 per cent (2013 est)
Religion – Christian (predominantly Protestant); Baha'i minority
Language – English (official)
National day – Second Saturday in June (birthday of Queen Elizabeth II)
Life expectancy (years) – 79.06 (2013 est)
Mortality rate – 7.22 (2013 est)
Birth rate – 10.19 (2013 est)
Infant mortality rate – 15.25 (2013 est)

ST HELENA
Area – 122 sq. km
Capital – Jamestown; population, 1000 (2009 est)
Currency – St Helena pound (£) of 100 pence
Population – 4,158 (2013 est)
Flag – British blue ensign with the coat of arms in the fly

CLIMATE AND TERRAIN
St Helena is a rugged and volcanic island, with sheer cliffs rising to a central plateau. Mt Actaeon, at 818m, is the highest elevation. The climate is tropical but mild, tempered by trade winds, and the average temperature is 18°C.

HISTORY AND POLITICS
St Helena is believed to have been discovered by the Portuguese navigator Joao da Nova in 1502. It was used as a port of call for vessels of all nations trading to the East until the late 19th century. From 1815 to 1821 the island was lent to the British government as a place of exile for Napoléon Bonaparte, who died there on 5 May 1821, and in 1834 it was annexed to the British crown. The Zulu chief Dinizulu was exiled to the island in 1890, and up to 6,000 Boer prisoners were held there between 1900 and 1903.

Under the 2009 constitution, government is administered by a governor, advised by an executive council comprising three *ex-officio* members (the chief secretary, financial secretary and attorney-general) and five elected members of the legislative council. The legislative council consists of 12 members elected for a four-year term, the three *ex-officio* members of the executive council and a speaker.

Governor, HE Mark Capes, *apptd* 2011

GOVERNMENT OF ST HELENA
16 Old Queen Street, London SW1H 9HP **T** 020-7031 0314

ECONOMY AND TRADE
The island has few natural resources and its economy is dependent on an annual grant from the UK. The main economic activities are agriculture, the sale of fishing licences, fish processing and tourism. The only significant exports are coffee and frozen, canned and dried fish.

Trade with UK	2012	2013
Imports from UK	£14,072,767	£15,488,515
Exports to UK	£233,654	£74,446

COMMUNICATIONS
Access is solely by sea to Jamestown port, provided by a regular supply ship. A long-promised international airport is scheduled for completion in 2016. St Helena has 138km of roads, most of which are single track. There are two local radio stations and two weekly newspapers.

ASCENSION ISLAND
Area – 88 sq. km
Capital – Georgetown
Currency – St Helena/Ascension pound (£) of 100 pence
Population – 880 (2011 est)

CLIMATE AND TERRAIN
The island is a rocky volcanic peak that lies in the South Atlantic Ocean some 1,200km north-west of St Helena. The highest point (Green Mountain, 859m) is covered with lush vegetation. It is an important breeding place for the green turtle and a number of seabird species.

HISTORY AND POLITICS
Ascension is said to have been discovered by Joao da Nova in 1501 and two years later it was visited on Ascension Day by

Alphonse d'Albuquerque, who gave the island its present name. As HMS *Ascension* it remained under the supervision of the Board of Admiralty until 1922, when it was made a dependency of St Helena. The island was an important logistical centre in both world wars and during the Falklands conflict, and it has a continuing role as a military air base and in broadcasting, telecommunications and satellite tracking.

In 2002 new constitutional arrangements introduced a measure of self-government, and in 2009 Ascension ceased to be a dependency of St Helena. The governor, who is resident in St Helena, retains responsibility for defence, external affairs, internal security and public services. The governor, represented locally by the island administrator, chairs the island council, which consists of five elected members and two *ex-officio* members (the director of resources and the attorney-general).

Administrator, Colin Wells, *apptd* 2011

ECONOMY
Before 2002 the island was administered and financed by the main commercial users (the BBC and Cable and Wireless) and the military. With the change in governance in 2002, a fiscal regime was introduced to finance public services through taxation. A private sector is developing following the sale of government-owned concerns to commercial operators and the establishment of a sports fishing industry.

COMMUNICATIONS
Georgetown is the only port and there are regular scheduled shipping services, as well as regular air links to the UK and the USA by military aircraft and occasional charter flights. Ascension has 40km of roads. Telecommunication services are provided via satellite links. There is a local radio station and a weekly newspaper.

TRISTAN DA CUNHA
Area – 98 sq. km
Capital – Edinburgh of the Seven Seas
Currency – Pound sterling (£) of 100 pence
Population – 263 (2014 est)
Flag – British blue ensign with the coat of arms in the fly

CLIMATE AND TERRAIN
Tristan da Cunha is the chief of a group of islands in the South Atlantic Ocean which lie some 2,333km south-west of St Helena. All of the islands are volcanic and steep-sided with cliffs or narrow beaches. The island is home to the highest peak in the South Atlantic, Queens Mary's Peak, which rises to 2,060m above sea-level. Gough and Inaccessible Islands are UNESCO World Heritage Sites.

HISTORY AND POLITICS
Tristan da Cunha was discovered in 1506 by the Portuguese navigator Tristao da Cunha. In 1816 the group was annexed to the British crown and a garrison was placed on Tristan da Cunha. When this force was withdrawn in 1817, four adults and two children remained at their own request and formed a settlement, which was joined in 1827 by five women from St Helena and afterwards by others from Cape Colony. Owing to its position on a major sea route the colony thrived, with an economy based on trade with passing ships, until the late 19th century, when the opening of the Suez Canal led to decline.

Tristan da Cunha and Inaccessible, Nightingale and Gough Islands were dependencies of St Helena from 1938 to 2009. They are administered by the governor of St Helena through a resident administrator, who is advised by an island council. This consists of eight members elected for a three-year term, of whom one must be a woman, and three appointed members.

Administrator, Alex Mitham, *apptd* 2013

ECONOMY
The island is almost financially self-sufficient; UK government aid finances training scholarships and a resident medical officer at the hospital. The main activities are crayfish fishing, fish processing, agriculture and the sale of postage stamps and coins.

COMMUNICATIONS
Communications with the outside world are by sea as there is no airport. Scheduled visits to the island are limited to about nine calls a year by fishing vessels from Cape Town and annual calls by a South African research vessel. Tristan da Cunha has 20km of roads, half of which are paved. There is a local radio station and a newspaper.

SOUTH GEORGIA AND THE SOUTH SANDWICH ISLANDS

For map *see* Falkland Islands entry.

Area – 3,903 sq. km
Capital – King Edward Point (administrative centre), on South Georgia
Currency – Pound sterling (£) of 100 pence
Population – There is no indigenous population. The British Antarctic Survey maintains two permanently staffed research stations, at King Edward Point and on Bird Island, to the north-west of South Georgia; in addition, there are the government officers at King Edward Point, and the curators of the museum at Grytviken, South Georgia
Flag – British blue ensign, with the coat of arms in the fly

CLIMATE AND TERRAIN
Over half of South Georgia is permanently ice-covered, with many large glaciers. The main mountain range is the Allardyce, and elevation extremes range from 2,934m (Mt Paget) to 0m (Atlantic Ocean). The South Sandwich Islands are a chain of 11 uninhabited volcanic islands some 350km long.

HISTORY AND POLITICS
South Georgia was used by whalers and sealers of many nationalities following its discovery by Captain Cook in 1775. Britain annexed South Georgia and the South Sandwich Islands in 1908 and since then they have been under continuous British occupation, apart from a brief period during the Falklands conflict in 1982; Argentina claims sovereignty over the territory. A small British army garrison was maintained on South Georgia until 2001, before being replaced by scientists from the British Antarctic Survey.

Under the present constitution, which came into effect in 1985, the commissioner is concurrently the governor of the Falkland Islands. A chief executive officer, also based in the Falklands Islands, is responsible for administration. Government officers are based in South Georgia.

Commissioner (non-resident), HE Colin Roberts, CVO, *apptd* 2014
Senior Executive Officer (non-resident), Martin Collins

ECONOMY
A conservation and management fishing zone was established around the islands in 1993 and a licensing regime

introduced for fishing vessels. Sale of fishing licences, passenger landing fees, harbour dues, and the sale of postage stamps and commemorative coins are the main sources of revenue. Tourism, especially wildlife tourism, is growing quickly, but prior permission to land on the islands must be sought.

TURKS AND CAICOS ISLANDS

Area – 430 sq. km
Capital – Cockburn Town, on Grand Turk; population, 4,831 (2012 est)
Currency – US dollar (US$) of 100 cents
Population – 47,754 rising at 2.87 per cent a year (2013 est)
Religion – Christian (Protestant 72.8 per cent, Roman Catholic 11.4 per cent) (est)
Language – English (official)
Population density – 33 per sq. km (2011 est)
Flag – British blue ensign with the coat of arms in the fly
National day – 30 August (Constitution Day)
Life expectancy (years) – 79.4 (2013 est)
Mortality rate – 3.06 (2013 est)
Birth rate – 17.05 (2013 est)
Infant mortality rate – 11.29 (2013 est)

CLIMATE AND TERRAIN
Around 40 islands and cays make up the the Turks and Caicos Islands, of which eight are permanently inhabited.

The climate is marine tropical, moderated by trade winds; the average annual temperature is 26°C. Flamingo Hill on East Caicos is the highest elevation, at 48m.

HISTORY AND POLITICS
The islands changed hands several times between the French, Spanish and British between their discovery in 1512 and the arrival of the first settlers, a group of Bermudans, in the 1670s. They achieved separate colonial status under the administration of the Bahamas in 1848, and since 1973 the territory has had its own governor and internal self-government.

A 2006 constitution provided for ministerial government and a partially elected legislature, with the governor retaining responsibility for defence, external affairs, internal security and the regulation of financial services. Following an inquiry into alleged political corruption in 2008–9, on 14 August 2009 the UK government suspended parts of the constitution, dismissed the House of Assembly and imposed direct rule by the governor for a period of at least two years, during which time legislative, administrative and financial reforms were implemented. A new constitution came into effect on 15 October 2012. The Progressive National Party (PNP) won elections held in November 2012, garnering eight seats to the People's Democratic Movement's seven, and elected government rule was reimplemented.
Governor, HE Peter Beckingham, *apptd* 2013

ECONOMY
The main industries are offshore financial services, fishing and tourism, with over one million people visiting the island in 2013. The USA is the main source of tourists.

Trade with UK	2012	2013
Imports from UK	£1,817,180	£1,789,452
Exports to UK	£13,900	£488,244

COMMUNICATIONS
The principal airports are on the islands of Grand Turk and Providenciales and provide international air links; the main seaports are on Grand Turk and Providenciales. The islands also have a total of 121km of roads, 24km of which are surfaced.

THE YEAR 2013–14

The year under review covers the period from 1 August 2013 to 31 July 2014

EVENTS OF THE YEAR 2013–14

UK AFFAIRS

AUGUST 2013

8. Two 18-year-old British women were attacked with acid while working as volunteers in Zanzibar, Tanzania. **13.** Trade unions protested at railway stations across England after the government announced an average 4.1 per cent increase in regulated rail fares from January 2014, with unregulated fares increasing by up to 9.1 per cent. **15.** A 21-year-old German intern, working for Bank of America Merrill Lynch in London, was found dead at his student residence, which prompted a debate concerning the culture of the industry; on 22 November 2013, a court was told the intern died from an epileptic fit which could not be proven to be linked to the 72-hour shift he had worked immediately before. **18.** Over 2,000 anti-fracking protestors marched through the West Sussex countryside at the beginning of a three-day campaign against exploratory drilling by the private company Cuadrilla, near the village of Balcombe. **19.** The Green MP for Brighton Pavilion, Caroline Lucas, was arrested along with her son and around 30 people at the continued anti-fracking demonstrations in Balcombe; campaigners also caused disturbances at the company's headquarters in Lichfield. **29.** The prime minister David Cameron definitively ruled out UK military action against Syrian president Bashar al-Assad's government following the defeat of a government motion by 285–272 votes; the UK government's motion supported military action if it was corroborated by evidence from UN weapons inspectors regarding a suspected chemical weapons attack near Damascus on 21 August, 2013.

SEPTEMBER 2013

2. In London, the building under construction at 20 Fenchurch Street, known as the Walkie-Talkie skyscraper due to its distinctive shape, reflected intense light onto the road below, which melted the bodywork on a Jaguar car. **5.** Over 130 vehicles were involved in a series of crashes on the Sheppey bridge crossing in Kent as a result of thick fog, leaving more than 60 people injured. **6.** Disclosures by Edward Snowden, a former American National Security Agency (NSA) contractor, alleged that the NSA, alongside the UK's GCHQ, cracked encryption codes protecting personal information such as emails and medical records of hundreds of millions of people. **10.** Nigel Evans, MP resigned as a House of Commons Deputy Speaker after he was charged with eight offences which included sexual assault, indecent assault and rape against seven men between 2002 and 2013; Mr Evans, the MP for Ribble Valley, denied any wrongdoing and called the claims 'incredulous' (*see* Crimes and Legal Affairs, 10 April). The Duke of Cambridge completed his tour as an RAF search and rescue pilot, which ended over seven years of military service and, with his family, moved from Anglesey to Kensington Palace, to turn his attention to royal duties and charity work. **14.** The Liberal Democrat Party conference took place in Glasgow, and saw the deputy prime minister Nick Clegg acclaimed by delegates after presenting a list of Conservative policies which had been blocked by his party. **20.** The UK Independence Party (UKIP) MEP Godfrey Bloom had the party whip removed after he joked that a 'women in politics' event at the party's annual conference was 'full of sluts'; the UKIP leader Nigel Farage stated that the comment required disciplinary action, while Mr Bloom was later filmed hitting the *Channel 4 News* reporter Michael

Crick on the head with a party brochure after being asked why there were no non-white faces on the leaflet. **21.** Five Britons died after Somalian al-Shabab militants stormed the Westgate shopping centre in the Kenyan capital Nairobi (*see* International Affairs, Africa). **22.** The Labour Party's annual conference began in Brighton and featured a pledge by the leader Ed Miliband to freeze electricity and gas prices for 20 months if elected in May 2015. **29.** In Manchester, the Conservative Party conference saw the prime minister deliver a speech which spoke of his ambition to make the UK 'a land of opportunity for all' and to win an overall majority in the 2015 general election.

OCTOBER 2013

8. The leader and founder of the English Defence League (EDL), Tommy Robinson, left the group after he expressed concern over the 'dangers of far-right extremism'; Mr Robinson was one of several senior figures to have quit the EDL. A passenger with no flying experience managed to land a plane after the pilot, the only other person on board, fell ill at the controls and was later pronounced dead; the plane landed safely at Humberside airport after the passenger was talked through the procedure by two flying instructors. **15.** The Royal Mail was listed on the London Stock Exchange after the government privatised the postal service company; 700,000 private investors applied for shares worth 330p each, which gave the company an initial flotation value of £3.3bn. **17.** The Duke of Cambridge conducted his first investiture ceremony in the Buckingham Palace ballroom during which he bestowed two knighthoods and presented the Wimbledon champion Andy Murray with an OBE. **21.** The government approved plans for a new nuclear station in Somerset, the first new nuclear power plant to be built in 20 years; Hinkley Point C, consisting of two pressurised water reactors, was planned to become operational in 2023 at a cost of £14bn to provide low-carbon power for 60 years. **23.** Prince George Alexander Louis of Cambridge was christened in the Chapel Royal at St James's Palace in London. **28.** Four people died and 625,000 homes were left without power after the worst storm to hit the UK since 2002 battered parts of southern Britain; flights, ferry services and railways were severely disrupted as winds reached speeds of more than 70mph, with the strongest gust of 99mph, recorded at Needles Old Battery, Isle of Wight. **29.** A Roman carved stone sculpture of an eagle clasping a serpent in its beak was discovered by archaeologists during a dig at a building site in the City of London; the eagle, in a state of 'outstanding preservation', was made in Britain in around 100AD.

NOVEMBER 2013

14. Grace Jones, the last living British person to be born in the 19th century, died at the age of 113. **17.** A British teacher was among 50 people killed when a Boeing 737 Russian passenger plane crashed at Kazan airport in Russia while attempting a second landing. **20.** Three British Greenpeace protestors, arrested by Russian authorities on 19 September 2013 while on board a boat in the Arctic, were released on bail at a cost of £38,000 having spent two months in prison. Hull was named the UK City of Culture from 2017 after it beat rival bids from Leicester, Dundee and Swansea Bay; Hull was the home of the poet Philip Larkin and is the site of the Ferens Art Gallery. **26.** Alex Salmond, the first minister of Scotland, launched a white paper setting out his government's case for Scottish independence in the referendum on 18 September 2014. **29.** Ten people died after a Police Scotland helicopter crashed into the roof of the Clutha pub in Glasgow, with three people on board the helicopter among the dead; around 120 people were in the pub on a busy Friday night, with 32 people taken to local hospitals for treatment.

DECEMBER 2013

5. The UK experienced the worst tidal surge in 60 years as more than 15,000 people on the east coast of England were forced to evacuate their homes, two people died and the Environment Agency issued over 60 severe flood warnings; the North Sea tidal surge was the biggest to hit the UK since 1953. **10.** David Cameron was criticised after he posed in a 'selfie' with US president Barack Obama and Denmark's prime minister Helle Thorning-Schmidt at the memorial service for the late South African president Nelson Mandela at the FNB stadium in Johannesburg. **16.** On a visit to Camp Bastion in Helmand, Afghanistan, David Cameron told UK troops they would be returning home the next year with their mission accomplished; the prime minister said a 'basic level of security' had been achieved in the country. **17.** The foreign office minister Hugh Robertson stated that Syrian authorities had 'in effect murdered' British orthopaedic doctor Abbas Khan only days before his expected release from jail; Syrian authorities claimed Mr Khan, 32, had committed suicide by hanging himself with his pyjamas. **18.** The Bank of England announced that plastic banknotes would be brought into UK circulation from 2016, replacing cotton paper notes, used in the UK for over 100 years. Ronnie Biggs, the former fugitive criminal who took part in the 1963 Great Train Robbery, died at the age of 84. **19.** During a performance of *The Curious Incident of the Dog in the Night-Time* at the Apollo Theatre in London, part of the ceiling collapsed, injuring 79 people, seven of those being serious injuries. **23.** A royal posthumous pardon was granted to the computer pioneer and codebreaker Alan Turing; Turing, who worked at the Bletchley Park codebreaking centre during the Second World War, committed suicide in 1954 after being chemically castrated for having an affair with a 19-year-old man. **25.** The Energy Networks Association confirmed that around 50,000 homes in the UK were without power on Christmas Day; flooding from stormy weather affected thousands of homes in southern England with over 100 people evacuated from their homes in Dorset after the river Stour burst its banks. **27.** Five Britons returned to the UK, having been imprisoned in Russia for 100 days after authorities seized their ship and arrested them during a Greenpeace environmental protest in the Arctic; the group, which consisted of 30 activists, was granted an amnesty from charges following their protests against Arctic oil drilling. **31.** In the New Year's Honours List, the actresses Angela Lansbury and Penelope Keith were made dames, while the sculptor Antony Gormley received a knighthood; women received more honours than men, with 611 women (51 per cent) making up the list.

JANUARY 2014

7. A United States Air Force HH-60G Pave Hawk helicopter crashed during a low-level training exercise at a nature reserve in Cley next the Sea in Norfolk, killing the crew of four. **21.** The UK's first motorway service station pub opened at junction two of the M40 at Beaconsfield, Buckinghamshire; the Wetherspoon chain's pub was licensed to serve alcohol from 9am and came under criticism from road safety and health campaigners including the charity Brake.

FEBRUARY 2014

1. The Radcliffe Meteorological Station at Oxford University revealed that rainfall in January 2014 was greater than any

month since the recording began in 1767, with a total of 146.9mm falling; the total eclipsed the previous 1914 record of 143.3mm. **3.** David Cameron overturned a Home Office decision to rule out extending pub opening hours during the 2014 FIFA World Cup; the pub industry requested extended hours during two weekends of the tournament, with the decision set to benefit the economy by up to £20m. **4.** Residents of the flood-hit Somerset Levels expressed anger at the slow response of the Environment Agency and the government, during a visit from the Prince of Wales; Prince Charles said there was 'nothing like a jolly good disaster to get people to do something'. Figures from a Public Health England report showed that Copeland in West Cumbria was the 'fattest' local authority area in England, with 75.9 per cent of the population classed as overweight or obese. **5.** David Cameron chaired a COBRA (Cabinet Office Briefing Room A) emergency committee concerning the flood response seeking £100m more for flood defences; the prime minister pledged 'no restrictions on help'. The Metropolitan police commissioner Sir Bernard Hogan-Howe, visited parliament to apologise to the former chief whip Andrew Mitchell after an off-duty police officer falsely claimed to have witnessed the Plebgate affair in September 2012 (*see* Crimes and Legal Affairs). **7.** David Cameron travelled by helicopter to the Somerset Levels six weeks after flooding began in the area; the prime minister blamed the previous Labour government for a pause in local river dredging in the 1990s and promised that there would be increased help from emergency services and the military. **13.** The former deputy head of the policy unit in Downing Street, Patrick Rock, was arrested in the middle of the night under allegations relating to child abuse imagery after resigning from his position in government the previous day. **14.** The Duke of Cambridge and Prince Harry worked with the armed forces in Datchet and Berkshire to help homeowners with the flood effort. **25.** John Downey, the man accused of killing four soldiers and seven horses in the 1982 Hyde Park bombing, was told he would not be prosecuted under the Good Friday peace agreement which guaranteed that he would not face trial; the decision could affect 186 others wanted for terror-related offences that took place during the Troubles.

MARCH 2014

10. The chief executive of the Co-operative Group, Euan Sutherland, resigned after details of his £6.6m pay deal for 2013 and 2014 were leaked; Sutherland claimed that individuals were attempting to undermine him and declared the organisation was 'ungovernable' and had 'lost its way'. **13.** A helicopter crashed in a field in Gillingham, Norfolk killing four people; on 3 April 2014, investigators stated that the crash was not due to technical malfunction but low visibility during intense fog. **15.** The Million Women Study, the biggest health research project in the UK, found that one in eight hospital admissions of women over 50 were due to excess weight or obesity. **19.** The chancellor George Osborne delivered the 2014 Budget to Parliament which included raising the income tax threshold to £10,500 from April 2015 and the cancellation of the fuel duty rise planned for September 2014. As part of the Budget, a new £1 coin was unveiled; it is to be introduced in 2017, replacing the current coin which was believed to have an estimated 45 million forgeries in circulation (*see* The Year 2013–14: Parliament). **26.** In a live TV and radio debate hosted by the radio station LBC, the deputy prime minister Nick Clegg and UKIP leader Nigel Farage clashed over Britain's future in the EU and immigration; a YouGov poll suggested 57 per cent of voters believed Mr Farage had performed better in the debate than Mr Clegg. **29.** The first same-sex weddings in England and Wales took place after gay marriage became legal at midnight;

David Cameron hailed the change as a declaration of equality 'whether gay or straight,' while a number of religious groups opposed the change in the law.

APRIL 2014

1. British-led military operations in Helmand province, Afghanistan ended after eight years of war and the loss of 448 British lives. **3.** The Queen and Prince Philip met Pope Francis for the first time after lunching with the Italian President, Giorgio Napolitano in Rome; in an exchange of gifts at the Vatican, the Queen gave the Pope a hamper including Balmoral whisky and chutney, while the Pontiff gifted a lapis lazuli orb for Prince George. **4.** The main railway line through Dawlish, Devon, was reopened at a cost of £34m after being partly destroyed during winter storms. **5.** The Queen Elizabeth Olympic Park opened to the public for the first time since the London 2012 Olympic Games; it was the biggest park opened in London for a century. **8.** At a state banquet at Windsor Castle, the Northern Ireland deputy first minister and former IRA leader Martin McGuinness joined in a toast to the Queen and stood for the national anthem; the occasion honoured the visit of the Irish President Michael D. Higgins, which was the first state visit to the UK by an Irish head of state. Prince George embarked on his first royal tour with his parents the Duke and Duchess of Cambridge; the family visited various places in Australia and New Zealand over a three-week period. **9.** The culture secretary Maria Miller resigned following a row over her parliamentary expenses, insisting it was her decision to step down and not a forced move by Downing Street; Conservative MP Sajid Javid was named the new culture secretary after Mrs Miller was cleared of using taxpayers' money to fund a home for her parents, but had to repay £5,800 of claimed expenses. **13.** Mark Shand, chair of the Elephant Family and the brother of the Duchess of Cornwall, died from a head injury after he sustained a fall in New York. **22.** The Prime Minister and the Chancellor announced £36 billion would be invested in more than 200 projects to improve UK infrastructure, including improvement of roads, rail services, broadband coverage and flood defences. **23.** The breast cancer drug Kadcyla was rejected by the NHS because it would be too expensive for routine use; Kadcyla can prolong the lives of women with advanced breast cancer by an average of six months.

MAY 2014

14. Nineteen-year-old teenage cancer fundraiser, Stephen Sutton, died after raising more than £3.2 million for charity. **22.** European and local council elections were held in England and Northern Ireland; Labour claimed the majority of councils with a total of 82 while UKIP won the European elections with 24 MEPs; the Liberal Democrats came sixth in the European elections with one MEP. **24.** A fire devastated the art-nouveau Charles Rennie Mackintosh Building at the Glasgow School of Art which was first opened in 1909. **30.** Google launched a service allowing Europeans to request the removal of personal data from online search results after a landmark European Union court ruling.

JUNE 2014

3. The Home secretary Theresa May accused the education secretary Michael Gove of failing to curb extremism in schools; the argument followed an investigation by Ofsted (the Office for Standards in Education), into a potential plot by Islamists to manipulate the administration and content of schools in the Birmingham and Bradford areas. **4.** The Queen delivered her speech at the State Opening of Parliament; one of the pageboys fainted and had to be carried from the chamber but was later declared to be fine. **5.** Robert Jenrick,

the Conservative candidate in the Newark by-election, won with forty-five per cent of the vote. **6.** The Queen began her three-day state visit to France by attending a commemoration ceremony in Normandy to mark the 70th anniversary of D-Day. **11.** Around 10,000 black-taxi drivers protested in central London against the lack of legal regulation of the ridesharing service Uber and other mobile phone apps that calculate taxi fares. **16.** The Foreign secretary William Hague announced that the British Embassy in Tehran, Iran would open to increase coordination in combatting the threat from the jihadist group Islamic State (IS, formerly known as ISIS) in Iraq; the embassy was closed in 2011 after a crowd of pro-regime demonstrators looted the building. **27.** Prince Harry began a six-day tour of Brazil and Chile. **29.** David Cameron was outvoted in his objection to the appointment of Luxembourgish president Jean-Claude Juncker as the next President of the European Commission, despite widespread scepticism about Juncker's suitability for the post.

JULY 2014

4. The Queen christened the HMS Queen Elizabeth at Rosyth Dockyard in Fife; the 280m aircraft carrier is the largest ever warship made in the UK. **9.** The member database of the Liberty tax strategy revealed that more than 1,600 people, many of them prominent celebrities, had taken part in one of Britain's most aggressive tax avoidance schemes; HMRC had investigated Liberty for over a decade. **14.** The Church of England approved the consecration of women bishops with an overwhelming majority; held at the University of York, the vote brought an end to a divisive and long-running debate within the church. A cabinet reshuffle saw thirteen ministers removed from their positions which included William Hague being replaced by Philip Hammond as foreign secretary and Owen Paterson replaced by Elizabeth Truss as environment secretary; Michael Gove was given the post of chief whip and was replaced by Nicky Morgan as education secretary. **16.** Employment figures hit a record high of 73.1 per cent from March to May 2014; in real terms, 30.6m people were employed and 2.1m remained unemployed. **28.** Hundreds of passport office workers went on strike over staff shortages resulting in a backlog of 450,000 applications; in 2010, the passport office included 3,700 staff but in 2013 that number had fallen to 3,333. **30.** Eastbourne's Victorian pier was destroyed when its main atrium caught fire; police believed that the blaze was not suspicious.

ARTS AND MEDIA

AUGUST 2013

4. Peter Capaldi, best known as the intimidating spin-doctor Malcolm Tucker in satirical political comedy *The Thick of It,* was revealed as the 12th actor to play the title role in *Doctor Who,* the world's longest running science fiction programme. **24.** The feminist comedian Bridget Christie won the 2013 Foster's Edinburgh Comedy award for her show, *A Bic for Her;* Christie, who was presented with the £10,000 prize by the actor Steve Coogan, was the first woman to win the award since 2005. **27.** The word 'omnishambles', originally coined in *The Thick of It* and subsequently used as a derogatory term by Labour leader Ed Miliband to describe the government's 2012 budget, was added to the Oxford Dictionaries online, along with such words as 'selfie', 'unlike' and 'digital detox'.

SEPTEMBER 2013

1. The broadcaster Andrew Marr returned to his Sunday morning politics and culture programme, *The Andrew Marr Show,* after he suffered a stroke in January 2013. **4.** A photograph of a lost *Sunflowers* painting by Vincent Van Gogh was recovered in a Japanese museum archive; *Six Sunflowers,* also known as *Vase with Five Sunflowers,* was painted in 1888 but destroyed in a fire after the US bombing of Osaka in the Second World War. **7.** At the Royal Albert Hall, Marin Alsop became the first female conductor to lead the Last Night of the Proms in the concert's 118-year history. **9.** A 25th anniversary revival of the musical *Miss Saigon* set a new one-day sales box-office record with takings of £4.4m, surpassing the previous record held by *The Book of Mormon,* which took £2.1m in March 2013; the play opened in May 2014, having previously run in the West End for ten years. **15.** The V&A museum displayed two prototypes of a working gun designed by a Texan law student; dubbed the 'Liberator', the controversial firearm was created using a 3D printer. The drama *12 Years a Slave,* directed by Briton Steve McQueen and based on the memoir of Solomon Northup, won the People's Choice award at the Toronto film festival. **17.** *Grand Theft Auto V,* the latest instalment in the controversial video game series, broke the UK record for first-day sales of a new console game, selling 1.57 million copies at a total of £65m. **25.** At London's Dorchester hotel, writer William Boyd launched his new James Bond novel, *Solo;* Boyd joined an exclusive list of authors to have penned Bond novels, including Sebastian Faulks and Jeffery Deaver. **26.** A radio producer revealed that the US poet Robert Frost's *Stopping by Woods on a Snowy Evening* was the most requested poem on BBC Radio 4's *Poetry Please,* having been read out 17 times since the programme began in 1979.

OCTOBER 2013
1. The Labour leader Ed Miliband accused the *Daily Mail* of lying about his father, Marxist academic Ralph Miliband, after the tabloid published an article calling him 'The man who hated Britain', for which the paper refused to apologise. **3.** *Shunga: Sex and Pleasure in Japanese Art* opened at the British Museum; the exhibition, which focused on the style of art prevalent from the 17th- to mid-19th century in Japan, was considered to be the most sexually explicit since the museum was founded in 1753. At the Museum of Modern Art in New York, a 1927 painting by the Belgian surrealist master René Magritte, *The Enchanted Pose,* which had been presumed to be lost or damaged, was discovered in sections beneath two of his other paintings, using X-rays and other imaging techniques. **10.** The Canadian author Alice Munro was awarded the 2013 Nobel Prize for Literature; the 82-year-old was described by the permanent secretary of the Swedish Academy as a 'master of the contemporary short story'. **12.** Linguistic analysis found that scenes and passages in three Elizabethan plays believed to have been written by other playwrights had William Shakespeare's input; *Arden of Faversham, The Spanish Tragedy* and *Mucedorus* were added to a major edition of collaborative plays bearing Shakespeare's name. **13.** The bronze sculpture *Standing Figure* by Henry Moore, was stolen from the Glenkiln Sculpture Park in south-west Scotland; the robbery followed the theft of another Moore sculpture, *The Sundial,* in Hertfordshire in November 2012. **15.** At 28, Eleanor Catton became the youngest winner of the £50,000 Man Booker Prize for her novel *The Luminaries;* the New Zealander's 832-page novel became the lengthiest work to win the literary award. **20.** The Polish director Pawel Pawlikowski's film *Ida* won the best film award at the BFI London Film Festival. **30.** The Barclaycard Mercury Prize for the best British or Irish album of the year was awarded to electronic artist James Blake for his second album, *Overgrown.*

NOVEMBER 2013
4. The Samuel Johnson Prize for Non-Fiction was presented to Lucy Hughes-Hallett for her book *The Pike,* a biography of the Italian poet and politician Gabriele D'Annunzio, a womaniser who became a national hero and fascist. **12.** A portrait of the jockey Katie Walsh by the photographer Spencer Murphy won the Taylor Wessing Photographic Prize and was later displayed at the National Portrait Gallery. **13.** Francis Bacon's *Three Studies of Lucian Freud* became the most expensive artwork ever sold at auction when it fetched £89m ($142m) in six minutes at Christie's in New York. **19.** Tate Britain was opened to the public following a £45m renovation which included the reopening of the gallery's Thames-facing entrance and a new spiral staircase with a revamped rotunda. **24.** Robbie Williams' big band album *Swings Both Ways* became the 1,000th number one record in the Official UK Album Chart; over 3,000 album charts were released between the first number one, Frank Sinatra's *Songs For Swingin' Lovers* in 1956, and Williams' record.

DECEMBER 2013
2. French installation artist Laure Prouvost won the Turner Prize for her piece *Wantee,* a film played in a room in the style of a tea party. **13.** The Ashmolean Museum in Oxford acquired one of the world's most significant collections of modern Chinese art; Professor Michael Sullivan, a Chinese art expert, donated around 400 works to the museum, many of which had never been seen in public. **17.** Apple Records released 59 rare and unheard Beatles recordings to stop their copyright protection expiring due to changes in EU laws. **23.** The former Manchester United manager Sir Alex Ferguson's memoir, *My Autobiography,* was confirmed as the bestselling print book of the year and the fastest selling non-fiction book on record with sales of 803,084 copies. **26.** Neil Gaiman's fantasy novel *The Ocean at the End of the Lane* won the Specsavers Book of the Year award. **29.** The Wellcome Library in Euston acquired a rare and tiny medieval medical almanac dating from the 15th century for £100,000; the almanac, consisting of a calendar, astrological chart and medical textbook, was illuminated in gold leaf and rich colours and was smaller than the palm of a hand.

JANUARY 2014
12. At the Golden Globe awards, the British–American film *12 Years a Slave* won best film drama; the other major winner was crime comedy-drama *American Hustle,* featuring the British actor Christian Bale, which won three awards. **13.** The inaugural Belfast Laureate, Sinead Morrissey, won the £15,000 T. S. Eliot Prize for Poetry for her collection 'Parallax'; Morrissey's writing was called 'politically, historically and personally ambitious' by the chair of judges. **14.** The British Museum announced that 2013 was its busiest year to date with 6.7 million visits, which surpassed the previous record of 6 million in 2008; the historic museum presented extremely popular exhibitions which included Pompeii and Ice Age Art. **28.** The Costa Book of the Year award was won by former mental health nurse Nathan Filer for his debut novel *The Shock of the Fall,* which beat works by four authors including the bestselling novelist Kate Atkinson's *Life After Life.*

FEBRUARY 2014
4. The social network site Facebook celebrated its tenth anniversary; at the end of 2013, there were 1.23 billion registered users, around 24 million of these were in the United Kingdom. A novella by comic entertainer Charlie Chaplin was published 66 years after it was written; the 70-page *Footlights* provided the basis for Chaplin's 1952 film *Limelight* and is the only known novella by the film star. **7.** The National Gallery acquired its first major painting by an

American artist after it paid £15.6m ($25.5m) for George Bellows' 1912 painting *Men of the Docks*, depicting a group of workers standing by the Brooklyn waterfront. *Gift Horse*, a skeletal horse by the German artist Hans Haacke, and *Really Good*, a 10m-high bronze thumb by David Shrigley, were chosen as the two works which would occupy the fourth plinth in Trafalgar Square from 2015 and 2016 respectively. **13.** A portrait by Francis Bacon became the most valuable work of art sold by Christie's auction house in Europe when it was bought by an anonymous telephone buyer for £42m; the 6ft-tall painting, *The Portrait of George Dyer Talking*, was painted in 1966 and portrayed a burglar who broke into Bacon's home and subsequently became his lover. **16.** At the British Academy of Film and Television Arts (BAFTA) awards in London, the space thriller *Gravity* collected six awards including outstanding British film and best director; the historical epic drama *12 Years a Slave* was named as best film with the British lead, Chiwetel Ejiofor, winning for best actor. **19.** David Bowie was named British male solo artist at the Brit Awards in London becoming, at 67, the oldest recipient of the music award; the Arctic Monkeys won two awards for British group and British album for *AM*. **27.** Vintage Books announced sales of E. L. James' erotic trilogy of novels, *Fifty Shades of Grey*, had passed the 100-million milestone with over 27 million copies sold in the UK and Commonwealth countries and over 45 million sold in the US.

MARCH 2014
2. At the 86th Academy Awards, *12 Years a Slave* won three Oscars including best picture, while the British-produced *Gravity*, which took five years to complete, won seven awards, most of them for technical achievement; the best actor award went to Matthew McConaughey for his role in *Dallas Buyers Club* and Cate Blanchett won the award for best actress for her part in Woody Allen's *Blue Jasmine*. **6.** As part of cost-cutting plans, the director general of the BBC, Lord Hall, announced the channel BBC Three would be dropped from television schedules and moved to an online only channel from autumn 2015. **10.** The American author George Saunders became the first recipient of the inaugural Folio Prize for his short story collection *Tenth of December* (Bloomsbury); the £40,000 prize was open to English-language writers from around the world. **13.** In a joint project with the Imperial War Museum, The National Archives published an online collection of 4,000 first-hand accounts of frontline events during the First World War, to mark the event's centenary.

APRIL 2014
13. A list compiled by Nielsen Book Research, published in *The Sunday Times*, revealed that *A Brief History of Time*, the bestseller by cosmologist Stephen Hawking had spent the longest time in the top 10 bestsellers list of any book over the past 40 years. **14.** At the 2014 Olivier Awards in central London, Rory Kinnear was named best actor for his portrayal of Iago in the National Theatre production of *Othello*, while the best actress award was presented to Lesley Manville for her performance in the Almeida Theatre production of *Ghosts*. **17.** An exhibition composed of one of the largest ever assembled collections of the French artist Henri Matisse's 'cut-out' artworks opened at Tate Modern, which included pieces such as *The Snail* and *Blue Nude*. **23.** William Shakespeare's 450th birthday was celebrated across the UK in a number of tributes and performances; a commemorative set of Royal Mail stamps was also released in his honour. **29.** The actors Harrison Ford, Carrie Fisher and Mark Hamill confirmed that they would reprise their respective roles as Han Solo, Princess Leia and Luke Skywalker in *Star Wars Episode VII*, scheduled for December 2015.

MAY 2014
7. Art collector Cornelius Gurlitt died leaving a collection worth around £850m to the Berne Art Museum; the bequest was controversial as Gurlitt's father had acquired many of the paintings from Jewish families during the Second World War. **14.** The Cannes Film Festival opened with a screening of *Grace of Monaco*, featuring Nicole Kidman in the title role; the film's release had previously been delayed due to an ongoing dispute between director Olivier Dahan and distributor Harvey Weinstein. **18.** At the BAFTA television awards, David Tennant and Olivia Coleman were awarded the leading actor and actress prizes for their roles in TV drama *Broadchurch*. Edward St Aubyn's novel *Lost for Words* was announced as the winner of the 2014 Bollinger Everyman Wodehouse Prize for comic fiction; a Gloucestershire old spot pig, named after the winning novel, was gifted to the author to honour his success. **21.** Bill Viola's video piece *Martyrs (Earth, Air, Fire, Water)* was displayed at St Paul's Cathedral and became the first moving-image artwork to be displayed in a British cathedral on a long-term basis. **22.** Matthew Warchus, best known for directing *Matilda* at the Royal Shakespeare Company, was announced to succeed Kevin Spacey as the next artistic director of the Old Vic. **24.** Timothy Spall won the best actor prize at the Cannes Film Festival for his portrayal of J. M. W. Turner in *Mr Turner*, directed by Mike Leigh; it was the first major award of his career despite receiving numerous nominations for major prizes. An exhibition by the Chinese artist Ai Weiwei opened in an 18th-century chapel in Yorkshire Sculpture Park, which consisted of 45 antique Chinese chairs alongside three of the artist's other sculptures. **29.** Peter Moore, 18, became the youngest member of the London Symphony Orchestra in its 110-year history when he was appointed as co-principal trombone; he was announced as the youngest ever winner of the BBC Young Musician competition earlier in 2014.

JUNE 2014
4. Eimear McBride was announced as the winner of the Baileys Women's Prize for Fiction for her novel, *A Girl is a Half-Formed Thing*; she originally wrote the book in 2003 and spent nine years trying to find a publisher. **9.** The Royal Academy opened its 246th annual Summer Exhibition; remaining the largest and most famous submission exhibition in the world. **18.** Jeremy Paxman presented *Newsnight* for the final time after 25 years as lead anchor; he became famous for his confrontational style and in one memorable 1997 interview, asked home secretary Michael Howard about his prison service 12 times in a row. **23.** Nicholas Penny, director of the National Gallery, announced that he would retire in the coming year; the National Gallery attracts 6 million visitors annually. **29.** Dolly Parton drew one of the biggest-ever crowds at the Glastonbury festival before Kasabian brought the music weekend to a close; other headline acts over the weekend included Metallica and Arcade Fire.

JULY 2014
1. Monty Python reunited on stage for the first time in 40 years to perform their Monty Python Live shows at the O2 arena; the show included famous sketches such as 'the Spanish Inquisition' and 'the Parrot Sketch'. **8.** A survey by the Authors' Licensing & Collecting Society revealed that authors' incomes had dropped to £11,000 per year, down from £15,540 in 2005, while just 11.5 per cent of professional authors could rely on writing as their sole source of income. **11.** The £20m remuneration package for Christopher Bailey, Burberry's new chief executive, was rejected by shareholders; it was only the sixth time that a FTSE 100 company had lost a remuneration vote since 2002. **15.** One of 18 surviving copies of *The Recuyell of the*

Historyes of Troye by William Caxton, the first book to be printed in the English language in 1473, was sold for £1,082,500 at auction at Sotheby's. **21.** Composer Judith Weir was appointed Master of the Queen's Music for a term of ten years; she became the first woman to hold the honorary position and succeeded Sir Peter Maxwell Davies.

CRIMES AND LEGAL AFFAIRS

AUGUST 2013
2. Magdalena Luczak and Mariusz Krezolek, the mother and partner respectively, each received life sentences with a minimum of 30 years for the murder of four-year-old Daniel Pelka, who was found to have been routinely tortured and starved; at the time of his death in March 2012, he weighed just 10.4kg. **5.** The Metropolitan Police issued an apology to the family of Ian Tomlinson and agreed an out-of-court settlement for his death in 2009; Mr Tomlinson was walking home from work when he died from an abdominal bleed shortly after he was struck with a baton and pushed to the ground by then-PC Simon Harwood during the G20 protests in the City. **6.** A Scottish woman, 19, and a Northern Irish woman, 20, were arrested at Lima airport, Peru, over suspected drug trafficking; the women admitted smuggling more than 24lb of cocaine, worth £1.5m, in their luggage, but claimed they had been forced at gunpoint to carry the bags. **7.** Domenico Rancadore, 64, wanted in Italy since the 1990s, was arrested in London; Italian police alleged that Mr Rancadore was the head of a crime family involved in extortion, racketeering and drug trafficking.

SEPTEMBER 2013
2. Two men were arrested on suspicion of conspiracy to commit burglary at Buckingham Palace; one of the men scaled 12 floors while his accomplice waited in the street. **23.** A police raid in Marshfield, South Wales, resulted in the arrest of four people, including a father and his two sons, on slavery charges; there were three alleged victims. **27.** At the Central Criminal Court, Michael Adebolajo, 29, and Michael Adebowale, 22, pleaded not guilty prior to their court appearance for the murder of Fusilier Lee Rigby outside Woolwich barracks in south-east London in May 2013; the two men were accused of hitting him with their car and hacking him to death with knives and a cleaver.

OCTOBER 2013
2. A disqualified driver, Aqab Hussain, was convicted of four counts of attempted murder and jailed for 20 years; Mr Hussain had deliberately run his car over four men following a minor dispute in Manchester in August 2013. **3.** Mother of eight Amanda Hutton was found guilty of manslaughter for allowing her four-year-old son, Hamzah Khan, to starve to death in December 2009; his mummified remains went undiscovered for nearly two years. **22.** A female couple received a 12-month suspended sentence for child cruelty after the eight-year-old daughter of one of the women wasted away to nearly 12.7kg. A 15-year-old boy was sentenced to 40 months in a young offender institution for robbing Barclays Bank in Liverpool with an imitation firearm, stealing £2,000 in the process. **25.** Three women were rescued from a house in South London after being held captive by a pair of non-British citizens for 30 years; a Malaysian woman, 69, an Irish woman, 57, and a British woman, 30, were discovered after a call from one of the women to the Freedom Charity which then contacted the police; the owners, who were not at home during the rescue, were later bailed until January 2014. Ukrainian student Pavlo Lapshyn was jailed for at least 40 years for the racially motivated murder of 82-year-old Mohammed Saleem in Birmingham, and for planting explosive devices near three Midlands mosques. **28.** At the Central Criminal Court, the trial of eight former employees of News International newspaper group began; the charges included phone-hacking, bribery of public officials and obstruction of justice.

NOVEMBER 2013
19. A trainee accountant was convicted of failing to stop and report an accident after knocking a cyclist off his bike while driving in Norfolk in May 2013; the incident came to light on Twitter after the driver wrote 'Definitely knocked a cyclist off his bike earlier...#Bloodycyclists'. **22.** Pilot Irfan Faiz was sentenced to nine months in prison at Leeds Crown Court after he was arrested in the cockpit of a commercial aircraft that he was due to fly to Islamabad, Pakistan; Mr Faiz was found to be three times over the legal alcohol level.

DECEMBER 2013
6. An army court martial sentenced Royal Marine sergeant Alexander Blackman to a minimum of ten years' imprisonment after finding him guilty of the murder of a badly wounded Taliban captive in Helmand province, Afghanistan, in September 2011. **9.** Two Damien Hirst paintings worth £33,000 were stolen from the Exhibitionist Gallery in Notting Hill, London; the works, *Pyronin Y* and *Oleoylsarcosine*, had only been on display for four days when they were taken. **10.** A gang of Sikh extremists were jailed after attacking Indian lieutenant-general Kuldip Singh Brar and his wife in central London in September 2012; the attackers sought revenge for a military raid on the sacred golden temple of Amritsar, India, in 1984, which was led by the general. **18.** Ian Watkins, the 36-year-old lead singer of the band Lostprophets, was sentenced to 35 years in prison for 13 child sex offences including the attempted rape of a baby; Watkins' two co-defendants, the mothers of the children he abused, were jailed for 14 and 17 years, as the judge, Mr Justice Royce, said the case 'plunged into new depths of depravity'. **19.** At the Central Criminal Court, Michael Adebolajo and Michael Adebowale were found guilty of the killing of soldier Lee Rigby; the two men stated that the murder was an act of war and they were 'soldiers of Islam' (*see* 27 September).

JANUARY 2014
8. The shooting of Mark Duggan on 4 August 2011, which sparked riots across England, was ruled lawful by a jury with a majority of eight to two at the Royal Courts of Justice; Duggan was shot and killed by police in Tottenham, North London, after they attempted to arrest him, believing him to be in possession of a handgun. **10.** The Metropolitan Police commissioner, Sir Bernard Hogan-Howe, apologised to the former Conservative chief whip Andrew Mitchell after one of his officers admitted to having fabricated a statement that Mitchell had referred to officers as 'plebs'; the September 2012 incident saw Mr Mitchell embroiled in a row with police officers when he was blocked from cycling through Downing Street's main gate. **18.** In Northampton, Lance Corporal Liam Culverhouse of the Grenadier Guards was jailed for six years for killing his 19-month-old daughter; Culverhouse was suffering from post-traumatic stress disorder following service in Afghanistan but admitted to having an aggressive temperament. **19.** The mother of the three-year-old boy Mikaeel Kular, who was reported missing from his Edinburgh home on 16 January, was charged in connection with his death after his body was found in Fife on 18 January. **23.** At Cardiff Crown Court, a landscape gardener was cleared of causing grievous bodily harm; Andrew Woodhouse caught two thieves attempting to steal petrol from his business, leaving one of them with two broken legs and a broken arm.

FEBRUARY 2014

19. During the phone-hacking trial which stemmed from the closure of the *News of the World* in 2011, the court saw an email from Rebekah Brooks, former editor of the paper and chief executive of News International, in which she claimed to have received advice from former prime minister Tony Blair; Mr Blair allegedly advised her to 'keep strong', take sleeping pills and avoid doing anything rash. **26.** The two men found guilty of the murder of Fusilier Lee Rigby in May 2013 were sentenced at the Central Criminal Court but were absent from the court after a fracas in the dock with security guards; Michael Adebolajo and Michael Adebowale were jailed for a whole-life term and a minimum of 45 years respectively (*see* 19 December). **28.** Serial killer Joanne Dennehy, who murdered three men in March 2013, became only the third woman in the UK to be given a whole-life sentence – after Myra Hindley and Rosemary West – as the judge, Mr Justice Spencer, described the 31-year-old as being 'cruel, calculating and manipulative'.

MARCH AND APRIL 2014

April 5-8. British millionaire Andrew Bush, 48, was shot dead in the Costa del Sol upon his return to the villa he rented in Estepona, Malaga; days later, Slovakian swimwear model Mayka Kukucova admitted shooting Bush, her former lover, in an act of self-defence after having requesting child maintenance. **9.** At the Central Criminal Court, Nicholas Jacobs was cleared of killing the police officer Keith Blakelock, who was stabbed 43 times at the Broadwater Farm riot in Tottenham in 1985; the prosecution collapsed when it emerged that two of the witnesses – who admitted kicking the officer as he was stabbed – received cash, hotel stays and other perks from police for testifying. **10.** The former deputy speaker of the House of Commons, Nigel Evans, MP, was cleared of several allegations of sexual abuse, including one of rape; several witness accounts were fraught with inconsistencies while others treated the alleged offenses with levity, resulting in the judge's suggestion halfway through the five-week trial held at Preston Crown Court, that the jury find Mr Evans 'not guilty' (*see* UK Affairs, 10 September 2013). **24.** Figures released by the Office for National Statistics revealed that the crime rate in England and Wales had fallen to its lowest recorded level since 1981; the crime rate fell by 15 per cent to an estimated 7.5m offences, a decline of 60 per cent since its peak in 1995. **28.** In Leeds, 61-year-old teacher Ann Maguire was stabbed to death by a 15-year-old male pupil in front of a full class.

MAY 2014

2. Celebrity publicist Max Clifford, 71, was sentenced to eight years' imprisonment after being found guilty of eight charges of indecent assault against women and girls as young as 15 between 1977 and 1985; his sentence was twice as long anticipated due to Mr Clifford's attitude during the trial, which Judge Anthony Leonard deemed 'quite extraordinary'. Constance Briscoe, one of Britain's first black female judges, was sentenced to 16 months in jail for perverting the course of justice. **15.** According to Ministry of Justice figures, the conviction rate for sex offences dropped suddenly by 6 per cent; the unexplained dip was not consistent with other kinds of crime. **23.** Former BBC Broadcaster Stuart Hall was sentenced to an extra two years and six months in prison for two counts of indecently assaulting a girl; the 84-year-old was already completing a 30-month term for similar crimes. **26.** A prisoner disappeared from HMP Hollesley Bay, the second escape from the prison in two days, despite the prison having a generally low rate of absconces. **27.** At the Central Criminal Court, Edward McKenzie-Green, the former head of counter-fraud at Oxfam was sentenced to two years and five months in prison; he was found guilty of defrauding the charity of nearly £65,000.

JUNE 2014

5. Gary Glitter was charged with sex offences against two girls as part of Scotland Yard's Operation Yewtree investigation; Mr Glitter faced eight charges relating to indecent assault, unlawful sexual intercourse and administering a drug to facilitate sexual intercourse. New figures revealed that 21 women out of 108 in the High Court and one in six of 654 circuit judges were female. **13.** Imran Khawaja, previously reported to have been killed in Syria, was arrested and charged with terrorism offences; Mr Khawaja was accused of preparing to commit terrorist acts and attending a place for terrorist training. **23.** At Nottingham Crown Court, Susan and Christopher Edwards were found guilty of the murder of Mrs Edwards' parents whose bodies lay undiscovered buried in their own back garden for 15 years; the couple proceeded to steal thousands of pounds from the murdered parents and sold their house before the bodies were discovered in October 2013. **24.** At the Central Criminal Court, Rebekah Brooks, the former chief executive of News International, was cleared of any wrongdoing in the phone-hacking scandal that led to closure of the *News of the World*; four co-defendants including her husband, Charlie Brooks, were also found not guilty but the paper's former editor Andy Coulson was found guilty of conspiracy to intercept voicemails. **27.** Michael Voudouri, one of Britain's most wanted tax fugitives, was sentenced to over 11 years imprisonment at Edinburgh High Court for an £11.6m tax fraud; Voudouri was extradited back to the UK for sentencing after he fled to Cyprus in 2012 after originally pleading guilty.

JULY 2014

2. New figures revealed that only 43 foreign nationals were transferred from jails in the UK to serve their sentences in their home countries in 2013; in July 2014 there were 10,695 foreign nationals in the UK prisons at a cost of £400m per year to the taxpayer. **4.** The 84-year-old Australian entertainer Rolf Harris was jailed for five years and nine months at Southwark Crown Court for twelve counts of indecent assault between 1969 to 1986 against four girls. At the Central Criminal Court, former Downing Street communications director, Andy Coulson, was sentenced to 18 months in prison for voicemail interception; the prime minister David Cameron issued an apology for hiring him (*see* 24 June). **6.** Figures revealed that the falling crime rates in London masked an increase in crime in areas outside of London as shoplifting was on the rise in 37 of 43 police force areas across England and Wales. **10.** At the Central Criminal Court, Paul Causer, an unlicensed cab driver, who drove a women to the Surrey countryside and raped her, was jailed for 11 years after being caught by her iPhone tracker app. **14.** Baroness Butler-Sloss, a former senior family judge, stood down as chairwoman of a landmark inquiry into child abuse just six days after being appointed; Baroness Butler-Sloss came under pressure following suggestions that her late brother, Michael Havers, had attempted to cover up sex abuse cases by those in powerful positions of responsibility. **16.** The National Crime Agency revealed that Operation Notarise, a police operation targeting online paedophile activity in Britain, identified 10,000 suspects; a total of 660 people were arrested in the previous six months leading to the statement. Asher Maslin was sentenced to life imprisonment at Gloucester Crown Court after stabbing his ex-girlfriend, Hollie Gazzard, 14 times; Ms Gazzard previously complained to the police and contemplated obtaining an injunction after receiving numerous violent threats from Maslin.

ENVIRONMENT AND SCIENCE

AUGUST 2013
5. The first lab-grown burger was cooked and eaten at a news conference in London; scientists from Maastricht University in the Netherlands took cells from a cow and formed them into strips of muscle, with researchers stating that the technology could be a sustainable method of fulfilling global demands for meat. **15.** The first new species of carnivore found in the western hemisphere in 35 years was discovered by scientists in the cloud forest of western Colombia and Ecuador; named the olinguito, the 35cm-long mammal is the smallest member of the animal family which includes raccoons. **21.** Studies conducted by Cancer Research UK concluded that men are 70 per cent more likely to die from skin cancer than women due to biological differences and a reluctance to receive medical attention.

SEPTEMBER 2013
5. A team from the University of Houston confirmed that Tamu Massif, an undersea volcano off the coast of Japan, was the largest in the world; the volcano covers an area of 120,000 sq. miles. **12.** NASA reported that the Voyager 1 probe, originally launched in 1977, had become the first man-made object to leave the solar system; the probe was calculated to have left the sun's gravitational pull on 12 August 2012. **13.** The US National Snow and Ice Data Centre (NSIDC) reported that Arctic sea ice had increased to 5.10 million sq. km from 3.41 million sq. km in 2012; the recovery was described as temporary. **19.** Research published in the journal *Astrobiology* estimated that all life on Earth would become extinct between 1.75bn and 3.25bn years in the future based on the planet's distance from the Sun and temperatures at which it would be possible to possess liquid water. **22.** Using the 2009 flu pandemic, scientists from Imperial College London created a 'blueprint' for a universal influenza vaccine; the results, which were published in the journal *Nature Medicine,* found that those of the 342 volunteers who avoided severe illness had more CD8 T cells – a virus-killing immune cell – at the outbreak of the pandemic.

OCTOBER 2013
8. Physicists Peter Higgs and Francois Englert were awarded the Nobel Prize in Physics for their discovery that particles acquire mass by interacting with an all-pervading field which is spread throughout the universe. The pharmaceutical company GlaxoSmithKline published results of a trial showing that its new vaccine for malaria, RTS,S, had some effectiveness in protecting children from the parasite; the trial in Africa involved nearly 15,000 children aged between five and 17 months at the time of vaccination, and resulted in a 46 per cent reduction in the number of infections. **24.** A Cambridge University study, published in the journal *Cell,* discovered the first obesity gene affecting fewer than one in 100 people; the mutated DNA, known as KSR2, reportedly slows down metabolism and increases the urge to eat. **26.** Scientists developed a new cancer treatment, which blocks the HSP90 'chaperone' molecule from aiding the development of cancer cells, thus preventing cancer proteins from functioning; the treatment could be more effective than previous treatments, as studies showed more aggressive cancers tend to be more reliant on the HSP90 molecule.

NOVEMBER 2013
8. Researchers at the Harvard Medical School, USA, discovered separate genes involved in tissue regeneration, which they believed could lead to the development of new drugs to speed healing processes in older people; the research, conducted on mice, showed the genes, Lin28a and IMP1,

were especially active during the foetal stage and gradually diminished during the ageing process. **13.** A 13-year study at the University of East Anglia indicated that, due to climate change, the hatching and migratory patterns of Icelandic seabirds had shifted by an average of two weeks. **26.** Figures released by the International Union for Conservation of Nature featured 21,286 species that were threatened with extinction, including the okapi (forest giraffe), which was classified as threatened. **27.** An implant, designed to mimic the effect of a gastric band was successfully tested on mice by a team of scientists at the Swiss Federal Institute of Technology in Zurich; the implant contained genetically engineered cells, designed to respond to fat in the bloodstream and produce a hormone signal to inform the brain that the need to eat was reduced.

DECEMBER 2013
3. After a five-year exploration below the surface of the Amundsen Sea off Pine Island Bay in Antarctica, marine biologists from the British Antarctic Survey identified 5,469 specimens from 275 species, which included 30 previously new and unclassified species. **5.** The journal *Nature* reported that researchers in Leipzig, Germany, had extracted and sequenced the oldest surviving human DNA from a femur discovered in a cave in northern Spain, believed to be around 400,000 years old; the mitochondrial DNA bore a resemblance to that found in the genome reconstructed from a 50,000-year-old bone fragment found in Siberia in 2010.

JANUARY 2014
2. Gambian pouched rats were used to successfully disarm nearly 2,500 landmines and 14,000 pieces of ordinance in Africa; the Department for International Development began funding nine-month training programmes for the rats. **8.** Parts of Britain's coast were destroyed by severe storms; a 150-million-year-old rock stack, known as Pom Pom rock, was washed away in Chiswell on the Isle of Portland, Dorset, while Chesil beach was dramatically reshaped. Research from the University of Reading revealed that Europe had 13.4 million too few honeybee colonies to properly pollinate its crops; the results, published in the journal *PLOS One,* showed that demand for insect pollination was growing five times faster than the number of honeybee colonies across the continent.

FEBRUARY 2014
3. Three Sumatran tiger cubs were born at London Zoo after the whole birth process was monitored using remote camera technology; at the time of the cubs' birth, there were believed to be around 300 Sumatran tigers left in the wild, compared with 1,000 in the 1970s. **5.** Mosquitoes were genetically engineered in Didcot, Oxfordshire, to outbreed mosquitoes in Panama, which were spreading dengue fever; the insects were engineered to be more attractive to female mosquitoes, but to produce offspring that died before reaching maturity. During continuing stormy weather in the UK, huge waves destroyed an 80m stretch of rail track on the mainline between London and Penzance, Cornwall, which was intended to reopen after engineering work (*see* UK Affairs, 4 April). Nine severe weather warnings were issued in coastal areas following waves of up to 22.7m. **6.** A Danish man became the first amputee to have a 'lifelike' sense of touch restored to a limb; Dennis Aabo Sorensen was the first patient to test a sensory-enhanced prosthetic hand, which allowed him to feel the size, shape and texture of objects. **10.** The river Thames burst its banks following heavy rain; up to 1,000 homes were flooded as a result. **24.** People were urged to look out for hedgehogs amid fears that many may have drowned in the floods; the People's Trust for Endangered Species and

the British Hedgehog Preservation Society warned that hedgehog populations had fallen by more than 33 per cent in ten years.

MARCH 2014

5. A clinical trial at the University of Pennsylvania, USA, of a radical gene therapy intended to fight HIV using genetically modified (GM) cells resistant to the virus, was declared a success; the results of the treatment, never before tested on humans, found that the disease-resistant cells multiplied in the patients' bodies and raised defences against the virus by replacing a number of their natural immune cells with GM versions. **12.** A diamond containing minerals of 1.5 per cent water found in a riverbed in Brazil, provided evidence of a 'wet zone' approximately 250–400 miles (410–660km) below the Earth's surface; published in the journal *Nature,* the research suggested there may be as much water trapped in the rocks as there is in all the Earth's oceans. **13.** A new species of tiny tyrannosaur was discovered by scientists in northern Alaska; named *Nanuqsaurus hoglundi,* the pygmy dinosaur measured 6m (20ft) long, approximately half the size of the Tyrannosaurus rex, according to a study in the journal *PLOS One.* **19.** American scientists in North and South Dakota discovered a new species of dinosaur, *Anzu wyliei,* nicknamed 'the chicken from hell', a bird-like creature the size of a small car with claws and feathers, a bony crest on its head and a long tail similar to a lizard. **30.** Scientists in the UK discovered a link between obesity and a gene which breaks down carbohydrates; the study found that people with fewer copies of the salivary amylase gene AMY1, which is responsible for carbohydrate breakdown, are more likely to be at risk of obesity. Forensic tests revealed 25 skeletons unearthed during excavations to build London Crossrail were victims of the Black Death pandemic; their graves at the edge of Charterhouse Square were dated between 1348–50.

APRIL 2014

9. Britain's first cloned dog was born after its owner won a competition which saw a South Korean company, who usually charged £60,000 to clone animals, reproduce the 12-year-old daschund Winnie for free, using her skin tissue. **14.** In a survey carried out by the Game and Wildlife Conservation Trust to record 11 bird species on the 'red list' of threatened wildlife, skylarks, yellowhammers and song thrushes showed signs of recovery from long-term decline on wildlife-protective farms; 500 farmers recorded birds on their land for 30 minutes in February 2014 with the most commonly spotted bird being the blackbird but only one lesser spotted wood-pecker was seen. **17.** Using NASA's Kepler space telescope, astronomers discovered a planet in the constellation Cygnus, 500 light years away, named Kepler-186f, that is the most Earth-like yet found in another solar system. **24.** A study funded by the Department for Environment, Food and Rural Affairs, published in the journal *PLOS One,* found that the authorised badger cull had seen hedgehog numbers more than double in some areas; the hedgehog population, which fell by a third in the previous decade, was prey to badgers and also competed with them for the same food such as slugs and worms.

MAY 2014

14. The discovery in the Yucatan of the skeleton of a 12,000 year old girl enabled scientists to draw direct links between modern Native Americans and the Paleoamericans who first inhabited the Americas after the most recent Ice Age. **15.** Scientists used the cloning technique that created Dolly the sheep to create human embryonic stem cells from adult tissue for the first time. **27.** It was announced that an immense

peatland, thought to contain billions of tonnes of peat, had been discovered in the Republic of Congo; scientists stated that investigations of the peatland could shed light on 10,000 years of environmental change within the region.

JUNE 2014

2. Astronomers at the Kepler space telescope discovered a 'mega-Earth' named Kepler-10c, 17 times the mass of Earth and about 560 light years away in the constellation Draco; its discovery overturned the long-held theory that a planet of its size would contain too much hydrogen and turn gaseous, therefore expanding the number of distant planets that may be capable of supporting life. **9.** A wireless pacemaker the size of a pill, thought to be the world's smallest, was inserted into the heart of a British patient at Southampton general hospital. **16.** The first Philippine crocodiles to be bred in the UK hatched at London Zoo; the five crocodiles weighed little more than 37 grams each but were expected to grow to around ten feet and weigh 33 pounds. **18.** British scientists found an 'Achilles' heel' in the cells of many drug-resistant superbugs such as E.coli and salmonella; the scientists used a chemical to block the LptD protein that allowed bacteria to create a protective shell and thus allowed the drugs to kill the bacteria. **23.** Researchers at Anglia Ruskin University discovered that the East Asian harlequin ladybird – a larger and more voracious species than British ladybirds – prey on the native British ten-spot and two-spot ladybirds which proved a strong contribution to the decline of these two species. **25.** Voters decided that antibiotic resistance would be the subject of the £10m Longitude Prize 2014; competitors were given five years to apply for the funding.

JULY 2014

8. Scientists developed a new type of blood test able to identify Alzheimer's disease before the worst symptoms appear in ninety per cent of cases; it was hoped that the test would become widely available within two years. **22.** Research published in *The Lancet* showed that the number of deaths related to HIV, tuberculosis and malaria had been reduced by one-third since 2005; the survey covered 188 countries from 1990 to 2013 and it was believed that most of the progress was due to treatments preventing children catching the conditions from their mothers. **25.** Scientists in the journal *PLoS Pathogens* described an endolysin enzyme which they had engineered and added to genetically modified yoghurt that could kill off the Clostridium difficile superbug; Jodi Lindsay, professor of microbiology at St George's, University of London, described the discovery as a breakthrough in the field of antibiotic resistance.

SPORT

AUGUST 2013

5. England retained the Ashes after drawing the third Test at Old Trafford as recurring showers stopped play with Australia in a commanding position; England had won the first two Tests at Trent Bridge and Lord's. **10.** Mo Farah became the first British man to win a 10,000m world title after he beat the 2011 champion Ibrahim Jeilan in a sprint finish at the World Athletics Championships in Moscow. **11.** Premier League winners Manchester United overcame FA Cup-holders Wigan 2–0 in the FA Community Shield at Wembley thanks to a brace from Robin van Persie, giving new manager David Moyes his first trophy. In Moscow, the six-time Olympic champion Usain Bolt regained the 100m world title with a season's best performance of 9.77 seconds. **12.** England sealed victory in the Ashes series with a 74-run win over Australia in the fourth Test at Durham, which saw Stuart Broad take six wickets for 20 runs in 45 balls. Christine

Ohuruogu became the first British woman to win two World Championship titles after she followed up her 2007 gold in the 400m with a record victory in the same distance in Moscow. **16.** Mo Farah became only the second man in history to complete the Olympic and world 'double-double' in distance races with victory in the 5,000m final in Moscow; Farah, who won double-gold at London 2012, equalled the record of the Ethiopian Kenenisa Bekele. **25.** Bad light ended the final day of the fifth Test of the Ashes at the Oval as England were denied a likely victory, needing 21 runs from 24 balls with five wickets remaining; the crowd watched England captain Alastair Cook lift the Ashes urn after the 3–0 series win. **30.** Britain's number one female tennis player Laura Robson was knocked out in straight sets in the third round of the US Open by the Chinese fifth seed Li Na.

SEPTEMBER 2013
1. Real Madrid signed the Tottenham Hotspur forward Gareth Bale for a world transfer record of £85.3m (€100m); the Welshman, who agreed a six-year deal worth £300,000 per week, was named the Professional Footballers' Association Player of the Year and Young Player of the Year in the previous season. **5.** The Swiss ninth seed Stanislas Wawrinka beat the reigning Wimbledon champion, Andy Murray, in the quarter-finals of the US Open. **8.** The American world number one, Serena Williams, won her fifth US Open title after beating Victoria Azarenka. **9.** Rafael Nadal defeated world number one Novak Djokovic in the US Open men's final in four sets; the victory, which included a 54-shot rally, marked Nadal's second US Open title and his 13th Grand Slam triumph. **19.** In cricket, Durham won their third County Championship title in six years after beating Nottinghamshire by eight wickets at Chester-le-Street. **22.** The cyclist Sir Bradley Wiggins claimed victory in the Tour of Britain, which finished after stage eight in London; the concluding stage was won by British road race champion Mark Cavendish. **25.** In one of sport's greatest comebacks the British sailor Sir Ben Ainslie and his Oracle Team USA won the America's Cup decider in San Francisco, having overhauled an 8–1 deficit to beat Team New Zealand by 44 seconds. The snooker player Stephen Lee was banned from the sport for 12 years after being found guilty of seven match fixing charges between 2008 and 2009, in what snooker's governing body described as 'the worst case of corruption' it had ever witnessed. **29.** The Kenyan long distance runner Wilson Kipsang Kiprotich broke the marathon world record by 15 seconds when he won the Berlin marathon in a time of 2 hours 3 minutes 23 seconds.

OCTOBER 2013
5. In rugby league, Wigan Warriors beat Warrington Wolves 30–16 in the Super League Grand Final at Old Trafford to complete a league and cup double after they defeated Hull FC in the Challenge Cup final on 24 August. **15.** England qualified for the 2014 FIFA World Cup in Brazil after a 2–0 victory over Poland at Wembley with goals from Wayne Rooney and Steven Gerrard. **27.** Red Bull's Sebastian Vettel secured his fourth consecutive Formula 1 World Championship following victory in the Indian Grand Prix; Red Bull also won the Formula 1 Constructors' Championship for the fourth year running.

NOVEMBER 2013
7. The jump jockey AP McCoy became the first person to ride 4,000 winners after he won his second race of the day at Towcester racecourse on Mountain Tunes; McCoy reached the milestone after competing in over 15,000 races and falling 1,000 times. **11.** The reigning champion, Novak Djokovic, won the ATP Tour Finals with a straight sets win

over world number one Rafael Nadal at London's O2 Arena. **16.** The India cricketer Sachin Tendulkar retired from international cricket following his 200th Test match, in which India beat West Indies; the 40-year-old batsman received a guard of honour and several awards after being dismissed for 74 in his final innings the previous day. **23.** New Zealand knocked England out of the Rugby League World Cup in the semi-final at Wembley as the Kiwis' Shaun Johnson scored a last-minute try and added the conversion to clinch a 20–18 victory. **24.** England collapsed in a humiliating defeat at The Gabba in Brisbane, Australia, in the first Test of the 2013–14 Ashes series; the tourists lost by 381 runs on the fourth day in what was, in terms of runs, their second biggest defeat in Ashes cricket in Australia. In rugby union, New Zealand defeated Ireland in Dublin to become the first side in the professional era to win every one of their 14 Tests in a calendar year. **27.** Two workers died in an accident at the Arena Corinthians stadium in Sao Paolo, Brazil, after a crane collapsed; the stadium was under construction for the opening ceremony of the 2014 FIFA World Cup.

DECEMBER 2013
15. Andy Murray was voted the 2013 BBC Sports Personality of the Year after a season which saw him become the first Briton in 77 years to win the Wimbledon men's singles title. **16.** Alastair Cook was dismissed for a golden duck in his 100th Test appearance as England laboured in the third Ashes Test at the WACA in Perth; the following day, Australia secured the Ashes trophy after winning the first three Tests. **22.** The England off-spinner Graeme Swann announced his retirement from international and first-class cricket, midway through the Ashes series in Australia. **26.** Trainer Paul Nicholls recorded an eighth win in the King George VI Chase at Kempton after his horse Silvinaco Conti finished first, with Nicholls' other horse Al Ferof in third. **29.** Michael Schumacher, the seven-time Formula 1 world champion, suffered a traumatic brain injury and was put into a medically induced coma after falling while skiing off-piste in Meribel, France.

JANUARY 2014
5. Australia completed a 5–0 Ashes whitewash after they defeated England within three days of the fifth Test in Sydney. **7.** Manchester United lost three games in a row for the first time since 2001 after Sunderland beat David Moyes' team 2–1 at the Stadium of Light in the first leg of the Capital One Cup semi-final. **8.** The former Aston Villa and Germany midfielder Thomas Hitzlsperger made an announcement in the German newspaper *Die Zeit* that he is gay; Hitzlsperger became the first former Premier League player to publicly reveal his homosexuality but stated he believed the issue was still taboo inside the dressing room. **13.** The Real Madrid and Portugal forward Cristiano Ronaldo won the 2013 FIFA Ballon d'Or; Ronaldo was named world player of the year for the first time since 2008 after Lionel Messi, the Barcelona forward, had won the award for the last four years. **14.** In tennis, organisers of the Australian Open were criticised after players were forced to compete in temperatures which rose to 42°C; the Canadian player Frank Dancevic needed medical attention after fainting on court and later stated it was 'inhumane' to play in the heat. **16.** Bernie Ecclestone stepped down from the board of Delta Topco, the company in charge of Formula 1, after his indictment on bribery charges in Germany; Mr Ecclestone, the chief executive of Formula 1, was accused of giving a $45m (£27.5m) bribe to a German banker who was jailed for accepting the payment. **18.** Manchester City became the first team in the Premier League era to score 100 goals before the end of January after they beat Cardiff City 4–2 at the Etihad Stadium. **20.** The West

Bromwich Albion sponsor Zoopla announced it would end its sponsorship at the end of the 2013–14 season because of a controversial gesture by the club's striker Nicolas Anelka after he scored against West Ham on 28 December 2013; the 'quenelle' gesture, described as an inverted Nazi salute and declared by some as having anti-Semitic connotations, was defended by Anelka as 'anti-system'. **22.** Andy Murray lost to Roger Federer in the quarter-finals at the Australian Open; the Swiss won in four sets after Murray saved two match-points in the third set tie-break. **24.** Official documents revealed that 185 Nepalese workers died in 2013 while building infrastructural projects for the 2022 World Cup in Qatar; Nepalese migrants made up one-sixth of Qatar's 2.2 million migrant worker population and the death toll was expected to rise. **25.** China's Li Na beat the Slovakian Dominika Cibulkova in the women's singles final at the Australian Open; Li, who won the tournament for the first time, appeared in her third Australian Open final while Cibulkova made her debut Grand Slam final. **26.** Stanislas Wawrinka won his first Grand Slam title when he beat an injured Rafael Nadal in the men's singles final in Melbourne; the 28-year-old Swiss won in four sets, becoming the first player outside the traditional 'big four' (Nadal, Roger Federer, Murray and Djokovic) to win a Grand Slam since Juan Martin Del Potro at the US Open in 2009. **29.** In Hobart, Australia, the England women's cricket team retained the Women's Ashes with a win in the first Twenty20 International to take an unassailable 10–4 lead in the multi-format series.

FEBRUARY 2014

1. In their opening game of the 2014 Rugby Six Nations Championship, England lost to France 26–24 in the Stade de France, Paris, after a last-gasp try from the French replacement Gael Fickou and the conversion from Maxime Machenaud. **2.** Great Britain progressed into the Davis Cup quarter-finals for the first time since 1986 after Andy Murray beat the American Sam Querrey in San Diego, USA. **4.** Kevin Pietersen, the 33-year-old batsman, was told he was no longer part of the England team's plans, thus ending his career with the national team; South African-born Pietersen, the team's all-time leading run-scorer across all formats (8,181 runs in 104 Tests), said that 'playing cricket for my country has been an honour'. **7.** The 22nd Winter Olympics, hosted in Sochi, Russia, began with an opening ceremony which saw athletes from 87 nations paraded in the Fisht Stadium as president Vladimir Putin declared the Games open; the £30bn Sochi Games were the most expensive Olympics in history but the build-up was eclipsed by concerns about the rights of sexual minorities, allegations of corruption and security fears. **9.** The snowboarder Jenny Jones made history at the Rosa Khutor Extreme Park when she won slopestyle bronze, which was Great Britain's first medal on snow in Winter Olympics history. **14.** Lizzy Yarnold, 25, became Great Britain's only gold medallist of Sochi 2014 when she won the women's skeleton with a dominant performance, finishing 0.97 seconds ahead of the silver medallist. **17.** The Indian embassy in Doha published figures suggesting that since January 2012, over 500 Indians had died working on infrastructure projects for the 2022 FIFA World Cup in Qatar, however, the embassy, along with Qatari officials, insisted the high death rate was not abnormal and the deaths were due to natural causes; human rights organisations stated the high level of deaths were 'horrendous' and gave 'an indication of an unfolding tragedy'. **19.** Great Britain's women's curling team won the bronze medal when they beat Switzerland 6–5. **21.** Team GB ended the Sochi Winter Olympics having matched their 1924 record of four medals, after the men's curlers claimed silver against Canada in the final. **22.** England beat Ireland in a thrilling match at

Twickenham to end the visitors' hopes of a Triple Crown; Danny Care scored England's only try as the home side came back from a seven-point deficit to win the match 13–10 and leave the Rugby Six Nations title race open. **27.** Nicolas Anelka was suspended by his club, West Bromwich Albion, after the FA banned him for five games and fined him £80,000 following his controversial 'quenelle' gesture during a match on 28 December 2013; the FA also ordered the French striker to attend a compulsory education course (*see* 20 January).

MARCH 2014

1. The Newcastle United manager Alan Pardew was sent off for head-butting the Hull City player David Meyler during a match at the KC Stadium; in an unprecedented incident, Pardew was fined £100,000 by Newcastle and given a formal warning. **2.** Manchester City beat Sunderland 3–1 in the League Cup final at Wembley as the Chilean manager Manuel Pellegrini secured his first trophy as the club's manager. **9.** At Twickenham, England beat Wales 29–18 in the Six Nations to claim their first Triple Crown in 11 years thanks to tries from Danny Care and Luther Burrell; the FA Cup holders, Wigan, ensured a return to Wembley after knocking out Manchester City 2–1 in the FA Cup quarter-final at the Etihad Stadium in a repeat of the previous year's final. **14.** In a photo-finish, Lord Windermere, ridden by Davy Russell, won the Cheltenham Gold Cup after beating On His Own over the line; the result meant Jim Culloty won the race as both trainer and jockey, having ridden to victory in three consecutive Gold Cups a decade previously. West Bromwich Albion sacked striker Nicolas Anelka for gross misconduct after the Frenchman announced he was quitting the club following fallout from a controversial incident on 28 December 2013 (*see* 20 January). **15.** Ireland won their second Six Nations title after beating France 22–20 at the Stade de France in Paris; the match marked the final appearance of Irish centre Brian O'Driscoll, who was playing in his 133rd Test. **22.** The Arsenal manager, Arsène Wenger, celebrated his 1,000th match in charge of the North London club, although the Frenchman experienced a day of mixed emotions as his side were thrashed 6–0 by Chelsea in a match which saw referee Andre Marriner incorrectly send off the wrong Arsenal player in a case of mistaken identity.

APRIL 2014

5. The 25–1 outsider Pineau De Re, ridden by Leighton Aspell, won the 167th Grand National at Aintree, with all horses and jockeys returning safely from the historic race. **6.** Having led 2–1 entering the final day, Great Britain failed to make the Davis Cup semi-final for the first time in 33 years; Italy fought back to win 3–2 in Naples and both Andy Murray and James Ward lost their singles matches. Oxford beat Cambridge by 11 lengths in the 160th Boat Race which saw Cambridge's Luke Juckett briefly fall from his seat after a clash of oars. **13.** On his London marathon debut, the British Olympic champion Mo Farah finished eighth while the Kenyan world-record-holder Wilson Kipsang Kiprotich won his second London marathon. **14.** In golf, the American left-hander, Bubba Watson, claimed his second green jacket in three years after he won the 78th Masters in Augusta, Georgia. **22.** David Moyes was sacked by Manchester United just ten months after succeeding Sir Alex Ferguson as manager; he was culpable for their worst home record since 1978, including two back-to-back 3–0 home defeats to Premier League rivals Manchester City and Liverpool in March, and a failure to qualify for the Champions League for the first time since the 1995–96 season. Leicester City clinched top spot of the Championship with two games left as they beat Bolton Wanderers 1–0. **27.** Yang Jian of China set a world record for a dive (a forward 4½ somersaults twice in one day) as he claimed the gold medal in the ten-metre platform event in the World Diving Series.

MAY 2014
3. League One champions Wolverhampton Wanderers set a new all-time points record of 103, surpassing the previous record of 101 held by Charlton Athletic in the 2012–13 season. **5.** Snooker player Mark Selby defeated Ronnie O' Sullivan 18–14 at the Crucible Theatre in Sheffield to claim his first World Championship triumph. **11.** Manchester City won the Premier League with 86 points after defeating West Ham United 2–0; it was their second title in three years. British Formula 1 driver Lewis Hamilton reached a personal milestone with four victories in succession after an initial victory in the Spanish Grand Prix. **13.** Cyclist Sir Bradley Wiggins won the second stage of the Tour of California; it was the second consecutive victory for a British cyclist after Mark Cavendish won the opening stage. **17.** Aaron Ramsey scored in the 19th minute of extra-time as Arsenal beat Hull City 3–2 in the FA Cup final at Wembley; the Arsenal manager Arsène Wenger became only the second manager in the modern era, after Sir Alex Ferguson, to win the FA Cup five times. **18.** Sir Bradley Wiggins was declared the overall winner of the Tour of California as Mark Cavendish claimed the stage win on the final day. **19.** Louis van Gaal was appointed the new manager of Manchester United while Ryan Giggs announced his retirement from professional football, after playing 963 games for the club and was appointed assistant manager (*see* 22 April). **25.** Golfer Rory McIlroy won the BMW PGA Championship at Wentworth, his first European Tour title in 18 months. **31.** Rugby union fly-half Johnny Wilkinson scored 15 points in his final career match in Toulon's 18–10 victory over Castres to win the French Championship; the previous week, he had won the Heineken Cup for the second time in his career.

JUNE 2014
8. Rafael Nadal won his ninth French Open (his fifth consecutively) at Roland Garros, after defeating Novak Djokovic in four sets in the final. Andy Murray announced the appointment of former Wimbledon champion, Amélie Mauresmo, as his new coach; becoming the first leading male tennis player to appoint a female coach. **12.** The 2014 FIFA World Cup began with Brazil beating Croatia 3–1 in the opening match at the Arena Corinthians, Sao Paulo. **14.** In Manaus, England lost their opening group game 2–1 to Italy after former Manchester City striker Mario Balotelli scored in the 50th minute. **15.** After Grigor Dimitrov won the Queen's Club tournament, tournament director Ross Hutchins and players including Andy and Jamie Murray, Heather Watson and Martina Hingis participated in the Rally for Bally held in memory of former British number one Elena Baltacha, who died of cancer in May 2014. **20.** England's exit from the World Cup was confirmed with a 2–1 defeat to Uruguay while Costa Rica beat Italy 1–0 the next day; the group-stage exit marked England's worst performance at a World Cup in 56 years. **23.** At Wimbledon, defending champion Andy Murray opened play on Centre Court as is tradition, with a straight sets win against David Goffin. **25.** Uruguay striker Luis Suárez was given a four-month global ban from 'any football-related activity' after biting Italian defender Giorgio Chiellini in Uruguay's 1–0 victory over Italy; the incident was the third time Suárez had bitten a player during his career.

JULY 2014
2. Andy Murray lost in straight sets 6–1 7–6 6–2 to Grigor Dimitrov in the Wimbledon quarter-final. **5.** The first stage of the Tour de France finished in Harrogate, England, as Mark Cavendish crashed out of the opening stage, dislocating his shoulder. **6.** Novak Djokovic won the Wimbledon men's singles title, defeating seven-time champion Roger Federer 6–7 6–4 7–6 5–7 6–4 a day after former champion Petra Kvitova beat Eugenie Bouchard 6–3 6–0 in the women's final in 55 minutes. Lewis Hamilton won the Formula 1 British Grand Prix at Silverstone to become the first British winner at the track since 2008. **8.** The hosts Brazil lost 7 (seven)–1 to Germany in the first semi-final of the World Cup, which was the worst defeat in Brazil's history; German striker Miroslav Klose scored his 16th goal in World Cup finals to surpass Ronaldo's record of 15. **9.** Defending Tour de France champion, Chris Froome, was forced to withdraw from the race after crashing out during stage five in Nice. **13.** Mario Götze scored in extra-time as Germany won the World Cup beating Argentina 1–0 in the final at the Maracanã stadium; it was their fourth World Cup victory, and the first since German reunification. Tournament hosts Brazil lost the 3rd place play-off 3–0 to the Netherlands the previous day. **20.** At 25, Rory McIlroy won the Open Championship at Hoylake, to become the third-youngest player in history to win three major titles after Jack Nicklaus and Tiger Woods. **23.** The Commonwealth Games Opening Ceremony took place at Hampden Park. **26.** Alistair and Jonny Brownlee, Jodie Stimpson and Vicky Holland won the triathlon mixed relay, the first to be held at a Commonwealth Games. **31.** England won their first International Test match in almost a year (*see* 12 August) with a 266-run victory over India in the third match of the five-Test series.

INTERNATIONAL AFFAIRS

AFRICA

AUGUST 2013
5. In Nigeria, 35 people were killed in the north-eastern state of Borno as a result of clashes between government troops and the extreme Islamist group Boko Haram. **7.** A large fire destroyed the arrivals hall of Jomo Kenyatta international airport in Nairobi, Kenya. **11.** At least 44 people were killed in an attack by Islamists on a mosque in the north-eastern Nigerian town of Kondunga; 12 people were shot dead in a linked attack in the nearby village of Ngom. In Mali, former prime minister Ibrahim Boubacar Keita was elected president with 77.6 per cent of the vote. **22.** Robert Mugabe was sworn in for a seventh five-year term as president of Zimbabwe; opposition candidate Morgan Tsvangirai disputed the result, citing allegations of vote-rigging and a lack of electoral transparency. **23.** Car bombs in Tripoli, Libya, killed at least 42 people and injured 500 outside two Sunni mosques. **27.** Liberia's main state-run university agreed to admit 1,800 new students after all 25,000 applicants failed the entrance exam. **29.** At least 41 people died in a bus crash near the Kenyan town of Narok. **30.** In the Democratic Republic of the Congo (DR Congo), M23 rebels called a unilateral ceasefire after a week of sustained fighting against the Congolese army and a UN intervention brigade in and around the border city of Goma.

SEPTEMBER 2013
10. The trial of Kenya's incumbent deputy president, William Ruto, accused of crimes against humanity in relation to the 1,100 people who died during post-election violence in 2007, commenced at the International Criminal Court in The Hague. **13.** President of the Central African Republic, Michel Djotodia, officially dissolved the Seleka alliance of rebels that brought him to power after two weeks of uncontrolled sectarian violence left several hundred people dead. **20.** In

north-east Nigeria around 160 people were killed by Boko Haram militants disguised as soldiers. **21–24.** In Kenya the Westgate shopping mall in Nairobi was attacked and around 1,000 people were taken hostage by the Islamist group al-Shabab; 75 people, including all four gunmen, died and a further 200 were wounded. **23–29.** In Sudan, at least 50 people died in violent protests after the government lifted fuel subsidies. **29.** Around 40 male students were shot dead in a college dormitory in north-east Nigeria; Boko Haram claimed responsibility for the attack.

OCTOBER 2013

3. The Gambian government announced that the country would be leaving the Commonwealth, branding it a 'neo-colonial institution'. **5.** The US Army's Delta Force abducted Abu Anas al-Liby, a senior member of al-Qaida, from a car in Tripoli; in a simultaneous raid, US Navy Seal Team 6 attempted and failed to capture Kenyan al-Shabab terrorist Abdulkadir Mohammed Abdulkadir at his home in Baraawe, Somalia. **7.** The former Ethiopian ambassador to Turkey, Mulatu Teshome, 55, was elected president of Ethiopia after a unanimous parliamentary vote. **18.** It was announced that Alpha Conde's Rally of the Guinean People party had won the Guinean legislative election with a total of 53 seats; the announcement came over three weeks after the election and was denounced as fraudulent by the opposition. **20.** Around 80 people were killed in a series of attacks by rebels in Jonglei state, South Sudan. **31.** In Niger, 92 immigrants were found dead after their vehicles broke down in the Sahara Desert.

NOVEMBER 2013

7. In the DR Congo, M23 rebels officially surrendered and announced that they would pursue their aims through 'purely political means'; the announcement ended 19 months of violent conflict that left at least 400 people dead. **19.** Around 20 construction workers died after a shopping mall collapsed in the South African town of Tongaat. **30.** A Mozambique Airlines aeroplane crashed in a national park in Namibia, killing all 34 people on board.

DECEMBER 2013

3. The Zimbabwean Justice Ministry reported that at least 100 prisoners had died of starvation during the year due to a lack of prison funding. **5.** South Africa's first black president, Nelson Mandela, died aged 95; a memorial service was held on 10 December and was attended by 52 presidents and 16 prime ministers. **5–7.** In the Central African Republic sectarian violence between Christian and Muslim militias escalated with almost 1,000 people reported dead after three days of fighting in the capital city of Bangui; the UN Security Council authorised French troops to join an expanded African peacekeeping force, numbering 1,600 and 4,000 troops respectively, and imposed an arms embargo in response. **15.** The state funeral for Nelson Mandela took place in his home village of Qunu, South Africa. In South Sudan, President Salva Kiir Mayardit alleged an attempted coup by his deputy Riek Machar; around 500 people died over the next three days as fighting spread from the capital, Juba, to surrounding cities. **25.** The UN doubled its peacekeeping force in South Sudan following reports of mass extra-judicial killings throughout the country. **30.** In the DR Congo, 103 people were reported dead after followers of the self-proclaimed prophet Paul Joseph Mukungubila attacked an army camp, the state broadcasting service and Ndjili international airport in the capital Kinshasa. **31.** In Johannesburg, South Africa, the prominent Rwandan exile Patrick Karegeya, 54, was poisoned and asphyxiated in a hotel room.

JANUARY 2014

9. Ali Larayedh resigned his position as Tunisian prime minister in line with an agreement to transition the government into a democracy; he was succeeded by Mehdi Jomaa. **10.** The Central African Republic's president Michel Djotodia and prime minister Nicolas Tiangaye resigned their positions at a regional summit in Chad; the announcement instigated a temporary ceasefire to the fighting between the countries Christian and Muslim militias. **12.** Around 300 people died when a boat carrying South Sudanese refugees sank while crossing the river Nile. **20.** Catherine Samba-Panza was elected interim president of the Central African Republic, becoming the first woman to hold the post. **24.** In South Sudan, an agreed ceasefire between President Salva Kiir Mayardit and rebel forces took effect; the truce sought to end an escalating ethnic conflict between the Dinka and Nuer peoples. **26.** Boko Haram militants killed 74 people in attacks on a marketplace and a church in the north-eastern Nigerian states of Borno and Adawama.

FEBRUARY 2014

11. An Algerian military plane crashed in the north-east province of Oum el-Bouaghi, killing 77 people. **15.** At least 106 people were killed after Boko Haram militants attacked the predominantly Christian village of Izghe in the Nigerian state of Borno. **24.** Ugandan president Yoweri Museveni signed new legislation penalising acts of 'aggravated homosexuality' and the 'promotion of homosexuality'; the maximum sentence for comiting 'acts of homosexuality' was extended to life in prison.

MARCH 2014

3. The murder trial of the South African paralympian Oscar Pistorius, 27, began at the High Court of Pretoria; Pistorius was accused of murdering his partner Reeva Steenkamp in February 2013. **11–16.** Approximately 170 people were killed in the northern Nigerian states of Katsina and Kaduna following organised attacks on villages by semi-nomadic Fulani herders. **24.** The World Health Organisation confirmed that an outbreak of Ebola had occurred in Guinea, with 59 people suspected of dying from the disease since December 2013.

APRIL 2014

5. In Rwanda a week of official mourning began in remembrance of the 800,000 victims of the 1994 Rwandan genocide. **14.** Around 230 school girls were abducted by Boko Haram militants in Borno, north-east Nigeria; in Abuja, Nigeria, 75 people were killed in Nigeria's capital when a bomb planted by Boko Haram members exploded on a bus. **15.** In South Sudan, around 200 civilians belonging to the Dinka ethnic group died when troops loyal to the former vice-president attacked the town of Bentiu.

MAY 2014

1. At least 12 people were killed by a car bomb in Abuja days before the city was due to host the World Economic Forum on Africa; Islamist group Boko Haram claimed responsibility. **2.** It was reported that the Republic of Congo expelled 50,000 citizens of the DR Congo; high crime rates had been linked by the government to illegal immigration. **5.** The military in Niger reported that human traffickers had abandoned 30 migrants in the Sahara desert without food or water; on 9 May, 13 members of the group were found dead in southern Algeria. **6.** Fifty people died and others were blinded after drinking from a batch of unlicensed alcohol in central and eastern Kenya. **7.** Gunmen suspected to be Boko Haram members killed 125 people in Gamburu, Nigeria. **15.** In Sudan, eight-months pregnant Dr Meriam Yahya

Ibrahim, 27, was sentenced to death for committing apostasy and adultery; Dr Ibrahim had converted to Christianity from Islam in order to marry a non-Muslim. **18.** Men suspected of being Boko Haram members attacked a work site in northern Cameroon killing at least one Cameroonian soldier and abducting ten Chinese workers. **24.** At least ten people were killed when the Islamist group al-Shabab attacked the Somali parliament in Mogadishu. In Djibouti at least two people were killed and 11 wounded when grenades were thrown into a restaurant in Djibouti City; no organisation claimed responsibility for the attack.

JUNE 2014

2. In Cameroon, two priests and a nun were released by Boko Haram after two months in captivity. **6.** In Gwoza, Nigeria, Boko Haram militants disguised as soldiers killed 200 civilians. In Mombasa, Kenya, £700,000 worth of illegal ivory was recovered from a warehouse; 2 people were arrested. **7.** A dispute over cattle in the south Kivu region of the DR Congo led to violence which killed 37 people. **11.** Sierra Leone closed its borders with Guinea and Liberia in an effort to halt the spread of the Ebola virus. **16.** In Bamako, Mali, two people died and 15 prisoners escaped when captured Islamist Mohamed Aly Ag Wadousene fought his way out of the capital's main prison. **17.** Wildfires in KwaZulu-Natal, South Africa destroyed thousands of hectares of forest and killed seven people. **23.** Kenyan fighter jets, acting on behalf of African Union Forces, killed 80 al-Shabab militants in Somalia. **25.** In South Africa, platinum miners returned to work after negotiating a wage deal, ending the longest and most costly strike in the country's history.

JULY 2014

1. In the Central African Republic, fighting between Ugandan troops and Muslim Seleka forces killed 17 people. **5.** The Nigerian army claimed to have killed 53 Boko Haram fighters after the Islamist group attacked a military base in Damboa, north-east Nigeria. **6.** Raids by Somali Islamists on two Kenyan coastal villages killed 29 people. **8.** In Somalia, members of the militant group al-Shabab stormed the presidential palace in Mogadishu; government forces recaptured the palace on the same day. **13.** In Mali, 30 people were killed in clashes between government forces and Tuareg rebels, days before scheduled peace talks. **17.** In Tunisia, 17 soldiers were killed when Islamist group the Okba Ibn Nafaa Brigade attacked a military checkpoint. **24.** Thousands of workers participated in a nationwide strike in Ghana protesting against rising inflation and the withdrawal of fuel subsidies; in Kaduna, Nigeria, 82 people were killed in two suicide bombings carried out by Boko Haram. Air Algeria flight AH5017 travelling from Ouagadougou to Algiers crashed in Mali due to poor weather; 116 passengers were killed. **25.** American citizen Patrick Sawyer, 40, a Liberian Ministry of Finance official, became the first person to die of the Ebola outbreak in Nigeria. **28.** In South Africa, a four week strike by 220,000 steel and construction workers ended when demands for higher pay were met by employers; the strike was thought to have cost the economy £17m per day. **30.** In Conakry, Guinea, 24 people died in a stampede at a beach party marking the end of Ramadan.

THE AMERICAS

AUGUST 2013

9. A Mexican court freed convicted killer and the former head of the Guadalajara Cartel, 60-year-old Rafael Caro Quintero, on a technicality; he then absconded without trace before a subsequent arrest warrant could be enforced. **21.** In the USA, mayor of San Diego, Bob Filner, resigned from his post following 18 separate allegations of sexual harrassment; former US soldier Private Chelsea Manning, aged 25, was sentenced to 35 years in prison and recieved a dishonourable discharge from the US Army after leaking sensitive intelligence documents to the online news organisation Wikileaks. **23.** A riot and gang fight in a Bolivian prison resulted in 31 deaths, including that of an 18-month-old child who lived in the jail. US Staff Sergeant Robert Bales was sentenced to life in prison by a military court for the murder of 16 Afghan civilians in Kandahar. **25.** In Mexico, six people were killed and 22 injured when a freight train carrying almost 300 illegal immigrants derailed. **28.** Nidal Hasan, a US colonel who went on a shooting spree, killing 13 and injuring 31 at Fort Hood military post in Texas, was sentenced to death by a military court.

SEPTEMBER 2013

2. Diana Nyad, 64, became the first person to swim from Cuba to Florida unassisted; the swim was her fifth attempt and took over 53 hours. **3.** In the USA, convicted kidnapper and rapist Ariel Castro, who was jailed in July 2013 for holding three women hostage for a decade, committed suicide in his cell at a state correctional facility in Ohio. **7–8.** In Brazil, more than 500 people across 40 cities were arrested during a weekend that saw thousands protest against the cost of staging the 2014 FIFA World Cup and 2016 Olympic Games. **16.** Former US naval reservist Aaron Alexis shot dead 12 people before being shot and killed by security forces at a naval base in Washington. **17.** Brazilian president Dilma Rousseff called off her state visit to the USA after leaked documents revealed her telephone and emails had been hacked by the National Security Agency. **30.** The US congress failed to pass a budget and agree a new debt ceiling before the end of the fiscal year, which resulted in some 700,000 federal workers being sent home without pay and most national parks, museums and federal buildings closing from 1 October; the shutdown lasted until 16 October when congress voted a deal through, extending borrowing authority until 7 February 2014.

OCTOBER 2013

1. US president Barack Obama's Patient Protection and Affordable Care Act, or 'Obamacare', came into effect; the website on which the initiative hinged suffered a series of technical glitches, leaving millions unable to access it. **3.** In Washington, D. C., a car rammed security barriers at the White House and was chased towards the Capitol by police; the driver, 34-year-old dental hygienist Miriam Carey, was shot dead while her one-year-old daughter, who was also in the vehicle, was unharmed. **7.** Argentine president Cristina Fernández de Kirchner, aged 60, was hospitalised and underwent successful brain surgery. **11.** Fifty-one people died when a cargo lorry careered off a mountain road in Cusco, Peru. **19.** The Mexican druglord and former head of the Tijuana Cartel, Francisco Rafael Arellano Félix, aged 63, was shot dead at a children's party in the resort of Cabo San Lucas by a man dressed as a clown.

NOVEMBER 2013

5. The mayor of Toronto, Rob Ford, admitted smoking crack cocaine while in office; in the weeks that followed, a series of motions stripped him of most mayoral powers. In the USA, Democrat Bill de Blasio was elected mayor of New York with 73 per cent of the vote. **20.** In Venezuela, President Nicolás Maduro was granted the power to govern by decree; the Enabling Law formed the latest development in a series of increasingly anti-capitalist economic reforms in Maduro's self-declared 'war' against private business, which included the arrest of around 100 businessmen for profiteering.

24. Juan Orlando Hernández, aged 45, of the Honduras National Party, was elected president of Honduras after receiving 36 per cent of the vote; the nearest rival, Xiomara Castro, who gained 29 per cent of the vote, alleged that the result was fraudulent.

DECEMBER 2013
1. In the USA, four people died and a further 63 were injured when a commuter train derailed in the Bronx, New York. An aeroplane crash in Alaska killed four people and injured six others. **3.** Detroit became the largest municipality to become bankrupt in US history when a judge ruled that it was unable to repay $18bn (£11bn) of debt. **10.** Nine people were killed and around 100 were injured when looters took advantage of a nationwide police strike in Argentina. **12.** US security forces arrested and strip-searched Indian diplomat Devyani Khobragade, aged 39, on charges of visa fraud relating to her Indian housekeeper; outrage in India escalated the arrest into an international dispute (*see* Asia, 17 December) and Khobragade was indicted and expelled from the US in January. **16.** Michelle Bachelet, 62, won the Chilean presidency with 62 per cent of the vote; her opponent, Evelyn Matthei, took 38 per cent.

JANUARY 2014
1. In the USA, Colorado became the first state to legalise the sale of recreational cannabis. Bill de Blasio was sworn in as mayor of New York, becoming the first Democratic mayor since 1993. **2–9.** A 'polar vortex' weather pattern caused record low temperatures in the eastern USA, with many states experiencing temperatures 15–25°C below average and snowfall of up to 61cm (24in); at least 21 people died from the cold. **6.** A former Miss Venezuela, Monica Spear, aged 29, and her partner Thomas Berry, 39, were shot dead by an armed gang near the town of Las Trincheras, Venezuela. **12.** In the south-eastern Brazilian city of Campinas, 12 men were shot dead by gunmen in a suspected revenge attack following the murder of an off-duty policeman. **23.** Around 32 elderly people died and a further 15 were injured in a fire at the L'Isle-Verte nursing home in Quebec, Canada.

FEBRUARY 2014
12–28. Daily anti-government marches protesting food shortages, rampant inflation and endemic violence were held throughout Venezuela; 18 protestors were shot dead. **22.** Mexican drug baron and leader of the prolific Sinaloa cartel, Joaquín 'El Chapo' Guzmán, was arrested in Mazatlan, Sinaloa, 13 years after his escape from a high-security prison.

MARCH 2014
12. Eight people died in a gas explosion in an apartment block in Harlem, New York City; around 60 others were injured by debris from the blast. **22.** At least 30 people died when a 54m-deep mudslide crushed 30 houses near the town of Oso in the US state of Washington. **23.** Venezuela's attorney-general, Luisa Ortega Díaz, announced the investigation of 60 cases of alleged human rights abuses, all of which occurred during ongoing anti-government protests (*see* 12–28 February) that injured 461 people and left a further 33 dead.

APRIL 2014
2. Ivan Lopez, 34, killed three people and injured 16 before taking his own life in a shooting at the Fort Hood military base in Texas. An 8.2 magnitude earthquake struck northern Chile; six people died, 2,600 homes were damaged and around 300 female prisoners absconded when a prison wall collapsed. **3.** A Brazilian court sentenced 15 police officers to

a total resolve of 48 years in prison; the men were convicted of killing four prisoners during a 1992 prison riot that left 111 people dead. **10.** In Peru, 28 people were arrested for belonging to the political wing of the Maoist insurgent group the Shining Path. **13.** In Brazil, strikes by 25,000 construction workers halted work on projects for the 2016 Rio Olympic Games. **25.** The Bolivian government dismissed 702 soldiers who had been protesting for better pay and conditions; the soldiers claimed that the army discriminates against indigenous Bolivians.

MAY 2014
1. In Tulsa, Oklahoma, convicted murderer Clayton Lockett took 43 minutes to die during a botched execution. In Florida, William Potts pleaded guilty to hijacking a plane and taking it to Cuba in 1984; Potts had already served a 13-year prison sentence for the crime in Cuba. **2.** In Venezuela, police arrested 58 foreign nationals accused of instigating civil unrest; 41 people had been killed during three months of political unrest. **12.** Michael Sam became the first openly gay athlete in the USA to play in the National Football League after signing for the St Louis Rams. **15.** Abu Hamza al-Masri was found guilty of 11 terrorism-related offences in New York; the Egyptian born cleric had lived in the UK for a number of years prior to being extradited to the USA in October 2012. **24.** British-born Elliott Rodger killed six people and wounded seven in a shooting in Santa Barbara, California. **31.** In Afghanistan, the American soldier Sgt Bowe Bergdahl, 28, was released by the Taliban after spending five years in captivity; Bergdahl's controversial release involved a prisoner swap with captured Taliban members.

JUNE 2014
4–7. Three members of the Royal Canadian Mounted police were shot dead by Justin Bourque, 24, in New Brunswick, Canada; Bourque was apprehended after a three-day manhunt. **6.** In Sao Paolo, approximately 10,000 homeless campaigners created a 135-mile traffic jam in protest of Brazil hosting the 2014 FIFA World Cup. **9–22.** Three prisoners escaped via helicopter from a detention centre in Montreal, Canada; the men were later arrested in Quebec. **10.** In Las Vegas, Nevada, Jared and Amanda Miller shot three people before killing themselves; six dancers from the Cuban National Ballet defected to the US, citing restrictions on artistic expression in Cuba. **11.** In Paraguay, 200,000 people were displaced by heavy flooding, with 75,000 people evacuated from the capital Asunción alone. **12.** In Virginia, Eric Cantor, the Republican house majority leader, was defeated in a shock result by Tea Party candidate David Brat in the Republican primary for Virginia's 7th congressional district. **27.** Jozef Wesolowski, the former papal envoy to the Dominican Republic, was convicted of sexual abuse by a Vatican tribunal and was subsequently stripped of his priesthood.

JULY 2014
4. Bolivia became the first country in the world to legalise child labour for minors as young as ten. **8.** In Boston, Azamat Tazhayakov, 20, was convicted of assisting Dzhokhar and Tamerlan Tsarnaev to bomb the Boston marathon in 2013. **10.** The former mayor of New Orleans, Ray Naggin, 58, was sentenced to 10 years in prison following a corruption scandal. **16.** Russia announced plans to re-open a military base in Cuba, one of the Soviet Union's largest during the Cold War; the former dictator of Panama, Manuel Noriega, 80, filed a lawsuit against Activision Entertainment over its alleged depiction of him in a number of video games. **17.** Shannon Richardson, 36, was sentenced to 18 years in prison for sending letters laced with the poison ricin to President Obama. **23.** In Caracas, soldiers and police evicted

thousands of squatters from a half-built skyscraper due to safety concerns. **24.** In Peru, doctors began searching for the Chitonahua tribe who made contact with a settled Amazonian community on July 7; it was feared the tribe's first interaction with the outside world would spread influenza, as the group had no immunity to the disease. **28.** In Virginia, a federal court struck down the state's 2006 ban on gay marriage, paving the way for the issue to be taken to the Supreme Court. **31.** Argentina defaulted on its national debt for the second time in 13 years when the country failed to reach an agreement with a number of American hedge funds to restructure its debt repayments. The US House of Representatives passed a resolution to sue President Obama for exceeding the executive power of the presidency.

ASIA

AUGUST 2013

9. In China, top economic official Liu Tienan was expelled from the Communist Party and removed from public office for accepting bribes as part of Chinese President Xi Jinping's crackdown on corruption. **14.** In India, 18 submariners were killed after INS *Sindhurakshak* exploded in a Mumbai dockyard due to an onboard accident. **24.** In north-west Myanmar, a Buddhist mob burned down over 40 shops and homes after a Muslim man was accused of sexual assault. **27.** A 15-year-old Kyrgyzstani herder, later named as Temirbek Isakunov, died of bubonic plague, the first case in the country for over 30 years.

SEPTEMBER 2013

2. A series of tornadoes hit eastern Japan, injuring 63 people. **8.** Tokyo, Japan, was announced as the host of the 2020 Olympic Games. **13.** In India, four men who gang raped and murdered 23-year-old Jyoti Singh on a bus in Delhi were sentenced to death; the verdict was widely supported within the country and followed months of protests and national anger. **9–27.** Over 100 people died in the Philippine city of Zamboanga when Muslim rebel faction the Moro National Liberation Front took over large parts of the city and attempted to declare an independent Muslim state. **20–25.** In Bangladesh, thousands of garment workers vandalised factories and clashed with police in protests for a rise in minimum wage. **22.** Former leading Chinese politician Bo Xilai was convicted of bribery, abuse of power and corruption, and sentenced to life imprisonment; this concluded a fall from power that began in February 2012 when former vice-mayor of Chongqing, Wang Lijun, sought asylum at the US consulate and implicated Mr Xilai and his wife, Gu Kailai, in the murder of British national Neil Heywood, which she later confessed to, receiving a suspended death sentence. At least 85 Pakistani Christians died in a church in Peshawar after two Taliban militants detonated suicide vests. **23.** China banned weapons-related exports to North Korea following the release of satellite imagery that suggested the country had resumed plutonium production. In Cambodia, Hun Sen was re-elected as prime minister for a sixth consecutive five-year term; the opposition alleged electoral fraud. **24.** A 7.7-magnitude earthquake hit the province of Balochistan in south-west Pakistan, killing approximately 825 people and injuring hundreds more. **26.** At least 17 people were killed after separatists attacked a police station in Indian-administered Kashmir. Around 60 people died when the Babu Genu Market building collapsed in Mumbai.

OCTOBER 2013

12–14. 45 people died in cyclone Phailin, a category-four tropical storm that struck the Indian states of Odisha and Andhra Pradesh. **13.** In India, around 115 people died when a crowd of Hindu pilgrims panicked and stampeded on a bridge near the Ratangarh temple in Madhya Pradesh. **15.** A 7.2-magnitude earthquake killed around 220 people on the Philippine islands of Bohol and Cebu. **16.** At least 17 people died in a landslide after a typhoon hit the Japanese island of Izu Oshima. In Laos, an aeroplane crashed into the Mekong River; all 44 passengers and crew died. **22.** The Sultan of Brunei, Hassanal Bolkiah, announced that the country would introduce Islamic Sharia law. **27–29.** In Bangladesh, at least nine people were killed and hundreds more injured after opposition candidate Khaleda Zia, leader of the Bangladesh National Party, called for strikes in response to incumbent prime minister Sheikh Hasina's refusal to hand over power to a neutral government in the run-up to elections. **28.** A suicide protest killed five people and injured 38 others in Tiananmen Square, Beijing, when a car was driven through crowds and into an ornamental bridge.

NOVEMBER 2013

1. The head of the Pakistan Taliban, Hakimullah Mehsud, was killed in a US drone strike. **5.** A court in Bangladesh sentenced 152 soldiers to death for their involvement in a 2009 mutiny in which 74 people died. India successfully launched its £45m Mars Orbiter Mission from the Satish Dhawan Space Centre. **7–9.** At least 4,000 people died and a further 4.4 million were displaced after typhoon Haiyan hit the Philippines; an estimated 707,000 buildings were damaged or destroyed and infrastructure was so severely affected that aid could not reach some areas for up to a week after the disaster. **11.** The International Court of Justice ruled that the Preah Vihear temple, an 11th century structure on the Thai–Cambodian border, belonged to Cambodia. **15–17.** Sri Lanka hosted the 23rd biennial Commonwealth Heads of Government Meeting; the prime ministers of Canada, India and Mauritius boycotted the summit in protest over Sri Lanka's human record. **24.** China created the 'East China Sea Air Defence Identification Zone' (ADIZ) and asserted military control over the airspace above the Japanese-controlled, uninhabited Senkaku islets; Japan refused to acknowledge the zone. **24–3 December.** In Thailand, over 100,000 people protested in the streets of Bangkok; initially provoked by a controversial, and swiftly revoked, amnesty bill that would have allowed influential former prime minister Thaksin Shinawatra to return to the country; the demonstrations soon focused on the leadership of his sister, Prime Minister Yingluck Shinawatra, with thousands occupying ministries and government headquarters in failed attempts to elicit her resignation.

DECEMBER 2013

3. In North Korea, 67-year-old Chang Song-thaek, the uncle of Kim Jong-un and his most powerful adviser, was removed from his post, the most drastic change in leadership since the death of Kim Jong-il in 2011; state media announced that he had been executed on 11 December. **8.** South Korea extended its East China Sea air defence zone into China's newly-established ADIZ (*see* 24 November) in a US-backed act of non-recognition. Around 400 migrant workers rioted in Singapore after a man was killed by a bus; the protests marked the first public disorder to hit Singapore in over 30 years. **9.** The prime minister of Thailand, Yingluck Shinawatra, dissolved parliament and announced an election following continuing large-scale protests and the mass resignation of the entire opposition (*see* 24 November). **11.** In India, the supreme court unexpectedly reinstituted a colonial-era law criminalising homosexual acts. **12.** In Bangladesh, at least five people were killed in street violence after the execution of Islamist opposition leader Abdul Quader Mollah for war crimes. **17.** In Delhi, India, staff removed security barriers protecting the US embassy and senior officials refused to meet a visiting US delegation in response to the arrest of an Indian diplomat in New York City (*see* The Americas, 12 December).

JANUARY 2014

3. In Phnom Penh, Cambodia, five people were killed and a further 20 injured when police fired on protesting garment makers. **5.** In Bangladesh, at least 18 people died and around 200 polling stations were burned down during widespread election violence. **6.** The spiritual leader of Kyrgyzstan, Grand Mufti Rakhmatulla-Hajji Egemberdiev, resigned after a leaked video recording showed him engaging in sexual intercourse with his illegal second wife. **9.** The head of Karachi's anti-terror unit, Chaudhry Aslam, 53, was killed in a suicide attack; the Pakistani Taliban claimed responsibility. **14.** In Rakhine, western Myanmar, at least 40 Rohingya Muslims were killed by security forces and local people; the attack was precipitated by the death of a policeman. **21.** In the wake of the protesters' 'shutdown' of Bangkok, the Thai government imposed a 60-day state of emergency and launched a spate of violent attacks on rallies and gatherings, injuring around 70 people and leaving several others dead. **26.** A Chinese court sentenced the prominent human rights activist Xu Zhiyong to four years in prison.

FEBRUARY 2014

2. Snap parliamentary elections were held in Thailand in an attempt to quell recent unrest (*see* 9 December), but violence and blockades instigated by the opposition prevented around 6 million people from voting. **11.** China and Taiwan held their first high-level talks since the end of the 1949 Chinese Civil War. **17.** The UN Commission of Inquiry on Human Rights in North Korea released its report concluding that the state was responsible for 'unspeakable atrocities' and that senior officials, including Kim Jong-un, should be prosecuted for crimes against humanity. **18.** In Gyeongju, South Korea, ten people died and around 100 others were injured when the snow-laden roof of an auditorium collapsed during a university ceremony; Thailand's National Anti-Corruption Commission announced it would charge prime minister Shinawatra with improperly handling the country's rice subsidy scheme.

MARCH 2014

1. Eight men armed with swords and meat cleavers killed 29 people and injured 130 others in an attack on a railway station in the south-western Chinese city of Kunming; officials blamed the attack on Uighur separatists. **8.** Malaysia Airlines flight MH370 disappeared en route from Kuala Lumpur to Beijing with 239 people aboard; searches were focused on the South China sea until, one week after the disappearance, satellite data revealed the plane had changed course mid-flight and the search was expanded to an area of 3 million miles, spanning from Kazakhstan to the southern Indian Ocean. **21.** Thailand's parliamentary elections (*see* 2 February) were ruled invalid and unconstitutional due to disruptions caused by the opposition. **24.** After more than two weeks of searching for flight MH370 (*see* 8 March) the Malaysian prime minister, Najib Razak, announced that data confirmed the aeroplane had crashed in the Indian Ocean and that was assumed 'beyond reasonable doubt' that there were no survivors. **27.** In the Philippines, the Moro Islamic Liberation Front rebel group signed a peace deal with the government to end four decades of separatist fighting; the agreement aimed to facilitate greater autonomy for the predominantly Muslim island of Mindanao.

APRIL 2014

16. Around 300 passengers and crew died when the South Korean ferry *Sewol* sank en route to Jeju island; the ferry's captain was later arrested and denounced by President Park Geun-hye for failing to evacuate his vessel and on 16 May prime minister Chung Hong-won resigned after claiming responsibility for the disaster. **11.** Newspapers in Myanmar printed black front pages in protest against the arrests of a number of journalists. **15.** In Shanghai, China 160 members of a criminal gang were arrested for fraud in relation to the creation of bogus medical clinics; it was estimated that 500 people were thought to have been cheated out of a total of 1.7m yuan (£161.8m). **24.** Sherpa mountain guides went on strike to demand better pay and working conditions in the wake of an avalanche which killed 16 guides in 2014; the strike led to the closure of the Nepalese section of Mt Everest.

MAY 2014

1. The Sultanate of Brunei became the first country in South East Asia to adopt Sharia law. **3.** In Afghanistan, 2,100 people died in mudslides in the Badakhshan region near the Tajik border. **7.** In China, police shot and wounded a man who stabbed six commuters at a railway station in the western city of Guangzhou; the attack was linked to Uighur separatists (*see* March). **7.** Prime minister Yingluck Shinawatra was dismissed from office by Thailand's Constitutional Court after reportedly appointing a relative to a position within the security services. **21.** A 21-year-old Taiwanese student stabbed three commuters to death and injured 25 others in an underground station in Taipei; Russia signed an agreement with China to supply the country with natural gas in a deal worth around $400bn (£237.1bn); the agreement was seen as an attempt to reduce Russia's reliance on western markets following the crisis in the Ukraine. The Pakistani military claimed to have killed at least 60 Islamists in North Waziristan. **27.** A Vietnamese fishing boat sank after colliding with a Chinese vessel in a disputed portion of the South China Sea; both countries blamed each other for the incident.

JUNE 2014

2. In India, Telegana was established as the country's 29th and newest state after a 60-year campaign. **5.** In Hong Kong, 100,000 people took part in a candlelit vigil to commemorate the Tiananmen Square massacre. **8.** In Karachi, Uzbek Islamists fighting the the Pakistani Taliban attacked the city's international airport; 39 people died, including all ten gunmen. **9.** The prime minister of Japan, Shinzo Abe, anounced plans to resume the controversial practice of hunting whales for scientific research; he preposed 210 whales a year be killed. **10.** In the Indian state of Himachal Pradesh, around 25 students were killed or missing after being caught in a flood that was caused by an accident at a hydroelectric dam. **11.** The Chinese government announced that it had made 800 arrests as part of a crackdown on illegal religous sects. **12.** In Uttar Pradesh, India, a 19-year-old was found hanged from a tree, the fourth woman to be found dead in such circumstances in the summer of 2014. **16.** In Aluthhama, Sri Lanka, three people died and 78 were injured when the millitant Buddhist group Bodu Bala Sena attacked a predominantly Muslim area of a village. **18.** In Japan, the possesion of child pornography was made illegal for the first time. **28.** North Korea conducted a short-range missile test ahead of a Chinese government visit to South Korea. **29.** In Tokoyo, a man set himself on fire in a busy area of the city in protest of the proposed changes to Japan's pacifist constitution.

JULY 2014

1. In Japan, legislation was passed to end the country's pacifist defence policy in place since the Second World War. **5.** In Hong Kong, police arrested five leaders of the island's largest pro-democracy protests since the territory reverted to China in 1997. **9–18.** Typhoom Ramasun caused widespread damage and loss of life in a number of Pacific nations; in the Philippines, at leat 94 people were killed and 41,000 homes were destroyed; in Hainan, China, 18 people were killed and in Vietnam, 27 were killed. **19.** Sampath Vidanapathirana, a member of Sri Lanka's ruling political party was sentenced to 20 years in prison with hard labour for the murder of British Red Cross worker Khuram Shaikh. **23.** The body of Yoo Bryung Wun, 73, the owner of the *Sewol* (*see* 15 April) was found in an orchard near the town of Suncheon; Yoo had been sought by police following the ferry's sinking. **22.** The city of Yumen in Ganso province, China, was placed under quarantine after a local man died from bubonic plague. **23.** In Magong airport on Pengchu Island, Taiwan, 48 people died when a TransAsia Airways plane crashed while attempting to land in poor weather. **28.** In Nagasaki, Japan, a 15-year-old girl was arrested by police on suspicion of killing and dismembering a classmate. On the island of Jolo in the Philippines, members of the Islamist group Abu Sayyaf killed 18 people in an attack on two vehicles.

AUSTRALASIA AND THE PACIFIC

AUGUST–SEPTEMBER 2013

7 September. Centre-right Liberal party leader Tony Abbott led the Liberal-National coalition to victory over Kevin Rudd's incumbent Labor party to become the 28th prime minister of Australia, with a majority of 88 seats to 57; he was sworn in on 18 September. **27.** Twenty-one asylum seekers drowned after a boat headed for Australia sank just off the coast of Indonesia.

OCTOBER 2013

13–25. A series of major bushfires in New South Wales killed two people, destroyed 248 buildings and 290,000 acres of land; the fires reflected an increase in temperature that made 2013 Australia's hottest year on record.

NOVEMBER–DECEMBER 2013

12 December. The Australian High Court overturned a law, implemented on 7 December, that allowed gay marriage in the Australian Capital Territory; the 27 couples who had wed since the ruling had their marriages nullified.

JANUARY 2014

2. In Commonwealth Bay, Antarctica, 52 passengers, including scientists and tourists, were rescued from the Australasian Antarctic Expedition aboard the Russian *Akademik Shokalskiy* after spending nine days trapped by pack ice. **13–18.** South-east Australia was hit by a 'significant multi-day heatwave', with temperatures reaching 49.2°C at their peak; the heat facilitated bushfires in Victoria state, which caused one death. **30.** A Salvadoran man, later named as José Salvador Alvarenga, was found washed up on a coral atoll of the Marshall Islands having spent 13 months stranded at sea.

FEBRUARY 2014

1. At least 15 people died after the Indonesian volcano, Mount Sinabung, unexpectedly erupted.

MARCH–APRIL 2014

1–10 April. Cyclone Ita moved across the Pacific killing 22 people and leaving 9,000 homeless in the Solomon Islands, destroying 1,159 homes in Papua New Guinea and damaging property in Australia and New Zealand. **3.** The Australian High Court ruled that the state of New South Wales must recognise a third 'non-specific' gender in addition to male and female classifications.

MAY 2014

2. The police minister of New South Wales, Mike Gallacher, resigned after it was alleged that he passed political donations to a construction firm. **29.** A remote area of sea off the west coast of Australia was searched after possible signals were thought to be detected from the missing Malaysia Airlines flight MH370; the search failed to locate any debris from the wreck of the missing plane (*see* Asia 8 March 2014).

JUNE 2014

10. In the Marshall Islands, costal erosion revealed the skeletons of approximately 20 Japanese soldiers dating from the Second World War.

JULY 2014

3. Tonga proposed exchanging the Minerva Reef with the Lau Island Group, owned by Fiji, in order to resolve a territorial dispute. **4.** The Anglican Church of Australia voted to allow priests to report crimes, including child abuse, exposed during religious confession. **5.** In Auckland, Korotangi Paki, 18, was acquitted of burglary, theft and drink driving by Judge Philippa Cunningham on the basis that a successful conviction would prevent him from becoming the Maori king of New Zealand; the present king being Paki's father, King Tuheita.

EUROPE

AUGUST 2013

1. The Italian Court of Cessation upheld the former Italian prime minister Silvio Berlusconi's four-year prison term for tax fraud; due to Berlusconi's age, the term was reduced to one year under house arrest. Russia granted asylum to fugitive US whistleblower Edward Snowden, allowing him to leave the Moscow airport transit zone he had occupied since June 2013. **19.** As part of a long-planned Royal Navy deployment to the Mediterranean and the Gulf, British frigate HMS *Westminster* sailed into the Port of Gibraltar; the ship's arrival followed several weeks of tensions between the UK and Spain over Gibraltar's construction of an artificial reef and Spain's introduction of tighter border controls.

SEPTEMBER 2013

5. In Deiningen and Woernitz, Germany, 40 children were seized and taken into care after police raids on the Christian Twelve Tribes sect. **13.** A fire in a psychiatric hospital in north-west Russia killed 37 people. **16.** The salvage of the wreck of the sunken cruise ship *Costa Concordia* began off the coast of Italy; 32 people died when the ship ran aground in January 2012. **18.** Greek anti-fascist rapper Pavlos Fyssas, was murdered by George Roupakias, a man with connections to the far-right political party Golden Dawn; the following weeks saw the party's headquarters raided and the arrest of several prominent members. **19.** Russian federal security force officers boarded the Greenpeace ship *Arctic Sunrise* and detained the 30 activists on board; all were subsequently charged with piracy. **22.** The incumbent chancellor of Germany, Angela Merkel, won a third term in office for the Christian Democratic Union/Christian Social Union; Merkel fell just short of an outright majority, winning 311 of the 316 seats needed, and thus formed a 'grand coalition' with the Social Democratic Party of Germany.

OCTOBER 2013
3. Around 359 African migrants drowned half a mile from the coast of the Italian island of Lampedusa after their boat caught fire and capsized; a further 50 died in a similar accident eight days later. **9.** In Azerbaijan, incumbent President Ilham Aliyev was re-elected with 84.6 per cent of the vote; opposition candidates and foreign regulatory bodies termed the election 'not free and fair', an allegation corroborated by a goverment election app that accidentally displayed the results a day before the election. **13.** Over 400 nationalist protestors were arrested in Moscow after they vandalised buildings and searched for migrants in reaction to the death of ethnic Russian Yegor Shcherbakov, 25, who was stabbed to death by a man of 'non-Slavic appearance'; police rounded up around 1,200 suspected illegal immigrants the following day. **15.** In Russia, a Dutch diplomat was beaten at his home in Moscow; the attack followed the arrest and alleged beating of a Russian diplomat in The Hague. **16.** In Greece, a blonde child named Maria was removed from a Roma camp in Farsala when police noticed she bore no resemblance to her parents and later concluded that the child was abducted; an international campaign was launched to trace her true parents and on 25 October, DNA tests proved the child was of Roma descent and was staying with the couple with the consent of her biological mother. **21.** A female suicide bomber killed six people and injured 33 others when she detonated a device on a bus in the Russian city of Volgograd. **27.** Giorgi Margvelashvili of the Georgian Dream-Democratic Georgia coalition won Georgia's presidential election, with 62.1 per cent of the vote.

NOVEMBER 2013
1. Two members of the Greek Golden Dawn Party (*see* 18 September) were shot dead outside their office; a newly formed far-left group, the Militant People's Revolutionary Forces, later claimed responsibility. **3.** In Germany, police revealed that they had seized a collection of around 1,500 Nazi-era looted artworks from the home of 80-year-old Cornelius Gurlitt; the paintings included works by Henri Matisse, Pablo Picasso and Marc Chagall. **8.** Ratings agency Standard & Poor downgraded France's credit rating from AAA to AA. **11.** Around 70 protestors were arrested in Paris after they booed French President François Hollande at an Armistice Day ceremony. **15.** Far-right politicians Marine Le Pen, leader of France's National Front, and Geert Wilders, leader of the Netherlands' Freedom Party, commenced a formal alliance. **17.** Fifty people died in a plane crash in the Russian city of Kazan. **18.** In France, a gunman, later named as 46-year-old Abdelhakim Dekhar, attacked two newspaper offices and a bank, injured one person and briefly held another hostage. **21.** Fifty-four people died when a supermarket roof collapsed in Riga, Latvia; six days later, prime minister Valdis Dombrovskis resigned and terminated his government. **21–7 December.** The Ukrainian government suspended imminent political and trade deals with the EU under alleged pressure from Russia, which sparked the largest protests since the Orange Revolution of 2004, with as many as 300,000 people attending rallies; the demonstrations were mostly peaceful with the exception of the violent removal of crowds from Kiev's Independence Square by police on 30 November, a move which drew international condemnation. **27.** Silvio Berlusconi was expelled from the senate and stripped of parliamentary immunity.

DECEMBER 2013
2. In Reykjavik, Iceland, officers shot dead a 50-year-old man in the country's first ever fatal police shooting. **3.** Twenty-nine-year-old Bolshoi dancer Pavel Dmitrichenko was convicted of partially blinding Sergei Filin, the theatre's

artistic director, in an organised acid attack in January 2013. **8–15.** Pro-EU protests in Ukraine continued to gain in severity and momentum with upwards of 200,000 people gathering in Independence Square, Kiev, each weekend. **17.** Angela Merkel was officially sworn in for a third term as chancellor of Germany. In Turkey, 52 people, including senior financial officials and the sons of several cabinet ministers, were arrested in a police-headed corruption investigation; reports suggested that the arrests were related to a feud between prime minister Recep Tayyip Erdogan and the self-exiled, influential Islamic scholar Fethullah Gulen. **19.** The Russian Duma approved a law granting amnesty to 20,000 prisoners; those pardoned included two members of the protest band Pussy Riot, the Greenpeace Arctic 30 (*see* 19 September) and the former oil tycoon Mikhail Khodorkovsky. **19–8 January.** In Turkey, over 400 members of the police force, including at least six chiefs, were removed from their posts in government reprisals for a police-led corruption inquiry. **29–30.** Two suicide bomb attacks killed 34 people and injured a further 95 in the Russian city of Volgograd; the explosions occured at the main railway station and on a trolleybus; Vilayat Dagestan, an Islamist group affiliated with the Causcasus Emirate, later claimed responsibility for the attacks.

JANUARY 2014
1. Latvia joined the eurozone, becoming the 18th member. The Palestinian ambassador to the Czech Republic, Jamal al-Jamal, died at the age of 56 after a safe containing undeclared firearms exploded at his residence in Prague. **10.** The French first lady, Valérie Trierweiler, was admitted to hospital following a gossip magazine's allegations that President François Hollande was having an affair with the actress Julie Gayet; Hollande announced his separation from Trierweiler 15 days later. **12.** In Dublin, Ireland, a 39-year-old Italian man confessed to killing his landlord and attempting to eat his heart after an argument over a chess game. **16–25.** The Ukrainian parliament eschewed normal voting procedure and implemented controversial and repressive anti-protest laws, including lengthy prison sentences, with a show of hands; previously peaceful protests became violent on December 19 2013, with hundreds of demonstrators and policemen injured and at least five people killed over the next ten days. **27.** Severe blizzards in southern Romania and northern Bulgaria left five people dead. **28.** The prime minister of Ukraine, Mykola Azarov, and his entire cabinet resigned their positions following escalating violence across the country; the following day, parliament also repealed new repressive protest legislation and offered an amnesty for protestors.

FEBRUARY 2014
9. In Switzerland, a controversial referendum to implement strict immigration quotas was backed by 50.3 per cent of the public, necessitating its passage into law. **14.** The last of 243 detained Ukrainian protestors was freed in accordance with a government amnesty (*see* 28 January). The Italian prime minister, Enrico Letta, resigned his position after losing a vote called by Democratic party leader Matteo Renz, 39; eight days later, Renzi was appointed as his successor, becoming the youngest man to ever hold the post. **15.** Turkish MPs brawled in parliament after prime minister Erdogan's Justice and Development party passed controversial reforms that put the supreme board of judges under ministry control; the reforms prevented inquiries into high-level government affairs (*see* 17 December). **18–21.** In Kiev, Ukraine, at least 88 people, including police officers, were killed and around 600 others injured when security forces cleared protest camps; President Viktor Yanukovych was removed from power by a

parliamentary vote just 24 hours after he announced a 'peace deal' and a reversion to the 2004 constitution, ending the fragile truce that was reached on 20 February. **24.** The interim government of Ukraine issued an international arrest warrant for former President Viktor Yanukovych, accusing him of 'the mass murder of peaceful citizens'. **27–28.** In Simferopol, Crimea, pro-Russian militia seized a number of government buildings following several days of unrest; plain-clothes Russian troops took over the airport at Sevastopol the following day.

MARCH 2014
1–6. Russian and Ukrainian troops engaged in tense stand-offs at a number of Ukrainian military bases in Crimea; some 16,000 Russian troops entered the region and thousands more conducted military exercises along Ukraine's eastern border. **3.** Belgium became the first country in the world to legalise child euthanasia. **4.** The Estonian prime minister Andrus Ansip resigned after nine years in office. **6.** Crimean politicians voted to join Russia after a parliamentary referendum. **18.** The Chechen Islamist group the Caucasus Emirate announced the 'martyrdom' of its leader Doku Umarov, one of Russia's most wanted men. **21.** Russian President Vladimir Putin formalised Crimea's union with Russia; the Turkish government implemented controversial new internet laws that blocked access to social media sites Twitter and YouTube; the restrictions followed the online publication of audio recordings purported to expose the prime minister engaging in corruption. **31.** The French interior minister Manuel Valls was named prime minister in a reshuffle prompted by severe losses for the Socialist Party in municipal elections.

APRIL 2014
3. Italian police arrested 24 armed men suspected of planning a violent attack on St Mark's Square, Venice; the group were thought to be secessionists seeking the independence of the Veneto region of Italy. **8.** A civil lawsuit against the Dutch government, filed by mothers and widows of men killed in the 1995 Srebrenica massacre, opened in the Hague District Court; The Mothers of Srebrenica, a group representing 6,000 women who lost family members during the massacre, originally filed the lawsuit in 2007, seeking compensation and international acknowledgement that UN-backed Dutch troops failed to prevent the killings. **11.** An anarchist group claimed responsibility for a car bomb which exploded outside the offices of the International Monetary Fund in Athens; windows were smashed but no injuries were caused. **15.** Silvio Berlusconi was sentenced to community service following a conviction for tax fraud. The acting Ukrainian President Olexander Turchynov announced the start of military operations against Russian separatists. **27.** Pope Francis canonised Popes John XXIII and John Paul II in St Peter's Square; the ceremony was attended by thousands of Roman Catholics from around the world. **30.** Fashion designers Domenico Dolce and Stefano Gabbana were issued with 18-month suspended sentences after they were convicted of concealing hundreds of millions of euros from Italian tax authorities.

MAY 2014
13. The European Court of Human Rights orderd Turkey to pay €90m (£73m) in compensation to Greek Cypriots displaced by Turkey's invasion in 1974; Isabel Carrasco, the leader of the provincial government in León, Spain, was shot dead; Spanish police arrested a mother and daughter in connection with the incident; an explosion at a coal mine in Soma, Turkey, killed 301 miners sparking strikes and demonstrations against poor safety standards in the mining industry. **14–18.** Major flooding left tens of thousands of people homeless and at least 35 people dead in Serbia, Bosnia and Hercegovina and Croatia. **19.** In Donetsk, eastern Ukraine, separatist militia occupied the local airport, and were subsequently engaged in a firefight with Ukrainian government forces; on 25 March, 50 separatists were killed and government forces regained control of the airport. **24.** The Italian navy rescued 435 migrants, including 264 children, on board a boat from North Africa. **25.** An unknown gunman killed three people and wounded one at a Jewish museum in Brussels, Belgium.

JUNE 2014
2. Juan Carlos I of Spain announced his intension to abdicate in favour of his son, Crown Prince Felipe. In Ankara, police clashed with around 500 demonstrators marking the death of a man killed by the police in 2013. Highly radioactive radium was found at a dump in the city of Bienne, Switzerland; the substance was left over from the manufacture of watch faces. **5.** The mayor of Venice, Giorgio Orsoni, was placed under house arrest following accusations that he stole €20m from the city's flood defence funds. **6.** Pope Francis dismissed the board of the Vatican bank, which was accused of corruption and money laundering. In Tuam, County Galway, the remains of 800 babies were found in a mass grave at the site of a former Catholic children's home. **18.** Former President of Turkey, Kenan Evren, was sentenced to life in prison for his part in the 1980 military coup. King Felipe VI became King of Spain by proclamation of the Spanish parliament's lower house. **20.** In Bulgaria, 12 people were killed in severe flash floods near the town of Varna. **28.** The 100th anniversary of the assassination of Arch-Duke Ferdinand, which sparked the First World War, was commemorated in Sarajevo.

JULY 2014
1. The European Court of Human Rights upheld the French government's ban of the Islamic full-face veil, the niqab, in public. In France, former President Nicholas Sarkozy was held for questioning over alleged corruption offences. **4.** In Greece, a strike held in protest of the privatisation of the energy sector led to power cuts on the mainland. **4–9.** In Germany, a member of the Bundesnachrichtendienst (BND), the German foreign intelligence agency, was arrested on suspicion of spying for the USA; a second person was later arrested. **15–22.** Protests against Israel's military actions in Gaza took place in a number of cities around the world; anti-semitic chanting was heard at rallies in France and Germany, with particularly violent demonstrations occurring in Paris. **16.** In the Hague, a Dutch court ruled that peace-keepers from the Netherlands were liable for the deaths of around 300 victims of the 1995 Srebrenica massacre; it was ruled that Dutch soldiers had failed to prevent Serbian soldiers murdering Bosnian civilians. **17.** Malaysia Airlines Flight 17 was shot down in eastern Ukraine by a surface to air missile, resulting in the death of 298 passengers and crew; the Ukrainian government and pro-Russian separatist groups blamed each other for the incident. **24.** Poland was ordered to pay damages worth £180,000 to two former Guantanamo Bay detainees after the European Court of Human Rights found they had been tortured by the CIA at a secret prison in Poland. **31.** The EU added several sanctions to Russian individuals and companies following the downing of Malaysia Airlines Flight 17; both the EU and the US had imposed increasingly stringent sanctions against Russia since May 2014, due to the on-going unrest in Ukraine.

MIDDLE EAST

AUGUST 2013

3. Interpol issued a global security alert following the escape of around 2,000 detainees from prisons in Iraq, Libya and Pakistan in late July; al-Qaida and its affiliates claimed responsibility for the prison breaks, which killed at least 30 members of the security forces. **4–13.** A terror alert in Yemen prompted the UK and USA to close their embassies and withdraw diplomatic staff; at least 30 suspected al-Qaida militants died in US drone attacks sanctioned by the Yemeni government, foiling a plot to seize ports and destroy oil pipelines. **14.** The first direct Israeli–Palestinian peace talks in three years commenced in Jerusalem. **14–18.** In Egypt, around 900 people were killed and thousands more wounded after security forces opened fire on crowds protesting the deposition of Islamist president Mohammed Mursi. **19.** Islamist militants killed 25 Egyptian police conscripts after dragging them from a bus in northern Sinai. **21.** In Syria, a reported 1,429 people were killed by sarin gas in the rebel-held Damascus suburbs; France, the UK and the USA blamed President Bashar al-Assad's government forces, while Russia placed responsibility with the rebel forces, but sniper attacks and a lack of government cooperation hampered UN investigators, leaving them unable to conclusively identify the perpetrator. **28.** At least 80 people were killed by a number of car bombings in predominantly Shia areas of Baghdad. A final 450 Ethiopian Jews arrived in Israel, officially concluding an operation begun three years previously when the Israeli government decided to airlift the last of the eligible Falash Mura, some 7,500 people, to Israel.

SEPTEMBER 2013

14. Syrian President Bashar al-Assad agreed a deal with the USA and Russia to remove and destroy Syria's chemical weapons stockpile by mid-2014. **16.** Lieutenant Negar, the most senior policewoman in Helmand, Afghanistan, died a day after gunmen attacked her near police headquarters; two female colleagues, including her predecessor, Islam Bibi, were killed in similar attacks in July 2013. **21.** Suicide bombers killed around 90 people at a Shia funeral in Sadr City, Iraq. **23.** In Egypt, a court outlawed the activities of Islamic political movement The Muslim Brotherhood and seized its assets; the ban followed months of violent protests by the organisation over the deposition of former President and Muslim Brotherhood member Mohammed Mursi in July 2013 (*see* 24 March).

OCTOBER 2013

5–6. Approximately 100 people died in suicide bomb attacks across Iraq, including 51 Shia pilgrims in Baghdad. **12.** Saudi Arabia turned down a two-year seat on the UN Security Council, citing 'double standards' among permanent members as the reason for its refusal. **14.** In Syria, a deal between the government and the Syrian Arab Red Crescent allowed 2,000 people to be evacuated from the besieged area of Moadamiyah where many had starved to death. **27.** Ten car bombs exploded in Shia areas of Baghdad, killing at least 40 people; the attacks reflected a marked increase in sectarian violence in Iraq since April 2013, with around 1,000 casualties recorded each month.

NOVEMBER 2013

15. Forty-three people were killed and around 300 others injured in Tripoli, Libya, when militias fired on crowds that were demonstrating in an anti-militia protest; the government responded by ordering all militia groups to leave by 24 November. **17.** In Damascus, Syria, around 31 people died in a bomb attack on a government building. **19.** In Lebanon,

around 23 people were killed and over 150 injured after two suicide bombs detonated outside the Iranian embassy in Beirut; the jihadist group Abdullah Azzam Brigades claimed responsibility for the attack. **23.** At least 40 people died in government airstrikes on the Syrian city of Aleppo. **24.** A six-month interim deal was struck between Iran and six major world powers; Iran agreed to halt uranium enrichment and submit to an intrusive nuclear inspection regime in exchange for access to around $4.2bn (£2.5bn) of frozen assets and an ease in international restrictions on certain trades. Egypt introduced a restrictive new law banning public protests without prior notification of the police.

DECEMBER 2013

2. In Syria, opposition fighters abducted 12 Greek Orthodox nuns from the town of Maaloula, then demanded that the regime release 1,000 female prisoners in exchange for their return. **4.** Hassan al-Laqqis, a commander of the Shia militant group Hezbollah, was assassinated in Beirut, Lebanon; two Sunni groups claimed responsibility for the murder. **5.** At least 56 people died in an attack by al-Qaida militants on a hospital in the Defence Ministry complex in the Yemeni capital, Sanaa. **12.** Fifteen people, at least 12 of whom were civilians, were killed after a US drone mistakenly targeted a wedding party near the town of Rada, Yemen. **15–24.** Hundreds of Syrian civilians were killed in indiscriminate 'barrel bomb' airstrikes by government forces in the city of Aleppo. **16.** Over 70 people died in four separate sectarian attacks across Iraq; many of those targeted were Shia pilgrims or members of the security forces. **24.** An explosion at a security building in the Egyptian city of Mansoura killed 12 people and injured around 100 others; Ansar Beit al-Maqdis, a group affiliated with al-Qaida, claimed responsibility, but the government blamed the Muslim Brotherhood and used the incident to justify further crackdowns. **25.** At least 35 people were killed in Christmas Day bomb attacks in Christian areas of the Iraqi capital, Baghdad. **27.** In the Lebanese capital, Beirut, a car bomb killed 62-year-old Mohamad Chatah, a senior adviser to prime minister Saad Hariri and vocal opponent of Shia Hezbollah; six other people died and around 50 were injured in the attack.

JANUARY 2014

1. The UN reported that 7,818 civilians were killed in Iraq over the course of 2013, the highest casualty rate since 2008. **3–9.** Around 500 rebel fighters died in Syria during factional fighting between the extremist group the Islamic State, IS, (formerly known as the Islamic State of Iraq and the Levant ISIL/ISIS) and a *de facto* alliance of other nationalist and Islamist opposition groups; IS was driven from its strongholds in Raqqa and Aleppo and at least 50 prisoners were freed. **4.** The Iraqi government lost control of areas of the Anbar province, including the city of Fallujah, to an insurgency by the al-Qaida-affiliated IS. **5–8.** Around 30,000 African asylum seekers, primarily from Sudan and Eritrea, protested in Tel Aviv, Israel, against the government's stance on immigration. **11.** The former prime minister of Israel, Ariel Sharon, died of organ failure at the age of 85 after spending eight years in a coma. **14–15.** Egypt held a referendum on a new constitution preserving the military government's power; despite campaigns against its adoption being suppressed, which resulted in at least nine deaths and 300 arrests, the vote saw a 38.6 per cent turnout with 98 per cent of voters backing the new constitution. **15.** At least 75 people died in a string of car bomb and suicide attacks across central Iraq. **17.** In Kabul, Afghanistan, 21 people died when a Taliban suicide bomber and several gunmen attacked the Taverna du Liban, a restaurant popular with foreign nationals. **22–31.** The Geneva II Conference on Syria was held in Switzerland with the aim of discussing the Geneva Communique, a political transition plan that aimed to end the ongoing civil war; the talks were largely unsuccessful with only the safe passage of women and children trapped in the besieged city of Homs agreed upon.

FEBRUARY 2014

10. Twenty-two men died after a device exploded in an extremist training camp in Baghdad; 23 others were arrested shortly afterwards. **10–15.** A second round of Syrian peace talks were held in Geneva, but no progress was made. **16.** Four tourists died in a militant attack on a bus in Egypt's Sinai peninsula; the terrorist organisation Ansar Beit al-Maqdis claimed responsibility. **20–25.** Pakistan launched a series of air strikes against militant hideouts in tribal North Waziristan on the Afghan border; around 45 militants were reported to have died in the attacks. **24.** Egypt's interim government unexpectedly resigned amid a series of strikes, although no official reason was given; three days later, Field Marshal Abdul Fattah al-Sisi resigned his position in order to stand for the presidency.

MARCH 2014

5. Saudi Arabia, Bahrain and the United Arab Emirates jointly withdrew their ambassadors from Qatar over its alleged interference in their internal affairs. **11.** The Libyan parliament dismissed prime minister Ali Zeidan after a tanker bearing the North Korean flag broke through a naval blockade erected to prevent the exporting of oil from rebel-held ports; Zeidan ignored a travel ban and fled the country. **16.** Syrian government forces retook the rebel-held town of Yabroud, effectively bringing the border between Syria and Lebanon under government control for the first time since 2011. **18–31.** At least 63 people died across Afghanistan in a string of Taliban suicide bombs and armed assaults designed to disrupt proceedings and deter voters from attending upcoming elections; the targets included a luxury hotel in Kabul and the headquarters of the election commission. **24.** An Egyptian court sentenced 528 members of the Muslim Brotherhood (see 23 September) to death in a mass trial; only 147 defendants were present at the hearing, while the rest were convicted in absentia.

APRIL 2014

3. The UN announced that the number of Syrian refugees in Lebanon had exceeded a total of 1 million. **4.** An estimated 20,000 Shia protestors marched in Bahrain to demand democratic reform days before the country's annual Formula 1 race. **9.** In Aleppo, Syria, the Carlton Hotel was bombed by the Islamic Front, killing a number of government forces; the hotel had been used by pro-Assad forces as a barracks. **11.** The government of Kuwait ordered a news blackout of a court case investigating an alleged attempt to overthrow the government. **13.** The former prime minister of Israel, Ehud Olmert was sentenced to six days in prison and fined 1m new shekels (£171,000) by an Israeli court for accepting an £86,000 bribe from the developers of two building projects. **20.** Yemini air strikes killed around 30 suspected al-Qaida members in the country's mountainous southern area. **22.** In Bahrain,12 men were sentenced to life in prison after being convicted of spying on behalf of Iran. **24.** Hamas and Fatah signed a reconciliation pact with the aim of establishing a single government for both Palestinian territories.

MAY 2014

3. In Egypt, 100 Muslim Brotherhood members were each sentenced to ten years in prison on charges ranging from killing to inciting violence. **7.** Raif Badawi, the founder of the Free Saudi Liberals website, was found guilty of insulting Islam and sentenced to ten years in prison, 1,000 lashes and orderd to pay a fine of 1m riyals. **21.** Former Egyptian president Hosni Mubarak and his two sons Alaa and Gamal were convicted of embezzling public funds and sentenced to three and four year jail terms respectively; Mubarak and his sons were all fined $3m and ordered to repay the $17.6m they allegedly stole. **25–26.** Pope Francis stirred up controversy during his visit to the Middle East when he prayed in front of an Israeli separation barrier seen by some as an obstacle to the free movement of ordinary Palestinians. **28.** In Libya, troops loyal to Khalifa Haftar bombed a government-funded Islamist militia in Benghazi; Haftar was a former army chief of staff under Col. Muanmar al-Gaddafi.

JUNE 2014

2. In Tehran, a sandstorm with wind speeds of up to 70mph killed four people and caused wide-spread power outages. **3.** In Saudi Arabia, authorities revealed that Middle East Respiratory Syndrome (MERS) has killed more people than 688 people since 2012, which was more than previously thought. In Iraq, at least 14 people died when a car bomb exploded outside a hospital in the predominately Shia city of Hilla. **5.** The Islamist group IS began a major offensive in Iraq, capturing the city of Samarra in the north; Iraq's second city Mosul was predominantly controlled by the group from 9 June. **8.** A wave of car bombings occurred across Iraq, killed 60 people; Anbar University in Ramadi, Iraq was seized by Sunni militants. **11.** In Iraq, IS captured Tikrit, the birth place of Saddam Hussein. **21.** Syrian government jets killed at least 16 Islamists near the border with Iraq. **12–30.** Three Israeli teenagers were kidnapped in the West Bank, instigating a major security operation by the Israeli Defence Force (IDF) that resulted in the recovery of the teenager's bodies on 30 June near Hebron; Israeli prime minister Bejamin Netanyahu blamed Hamas for the deaths. **27.** In Syria, 140 schoolboys aged 14 to 16 were abducted by IS militants to serve as child soldiers. **28.** Between 160 and 190 mainly Shia civilians were executed by IS militants in Tikrit. **29.** IS declared the establishment of an Islamic caliphate after capturing Syrian and Iraqi territory; the group's leader Abu Bakr al-Baghdadi was proclaimed the 'caliph'.

JULY 2014

1. The USA deployed additional helicopters, drones and 300 soldiers in Iraq due to mounting security concerns. **2.** Approximately 45 people were killed in clashes between Iraqi security forces and followers of Shia cleric Mahmoud al-Sarkhi in the city of Karbala. **2–5.** The body of a 16-year-old Palestinian child was found in a forest near east Jerusalem; the murder was thought to be a revenge attack relating to the killing of 3 Israeli boys in June. **5.** In Yemen, government forces bombed Shia insurgents, killing 70 people. **8–29.** The IDF launched operation Protective Edge on Gaza to find the killers of the three Israeli teenagers (see June 30); Hamas reacted to the military incursion by firing rockets into Israeli civilian areas and by July 29, the conflict had killed over a thousand people, with the vast majority being civilians. **25.** At least 13 Palestinians died and 200 were injured after a UN school was attacked in error; both Israel and Hamas denied attacking the school. **28.** In Libya, heavy fighting between government forces and rebel groups created two large fires in a 1.6 million gallon petrol storage facility; the Libyan government requested international assistance to prevent an explosion. **30.** In Gaza, a second UN school used by Palestinian refugees was hit by an airstrike killing 15; Israel accused Hamas of deliberately fighting near civilian areas.

OBITUARIES 2013–14

Ashcombe (4th), Lord, aged 89 – *b*. 31 March 1924, *d*. 4 December 2013

Attenborough, Lord, CBE, actor and Oscar-winning film director and producer, aged 90 – *b*. 29 August 1923, *d*. 24 August 2014

Avery, James, American actor, aged 68 – *b*. 27 November 1945, *d*. 31 December 2013

Awoonor, Kofi, Ghanian poet, teacher and diplomat, aged 78 – *b*. 13 March 1935, *d*. 21 September 2013 in the Nairobi Westgate Mall terrorist attack

Ballyedmond, Lord, OBE, entrepreneur and politician, aged 70 – *b*. 5 January 1944, *d*. 13 March 2014

Baltacha, Elena, Ukrainian-born tennis player, aged 30 – *b*. 14 August 1983, *d*. 4 May 2014

Banerjee, Sushmita, Indian writer and activist who documented the plight of Afghan women under the Taliban, aged 49 – *b*. 1963/4, *d*. 5 September 2013

Bannside, Revd Lord (Ian Paisley), PC, leader of the Democratic Unionist Party (1971–2008); First Minister of Northern Ireland (2007–8), aged 88 – *b*. 6 April 1926, *d*. 12 September 2014

Barry, Kate, photographer, aged 46 – *b*. 8 April 1967, *d*. 11 December 2013

Batten, Sir John, KCVO, specialist in chest diseases and cystic fibrosis and Physician to the Queen (1974–89), aged 89 – *b*. 11 March 1924, *d*. 7 October 2013

Bellany, John, CBE, Scottish painter, aged 71 – *b*. 18 June 1942, *d*. 28 August 2013

Benn, Tony (Anthony Wedgwood), politician: Labour MP for Bristol South East (1950–60, 1963–83) and Chesterfield (1984–2001); Secretary of State for Industry (1974–5) and Energy (1975–9), aged 88 – *b*. 3 April 1925, *d*. 14 March 2014

Biggs, Ronnie, thief who was convicted for his part in the Great Train Robbery (1963) but escaped prison and was a fugitive until 2001 when he returned to the UK, aged 84 – *b*. 8 August 1929, *d*. 18 December 2013

Bilston, Lord, Labour Co-op MP for Wolverhampton South East (1987–2005), aged 71 – *b*. 26 August 1942, *d*. 25 February 2014

Black, Charles, chair of A & C Black publishers (1973–2000), aged 76 – *b*. 4 May 1937, *d*. 9 October 2013

Boscawen, Robert, PC, Conservative MP for Wells (1970–83), Somerton and Frome (1983–92); Lord Commissioner of HM Treasury (1981–3); Vice-Chamberlain of HM Household (1983–6) and Comptroller (1986–8), aged 90 – *b*. 17 March 1923, *d*. 28 December 2013

Brabham, Sir John (Jack), OBE, Australian racing driver and Formula 1 champion (1959, 1960 and 1966), aged 88 – *b*. 2 April 1926, *d*. 19 May 2014

Butler, Sir Michael, GCMG, Ambassador and Permanent UK Representative to European Communities, Brussels (1979–85), aged 86 – *b*. 27 February 1927, *d*. 24 December 2013

Caro, Sir Anthony, OM, CBE, sculptor, aged 89 – *b*. 8 March 1924, *d*. 24 October 2013

Chevron, Philip, musician, aged 56 – *b*. 17 June 1957, *d*. 8 September 2013

Christie, Sir George, opera festival director; chair of Glyndebourne (1958–99), aged 79 – *b*. 31 December 1934, *d*. 7 May 2014

Clancy, Tom, American author, aged 66 – *b*. 12 April 1947, *d*. 1 October 2013

Coase, Prof. Ronald, DSc, economist and winner of the Nobel Prize in Economic Sciences (1991), aged 102 – *b*. 29 December 1910, *d*. 2 September 2013

Coleman, David, OBE, sports presenter and commentator, aged 87 – *b*. 26 April 1926, *d*. 21 December 2013

Cross, Ulric, DSO, DFC, Trinidadian wartime RAF navigator, judge and diplomat (High Commissioner in London, 1990–3), aged 96 – *b*. 1 May 1917, *d*. 4 October 2013

Curtiss, Air Marshal Sir John, KCB, aged 88 – *b*. 6 December 1924, *d*. 14 September 2013

Curwen, Sir Christopher, KCMG, Chief of the Secret Intelligence Service (MI6) (1985–8), aged 84 – *b*. 9 April 1929, *d*. 18 December 2013

Dolby, Ray, American audio engineer who invented his eponymous NR (noise reduction) technology eliminating the background hiss on tape recordings, aged 80 – *b*. 18 January 1933, *d*. 12 September 2013

Domínguez, Oralia, Mexican operatic contralto, aged 88 – *b*. 25 October 1925, *d*. 25 November 2013

Eusebio (Eusebio da Silva Ferreira), Mozambican-born Portuguese footballer, aged 71 – *b*. 25 January 1942, *d*. 5 January 2014

Everly, Phil, American singer, aged 74 – *b*. 19 January 1939, *d*. 4 January 2014

Finney, Sir Thomas (Tom), CBE, footballer, aged 91 – *b*. 5 April 1922, *d*. 14 February 2014

Fontaine, Joan, British-American actor, aged 96 – *b*. 22 October 1917, *d*. 16 December 2013

Fortune, John, satirist and actor, aged 74 – *b*. 30 June 1939, *d*. 31 December 2013

Fox, Frederick, LVO, royal milliner, aged 82 – *b*. 2 April 1931, *d*. 11 December 2013

Fyjis-Walker, Richard, CMG, CVO, diplomat, Ambassador to Sudan (1979–84) and Pakistan (1984–7); chair of the Commonwealth Institute (1988–93), aged 86 – *b*. 19 June 1927, *d*. 17 September 2013

Giger, H. R. (Hans Ruedi), Swiss Surrealist painter, sculptor and set designer, aged 74 – *b*. 5 February 1940, *d*. 12 May 2014

Goggins, Paul, PC, Labour MP for Wythenshawe and Sale East (1997–2014); Parliamentary Under-Secretary of State: Home Office (2003–6), Northern Ireland Office (2006–7); Minister of State, Northern Ireland Office (2007–10), aged 60 – *b*. 16 June 1953, *d*. 7 January 2014

Hallam, Chris, Paralympic athlete, aged 49 – *b*. 1 January 1964, *d*. 16 August 2013

Hamilton, Chico, American jazz drummer, aged 92 – *b*. 21 September 1921, *d*. 25 November 2013

Hancock, Sir David, KCB, civil servant, aged 79 – *b*. 27 March 1934, *d*. 5 September 2013

Hayhoe, Lord, life peer and Conservative MP for Heston and Isleworth (1970–4); Brentford and Isleworth (1974–92), aged 88 – *b*. 8 August 1925, *d*. 7 September 2013

Hitchen, Brian, journalist; editor of the *Daily Star* (1987–94), aged 77 – *b*. 8 July 1936, *d*. 2 December 2013

Hoggart, Simon, journalist and broadcaster, aged 67 – *b*. 26 May 1946, *d*. 5 January 2014

Hornby, Sir Derek, businessman, chair of Rank-Xerox (UK) (1984–90), aged 83 – *b*. 10 January 1930, *d*. 16 December 2013

Hoskins, Bob, actor, aged 71 – *b*. 26 October 1942, *d*. 29 April 2014

Howard, Elizabeth Jane, novelist, aged 90 – *b*. 26 March 1923, *d*. 2 January 2014

Hubel, David, Canadian-American neurophysiologist; joint winner of the Nobel Prize for Physiology or Medicine (1981), aged 87 – *b*. 27 February 1926, *d*. 22 September 2013

Inglis, Brand, antique silver dealer and expert on the *Antiques Roadshow*, aged 74 – *b*. 31 May 1939, *d*. 18 August 2013

Jacobs, David, CBE, broadcaster; presenter of BBC television series *Juke Box Jury* (1959–67), aged 87 – *b*. 19 May 1926, *d*. 2 September 2013

Kagan, Saul, Lithuanian-born executive director of the Conference on Jewish Material Claims Against Germany (1952–98), aged 91 – *b*. 20 July 1922, *d*. 8 November 2013

Kavanagh, Patrick, CBE, QPM, Deputy Commissioner, Metropolitan Police (1977–83), aged 90 – *b*. 18 March 1923, *d*. 11 December 2013

Kiel, Richard, American actor best known for his role as 'Jaws' in the *James Bond* films, aged 74 – *b*. 13 September 1939, *d*. 10 September 2014

Kilar, Wojciech, Polish composer and film score writer, aged 81 – *b*. 17 July 1932, *d*. 29 December 2013

Kimball, Lord, Conservative MP for Gainsborough (1956–83), aged 85 – *b*. 18 October 1928, *d*. 26 March 2014

Kindersley (3rd), Lord, merchant banker, aged 84 – *b*. 18 August 1929, *d*. 9 October 2013

Kingsdown, Lord, KG, PC, Governor of the Bank of England (1983–93), aged 86 – *b*. 5 January 1927, *d*. 24 November 2013

Klein, Lawrence, economist; winner of the Nobel Prize in Economic Sciences (1980), aged 93 – *b*. 14 September 1920, *d*. 20 October 2013

Le Quesne, Sir Godfray, QC, judge of Courts of Appeal of Jersey (1964–97); Chair, Monopolies and Mergers Commission (1975–87), aged 89 – *b*. 18 January 1924, *d*. 2 October 2013

Lessing, Doris, CH, author and winner of the Nobel Prize for Literature (2007), aged 94 – *b*. 22 October 1919, *d*. 17 November 2013

Lloyd-Pack, Roger, actor, best known for his role as 'Trigger' in TV sitcom *Only Fools and Horses,* aged 69 – *b*. 8 February 1944, *d*. 15 January 2014

Mandela, Nelson, OM, South African anti-apartheid revolutionary and politician: President, African National Congress, 1991–7; President of South Africa, 1994–9 and Nobel Peace Prize laureate (1993), aged 95 – *b*. 18 July 1918, *d*. 5 December 2013

Mayall, Rik, comedian and actor, aged 56 – *b*. 7 March 1958, *d*. 9 June 2014

Mera, Rosalía, seamstress who co-founded the Spanish fashion chain Zara, aged 69 – *b*. 28 January 1944, *d*. 15 August 2013

Morley, Lewis, photographer, aged 88 – *b*. 16 June 1925, *d*. 3 September 2013

Neuberger, Prof. Michael, immunologist, aged 59 – *b*. 2 November 1953, *d*. 26 October 2013

Sumner, Sir Christopher, High Court judge (1996–2008), aged 73 – *b*. 28 August 1939, *d*. 12 August 2013

O'Toole, Peter, actor, aged 81 – *b*. 2 August 1932, *d*. 14 December 2013

Parker, Eleanor, American actor, aged 91 – *b*. 26 June 1922, *d*. 9 December 2013

Pillinger, CBE, planetary scientist known for his 2003 attempt to land the *Beagle 2* probe on Mars, aged 70 – *b*. 9 May 1943, *d*. 7 May 2014

Pollock, Charles, American industrial designer, aged 83 – *b*. 20 June 1930, *d*. 20 August 2013

Pollock, Ida, romantic novelist, aged 105 – *b*. 12 April 1908, *d*. 3 December 2013

Ramis, Harold, American actor, aged 69 – *b*. 21 November 1944, *d*. 24 February 2014

Réchatin, Henri, French funambulist, aged 81 – *b*. 12 March 1931, *d*. 27 December 2013

Reed, Lou, singer and songwriter, aged 71 – *b*. 2 March 1942, *d*. 27 October 2013

Rees, Prof. David, FRS, mathematician, aged 95 – *b*. 29 May 1918, *d*. 16 August 2013

Resnik, Regina, operatic soprano and mezzo-soprano, aged 90 – *b*. 30 August 1922, *d*. 8 August 2013

Rivers, Joan, American actor and comedian, aged 81 – *b*. 8 June 1933, *d*. 4 September 2014

Roberts of Conwy, Lord, PC, Welsh Conservative MP for Conway (1970–83) and Conwy (1983–97); Parliamentary Under Secretary of State (1979–87), Minister of State (1987–94) Welsh Office, aged 83 – *b*. 10 July 1930, *d*. 13 December 2013

Rogers, Paul, actor, aged 96 – *b*. 22 March 1917, *d*. 6 October 2013

Rosenthal, Tom, publisher, aged 78 – *b*. 16 July 1935, *d*. 3 January 2014

Sanger, Dr Frederick, OM, CH, CBE, FRS, biochemist who twice won the Nobel Prize for Chemistry (1958, 1980), aged 95 – *b*. 13 August 1918, *d*. 19 November 2013

Seymour Hoffman, Philip, American actor, aged 46 – *b*. 23 July 1967, *d*. 2 February 2014

Sharon, Ariel, Prime Minister of Israel (2001–6), aged 85 – *b*. 26 February 1928, *d*. 11 January 2014

Sharp, Martin, Australian artist famed for his 1960s psychedelic album covers, aged 71 – *b*. 21 January 1942, *d*. 1 December 2013

Shaw, Sir Run Run, CBE, Chinese-born Hong Kong film and television mogul, aged 106 – *b*. 23 November 1907, *d*. 7 January 2014

Siebert, Muriel, financial dealer and first female board member of the New York Stock Exchange (1967), aged 80 – *b*. 12 September 1932, *d*. 24 August 2013

Sinden, Sir Donald, CBE, actor, aged 90 – *b*. 9 October 1923, *d*. 11 September 2014

Soames, Lady, KG, DBE, aged 91 – *b*. 15 September 1922, *d*. 31 May 2014

Sollit, Brian, chocolatier who invented the After Eight mint, aged 74 – *b*. 16 November 1938, *d*. 16 July 2013

Stoker, Sir Michael, CBE, FRS, virologist and cancer biologist, aged 95 – *b*. 4 July 1918, *d*. 13 August 2013

Szarewski, Dr Anne, clinician and researcher who made key advances in preventing, researching and raising awareness of cervical cancer, aged 53 – *b*. 1 September 1959, *d*. 24 August 2013

Tavener, Sir John, composer, aged 69 – *b*. 28 January 1944, *d*. 12 November 2013

Temple, Shirley, American actor, aged 85 – *b*. 23 April 1928, *d*. 10 February 2014

Templeman, Lord, MBE, PC, Lord of Appeal in Ordinary (1982–94), aged 94 – *b*. 3 March 1920, *d*. 4 June 2014

Torday, Paul, author, aged 67 – *b*. 1 August 1946, *d*. 18 December 2013

Townsend, Sue, author, best known for creating the character of Adrian Mole, aged 68 – *b*. 2 April 1946, *d*. 10 April 2014

Tracey, Stan, OBE, jazz pianist and composer, aged 86 – *b*. 30 December 1926, *d*. 6 December 2013

Twisk, Russell, editor of BBC magazine *The Listener* (1981–7) and UK *Reader's Digest* (1988–2006), aged 71 – *b*. 24 August 1941, *d*. 4 August 2013

Vo Nguyen Giap, Gen., Vietnamese military leader, aged 102 – *b*. 25 August 1911, *d*. 4 October 2013

Wheeler, Geoffrey, television presenter who presented *Songs of Praise* (1965–85), aged 83 – *b*. 24 September 1930, *d*. 30 December 2013

Wheldon, Dame Juliet, DCB, QC, Treasury Solicitor and Head of the Government Legal Service (2000–6), aged 63 – *b*. 26 March 1950, *d*. 2 September 2013

Williams, Robin, American actor and comedian, aged 63 – *b*. 21 July 1951, *d*. 11 August 2014

Wilkes, Gen. Sir Michael, KCB, CBE, Adjutant-General (1990–5), aged 73 – *b*. 11 June 1940, *d*. 27 October 2013

Woodland, Rae, operatic soprano, aged 91 – *b*. 9 April 1922, *d*. 12 December 2013

Zaentz, Saul, American Oscar-winning film producer and record company owner, aged 92 – *b*. 28 February 1921, *d*. 3 January 2014

ARCHAEOLOGY

Dr Nadia Durrani and Dr Neil Faulkner

THE FIRST FOOTPRINTS

Excavations by the Ancient Human Occupation of Britain Project at Happisburgh on the Norfolk coast have continued to astonish. Boxgrove in Sussex was an archaeological sensation half a generation ago with the discovery of hominid remains predating the great Anglian glaciation of c. 478,000 to 424,000 BC; it was believed that there had been no hominid presence in the British Isles until after this. Then came fresh discoveries at Happisburgh that virtually *doubled* the antiquity of the earliest hominid presence. Now the same site – where excavations are ongoing – has revealed no fewer than 49 certain footprints of hominids preserved in soft estuarine clay that has been exposed on an eroding shoreline. In at least one case, four of the individual's five toes can be made out, and at least five individuals are represented, both adults and children; 80 flint tools have been recovered nearby, and the dating evidence for these is between 850,000 and 950,000 BC.

The site is located at the former estuary of the Thames, dating from a time when it followed a radically different route from today, passing across East Anglia. But who were these early Thames mudlarks? The Natural History Museum's Chris Stinger says there are only two known candidate species: *Homo erectus* and *Homo antecessor*. The former is mainly a species of the Far East, whereas remains of the latter have been found at Atapuerca in Spain dating from around 800,000 BC. So, based on the present stage of knowledge, the likelihood is that the Happisburgh footprints, and the associated flint tools, were made by a group of *Homo antecessor* hunter-gatherers. They were present during a relatively warm phase – soon after, Britain would have become too cold and inhospitable for early hominids and the descendants of the Happisburgh group would have retreated southwards and eastwards. Only very much later, with the development of the cold-adapted and culturally inventive Neanderthals, would it become possible for hominids to remain permanent residents so far north.

Fast forward to 400,000 BC – still very much in what counts as 'Lower Palaeolithic' (pre-Neanderthal) – and archaeologists have other news to report. After nine years of research on a site excavated at Ebbsfleet in advance of the High Speed 1 railway from St Pancras to the Channel Tunnel, the most sensational discovery was the skeleton of an elephant, found associated with the flints used by local hominids to butcher the animal. The event occurred during the Hoxnian Interglacial, a warm spell around 425,000 to 375,000 BC. As well as 80 or so flints found in close association with the elephant, there were approximately 1,900 more in the immediate vicinity, along with thousands of other animal bones – rhinoceros, lion, red deer, roe deer, early wild cattle, even macaque monkey. The killers were almost certainly members of the *Homo heidelbergensis* species, a close cousin of *Homo erectus*. What the Ebbsfleet project has demonstrated is the previously unsuspected intensity of Lower Palaeolithic activity in Britain, and the determination with which early hominids organised and equipped themselves to pursue, kill and butcher some of the biggest and most formidable beasts of their age.

THE ORIGINS OF STONEHENGE AND SILBURY

In May 2000 it was discovered that a huge hole had opened at the top of Silbury Hill, the famous Neolithic mound near Avebury in Wiltshire. This subsequently widened alarmingly, and it became clear that it represented the top of the vertical shaft into the mound that had been dug by Colonel Edward Drax, an antiquarian scholar, in 1776. This in turn alerted the English Heritage authorities to the possibility that other cuttings into the mound over the years might also represent structural weaknesses. Between 1968 and 1970, for example, prehistorian and archaeologist Richard Atkinson had dug a horizontal tunnel across the base of the mound, eventually connecting at the centre-point with Drax's vertical shaft. Sure enough, when the locked door of Atkinson's tunnel was opened, it was found that back-filling had been rudimentary. Effective sealing of the openings became an urgent priority to prevent the possible collapse of Silbury Hill.

This, though, provided an opportunity for reinvestigation of the interior of the monument, and the results of this are now available. Two remarkable discoveries were made. First, from the carefully observed stratigraphic sequence along the line of the Atkinson tunnel, it is now clear that the mound was created incrementally, rather than being a single monumental construction project, and that there appears to have been no original intention of creating something the form and size that we see today. This observation seems confirmed by a second discovery, based on a new analysis of the dating, which has shown that work on Silbury Hill continued for between 55 and 155 years. The lesson seems to be that, in relation to prehistoric ritual monuments, process was more important than outcome. Each visit – once or twice a year, perhaps at critical moments in the annual cycle – seems to have left its residue of building activity at the site, without this necessarily ever being part of some grand plan to create a prestige monument.

There is news, too, from nearby Stonehenge. The main monument stands, of course, within an extensive ritual land-scape to the west of the River Avon. Recent excavations at Blick Mead, an ancient spring and pool beside the river, have produced startling evidence for activity long predating the Neolithic/Early Bronze Age main phases at Stonehenge. An extraordinary haul of more than 30,000 pieces of Mesolithic worked flint in a small area of sample excavation – representing a density of well over 1,000 pieces per square metre – have been recovered. In addition, over 1,000 fragments of animal bone, 60 per cent of it aurochs, an extinct species of giant wild cattle, had confirmed the site as one of feasting. The date range of the material covers much of the Mesolithic, the radiocarbon determinations extending from 7596–7542 BC to 4803–4702 BC. Moreover, in addition to the everyday flint-work, the assemblage includes some special finds: a unique red sandstone object worked on all sides and a Horsham point made from green slate. Both use material alien to the site and this, combined with a curious characteristic of the water in the pool, makes it likely that ritual activity took place here. A combination of dappled light, algae and the water's unusually constant temperature of 10–14°C causes submerged stones to take on a striking, bright pink hue. Perhaps the site was multi-dimensional: the water and vegetation attracting wild animals, the hunters lying in wait here to make their kills, and the whole community gathering periodically to feast on aurochs and make sacrifice to the spirits of the spring.

Meantime, Tim Darvill and Geoffrey Wainwright have been continuing their explorations on the Preseli Hills in Wales, the place from which Stonehenge's famous bluestones' were transported more than 200km. For some time, their ideas have been throwing new light on the complex layers of meaning represented by Europe's greatest prehistoric monument. The stones, they maintain, come from a wide area of the hills, but always from locations associated with springs and watercourses, many of which were believed to have healing properties in medieval and later times. Darvill and Wainwright contend that the 'bluestone phase' in the development of Stonehenge – which post-dates the erection of the famous sarsens – implies its conversion from cremation cemetery into healing sanctuary. They are not implying a radical and clearly defined change of purpose, rather a gradual change of emphasis, all perhaps under the aegis of the same deities, the gods of sun and moon in relation to whose movements the great monoliths appear to be arranged.

THE FIRST FARMERS

Neolithic houses are relatively rare discoveries, so the results from a 34-hectare investigation at Kingsmead Quarry near Horton in Berkshire by Wessex Archaeology, which uncovered four (possibly five) Early Neolithic examples, are of national importance. Only two dozen or so houses of this date are otherwise known to British archaeology. Two construction styles are represented. Two of the Horton houses are no more than groups of post-holes, while two others have beam-slots. The houses ranged in size from 7.7m by 5.5m to 15m by 7.5m, appear to have had internal partitions and the associated finds strongly imply that they were used for domestic occupation, since potsherds, worked flints and animal-fragments were found in the beam-slots, as if swept there in domestic cleaning. Dating was done using radiocarbon determinations taken from the charred remains of cereals and nuts found in one of the houses, and these came out at 3710–3650 BC.

The Horton discoveries will no doubt take their place in the data sets at the heart of a major argument about the British Neolithic triggered by the publication of *Gathering Time*, a collection of fine-tuned radiocarbon date determinations based on the use of Bayesian statistics. Alex Bayliss, Frances Healy, Alasdair Whittle and many other contributors to the new dating now see the British Neolithic as the result of an intrusion by a relatively small number of migrants arriving in Kent in the years around 4100 BC. Within 8–12 generations, they argue, people all over the British Isles had adopted domesticated plants and animals, learned how to make pots, to mine flint and stone (rather than collecting it on the surface), to make leaf-shaped arrowheads and polished axeheads, to build rectangular buildings and to construct cairns, barrows and ditched enclosures.

This conclusion has, however, been challenged by Scottish archaeologist Alison Sheridan, who argues that no single, simple, linear process of change can account for all the data, including data generated by the Gathering Time authors themselves. For example, there is clear evidence for the use on sites far distant from Kent of domesticated cattle and continental-style pottery and burial monuments several generations before the supposed arrival of the Neolithic 'pioneers'. Sheridan's view is that there never was a single 'founding migration', but that instead, between c. 4300 and 3800 BC, a whole series of separate small-scale migrations took place, some resulting in successful Neolithic colonisation, others in failure. Not only that but, in a strange echo of other debates about whether the cross-Channel route or the Western-coasts route was decisive in terms of

continental influence on developments in the British Isles, Sheridan argues that some of the earliest settlers established themselves at locations like Ferriter's Cove on the westernmost point of the Dingle Peninsula in Ireland's County Kerry. The debate erupted at a debate on the origins of the British Neolithic hosted by the Royal Archaeological Institute in January 2014 and looks set to run and run.

THE NEW FACE OF SILCHESTER

Silchester *(Calleva Atrebatum)* is one of Roman Britain's most important sites. Major excavations between 1890 and 1909 produced a famous plan of all the stone buildings in the town – though the excavators were later criticised by Mortimer Wheeler (indefatigable archaeologist of 'Animal, Vegetable, Mineral' fame) for having 'dug it like potatoes'. Since 1997 it has been the subject of another long-term research project, this time led by Mike Fulford and Amanda Clarke of Reading University, and this mammoth investigation of a single *insula* (town block) ended this summer. The project has transformed understanding of the origins and development of the Roman town, and thrown fresh light on Romano–British urbanism as a whole.

Silchester is a green-field site: it has never been built on since it was abandoned around AD 400. This means that entire areas can be opened to excavation; archaeologists are not dependent on the accidental snapshots of buried evidence permitted by redevelopment in modern urban centres. The medieval and modern replacement for Silchester is Reading, so the site is in the local university's backyard and has been mainly a summer student dig. Modern research excavation is painstaking, aiming to maximise data recovery, so despite spending a total of 108 weeks digging over 18 years, with up to 130 participants at any one time, the excavators have uncovered only about a quarter of one *insula* (Insula IX) – effectively the area of one large building (House 1) and its immediate environs. But the quality of data recovered is unsurpassed for its intimate detail.

Insula IX was chosen because House 1 was known to be misaligned with the Roman street-grid, while others conformed to it. Why might this have been so? Were the apparently empty areas on the 1890–1909 excavation plan really empty or had the earlier work missed all the timber buildings? And it was in Insula IX that a famous stone dating from some time after AD 400 and inscribed with the name Tebicatus in Ogham script had been found. What was it doing there, and might the find-spot shed light on the little-known 5th century history of the site? An additional aim was to recover information about the Iron Age (pre-Roman) activity of the settlement, as Silchester was a major Late Iron Age *oppidum* – an extensive defended settlement – that was even bigger than the Roman town. What was it like, and how did the transition from Iron Age *oppidum* to Roman town happen?

Only in the last few years have the excavations reached these lower levels and allowed an opportunity to answer these questions. Archaeologists have discovered a succession of three great timber halls, the last measuring 23m by 12m, and the second (still under excavation) at least 44m in length, and dating from turn of the 1st century BC/1st century AD. What is more, the excavations in Insula IX have confirmed the impression from earlier work by Mike Fulford (carried out in the 1980s on the site of the forum-basilica complex in the town centre) that the Iron Age town was laid out on a regular grid of straight streets and right-angled corners. The implication is that pre-Roman *Calleva* – the seat, presumably, of a Celtic ruler – was a highly organised and relatively sophisticated community, with large rectangular halls placed within a symmetrical arrangement of thoroughfares and side-streets.

The Iron Age town clearly influenced the layout of the Roman town. It has long been known that the later Roman walls mirror the lines of earlier earthworks. What is now apparent is that House 1 in Insula IX is misaligned with the Roman street-grid but is on the same alignment as its timber predecessors. House 1, in other words, is a replication in stone of Iron Age timber halls. No less curious is the fact that all the timber round-houses known so far at Silchester *post-date* the Roman Conquest; archaeologists have yet to show that a single one existed beforehand. In a sense, in the late 1st century and into the early 2nd century, Silchester seems to have become more characteristically 'native' in its appearance than before. Worth noting too is the seeming continuity of Iron Age ritual practice. Complete pots, sometimes deliberately pierced (to 'kill' them and allow them to pass to 'the other side'?), were placed in the bottoms of wells in the Iron Age and the same practice seems to have continued throughout the Roman period. Indeed, the famous Ogham stone had been placed at the bottom of a well, alongside a pierced pewter flagon, perhaps as late as the early 6th century.

One major result of the 1997–2014 Silchester excavations, therefore, is a blurring of the cultural lines, a breakdown of the former sharp distinction between Iron Age/Celtic culture and Roman 'civilisation' in Britain. The implications of this massive (and massively important) project will be the stuff of conference debates for years to come.

THE MAKING OF ENGLAND

Since its discovery by a metal-detectorist in 2009, the Staffordshire Hoard, a fabulous assemblage of almost 4,000 pieces of 7th-century metalwork, has intrigued archaeologists. Does this cache of weapons and ornaments, finely fashioned by top craftsmen in gold, silver and garnets, represent a magnificent votive offering, a chieftain's war-chest, or even the lost hoard of a metalworker who suffered some fate that precluded his return to recover it? A two-year intensive programme of conservation, cataloguing and detailed study, funded by English Heritage, National Geographic and the hoard's joint owners, Birmingham Museums Trust and the Potteries Museum and Art Gallery in Stoke-on-Trent, may finally be shedding light on this question.

Many of the objects bear unmistakable evidence of violence. Some fragments have been chopped up with little regard for their decoration. Some garnets are snapped in half. Many pieces reveal knife-marks where they have been prised from rivets. A silver bracket has been cleft in two with a sword or an axe. Hilt plates and sword pommels appear to have been wrenched off. Also telling is that the assemblage appears to have accumulated over time, representing not a single event, but a series of events, perhaps a succession of victorious battles during which rich booty had been taken. Combined with the lack of skill and method represented by the damage, the impression now is that the Staffordshire Hoard is a warrior lord's haul of spoil. This, though, does not rule out a ritual purpose in its deposition. The very fact that it was placed in the ground and never recovered may imply a deliberate intent to leave it there, perhaps as an offering to a deity, even a war deity, to whom honour was due in the twilight of Early Anglo-Saxon paganism, before the final triumph of the Christian Church.

Sutton Hoo is also associated with Anglo-Saxon treasure, but in this case we know the reason: it is the burial place of the first English kings – for Raedwald, the occupant of the famous ship burial with its fabulous treasure, was not only King of East Anglia but also *Bretwalda* ('Overking') of all the English. The early 7th-century burial was excavated in 1939 and, to mark the 75th anniversary, the newly reopened British Museum's Early Medieval Europe gallery has given the Sutton Hoo treasure pride of place. The assemblage is rich in anthropological significance, the rank and status of the owner symbolised by the wealth of material, the quality of the craftsmanship, the diversity of the places from which it had been imported and for the distinctive *Romanitas* of so much of it. Early Medieval rulers liked to dress up as Romans. Raedwald covered himself – in life and in death – in Roman bling.

But where was the grand residence? Where was the court? Anglo-Saxon sources refer to a 'royal village' at Rendlesham, and the Venerable Bede informs us that King Swithelm was baptised there in the mid 7th century. Rendlesham still exists, and near the modern village lies plough-land which has become a magnet for 'night-hawks' – looters with metal-detectors working illegally. Alerted to this by the local landowner, Suffolk County archaeologists organised a systematic investigation of the site. Over five years, an official metal-detecting team spent almost 200 days surveying the site. Finds were plotted, retrieved, and identified. What they indicated was a high-status community of 6th to 8th century date occupying a settlement area of up to 50 hectares. Small-scale trial excavations then confirmed the presence of Anglo-Saxon buildings. It now seems certain that archaeology has located the site of the first English royal court.

Rendlesham can now take its place in a map of Middle Anglo-Saxon settlement archaeology that is perhaps becoming somewhat less obscure. The period has for a long time been plagued by a desperate lack of clear thinking, with specialists refusing to interpret evidence and generate hypotheses, and instead falling back on such meaningless terminology as 'productive sites' (ie, sites from which large quantities of metalwork have been recovered). To be fair, part of the problem has been the sheer quantity of excavation data locked away in the under-researched – and quite often literally inaccessible – 'grey literature' created by commercial rescue-archaeology. Oxford University's John Blair has been trawling through this literature, recovering plans of Anglo-Saxon settlement sites, and among his findings is strong evidence for the systematic use of standard measures in the layout of settlement grids and the design of buildings. The measures in question were the perch and the four-perch module. The perch measured 15ft in Kent and East Anglia and 18ft in Wessex (and then became 16.5ft by way of compromise later). Blair has revealed that an astonishing number of settlements seem to have been laid out in this way, implying that official surveyors were at work, Anglo-Saxon equivalents of the more familiar Roman *agrimensores*.

Blair's work seems to complement that of University College London's Andrew Reynolds, who has argued that settlement grids are a feature of the Middle Anglo-Saxon period and that this reflects a growing concern with the definition of property and personal obligations, tighter elite control over land, labour and resources, and an increasingly complex, top-down, class-based society. Thus Anglo-Saxon settlement archaeologists are beginning to fill out the picture of how, especially during the 7th, 8th and 9th centuries, the creation of the Anglo-Saxon kingdoms, the rise of the Christian Church and the parcelling out of land in the form of great estates remodelled the English landscape and gave it its distinctive medieval form.

RICHARD III REVISITED

Summer 2014 saw the opening of Leicester's £4m King Richard III Visitor Centre. The new venue is the centrepiece of a series of local regeneration projects linked to the 2012 discovery of a body, believed 'beyond reasonable doubt' to be that of Richard III. Occupying the old Leicester Grammar

School, the centre tells the story of the last medieval king and of the archaeological detective work – including DNA analysis of Richard's 17th-generation nephew, Michael Ibsen – that led to the body's identification. The centre overlooks Leicester Social Services' former car park, where the king's body was found, and this is cleverly harnessed by the Centre: down a series of stairs, a new extension has been built right over the findspot, allowing visitors to view the still-open grave, preserved beneath a ventilated Perspex floor. The grave itself has been artfully flanked by modern bronze plaques engraved with extracts of a prayer from the Lambeth Book of Hours, thought to have been composed by Richard, and said to have once adorned a now-lost monument erected by Henry VII over the grave of his defeated foe. This makes for a poignant reminder that, behind the dramatic events of the Wars of the Roses, and the equally remarkable story of Leicester's Grey Friars 'Car Park King' excavation, there lies a human being.

It is exceedingly rare for archaeologists to find a named individual such as Richard III. And this has led to no end of questions about what should be done with the body or where it should be buried. After months of heated Judicial Review, it has been ruled that Richard III will be reburied in Leicester Cathedral in 2015. Richard's new tomb is currently being designed by architects van Heyningen and Haward, and shall be hewn from a block of Swaledale fossil stone, quarried in North Yorkshire. Roughly the size and shape of a sarcophagus, it will be mounted on a plinth of darker Kilkenny marble, decorated with the details of Richard's name, dates, coat of arms and his personal motto, *loyaulte me lie* ('loyalty binds me'). Richard is due to attract an estimated 100,000 visitors per year, making him perhaps one of our hardest-working royals.

THE NEW SAINSBURY EXHIBITIONS GALLERY AND THE VIKINGS
The British Museum opened its new Sainsbury Exhibitions Gallery, the museum's first purpose-built venue for major displays. Tucked unobtrusively into the far corner of the museum's magnificent Great Court, the gallery space is essentially a blank canvas of unembellished walls, which can be adapted to any new exhibition. The first exhibition to be featured there was 'Vikings: Life and Legend', the museum's first major treatment of the Vikings for 30 years. There was no wild innovation in the way that the objects were displayed within the new Gallery – largely inside glass boxes and with overly small information panels – however, the recreation of an entire Viking boat, Roskilde 6, right in the centre of the exhibition was undeniably impressive. Found in the late 1990s, enough of the keel survived to calculate an original length of 37m; though only portions of the boat's keel and hull survive, the remainder was evoked in metal, providing a potent impression of the ship's original scale and appearance.

In other Viking news, work on an extremely rare Viking cemetery at Cumwhitton, in Cumbria, came to an end with the publication of the post-excavation report by Oxford Archaeology. The cemetery was found in 2004 thanks to a metal detectorist, Peter Adams, who was out scanning farm land, with permission, when he found an unusual brooch. The local governmental Portable Antiquities Scheme officer identified it as a very rare Viking era brooch, of a type that is usually found in a pair and in the grave of women. A team from Oxford Archaeology therefore went to explore the site further. True to form, they found the grave. Unfortunately, the local Cumbrian soil is extremely acidic so the grave contained almost no bone. However, based on the grave goods – which included a maplewood box containing objects associated with textiles – they concluded that the burial was indeed almost certainly that of a high status female. The team then found a second grave containing 'female' grave goods, plus three other burials that contained a large number of weapons, and have been interpreted as men's graves. Analysis of the material suggests one, maybe two, generations of incoming Vikings. A single Viking-era grave is almost unknown from England, so to find a cemetery of five graves came as a complete surprise.

ARCHITECTURE

John Hitchman

STONEHENGE VISITOR CENTRE, NR AMESBURY, WILTSHIRE
Architect: Denton Corker Marshall

Decades after the visitor facilities at Stonehenge, built in 1968, had earned their derogatory description as 'woefully inadequate' and 'a national disgrace', and after four architectural competitions and a catalogue of negotiations, planning setbacks and funding failures, England's premier ancient monument finally acquired a new visitor centre worthy of its designation as a UNESCO World Heritage Site. The Stonehenge site has long suffered from the damaging immediacy of the traffic-laden A303 and A344 roads, the latter only narrowly missing the Heel Stone while cutting through the Avenue, the ancient processional way leading to the stone circle. This has now been partially addressed by the closure of the A344 and the site's reversion to a grassy downland landscape, coupled with the relocation of the visitor facilities and car park to a new site 1.5 miles away. The ambience of the location and the quality of the visitor experience has been transformed, although the A303 still remains at a slightly further distance, resistant to all attempts to hide it in a tunnel.

Edward Cullinan won the first architectural competition in 1992 with an earth-sheltered scheme located on military land to the north, but this did not find favour with the Ministry of Defence and the idea was shelved. After a second competition was abandoned at shortlist stage, a third was held in 2001 and won by Denton Corker Marshall with a scheme which relied for its funding on sinking the A303 trunk road into a tunnel. Predictably however, the tunnel failed to gain approval on cost grounds and in 2007 the proposed centre was consequently abandoned. Finally a fourth attempt was made in 2009 and this was also won by Denton Corker Marshall, resulting in the now-completed centre, located on a new site to the north-west of Stonehenge.

The new building sits in a hollow dip in the rolling landscape, completely isolated from the ancient stones. The design was heavily influenced by English Heritage's desire for a building that could be removed from the site with minimal disruption if the need arose, and the approach was also aimed at inflicting the least possible disturbance on an archaeologically rich landscape. Consequently, the centre sits lightly on the ground beneath an undulating and oversailing roof propped up on multiple slender steel columns, many of which are gently inclined as though to mimic the trunks of a grove of trees.

The building rises from a stone pavement of local limestone set on top of a concrete raft, to minimise the depth and penetration of the foundations. Sheltering clear beneath the oversailing roof and seemingly pinned in place by the proliferating roof supports, the centre's facilities occupy three stand-alone and contrasting blocks of accommodation. Two large pavilions – one glazed, the other solid –both square on plan but set slightly off-grid to one another, to counter any feeling of formal symmetry, contain the majority of the accommodation; in the space between the two, a much smaller kiosk houses the ticketing office and audio distribution point. Juxtaposing the different functions within three separate pavilions helps to reduce the visual scale of the centre and frees up the circulation patterns for visitors.

The glazed pavilion houses a large café, offering internal and external seating, a substantial shop and an education centre, all benefiting from expansive views to the east and west through full-height windows. These comprise floor-to-ceiling panes of clear low-iron glass, an expensive material which repays the investment by eliminating the green tinge characteristic of more conventional glasses.

The solid pavilion is primarily an inwardly focused museum, exhibition space and interpretative centre. The exhibition areas offer displays of artefacts from the site and a circular ante-room provides visitors with a 360° projection, simulating the view from the centre of the stones – an experience long since denied to most visitors. This opens out into the permanent exhibition tracing the history of Stonehenge and thence into a corner gallery housing temporary exhibitions. Externally, the pavilion is clad in vertical planks of pre-weathered sweet chestnut, a robust natural material handled very simply, except with openings treated as slightly bizarre punched holes capped by a ragged and uneven termination of the planks.

Overhead, the delicate steel-framed roof structure, notable for the thinness of its section, is clad with zinc sheeting on its underside and the outermost section around the perimeter is perforated with a random frit of punctured openings, a further visual metaphor for a canopy of trees, suggesting the dappled effect of sunlight through the leaf canopy.

The low-key simplicity of the pavilions, nestling under the almost tent-like roof, propped up on its forest of supports (211 in total), give the centre a self-effacing character almost to the point of being 'non-architectural'. This reflects entirely the thinking of English Heritage, which did not wish to see the centre become either an attraction in its own right or a challenge to the visual primacy of the ancient monument. It acts very much as a transition point where visitors are encouraged to step out of the modern world and take time to acclimatise to the landscape and contemplate the significance of one of the most famous historical sites in the world.

Visitors can approach the monument either on foot or by using a shuttle service, the route to the stones following the former line of the A344, now closed to traffic, reduced to a single track and integrated into the landscape. The National Trust-owned Fargo Plantation provides a half-way stop and is being developed into an information viewpoint from which to understand more about the dozens of earthworks visible in the immediate landscape.

The completed centre was an immediate success and appears to function well. It has seen a substantial increase in the number of visitors since opening in December 2013. The overall project cost of £27m covers a wide range of architectural and civil engineering elements, but included £6.9m for the centre itself, £1.1m for an ancillary building adjacent to the nearby coach park and £1.2m for works to the A344 access route and a security hub. Substantial support funding was received from the Heritage Lottery Fund, with further contributions from the Garfield Weston Foundation, the Wolfson Foundation and the Linbury Trust. Perhaps the only regret is that all the money spent and wasted during the project's grossly extended gestation period could have solved the problem of the intrusion of the nearby A303.

Fig. 1. Serpentine Sackler Gallery (south elevation), Zaha Hadid Architects

SERPENTINE SACKLER GALLERY, HYDE PARK, LONDON

Architect: Zaha Hadid Architects
Historic building work / restoration: Julian Harrap Architects and Liam O'Connor Architects

The temporary exhibition pieces occupying the area in front of the main Serpentine Gallery in London's Hyde Park and designed by signature names from the world of architecture have become an increasingly familiar summertime attraction since Zaha Hadid was selected for the Gallery's first such commission in 2000. The Gallery's companion building, The Magazine, has now undergone its own permanent transformation with the completion of a historic renovation and new extension project. This completes a 13-year cycle by virtue of Zaha Hadid again being responsible for design, this time for the major new intervention in the form of an extension wing that now houses a restaurant.

The Magazine, dating from 1805 and built originally as a gunpowder store amid fears of invasion during the Napoleonic War, comprised two massive brick barrel-vaulted spaces surrounded by a neo-classical façade, with corner pavilions and a colonnaded entrance. Formerly open, the spaces around the central Magazine have been roofed over and provided with long linear roof-lights, fitted with black-out blinds and external solar control louvres, to create a new wrap-around circuit of crisp white exhibition and gallery spaces opening into the vaulted volumes of the central brickwork core.

To the rear of the gallery, a new wing has been added in matching neo-classical style to accommodate office space, new toilets and service facilities. In order to maintain the integrity and cohesiveness of the circuit of galleries, an internal corridor passing through the new wing via an opening at the rear provides the only internal access route through to the project's main event, the new restaurant extension. There is thus no direct link between the two.

Compared with the classical restraint and symmetry of the Magazine's elevations, the new extension is a complete contrast, its voluptuous tent-like form oozing up and down around the perimeter and snuggling up to but not quite enveloping its historic counterpart. In that it appears lightweight and its enclosure is typical of tented forms of canopy, it in some ways maintains the established Serpentine formula of a contrast between the permanent and the temporary; if this latter impression is gained, it is because the considerable complexity and weight of the structural elements are cleverly concealed *(Fig. 1).*

The structure of the extension is an essay in tensile membrane construction, with the fabric envelope stretched between a wandering perimeter ring-beam and a series of internal upward-thrusting column supports to create a continuously undulating surface, both internally and externally. The volume is supported by five internal columns. However, these are no ordinary columns but are unique sculptural forms expanding as they rise from the floor and swelling into hollow oval forms as they punch through the inner ceiling membrane to form large sky-lights, allowing north-light to flood down through fritted glazing into the

restaurant. Prefabricated from a steel framework and finished in a smooth white fibre-reinforced plastic cladding, their form is reminiscent of white ceramic Chinese spoons, upended on their handles, each column held at an inclined angle by the tension exerted through the structural external membrane.

The perimeter ring beam is constructed from a variable-width ladder truss comprising two circular hollow steel beams connected by a series of struts. The ring beam structure is clad with a fibre-reinforced plastic over-cladding with a bull nose leading edge, like an aerofoil section, expanding and contracting as it snakes up and down in its progress around the perimeter. The leading edge touches the ground at three points, once each on the south, west and north faces, providing secure points of anchorage into piled foundations. There is a powerfully organic quality to the form and the shiny white undulations of the overhanging soffit, especially under certain lighting conditions.

Where the edge beam sweeps up to reveal the interior, a full-height glazed wall follows the curved profile of the plan as it swells out from the exposed brick facing of the Magazine's side wall to enclose the restaurant space. Constructed from low-iron glazing and braced by a sequence of low-iron laminated vertical glass fins, it provides unrestricted views, although these are not as extensive as they might ideally have been, given the substantial hedge that encloses the site at close quarters. As the membrane roof rises to offer a protective wing sheltering the original building, a narrow clerestory runs along the top of the gallery's external wall, providing a clear visual separation between the solidity of the restored historical core and the energy and exuberance of the extension.

While it is a pity that only the tent-like tops of the roof-light columns are visible from the park, the open frontage to the roadway as it crosses the Serpentine certainly allows the new extension to realise its dramatic impact to the full. This highly distinctive structure provides a valuable addition to the park's facilities and will no doubt add considerable impetus to the Serpentine Gallery's programme of exhibitions. Construction started on site in November 2011; the project cost £14.5m and was completed in September 2013.

THE REID BUILDING FOR GLASGOW SCHOOL OF ART, RENFREW STREET, GLASGOW

Architect: Stephen Noll Architects

Glasgow's city centre is home to many fine Victorian and early 20th-century buildings, but few can lay claim to quite such a high degree of familiarity and affection as Charles Rennie Mackintosh's celebrated School of Art. Perched on the hillside above Sauchiehall Street, with its famous tall-windowed sandstone elevations and wonderfully handcrafted wrought ironwork, facing onto Renfrew Street, it has long been the beating heart of one of the UK's most highly regarded art colleges. Facing it across the street, the run-down accommodation provided by the 1960s Newbery Tower and Foulis Building had, years earlier, been earmarked for redevelopment. A controversial architectural competition launched in 2009 for a replacement building on the site, thereby laying down a daunting challenge for would-be architects to design a substantial new building on a site of considerable sensitivity and significance.

The competition was won by US practice Stephen Holl Architects. The winning presentation and proposals derived considerable inspiration from Mackintosh's handling of light and Holl's approach to design, which typically focuses on the use of light internally. The resulting building, completing the first phase of the college's master plan for the campus, opened its doors in April 2014. Shortly afterwards, Mackintosh's masterpiece was cruelly devastated by fire (though thankfully it seems that the damage is not irreparable). Despite significant and irreplaceable losses, the weather-beaten sandstone façade of the old building has survived and will continue to provide robust visual contrast in opposition to its unrelentingly slick, smoothly engineered and rather overbearing new counterpart across the street.

The new building rises to five storeys, with a two-storey basement, and accommodates a variety of studios and workshops, teaching facilities and seminar rooms, an auditorium, exhibition areas, offices, and dining and catering facilities. Its undeniable bulk, concealed behind glass-skinned elevations, looms over the street in a no-nonsense confrontation of scale and form and, despite some bold modelling of the façade, makes no concessions to the immediate context, set against the presence of the Art Nouveau building opposite.

Given a demanding brief and with a large amount of accommodation to cram onto the site, daylight, and the means of securing its penetration deep into the interior, was one of the major determinants of the building's internal organisation. The major spaces of the studios and workshops are placed mainly along the north side, with large banks of sloping windows taking advantage of the north light, while other key areas such as the refectory, public cafe and exhibition areas are ranged along the south-facing Renfrew Street frontage. Occupying the mid-zone, a central circuit of routes links all the component elements through a complex interweaving of voids, balconies, ramps and stairs, providing a meandering route up and through the various levels. Functioning in many ways like a very linear form of atrium, the space is punctuated by three regularly spaced inclined cylinders of concrete, described by the architect as 'driven voids of light'.

Rising full height from ground to roof level, these coincide with the major structural system of concrete cross-walls, spaced apart at centres reflecting the studio module width of 15m. The underlying simplicity of the structural order is subverted by the many slots and openings cut into the tightly curved walls of the 'voids' and the cut-away sections of the cross-walls themselves. The circulation route rises through the levels via a mix of horizontal balconies, gently sloping ramps or flights of stairs. As the concrete enclosures to the 'voids' penetrate the roof plane, they are cut back on the south side and the sides and top are glazed, enabling more daylight than would penetrate through a flat skylight to be funnelled down to the lower levels.

The interior is an exciting and visually stimulating experience, with the 'circuit of connection' (as the architect describes it) linking all the different functions and providing multiple opportunities for overlooking and social interaction as it wends its way up through the central void. As it engages with the refectory areas in the middle layers, the cut-back frontage provides views out over the old School and daylight floods the central zone. Wall surfaces are white, and three different patterns of balustrade are utilised. These include simple metal mesh panels, solid white concrete

upstand walls and, most distinctively, unframed vertically cantilevered glass panels of a luminous turquoise hue with stainless steel patch fixings supporting the handrails. The flying soffits of staircase elements are enlivened with a stepped profile, mirroring the steps.

Daylight never reaches the lowest levels however, as the tubular voids are floored over at ground level, though the structural elements continue their path through the basement levels, albeit with the angle of inclination reversed, where they continue to exert an influence on the internal planning.

Externally, the building's appearance is a complete contrast to its famous counterpart, a smooth pale blue/grey glazed skin wrapped around the underlying volumes, devoid of detail or architectural references. Four different types of glass are used to provide varying degrees of transparency and translucency, and different responses to both daylight and artificial light. On the Renfrew Street façade, the frontage at second- and third-floor levels is substantially recessed. The heavy modelling is introduced partly as a means of reducing the overall scale, and also enables the refectory/dining areas to enjoy generous views out over a landscaped terrace towards the studio windows of the Mackintosh building.

The main entrance is off-centre, recessed and tucked in beside the other unusual feature of the new development – the retained 1930s Keppie and Henderson-designed Student Assembly Building. Now a Student Union bar and entertainment venue, its articulated stone façades are now firmly enveloped within the oversailing glazed embrace of the new Reid building as the upper floors project over the top. At the western extremity, a section of the glazed façade extends down in front of the building to pavement level in order to provide a line of structural support that conceals an escape staircase.

The recessed modelling of the front façade, together with the inclined north-facing windows of the studios, find expression on the gable elevations at either end, which give a strong pointer to the internal cross-section and the organisation of spaces, but the elevations otherwise remain inscrutable, all being concealed behind the ubiquitous glass rain-screen cladding. Despite considerable controversy surrounding the design, an inevitable consequence of its size and historical context, there can be no doubt that the future well-being of the college has been assured by the facilities offered within Stephen Holl's confident and thoroughly contemporary design.

SAW SWEE HOCK STUDENT CENTRE, LSE, SHEFFIELD STREET, LONDON
Architect: O'Donnell + Tuomey Architects

Despite its international reputation as a prominent London institution, the disparate collection of buildings occupied by the London School of Economics (LSE) has not hitherto seen the School's academic distinction reflected in the quality of its architecture. This has changed with the addition of this new student centre, named after its generous benefactor. It is a visually stunning and distinctive, if eccentric, intervention into the tightly knit streetscape to be found lying just behind the major urban arteries of Aldwych and Kingsway.

The design emerged as a result of an architectural competition held in 2009, with a brief to design 'the best student building in the UK'. The finished article has faithfully delivered what was proposed in the winning design: a highly sculpted form, its sloping surfaces clad in red hand-made bricks, its folded shape derived from the three-dimensional contours of space prescribed by the requirements of rights-to-light envelopes originating from the neighbouring buildings. Its abstract form is thus a direct response to context, though not in a visible way, and the

Fig 2. Saw Swee Hock Student Centre, LSE (east elevation), O'Donnell + Tuomey Architects

material used is a familiar one, but its treatment is anything but traditional in its detailing, with conventional situations such as window openings being handled in unconventional ways, and the cladding material being asked to perform in ways it is not normally required to.

The folded inclined planes of the brick façade enclose a complex and multi-functional interior comprising a wide array of different uses, arranged over seven storeys above ground and a double-height basement storey with mezzanine. The different uses accommodated reflect the full range of non-academic functions that are a necessary corollary of student life. They include a pub, café, media centre, prayer rooms, student union office, gym, roof-level coffee bar and roof garden terrace.

All these disparate functions find their various niches in a series of apparently chaotic floor plans that are substantially different at every floor level. A free-form central core of circulation and meeting spaces links the floors together, with a generous angular winding staircase providing visual interest as it progresses up through the interior. Brightly lit and with glazed screens offering views both into different parts of the building and out into the streets, the staircase is anchored by the core of two lifts, which provides the one constant orientating element running the height of the building. The absence of any clearly defined structural or organisational order renders the interior very much like a microcosm of the wider London scene, with its organic street pattern and accidental angles and shifts of axis, the vagaries of the public realm finding an equivalence in the permeability and apparent un-plannedness of the interior spaces.

The transition from public to non-public domain is moderated by the utilisation of hard, workmanlike materials and a mix of finishes designed to resist the predictable degradations of heavy use. The main stair is paved with terrazzo, within concrete balustrades, while the lift shaft core is encased in multi-coloured vitreous enamel panels capable of resisting the inevitable rash of notices and posters. Elsewhere, hardwood flooring provides a robust but warm finish and exposed brickwork reappears in some areas. Given the diversity of the plans, the structure is a pragmatic mix of systems, including prefabricated concrete panels, *in situ* concrete floors and tubular steel columns, with deep steel trusses providing the transfer structure necessary to achieve the clear spans required for the basement-level events space and for the gym on the fourth floor.

The real tour de force of this imaginative design lies in the folded angular planes of the external brickwork skin. The design of this has received an obsessive amount of detailed attention to ensure that the complex geometry could be achieved. The task required the creation of some 88 'specials' and 'special specials', bricks other than standard that were designed to deal with particular angles and complex junctions *(Fig. 2)*.

The resulting construction includes not only plain solid brickwork, laid to Flemish bond, but incorporates panels of hit-and-miss stretcher work, forming a brise-soleil screen in front of windows set back within the internal substructure and at other points turned into blind panels, the hit-and-miss design infilled with recessed bricks to create a patterned effect.

The main entrance sits within a triangular recess created by a series of inward turning folds in the external skin and is sheltered by a tall sloping glazed canopy, again triangular in shape and supported by pairs of dark-red painted tubular steel struts. Behind the canopy, the interiors are opened up to public view and daylight through timber-framed and slatted glazed screens that emerge above the canopy line in a triangular infill that continues right through to the top floor. The relatively few but substantial areas of window wall, cut into the folds of masonry, comprise the only alternative external finish to the brickwork. The design generates a sense of dramatic purposefulness as a result, a coherent and unified concept carried through with conviction.

Completed in December 2013, after a two-and-a-half year construction period, the centre cost £24m. Along with the undisputed quality and originality of the design, the building achieved the other major strand of the client's brief by gaining a BREEAM 'outstanding' environmental rating. This highly distinctive and sophisticated building is popular with students and has raised the architectural profile of the LSE.

CITY LIBRARY, CENTENARY SQUARE, BIRMINGHAM
Architect: Mecanoo

Proposals for a new City Library for Birmingham were first aired in 1998, at a time when significant changes were being implemented throughout the city. The Dutch firm, Mecanoo, was appointed in 2008 to develop proposals for a new library on a site on Centenary Square, formerly a car park, immediately next to the Birmingham Repertory Theatre.

After a four-month period for transfer of the library contents and staff relocations, the finished building opened to the public in September 2013 and is set to join some other notable Birmingham structures that have acquired iconic status, such as the silver disc covered Selfridges Store at the Bullring and the infamous Spaghetti Junction confluence of motorways. Viewed from the paved expanses of Centenary Square, the controversial and unconventional design looks like a pile of gaudily wrapped gifts. A series of simple box-like volumes, piled on top of each other, is enveloped in an all-encompassing skin of layered gold and blue/grey cladding overlaid with a persistent patterned mesh of black and silver aluminium rings, and topped off with a golden drum-shaped 'pill-box' hat. The jazzy elevations certainly generate a contrasting ambience to that of its immediate neighbours, the gently swelling concrete and glass façade of the 1971 Repertory Theatre, with which it is contiguous, to the west, and the neo-classical solemnity of the 1938 Baskerville House across the road to the east. Nevertheless, the new addition succeeds in tying the three major buildings together in a more unified manner than was previously the case.

The new library, which many have suggested might be the last of its kind in view of its size and the ever-more influential impact of technology on the way we access information, is huge, containing 35,000m^2 of floor space, and was realised at a project cost of around £190m. This figure includes costs of refurbishment of the auditorium and new back-of-house facilities for the Repertory Theatre as well as a new shared 300-seat studio theatre in a joint redevelopment that fully integrates the new library with the existing theatre building. The library accommodation is spread over ten floors, with a number of mezzanine levels adding complexity to the section. Consistent with the external image of piled up boxes, the floor plates diminish in area at the upper floor levels, forming a loose asymmetrical ziggurat.

The internal space is organised around a substantial and dramatic circular atrium, its voids varying in size and disposition at differing levels to create a dynamic and spectacular interior as it rises through the full height of the building towards a large skylight. The principal feature of this space is the book rotunda, occupying the middle levels, where full-height book shelves line the circular space which is accessed from galleried walkways with interconnecting steel stairs. The extensive floor plates around the rotunda provide areas for study, with open-access book stacks, group and private study areas, a gallery and reading lounges. At level three, the building steps back on two sides to create a landscaped roof terrace with views of the city.

Much attention has been given to the lower levels, with the exploitation of intermediate mezzanine 'terraces' to make the transitions up and down easier and to integrate the double-height ground floor foyer area with the basement accommodation. Entering the library through the double-height glazed screen fronting the Square, sheltered under the cantilevered overhanging projection of the lowest of the stack of 'boxes', the visitor is confronted by a double bank of escalators directly ahead, climbing through the circular opening of the atrium to the first floor.

The sequence of descending terraces continues with further escalators down to the children's library and music library, which by now is extending out underneath the paved surface of Centenary Square. At the end of this sequence of library areas, a circular amphitheatre has been cut through to the square above, with an adjoining performance space and a sequence of music practice rooms. The library thus cleverly reconnects with the public realm

through the large open well created in the square, enabling non-users to interact with activities generated from within.

Above the book rotunda, two levels of archive space encircle a different configuration of the atrium. These floors provide a climate-controlled environment for the storage of artefacts and the library's massive archive of rare books, photographs and documents. These floors are expressed externally as the 'golden box' where the colour of the underlying cladding panels changes from the more widespread blue/grey colour to a bright golden hue.

Two further storeys, set back from the floor below on two sides to create another high level landscaped garden terrace, contain a floor for staff facilities and an upper level containing mechanical and air handling plant rooms. This topmost box is surmounted by the golden drum, which contains the Shakespeare Memorial Room, a reconstructed original interior from the 1882 Central Library, designed in High Victorian style by John Henry Chamberlain with a decorative vaulted plasterwork ceiling and timber panelled walls. A cylindrical glass wall climber lift rises within the upper atrium, providing access from level four to these upper levels.

The building combines many different functions within an overarching 'library' context and provides a wide range of internal environments whose utilitarian qualities are offset by the spectacular theatricality of the central void. This functions as a cleverly orchestrated device for bringing light to the lowest levels and playing spatial games with the primary circulation routes, as expressed through the flying escalators and bridge links criss-crossing the space.

Externally, the many functions have been unified through the use of the decorative filigree wrapping of layers of concentric aluminium circles, an inner layer of smaller silver circles overlaid with another of larger black ones, set against the regular modular panelled cladding. There is a diaphanous quality to the exterior, a blurring of edges that sets it apart from its more prosaic neighbours. Whether or not one accepts the validity of suggested symbolic associations with Birmingham's metal working and jewellery traditions, it is unlike any other library building and is totally distinctive.

AWARDS

THE RIBA STIRLING PRIZE 2013
Astley Castle, Nuneaton, Warwickshire (Restoration/Landmark Trust house); Witherford Watson Mann Architects

The Stirling Shortlist
University of Limerick Medical School; Grafton Architects
Park Hill, Sheffield (Housing); Hawkins/Brown with Studio Egret West
Newhall Be, Harlow, Essex (Housing); Alison Brooks Architects
Giant's Causeway Visitor Centre, County Antrim, Northern Ireland; Heneghan Peng Architects
Bishop Edward King Chapel, Ripon College, Cuddesdon; Niall McLaughlin Architects

RIBA LUBETKIN PRIZE 2013
Gardens by the Bay Cooled Conservatories, Singapore; Wilkinson Eyre

RIBA SPECIAL AWARDS 2013
The Manser Medal – Slip House, Brixton, London; Carl Turner
The Stephen Lawrence Prize – Montpelier Community Nursery, Kentish Town, London; AY Architects

BRITISH CONSTRUCTION INDUSTRY AWARDS 2013

Prime Minister's Better Public Building Award – Manchester Metropolitan University Business School & Student Hub; Feilden Clegg Bradley Studios

Major Project Award – The Shard, London Bridge; Renzo Piano Building Workshop/WSP Group

Building Award – Newlands School, Southwark, London; Wright & Wright Architects

Small Building Award – Bishop Edward King Chapel, Ripon College, Cuddesdon; Niall McLaughlin Architects

Sustainability Award – The Hive, Worcester University; Feilden Clegg Bradley Studios

RIAS AWARDS 2013

RIAS Andrew Doolan Best Building in Scotland Award – WASPS South Block, Glasgow; NORD Architecture

RIBA SPECIAL AWARDS 2014

Royal Gold Medal – Joseph Rykwert

CIVIC TRUST AWARDS 2014

Pro Tem Special Award – The Shed, City of London; Haworth Tompkins

Special Award for Sustainability – Halley VI Antarctic Research Station, British Antarctic Territory; Hugh Broughton Architects

Michael Middleton Award (Conservation) – Mary Rose Museum, Portsmouth; Wilkinson Eyre

Special Award for Community Engagement – Scale Lane Bridge, Kingston-Upon-Hull; McDowell + Benedetti

Special Award for Scotland – Notre Dame Primary School, Glasgow; Project Management & Design, GCC

National Panel Special Award – Bishop Edward King Chapel, Ripon College, Cuddesdon; Niall McLaughlin Architects

ART

Eddy Frankel

AUCTION HEROES

Auction houses proved themselves to be near enough recession-proof last year as they continued to smash all previous records while almost everyone else in the western world floundered and swam against the financial tide. Slight wobbles in the art market near the middle of 2013 led many to believe that the waves of the recession were finally lapping at the art world's shores. But how wrong they were. As the downturn cooled, profits at the big auction houses once again eclipsed everything that had come before and paintings sold for ever-more astronomical sums. In January, Christie's announced that its auction revenue for 2013 had come in at a shade above $5.9bn (£3.6bn), a record year with a 16 per cent increase on 2012 and a cool $800m (£481m) more profit than its main rivals, Sotheby's. That difference did not stop this from being Sotheby's most profitable year since the heady pre-recession days of 2007, though.

The big ticket sales of impressionist, modern and old master paintings may have been the headline news, but this year's good tidings came from the east. Both Sotheby's and Christie's held their first auctions in mainland China this year – previously, all sales in the region had taken place in Hong Kong – with each auction house pulling in close to $1bn (£600m) in Asia, a sharp increase on last year.

Private sales also helped to make this a record year, with Christie's reporting a 20 per cent revenue increase from the sector compared with 2012. Collaboration with independent dealers, such as Kenny Schachter, Louisa Guinness and Steve Lazarides, also reached unprecedented levels, with auction houses expanding their interests to cover parts of the market previously reserved for galleries.

But who needs clever overseas dealings and ingenious private sales when you can sell a Francis Bacon triptych for $142m (85m), as Christie's New York managed to do in November? The *Three Studies of Lucian Freud* – a series of stunning yellow and brown canvases depicting Bacon's good pal Freud in three similarly contorted poses – became the most expensive work of art ever sold at auction, reaching almost double its estimate. That night, Christie's topped $782m (£471m) (and managed to break another record when a Jeff Koons balloon dog went for $58.4m (£3.5m)), making it the most expensive work of art sold at auction by a living artist. Investing in Francis Bacon looks to be pretty much the shrewdest move that any art investor has ever managed as, only months later in February, a 6ft portrait of Bacon's lover, George Dyer, sold at Christie's in London for £42m; this also almost doubled its estimate, and it became the most expensive work of art ever auctioned in Europe.

It wasn't all record-breaking cheeriness though. Sotheby's found itself all in a tizzy as hedge fund manager Daniel Loeb took over a substantial stake of the company's shares and proceeded to attempt to shake some life into it by calling for CEO William Ruprecht to step down and overseeing the departure of the head of contemporary art, Tobias Meyer. Ruprecht held on for dear life, however, and the shake-up continues to reverberate.

Elsewhere, an 'unauthorised' sale of murals by cheeky British street artist Banksy raised all sorts of ethical questions, with the artist himself decrying the sale and exhibition of his works as nothing short of 'disgusting'.

Auction records for other younger artists varied wildly across the board as people opted for the safer 'blue chip' work of the likes of Bacon and Koons, making the art market seem like a trickier place to invest than many had thought. Other grumbles could be heard in West London when art collector Charles Saatchi decided to make the risky move of selling chunks of his collection without reserves or estimates. The gamble didn't pay off, with works by the Chapman Brothers among others being snapped up for what many considered to be a steal. Mere months later however and Saatchi's decision to sell Tracey Emin's famously unmade bed seemed like a smarter move as Jay Jopling, the founder of White Cube gallery, stepped in to purchase it for no less than £2.2m – close to double the estimate – prompting many clever curmudgeons to offer Jopling their own filthy mattresses for a fraction of the price. That evening's sale of contemporary art, which saw auction records for artists such as Michelangelo Pistoletto and Jean Dubuffet, marked a 42 per cent increase in profits from a similar sale last year.

The auction world, and the art market with it, emerged from the recession in rude health – a few bumps along the road seem to have done little to dent its fortunes. Can next year get even better? Or will the bubble pop?

GALLERY GAMES

There was turbulence in London last year as the recession's effects were felt in the commercial art world – galleries started falling like dominoes. But a reversal of fortunes this year has led to a more stable 12 months for most involved.

There were no major closures to report, but plenty of expansions. Big-shot New York dealer Marian Goodman announced plans for her first UK venture with a major new space in London's Golden Square, while the art world behemoth that is Larry Gagosian gave the go-ahead to start work on his third London gallery, a new 22,000ft^2 space at Grosvenor Hill. The London-based Lisson Gallery, meanwhile, decided that it was time to look Stateside, with plans to expand into New York for the first time. While everyone else was announcing and planning, Sadie Coles HQ actually made good on its intentions and opened an absolutely immense new gallery space in a former nightclub in the West End with a show of gooey-looking paintings by American artist Ryan Sullivan. Victoria Miro opened a new space in Mayfair to accompany her gargantuan gallery near Old Street.

The real talk of the town, however, was on the shifting centre of London's art world; the capital's galleries seem to move like the tides. Only last year, everyone was decrying the death of the East End as all of Hoxton and Bethnal Green's hip galleries were forced to move to the West End (poor them!) by rising rents and gentrification. Now, they all seem to have realised that central London is actually quite expensive too, and are tentatively feeling around town for new homes.

No one represents the shifting face of the London gallery scene quite like the aforementioned Victoria Miro. Starting out in Cork Street in 1985 – a road once lined with the best galleries in town and now lined with hotels and shops, mainly – she moved in 2000 to her warehouse space in trendy Hoxton and, in October 2013, back to Mayfair with a new space behind Sotheby's. The truth is, London's gallery scene is currently epicentre-less – though the fact that galleries are continuing to thrive in west, east and south London probably goes to show how healthy things are in the commercial art world right now.

It's not just London which was the recipient of a clutch of new galleries – the rest of England benefited too. Zurich- and London-based Hauser & Wirth opened a quaint space in Somerset in July with a show of works by Phyllida Barlow while, in November, Oxford became home to OCCA, a new gallery of contemporary Chinese art.

There was some rough to go with all that smooth, however, as art space The Wapping Project decided to shut up shop in December for rather depressing reasons – no, not rising rents, but a change of clientele due to the gentrification of the area, which had led to complaints from new neighbours about any sort of outdoor activities or exhibitions at the venue. Gallery director Jules Wright threw in the towel and decried that they simply could not operate as they were once able. Other bad news came in the form of London's most famous gallerist, Charles Saatchi, being photographed grabbing his TV-chef wife Nigella Lawson by the throat in a London restaurant. The ensuing media fallout put Saatchi in the spotlight for all the wrong reasons and left the art world squirming uncomfortably every time his patronage of the arts was mentioned.

CRIME AND PUNISHMENT

Art, as ever, reflected the strife, crime and scandal of everyday society during the year under review. In December, two Damien Hirst spot paintings, worth a combined £33,000, were stolen from a Notting Hill gallery in an audacious 3am raid. The suspect fled with his haul and is yet to be apprehended. Over in Folkestone, authorities managed to collar one of the prime suspects in 2012's Kunsthal Rotterdam heist of works by Gauguin, Picasso and Freud, among others, as he attempted to escape via Eurotunnel.

In France, it was decided that a forged Marc Chagall painting, owned by a British property developer and featured on the BBC's *Fake or Fortune?* programme, was to be burned like a witch, despite the fact that the owner was absolutely fine with it being a fake and really just wanted his painting back. The French said *'c'est impossible'* and took a torch to it anyway.

Restitution cases also loomed large over UK institutions this year as the Victoria and Albert Museum was ordered to return three Meissen porcelain figures to the heirs of the Hamburg-based Jewish collector who had originally owned them. The Tate was similarly told to return a Nazi-looted John Constable painting in March to the family of its original Hungarian owner.

The value of Rolf Harris' art, meanwhile, plummeted after the Australian entertainer's conviction on child abuse charges. Online auction site eBay was flooded with paintings by the disgraced artist, with some going for as little as £250.

The most shocking act of destruction of the year was accidental, as the Glasgow School of Art caught fire just before the end-of-year shows. Costs of restoring the iconic Charles Rennie Mackintosh building look set to exceed £35m, though students were offered a £750,000 fund towards replacing their lost work. There was, though, some good news for art lovers as the Mark Rothko painting which was senselessly vandalised in 2012 finally went back on display at Tate Modern following an 18-month, £200,000 restoration. A victory for paint over permanent markers.

MONEY TALKS

The most saddening news of the year came in the form of *The Guardian's* January announcement that 33,000 works of art and other culturally significant items had been lost to rich foreign buyers in the past year alone. Chief among these was Pablo Picasso's blue-period masterpiece *Child with a Dove*, on loan to the National Gallery and sold for a mere £50m to a Qatari investor. British institutions have long had to fight to save significant works of art from the hands of the rich – the National Gallery's successful, and hugely expensive, campaign to save Raphael's *Madonna of the Pinks* in 2004 for example, or the National Portrait Gallery managing to save a pivotal Van Dyck portrait only this May – but this year it looked like it was a battle that they may be starting to lose.

There was other bad news as the tightening of cultural belts continued to pinch at the waists of the UK's museums, institutions and local councils. The Royal Geographical Society was forced to sell paintings by Thomas Baines valued at £4.2m in order to plug a gaping hole in its pensions scheme, while Croydon Council hawked its collection of Chinese ceramics for £8m in a Hong Kong auction, supposedly to pay for renovations to its Fairfields Hall arts centre – though the Museums Association was quick to accuse the council of 'asset stripping'. Northampton Council similarly sold off a 2,000-year-old Egyptian statue for a whopping £16m at the start of July. More bad news came creeping in over the Irish sea, as plans were announced to convert the former barracks that played host to 2013's Turner Prize exhibition in Derry into an office block. Protests were ineffective. So much for the legacy of being named a UK City of Culture.

Controversy abounded at the Serpentine Gallery in Hyde Park when it announced new plans around Christmas for a full-time unpaid position. As if that wasn't bad enough, it was declared that same week that the gallery's two directors – Hans Ulrich Obrist and Julia Peyton-Jones – were to be awarded hefty pay rises. Protests were held against the free-labour plans (truly one of the most barbaric of art world practices) and the gallery duly capitulated; a good old-fashioned PR nightmare did the trick.

More positive news came in the form of various openings, re-openings and refurbishments. The Imperial War Museum re-opened in July after a £40m revamp with two exhibitions dedicated to its art collection, from stunning early 20th-century images by the likes of Wyndham Lewis to contemporary work by artists and photographers such as Mark Neville. The Serpentine inaugurated its impressive Zaha Hadid-designed Sackler Gallery in the autumn of 2013 with a show by those naughty provocateurs of the art-loving public, the Chapman Brothers, while in November, Leeds became home to The Tetley, a new contemporary art space housed in a former brewery. Tate Britain's £45m renovations, overseen by architecture firm Caruso St John, were completed in November with new classrooms, event spaces and a spiral staircase in the oldest part of the museum.

This year also saw Tate Britain conduct an ambitious rehang of its permanent collection that involved displaying work chronologically and doing away with explanatory wall panels, much to the consternation of the press and a great swathe of the visiting public. But few were as annoyed by this daring/stupid (delete as applicable) move as *The Sunday Times* art critic Waldemar Januszczak who, by April, had simply had enough, and published a scathing two-page missive calling for the head of gallery director Penelope Curtis.

Januszczak had facts to back up his attack, namely a 10 per cent drop in visitors, with Tate Britain dropping from 26th to 38th in the global visitor figures for 2013 (though the museum insisted that the decrease was due to the almost year-long refurbishment). But British institutions, including Tate Britain's younger sibling Tate Modern, still featured heavily in the top ten most visited museums in 2013, with the British Museum second only to the Louvre with

6.7 million visitors and the National Gallery not far behind with 6 million, according to *The Art Newspaper*. The UK's most popular paid exhibitions were the Royal Academy's survey of French master Edouard Manet's portraits, which brought in a grand total of 344,323 art lovers, and Tate Modern's survey of pop art pioneer Roy Lichtenstein's work, which attracted 315,814 visitors. Healthy viewing figures all round, despite the complaints of some critics.

Meanwhile, north of the capital, the Yorkshire Sculpture Park was awarded the £100,000 Museum of the Year prize by the Arts Fund thanks to a brilliant programme of exhibitions from the likes of Yinka Shonibare, Lynne Chadwick and Ai Weiwei. Out in the wild west of the country, Bristol City Museum became the recipient of a stencilled work of street art by Banksy – though for how long, it remains to be seen. The artist has stated that the image now belongs to the youth club on whose door it was painted, and they can do with it as they please. They plan to sell the work to raise much-needed funds for the club after having it valued (at around £400,000) by that ever-reliable old friend, *Antiques Roadshow*.

There was plenty of moving and shaking in the upper echelons of the art world this year with the announcement that the directors of the National Gallery and the National Portrait Gallery (Nicholas Penny and Sandy Nairne, respectively) were to step down. This still failed to top the biggest vacancy story of the year, as culture secretary Maria Miller was forced to relinquish her grip on the arts thanks to an ongoing, and very embarrassing, expenses scandal. The art world, however, was up in arms at her replacement, ex-banker Sajid Javid. Authors, playwrights and artists all raised their voices to question Javid's qualifications, with some calling him too 'uncultured' for the job of culture secretary. The last laugh, so far, was his though when, in June, Javid used a speech in Bristol to accuse the art world of elitism. Like a playground scuffle, all we can hope is that nothing much comes of it all.

ALL THE FUN OF THE FAIRS, AND THE FESTIVALS TOO

The answer to the seemingly eternal question of 'have we got enough art fairs yet?' remained a resounding 'not quite', as yet more temporary art bazaars popped up in the capital this year. New fairs included Start Art Fair at the Saatchi Gallery and the inaugural 1:54 fair of contemporary African art at Somerset House. Last year's Art13 morphed cleverly into Art14 and attracted a record number of visitors, while old favourites like Multiplied, PAD, Sunday and Masterpiece all continued apace.

Frieze, the biggest and sleekest name in the annual fairs calendar, held its second installation of the Frieze Masters sub-fair this year – dedicated to everything from old masters to the best modern art – to the usual applause alongside its regular contemporary art fair. The fair also announced plans to dedicate a section of next year's event to that most unsellable of art forms, performance, which should prove to be intriguing. But surely that's as far as it can go; surely we've reached art fair capacity? Nope, not if plans for a new photography fair next year, imaginatively titled Photo London, are to be believed, and we can certainly expect even more fairs to be announced over the coming months.

On the non-commercial end of the scale, the UK played host to two major art festivals this year. The 8th edition of the Liverpool Biennial saw an exhibition of esoteric works by the great 19th century American painter James McNeill Whistler alongside more contemporary offerings across the city and at Tate Liverpool. Glasgow International meanwhile went even further in cementing the Scottish city's status as the UK's 'other' centre of art – all but one artist on this year's Turner Prize shortlist went to the Glasgow School of Art – with a city-wide festival of starkly cutting edge art from the likes of Jordan Wolfson, Claudia Comte and David Shrigley.

WHO'D BECOME AN ARTIST?

It was a topsy turvy year for artists. The most amusing news came as Morrisons, the supermarket chain, received heavy criticism for projecting an image of a baguette onto the wingspan of Antony Gormley's iconic Angel of the North sculpture in an advertising campaign, with the artist himself describing the move as 'shocking and stupid'. The company soon apologised.

Grayson Perry became the first artist to deliver the BBC's annual Reith Lectures, using the opportunity to wax lyrical on what the art world is all about. The potter also received a CBE alongside various other illustrious awards to top off a watershed year. Other recipients of rewards during the year under review included Corin Sworn, who was awarded the Max Mara Art Prize for Women, while last year's winner, the UK-based French artist Laure Prouvost, was awarded the prestigious and always controversial Turner Prize. Last year's Turner Prize-winner Elizabeth Price won the Contemporary Art Society's annual award. All in all, a good year for women in an art world that is still largely male-dominated.

In public sculpture news, David Shrigley was announced as the 11th artist to be allowed to stake a claim on Trafalgar Square's fourth plinth with his giant thumbs-up design, while Richard Wilson unveiled his immense metallic sculpture *Slipstream* to the weary travellers of Heathrow's Terminal 2.

It just wouldn't be a year in art without a handful of plagiarism accusations. Damien Hirst had the copycat finger pointed at him by artist Jim Starr, who believed that Hirst stole his ideas when he styled Rihanna as Medusa for the cover of GQ. Everyone's favourite performance artist, Marina Abramovic, came to London this year to stage her new show, 512 Hours, at the Serpentine, and even before the doors had opened, was criticised for failing to acknowledge the 'inspiration' taken for the show from artist Mary Ellen Carroll. The problem is, Abramovic isn't actually doing anything in 512 Hours ... it's a show about nothing, literally. So can an artist own 'nothing'? It's just one of the many quite ridiculous questions that makes the art world so entertaining year after year.

BUSINESS AND FINANCE

Lisa Carden

Over the past 12 months, the UK economy has begun to gently shake off the cobwebs that have accumulated since 2007. The Coalition government's austerity agenda remains unpopular in many quarters, but there are signs of recovery. GDP has been on an upward trend and, as of April 2014, there were five consecutive quarters of growth. While the UK has not yet made up all of the ground lost during the financial downturn, it is now on course to do so in the next six months and the International Monetary Fund (IMF) expects UK growth to be 2.9 per cent in 2014 and 2.5 per cent in 2015.

There are still risks ahead, though. All parties are keen on a 'broad-based' recovery yet there is concern that 'bubbles' in some sectors, particularly the housing market in London and the South East, may be dangerous. House prices have been on such a steep upward curve in the past year – in July 2014 they passed their 2007 peak – that both the government and the Bank of England have stepped in to cool the situation: the Help to Buy scheme, which set out to help prospective purchasers of newly built houses up to the value of £600,000, has been pared back, and lenders have been told to limit the number of mortgages that are more than four-and-a-half-times the size of borrowers' salaries. Interest rates remain at a record low – they have been at 0.5 per cent for more than five years – but there have been intimations from the Bank of England that they may rise towards the end of 2014. Such a move would undoubtedly be a relief for savers and may help to put the brakes on what could be construed as a 'two-speed' recovery in which the more affluent areas of the UK, particularly London and the South East, are leaving the rest of the country for dust.

This situation is starkly illustrated by those households whose budgets have been stretched to breaking point, and particularly by the families that have turned to food banks for support. According to the charity that runs food banks, the Trussell Trust, more than 900,000 people used them during 2013–14; more than a third of those fed were children.

Leading food retailers have been buffeted by previously loyal shoppers looking for a better deal elsewhere, with Tesco suffering the most precipitous drop in popularity: profits fell for the second year in a row and its market share was the lowest for a decade at 28.6 per cent, according to industry data. Sainsbury's has had a roller-coaster year – quarterly sales fell in March 2014 but had regained their verve by June – while Morrisons limped from profit warning to profit warning. While all the major supermarkets have been rolling out a number of 'price-busting' offers, they are barely making a dent in the ongoing popularity of their low-cost continental rivals, Aldi and Lidl.

Unemployment has been on a general downward trend over the past year. As of the three months to the end of March 2014, 2.16 million people were out of work (6.6 per cent); rates for the previous two quarters had been 6.9 per cent and 7.1 per cent respectively. The relatively fragile nature of the economic recovery was manifest in seesawing news over the year regarding job losses and opportunities: for example, while Asda plans to create more than 12,000 positions as part of long-term expansion plans, Morrisons will shed more than 2,000 managerial roles. The finance industry continues to be turbulent on the job front; the investment arm of Barclays bank is axeing a staggering

19,000 jobs globally, with more than 7,000 of those redundancies to come in the UK by 2016.

One of the most important recent employment trends has been the rise of 'zero-hours' contracts, a hiring arrangement under which employers are not obliged to offer employees a minimum number of hours' work, but where employees agree to provide their services as needed and to be paid only for hours worked. In April 2014, data from the Office for National Statistics (ONS) showed that more than 1.4 million people were employed in this way in the UK, more than double the number previously thought. While the ONS estimates that 13 per cent of employers use zero-hours contracts, they are much more prevalent in some industries than others (they are particularly common among workers in the food and tourism sectors, for example).

While some view them as a way of working flexibly, they are far from universally popular: the Trades Union Congress is uneasy about their impact on career progression and fears that they will trap people (particularly the young) in poorly paid positions. There has been increasing disquiet about them in the Coalition government – Business Secretary Vince Cable recently introduced legislation to remove the exclusivity element of such contracts (ie, to allow staff working under such contracts to sign up for more than one employer) while the Labour Opposition is vehemently opposed to them; indeed, if the Labour Party returns to power at the 2015 General Election, zero-hours contracts will be outlawed.

A MIXED PICTURE ON THE HIGH STREET

Some of the best-known names in retail have had a mixed 12 months. Next, which was launched in its current incarnation in 1982, reached a milestone in March 2014 when its results showed that it was about to overtake the venerable Marks & Spencer in terms of profit for the first time. Next's annual profits were up by more than 10 per cent to £695m, while M&S's pre-tax figure was £623m. While M&S has again struggled to entice customers to anywhere other than the food hall, Next's decision to mix fashion with homeware and – crucially – to offer a range of other top brands' merchandise as part of its online operations – has left its rivals spluttering. Debenhams also had a turbulent year: a difficult Christmas and below-forecast clothing sales both contributed to a huge 25 per cent fall in half-year profits as of the end of March 2014.

As the brick and mortar stalwarts struggle to differentiate themselves from the immense source of choice represented on the internet, M&S has been attempting to catch up with its nimbler next-door neighbour. It has recently opened a new e-commerce distribution centre, radically revamped its website and, in June 2014, appointed its head of e-commerce, Laura Wade-Gery, as head of its UK retail stores.

March 2014 saw a worrying low for independent bookshops, which numbered fewer than 1,000 for the first time. High rents were thought to be one of the main reasons for the news, but the inexorable rise of online retailers and their competitiveness on price have clearly also played a role. Sales of printed books fell in 2013 – down almost £100m (6.5 per cent on 2012) – but two pieces of good news in the late spring brightened the picture considerably. First, the record-breaking crime author, James Patterson, announced a donation of £250,000 to independent bookshops in the UK and Ireland; Mr Patterson had previously donated

$1m (£600,000) to a similar scheme in the US. Second, Foyles, one of the biggest and best-known names in bookselling, opened a new flagship store in central London in June 2014. Spread over four storeys and 37,000 square feet, the new shop represents a bold statement of commitment to books and readers for many years to come.

A similarly bold move – albeit in a different sector – was announced by the clothing retailer, Primark, in June 2014 when it revealed plans to buy an entire shopping centre in Birmingham and turn it into one massive store. Popular with its young, cash-conscious and fashion-savvy customer base, Primark was founded in Dublin in 1969 but began operating in the UK two years later, where it now has more than 270 shops. It has expanded across Europe in recent years and is due to open a number of US stores by 2016. The chain's rapid growth has not been without controversy, however: despite joining the Ethical Trading Initiative in 2006, concerns have been raised about working conditions in some of its overseas suppliers' premises. In 2013, more than 1,000 workers died in a fire at a factory supplying Primark and other retailers, and the company contributed more than £7m to victims' families and the injured.

Another discount retailer, Poundland, is also eyeing bigger opportunities. One of the UK's fastest growing companies – and named 'Variety Discounter of the Year' at The Grocer Gold Awards – it reported sales of £758m over the 39 weeks to the end of December 2013. Upon its flotation on the London stock market in March 2014, its market value rose from £750m to £900m. Customer numbers have risen in recent years as consumers have attempted to make their money go further, and store openings in affluent locations such as Stratford-upon-Avon, Bath and Cambridge have shown that Middle England is not immune to the lure of 'everything for £1'.

Despite encouraging signs, the British retail sector is not yet fully out of the woods: the Confederation of British Industry announced in late June 2014 that sales were slowing, again prompting fears that the UK's recovery was still shaky. While the World Cup has provided a boost in some areas – TV sales have jumped, for example – there is a long road ahead.

A BITTER PILL
While mergers and acquisitions are a common feature of the economic landscape, rarely do they spill over into the political domain. That is exactly what happened in spring 2014, however, during the repeated attempts by the US pharmaceuticals giant Pfizer to buy the British–Swedish company AstraZeneca (AZ). While Pfizer is home to a stable of market-dominating drugs such as Zoloft, Viagra and Lipitor, it has been keen to shore up its pipeline (ie, potential future products) and had zeroed in on AZ as a means of doing that (particularly as the patents on several of Pfizer's products are about to lapse and the next best-selling alternatives are produced by AZ). A merger would have created the world's biggest pharmaceuticals company, but there was much anxiety about the potential sale from a variety of quarters. Unions were worried that UK jobs would be lost – while AZ has operations globally, it employs thousands of research and development staff in the UK – and Pfizer was unable to give a firm guarantee about their security; industry experts explained AZ's strategic importance for the British economy – it accounts for more than 2 per cent of the UK's total goods exports, selling billions of pounds worth of its products overseas annually; research scientists were alarmed at the potential loss of valuable research and development and intellectual property; and economists pointed out how much tax revenue would be lost if AZ were subsumed into a larger, US-based entity.

As offer and counter-offer were traded, the politicians stepped (or were dragged) in: the Coalition seemed to be at loggerheads – a spokesman for Prime Minister David Cameron stated that the government had no objections to a foreign buy-out of a British firm but Business Secretary Vince Cable said that intervention was not unthinkable – while the Labour Opposition suggested that the merger should proceed only if Pfizer undertook to safeguard jobs, protect research and development and invest for the long term in the UK. Ultimately, all the hot air was to no avail: the final Pfizer offer of £63bn was rejected by the AZ board at the end of April. It may not be the last that the company has seen of its international admirers, however.

Less contentious has been the merger of the electronics retailer Dixons and Carphone Warehouse, the mobile phone company. Bringing together high street stores with larger premises, typically on retail parks, Dixons Carphone (as the new entity will be known) looks set to capitalise on technical innovations and the public's continuing appetite for a range of mobile devices. The deal was rubber-stamped by the European Commission in late June 2014 and prior to signing the final contracts, both partners were thriving: Dixons, which also operates PC World and Currys stores, enjoyed a 53 per cent rise in pre-tax profits to the end of April of £133m; Carphone Warehouse's profits over approximately the same period were £67m, up 3 per cent on the previous year.

(COFFEE) GROUNDS FOR CELEBRATION … AND COMPLAINT
The British have never needed much of an excuse to take solace in a hot beverage. Our love of tea is well known, but coffee has been popular since the heyday of the London coffee houses in the 17th and 18th centuries. Today, thanks to our predilection for flat whites, double espressos and flavoured lattes (to name but a few), it's bigger business than ever. According to the Project Café 13 report by the market research company Allegra Strategies, there are more than 16,000 coffee outlets across the UK, with a combined turnover of £6.2bn. One major player, Costa Coffee, served more than 400 million cups of coffee during the 2013–14 financial year and reported revenues of £110m. The company plans to open around 400 new stores by 2018 and may also continue its recent expansion into China and France.

Caffè Nero has also grown rapidly in recent years, and now has more than 500 shops across the UK. Although a British success story in many regards, its expansion has had a cool reception as – like a number of other multinational businesses – it has not paid any corporation tax since 2007. While the company has defended its position and has not acted illegally, it has attracted a good deal of criticism. Amazon continues to be one of the bêtes noires of the House of Commons' Public Accounts Committee in this regard; despite selling more than £4bn worth of products in 2013, it paid just £4.2m in tax. Margaret Hodge, chair of the Committee, went on the record to encourage shoppers to use other retailers; when faced with similar consumer dissatisfaction in 2013, Starbucks paid corporation tax for the first time in five years.

THE CREATIVE INDUSTRIES: PLAYING A STARRING ROLE IN THE ECONOMY
The UK's creative industries have a stellar reputation worldwide, and they also play a vital role in the economy. As outlined by the January 2014 report from the Department for Culture, Media and Sport, they contribute £71bn annually to the country – more than £8m per hour. The film and TV industries in particular have been enjoying a revival.

Game of Thrones, one of the most popular television programmes globally, is filmed predominantly in Northern Ireland and is one of a number of productions taking advantage of a TV drama tax credit introduced by George Osborne, Chancellor of the Exchequer, whereby qualifying productions – those with a budget of at least £1m per hour as well as TV shows with episodes of 30 minutes' duration or less – receive a government rebate of 20 per cent on UK expenditure. The scheme has proved popular thus far and according to the British Film Commission provided more than £200m of support to 320 films in 2011–12.

Similar tax incentives have also had a positive impact on British-made films. Science-fiction fans were thrilled when work began on a new generation of Star Wars films at Pinewood Studios near London. (Parts of the original three movies were also filmed in England, at Elstree Studios, and the entire six-picture series has gone on to gross more than $4bn (£2.4bn) worldwide.) Star Wars: Episode VII is due for release in 2015, but in June 2014, Mr Osborne announced that a new standalone film would also be filmed in the UK, again bringing welcome revenue.

Visiting the cinema remains a popular leisure activity in the UK, despite continuing pressure on household incomes. The British Film Institute reported that more than 39 million cinema tickets were sold in the first quarter of 2014; the biggest grossing release in the same period, The Lego Movie, brought in more than £33m alone.

ANOTHER DAY, ANOTHER DOLLAR

Forbes magazine is a regular barometer of the fortunes of the world's wealthiest people. Its 2014 World Almanac of Wealth – a comprehensive listing of global billionaires – was notable for having a record number of women, however, and one of them was British. Denise Coates founded Bet365, an online betting and gaming company, in 2000 while operating from a Portakabin in Stoke-on-Trent, where the business is still based. It now has more than 2,000 employees and is licensed in the UK, Gibraltar and Australia. According to Forbes, Ms Coates – one of the few self-made tycoons on the list – is worth more than $1.5bn (£900m).

John Robert, founder of the online white goods supplier AO.com, also had a good day at the office in 2014; his Bolton-based business floated on the London Stock Exchange in February and he went home £86m to the good after cashing in some of his stock.

OILING THE WHEELS OF INDUSTRY

China, arguably the world's last remaining economic superpower, has long been an important export market for the UK. Luxury cars continue to be in demand and 2013 was an extremely successful year for both Jaguar Land Rover – which sold 95,000 cars in China, which is now its largest market – and Rolls Royce, whose sales shot up by 11 per cent.

Figures compiled by the Foreign Office's economics unit show us the broader picture, however. UK exports to China quadrupled between 2002 and 2013 to £12.5bn but given that China's potential import market could be worth as much as £3 trillion by 2020, according to IMF forecasts, there is clearly room for improvement. The UK government has been lobbying for Britain to become China's preferred trading partner in Europe, and in December 2013 David Cameron and over 100 business leaders formed a trade delegation to Beijing to explore opportunities. (A change to visa regulations for Chinese visitors to the UK had been announced by the Chancellor in October of that year, softening up the ground somewhat.) A return visit to London by Chinese Premier Li Keqiang in June 2014 proved to be fruitful, and £18bn worth of deals were announced. Among the highest profile were two deals for leading oil companies: Shell will be working with the China National Offshore Oil Corporation on a variety of energy projects, while BP will be supplying £5bn worth of liquefied natural gas to China.

THE GREAT UNKNOWN

Perhaps the business story of 2014 with the most significant potential ramifications will emerge on the morning of 19 September, when the results of the Scottish independence referendum are in. The arguments for and against independence have become ever more heated over the past year, but there remain many unanswered questions. One of the most crucial is what currency an independent Scotland would use – the pound, the euro or something entirely different? – and indeed whether it may need to join a currency union with the remaining members of the UK. Scotland is currently home to a number of leading financial institutions, and there has been some debate about whether they would need to relocate following a 'yes' vote. The Royal Bank of Scotland, for example, is based in Edinburgh and has more than 3,000 employees. In 2008–9, however, it was bailed out by UK taxpayers to the tune of £46bn, and a number of Westminster-based politicians have suggested that a move south would be inevitable if Scotland goes solo.

CONSERVATION

THE NATURAL ENVIRONMENT

Peter Marren

THE BIRD ATLAS

The Bird Atlas 2007–11 is the most ambitious British wildlife mapping project so far. Some 40,000 observers took part and sent in a total of 19 million records during the five years of the project, organised by the British Trust for Ornithology (BTO) in partnership with Birdwatch Ireland and the Scottish Ornithologists' Club. This atlas was the first to map the distribution of both breeding and wintering birds. It was also the first to make full use of the internet to gather data and then feed the results back to the participants. With three preceding bird atlases monitoring birds since the late 1960s, there is now a 40-year run of data on the changing patterns of bird distribution and numbers.

The period of the new atlas covers a time of rapid change. It has seen the rise and rise of little egrets, red kites and ring-tailed parakeets, the colonisation of Ireland by the great spotted woodpecker and the northward spread of goldfinches and jays. Several birds have nested for the first time, including great white egret, cattle egret, purple heron and little bittern. Less happily, the period has seen the decline of many once familiar birds, including grey partridge, turtle dove and corn bunting on farmland, lesser spotted woodpecker and willow tit in woodland and upland birds such as ring ousel and curlew. It has also seen the separation of the herring gull into three species, the other two being the yellow-legged gull and Caspian gull, and the separation of the Balearic shearwater from the Manx shearwater.

The scientific quality of this atlas sets a new benchmark for recording schemes. This time around, the data has enabled the mappers to chart the relative abundance of birds and local changes in their numbers, as well as their broad distribution. It represents another success for the BTO following its tracking of cuckoos on their migratory journeys to and from central Africa. The atlas project has also strengthened the ties between the BTO and the 50-plus local and county bird clubs in Britain.

THE BEAVER RETURNS

The European beaver is a native British mammal that died out during the Middle Ages, probably because of unsustainable levels of trapping and hunting. Once an endangered species in Europe, it has been successfully reintroduced into many parts of its former range. Ecologists believe that beavers bring many advantages to the natural functioning of wild habitats, for example by creating ponds and improving water quality. Almost uniquely among wild animals, the beaver creates its own habitat by controlling the flow of water and gnawing down young trees that subsequently regenerate as 'beaver coppice'.

In Britain, the gradual return of the beaver officially began with the Scottish Beaver Trial when a family of four was introduced to a remote area of forests and lakes in Argyll in May 2009. Since then four more families have been introduced, all but one of which has survived. Around 14 baby beavers, or kits, have been raised by the families and the health and activity of the animals has been closely monitored. The trial period is now complete. Its findings are currently being written up and will be presented to the Scottish government by May 2015. The politicians will then decide whether or not to proceed with the plan to reintroduce beavers to Argyll and perhaps other suitable localities in Scotland.

Wales too is investigating the feasibility of introducing beavers, where they once thrived on a few rivers before dying out. The Welsh Beaver Project, led by the Wildlife Trusts, has found suitable reintroduction sites on a number of Welsh rivers including the Dee, Rheidol, Teifi and Cleddau. After much consultation and discussion, release sites have been finalised at the Bwlch Nant yr Arian visitor centre and on the upper reaches of the Afon Merin in central Wales – both owned and managed by Natural Resources Wales. The plan aims to introduce and monitor 30 to 40 young animals from Norwegian and British collections.

The government has to balance the desires of wildlife and 'rewilding' enthusiasts, with positive public opinion behind them, with the fear of landowning representatives and the Angling Trust that the scheme may have negative impacts on the local economy. There is a small chance that the beavers could introduce a tapeworm parasite to Britain. European experience indicates that the activity of beavers can result in localised flooding and so damage crops and trees. However in most places people have learned to live with beavers and support them. Public opinion seems to be in favour of the beavers.

The situation in Britain has been complicated by escapes or illegal releases of captive beavers. There is already a wild population of beavers living on the River Tay in Scotland. For the time being, the Scottish government has suspended its attempts to round them up by trapping. In 2014 three beavers were filmed on the River Otter in Devon. Environment minister George Eustice promptly announced his intention to have them removed and 'rehoused'. Beavers are also kept within a fenced environment on various nature reserves and wildlife collections.

In the end, the success or failure of the beaver projects will depend on our tolerance to this large and captivating animal. Whether or not a successful reintroduction will be followed by attempts to reintroduce other lost animals such as the lynx remains to be seen.

STORMS AND FLOODS

The wild weather of last winter created serious problems for farmers, local authorities and railway managers as well as flooding many homes. Its impact on wildlife was less reported. Information from county wildlife trusts around England suggests that some species of wildlife had a hard time too. Barn owls, for example, were unable to hunt in wet weather since rain waterlogs their delicate plumage. There were reports of flooded water vole burrows, with their residents presumably swept away by the current. Seals and seabirds took a beating from the crashing waves. The cloudy floodwaters made life hard for fish-eating birds such as heron and kingfisher. Some of the eggs of salmon and trout, laid in late autumn and winter, were detached from their beds and taken away in the flow.

Many coastal properties that are managed as nature reserves were damaged. The spits at Spurn Point and Dawlish Warren were engulfed by waves. Entire beaches were blown away at the Gower and elsewhere. The sea breached the walls at many points along the coast of East Anglia, inundating inland marshes and lagoons with saltwater. Huge numbers of cockles, mussels and other bivalves were reported to be stranded. The storms have effectively reshaped parts of the coast. On top of that, there was much reported damage to bridges, boardwalks, hides and other constructions on coastal nature reserves.

Flooding and storms are natural phenomena and wildlife has recovered from similar or even worse events in the past. What exacerbated the recent floods was poorly planned agriculture. In the clamour to dredge the flooding rivers, the origin of their heavy loads of silt was often overlooked – most silt is washed from ploughed fields. For example, most of the silt in the rivers Culm and Tone is said to have come from catchment land inappropriately used to grow forage maize. As the writer George Monbiot expressed it, it might be cheaper in the long run to buy and reforest sources of the Severn and Wye than to keep on paying out for carpets in Tewkesbury. The water-holding power of lakes and gravel pits also helps. Those at Langford in Wiltshire may have saved the nearby villages from flooding, just as natural marshland, such as that at Potteric Carr in Yorkshire, acting as a giant sponge, helped to limit the flooding there.

The Wildlife Trusts have urged the government to review its flood defence strategy by investing in projects that 'slow down water and reconnect rivers with their floodplains'. As well as lowering the risk of flooding, the benefits could also include soil conservation, carbon storage and more wildlife habitat. The Trusts also advocate the creation of more coastal marshland, if necessary by removing sea walls, to create a natural buffer between the sea and the arable land. This has already been done successfully on a number of Trust nature reserves in East Anglia.

If the storms of last winter are connected with climate change, as many believe, we will have to face many more of a similar magnitude. Even dredged rivers will flood given enough rain. It is better to work with nature, argue the Trusts, than against it.

OFFSETTING NATURE

In its 2011 White Paper on the Natural Environment, the government introduced the idea of biodiversity offsetting or 'habitat banking'. This approach aims to compensate for species and habitats lost to development with an equivalent area of land 'enhanced or restored' for nature. Hence in theory any negative impacts would be 'offset' and at the developer's cost.

A pilot scheme to test the idea was begun in 2011 but before the results were complete, the government decided to press on with the idea anyway. Its 2013 Green Paper provided an overview of offsetting, how the scheme might operate and the key issues that it has to address. Chief among these is whether it is always possible to find a substitute area for the one that was destroyed. Wildlife habitats such as ancient woodland and natural grassland have taken centuries to develop and do not acquire their full biodiversity overnight. Hence a group of planted trees is no substitute for a wood that has been in place since the Middle Ages.

The conservation bodies are in a bind. On the one hand they are dubious about whether the principle of offsetting really addresses the root causes of wildlife decline: the loss and degradation of habitats. Moreover, natural ecosystems are dynamic; birds and other animals are mobile, and rarely conform to the static notions of the planner. On the other hand, offsetting can offer financial advantages. For example, the developer Taylor Wimpey offered £51,000 to the Earth Trust to fund the restoration of scrubbed-up chalk downland on land near Wallingford owned by the Trust. In exchange it was allowed to build 98 houses at Southmoor in the Vale of the White Horse District of Oxfordshire on wild land that was already surrounded by houses and a road, and hence considered a write-off. This was regarded overall as a conservation benefit.

Responses to offsetting have varied. Friends of the Earth dismissed it out of hand, complaining that the measure weakens planning laws without any evidence that it actually works. The Royal Society for the Protection of Birds (RSPB) was worried that offsetting could easily become 'a license to trash' and hoped that it would be a last rather than a first resort. The Wildlife Trusts want an exemption for high-quality sites such as Sites of Special Scientific Interest (SSSIs) which, almost by definition, are unique and therefore cannot be compensated for. Others commented that local authorities lack the expertise and knowledge necessary for weighing outcomes. On the other hand, some at least regard offsetting as a potential improvement on the earlier policy of wildlife 'mitigation', the results of which have been consistently poor.

DEVELOPMENT VERSUS BIRDS

Two cases in which populations of birds were threatened by proposed development came to national prominence in 2014. Lodge Hill, a former army base on the Hoo peninsula in Kent, holds the greatest density of breeding nightingales in Britain: 85 singing males were counted, representing about 1.3 per cent of the national population. The site also contains other scarce species as well as grassland and woodland of scientific interest. The Ministry of Defence owns the site and wants to sell it to developers. In this it had the support of the local authority, Medway Council. Some 5,000 new homes along with shops, offices and schools were to be built on the site, effectively destroying its viability as a habitat for wildlife.

At first the question was whether alternative habitat could be provided elsewhere. The council's contractor said 'yes'; the Kent Wildlife Trust said 'no'. However, once the data on nightingales became known, Natural England stepped in and declared Lodge Hill an SSSI. While such designation does not protect the site from development – that decision is still the prerogative of Medway Council – it places a formidable obstacle in the way of the application.

Medway Council objected, but an independent inspector found its development plan 'unsound' in that it hinged on a dogged determination to build a new town on what was now an SSSI. As a consequence, the council reluctantly withdrew its housing plan. Even so, the Ministry of Defence has not given up the fight. Its developer, Land Securities, has submitted a revised application to build on the site and the final outcome is likely to rest in the hands of the Secretary of State.

In Derby, the fate of a ten-hectare patch of rough ground known as The Sanctuary became the subject of a brief but heated debate. Although the place was designated as a Local Nature Reserve for its sand martins, little ringed plover and other birds, Derby's council had other plans for it. It wished to build a cycling race track there, linked to the new velodrome nearby. This was the first time that a local authority had given itself planning permission to damage its own nature reserve. That might have set an unfortunate precedent for other local authorities to follow if they wished. Compensation in the form of a patch of scrubland was offered but, as local birdwatchers pointed out, this was hardly an equivalent area; it was not even the same habitat.

Derby Wildlife Trust also objected. It took legal advice and obtained an injunction that brought the preliminary clearance work to a halt. This threw the council's tight timetable into disarray and shortly afterwards it reversed its decision. For now, The Sanctuary's sand martins can breathe easy again.

DISAPPEARING MOTHS
Since 2007, a growing number of enthusiasts have been contributing observations to the National Moth Recording Scheme, which monitors the changing fortunes of larger moths across the UK. Data from this and earlier schemes has now been analysed by scientists at the Butterfly Conservation charity, the Centre for Ecology and Hydrology and the University of York.

Of the 673 species of larger moths, they found that around two-thirds have shown 'significant change' over the past 40 years. Unfortunately, those that seem to have decreased outnumber those that have increased. Some 260 species have declined and 160 species have increased over the period. In looking for possible causes, the researchers noted that moths are declining faster in the south than the north, which strongly suggests a link with intensive agriculture. Furthermore, declines have been greatest in species confined to 'nitrogen-poor' habitats such as chalk downland. Hence the fall-out of nitrogen from farm fertilisers and vehicle emissions could well be affecting our moths and other insects.

Moths are also responding to the changing climate. Some species, such as the flamboyant Jersey tiger-moth and the piebald dark arches, are spreading northwards while moths of cooler climates, such as moorland and mountains, seem to be decreasing in number.

GROUSE MOORS AND BIRDS OF PREY
Many of the heather-covered moors of northern England and Scotland are managed for one species: the red grouse. When the shooting season opens in August, the grouse are driven over a line of guns. In order to support the maximum number of grouse, the moors have to be managed. The heather is burned during the winter to promote nutritious young shoots for the birds. The wetter areas are often drained, since heather requires relatively dry conditions. Tracks are built to carry all-terrain vehicles, sometimes on a layer of ballast brought in for the purpose. Medicated grit is used to control parasitic worms. 'Vermin' species such as stoats and crows that eat grouse and their eggs are controlled. This activity is legal, but the killing of birds of prey is not. Nevertheless, it is known that birds of prey are widely persecuted on grouse moors. The worst affected species is the hen harrier. In 2013, this bird failed to raise a single chick in England although the RSPB estimates that there is room on the moors for about 300 breeding pairs.

Coexistence between hen harriers and red grouse is possible but it requires diverting the former by way of artificial feeding with day-old chicks – a technique demonstrated at the Langholm estate in Dumfries. Even so, it is clear that most grouse moors in England prefer outright extermination even though the hen harrier is a legally protected species. There are also complaints from conservation bodies about intensive moor management that destroys wetland habitats and hence the natural ecology of the moor. Matters came to a head at Walshaw Moor near Hebden Bridge in Yorkshire, an SSSI, where Natural England attempted to halt the burning of blanket bog and other harmful practices. An attempted prosecution for 45 instances of alleged damage was brought by Natural England but then suddenly dropped. The outcome was a new agreement which will pay the estate £2.5m out of public funds over the next 25 years. The RSPB made a formal complaint to the European Commission. The UK government duly responded and the Commission is currently considering its findings.

Meanwhile a public backlash against the persecution of hen harriers seems to be gathering pace. A series of 'Hen Harrier Days' were organised in 2014 to coincide with the opening of the grouse season. A boycott of goods associated with grouse moor owners was urged by *Ethical Consumer* magazine. The RSPB has called for a licensing system to 'govern grouse moor management to deliver environmental outcomes'. Some want to go further; an e-petition to ban driven grouse shooting in England received 7,000 signatures in three weeks. There is a sense that 'our' protected birds are being persecuted by a rich and selfish minority.

Another likely victim is the unprotected mountain hare, most of which live in the Scottish Highlands. Because the hare shares the same food – heather – and habitat as the grouse, it used to be found in large numbers on grouse moors. Estates traditionally ran hare shoots for the keepers after the grouse season was over. Unfortunately for the hare, it is blamed for spreading a tick-related virus, louping-ill, that affects grouse. The result has been a wholly unsustainable cull of mountain hares. According to a survey commissioned by Scottish Natural Heritage, some 24,500 hares were shot or snared on 90 sporting estates in one year alone. Hares have now disappeared from 43 per cent of their former range and there are indications that they are being deliberately wiped out on many estates.

FRACKING AND WILDLIFE
Fracking (which is shorthand for 'hydraulic fracturing') is a means of tapping natural gas from the depths of the earth. The process entails drilling into the rock layer. Fluid – a mixture of water, sand and chemicals such as acids – is then injected under high pressure to shatter the soft shale rock and release the gas, which then flows out to the well-head. In the United States, fracking has boosted domestic oil production and driven down oil prices. In Britain, drilling companies have found what may be trillions of cubic feet of shale gas, especially in northern England. If fully exploited, this will have a significant impact on the landscape. Northern England alone has enough gas reserves to support 5,000 fracking sites and 100,000 well-heads.

The environmental concerns raised by fracking are essentially twofold. The process requires vast amounts of water – which will inevitably impact on rivers and groundwater – and there is also some risk of chemical contamination, especially to groundwater around the site. The construction of well-heads and approach roads will be noisy and drilling may induce earth tremors or subsidence. Lights at night may confuse bats and migratory birds. And of course shale gas is a fossil fuel which, like coal, releases carbon and contributes to climate change. Campaigners say that the potential fracking bonanza will distract the government from pursuing renewable forms of energy such as through wind, solar and tidal sources.

A report by six conservation bodies including the RSPB and the Angling Trust titled *Are We Fit to Frack?* contains proposals intended to limit the environmental impact of the process (they see the actuality of fracking as inevitable and unavoidable). Given the current lack of regulation, fracking could impact on a range of threatened species including Atlantic salmon, geese and bats. In southern England, there is a risk of pollution to the crystal-clear chalk streams. The report urges the government to create 'frack-free zones' in the most sensitive areas such as National Parks, including the whole of the North York Moors where considerable reserves of shale-gas lie. Environmental impact assessments should be carried out for each drilling proposal, which the industry should pay for. It should also be made to pay for any clean-up operations.

The RSPB has already objected to a fracking proposal near Blackpool, close to a protected area used by wintering geese and swans, on the grounds that the noise will disturb the birds. Wildlife bodies also joined the public protest at Balcombe in West Sussex since no environmental assessment had been made. Expect many more such cases to follow in the coming years.

COMMON AGRICULTURAL POLICY REFORM DISAPPOINTS

In June 2014, DEFRA (the Department for Environment, Food and Rural Affairs) announced its plans on how to implement farming reforms introduced by the European Commission last year. In future, arable farmers will have to set aside 5 per cent of their land as 'Ecological Focus Areas' in order to receive the full Basic Payment of government support. Clearly the general idea is to benefit the environment but, in practice, the inducements are meagre. The farmer has the option of leaving the land fallow, of creating 'buffer strips' of grass around a field or planting crops that are deemed to be environment-friendly, such as peas or beans. The government decided that hedges can be included in the scheme but that wildlife-rich grassland cannot. The scheme will cost the taxpayer around £3bn per year to operate in the UK.

The decision has disappointed environmental bodies. Stephen Trotter, Director of the Wildlife Trusts in England, believes that an 'opportunity for a greener, fairer and better-value Common Agricultural Policy has been lost'. By excluding grassland, the farm habitat most at risk receives no extra protection. Experts are divided as to whether planting beans offers much, or any, benefit to insect pollinators such as bees when there is no provision to reduce the use of pesticides and fertiliser. Trotter concludes that the announcement is 'bad news for nature, fails the taxpayer and fails those farmers who do the right thing and really understand the connection between the future of their industry and the wildlife on their farms'.

BUILT HERITAGE

Matthew Saunders

THE DIVISION OF ENGLISH HERITAGE

At the time of writing in summer 2014, there had still been no formal government commitment to the projected split of English Heritage into a body of the same name which would oversee the 420 properties presently in government care and Historic England, which would do everything else – designation, advocacy and grant aid (albeit with a much reduced budget). However, the expectation is that the two bodies remain on course to be launched on 1 April 2015 and that the new English Heritage will be given £80m from HM Treasury to tackle the backlog of repairs and to give it a fighting chance of being self-sufficient some eight years after its launch. Despite the plans, ongoing reductions in public expenditure were continuing to threaten the effectiveness of the present organisation.

Fortunately, one anticipated casualty of the split has been saved: the Survey of London, a hugely ambitious exercise to record the architectural history of the capital, which launched in 1894 and migrated to English Heritage after the demise of the London County Council, is to be moved with all seven staff to the Bartlett Faculty of the Built Environment at University College London.

Financial cuts accompanied continuing government attempts at simplification and reductions in bureaucracy. The advent of the Scrap Metal Dealers Act 2013 seemed to have a positive effect, reducing the instances of metal theft from

churches and other historic buildings, and the Enterprise and Regulatory Reform Act 2013 began gradual implementation during 2014. This authorised the establishment of Heritage Partnership Agreements and Local and National Building Consent Orders, both of which were intended to reduce the need for repetitive applications for listed building consent. They also dealt with the abolition of conservation area consent as a separate permission, the ability to differentiate with greater clarity between protected and unprotected elements within a listed building and provided the opportunity to apply for a Certificate of Immunity from listing at any time.

The government continued along these lines with further measures to extend Permitted Development Rights, which were set to allow any agricultural building to be converted into up to three houses without formal planning permission (although there would be a need for 'prior approval'). The government's intentions to relax the existing controls, even where the buildings were listed, or in a Conservation Area, a National Park or an Area of Outstanding Natural Beauty, were dropped after an adverse reaction from the public during the consultation period.

In Wales, the plan to merge the Royal Commission on the Ancient and Historical Monuments of Wales, which records historic sites, with Cadw, the body that owns, designates and provides grant aid to historic buildings, was shelved. The decision came after a mixed consultation response to the proposals and was, according to Heritage Minister John Griffiths, made 'to avoid financial costs, organisational risks and disruption to the sector at a time when public resources are scarce'.

CASH IS KING

The Heritage Lottery Fund (HLF) continued to flourish, buoyed by income from the National Lottery, which is expected to reach £425m annually. It has made many grants available with some exceptional results – Astley Castle in Warwickshire, recreated for the Landmark Trust on the back of a substantial HLF grant, won the prestigious 2013 Stirling Prize for New Architecture, while another recipient, the William Morris Gallery in Walthamstow, was declared 'Museum of the Year 2013' by the Art Fund.

Some of the biggest grants announced in the year went to: the Harland and Wolff Drawing Office in the Titanic Quarter in Belfast (£5m), which will become a boutique hotel; the Globe Theatre in Stockton (£4m), a grant which will reopen an art deco super theatre closed since 1997; St Peter's Church, Northampton (£1.7m) to allow the Churches Conservation Trust to provide a 'Heritage Gateway' in the city; John Wesley's New Room in Bristol (£2.3m) to facilitate a considerable extension to the attractions offered by this Methodist 'shrine'; the National Conservation Centre for Historic Scotland (£3.5m) to create a single Centre for Conservation at Stirling; Middlesbrough Town Hall (£4m) to transform the late 19th-century civic complex into the artistic heart of the community; the Montgomery Canal (£3.9m) to allow the reopening of 2km presently closed; the Boat Building and Heritage Skills Training Centre at Portsmouth (£3.8m); 'Salisbury Cathedral from the Meadows' (£15.8m) to allow this iconic view of Salisbury Cathedral painted by John Constable in 1831 to be purchased by the Tate; St Peter's College, Cardross near Helensburgh (£4.3m) to rescue one of the great modernist ruins, built by Jack Coia between 1958 and 1968; and Highcliffe Castle Christchurch, Hampshire (£2.8m) to complete the programme of repairs at one of the longest-standing of all Buildings at Risk. (The sums shown in parentheses would only become available once a 'second round pass' had been confirmed.)

Grants offered usually lead, in the end, to projects completed. The principal HLF-funded schemes which were completed during the year included: the Picton Library, Liverpool (May 2013); Torre Abbey, Torquay (July 2013); the Benjamin Britten and Peter Pears Archive at Aldeburgh (June 2013); the new Visitor Centre at Stonehenge (December 2013); Cheltenham Art Gallery and Museum's substantial new extension (October 2013); Bentley Priory at Stanmore in Middlesex, the headquarters of Fighter Command during the Battle of Britain (September 2013); Kenwood House, Highgate in North London (November 2013); the London Museum of Water and Steam, formerly the Kew Bridge Steam Museum (March 2014); and Llanelly House, Llanelli in Carmarthenshire and the huge Conservatory at Wentworth Castle in South Yorkshire, both of which opened their doors to visitors early in 2014.

Among historic churches, the most unexpected bonus was the announcement in the government's 2014 Budget of a direct grant of £20m for the 'repair and enhancement of England's cathedrals'. The Church of England in general and the Churches Conservation Trust in particular both announced the launch of grant schemes for church fittings, while the Church Commissioners backed down over plans to sell the Bishop's Palace at Wells. One of the greatest Roman Catholic complexes, the Seminary at Ushaw in Durham with its five chapels, was saved largely through a partnership with the University of Durham. Long-standing redundant churches of importance at Freeby in Lincolnshire and Ufford in Huntingdonshire were passed for preservation intact to the Churches Conservation Trust, a body which suffered a major blow in the course of the year with the destruction by fire of its Grade I 17th-century church at Goltho in Lincolnshire. The HLF continued to allocate £30m a year towards the repair of church buildings.

FOR SALE: ONE USED CASTLE

The cuts in public expenditure continued to throw scores of historic buildings onto the open market, among the most important being Lancaster Castle, where the prison has been closed, and the great Jacobean house at Bramshill in Hampshire, which had served as the main training centre for the police since 1960. The cuts in personnel were just as severe – since 2006 there has been a drop of 18 per cent in archaeological officers and 33 per cent in conservation officers among local authorities and this from a base point where, in the same year, one in three planning authorities

had no conservation staff at all. General economic conditions continued to claim victims – in contrast to the good news that the historic Axminster Carpet Factory had been saved by a consortium of local businessmen, Nimbus Conservation (one of the most important private firms offering conservation skills), set up in Frome in 1991, was placed in voluntary liquidation in April 2014. Some 40 people lost their jobs. It was equally sad that, as a result of the National Trust's decision not to buy it, Sir Albert Richardson's house and contents at Avenue House, Ampthill in Bedfordshire, were sold off in September and November 2013.

In other developments during the year under review, the Castle Studies Trust was established in order to offer grants for research into fortresses and castles; a new society was formed to study the works of the pioneering 19th-century designer, Christopher Dresser; the Cumbria Vernacular Buildings Group began operations in June 2013; the East End (of London) Preservation Society was launched; and the Leadwork Conservation Network Group was set up.

In the area of published scholarship, there have been major new biographies of the architects William Burges, William Kent and Sir Charles Nicholson, and the architectural writer, Ian Nairn. The Shell County Guide series, begun by John Betjeman and John Piper, is to be relaunched on the initiative of the outgoing Bishop of Wakefield, while new Pevsners in the Buildings of England, Wales and Scotland volumes have been issued on Cornwall, Kent East, Sussex East, Northamptonshire and Powys. There has also been a significant primary assessment of architectural murals created between 1920 and 1960 (*British Murals & Decorative Painting 1920–1960*, edited by Alan Powers) and a history of the protection of historic buildings by Whitehall officials in *Men from the Ministry*, written by the Chief Executive of English Heritage, Dr Simon Thurley.

Formal protection of historic buildings continues to be enacted primarily through the device of listing – the biggest example to be given protection in the course of the year was the headquarters of the Halifax Building Society in the town that bears its name, constructed in 1974 and eligible for listing under the rolling 30-year rule. The right of a community to be given first refusal on the purchase of redundant buildings, many of them historic – 'assets of community value' – which was granted under the provisions of the Localism Act 2011, is proving particularly effective, especially in the protection of historic pubs.

DANCE

Hanna Weibye

In a funding climate that continues to be difficult for the arts, most of the UK's dance companies had reason to be cautiously pleased, as July 2014 saw Arts Council England announce a 9.4 per cent increase in its dance funding for the period 2015–18, despite an overall cut to the council's budget of £1.9m. The big ballet companies remained the largest beneficiaries, although after the Arts Council reviewed its investment in the 'big seven' opera and ballet companies there was some redistribution of funds among them. The Royal Opera House was told it would receive a 3.7 per cent cut in real terms over the three years of the next funding period, while English National Ballet received stand-still funding. An extra £500,000 a year was awarded to Birmingham Royal Ballet and Northern Ballet to enable them to tour more and commission new choreography, and to support the development of regional dance hubs in Birmingham and Leeds.

Touring, dance in the regions and outreach were a priority for the Arts Council, which instructed the major ballet companies to plan 'audience development iniatives' and rewarded companies undertaking good educational work. Akram Khan Company's grant was increased by 122 per cent in real terms to allow it to produce more work in Leicester and Manchester, and Jasmin Vardimon received £3m towards a new international dance centre in Kent. The council's greater emphasis on the English regions was seen as a response to reports that Londoners benefit disproportionately from arts subsidies, and to the cutting of arts budgets by local councils in recent years.

Several dance companies were added to the National Portfolio, including Mark Bruce Company, Shobana Jeyasingh Company and Matthew Bourne's New Adventures, the latter receiving £1.2 m; the Arts Council commended his educational programme after his *Lord of the Flies* tour involved 6,500 boys in dance workshops around the UK.

The culture secretary Maria Miller resigned in April 2014 after what was generally considered to be an uninspiring tenure, but a programme she had set in motion – of significant investment in cultural commemoration of the centenary of the First World War – dominated the arts in summer 2014 just as the Cultural Olympiad had in 2012. The main beneficiary in the dance world was Michael Nunn and William Trevitt's company BalletBoyz, which received funding from the 14–18NOW initiative to create a new full-length work. *Young Men,* with choreography by Iván Pérez and music by Keaton Heston, will premiere at Sadler's Wells in January 2015.

A short ballet season on the BBC2 and BBC4 television channels in February 2014 added to the impression that dance's star is rising in the public's perceptions. It featured programmes on ballet history presented by Darcey Bussell and David Bintley, an archive film of a 1959 *Sleeping Beauty* performance with Margot Fonteyn, and a profile of Tamara Rojo preparing to dance *Swan Lake,* in which the telegenic director of English National Ballet continued her charm offensive on the public.

Gailene Stock, director of the Royal Ballet School, died on 29 April 2014 after suffering from cancer. Stock had headed the school for 15 years, during which time the Upper School relocated from west London to Covent Garden and employment rates for graduates rose from 48 per cent to almost 100 per cent. Having danced as principal for Australian Ballet, National Ballet of Canada and Royal Winnipeg Ballet, she ran the school with an emphasis on competition, increasing the number of public performances, tours and overseas exchanges. She was succeeded by Jay Jolley, formerly her assistant director.

Birmingham Royal Ballet's director, David Bintley, stepped down from his directorship of the National Ballet of Japan in June 2014, to be replaced by Noriko Ohara. Johann Kobborg, a former Royal Ballet principal, and the partner of Romanian ballerina Alina Cojocaru, became director of the National Ballet of Romania.

THE ROYAL BALLET

The Royal Ballet performed 11 bills in the 2013–14 season (compared to 12 in 2012–13): six story ballets (including two new productions) and four mixed bills, with one programme devoted to George Balanchine's tripartite abstract ballet *Jewels*. All four mixed bills featured a mix of older and newer works – the all-Ashton, all-MacMillan or all-contemporary evenings seen under Monica Mason seem to have fallen out of favour, perhaps for reasons of box-office safety – and three bills included new pieces, by David Dawson, Wayne McGregor and Alastair Marriott.

The season opened in starry style with Carlos Acosta's version of *Don Quixote*. A colourful attempt to breathe life into one of the less accessible 19th-century classics, its ingenious sets (by Tim Hatley) and Acosta's judicious modifications to Petipa's choreography produced an appealing, jolly vision of Spain, and Marianela Nuñez sparkled admirably as Kitri. The other big new ballet of the season was Christopher Wheeldon's adaptation of Shakespeare's *The Winter's Tale*. The original score by Joby Talbot and fantastical designs by Bob Crowley both successfully evoked the very different settings of the court at Sicilia and the merry landscape of Bohemia. Wheeldon showed that his maturing choreographic talent can more than carry a story of this complexity and emotional depth, and he elicited powerful performances from Lauren Cuthbertson as Hermione and Edward Watson as Leontes.

Dawson's creation, *The Human Seasons,* was the odd one out among the three short premieres: its lyrical, gentle choreographic style was in contrast to the extreme extensions and intricate, twisting partnering which has become a McGregor trademark and had also clearly influenced Alastair Marriott. McGregor's *Tetractys* was decorated with angular fluorescent light tubes arranged in what their creator, American artist Tauba Auerbach, called glyphs. Both Auerbach's designs and McGregor's choreography were responding to the geometrical intricacies of the score, excerpts from J. S. Bach's *The Art of Fugue,* but the effect was more inscrutable than illuminating. McGregor used a stellar cast of principals, but his decision not to train a second cast was roundly criticised after Natalia Osipova was injured during the first performance, meaning that the second scheduled performance could not be given. Osipova's role was subsequently taken over by Olivia Cowley. *Connectome,* by the Royal Ballet's senior character artist Alastair Marriott, also used lighting effects, hi-spec design and the impressive flexibility of Osipova, but the mood of the piece, aided by its Arvo Pärt score, was more contemplative than *Tetractys*.

After last year's exodus of principals, there were some new stars at Covent Garden, including the rather colourless

Matthew Golding from Dutch National Ballet and Vadim Muntagirov, who joined in March from English National Ballet. In her first season with the company, Natalia Osipova showed herself more than capable of dancing 'English' staples as well as contemporary creations, making her company debut in Kenneth MacMillan's *Romeo and Juliet* (opposite Carlos Acosta) to high praise, and subsequently playing Titania in Frederick Ashton's *Dream*. Her intense, dramatic *Giselle* was one of the performances of the season.

The Opera House expanded its programme of cinema broadcasts, with five ballet performances – all story ballets *(Don Quixote, Nutcracker, Giselle, Sleeping Beauty and Winter's Tale)* – beamed live to cinemas all over Britain and around the world. This programme is likely to continue as the Arts Council has instructed companies to include screenings as one of their 'success measures' in the 2015–18 funding period.

The Linbury Studio Theatre hosted a second run of Liam Scarlett's 2013 *Hansel and Gretel*. A dark work portraying abuse, neglect and paedophilia, it played to packed houses, with powerful performances by Leanne Cope, Bennet Gartside, James Hay and Laura Morera. Young choreographer Alexander Whitley used Royal Ballet dancers in an evening of his own choreography, his piece *The Measures Taken* following the recent trend (led by Wayne McGregor) for 'intelligent' digital sets and lighting (by Marshmallow Laser Feast) which interact with the dancers.

Wendy Whelan, a principal dancer with the New York City Ballet, presented a new programme of duets created for her by four young male choreographers, widely seen as a sign of her intention to move into contemporary dance after she retires from NYCB. Unfortunately, the four pieces presented were dark and monotonous, and a sad underuse of Whelan's considerable talents.

Other visitors to the Linbury included Ballet Black, Dutch National Ballet's Junior Company, and Northern Ballet.

ENGLISH NATIONAL BALLET

The confidence Tamara Rojo has injected into English National Ballet really began to show as she entered her second full season as director. As ever with ENB, resources were tight, but Rojo deployed them cannily, presenting four box-office friendly story ballets with style, and one exciting and timely mixed bill.

The season opened in Milton Keynes with a new *Le Corsaire*, a 19th-century narrative ballet never before staged in its entirety in the UK. With a barrel-organ-worthy score by a mix of composers, including Minkus and Delibes, and a fantastical plot loosely based on a Byron poem, it was never going to gain plaudits for seriousness and the company embraced the fun, giving sparkling performances much aided by Bob Ringwood's splendid technicolour designs. Alina Cojocaru, formerly of the Royal Ballet, made her company debut as Medora on the opening night, partnered by Vadim Muntagirov.

In April 2014, the company presented *Lest We Forget,* an evening of new works to mark 2014's First World War centenary. In a gamble that paid off, Rojo had evidently put most of her new ballet funds into one basket: three top choreographers – rising Royal Ballet star Liam Scarlett and established contemporary greats Akram Khan and Russell Maliphant – created works with original scores, and all three were fluent, haunting and strongly styled. Khan's piece, *Dust,* was notable for having the choreographer himself perform an intimate, virtuosic *pas de deux* with Tamara Rojo, the first time these two powerful artists have been seen on stage together. A restaging of the 2012 *Firebird* by young ENB choreographer George Williamson was the odd piece out thematically, but signalled Rojo's commitment to encouraging in-house talent. The choice of the Barbican

venue suggested an unwillingness to gamble on filling the Coliseum for contemporary works, but the programme had an enthusiastic reception and played to sold-out houses. Both its vision and the quality of the dancing made an extremely positive impression, giving Rojo the greatest possible bang for her buck. Williamson curated *Choreographics,* another evening at the Barbican, in which four ENB dancers presented their own short (ten-minute) pieces on a First World War theme, with original scores by young composers; all were of impressively high quality.

English National Ballet lost two valuable principals when Daria Klimentová retired after 18 years with the company, and her partner, Vadim Muntagirov, was snapped up by the Royal Ballet. The two gave an emotional farewell performance in Derek Dean's *Romeo and Juliet* at the Royal Albert Hall on 22 June. That run boasted a feast of star principals, having opened with Tamara Rojo and Carlos Acosta in the title roles, and also featuring Alina Cojocaru, whose two magisterial performances with guest star Friedemann Vogel (of Stuttgart Ballet) were hailed as the start of a phenomenal new partnership. The summer run of *Coppélia,* by contrast, featured home-grown talent, as Rojo allowed the newly promoted young dancers Shiori Kase and Yonah Acosta to make their debuts in the principal roles on opening night. The threadbare sets of this 30-year-old production were proof of the company's limited funds, but the dancers carried it off with a charm, confidence and commitment to quality that suggests Rojo as director is doing a good job of keeping up morale.

IN THE REGIONS

Birmingham Royal Ballet mounted four story ballets: revivals of *The Sleeping Beauty, The Nutcracker* and *La fille mal gardée,* and the British premiere of director David Bintley's *The Prince of the Pagodas,* which was created for the National Ballet of Japan in 2011. The renowned theatre designer Rae Smith created a stunning fairytale Japanese setting, with a stylised Mount Fuji as backdrop and lots of creatures in compellingly weird, colourful masks and costumes. Bintley changed the story of the Britten-scored ballet, making the salamander prince the brother rather than the fiancé of the princess who must search for him; while this allowed for some affecting scenes of childhood happiness, the removal of any hint of sexuality makes the princess's journey through magical lands just a series of fabulous episodes rather than an allegory for growing up. It made for a much more family-friendly experience, however, than the Royal Ballet's sombre and often inscrutable Kenneth MacMillan production.

The company also performed three mixed bills at the Birmingham Hippodrome. One featured three of David Bintley's own ballets, *E=mc²*, *Tombeaux* and *Still Life at the Penguin Café,* and another the work of three renowned 20th-century choreographers, John Cranko's *Card Game,* George Balanchine's *Slaughter on Tenth Avenue* and Kenneth MacMillan's *Elite Syncopations.* Bintley continued to demonstrate that he and the BRB are just as much keepers of the English ballet tradition as the Royal Ballet by mounting a triple bill of early Ashton works. The company's dancers executed *Les Rendezvous* and *Façade* – frothy, funny little vignettes – with panache in Anthony Ward's candy-coloured costumes, but *Dante Sonata,* an iconic 1940 piece whose revival from oblivion Bintley had masterminded in 2000, failed to repeat the emotional impact it had in its original wartime context. New short works, *Kin* by Alexander Whitley and *Quatrain* by company dancer Kit Holder, were performed at the International Dance Festival in Birmingham and on the company's spring tour.

As well securing more direct funding for the next three years, Birmingham Royal Ballet also obtained a capital grant of £1.85 million from Arts Council England, enabling it to embark on a renovation and modernisation of its Birmingham city centre premises.

Scottish Ballet performed at the Edinburgh International Festival 2013 in a mixed programme that included Twyla Tharp's *Fugue* and pieces by Jiří Kylián. New director Christopher Hampson presented two of his own choreographies: 2011's *Rite of Spring,* in an autumn mixed bill with MacMillan's *Elite Syncopations,* and his new full-length *Hansel and Gretel* at Christmas 2013. The latter was a pleasing piece of storytelling, with its stylised 1950s setting and delightfully scary witch (Eve Mutso), but the choreography appeared cramped, particularly for the *corps de ballet*. Despite the Scottish public's love of the witty, pacy Christmas ballets created by Hampson's predecessor, Ashley Page, there was further evidence of the bad blood between Page and the company's board in the announcement that Christmas 2014 will see a revival of Peter Darrell's 1973 production of *The Nutcracker,* instead of the popular 2005 Page version currently in the repertoire.

Mark Bruce Company introduced a new version of *Dracula* which presented a deeply chilling and gory vision of the undead. Its star, Jonathan Goddard, was much praised for the power of his performance as the Count.

Northern Ballet produced a new *Cinderella* by artistic director David Nixon, and also toured a mixed programme featuring works by Lar Lubovitch, Hans van Manen, and two new creations by a young choreographer, Kenneth Tindall. Tindall's *The Architect* was on the bill in Leeds, and his *Luminous Junc•ture* was given at the Linbury Studio Theatre when the company toured to London.

CONTEMPORARY DANCE

Sadler's Wells continued to demonstrate impressive commerical viability in staging large numbers of contemporary dance productions, alongside flamenco, breakdancing and children's shows.

Wayne McGregor's company, Random Dance, premiered a new piece, *Atomos,* at Sadler's Wells in October 2013. Continuing McGregor's interest in cognitive science and computer programs to aid choreography, it wrapped his usual highly fluent movement language (and his more than competent company) in swathes of 'concept' talk that for most people only detracted from the dance's intrinsic high quality.

Hofesh Schechter and his company went from strength to strength, with a new piece, *Sun,* which premiered at Sadler's Wells in late October, garnering plaudits for its violent energy. *Sun* was performed again at the Brighton Festival, of which Schechter was guest director.

As usual, a large number of foreign companies visited Sadler's Wells. A high point of the year was the visit in February 2014 of Tanztheater Wuppertal Pina Bausch, who performed *1980,* a three-hour feast of a work that had caused a sensation at its first London performance in 1982 and was just as ecstatically received this time. The Canadian dancer Crystal Pite was added to the Wells roster of Associate Artists, and her company, Kidd Pivott, performed *The Tempest Replica* at the Wells in March. This retelling of Shakespeare's *The Tempest* used mime and faceted white masks by Nancy Bryant to create a magical atmosphere, and a contrasting powerfully kinetic dance style to evoke the violence and danger in Shakespeare's play.

Sadler's Wells Associate Artist Sylvie Guillem reprised her solo show *6000 Miles Away* at the International Dance Festival in Birmingham. In July the Coliseum saw Guillem and Russell Maliphant gave the last London performances of their joint work *PUSH,* a virtuosic display of their talents and

the lighting designs of Michael Hulls (who had won the 2014 Olivier Award for Lifetime Achievement in Dance).

Rambert performed two mixed bills at Sadler's Wells, the October 2013 bill including the premiere of Ashley Page's piece *Subterrain* with music by Mark-Anthony Turnage, and the London premiere of *The Castaways* by American choreographer Barak Marshall. The company moved from Chiswick to a new building on the South Bank in November 2013, enabling it to increase the number of classes and workshops it offers by 40 per cent and to practise with its own orchestra.

In November 2013 the Richard Alston Dance Company marked the centenary of Benjamin Britten's birth with a quadruple bill of works set to Britten's music, performed by the Britten Sinfonia at the Barbican. A new work created for the occasion, *Phaedra,* was subsequently nominated for an Olivier Award.

VISITORS

On a brief visit in August 2013, Shanghai Ballet presented its version of *Jane Eyre* at the Coliseum, but its transformation of Brontë's very specific fictional setting into a kind of timeless love triangle failed to excite either audiences or critics. Much more exciting was the visit in October of Stuttgart Ballet to Sadler's Wells. A smorgasbord programme of 13 short pieces displayed many exciting talents among its German choreographers (Marco Goecke, Demis Volpi) and the company's dancers (Friedemann Vogel). Its production of John Cranko's *The Taming of the Shrew* was less appealing, however, with both the design and Cranko's style of narrative choreography appearing dated.

The controversial Russian choreographer Boris Eifman returned to the Coliseum with his own company. Having spent years outside the dance establishment in Russia, Eifman now finds himself fêted and honoured at home, but his new creation, *Rodin,* drew mixed reactions in Britain. While its recreation of real sculptures through the living bodies of its dancers was extremely impressive, many found its treatment of sculptor Camille Claudel's mental illness both facile and offensive.

Andris Liepa's *Saisons Russes,* once considered to be a vanity project, impressed audiences and critics alike at the Coliseum with the fine musicians and dancers (of Natalia Sats Children's Theatre) 'recreating' pieces from the golden days of Diaghilev's Ballets Russes, including Rimsky-Korsakov's opera-ballet *Le Coq d'Or,* with dubious authenticity but undeniable verve and flair.

After an absence from London of three years, the Mariinsky Ballet returned in July 2014 to the Royal Opera House under the aegis of impresarios Victor and Lilian Hochhauser. Its programme balanced heritage works – the 1940 Lavrovsky *Romeo and Juliet,* the 1950 Sergeyev *Swan Lake* – with newer pieces, in particular works by former director Alexei Ratmansky that had never been seen in London, his *Concerto DSCH* (2011) and his *Cinderella* (2002).

NEW PRODUCTIONS

ROYAL BALLET
Founded 1931 as the Vic-Wells Ballet
Royal Opera House, Covent Garden, London WC2E 9DD

Don Quixote (Carlos Acosta after Petipa), 30 September 2013. *Music,* Ludwig Minkus, arranged Martin Yates; *design,* Tim Hatley; *lighting design,* Hugh Vanstone. Cast led by Carlos Acosta and Marianela Nuñez

The Human Seasons (David Dawson), 9 November 2013. A one-act work. *Music,* Greg Haines; *set design,* Eno Henze; *costume design,* Yumiko Takeshima; *lighting design,* Bert Dalhuysen. Cast led by Federico Bonelli, Lauren

Cuthbertson, Steven McRae, Marianela Nuñez and Edward Watson

Tetractys – The Art of Fugue (Wayne McGregor), 7 February 2014. A one-act work. *Music,* J. S. Bach's The Art of Fugue, arranged by Michael Berkeley; *set and costume design,* Tauba Auerbach; *lighting design,* Lucy Carter. Cast: Federico Bonelli, Lauren Cuthbertson, Nicol Edmonds, Paul Kay, Sarah Lamb, Steven McRae, Marianela Nuñez, Natalia Osipova, Thiago Soares, Akane Takada, Eric Underwood and Edward Watson

The Winter's Tale (Christopher Wheeldon), 10 April 2014. *Music,* Joby Talbot; designs, Bob Crowley; *lighting design,* Natasha Katz; *silk effects design,* Basil Twist; *projection design,* Daniel Brodie. Cast led by Lauren Cuthbertson, Sarah Lamb, Steven McRae and Edward Watson

Connectome (Alastair Marriott), 31 May 2014. A one-act work. *Music,* Arvo Pärt; *costume design,* Jonathan Howells; *set design,* Es Devlin; *lighting design,* Bruno Poet; *projection design,* Luke Halls. Cast led by Steven McRae, Natalia Osipova and Edward Watson

BIRMINGHAM ROYAL BALLET
Founded 1946 as the Sadler's Wells Opera Ballet
Birmingham Hippodrome, Thorp Street, Birmingham B5 4AU

The Prince of the Pagodas (David Bintley), 30 January 2014. UK premiere; revision of 2011 full-length work created for National Ballet of Japan. *Music,* Benjamin Britten; *designs,* Rae Smith; *lighting design,* Peter Teigen. Cast led by Joseph Caley and Momoko Hirata

ENGLISH NATIONAL BALLET
Founded 1950 as Festival Ballet
Markova House, 39 Jay Mews, London SW7 2ES

Le Corsaire (Anna-Marie Holmes after Petipa and Sergeyev), 17 October 2013. *Music,* various; libretto, Saint-Georges and Mazilier in a version by Anna-Marie Holmes; *set and costume design,* Bob Ringwood; *lighting design,* Neil Austin. Cast led by Alina Cojocaru and Vadim Muntagirov

No Man's Land (Liam Scarlett), 2 April 2014. A one-act work. *Music,* Liszt, arranged by Gavin Sutherland; *designs,* Jon Bausor; *lighting design,* Paul Keogan

Second Breath (Russell Maliphant), 2 April 2014. A one-act work. *Music,* Andy Cowton, orchestrated by Ben Foskett; *lighting design,* Michael Hulls; *costume design,* Stevie Stewart

Dust (Akram Khan), 2 April 2014. A one-act work. *Music,* Jocelyn Pook; *costume design,* Kimie Nakano; *lighting design,* Fabiana Piccioli; *set design,* Sander Loonen

NORTHERN BALLET
Founded 1969 as Northern Ballet Theatre
2 St Cecilia Street, Quarry Hill, Leeds LS2 7PA

Cinderella (David Nixon), 17 December 2013. A full-length work. *Music,* Philip Feeney; *costume design,* David Nixon; *lighting design,* Tim Mitchell. Cast led by Tobias Batley and Martha Leebolt

SCOTTISH BALLET
Founded 1956 as the Western Theatre Ballet, Bristol; moved to Glasgow as Scottish Theatre Ballet 1969
Tramway, 25 Albert Drive, Glasgow G41 2PE

Hansel and Gretel (Christopher Hampson), 10 December 2013. *Music,* Engelbert Humperdinck; *design,* Gary Harris; *lighting design,* George Thompson. Cast led by Sophie Martin, Eve Mutso and Constant Vigier

RAMBERT
Founded 1926 as the Marie Rambert Dancers
94 Chiswick High Road, London W4 1SH

Subterrain (Ashley Page), 22 October 2013. A one-act work. *Music,* Aphex Twin, Mark-Anthony Turnage; *design,* Jon Morrell; *lighting design,* Peter Mumford

SADLER'S WELLS – LONDON'S DANCE HOUSE
Rosebery Avenue, London EC1R 4TN

Atomos (Wayne McGregor/Random Dance), 9 October 2013. *Music,* A Winged Victory for the Sullen; *lighting design,* Lucy Carter; *film and set photography,* Ravi Deepres; *costume design,* Studio XO

Sun (Hofesh Shechter/Hofesh Shechter Company), 30 October 2013. *Music,* Hofesh Shechter; *set design,* Merle Hensel; *lighting design,* Lee Curran; *costume design,* Christina Cunningham

Mȷlonga (Sidi Larbi Cherkaoui/Eastman), 6 November 2013. UK premiere of a full-length work. *Music,* Fernando Marzan, Szymon Brzóska, Olga Wojciechowska; *costume design,* Tim van Steenbergen; *set design and video design,* Eugenio Szwarcer; *lighting design,* Adam Carrée

The Rashomon Effect (Akram Khan/Andrej Petrovic, National Youth Dance Company), 16 April 2014. A one-act work. *Music,* Vincenzo Lamagna; *costume design,* Kimie Nakano

MARK BRUCE COMPANY

Dracula (Mark Bruce), 25 September 2013. *Music,* various, arranged by Chris Samuels; *lighting design,* Guy Hoare; *design,* Phil Edolls; *costume design,* Dorothee Brodrueck; *puppet and mask design,* Pickled Image. Cast led by Jonathan Goddard

AWARDS

CRITICS' CIRCLE NATIONAL DANCE AWARDS 2013
Best Classical Choreography – Christopher Wheeldon for *Aeternum* (Royal Ballet)

Best Modern Choreography – Russell Maliphant for *Fallen* (BalletBoyz: The Talent)

Outstanding Male Performance (Classical) – Nicolas Le Riche for *Le Jeune Homme et la Mort* (English National Ballet)

Outstanding Female Performance (Classical) – Yuan Yuan Tan for *RAkU* (San Francisco Ballet)

Dancers Pro Award for Outstanding Modern Performance (Male) – Paul White for *The Oracle* (Meryl Tankard)

Dancers Pro Award for Outstanding Modern Performance (Female) – Julie Cunningham for *New Works 2012* (Michael Clark Company)

Jane Attenborough Dance Industry UK Award – Amanda Chinn, general manager of Scottish Dance Theatre

Grishko Award for Best Independent Company – BalletBoyz: The Talent

Stef Stefanou Award for Outstanding Company – Mikhailovsky Ballet

Dancing Times Award for Best Male Dancer – Dane Hurst (Rambert Dance Company)

Grishko Award for Best Female Dancer – Natalia Osipova (Mikhailovsky Ballet)

Du Valois Awards for Outstanding Achievement – Leanne Benjamin; Matthew Bourne

ROYAL ACADEMY OF DANCE 2013
Queen Elizabeth II Coronation Award – The Royal Ballet

YOUNG BRITISH DANCER OF THE YEAR 2014
Erik Woolhouse

LAURENCE OLIVIER AWARDS 2014 (DANCE)
See Theatre Awards

FILM

Omer Ali

Ahead of the annual awards season, winter 2013 saw the release of such heavyweight cinema fare as *Gravity* and *12 Years a Slave*, while spring 2014 was a time for monsters and superheroes, particularly inhabitants of the Marvel Universe. Transcending them all was the stand-out success of *Frozen*, Walt Disney's 95th animated theatrical release.

HAIL DISNEY
Loosely based on Hans Christian Andersen's *The Snow Queen*, *Frozen's* central royal princesses, Elsa and Anna, are left orphaned when their parents are killed at sea; Elsa's coronation precedes the revelation of her dark secret: she has the ability to produce terrible snow storms, which envelop the kingdom of Arendelle. Elsa flees to a stunning, self-built ice palace; sister Anna sets off after her. The film boasts beautifully realised Nordic backdrops and ice effects, as well as a diverting roster of characters, including romantic Anna's competing paramours, Prince Hans and dopey iceman Kristoff, plus the latter's reindeer, Sven; a goofy snowman, Olaf, surely one of the least likely stuffed merchandising opportunities of recent times; and Oaken, owner of Wandering Oaken's Trading Post and Sauna, popular for his 'Big summer blowout!' sales patter, and the subject of a raft of internet rumours concerning his sexuality.

Frozen was attacked by US Christian pastor and talk-show host Kevin Swanson for encouraging homosexuality (and even bestiality), gaining support from Mormon blogger Kathryn Skaggs; indeed, the film's Oscar-winning showstopper 'Let It Go' has become something of an LGBT anthem ('Conceal, don't feel, don't let them know/Well, now they know!'). But *Frozen's* strong central female characters and message of self-reliance are guaranteed to melt hearts and have led to its huge popularity among young women, though the film's feminist credentials could be tested by Elsa's icy transformation into sexy vamp. Released in the USA in late November 2013, and the UK one week later, within six months it had become the highest-grossing animation of all time, and by the end of May 2014 it was the fifth-biggest film in box office history, taking $1.22bn (£700m) worldwide, pulling ahead of 2013's *Iron Man 3*.

Frozen was named best animated film at both the Oscars and BAFTAs, where UK talent was well represented among the favourites for 2014's big awards. Mexican filmmaker Alfonso Cuarón was lavish in his praise of the London-based Framestore team behind the special effects for his 3D space spectacular, *Gravity*. It stars Sandra Bullock as a medical engineer trying to make her way back to Earth when her space shuttle is destroyed, with able support from George Clooney, apparently channeling the airy charm of *Toy Story's* Woody. Interpretations ranged from spectacular thriller to metaphysical dream – with nods to Pixar's *WALL-E*.

BRITS AND AMERICANS
Turner Prize-winning British director Steve McQueen followed up his 2011 sex-addiction movie, *Shame*, with a heartfelt adaptation of free man Solomon Northup's harrowing tale of kidnapping and servitude in mid-19th century America. London-born Chiwetel Ejiofor was rightly recognised for his powerful central performance, alongside outstanding displays from McQueen favourite Michael

Fassbender, Brad Pitt (one of the film's producers) and newcomer Lupita Nyong'o.

British man of the moment was Steve Coogan, whose presence seemed to dominate cinemas this year. *Alan Partridge: Alpha Papa*, the big-screen debut for Coogan's popular TV comedy character, premiered in Norwich, the fictional radio DJ's hometown; then Coogan appeared alongside Julianne Moore in Henry James adaptation *What Maisie Knew*. But his most celebrated appearance came in the self-scripted *Philomena* – the moving tale of an unmarried woman, played by Judi Dench, whose baby is taken away from her. Directed by Stephen Frears and based on the biographical book written by journalist Martin Sixsmith, *Philomena* earned Coogan a number of best adapted screenplay nominations.

US awards competition was led by David O. Russell's hugely entertaining *American Hustle*. Based on a true story, it's a tale of two con artists – played by Christian Bale and Amy Adams – who are coerced by an ambitious FBI agent (Bradley Cooper) to take part in a sting targeting corrupt politicians. Jennifer Lawrence (fresh from *The Hunger Games: Catching Fire*), Jeremy Renner, Louis C.K. and a typically menacing Robert De Niro are among the film's other pleasurable turns.

Another contender was Martin Scorsese's *The Wolf of Wall Street*, based on disgraced New York stockbroker Jordan Belfort's memoir and starring Scorsese's current muse, Leonardo DiCaprio. At a time of near-universal austerity, it came as a surprise to witness such an uncritical depiction of financial scamming and the freewheeling, drug-fuelled lifestyle that accompanied it, with its miserable treatment of women.

After an oddball turn as Belfort's early mentor in *The Wolf of Wall Street*, Matthew McConaughey could truly flex his acting muscles in *Dallas Buyers Club*, another true-life tale. The film was adapted from the story of AIDS patient Ron Woodruff, who treated his symptoms with unapproved drugs which he smuggled into Texas from Mexico and supplied to other HIV-positive patients. Jared Leto turned in a captivating performance in a supporting role as Rayon, a transgender woman.

The most overlooked performance of the period under review was arguably Tom Hanks' understated starring role in *Captain Phillips*. Director Paul Greengrass uses his trademark handheld camerawork and exceptional sound design to recount the real-life hijacking of a cargo ship in the Indian Ocean by Somali pirates in 2009. Phillips is portrayed as the taciturn catalyst of the film's action, which is resolved in a moment of heartbreaking release from Hanks. Co-star Barkhad Abdi was recognised for his portrayal of one of the young, frantic, khat-chewing hijackers. Hanks went on to star in *Saving Mr Banks*, where he plays Walt Disney, desperate to persuade Emma Thompson's P.L. Travers to allow her Mary Poppins to be adapted by the studio.

Cate Blanchett always led the best actress nominations for her role as a spoilt divorcee in *Blue Jasmine*, Woody Allen's latest return to form. Despite much carping over the writer/director's recent output, for nearly his 50th feature film he produced a nuanced narrative of a desperate woman who descends on her impoverished sister in San Francisco – Sally Hawkins in typically admirable form – as she tries to come to terms with the misguided decisions she's made in life, not least marrying fraudster Hal (the charismatic Alec

Baldwin). It's a humane antidote to the macho misanthropy of Scorsese's *The Wolf of Wall Street* and drew many favourable comparisons to Tennessee Williams' *A Streetcar Named Desire*.

FOREIGN AFFAIRS

The year's most attention-grabbing female performances, though, came from the duo at the centre of Tunisian-French director Abdellatif Kechiche's *Blue is the Warmest Colour*: Léa Seydoux and Adèle Exarchopoulos. Adapted from Julie Maroh's graphic novel, the film attracted controversy before it even opened in the UK due to its supposedly explicit sexual content; Maroh complained that the depiction of the film's central lesbian relationship was unrealistic. At Cannes, Kechiche accepted the Palme d'Or 2013 alongside Seydoux and Exarchopoulos, but later his leads complained about the intensity of his filming methods. Despite this war of words, *Blue is the Warmest Colour* is a remarkable achievement: a touching portrayal of emerging sexuality and maturing relationships set against a backdrop of class and race in small-town France. (It was a pleasure to see a major French film that eschews a Paris setting.)

Oddly, possibly due to a miscalculation, the film was not eligible for the 2014 Academy Awards, which left the way clear for Italian writer/director Paolo Sorrentino's *The Great Beauty* to scoop up the Best Foreign Language Film Oscar. Toni Servillo is the cynical writer at the centre of this prolonged wander through a corrupt, contemporary Rome. Set in a pop video style, its bizarre cast features a foolish performer, a mummified icon, politicking priests and sexual intrigue – a perfect summation of the Berlusconi era.

Unfairly overlooked for the Best Documentary Oscar, in June 2014 director Joshua Oppenheimer's *The Act of Killing* achieved another kind of record: his remarkable film about Indonesia's anti-communist purge in 1965–66 played for 52 consecutive weeks at London's ICA cinema. Although many of the screenings were on Sunday afternoons, it was testament nonetheless to Oppenheimer's trenchant, often surrealist look at some of those involved in the killing of more than 500,000 people.

For the year's most controversial, sexual film, you need look no further than arch provocateur Lars von Trier. Unbowed by the furore surrounding 2009's explicit *Antichrist* and 2011's *Melancholia*, the Dane served up *Nymphomaniac*. Saved from an attack by bookish virgin Seligman (Stellan Skarsgård), self-diagnosed nymphomaniac Joe (Charlotte Gainsbourg) recounts her erotic biography in eight chapters. Volume I, starring newcomer Stacy Martin as the younger Joe, is the more successful of the film's two parts, bearing von Trier's hallmark wry humour amid episodes drawn from soft-porn fiction. That promise evaporates in the second volume, which develops Joe's relationship with supposedly mercurial partner Jerome (Shia LaBeouf, looking out of his depth) and her unpleasant treatment at the hands of sadist K (Jamie Bell). It all gets predictably silly and leaves a bitter taste.

A welcome return was made by Sweden's Lukas Moodysson. The director had lost his way with the experimental *A Hole in My Heart* and *Container*, alongside English-language outing *Mammoth* – it took his wife Coco's comic book to revive the warm-hearted, witty feel of *Together* and *Show Me Love* with which we'd previously associated him; *We Are the Best!* is an ebullient portrayal of three girls in 1982 Stockholm who form a punk band.

OFFBEAT GEMS

There were more new offerings from other iconic filmmakers. Inspired by writer Stefan Zweig's stories chronicling the Weltschmerz evoked by the end of the Austria–Hungary Empire, Wes Anderson delivered *The Grand Budapest Hotel*. Like its eponymous home, the film is a gorgeous folly, held together by Ralph Fiennes' concierge, on the run through Mitteleuropa's fictional Zubrowka with trainee Zero (Tony Revolori) in tow. Adrien Brody, Willem Dafoe and Edward Norton are the pursuers; Tilda Swinton, Saoirse Ronan, Harvey Keitel, Léa Seydoux, Jude Law and, of course, Anderson stalwarts Bill Murray and Owen Wilson all join in. The director fills every frame of his movie with lush visuals and quirky narration, leaving little space for the viewer to be moved or reflect, only to be swept along with a kind of architectural wonder.

Swinton is the star of Jim Jarmusch's leisurely take on the vampire movie vogue, set in defunct, derelict Detroit, *Only Lovers Left Alive*. Swinton and musician partner Tom Hiddleston are forced out of their respective retreats when their supply of the red stuff dries up; sucked clean by Swinton's sister, played by Mia Wasikowska, they turn to John Hurt's playful Christopher Marlowe in Tangier. It's a beautiful ode to creativity and the limited pleasures of solitude.

The Coen brothers paid tribute to musicianship, riffing on the early legend of Bob Dylan, for *Inside Llewyn Davies*. Set in New York's Greenwich Village, Oscar Isaac is the folk musician trying to make it in a scene more in thrall to a cutesy duo played by pop star Justin Timberlake and Carey Mulligan, before heading out on a road trip with a sinister John Goodman and his beat poet driver, Garrett Hedlund. All the time, Llewyn is stuck with his best friends' escaped cat.

Having set and filmed his 'Before' trilogy nine years apart, US indie favourite Richard Linklater finally unveiled *Boyhood,* a remarkable family tale shot over 12 years, in which he revisited stars Patricia Arquette, Ethan Hawke, the director's daughter Lorelei Linklater and the young Ellar Coltrane, starting aged six. Practical considerations aside, the *Guardian's* Peter Bradshaw saw in it 'a kind of Bildungsroman for modern American cinema, conducted at a superbly intelligent, low-key level. . . one of the great films of the decade.'

Many film fans were drawn to writer/director Shane Carruth's offbeat second feature, nearly a decade after his cerebral time-travel debut *Primer*. *Upstream Color* is no less complex: a wandering drama of a woman infected with hallucinogenic, worm-like parasites, it leans on Thoreau's *Walden* and the work of Terrence Malick, and stars Carruth himself.

No less opaque, though infinitely more rewarding, is British director Jonathan Glazer's impressive sci-fi flick *Under the Skin*. Drawn from the novella by Michel Faber, it stars an impassive Scarlett Johansson as an alien driving the streets of Glasgow in search of male prey; struck by one encounter (with Adam Pearson, who has neurofibromatosis, which causes tumours to grow on his face) she flees to the Highlands, a motorcycle-driving associate and predatory truck driver in pursuit. Glazer employed hidden cameras to film Johansson picking up unsuspecting passers-by, providing a double frisson to many scenes.

HEROES AND BEASTS

Marvel's superheroes put their powers to dramatic effect in a host of films, including *Thor: The Dark World*, starring *Rush's* Chris Hemsworth alongside Natalie Portman, while *Captain America: The Winter Soldier* had Chris Evans – in the title role – and Scarlett Johansson (as the Black Widow) trying to uncover a sinister plot within Samuel L. Jackson's S.H.I.E.L.D.

Equally eagerly anticipated was the return of Andrew Garfield in *The Amazing Spider-Man 2*; Peter Parker has split up with Gwen Stacy (played by Emma Stone in some of the film's best scenes) and sets off for England to battle putative supervillains Harry Osborn and Electro (Dane DeHaan and Jamie Foxx, respectively). It's tidily played by the film's youngish cast of contemporaries but bigger thrills came in Marvel's latest franchise reboot: *X-Men: Days of Future Past*. From a furious opening set in the future, director Bryan Singer sends Hugh Jackman's Wolverine back to 1973 to confront Jennifer Lawrence's Mystique, a task for which he must recruit the younger Magneto and Xavier (James McAvoy and Michael Fassbender). Stalwart support from an all-star cast including Sir Patrick Stewart, Sir Ian McKellen, Halle Berry, Anna Paquin and Ellen Page pulls the complicated plot along apace.

There was a bigger villain to face in Gareth Edwards' Hollywood debut, *Godzilla*. Edwards had made only one previous feature – the self-penned *Monsters* back in 2010 – and here he marshalled a cast including Aaron Taylor-Johnson, Elizabeth Olsen and *Breaking Bad's* Bryan Cranston to battle the giant spawned from post-WWII Japanese nightmares, but the British director seemed to be over-whelmed by the weighty beast and the result proves no more illuminating than 1998's version.

Having shown how adept he is with digital effects in *Black Swan* (2010), director Darren Aronofsky aimed to provide spectacle on a giant scale in oddball choice *Noah*. Russell Crowe is the biblical hero in Aronofsky's pre-apocalyptic myth, pitted against Ray Winstone and the massed hordes who all want a place on his ark, alongside Sir Anthony Hopkins, Jennifer Connelly and Emma Watson. It was banned on religious grounds in several Gulf states as well as Malaysia and Indonesia for its depiction of *Noah*, an important figure in Islam.

Meanwhile, *Dawn of the Planet of the Apes* imagines a very different world where the intelligent primates, led by Andy Serkis' Caesar, are threatened by a band of surviving humans under Dreyfus (Gary Oldman). The ensuing ape infighting is vividly rendered, although much of the humanity of 2011's predecessor is lost amid the tremendous effects.

ANIMATION AND PUPPETS

Two contrasting, retro, kids' franchises made their mark in 2014: the Muppets built on the tentative box-office promise of 2011's eponymous outing with Amy Adams and Jason Segal for *Muppets Most Wanted*, a full-on jewellery-heist caper featuring a duplicitous Kermit double and starring comedy talents Tina Fey and Ricky Gervais. And toy manufacturer Lego made a surprisingly successful next leap for its expanding brand from building bricks, through electronic games to the big screen: in *The Lego Movie* directors Phil Lord and Christopher Miller (*Cloudy with a Chance of Meatballs*) created a sparky take on the everyman-has-to-save-the-world genre, with a nice line in self-effacing humour and plenty for adults to enjoy.

Hayao Miyazaki, film director, animator and co-founder of Studio Ghibli, announced that he was bowing out after more than 50 years in the film industry with *The Wind Rises*. A typically beautiful anime inspired by aircraft designer Jiro Horikoshi, the film is never explicit about the engineer's planes' ultimate use – as kamikaze bombers – but it's yet another testament to imagination, and a fitting curtain call.

In summer 2014, Walt Disney Pictures revisited Charles Perrault's *Sleeping Beauty* fairy tale for the live action *Maleficent*, nearly two years after principal photography on the feature began. Poor reviews notwithstanding, it proved to be Angelina Jolie's biggest box office hit yet, breaking the $500m (£300m) barrier. What a year for Disney.

AWARDS

70TH VENICE INTERNATIONAL FILM FESTIVAL
Golden Lion – *Sacro Gra* (Gianfranco Rosi)
Grand Jury Prize – *Jiao you* (Tsai Ming-liang)

BRITISH ACADEMY FILM AWARDS 2014
Best Film – 12 Years a Slave (Steve McQueen)
Director – Alfonso Cuarón *(Gravity)*
Outstanding British Film – *Gravity* (Alfonso Cuarón)
Outstanding Debut by a British Writer, Director or Producer – Kieran Evans (*Kelly* + Victor)
Documentary – *The Act of Killing* (Joshua Oppenheimer)
Original Screenplay – *American Hustle* (David O. Russell and Eric Warren Singer)
Adapted Screenplay – *Philomena* (Steve Coogan and Jeff Pope)
Film Not in the English Language – *The Great Beauty* (Paolo Sorrentino)
Animated Film – *Frozen* (Chris Buck and Jennifer Lee)
Leading Actor – Chiwetel Ejiofor *(12 Years a Slave)*
Leading Actress – Cate Blanchett *(Blue Jasmine)*
Supporting Actor – Barhad Abdi *(Captain Phillips)*
Supporting Actress – Jennifer Lawrence *(American Hustle)*
Fellowship – Dame Helen Mirren
Outstanding British Contribution to Cinema – Peter Greenaway

64TH BERLIN INTERNATIONAL FILM FESTIVAL
Golden Bear – *Black Coal, Thin Ice* (Yi'nan Diao)
Grand Jury Prize – *The Grand Budapest Hotel* (Wes Anderson)
Silver Bear for Best Director – *Boyhood* (Richard Linklater)

86TH ACADEMY AWARDS
Best Picture – *12 Years a Slave* (Steve McQueen)
Director – Alfonso Cuarón *(Gravity)*
Actor in a Leading Role – Matthew McConaughey *(Dallas Buyers Club)*
Actress in a Leading Role – Cate Blanchett *(Blue Jasmine)*
Actor in a Supporting Role – Jared Leto *(Dallas Buyers Club)*
Actress in a Supporting Role – Lupita Nyong'o *(12 Years a Slave)*
Animated Feature Film – *Frozen* (Chris Buck and Jennifer Lee)
Writing (Original Screenplay) – *Her* (Spike Jonze)
Writing (Adapted Screenplay) – *12 Years a Slave* (John Ridley)
Foreign Language Film – *The Great Beauty* (Paolo Sorrentino)
Documentary Feature – *20 Feet from Stardom* (Morgan Neville)

CANNES FILM FESTIVAL 2014
Palme d'Or – *Winter Sleep* (Nuri Bilge Ceylan)
Grand Prix – *Le Meraveglie* (Alice Rohrwacher)
Jury Prize – *Mommy* (Xavier Dolan)
Best Director – Bennett Miller *(Foxcatcher)*
Best Actor – Timothy Spall *(Mr. Turner)*
Best Actress – Julianne Moore *(Maps to the Stars)*
Best Screenplay – Andrey Zvyagintsev and Oleg Negin *(Leviathan)*
Caméra d'Or – *Party Girl* (Samuel Theis, Claire Burger and Marie Amachoukel)
Un Certain Regard – *Fehér Isten* (Kornél Mundruczó)

LITERATURE

Nick Rennison

FICTION

In a lecture given in Oxford in May 2014, Will Self lamented the decline of literary fiction, suggesting that 'the literary novel as an art work and a narrative art form central to our culture is indeed dying before our eyes', largely because 'the hallmark of our contemporary culture is an active resistance to difficulty in all its aesthetic manifestations'. Is Self correct? The 'death of the novel' has been proclaimed often enough before and yet writers still continue to produce demanding and complex fiction and readers continue to buy it and read it.

There was certainly no shortage of interesting titles published in the period under review. Philip Hensher's *The Emperor Waltz* (Fourth Estate) wove together three narrative strands from three different time periods to create a satisfying whole. In Sebastian Barry's *The Temporary Gentleman* (Faber), the Irish narrator, a former soldier, sits in exile in Africa and guiltily reviews his past. Helen Dunmore's *The Lie* (Hutchinson) focused on a young man, traumatised by his experiences in the First World War, who returns to his native Cornwall. Nicola Barker's characteristically offbeat *In the Approaches* (Fourth Estate) was another of her linguistically inventive works of comic fiction. *Arctic Summer* (Atlantic), by the South African novelist Damon Galgut, borrowed its title from an unfinished novel by E. M. Forster and followed that author on his own life-changing passage to India. Twice shortlisted for the Booker Prize, Australian Tim Winton published *Eyrie* (Picador), the story of a man emerging from self-imposed isolation in a high-rise tower block.

Two former *enfants terribles* of British literature have entered middle age determined to remain provocative. Irvine Welsh produced a blackly subversive, profanity-filled story of fitness, fatness and murder in Miami in *The Sex Lives of Siamese Twins* (Cape) and Hanif Kureishi's *The Last Word* (Faber) was the comic tale of a young man commissioned to pen the biography of a famous writer. Sebastian Faulks left his own style behind and tried his hand at Wodehousian prose in *Jeeves and the Wedding Bells* (Hutchinson). It was a successful pastiche but, no doubt gallingly for Faulks, his book failed to win the Bollinger Everyman Wodehouse Prize, which was awarded instead to Edward St Aubyn's *Lost for Words* (Picador), a satire on literary prizes.

Perhaps the clearest indication that Will Self was overstating the dangers to the future of the novel was that some of the year's most exciting fiction came from writers under the age of 40. *In the Wolf's Mouth* (Cape) by Adam Foulds was a powerful story set in North Africa and Sicily during the Second World War. Several other authors who, like Foulds, had been on Granta's 2013 'Best of Young British Novelists' list, produced new works. Ned Beauman's third novel, *Glow* (Sceptre), was a fast-moving, cleverly plotted thriller; *Boy, Snow, Bird* (Picador) by Helen Oyeyemi was an idiosyncratic, modern retelling of the story of Snow White; and Kamila Shamsie's *A God in Every Stone* (Bloomsbury) was a multi-layered historical novel which explored ideas of empire and individual destiny.

In the USA, Donna Tartt's *The Goldfinch* (Little, Brown) was only her third novel in 20 years. The story of a boy whose life is turned upside down by a terrorist bomb at an art exhibition hoovered up awards as effectively as the previous two, winning the 2014 Pulitzer Prize for Fiction. Joshua Ferris' *To Rise Again at a Decent Hour* (Viking) was a comic novel about a New York dentist whose sense of his own identity begins to slip. Michael Cunningham, author of *The Hours,* published his sixth novel, *The Snow Queen* (Fourth Estate), about two brothers finding different paths to transcendence and a meaningful life. *The Days of Anna Madrigal* (Doubleday), was the latest (and probably last) in Armistead Maupin's 'Tales of the City'. Thomas Pynchon's *Bleeding Edge* (Cape) was the reclusive author's idiosyncratic take on the thriller genre and E. L. Doctorow published a new novel, *Andrew's Brain* (Little, Brown).

In shorter fiction, A. L. Kennedy's *All the Rage* (Cape) was a collection of the Scottish writer's recent work and *England and Other Stories* (Simon & Schuster) was Graham Swift's first volume of stories in more than 30 years. Two brilliant American exponents of the short story-writer's art also produced new collections: Lorrie Moore's *Bark* (Faber) was her first in 16 years; Lydia Davis' *Can't and Won't* (Hamish Hamilton) was her first since she won the 2013 Man Booker International Prize. An American writer was also the winner of what has swiftly established itself as one of the most prestigious prizes for short stories, The Sunday Times EFG Short Story Award. Adam Johnson became the award's fifth winner with his story 'Nirvana'.

Turning from short stories to one very long narrative, Norwegian writer Karl Ove Knausgaard has written a six-volume, 3,500-page work, straddling the disputed border between autobiography and fiction, which has been an extraordinary bestseller in his own country. It has recently begun to appear in English translation and the third book, *Boyhood Island* (Harvill Secker), was published in March 2014. Opinion on Knausgaard's work seems divided between those who consider it a masterpiece and those who regard it as overwritten and overpraised.

In British crime fiction, a convincing sense of place has long been central to some of the best writing in the genre and this year there were additions to a number of series which prove the point. *Want You Dead* (Macmillan) was a new title by Peter James featuring Brighton detective Roy Grace; John Harvey's *Darkness, Darkness* (Heinemann) was the last outing for his Nottingham detective Charlie Resnick; and Peter Lovesey's *The Stone Wife* (Sphere) had Bath-based policeman Peter Diamond investigating the attempted robbery of a medieval carving of the Wife of Bath, a botched crime resulting in murder. *The Silkworm* (Sphere) was the second crime novel that J. K. Rowling published under the *nom de plume* of Robert Galbraith. Under his own alias of Benjamin Black, John Banville caught at least something of Raymond Chandler's often-imitated but rarely matched prose style in *The Black-Eyed Blonde* (Mantle), a new case for private eye Philip Marlowe. Simon Kernick's *Stay Alive* (Century) was an adrenaline-fuelled thriller about a woman on the run from a serial killer; *Wolf* (Bantam) was the latest of Mo Hayder's brutally compelling crime novels featuring her recurring character Jack Caffery; and Tony Parsons reinvented himself as a crime writer in *The Murder Bag* (Century).

One of 2014's most successful thrillers was *The Truth About the Harry Quebert Affair* (Maclehose Press) by Swiss first-time novelist Joel Dicker, an ingeniously contrived story of a decades-old murder and two writers involved in it. Other

European crime fiction found a place on British bookshelves. So-called 'Scandi Noir' continued to have its devotees and *The Son* (Harvill Secker) was the latest bestseller from Norwegian novelist Jo Nesbo. Italy was the setting for new adventures for two much-loved fictional detectives: in Andrea Camilleri's *Angelica's Smile* (Mantle), Sicilian Inspector Montalbano becomes obsessed by a beautiful woman who has been one of the victims in a series of burglaries; *By Its Cover* (Heinemann) was the 23rd instalment in Donna Leon's series about the Venetian Commissario Brunetti.

Across the Atlantic, John Grisham's *Sycamore Row* (Hodder) was a sequel to the author's very first novel, *A Time to Kill,* and featured the same protagonist in Jake Brigance. Stephen King's *Mr Mercedes* (Hodder) was a suspense thriller, without any of the supernatural trappings for which the author is famous. Other well-known American crime writers with new titles to their name included Harlan Coben, whose *Missing You* (Orion) was the story of a New York policewoman releasing skeletons from closets when she contacts a former fiancé through an online dating agency; Karin Slaughter, whose *Cop Town* (Century) was a powerful story of two policewomen in pursuit of a killer in 1970s Atlanta; and Michael Connelly, whose *The Gods of Guilt* (Orion) was another in his series featuring the LA lawyer Mickey Haller.

In science fiction, the Arthur C. Clarke Award for 2014 was won by a debut novelist, the American Ann Leckie, whose sophisticated space opera *Ancillary Justice* (Orbit) was the first in a proposed trilogy. Leckie's novel also won the British Science Fiction Association Award for 2013, sharing it with Gareth L. Powell's *Ack-Ack Macaque.* Powell's *Hive Monkey* (Solaris), the sequel to his prize-winner, was published in January 2014. Other noteworthy SF novels included Ken MacLeod's *Descent* (Orbit), *Tigerman* (Heinemann), a compelling mix of thriller, pulp fiction and environmentalist fable by Nick Harkaway, Charles Stross' *The Rhesus Chart* (Orbit), a further instalment in his supernatural espionage series known collectively as 'The Laundry Files' and Adam Roberts' knowing and enjoyable take on Jules Verne, *Twenty Trillion Leagues Under the Sea* (Gollancz). Andy Weir's *The Martian* (Del Rey), the story of a Robinson Crusoe-like astronaut stranded on the red planet, was self-published in 2012. Taken up by mainstream publishers in the US and the UK, it became a major bestseller. Terry Pratchett, still battling against what he has long termed the 'embuggerance' (the diagnosis of his early onset Alzheimer's disease), nonetheless published two new books – *Raising Steam* (Doubleday), a Discworld novel, and, with Stephen Baxter, *The Long Mars* (Doubleday), a further volume in an unfolding series about parallel Earths.

Amid the ongoing obsession with George R. R. Martin's 'A Game of Thrones', which (thanks to the TV series) continued to dominate the genre's bestseller charts, it was easy to forget that fantasy novels were being published which weren't set on Westeros. But other writers in the genre did indeed produce interesting work. Joe Abercrombie, author of 'The First Law' stories, began a new series with *Half a King* (Harper Voyager); Stephen Hunt also launched a new series with *In Dark Service* (Gollancz); *The Book of Life* (Headline) concluded Deborah Harkness's trilogy about witches, vampires and forbidden love in past and present times; and *Tower Lord* (Orbit) was the second volume in Anthony Ryan's 'Raven's Shadow' series.

NON-FICTION

The centennial year of the outbreak of the First World War unsurprisingly saw a flood of books on the subject. Among the best titles in the small library that was published in 2014 were Max Hastings' *Catastrophe: Europe Goes to War 1914*

(HarperCollins), Mark Bostridge's *The Fateful Year: England 1914* (Viking) and *The Long Shadow* (Simon & Schuster) by David Reynolds. Jerry White's *Zeppelin Nights* (Bodley Head) was a study of London life during the war; Tim Butcher's *The Trigger* (Chatto) followed the author's journey into the Balkans in search of the story of Gavrilo Princip, the man who assassinated Archduke Ferdinand. Other significant historical works included Philip Parker's *The Northmen's Fury* (Cape), a wide-ranging survey of the Viking world; *God's Traitors* (Bodley Head) by Jessie Childs, which examined Catholicism in Elizabethan England through the experiences of one particular family; and *World Without End* (Allen Lane), which concluded Hugh Thomas' magisterial, three-volume history of the Spanish Empire. In addition, two historians already successfully embarked on careers in politics had new books out in 2014. Tory MP Kwasi Karteng published *War and Gold* (Bloomsbury), an ambitious study of the links between money and the rise and fall of empires; *Ten Cities That Made an Empire* (Allen Lane) was written by Tristram Hunt, Labour's shadow education secretary.

Significant political biographies included John Campbell's *Roy Jenkins* (Cape), a substantial portrait of the Labour home secretary and chancellor of the exchequer sometimes called 'the best prime minister post-war Britain never had', and Michael Jago's *Clement Attlee* (Biteback), the life of another, even more important figure in Labour's history. Adam Begley's *Updike* (Harper) was a well-reviewed biography of the American novelist who died in 2009; Ben Macintyre's *A Spy Among Friends* (Bloomsbury) was the story of Soviet agent Kim Philby; and *Charlie Chaplin* (Chatto) was the latest Londoner to undergo the biographical scrutiny of Peter Ackroyd.

Morrissey's *Autobiography* appeared, to many people's horror, as an instant Penguin Classic (as per the singer's demand) but it did not receive uniformly adulatory reviews. One of the cruellest, by A. A. Gill in *The Sunday Times* – which dismissed the book as 'a potential firelighter of vanity, self-pity and logorrhoeic dullness' – won Hatchet Job of the Year, awarded by 'The Omnivore' website. Some of the most original autobiographical works of the year examined authors' own relationships with literature. In *The Unexpected Professor* (Faber) John Carey, emeritus professor of English literature at Oxford University and chief book reviewer of *The Sunday Times,* looked back on his life. *The Year of Reading Dangerously* (Fourth Estate) was a very funny, often touching account of Andy Miller's encounters with books and the memories of his life they stirred; Rebecca Mead's *The Road to Middlemarch* (Granta) mixed memoir, biography and criticism in its exploration of what George Eliot's book has meant to *The New Yorker* writer; and *The Mighty Dead* (HarperCollins) by Adam Nicolson, subtitled 'Why Homer Matters', journeyed much further into the literary past to provide a personal view of the continuing importance of the Ancient Greek poet. However, the accolade for most unusual autobiography of the year undoubtedly went to broadcaster, architectural critic, novelist and prodigious polymath Jonathan Meades, who produced a memoir unlike any other in *An Encyclopaedia of Myself* (Fourth Estate).

POETRY

Jeremy Paxman, chair of the judges for the 2014 Forward Prizes, caused a stir when he claimed, on announcing the shortlist in June (which included collections by John Burnside, Colette Bryce and Hugo Williams), that poetry 'has connived at its own irrelevance' and that poets should 'aim to engage with ordinary people much more'. The previous October, Michael Symmons Roberts had won the 2013 Forward Prize for Best Collection with *Drysalter* (Cape).

January 2014 saw the announcement of the winner of the other major UK poetry award, the T. S. Eliot Prize. Sinéad Morrissey took it for *Parallax* (Carcanet), a collection of poems in which films, paintings, maps and photographs were the starting points for deft examinations of human perception and the nature of art.

Other significant collections this year included *All One Breath* (Cape), a further demonstration of the elegiac and lyric talents of the Scottish poet John Burnside; *Byssus* (Picador), the third book by Jen Hadfield; Hugo Williams' *I Knew the Bride* (Faber); and *The Cartographer Tries to Map a Way to Zion* (Carcanet) by Kei Miller, a Jamaican poet now resident in the UK. *Learning to Make an Oud in Nazareth* (Chatto) by Ruth Padel explored the conflict in the Middle East in a series of powerful new poems. *The Poems of Rowan Williams* (Carcanet) was a volume of work by the former Archbishop of Canterbury. In *A Double Sorrow* (Faber), Lavinia Greenlaw took Chaucer's long poem *Troilus and Criseyde* as the starting point for her own version of the story of doomed lovers in the Trojan War. *The Moon Before Morning* (Bloodaxe) was a new collection by the much-admired elder statesman of American poetry, W. S. Merwin. And finally, November 2013 saw the publication of *Broken Hierarchies* (Oxford UP), the collected poems of Geoffrey Hill. To some people, Hill, with all his complexity, is probably the embodiment of Paxman's strictures on modern poetry; to others he is the greatest living British poet.

CHILDREN'S

Controversy attended the announcement of the winner of one of the major awards in children's literature, Kevin Brooks' *The Bunker Diary* (first published by Penguin early in 2013 but chosen as the winner of the 2014 Carnegie Medal in the period under review). For every voice raised in praise of this disturbing story of kidnapped children, there was another condemning it as an unsuitable winner. Brooks' novel was aimed at young adults and the author was already known for the dark edginess of his fiction but the debate about what is and is not appropriate subject matter for children's literature has been going on for many years and will probably continue for many more.

Despite reasonable calls from writers like Children's Laureate Malorie Blackman for more ethnic diversity in children's books, the sheer range of fiction published for children and young adults remains impressive and a small selection can only hint at the richness and variety of the titles on offer. Candy Gourlay's *Shine* (David Fickling) told the story of a young girl from a mysterious, rain-drenched island who is shunned by her fellow islanders because of an odd medical condition from which she suffers; *The Dark Wild* (Quercus) by Piers Torday, a sequel to *The Last Wild*, followed the further adventures of Kester Jaynes in a dystopian world where both humans and animals need a saviour; and Marcus Sedgwick's *She Is Not Invisible* (Indigo) was the tale of a blind girl and her young brother, travelling to America in search of their missing father. *Brilliant* (Macmillan) was another of Roddy Doyle's thoroughly engaging novels for children. *Allegiant* (HarperCollins) brought to a conclusion the 'Divergent' SF trilogy by Veronica Roth and E. Lockhart's *We Were Liars* (Hot Key Books) was a cunningly constructed suspense novel for young adults about a wealthy family with dark secrets to hide. David Walliams, a celebrity who has proved to be a genuine success as a children's writer, published *Demon Dentist* (HarperCollins), his sixth comic novel. Of recently published picture books none was more eagerly anticipated than *The Scarecrows' Wedding* (Scholastic), the latest collaboration between Julia Donaldson and Axel Scheffler.

NEWS AND FAREWELLS

News from the book trade continued to be the usual mixture of good and bad, with commentators often unable to agree on which was which. Was the decline in independent bookshops (the Booksellers' Association reported in February that there were fewer than 1,000 trading in the UK) an unmitigated disaster or did it mean that those which survived were those better equipped to face the challenges of the future? Was the continuing rise in sales of ebooks (up 20 per cent in 2013, according to industry figures) reason for celebration because literature of all kinds was so much in demand? Or was it reason for despair because the traditional printed book is under threat?

The biggest book retailer, of course, is Amazon but its dominance led to disputes, the most significant of which was probably the ongoing battle with the French-owned publishing group Hachette over ebook margins. There were other signs that Amazon, although continuing to be by far the most important player in the books market, was not always endearing itself to publishers, authors and readers. The controversy about how much tax the company had paid or should pay did not go away. Campaigners calling on Amazon to improve the pay and conditions of its workers gathered tens of thousands of signatures on a petition they presented to the company's London offices and briefly had a spoof book entitled *A Living Wage for All Amazon Workers* featured on its website. Veteran children's author Allan Ahlberg even turned down a Booktrust award for lifetime achievement because of its connection with Amazon.

On the high street rather than online, the news was in some ways encouraging. Waterstones opened its first shop in a new location in eight years in April. At the time of the opening in the Furlong Centre in Ringwood, Hampshire, Waterstones' managing director James Daunt promised new shops in other locations around the country and one in Lewes soon followed. Meanwhile Foyles, still arguably the most famous of all London bookshops, relocated from one site in Charing Cross Road to another in June. The company released an eye-opening timelapse video of the staff crating up some of the 500,000 books in stock and shifting them to their new store.

For many of the authors producing some of those half a million books, recent news has not been good. A survey commissioned by the Authors' Licensing and Collecting Society, published in July, revealed just how poorly most writers are rewarded for their work. The median income of a professional author turned out to be just £11,000, a figure which had dropped by 29 per cent in the nine years since the last such survey, and a mere 11.5 per cent of writers were able to live on the money earned from their writings alone. With reductions in both royalties and advances, many authors were clearly struggling to survive and the output of new titles in the future will surely reflect this.

As fierce argument about the funding of libraries continued, books were at the centre of other political controversies in the year. Justice minister Chris Grayling aroused the wrath of many when regulations were introduced in November 2013 which prevented people from sending books to prisoners in England and Wales. Author Philip Pullman, who described it as 'one of the most disgusting, mean, vindictive acts of a barbaric government' was by no means the only one to be appalled by the decision. In the spring of 2014, it was the turn of education minister Michael Gove to come under attack, amid claims that he was trying to ban such American classics as *Of Mice and Men* from the GCSE syllabus. Gove denied that he was doing anything of the sort but arguments over what should and should not be set as GCSE texts continued to rage. It sometimes seemed as if no story from the books world was entirely good news.

Even the unveiling of a statue in Portsmouth of Charles Dickens was tainted slightly by the fact that the subject had stipulated in his will that he should not be commemorated by any monument. However, looking at Martin Jennings' lively representation of the Victorian novelist, it was hard to see it as anything other than a welcome addition to the city's streets.

The world lost four winners of the Nobel Prize for Literature in the period under review. In August 2013, the Irish poet Seamus Heaney died in a Dublin clinic, reportedly soon after texting the words 'Noli timere' ('Do not fear') to his wife. In November, Doris Lessing, author of *The Golden Notebook* and the sequence of five novels known collectively as 'Children of Violence', passed away and, in April 2014, so too did the Colombian Gabriel Garcia Marquez, author of *One Hundred Years of Solitude* and one of the giants of South American and world literature. In July, the death of Nadine Gordimer, the South African novelist and short story-writer, was announced. The year from August 2013 to July 2014 also saw the losses of several other much-admired writers. The American crime novelist Elmore Leonard, once dubbed 'The Dickens of Detroit', died at the age of 87. Maya Angelou, poet and author of the sequence of autobiographical works that began with *I Know Why the Caged Bird Sings*, was a year younger when she passed away. In Britain, Sue Townsend, creator of hapless diarist Adrian Mole, succumbed to a stroke after many years of ill health.

Others who died in these 12 months included the American SF authors Frederik Pohl and Lucius Shepard; the writer and broadcaster Tom Vernon; the crime novelist Robert Barnard; Tom Clancy, whose thrillers featuring CIA man Jack Ryan were worldwide bestsellers; the Scottish historian and writer Andro Linklater; Paul Torday, author of *Salmon Fishing in the Yemen* and other novels; Leslie Thomas, the writer of *The Virgin Soldiers* and many other novels; Colin Wilson, who had begun his career as an Angry Young Man with the publication of *The Outsider* in 1956 and gone on to write many novels and books on true crime, mysticism and the occult; the novelist Elizabeth Jane Howard, author of the multi-volume 'Cazalet Chronicle'; the poets Sebastian Barker, Gerard Benson, John Hartley Williams and Rosemary Tonks; Richard Hoggart, author of *The Uses of Literacy*, who survived his son Simon Hoggart, the journalist and humorous writer, by three months; the beat writer and muse Carolyn Cassady; the Canadian short story-writer and novelist Mavis Gallant; Daniel Keyes, the author of *Flowers for Algernon;* Peter Matthiessen, novelist, co-founder of *The Paris Review* and travel writer; Mary Stewart, writer of a sequence of Arthurian novels; the children's writer and illustrator Eric Hill; the Canadian novelist Alistair Macleod; the literary agent Deborah Rogers; Dermot Healy, the Irish novelist and poet who wrote *A Goat's Song;* the children's writer Josephine Pullein-Thompson; and the literary scholar P. N. Furbank, biographer of E. M. Forster.

AWARDS

MAN BOOKER PRIZE 2013
Eleanor Catton – *The Luminaries*

SHORTLIST
NoViolet Bulawayo – *We Need New Names*
Jim Crace – *Harvest*
Jhumpa Lahiri – *The Lowland*
Ruth Ozeki – *A Tale for the Time Being*
Colm Tóibín – *The Testament of Mary*

COSTA BOOK AWARDS 2013
Book of the Year Award, Nathan Filer – *The Shock of the Fall*
First Novel Award, Nathan Filer – *The Shock of the Fall*
Novel Award, Kate Atkinson – *Life after Life*
Children's Book Award, Chris Riddell – *Goth Girl and the Ghost of a Mouse*
Poetry Award, Michael Symmons Roberts – *Drysalter*
Biography Award, Lucy Hughes-Hallett – *The Pike*

BAILEYS WOMEN'S PRIZE FOR FICTION 2014
Eimear McBride – *A Girl is a Half-Formed Thing*

SHORTLIST
Chimamanda Ngozi Adichie – *Americanah*
Hannah Kent – *Burial Rites*
Jhumpa Lahiri – *The Lowland*
Audrey Magee – *The Undertaking*
Donna Tartt – *The Goldfinch*

CARNEGIE MEDAL IN CHILDREN'S LITERATURE 2014
Kevin Brooks – *The Bunker Diary*

SHORTLIST
Julie Berry – *All The Truth That's in Me*
Rachel Campbell-Johnston – *The Child's Elephant*
Susan Cooper – *Ghost Hawk*
Anne Fine – *Blood Family*
Katherine Rundell – *Rooftoppers*
Rebecca Stead – *Liar & Spy*
William Sutcliffe – *The Wall*

MEDIA

Steve Clarke

TELEVISION

For all the talk of Twitter, the ubiquity of Facebook and people's love of their smartphones and tablets, it is sometimes forgotten that television remains the dominant medium of entertainment. Not only that, but our TV watching remains largely conservative. More than 90 per cent of viewing is of traditional 'linear' TV, rather than of catch-up services like the BBC's iPlayer. In 2014, on average, UK adults spent 221 minutes per day watching live TV plus a further 26 minutes watching previously recorded TV, according to Enders Analysis. Consumption patterns among younger adults were different, with 16–34-year-olds spending more time online than watching live TV.

WORLD CUP SCORES RATINGS GOAL
The summer's World Cup once again demonstrated the popularity of TV (despite England's failure to progress beyond the group stage). Over 20 million viewers watched Germany's extra time win over Argentina in the final, the vast majority of them on BBC One; the BBC's audience hit 16.7 million while ITV's peaked at 3.8 million.

Overall, during the period under review the BBC often appeared to be on the back foot while ITV was in expansionist mode. Not that the BBC failed to please audiences and reviewers. On the contrary, the year's programme highlights featured a number of obvious winners that, arguably, entertained very different audiences. There was the *Doctor Who* 50th anniversary special, 'Day of the Doctor' (watched by more than 10 million viewers in the UK alone), the second and third parts of David Hare's spell-binding spy story, *The Worricker Trilogy* starring Bill Nighy, and the much-praised crime series *Happy Valley*, containing a brilliant performance from Sarah Lancashire. In January 2014, the BBC screened the first of its programmes from the marathon First World War season designed to commemorate the conflict's centenary, the much-admired Jeremy Paxman documentary *Britain's Great War*.

As the Corporation struggled to move on from the impact of the Jimmy Savile affair and the cuts imposed by an earlier decision by the Coalition government to freeze the licence fee during the year under review, ITV was looking to grow.

In June it launched the drama repeats channel, ITV Encore, for Sky subscribers, while another new service, ITVBe, aimed at female viewers, would debut before the end of 2014. For the first time in a decade, ratings for the main ITV channel increased year on year, admittedly from a low base – from 15.7 per cent to 16.5 per cent, including the broadcaster's time-shift services.

THE CULLING OF BBC THREE
The perennial calls from distinguished broadcasters – often ex-BBC people – for the BBC to cut the number of services that it provides finally drew blood. In March, in a re-balancing of budgets, director-general Tony Hall announced that BBC Three would close as a TV station, subject to approval from the BBC Trust. The 'savings' of more than £50m would help to fund drama on BBC One. Killing off BBC Three was the first time in the Corporation's history that a TV channel had been axed.

From the autumn of 2015 the youth-friendly network would move to an online-only service. The BBC admitted that the decision was premature and said that '96 per cent of the consumption' of BBC Three was via traditional TV. There was immediate criticism of the decision. Comedy producer Ash Atalla said: 'It feels like a 60-year-old man walked into a really good nightclub and turned the music off so he can hear more Mozart next door.' Not everyone agreed. Actor James Corden suggested that scrapping BBC Three as a TV channel and moving it online made sense. The move showed that the BBC 'still had a commitment to BBC Three as a channel' and a willingness to provide a platform for young writers and performers.

PAXMAN EXITS *NEWSNIGHT* WITH BBC BLAST
There was stern criticism of the broadcaster's corporate culture from Jeremy Paxman, the 64-year-old presenter who in April surprised commentators when he announced that he was quitting *Newsnight;* three months later his successor was named as Evan Davis, the *Today* presenter.

Interviewed around this time by *The Guardian*, Paxman said: 'I love the BBC in many ways, but at the same time it has made me loathe aspects of it, and that's a very odd state of affairs. When I see people being given £1m merely for walking out of the door, when I see £100m being blown on that DMI [digital media initiative] thing, a stupid technical initiative like that, I start wondering: how much longer are we going to test the public's patience?'

Paxman's 25-year reign at *Newsnight* was drawing to a close, but elsewhere he was ubiquitous, continuing as the regular presenter of *University Challenge* and fronting *Britain's Great War*, which he also wrote. Cynics regarded the programme as a lengthy plug for his latest book, *Great Britain's Great War*, but others welcomed what they saw as a fresh, enquiring take on a very familiar subject.

For all its travails, the BBC's ability to laugh at itself was evident in a short new comedy series, *W1A*, from John Morton, the writer of the London Olympics satire, *Twenty Twelve*. Some BBC insiders felt that the programme's depiction of the BBC as a maddening, politically correct and bureaucratically over-blown institution was a little too closely observed for comfort.

BBC COMMEMORATES THE FIRST WORLD WAR
Overall, the BBC planned to broadcast 130 specially commissioned programmes commemorating the 100th anniversary of the First World War over the next four years. Alongside *Britain's Great War*, two of the first programmes broadcast were a drama documentary, *37 Days*, based on the European political crisis of July 1914, and *Crimson Field*, a drama set in a field hospital. Reviewers complained that the latter was predictable and it failed to win a second series.

They were more impressed by *37 Days*. 'What a cast, what costumes, and what talk', wrote Clive James in *The Daily Telegraph*. A BBC Two documentary examining the complex family relationships between the main European royal families in the years prior to 1914, *Royal Cousins at War*, was also admired.

Mass appeal entertainment shows like BBC One's *Strictly Come Dancing* retained their place in channel line-ups during the year under review. For the show's 86-year-old presenter, Bruce Forsyth, the 2014 season would be his last. In April he announced that he was quitting the series after a decade in charge of proceedings.

SHERLOCK RETURNS TO SOLVE RATINGS PUZZLE

The TV schedules remained addicted to crime stories. The return of *Sherlock* to BBC One in January was welcomed by viewers and critics alike as almost 10 million tuned in to the opening story, 'The Empty Hearse', the show's biggest audience to date. 'The third series of *Sherlock* has been event TV. Its lead actors are now at the top of their game. Together, Benedict Cumberbatch (statesman-like, hypnotic) and Martin Freeman (humble, deeply sympathetic) prove that charisma can come in very different forms', noted *The Telegraph's* Serena Davies. In the spring ITV's gritty new thriller, *Prey*, starring Rosie Cavaliero as DCI Susan Reinhardt, won many admirers.

However, it was another female detective, Sgt Catherine Cawood played by Sarah Lancashire, in BBC One's frequently violent *Happy Valley*, scripted by Sally Wainwright, which thrilled reviewers. Opined Mark Lawson in *The Guardian:* 'Some of Lancashire's close-ups in this show – especially her bloodied face after nearly being beaten to death by her daughter's nemesis – have provoked complaints to newspapers and the TV regulator, OFCOM. But the violence can be justified by the series' recurrent theme of violence, physical and mental, suffered by women.'

Another crime series focusing on a female detective, BBC Two's *Line of Duty*, prompted the *Daily Mail* columnist Jan Moir to ask if the programme was the best cop show ever. Writer Jed Mercurio's complex plotting won plaudits, as did Keeley Hawes' depiction of the mysterious Detective Inspector Lindsay Denton.

Earlier in the year, Inspector Hercule Poirot solved his final case when David Suchet made his last appearance in the long-running ITV series. Over almost 25 years *Poirot* had run to 70 episodes. Not everyone was pleased by the prevalence of crime drama and regarded it as a welcome relief when TV drama left the crime scene to instead investigate other parts of the fictional universe.

DOCTOR WHO TRIO REGENERATES

The success of 'The Day of the Doctor', featuring three doctors – Matt Smith, David Tennant and John Hurt, plus a cameo by Tom Baker – confirmed audiences' appetites for one of TV's most enduring brands. The *Doctor Who* 50th anniversary special set a Guinness world record as 'the world's largest-ever simulcast of a TV drama'. The episode was aired in 94 countries and was a big iTunes seller too.

Turning from fantasy to drama based on the lives of real celebrities, ITV's *Tommy Cooper: Not Like That, Like This* generated mixed reviews, but most critics agreed that David Threlfall's portrayal of one of Britain's most-loved comedians was exceptional. Tom Hollander received plaudits for his depiction of Dylan Thomas (and especially his readings of the poet's work) during a visit to Manhattan in 1953, in BBC Two's *A Poet in New York*. Technical standards in TV drama are generally high but when BBC One broadcast an adaptation of Daphne du Maurier's *Jamaica Inn*, viewers complained that the actors were mumbling. The show quickly became known as Jamaica Inn-audible.

'POVERTY PORN' GETS THE NATION TALKING

Television's ability to spark a national conversation and keep newspapers interested for days at a time was demonstrated by a new Channel 4 documentary, *Benefits Street*, which gave the broadcaster a much-needed hit. It was filmed in James Turner Street in Birmingham, where claiming state benefits was the norm. The series resonated with opinion formers and audiences partly because the programme attempted to engage with the government's highly controversial welfare reform agenda.

Several of the residents were unhappy about how *Benefits Street* depicted them. They complained that the film makers had misled them. Others, like the writer Owen Jones, insisted that *Benefits Street* was another attempt by television to demonise society's underprivileged. Writing in *The Independent*, he said: 'This is just the latest such programme – Channel 4's *Skint*, Channel 5's *On Benefits and Proud*, BBC Three's *People Like Us* being others – which present an entirely distorted picture of what our welfare state is, much to the benefit of our political elite.' The only clear winner from the furore over *Benefits Street* was Channel 4, which secured its highest audience since 2012 as more than 5 million tuned in.

Another Channel 4 show that made an impact during the year under review was *Gogglebox*, the latest reality hit from the creator of *Wife Swap*, Stephen Lambert. The reactions of a cross-section of people as they relaxed in their living rooms watching TV proved oddly compelling. Once again Lambert's team had worked hard to find a group of characters that provided compulsive viewing.

Educating Yorkshire, also broadcast by Channel 4, won a lot of fans. Once more, the heart of the show's appeal was its characters, pupils and teachers working at a tough comprehensive school in Dewsbury, West Yorkshire. 'Going into *Educating Yorkshire* wasn't a snap decision', wrote assistant head Mr Burton. 'We wanted to show that we're proud of who we are, that we offer a high standard of education, and that we work damned hard for every child who comes to us. We wanted to make sure that people see exactly what teachers do for your kids – whether it's in Yorkshire, Yeovil, Liverpool, Lincoln, Cornwall or Cardiff – and how they perform minor miracles on a daily basis.' Few who saw the programme would disagree.

The year under review saw the launch of a new wave of local TV services, led by *London Live* in the capital. The station is run by the owners of the *Evening Standard* and *The Independent*, the Lebedevs. Critics admired the fact that, unusually for a British TV channel, *London Live* looked determined to reflect the diversity of its target audience. But low viewing figures cast doubt on the venture's long-term financial viability. Another sign of how increasingly key parts of UK television are owned by foreign companies – often US giants – became clear in May when Richard Desmond, publisher of the *Daily Express*, sold Channel 5 to US media behemoth Viacom, the assets of which include MTV and Comedy Central.

RADIO

For many years, British commercial radio has languished under the shadow cast by the mighty BBC Radio. During the year under review there were signs that the tide may be turning, at least in London where the surge in listening to speech station LBC was compared to the rise of UKIP across parts of the UK during local and European elections.

THE RISE AND RISE OF LBC

At the Radio Academy's awards in May, LBC received the Special Award for two programmes, *Call Clegg* and *Ask Boris*, hosted respectively by Nick Clegg and Boris Johnson. In February, following 40 years of broadcasting, LBC finally went national thanks to digital transmission. The veteran *Daily Telegraph* radio reviewer Gillian Reynolds gleefully suggested that LBC's approach owed nothing to the BBC: 'You won't find a show like *Call Clegg* on the BBC. This is rough, bold radio, the old familiar phone-in format turned into a bustling on-air boxing booth.'

Now billed as 'Leading Britain's Conversation' (the station's original name was the London Broadcasting

Company), Reynolds was not the only commentator to praise the station's no-nonsense approach that avoided political correctness. Presenters Nick Ferrari and James O'Brien were singled out for praise; the Broadcasting Press Guild named Ferrari as radio broadcaster of the year and O'Brien's interview with UKIP leader Nigel Farage in May won admiration from all sides of the political spectrum. 'Nigel Farage was mauled live on air by LBC's James O'Brien this morning, in over 22 painful minutes of questioning over whether his party is racist, how comfortable he is with his wife speaking German, and his financial arrangements', said the left-wing *New Statesman*. The contrast between O'Brien's aggressive approach and the relatively gentle treatment handed out by Jeremy Paxman on the BBC's *Newsnight* to the UKIP chairman was widely remarked upon.

In London, the station had a greater market share than its nearest rival, BBC 5 Live (5.6 per cent to 4.3 per cent). And in the past five years, LBC had expanded its reach by 67 per cent compared with 5 Live's 7 per cent. The reason for LBC's newfound prominence? Look no further than the presenters, advised *The Observer's* Rachel Cooke. She described their style as being as 'fervent as evangelists'. Cooke added: 'They run a kind of radio confession box, and this involves a certain kind of devotion, one they seem to have in spades.'

RADIO 2 SCALES NEW HEIGHTS

Of course, LBC's audience was small compared with the BBC's listening figures for its own national stations. The year under review saw further gains by Britain's most popular radio station, Radio 2. When the RAJAR statistics were published in May, Radio 2 – named UK station of the year at the Radio Academy awards – was ahead of the pack, registering 15.6 million listeners a week in the first quarter of 2014. It was another new high for the station. There were record ratings for DJs Chris Evans, Ken Bruce, Steve Wright and Graham Norton. Evans attracted 9.83 million listeners; Norton drew 4.3 million listeners; Ken Bruce had a weekly reach of 8.4 million; and 8.1 million people tuned into Steve Wright's afternoon show.

OPERATION YEWTREE STRIKES AGAIN

Not everything was going to plan at Radio 2, however. One notable absentee from its schedules was veteran broadcaster Paul Gambaccini. Since his arrest in October, on suspicion of sexual offences, by officers from Operation Yewtree (set up following the Jimmy Savile scandal), he had decided it was best if he remained off air for the time being.

During the period under review, Radio 1 was urged by the BBC Trust to connect more strongly with younger audiences. The policy appeared to be working. Even though DJ Nick Grimshaw was losing listeners – 5.85 million during the first three months of 2014 compared with his predecessor Chris Moyles' final audience of 6.7 million – Radio 1 said that the show had gained 130,000 listeners aged 24 and under and shed more than half a million over-25s.

In an online age, another way for Radio 1 to potentially increase its popularity with young people was to offer video streams. In October, the BBC announced that Radio 1 would have its own iPlayer channel to allow fans to watch exclusive performances and interviews not broadcast elsewhere.

Catering to older radio lovers, Radio 4's listening levels were marginally down – by 2.2 per cent to 10.9 million in the first three months of 2014. One of the station's prominent presenters, Mark Lawson, host of the arts review *Front Row,* announced in March that he would be leaving the programme after 16 years for 'personal reasons'. There were reports alleging bullying by members of the programme's team, which Lawson was understood to have denied.

TODAY FINALLY DELIVERS ALL-FEMALE LINE-UP

Radio 4's flagship *Today* programme continued to generate headlines. In October, the show's keenly anticipated new female presenter, Mishal Husain, made her debut. *The Observer's* Miranda Sawyer remarked: 'On Thursday morning the *Today* programme was presented by two women, Sarah Montague and Mishal Husain. There was also a female newsreader, Corrie Cofield, and a woman sports presenter, Alison Mitchell. It should be noted that the sky did not fall in.' Husain told *The Guardian* that her new job was highly demanding: 'I felt so drained, and I remember I looked across at John [Humphrys] and said, "I can't believe we've only been on air for half an hour!"'

There was surprise in the arts community, and among listeners, when in the spring it emerged that Roger Wright, controller of Radio 3 and director of the Proms, had resigned. It was reported that Wright had been passed over as the BBC's new director of music in favour of Bob Shennan, controller of Radio 2. 'It is a clear snub to Wright, whose Radio 3 remains a daily demonstration of the power of great music to lift the soul, and whose Proms seasons have been the most imaginative and successful for decades', remarked *Sunday Times* columnist Paul Donovan.

THE PRESS

Newspaper ethics dominated the year under review. For much of the period, the eight-month phone hacking trial was centre stage. The jury heard that phone hacking took place on 'an industrial scale' at the now-defunct *News of the World*. Many thousands of messages on the phones of up to 5,500 people were illegally accessed. However, the jury at the Old Bailey failed to convict ex-*News of the World* editor Rebekah Brooks of phone hacking and bribing public officials.

EX-*NEWS OF THE WORLD* EDITOR CONVICTED

Her former colleague and lover, Andy Coulson, David Cameron's former communications chief, was however found guilty of phone hacking and sentenced to two years' imprisonment. The jury was dismissed after it failed to reach a verdict on whether Coulson conspired to commit misconduct in a public office. It had been alleged that Coulson paid police officers for two royal phone directories.

The verdicts triggered widespread debate over a range of issues. These included whether it had been right to spend so much money and time investigating criminal activity at the *News of the World*, and what the trial said about the way that power elites operate in modern Britain; it was estimated that the trial cost almost £100m, making it one of the most expensive in British history.

Apart from the revelation of Brooks and Coulson's six-year on-off affair, one of the most telling pieces of evidence to emerge at the trial, in the minds of many opinion formers, was that the former prime minister Tony Blair gave advice to Brooks at the height of the phone hacking crisis in July 2011. In an hour-long phone call with Brooks, Blair offered his personal guidance on how to deal with the storm engulfing her. He also said that he was available in an unofficial capacity to help Rupert Murdoch and his son James, then running the *News of the World's* publisher, News International.

THE POWER OF THE PRESS TO HIRE TOP LAWYERS

Some commentators, including the *Daily Mail,* implied that the trial was part of an attack on press freedom and a waste of public money. Others, like *The Guardian,* pointed out that the prosecution's case was hampered by austerity-style legal budgets which had to compete with the 'Rolls Royce' legal teams employed by Brooks and paid for by Rupert Murdoch.

Writing in the *London Review of Books* in July, the co-author of *Dial M for Murdoch – News Corporation and the Corruption of Britain,* Martin Hickman, observed: 'What have we learned? That, as the *News of the World* knew, if you want to prove somebody has done something wrong, you need good evidence. And that QCs earn every penny.'

One of the myths that rapidly grew up around the trial was that only Coulson was convicted for phone hacking. In fact, as Roy Greenslade reminded readers in *The Guardian,* three senior *News of the World* executives, Greg Miskiw, James Weatherup and Neville Thurlbeck, plus reporter Dan Evans and private investigator Glenn Mulcaire, all pleaded guilty at the Old Bailey.

HOW 'INDEPENDENT' IS NEW PRESS WATCHDOG?
During the year under review, the related and highly vexed topic of press regulation concentrated the minds of national newspaper editors and owners. A new press regulator, the Independent Press Standards Organisation (IPSO), supported by the *Mail,* the Murdoch press and *The Daily Telegraph,* will be set up in the autumn to replace the widely discredited Press Complaints Commission. The body will have more powers to investigate and levy fines than its predecessor, but there will be no independent oversight of its workings backed by Royal Charter. Some papers such as the *Financial Times* declined to join IPSO and would instead rely on their own complaints processes. *The Guardian* and *The Independent* were still considering their options.

The Hacked Off campaign, whose supporters included J. K. Rowling and the parents of Milly Dowler, whose phone was hacked by the *News of the World,* dismissed IPSO as another watchdog policed by the papers that it is supposed to regulate. Hacked Off's executive director Joan Smith opined: 'The press industry's self-regulator failed to work because, as always, such regulators are controlled by the big newspapers they are supposed to oversee. The Press Complaints Commission – much like its latest incarnation, IPSO – was designed from the outset to be powerless to investigate, powerless to sanction and thus powerless to prevent unethical, even criminal, behaviour. Even as journalists are being jailed, some newspapers refuse to accept that they must change their culture, or that they must implement [Lord] Leveson's recommendations for effective, independent regulation. Until they do, the public at large – and the journalists who work for these companies – remain at risk from unethical and unlawful newspaper conduct, without adequate remedy.'

NEWSPAPER SALES CONTINUE TO SLIDE
Circulation figures for national newspapers published in June showed that the overall daily newsprint market was falling at a rate of more than 8 per cent a year. Figures produced by the Audit Bureau of Circulation suggested that the Sunday market, which now sells some 570,000 fewer copies than the weekday issues, was declining slightly faster at over 9 per cent a year.

Some newspapers were holding their own, though. *The Times* enjoyed a slight year-on-year increase, of 0.66 per cent, while *The Guardian* recorded a drop of just 0.9 per cent. *The Daily Telegraph,* whose sales fell by 5.94 per cent, and *i,* with a 5.5 per cent fall, fared better than some of their competitors. The *Financial Times* saw sales fall by 14.68 per cent as the paper concentrated on building digital subscriptions, while *The Independent* was down 13.08 per cent.

Sales of the red-top tabloids were down too. The *Daily Star* lost 75,000 buyers during the year (a decrease of 13.67 per cent) while *The Sun* fell 9.37 per cent. The *Daily Mirror*

decreased by 7.71 per cent, the *Daily Mail* dropped 7.36 per cent and the *Daily Express* suffered an 8.15 per cent decline.

In autumn 2013, Labour leader Ed Miliband was involved in a dispute with the *Daily Mail* over a claim that his late father, Ralph, a much-admired Marxist academic, was 'a man who hated Britain'. The politician refuted the smear by pointing out in a subsequent *Mail* article that his father loved Britain and had served his adopted country in the Royal Navy during the Second World War.

THE INTERNET

During the year under review, the internet celebrated its 25th anniversary. To coincide with this milestone, the founder of the worldwide web, Sir Tim Berners-Lee, pinpointed the challenges facing a means of communication synonymous with social media services such as Twitter and Facebook, and the ubiquitous search engine Google.

In March, Berners-Lee wrote: 'As the Web enters its next quarter century, we urgently need even more data to inform the current debate on what it will take to enhance and defend the Web. The Web community – and the world at large – are wrestling with tough issues around security, surveillance, privacy, open infrastructure, net neutrality, content protection, and more. These global decisions must be made based on the best possible information.'

FACEBOOK MANIPULATES OUR EMOTIONS
Undoubtedly issues concerning security, surveillance and privacy were foremost in 2013–14. In the summer it emerged that Facebook had conducted an experiment in January 2012 in which it had deliberately skewed what 689,000 Facebook users saw when they logged in. Some of the service's users saw content containing a lot of positive and happy words, while others were shown content with more negative or sadder sentiments. The study showed that, when the experimental week was over, the unwitting guinea-pigs were more likely to post status updates and messages that were (respectively) positive or negative in tone.

'Statistically, the effect on users was relatively small, but the implications were obvious: Facebook had shown that it could manipulate people's emotions', wrote *The Observer's* John Naughton, who was not surprised by Facebook's actions. 'When the story of this period comes to be written, one thing that will astonish historians is the complaisant ease with which billions of apparently sane people allowed themselves to be monitored and manipulated by government security agencies and giant corporations.'

However, there were signs that perhaps the Facebook bubble was set to burst. In January, it was reported that the social networking behemoth would eventually die out 'like the bubonic plague'. US scientists at Princeton University argued that the site had spread like an infectious disease, but users were slowly becoming immune to its appeal.

They predicted that Facebook would be largely abandoned by 2017 after comparing the growth curve of epidemics like the plague to those of social networks. Facebook, which celebrated its tenth birthday in February, was forecast to lose 80 per cent of its users within the next three years. But there was a catch – researchers John Cannarella and Joshua Spechler based their prediction on the number of times that Facebook is typed into Google as a search term.

They discovered that Facebook searches peaked in December 2012 and have begun to tail off. According to estimates, 870 million people use Facebook via their smartphones each month, which could explain the drop in Google searches. Users accessing the site no longer do so by typing the name of the site into Google but by accessing it directly from their phones via the Facebook app.

In any case, in 2013–14 Facebook's share price reached record highs as the company was valued at £85bn. It also splashed the cash. In February, Facebook made its biggest acquisition to date when it bought messaging app WhatsApp for £11.4bn, paying in cash and shares. Several commentators wondered if the purchase would end badly. The BBC's North America technology correspondent, Richard Taylor, commented: 'Some are seeing the $19bn price tag as further evidence of swollen valuations of companies as the sector experiences what may yet prove to be another dotcom bubble. WhatsApp does give [Facebook founder] Mark Zuckerberg inroads into international markets and, as importantly, to a younger demographic. But what is less clear is whether the finances will add up in the long term.'

ALL A-TWITTER AS SOCIAL NETWORKING SITE FLOATS

Those looking for signs of a repeat of the 2000 dotcom bubble needed to look no further than the November stock market launch of Twitter. On the day of the flotation, the shares opened at $26 and closed at $44.90, valuing the company at around $31bn. Analysts warned that the valuation was unsustainable. As the year progressed, Twitter duly struggled to live up to investor expectations, while Facebook outperformed predictions.

Whatever the future holds for these social networking giants, during the year under review their popularity was much in evidence at events like the summer's World Cup football tournament. Pundits described the competition as 'the first real Twitter World Cup'. A total of 12.2 million tweets were sent from 150 countries during the opening match between Brazil and Croatia. The semi-final featuring Germany and Brazil set a new record for the most tweets about a single sporting event with 35.6 million posts on Twitter; Germany's 1-0 victory in the final peaked at 618,725 tweets a minute, with a total of 32.1 million tweets sent during the game.

The competition exposed the shortcomings of the internet too. Coverage of the first match on the ITV Player was interrupted when the streaming service broke down due to unprecedented numbers of people watching it. Inevitably, angry viewers used social media to express their frustration.

ONLINE NEWS OVERTAKES PRINT

In 2013–14 there was fresh evidence that online news was more popular than traditional newspapers. Research by OFCOM showed that 41 per cent of people said that they accessed news online. This was marginally ahead of those who preferred to receive their news in the form of print – 40 per cent – the same figure as the previous year when the percentage of readers whose preference for online news via websites or apps was 32 per cent. Among younger people (16–34-year-olds) the statistics for online news consumption were more impressive still. OFCOM found that receiving news through any online medium was three times higher for those in the 16–24 age group (60 per cent) than in the 55 and over age group (21 per cent).

However, despite TV news seeing a small decrease year on year, it remained far and away the most popular media platform for people to access the news. The BBC website or app was the third-most used news source in the UK, according to OFCOM.

CLASSICAL MUSIC AND OPERA

Leonora Dawson Bowling

ANNIVERSARIES

The 2013–14 classical music season continued to celebrate the 2013 bicentenaries of Verdi and Wagner across the country. The Royal Opera House put on a new production of Verdi's *Les Vêpres Siciliennes* while the Hallé and Sir Mark Elder undertook an exploration of Verdi's last three operas, *Simon Boccanegra, Falstaff* and *Otello.* The Royal Opera House also staged a new production of Wagner's *Parsifal* and, most notably, the 2013 BBC Proms programmed the entire *Ring* cycle and three further Wagner operas.

Britten's centenary was also celebrated through to the end of 2013. Opera North devoted its entire autumn season to productions of *Peter Grimes, A Midsummer Night's Dream* and *Death in Venice;* the Hallé opened its season with the first complete performance in the UK of a sequence of Britten pieces written for American radio in 1942; the London Philharmonic Orchestra presented *Peter Grimes,* the *War Requiem* and a number of rarely performed orchestral works over three concerts as part of the festival 'The Rest Is Noise'; the Royal Scottish National Orchestra also performed the *War Requiem* during Remembrance Week as part of its centenary celebrations while the BBC Scottish Symphony Orchestra explored Britten's fascination with Mahler's work; Aldeburgh Music hosted a bursting centenary weekend surveying the diversity of Britten's music, particularly the development of the string quartet and choral works, as well as mounting performances of the *Spring Symphony, Serenade for Tenor, Horn and Strings,* the *Four Sea Interludes* (from *Peter Grimes*), *Noye's Fludde* and *The Young Person's Guide to the Orchestra;* the latter work was also the centrepiece of the 'Britten 100' series run by the Royal Liverpool Philharmonic, which originally played its world premiere in October 1946.

With the start of 2014 came the 150th anniversary of Richard Strauss' birth. The Royal Opera House mounted productions of *Die Frau ohne Schatten* and *Elektra* while Glyndebourne staged *Der Rosenkavalier;* the Philharmonia Orchestra ran a series of Strauss concerts including his *Four Last Songs,* which the orchestra had originally premiered in 1950; the Liverpool Philharmonic 'Strauss Edition' series featured his *Horn Concerto No. 2, Ein Heldenleben, Don Quixote* and *Don Juan;* and, most exceptionally, the three professional Manchester orchestras, the Hallé, BBC Philharmonic Orchestra and Manchester Camerata, together covered a range of Strauss' work during the eight-week 'Strauss Voice' festival at the Bridgewater Hall, a festival which included a complete cycle of his orchestral songs and a mighty joint performance by the Hallé and the BBC Philharmonic of his *Alpine Symphony.*

The 300th anniversary of the birth of C. P. E. Bach, son of J. S. Bach and prolific composer in his own right, was celebrated by several chamber groups, orchestras and choirs in 2014. In particular, the Orchestra of the Age of Enlightenment focused on his symphonies as part of the 'Gamechangers' series in a concert entitled 'The Forgotten Revolutionary'; the Bournemouth Symphony Orchestra (BSO) and the BBC Singers united to give what is thought to be the first-ever performance of C. P. E. Bach's *St John Passion* after the BSO's chief conductor, Kirill Karabits, discovered the lost manuscript in a Kiev archive and transcribed it.

Other composer anniversaries in 2014 included Andrzej Panufnik's 100th anniversary (birth), Rameau's 250th anniversary (death), Gluck's 300th anniversary (birth), Lully's 350th anniversary (birth) and Hassler's 450th anniversary (birth).

The Academy of Ancient Music, the Taverner Consort, the English Concert and the Scottish Chamber Orchestra all celebrated their 40th birthdays while Glyndebourne Opera celebrated its 80th.

2014 also saw numerous commemorative concerts looking back 100 years to the outbreak of the First World War with performances of works composed at the time, including several by those who fought and, in some cases, died in the conflict.

OTHER HIGHLIGHTS

There was a strong thematic vein of personal and political influences on music running through the 2013–14 classical season. The London Symphony Orchestra (LSO) focused primarily on the influence of conductors in its two separate themes: 'Music Alchemists: Journeys with Great Conductors' featured ten concerts conducted by Bernard Haitink, Michael Tilson Thomas, Sir John Eliot Gardiner, Sir Mark Elder and Sir Simon Rattle; and 'The LSO invites...' featured eight conductors who were new to the orchestra, if well-established in the world of classical music. The Orchestra of the Age of Enlightenment (OAE) and Wigmore Hall both explored composers: the OAE's new series 'Gamechangers' examined composers and works that broke the mould and were pivotal in shaping musical history while Wigmore Hall's 'Songlives' series considered either works from a single specific year or works across the evolution of a single composer's life, including works by Schumann, Debussy, Duparc and Richard Strauss.

Cellist Steven Isserlis' thoughtful 'Music in the Shadow of War' series at Wigmore Hall contemplated the artistic record of haunting and prophetic musical responses to the two World Wars and the oppressive onset of both fascism and Soviet communism. Similarly, the City of London Sinfonia's series 'Hot Tunes, Cold War' reflected on the shaping of and influence on classical music by political events of the 20th century and the eruption of jazz and swing with works by Britten, Shostakovich and Copland. The final months of 'The Rest Is Noise' festival at the Southbank Centre explored events of the latter half of the 20th century and related contemporaneous music by Britten, Berio, Stockhausen, Glass, Gubaidulina and Adams among others.

At Kings Place, having 'unwrapped' the chamber music of four individual composers (Chopin, Mozart, Brahms and Bach) in previous years, the 'Unwrapped' series placed the whole genre of chamber music under the spotlight in 2014 and involved audiences in deciding which chamber works they would like to hear.

Elsewhere, piano works by Beethoven took centre stage across the season: the BBC Scottish Symphony Orchestra continued its cycle of Beethoven piano concertos, featuring Scottish pianist Steven Osborne, while Saleem Ashkar commenced his journey through Beethoven's complete piano sonatas at the Sage, Gateshead. Renowned Beethoven interpreter John Lill meanwhile celebrated his 70th birthday by performing all 32 of Beethoven's piano sonatas at the Cadogan Hall.

The works of Brahms also appeared prevalent in the UK's orchestral powerhouses: the BSO performed an entire Brahms symphony cycle and the Philharmonia presented a complete Brahms symphony and concerto series, which also culminated in his *Ein Deutsches Requiem*. The Hallé Orchestra and Chorus also came together to perform the *Requiem* as did the BBC National Orchestra and Chorus of Wales, which also performed the Poulenc *Gloria* and Fauré *Requiem* in a season which celebrated the chorus' 30th year.

The Fauré *Requiem* also featured as part of the BBC Symphony Orchestra season, which had strong French tendencies with programmes encompassing Poulenc's richly lush *Concerto for Two Pianos* and surreal opera *Les Mamelles de Tirésias*, and Ravel's *Mother Goose Suite*.

The Philharmonia Orchestra started a three-year exploration of Berlioz's music under the guidance of Esa-Pekka Salonen with performances of *The Damnation of Faust* and his *Symphonie Fantastique*, while the LSO under Valery Gergiev also staged 11 concerts interpreting the works of Berlioz alongside Scriabin's complete orchestral works. The Philharmonia furthermore produced a major new project entitled 'Bohemian Legends' under Czech conductor Jakub Hrůša, celebrating the musical legacy of Dvořák and his associates. The Scottish Chamber Orchestra similarly undertook an exploration of a number of Dvořák's works as well as a complete Schumann symphony cycle.

British music provided a central focus for several orchestras, with the BBC Scottish Symphony Orchestra concluding its cycle of Vaughan Williams symphonies with his *Sea Symphony*, the same symphony also performed by the Hallé, while the LSO's 'Sounds British' series featured works by Britten, Walton and Elgar as well as Panufnik, Maxwell Davies, Huw Watkins and Harrison Birtwistle.

In contrast, the BBC Scottish Symphony Orchestra looked across the pond for a major exploration of American composers including Copland, Gershwin, Ives, Barber and Adams. The BBC National Orchestra of Wales similarly plumbed the music of Barber, Copland, Bernstein and Adams amongst lesser-known composers in its 'Americana' concerts as well as presenting an overview of 100 years of film score music in 'America at the Movies'. The Royal Liverpool Philharmonic also took up the notion of film music with its 'Great Movie Themes' and 'Classical Music Goes to the Movies' concerts.

Russian big-hitters also appeared frequently in the concert hall: the BSO featured a Rachmaninov focus alongside other Russian repertoire, including Prokofiev's *Sinfonia Concertante* and *Symphony No. 2*. The Royal Liverpool Orchestra presented music by some of the 'great Russian composers', foregrounding Stravinsky, Shostakovich, Prokofiev, Tchaikovsky, Rachmaninov and Rimsky-Korsakov while the BBC National Orchestra of Wales also focused on works by Shostakovich, Rachmaninov and Prokofiev alongside those of Bartók, Brahms and Szymanowski.

The City of London Sinfonia embarked on the performance of music that it felt represented science versus religion, nature versus the mystical, in its 'Natural/Supernatural' series with works ranging from Mozart's *Magic Flute* overture and Beethoven's *Symphony No. 6* ('Pastoral') to Arvo Pärt's *Litany and Fratres* and John Tavener's *Supernatural Songs* and *The Protecting Veil* (along with a host of other Tavener works at a concert intended to be a celebration of his 70th birthday – see 'Obituaries').

The Royal Festival Hall celebrated having its organ restored and fully working with its 'Pull Out All the Stops' festival, including an opening gala concert, celebrity recitals from John Scott, Thomas Trotter and Olivier Latry, and performances of major organ works such as Saint-Saëns' *Organ Symphony* (London Philharmonic Orchestra) and Janáček's *Glagolitic Mass* (Philharmonia). The festival also revealed eight new Southbank Centre organ commissions by Tavener, Maxwell Davies, Neil Hannon, Martin Creed, Lynette Wallworth, Simon Holt, Kaija Saariaho and Terry Riley.

The discovery of newer music was a clear priority for several of the nation's orchestras as well. The Royal Northern Sinfonia staged an exploration of the music of John Casken while the Hallé performed the world premiere of Casken's oboe concerto *Apollinaire's Bird* along with the premiere of Ryan Wigglesworth's revised *Violin Concerto*. The Royal Liverpool Philharmonic also gave the world premiere of Steve Copland's percussion concerto *Poltroons in Paradise* while the London Philharmonic Orchestra premiered James MacMillan's *Viola Concerto* and Górecki's much-anticipated *Symphony No. 4*, the composer's last work.

FESTIVALS

The 119th season of the BBC Proms during the summer of 2013 made history by being the first season ever to have the famous Last Night of the Proms concert conducted by a female conductor, Marin Alsop. The festival also hosted its first-ever free concert, where the National Youth Orchestra of Great Britain performed Beethoven's *Symphony No. 9* along with Mark-Anthony Turnage's response to the latter, *Frieze*. True to the festival's pledge to reach out to all audiences, 2013 saw the first 'urban classical' prom, and Nigel Kennedy's jazzified interpretation of Vivaldi's *Four Seasons* also drew delighted crowds and dissent in equal measure.

The season also included 18 premieres, among them Thomas Adès's *Totentanz* and Frederic Rzweski's *Piano Concerto*. Featured composers included Sir Granville Bantock, his work somewhat neglected and forgotten, Sir Michael Tippett, most notably his opera *The Midsummer Marriage*, and Tchaikovsky's entire symphony cycle was performed. Britten's centenary was marked with works throughout the series including the opera *Billy Budd* as well as a world premiere of his youthful *Elegy for Strings*. In their bicentenary years, there was a small nod to Verdi while Wagner formed the central focus of the festival; the entire stupendous *Ring* cycle was performed by the Staatskapelle Berlin under the baton of Daniel Barenboim and, not doing anything by halves, the Proms also programmed *Tristan und Isolde* (BBC Symphony Orchestra under Semyon Bychkov), *Tannhäuser* (BBC Scottish Symphony under Donald Runnicles) and *Parsifal* (Hallé under Sir Mark Elder). Audiences also enjoyed a selection of more rarely performed piano concertos including Malcolm Arnold's *Concerto for Two Pianos (Three Hands)*, Glazunov's *Piano Concerto No. 2* and Stravinsky's *Concerto for Piano and Wind Instruments*.

The 67th Edinburgh International Festival over the last three weeks of August played host to a good selection of 20th-century and contemporary music with works by Berio, Varèse, Kurtág and Stockhausen, and a re-interpreted version of Berg's unfinished opera *Lulu* by Olga Neuwirth; performers included Ensemble MusikFabrik, Philip Glass, Pierre-Laurent Aimard and Marco Stroppa. Other central focuses were double bills by: the Bavarian Radio Symphony Orchestra with two symphonic greats, Tchaikovsky *Symphony No. 6* and Mahler *Symphony No. 2;* the Chamber Orchestra of Europe combining Strauss vignettes with Classical works they hark back to, including two Beethoven symphonies; the Russian National Orchestra performing Rachmaninov's *Piano Concertos Nos. 2 and 3;* Les Musiciens du Louvre Grenoble exploring five Schubert symphonies; and the Zurich Tonhalle presenting an all-Brahms programme. Oper Frankfurt delved into the theme of 'desire, obsession and doomed love' in Purcell's *Dido and Aeneas* and Bartók's *Bluebeard's Castle*. The Opéra de Lyon's performance of Beethoven's *Fidelio* explored the broader festival theme of technological innovation and its impact, setting the action in the future on a doomed spacecraft hurtling towards infinity.

Running throughout the ten-day 36th Huddersfield Contemporary Music Festival in November 2013 was the complex but melodic compositional output of Spanish composer-in-residence Hèctor Parra. Other highlights among the 31 world premieres and 92 UK premieres included an unconventional 'piano duo day' (including a piece for handcuffed pianists), audio-video installations by Irish art collective Grúpat and new works from Brian Ferneyhough as part of his 70th birthday celebration. There were also political statements in the form of Georg Friedrich Hass' tormented microtonal soundworld *In Vain,* composed following the rise of the right-wing Freedom Party in Austria, and Cecilia Ore's *Come to the Edge!,* which set parts of the transcripts from the controversial Pussy Riot trials.

Garsington Opera, running from June to July, celebrated its 25th anniversary with productions of Offenbach's comedy *Vert-Vert* (British premiere), Janáček's *The Cunning Little Vixen* (Wormsley's woodland providing a perfect backdrop) and a revival of the Garsington Opera Fidelio by Beethoven. The latter opera also formed part of a commemorative weekend, 'Peace in our Time?', marking 100 years since the outbreak of the First World War. The weekend also featured other music and poetry on the themes of justice, self-sacrifice and the brotherhood of mankind, culminating in a performance of Beethoven's *Symphony No. 9.*

Concurrently, Grange Park Opera's 2014 summer festival featured Verdi's *La Traviata,* Britten's *Peter Grimes,* a revival production of Tchaikovsky's *Queen of Spades* and Massenet's *Don Quixote.* July's Longborough Festival Opera presented Handel's *Rinaldo,* Rossini's *The Barber of Seville* and Puccini's *Tosca.* The festival also programmed the concert entitled 'On the Road to *Tristan und Isolde*' featuring works by Weber, Beethoven and early Wagner ahead of 2015's planned production of the opera.

To mark 100 years since the start of the First World War, the central focus of the 67th Aldeburgh Festival was Britten's rarely performed pacifist opera *Owen Wingrave* in a new production along with a screening of the original BBC television production for which it was written. The June festival also focused on works by featured composer Tristan Murail as well as those of Ligeti and Janáček. Other highlights included performances by Ian Bostridge, Richard Goode, Mark Padmore, Thomas Adès and the City of Birmingham Symphony Orchestra, and the resident Chamber Orchestra of Europe.

As part of the 70th Cheltenham Music Festival in July, the first-ever Town Hall Festival Proms series was launched, aiming to bring classical music to audiences in a more relaxed, festive spirit. In recognition of its birthday, the festival's first-night orchestral concert opened and closed with the same works as the inaugural concert 70 years earlier, Beethoven's *Leonore Overture No. 3* and Elgar's *Enigma Variations,* and featured artist-in-residence violinist Nicola Benedetti's piano trio in Beethoven's triple concerto. Amongst the broad offerings of the festival, highlights included a concert commemorating the outbreak of the First World War, a thread of works by Andrzej Panufnik in his centenary year and by his daughter, Roxanna. In the final concert, Richard Blackford's *The Great Animal Orchestra* married animal sound recordings with orchestral motifs, particularly using the 44-note melody of the 'musician wren' as the theme for a set of variations. The work urged mankind to understand and respect the natural world.

The Buxton Festival in July also commemorated the start of the First World War with recitals of songs from the period and songs about the Great War performed by Joshua Elliot and Roderick Williams respectively, the former interspersed with personal war letters. The Huddersfield Choral Society also sang a commemorative programme of works by Parry, Quilter and Elgar. The season's chosen operas, the centrepiece of the festival, were Dvořák's much-underrated *The*

Jacobin, Gluck's *Orfeo ed Euridice,* H. K. Gruber's quirky 'cabaret opera' *Gloria – A Pigtale* and concert performances of Rossini's *Otello.*

OBITUARIES

In November 2013, English composer Sir John Tavener died aged 69 after a series of heart problems. Originally a talented pianist, his earlier compositions could be extravagantly avant-garde although his style moved towards more minimalist tendencies and often reflected the spiritual journey he himself was making; in 1977 he was received into the Orthodox Church and for many years Mother Thekla, abbess of an Orthodox Yorkshire monastery, was his spiritual advisor, librettist and collaborator. He latterly adopted a more universalist religious approach and set Islamic, Hindu, Sufi, Christian and Jewish texts and the music of the Native Americans. Recurrent motifs in his work were a preoccupation with death, the fall from grace and loss of childhood innocence, and the transition from darkness to light.

In January the following year, conductor Claudio Abbado lost a long battle to stomach cancer aged 80. The introspective but uncompromising Italian conductor worked with La Scala (in his native Milan), the LSO and the Berlin Philharmonic amongst many others and strove to teach orchestras to listen and attune to each other, learning to play together like chamber groups. He also pushed orchestras beyond the comfortable boundaries of familiar repertoire and set up the European Union Youth Orchestra, the Mahler Jugendorchester and the Orchestra Mozart, as well his very own Lucerne Festival Orchestra, filled from the ranks of the very best orchestras and passionately revered by them in return. He believed strongly in culture as part of the lives of local people, championing concerts in schools, factories and opening La Scala out of season for free viewings of films of recent opera productions. He considered music to be a constant journey of discovery to the end of his life.

In June, Spanish-German conductor Rafael Frühbeck de Burgos, who had strong associations with the Philharmonia Orchestra and the Philadelphia Orchestra, died aged 80. A strong proponent of Spanish music, particularly Manuel de Falla, he also allegedly brought the first performance of Bach's *St Matthew Passion* to Spain. Diagnosed with cancer only a couple of months before he died, he may not have been rewarded with posts due a conductor of his calibre but he had the gift for obtaining high standards from lesser orchestras and he was held in affection and respect by audiences and fellow musicians alike.

In July, conductor Lorin Maazel died aged 84 having conducted 111 concerts only the previous year. Born in France to Jewish-American parents and brought up in the US, the child prodigy violinist and conductor was assisted by Toscanini in obtaining his first steady conducting job at the ripe age of 12. Eventually chief conductor of the Deutsche Oper and Berlin Radio Symphony Orchestra and later music director of the Cleveland Orchestra and the Orchestre National de France, he also worked with many other orchestras and was the associate conductor of the Philharmonia Orchestra in London for over 40 years from 1971. He was notably the first American, the youngest conductor and the first Jew since the Second World War to conduct at the Bayreuth Wagner festival in Germany (in 1960). A conductor who loved exploring and interpreting music that challenged him and was frustrated with music that did not, he was also a talented violinist, a composer (including an opera based on Orwell's *Nineteen Eighty-Four*) and opera director, and actively supported UNESCO, the Red Cross and the World Wide Fund for Nature.

Alexander Ivashkin, cellist, founder of the Bolshoi Soloists and promoter of Russian music, known for his writing on

Alfred Schnittke, died of cancer aged 64; Bryan Fairfax, who conducted the first English performances of works by Mahler, Shostakovich, Bruckner and Schmidt and a bold early performance of Havergal Brian's *Gothic Symphony*, died aged 88; Franz-Paul Decker, former conductor of the Orchestre Symphonique de Montréal, died aged 90; Gerd Albrecht, the former principal conductor of the Czech Philharmonic Orchestra, renowned for championing new music and the music of Jews who died in the Holocaust, died aged 78; Bulgarian operatic basso profundo Nicola Ghiuselev died aged 77; Patrice Chéreau, film, opera and stage director known particularly for his Bayreuth *Ring* cycle production in 1976, died from lung cancer at 68; Polish serialist and later minimalist composer Wojciech Kilar, best known for his film scores – particularly *Bram Stoker's Dracula* and *The Pianist* – died from cancer aged 81; and Italian operatic tenor Carlo Begonzi, remembered for his interpretations of Donizetti, Verdi and Puccini, died aged 90.

NEW APPOINTMENTS AND HONOURS
Having been made chief conductor designate in 2012, Sakari Oramo conducted his first concert as chief conductor of the BBC Symphony Orchestra as part of the 2013 BBC Proms festival. In September 2013, Bury-born conductor Stephen Bell took up his two-year post as the first associate conductor of the Hallé Pops Series at the Bridgewater Hall. The 2013–14 season also saw Simon Halsey take up the position of London Symphony Chorus director while, in May 2014, the LSO appointed its youngest-ever member, 18-year-old trombonist Peter Moore, who won the BBC Young Musician competition in 2008 aged only 12 and who has more recently been part of the LSO's Academy project.

In January, Robin Ticciati, already former Glyndebourne Tour director, took up the post of music director of Glyndebourne Opera. In February, Jean-Claude Picard performed his first concert as the assistant conductor of the Royal Scottish National Orchestra. The season also saw Hywel Davies embark on his first year of three as composer-in-residence with the Bournemouth Symphony Orchestra's contemporary group, Kokoro.

Following hot on the heels of the appointment and almost immediate departure of music director Emmanuel Joel-Hornak at the start of the season, Scottish Opera appointed baritone Sir Thomas Allen as music advisor to provide high-level guidance on musical and artistic matters while it continued its search for a new music director.

In the New Year's and Queen's Birthday Honours, conductor Sir Simon Rattle joined the 24-member Order of Merit while composer Sir Peter Maxwell Davies was made a Companion of Honour and András Schiff (pianist) was presented with a knighthood. CBEs were awarded to Stephen Hough (pianist), John Copley (opera director), John Berry (artistic director, English National Opera) and Susan Bullock (soprano), and OBEs to Katherine Jenkins (singer) and Loretta Tomasi (departing chief executive, English National Opera). In June 2014, Judith Weir was also revealed as the new 'Master of the Queen's Music' after the conclusion of Sir Peter Maxwell Davies' ten-year tenure.

COMPETITIONS
In March 2014, the Handel Singing Competition at St George's Hanover Square was won by Polish mezzo-soprano coloratura Ewa Gubańska. Both Second Prize and Audience Prize were carried away by Estonian soprano Maria Valdmaa. Further prizes were awarded to soprano Susanna Fairbairn and baritones Edward Grint and Timothy Nelson.

The following month, First Prize at the Wigmore Hall-based Ferrier Competition was won by Austrian soprano Christina Gansch and Second Prize was awarded to soprano Sarah-Jane Lewis. The Loveday Song Prize went to

soprano Jennifer France. In May, 17-year-old pianist Martin James Bartlett won the BBC Young Musician of the Year Competition at the Usher Hall, beating the two other finalists, percussionist Elliott Gaston-Ross, 15, and recorder-player Sophie Westbrooke, 15.

OPERA PRODUCTIONS

The list below summarises each opera company's activities and the date in parentheses indicates the year that the current production entered their repertory.

ROYAL OPERA
Founded 1946
W www.roh.org.uk

REPERTORY: *La Bohème* (1974), *Turandot* (1984), *La Traviata* (1994), *Wozzeck* (2002), *Ariadne auf Naxos* (2002), *Elektra* (2003), *Faust* (2004), *Le Nozze di Figaro* (2006), *Tosca* (2006), *Carmen* (2006), *La Fille du Regiment* (2007), *Manon* (2010)
NEW PRODUCTIONS: *Les Vêpres Siciliennes* (Verdi), 17 October 2013. Conductor, Antonio Pappano; director, Stefan Herrheim. Marina Poplavskaya (Helene), Bryan Hymel (Henri), Erwin Schrott (Procida), Michael Volle (Guy de Montfort)
Parsifal (Wagner), 30 November 2013. Conductor, Antonio Pappano; director, Stephen Langridge. Simon O'Neill (Parsifal), Angela Denoke (Kundry), René Pape (Gurnemanz), Gerald Finley (Amfortas), Willard White (Klingsor)
Don Giovanni (Mozart), 1 February 2014. Conductor, Nicola Luisotti; director, Kasper Holten. Mariusz Kwiecien (Don Giovanni), Alex Esposito (Leporello), Malin Byström (Donna Anna), Véronique Gens (Donna Elvira), Antonio Poli (Don Ottavio), Elizabeth Watts (Zerlina), Dawid Kimberg (Masetto), Alexander Tsymbalyuk (Commendatore)
Die Frau ohne Schatten (Richard Strauss), 14 March 2014. Conductor, Sermyon Bychkov; director, Claus Guth. Johan Botha (The Emperor), Emily Magee (The Empress), Michaela Schuster (The Nurse), Johan Reuter (Barak), Elena Pankratova (Barak's Wife)
Dialogues des Carmélites (Poulenc), 29 May 2014. Conductor, Simon Rattle; director, Robert Carsen. Sally Matthews (Blanche), Anna Prohaska (Constance), Emma Bell (Madame Lidoine), Sophie Koch (Mère Marie), Deborah Polaski (Madame de Croissy), Thomas Allen (Marquis de la Force), Yann Beuron (Chevalier de la Force)
Manon Lescaut (Puccini), 17 June 2014. Conductor, Antonio Pappano; director, Jonathan Kent. Kristine Opolais (Manon Lescaut), Christopher Maltman (Lescaut), Jonas Kaufmann (Chevalier des Grieux), Maurizio Muraro (Geronte de Ravoir), Benjamin Hulett (Edmondo)
Maria Stuarda (Donizetti), 5 July 2014. Conductor, Bertrand de Billy; directors, Moshe Leiser and Patrice Caurier. Joyce DiDonato (Maria), Carmen Giannattasio (Elisabetta), Charles Castronovo (Roberto), Jeremy Carpenter (Lord Cecil), Matthew Rose (Giorgio)

ENGLISH NATIONAL OPERA
Founded 1931
W www.eno.org

REPERTORY: *Madam Butterfly* (2005), *Satyagraha* (2007), *Peter Grimes* (2009), *The Pearl Fishers* (2010)
NEW PRODUCTIONS: *Fidelio* (Beethoven), 25 September 2013. Conductor, Edward Gardner; director, Calixto Bieito. Emma Bell (Leonore), Stuart Skelton (Florestan), Philip Horst (Don Pizarro), James Creswell (Rocco), Sarah Tynan (Marzelline), Adrian Dwyer (Jaquino), Roland Wood (Don Fernando)

Die Fledermaus (Johann Strauss II), 30 September 2013. Conductor, Eun Sun Kim; director, Christopher Alden. Tom Randle (Eisenstein), Julia Sporsén (Rosalinde), Jennifer Holloway (Orlofsky), Rhian Lois (Adele), Richard Burkhard (Falke), Edgaras Montvidas (Alfred), Simon Butteriss (Blind), Andrew Shore (Frank), Jon Pohl (Frosch)

The Magic Flute (Mozart), 7 November 2013. Conductor, Gergely Madaras; director, Simon McBurney. Ben Johnson (Tamino), Devon Guthrie (Pamina), Roland Wood (Papageno), Mary Bevan (Papagena), Cornelia Götz (Queen of the Night), James Creswell (Sarastro), Brian Galliford (Monostatos)

Rigoletto (Verdi), 13 February 2014. Conductor, Graeme Jenkins; director, Christopher Alden. Quinn Kelsey (Rigoletto), Barry Banks (Duke of Mantua), Anna Christy (Gilda), Peter Rose/Matthew Treviño (Sparafucile), Justina Gringyte (Maddalena), David Stout (Monterone), George Humphreys (Marullo), Anthony Gregory (Borsa), Barnaby Rea (Ceprano), Diana Montague (Giovanna)

Rodelinda (Handel), 28 February 2014. Conductor, Christian Curnyn; director, Richard Jones. Rebecca Evans (Rodelinda), Iestyn Davies (Bertarido), John Mark Ainsley (Grimoaldo), Susan Bickley (Eduige), Christopher Ainslie (Unulfo), Richard Burkhard (Garibaldo)

Powder Her Face (Thomas Adès), 2 April 2014. Conductor, Timothy Redmond; director, Joe Hill-Gibbins. Amanda Roocroft (Duchess), Clare Eggington (Maid), Alan Ewing (Hotel Manager), Alexander Sprague (Electrician)

Thebans (Julian Anderson), 3 May 2014, world premiere. Conductor, Edward Gardner; director, Pierre Audi. Roland Wood (Oedipus), Peter Hoare (Creon), Julia Sporsén (Antigone), Matthew Best (Tiresias), Susan Bickley (Jocasta), Christopher Ainslie (Messenger), Anthony Gregory (Haemon), Jonathan McGovern (Polynices)

Così Fan Tutte (Mozart), 16 May 2014. Conductor, Ryan Wigglesworth; director, Katie Mitchell. Kate Valentine (Fiordiligi), Christine Rice (Dorabella), Norman Reinhardt (Ferrando), Marcus Farnsworth (Guglielmo), Roderick Williams (Don Alfonso), Mary Bevan (Despina)

Benvenuto Cellini (Berlioz), 5 June 2014. Conductor, Edward Gardner; director, Terry Gilliam. Michael Spyres (Benvenuto Cellini), Corinne Winters (Teresa), Pavlo Hunka (Balcucci), Nicky Spence (Francesco), Paula Murrihy (Ascanio), Willard White (Pope Clement VII), Richard Burkhard (Fieramosca)

OPERA NORTH
Founded 1978
W www.operanorth.co.uk

REPERTORY: *La Bohème* (1993), *Peter Grimes* (2006), *A Midsummer Night's Dream* (2008), *Macbeth* (2008)
NEW PRODUCTIONS: *Death in Venice* (Britten), 17 October 2013. Conductor, Richard Farnes; director, Rob Kearley. Alan Oke (Gustav von Aschenbach), Peter Savidge (Traveller/Elderly Fop/Old Gondolier/Hotel Manager/Hotel Barber/Leader of the Players/Voice of Dionysus), Christopher Ainslie/James Laing (Voice of Apollo), Damian Thantrey (English Clerk)

La Fanciulla del West (Puccini), 21 January 2014. Conductor, Richard Farnes; director, Aletta Collins. Alwyn Mellor (Minnie), Robert Hayward (Jack Rance), Rafael Rojas (Dick Johnson), Bonaventura Bottone (Nick), Gaeme Danby (Ashby), Eddie Wade (Sonora), Adrian Dwyer (Trin), Gavan Ring (Jake Wallace), Dean Robinson (José Castro), Jeremy Peaker (Sid), Nicholas Butterfield (Jim Larkens)
CONCERT PERFORMANCES: *Götterdämmerung* (Wagner), 14 June 2013. Conductor, Richard Farnes. Alwyn Mellor (Brünnhilde), Mati Turi (Siegfried), Mats Almgren (Hagen),

Orla Boylan (Gutrune), Eric Greene (Gunther), Jo Pohlheim (Alberich), Susan Bickley (Waltraute)

SCOTTISH OPERA
Founded 1962
W www.scottishopera.co.uk

REPERTORY: *Madama Butterfly* (2000), *Macbeth* (2005), *The Seven Deadly Sins* (2011), *Last One Out* (2012)
NEW PRODUCTIONS: *American Lulu* (Olga Neuwirth after Berg's Lulu), 16 August 2013, UK premiere. Conductor, Gerry Cornelius; director, John Fulljames. Angel Blue (Lulu), Jacqui Dankworth (Eleanor), Donald Maxwell (Dr Bloom), Robert Winslade Anderson (Clarence), Jonathan Stoughton (Jimmy), Paul Curievici (Painter/Young Man), Simon Wilding (Athlete), Paul Reeves (Professor/Banker/Commissioner)

Rodelinda (Handel), 26 September 2013. Director, Chris Rolls. Sarah Power (Rodelinda), Andrew Radley (Bertarido), Reno Troilus (Unulfo), Richard Rowe (Grimoaldo), Andrew McTaggart (Garibaldo), Sioned Gwen Davies (Eduige)

Don Giovanni (Mozart), 15 October 2013. Conductors, Speranza Scappucci/James Grossmith; director, Thomas Allen. Jacques Imbrailo (Don Giovanni), Péter Kálmán (Leporello), Susan Gritton (Donna Anna), Johann Saevarsson (Commendatore), Ed Lyon (Don Ottavio), Lisa Milne (Donna Elvira), Anna Devin/Ruth Jenkins (Zerlina), Barnaby Rea (Masetto)

Don Pasquale (Donizetti), 24 January 2014. Conductor, Francesco Corti; director, Renaud Doucet. Bruno Praticò (Don Pasquale), Nicholas Lester (Dr Malatesta), Colin Lee (Ernesto), Ruth Jenkins (Norina), Andrew McTaggart (A Notary)
CONCERT PERFORMANCES: *Turandot* (Puccini), 30 March 2014. Conductor, Francesco Corti. Claire Rutter (Princess Turandot), Altoum Ryland Davies (The Emperor), Willard White (Timur), José Ferrero (Unknown Prince), Eleanor Dennis (Liù), Nicholas Lester (Ping), Andrew Kennedy (Pang), Christopher Turner (Pong), Jonathan May (A Mandarin)

WELSH NATIONAL OPERA
Founded 1946
W www.wno.org.uk

REPERTORY: *Tosca* (1992), *La Traviata* (2009), *Greek* (2011)
NEW PRODUCTIONS: *Paul Bunyan* (Britten), 23 August 2013. Conductor, Alice Farnham; director, Martin Constantine; WNO Youth Opera

Anna Bolena (Donizetti), 7 September 2013. Conductors, Daniele Rustioni/Andrew Greenwood; director, Alessandro Talevi. Serena Farnocchia/Linda Richardson (Anne Boleyn), Alastair Miles (Henry VIII), Katharine Goeldner (Jane Seymour), Robert McPherson (Lord Percy), Faith Sherman (Smeaton), Daniel Grice (Lord Rocheford), Robert Lyn Evans (Lord Hervey)

Maria Stuarda (Donizetti), 13 September 2013. Conductors, Graeme Jenkins/Robin Newton; director, Rudolf Frey. Adina Nitescu/Camilla Roberts (Queen Elizabeth), Judith Howarth (Mary Stuart), Bruce Sledge (Leicester), Alastair Miles (Talbot), Gary Griffiths (Cecil)

Roberto Devereux (Donizetti), 2 October 2013. Conductors, Daniele Rustioni/Christian Capocaccia; director, Alessandro Talevi. Leonardo Capalbo (Roberto Devereux), Alexandra Deshorties (Queen Elizabeth), Leah-Marian Jones (Sara the Duchess of Nottingham), David Kempster (Duke of Nottingham), William Robert Allenby (Walter Raleigh), Geraint Dodd (Cecil)

Manon Lescaut (Puccini), 8 February 2014. Conductor, Lothar Koenigs; director, Mariusz Trelinski. Chiara Taigi (Manon Lescaut), David Kempster (Lescaut), Gwyn Hughes

Jones (Chevalier des Grieux), Stephen Richardson (Geronte di Ravoir/Naval Captain), Simon Crosby Buttle (Edmondo) *Boulevard Solitude* (Henze), 26 February 2014. Conductor, Lothar Koenigs; director, Mariusz Trelinski. Sarah Tynan (Manon Lescaut), Jason Bridges (Armand des Grieux), Benjamin Bevan (Lescaut), Adrian Thompson (Lilaque Pere) *Moses und Aron* (Schoenberg), 24 May 2014. Conductor, Lothar Koenigs; directors, Jossi Wieler and Sergio Morabito. Sir John Tomlinson (Moses), Rainer Trost (Aron), Elizabeth Atherton (A Young Maiden/First Naked Virgin), Alexander Sprague (A Young Man), Daniel Grice (Another Man/Ephraimite), Richard Wiegold (A Priest) *Nabucco* (Verdi), 31 May 2014. Conductors, Xian Zhang/Simon Philippo; director, Rudolf Frey. David Kempster (Nabucco), Mary Elizabeth Williams (Abigaille), Kevin Short (Zaccaria), Justina Gringyte (Fenena), Robyn Lyn Evans (Ismaele), James Platt (High Priest)

GLYNDEBOURNE
Founded 1934
W www.glyndebourne.com

REPERTORY: *Eugene Onegin* (1994), *Don Giovanni* (2010), *Rinaldo* (2011)
NEW PRODUCTIONS: *Der Rosenkavalier* (Richard Strauss), 17 May 2014. Conductor, Robin Ticciati; director, Richard Jones. Tara Erraught (Octavian), Kate Royal (The Marschallin), Lars Woldt (Baron Ochs auf Lerchenau), Teodora Gheorghiu (Sophie), Michael Kraus (Herr von Faninal), Miranda Keys (Marianne Leitmetzerin), Christopher Gillett (Valzacchi), Helene Schneiderman (Annina)
La Finta Giardiniera (Mozart), 28 June 2014. Conductor, Robin Ticciati; director, Frederic Wake-Walker. Wolfgang Ablinger-Sperrhacke (Don Anchise – Il Podestà), Christiane Karg (Sandrina – La Marchesa Violante), Nicole Heaston (Arminda), Joel Prieto (Count Belfiore), Rachel Frenkel (Ramiro), Joélle Harvey (Serpetta), Gyula Orendt (Nardo – Roberto)
La Traviata (Verdi), 17 July 2014. Conductors, Mark Elder/David Afkham; director Tom Cairns. Venera Gimadieva (Violetta Valéry), Michael Fabiano (Alfredo Germont), Tassis Christoyannis (Giorgio Germont), Emanuele d'Aguanno (Gastone de Letorières), Graeme Broadbent (Doctor Grenvil)
GLYNDEBOURNE TOUR: *L'Elisir d'Amore* (2007), *Hänsel und Gretel* (2008), *The Rape of Lucretia* (2013)

AWARDS

GRAMOPHONE AWARDS 2013
SPECIAL AWARDS
Artist of the Year – Alison Balsom (trumpet)
Label of the Year – Decca
Lifetime Achievement – Julian Bream (guitar)
Special Achievement – Alain Lanceron
Young Artist of the Year – Jan Lisiecki (piano)
RECORDING AWARDS
Baroque Instrumental – *...Pour Passer la Mélancolie:* keyboard works by Froberger, d'Anglebert, Fischer, Couperin, Clérambault, Muffat: Andreas Staier
Baroque Vocal – Bach *Motets:* Monteverdi Choir/Sir John Eliot Gardiner
Chamber – Bartók *Sonatas for Violin and Piano, 1 & 2; Sonata for Solo Violin:* Barnabás Kelemen, Zoltán Kocsis
Choral – Elgar *The Apostles:* Soloists; Hallé Choir, Youth Choir and Orchestra/Sir Mark Elder
Concerto (Recording of the Year) – Bartók, Eötvös, Ligeti *Violin Concertos:* Patricia Kopatchinskaja, HR-SO & Ensemble Modern/Peter Eötvös

Contemporary – Dutilleux *Correspondances; Tout un Monde Lointain; The Shadows of Time:* Barbara Hannigan, Anssi Karttunen, Orchestre Philharmonique de Radio France/Esa-Pekka Salonen
Early – *A New Venetian Coronation:* Gabrieli Consort & Players/Paul McCreesh
Instrumental – Mussorgsky *Pictures at an Exhibition;* Prokofiev *Visions fugitives, Five Sarcasms:* Steven Osborne
Opera – Puccini *Il Trittico:* Soloists; Chorus and Orchestra of the Royal Opera House, Covent Garden; Antonio Pappano (dir. Richard Jones)
Orchestral – Suk *Prague, A Summer's Tale:* BBC Symphony Orchestra/Jiří Bělohlávek
Vocal – Wagner *Arias:* Jonas Kaufmann, Orchestra of the Deutsche Oper/Donald Runnicles

BBC MUSIC MAGAZINE AWARDS 2014
Concerto Award and Recording Of The Year – Elgar, Carter *Cello Concertos:* Alisa Weilerstein (cello) Staatskapelle Berlin/Daniel Barenboim
Orchestral Award – Brahms *Symphonies Nos. 1–4* etc: Gewandhaus Orchestra Leipzig/Riccardo Chailly
Chamber Award – Felix & Fanny Mendelssohn *String Quartets No. 2, Op. 13; No. 6, Op. 80 and Eb Major:* Quatuor Ebène
Instrumental Award – *Guardian Angel* – works by Bach, Biber, Tartini, Pisendel: Rachel Podger (violin)
Opera Award – Britten *Peter Grimes:* Alan Oke, Giselle Allen, David Kempster, Catherine Wyn-Rogers etc. Chorus of Opera North, Guildhall School of Music, Britten-Pears Orchestra/Steuart Bedford
Vocal Award – Wagner *Arias from Lohengrin, Die Walküre, Tannhäuser; Wesendonck Lieder:* Jonas Kaufmann (tenor), Orchester der Deutschen Oper Berlin/Donald Runnicles
Choral Award – Britten *War Requiem:* Gabrieli Consort and Players; Wroclaw Phil. Choir, New College trebles, John Mark Ainsley, Christopher Maltman, Susan Gritton/Paul McCreesh
App Award (new) – Beethoven's *Ninth Symphony:* Touch Press/DG
JURY AWARDS
Newcomer Award – Beethoven *The Late Sonatas:* Igor Levit (piano)
Premiere Award – George Benjamin *Written on Skin:* Christopher Purves, Barbara Hannigan, Bejun Mehta/Mahler Chamber Orchestra
DVD (Performance) – Puccini *Tosca:* Angela Gheorghiu, Jonas Kaufmann, Bryn Terfel etc. Chorus and Orchestra of Royal Opera House/Sir Antonio Pappano
DVD (Documentary) – *The Genius of Cavaillé-Coll* presented by Gerard Brooks

ROYAL PHILHARMONIC SOCIETY AWARDS 2014
Audiences and Engagement – Britten100 (Britten-Pears Foundation)
Chamber Music and Song – Champs Hill
Chamber-Scale Composition – Harrison Birtwistle *The Moth Requiem*
Concert Series and Festivals – The Rest Is Noise (Southbank Centre)
Conductor – Daniel Barenboim
Creative Communication – Touch Press: classical music iPad apps
Ensemble – London Philharmonic Orchestra
Instrumentalist – Patricia Kopatchinskaja
Large-Scale Composition – George Benjamin *Written on Skin*
Learning and Participation – Imago (Glyndebourne)
Opera and Music Theatre – Welsh National Opera
Singer – Joyce DiDonato
Young Artists – Igor Levit

POP MUSIC

Piers Martin

THE YEAR OF PHARRELL

In the same way that the British singer Adele dominated the last two years of pop music, so this year could be said to belong to one man: the American singer, songwriter and producer Pharrell Williams. A benign and ubiquitous presence, the 41-year-old was involved in three of the year's biggest selling and most streamed singles – his own 'Happy', Daft Punk's 'Get Lucky' and Robin Thicke's 'Blurred Lines' – each of which contributed to the considerable success of his second solo album, Girl, a funky neo-soul set that entered the UK charts – and those of several other countries – at number one in March 2014.

Williams, who came to prominence as an innovative hip-hop and pop producer in the early 2000s before somewhat fading from fashion, rediscovered his golden touch when he co-wrote and sang on both 'Get Lucky' and 'Blurred Lines', which between them sold nearly 3 million copies in the UK. In April, 'Blurred Lines' was declared the biggest selling download in UK history by the Official Charts Company, having sold 1.54 million copies since its release in May 2013, while the Daft Punk song was named the most streamed track of 2013 via data collected by popular streaming sites such as Spotify and Deezer. 'Happy' eclipsed the performance of both tracks, however, selling over 1.8 million copies in the UK in the seven months since its release in December 2013 and becoming 2014's most streamed song.

The positive message of 'Happy', an upbeat disco number initially released to promote the film Despicable Me 2, gained such traction around the world that its video, which notched up over 380 million YouTube views, spawned more than 1,500 fan-made tribute videos. 'Happy' also led to Williams becoming the second artist in UK chart history – after The Beatles – to have three million-selling singles in under 12 months, the Official Charts Company noted, and only the third act in UK chart history to score three million-sellers after The Beatles, who have six, and Rihanna, with four.

'BLURRED LINES'

The more popular that Robin Thicke's 'Blurred Lines' became, the more controversy the song attracted. In the US, the family of the late soul singer Marvin Gaye filed but later dropped a lawsuit against the song's publisher, Sony/ATV, which claimed 'Blurred Lines' copied Gaye's 1977 hit 'Got To Give It Up'. Closer to home, the track's suggestive lyrics – which, some argued, glorified sexual harassment, violent sex and even rape – and its video featuring topless women, ensured that the song became one of the more notorious hits of recent times and saw Thicke named 'Sexist of the Year' by Britain's End Violence Against Women Coalition.

Unable to convincingly defend lyrics such as 'I know you want it' and 'Just let me liberate you' (in addition to even more explicit lines delivered by guest rapper T.I.), Thicke, a Los Angeles-based R&B journeyman, found himself pilloried by the media. By November, more than 20 British university student unions had banned 'Blurred Lines' from being played at functions on campus on the grounds that the song was degrading to women. Speaking to BBC Radio 1 in October, Thicke explained that the song was actually about his actress wife of 20 years, Paula Patton. By July, the couple's marriage was reported to be over and Thicke's latest album, Paula, dedicated to his ex, had sold a mere 530 copies in the UK.

SALES SLIP

'Blurred Lines' joined three other singles – Daft Punk's 'Get Lucky', Swedish dance star Avicii's 'Wake Me Up' and 'Let Her Go' by British balladeer Passenger – that each sold over 1 million copies in 2013, spearheading an ultimately disappointing year for the format which saw a 3.6 per cent drop in sales to 182.2 million units, figures for the British Phonographic Industry (BPI) revealed. As the digital download celebrated its tenth birthday in 2014 – the format came of age in 2004 when iTunes launched in June of that year – new figures showed that this year digital formats accounted for 99.7 per cent of all singles sales.

Robin Thicke was not alone in his predicament of selling numerous copies of a single track and comparatively few of an album. Although industry income in 2013 rose by 1.9 per cent to £730m – the first increase since 2009 – overall in 2013, UK album sales continued their downward trajectory, falling by 6.4 per cent to 94 million and so slipping below 100 million for the first time since 1995, the BPI noted.

Although CDs still accounted for 64 per cent of album sales, this figure was down 12.8 per cent on the previous year, and while the growth of digital albums sales had slowed – up 6.8 per cent to 32.6 million – the BPI reported that sales of artist albums were down 9.1 per cent. In contrast, the biggest selling albums of 2013, as in 2012, were the latest instalments of the long-running Now series of compilations of current hits. November's Now That's What I Call Music 86 was the best seller of 2013 and the only album to sell over 1 million copies in the UK. As music streaming accelerates in growth and user-created playlists gradually replace the album in popularity, these Now compilations, which round up the latest radio and online hits, are the closest that many music fans get to purchasing a ready-made playlist that accurately reflects contemporary listening habits.

STREAMING KILLING THE ALBUM?

With sales dwindling in the face of streaming, many industry experts questioned the long-term viability of the album as a format, pointing to consistently poor first-week sales of new albums by high-profile stars and to the increasing prevalence of playlists on streaming sites. In February, for example, London indie outfit Bombay Bicycle Club's So Long, See You Tomorrow entered the chart at number one with first-week sales of 19,645, the lowest chart-topping total in history, while heavily promoted albums by major acts such as Lily Allen (Sheezus, 35,000 copies sold in its first week) and Lana Del Rey (Ultraviolence, 48,000) also performed poorly yet still entered the charts at number one. British boyband One Direction's Midnight Memories, released in November after blanket promotion that culminated in the global 1D Day event on the album's release day, was the biggest selling artist album of 2013, shifting 685,000 copies. Yet compare this with the 1.4 million copies of 2012's top selling album, Emeli Sandé's Our Version of Events – the only LP to pass a million last year – and then that with 2011, when four albums sold more than a million copies, and the decline appears pronounced.

There were still respectable showings in 2014 – Coldplay's Ghost Stories, Paolo Nutini's Caustic Love and In The Lonely Hour by soulful newcomer Sam Smith, winner of the Brits' Critics' Choice award, each sold over 100,000 in their first week – but even so, many concurred with George Ergatoudis, the influential head of music at BBC Radio 1 and 1Xtra, when he took to Twitter in July: 'Make no mistake.

With very few exceptions, albums are edging closer to extinction. Playlists are the future.' By this he meant that streaming, where consumers effectively rent the music they want to listen to by subscribing to a site such as Spotify, the market leader, Deezer or Napster, is slowly but surely replacing the consumer's need to purchase, or own, albums and singles. As well as albums, streaming sites contain numerous playlists of songs put together by listeners, bands, labels, brands and so on, which reflect trends and themes and often shed light on lesser-known material from artists' catalogues.

On Spotify, for example, there are 1.4 million albums but some 1.5 billion playlists. As an indication of streaming's growing popularity, the BPI reported that 7.4 billion songs were streamed in the UK in 2013, twice that of 2012, while in the first half of 2014, nine different tracks were streamed more than a million times in a week, with 'Happy' notching up 25 million streams in total.

Furthermore, a survey conducted by Ofcom found that 30 per cent of 16–24-year-olds prefer to listen to music on streaming sites, compared with 24 per cent who choose radio. Taking this into consideration, the Official Charts Company announced in June that for the first time streams of tracks would count towards official placings in the UK singles chart. To qualify, a track would have to be played for more than 30 seconds and 100 streams would equate to one download or physical format sale.

Despite streaming accounting for 10 per cent of music industry trade in 2013, Spotify came under fire from musicians and unions for paying low royalties. In October, Radiohead singer Thom Yorke removed his solo album *The Eraser* and side-project Atoms For Peace from the site in protest at the amount that Spotify pays artists, stating on Twitter that he was 'standing up for our fellow musicians' and describing Spotify in an interview as 'the last desperate fart of a dying corpse'.

Others countered that Spotify gives valuable exposure to new bands. In December, the company revealed that it pays rights holders between $0.006 and $0.0084 (around £0.005) per play. One act came up with a novel way to make money from Spotify this year; the Los Angeles funk band Vulfpeck released an album of ten silent tracks (named 'Zz', 'Zzz', 'Zzzz' etc) on the site and then asked fans to play the record on repeat overnight. The album, entitled *Sleepify,* was eventually pulled by Spotify after seven weeks, but during that period the album was played around 5.5 million times, *Billboard* reported, resulting in a final payout of $19,655 (almost £12,000), which Vulfpeck promised would be put towards a US tour.

VINYL REVIVAL

Just as streaming experienced twofold growth this year, so UK sales of vinyl LPs also doubled in 2013. Albums by Daft Punk *(Random Access Memories),* Arctic Monkeys *(AM)* and David Bowie *(The Next Day)* helped to boost annual sales of this once-doomed format to 781,000, up 101 per cent on 2012, the BPI reported. This was the vinyl LP's highest sales tally since 1997, but still it accounted for just 0.8 per cent of 2013's total albums sales. Nevertheless, at grassroots level, the vinyl revival continued apace, with a growing number of specialist record shops opening across the country and reports of vinyl pressing plants in the US and Europe expanding operations to meet demand as more music consumers looked to acquire a tangible product rather than an invisible file. However, research conducted by ICM showed that a quarter of 18–24-year-olds who buy physical records have no intention of playing them and would prefer to show off or display the records. Of all those surveyed,

53 per cent claimed to have bought a vinyl record and never listened to it.

In the US, sales of former White Stripes rocker Jack White's latest solo LP, *Lazaretto,* released in June 2014, topped 60,000 copies, making it, in just two months, the best-selling vinyl LP since Pearl Jam's *Vitalogy* in 1994. White, a vinyl enthusiast, also released the world's fastest record on Record Store Day in April, recording two songs in his Nashville studio then pressing and releasing the 7-inch in under four hours.

IT PAYS TO SURPRISE

In February, Prince delighted fans by staging a string of intimate shows in London and Manchester – dubbed the Hit and Run tour – that were announced on the day of the performance. Such was the demand for these pop-up gigs that the singer sometimes played two sets in one night to accommodate those fortunate enough to have secured £35 tickets after queueing for hours. More used to playing arenas for upwards of 20,000 people, Prince and his new band, 3rd Eye Girl, whose album these stunts aimed to promote, began their run of impromptu shows in the living room of his friend, the singer Lianne La Havas, in her home in Leyton, before appearing at London venues such as Ronnie Scott's Soho jazz club, the Electric Ballroom and Shepherd's Bush Empire. Having generated enough excitement, Prince then announced a more formal run of arena shows in May.

Another pop star who understood the value of surprise in an era of information overload was the American R&B singer Beyoncé, who, out of the blue, released her self-titled fifth album overnight on December 13. Described as a 'visual album', the record contained 14 songs and 17 videos and became the fastest-ever selling album on iTunes, with 828,772 copies sold around the world in three days, according to *Billboard.* Released into the busy Christmas market, the album made a big splash but the pedestrian nature of the material meant that the record was soon passed over.

In contrast, the protracted run-up to the November release of Lady Gaga's third album, *Artpop,* seemed to smother any element of surprise that the music might have provided. With hopes for the record inflated by sponsorship deals and brand partnerships, not to mention Gaga's standing as the world's biggest pop star, it was perhaps inevitable that the album would struggle to match expectations. In trying to appeal to her vast fanbase, Gaga spread herself thinly across the realms of music, fashion, social media and art (US artist Jeff Koons created the album's cover), and by the time of *Artpop*'s release she cut a confused figure. The album sold respectably, but the songs' generic high-energy techno-pop style asked questions of her integrity. Tellingly, at this time she also split with her long-term manager Troy Carter, citing creative differences.

A potential contender to Gaga's crown emerged in the form of Lorde, the 16-year-old New Zealander who scored a number one hit on both sides of the Atlantic with her enchanting debut single 'Royals'. Lorde became the youngest solo artist to reach the UK top spot since 15-year-old Billie Piper's 'Because We Want To' in 1998 and in February scooped the Brit for International Female Solo Artist, all the while appearing remarkably unfazed by her success.

Scruffy Britpop troubadour Ed Sheeran doled out more skewed home truths on his second album *X,* which became the UK's fastest selling album of 2014 when it sold 182,000 copies in one week in June. The 23-year-old also topped the American charts with *X,* selling an impressive 210,000 copies in its first week there and securing his first US number one. At number two that same week was Sam Smith's debut *In The Lonely Hour,* the first time in over 20 years that two British artists have claimed the top two places in the US album chart, a feat last managed by Sting and Eric Clapton.

IN MEMORIAM

This year saw the passing of the American rock musician Lou Reed in October at the age of 71 from liver disease. In his groundbreaking songs, first in the Velvet Underground with John Cale in the late 1960s, and then throughout his long and chequered solo career, Reed pushed the notion of pop music into places few others were prepared to take it. To many, with his shades, cigarette, black leather jacket and grumpy demeanour, he epitomised the seamy 1970s New York street poet, at times sketchy and wired, at others funny and profound. He will be remembered for songs such as 'Perfect Day' and 'Walk On The Wild Side', the sugary icing on a formidable body of work, and his influence will be felt for decades to come.

In April, the American DJ Frankie Knuckles, dubbed the godfather of house music, died unexpectedly at the age of 59 in Chicago. In the early 1980s, Knuckles began DJing his homemade extended edits of soul and R&B tracks at a Chicago nightclub called the Warehouse, which led to clubgoers coining the phrase 'house music'. As his reputation spread and this style of dance music became popular throughout Chicago and beyond, Knuckles moved to the Power Plant club and produced classic tracks such as 'Your Love' and 'Baby Wants To Ride'.

In June, the legendary US soul singer Bobby Womack died aged 70. Nicknamed the 'soul survivor' due to his eventful life, his music spanned six decades – the Rolling Stones covered his group the Valentinos' 1964 hit 'It's All Over Now' – and he enjoyed recent acclaim for his 2013 solo album *The Bravest Man in the Universe,* a spare, emotional set produced by Damon Albarn and Richard Russell of XL Recordings.

AWARDS

BRIT AWARDS 2014
British Male Solo Artist – David Bowie
British Female Solo Artist – Ellie Goulding
British Group – Arctic Monkeys
British Single – Rudimental, 'Waiting All Night'
British Album – Arctic Monkeys, *AM*
Critics' Choice – Sam Smith
International Male Solo Artist – Bruno Mars
International Female Solo Artist – Lorde
British Breakthrough Act – Bastille
British Live Act – Coldplay
International Group – Daft Punk

British Global Success – One Direction
British Producer – Flood and Alan Moulder

MERCURY MUSIC PRIZE 2013
James Blake, *Overgrown*

NME AWARDS 2014
British Band – Arctic Monkeys
Album – Arctic Monkeys, *AM*
Track – Disclosure, 'White Noise'
Solo Artist – Lily Allen
Live Band – Arctic Monkeys
New Band – Drenge
International Band – HAIM
Festival – Glastonbury
Worst Band – The 1975
Villain of the Year – Harry Styles

MUSIC OF BLACK ORIGIN (MOBO) AWARDS 2013
Best Female – Laura Mvula
Best Male – Wiley
Best Song – Naughty Boy, 'La La La'
Best Album – Rudimental, *Home*
Best Newcomer – Rita Ora
Best International – Krept and Konan
Best Gospel – Lurine Cato
Best Jazz – Sons Of Kemet
Best Reggae – Sean Paul
Best African Act – D'Banj
Best R&B/Soul – Laura Mvula
Best Hip-Hop/Grime – Tinie Tempah

IVOR NOVELLO AWARDS 2014
PRS for Music Most Performed Work – Passenger, 'Let Her Go'
Best Television Soundtrack – Dominik Scherrer, *Ripper Street*
Best Contemporary Song – James Blake, 'Retrograde'
International Achievement – Mumford & Sons
Best Original Film Score – Simon Fisher Turner, *The Epic of Everest*
The Ivors Inspiration Award – Jerry Dammers
Album Award – Nick Cave & The Bad Seeds, *Push the Sky Away*
PRS for Music Outstanding Contribution to British Music – Jeff Beck
Best Song Musically and Lyrically – London Grammar, 'Strong'
Songwriter of the Year – Tom Odell
Outstanding Song Collection – The Chemical Brothers
Lifetime Achievement – Christine McVie
PRS for Music Special International Award – Nile Rodgers

PARLIAMENT

Patrick Robathan

The year 2013–14 saw the start of the final session of the 2010 parliament, and while tensions remained within the coalition, the number of backbench rebellions was much lower than in previous years. Even in the Lords, which had previously given the coalition the most trouble, government defeats were down to 13 on bills, although some were large: a 128-vote defeat on anti-social behaviour, crime and policing bill on 8 January 2014 and a 98-vote defeat on the immigration bill on 7 April. Speaker John Bercow continued to grant urgent questions (some 34) but his relationship with MPs seemed to be becoming more strained.

Returning after the conference recess on 8 October, Foreign Secretary William Hague updated MPs on the Middle East peace process, Syria and Iran. Culture secretary Maria Miller updated the Commons on progress with press self-regulation: 'we have an opportunity to take a final look at our charter, bring all parties together and ensure that the final charter is both workable and effective. We have a once-in-a-generation opportunity to get it right.'

On 14 October, Schools minister David Laws made a statement on the future of secondary school accountability. On 17 October he responded to an urgent question from his Labour shadow Tristram Hunt about the Al-Medinah Free School in Derby, accused by Ofsted of being dysfunctional and inadequate. This was followed by the quarterly update on the government's progress in Afghanistan from the international development secretary Justine Greening.

On 21 October, energy secretary Ed Davey made a statement on the UK's nuclear energy programme, having reached broad commercial agreement on the key terms of a proposed investment contract, for a new nuclear power station at Hinkley Point, Somerset. He returned to the House on 23 October to answer an urgent question from his Labour shadow Caroline Flint on disruption at the Grangemouth refinery, confirming that there were robust contingency plans in place to ensure that supplies of fuels would continue to be available.

On 28 October prime minister David Cameron reported on the European Council meeting, which had discussed regulation, competitiveness, monetary union and migration policy. He also paid tribute to the emergency services, working to clear up after one of the worst storms for many years. Leader of the Opposition Ed Miliband felt 'the truth is that nothing is different after this summit from what it was before'. On 30 October, health secretary Jeremy Hunt made a statement on the shaping a healthier future programme, a locally led review of NHS services in north-west London, prompting his Labour shadow Andy Burnham to comment: 'has it ever been clearer than it is today that people simply cannot trust the Tories with the NHS?' On 31 October Ed Davey delivered the annual energy statement, claiming to be 'creating one of the most competitive and attractive electricity investment markets in the world; improving security and affordability, boosting home-grown clean energy, and providing jobs'. Caroline Flint asked: 'why are this government too weak to stand up to the energy companies?'

On 4 November, home secretary Theresa May made a statement on Mohammed Ahmed Mohamed who, despite being subject to a terrorism prevention and investigation measure, had absconded from his controls. Her Labour shadow Yvette Cooper felt the home secretary had been irresponsible: 'she was warned about changing the law and weakening controls . . . but did not act'. On 6 November, defence secretary Philip Hammond made a statement on aircraft carriers and UK shipbuilding; following 18 months of 'complex negotiations' with industry, they had reached heads of terms to address the flaws in the contract, and the total capital cost of procuring the carriers would be £6.2bn, with any variation to be shared on a 50:50 basis. To make best use of the labour force, the government had signed an agreement in principle with BAE Systems to order three new offshore patrol vessels. His Labour shadow Vernon Coaker expressed the hope that 'the unique abilities of our skilled workforce, particularly in Portsmouth, are not lost'. On 7 November the Liberal Democrat MP Simon Hughes made a personal statement apologising unreservedly to the House after an investigation by the Parliamentary Commissioner for Standards found that he had failed to observe the code of conduct for MPs and did not sufficiently seek advice from the registrar. On 8 November the European (referendum) bill, a private member's bill sponsored by James Wharton (Conservative), returned for consideration at report stage but only eventually received its third reading on 29 November.

On 11 November William Hague updated the House on developments in the Iran nuclear negotiations and work towards a peace conference on Syria. This was followed by a personal statement from Conservative MP Nadine Dorries apologising fully and unreservedly for her 'inadvertent breach of the rules' as the Committee on Standards in Public Life report on her declaration in the register of members' financial interests had concluded that she had breached the rules. On 12 November Jeremy Hunt replied to an urgent question from Andy Burnham on the urgent and emergency care review by Professor Sir Bruce Keogh, whose preliminary report would be published the next day. In the Lords, Foreign and Commonwealth Office (FCO) minister Baroness Northover replied to a private notice question from Baroness Symons of Vernham Dean on emergency aid to the people of the Philippines.

Returning after a short break, on 18 November David Cameron updated MPs on the disaster in the Philippines and the Commonwealth heads of state meeting in Sri Lanka, which had reached important conclusions on poverty, human rights and trade; he defended his decision to attend as it allowed him 'to advance UK interests with Commonwealth partners and shine a spotlight on the international concerns about Sri Lanka'. Welsh secretary David Jones made a statement on the Silk commission on devolution in Wales, unveiling a package of financial powers that would be devolved to the National Assembly for Wales and the Welsh government. On 19 November, justice secretary Chris Grayling replied to an urgent question from Bill Cash (Conservative), chair of the European scrutiny committee on the EU charter of fundamental rights, on a recent ruling by Mr Justice Mostyn in the High Court, confirming that he did not agree with that analysis of the case and intended to find another case at the earliest opportunity to clarify beyond doubt the legal effects of the charter. This was followed by a statement from Jeremy Hunt on the response to the public inquiry into the Mid Staffordshire NHS Foundation Trust, which he said gave confidence to patients that after the Mid Staffs scandal, 'the NHS has listened, the NHS has learned and the NHS will not rest until it is delivering the safest, most effective and most compassionate care anywhere in the world'. Andy Burnham replied that 'Mid Staffs was a betrayal of the NHS and its values. The previous government rightly apologised, but now is the time to back our words with action.' On 30 November, FCO minister Mark Simmonds replied to an urgent question from Bob Neill (Conservative) on the unauthorised incursion of a Spanish naval vessel into British territorial waters at Gibraltar harbour. Minister for skills and enterprise, Matthew Hancock, made a statement on start-up loans, suggesting that 'our future prosperity rests on the entrepreneurial aspirations of the British people . . . we support those who want to work hard and get on.'

On 25 November William Hague reported on the negotiations with Iran, addressing concerns about its nuclear programme. On 27 November, Europe minister David Lidington answered an urgent question from Nigel Evans (Conservative) on diplomatic relations between the UK and Spain in the light of escalating events in Gibraltar, including the searching of a diplomatic bag. Theresa May answered an urgent question from Yvette Cooper on controls on free movement within the EU, due to end on 1 January 2014, after which Romanians and Bulgarians would have the right to largely unrestricted free movement across Europe: 'in the long term there is much more we need to do.' Consumer affairs minister Jo Swinson made a statement on the Post Office, announcing a '£640m investment . . . establishing the platform for a vibrant, commercially sustainable post office network with a mutual future'. Her Labour shadow Ian Murray felt 'it is clear that the government have created chaos in our postal services'. On 28 November, public health minister Jane Ellison answered an urgent question from her Labour shadow Luciana Berger on standardised packaging of tobacco products, appointing Sir Cyril Chantler to carry out an independent review. William Hague made a statement about preventing sexual violence in conflict, and Justine Greening made one on the UK's response to Typhoon Haiyan in the Philippines.

On 2 December Ed Davey made a statement about reducing the impact of government policies on energy bills: 'help for people with energy bills while we maintain and extend support for the fuel-poor and continue to back green energy and boost energy efficiency'. Caroline Flint asked 'does he accept that the sum total of everything he said, which includes spending £600m of taxpayers' money . . . is that the energy companies will still be allowed to put up people's bills this winter? Does he really think that is a good deal for consumers?' Scotland secretary Alistair Carmichael made a statement updating the House on a helicopter crash in Glasgow. On 3 December, education secretary Michael Gove made a statement about the Programme for International Student Assessment (PISA) league tables of educational performance published by the Organisation for Economic Cooperation and Development, which he felt underlined the need to press ahead with further reform to the UK education system. Tristram Hunt hoped he would take 'the opportunity provided by the PISA data to pursue excellence for all, academic and vocational, in all our schools'. On 4 December, Chief Secretary to the Treasury Danny Alexander answered an urgent question from his Labour shadow Chris Leslie on the national infrastructure plan, which 'demonstrates a long-term vision for our energy, transport and digital networks. It is a plan that is helping to secure long-term investment and that will lead to sustainable, strong long-term growth.'

AUTUMN STATEMENT

Chancellor George Osborne delivered his fifth Autumn Statement on 5 December. The main points were:

- people now in their 40s to get the state pension at age 68, people now in their 30s at age 69; the state pension to rise by £2.95 a week
- predicted economic growth of 1.4 per cent in 2013–14, and 2.4 per cent in 2014–15
- an additional £1bn to be cut from government departmental budgets for each of the next three years
- car tax discs to be scrapped and replaced by an electronic vehicle excise duty system
- the planned increase of 2p a litre in fuel tax to be scrapped
- a major crackdown on tax evasion and avoidance to recoup £9bn over five years
- employers' National Insurance contributions for workers under 21 and earning less than £42,285 to be scrapped from April 2015
- tax breaks to be introduced to encourage 'fracking' for gas
- a cap on total government welfare spending to start in 2015
- an extra £150m to be made available to update and build kitchens and dining rooms in English primary schools
- a move to subsidise offshore instead of onshore wind farms
- plans for £375bn of investment in energy, transport, communications and water projects
- the sale of the government's 40 per cent stake in the Eurostar rail service

Mr Osborne began his 50-minute statement by saying the UK's economy was now growing faster than any other major economy, but stressed that he wanted a 'responsible recovery', warning of 'more difficult decisions' to come on spending. 'The hard work of the British people is paying off and we will not squander their efforts . . . The plan is working. The job is not yet done but Britain is moving again – let's keep going.' Shadow Chancellor Ed Balls said that 'for all his complacent boasts, for three damaging and wasted years, for most people there is no recovery at all'.

Following the death of former South African president Nelson Mandela, David Cameron led tributes to him on 9 December, when all other business was postponed. He described Mr Mandela as 'a towering figure in our lifetime, a pivotal figure in the history of South Africa and the world'. Ed Miliband called him 'an enduring and unique symbol of courage, hope and the fight against injustice'. Deputy prime minister Nick Clegg thought he 'appeared to be free of all the pettiness of politics'. On 10 December, Work and Pensions secretary Iain Duncan Smith responded to an urgent question from his Labour shadow Rachel Reeves about plans for the next stage of implementing the universal credit. Philip Hammond made a statement on the government's plans for reform of defence procurement, which 'will drive significant incremental improvements in DE&S [Defence Equipment and Support]', delivering the mechanisms that will allow the Ministry of Defence (MoD) 'to retest the market's appetite for continuing the DE&S evolution into a government-owned, contractor-operated model – a GoCo – and its ability to deliver value for money against a significantly enhanced public sector comparator'.

On 16 December, FCO minister Hugo Swire answered an urgent question from Fiona Bruce (Conservative) on North Korea following the execution of Jang Sung-taek, 'another example of the horrifying and surreal brutality of the North Korean regime'. On 17 December, transport secretary Patrick McLoughlin made a statement on the work of the Airports Commission and Network Rail's recent reclassification, which would 'deliver vital improvements to all modes of transport so that transport can remain the engine for economic growth that it is'. On 18 December, Communities and Local Government minister Brandon Lewis replied to an urgent question from Hilary Benn, Labour Communities and Local Government spokesperson, on the provisional local government finance settlement. On 19 December, Minister without Portfolio Kenneth Clarke made a statement on the report on the treatment of detainees published by the Rt. Hon. Sir Peter Gibson.

Returning on 6 January after the Christmas break, environment secretary Owen Paterson made a statement about flooding over the Christmas and New Year period, reiterating the 'government's commitment to continue to invest in our flood defences to help us to continue to respond effectively to any future flooding'. On 7 January David Lidington responded to an urgent question from Gisela Stuart (Labour) on the European Council meeting of 19–20 December 2013. The Council had focused on three things: defence; economic and monetary union; and EU enlargement and association agreements. On 8 January, Northern Ireland secretary Theresa Villiers updated MPs on the Haass talks, cross-party negotiations in Belfast that had failed to reach a comprehensive agreement. On 10 January the European Union (referendum) bill had its second reading in the House of Lords.

On 13 January William Hague updated MPs on developments on nuclear issues with Iran and preparations for the Geneva II peace negotiations concerning Syria. On 14 January Philip Hammond replied to an urgent question from Vernon Coaker (Labour) on the performance of MoD IT systems run by Capita and the effect on army recruitment.

On 20 January, immigration minister Mark Harper replied to an urgent question from Yvette Cooper (Labour) on the UN settlement programme for Syrian refugees, confirming that the government would continue 'playing our full part in the international response to the humanitarian crisis in Syria'. On 23 January Philip Hammond made a statement on the final part of the armed forces redundancy programme, which would give 'certainty about the future size and shape of our armed forces, and confidence that they will have the kit, equipment and platforms they need'. On 24 January the European Union (referendum) bill began its committee consideration in the Lords, with the House sitting for some eight hours but making very little progress as peers attempted to 'talk out' the bill.

On 29 January Theresa May made a statement regarding the government's proposal to relocate refugees who had fled the conflict in Syria: 'we are granting asylum to those who need it, consistent with this country's proud tradition of giving help to those who need it most, and through the relocation scheme will be providing emergency sanctuary to the people who are most at risk, including victims of torture and violence'.

On 3 February Owen Paterson replied to an urgent question from his Labour shadow Maria Eagle on flooding in Somerset. On 4 February William Hague made a statement about the Cabinet Secretary's report on the Indian operation at Sri Harmandir Sahib (the Golden Temple) in Amritsar in June 1984: 'the nature of the UK's assistance was purely advisory, limited and provided to the Indian government at an early stage; it had limited impact on the tragic events that unfolded at the temple three months later; there was no link between the provision of that advice and defence sales; and there is no record of the government receiving advance notice of the operation.' On 6 February, communities and local government secretary Eric Pickles, standing in for environment secretary Owen Paterson (who was in hospital), updated the House on the action taken in the light of the recent floods and extreme weather: 'we cannot control the weather, but we can and will provide the security that hard-working families deserve to allow them to get on with their daily lives.'

On 10 February Eric Pickles replied to an urgent question from Maria Eagle on the government's response to the flooding in Somerset, clarifying his comments accusing the Environment Agency of giving poor advice. Philip Hammond updated MPs on Afghanistan, looking forward to the completion of Operation Herrick at the end of 2014. On 12 February Theresa May updated the House on progress in the new inquests by Lord Justice Golding on the victims of the Hillsborough stadium tragedy, and the two related investigations by the Independent Police Complaints Commission and Operation Resolve, led by Jon Stoddart; she stressed her 'continuing commitment to do everything to ensure that the process of disclosing the truth . . . is followed by the process of justice'. On 13 February Patrick McLoughlin replied to an urgent question from his Labour shadow Mary Creagh on the transport disruption caused by the floods, pledging that 'the government are committed to providing all the practical support and assistance that is needed'.

On 24 February William Hague made a statement on the situation in Ukraine and in Syria and on relations with Iran, promising to 'maintain intensive diplomatic activity to ensure a more peaceful and stable world'. On 26 February the Attorney-General, Dominic Grieve, responded to an urgent question from Laurence Robertson (Conservative), chair of the Northern Ireland committee, on the background to the judgment in the case of former IRA member John Downey, which had been thrown out after he had produced a letter stating that he was free to enter the UK without fear of arrest. 'It was clear that its assurances were wrongly given, it was right that the matter should be tested in court . . . the judgment has now been given, and the CPS and I accept that judgment entirely and we do not consider that it gives rise to any prospect of a successful appeal.'

On 4 March William Hague updated MPs on the situation in Ukraine: 'we have a direct national interest in maintenance of international law, upholding of treaty obligations, sovereignty and territorial integrity of independent nations, and the diplomatic resolution of conflicts that affect the peace and security of us all.' On 5 March junior minister Matthew Hancock made a statement on the publication of the reform plan for vocational qualifications. On 6 March Theresa May made a statement on the Ellison review examining allegations of corruption surrounding the initial investigation into the murder of Stephen Lawrence and evidence of corruption within the Metropolitan Police, outlining plans for improving standards of integrity in the police. Philip Hammond made a statement on the decision to refuel the nuclear reactor in HMS Vanguard, one of the UK's four ballistic missile submarines, during its planned deep-maintenance period, scheduled to begin in 2015.

On 10 March David Cameron reported on the emergency European Council on Ukraine: 'we must stand up to aggression, uphold international law and support the Ukrainian government and people, who want the freedom to choose their own future'. Ed Miliband pledged to 'provide him with all the necessary support as he seeks to achieve that'. On 13 March David Laws made a statement on funding in English schools, with a £350m increase 'representing a huge step forward towards fair funding in English schools that will make a real difference on the ground'.

THE BUDGET 2014

Chancellor George Osborne delivered his fifth budget statement on 19 March. The main points included:

- an increase in the personal allowance (the amount earned before income tax is due) by £500 to £10,500
- extending the Help to Buy scheme for aspiring home owners until 2020
- a five-year cap on structural welfare spending from 2015, starting at £119bn and rising in line with inflation, excluding pensions and jobseeker's allowance

- an increase in the duty on cigarettes by 2 per cent above inflation
- freezing the 'carbon floor' price paid by businesses
- an increase in stamp duty on homes worth more than £500,000 to 15 per cent for properties bought by companies
- a scheme to boost exports, doubling the amount of finance available to £3bn
- an additional £140m for repairs to and maintenance of flood defences and £200m to repair potholes
- scrapping inheritance tax for members of the emergency services who 'give their lives protecting us'
- the reform of air passenger duty so that all long-haul flights carry the tax rate currently charged for flights to the USA
- a freeze in the duty on petrol, spirits and cider, and cuts in the duty on a pint of beer by 1p and the tax on bingo from 20 per cent to 10 per cent

In his 55-minute speech Mr Osborne told MPs: 'The message from this Budget is: you have earned it, you have saved it, and this government is on your side, whether you're on a low or middle income, whether you're saving for your home, for your family or for your retirement . . . This is a Budget for the makers, the doers, and the savers.' In response Labour leader Ed Miliband said, 'The chancellor did not mention one central fact – the working people of Britain are worse off under the Tories . . . Whose recovery is it? Under the Tories it is a recovery for the few, not the many. We know what their long term plan is, tax cuts for the richest whilst everyone else gets squeezed.' After four days of debate the Budget was passed by 305 votes to 252. The finance bill was introduced on 25 March and had its second reading in the Commons on 1 April, when it was approved by 292 votes to 235. It passed its third reading on 2 July by 289 votes to 228, and gained royal assent on 17 July.

On 20 March MPs paid tribute to former Labour MP and minister Tony Benn, who had died. Pensions minister Steve Webb set out the government's strategy for future pension provision in the light of the chancellor's Budget, with plans for liberalisation of the retirement savings market with effect from April 2015, giving pensioners the flexibility to choose how best to use their savings in the way that suits their personal circumstances.

On 24 March, work and pensions minister Esther McVey replied to an urgent question from Chris Bryant (Labour) regarding the exemption of those who have inherited social housing tenancies from paying the under-occupancy charge. Patrick McLoughlin made a statement on ensuring the High Speed 2 rail line was built better, brings benefits to the north sooner and supports job creation and economic growth. On 26 March David Cameron reported on the European Council and the nuclear security summit of G7 leaders, which had taken place without Russia in The Hague. On 27 March Ed Davey made a statement on competition in the energy markets to coincide with publication of the first annual assessment of competition from OFGEM, the Office of Fair Trading and the Competition and Markets Authority. Caroline Flint wondered: 'instead of defending the big six and asking for their co-operation, why does he not just enforce a price freeze now?' Steve Webb set out the actions being taking to ensure that pension schemes into which workers are enrolled are of high quality and provide value for money.

On 31 March Security and Immigration minister James Brokenshire replied to an urgent question from shadow home secretary Yvette Cooper on the death of a detainee at Yarl's Wood Immigration Centre. On 1 April, business secretary Vince Cable responded to an urgent question from his Labour shadow Chuka Umunna on the price at which Royal Mail had been privatised in the light of a recent National Audit Office report: 'the report confirms that we achieved our primary objective of securing a sale of shares, allowing Royal Mail to access the private capital it needs to invest and thrive'. Mr Umunna disagreed: 'the report delivers a damning verdict on the government's botched privatisation, which has left the taxpayer disgracefully short-changed to the tune of hundreds of millions of pounds'. On 3 April Jane Ellison made a statement about the publication of Sir Cyril Chantler's report on standardised packaging of tobacco products, announcing a final, short consultation on views on anything new that had arisen since the last full public consultation. Luciana Berger asked 'Why is the minister now kicking the matter into the long grass? . . . is this not yet another example of how her government are caving in to vested interests and standing up for the wrong people?' This was followed by a very short personal statement from culture secretary Maria Miller, apologising to the House for her attitude to the Commissioner's inquiries into allegations against her as recommended by the Committee on Standards. Owen Paterson made a statement on the publication of the government's strategy for achieving officially TB-free status for cattle in England, including a second year of badger culling in Gloucestershire and Somerset with the 'aim for England to be free of TB by 2038, with healthy cattle living alongside healthy badgers'. Maria Eagle felt this 'completely ignored the will of the House, which only three weeks ago voted overwhelmingly [219 to 1] to oppose his plans, to cancel the culls, and to seek alternative ways of dealing with the problem'.

On 8 April the Leader of the House of Commons, Andrew Lansley, answered an urgent question from John Mann (Labour) on parliamentary standards, giving greater detail of possible changes to the role of two committees which regulate complaints about fellow MPs. On 10 April James Brokenshire replied to an urgent question from Sarah Teather (Lib Dem) on support to meet the essential living needs of asylum seekers under sections 95 and 98 of the Immigration and Asylum Act 1999, stressing that 'asylum seekers are supported by the Home Office if they are destitute'.

On 28 April William Hague updated the House on developments in Ukraine. On 30 April Theresa May made a statement on the use of stop-and-search powers by the police, emphasising that where officers are not using their powers properly they would be subject to formal performance or disciplinary proceedings. Yvette Cooper thought this 'did not match up to her previous promises nor go far enough'. On 1 May, Care Services minister Norman Lamb responded to an urgent question from Nick Smith (Labour) on the Oban House care home and the government's policy for safeguarding residents in care homes: 'we are putting in place, through reform of the Care Quality Commission, a range of measures to improve the regulation of care homes, to hold to account providers that are responsible for unacceptable care, and to improve the quality of social care.'

On 6 May Vince Cable answered an urgent question from Julian Huppert (Lib Dem) on Pfizer's bid for AstraZeneca, reassuring the House that 'we are alive to the national interest considerations. We see the future of the UK as a knowledge economy, not a tax haven. Our focus is on what is best for the UK.'

On 12 May Michael Gove responded to an urgent question from Tristram Hunt on the allocation of funding for the free school programme, whose costs were 'significantly lower than under the last government's school building programme'. On 13 May Justine Greening updated the House on developments in Afghanistan before the House was prorogued, signalling the end of the 2013–14 session of Parliament.

STATE OPENING OF PARLIAMENT AND THE QUEEN'S SPEECH

The Queen's Speech on 4 June 2014 marked the start of the fourth and final session of the 2010 Parliament. It contained proposals for 11 new bills and three that had been published in draft form for pre-legislative scrutiny. In addition, six bills were carried over from the 2013–14 parliamentary session. Prime minister David Cameron described it as 'a packed programme of a busy and radical government . . . the long-term economic plan is working but there is much, much more to do.' Labour leader Ed Miliband said the speech failed to match the scale of the challenges Britain faces and that 'we would have a Queen's Speech with legislation which would make work pay, reform our banks, freeze energy bills and build homes again . . . a new direction for Britain, not one which offers more of the same.' After six days of debate the speech was approved on 12 June by 270 votes to 231.

On 9 June, home secretary Theresa May replied to an urgent question from her Labour shadow Yvette Cooper on her conduct regarding the government's action on preventing extremism. Ms May confirmed that following unauthorised comments to the media about the government's approach and the Cabinet Secretary's review, 'the education secretary apologised . . . and my special adviser Fiona Cunningham resigned'. Education secretary Michael Gove made a statement on schools in Birmingham following allegations in the so-called 'Trojan horse' letter that children were not being kept safe; Ofsted and the Education Funding Agency had investigated the allegations and found that governors 'are trying to impose and promote a narrow faith-based ideology in what are non-faith schools'. He was taking decisive action: 'Schools that are proven to have failed will be taken over, put under new leadership and taken in a fresh new direction. Any school could now be subject to rigorous, on-the-spot inspections with no advance warning and no opportunities to conceal failure.' On 11 June David Cameron reported on the G7 summit in Brussels and the commemoration of the 70th anniversary of D-Day in Normandy. On 12 June Theresa May answered an urgent question from Yvette Cooper on delays at HM Passport Office, which was receiving 350,000 more passport applications and renewals than normal for the time of year. She had asked the Home Office's permanent secretary, Mark Sedwill, to conduct two reviews: first, to ensure that HM Passport Office works as efficiently as possible; and secondly, to consider whether its agency status should be removed.

On 16 June, justice secretary Chris Grayling replied to an urgent question from his Labour shadow Sadiq Khan on the government's response to the prison overcrowding crisis: 'we do not have a prison overcrowding crisis . . . we have more than 1,000 spare places across the prison estate.' William Hague made a statement on Iraq, and updated the House on the outcome of the recent global summit on ending sexual violence in conflict.

On 24 June, Jeremy Hunt responded to an urgent question from Andy Burnham on the package of measures he had announced to boost safety, transparency and openness in the NHS. James Brokenshire made a statement on student visas, outlining plans to show that 'we will not hesitate to take firm action against those – students, colleges and universities – who do not abide by their legal responsibilities, and we will resolutely pursue organised criminality to bring those responsible to justice.' On 26 June Jeremy Hunt made a statement on NHS investigations into Jimmy Savile; 28 investigations had been published, including two larger reports on Leeds Infirmary and Broadmoor Hospital, which 'reveal a litany of disturbing accounts of rape and sexual abuse committed by Savile on vulnerable children and adults

over a period of decades'. He apologised on behalf of the government and the NHS to all the victims. The House then went on to debate the commemoration of the First World War.

On 30 June David Cameron reported on the European Council meeting, which had discussed the appointment of the next president of the European Commission. He had 'firmly believed that it should be for the European Council to propose the president of the European Commission. It should not be for the European Parliament to try and dictate that choice to the Council. That is a point of principle on which I was not prepared to budge'; in the event, Jean-Claude Juncker was put forward by the Council by 26 votes to two. On 1 July FCO minister Hugh Robertson answered an urgent question from Peter Bone (Conservative) on the effect that the murder of three Israeli teenagers abducted by Palestinians would have on the Middle East peace process, condemning the deaths as 'an appalling act of terror'.

On 7 July Theresa May made a statement about the sexual abuse of children and allegations that evidence of abuse was suppressed by people in positions of power, announcing the appointment of Peter Wanless, chief executive of the NSPCC, to lead a review. Cities minister Greg Clark made a statement on local growth deals: 'no longer will Whitehall monopolise decision making and shut out the role of local economic leadership . . . we are reviving the spirit of local leadership and entrepreneurship on which our nation's prosperity depends.' On 9 July Iain Duncan Smith replied to an urgent question from Chris Bryant (Labour) on whether the Department for Work and Pensions' business case for the implementation of universal credit has been approved by the chancellor, confirming that the Treasury had approved funding for the universal credit programme in 2013–14 and 2014–15 but that discussions were ongoing on the final sign-off of the business case covering the full programme. On 10 July Theresa May made a statement about the use of communications data and interception by the police, law enforcement agencies and the security and intelligence agencies and, in order to address the difficulties they faced, said she was introducing the data retention and investigatory powers bill, to be fast-tracked into law before the summer recess. Minister for the Cabinet Office Francis Maude updated the House on the day's industrial action called by some public-sector unions.

On 16 July Jeremy Hunt made a statement about hospitals in special measures and the next steps for rolling out a new inspection regime in the social care sector, following the Keogh report into NHS hospitals with the highest mortality rates; these included bringing back expert-led inspections for adult social care, to ensure that ongoing abuse and neglect in residential care homes and domiciliary care services is 'stamped out once and for all'. On 17 July Theresa May answered an urgent question from Yvette Cooper about child abuse, announcing progress since her last statement, but also that Baroness Butler-Sloss had stood down from her appointment as chair of an independent panel inquiry to consider whether public bodies and non-state institutions had taken seriously their duty of care to protect children from sexual abuse, having come to the conclusion that she should not chair the inquiry. Theresa Villiers made a statement on the publication of the report by Lady Justice Hallett into the scheme providing so-called 'on-the-runs' with immunity from prosecution; she had concluded that 'the administrative scheme did not amount to an amnesty for terrorists . . . Suspected terrorists were not handed a "get out of jail free" card.' On 18 July the Lords held the second reading of the assisted dying bill, a private member's bill introduced by Lord Falconer of Thoroton; some 130 peers spoke and the House sat for over ten hours, but the bill will progress to committee consideration later in 2014.

On 21 July David Cameron updated the House before it rose for the summer recess on the loss of Malaysia Airlines flight MH17 and the ongoing crisis in Israel and Gaza: 'it is only by securing a ceasefire that the space can be created to address the underlying issues and return to the long and painstaking task of building the lasting and secure peace that we all want to see'. On 22 July, the final day before rising for the recess, Nicky Morgan, appointed education secretary in the Cabinet reshuffle on 15 July, made a statement on the publication of Peter Clarke's report into allegations concerning Birmingham schools, presenting 'compelling evidence of a determined effort by people with a shared ideology to gain control of the governing bodies of a small number of schools in Birmingham'. Home secretary Theresa May made a statement on standards of integrity in the police, outlining measures to overhaul the systems that hold police officers to account that 'will build on our radical programme of police reform, and they will help to ensure that police honesty and integrity are protected, and that corruption and misconduct are rooted out'.

The House of Lords, which will not return for a short session in September 2014, continued to sit until 30 July. On 28 July the former Commons Speaker Baroness Boothroyd moved a motion regretting the decision of the prime minister to diminish the standing of the House of Lords by failing to make the new Leader of the House (Baroness Stowell of Beeston) a full member of the cabinet. Despite Baroness Stowell herself trying to make light of the matter, calling herself 'the Beyoncé of your Lordships' House', the motion was passed by 177 votes to 29.

PUBLIC ACTS OF PARLIAMENT

Public acts included in this list are those which received the royal assent after 20 July 2013. The date stated after each act is the date on which it came into operation. For further information *see* W www.legislation.gov.uk

Highspeed Rail (Preparation) Act 2013 ch. 31 (21 November 2013) makes provisions authorising expenditure in preparation for a high speed railway transport network.

Energy Act 2013 ch. 32 (18 December 2013) makes provision for the setting of a decarbonisation target range and duties in relation to it; for or in connection with reforming the electricity market for purposes of encouraging low carbon electricity generation or ensuring security of supply; for the establishment and functions of the Office for Nuclear Regulation; about the government pipe-line and storage system and rights exercisable in relation to it; about the designation of a strategy and policy statement; about domestic supplies of gas and electricity; for extending categories of activities for which energy licences are required; for the making of orders requiring regulated persons to provide redress to consumers of gas or electricity; about offshore transmission of electricity during a commissioning period; for imposing fees in connection with certain costs incurred by the Secretary of State; about smoke and carbon monoxide alarms; and for connected purposes.

Financial Services (Banking Reform) Act 2013 ch. 33 (18 December 2013) makes further provision about banking and other financial services, including provision about the Financial Services Compensation Scheme; to make provision for the amounts owed in respect of certain deposits to be treated as a preferential debt on insolvency; to make further provision about payment systems and securities settlement systems; to make provision about the accounts of the Bank of England and its wholly owned subsidiaries; to make provision in relation to persons providing claims management services; and for connected purposes.

Mesothelioma Act 2014 ch. 1 (30 January 2014) establishes a Diffuse Mesothelioma Payment Scheme and makes related provision; and to make provision about the resolution of certain insurance disputes.

Local Audit and Accountability Act 2014 ch. 2 (30 January 2014) makes provision for and in connection with the abolition of the Audit Commission for Local Authorities and the National Health Service in England; to make provision about the accounts of local and certain other public authorities and the auditing of those accounts; to make provision about the appointment, functions and regulation of local auditors; to make provision about data matching; to make provision about examinations by the Comptroller and Auditor General relating to English local and other public authorities; to make provision about the publication of information by smaller authorities; to make provision about compliance with codes of practice on local authority publicity; to make provision about access to meetings and documents of local government bodies; to make provision about council tax referendums; to make provision about polls consequent on parish meetings; and for connected purposes.

European Union (Approvals) Act 2014 ch. 3 (30 January 2014) makes provision approving for the purposes of section 8 of the European Act 2011 certain draft decisions under Article 352 of the Treaty on the Functioning of the European Union.

Transparency of Lobbying, Non-Party Campaigning and Trade Union Administration Act 2014 ch. 4 (30 January 2014) makes provision for establishing and maintaining a register of persons carrying on the business of consultant lobbying and to require those persons to be entered in the register; to make provision about expenditure and donations for political purposes; to make provision about the Electoral Commission's functions with respect to compliance with requirements imposed by or by virtue of enactments; to make provision relating to a trade union's duty to maintain a register of members under section 24 of the Trade Union and Labour Relations (Consolidation) Act 1992; and for connected purposes.

Supply and Appropriation (Anticipation and Adjustments) Act 2014 ch. 5 (13 March 2014) authorises the use of resources for the years ending with 31 March 2008, 31 March 2009, 31 March 2010, 31 March 2011, 31 March 2012, 31 March 2013, 31 March 2014 and 31 March 2015; to authorise the issue of sums out of the Consolidated Fund for the years ending 31 March 2013, 31 March 2014 and 31 March 2015; and to appropriate the supply authorised by this Act for the years ending with 31 March 2008, 31 March 2009, 31 March 2010, 31 March 2011, 31 March 2012, 31 March 2013 and 31 March 2014.

Children and Families Act 2014 ch. 6 (13 March 2014) makes provision about children, families, and people with special educational needs or disabilities; to make provision about the right to request flexible working; and for connected purposes.

National Insurance Contributions Act 2014 ch. 7 (13 March 2014) makes provision in relation to national insurance contributions; and for connected purposes.

Citizenship (Armed Forces) Act 2014 ch. 8 (13 March 2014) makes provision in connection with applications for naturalisation as a British citizen made by members or former members of the armed forces.

International Development (Gender Equality) Act 2014 ch. 9 (13 March 2014) promotes gender equality in the provision by the Government of development assistance and humanitarian assistance to countries outside the United Kingdom; and for connected purposes.

Leasehold Reform (Amendment) Act 2014 ch. 10 (13 March 2014) amends the Leasehold Reform, Housing and Urban Development Act 1993 in relation to the permitted signatories of notices; and for connected purposes.

Offender Rehabilitation Act 2014 ch. 11 (13 March 2014) makes provision about the release, and supervision after release, of offenders; to make provision about the extension period for extended sentence prisoners; to make provision about community orders and suspended sentence orders; and for connected purposes.

Anti-social Behaviour, Crime and Policing Act 2014 ch. 12 (13 March 2014) makes provision about anti-social behaviour, crime and disorder, including provision about recovery of possession of dwelling-houses; to make provision amending the Dangerous Dogs Act 1991, the Police Act 1997, Schedules 7 and 8 to the Terrorism Act 2000, the Extradition Act 2003, and Part 3 of the Police Reform and Social Responsibility Act 2011; to make provision about firearms, about sexual harm and violence and about forced marriage; to make provision about the police, the Independent Police Complaints Commission and the Serious Fraud Office; to make provision about invalid travel documents; to make provision about criminal justice and court fees; and for connected purposes.

Northern Ireland (Miscellaneous Provisions Act) 2014 ch. 13 (13 March 2014) makes provision about donations, loans and related transactions for political purposes in connection with Northern Ireland; to amend the Northern Ireland Assembly Disqualification Act 1975 and the Northern Ireland Act 1998; to make provision about the registration of electors and the administration of elections in Northern Ireland; and to make miscellaneous amendments in the law relating to Northern Ireland.

Cooperative and Community Benefit Societies Act 2014 ch. 14 (14 May 2014) consolidates certain enactments relating to cooperative societies, community benefit societies and other societies registered or treated as registered under the Industrial and Provident Societies Act 1965, with amendments to give effect to recommendations of the Law Commission and the Scottish Law Commission.

Deep Sea Mining Act 2014 ch. 15 (14 May 2014) makes provision about deep sea mining; and for connected purposes.

Inheritance and Trustees' Powers Act 2014 ch. 16 (14 May 2014) makes further provision about the distribution of estates of deceased persons and to amend the law relating to the powers of trustees.

Gambling (Licensing and Advertising) Act 2014 ch. 17 (14 May 2014) makes provision about the licensing and advertising of gambling.

Intellectual Property Act 2014 ch. 18 (14 May 2014) makes provision about intellectual property.

Pensions Act 2014 ch. 19 (14 May 2014) makes provision about pensions and about benefits payable to people in connection with bereavement; and for connected purposes.

Defence Reform Act 2014 ch.20 (14 May 2014) makes provision in connection with any arrangements that may be made by the Secretary of State with respect of the provision to the Secretary of State of defence procurement services; to make provision relating to defence procurement contracts awarded, or amended, otherwise than as the result of a competitive process; to make provision in relation to the reserve forces of the Crown; and for connected purposes.

Water Act 2014 ch. 21 (14 May 2014) makes provision about the water industry; about compensation for modification of licenses to abstract water; about main river maps; about records of waterworks; for the regulation of the water environment; about the provision of flood insurance for household premises; about internal drainage boards; about Regional Flood and Coastal Committees; and for connected purposes.

Immigration Act 2014 ch. 22 (14 May 2014) makes provision about immigration law; to limit, or otherwise make provision about, access to services, facilities and employment by reference to immigration status; to make provision about marriage and civil partnership involving certain foreign nationals; to make provision about the acquisition of citizenship by persons unable to acquire it because their fathers and mothers were not married to each other and provision about the removal of citizenship from persons whose conduct is seriously prejudicial to the United Kingdom's vital interests; and for connected purposes.

Care Act 2014 ch. 23 (14 May 2014) makes provision to reform the law relating to care and support for adults and the law relating to support for carers; to make provision about safeguarding adults from abuse or neglect; to make provision about care standards; to establish and make provision about Health Education England; to make provision about the Health Research Authority; to make provision about integrating care and support with health services; and for connected purposes.

House of Lords Reform Act 2014 ch. 24 (14 May 2014) makes provision for resignation from the House of Lords; and to make provision for the expulsion of Members of the House of Lords in specified circumstances.

Supply and Appropriation (Main Estimates) Act 2014 ch. 25 (17 July 2014) authorises the use of resources for the year ending with 31 March 2015; to authorise both the issue of sums out of the Consolidated Fund and the application of income for that year; and to appropriate the supply authorised that year by this Act and by the Supply and Appropriation (Anticipation and Adjustments) Act 2014.

Finance Act 2014 ch. 26 (17 July 2014) grants certain duties, to alter other duties, and to amend the law relating to the National Debt and the Public Revenue, and to make further provision in connection with finance.

Data Retention and Investigatory Powers Act 2014 ch. 27 (17 July 2014) makes provision, in consequence of a declaration of invalidity made by the Court of Justice of the European Union in relation to Directive 2006/24/EC, about the retention of certain communications data; to amend the grounds for issuing interception warrants, or granting or giving certain authorisations or notices, under Part 1 of the Regulation of Investigatory Powers Act 2000; to make provision about the extra-territorial application of that Part and about the meaning of 'telecommunications service' for the purposes of that Act; to make provision about additional reports by the Interception of Communications Commissioner; to make provision about a review of the operation and regulation of investigatory powers; and for connected purposes.

SCIENCE AND DISCOVERY

Storm Dunlop

SIGNALS FROM THE BEGINNING OF TIME?

On 17 March 2014, widespread media interest and excitement was generated by the announcement from an international team, led by the Harvard-Smithsonian Center for Astrophysics, that it had detected definite evidence of cosmic inflation, the exponential expansion of the universe immediately after the Big Bang, 13.82 billion years ago. The implications of this result, if confirmed, would have far-reaching consequences for cosmology and physics. The discovery would be the first detection of, and first evidence for, gravitational waves, which produced what is termed the cosmic gravitational-wave background (CGB) about one trillionth, trillionth, trillionth (10^{-36}) of a second after the Big Bang. The evidence is the expected complex polarisation pattern that the CGB later superimposed on the cosmic microwave background (CMB) radiation that actually arose about 380,000 years after the Big Bang, when the universe became transparent.

The first evidence of gravitational waves was expected to come from waves produced by collapsing or merging ultra-dense stars or black holes. The detection of CGB waves would imply the existence of a particle known as the graviton and, further, that this particle is subject to quantum effects. To date, quantum mechanics, which successfully account for the other three fundamental forces, have been unable to incorporate the gravitational force. The results therefore would imply that gravity is a quantum phenomenon, encouraging the search for a complete theory of quantum gravity.

The simplest explanation of inflation also implies the existence of a particle, the inflaton, that produces the required repulsive effect, but which decays rapidly over time. However, current theories predict that if there is such a particle as the inflaton, then it also implies the existence of what is collectively known as the multiverse (multiple universes, all probably with different physical properties from our own). In July 2014, Matthew Johnson of Canada's Perimeter Institute for Theoretical Physics and colleagues revealed how they are working to devise computer simulations that can test any multiverse hypothesis. Contact between two different universes, for example, might show as a circular feature in the CMB radiation. This programme has reached the point where it can rule out certain potential forms of multiverse.

The results from the BICEP2 (Background Imaging of Cosmic Extragalactic Polarization) experiment at the South Pole seemed unambiguous, but appeared to show a very strong signal, greatly at variance with other experiments, which have not detected even a weak effect. The discrepancy may be resolved when results from other experiments (such as one using the South Pole Telescope and the POLARBEAR experiment in the Atacama desert of Chile) are available, including data relating to the contribution to the polarisation by interstellar dust, obtained by the Planck spaceprobe, operated by the European Space Agency (ESA), to be released in October 2014. On 24 June, at a meeting of the Royal Astronomical Society, a team from King's College London announced that its calculations, using new data about the properties of the Higgs boson, showed that if the BICEP results were correct, the universe would have collapsed (in what is called the Big Crunch) within a fraction of a second after inflation. An unknown process and new particle physics would be required to prevent such a collapse. The original BICEP research team finally published its

work on 19 June, in *Physical Review Letters*. Although still maintaining that the results detected gravitational waves, the team acknowledges that the signal from interstellar dust may be larger than assumed.

YES, IT IS A HIGGS BOSON

Following the discovery of the Higgs boson in 2012, there was some doubt about its exact properties. New research carried out at the Large Hadron Collider (LHC) at CERN has definitively established that the mass of the Higgs is 125 GeV (gigaelectronvolts). Additional confirmation of its properties came in a paper published on 23 June 2014 in *Nature Physics* by a team from Rice University in Texas and colleagues. Using the CMS (Compact Muon Solenoid) detector at CERN, they have established that, as predicted, the Higgs may decay into a pair of photons and, in addition, there is evidence that it also decays into what are known as fermion particles. This firmly establishes that the Higgs boson behaves as predicted by the Standard Model in theoretical physics. A team using the ATLAS detector at CERN has also obtained positive evidence of the decay into fermions, but has yet to publish the results.

A NEW SPECIMEN IN THE PARTICLE ZOO

On 9 April 2014, scientists working with the LHC at CERN confirmed that they had discovered a new form of matter, previously suspected but not fully established experimentally. The discovery does not fit the traditional quark model, in which multiple quarks are believed to form particles known as hadrons that take part in the strong interaction (quarks cannot be observed directly, but are inferred from the properties of other particles.) Previously, it was known that three quarks combine to form certain particles (known as baryons), notably the proton and neutron, and that two form various mesons. Work by the Large Hadron Collider beauty (LHCb) collaboration has established the existence of an exotic particle, known as Z(4430), consisting of four quarks. Hints of this particle were first detected by the Belle Collaboration in 2008, but a later experiment by an international team called BaBar cast doubt upon the result. Later re-analysis by the Belle scientists put the result on a more substantial basis, but the latest findings are unambiguous and Z(4430) definitely exists.

GAIA

Building on the highly successful Hipparcos mission (1989–93), which determined the positions of over 100,000 stars and more than one million to a lesser accuracy, on 19 December 2013, the ESA launched the Gaia space telescope, designed to obtain precise information on the location of some one billion stars (about 1 per cent of the stars within our galaxy). In mid-June 2014, it was announced that initial tests had found that some unexpected stray light was likely to affect observation of the very faintest stars, reducing the accuracy of some measurements, although it may be possible to remedy the situation if the mission can be extended beyond the proposed five-year duration.

KEPLER IS REVIVED

NASA's Kepler space telescope, which has been so successful in discovering many hundreds of actual and candidate extrasolar planets, had been crippled by the failure in May 2013 of the second of its four reaction wheels that enabled it to maintain its pointing in space (a minimum of three wheels was required to position it in three dimensions). In June 2014, it was announced that a method of stabilising the spacecraft had been developed and an extended mission (known as K2) had been authorised by NASA on 16 May. The radiation pressure exerted by sunlight on the spacecraft's solar panels would be used in conjunction with the two functioning reaction wheels. Because of the constraints on positioning, observations would be possible only along the plane of the ecliptic (the Earth's orbit in space). The constraints are such that the telescope is limited to a number of 'windows', each with a duration of about 80 days, during which it will point in a single direction, before re-orientation of the spacecraft is required.

DISCOVERY IN THE OUTER SOLAR SYSTEM

In *Nature* on 26 March 2014, Chadwick A. Trujillo (Gemini Observatory, Hawaii) and Scott S. Sheppard (Carnegie Institution of Science, Washington DC) announced the discovery of a dwarf planet orbiting in the outer reaches of the solar system. The planet, currently known as 2012 VP_{113}, is believed to be about 450km in diameter and is probably an icy body. Only one other body, a dwarf planet known as Sedna discovered in 2004, with a diameter of about 1,000km, has such an extreme orbit, with perihelion (closest approach to the Sun) in a region of space beyond the major planets and the belt of small, icy bodies (known as Trans-Neptunian Objects, of which Pluto is one) that are members of the Kuiper Belt. Perihelion for Sedna is 76 astronomical units (au) – 1au is the average distance of the Earth from the Sun. 2012 VP_{113} has a perihelion of 80au and aphelion (farthest distance from the Sun) is estimated to be about 450au. Expressed in kilometres, these distances are approximately 12 billion km and an incredible 67 billion km. The orbital period of VP_{113} is approximately 4,300 years. For comparison, the farthest major planet, Neptune, orbits at about 4.5 billion km with a period of 164.8 years. Sedna and VP_{113} have extremely eccentric orbits and are thought to be a possible link between the Kuiper-Belt objects and the hypothesised Oort Cloud – the origin of many comets – that lies at a distance of some 50,000au.

ROSETTA AWAKES

On 20 January 2014, the ESA's Rosetta spaceprobe ended its state of hibernation, which had lasted for nearly three years, imposed to conserve its energy supplies. Rosetta, launched on 2 March 2004, is a complex, ambitious mission, scheduled to enter orbit around Comet 67P/Churyumov-Gerasimenko on 6 August 2014, when the comet and probe are approximately halfway between the orbits of Mars and Jupiter. (Although still far from the Sun, the comet displayed episodes of activity in spring 2014.) Rosetta will survey the comet's nucleus in order to find a site to land a probe (named Philae) on 11 November 2014. In early July 2014, it was found that the comet has a strange shape, apparently consisting of two bodies in contact with one another, which will make site selection more complicated. Because of the comet's feeble gravity, Philae will use a harpoon and ice screws to anchor itself in position. It will drill into the surface and obtain in-situ measurements of the material and properties of the nucleus. The main spacecraft will eventually leave cometary orbit, but (still acquiring data) will accompany the comet, within the coma of gas and dust ejected from the nucleus, for many months as it approaches perihelion. This lies between the orbits of Earth and Mars, and after perihelion (on 13 August 2015) the comet and Rosetta will begin to recede from the Sun. The mission provisionally ends on 31 December 2015.

COMET SIDING SPRING AND MARS

On 19 June 2014, a team of astronomers led by Dennis Bodewits (University of Maryland College Park) announced that a rare astronomical event will occur on 19 October 2014, when the Comet Siding Spring (C/2013A1) will brush past Mars. NASA's Swift satellite imaged the comet, finding it already active, producing water and dust. Based on the rate at which water is released, the team estimates that the comet's nucleus is about 700m across. The observations also enabled the orbit to be refined. The comet will pass just 138,000km from Mars; so close that the outer reaches of the comet's coma of gas and dust that it has shed will interact with the Martian atmosphere. The comet is thought to be 'fresh' from the reservoir known as the Oort Cloud, making its first approach to the inner solar system.

CHINESE LUNAR PROBE

On 14 December 2013, the Chinese lunar probe Chang'e landed on the Moon in Mare Imbrium, the first soft landing since the Soviet Union's Luna 24 mission in 1976. The lander carried a small rover, called Yutu or 'Jade Rabbit' (associated with the Moon goddess Chang'e in Chinese mythology). The rover carried out tests on the lunar soil before being shut down for the duration of lunar darkness. It was revived on 11 January, but suffered some form of breakdown and is no longer operational. No details have been released about whether the scientific instruments on the landing stage have continued to operate, although the mission was intended to have a one-year lifetime.

WATER, WATER (NEARLY) EVERYWHERE

The existence of water within or on celestial bodies is of fundamental interest. Not only is water considered essential for all life-forms, it also plays a major part in geology, helping to explain the origin of planets and satellites and their internal structure.

In January 2014, a team of scientists from the ESA announced in *Nature* that, using the Herschel infrared space telescope, it had unequivocally detected water vapour around the dwarf planet Ceres. The vapour is believed to result from plumes released when certain areas of the surface warm slightly. Ceres is thought to be a rocky body surrounded by a thick mantle of ice – possibly containing more fresh water than present on Earth. NASA's Dawn spaceprobe will arrive at Ceres in February 2015, mapping the surface and providing data until the end of the mission in July 2015.

In April 2014, an international team of scientists announced in *Science* that gravity measurements using the Cassini spaceprobe indicate the presence of a large, possibly regional, body of water beneath the icy crust of Enceladus, one of Saturn's satellites. A sub-surface ocean is assumed to be the source of the water observed to be emerging in plumes from fractures in the icy crust in the south polar region.

Similar additional results from Cassini were reported by an international team led by Giuseppe Mitri of the University of Nantes, in *Icarus* for July 2014. Gravity and topography measurements revealed the presence of an extremely salty oceanic layer beneath the icy surface of Titan, Saturn's largest satellite. The brine probably contains salts of sulphur, sodium and potassium with an overall content similar to the Dead Sea. The outermost shell of ice varies in thickness, probably as the result of localised freezing of water from the underlying brine onto the lower surface of the icy crust.

A team from the University of Gothenburg in Sweden, led by Andreas Johnsson, reported in the journal *Icarus* in April 2014 that liquid water had flowed on the surface of Mars some 200,000 years ago – extremely recent in geological terms – and long after the global ice age that is believed to have ended 400,000 years ago. The evidence for liquid water includes water-cut gullies and debris-flow deposits. In July 2014, however, a team headed by Colin Dundas of the US Geological Survey's Astrogeology Science Center, Arizona, published findings online in *Icarus* that gullies formed in the present day, previously thought to be signs of liquid water, are actually being created by the freezing and sublimation of carbon dioxide.

Water is significant in the history of the Moon. When, in 2010, considerable amounts of water were discovered in orange soil and other samples returned by Apollo astronauts, it cast doubt on the leading theory for the Moon's formation (that it resulted from the consolidation of debris from the collision of a Mars-sized body, known as Theia, with the early Earth). Such a collision would have vaporised most of the volatile materials (including water), giving a depletion on the Moon. Any water on the Moon was assumed to have derived from later cometary impacts. In April 2014, a team from the University of California Department of Planetary and Space Sciences announced in the online version of *Science* that the hydrogen in hydrogen-rich lunar rocks did not form in a water-rich environment, as was supposed. In late May 2014, a team from the University of Hawaii announced that it had found considerable regional variations in the water-content in the Moon's interior, suggesting that the body's formation was more complex than previously expected. Because both the Earth and Moon are assumed to have undergone a similar bombardment by cometary and other bodies, the findings have implications for the early history of Earth.

Two recent studies suggest that an extremely large amount of water is bound into rocks in Earth's upper mantle. In March 2014, a team led by Professor Graham Pearson (University of Alberta, Canada) published the results of an examination of ringwoodite inclusions in a diamond from the transition zone between the upper and lower mantle. Ringwoodite is thought to form at depths of 410 to 660km, and is a major component of the mantle. Although the inclusions contained just 1 per cent water, overall, a vast amount of water is involved.

This finding is confirmed by another study, published in June 2014 in Science, by Steven Jacobsen (Northwestern University, Illinois) and Brandon Schmandt (University of New Mexico). The team examined seismic data and found deep pockets of magma, presumably produced by partial melting of rock in the presence of water. These two results, obtained in completely different ways, suggest that large quantities of water are present in the mantle. The water present on Earth's surface may have been present when the planet originally formed and subsequently emerged from the deep interior. It may not have been accreted from cometary material, as has been assumed for many years.

THE ORIGIN OF THE EARTH AND MOON
Although the favoured theory for the formation of the Moon envisaged it being formed from debris produced by a planet-sized body (Theia) colliding with the early Earth, one major problem was that the composition of lunar rocks appeared to be identical to terrestrial rocks. On 6 June 2014, however, a team led by Dr Daniel Herwartz (University of Göttingen, Germany) presented evidence in *Science* that material from Theia could be detected from the subtle difference in the ratio between the two oxygen isotopes ^{17}O and ^{16}O found in lunar and terrestrial samples. This suggests that Theia's material closely resembled the meteorites known as E-type chondrites.

On 9 June 2014, a team of scientists from Harvard University reported that a previously unexplained isotopic anomaly in Earth's mantle rocks probably indicates that only a portion of the ancient Earth was melted and fragmented by

the impact of Theia, and that remnants of the ancient Earth persist within the mantle. Two days later, on 11 June 2014, Guillaume Avice and Bernard Marty from the University of Lorraine in France announced that isotopic analysis of xenon gas within quartz crystals from South Africa and Australia strongly suggested that the Earth–Moon impact occurred some 60 million years earlier than had been previously thought. This suggests that the impact occurred only 40 million years after the formation of the solar system itself.

NEW DANGERS TO THE OZONE LAYER
On 9 March 2014, a team from the University of East Anglia published results in *Nature Geoscience* of its findings that four previously undetected gases posed a potential threat to the ozone layer. The detection in 1985 that gases known as chlorofluorocarbons (CFCs) were causing ozone holes led to rapid action and the implementation in 1987 of the Montreal Protocol, which limited their use, and a complete ban on production in 2010. The newly discovered gases are three CFCs and one hydrochlorofluorocarbon (HCFC). They were discovered by studies of the atmospheric gases trapped within snow firn, which is the perennial snow pack. The gases were not present before the 1960s, suggesting that they are all of man-made origin. Although currently at low levels, these gases have the potential to contribute to ozone depletion. Of immediate concern is the fact that their sources are currently unknown.

PRODUCTIVITY OF PLANT ECOSYSTEMS NOT CONTROLLED BY CLIMATE
In a surprise finding, University of Arizona researchers and collaborators announced online in *Nature* on 20 July 2014 that they had established that climate is not a major factor in the productivity of plants, when whole ecosystems are considered, as had previously been assumed. This should lead to a great improvement in models of how climate (and climate change) affects ecosystems. Although warmth and water allow individual plants' metabolism to function at a higher rate than in colder and drier environments, it appears that when a whole ecosystem is considered, temperature and precipitation have a minor effect on the system's overall productivity and carbon sequestration. The size and age of plants proves to be of greater significance.

EARLIEST EVIDENCE OF HUMAN DEXTERITY
On 16 December 2013, an international team of researchers announced in *Proceedings of the National Academy of Sciences* that it had recovered a hand bone from a human ancestor present in East Africa about 1.42 million years ago. A particular projection on the bone (known as the styloid process) is an anatomical feature that enhances dexterity and enables humans to have both a powerful and a precise grip, greatly facilitating making and using stone tools. Such a feature is absent in apes and hominids such as the various *Australopithecus* species. The bone was found at the Kaitio site in West Turkana, Kenya. It is believed to have belonged to an individual of the *Homo erectus* species, and is the earliest evidence for a human-like hand, over 500,000 years earlier than previously known. The bone was found near sites where the earliest shaped tools (known as Acheulian) have been recovered, dating back about 1.6 million years.

THE DENISOVANS, NEANDERTHALS AND US
In December 2013, researchers at the Max Planck Institute for Evolutionary Anthropology in Germany announced in *Nature* that they had obtained the almost complete mitochondrial genome from a hominin femur that is some 400,000 years old. The bone is from a deposit in the Sima de los Huesos ('Cave of Bones') in northern Spain that is

the world's largest collection of Middle Pleistocene fossils. The human species at Sima de los Huevos is classed as *Homo heidelbergensis*, but has many traits in common with *Homo neanderthalensis*. The recovered genome was compared with that from present-day human groups, apes, Neanderthals and the extinct, relatively poorly understood human species known as Denisovans, who were apparently related to Neanderthals. The specimen from Sima de los Huevos suggests that there was a common ancestor to both the Denisovans and Neanderthals. Another possibility is that an unknown human group provided the Denisovan-like mtDNA to the hominins found in Spain.

The extent to which the mysterious Denisovans contributed to modern-day populations remains of considerable interest. In October 2013, Professor Alan Cooper of the University of Adelaide and Professor Chris Stringer of the Natural History Museum in London pointed out in an article in *Science* that, nowadays, major traces of Denisovan DNA are to be found only in human populations in New Guinea, Australia and nearby areas. This suggests that the Denisovans crossed the famous biogeographical barrier known as Wallace's Line, partly defined by a very strong oceanic current on the east coast of Borneo. The Line separates European and Asian mammals on the north and west from Australasian marsupials to the south and east. Modern humans did not colonise New Guinea and Australia until about 50,000 years ago, but must at some stage have interbred with the Denisovans, who have left no significant traces of their presence north and west of Wallace's Line.

A further twist to the story of the Denisovans was revealed in an article in *Nature* in early July 2014. A team from the University of California investigated the relationship between the presence in modern-day Tibetans of the gene known as EPAS1, which is part of the system that enables the body to cope with low levels of oxygen. Tibetans are known to have certain specific adaptations that enable them to live comfortably at high altitudes; they have a variant of the EPAS1 gene not found elsewhere in the world. The team compared the DNA from Tibetans with a wide range of modern populations and from known extinct groups. The only group to show the same variant were the Denisovans, who presumably contributed this important adaptation directly or indirectly to the Tibetan lineage.

On 19 December 2013, a large international team led by Svante Pääbo, of the Max Planck Institute for Evolutionary Anthropology in Leipzig, published in *Nature* its success in obtaining the complete genome from a Neanderthal bone from the Altai region in Siberia that is dated to about 50,000 years ago. The results have far-reaching implications about the interrelationships between the various species of hominin. In particular, they reveal the genetic links between the Neanderthals, Denisovans and modern humans. They also apparently reveal the presence of an earlier, unknown human species ancestral to all the groups. It shows that the Neanderthals and Denisovans were closely related until about 300,000 years ago, with their common ancestor splitting from the ancestor of modern humans some 400,000 years ago. It is estimated that between 1.5 and 2.1 per cent of the genome of modern non-Africans may be traced to Neanderthals. The Denisovan genome may be traced in some 6 per cent of Oceanic and Asian populations. However, only about 0.2 per cent of the genome in modern Han Chinese and other Asian populations arises from the Denisovans. There is also evidence that the Denisovans interbred with an unknown early group of humans. This latter group became distinct about one million years ago and may be the species known as *Homo erectus*.

On 7 July 2014, an international team described a surprise finding, detailed in the *Proceedings of the National Academy of Sciences*, of the results of a micro-CT scan of a very early human skull excavated during the 1970s at the Xujiayo site in the Nihewan Basin of northern China. The skull, some 100,000 years old, proved to have an inner-ear formation that had previously been considered to have occurred exclusively in Neanderthals, and indeed this particular pattern of the semicircular canals in the temporal labyrinth was used to positively differentiate Neanderthal skulls from other earlier or later human species. The implications of this finding, given the great distances separating the Neanderthals of central and western Europe from the archaic humans of eastern Asia, are unclear.

All these findings indicate the existence of considerable interbreeding between the various hominin species over time, and that the distinctions between the species are not as clear-cut as has long been believed. This view is bolstered by the results of work by psycholinguistic researchers from the Max Planck Institute, who published on 9 July 2013 in *Frontiers in Language Sciences* their finding that certain characteristics of modern language and speech may be traced back to the last common ancestor that modern humans share with the Neanderthals.

Acceptance of the idea that Neanderthals used speech was enhanced by a study, published by an international team in *PLoS One* in December 2013, on the structure of the hyoid bone found in a Neanderthal skeleton in 1989. The hyoid bone, which supports the base of the tongue, is rarely found in fossil skeletons, but is essential for speech in humans; in non-human primates it is not placed in such a way to allow vocalisation. Computer modelling of the bone's function showed that it was used in a similar way to that of modern-day humans.

EARLIEST FOOTPRINTS OUTSIDE AFRICA

In February 2014, a team of scientists from Queen Mary University, the British Museum and the Natural History Museum published in *PLoS ONE* details of the discovery of ancient footprints on the shore at Happisburgh in Norfolk. The prints are more than 800,000 years old, and are the earliest human footprints found outside Africa, and indeed the earliest evidence of humans in Europe. (The only other known footprints are at Laetoli in Tanzania, dated to about 3.5 million years ago, and at Ileret and Koobi Fora in Kenya, formed about 1.5 million years ago.) The hollows, exposed by beach erosion, were hastily photographed and recorded under difficult conditions before being destroyed by wave action. Analysis of the 3D images by Dr Isabelle De Groote of Liverpool John Moores University confirmed the hollows as human footprints, made by possibly five people, including one adult male and some children. The species is uncertain but may have been *Homo antecessor;* stone tools used by the same people were discovered locally in 2010. The climate deteriorated shortly after 800,000 before present (BP), and evidence of human occupation only recurs around 300,000 years later, with the appearance of *Homo heidelbergensis*, which evolved into the Neanderthals around 400,000 BP, and were replaced by modern *Homo sapiens* about 40,000 BP.

WHERE DID NATIVE AMERICANS ORIGINATE?

The origin of Native Americans has long posed a problem to researchers. The generally held view was that they derived from eastern Asians who migrated across Beringia, a land bridge which was dry during the Ice Age, but now submerged below the Bering Strait. The overall picture, however, was called into question by the genetic analysis of a bone from a child (known as the Mal'ta boy) buried in south-central Siberia, near Lake Baikal, some 24,000 years ago during the Ice Age. On 20 November 2013, Eske Willerslev, a geneticist at the Natural History Museum of Denmark, and colleagues reported in *Nature* that their examination of DNA from the arm bone revealed closer links with western and central Europeans and western Asians, than with present-day eastern Asians. Analysis of DNA from another skeleton, 17,000 years old, is genetically similar to that of the Mal'ta boy, suggesting, unexpectedly, that his people inhabited the area throughout the Ice Age. It appears that between 14 and 38 per cent of Native American ancestry may be traced back to the boy's people. At some stage they appear to have interbred with eastern Asians to give modern-day Native Americans, but there is no indication of whether this occurred in Asia or after the migration to North America.

In the issue of *Nature* for 13 February 2014, an international team published analysis of the DNA from another child, one year old, buried between 12,707 and 12,556 years ago in Montana. Associated with the burial were more than 100 bone and stone tools characteristic of the Clovis people, an early culture widespread in North America. This is the only known Clovis burial. The results of the analysis suggests that the Clovis people were the ancestors of all modern Native Americans. The Clovis baby, known as Anzick-1, traces part of his ancestry to the Siberian Mal'ta child. About 80 per cent of current Native Americans, primarily those of Central and South America, are direct descendants of the Anzick-1 baby's people. Other Native Americans, such as those in Canada, are also closely related to the Clovis people, but come from a different branch of the family. No data is available from Native Americans in the area now covered by the United States, so their precise relationship remains unknown.

Additional evidence of the early origins of Native Americans was provided by the discovery of the skeleton of a teenage girl in a flooded limestone cavern on the Yucatan peninsula. The age of the skeleton is at least 12,000 years. The earliest skeletons discovered in North America show slender features, which are distinct from those shown by the majority of modern Native Americans. This had suggested that there were multiple migrations of different peoples across the Beringia land bridge. However, the features of the teenage girl are slender, resembling the earliest Americans (Palaeoamericans), but her DNA closely matches that of modern Native Americans. This suggests that the differences arose after the gene pool of the inhabitants of Beringia became isolated from Asian peoples.

ANCIENT GIANT VIRUS RETURNS TO LIFE
On 4 March 2014, French scientists of the Centre National de Recherche Scientifique (CNRS) at the University of Aix-Marseille reported in *Proceedings of the National Academy of Sciences* that they had brought an ancient virus back to life after it had been frozen for 30,000 years. The giant virus, named *Pithovirus sibericum*, is 1.5 micrometres in size and is the largest ever recorded; large enough to be seen easily with a standard laboratory microscope. (The previous record-holder, *Pandoravirus salinus,* about one micrometre in size, was discovered in sea-floor deposits off Chile in 2013.) The new virus was recovered from a depth of 30m in Siberian permafrost, but became active once thawed. Although this virus, like other known giant viruses, infects amoebae, and poses no threat to humans, researchers are concerned that other, possibly dangerous, viruses entombed in permafrost may be released as a result of global warming.

GENETIC ORIGINS OF CANCER ARE IDENTIFIED
On 14 August 2013, a large team of researchers from the Wellcome Trust Sanger Institute announced in *Nature* that it had identified 21 mutations in cellular DNA that are involved in some 30 types of common tumours. Disruptions in the genetic code accounted for 97 per cent of these 30 cancers. This major insight into the exact structure of the various cancer genomes provides information as to why and how cancers occur. Most significantly, the findings reveal new previously unsuspected, processes involved in causing cells to become cancerous. As examples, two mutations underlie ovarian cancer, and six are involved in liver cancer. Although the involvement of certain factors in particular cancers was already known – such as smoking and lung cancer, and prolonged exposure to ultraviolet light and skin cancer – most mutation-inducing processes, whether caused by environmental factors or the response to viral infections, remain unknown. A knowledge of the processes at work offers the hope that more effective means of prevention and treatment may be devised.

TOWARDS A UNIVERSAL FLU VACCINE?
On 22 September 2013, a team of scientists from Imperial College London announced in *Nature Medicine* that it had made a major advance towards creating a vaccine that would be effective against all forms of influenza. The virus responsible is highly variable, in that it readily, and frequently, changes the proteins carried on its surface. Current vaccines target these proteins to produce an antibody response. Because of the virus' variability, however, seasonal vaccines are based on the 'best guess' of the form most likely to be prevalent during a coming winter. Such vaccines cannot be produced rapidly enough to counter the threat posed by pandemics. Working with cases of the swine flu pandemic, the team identified a specific form of the cells, known as T-cells, that are produced by the immune system. This form of T-cell targets the body of the virus itself, rather than its surface proteins. Eventual development of a vaccine using this information – a prize some years away – should help to contain seasonal influenza outbreaks and, more importantly, would be a major weapon against any future pandemics.

ATTACKING ANTIBIOTIC-RESISTANT BACTERIA AND THE LONGITUDE PRIZE
The growth in the number of antibiotic-resistant bacteria is becoming a serious problem in medicine. A new, promising approach has been found for attacking gram-negative bacteria (which include many that are showing antibiotic resistance and cause serious infections). The work was published in *Nature* on 19 June 2014 by researchers at the University of East Anglia's Norwich Medical School. Using the intense X-rays produced by the Diamond Light Source in Oxfordshire, the team determined the structure of a key dual-protein molecule (known as LptDE) that the bacteria use to construct their outer membrane. The protein transports lipopolysaccharide units from inside the bacterium and inserts them in the cell wall, by means of a 'path' and a 'gate'. Although the research is at an early stage, it offers the prospect of developing a means of blocking either the path or the gate and thus preventing the bacterium from constructing its outer membrane, making it more vulnerable to drugs that can act on bacteria from outside, rather than having to penetrate the interior. It would also make the bacteria prone to attack by the immune system.

In 1714 the Longitude Prize was offered for a solution to the problem of accurately determining longitude at sea. To mark the bicentenary of the original prize, a new Longitude Prize of £10m has been established in order to tackle a major present-day challenge. In June 2014, a public vote chose antibiotic resistance as the focus for the prize. The exact details of the competition are yet to be announced but, apart from any direct attack on bacteria, could include an improved method of determining whether an infection is caused by a bacterium or by a virus.

SPORTS RESULTS

ALPINE SKIING

WORLD CUP 2013–14

MEN
Downhill: Aksel Lund Svindal (Norway), 570pts
Slalom: Marcel Hirscher (Austria), 565pts
Giant Slalom: Ted Ligety (USA), 560pts
Super G: Aksel Lund Svindal (Norway), 346pts
Combined: Ted Ligety (USA)/Alexis Pinturault (France),
both 180pts
Overall: Marcel Hirscher (Austria), 1,222pts

WOMEN
Downhill: Maria Hoefl-Reisch (Germany), 504pts
Slalom: Mikaela Shiffrin (USA), 638pts
Giant Slalom: Anna Fenninger (Austria), 518pts
Super G: Lara Gut (Switzerland), 448pts
Combined: Marie-Michèle Gagnon (Canada), 100pts
Overall: Anna Fenninger (Austria), 1,371pts

AMERICAN FOOTBALL

AFC Championship 2013–14: Denver Broncos beat New
England Patriots 26–16
NFC Championship 2013–14: Seattle Seahawks beat San
Francisco 49ers 23–17
XLVIII Superbowl: Seattle Seahawks beat Denver Broncos
43–8

ANGLING

NATIONAL CHAMPIONSHIPS 2014
Individual: Kevin Hall
Individual (ladies): Kayleigh Smith

TEAMS
Division 1: Barnsley and District
Division 2: Wigan Match Group

ASSOCIATION FOOTBALL

LEAGUE COMPETITIONS 2013–14

ENGLAND AND WALES
Premier League
1. Manchester City, 86pts
2. Liverpool, 84pts
3. Chelsea, 82pts
4. Arsenal, 79pts
Relegated: Norwich City, Fulham, Cardiff City

Championship
1. Leicester City, 102pts
2. Burnley, 93pts
Play-off winner and third promotion place: Queens Park
Rangers
Relegated: Doncaster Rovers, Barnsley, Yeovil Town

League One
1. Wolverhampton Wanderers, 103pts
2. Brentford, 94pts
Play-off winner and third promotion place: Rotherham United
Relegated: Tranmere Rovers, Carlisle United, Shrewsbury
Town, Stevenage

League Two
1. Chesterfield, 84pts
2. Scunthorpe United, 81pts
3. Rochdale, 81pts
Play-off winner and fourth promotion place: Fleetwood Town
Relegated: Bristol Rovers, Torquay United

Football Conference
1. Luton Town, 101pts
Play-off winner and second promotion place: Cambridge
United
Relegated: Salisbury City★, Hereford United, Tamworth, Hyde
★Relegated due to financial irregularities

Welsh Premier League
1. The New Saints, 73pts
2. Airbus UK Broughton, 59pts
3. Carmarthen Town, 48pts

SCOTLAND
Scottish Premier League
1. Celtic, 99pts
2. Motherwell, 70pts
Relegated: Heart of Midlothian

Scottish Championship
1. Dundee, 69pts
Relegated: Greenock Morton

Scottish League One
1. Rangers, 102pts
Relegated: Arbroath

Scottish League Two
1. Peterhead, 76pts
Also promoted: Stirling Albion
Bottom: Queens Park

NORTHERN IRELAND
NFIL Premiership
1. Cliftonville, 85pts
2. Linfield, 79pts
3. Crusaders, 66pts

REPUBLIC OF IRELAND
2013 League of Ireland: 1. St Patrick's Athletic, 71pts;
2. Dundalk, 68pts; 3. Sligo Rovers, 66pts

FRANCE
Ligue 1: 1. Paris SG, 89pts; 2. Monaco, 80pts; 3. Lille, 71pts

GERMANY
Bundesliga: 1. Bayern Munich, 90pts; 2. Borussia Dortmund,
71pts; 3. Shalke 04, 64pts

ITALY
Serie A: 1. Juventus, 102pts; 2. Roma, 85pts; 3. Napoli, 78pts

NETHERLANDS
Eredivisie: 1. Ajax, 71pts; 2. Feyenoord, 67pts; 3. FC Twente,
63pts

SPAIN
La Liga: 1. Atletico Madrid, 90pts; 2. Barcelona, 87pts;
3. Real Madrid, 87pts

CUP COMPETITIONS 2013–14

ENGLAND
FA Cup final 2014: Arsenal beat Hull City 3–2
League Cup final 2014: Manchester City beat Sunderland 3–1
Football League Trophy final 2014: Peterborough United beat
   Chesterfield 3–1
FA Vase final 2014: Sholing beat West Auckland Town 1–0
FA Trophy final 2014: Cambridge United beat Gosport
   Borough 4–0
Community Shield 2014: Arsenal beat Manchester City 3–0

WOMEN
FA Cup final 2014: Arsenal beat Everton 2–0
Women's Super League 2013: 1. Liverpool, 36pts; 2. Bristol
   Academy, 31pts; 3. Arsenal, 30pts
Premier League Cup final 2014: Sheffield beat Cardiff City
   6–2

WALES
FAW Welsh Cup final 2014: The New Saints beat
   Aberystwyth Town 3–2
Welsh League Cup final 2014: Carmarthen Town beat Bala
   Town 3–1 on penalties (0–0 aet)

SCOTLAND
Scottish Cup final 2014: St Johnstone beat Dundee United
   2–0
League Cup final 2014: Aberdeen beat Inverness Caledonian
   Thistle 4–2 on penalties (0–0 aet)

NORTHERN IRELAND
Irish Cup final 2014: Glenavon beat Ballymena United 2–1

EUROPE
Champions League final 2014: Real Madrid beat Atletico
   Madrid 4–1
Europa League final 2014: Sevilla beat Benfica 4–2 on
   penalties (0–0 aet)

FIFA BALLON D'OR*
2014 – Cristiano Ronaldo (Portugal)
2013 – Lionel Messi (Argentina)
2012 – Lionel Messi (Argentina)
2011 – Lionel Messi (Argentina)
2010 – Lionel Messi (Argentina)
2009 – Lionel Messi (Argentina)
2008 – Cristiano Ronaldo (Portugal)
2007 – Kaká (Brazil)
2006 – Fabio Cannavaro (Italy)
2005 – Ronaldinho (Brazil)
2004 – Ronaldinho (Brazil)
2003 – Zinedine Zidane (France)
2002 – Ronaldo (Brazil)
2001 – Luís Figo (Portugal)
2000 – Zinedine Zidane (France)
1999 – Rivaldo (Brazil)
1998 – Zinedine Zidane (France)
1997 – Ronaldo (Brazil)

* Pre-2010, known as the FIFA World Player of the Year award

2014 FIFA WORLD CUP FINALS
Brazil, 12 June–13 July

GROUP A

	P	W	D	L	F	A	GD	PTS
Brazil	3	2	1	0	7	2	5	7
Mexico	3	2	1	0	4	1	3	7
Croatia	3	1	0	2	6	6	0	3
Cameroon	3	0	0	3	1	9	−8	0

Brazil beat Croatia 3–1
Mexico beat Cameron 1–0
Brazil drew with Mexico 0–0
Croatia beat Cameroon 4–0
Brazil beat Cameroon 4–1
Mexico beat Croatia 3–1

GROUP B

	P	W	D	L	F	A	GD	PTS
Netherlands	3	3	0	0	10	3	7	9
Chile	3	2	0	1	5	3	2	6
Spain	3	1	0	2	4	7	−3	3
Australia	3	0	0	3	3	9	−6	0

Netherlands beat Spain 5–1
Chile beat Australia 3–1
Netherlands beat Australia 3–2
Chile beat Spain 2–0
Spain beat Australia 3–0
Netherlands beat Chile 2–0

GROUP C

	P	W	D	L	F	A	GD	PTS
Colombia	3	3	0	0	9	2	7	9
Greece	3	1	1	1	2	4	−2	4
Ivory Coast	3	1	0	2	4	5	−1	3
Japan	3	0	1	2	2	6	−4	1

Colombia beat Greece 3–0
Ivory Coast beat Japan 2–1
Colombia beat Ivory Coast 2–1
Japan drew with Greece 0–0
Greece beat Ivory Coast 2–1
Colombia beat Japan 4–1

GROUP D

	P	W	D	L	F	A	GD	PTS
Costa Rica	3	2	1	0	4	1	3	7
Uruguay	3	2	0	1	4	4	0	6
Italy	3	1	0	2	2	3	−1	3
England	3	0	1	2	2	4	−2	1

Costa Rica beat Uruguay 3–1
Italy beat England 2–1
Uruguay beat England 2–1
Costa Rica beat Italy 1–0
England drew with Costa Rica 0–0
Uruguay beat Italy 1–0

GROUP E

	P	W	D	L	F	A	GD	PTS
France	3	2	1	0	8	2	6	7
Switzerland	3	2	0	1	7	6	1	6
Ecuador	3	1	1	1	3	3	0	4
Honduras	3	0	0	3	1	8	−7	0

Switzerland beat Ecuador 2–1
France beat Honduras 3–0
France beat Switzerland 5–2
Ecuador beat Honduras 2–1
Ecuador drew with France 0–0
Switzerland beat Honduras 3–0

GROUP F

	P	W	D	L	F	A	GD	PTS
Argentina	3	3	0	0	6	3	3	9
Nigeria	3	1	1	1	3	3	0	4
Bosnia and Hercegovina	3	1	0	2	4	4	0	3
Iran	3	0	1	2	1	4	−3	1

Argentina beat Bosnia and Hercegovina 2–1
Iran drew with Nigeria 0–0
Argentina beat Iran 1–0
Nigeria beat Bosnia and Hercegovina 1–0
Bosnia and Hercegovina beat Iran 3–1
Argentina beat Nigeria 3–2

GROUP G

	P	W	D	L	F	A	GD	PTS
Germany	3	2	1	0	7	2	5	7
USA	3	1	1	1	4	4	0	4
Portugal	3	1	1	1	4	7	–3	4
Ghana	3	0	1	2	4	6	–2	1

Germany beat Portugal 4–0
USA beat Ghana 2–1
Germany drew with Ghana 2–2
USA drew with Portugal 2–2
Portugal beat Ghana 2–1
Germany beat USA 1–0

GROUP H

	P	W	D	L	F	A	GD	PTS
Belgium	3	3	0	0	4	1	3	9
Algeria	3	1	1	1	6	5	1	4
Russia	3	0	2	1	2	3	–1	2
South Korea	3	0	1	2	3	6	–3	1

Belgium beat Algeria 2–1
Russia drew with South Korea 1–1
Belgium beat Russia 1–0
Algeria beat South Korea 4–2
Algeria drew with Russia 1–1
Belgium beat South Korea 1–0

LAST 16
Brazil beat Chile 3–2 on penalties (1–1 aet)
Colombia beat Uruguay 2–0
France beat Nigeria 2–0
Germany beat Algeria 2–1 (aet)
Netherlands beat Mexico 2–1
Costa Rica beat Greece 5–3 on penalties (1–1 aet)
Argentina beat Switzerland 1–0 (aet)
Belgium beat USA 2–1 (aet)

QUARTER-FINALS
Brazil beat Colombia 2–1
Germany beat France 1–0
Netherlands beat Costa Rica 4–3 on penalties (0–0 aet)
Argentina beat Belgium 1–0

SEMI-FINALS
Germany beat Brazil 7–1
Argentina beat Netherlands 4–2 on penalties (0–0 aet)

3RD PLACE PLAY-OFF
Netherlands beat Brazil 3–0

FINAL
Germany beat Argentina 1–0 (aet)

PLAYER AWARDS
Player of the Tournament: Lionel Messi (Argentina)
Golden Boot: James Rodriguez – 6 goals, 2 assists (Colombia)
Golden Glove: Manuel Neuer (Germany)

ATHLETICS

EUROPEAN CROSS COUNTRY CHAMPIONSHIPS
Belgrade, Serbia, 8 December 2013

SENIOR MEN (10,000m)
Individual: Alemayehu Bezabeh (Spain), 29min 11sec
Team: Spain, 31pts

U23 MEN (8,000m)
Individual: Peter-Jan Hannes (Belgium), 24min 02sec
Team: Great Britain, 40pts

U20 MEN (6,000m)
Individual: Ali Kaya (Turkey), 17min 49sec
Team: France, 48pts

SENIOR WOMEN (8,000m)
Individual: Sophia Duarte (France), 26min 34sec
Team: Great Britain, 35pts

U23 WOMEN (6,000m)
Individual: Sifan Hassan (Netherlands), 19min 40sec
Team: Great Britain, 19pts

U20 WOMEN (4,000m)
Individual: Emelia Gorecka (Great Britain), 13min 06sec
Team: Great Britain, 24pts

ENGLISH NATIONAL CROSS COUNTRY
CHAMPIONSHIPS
Wollaton Park, Nottingham, 22 February 2014

SENIOR MEN
Individual: Steven Vernon (Stockport Harriers), 36min 23sec
Team: Bedford and County, 265pts

JUNIOR MEN
Individual: Jonathan Davies (Reading), 31min 15sec
Team: Tonbridge, 67pts

SENIOR WOMEN
Individual: Gemma Steel (Charnwood), 27min 42sec
Team: Aldershot Farnham & Dist, 21pts

JUNIOR WOMEN
Individual: Georgia Taylor-Brown (Aldershot Farnham &
Dist), 21min 03sec
Team: Aldershot Farnham & Dist, 17pts

LONDON MARATHON
London, 13 April 2014

Men: Wilson Kipsang Kiprotich (Kenya), 2hr 04min 29sec
(Record)
Women: Edna Kiplagat (Kenya), 2hr 20min 21sec

BRITISH CHAMPIONSHIPS
Alexander Stadium, Birmingham, 27–29 June 2014

MEN
100m: Dwain Chambers (Belgrave), 10.12sec
200m: Danny Talbot (Birchfield), 20.42sec
400m: Martyn Rooney (Croydon), 45.78sec
800m: Michael Rimmer (Liverpool), 1min 48.00sec
1500m: Charlie Grice (Brighton), 3min 46.97sec
5000m: Thomas Farrell (Border), 13min 51.43sec
3000m Steeplechase: James Wilkinson (Leeds), 8min 37.36sec
110m Hurdles: William Sharman (Belgrave), 13.18sec
400m Hurdles: Niall Flannery (Newham), 49.54sec

5000m Walk: Dane Bird-Smith (Australia), 19min 14.53sec
High Jump: Allan Smith (Shaftesbury), 2.24m
Pole Vault: Steve Lewis (Newham), 5.55m
Long Jump: JJ Jegede (Newham), 7.83m
Triple Jump: Julian Reid (Birchfield), 16.82m
Shot: Scott Rider (Birchfield), 18.34m
Discus: Zane Duquemin (Shaftesbury), 60.38m
Hammer: Nick Miller (Border), 73.96m
Javelin: Lee Doran (Sheffield), 70.71m

WOMEN
100m: Asha Philip (Newham), 11.11sec
200m: Rachel Dickens (Blackheath), 24.35sec
400m: Kelly Massey (Sale), 52.42sec
800m: Lynsey Sharp (Edinburgh), 2min 01.40sec
1500m: Laura Weightman (Morpeth), 4min 09.77sec
5000m: Emelia Gorecka (Aldershot Farnham & Dist),
    15min 40.65sec
3000m Steeplechase: Eilish McColgan (Dundee),
    9min 50.06sec
100m Hurdles: Tiffany Porter (Woodford), 12.85sec
400m Hurdles: Eilidh Child (Pitreavie), 55.58sec
5000m Walk: Heather Lewis (Liverpool), 22min 09.87sec
High Jump: Isobel Pooley (Aldershot Farnham and Dist.),
    1.90m
Pole Vault: Sally Peake (Birchfield), 4.30m
Long Jump: Katarina Johnson-Thompson (Liverpool), 6.81m
Triple Jump: Yamile Aldama (Shaftesbury), 13.60m
Shot: Eden Francis (Birchfield), 16.66m
Discus: Eden Francis (Birchfield), 55.93m
Hammer: Sophie Hitchon (Blackburn), 65.56m
Javelin: Goldie Sayers (Belgrave), 62.75m

EUROPEAN ATHLETICS CHAMPIONSHIPS
Zurich, Switzerland, 12–17 August 2014

MEN
100m: James Dasaolu (Great Britain), 10.06sec
200m: Adam Gemili (Great Britain), 19.98sec
400m: Martyn Rooney (Great Britain), 44.71sec
800m: Adam Kszczot (Poland), 1min 44.15sec
1500m: Mahiedine Mekhissi-Benabbad (France),
    3min 45.60sec
5000m: Mohamed Farah (Great Britain), 14min 05.82sec
10,000m: Mohamed Farah (Great Britain), 28min 08.11sec
3000m Steeplechase: Yoann Kowal (France), 8min 26.66sec
110m Hurdles: Sergey Shubenkov (Russia), 13.19sec
400m Hurdles: Kariem Hussein (Switzerland), 48.96sec
4 × 100m: Great Britain, 37.93sec
4 × 400m: Great Britain, 2min 58.79sec
20km Walk: Miguel Angel Lopez (Spain), 1hr 19min 44sec
50km Walk: Yohann Diniz (France), 3hr 32min 33sec
Marathon: Daniele Meucci (Italy), 2hr 11min 08sec
High Jump: Bohdan Bondarenko (Ukraine), 2.35m
Pole Vault: Renaud Lavillenie (France), 5.90m
Long Jump: Greg Rutherford (Great Britain), 8.29m
Triple Jump: Benjamin Compaore (France), 17.46m
Shot: David Storl (Germany), 21.41m
Discus: Robert Harting (Germany), 66.07m
Hammer: Krisztian Pars (Hungary), 82.69m
Javelin: Anti Ruuskanen (Finland), 88.01m

WOMEN
100m: Dafne Schippers (Netherlands), 11.12sec
200m: Dafne Schippers (Netherlands), 22.03sec
400m: Libania Grenot (Italy), 51.10sec
800m: Maryna Arzamasova (Belarus), 1min 58.15sec
1500m: Sifan Hassan (Netherlands), 4min 04.18sec
5000m: Meraf Bahta (Sweden),15min 31.39sec
10,000m: Jo Pavey (Great Britain), 32min 22.39sec

Marathon: Christelle Daunay (France), 2hr 25min 14sec
3000m Steeplechase: Antje Moldner-Schmidt (Germany),
    9min 29.43sec
100m Hurdles: Tiffany Porter (Great Britain), 12.76sec
400m Hurdles: Eilidh Child (Great Britain), 54.48sec
4 × 100m: Great Britain, 42.24sec
4 × 400m: France, 3min 24.27sec
20km Walk: Elmira Alembekova (Russia), 1hr 27min 56sec
High Jump: Ruth Beitia (Spain), 2.01m
Pole Vault: Anzhelika Sidorova (Russia), 4.65m
Long Jump: Éloyse Lesueur (France), 6.85m
Triple Jump: Olha Saladukha (Ukraine), 14.73m
Shot: Christina Schwanitz (Germany), 19.90m
Discus: Sandra Perkovic (Croatia), 71.08m
Hammer: Anita Wlodarczyk (Poland), 78.76m
Javelin: Barbara Spotakova (Czech Rep.), 64.41m

BADMINTON

WORLD CHAMPIONSHIPS 2014
Copenhagen, Denmark, 25–31 August

Men's Singles: Chen Long (China) beat Lee Chong Wei
    (Malaysia) 2–0
Women's Singles: Carolina Marin (Spain) beat Li Xuerui
    (China) 2–1
Men's Doubles: Ko Sung-Hyun and Shin Baek-Choel (South
    Korea) beat Lee Yong-Dae and Yoo Yeon-Seong (South
    Korea) 2–1
Women's Doubles: Tian Qing and Zhao Yunlei (China) beat
    Wang Xiaoli and Yu Yang (China) 2–0
Mixed Doubles: Zhang Nan and Zhao Yunlei (China) beat
    Xu Chen and Ma Jin (China) 2–1

ALL-ENGLAND CHAMPIONSHIPS 2014
Birmingham, March

Men's Singles: Lee Chong Wei (Malaysia) beat Chen Long
    (China) 2–0
Women's Singles: Wan Shixian (China) beat Li Xuerui (China)
    2–1
Men's Doubles: Mohammed Ahsan and Hendra Setiawan
    (Indonesia) beat Hiroyuki Endo and Kenichi Hayakawa
    (Japan) 2–0
Women's Doubles: Wang Xiaoli and Yu Yang (China) beat Ma
    Jin and Tang Yuanting (China) 2–1
Mixed Doubles: Tontowi Ahmad and Lilyana Natsir
    (Indonesia) beat Zhang Nan and Zhao Yunlei (China) 2–0

ENGLISH NATIONAL CHAMPIONSHIPS 2014
Milton Keynes, February

Men's Singles: Rajiv Ouseph beat Sam Parsons 2–0
Women's Singles: Sarah Walker beat Elizabeth Cann 2–1
Men's Doubles: Chris Adcock and Andrew Ellis beat Chris
    Langridge and Peter Mills 2–0
Women's Doubles: Gabrielle Adcock and Lauren Smith beat
    Heather Olver and Kate Robertshaw 2–0
Mixed Doubles: Chris Adcock and Gabrielle Adcock beat
    Chris Langridge and Heather Olver 2–0

SCOTTISH NATIONAL CHAMPIONSHIPS 2014
Perth, February

Men's Singles: Keiran Merrilees beat Matthew Carder 2–0
Women's Singles: Kirsty Gilmour beat Holly Newall 2–0
Men's Doubles: Robert Blair and Paul van Rietvelde beat
    Martin Cambell and Patrick MacHugh 2–1

Women's Doubles: Imogen Bankier and Kirsty Gilmour beat Sarah Bok and Jillie Cooper 2–0
Mixed Doubles: Robert Blair and Imogen Bankier beat Paul van Rietvelde and Jillie Cooper 2–1

WELSH NATIONAL CHAMPIONSHIPS 2014
Cardiff, February

Men's Singles: Daniel Font beat Tsung Fong Mo 2–0
Men's Singles (Plate): Adam Stewart beat Scott Oakes by Walkover
Women's Singles: Carissa Turner beat Aimee Moran 2–0
Men's Doubles: Daniel Font and Oliver Gwilt beat Joe Morgan and Nic Strange 2–0
Women's Doubles: Sarah Thomas and Carissa Turner beat Vikki Jones and Aimee Moran 2–0
Mixed Doubles: Daniel Font and Sarah Thomas beat Nic Strange and Jordan Hart 2–0

BASEBALL

American League Championship Series 2013: Boston Red Sox beat Detroit Tigers 4–2
National League Championship Series 2013: St Louis Cardinals beat Los Angeles Dodgers 4–2
World Series 2013: Boston Red Sox beat St Louis Cardinals 4–2

BASKETBALL

BRITISH

MEN
BBL Play-off final 2014: Worcester Wolves beat Newcastle Eagles 90–78
BBL Trophy final 2014: Worcester Wolves beat Glasgow Rocks 83–76
BBL Cup final 2014: Leicester Riders beat Newcastle Eagles 72–69
BBL Champions 2013–14: Newcastle Eagles

WOMEN
EBL Division 1 2013–14: Sheffield Hatters
EBL Division 1 Play-off final 2013–14: Loughborough Riders beat Sheffield Hatters 68–63
National Cup final 2014: Team Northumbria beat Cardiff Archers 66–64

USA – NATIONAL BASKETBALL LEAGUE (NBA)
Eastern Conference final 2014: Miami Heat beat Indiana Pacers 4–2
Western Conference final 2013: San Antonio Spurs beat Oklahoma City Thunder 4–2
NBA final 2014: San Antonio Spurs beat Miami Heat 4–1

BOWLS—INDOOR

WORLD CHAMPIONSHIPS 2014
Hopton, Norfolk, January

Men's Singles: Darren Burnett (Scotland) beat Mervyn King (England) 2–1
Women's Singles: Katherine Rednall (England) beat Rebecca Field (England) 2–0
Men's Pairs: Nicky Brett and Greg Harlow (England) beat Paul Foster and Alex Marshall (Scotland) 1½ –1½
Mixed Pairs: Paul Foster and Laura Thomas (Scotland/Wales) beat Andy Thompson (England) and Katherine Rednall (England) 2–0

BRITISH ISLES INDOOR BOWLS CHAMPIONSHIPS 2014
Stanley, March

Singles: M. Dawes (England) beat T. Priaulx (Channel Islands) 21–9
Pairs: Scotland beat Wales 23–15
Triples: England beat the Channel Islands 19–12
Fours: Wales beat Scotland 28–21

ENGLISH NATIONAL CHAMPIONSHIPS 2014
Melton & District IBC, Melton Mowbray , March–April

Singles: J. Walker beat D. Hubbard 21–18
Pairs: Kingsthorpe beat Chawton Park 22–17
Triples: Spalding beat Angel 20–4
Fours: Swail beat Desborough 19–12
Liberty Trophy (Inter-County Championship) final: Kwnt beat Cambridgeshire 112–103
Champion of Champions (Warner Lakeside, January–February): R. K. Atkins beat C.Daniels 21–16

SCOTTISH NATIONAL CHAMPIONSHIPS 2014
Prestwick, March

Singles: Blantyre beat Garioch 14–21
Pairs: Midlothian beat Turriff 23–10
Triples: Blantyre beat Berwickshire 20–6
Fours: Elgin beat Auchinleck 16–15

BOWLS—OUTDOOR

BRITISH ISLES CHAMPIONSHIPS 2014
Leamington Spa, June

Singles: Wales beat Ireland 21–13
Pairs: Scotland beat Ireland 23–16
Triples: Scotland beat Wales 21–18

ENGLISH NATIONAL CHAMPIONSHIPS 2014
Worthing, August

Singles: Gloucestershire beat Devon 21–18
Pairs: Warwickshire beat Lincolnshire 22–4
Triples: Wiltshire beat Oxfordshire 15–14
Fours: Durham beat Yorkshire 21–19
Inter-County Championship: Hampshire beat Norfolk 127–106

WELSH NATIONAL CHAMPIONSHIPS 2014
Llandrindod Wells, August

Singles: Penarth beat Machynlleth 21–16
Pairs: Caldicot beat Cross Keys 20–12
Triples: Presteigne beat Beaufort 20–13
Fours: Graig Merthyr beat RTB Ebbw Vale 22–20

BOXING

WORLD CHAMPIONS
as at 17 August 2014

WORLD BOXING COUNCIL (WBC)
Heavy: Bermane Stiverne (Haiti)
Cruiser: Krzysztof Wlodarczyk (Poland)
Light-heavy: Adonis Stevenson (Canada)
Supermiddle: Sakio Bika (Cameroon)
Middle: Miguel Cotto (Puerto Rico)
Interim Middle: Marco Antonio Rubio (Mexico)
Superwelter: Floyd Mayweather Jr (USA)

Welter: Floyd Mayweather Jr (USA)
Superlight: Danny Garcia (USA)
Light: Omar Figueroa (USA)
Superfeather: Takashi Miura (Japan)
Feather: Jhonny Gonzalez (Mexico)
Superbantam: Leo Santa Cruz (Mexico)
Bantam: Shinsuke Yamanaka (Japan)
Superfly: Carlos Cuadras (Mexico)
Fly: Akira Yaegashi (Japan)
Lightfly: Naoya Inoue (Japan)
Straw: Oswaldo Novoa (Mexico)

WORLD BOXING ASSOCIATION (WBA)
Heavy: Wladimir Klitschko (Ukraine)
Cruiser: Dennis Lebedev (Russia)
Light-heavy: Bernard Hopkins (USA)
Supermiddle: Andre Ward (USA)/Carl Froch (Great Britain)
Middle: Gennady Golovkin (Kazakhstan)
Superwelter: Floyd Mayweather Jr (USA)
Welter: Floyd Mayweather Jr (USA)
Superlight: Danny Garcia (USA)
Light: Richard Abril (Cuba)
Superfeather: Takashi Uchiyama (Japan)
Feather: Nonito Donaire (Philippines)
Superbantam: Guillermo Rigondeaux (Cuba)
Bantam: Anselmo Moreno (Panama)
Superfly: Kohei Kono (Japan)
Fly: Juan Francisco Estrada (Mexico)
Lightfly: Alberto Rossel (Peru)
Minimum: Hekkie Budler (South Africa)

WORLD BOXING ORGANISATION (WBO)
Heavy: Wladimir Klitschko (Ukraine)
Junior-heavy: Marco Huck (Germany)
Light-heavy: Sergey Kovalev (Russia)
Supermiddle: Arthur Abraham (Armenia)
Middle: Peter Quillin (USA)
Junior-middle: Demetrius Andrade (USA)
Welter: Manny Pacquiao (Philippines)
Junior-welter: Chris Algieri (USA)
Light: Terence Crawford (USA)
Junior-light: Mikey Garcia (USA)
Feather: Vasyl Lomachenko (Ukraine)
Junior-feather: Guillermo Rigondeaux (Cuba)
Bantam: Tomoki Kameda (Japan)
Junior-bantam: Omar Narvaez (Argentina)
Fly: Juan Francisco Estrada (Mexico)
Junior-fly: Donnie Nietes (Philippines)
Mini-fly: Francisco Rodriguez Jr (Mexico)

INTERNATIONAL BOXING FEDERATION (IBF)
Heavy: Wladimir Klitschko (Ukraine)
Cruiser: Yoan Pablo Hernandez (Cuba)
Light-heavy: Bernard Hopkins (USA)
Supermiddle: Carl Froch (Great Britain)
Middle: Sam Soliman (Australia)
Junior-middle: Carlos Molina (Mexico)
Welter: Shawn Porter (USA)
Junior-welter: Lamont Peterson (USA)
Light: Miguel Vasquez (Mexico)
Feather: Evgeny Gradovich (Russia)
Junior-feather: Kiko Martinez (Spain)
Bantam: vacant
Fly: Amnat Ruenroeng (Thailand)
Junior-fly: vacant
Mini-fly: Francisco Rodriguez (Mexico)

BRITISH CHAMPIONS
Heavy: Tyson Fury
Cruiser: Ola Afolabi
Light-heavy: Enzo Maccarinelli

Super-middle: Carl Froch
Middle: Martin Murray
Light-middle: Brian Rose
Welter: Amir Khan
Light-welter: Lenny Daws
Light: Ricky Burns
Super-feather: Stephen Smith
Feather: Lee Selby
Super-bantam: Carl Frampton
Bantam: Jamie McDonnell
Super-fly: Kal Yafai
Fly: Kevin Satchell

CHESS

FIDE World Champion 2013: Magnus Carlsen (Norway)
British Champion 2014: David Howell and Jonathan Hawkins*
British Women's Champion 2014: Amy Hoare

* Shared title

CRICKET

TEST SERIES

AUSTRALIA V ENGLAND (THE ASHES)
Brisbane (21–25 November): Australia beat England by 381 runs. Australia 295 and 401–7; England 136 and 179
Adelaide (1–5 December): Australia beat England by 218 runs. Australia 570–9 dec. and 172–3 dec.; England 172 and 312
Perth (13–18 December): Australia beat England by 150 runs. Australia 385 and 369–6 dec.; England 251 and 353
Melbourne (26–28 December): Australia won by 8 wickets. Australia 204 and 231–2; England 255 and 179
Sydney (3–5 January): Australia beat England by 281 runs. Australia 326 and 276; England 155 and 166

ENGLAND VS SRI LANKA
Lord's (12–16 June): England drew with Sri Lanka. England 575–9 dec. and 267–8 dec.; Sri Lanka 453 and 201–9
Headingley (16–20 June): Sri Lanka beat England by 100 runs. England 365 and 249; Sri Lanka 257 and 457

ENGLAND V INDIA
Trent Bridge (5–9 July): England drew with India. England 496; India 457 and 391–9
Lord's (13–17 July): India beat England by 95 runs. India 295 and 342; England 319 and 223
Ageas Bowl (23–27 July): England beat India by 266 runs. England 569–7 dec. and 205–4 dec.; India 330 and 178
Old Trafford (5–7 August): England beat India by an innings and 54 runs. England 367; India 154 and 161
Kia Oval (15–19 August): England beat India by an innings and 244 runs. England 486; India 148 and 94

ONE-DAY INTERNATIONALS

ENGLAND V AUSTRALIA
Headingley (6 September): Match abandoned due to rain
Old Trafford (8 September): Australia won by 88 runs. Australia 315–7; England 227
Edgbaston (11 September): Match abandoned due to rain
Cardiff (14 September): England beat Australia by 3 wickets. England 231–7; Australia 227
Ageas Bowl (16 September): Australia beat England by 49 runs. Australia 298; England 249

AUSTRALIA V ENGLAND
Melbourne (12 January): Australia beat England by 6 wickets. Australia 270–4; England 269–7
Brisbane (17 January): Australia beat England by 1 wicket. Australia 301–9; England 300–8
Sydney (19 January): Australia beat England by 7 wickets. Australia 244–3; England 243–9
Perth (24 January): England beat Australia by 57 runs. Australia 259; England 316–8
Adelaide (26 January): Australia beat England by 5 runs. Australia 217–9; England 212

WEST INDIES V ENGLAND
Antigua (28 February): West Indies beat England by 15 runs. West Indies 269–6; England 254–6
Antigua (2 March): England beat West Indies by 3 wickets. England 163–7; West Indies 159
Antigua (23 February): England beat West Indies by 25 runs.. England 303–6; West Indies 278

SCOTLAND V ENGLAND
Aberdeen (9 May): England beat Scotland by 39 runs (D/L method). England 167–6; Scotland 133–9

ENGLAND V SRI LANKA
Kia Oval (22 May): England beat Sri Lanka by 81 runs (D/L method). England 247–6; Sri Lanka 144
Chester-le-Street (25 May): Sri Lanka beat England by 157 runs. Sri Lanka 256–8; England 99
Old Trafford (28 May): England beat Sri Lanka by 10 wickets. England 73–0; Sri Lanka 67
Lord's (31 May): Sri Lanka beat England by 7 runs. Sri Lanka 300–9; England 293–8

ENGLAND V INDIA
Bristol (25 August): Abandoned due to rain
Cardiff (27 August): India beat England by 133 (D/L method). India 304–6; England 161
Trent Bridge (30 August): India beat England by 6 wickets. India 228–4; England 227
Egbaston (2 September): India beat England by 9 wickets. India 212–1; England 206
Headingley (5 September): England beat India by 3 runs. England 180–7; India 177–5

TWENTY20 INTERNATIONALS

AUSTRALIA V ENGLAND
Hobart (29 January): Australia beat England by 13 runs. Australia 213; England 200–9
Melbourne (31 January): Australia beat England by 8 wickets. Australia 131–2; England 130–9
Sydney (2 February): Australia beat England by 84 runs. Australia 195–6; England 111

WEST INDIES V ENGLAND
Bridgetown (9 March): West Indies beat England by 27 runs. West Indies 170–3; England 143–9
Bridgetown (11 March): West Indies beat England by 5 wickets. West Indies 155–5; England 152–7
Bridgetown (13 March): England beat West Indies by 5 runs. England 165–6; West Indies 160–7

ENGLAND V SRI LANKA
Kia Oval (20 May): Sri Lanka beat England by 9 wickets. Sri Lanka 183–7; England 174–7

ENGLAND V INDIA
Edgbaston (7 September): England beat India by 3 runs. England 180–7; India 177–5

ICC WORLD TWENTY20
Bangladesh, March–April 2014

Group A

	Matches	Won	Lost	N/R	Pts	Net RR
Bangladesh	3	2	1	0	4	+1.466
Nepal	3	2	1	0	4	+0.933
Afghanistan	3	1	2	0	2	−0.981
Hong Kong	3	1	2	0	2	−1.455

Group B

	Matches	Won	Lost	N/R	Pts	Net RR
Netherlands	3	2	1	0	4	+1.109
Zimbabwe	3	2	1	0	4	+0.957
Ireland	3	2	1	0	4	−0.701
United Arab Emirates	3	0	3	0	0	−1.541

Super Tens stage
Group 1

	Matches	Won	Lost	N/R	Pts	Net RR
Sri Lanka	4	3	1	0	6	+2.233
South Africa	4	3	1	0	6	+0.075
New Zealand	4	2	2	0	4	−0.678
England	4	1	3	0	2	−0.776
Netherlands	4	1	3	0	2	−0.866

Group 2

	Matches	Won	Lost	N/R	Pts	Net RR
India	4	4	0	0	8	+1.280
West Indies	4	3	1	0	6	+1.971
Pakistan	4	2	2	0	4	−0.384
Australia	4	1	3	0	2	−0.857
Bangladesh	4	0	4	0	0	−2.072

Semi-finals
Mirpur (3 April): Sri Lanka beat West Indies by 27 runs (D/L method). Sri Lanka 160–6; West Indies 80–4
Mirpur (4 April): India beat South Africa by 6 wickets. India 176–4; South Africa 172–4
Final
Mirpur (6 April): Sri Lanka beat India by 6 wickets. Sri Lanka 134–4; India 130–4

ENGLAND AND WALES DOMESTIC COMPETITIONS
LV County Championship 2014, Division 1: Yorkshire, 246pts; *Relegated* Lancashire, 143pts; Northamptonshire, 67pts – *Division 2:* Worcestershire, 235pts; *Promoted* Hampshire, 207pts
Royal London One-Day Cup final 2014: Durham beat Warwickshire Bears by 3 wickets. Durham 166–7; Warwickshire Bears 165
Natwest t20 Blast: Birmingham Bears beat Lancashire Lighhtning by 4 runs. Birminigham Bears 181–5; Lancashire Lightning 177–8

OTHER INTERNATIONAL DOMESTIC CHAMPIONSHIPS
Australia: Sheffield Shield final 2013–14: New South Wales drew with Western Australia. New South Wales 447; Western Australia 180. *Ryobi One-Day Cup final 2013–14:* Queensland beat New South Wales by 5 wickets. Queensland 319–5; New South Wales 317–6. *Twenty20 Big Bash League final 2013–14*: Perth Scorches beat Hobart Hurricanes by 39 runs. Perth Scorchers 191–4; Hobart Hurricanes 152–7
Bangladesh: BCL 2013–14 final: South Zone beat North Zone by 213 runs. South Zone 271 and 536; North Zone 235 and 359. *Bangladesh Premier League final 2014:* Dhaka Gladiators beat Chittagong Kings by 43 runs. Dhaka Gladiators 172–9; Chittagong Kings 129
India: Irani Cup final 2013–14: Karnataka beat Rest of India

by an innings and 222 runs. Karnataka 606; Rest of
India 201 and 183. *BCCI Corporate Trophy 2013–14:*
Comptroller and Auditor General beat Chemplast by 32
runs. Comptroller 210; Chemplast 178. *NKP Salve
Challenger Trophy 2013–14:* India Blue beat Delhi by
50 runs. India Blue 274; Delhi 224. *Deodhar Trophy
2013–14:* West Zone beat North Zone by 133 runs. West
Zone 281–3; North Zone 148. North Zone vs South
Zone. Match abandoned due to rain. *Ranji Trophy Elite
final 2013–14:* Karnataka beat Maharashtra by 7 wickets.
Karnataka 515 and 157–3; Maharashtra 305 and 366.
Syed Mushtaq Ali Trophy 2013–14: Baroda beat Uttar
Pradesh by 3 runs. Baroda 144; Uttar Pradesh 141. *Vijay
Hazare Trophy final 2013–14:* Karnataka beat Railways by
4 wickets. Karnataka 158–6; Railways 157. *Indian Premier
League Twenty20 final 2014:* Kolkata Knight Riders beat
King's XI Punjab by 3 wickets. Kolkata Knight Riders
200–7; King's XI Punjab 199–4
New Zealand: Plunket Shield 2013–14: Canterbury 106pts.
Ford Trophy final 2013–14: Wellington beat Northern
Districts by 4 wickets. Wellington 233–6; Northern
Districts 232–9. *HRV Cup final 2013–14:*
Northern Districts beat Otago by 5 wickets. Northern
Districts 144–5; Otago 143–5
Pakistan: Quaid-e-Azam Trophy final 2013–14: Rawalpindi
beat Islamabad by 228 runs. Rawalpindi 211 and 398;
Islamabad 175 and 206. *Faysal Bank One-Day Cup final
2012–13:* Match abandoned due to rain; title shared
between Lahore Lions and Karachi Zebras. *Faysal Bank
Twenty20 Cup final 2013–14:* Lahore Lions beat
Faisalabad Wolves by 3wickets. Lahore Lions 131–7;
Faisalabad Wolves 130–9. *President's Trophy final
2013–14:* Sui Northern Gas Pipelines Ltd beat United
Bank Ltd by 278 runs. Sui Northern Gas Pipelines Ltd
386 and 262; United Bank Ltd 144 and 226
South Africa: Sunfoil Series 2013–14: Cape Cobras,
137.88pts. *Momentum One-day Cup final 2013–14:* Match
abandoned due to rain; title shared between Cape Cobras
and Titans. *Ram Slam T20 Challenge final 2013–14:*
Dolphins beat Cape Cobras by 2 runs. Dolphins 146–8;
Cape Cobras 144–7
Sri Lanka: Premier Limited Overs Tournament 2013–14:
Sinhalese Sports Club beat Nondescript CC by 54 runs.
Sinhalese Sports Club 278–9; Nondescripts 224
West Indies: NagicoSuper50 final 2013–14: Barbados beat
Trinidad and Tabago by 17 runs. Barbados 252; Trinidad
and Tabago 235. *Regional 4-Day Tournament 2013–14:*
Match drawn between Jamaica and Windward Islands,
Jamaica won due to first innings total; Jamaica 392 and
200; Windward Islands 217 and 204–6. *Caribbean
Premier League T20 final 2013–14:* Barbados Tridents beat
Guyana Amazon Warriors by 8 runs (D/L method).
Barbados Tridents 152–6; Guyana Amazon Warriors
107–4
Zimbabwe: Pro50 Championship final 2013–14:
Mountaineers beat Southern Rocks by 7 wickets.
Mountaineers 178–3; Southern Rocks 174

CURLING

MEN'S WORLD CHAMPIONSHIP 2014
Beijing, China, March–April

Final: Norway beat Sweden 8–3

WOMEN'S WORLD CHAMPIONSHIP 2014
St John, New Brunswick, Canada, March

Final: Switzerland beat Canada 9–5

CYCLING

Vuelta a España 2013: Chris Horner (USA)
Giro d'Italia 2014: Nairo Quintana (Colombia)
Tour de France 2014: Vincenzo Nibali (Italy)

UCI ROAD WORLD CHAMPIONSHIPS 2013
Tuscany, Italy, September

MEN
Elite Time Trial: Tony Martin (Germany)
Road Race: Rui Costa (Portugal)

WOMEN
Elite Time Trial: Ellen van Dijk (Netherlands)
Road Race: Marianne Vos (Netherlands)

BRITISH NATIONAL ROAD RACE CHAMPIONSHIPS
2014
Monmouthshire, June

MEN
Road Race: Peter Kennaugh

WOMEN
Road Race: Laura Trott

UCI TRACK CYCLING WORLD CHAMPIONSHIPS
2014
Cali, Colombia, February–March

MEN
Points Race: Edwin Ávila (Colombia)
Sprint: François Pervis (France)
1km Time Trial: François Pervis (France)
Individual Pursuit: Alex Edmondson (Australia)
Scratch Race: Ivan Kovalev (Russia)
Keirin: François Pervis (France)
Team Pursuit: Australia
Madison: David Muntaner and Albert Torres (Spain)
Team Sprint: New Zealand
Omnium: Thomas Boudat (France)

WOMEN
Points Race: Amy Cure (Australia)
Sprint: Kristina Vogel (Germany)
500m Time Trial: Miriam Welte (Germany)
Individual Pursuit: Joanna Rowsell (Great Britain)
Scratch Race: Kelly Druyts (Belgium)
Keirin: Kristina Vogel (Germany)
Team Pursuit: Great Britain
Team Sprint: Germany
Omnium: Sarah Hammer (USA)

DARTS

BDO World Championship 2014: Stephen Bunting (England)
beat Alan Norris (England) 7–4
PDC World Championship 2014: Michael van Gerwen
(Netherlands) beat Peter Wright (Scotland) 7–4

EQUESTRIANISM

Burghley Horse Trials 2013: Andrew Nicholson (New
Zealand) on Avebury
Badminton Horse Trials 2014: Sam Griffiths (Australia) on
Paulank Brockagh
British Open Horse Trials 2014 (Gatcombe Park): Andrew
Nicholson (New Zealand) on Avebury

ETON FIVES

Amateur Championship (Kinnaird Cup) final 2014: Tom
  Dunbar and Seb Cooley beat James Toop and Matthew
  Wiseman 3–0
Alan Barber Cup final 2014: Old Olavians beat Old Salopians
  2–1
Schools' Championship 2014: Eton 1 beat Highgate 1 3–2
Preparatory Schools' Tournament 2014: Highgate 2 beat
  Highgate 1 2–1
National Ladies' Championships 2014 final: Charlotta Cooley
  and Karen Hird beat Eve Smith-Bingham and Amira
  Reimer 3–0

FENCING

BRITISH CHAMPIONSHIPS 2013
Sheffield, December

MEN
Individual Foil: Alex Tofalides
Individual Epée: David Gregory
Individual Sabre: James Honeybone

WOMEN
Individual Foil: Dominique Szokolovics
Individual Epée: Corinna Lawrence
Individual Sabre: Sophie Williams

EUROPEAN CHAMPIONSHIPS 2014
Strasbourg, France, June

MEN
Individual Foil: James-Andrew Davis (Great Britain)
Individual Epée: András Rédli (Hungary)
Individual Sabre: Aleksey Yakimenko (Russia)
Team Foil: France
Team Epée: Switzerland
Team Sabre: Italy

WOMEN
Individual Foil: Elisa Di Francisca (Italy)
Individual Epée: Bianca Del Carretto (Italy)
Individual Sabre: Olha Kharlan (Ukraine)
Team Foil: Italy
Team Epée: Romania
Team Sabre: Russia

WORLD CHAMPIONSHIPS 2014
Kazan, Russia, 15–23 July

MEN
Individual Foil: Aleksey Cheremisinov (Russia)
Individual Epée: Ulrich Robeiri (France)
Individual Sabre: Nikolay Kovalev (Russia)
Team Foil: France
Team Epée: France
Team Sabre: Germany

WOMEN
Individual Foil: Arianna Errigo (Italy)
Individual Epée: Rossella Fiamingo (Italy)
Individual Sabre: Olha Kharlan (Ukraine)
Team Foil: Italy
Team Epée: Russia
Team Sabre: USA

FIGURE SKATING

BRITISH CHAMPIONSHIPS 2013/14
Sheffield, November 2013

Men: Matthew Parr
Women: Jenna McCorkell
Pairs: Amani Fancy and Christopher Boyadji
Ice Dance: Penny Coomes and Nicholas Buckland

EUROPEAN CHAMPIONSHIPS 2014
Budapest, Hungary, January

Men: Javier Fernández (Spain)
Women: Yulia Lipnitskaya (Russia)
Pairs: Tatiana Volosozhar and Maxim Trankov (Russia)
Ice Dance: Anna Cappellini and Luca Lanotte (Italy)

WORLD CHAMPIONSHIPS 2014
Saitama, Japan, March

Men: Yuzuru Hanyu (Japan)
Women: Mao Asada (Japan)
Pairs: Aliona Savchenko and Robin Szolkowy (Germany)
Ice Dance: Anna Cappellini and Luca Lanotte (Italy)

GOLF (MEN)

THE MAJOR CHAMPIONSHIPS 2014
US Masters (Augusta, 10–13 April): Bubba Watson (USA), 280
US Open (Merion, 12–15 June): Martin Kaymer (Germany),
  271
The Open (Muirfield, 17–20 July): Rory McIlroy (Northern
  Ireland), 271
US PGA Championship (Oak Hill Country Club, 7–10
  August): Rory McIlroy (Northern Ireland), 268

WORLD RANKINGS
as at 10 August 2014

1. Rory McIlroy (Northern Ireland); 2. Adam Scott
  (Australia); 3. Henrik Stenson (Sweden); 4. Sergio García
  (Spain); 5. Justin Rose (England)

PGA EUROPEAN TOUR 2013
The South African Open (Ekurhuleni, South Africa): Morten
  Ørum Madsen (Denmark), 269
Alfred Dunhill Championship (Mpumalanga, South Africa):
  Charl Schwartzel (South Africa), 271
Nedbank Golf Challenge (Sun City, South Africa): Thomas
  Bjrn (Denmark), 268
Hong Kong Open (Hong Kong Golf Club): Miguel Ángel
  Jiménez (Spain), 268
Nelson Mandela Championship (Durban): Dawie van der Walt
  (South Africa), 195

TEAM CHAMPIONSHIPS
Vivendi Seve Trophy 2013 (Saint-Nom-La-Breteche, France):
  Continental Europe beat Great Britain and Ireland, 15–13
2013 ISPS Handa World Cup of Golf (Melbourne, Australia):
  Australia
2014 EurAsia Cup: (Glenmarie Golf and Country Club,
  Malaysia) Europe and Asia tied 10–10

EUROPEAN TOUR RACE TO DUBAI 2013*
1. Henrik Stenson (Sweden); 2. Ian Poulter (England);
  3. Justin Rose (England); 4. Graeme McDowell
  (Northern Ireland); 5. Jamie Donaldson (Wales)

* Formerly known as the European Tour Order of Merit

PGA EUROPEAN TOUR 2014
Volvo Golf Champions (Durban CC, South Africa): Louis Oosthuizen (South Africa), 276
Abu Dhabi HSBC Golf Championship (Abu Dhabi GC): Pablo Larrazábal (Spain), 274
Commercial Bank Qatar Masters (Doha GC): Sergio Gracia (Spain), 272
Omega Dubai Desert Classic (Emirates): Stephen Gallacher (Scotland), 272
Joburg Open (Royal Johannesburg and Kensington): George Coetzee (South Africa), 268
Africa Open (East London): Thomas Aiken (South Africa), 264
WGC – Accenture Match Play Championship (Dove Mountain, USA): Jason Day (Australia)
Tshwane Open (Copperleaf, South Africa): Ross Fisher (England), 268
WGC – Cadillac Championship (Doral, USA): Patrick Reed (USA), 284
Trophée Hassan II (Agadir, Morocco): Alejandro Cañizares (Spain), 269
NH Collection Open (La Reserva de Sotogrande Club de Golf, Cadiz): Marco Crespi (Italy), 278
Maybank Malaysian Open (Kuala Lumpur): Lee Westwood (England), 270
Volvo China Open (Genzon GC, China): Alexander Levy (France), 269
The Championship at Laguna National (Laguna National GC, Singapore): Felipe Aguilar (Chile), 266
Madeira Islands Open (Clube de Golf do Santo da Serra, Portugal): Daniel Brooks (England), 135
Open de España (Parador de El Saler): Miguel Ángel Jiménez (Spain), 284
BMW PGA Championship (Wentworth, England): Rory McIlroy (Northern Ireland), 274
Nordea Masters (PGA Sweden National GC, Sweden): Thongchai Jaidee (Thailand), 272
Lyoness Open (Diamond CC, Austria): Mikael Lundberg (Sweden), 276
Irish Open (Fota Island): Mikko Ilonen (Finland), 271
BMW International Open (Golf Club Gut Lärchenhof, Germany): Fabrizio Zanotti (Paraguay), 269
Alstom Open de France (Le Golf National): Graeme McDowell (Northern Ireland), 279
Aberdeen Asset Management Scottish Open (Royal Aberdeen GC): Justin Rose (England), 268
M2M Russian Open (Tseleevo): David Horsley (England), 275
WGC – Bridgestone Invitational (Firestone, USA): Rory McIlroy (Northern Ireland), 265
Made in Denmark (Himmerland): Mark Warren (Scotland), 275
D+D Real Czech Masters (Prague): Jamie Donaldson (Wales), 274
Italian Open (Turin): Hennie Otto (South Africa), 268
Omega European Masters (Grans-sur-Sierre): David Lipsky (USA), 262
KLM Open (Netherlands): Paul Casey (England), 266

AMATEUR CHAMPIONSHIPS 2014
British Amateur Championship (Royal Portrush GC): Bradley Neil (Scotland)
English Amateur Championship (Saunton): Nick Marsh
Brabazon Trophy (English Open Strokeplay) (Seaton): Ben Stow (England), 278
Scottish Amateur Championship (Downfield): Chris Robb
Scottish Open Amateur Stroke Play Championship (Southerness): Gavin Moynihan (Ireland), 275

Welsh Amateur Championship (Pyle and Kenfig): Evan Griffith
Welsh Open Stroke Play (Conwy GC): Jamie Dick (England) and Toby Tree (England), 202
Irish Amateur Open Championship (Royal Dublin): Jamie Savage (Scotland), 288
Irish Amateur Close Championship (Seaport GL): John-Ross Galbraith 154
Lytham Trophy (Royal Lytham Golf Club): Thriston Lawrence (South Afica), 281
Berkshire Trophy (The Berkshire): Ryan Cornfield (England), 280

GOLF (WOMEN)

THE MAJOR CHAMPIONSHIPS 2014
Kraft Nabisco Championship (Rancho Mirage, USA, 3–6 April): Lexi Thompson (USA), 274
Wegmans LPGA Championship (Pittsford, USA, 14–17 August): Inbee Park (South Korea), 277
US Women's Open (Pinehurst, USA, 19–22 June): Michelle Wie (USA), 278

EUROPEAN LPGA TOUR 2013
Helsingborg Open (Sweden): Rebecca Artis (Australia), 280
The Evian Championship (Evian, France) Suzann Petterson (Norway), 203
Lacoste Ladies Open De France (Chantaco): Azahara Munoz (Spain), 266
Sanya Ladies Open (Yalong Bay, China): Lee-Anne Pace (South Africa), 203
China Suzhou Taihu Open (Suzhou): Gwladys Nocera (France), 201
Hero Women's Indian Open (DLF Golf and Country Club): Thidapa Suwannapura (Thailand), 208
Omega Dubai Ladies Masters (Emirates GC): Pornanong Phatlum (Thailand), 273

EUROPEAN LPGA TOUR ORDER OF MERIT 2013
1. Suzann Pettersen (Norway); 2. Lee-Anne Pace (South Africa); 3. Lexi Thompson (USA); 4. Gwladys Nocera (France); 5. Carlota Ciganda (Spain)

EUROPEAN LPGA TOUR 2014
ISPS HANDA New Zealand Women's Open (Clearwater): Mi Hyang Lee (South Korea), 207
Volvik RACV Ladies' Masters (Royal Pines, Australia): Cheyenne Woods (USA), 276
ISPS HANDA Women's Australian Open (Victoria GC): Karrie Webb (Australia), 276
World Ladies' Championship (Mission Hills, China): Inbee Park (South Korea), 268
Lalla Meryem Cup (Golf de l'Ocean, Morocco): Charley Hull (England), 269
Turkish Airlines Ladies Open (National Golf Club, Antalya): Valentine Derrey (France), 212
Deloitte Ladies Open (The International, Netherlands): Kylie Walker (Scotland), 213
Allianz Ladies Slovak Open (Golf Resort Tale): Camilla Lennarth (Sweden), 277
Italian Ladies Open (GC Perugia, Italy): Florentyna Parker (England), 209
ISPS HANDA Ladies European Masters (Buckinghamshire GC, England): I.K. Kim (South Korea), 270
Ricoh British Open (Royal Birkdale): Mo Martin (USA), 287
Ladies' German Open (Wörthsee GC, Germany): Kylie Walker (Scotland), 263
Sherbank Golf Masters (Golf Park Plzeň, Czech Republic): Julie Greciet (French), 196

Aberdeen Asset Management Ladies Scotland Open (Archerfield Links, Scotland): Trish Johnson (England), 209
Evian Championship (Evian-les-Bains, France): Hyo Joo Kim (South Korea), 273

TEAM CHAMPIONSHIPS 2014
Curtis Cup (St Louis Country Club, USA): USA beat Great Britain and Ireland 13 to 7

AMATEUR CHAMPIONSHIPS 2014
British Open Championship (Royal St George's GC): Emily Pedersen (Denmark)
Ladies' British Open Stroke Play Championship (Prestwick):
English Close Championship (St Enodoc GC): Bronte Law, 291
English Open Stroke Play Championship (Tandridge): Hayley Davis (England), 280
Helen Holm (Scottish Open Stroke Play Championship) (Troon): Annabell Dimmock (England), 214
Scottish Ladies Close Championship (Longniddry): Connie Jaffrey
Welsh Open Stroke Play Championship (Prestatyn): Eilidh Briggs (Scotland), 216
Welsh Close Match Play Championship (Monmouthshire GC): Katie Bradbury
Irish Open Strokeplay Championship (Douglas GC): Lucy Goddard (England), 217
Irish Close Championship (Enniscrone GC): Mary Doyle

GREYHOUND RACING

2013
Grand National (Sittingbourne): Mad Mash Snowy
Williamhill.com St Leger (Wimbledon): Farloe Tango

2014
The Coral Regency (Hove): Boltatwelldigger
Ladbrokes Golden Jacket (Crayford): Hometown Honey
The Williamhill.com Derby (Wimbledon): Salad Dodger

GYMNASTICS

EUROPEAN ARTISTIC CHAMPIONSHIPS 2014
Sofia, Bulgaria, May

MEN
All-Around: Oleg Verniaiev (Ukraine)
Floor: Max Whitlock (Great Britain)
Pommel Horse: Max Whitlock (Great Britain)
Rings: Denis Abliazin (Russia)
Vault: Oleg Verniaiev (Ukraine)
Parallel Bars: Oleg Verniaiev (Ukraine)
Horizontal Bar: Epke Zonderland (Netherlands)

WOMEN
All-Around: Larisa Iordache (Romania)
Floor: Larisa Iordache (Romania)
Beam: Larisa Iordache (Romania)
Vault: Giulia Steingruber (Switzerland)
Uneven Bars: Rebecca Downie (Great Britain)

BRITISH CHAMPIONSHIPS 2014
Liverpool, March

MEN
All-Around: Max Whitlock
Floor: Max Whitlock
Pommel Horse: Max Whitlock
Rings: Daniel Purvis
Vault: Kristian Thomas

Parallel Bars: Daniel Keatings
High Bar: Sam Oldham

WOMEN
All-Around: Rebecca Tunney
Floor: Claudia Fragapane
Beam: Hannah Whelan
Vault: Claudia Fragapane
Uneven Bars: Rebecca Tunney

HOCKEY

MEN
England Hockey League 2013–14: Premier Division: East Grinstead Men's 1s, 44pts; *Conference East:* Southgate Men's 1s, 47pts; *Conference North:* Brooklands MU Men's 1s, 46pts; *Conference West:* Cardiff & Met Men's 1s, 44pts
England Hockey League Championship final 2014: Beeston drew with East Grinstead. Beeston won 3–1 after extra time and penalty shuffles
England Hockey League Cup final 2013–14: Cannock drew with Brooklands MU 2–2. Cannock won 5–4 after extra time and penalty strokes
County Championship 2013–14: A Division: Staffordshire beat Sussex 4–2; *B Division:* Yorkshire beat Norfolk 8–3; *C Division:* Devon drew 4–4 with Cheshire, Devon won 4–3 after extra time and penalty shuffles

WOMEN
England Hockey League 2013–14: Premier Division: Canterbury, 44pts; *Conference East:* Holcombe, 48pts; *Conference North:* Brooklands Poynton, 47pts; *Conference West:* Buckingham, 48pts
England Hockey League Championship final 2013–14: Surbiton beat Canterbury 3–0
England Hockey League Cup final 2013–14: Subrbiton beat Hampstead and Westminster 7–1

HORSE RACING

NATIONAL HUNT
HENNESSY GOLD CUP
(1957) Newbury, 3 miles and about 2½ f

2009 Denman (9y), R. Walsh
2010 Diamond Harry (7y), D. Jacob
2011 Carruthers (8y), M. Batchelor
2012 Bobs Worth (7y), B. Geraghty
2013 Triolo D'Alene (6y), B. Geraghty

TINGLE CREEK CHASE
(1957) Sandown, 2 miles

2009 Twist Magic (7y), R. Walsh
2010 Master Minded (7y), N. Fehily
2011 Sizing Europe (9y), A. E. Lynch
2012 Sprinter Sacre (6y), B. Geraghty

KING GEORGE VI CHASE
(1937) Kempton, about 3 miles

2009 Kauto Star (9y), R. Walsh
2010 Long Run (6y), S. Waley-Cohen*
2011 Kauto Star (11y), R. Walsh
2012 Long Run (7y), S. Waley-Cohen
2013 Sire de Grugy (7y), J. Moore
* Race took place on 15 January 2011, after original meeting was postponed due to snow and frost

CHAMPION HURDLE
(1927) Cheltenham, 2 miles and about ½ f

2010 Binocular (6y), A. P. McCoy
2011 Hurricane Fly (7y), R. Walsh
2012 Rock On Ruby (7y), N. Fehily
2013 Hurricane Fly (9y), R. Walsh
2014 Jezki (6y), B. Geraghty

QUEEN MOTHER CHAMPION CHASE
(1959) Cheltenham, about 2 miles

2010 Big Zeb (9y), B. Geraghty
2011 Sizing Europe (9y), A. E. Lynch
2012 Finian's Rainbow (9y), B. Geraghty
2013 Sprinter Sacre (7y), B. Geraghty
2014 Sire de Grugy (8y), J. Moore

CHELTENHAM GOLD CUP
(1924) 3 miles and about 2½ f

2010 Imperial Commander (9y), P. Brennan
2011 Long Run (6y), S. Waley-Cohen
2012 Synchronised (9y), A. P. McCoy
2013 Bobs Worth (8y), B. Geraghty
2014 Lord Windermere (8y), D. Russell

GRAND NATIONAL
(1837) Liverpool, 4 miles and about 4 f

2010 Don't Push It (10y), A. P. McCoy
2011 Ballabriggs (10y), J. Maguire
2012 Neptune Collonges (11y), D. Jacob
2013 Auroras Encore (11y), R. Mania
2014 Pineau de Re (11y), L. Aspell

BET365 GOLD CUP
(1957) Sandown, 3 miles and about 5 f

2010 Church Island (11y), A. Heskin
2011 Poker De Sivola (8y), T. Murphy
2012 Tidal Bay (11y), D. Jacob
2013 Quentin Collonges (9y), A. Tinkler
2014 Hadrians Approach (7y), B. Geraghty

STATISTICS
WINNING NATIONAL HUNT TRAINERS 2013–14

P. F. Nicholls	£2,228,836
N. J. Henderson	1,905,541
J. J. O'Neil	1,488,305
P. J. Hobbs	1,483,195
D. E. Pipe	1,344,087
N. A. Twiston-Davies	1,103,880
V. Williams	1,038,364
A. King	1,033,448
R. Newland	915,161
D. McCain	914,687

WINNING NATIONAL HUNT JOCKEYS 2013–14

	1st	2nd	3rd	Unpl.	Total mts
A. P. McCoy	218	149	119	417	903
R. Johnson	155	126	119	431	831
J. Maguire	130	108	85	338	661
N. Fehily	127	73	78	315	593
S. Twiston-Davies	115	112	99	448	774
T. Scudamore	100	91	68	370	629
A. Coleman	97	97	80	373	647
B. Hughes	86	97	99	335	617
P. Brennan	77	77	60	313	527
T. O'Brien	74	75	54	326	529

The above statistics have been provided by *Timeform*, publishers of the *Racehorses* and *Chasers and Hurdlers* annuals

---

THE FLAT

THE CLASSICS
ONE THOUSAND GUINEAS
(1814) Rowley Mile, Newmarket, for three-year-old fillies

Year	Winner	Betting	Owner	Jockey	Trainer	Runners
2009	Ghanaati	20–1	H. Al Maktoum	R. Hills	B. Hills	19
2010	Special Duty	9–2	K. Abdulla	S. Pasquier	Mrs C. Head-Maarek	17
2011	Blue Bunting	16–1	Godolphin	F. Dettori	M. Al Zarooni	18
2012	Homecoming Queen	25–1	Mrs J. Magnier, M. Tabor and D. Smith	R. Moore	A. O'Brien	17
2013	Sky Lantern	9–1	B. Keswick	R. Hughes	R. Hannon	15
2014	Miss France	7–1	Ballymore Thoroughbred	M. Guyon	A. Fabre	17

TWO THOUSAND GUINEAS
(1809) Rowley Mile, Newmarket, for three-year-olds

Year	Winner	Betting	Owner	Jockey	Trainer	Runners
2009	Sea the Stars	8–1	C. Tsui	M. Kinane	M. Oxx	16
2010	Makfi	33–1	M. Offenstadt	C-P. Lemaire	M. Delzangles	19
2011	Frankel	1–2	K. Abdulla	T. Queally	Sir H. Cecil	13
2012	Camelot	15–8	D. Smith	J. P. O'Brien	A. O'Brien	18
2013	Dawn Approach	11–8	Godolphin	K. Manning	J. S. Bolger	13
2014	Night of Thunder	40–1	S. Manana	K. Fallon	R. Hannon Jr	14

THE DERBY
(1780) Epsom, 1 mile and about 4 f, for three-year-olds

The first winner was Sir Charles Bunbury's Diomed in 1780. The owners with the record number of winners are Lord Egremont, who won in 1782, 1804, 1805, 1807, 1826 (also won five Oaks); and Aga Khan III, who won in 1930, 1935, 1936, 1948, 1952. Other winning owners are: Duke of Grafton (1802, 1809, 1810, 1815); Mr J. Bowes (1835, 1843, 1852, 1853); Sir J. Hawley (1851, 1858, 1859, 1868); the 1st Duke of Westminster (1880, 1882, 1886, 1899); and Sir Victor Sassoon (1953, 1957, 1958, 1960).

The Derby was run at Newmarket in 1915–18 and 1940–5.

Year	Winner	Betting	Owner	Jockey	Trainer	Runners
2009	Sea the Stars	11–4	C. Tsui	M. Kinane	M. Oxx	12
2010	Workforce	6–1	K. Abdulla	R. Moore	M. Stoute	12
2011	Pour Moi	4–1	Mrs J. Magnier, M. Tabor and D. Smith	M. Barzalona	A. Fabre	13
2012	Camelot	8–13	D. Smith	J. P. O'Brien	A. P. O'Brien	9
2013	Ruler Of The World	7–1	Mrs J. Magnier, M. Tabor and D. Smith	R. Moore	A. P. O'Brien	12
2014	Australia	11–8	D. Smith, S. Magnier, M. Tabor and T. Ah Khing	J. O'Brien	A. P. O'Brien	16

THE OAKS
(1779) Epsom, 1 mile and about 4 f, for three-year-old fillies

Year	Winner	Betting	Owner	Jockey	Trainer	Runners
2009	Sariska	9–4	Michael Bell	Jamie Spencer	Lady Bamford	12
2010	Snow Fairy	9–1	Anamoine Ltd.	R. Moore	E. A. L. Dunlop	15
2011	Dancing Rain	20–1	M. J. and L. A. Taylor	J. Murtagh	W. Haggas	13
2012	Was	20–1	D. Smith, Mrs J. Magnier and M. Tabor	S. Heffernan	A. O'Brien	12
2013	Talent	20–1	J. L. Rowsell and M. H. Dixon	R. Hughes	R. Beckett	11
2014	Taghrooda	5–1	H. Al Maktoum	P. Hanagan	J. Gosden	17

ST LEGER
(1776) Doncaster, 1 mile and about 6 f, for three-year-olds

Year	Winner	Betting	Owner	Jockey	Trainer	Runners
2008	Conduit	8–1	Sir Michael Stoute	L. Dettori	Ballymacoll Stud	14
2009	Mastery	14–1	Godolphin	T. Durcan	S. Bin Suroor	8
2010	Arctic Cosmos	12–1	Ms R. Hood and R. Geffen	W. Buick	J. Gosden	10
2011	Masked Marvel	15–2	B. E. Neilsen	W. Buick	J. Gosden	9
2012	Encke	25–1	Godolphin	M. Barzalona	M. Al Zarooni	9
2013	Leading Light	7–2	D. Smith, S. Magnier and M. Tabor	J. O'Brien	A. P. O'Brien	11

RESULTS

CAMBRIDGESHIRE HANDICAP
(1839) Newmarket, 1 mile and 1 f

2009 Supaseus (6y), T. Block
2010 Credit Swap (5y), J. Crowley
2011 Prince of Johanne (5y), J. Fahy
2012 Bronze Angel (3y), W. Buick

PRIX DE L'ARC DE TRIOMPHE
(1920) Longchamp, Paris, 1½ miles

2009 Sea the Stars (3y), M. J. Kinane
2010 Workforce (3y), R. Moore
2011 Danedream (3y), A. Starke
2012 Solemia (4y), O. Peslier
2013 Educate (4y) J. Murtagh

CESAREWITCH
(1839) Newmarket, 2 miles and about 2 f

2009 Darley Sun (3y), A. Atzeni
2010 Aaim To Prosper (6y), L-P. Beuzelin
2011 Never Can Tell (4y), L. Dettori
2012 Aaim To Prosper (8y), K. Fallon

CHAMPION STAKES
(1877) Newmarket, 1 mile and 2 f

2009 Twice Over (4y), T. Queally
2010 Twice Over (5y), T. Queally
2011 Cirrus des Aigles (5y), C. Soumillon
2012 Frankel (4y), T. Queally
2013 Scatterdice (4y), S. de Sousa

DUBAI WORLD CUP
(1996) Dubai, 1 mile and 2 f

2010 Gloria de Campeao (7y), T. Pereira
2011 Victoire Pisa (4y), M. Dimuro
2012 Monterosso (5y), M. Barzalona
2013 Animal Kingdom (5y), J. Rosario
2014 African Story (7y), S. de Sousa

LINCOLN HANDICAP
(1965) Doncaster, 1 mile

2010 Penitent (4y), J. Murtagh
2011 Sweet Lightning (6y), J. Murtagh
2012 Brae Hill (6y), T. Hamilton
2013 Levitate (5y), D. Egan
2014 Ocean Tempest (5y), A. Kirby

JOCKEY CLUB STAKES
(1894) Newmarket, 1½ miles

2010 Jukebox Jury (4y), R. Ffrench
2011 Dandino (5y), P. Mulrennan
2012 Al Kazeem (4y), J. Doyle
2013 Universal (4y), J. Fanning
2014 Gospel Club (5y), R. Moore

PRIX DU JOCKEY CLUB
(1836) Chantilly, 1 mile and about 2½ f, for three-year-olds

2010 Lope de Vega, M. Guyon
2011 Reliable Man, G. Mosse
2012 Saonois, A. Hamelin
2013 Intello, O. Peslier
2014 The Grey Gatsby (3y), R. Moore

ASCOT GOLD CUP
(1807) Ascot, 2 miles and about 4 f

2010 Rite of Passage (6y), P. J. Smullen
2011 Fame and Glory (5y), J. Spencer
2012 Colour Vision (4y), L. Dettori
2013 Estimate (4y), R. Moore
2014 Leading Light (4y), J. O'Brien

IRISH DERBY
(1866) Curragh, 1½ miles, for three-year-olds

2010 Cape Blanco, J. Murtagh
2011 Treasure Beach, C. O'Donoghue
2012 Camelot, J. P. O'Brien
2013 Trading Leather, K. Manning
2014 Australia, J. O'Brien

ECLIPSE STAKES
(1886) Sandown, 1 mile and about 2 f

2010 Twice Over (5y), T. Queally
2011 So You Think (5y), S. Heffernan
2012 Nathaniel (4y), W. Buick
2013 Al Kazeem (5y), J. Doyle
2014 Mukhadram (5y), P. Hanagan

KING GEORGE VI AND QUEEN ELIZABETH
DIAMOND STAKES
(1952) Ascot, 1 mile and about 4 f

2010 Harbinger (4y), O. Peslier
2011 Nathaniel (3y), W. Buick
2012 Danedream (4y), A. Starke
2013 Novellist (4y), J. Murtagh
2014 Taghrooda (3y), P. Hanagan

GOODWOOD CUP
(1812) Goodwood, about 2 miles

2010 Illustrious Blue (7y), J. Crowley
2011 Opinion Poll (5y), L. Dettori
2012 Saddler's Rock (4y), J. Murtagh
2013 Brown Panther (5y), R. Kingscote
2014 Cavalryman (8y), K. Fallon

STATISTICS

WINNING FLAT OWNERS 2013

Godolphin	£3,854,819
Hamdan Al Maktoum	1,448,893
Mrs J. Magnier, M. Tabor and D. Smithr	1,276,248
Sheikh Hamdan bin Mohammed Al Maktoum	1,245,979
HE Sh Joann bin Hamad Al Thani	1,027,349
Mr. K. Abdullah	1,007,993
D Smith, Mrs J. Magnier and M. Tabor	990,070
Dr Marwan Koukash	867,635
D. J. Deer	675,364
B. Keswick	619,665

WINNING FLAT TRAINERS 2013

R. Hannon	£4,193,816
A. P. O'Brien	3,503,906
M. Johnston	2,518,875
S. bin Suroor	2,458,615
R. A. Fahey	2,238,590
J. Gosden	1,765,938
W. Haggas	1,713,514
Sir Michael Stoute	1,549,710
K. Ryan	1,498,930
R. Varian	1,238,635

WINNING FLAT SIRES 2013

	Races won	Stakes
Galileo by Sadler's Wells	75	£1,869,097
New Approach by Galileo	41	1,517,913
Pivotal by Polar Falcon	95	1,428,726
Dubawi by Dubai Millennium	70	1,398,307
Dark Angel by Acclamation	76	1,317,317
Oasis Dream by Green Desert	130	1,315,676
War Front (Danzig)	5	1,084,119
Dansili by Danehill	97	1,044,425
Cape Cross by Green Desert	119	937,391
Shamardal by Giant's Causeway	99	913,958

WINNING FLAT JOCKEYS 2013

	1st	2nd	3rd	Unpl.	Total mts
R. Hughes	208	171	136	497	1,012
R. Moore	194	135	135	435	899
A. Kirby	168	138	139	579	1,024
L. Morris	168	161	190	887	1,406
S. de Sousa	160	107	86	468	821
J. Fanning	156	158	151	714	1,179
J. Crowley	137	113	107	553	910
G. Lee	127	124	127	721	1,099
A. Atzeni	120	133	89	472	814
W. Buick	116	97	75	370	658

The above statistics have been provided by *Timeform*, publishers of the *Racehorses* and *Chasers and Hurdlers* annuals

ICE HOCKEY

MEN'S WORLD CHAMPIONSHIP 2014
Minsk, Belarus, May
Final: Russia beat Finland 5–2

DOMESTIC COMPETITIONS
Elite League Champions 2013–14: Belfast Giants
Play-off Champions 2014: Sheffield Steelers
Challenge Cup final 2013–14: Nottingham Panthers beat
    Belfast Giants 1–0 in a penalty shootout 6–6 (agg)

NATIONAL HOCKEY LEAGUE
Stanley Cup final 2013–14: Los Angeles Kings beat New
    York Rangers 4–1

JUDO

EUROPEAN CHAMPIONSHIPS 2014
Montpellier, France, April

MEN
Heavyweight (over 100kg): Teddy Riner (France)
Light-heavyweight (100kg): Lukas Krpalek (Czech Republic)
Middleweight (90kg): Varlam Liparteliani (Georgia)
Welterweight (81kg): Avtandil Tchrikishvili (Georgia)
Lightweight (73kg): Dex Elmont (Netherlands)
Junior Lightweight (66kg): Loïc Korval (France)
Bantamweight (60kg): Beslan Mudranov (Russia)

WOMEN
Heavyweight (over 78kg): Émilie Andéol (France)
Light-heavyweight (78kg): Audrey Tcheumeo (France)
Middleweight (70kg): Kim Polling (Netherlands)
Welterweight (63kg): Clarisse Agbegnenou (France)
Lightweight (57kg): Automne Pavia (France)
Junior Lightweight (52kg): Majlinda Kelmendi (Kosovo)
Bantamweight (48kg): Éva Csernoviczki (Hungary)

BRITISH OPEN CHAMPIONSHIPS 2013
Sheffield, December

MEN
Heavyweight (over 100kg): Christopher Sherrington
Light-heavyweight (100kg): Benjamin Fletcher
Middleweight (90kg): David Groom
Welter (81kg): Owen Livesey
Lightweight (73kg): Jan Gosiewski
Junior Lightweight (66kg): Colin Oates
Bantamweight (60kg): Ashley McKenzie

WOMEN
Heavyweight (over 78kg): Sarah Adlington
Light-heavyweight (78kg): Natalie Powell
Middleweight (70kg): Sally Conway
Welter (63kg): Gemma Howell
Lightweight (57kg): Nekoda Davis
Junior Lightweight (52kg): Kelly Edwards
Bantamweight (48kg): Hayley Willis

MOTORCYCLING

MOTOGP 2013
Qatar (Doha): Jorge Lorenzo (Spain), Yamaha
USA (Austin): Marc Marquez (Spain), Honda
Spain (Jerez): Dani Pedrosa (Spain), Honda
France (Le Mans): Dani Pedrosa (Spain), Honda
Italy (Mugello): Jorge Lorenzo (Spain), Yamaha
Catalonia (Barcelona): Jorge Lorenzo (Spain), Yamaha
Netherlands (Assen): Valentino Rossi (Italy), Yamaha
Germany (Sachsenring): Marc Marquez (Spain), Honda
USA (Mazda Raceway): Marc Marquez (Spain), Honda
USA (Indianapolis): Marc Marquez (Spain), Honda
Czech Republic (Brno): Marc Marquez (Spain), Honda
Britain (Silverstone): Jorge Lorenzo (Spain), Yamaha

MOTOGP 2014
Qatar (Doha): Marc Marquez (Spain), Honda
USA (Austin): Marc Marquez (Spain), Honda
Spain (Jerez): Marc Marquez (Spain), Honda
France (Le Mans): Marc Marquez (Spain), Honda
Italy (Mugello): Marc Marquez (Spain), Honda
Catalonia (Barcelona): Marc Marquez (Spain), Honda

Netherlands (Assen): Marc Marquez (Spain), Honda
Germany (Sachsenring): Marc Marquez (Spain), Honda
USA (Indianapolis): Marc Marquez (Spain), Honda
Czech Republic (Brno): Dani Pedrosa (Spain), Honda
Britain (Silverstone): Marc Marquez (Spain), Honda
San Marino (Misano): Valentino Rossi (Italy), Yamaha

MOTO2 2013
Qatar (Doha): Pol Espargaro (Spain), Kalex
USA (Austin): Nicolas Terol (Spain), Suter
Spain (Jerez): Esteve Rabat (Spain), Kalex
France (Le Mans): Scott Redding (Great Britain), Kalex
Italy (Mugello): Scott Redding (Great Britain), Kalex
Catalonia (Barcelona): Pol Espargaro (Spain), Kalex
Netherlands (Assen): Pol Espargaro (Spain), Kalex
Germany (Sachsenring): Jordi Torres (Spain), Suter
USA (Indianapolis): Esteve Rabat (Spain), Kalex
Czech Republic (Brno): Mika Kallio (Finland), Kalex
Riders' Championship 2013: 1. Pol Espargaro (Spain), Tuenti HP 40, 265pts; 2. Scott Redding (Great Britain), Marc VDS Racing Team, 225pts; 3. Esteve Rabat, Tuenti HP 40, 215pts

MOTO2 2014
Qatar (Doha): Esteve Rabat (Spain), Kalex
USA (Austin): Maverick Viñales (Spain), Kalex
Argentina (Santiago del Estero): Esteve Rabat (Spain), Kalex
Spain (Jerez): Mika Kallio (Finland), Kalex
France (Le Mans): Mika Kallio (Finland), Kalex
Italy (Mugello): Esteve Rabat (Spain), Kalex
Catalonia (Barcelona): Esteve Rabat (Spain), Kalex
Netherlands (Assen): Anthony West (Australia), Speed Up
Germany (Sachsenring): Dominique Aegerter (Switzerland), Suter
USA (Indianapolis): Mika Kallio (Finland), Kalex
Czech Republic (Brno): Esteve Rabat (Spain), Kalex
Britain (Silverstone): Esteve Rabat (Spain), Kalex
San Marino (Misano): Esteve Rabat (Spain), Kalex

MOTO3 GRAND PRIX 2013
Qatar (Doha): Luis Salom (Spain), KTM
USA (Austin): Alex Rins (Spain), KTM
Spain (Jerez): Maverick Viñales (Spain), KTM
France (Le Mans): Maverick Viñales (Spain), KTM
Italy (Mugello): Luis Salom (Spain), KTM
Catalonia (Barcelona): Luis Salom (Spain), KTM
Netherlands (Assen): Luis Salom (Spain), KTM
Germany (Sachsenring): Alex Rins (Spain), KTM
USA (Indianapolis): Alex Rins (Spain), KTM
Czech Republic (Brno): Luis Salom (Spain), KTM
Riders' Championship 2013: 1. Maverick Viñales (Spain), JHK, 325pts; 2. Alex Rins (Spain), Estrella Galicia, 311pts; 3. Luis Salom (Spain), KTM, 302pts

MOTO3 GRAND PRIX 2014
Qatar (Doha): Jack Miller (Australia), KTM
USA (Austin): Jack Miller (Australia), KTM
Argentina (Santiago del Estero): Romano Fenati (Italy), KTM
Spain (Jerez): Romano Fenati (Italy), KTM
France (Le Mans): Jack Miller (Australia), KTM
Italy (Mugello): Romano Fenati (Italy), KTM
Catalonia (Barcelona): Álex Márquez (Spain), Honda
Netherlands (Assen): Álex Márquez (Spain), Honda
Germany (Sachsenring): Jack Miller (Australia), KTM
USA (Indianapolis): Efren Vazquez (Spain), Honda
Czech Republic (Brno): Alexis Masbou (France), Honda
Britain (Silverstone): Alexis Rins (Spain), Honda
San Marino (Misano): Alexis Rins (Spain), Honda

ISLE OF MAN TOURIST TROPHY 2014
Senior: Michael Dunlop (Northern Ireland), BMW
Supersport: Race 1 – Gary Johnson (England), Triumph; Race 2 – Gary Johnson (England), Triumph

WORLD SUPERBIKES 2013
Australia (Phillip Island): Race 1 – Sylvain Guintoli (France), Aprilia; Race 2 – Eugene Laverty (Ireland), Aprilia
Spain (Aragon): Race 1 – Chaz Davies (Great Britain), BMW; Race 2 – Chaz Davies (Great Britain), BMW
Netherlands (Assen): Race 1 – Tom Sykes (Great Britain), Kawasaki; Race 2 – Eugene Laverty (Ireland), Aprilia
Italy (Monza): Race 1 – Marco Melandri (Italy), BMW; Race 2 – Eugene Laverty (Ireland), Aprilia
Great Britain (Donington): Race 1 – Tom Sykes (Great Britain), Kawasaki; Race 2 – Tom Sykes (Great Britain), Kawasaki
Portugal (Portimao): Race 1 – Marco Melandri (Italy), BMW; Race 2 – Eugene Laverty (Ireland), Aprilia
Italy (Imola): Race 1 – Tom Sykes (Great Britain), Kawasaki; Race 2 – Tom Sykes (Great Britain), Kawasaki
Russia (Moscow): Race 1 – Marco Melandri (Italy), BMW; Race 2 – Cancelled
Great Britain (Silverstone): Race 1 – Jonathan Rea (Great Britain), Honda; Race 2 – Loris Baz (France), Kawasaki
Germany (Nürburgring): Race 1 – Tom Sykes (Great Britain), Kawasaki; Race 2 – Chaz Davies (Great Britain), BMW
Turkey (Istanbul Park): Race 1 – Eugene Laverty (Ireland), Aprilia; Race 2 – Eugene Laverty (Ireland), Aprilia
USA (Monterey): Race 1 – Tom Sykes (Great Britain), Kawasaki; Race 2 – Eugene Laverty (Ireland), Aprilia
France (Magny-Cours): Race 1 – Tom Sykes (Great Britain), Kawasaki; Race 2 – Tom Sykes (Great Britain), Kawasaki
Spain (Jerez): Race 1 – Eugene Laverty (Ireland), Aprilia Racing Team; Race 2 – Eugene Laverty (Ireland), Aprilia
Rider's World Championship 2013: 1. Tom Sykes (Great Britain), Kawasaki, 447pts; 2. Eugene Laverty (Ireland), Aprilia, 424pts; 3. Sylvain Guintoli (France), Aprillia, 402pts

WORLD SUPERBIKES 2014
Australia (Phillip Island): Race 1 – Eugene Laverty (Ireland), Voltcom Crescent Suzuki; Race 2 – Sylvain Guintoli (France), Aprilia
Spain (Aragon): Race 1 – Tom Sykes (Great Britain), Kawasaki; Race 2 – Tom Sykes (Great Britain), Kawasaki
Netherlands (Assen): Race 1 – Sylvain Guintoli (France), Aprillia; Race 2 – Jonathan Rea (Great Britain), Pata Honda World Superbike
Italy (Imola): Race 1 – Jonathan Rea (Great Britain), Pata Honda World Superbike; Race 2 – Jonathan Rea (Great Britain), Pata Honda World Superbike
Great Britain (Donington): Race 1 – Tom Sykes (Great Britain), Kawasaki; Race 2 – Tom Sykes (Great Britain), Kawasaki
Malaysia (Sepang): Race 1 – Marco Melandri (Italy), Aprilia; Race 2 – Marco Melandri (Italy), Aprilia
Italy (Rimini): Race 1 – Tom Sykes (Great Britain), Kawasaki; Race 2 – Tom Sykes (Great Britain), Kawasaki
Portugal (Algarve): Race 1 – Tom Sykes (Great Britain), Kawasaki; Race 2 – Jonathan Rea (Great Britain), Pata Honda World Superbike
USA (Monterey): Race 1 – Marco Melandri (Italy), Aprilia; Race 2 – Tom Sykes (Great Britain), Kawasaki
Spain (Jerez): Race 1 – Marco Melandri (Italy), Aprilia; Race 2 – Marco Melandri (Italy), Aprilia

MOTOR RACING

FORMULA 1 GRAND PRIX 2013
Australia (Melbourne): Kimi Raikkonen (Finland), Lotus-Renault
Malaysia (Sepang): Sebastian Vettel (Germany), RBR-Renault
China (Shanghai): Fernando Alonso (Spain), Ferrari
Bahrain (Sakhir): Sebastian Vettel (Germany), RBR-Renault
Spain (Barcelona): Fernando Alonso (Spain), Ferrari
Monaco (Monte Carlo): Nico Rosberg (Germany), Mercedes
Canada (Montreal): Sebastian Vettel (Germany), RBR-Renault
Great Britain (Silverstone): Nico Rosberg (Germany), Mercedes
Germany (Nürburgring): Sebastian Vettel (Germany), RBR-Renault
Hungary (Hungaroring): Lewis Hamilton (Great Britain), Mercedes
Belgium (Spa): Sebastian Vettel (Germany), RBR-Renault
Italy (Monza): Sebastian Vettel (Germany), RBR-Renault
Singapore (Morina Bay): Sebastian Vettel (Germany), RBR-Renault
Korea (Yeongam): Sebastian Vettel (Germany), RBR-Renault
Japan (Suzuka): Sebastian Vettel (Germany), RBR-Renault
India (Buddh): Sebastian Vettel (Germany), RBR-Renault
Abu Dhabi (Yas Marina): Sebastian Vettel (Germany), RBR-Renault
USA (Austin): Sebastian Vettel (Germany), RBR-Renault
Brazil (Sao Paulo): Sebastian Vettel (Germany), RBR-Renault
Drivers' World Championship 2013: 1. Sebastian Vettel (Germany), RBR-Renault, 397pts; 2. Fernando Alonso (Spain), Ferrari, 242pts; 3. Mark Webber (Australia), RBR-Renault, 199pts
Constructors' World Championship 2013: 1. RBR-Renault, 596pts; 2. McLaren-Mercedes, 360pts; 3. Ferrari, 354pts

FORMULA 1 GRAND PRIX 2014
Australia (Melbourne): Nico Rosberg (Germany), Mercedes
Malaysia (Sepang): Lewis Hamilton (Great Britain), Mercedes
Bahrain (Sakhir): Lewis Hamilton (Great Britain), Mercedes
China (Shanghai): Lewis Hamilton (Great Britain), Mercedes
Spain (Barcelona): Lewis Hamilton (Great Britain), Mercedes
Monaco (Monte Carlo): Nico Rosberg (Germany), Mercedes
Canada (Montreal): Daniel Ricciardo (Australia), RBR-Renault
Austria (Spielberg): Nico Rosberg (Germany), Mercedes
Great Britain (Silverstone): Lewis Hamilton (Great Britain), Mercedes
Germany (Nürburgring): Nico Rosberg (Germany), Mercedes
Hungary (Hungaroring): Daniel Ricciardo (Australia), RBR-Renault
Belgium (Spa): Daniel Ricciardo (Australia), RBR-Renault
Italy (Monza): Lewis Hamilton (Great Britain), Mercedes

INDIANAPOLIS 500 2014
Indianapolis, USA, 25 May
Ryan Hunter-Reay (USA), Andretti Autosport

LE MANS 24-HOUR RACE 2014
Le Mans, France, 11–15 June
André Lotterer (Germany), Marcel Fässler (Switzerland) and Benoêt Tréluyer (France), Audi Sport Team Joest

MOTOR RALLYING

WORLD RALLY CHAMPIONSHIP 2013
Monte Carlo: Sébastien Loeb (France), Citroën
Sweden: Sébastien Ogier (France), Volkswagen

Mexico: Sébastien Ogier (France), Volkswagen
Portugal: Sébastien Ogier (France), Volkswagen
Argentina: Sébastien Loeb (France), Citroën
Greece: Jari-Matti Latvala (Finland), Volkswagen
Italy: Sébastien Ogier (France), Volkswagen
Finand: Sébastien Ogier (France), Volkswagen
Germany: Dani Sordo (Spain), Citroën
Australia: Sébastien Ogier (France), Volkswagen
France: Sébastien Ogier (France), Volkswagen
Spain: Sébastien Ogier (France), Volkswagen
Great Britain: Sébastien Ogier (France), Volkswagen
Drivers' World Championship 2013: 1. Sébastien Ogier
(France), Volkswagen, 290pts; 2. Thierry Neuville
(Belgium), Qatar WRT, 176pts; 3. Jari-Matti Latvala
(Finland), Volkswagen, 162pts
Manufacturers' World Championship 2013: 1. Volkswagen,
425pts; 2. Citroën, 280pts; 3. Qatar M-Sport , 190pts

WORLD RALLY CHAMPIONSHIP 2014
Monte Carlo: Sébastien Ogier (France), Volkswagen
Sweden: Jari-Matti Latvala (Finland), Volkswagen
Mexico: Sébastien Ogier (France), Volkswagen
Portugal: Sébastien Ogier (France), Volkswagen
Argentina: Jari-Matti Latvala (Finland), Volkswagen
Italy: Sébastien Ogier (France), Volkswagen
Poland: Sébastien Ogier (France), Volkswagen
Finland: Jari-Matti Latvala (Finland), Volkswagen

BRITISH RALLY CHAMPIONSHIP 2014
Pirelli Carlisle RB Foundation Rally: Osian Pryce (Great
Britain), Citroën
Jim Clark International: Daniel McKenna (Ireland),
Citroën
RSAC Scottish Rally: Daniel McKenna (Ireland), Citroën
Todds Leap Ulster Rally: Cancelled
Rally Isle of Man: Daniel McKenna (Ireland), Citroën
Drivers' Championship 2014: 1. Daniel McKenna (Ireland),
Citroën, 108pts; 2. Osian Pryce (Great Britain), Citroën,
97pts; 3. Dean Raftery (Ireland), Ford, 88pts

DAKAR RALLY RAID 2014
Argentina, Chile, 5–18 January

Motorcycle: Marc Coma (Spain), KTM
Quad: Ignacio Casale (Chile), Yamaha
Car: Nani Roma (Spain), Mini
Truck: Andrey Karginov (Russia), Kamaz

NETBALL

Superleague Grand Final 2014: Manchester Thunder beat
Surrey Storm 49–48

NORDIC EVENTS

BIATHLON WORLD CUP 2013–14

MEN
Overall: Martin Fourcade (France), 928pts

WOMEN
Overall: Kaisa Mäkäräinen (Finland), 860pts

NORDIC WORLD CUP 2013–14
World Cup: Eric Frenzel (Germany), 1,031pts
Nation Cup: Germany, 4,123pts

POLO

Prince of Wales Trophy 2014: La Indiana beat HB Polo 10–8
Queen's Cup final 2014: Zacara beat Talendaracas 10–7
Warwickshire Cup 2014: Halcyon Gallery beat Black Bears
10–8
Gold Cup (British Open) final 2014: Dubai beat King Power
13–11

RACKETS

Noel Bruce Cup 2013: Charlie Danby and Alex Titchener-
Barrett (Harrow I) beat Nick James and Ben Snell
(Cheltenham I) 4–1
Amateur Singles Championship final 2013: Alex Titchener-
Barrett beat James Coyne 3–2
The Foster Cup final 2013 (public schools' singles
championship): T. Morales (Eton) beat R. White (Harrow)
3–2
British Professional Singles Championship final 2014: Will
Hopton beat Mark Hubbard 3–0
British Open Singles Championship final 2013: Will Hopton
beat Alex Titchener-Barrett 4–3
British Open Doubles Championship final 2014: Christian
Portz and Alex Titchener-Barrett beat James Coyne and
Mike Bailey 4–1
Amateur Doubles Championship 2014: Harry Foster and Mark
Hue Williams beat James Coyne and Mike Bailey 3–1

REAL TENNIS

MEN
British Open Singles final 2013: Steve Virgona (Australia) beat
Bryn Sayers (Great Britain) 3–2
British Open Doubles final 2013: Tim Chisholm (USA) and
Bryn Sayers (Great Britain) beat Rob Fahey (Australia) and
Steve Virgona (Australia) 3–2
Henry Leaf Cup final 2014 (public schools' old boys' doubles
championship): Matt Ronaldson and David Sloan
(Canford) beat Harry Eddis and Horatio Carey (Eton) 2–1
World Championship 2014: Rob Fahey (Australia) beat
Camden Riviere (USA) 7–3

WOMEN
British Open Singles Championship final 2014 Claire Vigrass
(Great Britain) beat Sarah Vigrass (Great Britain) 2–0
British Open Doubles Championship final 2014: Karen Hird
(Great Britain) and Freddy Adam (USA) beat Claire Vigrass
(Great Britain) and Sarah Vigrass (Great Britain) 2–1

ROWING

HENLEY ROYAL REGATTA 2014
Grand Challenge Cup: Leander Club and University of
London beat Club France (France) by 1½ lengths
Stewards' Challenge Cup: Molsey Boat Club and Leander Club
beat Club France 'B' (France) by 3½ lengths
Queen Mother Challenge Cup: Leander Club and Agecroft
Rowing Club beat National Training Centre (Australia) by
1 length
Silver Goblets and Nickalls' Challenge Cup: J.P.B. Bahain and
M. Steenman (Netherlands) beat S.B. Keeling & V.A. Breet,
(South Africa) by 2 lengths
Double Sculls Challenge Cup: S. Delayre and J.Azou (France)
beat J.E. Collins & J.F.L. Walton by 3 feet
Diamond Challenge Sculls: A.M.O Drysdale (New Zealand)
beat R. Braas (Netherlands) by 5 lengths
Remenham Challenge Cup: Leander Club and Imperial College
London beat Hollandia Roeiclub (Netherlands) by ⅔ of a
length

Princess Grace Challenge Cup: Leander Club and Gloucester Rowing Club beat Gloucester Rowing Club and Northwich Rowing Club by 3¼ lengths
Princess Royal Challenge Cup: M. Knapkova (Czech Republic) heat K. Gyimes by 4½ lengths
Ladies' Challenge Plate: University of California, Berkeley (USA) beat Leander Club by 3 feet
Visitors' Challenge Cup: Harvard University (USA) beat Leander Club by 2¼ lengths
Prince of Wales Challenge Cup: Leander Club beat Rudern, Tennis und Hockey Club Bayer Leverkusen and Ruderverein Berlin v.1878 (Germany) by 2¾ lengths
Thames Challenge Cup: Frankfurter Rudergesellschaft Germania von 1869 e.V. (Germany) beat Sport Imperial Boat Club by a canvas
Wyfold Challenge Cup: Upper Thames Rowing Club 'A' beat The Tideway Scullers' School 'A' by disqualification
Britannia Challenge Cup: Upper Thames Rowing Club 'A' beat Frankfurter Rudergesellschaft Germania von 1869 e.V. (Germany) by 2 lengths
Temple Challenge Cup: Oxford Brookes University 'A' beat Brown University (USA) by 2¾ lengths
Prince Albert Challenge Cup: Newcastle University 'A' beat Harvard University (USA) 3½ lengths
Princess Elizabeth Challenge Cup: Eton College beat St Edward's School by 1¼ lengths
Fawley Challenge Cup: Sir William Borlase's Grammar School beat The Windsor Boys' School by 2¾ lengths

THE 160TH UNIVERSITY BOAT RACE
Putney–Mortlake, 4 miles, 1 f, 180 yd, 6 April 2014

Oxford beat Cambridge by 11 lengths; 18min 36sec
Cambridge have won 81 times, Oxford 78 and there has been one dead heat. The record time is 16min 19sec, rowed by Cambridge in 1998.

BRITISH ROWING SENIOR CHAMPIONSHIPS 2013
Nottingham, October
Gold Medal Winners
Open Double Skulls: Leander Club
Women's Double Skulls: Leander Club
Open Coxless Fours: Leander Club
Women's Coxless Fours: Leander Club
Open Quadruple Skulls: Leander Club
Women's Quadruple Skulls: Hollingworth Lake Rowing Club and Tees Rowing Club
Open Eights: Leander Club
Women's Eights: Leander Club
Open Legs, Trunk and Arms Single Skulls: Samuel Murray (Henley Rowing Club)
Open Trunks and Arms Single Skulls: Laurence Whiteley (Tees Rowing Club)
Women's Trunk and Arms Single Skulls: Sophie Brown (Sudbury Rowing Club)
Open Arms and Shoulders Single Skulls: Thomas Aggar (Royal Docks Rowing Club)
Women's Arms and Shoulders Single Skulls: Caroline MacDonald (Tees Rowing Club)

OTHER ROWING EVENTS
Wingfield Sculls 2013: Men, Alan Campbell (Tideway Scullers School); *Women,* Imogen Walsh (London Rowing Club)
Oxford Summer Eights 2014: Men, Oriel; *Women,* Wadham
Head of the River 2014: Men, N/A*; *Women,* Imperial College Boat Club 'A'

Abandoned due to poor weather

RUGBY FIVES

National Open Singles Championship final 2013: D. Tristao beat W. Ellison 2–0
National Ladies' Singles Championship final 2013: K. Briedenhann beat A. Steel 2–0
National Ladies' Doubles Championship final 2013: K. Briedenhann and T. Mills beat A. Steel and K.Hird 2–0
National Open Doubles Championship final 2014: W. Ellison and C. Brooks beat D. Grant and D. Tristao 2–1
National Club Championship final 2014: Old Paulines I beat Wessex 107–84
National Schools' Singles Championship final 2014: B. Beltrami (St Paul's) beat O. Arnold (St Paul's) 2–0
National Schools' Doubles Championship final 2014: St Paul's I beat St Paul's II 2–0
Varsity Match 2014: Cambridge Sparrows beat Oxford Beavers 146–117

RUGBY LEAGUE

Super League Grand Final 2013: Wigan Warriors beat Warrington Wolves 30–16
Tetley's Challenge Cup final 2014: Leeds Rhinos beat Castleford Tigers 23–10
World Club Challenge 2014: Sydney Roosters beat Wigan Warriors 26–14

AMATEUR COMPETITIONS 2013
National Conference League Premier Division Grand Final: Wath Brow Hornets beat West Hull 16–12
Division One Champions: East Leeds
Division Two Champions: Normanton Kinghts
BARLA National Cup final: Sharlston Rovers beat Hunslet Old Boys 26–16
Varsity Match 2014: Oxford beat Cambridge 40–0

RUGBY UNION

SIX NATIONS' CHAMPIONSHIP 2014

1 February	Cardiff	Wales beat Italy 23–15
	Saint-Denis	France beat England 26–24
2 February	Dublin	Ireland beat Scotland 28–6
8 February	Dublin	Ireland beat Wales 26–3
	Edinburgh	England beat Scotland 20–0
9 February	Saint-Denis	France beat Italy 30–10
21 February	Cardiff	Wales beat France 27–6
22 February	Rome	Scotland beat Italy 21–20
	Twickenham	England beat Ireland 13–10
8 March	Dublin	Ireland beat Italy 46–7
	Edinburgh	France beat Scotland 19–17
9 March	Twickenham	England beat Wales 29–18
15 March	Rome	England beat Italy 52–11
	Cardiff	Wales beat Scotland 51–3
	Saint-Denis	Ireland beat France 22–20

Final standings: 1. Ireland, 8pts; 2. England, 8pts; 3. Wales, 6pts; 4. France, 6pts; 5. Scotland, 2pts; 6. Italy, 0pts

EUROPEAN COMPETITIONS 2013–14
Heineken European Cup final: Toulon beat Saracens 23–6
European Challenge Cup final: Northampton Saints beat Bath 30–16

DOMESTIC COMPETITIONS 2013–14

ENGLAND
Aviva Premiership: Saracens, 78pts
Aviva Premiership final: Northampton Saints beat Saracens 24–20

RFU Championship: London Welsh, 88pts
RFU Championship final: London Welsh beat Bristol Rugby 27–8 (at London Welsh); London Welsh beat Bristol Rugby 21–20 (at Bristol). London Welsh promoted to the Premiership
National League: Division 1, Doncaster Knights, 122pts; *Promotion from Division 2 (North):* Macclesfield; *Promotion from Division 2 (South):* Hartpury College
British and Irish Cup final: Leinster 'A' beat Leeds Carnegie 44–17
County Championship final (Bill Beaumont Cup): Lancashire beat Cornwall 36–26
County Shield final: Surrey beat Leicestershire 39–12
132nd Varsity Match: Oxford beat Cambridge 33–15

ANGLO-WELSH
LV Cup final: Exeter Chiefs beat Northampton Saints 15–8

CELTIC
RaboDirect Pro12: Leinster, 82pts
RaboDirect Pro12 final: Leinster beat Glasgow Warriors 34–12

SCOTLAND
Premiership champions: Melrose; *National League champions:* Biggar RFC
RBS Cup final: Heriots beat Glasgow Hawks 31–10

WALES
Premiership: Pontypridd, 78pts; *National League:* League 1 (East), Merthyr RFC, 87pts; (West), Glynneath RFC, 98pts; (North) Bala RFC, 69pts
WRU Challenge Cup final: Pontypridd beat Cross Keys 21–8

IRELAND
All Ireland League: Division 1A, Clontarf, 64pts; Division 1B, Terenure College, 82pts; Division 2A, Galwegians, 64pts; Division 2B, Nenagh Ormond, 64pts

SHOOTING

145TH NATIONAL RIFLE ASSOCIATION IMPERIAL MEETING
Bisley, 5–19 July 2014

Queen's Prize: R. C. T. Jeens, 297.44 v-bulls
Grand Aggregate: P. G. Kent, 700.102 v-bulls
Prince of Wales Prize: D. R. Armstrong, 75.13 v-bulls
St George's Vase: J. P. Bailey, 150.25 v-bulls
All Comers' Aggregate: J. D. Warburton, 373.62 v-bulls
Kolapore Cup: Great Britain, 1192.177 v-bulls
Chancellor's Trophy: Oxford University, 1141.99 v-bulls
National Trophy: England, 2087.278 v-bulls
Musketeers Cup: Edinburgh University, 581.60 v-bulls
County Championship Long Range: Hertfordshire, 587.55 v-bulls
Mackinnon Challenge Cup: England, 1188.149 v-bulls
The Albert: C. N. Tremlett, 221.31 v-bulls
Hopton Challenge Cup: R. J. Lygoe, 1003.129 v-bulls

SNOOKER

2013–14
Shanghai Masters: Ding Junhui (China) beat Xiao Guodong (China) 10–6
World Open (Haikou, China): Shaun Murphy (England) beat Mark Selby (England) 10–6
UK Championship (York): Neil Robertson (Australia) beat Mark Selby (England) 10–7

Masters (Wembley): Ronnie O'Sullivan (England) beat Mark Selby (England) 10–4
Welsh Open (Newport): Ronnie O'Sullivan (England) beat Ding Junhui (China) 9–7
German Masters (Berlin): Ding Junhui (China) beat Judd Trump (England) 9–5
China Open (Beijing): Ding Junhui (China) beat Neil Robertson (Australia) 10–5
World Championship (Sheffield): Mark Selby (England) beat Ronnie O'Sullivan (England) 18–14
Australian Open (Bendigo): Judd Trump (England) beat Neil Robertson (Australia) 9–5
Players Tour Championship (Galway, Ireland): Barry Hawkins (England) beat Gerard Greene (Northern Ireland) 4–0
Wuxi Classic (China): Neil Robertson (Australia) beat Joe Perry (England) 10–9
International Championship (Chengdu, China): Ding Junhui (China) beat Marco Fu (Hong Kong) 10–9

SPEED SKATING

WORLD ALL-ROUND CHAMPIONSHIPS 2014
Heerenveen, Netherlands, 22–23 March

MEN
Gold: Koen Verweij (Netherlands); *Silver:* Jan Blokhuijsen (Netherlands); *Bronze:* Denis Yuskov (Russia)
500m: Konrad Niedźwiedzki (Poland), 35.91sec
1,500m: Denis Yuskov (Russia), 1min 46.12sec
5,000m: Jan Blokhuijsen (Netherlands), 6min 17.78sec
10,000m: Jan Blokhuijsen (Netherlands), 13min 13.93sec

WOMEN
Gold: Ireen Wüst (Netherlands); *Silver:* Olga Graf (Russia); *Bronze:* Yvonne Nauta (Netherlands)
500m: Ireen Wüst (Netherlands), 38.86sec
1,500m: Ireen Wüst (Netherlands), 1min 54.13sec
3,000m: Ireen Wüst (Netherlands), 3min 58.83sec
5,000m: Yvonne Nauta (Netherlands), 6min 57.59sec

EUROPEAN ALL-ROUND CHAMPIONSHIPS 2014
Hamar, Norway, 11–12 January

MEN
Gold: Jan Blokhuijsen (Netherlands); *Silver:* Koen Verweij (Netherlands); *Bronze:* Havard Bokko (Norway)
500m: Havard Bokko (Norway), 35.99sec
1,500m: Koen Verweij (Netherlands), 1min 45.93sec
5,000m: Jan Blokhuijsen (Netherlands), 6min 15.89sec
10,000m: Jan Blokhuijsen (Netherlands), 13min 07.22sec

WOMEN
Gold: Ireen Wüst (Netherlands); *Silver:* Yvonne Nauta (Netherlands); *Bronze:* Martina Sáblíková (Czech Republic)
500m: Ireen Wüst (Netherlands), 38.77sec
1,500m: Ireen Wüst (Netherlands), 1min 54.87sec
3,000m: Ireen Wüst (Netherlands), 4min 02.02sec
5,000m: Martina Sáblíková (Czech Republic), 6min 58.13sec

WORLD SHORT TRACK CHAMPIONSHIPS 2014
Montreal, Canada, 14–16 March

MEN
500m: Dajing Wu (China), 40.158sec
1,000m: Victor An (Russia), 1min 25.055sec
1,500m: Charles Hamelin (Canada), 2min 12.071sec
3,000m: J. R. Celski (USA), 4min 59.528sec
5,000m relay: Netherlands, 6min 45.064sec
Overall: Victor An (Russia), 63pts

WOMEN
500m: Park Seung Hi (Rep. of Korea), 42.792sec
1,000m: Shim Suk Hee (Rep. of Korea), 1min 30.488sec
1,500m: Shim Suk Hee (Rep. of Korea), 2min 27.791sec
3,000m: Shim Suk Hee (Rep. of Korea), 4min 50.829sec
3,000m relay: China, 4min 08.811sec
Overall: Shim Suk Hee (Rep. of Korea), 102pts

EUROPEAN SHORT TRACK CHAMPIONSHIPS 2014
Dresden, Germany, 17–19 January

MEN
500m: Victor An (Russia), 40.627sec
1,000m: Victor An (Russia), 1min 24.940sec
1,500m: Semen Elistratov (Russia), 2min 14.541sec
3,000m: Victor An (Russia), 4min 47.462sec
5,000m relay: Russia, 6min 45.803sec
Overall: Victor An (Russia), 102pts

WOMEN
500m: Arianna Fontana (Italy), 43.658sec
1,000m: Elise Christie (Great Britain), 1min 29.811sec
1,500m: Jorien Ter Mors (Netherlands), 2min 22.995sec
3,000m: Jorien Ter Mors (Netherlands), 5min 53.121sec
3,000m relay: Netherlands, 4min 13.473sec
Overall: Jorien Ter Mors (Netherlands), 107pts

SQUASH

MEN
European Individual Closed Championship 2014: Gregory
   Gaultier (France) Laurens Jan Anjema (Netherlands) 3–1
European Team Championship 2014: England beat France
   3–0
British National Championship 2014: Nick Matthew
   (England) beat James Willstrop (England) 3–1

WOMEN
European Individual Closed Championship 2014: Camille
   Serme (France) beat Line Hansen (Denmark) 3–0
European Team Championship 2014: England beat France
   2–1
British National Championship 2014: Alison Waters (England)
   beat Madeline Perry (England) 3–0

SWIMMING

BRITISH CHAMPIONSHIPS 2014
Glasgow, 10–15 April

MEN
50m freestyle: Adam Brown (Hatfield), 22.27sec
100m freestyle: Adam Brown (Hatfield), 49.35sec
200m freestyle: James Guy (Millfield), 1min 47.54sec
400m freestyle: James Guy (Millfield), 3min 45.15sec
1,500m freestyle: Daniel Fogg (Loughborough University),
   14min 59.86sec
100m backstroke: Chris Walker-Hebborn (Ellesmere College),
   53.82sec
200m backstroke: Charlie Boldison (University of Stirling),
   1min 59.40sec
100m breaststroke: Ross Murdoch (University of Stirling),
   59.56sec
200m breaststroke: Michael Jamieson (Bath University),
   2min 07.79sec
100m butterfly: James Guy (Millfield), 52.55sec
200m butterfly: Roberto Pavoni (Loughborough University),
   1min 57.20sec

200m medley: Roberto Pavoni (Loughborough University),
   1min 59.08sec
400m medley: Roberto Pavoni (Loughborough University),
   4min 12.24sec

WOMEN
50m freestyle: Francesca Halsall (Loughborough University),
   24.51sec
100m freestyle: Stephanie Slater (Preston), 1 min 07.20sec
200m freestyle: Siobhan-Marie O'Connor (Bath University),
   1min 56.59sec
400m freestyle: Jazmin Carlin (Swansea University), 4min
   04.68sec
800m freestyle: Jazmin Carlin (Swansea University), 8min
   18.36sec
100m backstroke: Georgia Davies (Loughbrough University),
   59.78sec
200m backstroke: Lauren Quigley (Stockport Metro SC),
   2min 09.79sec
100m breaststroke: Sophie Taylor (City of Leeds SC), 1min
   07.08sec
200m breaststroke: Sophie Taylor (City of Leeds SC), 2min
   24.46sec
100m butterfly: Rachael Kelly (Loughborough University),
   58.40sec
200m butterfly: Aimee Willmott (Middlesborough ASC),
   2min 07.97sec
200m medley: Siobhan-Marie O'Connor (Bath University),
   2min 09.71sec
400m medley: Aimee Willmott (Middlesborough ASC),
   4min 35.94sec

TABLE TENNIS

WORLD CHAMPIONSHIPS 2014: TEAM
Tokyo, Japan, 28 April–5 May

Men's team: China beat Germany 3–1
Women's team: China beat Japan 3–0

ENGLISH NATIONAL CHAMPIONSHIPS 2013–14
Men's singles: Liam Pitchford beat Paul Drinkhall 5–1
Women's singles: Joanna Drinkhall beat Kelly Sibley 4–2
Men's doubles: L. Pitchford and P. Drinkhall beat A. Baggaley
   and D. Knight 3–2
Women's doubles: K. Sibley and J. Drinkhall beat T. Ho and
   M. Tsaptsinos 3–1
Mixed doubles: S. Walker and T. Ho beat D. McBeath and
   E. Vickers 3–0

TENNIS

AUSTRALIAN OPEN CHAMPIONSHIPS 2014
Melbourne, 13–26 January

Men's Singles: Stanislas Wawrinka (Switzerland) beat Rafael
   Nadal (Spain) 6–3, 6–2, 3–6, 6–3
Women's Singles: Li Na (China) beat Dominika Cibulková
   (Slovakia) 7–6, 6–0
Men's Doubles: Łukasz Kubot (Poland) and Robert Lindstedt
   (Sweden) beat Eric Butorac (USA) and Raven Klaasen
   (South Africa) 6–3, 6–3
Women's Doubles: Sara Errani (Italy) and Roberta Vinci (Italy)
   beat Ekaterina Makarova (Russia) and Elena Vesnina
   (Russia) 6–3, 3–6, 7–5
Mixed Doubles: Kristina Mladenovic (France) and Daniel
   Nestor (Canada) beat Sania Mirza (India) and Horia Tecău
   (Romania) 6–3, 6–2

FRENCH OPEN CHAMPIONSHIPS 2014
Paris, 25 May–8 June

Men's Singles: Rafael Nadal (Spain) beat Novak Djokovic (Serbia) 3–6, 7–5, 6–2, 6–4
Women's Singles: Maria Sharapova (Russia) beat Simona Halep (Romania) 6–4, 6–7, 6–4
Men's Doubles: Julien Benneteau (France) and Édouard Roger-Vasselin (France) beat Marcel Granollers (Spain) and Marc López (Spain) 6–3, 7–6
Women's Doubles: Hsieh Su-wei (Chinese Taipei) and Peng Shuai (China) beat Sara Errani (Italy) and Roberta Vinci (Italy) 6–4, 6–1
Mixed Doubles: Anna-Lena Grönefeld (Germany) and Jean-Julien Rojer (Netherlands) beat Julia Görges (Germany) and Nenad Zimonjić (Serbia) 4–6, 6–2, 10–7

ALL-ENGLAND CHAMPIONSHIPS 2014
Wimbledon, 23 June–6 July

Men's Singles: Novak Djokovic (Serbia) beat Roger Federer (Switzerland) 6–7, 6–4, 7–6, 5–7, 6–4
Ladies' Singles: Petra Kvitová (Czech Republic) beat Eugenie Bouchard (Canada) 6–3, 6–0
Men's Doubles: Vasek Pospisil (Canada) and Jack Sock (USA) beat Bob Bryan (USA) and Mike Bryan (USA) 7–6, 6–7, 6–4, 3–6, 7–5
Ladies' Doubles: Sara Errani (Italy) and Roberta Vinci (Italy) beat Tímea Babos (Hungary) and Kristina Mladenovic (France) 6–1, 6–3
Mixed Doubles: Nenad Zimonjić (Serbia) and Samantha Stosur (Australia) beat Max Mirnyi (Belarus) and Chan Hao-ching (Taipei) 6–4, 6–2

US OPEN CHAMPIONSHIPS 2014
New York, 25 August–8 September

Men's Singles: Marin Cilic (Croatia) beat Kei Nishikori (Japan) 6–3, 6–3, 6–3
Women's Singles: Serena Williams (USA) beat Caroline Wozniacki (Denmark) 6–3, 6–3
Men's Doubles: Bob Bryan and Mike Bryan (USA) beat Marcel Granollers and Marc Lopez (Spain) 6–3, 6–4
Women's Doubles: Ekaterina Makarova and Elena Vesnina (Russia) beat Martina Hingis (Switzerland) and Flavia Pennetta (Italy) 2–6, 6–3, 6–2
Mixed Doubles: Sania Mirza (India) and Bruno Soares (Brazil) beat Abigail Spears (USA) and Santiago Gonzalez (Mexico) 6–1, 2–6, 11–9

TEAM CHAMPIONSHIPS
Davis Cup final 2013: Czech Republic beat Serbia 3–2
Fed Cup final 2013: Italy beat Russia 4–0

2014 (XXII) WINTER OLYMPICS

Sochi, Russia, 7–23 February

ALPINE SKIING

MEN
Downhill: Matthias Mayer (Austria), 2min 06.23sec
Slalom: Mario Matt (Austria), 1min 41.84sec
Giant Slalom: Ted Ligety (USA), 2min 45.29sec
Super G Slalom: Kjetil Jansrud (Norway), 1min 18.14sec
Combination: Sandro Viletta (Switzerland), 2min 45.20sec

WOMEN
Downhill: Tina Maze (Slovenia), 1min 41.57sec
Slalom: Mikaela Shiffrin (USA), 1min 44.54sec
Giant Slalom: Tina Maze (Slovenia), 2min 36.87sec
Super G Slalom: Anna Fenninger (Austria), 1min 25.52sec
Combination: Maria Hoefl-Riesch (Germany), 2min 34.62sec

BIATHLON

MEN
10km Sprint: Ole Einar Bjoerndalen (Norway), 24min 33.5sec
12.5km Pursuit: Martin Fourcade (France), 33min 48.6sec
15km Mass Start: Emil Hegle Svendsen (Norway), 42min 29.1sec
20km: Martin Fourcade (France), 49min 31.7sec
4 × 7.5km Relay: Russia, 1hr 12min 15.9sec

WOMEN
7.5km Sprint: Anastazia Kuzmina (Slovakia), 21min 06.8sec
10km Pursuit: Darya Domracheva (Belarus), 29min 30.7sec
12.5km Mass Start: Darya Domracheva (Belarus), 35min 25.6sec
15km: Darya Domracheva (Belarus), 43min 19.6sec
4 × 6km Relay: Ukraine, 1hr 10min 02.5sec

MIXED
Relay: Norway, 1hr 09min 17.0sec

BOBLSEIGH

MEN
Two-man: Russia, 3min 45.39sec
Four-man: Russia, 3min 40.60sec

WOMEN
Two-woman: Canada, 3min 50.61sec

CROSS COUNTRY SKIING

MEN
15km: Dario Cologna (Switzerland), 38min 29.7sec
30km Skiathlon: Dario Cologna (Switzerland), 1hr 08min 15.4sec
50km Freestyle: Alexander Legov (Russia), 1hr 46min 55.2sec
4 × 10km Relay: Sweden, 1hr 28min 42.0sec
Sprint: Ola Vigen Hattestad (Norway), 3min 38.39sec
Team Sprint: Finland, 23min 14.89sec

WOMEN
10km: Justyna Kowalczyk (Poland), 28min 17.8sec
15km Skiathon: Marit Bjoergen (Norway), 38min 33.6sec
30km Freestyle: Marit Bjoergen (Norway), 1hr 11min 05.2sec
4 × 5km Relay: Sweden, 53min 02.7sec
Sprint: Maiken Caspersen Falla (Norway), 2min 32.07sec
Team Sprint: Norway, 16min 04.5sec

CURLING
Men: Canada
Women: Canada

FIGURE SKATING
Men: Yazuru Hanyu (Japan), 280.09pts
Women: Adelina Sotnikova (Russia), 224.59pts
Pairs Mixed: Tatiana Volosozhar and Maxim Trankov (Russia), 236.86pts
Ice Dancing Mixed: Meryl Davis and Charlie White (USA), 195.52pts
Team Mixed: Russia, 75pts

FREESTYLE SKIING

MEN
Moguls: Alexandre Bilodeau (Canada), 26.31pts
Aerials: Anton Kushnir (Belarus), 134.5pts
Halfpipe: David Wise (USA), 92pts
Slopestyle: Joss Christensen (USA), 95.8pts
Ski Cross: Jean Frederic Chapuis (France)

WOMEN
Moguls: Justine Dufour-Lapointe (Canada), 22.44pts
Aerials: Alla Tsuper (Belarus), 98.01pts
Halfpipe: Maddie Bowman (USA), 89pts
Slopestyle: Dara Howell (Canada), 94.2pts
Ski Cross: Marielle Thompson (Canada)

ICE HOCKEY
Men: Canada
Women: Canada

LUGE
Men's Singles: Felix Loch (Germany), 3min 27.526sec
Men's Doubles: Germany, 1min 38.933sec
Women's Singles: Natalie Geisenberger (Germany), 3min 19.768sec
Mixed Relay: Germany, 2min 45.649sec

NORDIC COMBINED
Individual Large Hill: Joergen Graabak (Norway), 23min 27.5sec
Individual Normal Hill: Eric Frenzel (Germany), 23min 50.2sec
Team 4 x 5km: Norway, 47min 13.5sec

SHORT TRACK SPEED SKATING

MEN
500m: Victor An (Russia), 41.312sec
1000m: Victor An (Russia), 1min 25.325sec
1500m: Charles Hamelin (Canada), 2min 14.985sec
5km Relay: Russia, 6min 42.10sec

WOMEN
500m: Li Jianrou (China), 45.263sec
1000m: Seung-Hi Park (Rep. of Korea), 1min 30.76sec
1500m: Zhou Yang (China), 2min 19.140sec
3km Relay: Rep. of Korea, 4min 09.5sec

SKELETON
Men: Alexander Tretiakov (Russia), 3min 44.29sec
Women: Elizabeth Yarnold (Great Britain), 3min 52.89sec

SKI JUMPING

MEN
Normal Hill: Kamil Stoch (Poland), 278.0pts
Large Hill: Kamil Stoch (Poland), 278.7pts
Team: Germany, 1,041.1pts

WOMEN
Normal Hill: Carina Vogt (Germany), 247.4pts

SNOWBOARDING

MEN
Halfpipe: Iouri Podladtchikov (Switzerland), 94.75pts
Slopestyle: Sage Kotsenburg (USA), 93.5pts
Snowboard Cross: Pierre Vaultier (France)
Parallel Giant Slalom: Vic Wild (Russia)
Parallel Slalom: Vic Wild (Russia)

WOMEN
Halfpipe: Kaitlyn Farrington (USA), 91.75pts
Slopestyle: Jamie Anderson (USA), 95.25pts
Snowboard Cross: Eva Samkova (Czech Rep.)
Parallel Giant Slalom: Patrizia Kummer (Switzerland)
Parallel Slalom: Julia Dujmovits (Austria)

SPEED SKATING

MEN
500m: Michael Mulder (Netherlands), 69.31sec
1000m: Stefan Groothuis (Netherlands), 1min 08.39sec
1500m: Zbigniew Brodka (Poland), 1min 45.006sec
5000m: Sven Kramer (Netherlands), 6min 10.76sec
10km: Jorrit Bergsma (Netherlands), 12min 44.45sec
Team Pursuit: Netherlands, 3min 37.71sec

WOMEN
500m: Lee Sang-Hwa (Rep. of Korea), 74.70sec
1000m: Zhang Hong (China), 1min 14.02sec
1500m: Jorien Ter Mors (Netherlands), 1min 53.51sec
3000m: Ireen Wust (Netherlands), 4min 00.34sec
5000m: Martina Sablikova (Czech Rep.), 6min 51.5sec
Team Pursuit: Netherlands, 2min 58.05sec

MEDAL TABLE

Country	G	S	B	Total
Russia	13	11	9	33
Norway	11	5	10	26
Canada	10	10	5	25
USA	9	7	12	28
Netherlands	8	7	9	24
Germany	8	6	5	19
Switzerland	6	3	2	11
Belarus	5	0	1	6
Austria	4	8	5	17
France	4	4	7	15
Poland	4	1	1	6
China	3	4	2	9
Rep. of Korea	3	3	2	8
Sweden	2	7	6	15
Czech Republic	2	4	2	8
Slovenia	2	2	4	8
Japan	1	4	3	8
Finland	1	3	1	5
Great Britain	1	1	2	4
Ukraine	1	0	1	2
Slovakia	1	0	0	1
Italy	0	2	6	8
Latvia	0	2	2	4
Australia	0	2	1	3
Croatia	0	1	0	1
Kazakhstan	0	0	1	1

2014 (XX) COMMONWEALTH GAMES

Glasgow, Scotland, 23 July–3 August

ATHLETICS

MEN

100m: Kemar Bailey-Cole (Jamaica), 10.00sec
110m Hurdles: Andrew Riley (Jamaica), 13.32sec
200m: Rasheed Dwyer (Jamaica), 20.14sec
400m: Kirani James (Grenada), 44.24sec
400m Hurdles: Cornel Fredericks (South Africa), 48.50sec
800m: Nijel Amos (Botswana), 1min 45.18sec
1500m: James Kiplagat Magut (Kenya), 3min 39.31sec
3000m St: Jonathan Ndiku (Kenya), 8min 10.44sec
5000m: Caleb Mwangangi Ndiku (Kenya), 13min 12.07sec
10,000m: Moses Kipsiro (Uganda), 27min 56.11sec
4 × 100m Relay: Jamaica, 37.58sec
4 × 400m Relay: England, 3min 00.46sec
Marathon: Michael Shelley (Australia), 2hr 11min 15sec
Decathlon: Damian Warner (Canada), 8,282pts
High Jump: Derek Drouin (Canada), 2.31m
Long Jump: Gregory Rutherford (England), 8.20m
Triple Jump: Khotso Mokoena (South Africa), 17.20m
Discus: Vikas Shive Gowda (India), 63.64m
Hammer: Jim Steacy (Canada), 74.16m
Javelin: Julius Kiplangat Yego (Kenya), 83.87m
Shot: O'Dayne Richards (Jamaica), 21.61m
Pole Vault: Steven Lewis (England), 5.55m

MEN'S PARA-SPORT

100m (T37): Fanie van der Merwe (South Africa), 11.65sec
1500m (T54): David Weir (England), 3min 21.67sec
Discus (F42/44): Dan Greaves (England), 59.21m

WOMEN

100m: Blessing Okagbare (Nigeria), 10.85sec
100m Hurdles: Sally Pearson (Australia), 12.67sec
200m: Blessing Okagbare (Nigeria), 22.25sec
400m: Stephanie McPherson (Jamaica), 50.67sec
400m Hurdles: Kaliese Spencer (Jamaica), 54.10sec
800m: Eunice Jepkoech Sum (Kenya), 2min 00.31sec
1500m: Faith Chepngetich Kibiegon (Kenya), 4min 08.94sec
3000m St: Purity Cherotich Kirui (Kenya), 9min 30.36sec
5000m: Mercey Cherono (Kenya), 15min 07.21sec
10,000m: Joyce Chepkirui (Kenya), 32min 09.4sec
4 × 100m Relay: Jamaica, 41.83sec
4 × 400m Relay: Jamaica, 3min 23.82sec
Marathon: Flomena Cheyech Daniel (Kenya), 2hr 26min 45sec
Heptathon: Brianne Theisen-Eaton (Canada), 6,597pts
High Jump: Eleanor Patterson (Australia), 1.94m
Long Jump: Ese Brume (Nigeria), 6.56m
Triple Jump: Kimberly Williams (Jamaica), 14.21m
Discus: Dani Samuels (Australia), 64.88m
Hammer: Sultana Frizell (Canada), 71.97m
Javelin: Kim Mickle (Australia), 65.96m
Shot: Valerie Adams (New Zealand), 19.88m
Pole Vault: Alana Boyd (Australia), 4.50m

WOMEN'S PARA-SPORT

100m (T12): Libby Clegg (Scotland), 12.20sec
1500m (T54): Angela Ballard (Australia), 3min 59.20sec
Long Jump (T37/38): Jodi Elkington (Australia), 4.39m

BADMINTON

Men's Singles: Kashyap Parupalli (India)
Women's Singles: Michelle Li (Canada)
Men's Doubles: Malaysia
Women's Doubles: Malaysia

Mixed Doubles: England
Mixed Team: England

BOWLS

MEN

Singles: Darren Burnett (Scotland)
Pairs: Scotland
Triples: South Africa
Fours: Scotland

WOMEN

Singles: Jo Edwards (New Zealand)
Pairs: South Africa
Triples: England
Fours: South Africa

PARA-SPORT

Mixed Pairs (B2/B3): South Africa
Open Triples (B6/B7/B8): South Africa

BOXING

MEN

Light flyweight (49kg): Paddy Barnes (N. Ireland)
Flyweight (52kg): Andrew Moloney (Australia)
Bantamweight (56kg): Michael Conlan (N. Ireland)
Lightweight (60kg): Charlie Flynn (Scotland)
Light welterweight (64kg): Josh Taylor (Scotland)
Welterweight (69kg): Scott Fitzgerald (England)
Middleweight (75kg): Antony Fowler (England)
Light heavyweight (81kg): David Nyika (New Zealand)
Heavyweight (91kg): Samir El-Mais (Canada)
Super heavyweight (91kg+): Joseph Joyce (England)

WOMEN

Flyweight (48–51kg): Nicola Adams (England)
Lightweight (57–60kg): Shelley Watts (Australia)
Middleweight (69–75kg): Savannah Marshall (England)

CYCLING

MEN

Time Trial: Alex Dowsett (England), 47min 41.8sec
Cross-country: Anton Cooper (New Zealand), 1hr 38min 26sec
Sprint: Sam Webster (New Zealand)
Team Sprint: New Zealand
Keirin: Matthew Glaetzer (Australia)
20km Scratch Race: Shane Archbold (New Zealand)
1000m Time Trial: Scott Sunderland (Australia), 1min 0.675sec
4000m Individual Pursuit: Jack Bobridge (Australia), 4min 19.65sec
4000m Team Pursuit: Australia, 3min 54.851sec
40km Points Race: Thomas Scully (New Zealand), 98pts
Road Race: Geraint Thomas (Wales), 4hr 13min 05sec

MEN'S PARA-SPORT

Sprint (B2) Tandem: Neil Fachie (Scotland)
1000m Time Trial (B2) Tandem: Neil Fachie (Scotland)

WOMEN

Time Trial: Linda Villumsen (New Zealand), 42min 25.5sec
Cross-country: Catharine Pendrel (Canada), 1hr 39min 29sec
Sprint: Stephanie Morton (Australia)
500m Time Trial: Anna Meares (Australia), 33.435sec
3000m Individual Pursuit: Joanna Rowsell (England), 3min 31.615sec
10km Scratch Race: Annette Edmondson (Australia)
25km Points Race: Laura Trott (England), 37pts
Road Race: Lizzie Armitstead (England), 2hr 38min 48sec

WOMEN'S PARA-SPORT
Sprint (B2) Tandem: Sophie Thornhill (England)
1000m Time Trial (B2) Tandem: Sophie Thornhill (England)

DIVING

MEN
1m Springboard: Jack Laugher (England), 449.90pts
3m Springboard: Ooi Tze Liang (Malaysia), 457.60pts
10 Platform: Tom Daley (England), 516.55pts
3m Springboard Synch: England, 431.94pts
10m Platform Synch: Australia, 399.54pts

WOMEN
1m Springboard: Jennifer Abel (Canada), 287.25pts
3m Springboard: Esther Qin (Australia), 347.25pts
10 Platform: Meaghan Benefeito (Canada), 372.65pts
3m Springboard Synch: England, 300.24pts
10m Springboard Synch: Canada, 310.65pts

GYMNASTICS – ARTISTIC

MEN
Team: England, 266.804pts
Individual All-Around: Max Whitlock (England), 90.631pts
Floor: Max Whitlock (England), 15.533pts
Horizontal Bar: Nile Wilson (England), 14.966pts
Parallel Bars: Daniel Purvis (Scotland), 15.533pts
Pommel Horse: Daniel Keatings (Scotland), 16.058pts
Rings: Scott Morgan (Canada), 15.100pts
Vault: Scott Morgan (Canada), 14.733pts

WOMEN
Team: England, 167.555pts
Individual All-Around: Claudia Fragapane (England),
   56.132pts
Beam: Elisabeth Black (Canada), 14.900pts
Floor: Claudia Fragapane (England), 14.541pts
Uneven Bars: Rebecca Downie (England), 14.666pts
Vault: Claudia Fragapane (England), 14.633pts

GYMNASTICS – RHYTHMIC
Team: Canada, 141.450pts
Individual All-Around: Patricia Bezzoubenko (Canada),
   59.175pts
Hoop: Patricia Bezzoubenko (Canada), 14.800pts
Ball: Patricia Bezzoubenko (Canada), 15.250pts
Clubs: Patricia Bezzoubenko (Canada), 15.350pts
Ribbon: Francesca Jones (Wales), 14.500pts

HOCKEY
Men: Australia
Women: Australia

JUDO

MEN
-60kg: Ashley Mckenzie (England)
-66kg: Colin Oates (England)
-73kg: Danny Williams (England)
-81kg: Owen Livesey (England)
-90kg: Zack Piontek (South Africa)
-100kg: Euan Burton (Scotland)
100kg+: Christopher Sherrington (SCotland)

WOMEN
-48kg: Kimberley Renicks (Scotland)
-52kg: Louise Renicks (Scotland)
-57kg: Nekoda Davis (England)

-63kg: Sarah Clark (Scotland)
-70kg: Megan Fletcher (England)
-78kg: Natalie Powell (Wales)
78kg+: Sarah Adlington (Scotland)

NETBALL
Women: Australia

RUGBY SEVENS
Men: South Africa

SHOOTING

MEN
10m Air Pistol: Daniel Repacholi (Australia), 199.5pts
10m Air Rifle: Abhinav Bindra (India), 205.3pts
25m Rapid Fire Pistol: David Chapman (Australia), 23pts
50m Pistol: Jitu Rai (India), 194.1pts
50m Rifle Prone: Warren Potent (Australia), 204.3pts
50m Rifle 3 Positions: Daniel Rivers (England), 452.9pts
Skeet: Georgios Achilleos (Cyprus)
Trap: Adam Vella (Australia)
Double Trap: Steven Scott (England)

WOMEN
10m Air Pistol: Shun Xie Teo (Singapore), 198.6pts
10m Air Rifle: Apurvi Chandela (India), 206.7pts
25m Pistol: Rahi Sarnobat (India), 8pts
50m Rifle Prone: Sally Johnston (New Zealand), 620.7pts
50m Rifle 3 Positions: Jasmine Ser (Singapore), 449.1pts
Skeet: Laura Coles (Australia)
Trap: Laetisha Scanlan (Australia)
Double Trap: Charlotte Kerwood (England)

QUEEN'S PRIZE
Individual: David Luckman (England)
Pairs: England

SQUASH
Men's Singles: Nick Matthew (England)
Men's Doubles: Australia
Women's Singles: Nicol David (Malaysia)
Women's Doubles: India
Mixed Doubles: Australia

SWIMMING

MEN
50m Backstroke: Ben Treffers (Australia), 24.67sec
50m Breaststroke: Cameron van der Burgh (South Africa),
   26.76sec
50m Butterfly: Benjamin Proud (England), 22.93sec
50m Freestyle: Benjamin Proud (England), 21.92sec
100m Backstroke: Chris Walker-Hebborn (England), 53.12sec
100m Breaststroke: Adam Peaty (England), 58.94sec
100m Butterfly: Chad le Clos (South Africa), 51.29sec
100m Freestyle: James Magnussen (Australia), 48.11sec
200m Backstroke: Mitch Larkin (Australia), 1min 55.83sec
200m Breaststroke: Ross Murdoch (Scotland), 2min 07.30sec
200m Butterfly: Chad le Clos (South Africa), 1min 55.07sec
200m Individual Medley: Daniel Tranter (Australia), 1min
   57.83sec
200m Freestyle: Thomas Fraser-Holmes (Australia), 1min
   45.00sec
400m Freestyle: Ryan Cochrane (Canada), 3min 43.46sec
400m Individual Medley: Daniel Wallace (Scotland),
   4min 11.20sec
1500m Freestyle: Ryan Cochrane (Canada), 14min 44.03sec
4 × 100m Freestyle Relay: Australia, 3min 13.44sec

4 × 100m Medley Relay: England, 3min 31.51sec
4 × 200m Freestyle Relay: Australia, 7min 07.38sec

WOMEN
50m Backstroke: Georgia Davies (Wales), 27.56sec
50m Breaststroke: Leiston Pickett (Australia), 30.59sec
50m Butterfly: Francesca Halsall (England), 25.20sec
50m Freestyle: Francesca Halsall (England), 23.96sec
100m Backstroke: Emily Seebohm (Australia), 59.37sec
100m Breaststroke: Sophie Taylor (England), 1min 06.35sec
100m Butterfly: Katerine Savard (Canada), 57.40sec
100m Freestyle: Cate Campbell (Australia), 52.68sec
200m Backstroke: Belinda Hocking (Australia), 2min 07.24sec
200m Breaststroke: Taylor McKeown (Australia), 2min 22.36sec
200m Butterfly: Audrey Lacroix (Canada), 2min 07.61sec
200m Freestyle: Emma McKeon (Australia), 1min 55.7sec
200m Individual Medley: Siobhan O'Connor (England), 2min 08.20sec
400m Freestyle: Lauren Boyle (New Zealand), 4min 04.47sec
400m Individual Medley: Hannah Miley (Scotland), 4min 31.76sec
800m Freestyle: Jazz Carlin (Wales), 8min 18.11sec
4 × 100m Freestyle Relay: Australia, 3min 30.98sec
4 × 100m Medley Relay: Australia, 3min 56.23sec
4 × 200m Freestyle Relay: Australia, 7min 49.90sec

MEN'S PARA-SPORT
100m Freestyle (S9): Rowan Crothers (Australia), 54.58sec
200m Individual Medley (SM8): Oliver Hynd (England), 2min 22.86sec
200m Freestyle (S14): Daniel Fox (Australia), 1min 57.89sec

WOMEN'S PARA-SPORT
100m Freestyle (S8): Maddison Elliott (Australia), 1min 05.32sec
100m Breaststroke (SB9): Sophie Pascoe (New Zealand), 1min 19.36sec
200m Individual Medley (SM10): Sophie Pascoe (New Zealand), 2min 27.74sec

TABLE TENNIS
Men's Singles: Jian Zhan (Singapore)
Men's Doubles: Singapore
Men's Team: Singapore
Women's Singles: Tianwei Feng (Singapore)
Women's Doubles: Singapore
Women's Team: Singapore
Mixed Doubles: England

TRIATHLON
Men: Alistrair Brownlee (England), 1hr 48min 50sec
Women: Jodie Stimpson (England), 1hr 58min 56sec
Mixed Team: England, 1hr 13min 24sec

WEIGHTLIFTING

MEN
56kg: Sukhen Dey (India), 248kg
62kg: Dimitris Minasidis (Cyprus), 276kg
69kg: Mohd Hafifi Mansor (Malaysia), 305kg
77kg: Sathish Sivalingam (India), 328kg
85kg: Richard Patterson (New Zealand), 335kg
94kg: Steven Kukuna Kari (Papua New Guinea), 349kg
105kg: David Katoatau (Kiribati), 348kg
105kg+: George Kobaladze (Canada), 400kg

WOMEN
48kg: Sanjita Khumukcham (India), 173kg
53kg: Dika Toua (Papua New Guinea), 193kg

58kg: Zoe Smith (England), 210kg
63kg: Olauwatoyin Adesanmi (Nigeria), 207kg
69kg: Marie Fegue (Cameroon), 234kg
75kg: Marie-Eve Beauchemin-Nadeau (Canada), 250kg
75kg+: Maryam Usman (Nigeria), 280kg

PARA-SPORT POWERLIFTING
Men's Lightweight: Paul Kehinde (Nigeria)
Men's Heavyweight: Abdulazeez Ibrahim (Nigeria)
Women's Lightweight: Esther Oyema (Nigeria)
Women's Heavyweight: Loveline Obiji (Nigeria)

WRESTLING

MEN
57kg: Amit Kumar (India)
61kg: David Tremblay (Canada)
65kg: Yogeshwar Dutt (India)
74kg: Sushil Kumar (India)
86kg: Tamerian Tagziev (Canada)
97kg: Arjun Gill (Canada)
125kg: Korey Jarvis (Canada)

WOMEN
48kg: Vinesh Phogat (India)
53kg: Odunayo Adekuoroye (Nigeria)
55kg: Babita Kumari (India)
58kg: Aminat Adeniyi (Nigeria)
63kg: Danielle Lappage (Canada)
69kg: Dori Yeats (Canada)
75kg: Erica Wiebe (Canada)

MEDAL TABLE

Country	G	S	B	Total
England	58	59	57	174
Australia	49	42	46	137
Canada	32	16	34	82
Scotland	19	15	19	53
India	15	30	19	64
New Zealand	14	14	17	45
South Africa	13	10	17	40
Nigeria	11	11	14	36
Kenya	10	10	5	25
Jamaica	10	4	8	22
Singapore	8	5	4	17
Malaysia	6	7	6	19
Wales	5	11	20	36
Cyprus	2	4	2	8
Northern Ireland	2	3	7	12
Papua New Guinea	2	0	0	2
Cameroon	1	3	3	7
Uganda	1	0	4	5
Grenada	1	0	1	2
Botswana	1	0	0	1
Kiribati	1	0	0	1
Trinidad and Tobago	0	3	5	8
Pakistan	0	3	1	4
Bahamas	0	2	1	3
Samoa	0	2	1	3
Namibia	0	1	2	3
Mauritius	0	1	1	2
Bangladesh	0	1	0	1
Isle of Man	0	1	0	1
Nauru	0	1	0	1
Sri Lanka	0	1	0	1
Ghana	0	0	2	2
Zambia	0	0	2	2
Barbados	0	0	1	1
Fiji	0	0	1	1
St Lucia	0	0	1	1

SPORTS RECORDS

ATHLETICS WORLD RECORDS
As at 1 September 2014

All the world records given below have been accepted by the International Amateur Athletic Federation. Fully automatic timing to 1/100th second is mandatory up to and including 400 metres. For distances up to and including 10,000 metres, records will be accepted to 1/100th second if timed automatically, and to 1/10th if hand timing is used.

MEN

TRACK EVENTS	hr	min	sec
100m			9.58
Usain Bolt (Jamaica), 2009			
200m			19.19
Usain Bolt (Jamaica), 2009			
400m			43.18
Michael Johnson (USA), 1999			
800m		1	40.91
David Rudisha (Kenya), 2012			
1000m		2	11.96
Noah Ngeny (Kenya), 1999			
1500m		3	26.00
Hicham El Guerrouj (Morocco), 1998			
1 mile		3	43.13
Hicham El Guerrouj (Morocco), 1999			
2000m		4	44.79
Hicham El Guerrouj (Morocco), 1999			
3000m		7	20.67
Daniel Komen (Kenya), 1996			
5000m		12	37.35
Kenenisa Bekele (Ethiopia), 2004			
10,000m		26	17.53
Kenenisa Bekele (Ethiopia), 2005			
20,000m		56	26.0
Haile Gebrselassie (Ethiopia), 2007			
21,285m	1	00	00.0
Haile Gebrselassie (Ethiopia), 2007			
25,000m	1	12	25.4
Moses Mosop (Kenya), 2011			
30,000m	1	26	47.4
Moses Mosop (Kenya), 2011			
Marathon	2	03	23
Wilson Kipsang Kiprotich (Kenya), 2013			
110m Hurdles (1.07m)			12.80
Aries Merritt (USA), 2012			
400m Hurdles (0.97m)			46.78
Kevin Young (USA), 1992			
3000m Steeplechase		7	53.63
Saif Saeed Shaheen (Qatar), 2004			

RELAYS		min	sec
4 × 100m			36.84
Jamaica, 2012			
4 × 200m		1	18.63
Jamaica, 2014			
4 × 400m		2	54.29
USA, 1993			
4 × 800m		7	02.43
Kenya, 2006			
4 × 1,500m		14	22.22
Kenya, 2014			

FIELD EVENTS	m	ft	in
High Jump	2.45	8	0½
Javier Sotomayor (Cuba), 1993			
Pole Vault	6.14	20	1¾
Sergei Bubka (Ukraine), 1994			
Long Jump	8.95	29	4½
Mike Powell (USA), 1991			
Triple Jump	18.29	60	0¼
Jonathan Edwards (Great Britain), 1995			
Shot	23.12	75	10¼
Randy Barnes (USA), 1990			
Discus	74.08	243	0
Jürgen Schult (GDR), 1986			
Hammer	86.74	284	7
Yuriy Sedykh (USSR), 1986			
Javelin	98.48	323	1
Jan Zelezny (Czech Rep.), 1996			
Decathlon†			9,039pts
Ashton Eaton (USA), 2012			

† Ten events comprising 100m, long jump, shot, high jump, 400m, 110m hurdles, discus, pole vault, javelin, 1500m

WOMEN

TRACK EVENTS	hr	min	sec
100m			10.49
Florence Griffith-Joyner (USA), 1988			
200m			21.34
Florence Griffith-Joyner (USA), 1988			
400m			47.60
Marita Koch (GDR), 1985			
800m		1	53.28
Jarmila Kratochvilova (Czechoslovakia), 1983			
1000m		2	28.98
Svetlana Masterkova (Russia), 1996			
1500m		3	50.46
Qu Yunxia (China), 1993			
1 mile		4	12.56
Svetlana Masterkova (Russia), 1996			
2000m		5	25.36
Sonia O'Sullivan (Ireland), 1994			
3000m		8	06.11
Wang Junxia (China), 1993			
5000m		14	11.15
Tirunesh Dibaba (Ethiopia), 2008			
10,000m		29	31.78
Wang Junxia (China), 1993			
20,000m	1	5	26.6
Tegla Loroupe (Kenya), 2000			
18,517	1	00	00.0
Dire Tune (Ethiopia), 2008			
25,000m	1	27	05.9
Tegla Loroupe (Kenya), 2002			
30,000m	1	45	50.0
Tegla Loroupe (Kenya), 2003			
Marathon	2	15	25
Paula Radcliffe (Great Britain), 2003			
100m Hurdles (0.84m)			12.21
Yordanka Donkova (Bulgaria), 1988			
400m Hurdles (0.76m)			52.34
Yuliya Pechonkina (Russia), 2003			

	8	58.81
3000m Steeplechase		
Gulnara Galkina (Russia), 2008		

RELAYS	*min*	*sec*
4 × 100m		40.82
USA, 2012		
4 × 200m	1	27.46
USA, 2000		
4 × 400m	3	15.17
USSR, 1988		
4 × 800m	7	50.17
USSR, 1984		

FIELD EVENTS	*m*	*ft*	*in*
High Jump	2.09	6	10¼
Stefka Kostadinova (Bulgaria), 1987			
Pole Vault	5.06	16	7¼
Yelena Isinbayeva (Russia), 2009			
Long Jump	7.52	24	8¼
Galina Chistyakova (USSR), 1988			
Triple Jump	15.50	50	10¼
Inessa Kravets (Ukraine), 1995			
Shot	22.63	74	3
Natalya Lisovskaya (USSR), 1987			
Discus	76.80	252	0
Gabriele Reinsch (GDR), 1988			
Hammer	79.58	261	1
Anita Wlodarczyk (Poland), 2014			
Javelin	72.28	237	2
Barbora Spotakova (Czech Rep.), 2008			
Heptathlon†			7,291pts
Jackie Joyner-Kersee (USA), 1988			

† Seven events comprising 100m hurdles, shot, high jump, 200m, long jump, javelin, 800m

ATHLETICS NATIONAL (UK) RECORDS
As at 1 September 2014

Records set anywhere by athletes eligible to represent Great Britain and Northern Ireland.

MEN

TRACK EVENTS	*hr*	*min*	*sec*
100m			9.87
Linford Christie, 1993			
200m			19.87
John Regis, 1994			
400m			44.36
Iwan Thomas, 1997			
800m		1	41.73
Sebastian Coe, 1981			
1000m		2	12.18
Sebastian Coe, 1981			
1500m		3	28.81
Mohamed Farah, 2013			
1 mile		3	46.32
Steve Cram, 1985			
2000m		4	51.39
Steve Cram, 1985			
3000m		7	32.79
David Moorcroft, 1982			
5000m		12	53.11
Mohamed Farah, 2011			
10,000m		26	46.57
Mohamed Farah, 2011			
20,000m		57	28.7
Carl Thackery, 1990			
20,855m	1	00	00.0
Carl Thackery, 1993			
25,000m	1	15	22.6
Ron Hill, 1965			
30,000m	1	31	30.4
Jim Alder, 1970			
Marathon	2	07	13
Steve Jones, 1985			
3000m Steeplechase		8	07.96
Mark Rowland, 1988			
110m Hurdles			12.91
Colin Jackson, 1993			
400m Hurdles			47.82
Kriss Akabusi, 1992			

RELAYS	*min*	*sec*
4 × 100m		37.73
GB team, 1999		
4 × 200m	1	21.29
GB team, 1989		
4 × 400m	2	56.60
GB team, 1996		
4 × 800m	7	03.89
GB team, 1982		

FIELD EVENTS	*m*	*ft*	*in*
High Jump	2.37	7	9¼
Steve Smith, 1993			
Robbie Grabarz, 2012			
Pole Vault	5.82	19	1
Steven Lewis, 2012			
Long Jump	8.51	27	11
Greg Rutherford, 2014			
Triple Jump	18.29	60	0¼
Jonathan Edwards, 1995			
Shot	21.92	71	11
Carl Myerscough, 2003			
Discus	68.24	223	10
Lawrence Okoye, 2012			
Hammer	77.54	254	5
Martin Girvan, 1984			
Javelin	91.46	300	1
Steve Backley, 1992			
Decathlon			8,847pts
Daley Thompson, 1984			

WALKING (TRACK)	*hr*	*min*	*sec*
20,000m	1	23	26.5
Ian McCombie, 1990			
30,000m	2	19	18
Christopher Maddocks, 1984			
50,000m	4	05	44.6
Paul Blagg, 1990			
26,037m	2	00	00.0
Ron Wallwork, 1971			

WOMEN

TRACK EVENTS	*min*	*sec*
100m		11.05
Montell Douglas, 2008		
200m		22.10
Kathy Cook, 1984		
400m		49.41
Christine Ohuruogu, 2013		
800m	1	56.21
Kelly Holmes, 1995		
1500m	3	57.90
Kelly Holmes, 2004		
1 mile	4	17.57
Zola Budd, 1985		

	min	sec
3000m	8	22.20
Paula Radcliffe, 2002		
5000m	14	29.11
Paula Radcliffe, 2004		
10,000m	30	01.09
Paula Radcliffe, 2002		
Marathon	2 15	25
Paula Radcliffe, 2003		
100m Hurdles		12.54
Jessica Ennis-Hill, 2012		
400m Hurdles		52.74
Sally Gunnell, 1993		
3000m Steeplechase	9	24.24
Barbara Parker, 2012		

RELAYS	min	sec
4 × 100m		42.21
GB team, 2014		
4 × 200m	1	29.61
GB team, 2014		
4 × 400m	3	20.04
GB team, 2007		
4 × 800m	8	13.46
GB team, 2013		

FIELD EVENTS	m	ft	in
High Jump	1.96	6	5
Isobel Pooley, 2014			
Pole Vault	4.71	15	6
Holly Bleasdale, 2012			
Long Jump	6.95	22	8
Shara Proctor, 2012			
Triple Jump	15.15	49	8½
Ashia Hansen, 1997			
Shot	19.36	63	6¼
Judy Oakes, 1988			
Discus	67.48	221	5
Margaret Ritchie, 1981			
Hammer	72.97	239	4
Sophie Hitchon, 2013			
Javelin	66.17	217	1
Goldie Sayers, 2012			
Heptathlon			6,955pts
Jessica Ennis-Hill, 2012			

SWIMMING WORLD RECORDS
As at May 2014

MEN	min	sec
50m Freestyle		20.91
Cesar Cielo Filho (Brazil), 2009		
100m Freestyle		46.91
Cesar Cielo Filho (Brazil), 2009		
200m Freestyle	1	42.00
Paul Biedermann (Germany), 2009		
400m Freestyle	3	40.07
Paul Biedermann (Germany), 2009		
800m Freestyle	7	32.12
Zhang Lin (China), 2009		
1,500m Freestyle	14	31.02
Sun Yang (China), 2012		
50m Breaststroke		26.67
Cameron Van Der Burgh (South Africa), 2009		
100m Breaststroke		58.46
Cameron Van Der Burgh (South Africa), 2012		

	min	sec
200m Breaststroke	2	07.01
Akihiro Yamaguchi (Japan), 2012		
50m Butterfly		22.43
Rafael Munoz (Spain), 2009		
100m Butterfly		49.82
Michael Phelps (USA), 2009		
200m Butterfly	1	51.51
Michael Phelps (USA), 2009		
50m Backstroke		24.04
Liam Tancock (Great Britain), 2009		
100m Backstroke		51.94
Aaron Peirsol (USA), 2009		
200m Backstroke	1	51.92
Aaron Peirsol (USA), 2009		
200m Medley	1	54.00
Ryan Lochte (USA), 2011		
400m Medley	4	03.84
Michael Phelps (USA), 2008		
4 × 100m Freestyle relay	3	08.24
USA, 2008		
4 × 200m Freestyle relay	6	58.55
USA, 2009		
4 × 100m Medley relay	3	27.28
USA, 2009		

WOMEN	min	sec
50m Feestyle		23.73
Britta Steffen (Germany), 2009		
100m Freestyle		52.07
Britta Steffen (Germany), 2009		
200m Freestyle	1	52.98
Federica Pellegrini (Italy), 2009		
400m Freestyle	3	59.15
Federica Pellegrini (Italy), 2009		
800m Freestyle	8	13.86
Katie Ledecky (USA), 2013		
1,500m Freestyle	15	36.53
Katie Ledecky (USA), 2013		
50m Breaststroke		29.48
Ruta Meilutyte (Lithuania), 2013		
100m Breaststroke	1	04.35
Ruta Meilutyte (Lithuania), 2013		
200m Breaststroke	2	19.11
Rikke Moeller-Pedersen (Denmark), 2013		
50m Butterfly		25.07
Therese Alshammar (Sweden), 2009		
100m Butterfly		55.98
Dana Vollmer (USA), 2012		
200m Butterfly	2	01.81
Liu Zigi (China), 2009		
50m Backstroke		27.06
Zhao Jing (China), 2009		
100m Backstroke		58.12
Gemma Spofforth (Great Britain), 2009		
200m Backstroke	2	04.06
Missy Franklin (USA), 2012		
200m Medley	2	06.15
Ariana Kukors (USA), 2009		
400m Medley	4	28.43
Ye Shiwen (China), 2012		
4 × 100m Freestyle relay	3	31.72
Netherlands, 2009		
4 × 200m Freestyle relay	7	42.08
China, 2009		
4 × 100m Medley relay	3	52.05
USA, 2012		

THEATRE

Matt Trueman

VINTAGE OR DECAYING?

On 19 December 2013, approximately half an hour into a performance of *The Curious Incident of the Dog in the Night-Time* in the West End, the Apollo Theatre's ceiling collapsed. Roughly 10m² of ornate plasterwork and masonry fell into the stalls, leaving 76 theatregoers injured. While not as severe as initial rumours suggested, the incident came as a major jolt to the industry. Commentators leapt to decry the state of the West End's Victorian theatres, with many questioning the fruits of the restoration levy added to every ticket. Only three months earlier, a matinee performance of *Top Hat* at the Aldwych had been abandoned after plasterwork from the proscenium arch fell onto the stage.

By March, it had been established that the 'principal cause was the deterioration of wadding ties which supported the ceiling'. Personal injury claims were expected to top £1m, while the National – which withdrew *Curious Incident,* one of its biggest hits, from the theatre and re-opened it, in July, at the Gielgud Theatre next door – could also claim for lost earnings. Investigations will likely stretch into 2016.

Architecture was not the only thing under scrutiny. When three major musicals closed within months of opening, some decreed the West End a spent force. Andrew Lloyd Webber's latest, *Stephen Ward*, about the Profumo Scandal, lasted only four months – a catastrophe by his standards. Even *Love Never Dies* managed a year and a half. 'I haven't had a hit in 20 years', the composer half-joked to *The Telegraph*. Lloyd Webber's former lyricist Tim Rice fared little better: his staid adaptation of *From Here to Eternity* limped to five months before shuttering. With two musical theatre legends misfiring, it felt like the end of an era.

They were not alone, though. Simon Cowell's much-vaunted £6m *X Factor* musical, *I Can't Sing,* the brainchild of comedian Harry Hill, closed after only six weeks – despite positive reviews proclaiming it a deranged crowd-pleaser. Though it followed a contestant with the saddest of sob stories – orphan, lives in a caravan, grandfather in an iron lung – to *X Factor* success, it was mostly about Hill's trademark surrealist silliness. Two theories behind its failure emerged: the sheer size of the Palladium (2,286 seats) and the musical's intention both to praise Cowell and to bury him.

Three new British musicals; all of them flops. What hope for the future? Tori Amos' long-awaited musical *The Light Princess* also stuttered; too sugary and drawn-out, despite brilliance from Rosalie Craig as the floating royal. Leicester Curve executive Fiona Allan, having seen the theatre's *Water Babies* demolished by critics, called for critical leniency and support. Rice, meanwhile, harrumphed that only jukebox musicals stood a chance: 'They just want old songs repackaged.'

Certainly, musicals that lasted the course had some degree of familiarity. Some 25 years after its premiere, *Miss Saigon* returned, claiming £4.4m in first-day sales. *The Commitments* and *Dirty Rotten Scoundrels* relied on well-known source materials to pull crowds, while Hampstead's Kinks musical *Sunny Afternoon* bagged a commercial transfer. Fresh hope, perhaps, came from Chichester's *The Pajama Game,* the first crowdfunded musical, suggesting a potential new seam of investment. The first new musical funded thus – Julian Fellowes doing *The Wind in the Willows* with George Styles

and Anthony Drewe – is currently in development. The model could revolutionise the commercial sector.

Does it need revolution? Not really. Theatreland mostly felt more vibrant and varied than it had in years; almost a throwback to its post-war zenith. There were stellar revivals of modern classics: Bill Nighy and Carey Mulligan in David Hare's *Skylight* which, with is tussle beneath wealth and welfare, seemed as direct as it did when Nighy first performed it in 1996; Ben Whishaw and Rupert Grint – making his stage debut – led an all-star cast for Jez Butterworth's *Mojo,* in which Soho slicksters seemed more like Lost Boys than gangsters. Meanwhile, there was some decent comedy: expenses scandal satire *The Duck House* provided topicality, star-vehicle romp Jeeves and Wooster instilled anarchy and Dame Edna Everage bade us farewell with *Eat, Pray, Laugh!,* showing Simon Cowell that packing the Palladium is still possible.

Edna wasn't the only Dame to tread the London boards. Angela Lansbury, included in the New Year's Honours List, elevated an otherwise mediocre *Blithe Spirit* with her first London stage performance in four decades. Her spritely Madame Arcati belied her 88 years. It was a far cry from Vanessa Redgrave and James Earl Jones, who played a pensionable Beatrice and Benedick in a doddery *Much Ado About Nothing.* The Old Vic has never seemed older; Earl Jones scarcely remembered his lines, Redgrave could barely be heard. Also past it, apparently, is director Trevor Nunn, whose three offerings – *Fatal Attraction, Relative Values* and *Scenes From a Marriage* – all faltered.

WHERE THERE'S A WILL

Even William Shakespeare made it into the West End with regularity, thanks to directors Michael Grandage and Jamie Lloyd and a selection of populist casting. David Walliams and Sheridan Smith led a trippy *Midsummer Night's Dream* for Grandage that – commendably – aimed at accessibility above all else. Grandage's 14-month season reached a total of 390,000 people, 30 per cent of whom were first-time theatregoers. It closed with Jude Law as Henry V – a classically heroic portrayal, all rousing speeches and bellowed battle cries.

Law also had to battle his way through fans at the stage door each night. He wasn't alone. December was all about starry Shakespeareans. After a Stratford-Upon-Avon start, David Tennant led the Royal Shakespeare Company (RSC) back into the Barbican with his Richard II. Wearing an awful, elfin wig, Tennant took his time with the role, before unleashing that trademark twitchiness and ascending into a brilliant, barefoot Christ-lite figure. At the Donmar Warehouse, almost drowned out by screaming fans, Tom Hiddleston helmed Josie Rourke's stripped-back, bare-brick *Coriolanus.* For some, Hiddleston was too obviously a war-virgin – more public school cadet than battle-hardened commander. For others, though, he went from 'emotionally stunted' to 'killing machine'.

In fact, 2014 sometimes seemed the year of the fan fraternity, with producers wising up to the power of stars' sway over social media. Martin Freeman, playing Richard III for Jamie Lloyd's second Trafalgar Transformed season, was routinely greeted with entrance applause, drowning out his opening speech. Set – somewhat literally – against the 1979 'winter of discontent', Lloyd's production was gung-ho and gory. Clarence was drowned in a fish tank, Lady Anne was strangled by a telephone cord and the front row got warnings about stage blood splatters.

No blood, but a startling moment of violence defined Simon Russell Beale's long-awaited King Lear at the National Theatre. In the initial grip of madness, he battered Adrian Scarborough's Fool to death in a bath. This off-piste deviation was all the more shocking by virtue of the tenderness of their relationship. For while Sam Mendes' Olivier Theatre production aimed for scale, it was its softer side, a delicate treatise on love, that won the day. Russell Beale began as a dictator, clenched and bullet-headed, leaning into a microphone to demand his daughters' love. Then, on the heath, wind-wracked and Christ-like, everything went quiet. Love, as Mendes defined it, meant standing back and watching over. Lear was allowed to babble and Gloucester to find his own way to the 'cliff'. They had space to act freely, without putting themselves at risk, thanks to the devotion of those around them.

Devotion, though, does not get much more ardent than the Globe's latest project: touring Hamlet to every country on the planet. Starting on home turf to mark Shakespeare's 450th birthday, Dominic Dromgoole's production will go on to play in over 200 nations over the next two years. Without a penny of public subsidy, Shakespeare's Globe has become a dominant force under Dromgoole and the past 12 months have, undoubtedly, been its strongest to date. Twelfth Night and Richard III, its 'original practices' double-bill, transferred to Broadway, winning eight Tony nominations that brought Mark Rylance best supporting actor (his third Tony) and Jenny Tiramani the award for best costume design. Jessica Swale's Blue Stockings, about Oxford University's first female undergraduates, was the theatre's first new play to win an Olivier nomination, and Dromgoole announced an ambitious four-strong season of new work themed around war for 2014, with writers including David Eldridge, Howard Brenton, Richard Bean and Simon Armitage. Average capacity for new plays was 71 per cent in 2013 – an astonishing figure for a 1,600 seat theatre; Shakespeare productions played to 96 per cent houses.

However, its crowning achievement was the opening of a second playing space, the Sam Wanamaker Auditorium, an indoor space lit exclusively with candles. It opened in January, with Eileen Atkins' self-penned solo about Ellen Terry, before Dromgoole's shadowy and thrillingly clandestine production of The Duchess of Malfi starring Gemma Arterton. It's an extraordinary space for theatre, intimate and immaculate, with a dim glow that draws the watcher right in. Since then, it's hosted Francis Beaumont's screwball comedy The Knight of the Burning Pestle, the opera L'Ormindo and John Marston's The Malcontent as performed by a company of child actors. Dromgoole announced that he would step down as artistic director in 2016.

SPLIT SUBSIDY

That announcement meant that Dromgoole was among the first to rule himself out of succeeding Nicholas Hytner at the National Theatre (NT) in March 2015. Many others did likewise, including Michael Grandage, Marianne Elliott, Sam Mendes, Danny Boyle and Tom Morris. On 15 October, Rufus Norris was announced as the organisation's sixth artistic director, the first non-Oxbridge graduate to take the role since Laurence Olivier. A loyal lieutenant to Hytner, having been an NT Associate since 2011, the London Road director was greeted by a lengthy standing ovation when staff were told the news.

The National marked its 50th anniversary in 2013, an event celebrated with a series of talks and a one-off gala in the Olivier Theatre, featuring some of the finest alumni and broadcast live on BBC2. Judi Dench returned to her Cleopatra and Maggie Smith to The Beaux Strategem. Simon Russell Beale reprised his Hamlet, and Derek Jacobi and Michael Gambon played a morsel of Pinter's No Man's Land. The night made a case for several revivals: Ralph Fiennes as Pravda's Lambert Le Roux and Andrew Scott and Dominic Cooper in Angels in America merited fresh-mounted productions. There was one sour note: the lack of female playwrights in the line-up, Alecky Blythe being the only example with the inclusion of London Road. The NT's defence was a historical deficit and Hytner's subsequent season announcement, his last, included eight new plays by female dramatists.

At the same press conference, Hytner dismissed the idea of an NT audience: 'There isn't one audience at the National Theatre … There are many audiences.' His programming bore that out more than ever, the primary split being between the temporary Shed Theatre, with its youthful focus, and more classical, conventional work indoors, in the Olivier and the Lyttleton. So much so that Bijan Sheibani's revival of A Taste of Honey, presumably intended to rectify the late Shelagh Stevenson's absence from the National, seemed to be staged in inverted commas, as a knowing piece of vintage.

Its biggest coup came with Richard Bean's phone-hacking farce Great Britain. Announced on a Wednesday, it opened the following Monday, after months of secret rehearsals, pending the outcome of Rebekah Brooks' and Andy Coulson's trials. News of its West End transfer followed two days later. Bean's play starred Billie Piper as Paige Britain, ambitious news editor of the Free Press, intent on hacking her way to the top. Though its plot was outstripped by reality, Great Britain once again proved Bean to be the nation's best comic playwright.

But the energy, time and again, seemed to be in the Shed, which proved a nimble political arena. Tim Price's Protest Song saw Rhys Ifans play a homeless man caught up in the Occupy movement at St Paul's. Nadia Fall's verbatim piece Home looked at the vulnerability of those staying in homeless hostels. The World of Extreme Happiness by Frances Ya-Chu Cowhig – flawed though it was – picked at the foundations on which contemporary Chinese society was built. Nick Payne and Carrie Cracknell devised a piece of feminist agit-prop that reclaimed 'Blurred Lines' from Robin Thicke. Even when it misfired, as with Polly Stenham's misguided post-colonial potshot Hotel, it did so with its heart on its sleeve and all guns blazing. Here was the National Theatre doing what it should: examining the nation and the world beyond.

There was a similar split, albeit less pronounced, at the RSC. Deputy artistic director Erica Whyman re-opened The Other Place, the legendary studio space founded by Buzz Goodbody 40 years earlier, with a 'festival of radical new work' called Midsummer Mischief, four plays by female writers responding to the following statement: 'Well-behaved women seldom make history'. The best, by far, was Alice Birch's Revolt. She said. Revolt again – an extraordinary freeform piece of writing that applied scrutiny to the linguistics of gender politics. Whyman also headed up 'The Roaring Girls' season at the Swan Theatre: three rarely seen Jacobean classics with women at their centre. Lisa Dillon led Dekker and Middleton's anarchic comedy The Roaring Girl, Sharon Small starred in the unattributed Arden of Faversham and Kirsty Bushell and Laura Elphinstone paired up for Webster's The White Devil, after Flamineo was given a sex-change.

And yet all of Stratford's determination to place women centre stage seemed somewhat undermined by the decision to devote the Royal Shakespeare Theatre itself to two of Shakespeare's blokiest works: Henry IV Parts 1 and 2, with Antony Sher as a superlative, aristocratic and exploitative

Falstaff, and *The Two Gentlemen of Verona,* getting its first main-stage run-out in 44 years.

NEW WORK
Arguably the most significantly development of the year, however, was a culture war that seemed to be the fruition of *Three Kingdoms* at the Lyric Hammersmith in 2012. This was the year that British theatre really embraced form and ambition.

It started with the Lyric's own Secret Theatre company, a 20-strong rep ensemble working together while the building underwent refurbishment. Secret Theatre was about a new, process-led model that allowed scope to experiment and fail. Each show would be presented without a title and the first pair opened in September. In one, Billy Seymour played Woyzeck attached to a bungee cord, circling the stage like a mill horse, incapable of escaping. Another wrenched Tennessee Williams' *A Streetcar Named Desire* out of its naturalist habitat. There were bowling balls and frozen joints of meat, balloon clouds and watermelons. It didn't all work, but you'd never seen a *Streetcar* quite like it: all swagger, sweat and Americana, and not a tenement block in sight. New writing followed: Caroline Bird's *Chamber Piece,* an Ortonesque farce about botched state executions, then Hayley Squires' *Glitterland,* which whizzed *The White Devil* with gangland chic. The final show, *A Series of Increasingly Impossible Acts,* was a live-devised game played out afresh each time, with its lead actor drawn from a hat.

Elsewhere, three theatres motored what felt like a theatrical revolution: the Young Vic, easily Britain's best theatre under David Lan, the Almeida and the Royal Court, rejuvenated under new artistic directors Rupert Goold and Vicky Featherstone respectively.

At the former, Ramin Gray and David Greig premiered *The Events,* a play inspired by the shootings at Utoya. It pitted liberalism against cultural isolationism. Claire, a lesbian vicar, runs a multicultural choir that was decimated by a gunman. Attempting to understand his motives and forgive, she becomes obsessed, seeming to see him everywhere. (One actor plays every other part, including her lover.) Greig's genius is to set her up as a symbol of the liberal elite, as removed from her choristers as the killer himself. Also at the Young Vic: Kander and Ebb's final musical *The Scottsboro Boys,* which deploys the framework of a minstrel show to eviscerate the case against the nine young black men sentenced to death in 1931 Alabama over false rape allegations. A West End transfer is due in late 2014.

The crowning glory, though, was Belgian director Ivo van Hove's astonishing staging of *A View From the Bridge.* He had already received widespread acclaim for *Scenes From a Marriage,* an exploded adaptation of Bergman's original that moved its audience as the central couple aged and their marriage disintegrated. Its final scene had three Mariannes and three Johans, swapping partners as if the years had swirled together. His Miller, again, tore through the play's naturalism. Mark Strong played Eddie Carbone on an empty white floor. With no other set, it purified the drama into a concentrated tragedy. The social critique, originally specific to New York's Meatpacking District, seemed all the more universal; immigrant communities packed into cramped ghettos until something gives. The final fatal fight was played under a shower of blood and men became meat.

The Almeida had hit a rich seam even before Goold took over. Michael Attenborough had programmed *Chimerica* and *American Pyscho: the Musical,* in collaboration with Goold's Headlong. The latter starred Matt Smith, in his first stage role since *Doctor Who* and, though it generated overnight queues, it never caught the blank horror of Brett Easton Ellis' novel. Between them was a crisp, compact version of

Henrik Ibsen's *Ghosts* by Richard Eyre, featuring a stand-out (and subsequently award-winning) performance from Lesley Manville as Mrs Alving. Come January, Goold started with Duncan Macmillan and Robert Icke's *1984,* another Headlong import, which shed new light on the surveillance state that seemed all the more prescient following Edward Snowden's revelations. His first premiere, Mike Bartlett's mock-Shakespearean history play *King Charles III,* imagined Charles's ascension to the throne. If it seemed trite, it built a huge head of steam, cutting through assumptions to reveal the real and arcane governing systems and pushing Britain to the brink of civil war. Its success meant four West End transfers out of five, with *Psycho* expected to complete the set.

That record stalled in June with *Mr Burns: a Post-Electric Play.* Already an off-Broadway hit, Anne Washburn's three-act piece imagines America after some disaster, its population more than decimated, its national grid knocked out. Most mainstream critics loathed it, though it found zealous defenders too, mostly online. (There was an overload of American writing in 2013–14: George Brant's monologue about drones, *Grounded,* and Dan O'Brien's knotty look at photojournalism, *The Body of an American,* both at the Gate; David Lindsay-Abaire's *Good People* and Gina Gionfriddo's *Rapture Blister Burn* at the Hampstead; *Other Desert Cities* at the Old Vic and Laurence Boswell's superlative programming at Bath's Ustinov Theatre.)

It felt like the pinnacle of Vicky Featherstone's daring start in Sloane Square. Her first year brought a string of plays that broke the usual 'good dramaturgy' rules. Dennis Kelly's sweeping economic satire *The Ritual Slaughter of Gorge Mastromas* made a Machiavellian out of its modest protagonist, as Gorge lied (and lied) his way to riches. Abby Morgan's *The Mistress Contract,* an adaptation of a real couple's guide to their happy adulterous arrangement, was staid, smug and academic, but became the biggest grossing show in the Court's history. Simon Stephens' *Birdland* followed suit, with a sell-out run, thanks partly to the presence of Andrew Scott (*Sherlock's* Moriarty) as an insanely charismatic rock star, so hell-bent on ascension to rock god status that he forgets his own humanity. Theatre in 2013–14 never let the audience do likewise.

AWARDS

2013 LAURENCE OLIVIER AWARDS
Best Actor – Rory Kinnear for *Othello* at the National Theatre
Best Actress – Lesley Manville for *Ghosts* at the Almeida Theatre and Trafalgar Studios
Best Actor in a Supporting Role – Jack Lowden for *Ghosts* at the Almeida Theatre and Trafalgar Studios
Best Actress in a Supporting Role – Sharon D Clarke for *The Amen Corner* at the National Theatre
Best New Play – *Chimerica* by Lucy Kirkwood at the Almeida and Harold Pinter theatres
Best Revival – *Ghosts* at the Almeida Theatre and Trafalgar Studios
Best Actor in a Musical – Gavin Creel for *The Book of Mormon* at the Prince of Wales Theatre
Best Actress in a Musical – Zrinka Cvitesic for *Sweeney Todd* at the Adelphi Theatre
Best Performance in a Supporting Role in a Musical – Stephen Ashfield for *The Book of Mormon* at the Prince of Wales Theatre
Best New Musical – *The Book of Mormon* at the Prince of Wales Theatre
Best Musical Revival – *Merrily We Roll Along* at the Harold Pinter Theatre
Best New Comedy – *Jeeves & Wooster in Perfect Nonsense* at the Duke of York's Theatre

Best New Dance Production – *Eastman* by Sidi Larbi Cherkaoui & Sadler's Wells for *Puz/zle* at Sadler's Wells

Outstanding Achievement in Dance – Michael Hulls for his body of lighting work including *Ballet Boys – The Talent* at Sadler's Wells

Best New Opera Production – *Les Vêpres Siciliennes* at the Royal Opera House

Outstanding Achievement in Opera – English Touring Opera for its brave and challenging touring productions at the Linbury Studio, Royal Opera House

Outstanding Achievement in an Affiliate Theatre – *Handbagged* at the Tricycle Theatre

Outstanding Achievement in Music – Martin Lowe, Glen Hansard and Markéta Irglová for *Once* at the Phoenix Theatre

Best Entertainment and Family – *The Wind in the Willows* at the Duchess Theatre

Best Director – Lyndsey Turner for *Chimerica* at the Almeida and Harold Pinter theatres

Best Theatre Choreographer – Casey Nicholaw for *The Book of Mormon* at the Prince of Wales Theatre

Best Set Design – Es Devlin for *Chimerica* at the Almeida and Harold Pinter theatres

Best Lighting Design – Paul Pyant and Jon Driscoll for *Charlie and the Chocolate Factory* at the Theatre Royal Drury Lane, Tim Lutkin and Finn Ross for *Chimerica* at the Almeida Theatre and Harold Pinter Theatre

Best Sound Design – Carolyn Downing for *Chimerica* at the Almeida and Harold Pinter theatres, Gareth Owen for *Merrily We Roll Along* at the Harold Pinter Theatre

Best Costume Design – Mark Thompson for *Charlie and the Chocolate Factory* at the Theatre Royal Drury Lane

BBC Radio 2 Audience Award – *Les Miserables* at the Queen's Theatre

Special Award – Nicholas Hytner and Nick Starr

Special Award – Michael White

CRITICS' CIRCLE AWARDS FOR 2013

Best Actor – Lenny Henry for *Fences* at the Theatre Royal, Bath and the Duchess Theatre

Best Actress – Lesley Manville for *Ghosts* at the Almeida Theatre and Trafalgar Studios

The John and Wendy Trewin Award for Best Shakespearean Performance – Rory Kinnear for *Othello* at the National Theatre

The Jack Tinker Award for Most Promising Newcomer – Kate O'Flynn for *Port* at the National Theatre

Best New Play – *Chimerica* by Lucy Kirkwood at the Almeida and Harold Pinter theatres

The Peter Hepple Award for Best Musical – *The Scottsboro Boys* at the Young Vic

Best Director – Lyndsey Turner for *Chimerica* at the Almeida and Harold Pinter theatres

Best Designer – Es Devlin for *Chimerica* at the Almeida and Harold Pinter theatres

Most Promising Playwright – Rory Kinnear for *The Herd* at the Bush Theatre and Phoebe Waller-Bridge for *Fleabag* at the Underbelly, Edinburgh Fringe and the Soho Theatre

Special Award – Shakespeare's Globe for the Globe to Globe festival

EVENING STANDARD THEATRE AWARDS FOR 2013

Best Actor – Rory Kinnear and Adrian Lester for *Othello* at the National Theatre

The Natasha Richardson Award for Best Actress – Helen Mirren for *The Audience* at the Gielgud Theatre

Best Musical Performance – Rosalie Craig for *The Light Princess* at the National Theatre

The Milton Shulman Award for Outstanding Newcomer – Seth Numrich for his performance in *Sweet Bird of Youth* at the Old Vic

Best Play – *Chimerica* by Lucy Kirkwood at the Almeida and Harold Pinter theatres

The Ned Sherrin Award for Best Musical – *Merrily We Roll Along* at the Menier Chocolate Factory and the Harold Pinter Theatre

Best Director – Richard Eyre for *Ghosts* at the Almeida Theatre

Best Design – Bob Crowley for *People* at the National Theatre, *The Audience* at the Gielgud and *Once* at the Phoenix

The Charles Wintour Award for Most Promising Playwright – Rachel De-lahay for *Routes* at the Royal Court

Emerging Talent Award – Cush Jumbo for *Josephine and I* at the Bush Theatre

Award for Comedy – David Walliams for his performance as Bottom in *A Midsummer Night's Dream*

Editor's Award – Kevin Spacey for his contribution to British theatre

The Lebedev Special Award – Andrew Lloyd Webber for his contribution to musical theatre

The London Evening Standard Theatre Icon Award – Maggie Smith for her contribution to the world stage

WEATHER

The main feature of the year 2013–14 was the record-breaking rainfall of the winter quarter (December, January and February). The quarter was exceptionally stormy and very mild too. The rains relented at the beginning of March (though they returned for a time in May), and the first six months of 2014 were all warmer than average. Using the England and Wales rainfall series extending back to 1766, we find that the winter quarter 2013–14 was the wettest on record:

2013–14	1994–95	1989–90	1914–15	1876–77	1868–69
447mm	407mm	416mm	423mm	418mm	381mm

It can be noted that the frequency of wet winters has increased: there were no really wet ones in the first hundred years of the series, but there have been three in the last 25 years. There was only one more cyclonic December than that in 2013 and that occurred in 1974. January and February 2014 both broke records for very low pressure, and February broke the record by a wide margin. Pressure was 5.5 millibars lower than the previous record which was set in February 1990. And, with a Central England Temperature of 6.2°C for the winter season, there were only five warmer winters since the record began in 1659, though two had the same mean temperature. Looking at the warm first six months of 2014, we only have to go back to 2007 since the last time this happened.

NEWSWORTHY EVENTS
There were three really hot days between July and September 2013 – July 22 when the temperature climbed to 33.5°C at both Heathrow airport and Northolt (Greater London), August 1 when 34.1°C was reached at Heathrow, and September 5 when the mercury rose to 30.2°C at Writtle (Essex). The last ten days of July were very thundery with some violent downpours of rain, and 92mm fell at Southwell (Notts) in just two hours. The first week of August was also thundery and thunderstorms returned during the fourth week of the month with torrential rain in Essex and the north coast of Kent; 101mm of rain fell on the 24th at Heybridge (Essex). On October 28 as an explosively deepening depression tracked along the south coast of England; gusts on the mainland of Britain reached 71 knots at Langdon Bay, near Dover (Kent), but gusts peaked at 91 knots at Sandettie Light Vessel in the Straits of Dover. This was the worst gale to hit Britain since January 19 2007, when 19 people died in the UK and over 60 across Europe, and this depression, too, went on to wreak havoc in the northern Netherlands, north Germany and Scandinavia.

In early December the east coast of England suffered the worst North Sea storm surge for over 60 years – since the infamous events of January 31/February 1 1953. Flooding was much less severe this time, but floods did occur at Boston (Lincs), Jaywick (Essex) and Rhyl (Flintshire), indicating perhaps how much sea defences have improved over the years. The strongest gust on December 5 was 81 knots at Altnaharra (Sutherland). The second half of December was remarkably wet, and December 23 was the wettest day of all, with 156mm of rain falling at Postbridge on Dartmoor (Devon). Early on the 24th the pressure fell to 936.8 millibars at Stornoway (Isle of Lewis), the lowest pressure in any month since December 1886. A severe gale hit Wales and the West Country overnight of the 26th and 27th with a highest gust of 95 knots at Aberdaron (Gwynedd).

The first week of January was very stormy with widespread damage done in Wales and southwest England by very high tides. January overall was the second wettest on record by the smallest of margins (177mm in 1948 against 176mm in 2014). Severe gales again struck much of England and Wales frequently during the first half of February; the maximum gust was 94 knots at Aberdaron (Gwynedd) early on the 12th, and there was widespread gale damage during the nights of 11th/12th and 13th/14th. There were only two warmer Aprils in the last 100 years and those occurred very recently – in 2007 and 2011, while Northern Ireland registered its dullest May since before 1929 with only 66 per cent of the long-term average sunshine. It was very cool on June 4 with a high of just 8.9°C at Tredegar (Monmouthshire), while 57mm of rain fell in less than five hours on June 26 at Boughton-under-Blean (Kent).

THE YEAR 2013

The Central England Temperature (CET) for the entire year was 9.7°C, which is 0.3°C below the average for the standard reference period 1981–2010, not as cold as 2010, but with the exception of that year there has been none colder since 1996. July was the warmest since 2006, and in the entire CET record which started in 1659 there have been only eight warmer. March, by contrast, was the coldest since 1962, May since 1996, while August was the warmest since 2004. Rainfall, averaged over England and Wales, totalled 904mm over the year, some 2 per cent below the 1981–2010 normal, and it was drier than 2012 but wetter than 2011. The sunshine aggregate of 1,647 hours, again averaged over England and Wales, was 4 per cent above the long-term average; January was the dullest since 2002, March the dullest since 2005, July the sunniest since 2006, October the dullest since 2005, and November the sunniest since 2006.

TEMPERATURE

After the longest run of poor or indifferent summers since the 1960s and early 1970s, summer 2013 turned out to be warm

WEATHER STATISTICS 2013

	Mean Temp. °C	Diff. from normal °C*	Rainfall mm	Percentage of normal*	Sunshine hours	Percentage of normal*
England	9.8	−0.2	896	99	1,647	104
Wales	9.1	−0.5	1,037	93	1,652	105
Scotland	8.6	+0.3	1,018	103	1418	104
Northern Ireland	9.2	+1.3	901	102	1,553	107
United Kingdom	9.7	0.0	948	98	1613	104

* The standard reference period ('normal') for 2011–20 is the average for the 30-year period 1981–2010

and sunny. The highest temperature of the year was 34.1°C at Heathrow on August 1 while the warmest night was that of July 22/23 with a minimum reading of 21.0°C, also at Heathrow. There was only one day during the entire winter when the temperature failed to exceed the freezing point and that was as early as December 6 and then only in northern Scotland, with −1.7°C logged at Lerwick and −1.5°C at Baltasound (both Shetland). The lowest minimum temperature came even earlier, on November 25, with −8.1°C registered at Braemar (Aberdeenshire). The next lowest minima were −7.7°C at Tyndrum (Stirlingshire) on November 22 and at Altnaharra (Sutherland) on February 17.

MEAN MONTHLY TEMPERATURE (°C)

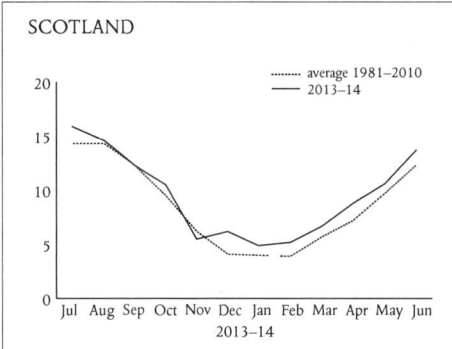

RAINFALL

A long, dry period in July lasted from the 4th to the 21st, but the weather became thundery thereafter and July's rainfall matched the long-term normal but August's rainfall was below average at 83 per cent of the normal amount. September's rainfall was also near average, but it was the wettest October since 2000 with 145 per cent of the long-term average. November had roughly 60 per cent of its average rain, while December was not quite as wet as December 2012, though it was 35 per cent wetter than average. January was second only to 1948 in a record stretching back to 1766, while February had two to three times the normal amount in all western parts of the country. March was 30 per cent drier than average while April had near normal rainfall, though May was the wettest since 2007, racking up 63 per cent of the normal amount. June was 25 per cent drier than usual, though not as dry as June 2013.

MEAN MONTHLY RAINFALL (MM)

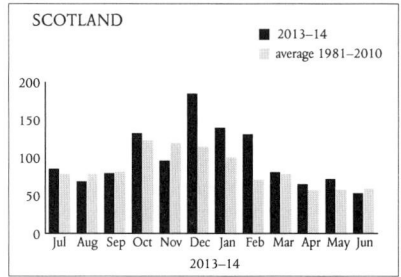

SUNSHINE

In July the sun shone for as much as 289 hours and only 2006 and 1911 were sunnier stretching back to 1876. August and September had near normal amounts of sunshine, but October had just 83 per cent of the average, while November had above average sunshine with about 120 per cent of the average. December the sun shone for just eight hours at Lerwick, contrasting with 90 hours at St Helier. March produced 156 hours over England and Wales, some 142 per cent of the normal amount, while sunshine in East Anglia during March exceeded the average by over 60 per cent. June was cloudy in Scotland and northeast England, but sunnier in Wales and southern England, exceeding 125.

MEAN MONTHLY SUNSHINE (HOURS)

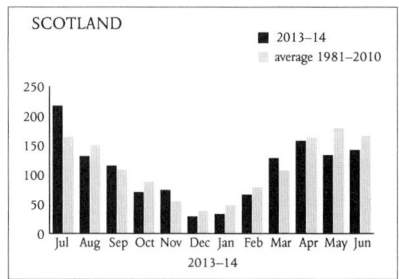

UK WEATHER STATIONS

Given below are temperature, rainfall and sunshine at selected climatological stations for July 2013 to June 2014.

Ht   height of station above mean sea-level

Temp.   mean monthly air temperature

Rain   total monthly rainfall

Sun   total monthly sunshine duration

	Ht	July 2013			August 2013			September 2013			October 2013		
	m	Temp. °C	Rain mm	Sun hrs	Temp. °C	Rain mm	Sun hrs	Temp. °C	Rain mm	Sun hrs	Temp. °C	Rain mm	Sun hrs
Stornoway	15	14.9	58	183	13.9	1.5	102	11.8	58	101	10.3	140	83
Aberdeen	65	16.3	98	179	15.3	63	143	12.7	34	125	10.5	94	61
Glasgow	59	17.3	99	223	15.2	62	119	12.7	80	95	11.0	216	58
Belfast	68	18.9	86	235	15.9	84	106	13.5	45	93	11.7	129	86
Durham	102	18.9	69	203	16.3	71	173	12.9	85	147	11.7	100	77
York	8	18.9	57	234	17.1	119	170	13.5	49	125	12.2	80	89
Manchester	69	18.9	69	253	16.8	48	133	13.6	52	99	12.7	100	68
Holyhead	10	18.6	58	311	16.1	68	163	14.3	76	101	13.5	174	73
Nottingham	117	18.7	111	234	17.2	25	166	13.9	34	138	12.4	132	72
Norwich	32	18.1	6	240	18.1	29	200	14.3	47	140	12.7	92	82
Birmingham	140	18.7	81	265	17.1	44	189	14.1	32	134	12.7	122	90
Cardiff	46	18.7	41	306	17.2	98	205	14.8	62	115	13.5	172	105
Bristol	42	19.7	55	309	17.7	39	146	14.9	42	112	13.3	161	97
London	137	20.0	35	235	18.3	49	163	14.5	78	104	12.9	125	65
Bournemouth	10	18.9	33	299	17.4	23	204	14.6	41	125	13.3	162	87
Camborne	86	17.4	49	278	16.6	88	170	14.9	62	115	13.9	161	77

	Ht	November 2013			December 2013			January 2014			February 2014		
	m	Temp. °C	Rain mm	Sun hrs	Temp. °C	Rain mm	Sun hrs	Temp. °C	Rain mm	Sun hrs	Temp. °C	Rain mm	Sun hrs
Stornoway	15	6.2	124	41	6.3	249	12	5.5	139	29	5.3	146	56
Aberdeen	65	5.7	67	89	6.2	70	40	4.7	164	31	5.3	104	76
Glasgow	59	4.9	121	67	6.5	292	26	4.7	201	21	5.3	204	37
Belfast	68	6.1	40	72	6.5	83	40	5.1	135	30	5.5	102	69
Durham	102	6	54	94	6.1	65	73	4.9	91	65	5.7	68	112
York	8	6.5	41	91	6.2	44	85	5.3	96	72	6.0	64	107
Manchester	69	6.2	54	77	6.7	76	56	6.0	116	39	6.5	66	63
Holyhead	10	8.6	36	49	8.6	131	35	7.3	159	34	7.3	103	72
Nottingham	117	6.4	32	87	6.3	37	64	5.4	114	62	6.1	50	77
Norwich	32	6.5	54	71	5.9	40	88	5.8	72	84	6.7	58	119
Birmingham	140	6.4	56	84	6.4	65	85	5.7	154	90	6.4	74	122
Cardiff	46	7.8	118	70	8.9	74	48	7	163	50	7.3	117	89
Bristol	42	7.1	78	74	7.1	95	51	6.5	152	56	6.9	128	79
London	137	6.7	71	77	6.3	112	58	6.1	198	78	6.8	103	85
Bournemouth	10	6.7	65	88	6.7	185	51	6.6	231	60	7.5	184	90
Camborne	86	8.9	94	60	8.5	176	45	7.7	218	43	7.2	194	85

	Ht	March 2014			April 2014			May 2014			June 2014		
	m	Temp. °C	Rain mm	Sun hrs	Temp. °C	Rain mm	Sun hrs	Temp. °C	Rain mm	Sun hrs	Temp. °C	Rain mm	Sun hrs
Stornoway	15	6.9	109	103	8.8	86	164	10.1	63	127	13.5	49	141
Aberdeen	65	7.2	35	133	8.5	45	139	10.7	56	143	14.0	53	116
Glasgow	59	6.7	126	100	9.3	98	134	11.5	95	107	14.7	45	166
Belfast	68	6.9	69	90	10.4	25	144	11.9	69	98	14.7	43	176
Durham	102	7.1	29	148	9.5	56	144	11.6	78	168	14.6	47	180
York	8	7.5	34	159	9.9	29	155	12.2	97	187	14.9	47	194
Manchester	69	7.5	44	124	10.5	29	110	12.2	94	121	15.1	32	155
Holyhead	10	8.2	49	122	10.4	36	176	12.2	93	158	14.9	44	263
Nottingham	117	7.8	23	146	10.5	20	124	12.5	80	145	15.4	52	165
Norwich	32	7.9	21	199	10.4	19	181	12.9	94	217	14.7	36	227
Birmingham	140	8.0	30	184	10.2	44	167	12.3	93	182	15.3	50	220
Cardiff	46	7.9	42	138	10.3	77	163	12.7	109	179	15.9	61	255
Bristol	42	7.9	23	123	10.7	60	132	13.1	84	165	16.5	33	219
London	137	8.9	30	158	11.4	35	143	13.2	80	141	16.5	31	187
Bournemouth	10	7.9	43	139	9.9	115	156	12.6	100	181	15.9	34	238
Camborne	86	8.1	57	95	9.9	81	155	11.7	70	183	14.7	66	266

METEOROLOGICAL OBSERVATIONS IN LONDON *(Hampstead Observatory)*

Maximum temperature is for the period 9am to 9pm; minimum temperature is for the period 9pm to 9am; the 'rainfall day' is the 24 hours starting at 9am on the day of entry; the 'wet hours' column counts all clock-hours during the rainfall day during which 0.2mm or more has fallen; sunshine is for the calendar day. All times are GMT.

July 2013

Day	Temperature Min °C	Max °C	Rain mm	Wet hours	Sun hours
1	12.4	20.4	0.0	0	7.2
2	11.0	16.7	1.2	3	0.9
3	13.5	19.6	0.0	0	0.8
4	11.5	23.6	0.0	0	3.5
5	12.2	25.1	0.0	0	11.5
6	12.6	27.8	0.0	0	11.8
7	14.8	28.0	0.0	0	12.5
8	13.2	26.1	0.0	0	12.1
9	10.0	25.9	0.0	0	12.5
10	11.8	23.3	0.0	0	10.5
11	10.1	22.7	0.0	0	10.3
12	9.9	24.9	0.0	0	6.9
13	15.0	30.5	0.0	0	10.7
14	17.7	29.4	0.0	0	10.6
15	16.1	30.6	0.0	0	11.5
16	16.4	30.8	0.0	0	7.9
17	17.4	31.2	0.0	0	8.9
18	16.0	28.6	0.0	0	12.1
19	13.9	28.4	0.0	0	11.8
20	15.0	22.6	0.0	0	2.2
21	15.4	26.5	0.9	1	5.8
22	15.7	33.2	4.4	2	9.6
23	18.7	26.5	2.2	2	3.7
24	14.6	27.4	3.4	3	8.3
25	16.3	25.3	0.0	0	6.0
26	13.8	26.5	0.0	0	5.8
27	14.4	28.4	6.2	5	6.2
28	14.0	23.3	4.4	2	5.7
29	15.0	22.8	6.2	3	5.4
30	14.2	20.2	6.0	6	0.9
31	15.6	23.2	0.0	0	1.2

August 2013

Day	Temperature Min °C	Max °C	Rain mm	Wet hours	Sun hours
1	16.2	33.1	0.4	1	10.5
2	15.9	24.8	1.5	1	3.2
3	14.1	23.6	0.0	0	5.4
4	13.6	23.0	0.2	2	5.7
5	16.4	22.9	7.9	3	2.8
6	10.8	22.2	0.0	0	6.2
7	13.4	22.5	0.0	0	6.5
8	11.0	24.4	1.5	3	8.6
9	14.5	23.8	0.0	0	4.2
10	11.8	21.8	0.0	0	3.8
11	14.9	22.9	0.0	0	5.7
12	12.6	20.6	0.0	0	4.0
13	9.8	19.9	0.0	0	5.1
14	10.3	22.8	0.3	2	6.0
15	15.2	22.8	0.9	3	1.8
16	15.7	21.7	0.7	3	1.3
17	13.2	19.5	0.2	2	3.1
18	15.1	23.0	0.0	0	3.6
19	11.2	22.9	0.0	0	6.8
20	11.3	24.4	0.0	0	7.4
21	12.1	26.6	4.1	4	8.3
22	15.7	20.0	1.2	2	0.2
23	15.4	26.6	1.1	2	6.1
24	16.4	17.9	29.1	20	0.0
25	11.6	22.9	0.0	0	3.9
26	14.4	25.2	0.0	0	6.7
27	11.1	22.9	0.0	0	5.0
28	11.4	23.9	0.0	0	8.2
29	13.6	24.1	0.0	0	8.0
30	14.0	24.5	0.0	0	6.0
31	12.2	20.1	0.0	0	9.0

September 2013

Day	Temperature Min °C	Max °C	Rain mm	Wet hours	Sun hours
1	9.1	21.3	0.0	0	6.3
2	10.6	25.8	0.0	0	9.8
3	14.3	23.7	0.0	0	3.4
4	14.9	27.4	0.0	0	8.9
5	15.0	29.1	1.1	2	8.8
6	13.5	17.1	2.3	3	1.1
7	10.5	18.1	0.0	0	4.0
8	9.1	17.5	2.7	2	5.0
9	8.2	12.1	9.2	6	0.3
10	7.7	15.7	0.6	2	3.2
11	10.9	16.0	2.9	5	1.2
12	11.6	17.8	3.8	5	1.3
13	14.7	17.2	41.0	17	0.0
14	7.8	12.8	0.3	2	0.0
15	6.4	14.5	3.5	4	2.1
16	6.6	13.9	1.6	2	4.9
17	6.2	12.6	6.5	6	1.7
18	9.1	15.6	0.0	0	3.1
19	6.7	15.1	1.9	4	0.6
20	8.9	18.9	0.0	0	4.9
21	9.4	17.5	0.0	0	0.1
22	15.4	18.6	0.0	0	0.0
23	13.4	19.0	0.1	0	1.2
24	10.9	21.8	0.1	0	5.4
25	13.2	21.0	0.0	0	4.9
26	12.3	19.0	0.0	0	5.6
27	9.2	17.3	0.0	0	6.0
28	10.9	18.5	0.4	2	1.9
29	11.9	17.6	0.0	0	5.2
30	12.2	18.4	0.0	0	2.8

October 2013

Day	Temperature Min °C	Max °C	Rain mm	Wet hours	Sun hours
1	10.3	16.4	2.2	5	0.8
2	12.2	18.4	0.0	0	0.7
3	12.6	17.9	1.8	3	0.7
4	15.6	20.1	0.0	0	2.3
5	12.3	17.6	0.0	0	0.1
6	8.9	19.3	0.0	0	6.0
7	10.0	18.9	0.0	0	3.0
8	12.5	19.6	0.0	0	3.3
9	12.3	16.0	0.0	0	1.1
10	5.7	11.2	4.1	6	1.9
11	7.1	12.1	11.4	13	1.3
12	8.2	13.2	7.5	6	3.8
13	8.7	10.1	7.3	7	0.0
14	7.6	9.8	2.8	3	0.6
15	7.3	13.6	0.2	2	2.1
16	6.2	14.4	5.8	5	0.8
17	10.8	17.3	0.0	0	3.5
18	10.7	17.5	1.3	2	0.8
19	12.5	16.5	4.7	4	0.4
20	11.6	16.0	14.0	6	3.0
21	11.8	16.4	1.1	3	0.0
22	15.1	17.2	20.6	5	0.4
23	12.6	17.1	0.0	0	4.0
24	7.1	17.3	2.2	4	5.1
25	12.0	17.4	0.3	1	2.5
26	13.1	16.1	4.5	4	0.7
27	9.8	15.6	27.7	12	3.6
28	10.3	13.9	2.6	2	2.8
29	6.2	13.2	0.0	0	4.1
30	3.0	13.4	2.1	4	5.5
31	10.9	11.6	0.6	2	0.0

November 2013

Day	Temperature Min °C	Max °C	Rain mm	Wet hours	Sun hours
1	10.2	13.0	0.2	1	0.1
2	9.2	14.4	1.0	1	2.5
3	6.2	11.8	20.2	13	4.9
4	4.3	9.6	7.1	4	6.5
5	3.2	11.1	3.2	5	0.7
6	8.0	13.9	5.1	7	0.0
7	7.7	10.4	0.0	0	0.9
8	5.1	11.6	9.8	6	0.8
9	2.4	6.6	4.9	6	0.9
10	3.1	9.6	0.8	2	7.1
11	2.9	11.8	7.7	16	0.0
12	8.6	11.3	0.0	0	1.5
13	1.6	9.8	0.6	2	6.4
14	6.0	9.2	0.0	0	4.8
15	2.4	9.0	0.0	0	6.3
16	1.0	9.3	0.0	0	5.0
17	6.6	8.5	1.8	9	0.0
18	7.3	8.1	0.2	2	0.0
19	0.4	5.4	0.7	2	5.3
20	−2.5	5.5	6.7	6	1.2
21	1.2	7.2	0.2	1	3.1
22	1.4	7.0	0.0	0	4.3
23	1.3	7.5	0.0	0	5.8
24	4.3	7.3	0.2	1	0.2
25	2.7	6.7	0.0	0	1.7
26	0.4	6.8	0.4	3	5.2
27	4.3	9.6	0.0	0	0.1
28	7.5	8.9	0.0	0	0.0
29	6.7	9.2	0.2	0	0.3
30	4.1	8.0	0.0	0	1.9

December 2013

Day	Temperature Min °C	Max °C	Rain mm	Wet hours	Sun hours
1	1.0	8.5	0.0	0	0.5
2	5.8	8.4	0.0	0	0.0
3	4.6	5.2	0.0	0	0.0
4	4.0	7.8	0.0	0	0.1
5	−0.2	9.4	2.5	2	0.7
6	1.2	7.3	0.0	0	2.6
7	5.1	7.9	0.0	0	0.0
8	4.0	10.5	0.0	0	3.5
9	4.9	10.9	0.2	0	5.9
10	3.7	8.4	0.1	0	0.9
11	0.0	7.6	0.2	0	4.6
12	2.8	8.1	0.6	2	2.3
13	7.0	10.9	2.2	3	0.0
14	2.8	10.2	2.3	4	2.9
15	7.4	11.4	8.8	11	1.0
16	10.4	11.7	13.3	14	0.0
17	3.2	5.8	3.3	6	0.5
18	4.2	9.1	7.2	5	2.4
19	3.5	8.0	4.0	2	2.5
20	1.3	8.8	3.8	11	5.8
21	8.4	10.8	7.4	5	0.0
22	6.3	9.3	0.0	0	3.3
23	3.3	10.2	29.8	22	0.0
24	6.7	8.2	7.6	4	0.4
25	2.6	6.1	3.9	4	2.2
26	2.2	4.6	3.5	4	0.3
27	4.7	9.4	0.0	0	0.9
28	2.9	7.8	0.0	0	5.2
29	−0.4	6.9	0.2	2	6.3
30	5.4	9.2	6.3	6	1.0
31	5.5	9.7	5.0	5	0.0

January 2014

Day	Temperature Min °C	Max °C	Rain mm	Wet hours	Sun hours
1	4.9	10.1	15.5	15	0.0
2	5.0	9.8	5.7	6	5.6
3	6.5	9.1	8.1	7	2.3
4	6.2	8.7	7.9	5	0.0
5	0.7	9.2	15.6	11	1.7
6	7.6	11.4	14.5	4	2.5
7	8.4	10.4	7.3	6	1.5
8	6.4	10.5	3.5	8	2.6
9	7.7	8.2	0.0	0	2.4
10	1.9	9.4	3.8	7	3.8
11	4.5	8.2	0.0	0	6.4
12	−0.2	7.3	2.8	3	2.9
13	4.4	8.9	7.0	2	4.0
14	0.4	6.6	6.1	9	5.8
15	4.7	10.0	3.3	3	0.4
16	6.6	9.8	18.5	10	2.6
17	5.4	8.0	2.5	2	2.4
18	5.9	8.9	1.4	3	1.2
19	6.1	7.8	0.0	0	3.8
20	1.9	8.4	0.2	0	5.1
21	2.0	7.3	8.7	6	4.2
22	4.9	9.6	0.5	1	1.7
23	2.4	7.7	3.2	3	2.8
24	1.4	7.2	6.3	8	1.2
25	6.1	10.6	6.7	1	3.0
26	2.9	8.2	6.3	7	0.2
27	0.9	6.9	1.4	3	2.7
28	3.3	8.8	6.1	9	4.8
29	3.3	3.3	17.0	21	0.0
30	2.0	4.9	1.0	3	0.0
31	1.6	6.9	17.6	15	1.4

February 2014

Day	Temperature Min °C	Max °C	Rain mm	Wet hours	Sun hours
1	3.5	7.6	0.0	0	0.2
2	4.8	9.6	0.0	0	0.2
3	4.7	7.5	0.2	1	4.1
4	3.3	8.3	10.8	7	4.3
5	4.4	8.7	1.7	2	1.7
6	5.7	8.8	20.6	14	0.0
7	2.3	8.3	5.9	4	2.6
8	6.1	8.6	1.1	2	4.8
9	5.4	7.2	1.6	3	1.2
10	3.3	8.7	1.3	2	2.0
11	1.2	8.2	2.5	3	2.7
12	1.4	7.5	8.9	6	0.6
13	2.7	7.4	0.2	1	4.6
14	2.1	10.9	11.1	7	0.0
15	7.1	9.9	0.4	1	4.7
16	1.4	9.9	0.0	0	6.6
17	4.7	10.0	4.8	3	0.8
18	6.7	9.8	10.0	7	2.5
19	3.9	9.6	1.1	1	2.0
20	7.9	12.3	1.1	2	1.2
21	1.9	9.6	0.0	0	5.6
22	3.1	11.3	0.0	0	5.6
23	6.6	11.0	0.0	0	0.1
24	6.9	13.8	2.7	2	4.2
25	6.9	9.5	2.9	3	1.7
26	2.9	11.2	3.7	3	5.7
27	4.9	11.7	4.3	4	4.2
28	2.5	6.5	5.7	4	0.8

March 2014

Day	Temperature Min °C	Max °C	Rain mm	Wet hours	Sun hours
1	1.0	8.2	1.1	2	3.5
2	1.9	9.3	10.1	8	2.4
3	2.2	8.4	2.7	2	4.8
4	0.3	10.6	0.0	0	4.7
5	0.9	13.2	0.0	0	7.2
6	5.1	13.1	0.0	0	7.1
7	6.0	16.5	0.0	0	3.5
8	6.6	15.6	0.0	0	7.1
9	8.5	19.7	0.0	0	8.4
10	7.1	12.1	0.0	0	4.6
11	4.9	10.7	0.0	0	0.6
12	2.5	15.0	0.0	0	8.8
13	3.9	17.5	0.0	0	9.2
14	4.9	16.6	0.0	0	8.3
15	6.2	18.0	0.0	0	6.4
16	6.2	19.6	0.0	0	8.6
17	5.4	14.1	0.0	0	4.7
18	6.2	13.7	0.0	0	3.0
19	6.6	16.2	0.0	0	3.3
20	5.7	13.3	2.4	6	3.6
21	5.3	12.1	5.7	4	5.6
22	2.7	10.9	0.2	1	5.2
23	1.0	10.2	0.0	0	6.2
24	−0.1	10.3	2.5	8	5.9
25	5.0	8.1	0.5	3	0.2
26	1.3	9.1	3.9	4	2.4
27	1.1	10.0	0.0	0	5.1
28	2.3	12.1	0.0	0	3.4
29	6.4	18.2	0.0	0	9.0
30	8.4	18.9	0.2	1	4.4
31	10.4	16.3	1.1	2	1.0

April 2014

Day	Temperature Min °C	Max °C	Rain mm	Wet hours	Sun hours
1	7.8	19.2	0.0	0	8.7
2	9.6	18.0	0.0	0	4.0
3	9.8	18.5	0.0	0	2.3
4	10.2	14.0	0.0	0	1.1
5	5.6	15.2	3.1	3	3.9
6	11.7	14.1	1.8	4	0.0
7	11.4	13.6	4.4	6	0.1
8	4.5	12.8	0.0	0	6.6
9	3.8	17.4	0.0	0	9.2
10	5.8	17.4	0.0	0	6.9
11	8.5	16.2	0.0	0	3.9
12	6.6	13.7	0.0	0	4.4
13	5.9	16.4	0.0	0	9.8
14	5.6	15.7	0.0	0	8.1
15	3.2	13.7	0.0	0	10.1
16	3.2	17.5	0.0	0	10.4
17	5.7	16.5	0.0	0	4.8
18	4.4	12.0	0.2	0	5.9
19	2.9	12.9	0.0	0	7.3
20	5.4	12.5	6.4	4	0.4
21	6.9	19.6	5.0	4	6.3
22	8.8	15.5	0.9	2	1.7
23	6.8	16.6	2.0	7	5.1
24	9.0	16.5	0.2	0	2.4
25	7.8	12.5	3.4	4	0.0
26	7.5	15.9	0.2	1	5.7
27	7.9	15.0	0.4	1	1.7
28	8.7	17.4	0.0	0	2.8
29	8.4	15.6	0.2	1	1.7
30	6.7	19.3	5.7	5	7.8

May 2014

Day	Min	Max	Rain	Wet	Sun
1	8.6	12.7	11.0	11	0.0
2	7.3	10.8	0.0	0	0.4
3	1.4	14.0	0.0	0	9.3
4	5.0	17.3	0.0	0	10.6
5	6.1	18.5	0.4	2	9.4
6	10.9	18.9	0.2	1	4.6
7	9.7	16.7	0.8	0	4.4
8	9.6	14.0	5.5	6	0.2
9	10.1	16.5	1.2	0	4.6
10	9.6	16.5	2.0	0	3.6
11	7.3	13.3	3.6	0	1.3
12	8.2	17.6	1.4	0	4.8
13	6.5	16.3	2.0	6	3.7
14	5.9	18.5	10.2	0	9.6
15	8.0	20.1	0.0	0	7.8
16	8.7	22.3	0.6	0	8.3
17	10.5	22.8	0.0	0	4.4
18	12.6	23.8	0.0	0	11.5
19	12.0	25.5	0.4	0	9.7
20	14.4	20.3	0.0	0	3.2
21	9.3	18.2	5.9	5	5.8
22	11.1	17.6	0.0	0	4.0
23	10.9	16.4	1.4	0	3.4
24	10.8	16.7	6.6	0	3.5
25	9.1	17.4	4.4	5	6.1
26	9.2	14.0	5.5	10	0.0
27	9.8	12.3	13.2	18	0.0
28	8.5	15.0	0.2	1	0.0
29	11.2	19.2	0.2	1	1.8
30	10.9	17.1	0.0	0	0.0
31	7.2	18.5	0.0	0	5.4

June 2014

Day	Min	Max	Rain	Wet	Sun
1	10.3	21.8	0.5	1	6.7
2	12.1	20.6	0.2	1	5.3
3	11.8	18.1	6.4	8	1.0
4	10.7	13.9	3.6	0	2.4
5	6.5	19.4	0.0	0	6.7
6	8.1	23.0	0.2	0	11.5
7	14.1	21.9	4.8	0	4.0
8	12.3	24.6	0.0	0	10.8
9	13.7	25.6	2.8	0	4.8
10	12.6	22.0	0.0	0	11.3
11	10.8	22.0	0.0	0	7.1
12	12.9	25.2	0.0	2	10.8
13	14.6	25.3	0.2	1	10.3
14	14.3	21.4	0.0	0	3.6
15	11.7	17.3	0.0	4	0.4
16	11.3	17.1	0.0	1	1.3
17	11.6	20.8	0.3	0	9.6
18	12.2	21.4	0.0	0	5.8
19	11.1	20.0	0.0	0	3.6
20	9.3	22.8	0.0	0	4.7
21	12.3	23.9	0.0	0	10.7
22	12.3	24.0	0.0	0	8.2
23	13.5	24.9	1.5	2	2.7
24	13.2	24.2	0.2	0	8.3
25	9.1	20.9	0.0	0	8.2
26	10.0	20.9	1.3	2	7.9
27	13.0	22.0	0.0	7	5.2
28	11.5	18.4	7.1	3	4.0
29	10.9	18.9	0.4	2	5.6
30	9.0	20.4	1.3	3	4.8

TIME AND SPACE

ASTRONOMY

The following pages give astronomical data for each month of the year 2015. There are four pages of data for each month. All data are given for 0h Greenwich Mean Time (GMT), ie at the midnight at the beginning of the day named. This applies also to data for the months when British Summer Time is in operation (for dates, *see* below).

The astronomical data are given in a form suitable for observation with the naked eye or with a small telescope. These data do not attempt to replace the *Astronomical Almanac* for professional astronomers.

A fuller explanation of how to use the astronomical data is given on pages 1115–1117.

CALENDAR FOR EACH MONTH

The calendar for each month comprises dates of general interest plus the dates of birth or death of well-known people. For key religious, civil and legal dates *see* page 7. For details of flag-flying days *see* page 19. For royal birthdays *see* pages 19 and 20–1. For public holidays *see also* pages 8 and 9.

Fuller explanations of the various calendars can be found under Time Measurement and Calendars.

The zodiacal signs through which the Sun is passing during each month are illustrated. The date of transition from one sign to the next, to the nearest hour, is given under Astronomical Phenomena.

JULIAN DATE

The Julian date on 2015 January 0.0 is 2457022.5. To find the Julian date for any other date in 2015 (at 0h GMT), add the day-of-the-year number on the extreme right of the calendar for each month to the Julian date for January 0.0.

BRITISH SUMMER TIME

British Summer Time is the legal time for general purposes during the period in which it is in operation (*see also* page 1120). During this period, clocks are kept one hour ahead of Greenwich Mean Time. The hour of changeover is 01h Greenwich Mean Time. The duration of Summer Time in 2015 is from March 29 01h GMT to October 25 01h GMT.

SEASONS

The seasons are defined astronomically as follows:

Spring from the vernal equinox to the summer solstice
Summer from the summer solstice to the autumnal equinox
Autumn from the autumnal equinox to the winter solstice
Winter from the winter solstice to the vernal equinox

The time when seasons start in 2015 are:

Northern Hemisphere

Vernal Equinox	March 20d 22h 45m GMT
Summer Solstice	June 21d 16h 38m GMT
Autumnal Equinox	September 23d 08h 21m GMT
Winter Solstice	December 22d 04h 48m GMT

Southern Hemisphere

Autumnal Equinox	March 20d 22h 45m GMT
Winter Solstice	June 21d 16h 38m GMT
Vernal Equinox	September 23d 08h 21m GMT
Summer Solstice	December 22d 04h 48m GMT

The longest day of the year, measured from sunrise to sunset, is at the summer solstice. The longest day in the UK will fall on 21 June in 2015.

The shortest day of the year is at the winter solstice. The shortest day in the UK will fall on 22 December in 2015.

The equinox is the point at which day and night are of equal length all over the world.

In popular parlance, the seasons in the northern hemisphere comprise the following months:

Spring	March, April, May
Summer	June, July, August
Autumn	September, October, November
Winter	December, January, February

The March equinox can fall as early as 19 March but this has not happened since 1796 and it will not happen again until 2044. This equinox in 2007 was on 21 March, however in 2008 it occurred on 20 March and will not revert to 21 March again until 2102.

In 2008 the June solstice occurred on 20 June, the first time since 1897. The June solstice in 1975 was on 22 June, but it will not occur on this date again until 2203.

JANUARY 2015

FIRST MONTH, 31 DAYS. *Janus,* god of the portal, facing two ways, past and future

1	*Thursday*	Mary Shelley's gothic horror novel *Frankenstein* is published in London 1818	day 1
2	*Friday*	Isaac Asimov, science fiction writer best known for his *Foundation Series b.* 1920	2
3	*Saturday*	The American writer Herman Melville sets sail for the Pacific on the whaler *Acushnet* 1841	3
4	*Sunday*	Albert Camus, the French Nobel Prize winning author, died in a car accident 1960	4

5	*Monday*	Samuel Beckett's play *Waiting for Godot* premiers at the Théâtre de Babylone, Paris 1953	week 1 day 5
6	*Tuesday*	Frances Burney, novelist and diarist who wrote the 1778 novel *Evelina d.* 1840	6
7	*Wednesday*	The inventor Henry Mill obtains a patent for the first typewriter 1714	7
8	*Thursday*	Andrei Bely, Russian novelist *d.* 1934	8
9	*Friday*	John Donne registers *Devotions upon Emergent Occasions* with the Stationers' Company 1624	9
10	*Saturday*	Georges Remi's comic book *The Adventures of Tintin* is published for the first time in Belgium 1929	10
11	*Sunday*	Thomas Hardy, Victorian novelist whose works include *Tess of the d'Urbervilles d.* 1928	11

12	*Monday*	Dame Agatha Christie, crime writer who created the character Miss Marple *d.* 1976	week 2 day 12
13	*Tuesday*	Emile Zola's *J'accuse* article on the Dreyfus Affair appears in the *L'Aurore* newspaper 1898	13
14	*Wednesday*	Anaïs Nin, French-born American author and diarist *d.* 1977	14
15	*Thursday*	Jean-Baptiste Poquelin, known by his stage name Molière, the French comedy playwright and actor *b.* 1622	15
16	*Friday*	The Spanish author Miguel de Cervantes' literary masterpiece *Don Quixote* is published 1605	16
17	*Saturday*	Anton Chekhov's final play *The Cherry Orchard* opens at the Moscow Art Theatre 1904	17
18	*Sunday*	Edward Bulwer-Lytton, novelist who coined the phrase 'the pen is mightier than the sword' *d.* 1873	18

19	*Monday*	Julian Barnes, who won the 2011 Man Booker Prize for *The Sense of an Ending b.* 1946	week 3 day 19
20	*Tuesday*	Robert Frost reads his poem 'The Gift Outright' at the inauguration of John F. Kennedy 1961	20
21	*Wednesday*	George Orwell, journalist and author who penned *Animal Farm* and *Nineteen Eighty-Four d.* 1950	21
22	*Thursday*	The poet Lord Byron, a flamboyant leading figure of the Romantic movement *b.* 1788	22
23	*Friday*	Derek Walcott, Saint Lucian poet who received the 1992 Nobel Prize in Literature *b.* 1930	23
24	*Saturday*	The poet Alfred, Lord Tennyson became the first person to be granted a peerage for writing 1883	24
25	*Sunday*	Virginia Woolf, modernist author of *Mrs Dalloway b.* 1882	25

26	*Monday*	The Belgian poet Maurice Maeterlinck's works are placed on the *Index Librorum Prohibitorum* 1916	week 4 day 26
27	*Tuesday*	The Italian-Jewish writer Primo Levi is liberated from Auschwitz concentration camp 1945	27
28	*Wednesday*	Jane Austen's romantic novel *Pride and Prejudice* is published 1813	28
29	*Thursday*	Edgar Allan Poe's narrative poem 'The Raven' is published in the *New York Evening Mirror* 1845	29
30	*Friday*	Jules Verne's adventure story *Around the World in Eighty Days* is published 1873	30
31	*Saturday*	Norman Mailer, American novelist who won the 1980 Pulitzer Prize for *The Executioner's Song b.* 1923	31

ASTRONOMICAL PHENOMENA

d h
3 24 Pluto in conjunction with the Sun
4 06 Earth at perihelion (147 million km)
8 08 Jupiter 5° N. of the Moon
14 21 Mercury at greatest elongation E.19°
16 12 Saturn 2° S. of the Moon
19 21 Neptune 0.2° N of Mars
21 18 Mercury 3° S. of the Moon
22 05 Venus 6° S. of the Moon
23 01 Neptune 4° S. of the Moon
23 05 Mars 4° S. of the Moon
25 12 Uranus 0.6° S. of the Moon
30 14 Mercury inferior conjunction with the Sun

MINIMA OF ALGOL

d	h	d	h	d	h
2	08.2	13	19.5	25	06.8
5	05.0	16	16.3	28	03.6
8	01.9	19	13.1	31	00.4
10	22.7	22	10.0		

CONSTELLATIONS

The following constellations are near the meridian at

	d	h		d	h
December	1	24	January	16	21
December	16	23	February	1	20
January	1	22	February	15	19

Draco (below the Pole), Ursa Minor (below the Pole), Camelopardalis, Perseus, Auriga, Taurus, Orion, Eridanus and Lepus

THE MOON

Phases, Apsides and Node		d	h	m
○	Full Moon	5	04	53
☾	Last Quarter	13	09	46
●	New Moon	20	13	14
☽	First Quarter	27	04	48

	d	h	m
Apogee (405,408km)	9	18	19
Perigee (359,645km)	21	20	08

Mean longitude of ascending node on 1st, 195°

THE SUN

s.d. 16′.3

Day	Right Ascension			Dec.		Equation of time		Rise 52°		Rise 56°		Transit		Set 52°		Set 56°		Sidereal time			Transit of first point of Aries		
	h	m	s	°	′	m	s	h	m	h	m	h	m	h	m	h	m	h	m	s	h	m	s
1	18	44	31	23	02	−3	11	8	08	8	31	12	03	15	59	15	36	6	41	19	17	15	51
2	18	48	56	22	58	−3	40	8	08	8	31	12	04	16	00	15	37	6	45	16	17	11	55
3	18	53	20	22	52	−4	08	8	08	8	31	12	04	16	01	15	38	6	49	12	17	07	59
4	18	57	44	22	46	−4	35	8	08	8	30	12	05	16	02	15	40	6	53	09	17	04	03
5	19	02	08	22	40	−5	02	8	07	8	30	12	05	16	03	15	41	6	57	05	17	00	07
6	19	06	31	22	33	−5	29	8	07	8	29	12	06	16	05	15	43	7	01	02	16	56	11
7	19	10	54	22	26	−5	55	8	07	8	29	12	06	16	06	15	44	7	04	58	16	52	15
8	19	15	16	22	18	−6	21	8	06	8	28	12	07	16	07	15	46	7	08	55	16	48	20
9	19	19	38	22	10	−6	46	8	06	8	27	12	07	16	09	15	47	7	12	52	16	44	24
10	19	23	60	22	02	−7	11	8	05	8	26	12	07	16	10	15	49	7	16	48	16	40	28
11	19	28	20	21	53	−7	35	8	04	8	26	12	08	16	12	15	50	7	20	45	16	36	32
12	19	32	41	21	44	−7	59	8	04	8	25	12	08	16	13	15	52	7	24	41	16	32	36
13	19	37	00	21	34	−8	22	8	03	8	24	12	09	16	15	15	54	7	28	38	16	28	40
14	19	41	19	21	24	−8	45	8	02	8	23	12	09	16	16	15	56	7	32	34	16	24	44
15	19	45	38	21	13	−9	07	8	01	8	22	12	09	16	18	15	58	7	36	31	16	20	48
16	19	49	56	21	02	−9	28	8	00	8	20	12	10	16	19	15	59	7	40	27	16	16	52
17	19	54	13	20	51	−9	49	8	00	8	19	12	10	16	21	16	01	7	44	24	16	12	56
18	19	58	29	20	39	−10	08	7	59	8	18	12	10	16	22	16	03	7	48	21	16	09	00
19	20	02	45	20	27	−10	28	7	58	8	17	12	11	16	24	16	05	7	52	17	16	05	05
20	20	07	00	20	14	−10	46	7	57	8	15	12	11	16	26	16	07	7	56	14	16	01	09
21	20	11	15	20	01	−11	04	7	55	8	14	12	11	16	28	16	09	8	00	10	15	57	13
22	20	15	28	19	48	−11	21	7	54	8	12	12	11	16	29	16	11	8	04	07	15	53	17
23	20	19	41	19	34	−11	37	7	53	8	11	12	12	16	31	16	13	8	08	03	15	49	21
24	20	23	53	19	20	−11	53	7	52	8	09	12	12	16	33	16	15	8	11	60	15	45	25
25	20	28	04	19	05	−12	07	7	51	8	08	12	12	16	35	16	17	8	15	56	15	41	29
26	20	32	15	18	51	−12	21	7	49	8	06	12	12	16	36	16	19	8	19	53	15	37	33
27	20	36	24	18	36	−12	34	7	48	8	04	12	13	16	38	16	22	8	23	50	15	33	37
28	20	40	33	18	20	−12	46	7	46	8	03	12	13	16	40	16	24	8	27	46	15	29	41
29	20	44	41	18	04	−12	58	7	45	8	01	12	13	16	42	16	26	8	31	43	15	25	45
30	20	48	48	17	48	−13	08	7	44	7	59	12	13	16	44	16	28	8	35	39	15	21	50
31	20	52	54	17	32	−13	18	7	42	7	57	12	13	16	45	16	30	8	39	36	15	17	54

DURATION OF TWILIGHT (in minutes)

Latitude	52°	56°	52°	56°	52°	56°	52°	56°
	1 January		11 January		21 January		31 January	
Civil	41	47	40	45	38	43	37	41
Nautical	84	96	82	93	80	90	78	87
Astronomical	125	141	123	138	120	134	117	130

THE NIGHT SKY

Mercury is at greatest eastern elongation on the 14th, and is visible for the first three weeks of the month. During this period it is an evening object, its magnitude fading from −0.8 to +1.0. Mercury is visible for a short while at the end of evening civil twilight, low in the south-western sky. After becoming lost in the evening twilight it passes through inferior conjunction on the 30th. On the evening of the 21st the very thin crescent Moon, 1.3 days old, is 8° above and to the right of Mercury, very low above the south-western horizon, though this will require very good conditions for successful observation. Just after sunset extremely low above the south-western horizon (altitude 5°), Mercury and Venus are less than 0.5° apart on 11th, magnitude −0.7.

Venus, magnitude −3.9, is visible in the evenings but will only be seen for a short while after sunset, low above the south-western horizon. It is slowly moving out from the Sun but even by the end of the month it is not visible for much more than an hour after sunset.

Mars is an evening object, magnitude +1.1, visible low in the south-western sky for about 2 hours after sunset. During the month Mars moves from Capricornus into Aquarius.

Jupiter is a brilliant object in the evening night sky. At the beginning of the month it is visible low in the eastern sky by about 22h. By the end of January it is visible for the greater part of the hours of darkness since it comes to opposition early in February. Its magnitude is −2.5. Jupiter is retrograding slowly in Cancer. On 8th Jupiter is 5° north of the Moon.

Saturn, magnitude +0.6, is a morning object in the constellation of Libra. It is visible low in the south-eastern sky before dawn. On the morning of the 16th the old crescent Moon will be seen approaching the planet.

Uranus is in Pisces, an evening object high in the south-western sky all evening. On 25th Uranus is a Moon's width south of the Moon.

THE MOON

Day	R.A. h m	Dec. °	Hor. Par. '	Diam. '	Sun's Co-Long. °	PA of Br. Limb °	Ph. %	Age d	Rise 52° h m	Rise 56° h m	Transit h m	Set 52° h m	Set 56° h m
1	3 16	+15.1	57.2	31.2	395	252	82	10.2	13 35	13 20	21 19	4 05	4 20
2	4 10	+17.2	56.7	30.8	407	255	90	11.2	14 17	14 00	22 11	5 10	5 27
3	5 04	+18.4	56.2	30.6	419	255	95	12.2	15 04	14 46	23 02	6 08	6 26
4	5 58	+18.6	55.7	30.4	432	251	98	13.2	15 58	15 40	23 53	6 59	7 17
5	6 50	+17.9	55.3	30.2	444	210	100	14.2	16 56	16 40	—	7 43	8 00
6	7 41	+16.4	54.9	30.0	96	128	99	15.2	17 56	17 43	0 42	8 20	8 34
7	8 31	+14.1	54.5	29.8	108	117	97	16.2	18 59	18 48	1 29	8 52	9 03
8	9 19	+11.3	54.3	29.6	120	114	93	17.2	20 01	19 54	2 14	9 19	9 27
9	10 05	+8.1	54.1	29.4	132	114	87	18.2	21 04	21 00	2 58	9 43	9 49
10	10 51	+4.5	54.1	29.4	144	114	80	19.2	22 07	22 06	3 40	10 06	10 08
11	11 36	+0.8	54.2	29.6	156	114	72	20.2	23 10	23 12	4 22	10 28	10 27
12	12 21	−3.0	54.5	29.6	169	114	64	21.2	—	—	5 05	10 50	10 46
13	13 07	−6.7	54.9	30.0	181	112	54	22.2	0 14	0 20	5 48	11 14	11 07
14	13 54	−10.2	55.5	30.2	193	111	44	23.2	1 19	1 28	6 34	11 41	11 31
15	14 44	−13.3	56.3	30.6	205	108	35	24.2	2 25	2 38	7 22	12 12	11 59
16	15 36	−15.9	57.1	31.2	217	105	25	25.2	3 31	3 47	8 13	12 50	12 34
17	16 32	−17.7	58.1	31.6	229	102	16	26.2	4 36	4 54	9 08	13 37	13 18
18	17 30	−18.5	59.0	32.2	242	100	9	27.2	5 38	5 56	10 05	14 33	14 14
19	18 30	−18.2	59.8	32.6	254	100	4	28.2	6 33	6 50	11 04	15 39	15 22
20	19 31	−16.7	60.5	33.0	266	114	1	29.2	7 20	7 35	12 04	16 54	16 40
21	20 32	−14.1	60.9	33.2	278	220	1	0.7	8 01	8 13	13 03	18 14	18 03
22	21 32	−10.5	61.0	33.2	290	241	3	1.7	8 36	8 44	14 00	19 35	19 29
23	22 30	−6.2	60.8	33.2	303	244	9	2.7	9 07	9 11	14 55	20 56	20 54
24	23 27	−1.6	60.3	32.8	315	245	17	3.7	9 35	9 35	15 49	22 15	22 17
25	0 22	+3.0	59.7	32.6	327	246	26	4.7	10 03	10 00	16 41	23 32	23 38
26	1 17	+7.3	59.0	32.2	339	248	37	5.7	10 32	10 25	17 33	—	—
27	2 10	+11.1	58.2	31.8	351	250	48	6.7	11 03	10 52	18 25	0 46	0 56
28	3 04	+14.3	57.5	31.4	363	253	59	7.7	11 38	11 24	19 16	1 57	2 10
29	3 58	+16.6	56.8	31.0	376	257	69	8.7	12 17	12 01	20 08	3 02	3 18
30	4 51	+18.0	56.1	30.6	388	260	78	9.7	13 02	12 45	20 59	4 02	4 20
31	5 44	+18.5	55.6	30.2	400	264	86	10.7	13 53	13 35	21 49	4 55	5 13

MERCURY

Day	R.A. h m	Dec °	Mag.	Diam. "	Phase %	Rise h m	Transit h m	Set h m
1	19 42.8	−23.5	−0.7	5	91	9 17	12 55	16 34
3	19 56.2	−22.8	−0.7	5	88	9 18	13 01	16 44
5	20 09.3	−22.1	−0.7	6	85	9 17	13 06	16 55
7	20 21.9	−21.3	−0.7	6	81	9 16	13 11	17 06
9	20 33.8	−20.3	−0.6	6	77	9 13	13 15	17 16
11	20 44.9	−19.4	−0.6	6	71	9 10	13 18	17 26
13	20 54.8	−18.4	−0.5	7	64	9 05	13 20	17 35
15	21 03.2	−17.4	−0.3	7	57	8 59	13 21	17 42
17	21 09.8	−16.4	−0.2	7	48	8 51	13 19	17 47
19	21 14.2	−15.5	+0.1	8	39	8 42	13 16	17 50
21	21 15.8	−14.8	+0.4	8	29	8 31	13 10	17 48
23	21 14.6	−14.2	+0.8	9	20	8 19	13 00	17 42
25	21 10.3	−13.9	+1.3	9	11	8 05	12 48	17 32
27	21 03.4	−13.9	+1.9	10	5	7 50	12 34	17 17
29	20 54.3	−14.1	+2.5	10	2	7 34	12 17	16 59
31	20 44.3	−14.5	+2.7	10	1	7 18	11 59	16 39

Rising and setting times are for latitude 54°

VENUS

Day	R.A. h m	Dec °	Mag.	Diam. "	Phase %	Rise h m	Transit h m	Set h m
1	19 55.3	−22.2	−3.3	10	96	9 20	13 08	16 56
6	20 21.7	−21.0	−3.3	10	96	9 17	13 15	17 12
11	20 47.6	−19.5	−3.3	11	95	9 13	13 21	17 28
16	21 12.9	−17.8	−3.3	11	94	9 07	13 26	17 46
21	21 37.8	−15.8	−3.3	11	94	9 00	13 31	18 03
26	22 02.0	−13.7	−3.3	11	93	8 51	13 36	18 21
31	22 25.8	−11.5	−3.3	11	92	8 42	13 40	18 38

MARS

Day	R.A. h m	Dec °	Mag.	Diam. "	Phase %	Rise h m	Transit h m	Set h m
1	21 34.4	−15.6	+1.3	5	94	10 14	14 47	19 20
6	21 49.7	−14.3	+1.3	5	95	10 01	14 42	19 24
11	22 04.8	−12.9	+1.3	5	95	9 48	14 38	19 27
16	22 19.7	−11.5	+1.3	5	95	9 34	14 33	19 31
21	22 34.4	−10.0	+1.4	5	95	9 21	14 28	19 35
26	22 49.0	−8.5	+1.4	4	96	9 07	14 23	19 39
31	23 03.4	−6.9	+1.4	4	96	8 53	14 18	19 42

SUNRISE AND SUNSET

d	London 0° 05'	51° 30'	Bristol 2° 35'	51° 28'	Birmingham 1° 55'	52° 28'	Manchester 2° 15'	53° 28'	Newcastle 1° 37'	54° 59'	Glasgow 4° 14'	55° 52'	Belfast 5° 56'	54° 35'
	h m	h m	h m	h m	h m	h m	h m	h m	h m	h m	h m	h m	h m	h m
1	8 06	16 02	8 16	16 12	8 18	16 04	8 25	16 00	8 31	15 49	8 47	15 54	8 46	16 08
2	8 06	16 03	8 16	16 13	8 18	16 05	8 25	16 01	8 31	15 50	8 47	15 55	8 46	16 10
3	8 06	16 04	8 15	16 14	8 18	16 06	8 25	16 02	8 31	15 51	8 47	15 56	8 46	16 11
4	8 05	16 05	8 15	16 15	8 18	16 08	8 24	16 04	8 30	15 52	8 46	15 57	8 45	16 12
5	8 05	16 06	8 15	16 16	8 17	16 09	8 24	16 05	8 30	15 54	8 46	15 59	8 45	16 13
6	8 05	16 07	8 15	16 18	8 17	16 10	8 23	16 06	8 29	15 55	8 45	16 00	8 44	16 15
7	8 04	16 09	8 14	16 19	8 16	16 11	8 23	16 08	8 29	15 57	8 45	16 02	8 44	16 16
8	8 04	16 10	8 14	16 20	8 16	16 13	8 22	16 09	8 28	15 58	8 44	16 03	8 43	16 18
9	8 04	16 11	8 13	16 22	8 15	16 14	8 22	16 10	8 28	16 00	8 43	16 05	8 43	16 19
10	8 03	16 13	8 13	16 23	8 15	16 16	8 21	16 12	8 27	16 01	8 43	16 07	8 42	16 21
11	8 02	16 14	8 12	16 24	8 14	16 17	8 21	16 13	8 26	16 03	8 42	16 08	8 41	16 22
12	8 02	16 16	8 12	16 26	8 14	16 19	8 20	16 15	8 25	16 04	8 41	16 10	8 40	16 24
13	8 01	16 17	8 11	16 27	8 13	16 20	8 19	16 17	8 24	16 06	8 40	16 12	8 39	16 26
14	8 00	16 19	8 10	16 29	8 12	16 22	8 18	16 18	8 23	16 08	8 39	16 13	8 39	16 27
15	7 59	16 20	8 09	16 30	8 11	16 23	8 17	16 20	8 22	16 10	8 38	16 15	8 38	16 29
16	7 59	16 22	8 08	16 32	8 10	16 25	8 16	16 22	8 21	16 11	8 37	16 17	8 37	16 31
17	7 58	16 23	8 08	16 33	8 09	16 26	8 15	16 23	8 20	16 13	8 35	16 19	8 35	16 33
18	7 57	16 25	8 07	16 35	8 08	16 28	8 14	16 25	8 19	16 15	8 34	16 21	8 34	16 34
19	7 56	16 27	8 06	16 37	8 07	16 30	8 13	16 27	8 18	16 17	8 33	16 23	8 33	16 36
20	7 55	16 28	8 05	16 38	8 06	16 32	8 12	16 28	8 17	16 19	8 31	16 25	8 32	16 38
21	7 54	16 30	8 04	16 40	8 05	16 33	8 11	16 30	8 15	16 21	8 30	16 27	8 31	16 40
22	7 53	16 32	8 02	16 42	8 04	16 35	8 09	16 32	8 14	16 23	8 29	16 29	8 29	16 42
23	7 51	16 33	8 01	16 43	8 03	16 37	8 08	16 34	8 12	16 25	8 27	16 31	8 28	16 44
24	7 50	16 35	8 00	16 45	8 01	16 39	8 07	16 36	8 11	16 27	8 26	16 33	8 26	16 46
25	7 49	16 37	7 59	16 47	8 00	16 40	8 05	16 38	8 09	16 29	8 24	16 35	8 25	16 48
26	7 48	16 39	7 58	16 49	7 59	16 42	8 04	16 40	8 08	16 31	8 22	16 37	8 23	16 50
27	7 46	16 40	7 56	16 50	7 57	16 44	8 02	16 42	8 06	16 33	8 21	16 39	8 22	16 52
28	7 45	16 42	7 55	16 52	7 56	16 46	8 01	16 43	8 05	16 35	8 19	16 41	8 20	16 54
29	7 44	16 44	7 53	16 54	7 54	16 48	7 59	16 45	8 03	16 37	8 17	16 43	8 19	16 56
30	7 42	16 46	7 52	16 56	7 53	16 50	7 58	16 47	8 01	16 39	8 15	16 46	8 17	16 58
31	7 41	16 47	7 51	16 58	7 51	16 51	7 56	16 49	8 00	16 41	8 14	16 48	8 15	17 00

JUPITER

Day	R.A. h m	Dec °	Mag.	Diam. "	Rise h m	Transit h m	Set h m
1	9 36.8	+15.1	−2.0	43	19 17	2 51	10 22
11	9 33.5	+15.4	−2.1	44	18 32	2 08	9 41
21	9 29.1	+15.8	−2.1	45	17 46	1 25	9 00
31	9 24.2	+16.2	−2.1	45	16 59	0 41	8 18

Equatorial Diam. 45″, Polar Diam. 42″

SATURN

Day	R.A. h m	Dec °	Mag.	Diam. "	Rise h m	Transit h m	Set h m
1	15 55.7	−18.4	+0.8	16	4 54	9 09	13 24
11	15 59.7	−18.6	+0.8	16	4 20	8 34	12 47
21	16 03.3	−18.7	+0.8	16	3 45	7 58	12 11
31	16 06.4	−18.9	+0.8	16	3 10	7 22	11 34

Equatorial Diam. 16″, Polar Diam. 14″
Rings – major axis 36″ minor axis 15″, Tilt 25°

URANUS

Day	R.A. h m	Dec °	Mag.	Diam. "	Rise h m	Transit h m	Set h m
1	0 46.7	+4.3	+6.2	4	11 32	18 02	0 29
11	0 47.1	+4.3	+6.2	4	10 53	17 24	23 46
21	0 47.9	+4.4	+6.2	3	10 14	16 45	23 08
31	0 49.0	+4.6	+6.2	3	9 35	16 07	22 31

NEPTUNE

Day	R.A. h m	Dec °	Mag.	Diam. "	Rise h m	Transit h m	Set h m
1	22 29.1	−10.3	+7.8	2	10 36	15 41	20 47
11	22 30.1	−10.2	+7.8	2	9 57	15 03	20 09
21	22 31.3	−10.1	+7.8	2	9 18	14 25	19 31
31	22 32.5	−10.0	+7.8	2	8 39	13 47	18 54

FEBRUARY 2015

SECOND MONTH, 28 or 29 DAYS. *Februa*, Roman festival of Purification

1	*Sunday*	Mary Ann Evans publishes *Adam Bede* under her new pen name of George Eliot 1859	day 32

2	*Monday*	The modernist Irish novelist and poet, James Joyce, who wrote *Ulysses b.* 1882	week 5 day 33
3	*Tuesday*	Johannes Gutenberg, German publisher who invented movable type printing *d.* 1468	34
4	*Wednesday*	James Fenimore Cooper's *The Last of the Mohicans*, set during the Seven Years' War, is published 1826	35
5	*Thursday*	Molière's theatrical comedy *Tartuffe* is first performed at the Palais-Royal Theatre, Paris 1669	36
6	*Friday*	John Steinbeck's novella *Of Mice and Men*, set during the Great Depression, is published 1937	37
7	*Saturday*	Charles Dickens, regarded as the greatest writer of the Victorian period, was born in Portsmouth 1812	38
8	*Sunday*	Halldór Laxness, the only Icelandic writer to have won the Nobel Prize in Literature *d.* 1998	39

9	*Monday*	The Russian novelist and essayist Fyodor Dostoyevsky who wrote *The Idiot d.* 1881	week 6 day 40
10	*Tuesday*	Aleksandr Pushkin, the Romantic Russian author and poet, dies after being shot in a duel 1837	41
11	*Wednesday*	The American poet and novelist Sylvia Plath commits suicide in her kitchen 1963	42
12	*Thursday*	George Meredith, novelist and poet of the Victorian era, is born in Portsmouth 1828	43
13	*Friday*	Part of the missing manuscript of *Adventures of Huckleberry Finn* is found in a trunk in Los Angeles 1991	44
14	*Saturday*	Ayatollah Ruhollah Khomeini of Iran issues a fatwa in response to Salman Rushdie's *The Satanic Verses* 1989	45
15	*Sunday*	The science fiction author H. G. Wells announces he has co-founded the Diabetics Association 1934	46

16	*Monday*	Thomas Gray's best known work *Elegy Written in a Country Churchyard* is published 1751	week 7 day 47
17	*Tuesday*	The Bohemian-Austrian poet Rainer Maria Rilke writes the first of his *Letters to a Young Poet* 1903	48
18	*Wednesday*	The Christian writer John Bunyan's *The Pilgrim's Progress*, started when he was in gaol, is published 1678	49
19	*Thursday*	The Norwegian author Knut Hamsun who won the 1920 Nobel Prize in Literature *d.* 1952	50
20	*Friday*	F. T. Marinetti publishes his *Futurist Manifesto* in the French newspaper *Le Figaro* 1909	51
21	*Saturday*	Karl Marx and Friedrich Engels' political manuscript *The Communist Manifesto* is published 1848	52
22	*Sunday*	The American short story writer Raymond Chandler's *Will You Please Be Quiet, Please?* is published 1976	53

23	*Monday*	The American civil rights activist W. E. B. Du Bois, who wrote *The Souls of Black Folk b.*1868	week 8 day 54
24	*Tuesday*	Nikolai Gogol, the Russian novelist, burns his manuscripts nine days before his death 1852	55
25	*Wednesday*	Victor Hugo's play *Hernani* premieres in Paris amidst huge demonstrations 1830	56
26	*Thursday*	The Romantic poet, playwright and novelist Victor Hugo, who authored *Les Misérables b.* 1802	57
27	*Friday*	The American pedagogue and Fireside Poet Henry Wadsworth Longfellow *b.* 1807	58
28	*Saturday*	The American-born literary realist Henry James who wrote *The Ambassadors* and *Daisy Miller d.* 1916	59

ASTRONOMICAL PHENOMENA

d　h
1　11　Neptune 0.8° N of Venus
4　09　Jupiter 5° N. of the Moon
6　18　Jupiter at opposition
12　24　Saturn 2° S. of the Moon
17　06　Mercury 4° S. of the Moon
19　13　Neptune 4° S. of the Moon
21　01　Venus 2° S. of the Moon
21　02　Mars 2° S. of the Moon
21　20　Mars 0.5° N of Venus
21　22　Uranus 0.3° S. of the Moon
24　16　Mercury at greatest elongation W.27°
26　05　Neptune in conjunction with the Sun

MINIMA OF ALGOL

d	h	d	h	d	h
2	21.3	14	08.6	25	19.8
5	18.1	17	05.4	28	16.7
8	14.9	20	02.2		
11	11.7	22	23.0		

CONSTELLATIONS
The following constellations are near the meridian at

	d	h		d	h
January	1	24	February	15	21
January	16	23	March	1	20
February	1	22	March	16	19

Draco (below the Pole), Camelopardalis, Auriga, Taurus, Gemini, Orion, Canis Minor, Monoceros, Lepus, Canis Major and Puppis

THE MOON

Phases, Apsides and Node	d	h	m
○　Full Moon	3	23	09
☾　Last Quarter	12	03	50
●　New Moon	18	23	47
☽　First Quarter	25	17	14
Apogee (406,150km)	6	06	27
Perigee (356,995km)	19	07	30

Mean longitude of ascending node on 1st, 193°

THE SUN

s.d. 16'.2

Day	Right Ascension h m s	Dec. ° '	Equation of time m s	Rise 52° h m	Rise 56° h m	Transit h h	Set 52° m h	Set 56° h m	Sidereal time h m s	Transit of first point of Aries h m s
1	20 57 00	17 15	-13 27	7 40	7 55	12 14	16 47	16 32	8 43 32	15 10 02
2	21 01 04	16 58	-13 35	7 39	7 54	12 14	16 49	16 34	8 47 29	15 06 06
3	21 05 08	16 41	-13 42	7 37	7 52	12 14	16 51	16 37	8 51 25	15 02 10
4	21 09 11	16 23	-13 49	7 36	7 50	12 14	16 53	16 39	8 55 22	14 58 14
5	21 13 13	16 05	-13 54	7 34	7 48	12 14	16 55	16 41	8 59 19	14 54 18
6	21 17 15	15 47	-13 59	7 32	7 46	12 14	16 57	16 43	9 03 15	14 50 22
7	21 21 15	15 28	-14 03	7 31	7 44	12 14	16 58	16 45	9 07 12	14 46 26
8	21 25 15	15 10	-14 06	7 29	7 41	12 14	17 00	16 48	9 11 08	14 42 30
9	21 29 14	14 51	-14 09	7 27	7 39	12 14	17 02	16 50	9 15 05	14 38 35
10	21 33 12	14 31	-14 10	7 25	7 37	12 14	17 04	16 52	9 19 01	14 34 39
11	21 37 10	14 12	-14 11	7 23	7 35	12 14	17 06	16 54	9 22 58	14 30 43
12	21 41 06	13 52	-14 11	7 21	7 33	12 14	17 08	16 56	9 26 54	14 26 47
13	21 45 02	13 32	-14 11	7 20	7 31	12 14	17 10	16 59	9 30 51	14 22 51
14	21 48 57	13 12	-14 10	7 18	7 28	12 14	17 11	17 01	9 34 48	14 18 55
15	21 52 52	12 52	-14 08	7 16	7 26	12 14	17 13	17 03	9 38 44	14 14 59
16	21 56 46	12 31	-14 05	7 14	7 24	12 14	17 15	17 05	9 42 41	14 11 03
17	22 00 39	12 10	-14 01	7 12	7 21	12 14	17 17	17 07	9 46 37	14 07 07
18	22 04 31	11 49	-13 57	7 10	7 19	12 14	17 19	17 10	9 50 34	14 03 11
19	22 08 23	11 28	-13 52	7 08	7 17	12 14	17 21	17 12	9 54 30	13 59 16
20	22 12 14	11 07	-13 47	7 06	7 14	12 14	17 23	17 14	9 58 27	13 55 20
21	22 16 04	10 45	-13 41	7 04	7 12	12 14	17 24	17 16	10 02 23	13 51 24
22	22 19 54	10 23	-13 34	7 02	7 10	12 14	17 26	17 18	10 06 20	13 47 28
23	22 23 43	10 02	-13 26	7 00	7 07	12 13	17 28	17 20	10 10 17	13 43 32
24	22 27 31	9 40	-13 18	6 57	7 05	12 13	17 30	17 23	10 14 13	13 39 36
25	22 31 19	9 17	-13 09	6 55	7 02	12 13	17 32	17 25	10 18 10	13 35 40
26	22 35 06	8 55	-12 60	6 53	7 00	12 13	17 34	17 27	10 22 06	13 31 44
27	22 38 53	8 33	-12 50	6 51	6 57	12 13	17 35	17 29	10 26 03	13 27 48
28	22 42 39	8 10	-12 39	6 49	6 55	12 13	17 37	17 31	10 29 59	13 23 52

DURATION OF TWILIGHT (in minutes)

Latitude	52°	56°	52°	56°	52°	56°	52°	56°
	1 February		11 February		21 February		31 February	
Civil	37	41	35	39	34	38	34	37
Nautical	77	86	75	83	74	81	73	80
Astronomical	117	130	114	126	113	124	112	124

THE NIGHT SKY

Mercury is unsuitably placed for observation from these latitudes.

Venus continues to be visible as a brilliant evening object, magnitude −3.9. The rapid motion of the planet northwards in declination makes it visible for longer each night and by the end of February it is still visible low in the western sky for over two hours after sunset. In fact from early this month until mid-May Venus can still be seen for a while after the end of astronomical twilight.

Mars is an evening object, magnitude +1.4, visible low above the west-south-western horizon for a short while in the early evenings. During February Mars moves from Aquarius into Pisces. On 21st Venus lies less than 0.5° below and to the left of Mars, the crescent Moon 9° above an to the left.

Jupiter, magnitude −2.6, is at opposition on 6th and therefore visible throughout the hours of darkness. By the end of the month it is visible low in the eastern sky shortly after sunset. Jupiter is retrograding slowly in the constellation of Cancer.

Saturn, magnitude +0.5, is visible in the mornings, low above the south horizon. The Last Quarter Moon will be seen near the planet on the mornings of the 13th.

Uranus lies 2.5° (five Moon's widths) above and to the left of the crescent Moon at 20h on 21st.

THE MOON

Day	R.A. h m	Dec. °	Hor. Par. '	Diam. '	Sun's Co-Long. °	PA of Br. Limb °	Ph. %	Age d	Rise 52° h m	Rise 56° h m	Transit h m	Set 52° h m	Set 56° h m
1	6 37	+18.1	55.1	30.0	412	266	92	11.7	14 48	14 32	22 38	5 41	5 58
2	7 28	+16.8	54.8	29.8	424	266	96	12.7	15 47	15 33	23 25	6 20	6 35
3	8 17	+14.8	54.5	29.6	436	259	99	13.7	16 49	16 37	—	6 54	7 06
4	9 06	+12.2	54.2	29.6	448	192	100	14.7	17 51	17 42	0 11	7 22	7 32
5	9 52	+9.1	54.1	29.4	101	127	99	15.7	18 54	18 48	0 55	7 48	7 55
6	10 38	+5.7	54.0	29.4	113	119	96	16.7	19 56	19 54	1 38	8 11	8 15
7	11 23	+2.0	54.0	29.4	125	116	92	17.7	20 59	21 00	2 20	8 34	8 34
8	12 08	−1.7	54.2	29.6	137	114	86	18.7	22 02	22 07	3 02	8 56	8 53
9	12 54	−5.4	54.4	29.6	149	113	79	19.7	23 06	23 13	3 45	9 19	9 13
10	13 40	−8.9	54.8	29.8	161	111	71	20.7	—	—	4 29	9 44	9 36
11	14 28	−12.1	55.4	30.2	173	108	62	21.7	0 10	0 21	5 15	10 13	10 01
12	15 18	−14.8	56.1	30.6	186	105	52	22.7	1 14	1 28	6 03	10 47	10 32
13	16 11	−16.9	56.9	31.0	198	101	42	23.7	2 18	2 35	6 55	11 28	11 10
14	17 06	−18.1	57.8	31.6	210	97	31	24.7	3 19	3 37	7 49	12 17	11 59
15	18 04	−18.4	58.8	32.0	222	93	22	25.7	4 16	4 34	8 45	13 16	12 58
16	19 03	−17.5	59.7	32.6	234	89	13	26.7	5 07	5 23	9 44	14 25	14 09
17	20 04	−15.4	60.6	33.0	246	87	6	27.7	5 51	6 05	10 43	15 42	15 29
18	21 04	−12.3	61.1	33.4	259	90	2	28.7	6 29	6 39	11 41	17 03	16 54
19	22 04	−8.3	61.4	33.4	271	162	0	0.2	7 03	7 09	12 39	18 26	18 22
20	23 03	−3.7	61.3	33.4	283	239	2	1.2	7 34	7 36	13 35	19 49	19 49
21	0 00	+1.0	61.0	33.2	295	245	6	2.2	8 04	8 01	14 30	21 10	21 14
22	0 57	+5.6	60.3	32.8	307	248	13	3.2	8 33	8 27	15 24	22 28	22 36
23	1 53	+9.8	59.5	32.4	320	251	22	4.2	9 05	8 55	16 18	23 43	23 55
24	2 49	+13.2	58.5	31.8	332	254	32	5.2	9 39	9 26	17 11	—	—
25	3 44	+15.8	57.6	31.4	344	258	43	6.2	10 18	10 02	18 04	0 52	1 07
26	4 38	+17.5	56.8	31.0	356	262	53	7.2	11 01	10 44	18 55	1 55	2 12
27	5 32	+18.3	56.0	30.6	368	266	63	8.2	11 50	11 33	19 46	2 51	3 09
28	6 24	+18.1	55.4	30.2	381	270	73	9.2	12 44	12 27	20 35	3 39	3 57

MERCURY

Day	R.A. h m	Dec °	Mag.	Diam. "	Phase %	Rise h m	Transit h m	Set h m
1	20 39.3	−14.7	+2.5	10	2	7 11	11 50	16 29
3	20 29.8	−15.3	+2.1	10	5	6 57	11 33	16 08
5	20 21.8	−15.8	+1.7	10	9	6 45	11 17	15 48
7	20 15.9	−16.4	+1.3	10	15	6 35	11 03	15 31
9	20 12.3	−16.9	+1.1	9	21	6 27	10 52	15 16
11	20 11.0	−17.4	+0.9	9	27	6 21	10 42	15 04
13	20 11.7	−17.7	+0.7	9	33	6 16	10 35	14 55
15	20 14.2	−18.0	+0.6	8	39	6 12	10 30	14 47
17	20 18.4	−18.2	+0.5	8	44	6 10	10 26	14 42
19	20 23.8	−18.3	+0.4	8	48	6 08	10 24	14 39
21	20 30.4	−18.3	+0.4	7	52	6 07	10 22	14 38
23	20 37.9	−18.2	+0.3	7	56	6 06	10 22	14 38
25	20 46.2	−18.1	+0.3	7	59	6 05	10 22	14 40
27	20 55.2	−17.8	+0.3	7	62	6 05	10 23	14 42

Rising and setting times are for latitude 54°

VENUS

Day	R.A. h m	Dec °	Mag.	Diam. "	Phase %	Rise h m	Transit h m	Set h m
1	22 30.5	−11.0	−3.3	11	92	8 40	13 41	18 42
6	22 53.7	−8.6	−3.4	11	91	8 29	13 44	18 59
11	23 16.6	−6.1	−3.4	11	90	8 18	13 47	19 17
16	23 39.2	−3.5	−3.4	12	89	8 07	13 50	19 34
21	0 01.6	−0.9	−3.4	12	88	7 55	13 57	19 51
26	0 23.9	+1.7	−3.4	12	87	7 43	13 59	20 08

MARS

Day	R.A. h m	Dec °	Mag.	Diam. "	Phase %	Rise h m	Transit h m	Set h m
1	23 06.3	−6.6	+1.4	4	96	8 50	14 16	19 43
6	23 20.6	−5.1	+1.4	4	96	8 36	14 11	19 46
11	23 34.8	−3.5	+1.4	4	97	8 22	14 06	19 49
16	23 48.9	−1.9	+1.4	4	97	8 08	14 00	19 52
21	0 03.0	−0.3	+1.5	4	97	7 53	13 58	19 55
26	0 17.0	+1.3	+1.5	4	97	7 39	13 53	19 58

SUNRISE AND SUNSET

	London 0° 05' 51° 30'		Bristol 2° 35' 51° 28'		Birmingham 1° 55' 52° 28'		Manchester 2° 15' 53° 28'		Newcastle 1° 37' 54° 59'		Glasgow 4° 14' 55° 52'		Belfast 5° 56' 54° 35'	
d	h m	h m	h m	h m	h m	h m	h m	h m	h m	h m	h m	h m	h m	h m
1	7 39	16 49	7 49	16 59	7 50	16 53	7 55	16 51	7 58	16 43	8 12	16 50	8 13	17 02
2	7 38	16 51	7 48	17 01	7 48	16 55	7 53	16 53	7 56	16 45	8 10	16 52	8 12	17 04
3	7 36	16 53	7 46	17 03	7 46	16 57	7 51	16 55	7 54	16 47	8 08	16 54	8 10	17 06
4	7 34	16 55	7 44	17 05	7 45	16 59	7 49	16 57	7 52	16 49	8 06	16 56	8 08	17 08
5	7 33	16 56	7 43	17 07	7 43	17 01	7 48	16 59	7 50	16 51	8 04	16 59	8 06	17 10
6	7 31	16 58	7 41	17 08	7 41	17 03	7 46	17 01	7 48	16 53	8 02	17 01	8 04	17 12
7	7 29	17 00	7 39	17 10	7 40	17 05	7 44	17 03	7 46	16 55	8 00	17 03	8 02	17 14
8	7 28	17 02	7 38	17 12	7 38	17 07	7 42	17 05	7 44	16 58	7 58	17 05	8 00	17 16
9	7 26	17 04	7 36	17 14	7 36	17 08	7 40	17 07	7 42	17 00	7 56	17 07	7 58	17 18
10	7 24	17 06	7 34	17 16	7 34	17 10	7 38	17 09	7 40	17 02	7 54	17 09	7 56	17 20
11	7 22	17 07	7 32	17 18	7 32	17 12	7 36	17 11	7 38	17 04	7 52	17 12	7 54	17 22
12	7 21	17 09	7 30	17 19	7 30	17 14	7 34	17 13	7 36	17 06	7 49	17 14	7 52	17 24
13	7 19	17 11	7 29	17 21	7 28	17 16	7 32	17 15	7 34	17 08	7 47	17 16	7 50	17 27
14	7 17	17 13	7 27	17 23	7 26	17 18	7 30	17 17	7 32	17 10	7 45	17 18	7 48	17 29
15	7 15	17 15	7 25	17 25	7 24	17 20	7 28	17 19	7 30	17 12	7 43	17 20	7 46	17 31
16	7 13	17 17	7 23	17 27	7 22	17 22	7 26	17 21	7 28	17 14	7 40	17 23	7 44	17 33
17	7 11	17 18	7 21	17 29	7 20	17 24	7 24	17 23	7 25	17 17	7 38	17 25	7 42	17 35
18	7 09	17 20	7 19	17 30	7 18	17 26	7 22	17 25	7 23	17 19	7 36	17 27	7 39	17 37
19	7 07	17 22	7 17	17 32	7 16	17 27	7 20	17 27	7 21	17 21	7 33	17 29	7 37	17 39
20	7 05	17 24	7 15	17 34	7 14	17 29	7 18	17 29	7 19	17 23	7 31	17 31	7 35	17 41
21	7 03	17 26	7 13	17 36	7 12	17 31	7 16	17 31	7 16	17 25	7 29	17 33	7 33	17 43
22	7 01	17 27	7 11	17 38	7 10	17 33	7 13	17 33	7 14	17 27	7 26	17 36	7 30	17 45
23	6 59	17 29	7 09	17 39	7 08	17 35	7 11	17 34	7 12	17 29	7 24	17 38	7 28	17 47
24	6 57	17 31	7 07	17 41	7 06	17 37	7 09	17 36	7 09	17 31	7 21	17 40	7 26	17 49
25	6 55	17 33	7 05	17 43	7 04	17 39	7 07	17 38	7 07	17 33	7 19	17 42	7 23	17 51
26	6 53	17 35	7 03	17 45	7 02	17 41	7 04	17 40	7 05	17 35	7 17	17 44	7 21	17 53
27	6 51	17 36	7 01	17 47	6 59	17 42	7 02	17 42	7 02	17 37	7 14	17 46	7 19	17 55
28	6 49	17 38	6 58	17 48	6 57	17 44	7 00	17 44	7 00	17 39	7 12	17 48	7 16	17 57

JUPITER

Day	R.A. h m	Dec °	Mag.	Diam. "	Rise h m	Transit h m	Set h m
1	9 23.7	+16.3	−2.1	45	16 54	0 36	8 14
11	9 18.4	+16.7	−2.1	45	16 07	23 52	7 32
21	9 13.3	+17.1	−2.1	45	15 20	23 07	6 51

Equatorial Diam. 45″, Polar Diam. 42″

SATURN

Day	R.A. h m	Dec °	Mag.	Diam. "	Rise h m	Transit h m	Set h m
1	16 06.7	−18.9	+0.7	16	3 06	7 18	11 30
11	16 09.1	−18.9	+0.7	16	2 30	6 41	10 52
21	16 11.0	−19.0	+0.7	17	1 53	6 04	10 15

Equatorial Diam. 17″, Polar Diam. 15″
Rings – major axis 38″ minor axis 16″, Tilt 25°

URANUS

Day	R.A. h m	Dec °	Mag.	Diam. "	Rise h m	Transit h m	Set h m
1	0 49.1	+4.6	+6.2	3	9 31	16 03	22 27
11	0 50.5	+4.7	+6.2	3	8 52	15 25	21 50
21	0 52.0	+4.9	+6.2	3	8 13	14 47	21 13

NEPTUNE

Day	R.A. h m	Dec °	Mag.	Diam. "	Rise h m	Transit h m	Set h m
1	22 32.7	−9.9	+7.8	2	8 36	13 43	18 50
11	22 34.0	−9.8	+7.8	2	7 57	13 05	18 13
21	22 35.5	−9.7	+7.8	2	7 18	12 27	17 36

MARCH 2015

THIRD MONTH, 31 DAYS. *Mars,* Roman god of battle

1	*Sunday*	The first recorded performance of Shakespeare's *Romeo and Juliet* occurs at Lincoln's Inn Fields 1662	day 60
2	*Monday*	The novelist D. H. Lawrence, author of *Sons and Lovers* and *The Rainbow* d. 1930	week 9 day 61
3	*Tuesday*	William Godwin, philosopher and novelist who wrote *An Enquiry Concerning Political Justice* b. 1756	62
4	*Wednesday*	The American modernist poet and doctor William Carlos Williams d. 1963	63
5	*Thursday*	The Welsh poet Dylan Thomas's radio drama *Under Milk Wood* is first published 1954	64
6	*Friday*	Gabriel García Márquez, Colombian writer whose novels include *Love in the Time of Cholera* b. 1927	65
7	*Saturday*	The French author Georges Perec, who wrote *La Vie mode d'emploi* (*Life A User's Manual*) b. 1936	66
8	*Sunday*	BBC Radio 4 first broadcasts Douglas Adams' comic series *The Hitchhiker's Guide to the Galaxy* 1978	67
9	*Monday*	Vita Sackville-West, author and poet affiliated with the Bloomsbury Group b. 1892	week 10 day 68
10	*Tuesday*	Mikhail Bulgakov, Russian author of the satirical novel *The Master and Margarita* d. 1940	69
11	*Wednesday*	John Wyndham, science fiction writer who authored the 1951 novel *The Day of the Triffids* d. 1969	70
12	*Thursday*	Jack Kerouac, American Beat Generation pioneer who wrote *On the Road* and *Big Sur* b. 1922	71
13	*Friday*	Flann O'Brien's *At Swim-Two-Birds* is published, most copies are later destroyed by Luftwaffe bombing 1939	72
14	*Saturday*	Alexandru Macedonski, poet and novelist who led the Romanian symbolist movement b. 1854	73
15	*Sunday*	The American horror writer H. P. Lovecraft, who penned *At the Mountains of Madness* d. 1937	74
16	*Monday*	The first female recipient of the Nobel Prize in Literature, Selma Lagerlof d. 1940	week 11 day 75
17	*Tuesday*	Patrick Hamilton, playwright and novelist who wrote *Hangover Square* and *Rope* b. 1904	76
18	*Wednesday*	John Updike, prolific novelist and two-times winner of the Pulitzer Prize b. 1932	77
19	*Thursday*	The American writer Edgar Rice Burroughs, author of *Tarzan of the Apes* d. 1950	78
20	*Friday*	Harriet Beecher Stowe's *Uncle Tom's Cabin*, the bestselling novel of the 19th century, is published 1852	79
21	*Saturday*	Robert Southey, Romantic poet who held the Poet Laureateship for 30 years d. 1843	80
22	*Sunday*	Thomas Carew, the 17th-century Cavalier poet who penned the erotic poem 'A Rapture' d. 1640	81
23	*Monday*	Marie-Henri Beyle, known by his pen name Stendhal, author of *The Red and the Black* d. 1842	week 12 day 82
24	*Tuesday*	Dario Fo, Italian actor-playwright and recipient of the 1997 Nobel Prize in Literature b. 1926	83
25	*Wednesday*	Arthur Conan Doyle's Sherlock Holmes novel *The Hound of the Baskervilles* is published 1902	84
26	*Thursday*	F. Scott Fitzgerald's debut novel, *This Side of Paradise*, is first published 1920	85
27	*Friday*	William Wordsworth completes the first part of his poem 'Ode: Intimations of Immortality' 1802	86
28	*Saturday*	Virginia Woolf commits suicide by filling her pockets with stones and walking into the River Ouse 1941	87
29	*Sunday*	William Godwin and Mary Wollstonecraft, the parents of Mary Shelley, marry 1797	88
30	*Monday*	The novelist Anna Sewell, author of the pioneering children's book *Black Beauty* b. 1820	week 13 day 89
31	*Tuesday*	Toni Morrison's novel *Beloved* wins the Pulitzer Prize for Fiction 1988	90

ASTRONOMICAL PHENOMENA

d	h	
3	08	Jupiter 5° N. of the Moon
4	20	Uranus 0.1° S of Venus
11	20	Uranus 0.3° S of Mars
12	08	Saturn 2° S. of the Moon
18	00	Neptune 2° N of Mercury
19	02	Neptune 4° S. of the Moon
19	05	Mercury 5° S. of the Moon
20	22	Equinox
20	09	Total solar eclipse
21	11	Uranus 0.1° S. of the Moon
21	22	Mars 1° N. of the Moon
22	20	Venus 3° N. of the Moon
30	10	Jupiter 6° N. of the Moon

MINIMA OF ALGOL

d	h	d	h	d	h
3	13.5	15	00.8	26	12.1
6	10.3	17	21.6	29	08.9
9	07.1	20	18.4		
12	04.0	23	15.2		

CONSTELLATIONS

The following constellations are near the meridian at

	d	h		d	h
February	1	24	March	16	21
February	15	23	April	1	20
March	1	22	April	15	19

Cepheus (below the Pole), Camelopardalis, Lynx, Gemini, Cancer, Leo, Canis Minor, Hydra, Monoceros, Canis Major and Puppis

THE MOON

Phases, Apsides and Node	d	h	m
○ Full Moon	5	18	05
☾ Last Quarter	13	17	48
● New Moon	20	09	36
☽ First Quarter	27	07	43

Apogee (406,385km)	5	07	34
Perigee (357,584km)	19	19	39

Mean longitude of ascending node on 1st, 192°

THE SUN

s.d. 16′.1

Day	Right Ascension h m s			Dec. ° ′		Equation of time m s		Rise 52° h m		Rise 56° h m		Transit h h		Set 52° m h		Set 56° h m		Sidereal time h m s			Transit of first point of Aries h m s		
1	22	46	25	−7	47	−12	28	6	47	6	52	12	12	17	39	17	33	10	33	56	13	19	56
2	22	50	09	−7	25	−12	17	6	44	6	50	12	12	17	41	17	35	10	37	52	13	16	01
3	22	53	54	−7	02	−12	05	6	42	6	47	12	12	17	43	17	38	10	41	49	13	12	05
4	22	57	38	−6	39	−11	52	6	40	6	45	12	12	17	44	17	40	10	45	46	13	08	09
5	23	01	21	−6	16	−11	39	6	38	6	42	12	12	17	46	17	42	10	49	42	13	04	13
6	23	05	04	−5	52	−11	25	6	36	6	40	12	11	17	48	17	44	10	53	39	13	00	17
7	23	08	47	−5	29	−11	12	6	33	6	37	12	11	17	50	17	46	10	57	35	12	56	21
8	23	12	29	−5	06	−10	57	6	31	6	35	12	11	17	52	17	48	11	01	32	12	52	25
9	23	16	11	−4	43	−10	42	6	29	6	32	12	11	17	53	17	50	11	05	28	12	48	29
10	23	19	52	−4	19	−10	27	6	27	6	29	12	10	17	55	17	52	11	09	25	12	44	33
11	23	23	34	−3	56	−10	12	6	24	6	27	12	10	17	57	17	54	11	13	21	12	40	37
12	23	27	14	−3	32	−9	56	6	22	6	24	12	10	17	59	17	56	11	17	18	12	36	41
13	23	30	55	−3	08	−9	40	6	20	6	22	12	10	18	00	17	59	11	21	15	12	32	46
14	23	34	35	−2	45	−9	24	6	17	6	19	12	09	18	02	18	01	11	25	11	12	28	50
15	23	38	15	−2	21	−9	07	6	15	6	16	12	09	18	04	18	03	11	29	08	12	24	54
16	23	41	55	−1	57	−8	51	6	13	6	14	12	09	18	06	18	05	11	33	04	12	20	58
17	23	45	35	−1	34	−8	34	6	11	6	11	12	08	18	07	18	07	11	37	01	12	17	02
18	23	49	14	−1	10	−8	17	6	08	6	09	12	08	18	09	18	09	11	40	57	12	13	06
19	23	52	53	−0	46	−7	59	6	06	6	06	12	08	18	11	18	11	11	44	54	12	09	10
20	23	56	32	−0	22	−7	42	6	04	6	03	12	08	18	12	18	13	11	48	50	12	05	14
21	0	00	11	+0	01	−7	24	6	01	6	01	12	07	18	14	18	15	11	52	47	12	01	18
22	0	03	50	+0	25	−7	06	5	59	5	58	12	07	18	16	18	17	11	56	44	11	57	22
23	0	07	29	+0	49	−6	49	5	57	5	55	12	07	18	18	18	19	12	00	40	11	53	26
24	0	11	08	+1	12	−6	31	5	54	5	53	12	06	18	19	18	21	12	04	37	11	49	31
25	0	14	46	+1	36	−6	13	5	52	5	50	12	06	18	21	18	23	12	08	33	11	45	35
26	0	18	25	+1	60	−5	55	5	50	5	48	12	06	18	23	18	25	12	12	30	11	41	39
27	0	22	03	+2	23	−5	37	5	47	5	45	12	05	18	25	18	27	12	16	26	11	37	43
28	0	25	41	+2	47	−5	18	5	45	5	42	12	05	18	26	18	29	12	20	23	11	33	47
29	0	29	20	+3	10	−5	00	5	43	5	40	12	05	18	28	18	31	12	24	19	11	29	51
30	0	32	58	+3	33	−4	42	5	40	5	37	12	05	18	30	18	33	12	28	16	11	25	55
31	0	36	37	+3	57	−4	24	5	38	5	34	12	04	18	31	18	35	12	32	13	11	21	59

DURATION OF TWILIGHT (in minutes)

Latitude	52° 1 March	56°	52° 11 March	56°	52° 21 March	56°	52° 31 March	56°
Civil	34	37	34	37	34	37	34	38
Nautical	73	80	73	80	74	81	75	84
Astronomical	112	124	113	125	115	128	120	135

THE NIGHT SKY

Mercury remains too close to the Sun for observation throughout the month.

Venus, magnitude −4.0, continues to be visible as a brilliant object in the evening skies and by the end of the month is visible for nearly three hours after sunset. On the evening of the 22nd the thin, waxing crescent Moon will be seen passing about 4° below Venus.

Mars, magnitude +1.5, may only be glimpsed with difficulty for a short while at around 19h low above the western horizon, early in the month. Later Mars becomes lost in the glare of the lengthening twilight and will not be seen again in these latitudes for about six months.

Jupiter, magnitude −2.4, is a conspicuous object in the eastern sky in the early evenings, and visible in the southern skies for several hours after midnight. Jupiter is moving very slowly retrograde in Cancer and observers with binoculars will get a pleasant surprise during March and April as Jupiter will be seen only a couple of degrees south-east of the open cluster Praesepe (the Beehive); which is just visible to the naked-eye as a misty patch of light.

Saturn is a morning object, magnitude +0.6, low above the south-eastern horizon. The Moon is 2° above Saturn on 12th.

Uranus and Mars are less than 0.25° apart at altitude 5° in the west on 11th at 19h30m (in twilight).

Total eclipse of the Sun will occur on 20th March. This is a very large partial eclipse for the British Isles and details will be found on page 1114.

THE MOON

Day	R.A. h	R.A. m	Dec. °	Hor. Par '	Diam. '	Sun's Co-Long. °	PA of Br. Limb °	Ph. %	Age d	Rise 52° h	Rise 52° m	Rise 56° h	Rise 56° m	Transit h	Transit m	Set 52° h	Set 52° m	Set 56° h	Set 56° m
1	7	16	+17.1	54.9	29.8	393	273	81	10.2	13	42	13	26	21	22	4	20	4	36
2	8	05	+15.3	54.5	29.6	405	276	88	11.2	14	42	14	29	22	08	4	55	5	09
3	8	54	+12.9	54.2	29.6	417	278	93	12.2	15	43	15	33	22	53	5	26	5	36
4	9	41	+9.9	54.0	29.4	429	278	97	13.2	16	45	16	39	23	36	5	52	6	00
5	10	27	+6.6	54.0	29.4	441	272	99	14.2	17	48	17	45	—		6	16	6	21
6	11	12	+3.0	54.0	29.4	93	150	100	15.2	18	51	18	51	0	19	6	39	6	41
7	11	57	-0.7	54.1	29.4	106	117	99	16.2	19	54	19	57	1	01	7	02	7	00
8	12	42	-4.4	54.3	29.6	118	113	96	17.2	20	57	21	04	1	44	7	25	7	20
9	13	28	-7.9	54.5	29.8	130	110	91	18.2	22	01	22	11	2	27	7	49	7	42
10	14	16	-11.2	54.9	30.0	142	107	85	19.2	23	04	23	17	3	12	8	17	8	06
11	15	05	-14.0	55.4	30.2	154	104	77	20.2	—		—		3	59	8	48	8	34
12	15	56	-16.2	56.0	30.6	166	100	68	21.2	0	07	0	23	4	48	9	25	9	09
13	16	49	-17.7	56.8	31.0	179	96	58	22.2	1	08	1	25	5	40	10	10	9	52
14	17	44	-18.3	57.6	31.4	191	92	47	23.2	2	05	2	23	6	33	11	03	10	45
15	18	41	-17.8	58.4	31.8	203	87	37	24.2	2	56	3	13	7	29	12	05	11	48
16	19	39	-16.3	59.3	32.4	215	83	26	25.2	3	42	3	57	8	26	13	15	13	01
17	20	38	-13.7	60.1	32.8	227	80	17	26.2	4	21	4	33	9	22	14	32	14	21
18	21	37	-10.2	60.8	33.2	240	77	9	27.2	4	57	5	05	10	19	15	53	15	46
19	22	35	-5.9	61.2	33.4	252	76	3	28.2	5	29	5	33	11	16	17	15	17	13
20	23	33	-1.2	61.3	33.4	264	82	0	29.2	5	59	5	59	12	12	18	38	18	40
21	0	31	+3.5	61.1	33.2	276	246	1	0.6	6	30	6	26	13	08	19	59	20	06
22	1	29	+8.0	60.6	33.0	288	251	4	1.6	7	01	6	53	14	03	21	18	21	29
23	2	26	+11.8	59.8	32.6	301	255	10	2.6	7	35	7	24	14	59	22	33	22	47
24	3	23	+14.9	58.9	32.0	313	258	18	3.6	8	13	7	59	15	54	23	41	23	58
25	4	20	+17.0	57.9	31.6	325	263	27	4.6	8	56	8	40	16	47	—		—	
26	5	15	+18.1	57.0	31.0	337	267	37	5.6	9	45	9	27	17	40	0	42	1	00
27	6	09	+18.2	56.1	30.6	349	271	47	6.6	10	38	10	20	18	31	1	35	1	52
28	7	02	+17.4	55.4	30.2	362	275	57	7.6	11	35	11	19	19	19	2	19	2	35
29	7	52	+15.8	54.8	29.8	374	279	66	8.6	12	34	12	21	20	06	2	56	3	10
30	8	41	+13.5	54.4	29.6	386	282	75	9.6	13	35	13	25	20	51	3	28	3	40
31	9	28	+10.7	54.2	29.6	398	285	83	10.6	14	37	14	29	21	34	3	56	4	04

MERCURY

Day	R.A. h	R.A. m	Dec °	Mag.	Diam. "	Phase %	Rise h	Rise m	Transit h	Transit m	Set h	Set m
1	21	04.7	-17.4	+0.2	7	65	6	04	10	25	14	46
3	21	14.7	-17.0	+0.2	6	68	6	03	10	27	14	51
5	21	25.0	-16.5	+0.2	6	70	6	02	10	30	14	57
7	21	35.7	-15.8	+0.1	6	72	6	01	10	32	15	04
9	21	46.7	-15.1	+0.1	6	75	6	00	10	36	15	12
11	21	58.0	-14.4	+0.0	6	77	5	58	10	39	15	20
13	22	09.5	-13.5	+0.0	6	79	5	56	10	43	15	29
15	22	21.2	-12.5	-0.1	6	80	5	54	10	46	15	39
17	22	33.1	-11.5	-0.1	5	82	5	52	10	50	15	49
19	22	45.2	-10.3	-0.2	5	84	5	50	10	55	16	00
21	22	57.4	-9.1	-0.3	5	86	5	47	10	59	16	11
23	23	09.9	-7.9	-0.4	5	88	5	44	11	03	16	23
25	23	22.6	-6.5	-0.5	5	89	5	41	11	08	16	35
27	23	35.4	-5.1	-0.6	5	91	5	38	11	13	16	48
29	23	48.5	-3.5	-0.7	5	93	5	35	11	18	17	02
31	0	01.9	-2.0	-0.9	5	95	5	32	11	28	17	16

Rising and setting times are for latitude 54°

VENUS

Day	R.A. h	R.A. m	Dec °	Mag.	Diam. "	Phase %	Rise h	Rise m	Transit h	Transit m	Set h	Set m
1	0	37.2	+3.2	-3.4	12	86	7	36	14	01	20	18
6	0	59.4	+5.8	-3.4	12	85	7	24	14	03	20	35
11	1	21.8	+8.3	-3.4	13	84	7	13	14	06	20	52
16	1	44.2	+10.8	-3.4	13	83	7	01	14	09	21	09
21	2	07.0	+13.2	-3.5	13	81	6	50	14	12	21	26
26	2	30.0	+15.4	-3.5	13	80	6	39	14	15	21	43
31	2	53.3	+17.5	-3.5	14	78	6	29	14	19	22	01

MARS

Day	R.A. h	R.A. m	Dec °	Mag.	Diam. "	Phase %	Rise h	Rise m	Transit h	Transit m	Set h	Set m
1	0	25.3	+2.2	+1.5	4	97	7	30	13	49	20	00
6	0	39.3	+3.8	+1.5	4	98	7	16	13	43	20	03
11	0	53.2	+5.3	+1.5	4	98	7	02	13	38	20	06
16	1	07.1	+6.8	+1.5	4	98	6	47	13	32	20	09
21	1	21.1	+8.3	+1.5	4	98	6	33	13	26	20	11
26	1	35.1	+9.7	+1.6	4	98	6	19	13	20	20	14
31	1	49.1	+11.1	+1.6	4	99	6	05	13	15	20	16

SUNRISE AND SUNSET

	London 0° 05'	51° 30'	Bristol 2° 35'	51° 28'	Birmingham 1° 55'	52° 28'	Manchester 2° 15'	53° 28'	Newcastle 1° 37'	54° 59'	Glasgow 4° 14'	55° 52'	Belfast 5° 56'	54° 35'
d	h m	h m	h m	h m	h m	h m	h m	h m	h m	h m	h m	h m	h m	h m
1	6 46	17 40	6 56	17 50	6 55	17 46	6 58	17 46	6 57	17 41	7 09	17 51	7 14	17 59
2	6 44	17 42	6 54	17 52	6 53	17 48	6 55	17 48	6 55	17 43	7 07	17 53	7 12	18 01
3	6 42	17 44	6 52	17 54	6 50	17 50	6 53	17 50	6 52	17 45	7 04	17 55	7 09	18 03
4	6 40	17 45	6 50	17 55	6 48	17 52	6 51	17 52	6 50	17 47	7 02	17 57	7 07	18 05
5	6 38	17 47	6 48	17 57	6 46	17 53	6 48	17 54	6 48	17 50	6 59	17 59	7 04	18 07
6	6 35	17 49	6 45	17 59	6 44	17 55	6 46	17 56	6 45	17 52	6 57	18 01	7 02	18 09
7	6 33	17 51	6 43	18 01	6 41	17 57	6 44	17 57	6 43	17 54	6 54	18 03	6 59	18 11
8	6 31	17 52	6 41	18 02	6 39	17 59	6 41	17 59	6 40	17 56	6 51	18 05	6 57	18 13
9	6 29	17 54	6 39	18 04	6 37	18 01	6 39	18 01	6 38	17 58	6 49	18 07	6 55	18 15
10	6 27	17 56	6 37	18 06	6 35	18 02	6 37	18 03	6 35	18 00	6 46	18 09	6 52	18 17
11	6 24	17 57	6 34	18 07	6 32	18 04	6 34	18 05	6 33	18 02	6 44	18 11	6 50	18 19
12	6 22	17 59	6 32	18 09	6 30	18 06	6 32	18 07	6 30	18 04	6 41	18 13	6 47	18 21
13	6 20	18 01	6 30	18 11	6 28	18 08	6 29	18 09	6 28	18 05	6 39	18 16	6 45	18 23
14	6 18	18 03	6 28	18 13	6 25	18 10	6 27	18 11	6 25	18 07	6 36	18 18	6 42	18 25
15	6 15	18 04	6 25	18 14	6 23	18 11	6 25	18 12	6 23	18 09	6 33	18 20	6 40	18 27
16	6 13	18 06	6 23	18 16	6 21	18 13	6 22	18 14	6 20	18 11	6 31	18 22	6 37	18 29
17	6 11	18 08	6 21	18 18	6 18	18 15	6 20	18 16	6 17	18 13	6 28	18 24	6 35	18 31
18	6 09	18 09	6 19	18 19	6 16	18 17	6 17	18 18	6 15	18 15	6 25	18 26	6 32	18 33
19	6 06	18 11	6 16	18 21	6 14	18 18	6 15	18 20	6 12	18 17	6 23	18 28	6 30	18 35
20	6 04	18 13	6 14	18 23	6 11	18 20	6 12	18 22	6 10	18 19	6 20	18 30	6 27	18 37
21	6 02	18 14	6 12	18 24	6 09	18 22	6 10	18 24	6 07	18 21	6 18	18 32	6 25	18 39
22	5 59	18 16	6 09	18 26	6 07	18 24	6 08	18 25	6 05	18 23	6 15	18 34	6 22	18 40
23	5 57	18 18	6 07	18 28	6 04	18 26	6 05	18 27	6 02	18 25	6 12	18 36	6 20	18 42
24	5 55	18 20	6 05	18 30	6 02	18 27	6 03	18 29	6 00	18 27	6 10	18 38	6 17	18 44
25	5 53	18 21	6 03	18 31	6 00	18 29	6 00	18 31	5 57	18 29	6 07	18 40	6 15	18 46
26	5 50	18 23	6 00	18 33	5 57	18 31	5 58	18 33	5 55	18 31	6 04	18 42	6 12	18 48
27	5 48	18 25	5 58	18 35	5 55	18 33	5 56	18 35	5 52	18 33	6 02	18 44	6 09	18 50
28	5 46	18 26	5 56	18 36	5 52	18 34	5 53	18 36	5 49	18 35	5 59	18 46	6 07	18 52
29	5 43	18 28	5 54	18 38	5 50	18 36	5 51	18 38	5 47	18 37	5 57	18 48	6 04	18 54
30	5 41	18 30	5 51	18 40	5 48	18 38	5 48	18 40	5 44	18 39	5 54	18 50	6 02	18 56
31	5 39	18 31	5 49	18 41	5 45	18 40	5 46	18 42	5 42	18 41	5 51	18 52	5 59	18 58

JUPITER

Day	R.A. h m	Dec °	Mag.	Diam. "	Rise h m	Transit h m	Set h m
1	9 09.6	+17.4	−2.1	45	14 43	22 32	6 17
11	9 05.6	+17.7	−2.0	44	13 58	21 49	5 36
21	9 02.7	+17.9	−2.0	43	13 14	21 06	4 55
31	9 01.0	+18.0	−1.9	42	12 32	20 25	4 15

Equatorial Diam. 43″, Polar Diam. 40″

SATURN

Day	R.A. h m	Dec °	Mag.	Diam. "	Rise h m	Transit h m	Set h m
1	16 12.0	−19.0	+0.7	17	1 22	5 33	9 44
11	16 12.6	−19.0	+0.6	17	0 44	4 54	9 05
21	16 12.5	−19.0	+0.6	17	24 00	4 15	8 26
31	16 11.7	−18.9	+0.5	18	23 20	3 35	7 46

Equatorial Diam. 17″, Polar Diam. 16″
Rings – major axis 40″ minor axis 17″, Tilt 25°

URANUS

Day	R.A. h m	Dec °	Mag.	Diam. "	Rise h m	Transit h m	Set h m
1	0 53.4	+5.0	+6.2	3	7 43	14 17	20 44
11	0 55.3	+5.2	+6.3	3	7 04	13 40	20 08
21	0 57.4	+5.5	+6.3	3	6 25	13 02	19 32
31	0 59.4	+5.7	+6.3	3	5 47	12 25	18 56

NEPTUNE

Day	R.A. h m	Dec °	Mag.	Diam. "	Rise h m	Transit h m	Set h m
1	22 36.6	−9.6	+7.8	2	6 47	11 57	17 06
11	22 38.0	−9.4	+7.8	2	6 09	11 19	16 29
21	22 39.4	−9.3	+7.8	2	5 30	10 41	15 52
31	22 40.7	−9.2	+7.8	2	4 51	10 03	15 15

APRIL 2015

FOURTH MONTH, 30 DAYS. *Aperire*, to open; Earth opens to receive seed.

1	*Wednesday*	Charles Dickens' shortest novel *Hard Times* begins its serialisation in *Household Words* 1854	day 91
2	*Thursday*	The Danish author Hans Christian Andersen, renowned for his fairy tales *b.* 1805	92
3	*Friday*	George Herbert, an Anglican priest, orator and one of the metaphysical poets *b.* 1593	93
4	*Saturday*	The American author Maya Angelou, famed for her biography *I Know Why the Caged Bird Sings b.* 1928	94
5	*Sunday*	Thomas Hobbes, political philosopher who penned the influential work *Leviathan b.* 1588	95
6	*Monday*	Italian Renaissance poet Petrarch saw 'Laura', the inspiration for his poetry, for the first time 1327	week 14 day 96
7	*Tuesday*	William Wordsworth, major poet of the Romantic Age and author of *The Prelude b.* 1770	97
8	*Wednesday*	Erik Axel Karlfeldt, Swedish poet and posthumous winner of the 1931 Nobel Prize in Literature *d.* 1931	98
9	*Thursday*	The French poet Charles Baudelaire, who wrote *Les Fleurs du mal* (*The Flowers of Evil*) *b.* 1821	99
10	*Friday*	Algernon Charles Swinburne, decadent novelist, poet and playwright who devised the roundel form *d.* 1909	100
11	*Saturday*	George Bernard Shaw's play *Pygmalion* opened at His Majesty's Theatre in London 1914	101
12	*Sunday*	Valentin Kataev, Russian novelist who developed the 'lyrical diary' style of writing *d.* 1986	102
13	*Monday*	Ian Fleming's first James Bond novel, *Casino Royale*, adapted for cinema in 2006, is published 1953	week 15 day 103
14	*Tuesday*	John Steinbeck's Pulitzer Prize winning novel *The Grapes of Wrath* is published 1939	104
15	*Wednesday*	J. M. Barrie presents the copyright of his *Peter Pan* works to Great Ormond Street Hospital in London 1929	105
16	*Thursday*	Aphra Behn, the first professional female writer in English literature and author of *Oroonoko d.* 1689	106
17	*Friday*	Geoffrey Chaucer is believed to have read his *Canterbury Tales* aloud in the court of King Richard II 1397	107
18	*Saturday*	The poet Ezra Pound is freed from St. Elizabeth's Hospital for the criminally insane 1958	108
19	*Sunday*	The final volume of the first edition of the *Oxford English Dictionary* is published 1928	109
20	*Monday*	The gothic writer Bram Stoker, who created the modern vampire in his novel *Dracula d.* 1912	week 16 day 110
21	*Tuesday*	Charlotte Brontë, who wrote *Jane Eyre* and was the eldest of the three Brontë sisters *b.* 1816	111
22	*Wednesday*	William Caxton produces the first translation of Ovid's *Metamorphoses* 1480	112
23	*Thursday*	William Shakespeare, poet and playwright *d.* 1616	113
24	*Friday*	The prolific Victorian novelist Anthony Trollope, who wrote the *Chronicles of Barsetshire b.* 1815	114
25	*Saturday*	Daniel Defoe publishes *Robinson Crusoe*, helping to popularise the novel form in England 1719	115
26	*Sunday*	Vicente Aleixandre, Spanish poet who was awarded the 1977 Nobel Prize in Literature *b.* 1898	116
27	*Monday*	Ralph Waldo Emerson, American poet *d.* 1882	week 17 day 117
28	*Tuesday*	Harold Pinter's second full-length play *The Birthday Party* premieres at the Arts Theatre, Cambridge 1958	118
29	*Wednesday*	The American writer Henry James' collection of travel pieces *Transatlantic Sketches* is published 1875	119
30	*Thursday*	Roman poet Marcus Annaeus Lucanus, known as Lucan, commits suicide after he is accused of treason AD 65	120

ASTRONOMICAL PHENOMENA

d	h	
4	12	Lunar eclipse (not UK)
6	14	Uranus in conjunction with the Sun
8	10	Uranus 0.5° N of Mercury
8	13	Saturn 2° S. of the Moon
10	04	Mercury superior conjunction with the Sun
15	13	Neptune 4° S. of the Moon
18	01	Uranus 0.04° N. of the Moon
19	11	Mercury 3° N. of the Moon
19	19	Mars 3° N. of the Moon
23	07	Mars 1° S of Mercury
26	18	Jupiter 5° N. of the Moon

MINIMA OF ALGOL

d	h	d	h	d	h
1	05.7	12	17.0	24	04.3
4	02.5	15	13.8	27	01.1
6	23.4	18	10.6	29	21.9
9	20.2	21	07.5		

CONSTELLATIONS

The following constellations are near the meridian at

	d	h		d	h
March	1	24	April	15	21
March	16	23	May	1	20
April	1	22	May	16	19

Cepheus (below the Pole), Cassiopeia (below the Pole), Ursa Major, Leo Minor, Leo., Sextans, Hydra and Crater

THE MOON

Phases, Apsides and Node	d	h	m
○ Full Moon	4	12	06
☾ Last Quarter	12	03	44
● New Moon	18	18	57
☽ First Quarter	25	23	55
Apogee (406,012km)	1	13	02
Perigee (361,023km)	17	03	49

Mean longitude of ascending node on 1st, 190°

THE SUN

s.d. 16′.0

Day	Right Ascension			Dec. +		Equation of time		Rise 52°		56°		Transit		Set 52°		56°		Sidereal time			Transit of first point of Aries		
	h	m	s	°	′	m	s	h	m	h	m	h	h	m	h	h	m	h	m	s	h	m	s
1	0	40	15	4	20	−4	06	5	36	5	32	12	04	18	33	18	38	12	36	09	11	18	03
2	0	43	54	4	43	−3	48	5	34	5	29	12	04	18	35	18	40	12	40	06	11	14	07
3	0	47	33	5	06	−3	30	5	31	5	26	12	03	18	37	18	42	12	44	02	11	10	11
4	0	51	12	5	29	−3	13	5	29	5	24	12	03	18	38	18	44	12	47	59	11	06	16
5	0	54	51	5	52	−2	55	5	27	5	21	12	03	18	40	18	46	12	51	55	11	02	20
6	0	58	30	6	15	−2	38	5	24	5	19	12	02	18	42	18	48	12	55	52	10	58	24
7	1	02	09	6	37	−2	21	5	22	5	16	12	02	18	43	18	50	12	59	48	10	54	28
8	1	05	49	6	60	−2	04	5	20	5	13	12	02	18	45	18	52	13	03	45	10	50	32
9	1	09	29	7	22	−1	47	5	18	5	11	12	02	18	47	18	54	13	07	42	10	46	36
10	1	13	09	7	45	−1	31	5	15	5	08	12	01	18	49	18	56	13	11	38	10	42	40
11	1	16	49	8	07	−1	15	5	13	5	06	12	01	18	50	18	58	13	15	35	10	38	44
12	1	20	30	8	29	−0	59	5	11	5	03	12	01	18	52	19	00	13	19	31	10	34	48
13	1	24	11	8	51	−0	43	5	09	5	01	12	01	18	54	19	02	13	23	28	10	30	52
14	1	27	52	9	13	−0	28	5	06	4	58	12	00	18	55	19	04	13	27	24	10	26	56
15	1	31	34	9	34	−0	13	5	04	4	56	12	00	18	57	19	06	13	31	21	10	23	01
16	1	35	16	9	56	+0	01	5	02	4	53	12	00	18	59	19	08	13	35	17	10	19	05
17	1	38	59	10	17	+0	16	5	00	4	51	12	00	19	00	19	10	13	39	14	10	15	09
18	1	42	41	10	38	+0	29	4	58	4	48	11	59	19	02	19	12	13	43	11	10	11	13
19	1	46	25	10	59	+0	43	4	56	4	46	11	59	19	04	19	14	13	47	07	10	07	17
20	1	50	08	11	20	+0	56	4	54	4	43	11	59	19	06	19	16	13	51	04	10	03	21
21	1	53	52	11	40	+1	08	4	51	4	41	11	59	19	07	19	18	13	55	00	9	59	25
22	1	57	37	12	01	+1	20	4	49	4	38	11	59	19	09	19	20	13	58	57	9	55	29
23	2	01	22	12	21	+1	32	4	47	4	36	11	58	19	11	19	22	14	02	53	9	51	33
24	2	05	07	12	41	+1	43	4	45	4	33	11	58	19	12	19	24	14	06	50	9	47	37
25	2	08	53	13	01	+1	54	4	43	4	31	11	58	19	14	19	26	14	10	46	9	43	42
26	2	12	39	13	20	+2	04	4	41	4	29	11	58	19	16	19	28	14	14	43	9	39	46
27	2	16	26	13	40	+2	14	4	39	4	26	11	58	19	17	19	30	14	18	40	9	35	50
28	2	20	13	13	59	+2	24	4	37	4	24	11	58	19	19	19	33	14	22	36	9	31	54
29	2	24	00	14	18	+2	32	4	35	4	22	11	57	19	21	19	35	14	26	33	9	27	58
30	2	27	49	14	36	+2	41	4	33	4	19	11	57	19	23	19	37	14	30	29	9	24	02

DURATION OF TWILIGHT (in minutes)

Latitude	52°	56°	52°	56°	52°	56°	52°	56°
	1 April		11 April		21 April		31 April	
Civil	34	38	35	39	37	42	39	44
Nautical	76	84	79	89	83	96	89	106
Astronomical	120	136	127	147	137	165	152	204

THE NIGHT SKY

Mercury passes through superior conjunction on the 7th and about fifteen days later becomes visible as an evening object, very low above the west-north-western horizon for a short while, around the end of evening civil twilight. During this period its magnitude fades from −1.2 to 0.0. This is the most favourable evening apparition of the year for observers in the latitudes of the British Isles.

Venus is still visible as a brilliant object in the evening sky, magnitude −4.1. By the end of April it is visible for well over three hours after sunset before setting over the west-north-west horizon. On 21st the Moon is 4° below Venus at 21h.

Mars is unsuitably placed for observation.

Jupiter continues to be visible as a bright object in the evening sky, magnitude −2.2, and can still be seen after midnight. Jupiter reaches its second stationary point on the 4th and then resumes its direct motion: it is in the constellation of Cancer.

Saturn, magnitude +0.4, is now visible for the greater part of the night, crossing the meridian well before dawn. The Moon will be seen 4° above Saturn at 01h on 8th.

THE MOON

Day	R.A. h	R.A. m	Dec. °	Hor. Par. '	Diam. '	Sun's Co-Long. °	PA of Br. Limb °	Ph. %	Age d	Rise 52° h	Rise 52° m	Rise 56° h	Rise 56° m	Transit h	Transit m	Set 52° h	Set 52° m	Set 56° h	Set 56° m
1	10	15	+7.5	54.0	29.4	410	287	89	11.6	15	39	15	35	22	17	4	21	4	26
2	10	60	+3.9	54.0	29.4	422	288	94	12.6	16	42	16	41	22	59	4	44	4	47
3	11	45	+0.3	54.1	29.4	435	289	98	13.6	17	45	17	47	23	42	5	07	5	06
4	12	31	−3.5	54.3	29.6	447	292	100	14.6	18	49	18	54	—		5	29	5	26
5	13	17	−7.1	54.6	29.8	99	102	100	15.6	19	53	20	02	0	26	5	54	5	47
6	14	04	−10.4	54.9	30.0	111	103	98	16.6	20	57	21	09	1	10	6	20	6	10
7	14	53	−13.4	55.3	30.2	123	101	94	17.6	22	01	22	15	1	57	6	51	6	38
8	15	44	−15.8	55.8	30.4	135	98	89	18.6	23	02	23	19	2	46	7	26	7	10
9	16	36	−17.4	56.3	30.6	148	95	81	19.6	23	59	—		3	36	8	08	7	50
10	17	31	−18.2	56.9	31.0	160	90	73	20.6	—		0	17	4	28	8	57	8	39
11	18	26	−18.0	57.5	31.4	172	86	63	21.6	0	50	1	09	5	22	9	55	9	38
12	19	22	−16.8	58.2	31.8	184	82	52	22.6	1	38	1	54	6	17	11	00	10	45
13	20	19	−14.6	58.9	32.2	196	78	41	23.6	2	18	2	32	7	12	12	12	12	00
14	21	16	−11.5	59.6	32.4	209	74	30	24.6	2	54	3	04	8	06	13	28	13	20
15	22	12	−7.6	60.2	32.8	221	72	20	25.6	3	26	3	32	9	01	14	47	14	43
16	23	09	−3.2	60.6	33.0	233	70	11	26.6	3	56	3	58	9	55	16	07	16	07
17	0	06	+1.4	60.7	33.0	245	68	5	27.6	4	26	4	24	10	50	17	29	17	33
18	1	03	+6.0	60.6	33.0	257	64	1	28.6	4	56	4	50	11	46	18	49	18	57
19	2	00	+10.2	60.3	32.8	270	284	0	0.1	5	29	5	19	12	42	20	07	20	19
20	2	58	+13.7	59.7	32.6	282	264	2	1.1	6	05	5	52	13	38	21	20	21	35
21	3	56	+16.2	58.9	32.0	294	265	7	2.1	6	47	6	31	14	34	22	27	22	44
22	4	54	+17.8	58.0	31.6	306	269	13	3.1	7	34	7	16	15	29	23	25	23	43
23	5	50	+18.3	57.1	31.2	319	273	22	4.1	8	26	8	08	16	22	—		—	
24	6	44	+17.8	56.3	30.6	331	277	31	5.1	9	23	9	07	17	12	0	14	0	31
25	7	37	+16.4	55.5	30.2	343	280	40	6.1	10	23	10	09	18	01	0	55	1	10
26	8	27	+14.3	54.9	30.0	355	284	50	7.1	11	25	11	13	18	47	1	29	1	42
27	9	15	+11.6	54.5	29.6	367	287	60	8.1	12	27	12	18	19	31	1	59	2	09
28	10	01	+8.5	54.2	29.6	380	289	69	9.1	13	29	13	23	20	14	2	25	2	31
29	10	47	+5.0	54.1	29.4	392	291	77	10.1	14	32	14	29	20	56	2	48	2	52
30	11	32	+1.4	54.2	29.6	404	292	85	11.1	15	34	15	35	21	39	3	11	3	12

MERCURY

Day	R.A. h	R.A. m	Dec °	Mag.	Diam. "	Phase %	Rise h	Rise m	Transit h	Transit m	Set h	Set m
1	0	08.4	−1.2	−0.9	5	95	5	34	11	34	17	27
3	0	22.2	+0.5	−1.1	5	97	5	31	11	40	17	42
5	0	36.2	+2.2	−1.3	5	98	5	27	11	46	17	57
7	0	50.6	+4.0	−1.4	5	99	5	24	11	53	18	14
9	1	05.2	+5.8	−1.6	5	100	5	20	12	00	18	31
11	1	20.2	+7.7	−1.7	5	100	5	17	12	07	18	48
13	1	35.5	+9.5	−1.7	5	99	5	14	12	14	19	06
15	1	50.9	+11.4	−1.6	5	98	5	10	12	22	19	25
17	2	06.5	+13.2	−1.5	5	95	5	07	12	29	19	43
19	2	22.2	+14.9	−1.4	5	92	5	04	12	37	20	02
21	2	37.6	+16.5	−1.2	6	87	5	01	12	44	20	20
23	2	52.8	+18.0	−1.0	6	81	4	58	12	52	20	37
25	3	07.5	+19.3	−0.8	6	75	4	56	12	59	20	53
27	3	21.6	+20.5	−0.6	6	69	4	54	13	05	21	08
29	3	35.0	+21.6	−0.4	6	62	4	51	13	10	21	21

Rising and setting times are for latitude 54°

VENUS

Day	R.A. h	R.A. m	Dec °	Mag.	Diam. "	Phase %	Rise h	Rise m	Transit h	Transit m	Set h	Set m
1	2	57.9	+17.8	−3.5	14	78	6	31	14	23	22	08
6	3	21.6	+19.7	−3.5	14	77	6	22	14	27	22	25
11	3	45.7	+21.3	−3.5	15	75	6	15	14	32	22	41
16	4	10.1	+22.8	−3.6	15	73	6	08	14	36	22	57
21	4	34.8	+24.0	−3.6	16	71	6	04	14	41	23	11
26	4	59.6	+24.9	−3.6	16	69	6	01	14	46	23	24

MARS

Day	R.A. h	R.A. m	Dec °	Mag.	Diam. "	Phase %	Rise h	Rise m	Transit h	Transit m	Set h	Set m
1	1	51.8	+11.3	+1.6	4	99	6	06	13	17	20	21
6	2	05.9	+12.7	+1.6	4	99	5	53	13	12	20	23
11	2	20.1	+14.0	+1.6	4	99	5	39	13	06	20	25
16	2	34.3	+15.2	+1.6	4	99	5	26	13	01	20	28
21	2	48.6	+16.3	+1.6	4	99	5	13	12	55	20	30
26	3	03.0	+17.4	+1.6	4	99	5	01	12	50	20	32

SUNRISE AND SUNSET

	London				Bristol				Birmingham				Manchester				Newcastle				Glasgow				Belfast			
	0° 05'		51° 30'		2° 35'		51° 28'		1° 55'		52° 28'		2° 15'		53° 28'		1° 37'		54° 59'		4° 14'		55° 52'		5° 56'		54° 35'	
d	h	m	h	m	h	m	h	m	h	m	h	m	h	m	h	m	h	m	h	m	h	m	h	m	h	m	h	m
1	5	37	18	33	5	47	18	43	5	43	18	41	5	43	18	44	5	39	18	43	5	49	18	54	5	57	19	00
2	5	34	18	35	5	44	18	45	5	41	18	43	5	41	18	45	5	37	18	45	5	46	18	56	5	54	19	02
3	5	32	18	36	5	42	18	46	5	38	18	45	5	39	18	47	5	34	18	47	5	44	18	58	5	52	19	03
4	5	30	18	38	5	40	18	48	5	36	18	47	5	36	18	49	5	32	18	49	5	41	19	00	5	50	19	05
5	5	28	18	40	5	38	18	50	5	34	18	48	5	34	18	51	5	29	18	51	5	38	19	02	5	47	19	07
6	5	25	18	41	5	35	18	51	5	31	18	50	5	31	18	53	5	27	18	53	5	36	19	04	5	45	19	09
7	5	23	18	43	5	33	18	53	5	29	18	52	5	29	18	55	5	24	18	54	5	33	19	06	5	42	19	11
8	5	21	18	45	5	31	18	55	5	27	18	53	5	27	18	56	5	22	18	56	5	31	19	08	5	40	19	13
9	5	19	18	46	5	29	18	56	5	25	18	55	5	24	18	58	5	19	18	58	5	28	19	10	5	37	19	15
10	5	16	18	48	5	27	18	58	5	22	18	57	5	22	19	00	5	17	19	00	5	25	19	12	5	35	19	17
11	5	14	18	50	5	24	19	00	5	20	18	59	5	20	19	02	5	14	19	02	5	23	19	14	5	32	19	19
12	5	12	18	51	5	22	19	01	5	18	19	00	5	17	19	04	5	12	19	04	5	20	19	17	5	30	19	21
13	5	10	18	53	5	20	19	03	5	15	19	02	5	15	19	05	5	09	19	06	5	18	19	19	5	27	19	23
14	5	08	18	55	5	18	19	05	5	13	19	04	5	13	19	07	5	07	19	08	5	15	19	21	5	25	19	24
15	5	06	18	56	5	16	19	06	5	11	19	06	5	10	19	09	5	04	19	10	5	13	19	23	5	23	19	26
16	5	03	18	58	5	13	19	08	5	09	19	07	5	08	19	11	5	02	19	12	5	10	19	25	5	20	19	28
17	5	01	19	00	5	11	19	10	5	07	19	09	5	06	19	13	5	00	19	14	5	08	19	27	5	18	19	30
18	4	59	19	01	5	09	19	11	5	04	19	11	5	03	19	15	4	57	19	16	5	05	19	29	5	15	19	32
19	4	57	19	03	5	07	19	13	5	02	19	13	5	01	19	16	4	55	19	18	5	03	19	31	5	13	19	34
20	4	55	19	05	5	05	19	15	5	00	19	14	4	59	19	18	4	52	19	20	5	00	19	33	5	11	19	36
21	4	53	19	06	5	03	19	16	4	58	19	16	4	57	19	20	4	50	19	22	4	58	19	35	5	08	19	38
22	4	51	19	08	5	01	19	18	4	56	19	18	4	54	19	22	4	48	19	24	4	56	19	37	5	06	19	40
23	4	49	19	10	4	59	19	20	4	54	19	20	4	52	19	24	4	45	19	26	4	53	19	39	5	04	19	42
24	4	47	19	11	4	57	19	21	4	52	19	21	4	50	19	26	4	43	19	28	4	51	19	41	5	02	19	44
25	4	45	19	13	4	55	19	23	4	49	19	23	4	48	19	27	4	41	19	30	4	48	19	43	4	59	19	46
26	4	43	19	15	4	53	19	25	4	47	19	25	4	46	19	29	4	39	19	31	4	46	19	45	4	57	19	47
27	4	41	19	16	4	51	19	26	4	45	19	27	4	44	19	31	4	36	19	33	4	44	19	47	4	55	19	49
28	4	39	19	18	4	49	19	28	4	43	19	28	4	42	19	33	4	34	19	35	4	41	19	49	4	53	19	51
29	4	37	19	20	4	47	19	30	4	41	19	30	4	39	19	35	4	32	19	37	4	39	19	51	4	50	19	53
30	4	35	19	21	4	45	19	31	4	39	19	32	4	37	19	36	4	30	19	39	4	37	19	53	4	48	19	55

JUPITER

Day	R.A.		Dec	Mag.	Diam.	Rise		Transit		Set	
	h	m	°		"	h	m	h	m	h	m
1	9	00.9	+18.0	−1.9	41	12	32	20	25	4	15
11	9	00.5	+18.0	−1.8	40	11	52	19	46	3	35
21	9	01.4	+17.9	−1.8	39	11	14	19	07	2	56

Equatorial Diam. 39", Polar Diam. 37"

SATURN

Day	R.A.		Dec	Mag.	Diam.	Rise		Transit		Set	
	h	m	°		"	h	m	h	m	h	m
1	16	11.6	−18.9	+0.5	18	23	20	3	35	7	46
11	16	10.2	−18.8	+0.5	18	22	38	2	54	7	06
21	16	08.1	−18.7	+0.4	18	21	56	2	13	6	25

Equatorial Diam. 18", Polar Diam. 17"
Rings – major axis 41" minor axis 17", Tilt 25°

URANUS

Day	R.A.		Dec	Mag.	Diam.	Rise		Transit		Set	
	h	m	°		"	h	m	h	m	h	m
1	0	59.6	+5.7	+6.3	3	5	47	12	25	18	56
11	1	01.8	+5.9	+6.3	3	5	09	11	48	18	20
21	1	03.9	+6.1	+6.3	3	4	30	11	11	17	44

NEPTUNE

Day	R.A.		Dec	Mag.	Diam.	Rise		Transit		Set	
	h	m	°		"	h	m	h	m	h	m
1	22	40.8	−9.2	+7.8	2	4	51	10	03	15	15
11	22	42.0	−9.0	+7.8	2	4	12	9	25	14	37
21	22	43.1	−8.9	+7.8	2	3	34	8	47	14	00

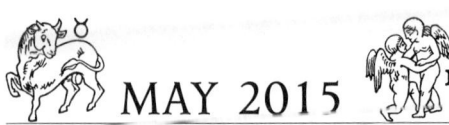

MAY 2015

FIFTH MONTH, 31 DAYS. *Maia*, goddess of growth and increase

1	*Friday*	Carol Ann Duffy becomes the first female Poet Laureate 2009	day 121
2	*Saturday*	The King James Bible, or Authorised Version, is published for the first time 1611	122
3	*Sunday*	Lord Byron swims from Europe to Asia across the Hellespont Strait 1810	123
4	*Monday*	Edith Nesbit, author who penned over 60 children's books including *The Railway Children d.* 1924	week 18 day 124
5	*Tuesday*	*The Examiner* publishes the Romantic poet John Keats' sonnet 'O Solitude' 1816	125
6	*Wednesday*	The American author Ayn Rand's bestselling novel *The Fountainhead* is published 1943	126
7	*Thursday*	Angela Carter, feminist novelist whose works include *The Magic Toyshop* and *Love b.* 1940	127
8	*Friday*	Gustave Flaubert, French novelist and mentor of Guy de Maupassant *d.* 1880	128
9	*Saturday*	The playwright and author Alan Bennett, whose work includes *The History Boys b.* 1934	129
10	*Sunday*	In Nazi Germany, the German Student Union incinerates around 25,000 'un-German' books 1933	130
11	*Monday*	C. S. Lewis and J. R. R. Tolkien meet for the first time at Merton College, Oxford 1926	week 19 day 131
12	*Tuesday*	Edward Lear, artist and poet whose nonsense poetry includes 'The Owl and the Pussycat' *b.* 1812	132
13	*Wednesday*	Daphne du Maurier, author and playwright who penned *Rebecca* and *The Birds b.* 1907	133
14	*Thursday*	*Mrs Dalloway*, Virginia Woolf's novel about a day in the life of a high-society woman, is published 1925	134
15	*Friday*	Alexander Pope's *An Essay on Criticism* is published anonymously 1711	135
16	*Saturday*	James Boswell's pioneering biography, *The Life of Samuel Johnson*, is published 1791	136
17	*Sunday*	L. Frank Baum's children's book *The Wonderful Wizard of Oz* is published 1900	137
18	*Monday*	George Meredith, Victorian novelist and poet who was a favourite of Oscar Wilde *d.* 1909	week 20 day 138
19	*Tuesday*	The Lost Man Booker Prize of 1970 is awarded to J. G. Farrell for *Troubles* 2010	139
20	*Wednesday*	John Clare, labouring-class Romantic poet known for his representations of rural England *d.* 1864	140
21	*Thursday*	Dame Barbara Cartland, romantic novelist *d.* 2000	141
22	*Friday*	The detective fiction writer Arthur Conan Doyle was born in Edinburgh 1859	142
23	*Saturday*	Robert Louis Stevenson's adventure novel *Treasure Island* is first published as a book 1883	143
24	*Sunday*	Joseph Brodsky, Russian poet who was awarded the 1987 Nobel Prize in Literature *b.* 1940	144
25	*Monday*	Oscar Wilde is convicted of gross indecency and sentenced to two years of hard labour 1895	week 21 day 145
26	*Tuesday*	Bram Stoker's gothic horror novel *Dracula*, which references *Whitaker's Almanack*, is published 1897	146
27	*Wednesday*	The American poet and author Edgar Allan Poe enlists as a private in the US Army 1827	147
28	*Thursday*	Anne Brontë, the youngest member of the literary family, dies of pulmonary tuberculosis 1849	148
29	*Friday*	Juan Ramón Jiménez, Spanish poet who received the 1956 Nobel Prize in Literature *d.* 1958	149
30	*Saturday*	The dramatist and poet Christopher Marlowe is stabbed to death 1593	150
31	*Sunday*	The final entry in the diary of Samuel Pepys 1669	151

ASTRONOMICAL PHENOMENA

d h
5 16 Saturn 2° S. of the Moon
7 05 Mercury at greatest elongation E.21°
12 21 Neptune 3° S. of the Moon
15 12 Uranus 0.2° N. of the Moon
18 16 Mars 5° N. of the Moon
19 07 Mercury 6° N. of the Moon
23 02 Saturn at opposition
24 07 Jupiter 5° N. of the Moon
27 15 Mars 2° N of Mercury
30 17 Mercury inferior conjunction with the Sun

MINIMA OF ALGOL

Algol is inconveniently situated for observation during May

CONSTELLATIONS

The following constellations are near the meridian at

	d	h		d	h
April	1	24	May	16	21
April	15	23	June	1	20
May	1	22	June	15	19

Cepheus (below the Pole), Cassiopeia (below the Pole), Ursa Minor, Ursa Major, Canes Venatici, Coma Berenices, Bootes, Leo, Virgo, Crater, Corvus and Hydra

THE MOON

Phases, Apsides and Node	d	h	m
○ Full Moon	4	03	42
◔ Last Quarter	11	10	36
● New Moon	18	04	13
◑ First Quarter	25	17	19
Perigee (366,024km)	15	00	19
Apogee (404,244km)	26	22	13

Mean longitude of ascending node on 1st, 189°

THE SUN

s.d. 15'.8

Day	Right Ascension			Dec. +		Equation of time		Rise 52°		Rise 56°		Transit		Set 52°		Set 56°		Sidereal time			Transit of first point of Aries		
	h	m	s	°	'	m	s	h	m	h	m	h	h	m	h	m	h	m	s	h	m	s
1	2	31	37	14	55	+2	49	4	31	4	17	11	57	19	24	19	39	14	34	26	9	20	06
2	2	35	26	15	13	+2	56	4	29	4	15	11	57	19	26	19	41	14	38	22	9	16	10
3	2	39	16	15	31	+3	03	4	27	4	13	11	57	19	28	19	43	14	42	19	9	12	14
4	2	43	06	15	48	+3	09	4	25	4	10	11	57	19	29	19	45	14	46	15	9	08	18
5	2	46	57	16	06	+3	15	4	24	4	08	11	57	19	31	19	47	14	50	12	9	04	22
6	2	50	49	16	23	+3	20	4	22	4	06	11	57	19	33	19	49	14	54	09	9	00	27
7	2	54	41	16	40	+3	25	4	20	4	04	11	57	19	34	19	51	14	58	05	8	56	31
8	2	58	33	16	56	+3	29	4	18	4	02	11	57	19	36	19	53	15	02	02	8	52	35
9	3	02	26	17	13	+3	32	4	17	4	00	11	56	19	37	19	54	15	05	58	8	48	39
10	3	06	20	17	29	+3	35	4	15	3	58	11	56	19	39	19	56	15	09	55	8	44	43
11	3	10	14	17	44	+3	37	4	13	3	56	11	56	19	41	19	58	15	13	51	8	40	47
12	3	14	09	17	60	+3	39	4	12	3	54	11	56	19	42	20	00	15	17	48	8	36	51
13	3	18	05	18	15	+3	40	4	10	3	52	11	56	19	44	20	02	15	21	44	8	32	55
14	3	22	01	18	30	+3	41	4	08	3	50	11	56	19	45	20	04	15	25	41	8	28	59
15	3	25	57	18	44	+3	40	4	07	3	48	11	56	19	47	20	06	15	29	38	8	25	03
16	3	29	54	18	58	+3	40	4	05	3	46	11	56	19	48	20	08	15	33	34	8	21	07
17	3	33	52	19	12	+3	38	4	04	3	44	11	56	19	50	20	10	15	37	31	8	17	12
18	3	37	51	19	26	+3	37	4	02	3	43	11	56	19	51	20	11	15	41	27	8	13	16
19	3	41	50	19	39	+3	34	4	01	3	41	11	56	19	53	20	13	15	45	24	8	09	20
20	3	45	49	19	52	+3	31	4	00	3	39	11	57	19	54	20	15	15	49	20	8	05	24
21	3	49	49	20	04	+3	28	3	58	3	38	11	57	19	56	20	17	15	53	17	8	01	28
22	3	53	50	20	16	+3	24	3	57	3	36	11	57	19	57	20	19	15	57	13	7	57	32
23	3	57	51	20	28	+3	19	3	56	3	34	11	57	19	59	20	20	16	01	10	7	53	36
24	4	01	52	20	40	+3	14	3	55	3	33	11	57	20	00	20	22	16	05	07	7	49	40
25	4	05	54	20	51	+3	09	3	53	3	31	11	57	20	01	20	24	16	09	03	7	45	44
26	4	09	57	21	02	+3	03	3	52	3	30	11	57	20	03	20	25	16	12	60	7	41	48
27	4	13	60	21	12	+2	56	3	51	3	29	11	57	20	04	20	27	16	16	56	7	37	52
28	4	18	03	21	22	+2	50	3	50	3	27	11	57	20	05	20	28	16	20	53	7	33	57
29	4	22	07	21	32	+2	42	3	49	3	26	11	57	20	06	20	30	16	24	49	7	30	01
30	4	26	12	21	41	+2	34	3	48	3	25	11	58	20	08	20	31	16	28	46	7	26	05
31	4	30	16	21	50	+2	26	3	47	3	24	11	58	20	09	20	33	16	32	42	7	22	09

DURATION OF TWILIGHT (in minutes)

Latitude	52°	56°	52°	56°	52°	56°	52°	56°
	1 May		11 May		21 May		31 May	
Civil	39	44	41	48	44	53	46	57
Nautical	89	106	97	120	106	141	115	187
Astronomical	152	204	176	TAN	TAN	TAN	TAN	TAN

THE NIGHT SKY

Mercury, its magnitude fading from 0.0 to +1.0, is visible as an evening object for the first week of the month, low above the west-north-western horizon for a short while around the end of evening civil twilight. There after it is too close to the Sun for observation, passing through inferior conjunction on the 30th.

Venus, magnitude −4.2, is still a splendid object in the evenings. It is visible until about 23h, before setting over the west-north-west horizon.

Mars is unsuitably placed for observation.

Jupiter, magnitude −2.0, continues to be visible as a brilliant object in the western sky in the evenings. On the evening of the 8th the Moon passes about 6 degrees south of the planet.

Saturn, magnitude +0.2, is at opposition on the 15th, and thus visible throughout the hours of darkness. On 5th the Moon passes close to Saturn in the south-east.

THE MOON

Day	R.A.		Dec.	Hor. Par.	Diam.	Sun's Co-Long.	PA of Br. Limb	Ph.	Age	Rise 52°		Rise 56°		Transit		Set 52°		Set 56°	
	h	m	°	'	'	°	°	%	d	h	m	h	m	h	m	h	m	h	m
1	12	17	−2.4	54.4	29.6	416	293	91	12.1	16	38	16	42	22	22	3	34	3	31
2	13	03	−6.1	54.6	29.8	428	294	96	13.1	17	42	17	50	23	07	3	57	3	52
3	13	51	−9.5	55.0	30.0	441	298	99	14.1	18	47	18	58	23	53	4	23	4	14
4	14	40	−12.7	55.4	30.2	93	345	100	15.1	19	52	20	06	—		4	52	4	40
5	15	30	−15.3	55.9	30.4	105	84	99	16.1	20	55	21	12	0	42	5	26	5	11
6	16	23	−17.1	56.4	30.8	117	89	96	17.1	21	55	22	13	1	32	6	06	5	49
7	17	18	−18.2	56.9	31.0	129	87	91	18.1	22	50	23	08	2	25	6	53	6	35
8	18	13	−18.2	57.4	31.2	141	84	85	19.1	23	38	23	55	3	19	7	49	7	31
9	19	10	−17.3	57.9	31.6	154	80	76	20.1	—		—		4	13	8	52	8	36
10	20	06	−15.3	58.4	31.8	166	76	66	21.1	0	20	0	34	5	07	10	01	9	48
11	21	02	−12.5	58.8	32.0	178	73	55	22.1	0	56	1	07	6	01	11	14	11	04
12	21	57	−8.9	59.2	32.2	190	70	44	23.1	1	28	1	36	6	54	12	30	12	24
13	22	52	−4.7	59.6	32.4	202	69	33	24.1	1	58	2	01	7	47	13	47	13	45
14	23	47	−0.2	59.8	32.6	215	67	22	25.1	2	26	2	26	8	39	15	06	15	08
15	0	42	+4.3	59.9	32.6	227	67	13	26.1	2	55	2	51	9	33	16	24	16	30
16	1	38	+8.6	59.8	32.6	239	66	6	27.1	3	25	3	17	10	27	17	42	17	52
17	2	34	+12.3	59.5	32.4	251	62	2	28.1	3	59	3	47	11	22	18	57	19	11
18	3	32	+15.3	59.1	32.2	264	19	0	29.1	4	37	4	23	12	18	20	07	20	24
19	4	30	+17.3	58.4	31.8	276	283	1	0.6	5	21	5	04	13	14	21	10	21	28
20	5	27	+18.3	57.7	31.4	288	278	4	1.6	6	12	5	54	14	09	22	05	22	23
21	6	23	+18.2	56.9	31.0	300	279	10	2.6	7	08	6	50	15	02	22	51	23	07
22	7	18	+17.2	56.2	30.6	313	282	17	3.6	8	08	7	52	15	52	23	29	23	43
23	8	09	+15.3	55.5	30.2	325	285	25	4.6	9	10	8	57	16	40	—		—	
24	8	59	+12.7	55.0	30.0	337	288	34	5.6	10	13	10	03	17	26	0	01	0	12
25	9	47	+9.7	54.6	29.8	349	290	43	6.6	11	16	11	09	18	10	0	28	0	36
26	10	33	+6.3	54.3	29.6	362	292	53	7.6	12	19	12	15	18	52	0	53	0	58
27	11	18	+2.7	54.2	29.6	374	293	62	8.6	13	21	13	21	19	35	1	15	1	17
28	12	03	−1.0	54.3	29.6	386	293	71	9.6	14	25	14	27	20	17	1	38	1	37
29	12	49	−4.8	54.6	29.8	398	293	79	10.6	15	29	15	35	21	01	2	01	1	56
30	13	35	−8.4	55.0	30.0	410	293	87	11.6	16	33	16	43	21	47	2	25	2	18
31	14	24	−11.6	55.5	30.2	423	293	93	12.6	17	39	17	52	22	35	2	52	2	42

MERCURY

Day	R.A.		Dec	Mag.	Diam.	Phase	Rise		Transit		Set	
	h	m	°		"	%	h	m	h	m	h	m
1	3	47.4	+22.4	−0.1	7	56	4	49	13	15	21	32
3	3	58.9	+23.1	+0.1	7	50	4	48	13	18	21	41
5	4	09.2	+23.6	+0.3	8	44	4	46	13	21	21	48
7	4	18.4	+24.0	+0.5	8	38	4	44	13	22	21	53
9	4	26.3	+24.3	+0.7	8	32	4	42	13	22	21	54
11	4	32.9	+24.3	+0.9	9	27	4	40	13	21	21	54
13	4	38.1	+24.3	+1.1	9	23	4	38	13	18	21	51
15	4	42.0	+24.1	+1.4	10	18	4	35	13	14	21	46
17	4	44.4	+23.9	+1.6	10	14	4	32	13	09	21	38
19	4	45.4	+23.5	+1.8	11	11	4	28	13	02	21	28
21	4	45.1	+23.0	+2.1	11	8	4	24	12	54	21	16
23	4	43.5	+22.4	+2.4	11	5	4	19	12	44	21	02
25	4	40.9	+21.8	+2.6	12	3	4	13	12	34	20	46
27	4	37.4	+21.1	+3.0	12	1	4	07	12	22	20	30
29	4	33.3	+20.3	+3.3	12	0	4	01	12	10	20	12
31	4	29.0	+19.6	+3.4	12	0	3	54	11	58	19	55

Rising and setting times are for latitude 54°

VENUS

Day	R.A.		Dec	Mag.	Diam.	Phase	Rise		Transit		Set	
	h	m	°		"	%	h	m	h	m	h	m
1	5	24.5	+25.5	−3.7	17	67	6	01	14	52	23	35
6	5	49.2	+25.9	−3.7	17	65	6	03	14	57	23	43
11	6	13.8	+26.0	−3.7	18	63	6	06	15	01	23	49
16	6	37.9	+25.9	−3.8	19	61	6	12	15	06	23	52
21	7	01.5	+25.5	−3.8	20	59	6	20	15	10	23	52
26	7	24.3	+24.8	−3.8	21	56	6	28	15	13	23	50
31	7	46.3	+23.9	−3.9	22	54	6	38	15	15	23	45

MARS

Day	R.A.		Dec	Mag.	Diam.	Phase	Rise		Transit		Set	
	h	m	°		"	%	h	m	h	m	h	m
1	3	17.5	+18.4	+1.7	4	100	4	49	12	45	20	33
6	3	32.1	+19.4	+1.7	4	100	4	37	12	40	20	35
11	3	46.7	+20.2	+1.7	4	100	4	26	12	35	20	36
16	4	01.4	+21.0	+1.7	4	100	4	15	12	30	20	37
21	4	16.2	+21.7	+1.7	4	100	4	05	12	25	20	37
26	4	31.1	+22.3	+1.7	4	100	3	55	12	20	20	37
31	4	45.9	+22.8	+1.7	4	100	3	46	12	15	20	36

SUNRISE AND SUNSET

d	London 0° 05' 51° 30' h m	h m	Bristol 2° 35' 51° 28' h m	h m	Birmingham 1° 55' 52° 28' h m	h m	Manchester 2° 15' 53° 28' h m	h m	Newcastle 1° 37' 54° 59' h m	h m	Glasgow 4° 14' 55° 52' h m	h m	Belfast 5° 56' 54° 35' h m	h m
1	4 33	19 23	4 43	19 33	4 37	19 33	4 35	19 38	4 27	19 41	4 34	19 55	4 46	19 57
2	4 31	19 25	4 41	19 35	4 35	19 35	4 33	19 40	4 25	19 43	4 32	19 57	4 44	19 59
3	4 29	19 26	4 39	19 36	4 33	19 37	4 31	19 42	4 23	19 45	4 30	19 59	4 42	20 01
4	4 27	19 28	4 38	19 38	4 32	19 39	4 29	19 43	4 21	19 47	4 28	20 01	4 40	20 03
5	4 26	19 29	4 36	19 39	4 30	19 40	4 27	19 45	4 19	19 49	4 26	20 03	4 38	20 04
6	4 24	19 31	4 34	19 41	4 28	19 42	4 25	19 47	4 17	19 51	4 24	20 05	4 36	20 06
7	4 22	19 33	4 32	19 43	4 26	19 44	4 24	19 49	4 15	19 52	4 21	20 07	4 34	20 08
8	4 20	19 34	4 31	19 44	4 24	19 45	4 22	19 50	4 13	19 54	4 19	20 09	4 32	20 10
9	4 19	19 36	4 29	19 46	4 22	19 47	4 20	19 52	4 11	19 56	4 17	20 11	4 30	20 12
10	4 17	19 37	4 27	19 47	4 21	19 49	4 18	19 54	4 09	19 58	4 15	20 13	4 28	20 14
11	4 15	19 39	4 26	19 49	4 19	19 50	4 16	19 56	4 07	20 00	4 13	20 15	4 26	20 15
12	4 14	19 41	4 24	19 50	4 17	19 52	4 14	19 57	4 05	20 02	4 11	20 17	4 24	20 17
13	4 12	19 42	4 22	19 52	4 16	19 53	4 13	19 59	4 03	20 04	4 09	20 18	4 22	20 19
14	4 11	19 44	4 21	19 53	4 14	19 55	4 11	20 01	4 01	20 05	4 07	20 20	4 21	20 21
15	4 09	19 45	4 19	19 55	4 12	19 57	4 09	20 02	4 00	20 07	4 06	20 22	4 19	20 22
16	4 08	19 47	4 18	19 56	4 11	19 58	4 08	20 04	3 58	20 09	4 04	20 24	4 17	20 24
17	4 06	19 48	4 16	19 58	4 09	20 00	4 06	20 06	3 56	20 11	4 02	20 26	4 15	20 26
18	4 05	19 50	4 15	19 59	4 08	20 01	4 05	20 07	3 55	20 12	4 00	20 28	4 14	20 28
19	4 03	19 51	4 14	20 01	4 07	20 03	4 03	20 09	3 53	20 14	3 59	20 29	4 12	20 29
20	4 02	19 52	4 12	20 02	4 05	20 04	4 02	20 10	3 51	20 16	3 57	20 31	4 11	20 31
21	4 01	19 54	4 11	20 04	4 04	20 06	4 00	20 12	3 50	20 17	3 55	20 33	4 09	20 33
22	4 00	19 55	4 10	20 05	4 02	20 07	3 59	20 13	3 48	20 19	3 54	20 35	4 08	20 34
23	3 58	19 57	4 09	20 06	4 01	20 09	3 57	20 15	3 47	20 21	3 52	20 36	4 06	20 36
24	3 57	19 58	4 07	20 08	4 00	20 10	3 56	20 16	3 45	20 22	3 51	20 38	4 05	20 37
25	3 56	19 59	4 06	20 09	3 59	20 11	3 55	20 18	3 44	20 24	3 49	20 40	4 04	20 39
26	3 55	20 01	4 05	20 10	3 58	20 13	3 54	20 19	3 43	20 25	3 48	20 41	4 02	20 40
27	3 54	20 02	4 04	20 12	3 56	20 14	3 53	20 21	3 41	20 27	3 46	20 43	4 01	20 42
28	3 53	20 03	4 03	20 13	3 55	20 15	3 51	20 22	3 40	20 28	3 45	20 44	4 00	20 43
29	3 52	20 04	4 02	20 14	3 54	20 16	3 50	20 23	3 39	20 30	3 44	20 46	3 59	20 44
30	3 51	20 05	4 01	20 15	3 53	20 18	3 49	20 25	3 38	20 31	3 43	20 47	3 57	20 46
31	3 50	20 07	4 00	20 16	3 52	20 19	3 48	20 26	3 37	20 32	3 41	20 49	3 56	20 47

JUPITER

Day	R.A. h m	Dec °	Mag.	Diam. "	Rise h m	Transit h m	Set h m
1	9 03.5	+17.8	-1.7	38	10 38	18 30	2 18
11	9 06.7	+17.5	-1.6	37	10 04	17 54	1 40
21	9 10.9	+17.2	-1.6	36	9 31	17 19	1 03
31	9 16.0	+16.8	-1.5	35	8 59	16 44	0 26

Equatorial Diam. 36", Polar Diam. 34"

SATURN

Day	R.A. h m	Dec °	Mag.	Diam. "	Rise h m	Transit h m	Set h m
1	16 05.6	-18.6	+0.3	18	21 14	1 31	5 44
11	16 02.7	-18.5	+0.3	18	20 30	0 49	5 03
21	15 59.7	-18.3	+0.2	19	19 47	0 06	4 22
31	15 56.6	-18.2	+0.3	19	19 04	23 24	3 40

Equatorial Diam. 19", Polar Diam. 17"
Rings – major axis 42" minor axis 17", Tilt 25°

URANUS

Day	R.A. h m	Dec °	Mag.	Diam. "	Rise h m	Transit h m	Set h m
1	1 05.9	+6.3	+6.3	3	3 52	10 34	17 08
11	1 07.9	+6.5	+6.3	3	3 13	9 56	16 32
21	1 09.7	+6.7	+6.2	3	2 35	9 19	15 55
31	1 11.3	+6.9	+6.2	3	1 56	8 41	15 18

NEPTUNE

Day	R.A. h m	Dec °	Mag.	Diam. "	Rise h m	Transit h m	Set h m
1	22 44.0	-8.8	+7.8	2	2 55	8 08	13 22
11	22 44.8	-8.8	+7.7	2	2 16	7 30	12 44
21	22 45.3	-8.7	+7.7	2	1 37	6 51	12 05
31	22 45.7	-8.7	+7.7	2	0 57	6 12	11 26

JUNE 2015

SIXTH MONTH, 30 DAYS. *Junius*, Roman *gens* (family)

1	Monday	Samuel Taylor Coleridge begins to publish *The Friend*, an eclectic weekly journal 1809	week 22 day 152
2	Tuesday	Thomas Hardy, poet and author whose novels include *Far from the Madding Crowd b.* 1840	153
3	Wednesday	Franz Kafka, existentialist writer whose works include *The Trial* and *The Metamorphosis d.* 1924	154
4	Thursday	E. M. Forster's prize-winning novel *A Passage to India* is published 1924	155
5	Friday	Ray Bradbury, American science fiction author of the dystopian novel *Fahrenheit 451 d.* 2012	156
6	Saturday	Alexander Pushkin, Russian poet and author of the verse novel *Eugene Onegin b.* 1799	157
7	Sunday	The novelist and essayist E. M. Forster, who penned the 1908 novel *A Room with a View d.* 1970	158

8	Monday	George Orwell's dystopian, political novel *Nineteen Eighty-Four* is first published 1949	week 23 day 159
9	Tuesday	Charles Dickens dies after suffering a stroke while writing *The Mystery of Edwin Drood* 1870	160
10	Wednesday	The author and essayist Mario Vargas Llosa loses his bid for the Peruvian presidency 1990	161
11	Thursday	Robert E. Howard, pulp fiction author who created the character Conan the Barbarian *d.* 1936	162
12	Friday	Anne Frank, Jewish diarist and Holocaust victim, is born in Frankfurt, Germany *b.* 1929	163
13	Saturday	W. B. Yeats, poet and the first Irishman to be awarded the Nobel Prize in Literature *b.* 1865	164
14	Sunday	Pope Paul VI abolishes the *Index Librorum Prohibitorum* (List of Prohibited Books) 1966	165

15	Monday	W. H. Auden marries Erika Mann, granting her a British passport to escape Nazi persecution 1935	week 24 day 166
16	Tuesday	The poets Ted Hughes and Sylvia Plath wed on Bloomsday at St George the Martyr, Holborn 1956	167
17	Wednesday	Joseph Addison, politician and poet who co-founded *The Spectator* magazine *d.* 1719	168
18	Thursday	The Portuguese writer José Saramago, author of *The Gospel According to Jesus Christ d.* 2010	169
19	Friday	Salman Rushdie, author of the Man Booker Prize winning novel *Midnight's Children b.* 1947	170
20	Saturday	Oscar Wilde's *The Picture of Dorian Gray* debuts in *Lippincott's Monthly Magazine* 1890	171
21	Sunday	Jean-Paul Sartre, French writer, political activist and existentialist philosopher *b.* 1905	172

22	Monday	Henry Miller's *Tropic of Cancer* is declared non-obscene by the US Supreme Court 1964	173
23	Tuesday	The Japanese novelist Haruki Murakami completes his first 100km ultramarathon 1996	week 25 day 174
24	Wednesday	Ambrose Bierce, American satirist, fabulist and compiler of *The Devil's Dictionary b.* 1842	175
25	Thursday	The American playwright Arthur Miller marries the actor Marilyn Monroe 1956	176
26	Friday	J. K. Rowling's *Harry Potter and the Philosopher's Stone* is first published by Bloomsbury 1997	177
27	Saturday	The English historian Edward Gibbon completes *The Decline and Fall of the Roman Empire* 1787	178
28	Sunday	The Italian novelist and dramatist Luigi Pirandello, winner of the 1934 Nobel Prize in Literature *b.* 1867	179

| 29 | Monday | London's Globe Theatre burns down during a performance of *Henry VIII* 1613 | week 26 day 180 |
| 30 | Tuesday | Margaret Mitchell's American Civil War-era novel *Gone with the Wind* is published 1936 | 181 |

ASTRONOMICAL PHENOMENA

d	h	
1	20	Saturn 2° S. of the Moon
6	19	Venus at greatest elongation E.45°
9	03	Neptune 3° S. of the Moon
11	20	Uranus 0.5° N. of the Moon
14	16	Mars in conjunction with the Sun
15	02	Mercury 0.04° N. of the Moon
16	13	Mars 6° N. of the Moon
20	11	Venus 6° N. of the Moon
20	24	Jupiter 5° N. of the Moon
21	16	Solstice
24	17	Mercury at greatest elongation W.23°
29	01	Saturn 2° S. of the Moon

MINIMA OF ALGOL

Algol is inconveniently situated for observation during June

CONSTELLATIONS

The following constellations are near the meridian at

	d	h		d	h
May	1	24	June	15	21
May	16	23	July	1	20
June	1	22	July	16	19

Cassiopeia (below the Pole), Ursa Minor, Draco, Ursa Major, Canes Venatici, Bootes, Corona, Serpens, Virgo and Libra

THE MOON

Phases, Apsides and Node	d	h	m
○ Full Moon	2	16	19
☾ Last Quarter	9	15	42
● New Moon	16	14	05
☽ First Quarter	24	11	03
Perigee (369,711km)	10	04	45
Apogee (404,132km)	23	17	01

Mean longitude of ascending node on 1st, 187°

THE SUN

s.d. 15'.8

Day	Right Ascension h m s	Dec. + ° '	Equation of time m s	Rise 52° h m	Rise 56° h m	Transit h m	Set 52° h m	Set 56° h m	Sidereal time h m s	Transit of first point of Aries h m s
1	4 34 22	21 59	+2 18	3 46	3 22	11 58	20 10	20 34	16 36 39	7 18 13
2	4 38 27	22 07	+2 09	3 46	3 21	11 58	20 11	20 35	16 40 36	7 14 17
3	4 42 33	22 15	+1 59	3 45	3 20	11 58	20 12	20 37	16 44 32	7 10 21
4	4 46 39	22 22	+1 49	3 44	3 20	11 58	20 13	20 38	16 48 29	7 06 25
5	4 50 46	22 29	+1 39	3 43	3 19	11 58	20 14	20 39	16 52 25	7 02 29
6	4 54 53	22 35	+1 29	3 43	3 18	11 59	20 15	20 40	16 56 22	6 58 33
7	4 59 01	22 42	+1 18	3 42	3 17	11 59	20 16	20 41	17 00 18	6 54 37
8	5 03 08	22 47	+1 07	3 42	3 16	11 59	20 17	20 42	17 04 15	6 50 42
9	5 07 16	22 53	+0 55	3 41	3 16	11 59	20 18	20 43	17 08 11	6 46 46
10	5 11 24	22 58	+0 44	3 41	3 15	11 59	20 18	20 44	17 12 08	6 42 50
11	5 15 33	23 02	+0 32	3 40	3 15	12 00	20 19	20 45	17 16 05	6 38 54
12	5 19 42	23 07	+0 19	3 40	3 14	12 00	20 20	20 46	17 20 01	6 34 58
13	5 23 51	23 10	+0 07	3 40	3 14	12 00	20 20	20 47	17 23 58	6 31 02
14	5 27 60	23 14	−0 06	3 40	3 13	12 00	20 21	20 47	17 27 54	6 27 06
15	5 32 09	23 17	−0 18	3 40	3 13	12 00	20 22	20 48	17 31 51	6 23 10
16	5 36 19	23 19	−0 31	3 39	3 13	12 01	20 22	20 48	17 35 47	6 19 14
17	5 40 28	23 22	−0 44	3 39	3 13	12 01	20 22	20 49	17 39 44	6 15 18
18	5 44 38	23 23	−0 57	3 39	3 13	12 01	20 23	20 49	17 43 40	6 11 22
19	5 48 48	23 25	−1 11	3 39	3 13	12 01	20 23	20 50	17 47 37	6 07 27
20	5 52 57	23 25	−1 24	3 40	3 13	12 02	20 23	20 50	17 51 34	6 03 31
21	5 57 07	23 26	−1 37	3 40	3 13	12 02	20 24	20 50	17 55 30	5 59 35
22	6 01 17	23 26	−1 50	3 40	3 13	12 02	20 24	20 50	17 59 27	5 55 39
23	6 05 26	23 26	−2 03	3 40	3 14	12 02	20 24	20 51	18 03 23	5 51 43
24	6 09 36	23 25	−2 16	3 41	3 14	12 02	20 24	20 51	18 07 20	5 47 47
25	6 13 45	23 24	−2 29	3 41	3 14	12 03	20 24	20 51	18 11 16	5 43 51
26	6 17 54	23 22	−2 42	3 41	3 15	12 03	20 24	20 51	18 15 13	5 39 55
27	6 22 04	23 20	−2 54	3 42	3 15	12 03	20 24	20 50	18 19 09	5 35 59
28	6 26 13	23 18	−3 07	3 42	3 16	12 03	20 24	20 50	18 23 06	5 32 03
29	6 30 21	23 15	−3 19	3 43	3 17	12 03	20 24	20 50	18 27 03	5 28 08
30	6 34 30	23 12	−3 31	3 43	3 17	12 04	20 23	20 49	18 30 59	5 24 12

DURATION OF TWILIGHT (in minutes)

Latitude	52°	56°	52°	56°	52°	56°	52°	56°
	1 June		11 June		21 June		31 June	
Civil	46	58	48	61	49	63	48	61
Nautical	116	TAN	124	TAN	127	TAN	124	TAN
Astronomical	TAN	TAN	TAN	TAN	TAN	TAN	TAN	TAN

THE NIGHT SKY

Mercury, is at greatest western elongation on the 24th, but the long duration of twilight renders observation impossible.

Venus, magnitude −4.3, continues to be visible as a brilliant object in the evening skies, though by the end of the month it w ill be lost to view over the west-north-west horizon before 22h.

Mars is unsuitably placed for observation, conjunction occurring on the 14th.

Jupiter, magnitude −1.9, is still a brilliant object in the western sky in the early evenings. Jupiter is in the constellation of Cancer. On 30th Jupiter and Venus are only a Moon's width apart in the evening summer twilight.

Saturn, magnitude +0.3, is visible for the greater part of the night low in the southern sky. Saturn is in Libra. The Moon passes very near the planet on the night of 1st/2nd and again on the 28th/29th.

Twilight. Reference to the section above shows that astronomical twilight lasts all night for a period around the summer solstice (ie in June and July), even in southern England. Under these conditions the sky never gets completely dark as the Sun is always less than 18 degrees below the horizon.

THE MOON

Day	R.A.		Dec.	Hor. Par.	Diam.	Sun's Co-Long.	PA of Br. Limb	Ph.	Age	Rise 52°		Rise 56°		Transit		Set 52°		Set 56°	
	h	m	°	'	'	°	°	%	d	h	m	h	m	h	m	h	m	h	m
1	15	14	−14.5	56.0	30.6	435	294	97	13.6	18	44	18	59	23	25	3	24	3	11
2	16	07	−16.7	56.6	30.8	447	307	99	14.6	19	46	20	04	—		4	02	3	46
3	17	02	−18.0	57.2	31.2	99	46	100	15.6	20	44	21	03	0	18	4	47	4	29
4	17	58	−18.4	57.7	31.4	111	74	98	16.6	21	36	21	54	1	12	5	40	5	22
5	18	55	−17.8	58.2	31.8	123	76	94	17.6	22	21	22	36	2	08	6	42	6	25
6	19	53	−16.1	58.6	32.0	136	74	87	18.6	23	00	23	12	3	03	7	51	7	36
7	20	49	−13.4	58.9	32.0	148	71	79	19.6	23	33	23	42	3	58	9	04	8	52
8	21	45	−9.9	59.1	32.2	160	69	69	20.6	—		—		4	51	10	19	10	12
9	22	40	−5.9	59.3	32.2	172	68	58	21.6	0	03	0	08	5	44	11	35	11	32
10	23	34	−1.5	59.3	32.4	184	67	46	22.6	0	31	0	32	6	35	12	52	12	53
11	0	28	+3.0	59.3	32.2	197	67	35	23.6	0	59	0	56	7	27	14	09	14	13
12	1	22	+7.3	59.2	32.2	209	67	24	24.6	1	27	1	21	8	19	15	25	15	33
13	2	17	+11.1	59.0	32.2	221	68	15	25.6	1	58	1	48	9	13	16	39	16	51
14	3	13	+14.4	58.6	32.0	233	69	8	26.6	2	33	2	20	10	07	17	50	18	06
15	4	09	+16.7	58.2	31.8	246	68	3	27.6	3	14	2	58	11	02	18	56	19	13
16	5	06	+18.1	57.7	31.4	258	52	1	28.6	4	01	3	43	11	57	19	54	20	12
17	6	03	+18.4	57.1	31.2	270	314	0	0.1	4	54	4	36	12	51	20	44	21	01
18	6	58	+17.8	56.5	30.8	282	291	3	1.1	5	52	5	35	13	42	21	26	21	41
19	7	51	+16.2	55.9	30.4	295	289	7	2.1	6	54	6	39	14	32	22	01	22	13
20	8	42	+13.9	55.3	30.2	307	290	12	3.1	7	57	7	46	15	19	22	31	22	40
21	9	31	+11.0	54.8	29.8	319	291	19	4.1	9	01	8	53	16	04	22	56	23	03
22	10	18	+7.7	54.5	29.6	331	292	28	5.1	10	04	9	59	16	48	23	20	23	24
23	11	03	+4.1	54.3	29.6	344	293	37	6.1	11	07	11	05	17	30	23	43	23	43
24	11	49	+0.4	54.3	29.6	356	293	46	7.1	12	10	12	11	18	12	—		—	
25	12	34	−3.3	54.4	29.6	368	293	55	8.1	13	13	13	18	18	55	0	05	0	02
26	13	19	−6.9	54.7	29.8	380	292	65	9.1	14	17	14	25	19	40	0	28	0	22
27	14	07	−10.4	55.2	30.0	393	291	74	10.1	15	22	15	33	20	26	0	54	0	45
28	14	56	−13.4	55.8	30.4	405	289	82	11.1	16	27	16	41	21	15	1	23	1	11
29	15	47	−15.9	56.4	30.8	417	288	89	12.1	17	31	17	48	22	07	1	57	1	42
30	16	42	−17.6	57.2	31.2	429	287	95	13.1	18	32	18	50	23	01	2	39	2	22

MERCURY

Day	R.A.		Dec	Mag.	Diam.	Phase	Rise		Transit		Set	
	h	m	°		"	%	h	m	h	m	h	m
1	4	26.8	+19.3	+3.3	12	0	3	50	11	52	19	46
3	4	22.6	+18.6	+3.0	12	1	3	43	11	40	19	30
5	4	18.9	+18.0	+2.7	12	3	3	35	11	29	19	14
7	4	16.0	+17.5	+2.4	12	5	3	27	11	18	19	00
9	4	13.9	+17.2	+2.2	11	7	3	20	11	08	18	48
11	4	12.8	+17.0	+1.9	11	10	3	13	10	59	18	37
13	4	12.9	+16.9	+1.7	11	13	3	05	10	51	18	29
15	4	14.2	+16.9	+1.5	10	17	2	58	10	45	18	23
17	4	16.6	+17.1	+1.3	10	20	2	52	10	39	18	18
19	4	20.3	+17.4	+1.2	9	24	2	46	10	35	18	16
21	4	25.1	+17.7	+1.0	9	28	2	40	10	32	18	16
23	4	31.1	+18.2	+0.8	8	33	2	35	10	30	18	17
25	4	38.3	+18.7	+0.7	8	37	2	31	10	29	18	20
27	4	46.6	+19.3	+0.5	8	42	2	27	10	30	18	24
29	4	56.1	+19.9	+0.3	7	47	2	24	10	31	18	30

Rising and setting times are for latitude 54°

VENUS

Day	R.A.		Dec	Mag.	Diam.	Phase	Rise		Transit		Set	
	h	m	°		"	%	h	m	h	m	h	m
1	7	50.6	+23.7	−3.9	22	53	6	40	15	15	23	43
6	8	11.4	+22.6	−3.9	23	50	6	50	15	16	23	35
11	8	31.0	+21.3	−4.0	25	47	7	00	15	16	23	25
16	8	49.3	+19.8	−4.0	26	44	7	09	15	15	23	13
21	9	06.2	+18.3	−4.1	28	41	7	17	15	12	23	00
26	9	21.5	+16.6	−4.1	30	38	7	24	15	08	22	44

MARS

Day	R.A.		Dec	Mag.	Diam.	Phase	Rise		Transit		Set	
	h	m	°		"	%	h	m	h	m	h	m
1	4	48.9	+22.9	+1.7	4	100	3	45	12	14	20	36
6	5	03.8	+23.4	+1.7	4	100	3	37	12	09	20	34
11	5	18.7	+23.7	+1.7	4	100	3	29	12	05	20	32
16	5	33.5	+23.9	+1.7	4	100	3	22	12	00	20	29
21	5	48.4	+24.1	+1.7	4	100	3	16	11	55	20	26
26	6	03.2	+24.1	+1.8	4	100	3	11	11	50	20	21

SUNRISE AND SUNSET

	London			Bristol			Birmingham			Manchester			Newcastle			Glasgow			Belfast		
	0° 05'		51° 30'	2° 35'		51° 28'	1° 55'		52° 28'	2° 15'		53° 28'	1° 37'		54° 59'	4° 14'		55° 52'	5° 56'		54° 35'
d	h m		h m	h m		h m	h m		h m	h m		h m	h m		h m	h m		h m	h m		h m
1	3 49		20 08	3 59		20 17	3 52		20 20	3 47		20 27	3 36		20 34	3 40		20 50	3 55		20 48
2	3 48		20 09	3 59		20 19	3 51		20 21	3 46		20 28	3 35		20 35	3 39		20 51	3 54		20 50
3	3 48		20 10	3 58		20 20	3 50		20 22	3 46		20 29	3 34		20 36	3 38		20 53	3 54		20 51
4	3 47		20 11	3 57		20 21	3 49		20 23	3 45		20 30	3 33		20 37	3 37		20 54	3 53		20 52
5	3 46		20 12	3 57		20 22	3 48		20 24	3 44		20 31	3 32		20 38	3 36		20 55	3 52		20 53
6	3 46		20 13	3 56		20 22	3 48		20 25	3 43		20 32	3 31		20 40	3 36		20 56	3 51		20 54
7	3 45		20 13	3 55		20 23	3 47		20 26	3 43		20 33	3 31		20 41	3 35		20 57	3 50		20 55
8	3 45		20 14	3 55		20 24	3 47		20 27	3 42		20 34	3 30		20 42	3 34		20 58	3 50		20 56
9	3 44		20 15	3 54		20 25	3 46		20 28	3 42		20 35	3 29		20 42	3 34		20 59	3 49		20 57
10	3 44		20 16	3 54		20 26	3 46		20 29	3 41		20 36	3 29		20 43	3 33		21 00	3 49		20 58
11	3 44		20 17	3 54		20 26	3 45		20 29	3 41		20 37	3 28		20 44	3 33		21 01	3 48		20 59
12	3 43		20 17	3 53		20 27	3 45		20 30	3 40		20 37	3 28		20 45	3 32		21 02	3 48		20 59
13	3 43		20 18	3 53		20 28	3 45		20 31	3 40		20 38	3 28		20 46	3 32		21 03	3 48		21 00
14	3 43		20 18	3 53		20 28	3 45		20 31	3 40		20 39	3 27		20 46	3 31		21 03	3 47		21 01
15	3 43		20 19	3 53		20 29	3 45		20 32	3 40		20 39	3 27		20 47	3 31		21 04	3 47		21 01
16	3 43		20 20	3 53		20 29	3 44		20 32	3 40		20 40	3 27		20 47	3 31		21 04	3 47		21 02
17	3 43		20 20	3 53		20 30	3 44		20 33	3 40		20 40	3 27		20 48	3 31		21 05	3 47		21 02
18	3 43		20 20	3 53		20 30	3 44		20 33	3 40		20 41	3 27		20 48	3 31		21 05	3 47		21 03
19	3 43		20 21	3 53		20 30	3 44		20 34	3 40		20 41	3 27		20 49	3 31		21 06	3 47		21 03
20	3 43		20 21	3 53		20 31	3 45		20 34	3 40		20 41	3 27		20 49	3 31		21 06	3 47		21 03
21	3 43		20 21	3 53		20 31	3 45		20 34	3 40		20 42	3 27		20 49	3 31		21 06	3 47		21 04
22	3 43		20 21	3 53		20 31	3 45		20 34	3 40		20 42	3 27		20 49	3 31		21 06	3 47		21 04
23	3 43		20 22	3 54		20 31	3 45		20 34	3 40		20 42	3 28		20 50	3 32		21 07	3 48		21 04
24	3 44		20 22	3 54		20 31	3 45		20 34	3 41		20 42	3 28		20 50	3 32		21 07	3 48		21 04
25	3 44		20 22	3 54		20 31	3 46		20 35	3 41		20 42	3 28		20 50	3 32		21 07	3 48		21 04
26	3 45		20 22	3 55		20 31	3 46		20 34	3 42		20 42	3 29		20 50	3 33		21 06	3 49		21 04
27	3 45		20 22	3 55		20 31	3 47		20 34	3 42		20 42	3 29		20 49	3 33		21 06	3 49		21 04
28	3 45		20 21	3 56		20 31	3 47		20 34	3 43		20 42	3 30		20 49	3 34		21 06	3 50		21 04
29	3 46		20 21	3 56		20 31	3 48		20 34	3 43		20 41	3 31		20 49	3 35		21 06	3 51		21 03
30	3 47		20 21	3 57		20 31	3 48		20 34	3 44		20 41	3 31		20 49	3 35		21 05	3 51		21 03

JUPITER

Day	R.A.		Dec	Mag.	Diam.	Rise		Transit		Set	
	h	m	°		"	h	m	h	m	h	m
1	9	16.6	+16.8	−1.5	35	8	56	16	41	0	22
11	9	22.5	+16.3	−1.5	34	8	26	16	08	23	42
21	9	29.0	+15.8	−1.4	33	7	56	15	35	23	06

Equatorial Diam. 33", Polar Diam. 31"

SATURN

Day	R.A.		Dec	Mag.	Diam.	Rise		Transit		Set	
	h	m	°		"	h	m	h	m	h	m
1	15	56.3	−18.2	+0.3	19	18	59	23	20	3	36
11	15	53.4	−18.1	+0.3	18	18	16	22	38	2	55
21	15	50.7	−17.9	+0.4	18	17	34	21	56	2	14

Equatorial Diam. 18", Polar Diam. 17"
Rings – major axis 42" minor axis 17", Tilt 24°

URANUS

Day	R.A.		Dec	Mag.	Diam.	Rise		Transit		Set	
	h	m	°		"	h	m	h	m	h	m
1	1	11.5	+6.9	+6.2	3	1	52	8	37	15	15
11	1	12.9	+7.0	+6.2	3	1	14	7	59	14	37
21	1	14.0	+7.1	+6.2	3	0	35	7	21	14	00

NEPTUNE

Day	R.A.		Dec	Mag.	Diam.	Rise		Transit		Set	
	h	m	°		"	h	m	h	m	h	m
1	22	45.7	−8.7	+7.7	2	0	54	6	08	11	23
11	22	45.8	−8.7	+7.7	2	0	14	5	29	10	43
21	22	45.8	−8.7	+7.7	2	23	31	4	49	10	04

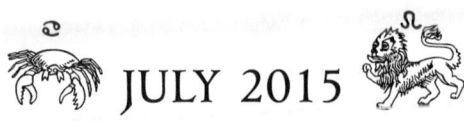

JULY 2015

SEVENTH MONTH, 31 DAYS. *Julius* Caesar, formerly *Quintilis*, fifth month of Roman pre-Julian calendar

1	*Wednesday*	The British Library is established as a result of the *British Library Act 1972*	day 182
2	*Thursday*	Ernest Hemingway, American author and Nobel Prize winner, committed suicide with a shotgun in Idaho 1961	183
3	*Friday*	Tom Stoppard, Czech-born British playwright *b.* 1937	184
4	*Saturday*	The first edition of *Leaves of Grass*, a poetry collection by the American poet Walt Whitman, is published 1855	185
5	*Sunday*	Jean Cocteau, French writer who wrote the 1929 novel *Les Enfants Terribles b.* 1889	186

6	*Monday*	William Faulkner, American author who penned the 1929 novel *The Sound and the Fury d.* 1962	week 27 day 187
7	*Tuesday*	Arthur Conan Doyle, crime fiction writer and creator of the character Sherlock Holmes *d.* 1930	188
8	*Wednesday*	Percy Bysshe Shelley, Romantic poet whose lyrical verses included *Ozymandias d.* 1822	189
9	*Thursday*	Ann Radcliffe, influential gothic writer, author of *The Mysteries of Udolpho b.* 1764	190
10	*Friday*	Alice Munro, Canadian author who was awarded the 2013 Nobel Prize in Literature *b.* 1931	191
11	*Saturday*	Harper Lee's Pulitzer Prize winning American novel *To Kill a Mockingbird* is published 1960	192
12	*Sunday*	The Chilean poet and politician Pablo Neruda *b.* 1904	193

13	*Monday*	William Wordsworth pens 'Lines Composed a few miles above Tintern Abbey' in 1798	week 28 day 194
14	*Tuesday*	Jacinto Benavente, Spanish dramatist, who was awarded the 1922 Nobel Prize for Literature *d.* 1954	195
15	*Wednesday*	Iris Murdoch, author whose novels include the Man Booker Prize winning *The Sea, The Sea b.* 1919	196
16	*Thursday*	J. D. Salinger's seminal novel *The Catcher in the Rye* is published 1951	197
17	*Friday*	Shmuel Yosef Agnon, a key figure of modern Hebrew fiction *b.* 1888	198
18	*Saturday*	The prolific novelist William Makepeace Thackeray is born in Calcutta, India 1811	199
19	*Sunday*	A. J. Cronin, novelist and physician who wrote the 1937 novel *The Citadel b.* 1896	200

20	*Monday*	Gavrila Derzhavin, Russian poet remembered for his odes dedicated to the Empress *d.* 1816	week 29 day 201
21	*Tuesday*	Robert Burns, Scottish poet and lyricist whose poems included 'Auld Lang Syne' *d.* 1796	202
22	*Wednesday*	James Whitcomb Riley, American author whose poetry included *The Raggedy Man d.* 1916	203
23	*Thursday*	The American detective fiction writer Raymond Chandler, author of *The Big Sleep b.* 1888	204
24	*Friday*	Alexandre Dumas, French writer of historical novels such as *The Count of Monte Cristo b.* 1802	205
25	*Saturday*	Elias Canetti, Bulgarian-born modern novelist and recipient of the 1981 Nobel Prize in Literature *b.* 1905	206
26	*Sunday*	Aldous Huxley, author of the 1932 dystopian novel *Brave New World b.* 1894	207

27	*Monday*	The soldier and poet Siegfried Sassoon is awarded the Military Cross 1916	week 30 day 208
28	*Tuesday*	Beatrix Potter, author and illustrator known for her children's books such as *The Tale of Peter Rabbit b.* 1866	209
29	*Wednesday*	The first volume in J. R. R. Tolkien's *The Lord of the Rings* trilogy is published 1954	210
30	*Thursday*	Ford Madox Ford enlists in the Welch Regiment, inspiring him to write *Parade's End* 1915	211
31	*Friday*	John Wilson published Robert Burns' *Poems, Chiefly in the Scottish dialect* 1786	212

ASTRONOMICAL PHENOMENA

d h
1 14 Jupiter 0.4° N of Venus
6 08 Neptune 3° S. of the Moon
6 16 Pluto at opposition
6 19 Earth at aphelion (152 million km)
9 03 Uranus 0.8° N. of the Moon
12 – Venus greatest brilliance (evening)
15 06 Mercury 6° N. of the Moon
15 09 Mars 6° N. of the Moon
16 05 Mars 0.1° N of Mercury
18 18 Jupiter 4° N. of the Moon
19 01 Venus 0.4° N. of the Moon
23 19 Mercury superior conjunction with the Sun
26 08 Saturn 2° S. of the Moon
31 20 Jupiter 6° N of Venus

MINIMA OF ALGOL

d	h	d	h	d	h
1	23.8	13	11.1	24	22.3
4	20.7	16	07.9	27	19.2
7	17.5	19	04.7	30	16.0
10	14.3	22	01.5		

CONSTELLATIONS

The following constellations are near their meridian at

	d	h		d	h
June	1	24	July	16	21
June	15	23	August	1	20
July	1	22	August	16	19

Ursa Minor, Draco, Corona, Hercules, Lyra, Serpens, Ophiuchus, Libra, Scorpius and Sagittarius

THE MOON

Phases, Apsides and Node		d	h	m
○	Full Moon	2	02	20
☾	Last Quarter	8	20	24
●	New Moon	16	01	24
☽	First Quarter	24	04	04
○	Full Moon	31	10	43

Perigee (367,093km)	5	18	53
Apogee (404,835km)	21	11	03

Mean longitude of ascending node on 1st, 185°

THE SUN

s.d. 15′.8

Day	Right Ascension			Dec. +		Equation of time		Rise 52°		Rise 56°		Transit		Set 52°		Set 56°		Sidereal time			Transit of first point of Aries		
	h	m	s	°	′	m	s	h	m	h	m	h	h	m	h	h	m	h	m	s	h	m	s
1	6	38	38	23	08	−3	43	3	44	3	18	12	04	20	23	20	49	18	34	56	5	20	16
2	6	42	46	23	04	−3	54	3	45	3	19	12	04	20	23	20	49	18	38	52	5	16	20
3	6	46	54	22	60	−4	05	3	46	3	20	12	04	20	22	20	48	18	42	49	5	12	24
4	6	51	02	22	55	−4	16	3	46	3	21	12	04	20	22	20	47	18	46	45	5	08	28
5	6	55	09	22	50	−4	27	3	47	3	22	12	05	20	21	20	47	18	50	42	5	04	32
6	6	59	16	22	44	−4	37	3	48	3	23	12	05	20	21	20	46	18	54	38	5	00	36
7	7	03	22	22	38	−4	47	3	49	3	24	12	05	20	20	20	45	18	58	35	4	56	40
8	7	07	29	22	32	−4	57	3	50	3	25	12	05	20	20	20	44	19	02	32	4	52	44
9	7	11	35	22	25	−5	06	3	51	3	26	12	05	20	19	20	43	19	06	28	4	48	48
10	7	15	40	22	18	−5	15	3	52	3	28	12	05	20	18	20	42	19	10	25	4	44	53
11	7	19	45	22	10	−5	24	3	53	3	29	12	05	20	17	20	41	19	14	21	4	40	57
12	7	23	50	22	02	−5	32	3	54	3	30	12	06	20	16	20	40	19	18	18	4	37	01
13	7	27	54	21	54	−5	40	3	55	3	32	12	06	20	16	20	39	19	22	14	4	33	05
14	7	31	58	21	45	−5	47	3	56	3	33	12	06	20	15	20	38	19	26	11	4	29	09
15	7	36	01	21	36	−5	54	3	58	3	34	12	06	20	14	20	37	19	30	07	4	25	13
16	7	40	04	21	27	−5	60	3	59	3	36	12	06	20	13	20	35	19	34	04	4	21	17
17	7	44	06	21	17	−6	06	4	00	3	37	12	06	20	12	20	34	19	38	01	4	17	21
18	7	48	08	21	07	−6	11	4	01	3	39	12	06	20	10	20	32	19	41	57	4	13	25
19	7	52	09	20	56	−6	15	4	03	3	41	12	06	20	09	20	31	19	45	54	4	09	29
20	7	56	10	20	45	−6	20	4	04	3	42	12	06	20	08	20	30	19	49	50	4	05	33
21	8	00	10	20	34	−6	23	4	05	3	44	12	06	20	07	20	28	19	53	47	4	01	38
22	8	04	09	20	22	−6	26	4	07	3	45	12	06	20	05	20	26	19	57	43	3	57	42
23	8	08	08	20	11	−6	28	4	08	3	47	12	06	20	04	20	25	20	01	40	3	53	46
24	8	12	07	19	58	−6	30	4	09	3	49	12	07	20	03	20	23	20	05	36	3	49	50
25	8	16	05	19	46	−6	31	4	11	3	51	12	07	20	01	20	21	20	09	33	3	45	54
26	8	20	02	19	33	−6	32	4	12	3	52	12	07	20	00	20	20	20	13	30	3	41	58
27	8	23	58	19	20	−6	32	4	14	3	54	12	07	19	58	20	18	20	17	26	3	38	02
28	8	27	54	19	06	−6	31	4	15	3	56	12	07	19	57	20	16	20	21	23	3	34	06
29	8	31	49	18	52	−6	30	4	17	3	58	12	06	19	55	20	14	20	25	19	3	30	10
30	8	35	44	18	38	−6	28	4	18	4	00	12	06	19	54	20	12	20	29	16	3	26	14
31	8	39	38	18	23	−6	26	4	20	4	01	12	06	19	52	20	10	20	33	12	3	22	18

DURATION OF TWILIGHT (in minutes)

Latitude	52°	56°	52°	56°	52°	56°	52°	56°
	1 July		11 July		21 July		31 July	
Civil	48	61	47	58	44	53	42	49
Nautical	124	TAN	117	TAN	107	146	98	123
Astronomical	TAN	TAN	TAN	TAN	TAN	TAN	182	TAN

THE NIGHT SKY

Mercury passes through superior conjunction on the 21st and therefore is unsuitably placed for observation throughout the month.

Venus, magnitude −4.5, attains its greatest brilliancy on the 12th. It is visible as a brilliant object in the western sky in the evenings but the period available for observation is shortening noticeably and it will be lost in the glare of sunset by the beginning of the last week in the month. Venus passes 0.5° south of Saturn on the 1st.

Mars is unsuitably placed for observation.

Jupiter, magnitude −1.8, is an evening object but only visible for a short while low above the western horizon. By the middle of the month it is lost to view in the gathering twilight.

Saturn is visible in the south-western sky, magnitude +0.4. By the end of the month it will be too low for observation long before midnight. The Moon is close to the planet on 26th.

THE MOON

Day	R.A. h	m	Dec. °	Hor. Par. '	Diam. '	Sun's Co-Long. °	PA of Br. Limb °	Ph. %	Age d	Rise 52° h	m	56° h	m	Transit h	m	Set 52° h	m	56° h	m
1	17	38	−18.4	57.9	31.6	441	291	98	14.1	19	28	19	46	23	57	3	29	3	10
2	18	36	−18.2	58.5	31.8	94	342	100	15.1	20	17	20	34	—		4	28	4	10
3	19	35	−16.8	59.1	32.2	106	59	99	16.1	20	59	21	13	0	54	5	35	5	19
4	20	33	−14.4	59.5	32.4	118	67	95	17.1	21	36	21	46	1	50	6	49	6	36
5	21	30	−11.1	59.7	32.6	130	67	89	18.1	22	08	22	14	2	46	8	05	7	56
6	22	27	−7.1	59.7	32.6	142	67	81	19.1	22	37	22	39	3	40	9	23	9	18
7	23	22	−2.8	59.6	32.4	154	66	71	20.1	23	05	23	03	4	33	10	41	10	40
8	0	16	+1.7	59.4	32.4	167	67	60	21.1	23	33	23	28	5	25	11	58	12	01
9	1	10	+6.1	59.1	32.2	179	68	48	22.1	—		23	54	6	17	13	14	13	21
10	2	04	+10.1	58.7	32.0	191	69	37	23.1	0	02	—		7	09	14	28	14	39
11	2	59	+13.5	58.3	31.8	203	72	27	24.1	0	35	0	23	8	02	15	39	15	53
12	3	54	+16.0	57.8	31.6	216	74	18	25.1	1	13	0	58	8	55	16	45	17	02
13	4	50	+17.7	57.4	31.2	228	77	10	26.1	1	56	1	39	9	49	17	45	18	03
14	5	46	+18.4	56.9	31.0	240	78	5	27.1	2	45	2	27	10	42	18	38	18	56
15	6	40	+18.1	56.4	30.8	252	73	1	28.1	3	41	3	23	11	34	19	23	19	39
16	7	34	+16.9	55.9	30.4	265	17	0	29.1	4	41	4	25	12	25	20	00	20	14
17	8	25	+14.8	55.4	30.2	277	305	1	0.5	5	44	5	30	13	13	20	32	20	43
18	9	15	+12.1	54.9	30.0	289	296	4	1.5	6	47	6	37	13	59	21	00	21	08
19	10	03	+9.0	54.6	29.8	301	295	8	2.5	7	51	7	44	14	43	21	25	21	29
20	10	49	+5.5	54.3	29.6	314	294	15	3.5	8	54	8	51	15	26	21	48	21	49
21	11	35	+1.8	54.2	29.6	326	294	22	4.5	9	57	9	57	16	08	22	10	22	08
22	12	19	−1.9	54.2	29.6	338	293	30	5.5	11	00	11	03	16	51	22	32	22	28
23	13	05	−5.5	54.4	29.6	350	292	39	6.5	12	02	12	09	17	34	22	57	22	49
24	13	51	−9.0	54.7	29.8	363	291	49	7.5	13	06	13	16	18	18	23	24	23	13
25	14	39	−12.1	55.2	30.0	375	288	58	8.5	14	10	14	22	19	05	23	55	23	41
26	15	28	−14.8	55.8	30.4	387	286	68	9.5	15	13	15	29	19	55	—		—	
27	16	21	−16.8	56.6	30.8	399	283	77	10.5	16	15	16	33	20	47	0	32	0	16
28	17	15	−18.1	57.5	31.4	411	279	85	11.5	17	13	17	32	21	42	1	17	0	59
29	18	13	−18.3	58.3	31.8	424	277	92	12.5	18	06	18	24	22	39	2	11	1	53
30	19	11	−17.5	59.1	32.2	436	277	97	13.5	18	53	19	08	23	36	3	15	2	58
31	20	11	−15.5	59.8	32.6	448	294	100	14.5	19	33	19	45	—		4	26	4	12

MERCURY

Day	R.A. h	m	Dec °	Mag.	Diam. "	Phase %	Rise h	m	Transit h	m	Set h	m
1	5	06.7	+20.6	+0.1	7	52	2	22	10	34	18	38
3	5	18.4	+21.2	−0.1	7	57	2	22	10	38	18	46
5	5	31.3	+21.8	−0.3	6	63	2	22	10	43	18	56
7	5	45.3	+22.3	−0.5	6	69	2	24	10	49	19	06
9	6	00.4	+22.8	−0.7	6	75	2	28	10	56	19	17
11	6	16.5	+23.2	−0.9	6	80	2	33	11	04	19	28
13	6	33.4	+23.4	−1.1	6	86	2	40	11	13	19	38
15	6	51.1	+23.4	−1.3	5	90	2	50	11	23	19	49
17	7	09.2	+23.3	−1.5	5	94	3	01	11	33	19	58
19	7	27.6	+23.1	−1.6	5	97	3	13	11	44	20	06
21	7	46.0	+22.6	−1.7	5	99	3	28	11	54	20	13
23	8	04.3	+21.9	−1.8	5	100	3	43	12	05	20	19
25	8	22.2	+21.2	−1.7	5	100	3	59	12	15	20	23
27	8	39.5	+20.2	−1.5	5	99	4	15	12	24	20	25
29	8	56.3	+19.2	−1.3	5	98	4	32	12	33	20	26
31	9	12.5	+18.0	−1.1	5	96	4	48	12	41	20	27

Rising to setting times are for latitude 54°

VENUS

Day	R.A. h	m	Dec °	Mag.	Diam. "	Phase %	Rise h	m	Transit h	m	Set h	m
1	9	34.9	+15.0	−4.1	32	34	7	28	15	01	22	27
6	9	46.3	+13.3	−4.2	35	30	7	30	14	53	22	08
11	9	55.4	+11.7	−4.2	38	26	7	29	14	43	21	48
16	10	01.8	+10.2	−4.2	41	22	7	25	14	29	21	25
21	10	05.1	+8.8	−4.1	44	17	7	17	14	13	21	01
26	10	05.0	+7.7	−4.0	48	13	7	04	13	53	20	35
31	10	01.1	+6.8	−3.9	51	8	6	45	13	30	20	06

MARS

Day	R.A. h	m	Dec °	Mag.	Diam. "	Phase %	Rise h	m	Transit h	m	Set h	m
1	6	17.9	+24.1	+1.8	4	100	3	06	11	45	20	16
6	6	32.6	+24.0	+1.8	4	100	3	02	11	40	20	10
11	6	47.1	+23.8	+1.8	4	100	2	58	11	35	20	04
16	7	01.5	+23.5	+1.9	4	100	2	55	11	30	19	56
21	7	15.8	+23.2	+1.9	4	100	2	53	11	24	19	48
26	7	29.9	+22.8	+1.9	4	100	2	50	11	19	19	39
31	7	43.9	+22.3	+1.9	4	99	2	49	11	13	19	29

SUNRISE AND SUNSET

	London 0° 05' 51° 30'		Bristol 2° 35' 51° 28'		Birmingham 1° 55' 52° 28'		Manchester 2° 15' 53° 28'		Newcastle 1° 37' 54° 59'		Glasgow 4° 14' 55° 52'		Belfast 5° 56' 54° 35'	
d	h m	h m	h m	h m	h m	h m	h m	h m	h m	h m	h m	h m	h m	h m
1	3 47	20 21	3 57	20 31	3 49	20 33	3 44	20 41	3 32	20 48	3 36	21 05	3 52	21 03
2	3 48	20 20	3 58	20 30	3 50	20 33	3 45	20 40	3 33	20 48	3 37	21 04	3 53	21 02
3	3 49	20 20	3 59	20 30	3 51	20 33	3 46	20 40	3 34	20 47	3 38	21 04	3 54	21 02
4	3 49	20 20	4 00	20 29	3 51	20 32	3 47	20 39	3 34	20 47	3 39	21 03	3 54	21 01
5	3 50	20 19	4 00	20 29	3 52	20 32	3 48	20 39	3 35	20 46	3 40	21 03	3 55	21 01
6	3 51	20 19	4 01	20 28	3 53	20 31	3 49	20 38	3 36	20 45	3 41	21 02	3 56	21 00
7	3 52	20 18	4 02	20 28	3 54	20 30	3 50	20 38	3 37	20 45	3 42	21 01	3 57	20 59
8	3 53	20 17	4 03	20 27	3 55	20 30	3 51	20 37	3 39	20 44	3 43	21 00	3 58	20 58
9	3 54	20 17	4 04	20 26	3 56	20 29	3 52	20 36	3 40	20 43	3 44	20 59	4 00	20 58
10	3 55	20 16	4 05	20 26	3 57	20 28	3 53	20 35	3 41	20 42	3 45	20 58	4 01	20 57
11	3 56	20 15	4 06	20 25	3 58	20 27	3 54	20 34	3 42	20 41	3 47	20 57	4 02	20 56
12	3 57	20 14	4 07	20 24	3 59	20 27	3 55	20 33	3 43	20 40	3 48	20 56	4 03	20 55
13	3 58	20 13	4 08	20 23	4 00	20 26	3 56	20 32	3 45	20 39	3 49	20 55	4 04	20 54
14	3 59	20 12	4 09	20 22	4 02	20 25	3 57	20 31	3 46	20 38	3 51	20 54	4 06	20 53
15	4 00	20 11	4 11	20 21	4 03	20 24	3 59	20 30	3 47	20 37	3 52	20 53	4 07	20 51
16	4 02	20 10	4 12	20 20	4 04	20 23	4 00	20 29	3 49	20 35	3 54	20 51	4 08	20 50
17	4 03	20 09	4 13	20 19	4 05	20 21	4 01	20 28	3 50	20 34	3 55	20 50	4 10	20 49
18	4 04	20 08	4 14	20 18	4 07	20 20	4 03	20 27	3 52	20 33	3 57	20 49	4 11	20 48
19	4 05	20 07	4 15	20 17	4 08	20 19	4 04	20 26	3 53	20 31	3 58	20 47	4 13	20 46
20	4 07	20 06	4 17	20 16	4 09	20 18	4 06	20 24	3 55	20 30	4 00	20 46	4 14	20 45
21	4 08	20 05	4 18	20 15	4 11	20 17	4 07	20 23	3 56	20 28	4 02	20 44	4 16	20 44
22	4 09	20 04	4 19	20 13	4 12	20 15	4 08	20 22	3 58	20 27	4 03	20 42	4 17	20 42
23	4 11	20 02	4 21	20 12	4 13	20 14	4 10	20 20	3 59	20 25	4 05	20 41	4 19	20 41
24	4 12	20 01	4 22	20 11	4 15	20 13	4 11	20 19	4 01	20 24	4 07	20 39	4 20	20 39
25	4 13	19 59	4 23	20 09	4 16	20 11	4 13	20 17	4 03	20 22	4 08	20 37	4 22	20 37
26	4 15	19 58	4 25	20 08	4 18	20 10	4 15	20 16	4 04	20 21	4 10	20 36	4 24	20 36
27	4 16	19 57	4 26	20 06	4 19	20 08	4 16	20 14	4 06	20 19	4 12	20 34	4 25	20 34
28	4 18	19 55	4 28	20 05	4 21	20 07	4 18	20 12	4 08	20 17	4 14	20 32	4 27	20 32
29	4 19	19 54	4 29	20 03	4 22	20 05	4 19	20 11	4 09	20 15	4 15	20 30	4 29	20 31
30	4 21	19 52	4 31	20 02	4 24	20 03	4 21	20 09	4 11	20 13	4 17	20 28	4 30	20 29
31	4 22	19 50	4 32	20 00	4 25	20 02	4 22	20 07	4 13	20 12	4 19	20 26	4 32	20 27

JUPITER

Day	R.A. h m	Dec °	Mag.	Diam. "	Rise h m	Transit h m	Set h m
1	9 36.0	+15.2	−1.4	32	7 28	15 03	22 30
11	9 43.5	+14.6	−1.3	32	7 00	14 31	21 54
21	9 51.3	+13.9	−1.3	31	6 33	13 59	21 18
31	9 59.3	+13.2	−1.3	31	6 06	13 28	20 42

Equatorial Diam. 32", Polar Diam. 30"

SATURN

Day	R.A. h m	Dec °	Mag.	Diam. "	Rise h m	Transit h m	Set h m
1	15 48.5	−17.9	+0.5	18	16 52	21 14	1 33
11	15 46.8	−17.8	+0.5	18	16 10	20 33	0 52
21	15 45.6	−17.8	+0.6	18	15 30	19 53	0 12
31	15 45.1	−17.8	+0.6	17	14 50	19 13	23 28

Equatorial Diam. 18", Polar Diam. 16"
Rings – major axis 40" minor axis 16", Tilt 24°

URANUS

Day	R.A. h m	Dec °	Mag.	Diam. "	Rise h m	Transit h m	Set h m
1	1 14.9	+7.2	+6.2	3	23 56	6 43	13 22
11	1 15.5	+7.3	+6.2	4	23 17	6 04	12 44
21	1 15.9	+7.3	+6.1	4	22 38	5 25	12 05
31	1 15.9	+7.3	+6.1	4	21 58	4 46	11 25

NEPTUNE

Day	R.A. h m	Dec °	Mag.	Diam. "	Rise h m	Transit h m	Set h m
1	22 45.5	−8.7	+7.7	2	22 52	4 10	9 24
11	22 45.0	−8.8	+7.7	2	22 12	3 30	8 44
21	22 44.4	−8.9	+7.7	2	21 33	2 50	8 04
31	22 43.7	−8.9	+7.7	2	20 53	2 10	7 23

AUGUST 2015

EIGHTH MONTH, 31 DAYS. *Augustus*, formerly *Sextilis*, sixth month of Roman pre-Julian calendar

1	Saturday	Roald Dahl's first published piece 'Shot Down Over Libya' appears in *The Saturday Evening Post*	day 213
2	Sunday	Wallace Stevens, American modernist poet who won the 1955 Pulitzer Prize for Poetry d. 1955	214

3	Monday	The Polish author Joseph Conrad whose most famous novels include *Heart of Darkness* d. 1924	week 31 day 215
4	Tuesday	George Bernard Shaw conceives the idea of the London School of Economics over breakfast 1894	216
5	Wednesday	Friedrich Engels, joint father of Marxist theory with Karl Marx d. 1895	217
6	Thursday	Ben Jonson, poet, playwright and satirist, known for his plays *The Alchemist* and *Volpone* d. 1637	218
7	Friday	The Italian writer Italo Calvino, who wrote *Invisible Cities*, leaves the Italian Communist Party 1957	219
8	Saturday	Shirley Jackson, American author of *The Lottery* and *The Haunting of Hill House* d. 1965	220
9	Sunday	The German Nobel Prize winning poet and novelist Hermann Hesse d. 1962	221

10	Monday	Laurence Binyon, poet and dramatist whose *For the Fallen* is used in Remembrance Day services b. 1869	week 32 day 222
11	Tuesday	Enid Blyton, the children's writer who created the character Noddy and wrote *The Famous Five* series b. 1897	223
12	Wednesday	Radclyffe Hall, who wrote the controversial 1928 novel *The Well of Loneliness* b. 1880	224
13	Thursday	H. G. Wells, science fiction author who penned *The Time Machine* and *The War of the Worlds* d. 1946	225
14	Friday	The Indian poet Rabindranath Tagore's Bengali collection of poems, *Gitanjali*, is published 1910	226
15	Saturday	Sir Walter Scott, historical novelist whose renowned works include *Ivanhoe* and *Rob Roy* b. 1771	227
16	Sunday	Georgette Heyer, pioneer of historical romance fiction, whose novels include *These Old Shades* b. 1902	228

17	Monday	George Orwell's allegorical and dystopian novel *Animal Farm* is published 1945	week 33 day 229
18	Tuesday	The French novelist and playwright Honoré de Balzac, author of *La Comédie humaine* d. 1850	230
19	Wednesday	John Dryden, influential poet and playwright who held the Poet Laureateship from 1688 onwards b. 1631	231
20	Thursday	John Milton's epic, biblical poem *Paradise Lost* is entered in the Stationers' Register 1667	232
21	Friday	Aubrey Beardsley, author and illustrator and a prominent proponent of aestheticism b. 1872	233
22	Saturday	The 1937 Nobel Prize for Literature winner, Roger Martin du Gard, who wrote *Les Thibault* d. 1958	234
23	Sunday	Willy Russell, lyricist and composer whose best known works include *Blood Brothers* and *Educating Rita* b. 1947	235

24	Monday	Jean Rhys, the novelist famed for *Wide Sargasso Sea*, is born in Dominica, British West Indies 1890	week 34 day 236
25	Tuesday	Martin Amis, novelist who won the 2000 James Tait Black Memorial Prize for his memoir *Experience* b. 1949	237
26	Wednesday	*On the Road*, a novel by the beat poet Jack Kerouac, based on his travels across America, is published 1957	238
27	Thursday	The poet James Thomson, who wrote the influential poem *The Seasons* 1730 d. 1748	239
28	Friday	Alexandre Dumas' *The Count of Monte Cristo* appears in print, serialised in the *Journal des Débats* 1844	240
29	Saturday	Oliver Wendell Holmes, American physician and author who wrote the 'Breakfast-Table' series b. 1809	241
30	Sunday	Seamus Heaney, Irish poet who was awarded the 1995 Nobel Prize in Literature d. 2013	242

31	Monday	Charles Baudelaire, French poet credited with coining the term 'modernity' d. 1867	week 35 day 243

ASTRONOMICAL PHENOMENA

d h
2 15 Neptune 3° S. of the Moon
5 09 Uranus 1° N. of the Moon
5 09 Venus 8° S of Mercury
7 04 Jupiter 0.6° S of Mercury
13 05 Mars 6° N. of the Moon
14 16 Venus 5° S. of the Moon
15 12 Jupiter 4° N. of the Moon
15 19 Venus inferior conjunction with the Sun
16 15 Mercury 2° N. of the Moon
22 17 Saturn 3° S. of the Moon
26 22 Jupiter in conjunction with the Sun
29 05 Mars 9° N of Venus
30 00 Neptune 3° S. of the Moon

MINIMA OF ALGOL

d	h	d	h	d	h
2	12.8	14	00.0	25	11.3
5	09.6	16	20.8	28	08.1
8	06.4	19	17.6	31	04.9
11	03.2	22	14.4		

CONSTELLATIONS

The following constellations are near their meridian at

	d	h		d	h
July	1	24	August	16	21
July	16	23	September	1	20
August	1	22	September	15	19

Draco, Hercules, Lyra, Cygnus, Sagitta, Ophiuchus, Serpens, Aquila and Sagittarius

THE MOON

Phases, Apsides and Node	d	h	m
☾ Last Quarter	7	02	03
● New Moon	14	14	53
☽ First Quarter	22	19	31
○ Full Moon	29	18	35

Perigee (362,139km)	2	10	04
Apogee (405,848km)	18	02	34
Perigee (358,290km)	30	15	23

Mean longitude of ascending node on 1st, 184°

THE SUN

s.d. 15′.8

Day	Right Ascension			Dec. +		Equation of time		Rise 52°		56°		Transit		Set 52°		56°		Sidereal time			Transit of first point of Aries		
	h	m	s	°	′	m	s	h	m	h	m	h	h	h	m	h	m	h	m	s	h	m	s
1	8	43	32	18	09	−6	23	4	21	4	03	12	06	19	50	20	08	20	37	09	3	18	23
2	8	47	24	17	54	−6	19	4	23	4	05	12	06	19	49	20	06	20	41	05	3	14	27
3	8	51	17	17	38	−6	15	4	24	4	07	12	06	19	47	20	04	20	45	02	3	10	31
4	8	55	08	17	23	−6	10	4	26	4	09	12	06	19	45	20	02	20	48	59	3	06	35
5	8	58	59	17	07	−6	04	4	27	4	11	12	06	19	44	20	00	20	52	55	3	02	39
6	9	02	50	16	50	−5	58	4	29	4	13	12	06	19	42	19	58	20	56	52	2	58	43
7	9	06	40	16	34	−5	52	4	31	4	15	12	06	19	40	19	56	21	00	48	2	54	47
8	9	10	29	16	17	−5	44	4	32	4	17	12	06	19	38	19	53	21	04	45	2	50	51
9	9	14	18	16	00	−5	36	4	34	4	18	12	06	19	36	19	51	21	08	41	2	46	55
10	9	18	06	15	43	−5	28	4	35	4	20	12	05	19	34	19	49	21	12	38	2	42	59
11	9	21	54	15	25	−5	19	4	37	4	22	12	05	19	32	19	47	21	16	34	2	39	03
12	9	25	41	15	08	−5	10	4	39	4	24	12	05	19	31	19	45	21	20	31	2	35	08
13	9	29	27	14	50	−4	60	4	40	4	26	12	05	19	29	19	42	21	24	28	2	31	12
14	9	33	13	14	31	−4	49	4	42	4	28	12	05	19	27	19	40	21	28	24	2	27	16
15	9	36	59	14	13	−4	38	4	43	4	30	12	05	19	25	19	38	21	32	21	2	23	20
16	9	40	44	13	54	−4	26	4	45	4	32	12	04	19	23	19	35	21	36	17	2	19	24
17	9	44	28	13	35	−4	14	4	47	4	34	12	04	19	20	19	33	21	40	14	2	15	28
18	9	48	12	13	16	−4	01	4	48	4	36	12	04	19	18	19	30	21	44	10	2	11	32
19	9	51	55	12	57	−3	48	4	50	4	38	12	04	19	16	19	28	21	48	07	2	07	36
20	9	55	38	12	37	−3	34	4	52	4	40	12	03	19	14	19	26	21	52	03	2	03	40
21	9	59	20	12	17	−3	20	4	53	4	42	12	03	19	12	19	23	21	55	60	1	59	44
22	10	03	02	11	57	−3	06	4	55	4	44	12	03	19	10	19	21	21	59	57	1	55	48
23	10	06	43	11	37	−2	50	4	56	4	46	12	03	19	08	19	18	22	03	53	1	51	53
24	10	10	24	11	17	−2	35	4	58	4	48	12	02	19	06	19	16	22	07	50	1	47	57
25	10	14	05	10	56	−2	19	5	00	4	50	12	02	19	04	19	13	22	11	46	1	44	01
26	10	17	45	10	36	−2	02	5	01	4	52	12	02	19	01	19	11	22	15	43	1	40	05
27	10	21	24	10	15	−1	45	5	03	4	54	12	02	18	59	19	08	22	19	39	1	36	09
28	10	25	04	9	54	−1	28	5	05	4	56	12	01	18	57	19	06	22	23	36	1	32	13
29	10	28	42	9	33	−1	10	5	06	4	58	12	01	18	55	19	03	22	27	32	1	28	17
30	10	32	21	9	11	−0	52	5	08	5	00	12	01	18	53	19	01	22	31	29	1	24	21
31	10	35	59	8	50	−0	33	5	09	5	02	12	00	18	50	18	58	22	35	26	1	20	25

DURATION OF TWILIGHT (in minutes)

Latitude	52°	56°	52°	56°	52°	56°	52°	56°
	1 August		11 August		21 August		31 August	
Civil	41	49	39	45	37	42	35	40
Nautical	97	121	90	107	84	97	79	90
Astronomical	179	TAN	154	210	139	168	128	148

THE NIGHT SKY

Mercury remains too close to the Sun for observation throughout the month.

Venus passes through inferior conjunction on the 15th and remains too close to the Sun for observation for almost the first three weeks of the month. Thereafter it might be glimpsed low in the eastern sky for a few minutes before sunrise. Its magnitude is −4.3.

Mars is unsuitably placed for observation at first but later in the month it gradually becomes visible as a morning object, magnitude +1.9, low above the east-north-eastern horizon shortly after 03h.

Jupiter passes through conjunction on the 26th and therefore remains too close to the Sun for observation throughout the month.

Saturn, magnitude +0.7, is an evening object, visible low in the south-western sky for several hours after sunset. Even in a small telescope the Rings of Saturn are a beautiful sight and they are now well open after the Earth's last passage through the ring plane in 2009.

Uranus is high in the south-eastern sky in Pisces, magnitude 5.7, theoretically visible to the unaided eye.

Meteors. The maximum of the famous Perseid meteor shower occurs on the 12th, and observers should expect to see most meteors during the early hours of the morning on that day. Consult the British Astronomical Association (W www.britastro.org) for the exact time of the maximum nearer the time.

THE MOON

Day	R.A. h	R.A. m	Dec. °	Hor. Par. '	Diam. '	Sun's Co-Long. °	PA of Br. Limb °	Ph. %	Age d	Rise 52° h	52° m	Rise 56° h	56° m	Transit h	Transit m	Set 52° h	52° m	Set 56° h	56° m
1	21	10	−12.5	60.3	32.8	100	47	100	15.5	20	08	20	16	0	34	5	43	5	33
2	22	08	−8.7	60.5	33.0	112	63	97	16.5	20	39	20	43	1	30	7	03	6	56
3	23	05	−4.3	60.5	33.0	124	65	91	17.5	21	08	21	09	2	25	8	23	8	21
4	0	01	+0.3	60.3	32.8	137	66	83	18.5	21	37	21	34	3	19	9	43	9	45
5	0	57	+4.8	59.8	32.6	149	68	73	19.5	22	07	22	00	4	13	11	01	11	07
6	1	52	+9.0	59.3	32.2	161	70	62	20.5	22	39	22	28	5	06	12	17	12	27
7	2	47	+12.5	58.6	32.0	173	73	51	21.5	23	15	23	01	5	59	13	30	13	43
8	3	42	+15.3	58.0	31.6	186	76	40	22.5	23	56	23	40	6	52	14	38	14	53
9	4	37	+17.2	57.3	31.2	198	80	30	23.5	—		—		7	45	15	39	15	57
10	5	32	+18.2	56.8	31.0	210	84	21	24.5	0	43	0	25	8	38	16	34	16	51
11	6	27	+18.2	56.2	30.6	222	87	13	25.5	1	35	1	18	9	30	17	21	17	37
12	7	20	+17.2	55.7	30.4	234	89	7	26.5	2	33	2	16	10	20	18	00	18	15
13	8	11	+15.4	55.3	30.2	247	89	3	27.5	3	34	3	20	11	08	18	34	18	46
14	9	01	+13.0	54.9	29.8	259	78	1	28.5	4	36	4	25	11	55	19	03	19	12
15	9	49	+10.0	54.5	29.8	271	325	0	29.5	5	40	5	32	12	40	19	29	19	35
16	10	36	+6.6	54.3	29.6	283	299	2	1.0	6	43	6	38	13	23	19	52	19	55
17	11	22	+3.0	54.1	29.4	296	295	5	2.0	7	46	7	44	14	05	20	15	20	15
18	12	07	−0.7	54.0	29.4	308	293	10	3.0	8	48	8	50	14	48	20	38	20	34
19	12	52	−4.3	54.1	29.4	320	292	17	4.0	9	51	9	56	15	30	21	01	20	55
20	13	37	−7.8	54.3	29.6	332	290	24	5.0	10	53	11	02	16	14	21	26	21	17
21	14	24	−11.0	54.6	29.8	345	288	33	6.0	11	56	12	07	16	59	21	55	21	43
22	15	12	−13.8	55.1	30.0	357	285	42	7.0	12	58	13	13	17	46	22	29	22	14
23	16	02	−16.0	55.8	30.4	369	281	52	8.0	14	00	14	16	18	36	23	09	22	52
24	16	55	−17.6	56.5	30.8	381	278	62	9.0	14	58	15	16	19	28	23	57	23	40
25	17	50	−18.2	57.4	31.2	393	274	72	10.0	15	53	16	10	20	23	—		—	
26	18	47	−17.8	58.4	31.8	406	269	81	11.0	16	42	16	58	21	19	0	55	0	37
27	19	45	−16.4	59.3	32.4	418	266	89	12.0	17	25	17	38	22	16	2	01	1	46
28	20	44	−13.9	60.1	32.8	430	264	95	13.0	18	02	18	12	23	14	3	15	3	03
29	21	43	−10.4	60.8	33.2	442	267	99	14.0	18	36	18	42	—		4	34	4	26
30	22	41	−6.2	61.1	33.4	94	37	100	15.0	19	07	19	09	0	10	5	56	5	51
31	23	39	−1.6	61.2	33.4	107	65	98	16.0	19	37	19	35	1	06	7	18	7	18

MERCURY

Day	R.A. h	R.A. m	Dec °	Mag.	Diam. "	Phase %	Rise h	Rise m	Transit h	Transit m	Set h	Set m
1	9	20.3	+17.4	−1.0	5	95	4	56	12	45	20	26
3	9	35.4	+16.1	−0.9	5	93	5	12	12	52	20	25
5	9	49.9	+14.8	−0.7	5	91	5	27	12	59	20	23
7	10	03.8	+13.4	−0.6	5	89	5	41	13	05	20	20
9	10	17.1	+12.0	−0.4	5	87	5	55	13	10	20	17
11	10	29.8	+10.6	−0.3	5	84	6	09	13	15	20	13
13	10	42.0	+9.1	−0.2	5	82	6	21	13	19	20	09
15	10	53.7	+7.7	−0.1	6	80	6	33	13	23	20	05
17	11	04.9	+6.3	+0.0	6	78	6	45	13	26	20	00
19	11	15.6	+4.8	+0.0	6	76	6	56	13	29	19	55
21	11	25.9	+3.4	+0.1	6	74	7	06	13	32	19	50
23	11	35.8	+2.1	+0.2	6	71	7	15	13	34	19	44
25	11	45.2	+0.7	+0.2	6	69	7	24	13	35	19	38
27	11	54.2	−0.6	+0.3	6	67	7	33	13	36	19	32
29	12	02.8	−1.9	+0.3	6	64	7	40	13	37	19	26
31	12	10.9	−3.1	+0.4	7	61	7	47	13	37	19	19

Rising and setting times are for latitude 54°

VENUS

Day	R.A. h	R.A. m	Dec °	Mag.	Diam. "	Phase %	Rise h	Rise m	Transit h	Transit m	Set h	Set m
1	9	59.9	+6.7	−3.8	52	7	6	41	13	24	20	01
6	9	51.7	+6.3	−3.6	55	4	6	15	12	57	19	30
11	9	40.8	+6.3	−3.3	57	2	5	45	12	26	19	00
16	9	28.6	+6.6	−3.1	58	1	5	11	11	54	18	30
21	9	16.7	+7.3	−3.3	57	2	4	36	11	23	18	02
26	9	07.0	+8.1	−3.6	55	5	4	02	10	53	17	37
31	9	00.7	+8.9	−3.9	52	8	3	31	10	27	17	16

MARS

Day	R.A. h	R.A. m	Dec °	Mag.	Diam. "	Phase %	Rise h	Rise m	Transit h	Transit m	Set h	Set m
1	7	46.7	+22.2	+1.9	4	99	2	48	11	12	19	27
6	8	00.5	+21.6	+1.9	4	99	2	47	11	06	19	17
11	8	14.1	+20.9	+1.9	4	99	2	46	11	00	19	06
16	8	27.6	+20.2	+2.0	4	99	2	45	10	53	18	55
21	8	40.8	+19.4	+2.0	4	99	2	44	10	47	18	43
26	8	53.9	+18.6	+2.0	4	99	2	43	10	40	18	30
31	9	06.9	+17.7	+2.0	4	99	2	42	10	34	18	17

SUNRISE AND SUNSET

	London 0° 05' 51° 30'		Bristol 2° 35' 51° 28'		Birmingham 1° 55' 52° 28'		Manchester 2° 15' 53° 28'		Newcastle 1° 37' 54° 59'		Glasgow 4° 14' 55° 52'		Belfast 5° 56' 54° 35'	
d	h m	h m	h m	h m	h m	h m	h m	h m	h m	h m	h m	h m	h m	h m
1	4 23	19 49	4 34	19 59	4 27	20 00	4 24	20 05	4 15	20 10	4 21	20 24	4 34	20 25
2	4 25	19 47	4 35	19 57	4 29	19 58	4 26	20 04	4 16	20 08	4 23	20 22	4 36	20 23
3	4 26	19 46	4 37	19 55	4 30	19 57	4 27	20 02	4 18	20 06	4 25	20 20	4 37	20 21
4	4 28	19 44	4 38	19 54	4 32	19 55	4 29	20 00	4 20	20 04	4 26	20 18	4 39	20 19
5	4 30	19 42	4 40	19 52	4 33	19 53	4 31	19 58	4 22	20 02	4 28	20 16	4 40	20 18
6	4 31	19 40	4 41	19 50	4 35	19 51	4 32	19 56	4 24	20 00	4 30	20 14	4 41	20 17
7	4 33	19 39	4 43	19 48	4 37	19 49	4 34	19 54	4 25	19 58	4 32	20 12	4 43	20 15
8	4 34	19 37	4 44	19 47	4 38	19 47	4 36	19 52	4 27	19 56	4 34	20 10	4 44	20 13
9	4 36	19 35	4 46	19 45	4 40	19 46	4 38	19 50	4 29	19 54	4 36	20 08	4 46	20 11
10	4 37	19 33	4 47	19 43	4 41	19 44	4 39	19 48	4 31	19 51	4 37	20 ??	4 48	20 09
11	4 39	19 31	4 49	19 41	4 43	19 42	4 41	19 46	4 33	19 49	4 38	20 05	4 50	20 07
12	4 40	19 29	4 51	19 39	4 45	19 40	4 43	19 44	4 35	19 47	4 40	20 03	4 52	20 05
13	4 42	19 27	4 52	19 37	4 46	19 38	4 44	19 42	4 37	19 45	4 42	20 01	4 53	20 03
14	4 44	19 25	4 54	19 35	4 48	19 36	4 46	19 40	4 38	19 43	4 44	19 59	4 55	20 01
15	4 45	19 23	4 55	19 33	4 50	19 34	4 48	19 38	4 40	19 40	4 46	19 56	4 57	19 59
16	4 47	19 21	4 57	19 31	4 51	19 32	4 50	19 36	4 42	19 38	4 48	19 54	4 59	19 56
17	4 48	19 19	4 58	19 29	4 53	19 29	4 51	19 34	4 44	19 36	4 50	19 52	5 01	19 54
18	4 50	19 17	5 00	19 27	4 55	19 27	4 53	19 32	4 46	19 34	4 52	19 49	5 03	19 52
19	4 52	19 15	5 02	19 25	4 56	19 25	4 55	19 29	4 48	19 31	4 53	19 47	5 04	19 50
20	4 53	19 13	5 03	19 23	4 58	19 23	4 57	19 27	4 50	19 29	4 55	19 45	5 06	19 47
21	4 55	19 11	5 05	19 21	5 00	19 21	4 58	19 25	4 52	19 27	4 57	19 42	5 08	19 45
22	4 56	19 09	5 06	19 19	5 01	19 19	5 00	19 23	4 53	19 24	4 59	19 40	5 10	19 43
23	4 58	19 07	5 08	19 17	5 03	19 17	5 02	19 20	4 55	19 22	5 01	19 37	5 12	19 40
24	5 00	19 05	5 10	19 15	5 05	19 14	5 04	19 18	4 57	19 19	5 03	19 35	5 14	19 38
25	5 01	19 03	5 11	19 13	5 06	19 12	5 05	19 16	4 59	19 17	5 05	19 32	5 15	19 36
26	5 03	19 01	5 13	19 11	5 08	19 10	5 07	19 14	5 01	19 15	5 07	19 30	5 17	19 33
27	5 04	18 58	5 14	19 08	5 10	19 08	5 09	19 11	5 03	19 12	5 09	19 27	5 19	19 31
28	5 06	18 56	5 16	19 06	5 11	19 06	5 11	19 09	5 05	19 10	5 11	19 25	5 21	19 28
29	5 07	18 54	5 18	19 04	5 13	19 03	5 12	19 07	5 06	19 07	5 13	19 22	5 23	19 26
30	5 09	18 52	5 19	19 02	5 15	19 01	5 14	19 04	5 08	19 05	5 15	19 20	5 25	19 24
31	5 11	18 50	5 21	19 00	5 16	18 59	5 16	19 02	5 10	19 02	5 17	19 17	5 26	19 21

JUPITER

Day	R.A. h m	Dec °	Mag.	Diam. "	Rise h m	Transit h m	Set h m
1	10 00.2	+13.1	−1.3	31	6 03	13 25	20 39
11	10 08.4	+12.4	−1.3	31	5 36	12 54	20 03
21	10 16.6	+11.6	−1.2	31	5 10	12 23	19 27
31	10 24.9	+10.9	−1.2	31	4 43	11 52	18 52

Equatorial Diam. 31", Polar Diam. 29"

SATURN

Day	R.A. h m	Dec °	Mag.	Diam. "	Rise h m	Transit h m	Set h m
1	15 45.1	−17.8	+0.6	17	14 46	19 09	23 24
11	15 45.3	−17.8	+0.7	17	14 07	18 30	22 44
21	15 46.2	−17.9	+0.7	17	13 29	17 51	22 05
31	15 47.7	−18.1	+0.8	16	12 52	17 13	21 27

Equatorial Diam. 17", Polar Diam. 16"
Rings – major axis 38" minor axis 16", Tilt 24°

URANUS

Day	R.A. h m	Dec °	Mag.	Diam. "	Rise h m	Transit h m	Set h m
1	1 15.9	+7.3	+6.1	4	21 54	4 42	11 22
11	1 15.6	+7.3	+6.1	4	21 15	4 02	10 42
21	1 15.0	+7.2	+6.1	4	20 35	3 22	10 01
31	1 14.1	+7.1	+6.1	4	19 56	2 42	9 21

NEPTUNE

Day	R.A. h m	Dec °	Mag.	Diam. "	Rise h m	Transit h m	Set h m
1	22 43.6	−8.9	+7.7	2	20 49	2 06	7 19
11	22 42.7	−9.0	+7.6	2	20 09	1 26	6 38
21	22 41.7	−9.1	+7.6	2	19 30	0 46	5 58
31	22 40.7	−9.2	+7.6	2	18 50	0 05	5 17

SEPTEMBER 2015

NINTH MONTH, 30 DAYS. *Septem* (seven), seventh month of Roman pre-Julian calendar

1	Tuesday	Ernest Hemingway's last major work of fiction, *The Old Man and the Sea*, is published 1952	day 244
2	Wednesday	J. R. R. Tolkien, author of *The Hobbit* and *The Lord of the Rings* d. 1973	245
3	Thursday	The American poet E. E. Cummings, whose work includes 2,900 poems and four plays d. 1962	246
4	Friday	Stocks from the printers and booksellers of Paternoster Row are destroyed during the Great Fire of London 1666	247
5	Saturday	Jack Kerouac's *On the Road*, a novel based on his travels across America, is published 1957	248
6	Sunday	Joseph Conrad becomes the captain of a steamer on the Congo, inspiring him to write *Heart of Darkness* 1890	249

7	Monday	The French poet Guillaume Apollinaire is mistakenly arrested for stealing the *Mona Lisa* 1911	week 36 day 250
8	Tuesday	Stella Gibbons' comic novel *Cold Comfort Farm*, satirising contemporary rural life, is published 1932	251
9	Wednesday	Dante Alighieri, Italian poet whose *Divine Comedy* is considered one of Italian literature's great works d. 1321	252
10	Thursday	The writer Mary Wollstonecraft dies shortly after giving birth to her daughter, Mary Shelley 1797	253
11	Friday	D. H. Lawrence, the novelist whose most famous works include the 1913 novel *Sons and Lovers* b. 1885	254
12	Saturday	The Victorian poets Robert Browning and Elizabeth Barrett are secretly married and leave for Italy 1846	255
13	Sunday	The children's novelist Roald Dahl, author of *James and the Giant Peach* and *Matilda* b. 1916	256

14	Monday	James Fenimore Cooper, the American author of the historical novel *The Last of the Mohicans* d. 1851	week 37 day 257
15	Tuesday	Agatha Christie, writer who wrote the world's bestselling mystery novel *And Then There Were None* b. 1890	258
16	Wednesday	Alfred Noyes, poet and playwright who wrote the 1906 ballad *The Highwayman* b. 1880	259
17	Thursday	*Lord of the Flies*, Nobel Prize winner William Golding's dystopian debut novel, is published 1954	260
18	Friday	The lexicographer Samuel Johnson, who compiled *A Dictionary of the English Language* in 1755 b. 1709	261
19	Saturday	Hartley Coleridge, poet and eldest son of Samuel Taylor Coleridge b. 1796	262
20	Sunday	Saint-John Perse, French poet who was awarded the 1960 Nobel Prize in Literature d. 1975	263

21	Monday	First recorded performance of William Shakespeare's *Julius Caesar*, at the Globe Theatre 1599	week 38 day 264
22	Tuesday	The satirical playwright Ben Jonson killed Gabriel Spenser in a duel in Hogsden Fields 1598	265
23	Wednesday	Wilkie Collins, novelist who wrote *The Woman in White* and a close friend of Charles Dickens d. 1889	266
24	Thursday	Dr. Seuss, American writer who published 46 children's books including *Green Eggs and Ham* d. 1991	267
25	Friday	Samuel Butler, poet and satirist who is primarily remembered for his poem *Hudibras* d. 1680	268
26	Saturday	T. S. Eliot, influential modernist poet, whose works include *The Waste Land* b. 1888	269
27	Sunday	Grazia Deledda, Italian writer who was awarded the 1926 Nobel Prize in Literature b. 1871	270

28	Monday	André Breton, French writer and founder of surrealism, author of the *Surrealist Manifesto* d. 1966	week 39 day 271
29	Tuesday	The German author Johann Wolfgang von Goethe publishes *The Sorrows of Young Werther* 1774	272
30	Wednesday	Louisa May Alcott's *Little Women*, a novel following the lives of four sisters, is published 1868	273

ASTRONOMICAL PHENOMENA

d	h	
1	04	Neptune at opposition
1	16	Uranus 1° N. of the Moon
4	10	Mercury at greatest elongation E.27°
10	06	Venus 3° S. of the Moon
10	23	Mars 5° N. of the Moon
12	06	Jupiter 3° N. of the Moon
13	06	Partial solar eclipse (not UK)
15	06	Mercury 5° S. of the Moon
19	03	Saturn 3° S. of the Moon
20	–	Venus greatest brilliance (morning)
23	08	Equinox
26	10	Neptune 3° S. of the Moon
28	02	Total Lunar eclipse
29	01	Uranus 1° N. of the Moon
30	15	Mercury inferior conjunction with the Sun

MINIMA OF ALGOL

d	h	d	h	d	h
3	01.7	14	12.9	26	00.2
5	22.5	17	09.7	28	21.0
8	19.3	20	06.6		
11	16.1	23	03.4		

CONSTELLATIONS
The following constellations are near their meridian at

	d	h		d	h
August	1	24	September	15	21
August	16	23	October	1	20
September	1	22	October	16	19

Draco, Cepheus, Lyra, Cygnus, Vulpecula, Sagitta, Delphinus, Equuleus, Aquila, Aquarius and Capricornus

THE MOON

Phases, Apsides and Node		d	h	m
☾	Last Quarter	5	09	54
●	New Moon	13	06	41
☽	First Quarter	21	08	59
○	Full Moon	28	02	51

Apogee (406,464km)	14	11	28
Perigee (356,877km)	28	01	47

Mean longitude of ascending node on 1st, 182°

THE SUN

s.d. 15′.9

Day	Right Ascension h	m	s	Dec. °	′	Equation of time m	s	Rise 52° h	m	Rise 56° h	m	Transit h	h	Set 52° m	h	Set 56° h	m	Sidereal time h	m	s	Transit of first point of Aries h	m	s
1	10	39	37	+8	28	−0	15	5	11	5	03	12	00	18	48	18	55	22	39	22	1	16	29
2	10	43	14	+8	07	+0	04	5	13	5	05	12	00	18	46	18	53	22	43	19	1	12	34
3	10	46	51	+7	45	+0	24	5	14	5	07	11	59	18	43	18	50	22	47	15	1	08	38
4	10	50	28	+7	23	+0	43	5	16	5	09	11	59	18	41	18	48	22	51	12	1	04	42
5	10	54	05	+7	01	+1	03	5	18	5	11	11	59	18	39	18	45	22	55	08	1	00	46
6	10	57	42	+6	38	+1	23	5	19	5	13	11	58	18	37	18	42	22	59	05	0	56	50
7	11	01	18	+6	16	+1	44	5	21	5	15	11	58	18	34	18	40	23	03	01	0	52	54
8	11	04	54	+5	54	+2	04	5	22	5	17	11	58	18	32	18	37	23	06	58	0	48	58
9	11	08	30	+5	31	+2	25	5	24	5	19	11	57	18	30	18	35	23	10	55	0	45	02
10	11	12	06	+5	08	+2	45	5	26	5	21	11	57	18	27	18	32	23	14	51	0	41	06
11	11	15	42	+4	46	+3	06	5	27	5	23	11	57	18	25	18	29	23	18	48	0	37	10
12	11	19	17	+4	23	+3	27	5	29	5	25	11	56	18	23	18	27	23	22	44	0	33	14
13	11	22	53	+3	60	+3	48	5	31	5	27	11	56	18	20	18	24	23	26	41	0	29	19
14	11	26	28	+3	37	+4	09	5	32	5	29	11	56	18	18	18	21	23	30	37	0	25	23
15	11	30	03	+3	14	+4	31	5	34	5	31	11	55	18	16	18	19	23	34	34	0	21	27
16	11	33	38	+2	51	+4	52	5	36	5	33	11	55	18	13	18	16	23	38	30	0	17	31
17	11	37	14	+2	28	+5	13	5	37	5	35	11	55	18	11	18	13	23	42	27	0	13	35
18	11	40	49	+2	05	+5	35	5	39	5	37	11	54	18	09	18	11	23	46	24	0	09	39
19	11	44	24	+1	41	+5	56	5	40	5	39	11	54	18	06	18	08	23	50	20	0	05	43
20	11	47	59	+1	18	+6	17	5	42	5	41	11	54	18	04	18	05	23	54	17	23	57	51
21	11	51	34	+0	55	+6	39	5	44	5	42	11	53	18	02	18	03	23	58	13	23	53	55
22	11	55	10	+0	31	+7	00	5	45	5	44	11	53	17	59	18	00	24	02	10	23	49	59
23	11	58	45	+0	08	+7	21	5	47	5	46	11	52	17	57	17	57	24	06	06	23	46	03
24	12	02	21	−0	15	+7	42	5	49	5	48	11	52	17	55	17	55	24	10	03	23	42	07
25	12	05	56	−0	39	+8	03	5	50	5	50	11	52	17	52	17	52	24	13	59	23	38	11
26	12	09	32	−1	02	+8	24	5	52	5	52	11	51	17	50	17	49	24	17	56	23	34	15
27	12	13	08	−1	25	+8	45	5	54	5	54	11	51	17	48	17	47	24	21	53	23	30	19
28	12	16	44	−1	49	+9	05	5	55	5	56	11	51	17	45	17	44	24	25	49	23	26	23
29	12	20	20	−2	12	+9	26	5	57	5	58	11	50	17	43	17	42	24	29	46	23	22	27
30	12	23	57	−2	35	+9	46	5	59	6	00	11	50	17	41	17	39	24	33	42	23	18	32

DURATION OF TWILIGHT (in minutes)

Latitude	52°	56°	52°	56°	52°	56°	52°	56°
	1 September		11 September		21 September		31 September	
Civil	35	39	34	38	34	37	34	37
Nautical	79	89	76	85	74	82	73	80
Astronomical	127	147	120	136	116	129	113	125

THE NIGHT SKY

Mercury is at greatest eastern elongation on the 4th and passes through inferior conjunction on the 30th, but continues to remain too close to the Sun for observation.

Venus is emerging from the morning twilight and is visible in the eastern sky before dawn. Venus attains its greatest brilliancy on the 20th with a magnitude of −4.6. On 10th at 04h the Moon will be close to both Mars and Venus in the eastern dawn skies.

Mars is a morning object, magnitude +2.0, visible low above the eastern horizon shortly after 03h.

Jupiter, magnitude −1.7, emerges from the morning twilight after the first week of the month, becoming visible above the eastern horizon before dawn.

Saturn, magnitude +0.8, is an evening object, visible low in the south-western sky.

Uranus is in Pisces visible all night at magnitude +5.7 theoretically visible to the unaided eye.

Neptune is at opposition on 1st in the constellation of Aquarius. It is not visible to the naked-eye since its magnitude is +7.8.

A total Lunar Eclipse is visible on 28th. The Moon enters the Earth's umbra at 01h 07m 12s; totality lasts from 02h 11m 11s to 03h 23m 07s; the Moon leaves the Earth's umbra at 04h 27m 06s. All times are UT (GMT).

THE MOON

Day	R.A.		Dec.	Hor. Par.	Diam.	Sun's Co-Long	PA of Br. Limb	Ph.	Age	Rise 52°		Rise 56°		Transit		Set 52°		Set 56°	
	h	m	°	'	'	°	°	%	d	h	m	h	m	h	m	h	m	h	m
1	0	37	+3.1	60.9	33.2	119	68	93	17.0	20	08	20	02	2	02	8	40	8	44
2	1	34	+7.5	60.4	32.8	131	71	85	18.0	20	40	20	31	2	57	10	00	10	08
3	2	31	+11.4	59.7	32.6	143	74	76	19.0	21	16	21	03	3	52	11	16	11	28
4	3	27	+14.5	58.9	32.0	155	77	66	20.0	21	56	21	40	4	47	12	27	12	42
5	4	24	+16.7	58.0	31.6	167	81	55	21.0	22	41	22	24	5	41	13	32	13	49
6	5	20	+17.9	57.2	31.2	180	85	44	22.0	23	32	23	15	6	35	14	30	14	47
7	6	14	+18.1	56.5	30.8	192	90	34	23.0	—		—		7	27	15	19	15	36
8	7	08	+17.4	55.8	30.4	204	94	24	24.0	0	28	0	11	8	17	16	01	16	16
9	7	59	+15.8	55.3	30.2	216	97	16	25.0	1	27	1	13	9	06	16	36	16	49
10	8	49	+13.6	54.8	29.8	229	100	10	26.0	2	29	2	17	9	53	17	06	17	16
11	9	37	+10.8	54.5	29.6	241	102	5	27.0	3	32	3	23	10	38	17	33	17	40
12	10	24	+7.5	54.2	29.6	253	102	2	28.0	4	34	4	29	11	21	17	57	18	01
13	11	10	+4.0	54.0	29.4	265	90	0	29.0	5	37	5	35	12	04	18	20	18	21
14	11	55	+0.3	54.0	29.4	277	295	1	0.5	6	40	6	40	12	46	18	43	18	41
15	12	40	-3.3	54.0	29.4	290	290	3	1.5	7	42	7	46	13	28	19	06	19	01
16	13	25	-6.9	54.1	29.4	302	288	7	2.5	8	45	8	52	14	12	19	31	19	22
17	14	11	-10.2	54.3	29.6	314	286	12	3.5	9	47	9	57	14	56	19	58	19	47
18	14	59	-13.0	54.6	29.8	326	283	19	4.5	10	49	11	02	15	42	20	29	20	15
19	15	48	-15.4	55.1	30.0	339	280	27	5.5	11	49	12	05	16	30	21	06	20	50
20	16	39	-17.1	55.7	30.4	351	277	36	6.5	12	48	13	05	17	20	21	50	21	32
21	17	32	-18.0	56.4	30.8	363	272	46	7.5	13	42	14	00	18	12	22	42	22	24
22	18	26	-18.0	57.2	31.2	375	268	57	8.5	14	32	14	49	19	05	23	42	23	26
23	19	22	-17.0	58.2	31.6	387	264	67	9.5	15	16	15	31	20	00	—		—	
24	20	19	-15.0	59.1	32.2	400	260	77	10.5	15	55	16	07	20	56	0	50	0	36
25	21	17	-12.0	60.0	32.6	412	256	86	11.5	16	30	16	39	21	52	2	05	1	54
26	22	15	-8.2	60.7	33.0	424	253	93	12.5	17	02	17	07	22	48	3	24	3	17
27	23	13	-3.7	61.2	33.4	436	251	98	13.5	17	33	17	33	23	44	4	46	4	44
28	0	11	+1.0	61.4	33.4	448	241	100	14.5	18	04	18	00	—		6	09	6	11
29	1	09	+5.6	61.3	33.4	100	75	99	15.5	18	36	18	28	0	41	7	32	7	38
30	2	08	+9.9	60.8	33.2	113	76	95	16.5	19	11	19	00	1	38	8	52	9	02

MERCURY

Day	R.A.		Dec	Mag.	Diam.	Phase	Rise	Transit	Set
	h	m	°		"	%	h m	h m	h m
1	12	14.7	-3.7	+0.4	7	60	7 50	13 37	19 16
3	12	22.0	-4.8	+0.4	7	57	7 56	13 36	19 09
5	12	28.8	-5.8	+0.5	7	54	8 01	13 35	19 02
7	12	34.8	-6.8	+0.5	7	51	8 04	13 34	18 55
9	12	40.2	-7.6	+0.6	8	47	8 07	13 31	18 47
11	12	44.6	-8.4	+0.6	8	43	8 07	13 28	18 40
13	12	48.2	-9.0	+0.7	8	39	8 07	13 23	18 32
15	12	50.6	-9.5	+0.8	9	34	8 04	13 18	18 24
17	12	51.7	-9.8	+0.9	9	29	7 59	13 11	18 15
19	12	51.4	-9.8	+1.1	9	24	7 51	13 03	18 07
21	12	49.5	-9.6	+1.3	10	18	7 40	12 53	17 58
23	12	46.1	-9.2	+1.6	10	13	7 26	12 38	17 50
25	12	41.1	-8.4	+1.9	10	8	7 09	12 25	17 41
27	12	34.8	-7.4	+2.3	10	4	6 49	12 11	17 33
29	12	27.6	-6.2	+2.7	10	1	6 27	11 56	17 25

Rising and setting times are for latitude 54°

VENUS

Day	R.A.		Dec	Mag.	Diam.	Phase	Rise	Transit	Set
	h	m	°		"	%	h m	h m	h m
1	8	59.9	+9.1	-3.9	52	9	3 25	10 23	17 12
6	8	58.3	+9.8	-4.1	48	13	3 00	10 02	16 56
11	9	00.7	+10.4	-4.2	45	18	2 39	9 44	16 42
16	9	06.6	+10.8	-4.2	41	22	2 23	9 31	16 30
21	9	15.5	+11.0	-4.3	38	27	2 11	9 20	16 21
26	9	27.0	+10.9	-4.2	36	31	2 03	9 08	16 12

MARS

Day	R.A.		Dec	Mag.	Diam.	Phase	Rise	Transit	Set
	h	m	°		"	%	h m	h m	h m
1	9	09.4	+17.6	+2.0	4	98	2 42	10 32	18 15
6	9	22.1	+16.6	+2.0	4	98	2 41	10 25	18 02
11	9	34.7	+15.7	+2.0	4	98	2 40	10 18	17 48
16	9	47.1	+14.6	+2.0	4	98	2 40	10 11	17 34
21	9	59.3	+13.6	+2.0	4	98	2 39	10 03	17 20
26	10	11.4	+12.5	+2.0	4	97	2 38	9 52	17 06

SUNRISE AND SUNSET

d	London 0° 05', 51° 30'		Bristol 2° 35', 51° 28'		Birmingham 1° 55', 52° 28'		Manchester 2° 15', 53° 28'		Newcastle 1° 37', 54° 59'		Glasgow 4° 14', 55° 52'		Belfast 5° 56', 54° 35'	
	h m	h m	h m	h m	h m	h m	h m	h m	h m	h m	h m	h m	h m	h m
1	5 12	18 48	5 22	18 57	5 18	18 56	5 17	19 00	5 12	19 00	5 19	19 15	5 28	19 19
2	5 14	18 45	5 24	18 55	5 20	18 54	5 19	18 57	5 14	18 57	5 21	19 12	5 30	19 16
3	5 15	18 43	5 26	18 53	5 21	18 52	5 21	18 55	5 16	18 55	5 23	19 09	5 32	19 14
4	5 17	18 41	5 27	18 51	5 23	18 50	5 23	18 52	5 18	18 52	5 25	19 07	5 34	19 11
5	5 19	18 39	5 29	18 49	5 25	18 47	5 24	18 50	5 19	18 50	5 27	19 04	5 36	19 09
6	5 20	18 36	5 30	18 46	5 26	18 45	5 26	18 48	5 21	18 47	5 28	19 02	5 37	19 06
7	5 22	18 34	5 32	18 44	5 28	18 43	5 28	18 45	5 23	18 45	5 30	18 59	5 39	19 04
8	5 23	18 32	5 33	18 42	5 30	18 40	5 30	18 43	5 25	18 42	5 32	18 56	5 41	19 01
9	5 25	18 29	5 35	18 39	5 31	18 38	5 31	18 40	5 27	18 40	5 34	18 54	5 43	18 59
10	5 27	18 27	5 37	18 37	5 33	18 36	5 33	18 38	5 29	18 37	5 36	18 51	5 45	18 56
11	5 28	18 25	5 38	18 35	5 35	18 33	5 35	18 35	5 31	18 35	5 38	18 49	5 47	18 54
12	5 30	18 23	5 40	18 33	5 36	18 31	5 37	18 33	5 33	18 32	5 40	18 46	5 48	18 51
13	5 31	18 20	5 41	18 30	5 38	18 28	5 38	18 31	5 34	18 29	5 42	18 43	5 50	18 49
14	5 33	18 18	5 43	18 28	5 40	18 26	5 40	18 28	5 36	18 27	5 44	18 41	5 52	18 46
15	5 35	18 16	5 45	18 26	5 41	18 24	5 42	18 26	5 38	18 24	5 46	18 38	5 54	18 44
16	5 36	18 13	5 46	18 23	5 43	18 21	5 44	18 23	5 40	18 22	5 48	18 35	5 56	18 41
17	5 38	18 11	5 48	18 21	5 45	18 19	5 45	18 21	5 42	18 19	5 50	18 33	5 58	18 39
18	5 39	18 09	5 49	18 19	5 46	18 17	5 47	18 18	5 44	18 17	5 52	18 30	5 59	18 36
19	5 41	18 06	5 51	18 16	5 48	18 14	5 49	18 16	5 46	18 14	5 54	18 28	6 01	18 34
20	5 43	18 04	5 53	18 14	5 50	18 12	5 51	18 13	5 47	18 11	5 56	18 25	6 03	18 31
21	5 44	18 02	5 54	18 12	5 51	18 09	5 52	18 11	5 49	18 09	5 58	18 22	6 05	18 29
22	5 46	18 00	5 56	18 10	5 53	18 07	5 54	18 09	5 51	18 06	5 59	18 20	6 07	18 26
23	5 47	17 57	5 57	18 07	5 55	18 05	5 56	18 06	5 53	18 04	6 01	18 17	6 09	18 23
24	5 49	17 55	5 59	18 05	5 56	18 02	5 58	18 04	5 55	18 01	6 03	18 14	6 10	18 21
25	5 51	17 53	6 01	18 03	5 58	18 00	5 59	18 01	5 57	17 59	6 05	18 12	6 12	18 18
26	5 52	17 50	6 02	18 00	6 00	17 58	6 01	17 59	5 59	17 56	6 07	18 09	6 14	18 16
27	5 54	17 48	6 04	17 58	6 01	17 55	6 03	17 56	6 01	17 54	6 09	18 06	6 16	18 13
28	5 55	17 46	6 05	17 56	6 03	17 53	6 05	17 54	6 02	17 51	6 11	18 04	6 18	18 11
29	5 57	17 44	6 07	17 54	6 05	17 51	6 06	17 51	6 04	17 48	6 13	18 01	6 20	18 08
30	5 59	17 41	6 09	17 51	6 06	17 48	6 08	17 49	6 06	17 46	6 15	17 58	6 21	18 06

JUPITER

Day	R.A. h m	Dec °	Mag.	Diam. "	Rise h m	Transit h m	Set h m
1	10 25.8	+10.8	−1.2	31	4 41	11 48	18 48
11	10 34.0	+10.0	−1.2	31	4 14	11 17	18 12
21	10 42.0	+9.2	−1.3	31	3 48	10 46	17 36

Equatorial Diam. 31", Polar Diam. 29"

SATURN

Day	R.A. h m	Dec °	Mag.	Diam. "	Rise h m	Transit h m	Set h m
1	15 47.9	−18.1	+0.8	16	12 49	17 10	21 23
11	15 50.1	−18.2	+0.8	16	12 12	16 33	20 45
21	15 52.8	−18.4	+0.8	16	11 37	15 56	20 07

Equatorial Diam. 16", Polar Diam. 15"
Rings – major axis 37" minor axis 15", Tilt 25°

URANUS

Day	R.A. h m	Dec °	Mag.	Diam. "	Rise h m	Transit h m	Set h m
1	1 14.0	+7.1	+6.1	4	19 52	2 38	9 17
11	1 12.9	+7.0	+6.1	4	19 12	1 58	8 36
21	1 11.6	+6.9	+6.1	4	18 32	1 17	7 54

NEPTUNE

Day	R.A. h m	Dec °	Mag.	Diam. "	Rise h m	Transit h m	Set h m
1	22 40.6	−9.3	+7.6	2	18 46	0 01	5 13
11	22 39.5	−9.4	+7.6	2	18 06	23 21	4 32
21	22 38.6	−9.5	+7.6	2	17 26	22 41	3 51

OCTOBER 2015

TENTH MONTH, 31 DAYS. *Octo* (eighth), eighth month of Roman pre-Julian calendar

1	*Thursday*	Gustave Flaubert's debut novel *Madame Bovary* is first serialised in *La Revue de Paris* 1856	day 274
2	*Friday*	*The Tale of Peter Rabbit*, written and illustrated by Beatrix Potter, is published for the first time 1902	275
3	*Saturday*	Edgar Allan Poe is found delirious in a gutter in Baltimore and dies four days later 1849	276
4	*Sunday*	William Wordsworth and Samuel Taylor Coleridge published their *Lyrical Ballads* 1798	277

5	*Monday*	Dante Gabriel Rossetti exhumes the coffin of Elizabeth Siddal to retrieve his manuscripts 1870	week 40 day 278
6	*Tuesday*	Elizabeth Bishop, Pulitzer Prize winning author and Poet Laureate of the United States d. 1979	279
7	*Wednesday*	The beat poet Allan Ginsberg's *Howl* is given its first public reading at the Six Gallery in San Francisco 1955	280
8	*Thursday*	Henry Fielding, satirical author who wrote *Tom Jones* and founded the Bow Street Runners d. 1754	281
9	*Friday*	Ivo Andrić, Yugoslav novelist who was awarded the 1961 Nobel Prize in Literature b. 1892	282
10	*Saturday*	The Nobel Prize winning playwright Harold Pinter, whose plays include *The Birthday Party* b. 1930	283
11	*Sunday*	Doris Lessing becomes the oldest recipient and eleventh woman to win the Nobel Prize in Literature 2007	284

12	*Monday*	The Australian academic and feminist Germaine Greer's *The Female Eunuch* is published 1970	week 41 day 285
13	*Tuesday*	Paddington Bear, the fictional character from Peru created by Michael Bond, first appeared 1958	286
14	*Wednesday*	A. A. Milne's iconic children's book *Winnie-the-Pooh* is first published 1926	287
15	*Thursday*	The Roman poet Virgil, who composed the *Eclogues, Georgics* and epic poem the *Aeneid* b. 70 BC	288
16	*Friday*	Charlotte Brontë's novel *Jane Eyre* is published by Smith, Elder & Co. under the pen name 'Currer Bell' 1847	289
17	*Saturday*	Hilary Mantel becomes the first woman to win the Booker Prize twice with *Bring Up the Bodies* 2012	290
18	*Sunday*	Thomas Love Peacock, novelist, poet and friend of Percy Bysshe Shelley b. 1785	291

19	*Monday*	Jonathan Swift, satirist and clergyman who wrote the 1726 novel *Gulliver's Travels* d. 1745	week 42 day 292
20	*Tuesday*	The prosecution of Penguin Books for the publication of D. H. Lawrence's *Lady Chatterley's Lover* begins 1960	293
21	*Wednesday*	The leading Victorian poet Gerald Manley Hopkins converts to Catholicism 1866	294
22	*Thursday*	Austrian psychoanalyst Sigmund Freud's *The Interpretation of Dreams* is first published 1899	295
23	*Friday*	The Nowell Codex, the only known manuscript of *Beowulf*, is damaged in a fire 1731	296
24	*Saturday*	William Prynne, author and polemicist who generated some 200 political and religious pamphlets d. 1669	297
25	*Sunday*	Geoffrey Chaucer, author and philosopher whose works include *Troilus and Criseyde* d. 1400	298

26	*Monday*	The South African writer J. M. Coetzee wins the Man Booker Prize for *Disgrace* 1999	week 43 day 299
27	*Tuesday*	Sylvia Plath, the American novelist and poet who wrote the semi-autobiographical novel *The Bell Jar* b. 1932	300
28	*Wednesday*	Evelyn Waugh, author who wrote the 1945 novel *Brideshead Revisited* and the satire *Decline and Fall* b. 1903	301
29	*Thursday*	The Russian author Boris Pasternak refuses the Nobel Prize in Literature 1958	302
30	*Friday*	A broadcast of Orson Welles' radio adaptation of H.G. Wells' novel *The War of the Worlds* causes panic 1938	303
31	*Saturday*	The first collection of Arthur Conan Doyle's *The Adventures of Sherlock Holmes* is published 1892	304

ASTRONOMICAL PHENOMENA

d h
8 21 Venus 0.7° N. of the Moon
9 17 Mars 3° N. of the Moon
9 24 Jupiter 3° N. of the Moon
11 12 Mercury 1° N. of the Moon
12 04 Uranus at opposition
16 03 Mercury at greatest elongation W.18°
16 13 Saturn 3° S. of the Moon
17 14 Jupiter 0.4° S of Mars
23 19 Neptune 3° S. of the Moon
26 07 Venus at greatest elongation W.46°
26 08 Jupiter 1° N of Venus
26 10 Uranus 0.9° N. of the Moon

MINIMA OF ALGOL

d	h	d	h	d	h
1	17.8	13	05.1	24	16.3
4	14.6	16	01.9	27	13.1
7	11.4	18	22.7	30	09.9
10	08.2	21	19.5		

CONSTELLATIONS

The following constellations are near their meridian at

	d	h		d	h
September	1	24	October	16	21
September	15	23	November	1	20
October	1	22	November	15	19

Ursa Major (below the Pole), Cepheus, Cassiopeia, Cygnus, Lacerta, Andromeda, Pegasus, Capricornus, Aquarius and Piscis Austrinus

THE MOON

Phases, Apsides and Node		d	h	m
☽	Last Quarter	4	21	06
●	New Moon	13	00	06
☽	First Quarter	20	20	31
○	Full Moon	27	12	05

Apogee (406,388km)	11	13	19
Perigee (358,463km)	26	13	02

Mean longitude of ascending node on 1st, 180°

THE SUN

s.d. 16′.1

Day	Right Ascension			Dec.		Equation of time		Rise 52°		Rise 56°		Transit		Set 52°		Set 56°		Sidereal time			Transit of first point of Aries		
	h	m	s	°	′	m	s	h	m	h	m	h	h	m	h	m	h	h	m	s	h	m	s
1	12	27	33	2	59	+10	05	6	00	6	02	11	50	17	38	17	36	24	37	39	23	14	36
2	12	31	10	3	22	+10	25	6	02	6	04	11	49	17	36	17	34	24	41	35	23	10	40
3	12	34	48	3	45	+10	44	6	04	6	06	11	49	17	34	17	31	24	45	32	23	06	44
4	12	38	26	4	08	+11	03	6	05	6	08	11	49	17	31	17	28	24	49	28	23	02	48
5	12	42	04	4	31	+11	21	6	07	6	10	11	49	17	29	17	26	24	53	25	22	58	52
6	12	45	42	4	54	+11	39	6	09	6	12	11	48	17	27	17	23	24	57	22	22	54	56
7	12	49	21	5	17	+11	57	6	10	6	14	11	48	17	25	17	21	25	01	18	22	51	00
8	12	53	00	5	40	+12	14	6	12	6	16	11	48	17	22	17	18	25	05	15	22	47	04
9	12	56	40	6	03	+12	31	6	14	6	18	11	47	17	20	17	15	25	09	11	22	43	08
10	13	00	20	6	26	+12	48	6	15	6	20	11	47	17	18	17	13	25	13	08	22	39	12
11	13	04	01	6	49	+13	04	6	17	6	22	11	47	17	16	17	10	25	17	04	22	35	17
12	13	07	42	7	11	+13	19	6	19	6	24	11	47	17	13	17	08	25	21	01	22	31	21
13	13	11	23	7	34	+13	34	6	21	6	26	11	46	17	11	17	05	25	24	57	22	27	25
14	13	15	05	7	56	+13	48	6	22	6	28	11	46	17	09	17	03	25	28	54	22	23	29
15	13	18	48	8	19	+14	02	6	24	6	30	11	46	17	07	17	00	25	32	51	22	19	33
16	13	22	31	8	41	+14	16	6	26	6	32	11	46	17	05	16	58	25	36	47	22	15	37
17	13	26	15	9	03	+14	29	6	27	6	35	11	45	17	03	16	55	25	40	44	22	11	41
18	13	29	59	9	25	+14	41	6	29	6	37	11	45	17	00	16	53	25	44	40	22	07	45
19	13	33	44	9	47	+14	53	6	31	6	39	11	45	16	58	16	50	25	48	37	22	03	49
20	13	37	30	10	08	+15	04	6	33	6	41	11	45	16	56	16	48	25	52	33	21	59	53
21	13	41	16	10	30	+15	14	6	35	6	43	11	45	16	54	16	46	25	56	30	21	55	57
22	13	45	03	10	51	+15	24	6	36	6	45	11	45	16	52	16	43	26	00	26	21	52	02
23	13	48	50	11	13	+15	33	6	38	6	47	11	44	16	50	16	41	26	04	23	21	48	06
24	13	52	38	11	34	+15	42	6	40	6	49	11	44	16	48	16	38	26	08	20	21	44	10
25	13	56	27	11	54	+15	49	6	42	6	51	11	44	16	46	16	36	26	12	16	21	40	14
26	14	00	16	12	15	+15	57	6	43	6	53	11	44	16	44	16	34	26	16	13	21	36	18
27	14	04	06	12	36	+16	03	6	45	6	56	11	44	16	42	16	31	26	20	09	21	32	22
28	14	07	57	12	56	+16	09	6	47	6	58	11	44	16	40	16	29	26	24	06	21	28	26
29	14	11	49	13	16	+16	14	6	49	7	00	11	44	16	38	16	27	26	28	02	21	24	30
30	14	15	41	13	36	+16	18	6	51	7	02	11	44	16	36	16	25	26	31	59	21	20	34
31	14	19	34	13	56	+16	21	6	52	7	04	11	44	16	34	16	22	26	35	55	21	16	38

DURATION OF TWILIGHT (in minutes)

Latitude	52°	56°	52°	56°	52°	56°	52°	56°
	1 October		11 October		21 October		31 October	
Civil	34	37	34	37	34	38	35	39
Nautical	73	80	73	80	74	81	75	83
Astronomical	113	125	112	124	113	124	114	126

THE NIGHT SKY

Mercury reaches greatest western elongation (18°) on the 16th and is visible as a morning object after the first week of the month, low above the east-south-eastern horizon around the time of morning civil twilight. During the last week of the month it is getting too close to the Sun to be detected, even though its magnitude has brightened to −1.0. This is the most favourable morning apparition of the year for observers in the latitudes of the British Isles. On the 11th the crescent Moon will be only 2° to the right and above Mercury.

Venus, magnitude −4.5 , is a magnificent morning object, visible in the eastern sky before 03h. By the end of the month it becomes visible low in the east almost four hours before sunrise. Around the 8th–10th of the month there is an interesting group of Venus, Mars and Jupiter with the Moon, Venus being around two degrees south of Regulus.

Mars is a morning object, magnitude +1.7, and may be seen in the eastern sky for several hours before it becomes invisible in the morning twilight. On 18th Mars and Jupiter will be less than 0.5° (less than a Moon's width apart).

Jupiter, magnitude −1.8, continues to be visible as a brilliant morning object in the eastern sky. By the end of the month it may be seen low in the east shortly after 02h. The four Galilean satellites are readily observable with a small telescope or even a good pair of binoculars provided that they are held rigidly.

Saturn is lost in the evening twilight and will not be visible again this year.

Uranus is at opposition on 12th, magnitude +5.7 and still high in the sky all night in Pisces

THE MOON

Day	R.A. (h m)	Dec. (°)	Hor. Par. (')	Diam. (')	Sun's Co-Long. (°)	PA of Br. Limb (°)	Ph. (%)	Age (d)	Rise 52° (h m)	Rise 56° (h m)	Transit (h m)	Set 52° (h m)	Set 56° (h m)
1	3 06	+13.4	60.1	32.8	125	79	88	17.5	19 51	19 36	2 35	10 09	10 23
2	4 05	+16.1	59.2	32.2	137	82	80	18.5	20 36	20 19	3 31	11 19	11 36
3	5 03	+17.6	58.3	31.8	149	87	70	19.5	21 26	21 08	4 27	12 22	12 39
4	5 59	+18.1	57.3	31.2	161	91	59	20.5	22 21	22 04	5 21	13 15	13 33
5	6 54	+17.7	56.5	30.8	173	95	49	21.5	23 20	23 05	6 13	14 00	14 16
6	7 47	+16.3	55.7	30.4	186	99	39	22.5	—	—	7 03	14 38	14 51
7	8 37	+14.2	55.1	30.0	198	103	29	23.5	0 22	0 09	7 50	15 10	15 21
8	9 26	+11.5	54.6	29.8	210	106	21	24.5	1 24	1 14	8 36	15 37	15 45
9	10 13	+8.3	54.3	29.6	222	108	14	25.5	2 27	2 20	9 20	16 02	16 07
10	10 58	+4.9	54.1	29.4	234	110	8	26.5	3 29	3 26	10 02	16 25	16 27
11	11 43	+1.3	54.0	29.4	247	112	4	27.5	4 32	4 31	10 45	16 48	16 47
12	12 28	-2.4	54.0	29.4	259	116	1	28.5	5 34	5 37	11 27	17 11	17 06
13	13 14	-6.0	54.0	29.4	271	201	0	29.5	6 37	6 43	12 10	17 35	17 27
14	13 60	-9.4	54.2	29.6	283	277	1	0.9	7 40	7 49	12 54	18 01	17 51
15	14 47	-12.4	54.5	29.6	296	279	4	1.9	8 42	8 54	13 40	18 31	18 18
16	15 36	-14.9	54.8	29.8	308	277	8	2.9	9 43	9 58	14 27	19 06	18 51
17	16 26	-16.8	55.2	30.0	320	274	14	3.9	10 42	10 59	15 16	19 47	19 30
18	17 18	-17.9	55.7	30.4	332	271	22	4.9	11 37	11 55	16 07	20 36	20 18
19	18 11	-18.2	56.4	30.8	344	267	31	5.9	12 28	12 45	16 58	21 31	21 14
20	19 06	-17.5	57.1	31.0	357	263	41	6.9	13 13	13 28	17 51	22 35	22 19
21	20 01	-15.8	57.9	31.6	369	259	52	7.9	13 52	14 05	18 45	23 44	23 32
22	20 56	-13.2	58.7	32.0	381	255	63	8.9	14 27	14 37	19 38	—	—
23	21 52	-9.8	59.5	32.4	393	252	73	9.9	14 59	15 05	20 32	0 59	0 50
24	22 48	-5.7	60.2	32.8	405	249	83	10.9	15 29	15 32	21 27	2 17	2 12
25	23 45	-1.2	60.8	33.2	417	247	91	11.9	15 59	15 58	22 22	3 37	3 37
26	0 42	+3.5	61.1	33.2	430	245	97	12.9	16 30	16 24	23 19	4 59	5 03
27	1 40	+8.0	61.1	33.4	442	231	100	13.9	17 03	16 54	—	6 21	6 29
28	2 39	+12.0	60.8	33.2	94	98	100	14.9	17 41	17 28	0 16	7 41	7 53
29	3 39	+15.1	60.2	32.8	106	88	97	15.9	18 24	18 08	1 14	8 57	9 12
30	4 39	+17.2	59.4	32.4	118	89	91	16.9	19 14	18 56	2 12	10 06	10 23
31	5 38	+18.2	58.5	31.8	130	93	84	17.9	20 09	19 51	3 09	11 06	11 23

MERCURY

Day	R.A. (h m)	Dec (°)	Mag.	Diam. (")	Phase (%)	Rise (h m)	Transit (h m)	Set (h m)
1	12 20.2	-4.7	+3.0	10	0	6 04	11 41	17 17
3	12 13.3	-3.3	+2.5	10	2	5 41	11 26	17 11
5	12 07.8	-2.0	+1.9	10	6	5 21	11 13	17 05
7	12 04.3	-0.9	+1.4	9	12	5 03	11 01	16 59
9	12 03.1	-0.1	+0.9	9	20	4 50	10 52	16 55
11	12 04.4	+0.4	+0.5	8	29	4 41	10 46	16 51
13	12 08.0	+0.5	+0.1	8	39	4 36	10 41	16 47
15	12 13.8	+0.2	-0.2	7	48	4 35	10 39	16 43
17	12 21.4	-0.3	-0.4	7	58	4 38	10 39	16 40
19	12 30.4	-1.1	-0.6	6	66	4 43	10 40	16 37
21	12 40.4	-2.1	-0.7	6	73	4 51	10 42	16 33
23	12 51.2	-3.3	-0.8	6	79	5 00	10 45	16 30
25	13 02.6	-4.5	-0.8	6	84	5 10	10 49	16 27
27	13 14.3	-5.8	-0.8	5	88	5 22	10 52	16 23
29	13 26.3	-7.1	-0.9	5	91	5 33	10 56	16 20
31	13 38.5	-8.5	-0.9	5	93	5 45	11 01	16 16

Rising and setting times are for latitude 54°

VENUS

Day	R.A. (h m)	Dec (°)	Mag.	Diam. (")	Phase (%)	Rise (h m)	Transit (h m)	Set (h m)
1	9 40.5	+10.6	-4.2	33	35	1 59	9 01	16 04
6	9 55.6	+10.0	-4.2	31	38	1 58	8 57	15 56
11	10 12.1	+9.2	-4.2	29	42	1 59	8 54	15 48
16	10 29.5	+8.2	-4.1	27	45	2 02	8 51	15 40
21	10 47.8	+7.0	-4.1	26	48	2 08	8 50	15 32
26	11 06.7	+5.7	-4.0	24	50	2 15	8 49	15 23
31	11 26.2	+4.1	-4.0	23	53	2 23	8 49	15 14

MARS

Day	R.A. (h m)	Dec (°)	Mag.	Diam. (")	Phase (%)	Rise (h m)	Transit (h m)	Set (h m)
1	10 23.4	+11.4	+2.0	4	97	2 37	9 44	16 52
6	10 35.2	+10.3	+2.0	4	97	2 35	9 36	16 37
11	10 46.9	+9.2	+2.0	4	97	2 34	9 28	16 22
16	10 58.5	+8.0	+1.9	4	96	2 33	9 20	16 08
21	11 09.9	+6.8	+1.9	4	96	2 31	9 12	15 53
26	11 21.3	+5.7	+1.9	4	96	2 29	9 04	15 38
31	11 32.6	+4.5	+1.9	4	95	2 28	8 55	15 23

SUNRISE AND SUNSET

	London 0° 05' / 51° 30'		Bristol 2° 35' / 51° 28'		Birmingham 1° 55' / 52° 28'		Manchester 2° 15' / 53° 28'		Newcastle 1° 37' / 54° 59'		Glasgow 4° 14' / 55° 52'		Belfast 5° 56' / 54° 35'	
d	h m	h m	h m	h m	h m	h m	h m	h m	h m	h m	h m	h m	h m	h m
1	6 00	17 39	6 10	17 49	6 08	17 46	6 10	17 47	6 08	17 43	6 17	17 56	6 23	18 03
2	6 02	17 37	6 12	17 47	6 10	17 43	6 12	17 44	6 10	17 41	6 19	17 53	6 25	18 01
3	6 04	17 34	6 14	17 44	6 11	17 41	6 13	17 42	6 12	17 38	6 21	17 51	6 27	17 58
4	6 05	17 32	6 15	17 42	6 13	17 39	6 15	17 39	6 14	17 36	6 23	17 48	6 29	17 56
5	6 07	17 30	6 17	17 40	6 15	17 36	6 17	17 37	6 16	17 33	6 25	17 45	6 31	17 53
6	6 08	17 28	6 18	17 38	6 17	17 34	6 19	17 35	6 18	17 31	6 27	17 43	6 33	17 51
7	6 10	17 25	6 20	17 35	6 18	17 32	6 21	17 32	6 20	17 28	6 29	17 40	6 35	17 48
8	6 12	17 23	6 22	17 33	6 20	17 30	6 22	17 30	6 21	17 26	6 31	17 38	6 36	17 46
9	6 13	17 21	6 23	17 31	6 22	17 27	6 24	17 28	6 23	17 23	6 33	17 35	6 38	17 43
10	6 15	17 19	6 25	17 29	6 24	17 25	6 26	17 25	6 25	17 21	6 35	17 33	6 40	17 41
11	6 17	17 17	6 27	17 27	6 25	17 23	6 28	17 23	6 27	17 18	6 37	17 30	6 42	17 38
12	6 19	17 14	6 29	17 24	6 27	17 20	6 30	17 20	6 29	17 16	6 39	17 27	6 44	17 36
13	6 20	17 12	6 30	17 22	6 29	17 18	6 32	17 18	6 31	17 13	6 41	17 25	6 46	17 34
14	6 22	17 10	6 32	17 20	6 31	17 16	6 33	17 16	6 33	17 11	6 43	17 22	6 48	17 31
15	6 24	17 08	6 34	17 18	6 32	17 14	6 35	17 14	6 35	17 09	6 45	17 20	6 50	17 29
16	6 25	17 06	6 35	17 16	6 34	17 12	6 37	17 11	6 37	17 06	6 47	17 17	6 52	17 26
17	6 27	17 04	6 37	17 14	6 36	17 09	6 39	17 09	6 39	17 04	6 49	17 15	6 54	17 24
18	6 29	17 02	6 39	17 12	6 38	17 07	6 41	17 07	6 41	17 01	6 51	17 12	6 56	17 22
19	6 30	16 59	6 40	17 09	6 40	17 05	6 43	17 05	6 43	16 59	6 53	17 10	6 58	17 19
20	6 32	16 57	6 42	17 07	6 41	17 03	6 45	17 02	6 45	16 57	6 55	17 08	7 00	17 17
21	6 34	16 55	6 44	17 05	6 43	17 01	6 46	17 00	6 47	16 54	6 57	17 05	7 02	17 15
22	6 36	16 53	6 46	17 03	6 45	16 59	6 48	16 58	6 49	16 52	7 00	17 03	7 03	17 12
23	6 37	16 51	6 47	17 01	6 47	16 57	6 50	16 56	6 51	16 50	7 02	17 00	7 05	17 10
24	6 39	16 49	6 49	16 59	6 49	16 55	6 52	16 54	6 53	16 47	7 04	16 58	7 07	17 08
25	6 41	16 47	6 51	16 57	6 50	16 52	6 54	16 52	6 55	16 45	7 06	16 56	7 09	17 06
26	6 43	16 45	6 53	16 55	6 52	16 50	6 56	16 49	6 57	16 43	7 08	16 53	7 11	17 03
27	6 44	16 43	6 54	16 53	6 54	16 48	6 58	16 47	6 59	16 41	7 10	16 51	7 13	17 01
28	6 46	16 41	6 56	16 52	6 56	16 46	7 00	16 45	7 01	16 39	7 12	16 49	7 15	16 59
29	6 48	16 40	6 58	16 50	6 58	16 44	7 02	16 43	7 03	16 36	7 14	16 46	7 17	16 57
30	6 50	16 38	7 00	16 48	6 59	16 43	7 03	16 41	7 05	16 34	7 16	16 44	7 19	16 55
31	6 51	16 36	7 01	16 46	7 01	16 41	7 05	16 39	7 07	16 32	7 18	16 42	7 21	16 53

JUPITER

Day	R.A. h m	Dec °	Mag.	Diam. "	Rise h m	Transit h m	Set h m
1	10 49.9	+8.4	−1.3	31	3 21	10 11	17 01
11	10 57.4	+7.7	−1.3	32	2 53	9 39	16 24
21	11 04.5	+7.0	−1.3	32	2 25	9 07	15 48
31	11 11.2	+6.3	−1.4	33	1 56	8 34	15 12

Equatorial Diam. 32", Polar Diam. 30"

SATURN

Day	R.A. h m	Dec °	Mag.	Diam. "	Rise h m	Transit h m	Set h m
1	15 56.1	−18.6	+0.8	16	11 02	15 16	19 30
11	15 59.8	−18.8	+0.8	16	10 28	14 40	18 53
21	16 03.9	−19.0	+0.8	15	9 54	14 05	18 16
31	16 08.3	−19.3	+0.7	15	9 21	13 30	17 39

Equatorial Diam. 16", Polar Diam. 14"
Rings – major axis 35" minor axis 15", Tilt 25°

URANUS

Day	R.A. h m	Dec °	Mag.	Diam. "	Rise h m	Transit h m	Set h m
1	1 10.1	+6.7	+6.0	4	17 48	0 32	7 13
11	1 08.6	+6.6	+6.0	4	17 08	23 52	6 31
21	1 07.1	+6.4	+6.0	4	16 28	23 11	5 49
31	1 05.7	+6.3	+6.1	4	15 48	22 30	5 08

NEPTUNE

Day	R.A. h m	Dec °	Mag.	Diam. "	Rise h m	Transit h m	Set h m
1	22 37.6	−9.5	+7.7	2	16 47	21 56	3 10
11	22 36.8	−9.6	+7.7	2	16 07	21 16	2 29
21	22 36.2	−9.7	+7.7	2	15 27	20 36	1 49
31	22 35.7	−9.7	+7.7	2	14 48	19 56	1 09

NOVEMBER 2015

ELEVENTH MONTH, 30 DAYS. *Novem* (nine), ninth month of Roman pre-Julian calendar

1	Sunday	William Shakespeare's tragedy *Othello* is performed for the first time at Whitehall Palace in London 1604	day 305

2	Monday	Odysseas Elytis, Greek romantic modernist poet who won the 1979 Nobel Prize in Literature *b.* 1911	week 44 day 306
3	Tuesday	Olympe de Gouges, French playwright and activist who penned the *Declaration of the Rights of Woman d.* 1793	307
4	Wednesday	War poet Wilfred Owen dies a week before the end of the First World War 1918	308
5	Thursday	*Catholicon,* a trilingual dictionary containing 6,000 entries, and the first French dictionary, is published 1464	309
6	Friday	George Eliot submits the first story from her book *Scenes of Clerical Life* to *Edinburgh Magazine* 1856	310
7	Saturday	The Algerian-French author and philosopher Albert Camus, who penned *The Plague* and *The Fall b.* 1913	311
8	Sunday	John Milton, poet and polemicist who wrote the epic poem *Paradise Lost d.* 1674	312

9	Monday	Ivan Turgenev, Russian author and playwright who wrote the novel *Fathers and Sons b.* 1818	week 45 day 313
10	Tuesday	Oliver Goldsmith, who wrote the novel *The Vicar of Wakefield* and the poem *The Deserted Village b.* 1730	314
11	Wednesday	The satirical novel *Catch-22* by the American author Joseph Heller is published 1961	315
12	Thursday	Elizabeth Gaskell, popular Victorian author whose best known novels include *Cranford d.* 1865	316
13	Friday	Robert Louis Stevenson, author of *Treasure Island, Kidnapped* and *Strange Case of Dr Jekyll and Mr Hyde b.* 1850	317
14	Saturday	Herman Melville's epic sea-tale *Moby-Dick; or, The Whale,* his sixth book, is first published in America 1851	318
15	Sunday	The murders of Herbert Clutter and his family, documented in Truman Capote's *In Cold Blood,* occur in Kansas 1959	319

16	Monday	The Nigerian novelist Chinua Achebe, author of the 1958 book *Things Fall Apart b.* 1930	week 46 day 320
17	Tuesday	Sylvia Beach, an American bookseller, opens the Shakespeare and Company bookstore in Paris 1919	321
18	Wednesday	Margaret Atwood, the Canadian author of *The Handmaid's Tale* and *The Blind Assassin b.* 1939	322
19	Thursday	Thomas Shadwell, English poet and playwright who was appointed Poet Laureate in 1689 *d.* 1692	323
20	Friday	Leo Tolstoy, the Russian author of *War and Peace* and *Anna Karenina,* dies at Astapovo train station 1910	324
21	Saturday	Isaac Bashevis Singer, Jewish-American author and winner of the 1978 Nobel Prize in Literature *b.* 1902	325
22	Sunday	André Gide, French author who was awarded the 1947 Nobel Prize in Literature *b.* 1869	326

23	Monday	John Milton's *Areopagitica,* a pamphlet condemning pre-publication censorship, is published 1644	week 47 day 327
24	Tuesday	Darwin's influential evolutionary work, *On the Origin of Species,* is published 1859	328
25	Wednesday	Agatha Christie's murder mystery play *The Mousetrap* opens in London and is still running today 1952	329
26	Thursday	Lewis Carroll's famed work of literary nonsense, *Alice's Adventures in Wonderland,* is published 1865	330
27	Friday	Alexandre Dumas, *fils,* a writer and dramatist, the son of the author Alexandre Dumas *d.* 1895	331
28	Saturday	William Blake, a seminal figure of the Romantic Age, who produced *The Marriage of Heaven and Hell b.* 1757	332
29	Sunday	The novelist, poet and academic C. S. Lewis, creator of *The Chronicles of Narnia* series *b.* 1898	333

30	Monday	Samuel Langhorne Clemens (Mark Twain) who wrote *Adventures of Huckleberry Finn b.* 1835	week 48 day 334

ASTRONOMICAL PHENOMENA

d h
3 16 Mars 0.7° N of Venus
6 16 Jupiter 2° N. of the Moon
7 10 Mars 2° N. of the Moon
7 14 Venus 1° N. of the Moon
11 08 Mercury 3° S. of the Moon
13 01 Saturn 3° S. of the Moon
17 15 Mercury superior conjunction with the Sun
20 02 Neptune 3° S. of the Moon
22 19 Uranus 0.9° N. of the Moon
25 13 Saturn 3° N of Mercury
30 00 Saturn in conjunction with the Sun

MINIMA OF ALGOL

d	h	d	h	d	h
2	06.7	13	18.0	25	05.3
5	03.6	16	14.8	28	02.1
8	00.4	19	11.6	30	22.9
10	21.2	22	08.5		

CONSTELLATIONS

The following constellations are near their meridian at

	d	h		d	h
October	1	24	November	15	21
October	16	23	December	1	20
November	1	22	December	16	19

Ursa Major (below the Pole), Cepheus, Cassiopeia, Andromeda, Pegasus, Pisces, Aquarius and Cetus

THE MOON

Phases, Apsides and Node	d	h	m
☾ Last Quarter	3	12	24
● New Moon	11	17	47
☽ First Quarter	19	06	27
○ Full Moon	25	22	44

Apogee (405,721km)	7	21	51
Perigee (362,817km)	23	20	08

Mean longitude of ascending node on 1st, 179°

THE SUN

s.d. 16′.2

Day	Right Ascension			Dec.		Equation of time		Rise				Transit		Set				Sidereal time			Transit of first point of Aries		
								52°		56°				52°		56°							
	h	m	s	°	′	m	s	h	m	h	m	h	h	h	m	h	m	h	m	s	h	m	s
1	14	23	28	14	15	+16	24	6	54	7	06	11	44	16	32	16	20	26	39	52	21	12	42
2	14	27	23	14	34	+16	26	6	56	7	08	11	44	16	30	16	18	26	43	49	21	08	47
3	14	31	19	14	53	+16	26	6	58	7	10	11	44	16	29	16	16	26	47	45	21	04	51
4	14	35	15	15	12	+16	27	7	00	7	12	11	44	16	27	16	14	26	51	42	21	00	55
5	14	39	12	15	30	+16	26	7	01	7	15	11	44	16	25	16	12	26	55	38	20	56	59
6	14	43	10	15	49	+16	24	7	03	7	17	11	44	16	23	16	10	26	59	35	20	53	03
7	14	47	09	16	07	+16	22	7	05	7	19	11	44	16	22	16	08	27	03	31	20	49	07
8	14	51	09	16	24	+16	19	7	07	7	21	11	44	16	20	16	06	27	07	28	20	45	11
9	14	55	10	16	42	+16	15	7	08	7	23	11	44	16	18	16	04	27	11	24	20	41	15
10	14	59	11	16	59	+16	10	7	10	7	25	11	44	16	17	16	02	27	15	21	20	37	19
11	15	03	14	17	16	+16	04	7	12	7	27	11	44	16	15	16	00	27	19	18	20	33	23
12	15	07	17	17	32	+15	57	7	14	7	29	11	44	16	14	15	58	27	23	14	20	29	28
13	15	11	21	17	49	+15	50	7	16	7	32	11	44	16	12	15	56	27	27	11	20	25	32
14	15	15	26	18	05	+15	41	7	17	7	34	11	44	16	11	15	55	27	31	07	20	21	36
15	15	19	32	18	20	+15	32	7	19	7	36	11	45	16	09	15	53	27	35	04	20	17	40
16	15	23	38	18	36	+15	22	7	21	7	38	11	45	16	08	15	51	27	39	00	20	13	44
17	15	27	46	18	51	+15	11	7	23	7	40	11	45	16	07	15	49	27	42	57	20	09	48
18	15	31	54	19	05	+14	60	7	24	7	42	11	45	16	05	15	48	27	46	53	20	05	52
19	15	36	03	19	20	+14	47	7	26	7	44	11	45	16	04	15	46	27	50	50	20	01	56
20	15	40	13	19	34	+14	34	7	28	7	46	11	46	16	03	15	45	27	54	47	19	58	00
21	15	44	23	19	47	+14	20	7	29	7	48	11	46	16	02	15	43	27	58	43	19	54	04
22	15	48	35	20	00	+14	05	7	31	7	50	11	46	16	01	15	42	28	02	40	19	50	08
23	15	52	47	20	13	+13	49	7	33	7	52	11	46	15	59	15	40	28	06	36	19	46	13
24	15	56	60	20	26	+13	33	7	34	7	54	11	47	15	58	15	39	28	10	33	19	42	17
25	16	01	14	20	38	+13	16	7	36	7	56	11	47	15	57	15	38	28	14	29	19	38	21
26	16	05	28	20	50	+12	58	7	38	7	57	11	47	15	56	15	37	28	18	26	19	34	25
27	16	09	43	21	01	+12	39	7	39	7	59	11	48	15	56	15	35	28	22	22	19	30	29
28	16	13	59	21	12	+12	19	7	41	8	01	11	48	15	55	15	34	28	26	19	19	26	33
29	16	18	16	21	23	+11	59	7	42	8	03	11	48	15	54	15	33	28	30	16	19	22	37
30	16	22	34	21	33	+11	38	7	44	8	04	11	49	15	53	15	32	28	34	12	19	18	41

DURATION OF TWILIGHT (in minutes)

Latitude	52°	56°	52°	56°	52°	56°	52°	56°
	1 November		11 November		21 November		31 November	
Civil	36	40	37	41	38	43	40	45
Nautical	75	84	78	87	80	90	82	93
Astronomical	115	127	117	130	120	134	123	138

THE NIGHT SKY

Mercury passes through superior conjunction on the 17th and thus remains too close to the Sun for observation throughout the month.

Venus continues to be visible as a magnificent object, completely dominating the south-eastern sky for several hours before dawn, magnitude −4.3. Shortly before the end of the month Venus passes nearly 5° south of Spica. Venus, Mars and Jupiter are close together in the morning skies from 1st–5th. Venus and Mars are closest on 1st being only 1° apart. The waning crescent Moon joins the trio on 8th and 9th.

Mars is a morning object, magnitude +1.7, and visible in the eastern sky by around 03h. During the month Mars moves from Leo into Virgo.

Jupiter, magnitude −1.9, continues to be visible in the eastern sky as a brilliant morning object. By the end of the month it should be visible very low in the east shortly after midnight.

Saturn is unsuitably placed for observation, conjunction occurring on the 30th.

THE MOON

Day	R.A. h m	Dec. °	Hor. Par. '	Diam. '	Sun's Co-Long. °	PA of Br. Limb °	Ph. %	Age d	Rise 52° h m	Rise 56° h m	Transit h m	Set 52° h m	Set 56° h m
1	6 35	+18.0	57.6	31.4	142	96	75	18.9	21 08	20 52	4 04	11 56	12 13
2	7 30	+16.9	56.7	30.8	155	100	65	19.9	22 11	21 57	4 56	12 37	12 52
3	8 22	+15.0	55.8	30.4	167	104	55	20.9	23 14	23 03	5 46	13 12	13 24
4	9 12	+12.4	55.2	30.0	179	107	45	21.9	—	—	6 33	13 41	13 50
5	9 60	+9.3	54.7	29.8	191	109	36	22.9	0 17	0 09	7 17	14 07	14 13
6	10 46	+5.9	54.3	29.6	203	111	27	23.9	1 20	1 15	8 00	14 30	14 33
7	11 31	+2.3	54.1	29.4	216	113	19	24.9	2 23	2 21	8 43	14 53	14 53
8	12 16	−1.4	54.0	29.4	228	114	12	25.9	3 25	3 27	9 25	15 15	15 12
9	13 01	−5.0	54.1	29.4	240	115	7	26.9	4 28	4 33	10 08	15 39	15 33
10	13 47	−8.5	54.3	29.6	252	118	3	27.9	5 31	5 39	10 51	16 04	15 55
11	14 35	−11.7	54.6	29.8	264	130	1	28.9	6 34	6 45	11 37	16 33	16 21
12	15 23	−14.4	54.9	29.8	277	230	0	0.4	7 36	7 51	12 24	17 06	16 52
13	16 14	−16.5	55.3	30.2	289	263	2	1.4	8 37	8 54	13 13	17 46	17 29
14	17 06	−17.8	55.7	30.4	301	265	5	2.4	9 34	9 52	14 04	18 32	18 14
15	17 59	−18.3	56.2	30.6	313	263	11	3.4	10 27	10 45	14 55	19 25	19 08
16	18 53	−17.9	56.7	30.8	325	260	18	4.4	11 13	11 30	15 48	20 26	20 10
17	19 48	−16.5	57.2	31.2	337	257	26	5.4	11 54	12 08	16 40	21 33	21 19
18	20 43	−14.2	57.8	31.6	350	254	36	6.4	12 29	12 41	17 33	22 44	22 34
19	21 37	−11.0	58.4	31.8	362	251	47	7.4	13 01	13 09	18 25	23 58	23 52
20	22 31	−7.2	59.1	32.2	374	249	58	8.4	13 31	13 35	19 17	—	—
21	23 25	−2.9	59.6	32.4	386	247	69	9.4	13 59	13 59	20 09	1 15	1 12
22	0 20	+1.6	60.1	32.8	398	246	79	10.4	14 28	14 24	21 03	2 33	2 35
23	1 16	+6.1	60.4	32.8	410	246	88	11.4	14 58	14 51	21 58	3 52	3 58
24	2 14	+10.3	60.4	33.0	423	245	95	12.4	15 33	15 22	22 55	5 12	5 22
25	3 12	+13.8	60.3	32.8	435	238	99	13.4	16 12	15 58	23 53	6 30	6 43
26	4 12	+16.4	59.9	32.6	447	161	100	14.4	16 58	16 41	—	7 43	7 59
27	5 12	+18.0	59.2	32.2	99	104	98	15.4	17 51	17 33	0 52	8 49	9 07
28	6 11	+18.4	58.5	31.8	111	101	94	16.4	18 50	18 33	1 49	9 45	10 03
29	7 08	+17.7	57.6	31.4	123	102	88	17.4	19 53	19 38	2 44	10 32	10 48
30	8 03	+16.0	56.8	31.0	135	105	81	18.4	20 58	20 45	3 36	11 11	11 24

MERCURY

Day	R.A. h m	Dec °	Mag.	Diam. ''	Phase %	Rise h m	Transit h m	Set h m
1	13 44.9	−9.2	−0.9	5	94	5 48	10 59	16 11
3	13 57.2	−10.5	−0.9	5	96	6 00	11 04	16 08
5	14 09.6	−11.9	−0.9	5	97	6 12	11 08	16 04
7	14 22.0	−13.1	−0.9	5	98	6 24	11 13	16 01
9	14 34.6	−14.4	−0.9	5	99	6 37	11 17	15 58
11	14 47.1	−15.6	−0.9	5	99	6 49	11 22	15 55
13	14 59.7	−16.7	−0.9	5	100	7 01	11 27	15 53
15	15 12.4	−17.8	−0.9	5	100	7 13	11 32	15 50
17	15 25.2	−18.9	−0.9	5	100	7 25	11 36	15 48
19	15 38.0	−19.9	−0.8	5	100	7 36	11 41	15 46
21	15 51.0	−20.8	−0.8	5	100	7 48	11 46	15 45
23	16 04.0	−21.6	−0.7	5	100	7 59	11 52	15 44
25	16 17.1	−22.4	−0.7	5	99	8 10	11 57	15 44
27	16 30.4	−23.1	−0.6	5	99	8 21	12 02	15 44
29	16 43.7	−23.7	−0.6	5	99	8 31	12 07	15 44

Rising and setting times are for latitude 54°

VENUS

Day	R.A. h m	Dec °	Mag.	Diam. ''	Phase %	Rise h m	Transit h m	Set h m
1	11 30.3	+3.8	−4.0	23	54	2 21	8 45	15 09
6	11 50.3	+2.1	−3.9	22	56	2 31	8 45	15 00
11	12 10.6	+0.3	−3.9	21	58	2 42	8 46	14 50
16	12 31.3	−1.7	−3.8	20	61	2 53	8 47	14 41
21	12 52.3	−3.6	−3.8	19	63	3 05	8 48	14 31
26	13 13.7	−5.6	−3.8	18	65	3 18	8 50	14 22

MARS

Day	R.A. h m	Dec °	Mag.	Diam. ''	Phase %	Rise h m	Transit h m	Set h m
1	11 34.9	+4.2	+1.9	4	95	2 24	8 50	15 16
6	11 46.1	+3.0	+1.9	4	95	2 22	8 41	15 01
11	11 57.2	+1.8	+1.8	4	95	2 20	8 33	14 46
16	12 08.3	+0.7	+1.8	4	94	2 18	8 24	14 30
21	12 19.3	−0.5	+1.8	5	94	2 15	8 15	14 15
26	12 30.2	−1.7	+1.8	5	94	2 13	8 07	14 00

SUNRISE AND SUNSET

	London 0° 05' 51° 30'		Bristol 2° 35' 51° 28'		Birmingham 1° 55' 52° 28'		Manchester 2° 15' 53° 28'		Newcastle 1° 37' 54° 59'		Glasgow 4° 14' 55° 52'		Belfast 5° 56' 54° 35'	
d	h m	h m	h m	h m	h m	h m	h m	h m	h m	h m	h m	h m	h m	h m
1	6 53	16 34	7 03	16 44	7 03	16 39	7 07	16 37	7 09	16 30	7 20	16 40	7 23	16 51
2	6 55	16 32	7 05	16 42	7 05	16 37	7 09	16 35	7 11	16 28	7 23	16 38	7 25	16 49
3	6 57	16 30	7 07	16 41	7 07	16 35	7 11	16 33	7 13	16 26	7 25	16 35	7 27	16 47
4	6 58	16 29	7 08	16 39	7 09	16 33	7 13	16 31	7 15	16 24	7 27	16 33	7 29	16 44
5	7 00	16 27	7 10	16 37	7 10	16 31	7 15	16 30	7 17	16 22	7 29	16 31	7 31	16 43
6	7 02	16 25	7 12	16 35	7 12	16 30	7 17	16 28	7 19	16 20	7 31	16 29	7 33	16 41
7	7 04	16 24	7 14	16 34	7 14	16 28	7 19	16 26	7 22	16 18	7 33	16 27	7 35	16 39
8	7 05	16 22	7 15	16 32	7 16	16 26	7 21	16 24	7 24	16 16	7 35	16 25	7 37	16 37
9	7 07	16 20	7 17	16 31	7 18	16 25	7 23	16 22	7 26	16 14	7 37	16 23	7 39	16 35
10	7 09	16 19	7 19	16 29	7 20	16 23	7 24	16 21	7 28	16 12	7 40	16 21	7 41	16 33
11	7 11	16 17	7 21	16 27	7 21	16 21	7 26	16 19	7 30	16 11	7 42	16 19	7 43	16 31
12	7 12	16 16	7 22	16 26	7 23	16 20	7 28	16 17	7 32	16 09	7 44	16 17	7 45	16 29
13	7 14	16 14	7 24	16 24	7 25	16 18	7 30	16 16	7 34	16 07	7 46	16 16	7 47	16 28
14	7 16	16 13	7 26	16 23	7 27	16 17	7 32	16 14	7 36	16 05	7 48	16 14	7 49	16 26
15	7 18	16 12	7 28	16 22	7 29	16 15	7 34	16 13	7 38	16 04	7 50	16 12	7 51	16 24
16	7 19	16 10	7 29	16 20	7 30	16 14	7 36	16 11	7 40	16 02	7 52	16 10	7 53	16 23
17	7 21	16 09	7 31	16 19	7 32	16 12	7 38	16 10	7 42	16 01	7 54	16 09	7 55	16 21
18	7 23	16 08	7 33	16 18	7 34	16 11	7 39	16 08	7 44	15 59	7 56	16 07	7 57	16 20
19	7 24	16 06	7 34	16 16	7 36	16 10	7 41	16 07	7 45	15 58	7 58	16 05	7 59	16 18
20	7 26	16 05	7 36	16 15	7 37	16 09	7 43	16 06	7 47	15 56	8 00	16 04	8 01	16 17
21	7 28	16 04	7 38	16 14	7 39	16 07	7 45	16 04	7 49	15 55	8 02	16 02	8 03	16 15
22	7 29	16 03	7 39	16 13	7 41	16 06	7 46	16 03	7 51	15 53	8 04	16 01	8 05	16 14
23	7 31	16 02	7 41	16 12	7 42	16 05	7 48	16 02	7 53	15 52	8 06	15 59	8 06	16 13
24	7 33	16 01	7 42	16 11	7 44	16 04	7 50	16 01	7 55	15 51	8 08	15 58	8 08	16 11
25	7 34	16 00	7 44	16 10	7 46	16 03	7 52	16 00	7 57	15 50	8 10	15 57	8 10	16 10
26	7 36	15 59	7 46	16 09	7 47	16 02	7 53	15 59	7 58	15 49	8 12	15 55	8 12	16 09
27	7 37	15 58	7 47	16 08	7 49	16 01	7 55	15 58	8 00	15 47	8 14	15 54	8 14	16 08
28	7 39	15 57	7 49	16 07	7 50	16 00	7 57	15 57	8 02	15 46	8 15	15 53	8 15	16 07
29	7 40	15 57	7 50	16 07	7 52	15 59	7 58	15 56	8 03	15 45	8 17	15 52	8 17	16 06
30	7 42	15 56	7 52	16 06	7 53	15 59	8 00	15 55	8 05	15 45	8 19	15 51	8 19	16 05

JUPITER

Day	R.A. h m	Dec °	Mag.	Diam. "	Rise h m	Transit h m	Set h m
1	11 11.9	+6.2	−1.4	33	1 49	8 27	15 04
11	11 18.0	+5.6	−1.4	34	1 19	7 53	14 28
21	11 23.3	+5.1	−1.5	35	0 48	7 19	13 51

Equatorial Diam. 34″, Polar Diam. 32″

SATURN

Day	R.A. h m	Dec °	Mag.	Diam. "	Rise h m	Transit h m	Set h m
1	16 08.8	−19.3	+0.7	15	9 14	13 23	17 32
11	16 13.5	−19.5	+0.7	15	8 41	12 48	16 56
21	16 18.4	−19.7	+0.7	15	8 08	12 14	16 20

Equatorial Diam. 15″, Polar Diam. 14″
Rings – major axis 34″ minor axis 15″, Tilt 25°

URANUS

Day	R.A. h m	Dec °	Mag.	Diam. "	Rise h m	Transit h m	Set h m
1	1 05.5	+6.3	+6.1	4	15 41	22 22	5 00
11	1 04.2	+6.1	+6.1	4	15 01	21 41	4 18
21	1 03.1	+6.0	+6.1	4	14 21	21 01	3 37

NEPTUNE

Day	R.A. h m	Dec °	Mag.	Diam. "	Rise h m	Transit h m	Set h m
1	22 35.7	−9.7	+7.7	2	14 40	19 49	1 01
11	22 35.4	−9.8	+7.7	2	14 01	19 09	0 21
21	22 35.3	−9.8	+7.7	2	13 21	18 30	23 38

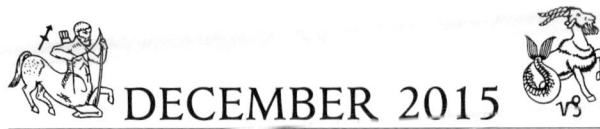

DECEMBER 2015

TWELFTH MONTH, 31 DAYS. *Decem* (ten), tenth month of Roman pre-Julian calendar

1	Tuesday	Victor Hugo misses the deadline to submit *The Hunchback of Notre-Dame* to his publisher 1830	day 335
2	Wednesday	The Marquis de Sade, a French aristocrat and revolutionary libertine, best known for his erotic works *d.* 1814	336
3	Thursday	The American playwright Tennessee Williams' play *A Streetcar Named Desire* opened on Broadway 1947	337
4	Friday	Omar Khayyám, Persian philosopher and poet who wrote around a thousand *rubáiyát* (four line verses) *d.* 1131	338
5	Saturday	Sir Edward Dering makes the earliest recorded purchase of Shakespeare's *First Folio* 1623	339
6	Sunday	The Russian novelist Vladimir Nabokov completes *Lolita*, considered his finest work in English 1953	340

7	Monday	Willa Cather, American author whose novels reflect upon life on the Great Plains *b.* 1873	week 49 day 341
8	Tuesday	*Baal*, the first play by Bertolt Brecht, is first performed at the Altes Theatre in Leipzig, Germany 1923	342
9	Wednesday	The poet and statesman John Milton is born on Bread Street, London, to a composer and his wife 1608	343
10	Thursday	Sully Prudhomme, the French poet and essayist, is awarded the first Nobel Prize in Literature 1901	344
11	Friday	Aleksandr Solzhenitsyn, Russian novelist who raised awareness of Soviet Union forced labour camps *b.* 1918	345
12	Saturday	The French writer Gustave Flaubert, famous for the novel *Madame Bovary* and his *Correspondence b.* 1821	346
13	Sunday	Heinrich Heine, 19th century German poet whose lyric poetry was set to music by Franz Schubert *b.* 1797	347

14	Monday	The German writer and academic W. G. Sebald, whose novels include *Vertigo* and *Austerlitz d.* 2001	week 50 day 348
15	Tuesday	The Institute of Russian Literature, known as Pushkin House, is established in St. Petersburg 1905	349
16	Wednesday	Jane Austen, romantic novelist, one of the most widely read authors in English literature *b.* 1775	350
17	Thursday	John Greenleaf Whittier, Quaker poet and abolitionist who penned *Snow-Bound b.* 1807	351
18	Friday	The first two volumes of Laurence Sterne's humorous novel *Tristram Shandy* are published 1759	352
19	Saturday	Charles Dickens' novella *A Christmas Carol*, featuring the miserly Ebenezer Scrooge, is published 1843	353
20	Sunday	The Brothers Grimm publish *Kinder- und Hausmärchen*, their first volume of fairy tales 1812	354

21	Monday	Norwegian playwright Henrik Ibsen's *A Doll's House* premieres in Copenhagen 1879	week 51 day 355
22	Tuesday	Mary Anne Evans, known by her pen name George Eliot, whose novels include *Middlemarch d.* 1880	356
23	Wednesday	The first ever edition of *Whitaker's Almanack* is published 1868	357
24	Thursday	William Makepeace Thackeray, prolific Victorian novelist eclipsed only by Charles Dickens *d.* 1863	358
25	Friday	Dorothy Wordsworth, author, poet and sister of the Romantic poet William Wordsworth *b.* 1771	359
26	Saturday	Henry Miller, controversial American author whose books were banned in the USA until 1961 *b.* 1891	360
27	Sunday	Charles Lamb, essayist who was once referred to as 'the most lovable figure in English literature' *d.* 1834	361

28	Monday	Susan Sontag, American writer and political activist whose works include *On Photography d.* 2004	week 52 day 362
29	Tuesday	Christina Rossetti, poet and artists' model who wrote the lyrics for *In the Bleak Midwinter* 1894	363
30	Wednesday	The Romantic poet Percy Bysshe Shelley marries the author Mary Shelley (née Godwin) 1816	364
31	Thursday	Aleksis Kivi, Finnish author who wrote *Seven Brothers*, the first significant Finnish language novel *d.* 1872	365

ASTRONOMICAL PHENOMENA

d h
4 06 Jupiter 2° N. of the Moon
6 03 Mars 0.1° N. of the Moon
7 17 Venus 0.7° S. of the Moon
10 14 Saturn 3° S. of the Moon
17 08 Neptune 3° S. of the Moon
20 01 Uranus 1° N. of the Moon
22 04 Solstice
29 03 Mercury at greatest elongation E. 20°
31 18 Jupiter 1° N. of the Moon

MINIMA OF ALGOL

d	h	d	h	d	h
3	19.7	15	07.0	26	18.3
6	16.6	18	03.8	29	15.1
9	13.4	21	00.6		
12	10.2	23	21.5		

CONSTELLATIONS

The following constellations are near their meridian at

	d	h		d	h
November	1	24	December	16	21
November	15	23	January	1	20
December	1	22	January	16	19

Ursa Major (below the Pole), Ursa Minor (below the Pole), Cassiopeia, Andromeda, Perseus, Triangulum, Aries, Taurus, Cetus and Eridanus

THE MOON

Phases, Apsides and Node		d	h	m
☾	Last Quarter	3	07	40
●	New Moon	11	10	29
☽	First Quarter	18	15	14
○	Full Moon	25	11	11

Apogee (404,799km)	5	14	57
Perigee (368,417km)	21	09	01

Mean longitude of ascending node on 1st, 177°

THE SUN

s.d. 16'.3

Day	Right Ascension			Dec.		Equation of time		Rise				Transit		Set				Sidereal time			Transit of first point of Aries		
								52°		56°				52°		56°							
	h	m	s	°	'	m	s	h	m	h	m	h	h	m	h	m	h	m	h	m	s	h	m	s
1	16	26	52	21	43	+11	17	7	45	8	06	11	49	15	52	15	31	28	38	09	19	14	45
2	16	31	11	21	52	+10	55	7	46	8	08	11	49	15	52	15	30	28	42	05	19	10	49
3	16	35	30	22	01	+10	32	7	48	8	09	11	50	15	51	15	30	28	46	02	19	06	53
4	16	39	50	22	09	+10	08	7	49	8	11	11	50	15	51	15	29	28	49	58	19	02	58
5	16	44	11	22	17	+9	44	7	50	8	12	11	50	15	50	15	28	28	53	55	18	59	02
6	16	48	32	22	25	+9	19	7	52	8	14	11	51	15	50	15	28	28	57	51	18	55	06
7	16	52	54	22	32	+8	54	7	53	8	15	11	51	15	49	15	27	29	01	48	18	51	10
8	16	57	16	22	39	+8	28	7	54	8	17	11	52	15	49	15	26	29	05	45	18	47	14
9	17	01	39	22	45	+8	02	7	55	8	18	11	52	15	49	15	26	29	09	41	18	43	18
10	17	06	02	22	51	+7	35	7	56	8	19	11	53	15	49	15	26	29	13	38	18	39	22
11	17	10	26	22	57	+7	08	7	58	8	21	11	53	15	49	15	25	29	17	34	18	35	26
12	17	14	50	23	02	+6	40	7	59	8	22	11	54	15	48	15	25	29	21	31	18	31	30
13	17	19	15	23	06	+6	12	8	00	8	23	11	54	15	48	15	25	29	25	27	18	27	34
14	17	23	40	23	10	+5	44	8	00	8	24	11	55	15	48	15	25	29	29	24	18	23	38
15	17	28	05	23	14	+5	15	8	01	8	25	11	55	15	49	15	25	29	33	20	18	19	43
16	17	32	31	23	17	+4	46	8	02	8	26	11	55	15	49	15	25	29	37	17	18	15	47
17	17	36	56	23	20	+4	17	8	03	8	27	11	56	15	49	15	25	29	41	14	18	11	51
18	17	41	22	23	22	+3	48	8	04	8	27	11	56	15	49	15	25	29	45	10	18	07	55
19	17	45	48	23	24	+3	18	8	04	8	28	11	57	15	49	15	26	29	49	07	18	03	59
20	17	50	14	23	25	+2	49	8	05	8	29	11	57	15	50	15	26	29	53	03	18	00	03
21	17	54	40	23	26	+2	19	8	06	8	29	11	58	15	50	15	26	29	56	60	17	56	07
22	17	59	07	23	26	+1	50	8	06	8	30	11	58	15	51	15	27	30	00	56	17	52	11
23	18	03	33	23	26	+1	20	8	07	8	30	11	59	15	51	15	27	30	04	53	17	48	15
24	18	07	59	23	25	+0	50	8	07	8	31	11	59	15	52	15	28	30	08	49	17	44	19
25	18	12	26	23	24	+0	20	8	07	8	31	12	00	15	53	15	29	30	12	46	17	40	23
26	18	16	52	23	23	+0	09	8	08	8	31	12	00	15	53	15	30	30	16	43	17	36	28
27	18	21	18	23	21	-0	39	8	08	8	31	12	01	15	54	15	30	30	20	39	17	32	32
28	18	25	44	23	18	-1	09	8	08	8	32	12	01	15	55	15	31	30	24	36	17	28	36
29	18	30	10	23	15	-1	38	8	08	8	32	12	02	15	56	15	32	30	28	32	17	24	40
30	18	34	36	23	12	-2	07	8	08	8	32	12	02	15	57	15	33	30	32	29	17	20	44
31	18	39	01	23	08	-2	36	8	08	8	31	12	03	15	58	15	34	30	36	25	17	16	48

DURATION OF TWILIGHT (in minutes)

Latitude	52°	56°	52°	56°	52°	56°	52°	56°
	1 December		11 December		21 December		31 December	
Civil	40	45	41	47	41	47	41	47
Nautical	82	93	84	96	85	97	84	96
Astronomical	123	138	125	141	126	142	125	141

THE NIGHT SKY

Mercury remains too close to the Sun for most of December. However, for the last week of the month it may be detected low above the south-western horizon around the end of evening civil twilight at magnitude −0.3.

Venus, magnitude −4.2, continues to be visible as a brilliant object in the south-eastern sky in the early mornings.

Mars is visible as a morning object, magnitude +1.6, in the constellation of Virgo, passing 4° north-east of Spica on the morning of the 24th.

Jupiter, magnitude −2.0, is a brilliant morning object, in the south-eastern sky. It is moving slowly eastwards in Leo. Mars and Jupiter are joined by the waxing Moon on 4th–6th.

Saturn is unsuitably placed for observation.

Meteors. The maximum of the well-known Geminid meteor shower occurs late on the 14th, although they can be seen in lesser numbers a few days either side. Consult the British Astronomical Association (W www.britastro.org) for the exact time of the maximum nearer the time.

THE MOON

Day	R.A. h	R.A. m	Dec. °	Hor. Par. ′	Diam. ′	Sun's Co-Long. °	PA of Br. Limb °	Ph. %	Age d	Rise 52° h	Rise 52° m	Rise 56° h	Rise 56° m	Transit h	Transit m	Set 52° h	Set 52° m	Set 56° h	Set 56° m
1	8	55	+13.6	56.0	30.4	148	108	72	19.4	22	03	21	53	4	26	11	43	11	54
2	9	45	+10.6	55.3	30.2	160	110	63	20.4	23	07	23	01	5	12	12	11	12	18
3	10	32	+7.3	54.8	29.8	172	112	53	21.4	—		—		5	57	12	35	12	40
4	11	18	+3.6	54.4	29.6	184	113	44	22.4	0	10	0	07	6	39	12	58	12	59
5	12	03	−0.1	54.2	29.6	196	114	35	23.4	1	13	1	13	7	22	13	20	13	19
6	12	48	−3.8	54.2	29.6	208	114	26	24.4	2	16	2	19	8	04	13	43	13	38
7	13	33	−7.3	54.3	29.6	221	113	18	25.4	3	18	3	25	8	47	14	07	13	59
8	14	20	−10.7	54.6	29.8	233	113	11	26.4	4	22	4	32	9	32	14	35	14	23
9	15	08	−13.6	55.0	30.0	245	113	6	27.4	5	25	5	38	10	18	15	06	14	52
10	15	59	−15.9	55.4	30.2	257	116	2	28.4	6	27	6	43	11	07	15	43	15	26
11	16	51	−17.6	55.9	30.4	269	140	0	29.4	7	27	7	45	11	58	16	27	16	09
12	17	45	−18.4	56.4	30.8	281	235	1	0.9	8	23	8	41	12	50	17	18	17	00
13	18	40	−18.2	56.9	31.0	294	252	3	1.9	9	12	9	30	13	44	18	18	18	01
14	19	35	−17.1	57.4	31.2	306	253	7	2.9	9	56	10	11	14	37	19	23	19	09
15	20	30	−15.0	57.8	31.6	318	252	14	3.9	10	34	10	46	15	30	20	34	20	22
16	21	25	−12.0	58.3	31.8	330	250	22	4.9	11	06	11	15	16	22	21	47	21	39
17	22	19	−8.4	58.6	32.0	342	248	32	5.9	11	36	11	42	17	14	23	02	22	58
18	23	13	−4.2	58.9	32.2	355	247	43	6.9	12	04	12	06	18	05	—		—	
19	0	06	+0.2	59.2	32.2	367	247	54	7.9	12	31	12	29	18	57	0	18	0	18
20	1	00	+4.6	59.4	32.4	379	247	66	8.9	13	00	12	54	19	49	1	35	1	39
21	1	55	+8.8	59.5	32.4	391	248	76	9.9	13	31	13	22	20	43	2	52	3	00
22	2	51	+12.5	59.5	32.4	403	249	85	10.9	14	06	13	54	21	39	4	08	4	20
23	3	49	+15.5	59.3	32.4	415	251	92	11.9	14	48	14	32	22	36	5	22	5	37
24	4	48	+17.5	59.0	32.2	427	249	97	12.9	15	36	15	19	23	33	6	30	6	47
25	5	47	+18.4	58.5	31.8	440	229	100	13.9	16	32	16	14	—		7	31	7	49
26	6	45	+18.2	57.9	31.6	92	130	100	14.9	17	33	17	16	0	29	8	23	8	40
27	7	41	+16.9	57.3	31.2	104	112	97	15.9	18	38	18	24	1	23	9	06	9	21
28	8	35	+14.8	56.6	30.8	116	111	93	16.9	19	44	19	33	2	15	9	42	9	55
29	9	26	+12.0	55.9	30.4	128	111	87	17.9	20	50	20	42	3	04	10	12	10	22
30	10	15	+8.8	55.3	30.2	140	112	79	18.9	21	55	21	50	3	50	10	39	10	45
31	11	02	+5.2	54.8	29.8	152	113	71	19.9	22	58	22	57	4	34	11	03	11	05

MERCURY

Day	R.A. h	R.A. m	Dec °	Mag.	Diam. ″	Phase %	Rise h	Rise m	Transit h	Transit m	Set h	Set m
1	16	57.1	−24.2	−0.6	5	98	8	41	12	13	15	46
3	17	10.6	−24.7	−0.6	5	97	8	50	12	19	15	48
5	17	24.2	−25.1	−0.6	5	96	8	58	12	24	15	51
7	17	37.8	−25.3	−0.5	5	96	9	06	12	30	15	54
9	17	51.5	−25.5	−0.5	5	94	9	14	12	36	15	58
11	18	05.1	−25.6	−0.5	5	93	9	20	12	42	16	03
13	18	18.7	−25.6	−0.5	5	91	9	26	12	47	16	09
15	18	32.2	−25.5	−0.5	5	90	9	31	12	53	16	15
17	18	45.5	−25.3	−0.5	5	87	9	34	12	58	16	22
19	18	58.6	−25.0	−0.5	6	85	9	37	13	03	16	30
21	19	11.3	−24.6	−0.5	6	81	9	39	13	08	16	38
23	19	23.4	−24.1	−0.5	6	77	9	39	13	12	16	46
25	19	34.9	−23.5	−0.5	6	73	9	38	13	16	16	54
27	19	45.4	−22.9	−0.4	6	67	9	36	13	19	17	02
29	19	54.7	−22.2	−0.3	7	61	9	32	13	20	17	08
31	20	02.4	−21.5	−0.2	7	53	9	26	13	20	17	13

Rising and setting times are for latitude 54°

VENUS

Day	R.A. h	R.A. m	Dec h	Mag.	Diam. ″	Phase %	Rise h	Rise m	Transit h	Transit m	Set h	Set m
1	13	35.5	−7.6	−3.7	17	67	3	31	8	52	14	12
6	13	57.7	−9.6	−3.7	17	69	3	45	8	54	14	04
11	14	20.3	−11.6	−3.7	16	70	4	00	8	57	13	55
16	14	43.4	−13.4	−3.6	16	72	4	14	9	01	13	47
21	15	07.0	−15.2	−3.6	15	74	4	29	9	05	13	40
26	15	31.0	−16.8	−3.6	15	75	4	44	9	09	13	34
31	15	55.7	−18.3	−3.5	14	77	4	58	9	14	13	29

MARS

Day	R.A. h	R.A. m	Dec °	Mag.	Diam. ″	Phase %	Rise h	Rise m	Transit h	Transit m	Set h	Set m
1	12	41.1	−2.8	+1.7	5	93	2	10	7	58	13	45
6	12	51.9	−4.0	+1.7	5	93	2	08	7	49	13	30
11	13	02.7	−5.1	+1.6	5	93	2	05	7	40	13	15
16	13	13.5	−6.2	+1.6	5	92	2	02	7	31	13	00
21	13	24.1	−7.2	+1.6	5	92	1	59	7	22	12	45
26	13	34.8	−8.3	+1.5	5	92	1	56	7	13	12	30
31	13	45.3	−9.3	+1.4	6	91	1	53	7	04	12	15

SUNRISE AND SUNSET

	London				Bristol				Birmingham				Manchester				Newcastle				Glasgow				Belfast		
	0° 05'		51° 30'		2° 35'		51° 28'		1° 55'		52° 28'		2° 15'		53° 28'		1° 37'		54° 59'		4° 14'		55° 52'		5° 56'		54° 35'
d	h	m	h	m	h	m	h	m	h	m	h	m	h	m	h	m	h	m	h	m	h	m	h	m	h	m	h	m
1	7	43	15	55	7	53	16	05	7	55	15	58	8	01	15	54	8	07	15	44	8	21	15	50	8	20	16	04
2	7	44	15	54	7	54	16	05	7	56	15	57	8	03	15	54	8	08	15	43	8	22	15	49	8	22	16	03
3	7	46	15	54	7	56	16	04	7	58	15	57	8	04	15	53	8	10	15	42	8	24	15	48	8	23	16	02
4	7	47	15	53	7	57	16	04	7	59	15	56	8	06	15	52	8	11	15	41	8	26	15	47	8	25	16	02
5	7	48	15	53	7	58	16	03	8	00	15	56	8	07	15	52	8	13	15	41	8	27	15	47	8	26	16	01
6	7	50	15	53	8	00	16	03	8	02	15	55	8	08	15	51	8	14	15	40	8	29	15	46	8	28	16	00
7	7	51	15	52	8	01	16	02	8	03	15	55	8	10	15	51	8	16	15	40	8	30	15	45	8	29	16	00
8	7	52	15	52	8	02	16	02	8	04	15	54	8	11	15	50	8	17	15	39	8	31	15	45	8	31	15	59
9	7	53	15	52	8	03	16	02	8	05	15	54	8	12	15	50	8	18	15	39	8	33	15	44	8	32	15	59
10	7	54	15	51	8	04	16	02	8	06	15	54	8	13	15	50	8	19	15	39	8	34	15	44	8	33	15	59
11	7	55	15	51	8	05	16	01	8	08	15	54	8	14	15	50	8	21	15	38	8	35	15	44	8	34	15	58
12	7	56	15	51	8	06	16	01	8	09	15	54	8	15	15	50	8	22	15	38	8	37	15	43	8	35	15	58
13	7	57	15	51	8	07	16	01	8	10	15	54	8	16	15	50	8	23	15	38	8	38	15	43	8	37	15	58
14	7	58	15	51	8	08	16	01	8	11	15	54	8	17	15	50	8	24	15	38	8	39	15	43	8	38	15	58
15	7	59	15	51	8	09	16	02	8	11	15	54	8	18	15	50	8	25	15	38	8	40	15	43	8	39	15	58
16	8	00	15	52	8	10	16	02	8	12	15	54	8	19	15	50	8	26	15	38	8	41	15	43	8	40	15	58
17	8	01	15	52	8	11	16	02	8	13	15	54	8	20	15	50	8	26	15	38	8	42	15	43	8	40	15	58
18	8	01	15	52	8	11	16	02	8	14	15	54	8	21	15	50	8	27	15	39	8	43	15	43	8	41	15	58
19	8	02	15	52	8	12	16	03	8	15	15	55	8	21	15	50	8	28	15	39	8	44	15	43	8	42	15	58
20	8	03	15	53	8	13	16	03	8	15	15	55	8	22	15	51	8	29	15	39	8	44	15	44	8	43	15	59
21	8	03	15	53	8	13	16	03	8	16	15	55	8	23	15	51	8	29	15	40	8	45	15	44	8	43	15	59
22	8	04	15	54	8	14	16	04	8	16	15	56	8	23	15	52	8	30	15	40	8	45	15	44	8	44	15	59
23	8	04	15	54	8	14	16	04	8	17	15	57	8	24	15	52	8	30	15	41	8	46	15	45	8	45	16	00
24	8	05	15	55	8	15	16	05	8	17	15	57	8	24	15	53	8	31	15	41	8	46	15	45	8	45	16	00
25	8	05	15	56	8	15	16	06	8	17	15	58	8	24	15	54	8	31	15	42	8	47	15	46	8	45	16	01
26	8	05	15	56	8	15	16	06	8	18	15	59	8	25	15	54	8	31	15	43	8	47	15	47	8	46	16	02
27	8	06	15	57	8	15	16	07	8	18	15	59	8	25	15	55	8	31	15	44	8	47	15	47	8	46	16	02
28	8	06	15	58	8	16	16	08	8	18	16	00	8	25	15	56	8	31	15	44	8	48	15	48	8	46	16	03
29	8	06	15	59	8	16	16	09	8	18	16	01	8	25	15	57	8	32	15	45	8	48	15	49	8	46	16	04
30	8	06	16	00	8	16	16	10	8	18	16	02	8	25	15	58	8	32	15	46	8	48	15	50	8	46	16	05
31	8	06	16	01	8	16	16	11	8	18	16	03	8	25	15	59	8	31	15	47	8	48	15	51	8	46	16	06

JUPITER

Day	R.A. h m	Dec °	Mag.	Diam. "	Rise h m	Transit h m	Set h m
1	11 27.9	+4.7	-1.5	36	0 16	6 45	13 13
11	11 31.6	+4.3	-1.6	37	23 38	6 09	12 36
21	11 34.3	+4.1	-1.7	38	23 03	5 32	11 58
31	11 35.9	+4.0	-1.7	39	22 26	4 55	11 19

Equatorial Diam. 37", Polar Diam. 35"

SATURN

Day	R.A. h m	Dec °	Mag.	Diam. "	Rise h m	Transit h m	Set h m
1	16 23.3	-19.9	+0.6	15	7 35	11 39	15 44
11	16 28.3	-20.1	+0.7	15	7 02	11 05	15 08
21	16 33.2	-20.3	+0.7	15	6 29	10 31	14 33
31	16 37.9	-20.5	+0.7	15	5 55	9 56	13 57

Equatorial Diam. 15", Polar Diam. 14"
Rings – major axis 34" minor axis 15", Tilt 26°

URANUS

Day	R.A. h m	Dec °	Mag.	Diam. "	Rise h m	Transit h m	Set h m
1	1 02.2	+5.9	+6.1	4	13 41	20 21	2 56
11	1 01.6	+5.9	+6.1	4	13 01	19 41	2 16
21	1 01.2	+5.8	+6.1	4	12 22	19 01	1 36
31	1 01.2	+5.8	+6.1	4	11 43	18 22	0 57

NEPTUNE

Day	R.A. h m	Dec °	Mag.	Diam. "	Rise h m	Transit h m	Set h m
1	22 35.5	-9.7	+7.7	2	12 42	17 50	22 59
11	22 35.9	-9.7	+7.7	2	12 03	17 12	22 20
21	22 36.4	-9.6	+7.7	2	11 24	16 33	21 42
31	22 37.2	-9.6	+7.8	2	10 45	15 54	21 04

TOTAL SOLAR ECLIPSE 2015

The solar eclipse on 20 March 2015 will be the first major eclipse visible in the UK since the annular eclipse of 2003 and the total eclipse of 1999, reaching a magnificent 98 per cent if viewed from the Outer Hebrides. The next eclipse whose magnitude is over 90 per cent when viewed from London will not be until 2026.

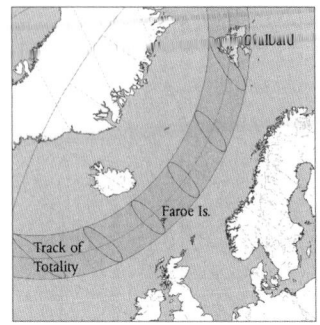

LOCAL CIRCUMSTANCES (UK & IRELAND)

	Start of eclipse			Maximum eclipse				End of eclipse		
Location	h	m	Alt.°	h	m	Mag.%	Alt.°	h	m	Alt.°
Aberdeen	8	33	18	9	38	94	25	10	46	30
Aird Uig, Isle of Lewis	8	32	15	9	36	98	22	10	43	27
Aran Island (Ireland)	8	26	14	9	29	95	22	10	37	29
Armagh	8	25	16	9	30	94	24	10	38	30
Birmingham	8	25	19	9	31	89	27	10	40	34
Bristol	8	23	19	9	28	88	27	10	38	34
Cambridge	8	26	20	9	32	88	28	10	42	35
Cardiff	8	23	18	9	28	89	27	10	37	34
Dublin (Ireland)	8	24	16	9	28	92	24	10	37	31
Edinburgh	8	30	17	9	35	94	25	10	43	31
Glasgow	8	29	17	9	34	94	24	10	42	30
London (Greenwich)	8	25	20	9	31	87	29	10	41	35
Herstmonceux	8	24	21	9	30	86	29	10	41	36
Inverness	8	32	16	9	37	96	23	10	44	29
Kirkwall	8	36	17	9	40	97	23	10	47	28
Lerwick	8	39	17	9	43	97	23	10	51	28
Liverpool	8	26	18	9	31	91	26	10	40	33
Newcastle	8	30	18	9	35	92	26	10	44	32
Penzance	8	19	17	9	24	88	26	10	33	34
Stornoway	8	32	15	9	36	97	22	10	43	28
York	8	28	19	9	34	90	27	10	43	33

Mag. shows the percentage of the Sun covered by the Moon.   Alt. is the height of the Sun above the horizon

THE AMOUNT OF THE SUN VISIBLE AT MAXIMUM ECLIPSE

| London | Glasgow | Stornaway | NW Ireland | Cardiff |

LOCATIONS EXPERIENCING TOTALITY

	Start of eclipse			Mid-totality					End of eclipse		
Location	h	m	Alt.°	h	m	s	Duration m	s	Alt.°	h	m	Alt.°
Torshavn, Faroe	8	39	14	9	41	51	2	2	20	10	48	25
Vagar, Faroe	8	38	14	9	41	0	1	26	20	10	47	25
Barentsburg, Svalbard	9	11	10	10	11	20	2	29	11	11	12	12
Longyearbyen, Svalbard	9	12	10	10	11	56	2	28	11	11	12	12
North Pole	9	22	0	10	17	12	1	58	0	11	12	0

ECLIPSES 2015

ECLIPSES

During 2015 there will be four eclipses, two of the Sun and two of the Moon.

1. A total eclipse of the Sun on March 20 is visible from only a few northern locations – notably Svalbard and the Faroe Islands. *See* page 1114 for full details.

2. A total eclipse of the Moon on April 4 is visible from eastern Australia, at moonrise from much of Asia, and from the Americas at moonset.

3. A partial eclipse of the Sun on September 13 is visible from southern Africa and Antarctica.

4. A total eclipse of the Moon on September 28 is visible from much of western Africa, Europe and South America. It is visible at moonset for eastern Europe and Asia, and at moonrise for North America.

MEAN AND SIDEREAL TIME

The length of a sidereal day in mean time is 23h 56m 04s.09. Hence 1h MT = 1h+9^s.86 ST and 1h ST = 1h − 9^s.83 MT.

Acceleration						Retardation					
h	m	s	m	s	s	h	m	s	m	s	s
1	0	10	0	00	0	1	0	10	0	00	0
2	0	20	3	02	1	2	0	20	3	03	1
3	0	30	9	07	2	3	0	29	9	09	2
4	0	39	15	13	3	4	0	39	15	15	3
5	0	49	21	18	4	5	0	49	21	21	4
6	0	59	27	23	5	6	0	59	27	28	5
7	1	09	33	28	6	7	1	09	33	34	6
8	1	19	39	34	7	8	1	19	39	40	7
9	1	29	45	39	8	9	1	28	45	46	8
10	1	39	51	44	9	10	1	38	51	53	9
11	1	48	57	49	10	11	1	48	57	59	10
12	1	58	60	00		12	1	58	60	00	
13	2	08				13	2	08			
14	2	18				14	2	18			
15	2	28				15	2	27			
16	2	38				16	2	37			
17	2	48				17	2	47			
18	2	57				18	2	57			
19	3	07				19	3	07			
20	3	17				20	3	17			
21	3	27				21	3	26			
22	3	37				22	3	36			
23	3	47				23	3	46			
24	3	57				24	3	56			

To convert an interval of mean time to the corresponding interval of sidereal time, enter the acceleration table with the given mean time (taking the hours and the minutes and seconds separately) and add the acceleration obtained to the given mean time. To convert an interval of sidereal time to the corresponding interval of mean time, take out the retardation for the given sidereal time and subtract.

The columns for the minutes and seconds of the argument are in the form known as critical tables. To use these tables, find in the appropriate left-hand column the two entries between which the given number of minutes and seconds lies; the quantity in the right-hand column between these two entries is the required acceleration or retardation. Thus the acceleration for 11m 26s (which lies between the entries 9m 07s and 15m 13s) is 2s. If the given number of minutes and seconds is a tabular entry, the required acceleration or retardation is the entry in the right-hand column above the given tabular entry, eg the retardation for 45m 46s is 7s.

Example – Convert 14h 27m 35s from ST to MT

	h	m	s
Given ST	14	27	35
Retardation for 14h		2	18
Retardation for 27m 35s			5
Corresponding MT	14	25	12

For further explanation *see* pages 1118 and 1120

EXPLANATION OF ASTRONOMICAL DATA

Positions of the heavenly bodies are given only to the degree of accuracy required by amateur astronomers for setting telescopes, or for plotting on celestial globes or star atlases. Where intermediate positions are required, linear interpolation may be employed.

Detailed definitions of the terms used cannot be given here. They must be sought in astronomical literature and textbooks.

A special feature has been made of the times when the Sun and Moon are visible in the British Isles. Since two columns, calculated for latitudes 52° and 56°, are devoted to risings and settings, the range 50° to 58° can be covered by interpolation and extrapolation. The times given in these columns are Greenwich Mean Times for the meridian of Greenwich. An observer west of this meridian must add his/her longitude (in time) and vice versa.

In accordance with the usual convention in astronomy, + and − indicate respectively north and south latitudes or declinations.

All data are, unless otherwise stated, for 0h Greenwich Mean Time (GMT), ie at the midnight at the beginning of the day named. Allowance must be made for British Summer Time during the period that this is in operation.

PAGE ONE OF EACH MONTH

The calendar for each month is explained on page 1065.

Under the heading Astronomical Phenomena will be found particulars of the more important conjunctions of the Sun, Moon and planets with each other, and also the dates of other astronomical phenomena of special interest.

Times of Minima of Algol are approximate times of the middle of the period of diminished light.

The Constellations listed each month are those that are near the meridian at the beginning of the month at 22h local mean time. Allowance must be made for British Summer Time if necessary. The fact that any star crosses the meridian 4m earlier each night or 2h earlier each month may be used, in conjunction with the lists given each month, to find what constellations are favourably placed at any moment.

The principal phases of the Moon are the GMTs when the difference between the longitude of the Moon and that of the Sun is 0°, 90°, 180° or 270°. The times of perigee and apogee are those when the Moon is nearest to, and farthest from, the Earth, respectively. The nodes or points of intersection of the Moon's orbit and the ecliptic make a complete retrograde circuit of the ecliptic in about 19 years. From a knowledge of the longitude of the ascending node and the inclination, whose value does not vary much from 5°, the path of the Moon among the stars may be plotted on a celestial globe or star atlas.

PAGE TWO OF EACH MONTH

The Sun's semi-diameter, in arc seconds, is given once a month.

The right ascension and declination (Dec.) is that of the true Sun. The right ascension of the mean Sun is obtained by applying the equation of time, with the sign given, to the right ascension of the true Sun, or, more easily, by applying 12h to the Sidereal Time. The direction in which the equation of time has to be applied in different problems is a frequent source of confusion and error. Apparent Solar Time is equal to the Mean Solar Time plus the Equation of Time. For example, at 12h GMT on August 8 the Equation of Time is −5m 44s and thus at 12h Mean Time on that day the Apparent Time is 12h − 5m 44s = 11h 54m 16s.

The Greenwich Sidereal Time at 0h and the Transit of the First Point of Aries (which is really the mean time when the sidereal time is 0h) are used for converting mean time to sidereal time and vice versa.

The GMT of transit of the Sun at Greenwich may also be taken as the local mean time (LMT) of transit in any longitude. It is independent of latitude. The GMT of transit in any longitude is obtained by adding the longitude to the time given if west, and vice versa.

DECLINATION
The distance in degrees from the ecliptic (the Sun's apparent path through the sky and the path that the planets closely follow) is termed its *declination (Dec.)*. For northern latitudes, higher positive declination means the object is higher in the sky.

LIGHTING-UP TIME
The legal importance of sunrise and sunset is that the Road Vehicles Lighting Regulations 1989 (SI 1989 No. 1796) as amended, make the use of front and rear position lamps on vehicles compulsory during the period between sunset and sunrise. Headlamps on vehicles are required to be used during the hours of darkness on unlit roads, on lit roads with a speed limit exceeding 30mph, or whenever visibility is seriously reduced. The hours of darkness are defined in these regulations as the period between half an hour after sunset and half an hour before sunrise.

In all laws and regulations 'sunset' refers to the local sunset, ie the time at which the Sun sets at the place in question. This common-sense interpretation has been upheld by legal tribunals.

MAGNITUDE
Magnitudes of astronomical objects are measured in what may be considered the reverse to the obvious. Magnitude +3 is brighter than +4, magnitude −2 is brighter than magnitude −1. So from brighter to dimmer: −4, −3, −2, −1, 0, +1, +2, +3 etc, with +6 being the dimmest considered visible with the naked eye in very dark skies. Each magnitude is roughly 2.5 times brighter than the next, so a magnitude +1 object is 100 times brighter than a magnitude +6 object.

SUNRISE AND SUNSET
The times of sunrise and sunset are those when the Sun's upper limb, as affected by refraction, is on the true horizon of an observer at sea-level. Assuming the mean refraction to be 34′, and the Sun's semi-diameter to be 16′, the time given is that when the true zenith distance of the Sun's centre is 90°+34′+16′ or 90° 50′, or, in other words, when the depression of the Sun's centre below the true horizon is 50′. The upper limb is then 34′ below the true horizon, but is brought there by refraction. An observer on a ship might see the Sun for a minute or so longer, because of the dip of the horizon, while another viewing the sunset over hills or mountains would record an earlier time. Nevertheless, the moment when the true zenith distance of the Sun's centre is 90° 50′ is a precise time dependent only on the latitude and longitude of the place, and independent of its altitude above sea-level, the contour of its horizon, the vagaries of refraction

or the small seasonal change in the Sun's semi-diameter; this moment is suitable in every way as a definition of sunset (or sunrise) for all statutory purposes.

(For further information, *see* footnote on page 1117.)

TWILIGHT
Light reaches us before sunrise and continues to reach us for some time after sunset. The interval between darkness and sunrise or sunset and darkness is called twilight. Astronomically speaking, twilight is considered to begin or end when the Sun's centre is 18° below the horizon, as no light from the Sun can then reach the observer. As thus defined twilight may last several hours; in high latitudes at the summer solstice the depression of 18° is not reached, and twilight lasts from sunset to sunrise.

The need for some sub-division of twilight is met by dividing the gathering darkness into four stages.

(1) *Sunrise or Sunset,* defined as above
(2) *Civil twilight,* which begins or ends when the Sun's centre is 6° below the horizon. This marks the time when operations requiring daylight may commence or must cease. In England it varies from about 30 to 60 minutes after sunset and the same interval before sunrise
(3) *Nautical twilight,* which begins or ends when the Sun's centre is 12° below the horizon. This marks the time when it is, to all intents and purposes, completely dark
(4) *Astronomical twilight,* which begins or ends when the Sun's centre is 18° below the horizon. This marks theoretical perfect darkness. It is of little practical importance, especially if nautical twilight is tabulated

To assist observers the durations of civil, nautical and astronomical twilights are given at intervals of ten days. The beginning of a particular twilight is found by subtracting the duration from the time of sunrise, while the end is found by adding the duration to the time of sunset. Thus the beginning of astronomical twilight in latitude 52°, on the Greenwich meridian, on March 11 is found as 06h 24m − 113m = 04h 31m and similarly the end of civil twilight as 17h 57m +34m = 18h 31m. The letters TAN (twilight all night) are printed when twilight lasts all night.

Under the heading The Night Sky will be found notes describing the position and visibility of the planets and other phenomena.

PAGE THREE OF EACH MONTH
The Moon moves so rapidly among the stars that its position is given only to the degree of accuracy that permits linear interpolation. The right ascension (RA) and declination (Dec.) are geocentric, ie for an imaginary observer at the centre of the Earth. To an observer on the surface of the Earth the position is always different, as the altitude is always less on account of parallax, which may reach 1°.

The lunar terminator is the line separating the bright from the dark part of the Moon's disk. Apart from irregularities of the lunar surface, the terminator is elliptical, because it is a circle seen in projection. It becomes the full circle forming the limb, or edge, of the Moon at New and Full Moon. The selenographic longitude of the terminator is measured from the mean centre of the visible disk, which may differ from the visible centre by as much as 8°, because of libration.

Instead of the longitude of the terminator the Sun's selenographic co-longitude (Sun's co-long.) is tabulated. It is numerically equal to the selenographic longitude of the morning terminator, measured eastwards from the mean centre of the disk. Thus its value is approximately 270° at New Moon, 360° at First Quarter, 90° at Full Moon and 180° at Last Quarter.

The Position Angle (PA) of the Bright Limb is the position

angle of the midpoint of the illuminated limb, measured eastwards from the north point on the disk. The Phase column shows the percentage of the area of the Moon's disk illuminated; this is also the illuminated percentage of the diameter at right angles to the line of cusps. The terminator is a semi-ellipse whose major axis is the line of cusps, and whose semi-minor axis is determined by the tabulated percentage; from New Moon to Full Moon the east limb is dark, and vice versa.

The times given as moonrise and moonset are those when the upper limb of the Moon is on the horizon of an observer at sea-level. The Sun's horizontal parallax (Hor. par.) is about 9″, and is negligible when considering sunrise and sunset, but that of the Moon averages about 57′. Hence the computed time represents the moment when the true zenith distance of the Moon is 90° 50′ (as for the Sun) minus the horizontal parallax. The time required for the Sun or Moon to rise or set is about four minutes (except in high latitudes). *See also* the footnote below.

The GMT of transit of the Moon over the meridian of Greenwich is given; these times are independent of latitude but must be corrected for longitude. For places in the British Isles it suffices to add the longitude if west, and vice versa. For other places a further correction is necessary because of the rapid movement of the Moon relative to the stars. The entire correction is conveniently determined by first finding the west longitude λ of the place. If the place is in west longitude, λ is the ordinary west longitude; if the place is in east longitude λ is the complement to 24h (or 360°) of the longitude and will be greater than 12h (or 180°). The correction then consists of two positive portions, namely λ and the fraction $\lambda/24$ (or $\lambda°/360$) multiplied by the difference between consecutive transits. Thus for Christchurch, New Zealand, the longitude is 11h 31m east, so λ = 12h 29m and the fraction $\lambda/24$ is 0.52. The transit on the local date 8 January 2015 is found as follows:

		d	h	m
GMT of transit at Greenwich	January	7	01	29
λ			12	29
0.52 × (02h 14m – 01h 29m)				23
GMT of transit at Christchurch		7	14	21
Corr. to NZ Standard Time			12	00
Local standard time of transit	January	8	02	21

As is evident, for any given place the quantities λ and the correction to local standard time may be combined permanently, being here 24h 29m.

Positions of Mercury are given for every second day, and those of Venus and Mars for every fifth day; they may be interpolated linearly. The diameter (Diam.) is given in seconds of arc. The phase is the illuminated percentage of the

SUNRISE, SUNSET, MOONRISE AND MOONSET
The tables have been constructed for the meridian of Greenwich and for latitudes 52° and 56°. They give Greenwich Mean Time (GMT) throughout the year. To obtain the GMT of the phenomenon as seen from any other latitude and longitude in the British Isles, first interpolate or extrapolate for latitude by the usual rules of proportion. To the time thus found, the longitude (expressed in time) is to be added if west (as it usually is in Great Britain) or subtracted if east. If the longitude is expressed in degrees and minutes of arc, it must be converted to time at the rate of 1° = 4m and 15′ = 1m.

The GMT at which the planet transits the Greenwich meridian is also given. The times of transit are to be corrected to local meridians in the usual way, as already described.

disk. In the case of the inner planets this approaches 100 at superior conjunction and 0 at inferior conjunction. When the phase is less than 50 the planet is crescent-shaped or horned; for greater phases it is gibbous. In the case of the exterior planet Mars, the phase approaches 100 at conjunction and opposition, and is a minimum at the quadratures.

To determine if a planet is visible or not, the transit time should be examined. If the transit time coincides with hours of darkness the planet should be easy to find, provided it is bright enough. If the time of transit is between 00h and 12h the planet should be visible above the eastern horizon; if between 12h and 24h, above the western horizon. The closer the transit time to midnight (0h) the longer it will be visible.

The inner planets – Mercury and Venus can never transit at midnight because they are too close to the Sun. If they transit close to noon (12h) then they will be too close to the Sun except during a large solar eclipse (like on March 20th). The rise or set times should be examined to see if either is near sunrise or sunset. If this also coincides with a large positive declination (Dec.) then conditions are favourable for viewing.

Consulting The Night Sky paragraphs will also help determine observability.

PAGE FOUR OF EACH MONTH

The GMTs of sunrise and sunset for seven cities, whose adopted positions in longitude (W.) and latitude (N.) are given immediately below the name, may be used not only for these phenomena, but also for lighting-up times (*see* page 1116 for a fuller explanation).

The particulars for the four outer planets resemble those for the planets on Page Three of each month, except that, because of the inferior brightness of Uranus and Neptune, these two planets require optical aids such as binoculars or a small telescope. The diameters given for the rings of Saturn are those of the major axis (in the plane of the planet's equator) and the minor axis respectively. The former has a small seasonal change due to the slightly varying distance of the Earth from Saturn, but the latter varies from zero when the Earth passes through the ring plane every 15 years to its maximum opening half-way between these periods. The rings were last open at their widest extent (and Saturn at its brightest) in 2002; this will occur again in 2017. The Earth passed through the ring plane in 2009.

TIME

From the earliest ages, the natural division of time into recurring periods of day and night has provided the practical time-scale for the everyday activities of the human race. Indeed, if any alternative means of time measurement is adopted, it must be capable of adjustment so as to remain in general agreement with the natural time-scale defined by the diurnal rotation of the Earth on its axis. Ideally the rotation should be measured against a fixed frame of reference; in practice it must be measured against the background provided by the celestial bodies. If the Sun is chosen as the reference point, we obtain Apparent Solar Time, which is the time indicated by a sundial. It is not a uniform time but is subject to variations which amount to as much as a quarter of an hour in each direction. Such wide variations cannot be tolerated in a practical time-scale, and this has led to the concept of Mean Solar Time in which all the days are exactly the same length and equal to the average length of the Apparent Solar Day.

The positions of the stars in the sky are specified in relation to a fictitious reference point in the sky known as the First Point of Aries (or the Vernal Equinox). It is therefore convenient to adopt this same reference point when considering the rotation of the Earth against the background of the stars. The time-scale so obtained is known as Apparent Sidereal Time.

GREENWICH MEAN TIME

The daily rotation of the Earth on its axis causes the Sun and the other heavenly bodies to appear to cross the sky from east to west. It is convenient to represent this relative motion as if the Sun really performed a daily circuit around a fixed Earth. Noon in Apparent Solar Time may then be defined as the time at which the Sun transits across the observer's meridian. In Mean Solar Time, noon is similarly defined by the meridian transit of a fictitious Mean Sun moving uniformly in the sky with the same average speed as the true Sun. Mean Solar Time observed on the meridian of the transit circle telescope of the Royal Observatory at Greenwich is called Greenwich Mean Time (GMT). The mean solar day is divided into 24 hours and, for astronomical and other scientific purposes, these are numbered 0 to 23, commencing at midnight. Civil time is usually reckoned in two periods of 12 hours, designated am (*ante meridiem*, ie before noon) and pm (*post meridiem*, ie after noon), although the 24 hour clock is increasingly being used.

UNIVERSAL TIME

Before 1925 January 1, GMT was reckoned in 24 hours commencing at noon; since that date it has been reckoned from midnight. To avoid confusion in the use of the designation GMT before and after 1925, since 1928 astronomers have tended to use the term Universal Time (UT) or Weltzeit (WZ) to denote GMT measured from Greenwich Mean Midnight.

In precision work it is necessary to take account of small variations in Universal Time. These arise from small irregularities in the rotation of the Earth. Observed astronomical time is designated UT0. Observed time corrected for the effects of the motion of the poles (giving rise to a 'wandering' in longitude) is designated UT1. There is also a seasonal fluctuation in the rate of rotation of the Earth arising from meteorological causes, often called the annual fluctuation. UT1 corrected for this effect is designated UT2 and provides a time-scale free from short-period fluctuations. It is still subject to small secular and irregular changes.

APPARENT SOLAR TIME

As mentioned above, the time shown by a sundial is called Apparent Solar Time. It differs from Mean Solar Time by an amount known as the Equation of Time, which is the total effect of two causes which make the length of the apparent solar day non-uniform. One cause of variation is that the orbit of the Earth is not a circle but an ellipse, having the Sun at one focus. As a consequence, the angular speed of the Earth in its orbit is not constant; it is greatest at the beginning of January when the Earth is nearest the Sun.

The other cause is due to the obliquity of the ecliptic; the plane of the equator (which is at right angles to the axis of rotation of the Earth) does not coincide with the ecliptic (the plane defined by the apparent annual motion of the Sun around the celestial sphere) but is inclined to it at an angle of 23° 26'. As a result, the apparent solar day is shorter than average at the equinoxes and longer at the solstices. From the combined effects of the components due to obliquity and eccentricity, the equation of time reaches its maximum values in February (−14 minutes) and early November (+16 minutes). It has a zero value on four dates during the year, and it is only on these dates (approximately April 15, June 14, September 1 and December 25) that a sundial shows Mean Solar Time.

SIDEREAL TIME

A sidereal day is the duration of a complete rotation of the Earth with reference to the First Point of Aries. The term sidereal (or 'star') time is a little misleading since the time-scale so defined is not exactly the same as that which would be defined by successive transits of a selected star, as there is a small progressive motion between the stars and the First Point of Aries due to the precession of the Earth's axis. This makes the length of the sidereal day shorter than the true period of rotation by 0.008 seconds. Superimposed on this steady precessional motion are small oscillations (nutation), giving rise to fluctuations in apparent sidereal time amounting to as much as 1.2 seconds. It is therefore customary to employ Mean Sidereal Time, from which these fluctuations have been removed. The conversion of GMT to Greenwich sidereal time (GST) may be performed by adding the value of the GST at 0h on the day in question (page two of each month) to the GMT converted to sidereal time using the table on page 1115.

Example – To find the GST at August 8d 02h 41m 11s GMT

	h	m	s
GST at 0h	21	06	40
GMT	2	41	11
Acceleration for 2h			20
Acceleration for 41m 11s			7
Sum = GST =	23	48	18

If the observer is not on the Greenwich meridian then his/her longitude, measured positively westwards from Greenwich, must be subtracted from the GST to obtain Local Sidereal Time (LST). Thus, in the above example, an observer 5h east of Greenwich, or 19h west, would find the LST as 4h 49m 16s.

EPHEMERIS TIME

An analysis of observations of the positions of the Sun, Moon and planets taken over an extended period is used in preparing ephemerides. (An ephemeris is a table giving the apparent position of a heavenly body at regular intervals of time, eg one day or ten days, and may be used to compare current observations with tabulated positions.) Discrepancies between the positions of heavenly bodies observed over a 300-year period and their predicted positions arose because the time-scale to which the observations were related was based on the assumption that the rate of rotation of the Earth is uniform. It is now known that this rate of rotation is variable. A revised time-scale, Ephemeris Time (ET), was devised to bring the ephemerides into agreement with the observations.

The second of ET is defined in terms of the annual motion of the Earth in its orbit around the Sun (1/31556925.9747 of the tropical year for 1900 January 0d 12h ET). The precise determination of ET from astronomical observations is a lengthy process as the requisite standard of accuracy can only be achieved by averaging over a number of years.

In 1976 the International Astronomical Union adopted Terrestrial Dynamical Time (TDT), a new dynamical time-scale for general use whose scale unit is the SI second (*see* Atomic Time, below). TDT was renamed Terrestrial Time (TT) in 1991. ET is now of little more than historical interest.

TERRESTRIAL TIME

The uniform time system used in computing the ephemerides of the solar system is Terrestrial Time (TT), which has replaced ET for this purpose. Except for the most rigorous astronomical calculations, it may be assumed to be the same as ET. During 2015 the estimated difference TT − UT is about 68 seconds.

ATOMIC TIME

The fundamental standards of time and frequency must be defined in terms of a periodic motion adequately uniform, enduring and measurable. Progress has made it possible to use natural standards, such as atomic or molecular oscillations. Continuous oscillations are generated in an electrical circuit, the frequency of which is then compared or brought into coincidence with the frequency characteristic of the absorption or emission by the atoms or molecules when they change between two selected energy levels. Since the 13th General Conference on Weights and Measures in October 1967, the unit of time, the second, has been defined in the International System of units (SI) as 'the duration of 9 192 631 770 periods of the radiation corresponding to the transition between the two hyperfine levels of the ground state of the caesium-133 atom'.

In the UK, the national time scale is maintained by the National Physical Laboratory (NPL), using an ensemble of atomic clocks based on either caesium or hydrogen atoms. In addition the NPL (along with several other national laboratories) has constructed and operates a caesium fountain primary frequency standard, which utilises the cooling of caesium atoms by laser light to determine the duration of the SI second at the highest attainable level of accuracy. Caesium fountain primary standards typically achieve an accuracy of around 1 part in 1,000 000 000 000 000, which is equivalent to one second in 30 million years.

Timekeeping worldwide is based on two closely related atomic time scales that are established through international collaboration. International Atomic Time (TAI) is formed by combining the readings of more than 250 atomic clocks located in about 55 institutes and was set close to the astronomically based Universal Time (UT) near the beginning of 1958. It was formally recognised in 1971 and since 1988 January 1 has been maintained by the International Bureau of Weights and Measures (BIPM). Civil time in almost all countries is now based on Coordinated Universal Time (UTC), which differs from TAI by an integer number of seconds and was designed to make both atomic time and UT available with accuracy appropriate for most users. On 1 January 1972 UTC was set to be exactly 10 seconds behind TAI, and since then the UTC time-scale has been adjusted by the insertion (or, in principle, omission) of leap seconds in order to keep it within ±0.9 s of UT. These leap seconds are introduced, when necessary, at the same instant throughout the world, either at the end of December or at the end of June. The last leap second occurred immediately prior to 0h UTC on 2012 July 1, and was the 25th leap second. All leap seconds so far have been positive, with 61 seconds in the final minute of the UTC month. The time 23h 59m 60s UTC is followed one second later by 0h 0m 00s of the first day of the following month. Notices concerning the insertion of leap seconds are issued by the International Earth Rotation and Reference Systems Service (IERS).

The computation of UTC is carried out monthly by the BIPM and takes place in three stages. First, a weighted average known as Echelle Atomique Libre (EAL) is calculated from all of the contributing atomic clocks. In the second stage, TAI is generated by applying small corrections, derived from the results contributed by primary frequency standards, to the scale interval of EAL to maintain its value close to that of the SI second. Finally, UTC is formed from TAI by the addition of an integer number of seconds. The results are published monthly in the BIPM Circular T in the form of offsets at 5-day intervals between UTC and the time scales of contributing organisations.

RADIO TIME-SIGNALS

UTC is made generally available through time-signals and standard frequency broadcasts such as MSF in the UK, CHU in Canada and WWV and WWVH in the USA. These are based on national time-scales that are maintained in close agreement with UTC and provide traceability to the national time-scale and to UTC. The markers of seconds in the UTC scale coincide with those of TAI.

To disseminate the national time-scale in the UK, special signals (call-sign MSF) are broadcast by the National Physical Laboratory. From April 1, 2007 the MSF service, previously broadcast from British Telecom's radio station at Rugby, has been transmitted from Anthorn radio station in Cumbria. The signals are controlled from a caesium beam atomic frequency standard and consist of a precise frequency carrier of 60 kHz which is switched off, after being on for at least half a second, to mark every second. The first second of the minute begins with a period of 500 ms with the carrier switched off, to serve as a minute marker. In the other seconds the carrier is always off for at least one tenth of a second at the start and then it carries an on-off code giving the British clock time and date, together with information identifying the start of the next minute. Changes to and from summer time are made following government announcements. Leap seconds are inserted as announced by the IERS and information provided by them on the difference between UTC and UT is also signalled. Other broadcast signals in the UK include the BBC six pips signal, the BT Timeline ('speaking clock'), the NPL telephone and internet time services for computers, and a coded time-signal on the BBC 198 kHz transmitters which is used for timing in the electricity supply industry. From 1972 January 1 the six pips on the BBC have consisted of five short pips from second 55 to second 59 (six pips in the case of a leap second) followed by one lengthened pip, the start of which indicates the exact minute. From 1990 February 5 these signals have been controlled by the BBC with seconds markers referenced to the satellite-based US navigation system GPS (Global Positioning System) and time and day referenced to the MSF transmitter. Formerly they were generated by the Royal Greenwich Observatory. The NPL telephone and internet time services are directly connected to the national time scale.

Accurate timing may also be obtained from the signals of international navigation systems such as the ground-based eLORAN, or the satellite-based American GPS or Russian GLONASS systems.

STANDARD TIME

Since 1880 the standard time in Britain has been Greenwich Mean Time (GMT); a statute that year enacted that the word 'time' when used in any legal document relating to Britain meant, unless otherwise specifically stated, the mean time of the Greenwich meridian. Greenwich was adopted as the universal meridian on 13 October 1884. A system of standard time by zones is used worldwide, standard time in each zone differing from that of the Greenwich meridian by an integral number of hours or, exceptionally, half-hours or quarter-hours, either fast or slow. The large territories of the USA and Canada are divided into zones approximately 7.5° on either side of central meridians.

Variations from the standard time of some countries occur during part of the year; they are decided annually and are usually referred to as Summer Time or Daylight Saving Time.

At the 180th meridian the time can be either 12 hours fast on Greenwich Mean Time or 12 hours slow, and a change of date occurs. The internationally recognised date or calendar line is a modification of the 180th meridian, drawn so as to include islands of any one group on the same side of the line, or for political reasons. The line is indicated by joining up the following coordinates:

Lat.	Long.	Lat.	Long.
90° S.	180°	48° N.	180°
51° S	180°	53° N.	170° E.
45° S.	172.5° W.	65.5° N.	169° W.
15° S.	172.5° W.	68° N.	169° W.
5° S.	180°	90° N.	180°

Changes to the date line would require an international conference.

BRITISH SUMMER TIME

In 1916 an Act ordained that during a defined period of that year the legal time for general purposes in Great Britain should be one hour in advance of Greenwich Mean Time. The Summer Time Acts 1922 and 1925 defined the period during which Summer Time was to be in force, stabilising practice until the Second World War.

During the Second World War (1941–5) and in 1947 Double Summer Time (two hours in advance of Greenwich Mean Time) was used for the period in which ordinary Summer Time would have been in force. During these years clocks were also kept one hour in advance of Greenwich Mean Time in the winter. After the war, ordinary Summer Time was invoked each year from 1948–68.

Between 1968 October 27 and 1971 October 31 clocks were kept one hour ahead of Greenwich Mean Time throughout the year. This was known as British Standard Time.

The most recent legislation is the Summer Time Act 1972, which enacted that 'the period of summer time for the purposes of this Act is the period beginning at two o'clock, Greenwich Mean Time, in the morning of the day after the third Saturday in March or, if that day is Easter Day, the day after the second Saturday in March, and ending at two o'clock, Greenwich Mean Time, in the morning of the day after the fourth Saturday in October.'

The duration of Summer Time can be varied by Order in Council and in recent years alterations have been made to synchronise the period of Summer Time in Britain with that used in Europe. The rule for 1981–94 defined the period of Summer Time in the UK as from the last Sunday in March to the day following the fourth Saturday in October and the hour of changeover was altered to 01h Greenwich Mean Time.

There was no rule for the dates of Summer Time between 1995–7. Since 1998 the 9th European Parliament and Council Directive on Summer Time has harmonised the dates on which Summer Time begins and ends across member states as the last Sundays in March and October respectively. Under the directive Summer Time begins and ends at 01hr Greenwich Mean Time in each member state. Amendments to the Summer Time Act to implement the directive came into force on 11 March 2002.

The duration of Summer Time in 2015 is:
March 29 01h GMT to October 25 01h GMT

MEAN REFRACTION

Alt.		Ref.	Alt.		Ref.	Alt.		Ref.
°	'	'	°	'	'	°	'	'
1	20		3	12		7	54	
1	30	21	3	34	13	9	27	6
1	41	20	4	00	12	11	39	5
1	52	19	4	30	11	15	00	4
2	05	18	5	06	10	20	42	3
2	19	17	5	50	9	32	20	2
2	35	16	6	44	8	62	17	1
2	52	15	7	54	7	90	00	0
3	12	14						

The refraction table is in the form of a critical table (*see* page 1115).

ASTRONOMICAL CONSTANTS

Solar parallax	8".794
Astronomical unit	149597870 km
Precession for the year 2006	50".291
Precession in right ascension	3^s.075
Precession in declination	20".043
Constant of nutation	9".202
Constant of aberration	20".496
Mean obliquity of ecliptic (2009)	23° 26' 17"
Moon's equatorial hor. parallax	57' 02".70
Velocity of light in vacuo per second	299792.5 km
Solar motion per second	20.0 km
Equatorial radius of the Earth	6378.137 km
Polar radius of the Earth	6356.752 km
North galactic pole (IAU standard)	
	RA 12h 51m (2000.0). Dec. +27°.1 N.
Solar apex	RA 18h 04m Dec. + 30°

Length of year (in mean solar days)

Tropical	365.24219
Sidereal	365.25636
Anomalistic (perihelion to perihelion)	365.25964
Eclipse	346.62003

Length of month (mean values)	d	h	m	s
New Moon to New	29	12	44	02.9
Sidereal	27	07	43	11.5
Anomalistic (perigee to perigee)	27	13	18	33.2

THE EARTH

The shape of the Earth is that of an oblate spheroid or solid of revolution whose meridian sections are ellipses not differing much from circles, while the sections at right angles are circles. The length of the equatorial axis is about 12,756 km, and that of the polar axis is 12,714 km. The mean density of the Earth is 5.5 times that of water, although that of the surface layer is less. The Earth and Moon revolve about their common centre of gravity in a lunar month; this centre in turn revolves round the Sun in a plane known as the ecliptic, that passes through the Sun's centre. The Earth's equator is inclined to this plane at an angle of 23.4°. This tilt is the cause of the seasons. In mid-latitudes, and when the Sun is high above the Equator, not only does the high noon altitude make the days longer, but the Sun's rays fall more directly on the Earth's surface; these effects combine to produce summer. In equatorial regions the noon altitude is large throughout the year, and there is little variation in the length of the day. In higher latitudes the noon altitude is lower, and the days in summer are appreciably longer than those in winter.

The average velocity of the Earth in its orbit is 30km a second. It makes a complete rotation on its axis in about 23h 56m of mean time, which is the sidereal day. Because of its annual revolution round the Sun, the rotation with respect to the Sun, or the solar day, is more than this by about four minutes. The extremity of the axis of rotation, or the North Pole of the Earth, is not rigidly fixed, but wanders over an area roughly 20 metres in diameter.

Perihelion is when the Earth is closest to the Sun, and *aphelion* when the Earth is furthest from the Sun:

Perihelion	January	4d 06h 36m
		(147,096,204km, 0.983277390au)
Aphelion	July	6d 19h 40m
		(152,093,481km, 1.016682122au)

TERRESTRIAL MAGNETISM

The Earth's main magnetic field corresponds approximately to that of a very strong small bar magnet near the centre of the Earth, but with appreciable smooth spatial departures. The origin of the main field is generally ascribed to electric currents associated with fluid motions in the Earth's core. As a result not only does the main field vary in strength and direction from place to place, but also with time. Superimposed on the main field are local and regional anomalies whose magnitudes may in places approach that of the main field; these are due to the influence of mineral deposits in the Earth's crust. A small proportion of the field is of external origin, mostly associated with electric currents in the ionosphere and magnetosphere. The configuration of the external field and the ionisation of the atmosphere depend on the incident particle and radiation flux from the Sun. There are, therefore, short-term and non-periodic as well as diurnal, 27-day, seasonal and 11-year periodic changes in the magnetic field, dependent upon the position of the Sun, the degree of solar activity and the magnetic field embedded in the solar wind.

A magnetic compass points along the horizontal component of a magnetic line of force. These lines of force converge on the 'magnetic dip-poles', the places where the Earth's magnetic field is vertical. These poles move with time, and their present approximate adopted mean positions are 86.1° N., 153.3° W. and 64.3° S., 136.7° E. Compasses do not point directly, ie via great circle routes, to the dip-poles.

There is also a 'magnetic equator', at all points of which the vertical component of the Earth's magnetic field is zero and a magnetised needle remains horizontal. This line runs between 2° and 12° north of the geographical equator in Asia and Africa, turns sharply south in the Atlantic Ocean and crosses South America south of the geographical equator; it re-crosses the geographical equator in mid-Pacific.

Reference has already been made to secular changes in the Earth's field. The following table indicates the changes in magnetic declination (or variation of the compass relative to true north). Declination is the angle in the horizontal plane between the direction of true north and that in which a magnetic compass points. Similar, though much smaller, changes have occurred in 'dip' or magnetic inclination. Secular changes differ throughout the world.

London			Greenwich		
1580	11°	15′ E.	1900	16°	29′ W.
1622	5°	56′ E.	1925	13°	10′ W.
1665	1°	22′ W.	1950	9°	07′ W.
1730	13°	00′ W.	1975	6°	39′ W.
1773	21°	09′ W.	1998	3°	32′ W.
1850	22°	24′ W.			

In the British Isles, lines of equal declination (isogonics) now run approximately north–northeast to south–southwest. Though there are considerable local deviations due to geological causes, a rough value of magnetic declination may be obtained by assuming that at 50° N. on the meridian of Greenwich, the value in 2015 is 0° 16′ west and allowing an increase of 11′ for each degree of latitude northwards and one of 26′ for each degree of longitude westwards. For example, at 53° N., 5° W., declination will be about 0° 16′ + 33′ + 130′, ie 2° 59′ west. The average annual change at the present time is about 12′ decrease. For navigation by compass using maps with the north lines from the British National Grid (as opposed to lines of equal longitude), account has to be taken of the difference between true north and grid north. This angle can be several degrees.

In 2014 the variation of the compass relative to grid north started to become easterly for the first time in 350 years.

The number of magnetic observatories is about 180, irregularly distributed over the globe. There are three in the UK, run by the British Geological Survey: at Hartland, north Devon; at Eskdalemuir, Dumfries and Galloway; and at Lerwick, Shetland Islands. The following are some recent annual mean values of the magnetic elements for Hartland.

Year	Declination West ° ′		Dip or inclination ° ′		Horizontal intensity nanoTesla (nT)	Vertical intensity nT
1960	9	58.8	66	43.9	18707	43504
1965	9	30.1	66	34.0	18872	43540
1970	9	06.5	66	26.1	19033	43636
1975	8	32.3	66	17.0	19212	43733
1980	7	43.8	66	10.3	19330	43768
1985	6	56.1	66	07.9	19379	43796
1990	6	15.0	66	09.7	19539	43886
1995	5	33.2	66	07.3	19457	43951
2000	4	43.6	66	06.9	19508	44051
2005	3	56.4	66	06.0	19576	44177
2013	2	37.8	66	00.7	19710	44296

The magnetic field is also observed by a series of specialised satellites, the latest being a mission called Swarm. Three satellites were successfully launched by the European Space Agency in November 2013, each equipped with magnetometers and star cameras for accurate orientation. With the data from these satellites it is hoped to map the Earth's magnetic field and to track its changes in time to unprecedented accuracy.

Reliance on the Earth's magnetic field for navigation by compass is not restricted to land, maritime or aeronautical navigation (in the latter two usually as a fail-safe back-up system). It also extends underground with the oil industry using magnetic survey tools when drilling well-bores. Very accurate estimates of the local magnetic field are required for this, taking into account the crustal and external fields.

MAGNETIC STORMS

Occasionally, sometimes with great suddenness, the Earth's magnetic field is subject for several hours to marked disturbance. During a severe storm in October 2003 the declination at Eskdalemuir changed by over 5° in six minutes. In many instances such disturbances are accompanied by widespread displays of aurorae, marked changes in the incidence of cosmic rays, an increase in the reception of 'noise' from the Sun at radio frequencies, and rapid changes in the ionosphere and induced electric currents within the Earth. These can adversely affect satellite operations, telecommunications and electric power transmission systems. The disturbances are caused by changes in the stream of ionised particles which emanates from the Sun and through which the Earth is continuously passing. Some of these changes are associated with eruptions on the Sun, usually in the region of sun-spots. There is some tendency for disturbances to recur after intervals of about 27 days, the period of rotation of the Sun on its axis as seen from the Earth. But the sources of many disturbances are shorter lived than this. Predicting such disturbances with any useful accuracy remains challenging. The year 2015 is expected to be one to two years after the most recent maximum of the approximate 11-year solar activity cycle. The peak in magnetic activity usually lags that in solar activity by at least two years.

ELEMENTS OF THE SOLAR SYSTEM

Orb	Mean distance from Sun (Earth = 1)	km 10^6	Sidereal period days	Synodic period days	Incl. of orbit to ecliptic ° '	Diameter km	Mass (Earth = 1)	Period of rotation on axis days
Sun	—	—	—	—	—	1,392,000	332,981	25–35*
Mercury	0.39	58	88.0	116	7 00	4,879	0.0553	58.646
Venus	0.72	108	224.7	584	3 24	12,104	0.8150	243.019r
Earth	1.00	150	365.3	—	—	12,756e	1.0000	0.997
Mars	1.52	228	687.0	780	1 51	6,794e	0.1074	1.026
Jupiter	5.20	778	4,334.4	399	1 18	142,984e / 133,708p	317.83	0.410e
Saturn	9.55	1429	10,787.9	378	2 29	120,536e / 108,728p	95.16	0.426e
Uranus	19.22	2875	30,773.3	370	0 46	51,118e	14.54	0.718r
Neptune	30.11	4504	60,349.2	367	1 46	49,528e	17.15	0.671
Pluto †	39.80	5954	91,708.2	367	17 09	2,390	0.002	6.387

e equatorial, p polar, r retrograde, * depending on latitude, † reclassified as a dwarf planet since August 2006

THE SATELLITES

Name		Star mag.	Mean distance from primary km	Sidereal period of revolution d	Name		Star mag.	Mean distance from primary km	Sidereal period of revolution d
EARTH					SATURN				
I	Moon	—	384,400	27.322	VII	Hyperion	14	1,481,000	21.277
					VIII	Iapetus	11	3,561,300	79.330
MARS					IX	Phoebe	16	12,952,000	550.48r
I	Phobos	11	9,378	0.319					
II	Deimos	12	23,459	1.262	URANUS				
					VI	Cordelia	24	49,770	0.335
JUPITER					VII	Ophelia	24	53,790	0.376
XVI	Metis	17	127,960	0.295	VIII	Bianca	23	59,170	0.435
XV	Adrastea	19	128,980	0.298	IX	Cressida	22	61,780	0.464
V	Amalthea	14	181,300	0.498	X	Desdemona	22	62,680	0.474
XIV	Thebe	16	221,900	0.675	XI	Juliet	21	64,350	0.493
I	Io	5	421,600	1.769	XII	Portia	21	66,090	0.513
II	Europa	5	670,900	3.551	XIII	Rosalind	22	66,940	0.558
III	Ganymede	5	1,070,000	7.155	XIV	Belinda	22	75,260	0.624
IV	Callisto	6	1,883,000	16.689	XV	Puck	20	86,010	0.762
XIII	Leda	20	11,165,000	240.92	V	Miranda	16	129,390	1.413
VI	Himalia	15	11,460,000	250.57	I	Ariel	14	191,020	2.520
X	Lysithea	18	11,717,000	259.22	II	Umbriel	15	266,300	4.144
VII	Elara	17	11,741,000	259.65	III	Titania	14	435,910	8.706
XII	Ananke	19	21,276,000	629.77r	IV	Oberon	14	583,520	13.463
XI	Carme	18	23,404,000	734.17r	XVI	Caliban	22	7,230,000	579.5r
VIII	Pasiphae	17	23,624,000	743.68r	XX	Stephano	24	8,002,000	676.5r
IX	Sinope	18	23,939,000	758.90r	XVII	Sycorax	21	12,179,000	1,283.4r
					XVIII	Prospero	23	16,418,000	1,992.8r
SATURN					XIX	Setebos	23	17,459,000	2,202.2r
XVIII	Pan	20	133,583	0.575					
XV	Atlas	18	137,640	0.602	NEPTUNE				
XVI	Prometheus	16	139,353	0.613	III	Naiad	25	48,230	0.294
XVII	Pandora	16	141,700	0.629	IV	Thalassa	24	50,080	0.311
XI	Epimetheus	15	151,422	0.694	V	Despina	23	52,530	0.335
X	Janus	14	151,472	0.695	VI	Galatea	22	61,950	0.429
I	Mimas	13	185,520	0.942	VII	Larissa	22	73,550	0.555
II	Enceladus	12	238,020	1.370	VIII	Proteus	20	117,650	1.122
III	Tethys	10	294,660	1.888	I	Triton	13	354,760	5.877
XIII	Telesto	19	294,660	1.888	II	Nereid	19	5,513,400	360.136
XIV	Calypso	19	294,660	1.888					
IV	Dione	10	377,400	2.737	PLUTO				
XII	Helene	18	377,400	2.737	I	Charon	17	19,600	6.387
V	Rhea	10	527,040	4.518					
VI	Titan	8	1,221,850	15.945					

Currently the total number of satellites of the outer planets are: Jupiter 67, Saturn 62, Uranus 27, Neptune 14, Pluto 3.

TIME MEASUREMENT AND CALENDARS

MEASUREMENTS OF TIME

Measurements of time are based on the time taken by the earth to rotate on its axis (day); by the Moon to revolve around the earth (month); and by the earth to revolve around the Sun (year). From these, which are not commensurable, certain average or mean intervals have been adopted for ordinary use.

THE DAY
The day begins at midnight and is divided into 24 hours of 60 minutes, each of 60 seconds. The hours are counted from midnight up to 12 noon (when the Sun crosses the meridian), and these hours are designated am *(ante meridiem);* and again from noon up to 12 midnight, which hours are designated pm *(post meridiem),* except when the 24-hour reckoning is employed. The 24-hour reckoning ignores am and pm, numbering the hours 0 to 23 from midnight.

Colloquially the 24 hours are divided into day and night, day being the time while the Sun is above the horizon (including the four stages of twilight defined in the Astronomy section). Day is subdivided into morning, ending at noon; afternoon, from noon to about 6pm; and evening, which may be said to extend from 6pm until midnight. Night begins at the close of astronomical twilight (*see* the Astronomy section) and extends beyond midnight to sunrise the next day.

The names of the days are derived from Old English translations or adaptations of the Roman titles.

Sunday	Sol	Sun
Monday	Luna	Moon
Tuesday	Tiw/Tyr (god of war)	Mars
Wednesday	Woden/Odin	Mercury
Thursday	Thor	Jupiter
Friday	Frigga/Freyja (goddess of love)	Venus
Saturday	Saeterne	Saturn

THE MONTH
The month in the ordinary calendar is approximately the twelfth part of a year, but the lengths of the different months vary from 28 (or 29) days to 31.

THE YEAR
The equinoctial or tropical year is the time that the earth takes to revolve around the Sun from equinox to equinox, ie 365.24219 mean solar days, or 365 days 5 hours 48 minutes and 45 seconds.

The calendar year usually consists of 365 days but a year containing 366 days is called a bissextile (*see* Roman calendar) or leap year, one day being added to the month of February so that a date 'leaps over' a day of the week. In the Roman calendar the day that was repeated was the sixth day before the beginning of March, the equivalent of 24 February.

A year is a leap year if the date of the year is divisible by four without remainder, unless it is the last year of the century. The last year of a century is a leap year only if its number is divisible by 400 without remainder, eg the years 1800 and 1900 had only 365 days but the year 2000 had 366 days.

THE SOLSTICE
A solstice is the point in the tropical year at which the Sun attains its greatest distance, north or south, from the Equator. In the northern hemisphere the furthest point north of the Equator marks the summer solstice and the furthest point south marks the winter solstice.

The date of the solstice varies according to locality. For example, if the summer solstice falls on 21 June late in the day by Greenwich time, that day will be the longest of the year at Greenwich, but it will fall on 22 June, local date, in Japan, and so 22 June will be the longest day there. The date of the solstice is also affected by the length of the tropical year, which is 365 days 6 hours less about 11 minutes 15 seconds. If a solstice happens late on 21 June in one year, it will be nearly 6 hours later in the next (unless the next year is a leap year), ie early on 22 June, and that will be the longest day.

This delay of the solstice does not continue because the extra day in a leap year brings it back a day in the calendar. However, because of the 11 minutes 15 seconds mentioned above, the additional day in a leap year brings the solstice back too far by 45 minutes, and the time of the solstice in the calendar is earlier, in a four-year pattern, as the century progresses. The last year of a century is in most cases not a leap year, and the omission of the extra day puts the date of the solstice later by about 6 hours. Compensation for this is made by the fourth centennial year being a leap year. The solstice has become earlier in date throughout the last century and, because the year 2000 was a leap year, the solstice will get earlier still throughout the 21st century. The date of the winter solstice, the shortest day of the year, is affected by the same factors as the longest day.

At Greenwich the Sun sets at its earliest by the clock about ten days before the shortest day. The daily change in the time of sunset is due in the first place to the Sun's movement southwards at this time of the year, which diminishes the interval between the Sun's transit and its setting. However, the daily decrease of the Equation of Time causes the time of apparent noon to be continuously later day by day, which to some extent counteracts the first effect. The rates of the change of these two quantities are not equal or uniform; their combination causes the date of earliest sunset to be 12 or 13 December at Greenwich. In more southerly latitudes the effect of the movement of the Sun is less, and the change in the time of sunset depends on that of the Equation of Time to a greater degree, and the date of earliest sunset is earlier than it is at Greenwich, eg on the Equator it is about 1 November.

THE EQUINOX
The equinox is the point at which the Sun crosses the Equator and day and night are of equal length all over the world. This occurs in March and September.

DOG DAYS
The days about the heliacal rising of the Dog Star, noted from ancient times as the hottest period of the year in the northern hemisphere, are called the Dog Days. Their incidence has been variously calculated as depending on the Greater or Lesser Dog Star (Sirius or Procyon) and their duration has been reckoned as from 30 to 54 days. A generally accepted period is from 3 July to 15 August.

CHRISTIAN CALENDAR

In the Christian chronological system the years are distinguished by cardinal numbers before or after the birth of Christ, the period being denoted by the letters BC (Before Christ) or, more rarely, AC *(Ante Christum),* and AD *(Anno Domini –* In the Year of Our Lord). The correlative dates of the epoch are the fourth year of the 194th Olympiad, the

753rd year from the foundation of Rome, AM 3761 in Jewish chronology, and the 4,714th year of the Julian period.

The system was introduced into Italy in the sixth century. Though first used in France in the seventh century, it was not universally established there until about the eighth century. It has been said that the system was introduced into England by St Augustine (AD 596), but it was probably not generally used until some centuries later. It was ordered to be used by the bishops at the Council of Chelsea (AD 816).

THE JULIAN CALENDAR
In the Julian calendar (adopted by the Roman Empire in 45 BC) all the centennial years were leap years, and for this reason towards the close of the 16th century there was a difference of ten days between the tropical and calendar years; the equinox fell on 11 March of the calendar, whereas at the time of the Council of Nicaea (AD 325), it had fallen on 21 March. In 1582 Pope Gregory ordained that 5 October should be called 15 October and that of the end-century years only the fourth should be a leap year.

THE GREGORIAN CALENDAR
The Gregorian calendar was adopted by Italy, France, Spain and Portugal in 1582, by Prussia, the Roman Catholic German states, Switzerland, Holland and Flanders on 1 January 1583, by Poland in 1586, Hungary in 1587, the Protestant German and Netherland states and Denmark in 1700, and by Great Britain and its Dominions (including the North American colonies) in 1752, by the omission of 11 days (3 September being reckoned as 14 September). Sweden omitted the leap day in 1700 but observed leap days in 1704 and 1708, and reverted to the Julian calendar by having two leap days in 1712; the Gregorian calendar was adopted in 1753 by the omission of 11 days (18 February being reckoned as 1 March). Japan adopted the calendar in 1872, China in 1912, Bulgaria in 1916, Turkey and Soviet Russia in 1918, Yugoslavia and Romania in 1919, and Greece in 1923.

In the same year that the change was made in England from the Julian to the Gregorian calendar, the start of the new year was also changed from 25 March to 1 January.

THE ORTHODOX CHURCHES
Some Orthodox churches still use the Julian reckoning but the majority of Greek Orthodox churches and the Romanian Orthodox Church have adopted a modified 'New Calendar', observing the Gregorian calendar for fixed feasts and the Julian for movable feasts.

The Orthodox Church year begins on 1 September. There are four fast periods and, in addition to Pascha (Easter), twelve great feasts, as well as numerous commemorations of the saints of the Old and New Testaments throughout the year.

EASTER DAYS AND DOMINICAL LETTERS 1500 TO 2035
Dates up to and including 1752 are according to the Julian calendar. For dominical letters in leap years, *see* note below

		1500–1599	1600–1699	1700–1799	1800–1899	1900–1999	2000–2035
March							
d	22	1573	1668	1761	1818		
e	23	1505/16	1600	1788	1845/56	1913	2008
f	24		1611/95	1706/99		1940	
g	25	1543/54	1627/38/49	1722/33/44	1883/94	1951	2035
A	26	1559/70/81/92	1654/65/76	1749/58/69/80	1815/26/37	1967/78/89	
b	27	1502/13/24/97	1608/87/92	1785/96	1842/53/64	1910/21/32	2005/16
c	28	1529/35/40	1619/24/30	1703/14/25	1869/75/80	1937/48	2027/32
d	29	1551/62	1635/46/57	1719/30/41/52	1807/12/91	1959/64/70	
e	30	1567/78/89	1651/62/73/84	1746/55/66/77	1823/34	1902/75/86/97	
f	31	1510/21/32/83/94	1605/16/78/89	1700/71/82/93	1839/50/61/72	1907/18/29/91	2002/13/24
April							
g	1	1526/37/48	1621/32	1711/16	1804/66/77/88	1923/34/45/56	2018/29
A	2	1553/64	1643/48	1727/38	1809/20/93/99	1961/72	
b	3	1575/80/86	1659/70/81	1743/63/68/74	1825/31/36	1904/83/88/94	
c	4	1507/18/91	1602/13/75/86/97	1708/79/90	1847/58	1915/20/26/99	2010/21
d	5	1523/34/45/56	1607/18/29/40	1702/13/24/95	1801/63/74/85/96	1931/42/53	2015/26
e	6	1539/50/61/72	1634/45/56	1729/35/40/60	1806/17/28/90	1947/58/69/80	
f	7	1504/77/88	1667/72	1751/65/76	1822/33/44	1901/12/85/96	
g	8	1509/15/20/99	1604/10/83/94	1705/87/92/98	1849/55/60	1917/28	2007/12
A	9	1531/42	1615/26/37/99	1710/21/32	1871/82	1939/44/50	2023/34
b	10	1547/58/69	1631/42/53/64	1726/37/48/57	1803/14/87/98	1955/66/77	
c	11	1501/12/63/74/85/96	1658/69/80	1762/73/84	1819/30/41/52	1909/71/82/93	2004
d	12	1506/17/28	1601/12/91/96	1789	1846/57/68	1903/14/25/36/98	2009/20
e	13	1533/44	1623/28	1707/18	1800/73/79/84	1941/52	2031
f	14	1555/60/66	1639/50/61	1723/34/45/54	1805/11/16/95	1963/68/74	
g	15	1571/82/93	1655/66/77/88	1750/59/70/81	1827/38	1900/06/79/90	2001
A	16	1503/14/25/36/87/98	1609/20/82/93	1704/75/86/97	1843/54/65/76	1911/22/33/95	2006/17/28
b	17	1530/41/52	1625/36	1715/20	1808/70/81/92	1927/38/49/60	2022/33
c	18	1557/68	1647/52	1731/42/56	1802/13/24/97	1954/65/76	
d	19	1500/79/84/90	1663/74/85	1747/67/72/78	1829/35/40	1908/81/87/92	
e	20	1511/22/95	1606/17/79/90	1701/12/83/94	1851/62	1919/24/30	2003/14/25
f	21	1527/38/49	1622/33/44	1717/28	1867/78/89	1935/46/57	2019/30
g	22	1565/76	1660	1739/53/64	1810/21/32	1962/73/84	
A	23	1508	1671		1848	1905/16	2000
b	24	1519	1603/14/98	1709/91	1859		2011
c	25	1546	1641	1736	1886	1943	

No dominical letter is placed against the intercalary day 29 February, but since it is still counted as a weekday and given a name, the series of letters moves back one day every leap year after intercalation. Thus, a leap year beginning with the dominical letter C will change to a year with the dominical letter B on 1 March

MOVEABLE FEASTS TO THE YEAR 2035

Year	Ash Wednesday	Easter	Ascension	Pentecost (Whit Sunday)	Advent Sunday
2015	18 February	5 April	14 May	24 May	29 November
2016	10 February	27 March	5 May	15 May	27 November
2017	1 March	16 April	25 May	4 June	3 December
2018	14 February	1 April	10 May	20 May	2 December
2019	6 March	21 April	30 May	9 June	1 December
2020	26 February	12 April	21 May	31 May	29 November
2021	17 February	4 April	13 May	23 May	28 November
2022	2 March	17 April	26 May	5 June	27 November
2023	22 February	9 April	18 May	28 May	3 December
2024	14 February	31 March	9 May	19 May	1 December
2025	5 March	20 April	29 May	8 June	30 November
2026	18 February	5 April	14 May	24 May	29 November
2027	10 February	28 March	6 May	16 May	28 November
2028	1 March	16 April	25 May	4 June	3 December
2029	14 February	1 April	10 May	20 May	2 December
2030	6 March	21 April	30 May	9 June	1 December
2031	26 February	13 April	22 May	1 June	30 November
2032	11 February	28 March	6 May	16 May	28 November
2033	2 March	17 April	26 May	5 June	27 November
2034	22 February	9 April	18 May	28 May	3 December
2035	7 February	25 March	3 May	13 May	2 December

NOTES

Ash Wednesday (first day in Lent) can fall at earliest on 4 February and at latest on 10 March

Mothering Sunday (fourth Sunday in Lent) can fall at earliest on 1 March and at latest on 4 April

Easter Day can fall at earliest on 22 March and at latest on 25 April

Ascension Day is forty days after Easter Day and can fall at earliest on 30 April and at latest on 3 June

Pentecost (Whit Sunday) is seven weeks after Easter and can fall at earliest on 10 May and at latest on 13 June

Trinity Sunday is the Sunday after Whit Sunday

Corpus Christi falls on the Thursday after Trinity Sunday

Sundays after Pentecost – there are not less than 18 and not more than 23

Advent Sunday is the Sunday nearest to 30 November

THE DOMINICAL LETTER

The dominical letter is one of the letters A–G which are used to denote the Sundays in successive years. If the first day of the year is a Sunday the letter is A; if the second, B; the third, C; and so on. A leap year requires two letters, the first for 1 January to 29 February, the second for 1 March to 31 December.

EPIPHANY

The feast of the Epiphany, commemorating the manifestation of Christ, later became associated with the offering of gifts by the Magi. The day was of great importance from the time of the Council of Nicaea (AD 325), as the primate of Alexandria was charged at every Epiphany feast with the announcement in a letter to the churches of the date of the forthcoming Easter. The day was also of importance in Britain as it influenced dates, ecclesiastical and lay, eg Plough Monday, when work was resumed in the fields, fell on the Monday in the first full week after Epiphany.

LENT

The Teutonic word *Lent,* which denotes the fast preceding Easter, originally meant no more than the spring season; but from Anglo-Saxon times, at least, it has been used as the equivalent of the more significant Latin term *Quadragesima,* meaning the 'forty days' or, more literally, the fortieth day. Ash Wednesday is the first day of Lent, which ends at midnight before Easter Day.

PALM SUNDAY

Palm Sunday, the Sunday before Easter and the beginning of Holy Week, commemorates the triumphal entry of Christ into Jerusalem.

MAUNDY THURSDAY

Maundy Thursday is the day before Good Friday, the name itself being a corruption of *dies mandati* (day of the mandate) when Christ washed the feet of the disciples and gave them the mandate to love one another.

EASTER DAY

Easter Day is the first Sunday after the full moon which happens on, or next after, the 21st day of March; if the full moon happens on a Sunday, Easter Day is the Sunday after.

This definition is contained in an Act of Parliament (24 Geo. II ch. 23) and explanation is given in the preamble to the Act that the day of full moon depends on certain tables that have been prepared. These tables are summarised in the early pages of the Book of Common Prayer. The moon referred to is not the real Moon of the heavens, but a hypothetical moon on whose 'full' the date of Easter depends, and the lunations of this 'calendar' moon consist of 29 and 30 days alternately, with certain necessary modifications to make the date of its full agree as nearly as possible with that of the real Moon, which is known as the Paschal Full Moon.

A FIXED EASTER

In 1928 the House of Commons agreed to a motion for the third reading of a bill proposing that Easter Day shall, in the calendar year next but one after the commencement of the Act and in all subsequent years, be the first Sunday after the second Saturday in April. Easter would thus fall on the second or third Sunday in April, ie between 9 and 15 April (inclusive). A clause in the bill provided that before it shall come into operation, regard shall be had to any opinion expressed officially by the various Christian churches. Efforts by the World Council of Churches to secure a unanimous choice of date for Easter by its member churches have so far been unsuccessful.

ROGATION DAYS
Rogation Days are the Monday, Tuesday and Wednesday preceding Ascension Day and from the fifth century were observed as public fasts with solemn processions and supplications. The processions were discontinued as religious observances at the Reformation, but survive in the ceremony known as 'beating the parish bounds'. Rogation Sunday is the Sunday before Ascension Day.

EMBER DAYS
The Ember days occur on the Wednesday, Friday and Saturday of the same week, four times a year. Used for the ordination of clergy, these days are set aside for fasting and prayer. The weeks in which they fall are: (a) after the third Sunday in Advent, (b) before the second Sunday in Lent, (c) before Trinity Sunday and (d) after Holy Cross day.

TRINITY SUNDAY
Trinity Sunday is eight weeks after Easter Day, on the Sunday following Pentecost (Whit Sunday). Subsequent Sundays are reckoned in the Book of Common Prayer calendar of the Church of England as 'after Trinity'.

Thomas Becket (1118–70) was consecrated Archbishop of Canterbury on the Sunday after Whit Sunday and his first act was to ordain that the day of his consecration should be held as a new festival in honour of the Holy Trinity.

HINDU CALENDAR

The Hindu calendar is a luni-solar calendar of 12 months, each containing 29 days, 12 hours. Each month is divided into a light fortnight (Shukla or Shuddha) and a dark fortnight (Krishna or Vadya) based on the waxing and waning of the Moon. In most parts of India the month starts with the light fortnight, ie the day after the new Moon, although in some regions it begins with the dark fortnight, ie the day after the full Moon.

The new year according to the civil calendar begins on the first day of the month of Chaitra (March/April) and ends in the month of Phalgun (March). The financial new year begins on the first day of Kartik (Diwali day). For most Hindus, the first day of Chaitra and the first day of Kartik are equally important.

The 12 months – Chaitra, Vaishakh, Jyeshtha, Ashadh, Shravan, Bhadrapad, Ashvin, Kartik, Margashirsh, Paush, Magh and Phalgun – have Sanskrit names derived from 12 asterisms (constellations). There are regional variations to the names of the months but the Sanskrit names are understood throughout India.

Every lunar month that has a solar transit is termed pure (*shuddha*). The lunar month without a solar transit is impure (*mala*) and called an intercalary month. An intercalary month occurs approximately every 32 lunar months, whenever the difference between the Hindu year of 360 lunar days (354 days 8 hours solar time) and the 365 days 6 hours of the solar year reaches the length of one Hindu lunar month (29 days 12 hours).

The leap month may be added at any point in the Hindu year. The name given to the month varies according to when it occurs but is taken from the month immediately following it. There is no leap month in 2015.

The days of the week are called Raviwar (Sunday), Somawar (Monday), Mangalwar (Tuesday), Budhawar (Wednesday), Guruwar (Thursday), Shukrawar (Friday) and Shaniwar (Saturday). The names are derived from the Sanskrit names of the Sun, the Moon and five planets, Mars, Mercury, Jupiter, Venus and Saturn.

Most fasts and festivals are based on the lunar calendar but a few are determined by the apparent movement of the sun, eg Makar Sankranti and Pongal (in southern India), which are celebrated on 14/15 January to mark the start of the Sun's apparent journey northwards and a change of season.

Festivals celebrated throughout India are Chaitra (the New Year), Raksha-bandhan (the renewal of the kinship bond between brothers and sisters), Navaratri (a nine-night festival dedicated to the goddess Parvati), Dussehra (the victory of Rama over the demon army), Diwali (a festival of lights), Makar Sankranti, Shivaratri (dedicated to Shiva), and Holi (a spring festival). British Hindus commonly celebrate the festival of Diwali as the start of the financial new year.

Regional festivals are Durga-puja (dedicated to the goddess Durga (Parvati)), Sarasvati Puja (dedicated to the goddess Sarasvati), Ganesh Chaturthi (worship of Ganesh on the fourth day (Chaturthi) of the light half of Bhadrapad), Ram Navami (the birth festival of the god Rama) and Krishna Janmashtami (the birth festival of the god Krishna).

The main festivals celebrated in Britain are Navaratri, Dussehra, Durga-puja, Diwali, Holi, Sarasvati Puja, Ganesh Chaturthi, Raksha-bandhan, Ram Navami and Krishna Janmashtami. For dates of the main festivals in 2015, *see* page 000.

JEWISH CALENDAR

The story of the Flood in the Book of Genesis indicates the use of a calendar of some kind and that the writers recognised 30 days as the length of a lunation. However, after the diaspora, Jewish communities were left in considerable doubt as to the times of fasts and festivals. This led to the formation of the Jewish calendar as used today. It is said that this was done in AD 358 by Rabbi Hillel II, though some assert that it did not happen until much later.

The calendar is luni-solar, and is based on the lengths of the lunation and the tropical year as found by Hipparchus (*c.*120 BC), which differ little from those adopted at the present day. The year AM 5775 (2014–15) is the 18th year of the 304th Metonic (Minor or Lunar) cycle of 19 years and the 7th year of the 207th Solar (or Major) cycle of 28 years since the Era of the Creation. Jews hold that the Creation occurred at the time of the autumnal equinox in the year known in the Christian calendar as 3760 BC (954 of the Julian period). The epoch or starting point of Jewish chronology corresponds to 7 October 3761 BC. At the beginning of each solar cycle, the Tekufah of Nisan (the vernal equinox) returns to the same day and hour.

The hour is divided into 1,080 minims, and the month between one new moon and the next is reckoned as 29 days 12 hours 793 minims. The normal calendar year, called a regular common year, consists of 12 months of 30 days and 29 days alternately. Since 12 months such as these comprise only 354 days, in order that each of them shall not diverge greatly from an average place in the solar year, a 13th month is occasionally added after the fifth month of the civil year (which commences on the first day of the month Tishri), or as the penultimate month of the ecclesiastical year (which commences on the first day of the month Nisan). The years when this happens are called Embolismic or leap years.

Of the 19 years that form a Metonic cycle, seven are leap years; they occur at places in the cycle indicated by the numbers 3, 6, 8, 11, 14, 17 and 19, these places being chosen so that the accumulated excesses of the solar years should be as small as possible.

A Jewish year is of one of the following six types:

minimal common	353 days
regular common	354 days
full common	355 days
minimal leap	383 days
regular leap	384 days
full leap	385 days

The regular year has alternate months of 30 and 29 days. In a full year, Marcheshvan, the second month of the civil year, has 30 days instead of 29; in minimal years Kislev, the third month, has 29 instead of 30. The additional month in leap years is called Adar Sheni (Adar II) and follows the month called Adar Rishon; the usual Adar festivals are observed in Adar Sheni. In a leap year Adar I has 30 days, in all other years it has 29. None of the variations mentioned are allowed to change the number of days in the other months, which still follow the alternation of the normal 12.

These are the main features of the Jewish calendar, which must be considered permanent because as a Jewish law it cannot be altered except by a Great Sanhedrin.

The Jewish day begins between sunset and nightfall. The time used is that of the meridian of Jerusalem, which is 2h 21m in advance of Greenwich Mean Time. Rules for the beginning of sabbaths and festivals were laid down for the latitude of London in the 18th century and hours for nightfall are fixed annually by the Chief Rabbi.

JEWISH CALENDAR 5775–76

AM 5775 is a regular common year of 12 months, 51 sabbaths and 354 days. AM 5776 is a full leap year of 13 months, 55 sabbaths and 385 days.

Month (length)	AM 5775	AM 5776
Tishri 1 (30)	25 September 2014	14 September 2015
Marcheshvan 1		
(29/30)	25 October	14 October
Kislev 1 (30/30)	23 November	13 November
Tebet 1 (29)	23 December	13 December
Shebat 1 (30)	21 January 2015	11 January 2016
*Adar 1 (29)	20 February	
Nisan 1 (30)	21 March	
Iyar 1 (29)	20 April	
Sivan 1 (30)	19 May	
Tammuz 1 (29)	18 June	
Ab 1 (30)	17 July	
Elul 1 (29)	16 August	

* Known as Adar Rishon in leap years (30 days)

JEWISH FASTS AND FESTIVALS

For dates of principal festivals in 2015, see page 000.

Tishri 1–2	Rosh Hashanah (New Year)
Tishri 3	*Fast of Gedaliah
Tishri 10	Yom Kippur (Day of Atonement)
Tishri 15–21	Succot (Feast of Tabernacles)
Tishri 21	Hoshana Rabba
Tishri 22	Shemini Atseret (Solemn Assembly)
Tishri 23	Simchat Torah (Rejoicing of the Law)
Kislev 25	Hanukkah (Dedication of the Temple) begins
Tebet 10	Fast of Tebet
†Adar 13	§Fast of Esther
†Adar 14	Purim
†Adar 15	Shushan Purim
Nisan 15–22	Pesach (Passover)
Sivan 6–7	Shavuot (Feast of Weeks)

Tammuz 17	*Fast of Tammuz
Ab 9	*Fast of Ab

* If these dates fall on the sabbath the fast is kept on the following day
† Adar Sheni in leap years
§ This fast is observed on Adar 11 (or Adar Sheni 11 in leap years) if Adar 13 falls on a sabbath

MUSLIM CALENDAR

The Muslim era is dated from the *Hijrah,* or flight of the Prophet Muhammad from Mecca to Medina, the corresponding date of which in the Julian calendar is 16 July AD 622. The lunar *hijri* calendar is used principally in Iran, Egypt, Malaysia, Pakistan, Mauritania, various Arab states and certain parts of India. Iran uses the solar hijri calendar as well as the lunar hijri calendar. The dating system was adopted about AD 639, commencing with the first day of the month Muharram.

The lunar calendar consists of 12 months of either 30 or 29 days, with the intercalation of one day at the end of the 12th month at stated intervals in each cycle of 30 years. The object of the intercalation is to reconcile the date of the first day of the month with the date of the actual new moon.

Some adherents still take the date of the evening of the first physical sighting of the crescent of the new moon as that of the first of the month. If cloud obscures the Moon the present month may be extended to 30 days, after which the new month will begin automatically regardless of whether the Moon has been seen. (Under religious law a month must have less than 31 days.) This means that the beginning of a new month and the date of religious festivals can vary from the published calendars.

In each cycle of 30 years, 19 years are common and contain 354 days, and 11 years are intercalary (leap years) of 355 days, the latter being called *kabisah*. The mean length of the Hijrah years is 354 days 8 hours 48 minutes and the period of mean lunation is 29 days 12 hours 44 minutes.

To ascertain if a year is common or kabisah, divide it by 30: the quotient gives the number of completed cycles and the remainder shows the place of the year in the current cycle. If the remainder is 2, 5, 7, 10, 13, 16, 18, 21, 24, 26 or 29, the year is kabisah and consists of 355 days.

MUSLIM CALENDAR 1436–37

Hijrah 1436 (remainder 26) is a kabisah year and Hijrah 1437 (remainder 27) is a common year. Calendar dates below are estimates based on calculations of moon phases.

Month (length)	1436 AH	1437 AH
Muharram 1		
(29/30)	25 October 2014	14 October 2015
Safar 1 (30/29)	23 November	13 November
Rabi' I 1 (29/30)	23 December	12 December
Rabi' II 1 (30/30)	21 January 2015	11 January 2016
Jumada I 1 (29)	20 February	
Jumada II 1 (30)	21 March	
Rajab 1 (29)	20 April	
Sha'ban 1 (30)	19 May	
Ramadan 1 (29)	18 June	
Shawwal 1 (30)	17 July	
Dhu'l Qa'da 1 (29)	16 August	
Dhu'l Hijjah 1 (30)	14 September	

MUSLIM FESTIVALS

Ramadan is a month of fasting for all Muslims because it is the month in which the revelation of the *Qur'an* (Koran) began. During Ramadan, Muslims abstain from food, drink and sexual pleasure from dawn until after sunset.

The two major festivals are *Eid-ul-Fitr* and *Eid-ul-Adha*. Eid-ul-Fitr marks the end of the Ramadan fast and is celebrated on the day after the sighting of the new moon of the following month. Eid-ul-Adha, the festival of sacrifice (also known as the great festival), celebrates the submission of the Prophet Ibrahim (Abraham) to God. Eid-ul-Adha falls on the tenth day of Dhu'l-Hijjah, coinciding with the day when those on *hajj* (pilgrimage to Mecca) sacrifice animals.

Other days accorded special recognition are:

Muharram 1	New Year's Day
Muharram 10	Ashura (the day Prophet Noah left the Ark and Prophet Moses was saved from Pharaoh (Sunni), the death of the Prophet's grandson Husain (Shi'ite))
Rabi'u-l-Awwal (Rabi' I) 12	Mawlid ul-Nabi (birthday of the Prophet Muhammad)
Rajab 27	Laylat ul-Isra' wa'l-Mi'raj (The Night of Journey and Ascension)
Ramadan*	Laylat ul-Qadr (Night of Power)

* Moveable feast

For dates of the major celebrations in 2014–15, *see* page 000.

SIKH CALENDAR

The Sikh calendar is a lunar calendar of 365 days divided into 12 months. The length of the months varies between 29 and 32 days.

There are no prescribed feast days and no fasting periods. The main celebrations are Baisakhi (the new year and the anniversary of the founding of the Khalsa), Diwali Mela (festival of light), Hola Mohalla Mela (a spring festival held in the Punjab), and the Gurpurbs (anniversaries associated with the ten Gurus).

For dates of the major celebrations in 2015, *see* page 000.

THAI CALENDAR

Thailand adopted the Suriyakati calendar, a modified version of the Gregorian calendar, during the reign of King Rama V in 1888, using 1 April as the first day of the year. In 1940 the date of the new year was changed to 1 January. The years are counted from the beginning of the Buddhist era (BE), which is calculated to have commenced upon the death of the Lord Buddha, taken to have occurred in 543 BC, so AD 2015 is BE 2558. The Chinese system of associating years with one of twelve animals is also in use in Thailand. The Chantarakati lunar calendar is used to determine religious holidays; the new year begins on the first day of the waxing moon in November or, if there is a leap month, in December.

CIVIL AND LEGAL CALENDAR

THE HISTORICAL YEAR

Before 1752, two calendar systems were used in England. The civil or legal year began on 25 March and the historical year on 1 January. Thus the civil or legal date 24 March 1658 was the same day as the historical date 24 March 1659; a date in that portion of the year is written as 24 March 1658/9, the earlier date showing the civil or legal year.

THE NEW YEAR

In England in the seventh century, and as late as the 13th, the year was reckoned from Christmas Day, but in the 12th century the Church in England began the year with the feast of the Annunciation of the Blessed Virgin ('Lady Day') on 25 March, and this practice was adopted generally in the 14th century. The civil or legal year in the British dominions (exclusive of Scotland) began with Lady Day until 1751. But in and since 1752 the civil year has begun with 1 January. New Year's Day in Scotland was changed from 25 March to 1 January in 1600.

Elsewhere in Europe, 1 January was adopted as the first day of the year by Venice in 1522, German states in 1544, Spain, Portugal and the Roman Catholic Netherlands in 1556, Prussia, Denmark and Sweden in 1559, France in 1564, Lorraine in 1579, the Protestant Netherlands in 1583, Russia in 1725, and Tuscany in 1751.

REGNAL YEARS

Regnal years are the years of a sovereign's reign and each begins on the anniversary of his or her accession, eg regnal year 64 of the present queen begins on 6 February 2015.

The system was used for dating Acts of Parliament until 1962. The Summer Time Act 1925, for example, is quoted as 15 and 16 Geo. V ch. 64, because it became law in the parliamentary session which extended over part of both of these regnal years. Acts of a parliamentary session during which a sovereign died were usually given two year numbers, the regnal year of the deceased sovereign and the regnal year of his or her successor, eg those passed in 1952 were dated 16 Geo. VI and 1 Elizabeth II. Since 1962 Acts of Parliament have been dated by the calendar year.

QUARTER AND TERM DAYS

Holy days and saints days were the usual means in early times for setting the dates of future and recurrent appointments. The quarter days in England and Wales are the feast of the Nativity (25 December), the feast of the Annunciation (25 March), the feast of St John the Baptist (24 June) and the feast of St Michael and All Angels (29 September).

The term days in Scotland are Candlemas (the feast of the Purification), Whitsunday, Lammas (Loaf Mass) and Martinmas (St Martin's Day). These fell on 2 February, 15 May, 1 August and 11 November respectively. However, by the Term and Quarter Days (Scotland) Act 1990, the dates of the term days were changed to 28 February (Candlemas), 28 May (Whitsunday), 28 August (Lammas) and 28 November (Martinmas).

RED-LETTER DAYS

Red-letter days were originally the holy days and saints days indicated in early ecclesiastical calendars by letters printed in red ink. The days to be distinguished in this way were approved at the Council of Nicaea in AD 325.

These days still have a legal significance, as judges of the Queen's Bench Division wear scarlet robes on red-letter days falling during the law sittings. The days designated as red-letter days for this purpose are:

Holy and saints days
The Conversion of St Paul, the Purification, Ash Wednesday, the Annunciation, the Ascension, the feasts of St Mark, SS Philip and James, St Matthias, St Barnabas, St John the Baptist, St Peter, St Thomas, St James, St Luke, SS Simon and Jude, All Saints, St Andrew.

Civil calendar (for dates, *see* page 000)
Includes the anniversaries of the Queen's accession, the Queen's birthday and the Queen's coronation, the Queen's official birthday, the birthday of the Duke of Edinburgh, the birthday of the Prince of Wales, St David's Day and Lord Mayor's Day.

PUBLIC HOLIDAYS

Public holidays are divided into two categories, common law and statutory. Common law holidays are holidays 'by habit and custom'; in England, Wales and Northern Ireland these are Good Friday and Christmas Day.

Statutory public holidays, known as bank holidays, were first established by the Bank Holidays Act 1871. They were, literally, days on which the banks (and other public institutions) were closed and financial obligations due on that day were payable the following day. The legislation currently governing public holidays in the UK, which is the Banking and Financial Dealings Act 1971, stipulates the days that are to be public holidays in England, Wales, Scotland and Northern Ireland.

If a public holiday falls on a Saturday or a Sunday then another day will be given in lieu, usually the following Monday. For dates of public holidays in 2015 and 2016, *see* pages 000–000.

CHRONOLOGICAL CYCLES AND ERAS

SOLAR (OR MAJOR) CYCLE

The solar cycle is a period of 28 years; in any corresponding year of each cycle the days of the week recur on the same day of the month.

METONIC (LUNAR, OR MINOR) CYCLE

In 432 BC, Meton, an Athenian astronomer, found that 235 lunations are very nearly, though not exactly, equal in duration to 19 solar years and so after 19 years the phases of the Moon recur approximately on the same days of the month. The dates of full moon in a cycle of 19 years were inscribed in figures of gold on public monuments in Athens, and the number showing the position of a year in the cycle is called the golden number of that year.

JULIAN PERIOD

The Julian period was proposed by Joseph Scaliger in 1582. The period is 7,980 Julian years, and its first year coincides with the year 4713 BC. The figure of 7,980 is the product of the number of years in the solar cycle, the Metonic cycle and the cycle of the Roman indiction ($28 \times 19 \times 15$).

ROMAN INDICTION

The Roman indiction is a period of 15 years, instituted for fiscal purposes about AD 300.

EPACT

The epact is the age of the calendar Moon, diminished by one day, on 1 January, in the ecclesiastical lunar calendar.

CHINESE CALENDAR

A lunar calendar was the sole calendar in use in China until 1911, when the government adopted the new (Gregorian) calendar for official and most business activities. The Chinese tend to follow both calendars, the lunar calendar playing an important part in personal life, eg birth celebrations, festivals, marriages; and in rural villages the lunar calendar dictates the cycle of activities, denoting the change of weather and farming activities.

The lunar calendar is used in Hong Kong, Singapore, Malaysia, Tibet and elsewhere in South-East Asia. The calendar has a cycle of 60 years. The new year begins at the first new moon after the sun enters the sign of Aquarius, ie the new year falls between 21 January and 19 February in the Gregorian calendar.

Each year in the Chinese calendar is associated with one of 12 animals: the rat, the ox, the tiger, the rabbit, the dragon, the snake, the horse, the sheep, the monkey, the chicken or rooster, the dog, and the pig.

The date of the Chinese new year and the astrological sign for the years 2015–18 are:

2015	19 February	Goat or Sheep
2016	8 February	Monkey
2017	28 January	Rooster
2018	16 February	Dog

COPTIC CALENDAR

In the Coptic calendar, which is used in parts of Egypt and Ethiopia, the year is made up of 12 months of 30 days each, followed, in general, by five complementary days. Every fourth year is an intercalary or leap year and in these years there are six complementary days. The intercalary year of the Coptic calendar immediately precedes the leap year of the Julian calendar. The era is that of Diocletian or the Martyrs, the origin of which is fixed at 29 August AD 284 (Julian date).

INDIAN ERAS

In addition to the Muslim reckoning, other eras are used in India. The Saka era of southern India, dating from 3 March AD 78, was declared the national calendar of the Republic of India with effect from 22 March 1957, to be used concurrently with the Gregorian calendar. As revised, the year of the new Saka era begins at the spring equinox, with five successive months of 31 days and seven of 30 days in ordinary years, and six months of each length in leap years. The year AD 2015 is 1937 of the revised Saka era.

The year AD 2015 corresponds to the following years in other eras:

Year 2072 of the Vikram Samvat era
Year 1422 of the Bengali San era
Year 1191 of the Kollam era
Year 5116 of the Kaliyuga era
Year 2558 of the Buddha Nirvana era

JAPANESE CALENDAR

The Japanese calendar is essentially the same as the Gregorian calendar, the years, months and weeks being of the same length and beginning on the same days as those of the Gregorian calendar. The numeration of the years is different, based on a system of epochs or periods, each of which begins at the accession of an emperor or other important occurrence. The method is not unlike the British system of regnal years, except that each year of a period closes on 31 December. The Japanese chronology begins about AD 650 and the three latest epochs are defined by the reigns of emperors, whose actual names are not necessarily used:

Epoch
Taisho – 1 August 1912 to 25 December 1926
Showa – 26 December 1926 to 7 January 1989
Heisei – 8 January 1989

The year Heisei 27 begins on 1 January 2015.

The months are known as First Month, Second Month, etc, First Month being equivalent to January. The days of the week are Nichiyobi (Sun-day), Getsuyobi (Moon-day), Kayobi (Fire-day), Suiyobi (Water-day), Mokuyobi (Wood-day), Kinyobi (Metal-day) and Doyobi (Earth-day).

THE MASONIC YEAR

Two dates are quoted in warrants, dispensations, etc, issued by the United Grand Lodge of England, those for the current year being expressed as *Anno Domini* 2015 – *Anno Lucis* 6015. This *Anno Lucis* (year of light) is based on the Book of Genesis 1:3, the 4,000-year difference being derived, in modified form, from *Ussher's Notation,* published in 1654, which places the Creation of the World in 4004 BC.

OLYMPIADS

Ancient Greek chronology was reckoned in Olympiads, cycles of four years corresponding with the Olympic Games held on the plain of Olympia, in Elis. The intervening years were the first, second, etc, of the Olympiad, which received the name of the victor at the Games. The first recorded Olympiad is that of Choroebus, 776 BC.

ZOROASTRIAN CALENDAR

Zoroastrians, followers of the Iranian prophet Zarathushtra (known to the Greeks as Zoroaster) are mostly to be found in Iran and in India, where they are known as Parsees.

The Zoroastrian era dates from the coronation of the last Zoroastrian Sasanian king in AD 631. The Zoroastrian calendar is divided into 12 months, each comprising 30 days, followed by five holy days of the Gathas at the end of each year to make the year consist of 365 days.

In order to synchronise the calendar with the solar year of 365 days, an extra month was intercalated once every 120 years. However, this intercalation ceased in the 12th century and the new year, which had fallen in the spring, slipped back to August. Because intercalation ceased at different times in Iran and India, there was one month's difference between the calendar followed in Iran (Kadmi calendar) and that followed by the Parsees (Shenshai calendar). In 1906 a group of Zoroastrians decided to bring the calendar back in line with the seasons again and restore the new year to 21 March each year (Fasli calendar).

The Shenshai calendar (new year in August) is mainly used by Parsees. The Fasli calendar (new year, 21 March) is mainly used by Zoroastrians living in Iran, in the Indian subcontinent, or elsewhere.

ROMAN CALENDAR

Roman historians adopted as an epoch the foundation of Rome, which is believed to have happened in the year 753 BC. The ordinal number of the years in Roman reckoning is followed by the letters AUC *(ab urbe condita)*, so that the year 2015 is 2768 AUC (MMDCCLXVIII). The calendar that we know has developed from one said to have been established by Romulus using a year of 304 days divided into ten months, beginning with March. To this Numa added January and February, making the year consist of 12 months of 30 and 29 days alternately, with an additional day so that the total was 355. It is also said that Numa ordered an intercalary month of 22 or 23 days in alternate years, making 90 days in eight years, to be inserted after 23 February.

However, there is some doubt as to the origination and the details of the intercalation in the Roman calendar. In the year 46 BC Julius Caesar found that the calendar had been allowed to fall into some confusion. He sought the help of Egyptian astronomer Sosigenes, which led to the construction and adoption (45 BC) of the Julian calendar, and, by a slight alteration, to the Gregorian calendar now in use. The year 46 BC was made to consist of 445 days and is called the Year of Confusion.

In the Roman (Julian) calendar the days of the month were counted backwards from three fixed points, or days, and an intervening day was said to be so many days before the next coming point, the first and last being counted. These three points were the Kalends, the Nones and the Ides. Their positions in the months and the method of counting from them will be seen in the table below. The year containing 366 days was called *bissextilis annus,* as it had a doubled sixth day *(bissextus dies)* before the March Kalends on 24 February – *ante diem sextum Kalendas Martias,* or a.d. VI Kal. Mart.

Present days of the month	*March, May, July, October have thirty-one days*	*January, August, December have thirty-one days*	*April, June, September, November have thirty days*	*February has twenty-eight days, and in leap year twenty-nine*
1	Kalendis	Kalendis	Kalendis	Kalendis
2	VI	IV ⎱ ante	IV ⎱ ante	IV ⎱ ante
3	V ⎱ ante	III ⎰ Nonas	III ⎰ Nonas	III ⎰ Nonas
4	IV ⎰ Nonas	pridie Nonas	pridie Nonas	pridie Nonas
5	III	Nonis	Nonis	Nonis
6	pridie Nonas	VIII	VIII	VIII
7	Nonis	VII	VII	VII
8	VIII	VI ⎱ ante	VI ⎱ ante	VI ⎱ ante
9	VII	V ⎰ Idus	V ⎰ Idus	V ⎰ Idus
10	VI ⎱ ante	IV	IV	IV
11	V ⎰ Idus	III	III	III
12	IV	pridie Idus	pridie Idus	pridie Idus
13	III	Idibus	Idibus	Idibus
14	pridie Idus	XIX	XVIII	XVI
15	Idibus	XVIII	XVII	XV
16	XVII	XVII	XVI	XIV
17	XVI	XVI	XV	XIII
18	XV	XV	XIV	XII
19	XIV	XIV	XIII	XI
20	XIII	XIII	XII	X ⎱ ante Kalendas
21	XII	XII	XI ⎱ ante Kalendas	IX ⎰ Martias
22	XI	XI ⎱ ante Kalendas	X ⎰ (of the month	VIII
23	X ⎱ ante Kalendas	X ⎰ (of the month	IX ⎰ following)	VII
24	IX ⎰ (of the month	IX ⎰ following)	VIII	*VI
25	VIII ⎰ following)	VIII	VII	V
26	VII	VII	VI	IV
27	VI	VI	V	III
28	V	V	IV	pridie Kalendas
29	IV	IV	III	Martias
30	III	III	pridie Kalendas	
31	pridie Kalendas (Aprilis, Iunias, Sextilis, Novembris)	pridie Kalendas (Februarias, Septembris, Ianuarias)	(Maias, Quinctilis, Octobris, Decembris)	

* Repeated in leap year

CALENDAR FOR ANY YEAR 1780–2040

To select the correct calendar for any year between 1780 and 2040, consult the index below

* leap year

1780 N*	1813 K	1846 I	1879 G	1912 D*	1945 C	1978 A	2011 M
1781 C	1814 M	1847 K	1880 J*	1913 G	1946 E	1979 C	2012 B*
1782 E	1815 A	1848 N*	1881 M	1914 I	1947 G	1980 F*	2013 E
1783 G	1816 D*	1849 C	1882 A	1915 K	1948 J*	1981 I	2014 G
1784 J*	1817 G	1850 E	1883 C	1916 N*	1949 M	1982 K	2015 I
1785 M	1818 I	1851 G	1884 F*	1917 C	1950 A	1983 M	2016 L*
1786 A	1819 K	1852 J*	1885 I	1918 E	1951 C	1984 B*	2017 A
1787 C	1820 N*	1853 M	1886 K	1919 G	1952 F*	1985 E	2018 C
1788 F*	1821 C	1854 A	1887 M	1920 J*	1953 I	1986 G	2019 E
1789 I	1822 E	1855 C	1888 B*	1921 M	1954 K	1987 I	2020 H*
1790 K	1823 G	1856 F*	1889 E	1922 A	1955 M	1988 L*	2021 K
1791 M	1824 J*	1857 I	1890 G	1923 C	1956 B*	1989 A	2022 M
1792 B*	1825 M	1858 K	1891 I	1924 F*	1957 E	1990 C	2023 A
1793 E	1826 A	1859 M	1892 L*	1925 I	1958 G	1991 E	2024 D*
1794 G	1827 C	1860 B*	1893 A	1926 K	1959 I	1992 H*	2025 G
1795 I	1828 F*	1861 E	1894 C	1927 M	1960 L*	1993 K	2026 I
1796 L*	1829 I	1862 G	1895 E	1928 B*	1961 A	1994 M	2027 K
1797 A	1830 K	1863 I	1896 H*	1929 E	1962 C	1995 A	2028 N*
1798 C	1831 M	1864 L*	1897 K	1930 G	1963 E	1996 D*	2029 C
1799 E	1832 B*	1865 A	1898 M	1931 I	1964 H*	1997 G	2030 E
1800 G	1833 E	1866 C	1899 A	1932 L*	1965 K	1998 I	2031 G
1801 I	1834 G	1867 E	1900 C	1933 A	1966 M	1999 K	2032 J*
1802 K	1835 I	1868 H*	1901 E	1934 C	1967 A	2000 N*	2033 M
1803 M	1836 L*	1869 K	1902 G	1935 E	1968 D*	2001 C	2034 A
1804 B*	1837 A	1870 M	1903 I	1936 H*	1969 G	2002 E	2035 C
1805 E	1838 C	1871 A	1904 L*	1937 K	1970 I	2003 G	2036 F*
1806 G	1839 E	1872 D*	1905 A	1938 M	1971 K	2004 J*	2037 I
1807 I	1840 H*	1873 G	1906 C	1939 A	1972 N*	2005 M	2038 K
1808 L*	1841 K	1874 I	1907 E	1940 D*	1973 C	2006 A	2039 M
1809 A	1842 M	1875 K	1908 H*	1941 G	1974 E	2007 C	2040 B*
1810 C	1843 A	1876 N*	1909 K	1942 I	1975 G	2008 F*	
1811 E	1844 D*	1877 C	1910 M	1943 K	1976 J*	2009 I	
1812 H*	1845 G	1878 E	1911 A	1944 N*	1977 M	2010 K	

A

	January	February	March
Sun.	1 8 15 22 29	5 12 19 26	5 12 19 26
Mon.	2 9 16 23 30	6 13 20 27	6 13 20 27
Tue.	3 10 17 24 31	7 14 21 28	7 14 21 28
Wed.	4 11 18 25	1 8 15 22	1 8 15 22 29
Thur.	5 12 19 26	2 9 16 23	2 9 16 23 30
Fri.	6 13 20 27	3 10 17 24	3 10 17 24 31
Sat.	7 14 21 28	4 11 18 25	4 11 18 25

	April	May	June
Sun.	2 9 16 23 30	7 14 21 28	4 11 18 25
Mon.	3 10 17 24	1 8 15 22 29	5 12 19 26
Tue.	4 11 18 25	2 9 16 23 30	6 13 20 27
Wed.	5 12 19 26	3 10 17 24 31	7 14 21 28
Thur.	6 13 20 27	4 11 18 25	1 8 15 22 29
Fri.	7 14 21 28	5 12 19 26	2 9 16 23 30
Sat.	1 8 15 22 29	6 13 20 27	3 10 17 24

	July	August	September
Sun.	2 9 16 23 30	6 13 20 27	3 10 17 24
Mon.	3 10 17 24 31	7 14 21 28	4 11 18 25
Tue.	4 11 18 25	1 8 15 22 29	5 12 19 26
Wed.	5 12 19 26	2 9 16 23 30	6 13 20 27
Thur.	6 13 20 27	3 10 17 24 31	7 14 21 28
Fri.	7 14 21 28	4 11 18 25	1 8 15 22 29
Sat.	1 8 15 22 29	5 12 19 26	2 9 16 23 30

	October	November	December
Sun.	1 8 15 22 29	5 12 19 26	3 10 17 24 31
Mon.	2 9 16 23 30	6 13 20 27	4 11 18 25
Tue.	3 10 17 24 31	7 14 21 28	5 12 19 26
Wed.	4 11 18 25	1 8 15 22 29	6 13 20 27
Thur.	5 12 19 26	2 9 16 23 30	7 14 21 28
Fri.	6 13 20 27	3 10 17 24	1 8 15 22 29
Sat.	7 14 21 28	4 11 18 25	2 9 16 23 30

B (LEAP YEAR)

	January	February	March
Sun.	1 8 15 22 29	5 12 19 26	4 11 18 25
Mon.	2 9 16 23 30	6 13 20 27	5 12 19 26
Tue.	3 10 17 24 31	7 14 21 28	6 13 20 27
Wed.	4 11 18 25	1 8 15 22 29	7 14 21 28
Thur.	5 12 19 26	2 9 16 23	1 8 15 22 29
Fri.	6 13 20 27	3 10 17 24	2 9 16 23 30
Sat.	7 14 21 28	4 11 18 25	3 10 17 24 31

	April	May	June
Sun.	1 8 15 22 29	6 13 20 27	3 10 17 24
Mon.	2 9 16 23 30	7 14 21 28	4 11 18 25
Tue.	3 10 17 24	1 8 15 22 29	5 12 19 26
Wed.	4 11 18 25	2 9 16 23 30	6 13 20 27
Thur.	5 12 19 26	3 10 17 24 31	7 14 21 28
Fri.	6 13 20 27	4 11 18 25	1 8 15 22 29
Sat.	7 14 21 28	5 12 19 26	2 9 16 23 30

	July	August	September
Sun.	1 8 15 22 29	5 12 19 26	2 9 16 23 30
Mon.	2 9 16 23 30	6 13 20 27	3 10 17 24
Tue.	3 10 17 24 31	7 14 21 28	4 11 18 25
Wed.	4 11 18 25	1 8 15 22 29	5 12 19 26
Thur.	5 12 19 26	2 9 16 23 30	6 13 20 27
Fri.	6 13 20 27	3 10 17 24 31	7 14 21 28
Sat.	7 14 21 28	4 11 18 25	1 8 15 22 29

	October	November	December
Sun.	7 14 21 28	4 11 18 25	2 9 16 23 30
Mon.	1 8 15 22 29	5 12 19 26	3 10 17 24 31
Tue.	2 9 16 23 30	6 13 20 27	4 11 18 25
Wed.	3 10 17 24 31	7 14 21 28	5 12 19 26
Thur.	4 11 18 25	1 8 15 22 29	6 13 20 27
Fri.	5 12 19 26	2 9 16 23 30	7 14 21 28
Sat.	6 13 20 27	3 10 17 24	1 8 15 22 29

EASTER DAYS

March 26	1815, 1826, 1837, 1967, 1978, 1989
April 2	1809, 1893, 1899, 1961
April 9	1871, 1882, 1939, 1950, 2023, 2034
April 16	1786, 1797, 1843, 1854, 1865, 1911, 1922, 1933, 1995, 2006, 2017
April 23	1905

EASTER DAYS

April 1	1804, 1888, 1956, 2040
April 8	1792, 1860, 1928, 2012
April 22	1832, 1984

C

Day	January	February	March
Sun.	7 14 21 28	4 11 18 25	4 11 18 25
Mon.	1 8 15 22 29	5 12 19 26	5 12 19 26
Tue.	2 9 16 23 30	6 13 20 27	6 13 20 27
Wed.	3 10 17 24 31	7 14 21 28	7 14 21 28
Thur.	4 11 18 25	1 8 15 22	1 8 15 22 29
Fri.	5 12 19 26	2 9 16 23	2 9 16 23 30
Sat.	6 13 20 27	3 10 17 24	3 10 17 24 31

Day	April	May	June
Sun.	1 8 15 22 29	6 13 20 27	3 10 17 24
Mon.	2 9 16 23 30	7 14 21 28	4 11 18 25
Tue.	3 10 17 24	1 8 15 22 29	5 12 19 26
Wed.	4 11 18 25	2 9 16 23 30	6 13 20 27
Thur.	5 12 19 26	3 10 17 24 31	7 14 21 28
Fri.	6 13 20 27	4 11 18 25	1 8 15 22 29
Sat.	7 14 21 28	5 12 19 26	2 9 16 23 30

Day	July	August	September
Sun.	1 8 15 22 29	5 12 19 26	2 9 16 23 30
Mon.	2 9 16 23 30	6 13 20 27	3 10 17 24
Tue.	3 10 17 24 31	7 14 21 28	4 11 18 25
Wed.	4 11 18 25	1 8 15 22 29	5 12 19 26
Thur.	5 12 19 26	2 9 16 23 30	6 13 20 27
Fri.	6 13 20 27	3 10 17 24 31	7 14 21 28
Sat.	7 14 21 28	4 11 18 25	1 8 15 22 29

Day	October	November	December
Sun.	7 14 21 28	4 11 18 25	2 9 16 23 30
Mon.	1 8 15 22 29	5 12 19 26	3 10 17 24 31
Tue.	2 9 16 23 30	6 13 20 27	4 11 18 25
Wed.	3 10 17 24 31	7 14 21 28	5 12 19 26
Thur.	4 11 18 25	1 8 15 22 29	6 13 20 27
Fri.	5 12 19 26	2 9 16 23 30	7 14 21 28
Sat.	6 13 20 27	3 10 17 24	1 8 15 22 29

EASTER DAYS

March 25	1883, 1894, 1951, 2035
April 1	1866, 1877, 1923, 1934, 1945, 2018, 2029
April 8	1787, 1798, 1849, 1855, 1917, 2007
April 15	1781, 1827, 1838, 1900, 1906, 1979, 1990, 2001
April 22	1810, 1821, 1962, 1973

E

Day	January	February	March
Sun.	6 13 20 27	3 10 17 24	3 10 17 24 31
Mon.	7 14 21 28	4 11 18 25	4 11 18 25
Tue.	1 8 15 22 29	5 12 19 26	5 12 19 26
Wed.	2 9 16 23 30	6 13 20 27	6 13 20 27
Thur.	3 10 17 24 31	7 14 21 28	7 14 21 28
Fri.	4 11 18 25	1 8 15 22	1 8 15 22 29
Sat.	5 12 19 26	2 9 16 23	2 9 16 23 30

Day	April	May	June
Sun.	7 14 21 28	5 12 19 26	2 9 16 23 30
Mon.	1 8 15 22 29	6 13 20 27	3 10 17 24
Tue.	2 9 16 23 30	7 14 21 28	4 11 18 25
Wed.	3 10 17 24	1 8 15 22 29	5 12 19 26
Thur.	4 11 18 25	2 9 16 23 30	6 13 20 27
Fri.	5 12 19 26	3 10 17 24 31	7 14 21 28
Sat.	6 13 20 27	4 11 18 25	1 8 15 22 29

Day	July	August	September
Sun.	7 14 21 28	4 11 18 25	1 8 15 22 29
Mon.	1 8 15 22 29	5 12 19 26	2 9 16 23 30
Tue.	2 9 16 23 30	6 13 20 27	3 10 17 24
Wed.	3 10 17 24 31	7 14 21 28	4 11 18 25
Thur.	4 11 18 25	1 8 15 22 29	5 12 19 26
Fri.	5 12 19 26	2 9 16 23 30	6 13 20 27
Sat.	6 13 20 27	3 10 17 24 31	7 14 21 28

Day	October	November	December
Sun.	6 13 20 27	3 10 17 24	1 8 15 22 29
Mon.	7 14 21 28	4 11 18 25	2 9 16 23 30
Tue.	1 8 15 22 29	5 12 19 26	3 10 17 24 31
Wed.	2 9 16 23 30	6 13 20 27	4 11 18 25
Thur.	3 10 17 24 31	7 14 21 28	5 12 19 26
Fri.	4 11 18 25	1 8 15 22 29	6 13 20 27
Sat.	5 12 19 26	2 9 16 23 30	7 14 21 28

EASTER DAYS

March 24	1799
March 31	1782, 1793, 1839, 1850, 1861, 1907, 1918, 1929, 1991, 2002, 2013
April 7	1822, 1833, 1901, 1985
April 14	1805, 1811, 1895, 1963, 1974
April 21	1867, 1878, 1889, 1935, 1946, 1957, 2019, 2030

D (LEAP YEAR)

Day	January	February	March
Sun.	7 14 21 28	4 11 18 25	3 10 17 24 31
Mon.	1 8 15 22 29	5 12 19 26	4 11 18 25
Tue.	2 9 16 23 30	6 13 20 27	5 12 19 26
Wed.	3 10 17 24 31	7 14 21 28	6 13 20 27
Thur.	4 11 18 25	1 8 15 22 29	7 14 21 28
Fri.	5 12 19 26	2 9 16 23	1 8 15 22 29
Sat.	6 13 20 27	3 10 17 24	2 9 16 23 30

Day	April	May	June
Sun.	7 14 21 28	5 12 19 26	2 9 16 23 30
Mon.	1 8 15 22 29	6 13 20 27	3 10 17 24
Tue.	2 9 16 23 30	7 14 21 28	4 11 18 25
Wed.	3 10 17 24	1 8 15 22 29	5 12 19 26
Thur.	4 11 18 25	2 9 16 23 30	6 13 20 27
Fri.	5 12 19 26	3 10 17 24 31	7 14 21 28
Sat.	6 13 20 27	4 11 18 25	1 8 15 22 29

Day	July	August	September
Sun.	7 14 21 28	4 11 18 25	1 8 15 22 29
Mon.	1 8 15 22 29	5 12 19 26	2 9 16 23 30
Tue.	2 9 16 23 30	6 13 20 27	3 10 17 24
Wed.	3 10 17 24 31	7 14 21 28	4 11 18 25
Thur.	4 11 18 25	1 8 15 22 29	5 12 19 26
Fri.	5 12 19 26	2 9 16 23 30	6 13 20 27
Sat.	6 13 20 27	3 10 17 24 31	7 14 21 28

Day	October	November	December
Sun.	6 13 20 27	3 10 17 24	1 8 15 22 29
Mon.	7 14 21 28	4 11 18 25	2 9 16 23 30
Tue.	1 8 15 22 29	5 12 19 26	3 10 17 24 31
Wed.	2 9 16 23 30	6 13 20 27	4 11 18 25
Thur.	3 10 17 24 31	7 14 21 28	5 12 19 26
Fri.	4 11 18 25	1 8 15 22 29	6 13 20 27
Sat.	5 12 19 26	2 9 16 23 30	7 14 21 28

EASTER DAYS

March 24	1940
March 31	1872, 2024
April 7	1844, 1912, 1996
April 14	1816, 1968

F (LEAP YEAR)

Day	January	February	March
Sun.	6 13 20 27	3 10 17 24	2 9 16 23 30
Mon.	7 14 21 28	4 11 18 25	3 10 17 24 31
Tue.	1 8 15 22 29	5 12 19 26	4 11 18 25
Wed.	2 9 16 23 30	6 13 20 27	5 12 19 26
Thur.	3 10 17 24 31	7 14 21 28	6 13 20 27
Fri.	4 11 18 25	1 8 15 22 29	7 14 21 28
Sat.	5 12 19 26	2 9 16 23	1 8 15 22 29

Day	April	May	June
Sun.	6 13 20 27	4 11 18 25	1 8 15 22 29
Mon.	7 14 21 28	5 12 19 26	2 9 16 23 30
Tue.	1 8 15 22 29	6 13 20 27	3 10 17 24
Wed.	2 9 16 23 30	7 14 21 28	4 11 18 25
Thur.	3 10 17 24	1 8 15 22 29	5 12 19 26
Fri.	4 11 18 25	2 9 16 23 30	6 13 20 27
Sat.	5 12 19 26	3 10 17 24 31	7 14 21 28

Day	July	August	September
Sun.	6 13 20 27	3 10 17 24 31	7 14 21 28
Mon.	7 14 21 28	4 11 18 25	1 8 15 22 29
Tue.	1 8 15 22 29	5 12 19 26	2 9 16 23 30
Wed.	2 9 16 23 30	6 13 20 27	3 10 17 24
Thur.	3 10 17 24 31	7 14 21 28	4 11 18 25
Fri.	4 11 18 25	1 8 15 22 29	5 12 19 26
Sat.	5 12 19 26	2 9 16 23 30	6 13 20 27

Day	October	November	December
Sun.	5 12 19 26	2 9 16 23 30	7 14 21 28
Mon.	6 13 20 27	3 10 17 24	1 8 15 22 29
Tue.	7 14 21 28	4 11 18 25	2 9 16 23 30
Wed.	1 8 15 22 29	5 12 19 26	3 10 17 24 31
Thur.	2 9 16 23 30	6 13 20 27	4 11 18 25
Fri.	3 10 17 24 31	7 14 21 28	5 12 19 26
Sat.	4 11 18 25	1 8 15 22 29	6 13 20 27

EASTER DAYS

March 23	1788, 1856, 2008
April 6	1828, 1980
April 13	1884, 1952, 2036
April 20	1924

G

	January	February	March
Sun.	5 12 19 26	2 9 16 23	2 9 16 23 30
Mon.	6 13 20 27	3 10 17 24	3 10 17 24 31
Tue.	7 14 21 28	4 11 18 25	4 11 18 25
Wed.	1 8 15 22 29	5 12 19 26	5 12 19 26
Thur.	2 9 16 23 30	6 13 20 27	6 13 20 27
Fri.	3 10 17 24 31	7 14 21 28	7 14 21 28
Sat.	4 11 18 25	1 8 15 22	1 8 15 22 29

	April	May	June
Sun.	6 13 20 27	4 11 18 25	1 8 15 22 29
Mon.	7 14 21 28	5 12 19 26	2 9 16 23 30
Tue.	1 8 15 22 29	6 13 20 27	3 10 17 24
Wed.	2 9 16 23 30	7 14 21 28	4 11 18 25
Thur.	3 10 17 24	1 8 15 22 29	5 12 19 26
Fri.	4 11 18 25	2 9 16 23 30	6 13 20 27
Sat.	5 12 19 26	3 10 17 24 31	7 14 21 28

	July	August	September
Sun.	6 13 20 27	3 10 17 24 31	7 14 21 28
Mon.	7 14 21 28	4 11 18 25	1 8 15 22 29
Tue.	1 8 15 22 29	5 12 19 26	2 9 16 23 30
Wed.	2 9 16 23 30	6 13 20 27	3 10 17 24
Thur.	3 10 17 24 31	7 14 21 28	4 11 18 25
Fri.	4 11 18 25	1 8 15 22 29	5 12 19 26
Sat.	5 12 19 26	2 9 16 23 30	6 13 20 27

	October	November	December
Sun.	5 12 19 26	2 9 16 23 30	7 14 21 28
Mon.	6 13 20 27	3 10 17 24	1 8 15 22 29
Tue.	7 14 21 28	4 11 18 25	2 9 16 23 30
Wed.	1 8 15 22 29	5 12 19 26	3 10 17 24 31
Thur.	2 9 16 23 30	6 13 20 27	4 11 18 25
Fri.	3 10 17 24 31	7 14 21 28	5 12 19 26
Sat.	4 11 18 25	1 8 15 22 29	6 13 20 27

EASTER DAYS

March 23	1845, 1913
March 30	1823, 1834, 1902, 1975, 1986, 1997
April 6	1806, 1817, 1890, 1947, 1958, 1969
April 13	1800, 1873, 1879, 1941, 2031
April 20	1783, 1794, 1851, 1862, 1919, 1930, 2003, 2014, 2025

I

	January	February	March
Sun.	4 11 18 25	1 8 15 22	1 8 15 22 29
Mon.	5 12 19 26	2 9 16 23	2 9 16 23 30
Tue.	6 13 20 27	3 10 17 24	3 10 17 24 31
Wed.	7 14 21 28	4 11 18 25	4 11 18 25
Thur.	1 8 15 22 29	5 12 19 26	5 12 19 26
Fri.	2 9 16 23 30	6 13 20 27	6 13 20 27
Sat.	3 10 17 24 31	7 14 21 28	7 14 21 28

	April	May	June
Sun.	5 12 19 26	3 10 17 24 31	7 14 21 28
Mon.	6 13 20 27	4 11 18 25	1 8 15 22 29
Tue.	7 14 21 28	5 12 19 26	2 9 16 23 30
Wed.	1 8 15 22 29	6 13 20 27	3 10 17 24
Thur.	2 9 16 23 30	7 14 21 28	4 11 18 25
Fri.	3 10 17 24	1 8 15 22 29	5 12 19 26
Sat.	4 11 18 25	2 9 16 23 30	6 13 20 27

	July	August	September
Sun.	5 12 19 26	2 9 16 23 30	6 13 20 27
Mon.	6 13 20 27	3 10 17 24 31	7 14 21 28
Tue.	7 14 21 28	4 11 18 25	1 8 15 22 29
Wed.	1 8 15 22 29	5 12 19 26	2 9 16 23 30
Thur.	2 9 16 23 30	6 13 20 27	3 10 17 24
Fri.	3 10 17 24 31	7 14 21 28	4 11 18 25
Sat.	4 11 18 25	1 8 15 22 29	5 12 19 26

	October	November	December
Sun.	4 11 18 25	1 8 15 22 29	6 13 20 27
Mon.	5 12 19 26	2 9 16 23 30	7 14 21 28
Tue.	6 13 20 27	3 10 17 24	1 8 15 22 29
Wed.	7 14 21 28	4 11 18 25	2 9 16 23 30
Thur.	1 8 15 22 29	5 12 19 26	3 10 17 24 31
Fri.	2 9 16 23 30	6 13 20 27	4 11 18 25
Sat.	3 10 17 24 31	7 14 21 28	5 12 19 26

EASTER DAYS

March 22	1818
March 29	1807, 1891, 1959, 1970
April 5	1795, 1801, 1863, 1874, 1885, 1931, 1942, 1953, 2015, 2026, 2037
April 12	1789, 1846, 1857, 1903, 1914, 1925, 1998, 2009
April 19	1829, 1835, 1981, 1987

H (LEAP YEAR)

	January	February	March
Sun.	5 12 19 26	2 9 16 23	1 8 15 22 29
Mon.	6 13 20 27	3 10 17 24	2 9 16 23 30
Tue.	7 14 21 28	4 11 18 25	3 10 17 24 31
Wed.	1 8 15 22 29	5 12 19 26	4 11 18 25
Thur.	2 9 16 23 30	6 13 20 27	5 12 19 26
Fri.	3 10 17 24 31	7 14 21 28	6 13 20 27
Sat.	4 11 18 25	1 8 15 22 29	7 14 21 28

	April	May	June
Sun.	5 12 19 26	3 10 17 24 31	7 14 21 28
Mon.	6 13 20 27	4 11 18 25	1 8 15 22 29
Tue.	7 14 21 28	5 12 19 26	2 9 16 23 30
Wed.	1 8 15 22 29	6 13 20 27	3 10 17 24
Thur.	2 9 16 23 30	7 14 21 28	4 11 18 25
Fri.	3 10 17 24	1 8 15 22 29	5 12 19 26
Sat.	4 11 18 25	2 9 16 23 30	6 13 20 27

	July	August	September
Sun.	5 12 19 26	2 9 16 23 30	6 13 20 27
Mon.	6 13 20 27	3 10 17 24 31	7 14 21 28
Tue.	7 14 21 28	4 11 18 25	1 8 15 22 29
Wed.	1 8 15 22 29	5 12 19 26	2 9 16 23 30
Thur.	2 9 16 23 30	6 13 20 27	3 10 17 24
Fri.	3 10 17 24 31	7 14 21 28	4 11 18 25
Sat.	4 11 18 25	1 8 15 22 29	5 12 19 26

	October	November	December
Sun.	4 11 18 25	1 8 15 22 29	6 13 20 27
Mon.	5 12 19 26	2 9 16 23 30	7 14 21 28
Tue.	6 13 20 27	3 10 17 24	1 8 15 22 29
Wed.	7 14 21 28	4 11 18 25	2 9 16 23 30
Thur.	1 8 15 22 29	5 12 19 26	3 10 17 24 31
Fri.	2 9 16 23 30	6 13 20 27	4 11 18 25
Sat.	3 10 17 24 31	7 14 21 28	5 12 19 26

EASTER DAYS

March 29	1812, 1964
April 5	1896
April 12	1868, 1936, 2020
April 19	1840, 1908, 1992

J (LEAP YEAR)

	January	February	March
Sun.	4 11 18 25	1 8 15 22 29	7 14 21 28
Mon.	5 12 19 26	2 9 16 23	1 8 15 22 29
Tue.	6 13 20 27	3 10 17 24	2 9 16 23 30
Wed.	7 14 21 28	4 11 18 25	3 10 17 24 31
Thur.	1 8 15 22 29	5 12 19 26	4 11 18 25
Fri.	2 9 16 23 30	6 13 20 27	5 12 19 26
Sat.	3 10 17 24 31	7 14 21 28	6 13 20 27

	April	May	June
Sun.	4 11 18 25	2 9 16 23 30	6 13 20 27
Mon.	5 12 19 26	3 10 17 24 31	7 14 21 28
Tue.	6 13 20 27	4 11 18 25	1 8 15 22 29
Wed.	7 14 21 28	5 12 19 26	2 9 16 23 30
Thur.	1 8 15 22 29	6 13 20 27	3 10 17 24
Fri.	2 9 16 23 30	7 14 21 28	4 11 18 25
Sat.	3 10 17 24	1 8 15 22	5 12 19 26

	July	August	September
Sun.	4 11 18 25	1 8 15 22 29	5 12 19 26
Mon.	5 12 19 26	2 9 16 23 30	6 13 20 27
Tue.	6 13 20 27	3 10 17 24 31	7 14 21 28
Wed.	7 14 21 28	4 11 18 25	1 8 15 22 29
Thur.	1 8 15 22 29	5 12 19 26	2 9 16 23 30
Fri.	2 9 16 23 30	6 13 20 27	3 10 17 24
Sat.	3 10 17 24 31	7 14 21 28	4 11 18 25

	October	November	December
Sun.	3 10 17 24 31	7 14 21 28	5 12 19 26
Mon.	4 11 18 25	1 8 15 22 29	6 13 20 27
Tue.	5 12 19 26	2 9 16 23 30	7 14 21 28
Wed.	6 13 20 27	3 10 17 24	1 8 15 22 29
Thur.	7 14 21 28	4 11 18 25	2 9 16 23 30
Fri.	1 8 15 22 29	5 12 19 26	3 10 17 24 31
Sat.	2 9 16 23 30	6 13 20 27	4 11 18 25

EASTER DAYS

March 28	1880, 1948, 2032
April 4	1920
April 11	1784, 1852, 2004
April 18	1824, 1976

K

	January	February	March
Sun.	3 10 17 24 31	7 14 21 28	7 14 21 28
Mon.	4 11 18 25	1 8 15 22	1 8 15 22 29
Tue.	5 12 19 26	2 9 16 23	2 9 16 23 30
Wed.	6 13 20 27	3 10 17 24	3 10 17 24 31
Thur.	7 14 21 28	4 11 18 25	4 11 18 25
Fri.	1 8 15 22 29	5 12 19 26	5 12 19 26
Sat.	2 9 16 23 30	6 13 20 27	6 13 20 27

	April	May	June
Sun.	4 11 18 25	2 9 16 23 30	6 13 20 27
Mon.	5 12 19 26	3 10 17 24 31	7 14 21 28
Tue.	6 13 20 27	4 11 18 25	1 8 15 22 29
Wed.	7 14 21 28	5 12 19 26	2 9 16 23 30
Thur.	1 8 15 22 29	6 13 20 27	3 10 17 24
Fri.	2 9 16 23 30	7 14 21 28	4 11 18 25
Sat.	3 10 17 24	1 8 15 22 29	5 12 19 26

	July	August	September
Sun.	4 11 18 25	1 8 15 22 29	5 12 19 26
Mon.	5 12 19 26	2 9 16 23 30	6 13 20 27
Tue.	6 13 20 27	3 10 17 24 31	7 14 21 28
Wed.	7 14 21 28	4 11 18 25	1 8 15 22 29
Thur.	1 8 15 22 29	5 12 19 26	2 9 16 23 30
Fri.	2 9 16 23 30	6 13 20 27	3 10 17 24
Sat.	3 10 17 24 31	7 14 21 28	4 11 18 25

	October	November	December
Sun.	3 10 17 24 31	7 14 21 28	5 12 19 26
Mon.	4 11 18 25	1 8 15 22 29	6 13 20 27
Tue.	5 12 19 26	2 9 16 23 30	7 14 21 28
Wed.	6 13 20 27	3 10 17 24	1 8 15 22 29
Thur.	7 14 21 28	4 11 18 25	2 9 16 23 30
Fri.	1 8 15 22 29	5 12 19 26	3 10 17 24 31
Sat.	2 9 16 23 30	6 13 20 27	4 11 18 25

EASTER DAYS

March 28	1869, 1875, 1937, 2027
April 4	1790, 1847, 1858, 1915, 1926, 1999, 2010, 2021
April 11	1819, 1830, 1841, 1909, 1971, 1982, 1993
April 18	1802, 1813, 1897, 1954, 1965
April 25	1886, 1943, 2038

M

	January	February	March
Sun.	2 9 16 23 30	6 13 20 27	6 13 20 27
Mon.	3 10 17 24 31	7 14 21 28	7 14 21 28
Tue.	4 11 18 25	1 8 15 22	1 8 15 22 29
Wed.	5 12 19 26	2 9 16 23	2 9 16 23 30
Thur.	6 13 20 27	3 10 17 24	3 10 17 24 31
Fri.	7 14 21 28	4 11 18 25	4 11 18 25
Sat.	1 8 15 22 29	5 12 19 26	5 12 19 26

	April	May	June
Sun.	3 10 17 24	1 8 15 22 29	5 12 19 26
Mon.	4 11 18 25	2 9 16 23 30	6 13 20 27
Tue.	5 12 19 26	3 10 17 24 31	7 14 21 28
Wed.	6 13 20 27	4 11 18 25	1 8 15 22 29
Thur.	7 14 21 28	5 12 19 26	2 9 16 23 30
Fri.	1 8 15 22 29	6 13 20 27	3 10 17 24
Sat.	2 9 16 23 30	7 14 21 28	4 11 18 25

	July	August	September
Sun.	3 10 17 24 31	7 14 21 28	4 11 18 25
Mon.	4 11 18 25	1 8 15 22 29	5 12 19 26
Tue.	5 12 19 26	2 9 16 23 30	6 13 20 27
Wed.	6 13 20 27	3 10 17 24 31	7 14 21 28
Thur.	7 14 21 28	4 11 18 25	1 8 15 22 29
Fri.	1 8 15 22 29	5 12 19 26	2 9 16 23 30
Sat.	2 9 16 23 30	6 13 20 27	3 10 17 24

	October	November	December
Sun.	2 9 16 23 30	6 13 20 27	4 11 18 25
Mon.	3 10 17 24 31	7 14 21 28	5 12 19 26
Tue.	4 11 18 25	1 8 15 22 29	6 13 20 27
Wed.	5 12 19 26	2 9 16 23 30	7 14 21 28
Thur.	6 13 20 27	3 10 17 24	1 8 15 22 29
Fri.	7 14 21 28	4 11 18 25	2 9 16 23 30
Sat.	1 8 15 22 29	5 12 19 26	3 10 17 24 31

EASTER DAYS

March 27	1785, 1842, 1853, 1910, 1921, 2005
April 3	1825, 1831, 1983, 1994
April 10	1803, 1814, 1887, 1898, 1955, 1966, 1977, 2039
April 17	1870, 1881, 1927, 1938, 1949, 2022, 2033
April 24	1791, 1859, 2011

L (LEAP YEAR)

	January	February	March
Sun.	3 10 17 24 31	7 14 21 28	6 13 20 27
Mon.	4 11 18 25	1 8 15 22 29	7 14 21 28
Tue.	5 12 19 26	2 9 16 23	1 8 15 22 29
Wed.	6 13 20 27	3 10 17 24	2 9 16 23 30
Thur.	7 14 21 28	4 11 18 25	3 10 17 24 31
Fri.	1 8 15 22 29	5 12 19 26	4 11 18 25
Sat.	2 9 16 23 30	6 13 20 27	5 12 19 26

	April	May	June
Sun.	3 10 17 24	1 8 15 22 29	5 12 19 26
Mon.	4 11 18 25	2 9 16 23 30	6 13 20 27
Tue.	5 12 19 26	3 10 17 24 31	7 14 21 28
Wed.	6 13 20 27	4 11 18 25	1 8 15 22 29
Thur.	7 14 21 28	5 12 19 26	2 9 16 23 30
Fri.	1 8 15 22 29	6 13 20 27	3 10 17 24
Sat.	2 9 16 23 30	7 14 21 28	4 11 18 25

	July	August	September
Sun.	3 10 17 24 31	7 14 21 28	4 11 18 25
Mon.	4 11 18 25	1 8 15 22 29	5 12 19 26
Tue.	5 12 19 26	2 9 16 23 30	6 13 20 27
Wed.	6 13 20 27	3 10 17 24 31	7 14 21 28
Thur.	7 14 21 28	4 11 18 25	1 8 15 22 29
Fri.	1 8 15 22 29	5 12 19 26	2 9 16 23 30
Sat.	2 9 16 23 30	6 13 20 27	3 10 17 24

	October	November	December
Sun.	2 9 16 23 30	6 13 20 27	4 11 18 25
Mon.	3 10 17 24 31	7 14 21 28	5 12 19 26
Tue.	4 11 18 25	1 8 15 22 29	6 13 20 27
Wed.	5 12 19 26	2 9 16 23 30	7 14 21 28
Thur.	6 13 20 27	3 10 17 24	1 8 15 22 29
Fri.	7 14 21 28	4 11 18 25	2 9 16 23 30
Sat.	1 8 15 22 29	5 12 19 26	3 10 17 24 31

EASTER DAYS

March 27	1796, 1864, 1932, 2016
April 3	1836, 1904, 1988
April 17	1808, 1892, 1960

N (LEAP YEAR)

	January	February	March
Sun.	2 9 16 23 30	6 13 20 27	5 12 19 26
Mon.	3 10 17 24 31	7 14 21 28	6 13 20 27
Tue.	4 11 18 25	1 8 15 22 29	7 14 21 28
Wed.	5 12 19 26	2 9 16 23	1 8 15 22 29
Thur.	6 13 20 27	3 10 17 24	2 9 16 23 30
Fri.	7 14 21 28	4 11 18 25	3 10 17 24 31
Sat.	1 8 15 22 29	5 12 19 26	4 11 18 25

	April	May	June
Sun.	2 9 16 23 30	7 14 21 28	4 11 18 25
Mon.	3 10 17 24	1 8 15 22 29	5 12 19 26
Tue.	4 11 18 25	2 9 16 23 30	6 13 20 27
Wed.	5 12 19 26	3 10 17 24 31	7 14 21 28
Thur.	6 13 20 27	4 11 18 25	1 8 15 22 29
Fri.	7 14 21 28	5 12 19 26	2 9 16 23 30
Sat.	1 8 15 22 29	6 13 20 27	3 10 17 24

	July	August	September
Sun.	2 9 16 23 30	6 13 20 27	3 10 17 24
Mon.	3 10 17 24 31	7 14 21 28	4 11 18 25
Tue.	4 11 18 25	1 8 15 22 29	5 12 19 26
Wed.	5 12 19 26	2 9 16 23 30	6 13 20 27
Thur.	6 13 20 27	3 10 17 24 31	7 14 21 28
Fri.	7 14 21 28	4 11 18 25	1 8 15 22 29
Sat.	1 8 15 22 29	5 12 19 26	2 9 16 23 30

	October	November	December
Sun.	1 8 15 22 29	5 12 19 26	3 10 17 24 31
Mon.	2 9 16 23 30	6 13 20 27	4 11 18 25
Tue.	3 10 17 24 31	7 14 21 28	5 12 19 26
Wed.	4 11 18 25	1 8 15 22 29	6 13 20 27
Thur.	5 12 19 26	2 9 16 23 30	7 14 21 28
Fri.	6 13 20 27	3 10 17 24	1 8 15 22 29
Sat.	7 14 21 28	4 11 18 25	2 9 16 23 30

EASTER DAYS

March 26	1780
April 2	1820, 1972
April 9	1944
April 16	1876, 2028
April 23	1848, 1916, 2000

GEOLOGICAL TIME

Era	Period	Epoch	Dates*	Evolutionary Stages
Cenozoic	Quaternary	Holocene	11,700 BP†–present	
		Pleistocene	2,588,000–11,700 BP	First humans
	Neogene	Pliocene	5.332–2.588 Mya ‡	} Majority of still existing species
		Miocene	23.03–5.332 Mya	
	Palaeogene	Oligocene	33.9–23.03 Mya	} First modern mammals
		Eocene	55.8–33.9 Mya	
		Palaeocene	65.5–55.8 Mya	
Mesozoic	Cretaceous		145.5–65.5 Mya	
	Jurassic		199.6–145.5 Mya	First birds
	Triassic		251–199.6 Mya	First mammals
Palaeozoic	Permian		299–251 Mya	First reptiles
	Carboniferous		359.2–299 Mya	} First traces of land-living creatures
	Devonian		416–359.2 Mya	
	Silurian		443.7–416 Mya	
	Ordovician		488.3–443.7 Mya	First fish
	Cambrian		542–488.3 Mya	First invertebrates
Precambrian	Proterozoic		2,500–542 Mya	First primitive life forms, eg algae and bacteria
	Archaean		3,800–2,500 Mya	} Earth uninhabited
	Hadean		4,600–3,800 Mya	

* approximate † BP = Before Present ‡ Mya = million years ago

PALAEOZOIC ('ANCIENT LIFE')

Cambrian – Mainly sandstones, slate and shales; limestones in Scotland. Shelled fossils and invertebrates, eg trilobites and brachiopods, and the earliest known vertebrates (jawless fish) appear

Ordovician – Mainly shales and mudstones, eg in north Wales; limestones in Scotland. First fish

Silurian – Shales, mudstones and some limestones, found mostly in Wales and southern Scotland

Devonian – Old red sandstone, shale, limestone and slate, eg in south Wales and the West Country

Carboniferous – Coal-bearing rocks, millstone grit, limestone and shale. First traces of land-living creatures

Permian – Marls, sandstones and clays. First reptile fossils

There were two great phases of mountain building in the Palaeozoic era: the Caledonian, characterised in Britain by NE–SW lines of hills and valleys; and the later Hercynian, widespread in west Germany and adjacent areas, and in Britain exemplified in E–W lines of hills and valleys.

The end of the Palaeozoic era was marked by the extensive glaciations of the Permian period in the southern continents and the decline of amphibians. It was succeeded by an era of warm conditions.

MESOZOIC ('MIDDLE FORMS OF LIFE')

Triassic – Mostly sandstone, eg in the W. Midlands; primitive mammals appear

Jurassic – Mainly limestones and clays, typically displayed in the Jura mountains, and in England in a NE–SW belt from Lincolnshire and the Wash to the Severn and the Dorset coast

Cretaceous – Mainly chalk, clay and sands, eg in Kent and Sussex

Giant reptiles were dominant during the Mesozoic era; marsupial mammals first appeared, as well as *Archaeopteryx lithographica,* the earliest known species of bird. Coniferous trees and flowering plants also developed during the era and, with the birds and the mammals, were the main species to survive into the Cenozoic era. The giant reptiles became extinct.

CENOZOIC ('RECENT LIFE')

Palaeocene } The emergence of new forms of life, including
Eocene existing species; primates appear

Oligocene – Fossils of a few still existing species

Miocene – Fossil remains show a balance of existing and extinct species

Pliocene } Fossil remains show a majority of still existing
Pleistocene species

Holocene – The present, post-glacial period. Existing species only, except for a few exterminated by humans

In the last 25 million years, from the Miocene through the Pliocene periods, the Alpine-Himalayan and the circum-Pacific phases of mountain building reached their climax. During the Pleistocene period ice-sheets locked up masses of water as land ice, lowering the sea-level by 100–200m. The glaciations and interglacials of the Ice Age are difficult to date and classify, but recent scientific opinion considers the Pleistocene period to have begun *c.*1.64 Mya. The last glacial retreat, merging into the Holocene period, was *c.*10,000 years ago.

HUMAN DEVELOPMENT

All members of the human race belong to one species of animal, *Homo sapiens,* the definition of a species being in biological terms that all its members can interbreed. As a species of mammal it is possible to group humans with other similar types, known as the primates. Amongst these is found a sub-group, the apes, which includes, in addition to humans, the chimpanzees, gorillas, orangutans and gibbons. All lack a tail, have shoulder blades at the back, and a Y-shaped chewing pattern on the surface of their molars, as well as showing the more general primate characteristics of four incisors, a thumb which is able to touch the fingers of the same hand, and finger and toe nails instead of claws. However, there once lived creatures, now extinct, which were closer to modern man than the chimpanzees and gorillas, and which shared with modern man the characteristics of having flat faces (ie the absence of a pronounced muzzle), being bipedal, and possessing large brains.

The debate surrounding evidence for the oldest human ancestors is ongoing. The earliest putative hominin for which there is significant fossil evidence is *Ardipithecus ramidus,* for which an almost complete skeleton, dating to at least 4.4 million years ago (Mya), was discovered in the Afar Rift, Ethiopia in 1992. Analysis of the *Ardipithecus ramidus* skeleton suggests the creature had characteristics of both humans and apes; able to climb trees and walk on two feet.

The subsequent Australopithecines have left more numerous remains in south and east Africa, among which sub-groups may be detected. Living between 4.2 and 1.5 Mya, they were relatives of modern humans in respect of the fact that they walked upright, did not have an extensive muzzle and had similar types of pre-molars. The first australopithecine remains were recognised at Taung in South Africa in 1924 and named *Australopithecus africanus,* dating between 3.3 and 2.3 Mya. The most impressive discovery was made at Hadar, Ethiopia, in 1974 when about half a skeleton of *Australopithecus afarensis,* known as 'Lucy', was found. Some 3.2 Mya, 'Lucy' (who is now considered to be male) certainly walked upright.

Also in east Africa, especially at Olduvai Gorge in Tanzania, between 2.5 and 1.8 Mya, lived a hominid group which not only walked upright, had a flat face, and a large brain case, but also made simple pebble and flake stone tools. Due to their distinctive characteristics, they have been grouped as a separate sub-species, now extinct, of the genus *Homo* and are known as *Homo habilis* or 'handy man'.

The use of fire, again a human characteristic, is associated with another group of extinct hominids whose remains, about a million years old, are found in south and east Africa, China, Indonesia, north Africa and Europe. The ability to make fire probably helped the colonisation of the colder northern areas and in this respect the site of Vertesszollos in Hungary is of particular importance. *Homo ergaster* in Africa and *Homo erectus* in Asia are the names given to this group of fossils and they relate to a number of famous individual discoveries, eg Solo Man, Heidelberg Man, and especially Peking Man who lived at the cave site at Choukoutien which has yielded evidence of fire and burnt bone.

The well-known group the Neanderthals, or *Homo neanderthalensis,* is an extinct form of human that lived between *c.*350,000 and *c.*24,000 years ago; spanning the last Ice Age and living alongside modern humans. The Neanderthals' ability to adapt to the cold climate on the edge of the ice-sheets is one of their characteristic features, with remains being found only in Europe, Asia and the Middle East. Complete Neanderthal skeletons were found during excavations at Tabun in Israel, together with evidence of tool-making and the use of fire. Distinguished by very large brains, it seems that Neanderthals were the first to develop recognisable social customs, especially deliberate burial rites. Why the Neanderthals became extinct is not clear but it may be connected with the climatic changes at the end of the Ice Ages, which would have seriously affected their food supplies; possibly they became too specialised for their own good.

The shin bone of Boxgrove Man found in 1993 – *Homo heidelbergensis* – and the Swanscombe skull are the best known early human fossil remains found in England. Some specialists prefer to group Swanscombe Man (or, more probably, woman) together with the Steinheim skull from Germany, seeing both as a separate sub-species. There is too little evidence as yet on which to form a final judgement.

Anatomically modern humans – *Homo sapiens sapiens* ('doubly wise man') – had evolved to our present physical condition and had colonised much of the world by about 40,000 years ago. There are many previously distinguished individual specimens, eg Cromagnon Man, the first early *Homo sapiens sapiens* of the European Upper Palaeolithic.

The discovery of the structure of DNA in 1953 has come to have a profound effect upon the study of human evolution. For example, it was claimed in 1987 that a common ancestor of all human beings was a person who lived in Africa some 200,000 years ago, thus encouraging the 'out of Africa' theory of hominid migration from east Africa to the Middle East and then throughout the world.

CULTURAL DEVELOPMENT

The Three Age system, whereby prehistory was divided into a Stone Age, a Bronze Age and an Iron Age, was devised by Christian Thomsen, curator of the National Museum of Denmark in the early 19th century, to facilitate the classification of the museum's collections. The adjectives referred to the materials from which the implements and weapons were made and came to be regarded as the dominant features of the societies to which they related. The Three Age system remains a generally accepted concept in the popular mind. However, it is now seen by archaeologists as an inadequate model for human development. Common sense suggests that there were no complete breaks between one so-called Age and another. Nor can the Three Age system be applied universally. In some areas it is necessary to insert a Copper Age, while in South Africa there would seem to be no Bronze Age at all; in Australia, Old Stone Age societies survived, while in South America, New Stone Age communities exist into modern times.

The concept of the 'Neolithic revolution', associated with the domestication of plants and animals, was a development of particular importance in the human cultural pattern. It reflected a gradual change from the hunter-gatherer economies to a more settled agricultural way of life and therefore, so the argument goes, made possible the development of urban civilisation. Though it appears that the cultivation of wheat and barley was first undertaken, together with the domestication of cattle and goats/sheep, around 10,000 years ago in the Fertile Crescent (the area bounded by the rivers Tigris and Euphrates), there is evidence that sorghum was first domesticated in Africa, rice was first deliberately planted and pigs domesticated in South East Asia, maize first cultivated in Central America and llamas first domesticated in South America. Cultural change took place independently in different parts of the world at different rates and different times.

The Neolithic period of cultural development has been difficult to date reliably because it took place long before writing was invented. With the development and refinement of radio-carbon dating and other scientific methods of producing absolute chronologies, it may eventually be possible to obtain a reliable chronological framework, in terms of years, against which the cultural development of any particular area may be set.

TIDES AND TIDAL PREDICTIONS

TIDES

Tides are the periodic rise and fall of the sea-level caused mainly by the gravitational pull of the Moon and the Sun. This generates the tide raising force (TRF), of which the Moon accounts for approximately 70 per cent and the Sun 30 per cent. When the Moon and the Sun are in line with the Earth they are said to be 'in conjunction' (or syzygy) and their combined TRFs are greatest. This produces the largest rise and fall of the tide, otherwise known as spring tides; they occur just after a full or new moon. The opposite effect, just after the Moon's first and last quarters, when the Sun and Moon form a right angle with the Earth, produces neap tides, with a relatively small tidal range between high water and low water.

A lunar day is about 24 hours and 50 minutes, giving two complete tidal cycles, with about 12 hours and 25 minutes between successive high waters. These are known as semi-diurnal tides and are applicable in the Atlantic Ocean and around the coasts of north-west Europe. Other parts of the world have diurnal tides, with only one high water and one low water each (lunar) day, or mixed tides which are partly diurnal and partly semi-diurnal.

Land and seabed conditions influence the tides locally. On the south coast of England, for example, double high waters occur between Swanage and Selsey Bill, and low water is much more sharply defined than high water. Tides can also be greatly affected by the Coriolis force, which is induced by the Earth's rotation and, in the northern hemisphere, tends to deflect any moving object to the right. Thus the easterly flood tidal stream in the English Channel is deflected towards the French coast causing higher high waters; on the ebb the opposite happens causing lower low waters. This, coupled with local geography, means that the mean spring range of the tide at St Malo is nearly 11m while the range on the English coast at Portland, 120 miles to the north, is a mere 2m.

Meteorological conditions also affect the tides. Prolonged strong winds and unusually high (or low) atmospheric pressure can significantly lower (or raise) the height of the tide; the wind alone can affect the predicted times of high and low water by as much as an hour. Variation of pressure by 34 millibars from the norm can cause a height difference of 0.3m. Intense minor depressions, line squalls, or other abrupt changes in the weather can cause wave oscillations known as seiches. The wave period of a seiche can vary from a few minutes to about 2 hours, with heights of up to a metre. Wick on the north-east coast of Scotland and Fishguard in south-west Wales are particularly prone to seiches.

TIDAL STREAMS
Tidal streams are the horizontal movements of water caused by the rise and fall of the tide. They normally change direction about every 6 hours. Tidal streams should not be confused with ocean currents, such as the Gulf Stream, which run indefinitely in the same direction. The rate, or set, of the stream at any particular place is proportional to the range of the tide. Thus, the rate during spring tides is greater than that at neaps. In the central English Channel the maximum spring rate is nearly 5 knots while the neap rate at the same position is just 3 knots. As with tidal heights, local geography plays a significant role in the rate of the tidal stream. For example, in the narrow waters of the Pentland Firth between mainland

Scotland and the Orkney Islands, rates of 16 knots have been recorded.

The tidal stream does not necessarily turn at the same time as high or low water. In the English Channel the stream turns at approximately high and low water at Dover. However, high water at Dover is at about the same time as low water at Plymouth, and vice versa.

Around the UK, the main flood tidal stream sets eastward up the English Channel, north-east into the Bristol Channel, and north up the west coasts of Ireland and Scotland. However, the flood sets south-east through the North Channel and south into the Irish Sea, where it meets the northerly flood through St George's Channel at the Isle of Man. Off the east coasts of Scotland and England the stream sets south as far as the Thames Estuary before meeting the north-going stream from the eastern part of the Dover Strait.

DEFINITIONS
Highest Astronomical Tide (HAT) and **Lowest Astronomical Tide (LAT)** are the highest and lowest tide levels predicted to occur under average meteorological, and any combination of astronomical, conditions. For a given area, **Chart Datum (CD)** is the level, as close as possible to LAT, below which charted depths are given. It is also the reference for tidal predictions: the total depth at a given time being equal to the charted depth plus the height of the tide. **Ordnance Datum (OD)** at Newlyn is the datum level of land survey on mainland England, Scotland and Wales, from which heights on UK land maps are measured. CD depends on the tidal range and varies around the UK from about 5m above OD to about 6.5m below. The differences are noted in tide tables, allowing comparison of the tide levels along the coast and reference to Ordnance Survey data. **Duration** of the tide is the interval between low water and the next high water. It can be used to calculate the approximate time of low water when only the time of high water is known. **Mean Sea Level (MSL or ML)** is the average level of the sea's surface over a long period, normally observed over 18.6 years. The **Range** of the tide is the difference in height between successive high and low waters. It is greatest at spring tides, least at neaps. The range may be indicated by **Tidal Coefficients** which are proportional to, but not the same as, the range on a particular day. A coefficient of 95 indicates an average spring tide, while 45 is an average neap tide.

PREDICTIONS

The following data are daily predictions of the time and height of high water at London Bridge, Liverpool, Greenock and Leith. The time of the data is Greenwich Mean Time; this applies also to data for the months when British Summer Time is in operation and the hour's time difference should be added. The datum of predictions for each port shows the difference of height, in metres, of CD from Ordnance datum (Newlyn).

Tidal predictions for London Bridge, Liverpool, Greenock and Leith © Crown Copyright and/or database rights. Reproduced by permission of the Controller of Her Majesty's Stationery Office and the UK Hydrographic Office (W www.ukho.gov.uk). The section was compiled with the assistance of Chris Stevens and Perrin Towler.

JANUARY 2015   *High Water*   GMT

		LONDON BRIDGE Datum of Predictions 3.20m below				LIVERPOOL (Gladstone Dock) Datum of Predictions 4.93m below				GREENOCK Datum of Predictions 1.62m below				LEITH Datum of Predictions 2.90m below			
		hr	m	ht hr	m	hr	m	ht hr	m	hr	m	ht hr	m	hr	m	ht hr	m
TH	1	10 21	6.4	23 02	6.4	07 56	8.1	20 20	8.4	09 06	3.1	21 43	3.2	11 33	5.0	23 59	5.0
F	2	11 28	6.5	—	—	08 56	8.4	21 18	8.6	10 10	3.3	22 44	3.3	12 32	5.1	—	—
SA	3	00 06	6.5	12 27	6.6	09 47	8.7	22 08	8.8	11 02	3.4	23 36	3.4	00 57	5.1	13 24	5.3
SU	4	00 59	6.6	13 17	6.8	10 30	9.0	22 51	8.9	11 46	3.5	—	—	01 47	5.2	14 08	5.4
M	5	01 44	6.7	14 00	6.9	11 10	9.1	23 30	9.0	00 23	3.4	12 27	3.6	02 31	5.3	14 49	5.5
TU	6	02 23	6.8	14 40	7.0	11 46	9.2	—	—	01 05	3.4	13 03	3.7	03 10	5.3	15 27	5.5
W	7	02 59	6.8	15 16	7.0	00 05	9.0	12 20	9.2	01 42	3.3	13 37	3.7	03 48	5.3	16 03	5.4
TH	8	03 31	6.8	15 49	6.9	00 39	8.9	12 53	9.1	02 16	3.3	14 11	3.7	04 23	5.3	16 38	5.3
F	9	04 01	6.7	16 21	6.8	01 13	8.8	13 26	8.9	02 51	3.3	14 46	3.7	04 58	5.2	17 12	5.2
SA	10	04 32	6.7	16 52	6.7	01 46	8.6	14 00	8.7	03 27	3.3	15 22	3.7	05 34	5.0	17 48	5.1
SU	11	05 03	6.5	17 25	6.5	02 22	8.3	14 35	8.4	04 05	3.2	16 00	3.6	06 13	4.9	18 27	4.9
M	12	05 36	6.4	18 01	6.3	03 01	8.0	15 15	8.0	04 45	3.1	16 40	3.4	06 55	4.7	19 11	4.7
TU	13	06 14	6.2	18 43	6.1	03 46	7.7	16 04	7.7	05 28	3.0	17 26	3.3	07 42	4.6	20 01	4.6
W	14	07 00	6.0	19 35	5.9	04 42	7.4	17 07	7.5	06 18	2.9	18 19	3.1	08 37	4.5	21 04	4.5
TH	15	07 58	5.8	20 50	5.8	05 52	7.4	18 22	7.4	07 20	2.9	19 22	3.0	09 41	4.5	22 14	4.5
F	16	09 29	5.8	22 10	6.0	07 05	7.6	19 35	7.7	08 36	2.9	20 34	3.0	10 47	4.6	23 22	4.6
SA	17	10 45	6.2	23 18	6.3	08 10	8.0	20 38	8.1	09 48	3.1	21 45	3.1	11 51	4.8	—	—
SU	18	11 47	6.6	—	—	09 06	8.5	21 33	8.6	10 43	3.3	22 47	3.3	00 25	4.9	12 48	5.1
M	19	00 18	6.7	12 44	6.9	09 56	9.1	22 22	9.1	11 29	3.4	23 41	3.4	01 19	5.2	13 37	5.4
TU	20	01 13	6.9	13 36	7.2	10 43	9.5	23 09	9.5	12 13	3.6	—	—	02 06	5.5	14 21	5.7
W	21	02 03	7.1	14 25	7.4	11 28	9.9	23 55	9.7	00 31	3.4	12 56	3.7	02 50	5.8	15 03	5.9
TH	22	02 50	7.2	15 13	7.5	12 14	10.1	—	—	01 20	3.5	13 39	3.8	03 33	5.9	15 46	6.0
F	23	03 35	7.3	15 59	7.5	00 41	9.8	13 01	10.1	02 07	3.5	14 23	3.9	04 18	5.9	16 31	6.0
SA	24	04 18	7.3	16 44	7.4	01 28	9.6	13 47	9.9	02 52	3.5	15 08	3.9	05 04	5.8	17 18	5.9
SU	25	05 01	7.2	17 30	7.2	02 14	9.3	14 35	9.6	03 36	3.5	15 53	3.8	05 53	5.6	18 07	5.7
M	26	05 45	7.0	18 18	6.9	03 02	8.9	15 25	9.1	04 19	3.4	16 39	3.6	06 45	5.3	19 02	5.4
TU	27	06 34	6.8	19 11	6.6	03 55	8.4	16 22	8.6	05 04	3.3	17 29	3.4	07 44	5.0	20 08	5.1
W	28	07 30	6.5	20 11	6.3	04 57	8.0	17 30	8.1	05 52	3.2	18 27	3.2	08 50	4.8	21 19	4.8
TH	29	08 37	6.3	21 16	6.1	06 11	7.7	18 46	7.8	06 52	3.0	19 50	3.0	09 58	4.7	22 31	4.7
F	30	09 48	6.2	22 31	6.1	07 30	7.7	20 02	7.9	08 22	2.9	21 28	3.0	11 09	4.7	23 44	4.7
SA	31	11 03	6.2	23 45	6.2	08 39	8.0	21 06	8.1	09 48	3.0	22 35	3.1	12 17	4.8	—	—

FEBRUARY 2015   *High Water*   GMT

		LONDON BRIDGE				LIVERPOOL (Gladstone Dock)				GREENOCK				LEITH			
SU	1	12 10	6.4	—	—	09 33	8.4	21 57	8.4	10 46	3.2	23 27	3.2	00 48	4.9	13 13	5.1
M	2	00 42	6.5	13 03	6.7	10 17	8.7	22 38	8.7	11 32	3.4	—	—	01 39	5.0	13 58	5.2
TU	3	01 28	6.7	13 47	6.8	10 55	9.0	23 14	8.9	00 12	3.2	12 13	3.5	02 20	5.2	14 37	5.4
W	4	02 08	6.8	14 25	6.9	11 29	9.1	23 47	9.0	00 52	3.3	12 49	3.6	02 56	5.2	15 12	5.4
TH	5	02 42	6.8	14 59	6.9	12 01	9.2	—	—	01 26	3.3	13 21	3.6	03 28	5.3	15 44	5.4
F	6	03 13	6.9	15 28	6.9	00 18	9.0	12 32	9.2	01 58	3.3	13 52	3.6	03 59	5.3	16 15	5.4
SA	7	03 41	6.9	15 56	6.9	00 49	8.9	13 02	9.1	02 29	3.3	14 24	3.6	04 31	5.2	16 47	5.3
SU	8	04 09	6.9	16 25	6.8	01 20	8.8	13 32	8.9	03 01	3.3	14 57	3.6	05 04	5.2	17 19	5.2
M	9	04 39	6.8	16 57	6.7	01 51	8.6	14 03	8.6	03 34	3.3	15 33	3.6	05 40	5.0	17 54	5.1
TU	10	05 11	6.6	17 31	6.5	02 24	8.3	14 36	8.3	04 08	3.2	16 11	3.5	06 18	4.9	18 32	4.9
W	11	05 46	6.4	18 09	6.3	03 02	8.0	15 16	8.0	04 45	3.1	16 52	3.3	07 00	4.7	19 16	4.7
TH	12	06 27	6.2	18 54	6.1	03 49	7.7	16 10	7.6	05 26	3.0	17 40	3.1	07 49	4.6	20 12	4.5
F	13	07 19	6.1	19 54	5.9	04 54	7.4	17 27	7.4	06 18	2.8	18 38	3.0	08 51	4.4	21 26	4.4
SA	14	08 31	5.9	21 24	5.9	06 17	7.4	18 55	7.5	07 32	2.8	19 52	2.9	10 04	4.5	22 46	4.5
SU	15	10 06	6.1	22 45	6.2	07 36	7.8	20 12	7.9	09 06	2.9	21 18	2.9	11 18	4.7	23 58	4.8
M	16	11 20	6.5	23 54	6.6	08 41	8.4	21 14	8.5	10 16	3.1	22 31	3.1	12 22	5.0	—	—
TU	17	12 23	6.9	—	—	09 36	9.0	22 06	9.1	11 08	3.3	23 28	3.3	00 57	5.2	13 16	5.3
W	18	00 53	6.9	13 19	7.2	10 25	9.6	22 54	9.6	11 55	3.5	—	—	01 47	5.5	14 01	5.7
TH	19	01 45	7.1	14 09	7.4	11 12	10.0	23 40	9.9	00 18	3.4	12 41	3.7	02 31	5.8	14 44	6.0
F	20	02 32	7.3	14 56	7.6	11 57	10.3	—	—	01 06	3.5	13 26	3.8	03 15	6.0	15 28	6.1
SA	21	03 17	7.5	15 41	7.6	00 24	10.0	12 43	10.3	01 51	3.5	14 10	3.8	03 59	6.0	16 13	6.1
SU	22	03 59	7.5	16 25	7.5	01 08	9.8	13 27	10.1	02 34	3.5	14 54	3.8	04 44	5.9	16 59	6.0
M	23	04 41	7.5	17 08	6.9	01 51	9.5	14 12	9.7	03 15	3.5	15 37	3.8	05 30	5.6	17 48	5.7
TU	24	05 23	7.2	17 51	6.9	02 35	9.1	14 59	9.1	03 55	3.5	16 20	3.6	06 20	5.3	18 41	5.4
W	25	06 07	6.9	18 37	6.5	03 23	8.5	15 51	8.5	04 35	3.4	17 05	3.3	07 15	5.0	19 43	5.0
TH	26	06 58	6.6	19 30	6.1	04 20	7.9	16 56	7.8	05 18	3.2	17 55	3.0	08 18	4.7	20 52	4.7
F	27	07 59	6.2	20 35	5.9	05 34	7.5	18 17	7.4	06 07	3.0	19 05	2.8	09 27	4.5	22 04	4.5
SA	28	09 13	6.0	21 55	5.8	06 59	7.4	19 41	7.5	07 19	2.8	21 14	2.7	10 40	4.5	23 23	4.5

MARCH 2015   *High Water*   GMT

		LONDON BRIDGE Datum of Predictions 3.20m below				LIVERPOOL (Gladstone Dock) Datum of Predictions 4.93m below				GREENOCK Datum of Predictions 1.62m below				LEITH Datum of Predictions 2.90m below			
		hr	m	hr	m	hr	m	hr	m	hr	m	hr	m	hr	m	hr	m
SU	1	10 35	6.0	23 17	6.0	08 15	7.7	20 49	7.8	09 20	2.9	22 21	2.9	11 56	4.6	—	—
M	2	11 48	6.3	—	—	09 13	8.1	21 39	8.2	10 24	3.1	23 10	3.0	00 34	4.7	12 56	4.9
TU	3	00 18	6.4	12 42	6.6	09 57	8.5	22 19	8.5	11 11	3.3	23 52	3.2	01 24	4.9	13 41	5.1
W	4	01 05	6.6	13 25	6.8	10 34	8.8	22 53	8.8	11 52	3.4	—	—	02 03	5.1	14 18	5.2
TH	5	01 44	6.8	14 03	6.8	11 07	9.0	23 24	9.0	00 29	3.2	12 28	3.4	02 35	5.2	14 51	5.3
F	6	02 19	6.9	14 35	6.9	11 37	9.1	23 54	9.0	01 03	3.2	13 00	3.5	03 05	5.3	15 21	5.4
SA	7	02 49	6.9	15 03	6.9	12 07	9.2	—	—	01 34	3.3	13 29	3.5	03 33	5.3	15 51	5.4
SU	8	03 17	7.0	15 29	7.0	00 23	9.1	12 37	9.1	02 03	3.3	13 59	3.5	04 04	5.3	16 22	5.4
M	9	03 45	7.0	15 59	6.9	00 53	9.0	13 06	9.0	02 32	3.3	14 32	3.5	04 36	5.2	16 53	5.3
TU	10	04 15	6.9	16 31	6.8	01 23	8.8	13 35	8.8	03 02	3.3	15 07	3.5	05 10	5.1	17 27	5.1
W	11	04 48	6.8	17 04	6.6	01 54	8.6	14 07	8.5	03 34	3.3	15 45	3.4	05 46	5.0	18 04	5.0
TH	12	05 23	6.6	17 41	6.4	02 30	8.3	14 47	8.2	04 08	3.2	16 24	3.3	06 26	4.8	18 47	4.8
F	13	06 03	6.5	18 25	6.2	03 15	8.0	15 38	7.8	04 45	3.1	17 09	3.1	07 12	4.7	19 41	4.6
SA	14	06 53	6.2	19 22	6.0	04 17	7.6	16 52	7.4	05 31	2.9	18 04	2.9	08 10	4.5	20 51	4.5
SU	15	08 01	6.0	20 46	5.9	05 41	7.5	18 25	7.4	06 37	2.8	19 18	2.8	09 25	4.4	22 16	4.5
M	16	09 36	6.1	22 15	6.1	07 06	7.8	19 48	7.9	08 24	2.8	20 56	2.9	10 46	4.6	23 32	4.8
TU	17	10 54	6.5	23 29	6.5	08 16	8.3	20 54	8.5	09 49	3.0	22 16	3.0	11 56	4.9	—	—
W	18	12 02	6.9	—	—	09 14	9.0	21 47	9.1	10 45	3.3	23 12	3.2	00 35	5.2	12 52	5.3
TH	19	00 31	6.9	12 59	7.2	10 05	9.6	22 35	9.6	11 34	3.5	—	—	01 25	5.5	13 39	5.7
F	20	01 24	7.2	13 49	7.4	10 52	10.0	23 20	9.9	00 01	3.4	12 22	3.6	02 10	5.8	14 23	6.0
SA	21	02 10	7.4	14 36	7.5	11 37	10.2	—	—	00 47	3.5	13 08	3.7	02 53	6.0	15 07	6.1
SU	22	02 54	7.6	15 19	7.5	00 03	10.0	12 22	10.2	01 30	3.5	13 53	3.8	03 37	6.0	15 53	6.1
M	23	03 36	7.7	16 02	7.4	00 46	9.9	13 06	10.0	02 11	3.5	14 37	3.7	04 21	5.9	16 40	6.0
TU	24	04 18	7.6	16 43	7.2	01 27	9.6	13 49	9.6	02 50	3.6	15 19	3.6	05 08	5.6	17 29	5.7
W	25	04 59	7.3	17 24	6.8	02 09	9.1	14 33	9.0	03 28	3.5	16 00	3.5	05 56	5.3	18 21	5.3
TH	26	05 42	7.0	18 06	6.4	02 54	8.5	15 23	8.3	04 07	3.4	16 43	3.2	06 48	5.0	19 19	4.9
F	27	06 29	6.6	18 52	6.1	03 47	8.0	16 24	7.7	04 49	3.2	17 31	2.9	07 48	4.7	20 23	4.6
SA	28	07 26	6.2	19 53	5.8	04 57	7.5	17 42	7.2	05 36	3.0	18 34	2.7	08 54	4.4	21 32	4.4
SU	29	08 37	5.9	21 12	5.7	06 20	7.3	19 08	7.2	06 37	2.8	20 43	2.6	10 04	4.4	22 49	4.4
M	30	09 57	5.9	22 36	5.8	07 39	7.5	20 19	7.6	08 30	2.8	21 54	2.8	11 21	4.5	—	—
TU	31	11 13	6.2	23 43	6.2	08 40	7.9	21 11	8.0	09 50	2.9	22 42	3.0	00 04	4.5	12 25	4.7

APRIL 2015   *High Water*   GMT

		LONDON BRIDGE				LIVERPOOL (Gladstone Dock)				GREENOCK				LEITH			
W	1	12 11	6.5	—	—	09 26	8.3	21 50	8.4	10 41	3.1	23 23	3.1	00 57	4.8	13 12	4.9
TH	2	00 32	6.5	12 56	6.7	10 04	8.6	22 24	8.7	11 22	3.3	23 59	3.2	01 35	5.0	13 50	5.1
F	3	01 14	6.7	13 33	6.8	10 38	8.8	22 55	8.9	11 59	3.3	—	—	02 07	5.1	14 23	5.2
SA	4	01 49	6.9	14 06	6.8	11 10	9.0	23 26	9.0	00 33	3.2	12 32	3.3	02 36	5.2	14 54	5.3
SU	5	02 21	7.0	14 34	6.9	11 40	9.0	23 56	9.1	01 06	3.3	13 02	3.4	03 06	5.3	15 25	5.4
M	6	02 50	7.0	15 03	7.0	12 10	9.0	—	—	01 35	3.3	13 33	3.4	03 37	5.3	15 57	5.3
TU	7	03 20	7.1	15 34	6.9	00 26	9.1	12 41	9.0	02 03	3.4	14 07	3.4	04 10	5.3	16 29	5.3
W	8	03 52	7.1	16 08	6.8	00 58	9.0	13 13	8.8	02 33	3.4	14 44	3.4	04 43	5.2	17 04	5.2
TH	9	04 27	6.9	16 43	6.6	01 32	8.8	13 48	8.6	03 05	3.4	15 22	3.4	05 20	5.1	17 43	5.1
F	10	05 04	6.8	17 21	6.4	02 10	8.5	14 30	8.3	03 39	3.3	16 03	3.3	06 00	5.0	18 29	4.9
SA	11	05 47	6.6	18 06	6.2	02 56	8.2	15 24	7.9	04 17	3.2	16 48	3.1	06 46	4.8	19 22	4.7
SU	12	06 38	6.4	19 03	6.0	03 58	7.9	16 36	7.6	05 02	3.0	17 43	2.9	07 43	4.6	20 30	4.6
M	13	07 46	6.2	20 22	5.9	05 19	7.7	18 03	7.6	06 05	2.9	18 55	2.8	08 56	4.5	21 51	4.6
TU	14	09 14	6.3	21 50	6.1	06 39	7.9	19 24	8.0	07 49	2.8	20 34	2.9	10 18	4.7	23 07	4.9
W	15	10 31	6.6	23 04	6.5	07 50	8.4	20 30	8.5	09 19	3.0	21 54	3.0	11 28	5.0	—	—
TH	16	11 39	6.9	—	—	08 50	9.0	21 25	9.1	10 20	3.3	22 50	3.0	00 09	5.2	12 26	5.3
F	17	00 07	6.9	12 38	7.2	09 42	9.5	22 13	9.5	11 11	3.5	23 39	3.4	01 05	5.5	13 15	5.6
SA	18	01 00	7.2	13 28	7.3	10 30	9.8	22 58	9.7	12 00	3.6	—	—	01 47	5.7	14 01	5.9
SU	19	01 47	7.4	14 14	7.4	11 16	10.0	23 41	9.8	00 24	3.4	12 48	3.6	02 31	5.9	14 48	6.0
M	20	02 31	7.5	14 57	7.4	12 01	9.9	—	—	01 07	3.5	13 34	3.6	03 15	6.0	15 35	6.0
TU	21	03 13	7.6	15 38	7.3	00 23	9.7	12 45	9.7	01 47	3.6	14 18	3.6	04 00	5.8	16 22	5.8
W	22	03 56	7.5	16 19	7.1	01 04	9.4	13 27	9.3	02 25	3.6	15 00	3.5	04 46	5.6	17 11	5.5
TH	23	04 37	7.3	16 58	6.7	01 45	9.1	14 11	8.8	03 03	3.5	15 42	3.3	05 33	5.3	18 02	5.2
F	24	05 20	6.9	17 38	6.4	02 28	8.6	14 57	8.2	03 42	3.4	16 25	3.1	06 23	5.0	18 55	4.9
SA	25	06 04	6.5	18 21	6.1	03 18	8.1	15 53	7.7	04 23	3.3	17 12	2.9	07 18	4.7	19 52	4.6
SU	26	06 55	6.1	19 14	5.8	04 20	7.6	17 01	7.3	05 09	3.1	18 10	2.7	08 18	4.5	20 53	4.4
M	27	08 00	5.9	20 27	5.6	05 34	7.3	18 19	7.2	06 04	2.9	19 32	2.6	09 22	4.4	21 58	4.3
TU	28	09 13	5.8	21 45	5.7	06 49	7.4	19 32	7.4	07 22	2.8	21 04	2.7	10 31	4.4	23 10	4.4
W	29	10 23	6.0	22 54	6.0	07 54	7.6	20 29	7.8	08 56	2.9	21 59	2.9	11 38	4.5	—	—
TH	30	11 26	6.3	23 51	6.4	08 46	8.0	21 13	8.1	09 57	3.0	22 44	3.0	00 11	4.6	12 32	4.7

MAY 2015   *High Water*   GMT

	LONDON BRIDGE — Datum of Predictions 3.20m below				LIVERPOOL (Gladstone Dock) — Datum of Predictions 4.93m below				GREENOCK — Datum of Predictions 1.62m below				LEITH — Datum of Predictions 2.90m below			
	hr	m	hr	m (ht)	hr	m	hr	m (ht)	hr	m	hr	m (ht)	hr	m	hr	m (ht)
F 1	12	16 6.5	—	—	09	28 8.3	21	49 8.5	10	43 3.1	23	23 3.2	00	55 4.8	13	14 4.9
SA 2	00	36 6.6	12	57 6.7	10	04 8.6	22	23 8.7	11	21 3.2	—	—	01	31 5.0	13	50 5.1
SU 3	01	16 6.8	13	33 6.8	10	39 8.8	22	56 8.9	00	00 3.2	11	57 3.2	02	04 5.2	14	25 5.2
M 4	01	50 6.9	14	06 6.9	11	12 8.9	23	28 9.1	00	35 3.3	12	30 3.3	02	37 5.3	14	59 5.3
TU 5	02	23 7.0	14	39 6.9	11	45 9.0	—	—	01	06 3.4	13	05 3.3	03	11 5.4	15	33 5.3
W 6	02	57 7.1	15	14 6.9	00	02 9.1	12	20 8.9	01	36 3.4	13	43 3.4	03	45 5.4	16	09 5.3
TH 7	03	33 7.1	15	51 6.8	00	38 9.1	12	57 8.9	02	07 3.5	14	23 3.4	04	21 5.3	16	46 5.3
F 8	04	11 7.0	16	28 6.7	01	16 9.0	13	37 8.7	02	42 3.5	15	05 3.4	04	59 5.2	17	28 5.2
SA 9	04	52 6.9	17	09 6.5	01	58 8.7	14	23 8.4	03	19 3.4	15	48 3.3	05	41 5.1	18	15 5.1
SU 10	05	37 6.7	17	55 6.3	02	47 8.5	15	18 8.1	03	59 3.3	16	35 3.2	06	29 5.0	19	09 4.9
M 11	06	30 6.5	18	52 6.2	03	48 8.2	16	26 7.9	04	46 3.2	17	30 3.0	07	25 4.8	20	14 4.8
TU 12	07	38 6.4	20	07 6.1	05	01 8.1	17	43 7.8	05	49 3.0	18	40 2.9	08	35 4.7	21	29 4.8
W 13	08	56 6.4	21	27 6.3	06	14 8.2	18	58 8.1	07	20 3.0	20	07 2.9	09	52 4.8	22	41 4.9
TH 14	10	08 6.6	22	38 6.5	07	24 8.5	20	04 8.5	08	48 3.1	21	25 3.0	11	01 5.0	23	43 5.1
F 15	11	15 6.8	23	42 6.8	08	25 8.9	21	01 8.9	09	54 3.2	22	24 3.2	12	00 5.3	—	—
SA 16	12	15 7.0	—	—	09	20 9.2	21	51 9.2	10	48 3.4	23	15 3.3	00	37 5.4	12	54 5.5
SU 17	00	37 7.0	13	07 7.1	10	10 9.5	22	37 9.4	11	39 3.5	—	—	01	25 5.6	13	43 5.7
M 18	01	26 7.2	13	53 7.1	10	57 9.6	23	21 9.5	00	00 3.4	12	28 3.5	02	11 5.7	14	31 5.8
TU 19	02	10 7.4	14	37 7.1	11	42 9.5	—	—	00	44 3.5	13	15 3.5	02	56 5.7	15	19 5.7
W 20	02	54 7.4	15	18 7.1	00	03 9.5	12	26 9.3	01	24 3.5	14	00 3.4	03	42 5.6	16	06 5.6
TH 21	03	36 7.4	15	58 6.9	00	44 9.3	13	08 9.0	02	02 3.6	14	43 3.3	04	27 5.5	16	54 5.4
F 22	04	18 7.2	16	37 6.7	01	24 9.0	13	49 8.7	02	40 3.6	15	24 3.2	05	13 5.3	17	41 5.2
SA 23	04	59 6.9	17	14 6.4	02	05 8.6	14	32 8.2	03	18 3.5	16	06 3.1	05	59 5.1	18	28 4.9
SU 24	05	41 6.5	17	53 6.2	02	49 8.2	15	20 7.8	03	59 3.4	16	52 2.9	06	48 4.8	19	17 4.7
M 25	06	25 6.2	18	37 5.9	03	42 7.8	16	17 7.5	04	42 3.2	17	43 2.8	07	40 4.6	20	09 4.5
TU 26	07	18 6.0	19	37 5.7	04	44 7.5	17	22 7.3	05	31 3.0	18	42 2.7	08	36 4.5	21	05 4.4
W 27	08	24 5.8	20	53 5.7	05	52 7.4	18	31 7.3	06	30 2.9	19	50 2.7	09	35 4.4	22	03 4.4
TH 28	09	30 5.9	22	02 5.9	06	58 7.5	19	34 7.5	07	41 2.9	20	58 2.8	10	36 4.4	23	04 4.5
F 29	10	32 6.1	23	02 6.2	07	56 7.7	20	26 7.9	08	54 2.9	21	55 3.0	11	36 4.6	—	—
SA 30	11	28 6.3	23	54 6.5	08	45 8.0	21	10 8.2	09	52 3.0	22	43 3.1	00	00 4.7	12	29 4.8
SU 31	12	17 6.5	—	—	09	28 8.3	21	49 8.6	10	38 3.1	23	26 3.2	00	48 4.9	13	14 4.9

JUNE 2015   *High Water*   GMT

	LONDON BRIDGE				LIVERPOOL (Gladstone Dock)				GREENOCK				LEITH			
M 1	00	39 6.7	13	00 6.7	10	07 8.6	22	26 8.8	11	18 3.2	—	—	01	30 5.1	13	55 5.1
TU 2	01	20 6.9	13	40 6.8	10	45 8.8	23	03 9.1	00	04 3.3	11	58 3.2	02	09 5.3	14	34 5.3
W 3	02	00 7.0	14	20 6.9	11	23 8.9	23	41 9.2	00	38 3.4	12	39 3.3	02	47 5.4	15	12 5.4
TH 4	02	39 7.1	15	00 6.9	12	02 9.0	—	—	01	12 3.5	13	22 3.3	03	24 5.4	15	50 5.4
F 5	03	20 7.2	15	40 6.9	00	21 9.3	12	44 9.0	01	47 3.5	14	06 3.2	04	02 5.5	16	31 5.4
SA 6	04	01 7.1	16	21 6.8	01	04 9.2	13	29 8.9	02	25 3.6	14	51 3.4	04	43 5.4	17	15 5.4
SU 7	04	45 7.0	17	03 6.6	01	50 9.1	14	17 8.7	03	05 3.6	15	37 3.3	05	27 5.4	18	03 5.3
M 8	05	31 6.9	17	50 6.5	02	40 8.9	15	11 8.5	03	48 3.5	16	26 3.2	06	15 5.2	18	56 5.1
TU 9	06	24 6.7	18	44 6.4	03	37 8.6	16	12 8.2	04	37 3.4	17	19 3.1	07	09 5.1	19	57 5.0
W 10	07	27 6.6	19	51 6.3	04	41 8.4	17	20 8.1	05	36 3.2	18	21 3.0	08	15 5.0	21	06 4.9
TH 11	08	36 6.5	21	04 6.4	05	49 8.4	18	31 8.1	06	52 3.1	19	35 3.0	09	28 4.9	22	14 4.9
F 12	09	44 6.6	22	12 6.5	06	57 8.4	19	38 8.6	08	17 3.1	20	52 3.0	10	37 5.0	23	18 5.0
SA 13	10	50 6.6	23	17 6.7	08	02 8.6	20	39 8.6	09	29 3.2	21	57 3.1	11	39 5.1	—	—
SU 14	11	54 6.7	—	—	09	01 8.8	21	32 8.9	10	29 3.3	22	52 3.3	00	15 5.2	12	37 5.3
M 15	00	16 6.8	12	50 6.8	09	53 9.0	22	20 9.1	11	23 3.3	23	40 3.4	01	08 5.4	13	30 5.4
TU 16	01	09 7.0	13	38 6.9	10	42 9.1	23	04 9.2	12	13 3.3	—	—	01	56 5.5	14	19 5.5
W 17	01	55 7.1	14	22 6.9	11	27 9.2	23	46 9.3	00	24 3.4	13	01 3.3	02	42 5.5	15	06 5.5
TH 18	02	39 7.2	15	03 6.9	12	09 9.1	—	—	01	05 3.5	13	46 3.2	03	26 5.5	15	51 5.4
F 19	03	21 7.2	15	41 6.9	00	26 9.2	12	49 8.9	01	43 3.5	14	26 3.2	04	10 5.4	16	34 5.3
SA 20	04	01 7.1	16	18 6.7	01	04 9.0	13	27 8.7	02	19 3.6	15	05 3.1	04	52 5.3	17	16 5.2
SU 21	04	40 6.8	16	52 6.5	01	41 8.8	14	06 8.4	02	56 3.5	15	44 3.1	05	33 5.2	17	58 5.0
M 22	05	16 6.6	17	27 6.4	02	20 8.5	14	46 8.1	03	34 3.5	16	23 3.0	06	15 5.0	18	40 4.8
TU 23	05	54 6.4	18	04 6.2	03	04 8.2	15	32 7.8	04	14 3.3	17	04 3.0	06	59 4.8	19	25 4.6
W 24	06	34 6.1	18	46 6.0	03	53 7.8	16	26 7.5	04	56 3.2	17	58 2.9	07	47 4.6	20	14 4.5
TH 25	07	25 5.9	19	44 5.8	04	51 7.5	17	27 7.3	05	45 3.0	18	52 2.8	08	41 4.5	21	09 4.4
F 26	08	31 5.8	21	04 5.7	05	55 7.4	18	32 7.4	06	42 2.9	19	53 2.8	09	39 4.4	22	06 4.5
SA 27	09	37 5.9	22	11 5.9	07	00 7.5	19	34 7.6	07	46 2.9	20	59 2.9	10	40 4.5	23	06 4.6
SU 28	10	39 6.1	23	10 6.2	08	00 7.7	20	28 8.0	08	53 2.9	22	00 3.0	11	41 4.6	—	—
M 29	11	37 6.4	—	—	08	52 8.0	21	16 8.4	09	53 3.0	22	51 3.1	00	04 4.8	12	37 4.8
TU 30	00	04 6.6	12	30 6.6	09	38 8.4	21	59 8.8	10	45 3.1	23	34 3.3	00	57 5.0	13	26 5.1

JULY 2015   *High Water*   GMT

		LONDON BRIDGE Datum of Predictions 3.20m below						LIVERPOOL (Gladstone Dock) Datum of Predictions 4.93m below						GREENOCK Datum of Predictions 1.62m below						LEITH Datum of Predictions 2.90m below					
		hr	m	ht	hr	m	ht	hr	m	ht	hr	m	ht	hr	m	ht	hr	m	ht	hr	m	ht	hr	m	ht
W	1	00	53	6.8	13	18	6.8	10	22	8.7	22	41	9.1	11	32	3.2	—		—	01	43	5.2	14	10	5.3
TH	2	01	39	7.0	14	03	6.9	11	04	9.0	23	23	9.4	00	13	3.4	12	19	3.3	02	25	5.4	14	52	5.5
F	3	02	24	7.2	14	48	7.0	11	48	9.2	—		—	00	51	3.5	13	05	3.3	03	05	5.6	15	33	5.6
SA	4	03	08	7.3	15	31	7.0	00	06	9.5	12	33	9.3	01	31	3.6	13	52	3.3	03	45	5.7	16	16	5.7
SU	5	03	52	7.3	16	13	7.0	00	52	9.6	13	19	9.2	02	12	3.7	14	39	3.3	04	27	5.7	17	00	5.6
M	6	04	37	7.3	16	56	6.9	01	39	9.5	14	06	9.1	02	54	3.7	15	26	3.3	05	12	5.6	17	48	5.5
TU	7	05	23	7.1	17	40	6.8	02	27	9.3	14	56	8.8	03	38	3.6	16	13	3.3	06	00	5.5	18	39	5.3
W	8	06	13	6.9	18	30	6.7	03	20	9.0	15	51	8.5	04	25	3.5	17	03	3.2	06	52	5.3	19	36	5.1
TH	9	07	09	6.7	19	29	6.6	04	18	8.7	16	53	8.2	05	18	3.3	17	56	3.1	07	54	5.1	20	41	4.9
F	10	08	12	6.5	20	37	6.5	05	22	8.4	18	03	8.0	06	23	3.2	18	58	3.0	09	05	5.0	21	49	4.9
SA	11	09	17	6.4	21	45	6.5	06	32	8.2	19	14	8.1	07	43	3.0	20	14	3.0	10	15	4.9	22	55	4.9
SU	12	10	25	6.4	22	54	6.5	07	43	8.3	20	21	8.3	09	07	3.0	21	31	3.0	11	23	5.0	23	58	5.0
M	13	11	34	6.5	23	59	6.6	08	47	8.4	21	18	8.6	10	16	3.1	22	34	3.2	12	26	5.1	—		—
TU	14	12	35	6.6	—		—	09	43	8.6	22	08	8.8	11	13	3.2	23	25	3.3	00	55	5.2	13	22	5.2
W	15	00	56	6.8	13	26	6.7	10	31	8.8	22	51	9.0	12	04	3.2	—		—	01	46	5.3	14	11	5.3
TH	16	01	45	7.0	14	10	6.8	11	14	8.9	23	31	9.1	00	10	3.4	12	50	3.2	02	30	5.4	14	54	5.4
F	17	02	28	7.1	14	49	6.9	11	53	8.9	—		—	00	50	3.5	13	32	3.2	03	12	5.5	15	34	5.4
SA	18	03	07	7.1	15	25	6.9	00	08	9.1	12	29	8.9	01	26	3.5	14	09	3.1	03	51	5.5	16	12	5.3
SU	19	03	44	7.0	15	58	6.8	00	43	9.1	13	03	8.8	02	00	3.5	14	43	3.1	04	29	5.4	16	49	5.2
M	20	04	17	6.9	16	29	6.7	01	16	8.9	13	37	8.6	02	34	3.5	15	18	3.1	05	05	5.3	17	25	5.1
TU	21	04	49	6.7	17	00	6.6	01	51	8.7	14	13	8.4	03	08	3.5	15	55	3.1	05	41	5.1	18	03	5.0
W	22	05	21	6.5	17	32	6.4	02	26	8.4	14	51	8.1	03	44	3.5	16	34	3.1	06	19	5.0	18	44	4.8
TH	23	05	54	6.3	18	07	6.2	03	05	8.1	15	33	7.8	04	23	3.3	17	15	3.0	07	01	4.8	19	29	4.7
F	24	06	32	6.1	18	48	6.0	03	51	7.7	16	25	7.5	05	06	3.2	18	01	2.9	07	49	4.6	20	19	4.5
SA	25	07	20	5.9	19	43	5.8	04	48	7.4	17	29	7.3	05	57	3.0	18	55	2.8	08	46	4.5	21	18	4.5
SU	26	08	31	5.7	21	10	5.8	05	59	7.3	18	41	7.4	06	57	2.9	19	59	2.8	09	51	4.4	22	21	4.5
M	27	09	51	5.9	22	26	6.0	07	13	7.4	19	48	7.8	08	05	2.9	21	13	2.9	10	58	4.5	23	26	4.7
TU	28	10	59	6.2	23	29	6.4	08	18	7.8	20	45	8.3	09	16	2.9	22	16	3.1	12	03	4.7	—		—
W	29	12	00	6.5	—		—	09	13	8.3	21	35	8.8	10	19	3.1	23	07	3.3	00	26	5.0	13	00	5.0
TH	30	00	26	6.8	12	56	6.8	10	02	8.7	22	21	9.2	11	13	3.2	23	50	3.4	01	18	5.2	13	49	5.3
F	31	01	19	7.1	13	45	7.0	10	48	9.1	23	06	9.6	12	02	3.3	—		—	02	03	5.5	14	32	5.6

AUGUST 2015   *High Water*   GMT

		LONDON BRIDGE						LIVERPOOL (Gladstone Dock)						GREENOCK						LEITH					
SA	1	02	07	7.3	14	31	7.2	11	32	9.4	23	50	9.9	00	33	3.5	12	51	3.3	02	45	5.7	15	14	5.8
SU	2	02	53	7.5	15	16	7.3	12	17	9.6	—		—	01	16	3.6	13	38	3.3	03	26	5.9	15	57	5.9
M	3	03	38	7.5	15	58	7.3	00	36	10.0	13	03	9.6	01	58	3.7	14	25	3.4	04	09	6.0	16	42	5.8
TU	4	04	23	7.4	16	40	7.3	01	22	9.9	13	49	9.4	02	42	3.8	15	10	3.4	04	54	5.9	17	28	5.7
W	5	05	07	7.2	17	23	7.1	02	09	9.9	14	36	9.1	03	26	3.7	15	54	3.4	05	42	5.8	18	18	5.5
TH	6	05	53	6.9	18	09	6.9	02	58	9.3	15	26	8.7	04	10	3.6	16	39	3.3	06	33	5.5	19	12	5.2
F	7	06	44	6.6	19	02	6.7	03	52	8.8	16	25	8.2	04	58	3.4	17	25	3.2	07	33	5.2	20	15	4.9
SA	8	07	42	6.4	20	06	6.5	04	55	8.3	17	35	7.9	05	53	3.2	18	19	3.1	08	44	4.9	21	24	4.8
SU	9	08	47	6.2	21	17	6.3	06	09	7.9	18	52	7.8	07	07	2.9	19	30	2.9	09	56	4.8	22	34	4.8
M	10	09	58	6.1	22	31	6.3	07	27	7.9	20	06	8.0	08	54	2.8	21	08	3.0	11	09	4.8	23	44	4.9
TU	11	11	14	6.2	23	43	6.5	08	38	8.1	21	07	8.4	10	10	3.0	22	19	3.1	12	19	4.9	—		—
W	12	12	19	6.6	—		—	09	34	8.4	21	56	8.7	11	05	3.1	23	11	3.3	00	45	5.1	13	16	5.1
TH	13	00	42	6.8	13	10	6.7	10	20	8.6	22	37	8.9	11	53	3.2	23	55	3.4	01	36	5.3	14	01	5.2
F	14	01	31	7.0	13	53	6.9	10	59	8.8	23	13	9.1	12	35	3.2	—		—	02	18	5.4	14	40	5.3
SA	15	02	12	7.0	14	31	6.9	11	38	8.9	23	46	9.2	00	33	3.5	13	13	3.2	02	55	5.5	15	14	5.3
SU	16	02	49	7.0	15	04	7.0	12	05	9.0	—		—	01	07	3.5	13	45	3.2	03	30	5.5	15	47	5.3
M	17	03	21	7.0	15	34	7.0	00	18	9.2	12	37	8.9	01	38	3.5	14	15	3.2	04	03	5.4	16	19	5.3
TU	18	03	50	7.0	16	02	6.9	00	49	9.1	13	08	8.8	02	09	3.6	14	47	3.2	04	35	5.4	16	53	5.2
W	19	04	18	6.9	16	31	6.8	01	20	8.9	13	40	8.6	02	41	3.6	15	20	3.2	05	09	5.3	17	28	5.1
TH	20	04	48	6.7	17	01	6.6	01	51	8.6	14	12	8.4	03	16	3.5	15	55	3.2	05	44	5.1	18	06	5.0
F	21	05	19	6.5	17	34	6.4	02	24	8.3	14	49	8.1	03	52	3.4	16	32	3.1	06	22	4.9	18	47	4.8
SA	22	05	54	6.3	18	12	6.2	03	02	8.0	15	33	7.7	04	32	3.3	17	14	3.0	07	06	4.7	19	34	4.6
SU	23	06	35	6.0	18	59	6.0	03	51	7.6	16	33	7.4	05	19	3.1	18	04	2.9	07	59	4.5	20	31	4.5
M	24	07	30	5.8	20	04	5.8	05	02	7.3	17	52	7.4	06	16	2.9	19	07	2.8	09	06	4.4	21	40	4.5
TU	25	08	56	5.7	21	41	5.9	06	29	7.3	19	11	7.7	07	27	2.8	20	26	2.9	10	21	4.5	22	51	4.6
W	26	10	21	6.0	22	56	6.4	07	48	7.7	20	26	8.2	08	47	2.9	21	44	3.0	11	33	4.7	23	57	4.9
TH	27	11	31	6.4	—		—	08	50	8.3	21	12	8.8	10	01	3.0	22	41	3.3	12	35	5.1	—		—
F	28	00	00	6.8	12	31	6.8	09	43	8.9	22	01	9.4	10	59	3.2	23	28	3.5	00	53	5.3	13	26	5.4
SA	29	00	57	7.2	13	23	7.1	10	30	9.4	22	46	9.8	11	48	3.3	—		—	01	40	5.6	14	11	5.7
SU	30	01	47	7.4	14	10	7.3	11	14	9.7	23	31	10.1	00	13	3.6	12	35	3.4	02	22	5.9	14	53	6.0
M	31	02	34	7.6	14	54	7.5	11	58	9.9	—		—	00	58	3.7	13	21	3.4	03	05	6.1	15	36	6.0

SEPTEMBER 2015   *High Water*   GMT

	LONDON BRIDGE Datum of Predictions 3.20m below				LIVERPOOL (Gladstone Dock) Datum of Predictions 4.93m below				GREENOCK Datum of Predictions 1.62m below				LEITH Datum of Predictions 2.90m below			
	hr	m (ht)	hr	m (ht)	hr	m (ht)	hr	m (ht)	hr	m (ht)	hr	m (ht)	hr	m (ht)	hr	m (ht)
TU 1	03 19	7.6	15 37	7.6	00 16	10.3	12 43	9.9	01 43	3.8	14 05	3.5	03 48	6.2	16 20	6.0
W 2	04 02	7.5	16 19	7.5	01 01	10.1	13 27	9.6	02 27	3.8	14 48	3.5	04 34	6.1	17 06	5.8
TH 3	04 45	7.3	17 01	7.3	01 47	9.8	14 12	9.2	03 10	3.8	15 29	3.5	05 22	5.9	17 54	5.5
F 4	05 29	6.9	17 45	7.1	02 34	9.3	14 59	8.7	03 53	3.6	16 11	3.4	06 14	5.6	18 48	5.2
SA 5	06 14	6.6	18 34	6.7	03 26	8.7	15 55	8.2	04 38	3.4	16 55	3.3	07 13	5.2	19 50	4.9
SU 6	07 08	6.2	19 34	6.4	04 29	8.0	17 06	7.7	05 27	3.1	17 45	3.1	08 23	4.9	20 59	4.7
M 7	08 12	6.0	20 47	6.2	05 47	7.6	18 29	7.6	06 34	2.8	18 48	2.9	09 37	4.7	22 11	4.7
TU 8	09 28	5.9	22 05	6.2	07 12	7.6	19 48	7.8	08 45	2.7	20 40	2.9	10 53	4.6	23 25	4.8
W 9	10 49	6.1	23 22	6.4	08 25	7.9	20 50	8.2	09 59	2.9	21 58	3.1	12 07	4.8	—	—
TH 10	11 56	6.4	—	—	09 19	8.3	21 37	8.6	10 50	3.1	22 50	3.3	00 29	5.0	13 03	5.0
F 11	00 22	6.8	12 48	6.7	10 02	8.6	22 16	8.9	11 34	3.2	23 33	3.4	01 18	5.2	13 45	5.2
SA 12	01 10	6.9	13 30	6.9	10 37	8.8	22 50	9.1	12 12	3.3	—	—	01 58	5.3	14 19	5.3
SU 13	01 49	7.0	14 06	6.9	11 09	9.0	23 21	9.2	00 10	3.5	12 47	3.3	02 33	5.4	14 50	5.3
M 14	02 24	7.0	14 38	7.0	11 39	9.1	23 52	9.2	00 43	3.5	13 17	3.3	03 05	5.5	15 19	5.4
TU 15	02 54	7.0	15 06	7.0	12 08	9.1	—	—	01 13	3.5	13 45	3.3	03 36	5.5	15 50	5.4
W 16	03 20	7.0	15 34	7.0	00 21	9.1	12 39	9.0	01 42	3.6	14 15	3.3	04 07	5.4	16 22	5.3
TH 17	03 47	6.9	16 03	7.0	00 51	9.0	13 09	8.8	02 14	3.6	14 46	3.4	04 39	5.3	16 56	5.2
F 18	04 17	6.8	16 34	6.8	01 21	8.8	13 40	8.6	02 49	3.6	15 19	3.4	05 13	5.2	17 32	5.1
SA 19	04 49	6.6	17 07	6.6	01 52	8.5	14 14	8.3	03 25	3.5	15 54	3.3	05 51	5.0	18 11	4.9
SU 20	05 23	6.4	17 45	6.4	02 28	8.1	14 56	8.0	04 05	3.4	16 33	3.2	06 33	4.8	18 56	4.8
M 21	06 02	6.1	18 30	6.2	03 16	7.7	15 53	7.6	04 48	3.2	17 19	3.0	07 24	4.6	19 51	4.6
TU 22	06 53	5.9	19 30	6.0	04 24	7.4	17 13	7.5	05 42	3.0	18 21	2.9	08 29	4.5	21 00	4.5
W 23	08 07	5.7	21 00	6.0	05 54	7.3	18 38	7.7	06 53	2.9	19 45	2.9	09 48	4.5	22 18	4.6
TH 24	09 44	5.9	22 25	6.4	07 20	7.7	19 50	8.3	08 22	2.9	21 12	3.1	11 04	4.8	23 28	4.9
F 25	11 00	6.4	23 33	6.9	08 27	8.3	20 48	8.9	09 45	3.1	22 14	3.3	12 09	5.1	—	—
SA 26	12 03	6.8	—	—	09 21	9.0	21 38	9.5	10 42	3.3	23 05	3.5	00 26	5.3	13 02	5.5
SU 27	00 32	7.2	12 57	7.2	10 09	9.5	22 25	10.0	11 30	3.4	23 52	3.7	01 14	5.7	13 47	5.8
M 28	01 23	7.5	13 45	7.4	10 53	9.9	23 10	10.3	12 15	3.5	—	—	01 58	6.0	14 29	6.0
TU 29	02 11	7.6	14 30	7.6	11 37	10.0	23 55	10.3	00 38	3.8	13 00	3.6	02 42	6.2	15 12	6.1
W 30	02 55	7.6	15 13	7.7	12 20	10.0	—	—	01 25	3.8	13 42	3.6	03 27	6.3	15 57	6.0

OCTOBER 2015   *High Water*   GMT

	LONDON BRIDGE				LIVERPOOL (Gladstone Dock)				GREENOCK				LEITH			
TH 1	03 38	7.5	15 55	7.6	00 39	10.2	13 04	9.7	02 09	3.8	14 24	3.6	04 14	6.1	16 43	5.8
F 2	04 21	7.3	16 37	7.4	01 25	9.8	13 47	9.3	02 53	3.8	15 04	3.6	05 03	5.9	17 31	5.6
SA 3	05 03	6.9	17 21	7.1	02 11	9.2	14 33	8.8	03 35	3.6	15 45	3.5	05 55	5.5	18 24	5.2
SU 4	05 46	6.5	18 09	6.7	03 02	8.5	15 27	8.2	04 19	3.4	16 28	3.4	06 54	5.1	19 24	4.9
M 5	06 33	6.1	19 04	6.3	04 03	7.9	16 36	7.7	05 08	3.1	17 16	3.2	08 01	4.8	20 33	4.7
TU 6	07 33	5.9	20 15	6.1	05 20	7.4	17 58	7.5	06 12	2.8	18 16	3.0	09 11	4.6	21 43	4.6
W 7	08 51	5.7	21 32	6.0	06 45	7.4	19 17	7.7	08 20	2.7	19 53	3.0	10 25	4.5	22 56	4.7
TH 8	10 13	5.9	22 49	6.3	07 59	7.7	20 21	8.1	09 35	2.9	21 24	3.1	11 40	4.7	—	—
F 9	11 23	6.2	23 52	6.6	08 54	8.1	21 10	8.5	10 24	3.1	22 19	3.3	00 01	4.9	12 37	4.9
SA 10	12 16	6.6	—	—	09 35	8.5	21 48	8.8	11 05	3.3	23 02	3.4	00 52	5.1	13 19	5.1
SU 11	00 40	6.8	12 59	6.8	10 08	8.8	22 23	9.0	11 42	3.4	23 40	3.5	01 32	5.3	13 52	5.2
M 12	01 20	6.9	13 36	6.9	10 41	9.0	22 54	9.1	12 15	3.4	—	—	02 06	5.4	14 22	5.3
TU 13	01 54	6.9	14 08	7.0	11 11	9.1	23 25	9.2	00 14	3.5	12 46	3.4	02 38	5.4	14 51	5.4
W 14	02 23	7.0	14 37	7.1	11 41	9.2	23 55	9.1	00 45	3.5	13 16	3.5	03 09	5.5	15 21	5.4
TH 15	02 50	7.0	15 05	7.1	12 11	9.1	—	—	01 15	3.6	13 45	3.5	03 40	5.4	15 53	5.4
F 16	03 19	7.0	15 36	7.1	00 25	9.0	12 42	9.0	01 49	3.6	14 15	3.5	04 13	5.4	16 27	5.3
SA 17	03 50	6.9	16 10	7.0	00 56	8.8	13 14	8.8	02 25	3.6	14 48	3.5	04 48	5.2	17 03	5.2
SU 18	04 24	6.7	16 45	6.8	01 29	8.6	13 50	8.6	03 03	3.5	15 23	3.5	05 26	5.1	17 42	5.1
M 19	04 59	6.5	17 24	6.6	02 08	8.3	14 33	8.3	03 43	3.4	16 02	3.4	06 10	4.9	18 26	4.9
TU 20	05 39	6.3	18 11	6.4	02 57	7.9	15 29	7.9	04 26	3.3	16 46	3.2	07 01	4.8	19 19	4.7
W 21	06 29	6.0	19 09	6.2	04 03	7.6	16 45	7.7	05 18	3.1	17 44	3.1	08 03	4.6	20 26	4.6
TH 22	07 37	5.9	20 32	6.1	05 28	7.5	18 08	7.9	06 26	3.0	19 07	3.0	09 20	4.6	21 46	4.7
F 23	09 10	6.0	21 56	6.4	06 52	7.8	19 21	8.4	07 57	3.0	20 38	3.1	10 36	4.9	22 58	5.0
SA 24	10 29	6.4	23 05	6.8	08 01	8.4	20 22	9.0	09 21	3.1	21 46	3.4	11 41	5.2	23 57	5.3
SU 25	11 34	6.8	—	—	08 57	9.0	21 15	9.5	10 20	3.4	22 40	3.6	12 35	5.5	—	—
M 26	00 06	7.2	12 30	7.1	09 46	9.5	22 03	9.9	11 09	3.5	23 30	3.7	00 48	5.7	13 22	5.8
TU 27	00 59	7.3	13 20	7.4	10 32	9.8	22 49	10.1	11 54	3.6	—	—	01 35	6.0	14 06	6.0
W 28	01 47	7.4	14 05	7.5	11 16	10.0	23 35	10.2	00 18	3.8	12 38	3.7	02 21	6.1	14 50	6.1
TH 29	02 32	7.4	14 49	7.6	11 59	9.9	—	—	01 06	3.8	13 20	3.7	03 08	6.2	15 35	6.0
F 30	03 16	7.4	15 33	7.6	00 20	10.0	12 42	9.7	01 52	3.8	14 01	3.8	03 56	6.0	16 21	5.8
SA 31	03 58	7.2	16 16	7.4	01 05	9.6	13 25	9.3	02 36	3.7	14 41	3.7	04 46	5.8	17 10	5.5

NOVEMBER 2015   *High Water*   GMT

Datum of Predictions — LONDON BRIDGE: 3.20m below; LIVERPOOL (Gladstone Dock): 4.93m below; GREENOCK: 1.62m below; LEITH: 2.90m below

Day	LONDON BRIDGE hr m	ht m	hr m	ht m	LIVERPOOL hr m	ht m	hr m	ht m	GREENOCK hr m	ht m	hr m	ht m	LEITH hr m	ht m	hr m	ht m
SU 1	04 39	6.9	17 00	7.1	01 51	9.1	14 10	8.9	03 19	3.6	15 22	3.7	05 38	5.5	18 01	5.2
M 2	05 20	6.5	17 46	6.7	02 39	8.5	15 00	8.3	04 03	3.3	16 04	3.5	06 34	5.1	18 58	5.0
TU 3	06 03	6.1	18 37	6.3	03 35	7.9	16 02	7.9	04 52	3.1	16 51	3.3	07 34	4.8	20 01	4.7
W 4	06 55	5.8	19 39	6.0	04 43	7.5	17 15	7.6	05 50	2.9	17 47	3.2	08 37	4.6	21 06	4.6
TH 5	08 06	5.7	20 51	5.9	06 00	7.3	18 31	7.6	07 16	2.8	18 59	3.1	09 43	4.5	22 13	4.6
F 6	09 24	5.7	22 02	6.0	07 15	7.5	19 38	7.8	08 49	2.9	20 29	3.1	10 53	4.6	23 19	4.7
SA 7	10 35	6.0	23 08	6.3	08 15	7.9	20 31	8.2	09 45	3.1	21 35	3.2	11 55	4.7	—	—
SU 8	11 34	6.3	—	—	09 00	8.3	21 14	8.5	10 28	3.3	22 24	3.4	00 14	4.9	12 42	4.9
M 9	00 01	6.6	12 22	6.6	09 38	8.6	21 52	8.7	11 07	3.4	23 05	3.4	00 58	5.1	13 18	5.1
TU 10	00 44	6.7	13 02	6.8	10 11	8.9	22 26	8.9	11 43	3.5	23 41	3.5	01 36	5.2	13 51	5.3
W 11	01 20	6.8	13 37	6.9	10 43	9.1	22 58	9.0	12 17	3.5	—	—	02 10	5.3	14 23	5.4
TH 12	01 52	6.9	14 09	7.0	11 15	9.2	23 31	9.1	00 15	3.5	12 49	3.6	02 43	5.4	14 55	5.5
F 13	02 23	6.9	14 41	7.1	11 47	9.2	—	—	00 50	3.5	13 20	3.6	03 17	5.4	15 29	5.5
SA 14	02 56	6.9	15 15	7.1	00 03	9.0	12 21	9.2	01 26	3.6	13 51	3.7	03 52	5.4	16 03	5.4
SU 15	03 30	6.9	15 51	7.0	00 38	8.9	12 56	9.0	02 05	3.6	14 25	3.7	04 28	5.3	16 40	5.4
M 16	04 06	6.7	16 29	6.9	01 15	8.7	13 35	8.8	02 45	3.5	15 02	3.6	05 08	5.2	17 19	5.2
TU 17	04 43	6.6	17 11	6.8	01 57	8.5	14 20	8.6	03 27	3.5	15 41	3.6	05 52	5.1	18 04	5.1
W 18	05 25	6.4	17 58	6.6	02 47	8.2	15 15	8.3	04 11	3.4	16 26	3.4	06 43	5.0	18 56	4.9
TH 19	06 15	6.2	18 56	6.4	03 49	7.9	16 23	8.1	05 02	3.2	17 21	3.3	07 42	4.8	19 58	4.8
F 20	07 17	6.1	20 10	6.3	05 04	7.8	17 39	8.1	06 04	3.1	18 35	3.2	08 53	4.8	21 15	4.9
SA 21	08 40	6.1	21 28	6.5	06 22	8.0	18 50	8.4	07 25	3.1	20 03	3.2	10 07	4.9	22 28	5.0
SU 22	09 58	6.4	22 37	6.7	07 32	8.4	19 55	8.9	08 50	3.2	21 17	3.4	11 13	5.2	23 30	5.3
M 23	11 05	6.7	23 40	6.9	08 32	8.8	20 52	9.3	09 54	3.3	22 17	3.6	12 09	5.4	—	—
TU 24	12 04	7.0	—	—	09 25	9.3	21 43	9.6	10 46	3.5	23 10	3.7	00 25	5.6	13 00	5.7
W 25	00 36	7.1	12 57	7.2	10 13	9.6	22 32	9.8	11 33	3.6	—	—	01 16	5.8	13 46	5.8
TH 26	01 27	7.2	13 45	7.3	10 58	9.7	23 19	9.8	00 00	3.7	12 18	3.7	02 05	5.9	14 31	5.9
F 27	02 13	7.2	14 31	7.5	11 42	9.8	—	—	00 50	3.7	13 01	3.8	02 53	5.9	15 17	5.9
SA 28	02 57	7.2	15 15	7.5	00 04	9.7	12 25	9.6	01 37	3.7	13 42	3.8	03 42	5.8	16 04	5.7
SU 29	03 39	7.1	15 59	7.3	00 49	9.4	13 07	9.3	02 21	3.6	14 22	3.8	04 30	5.7	16 51	5.5
M 30	04 20	6.8	16 42	7.0	01 32	9.0	13 49	9.0	03 04	3.5	15 02	3.7	05 19	5.4	17 39	5.3

DECEMBER 2015   *High Water*   GMT

Day	LONDON BRIDGE hr m	ht m	hr m	ht m	LIVERPOOL (Gladstone Dock) hr m	ht m	hr m	ht m	GREENOCK hr m	ht m	hr m	ht m	LEITH hr m	ht m	hr m	ht m
TU 1	04 59	6.5	17 24	6.7	02 16	8.5	14 34	8.6	03 47	3.3	15 44	3.6	06 09	5.1	18 29	5.1
W 2	05 37	6.3	18 08	6.3	03 03	8.1	15 25	8.1	04 33	3.2	16 28	3.5	07 00	4.9	19 23	4.8
TH 3	06 19	6.0	18 58	6.1	03 58	7.7	16 25	7.8	05 23	3.0	17 16	3.3	07 54	4.6	20 21	4.7
F 4	07 12	5.8	20 00	5.9	05 02	7.4	17 32	7.6	06 22	2.9	18 12	3.2	08 51	4.5	21 21	4.6
SA 5	08 27	5.6	21 06	5.9	06 12	7.3	18 40	7.6	07 30	2.9	19 18	3.1	09 50	4.5	22 22	4.6
SU 6	09 39	5.7	22 10	6.0	07 20	7.5	19 43	7.8	08 42	3.0	20 31	3.1	10 51	4.5	23 22	4.7
M 7	10 42	6.0	23 09	6.2	08 15	7.9	20 35	8.1	09 41	3.2	21 34	3.2	11 49	4.7	—	—
TU 8	11 38	6.3	—	—	09 01	8.3	21 19	8.4	10 29	3.3	22 25	3.3	00 15	4.8	12 37	4.9
W 9	00 01	6.5	12 25	6.6	09 40	8.6	21 58	8.6	11 12	3.4	23 08	3.4	01 02	5.0	13 18	5.1
TH 10	00 46	6.7	13 06	6.8	10 16	8.9	22 34	8.8	11 50	3.5	23 48	3.4	01 44	5.2	13 56	5.3
F 11	01 25	6.8	13 44	6.9	10 52	9.1	23 10	9.0	12 25	3.6	—	—	02 20	5.3	14 33	5.4
SA 12	02 02	6.9	14 21	7.0	11 27	9.3	23 46	9.0	00 27	3.5	12 58	3.7	02 57	5.4	15 08	5.5
SU 13	02 40	6.9	14 59	7.1	12 04	9.3	—	—	01 07	3.5	13 32	3.7	03 34	5.4	15 44	5.5
M 14	03 18	6.9	15 38	7.1	00 25	9.1	12 43	9.3	01 48	3.5	14 08	3.7	04 12	5.5	16 22	5.5
TU 15	03 56	6.8	16 19	7.1	01 06	9.0	13 25	9.2	02 30	3.5	14 47	3.7	04 53	5.4	17 02	5.4
W 16	04 35	6.7	17 02	7.0	01 49	8.8	14 11	9.0	03 13	3.5	15 28	3.7	05 37	5.3	17 47	5.3
TH 17	05 17	6.6	17 49	6.8	02 38	8.6	15 02	8.8	03 58	3.4	16 13	3.6	06 26	5.2	18 37	5.2
F 18	06 04	6.5	18 42	6.6	03 33	8.3	16 02	8.5	04 46	3.3	17 04	3.5	07 21	5.0	19 34	5.1
SA 19	07 00	6.3	19 49	6.4	04 38	8.1	17 09	8.4	05 41	3.2	18 07	3.3	08 26	4.9	20 44	5.0
SU 20	08 11	6.3	21 01	6.4	05 50	8.0	18 19	8.4	06 48	3.1	19 26	3.3	09 37	4.9	21 59	5.0
M 21	09 29	6.3	22 10	6.5	07 03	8.2	19 29	8.6	08 11	3.1	20 47	3.3	10 45	5.0	23 06	5.1
TU 22	10 38	6.5	23 16	6.6	08 09	8.5	20 32	8.9	09 26	3.2	21 56	3.4	11 46	5.2	—	—
W 23	11 42	6.7	—	—	09 07	8.9	21 29	9.1	10 26	3.4	22 55	3.5	00 07	5.3	12 42	5.4
TH 24	00 18	6.8	12 40	6.9	09 58	9.2	22 20	9.3	11 17	3.5	23 49	3.5	01 03	5.5	13 32	5.6
F 25	01 12	6.9	13 31	7.1	10 45	9.4	23 08	9.4	12 03	3.7	—	—	01 54	5.6	14 19	5.7
SA 26	02 00	7.0	14 18	7.2	11 29	9.5	23 52	9.4	00 39	3.6	12 46	3.7	02 43	5.7	15 04	5.7
SU 27	02 44	7.0	15 02	7.2	12 11	9.5	—	—	01 26	3.5	13 27	3.8	03 29	5.6	15 49	5.7
M 28	03 25	7.0	15 45	7.2	00 34	9.2	12 51	9.4	02 09	3.5	14 06	3.8	04 14	5.5	16 33	5.6
TU 29	04 03	6.9	16 24	7.0	01 14	9.0	13 29	9.1	02 49	3.4	14 44	3.8	04 58	5.4	17 16	5.4
W 30	04 39	6.7	17 02	6.7	01 52	8.7	14 07	8.8	03 28	3.3	15 23	3.7	05 41	5.2	17 58	5.2
TH 31	05 13	6.5	17 38	6.5	02 31	8.4	14 48	8.4	04 08	3.2	16 03	3.6	06 23	4.9	—	—

ABBREVIATIONS AND ACRONYMS

A

AAA — Amateur Athletic Association
ABA — Amateur Boxing Association
abr — abridged
ac — alternating current
AC — *(ante Christum)* before Christ
  Companion, Order of Australia
ADC — Aide-de-Camp
ADC (P) — Personal ADC to the Queen
Adj. — Adjutant
Adj. Gen. — Adjutant General
Adm. — Admiral
AE — Air Efficiency award
AEM — Air Efficiency Medal
aet — after extra time
AFC — Air Force Cross
AFM — Air Force Medal
AG — Attorney-General
AH — *(anno Hegirae)* in the year of the Hegira
AM — Assembly Member (Wales)
ANC — African National Congress
AO — Air Officer
  Officer, Order of Australia
AOC — Air Officer Commanding
apptd — appointed
APR — annual percentage rate
ASBO — antisocial behaviour order
AUC — *(ab urbe condita)* from the foundation of Rome
  (anno urbis conditae) from the founding of the city

B

b. — born
  bowled (cricket)
BAF — British Athletics Federation
BAFTA — British Academy of Film and Television Arts
BAS — Bachelor in Agricultural Science
  British Antarctic Survey
BBA — British Bankers' Association
BBFC — British Board of Film Classification
BCH (D) — Bachelor of (Dental) Surgery
BCL — Bachelor of Civil Law
BCOM — Bachelor of Commerce
BD — Bachelor of Divinity
BDA — British Dental Association
BDS — Bachelor of Dental Surgery
BED — Bachelor of Education
BEM — British Empire Medal
BENG — Bachelor of Engineering
BFPO — British Forces Post Office
BLIT — Bachelor of Literature
BLITT — Bachelor of Letters
BM — Bachelor of Medicine
BMA — British Medical Association
BMUS — Bachelor of Music
Bp — Bishop
BPHARM — Bachelor of Pharmacy
BPHIL — Bachelor of Philosophy
BPS — British Psychological Society

Brig. — Brigadier
BSI — British Standards Institution
BST — British Summer Time
Bt. — Baronet
BTEC — Business and Technology Education Council
BVMS — Bachelor of Veterinary Medicine and Surgery

C

c. — *(circa)* about
C. — Conservative
Cantuar: — of Canterbury (Archbishop)
Capt. — Captain
Carliol — of Carlisle (Bishop)
CB — Companion, Order of the Bath
CBE — Commander, Order of the British Empire
CC — Companion, Order of Canada
CCF — Combined Cadet Force
CCHEM — chartered chemist
CD — Civil Defence
  Corps Diplomatique
Cdr — Commander
Cdre — Commodore
CDS — Chief of the Defence Staff
CE — civil engineer
  Common (or Christian) Era
CENG — chartered engineer
Cestr: — of Chester (Bishop)
CET — Central European Time
cf — *(confer)* compare
CGC — Conspicuous Gallantry Cross
CGEOL — chartered geologist
CGM — Conspicuous Gallantry Medal
CGS — Chief of General Staff
CH — Companion of Honour
CHB/M — Bachelor/Master of Surgery
CI — Channel Islands
Cicestr: — of Chichester (Bishop)
CID — Criminal Investigation Department
CIE — Companion, Order of the Indian Empire
C-in-C — Commander-in-Chief
CILIP — Chartered Institute of Library and Information Professionals
CIPFA — Chartered Institute of Public Finance and Accountancy
CIS — Commonwealth of Independent States
CLJ — Commander, Order of St Lazarus of Jerusalem
CM — *(Chirurgiae Magister)* Master of Surgery
CMG — Companion, Order of St Michael and St George
CO — Commanding Officer
C of E — Church of England
Col. — Colonel
cons. — consecrated
Cpl. — Corporal
CPM — Colonial Police Medal

CPS — Crown Prosecution Service
CSI — Companion, Order of the Star of India
CVO — Commander, Royal Victorian Order

D

d — *(denarius)* penny
d. — died
DAB — Digital Audio Broadcasting
DBE — Dame Commander, Order of the British Empire
DCB — Dame Commander, Order of the Bath
D CH — *(Doctor Chirurgiae)* Doctor of Surgery
DCL — Doctor of Civil Law
DCM — Distinguished Conduct Medal
DCMG — Dame Commander, Order of St Michael and St George
DCVO — Dame Commander, Royal Victorian Order
DD — Doctor of Divinity
DDS — Doctor of Dental Surgery
DDT — dichlorodiphenyl trichloroethane
DFC — Distinguished Flying Cross
DFM — Distinguished Flying Medal
DIP ED — Diploma in Education
DIP HE — Diploma in Higher Education
DL — Deputy Lieutenant
DLIT — Doctor of Literature
DLITT — Doctor of Letters
DLR — Docklands Light Railway
DMUS — Doctor of Music
DNA — deoxyribonucleic acid
DPH *or* — Doctor of Philosophy
DPHIL
DPP — Director of Public Prosecutions
DSC — Distinguished Service Cross
DSc — Doctor of Science
DSM — Distinguished Service Medal
DSO — Companion, Distinguished Service Order
Dunelm: — of Durham (Bishop)
DUP — Northern Ireland Democratic Unionist Party

E

Ebor: — of York (Archbishop)
EC — Elizabeth Cross
  European Community
ECG — electrocardiogram
ED — Efficiency Decoration
EEG — electroencephalogram
EIB — European Investment Bank
ER — *(Elizabetha Regina)* Queen Elizabeth
ERM — exchange rate mechanism
ESA — European Space Agency
ETA — *(Euzkadi ta Askatasuna)* Basque separatist organisation

et seq	*(et sequentia)* and the following	
Exon:	of Exeter (Bishop)	
F		
FANY	First Aid Nursing Yeomanry	
FAQ	frequently asked questions	
FARC	*(Fuerzas Armadas Revolucionarias de Colombia)* Revolutionary Armed Forces of Colombia	
FBA	Fellow, British Academy	
FBAA	Fellow, British Association of Accountants and Auditors	
FBS	Fellow, Botanical Society	
FBU	Fire Brigades Union	
FCA	Fellow, Institute of Chartered Accountants in England and Wales	
FCCA	Fellow, Chartered Association of Certified Accountants	
FCGI	Fellow, City and Guilds of London Institute	
FCIA	Fellow, Corporation of Insurance Agents	
FCIARB	Fellow, Chartered Institute of Arbitrators	
FCIB	Fellow, Chartered Institute of Bankers	
	Fellow, Corporation of Insurance Brokers	
FCIBSE	Fellow, Chartered Institution of Building Services Engineers	
FCII	Fellow, Chartered Insurance Institute	
FCIPS	Fellow, Chartered Institute of Purchasing and Supply	
FCIS	Fellow, Institute of Chartered Secretaries and Administrators	
FCIT	Fellow, Chartered Institute of Transport	
FCMA	Fellow, Chartered Institute of Management Accountants	
FCP	Fellow, College of Preceptors	
FD	*(Fidei Defensor)* Defender of the Faith	
FE	further education	
FFA	Fellow, Faculty of Actuaries (Scotland)	
	Fellow, Institute of Financial Accountants	
FFAS	Fellow, Faculty of Architects and Surveyors	
FFCM	Fellow, Faculty of Community Medicine	
FFPHM	Fellow, Faculty of Public Health Medicine	
FGS	Fellow, Geological Society	
FHS	Fellow, Heraldry Society	
FHSM	Fellow, Institute of Health Service Management	
FIA	Fellow, Institute of Actuaries	
FIBIOL	Fellow, Institute of Biology	
FICE	Fellow, Institution of Civil Engineers	

FICS	Fellow, Institution of Chartered Shipbrokers	
FIEE	Fellow, Institution of Electrical Engineers	
FIERE	Fellow, Institution of Electronic and Radio Engineers	
FIM	Fellow, Institute of Metals	
FIMGT	Fellow, Institute of Management	
FIMM	Fellow, Institution of Mining and Metallurgy	
FINSTF	Fellow, Institute of Fuel	
FINSTP	Fellow, Institute of Physics	
FIQS	Fellow, Institute of Quantity Surveyors	
FIS	Fellow, Institute of Statisticians	
FJI	Fellow, Institute of Journalists	
FLS	Fellow, Linnean Society	
FMEDSCI	Fellow, Academy of Medical Sciences	
fo	folio	
FPHS	Fellow, Philosophical Society	
FRAD	Fellow, Royal Academy of Dancing	
FRAES	Fellow, Royal Aeronautical Society	
FRAGS	Fellow, Royal Agricultural Societies	
FRAI	Fellow, Royal Anthropological Institute	
FRAM	Fellow, Royal Academy of Music	
FRAS	Fellow, Royal Asiatic Society	
	Fellow, Royal Astronomical Society	
FRBS	Fellow, Royal Botanic Society	
	Fellow, Royal Society of British Sculptors	
FRCA	Fellow, Royal College of Anaesthetists	
FRCGP	Fellow, Royal College of General Practitioners	
FRCM	Fellow, Royal College of Music	
FRCO	Fellow, Royal College of Organists	
FRCOG	Fellow, Royal College of Obstetricians and Gynaecologists	
FRCP	Fellow, Royal College of Physicians, London	
FRCPATH	Fellow, Royal College of Pathologists	
FRCPE *or* FRCPED	Fellow, Royal College of Physicians, Edinburgh	
FRCPI	Fellow, Royal College of Physicians, Ireland	
FRCPSYCH	Fellow, Royal College of Psychiatrists	
FRCR	Fellow, Royal College of Radiologists	
FRCS	Fellow, Royal College of Surgeons of England	
FRCSE *or* FRCSED	Fellow, Royal College of Surgeons of Edinburgh	
FRCSGLAS	Fellow, Royal College of Physicians and Surgeons of Glasgow	

FRCSI	Fellow, Royal College of Surgeons in Ireland	
FRCVS	Fellow, Royal College of Veterinary Surgeons	
FRECONS	Fellow, Royal Economic Society	
FRENG	Fellow, Royal Academy of Engineering	
FRGS	Fellow, Royal Geographical Society	
FRHISTS	Fellow, Royal Historical Society	
FRHS	Fellow, Royal Horticultural Society	
FRIBA	Fellow, Royal Institute of British Architects	
FRICS	Fellow, Royal Institution of Chartered Surveyors	
FRMETS	Fellow, Royal Meteorological Society	
FRMS	Fellow, Royal Microscopical Society	
FRNS	Fellow, Royal Numismatic Society	
FRPHARMS	Fellow, Royal Pharmaceutical Society	
FRPS	Fellow, Royal Photographic Society	
FRS	Fellow, Royal Society	
FRSA	Fellow, Royal Society of Arts	
FRSC	Fellow, Royal Society of Chemistry	
FRSE	Fellow, Royal Society of Edinburgh	
FRSH	Fellow, Royal Society of Health	
FRSL	Fellow, Royal Society of Literature	
FRTPI	Fellow, Royal Town Planning Institute	
FSA	Fellow, Society of Antiquaries	
FSS	Fellow, Royal Statistical Society	
FSVA	Fellow, Incorporated Society of Valuers and Auctioneers	
FTI	Fellow, Textile Institute	
FTII	Fellow, Chartered Institute of Taxation	
FZS	Fellow, Zoological Society	
G		
GBE	Dame/Knight Grand Cross, Order of the British Empire	
GC	George Cross	
GCB	Dame/Knight Grand Cross, Order of the Bath	
GCLJ	Knight Grand Cross, Order of St Lazarus of Jerusalem	
GCMG	Dame/Knight Grand Cross, Order of St Michael and St George	
GCSI	Knight Grand Commander, Order of the Star of India	
GCVO	Dame/Knight Grand Cross, Royal Victorian Order	
Gen.	General	
GHQ	general headquarters	
GLA	Greater London Authority	
GM	George Medal	

GMB	Britain's General Union
GOC	General Officer Commanding
Gp Capt.	Group Captain
GPS	Global Positioning System
H	
HB	His Beatitude
HBM	Her/His Britannic Majesty('s)
HCF	Honorary Chaplain to the Forces
HE	Her/His Excellency
	higher education
	His Eminence
HH	Her/His Highness
	Her/His Honour
	His Holiness
HIM	Her/His Imperial Majesty
HJS	*(hic jacet sepultus)* here lies buried
HM	Her/His Majesty('s)
HMAS	Her/His Majesty's Australian Ship
HMC	Headmasters' and Headmistresses' Conference
HMI	Her/His Majesty's Inspector
HMS	Her/His Majesty's Ship
Hon.	Honorary
	Honourable
HRH	Her/His Royal Highness
HRT	hormone replacement therapy
HSE	*(hic sepultus est)* here is buried
HSH	Her/His Serene Highness
I	
IB	International Baccalaureate
IBF	International Boxing Federation
ICC	International Cricket Council
	International Criminal Court
ICJ	International Court of Justice
id	*(idem)* the same
IP	intellectual property
	internet protocol
IPSA	Independent Parliamentary Standards Authority
iPSC	induced pluripotent stem cell
IRA	Irish Republican Army
IRB	International Rugby Board
IRC	International Rescue Committee
Is	Islands
ISO	Imperial Service Order
	International Organisation for Standardisation
ISP	internet service provider
ISSN	International Standard Serial Number
ITU	International Telecommunication Union
J	
J	Judge
	Justice
JP	Justice of the Peace

K	
KBE	Knight Commander, Order of the British Empire
KCB	Knight Commander, Order of the Bath
KCLJ	Knight Commander, Order of St Lazarus of Jerusalem
KCMG	Knight Commander, Order of St Michael and St George
KCSI	Knight Commander, Order of the Star of India
KCVO	Knight Commander, Royal Victorian Order
KG	Knight of the Garter
KGB	*(Komitet Gosudarstvennoi Bezopasnosti)* Committee of State Security (USSR)
KLJ	Knight, Order of St Lazarus of Jerusalem
KP	Knight, Order of St Patrick
KStJ	Knight, Order of St John of Jerusalem
Kt.	Knight
KT	Knight of the Thistle
L	
Lab.	Labour
Lat.	Latitude
lbw	leg before wicket (cricket)
lc	lower case (printing)
LCJ	Lord Chief Justice
LCM	least/lowest common multiple
LD	Liberal Democrat
LDS	Licentiate in Dental Surgery
LHD	*(Literarum Humaniorum Doctor)* Doctor of Humane Letters/Literature
Lib.	Liberal
LITT D	Doctor of Letters
LJ	Lord Justice
LLB	Bachelor of Laws
LLD	Doctor of Laws
LLM	Master of Laws
loc cit	*(loco citato)* in the place cited
Londin:	of London (Bishop)
Long.	longitude
lsd	*(librae, solidi, denarii)* pounds, shillings and pence
Lt	Lieutenant
LTA	Lawn Tennis Association
LVO	Lieutenant, Royal Victorian Order
M	
m.	married
M	Monsieur
Maj.	Major
MB	*(Medicinae Baccalaureus)* Bachelor of Medicine
MBA	Master of Business Administration
MBC	Metropolitan Borough Council
MBE	Member, Order of the British Empire
MBO	management buy-out
MC	Master of Ceremonies
	Military Cross
MCB	Muslim Council of Britain
MCC	Marylebone Cricket Club

MCH(D)	Master of (Dental) Surgery
MDS	Master of Dental Surgery
ME	Middle English
	myalgic encephalomyelitis
MED	Master of Education
Mgr	Monsignor
MIT	Massachusetts Institute of Technology
MLA	Member of Legislative Assembly (NI)
	Museums, Libraries and Archives Council
MLITT	Master of Letters
Mlle	Mademoiselle
MM	Military Medal
Mme	Madame
MMR	measles, mumps and rubella (vaccine)
MN	Merchant Navy
MPHIL	Master of Philosophy
MR	Master of the Rolls
MRI	magnetic resonance imaging
MRSA	methicillin-resistant staphylococcus aureus
MS	manuscript (*pl* MSS)
	Master of Surgery
	multiple sclerosis
MSP	Member of Scottish Parliament
MUSB/D	Bachelor/Doctor of Music
MVO	Member, Royal Victorian Order
N	
NAAFI	Navy, Army and Air Force Institutes
NAFTA	North American Free Trade Agreement
NAO	National Audit Office
NCO	non-commissioned officer
NDPB	non-departmental public body
NFU	National Farmers' Union
non seq	*(non sequitur)* it does not follow
Norvic:	of Norwich (Bishop)
NP	Notary Public
NSW	New South Wales (Australia)
NUJ	National Union of Journalists
NUS	National Union of Students
NUT	National Union of Teachers
O	
Ob *or* obit	died
OBE	Officer, Order of the British Empire
OBR	Office for Budget Responsibility
OE	Old English
OED	*Oxford English Dictionary*
OHMS	On Her/His Majesty's Service
OM	Order of Merit
ono	or near(est) offer
op	*(opus)* work
op cit	*(opere citato)* in the work cited
OS	Ordnance Survey
OStJ	Officer, Order of St John of Jerusalem

P

PC	Plaid Cymru
	Police Constable
	Privy Counsellor
Petriburg:	of Peterborough (Bishop)
PG	parental guidance
	postgraduate
PHD	Doctor of Philosophy
pl	plural
PLO	Palestine Liberation Organisation
PM	post mortem
	Prime Minister
PO	Petty Officer
	Pilot Officer
	post office
	postal order
	(per procurationem) by proxy
PPS	Parliamentary Private Secretary
PR	proportional representation
PRA	President of the Royal Academy
pro tem	*(pro tempore)* for the time being
prox	*(proximo)* next month
PRS	President of the Royal Society
PRSE	President of the Royal Society of Edinburgh
Pte.	Private

Q

QBD	Queen's Bench Division
QC	Queen's Counsel
QE	quantitative easing
QED	*(quod erat demonstrandum)* which was to be proved
QGM	Queen's Gallantry Medal
QHC	Queen's Honorary Chaplain
QHDS	Queen's Honorary Dental Surgeon
QHNS	Queen's Honorary Nursing Sister
QHP	Queen's Honorary Physician
QHS	Queen's Honorary Surgeon
QMG	Quartermaster-General
QPM	Queen's Police Medal
QSO	quasi-stellar object *(quasar)*
	Queen's Service Order
quango	quasi-autonomous non-governmental organisation
qv	*(quod vide)* which see

R

r.	*(recto)* on the right-hand page
R	*(Regina)* Queen
	(Rex) King
RA	Royal Academy/Academician
	Royal Artillery
RAC	Royal Armoured Corps
	Royal Automobile Club
RADA	Royal Academy of Dramatic Art
RADC	Royal Army Dental Corps
RAEC	Royal Army Educational Corps
RAES	Royal Aeronautical Society
RAM	Royal Academy of Music

RAMC	Royal Army Medical Corps
RAN	Royal Australian Navy
RAOC	Royal Army Ordnance Corps
RAPC	Royal Army Pay Corps
RAVC	Royal Army Veterinary Corps
RBS	Royal Society of British Sculptors
RC	Red Cross
	Roman Catholic
RCN	Royal College of Nursing
RCT	Royal Corps of Transport
RD	Royal Naval and Royal Marine Forces Reserve Decoration
	Rural Dean
RE	Royal Engineers
REME	Royal Electrical and Mechanical Engineers
Rep	Republican
Rep.	Republic
Revd	Reverend
RGS	Royal Geographical Society
RHS	Royal Horticultural Society
RI	Royal Institute of Painters in Watercolours
	Royal Institution
RIR	Royal Irish Regiment
RM	Royal Marines
RMA	Royal Military Academy
RMT	National Union of Rail, Maritime and Transport Workers
RNIB	Royal National Institute of Blind People
RNID	Royal National Institute for Deaf People
RNR	Royal Naval Reserve
RNVR	Royal Naval Volunteer Reserve
RNXS	Royal Naval Auxiliary Service
Roffen:	of Rochester (Bishop)
RPA	Rural Payments Agency
RSA	Royal Scottish Academician
	Royal Society of Arts
RSC	Royal Shakespeare Company
RSE	Royal Society of Edinburgh
Rt. Hon.	Right Honourable
RUC	Royal Ulster Constabulary

S

s	section (Public Acts)
	(solidus) shilling
Salop	Shropshire
Sarum:	of Salisbury (Bishop)
SCD	Doctor of Science
SDLP	Social Democratic and Labour Party
SEAQ	Stock Exchange Automated Quotations system
SEN	special educational needs
	State Enrolled Nurse
SF	Sinn Fein
SFO	Serious Fraud Office
SI	statutory instrument
	(Système International d'Unités) International System of Units

sic	*(sic)* so written
sig	signature
	Signor
SLD	Social and Liberal Democrats
SOE	Special Operations Executive
sp	*(sine prole)* without issue
Sr	Senior
	Sister (title)
SS	steamship
SSN	standard serial number
stet	*(stet)* let it stand (printing)
Sub Lt.	sub-lieutenant

T

TD	Territorial Decoration
TEFL	teaching English as a foreign language
TNT	trinitrotoluene (explosive)
trans.	translated
TRH	Their Royal Highnesses
trs	transpose (printing)

U

U	Unionist
uc	upper case (printing)
UDA	Ulster Defence Association
UDR	Ulster Defence Regiment
UG	undergraduate
USB	universal serial bus
UTC	*(Temps Universel Coordonné)* coordinated universal time
UVF	Ulster Volunteer Force

V

v	*(versus)* against
v.	*(verso)* on the left-hand page
	Victoria and Albert Order
VAD	Voluntary Aid Detachment (nursing)
VC	Victoria Cross
VD	Volunteer Officers' Decoration
Ven.	Venerable
VRD	Royal Naval Volunteer Reserve Officers' Decoration
VSO	Voluntary Service Overseas

W

w.	widowed
WBC	World Boxing Council
WBO	World Boxing Organisation
WCC	World Council of Churches
WFTU	World Federation of Trade Unions
Winton:	of Winchester (Bishop)
WO	Warrant Officer
WRAC	Women's Royal Army Corps
WRAF	Women's Royal Air Force
WRNS	Women's Royal Naval Service
WRVS	Women's Royal Voluntary Service
WS	Writer to the Signet

Y

YMCA	Young Men's Christian Association
YWCA	Young Women's Christian Association

Z

ZANU-PF	Zimbabwean African National Union-Patriotic Front

INDEX